D0788393

Novel Openers

First Sentences of 11,000 Fictional Works, Topically Arranged with Subject, Keyword, Author and Title Indexing

by Bruce L. Weaver

McFarland & Company, Inc., Publishers
Jefferson, North Carolina, and London

British Library Cataloguing-in-Publication data are available

Library of Congress Cataloguing-in-Publication Data

Weaver, Bruce L.
    Novel openers : first sentences of 11,000 fictional works, topically
arranged with subject, keyword, author and title indexing / by Bruce
L. Weaver.
      p. cm.
    ISBN 0-7864-0050-1 (lib. bdg. : 45# alk. paper) ∞
    1. Fiction—Indexes.   2. Openings (Rhetoric)—Indexes.
3. Quotations, English.   I. Title.
Z5916.W43   1995
[PN3365]
016.80883—dc20   94-41653
                                                  CIP

Manufactured in the United States of America

McFarland & Company, Inc., Publishers
  Box 611, Jefferson, North Carolina 28640

Acknowledgments

My deepest gratitude goes to the library staffs who graciously tolerated my irritating presence for so many months. Making great contributions to the completion of this collection were the Warsaw Community Public Library in Warsaw, Indiana, the Helmke Library at Indiana University–Purdue University in Fort Wayne, Indiana, and the Hesburgh Library at the University of Notre Dame in South Bend, Indiana.

The Allen County Public Library in Fort Wayne, Indiana, deserves special mention. Bearing the brunt of my relentless onslaught, its compassionate and patient personnel were ever ready to offer assistance and moral support whenever I needed it. They are a fine crew, and I recommend them to anyone searching for a large library with ample resources and small-town friendliness.

Table of Contents

Acknowledgments v

The Openers 1

Ability   6
Accidents   6
Adversity   7
Age   9
Agedness   9
Ailments   10
Air   12
Aircraft and Aviation   13
Ambition   15
America   16
Amusement   17
Anatomy   19
Ancestry   20
Anger   21
Animals   22
Art and Artists   25
Astronomy   26
Babies   27
Bathing   28
Beginnings   29
Behavior   31
Bells   31
Bewilderment   32
Biography   33
Birds   34
Birth   36
Birthdays   39
Bombs and Explo-
   sions   40
Books   41
Boredom   42
Boys   43

Business   46
Calls   50
Captivity   52
Castles   53
Cemeteries   53
Ceremonies and
   Rites   54
Chance and Luck   55
Change   56
Childhood   57
Children   58
Churches   58
Cinema   59
Cities and Towns   60
Clergymen   67
Cold   69
Coming and Going   70
Compassion   78
Confession   79
Conflict   79
Construction   80
Cookery   81
Corpses   82
Correspondence   83
Couples   85
Crime and
   Criminals   87
Crying   89
Curiosity   90
Dance   90
Darkness   91
Days   91

Daytime and Night-
   time   93
Death   97
Decisions   104
Depression   105
Desire   106
Diaries   106
Disappearance   107
Disappointment   109
Disaster   109
Discovery   109
Divinities   110
Divorce   111
Doors and Windows   113
Doubt   114
Dreams   115
Dress   118
Drink   120
Driving   123
Drugs   128
Dwellings   128
Education   137
Elevators   138
Emotions   138
Employers and
   Employees   139
Endings   140
Environment   140
Eras   141
Escape   143
Establishments   144
Events   144

Evidence   145
Excitement   146
Exercise   146
Experiences   147
Failure   148
Fame   148
Families   149
Farming   153
Fate   155
Fatigue   156
Fear   156
Finance   158
Fire and Smoke   159
Flowers   160
Food   161
Forests   164
Friends   164
Funerals   165
Gambling   166
Gardens   167
Gatherings   167
Geography   169
Ghosts   173
Gifts   174
Girls   175
Greetings   178
Grief   178
Growing Up   179
Guns   179
Habits   180
Hair   181
Hangouts   181
Happiness   183
Hatred   184
Heat   185
Heredity   187
Heritage   188
Heroes and
   Heroines   188
Hiding   190
History   190
Holidays   191
Home   192
Homecoming   193
Hope   195
Hospitals   195
Hotels and Motels   196
Humor   197
Hunger and Thirst   198

Hunting and Fish-
   ing   198
Ideas   199
Identity   200
Ignorance   205
Imagination   205
Impatience   206
Inheritance   207
Insanity   207
Insects   208
Insults   209
Intelligence   210
Islands   210
Knowledge   212
Lakes   213
Landmarks   213
Landscape   215
Laughter   218
Law   219
Legends   220
Lies and Liars   221
Life   221
Lifestyles   222
Light and Lights   224
Likes and Dislikes   225
Literature   227
Lives   235
Lost   237
Lounging   238
Love   239
Machinery   241
Mankind   241
Maps   242
Marriage   243
Meetings   245
Men   249
Messages   254
Mistakes   255
Motives   255
Mountains   256
Moving   258
Murder   262
Music   263
Nations of the
   World   265
Neighborhoods   266
Neighbors   267
News   268
Newspapers   270

Nights   270
Nudity   271
Occupations   272
Offices   276
Offspring   277
Outings   278
Pain   280
Parents   280
Parties   287
The Past   288
Peace   289
People   289
Philosophy   290
Photographs   291
Physicians   292
Physics   293
Places   293
Plans   294
Police   295
Politics   296
Portent   298
Poverty   298
Pranks and Tricks   299
Pregnancy and Child-
   birth   299
Presence   302
Pride   302
Prison   303
Problems   304
Psychology   304
Punishment   305
Questions   305
Quests   306
Railroads   307
Rain   309
Reading   311
Recollection   312
Recovery   316
Reflections   316
Regret   317
Religion   318
Reproach   321
Restaurants   321
Reticence   322
Riding   323
Rivers   325
Romance   328
Rooms   329
Rulers   331

Rules   332
Rumors   333
Running   334
Scandal   335
Schools   335
The Sea   337
Secrets   338
Self-Knowledge   339
Sex   340
Shadows   342
Shaving   342
Ships and Boats   343
Shock and Surprise   348
Siblings   349
Sight   351
Signs   353
Silence   354
Sitting   354
The Sky   356
Sleep   359
Sleeplessness   360
Smells   361
Smiles   363
Smoking   363
Snow   364
Socializing   366
Soldiers and Sailors

367
Solitude   370
Song   371
Sounds   372
Speech   375
Spies   378
Sports   378
Statues   379
Stories   380
Storms   385
Strangers   386
Streets and Roads   387
Structures   391
Success   393
Suffering   394
Suicide   394
Suspicion   395
Swearing   396
Swimming   396
Tardiness   396
Teatime   397
Television and Radio
    398
Theater   398
Thoughts   400
Time   402
Travel   404

Trees and Plants   410
Trust   412
Truth   412
Upbringing   412
Vacations   413
Valleys   414
Vehicles   415
Violence   418
Visitors   419
Voices   424
Waiting   426
Waking   429
Walking   437
War   443
Warnings   447
Wealth   447
Weather and Seasons
    448
Weddings   451
Wind   452
Wisdom   455
Women   456
Words   462
Work   462
Worry   464
Years   465
Youth   466

Index of Subjects, Key Words and Key Phrases   467
Index of Authors and Titles   903

The Openers

Preface

Opening lines of fictional art are the thresholds that take us into different worlds. They are distinct pieces of prose, discrete and usually brief combinations of words that are, conceivably, the most important pieces of writing that an author must produce. Not only must the opener function as a convincing starting place, but it must somehow appeal to the reader, both esthetically and functionally, and in some manner drag or push the reader into the author's tale. As this collection demonstrates, though there are countless methods that serve these purposes, an opener—like any other piece of writing—may contain identifiable topics, obscure as well as obvious relationships to other works, reflections upon contemporary affairs and philosophies, and, of course, memorable prose.

The best way to capture readers with fiction is to put them, instantly, somewhere else, and in the same breath pique their curiosity. The first words that a reader encounters in any piece of writing are special in that they are the initial confrontation between the two participants of what, ideally, will be a gratifying experience for the reader. Fiction, perhaps more so than other types of literature, is an intensely personal interaction between author and reader. If they do nothing else, opening lines of fiction must succeed in forming this link between the participants.

It is easy to understand why authors *should* expend more effort on the first line or two than on any other piece of writing in

their works. It is the part which is most readily accessible to browsers, and that which can instantly dissuade a prospective reader from taking a book home. "To a reader," say Hallie and Whit Burnett in their *Fiction Writer's Handbook*, "the writer must seem to have all the requisite knowledge of the experience, he must seem to be the master of the beginning; the end, with the sense of inevitability, should take care of itself" (Burnett, page 108). Though endings can help make books memorable and ultimately satisfying, openers, by quickly exhibiting an author's mastery, can sell them.

How a fictional narrative begins depends upon the author's selection of his or her tool for implementing it. Is the reader best served by being given a history of events before the action starts? Is it better to start with dialogue, allowing the reader to be present when characters are interacting and exhibiting some conflict? Does the tale hinge upon a specific action, such as a storm or a battle, that might supply the proper beginning? Is the story's setting so important that it should come first? Should a character be described, physically and or psychologically, to prepare us for that character's further treatment? Is it best to offer a quotation (from a real or fictional work) first, either as background information or as philosophical hypothesis? There are, obviously, many things for an author to consider about the beginning.

Irish novelist Elizabeth Bowen (see entries 727, 1589, 2954, 5143, 6220, 6913, 8770, 10382, and 10646) once suggested that

1

an author should simply "Bring all your intelligence to bear on your beginning" (Burnett, page 145). Jack Hodgins (8749) in *A Passion for Narrative* writes, "In the best fiction, there is a sense that the entire story, including its ending, somehow grows out of the first sentence, that everything is organically related to the first cluster of words the reader encounters" (Hodgins, page 167). Yet the writer must use some discretion in attempts to impress the reader or to offer a beginning that is perhaps too outlandish. "But be careful," warns A. B. Guthrie, Jr. (see entries 1667, 1713, 2048, 4358, 6184, 6961, 7298, 8781, 8862, 9240) in *A Field Guide to Writing Fiction*. "You can overdo it and strain the reader's credulity. And don't be upset if you can't come upon a novel beginning. If your story is good, a clear beginning is enough" (Guthrie, page 46).

Perhaps the most awesome aspect of opening lines for the author relates to what Jack Hodgins said. Everything else must come, in some orderly fashion, after them. Joan Didion (2267, 3462, 7169, 8796), in an interview with *The Paris Review*, amplifies this thought: "What's so hard about the first sentence is that you're stuck with it. Everything else is going to flow out of that sentence. And by the time you've laid down the first *two* sentences, your options are all gone" (Plimpton, page 68). Of course, opening lines can be reworked. Strategies can be revised and even discarded. Sometimes, however, authors are content with their first choice for an opening. Joseph Heller (509, 2705, 5486, 5651, 8006) has said that the opening line of *Catch-22* came to his mind first, and the rest of the book was planned and completed based upon that one inspiration only, with his opening sentence remaining intact (Plimpton, page 75).

Although many of the same considerations apply to all types of fiction, there can be a functional difference between the openers of short stories and those of novels. "Runners of the hundred-yard dash," writes John Gardner (340, 434, 1187, 2039, 3749, 5292, 5577, 5838, 7631) in *The Art of Fiction*, "do not take off in the same way runners of the marathon do. If the opening pages of a thousand-page novel would serve equally well as the opening pages of a short story, the likelihood is that the novel-opening is wrong" (Gardner, page 56). Each opener, regardless of its quality or the quality of the work as a whole, serves a purpose. Each one is an entity in itself. This collection offers a chance to view and compare 11,004 of them, and to judge them on their own, separated from what follows them but standing amongst their counterparts from the hands and minds of thousands of authors spanning four centuries.

Given the staggering number of fictional works that have been written, no book of this kind can aspire to true comprehensiveness. A reasonable and systematic strategy of inclusiveness, therefore, had to be developed. The first step in narrowing the field of study was to focus only on the novel and related forms of long fiction, and only on those works written in English. The next method for restriction was to search out as many essentially *literary* works as possible, while generally ignoring those without literary pretension. The obvious initial task in assembling this collection, then, was to gather the openers of the classics of the English language. Since the authors of those classics are well known and, in most circles, highly regarded, the next step was to add their lesser-known works. Even mediocre novels written by world-class writers often begin with classic openers. Next, a long list was compiled of works by authors of the past whose reputations have faded or been tarnished. Many of those writers have slipped out of print or, perhaps even worse, out of favor. Changing tastes in fiction cannot, however, diminish the impact these writers had on their contemporaries, and cannot detract from the wit or the historical significance of their opening lines. To round out the collection, a generous number of contemporary works were added. Author reputation was not necessarily used as the primary criterion

for selecting the more recent works, but instead a view toward content and reasonable literary merit. Finally, although the method of harvesting the openers tended to bypass genre fiction, some of the best such works were sought out in order to present a more balanced view and to recognize worthy contributions from respected authors that would otherwise have been overlooked. Thus a limited number of science fiction novels, thrillers, mysteries, romances, and westerns are represented in this collection.

It should be an easy task to locate the opening lines of any work of fiction — all you need to do is find the beginning. But where does a novel start? Some novels have introductions, some have prologues, some have proems, some have a paragraph or two after the title page and before Chapter 1 with no identifying heading. To deal evenly with those volumes having several possible beginnings, a strategy was devised. The first lines that contained fiction or that spoke to the reader from the viewpoint of the narrator rather than of the author were selected as the lines to be used for this collection.

Having settled on where an opener *begins*, the next problem was to identify where it *ends*. Does it stop at the first period? At the end of the first paragraph? Since the selections were to be grouped under topic headings, and since brevity, in most cases, both enhances the impact of a selection and narrows the subject matter, the end of the opener for our purposes is at the culmination of a complete thought or idea or image. In some cases this means only a word is enough, in others a complete sentence is needed, and in others it takes a full paragraph. Brevity is disregarded when a succession of sentences is required to bring us to the punchline of a joke or to the worthwhile climax of an interchange between characters, or when, caught up in a rambling narrative, an author nearly loses the reader before finding a period. In most cases, however, the opener ends if, after a period, the subject matter changes. There are even a few that end without a period.

A technical problem was encountered in some of those selections that contain dialogue. If the quoted speech continues past the natural end (as defined above) of the opener, there is no good way of ending the text without violating editorial practice. To show that there is an ending quotation mark somewhere, and that only a portion of the speech of the character has been extracted, three ellipsis points have been added behind the period at the end of those sentences, with the ending quotation mark following them. The drawback of this technique is that it may create the impression that the actual text contained ellipsis points. In all but one or two cases, those selections that actually do contain ellipsis points in the original text do not include a period immediately after the last enclosed word. The presence of that period must serve as the indicator that, in all likelihood, the ellipsis points have been added, and that more words lie between the period and the ending quotation mark in the original text.

Some novels have opened with special typography, which cannot be duplicated in the present work. Such simple devices as italics, all capital letters and the like are, however, faithfully reproduced, but space limitations prevented, for example, the mimicking of geometric shapes into which some openers were formed on the page. In such cases the original line endings are represented by a virgule (/); the same character more commonly shows ordinary paragraph breaks, and in some cases line breaks in verse.

The openers are arranged under topic headings. Under each topic, the entries are ordered chronologically by year published, and then alphabetically by author. Some authors appear with their pseudonymous names if that is generally how they are to be found in reference volumes. Others appear under their real names, with mention, if applicable, of pseudonyms.

The topic headings themselves and the numbers of openers under each are indicators of the utility of openers and the re-

curring themes at work in fiction. What simpler way to start a story (both technically and symbolically) than by *waking* a character? What easier way to introduce a conflict than by the mention of troublesome members of *families*? How better to set a scene than by describing a *dwelling*? Each of these is an example of the more than 300 topic headings listed in the Table of Contents. The openers are each located under the one heading that best identifies the essential topic of the sentence.

A few selections are included that were written first in other languages but were later translated into English by the authors, such as novels by Samuel Beckett and Vladimir Nabokov. Novels make up the great majority of sources, but a number of works of shorter length were used also. Titles of works that are commonly considered full-fledged novels and other major works that have been published as separate volumes appear with titles in italics. Titles of works that are generally considered something else (e.g. novellas, novelettes, and short novels) and have been published within volumes along with other works, appear in quotes.

Titles of famous works from centuries ago have, in many cases, evolved through the years. Long and often difficult to remember, many of them have been shortened and simplified through the years. The titles used in this volume are, for the most part, the most easily recognized versions.

Not only do titles of works evolve, but so too may the text itself. Many works written in the eighteenth century have been revised in later editions by editors attempting to make them suitable for modern readers. An effort was made here to provide text closest to the original versions in as many of those works as possible, although a few selections were found only in edited versions.

The years shown in the main entries behind the authors' names are publishing dates. The earliest discovered publishing dates were used, regardless of where publication occurred. Since the research for this

book took place in the United States, U.S. publishing dates for some selections were the only dates available. In a few entries, the date given is the date of authorship, with the date of publishing included in parentheses. This was done in those cases where works were published a considerable time after creation.

It is interesting to note that many openers are remarkably similar, and a few are even identical. Often, similar openers appear under the same topic, but occasionally they are similar in aspects of structure and not subject matter. Others have intentionally been written to mimic openers of previous and more famous books. (For some examples of this phenomenon, see entries 1114, 4713, 4765, 4791, 4798, and 4815.) Authors are influenced by other authors, and they often echo sentiments or techniques they have admired in predecessors or contemporaries.

There are two indexes to aid the reader, each citing entry numbers rather than page numbers. The second, the Index of Authors and Titles, is self-explanatory; the first, the Index of Subjects, Key Words and Key Phrases (hereafter referred to as the subject index), combines several functions. One is to list subject matter that appears in an entry but that differs from the topic heading under which the entry is located. Some such subjects are identical to other topic headings (i.e., those under which the book is not found), but generally they are narrower and more specific than the topic headings. Subjects may also be names of real persons, countries, institutions, and states.

A second major element of the subject index is a thorough listing of keywords-in-context. Keyword entries in the index are identified by quotation marks. The keyword itself is listed first, followed by trailing words, then by a comma, then by the words preceding the keyword in the text. The use of commas to separate the keywords from their preceding words unfortunately necessitated the deletion of natural commas from some entries, but the instances in which this

minor surgery was performed are fairly obvious and do not significantly damage the authors' intents.

For years that are keywords, numerals are used exclusively in the index regardless of the form used in the opener. (In the body of the book, however, years are spelled out if the opener renders them that way.)

The various strategies used in the building of the subject index afford even further insight into the methods and techniques of writing opening lines of fiction. The authors in this collection are ingenious in their attempts to lure the reader, and do so by using the best weapons at their disposal: their wits and the English language. The subject index, if nothing else, is a striking illustration of the nearly limitless utility of our language and of the ingenuity of many of our best writers. Openers, as you will see within, provide them with a challenging way to exhibit their very best skills.

A Note on the Purity of Text

Observant readers will occasionally note what appear to be typographical errors in the quoted opening lines. It would be folly to warrant that the present volume is entirely free of mistakes, but as a rule the reader may safely assume that these eccentricities of spelling, grammar and punctuation have been faithfully reproduced from the novels. Many are rather easily identified as archaic forms, deliberately peculiar stylistic choices, or errors designed to reveal something about the speaker or narrator; see, for example, the opening of Mary Roberts Rinehart's 1917 novel *Bab*: "I have decided to relate with Presision what occurred during my recent Christmas holaday." Others look more like simple typos: "Most of my life Ive been confused" (*Snakes*, Al Young, 1970) or "...dressed in a suit of black garbardine" (*The Missolonghi Manuscript*, Frederic Prokosch, 1968). And a few might even be true errors: "'It's going to a

great nuisance for both of us,' said Freddy" (Robertson Davies, *Tempest-Tost*, 1951) or "...a great and goodly city by the sea which had to name Langton on Holm" (*The Wood Beyond the World*, William Morris, 1894). But all of these, and numerous other suspicious-looking examples, are true to the actual novels, each of which was physically pulled from a shelf and scrutinized. Those selections that appeared defective in some way, upon subsequent readings of the transcriptions, were double-checked for accuracy. It is important to note, however, that later editions of a book may either introduce errors or correct old ones, so the opening lines as rendered here may not match all editions of the novels. The original edition or a facsimile, as noted earlier, was used as the source whenever possible. All British spellings have been left intact, except for the addition of periods behind abbreviations and the use of double quotes instead of single. This effort to remain as close as possible to the original versions may perpetuate some unintended oddities, but it seemed the most ethical and efficient method of eliminating subjectivity and avoiding editorial intrusions in those cases, not always certain, when the errors were introduced to serve a literary purpose. The result is the truest possible rendition of the novel openers.

References

Burnett, Hallie, and Whit Burnett. *Fiction Writer's Handbook*. New York: Harper & Row, 1975.

Gardner, John. *The Art of Fiction*. New York: Alfred A. Knopf, 1984.

Guthrie, A. B., Jr. *A Field Guide to Writing Fiction*. New York: HarperCollins, 1991.

Hodgins, Jack. *A Passion for Narrative*. New York: St. Martin's, 1994.

Plimpton, George, ed. *The Writer's Chapbook*. New York: Viking Penguin, 1989.

Ability

1 When Warren Hastings became Governor-General of India in the year 1773, he had among his associates a young man whose abilities, if somewhat less than those of his chief, were so peculiarly marked that Hastings soon found it necessary to decide whether this person was to be broken as an enemy or raised to the illustrious eminence of a friend. — *Jennifer Lorn*, Elinor Wylie, 1923.

2 "Brilliant performance," said the brown man, expansively. — *The Blackmailer*, Isabel Colegate, 1958.

3 "Is this chap really as good as you say?" asked Harold Meers. — *Girl, 20*, Kingsley Amis, 1972.

4 Mr. Skelding was doing what some men would have found more difficult. — *In Their Wisdom*, C. P. Snow, 1974.

5 He was the greatest natural talent I've ever seen. — *A Star in the Family*, Irvin Faust, 1975.

6 Dear Rob,/ I just asked Miss Appleton to put us on the same team for the spelling bee. Since we're the only two people in the fourth grade who can spell "perspicacious," our team is sure to win. — *A Woman of Independent Means*, Elizabeth Forsythe Hailey, 1978.

7 No one else could have done the job. — *Damages*, Helena Harlow Worthen, 1986.

8 It's Frank's turn. He's really good. — *How Old Was Lolita?*, Alan Saperstein, 1987.

9 The man is fast. The fastest fucker in town, no lie. — *Home Boy*, Jimmy Chesire, 1989.

10 Lord, Wylie thought, the dive Amos "Pinky" Cody could do, a slow half gainer off the high board at the Pinnacle Rock Club, the dive a work of art, a sculpturing of flesh over a shimmering turquoise plane. — *Furors Die*, William Hoffman, 1989.

11 When Michael's mother said her three nieces could have been hotel girls, she didn't mean anything cheap. — *The Incubator Ballroom*, John Rolfe Gardiner, 1991.

12 Father Gunn knew that their housekeeper Mrs. Kennedy could have done it all much better than he would do it. — *The Copper Beech*, Maeve Binchy, 1992.

13 I type easily. — "Helen," Hollis Summers, 1992.

Accidents

14 A gentleman, noteworthy for a lively countenance and a waistcoat to match it, crossing London Bridge at noon on a gusty April day, was almost magically detached from his conflict with the gale by some sly strip of slipperiness, abounding in that conduit of the markets, which had more or less adroitly performed the trick upon preceding passengers, and now laid this one flat amid the shuffle of feet, peaceful for the moment as the uncomplaining who have gone to Sabrina beneath the tides. — *One of Our Conquerors*, George Meredith, 1891.

15 On Friday noon, July the twentieth, 1714, the finest bridge in all Peru broke and precipitated five travellers into the gulf below. — *The Bridge of San Luis Rey*, Thornton Wilder, 1927.

16 Her right ankle turned under her and she fell. — *Woman in the Dark*, Dashiell Hammett, 1933.

17 "Was anyone hurt?"/ "No one I am thankful to say," said Mrs. Beaver, "except two housemaids who lost their heads and jumped through a glass roof into the paved court. . . ." — *A Handful of Dust*, Evelyn Waugh, 1934.

18 Peter guessed that he must have been hurt in the accident though he could not remember very much from the time he had left the safety of Scotch Nanny's side and run out across the street to get to the garden in the square, where the tabby striped kitten was warming herself by the railing and washing in the early spring sunshine. — *The Abandoned*, Paul Gallico, 1950.

19 The traffic policemen and the two detectives from the homicide squad examined the tracks of the car and were convinced that a soft shoulder of the road had given way. — *World So Wide*, Sinclair Lewis, 1951.

20 John Sinnott cut his hand trying to raise a stuck window in the downstairs bathroom. — *A Charmed Life*, Mary McCarthy, 1955.

21 That afternoon Mr. Surujpat Harbans nearly killed the two white women and the black bitch. — *The Suffrage of Elvira*, V. S. Naipaul, 1958.

22 When he was nearly thirteen, my brother Jem got his arm badly broken at the elbow. — *To Kill a Mockingbird*, Harper Lee, 1960.

23 "She fell down." — *Kate and Emma*, Monica Dickens, 1964.

24 He came tumbling down the stairs head over heels cursing as his skull collided with each angled joining of riser and tread, wincing whenever a new step rushed up to meet him, and thinking all the while How *dare* he do this to me,

a good old friend like me? — *A Horse's Head*, Evan Hunter, 1967.

25 Arkansas. On that day, many years ago, a truck carrying a number of migratory workers collided with a car on a country highway. — *A Garden of Earthly Delights*, Joyce Carol Oates, 1967.

26 In those days, if you got something in your eye, you headed for the nearest drugstore. — *A Thousand Summers*, Garson Kanin, 1973.

27 Brenda was six when she fell out of the apple tree. — *The Executioner's Song*, Norman Mailer, 1979.

28 Once, such a long time ago his mother was still a little girl, a man came by to pick the cherry tree and as soon as he climbed up into the limbs, he began tasting the cherries and making faces and he told the little girl and her mother the cherries were sour and he would have to come back another time when the cherries were ripe — but he didn't come down, he stayed up there tasting cherries a long time, and with all the weight he was putting on by tasting all those cherries he broke a limb, and that broke the mother's heart and she yelled, and the man fell out of the tree and limped away with red juice on his chin and he never came back — and since that time such a long time ago, no one has ever been allowed to climb the cherry tree. — *Young Heart*, William Harry Harding, 1903.

29 Not many miles from the hill on which I stood they were prying great chunks of concrete off the mangled bodies of children. — *Prince of Peace*, James Carroll, 1984.

30 The accident happened on one of the few sunny mornings during the otherwise wet and windy summer of 1931. — *The Raging of the Sea*, Charles Gidley, 1984.

31 Henry got hit about six A.M. — *Opening Nights*, Janet Burroway, 1985.

32 "On March 21, 19–, as he raced down a path in the outlying hills of the Whale Back, a man lost his footing. His fall from the footholds cut into the rock high above the bay left him unconscious and terribly mutilated. . . ." — *Face*, Cecile Pineda, 1985.

33 Trapped. Crushed. Weight coming from all directions, entangled in the wreckage (you have to become one with the machine). — *The Bridge*, Iain Banks, 1986.

34 I don't know how I missed him from two inches away, but I did. Still, that gunshot scared the hell out of him and he jumped back, then lost his balance and fell backwards, cracking the back of his head on the corner of the hi-fi console. I found out the next day that he was in the hospital for being a vegetable. — *Experiments with Life and Death*, Chuck Rosenthal, 1987.

35 Within one hour of arriving in Pickett,

Philip Pearl almost broke his neck. — *Pearl's Progress*, James Kaplan, 1989.

36 When the man was injured so near their gate, the nuns said it was God's will. — *The Age of Miracles*, Catherine MacCoun, 1989.

37 Just before noon on Friday, the scaffolding snapped. — *Sleepwalker*, Michael Cadnum, 1991.

38 The sky collapsed like an old roof in an avalanche of rock and boulder, cracking me on the noggin and crushing me to the pavement. — *China Boy*, Gus Lee, 1991.

39 Tip of my shoe just snapped off. Cracked like an eggshell. — *Topless*, D. Keith Mano, 1991.

40 The rented Toyota, driven with such impatient exuberance by The Senator, was speeding along the unpaved unnamed road, taking the turns in giddy skidding slides, and then, with no warning, somehow the car had gone off the road and had overturned in black rushing water, listing to its passenger's side, rapidly sinking. — *Black Water*, Joyce Carol Oates, 1992.

41 Because he wasn't wearing his spectacles, he didn't see her pedalling painfully along the gutter beside him in the dark and the rain, and in consequence, he knocked her gently off her bicycle. — *The Men and the Girls*, Joanna Trollope, 1992.

42 *It isn't until several days after the accident that Lottie lets herself — makes herself — think about it.* — *For Love*, Sue Miller, 1993.

Adversity

43 I was born in 1843. Since then I have endured many perils, of which I shall try to tell you. — *The Hand-Made Gentleman*, Irving Bacheller, 1909.

44 "Unexpected obstacle. Please don't come till thirtieth. Anna." — *The Reef*, Edith Wharton, 1912.

45 How many swords had Lady Beveridge in her pierced heart! Yet there always seemed room for another. — "The Ladybird," D. H. Lawrence, 1923.

46 More acutely than ever before Emma Lou began to feel that her luscious black complexion was somewhat of a liability, and that her marked color variation from the other people in her environment was a decided curse. — *The Blacker the Berry . . .*, Wallace Thurman, 1929.

47 It was clearly going to be a bad crossing. — *Vile Bodies*, Evelyn Waugh, 1930.

48 "No, not really," Mary was saying. "No, it

didn't really help things much." — *The Memorial*, Christopher Isherwood, 1932.

49 Things were going none too well this morning, the vicar thought. — *The Shadow Flies*, Rose Macaulay, 1932.

50 In order to pay off an old debt that some-one else had contracted, Austin King had said yes when he knew that he ought to have said no, and now at five o'clock of a July afternoon he saw the grinning face of trouble everywhere he turned. — *Time Will Darken It*, William Maxwell, 1948.

51 "It's going to a great nuisance for both of us," said Freddy. "Couldn't you make a fuss about it, Tom?" — *Tempest-Tost*, Robertson Davies, 1951.

52 "I cannot be patriotic, God, because I have been through it all before." — *Song in the Night*, Josephine Lawrence, 1952.

53 It takes courage to be courageous said Mrs. Reynolds. — *Mrs. Reynolds*, Gertrude Stein, 1952.

54 *She wore her trauma like a plume.* — *The Judgment of Paris*, Gore Vidal, 1952.

55 When the winds of Heaven blow, men are inclined to throw back their heads like horses, and stride ruggedly into the gusts, pretending to be much healthier than they really are; but women tend to creep about, shrunk into their clothes, and clutching miserably at their hats and hair. — *The Winds of Heaven*, Monica Dickens, 1955.

56 When it came to concealing his troubles, Tommy Wilhelm was not less capable than the next fellow. — "*Seize the Day*," Saul Bellow, 1956.

57 When I was a young boy, if I was sick or in trouble, or had been beaten at school, I used to remember that on the day I was born my father had wanted to kill me. — *The Last of the Wine*, Mary Renault, 1956.

58 I cannot read, I cannot think, I cannot write. — *The Woman of My Life*, Ludwig Bemelmans, 1957.

59 For the first time in months Blainey was held up at the dock gates. He sat in his little Italian car, looking into the soldier's face. — *Revolution and Roses*, P. H. Newby, 1957.

60 *Nothing ever goes right.* — *Pinktoes*, Chester Himes, 1961.

61 They say when trouble comes close ranks, and so the white people did. — *Wide Sargasso Sea*, Jean Rhys, 1966.

62 Did things ever get so outlandishly rock-bottom rotten that you went around muttering, not necessarily out loud, but muttering nonetheless: *I don't believe it!* — *P.S. Your Cat Is Dead!*, James Kirkwood, 1972.

63 The worst week in my life began that morning in 1948 when I got rid of Janice: as rid of Janice as I am ever going to be. — *A Good Confession*, Elizabeth Savage, 1975.

64 Everything began to go wrong for Janice Wilder in the late summer of 1960. — *Disturbing the Peace*, Richard Yates, 1975.

65 Out of the woods. / How do I feel? — *Half a Marriage*, Violet Weingarten, 1976.

66 It was a bad time. — *Going After Cacciato*, Tim O'Brien, 1978.

67 The troubles began in January, in the cold, dark part of the year. — *Rachel, the Rabbi's Wife*, Silvia Tennenbaum, 1978.

68 "I do not need this shit," Terry Mooney said. — *The Rat on Fire*, George V. Higgins, 1981.

69 God don't give you more than you can bear, I say. — *The Wine of Astonishment*, Earl Lovelace, 1982.

70 On the Ides of March, in his forty-fifth year, the neutral if not cooperative world turned on Mr. Raleigh W. Hayes as sharply as if it had stabbed him with a knife. — *Handling Sin*, Michael Malone, 1986.

71 Anyways ... my name is Lisa Perlman, and you don't know what I've been through. — *So Long, Princess*, Barbara Brooker, 1987.

72 Last week was a killer-diller! — *Such Was the Season*, Clarence Major, 1987.

73 Jesus Christ what a fucking wreck I am, my face looks a hundred years old, people would scream if I went out on the streets, my hair's all falling out, there's a woman from the Milk Marketing Board trying to kill me. — *Milk, Sulphate and Alby Starvation*, Martin Millar, 1987.

74 "And then say what? Say, 'Forget you're hungry, forget you got shot inna back by some racist cop — Chuck was here? Chuck come up to Harlem —'" — *The Bonfire of the Vanities*, Tom Wolfe, 1987.

75 I was trying to survive. Every night was a torment to me during which I prayed God not to let me jump out of the window and kill myself. — *Don Juan in the Village*, Jane DeLynn, 1990.

76 Now that the dust has settled, we can begin to look at our situation. — *A Place of Greater Safety*, Hilary Mantel, 1992.

77 I have been in the avant-garde in New York — the avant-garde of losing money. A front-runner of the downwardly mobile. Precocious in tragedy — first on the block to reach widowhood. — *Smart Hearts in the City*, Barbara Probst Solomon, 1992.

78 The snow in the mountains was melting and Bunny had been dead for several weeks before we came to understand the gravity of our situation. — *The Secret History*, Donna Tartt, 1992.

Age

79 Frau von Sigmundskron was not really much past middle age, though the people in the village generally called her the old baroness. — *Greifenstein*, F. Marion Crawford, 1889.

80 Miss Elizabeth Mapp might have been forty, and she had taken advantage of this opportunity by being just a year or two older. — *Miss Mapp*, E. F. Benson, 1922.

81 Until Alwyn Tower grew to manhood he never forgot that everyone was older than he. — *The Grandmothers*, Glenway Wescott, 1927.

82 "Well, Buttermere, this is a day that is good to live and breathe in, that makes a man feel in his prime. Standing here in front of my house, I feel as young as when I moved into it thirty years ago, in the year eighteen hundred and fifty-nine. What aged man would you take me to be, as I step as it were casually into your view?" — *Men and Wives*, Ivy Compton-Burnett, 1931.

83 He was at the prayer age. — *Knock on Any Door*, Willard Motley, 1947.

84 She had reached the age when in these ridiculous times you are required to stop instanter whatever you have been doing, no matter how well you did it yesterday, if it is anything anyone younger wants to do, or for which he wants the pay and the prestige. — *The Road Grows Strange*, Gladys Hasty Carroll, 1965.

85 In spite of his age, Avrom Glickman was still upright and slender. — *The Beginners*, Dan Jacobson, 1966.

86 Devar Moragoda was fifty-four years old, and that is a very decisive time if a man is suddenly obliged to examine his life. — *Lion in the Stone*, Henrietta Buckmaster, 1968.

87 The social worker was older than she had expected; perhaps the nameless official who arranged these matters thought that graying hair and menopausal plumpness might induce confidence in the adopted adults who came for their compulsory counseling. — *Innocent Blood*, P. D. James, 1980.

88 He was a young man in his late twenties, but looked younger. — *Threat*, Richard Jessup, 1981.

89 I am a child of my century and as old as the century. — *Byzantium Endures*, Michael Moorcock, 1981.

90 My mother said: "Tell me how old I am!" — *Scenes from Later Life*, William Cooper, 1983.

91 By age thirty-eight, I had reached my stride and was lucky enough to know it. — *Coming Back Up*, Suzanne Lipsett, 1985.

92 I am the vampire Lestat. I'm immortal. More or less. The light of the sun, the sustained heat of an intense fire — these things might destroy me. But then again, they might not. — *The Vampire Lestat*, Anne Rice, 1986.

93 The teak from which the chair was cut was old when China was young. — *Born Burning*, Thomas Sullivan, 1989.

94 The machinery's rusty, I acknowledge to my half-expected guest, but it hasn't seized up altogether. — *The Last Voyage of Somebody the Sailor*, John Barth, 1991.

95 *Wait a minute, he said, how old are you?* — *Slow Poison*, Sheila Bosworth, 1992.

Agedness

96 Although I am an old man, night is generally my time for walking. — *The Old Curiosity Shop*, Charles Dickens, 1840.

97 I am an old woman now, and things are very different to what they were in my youth. — *My Lady Ludlow*, Elizabeth Gaskell, 1859.

98 "I believe I am old," said the Doctor, pushing his straight-backed wooden chair from the table, and turning from his books to look out of his small window. "Yes, I am certainly very old," he said again, rapping absently on the arm of the chair with the pen he held. — *Doctor Claudius*, F. Marion Crawford, 1883.

99 The Reverend Augustin Ambrose would gladly have given up taking pupils. He was growing old and his sight was beginning to trouble him; he was weary of Thucydides, of Homer, of the works of Mr. Todhunter of which the green bindings expressed a hope still unrealised, of conic sections — even of his beloved Horace. — *A Tale of a Lonely Parish*, F. Marion Crawford, 1886.

100 The writer, an old man with a white mustache, had some difficulty in getting into bed. — *Winesburg, Ohio*, Sherwood Anderson, 1919.

101 "Old age will be served," said Mrs. Carteret grimly. "But I suppose you think I am a long time dying." — *The Crystal Cup*, Gertrude Atherton, 1925.

102 Henry Lyulph Holland, first Earl of Slane, had existed for so long that the public had begun to regard him as immortal. — *All Passion Spent*, V. Sackville-West, 1931.

103 When you are getting on in years (but not ill, of course), you get very sleepy at times, and the hours seem to pass like lazy cattle moving across a landscape. — *Good-bye, Mr. Chips*, James Hilton, 1934.

104 I am old now and have not much to fear from the anger of gods. — *Till We Have Faces*, C. S. Lewis, 1956.

105 Karl Mueller was an old-timer in the deep south-west of Western Australia. — *Bony and the White Savage*, Arthur W. Upfield, 1961.

106 I have been young and now am old. — *Morning Noon and Night*, James Gould Cozzens, 1968.

107 I am not mad, only old. — *As We Are Now*, May Sarton, 1973.

108 Nothing is more shocking about old age than the speed with which even the most famous persons are isolated and forgotten. — *The House of the Prophet*, Louis Auchincloss, 1980.

109 Elizabeth was not crazy, she was old. — *Kill Memory*, William Herrick, 1983.

110 As she is perfectly well aware, they look at her as they would look at a relic, with the same rude wonder they might feel for the knucklebone of St. So-and-so in its gorgeous gem-encrusted receptacle of tarnished silver. — *Alice at 80*, David R. Slavitt, 1984.

111 "No point in being eighty, is there?" said Liza. "If you can't be a bit outrageous?" — *The Century's Daughter*, Pat Barker, 1986.

112 Mrs. Exley felt doomed, but she also felt good about it. — *The Forest of Arden*, Don Robertson, 1986.

113 My mother lived to be old, although she always said she would die young. — *Her Mother's Daughter*, Marilyn French, 1987.

114 The old woman — eighty if she's a day — distorts perspective, throws off scale. — *Mamaw*, Susan Dodd, 1988.

115 In isolated rural areas there are many elderly people who have difficulty getting their toenails cut. — *Taking the Biscuit*, Faith Addis, 1989.

116 Until this afternoon Bet had looked forward to a ripe old senility, to playing hide-and-seek with words and memories in a mist of pleasant confusion. — *In Full Possession*, Helen Flint, 1989.

117 Now that I am old and often still, I no longer believe what I once believed, that motion is the opposite of stillness. — *The Dance of the Mothers*, Millicent Dillon, 1991.

118 The old Gullah granny woman was an ancient thing, as old, it almost seemed, as Tawabaw Island itself. — *Looker*, Michael Kilian, 1991.

119 Oliver Oliphant was one hundred years old and his mind was as clear as a bell. Unfortunately for him. — *The Fourth K*, Mario Puzo, 1991.

Ailments

120 It was about the Beginning of *September* 1664, that I, among the Rest of my Neighbours, heard in ordinary Discourse, that the Plague was return'd again in *Holland*; for it had been very violent there, and particularly at *Amsterdam* and *Roterdam*, in the Year 1663, whither *they say*, it was brought, some said from *Italy*, others from the *Levant* among some Goods, which were brought home by their Turkey Fleet; others said it was brought from *Candia*; others from *Cyprus*. It matter'd not, from whence it come; but all agreed, it was come into *Holland* again. — *A Journal of the Plague Year*, Daniel Defoe, 1722.

121 I put on my hat, and walked at once to the Doctor's house. "Yes," said I, musingly, "I am certainly in a consumption. I may as well, like Colonel Jones, leave my poor remains to the surgeons at once, and enjoy the newspaper credit of my generosity before I die. . . ." — *Asmodeus at Large*, Edward Bulwer-Lytton, 1833.

122 In default of a screen, a gown and a red petticoat had been thrown over a clothes-horse, and these had shaded the glare of the lamp from the eyes of the sick man. — *A Mummer's Wife*, George Moore, 1885.

123 "Stay here beside her, major. I shall not be needed for an hour yet. Meanwhile I'll go downstairs and snatch a bit of sleep, or talk to old Jane." — *The Marrow of Tradition*, Charles Waddell Chesnutt, 1901.

124 "But the man's almost dead." — *The Heritage of the Desert*, Zane Grey, 1910.

125 Because Edith had not been feeling very well, that seemed no reason why she should be the centre of interest; and Bruce, with that jealousy of the privileges of the invalid and in that curious spirit of rivalry which his wife had so often observed, had started, with enterprise, an indisposition of his own, as if to divert public attention. — *Tenterhooks*, Ada Leverson, 1912.

126 The bishop was feeling rather sea-sick. Confoundedly sea-sick, in fact. — *South Wind*, Norman Douglas, 1917.

127 Neither her Gaudiness the Mistress of the Robes nor her Dreaminess the Queen were feeling quite themselves. — *The Flower Beneath the Foot*, Ronald Firbank, 1923.

128 I have wrenched my knee, and for the past two weeks my days have consisted of three trays, two of them here in the library, a nurse at ten o'clock each morning with a device of infernal origin which is supposed to bake the pain out of my leg, and my thoughts for company. — *The Door*, Mary Roberts Rinehart, 1930.

129 Although she herself was ill enough to justify being in bed had she been a person weak-minded enough to give up, Rose Sayer could see that her brother, the Reverend Samuel Sayer, was far more ill. — *The African Queen*, C. S. Forester, 1935.

130 Katherine knew, before the first act was half over, that something was wrong with Manya. — *Prelude*, Madeleine L'Engle, 1945.

131 The bulky ambulance-driver pushed a thin pillow beneath Eric's head and covered his long body with a clean white sheet. — *Boy Almighty*, Frederick Manfred *as* Feike Feikema, 1945.

132 Ralph was ten and Molly was eight when they had scarlet fever. — *The Mountain Lion*, Jean Stafford, 1947.

133 It happens to millions. — *Opus 21*, Philip Wylie, 1949.

134 A minute or two before or after two-thirty on the afternoon of the twenty-second of June, Avery Bullard suffered what was subsequently diagnosed as a cerebral hemorrhage. — *Executive Suite*, Cameron Hawley, 1952.

135 Like all Frenchmen who have to earn their living, Pierre Deschamps was never happy unless his wife was working at his side, and so this thirteenth day of July, 1870, his twenty-sixth birthday, he spent in a sense of vague uneasiness because his wife Anne was unwell. *A Rose for Marianne*, F. T. Giles, 1955.

136 It was all right till the bus had to stop for the first freight train, but after that, Max Fallon knew he was going to be sick. — *Rock*, David Wagoner, 1958.

137 This morning — cold and fresh with a pale sun reluctantly administering sudden jabs of heat — Dick felt the whole burden of his illness like an enemy triumphantly straddling his chest. — *The Vodi*, John Braine, 1959.

138 A week after Lucy got her scholarship to Oxford, her uncle, Bob Low, had a stroke. — *Glass Slippers Always Pinch*, Nina Bawden, 1960.

139 In the calefactory Brother Thomas's illness was discussed with a certain restraint, since nobody seemed quite sure how far one could go in anticipating his death with good taste. — *The Foxglove Saga*, Auberon Waugh, 1960.

140 "You know anybody in Arizona?" the doctor said./ "No," Roak Garfield said. — *The Garfield Honor*, Frank Yerby, 1961.

141 Suspecting myself of a cardiac disease, I went one morning to Harley Street to see Setter who had been recommended to me by my doctor. — *An Error of Judgement*, Pamela Hansford Johnson, 1962.

142 At first, Hilda, one hand pressed against the wall, had only retched. Three spasms had shaken her, brought her head down before the finger of bone foreshortened on the scaling plaster, the skull faded from white to gray in its monk's cowl. Then she had leaned across the railing to puke. — *The Second Stone*, Leslie Fiedler, 1963.

143 As Roy Dillon stumbled out of the shop his face was a sickish green, and each breath he drew was an incredible agony. — *The Grifters*, Jim Thompson, 1963.

144 The heart attack was strange — fear is strange. — *Tell Me How Long the Train's Been Gone*, James Baldwin, 1968.

145 Daniel Kaminer was suddenly taken ill. — *The Estate*, Isaac Bashevis Singer, 1969.

146 I am a sick man, I am a spiteful man. I think my life is diseased. — *Nightspawn*, John Banville, 1971.

147 The old woman's head was barely fretting against the pillow. She could have moaned slightly. — *The Eye of the Storm*, Patrick White, 1973.

148 "How's your leg this morning, Bernard?" asked Adela Bastable. — *Ending Up*, Kingsley Amis, 1974.

149 You know how long Mama was sick. — *The Mystic Adventures of Roxie Stoner*, Berry Morgan, 1974.

150 A womaniser approaching eighty, especially one who has womanised for far longer than appears credible, let alone decent, cannot be surprised when medical opinion pronounces him practically off the hooks. — *The Faithful Servants*, Margery Sharp, 1975.

151 The boy, Diego Fernández, lifted the woman's stocking he was wearing over his face just high enough to free his left eye. Thin as the nylon was, seeing through it on a dark Parisian street at two o'clock in the morning wasn't easy. Breathing through it wasn't either, especially when you were dog sick and shaking and trying not to throw up. — *A Rose for Ana María*, Frank Yerby, 1976.

152 By now, my friend August was flat as a man of gingerbread, buckled at the knees and curled at the feet by too hot an oven, nibbled cruelly up and down his long limbs and sides. — *Going Blind*, Jonathan Penner, 1977.

153 "Oliver, you're sick." — *Oliver's Story*, Erich Segal, 1977.

154 He came to me from the sea and for many days it was all I knew of him or thought that I might ever know, he was so near to death when I found him. — *The Burning Woman*, Margaret Ritter, 1979.

155 In December, when the others, the lucky ones, were advancing on Tripoli, Simon Boulderstone was sent to the hospital at Helwan. — *The Sum of Things*, Olivia Manning, 1980.

156 Every summer Dinah was sick in this house she rented. — *Dale Loves Sophie to Death*, Robb Forman Dew, 1981.

157 I don't think, after all, that the Wednesday morning in April when it rained and I caught the cold was the beginning of it. — *Bed Rest*, Rita Kashner, 1981.

158 Naomi Silverstein suffered mostly from weak eyesight and poor feet. — *Reconciliations*, Elizabeth Klein, 1982.

159 Because his father had suffered a heart attack, Max Berenson was called away to Miami at the beginning of August 1956. — *Midnight Suppers*, Susan Monsky, 1983.

160 Frank Joiner first notices it when he goes to his right and makes backhand snags of ground balls hit hard down the line. — *The Greatest Slump of All Time*, David Carkeet, 1984.

161 Edith Goodnough isn't in the country anymore. She's in town now, in the hospital, lying there in that white bed with a needle stuck in the back of one hand and a man standing guard in the hallway outside her room. — *The Tie That Binds*, Kent Haruf, 1984.

162 "Mr. . . .'"; the doctor paused and had a quick look at his notes, the subject being inescapably personal. "Mr. Keller. Sorry. Mr. Kestler. You have no living relatives then, is that right? No brother? No sister? A close friend perhaps? . . ." — *The Cabalist*, Amanda Prantera, 1985.

163 Dr. Liat Bloom looked at her watch again, then reappraised the recalcitrant heart. — *Bread and Stones*, Ellen Alexander Conley, 1986.

164 Every time they got a call from the leper hospital to pick up a body Jack Delaney would feel himself coming down with the flu or something. — *Bandits*, Elmore Leonard, 1987.

165 For some time now I have noticed that something strange is occurring in our region. — *The Thanatos Syndrome*, Walker Percy, 1987.

166 *Ever since the family doctor, during a routine checkup, discovered an abnormality on his EKG and he went in overnight for the coronary catheterization that revealed the dimensions of the disease, Henry's condition had been successfully treated with drugs, enabling him to work and to carry on his life at home exactly as before.* — *The Counterlife*, Philip Roth, 1987.

167 In the spring of that year an epidemic of rabies broke out in Ether County, Georgia. — *Paris Trout*, Pete Dexter, 1988.

168 He lies there. *Hic jacet*, for indeed he looks like one of those figures carved in marble on a catafalque. — *Salazar Blinks*, David R. Slavitt, 1988.

169 In thirteen forty-nine plague stalked Europe, skull-visaged, gibbering. — *The Love Knot*, Catherine Darby, 1989.

170 Maggie Sullivan was not a well woman. — *Tangled Up in Blue*, Larry Duplechan, 1989.

171 The new epidemic spreads like spilt quicksilver from tip to tip of the island, from the sierras to the bays. — *Latin Jazz*, Virgil Suarez, 1989.

172 KORRHEA: (also *co-rhea*) a particularly pernicious combination of dysentery and the clap contracted during a single debauch. — *Perchan's Chorea*, Robert Perchan, 1991.

173 "You don't remember polio, do you?" Juanita wants to know. — *In the Spanish Ballroom*, Doris Rochlin, 1991.

174 When we were eleven, Helen Walsh fell sick with something I'd never heard of, something that would be with her, inside of her, for the rest of her life. — *Augusta Cotton*, Margaret Erhart, 1992.

Air

175 A cloudy day: do you know what that is in a town of iron-works? The sky sank down before dawn, muddy flat, immovable. The air is thick, clammy with the breath of crowded human beings. It stifles me. — *Life in the Iron Mills*, Rebecca Harding Davis, 1861.

176 As Clayton rose to his feet in the still air, the tree-tops began to tremble in the gap below him, and a rippling ran through the leaves up the mountain-side. — *A Mountain Europa*, John Fox, Jr., 1899.

177 There had been much rain during the night, and the morning air was still saturated with moisture, heavy and oppressive, and yet with a suspicion of chill about it, enough to make flies sluggish and men and women slow in their movements. — *The Sky and the Forest*, C. S. Forester, 1948.

178 Snow from yesterday's fall still lay in patches and the morning air was glacial. — *The Valley of Bones*, Anthony Powell, 1964.

179 The first thing I noticed was the clarity of the air, and then the sharp green colour of the land. — *The House on the Strand*, Daphne du Maurier, 1969.

180 "Smell that air," said Major Mann. — *Catch a Falling Spy*, Len Deighton, 1976.

181 The night air above nine thousand feet was black and cold and very smooth. — *The Herald*, Michael Shaara, 1981.

182 Once every summer a mass of humid air settled over Lunsbury, Missouri. — *The Time of Her Life*, Robb Forman Dew, 1984.

183 The air was getting thick—if you like calling a garotte of diesel and greasy dirt "air"—and so before the burning rain began I stepped into the McDonald's. — *The Stars at Noon*, Denis Johnson, 1986.

184 What was that cold rush of air, frightening the papers on my table so that they rustled and fluttered?—*A Mirror for Princes*, Tom De Haan, 1987.

185 The air lay as heavy as water in the square dark rooms of the farmhouse. — *Eden Close*, Anita Shreve, 1989.

186 *If you come as most do, down 17, it's around Elizabeth City that the air gets the first sting of salt and handfuls of lost and disoriented gulls circle dumpsters.* — *Up Through the Water*, Darcey Steinke, 1989.

187 I spent my time in the frozen air. — *Calm at Sunset, Calm at Dawn*, Paul Watkins, 1989.

188 The cool air was a welcome shock. — *Mirage*, Pauline Gedge, 1990.

189 Between them, pure alcohol coiled from the turned-back lid; the air curled with its distortion. Vaporous, the face stretched longer and thinner than the pillar it began. The shimmer off the vat worried his expression, tortured his eyebrows in the heat, further emphasizing a figure already overdrawn: too wild, too skinny, too tall. — *The Bleeding Heart*, Lionel Shriver, 1990.

190 The atmosphere in the sickroom was stifling. — *The Peculiar People*, Jan de Hartog, 1992.

191 The air in the cave was quiet. — *The Horsemasters*, Joan Wolf, 1993.

Aircraft and Aviation

---

192 "VICTORY! It flies! I am master of the Powers of the Air at last!" — *The Angel of the Revolution*, George Griffith, 1894.

193 High up in the pale Flemish sky aeroplanes were wheeling and darting like bright-coloured insects, catching from one moment to another the glint of sun on metallic body or translucent wing. — *The Crime at Vanderlynden's*, R. H. Mottram, 1926.

194 How wonderful was that first day on the great airship.—*Swiss Family Manhattan*, Christopher Morley, 1932.

195 We swooped down and hit the concrete alongside the Potomac at 1:20 P.M. on a raw Monday in early March. — "Not Quite Dead Enough"—Rex Stout, 1942.

196 I came into aviation the hard way. I was never in the R.A.F., and my parents hadn't got fifteen hundred pounds to spend on pilot training for me at a flying school. — *Round the Bend*, Nevil Shute, 1951.

197 There was a layer of cumulus, about seven-tenths, with tops at about five thousand feet as we came to Essendon airport; we broke out of it at two thousand and we were on the circuit downwind, with the aerodrome on our starboard wing. — *The Breaking Wave*, Nevil Shute, 1955.

198 The weekly Dakota from Selampang had never been known to arrive at the valley airstrip before noon, or to leave on the return journey before one. — *The Night-Comers*, Eric Ambler, 1956.

199 The plane, a shabby old Dakota, bumped twice in the noon-day heat, then settled down on its steady course. — *The Tribe That Lost Its Head*, Nicholas Monsarrat, 1956.

200 The Chinese captain and the Malay second pilot worked stolidly through the check-list. — *The Enemy in the Blanket*, Anthony Burgess, 1958.

201 Suddenly the land was no longer there, and the airliner had lifted itself like a cripple grown used to his crutches. — *Of Age and Innocence*, George Lamming, 1958.

202 John Pascoe must have created something like a record for a pilot in civil aviation, because he went on flying a DC-6B across the Pacific from Sydney to Vancouver as a senior captain of AusCan Airways till he was sixty years old. — *The Rainbow and the Rose*, Nevil Shute, 1958.

203 Sam Hassoon watched his friend Captain Ali Zareef, an Egyptian and also a Mohammedan, landing a small Auster. Zareef's flying was rather like Zareef himself—rounded and friendly and professional. — *The Last Exile*, James Aldridge, 1961.

204 We left Kelly Field in a bucket-seat C-47, nineteen officers in all, I alone headed for Colfax. — *Captain Newman, M.D.*, Leo Rosten, 1961.

205 A Dakota of the Royal Air Force Transport Command flying over the polar ice along the 87th meridian, north of Grant Land, had sighted a strange incandescent blue stain on the sun-soaked ice. — *A Captive in the Land*, James Aldridge, 1962.

206 At last and finally! Iris thought when the plane sped away from Boston, where they had been forced to land because of fog in New York. — *Sissie*, John A. Williams, 1963.

207 If the Bastard hadn't been behaving herself, I wouldn't have had time to look out for the girl. But that afternoon, the Bastard acted like a lady, and I had never flown so well. — *Sword of Honour*, David Beaty, 1965.

208 At a quarter past twelve on a night in the early spring of 1962 a jet sighed tiredly and fell silent near a shed that reached toward the runways of Idlewild Airport. — *They Both Were Naked*, Philip Wylie, 1965.

209 *All day long the sleek little planes and the clumsy-looking helicopters had criss-crossed the hills, flying low and yet out of reach of possible rifle shot.* — *This Island, Now*, Peter Abrahams, 1967.

210 Because even if Lightnings are faster than Grummans I wouldn't fly in an Army plane. — *American Scrapbook*, Jerome Charyn, 1969.

211 Molly would have preferred a day flight (when she was with Mike, they always tried to save time by flying at night) because streaking through the trackless dark gave her a sense of circling from nowhere to nowhere. — *A Loving Wife*, Violet Weingarten, 1969.

212 A military plane crashed that winter on Mount Vesuvius. — *The Bay of Noon*, Shirley Hazzard, 1970.

213 "Your aircraft, sah, will be landing in two hours' time." — *The Temple Tree*, David Beaty, 1971.

214 It was nine-thirty and Virgil Haynes and Agnes McCoy were parked on top of Needle Hill watching the Piedmont and Delta flights coming in from Atlanta. — *Ruby Red*, William Price Fox, 1971.

215 Aimed at vacancy and unimpeachably erect, the space pencil belched and lifted free. As if for all time. — *Colonel Mint*, Paul West, 1972.

216 High, high above the North Pole, on the first day of 1969, two professors of English Literature approached each other at a combined velocity of 1200 miles per hour. — *Changing Places*, David Lodge, 1975.

217 Early one evening in September of 1974 a small twin-engine plane, silver and black, sailed down onto a secondary runway at São Paulo's Congonhas Airport, and slowing, turned aside and taxied to a hangar where a limousine stood waiting. — *The Boys from Brazil*, Ira Levin, 1976.

218 The little plane circled prettily over Boonton, Vermont, no butterfly acoustically or in its purpose, though some were pleased to see it, for various reasons. — *Gloria Mundi*, Eleanor Clark, 1979.

219 The twin-engined Mitsubishi Zero-1 medium bomber, called a "Betty" by American forces, cruised on a westerly course across the southern end of the Gulf of Leyte. — *Silent Sea*, Harry Homewood, 1981.

220 As Jason stepped into the body of the aeroplane he thought — What does this remind me of? this hollow containing people staring at a blank wall: some image of the mind that for thousands of years has been in the mind: Plato's cave, where people sit with their backs to the sun and see the shadows cast on the wall in front; their intimations of reality. — *Serpent*, Nicholas Mosley, 1981.

221 He arrived in Korea in a snowstorm on a huge big-bellied aircraft named the *Thin Man*.

— *The Book of Lights*, Chaim Potok, 1981.

222 Under the pale outrage of a breaking sky, the plane thuds. — *The Tent Peg*, Aritha van Herk, 1981.

223 A March noon, and the Central European heaven full not only of grey scud but of aircraft of the Third Reich in a menacing dance celebratory of the wholly beneficent ends of the *Anschluss*: tranquillity, order, uniformity, protection from free thought, that sort of thing. — *The End of the World News*, Anthony Burgess, 1982.

224 All morning, far over to his left where the light of the swamp ended and farmlands began, a clumsy shape had been lifting itself out of an invisible paddock and making slow circuits of the air, climbing, dipping, rolling a little, then disappearing below the trees. — "The Bread of Time to Come" — David Malouf, 1982.

225 The Freedom Bird grew from a silver speck in the sun and landed with a jarring shock and the stink of rubber. — *De Mojo Blues*, Arthur Flowers, 1985.

226 He was flying. — *Selling Out*, Dan Wakefield, 1985.

227 The single-engine Cessna 172 was a tiny blip on the radar screen at San Diego's Lindbergh Field. — *The Secrets of Harry Bright*, Joseph Wambaugh, 1985.

228 I was at McMurdo Station, the American base on Ross Island in Antarctica, when I received a radio communication from Kiwi Airways of New Zealand. It suggested that I be the flight commentator for their Flight Five Zero, scheduled for 29 November 1979 to commemorate the fiftieth anniversary of Richard E. Byrd's flight over the South Pole. — *Overflight*, Charles Neider, 1986.

229 The Jenny's engine coughed and missed all the way north from Hermosillo. — *A Time for Heroes*, Will Bryant, 1987.

230 One of the new Sikorsky gunships, an element of the First Air Cavalry with the words *Whispering Death* painted on its side, gave Mingolla and Gilbey and Baylor a lift from the Ant Farm to San Francisco de Juticlan, a small town located inside the green zone, which on the latest maps was designated Free Occupied Guatemala. — *Life During Wartime*, Lucius Shepard, 1987.

231 My husband, Nick Symonds, commuted to work in a seaplane. — *Crazy in Love*, Luanne Rice, 1988.

232 When I landed at Heathrow, the terminal was being remodeled. — *The Tormenting of Lafayette Jackson*, Andrew Rosenheim, 1988.

233 The best way to get a view of the Historic Museum Village of Copperfield is to hire a Fly-By-Nite helicopter. — *The Bluebird Café*, Carmel Bird, 1990.

234 Halifax flew in from the desert, a thousand feet above the sand. — *In the Blue Light of African Dreams*, Paul Watkins, 1990.

235 As the jetliner flew toward Cebu, it rattled like an old Ford on the freeway. — *Cebu*, Peter Bacho, 1991.

236 Blackout. Julian stares at the ceiling while the noise of a patrol helicopter drums into the room. — *The Cutter*, Virgil Suarez, 1991.

Ambition

237 There is nothing that human imagination can figure brilliant and enviable, that human genius and skill do not aspire to realize. — *St. Leon*, William Godwin, 1799.

238 Mrs. Stanhope, a well-bred woman, accomplished in that branch of knowledge which is called the art of rising in the world, had, with but a small fortune, contrived to live in the highest company. — *Belinda*, Maria Edgeworth, 1801.

239 You must go back with me to the autumn of 1827. My father, as you know, was a sort of gentleman farmer in ——shire; and I, by his express desire, succeeded him in the same quiet occupation, not very willingly, for ambition urged me to higher aims, and self-conceit assured me that, in disregarding its voice, I was burying my talent in the earth, and hiding my light under a bushel. — *The Tenant of Wildfell Hall*, Anne Brontë, 1848.

240 "Want to be a school-master, do you? You?..." — *The Hoosier School-Master*, Edward Eggleston, 1871.

241 Bunker Bean was wishing he could be different. — *Bunker Bean*, Harry Leon Wilson, 1913.

242 It had just occurred to Rob Ashton that for a young fellow of twenty-seven he had recently bitten off a big mouthful. — *Three Harbors*, F. van Wyck Mason, 1938.

243 The urgent whistle of the Manhattan Flyer woke the boy, and his square face moved with smiling as in half-dreams he was certain that some day he would take that train and be welcomed in lofty rooms by millionaires and poets and actresses. — *Gideon Planish*, Sinclair Lewis, 1943.

244 "When I grow up I want to be an American," Giustina said. We looked at our sister; it was something none of us had ever said. — *Mount Allegro*, Jerre Mangione, 1943.

245 I am an American, Chicago born — Chicago, that somber city — and go at things as I have taught myself, free-style, and will make the record in my own way: first to knock, first admitted; sometimes an innocent knock, sometimes a not so innocent. — *The Adventures of Augie March*, Saul Bellow, 1953.

246 We were sitting side by side on the rails of the training track fence: John Callant with his long upper lip moving up and down over his chew of tobacco, Doone's gold watch in his fist, and his impudent blue eyes following the prances of Blue Dandy as Doone limbered him up along the backstretch; and myself, a boy of twelve, bare-legged, dividing my attention between the horse and John Callant's mouth, for he had a neat way of spitting that someday I intended to master, just as I dreamed someday of being old enough to hold the lines over the back of one of Uncle Ledyard's trotters. — *The Boyds of Black River*, Walter D. Edmonds, 1953.

247 In his pale-blue distempered office Alan Wint, First Secretary and Head of Chancery, sat white-shirted, smoking, and dreaming in the Asian alpine sunshine of the day when, silver-haired and knighted, he would preside as His Excellency over some great embassy, in Washington, say, or Paris, or even Bonn. — *Dust on the Paw*, Robin Jenkins, 1961.

248 The year Aunt Hat came to us, my main ambition — apart from rescuing someone from drowning or winning the Victoria Cross — was to go down to Jock's Icecream Parlour in the main street of Monks Ford and eat as many Knickerbocker Glories as I could pay for. — *A Little Love, a Little Learning*, Nina Bawden, 1965.

249 Not many go to the ends of the earth for their heart's desire; not many make new ways. — *The Outcasts*, Stephen Becker, 1967.

250 Not to be rich, not to be famous, not to be mighty, not even to be happy, but to be civilized — that was the dream of his life. — *When She Was Good*, Philip Roth, 1967.

251 At that time of life and for a little while in that summer of 1921, my cousin Max was everything I wished I were. — *Everything to Live For*, Paul Horgan, 1968.

252 When Carol Prince was fourteen she wrote in her diary: "Someday I am going to be important." She did become important, but in a way she least expected. — *The Other Woman*, Rona Jaffe, 1972.

253 It is time to tell you of Faith and the Good Thing. People tell her tale in many ways — conjure men and old gimped grandmothers whisper it to make you smile — but always Faith Cross is a beauty, a brown-sugared soul sister seeking the Good Thing in the dark days when the Good Thing was lost or, if the bog-dwelling Swamp Woman did not lie, was hidden by the gods to torment mankind for sins long forgotten. — *Faith and the Good Thing*, Charles Johnson, 1974.

254 On the green April morning when I leave for Montreal to be interviewed for a teaching job, I have in fact two objectives. One, of course, is to get the job: I've always wanted to teach. The other is to marry somebody as promptly as possible — or at the very least to have an affair. — *A Population of One*, Constance Beresford-Howe, 1977.

255 Michael, my twin brother, and I always wanted something other — better — than we had. — *Three Continents*, Ruth Prawer Jhabvala, 1987.

256 Every man says he wants to change the future but no he don't. — *The Bamboo Cannon*, Donald McCaig, 1989.

257 I have decided to be a famous author when I grow up. — *Fathers*, Virginia Budd, 1990.

258 His heart was full of dreams, his head was full of schemes. — *Toward What Bright Glory?*, Allen Drury, 1990.

259 Nagaraj fancied himself a man with a mission. — *The World of Nagaraj*, R. K. Narayan, 1990.

260 There is nothing sadder than the sight of a clever, nervy young man, agulp with ambitions enormous and vague as a headache and flaming with an almost chivalric love of a world he hasn't yet met, relinquishing his urgent purposes almost imperceptibly, slowing down, retreating, and fizzling out like a planet still shining but dead. — *Isaac and His Devils*, Fernanda Eberstadt, 1991.

261 Just to give you an idea of Susie. What a go-getter she was, right from the start. — *To Die For*, Joyce Maynard, 1992.

America

---

262 Much was said and written, at the time, concerning the policy of adding the vast regions of Louisiana, to the already immense, and but half-tenanted territories of the United-States. — *The Prairie*, James Fenimore Cooper, 1827.

263 The incidents of this tale must be sought in a remote period of the annals of America. A colony of self-devoted and pious refugees from religious persecution had landed on the rock of Plymouth, less than half a century before the time at which the narrative commences; and they, and their descendants, had already transformed many a broad waste of wilderness into smiling fields and cheerful villages. — *The Wept of Wish-Ton-Wish*, James Fenimore Cooper, 1829.

264 There is a widespread error on the subject of American scenery. — *Wyandotté*, James Fenimore Cooper, 1843.

265 It is easy to foresee that this country is destined to undergo great and rapid changes. — *Satanstoe*, James Fenimore Cooper, 1845.

266 There is nothing in which American liberty, not always as much restrained as it might be, has manifested a more decided tendency to run riot, than in the use of names. — *The Crater*, James Fenimore Cooper, 1847.

267 While there is less of that high polish in America that is obtained by long intercourse with the great world, than is to be found in nearly every European country, there is much less positive rusticity also. — *The Sea Lions*, James Fenimore Cooper, 1849.

268 In the United States of America there was, in the early decades of this century, a very widely spread excitement of a religious sort. — *The Mormon Prophet*, Lily Dougall, 1899.

269 In the fall of 1860 a stranger visiting the United States would have thought that nothing short of a miracle could preserve the union of states so proudly proclaimed by the signers of the Declaration of Independence, and so gloriously maintained by the gallant Washington. — *Hagar's Daughter*, Pauline Hopkins, 1901-1902.

270 When history has granted him the justice of perspective, we shall know the American Pioneer as one of the most picturesque of her many figures. — *The Blazed Trail*, Stewart Edward White, 1902.

271 I ask you to look at this splendid tool, the American ax, not more an implement of labor than an instrument of civilization. If you can not use it, you are not American. If you do not understand it, you can not understand America. — *The Way to the West*, Emerson Hough, 1903.

272 All about, in the cities and in the villages, the country was being built. — *The Bishop's Wife*, Robert Nathan, 1928.

273 The twentieth century/ is for ever man a time of trials./ The American People/ entered their time of trials/ with very little preparation. — *Adventures of a Young Man*, John Dos Passos, 1939.

274 A man can derive a certain ill-natured pleasure from tallying up the number of Old World writers who have noted America's shallowness of background in human history, and then considering how many of the human histories they long ago wrote off as ended did not end at all, but merely shifted from places like the Loire and Isar and Tweed and Tagus to new settings along the Platte and French Broad and Orinoco, there to continue through their dips, spurs, angles, crises, amendments, reconciliations and backslidings exactly as they had been doing from their beginnings, only with less self-consciousness and mostly less tragically. — *Harp of a Thousand Strings*, H. L. Davis, 1947.

275 *It is a young nation, florid and loud and innocent, free of rot. Then it attempts to devour itself. It loses its innocence. It acquires rot. It is no longer young. It learns all the corrupt wisdoms. It acquires sadness and wrinkles. It becomes civilized.* — *The River and the Wilderness*, Don Robertson, 1962.

276 The airport is not yet New York, U.S.A., to Anika. — *The Fanatic*, Meyer Levin, 1963.

277 The first thing he thought of as he set his feet upon American soil was the weather! — *The King's Orchard*, Agnes Sligh Turnbull, 1963.

278 The small town of Party lies in the American heartland somewhere near the point where the various wests collide — where the middle west meets the far west and the southwest the northwest. — *Stepping Westward*, Malcolm Bradbury, 1965.

279 Nobody knows, from sea to shining sea, why we are having all this trouble with our republic... — *Ninety-Two in the Shade*, Thomas McGuane, 1973.

280 California, named for the negro/ Queen Califia/ California, The Out-Yonder State/ California, refuge for survivors/ of the ancient continent of/ Lemuria/ California, Who, one day, prophets/ say will also sink — *The Last Days of Louisiana Red*, Ishmael Reed, 1974.

281 You, Walt Whitman,/ who rose out of fish-shape Paumanok/ to go crying, like the spotted hawk,/ your barbaric yawp over the roofs,/ to utter "the password primeval,"/ and strike up for a new world;/ what would you say, Walt, here, now, today,/ of these States that you loved,/ Walt Whitman, what would you say? — *Century's Ebb*, John Dos Passos, 1975.

282 It was a peculiarly American thing, the paradox of success that destroys. — *The Big Nickel*, Calder Willingham, 1975.

283 "There's gold, Wayne, gold dust everywhere! Wake up! The streets of America *are* paved with gold!" — *Hello America*, J. G. Ballard, 1981.

284 In America they would have a toilet for each member of the family, maybe even a day one and a night one, plus a holiday one, and a thickly shining pipe to carry the bad stuff far away from where people walked. — *Family*, Herbert Gold, 1981.

285 When I was a boy, everybody but the Wobblies knew that America and God had gone into business together. — *Un-American Activities*, Richard Kluger, 1982.

286 We drove past Tiny Polski's mansion house to the main road, and then the five miles into Northampton, Father talking the whole way about savages and the awfulness of America — how it got turned into a dope-taking, door-locking, ulcerated danger zone of rabid scaven-gers and criminal millionaires and moral sneaks. — *The Mosquito Coast*, Paul Theroux, 1982.

287 The Russians had been a threat to California for many years. — *The Sunset Dream*, Catherine Gavin, 1983.

288 To say the truth, it was not how I expected — stepping off toward America past a drowned horse. — *Dancing at the Rascal Fair*, Ivan Doig, 1987.

289 Moving on, according to the Poet, was the American way. — *The Circle Tour*, William Wiser, 1988.

290 Here they come, marching into American sunlight. — *Mao II*, Don DeLillo, 1991.

291 A remote and desolate corner of America. — *Crazy Cock*, Henry Miller, 1991.

Amusement

292 "Clear the lulla!" was the general cry on a bright December afternoon, when all the boys and girls of Harmony Village were out enjoying the first good snow of the season. — *Jack and Jill*, Louisa May Alcott, 1880.

293 The forty-sixth annual fair of the Pymantoning County Agricultural Society was in its second day. — *The Coast of Bohemia*, William Dean Howells, 1893.

294 One day Mrs. Morton, wife of the city manager, came to the offices and in polite brigandage compelled each man in the room to pay fifty cents for a ticket to the charity entertainment. — *Artie*, George Ade, 1896.

295 Drake called for two cards, and with an abortive attempt at carelessness, signalled for a whiskey. — *Life's Lure*, John G. Neihardt, 1914.

296 During the daylight hours of several autumn Saturdays there had been severe outbreaks of cavalry in the Schofield neighbourhood. — *Penrod and Sam*, Booth Tarkington, 1916.

297 "Carnac! Carnac! Come and catch me, Carnac!" — *Carnac's Folly*, Gilbert Parker, 1922.

298 It was Tuesday evening and so William's friend, Greenlaw, from the Buntingham Grammar School, was there. When William dropped the stub of his cigarette into his coffee cup and said, "Well, what about a game?" Greenlaw nodded and then replied solemnly: "Let us play at the pieces." — *Faraway*, J. B. Priestley, 1932.

299 Slow yellow river flowing, willows that gesture in tepid August airs, and four children playing at greatness, as, doubtless, great men themselves must play. — *Ann Vickers*, Sinclair Lewis, 1933.

300 The theater in Chinatown was crowded to the doors. — *Kinfolk*, Pearl S. Buck, 1949.

301 Joan Mitchell sat in the green painted gazebo that stood in the far corner of her great-aunt's lawn, the corner overlooking the Gulf. She had been there most of the afternoon, playing one game of solitaire after the other, shuffling the cards in fancy river-boat gambler fashion. — *The House on Coliseum Street*, Shirley Ann Grau, 1961.

302 Jim had this tennis ball he found at the hospital, in the grass near the tennis courts. He walked around bouncing it off the sidewalks and off walls. He bounced it in the library and bugged everybody. He was wearing an imaginary baseball cap until he could get a real one. — *The Butterfly*, Michael Rumaker, 1962.

303 The plastic butterflies were the size of birds. They clung to the wall on suction cups and quivered if one touched them. — *The Leader*, Gillian Freeman, 1965.

304 The merry-go-round had a center post of cast iron, reddened a little by the salt air, and of a certain ornateness: not striking enough to attract a casual eye, but still, to an eye concentrated upon it (to the eye, say, of a lover of the merry-go-round, a child) intriguing in its transitions. — *The Merry-go-round in the Sea*, Randolph Stow, 1965.

305 Lying back in the chair I swing young Bobby off my knee and high over my head, holding him at the end of my stiff arms, my hands round his deep little chest and shaking him. — *The Watchers on the Shore*, Stan Barstow, 1966.

306 As far as it was possible for an elderly gentleman suffering from dyspepsia and a particularly violent attack of gout to take pleasure in anything but the alleviation of his various pains the Earl of Wroxton was enjoying himself. — *Charity Girl*, Georgette Heyer, 1970.

307 A city's blank white concrete slabs, the giant ones ringed by the less giant, gave space in their midst to a broad pink-floored plaza, a playground in which some two hundred young children played and exercised under the care of a dozen supervisors in white coveralls. — *This Perfect Day*, Ira Levin, 1970.

308 Harry the Goth, seated gingerly on his Sandy The Sea Serpent rubber lifesaver, buzzed and clicked the deck of cards. — *The Death and Life of Harry Goth*, D. Keith Mano, 1971.

309 *Dinosauric, obsolete, functions and powers atrophied, dressed in sport shirts from Sulka and Cardin, they sat across from each other at small tables in airy rooms overlooking the changing sea and dealt and received cards just as they had done in the lush years in the rainfall forest of the West Coast when in all seasons they had announced the law in the banks, the board rooms, the Moorish mansions, the chateaux, the English castles, the* Georgian town houses of Southern California. — *Evening in Byzantium*, Irwin Shaw, 1973.

310 A dismal Autumn afternoon in the country. Without, a soft drizzle falling on yellow leaves & damp ground; within, two people playing chess by the window of the fire-lighted drawing-room at Holly Lodge. — "Fast and Loose" — Edith Wharton *as* David Olivieri, 1977.

311 Below our tiny house, on the soccer field, my sons, Ari and Hanan, are kicking a ball. — *Holocaust*, Gerald Green, 1978.

312 Lilian was not giving her mind to the game, I could tell. — *Flowers for Lilian*, Anna Gilbert, 1980.

313 A bowling ball goes thundering down the alley. It smashes the pins for a ten-strike! — *Everything That Moves*, Budd Schulberg, 1980.

314 There used to be an Easter Fair at the Presbyterian church every year. — *Morgan's Passing*, Anne Tyler, 1980.

315 Six North Africans were playing *boules* beneath Flaubert's statue. — *Flaubert's Parrot*, Julian Barnes, 1984.

316 On the day of the Lendrick Mills Parade at the Grand Hotel, Charbury, in the last year of the Sixties and the last week of March, for once in the West Riding of Yorkshire spring had arrived at the appointed date and had settled down to hand out its special gift of a brisk euphoria. — *The Two of Us*, John Braine, 1984.

317 Fine sport yesterday at our notary's house. — *The Notebook of Gismondo Cavalletti*, R. M. Lamming, 1985.

318 "No bid."/ "One spade."/ "No bid."/ "One no-trump." — *Hugger Mugger*, Max Davidson, 1986.

319 *Nobody ever won a game of anything from Harry Fisher.* That was something he wrote down years later, hoping it would turn into a cautionary tale he could tell his children. — *Greencastle and the Denizens of the Sacred Crypt*, Lloyd Kropp, 1986.

320 I was too old to play kick-the-can anymore so I was just standing there watching when Jimmy T. came running in from behind our house. — *Kick the Can*, Jim Lehrer, 1988.

321 Asel watches wrestling on Saturday nights. — *Soft Water*, Robert Olmstead, 1988.

322 My father, unlike so many of the men he served with, knew just what he wanted to do when the war was over. He wanted to drink and whore and play the horses. — *The Risk Pool*, Richard Russo, 1988.

323 *A good miniature is a sugarplum.* — *The Trotter-Nama*, I. Allan Sealy, 1988.

324 Stealthily he prowled among the skeleton trees, sickened by the miasma of their hideous parasite growth. On either side, sharp disembodied eyes spied on him through the swaying

vapours of the land of the Undead. —*Enchantment*, Monica Dickens, 1989.

325 Ambrose Flood had a model railway, but none of us ever saw it, for it was under the floorboards of his bedroom. — *Out After Dark*, Hugh Leonard, 1989.

326 My master beat Galileo at marbles. — *The Palace of Wisdom*, Bob Marshall-Andrews, 1989.

327 We played our games in the heat of summer. — *The Last of the Golden Girls*, Susan Swan, 1989.

328 After the Tarzan serial at the movies every Saturday afternoon, my friend Hutch and I would climb the mimosa tree in his back yard and take off our shirts and eat bananas. — *The Revolution of Little Girls*, Blanche McCrary Boyd, 1991.

329 We used to play hide-and-seek underneath Great-Grandfather's house, where the sand was soft and the dark wove threads like cool smoke, and stone pillars glimmered smooth white at the edges of the dark. — *The Scent of the Gods*, Fiona Cheong, 1991.

330 The river was crowded, and the lawns that sloped down to the river, there were young people everywhere, and the sun shone, as it properly should on such a scene, as it shines in stories, sparkled on the water and on the upturned young faces, and the parasols (for parasols were once again in fashion). And then, suddenly, there was a stir in the midst of it all, where the crowd was thickest, and some of the young men raised a boat high, high above their heads, to a great shout . . . "Hurrah" . . . "rah" . . . "rah," and water cascaded out of it onto their heads and shoulders and down their arms, in a brief silver stream. —*Air and Angels*, Susan Hill, 1991.

331 On an autumn afternoon in 1915 in a small, bleached town in South Carolina, not too far from Charleston, in a tent on a lot near the town square, a group of men called Tiny Cleveland's Minstrels sat in a solemn, unblinking row and faced their audience. —*Jim Dandy*, Irvin Faust, 1994.

Anatomy

332 In the firelight the face of Julien De Medici appeared like a gray and scarlet mask of ennui. — *The Florentine Dagger*, Ben Hecht, 1923.

333 Samuel Spade's jaw was long and bony, his chin a jutting v under the more flexible v of his mouth. His nostrils curved back to make another, smaller, v. His yellow-grey eyes were horizontal. The v *motif* was picked up again by thickish brows rising outward from twin creases above a hooked nose, and his pale brown hair grew down—from high flat temples—in a point on his forehead. He looked rather pleasantly like a blond satan. — *The Maltese Falcon*, Dashiell Hammett, 1930.

334 Simon Grant, who had handled many skulls in his time, was immediately taken by the shape of the head, the colouring, and the fineness of the features. — *The Silver Bough*, Neil M. Gunn, 1948.

335 Lois would not have noticed him if it had not been for his eyes. —*A Wreath for Udomo*, Peter Abrahams, 1956.

336 Régis Loisel's black eyes had been studying their bearded faces, his gaze lingering on the strong jutting jaw of William Clark, on the changing lights in the slate-gray eyes of Meriwether Lewis. — *Tale of Valor*, Vardis Fisher, 1958.

337 My name is Mary Katherine Blackwood. I am eighteen years old, and I live with my sister Constance. I have often thought that with any luck at all I could have been born a werewolf, because the two middle fingers on both my hands are the same length, but I have had to be content with what I had. — *We Have Always Lived in the Castle*, Shirley Jackson, 1962.

338 Rose McConnell said to her husband, William, turning a ring around on her finger, "I never look at this emerald without thinking how its color resembles Grandmother's eyes. . . ." — *Grandmother and the Priests*, Taylor Caldwell, 1963.

339 "Blue Eyes."/ She was indebted to the gouges in his face, high cheeks that could blunt a scary color. —*Marilyn the Wild*, Jerome Charyn, 1976.

340 In a certain kingdom, in a certain land, there lived a dwarf who had an evil reputation, for he was humpbacked and ugly, with teeth like a saw's and skin like a mushroom's, and his legs were crooked and his eyebrows were hairy, as were his nostrils and ears, and the eyes that peered out from the shadow of those eyebrows were as mottled and devoid of vitality as two dead mackerels. — *In the Suicide Mountains*, John Gardner, 1977.

341 "How tall are you?" he asked./ "One and a half feet," I said, and then added, "Sorry." —*Lucky to Be Alive?*, Alice Cromie, 1978.

342 "Why are so many tennis players pigeon-toed?" said Prue. "They're very sexy-looking till you get to their feet." — *The Beaufort Sisters*, Jon Cleary, 1979.

343 Now. Right here. Yes. You're touching it—this tiny flowershaped freckle between my legs, a few centimeters from my vulva, in the soft

ribbon of white skin between hairline and thigh.
— *Ancient Lights*, Davis Grubb, 1982.

344 Two seats away is a guy with a huge Adam's apple and blue eyes like two line drives. — *F.N.G.*, Donald Bodey, 1985.

345 See her with the king's eyes. — *After Goliath*, R. V. Cassill, 1985.

346 Us Poles have big pricks!!! — *Mortadella*, Justin Wintle, 1985.

347 Against the heavenly windowlight, a New England profile: solid line of brow and nose, mouth a little soft, soft eyes, brown. — *November*, Janet Hobhouse, 1986.

348 My father's right arm ended not in a hand but, at the elbow, in a bony swelling. — *The Gift of Stones*, Jim Crace, 1988.

349 **April 3** You see a lot of penises in my line of work: short ones, stubby ones, hard ones, soft ones. Circumcised and uncircumcised; laid-back and athletic. — *Squeeze Play*, Jane Leavy, 1990.

350 On a day like this the big toe of Zivanias had failed him. — *Philadelphia Fire*, John Edgar Wideman, 1990.

351 On the desk in front of me lie two human hands. — *A Landing on the Sun*, Michael Frayn, 1991.

352 A perfect combination of raised blue veins on Martin's right foot spelled *M*. — *O Beautiful*, Jesse Green, 1992.

Ancestry

353 As it is usual for great Persons whose Lives have been remarkable, and whose Actions deserve Recording to Posterity, to insist much upon their Originals, give full Accounts of their Families, and the Histories of their Ancestors: So, that I may be methodical, I shall do the same, tho' I can look but a very little Way into my Pedigree as you will see presently. — *Captain Singleton*, Daniel Defoe, 1720.

354 Of the goodness and antiquity of the name and family of this gentleman, nobody can ever make any question. He is a Campbell, lineally descended from the house of Argyll, and bears a distant relation to the present duke of that name in Scotland, and who is now constituted a duke of England, by the style and title of Duke of Greenwich. — *Duncan Campbell*, Daniel Defoe, 1720.

355 This *John Sheppard*, a Youth both in Age and Person, tho' an old Man in Sin; was Born in the Parish of *Stepney* near *London*, in the Year 1702, a Son, Grandson, and great Grandson of a

Carpenter: His Father died when he was so very Young that he could not recollect that ever he saw him. — *The History of the Remarkable Life of John Sheppard*, Daniel Defoe, 1724.

356 I derive my birth from one of the first emigrants to New England, being lineally descended from Captain John Underhill, who came into the Massachusetts in the year 1630; of whom honorable mention is made by that elegant, accurate, and interesting historian, the Reverend Jeremy Belknap, in his *History of New Hampshire*. — *The Algerine Captive*, Royall Tyler, 1797.

357 The Mailings have long occupied a distinguished place in the laws and annals of Scotland. That they were of Celtic origin many learned antiquaries shrewdly suspect, nor are we disposed to controvert the opinion; although it must be allowed they have never been without a taint of Saxon blood in their veins, being from time immemorial regarded as of intimate propinquity with the Pedigrees, whose eminent merits and great actions are so worthily celebrated in the chronicles of venerable virginity. — *The Last of the Lairds*, John Galt, 1826.

358 My birth was unpropitious. I came into the world, branded and denounced as a vagrant, not littered by a drab in a ditch but still worse; for I was a younger son of a family, so proud of their antiquity, that even gout and mortgaged estates were traced, many generations back, on the genealogical tree, as ancient heir-looms of aristocratic origin, and therefore reverenced. — *Adventures of a Younger Son*, Edward John Trelawny, 1831.

359 As no lady or gentleman, with any claims to polite breeding, can possibly sympathise with the Chuzzlewit Family without being first assured of the extreme antiquity of the race, it is a great satisfaction to know that it undoubtedly descended in a direct line from Adam and Eve; and was, in the very earliest times, closely connected with the agricultural interest. — *Martin Chuzzlewit*, Charles Dickens, 1844.

360 To plague my wife, who does not understand pleasantries in the matter of pedigree, I once drew a fine family tree of my ancestors, with Claude Duval, captain and highwayman, *sus. per coll.* in the reign of Charles II., dangling from a top branch. But this is only my joke with her High Mightiness my wife, and his Serene Highness my son. None of us Duvals have been *supercollated* to my knowledge. — *Denis Duval*, William Makepeace Thackeray, 1864.

361 I am a native of ————, in the United States of America. My ancestors migrated from England in the reign of Charles II, and my grandfather was not undistinguished in the War of Independence. My family, therefore, enjoyed

a somewhat high social position in right of birth. — *The Coming Race*, Edward Bulwer-Lytton, 1871.

362 We Caskodens take great pride in our ancestry. Some persons, I know, hold all that to be totally un–Solomonlike and the height of vanity, but they, usually, have no ancestors of whom to be proud. — *When Knighthood Was in Flower*, Charles Major, 1898.

363 When Napoleon was about to crown himself — so I have somewhere read — they submitted to him the royal genealogy they had faked up for him. He crumpled the parchment and flung it in the face of the chief herald, or whoever it was. "My line," said he, "dates from Montenotte." — *The Deluge*, David Graham Phillips, 1905.

364 We had known General Conyers immemorially not because my father had ever served under him but through some long-forgotten connexion with my mother's parents, to one or other of whom he may even have been distantly related. — *At Lady Molly's*, Anthony Powell, 1957.

365 His name was Jai Vedh./ There was some Hindi in the family, way back — a father, for they still used fathers' names — but he did not look it, being yellow-haired with blue eyes and a dark yellow beard, a streaked beard, as if stained or dyed. — *And Chaos Died*, Joanna Russ, 1970.

366 Lest anyone should suppose I am a son of nobody, sold off by some peasant father in a drought year, I may say our line is an old one, though it ends with me. — *The Persian Boy*, Mary Renault, 1972.

367 Cletus Hayworth was the grandson, on his father's side, of a noted theologian and convicted rapist. — *The Fabricator*, Hollis Hodges, 1976.

368 Some folk who lived among the mule deer and the long-tailed curlews when Jason Crockett first emerged on the northwestern scene — modestly as a state's treasurer — assumed he was one of the Crocketts descended from the fabulous Davy Crockett. — *Strike the Bell Boldly*, Stephen Longstreet, 1977.

369 This is what Abhor, who's my partner, part robot, and part black; told me was her childhood:/ **My Grandmother**/ She's my father's mother. He came out of her. And she came out of a German-Jewish family which was real wealthy. — *Empire of the Senseless*, Kathy Acker, 1988.

370 My grandmother, Lorna Huber, was born in Chacallit, New York, fifty miles or so northwest of Albany, in the valley of the Whatsit River, a tributary of the Mohawk. — *Herb 'n' Lorna*, Eric Kraft, 1988.

371 My grandmother belonged to Thomas Jefferson. — *My Thomas*, Roberta Grimes, 1993.

Anger

372 Why Stub McKay turned out such a devil he himself hardly knew; he himself did not understand what thing had embittered him. — *Somebody in Boots*, Nelson Algren, 1935.

373 The old brick palace at Williamsburg was in a tumult. The Governor tore off his wig and stamped it under foot in rage. — *The Conquest*, Eva Emery Dye, 1936.

374 One night when I had tasted bitterness I went out on to the hill. — *Star Maker*, Olaf Stapledon, 1937.

375 All night long there was a cold bitterness in the air like the unexpected coming of winter after a day of warm sunshine. — *All Night Long*, Erskine Caldwell, 1942.

376 She swept into the reception room of Miss English's Academy, her hazel eyes bright with anger, the rustle of her taffeta gown raised from a crisp whisper to a cry by the vigor of her movements. — *Immortal Wife*, Irving Stone, 1944.

377 "My dear Philip," he said, "you mustn't get bitter," he said. He was all right. These were his rooms, oak-panelling, books, sherry and all the time in the world. — *A Man's Estate*, Emyr Humphreys, 1955.

378 Like an echo bounding from a distant object and returning to its source, the sound of Roy Complain's beating heart seemed to him to fill the clearing. He stood with one foot on the threshold of his compartment, listening to the rage hammering through his arteries. — *Starship*, Brian W. Aldiss, 1958.

379 Like most irritable people I rarely lose my temper (a dog that's let out for regular exercise isn't as apt to run away when it does escape), but I was losing it this morning. — *The Mackerel Plaza*, Peter De Vries, 1958.

380 He could feel the rage suddenly flaring in him. He liked to feel rage, for it meant not only a quick warm flooding about his loins, a hot, watery flooding, but also an intense inner excitement that made him experience a voluptuous heightening of all senses. — *Wicked Angel*, Taylor Caldwell, 1965.

381 A pretty sight, the confrontation of Dorothy Merlin and her new doctor. They glared at each other, rampant, like supporters on a coat of arms, with the desk as shield between them. — *Cork Street, Next to the Hatter's*, Pamela Hansford Johnson, 1965.

382 The red flag was up when he drove up to the house. — *Voices of a Summer Day*, Irwin Shaw, 1965.

383 Robert Bruce chewed at his lip — partly

to hold back hot words. — *Robert the Bruce*, Nigel Tranter, 1971.

384 Every time he drove through Yorkville, Rosenbaum got angry, just on general principles. —*Marathon Man*, William Goldman, 1974.

385 Rose smelt the air, considering what she smelt; a miasma of unspoken criticism and disparagement fogged the distance between us. — *Good Behaviour*, Molly Keane, 1981.

386 Daddy was livid at breakfast. — *Domestic Arrangements*, Norma Klein, 1981.

387 I used to try not to lose my temper, for fear of saying something that would haunt me. —*A Change of Scene*, Elizabeth Cullinan, 1982.

388 Fury was a constant state of being for His Honor Judge Guthrie Scaggs. — *The Barefoot Brigade*, Douglas C. Jones, 1982.

389 *Mincemeat. They could make mincemeat out of her.* — *Forgiving*, Shelley List, 1982.

390 *Anger's my meat, I'll sup upon myself. . . ./* Lately lines from *Coriolanus* and *Timon of Athens* and *Macbeth*, the angry plays, had begun to surface in his mind like breath-starved divers rocketing up for air. — *The Tiger in the Tiger Pit*, Janette Turner Hospital, 1983.

391 A tuba blast of anger and lust shattered the silence and echoed through the hills. — *Thirteen O'Clock*, Thurston Clarke, 1984.

392 A bitter shaft blew from the firth. — *Banners of Gold*, Pamela Kaufman, 1986.

393 She rages against junk. — *The Last to Go*, Rand Richards Cooper, 1988.

394 Geoffrey Danes wasn't obviously mad. —*Suddenly, in Rome*, Max Davidson, 1988.

395 What it begins with, I know finally, is the kernel of meanness in people's hearts. — *The Book of Ruth*, Jane Hamilton, 1988.

396 Normalyn crumpled the single sheet with the two handwritten entries and threw it down. —*Marilyn's Daughter*, John Rechy, 1988.

397 "You broke my heart and now I'm pissed." — *Night Over Day Over Night*, Paul Watkins, 1988.

398 OBI Director C. Harry Hayes was clearly angry with me, his best friend in the government of Oklahoma. — *The Sooner Spy*, Jim Lehrer, 1990.

Animals

399 The dog Crusoe was once a pup. Now do not, courteous reader, toss your head contemptuously and exclaim: "Of course he was; I could have told *you* that."— *The Dog Crusoe*, R. M. Ballantyne, 1869.

400 Buck did not read the newspapers, or he would have known that trouble was brewing, not alone for himself, but for every tidewater dog, strong of muscle and with warm, long hair, from Puget Sound to San Diego. — *The Call of the Wild*, Jack London, 1903.

401 The Mole had been working very hard all the morning, spring cleaning his little home. — *The Wind in the Willows*, Kenneth Grahame, 1908.

402 I stood watching the shadowy fish slide through the gloom of the millpond. — *The White Peacock*, D. H. Lawrence, 1911.

403 Kazan lay mute and motionless, his gray nose between his forepaws, his eyes half closed. —*Kazan*, James Oliver Curwood, 1914.

404 With the silence and immobility of a great reddish-tinted rock, Thor stood for many minutes looking out over his domain. — *The Grizzly King*, James Oliver Curwood, 1916.

405 Not until *Mister* Haggin abruptly picked him up under one arm and stepped into the sternsheets of the waiting whaleboat, did Jerry dream that anything untoward was to happen to him. —*Jerry of the Islands*, Jack London, 1917.

406 But Michael never sailed out of Tulagi, nigger-chaser on the *Eugénie.* — *Michael, Brother of Jerry*, Jack London, 1917.

407 It was late in the month of March, at the dying-out of the Eagle Moon, that Neewa the black bear cub got his first real look at the world. —*Nomads of the North*, James Oliver Curwood, 1919.

408 She was beautiful. And she had a heart and a soul—which were a curse. —*Bruce*, Albert Payson Terhune, 1920.

409 She was a mixture of the unmixable. —*Buff*, Albert Payson Terhune, 1921.

410 The sharp splat of the bullet and the downward glide of a ribbon of dry sand checked the forward surge of the bay mare and she arose on her trim hind hoofs, hung perilously in the balance while one might count five, and then, whirling like a dancer, dropped down facing the way she had come and leaped ahead like a missile from a catapult. —*Rustlers' Valley*, Clarence E. Mulford, 1924.

411 The bay mare had had a bad night. —*Father Abraham*, Irving Bacheller, 1925.

412 Down the winding and oak-shaded furlong of driveway between Sunnybank House and the main road trotted the huge mahogany-and-snow collie. He was mighty of chest and shoulder, heavy of coat, and with deepset dark eyes in whose depths lurked a Soul. — *Lad of Sunnybank*, Albert Payson Terhune, 1929.

413 She had begun life, as far as any record can be found, tucked under the right arm of a mangy-looking man. —*A Dog Named Chips*, Albert Payson Terhune, 1931.

414 From the top of the bank, behind a sparse hedge of thorn, the lioness stared at the Hertfordshire road. — *The Place of the Lion*, Charles Williams, 1933.

415 A small and scattered herd grazed over the False Divide between Plomo and Horsethief, and turned down into Gridiron; something around six hundred head of cattle. — *The Trusty Knaves*, Eugene Manlove Rhodes, 1934.

416 Tapiola was a Yorkshire terrier. His body, which was about twelve inches long, and felt to the touch like a squab or a young bird, was covered with blue and silver hair; and he usually wore a little ribbon on top of his head. — *Journey of Tapiola*, Robert Nathan, 1938.

417 Tapiola was worried. Life did not seem the same to him any more. — *Tapiola's Brave Regiment*, Robert Nathan, 1941.

418 "We had a mouse last night," said Cassilis. — *Winter Quarters*, Pamela Hansford Johnson, 1943.

419 I dreamed a fellow asked me if I wanted a dog and I said yeah, I'd like to have a dog and he went off and came back with a little black dog with stiff black gold-tipped hair and sad eyes that looked something like a wire-haired terrier. — *If He Hollers Let Him Go*, Chester Himes, 1945.

420 All day the sheep had been skittish with mating, but now it was night and the last of the stragglers had been dragged back under the first of the stars. — *David the King*, Gladys Schmitt, 1946.

421 As Carlo Boldesca moved across the Piazza San Marco a muzzled dog ran out from the shadow of a café table, barked at the pigeons which strutted about the great flagstones that lay lemon-colored under the pale April sunlight. — *Bird of Prey*, Victor Canning, 1950.

422 Thomas Tracy had a tiger./ It was actually a black panther, but that's no matter, because he *thought* of it as a tiger. — *Tracy's Tiger*, William Saroyan, 1951.

423 Radiant and full-leafed, the Park was alive with the murmuring vibration of the species which made it its preserve. — *Hackenfeller's Ape*, Brigid Brophy, 1953.

424 In the last days of Narnia, far up to the west beyond Lantern Waste and close beside the great waterfall, there lived an Ape. — *The Last Battle*, C. S. Lewis, 1956.

425 When he was about two years old, and had been a Cat About Town for some time, glorious in conquests, but rather too thin for comfort, the Fur Person decided that it was time he settled down. — *The Fur Person*, May Sarton, 1957.

426 I was dreaming about a hairless ape who lived in a cage by himself. His trouble was that people were always trying to get in. It kept the ape in a state of nervous tension. — *The Doomsters*, Ross Macdonald, 1958.

427 There are, it appears to us, though living in London as we do we really know very little about it, far more ponies in the world than there used to be. — *Love at All Ages*, Angela Thirkell, 1959.

428 Through broken reeds the creature moved. It was not alone; its mate followed, and behind her five youngsters, joining the hunt with eagerness. — *Greybeard*, Brian W. Aldiss, 1964.

429 The big half-bred bloodhound lay in his barrel kennel and dreamed he was deer hunting. — *The Fox and the Hound*, Daniel P. Mannix, 1967.

430 The unicorn lived in a lilac wood, and she lived all alone. — *The Last Unicorn*, Peter S. Beagle, 1968.

431 Mother says there are rats in the rockery. — *Willard*, Stephen Gilbert, 1968.

432 Hazard had to get hold of a mare. — *The Studhorse Man*, Robert Kroetsch, 1969.

433 There had always been horses on the island, a wandering fluid band which had additions at times when a pony broke its hobbles and was away to them, and no-one bothered to go and catch it when an ass is better, all told. Or the tinkers' piebalds would join them, and these being usually entires it was pretty sure next year there'd be some magpie foals with some of the mares. — *The Horse of Selene*, Juanita Casey, 1971.

434 The old ram stands looking down over rockslides, stupidly triumphant. — *Grendel*, John Gardner, 1971.

435 Current-borne, wave-flung, tugged hugely by the whole might of ocean, the jellyfish drifts in the tidal abyss. — *The Lathe of Heaven*, Ursula K. Le Guin, 1971.

436 Almost a hundred years before Breck Hord was born, a dog appeared by a nameless branch of Poor Fork, which is one of the three sources of the Cumberland River. — *Stand Like Men*, James Sherburne, 1973.

437 In the tall weeds of the borrow pit, I took a leak and watched the sorrel mare, her colt beside her, walk through burnt grass to the shady side of the log-and-mud cabin. — *Winter in the Blood*, James Welch, 1974.

438 The octopus lived in a square plastic box with holes for his arms. — *The Realms of Gold*, Margaret Drabble, 1975.

439 Shortly before two o'clock the blues began to work the baitfish in toward the shore at Madaket. — *A City on a Hill*, George V. Higgins, 1975.

440 She was standing in the middle of the railroad tracks. Her head was bowed and her right front hoof was raised as if she rested. Her reins hung down to the ground and her saddle

had slipped to one side. — *The Wars*, Timothy Findley, 1977.

441 There were no lions any more. — *The Lion of Boaz-Jachin and Jachin-Boaz*, Russell Hoban, 1977.

442 The moment a tiny gray verdin piped its danger signal, the old dog crouched low on the ground, mute and motionless. — *Something on the Wind*, Barbara Moore, 1978.

443 "Please, no dog in the manger," Steadman said. — *The Blood of Paradise*, Stephen Goodwin, 1979.

444 Musco whaled a boom of delight, as happy Blue whales do. — *The Last Blue Whale*, Vincent Smith, 1979.

445 Drat that camel! He was chewing the walls again, and I figured the veranda would break. — *Darlin' Bill*, Jerome Charyn, 1980.

446 "Tell you what, Cassandra. Get it over with, and I'll fill your bin." — *The Horsemaster*, T. Alan Broughton, 1981.

447 He was born in Ireland in the early thirties, a big foal even longer-legged than usual, legs that were slender but strong, already showing incipient power. — *The Dark Horse*, Rumer Godden, 1981.

448 The yellow dog named Daniels lay dreaming. — *In a High Place*, Joanne Meschery, 1981.

449 There were sometimes snakes on Ruth's lawns at night, out from the pushed-back jungle edging the estate to the short grass still holding the sun's warmth. — *The Blazing Air*, Oswald Wynd, 1981.

450 Aunt Frances' white cat Matilda was reflected in the sideboard when he passed through the dining room into the parlor after supper. — *First Wine*, Jack Dunphy, 1982.

451 Killing the animals was the hard part. — *Magnetic Field(s)*, Ron Loewinsohn, 1983.

452 "No, sir, I'm afraid I don't. There's hardly any demand for rats just now. . . ." — *A Prayer for Fair Weather*, John Broderick, 1984.

453 A stillborn calf had been tied into the membrane of the sac with plaited straw, and hung up by a nail over the stall above the head of its mother. — *Sunrising*, David Cook, 1984.

454 Coyotes were sneaking into the neighborhood like unwanted guests at a party. — *Golden States*, Michael Cunningham, 1984.

455 *Road there is none, but only the river's passage through the impenetrable reaches of this Toro y Plata domaine, wherein flora and fauna of a most exquisite and rare beauty flourish in unimaginable abundance.* — *Jewels*, Jill Tweedie, 1984.

456 Together, as if in prayer, the small hooves came first, glistening in the sunlight that stippled the floor of the pine grove. — "The Pull of the Earth," Alfred Alcorn, 1985.

457 In the waters of these islands there is a certain fish whose eyes, like the eyes of the chameleon, are able to look in opposite directions at the same time. — *Beachmasters*, Thea Astley, 1985.

458 He was only a small rat, but bolder than most, with a disproportionately long tail which curled behind him on the stone floor, losing itself in the half-gloom of a solitary candle's light. — *Legacy*, Susan Kay, 1985.

459 When Augustus came out on the porch the blue pigs were eating a rattlesnake — not a very big one. — *Lonesome Dove*, Larry McMurtry, 1985.

460 When Tor Anwari came into the stable his horse pawed the floor, then stood with forelegs splayed, ears quivering in anticipation. — *Kabul*, M. E. Hirsh, 1986.

461 MouMou found her. — *Murder on Clam Pond*, Douglas Kiker, 1986.

462 The dog was a tan fice — cowlicked, thin pointed sticks for legs, a pointed little face with powerful whiskers, one ear flopped and one straight. — *Walking Across Egypt*, Clyde Edgerton, 1987.

463 Just before daybreak the old lioness stirs in her bed of sweet clover hay under the low eaves of her wooden stall. — *Suite for Calliope*, Ellen Hunnicutt, 1987.

464 The black horse was first to know. It came to him across the frost of the open field, the smell of unfamiliar men. — *Home Fires Burning*, Robert Inman, 1987.

465 "I'd say we've seen the last of the elephant, eh, Johnny?" said one of the soldiers in blue. — *Spangle*, Gary Jennings, 1987.

466 The bear was huge. — *The Perfect Sonya*, Beverly Lowry, 1987.

467 Baal, the cat, King of the Invisible. — *Rose Theatre*, Gilbert Sorrentino, 1987.

468 Traveller died of lockjaw two years after Robert E. Lee died. — *Lincoln's Dreams*, Connie Willis, 1987.

469 The dogs breathe in my face. — *The Floatplane Notebooks*, Clyde Edgerton, 1988.

470 Sometimes, in Southern California, if you're a dog trainer, you go looking for a certain dog, and you have to do this knowing that maybe there isn't such a dog, although there's no reason why not. — *The White German Shepherd*, Vicki Hearne, 1988.

471 He kicked viciously./ The foal was resisting his birth. — *The Horse Hunters*, Robert Newton Peck, 1988.

472 They put the behemoths in the hold along with the rhinos, the hippos and the elephants. — *A History of the World in 10½ Chapters*, Julian Barnes, 1989.

473 The great white catfish of Amazonia was

first reported by the reflective Spanish explorer Don Hipólito Baldo in 1684, although for almost three hundred years just which of the many tributaries of the Amazon actually harbored the leviathan remained a mystery. — *Darwin's Secret*, Richard Hoyt, 1989.

474 The lizard again. The self-consuming bile-green lizard with the bird-of-prey's beak, whose forking segmented tails regenerate two sections for every one snapped off and swallowed. — *Triangulation*, Jack Stephens, 1989.

475 Hilda drops clumsily out of an acacia tree, recovers her balance, and skitters across the clearing, hair bristling, lips drawn back, teeth a white scar of warning on a black face. — *After Roy*, Mary Tannen, 1989.

476 Yesterday, while mousing in the meadow, Ezra saw a car drift down the road and, remembering that cars now carried men with guns, he ran toward the barn. — *The Predator*, Linda Grace Hoyer, 1990.

477 He understood what they were thinking and saying: Old man that he is, what's to become of him? — *To Dance with the White Dog*, Terry Kay, 1990.

478 A dog—it was a dog I saw for certain. — *The Sweet Hereafter*, Russell Banks, 1991.

479 Some lions roaring in the park: Maw Maw Maw! — *Tar Beach*, Richard Elman, 1991.

480 *Each year the whales went to the great bay.* — *Cape Cod*, William Martin, 1991.

481 They had taken her kitten, whose name was Mopsy. — *The Night Travellers*, Elizabeth Spencer, 1991.

482 He sat on his haunches, his breath clouding the glass on the inside of the front door, his brown eyes intent on the far corner of the laurel hedge past the driveway, where he might first catch sight of his master returning. — *Book*, Robert Grudin, 1992.

483 Balancing on the bars of the fire escape, a blue cat peered in through the French window. For the few minutes it took the sun to sink below the skyline, the cat could see nothing but molten light reflected on glass. Once the glass had cooled, the cat saw what it had come to see, what it had seen once before and wanted to see again. — *The Courage of Girls*, Jean McGarry, 1992.

Art and Artists

484 A young lady sat pricking a framed canvas in the drawing-room of Kent Villa, a mile from Gravesend; she was making, at a cost of time and tinted wool, a chair-cover, admirably unfit to be sat upon—except by some severe artist, bent on obliterating discordant colours. — *A Simpleton*, Charles Reade, 1873.

485 One August afternoon the people who drove along the east road of a pleasant Sussex County town were much interested in the appearance of a young man who was hard at work before a slender easel near the wayside. — *A Marsh Island*, Sarah Orne Jewett, 1885.

486 Two years of service in the Zouaves had wrought a change in Anastase Gouache, the painter. — *Sant' Ilario*, F. Marion Crawford, 1888.

487 The picture hangs at my lodgings here at Avignon, a stone's-throw from the Porte de la Ligne, and within the shadow of Notre Dame des Doms, though its intended housing-place was the great gallery of Blackladies. — *Lawrence Clavering*, A. E. W. Mason, 1897.

488 "I cannot help it," said Filmore Durand quietly. "I paint what I see. If you are not pleased with the likeness, I shall be only too happy to keep it." — *The White Sister*, F. Marion Crawford, 1909.

489 Felix Brun, perched like a little bird, on the steps of the Rede Art Gallery, gazed up and down Bond Street, with his sharp eyes for someone to whom he might show Yale Ross's portrait of the Duchess of Wrexe. — *The Duchess of Wrexe*, Hugh Walpole, 1914.

490 A portrait, a painting? You cannot paint today as you painted yesterday. You cannot paint tomorrow as you paint today. — *Paint It Today*, Hilda Doolittle *as* H. D., 1921.

491 John Campton, the American portrait-painter, stood in his bare studio in Montmartre at the end of a summer afternoon contemplating a battered calendar that hung against the wall. — *A Son at the Front*, Edith Wharton, 1923.

492 Mr. Conrad Pybus collected pictures, and being the possessor of two "Constables," and three "Cotmans," he had some right to stretch out a large hand and to indicate the picture that was hung against the blue horizon. — *Old Pybus*, Warwick Deeping, 1928.

493 "Ah, but what a sense of order they had!" exclaimed Mrs. Livermore as she bent down to examine the detail of a large portrait of the *Grand Dauphin* and his family. — *The Indifferent Children*, Louis Auchincloss, 1947.

494 The last time I saw any examples of Mr. Deacon's work was at a sale, held obscurely in the neighbourhood of Euston Road, many years after his death. — *A Buyer's Market*, Anthony Powell, 1952.

495 A child's hand and a piece of chalk had made it: a careful, child's scrawl of white lines on the red bricks of the wall beside Jander's Livery Stable: a crude pair of sticks for the gallows tree, a thick broken line for the rope and then the

scarecrow of the hanging man. — *The Night of the Hunter*, Davis Grubb, 1953.

496 Exactly a year later Francis learned the truth about the slashed portrait — by then, of course, restored with expert care. — *The Seraglio*, James Merrill, 1957.

497 It was two or three months ago that I first met Davie, the young coal miner from South Yorkshire. He was, and is, a lonely, temperamental, impulsive boy, a miner who paints under circumstances which shame me. — *Weekend in Dinlock*, Clancy Sigal, 1960.

498 He sat before the mirror of the second-floor bedroom sketching his lean cheeks with their high bone ridges, the flat broad forehead, and ears too far back on the head, the dark hair curling forward in thatches, the amber-colored eyes wide-set but heavy-lidded. — *The Agony and the Ecstasy*, Irving Stone, 1961.

499 There was no reason why I should not be a painter of note, one of those riding high and comfortably on the wave of public interest in arts and artists. — *The Shape of Illusion*, William E. Barrett, 1972.

500 "Ordinary things show up in extraordinary dimensions when one lives this close to an artist of Goss's stature," Susan Vail would write. — *The Goss Women*, R. V. Cassill, 1974.

501 I am a painter. — *Violet Clay*, Gail Godwin, 1978.

502 *My name is Ahmoud Hussein./ I am a sculptor.* — *Popo*, Rosser Reeves, 1980.

503 James O'Brien, painter of saints, madonnas, martyrs, and Stations of the Cross for the interiors of parish churches, not to mention an occasional civic mural of Osage Indians presenting corn to a French settler — he who had never in his career entered an expensive restaurant by the front door — should not have undertaken Tony Faust's Four Seasons. — *Anne's Head*, Carol O'Brien Blum, 1982.

504 Jake McKay was drawn to the clown portraits by Rouault because he was eighteen years old. — *Family Trade*, James Carroll, 1982.

505 35. BOY ON VENICE BLVD./ **Los Angeles, 1959**/ Paper, twigs, string, gold stars on cardboard/ Size: 9 x 12 inches/ Coll. Mrs. M. Dorfman, New York/ *Venice is burning.* — *Heart Payments*, Gerald Jay Goldberg, 1982.

506 It's very tricky being an artist in the system. — *The Return of Mr. Hollywood*, Josh Greenfeld, 1984.

507 "It's a fake," said the Russian leader, staring down at the small exquisite painting he held in his hands. — *A Matter of Honor*, Jeffrey Archer, 1986.

508 Quite soon after he began what was at the time just a drawing of an American eating in a restaurant in France, Vincent Booth realized

he would make a painting of it. — *The Lap of Luxury*, William Hamilton, 1988.

509 Aristotle contemplating the bust of Homer thought often of Socrates while Rembrandt dressed him with paint in a white Renaissance surplice and a medieval black robe and encased him in shadows. — *Picture This*, Joseph Heller, 1988.

510 People who tour the Norman Rockwell Museum in Stockbridge, Massachusetts, find that when they leave the building and walk down Main Street many people seem to look familiar. — *Norman Rockwell's Greatest Painting*, Hollis Hodges, 1988.

511 Sunday afternoon. Opening of Myrtle Wood's one-woman pottery show at a modest gallery in Larchmont, New York. — *The Story of a Happy Woman*, Elizabeth Levin, 1988.

512 Before that day, painting had always been a simple act of control for me: look, visualize, and transfer that barn, that face, that flower. — *Points of Light*, Linda Gray Sexton, 1988.

513 I'm learning to pose. — *Owning Jolene*, Shelby Hearon, 1989.

514 Before the beginning, blanker than an eggshell, blanker than the blankest scroll, blanker than all the hungry wordless pages in the hungry word-filled dynasties of what will someday be the future, is the uncarved block./ And then there is Nu Wa. Who gets bored. — *Silk Road*, Jeanne Larsen, 1989.

515 They were young lovers, and married; and hand in hand, that first summer in Europe, they saw, among other inevitable sights, Michelangelo's "Creation of the World" in the Sistine Chapel; and after an hour stumbled back out into the traffic-clogged streets of Rome, into the blinding midday sun, each with a mild headache and not much to say, but smiling, dazed: no longer hand in hand. — *American Appetites*, Joyce Carol Oates, 1989.

516 On the wall behind a table was a big mural labeled *Civilization Teeters*. Dogs chased half-naked women, columns tumbled. — *The Colorist*, Susan Daitch, 1990.

517 At first, I thought I would study art. — *How to Make an American Quilt*, Whitney Otto, 1991.

518 Before I lost my ability to paint, I spent hours each day slamming and smudging colorful oils onto canvas in patterns that appealed to me. — *Recital of the Dog*, David Rabe, 1993.

Astronomy

519 No one would have believed in the last years of the nineteenth century that this world

was being watched keenly and closely by intelligences greater than man's and yet as mortal as his own; that as men busied themselves about their various concerns they were scrutinised and studied, perhaps almost as narrowly as a man with a microscope might scrutinise the transient creatures that swarm and multiply in a drop of water. — *The War of the Worlds*, H. G. Wells, 1898.

520 An old man sat in the shadows of the summer night. From a veranda chair he looked at the stars. — *Erik Dorn*, Ben Hecht, 1921.

521 There was a large, brilliant evening star in the early twilight, and underfoot the earth was half frozen. It was Christmas Eve. — *Aaron's Rod*, D. H. Lawrence, 1922.

522 A heavy cloud passed swiftly away before the wind that came with the night, and far in a clear sky the evening star shone with pure brightness, a gleaming world set high above the dark earth and the black shadows in the lane. — *The Secret Glory*, Arthur Machen, 1922.

523 Night. Dark spaces. A pantomime of stars. The half wheel of the sky rolled slowly into the shadows. — *Humpty Dumpty*, Ben Hecht, 1924.

524 Mavrozomes pushed back the flap of his tent and looked at the stars. — *Durandal*, Harold Lamb, 1926.

525 Enveloped in the gaseous film of the atmosphere, half-covered by a skim of water forming the oceans — the great sphere of the earth spun upon its axis and moved inflexibly in its course around the sun. — *Storm*, George R. Stewart, 1941.

526 *Upon the geography of space, there are no boundaries where all is infinite, nor age where time is only the measure of change within the changeless, nor death where life is the indestructible pulse of energy in the hot and the cold.* — *Darkness and the Deep*, Vardis Fisher, 1943.

527 He lay rolled in his blanket, watching the North Star brighten. — *The Passionate Journey*, Irving Stone, 1949.

528 They say that Andromeda lies far off in the remote fastnesses of space, beyond the mind's reach. And beyond Andromeda are other systems still, each a universe like our own; and beyond these, still others, in all directions. — *The Married Look*, Robert Nathan, 1950.

529 The Milky Way was so bright and long that you could see why the Navajos call it a giant sacred snake, and the three big stars of the constellation Orion were lined up like surveyor's stakes to show me the way over the mountain directly ahead in the east. — *Unholy Uproar*, Clyde Brion Davis, 1957.

530 This was the third nightfall since he began to look for signs of the new moon. — *Arrow of God*, Chinua Achebe, 1969.

531 *The satellite whirled around the globe, a tiny silver bubble lost in the sky's infinitude.* — *The Throne of Saturn*, Allen Drury, 1971.

532 On 24 October 1944 Planet Earth was following its orbit about the sun as it has obediently done for nearly five billion years. — *Space*, James A. Michener, 1982.

533 A shooting star of unusual brilliance and duration streaked across the southern sky, and disappeared beyond the west bank of the Little Miami River of Ohio. — *Counterpoint*, James Huston, 1987.

534 Bellatrix./ Betelgeuse./ Aldebaran. — *Lucid Stars*, Andrea Barrett, 1988.

535 The spring sign of the Ram is, of course, the earliest in the Zodiac; and Aries relates to the first House in the Wheel. You will have read the Divine Ptolemy on the subject. — *The Spring of the Ram*, Dorothy Dunnett, 1988.

536 *Somewhere, my father is teaching us the names of the constellations.* — *Prisoner's Dilemma*, Richard Powers, 1988.

537 It was a private light: modest, unblinking, a cold eye pale and pasty above the silhouetted bungalows; and during the months that I drove in the dark to Manhattan, to my job at Denny Meat Packing Company, I came to think of the planet Venus as my secret morning companion, silent, untouchable, demanding nothing. — *Straight Through the Night*, Edward Allen, 1989.

538 It was the summer that men first walked on the moon. — *Moon Palace*, Paul Auster, 1989.

539 "They say it's the greatest advance in lunar astronomy since Galileo! Four thousand fucking close-up pictures of the moon radioed to Earth … just like *that* in a matter of minutes!" — *Miracles*, Susan Hufford, 1989.

Babies

540 "It's a Holy Terror," said Betsy Barnacle, the monthly nurse. "I never heard such a baby. Scream and scream it does. *And* its little fists!" — *The Holy Terror*, H. G. Wells, 1938.

541 It is said that when the new Queen saw the old Queen's baby daughter, she told the King that the brat must be got rid of at once. And the King, who by now had almost forgotten the old Queen and had scarcely looked at the baby, agreed and thought no more about it. And that would have been the end of that baby girl, but that her nurse, Matulli, came to hear of it. — *Travel Light*, Naomi Mitchison, 1952.

542 On Tuesday Ben gave the Tabors' baby girl the first of her typhus and typhoid shots. — *Pretty Leslie*, R. V. Cassill, 1963.

543 It was early morning in Western Maryland and already the whole Murdoch clan had been in to see the twins. That is, all except Granpap. He wouldn't come down from his shanty along the run. He acted mad every time a new baby turned up, let alone two. — *The Grandfathers*, Conrad Richter, 1964.

544 "This one is different." — *Sacred and Profane*, David Weiss, 1968.

545 "It looks like it has some sort of contagious disease." — *Coming to Life*, Norma Klein, 1974.

546 There is at the moment a baby with bowlegs standing on my lap. — *Babble*, Jonathan Baumbach, 1976.

547 Patrick Silver left the baby in the lobby of the Plaza Hotel. The baby, who was forty-four, sat in an upholstered chair, with his knuckles in his lap. — *The Education of Patrick Silver*, Jerome Charyn, 1976.

548 First you are very small and the color is old-rose and pink, and you are kept very warm. — *God and Sarah Pedlock*, Stephen Longstreet, 1976.

549 "It's not a nose, it's a snout," said Professor Corbett./ "I daresay it'll change," said Mrs. Corbett in a nursing home, wrapping her new-born son's face away in a shawl./ "Change! No change for the better happens now." — *The Cutting Edge*, Penelope Gilliatt, 1978.

550 *Like a baby with a meatless bone in his mouth, a bone given him by his mother to suck while she is in the kitchen minding the pot which has now begun to sing....* — *Sweet and Sour Milk*, Nuruddin Farah, 1979.

551 "Just what do you do with these babies, anyway?" — *Double Negative*, David Carkeet, 1980.

552 "Mommy, where do babies come from?" — *Expecting Miracles*, Linda U. Howard, 1980.

553 I am told that I was an extremely interesting baby. — *Fortunoff's Child*, Leslie Tonner, 1980.

554 Eduard Wertheim thought all babies ugly and never failed to pass this information on to their mothers. — *Yesterday's Streets*, Silvia Tennenbaum, 1981.

555 The baby shouted, a hearty male cry of protest. — *The Garish Day*, Rachel Billington, 1985.

556 In the hospital of the orphanage — the boys' division at St. Cloud's, Maine — two nurses were in charge of naming the new babies and checking that their little penises were healing from the obligatory circumcision. — *The Cider House Rules*, John Irving, 1985.

557 Leila pulled the baby boy even closer to her body. He was hungry and tired but she could not feed him here. — *The Final Passage*, Caryl Phillips, 1985.

558 They is many a way to mark a baby while it is still yet in the womb. — *Storming Heaven*, Denise Giardina, 1987.

559 The baby arrived in the middle of an August night, and announced himself unequivocally as himself. — *Onion*, Kate Braestrup, 1990.

560 Now that the baby was two months old, she seemed to be waking up at least twice a night. — *Slow Motion Riot*, Peter Blauner, 1991.

561 In the seventh year of the People's Republic of China (1956), in a remote village in Yunnan Province, Kuo Hsiao-mei gave birth to a son with extraordinarily well developed earlobes. — *The Laughing Sutra*, Mark Salzman, 1991.

Bathing

562 Among all the pleasant established circumstances of Nina Henry's life she liked her bath the most. — *The Party Dress*, Joseph Hergesheimer, 1930.

563 Julia, by marriage Mrs. Packett, by courtesy Mrs. Macdermot, lay in her bath singing the Marseillaise. — *The Nutmeg Tree*, Margery Sharp, 1937.

564 Hilda Adams was going through her usual routine after coming off a case. She had taken a long bath, using plenty of bath salts, shampooed her short, slightly graying hair, examined her feet and cut her toenails, and was now carefully rubbing hand lotion into her small but capable hands. — *The Haunted Lady*, Mary Roberts Rinehart, 1942.

565 Captain Sir Horatio Hornblower sat in his bath, regarding with distaste his legs dangling over the end. — *Commodore Hornblower*, C. S. Forester, 1945.

566 For the second morning in succession Cass Murray stood in the rear doorway of his livery and watched the young man washing up at the water trough by the corral. — *Play a Lone Hand*, Luke Short, 1951.

567 As I sat in the bath-tub, soaping a meditative foot and singing, if I remember correctly, "Pale Hands I Loved Beside the Shalimar," it would be deceiving my public to say that I was feeling boomps-a-daisy. — *Jeeves and the Feudal Spirit*, P. G. Wodehouse, 1954.

568 Charles Swallow was taking a bath, and as was his custom on such occasions, he had undressed before climbing into the tub. — *The Tents of Wickedness*, Peter De Vries, 1959.

569 The bathers in Baden in summer were few and fat. — *Pawn in Frankincense*, Dorothy Dunnett, 1969.

570 Commander "Rich" Richardson, commanding officer of the United States Ship *Eel*, was luxuriously soaping himself in the cramped officers' shower stall in the after starboard corner of the submarine's forward torpedo room. — *Dust on the Beach*, Edward L. Beach, 1972.

571 My attention was drawn to the spots on my chest when I was in my bath, singing, if I remember rightly, the "Toreador Song" from the opera *Carmen*. — *The Cat-Nappers*, P. G. Wodehouse, 1974.

572 On the day Don Juan was conceived, as on every other day, his mother, the duchess, took a bath. — *The Education of Don Juan*, Robin Hardy, 1980.

573 Margo slid open the glass door leading to the patio outside her bedroom. She set the Jacuzzi pump for twenty minutes, tested the temperature of the water with her left foot, tossed her robe onto the redwood platform, then slowly lowered herself into the hot tub, allowing the swirling water to surround her body. — *Smart Women*, Judy Blume, 1983.

574 Paul lay in the bath and sipped a whisky and soda. — *The Wolf*, Max Davidson, 1983.

575 His mother's fingers were like steel digging into his scalp and he kept his eyes tight shut as soapy water ran down his face. — *Another Street, Another Dance*, Clifford Hanley, 1983.

576 Duane was in the hot tub, shooting at his new doghouse with a .44 Magnum. — *Texasville*, Larry McMurtry, 1987.

577 He opened the bathroom door and saw his daughter's head go under water. — *The Native*, David Plante, 1987.

578 There was something powerful emanating from the bathtub, something magical churning there in the primordial Mr. Bubble sea. — *The Whistling Song*, Stephen Beachy, 1991.

Beginnings

579 The first day of term cannot be considered a cheerful occasion. — *Jack Archer*, G. A. Henty, 1883.

580 In accordance with many most excellent precedents, I might begin by claiming the sympathy due to an orphan alone in the world. — *The Indiscretion of the Duchess*, Anthony Hope, 1894.

581 I scarcely know where to begin, though I sometimes facetiously place the cause of it all to Charley Furuseth's credit. — *The Sea Wolf*, Jack London, 1904.

582 When the Reverend Jerry Catlin and Professor J. Adlee Petrie fell into conversation on the southbound train going into Florence, Alabama, it began for them their disturbed, uncomfortable, and mutually disparaging acquaintance which lasted for the rest of their lives. — *Unfinished Cathedral*, T. S. Stribling, 1934.

583 Wolfe and I sat in the office Friday afternoon. As it turned out, the name of Paul Chapin, and his slick and thrifty notions about getting vengeance at wholesale without paying for it, would have come to our notice pretty soon in any event; but that Friday afternoon the combination of an early November rain and a lack of profitable business that had lasted so long it was beginning to be painful, brought us an opening scene — a prologue, not a part of the main action — of the show that was about ready to begin. — *The League of Frightened Men*, Rex Stout, 1935.

584 Of origins, which grow and change and mean all ways in life, people, living in the flat outland countries of America, might say, as of a storm coming on the horizon, "A cloud no bigger'n a man's hand." — *Main Line West*, Paul Horgan, 1936.

585 It all started one afternoon, early in May, when I came out of the House of Commons with Tommy Deloraine. — *The Power-House*, John Buchan, 1941.

586 It all began the second day of the Moon of Fattening, June 2, 1823. — *Lord Grizzly*, Frederick Manfred, 1954.

587 As far as I know it started when I was about eleven. — *Make Me an Offer*, Wolf Mankowitz, 1955.

588 My adventure began with a legacy, a very small legacy — just under a hundred pounds, in fact. But then it was only an intellectual adventure. — *The Dear Deceit*, Christine Brooke-Rose, 1960.

589 The case began quickly, on the women's floor of the county jail. — *The Ferguson Affair*, Ross Macdonald, 1960.

590 How to make a beginning with them, that was the problem. — *The Limits of Love*, Frederic Raphael, 1960.

591 How did it all begin? These days with everything so fogged up, it's like feeling around in a sack of wool and getting only short broken strands.... — *Four Voices*, Isobel English, 1961.

592 At first I wasn't sure at all where to begin. — *Hombre*, Elmore Leonard, 1961.

593 What led you, just now, to glance at this page? To make a beginning, right? — *Cause for Wonder*, Wright Morris, 1963.

594 Since it was the deciding factor, I might as well begin by describing it. — *The Doorbell Rang*, Rex Stout, 1965.

595 I suppose it all began when that beautiful Pan American hostess put a breakfast tray in front of me and I sat up to reach for the orange

juice. — *The End of the Rug*, Richard Llewellyn, 1968.

596 A man with binoculars. That is how it began: with a man standing by the side of the road, on a crest overlooking a small Arizona town, on a winter night. — *Andromeda Strain*, Michael Crichton, 1969.

597 It was Georg Kerenyi who brought into my life both Lali, my wife, and Julia Homburg. So that it seems only fair to begin at the beginning, with his appearance. — *A Place in the Country*, Sarah Gainham, 1969.

598 It begins on a June afternoon in Majorca, on the beach in front of the Hotel Prado. — *The Red-Haired Bitch*, Clifford Hanley, 1969.

599 I don't know exactly when the restlessness began. I think it must have been round about September. — *The Backward Shadow*, Lynne Reid Banks, 1970.

600 It began oddly. But could it have begun otherwise, however it began? — *The Breast*, Philip Roth, 1972.

601 In the beginning was the word, and Adam was the Printer's Devil. — *Raw Material*, Alan Sillitoe, 1972.

602 Well you cannot hold back any longer. Close your eyes, hold your nose, grab air and jump. — *Foreign Devils*, Irvin Faust, 1973.

603 "You have begun another fashion I fear, my dear." — *The Hollow Lands*, Michael Moorcock, 1974.

604 I can be precise about the day it began. — *The Front Runner*, Patricia Nell Warren, 1974.

605 All beginnings are hard. — *In the Beginning*, Chaim Potok, 1975.

606 At first it had no name. — *Doctor Copernicus*, John Banville, 1976.

607 I made the first incision at 7:15 A.M. It was an important step. — *Moving Parts*, Steve Katz, 1977.

608 Begin at the beginning. — "By the Sea," Martha Gellhorn, 1978.

609 Begin. Again. Begin again, little pig. Begin with who I am, and then the harrowing of hell. — *Merlin*, Robert Nye, 1978.

610 I was there at the beginning. — *Letter to Sister Benedicta*, Rose Tremain, 1978.

611 Where to begin? — *Kalki*, Gore Vidal, 1978.

612 In the beginning there was no beginning, only an emptiness in the midst of which quivered a black egg full of very small things. — *The Sacred Hoop*, Bill Broder, 1979.

613 I have to get this right. I've started it three times. Here is the fourth . . . — *Newsreel*, Irvin Faust, 1980.

614 Let's say it began that afternoon when I exposed myself to Mina Meintjies. — *A Separate Development*, Christopher Hope, 1980.

615 It all began so quietly, so very ordinarily — a routine job, something any junior in an estate agent's office could have handled. — *Solomon's Seal*, Hammond Innes, 1980.

616 1st   To begin with, there is no earthly reason to begin. Heaven knows. — *Creator*, Jeremy Leven, 1980.

617 When had it all begun? — *Silent Song*, Mary Vigliante Szydlowski, 1980.

618 *Before the beginning there was chaos.* — *Spring Moon*, Bette Bao Lord, 1981.

619 Who knows how things begin. Consequences are what we have to live with anyway. — *The Woman Driver*, Jean Thompson, 1985.

620 Now, as it happened, most of the trouble got started because Chick Devine lowered his standards. — *Vacationland*, Christopher Corbett, 1986.

621 It's hard to get started, but the nights are long here, so I've got plenty of time. — *Vic Holyfield and the Class of 1957*, William Heyen, 1986.

622 Miriam says, "Begin *sotto voce*." — *Shoulders*, Georgia Cotrell, 1987.

623 So it begins. — *The Bad Angel*, Ernest K. Gann, 1987.

624 I figure this is one of those things you have to ease into very slowly. No rush, take your time, move around a little, no sense *forcing* things. Feel out the terrain, as it were. — *Class Porn*, Molly Hite, 1987.

625 It was Jasmin who made the first move, not Lacy. That was the awkward but undeniable truth. — *The People in the Picture*, Haydn Middleton, 1987.

626 It's hard to know where to begin. — *The Human Season*, Sarah Rossiter, 1987.

627 All this began long before I died and they cut out my brain to keep it functioning. — *Lindbergh's Son*, John Vernon, 1987.

628 The trouble started on Sunday. — *A Craving for Women*, Sybil Claiborne, 1988.

629 In the beginning was nothing much. — *Joan Makes History*, Kate Grenville, 1988.

630 "All right, all right. Let's get started, ladies and gentlemen. Come on. Find your seats." — *Settling the Score*, Michael Levin, 1989.

631 I place the start of this trouble not with a date, rather with a clever, loving governess named Rosie. — *Walking the Cat*, John Calvin Batchelor, 1991.

632 You know how it begins. Don't you? — *Gojiro*, Mark Jacobson, 1991.

633 If this story has a beginning, a moment at which a single gesture broke the surface of events like a stone thrown into the sea, the ripples cresting away endlessly, then that beginning occurred on a hot July day in the year 1960, in the village of Valle del Sole, when my mother was bitten by a snake. — *The Book of Saints*, Nino Ricci, 1991.

634 I began with what Mom called "sweet dreams": the silver wrappings of chocolate kisses, the glossy yellow and red cartoons from Double Bubble gum, and the cowboy pictures on the underside of Dixie Cup lids. — *Home and Away*, Peter Filene, 1992.

635 Things started with Cynthia in October. — *Praise*, Andrew McGahan, 1992.

636 Begin with beauty. — *The Dork of Cork*, Chet Raymo, 1993.

Behavior

637 I had noticed for some time that Josiah Allen had acted queer. — *Samantha at the St. Louis Exposition*, Marietta Holley *as* Josiah Allen's Wife, 1904.

638 Energy and action may be of two sorts, good or bad; this being as well as we can phrase it in human affairs. — *The Story of the Outlaw*, Emerson Hough, 1907.

639 Much was said in the days of Monica's early youth about being good. — *Thank Heaven Fasting*, E. M. Delafield, 1932.

640 I often meet people who ask me why it happened. Who say they could understand kids from the slums behaving that way, but the sons and daughters of our best families—why them? — *Poorboy at the Party*, Robert Gover, 1966.

641 All week Gus had been fussed by Matilda's unusual activity. — *Jumping the Queue*, Mary Wesley, 1983.

642 Like so much brain damage, the first symptoms mine produced were almost indistinguishable from normal behavior. — *Memories of Amnesia*, Lawrence Shainberg, 1988.

643 "I've told you not to do that before." — *Lion at the Door*, David Attoe, 1989.

644 My behavior slipped after Daddy died and went to San Francisco. — *Sorrow Floats*, Tim Sandlin, 1992.

Bells

645 The sweet bells of Helstonleigh Cathedral were ringing out in the summer's afternoon. — *The Channings*, Mrs. Henry Wood, 1862.

646 The bell of the North Liberty Second Presbyterian Church had just ceased ringing. — *The Argonauts of North Liberty*, Bret Harte, 1888.

647 On a certain afternoon, in the late springtime, the bell upon Tunstall Moat House was heard ringing at an unaccustomed hour. — *The Black Arrow*, Robert Louis Stevenson, 1888.

648 The great bell of Beaulieu was ringing. Far away through the forest might be heard its musical clangor and swell. — *The White Company*, Arthur Conan Doyle, 1891.

649 All the bells were ringing the Angelus. — *The Master-Christian*, Marie Corelli, 1900.

650 From the valley, borne aloft on the wings of the evening breeze, rose faintly the tolling of an Angelus bell, and in a goat-herd's hut on the heights above stood six men with heads uncovered and bowed, obeying its summons to evening prayer. — *Love at Arms*, Rafael Sabatini, 1907.

651 Sylvia was reading in her grandfather's library when the bell tinkled. — *A Hoosier Chronicle*, Meredith Nicholson, 1912.

652 The clangour of bells grew insistent. In uncontrollable hilarity pealed S. Mary, contrasting clearly with the subdued carillon of S. Mark. From all sides, seldom in unison, resounded bells. S. Elizabeth and S. Sebastian, in Flower Street, seemed in loud dispute, while S. Ann "on the Hill," all hollow, cracked, consumptive, fretful, did nothing but complain. Near by S. Nicaise, half paralysed and impotent, feebly shook. Then, triumphant, in a hurricane of sound, S. Irene hushed them all. — *Caprice*, Ronald Firbank, 1917.

653 On Sunday the church bells of Hillsboro rang out across the ripening fields with a grave and holy sound, and again at evening knocked faintly, with quiet sorrow, at doors where children watched for the first star, to make their wishes. — *Autumn*, Robert Nathan, 1921.

654 Mr. Sutherland rang the bell once, in his private sitting-room at the Hotel Splendide, and expected the prompt arrival of the waiter. — *The Vanguard*, Arnold Bennett, 1927.

655 It was midnight of the third day of July, 1775. The bells of Boston were ringing. — *The Master of Chaos*, Irving Bacheller, 1932.

656 I reached out a hand from under the blankets and rang the bell for Jeeves. — *The Code of the Woosters*, P. G. Wodehouse, 1938.

657 "There goes the bell," said Sim. "I told you we should a gone." — *Evening in Spring*, August Derleth, 1941.

658 A bell clanged. Brazen, insistent, maddening. — *Miss Pym Disposes*, Elizabeth Mackintosh *as* Josephine Tey, 1947.

659 The shrill clamoring of the dismissal bell in the hallway was like a long-sought wish that finally comes true. — *Episode in Palmetto*, Erskine Caldwell, 1950.

660 Snowy Weeks was drying himself in the wash house under the tower, listening to noon chiming on two bells, a big one that called across the rooftops of Torre Fiore in a hearty bellow and no nonsense about it, and a little one that followed a long time afterward, creeping out among the glory still afloat with a little clonk from the side of its mouth. — *A Few Flowers for Shiner*, Richard Llewellyn, 1950.

661 At four o'clock in the afternoon, the bell ringers of Hungerford, celebrating Christmas, dropped round globes of sound, clear exclamations of joy from the church tower, to sail free on the cold and brilliant air. — *My Lady Greensleeves*, Constance Beresford-Howe, 1955.

662 On the day when I first learned of my father's journey, I had come back with two companions from a satisfactory afternoon in the weeds near Kay's Bell Foundry, shooting a slingshot at the new bells, which were lying out in the yard and strung up on rafters. — *The Travels of Jaimie McPheeters*, Robert Lewis Taylor, 1958.

663 The bell in the rusty tower of the courthouse struck nine while one of the Cloud boys was filling the gas tank. — *The Winter Rider*, Berry Fleming, 1960.

664 In the evening quiet that had fallen, a bell from far up on Cade's Ridge could be dimly heard. — *A Buried Land*, Madison Jones, 1963.

665 The sound of the Angelus bell floated in the air above the little town of Parish between the hills and the sea. — *The Devil with Love*, Robert Nathan, 1963.

666 The great bell of Cleeve Abbey boomed out over the dank, cold fields. — *Path of Dalliance*, Auberon Waugh, 1963.

667 In the mild January night, a young man was waiting outside his father's house. A single bell rang, and kept on ringing, from the cathedral tower. — *The Malcontents*, C. P. Snow, 1972.

668 When someone pushes the button at the front door of the old brownstone, bells ring in four places: in the kitchen, in the office, down in Fritz's room, and up in my room. — *A Family Affair*, Rex Stout, 1975.

669 A bell clanged somewhere in the dusty distance. — *A More Innocent Time*, Eugenie Hill, 1979.

670 Jason Aloysius Garrity was awakened rudely, as usual, by the clamor of the 5:30-A.M. bells of the little church almost next door: St. John the Baptist Church. — *Answer as a Man*, Taylor Caldwell, 1980.

671 The dogs in my dreams are lulled to sleep by the tolling of tape-recorded bells from a nearby church with loudspeakers in its steeple. — *Dogs, Dreams, and Men*, Joan Kaufman, 1988.

672 Laura brought that child in with her again today, backing through the swing doors dragging the pushchair as the nine o'clock bell rang. — "Darker Days Than Usual" — Suzannah Dunn, 1990.

673 The sound of church bells clamoured down the soft wind of mid June and disturbed the sleeper in the high old bed. — *The Native Air*, Sarah Woodhouse, 1990.

674 The chimes of San Salvatore broke into Josef Breuer's reverie. — *When Nietzsche Wept*, Irvin D. Yalom, 1992.

Bewilderment

675 I am eight years older now. It had never occurred to me that I am advancing in life and experience until, in setting myself to recall the various details of the affair, I suddenly remembered my timid confusion before the haughty mien of the clerk at Keith Prowse's. — *The Ghost*, Arnold Bennett, 1907.

676 "But I can't understand why -"/ "Why what?" said the man called Petrov repressively. — *The Sad Variety*, Cecil Day-Lewis *as* Nicholas Blake, 1964.

677 "I don't see the connection!" — *White Figure, White Ground*, Hugh Hood, 1964.

678 I still haven't figured out my accident. — *The Arrangement*, Elia Kazan, 1967.

679 Most of my life Ive been confused. — *Snakes*, Al Young, 1970.

680 It was a queer, sultry summer, the summer they electrocuted the Rosenbergs, and I didn't know what I was doing in New York. — *The Bell Jar*, Sylvia Plath, 1971.

681 "Swear to God, Matt," Monroe Parks said to his brother Matthew, "I don't know why you bought this here nigger. I plumb downright plain don't know." — *The Dahomean*, Frank Yerby, 1971.

682 Wendell Black, chief surgeon, USVA Hospital, Spruce Harbor, Maine, was mildly perplexed. — *M*A*S*H Goes to Maine*, Richard Hooker, 1972.

683 Their instruments picked up the massive outline long before they saw it. That was to be expected. What baffled Carlsen was that even when they were a thousand miles away, and the braking rockets had cut their speed to seven hundred miles an hour, it was still invisible. — *The Space Vampires*, Colin Wilson, 1976.

684 Celia could never understand how or why she persuaded Nick to take her to Bally C that summer. — *The Out-haul*, Alannah Hopkin, 1985.

685 My mind didn't register for a moment. — *High Stand*, Hammond Innes, 1985.

686 They lay on the hardstand under the wing of *Archangel*, more or less uncertain as to what they were supposed to be doing. — *Paper Doll*, Jim Shepard, 1986.

687 Even at the end of things she is still looking for a reason as she had at the beginning, puzzling in a muddleheaded way while she watches that fool of a Reever, legs dangling from fifty feet up where he has lashed himself for the third day into the crown of a celerywood tree. — *It's Raining in Mango*, Thea Astley, 1987.

688 After all she was not so sure what had happened, or when it had started. — *Women and Men*, Joseph McElroy, 1987.

689 In all probability it's October. Mid October. I guess it could possibly be September. Or November even. I don't know. — *Riding the Dolphin*, Amanda Thomas, 1987.

690 Why I didn't know. — *His Vision of Her*, G. D. Dess, 1988.

691 Nora never did figure out how she ended up in the bedroom of that moribund Amtrak sleeping car with Max Miller. — *Looking for Love*, Ellen Feldman, 1990.

692 "What do they see in it, eh? What do they see in it?" — *Paradise News*, David Lodge, 1991.

693 Dear Reader,/ You are traveling. You are perplexed. You want to know. — *A Guide for the Perplexed*, Jonathan Levi, 1992.

Biography

694 Having, out of friendship for the family, upon whose estate, praised be Heaven! I and mine have lived rent-free time out of mind, voluntarily undertaken to publish the MEMOIRS OF THE RACKRENT FAMILY, I think it my duty to say a few words, in the first place, concerning myself. — *Castle Rackrent*, Maria Edgeworth, 1800.

695 I have heard it remarked, that he who writes his own history ought to possess Irish humour, Scotch prudence, and English sincerity; — the first, that his work may be read; the second that it may be read without injury to himself; the third, that the perusal of it may be profitable to others. — *Discipline*, Mary Brunton, 1814.

696 Professor Joslin, who, as our readers are doubtless aware, is engaged in writing the life of Mrs. Aubyn, asks us to state that he will be greatly indebted to any of the famous novelist's friends who will furnish him with information concerning the period previous to her coming to En-

gland. Mrs. Aubyn had so few intimate friends, and consequently so few regular correspondents, that letters will be of special value. Professor Joslin's address is 10 Augusta Gardens, Kensington, and he begs us to say that he will promptly return any documents entrusted to him.

Glennard dropped the *Spectator* and sat looking into the fire. — "The Touchstone," Edith Wharton, 1900.

697 It may seem presumptuous that so young a man as myself should propose to write his life and memoirs, for, as a rule, one waits until he has accomplished something in the world, or until he has reached old age, before he ventures to tell of the times in which he has lived, and of his part in them. — *Captain Macklin*, Richard Harding Davis, 1902.

698 Since I play no mean part in the events of this chronicle, a few words concerning my own history previous to the opening of the story I am about to tell you will surely not be amiss, and they may help you to a better understanding of my narrative. — *Dorothy Vernon of Haddon Hall*, Charles Major, 1902.

699 It is strange that I can never think of writing any account of my life without thinking of Pauline Mills and wondering what she will say of it. — *A Woman of Genius*, Mary Austin, 1912.

700 Somewhere in this book I must write a paragraph exclusively about myself. — *Gold*, Stewart Edward White, 1913.

701 Hubbard speaks of this story as a biography, but perhaps it is more in the nature of an encyclopædia, or encyclical. — *Human Being*, Christopher Morley, 1932.

702 When I told John that I intended to write his biography, he laughed. — *Odd John*, Olaf Stapledon, 1935.

703 When Mr. William Faraday sat down to write his memoirs after fifty-eight years of blameless inactivity he found the work of inscribing the history of his life almost as tedious as living it had been, and so, possessing a natural invention coupled with a gift for locating the easier path, he began to prevaricate a little upon the second page, working up to downright lying on the sixth and subsequent folios. — *Dancers in Mourning*, Margery Allingham, 1937.

704 This is the story of the lives and loves of Timothy Hazard, and so, indirectly, a token biography of Reno, Nevada, as well. — *The City of Trembling Leaves*, Walter Van Tilburg Clark, 1945.

705 When Martin Crystal's publishers first asked me to write his biography I refused. But they would ask no one else, and others who might with some justification have offered themselves held back, certain that I must be about to publish one. — *The Heart in the Desert*, Gilbert Phelps, 1954.

706 Now, at last, I'm ready to write about Mr. Lancaster. For years I have been meaning to, but only rather halfheartedly; I never felt I could quite do him justice. — *Down There on a Visit*, Christopher Isherwood, 1962.

707 You do me great honor, my friends, in asking me to write down, for the instruction of future ages, some account of the thoughts and actions of Pericles the Athenian, the news of whose death we have just heard. — *Pericles the Athenian*, Rex Warner, 1963.

708 how it was I quote before Pim with Pim after Pim how it is three parts I say it as I hear it — *How It Is*, Samuel Beckett, 1964.

709 I originally wrote the story of Rupert Royce in a more conventional form, using a series of events put together chronologically to show what happened to him in the short time I knew him so well. — *The Statesman's Game*, James Aldridge, 1966.

710 I have been sitting here at my desk with the last page of my book in front of me — my book, still untitled, the biography of the novelist Edward Granville. — *Stonecliff*, Robert Nathan, 1967.

711 In any memoir it is usual for the first sentence to reveal as much as possible of your subject's nature by illustrating it in a vivid and memorable motto, and with my own first sentence now drawing to a finish I see I have failed to do this! — *Saint Jack*, Paul Theroux, 1973.

712 Three full-length books and a variety of articles have been written about Paul Stafford attempting to evaluate his life and work. — *The Merciless Ladies*, Winston Graham, 1979.

713 In accordance with the last will and testament of my ancestor, Malachi Desmond Murfy, Ensign, First Rhode Island Regiment of the Continental Army, I do today, on the 200th anniversary of the Battle of Rhode Island (also called the Battle of Newport), make public his memoirs. — *Murfy's Men*, Gerald Green, 1981.

714 In the preparation of my study on Narita Reyes, I am indebted to my colleagues, particularly to my former teachers, Professors Alejo Orina and M. D. Guerzon who read the manuscript and gave valuable advice. — "Cadena de Amor" — F. Sionil José, 1981.

715 It was Lord Hervey who persuaded me to embark on these memoirs. — *Exit Lady Masham*, Louis Auchincloss, 1983.

716 Our projected study of John Ruskin's last years, a joint venture by my cousin and myself, subtitled, "An Experiment in Biography," was based on shorthand notes of conversations with people who had known Ruskin at the end of his life. — *Brantwood*, Peter Hoyle, 1986.

717 After Mrs. Gray's death I was asked by her daughter Hilda to edit the memoirs Alex had kept locked in a morocco writing case, behind arabesques in faded gilt, the work of some Turkish craftsman, which Grandfather Gray had brought back from Constantinople. — *Memoirs of Many in One*, Patrick White, 1986.

718 I am not going to pretend that hordes of my contemporaries urged me to write this memoir. — *Garish Days*, Lynn Caraganis, 1988.

Birds

719 A crow, who had flown away with a cheese from a dairy window, sate perched on a tree looking down at a great big frog in a pool underneath him. — *The Newcomes*, William Makepeace Thackeray, 1854-1855.

720 It is surely an early hour for the whippoor-will to begin her monotonous plainings, sitting on her accustomed hawthorn, just on the edge of the swamp. — *Eutaw*, William Gilmore Simms, 1856.

721 "My poor pets!" a lady exclaimed sorrowfully; "it is too bad. They all knew me so well, and ran to meet me when they saw me coming, and seemed really pleased to see me even when I had no food to give them." — *For Name and Fame*, G. A. Henty, 1886.

722 A green and yellow parrot, which hung in a cage outside the door, kept repeating over and over:/ "Allez vous-en! Allez vous-en! Sapristi! That's all right!" — *The Awakening*, Kate Chopin, 1899.

723 He darted through the orange orchard searching for slugs for his breakfast, and between whiles he rocked on the branches and rang over his message of encouragement to men. — *The Song of the Cardinal*, Gene Stratton-Porter, 1902.

724 *Over this country, when the giant Eagle flings the shadow of his wing, the land is darkened. So compact is it that the wing covers all its extent in one pause of the flight. The sea breaks on the pale line of the shore; to the Eagle's proud glance waves run in to the foot of the hills that are like rocks planted in green water.* — *Rogue Herries*, Hugh Walpole, 1930.

725 When the peacock comes out of his little house to walk among the old tombstones in the churchyard on the corner, then everyone up and down the block knows that spring has really come. — *Just Across the Street*, Rachel Field, 1933.

726 A redbird trilled from the coral honeysuckle on the white-washed fence of the burying-ground. — *Golden Apples*, Marjorie Kinnan Rawlings, 1935.

727 That morning's ice, no more than a brittle film, had cracked and was now floating in segments. These tapped together or, parting, left channels of dark water, down which swans in slow indignation swam. — *The Death of the Heart*, Elizabeth Bowen, 1938.

728 The gulls swept over Dover. — *The Confidential Agent*, Graham Greene, 1939.

729 High in the reaches of wet sky a buzzard lazed, still-winged — an amazing queer thing for him to do in this cold drizzle. — *Lebanon*, Caroline Miller, 1944.

730 Shy flocks of small banana-green parrots had begun to come back to the pipal trees about the bombed pagoda. But across the rice fields, scorched and barren now from the long dry season, only a few white egrets stepped daintily like ghostly cranes about the yellow dust in the heat haze. — *The Purple Plain*, H. E. Bates, 1947.

731 The cocks were crowing in the cool glassy darkness before the dawn. — *Return to Night*, Mary Renault, 1947.

732 No gulls escorted the trawlers going out of the harbour, at tea-time, as they would on the return journey; they sat upon the rocking waters without excitement, perching along the sides of little boats, slapped up and down by one wake after another. — *A View of the Harbour*, Elizabeth Taylor, 1947.

733 Fog was so dense, bird that had been disturbed went flat into a balustrade and slowly fell, dead, at her feet. — *Party Going*, Henry Green *as* H. V. Yorke, 1951.

734 "Oh, dear, oh, dear!" said Henry Clare./ His sister glanced in his direction./ "They are pecking the sick one. They are angry because he is ill." — *The Present and the Past*, Ivy Compton-Burnett, 1953.

735 The ducks swam through the drawing-room windows. — *Who Was Changed and Who Was Dead*, Barbara Comyns, 1954.

736 The swannery had been established there, just on the edge of Lord Glourie's grounds, because it was here the swans had come of themselves since years, since centuries maybe, to feed on the weeds and to lead their own strong violent life in the lagoon. — "The Bridegroom's Body," Kay Boyle, 1958.

737 The barnacle goose was instantly awake, for even in sleep his senses had detected the change in the behavior of the sea. — *The Strange One*, Fred Bodsworth, 1959.

738 There was something wrong with the swans that May afternoon. — *The Widow's Cruise*, Cecil Day-Lewis *as* Nicholas Blake, 1959.

739 Only the steady creaking of a flight of swans disturbed the silence, labouring low overhead with outstretched necks towards the sea. — *The Fox in the Attic*, Richard Hughes, 1961.

740 If Melba interrupts her South American love song and squawks, "Wurrah Yadoor-a!" I take no notice, simply carry on with whatever I happen to be doing, but if the squawk is followed by the tinny sound she makes with her beak and claws when she tangles with the wire netting of her cage I leave the hut and go into the clearing to calm her down by tickling her stomach and ruffling the top of her head. — *The Birds of Paradise*, Paul Scott, 1962.

741 A family of wild swans skimmed across Skywater. — *Scarlet Plume*, Frederick Manfred, 1964.

742 There had been no surf: only the yellow-brown waters becoming imperceptibly yellow-brown mud; and overhead the sudden inruption of landbirds, the quick nervous flutter of flycatchers skittering across the smooth swoop of the gulls. — *Back to China*, Leslie Fiedler, 1965.

743 "May Liza, how come you so restless and uneasy? You must be restless in your mind."/ "I is. I is. That old screech owl is making me nervous." — *Jubilee*, Margaret Walker, 1966.

744 The birds flew around for nothing but the hell of it. — *An Expensive Place to Die*, Len Deighton, 1967.

745 He left Phoenix in the morning, in the early dawning moments when the world is purple; and he saw, on the highway, bands of spectral birds clustered on the pavement searching for God knows what — certainly not food, not on the bare highway and so near the sleeping city. — *Numbers*, John Rechy, 1967.

746 The large nest of a sparrow was built in the taller branches of a pear tree. — *The Slipway*, Graham Billing, 1969.

747 Sea-birds that ride on the ninth wave from shore are the souls of the dead, sailors say. — *Consider Sappho Burning*, Nicholas Delbanco, 1969.

748 He came out of a tumultuous sky into a captive flock of his own kind, and while waiting out the storm among the manmade ponds which floated earthbound geese, took one of them as his mate. — *Wild Goose, Brother Goose*, Mel Ellis, 1969.

749 In the Wild Life Sanctuary, the Great Horned Owl had died. — *Birds of America*, Mary McCarthy, 1971.

750 Beneath our windows I can hear the crows cawing in the stableyard. — *The Barrier*, Robin Maugham, 1973.

751 Pale freckled eggs. — *The Conservationist*, Nadine Gordimer, 1974.

752 The eagle Sun was named Sun by the Indians because each day their final eagle, doomed by the dam, circled this part of the Navajo Nation in northern New Mexico like the clock of sun. — *Dancers in the Scalp House*, William Eastlake, 1975.

753 Duck, flying in from the south, ignored four or five ponderous explosions over at the quarry. — *Hearing Secret Harmonies*, Anthony Powell, 1975.

754 On a Wednesday in the second half of November, a pheasant, flying over Anthony Keating's pond, died of a heart attack, as birds sometimes do: it thudded down and fell into the water, where he discovered it some hours later. — *The Ice Age*, Margaret Drabble, 1977.

755 From behind a clump of prickly pear, a road runner flew onto the blacktop, and with comic determination began to race the right front tire of the jeep. — *An American Prophet*, Gerald Green, 1977.

756 The seabird was flying east, warned inland by the storm in his cool, hasty blood. — *Crown in Candlelight*, Rosemary Hawley Jarman, 1978.

757 High above the yellowing plain, too high for a shadow, an eagle pair climbed the mid-morning sky, their soaring, spiral flight and a slow-spreading white cloud the only perceptible movement in the clearness overhead. — *Hanta Yo*, Ruth Beebe Hill, 1979.

758 The koels began to call before daylight. — *Clear Light of Day*, Anita Desai, 1980.

759 The swallows were back. — *In Her Garden*, Jon Godden, 1981.

760 *Haforn, the first sea eagle, was born when the skies still hung red with fire and volcanic dust, and the oceans ran wild with stress and hate.* — *The Stonor Eagles*, William Horwood, 1982.

761 But when you raise your head, when you see the trees standing there as they always have, when you see a goose up in the sky and you feel the freezing air hardening the deep insides of your nostrils, you realize the goose, seemingly hanging in front of a cloud, is flying, actually straining to fly at the moment. — *Fisher's Hornpipe*, Todd McEwen, 1983.

762 The cage was too small for the eagle to spread his wings for balance as the journey continued southwards. He was tossed and thrown from one side to another with the frightening vibrations of the great unnatural machine that carried him as his only company. — *Callanish*, William Horwood, 1984.

763 The bird, a pigeon was it? or a dove (she'd found there were doves here) flew through the air, its colour lost in what light remained. — *Carpenter's Gothic*, William Gaddis, 1985.

764 The bird had died. — *The Beacon at Alexandria*, Gillian Bradshaw, 1986.

765 The bitter cold weather set in during the third week of January. Until then the female dunnock's first winter had been relatively easy. — *The Heart of the Valley*, Nigel Hinton, 1986.

766 A night bird winging back to one of the islands made a harsh sobbing cry as it passed near a small cruiser anchored well to the south of the channel. — *Barrier Island*, John D. MacDonald, 1986.

767 I was at my desk by my window in my bedroom when a sparrow appeared on the sill. — *Lovingkindness*, Anne Roiphe, 1987.

768 Last summer, at this bridge, Hugo and I had seen a kingfisher. — *The Cartomancer*, Anne Spillard, 1987.

769 The scout crow, lean in winter, makes a sweep over the outer ring of wrecks and junks. — *Letourneau's Used Auto Parts*, Carolyn Chute, 1988.

770 The pond on the Common froze in the night. Thirteen ducks were caught by their feet. The big dog came along and bit each bird off at the knee. Later, the sight of a stubble of duck stumps poking through the ice like a five o'clock shadow was to fracture Hazel's morning. — *Ducks*, Helen Hodgman, 1988.

771 Three greasy brother crows wheel, beak to heel, cutting a circle into the bruised and troubled sky, making fast, dark rings through the thicksome bloats of smoke. — *And the Ass Saw the Angel*, Nick Cave, 1989.

772 One morning—during the record cold spell of 1851—a big menacing black bird, the likes of which had never been seen before, soared over the crude mill town of Magog, hard by the Vermont border, swooping low again and again. — *Solomon Gursky Was Here*, Mordecai Richler, 1989.

773 *The old woman remembered a swan she had bought many years ago in Shanghai for a foolish sum. This bird, boasted the market vendor, was once a duck that stretched its neck in hopes of becoming a goose, and now look!—it is too beautiful to eat.* — *The Joy Club*, Amy Tan, 1989.

774 Sea birds are aloft again, a tattered few. — *Killing Mister Watson*, Peter Matthiessen, 1990.

775 Late in August, three crows took up residence in the chimney of the corner house on Hemlock Street. — *Seventh Heaven*, Alice Hoffman, 1991.

776 She saw, that afternoon, on Oxford Street, a woman crushing ice cream cones with her heels to feed the pigeons. — *Memories of Rain*, Sunetra Gupta, 1992.

777 Behind the house a crow cawed irritably as the rains began. — *Shadow Play*, Charles Baxter, 1993.

Birth

778 It may suffice the Reader, without being very inquisitive after my Name, that I was born

in the County of *SALOP*, in the Year 1608; under the Government of what Star I was never Astrologer enough to examine; but the Consequences of my Life may allow me to suppose some extraordinary Influence affected my Birth. — *Memoirs of a Cavalier*, Daniel Defoe, 1720.

779 Among other public buildings in a certain town, which for many reasons it will be prudent to refrain from mentioning, and to which I will assign no fictitious name, there is one anciently common to most towns, great or small: to wit, a workhouse; and in this workhouse was born; on a day and date which I need not trouble myself to repeat, inasmuch as it can be of no possible consequence to the reader, in this stage of the business at all events; the item of mortality whose name is prefixed to the head of this chapter. — *Oliver Twist*, Charles Dickens, 1838.

780 I was born in a valley not very remote from the sea. — *Afloat and Ashore*, James Fenimore Cooper, 1844.

781 In the ancient city of London, on a certain autumn day in the second quarter of the sixteenth century, a boy was born to a poor family of the name of Canty, who did not want him. — *The Prince and the Pauper*, Mark Twain, 1882.

782 I first saw the light in the city of Boston in the year 1857. — *Looking Backward*, Edward Bellamy, 1888.

783 I was born under the Blue Ridge, and under that side which is blue in the evening light, in a wild land of game and forest and rushing waters. — *The Crossing*, Winston Churchill, 1904.

784 Edward Henry Machin first saw the smoke on the 27th May 1867, in Brougham Street, Bursley, the most ancient of the Five Towns. — *The Card*, Arnold Bennett, 1911.

785 More than thirty years ago two atoms of the eternal Energy sped forth from the heart of it which we call God, and incarnated themselves in the human shapes that were destined to hold them for a while, as vases hold perfumes, or goblets wine, or as sparks of everlasting radium inhabit the bowels of the rock. — *Love Eternal*, H. Rider Haggard, 1918.

786 I was born at Restwell, two miles from the small town of Whitechurch, in the county of —— in Virginia. The night of my birth, by going to the top of Lone Tree Hill behind Restwell, one might see the smoke and flare of a dying battle and hear in diminuendo the guns of North and South. — *Michael Forth*, Mary Johnston, 1919.

787 Adam Brandon was born at Little Empton in Kent in 1839. — *The Cathedral*, Hugh Walpole, 1922.

788 Oliver Baxter, junior, was born on a vile October day in 1890 — at seven o'clock in the morning, to be exact. — *Oliver October*, George Barr McCutcheon, 1923.

789 The god of the great Osages was still dominant over the wild prairie and the blackjack hills when Challenge was born. — *Sundown*, John Joseph Mathews, 1934.

790 George William Apley was born in the house of his maternal grandfather, William Leeds Hancock, on the steeper part of Mount Vernon Street, on Beacon Hill, on January 25, 1866. — *The Late George Apley*, John P. Marquand, 1937.

791 Sebastian Knight was born on the thirty-first of December, 1899, in the former capital of my country. — *The Real Life of Sebastian Knight*, Vladimir Nabokov, 1941.

792 Jim Pignatelli was born in the year of victories. — *Chosen Country*, John Dos Passos, 1951.

793 First off I must tell you something about myself, Henry Wiggen, and where I was born and my folks. — *The Southpaw*, Mark Harris, 1953.

794 Mr. Kaplan was born one Sunday night, over twenty years ago, quite unexpectedly and full-grown as Athene, to an earnest young man who was lost in solemn research for a book about the Washington correspondents. — *The Return of H*Y*M*A*N K*A*P*L*A*N*, Leo Rosten, 1959.

795 Lucky for me I was born at all really, I mean she could have decided not to bother. — *That's How It Was*, Maureen Duffy, 1962.

796 I was born before my time. When my time came, the place was occupied by someone else; all the good things of life for which I was now fit had suddenly become unfit. — *Before My Time*, Niccolò Tucci, 1962.

797 He was born in Paris in a big white house on a little square off Avenue Foch. Of a mother blond and beautiful and a father quiet and rich. — *The Beastly Beatitudes of Balthazar B*, J. P. Donleavy, 1968.

798 Peter's uncle had been born in 1845, the same year as Ludwig who was to become his lover and, of course, his king. — *The Alabaster Egg*, Gillian Freeman, 1970.

799 No one remembers her beginnings. — *Rubyfruit Jungle*, Rita Mae Brown, 1973.

800 Of the many previous existences that my soul has memory of, none gives me greater pleasure to reflect upon than the one that saw me born of a Brazilian father and an English mother in Rio Grande do Sul in 1851. — *The Beautiful Empire*, Zulfikar Ghose, 1975.

801 I was born. It was born. So it began. It continues. It will outlive me. — *The Assassins*, Joyce Carol Oates, 1975.

802 Gary Cooper White was born in Jersey City, New Jersey. — *Looking for Mr. Goodbar*, Judith Rossner, 1975.

803 I was born on a farm on Whileaway. — *The Female Man*, Joanna Russ, 1975.

804 Early in the spring of 1750, in the village of Juffure, four days upriver from the coast of The Gambia, West Africa, a manchild was born to Omoro and Binta Kinte. — *Roots*, Alex Haley, 1976.

805 I was begotten on the giant of Cerne Abbas. — *Falstaff*, Robert Nye, 1976.

806 Once upon a time, long long ago, but not so far away, George Abraham Carver was born in a place called Georgia. — *The True American*, Melvin Van Peebles, 1976.

807 I was born on July 1, 1880, in a farmhouse about a hundred and thirty miles northeast of the city of Toronto in Ontario, Canada. My mother died giving birth to me and they buried her two days later in the Anglican churchyard here in Craven Falls, not a hundred yards from where I'm sitting at this very moment. — *Farthing's Fortunes*, Richard B. Wright, 1976.

808 I, Edward Milton Henley, was born Saturday, May 26, 1883, in the front bedroom of my family's five-storied brick townhouse. — *Evidence of Love*, Shirley Ann Grau, 1977.

809 I was born in the town of Vliss, up in the north. It is a place of no importance. — *The Confessions of Josef Baisz*, Dan Jacobson, 1977.

810 Ashton Hilary Akbar Pelham-Martyn was born in a camp near the crest of a pass in the Himalayas, and subsequently christened in a patent canvas bucket. — *The Far Pavilions*, M. M. Kaye, 1978.

811 I was born in the city of Bombay ... once upon a time. — *Midnight's Children*, Salman Rushdie, 1981.

812 Surprisingly enough, our Carolyn Kingston was not born at twenty after six. — *Delicate Geometry*, Ken Chowder, 1982.

813 As with most of those who enter this world, Max Britsky did so violently and unwillingly, and once life had been smacked into his small red behind, he screamed out his anger and resentment with a voice and strength that surprised Dr. Segal, who held him upside down by his two small feet. — *Max*, Howard Fast, 1982.

814 I was born in 1950 in a rather odd part of Los Angeles that not very many people know about. — *Screenplay*, MacDonald Harris, 1982.

815 I was born the year of the Crash — a few months earlier than Black Friday — but my farmer parents had done their crashing well before their urban neighbors and were well adjusted to the Great Depression by the time I arrived. — *The Sailing Out*, Julie McDonald, 1982.

816 She was born on the Nunnery Grounds. — *Missed Connections*, Elaine Ford, 1983.

817 "Lor' love you, sir!" Fevvers sang out in a voice that clanged like dustbin lids. "As to my place of birth, why, I first saw light of day right here in smoky old London, didn't I! Not billed the 'Cockney Venus', for nothing, sir, though they could just as well 'ave called me 'Helen of the High Wire', due to the unusual circumstances in which I come ashore — for I never docked via what you might call the *normal channels*, sir, oh, dear me, no; but, just like Helen of Troy, was *hatched*...." — *Nights at the Circus*, Angela Carter, 1984.

818 Alan Mulvanney was born on 10 December 1919. — *A Curious Street*, Desmond Hogan, 1984.

819 I was born on January 6, 1939. — *Growing Up Bronx*, Gerald Rosen, 1984.

820 I was born on Clinton Street in the Lower East Side. — *World's Fair*, E. L. Doctorow, 1985.

821 David Treadup was born in the incorporated village of Salt Branch, New York, on July 7, 1878, at 4:36 P.M., or 5:17 P.M., or 5:23 P.M. — *The Call*, John Hersey, 1985.

822 Way a wee screwed up protestant face an' a head of black hair a was born, in a state of original sin. — *No Mate for the Magpie*, Frances Molloy, 1985.

823 How do I know when I was born? — *Slave*, William Malliol, 1986.

824 I was born in *Cumbria*, near the border with *Scotland*, or so my aunt and uncle told me. — *The Adventures of Robina*, Emma Tennant, 1986.

825 Erc said the night the boy was born he saw the woods by the boy's house catch fire. — *Brendan*, Frederick Buechner, 1987.

826 Langston James McHenry was born in a two-room sharecropper's cabin outside Whippet, Georgia, on the night of July 4, 1922. — *Angel Child*, Mark Steadman, 1987.

827 It was neither the best time nor the best place to be reborn. — *Gabo Djara*, B. Wongar, 1987.

828 My first act on entering this world was to kill my mother. — *The New Confessions*, William Boyd, 1988.

829 A destiny, you might call it, began — according to the weather report in a yellowed newspaper clipping — on a drizzling February afternoon in 1943, when James Payton "Beau" Gunn II officially arrived on earth and was certified a human being of American citizenship. — *Gone the Sun*, Winston Groom, 1988.

830 Daniel Pearse was born on the rainy dawn of March 15, 1966. — *Stone Junction*, Jim Dodge, 1990.

831 I was born the illegitimate son of a Palestinian mother and a French father in a squalid little village on the West Bank of the Jordan River. — *The Perpignon Exchange*, Warren Kiefer, 1990.

832 When Hung Shiu-Ch'uan was letting out his first cry in a midwife's hands on a summer night in 1812, a comet flashed across the evening sky. — *The Second Son of Heaven*, C. Y. Lee, 1990.

833 The sixteen years of Janet's life began in wartime on a fogbound winter night in Edinburgh. — *O Caledonia*, Elspeth Barker, 1991.

Birthdays

834 George Augustus Frederick, Duke of St. James, completed his twenty-first year, an event which created almost as great a sensation among the aristocracy of England as the Norman Conquest. — *The Young Duke*, Benjamin Disraeli, 1831.

835 It was on the night of my thirteenth birthday, I know, that the old farm-house was burned over our heads. — *The Copperhead*, Harold Frederic, 1893.

836 Neville, at five o'clock (nature's time, not man's) on the morning of her birthday, woke from the dream-broken sleep of summer dawns, hot with the burden of two sheets and a blanket, roused by the multitudinous silver calling of a world full of birds. — *Dangerous Ages*, Rose Macaulay, 1921.

837 Because it was his fourteenth birthday they had allowed him a day off from school, his mother doubtfully, his uncles Alan and Robin with their understanding grin. — *The Wind Bloweth*, Donn Byrne, 1922.

838 It was Gerane's birthday. Not very many people were aware of it, to be sure, but few as they were they went a long way toward making up the population of the entire world as far as it was known to the sprightly young woman who was turning nineteen that day. — *The Inn of the Hawk and Raven*, George Barr McCutcheon, 1927.

839 Though we came to Bruges when I was eleven it was not until my thirteenth birthday that Father would give me a boat, and when he did buy it, it was only a second-hand one, broad and flat-bottomed, with little thick oars. — *Too Dear for My Possessing*, Pamela Hansford Johnson, 1940.

840 That was the first time that anyone ever called her an actress — June 1, 1922, Bethel's sixth birthday. — *Bethel Merriday*, Sinclair Lewis, 1940.

841 It was January 6th of the year 1641, being the last of the twelve days of Christmas, and my fifteenth birthday. — *Wife to Mr. Milton*, Robert Graves, 1943.

842 It was her fortieth birthday. — *Pavilion of Women*, Pearl S. Buck, 1946.

843 The occasion was Charmian's twenty-fourth birthday. — *A Summer to Decide*, Pamela Hansford Johnson, 1948.

844 Rain, rain, rain ... my mother put her head through the window to let the neighbour know that I was nine, and they flattered me with the consolation that my birthday had brought showers of blessing. — *In the Castle of My Skin*, George Lamming, 1953.

845 "Happy birthday," my father said./ He brought a book out of his coat pocket and handed it to me. — *Papa You're Crazy*, William Saroyan, 1957.

846 It was the morning of my hundredth birthday. — *The Billion Dollar Brain*, Len Deighton, 1966.

847 On the morning of his seventieth birthday, in the Jubilee month of June, 1897, Adam Swann, one-time cavalryman, subsequently haulier extraordinary, now landscaper and connoisseur, picked up his *Times*, turned his back on an erupting household and stumped down the curving drive to his favourite summer vantage point, a knoll sixty feet above the level of the lake overlooking the rustic building entered on the "Tryst" estate map as "The Hermitage." — *Give Us This Day*, R. F. Delderfield, 1973.

848 I am twenty today. There is only Thankful Perkins to tell it to, but Thankful is asleep. — *Prisons*, Mary Lee Settle, 1973.

849 "Goodnight, Mr. Potter, and happy birthday." — *The Rainbow*, Pearl S. Buck, 1974.

850 It began one day in May. It was my fiftieth birthday. — *Tear His Head Off His Shoulders*, Nell Dunn, 1974.

851 On December 8th, 1915, Meggie Cleary had her fourth birthday. After the breakfast dishes were put away her mother silently thrust a brown paper parcel into her arms and ordered her outside. — *The Thorn Birds*, Colleen McCullough, 1977.

852 *Happy birthday to you,/ Squashed bananas and stew!/ You look like a monkey,/ Go back to the zoo!/* Johnnie Bedworth sang this as lustily as any of his guests. — *The Madonna of the Astrolabe*, J. I.M. Stewart, 1977.

853 I was sick yesterday on my birthday, after not having been sick crossing the Bay of Biscay and even in the storm off Malta. — *The Ginger Tree*, Oswald Wynd, 1977.

854 His thirtieth birthday tomorrow. He would, of course, go home to his mother who, rosy and refulgent with leaning over a hot stove, would have made him all the things he liked best to eat — or, more precisely, some of the things he no longer cared to eat. — *The Good Husband*, Pamela Hansford Johnson, 1978.

855 Today is my birthday, today I am thirty-seven. And look, here is my face floating in the

polished silver mirror. — *Magdalene*, Carolyn Slaughter, 1978.

856 It was the afternoon of my eighty-first birthday, and I was in bed with my catamite when Ali announced that the archbishop had come to see me. — *Earthly Powers*, Anthony Burgess, 1980.

857 On my naming day when I come 12 I gone front spear and kilt a wyld boar he parbly ben the las wyld pig on the Bundel Downs any how there hadnt ben none for a long time befor him nor I aint looking to see none agen. — *Riddley Walker*, Russell Hoban, 1980.

858 "Happy birthday, Bessie." — *The Wine and the Music*, David A. Kaufelt, 1981.

859 Today I remembered my hamster: my pet hamster, Sammy, a gift for my tenth birthday. It is over twenty years since my tenth birthday, since my hamster came to live in our house, but today I remembered it as if it still existed. — *Shuttlecock*, Graham Swift, 1981.

860 The day before yesterday was my birthday and Josh boiled two lobsters in seawater and then baked a chocolate cake for the party later, so rich I wanted to eat it in tissue-paper slices. — *Braided Lives*, Marge Piercy, 1982.

861 She was thinking that it was exactly what she needed, a birthday party. — *The Immigrant's Daughter*, Howard Fast, 1985.

862 I rose early that day, half an hour before the alarm went off. It was my birthday. — *Love Life*, James D. Houston, 1985.

863 I signalized my birthday by giving myself a present since no one else seemed inclined to! — *Close Quarters*, William Golding, 1987.

864 On his sixty-fifth birthday Frank Kellerman locked himself inside an old stone schoolhouse filled with honey bees. — *The Automotive History of Lucky Kellerman*, Steve Heller, 1987.

865 I am now in my twenty-second year and yet the only birthday which I can clearly distinguish among all the rest is my twelfth, for it was on that damp and misty day in September I met the Captain for the first time. — *The Captain and the Enemy*, Graham Greene, 1988.

866 A week before Isobel Callaghan's ninth birthday, her mother said, in a tone of mild regret, "No birthday presents this year! We have to be very careful about money this year." — *I for Isobel*, Amy Witting, 1989.

867 Edward Tyler remembered his forty-first birthday: his brother came back from the woodshed but wasn't carrying any wood, and told Tyler they had better go back down to the shed together. — *The Wars of Heaven*, Richard Currey, 1990.

868 It's my brother Mack's birthday. — *Family Pictures*, Sue Miller, 1990.

869 As dusk fell on her eighteenth birthday,

with only the wood fire for light, Susan Garth, alone in her silent house in a wild part of Arizona, read the two cards she had had that day. — *Silver Light*, David Thompson, 1990.

870 Jessie remembered her sixth birthday well. — *Jessie and Jesus*, Raymond Andrews, 1991.

871 He was twelve twice and later he was nineteen twice. — "Tinian" — Charles Smith, 1991.

Bombs and Explosions

872 *Explosion! Concussion! The vault doors burst open. And deep inside, the money is racked ready for pillage, rapine, loot.* — *The Demolished Man*, Alfred Bester, 1953.

873 When the first bombs lit at Wheeler Field on December 7, 1941, Pfc Richard Mast was eating breakfast. — "The Pistol," James Jones, 1958.

874 When the blast finally came it came foreseen, like the end of the world. — *Men Die*, H. L. Humes, 1959.

875 — Bombs? You're out of your mind. — *The Bombardier*, John William Corrington, 1970.

876 The bearded Anarchist, dressed in a coat three sizes too large and inhabiting the crepuscular frames of an old newsreel, paces restlessly up an unwatched street, holding a homemade bomb deep in one pocket, and a fistful of sulphur matches deep in the other. — *The Tale of Asa Bean*, Jack Matthews, 1971.

877 In his fifty-third year a chemical blast burned the beard from the Colonel's face, and gave to his eyes their characteristic powdery blue. — *War Games*, Wright Morris, 1972.

878 At the crest he could hear the first eee-thud, eee-thud of the mortars. — *The Bridge*, D. Keith Mano, 1973.

879 It all comes together. Don't fall. Each of us carries a stick of dynamite. Concealed on his person. That does several things. One it forms a bond. Two it makes you feel special. Three it's mute articulation of the conditions we live in today I mean not only us but everybody the *zeitgeist* you might say if not the human condition itself and keeps you in touch with reality. — *Out*, Ronald Sukenick, 1973.

880/881 It is a silent flash there in the city's grid, and as I happen to look down at that precise point I am thinking of real estate prices. — *Lookout Cartridge*, Joseph McElroy, 1974.

882 When the bank blew up, I had just got to the part in "Old MacDonald Had a Farm" where it was an *Oink Oink here and an Oink Oink there* (it's easier to grunt on a mouth-harp than do most anything else, so I was stretching it out a little to

make up for spoiling it later on when the *Gobble Gobbles* commenced), and at first I thought I'd busted my eardrums from blowing too hard. — *Tracker*, David Wagoner, 1975.

883 The Tartan Army had planted a bomb at Heathrow, and Julia Stretton, who had gone the long way round past the airport to avoid the usual congestion on the approach-roads to the M3, had been delayed for two hours by police and army checkpoints. — *The Perfect Lover*, Christopher Priest, 1977.

884 The warning message arrived on Monday, the bomb itself on Wednesday. — *The Care of Time*, Eric Ambler, 1981.

885 Fireworks went off behind me and I jumped into a construction ditch. — *On the Way Home*, Robert Bausch, 1982.

886 Lee was in the ladies' room when the bomb went off. — *Dutch Shea, Jr.*, John Gregory Dunne, 1982.

887 Something odd happened; the light was exploding. — *The Address Book*, Anne Bernays, 1983.

888 Darrell Reeves looked to the south when he heard the bombs falling, south down the trackless Jornada del Muerto, the journey of the dead, where the mesquite sucked deep into the desert soil. — *Countrymen of Bones*, Robert Olen Butler, 1983.

889 On a clear night in 1942 a hand grenade exploded in a Cairo slum, killing one man instantly. — *Nile Shadows*, Edward Whittemore, 1983.

890 The first bomb goes off at Heathrow the night before their departure. — *The Italian Lesson*, Janice Elliott, 1985.

891 I thought of the breaking glass. Then of his face, and how it must have looked — the "O" my father's lips pucker into when he is caught unaware — at the sound of the explosion. — *A Boy's Pretensions*, Anthony Giardina, 1988.

892 Chris Mankowski's last day on the job, two in the afternoon, two hours to go, he got a call to dispose of a bomb. — *Freaky Deaky*, Elmore Leonard, 1988.

893 It rose, swelled, then burst and dispersed in a great clatter of sound. — *The High Road*, Edna O'Brien, 1988.

Books

894 Alice was beginning to get very tired of sitting by her sister on the bank, and of having nothing to do: once or twice she had peeped into the book her sister was reading, but it had no pictures or conversations in it, "and what is the use of a book," thought Alice, "without pictures or conversations?" — *Alice's Adventures in Wonderland*, Lewis Carroll, 1865.

895 Subtraction is the hardest "ciphering" in the book. — *The Circuit Rider*, Edward Eggleston, 1874.

896 You don't know about me without you have read a book by the name of *The Adventures of Tom Sawyer*; but that ain't no matter. — *Huckleberry Finn*, Mark Twain, 1884.

897 This book might be called also *The Triumph of Love*. — *Mrs. Craddock*, W. Somerset Maugham, 1902.

898 It was on his fourteenth birthday that Keith Burton discovered the Great Terror, though he did not know it by that name until some days afterward. He knew only, to his surprise and distress, that the "Treasure Island," given to him by his father for a birthday present, was printed in type so blurred and poor that he could scarcely read it. — *Dawn*, Eleanor H. Porter, 1919.

899 A bottle, half full of moonshine whisky, stood on the table./ Beside it, there was a corncob pipe and a library book, held open by a sack of black St. Louis tobacco at an essay called *The American Consciousness*. — *American Dream*, Michael Foster, 1937.

900 I put the 1938-39 edition of *Who's Who in America*, open, on the leaf of my desk, because it was getting too heavy to hold on a hot day. — *Where There's a Will*, Rex Stout, 1940.

901 "The barometer of his emotional nature was set for a spell of riot."/ These words on the printed page had the unsettling effect no doubt intended, but with a difference. At once he put the book aside: closed it, with his fingers still between the pages; dropped his arm over the edge of the chair and let it hang, the book somewhere near the floor. — *The Lost Weekend*, Charles Jackson, 1944.

902 A few mornings ago a large parcel of books and papers came from town for my husband. — *Coronation Summer*, Angela Thirkell, 1953.

903 The graceful and grey, long-legged and small-headed Jane swung back to caress the famous names lined up upon her shelves. — *The Red Priest*, Wyndham Lewis, 1956.

904 I've always liked the idea of books with titles for chapters, such as "Another Adventure Ensues." That's the way all the books used to begin when I was a girl. — *The Weather of February*, Hollis Summers, 1957.

905 It all began one day in April when I went round to change a library book. — *The Color of Murder*, Julian Symons, 1957.

906 I have walked by stalls in the market-place where books, dog-eared and faded from

their purple, have burst with a white hosanna. — *Free Fall*, William Golding, 1959.

907 I divide the books Nero Wolfe reads into four grades: A, B, C, and D. — *Plot It Yourself*, Rex Stout, 1959.

908 You've never heard of me but you've probably read some of my books. — *Amanda*, Paula Christian, 1965.

909 Though it was past nine o'clock, library closing time, the lank, disjointed young man in the duffel coat did not go to the desk to have his books checked out. He went on turning slowly, staring up, knitting his pale eyebrows over the condition of the ceiling. — *Catch a Brass Canary*, Donna Hill, 1965.

910 I've got the whole state of Jewish affairs right between my fingers! — *Thou Worm Jacob*, Mark Mirsky, 1967.

911 Shortly after dawn, or what would have been dawn in a normal sky, Mr. Artur Sammler with his bushy eye took in the books and papers of his West Side bedroom and suspected strongly that they were the wrong books, the wrong papers. — *Mr. Sammler's Planet*, Saul Bellow, 1970.

912 More than twenty-five years have gone by since a guidebook to Nihilon was published. — *Travels in Nihilon*, Alan Sillitoe, 1971.

913 "Books!" said Tuppence./ She produced the word rather with the effect of a bad-tempered explosion. — *Postern of Fate*, Agatha Christie, 1973.

914 This is my favorite book in all the world, though I have never read it. — *The Princess Bride*, William Goldman, 1973.

915 The book of ballads published by Von Humboldt Fleisher in the Thirties was an immediate hit. — *Humboldt's Gift*, Saul Bellow, 1975.

916 They say that every man has a book somewhere inside him, a sort of credo, or confession. — *The Katana*, George MacBeth, 1981.

917 He signed the Friend's Book in his elegant handwriting: Alexander Wedderburn, January 22, 1980. — *Still Life*, A. S. Byatt, 1985.

918 "The book must be dropped." — *What's Bred in the Bone*, Robertson Davies, 1985.

919 At the end of the room, the books were arranged in a tall pyramid on a long table. — *Elena*, Thomas H. Cook, 1986.

920 I am afraid my father's account of his Gallic Wars is among the dullest books ever written. — *Let the Emperor Speak*, Allan Massie, 1987.

921 Perhaps a question will open the way to resolution, for instance: Why does this old A & P supermarket, with its wooden floors, narrow aisles, and overabundance, or so some think, of house-brand canned goods and bakery products, display, as if carelessly forgotten atop a binful of Granny Smith apples, a seemingly well-read paperback copy of *Absalom! Absalom!*? — *Misterioso*, Gilbert Sorrentino, 1989.

922 The book was thick and black and covered with dust. — *Possession*, A. S. Byatt, 1990.

923 I slipped a bookmark into *Psychological Correspondences*. — *Lying Together*, D. M. Thomas, 1990.

924 The black-bound book is about the size of an open hand. — *My Life with Darwin*, Molly Best Tinsley, 1991.

925 With her index finger, Veronica Melendez shoved the paperback volume of Latina short stories across the table's weathered surface. — *Margins*, Terri de la Peña, 1992.

926 Montague Fox flipped open the magazine, exposing the book concealed inside it. They were a study in stark contrast — the glossy, clay-and-glucose-sprayed magazine with its beautiful half-tone illustrations framing the small, yellow-paged book in its dull and distressed leather binding. — *The Book of Common Dread*, Brent Monahan, 1993.

Boredom

927 Everybody has heard of the beautiful Countess of Cressett, who was one of the lights of this country at the time when crowned heads were running over Europe, crying out for charity's sake to be amused after their tiresome work of slaughter: and you know what a dread they have of moping. — *The Amazing Marriage*, George Meredith, 1895.

928 "I wish most heartily that something would happen," Harry Parkhurst, a midshipman of some sixteen years of age, said to his chum, Dick Balderson, as they leaned on the rail of her majesty's gun-boat *Serpent*, and looked gloomily at the turbid steam that rolled past the ship as she lay at anchor. — *Among Malay Pirates*, G. A. Henty, 1897.

929 "What we want," said Harris, "is a change." — *Three Men on Wheels*, Jerome K. Jerome, 1900.

930 "If anything really interesting should happen to me I think I should drop dead," declared Ardmore as he stood talking to Griswold in the railway station at Atlanta. — *The Little Brown Jug at Kildare*, Meredith Nicholson, 1908.

931 "Hole!" said Mr. Polly, and then for a change, and with greatly increased emphasis: "Ole!" He paused, and then broke out with one of his private and peculiar idioms. "Oh! Beastly Silly Wheeze of a Hole!" — *The History of Mr. Polly*, H. G. Wells, 1909.

932 Mr. Barnstaple found himself in urgent need of a holiday, and he had no one to go with

and nowhere to go.—*Men Like Gods*, H. G. Wells, 1923.

933 Looking gloriously bored, Miss Miami Mouth gaped up into the boughs of a giant silk-cotton-tree.—*Prancing Nigger*, Ronald Firbank, 1924.

934 Cleopatra yawned.—*Queen Cleopatra*, Talbot Mundy, 1929.

935 I am living at the Villa Borghese. There is not a crumb of dirt anywhere, nor a chair misplaced. We are all alone here and we are dead. —*Tropic of Cancer*, Henry Miller, 1934.

936 I am in perfect health, work at a job that pays me back, am encircled by friends. Nothing is wrong with my days but they are pallid and dull me.—*Acrobat Admits*, Alfred Grossman, 1959.

937 I've got to have something to do. This place is getting me down.—*The Wolves Were in the Sledge*, Stella Gibbons, 1964.

938 It was the end of August and the children were getting bored with their summer freedom. They had spent too many hours at the mercy of their own desires.—*The Fiend*, Margaret Millar, 1964.

939 Sunday mornings at the American Embassy in Port Amitié were usually quiet. And dull.—*A Thunder at Dawn*, Jack Hoffenberg, 1965.

940 Al Dooley, graduate student in sociology at the University of California, and bored, sick of being bored, bored with being bored, had thought that his service in the army would provide a nice, unpleasant break in the easy slide of his life. Well, it didn't.—*The Great American Jackpot*, Herbert Gold, 1970.

941 Duty aboard a U.S. Navy nuclear ballistic missile submarine can be boring.—*Torpedo!*, Harry Homewood, 1982.

942 Captain Bill Miller leaned back in his chair and tried to stifle a yawn.—*High Command*, John Masters, 1983.

943 Nothing was ever so interesting again after Mamma and Richard Quin died.—*Cousin Rosamund*, Rebecca West, 1985.

944 "I'm being buried alive."—*The Innocents*, Carolyn Slaughter, 1986.

945 "Errol, I'm tired of being a character." —*The Female of the Species*, Lionel Shriver, 1987.

946 Precious little was happening in the Holloway street.—*Nothing for You, Love*, Helen Muir, 1988.

Boys

947 When I was a little boy of about six years old, I was standing with a maid-servant in the balcony of one of the upper rooms of my father's house in London—it was the evening of the first day that I had ever been in London, and my senses had been excited, and almost exhausted, by the vast variety of objects that were new to me.—*Harrington*, Maria Edgeworth, 1817.

948 In the twentieth year of the reign of the right high and puissant king Henry the Eighth, namely, in 1529, on the twenty-first of April, and on one of the loveliest evenings that ever fell on the loveliest district in England, a fair youth, having somewhat the appearance of a page, was leaning over the terrace-wall on the north side of Windsor Castle, and gazing at the magnificent scene before him.—*Windsor Castle*, William Harrison Ainsworth, 1843.

949 It was a bright May morning some twelve years ago, when a youth of still tender age, for he had certainly not entered his teens by more than two years, was ushered into the waiting-room of a house in the vicinity of St. James's Square, which, though with the general appearance of a private residence, and that too of no very ambitious character, exhibited at this period symptoms of being occupied for some public purpose.—*Coningsby*, Benjamin Disraeli, 1844.

950 When Francis, fourth Viscount Castlewood, came to his title, and presently after to take possession of his house of Castlewood, County Hants, in the year 1691, almost the only tenant of the place besides the domestics was a lad of twelve years of age, of whom no one seemed to take any note until my Lady Viscountess lighted upon him, going over the house with the housekeeper on the day of her arrival.—*The History of Henry Esmond*, William Makepeace Thackeray, 1852.

951 Martin Rattler was a very bad boy. At least his aunt, Mrs. Dorothy Grumbit, said so; and certainly she ought to have known, if anybody should, for Martin lived with her, and was, as she herself expressed it, "the bane of her existence,—the very torment of her life."—*Martin Rattler*, R. M. Ballantyne, 1858.

952 "I remember him a little boy," said the Duchess, "a pretty little boy, but very shy. His mother brought him to us one day. She was a dear friend of mine; you know she was one of my bridesmaids?"—*Lothair*, Benjamin Disraeli, 1870.

953 "Please, sir, is this Plumfield?" asked a ragged boy of the man who opened the great gate at which the omnibus left him.—*Little Men*, Louisa May Alcott, 1871.

954 You would have known that it was a holiday in the county-seat village of Luzerne, had you fallen in with a party of country boys dressed in white cotton shirts and trousers of blue jeans, who hurried along the road at sun rise, to the

summit of the hill that overlooks the town.
— *Roxy*, Edward Eggleston, 1878.

955 While the larger boys in the village school of Greenbank were having a game of "three old cat" before school-time, there appeared on the playground a strange boy, carrying two books, a slate, and an atlas under his arm. — *The Hoosier School-Boy*, Edward Eggleston, 1883.

956 "Dreaming, John, as usual? I never saw such a boy. You are always in extremes, either tiring yourself out or lying half-asleep." — *For the Temple*, G. A. Henty, 1888.

957 A very little boy stood upon a heap of gravel for the honor of Rum Alley. He was throwing stones at howling urchins from Devil's Row who were circling madly about the heap and pelting at him. — *Maggie*, Stephen Crane, 1893.

958 There grows in the North Country a certain kind of youth of whom it may be said that he is born to be a Londoner. — *A Man from the North*, Arnold Bennett, 1898.

959 The woods were as the Indians had left them, but the boys who were playing there did not realize, until many years afterwards, that they had moved in as the Indians moved out. Perhaps, if these boys had known that they were the first white boys to use the Indians' playgrounds, the realization might have added zest to the make-believe of their games; but probably boys between seven and fourteen, when they play at all, play with their fancies strained, and very likely these little boys, keeping their stick-horse livery-stable in a wild-grape arbour in the thicket, needed no verisimilitude. — *A Certain Rich Man*, William Allen White, 1909.

960 At the beginning of the long twilight of a summer evening, Sam McPherson, a tall big-boned boy of thirteen, with brown hair, black eyes, and an amusing little habit of tilting his chin in the air as he walked, came upon the station platform of the little corn-shipping town of Caxton in Iowa. — *Windy McPherson's Son*, Sherwood Anderson, 1916.

961 Once upon a time and a very good time it was there was a moocow coming down along the road and this moocow that was coming down along the road met a nicens little boy named baby tuckoo.... — *A Portrait of the Artist as a Young Man*, James Joyce, 1916.

962 In the spring of 1893 Strindberg had just published "A Fool's Confession," D'Annunzio was employing all the multi-colored glory of his style to prove "The Triumph of Death"; Hardy was somberly mixing on his palette the twilight grays and blacks and mourning purples of "Jude the Obscure"; Nordau, gnashing his teeth, was bellowing "Decadent" at his contemporaries who smirked a complacent acceptance of the epithet

... and, all unconscious of the futility and sordidness of the world, Neale Crittendon swaggered along Central Avenue, brandishing his shinny stick. — *Rough-Hewn*, Dorothy Canfield Fisher, 1922.

963 I dreamed of a boy who was born in the land of Puritania and his name was John. And I dreamed that when John was able to walk he ran out of his parents' garden on a fine morning on to the road. — *The Pilgrim's Regress*, C. S. Lewis, 1933.

964 On a warm and bright Saturday morning in May, Master Orvard Stone, a large-headed, partly toothless little boy not yet eight years old, was being dressed in his best by Corbena, the indulgent colored woman more usually familiar to his sight against a background of kitchen. — *Little Orvie*, Booth Tarkington, 1934.

965 Children were chasing an idiot boy up the village street to the churchyard. — *Vein of Iron*, Ellen Glasgow, 1935.

966 An undersized boy, in a neat brown suit, stood in the farmyard. — *Charley Is My Darling*, Joyce Cary, 1940.

967 The first time I saw him he couldn't have been much more than sixteen years old, a little ferret of a kid, sharp and quick. — *What Makes Sammy Run?*, Budd Schulberg, 1941.

968 The little boy named Ulysses Macauley one day stood over the new gopher hole in the backyard of his house on Santa Clara Avenue in Ithaca, California. — *The Human Comedy*, William Saroyan, 1943.

969 Sebastian Barnack came out of the reading room of the public library and paused in the vestibule to put on his shabby overcoat. Looking at him, Mrs. Ockham felt a sword in her heart. This small and exquisite creature with the seraphic face and the pale curly hair was the living image of her own, her only, her dead and vanished darling. — *Time Must Have a Stop*, Aldous Huxley, 1944.

970 On a golden May morning in the sixth year of Calvin Coolidge's presidency, a stout little dark-haired boy named Herbert Bookbinder, dressed in a white shirt, a blue tie and gray knee breeches, sat at a desk in Public School 50 in the Bronx, suffering the pain of a broken heart. — *The City Boy*, Herman Wouk, 1948.

971 Wheeler, or the Ha'penny Bit, as his countrymen ever after were to speak of him, makes his entrance into history at the fall of a November evening in the thirty-ninth year of Victoria's reign, and stands in front of Windsor Castle in a thick Thames fog. — *The Mudlark*, Theodore Bonnet, 1949.

972 Titus is seven. His confines, Gormenghast. — *Gormenghast*, Mervyn Peake, 1950.

973 The boy and the dog followed a cow path

through the woods, the boy's eyes taking in the slick, shiny green of gum and sassafras bushes, the red spray of sumac, the heavy veins of dogwood seedlings. — *Miss Willie*, Janice Holt Giles, 1951.

974 The boy was about fifteen years old. — *The Light in the Forest*, Conrad Richter, 1953.

975 Burr Fuller/ *On His 17th Birthday/ (Seventeen)/ 2 May 1941/ 1. Try to be secretive (cannot). Try to be strong, silent, and hold tongue (no luck at all so far).* — *The Optimist*, Herbert Gold, 1959.

976 Brian, watched by his mother, stood in the paddling-pool without becoming part of the fray. His vacant blue eyes were caught by the broad elbow of the river, though he couldn't be entirely captivated by its movement, and he clutched a mouth-organ as knuckle-duster in case the flying bolts of screamed-up kids should on purpose or accidentally jolt him face down into the gritty water. — *Key to the Door*, Alan Sillitoe, 1961.

977 The boys, as they talked to the girls from Marcia Blaine School, stood on the far side of their bicycles holding the handlebars, which established a protective fence of bicycle between the sexes, and the impression that at any moment the boys were likely to be away. — *The Prime of Miss Jean Brodie*, Muriel Spark, 1961.

978 First of all, it was October, a rare month for boys. Not that all months aren't rare. But there be bad and good, as the pirates say. — *Something Wicked This Way Comes*, Ray Bradbury, 1962.

979 A boy and a horse./ A thin knobby boy, coming sixteen, all long bone and stringy muscle, not yet grown up to knuckly hands and seeming oversize feet, and a big gaunt old draft horse, rough-coated, heavy-fetlocked. — *Monte Walsh*, Jack Schaefer, 1963.

980 The fifteen-year-old boy, Mario, stands on the yellow-gold beach in the early morning, in the butter-colored sunlight, the long, blue-green lip of the sea licking at his bare brown ankles in rippling, lacelike surf, and retreating, to come again and invade, seize, hold for a moment those copper-colored ankles in handcuffs of seawater. — *Let Noon Be Fair*, Willard Motley, 1966.

981 "Mickey Balloon! Mickey Balloon, come down!"/ A little boy, aged four, stood screaming on the verge of the platform. — *The Butterfly Plague*, Timothy Findley, 1969.

982 Gilda Hooper, wedged with her Best Friend into a small front desk, was comparing the boys of Camperlea. She spoke as an authority on male shortcomings. — *The Camperlea Girls*, Olivia Manning, 1969.

983 One evening toward sunset a lonely boy was skating on a pond. His arms were spread like a dancer's and his muffler danced in the wind. The dazzle of the sun turned the snow into molten gold and the lines left by the skater shone like a tangle of red-hot wires. — *America, My Wilderness*, Frederic Prokosch, 1971.

984 The small boy was Aboriginal — distinctly so by cast of countenance, while yet so lightly coloured as to pass for any light-skinned breed, even tanned Caucasian. — *Poor Fellow My Country*, Xavier Herbert, 1975.

985 His visiting grandsons, lounging on the living room rug like young animals resting in the heat of the day, asked him to tell about a shooting he was mixed up in, but he would not accommodate them. — *Hardcastle*, John Yount, 1980.

986 Mick's class filed into the hall and a teacher showed them where to sit. As the boys shuffled along the rows, their feet clanged against the metal legs of the chairs and the Deputy Headmaster, who was supervising the seating arrangements from the platform, shouted at them to make less noise in a voice that implied they were kicking the furniture on purpose. — *Looks and Smiles*, Barry Hines, 1981.

987 The six-year-old boy, Peter, Pete, Peterkin, Petal, Pet, sprawls on his stomach, chin propped on hands, and stares down at the copy of the *Illustrated London News* in an attempt to decipher what is written below the photograph of the Indian Army officer whom he has always known as Uncle Jack. — *Act of Darkness*, Francis King, 1983.

988 Down in Awful Alley, many years ago when the sun was higher in the sky and a much brighter yellow, there lived a strange small boy called Pinfold. — *Funny Papers*, Tom De Haven, 1985.

989 The two boys snickered nervously, each unobtrusively trying to maneuver himself so that the other would be first to enter Old Man Gant's farmhouse. — *The Scarlet Mansion*, Allan W. Eckert, 1985.

990 "Burnes?" Mrs. Jencks enquired generally of the small room filled with six beds, six eight-year-old boys scurrying to get dressed, and odd pieces of clothing on the beds, on the boys, in the air, on the floor, underfoot and in hand as weapons. — *Safekeeping*, Gregory Mcdonald, 1985.

991 The boy had no sooner arrived, people said afterwards, than Balaram had run into the house to look for the Claws. — *The Circle of Reason*, Amitav Ghosh, 1986.

992 The boy squatted in the crow's nest, feeling both lonely and splendid, separated so totally from the men below. — *American Tropic*, David A. Kaufelt, 1986.

993 Thorns and thistles! the boy cried, like a crazy thing, thorns and thistles! — *Behold the Man*, N. Richard Nash, 1986.

994 In the autumn of the year 1842 an active boy might have been observed ascending a hillside in the Western Highlands of Scotland, whilst a rough-coated little dog of the terrier kind dragged along on a length of twine at his heels. — *Captain Vinegar's Commission*, Philip Glazebrook, 1987.

995 If he is awake early enough the boy sees the men walk past the farmhouse down First Lake Road. — *In the Skin of a Lion*, Michael Ondaatje, 1987.

996 "See me," Joe said, in his pajamas and slippers now, coming into the living room to say good night to the party people again. — *Wheat That Springeth Green*, J. F. Powers, 1988.

997 My first night in the foster home, a boy named Sylvester Snell decided that I belonged to him. — *The Year of the Zinc Penny*, Rick DeMarinis, 1989.

998 *There's a boy in the river.* — *A Place in Mind*, Sydney Lea, 1989.

999 Down the slope of the knoll by the river six boys herded a seventh. — *The Drummer of the Eleventh North Devonshire Fusiliers*, Guy Davenport, 1990.

1000 The boy on a bicycle swerved with a flourish into the shadowy drive. — *Changes and Chances*, Stanley Middleton, 1990.

1001 On Poughkeepsie's Main Street, the pedestrian mall, a boy sits. — *The Salt Point*, Paul Russell, 1990.

1002 Peter Flood is eight years old, dressed in tennis shoes and a jacket that is too light against the cold and the wind. — *Brotherly Love*, Pete Dexter, 1991.

1003 Jack Dempsey Cliff sits in cab sixteen outside the Beachcomber Bar, watching two teenage Filipino boys wander out the door carrying spaghetti on paper plates. — *Hunger in America*, David Cates, 1992.

1004 I'm a very dangerous boy. — *Right by My Side*, David Haynes, 1993.

Business

1005 Hillsborough and its outlying suburbs make bricks by the million, spin and weave both wool and cotton, forge in steel from the finest needle up to a ship's armour, and so add considerably to the kingdom's wealth. — *Put Yourself in His Place*, Charles Reade, 1870.

1006 Everybody who has any connection with Birmingham will be acquainted with the vast publishing establishment still known by the short title of "Meeson's," which is perhaps the

most remarkable institution of the sort in Europe. — *Mr. Meeson's Will*, H. Rider Haggard, 1888.

1007 It was a dull evening in the month of September, 1728. The apprentices had closed and barred the shutters and the day's work was over. — *Bonnie Prince Charlie*, G. A. Henty, 1888.

1008 The approach to the offices of Girdlestone and Co. was not a very dignified one, nor would the uninitiated who traversed it form any conception of the commercial prosperity of the firm in question. — *The Firm of Girdlestone*, Arthur Conan Doyle, 1890.

1009 Charon, the Ferryman of renown, was cruising slowly along the Styx one pleasant Friday morning not long ago, and as he paddled idly on he chuckled mildly to himself as he thought of the monopoly in ferriage which in the course of years he had managed to build up. — *A House-Boat on the Styx*, John Kendrick Bangs, 1896.

1010 Mr. Verloc, going out in the morning, left his shop nominally in charge of his brother-in-law. It could be done, because there was very little business at any time, and practically none at all before the evening. — *The Secret Agent*, Joseph Conrad, 1907.

1011 I passed from the street between two lackeys who might have been the lackeys of Marie Antoinette into the curtained and velvety calm of those vast suites which a merchant designed in order to flatter the lust of eyes like mine. — *The Glimpse*, Arnold Bennett, 1909.

1012 In the days when New York's traffic moved at the pace of the drooping horse-car, when society applauded Christine Nilsson at the Academy of Music and basked in the sunsets of the Hudson River School on the walls of the National Academy of Design, an inconspicuous shop with a single show-window was intimately and favourably known to the feminine population of the quarter bordering on Stuyvesant Square. — "Bunner Sisters" — Edith Wharton, 1916.

1013 If you are ever in Brooklyn, that borough of superb sunsets and magnificent vistas of husband-propelled baby-carriages, it is to be hoped you may chance upon a quiet by-street where there is a very remarkable book-shop. — *The Haunted Bookshop*, Christopher Morley, 1919.

1014 No well informed resident of Millsburgh, when referring to the principal industry of his little manufacturing city, ever says "the mills" — it is always "the Mill." — *Helen of the Old House*, Harold Bell Wright, 1921.

1015 Messrs. Frobisher & Haslitt, the solicitors on the east side of Russell Square, counted amongst their clients a great many who had

undertakings established in France; and the firm was very proud of this branch of its business. — *The House of the Arrow*, A. E. W. Mason, 1924.

1016 When the Stippled Silver Kennel, Inc., went into the wholesale raising of silver foxes for a world market, its two partners brought to the enterprise a comfortable working capital and an uncomfortable ignorance of the brain-reactions of a fox. — *The Heart of a Dog*, Albert Payson Terhune, 1924.

1017 The antique shop is very still now. Theobold and I have it all to ourselves, for the cuckoo clock was sold day before yesterday and Theobold has been so industrious of late there are no more mice to venture out from behind the woodwork. — *Hitty*, Rachel Field, 1929.

1018 The Monkey Nest coal mine tipple stood twenty years; its dirt dump grew from a diminutive hillock among the scrub oaks to the height of a young mountain. — *The Disinherited*, Jack Conroy, 1933.

1019 That was the year business failed, and many families, investors, and business houses were ruined. — *One More Spring*, Robert Nathan, 1933.

1020 San Francisco's watery afternoon sunshine was slanting in through the slats of the Venetian blinds which screened the windows of the Harnsworth Furniture Company. — *Zest*, Charles G. Norris, 1933.

1021 It had not taken Wilson Hitchings long to realize that the firm of Hitchings Brothers had its definite place in the commercial aristocracy of the East, and that China had retained a respect for mercantile tradition which had disappeared from the Occidental world. — *Think Fast, Mr. Moto*, John P. Marquand, 1937.

1022 It was fur that made our lives what they were. Fur, and the people who lived by it. — *The Loon Feather*, Iola Fuller, 1940.

1023 I drove out to Glendale to put three new truck drivers on a brewery company bond, and then I remembered this renewal over in Hollywood. — *Double Indemnity*, James M. Cain, 1943.

1024 Spence Douthit had spent the whole day trying to buy a bottle of Maud's favorite stomach tonic on credit somewhere. — *Tragic Ground*, Erskine Caldwell, 1944.

1025 Toward the end of the last century, a time already remote enough to make fables seem possible yet near enough our day to share its commonplaces, a druggist by the name of Timothy Partridge kept a modest shop, too modestly tucked away in a narrow side street. — *Great Mischief*, Josephine Pinckney, 1948.

1026 The store was there, just as Major Fawn-Cochley had said in his letter. — *The Year of the Lion*, Gerald Hanley, 1953.

1027 A market of fat stock has been held in Ashersham market-place, in front of the Shambles, for six centuries. — *The Slaughterhouse Informer*, Edward Hyams, 1955.

1028 The Hudson River Trust Company, at 65 Wall Street, was one of the oldest business structures in the financial area. — *Venus in Sparta*, Louis Auchincloss, 1958.

1029 The office of Conger & Way was on the second floor of a building that once stood on Commerce Street in Cincinnati, not far from the then-famous Suspension Bridge that leads across the wide, muddy Ohio River to Covington, Kentucky. — *The Office*, Frederic Brown, 1958.

1030 "Sir, with respect . . . may the model be handled carefully? It has cost the company whose brief I hold a considerable expenditure of time and money." — *Cone of Silence*, David Beaty, 1959.

1031 Carrie Anderson walked out of the Daitch Shopwell on the Shore Road to her small blue Volkswagen and unloaded her groceries on the back seat. — *The Other Side of Desire*, Paula Christian, 1965.

1032 "Breadth of vision" was a peculiarity much recommended at Amalgamated Television, and from the Chairman's suite in the penthouse on top of Amalgatel House the vision was as broad in every direction as the industrial haze would allow. — *The Tin Men*, Michael Frayn, 1965.

1033 Elgar Enders patted the four new, crisp rent books in his pocket with tender satisfaction. At last he had a business: Real Estate. — *The Landlord*, Kristin Hunter, 1966.

1034 Not many people remember Lamprias now in Athens. But his company is still talked about in the Peloponnese. — *The Mask of Apollo*, Mary Renault, 1966.

1035 Two people had come to buy a desk. — *A Weekend with Claude*, Beryl Bainbridge, 1967.

1036 The seed bins are empty, the counters and rows of shelves along the walls stripped of merchandise, containing only slanting shadows and the slanting rainy light from the front windows. — *A Place on Earth*, Wendell Berry, 1967.

1037 Now folks today we're going to auction off Missus Pimber's things. — *Omensetter's Luck*, William H. Gass, 1967.

1038 When the Shah brothers began to buy land around the small but increasingly flourishing town of Kalapur, where they had established two textile mills, most of the landlords in this part of the Punjab were glad to sell. — *The Murder of Aziz Khan*, Zulfikar Ghose, 1967.

1039 From Los Angeles to Santa Barbara, a paradisal coast bears the permanent exhaust of the automobile: shack towns, oil pumps, drive-ins, Tastee-Freeze bars, motels, service stations. — "Veni, Vidi . . . Wendt" — Richard G. Stern, 1968.

1040 The grocery store on Uhuru Avenue (formerly Queensway) was owned by Sam Fong, a Chinese immigrant. — *Fong and the Indians*, Paul Theroux, 1968.

1041 Men emerge pale from the little printing plant at four sharp, ghosts for an instant, blinking, until the outdoor light overcomes the look of constant indoor light clinging to them. — *Rabbit Redux*, John Updike, 1971.

1042 "As you know," the Governor of the Province said, "there are still opportunities for a little capitalism in Egypt. Cotton now; I have interest still in cotton. The President entrusts me with something under half, a moiety I should say, of. . ." — "New Queens for Old," Gabriel Fielding, 1972.

1043 "Yes," Dortmunder said. "You can reserve all this, for yourself and your family, for simply a ten-dollar deposit." — *Bank Shot*, Donald E. Westlake, 1972.

1044 The Skelly service station is one mile south of Zimmerdale, on the west side of Route 81, going straight down to Wichita. — *Pictures of the Journey Back*, Jack Matthews, 1973.

1045 The street that led to the hotel was crowded, the narrow pavement cluttered with stalls and people striving to sell things; small articles of daily use. — *Mooncranker's Gift*, Barry Unsworth, 1973.

1046 Albert Handley left his car in a meter-bay behind Oxford Street, and went into a shop to buy a transistor radio. — *The Flame of Life*, Alan Sillitoe, 1974.

1047 When Buddy Sandifer drove onto his used-car lot he saw that both Leo, his full-time salesman, and Jack, a schoolteacher who sold cars only on Saturday, had clients in hand, while several other potential customers were roaming unsupervised, opening driver's-side doors and peering at the prices whitewashed on windshields. — *Sneaky People*, Thomas Berger, 1975.

1048 The boss came in, walking fast past the waiting customers to the other side of the counter behind the burly bespectacled white cashier, who was busy writing, receiving money through the steel bars and giving customers receipts. He asked the cashier, "What's going on here, Pont? Why is the shop so full?" — *Muriel at Metropolitan*, Miriam Tlali, 1975.

1049 The Eke Market was the centre of all that mattered in Ibuza. — *The Slave Girl*, Buchi Emecheta, 1977.

1050 My maternal uncle, Sean Bookless, was sole proprietor of this little business, Bone having departed some years before to the great knackery in the sky. — *Pagan's Pilgrimage*, John Herdman, 1978.

1051 Inside Broadcasting House, the Department of Recorded Programmes was some-times called the Seraglio, because its Director found that he could work better when surrounded by young women. — *Human Voices*, Penelope Fitzgerald, 1980.

1052 "How much did you pay for me?" I yelled at Noah York as he paddled the dugout across Sitka Bay. — *Alaska*, Jana Harris, 1980.

1053 On the whole Wallace avoided intimate dealings with the Chinese. — *The Monkey King*, Timothy Mo, 1980.

1054 AAA CON is the first name in the phone book of most large American cities. This outfit arranges drive-aways; searches out people to drive cars for delivery from one place to another. — *Dad*, William Wharton, 1981.

1055 When I reached Crownflights in Baker Street that Tuesday afternoon, walking through pouring rain without an umbrella, I was surprised to find it open. — *Travels to the Enu*, Jakov Lind, 1982.

1056 The dust was thick. It obscured the four small white stores of town when a car passed. The dust slid down the grooves in their tin roofs. — *County Woman*, Joan Williams, 1982.

1057 One Saturday morning in the middle of October, Dolf Beeler, a burly, beer-bellied foreman at the plant in Millville, but who lived in the neighboring town of Hornbeck, came over to Bud's Hardware in Millville to buy paint remover and steel wool for the purpose of stripping a supposedly solid-walnut dresser to the wood that underlay the many coats of varnish. — *The Feud*, Thomas Berger, 1983.

1058 The seed bins are empty. — *A Place on Earth (Revised)*, Wendell Berry, 1983.

1059 Not far from the Jerusalem wall are vineyards with grapes of a very special flavor, and that first time in Judea when I was the senator's agent buying wine and olives for shipment to Rome, I used to think the Jews were like these grapes. — *A Time for Judas*, Morley Callaghan, 1983.

1060 This Chicago business — damn it to hell for all it's done and all it's caused, damn it double for refusing to end. — *The Secret Annie Oakley*, Marcy Heidish, 1983.

1061 Every year Judson Baker and some other boys sold Christmas trees, using the empty lot next door to Nancy Farr's house. — *The Class of '49*, Don Carpenter, 1985.

1062 The Poison Trade. . . — *White Poppy*, Margaret Gaan, 1985.

1063 The flea market in Saint-Ouen: war medals, glass taxidermists' eyes, a bicycle wheel, a leopard's skin, a pack of cards, an acrobat's costume (for Hélène?) with half the pink sequins gone. — *The Dream Years*, Lisa Goldstein, 1985.

1064 Terry Delaney's father often remarked on the state of Main Street, Penrith, in the hard

times of the 1980s. "The shops that sell real things close down," he said, "and in their place you get the bloody juju medicine stalls." — *A Family Madness*, Thomas Keneally, 1985.

1065 It is a pleasant place to work, Viatech, a new bioengineering company in Manhattan, staffed by fairly young biochemists and molecular biologists and geneticists. — *Recombinations*, Perri Klass, 1985.

1066 An inventory of my Business, owing to & by me, Thomas Keene, taken this Day; is as follows, viz. — *The Tree of Life*, Hugh Nissenson, 1985.

1067 Chapman's Yankee Trader, Rte. 45. Gas. Foodstuffs. Sandwiches. Drugstore products (hair spray, toothpaste, band-aids) without a pharmacist. Local papers in the front, beneath a row of paperback books which are gathering dust. — *From My Father, Singing*, David Bosworth, 1986.

1068 The St. Joseph's Laundry, business headquarters for the Prizzi family, was a large, low, triangular building that occupied a pie-cut block in central Flatbush. — *Prizzi's Family*, Richard Condon, 1986.

1069 From Venice to Cathay, from Seville to the Gold Coast of Africa, men anchored their ships and opened their ledgers and weighed one thing against another as if nothing would ever change. — *Niccolò Rising*, Dorothy Dunnett, 1986.

1070 When Wabash Steel had orders and there was work, the fine, black soot from the mill lay on the porch steps each morning like an overnight snow. — *Wabash*, Robert Olen Butler, 1987.

1071 Vartan gave the Ford dealer a check for a little over three thousand. — *Stolen Goods*, Susan Dworkin, 1987.

1072 For many years now I haven't been able to stop the Factory. — *Crosstown Sabbath*, Frederic Morton, 1987.

1073 Early in December, 1985, a rotten day otherwise, Charley Partanna, CEO of the Prizzi family, sat behind his desk in the St. Gabbione Laundry, the family's executive offices for street operations, in central Brooklyn, and listened, over the sloshing roar of the laundry vats turning outside his office door, to a proposal by Sylvan Robbins, president of the hotel company that ran the three Prizzi casinos in Atlantic City. — *Prizzi's Glory*, Richard Condon, 1988.

1074 Luke trades big. — *The Broken Bubble*, Philip K. Dick, 1988.

1075 An old woman came round the streets of a Saturday morning, calling, "Wee lambs to sell, all nicely done! Ask your mother to buy you one!" — *A Chelsea Girl*, Barbara Hanrahan, 1988.

1076 My great-grandfather sometimes painted his face yellow and black and went out to capture a few Caddos to sell to the French.

— *Remember Santiago*, Douglas C. Jones, 1988.

1077 Exec-Career is a head hunting firm, of the modern white-collar tribe of head hunters, specializing in the well-trimmed head of the stockbroker. — *The Last Room in Manhattan*, Kathleen Rockwell Lawrence, 1988.

1078 Guts Gallimore turned out the light in the Blue Flame and stepped out onto the concrete apron that marked the entrance to his establishment. — *The Avenue, Clayton City*, C. Eric Lincoln, 1988.

1079 Inkpen sent me to her to make her more commercial, to get her to switch to electric. — *Painted Turtle*, Clarence Major, 1988.

1080 The service station was one of those lonely, run-down places along the highway, a sun-blistered garage and cafe with two gas pumps out front under a wooden canopy. — *Long Road Home*, Ronald B. Taylor, 1988.

1081 Says he: "*Sensei*, I am astounded!"/ Says I: "Reet. But can you hack it? Is the price not right? Do you dig the concept?" — *The Eight Corners of the World*, Gordon Weaver, 1988.

1082 Along the length of Main Street, the business people of Carson City had come out to sweep the sidewalks in front of their shops and stores and little hotels. — *The Basque Hotel*, Robert Laxalt, 1989.

1083 Pete's gas station was located on Staten Island alongside the world's largest garbage dump. — *The Summer of the Paymaster*, Alfred Nielsen, 1990.

1084 When in Rome (said Sandor) you have to walk down the Via Condotti and look at the shops. That is where the money is, and the windows full of beautiful things. — *Gallowglass*, Ruth Rendell *as* Barbara Vine, 1990.

1085 "I don't offer you these for tuppence," my granpa would shout, holding up a cabbage in both hands, "I don't offer 'em for a penny, not even a ha'penny. No, I'll give 'em away for a farthin'." — *As the Crow Flies*, Jeffrey Archer, 1991.

1086 In September, which to him had always meant the fresh start of a new year, Boomfell sold his first house for Odyssey, and on a Saturday night, in the grip of a prodigal mood, he took his wife to Cyrano's. — *Boomfell*, Douglas Hobbie, 1991.

1087 The case of curiosities came into my possession at a Paris auction in the spring of 1983. — *A Case of Curiosities*, Allen Kurzweil, 1992.

1088 The shops stand three across: mine in the middle, Dennis Vaughan's to my left and Libby Getchel's to my right, fronting on Main Street in Harrow, Massachusetts. — *The Way Men Act*, Elinor Lipman, 1992.

1089 It is the entrance to a flea market. No charge. Admittance free. Sloppy crowds. Vulpine, larking. Why enter? — *The Volcano Lover*, Susan Sontag, 1992.

1090 A number of years ago in the town of La Luz, on an August day half of hot sun, half of rain, Don Enrique Ortiz de León prepared to sell his ancestral estate to an American gentleman and an American lady. — *Consider This, Señora*, Harriet Doerr, 1993.

1091 When Saks opened its doors to the morning crowd, Nancy Whittredge was the second customer into the store. — *Orion*, Ralph Graves, 1993.

Calls

1092 "You're wanted on the telephone, sir." — *The Loot of Cities*, Arnold Bennett, 1911.

1093 Slowly, amidst intolerable noises from, on the one hand the street and, on the other, from the large and voluminously echoing playground, the depths of the telephone began, for Valentine, to assume an aspect that, years ago it had used to have — of being a part of the supernatural paraphernalia of inscrutable Destiny. — *A Man Could Stand Up —*, Ford Madox Ford, 1926.

1094 I have noticed that when someone asks for you on the telephone and, finding you out, leaves a message begging you to call him up the moment you come in, and it's important, the matter is more often important to him than to you. — *Cakes and Ale*, W. Somerset Maugham, 1930.

1095 It seemed to me that I had just gone to bed that Monday night when I heard the telephone ringing and had to crawl out again. — *Miss Pinkerton*, Mary Roberts Rinehart, 1932.

1096 Ernest let the telephone ring, peal on impatient peal, while he searched for a cigarette. — *Men and Brethren*, James Gould Cozzens, 1936.

1097 He wished the phone would stop ringing. — *Johnny Got His Gun*, Dalton Trumbo, 1939.

1098 The telephone rang, and it chanced to be answered by the lame butler whom Lanny had hired in Spain. "Someone for you, Monsieur Lanny. He says his name is Branting." — *Dragon Harvest*, Upton Sinclair, 1945.

1099 Two years after the end of the war, I received a telephone call from a stranger describing himself as Sergeant Burke. — *Mr. Smith*, Louis Bromfield, 1951.

1100 One Saturday in late August when my friend Olwen Taylor's mother telephoned to say that Olwen would not be able to go to the bioscope because she was going to a wedding, I refused to go with Gloria Dufalette (I heard Mrs. Dufalette's call, out the back door in the next house — Gloriah, Gloriah!) or with Paddy Connolly. — *The Lying Days*, Nadine Gordimer, 1953.

1101 The waiter, who had slipped out to make a quick telephone call, came back into the coffee-room of the Goose and Gherkin wearing the starry-eyed look of a man who has just learned that he has backed a long-priced winner. — *The Return of Jeeves*, P. G. Wodehouse, 1953.

1102 The lie detector was asleep when he heard the telephone ringing. — *A Spy in the House of Love*, Anaïs Nin, 1954.

1103 Me and Holly were laying around in bed around 10 A.M. on a Wednesday morning when the call come. — *Bang the Drum Slowly*, Mark Harris, 1956.

1104 I suppose it must have been the shock of hearing the telephone ring, apparently in the church, that made me turn my head and see Piers Longridge in one of the side aisles behind me. — *A Glass of Blessings*, Barbara Pym, 1958.

1105 "Lois? This is Belle! I simply *had* to ring." — *The Cautious Heart*, William Sansom, 1958.

1106 If it hadn't been raining and blowing that raw Tuesday morning in March I would have been out, walking to the bank to deposit a couple of checks, when Austin Byne phoned me, and he might have tried somebody else. — *Champagne for One*, Rex Stout, 1958.

1107 "I dealt with the young person from *Life* on the long distance telephone," Mrs. B. D. Starkey said. — *Dear Beast*, Nancy Hale, 1959.

1108 *Call Aubrey George Grant! Aubrey George Grant!/* The moment had come. — *The Doomed Oasis*, Hammond Innes, 1960.

1109 At slow but regular intervals, in the rhythm of a Roman water-clock that knew the Empire would last for ever, the gathered globule of sweat at the end of his nose fell into the telephone mouthpiece. — *Devil of a State*, Anthony Burgess, 1961.

1110 Arthur Sears came out of the telephone box with a sliding twist, and looked quickly from side to side without moving his head. — *The Heart of London*, Monica Dickens, 1961.

1111 Lashed in the twisted phone wire, Norman was a victim of his own tendency to fool around, but, finally anchored, he became quiet. — *The Tenants of Moonbloom*, Edward Lewis Wallant, 1963.

1112 Possessed with dread that his wife somehow knew what he had been doing, Joe Talbot stopped his car on the road from Central London and dialled his own number at Twickenham. — *One by One*, Penelope Gilliatt, 1965.

1113 The afternoon sun was hot on Martha's back, but not steadily so; she had become conscious of a pattern varying in impact some minutes ago, at the start of a telephone conversation that seemed as if it might very well go on for hours yet. — *Landlocked*, Doris Lessing, 1965.

1114 Call me, Ishmael. Feel absolutely free to. — *The Vale of Laughter*, Peter De Vries, 1967.

1115 It was in the afternoon when the phone call came from Europe, one of those long shimmering afternoons of high summer when the distant reaches of the avenue dissolved into a haze and the heat was locked into the streets by the tall buildings. — *Call in the Night*, Susan Howatch, 1967.

1116 The telephone in Ben Powers's hotel room rang at a little after ten in the morning. — *Janus Island*, Sloan Wilson, 1967.

1117 The telephone rang. — *The New Year*, Pearl S. Buck, 1968.

1118 Towards morning the teleprinter's bell sounded. A whole night could pass without a summons of that sort, for here, unlike the formations, was no responsibility to wake at four and take dictation — some brief unidentifiable passage of on the whole undistinguished prose — from the secret radio *Spider*, calling and testing in the small hours. — *The Military Philosophers*, Anthony Powell, 1968.

1119 The phone's first ring pierced his study door, a klaxon vs. cheap birch veneer. — *Love and Work*, Reynolds Price, 1968.

1120 I was on my third cup of coffee when the telephone began to ring. I let it ring. You wait three years for a phone call, you can wait thirty seconds more. — *The Inheritors*, Harold Robbins, 1969.

1121 "Mama?"/ Sam's quiet voice, which he'd affected since he was at Oxford, murmured in her ear. — *The Sixth Seal*, Mary Wesley, 1969.

1122 Today there are three telephone messages on my desk when I return from my lunch-hour walk around the Shopping Plaza: three small yellow slips, rectangular in shape, and each entitled "Someone Called While You Were Out." — *The Weekend Man*, Richard B. Wright, 1971.

1123 The call had come at 6:12 precisely. It was second nature to him now to note the time by the illuminated dial of his electric bedside clock before he had switched on his lamp, a second after he had felt for and silenced the raucous insistence of the telephone. — *Death of an Expert Witness*, P. D. James, 1977.

1124 "Terry speaking," I said. — *Success*, Martin Amis, 1978.

1125 I was sleeping when Betaut called. — *Death of a Politician*, Richard Condon, 1978.

1126 The bureau clerk was telephoning to the Pensione Sofia while Robert Leaver watched the water-traffic at the ferry and the off-season visitors arriving in Venice. — *Territorial Rights*, Muriel Spark, 1979.

1127 The phone rang. — *The Blue Guitar*, Nicholas Hasluck, 1980.

1128 The telephone rang, waking him. — *Cold Comfort*, David R. Slavitt, 1980.

1129 Sometimes you can hear the wire, hear it reaching out across the miles; whining with its own weight, crying from the cold, panting at the distance, humming with the phantom sounds of someone else's conversation. — *The Chaneysville Incident*, David Bradley, 1981.

1130 Chuck Deering called Silky Monahan at the network. — *The Year of the Mongoose*, William Hogan, 1981.

1131 Donald reached for the phone at the end of its first ring, and at the same time his eye caught the clock on the small night-table. — *Love in All Its Disguises*, Norman Rosten, 1981.

1132 I/ was/ certainly/ wide awake enough/ after shouting "All right,/ Paul!" three times in succession/ and banging down the phone hard enough/ to wake the poor people trying to sleep in/ the rooms on either side of me. — *Death by Dreaming*, Jon Manchip White, 1981.

1133 The phone rang for a long time. She had that chance to reconsider but she continued to stand there with the receiver pressed against her ear. — *Other Halves*, Sue McCauley, 1982.

1134 She should have hung up instantly. — *Radiance*, N. Richard Nash, 1983.

1135 "Call me the minute you get there, okay?" — *Lovers*, Norma Klein, 1984.

1136 I finally forced myself to call Agios. — *I, Giorghos*, William J. Lederer, 1984.

1137 The phone woke him. — *Slow Fade*, Rudolph Wurlitzer, 1984.

1138 It was a wrong number that started it, the telephone ringing three times in the dead of night, and the voice on the other end asking for someone he was not. — *City of Glass*, Paul Auster, 1985.

1139 A month after the military coup in Chile we received a phone call from our friend Marshall Berringer, who for the third time in ten days was escorting a Chilean refugee from New York to Canada. — *Luisa Domic*, George Dennison, 1985.

1140 Mereth replaced the phone receiver as though fearful of hurting it. — *Warrick*, Marilyn Harris, 1985.

1141 Would he accept a collect call from Daisy? — *Clemmons*, Hilary Masters, 1985.

1142 The call came a few days before Christmas, while my wife, Sylvia, and I were having one of our Darby-and-Joan tiffs, the usual result of our being under pressure. — *The Commodore*, Jan de Hartog, 1986.

1143 "Aaron Lebow calling, fresh from his overnight at Our Lady of the Vapors. Come for a drink, Willy. At seven-thirty. I bought the new Boulez *Parsifal*. I'll play some for you and then we'll go for a pleasant dinner to Bobby Van's.

Come. I need you, Willy." — *Privates*, Gene Horowitz, 1986.

1144 Peggy picked up the receiver, but there was no dial tone. — *Their Pride and Joy*, Paul Buttenwieser, 1987.

1145 My ordeal began one summer afternoon when I received a telephone call from the Archbishop of Canterbury. — *Glittering Images*, Susan Howatch, 1987.

1146 It was my first middle-of-the-night crisis call in three years. — *Over the Edge*, Jonathan Kellerman, 1987.

1147 Obadiah Wheeler returned the receiver to its cradle and exhaled. — *Unassigned Territory*, Kem Nunn, 1987.

1148 I walked into the empty old house in Tampa and the phone was ringing. — *Home Again*, Jose Yglesias, 1987.

1149 Debbie telephoned this morning, as she does every morning. Debbie is a volunteer, a member of a group of charitable people that has taken it upon itself to phone old men and women who live alone to make sure they are still alive. — *"M.H." Meets President Harding*, Michael Zagst, 1987.

1150 A couple of days later Pinchot phoned. — *Hollywood*, Charles Bukowski, 1989.

1151 One of those distant Tampa cousins called and told Tristan's mom (his dad was in the hospital for one more day) that Grandpa was dead. — *Tristan and the Hispanics*, Jose Yglesias, 1989.

1152 One day I get a call to pick up a customer in front of the Green Leaf Tavern in Woodside. — *Me and Brenda*, Philip Israel, 1990.

1153 It's ten below out there, snow blowing around like a bastard, when we receive a call from a father concerned about his twelve-year-old son. — *Triphammer*, Dan McCall, 1990.

1154 In the months — more than a year now — since her mother had passed on, the telephone seldom rang in Ruby's apartment. — "The Woman Who Read Novels" — Constance Urdang, 1990.

1155 On Alter's desk the telephone rang, an unwelcome alarm. — *Biography*, Celia Gittelson, 1991.

1156 The telephone gave a faint tingle. — *Horses of War*, Duff Hart-Davis, 1991.

1157 Four and a half months before his wedding, my younger brother called me from Chicago at one in the morning. — *The Easy Way Out*, Stephen McCauley, 1992.

1158 When they called from the Home and said they were making arrangements to send Sister home for Christmas and needed to know which bus she should take, I didn't know what to say. — *Home Truth*, Janis Stout, 1992.

1159 I learned about the other Philip Roth in January 1988, a few days after the New Year, when my cousin Apter telephoned me in New York to say that Israeli radio had reported that I was in Jerusalem attending the trial of John Demjanjuk, the man alleged to be Ivan the Terrible of Treblinka. — *Operation Shylock*, Philip Roth, 1993.

Captivity

1160 Well, it was the next spring after me and Tom Sawyer set our old nigger Jim free the time he was chained up for a runaway slave down there on Tom's uncle Silas's farm in Arkansaw. — *Tom Sawyer, Detective*, Mark Twain, 1896.

1161 It was in the month of May, 1813, that I was so unlucky as to fall at last into the hands of the enemy. — *St. Ives*, Robert Louis Stevenson, 1897.

1162 The weather was very bad, the rain pelting in at the open windows; we were saucy and improvident enough on the first night to tear down some of the rafters to keep the fire alive in the grate — an act for which our guards greatly abused us. — *Proceed, Sergeant Lamb*, Robert Graves, 1941.

1163 To live under the threat of death ennobles some people. Unfortunately it does nothing of the sort for me. — *The Way to the Lantern*, Audrey Erskine Lindop, 1961.

1164 *Jaime will get him. No, Alejo will have him delivered.* — *The Prince*, R. M. Koster, 1971.

1165 The main entrance to Falconer — the only entrance for convicts, their visitors and the staff — was crowned by an escutcheon representing Liberty, Justice and, between the two, the sovereign power of government. — *Falconer*, John Cheever, 1977.

1166 The old man was seated on a wooden table, his scrawny legs spread wide in a V, his ankles lashed at the corners with loops of synthetic cord. He was naked and a knife, the kind the Americans called a K-bar, had been stuck through his scrotum, down low and away from the testes where the skin was loose and wattled like the skin on the neck of a chicken. The point of the blade fixed the old man to the table as surely as a pin held an insect to a collector's board. It was not as painful as it looked; it was the *idea* of it that hurt so. — *The Embassy House*, Nicholas Proffitt, 1986.

1167 He brings me writing materials without asking for money but he does not speak, I cannot be sure what his motives are, whether he has

seen my worth and wishes sincerely to help me or whether he is merely acting on orders from his superiors or it is possible he has believed my promises to reward him when I get out of this hole, but whatever the truth of it I take this chance of reaching you, noble lord. — *Stone Virgin*, Barry Unsworth, 1986.

1168 Winter entered the prison cell unprepared for the change that the short period of imprisonment had brought to his friend. — *Winter*, Len Deighton, 1987.

1169 Sally Gaither had been waiting to be found for a day and a night, sitting naked, wired to her folding chair in a small, shifting storm of steam and hot water, the pink spauldeen bulging fat between her teeth. — *Daydreams*, Mitchell Smith, 1987.

1170 He lies naked on a bed with his wrists bound, legs splayed, ankles secured to the corners. — *Frisk*, Dennis Cooper, 1991.

Castles

1171 On the north-east coast of Scotland, in the most romantic part of the Highlands, stood the castle of Athlin; an edifice built on the summit of a rock whose base was in the sea. This pile was venerable from its antiquity, and from its Gothic structure; but more venerable from the virtues which it enclosed. — *The Castles of Athlin and Dunbayne*, Ann Radcliffe, 1789.

1172 It was a bright morning in the month of August, when a lad of some fifteen years of age, sitting on a low wall, watched party after party of armed men riding up to the castle of the Earl of Evesham. — *The Boy Knight*, G. A. Henty, 1882.

1173 A few miles to the south of Bray Head, on the crest of a hill falling sharply down to the sea, stood Castle Davenant, a conspicuous landmark to mariners skirting the coast on their way back from Cork or Waterford to Dublin Bay. — *Orange and Green*, G. A. Henty, 1888.

1174 Tall, massive, and noble, upon its own cliff, stood — as long may it stand — the grand Castle of Dover, ruling over the Strait that links two seas together, and looking to the opposite coast, whence, happily for herself, Great Britain must have been torn in some long past convulsion of nature. — *The Constable's Tower*, Charlotte Mary Yonge, 1891.

1175 riverrun, past Eve and Adam's, from swerve of shore to bend of bay, brings us by a commodius vicus of recirculation back to Howth Castle and Environs. — *Finnegans Wake*, James Joyce, 1939.

1176 From where they stood, they could see the castle. — *The Saracen Blade*, Frank Yerby, 1952.

1177 The delicate sunshine of an English spring shone through the tall and mullioned windows of the castle. — *Death in the Castle*, Pearl S. Buck, 1965.

1178 The summer day was drawing to a close and dusk had fallen on Blandings Castle, shrouding from view the ancient battlements, dulling the silver surface of the lake and causing Lord Emsworth's supreme Berkshire sow, Empress of Blandings, to leave the open-air portion of her sty and withdraw into the covered shed where she did her sleeping. A dedicated believer in the maxim of early to bed and early to rise, she always turned in at about this time. — *No Nudes Is Good Nudes*, P. G. Wodehouse, 1970.

1179 They don't often invite me to Balmoral nowadays, which is a blessing; those damned tartan carpets always put me off my food, to say nothing of the endless pictures of German royalty and that unspeakable statue of the Prince Consort standing knock-kneed in a kilt. — *Flashman in the Great Game*, George MacDonald Fraser, 1975.

1180 The big house in East Anglia, half-rectory half-manor, had been in the hands of the Tabors for some two hundred years before old John Henry Braithwaite bought it from the last of the line in the 1850s; it was he who made the place absurd by attempting to add the more striking features of a mediaeval castle — crenellating the roof, digging a moat, and throwing three ground floor rooms into one to make a great hall complete with minstrels' gallery. — *Summer Visits*, Margery Sharp, 1977.

1181 In the late afternoon of May 2, 1851, having left the mildness of spring behind in London, in a cold rain, Elizabeth looked up to see the gray silhouette of Eden Castle in the distance. — *The Eden Passion*, Marilyn Harris, 1979.

1182 *THE DUNGEON.* The dungeon is said to be located so far beneath the lowest subterranean chambers of the castle that a question naturally arises: is the dungeon part of the castle itself? — "The Princess, the Dwarf, and the Dungeon," Steven Millhauser, 1993.

Cemeteries

1183 A narrow grave-yard in the heart of a bustling, indifferent city, seen from the windows of a gloomy-looking inn, is at no time an object of enlivening suggestion; and the spectacle is not

at its best when the mouldy tombstones and funeral umbrage have received the ineffectual refreshment of a dull, moist snow-fall. — *The Europeans*, Henry James, 1878.

1184 In the troubled twilight of a March evening ten years ago, an old man, whose equipment and bearing suggested that he was fresh from travel, walked slowly across Clerkenwell Green, and by the graveyard of St. James's Church stood for a moment looking about him. — *The Nether World*, George Gissing, 1889.

1185 Yesterday, an old man nearing my end, I stood by the grave of a noble woman, one of the three noblest I have ever known, my mother, my sister, my wife. — *Except the Lord*, Joyce Cary, 1953.

1186 Three crows flew low over the fresh mound in the Linden burying-ground, dark as the thoughts of the three unmourning mourners. — *The Sojourner*, Marjorie Kinnan Rawlings, 1953.

1187 A country cemetery in upstate New York. — *The Resurrection*, John Gardner, 1966.

1188 Mounds of moist earth were piled around the edge of the grave that had been dug at dawn in St. David's churchyard at Radnor, Pennsylvania, but it dried as the sun rose higher all through the hot morning of July 4, 1809. — *I'll Storm Hell*, Noel B. Gerson, 1967.

1189 Let me tell you./ In the Mount Pleasant Cemetery in Seattle there were three new graves in a row. — *Joe Hill*, Wallace Stegner, 1969.

1190 The giantess was buried in the cemetery by the Lutheran church. It was the expressed wish of the deceased that her remains should be conveyed to their last resting place in the spring cart in which she used to travel about the country when on tour. — *Dove*, Barbara Hanrahan, 1982.

1191 Riding up the winding road of Saint Agnes Cemetery in the back of the rattling old truck, Francis Phelan became aware that the dead, even more than the living, settled down in neighborhoods. — *Ironweed*, William Kennedy, 1983.

1192 *The Arawaks, the first inhabitants of Jamaica, buried their dead in secluded, tranquil places not easily reached.* — *The View from Coyaba*, Peter Abrahams, 1985.

1193 Marc Williams passed through the blighted gate of the cemetery and turned right. — *Mummy*, Daniel Curley, 1987.

1194 The stones lay before him, dappled in the early morning sunfall, stretching far away down the slope and across the river. The aroma of gardenias, rich and pungent, drifted from the overgrown graves along the hill, and Daniel Mitchell knelt beneath a cool oak and pulled the vines back from a marker that had a single word: BABY. — *The Song of Daniel*, Philip Lee Williams, 1989.

1195 They stand still. "And Kafka?" Howard says./ "Kafka is not buried here." — *Frog*, Stephen Dixon, 1991.

Ceremonies and Rites

1196 On the 10th of July 1553, about two hours after noon, a loud discharge of ordnance burst from the turrets of Durham House, then the residence of the Duke of Northumberland, grandmaster of the realm, and occupying the site of the modern range of buildings known as the Adelphi; and at the signal, which was immediately answered from every point along the river where a bombard or culverin could be planted — from the adjoining hospital of the Savoy; the old palace of Bridewell, recently converted by Edward VI., at the instance of Ridley, Bishop of London, into a house of correction; Baynard's Castle, the habitation of the Earl of Pembroke; the gates of London Bridge; and, lastly, from the batteries of the Tower — a gallant train issued from the southern gateway of the stately mansion above named, and descended the stairs leading to the water's edge, where, appointed for their reception, was drawn up a squadron of fifty superbly gilt barges, some decorated with banners and streamers, some with cloth-of-gold and arras, embroidered with the devices of the civic companies, others with innumerable silken pennons to which were attached small silver bells, "making a goodly noise and a goodly sight as they waved in the wind," while others, reserved for the more important personages of the ceremony, were covered at the sides with shields gorgeously emblazoned with the armorial bearings of the different noblemen and honourable persons composing the privy-council, amid which the cognisance of the Duke of Northumberland — a lion rampant, *or*, double quevée, *vert* — appeared proudly conspicuous. — *The Tower of London*, William Harrison Ainsworth, 1840.

1197 Before my coronation there was no event in childhood that impressed itself on my memory with marked or singular distinction. — *The King's Mirror*, Anthony Hope, 1899.

1198 Huddled up in a cope of gold wrought silk he peered around. Society had rallied in force. A christening — and not a child's. — *Concerning the Eccentricities of Cardinal Pirelli*, Ronald Firbank, 1926.

1199 As Mr. Horace Sewall cleared his bearded throat, pushed back his carved armchair, placed his damask napkin on the row of

forks beside his Royal Crown Derby plate, picked up his champagne glass and rose to his feet, the eyes of Sally, his sixteen-year-old daughter, met those of her grandmother across the candlelit table with a little gleam of half-humorous, half-deprecatory sympathy. — *Within This Present*, Margaret Ayer Barnes, 1933.

1200 The Principal had told him to reserve the three center rows. — *Valedictory*, MacKinlay Kantor, 1939.

1201 On the morning of the eleventh of November, 1937, precisely at eleven o'clock, some well-meaning busybody consulted his watch and loudly announced the hour, with the result that all of us in the dining car felt constrained to put aside drinks and newspapers and spend the two minutes' silence in rather embarrassed stares at one another or out of the window. — *Random Harvest*, James Hilton, 1941.

1202 Joe and I sat on the front seat of the church with Mother. Mother's face was red; she kept her head bowed during most of the dedication service, but her eyes were open. — *Brighten the Corner*, Hollis Summers, 1952.

1203 When Patrick suggested throwing their champagne glasses over their shoulders, only Helen threw. — *The Project*, Andrew Sinclair, 1960.

1204 Restraint is the keynote of the Warrington School commencement exercises. — *The Fit*, William Wood, 1960.

1205 *Dost thou, in the name of this Child, renounce the devil and all his works, the vain pomp and glory of the world, with all covetous desires of the same, and the carnal desires of the flesh, so that thou wilt not follow nor be led by them?* — *The Godmother*, Janice Elliott, 1966.

1206 On the second Sunday after the war in Europe ended, we had a service in the school chapel in memory of the dead. — *Fielding Gray*, Simon Raven, 1967.

1207 "Room!" Peter Ringkoping said, reaching his hands out as far as they would go to either side. — *The Entrance to Porlock*, Frederick Buechner, 1970.

1208 The Coleses got up at a quarter to four in the morning so that they might be among the first people to cross the Bridge when the ribbon was cut. — *Water Under the Bridge*, Sumner Locke-Elliott, 1977.

1209 Anthropologists explain how the rituals and totems of primitive people are expressions of ambiguities that a person feels but cannot readily comprehend — himself as an individual and yet a member of a group, as part of both a natural environment and a culture, as possessing instincts for self-preservation and yet for self-sacrifice for a whole. — *Catastrophe Practice*, Nicholas Mosley, 1979.

1210 On this autumn day in Vienna, my mother allowed me to carry the candle to the altar of the Virgin for the first time. — *The Water Castle*, Ingeborg Lauterstein, 1980.

1211 I shall clasp my hands together and bow to the corners of the world. — *Bridge of Birds*, Barry Hughart, 1984.

1212 *In a hollow of the crudely heaped pile of stones some juniper was smoldering, scenting the icy air and casting a red, pulsing glow over the cracked porcelain cup next to it, which held an offering of blood and milk out to the east.* — *Fragments of Light*, Charles LeBaron, 1984.

1213 It did help some to keep his eyes closed, let his mind limber up before starting out through the arctic dark to discover what had been caught in the body trap-line overnight. — *Since Daisy Creek*, W. O. Mitchell, 1984.

1214 Six months after Martin Luther King was shot, four months after Bobby, six days after the 1968 Democratic National Convention shook Chicago, upperclassmen at New York's Ridgedale College for Women gathered in the dining hall to participate in an arcane ritual that everyone agreed was not only sexist but delightfully kinky as well. — *Give Me Time*, Linnea A. Due, 1985.

1215 At six A.M., after a two-hour stand on a cold floor, the enlistees were ordered down to the basement of the water tower and told to strip to their skivvies. — *Brave Talk*, Stephen Molton, 1987.

1216 In the light of coming darkness, on a beach just south of Ensenada, Michael commanded Ginny to bow her head while he crowned her with a broken starfish and christened her *Queen of the World*. — *King of the World*, Merrill Joan Gerber, 1989.

1217 In a cypress grove just beyond Point Reyes there is a shrine where for centuries survivors of shipwreck, fire, and earthquake have given thanks for their escape from death and, to commemorate their moment of salvation, have offered some token: a piece of driftwood that bore them to shore, the charred blanket that put the fire out, the fallen tile, the shattered glass, sometimes the riven stone itself. — *The Shrine at Altamira*, John L'Heureux, 1992.

1218 I was baptized in blood. — *Acts of Faith*, Erich Segal, 1992.

Chance and Luck

1219 As I sit down to write here amidst the shadows of vine-leaves under the blue sky of

southern Italy it comes to me with a certain quality of astonishment that my participation in these amazing adventures of Mr. Cavor was, after all, the outcome of the purest accident. — *The First Men in the Moon*, H. G. Wells, 1901.

1220 Goddess Fortune seems to delight in smiling on a man who risks his all, including life, perhaps, on a desperate chance of, say one to one hundred. — *The Touchstone of Fortune*, Charles Major, 1912.

1221 A destiny that leads the English to the Dutch is strange enough; but one that leads from Epsom into Pennsylvania, and thence into the hills that shut in Altamont over the proud coral cry of the cock, and the soft stone smile of an angel, is touched by that dark miracle of chance which makes new magic in a dusty world. — *Look Homeward, Angel*, Thomas Wolfe, 1929.

1222 A Frenchman named Chamfort, who should have known better, once said that chance was a nickname for Providence. — *The Mask of Dimitrios*, Eric Ambler, 1939.

1223 It could just as well have been any other town but Forks, and any other afternoon but Saturday, but that was the way it happened. — *Bounty Guns*, Luke Short, 1940.

1224 "We are fortunate," Pierce Delaney said to his wife. — *The Angry Wife*, Pearl S. Buck *as* John Sedges, 1947.

1225 The way the thing turned out in the end, it was lucky for all of us: fairly lucky for me, luckier for Donnington, luckiest of all, I suppose, for Barraclough and the five other airmen in his crew. — *The Donnington Legend*, David Beaty, 1949.

1226 As a lot of people in Palmyra had often said, some of them mystified and baffled and many more of them envious, Native Hunnicutt was undoubtedly the luckiest man in town. — *Close to Home*, Erskine Caldwell, 1962.

1227 There were no taxis in the station yard when he came through, but while he stood hesitating, wondering whether to inquire directions and start walking, one returned to the rank. This was lucky. — *The Practice*, Stanley Winchester, 1967.

1228 It is an ill-fortune to be born ill-favoured, that stout limbs and a fair wit scarce redeem. — *Three Years to Play*, Colin MacInnes, 1970.

1229 Potter was lucky; everyone told him so. — *Starting Over*, Dan Wakefield, 1973.

1230 One could imagine that it happened this way:/ in the beginning/ words scattered/ by chance/ and in all directions! — *Take It or Leave It*, Raymond Federman, 1976.

1231 Prem Naran knew himself to be lucky, because the Guru had told him so, that Saturday. — *At Sunrise, the Rough Music*, Richard Llewellyn, 1976.

1232 One suspects that coincidence, made routine by repetition, is the origin of superstition. — *The Monumental Sculptor*, Arthur A. Cohen, 1978.

1233 It was by chance that he met Dunky Aldridge on Thursday on Fifth Avenue after work. — *The Top of the Hill*, Irwin Shaw, 1979.

1234 I have no way of knowing if it is true for others, but for me, things seem to work out for the best. — *Smash*, Garson Kanin, 1980.

1235 Fortune, when not smiling on you, may be grinning at you. — *Sauce for the Goose*, Peter De Vries, 1981.

1236 It was luck, the twins said to everyone, although they did not believe that luck had very much to do with the matter. — *Finders Keepers*, Lucienne S. Bloch, 1982.

1237 I couldn't believe our luck. It was like being in a movie. — *Our Deal*, Norman Levy, 1983.

1238 Chance was in the beginning. — *Mefisto*, John Banville, 1986.

1239 "Can you tell me, Octavia, why our luck never seems to change for the better?" asked Mrs. Drusilla Wright of her sister, adding with a sigh, "We need a new roof." — *The Ladies of Missalonghi*, Colleen McCullough, 1987.

1240 My bad luck started just before Christmas 1985. — *Legacy*, James A. Michener, 1987.

1241 As luck would have it, I didn't meet Sonya on the way to school. — *That's My Baby*, Norma Klein, 1988.

1242 Elaine Netherlands had a change of luck on the day she made a wrong turn in Danbury, Connecticut. — *A Change of Luck*, Julia Markus, 1991.

1243 I don't know if it was luck or providence that put me in Rose Looney's hotel room the day after her wedding. — *Sugar Cage*, Connie May Fowler, 1992.

Change

1244 The old men say their fathers told them that soon after the fields were left to themselves a change began to be visible. It became green everywhere in the first spring, after London ended, so that all the country looked alike. — *After London*, Richard Jefferies, 1885.

1245 "If anyone had told me what wonderful changes were to take place here in ten years, I wouldn't have believed it," said Mrs. Jo to Mrs. Meg, as they sat on a piazza at Plumfield one summer day, looking about them with faces full

of pride and pleasure. — *Jo's Boys*, Louisa May Alcott, 1886.

1246 Sometimes, when I think of my past in a superficial, casual way, the metamorphosis I have gone through strikes me as nothing short of a miracle. — *The Rise of David Levinsky*, Abraham Cahan, 1917.

1247 It is odd, how one's ideas can change. — *The Wall*, Mary Roberts Rinehart, 1938.

1248 Nothing was the same now. — *The Darker Brother*, Bucklin Moon, 1943.

1249 *Plus ça change, plus c'est la même chose.* — *Then and Now*, W. Somerset Maugham, 1946.

1250 Stepping off the bus at Montmartre Djuna arrived in the center of the ambulant Fair and precisely at the moment when she set her right foot down on the cobble-stones the music of the merry-go-round was unleashed from its mechanical box and she felt the whole scene, her mood, her body, transformed by its gaiety exactly as in her childhood her life in the orphan asylum had been suddenly transformed from a heavy nightmare to freedom by her winning of a dance scholarship. — *Children of the Albatross*, Anaïs Nin, 1947.

1251 As Finch Whiteoak was dressing that morning he noticed the change in his hands. — *The Whiteoak Brothers*, Mazo de la Roche, 1953.

1252 *Je rêve donc je suis!* If only I could explain to you how changed I am since those days! — *The Benefactor*, Susan Sontag, 1963.

1253 All around us everything was changing in the order of things we had fashioned for ourselves. — *The Promise*, Chaim Potok, 1969.

1254 Comics, before they are permitted to pass into camp ground — I think to some extent of W. C. Fields and Lenny Bruce — must suffer a sea change. — *You Could Live If They Let You*, Wallace Markfield, 1974.

1255 The staircase had changed in the twenty years and more elapsed since my last view of it. — *The Gaudy*, J. I. M. Stewart, 1974.

1256 "When did you first notice something was wrong?" — *Jake's Thing*, Kingsley Amis, 1978.

1257 When my aunt Zita came, there were changes everywhere. — *Wild Nights*, Emma Tennant, 1979.

1258 "Everything's changing so fast," she said. "Isn't it stunning to wake up every morning and feel that the whole world's brand-new again, a present waiting for you to unwrap it?" — *A Summer in the Twenties*, Peter Dickinson, 1981.

1259 I'm looking at a hot dog bun, and it reminds me of a finger that has undergone a transformation and become a bad thing. — *Physical Culture*, Hillary Johnson, 1989.

1260 When Junior interrupted him, Bobby Sauls had finally seen how the world would be beautifully changed. — *Walls of Blue Coquina*, Sam Harrison, 1990.

1261 The week that Claudia became obsessed with waste, nothing unusual happened. — *Biodegradable Soap*, Amy Ephron, 1991.

1262 This city has changed, and not for the better. — *The Autobiography of My Body*, David Guy, 1991.

1263 "I am getting small," Emmet noted with pleasure as he reached for the keys to his apartment. — *Force of Gravity*, R. S. Jones, 1991.

1264 Bagese, as you must have heard by now, became a bear last year in the city. — *Dead Voices*, Gerald Vizenor, 1992.

Childhood

1265 We are not aware that the infancy of Vivian Grey was distinguished by any extraordinary incident. — *Vivian Grey*, Benjamin Disraeli, 1826.

1266 To begin with the old rigmarole of childhood. — *Wives and Daughters*, Elizabeth Gaskell, 1866.

1267 Of my childhood in this Olaf life I can regain little. — *The Wanderer's Necklace*, H. Rider Haggard, 1914.

1268 My childhood was a queer and not altogether happy one. — *Memoirs of a Fox-Hunting Man*, Siegfried Sassoon, 1929.

1269 As a child, on the Red River plantation where he was born, Little Augie was not required to chop cotton or work in the rice swamp like the other boys of his age. He was considered too frail for hard labor. Instead it became his duty to mind the cows when they grazed in the clover fields and to lead the horses to the watering-place. — *God Sends Sunday*, Arna Bontemps, 1931.

1270 *We are talking now of summer evenings in Knoxville, Tennessee in the time that I lived there so successfully disguised to myself as a child.* — *A Death in the Family*, James Agee, 1957.

1271 When we were very little, I and my brother Hugo, who was a year older, loved our rabbits, turtle, and toys. — *Are You Hungry Are You Cold*, Ludwig Bemelmans, 1963.

1272 Once, when he was five, a Negro woman had been assigned to watch him through the summer, allowing him to wander only twenty paces in each direction. — *A Mother's Kisses*, Bruce Jay Friedman, 1964.

1273 A happy childhood can't be cured. Mine'll hang around my neck like a rainbow, that's all, intead of a noose. In today's world, Miss Piranesi, who doesn't know which is more practical? — *Queenie*, Hortense Calisher, 1971.

1274 My childhood lies behind me muted, opaque and drab, the color of gruel and of woolen gaiters, its noises muted and monotonous as a sleeper's pulse. — *Lovers and Tyrants*, Francine du Plessix Gray, 1976.

1275 As a child I used to think I would never live to be seventy. — *One Last Mirror*, Andrew Harvey, 1985.

1276 I have been trying to remember where it began, thinking about my early childhood and wondering if anything might have happened that made me become what I am. — *The Glamour*, Christopher Priest, 1985.

1277 As the Korean war ended and our uncles began to come home, my cousin Tucker noted that the last of the war marked our last summer as children, being we were twelve years old at the start of it and we'd be teenagers at the end. — *Just Before Daybreak*, Audrey Couloumbis, 1987.

1278 No wonder Victor never fell in love. A childhood like the one he had would make ice cubes of us all. — *Arcadia*, Jim Crace, 1991.

1279 Back during the Civil War Kyle Nitburg was just twelve years old. — *Never Die*, Barry Hannah, 1991.

1284 In the dream in the dream/ the child played a poem/ protected by mild adjectives/ gentle verbs and the two/ pronouns teaching the/ division of earth and sky/ night and day/ object and show; and the separating/ personal eye. — *Intensive Care*, Janet Frame, 1970.

1285 As a child of eight that summer of 1918 he took for granted that all people in the world existed for his delight. — *A Would-Be Saint*, Robin Jenkins, 1978.

1286 *When I first saw the child I cannot say.* — *An Imaginary Life*, David Malouf, 1978.

1287 See the child. He is pale and thin, he wears a thin and ragged linen shirt. — *Blood Meridian*, Cormac McCarthy, 1985.

1288 To a child, nothing that is familiar in her world — not earthquakes or revolutions, slavery or sodomy, poverty or riches — seems either exotic or wicked. — *Home Ground*, Lynn Freed, 1986.

1289 Let's start here: the eyes of the child looking. — *The Rising*, Edgar White, 1988.

1290 There is a special curse on the child of a great love. — *The Grotto*, Coral Lansbury, 1989.

1291 The children are fighting in the back seat. — "Peacetime," Constance Urdang, 1990.

Children

1280 The yard was all silent and empty under the burning afternoon heat, which had made its asphalt springy like turf, when suddenly the children threw themselves out of the great doors at either end of the Sunday-school — boys from the right, girls from the left — in two howling, impetuous streams, that widened, eddied, intermingled and formed backwaters until the whole quadrangle was full of clamour and movement. — *Anna of the Five Towns*, Arnold Bennett, 1902.

1281 "That's the child — that's Cherry," Sister Seraphine said in her serene voice. — *The Secret of the Marshbanks*, Kathleen Norris, 1940.

1282 Once there were four children whose names were Peter, Susan, Edmund and Lucy. This story is about something that happened to them when they were sent away from London during the war because of the air-raids. — *The Lion, the Witch and the Wardrobe*, C. S. Lewis, 1950.

1283 Once there were four children whose names were Peter, Susan, Edmund and Lucy, and it has been told in another book called *The Lion, the Witch and the Wardrobe* how they had a remarkable adventure. — *Prince Caspian*, C. S. Lewis, 1951.

Churches

1292 Scarcely had the abbey-bell tolled for five minutes, and already was the church of the Capuchins thronged with auditors. Do not encourage the idea, that the crowd was assembled either from motives of piety or thirst of information. But very few were influenced by those reasons; and in a city where superstition reigns with such despotic sway as in Madrid, to seek for true devotion would be a fruitless attempt. — *The Monk*, Matthew G. Lewis, 1796.

1293 About the year 1764, some English travellers in Italy, during one of their excursions in the environs of Naples, happened to stop before the portico of the *Santa Maria del Pianto*, a church belonging to a very ancient convent of the order of *Black Penitents*. The magnificence of this portico, though impaired by time, excited so much admiration, that the travellers were curious to survey the structure to which it belonged, and with this intention they ascended the marble steps that led to it. — *The Italian*, Ann Radcliffe, 1797.

1294 At a quarter to one o'clock, on a wet Sunday afternoon, in November, 1837, Samuel Snoxell, page to Mr. Zachary Thorpe, of Baregrove Square, London, left the area gate with

three umbrellas under his arm, to meet his master and mistress at the church door, on the conclusion of morning service. — *Hide and Seek*, Wilkie Collins, 1854.

1295 The new church of St. John's, on Fifth Avenue, was thronged the morning of the last Sunday of October, in the year 1880. — *Esther*, Henry Adams, 1884.

1296 A great mulititude of people filled the church, crowded together in the old black pews, standing closely thronged in the nave and aisles, pressing shoulder to shoulder even in the two chapels on the right and left of the apse, a vast gathering of pale men and women whose eyes were sad and in whose faces was written the history of their nation. — *The Witch of Prague*, F. Marion Crawford, 1891.

1297 It was very still in the small neglected chapel. — *The Valley of Decision*, Edith Wharton, 1902.

1298 Why pounce upon the cathedral? There it stood, amidst its town, awaiting them, three little people about to join the millions over whom in its long life it had cast its shelter and its spell. — *Dimple Hill*, Dorothy M. Richardson, 1938.

1299 When you are still several miles outside the town of Castlerampart you can see the spire of the church pricking the distant clouds. — *The House in Clewe Street*, Mary Lavin, 1945.

1300 Lady Nelly came out from the cool, porphyry-tinted twilight of St. Mark's into the strong white sunshine of the Piazza. — *Eustace and Hilda*, L. P. Hartley, 1947.

1301 The church was cold. It was October, too early for the heating to be on. Outside, the sun gave a watery promise of warmth and good cheer, but here within the chill grey stone there was only dampness and a sure foreknowledge of winter. — *The Burden*, Agatha Christie *as* Mary Westmacott, 1956.

1302 Many people had gathered, either ironically or sentimentally: the air was slashed by modish dresses and fierce make-up at mouth and eye, so at odds with the elephantine pillars and arches and the calm windows with their miracles, lilies and turbaned, disconsolate seekers in the desert, together with Christ walking on waves in an off-hand way. — *Orders of Chivalry*, Peter Vansittart, 1958.

1303 It had been a lucky day for the Order of St. Clement the day Mr. Billy Cosgrove entered the sacristy of a suburban church after Mass and shook the hand of Father Urban. — *Morte d'Urban*, J. F. Powers, 1962.

1304 It was a pretty churchyard. An ugly church, monstrous and vulgar as the cloth merchants who had built it. — *Gentleman and Ladies*, Susan Hill, 1968.

1305 An explosion of chrysanthemums, candlelight, Oriental carpets, Byzantine eyes. Plumes of incense rising between two a cappella choirs, blown heavenward by chanting voices. — *The Black Marble*, Joseph Wambaugh, 1978.

1306 The very size of the Cathedral was a surprise. — *A Severed Wasp*, Madeleine L'Engle, 1982.

1307 This morning I visited once again the little church of St. Julien-le-Pauvre. — *The Last Testament of Oscar Wilde*, Peter Ackroyd, 1983.

1308 If you should ever happen to make the trip to Slaka, that fine flower of middle European cities, capital of commerce and art, wide streets and gipsy music, then, whatever else you plan to do there, do not, as the travel texts say, neglect to visit the Cathedral of Saint Valdopin: a little outside the town, at the end of the tramway-route, near to the power station, down by the slow, marshy, mosquito-breeding waters of the great River Niyt. — *Rates of Exchange*, Malcolm Bradbury, 1983.

1309 About six, one wet Friday evening in March, Bridget Mayor was preparing for her first (and as it was to turn out her only) visit to the Apostolic Church of the Children of Sinai, where she wrongly thought her vicar had urged her to go as part of the ecumenical services in the district. — *Behaving Badly*, Catherine Heath, 1985.

1310 The bruise-coloured steeple of St. Augustine's was visible for miles around on the hill of South Hobart: a watch-tower over a camp of fear. — *The Doubleman*, C. J. Koch, 1985.

1311 As the brothers left the chapel, Luke lingered behind on the pretext of hanging some hassocks back on their hooks. — *Little Bits of Baby*, Patrick Gale, 1989.

1312 Upstate New York./ August 1906./ Half-moon and a wrack of gray clouds./ Church windows and thirty nuns singing the Night Office in Gregorian chant. Matins. Lauds. And then silence. — *Mariette in Ecstasy*, Ron Hansen, 1991.

Cinema

1313 The ticket-taker of the Nickelorion Moving-Picture Show is a public personage, who stands out on Fourteenth Street, New York, wearing a gorgeous light-blue coat of numerous brass buttons. — *Our Mr. Wrenn*, Sinclair Lewis, 1914.

1314 It has been interesting to watch the elegant and dignified traditions of the world of literature and cultivated appreciation, under the stresses and thrusts produced by the development of rapid photography during the past half-

century. — *The King Who Was a King*, H. G. Wells, 1929.

1315 As the earlier of the two afternoon programs at the Garfield Avenue Theater was completed and a sparse procession of patrons emerged to the sidewalk, an imported closed automobile stopped before the entrance and a colored chauffeur, neat in dark grey, opened the door of the rear compartment. — *The Lorenzo Bunch*, Booth Tarkington, 1936.

1316 Though I haven't ever been on the screen I was brought up in pictures. — *The Last Tycoon (Unfinished)*, F. Scott Fitzgerald, 1941.

1317 Stella sat in a small, dark room and watched her own figure acting on the screen. — "Stella," Anaïs Nin, 1945.

1318 The first time that Margaret Pennefather saw Colum McInnes on the films she was not attracted by him, indeed she was repelled, even more sharply repelled than she expected to be. — *My Fellow Devils*, L. P. Hartley, 1951.

1319 The owner-manager was also the ticket seller and ticket taker and would have been his own projectionist, too, if labor regulations had not forced him to hire a licensed one. — *The Morning and the Evening*, Joan Williams, 1961.

1320 All through that year the kinemas showed scenes from the Wild West Exhibition in London on Gaumont Graphic or Pathé Pictorial (for the cowboys much *largo* to express wide open spaces; but for the little geisha girls the piano sounded a touching staccato). — *No Laughing Matter*, Angus Wilson, 1967.

1321 They were watching Ryan beat up the Mexican crew leader on 16mm Commercial Ektachrome. — *The Big Bounce*, Elmore Leonard, 1969.

1322 Look and tell, I heard as the first movie began to roll. — *Caliban's Filibuster*, Paul West, 1971.

1323 I sat there in that pitch-dark movie house — something was wrong with the projector, so even the screen was abnormally dark — half the time fascinated by *The Maltese Falcon* and half the time fascinated by Rhoda biting the polish off her nails. — *Six Months with an Older Woman*, David A. Kaufelt, 1973.

1324 As always when the weather was not unusual the Californian sun shone brightly down on the Superba-Llewellyn motion-picture studio at Llewellyn City. — *The Plot That Thickened*, P. G. Wodehouse, 1973.

1325 Certain melodramatic situations derived from the detective story and the thriller have been so done to death by the cinema and television that I suspect a new and nonsensical law of inverse probability has been established — the more frequently one of these situations is shown on the screen, the less chance there is of

its taking place in the viewer's real life. — "Poor Koko," John Fowles, 1974.

1326 It will be remembered that during his transatlantic flight Victor England watches a Western. — *California Time*, Frederic Raphael, 1975.

1327 Skin flick. My skin. Open scene inside my head. Deep nothing. — *Blue Skies, No Candy*, Gael Greene, 1976.

1328 She says, "This movie's much too violent for me, I've got to leave." — *Too Late*, Stephen Dixon, 1978.

1329 When her last movie was being promoted Kelly Rayburn told an interviewer she had stayed with her career for the long haul of more than thirty-five years and more than that number of pictures because before it all began a fortune teller's Tarot cards had predicted she was going to be a big star. — *Flame*, R. V. Cassill, 1980.

1330 It was intended to be the pivotal scene in the film in which the protagonist becomes suddenly aware of the conspiracy into which he is being drawn. — *The Man from Marseille*, J. P. Smith, 1985.

1331 I'm going to run the home movie again. Unlike the Egyptian mummy, I ain't pressed for time. — *Scorpio Rising*, R. G. Vliet, 1985.

1332 I should have known: When a star like Vico disappears, the spotlight he lived under spills into headlines, and anyone caught there tastes the actor's secret vice. — *The Last Film of Emile Vico*, Thomas Gavin, 1986.

1333 The philosopher loved the flicks, periodically needing to empty himself in that laving river of light in which he could openly gape and forget. — *The World As I Found It*, Bruce Duffy, 1987.

Cities and Towns

1334 In one respect, there is a visible improvement in the goodly town of Manhattan, and that is in its architecture. — *The Ways of the Hour*, James Fenimore Cooper, 1850.

1335 There is an assize-town in one of the eastern counties which was much distinguished by the Tudor sovereigns, and, in consequence of their favour and protection, attained a degree of importance that surprises the modern traveller. — *Ruth*, Elizabeth Gaskell, 1853.

1336 All who have travelled through the delicious scenery of North Devon must needs know the little white town of Bideford, which slopes upwards from its broad tide-river paved

with yellow sands, and many-arched old bridge where salmon wait for Autumn floods, toward the pleasant upland on the west. — *Westward Ho!*, Charles Kingsley, 1855.

1337 It is the London season: come into the country! It is hot, and dusty, and muddy here; and this opening of all the drains, which is to bridle all the disorders by and by, poisons us dead meanwhile, O Board of Health! Come into the country! — *Clouds and Sunshine*, Charles Reade, 1855.

1338 On the north-eastern shores of England there is a town called Monkshaven, containing at the present day about fifteen thousand inhabitants. There were, however, but half the number at the end of the last century, and it was at that period that the events narrated in the following pages occurred. — *Sylvia's Lovers*, Elizabeth Gaskell, 1863.

1339 The time was the year of grace 1779; the locality, Morristown, New Jersey. — "Thankful Blossom," Bret Harte, 1877.

1340 I never could understand why anybody should ever have begun to live at Dillsborough, or why the population there should have been at any time recruited by new comers. — *The American Senator*, Anthony Trollope, 1877.

1341 The village stood on a wide plain, and around it rose the mountains. — *A Modern Instance*, William Dean Howells, 1882.

1342 There are two Romes. There is the Rome of the intelligent foreigner, consisting of excavations, monuments, tramways, hotels, typhoid fever, incense, and wax candles; and there is the Rome within, a city of antique customs, good and bad, a town full of aristocratic prejudices, of intrigues, of religion, of old-fashioned honour and new-fashioned scandal, of happiness and unhappiness, of just people and unjust. — *To Leeward*, F. Marion Crawford, 1883.

1343 In the year 1865 Rome was still in a great measure its old self. — *Saracinesca*, F. Marion Crawford, 1887.

1344 Most of the towns standing on our seacoast have suffered a radical change in the course of the last century. Railways and the fashion of summer holiday-making have transformed them altogether, and great towns have sprung up where fishing villages once stood. — *With Wolfe in Canada*, G. A. Henty, 1887.

1345 The sun was blazing down upon a city on the western shore of the Caspian. It was a primitive city, and yet its size and population rendered it worthy of the term. It consisted of a vast aggregation of buildings, which were for the most part mere huts. — *The Cat of Bubastes*, G. A. Henty, 1889.

1346 Rotherhithe in the year of 1572 differed very widely from the Rotherhithe of to-day. It was then a scattered village, inhabited chiefly by a seafaring population. — *By Pike and Dyke*, G. A. Henty, 1890.

1347 *Not here in our London Ghetto the gates and gaberdines of the olden Ghetto of the Eternal City; yet no lack of signs external by which one may know it, and those who dwell therein.* — *Children of the Ghetto*, Israel Zangwill, 1892.

1348 A while ago there was a young man dwelling in a great and goodly city by the sea which had to name Langton on Holm. — *The Wood Beyond the World*, William Morris, 1894.

1349 The scene of this chronicle is the town of Dawson's Landing, on the Missouri side of the Mississippi, half a day's journey, per steamboat, below St. Louis./ In 1830 it was a snug little collection of modest one- and two-story frame dwellings whose whitewashed exteriors were almost concealed from sight by climbing tangles of rose-vines, honeysuckles and morning-glories. — *Pudd'nhead Wilson*, Mark Twain, 1894.

1350 There was something about the coast town of Dunnet which made it seem more attractive than other maritime villages of eastern Maine. — *The Country of the Pointed Firs*, Sarah Orne Jewett, 1896.

1351 It was the full "season" in Cairo. The ubiquitous Britisher and the no less ubiquitous American had planted their differing "society" standards on the sandy soil watered by the Nile, and were busily engaged in the work of reducing the city, formerly called Al Kahira or The Victorious, to a more deplorable condition of subjection and slavery than any old-world conqueror could ever have done. — *Wormwood: The Problem of a Wicked Soul*, Marie Corelli, 1897.

1352 The time was in or about the year 1544, when the Emperor Charles V. ruled the Netherlands, and our scene the city of Leyden./ Any one who has visited this pleasant town knows that it lies in the midst of wide, flat meadows, and is intersected by many canals filled with Rhine water. — *Lysbeth*, H. Rider Haggard, 1901.

1353 Rome had passed the summits and stood looking into the dark valley of fourteen hundred years. — *Vergilius*, Irving Bacheller, 1904.

1354 Since money is the fount of all modern romantic adventure, the City of London, which holds more money to the square yard than any other place in the world, is the most romantic of cities. — *Teresa of Watling Street*, Arnold Bennett, 1904.

1355 In the time of Spanish rule, and for many years afterwards, the town of Sulaco — the luxuriant beauty of the orange gardens bears witness to its antiquity — had never been commercially anything more important than a coasting port with a fairly large local trade in ox-hides and indigo. — *Nostromo*, Joseph Conrad, 1904.

1356 London, — and a night in June. London, swart and grim, semi-shrouded in a warm close mist of mingled human breath and acrid vapour streaming up from the clammy crowded streets, — London, with a million twinkling lights gleaming sharp upon its native blackness, and looking, to a dreamer's eye, like some gigantic Fortress, built line upon line and tower upon tower, — with huge ramparts raised about it frowningly as though in self-defence against Heaven. — *The Treasure of Heaven*, Marie Corelli, 1906.

1357 Sibley Junction is in the sub-tropic zone of Colorado. It lies in a hot, dry, but immensely productive valley at an altitude of some four thousand feet above the sea, a village laced with irrigating ditches, shaded by big cotton-wood-trees, and beat upon by a genial, generous-minded sun. — *Money Magic*, Hamlin Garland, 1907.

1358 The suburb of Saffron Park lay on the sunset side of London, as red and ragged as a cloud of sunset. — *The Man Who Was Thursday*, G. K. Chesterton, 1908.

1359 The Philadelphia into which Frank Algernon Cowperwood was born was a city of two hundred and fifty thousand and more. — *The Financier*, Theodore Dreiser, 1912.

1360 With few exceptions, the incidents recorded in these pages take place in one of the largest cities of the United States of America, and of that portion called the Middle West, — a city once conservative and provincial, and rather proud of these qualities; but now outgrown them, and linked by lightning limited trains to other teeming centers of the modern world: a city overtaken, in recent years, by the plague which has swept our country from the Atlantic to the Pacific — Prosperity. — *The Inside of the Cup*, Winston Churchill, 1913.

1361 North of east, in the bottom, where the road drops from the High Moor, is the village of Garth in Garthdale. — *The Three Sisters*, May Sinclair, 1914.

1362 In the year 1892 Bleakridge, residential suburb of Bursley, was still most plainly divided into old and new, — that is to say, into the dull red or dull yellow with stone facings, and the bright red with terra-cotta gimcrackery. Like incompatible liquids congealed in a pot, the two components had run into each other and mingled, but never mixed. — *These Twain*, Arnold Bennett, 1915.

1363 This story has its beginnings in the town of Alexandria, Illinois, between 1884 and 1889, at the time when the place had a population of somewhere near ten thousand. — *The "Genius,"* Theodore Dreiser, 1915.

1364 There is a midland city in the heart of fair, open country, a dirty and wonderful city nesting dingily in the fog of its own smoke. — *The Turmoil*, Booth Tarkington, 1915.

1365 The town of Pedro stood on the edge of the mountain country; a straggling assemblage of stores and saloons from which a number of branch railroads ran up into the canyons, feeding the coal-camps. — *King Coal*, Upton Sinclair, 1917.

1366 Paris hints of sacrifice. — *Tarr*, Wyndham Lewis, 1918.

1367 The village of West Meadows climbed the sunny flank of one of Vermont's green mountains. — *The Promises of Alice*, Margaret Deland, 1919.

1368 The city turned its dreariest aspect toward the railway station; blackened walls, irregular and ill-paved streets, gloomy warehouses, and over all a gray, smoke-laden atmosphere which gave it mystery and often beauty. — *A Poor Wise Man*, Mary Roberts Rinehart, 1920.

1369 Except for the Marabar Caves — and they are twenty miles off — the city of Chandrapore presents nothing extraordinary. — *A Passage to India*, E. M. Forster, 1924.

1370 New York was almost still, that night. — *The Avalanche*, Ernest Poole, 1924.

1371 "Oh, but you can't know *Paris*," murmured the nice lady sitting opposite Mr. Haddock in the first-class railroad compartment, "unless you live on the *rive gauche*." — *Mr. and Mrs. Haddock in Paris, France*, Donald Ogden Stewart, 1926.

1372 The city lies in a plain, ornamented with mountains. — *The Childermass*, Wyndham Lewis, 1928.

1373 Late on a late autumn afternoon in the year 1903 the village of Denboro, in the Commonwealth of Massachusetts, was undergoing inspection and appraisal. It did not know that it was undergoing anything of the kind, nor would it have been in the least troubled if it had known. — *Silas Bradford's Boy*, Joseph C. Lincoln, 1928.

1374 Our town of Arundel, at the mouth of the Arundel River in the Province of Maine, halfway between Portsmouth and Portland, is a small place; and those who live there think that nothing happens in it, ever. — *The Lively Lady*, Kenneth Roberts, 1931.

1375 Even as late as 1890 the little ancient town of Bowport down on the Maine coast was still, except for the summer residents on Blacknose Point, unspotted from the world. — *Captain Archer's Daughter*, Margaret Deland, 1932.

1376 The village, in the hollow below the house, is picturesque, unhygienic: it has more atmosphere than form, than outline: huddled shapes of soft red brick sag towards gardens

massed with sunflowers, Canterbury bells, sweet-williams. — *Invitation to the Waltz*, Rosamond Lehmann, 1932.

1377 In 1846 the prairie town of Oak River existed only in a settler's dream. — *Miss Bishop*, Bess Streeter Aldrich, 1933.

1378 "Here is the metropolis of idiocy," said my friend as we stopped the car. — *Uncle Peel*, Irving Bacheller, 1933.

1379 Clear, pale October sunlight was shining down on the slanting intersection of Broadway and Seventh Avenue, illuminating with the uncompromising clarity of mid-morning the restless ugliness of the crowded streets. — *Edna His Wife*, Margaret Ayer Barnes, 1935.

1380 It is Earth's most famous town, so it belongs to everybody, and to all times at once. — *The Trojan Horse*, Christopher Morley, 1937.

1381 Our village — I don't think you have ever heard about it — Kanthapura is its name, and it is in the province of Kara. — *Kanthapura*, Raja Rao, 1938.

1382 In the evening sun of September the capital city lay along the bed of the Little Grand River like a cluster of lice along the vein of a yellowing leaf. — *Capital City*, Mari Sandoz, 1939.

1383 The hamlet stood on a gentle rise in the flat, wheat-growing north-east corner of Oxfordshire. — *Lark Rise*, Flora Thompson, 1939.

1384 Scientific digging into buried towns sometimes finds previous foundations, one beneath another, making it clear that the ancient communities had every one in turn been overwhelmed by a newer that built upon the ruins. — *The Heritage of Hatcher Ide*, Booth Tarkington, 1941.

1385 It was in the little agricultural town of Amorra, East Bengal, India. — *Breakfast with the Nikolides*, Rumer Godden, 1942.

1386 The town itself is dreary; not much is there except the cotton mill, the two-room houses where the workers live, a few peach trees, a church with two colored windows, and a miserable main street only a hundred yards long. — "The Ballad of the Sad Café," Carson McCullers, 1943.

1387 The plaza of Santa Luz was flanked on three sides by wooden-awninged stores. Only three things distinguished it from its sister towns of the Territory: it was the capital; it had a Governor's Palace that made up the fourth side of the plaza; and it had six good saloons on the other three sides. — *Bought with a Gun*, Luke Short, 1943.

1388 Serene was a word you could put to Brooklyn, New York. — *A Tree Grows in Brooklyn*, Betty Smith, 1943.

1389 The town had a name but no shape, no street, no core. — *Bugles in the Afternoon*, Ernest Haycox, 1944.

1390 The city which was to be the scene of the telling of this tale was neither Flint nor Lansing nor Pontiac; the state need not be Michigan. But it was a city of that kind, a Midwestern industrial city with its noisy, haphazard but to the inhabitants very homelike business section, its bleaker factory areas, its flat and green semi-suburban avenues lined by smaller and larger examples of that incomparable achievement of modern America, its domestic architecture. — *Breathe Upon These*, Ludwig Lewisohn, 1944.

1391 There was too much of everything. But not for Vaughan Melendy. Himself of heroic stature, he fitted well into the gorgeous and spectacular setting that was the city of Seattle. — *Great Son*, Edna Ferber, 1945.

1392 The city was unlike any other either in the New or the Old World, for in a few feverish years it had grown from a tiny Spanish settlement into the principal port of the Pacific Coast. — *The World in His Arms*, Rex Beach, 1946.

1393 *Blakesburg is a town beneath the Southern sun, fenced in by two rivers, a mountain, and the wind.* — *Foretaste of Glory*, Jesse Stuart, 1946.

1394 Sawley, the town, is in west Florida, on the famous Suwanee River. — *Seraph on the Suwanee*, Zora Neale Hurston, 1948.

1395 The Oxfordshire village of Restharrow has changed little in outward appearance during the last fifty years. — *Still Glides the Stream*, Flora Thompson, 1948.

1396 In giving the village of Aspen in Tyrol face, and telling part of its chronicle to Americans, one will first state that it lies atop the Arlberg, at an altitude of three thousand four hundred and sixty feet, at the foot of a pinnacle of triangular shape called "the Eye of God"; that its fauna, flora, and landscape are like that of its namesake, Aspen, Colorado; and that its people — in character, appearance, and way of life — are a kind of well-to-do Kentucky mountaineers. — *The Eye of God*, Ludwig Bemelmans, 1949.

1397 No words can convey an adequate impression of the small settlement known as Ville Marie de Montréal as it was in the final years of the seventeenth century. — *High Towers*, Thomas B. Costain, 1949.

1398 The city of Cuenca is rimmed around three sides by blue mountains. It sits down in a valley cup, mellow in the sunshine of Mexican December. — *The Brave Bulls*, Tom Lea, 1949.

1399 It was a gray day. Dark rain-clouds moved slowly in from the west, grazing the tops of the tall buildings downtown. The huge, sprawling Midwestern city by the river looked dirty, bleak, and ugly under a steady drizzle. — *Little Men, Big World*, W. R. Burnett, 1951.

1400 The courthouse is less old than the town, which began somewhere under the turn of the century as a Chickasaw Agency trading-post and so continued for almost thirty years before it discovered, not that it lacked a depository for its records and certainly not that it needed one, but that only by creating or anyway decreeing one, could it cope with a situation which otherwise was going to cost somebody money; — *Requiem for a Nun*, William Faulkner, 1951.

1401 The city of Tolland, New York, is of industrial importance far beyond its population of 77,861. It also is not without its cultural renown. It has given the world several sons and daughters who have gained prominence in varied fields. But we of Tolland are conscious that our beloved city is particularly and peculiarly associated with the name Thudbury almost as closely as is Mount Vernon with George Washington. — *Thudbury*, Clyde Brion Davis, 1952.

1402 Springfield Illinois. 1879. Twenty thousand persons. Abraham Lincoln is fourteen years dead. — *City of Discontent*, Mark Harris, 1952.

1403 Ilium, New York, is Divided Into Three Parts. — *Player Piano*, Kurt Vonnegut, 1952.

1404 The city faced the bay. — *The City of Anger*, William Manchester, 1953.

1405 *Hong Kong is a pore upon the body of Asia.* — *Soldier of Fortune*, Ernest K. Gann, 1954.

1406 This is the story of a town that refused to die. — *Runner in the Sun*, D'Arcy McNickle, 1954.

1407 Across the Hudson River from the grubby harbor town of Bohegan little squares of light were coming on all over the seaport metropolis. — *Waterfront*, Budd Schulberg, 1955.

1408 As it is some time since we were at Hatch End, we will take this opportunity of reminding our Reader (the one who says our books are so nice because it doesn't matter which you read or where you open it as they are all exactly the same — as indeed they are, with a difference) that it is a small village in the valley of the Rising, which here flows through water-meadows. — *Enter Sir Robert*, Angela Thirkell, 1955.

1409 From the noise-bound cockpit of an aircraft, the wide circle of London on an early spring evening looked as quiet as a bank of windflowers. — *The Proving Flight*, David Beaty, 1956.

1410 Greenwich, for all its faults, was a fascinating place, and I always left it with regret, especially at Trinity Term, to go up to Oxford. — *Boon Island*, Kenneth Roberts, 1956.

1411 St. Botolphs was an old place, an old river town. — *The Wapshot Chronicle*, John Cheever, 1957.

1412 The town lay sprawled at his feet. — *At Fever Pitch*, David Caute, 1959.

1413 It was a Sunday. Shade Motley stood tall and forked on the mountain to the east and looked down on Macedonia; and he saw the creek curving there, and the two red ribbons of dirt road, and the friendly cluster of houses. — *The Insolent Breed*, Borden Deal, 1959.

1414 Dear Janey:/ Good morning, New York! — *Affectionately, Eve*, Upton Sinclair, 1961.

1415 *August, 1931* — The port town of Veracruz is a little purgatory between land and sea for the traveler, but the people who live there are very fond of themselves and the town they have helped to make. — *Ship of Fools*, Katherine Anne Porter, 1962.

1416 The gravel pits circled the town, turning it at night into a suburban Venice, glimmering over a waste of water. — *Tortoise by Candlelight*, Nina Bawden, 1963.

1417 Marrakech is just what the guide-books say it is. Marrakech is an ancient walled city surrounded with olive groves and palm trees. — *Horse Under Water*, Len Deighton, 1963.

1418 Clarksville is in Texas — but only barely. — *The Ordways*, William Humphrey, 1965.

1419 You stand there on the top-floor landing of the three-storeyed tenement building on Webber Street, look out at the city of Port of Spain. — *While Gods Are Falling*, Earl Lovelace, 1965.

1420 Johannesburg from the air is *not* like a miniature New York, whatever the South African Tourist Corporation may claim; but its compactness and modestly tall buildings do vaguely recall a stunted Manhattan Island surrounded by sand castles. The sand castles, of course, are grown-up toys; they are mine-dumps, to be exact, the yellow dross of a full half century's frenetic burrowing for gold. For the rest, it is a sprung-up, counter-jumping town, as brash, nervous, and noisy as its newest millionaire. — *The Pillow Fight*, Nicholas Monsarrat, 1965.

1421 In a little valley on the shore of a great bay, set between a beautiful sound and a chain of offshore islands, lies the village of Caplin Bight, where the boy Eli was born. — *Tomorrow Will Be Sunday*, Harold Horwood, 1966.

1422 It was the second week of June in Unionville, a town of almost five thousand people in the northwestern corner of Tennessee and not far from Kentucky, where I had gone to spend two months of the summer. — *Summertime Island*, Erskine Caldwell, 1968.

1423 Enigma, Georgia, was a dead end. — *The Gospel Singer*, Harry Crews, 1968.

1424 They'd been rioting in city after city across the nation, but not here. — *J C Saves*, Robert Gover, 1968.

1425 There is a certain type of American county seat town which just escapes being an overgrown village by the presence of a usually

ornate stone courthouse in its midst. —*Many a Green Isle*, Agnes Sligh Turnbull, 1968.

1426 The city was open to the nomad. — *Barefoot in the Head*, Brian W. Aldiss, 1969.

1427 The little Baralong village swept right up to the border fence. — *When Rain Clouds Gather*, Bessie Head, 1969.

1428 Whitechapel appeared more squashed than usual. — *By the Waters of Whitechapel*, Bernard Kops, 1969.

1429 *As well as Timbuctoo on the river Niger there are Timbuctoos, some of them in specific places and some, entirely of the mind, being void of storks and lions and quite unreachable by camel caravan. And there are others which, specifically placed, seem also to be of the mind, so much so that the mind cannot divide what it sees from what it invents and therefore boosts itself with homemade miracles, like snowmen found in the Sahara. . . .* — *I'm Expecting to Live Quite Soon*, Paul West, 1970.

1430 Piemburg is deceptive. Nothing about it is entirely what it seems to be. — *Riotous Assembly*, Tom Sharpe, 1971.

1431 Rome. Syracuse. Ithaca. Troy. Years later I was to wonder what scholar-gypsy had wandered through our state, bestowing such illustrious names on places (which seemed to me then, years later) so singularly lacking in luster. Vestal. Nineveh. Oxford. Delhi. Cincinnatus. —*Songs My Mother Taught Me*, Audrey Thomas, 1971.

1432 The Welcome Wagon lady, sixty if she was a day but working at youth and vivacity (Ginger hair, red lips, a sunshine-yellow dress), twinkled her eyes and teeth at Joanna and said, "You're really going to like it here! It's a nice town with nice people! You couldn't have made a better choice!" — *The Stepford Wives*, Ira Levin, 1972.

1433 In the early morning it was barely visible within the shelter of the deep, round valley. Under the bluish tint of the first light of dawn it seemed like a small, weightless city floating near the surface of a bottomless pool of clouds. A silent, dead city. —*Die the Long Day*, Orlando Patterson, 1972.

1434 "There it is—that glorious skyline—the greatest in the world!" —*All Under Heaven*, Pearl S. Buck, 1973.

1435 Oxford, like all great cities, is ruined once in every generation. —*Sarsen Place*, Gwendoline Butler, 1973.

1436 "But Dunwich is only a depot. Don't judge us by a depot. Wait, my dear Miss O'Beirne, wait till we get to the settlement. . . ." — *The Commandant*, Jessica Anderson, 1975.

1437 *A summer's dusk in Washington, a city built of magnet; the air was auspicious, the night filled with promise.* —*Nicholson at Large*, Ward Just, 1975.

1438 When spring came she looked westward. Down the sliding road, over the hills, to where Galway city lay. — *The Ikon Maker*, Desmond Hogan, 1976.

1439 The village of Kravasaras was situated on a plain dominated by the towering peaks of the ancient, holy mountain, Parnassus, separated from Attica by rock-ribbed ranges and divided from the Peloponnesus to the south by the Gulf of Corinth. — *The Hour of the Bell*, Harry Mark Petrakis, 1976.

1440 Dynmouth nestled on the Dorset coast, gathered about what was once the single source of its prosperity, a small fishing harbour. — *The Children of Dynmouth*, William Trevor, 1976.

1441 "That is New York." I pointed to the waterfront just ahead as if the city were mine. —*1876*, Gore Vidal, 1976.

1442 *It was a cowtown compared to London, Paris, or Berlin, a carbuncle south of Baltimore, created by George Washington, the first American king, to house a squalid little government that was frightened of its thirteen constituent states.* — *The Franklin Scare*, Jerome Charyn, 1977.

1443 The city of Singapore was not built up gradually, the way most cities are, by a natural deposit of commerce on the banks of some river or at a traditional confluence of trade routes. It was simply invented one morning early in the nineteenth century by a man looking at a map. —*The Singapore Grip*, J. G. Farrell, 1978.

1444 I sit in my little cottage in the village of Forchheim, from which Carolingian princes led forth the Frankish tribes to crown a German as Emperor of the Holy Roman Empire a thousand years before the Anglo-Saxon doctrine of democracy and self-emasculation was ever dreamed of. — *Night of the Aurochs*, Dalton Trumbo, 1979.

1445 Demera had never grown much beyond its Civil War boundaries. —*Real Presence*, Richard Bausch, 1980.

1446 It is hard to imagine a place less important than the village of Chakrata. —*Shaitan*, Max Ehrlich, 1981.

1447 During the reign of Julian the Apostate, when Milan was an imperial capital, the city was renowned for its clean breezes and its wealth of clear water. —*Just Causes*, Malcolm McConnel, 1981.

1448 Once there was a candy-counter City of Limitless Options, where it was possible (if one was driven and romantic enough) to synthetically sweeten all values indefinitely. — *Unapparent Wounds*, Gloria Nagy, 1981.

1449 *A great city is nothing more than a portrait of itself, and yet when all is said and done, its arsenals of scenes and images are part of a deeply moving plan.* — *Winter's Tale*, Mark Helprin, 1983.

1450 So this is Venice! —*Sweethearts*, A. M. Krich, 1983.

1451 *Duluth! Love it or loathe it, you can never leave it or lose it.* —*Duluth*, Gore Vidal, 1983.

1452 Signs are, even to my drugged eye, that the village is finally coming out of winter. I am not witnessing a return to robustness and sanity exactly—that's too much to expect down here, so far from the soundness of cities, so deep into the obsessional neurosis of Nature—but there is an atmosphere of fragile convalescence abroad, as if the patients have been allowed their first unaccompanied turn around the walled gardens of the institution. —*Peeping Tom*, Howard Jacobson, 1984.

1453 I stood in the middle of downtown renovation, watching frat boys push their sorority sisters around the only block the Refurbishment Project hadn't turned into rubble. —*Heroes*, David Shields, 1984.

1454 Venice, California, in the old days had much to recommend it to people who liked to be sad. —*Death Is a Lonely Business*, Ray Bradbury, 1985.

1455 Washington is a market. —*The Floating Island*, Garrett Epps, 1985.

1456 Cobargo was a terribly dull place in 1935. —*A Long Time Dying*, Olga Masters, 1985.

1457 In Kansas there is a town called Valley Forge. —*Heart of the Country*, Greg Matthews, 1985.

1458 For a third of a century, I got by nicely without Detroit. —*Three Farmers on Their Way to a Dance*, Richard Powers, 1985.

1459 Some people say that Philadelphia is a place where nothing ever really happens. —*Sorcerers*, Jacob Needleman, 1986.

1460 In the Old West, when a man's destiny was open to whatever chances he could or would take, Agatite, Texas, sprang up on the north central plains as a major railhead and agricultural and ranching center. —*Agatite*, Clay Reynolds, 1986.

1461 Constantinople was bigger than he had ever imagined. —*The Bearkeeper's Daughter*, Gillian Bradshaw, 1987.

1462 The village square of Owensville, Vermont wasn't a square at all—it was a small triangle created by the fork of Clayborne Road dead-ending into the curve of Route 363. —*Look Under the Hawthorn*, Ellen Frye, 1987.

1463 It was a town of no significance. —*The Hussar*, David R. Slavitt, 1987.

1464 Jerusalem in the early twentieth century was a vibrant little city only newly awakened from medieval obscurity by the coming of the British at the end of the First World War—a dream from antiquity suddenly stirring to life after four hundred years of slumber under the stupefying decadence of the Ottoman Empire. —*Jericho Mosaic*, Edward Whittemore, 1987.

1465 Early spring, 1866. Lexington, Virginia: a small town in a rocky upland valley below the Blue Ridge Mountains. It is a lonely, remote place, difficult of access, the choice lying between a twenty-three-mile journey on a bad road from the railroad station at Goshen, and twelve hours by boat from Lynchburg along the James River and Kanawha Canal. —*Traveller*, Richard Adams, 1988.

1466 Billarooby was a small community on the Lachlan River, a few miles northwest of Wudgewunda in New South Wales, Australia. —*Billarooby*, Jim Anderson, 1988.

1467 When they ask me to become president of the United States I'm going to say, "Except for Washington, D.C." —*Spy Hook*, Len Deighton, 1988.

1468 Grayling, Montana, was incorporated at a small celebration in 1890. —*The Corner of Rife and Pacific*, Thomas Savage, 1988.

1469 Once upon a time there were two cities within a city. One was light and one was dark. One moved restlessly all day while the other never stirred. One was warm and filled with ever-changing lights. One was cold and fixed in place by stones. —*A Graveyard for Lunatics*, Ray Bradbury, 1989.

1470 Every city should be so beautiful, every hill should have such a gleaming pinnacle. —*Firebird*, James Carroll, 1989.

1471 Athens is a large city situated in the middle part of the country we call Greece. —*Goatsong*, Tom Holt, 1989.

1472 Perhaps San Francisco existed outside the weather. —*Loss of Flight*, Sara Vogan, 1989.

1473 In the center of Italy, surrounded by the rolling hills of Umbria, there is a city built on top of a hill. —*Franky Furbo*, William Wharton, 1989.

1474 You want to know about Butte, you go over to the twenty-four-hour Jim Hill Cafe & Cigar Store on Silver Street and ask for me and Whippy Bird. —*Buster Midnight's Cafe*, Sandra Dallas, 1990.

1475 Yalta, in troubled times. —*Chekhov's Sister*, W. D. Wetherell, 1990.

1476 Q. Why is London like Budapest?/ A. Because it is two cities divided by a river. —*Wise Children*, Angela Carter, 1991.

1477 In Scarsdale, the men do not tinker beneath their car hoods on hot summer Saturdays or spend winter mornings doing small fix-it jobs in their basement shops, and the women do not clean their own houses or do their own nails. —*Private Acts*, Linda Gray Sexton, 1991.

1478 It is seven years now since I came to this town, this sluggish hot-smelling sprawl of a place, immodestly supine like a woman with her

skirts hitched up, along the banks of the river. —*Inventing the Weather*, Thea Astley, 1992.

1479 The Silver Smile, New Orleans, ringed all around them now that the tug was pushing midriver. —*Divining Blood*, Maureen McCoy, 1992.

1480 See a town stucco-pink, fishbelly-white, done up in wisteria and swaying palms and smelling of rotted fruits broken beneath trees: mango, papaya, delicious tangerine; imagine this town rising from coral shoals bleached and cutting upward through bathwater seas: the sunken world of fish. —*Elect Mr. Robinson for a Better World*, Donald Antrim, 1993.

1481 At five-thirty on Friday afternoon the eight-block crescent of downtown Bay St. Louis, Mississippi, looked like an airport postcard of a Mediterranean seaside village, one of those bathed-in-light towns, high off the sparkling water, trees bent with wind, everything going red against a swelling sky. —*The Brothers*, Frederick Barthelme, 1993.

1482 Some said Mount Hope was founded on love, and some said it was founded on war. —*Blue Moon*, Luanne Rice, 1993.

Clergymen

1483 In the same year, and on the same day of the same month, that his Sacred Majesty King George, the third of the name, came to his crown and kingdom, I was placed and settled as the minister of Dalmailing. —*Annals of the Parish*, John Galt, 1821.

1484 Of late years, an abundant shower of curates has fallen upon the north of England: they lie very thick on the hills; every parish has one or more of them; they are young enough to be very active, and ought to be doing a great deal of good. —*Shirley*, Charlotte Brontë, 1849.

1485 In the four hundred and thirteenth year of the Christian era, some three hundred miles above Alexandria, the young monk Philammon was sitting on the edge of a low range of inland cliffs, crested with drifting sand. —*Hypatia*, Charles Kingsley, 1853.

1486 The Rev. Septimus Harding was, a few years since, a beneficed clergyman residing in the cathedral town of ——; let us call it Barchester. Were we to name Wells or Salisbury, Exeter, Hereford, or Gloucester, it might be presumed that something personal was intended; and as this tale will refer mainly to the cathedral dignitaries of the town in question, we are anxious that no personality may be suspected. —*The Warden*, Anthony Trollope, 1855.

1487 In the latter days of July in the year 185-, a most important question was for ten days hourly asked in the cathedral city of Barchester, and answered every hour in various ways—Who was to be the new Bishop? —*Barchester Towers*, Anthony Trollope, 1857.

1488 It is natural to suppose that the arrival of the new Rector was a rather exciting event for Carlingford. —*The Rector*, Margaret Oliphant *as* Mrs. Oliphant, 1863.

1489 "Then I say once for all, that priest shall never darken my doors again."/ "Then I say they are my doors and not yours, and that holy man shall brighten them whenever he will." —*Griffith Gaunt*, Charles Reade, 1866.

1490 Parson Wibird Hawkins was in trouble. —*Prudence Palfrey*, Thomas Bailey Aldrich, 1874.

1491 In the year 1835, the Rev. Philip Penniloe was Curate-in-charge of Perlycross, a village in a valley of the Blackdown Range. —*Perlycross*, R. D. Blackmore, 1894.

1492 Harold was about ten years of age when his father, the Rev. Mr. Excell, took the pastorate of the First Church in Rock River. —*The Eagle's Heart*, Hamlin Garland, 1900.

1493 A Mr. Dobie, a clergyman, wearying of his job, relinquished it, ostensibly on the grounds that he did not care to bury dissenters or to baptise illegitimate infants, but in reality because he was tired of being so busy, so sociable, and so conversational, of attending parish meetings, sitting on committees, calling on parishioners and asking them how they did—an inquiry the answer to which he was wholly indifferent. —*Crewe Train*, Rose Macaulay, 1926.

1494 One summer evening in the year 1848, three Cardinals and a missionary Bishop from America were dining together in the gardens of a villa in the Sabine hills, overlooking Rome. —*Death Comes for the Archbishop*, Willa Cather, 1927.

1495 Though the Reverend Timothy Fortune had spent three years in the island of Fanua he had made but one convert. —*Mr. Fortune's Maggot*, Sylvia Townsend Warner, 1927.

1496 One foggy morning in November a little old clergyman in a shabby black coat got into a third-class compartment of a train waiting in Queen Street Station, Glasgow, disposed his ancient brown bag on the rack, sat down, shut his tired old eyes the better to rid himself of the world, and began to meditate upon the folly of all human ambition and the wisdom of Almighty God and of the love of Our Lord Jesus Christ and of the way that the Holy Ghost went about the world, now blowing like a wind, now taking the form of a flower and glowing in gorgeous reds and yellows. —*Father Malachy's Miracle*, Bruce Marshall, 1931.

1497 In the frontierland of western New York, Palmyra was only a small town, but more itinerant evangelists had come to it than the pious Smiths could remember. — *Children of God*, Vardis Fisher, 1939.

1498 Late one afternoon in September 1938 old Father Francis Chisholm limped up the steep path from the church of St. Columba to his house upon the hill. — *The Keys of the Kingdom*, A. J. Cronin, 1941.

1499 As he freewheeled down the long hill, Father Smith remembered with irritation that, as a member of the League of Saint Columba, he had promised to say a Pater, an Ave, and a Gloria daily for the conversion of Scotland. — *The World, the Flesh, and Father Smith*, Bruce Marshall, 1945.

1500 In September, 1947, the Reverend Gerald Seddon, of St. Frideswide, Hoxton, paid his annual visit to the Reverend Samuel Bott, of St. Sody, North Cornwall. — *The Feast*, Margaret Kennedy, 1950.

1501 The new curate seemed quite a nice young man, but what a pity it was that his combinations showed, tucked carelessly into his socks, when he sat down. — *Some Tame Gazelle*, Barbara Pym, 1950.

1502 Everyone had always said that John would be a preacher when he grew up, just like his father. — *Go Tell It on the Mountain*, James Baldwin, 1953.

1503 The Bishop always shaved on holy days, and he was still looking clean when his chaplain entered his study in the afternoon. — *The Fair Bride*, Bruce Marshall, 1953.

1504 "Nice of you to come to the station, Father," Bishop Soutar said as he shook hands with the young priest. — *Girl in May*, Bruce Marshall, 1956.

1505 The Rev. Mr. Syson, having been sentenced to six months in gaol, had his eye cut by a broken bottle as they tried to smuggle him out of court by a back way. — *The Captive and the Free*, Joyce Cary, 1959.

1506 The Archbishop was leaving for Paris the same morning and had to make his new priests quickly. — *Satan and Cardinal Campbell*, Bruce Marshall, 1959.

1507 It was his profession to prepare other men for death; it shocked him to be so unready for his own. — *The Devil's Advocate*, Morris West, 1959.

1508 "Bloody funny Bishop, that Bishop," said Pemberton. — *The Fourth of June*, David Benedictus, 1962.

1509 The Pope was dead. — *The Shoes of the Fisherman*, Morris West, 1963.

1510 Father Finnocchino canvassed the apartments on both sides of the court at least

three times, but he did not have much success with the Catholic boys in the building. — *On the Darkening Green*, Jerome Charyn, 1965.

1511 Now it was Father O'Flynn's turn, Mrs. Beneker thought. — *Mrs. Beneker*, Violet Weingarten, 1967.

1512 The first time that preacher came he got tangled up with Nebuchadnezzar and old Belshazzar and they had to take twelve stitches in his head. — *Shady Grove*, Janice Holt Giles, 1968.

1513 One Saturday evening, Maitland had to say Mass on a headland for a guild of graduates. — *Three Cheers for the Paraclete*, Thomas Keneally, 1968.

1514 Interviews always make me nervous. When I presented myself at CACTM to be accepted as a candidate, the first question they asked me was why I wanted to become a priest. I replied: "Because I like meeting people." — *Consider the Lilies*, Auberon Waugh, 1968.

1515 The Reverend B. Jonas Carlson had set up one of those storefront addict centers on Lowery Street in Sunnyside, Queens, New York's unknown borough. — *The File on Stanley Patton Buchta*, Irvin Faust, 1970.

1516 "Do you believe in God?"/ "Very deeply," said Dr. Baird. "Don't you?"/ "Hell, no!" said Reverend Becker. — *The Couch Trip*, Ken Kolb, 1970.

1517 Toward four o'clock of an afternoon in middle May, the priest appeared, and the following day the whole thing began. — *The Hessian*, Howard Fast, 1972.

1518 In the year 1840 my great-great-grandfather, the Reverend Mr. Nathaniel Nye, who was then the minister of the Baptist Chapel at Barnoldswick in the West Riding of Yorkshire, received a call from God to go to the New World, and go he did. — *The Dead of the House*, Joanne Greenberg *as* Hannah Green, 1972.

1519 In the spring of 1937 a curate was admitted to the Charing Cross Hospital in London for the removal of a stone from his bladder. — *The Upstart*, Piers Paul Read, 1973.

1520 Forgive me my denomination and my town; I am a Christian minister, and an American. — *A Month of Sundays*, John Updike, 1975.

1521 The pastor pointed out his toes to the limit of extension, spread his arms like wings, and lifted his head in an utmost pose of rapture, his old face exalted, his eyes staring as if with ecstasy at the mildewed white ceiling of his church. — *Ceremony of the Innocent*, Taylor Caldwell, 1976.

1522 It was not the Bishop of Rochester. — *The Book of Merlyn*, T. H. White, 1977.

1523 In a cavernous seventeenth-century Roman palazzo on a narrow cobblestone street

near the Vatican, Monsignor Hans Weiller sat motionless and inscrutable as a Buddha. — *Provenance*, Frank McDonald, 1979.

1524 The priest's face was wrapped from the edge of his eyes to the edge of his collar in a dirty cotton-white beard, and his breath stunk to high heaven. — *The Parachutists*, Edward Klein, 1981.

1525 In the seventh year of his reign, two days before his sixty-fifth birthday, in the presence of a full consistory of Cardinals, Jean Marie Barette, Pope Gregory XVII, signed an instrument of abdication, took off the Fisherman's ring, handed his seal to the Cardinal Camerlengo and made a curt speech of farewell. — *The Clowns of God*, Morris West, 1981.

1526 "Preacher!" The hoarsely whispered shout hung heavily in the shadowed humid jungle air. — *Spellbinder*, Harold Robbins, 1982.

1527 "Our friend Rich," the Archdeacon of Oxford had been known to say, "is inclined to view his sacerdotal function through somewhat antique spectacles. He might come straight out of *Mansfield Park*." — *A Villa in France*, J. I. M. Stewart, 1982.

1528 I am Franco Ellera, who has been the chamberlain, companion, bodyguard, and counselor to a pope. — *A Trembling Upon Rome*, Richard Condon, 1983.

1529 Rabbi David Hartman came to Leighton Ridge in the spring of 1946, six months after his discharge from the United States Army, where he had served as a chaplain in the infantry. — *The Outsider*, Howard Fast, 1984.

1530 As I walked through the wilderness of what remained of the world of Father Lynch and his "little guild," I saw much to disturb me. — *Kruger's Alp*, Christopher Hope, 1984.

1531 *The Reverend Joshua Smith, Sr. was born November 5, 1900 in Ouichitta, Mississippi/* He stared at what he'd written. — *Do Lord Remember Me*, Julius Lester, 1984.

1532 The Reverend Doctor John Tinker Meadows stood silent and motionless at the pulpit of the great Tabernacle of the Eternal Church of the Believer, staring at the stained-glass window at the far end of the building, listening to the murmur and rustle of the enormous congregation as the sounds slowly diminished. — *One More Sunday*, John D. MacDonald, 1984.

1533 Reverend Lilley was never to become a popular minister of the gospel in the town of Fonthill (population 13,854 in 1930, when this story takes place), for the precise reason that the congregation always felt the preacher was singling a particular person out for condemnation in the sermon. — *On Glory's Course*, James Purdy, 1984.

1534 Brother Anselm had come into the chapel early. — "Blessed Art Thou," Rachel Ingalls, 1985.

1535 If there was a bishop, my mother would have him to tea. — *Oscar and Lucinda*, Peter Carey, 1988.

1536 It had not taken long for young Reverend Weir Snape to realise how infirm the old rector was. — *The Bathing Machine Called the Twentieth Century*, Nigel Krauth, 1988.

1537 The priest had been lacerated from his scalp to his ankles by at least nine different leopards. — *Gondar*, Nicholas Luard, 1988.

1538 I started remembering all the things that happened to me that day when I overheard Dave Bulkley preaching a sermon over the prostitute's dead child. — *Annie Chambers*, Lenore Carroll, 1989.

1539 The priest rarely masturbated during confession. — *Eighty-Sixed*, David B. Feinberg, 1989.

1540 My father was a Methodist minister, but since he was never a strong "pulpit man," he rose quite slowly in the heirarchy of Southern Methodism. — *The Kneeling Bus*, Beverly Coyle, 1990.

1541 At five minutes to twelve on Christmas Eve, 1929, Father Hattersley knelt in the corner of his vestry and prayed for the strength to say the Midnight Mass. — *The Maker's Mark*, Roy Hattersley, 1990.

1542 *Try*, the old priest told himself. — *Kahuna*, Joanna Higgins, 1993.

Cold

1543 Cold winter lay deep in the Canadian wilderness. — *The Wolf Hunters*, James Oliver Curwood, 1908.

1544 The man standing in the shadow of the doorway turned up the collar of his overcoat and stamped his numb feet gently on the damp stones. — *Cause for Alarm*, Eric Ambler, 1938.

1545 It was one of those December nights of dazzling starlight that we have in New York, a night so cold that the frost had gone deep into the streets, and made the iron of the horses' shoes ring upon the cobblestones like metal on metal. — *An Actor's Daughter*, Aline Bernstein, 1941.

1546 The sun was going down and there was a late October chillness in the air. — *This Very Earth*, Erskine Caldwell, 1948.

1547 Outside the house it was so cold that the earth rang like slag. — *Blandings' Way*, Eric Hodgins, 1950.

1548 The chill of the high country spring was in the night, so that when Owen Daybright stepped out of the warm Burke House bar onto Stobie's main street, he fumbled out of habit for the long-gone buttons of his sheepskin. — *Vengeance Valley*, Luke Short, 1950.

1549 The seat in the shady side of the bull-ring made McKee cold. — *The Field of Vision*, Wright Morris, 1955.

1550 It was a gray, cold day, without wind. — *Two Weeks in Another Town*, Irwin Shaw, 1960.

1551 It was cold outside the Bachelor Officers Quarters — too cold to snow. — *P. S. Wilkinson*, C. D. B. Bryan, 1965.

1552 "Pattie."/ "Yes."/ "Have you lit a fire in Miss Elizabeth's room?"/ "Yes."/ "It's so cold."/ "What did you say?"/ "It's so cold."/ "Yes." — *The Time of the Angels*, Iris Murdoch, 1966.

1553 The worst thing is the cold. I've always hated being cold — maybe they know that. Outrage, humiliation and dread have all been absorbed into this one, final, petty discomfort. — *Up*, Ronald Sukenick, 1968.

1554 It was a golden morning with a chilly breeze. The birds bobbed like clothespins on the telephone line; the two old people on the cement porch wore sweaters. — *Happy Ending*, Elizabeth Savage, 1972.

1555 It is cold where he sits. The big house too is cold, but there at least they can set fires. — *Possession*, Nicholas Delbanco, 1977.

1556 She shivered, despite the heat of the hearth, and glanced again toward the sunny rectangle of the cabin door. — *Follow the River*, James Alexander Thom, 1981.

1557 It was cold in that bed-sitter in Bethnal Green. — *Ridge of Gold*, James Ambrose Brown, 1983.

1558 This Sunday morning the first chill of fall had risen from the land like the delicate silver frost on a plum. — *Bodies and Souls*, Nancy Thayer, 1983.

1559 So cold. — *Mill Song*, William Harry Harding, 1984.

1560 "Camping! Overnight? in this weather? It's freezing! Marilyn, you're pulling my leg." — *Camping Out*, Eleanor Clark, 1986.

1561 Clarise reach New York early March when it cold like dog-nose and she shivering and lonely. — *Clarise Cumberbatch Want to Go Home*, Joan Cambridge, 1987.

1562 I'd forgotten how cold Brisbane can be in August. — *The Estuary*, Georgia Savage, 1987.

1563 The record-breaking winter had frozen everyone's spirits. — *The Shepherd*, Joseph F. Girzone, 1990.

1564 It was cold when I arrived in Delhi. — *Playing the Game*, Ian Buruma, 1991.

Coming and Going

1565 The cornets sounded a final flourish as the Prince of the Captivity dismounted from his white mule; his train shouted as if they were once more a people; and, had it not been for the contemptuous leer which played upon the countenances of the Moslem bystanders, it might have been taken for a day of triumph rather than of tribute. — *Alroy*, Benjamin Disraeli, 1833.

1566 It was in the middle of a bright tropical afternoon that we made good our escape from the bay. — *Omoo*, Herman Melville, 1847.

1567 At sunrise on a first of April, there appeared, suddenly as Manco Capac at the lake Titicaca, a man in cream-colors, at the water-side in the city of St. Louis. — *The Confidence-Man*, Herman Melville, 1857.

1568 If the reader will excuse me, I will say nothing of my antecedents, nor of the circumstances which led me to leave my native country; the narrative would be tedious to him and painful to myself. Suffice it, that when I left home it was with the intention of going to some new colony, and either finding, or even perhaps purchasing, waste crown land suitable for cattle or sheep farming, by which means I thought that I could better my fortunes more rapidly than in England. — *Erewhon*, Samuel Butler, 1872.

1569 It was a rich, warm night, at the beginning of August, when a gentleman enveloped in a cloak, for he was in evening dress, emerged from a club-house at the top of St. James' Street, and descended that celebrated eminence. — *Endymion*, Benjamin Disraeli, 1880.

1570 I will begin the story of my adventures with a certain morning early in the month of June, the year of grace 1751, when I took the key for the last time out of the door of my father's house. — *Kidnapped*, Robert Louis Stevenson, 1886.

1571 After the death of Judge Kilburn his daughter came back to America. — *Annie Kilburn*, William Dean Howells, 1889.

1572 On a certain fine evening of early autumn — I will not say how many years ago — I alighted from a green gig, before the door of a farm-house at West Poley, a village in Somersetshire. — *Our Exploits at West Poley*, Thomas Hardy, 1892–1893.

1573 At half past six o'clock on Sunday night Barnabas came out of his bedroom. — *Pembroke*, Mary E. Wilkins Freeman, 1894.

1574 At eight o'clock on Sunday morning, Arthur Peachey unlocked his front door, and quietly went forth. — *In the Year of Jubilee*, George Gissing, 1894.

1575 She stood on the platform watching the receding train. — *Esther Waters*, George Moore, 1894.

1576 Once upon a time, as the story-books say, a boy came over a ridge of hill, from which a shallow vale ran out into the sunset. — "Fountainblue," John Buchan, 1901.

1577 Mr. Grenfall Lorry boarded the eastbound express at Denver with all the air of a martyr. — *Graustark*, George Barr McCutcheon, 1901.

1578 "I'll catch the first train back this evening, Graves. Wouldn't go down there if it were not absolutely necessary; but I have just heard that Mrs. Delaney is to leave for New York tonight, and if I don't see her to-day there will be a pack of troublesome complications. Tell Mrs. Graves she can count me in on the box party tonight." — *The Day of the Dog*, George Barr McCutcheon, 1904.

1579 When Hank Clery left the switch-yards in the outskirts of Chicago he took the street car and went down town. He was going to the county jail on the north side of the river. — *An Eye for an Eye*, Clarence Darrow, 1905.

1580 A tall young man sped swiftly up the wide stone steps leading to the doorway of a mansion in one of Chicago's most fashionable avenues. — *Nedra*, George Barr McCutcheon, 1905.

1581 Lee Virginia Wetherford began her return journey into the mountain West with exultation. — *Cavanagh: Forest Ranger*, Hamlin Garland, 1910.

1582 Two tired but happy punchers rode into the coast town and dismounted in front of the best hotel. — *Bar-20 Days*, Clarence E. Mulford, 1911.

1583 "Bel, come here!" — *The Harvester*, Gene Stratton-Porter, 1911.

1584 When Madeline Hammond stepped from the train at El Cajon, New Mexico, it was nearly midnight, and her first impression was of a huge dark space of cool, windy emptiness, strange and silent, stretching away under great blinking white stars. — *The Light of Western Stars*, Zane Grey, 1914.

1585 A girl came out of lawyer Royall's house, at the end of the one street of North Dormer, and stood on the doorstep. — *Summer*, Edith Wharton, 1917.

1586 Soames Forsyte emerged from the Knightsbridge Hotel, where he was staying, in the afternoon of the 12th of May, 1920, with the intention of visiting a collection of pictures in a Gallery off Cork Street, and looking into the Future. — *To Let*, John Galsworthy, 1921.

1587 "Well, Mother," I said as I took my seat at the breakfast table the second day after our Thanksgiving dinner, "I must return to Chicago. I have some lectures to deliver and besides I must get back to my writing." — *A Daughter of the Middle Border*, Hamlin Garland, 1921.

1588 "So of course," wrote Betty Flanders, pressing her heels rather deeper in the sand, "there was nothing for it but to leave." — *Jacob's Room*, Virginia Woolf, 1922.

1589 Miss Fitzgerald hurried out of the Hotel into the road. Here she stood still, looking purposelessly up and down in the blinding sunshine and picking at the fingers of her gloves. — *The Hotel*, Elizabeth Bowen, 1927.

1590 It was not till the beginning of September that R. Ashenden, a writer by profession, who had been abroad at the outbreak of the war, managed to get back to England. — *Ashenden*, W. Somerset Maugham, 1928.

1591 Mr. Nelson Smock, arriving at his cottage in Maine on Friday afternoon for his weekly recuperation from Wall Street, paused in the hall and looked into the living room before going on in search of his wife. — *Claire Ambler*, Booth Tarkington, 1928.

1592 Bridesley, Birmingham/ Two o'clock. Thousands came back from dinner along streets. — *Living*, Henry Green, 1929.

1593 It was no mere chance that, during the first decade of the new century, brought Mamba out of the darkness of the underworld into the light of the Wentworths' kitchen. — *Mamba's Daughters*, Du Bose Heyward, 1929.

1594 *He had closed the door carefully, silently, behind him, and was in the dim hall with his foot on the first step of the familiar stairs.* — *How Like a God*, Rex Stout, 1929.

1595 Evelyn came down by the lift into the great front-hall. — *Imperial Palace*, Arnold Bennett, 1930.

1596 At four o'clock in the evening of the shortest day in the year 1878 a young man passed from a main street in Islington into a quadrangle through an arch, over which was an iron plate inscribed *Dodd's Buildings*. — *Immaturity*, George Bernard Shaw, 1930.

1597 Bonthorn closed the gate. — *The Ten Commandments*, Warwick Deeping, 1931.

1598 1743 and a fine June morning. Blue water, wind from the southwest, and Marguerite Ledoux taking her last sight of Marblehead as she crouched at the low railing of the *Isabella B.* — *Calico Bush*, Rachel Field, 1931.

1599 "Good," Harriette said to herself when Verheiden got in the yellow station-wagon and drove away. — *Ambrose Holt and Family*, Susan Glaspell, 1931.

1600 Shortly after midnight on Sunday, June 21st, Francis Ferriter left the offices of the *Morning Star* in O'Connell Street, Dublin, and returned

to his lodgings in Lower Gardiner Street. — *The Puritan*, Liam O'Flaherty, 1931.

1601 In the thick darkness of the warm spring night he slipped as he stepped from the window-sill to the tin roof of the shed just below and one of the heavy shoes dropped from his hand and fell into the grass and bushes of the garden. — *A Modern Hero*, Louis Bromfield, 1932.

1602 Cean turned and lifted her hand briefly in farewell as she rode away beside Lonzo in the ox-cart. Her mother and father and Jasper and Lias stood in front of the house, watching her go. — *Lamb in His Bosom*, Caroline Miller, 1933.

1603 It was half past eight of a sultry August night when Felix Hollister left the Exeter Country Club. — *Lost Morning*, Du Bose Heyward, 1936.

1604 Jeff Gilman came out of the house from saying goodbye to the womenfolk. He carried two battered brown leather bags, and his small curtained touring car stood waiting for him in the driveway. — *Neighbor to the Sky*, Gladys Hasty Carroll, 1937.

1605 The door opened and Michael Gosselyn looked up. Julia came in. — *Theatre*, W. Somerset Maugham, 1937.

1606 . . . Light came and went and came again, the booming strokes of three o'clock beat out across the town in thronging bronze, light winds of April blew the fountain out in rainbow sheets, until the plume returned and pulsed, as Grover turned into the Square. — "The Lost Boy," Thomas Wolfe, 1937 (pub. 1992).

1607 I am going to pack my two shirts with my other socks and my best suit in the little blue cloth my mother used to tie round her hair when she did the house, and I am going from the Valley. — *How Green Was My Valley*, Richard Llewellyn, 1939.

1608 Kenthill at last, and the bus stopping at East and Market streets! — *Lost Sunrise*, Kathleen Norris, 1939.

1609 One morning last autumn a little man with a large sad face turned out of Midland Street, Birchester, and climbed the stairs next to the sewing-machine shop. — *Let the People Sing*, J. B. Priestley, 1939.

1610 The door of the Drones Club swung open, and a young man in form-fitting tweeds came down the steps and started to walk westwards. An observant passer-by, scanning his face, would have fancied that he discerned on it a keen, tense look, like that of an African hunter stalking a hippopotamus. — *Uncle Fred in the Springtime*, P. G. Wodehouse, 1939.

1611 On a day of early November in the mid-1920's Francis Ellery was leaving Florence. — *Ask Me Tomorrow*, James Gould Cozzens, 1940.

1612 They say that it was a gay train which carried Cristo Lorenzo Rodriguez into Calumet when first he came there. — *Cuba Libre*, MacKinlay Kantor, 1940.

1613 The cat got into the milk at the same moment that Uncle Dan arrived from America. — *Thorofare*, Christopher Morley, 1942.

1614 On a certain cold gray morning, wet and misty, (December 15, 1850, in fact) a young man of about eighteen years turned in at Russell Square, whistling abstractedly to himself. — *The Turnbulls*, Taylor Caldwell, 1943.

1615 On the third of March, 1820, John Brodrick set out from Andriff to Doonhaven, intending to cover the fifteen miles of his journey before nightfall. — *Hungry Hill*, Daphne du Maurier, 1943.

1616 The train was/ rocking through/ wide open country/ before Elsa was able to/ put off the misery of leaving/ and reach out for the freedom/ and release that were hers now. — *The Big Rock Candy Mountain*, Wallace Stegner, 1943.

1617 Laura sat up beside her father on the high front seat of the spring cart and waved to the neighbours. — *Candleford Green*, Flora Thompson, 1943.

1618 Holding Mama's hand tightly, I came out of the dark arches of the railway station and into the bright streets of the strange town. — *The Green Years*, A. J. Cronin, 1944.

1619 On our way out of the house — his house, which was also his office, on West 35th Street over near the North River — Nero Wolfe, who was ahead of me, stopped so abruptly that I nearly bumped into him. — "Booby Trap," Rex Stout, 1944.

1620 A country bus drew up below the church and a young man got out. This he had to do carefully because he had a peg leg. — *Back*, Henry Green, 1946.

1621 The cleaner rose from her knees, collecting bucket, brush and duster, and creaked toward the door. There, as usual, she turned, beamed, said, "Ta-ta, Mr. Strangeways, be good," before clanking off to do the deputy director. — *Minute for Murder*, Cecil Day-Lewis *as* Nicholas Blake, 1947.

1622 The day was breaking when the woman came out of the house. — *The Enchanted*, Martin Flavin, 1947.

1623 It took all of April and May to get out of the jungle. — *The Wind Cannot Read*, Richard Mason, 1947.

1624 When the train reached Westport, Gifford Maxim gave not the slightest sign that he had come to his destination. — *The Middle of the Journey*, Lionel Trilling, 1947.

1625 I got out of a cab on Rockefeller Plaza. — *The Dream Merchants*, Harold Robbins, 1949.

1626 On every ordinary weekday in term-

time, Claude Batchelor stepped out of his house at exactly twenty minutes past nine, slammed the door and set off at a furious pace in the direction of St. Mark's School. — *The Lost Traveller*, Antonia White, 1950.

1627 On a rainy day, Peter Manderson Perry and his small son Joey left Paradise. — *The Pedlocks*, Stephen Longstreet, 1951.

1628 Land was left behind. — *The Viking*, Edison Marshall, 1951.

1629 On a bleak and gusty Saturday afternoon in March, the 2:45 bus from Market Square, Farbridge, arrived at the corner of Mayton Park Avenue, and stopped just long enough to allow a young woman carrying a portable typewriter to descend, which she did gracefully but grumpily. — *Festival at Farbridge*, J. B. Priestley, 1951.

1630 Ann Prentice stood on the platform at Victoria, waving. — *A Daughter's a Daughter*, Agatha Christie *as* Mary Westmacott, 1952.

1631 They arrived in Bulinga late on a Friday afternoon. — *The Sundowners*, Jon Cleary, 1952.

1632 They gripped the spokes of the two-wheeled timber cart and threw their bodies forward. — *Crown Jewel*, Ralph de Boissiere, 1952.

1633 Hugo Fletcher had scarcely drawn a breath of Coldmouth air when he asked himself what had brought him back here. — *A Different Face*, Olivia Manning, 1953.

1634 It was only a little after nine o'clock in the evening, but already the horde had gone rampaging away. — *God and My Country*, MacKinlay Kantor, 1954.

1635 It was just about midnight when Stenham left Si Jaffar's door. — *The Spider's House*, Paul Bowles, 1955.

1636 "I shall leave the house tomorrow morning." — *The Hidden River*, Storm Jameson, 1955.

1637 So many were leaving, so many and mostly so young. — *The Sixth of June*, Lionel Shapiro, 1955.

1638 When Dave Borthen walked into the lighted lobby of the old hotel, Bowie Sutton, the elevator operator, was the first to spot him. — *Rimrock*, Luke Short, 1955.

1639 *Now he was here.* Fate Laird placed the worn cardboard suitcase carefully in the dusty road and lifted his head. Until this moment of arrival at the place where the dirt road twisted out of the pines and the hill fell away to the right he had not let himself look, saving it until he could have all of the seeing at once. — *Walk Through the Valley*, Borden Deal, 1956.

1640 It was spring when I came back to the river. I had traveled a long way to reach it, by bush plane out of northern Ontario, by Trans-Canada Air to the Atlantic coast, and then the train crawling down the shore. — *The Wings of Night*, Thomas H. Raddall, 1956.

1641 Eric entered the room quietly and stood for a moment beside the table so that I could not see his face. — *The Game and the Ground*, Peter Vansittart, 1956.

1642 I came to Warley on a wet September morning with the sky the grey of Guiseley sandstone. — *Room at the Top*, John Braine, 1957.

1643 "Take my camel, dear," said my aunt Dot, as she climbed down from this animal on her return from High Mass. — *The Towers of Trebizond*, Rose Macaulay, 1957.

1644 Coming back was worse, much worse, than Martin Stone had anticipated. — *The Lost Europeans*, Emanuel Litvinoff, 1959.

1645 Ruth Whiting stepped out of the high train directly it stopped. — *Cave of Ice*, Penelope Mortimer, 1959.

1646 "So you're leaving us, sir?" said the R.S.M./ "Yes," said Jacinth Crewe. "That is to say, I'm going on leave tomorrow until such time as my resignation is gazetted. I shan't be back." — *Brother Cain*, Simon Raven, 1959.

1647 Young Sam Price stepped out of a patch of gray-dusty, dry-scraggly mesquite. — *Poor No More*, Robert Ruark, 1959.

1648 He sprang from the gritty iron of the Pullman car step and caught his balance upon the dim whiteness that covered the ground. His feet felt the snow. His pounding heart felt it. — *The Primal Yoke*, Tom Lea, 1960.

1649 She got out of the train and walked slowly across the platform. — *The Fugitives*, John Broderick, 1962.

1650 It was noon. Time to go. — *Seconds*, David Ely, 1963.

1651 The double doors at the end of the ballroom were thrust open. Some of the people into whose backs they were thrust resisted and resented for a moment and then, understanding, made way. A space was created and at the same time a pause, as though someone very important or very fat was about to enter and nothing of smaller weight could command attention meanwhile. At last a sedan chair was carried in at a run. — *The Snow Ball*, Brigid Brophy, 1964.

1652 When Brother got out of the car, the two Cajuns sitting on the porch turned to look at him. — *Catherine Carmier*, Ernest J. Gaines, 1964.

1653 One morning late in September of the year 1955 a man stepped out of a taxi in front of a hotel in New York, paid the driver, and arranged three pieces of luggage on the sidewalk. — *One Day in the Afternoon of the World*, William Saroyan, 1964.

1654 Eric Taylor, returning home to lunch, after the French fashion, from his morning's work at the City of London (Paris branch) Bank,

paused as usual outside the concierge's lodge. — *Martha, Eric and George*, Margery Sharp, 1964.

1655 I stopped the taxi at the corner of Lord North Street. — *Corridors of Power*, C. P. Snow, 1964.

1656 "Bluebeard has gone away. He came in while you were still asleep, and he kissed your eyes." — *The Final Beast*, Frederick Buechner, 1965.

1657 Here they come now, walking in right after we open up, two of them. — *Do, Lord, Remember Me*, George Garrett, 1965.

1658 Andrew Lingard came to kiss his wife good morning and good-bye; he was off as usual to the British Museum Reading Room. — "A Promising Career," Martha Gellhorn, 1965.

1659 The wrought-iron gate of the villa swung open easily. The young man shut it behind him, put his suitcase down on the sandy path, and stood with his hands on his hips looking around. — *In the Sun*, Jon Godden, 1965.

1660 George Raymond was on time, arriving to pick up Eddie Ryan at seven-thirty. — *Lonely for the Future*, James T. Farrell, 1966.

1661 "Come again *soon*," Julia said, arresting them again at the top of the stairs, smiling and pleading. — *The Game*, A. S. Byatt, 1967.

1662 As she passed the front window downstairs, carrying a box of paint, Stacey noticed the children outside, grouped round the rear end of the Land Rover and poking at the luggage to make it fit better. — *The Hot Month*, Clifford Hanley, 1967.

1663 Sundy breathed a sigh of relief as she slammed the door shut. — *The Anarchy of Love*, Colin Spencer, 1967.

1664 It is too late, of course. They are expecting me by seven o'clock and it is nearly six now. So I will go. — *Listen Ruben Fontanez*, Jay Neugeboren, 1968.

1665 On returning to the Fitzjohn's Avenue flat after a few days in Suffolk, Joanna always half expected to find someone there. — *Someone Else*, Gillian Tindall, 1969.

1666 Each thing that goes away returns and nothing in the end is lost. — *Fragments*, Ayi Kwei Armah, 1970.

1667 Benton Collingsworth stepped off the train, turned and helped little Mary Jess down and then gave a hand to May, who was carrying Tommie. — *Arfive*, A. B. Guthrie, Jr., 1970.

1668 In his rear-view mirror the bridge fell away, and behind the bridge the city, where his mistress dwelled. — *The Goy*, Mark Harris, 1970.

1669 *Farewell, Farewell, Farewell, Eight Bells, Wywurk, The Wicket Gate. The little house looked all right. So we love forever, taking leave.* — *October Ferry to Gabriola*, Malcolm Lowry, 1970.

1670 Brownfield stood close to his mother in the yard, not taking his eyes off the back of the receding automobile. — *The Third Life of Grange Copeland*, Alice Walker, 1970.

1671 It was already evening when I approached Stonehenge, and the tourist bus was pulling away for its return to Salisbury. — *The Elixir*, Robert Nathan, 1971.

1672 *A figure appears.* — *Wonderland*, Joyce Carol Oates, 1971.

1673 The other servants fall silent as Lister enters the room. — *Not to Disturb*, Muriel Spark, 1971.

1674 Mrs. Palfrey first came to the Claremont Hotel on a Sunday afternoon in January. — *Mrs. Palfrey at the Claremont*, Elizabeth Taylor, 1971.

1675 He arrived in town with his pajamas, his slippers, three NōDōz pills, and an uneasy feeling that he had known himself in better times. — *John-Juan*, Douglas Woolf, 1971.

1676 On March 17, 197-, at half-past ten o'clock in the morning, Pierce Davis set out from his home town of Spark, Iowa, to walk around the world. — *Walking Davis*, David Ely, 1972.

1677 They were flying out the next morning, and Master Sergeant Cesario Flores had a farewell word to say. — *The Assassins*, Elia Kazan, 1972.

1678 The cab dropped him at the Place Pigalle. — *Strangers and Journeys*, Maurice Shadbolt, 1972.

1679 It was two days after Christmas when they drove us out of Berea. — *The Way to Fort Pillow*, James Sherburne, 1972.

1680 They came like a caravan of carnival folk up through the swales of broomstraw and across the hill in the morning sun, the truck rocking and pitching in the ruts and the musicians on chairs in the truckbed teetering and tuning their instruments, the fat man with guitar grinning and gesturing to others in a car behind and bending to give a note to the fiddler who turned a fiddlepeg and listened with a wrinkled face. — *Child of God*, Cormac McCarthy, 1973.

1681 Naked to the waist and seven thousand feet high, he stepped from his house. — *Luck and Pluck*, Glendon Swarthout, 1973.

1682 There is in me a thing that when I go, I go for good and all. — *The Other Room*, Borden Deal, 1974.

1683 He walked out of the cottage and into the night. — *The Reincarnation of Peter Proud*, Max Ehrlich, 1974.

1684 The truth is, if old Major Dover hadn't dropped dead at Taunton races Jim would never have come to Thursgood's at all. — *Tinker, Tailor, Soldier, Spy*, John Le Carré, 1974.

1685 He has come to Chicago. He has come on foot, in the company of night. — *The Death of the Detective*, Mark Smith, 1974.

1686 I'd probably have went Pikes-Peak-or-Busting without no extra help or discouragement, but what made it certain sure was my old man cussing our farm. — *The Road to Many a Wonder*, David Wagoner, 1974.

1687 Mr. Ephraim Trout of Trout, Wapshott and Edelstein, one of the many legal firms employed by Ivor Llewellyn, head of the Superba-Llewellyn studio of Llewellyn City, Hollywood, was seeing Mr. Llewellyn off at the Los Angeles airport. — *Bachelors Anonymous*, P. G. Wodehouse, 1974.

1688 I arrived in New Orleans in the rain at 5 o'clock in the morning. — *Factotum*, Charles Bukowski, 1975.

1689 Shortly after Olivia went away with the Nawab, Beth Crawford returned from Simla. — *Heat and Dust*, Ruth Prawer Jhabvala, 1975.

1690 I am back. After several years coming down — maneuvering like a weightless astronaut in space — I'm on earth again. — *Zone of the Interior*, Clancy Sigal, 1976.

1691 Herbert of Bosham, Master in the study of Holy Writ in the diocese of Canterbury, came to the Abbey of Clair-Marais in Flanders only a few days after Richard de Luci, King Henry's Justiciar, having failed to persuade the fugitive Archbishop of Canterbury to return to England, had departed from it in anger. — *The Lion of Christ*, Margaret Butler, 1977.

1692 Tamsin came yesterday. I knew she would. She's in a phase of needing to be with me, I don't know why. — *Nobody's Fault*, Mervyn Jones, 1977.

1693 We got the word that the four of them were coming a month before they arrived. — *Whistle*, James Jones, 1978.

1694 Simon Boulderstone, coming into Cairo on leave, passed the pyramids at Giza when they were hazed over by mid-day heat. — *The Battle Lost and Won*, Olivia Manning, 1978.

1695 I got my things and left. — "The House of Hunger," Dambudzo Marechera, 1978.

1696 Autumn, after all, is not a good time to leave. — *On the Verge*, Dikkon Eberhart, 1979.

1697 Nnu Ego backed out of the room, her eyes unfocused and glazed, looking into vacancy. — *The Joys of Motherhood*, Buchi Emecheta, 1979.

1698 In the winter of 1918-1919, on a day when the wind was blowing, I. C. Trumpelman arrived in our town. — *King of the Jews*, Leslie Epstein, 1979.

1699 Gabriel Michelson stepped out of the Air Terminal building at Kennedy Airport and hailed a taxi. — *Love Affair*, Seymour Epstein, 1979.

1700 MacCarthy was light-headed that night when he set out from Judy Conlon's cabin in the Acres of Killala. — *The Year of the French*, Thomas Flanagan, 1979.

1701 I was shoveling the snow down the driveway when Holly arrived home from work, climbing out of her car and saying, "Henry, can I see you for 1 minute?" — *It Looked Like For Ever*, Mark Harris, 1979.

1702 One morning early in October, a man called Ashburner, tightly buttoned into a black overcoat and holding a suitcase, tried to leave his bedroom on the second floor of a house in Beaufort Street. — *Winter Garden*, Beryl Bainbridge, 1980.

1703 When the train stopped I stumbled out, nudging and kicking the kitbag before me. — *A Month in the Country*, J. L. Carr, 1980.

1704 The Masked Rider of the plains reined up in back of the tailor shop, his mighty horse raising the dust in the road. — *Jack in the Box*, William Kotzwinkle, 1980.

1705 One of the valet parking attendants at Hazel Park Racecourse would remember the judge leaving sometime after the ninth race, about 1:00 A.M., and fill in the first part of what happened. — *City Primeval*, Elmore Leonard, 1980.

1706 It was many years ago in that dark, chaotic, unfathomable pool of time before Germaine's birth (nearly twelve months before her birth), on a night in late September stirred by innumerable frenzied winds, like spirits contending with one another — now plaintively, now angrily, now with a subtle cellolike delicacy capable of making the flesh rise on one's arms and neck — a night so sulfurous, so restless, so swollen with inarticulate longing that Leah and Gideon Bellefleur in their enormous bed quarreled once again, brought to tears because their love was too ravenous to be contained by their mere mortal bodies; and their groping, careless, anguished words were like strips of raw silk rubbed violently together (for each was convinced that the other did not, *could* not, be equal to his love — Leah doubted that any man was capable of a love so profound it could lie silent, like a forest pond; Gideon doubted that any woman was capable of comprehending the nature of a man's passion, which might tear through him, rendering him broken and exhausted, as vulnerable as a small child): it was on this tumultuous rain-lashed night that Mahalaleel came to Bellefleur Manor on the western shore of the great Lake Noir, where he was to stay for nearly five years. — *Bellefleur*, Joyce Carol Oates, 1980.

1707 This is how I got here, says Rennie. — *Bodily Harm*, Margaret Atwood, 1981.

1708 "Parlabane is back." — *The Rebel Angels*, Robertson Davies, 1981.

1709 I have returned. — *Summon the Bright Water*, Geoffrey Household, 1981.

1710 No one knew or cared where the Newspaper of Claremont Street went in her spare time. — *The Newspaper of Claremont Street*, Elizabeth Jolley, 1981.

1711 He believed he was safe. He stood at the railing of H.M.S. *Stor Konigsgaarten* and sucked in great gulps of air, his heart pounding in sweet expectation as he stared at the harbor. — *Tar Baby*, Toni Morrison, 1981.

1712 It was after five o'clock when he left the courthouse. — *Second Heaven*, Judith Guest, 1982.

1713 Dick Summers climbed the ridge from a channeled valley, glad enough to be leaving Oregon behind him. — *Fair Land, Fair Land*, A. B. Guthrie, Jr., 1982.

1714 In Poland's deepest autumn, a tall young man in an expensive overcoat, double-breasted dinner jacket beneath it and — in the lapel of the dinner jacket — a large ornamental gold-on-black-enamel *Hakenkreuz* (swastika) emerged from a fashionable apartment building in Straszewskiego Street, on the edge of the ancient center of Cracow, and saw his chauffeur waiting with fuming breath by the open door of an enormous and, even in this blackened world, lustrous Adler limousine. — *Schindler's List*, Thomas Keneally, 1982.

1715 Lydia Sinclair was just seventeen when she arrived on her husband's estate in the Andes, and from the first day she felt that she belonged there. She had never felt that she belonged anywhere before that. — *The Long Way Home*, Lisa St. Aubin de Terán, 1982.

1716 I dropped off Leah at dawn on the tenth day of summer. She wouldn't let me help her with the suitcases. — *Last Resort*, Scott Summer, 1982.

1717 Like a lady. That's how I stepped onto that train. — *A Measure of Time*, Rosa Guy, 1983.

1718 He hopes his own death will take him somewhere else, but the deaths of others always bring him back here. — *Job's Year*, Joseph Hansen, 1983.

1719 "Are you sure, darling, you won't come with us after all?" — *False Premises*, Winthrop Knowlton, 1983.

1720 Sometimes — once or twice a year — the Amerindians would come into Charlestown. — *Love and Death in a Hot Country*, Shiva Naipaul, 1983.

1721 Jacob came to Sweetwater, Tennessee, by train. — *Familiar Ground*, Elizabeth Cox, 1984.

1722 Rachel Kane arrived in Jerusalem after a sleepless eleven-hour flight from New York, and insisted on going directly to the Western Wall. — *The Lives of Rachel*, Joel Gross, 1984.

1723 My heel caught as I stepped off the train. — *If the Old Could . . .*, Doris Lessing *as* Jane Somers, 1984.

1724 On a cold blowy February day a woman is boarding the ten A.M. flight to London, followed by an invisible dog. — *Foreign Affairs*, Alison Lurie, 1984.

1725 Lonnie Baer arrived at Los Angeles International as a ward of the court. — *Hot Wire*, James Brown, 1985.

1726 One bright fresh summer morning, in a prosperous decade between two disastrous economic depressions, a thin young man disembarked in Victoria Coach Station from one of the buses plying between Scotland and London. — *The Fall of Kelvin Walker*, Alasdair Gray, 1985.

1727 On the night before Christmas, a snowy night with wind in the forecast, Janet Raft arrived at Agatha McGee's house on River Street. — *A Green Journey*, Jon Hassler, 1985.

1728 Did he think I wouldn't come? — *White Water*, Joyce Reiser Kornblatt, 1985.

1729 Stone telling is my last name. It has come to me of my own choosing, because I have a story to tell of where I went when I was young; but now I go nowhere, sitting like a stone in this place, in this ground, in this Valley. I have come where I was going. — *Always Coming Home*, Ursula K. Le Guin, 1985.

1730 Sybill parks carefully at the curb in front of the hypnotist's house and stares at it for some time without getting out of the car, without even turning off the motor or the air conditioner. — *Family Linen*, Lee Smith, 1985.

1731 Again he struck out due west. She watched his predatory, slightly uneven gait and once more puzzled over whether he was foolish or bold. — *The Maid of Buttermere*, Melvyn Bragg, 1986.

1732 Just at the moment of dawn, Milos appeared out of the darkness at the edge of the town square and walked toward the depot. — *The Dispossessed*, Don Carpenter, 1986.

1733 Hello Camille!/ I suppose we fled the South. — "Deaths at Sea," Andre Dubus, 1986.

1734 I got out late winter. — *Rubicon Beach*, Steve Erickson, 1986.

1735 The Cheyenne had come twice already, straight down the streambed toward the island, their charge splitting at the last moment to pass on either side. — *Roman*, Douglas C. Jones, 1986.

1736 In the small hours of a blustery October morning in a south Devon coastal town that seemed to have been deserted by its inhabitants, Magnus Pym got out of his elderly country taxicab and, having paid the driver and waited till he had left, struck out across the church square. — *A Perfect Spy*, John Le Carré, 1986.

1737 No Latino villager ever hurries, for, after all, where is there to go? — *Pasaquina*, Erin O'Shaughnessy, 1986.

1738 The man of startling redness lumbers

towards the three new arrivals from Port, and the train starts pulling out of the camp. And as the last carriage passes, a bundle of blankets is tossed out of the door. — *The Canberran*, Rupert Parsons, 1986.

1739 "Brucie, we gotta get in. I told Joyce we was gonna get in." — *Social Disease*, Paul Rudnick, 1986.

1740 I went back to Oxford recently. — *The Last Romantics*, Caroline Seebohm, 1986.

1741 Sarah Williams left for Minneapolis with our life together in the worst possible repair. — *Waking the Dead*, Scott Spencer, 1986.

1742 *Someone. . . ,/ "Hey, hey, . . ."/ coming down the Quarters./ ". . . sweet mamma."*, — *Dessa Rose*, Sherley Anne Williams, 1986.

1743 Able to bear it no longer he, Xman, at last decided to depart for good, this time with no turning back. — *Xman*, Michael Brodsky, 1987.

1744 When the trial began, we left the country. — *The Red White and Blue*, John Gregory Dunne, 1987.

1745 It took them an hour to leave the house. — "Friends in the Country," Rachel Ingalls, 1987.

1746 It was late, almost eleven-thirty, when Cyrus Irani left Carnegie Hall with the crowd at the end of Bach's Saint Matthew Passion. — *The Rug Merchant*, Phillip Lopate, 1987.

1747 He was dead set against me going, but there was nothing he could do. — *Life in the Land of the Living*, Daniel Vilmure, 1987.

1748 At almost one o'clock I entered the lobby of the building where I worked and turned toward the escalators, carrying a black Penguin paperback and a small white CVS bag, its receipt stapled over the top. — *The Mezzanine*, Nicholson Baker, 1988.

1749 Terri DiFranco closed the front door of the rowhouse and hurried down the steps. — *The Seduction*, Art Bourgeau, 1988.

1750 Catherine de Rochefauld climbed aboard the Simplon-Orient Express in Paris at the Gare de l'Est. — *A Woman of Singular Occupation*, Penelope Gilliatt, 1988.

1751 I was at the office window, looking out over the still waters of the harbour and watching a small boat break the reflection of Bloody Island's hospital ruins, when he drove up. — *Medusa*, Hammond Innes, 1988.

1752 Ulysses Turner Fraser, my father, came from the dark bedroom into the morning light of the upstairs landing. — *Three Nights in the Heart of the Earth*, Brett Laidlaw, 1988.

1753 O clocked off at exactly half past three. — *Shifts*, Christopher Meredith, 1988.

1754 No, this third time she would be gone. An afternoon, a weekday bleached by summer light, would see her taken from him. — *Blair*, John A. Scott, 1988.

1755 Yesterday, I went back to Ivers. — *The Timeless Moment*, Pamela Street, 1988.

1756 The brothers Moon were kicked out of England in 1767. — *The Phases of Harry Moon*, Thomas Sullivan, 1988.

1757 June 1984. Storm clouds gathered in the sky above Bombay's Victoria Station as David Spencer Bruce, former Captain, Indian Army, Burma, a graying centurion with an athletic stride, and his wife Philippa got down from a taxi. — *Then Spoke the Thunder*, Elwyn Chamberlain, 1989.

1758 On Monday March 28, 1966, Sir Walter Springfellow, Director-General of the Australian Security Intelligence Organization, left his home in Mosman in the city of Sydney to return to Melbourne and the then headquarters of ASIO. — *Babylon South*, Jon Cleary, 1989.

1759 Joe Cullen came in out of the rain, his hat soaked, his trench coat sodden across the shoulders, and leaned his weight against the bar and waited for Billy Sullivan to look at him and recognize him. — *The Confession of Joe Cullen*, Howard Fast, 1989.

1760 Lila Mae splayed her fingers and waved her hand gently in the air. — *The Book of Marvels*, Christopher T. Leland, 1989.

1761 Had they still been a possibility in England, Mr. Baldwin would have sent his other children telegrams to announce his return. — *Family Planning*, Tim Parks, 1989.

1762 Borne on the breezy sweep of sunlight, Professor Jonathan was trying to cross Avenida Atlântica to get to the beach. — *The Sun in Capricorn*, Paul Rosenblatt, 1989.

1763 *And all the people saw the thunderings, and the lightnings, and the noise of the trumpet, and the mountain smoking: and when the people saw it, they removed, and stood afar off. And they said unto Moses, Speak thou with us, and we will hear: but let not God speak with us, lest we die. And Moses said unto the people, Fear not: for God is come to prove you, and this his fear may be before your faces, that ye sin not. And the people stood afar off, and Moses drew near unto the thick darkness where God was./* "Is he going to come back?" I whispered to my mother. "Wait and see," she replied. — *Cosmetic Effects*, Clive Sinclair, 1989.

1764 They appeared with the sun at their backs on the crest of the hill after daybreak, black figures, threading their way toward the sea through the gray rocks and heather into the town of St. Ives. — *John Dollar*, Marianne Wiggins, 1989.

1765 The screen door slammed shut as she raced to the front gate. Freedom at last. She clasped her bookbag to her chest and suddenly it became her illegitimate child. — *The Past Is Another Country*, Lois Battle, 1990.

1766 David was the first person to arrive at Lillian's spring cocktail party. — *Leap Year*, Peter Cameron, 1990.

1767 When they got out of the limousine at the Library (the invitation asked the honorees and their guests to please use the Forty-second Street entrance rather than the Fifth Avenue steps between the lions), the first thing that Seaton noticed was that Gin was standing halfway up the steps under a steetlight. — *Fairyland*, Summer Locke Elliott, 1990.

1768 In the end Jack Burdette came back to Holt after all. — *Where You Once Belonged*, Kent Haruf, 1990.

1769 Finally, I see Gordon: dropping the screen door against the frame of his mother's side porch and checking his pocket for the key to his Mercury. — *Dying Young*, Marti Leimbach, 1990.

1770 Thickening twilight as the night nurse came stealing. — *The Charnel House*, Eamonn McGrath, 1990.

1771 The bus stops. I get on. — *I Get on the Bus*, Reginald McKnight, 1990.

1772 Marylou Jackson, the other girl in the office who lives over Steadman's Drugstore down the street with her two preschoolers, has just left. — *Sweet Eyes*, Jonis Agee, 1991.

1773 . . . and we are on our way. — *Otherwhere*, Margaret Wander Bonanno, 1991.

1774 About sixty people have left an apartment building east of Washington Square Park in New York City. — *Mister Touch*, Malcolm Bosse, 1991.

1775 The auctioneer was waiting when the farm truck full of Woolsey-Beans and their valuables came bobbing into view like flotsam from a shipwreck. — *Wild Apples*, Lucinda Franks, 1991.

1776 She was back now. — *Family Fictions*, Richard Hall, 1991.

1777 She pulled on her coat and boots, closed the pantry door and slipped away before anyone saw her disappear. — *Asya*, Michael Ignatieff, 1991.

1778 He came there in the off-season. So much was off. All bets were off. The last deal was off. His timing was off, or he wouldn't have come here at this moment, and also every second arc lamp along the peninsular highway was switched off. — *Resuscitation of a Hanged Man*, Denis Johnson, 1991.

1779 After a month's journey across Europe the royal procession of litters, sumpter horses, and carts finally arrived at the King's camp in Normandy. — *The Fatal Crown*, Ellen Jones, 1991.

1780 It was a time of returning. — *Pettibone's Law*, John Keene, 1991.

1781 You can never go back. — *Turning Back the Sun*, Colin Thubron, 1991.

1782 Lao Li's wife slipped out the back door of her house. — *Bittersweet*, Leslie Li, 1992.

1783 Frank Copenhaver put his wife Gracie's suitcases in the back of the Electra and held the door for her. — *Nothing But Blue Skies*, Thomas McGuane, 1992.

1784 At the moment Monroe was ready to unlock his front door, the girl next door called to him, and then fell in the grass, and a dog, coming from down the street, turned around, and went home. — *Taller Women*, Lawrence Naumoff, 1992.

1785 Even before he got up he knew he was on his way. — *Postcards*, E. Annie Proulx, 1992.

1786 He appeared on the hill at first light. — *Ulverton*, Adam Thorpe, 1992.

1787 On the morning of August 8, 1965, Robert Kincaid locked the door to his small two-room apartment on the third floor of a rambling house in Bellingham, Washington. — *The Bridges of Madison County*, Robert James Waller, 1992.

Compassion

1788 "All is well," Judith said quietly, coming forward and stroking the red apples of the sofa. "I shall not leave you, Jennifer. It is better I remain." — *The Fortress*, Hugh Walpole, 1932.

1789 You would think I care, and I did for a while, but not now. — *The God Boy*, Ian Cross, 1957.

1790 It wasn't any lack of human feeling. There were people in the town who said it was that, but it wasn't. — *The Exhibitionist*, David R. Slavitt *as* Henry Sutton, 1967.

1791 Consider Arkie. (But it breaks your heart.) — *The Gaudy Place*, Fred Chappell, 1973.

1792 The first thing Helen did was to walk swiftly across the room and put her strong arm, her tennis arm, around Targ's shoulder and squeeze fiercely and guide his head to between her breasts. "It's all right. It's all right," she whispered. — *An Island Death*, Sol Yurick, 1975.

1793 "Are you sure you're going to be all right?" — *Winter Doves*, David Cook, 1979.

1794 "What is it, Rick? What's wrong?"/ "Nothing." — *Untold Millions*, Laura Z. Hobson, 1982.

1795 "You're sure that you'll be all right?" Claire asked for the third time. — *Memorial Day*, Karen Brownstein, 1983.

1796 "Easy."/ Dropping a hand to Hale's shoulder, Diana pressed lightly. — *Breaking Gentle*, Beverly Lowry, 1988.

1797 Let me be sorry for myself, just a little, just at the start. Please. — *The Antique Collector*, Glyn Hughes, 1990.

1798 Sally Marble would give her the shirt off her back and had, on occasion. — *Joy Baby*, Linda Ashour, 1992.

1799 Remedios, *la curandera*, stands at the edge of the sea. The old healer is weary, a result, in part, of the countless times she has cocked her head in the direction of someone's story. — *A Place Where the Sea Remembers*, Sandra Benítez, 1993.

Confession

1800 I admit I kissed her. — *The Way of a Man*, Emerson Hough, 1907.

1801 I ought to tell you at the beginning that I am not quite normal having had a violent experience at the age of nine. I will make this clear at once because I have noticed that if things seep out slowly through a book the reader is apt to feel let down or tricked in some way when he eventually gets the point. — *A Long Way from Verona*, Jane Gardam, 1971.

1802 Dear Mama,/ I'm sorry about all the rows during vacation, and I have something to tell you that I guess I better not put off any longer. — *Consenting Adult*, Laura Z. Hobson, 1975.

1803 "Bless me, Father, for I have sinned. It has been four days since my last confession." — *Brothers Keepers*, Donald E. Westlake, 1975.

1804 "You want to hear a good confession, Mac?" Chatworth leaned against the armrest breathing a stream of friendly booze. — *Transatlantic Blues*, Wilfrid Sheed, 1978.

1805 *You better not never tell nobody but God. It'd kill your mammy.* — *The Color Purple*, Alice Walker, 1982.

1806 I will arise and go to my father, and will say unto him, Father I have sinned against heaven and before thee, and am no more worthy to be called thy son. — *The Good Apprentice*, Iris Murdoch, 1985.

1807 Go and sin no more. A jingle of brass rings as the priest pulled the little curtain. — *Expensive Habits*, Maureen Howard, 1986.

1808 "Bless me, Father, for I have sinned." — *The Rising of the Moon*, William Martin, 1987.

1809 "Declare yourself." — *Sting of the Bee*, Seth Rolbein, 1987.

1810 The need has come to explain myself to someone. — *Sex and Sunsets*, Tim Sandlin, 1987.

1811 "Bless me Father, for I have sinned...." — *Lapsing*, Jill Paton Walsh, 1987.

1812 There were crows in his eyes when he came right out with it, confessing that he had been the murderer. You could see them flapping

in there. And now and again the glint of a beak. You can't tell me anything about crows I don't already know at eighty. Nor about him, either. — *Captivity Captive*, Rodney Hall, 1988.

1813 I don't reckon Lucas will mind me telling about us, at least he never told me not to. — *All the Western Stars*, Philip Lee Williams, 1988.

1814 Time and again Emilia had been on the verge of telling him, but each time she had pulled back. — *Night of the Broken Glass*, Peter Broner, 1991.

1815 I promised to confess so I guess I'll have to tell you about the real Rose. — *Rose Reason*, Mary Flanagan, 1991.

1816 Let me confess to you at once that if I had not, on the spur of the moment, picked up my pen and scribbled a note to George Smiley inviting him to address my passing-out class on the closing evening of their entry course — and had Smiley not, against all my expectations, consented — I would not be making so free to you with my heart. — *The Secret Pilgrim*, John Le Carré, 1991.

1817 I shouldn't have thought I'd have gone public like this. Well, to begin with, there's the question of our musty old laws, isn't there? — "*Town Crier* Exclusive," Stanley Elkin, 1993.

1818 *It is an old sin, several years old.* — *Midnight Lemonade*, Ann Goethe, 1993.

1819 Never never tell, Maddy-Monkey, they warned me, it's Death if you tell any of Them but now after so many years I am going to tell, for who's to stop me? — *Foxfire*, Joyce Carol Oates, 1993.

Conflict

1820 Now that we are cool, he said, and regret that we hurt each other, I am not sorry that it happened. — *Green Mansions*, W. H. Hudson, 1904.

1821 The opinions of Owen Powell marked a sharp difference between him and most of his fellow-townsmen in the town of the Middle West, where he lived sixty years ago. — *New Leaf Mills*, William Dean Howells, 1913.

1822 "My dear," said Mr. Blithers, with decision, "you can't tell me." — *The Prince of Graustark*, George Barr McCutcheon, 1914.

1823 It was a scene of bitter disputation. — *The Soul of a Bishop*, H. G. Wells, 1917.

1824 Margaret and I quarrelled because she would not let me sink her makeshift boat in the marsh pool, in which a fine steep sea could be

worked up by hand in a few seconds. — *Ordinary Families*, E. Arnot Robertson, 1933.

1825 The agon, then. It begins. — *The Black Book*, Lawrence Durrell, 1938.

1826 Lucia Pillson, the Mayor-elect of Tilling, and her husband Georgie were talking together one October afternoon in the garden room at Mallards. The debate demanded the exercise of their keenest faculties. — *Trouble for Lucia*, E. F. Benson, 1939.

1827 She had often heard her mother say that freeing Negroes made them impudent, and for a moment she thought that the packet-boat stewardess was going to be distressingly impertinent. — *The Wedding Journey*, Walter D. Edmonds, 1947.

1828 From her resting place in the broom closet Consuela could hear the two American ladies in 404 arguing. — *The Listening Walls*, Margaret Millar, 1959.

1829 For three or four weeks Obi Okonkwo had been steeling himself against this moment. And when he walked into the dock that morning he thought he was fully prepared. — *No Longer at Ease*, Chinua Achebe, 1960.

1830 They almost had a blisterer in the taxi on the way to St. Paul's. — *The Thing of It Is . . .*, William Goldman, 1967.

1831 One fine day in the middle of the night, two dead men got up to fight, two blind men looking on, two cripples running for the priest, and two dummies shouting Hurry on. That's how it is. Topsy-turvy. — *Night*, Edna O'Brien, 1972.

1832 In Bangkok there had been some argument about whether or not they wanted to go journeying up *klongs* with the rest of the tourists. — *The Children Sing*, MacKinlay Kantor, 1973.

1833 *From Dr. A.B.W. Munday./* Sir, It is to be regretted that your correspondent ("Tribal War in Western Uganda," 25 Oct.) did not trouble himself to probe more deeply into the conflict between the Bwamba and Batoro peoples, and saw fit only to repeat the confused observations of a generation of misfit District Commissioners. — *The Black House*, Paul Theroux, 1974.

1834 Afterwards, in the dusty little corners where London's secret servants drink together, there was argument about where the Dolphin case history should really begin. — *The Honourable Schoolboy*, John Le Carré, 1977.

1835 "I'm gonna smash yer ter bits." — *The Storyteller*, Alan Sillitoe, 1979.

1836 As usual they were arguing — it was always about money or women or something that had happened in the dim forgotten past, and half the time it was a combination of all three. — *Nighthawk Blue*, Peter Guralnick, 1980.

1837 By midsummer it had begun to look as though the Angles would never make up in time to have their party before the fall. — *The Delphinium Girl*, Mark Smith, 1980.

1838 Armstrong was sitting in a rum shop at the corner of Princess and Lombard Streets. A grey, three-day stubble grew from his chin and, in parts, from his face, which had been only partly shaven that day. He had quarrelled with his barber in the American barber shop and had walked out without waiting to have the job finished. — *One Generation*, Roy A. K. Heath, 1981.

1839 She wanted to win this fight. She would win it at any cost. — *Sweetsir*, Helen Yglesias, 1981.

1840 "How about Bunny Turnbull chewing the rag?" Banana Mae started up. — *Southern Discomfort*, Rita Mae Brown, 1982.

1841 The women were quarreling at his bedside. — *The False Messiah*, Leonard Wolf, 1982.

1842 No! she said stubbornly and hung on by her teeth. — *Floaters*, Tish O'Dowd Ezekiel, 1984.

1843 I would not have remembered that particular row with my husband, if the phone call hadn't interrupted it. — *Casualties*, Lynne Reid Banks, 1986.

1844 Even before their last kiss something, not time or place or that vicious circumstance, divided them. — *Supply of Heroes*, James Carroll, 1986.

1845 We fought. When my mother and I crossed state lines in the stolen car, I'd sit against the window and wouldn't talk. — *Anywhere But Here*, Mona Simpson, 1987.

1846 My mother always kept plastic plants because they were easier to move and my father always watered them after each senseless fight. — *Blueprints*, Sara Vogan, 1990.

1847 Sarah pleaded with her eyes for Larry to be civil. — *Plain Grief*, Maxine Chernoff, 1991.

1848 Eddie was twenty-six years old, and he was thinking about how he didn't really mind these arguments with Betty. — *Ten Seconds*, Louis Edwards, 1991.

Construction

1849 The upper lattices of a tall, narrow window were open, and admitted the view, of, first, some richly tinted vine leaves and purpling grapes, then, in dazzling freshness of new white stone, the lacework fabric of a half-built minster spire, with a mason's crane on the summit, bending as though craving for a further supply of materials; and beyond, peeping through every crevice of the exquisite open fretwork, was the

intensely blue sky of early autumn. — *The Dove in the Eagle's Nest*, Charlotte Mary Yonge, 1866.

1850 Great are the toils and terrible the hardships that go to the building up of a frontier farm; inconceivable to those who have not done the task or watched its doing. — *Zury: The Meanest Man in Spring County*, Joseph Kirkland, 1887.

1851 The careful Dutch had built a fragment of Holland on the north arm of Hirado Bay. — *Venture in the East*, Bruce Lancaster, 1951.

1852 We — that is my Uncle Francis and I — finished the building of Tom Rowhedge's new house at Merravay on the last Sunday in October in the year 1577. — *Bless This House*, Norah Lofts, 1954.

1853 On Sunday afternoons people would drive out to have a look at George Lockwood's wall, and sometimes they would see, from a distance, George Lockwood doing the same thing they were doing. — *The Lockwood Concern*, John O'Hara, 1965.

1854 On a recent clear September morning, marred by only a trace of saffron haze suspended in the air over Manhattan Island, James Kittering sat at his desk in a large office and made a little paper airplane. — *Providence Island*, Calder Willingham, 1969.

1855 There was a wall. It did not look important. It was built of uncut rocks roughly mortared. — *The Dispossessed*, Ursula K. Le Guin, 1974.

1856 The early suburb of Southview Gardens was constructed by a man who thought flatteringly of himself as a jerry builder. — *The Replay*, Michael Curtin, 1981.

1857 I built the box real careful with scraps out of the kindling pile. — *Bone of My Bones*, Sylvia Wilkinson, 1982.

1858 Ray Bannister started to build the guillotine the day Jerry Renault returned to Monument. — *Beyond the Chocolate War*, Robert Cormier, 1985.

1859 They stand near the top of the hill looking down at the unfinished house. The setting sun turns the 2X4 skeleton gold. He tells her he couldn't have done it without her. She smiles, tears in her eyes. — *Terre Haute*, Will Aitken, 1989.

Cookery

1860 Abigail Bennet stood by the kitchen table, her mixing-bowl before her. She hummed a little under her breath, as she paused, considering what to make. — *The County Road*, Alice Brown, 1906.

1861 Andrew Harlan stepped into the kettle. — *The End of Eternity*, Isaac Asimov, 1955.

1862 *Joseph said*: Cocoa needs cooking in a saucepan. — *Albert Angelo*, B. S. Johnson, 1964.

1863 Roarty was making an omelette with the mushrooms Eamonn Eales had collected in Davy Long's park that morning. They were good mushrooms, medium sized and delicately succulent, just right for a special omelette, an omelette surprise. He had chosen the best mushrooms for his own omelette; the one he was making for Eales was special because it contained not only mushrooms from Davy Long's park but also a handful of obnoxious, black-gilled toadstools which he himself had picked on the dunghill behind the byre. — *Bogmail*, Patrick McGinley, 1978.

1864 Hodges sat against a wet, grassy paddy dike and lazily stirred a can of Beef and Potatoes with a dirty plastic spoon. — *Fields of Fire*, James Webb, 1978.

1865 Reinhart was preparing brunch for his daughter and his new girl friend. — *Reinhart's Women*, Thomas Berger, 1981.

1866 I look out at the yard and I am smitten by the sight of a lurking, charcoal-soiled, freewheeling, easy-cook, superchef barbecue grill. — *The Family Man*, Joseph Monninger, 1982.

1867 Two hours ago I decided to surrender to the stickiness. Now every hair on my arms is encased in a thin layer of peach glue. — *Moondreamer*, Zoë Kamitses, 1983.

1868 Martin Morley poured custard over his bilberry pie and smashed it into a mauve pulp. — *The Summer Boy*, Don Bannister, 1984.

1869 Ann sat in the kitchen, larger by half than her own studio, and listened to Elaine grumble over pie crust. — *Columbus Avenue*, Alan Gelb, 1984.

1870 A child is standing on a chair pulled up to the kitchen counter, watching her grandmother, whose fingers are clenched around a sharp cleaver, as she chops onions in a wooden bowl. — *Surviving the Seasons*, Fern Kupfer, 1987.

1871 Elise stood at the kitchen counter and forced herself to concentrate on the onion she was cutting into small, regular cubes. — *Appetites*, Tom Murphy, 1987.

1872 It was Napoleon who had such a passion for chicken that he kept his chefs working around the clock. — *The Passion*, Jeanette Winterson, 1987.

1873 Mary was sucking cream off her right index finger. — *Loving Attitudes*, Rachel Billington, 1988.

1874 Bunty Streetfield poured boiling water from the electric kettle on to the bowl of dried apricots destined for tomorrow's breakfast. — *The Folks That Live on the Hill*, Kingsley Amis, 1990.

1875 I watched my grandmother make ravioli once, but I didn't pay much attention. — *In Search of the Perfect Ravioli*, Paul Mantee, 1991.

1876 She liked to make things: cookies, pie crust, Hallowe'en costumes, bread. — *The Return of the Goddess*, Elizabeth Cunningham, 1992.

Corpses

1877 It was the parlor-maid who found Old Josiah in the morning, seated at his desk, his head fallen forward upon his arms. — *Boston*, Upton Sinclair, 1928.

1878 "Red, I tell you, when I saw poor Shrimp Haggerty laid out in the coffin, I got a damn snaky feeling," Stan Simonsky, riding backward by the window, morosely said, turning to Red Kelly beside him. — *Judgment Day*, James T. Farrell, 1935.

1879 One noon, in the blaze of a cloudless Carolina summer, what was left of eight dead boys lay strewn about the landscape, among the poison ivy and the pine needles and loblolly saplings. — *The Long March*, William Styron, 1956.

1880 The body lay in the next room, under a dirty tablecloth. — "Till Death Us Do Part," Martha Gellhorn, 1958.

1881 Man found dead in plastic wardrobe. That's the way you'll finish up if you're not careful, I tell myself. — *Jubb*, Keith Waterhouse, 1963.

1882 The dead man drifted along in the breeze. He walked upright on his hind legs like a performing nanny goat, as he had in life, nothing improper, farther beyond the reach of ideology, nationality, hardship, inspiration, than he had ever been in life. — *Earthworks*, Brian W. Aldiss, 1966.

1883 The corpse without hands lay in the bottom of a small sailing dinghy drifting just within sight of the Suffolk coast. — *Unnatural Causes*, P. D. James, 1967.

1884 My mother's body disappeared three weeks ago from the Peretz Memorial Hospital in the Borough of Queens. — *Last Respects*, Jerome Weidman, 1971.

1885 Before they reached the river, the horses had grown used to the corpse. Tacs had not. — *The Death of Attila*, Cecelia Holland, 1973.

1886 There were many bodies in the street that winter, and Aunt Chi reported an unusual number of virgins sold into the penny brothels. — *The Last Mandarin*, Stephen Becker, 1979.

1887 The last time I saw my father, he was lying quietly on his back in his coffin, his eyes closed, an unaccustomed blandness on his strong features, his thick white hair and heavy eyebrows neatly brushed. — *Memories of Another Day*, Harold Robbins, 1979.

1888 He lay on his bed trying to see, as if reflected in the air above him, a body. — *The Woods*, David Plante, 1982.

1889 On Wednesday 23rd March 1983 there appeared in the *Guardian* the following report:/ An inquest is to be held on the two elderly women whose bodies were found on Monday in the dilapidated North London house they shared with a man who was the brother of one of them and the brother-in-law of the other. Post-mortem examinations yesterday revealed that they had both died from natural causes — but that the older woman had been dead for up to a year. — *When I Was Otherwise*, Stephen Benatar, 1983.

1890 Not one of us noticed the body at first. — *Gerald's Party*, Robert Coover, 1986.

1891 The bodies were discovered at eight forty-five on the morning of Wednesday 18 September by Miss Emily Wharton, a sixty-five-year-old spinster of the parish of St. Matthew's in Paddington, London, and Darren Wilkes, aged ten, of no particular parish as far as he knew or cared. — *A Taste for Death*, P. D. James, 1986.

1892 Late one April evening, in the middle-1950s/ *The body of the man was lying face-down in the glistening dew, Leadbetter saw by the headlights of the police car parked on the verge.* — *Sandmouth*, Ronald Frame, 1987.

1893 The day Elsdon Bird found the dead baby began no differently from any other. — *The Redemption of Elsdon Bird*, Noel Virtue, 1987.

1894 *The body of Rebecca Carpenter was found late one October night at an overlook in Woodedge that was popular with teenage neckers who drove there from Nestor or Walmouth.* — *The Immediate Prospect of Being Hanged*, Walter Walker, 1989.

1895 The man lay curled up on the beach like a grotesque grey ball with its air booted out. — *Love, Bones and Water*, Adam Zameenzad, 1989.

1896 "Little Red" Garlock, sixteen years old, skull smashed soft as a rotted pumpkin and body dumped into the Cassadaga River near the foot of Pitt Street, must not have sunk as deep as he'd been intended to sink, or floated as far. — *Because It Is Bitter, and Because It Is My Heart*, Joyce Carol Oates, 1990.

1897 My father has been dead 101 days./ I bet he is rotten. Amelia is rotten. — *Many Things Have Happened Since He Died and Here Are the Highlights*, Elizabeth Dewberry Vaughn, 1990.

1898 I don't know who saw them first. — *Finding Brendan*, Philip F. O'Connor, 1991.

1899 "I say it was a body." — *Something Like a Love Affair*, Julian Symons, 1992.

1900 "Daddy, there's a dead man floating in our pool." — *Dark Summer*, Jon Cleary, 1993.

Correspondence

1901 On New Year's Day Doctor Pringle received a letter from India informing him that his cousin, Colonel Armour, had died at Hyderabad and left him his residuary legatee. — *The Ayrshire Legatees*, John Galt, 1821.

1902 This is Valoroso XXIV., King of Paflagonia, seated with his Queen and only child at their royal breakfast-table, and receiving the letter which announces to His Majesty a proposed visit from Prince Bulbo, heir of Padella, reigning King of Crim Tartary. — *The Rose and the Ring*, William Makepeace Thackeray, 1855.

1903 The other day, in looking over my papers, I found in my desk the following copy of a letter, sent by me a year since to an old school-acquaintance. — *The Professor*, Charlotte Brontë, 1857.

1904 "Cephas! here is a letter for you, and it is from Shady Dale! I know you will be happy now!" — *Gabriel Tolliver*, Joel Chandler Harris, 1902.

1905 Pickering's letter bringing news of my grandfather's death found me at Naples early in October. — *The House of a Thousand Candles*, Meredith Nicholson, 1905.

1906 One may as well begin with Helen's letters to her sister. — *Howards End*, E. M. Forster, 1910.

1907 The two old men sat in the library, eyeing the unresponsive blue envelope that lay on the end of the long table nearest the fireplace, where a merry but unnoticed bed of coals crackled fiercely in the vain effort to cry down the shrieks of the bleak December wind that whistled about the corners of the house. — *Black Is White*, George Barr McCutcheon, 1914.

1908 Billy Deering let himself into his father's house near Radford Hills, Westchester County, and with a nod to Briggs, who came into the hall to take his hat and coat, began turning over the letters that lay on the table. — *The Madness of May*, Meredith Nicholson, 1917.

1909 The train was late that day, and when the old leather mail pouch was brought in, dripping wet, by Jonas, the negro driver, Mrs. Meade put down the muffler she was knitting, and received it reluctantly. — *The Builders*, Ellen Glasgow, 1919.

1910 Now a letter makes dull enough reading to outsiders. Most of all when its writer has been dead for some hundred-and-twenty-odd years. — *The Faith of a Collie*, Albert Payson Terhune, 1926.

1911 She found the letter when she returned to the slate-colored house from the regular monthly meeting of the Augusta Simpson Branch of the Woman's Christian Temperance Union. — *A Good Woman*, Louis Bromfield, 1927.

1912 On the ground where Number Two bonded warehouse of Bird & Son's Old Blockhouse Distilling Company would one day stand, the first of the Birds to come through the Gap and along the Wilderness Trail into this virgin country, past the mountains, sat down by his door, it being a fine spring morning, and wrote a letter to the young governor of the young state. — *Red Likker*, Irvin S. Cobb, 1929.

1913 It was the last letter in Irene Redfield's little pile of morning mail. — *Passing*, Nella Larsen, 1929.

1914 *July 7th.* — Incredulous astonishment on receiving by second post—usually wholly confined to local bills and circulars concerning neighboring Garden Fêtes—courteous and charming letter from publishers in America. — *The Provincial Lady in America*, E. M. Delafield, 1934.

1915 At the top of Allen Southby's letter was engraved MARTIN HOUSE STUDY, and to the left in smaller type DR. SOUTHBY. — *Wickford Point*, John P. Marquand, 1939.

1916 Miss Isobel Seton settled her chin into the collar of her sable coat and, as was her custom in moments of stress, mentally composed an abusive letter. — *Fire Will Freeze*, Margaret Millar, 1944.

1917 Today there arrived a letter from underground France. — "The End of the Road," Louis Bromfield, 1946.

1918 Number Eight was a drawing of an envelope addressed to Mr. John Brown, 114 West 78th., New York, N.Y. — *Turvey*, Earle Birney, 1949.

1919 There I stood, looking at the letter. — *The Trap*, Dan Billany, 1950.

1920 When Henry Mulcahy, a middle-aged instructor of literature at Jocelyn College, Jocelyn, Pennsylvania, unfolded the President's letter and became aware of its contents, he gave a sudden sharp cry of impatience and irritation, as if such interruptions could positively be brooked no longer. — *The Groves of Academe*, Mary McCarthy, 1952.

1921 Once in a way, perhaps as often as every eighteen months, an invitation to Sunday afternoon tea at the Ufford would arrive on a postcard addressed in Uncle Giles's neat, constricted handwriting. — *The Acceptance World*, Anthony Powell, 1955.

1922 I found your letter awaiting me. — *A Slanting Light*, Gerda Charles, 1963.

1923 She sat in the center of the bed she shared with her old sister Mary, slim legs tucked beneath her, enjoying the early October sunlight as her hand moved across the letter paper. — *Those Who Love*, Irving Stone, 1965.

1924 Blix's letter came addressed to my maiden name, Tasmania Murphy. — *A Matter of Time*, Jessamyn West, 1966.

1925 After my interview with the company president, the letter from my cousin Abel in Cuba, which my secretary had placed on top of the day's incoming mail, was only a minor shock. — *An Orderly Life*, Jose Yglesias, 1967.

1926 When young Robert Sylvester Morgan had occasion to write his mother he always made what he wryly called "a first draft." — *Testimony of Two Men*, Taylor Caldwell, 1968.

1927 The express letter came late in the afternoon. — *A Pocketful of Rye*, A. J. Cronin, 1969.

1928 "Anything important in the mail?" the Vicar General asked the Bishop's secretary. — *The Bishop*, Bruce Marshall, 1970.

1929 This is not a letter. I wrote you for the last time over a year ago to offer the little understanding I had, to say good-by. — *This Is Not for You*, Jane Rule, 1970.

1930 Among my father's papers in Bithoor was a copy of Maharaja Pratap's appeal to Lord Hardinge, the East India Company's Governor-General in India. — *The Devil's Wind*, Manohar Malgonkar, 1972.

1931 Boysie began writing letters to the newspapers to voice his opinion on matters such as pollution, urban development and high-rise apartments in the downtown area where he lived. — *The Bigger Light*, Austin Clarke, 1975.

1932/1933 For weeks now I have been sitting in my apartment, which has a panoramic view of the splendours and squalors of Manhattan, and I have been writing letters in my head . . . — *The Stepdaughter*, Caroline Blackwood, 1976.

1934 One early July day in 1934 Peter Piatkov entered his office suite on the third floor of the Lubianka and fell into an ambush. A square envelope embossed with the familiar OGPU emblem, a serpent struck down by a sword, lay on top of the neat stack of papers on his desk. — *The Face of Terror*, Emanuel Litvinoff, 1978.

1935 Two weeks ago I had a letter from Beatrice. — *The Opportunity of a Lifetime*, Emma Smith, 1978.

1936 Two postcards of the holiday town in the south-west of England. — *The Past*, Neil Jordan, 1980.

1937 When I was writing my usual Christmas letter home, I noticed that the shapes of my letters were changing. — *Meeting Rozzy Halfway*, Caroline Leavitt, 1980.

1938 "What do you mean there's no room for her?" Bernard said. "Didn't you get my letter?" — *The Temptation of Eileen Hughes*, Brian Moore, 1981.

1939 Dear Mr. Jones,/ I have received your letter of the 7th. I am afraid I must say categorically that I cannot grant your request. — *Two Women and Their Man*, Mervyn Jones, 1982.

1940 Just today I came upon the picture postcard. It fell out of a book that I had not opened for years. — *Arcadio*, William Goyen, 1983.

1941 This is the twelfth start of the letter I am sending. — *Dear Mr. Capote*, Gordon Lish, 1983.

1942 "My dear Gloria," Russell wrote in a memo as he sat hunched over the desk in his windowless office, regimental striped tie askew. — *Double Vision*, Linsey Abrams, 1984.

1943 Patrick did not read the letter again until after take-off. — *Short of Glory*, Alan Judd, 1984.

1944 "You'd better be after getting the mail," Annie Doherty told him. — *The South African Quirt*, Walter D. Edmonds, 1985.

1945 Dear Miss Pencraft,/ I am delighted to receive your charming letter inviting me to participate in your January School. — *Foxybaby*, Elizabeth Jolley, 1985.

1946 "Hebe," the old man called./ "Yes."/ "Take these letters to the post for me." — *Harnessing Peacocks*, Mary Wesley, 1985.

1947 Maudie Nettleship had two letters that day, but she read them in silence over the breakfast table, and did not communicate their disturbing contents to her mother and father. — *Gentlemen in England*, A. N. Wilson, 1985.

1948 The letter came to his office. Its writing in pencil, wobbled diagonally across the envelope, fell over the edge, came back on a new track. — *Red Earth, White Earth*, Will Weaver, 1986.

1949 The letter arrived in early October on a Paris morning so full and clear I had no desire to open it but let it lie on my desk until lunchtime soaking up the autumn sun. — *The Web*, Andrew Harvey, 1987.

1950 *Professor of the Year.* Sanford Clapp stood before his mailbox and reread the letter bearing the unexpected news. — *The Socratic Method*, Michael Levin, 1987.

1951 Louise Kahan, aka Annette Hollander Sinclair, sorted her mail in the foyer of her apartment. — *Gone to Soldiers*, Marge Piercy, 1987.

1952 Arthur Smollett, in work clothes, a shaggy moustache concealing his mouth, sat at the table in his bedroom, writing to Emma Howe. — *Courting Emma Howe*, Margaret A. Robinson, 1987.

1953 Rachel waited two weeks to get his first letter. — *Painting on Glass*, Jessica Auerbach, 1988.

1954 The woman holding, then handing over the letter to this poised, dumbfounded fifteen-year-old: is the letter also *hers*? — *The Letter Left to Me*, Joseph McElroy, 1988.

1955 *In the name of Allah, the Compassionate, the Merciful, VICTORY!,* I have written to you earlier, my uncle, in terms I now wish you to erase from your memory. — *Chinese Whispers*, Robert Sproat, 1988.

1956 *Dear Charles, / I had put off writing to you for a few days because I wasn't sure of your address; that is, if you were still there.* — *Born Brothers*, Larry Woiwode, 1988.

1957 My darling son Davie, / I'm sitting here in the airplane, flying back to New York, and writing to you this letter. And even while I'm writing it I know I'm not going to send it. — *A Nice Murder for Mom*, James Yaffe, 1988.

1958 This time Hadi Besharat would write the letter on onionskin paper. — *The Pilgrim's Rules of Etiquette*, Taghi Modarressi, 1989.

1959 Wilson sat up very straight. This was the first letter she had ever written in her life and she wished it to be correct in every particular. — *Lady's Maid*, Margaret Forster, 1990.

1960 One cold night in November, three years ago, I was a normal person opening his mail. — *Almighty Me*, Robert Bausch, 1991.

1961 "My Dear Lizzie," (she wrote), / "No doubt you will be surprised to hear from me after all this time, and from such a strange place. . . ." — *A Closed Eye*, Anita Brookner, 1991.

1962 Thank you for your letters. — *Company Man*, Brent Wade, 1992.

1963 *Dear James*, she wrote in blue ink on a page of cream stationery. — *Dear James*, Jon Hassler, 1993.

Couples

1964 The various accidents which befell a very worthy couple after their uniting in the state of matrimony will be the subject of the following history. — *Amelia*, Henry Fielding, 1752.

1965 The Kentons were not rich, but they were certainly richer than the average in the pleasant county-town of the Middle West where they had spent nearly their whole married life. — *The Kentons*, William Dean Howells, 1902.

1966 It is a tale which they narrate in Poictesme, saying; In the old days lived a pawnbroker named Jurgen; but what his wife called him was very often much worse than that. — *Jurgen*, James Branch Cabell, 1919.

1967 "She was *bad* . . . always. They used to meet at the Fifth Avenue Hotel," said my mother, as if the scene of the offence added to the guilt of the couple whose past she was revealing. — "New Year's Day (The 'Seventies)," Edith Wharton, 1924.

1968 Elsie and her husband Joe were working in the kitchen of Dr. Raste's abode at the corner of Myddelton Square and Cheval Street, Clerkenwell, E.C.1. — *Elsie and the Child*, Arnold Bennett, 1925.

1969 Once upon a time in Colorado lived a man named Abednego Danner and his wife, Matilda. — *Gladiator*, Philip Wylie, 1930.

1970 The owner of the touring car was interested in the filling station from which he was getting a fresh supply of gasoline, but his wife was more interested in the young man who was attending to their wants. — *Whiteoak Harvest*, Mazo de la Roche, 1936.

1971 "My dear, good wife!" said Sir Roderick Shelley. — *Two Worlds and Their Ways*, Ivy Compton-Burnett, 1949.

1972 Sometimes at night I think that my husband is with me again, coming gently through the mists, and we are tranquil together. — *Nectar in a Sieve*, Kamala Markandaya, 1954.

1973 I was Janet Shirley, *née* Barnes, and my husband was Howard Shirley, and in this story he was nearly twenty-seven and I was just gone twenty-three. — *One Hand Clapping*, Anthony Burgess, 1961.

1974 Marcus knew that people must wonder what Nancy saw in him. — *Flesh*, Brigid Brophy, 1962.

1975 "To the happy couple!" — *Textures of Life*, Hortense Calisher, 1963.

1976 First to arrive were Wicklow and Diana Thayer, which was like them. — *Memories of the Future*, Paul Horgan, 1966.

1977 This book is addressed to young men and dedicated to older women — and the connection between the two is my proposition. — *In Praise of Older Women*, Stephen Vizinczey, 1966.

1978 Mr. and Mrs. Beresford were sitting at the breakfast table. They were an ordinary couple. Hundreds of elderly couples just like them were having breakfast all over England at that particular moment. — *By the Pricking of My Thumbs*, Agatha Christie, 1968.

1979 "What did you make of the new couple?" — *Couples*, John Updike, 1968.

1980 Her husband folded his arms over his chest and rocked back on his heels. — *Glass People*, Gail Godwin, 1972.

1981 "I think she'll be absolutely right for Danny," Virginia Playfair said. "She's pretty, she's intelligent and she admires everything he's

done." — *April, June and November*, Frederic Raphael, 1972.

1982 A True Sport, the Mayor of New Orleans, spiffy in his patent-leather brown and white shoes, his plaid suit, the Rudolph Valentino parted-down-the-middle hair style, sits in his office. Sprawled upon his knees is Zuzu, local doo-wack-a-doo and voo-do-dee-odo fizgig. A slatternly floozy, her green, sequined dress quivers. — *Mumbo Jumbo*, Ishmael Reed, 1972.

1983 Eugene Shore and his wife lived in a big house near the footbridge over a ravine. — *A Fine and Private Place*, Morley Callaghan, 1975.

1984 *And they lived happily ever after. Well, not exactly. Actually, not at all. As a matter of fact, miserably. To tell the truth, their life together was sheer hell, and their struggles to free themselves from each other were disastrous.* — *Love, etc.*, Bel Kaufman, 1979.

1985 In the second year of the war, Mrs. Ephephtha Bumpass saw her husband Usaph unexpectedly one cold March night. — *Confederates*, Thomas Keneally, 1979.

1986 Rosanna had moved in to live with me seven days previously. It was rewarding but still prickly, probationary, on both sides, and wild, tender and distant by turns. — *Tetrarch*, Alex Comfort, 1980.

1987 The two of them celebrated Saturday morning as best they could. — *He/She*, Herbert Gold, 1980.

1988 The first time Graham Hendrick watched his wife commit adultery he didn't mind at all. — *Before She Met Me*, Julian Barnes, 1982.

1989 They represented the collision of two very different cultures. — *This Promised Land*, Robert Easton, 1982.

1990 She tried to nestle against him, to lean her head on his shoulder, but his hand moved just then to start the windshield wipers and blocked her. — *The Love of Elspeth Baker*, Myron S. Kaufmann, 1982.

1991 Stan Binstead and his wife, Millie, reached London early in the morning. — *Binstead's Safari*, Rachel Ingalls, 1983.

1992 From inside his office, the newly repaired air conditioner clanking in the background, Misha Edelman looked out at the teenage couple wandering around the lot where he sold used cars. — *The Swap*, Norma Klein, 1983.

1993 You can see them in public places, if you know where to look. — *Ask for Nothing More*, James Elward, 1984.

1994 Marjorie should have known that there were rough times ahead when her husband announced, over ordinary coffee, that he felt like God. — *A Little Bit Married*, Gail Parent, 1984.

1995 We get married in two days: Charles and me. — *Raney*, Clyde Edgerton, 1985.

1996 Barry picks me up to carry me over the

threshold. "Oof," he says and kicks open the door. — *Wild Bananas*, Sandra Thompson, 1985.

1997 Maybe I expected too much from Roger Halpern and our live-together trial. — *Alamo House*, Sarah Bird, 1986.

1998 KATHERINE SHERRITT SAGAMORE, 39 YEARS OLD AND 8 1/2 MONTHS PREGNANT, BECALMED IN OUR ENGINELESS SMALL SAILBOAT AT THE END OF A STICKY JUNE CHESAPEAKE AFTERNOON AMID EVERY SIGN OF THUNDERSTORMS APPROACHING FROM ACROSS THE BAY, AND SPEAKING AS SHE SOMETIMES DOES IN VERSE, SETS HER HUSBAND A TASK. — *The Tidewater Tales*, John Barth, 1987.

1999 I've forgotten how long we've been together but there's hardly a night when I ask myself why I don't do her in. — *The Companion*, Chaim Bermant, 1987.

2000 Sometime in the next few days my husband will have put me to death. — *Palu*, Louis Nowra, 1987.

2001 Edward Lasco was on the screened porch of his rented house in a comfortable but not elegant older section of the town where he'd lived for the past fifteen years when his wife, Elise, who six months before had left him and moved to a nearby city to work in a psychiatric hospital, came around the side of the house and stood beside the screen looking in. — *Two Against One*, Frederick Barthelme, 1988.

2002 A man and a woman are alone in bed. — *The Anna Papers*, Ellen Gilchrist, 1988.

2003 Jack is the church I have joined, but he is a church without ceremony. — *A Farm Under a Lake*, Martha Bergland, 1989.

2004 Scouting was a funny thing for me to get into, the way both Alice and I felt about travel. — *Prospect*, Bill Littlefield, 1989.

2005 Caroline Carter and her husband, Ralph, as a couple are impressive, even imposing: perched at the top of the broad concrete flight of stairs, in one of San Francisco's prettiest, greenest, and most elevated parks (the view is marvelous, hills and tall buildings, church spires and the further high green parks), they draw a lot of attention from the stray passers-by, the dog walkers and strollers, on this bright April Sunday. — *Caroline's Daughters*, Alice Adams, 1991.

2006 Observing the two of them stroll hand in hand through the Cape that late summer's day — Kirstenbosch, the Gardens, up the Mountain, across the burning sand of Camp's Bay, through the alleys of the Malay Quarter and downhill again, across the Parade (past the Castle), to the bare grassy slope where only a few desolate churches and mosques remained as witnesses to the long-vanished boisterous life of

District Six—no one could have imagined, not even in an outrageous fantasy, that next day they would take part in a bomb attack. —*An Act of Terror*, André Brink, 1991.

2007 "I don't love you anymore," William told Molly one Sunday afternoon as they sat together in the den. — *The Ragged Way People Fall Out of Love*, Elizabeth Cox, 1991.

2008 The power of Rachel Arkwright to annoy her husband Thomas, always active, was particularly strong at eight in the morning. —*Invitation to the Married Life*, Angela Huth, 1991.

2009 Luther Wallace, the speaker of our Oklahoma House of Representatives, said goodbye to his wife, Annabel, at their house in the Nichols Hills section of Oklahoma City at 7:25 A.M. —*Lost and Found*, Jim Lehrer, 1991.

2010 Billy found Ruby. —*The Lady with the Alligator Purse*, Ernest J. Finney, 1992.

2011 Sandra and her boyfriend, Bert, worked for the same firm. —"Be My Guest," Rachel Ingalls, 1992.

2012 In 1957, Laszlo Horvath arrived in England with his beloved Moura. —*Lip Service*, Russell Lucas, 1992.

2013 *The last time I saw Russell and Corrine together was the weekend of the final softball game between the Addicts and the Depressives.* —*Brightness Falls*, Jay McInerney, 1992.

Crime and Criminals

2014 "Hija of a thief! Carmelita Banditita! Go finda your father and robba the stage! Go taka the gold and cutta the throat! Where your mother? Who was she? Who marrying her? Caramba! little black bandit, go steal for the books. We no wanting you here." —*Los Cerritos*, Gertrude Atherton, 1890.

2015 When he stepped off the straight and narrow path of his peculiar honesty, it was with an inward assertion of unflinching resolve to fall back again into the monotonous but safe stride of virtue as soon as his little excursion into the wayside quagmires had produced the desired effect. —*An Outcast of the Islands*, Joseph Conrad, 1896.

2016 The House-boat of the Associated Shades, formerly located upon the River Styx, as the reader may possibly remember, had been torn from its moorings and navigated out into unknown seas by that vengeful pirate Captain Kidd, aided and abetted by some of the most ruffianly inhabitants of Hades. —*The Pursuit of the House-Boat*, John Kendrick Bangs, 1897.

2017 He sat, in defiance of municipal orders, astride the gun Zam-Zammah on her brick platform opposite the old Ajaib-Gher—the Wonder House, as the natives call the Lahore Museum. —*Kim*, Rudyard Kipling, 1901.

2018 This is the story of how a middle-aged spinster lost her mind, deserted her domestic gods in the city, took a furnished house for the summer out of town, and found herself involved in one of those mysterious crimes that keep our newspapers and detective agencies happy and prosperous. —*The Circular Staircase*, Mary Roberts Rinehart, 1908.

2019 My name is Rudolph Schnaubelt. I threw the bomb which killed eight policemen and wounded sixty in Chicago in 1886. Now I lie here in Reichholz, Bavaria, dying of consumption under a false name, in peace at last. —*The Bomb*, Frank Harris, 1909.

2020 The judge, when he sent me to prison, said that I had behaved like a woman without any moral sense. —*Herself Surprised*, Joyce Cary, 1941.

2021 Last month I suffered a great misfortune in the loss of my housekeeper, Mrs. Jimson. She was sent to prison for pawning some old trinkets which I had long forgotten. —*To Be a Pilgrim*, Joyce Cary, 1942.

2022 It was just noon that Sunday morning when the sheriff reached the jail with Lucas Beauchamp though the whole town (the whole county too for that matter) had known since the night before that Lucas had killed a white man. —*Intruder in the Dust*, William Faulkner, 1948.

2023 The middle years—the eighteen-seventies, 'eighties, 'nineties—were a time of moral bankruptcy when men stole millions by a stroke of the pen or by the simple expedient of printing tons of worthless paper. —*Pride's Castle*, Frank Yerby, 1949.

2024 In the late spring of 1916, after the bloody and abortive Easter Rising in Dublin, four men on the run from the police and the military reached the outskirts of a small village called Cloncraig, in the county of Wexford in southern Ireland. —*The Story of Esther Costello*, Nicholas Monsarrat, 1953.

2025 The Baltic aunt smiled mischievously and reported that she, the gardener and the cobbler had stolen a horse from the Germans and taken it to the hills to the Partigiani. —"For Better for Worse," Martha Gellhorn, 1958.

2026 All that Mr. Wright, the rubber-estate manager, ever knew of the business was that an army patrol had ambushed a band of terrorists within a mile of his bungalow, that five months later his Indian clerk, Girija Krishnan, had reported the theft of three tarpaulins from the curing sheds, and that three years after that some-

one had removed the wheels from an old scooter belonging to one of his children. — *Passage of Arms*, Eric Ambler, 1959.

2027 The jury said "Guilty" and the Judge said "Life" but he didn't hear them. — *The Mansion*, William Faulkner, 1959.

2028 I was at my place in Perelkop when the Prime Minister was shot in Johannesburg. — *The Greyling*, Daphne Rooke, 1962.

2029 He'd first begun to steal when he was eleven. — *The Slow Natives*, Thea Astley, 1965.

2030 dont you think if a thief wants to come in, a locked door wont make any difference;/ he takes a walk,/ he goes flying,/ he crouches and he creeps — *Milkbottle H*, Gil Orlovitz, 1967.

2031 I was a child murderer. — *Expensive People*, Joyce Carol Oates, 1968.

2032 *"Do you know what treason is, Bell?"/ "No,"* Bell said. — *Poor Devils*, David Ely, 1970.

2033 The most dangerous criminal I ever met was not confined in the top security wing of Durham Jail; he was in the Rose Hill experimental prison near Sedgefield — an open prison run along Swedish lines, where the seventy-five internees are given the minimum of supervision. — *Lingard*, Colin Wilson, 1970.

2034 I become a murderess. — *The Childlike Life of the Black Tarantula*, Kathy Acker, 1973.

2035 Premeditated crime: the longer the meditation, the dreaming, the more triumphant the execution! — *Do With Me What You Will*, Joyce Carol Oates, 1973.

2036 The problem is this: when you commit a crime, pull off a big one — especially if it's not and never has been your line of work — there is one fierce compulsion to tell about it. — *Some Kind of Hero*, James Kirkwood, 1975.

2037 The crimes known to the press first as the Karate Killings and then as Sherlock Holmes's Last Case began one New Year's Eve. — *A Three-Pipe Problem*, Julian Symons, 1975.

2038 She had offered no defence. There could have been none. — *The Rabbi's Wife*, David Benedictus, 1976.

2039 "Corruption? *I'll* tell you about corruption, sonny!" — *October Light*, John Gardner, 1976.

2040 Garp's mother, Jenny Fields, was arrested in Boston in 1942 for wounding a man in a movie theater. — *The World According to Garp*, John Irving, 1978.

2041 The extraordinary series of crimes popularly called the Blackheath Poisonings took place in the early 1890s, at a time when the Mortimer family had lived in that suburb on the edge of London for nearly half a century. — *The Blackheath Poisonings*, Julian Symons, 1978.

2042 In the first place, why did I steal the aircraft? — *The Unlimited Dream Company*, J. G. Ballard, 1979.

2043 The manner of executing a criminal in those days, as I have seen too often with my own eyes, was somewhat in the manner I shall now describe. — *Man of Nazareth*, Anthony Burgess, 1979.

2044 Eustace Dench, master criminal, paid the cabby with a legitimate five pound note, accepted his change, gave the man a twenty pence tip — not enough; the chap did *not* touch his cap — and turned away to take the delectable Lida's slender arm. — *Castle in the Air*, Donald E. Westlake, 1980.

2045 Shortly before nine o'clock the sheriff marched into court with my client, jaw resolutely jutting, one hand resting with casual vigilance on the butt of his pistol, following so closely behind his prisoner that I helplessly thought of an eye-rolling cigar-puffing Groucho avidly stalking a dame in one of his old movies, the scene conveying a memorable picture of law and order triumphant. — *People Versus Kirk*, Robert Traver, 1981.

2046 The security system was on the blink. — *In the City of Fear*, Ward Just, 1982.

2047 At 8.45 one night, on the pitted track which led from the shanty-town to the house above it where the nuns lived, Sister Katherine Elizabeth was raped by two men, (probably) members of, or paid by, the National Security Forces. — *Virgin Territory*, Sara Maitland, 1984.

2048 "It's not the rape that distresses me so much," Madame Simone said to me. — *Playing Catch-Up*, A. B. Guthrie, Jr., 1985.

2049 *This is the pencil that I managed to steal from Olga.* — *Rare Earth*, Mary Lee Grisanti, 1986.

2050 Lila Futuransky always knew she was an outlaw, but she could never figure out which one. — *Girls, Visions, and Everything*, Sarah Schulman, 1986.

2051 It was the fall before my captivity at the hands of King Philip that I discovered my wife was stealing from me. — *The Devil in the Dooryard*, Gregory Blake Smith, 1986.

2052 They were the Bandidos, lunatics and murderers Castro had let out of his jails and shoveled onto the boats at Mariel harbor. — *Paradise Man*, Jerome Charyn, 1987.

2053 You asked me about their corruption. — *The American Ambassador*, Ward Just, 1987.

2054 Rape. My child, Persephone, a virgin. — *The Goddess Letters*, Carol Orlock, 1987.

2055 It was gone. — *Queen Dolley*, Dorothy Clarke Wilson, 1987.

2056 Wanda Zbyszek was not a virgin when three boys from her village raped her that beautiful spring day in May 1939. — *A Mother's Secret*, Carolyn Haddad, 1988.

2057 On his way to the VFW lodge, where he went every Thursday night to drink and play

cards and discuss the sorry state of civilization with other old soldiers, Big Joe Kohler stopped by his grocery store to pick up a roll of antacid tablets and discovered he was being robbed. — *Serious Living*, Tom Lorenz, 1988.

2058 It's been two days since the mugging. — *Intimacy*, Susan Chace, 1989.

2059 Breaking and entering. She would never have thought herself capable of it. — *The Journey from Prague Street*, Nana Demetz, 1990.

2060 When she discovered that the beads, which she had been saving for so many years, were missing, Rivke at first could not do anything at all. — *Missing*, Michelle Herman, 1990.

2061 The first bill of Bim Auctor's currency to enter the economy came into the hands of a temporarily unemployed housepainter named Wayne Paschke, who lived with his wife and daughter in Santa Venetia — which is before Terra Linda, one exit north of San Rafael and out San Pedro Road past the La Brea apartments. — *Ordinary Money*, Louis B. Jones, 1990.

2062 When Chili first came to Miami Beach twelve years ago they were having one of their off-and-on cold winters: thirty-four degrees the day he met Tommy Carlo for lunch at Vesuvio's on South Collins and had his leather jacket ripped off. — *Get Shorty*, Elmore Leonard, 1990.

2063 "This is rape!" His voice was reaching a pitch it had never reached before and went higher still as he surveyed the wreckage. "This is violation!" — *Symposium*, Muriel Spark, 1990.

2064 Early Easter Sunday, Edith Schmertz set the clocks in her house back two hours and went outside, carrying a small parachute she'd stolen from her wicked sister-in-law. — *The Planets*, James Finney Boylan, 1991.

2065 Dale Crowe Junior told Kathy Baker, his probation officer, he didn't see where he had done anything wrong. — *Maximum Bob*, Elmore Leonard, 1991.

2066 Consider fascia, a transparent membrane — a caul for muscles, one you could pull thin and taut, something burglars could wear over their faces to distort and disguise the nose, the mouth, the eyes. — *The Late Night Muse*, Bette Pesetsky, 1991.

2067 On my book tours, I am often asked a number of questions: Did he really do it? Do I think that he was justified? Did they do it for the money or for love? — *Strange Fits of Passion*, Anita Shreve, 1991.

2068 Maximilian Nutmeg was a mildly incompetent, mostly harmless petty crook, always hustling for money. — *Cooler by the Lake*, Larry Heinemann, 1992.

2069 The last major crime in the town of Verity was in 1958, when one of the Platts shot his brother in an argument over a Chevy Nomad they had bought together on time. — *Turtle Moon*, Alice Hoffman, 1992.

Crying

2070 Rose sat all alone in the big best parlor, with her little handkerchief laid ready to catch the first tear, for she was thinking of her troubles, and a shower was expected. — *Eight Cousins*, Louisa May Alcott, 1874.

2071 It was not because life was not good enough that Ellen Melville was crying as she sat by the window. — *The Judge*, Rebecca West, 1922.

2072 Peter Innocent Bon was about to return to the Republic of Venice; although he had that very day entered upon the eighty-first year of his age, his eyes, blue as veronica flowers, were even now full of a child's tears. — *The Venetian Glass Nephew*, Elinor Wylie, 1925.

2073 When Sam Hartley took his wife Lulah to the window of their new apartment to look at the white cliffs of Park Avenue she broke down and cried. — "The Abiding Vision," Rebecca West, 1935.

2074 Molly and Lily went home after the funeral and pulled down the shades in the parlor and had a good long cry together. — *The Sure Hand of God*, Erskine Caldwell, 1947.

2075 Arthur was the first in the Bridges' ranch house to hear the far-away crying, like muted horns a little out of tune. — *The Track of the Cat*, Walter Van Tilburg Clark, 1949.

2076 I told Helen my story and she went home and cried. — *Our Spoons Came from Woolworths*, Barbara Comyns, 1950.

2077 It was a dull autumn day and Jill Pole was crying behind the gym. — *The Silver Chair*, C. S. Lewis, 1953.

2078 "Stop crying, anyway. Try to, that is." — *As Music and Slendour*, Kate O'Brien, 1958.

2079 The beautiful young mother came weeping to look upon her child, Aspasia. — *Glory and the Lightning*, Taylor Caldwell, 1974.

2080 They embrace and face Jordan. They are turned golden in the evening light, like the stone. There are several of them. The weeping one will not turn to salt. In fact, she drinks her tears. She is a full-bellied sabra and her fruit is sucking away inside her. — *A Weave of Women*, E. M. Broner, 1978.

2081 There was a baby crying. — *The House of Cards*, Leon Garfield, 1982.

2082 Liz was the only one crying that hot September morning. — *Blood Sisters*, Valerie Miner, 1982.

2083 Late on a late spring afternoon, Chub, ambling across the Oberlin campus, was astonished to see the girl of his dreams break into tears. — *The Color of Light*, William Goldman, 1984.

2084 When the girl found me I was perched in my favorite kapok tree, sobbing softly and moaning a tuneless funeral croon. — *A Cannibal in Manhattan*, Tama Janowitz, 1987.

2085 When the fire curtain had been lowered and the doors were at last closed, Meredith thought he heard a child crying. — *An Awfully Big Adventure*, Beryl Bainbridge, 1989.

2086 *"Here is this baby, crying in my arms, and don't he know just when to stop?..."* — *Martin and John*, Dale Peck, 1993.

Curiosity

2087 It was in the beginning of the month of November, 17—, when a young English gentleman, who had just left the university of Oxford, made use of the liberty afforded him, to visit some parts of the north of England; and curiosity extended his tour into the adjacent frontier of the sister country. — *Guy Mannering*, Sir Walter Scott, 1815.

2088 There is a handsome parish church in the town of Woodstock, — I am told so, at least, for I never saw it, having scarce time, when at the place, to view the magnificence of Blenheim, its painted halls and tapestried bowers, and then return in due season to dine in hall with my learned friend, the provost of ——; being one of those occasions on which a man wrongs himself extremely, if he lets his curiosity interfere with his punctuality. — *Woodstock*, Sir Walter Scott, 1826.

2089 Miss Thangue, who had never seen her friend's hand tremble among the teacups before, felt an edge on her mental appetite, stimulating after two monotonous years abroad. — *Ancestors*, Gertrude Atherton, 1907.

2090 "What now? What now? What now?" said Old Hector, spreading his legs. — *Young Art and Old Hector*, Neil M. Gunn, 1942.

2091 And don't forget, my dear Harold, to find out about Irma for me, if you can. If I didn't live so far away, I would rout her out myself./ Yours ever,/ Alec — *A Perfect Woman*, L. P. Hartley, 1955.

2092 "What's this?" — *The Poorhouse Fair*, John Updike, 1959.

2093 "Father, who were the Mongols?" — *The Siege*, Peter Vansittart, 1963.

2094 "What's up, darling?" Castleton wants to know. — *The Sioux*, Irene Handl, 1965.

2095 Old Pete, out chopping wood beside his shack, saw the two women go past down the dirt road toward the brook and watched them, as he watched everything within range, with lively curiosity. — *Kinds of Love*, May Sarton, 1970.

2096 "Look, Thomas, I know you've probably been asked this question a million times before, but what was it really like to be Stephen Abbey's ——" — *The Land of Laughs*, Jonathan Carroll, 1980.

2097 "What are you trying to climb into the freezer for?" George wanted to know. — *Her Victory*, Alan Sillitoe, 1982.

2098 "Who's those?" — *The Founding Father*, Jo Haring, 1984.

2099 "Anything strange?" asked Pop. — *Fighting with Shadows*, Dermot Healy, 1984.

2100 "Why threes, Mom?" Charlotte was asking. — *Failure to Zigzag*, Jane Vandenburgh, 1989

Dance

2101 "One, two, three, four, one, two, three, four — turn to your lady; one, two, three, four — now a deep reverence. Now you take her hand; no, not her whole hand — the tips of her fingers; now you lead her to her seat; now a deep bow, so. That will do. You are improving, but you must be more light, more graceful, more courtly in your air; still, you will do. Now run away, Mignon, to the garden; you have madam's permission to gather fruit. Now, M. Rupert, we will take our lesson in fencing." — *The Cornet of Horse*, G. A. Henty, 1881.

2102 "You hear me, Saxon? Come on along. What if it is the Bricklayers'? I'll have gentlemen friends there, and so'll you. The Al Vista band'll be along, an' you know it plays heavenly. An' you just love dancin' ——" — *The Valley of the Moon*, Jack London, 1913.

2103 Nadina, the Russian dancer who had taken Paris by storm, swayed to the sound of the applause, bowed and bowed again. — *The Man in the Brown Suit*, Agatha Christie, 1924.

2104 The aristocracy of Zenith were dancing at the Kennepoose Canoe Club. — *Dodsworth*, Sinclair Lewis, 1929.

2105 There was a slight, a frigid, mist, but in the monstrous starlight, fading but still visible, something like a scene in a ballet was in progress. — *Malign Fiesta*, Wyndham Lewis, 1956.

2106 The Six Boys were playing the Fire Highlife, playing it with a beat urgent as love.

And Johnnie Kestoe, who didn't like Africans, was dancing the highlife with an African girl. — *This Side Jordan*, Margaret Laurence, 1960.

2107 Look listless. Pretend the girl is an inanimate object such as a door or a telephone pole. Curve your right arm about her torso and hang your right hand high between her shoulderblades. Apply your left palm to her right, aloofly, and extend your arm and hers to make a crowd-cutter. Stand side-by-side and glide up and glide her up and down the floor in long, undulant steps. — *Loveland*, Glendon Swarthout, 1968.

2108 Marie Laveau is dancing with a cobra in Congo Square. — *Marie Laveau*, Francine Prose, 1977.

2109 Disco was dead. — *Playing Tahoe*, Sandra Hochman, 1981.

2110 When I first lived in New York my object was to sleep through Sundays in winter — there was nothing to do with them anyway, so we stayed out Saturday night dancing. — *Nights in Aruba*, Andrew Holleran, 1983.

2111 In memory it seems someone else, a boy in a glen plaid suit and a lime green shirt chewing gum with a cigarette behind his ear while he danced awkwardly with a girl who made his stomach buzz, and Frankie Laine sang "Black Lace" on the record player. — *Love and Glory*, Robert B. Parker, 1983.

2112 Jack Daley and Kitty Price were the best dancers in Buffalo. — *The Snow Ball*, A. R. Gurney, Jr., 1984.

2113 John Grape decided to go to the ballet, after all. — *Walking Papers*, Jay Cronley, 1988.

2114 Danny Kachiah smelled the burning fires as he watched the Pi-Ume-Sha dancers circle through the hazy air. — *River Song*, Craig Lesley, 1989.

2115 Who would believe anyone named Donald Duk dances like Fred Astaire? — *Donald Duk*, Frank Chin, 1991.

2116 The first thing I remember is dancing with my brother. — *Life Drawing*, Michael Grumley, 1991.

2117 "You must dance, Mr. Adamson," said Lady Alabaster from her sofa. "It is very kind of you to sit by me, and fetch glasses of lemonade, but I really do think you must dance. Our young ladies have made themselves beautiful in your honour, and I hope their efforts will not have been in vain." — "Morpho Eugenia," A. S. Byatt, 1992.

2118 The formal ball usually begins with the *rigodón de honor*, a quadrille by seven couples, six along the hall's length and one in the middle, underneath a ball of mirrors spinning on its axis, piercing space with the pink, blue, yellow, and purple of reflected light, reflected images, its harsh brilliance an insubstantial waterfall spilling upon the dancing pairs, all drawn from high society, provided of course there are enough who can dance without tripping on their feet or causing the help to titter under their breath, otherwise dancers will have to be pulled in from the Women's School, where they train future society-page ladies and discreet prostitutes. — *Twice Blessed*, Ninotchka Rosca, 1992.

Darkness

2119 Our tale begins in darkness and ends in darkness. The dark of the end is an autumn dusk, a withering away of heat and brightness. The dark of the beginning is dawn: a cool, foglit stillness. — *A Tale for Midnight*, Frederic Prokosch, 1955.

2120 "It's so dark in here," Paul Cattleman said. "Don't you want me to open the window?" — *The Nowhere City*, Alison Lurie, 1965.

2121 Imagine darkness. — *City of Illusions*, Ursula K. Le Guin, 1967.

2122 He was conscious of the dark stillness in the corridor. — *The Room*, Hubert Selby, Jr., 1971.

2123 Moke, small, comely and brown, came out only at dark, like a nocturnal fish. — *The Rap*, Ernest Brawley, 1974.

2124 So great and deep a cave, of course, had to be dark. — *A Far Off Place*, Laurens van der Post, 1974.

2125 Everything was a mess, especially in the dark. — *Barn Blind*, Jane Smiley, 1980.

2126 With the rushing of wings, darkness gathered in the forest behind him. — *Perpetual Motion*, Graeme Gibson, 1982.

2127 It was dark. — *Days Without Weather*, Cecil Brown, 1983.

2128 I return home. I shut the door and keep out the darkness. — *A Revolutionary Woman*, Sheila Fugard, 1983.

2129 We had candles in the cellar rooms, but Grandmother, in her fever, spilled wine over our matches. "NOW," she cheerfully said, "we're invisible." — *Vienna Girl*, Ingeborg Lauterstein, 1986.

2130 9:27 P.M. Everyone's story begins and ends in the dark. — *One Big Bed*, John Krich, 1987.

Days

2131 It was the first day of Carnival. — *Pascarel*, Ouida, 1873.

2132 It was a fine, sunny, showery day in April. — *Trilby*, George du Maurier, 1894.

2133 The sun was setting on the fifth day of May, in the year of our Lord's grace eleven hundred and forty-five. — *Via Crucis*, F. Marion Crawford, 1899.

2134 Such a day made glad the heart. — *Saint's Progress*, John Galsworthy, 1919.

2135 It was not Wolf's day. Few days were Wolf's days. — *Wolf*, Albert Payson Terhune, 1925.

2136 This was going to be another of those fine September days. — *The Folks*, Ruth Suckow, 1934.

2137 It was the morning of the twentieth of July, 1900. — *Moment in Peking*, Lin Yutang, 1939.

2138 The Texas January day was all blue and gold and barely crisp. — *Hold Autumn in Your Hand*, George Sessions Perry, 1941.

2139 The day promised to be hot. — *One Fine Day*, Mollie Panter-Downes, 1947.

2140 It was a great day for the city of Castel Rodriguez. — *Catalina*, W. Somerset Maugham, 1948.

2141 *March fourth dawned dark that year.* — *The Grand Design*, John Dos Passos, 1949.

2142 The day had been a hard one. — *In a Summer Season*, Ludwig Lewisohn, 1955.

2143 The year is 1950, the month is September, and the day the twenty-fifth. — *Letter from Peking*, Pearl S. Buck, 1957.

2144 It was a hot, peaceful, optimistic sort of day in September. — *The Dud Avocado*, Elaine Dundy, 1958.

2145 Lunaday, the 31st of June, brought to Peradore the kind of summer morning we all remember from years ago but seem to have missed ever since. — *The 31st of June*, J. B. Priestley, 1961.

2146 The day on which Emily Stockwell Turner fell out of love with her husband began much like other days. — *Love and Friendship*, Alison Lurie, 1962.

2147 Seldom, decided Lieutenant-Colonel John Sevier, had he more throughly appreciated the beauties of such a fine, warm and crystal-clear September day. — *Wild Horizon*, F. van Wyck Mason, 1966.

2148 My story begins with the day little Dunwoodie Keogh ran away. — *Man on the Mountain*, Gladys Hasty Carroll, 1969.

2149 On December 22, 1958, only two days before, they had been safe in London. — *Mile High*, Richard Condon, 1969.

2150 It had been a dark, wet day, as though under the aegis of Saint Swithin, until suddenly in the late afternoon the spell was broken, the rain ceased, the June sky cleared rapidly and then burst into flaming gold and red. — *Whistle and I'll Come to You*, Agnes Sligh Turnbull, 1970.

2151 It was a day something like right now, dry, hot, and dusty dusty. — *The Autobiography of Miss Jane Pittman*, Ernest J. Gaines, 1971.

2152 It was a gorgeous Wednesday in August, of which there had not been too many in New York this summer. — *Every Little Crook and Nanny*, Evan Hunter, 1972.

2153 The day, as Clarissa Maynard never forgot, was Thursday, the thirteenth of September, 1928, scarcely a fortnight after her thirty-second birthday. — *Rosalind Passes*, Frank Swinnerton, 1973.

2154 If Bart were alive tonight, he would say, "Well — tomorrow is First Pasturing Day." — *Next of Kin*, Gladys Hasty Carroll, 1974.

2155 Eddie Ryan looked at the calendar on his desk. January 1, 1946. What a way to start a new year. — *The Death of Nora Ryan*, James T. Farrell, 1978.

2156 It was a drowsy, buzzing day in July, the sort of day when you could believe that summer was perpetual and everything in it perfect and immutable, fixed in time under glass like the vivid butterfly collection that adorned Doc Thompson's otherwise dingy waiting room. — *The Lakestown Rebellion*, Kristin Hunter, 1978.

2157 It was going to be a beautiful June day, Jeannie Laird Colter thought. — *The Beauty Queen*, Patricia Nell Warren, 1978.

2158 Momentous day. The sun is shining. That in itself is not momentous, merely, for August, surprising. — *The Old Jest*, Jennifer Johnston, 1979.

2159 This is his greatest day, they were telling me. — *My Friend, My Father*, Stanley Burnshaw, 1981.

2160 It was a beautifully clear day for an ambush. — *The Faraway Drums*, Jon Cleary, 1981.

2161 The time was six o'clock in the morning. The date was the seventh of January, 1929. The place was the White House. — *The Big Boys*, Max Ehrlich, 1981.

2162 The day that Barney Snow saw the Bumblebee for the first time (although he didn't know it was the Bumblebee, of course) was also the day that Mazzo got the telephone installed in his room and Ronson received the merchandise for the Ice Age. — *The Bumblebee Flies Anyway*, Robert Cormier, 1983.

2163 The day Um Mona dreaded dawned clear. — *Nile*, Laurie Devine, 1983.

2164 The first day I did not think it was funny. — *Heartburn*, Nora Ephron, 1983.

2165 That glowing day in autumn gave no warning of being different from many other days Manolis and Aleko had shared. — *Days of Vengeance*, Harry Mark Petrakis, 1983.

2166 Tomorrow was Friday. — *Crumbs Under the Skin*, Carol Bruggen, 1984.

2167 It began as such an ordinary day. —*Among Friends*, L. R. Wright, 1984.

2168 It was only for them that the day broke unlike any other. — *The Bread of Exile*, Karen Gershon, 1985.

2169 *Yesterday was a shocker.* — *Rainbow Walkers*, Doris Schwerin, 1985.

2170 The day started badly and then got worse. — *The Trap*, John Treherne, 1985.

2171 That morning was not much different from any other morning as far as Nicky was concerned, except that at least it was Friday and another stinking week of torture was ended. —*Blanche and Nicky*, Elliot West, 1985.

2172 He had missed yet another day of summer. — *The Adventures of Goodnight and Loving*, Leslie Thomas, 1986.

2173 On the north-east coast of Scotland in the last days of September there can be a sequence of halcyon days. — *The Upper Hand*, Stuart Hood, 1987.

2174 Strange days indeed! —"The Rules of Life," Fay Weldon, 1987.

2175 Who can tell us what my father was doing at three o'clock in the morning of a balmy May Friday in 1946? — *Brighten the Corner Where You Are*, Fred Chappell, 1989.

2176 It was one o'clock in the morning, the Saturday after Labor Day. Clouds scudded across a half moon. — *Father and Son*, Peter Maas, 1989.

2177 Though more than a year has passed and we've gone through enough turmoil and self-destruction to last a lifetime, I've forgotten nothing of that hot, August Thursday. — *Brief Candle*, Martin Boris, 1990.

2178 It was a perfect day for aviators, bird watchers, photographers and sniping murderers. —*Murder Song*, Jon Cleary, 1990.

2179 The day my father was arrested, Roger Maris hit his sixty-first home run. —*A Stone of the Heart*, Tom Grimes, 1990.

2180 It was my first day. —*Lucy*, Jamaica Kincaid, 1990.

2181 Saturday was changeover day at Patna Hall. — *Coromandel Sea Change*, Rumer Godden, 1991.

2182 It was a bright sunny day, without fog. —*Pacific Street*, Cecelia Holland, 1992.

2183 It is Saturday, July twenty-sixth, 1958, the sun will rise in about twenty-five minutes, the air is still, and even the birds are not yet awake on Colonie Street. — *Very Old Bones*, William Kennedy, 1992.

2184 *Saturdays was the best day.* — *Crossover*, Dennis A. Williams, 1992.

2185 There was no reason why anyone, least of all William Bradley, should have known that 18 September 1589 was to be the last day of his life. — *The Slicing Edge of Death*, Judith Cook, 1993.

Daytime
and Nighttime

2186 It was growing dark in the city. — *The Lamplighter*, Maria Susanna Cummins, 1854.

2187 It was five o'clock in the afternoon. There can be no doubt whatever as to that. — *The Gorilla Hunters*, R. M. Ballantyne, 1861.

2188 March 15, 1862. —On board the small Siamese steamer *Chow Phya*, in the Gulf of Siam./ I rose before the sun, and ran on deck to catch an early glimpse of the strange land we were nearing; and as I peered eagerly, not through mist and haze, but straight into the clear, bright, many-tinted ether, there came the first faint, tremulous blush of dawn, behind her rosy veil; and presently the welcome face shines boldly out, glad, glorious, beautiful, and aureoled with flaming hues of orange, fringed with amber and gold, wherefrom flossy webs of colour float wide through the sky, paling as they go. — *The English Governess at the Siamese Court*, Anna Leonowens, 1870.

2189 A Saturday afternoon in November was approaching the time of twilight, and the vast tract of unenclosed wild known as Egdon Heath embrowned itself moment by moment. — *The Return of the Native*, Thomas Hardy, 1878.

2190 On an early winter afternoon, clear but not cold, when the vegetable world was a weird multitude of skeletons through whose ribs the sun shone freely, a gleaming landau came to a pause on the crest of a hill in Wessex. — *Two on a Tower*, Thomas Hardy, 1882.

2191 Along the entire river front of Montreal camp-fires faded as the amphitheatre of night gradually dissolved around them. — *The Story of Tonty*, Mary Hartwell Catherwood, 1890.

2192 The autumn afternoon was fading into evening. —*Beatrice*, H. Rider Haggard, 1890.

2193 It is a matchless morning in rural England. — *The American Claimant*, Mark Twain, 1892.

2194 The middle of a fragrant afternoon of May in the green wilderness of Kentucky: the year 1795. — *The Choir Invisible*, James Lane Allen, 1897.

2195 The sun was going down on the Black Spur Range. The red light it had kindled there was still eating its way along the serried crest, showing through gaps in the ranks of pines, etching out the interstices of broken boughs, fading

away and then flashing suddenly out again like sparks in burnt-up paper. — *Three Partners*, Bret Harte, 1897.

2196 The short winter's day was drawing to its close, and twilight, the steel and silver twilight of a windless frost, was falling in throbs of gathered dusk over an ice-bound land. — *The Luck of the Vails*, E. F. Benson, 1901.

2197 The day broke gray and dull. — *Of Human Bondage*, W. Somerset Maugham, 1915.

2198 Dusk, like soft blue smoke, fell with the dying spring air and settled upon the northern French village. — *Through the Wheat*, Thomas Boyd, 1923.

2199 The horizon was cloudless that evening, and over the ocean, beyond the ridge of Toros Point, a glimmer of daylight lingered in the sky. The gorges of the San Benito Hills were filled with a purplish haze; little by little, with a change relentless and imperceptible as the approach of age, purple shadows turned gray and gray turned black, while the afterglow illuminating the summits of the range faded and was swallowed up in the dusk. — *Pícaro*, Charles Nordhoff, 1924.

2200 Dusk — of a summer night. — *An American Tragedy*, Theodore Dreiser, 1925.

2201 It was a morning when all nature shouted "Fore!" — *The Heart of a Goof*, P. G. Wodehouse, 1926.

2202 The earth sighed as it turned in its course; the shadow of night crept gradually along the Mediterranean, and Asia was left in darkness. — *The Woman of Andros*, Thornton Wilder, 1930.

2203 The sun had not yet risen. — *The Waves*, Virginia Woolf, 1931.

2204 The morning seemed to herald a glorious day. — *The Rash Act*, Ford Madox Ford, 1933.

2205 Night entered the clearing from the scrub. The low tangled growth of young oak and pine and palmetto fell suddenly black and silent, seeming to move closer in one shadowy spring. — *South Moon Under*, Marjorie Kinnan Rawlings, 1933.

2206 "What a beautiful evening!" Fanny Carlisle said to the little lady who was standing beside her. — *Captain Nicholas*, Hugh Walpole, 1934.

2207 The morning, drawing within itself, moved in sun and shadow over the Common and through the pond till it came to the houses. — *This Bed Thy Centre*, Pamela Hansford Johnson, 1935.

2208 At last it was evening. — *In Dubious Battle*, John Steinbeck, 1936.

2209 It was the hour of the day that Ransome loved best and he sat on the verandah now, drinking brandy and watching the golden light flood all the banyan trees and the yellow-gray

house and the scarlet creeper for one brilliant moment before the sun, with a sudden plunge, dropped below the horizon and left the whole countryside in darkness. — *The Rains Came*, Louis Bromfield, 1937.

2210 You know how it is there early in the morning in Havana with the bums still asleep against the walls of the buildings; before even the ice wagons come by with ice for the bars? — *To Have and Have Not*, Ernest Hemingway, 1937.

2211 It was a glorious morning of blue and gold, of fleecy clouds and insects droning in the sunshine. — *Summer Moonshine*, P. G. Wodehouse, 1937.

2212 The twilight was like deep pale water standing movelessly over the countryside and the long low hills. It was a medium that held everything motionless and transfixed, not a rigid motionlessness, but a sleeping quiescence, or as though all things had lost the robust body of the day and had become liquid and vaporous dreams, that, should the pale medium that held them be disturbed by even a ripple of air, they would blur together, dissolve, dissipate into silent and spreading rings of water. — *Dynasty of Death*, Taylor Caldwell, 1938.

2213 Here in the city the mild October day is drawing to its close. — *Winter in April*, Robert Nathan, 1938.

2214 A faint glow in the east caught the weather vane of Town Hall and gilded the spire of St. Paul's, rising above the leafless trees. — *Raleigh's Eden*, Inglis Fletcher, 1940.

2215 The spring dusk of the Indian Nations was settling swiftly, and behind him Frank Christian could hear the uneasy bawling of the thirsty trail herd. — *War on the Cimarron*, Luke Short, 1940.

2216 That long-ago midsummer morning shone hot and clear. — *New Hope*, Ruth Suckow, 1942.

2217 The morning of the big day dawned bright and clear. — *Barefoot Boy with Cheek*, Max Shulman, 1943.

2218 Always, somewhere, it is morning. That bright streak of dawn extending from the arctic to the antarctic, the glittering boundary between day and night on this whirling sphere of ours, is always there. — *Bedford Village*, Hervey Allen, 1944.

2219 One by one, the lights went up in the May evening. The streetlights burst into radiance all over the village, and windows began to show yellow, pale in the twilight. — *The Shield of the Valiant*, August Derleth, 1945.

2220 At daybreak Billy Buck emerged from the bunkhouse and stood for a moment on the porch looking up at the sky. — *The Red Pony*, John Steinbeck, 1945.

2221 It was a calm, early summer noon in the southern mountains of Arabia. — *The Big Fisherman*, Lloyd C. Douglas, 1948.

2222 The day was dying. — *Roanoke Hundred*, Inglis Fletcher, 1948.

2223 When the young gentleman strolling through the park with his gun on his shoulder and an elderly spaniel at his heels came within sight of the house it occurred to him that the hour must be further advanced than he had supposed, for the sun had sunk below the great stone pile, and an autumnal mist was already creeping over the ground. — *The Foundling*, Georgette Heyer, 1948.

2224 Night in the dark New England hills, night and the winter stillness. — *The God-Seeker*, Sinclair Lewis, 1949.

2225 At five o'clock in the afternoon, which was late in March, the stainless blue of the sky over Rome had begun to pale and the blue transparency of the narrow streets had gathered a faint opacity of vapor. Domes of ancient churches, swelling above the angular roofs like the breasts of recumbent giant women, still bathed in gold light, and so did the very height of that immense cascade of stone stairs that descended from the Trinita di Monte to the Piazza di Spagna. — *The Roman Spring of Mrs. Stone*, Tennessee Williams, 1950.

2226 Dawn broke somewhere up the line, pearly under a drizzle of rain, but presently the rain left off and the flat eastern rim of earth was tinted rose. — *Jordan County*, Shelby Foote, 1954.

2227 BY JUNE THE ARCTIC NIGHT HAS DWINDLED TO A BRIEF INTERVAL OF GREY DUSK AND THROUGHOUT THE LONG DAYS MOSQUITOES SWARM UP LIKE CLOUDS OF SMOKE FROM THE POTHOLES OF THE THAWING TUNDRA. — *Last of the Curlews*, Fred Bodsworth, 1955.

2228 Afternoon had turned to evening and all the sweep and movement of the Downs lay still, bathed in pearly light. — *A Thing of Beauty*, A J Cronin, 1955.

2229 At half-past three the long winter night, like an Arctic season, had already begun. — *The Bright Prison*, Penelope Mortimer, 1956.

2230 *The day is early with birds beginning and the wren in a cloud piping like the child in the poem, drop thy pipe, thy happy pipe.* — *Owls Do Cry*, Janet Frame, 1957.

2231 It was not so dark as it had been a moment before. — *Gate to the Sea*, Bryher, 1958.

2232 Early morning is the best time of the day along the Barricades. — *The Eye of the Storm*, John Hearne, 1958.

2233 Monday morning./ Gray October, and an early-morning chill in the house and a sullen sky pressing against the windowpanes. — *Strangers When We Meet*, Evan Hunter, 1958.

2234 The afternoon of the October day was approaching the hour of sundown and twilight, and already the distances were lost in a pale, lavender haze. — *The Hills Stand Watch*, August Derleth, 1960.

2235 As though twilight had been forgotten in the hasty changing of the season, nightfall was coming with a sudden onrush of darkness that day in October. — *Jenny by Nature*, Erskine Caldwell, 1961.

2236 It was a bright noon, high summer, in the upland valleys of Tuscany: a torpid time, a season of dust and languor, of stripped flax and larks in the wheat stubble, and new wines coming to vintage in the country of the Elder Gods. — *Daughter of Silence*, Morris West, 1961.

2237 *Morning rose above the hills of Moab, swept across the sea to Cyprus, and lifted the shadows from the ruins of Berlin and Nuremberg.* — *A Star in the Wind*, Robert Nathan, 1962.

2238 The afternoon of the 9th of September was exactly like any other afternoon. — *The Clocks*, Agatha Christie, 1963.

2239 There is a short spell during the year in Trinidad when a kind of twilight comes between the sudden shift from light to dark. Actually, there is no such thing as twilight in the island, but for a week or so before the rainy season starts the daylight lingers for an extra hour. — *I Hear Thunder*, Samuel Selvon, 1963.

2240 November evenings are quiet and still and dry. — *The Keepers of the House*, Shirley Ann Grau, 1964.

2241 This autumn evening in Escondido seems no different than countless others. — *One Day*, Wright Morris, 1965.

2242 The morning had brought him out. He liked the clear beginnings that only June had when the gray sky crinkled into a rose colored hollow at its edge like the shells he had so often kicked into the water on his native beaches. — *This January Tale*, Bryher, 1966.

2243 The morning tastes bitterly of cream and jam and flaky pastry as Rappaport gets out of his car. — *Rappaport*, Morris Lurie, 1966.

2244 Spring of the year. A morning in early April like a knife driven suddenly into the cold strong heart of winter. — *A Dream of Kings*, Harry Mark Petrakis, 1966.

2245 The sky grew darker and darker as the morning wore on. By the time the coffee came round it was like a winter evening, and there were lights in all the windows that looked down on Hand and Ball Court. — *Against Entropy*, Michael Frayn, 1967.

2246 Ten minutes to midnight: a pious Friday evening in May and a fine river mist lying

in the market square. — *A Small Town in Germany*, John Le Carré, 1968.

2247 It is always night. — *Nightclimber*, Jon Manchip White, 1968.

2248 It was past midnight. — *The Three Daughters of Madame Liang*, Pearl S. Buck, 1969.

2249 The morning was Roxy's good time of day. She did not always rise early, but she felt better within herself when she did, as though her soul took a better grasp upon the world. — *Interstate*, Borden Deal, 1970.

2250 Mornings were still shivering cold with May just begun, but nothing like the winter mornings had been. He used to wake up cold, but now he was so cozy snug in his blanket cocoon that he wished it were Saturday and he could stay there awhile. — *Lonesome Traveler*, Weldon Hill, 1970.

2251 There was a thin robin's-egg-blue dawn coming up over Tel Aviv when the intelligence analyst finished typing his report. — *The Odessa File*, Frederick Forsyth, 1972.

2252 Daybreak. — *Far Tortuga*, Peter Matthiessen, 1975.

2253 To whom it may concern:/ It is springtime. It is late afternoon. — *Slapstick*, Kurt Vonnegut, 1976.

2254 He never called her down in mid-afternoon. — *Colliers Row*, Jan Webster, 1977.

2255 The dawn came early, tinting a cloudless sky the palest shade of green. — *The Passing Bells*, Phillip Rock, 1978.

2256 Night had come. — *City of God*, Cecelia Holland, 1979.

2257 As the arc of dawn passes over the steppes of Russian Asia it moves swiftly westward to pour its warmth on a royal and long-established continent — Europe. — *Now, God Be Thanked*, John Masters, 1979.

2258 Between eight and nine on a June night in the highest corner of the Berkshire Hills, there is still some light to see by. — *Sister Wolf*, Ann Arensberg, 1980.

2259 Dearest, it's midnight. — *Palomino*, Elizabeth Jolley, 1980.

2260 Mornings slice their way into being. — *If Birds Are Free*, Evelyn Wilde Mayerson, 1980.

2261 Night comes as a surprise in the tropics. — *Basic Black with Pearls*, Helen Weinzweig, 1980.

2262 As the arc of night passes westward over Europe, its veil of darkness is drawn across a continent in ruins. — *By the Green of the Spring*, John Masters, 1981.

2263 "Imagine a humid July afternoon." — *Bad Guy*, Rosalyn Drexler, 1982.

2264 After a long run of raw weather, on the fifteenth of October the continent of Europe woke to a morning of warm and balmy sunshine.

— *A Private Life*, Cynthia Propper Seton, 1982.

2265 Dusk dropped into the air like whiskey into water in a glass. — *Invisible Mending*, Frederick Busch, 1984.

2266 It was getting dark. The trees at the back of the yard seemed to be reaching upward as if to join the descending night and form a wall, cutting Noah off from the river, the woods and the solitary mountain beyond. — *The Deer at the River*, Joseph Caldwell, 1984.

2267 The light at dawn during those Pacific tests was something to see. — *Democracy*, Joan Didion, 1984.

2268 This morning like this evening, night, aint no difference way I see it. — *This Place*, Andrea Freud Loewenstein, 1984.

2269 The slit of dark grey in the gap between my bedroom curtains had lightened and then it'd gone black: the false dawn. — *When the Boys Came Out to Play*, Ray Salisbury, 1984.

2270 She was standing at the bottom of the government wharf and it was very early in the morning. — *Intertidal Life*, Audrey Thomas, 1984.

2271 Morning is rising in silence. — *The Heart of a Distant Forest*, Philip Lee Williams, 1984.

2272 It was a wet Sunday afternoon in North Oxford at the beginning of October. — *Crampton Hodnet*, Barbara Pym, 1985.

2273 It was a shadowless London morning; a grudged measure of twilight between darknesses. — *Foreign Land*, Jonathan Raban, 1985.

2274 The motion of the earth no longer seemed synchronous with the movements of the clock. — *Indian Country*, Philip Caputo, 1987.

2275 Late in August, nights at the farm became cooler, and the morning grass, wet with diamonds of dew. — *Cliff Walk*, Margaret Dickson, 1987.

2276 It was that lingering time between day and evening that Parisians called *l'heure bleue*. — *Dance on a Sinking Ship*, Michael Kilian, 1988.

2277 It was one of those May mornings, cloudless, warm, and fragrant: a morning not to be trusted. — *Curtain Going Up*, Carolyn Scott, 1988.

2278 During the mystery-laden time of day when, in the words of the passover song, it was "neither day nor night," and the milk white nolight might have been dawn or dusk, so tenuous, so precarious, was the silver balance between light and darkness, Nachman of Bratslav, the great-grandson of the holy Baal Shem Tov, walked to the river, alone in the world. — *The Man Who Thought He Was Messiah*, Curt Leviant, 1990.

2279 Darling Jane-/ Here I sit, in the evening dews — you'll get some sopping big ones up here on the Yellowstone. — *Buffalo Girls*, Larry McMurtry, 1990.

2280 On the ninth of August, 1964, Rome lay asleep in afternoon light as the sun swirled in a blinding pinwheel above its roofs, its low hills, and its gilded domes. — *A Soldier of the Great War*, Mark Helprin, 1991.

2281 An April morning in Lombardy in all its brilliance. — *Antonietta*, John Hersey, 1991.

2282 There was dark, and there was light, and the light was losing. — *Ghostwright*, Michael Cadnum, 1992.

2283 The dawn had not yet begun. — *Cold Times*, Elizabeth Jordan Moore, 1992.

2284 It can only be late afternoon. — *The Discovery of Light*, J. P. Smith, 1992.

2285 It was early to be seeing a sailboat — still more night than morning, the pale first light all in the east behind the dunes. — *The Big Score*, Michael Kilian, 1993.

Death

2286 On the first of *December* 1741, I departed this Life, at my Lodgings in *Cheapside*. My Body had been some time dead before I was at liberty to quit it, lest it should by any accident return to Life: this is an Injunction imposed on all Souls by the eternal Law of Fate, to prevent the Inconveniencies which would follow. — *A Journey from This World to the Next*, Henry Fielding, 1743.

2287 After a long and painful journey thro' life, with a heart exhausted by various afflictions, and eyes which can no longer supply tears to lament them, I turn my every thought toward that grave on the verge of which I hover. — *The Recess*, Sophia Lee, 1783-1785.

2288 Marley was dead, to begin with. — *A Christmas Carol*, Charles Dickens, 1843.

2289 "Will she last out the night, I wonder?" — *The Dead Secret*, Wilkie Collins, 1857.

2290 Long after the hours when tradesmen are in the habit of commencing business, the shutters of a certain shop in the town of Lymport-on-the-Sea remained significantly closed, and it became known that death had taken Mr. Melchisedec Harrington, and struck one off the list of living tailors. — *Evan Harrington*, George Meredith, 1861.

2291 In the matter of Jezebel's Daughter, my recollections begin with the deaths of two foreign gentlemen, in two different countries, on the same day of the same year. — *Jezebel's Daughter*, Wilkie Collins, 1880.

2292 When Egbert Dormer died he left his two daughters utterly penniless upon the world, and it must be said of Egbert Dormer that noth-ing else could have been expected of him. — *Ayala's Angel*, Anthony Trollope, 1881.

2293 They have a fashion across the water, particularly on the Continent, of making much of their dead. — *From Ponkapog to Pesth*, Thomas Bailey Aldrich, 1883.

2294 I, who write this, am a dead man. Dead legally — dead by absolute proofs — dead and buried! — *Vendetta*, Marie Corelli, 1886.

2295 When Jérôme Lafirme died, his neighbors awaited the results of his sudden taking off with indolent watchfulness. — *At Fault*, Kate Chopin, 1890.

2296 "O God, take ker o' Dick! He'll sure have a tough time when I'm gone — an' I'm er goin' — mighty fast I reckon. . . ." — *That Printer of Udell's*, Harold Bell Wright, 1903.

2297 The death of Taswell Skaggs was stimulating, to say the least, inapplicable though the expression may seem. — *The Man from Brodney's*, George Barr McCutcheon, 1908.

2298 "The child's dead," said Nora, the nurse. — *Susan Lenox*, David Graham Phillips, 1917.

2299 Death leapt upon the Rev. Charles Cardinal, Rector of St. Dreots in South Glebeshire, at the moment that he bent down towards the second long drawer of his washing-stand; he bent down to find a clean collar. It is in its way a symbol of his whole life, that death claimed him before he could find one. — *The Captives*, Hugh Walpole, 1920.

2300 There are Alards buried in Winchelsea church — they lie in the south aisle on their altar tombs, with lions at their feet. — *The End of the House of Alard*, Sheila Kaye-Smith, 1923.

2301 That was the spring poor Ezra Adams died. — *The Woodcutter's House*, Robert Nathan, 1927.

2302 When old Lucius Dowling lay dying he sent for his will and reread it. — *Lost Ecstacy*, Mary Roberts Rinehart, 1927.

2303 As usual, old man Falls had brought John Sartoris into the room with him, had walked the three miles in from the county Poor Farm, fetching, like an odor, like the clean dusty smell of his faded overalls, the spirit of the dead man into that room where the dead man's son sat and where the two of them, pauper and banker, would sit for a half an hour in the company of him who had passed beyond death and then returned. — *Sartoris*, William Faulkner, 1929.

2304 Jim Watson had died: specifically, he had been hanged, and hanged by his best friend, the sheriff; and thereby the hand was played out, the loser lost, and the game was ended; and no one believed that a new game was to start, that the dead man would start it after his death. Sardonic when alive, he was as sardonic dead. — *Me an' Shorty*, Clarence E. Mulford, 1929.

2305 I have said that Spring arrived late in 1916, and that up in the trenches opposite Mametz it seemed as though Winter would last for ever. I also stated that *as for me, I had more or less made up my mind to die* because *in the circumstances there didn't seem anything else to be done.* — *Memoirs of an Infantry Officer*, Siegfried Sassoon, 1930.

2306 For a time Mr. Parham was extremely coy about Sir Bussy Woodcock's invitation to assist at a séance. — *The Autocracy of Mr. Parham*, H. G. Wells, 1930.

2307 The Bishop of Porthminster was sinking fast; they had sent for his four nephews, his two nieces and their one husband. — *Maid in Waiting*, John Galsworthy, 1931.

2308 Mungo Park walked on in the belief, absurd as he knew it to be, that he had died. — *Park*, John Gray, 1931.

2309 Wang Lung lay dying. — *Sons*, Pearl S. Buck, 1932.

2310 "Whereas, the Creator," Malcolm Bedford wrote, "has seen fit to remove from the earthly scene our beloved friend, Hugh McGehee, and, whereas, Zachary Taylor, President of the United States of America, stated that Edward McGehee of Woodville, brother of the deceased, was the best man he ever knew, making him, furthermore, executor of his estate, it is the opinion here that the virtues of said Hugh McGehee were no less great." — *So Red the Rose*, Stark Young, 1934.

2311 Stoner Drake made a vow, solemnly spoken, weighted with passionate words. If Joan Drake should die he would never set his foot on God's earth again. — *He Sent Forth a Raven*, Elizabeth Madox Roberts, 1935.

2312 DEAR GREAT-AUNT HENRIETTA,/ Although I never knew you in life, as a child I often cracked butternuts on your tombstone. — *All This, and Heaven Too*, Rachel Field, 1938.

2313 When I was six years old I thought it would be a good thing if my Aunt Christine died. I never spoke of this to anyone, but I thought she would be much happier dead. I thought I should be happier too, because I didn't like the idea of Tom Brooks coming to our house. — *Nebraska Coast*, Clyde Brion Davis, 1939.

2314 Once you have given up the ghost, everything follows with dead certainty, even in the midst of chaos. — *Tropic of Capricorn*, Henry Miller, 1939.

2315 Jules Bouchard, of Bouchard & Sons, munitions manufacturers, knew he was dying. He had been dying for a long time, ever since his beloved cousin, Honore Bouchard, had died on the *Lusitania*, while on a secret mission to the Allies. — *The Eagles Gather*, Taylor Caldwell, 1940.

2316 Once upon a day an old butler called Eldon lay dying in his room attended by the head housemaid, Miss Agatha Burch. — *Loving*, Henry Green, 1945.

2317 "Did the old man die here? What do you think?" Julia asked, as her husband began to come upstairs. — *At Mrs. Lippincote's*, Elizabeth Taylor, 1945.

2318 But old Mrs. Goodman did die at last. — *The Aunt's Story*, Patrick White, 1948.

2319 Persis Bradford died a few days before Christmas in the house on Mt. Vernon Street in Boston where her mother had died before her, at almost exactly the same age, in her early sixties. — *Shadow of a Man*, May Sarton, 1950.

2320 Major Malcolm Barcroft was sixty-seven when he died, the last male of his line. — *Love in a Dry Season*, Shelby Foote, 1951.

2321 I never knew the Holt brothers, which seems strange because within a few weeks of their deaths I felt that nobody else could have known them so well. — *My Brother's Keeper*, Marcia Davenport, 1954.

2322 That was the one and only time Nero Wolfe has ever seen the inside of the morgue. — *The Black Mountain*, Rex Stout, 1954.

2323 When my childhood had slipped by, and the days no longer seemed eternal but had shrunk to twelve hours or less, I began to think seriously about death. — *Homer's Daughter*, Robert Graves, 1955.

2324 I shall soon be quite dead at last in spite of all. — *Malone Dies*, Samuel Beckett, 1956.

2325 The tree./ The tree fell./ Fell and killed Captain Joe Cree. — *The Velvet Horn*, Andrew Lytle, 1957.

2326 Augustus Grimshawe, by dying in the night, caught us off our guard. — *Splendid in Ashes*, Josephine Pinckney, 1958.

2327 *The circus celebrating death was shaking Central Avenue and coming to our flat.* — *Three Circles of Light*, Pietro di Donato, 1960.

2328 When the old captain died the family went strange and it wasn't with grief, and if you want to know why, you should talk to somebody who knew the old captain. — *The Captain with the Whiskers*, Benedict Kiely, 1960.

2329 Francis Marion Tarwater's uncle had been dead for only half a day when the boy got too drunk to finish digging his grave and a Negro named Buford Munson, who had come to get a jug filled, had to finish it and drag the body from the breakfast table where it was still sitting and bury it in a decent and Christian way, with the sign of its Saviour at the head of the grave and enough dirt on top to keep the dogs from digging it up. — *The Violent Bear It Away*, Flannery O'Connor, 1960.

2330 Old Mrs. Quin died in her sleep in the

early hours of an August morning. — *China Court*, Rumer Godden, 1961.

2331 Death is always the same, but each man dies in his own way. — *Clock Without Hands*, Carson McCullers, 1961.

2332 Death had spared Arnold Soby — as it had also deprived him — of the academic wife who gave teas to freshmen, saw that the wall flowers at the parties were watered, and played cards in the foyer while the seniors danced. — *What a Way to Go*, Wright Morris, 1962.

2333 The morning I found her dead was gray, and the toast at breakfast had been burnt. — *The Garden*, Kathrin Perutz, 1962.

2334 First Lois and then Ernie, her daughter, her husband, and no wonder everything had run downhill since then. — *A Little Raw on Monday Mornings*, Robert Cormier, 1963.

2335 Mother died at five fifty-eight. Her last act was to reach out for the gold fob watch that lay on the bedside table. Unsurely grasped in the thin fingers the watch fell and its soft rhythm ceased, marking the precise minute as if in evidence of some crime. — *Our Mother's House*, Julian Gloag, 1963.

2336 Gerard Duluoz was born in 1917 a sickly little kid with a rheumatic heart and many other complications that made him ill for the most part of his life which ended in July 1926, when he was 9, and the nuns of St. Louis de France Parochial School were at his bedside to take down his dying words because they'd heard his astonishing revelations of heaven delivered in catechism class on no more encouragement than that it was his turn to speak — Saintly Gerard, his pure and tranquil face, the mournful look of him, the piteousness of his little soft shroud of hair falling down his brow and swept aside by the hand over blue serious eyes. — *Visions of Gerard*, Jack Kerouac, 1963.

2337 When you were young and a friend died, Solomon Stark reflected as he steered absently through the slush on the road to the municipal airport, you wept; but when you were past seventy, the tears did not come so easily, even though the loss was correspondingly greater. Instead you felt the shuddering wind that was building up to gale force to blow you down too, in your turn; and, driven onward by the wind, a swirling flood of reminiscence. — *The Will*, Harvey Swados, 1963.

2338 Everybody dies, everybody. Sure. And there's neither heaven nor hell. — *Boswell*, Stanley Elkin, 1964.

2339 Edward Thornhill died on the night of October 20, 1962, when the car he was driving was carried away with the bridge near the village of Toroella de Sta. Barbara during the floods that devastated many parts of Catalonia in that

month. — *The Corrida at San Feliu*, Paul Scott, 1964.

2340 WICKENBURG — *Mrs. Jeanette Champie, 93, Arizona pioneer, died Tuesday in Phoenix.* — *The Cadillac Cowboys*, Glendon Swarthout, 1964.

2341 She besieged the whole countryside between Gerona and Barcelona, and her whole family, from Paris down to Sicily, to Venezuela, Chile and Colombia, Paraguay and Peru, with the idea of death as represented by her person almost as a commercial enterprise. — *Unfinished Funeral*, Niccolò Tucci, 1964.

2342 He was a pattern of amiability when he fell flat on the gravel. — *Christopher Homm*, C. H. Sisson, 1965.

2343 "I am dying," said William Wagner Bird on the night of August 13th, turning his face towards the wall for privacy, sighing at the little bunches of forget-me-not on the wallpaper. — *The Boarding-House*, William Trevor, 1965.

2344 *They buried old Harry this morning.* — *Diary of an Old Man*, Chaim Bermant, 1966.

2345 Elvira — that was his mother — had at least enjoyed her dying. — *Eyes*, Janet Burroway, 1966.

2346 And I think by now you must be earth, earth or slime. — *The Microcosm*, Maureen Duffy, 1966.

2347 *In my end is my beginning. . . .* That's a quotation I've often heard people say. It sounds all right — but what does it really mean? — *Endless Night*, Agatha Christie, 1967.

2348 In the yellow sunshine that was just beginning to warm the morning, Miss Winifred Grainger sat in the last of the lawn chairs that had not yet been put away for the winter, holding in her hand, which lay in the lap of her corduroy skirt, a black-bordered announcement. — *A Second-Hand Life*, Charles Jackson, 1967.

2349 Wanting her to have what was right, after a life in which much had gone wrong, I would not let my wife go with the red-haired undertaker before Julia came home. — *The Landlord's Daughter*, Monica Dickens, 1968.

2350 Nero is dead. — *The Imperial Governor*, George Shipway, 1968.

2351 He had seen it before, in the movies, or on television. Or maybe the movie was on television, because he had been drinking beer from a bottle, which Ruth disapproved of. Anyway, he remembered seeing the doctor pull the sheet up over the face of the man on the bed, shake his head, and snap his black bag shut. Dead. And Bernie had taken a swig of the beer, feeling suddenly as cold as the beer, because, for an instant, he was that dead man. — *Feel Free*, David R. Slavitt, 1968.

2352 The sound filled the narrow bedroom, breath after long harsh breath, each of them

drawn out, running into the next, as though there at the end Mrs. Devlin meant to get all she could from every one since that was what she was reduced to now—lying there in her narrow walnut bed, breathing. —*House of Gold*, Elizabeth Cullinan, 1969.

2353 When Auntie Edna fell off the bus, she landed on her pate and remained unconscious for sixty-three days. At the end of this period she died, and they had a funeral. —*A Touch of Daniel*, Peter Tinniswood, 1969.

2354 *When my body is found people may wonder who I really was and why I did these things. Suicide? Accident? Murder? My death may be all three.* —*Strange Alphabet*, Alexis Lykiard, 1970.

2355 What can you say about a twenty-five-year-old girl who died? —*Love Story*, Erich Segal, 1970.

2356 Dying, he groped for others to take with him—landlords denying heat, dentists drilling too deep, specific faces that had sneered, ranted, laughed at him. —*Pocock and Pitt*, Elliott Baker, 1971.

2357 The old Colonel died at five minutes to three, on the morning of January the nineteenth, 1879. —*Theirs Was the Kingdom*, R. F. Delderfield, 1971.

2358 "Get up, Herman Redpath," my father-in-law Leo Bebb said. —*Open Heart*, Frederick Buechner, 1972.

2359 On the morning of Bernie Pryde's death—or it may have been the morning after, since Bernie died at his own convenience, nor did he think the estimated time of his departure worth recording—Cordelia was caught in a breakdown of the Bakerloo Line outside Lambeth North and was half an hour late at the office. —*An Unsuitable Job for a Woman*, P. D. James, 1972.

2360 Edwin Abraham Mullhouse, whose tragic death at 1:06 A.M. on August 1, 1954, deprived America of her most gifted writer, was born at 1:06 A.M. on August 1, 1943, in the shady town of Newfield, Connecticut. —*Edwin Mullhouse*, Steven Millhauser, 1972.

2361 Vaughan died yesterday in his last car-crash. —*Crash*, J. G. Ballard, 1973.

2362 Life is a riddle but death is no answer, and a soldier alone walks in fear because there is no one with him to die instead. —*Dog Tags*, Stephen Becker, 1973.

2363 Hamnet was dying. The physician had bled and purged the boy till all strength was gone, and the family now awaited the end. —*You, My Brother*, Philip Burton, 1973.

2364 Between midnight and dawn, while his fellow Romans were celebrating the end of Carnival, Massimo Count Pantaleone, General of the Military Staff, died in his bed. —*The Sala-*

mander, Morris West, 1973.

2365 The hearse stood outside the block of flats, waiting for the old lady. —*The Bottle Factory Outing*, Beryl Bainbridge, 1974.

2366 My family has always been into death. —*Kinflicks*, Lisa Alther, 1975.

2367 *The Dead Father's head. The main thing is, his eyes are open.* —*The Dead Father*, Donald Barthelme, 1975.

2368 My husband died sailing off the coast of Maine, leaving me a widow at the age of twenty-seven. —*Shine On, Bright and Dangerous Object*, Laurie Colwin, 1975.

2369 "I really don't think he's dead," I said to my three very old friends. —*Legs*, William Kennedy, 1975.

2370 Trace back the violent death of a friend and see how it happened. —*Murder at the ABA*, Isaac Asimov, 1976.

2371 Something was wrong about this funeral. —*The Last Chance*, Rona Jaffe, 1976.

2372 Amoebae leave no fossils. —*Even Cowgirls Get the Blues*, Tom Robbins, 1976.

2373 When Tusker Smalley died of a massive coronary at approximately 9.30 A.M. on the last Monday in April, 1972, his wife Lucy was out, having her white hair blue-rinsed and set in the Seraglio Room on the ground floor of Pankot's new five-storey glass and concrete hotel, The Shiraz. —*Staying On*, Paul Scott, 1977.

2374 I was the only boy, or girl either, in the public school of the town of Dugton, Claxford County, Alabama, whose father had ever got killed in the middle of the night standing up in the front of his wagon to piss on the hindquarters of one of a span of mules and, being drunk, pitching forward on his head, still hanging on to his dong, and hitting the pike in such a position and condition that both the left front and the left rear wheels of the wagon rolled, with perfect precision, over his unconscious neck, his having passed out being, no doubt, the reason he took the fatal plunge in the first place. Throughout, he was still holding on to his dong. —*A Place to Come To*, Robert Penn Warren, 1977.

2375 It is the winter of 1899. I have been here a short while and shortly will be here no longer. —*The Mutual Friend*, Frederick Busch, 1978.

2376 *He had never laughed over her bones. The dead had their rights.* —*Halloween*, Ben Greer, 1978.

2377 Midnight/ The Deep South/ Ecstasy,/ *It's finally spring down here on the Chattahoochee —the azaleas are in bloom, and everyone is dying of cancer.* —*Dancer from the Dance*, Andrew Holleran, 1978.

2378 *The human embryo is curled up in a ball with the nostrils placed between the two knees./ At death the pupil opens wide.* —*Narrow Rooms*, James Purdy, 1978.

2379 There's a sentence which used to fascinate me when I overheard it in bus queues, shops, in the street: "I've buried two husbands, you know." — *Living in the Maniototo*, Janet Frame, 1979.

2380 Papa Francesco was dead. — *The Vicar of Christ*, Walter F. Murphy, 1979.

2381 There was a lover of mine who worshipped me, and became wreckless with his life, which was soon taken from him — more abruptly than I would have wished, and more cruelly; for I came to pity him in the end. — *Cybele*, Joyce Carol Oates, 1979.

2382 Jake told me once that when he died he wanted to be stuffed. — *The Petting Zoo*, Brett Singer, 1979.

2383 Often, cloaked like trick or treaters in the casual disguises of philosophical gossip, we wonder about the ultimate meaning of a man's life, and today I'm thinking about Joseph Francl: a man who brought his future to America, God only knows why, from Czechoslovakia in 1851, and completely used up that future to lie dead, facedown in the snow, not unhappy in early December 1875, and then to be buried at Fort Klamath, Oregon, in a grave that was lost forever. — *The Tokyo-Montana Express*, Richard Brautigan, 1980.

2384 From the edge, near the road, looking to the fenced end of the graveyard, where pasture began, Silver saw his son's coffin. It was a metal lozenge. It was an oblong medicated tablet. It was going to be swallowed, he thought. — *Rounds*, Frederick Busch, 1980.

2385 The bitter cold morning of the ninth day of January, 1806, signalled a most curious division between great and small in much of southern England, and also gave ample evidence of a shared bereavement. — *Darken Ship*, Nicholas Monsarrat, 1980.

2386 In late March 1922, the following item appeared in the columns of the *Gaelic American*, a journal published in New York City, price 5 cents:/ AMERICAN CITIZEN/ LATEST MARTYR TO IRISH CAUSE/ Word has been received by relatives in New York and by The Friends of Irish Freedom of the death of one of their delegates to the Old Land. John Chrysostom Spartacus (Sparky) Driscoll was killed while performing his mission which was to observe the fighting being fomented in Ulster by agents of the Crown. — *No Country for Young Men*, Julia O'Faolain, 1980.

2387 She was dead even before I became aware of her existence. — *The Fate of Mary Rose*, Caroline Blackwood, 1981.

2388 On Friday afternoon, Alice watched her husband die on television. — *Callbacks*, Margaret Wander Bonanno, 1981.

2389 Harry Joy was to die three times, but it was his first death which was to have the greatest effect on him, and it is this first death which we shall now witness. — *Bliss*, Peter Carey, 1981.

2390 The President died at 6:27 P.M. on Monday, the Fourth of July. — *The Hill of Summer*, Allen Drury, 1981.

2391 Sam Bhengu knew that he was dying. — *Store Up the Anger*, Wessel Ebersohn, 1981.

2392 The priest phoned to tell me Sutton was dead. — *Meg*, Maurice Gee, 1981.

2393 It is on a windy morning in early March, a day of high scudding dizzy clouds, some nine months after their father's ignoble death, that his only children, Owen and Kirsten, make a pact to revenge that death. — *Angel of Light*, Joyce Carol Oates, 1981.

2394 My mother told me I would cut off my nose to spite my face, and, when I was thirty-three, to prove it she died. — *Lessons*, Lee Zacharias, 1981.

2395 I didn't know that afternoon that the ground was waiting to become another grave in just a few short days. — *So the Wind Won't Blow It All Away*, Richard Brautigan, 1982.

2396 Watching Father Die/ has not yet begun. — "Watching Father Die," B. H. Friedman, 1982.

2397 My first thought was that in a world where there was any mercy I should have been killed cleanly then and there, for I had no doubt that a more protracted death after days and nights of agony awaited me. — *Rogue Justice*, Geoffrey Household, 1982.

2398 Stavros Topouzoglou, the Anatolian, first son of Isaac Topouzoglou, lay in state, his arms folded across his chest, his head supported by an old-country bolster, his face open to the ceiling, not a dead king but the prince of a divided family, their hope on earth. — *The Anatolian*, Elia Kazan, 1982.

2399 The Reverend Peter Murchison peered into the mirror and thought, "It is true. I am going to die. My face is thinner than it was a week ago. I feel lighter and more frail. It is not that I'm afraid of dying, it is rather that I've lost my faith. Not only that. But I feel that I've not lived, I do not understand the world." — *A Field Full of Folk*, Iain Crichton Smith, 1982.

2400 They talked about death as if it were a country in Europe. — *Sleepwalking*, Meg Wolitzer, 1982.

2401 Leon Hubbard died ten minutes into lunch break on the first Monday in May, on the construction site of the new one-story trauma wing at Holy Redeemer Hospital in South Philadelphia. — *God's Pocket*, Pete Dexter, 1983.

2402 Gerald Muspratt gave no indication of what he was about to do. He walked over to the french windows in the dining room to inspect the

weather and, without even turning around, died. — *The Handyman*, Penelope Mortimer, 1983.

2403 In literal truth each of us has only one life to live, one death to die, yet there is a sense in which it could be said that Annabel Lee died twice. — *The Name of Annabel Lee*, Julian Symons, 1983.

2404 Did I ask to die? — *My Death My Life*, Kathy Acker, 1984.

2405 The dusk was cold. March snow had fallen. For three days, the great man had lain unconscious, his still-powerful lungs breathing an ominous death rattle that defied the dissolution of his ravaged frame. — *The Beethoven Conspiracy*, Thomas Hauser, 1984.

2406 Just before noon, there was a little bang and, weeping, the man fell dead. — *In the Middle of Nowhere*, Fanny Howe, 1984.

2407 My father died suddenly when he was forty and I was twelve. — *In Another Country*, Susan Kenney, 1984.

2408 Evelyn, the mother of Small Henry, succumbed to a kidney disease and died hours after he was born. — *Loving Daughters*, Olga Masters, 1984.

2409 *I think I am dead. I think I have been dead for a long time now.* — *Unexplained Laughter*, Alice Thomas Ellis, 1985.

2410 For a short while during the year I was ten, I thought only people I did not know died. — *Annie John*, Jamaica Kincaid, 1985.

2411 Constantinople, August 15, 1817./ The Sultane Valide is dead. — *Valide*, Barbara Chase-Riboud, 1986.

2412 *My Dear Catherine:*/ I am dying. — *The Autobiography of Henry VIII*, Margaret George, 1986.

2413 *Father is dead.* — *Lenin*, Alan Brien, 1987.

2414 My Aunt Vida was six years old when she began collecting dead people. — *A Coven of Women*, Jean Brody, 1987.

2415 When I was told they were dead, the first thing I did was move into their room. — *Renifleur's Daughter*, Candida Fraze, 1987.

2416 In a house in Tangier one night, David Becker thought he was about to die. — *Reasons of the Heart*, Henry Giniger, 1987.

2417 There are as many versions of my parents' deaths as I had hours to invent them. — *The Part of Fortune*, Laurel Goldman, 1987.

2418 In those days I had never given a thought to poisoning and I can be sure of this, that I had nothing to do with our mother's death. — *Heartstones*, Ruth Rendell, 1987.

2419 "Our father died in childbirth," wrote David Crown, bearer of bad news (retired), as he sat with his hearing aid turned off at his desk in what had been the ironing room in the basement of his own house. — *Memory Board*, Jane Rule, 1987.

2420 Ned was dead a year; his bed was cold and silent. — *The Red Truck*, Rudy Wilson, 1987.

2421 Perdita Whitney was twenty-six when she went out to India to die. — *The Distant Kingdom*, Daphne Wright, 1987.

2422 On shore, Eugene Goessler licked his index finger and dipped it into the envelope marked "Clara." It contained his third of his mother's ashes. — *River Road*, C. F. Borgman, 1988.

2423 The Sunday Char died I wondered if things would ever be the same again. — *Running to Paradise*, Virginia Budd, 1988.

2424 An hour before dawn on March 7th 1974, Kaspar Joachim Utz died of a second and long-expected stroke, in his apartment at No. 5 Široká Street, overlooking the Old Jewish Cemetery in Prague. — *Utz*, Bruce Chatwin, 1988.

2425 We started dying before the snow, and like the snow, we continued to fall. — *Tracks*, Louise Erdrich, 1988.

2426 "Drink your ginger ale, Nino, it's getting warm," Laura said, grumpily turning to shake her finger at Maria's body. "Even dead," she accused, "you're giving us trouble." — *The Right Thing to Do*, Josephine Gattuso Hendin, 1988.

2427 "To be born again," sang Gibreel Farishta tumbling from the heavens, "first you have to die." — *The Satanic Verses*, Salman Rushdie, 1988.

2428 The South killed Lucy Bondurant Chastain Venable on the day she was born. It just took her until now to die. — *Peachtree Road*, Anne Rivers Siddons, 1988.

2429 Her eyes in the final spasm had this far-beyond-it-all and happy look: well, if not exactly happy, then at least resigned, as if she was glad it was over and done with for this lifetime anyway, all because of a fluke. — *The Place in Flowers Where Pollen Rests*, Paul West, 1988.

2430 Once you know your days are numbered, you dont waste too much time foolin around — not if you got any sense. — *Seduction by Light*, Al Young, 1988.

2431 Let me be drawn up into the immensity. Into the darkness, where nothing can be known. — *First Light*, Peter Ackroyd, 1989.

2432 Spring 1957/ I had stepped over to the closet hoping to get a look at the embroidered silk jackets that she knew I coveted when Lam Fan opened one eye and said, "Get away from there you silly boy," scratched at the bedspread with her long red nails, and died. — *To All Appearances a Lady*, Marilyn Bowering, 1989.

2433 Died on me finally. He had to. — *Oldest Living Confederate Widow Tells All*, Allan Gurganus, 1989.

2434 Just because I've outlived practically everybody don't mean I'm in a hurry to die. — *Outlaw*, Warren Kiefer, 1989.

2435 The first time Louise thought she was dying she called Danny and April to the side of her hospital bed and said, "Listen, kids, there's something I want to say to you both." — *Equal Affections*, David Leavitt, 1989.

2436 Mama didn't want Daddy taking Little Brother to Arkansas. How would she visit the grave, see that it was kept clean. — *The Lost Sister*, Robert Love Taylor, 1989.

2437 Being dead is the best high I've ever seen. Except that being dead doesn't settle anything. — *Night Time Losing Time*, Michael Ventura, 1989.

2438 Julia died. — *Brief Lives*, Anita Brookner, 1990.

2439 Brother   When the telephone rings, I know. He is gone, Brother says. I held a mirror to the mouth. Will you come on? — *The Last Man Standing*, George Chambers, 1990.

2440 The morning Dinah died was cold. — *Bird of Paradise*, Vicki Covington, 1990.

2441 In the early spring of 1941, thirteen years after he'd left home, my father, Lincoln Bynum, died far away from my mother and me in a seaside village in northern California. — *The God of Nightmares*, Paula Fox, 1990.

2442 "He may be alive or he may be dead," Arnold said. "There's no way of knowing." — *Of Desire*, David Helwig, 1990.

2443 Rupert Van Leer, celebrated architect, knight of the realm, was buried at a church of his own design on 13th January 1987, the second day of a week that was already being called the Big Freeze. — *The Poison Heart*, Amanda Hemingway, 1990.

2444 Waiting so long for death has put me in poor spirits. — *Portrait of the Artist with My Wife*, Simon Mason, 1990.

2445 If everyone hadn't died at the same time, none of this would have happened. — *Afterlife*, Paul Monette, 1990.

2446 I'm as peaceful a man as you're likely to meet in America now, but this is about a death I may have caused. — *The Tongues of Angels*, Reynolds Price, 1990.

2447 Standing amid the tan, excited post-Christmas crowd at the Southwest Florida Regional Airport, Rabbit Angstrom has a funny sudden feeling that what he has come to meet, what's floating in unseen about to land, is not his son Nelson and daughter-in-law Pru and their two children but something more ominous and intimately his: his own death, shaped vaguely like an airplane. — *Rabbit at Rest*, John Updike, 1990.

2448 The day Tommy died it was raining.

— *Day of Atonement*, A. Alvarez, 1991.

2449 When the doctor told her there were less than six months of life left in her body she, figuring she could deal with death better from her house than from the formality of the hospital, told him she wanted to go home and die in her own bed. — *Cousin Claire*, Raymond Andrews, 1991.

2450 In the summer of my thirty-seventh year, when the air began leaking so conspicuously from my life that remaining oblivious to it soon required my full attention, my father fell into a pig-rendering fire and, of his unspeakable injuries, perished. — *Blue Ruin*, Brendan Boyd, 1991.

2451 Miss Sabina Taheny, Canon Sharkey's housekeeper, died suddenly one morning in May 1934 at a very awkward time. — *The Irish Magdalen*, John Broderick, 1991.

2452 Even before the earthquake my grandmother liked to say how wonderful it would be if we could all die together. — *After Shocks/Near Escapes*, Stephen Dobyns, 1991.

2453 The last thing Raymond Gaver expected was that he would die with a key to the Beverly Hills Hotel in his pocket. — *Domestic Pleasures*, Beth Gutcheon, 1991.

2454 Cassie Raintree was dying of brain cancer every afternoon at two thirty. — *Bones of Coral*, James W. Hall, 1991.

2455 Molly said, "She died standing up." — *Interviewing Matisse*, Lily Tuck, 1991.

2456 The night before her great-grandson Daniel was to be buried, old Marie Dufore sat alone by the woodstove and kept him company on his last night among the living. She was over ninety, and felt closer to the dead these days, anyway. — *The Wives' Tale*, Alix Wilber, 1991.

2457 "Randy's ashes came today." — *Sweetheart*, Peter McGehee, 1992.

2458 Sara stood on the fox until it died. — *Due North*, Mitchell Smith, 1992.

2459 I did not realize for a long time that I was dead. — *Possessing the Secret of Joy*, Alice Walker, 1992.

2460 "Dying's not so bad. At least I won't have to answer the telephone." — *Venus Envy*, Rita Mae Brown, 1993.

2461 I was five years old when I saw my father hanged for a thief in front of Canterbury Cathedral with the priest reading Scripture and a crowd watching. — *Nicholas Cooke*, Stephanie Cowell, 1993.

2462 I've lived with Lauro for five years, and I still admire him. He doesn't seem to be afraid of death. — "Living at Home," Mary Gordon, 1993.

2463 That night, you dreamt, that instead of dying fresh as a blade of grass, last year, one

winter afternoon, your sister had lingered, until her flesh had blackened so that the moonstone on her finger stood a monstrous white against her charred skin, and the whitewashed walls beside her bed, where, in your dream, she fought grimly with death, the whitewashed walls, in your dream, spread with stains of old blood at the touch of her fingers, as death sliced into her gums like the sharp thread with which the two of you would floss your teeth after a meal of rubbery mutton. — *The Glassblower's Breath*, Sunetra Gupta, 1993.

2464 It is bad form to come right out and express one's desire that an elderly relative should stop wasting everyone's time already and pack it in. — *Alive and Kicking*, Michael Levin, 1993.

2465 What did Jewel's mother die of? For two months, Jewel had tried to stop wondering. — *End of the Empire*, Denise Ohio, 1993.

Decisions

2466 The title of this work has not been chosen without the grave and solid deliberation which matters of importance demand from the prudent. — *Waverly*, Sir Walter Scott, 1814.

2467 As the train sped through the night Grace Durland decided that after all it didn't matter so much! — *Broken Barriers*, Meredith Nicholson, 1922.

2468 It was on the second of May, in the morning, that Robert Whittle, Professor of History at Caraway College, decided that the world was coming to an end. — *Mr. Whittle and the Morning Star*, Robert Nathan, 1947.

2469 It rained lightly on the morning of Wednesday, July 4, 1917, and the Festival Committee met to decide whether to postpone the Festival until the following Saturday. — *A Rage to Live*, John O'Hara, 1949.

2470 One day last fall I ordered the swimming pool destroyed. — *The Swimming Pool*, Mary Roberts Rinehart, 1952.

2471 It was about three o'clock on a Friday afternoon when Annette decided to leave school. — *Flight from the Enchanter*, Iris Murdoch, 1956.

2472 It was early in August when Frank Skeffington decided — or rather, announced his decision, which actually had been arrived at some months before — to run for re-election as mayor of the city. — *The Last Hurrah*, Edwin O'Connor, 1956.

2473 "What's it going to be then, eh?" — *A Clockwork Orange*, Anthony Burgess, 1962.

2474 The decision to withdraw the Unit from Laerg was taken early in October. — *Atlantic Fury*, Hammond Innes, 1962.

2475 I have decided to report the Ambassador to the Department in Pretoria. — *The Ambassador*, André Brink, 1964.

2476 It was the breaking of the cup which caused her final decision. — *The Wedding Bargain*, Agnes Sligh Turnbull, 1966.

2477 When did you decide you should come to Zürich, Mr. Staunton?/ "When I heard myself shouting in the theatre." — *The Manticore*, Robertson Davies, 1972.

2478 Dr. Wicker was debating whether to buy one or two air-flight insurance policies when a soft-voiced man in a gray suit appeared at his elbow. — *Tourist*, Gerald Green, 1973.

2479 . . . and, further, I decided today to abandon, once and for all, the God-damned Tumulty project. — *One Hell of an Actor*, Garson Kanin, 1977.

2480 It was when Ponsonby saw the brand new Family Planning Clinic at the end of a dirt-track in the middle of the Javanese countryside, that he decided that something had to be done. And quickly. — *The Ponsonby Post*, Bernice Rubens, 1977.

2481 I decided to take Grace with me to Europe for one reason: cowardice. — *Spend It Foolishly*, Mary Gallagher, 1978.

2482 Fabian decided to get a haircut. — *Passion Play*, Jerzy Kosinski, 1979.

2483 What do you do? Angela Lee asks herself. — *Love and Work*, Gwyneth Cravens, 1982.

2484 With a strength born of the decision that had just come to her in the middle of the night, Avey Johnson forced the suitcase shut on the clothes piled inside and slid the lock into place. — *Praisesong for the Widow*, Paule Marshall, 1983.

2485 King Charles III made the final decision. — *First Among Equals*, Jeffrey Archer, 1984.

2486 It was on a Sunday in May 1870 that Aaron Abrahams finally decided he could no longer live with his wife, Annie, nor put up with the inscrutable gaze of his daughter Mary. — *The Highly Flavoured Ladies*, Patricia Angadi, 1987.

2487 "And you want to know -"/ "If I should take it." — *Second Sight*, Mary Tannen, 1988.

2488 . . . and so, I decided to devote myself exclusively to the pursuit of women. — *Memoirs of a Dance-Hall Romeo*, Jack Higgins, 1989.

2489 "Do you know what you're going to tell Dean Roskov about what you've decided on?" my father asked as we neared Cobbton where the college lingered gently out from the town's north edge into the wide estates and farms. — *The Tangerine Tango Equation*, Barry Targan, 1990.

2490 Why did you decide to live in Kreis-

wald?—*Tales of the Master Race*, Marcie Hershman, 1991.

2491 In the month of April of the year 1912, First Lord of the Admiralty Winston Churchill announced that all British ships of war would in the future be powered by oil. It was a critical decision. "He who owns the oil," the French premier, Georges Clemenceau, declared, "will own the world."—*Beyond the Aegean*, Elia Kazan, 1994.

Depression

2492 "I tell you, Clarence Howard, that there is a—hell!" exclaimed the young lord, leaning over the oaken table, while his face glowed in the light of the lamp beams—"a dark, a fearful, and an eternal hell—far more dread, far more terrible, than the flames of a never-ending fire, imagined by priests, or taught by the dogmas of superstition! Aye—curl your lip with that incredulous smile, and laugh in my face, if it pleases you! But, Clarence, there is a hell—dark, fearful, and terrible. That hell is here—*the hell of a blighted heart!*"—*Blanche of Brandywine*, George Lippard, 1846.

2493 Lonely Mag Smith! See her as she walks with downcast eyes and heavy heart. — *Our Nig*, Harriet E. Wilson, 1859.

2494 Mr. Robert Pagebrook was "blue."—*A Man of Honor*, George Cary Eggleston, 1873.

2495 She did not wish any supper and she sank forgetfully back into the stately oak chair. — *The Mettle of the Pasture*, James Lane Allen, 1903.

2496 "And yet," Edward Henry Machin reflected as at six minutes to six he approached his own dwelling at the top of Bleakridge, "and yet—I don't feel so jolly after all!"—*The Regent*, Arnold Bennett, 1913.

2497 Penrod sat morosely upon the back fence and gazed with envy at Duke, his wistful dog. — *Penrod*, Booth Tarkington, 1914.

2498 The morning was gray and I sat by the sea near Palos in a gray mood. — *1492*, Mary Johnston, 1922.

2499 Yes, I certainly was feeling depressed. — *Diary of a Drug Fiend*, Aleister Crowley, 1923.

2500 It had been an unhappy day for little Kay Harker. — *The Midnight Folk*, John Masefield, 1927.

2501 Mr. Virginius Curle Littlepage, who had his reason apart from the weather for a melancholy view of life, stood at the window of his law office and looked out upon a depressing

afternoon in November.—*They Stooped to Folly*, Ellen Glasgow, 1929.

2502 Plaxy and I had been lovers; rather uneasy lovers, for she would never speak freely about her past, and sometimes she withdrew into a cloud of reserve and despond.—*Sirius*, Olaf Stapledon, 1944.

2503 Abrupt as anger, depression plunged through him. — *Gentleman's Agreement*, Laura Z. Hobson, 1947.

2504 To think that Christmas should ever come to be sad, and make her heart heavy! —"One Red Rose for Christmas," Paul Horgan, 1952.

2505 When I brought the stage into Goshen that day I was feeling sorry for myself. — *First Blood*, Jack Schaefer, 1953.

2506 Later that summer, when Mrs. Penmark looked back and remembered, when she was caught up in despair so deep that she knew there was no way out, no solution whatever for the circumstances that encompassed her, it seemed to her that June seventh, the day of the Fern Grammar School picnic, was the day of her last happiness, for never since then had she known contentment or felt peace. — *The Bad Seed*, William March, 1954.

2507 Gerald Middleton was a man of mildly but persistently depressive temperament. Such men are not at their best at breakfast, nor is the week before Christmas their happiest time. —*Anglo-Saxon Attitudes*, Angus Wilson, 1956.

2508 What with his wife so ill these past few weeks and the prospect of three more days of teaching before the weekend break, Mr. MacPherson felt unusually glum. — *The Apprenticeship of Duddy Kravitz*, Mordecai Richler, 1959.

2509 Not long ago Kate Brady and I were having a few gloomy gin fizzes up London, bemoaning the fact that nothing would ever improve, that we'd die the way we were—enough to eat, married, dissatisfied. — *Girls in Their Married Bliss*, Edna O'Brien, 1964.

2510 One year, when I was a boy—eleven, going on twelve—my father took me to Ireland. We went because of a tragedy, a family tragedy which was really my first experience with sadness of any kind. —*All in the Family*, Edwin O'Connor, 1966.

2511 The afternoon sun poured brightly into the office of the manager of Guildenstern's Stores, Madison Avenue, New York, but there was no corresponding sunshine in the heart of Homer Pyle, the eminent corporation lawyer, as he sat there. — *The Girl in Blue*, P. G. Wodehouse, 1971.

2512 I get depressed on Sundays. When I was a kid I got depressed on Sundays and over the years I've found no valid reason for not getting

depressed on Sundays. — *The Bradley Beach Rumba*, David A. Kaufelt, 1974.

2513 The old General felt it coming at sunset on that fine cool evening, while he sat on the porch of his log house on the bluff overlooking the Ohio: a greater melancholy than any he had faced in the thirty years of his decline. — *Long Knife*, James Alexander Thom, 1979.

2514 By Christmas he knew he'd be ready for an oxygen tent. — *Ask Me Now*, Al Young, 1980.

2515 Mr. Godfrey was depressed — more depressed than he'd been at any other time in his life. — *Address Unknown*, Malcolm Hutton, 1981.

2516 In late April of the year 1890, T., who had been undergoing a depression so severe that his most recent biographer believes he might have been nearing a breakdown, left his home in Moscow for the penal colony on the island of Sakhalin, a journey of over sixty-five hundred miles, or more than a quarter of our planet's circumference. — *To a Distant Island*, James McConkey, 1984.

2517 "Cheer up, Werner. It will soon be Christmas," I said. — *London Match*, Len Deighton, 1985.

2518 On Tuesday, October 10, 1967, the day the surgical resident advertised him as the German who just came down from McGill, Dr. Josef Bernhardt realized he had been in a depression since the end of the war. — *Berlin Wild*, Elly Welt, 1986.

2519 There are no new days ahead of me. — *Fool's Sanctuary*, Jennifer Johnston, 1987.

2520 After Kitty fell out of the window I fell into the abyss. — *Make-Believe Ballrooms*, Peter J. Smith, 1989.

Desire

2521 I no longer have the desire, on this immense and silent winter's night, to dissemble, to fabricate tales. — *Crossroads*, James McConkey, 1968.

2522 I was ten years old when I first saw the Inheritance and twenty years old when I first saw Janna Roslyn, but my reaction to both was identical. I wanted them. — *Penmarric*, Susan Howatch, 1971.

2523 Here's the person I want. — *Transparent Things*, Vladimir Nabokov, 1972.

2524 Wasn't it miraculous, that she could feel this way after so long? Desire, she meant, and its fulfillment. — *Rough Strife*, Lynne Sharon Schwartz, 1980.

2525 LAST SEASON'S BESTSELLER WAS *GREED*. — *The Hanky of Pippin's Daughter*, Rosmarie Waldrop, 1986.

2526 Lowell Perry wanted a new car. — *A Boat Off the Coast*, Stephen Dobyns, 1987.

2527 All Quinn wanted was a little peace. And some money, a lot of money. And a job. And to write a novel that would make all those smug bastards at Williams choke with envy. — *A Woman Run Mad*, John L'Heureux, 1988.

2528 "Come on, Elizabeth," said Oscar Lemoine. "Stop drooling." — *The Cover Artist*, Paul Micou, 1990.

2529 Walking along the Seine, close to the swiftly moving but heavy water that slithered against the quai, walking round the couples sitting at the edge with their arms about each other, one young man with his hand inside the unbuttoned blouse of a young woman and holding her breast, I longed for what I felt couldn't be fulfilled even by making love, only by throwing myself into the river, not to die, but to be taken somewhere else on its current, which, out at the center, streamed in smooth, shiny, infolding waves. — *The Accident*, David Plante, 1991.

2530 In Africa, you want more, I think. — *Mating*, Norman Rush, 1991.

Diaries

2531 Diary of John Haye, Secretary to the Noat Art Society, and in J.W.P.'s House at the Public School of Noat./ *6 July (about)*,/ It has only just struck me that a kind of informal diary would be rather fun. — *Blindness*, Henry Green, 1926.

2532 *September 1st, 1939*. — Enquire of Robert whether he does not think that, in view of times in which we live, diary of daily events might not be of ultimate historical value to posterity. He replies that It Depends. — *The Provincial Lady in Wartime*, E. M. Delafield, 1940.

2533 Seventy-five years ago a young woman kept a diary in which she wrote some of her innermost thoughts, many of the daily happenings, and all of the weather. — *The Lieutenant's Lady*, Bess Streeter Aldrich, 1942.

2534 The girls kept diaries, but you never had a chance to read them. — *A Woman of Means*, Peter Taylor, 1950.

2535 The cabin-passenger wrote in his diary a parody of Descartes: "I feel discomfort, therefore I am alive," then sat pen in hand with no more to record. — *A Burnt-Out Case*, Graham Greene, 1961.

2536 I cannot and do not wish to sleep again and so, for want of anything better, I have taken up this diary, neglected since I came to Japan, and am hunched over it in the *roka*, the glassed-in porch which separates my quarters from the garden. — *The Custom House*, Francis King, 1961.

2537 September 10, 1939. I have always wanted to keep a journal, but whenever I am about to start one, I am dissuaded by the idea that it is too late. — *The Rector of Justin*, Louis Auchincloss, 1964.

2538 *March, 1963.* Looking back through my diary, as I begin this account of the strange means by which the prosperity of the company I now serve was founded, I find it difficult to realize that there was a time when I had never been to the Maldives, had scarcely ever heard of Addu Atoll. — *The Strode Venturer*, Hammond Innes, 1965.

2539 *Paris. Early December 1966/* When we were young, Fanny and I both kept diaries. Now, I can't think why, for our lives were, contrary to the romantic myth about vivid, painful adolescence, quite extraordinarily dull. — *Fly Away Home*, Gillian Tindall, 1971.

2540 *Monday, September 20, 1943* — This seems like as good a time as any to start this diary. — *A Necessary End*, Nathaniel Benchley, 1976.

2541 Father you had to go away,/ And sadly I have had to stay./ I am sad we had to part./ I will miss you in my heart./ He chewed the end of his pen and tried to visualize the words printed in the *Journal*, even perhaps with the importance of a thick black line around them, presenting them to the world. — *Shadows on Our Skin*, Jennifer Johnston, 1977.

2542 FROM BILLY ABBOTT'S NOTE-BOOK — / I AM WORTHLESS, MONIKA SAYS. — *Beggarman, Thief*, Irwin Shaw, 1977.

2543 Having had a day of calm weather now after the strong gale at South which forced me to stand to the Westward, I have an opportunity to begin this personal history, or Diary, of the Voyage on which we are embarked. — *The Last Voyage*, Hammond Innes, 1978.

2544 Odd to say it, but I can still *see* my sister's diary, only then we called it her "personal." — *Time in Its Flight*, Susan Fromberg Schaeffer, 1978.

2545 Honoured godfather,/ With those words I begin the journal I engaged myself to keep for you — no words could be more suitable! — *Rites of Passage*, William Golding, 1980.

2546 I forgot to bring my journal with us. — *A Sense of Shadow*, Kate Wilhelm, 1981.

2547 Throughout her life, Peggy kept a journal. — *Peggy Salté*, Page Edwards, 1983.

2548 I have been working such long hours on this last corporate takeover that I have hardly made an entry in my journal for six weeks. — *Diary of a Yuppie*, Louis Auchincloss, 1986.

2549 Julia darling,/ I've been awake all night trying to write you a letter, but after half a dozen futile attempts, I've decided to leave you these journals instead. — *Joanna's Husband and David's Wife*, Elizabeth Forsythe Hailey, 1986.

2550 Having written "The End" to this story of my life, I find it prudent to scamper back here to before the beginning, to my front door, so to speak, and to make this apology to arriving guests: "I promised you an autobiography, but something went wrong in the kitchen. It turns out to be a *diary* of this past troubled summer, too! We can always send out for pizzas if necessary. Come *in*, come *in*." — *Bluebeard*, Kurt Vonnegut, 1987.

2551 Cassie picked up her journal. — *To Hear a Nightingale*, Charlotte Bingham, 1988.

2552 Dear Father,/ I shall never see you again. As a gesture of farewell, I am sending you this account of all that I have seen and done since leaving Japan. — *Blue Fruit*, Adam Lively, 1988.

2553 The pages from the journal of Samuel Himmelhoch were found under a jerrycan in the tomb of Hannah and her seven sons. — *Master of the Return*, Tova Reich, 1988.

2554 When Lydia Franklin married George Webster in 1909, she took her journals with her from the dark brownstone on East Thirty-eighth Street to the plain white farmhouse in Northington, Connecticut. — *In My Mother's House*, Elizabeth Winthrop, 1988.

2555 The journals of the Black-Gowns, submitted once a year to their superiors in Québec and Montréal, and thence forwarded to France, were published in duodecimal volumes known to book-worms and book-lice as Cramoisys, but the pious thousands called them simply *Jesuit Relations*. — *Fathers and Crows*, William T. Vollmann, 1992.

2556 I don't know how much to include and how much to leave out. — *Diary of a Lost Boy*, Harry Kondoleon, 1994.

Disappearance

2557 The story of the little man, sometimes a stockbroker, sometimes a tea merchant, but always something in the City, who walked out of his suburban house one sunny morning and vanished like a puff of grey smoke in a cloudless sky, can be recalled by nearly everyone who lived in Greater London in the first years of the century. — *Flowers for the Judge*, Margery Allingham, 1936.

2558 The death—or rather, the disappearance—of Don Juan de Tenorio took place at Seville in the seventh decade of the eighteenth century. —*After the Death of Don Juan*, Sylvia Townsend Warner, 1938.

2559 The female of the species vanished on the afternoon of the second Tuesday of February at four minutes and fifty-two seconds past four o'clock, Eastern Standard Time. — *The Disappearance*, Philip Wylie, 1951.

2560 In August, 1945, in a small Southern town which still cannot be named, a First Lieutenant Allerd Pennington, a young scientist, disappeared from an inconspicuous Army installation. — *The Hound of Earth*, Vance Bourjaily, 1955.

2561 The last time his wife saw Ron Galloway was on a Saturday evening in the middle of April. —*An Air That Kills*, Margaret Millar, 1957.

2562 . . .*His first moment of feeling invisible occurred the morning of the day before he ran away.* — *Has Anybody Seen My Father?*, Harrison Kinney, 1960.

2563 It was on May 31 of last year, at Geneva's Cointrin airport, that the man who called himself Charles Latimer disappeared. — *The Intercom Conspiracy*, Eric Ambler, 1969.

2564 In Devon's dream they were searching the reservoir again for Robert. —*Beyond This Point Are Monsters*, Margaret Millar, 1970.

2565 The commonest kind of missing person is the adolescent girl, closely followed by the teen-age boy. —"The Enigma," John Fowles, 1974.

2566 Lucy Bear and Rainbo Woman have disappeared. —*Riverfinger Women*, Elana Nachman, 1974.

2567 *Extract of a letter from Mrs. Eudora Hilliard, dated New York, June 17th, 1974/* Yes, I agree with you. It is now nearly ten years since my nephew disappeared and we can try to clear his name without either of us having much fear of prosecution. But you should write the story, not I. — *Red Anger*, Geoffrey Household, 1975.

2568 In the spring of 1980 a bright, gifted student at Grant University in Pequod, Pennsylvania, mysteriously disappeared. —*Mazes and Monsters*, Rona Jaffe, 1981.

2569 Long after Daniel had disappeared, Isadora haunted the obituaries. —*Lifelines*, Caroline Leavitt, 1982.

2570 "*Ruina! Ruina!*" my grandfather, Isidro Sanchez, had scrawled at the end of his farewell note to my grandmother, which, she recounted, in a voice still astonished after all the passing years, he had written only an arm's length from where she sat mending a tear in the shirt he was to wear the next morning when he had been summoned to see Antonio de la Cueva, the proprietor of the sugar plantation of Malagita, to answer, among other serious questions, why he

had not fulfilled his cane quota and therefore could not guarantee his rent for the coming year. —*A Servant's Tale*, Paula Fox, 1984.

2571 The gravel crackled as the General's boot scuffed it. "Where the hell have they got to?" he muttered. — *Coup d'Etat*, John Harvey, 1985.

2572 The day the child disappeared, the fog came up early and by midday it seemed as if the forest was covered in a thick white cloud. — *Fiela's Child*, Dalene Matthee, 1986.

2573 My mother's name was Lise Hurwitz Branson. The day after she disappeared, my brother Gil and I went to stay with our aunt and uncle in the next town. — *The Dream Dredger*, Roberta Silman, 1986.

2574 First Ralph heard again how Harry had—one evening in the settlement's first days—discovered Duckling's absence from her tent across the stream. — *The Playmaker*, Thomas Keneally, 1987.

2575 If I haven't vanished from this earth altogether, dear Boris, I have reached its outer rim from where it's but a small step to enter the void. — *The Inventor*, Jakov Lind, 1987.

2576 My son, Davy Chadwick, was abducted from my house in southern Italy in the late afternoon of 15 December 1984. —*Davy Chadwick*, James Buchan, 1988.

2577 *May is missing. She is somewhere in Southeast Asia, possibly she made it into Saigon on one of the last flights, we can't be sure.* — *Gift of the Golden Mountain*, Shirley Streshinsky, 1988.

2578 This is the story of my older brother's strange criminal behavior and his disappearance. No one urged me to reveal these things; no one asked me not to. —*Affliction*, Russell Banks, 1989.

2579 *It's a good name, you once said, for a vanishing act.* —*In the Night Café*, Joyce Johnson, 1989.

2580 I lose people. —*Boys Like Us*, Peter McGehee, 1991.

2581 The facts, as far as they could be ascertained, were as follows. Miss Durant, a woman in middle years, living alone in apparently comfortable circumstances, had been missing for some four months, although no-one had seen her leave her flat in South Kensington, and her cleaner, who had a key, and who was used to finding the flat empty, thought little about the matter until the money, which was usually left on the kitchen table, was not replaced. —*Fraud*, Anita Brookner, 1993.

2582 I was walking on Brattle Street when I noticed for the first time that I had become invisible. —*Peachy*, Fredrica Wagman, 1993.

2583 In the weeks preceding her fortieth birthday Kiki Shaw made the uncomfortable discovery that she was disappearing. — *Now You See Her*, Whitney Otto, 1994.

Disappointment

2584 Jonah Wood was bitterly disappointed in his son. — *The Three Fates*, F. Marion Crawford, 1891.

2585 The weak bubble of the mission's water fountain and its flat, swimming-hole taste washed away the dull satisfaction that had been Acel Stecker's on reaching the free shelter. — *Hungry Men*, Edward Anderson, 1935.

2586 I was twelve that Christmas, too old for Santa Claus, but still too young to take a great disappointment with any grace. — *Hound-dog Man*, Fred Gipson, 1949.

2587 This was the day before the night when the knives of official disappointment struck. — *The Wanting Seed*, Anthony Burgess, 1962.

2588 The man had been eyeing me most of the way home, and even happened to leave the bus at the same stop; but as soon as I got off he lost interest and walked away hunching his shoulders against the disappointment and the rain. — *The Walking Stick*, Winston Graham, 1967.

2589 "It's," said this customer at the bar, "what I personally would want to call — and anyone else can call it what the hell they like for all I care —" Hogg listened respectfully, half-bowed, wiping dry a glass from which a very noisy woman, an actress or something, had drunk and eaten a Pimm's Number One. "But it's what I, speaking for myself, would call —" Hogg burnished an indelible veronica of lipstick, waiting for some highly idiosyncratic pay-off, not just the just word but the word just with just this customer's personal brand of justness. "A barefaced liberty." Hogg bowed deeper in tiny dissatisfaction. — *Enderby Outside*, Anthony Burgess, 1968.

2590 She was disappointed. She had expected the back of the limousine to be luxurious, to make her feel aristocratic and rich, coddled and protected. — *Late Bloomer*, David A. Kaufelt, 1979.

2591 Halley's comet had been a big disappointment the year before. — *The World Around Midnight*, Patricia Browning Griffith, 1991.

Disaster

2592 A succession of national disasters led to the downfall of Count Kornowski. The droughts of 1924 and 1925 halved the crop from his estates at Jezow; a fall in the world price of timber and sugar meant lower prices for what he could sell; and finally, in the middle of 1925, came the German tariff war against Poland which cut him off from his best customers. — *Polonaise*, Piers Paul Read, 1976.

2593 Ever since I can remember I have thought the grown-up world to be mad; its way of talking to itself and being outraged at the answers; the bright look in its eye as it goes off to feed on disaster. — *Imago Bird*, Nicholas Mosley, 1980.

2594 I came to grief late in life — when I was forty, in Minnesota. — *Gabriel's Lament*, Paul Bailey, 1986.

2595 A minute away from disaster, as he was thinking that nothing was the same any more, and that nothing could ever again be as sweet as it used to be, the tall and sharp-boned traveller in the corner seat let out the sigh of his body's premonition, shifted awkwardly as though his limbs were hurting him, and stared out through the dining-car window. — *Ticket to Ride*, Dennis Potter, 1986.

2596 Sybil and I were discussing disastrous attachments. — *The Bride Who Ran Away*, Diana O'Hehir, 1988.

2597 I never meant to return to the scene of my great disaster. — *Scandalous Risks*, Susan Howatch, 1990.

2598 Of all the things that drive men to sea, the most common disaster, I've come to learn, is women. — *Middle Passage*, Charles Johnson, 1990.

2599 Max lived scared, always alert to the threat of disaster, and yet when disaster finally arrived he was relaxed. — *Fearless*, Rafael Yglesias, 1993.

Discovery

2600 In the year 1817, I projected a voyage of discovery, in the hope of finding a passage to a new and untried world. I flattered myself that I should open the way to new fields for the enterprise of my fellow-citizens, supply new sources of wealth, fresh food for curiosity, and additional means of enjoyment; objects of vast importance, since the resources of the known world have been exhausted by research, its wealth monopolized, its wonders of curiosity explored, its every thing investigated and understood! — *Symzonia*, John Cleves Symmes *as* Captain Adam Seaborn, 1820.

2601 There was no mistake this time: he had struck gold at last! — "A Millionaire of Rough-and-Ready," Bret Harte, 1887.

2602 It was a diamond all right, shining in the grass half a dozen feet from the blue brick walk. — *The Dain Curse*, Dashiell Hammett, 1929.

2603 While walking in the tall grass that has sprung up around the city of Troy, Balso Snell came upon the famous wooden horse of the Greeks. — *The Dream Life of Balso Snell*, Nathanael West, 1931.

2604 One sunny day in the summer after the end of the war, a search party found the Levinson Archive buried in seventeen iron boxes and a number of small parcels, the latter wrapped in rags and old clothes, under the sites of what had been, before the razing of the entire Warsaw ghetto, Nowolipki Street 68 and Swientojerska Street 34. — *The Wall*, John Hersey, 1950.

2605 Those of you who have followed the work of our archaeologists along the east and west coasts of the Great West, or Salt, Continent, and in the interior deserts, know that the Kenya and Uganda expeditions have recently discovered traces of a lost people of prehistory among the mounds and tumuli of that unexplored waste. — *The Weans*, Robert Nathan, 1960.

2606 Young Lance first noticed the small track in the fan of earth below a washout. — *The Story Catcher*, Mari Sandoz, 1963.

2607 I knew it! — I knew if I searched long enough, high and low and far and wide, that I was bound to discover something underground today; because when I receive those wavelengths of hidden pressures and intangible tensions along my spine and up and down my left leg and arm, as sure a weathercock as an ill-mended bone is for dirty weather, something's here all right, it's always here. — *The Middleman*, Mark Smith, 1967.

2608 Mrs. Sidney Shallop would discover the instigation of passion and doom on this day. — *Beauty Beast*, MacKinlay Kantor, 1968.

2609 The magician's underwear has just been found in a cardboard suitcase floating in a stagnant pond on the outskirts of Miami. — *Another Roadside Attraction*, Tom Robbins, 1971.

2610 *It was a brown box, a dispatch box, of decayed dark brown leather with brass reinforced corners.* — "V. R. T.," Gene Wolfe, 1972.

2611 I have just discovered I can magnify objects by a slight pressure on the lids of my eyes. — *The Fork River Space Project*, Wright Morris, 1977.

2612 Some discoveries set you free, but most just complicate your life. — *Love and Other Natural Disasters*, Allen Hannay, 1982.

2613 The children were the first to see one of them. — *Baby Sweet's*, Raymond Andrews, 1983.

2614 Today, going through some dusty boxes in Jack's closet, I found that awful stuffed alligator. — *Not in Vain*, Gerald Green, 1984.

2615 Ilka had been three months in this country when she went West and discovered her first American sitting on a stool in a bar in the desert, across from the railroad. — *Her First American*, Lore Segal, 1985.

2616 The sequence of events that transformed Dr. Charles Peruzzi from an overworked general practitioner into one of the most remarkable medical discoverers of our time began in a corridor of the Park View Hotel in central London, on a mild Friday afternoon in late September 1978. — *The Personality Surgeon*, Colin Wilson, 1985.

2617 There was nothing out of the way about the package. — *Louisiana Black*, Samuel Charters, 1986.

2618 She found the roll of film cleaning out the freezer, crooked behind a mound of ice trays frosted together, jumbled in with all the Unidentified Frozen Objects of the year so far. — *Save Me, Joe Louis*, Madison Smartt Bell, 1993.

Divinities

2619 We have heard of those who fancied that they beheld a signal instance of the hand of the Creator in the celebrated cataract of Niagara. — *The Oak Openings*, James Fenimore Cooper, 1848.

2620 Two eternal beings, magnificently enhaloed, the one in a blinding excess of white radiance and the other in a bewildering extravagance of colours, converse amidst stupendous surroundings. — *The Undying Fire*, H. G. Wells, 1919.

2621 All things touching their people flowed through the minds of the War Gods in their high place. — *The Enemy Gods*, Oliver La Farge, 1937.

2622 Peter Hamilton, who was no fool, often remarked at "Good Book readin' time" that there was nothing in the Bible, not even in Genesis, that indicated God "thought." God "did." — *Maggie — Her Marriage*, Taylor Caldwell, 1953.

2623 There was then in heaven a Calling-Together, or Convocation of the saints, they being vexed and worried at the look of things below and anxious for the world about which they received reports from time to time from angelic messengers who traveled between heaven and earth, descending like doves to the green continents and rising again like herring gulls above the glowing blue oceans. — *The Rancho of the Little Loves*, Robert Nathan, 1956.

2624 It was all a matter of a goddess — dark, hidden, deadly, horribly desirable. — *Nothing Like the Sun*, Anthony Burgess, 1964.

2625 It was the sort of morning when you might expect to find the Heavenly Father off in a corner and doubting His Own Self, and nothing to be done but wait, God love Him, and His Own patience save us all. — *Sweet Morn of Judas' Day*, Richard Llewellyn, 1964.

2626 Salutations to the Lord God of Hosts, the Father Almighty, Creator of Heaven and worlds and suns, the Holy of Holies, the Ineffable One, the Serenity of Universes, the Splendor of Life, the Progenitor of archangels, angels, cherubim and seraphim, Powers and Dominions, Princes and Principalities, the Triune God, the Perpetrator of men — and my Father. — *Dialogues with the Devil*, Taylor Caldwell, 1967.

2627 Today was Friday and the day of sacrifice for the great god Tano. — *A Woman in Her Prime*, Asare Konadu, 1967.

2628 On a certain afternoon — one of those which cannot be measured on any calendar devised by man — Zeus, the Father of Gods and Men, ascended to the highest peak of Mount Olympus. — *The Glory of Hera*, Caroline Gordon, 1972.

2629 "As I've said before," said Voltaire (*né* F. M. Arouet), "if God did not exist, it would be necessary to invent him." — *The Adventures of God in His Search for the Black Girl*, Brigid Brophy, 1973.

2630 I have seen God creating the cosmos, watching its growth, and finally destroying it. — *Nebula Maker*, Olaf Stapledon, 1976.

2631 1. There was a Master come unto the earth, born in the holy land of Indiana, raised in the mystical hills east of Fort Wayne. — *Illusions*, Richard Bach, 1977.

2632 There was Eru, the One, who in Arda is called Ilúvatar; and he made first the Ainur, the Holy Ones, that were the offspring of his thought, and they were with him before aught else was made. — *The Silmarillion*, J.R.R. Tolkien, 1977.

2633 You remember the old myth about Eden. How Adam and Eve ate of "the tree of the knowledge of good and evil," and how the Ancient of Days, the Cosmic Link, the Substantial Boss, God Himself was pained at them for touching *that* tree of all those in the forest. — *Passenger*, Thomas Keneally, 1979.

2634 Vanity, the angel said. Waste and vanity./ That, later, seemed the main message. — *The Lovelock Version*, Maurice Shadbolt, 1980.

2635 Above the twelve heavens, it is said, is Omeyocan, the Place of Duality. Here is the abode of Ometeotl, the Creator of All Things, the god both male and female, known to the people as Ometecuhtli and Omecihuatl, the Lord and the Lady of the Duality. And out of himself, Ometeotl created four sons, one to rule over each of the directions upon the earth. — *The Luck of Huemac*, Daniel Peters, 1981.

2636 The ziggurat of Bel-Marduk had been half ruinous for a century and a half, ever since Xerxes had humbled the gods of rebellious Babylon. — *Funeral Games*, Mary Renault, 1981.

2637 *Darling!/ What do you imagine the serpent looked like before God cursed it?* — *Secret Understandings*, Morris Philipson, 1983.

2638 In Paradise, on the banks of the River of Time, the Lord of the Universe is playing ball with His archangels. — *Things Invisible to See*, Nancy Willard, 1984.

2639 There were angels in the glass, two four six many of them, each one shuffling into his place in line like an alderman at the Lord Mayor's show. — *Ægypt*, John Crowley, 1987.

2640 Veronica Smiles was crossing the Sahara desert, minding her own business, when she ran into God. — *Our Father*, Bernice Rubens, 1987.

2641 God puts His finger through the dust of the earth and into this channel He spits. — *Black Baby*, Clare Boylan, 1988.

2642 In the beginning there was Accompong, a being of infinite goodness. — *The Fablesinger*, Judith Woolcock Colombo, 1989.

2643 "Lord, Lord, Lord," she said. — *A Visitation of Spirits*, Randall Kenan, 1989.

2644 One day, when the Son of God had been long wandering through the halls of heaven, he stopped to rest beside an aged man on a bench of alabaster. — *Plain Song*, Deborah Grabien, 1990.

2645 God's heart is not easily swayed. — *In the Falcon's Claw*, Chet Raymo, 1990.

2646 I'd just bitten the hand that fed me when God called, again. — *Outside the Dog Museum*, Jonathan Carroll, 1991.

2647 Atlas Malone saw the angel again, this time down by the horse chestnut tree. — *The Man in the Window*, Jon Cohen, 1992.

Divorce

2648 They first met in Boston, but the match was made in Europe, where they afterwards saw each other; whither, indeed, he followed her; and there the match was also broken off. — *Their Wedding Journey*, William Dean Howells, 1872.

2649 The litigation had seemed interminable and had in fact been complicated; but by the decision on the appeal the judgement of the divorce-court was confirmed as to the assignment

of the child. — "What Maisie Knew," Henry James, 1897.

2650 "It's perfectly terrible, but it's no more terrible than I knew it would be," said Isabel Bridges. — *Wisdom's Gate*, Margaret Ayer Barnes, 1938.

2651 "He's just a pore lonesome wife-left feller," the more understanding said of Fitz Linkhorn, "losin' his old lady is what crazied him." — *A Walk on the Wild Side*, Nelson Algren, 1956.

2652 Dora Greenfield left her husband because she was afraid of him. — *The Bell*, Iris Murdoch, 1958.

2653 Immediately after her divorce from Zeke Daniels, Anne Duncan Daniels went to Chicago. — *A Brand New Life*, James T. Farrell, 1968.

2654 Within a single hour her absence was opaque. — *Echoes of Celandine*, Derek Marlowe, 1970.

2655 The point at which it all starts is when Deirdre walked — or rather ran — out of my house. — *The Queen of a Distant Country*, John Braine, 1972.

2656 What I'm doing in this car flying down these screaming highways is getting my tail to Juarez so I can legally rid myself of a crummy son-of-a-bitch who promised me a tomorrow like a yummy fruitcake and delivered instead wilted lettuce, rotted cucumber, a garbage of a life. — *Long Division*, Anne Roiphe, 1972.

2657 I left Claude, the French rat. — *After Claude*, Iris Owens, 1973.

2658 Ursula is leaving. Dressed in her severe gray suit, her gardening hat, her girdle, her negligee, her sullen silk dress, her black blouse, her stockings, her red pumps, and carrying a carefully packed straw suitcase in either hand, thus she is leaving me. — *Death, Sleep & the Traveler*, John Hawkes, 1974.

2659 *Today, Tuesday, the day that Penelope has chosen to leave her husband, is the first really warm day of spring.* — *Afternoon of a Good Woman*, Nina Bawden, 1976.

2660 One night last September my brother phoned from San Elmo to report that Mama and Papa were again talking about divorce. — *The Brotherhood of the Grape*, John Fante, 1977.

2661 I left my husband on Thanksgiving Day. — *How to Save Your Own Life*, Erica Jong, 1977.

2662 The marriage wasn't going well and I decided to leave my husband. — *Earthly Possessions*, Anne Tyler, 1977.

2663 Before James told his wife that he was leaving her, he took her out to dinner. — *Familiar Passions*, Nina Bawden, 1979.

2664 My wife Norma had run off with Guy Dupree and I was waiting around for the credit card billings to come in so I could see where they had gone. — *The Dog of the South*, Charles Portis, 1979.

2665 "Do you really want to know why we were divorced? . . ." — *Living Alone*, John Givens, 1981.

2666 It's divorce that did it, his father had said last night. — *Voices from the Moon*, Andre Dubus, 1984.

2667 My father left my mother when I was twelve and went back to London. — *Low Tide*, Fernanda Eberstadt, 1985.

2668 It would be a breeze leaving Judd. — *Walking After Midnight*, Maureen McCoy, 1985.

2669 I waited and waited and waited for Rambeau to leave me. — *Available Light*, Ellen Currie, 1986.

2670 When Claire's husband left her and their daughter, she was twenty-five years old and Molly was three. — "Molly," Andre Dubus, 1986.

2671 "I have never understood," Emily Brandt said, "why people who couldn't get along in marriage expect to become the best of friends during divorce." — *Conjugal Rites*, Ellen Feldman, 1986.

2672 When Carla's marriage broke up, everyone from her father's branch of the family felt obliged to load her with so much pity and advice that she didn't think she'd be able to last out the summer with them. — "Inheritance," Rachel Ingalls, 1986.

2673 On parting with Edmund, Poppy Carew sank into a state of mind where physical need and emotion ceased as though she had been pole-axed. — *The Vacillations of Poppy Carew*, Mary Wesley, 1986.

2674 I suppose it all began three years ago when Jack left me. — *Pause Between Acts*, Mavis Cheek, 1988.

2675 One night in August, understanding all at once why I'd been so sad, I decided to leave Howard. — *Silver*, Hilma Wolitzer, 1988.

2676 Long after my husband left me, I still thought about him. — *The Chinchilla Farm*, Judith Freeman, 1989.

2677 "He waited until the kids were in bed one night, and then he said: 'Becky, I'm leaving you. I'm in love with another woman and I'm moving in with her.' And Becky says not but one night before they were walking by the creek together, watching the stars in the heavens and holding hands in the cold. So when he said he was leaving her, she ran into the downstairs bathroom and upchucked. It was that much of a shock. She just threw up." — *How I Got Him Back*, Valerie Sayers, 1989.

2678 Joe McKay got what he wanted for his sixtieth birthday in April, a request for a divorce

from the lady he had dumbass married five years earlier. — *Old Soldier*, Vance Bourjaily, 1990.

2679 One of the things that I had *not* considered in the traumatic change from family status to single parenthood was dogs. — *Dog Days*, Mavis Cheek, 1990.

2680 If she should return now, of course, or even five minutes from now, it would still be all right. — *Into the Blue*, Robert Goddard, 1990.

2681 In the bicentennial year of our country's independence from Great Britain, a time when I imagined the American masses celebrative and awash with a sense of history and continuity, my wife of only four years decided it would be best for both of us if she moved in with her mother for a while — a trial separation, she said, though we both were so immediately relieved by the *idea* of parting, the real thing was bound to endure. — *The Music Room*, Dennis McFarland, 1990.

2682 Josh, Shira's ex-husband, sat immediately in front of her in the Hall of Domestic Justice as they faced the view screen, awaiting the verdict on the custody of Ari, their son. — *He, She and It*, Marge Piercy, 1991.

2683 My Darling,/ I have to leave you tonight, and it could be for good if fate says *Quit*. — *Blue Calhoun*, Reynolds Price, 1992.

2684 After his wife stole the gangster's money and split on him, she wanted to rub his nose in her deed, so she sent him a note. — *The Ones You Do*, Daniel Woodrell, 1992.

2685 "All I can say," Schiff told Claire, "is you've got a hell of a sense of timing, a *hell* of a sense of timing. You've got a sense of timing on you like last year's calendar." — "Her Sense of Timing," Stanley Elkin, 1993.

Doors and Windows

2686 It was the sort of window which was common in Paris about the end of the seventeenth century. It was high, mullioned, with a broad transom across the centre, and above the middle of the transom a tiny coat of arms — three caltrops gules upon a field argent — let into the diamond-paned glass. — *The Refugees*, Arthur Conan Doyle, 1893.

2687 "Whas the mather with the latch!" — *The Traitor*, Thomas Dixon, Jr., 1907.

2688 The one opened the door with a latchkey and went in, followed by a young fellow who awkwardly removed his cap. — *Martin Eden*, Jack London, 1909.

2689 There was a certain window between the kitchen and the pantry that was Hamlet's

favourite. — *Jeremy and Hamlet*, Hugh Walpole, 1923.

2690 For a full minute Jiggs stood before the window in a light spatter of last night's confetti lying against the windowbase like spent dirty foam, lightpoised on the balls of his greasestained tennis shoes, looking at the boots. — *Pylon*, William Faulkner, 1935.

2691 The cottage door stood open, as it did all summer, and most of the spring when the sun was warm. — *Flowers on the Grass*, Monica Dickens, 1945.

2692 From my desk I can look out through the old bubbly glass panes in the window. — *Still meadow Seasons*, Gladys Taber, 1950.

2693 Old Lanscombe moved totteringly from room to room, pulling up the blinds. Now and then he peered with screwed up rheumy eyes through the windows. — *Funerals Are Fatal*, Agatha Christie, 1953.

2694 At a touch, silently, the door swung open. — *The Day the Money Stopped*, Brendan Gill, 1957.

2695 Mrs. Harley sat at the open window of her bedroom at Hardpan Farm, in a flood of morning sunshine. — *Heaven and Hardpan Farm*, Nancy Hale, 1957.

2696 Come to the window. The one at the rear of the Lone Tree Hotel. — *Ceremony in Lone Tree*, Wright Morris, 1960.

2697 It was a good shop. Even without looking in the windows, one could tell by the door. It was all glass with a copper handle shaped like a boomerang, and as I pushed it open it made a very polite squeak, like a fat rich woman being pinched and liking it. — *House of Hope*, Lynne Reid Banks, 1962.

2698 I pressed the door gently. — *The Italian Girl*, Iris Murdoch, 1964.

2699 Sir George stared for a moment or two at his tall windows overlooking Russell Square. — *Sir Michael and Sir George*, J. B. Priestley, 1964.

2700 Behind the moldy green filing cabinets was a door marked FIRE EXIT, with a red light over it. Nobody ever went out that way, it would have been quite pointless. — *Office Politics*, Wilfrid Sheed, 1966.

2701 Hornblower was expecting the knock on the door, because he had seen through his cabin window enough to guess what was happening outside. — *Hornblower During the Crisis*, C. S. Forester, 1967.

2702 At four o'clock on the afternoon of July 16, 1818, Prill Converse went to the back door of her home in Blue Grass, Ohio. — *Leafy Rivers*, Jessamyn West, 1967.

2703 In front of Martha was grimed glass, its lower part covered with grimed muslin. — *The Four-Gated City*, Doris Lessing, 1969.

2704 It was through the north window that they would see the killers when they came, but Cal had long since moved his chair away from that cracked and dusty square of winter sundown and now sat by the hearth staring through the queer light at his mother. — *The Barefoot Man*, Davis Grubb, 1971.

2705 I get the willies when I see closed doors. —*Something Happened*, Joseph Heller, 1974.

2706 She closed the door behind her, and then it was quite silent, quite dark. — *In the Springtime of the Year*, Susan Hill, 1974.

2707 Elizabeth Khan closed the door of the surgery, and locked it. — *The Inverted World*, Christopher Priest, 1974.

2708 Aku-nna fitted the key into the keyhole, turned it this way and that, pushed open the whitewashed door, then stood there, very still. — *The Bride Price*, Buchi Emecheta, 1976.

2709 Virginia Colar was standing in the kitchen looking out of the window at the rain when she heard the knocking at the front door. —*In My Father's House*, Ernest J. Gaines, 1978.

2710 Chester Simmons sat at the desk that occupied one corner of his embalming room and stared glumly out the window at the growing city of Washington. — *Portrait of a Scoundrel*, Nathaniel Benchley, 1979.

2711 A fellow knows his own door on Princess Street and doesn't examine it before entering. —*Slave Trade*, Herbert Gold, 1979.

2712 Alone in the kitchen while the lives of her children went on around her in the other rooms of the house, Jennifer stood for a moment and looked out the window where the last light of the early autumn day was gathered in the pale streaks of the cloudy sky. — *Jennifer*, David Helwig, 1979.

2713 In her haste to get out, Leah forgot about the catch on the screen door. — *Passing Through*, Guida Jackson, 1979.

2714 Charlie looked toward the door, thinking he could slam it closed behind him just hard enough to tilt the little print hanging beside it, then call her from work later and apologize. — *The Pope of Greenwich Village*, Vincent Patrick, 1979.

2715 There was a square of cardboard in the window where the glass had been smashed. — *Union Street*, Pat Barker, 1982.

2716 The windows of the room looked over Parliament Square. I was the first to arrive for the meeting, so I went and looked through them. —*Scenes from Metropolitan Life*, William Cooper, 1982.

2717 The window means so much to me. — *A Book of Songs*, Merritt Linn, 1982.

2718 From the window all that could be seen was a receding area of grey. — *Hotel du Lac*, Anita Brookner, 1984.

2719 She stands looking out the long window, the toe of her silk slipper hard against the sill. — *The Ladies*, Doris Grumbach, 1984.

2720 As Latchmer took hold of the knob of the front door of the apartment house, the doorman on the other side smartly yanked it open. —*Cold Dog Soup*, Stephen Dobyns, 1985.

2721 Dortmunder opened the door and a distant burglar alarm went CLANG*angangangangang* ... "Hell," Dortmunder said, and shut the door again, but the *angangangang* went on and on and on. — *Good Behavior*, Donald E. Westlake, 1985.

2722 Brian McGuire stood at the classroom window looking out to the sad little clump of trees at the east end of the playground. — *Jeffrey County*, Kathleen Ford, 1986.

2723 Even today, I don't have the faintest idea how long I stood staring in through my living room window at Genie. — *Strange Ailments; Uncertain Cures*, Bruce Goldsmith, 1986.

2724 The back door to the Mohawk Grill opens on an alley it shares with the junior high. —*Mohawk*, Richard Russo, 1986.

2725 The door had been forced. — *Perfect Gallows*, Peter Dickinson, 1988.

2726 Job Turner, a widower, closed the front door behind his daughter and then, wrestling with the catch, immediately jerked it open again. —*Recovery*, Stanley Middleton, 1988.

2727 Come close, so close your breath might fog the blue-moon window on the black door, shining like patent leather in the afternoon sun. — *The Bar Stories*, Nisa Donnelly, 1989.

2728 At six o'clock that evening, Laura stood up from her desk and walked to the window. —*Remember This*, Dinitia Smith, 1989.

2729 A door slammed shut at the back of the house. —*Even Now*, Michelle Latiolais, 1990.

2730 From her window she could see the beach below, but to reach it seemed impossible, as if the sea and sand and rocks were part of a picture postcard. — *News from a Foreign Country Came*, Alberto Manguel, 1991.

2731 Delicate features distinguished the brown faces of the carved angels sounding trumpets from the opulent baroque doorway of the royal palace in the City of Mexico. — *The Rag Doll Plagues*, Alejandro Morales, 1992.

Doubt

2732 "I can never bring myself to believe it, John," said Mary Walker, the pretty daughter of

Mr. George Walker, attorney, of Silverbridge. — *The Last Chronicle of Barset*, Anthony Trollope, 1867.

2733 Such previous landings of mermaids as have left a record, have all a flavour of doubt. — *The Sea Lady*, H. G. Wells, 1902.

2734 Because it all seems so improbable — so horribly impossible to me now, sitting here safe and sane in my own library — I hesitate to record an episode which already appears to me less horrible than grotesque. Yet, unless this story is written now, I know I shall never have the courage to tell the truth about the matter — not from fear of ridicule, but because I myself shall soon cease to credit what I now know to be true. — *In Search of the Unknown*, Robert W. Chambers, 1904.

2735 I would never believe that my father had run away with the money. — *The Lady*, Conrad Richter, 1957.

2736 Arthur Bulow's disenchantment took shape so that he was aware of it as the dispelling of a doubt about a doubt — in a quarter where he did not reckon to have any. — "A Likely Story," A. L. Barker, 1963.

2737 You won't believe it. But I wish you would. For what is written about me in these pages did, God help me, happen. — *A Most Private Intrigue*, Leo Rosten, 1967.

2738 "I hope we've done right," Clara Tilney said. From her, this was an unusual remark — she seldom doubted her actions, nor expected her husband to share the responsibility when she did — but the occasion was exceptional. — *The Birds on the Trees*, Nina Bawden, 1970.

2739 "Credible?" he asked, swivelling his dark glasses round on the chair where he had supposed Neilsen to be sitting. — *The Acolyte*, Thea Astley, 1972.

2740 When in doubt, Karl Glogauer would always return to Derry and Toms. — *Breakfast in the Ruins*, Michael Moorcock, 1972.

2741 I have learned to mistrust symmetry and the decimal system. — *Memoirs of an Ex-Prom Queen*, Alix Kates Shulman, 1972.

2742 Don't believe everything you hear. — *Witnesses*, Marcy Heidish, 1980.

2743 *Never believe anything anyone promises you at The Four Seasons.* — *Getting Together*, Toby Stein, 1980.

2744 Already there are many who find our voyage hard to believe. — *Surviving the Flood*, Steven Minot, 1981.

2745 "I don't believe it, of course," said Golan Trevize, standing on the wide steps of Sedon Hall and looking out over the city as it sparkled in the sunlight. — *Foundation's Edge*, Isaac Asimov, 1982.

2746 She is almost beginning to believe him.

— *A Bigamist's Daughter*, Alice McDermott, 1982.

2747 Stephen couldn't believe it. — *A Moment in the Sun*, Ann Pinchot, 1984.

2748 Virginia says: "I simply can't *believe* it." — *Shake Down the Stars*, Frances Donnelly, 1988.

2749 I'm like, I don't believe this shit. — *Story of My Life*, Jay McInerney, 1988.

2750 I can't believe I'm doing this. — *Show Business*, Shashi Tharoor, 1992.

Dreams

2751 As I walk'd through the wilderness of this world, I lighted on a certain place where there was a Den, and laid me down in that place to sleep; and as I slept I dreamed a Dream. I Dreamed, and behold I saw a man clothed with Rags, standing in a certain place, with his face from his own house, a Book in his hand, and a great Burden upon his back. I looked, and saw him open the Book, and read therein; and as he read, he wept and trembled; and not being able longer to contain, he brake out with a lamentable cry, saying, What shall I do? — *The Pilgrim's Progress*, John Bunyan, 1678.

2752 He wakened from a charming dream, in which the hat had played a conspicuous part. — *Hugo*, Arnold Bennett, 1906.

2753 Pictures! Pictures! Pictures! Often, before I learned, did I wonder whence came the multitudes of pictures that thronged my dreams; for they were pictures the like of which I had never seen in real wake-a-day life. — *Before Adam*, Jack London, 1906.

2754 Edward Darnell awoke from a dream of an ancient wood, and of a clear well rising into grey film and vapour beneath a misty, glimmering heat; and as his eyes opened he saw the sunlight bright in the room, sparkling on the varnish of the new furniture. — *A Fragment of Life*, Arthur Machen, 1906.

2755 Last night I dreamt I went to Manderley again. — *Rebecca*, Daphne du Maurier, 1938.

2756 June morning sunshine brightening hotly on the lowered window shades of Mrs. Little's bedroom woke her from a dream that she was still beautiful Wilma Filmer, unmarried and being chased by a Russian choir. — *The Fighting Littles*, Booth Tarkington, 1941.

2757 Mrs. Bantry was dreaming. Her sweet peas had just taken a First at the flower show. The vicar, dressed in cassock and surplice, was giving out the prizes in church. His wife wandered past, dressed in a bathing suit, but, as is the blessed habit of dreams, this fact did not

arouse the disapproval of the parish in the way it would assuredly have done in real life. Mrs. Bantry was enjoying her dream a good deal. — *The Body in the Library*, Agatha Christie, 1942.

2758 Roma Smith, known to the entertainment profession as Romelle LaRue, was lying in the rickety wall-bed of a cheap one-room bachelor apartment just off Vine Street — dreaming. — *Romelle*, W. R. Burnett, 1946.

2759 *You stirred in your sleep tonight, and said: —/ "Wait! Where are the . . ."/ A loud clear word, and a fragment of a question fading with the uneasy breath of a dream. From the seat you helped me build around the trunk of the big maple, I listened: you did not speak again.* — *House Above the River*, Michael Foster, 1946.

2760 In my dreams I was reaching right through the glass of the window of a hockshop. — *The Fabulous Clipjoint*, Frederic Brown, 1948.

2761 In this dream Mr. Ormsby stood in the room — at the edge of the room where the floor was bare — and gazed at the figure that seemed to hover over the yard. — *Man and Boy*, Wright Morris, 1951.

2762 The third day he awoke in some confusion after a dream about the Prison. — *Eight Days*, Gabriel Fielding, 1958.

2763 No live organism can continue for long to exist sanely under conditions of absolute reality; even larks and katydids are supposed, by some, to dream. — *The Haunting of Hill House*, Shirley Jackson, 1959.

2764 No matter how hard he squinted his eyes and craned his neck, he could not see the top of the steps. But somebody was calling and he had to go up. — *Lawd Today!*, Richard Wright, 1963.

2765 "Milo. Son?" Emma Mustian spoke from the foot of the steps for the third time that morning, still not raising her voice, trusting her natural power to wake him. But it had not and did not. It was Saturday, no school and Milo was dreaming, and because he so rarely dreamed — waking or sleeping — he clung to it now, her his dream, like money smuggled into his head, chest, hips and abandoned there, sudden and perilous. — *A Generous Man*, Reynolds Price, 1966.

2766 Again Bailey dreamed, just before opening his eyes, of an essential oil that when massaged on eyelids became the quicksilver of the brain. — *The Ink Truck*, William Kennedy, 1969.

2767 In the little death of sleep it was a marvelous dream and did not, as so many of his dreams, turn to mockery or abasement of spirit. — *Pedlock Saint, Pedlock Sinner*, Stephen Longstreet, 1969.

2768 A nightmare is terrifying because it can never be undone. — *Nine Months in the Life of an Old Maid*, Judith Rossner, 1969.

2769 Nicola was dreaming. She was alone by the sea and before her stretched miles of empty sands. — *The Devil on Lammas Night*, Susan Howatch, 1970.

2770 "I dreamed about fish last night, Francie," Mrs. Mackey said, sliding back the chain and opening the door to admit me. — *Daddy Was a Number Runner*, Louise Meriwether, 1970.

2771 Often, in the long-ago summer, he had lain wanting only to daydream. But when he sought sleep without dreams, Poppa intruded again. — *The Wintering*, Joan Williams, 1971.

2772 Billy Bowan was dreaming of soft-bodied women with ivory skin and fine dark hair, when the sun cracked the day open and hit him in the eye. — *The Man Who Loved Cat Dancing*, Marilyn Durham, 1972.

2773 One morning in late March, a Friday, Freddy Landon awakened from a dream about his daughter. It was a weird dream in which he watched helplessly while his daughter and a young man named Ralph Chamberlain set fire to his apartment building. They were both naked as babes and they laughed wildly as he roasted in the flames. — *In the Middle of a Life*, Richard B. Wright, 1973.

2774 It had all begun like a dream. You know, that sort of dream which seems to have originated from nowhere, yet one was always aware of its existence. — *Second-Class Citizen*, Buchi Emecheta, 1974.

2775 April 15 Dreaming. Dreamt I was dreaming. — *Celebration*, Harvey Swados, 1975.

2776 That final year of my life, I often dreamed of Evangeline in her attic room, asleep in her high wind-rocked moon-haunted bed, in that rotting farmhouse on the river: my teeth grinding as hers did, my voice guttural and sleep-stricken. — *Childwold*, Joyce Carol Oates, 1976.

2777 Last night I dreamt of Caroline again. — *Caroline, Caroline*, Margaret Ritter, 1976.

2778 In his dream he could see the sun and feel its heat on his face. — *War Story*, Gordon McGill, 1979.

2779 His dream is incomplete, and he knows this even as he loses it. — *Stillness*, Nicholas Delbanco, 1980.

2780 Many people dream of country cottages. — *Puffball*, Fay Weldon, 1980.

2781 Somewhere on the frontier between darkness and light, I was detained by a dream. — *The Marriage Bed*, Constance Beresford-Howe, 1981.

2782 Solomon awake now, but breath still coming rapidly, that dream again, familiar, the glittery underwater light, something awful coming toward him, what is it? — *Solomon's Daughter*, C. E. Poverman, 1981.

2783 Last night, Karen Wendell had a dream about God. — *Expensive Habits*, Robin Vigfusson, 1981.

2784 She had been dreaming of men screaming and dying with open, untended wounds when the pounding sounded at the door and awakened her and she realized she was cold. — *Eden Rising*, Marilyn Harris, 1982.

2785 He was having a pleasant dream when the bedroom telephone extension awoke him. — *Acceptable Losses*, Irwin Shaw, 1982.

2786 Galloping for all she might in the last quarter of our benighted century, Lady Corfe of Northumberland said mutely in her sleep at five in the morning, "We're not in *Northumberland*, we're being hauled to London. They're moving the house and all of us in it." — *Mortal Matters*, Penelope Gilliatt, 1983.

2787 In his dream, Paul Christopher, thirteen years old, wore a thick woolen sweater with three bone buttons on the left shoulder. — *The Last Supper*, Charles McCarry, 1983.

2788 Hey Bruh./ Hey man./ What you thinking, man?/ I had this dream. This real bad dream. — *Sent for You Yesterday*, John Edgar Wideman, 1983.

2789 He had seen the dream many times before. — *Sam Bass*, Bryan Woolley, 1983.

2790 An hour and a half earlier, in total darkness, the crowing of roosters had raked the dreams of the sleeping and shouted down all the lesser choruses of the night, until, when the roosters ceased at last, every creature was subdued and hushed, and the night was mute and black as ether between the stars. — *Toots in Solitude*, John Yount, 1984.

2791 Last night I dreamed of Ursula DeVane. — *The Finishing School*, Gail Godwin, 1985.

2792 "I had a disagreeable dream," the old man said. — *Paradise Postponed*, John Mortimer, 1985.

2793 After the women had gone Simon began dreaming with new intensity. — *Paradise*, Donald Barthelme, 1986.

2794 Nadia was flying home to Leningrad. Drowsy, she was dreaming that Alexander Pushkin was beside her, they were in a troika heading for the sacred early Christian city of Kitezh. The poet was trying successfully to seduce her. — *Summit*, D. M. Thomas, 1987.

2795 I dreamed about Alma Crescent last night, Marius, a tribute from my fantasy to the shock of seeing you after all this time. — *Revisiting Empty Houses*, Una Flett, 1988.

2796 *Sometimes in my dreams you rise up as if from a swamp, whole, younger than I remember, dazzling, jagged, and I follow you into smoky rooms, overwhelmed by the sense of being in the presence of an untamed thing, full of light, impossible to control.* — *Velocity*, Kristin McCloy, 1988.

2797 I, William Stewart, or you might spell that Stuart, if you wish, lay dreaming in the heather. — *Running West*, James Houston, 1989.

2798 The night before we learned of the drowning, I dreamed that Billy couldn't breathe. — *The Waterline*, Joseph Olshan, 1989.

2799 The dreams stood around her cot again, the golems, the dybbuks, grotesque gargoyles waiting for her to sleep, so that they could gorge themselves on the flesh of her heart, the blood of her veins. — *Our Choice of Gods*, Richard Parrish, 1989.

2800 Sometimes I still dreamed of him, but in my daily life I rarely thought of Cary anymore. — *Early from the Dance*, David Payne, 1989.

2801 An old man lay asleep in his bed. This was his dream: — *Homesick*, Guy Vanderhaeghe, 1989.

2802 Nothing of the dream remained. — *The Gates of Paradise*, Gwyneth Cravens, 1990.

2803 Worry furrows creased Cahuom Chhuon's forehead. He was trapped, held in an amorphous iridescent blue, almost black, dream. — *For the Sake of All Living Things*, John M. Del Vecchio, 1990.

2804 The Doctor woke up afraid. He had been dreaming of the old house in New Orleans again. He had seen the woman in the rocker. He'd seen the man with the brown eyes. — *The Witching Hour*, Anne Rice, 1990.

2805 Eve had thought about Donald Furey at supper and into the final evening hours aboard ship, until he entered her dreams that night: He was walking through a deep exhibition hall, surrounded by student work, picking up a plate here, a vase there, stooping before a black sculptured amphora as heavy as stone. — *The Clay That Breathes*, Catherine Browder, 1991.

2806 Jacob Balthus dreamed again of the Café Stieckus. — *The Good Republic*, William Palmer, 1991.

2807 The first time Nathan had the dream, he was staying at his aunt's house on the Cape. — *The Five Gates of Hell*, Rupert Thompson, 1991.

2808 A daydream: Bud Wiggins was awash in clay. — *Force Majeure*, Bruce Wagner, 1991.

2809 The coldness crept upon Morgana, as did the man in her dream. — *Heartbeat Drumbeat*, Irene Beltrán Hernández, 1992.

2810 Ike Sallas was asleep when it began, in a red aluminum Galaxxy, not all that far away and only a short skip into the future. — *Sailor Song*, Ken Kesey, 1992.

2811 When the ringing cut into his dream, Danny was walking down a bombed-out block in what looked like some war-torn, Middle Eastern capital. — *The Blue Streak*, Ellen Lesser, 1992.

2812 When I see her, I know her from my

dreams. — *Dreams of Long Lasting*, Mark Medoff, 1992.

2813 It was a nightmare. But Lauren Wagner did not know that. It's often that way with bad dreams. — *The Season of Passage*, Christopher Pike, 1992.

2814 Lily wakes, as she always does, at five. The dream she was having evaporates, leaving a salt trace of anxiety, a feeling that something must be done. — *Easy Keeper*, Mary Tannen, 1992.

2815 "Ten thousand dreams a night," a Dallas psychologist told me, when I dined with her and her black lover, "are dreamt about Kennedy's assassination." — *Flying in to Love*, D. M. Thomas, 1992.

2816 I sleep with Connie whenever I want to dream. Put more precisely, I sleep with Connie whenever I want to remember my dreams. — *The House of Real Love*, Carla Tomaso, 1992.

2817 In the beginning was the nightmare, and the knife was with Saint Paul, and the circumcision was a Jewish notion and definitely not mine. — *Live from Golgotha*, Gore Vidal, 1992.

2818 My dreams still take place here, most of them, half of them, over half. — "Doing and Undoing," Jonathan Strong, 1993.

Dress

2819 It was not a *very* white jacket, but white enough, in all conscience, as the sequel will show. — *White-Jacket*, Herman Melville, 1850.

2820 "I don't say but what he's difficult to please with his Tops," said Mr. Rake, factotum to the Hon. Bertie Cecil, of the First Life Guards, with that article of hunting toggery suspended in his right hand as he paused, before going up stairs, to deliver his opinions with characteristic weight and vivacity to the studgroom, "he is uncommon particular about 'em; and if his leathers ain't as white as snow, he'll never touch 'em, tho' as soon as the pack come nigh him at Royallieu, the leathers might just as well never have been cleaned, them hounds jump about him so; old Champion's at his saddle before you can say Davy Jones. . . ." — *Under Two Flags*, Ouida, 1867.

2821 "Tak your hat, Louie! Yo're allus leavin summat behind yer." — *The History of David Grieve*, Mary Augusta Ward *as* Mrs. Humphry Ward, 1892.

2822 A shrunken sallow old lady, dressed in rusty ill-shaped black and adorned with an evidently false "front" of fair hair, sat in a tiny flat whose windows overlooked Hyde Park from south to north. — *Quisanté*, Anthony Hope, 1900.

2823 At 6:30 in our Paris apartment I had finished the Honourable George, performing those final touches that make the difference between a man well turned out and a man merely dressed. — *Ruggles of Red Gap*, Harry Leon Wilson, 1915.

2824 It has occurred to the writer to call this unimportant history The Green Hat because a green hat was the first thing about her that he saw: as also it was, in a way, the last thing about her that he saw. — *The Green Hat*, Michael Arlen, 1924.

2825 Fifty-five. Tallish — but stoutish. Dressed like the country gentleman which he was not and never would be. — *Lord Raingo*, Arnold Bennett, 1926.

2826 The first morning I ever saw her she wore a shell-pink organdie gown, a white flowered scarf across her breast, cross-strapped slippers of a rose colour, and a gauze cap; and she carried a market basket tied with rosy ribbons. — *The Happy Parrot*, Robert W. Chambers, 1929.

2827 Studs Lonigan, on the verge of fifteen, and wearing his first suit of long trousers, stood in the bathroom with a Sweet Caporal pasted in his mug. — *Young Lonigan*, James T. Farrell, 1932.

2828 Once I was sitting on a bench in Boston Common and a crazy man came down the path from that Civil War memorial. He was an old man about fifty or sixty and the lapels of his coat were covered with celluloid buttons that said, "O, You Kid," "Keep Cool With Coolidge," "Cow Brand Soda," "The Jolly Chums Club," and things like that. — *The Anointed*, Clyde Brion Davis, 1937.

2829 At the ten-second warning to the evening's first preliminary, a newspaperman on the apron of the ring stood up to get his slicker off. — *Never Come Morning*, Nelson Algren, 1942.

2830 Twenty-four black silk stockings all in a row! — *The Horn of Life*, Gertrude Atherton, 1942.

2831 He stood at the window in a long flannel nightgown, brushing his suit carefully so that the dust would fly into the open air of Wabash Street. — *Adversary in the House*, Irving Stone, 1947.

2832 In her tight-fitting Persian dress, with turban to match, she looked ravishing. — *Plexus*, Henry Miller, 1953.

2833 Peter McKenzie stripped off his faded shorts and his green drill shirt and reached for a bowl of ocher mud which had been softened to a pliant paste with water. He smeared the mud over his face, neck, and shoulders, until his sun-

burned skin was dyed a deep coppery red. — *Something of Value*, Robert Ruark, 1955.

2834 Young Patrick Dennis Moore wore the tightest pants in all of County Kilkenny. — *Maggie-Now*, Betty Smith, 1958.

2835 They were number X-362 in the Monkey-Ward catalogue, genuine cowhide, prime leather, expertly tanned, made to our specifications, on our special last, ten inches high, brass eyelets, top strap with brass buckle, worn and admired by sportsmen everywhere, size 9½ B — which is not a big foot or a little one, for a man. But the man was not there. — *The Cave*, Robert Penn Warren, 1959.

2836 In Los Angeles, Mrs. Sylvester Perkins was dressing. — *South of the Angels*, Jessamyn West, 1960.

2837 I went out in the woods to a fallen-down sycamore I knew and reached in a hollow place and pulled out Uncle Jim's costume for the Ku Klux Klan. It didn't amount to much for such an almighty secret and desperate society; even a boy could see that. — *A Journey to Matecumbe*, Robert Lewis Taylor, 1961.

2838 Afterwards, when he looked at the photographs, he noticed that his morning coat was getting tight. — *The Great Occasion*, Isabel Colegate, 1962.

2839 Christmas Eve, 1955, Benny Profane, wearing black levis, suede jacket, sneakers and big cowboy hat, happened to pass through Norfolk, Virginia. — *V.*, Thomas Pynchon, 1963.

2840 Ted laid out the suit on his bed. The trousers were creased, in spite of the new plastic coat hangers that were supposed to make sure they remained in the rigid folds he arranged with such loving care. — *Georgy Girl*, Margaret Forster, 1965.

2841 When, at the start of the whole business, I bought an army greatcoat, it was at one of those places in the neighbourhood of Shaftesbury Avenue, where, as well as officers' kit and oufits for sport, they hire or sell theatrical costume. — *The Soldier's Art*, Anthony Powell, 1966.

2842 He left the carriage, ascended the short flight of steps and walked briskly past the dozing porter sitting in the deep shade of the portico; a small, neat man, in dark, well-cut clothes and glossy topper. — *Long Summer Day*, R. F. Delderfield, 1967.

2843 Here he is. In the doorway, going to his first interview with Leonard. Badly dressed. — *Orlando King*, Isabel Colegate, 1968.

2844 "Look!"/ "It's beautiful."/ Frances Garland touched the bracelet, made in the shape of two linked serpents, with her pointed fingers. — *Angels Falling*, Janice Elliott, 1969.

2845 "And the material doesn't stain," the salesgirl says. — *The Driver's Seat*, Muriel Spark, 1970.

2846 On a lovely late-March evening she strolled along Park Avenue wearing a palomino mink car coat and a beaded bag which a beautiful man (who turned out to have acne on his back) had given her in Paris when her husband had been alive. — *The Vertical Smile*, Richard Condon, 1971.

2847 Kathy sat in the old Westland helicopter watching MacGregor struggling with the greasy, padded flying suit. — *Mockery in Arms*, James Aldridge, 1974.

2848 Amato in a gray suit with a muted red stripe, textured pink shirt with his initials on the left French cuff, a maroon and gold tie, sat at the kidney-shaped, walnut veneer desk and stared. — *Cogan's Trade*, George V. Higgins, 1974.

2849 I am wearing pink today and it doesn't suit me. — *The Mandrake Root*, Joy Cowley, 1975.

2850 "A sombrero fell out of the sky and landed on the Main Street of town in front of the mayor, his cousin and a person out of work." — *Sombrero Fallout*, Richard Brautigan, 1976.

2851 She felt the snake between her breasts, felt him there, and loved him there, coiled, the deep tumescent S held rigid, ready to strike. She loved the way the snake looked sewn onto her V-neck letter sweater, his hard diamondback pattern shining in the sun. — *A Feast of Snakes*, Harry Crews, 1976.

2852 Dressed in slacks, shirt, and sweater, Bubbles Wiggins placed his package of freshly laundered work clothes on the avocado kitchen table. Over the years he'd learned that this was the way to remember them. — *The Junior Bachelor Society*, John A. Williams, 1976.

2853 In her black slip and her fluffy mules, Grooters was ironing a shirt. — *The Chelsea Murders*, Lionel Davidson, 1978.

2854 It was from the Woman taken in the raid on Santa Rosa that Sanjak obtained the amulet he called his Medicine. — *The Kiowa*, Elgin Groseclose, 1978.

2855 Here they are. They're entirely in black, with belted tabards over something like long underwear that make them look like the cards in *Alice*, though nobody here has heard about that. — *The Two of Them*, Joanna Russ, 1978.

2856 Perhaps it was right that Lise should first see the beads as they lay in the dirt and debris of a table outside the cheapest kind of café among the rubbish of the Paris night. — *Five for Sorrow, Ten for Joy*, Rumer Godden, 1979.

2857 I have never seen anything like it: two little discs of glass suspended in front of his eyes in loops of wire. — *Waiting for the Barbarians*, J. M. Coetzee, 1980.

2858 I wear the ring. — *The Lords of Discipline*, Pat Conroy, 1980.

2859 A green hunting cap squeezed the top of the fleshy balloon of a head. The green earflaps, full of large ears and uncut hair and the fine bristles that grew in the ears themselves, stuck out on either side like turn signals indicating two directions at once. — *A Confederacy of Dunces*, John Kennedy Toole, 1980.

2860 "I really don't know what to wear," Andrew said, just before eight o'clock on that Saturday morning. — *Walking Naked*, Nina Bawden, 1981.

2861 Lying in the jeweler's case is my emerald-and-diamond ring. — *Something for Nothing*, Kathryn Kilgore, 1981.

2862 Darconville, the schoolmaster, always wore black. — *Darconville's Cat*, Alexander Theroux, 1981.

2863 It was always worse for Reba on a Saturday night, because that was the night when she and Billy Fain would get dressed up in the new clothes she had bought with her insurance money, he in his satin-lapel tuxedo, she in one of her chiffon gowns. — *Summer Dreams and the Kleig Light Gas Company*, Cynthia Applewhite, 1982.

2864 The dress she would wear was blue, sewn by the same dressmaker who had made her mother's, and her underclothes were white, bought in the same fine store on Fifth Avenue where her mother had bought hers. — *Family Ties*, Syrell Rogovin Leahy, 1982.

2865 The austere, antique civility preserved in Edgar's London tailor's rooms made a new suit seem more like a dignified responsibility than an indulgence. — *The Charlatan*, William Hamilton, 1985.

2866 So Biddy Hogan did, after all, wear vests. — *The Hottentot Room*, Christopher Hope, 1986.

2867 That day Margaret Hollander saw two people dressed as chickens on Manhattan's Ninety-first Street. — *Portrait of a Married Woman*, Sally Mandel, 1986.

2868 "What jewels will you be wearing tonight, Mother?" — *An Academic Question*, Barbara Pym, 1986.

2869 When Grady Durant's husband, Andy, was killed holding up a gas station, he was wearing a mask made from the stockings Grady bought to go with the black dress she wore when she sang in the Christmas Cantata at Holy Apostles Church. — *Under the Dog Star*, Joseph Caldwell, 1987.

2870 From the back of the office I watched my aunt Marie at the counter, waiting on two men dressed like women. — *On Other Days While Going Home*, Michelle Carter, 1987.

2871 "David Crimond is here in a *kilt!*" — *The Book and the Brotherhood*, Iris Murdoch, 1987.

2872 As recently as two years ago, when I was twenty-six, I dressed in ratty jeans and a sweatshirt with lettering across the chest. That's where I was. — *Swann*, Carol Shields, 1987.

2873 It took eight tries to put my pants on. — *A Short Dance in the Sun*, George Benet, 1988.

2874 From where he sat on a low stool, the boy — whose name was Eugene Talmadge Biggs, but who was often called Knockout or K.O. or Knocker — had counted the suits hanging in the open closet three times. — *The Knockout Artist*, Harry Crews, 1988.

2875 She usually wore tight blue jeans low on her hips, frayed tennis shoes, and a stethoscope around her neck, its listening end tucked into a pocket of her loose khaki shirt. — *Three Hunters*, William Harrison, 1989.

2876 Wally's arms were folded over his chest in a straight jacket. He wore nothing else except a towel in his mouth. — *Escape from Dade City*, Rippeth Merington, 1989.

2877 "I told you already. It says: 'Take a bow.' See the girl in the picture? Doesn't she have a nice dress? See what it says: 'Be nice.'..." — *Ordinary Time*, A. G. Mojtabai, 1989.

2878 My mother, Gertie Neelan, wore a hunting costume. — *The Port of Missing Men*, Mary-Ann Tirone Smith, 1989.

2879 B.J. McGrath stood in her postage-stamp bathroom, pressed between the sink and a rack crowded with her roommate's designer towels, touching up her makeup. — *Wonkers*, Layne Littlepage, 1990.

2880 Maggie Hatch's printed skirt had a raspberry stain. — *Well and Truly*, Evelyn Wilde Mayerson, 1990.

2881 We all wore bras in 1954. — *Is This What Other Women Feel Too?*, June Akers Seese, 1991.

2882 "What are you wearing?" he asked. — *Vox*, Nicholson Baker, 1992.

2883 It is a Sunday morning in July. The year is 1943. Hoyt is dressing up. Not in this room, where trees reach in the windows. In other rooms. — *Living Upstairs*, Joseph Hansen, 1993.

2884 As the taxi cuts through the rain, Ann struggles out of her black skirt, keeping her eyes on the driver as she hurries to free the heel of her black satin pump. — *Exposure*, Kathryn Harrison, 1993.

Drink

2885 "What! no music, no dancing at Castle Hermitage to-night; and all the ladies sitting in

a formal circle, petrifying into perfect statues?" cried Sir Ulick O'Shane as he entered the drawing-room, between ten and eleven o'clock at night, accompanied by what he called his *rearguard*, veterans of the old school of good fellows, who at those times in Ireland—times long since past—deemed it essential to health, happiness, and manly character, to swallow, and show themselves able to stand after swallowing, a certain number of bottles of claret per day or night. —*Ormond*, Maria Edgeworth, 1817.

2886 Late in the afternoon of a chilly day in February, two gentlemen were sitting alone over their wine, in a well-furnished dining-parlor, in the town of P—, in Kentucky. —*Uncle Tom's Cabin*, Harriet Beecher Stowe, 1852.

2887 On the very day when Charles I. was crowned with due rejoicings—Candlemasday, in the year of our Lord 1626—a loyalty, quite as deep and perhaps even more lasting, was having its beer at Ley Manor in the north of Devon. —"Frida," R. D. Blackmore, 1895.

2888 "That's my last dime," said young Redpath, as he deposited the coin with elaborate precision upon the shiny surface of the bar. As the bartender slid the glass and the bottle in front of him, he added, unsteadily: "And this is my last drink."—*Sherry*, George Barr McCutcheon, 1919.

2889 Elmer Gantry was drunk. He was eloquently drunk, lovingly and pugnaciously drunk. —*Elmer Gantry*, Sinclair Lewis, 1927.

2890 From beyond the screen of bushes which surrounded the spring, Popeye watched the man drinking. —*Sanctuary*, William Faulkner, 1931.

2891 Charley Anderson lay in his bunk in a glary red buzz. —*The Big Money*, John Dos Passos, 1936.

2892 What a grand guy. Sometimes he used to sneak a slug of whiskey in the forenoon, against doctor's orders. —*Kitty Foyle*, Christopher Morley, 1939.

2893 There was a bottle of Robinson's B.E.B. right in Lou's bag but Jay Oliver wasn't interested. —*Angels on Toast*, Dawn Powell, 1940.

2894 It would be difficult to overestimate the importance to me of the events which had taken place previous to the hour (it was shortly after ten o'clock in the evening) when I was lying in the marsh near the small pond at the bottom of Gurney's meadow, my face in the mud and the black mud beginning to ooze through the spaces between the fingers of my outstretched hands, drunk, but not blindly so, for I seemed only to have lost the use of my limbs. —*The Aerodrome*, Rex Warner, 1941.

2895 Mr. Jones, of the Manor Farm, had locked the hen-houses for the night, but was too drunk to remember to shut the popholes. —*Ani-*

mal Farm, George Orwell, 1945.

2896 When I came into the story I was having a quiet conversation over a bottle of Old Taylor with my friend Charles the bartender at Mickey Walker's, the place Mickey hasn't got any more at 50th and Eighth Avenue, right across the street from the Garden. —*The Harder They Fall*, Budd Schulberg, 1947.

2897 The captain never drank. —*The Man with the Golden Arm*, Nelson Algren, 1949.

2898 Rose was on the skids again. Everyone in the boarding house knew it. —*Rose's Last Summer*, Margaret Millar, 1952.

2899 The first time I laid eyes on Terry Lennox he was drunk in a Rolls-Royce Silver Wraith outside the terrace of The Dancers. —*The Long Goodbye*, Raymond Chandler, 1954.

2900 Will Gannon sat with his back against the log wall and watched the stage driver get drunk. —*The Whip*, Luke Short, 1957.

2901 The rowdy gang of singers who sat at the scattered tables saw Arthur walk unsteadily to the head of the stairs, and though they must all have known that he was dead drunk, and seen the danger he would soon be in, no one attempted to talk to him and lead him back to his seat. With eleven pints of beer and seven small gins playing hide-and-seek inside his stomach, he fell from the top-most stair to the bottom. —*Saturday Night and Sunday Morning*, Alan Sillitoe, 1958.

2902 The day the revolution started my Aunt Natasha was drunk. —*Sigh for a Strange Land*, Monica Stirling, 1958.

2903 At the Blackhawk railway station, where Janet and I picked Clem up, we found him being helped from the train like an invalid V.I.P. by a porter twice his age. Clem was drunk—"Already," Janet whispered. In that moment of seeing him come back to us like a battered refugee from time, it seemed to me no early indulgence that we were witnessing. "Still," I said. —*Clem Anderson*, R. V. Cassill, 1960.

2904 The Man from Bodie drank down a half bottle of the Silver Sun's best; that cleared the dust from his throat and then when Florence, who was redhead, moved along the bar to him, he turned and grinned down at her. —*Welcome to Hard Times*, E. L. Doctorow, 1960.

2905 David Hillary, still half-stuporous from the bad whisky he had had that morning, stepped slowly into the pawnshop. —*Night Song*, John A. Williams, 1961.

2906 The church is blowing a sad windblown "Kathleen" on the bells in the skid row slums as I wake up all woebegone and goopy, groaning from another drinking bout and groaning most of all because I'd ruined my "secret return" to San Francisco by getting silly drunk while hiding in the alleys with bums and then marching forth

into North Beach to see everybody altho Lorenz Monsanto and I'd exchanged huge letters outlining how I would sneak in quietly, call him on the phone using a code name like Adam Yulch or Lalagy Pulvertaft (also writers) and then he would secretly drive me to his cabin in the Big Sur woods where I would be alone and undisturbed for six weeks just chopping wood, drawing water, writing, sleeping, hiking, etc. etc. — *Big Sur*, Jack Kerouac, 1962.

2907 No matter what, you always feel bad in the morning, anyway. — *The Liberation of Lord Byron Jones*, Jesse Hill Ford, 1965.

2908 Here it was the twenty-eighth of December and he still wasn't sober. In fact, he was drunker than ever. — *Run Man Run*, Chester Himes, 1966.

2909 The policeman was watching him. He let go of the railing and walked as steadily as he could to the unlit turning in the road and waited. When he walked on the policeman followed; he had big boots on: probably a sergeant. — *A Handful of Rice*, Kamala Markandaya, 1966.

2910 Pfffrrrummmp./ And a very happy New Year to you too, Mr. Enderby! — *Inside Mr. Enderby*, Anthony Burgess, 1967.

2911 The day before, Rheinhardt had bought a pint of whiskey in Opelika and saved it all afternoon while the bus coursed down through red clay and pine hills to the Gulf. Then, after sundown, he had opened the bottle and shared it with the boy who sold bibles, the blond gangling country boy in the next seat. — *A Hall of Mirrors*, Robert Stone, 1967.

2912 It was a late afternoon in the middle of May and Max Reddick was sitting in an outdoor cafe on the Leidseplein toying with a Pernod. — *The Man Who Cried I Am*, John A. Williams, 1967.

2913 Waned, I wined and, whining, wound my fingers hundredfold, found hair. — *Grasse 3/23/66*, Nicholas Delbanco, 1968.

2914 Of the three men at the table, all dressed in black business suits, two must have been stone drunk. — *Tunc*, Lawrence Durrell, 1968.

2915 Afterwards she went through into the little front room, the tape measure still dangling about her neck, and allowed herself a glass of port. — *The Secret Glass*, Beryl Bainbridge, 1973.

2916 "The Guernica network!" said Steve Champion, holding up his glass. — *Yesterday's Spy*, Len Deighton, 1975.

2917 He fixed daiquiris for us while I leaned against the open shutter-door and watched. — *All the Time There Is*, Toby Stein, 1977.

2918 When Luke Hardy took to the bottle, everyone understood. — "In the Highlands," Martha Gellhorn, 1978.

2919 There was a young woman sitting in the bar. Her name was Pearl. She was drinking gin and tonics and she held an infant in the crook of her right arm. The infant was two months old and his name was Sam. — *The Changeling*, Joy Williams, 1978.

2920 "It would have been nice," said Earl Keese to himself as much as to the wife who sat across the coffee table from him, "to have asked them over for a drink." — *Neighbors*, Thomas Berger, 1980.

2921 "No, thanks." Vida placed her hand over the top of the tulip-shaped wineglass. "No more for me. Thank you." — *Vida*, Marge Piercy, 1980.

2922 "Good man," said Dalmire, gratefully accepting the gin Morgan Leafy offered him, "Oh, good man." — *A Good Man in Africa*, William Boyd, 1981.

2923 I will call this drink the Flowers of Summer, the Magician says. — *Crystal Vision*, Gilbert Sorrentino, 1981.

2924 Father Egan left off writing, rose from his chair and made his way — a little unsteadily — to the bottle of Flor de Cana which he had placed across the room from his desk. — *A Flag for Sunrise*, Robert Stone, 1981.

2925 Tito Solivan took a pint bottle of whiskey out of the hip pocket of his baggy brown pants, swigged it and then spoke while his lips still glistened with drink. — *Forsaking All Others*, Jimmy Breslin, 1982.

2926 Craddock could remember a time when his hangovers were trivially unpleasant: thick head, loose bowels and a feeling of self-reproach, all of which could be adequately treated with plenty of tap water and a day's abstinence from alcohol. — *Mid-Century Men*, Arthur Hopcraft, 1982.

2927 Miguel Semana lifted a cut crystal glass full of golden brandy to his moustachioed lips. — *Sudden Death*, Rita Mae Brown, 1983.

2928 The room was swaying. Remmnant struggled to his feet. — *A Sound Like Laughter*, David Helwig, 1983.

2929 They had come back from dancing at four o'clock and were still up drinking brandy. — *Dancing in the Dark*, Janet Hobhouse, 1983.

2930 It was the summer before that first big summer of weddings because Adam was in London; and not simply in London this first early summer evening but hesitating before the closed front door of a house in Hans Place and quite drunk. — *A Parish of Rich Women*, James Buchan, 1984.

2931 When Ben Jonson was let out of jail he went straight to William Shakespeare's lodgings in Silver Street and said: "Let us drink." — *Enderby's Dark Lady*, Anthony Burgess, 1984.

2932 It was a cold night, and I was drunk.

—"Land Where My Fathers Died," Andre Dubus, 1986.

2933 Bubble Riley decided to drink all the wine in the world the night Billy cut the soldier's lung in half. — *The Acorn Plan*, Tim McLaurin, 1988.

2934 In early June of 1976, in the weeks after his one daughter and only child, at the age of nineteen, walked out of the house with someone like Cole Gilbertson—undoing, he believed, everything he had tried to accomplish in the years of raising her by himself, and heading with unbelievable placid recklessness toward disaster—James Field began drinking in the evenings just to get himself calm enough to sleep. — *Mr. Field's Daughter*, Richard Bausch, 1989.

2935 The Blackbird told himself he was drinking too much because he lived in this hotel and the Silver Dollar was close by, right downstairs. — *Killshot*, Elmore Leonard, 1989.

2936 The regulars at the Idle Hour Bar & Grill, beer drinkers except for Joe Becker, who preferred stronger stuff and could afford it, and Molly McShane, who always drank sherry wine, were either too old for the service, medically disqualified, or, as in the case of Molly and her pal Gladys, of the wrong sex. — *Orrie's Story*, Thomas Berger, 1990.

2937 Raymond McCreary sits in the belfry sipping Jose Cuervo by the capful. — *Buffalo*, Sydney Blair, 1991.

2938 I was drinking a lot in those days. — *How Boys See Girls*, David Gilmour, 1991.

2939 Alexander Carew put the flask to his mouth and let the last of the brandy trickle over his tongue. — *The Killing Frost*, Thomas Hayden, 1991.

2940 Alice was trying to wriggle through a crowd of people to the drinks table when her way was barred by a broad, green-sweatered back. — *Not in Newbury*, Mary Scott, 1992.

2941 Was it the bourbon or the dye fumes that made the pink walls quiver like vaginal lips? — *Suicide Blonde*, Darcey Steinke, 1992.

2942 *"Watchman, what of the night?!"* It was his tipsy father's inscrutable war cry on leaving a fun party, say, a beaker of martinis under his belt, yet barring his pretty wife from any proximity to the steering wheel. — *City of Light*, Cyrus Colter, 1993.

Driving

2943 A gentleman and a lady travelling from Tunbridge towards that part of the Sussex coast which lies between Hastings and Eastbourne, being induced by business to quit the high road and attempt a very rough lane, were overturned in toiling up its long ascent, half rock, half sand. — *Sanditon*, Jane Austen, 1817.

2944 It was late in the autumn, and I was skimming along, through a rich English county, in a postchaise, among tall hedgerows gilded, like all the landscape, with the slanting beams of sunset. — *Wylder's Hand*, J. Sheridan LeFanu, 1864.

2945 Day was drooping on a fine evening in March as a brown barouche passed through the wrought-iron gates of Hare-Hatch House on to the open highway. — *Valmouth*, Ronald Firbank, 1919.

2946 When the windshield was closed it became so filmed with rain that Claire fancied she was piloting a drowned car in dim spaces under the sea. When it was open, drops jabbed into her eyes and chilled her cheeks. — *Free Air*, Sinclair Lewis, 1919.

2947 Mr. James Sandage, overseer of the county poor farm, jolted monotonously against his steering wheel, against the standards of his car top, against the youth in the seat beside him as he ground along in low gear over the stony rut-lined trail which represented a public road in Lane County, Tennessee, in summer weather. — *Teeftallow*, T. S. Stribling, 1926.

2948 "Will you stop," said William Demarest, leaning his head out of the taxi window, "at the corner drug store?"— *Blue Voyage*, Conrad Aiken, 1927.

2949 Out of a blue wide valley, Dock Hunter, with his young wife sitting by him on a rickety seat, took his slow way up and over dusty foothills, following a gray wagon road, one track of which had once been an old cattle trail; going over round-backed hills and down into arid gullies and across the flat and lonely waste of desert and sagebrush. — *Toilers of the Hills*, Vardis Fisher, 1928.

2950 Old True Baldwin and his daughter Candace were whirling up the brisk little hills and swooping down into the rich green valleys of that spectacular part of Connecticut through which the Still River flows, and the storied Housatonic. —*American Beauty*, Edna Ferber, 1931.

2951 They drove uncertainly along the avenue that led to the house, through the bars of light that fell between the tree-trunks and made the shadows of the lime-trees strike obliquely across the gravel. — *From a View to a Death*, Anthony Powell, 1933.

2952 Driving from Carson to Reno, Lily Tennant saw the sullen banner of dust boil up in the valley and cross the highway like smoke from

a grass fire. — *The Silver Desert*, Ernest Haycox, 1935.

2953 Alice Pemberton had not expected to enjoy the motor-drive home, since because of it, the previous afternoon, she had received a bitter hurt. — "The Salt of the Earth," Rebecca West, 1935.

2954 In a taxi skidding away from the Gare du Nord, one dark greasy February morning before the shutters were down, Henrietta sat beside Miss Fisher. — *The House in Paris*, Elizabeth Bowen, 1936.

2955 In the darkness of the country road after midnight, the car was speeding, but the three young men jammed together in the one seat did not worry. — *The Prodigal Parents*, Sinclair Lewis, 1938.

2956 Early in the twentieth century, when Roy Earle was a happy boy on an Indiana farm, he had no idea that at thirty-seven he'd be a pardoned ex-convict driving alone through the Nevada-California desert towards an ambiguous destiny in the Far West. — *High Sierra*, W. R. Burnett, 1940.

2957 One winter day, in the nineteen-twenties, the physician Peter Rush was driving carefully through a cold sandstorm that was blowing off the mountains, across the mesa, and down upon the town of Albuquerque. — *The Common Heart*, Paul Horgan, 1942.

2958 Lanny Budd's heart was high as he drove northward along the Palisades. — *Presidential Mission*, Upton Sinclair, 1947.

2959 The dark outline of the heavy wagon and its cart trailing a long shadow, the stark silhouette of the two outriders, one behind and one before, passed in slow procession through the bare trees, plodding eastward along the rocky Pennsylvania road between Fort Bedford and Fort Lyttleton. — *Toward the Morning*, Hervey Allen, 1948.

2960 After the death of their elder brother the two Aspen sisters came back to Evensford at the end of February, driving in the enormous brown coachwork Daimler with the gilt monograms on the doors, through a sudden fall of snow. — *Love for Lydia*, H. E. Bates, 1952.

2961 Tim Archer got into the utility and drove it from the Banbury Feed and General Supply Pty. Ltd., down the main street of the town. — *The Far Country*, Nevil Shute, 1952.

2962 I pulled the old Ford into the curb and cut off the motor. — *Roughneck*, Jim Thompson, 1954.

2963 Mrs. Radha Chakravarty and her daughter Amrita sat in a tonga. Two ladies unmoving and passive, yet jerking up and down, backward and forward with grave faces, as the carriage rattled over the street. — *Amrita*, Ruth Prawer Jhabvala, 1956.

2964 Nigel Strangeways turned into Adelphi, and soon arrived at the distinguished backwater of Angel Street, the Strand traffic roaring softly behind him like a weir. — *End of Chapter*, Cecil Day-Lewis *as* Nicholas Blake, 1957.

2965 Alone in the back of his brother-in-law's car, Rigden gave himself up to the pleasure of being driven through a countryside seemingly empty, and so smooth that it gave the impression of being more civilized than a capital city. — *A Cup of Tea for Mr. Thorgill*, Storm Jameson, 1957.

2966 Far away, on the precarious underside of the world, a young woman was driving along the broad federal highway that approached a city. — *The Animal Game*, Frank Tuohy, 1957.

2967 Because Mr. Blankhard believes only in horses, my father had to drive up to the Junction to pick up Rodney, Mr. Blankhard's nephew, from the train. It's about thirty miles from the Hill to the Junction, and this was in June, and nobody in Alabama drives sixty miles in June by horse and buggy any more, even if they got the time, and if that's all they got to drive by. — *The Rain and the Fire and the Will of God*, Donald Wetzel, 1957.

2968 The mine whistles were tooting midnight as I drove down Main Street hill. — *Anatomy of a Murder*, Robert Traver, 1958.

2969 They had left the lowlands and were climbing steadily on the narrow road that wound dangerously round the high flank of the mountain. — *The Second Victory*, Morris West, 1958.

2970 A little after one, Jack Trudel turned his cab into Hillton Road and began to drive slowly down its slope. — *The Pyx*, John Buell, 1959.

2971 All the flags were out in front of the houses and stores in Rainbow Center on Memorial Day, as Boyd Mason drove his Buick back from a real-estate trip to Kentucky, and parked on the east corner of Peninsula Drive and Crest Ridge Road, at the side of his sister Alma's house, where he had lived since his wife's death twenty years before. — *The Nephew*, James Purdy, 1960.

2972 All night and most of the day they had been driving, through mountains, and desert, and now mountains again. The old car was beginning to act skittish, the driver was getting irritable, and Quinn, to escape both, had gone to sleep in the back seat. — *How Like an Angel*, Margaret Millar, 1962.

2973 Just with his body and from inside like a snake, leaning that black motorcycle side to side, cutting in and out of the slow line of cars to get there first, staring due-north through goggles towards Mount Moriah and switching coon tails in everybody's face was Wesley Beavers, and laid

against his back like sleep, spraddle-legged on the sheepskin seat behind him was Rosacoke Mustian who was maybe his girl and who had given up looking into the wind and trying to nod at every sad car in the line, and when he even speeded up and passed the truck (lent for the afternoon by Mr. Isaac Alston and driven by Sammy his man, hauling one pine box and one black boy dressed in all he could borrow, set up in a ladder-back chair with flowers banked round him and a foot on the box to steady it) — when he even passed that, Rosacoke said once into his back "Don't" and rested in humiliation, not thinking but with her hands on his hips for dear life and her white blouse blown out behind her like a banner in defeat. — *A Long and Happy Life*, Reynolds Price, 1962.

2974 He crawled into the car, took off his gloves and gave the ignition a resigned twitch. The radio, still half-alive from the night before, resumed its mumble of vague, weekend music. He slid around the corner and turned off the motor; popped, flipped, aimed a cigarette at his mouth; rolled the window down; wrapped the tails of his overcoat round his knees; yawned. — *The Hack*, Wilfrid Sheed, 1963.

2975 Grundy's hands, large, strong and hairy, rested on the steering wheel. — *The End of Solomon Grundy*, Julian Symons, 1964.

2976 Mrs. Hapgood, a woman noted for her sense of order, drove aimlessly through the Loire valley. — "The Fall and Rise of Mrs. Hapgood," Martha Gellhorn, 1965.

2977 Spring sunlight cut through the windshield and nicked me into facets, like a diamond; mirages of creeks and ditches, ponds and puddles glittered in the road's blacktop ahead of me. — *Toyland*, Mark Smith, 1965.

2978 We turned off the Turnpike onto a macadam highway, then off the macadam onto a pink dirt road. — *Of the Farm*, John Updike, 1965.

2979 They were speeding along the new throughway down the valley at three in the morning under a wet full moon. — *Too Far to Walk*, John Hersey, 1966.

2980 He drove with his moist palms gripping the wheel of the jeep wagon. — *The Zinzin Road*, Fletcher Knebel, 1966.

2981 Although he didn't ask himself what time it was, Ned Ingles must have driven in to the place about five in the afternoon. — *Pursuit*, Berry Morgan, 1966.

2982 I stopped the car at the top of the hill and looked down the broad cleft to the sea. I braked without knowing why, obeying a kind of reflex, so that it took me a moment or two to recall that this was the exact spot I had stopped for a last look back on the way out of Redcliffe

Bay, more than thirty years ago. — *Return Journey*, R. F. Delderfield, 1967.

2983 From my gallery I could see that dust coming down the quarter, coming fast, and I thought to myself, "Who in the world would be driving like that?" — *Of Love and Dust*, Ernest J. Gaines, 1967.

2984 The little Daimler buzzed out of its garage between the rhododendrons and rolled across the raked pebbles in front of the house. The next Linda saw of it, Jeremy had turned up the gravel path past the tennis court and was heading for the gap in the rosy brick wall which squared the kitchen garden. — *Orchestra and Beginners*, Frederic Raphael, 1967.

2985 Puffs of warm July wind came through the car to fan George Gallion's face and his woolly arm that rested on the open window. — *Mr. Gallion's School*, Jesse Stuart, 1967.

2986 There was light early morning traffic on Sepulveda. As I drove over the low pass, the sun came up glaring behind the blue crags on the far side of the valley. For a minute or two, before regular day set in, everything looked fresh and new and awesome as creation. — *The Instant Enemy*, Ross Macdonald, 1968.

2987 Dino Tomasso braked before the high, familiar gates with the coupling snakes woven into the wrought iron. — *Cocksure*, Mordecai Richler, 1968.

2988 At the beginning of his sixty-third, decisive summer, Alec Ramsey drove down from his university town on the tableland to the wheat, sheep, and cattle towns on the inland plains. — *The Survivor*, Thomas Keneally, 1969.

2989 It was close to the end of the day. They drove through the woods, up the incline of the narrow clay road — the front tires taking their own erratic paths in the deep ruts eroded by spring storms — and came over the crest of the hill and onto a sight so arresting that the young man who was at the wheel went for the brake. — *What I'm Going to Do, I Think*, Larry Woiwode, 1969.

2990 There was very little talk between them as Lily drove. Earlier in the day there had been rain and the night frost now made the road slippery in places so that most of Lily's attention was on her driving. — *Firecrest*, Victor Canning, 1971.

2991 Cassidy drove contentedly through the evening sunlight, his face as close to the windshield as the safety belt allowed, his foot alternating diffidently between accelerator and brake as he scanned the narrow lane for unseen hazards. — *The Naive and Sentimental Lover*, John Le Carré, 1971.

2992 They decided to pull in at the Howard Johnson's. — *The Shrewsdale Exit*, John Buell, 1972.

2993 A man sits in his car at the traffic lights, waiting for them to go green. — *Sweet Dreams*, Michael Frayn, 1973.

2994 Larry Berlin is driving north on Route 27 when he spots the car. — "Noise of Strangers," George Garrett, 1973.

2995 The taxi taking me from the Athens Hilton to the Piraeus ferry dock roared around the last cloverleaf of new road and slid in against the high curb like a scared baserunner with his cleats bared. — *A Touch of Danger*, James Jones, 1973.

2996 The miles were draining away. They were down to single figures when the traffic began to slow and thicken ahead of her. — *Richard's Things*, Frederic Raphael, 1973.

2997 Peter Colby was a cautious man. He drove north along the South Dixie Highway, alert, habitually careful, scanning the traffic for the erratic behavior of knaves and fools who roared around, changing lanes, beating lights, passing in reckless ways and at the wrong times. — *The Liberated*, David R. Slavitt *as* Henry Sutton, 1973.

2998 Soon after three o'clock on the afternoon of April 22nd 1973, a 35-year-old architect named Robert Maitland was driving down the high-speed exit lane of the Westway interchange in central London. — *Concrete Island*, J. G. Ballard, 1974.

2999 She sat next to Jamie, in the vinyl bucket seat of his 380-hp copper Cougar, speeding along Memorial Drive on the way to his apartment. — *Miriam at Thirty-four*, Alan Lelchuk, 1974.

3000 After lunch Jane and Roche left their house on the Ridge to drive to Thrushcross Grange. — *Guerrillas*, V. S. Naipaul, 1975.

3001 Past the orange roof and turquoise tower, past the immense sunburst of the green and yellow sign, past the golden arches, beyond the low buff building, beside the discrete hut, the dark top hat on the studio window shade, beneath the red and white longitudes of the enormous bucket, coming up to the thick shaft of the yellow arrow piercing the royal-blue field, he feels he is home. — *The Franchiser*, Stanley Elkin, 1976.

3002 Driving the Ford into the parking field, Trask found his access blocked by a Sanitation Department truck. — *The Hostage Heart*, Gerald Green, 1976.

3003 Where was he going? — *Night Swimmers*, Nancy Hallinan, 1976.

3004 No, no, Henri. Hands off the wheel. Please. It is too late. — *Travesty*, John Hawkes, 1976.

3005 I drove up to the house on a private road that widened at the summit into a parking apron. — *The Blue Hammer*, Ross Macdonald, 1976.

3006 "Ali! Ali! Ali!" shouts the surging crowd as my Austin Minimoke tries to wind its way through the people. — *The Last Duty*, Isidore Okpewho, 1976.

3007 Truman Held drove slowly into the small town of Chicokema as the two black men who worked at the station where he stopped for gas were breaking for lunch. — *Meridian*, Alice Walker, 1976.

3008 They stopped the car by the gateway in the wall on the lower coast road. Then, after a moment or two, the three of them climbed out stiffly, their shirts clinging to their backs. — *The Siege of the Villa Lipp*, Eric Ambler, 1977.

3009 Six sweat-lathered, black horses raced ahead of the billowing cloud of dust. In the middle of it bounced and jerked the coach from Port Glasgow with Will Bramstone, better known as Old Brimstone, clutching the reins and cracking his whip as he goaded the horses on to greater effort. — *Scorpion in the Fire*, Margaret Thomson Davis, 1977.

3010 Anne Linton drove north to Lichfield through the morning. — *The Road to Lichfield*, Penelope Lively, 1977.

3011 The wet black road twisted and flowed before him, a rippling black river, glittering in the bouncing headlights of his car. — *Bright Flows the River*, Taylor Caldwell, 1978.

3012 A woman drove me back to Rio. Yes, I admit — it was madness! — *A Different World*, Zulfikar Ghose, 1978.

3013 Mickey said, "I'll drive. I'd really like to." — *The Switch*, Elmore Leonard, 1978.

3014 *You think, perhaps, you will turn off and drive through the town.* — *Season of the Owl*, Miles Wolff, Jr., 1980.

3015 He drove up to Flanders in the early summer of 1921 knowing that it would be for the last time. — *Circles of Time*, Phillip Rock, 1981.

3016 The road snakes uphill, mostly clear of snow but wet, with icy patches glittering in the headlights' beam. — *Chance*, Sara McAulay, 1982.

3017 Christmas is always like this, Nan complained to herself as she steered through the last-minute shoppers on Mission Boulevard. — *Murder in the English Department*, Valerie Miner, 1982.

3018 Dr. Levaster drove the Lincoln. — *The Tennis Handsome*, Barry Hannah, 1983.

3019 Harmony is driving home, eastward out of Las Vegas, her spirits high, her head a clutter of memories. — *Desert Rose*, Larry McMurtry, 1983.

3020 Joe The Engineer and Joe Flushing Avenue are driving out to Howard Beach, the neighborhood whose water meters they were assigned to read that morning. — *Joe the Engineer*, Chuck Wachtel, 1983.

3021 "Some of these people *want* to get killed," said Dicky Cruyer, as he jabbed the brake pedal to avoid hitting a newsboy. — *Mexico Set*, Len Deighton, 1984.

3022 Mark Lamming, driving from London to Dorset to visit a young woman he had not met, thought about her grandfather. — *According to Mark*, Penelope Lively, 1984.

3023 At midafternoon of July 3, 1957, a truck driver stopped on a highway southwest of Milwaukee and walked into the woods to take a leak. — *Final Harbor*, David Martin, 1984.

3024 He was driving along the road in France from St. Dié to Nancy in the district of Meurthe; it was straight and almost white, through thick woods of fir and birch. — *The Only Problem*, Muriel Spark, 1984.

3025 "I have to stop again, hon," Sam's grandmother says, tapping her on the shoulder. Sam Hughes is driving, with her uncle, Emmett Smith, half asleep beside her. — *In Country*, Bobbie Ann Mason, 1985.

3026 Steven hummed along with an aria soaring out of the car's tape deck as he navigated the old road from the highway. — *Wolf Tickets*, Edward Hower, 1986.

3027 As a rule, Gina Heriot liked driving; but she was not liking this. — *Closing*, Zoë Fairbairns, 1987.

3028 "Whose turn?" asks Jude, the sister who is driving. — *Mother Love*, Candace Flynt, 1987.

3029 I pulled on the headlights; there was nothing for them to penetrate; the dark had barely gathered the first gray beginnings of itself. — *Boats Against the Current*, John Logue, 1987.

3030 Emma sat stiffly on the big plush seat of the Cadillac, looking small and faint, hugging the little suitcase as though it could protect her. "Are they still following us?" — *Island*, Thomas Perry, 1987.

3031 The light turned red when I was halfway across Forty-third Street, forcing me to mark time on the traffic island separating Broadway and Seventh Avenue. — *The Lost World*, Edwin McDowell, 1988.

3032 On a July afternoon as hot as they come, when the river that runs through Lethem lies flat as a mirror (two sets of trees, two skies), and the katydids saw and saw as if they could sever this hour from the rest of the day, Katherine Watters pulls into Tano's Shop-Rite parking lot behind Main Street. — *Home Bodies*, Alicia Miller, 1988.

3033 "Stop the car!" — *Family Business*, Anna Murdoch, 1988.

3034 Swain hits the brakes and all the books on the car seat beside him shoot forward onto the floor. — *Revelation*, Peggy Payne, 1988.

3035 Here's Yozip rattling around in his rusty wagon. — *The People*, Bernard Malamud, 1989.

3036 Hudson's brown Volvo took the last curve in the rutted Vermont dirt road, and within a few yards the public road narrowed to a private lane overgrown with sumac, grasses, laurel bushes, and maple saplings. — *My Dearest Friend*, Nancy Thayer, 1989.

3037 For one whole year he did nothing but drive, traveling back and forth across America as he waited for the money to run out. — *The Music of Chance*, Paul Auster, 1990.

3038 The St. Louis Arch loomed into view through Jeremy Cook's bug-spattered windshield. — *The Full Catastrophe*, David Carkeet, 1990.

3039 I'm driving my son to college. — *Riding in Cars with Boys*, Beverly Donofrio, 1990.

3040 On the way home, Caroline and Richard passed a pickup truck coming from the opposite direction, and as it passed, a pig rose up out of nowhere in the passenger seat, stuck its head out the window, looked around and then quickly disappeared. — *Rootie Kazootie*, Lawrence Naumoff, 1990.

3041 The Labor Day traffic was legendary, bumper to bumper from the Chinatown ramp in Boston to Hyannisport on Cape Cod. — *Postcards from Pinsk*, Larry Duberstein, 1991.

3042 Thomas Cuss turned carefully off the main road and drove slowly through the open countryside of Dirrabeg. — *The Bodhrán Makers*, John B. Keane, 1992.

3043 On their monthly visits to the prison, Aurora drove going and Rosie drove home. — *The Evening Star*, Larry McMurtry, 1992.

3044 Guthrie. Mulhall. Orlando, Perry, Ceres, Three Sands, and Tonkawa. Blackwell. He liked the flat land in between, the gray farmhouses, the long straight road lined with dark telephone poles, the wires rising and falling in sweet regular curves from pole to pole like moving arcs that would make circles if they could, a lot of perfect circles across the dull sky. — *Lady of Spain*, Robert Love Taylor, 1992.

3045 When Cody swerved the truck to avoid the splash of sparrows ahead of them, the horses in the trailer shifted their weight and rocked the stock trailer back and forth. — *Strange Angels*, Jonis Agee, 1993.

3046 Professor Hengist Morton Embry was at the wheel, gliding along through Fort Lauderdale, pointing out the sights to his English visitor. — *Remembrance Day*, Brian W. Aldiss, 1993.

Drugs

3047 Sherlock Holmes took his bottle from the corner of the mantel-piece, and his hypodermic syringe from its neat morocco case. With his long, white, nervous fingers he adjusted the delicate needle, and rolled back his left shirt-cuff. For some little time his eyes rested thoughtfully upon the sinewy forearm and wrist, all dotted and scarred with innumerable puncture-marks. Finally, he thrust the sharp point home, pressed down the tiny piston, and sank back into the velvet-lined armchair with a long sigh of satisfaction. — *The Sign of Four*, Arthur Conan Doyle, 1890.

3048 "When do you take it?" said Atwater./ Pringle said: "You're supposed to take it after every meal, but I only take it after breakfast and dinner. I find that enough." — *Afternoon Men*, Anthony Powell, 1931.

3049 My first experience with junk was during the War, about 1944 or 1945. — *Junky*, William S. Burroughs, 1953.

3050 I can feel the heat closing in, feel them out there making their moves, setting up their devil doll stool pigeons, crooning over my spoon and dropper I throw away at Washington Square Station, vault a turnstile and two flights down the iron stairs, catch an uptown A train ... Young, good looking, crew cut, Ivy League, advertising exec type fruit holds the door back for me. — *The Naked Lunch*, William S. Burroughs, 1959.

3051 *Dear Gabe,/ The drugs help me bend my fingers around a pen.* — *Letting Go*, Philip Roth, 1962.

3052 Three bottles stood beside the telephone, on the table between the beds. — *The Camera Always Lies*, Hugh Hood, 1967.

3053 Seated on a cushion at the upstairs window of the tall house, Hood raised the cigarette to the sun and saw that it was half full of the opium mixture. — *The Family Arsenal*, Paul Theroux, 1976.

3054 Just about the last kind of madness I ever thought I would get mixed up in is the drug-smuggling trade. — *The Greatest Crime*, Sloan Wilson, 1980.

3055 I received the elixir from the Wandering Jew. — *Snail*, Richard Miller, 1984.

3056 *Lying under the burnt-out truck, head still bleeding and cocaine still rampaging around his body, Lux the Poet begins to ramble.* — *Lux the Poet*, Martin Millar, 1988.

3057 We all know the story of the whore who, finding her China white to be less and less reliable a friend no matter how much of it she injected into her arm, recalled in desperation the phrase "shooting the shit," and so filled the needle with her own watery excrement and pumped it in, producing magnificent abscesses. — *Whores for Gloria*, William T. Vollmann, 1991.

Dwellings

3058 Nightmare Abbey, a venerable family-mansion, in a highly picturesque state of semi-dilapidation, pleasantly situated on a strip of dry land between the sea and the fens at the verge of the county of Lincoln, had the honour to be the seat of Christopher Glowry, Esquire. — *Nightmare Abbey*, Thomas Love Peacock, 1818.

3059 Some ten years before the revolt of our American colonies, there was situate in one of our midland counties, on the borders of an extensive forest, an ancient hall that belonged to the Herberts, but which, though ever well preserved, had not until that period been visited by any member of the family, since the exile of the Stuarts. — *Venetia*, Benjamin Disraeli, 1837.

3060 Half-way down a by-street of one of our New England towns, stands a rusty wooden house, with seven acutely peaked gables facing towards various points of the compass, and a huge clustered chimney in the midst. — *The House of the Seven Gables*, Nathaniel Hawthorne, 1851.

3061 My godmother lived in a handsome house in the clean and ancient town of Bretton. — *Villette*, Charlotte Brontë, 1853.

3062 The house was a neat, though a lowly one. — *Ticonderoga*, George P. R. James, 1854.

3063 Of course there was a Great House at Allington. How otherwise should there have been a Small House? — *The Small House at Allington*, Anthony Trollope, 1864.

3064 The school-room at Roselands was a very pleasant apartment; the ceiling, it is true, was somewhat lower than in the more modern portion of the building, for the wing in which it was situated dated back to the old-fashioned days prior to the Revolution, while the larger part of the mansion had not stood more than twenty or thirty years; but the effect was relieved by windows reaching from floor to ceiling, and opening on a veranda which overlooked a lovely flower-garden, beyond which were fields and woods and hills. — *Elsie Dinsmore*, Martha Finley, 1868.

3065 The elm-tree avenue was all overgrown, the great gate was never unlocked, and the old

house had been shut up for several years. — *Under the Lilacs*, Louisa May Alcott, 1877.

3066 Some years ago it matters not how many, the old Earl of Scroope lived at Scroope Manor in Dorsetshire. The house was an Elizabethan structure of some pretensions, but of no fame. — *An Eye for an Eye*, Anthony Trollope, 1879.

3067 Very bright and pretty, in the early springtime of the year 1857, were the British cantonments of Sandynugghur. — *In Times of Peril*, G. A. Henty, 1881.

3068 A low hut built of turf roughly thatched with rushes and standing on the highest spot of some slightly raised ground. — *The Dragon and the Raven*, G. A. Henty, 1886.

3069 There was a wide entrance gate to the old family mansion of Midbranch, but it was never opened to admit the family or visitors; although occasionally a load of wood, drawn by two horses and two mules, came between its tall chestnut posts, and was taken by a roundabout way among the trees to a spot at the back of the house, where the chips of several generations of sturdy wood-choppers had formed a ligneous soil deeper than the arable surface of any portion of the nine hundred and fifty acres which formed the farm of Midbranch. — *The Late Mrs. Null*, Frank R. Stockton, 1886.

3070 On the outskirts of the pretty town of N—, among neat vine-covered homes, like a blot upon a beautiful picture, there stood a weather-beaten, tumble-down cottage. — *Clarence and Corinne*, Mrs. A. E. Johnson, 1890.

3071 Don Orsino Saracinesca is of the younger age and lives in the younger Rome, with his father and mother, under the roof of the vast old palace which has sheltered so many hundreds of Saracinesca in peace and war, but which has rarely in the course of the centuries been the home of three generations at once during one and twenty years. — *Don Orsino*, F. Marion Crawford, 1891.

3072 King's-Hintock Court (said the narrator, turning over his memoranda for reference) — King's-Hintock Court is, as we know, one of the most imposing of the mansions that overlook our beautiful Blackmoor, or Blakemore, Vale. — *A Group of Noble Dames*, Thomas Hardy, 1891.

3073 My dear wife Carrie and I have just been a week in our new house, "The Laurels," Brickfield Terrace, Holloway — a nice six-roomed residence, not counting basement, with a front breakfast-parlour. — *The Diary of a Nobody*, George and Weedon Grossmith, 1892.

3074 Away back in the "twenties," when Indiana was a baby state, and great forests of tall trees and tangled underbrush darkened what are now her bright plains and sunny hills, there

stood upon the east bank of Big Blue River, a mile or two north of the point where that stream crosses the Michigan road, a cozy log cabin of two rooms — one front and one back. — *The Bears of Blue River*, Charles Major, 1901.

3075 Fiction has said so much in regret of the old days when there were plantations and overseers and masters and slaves, that it was good to come upon such a household as Berry Hamilton's, if for no other reason than that it afforded a relief from the monotony of tiresome iteration. — *The Sport of the Gods*, Paul Laurence Dunbar, 1902.

3076 The old red-brick house, on a southern slope of the Surrey hills, was glowing from a dark forest depth of pines with the warmth of a rare jewel. — *The Four Feathers*, A. E. W. Mason, 1902.

3077 It was a plain brick house, three full stories, with four broad chimneys, and overhanging eaves. — "The Master of the Inn," Robert Herrick, 1908.

3078 It was one of the top-floor-rear flats in the Wyandotte, not merely biggest of Washington's apartment hotels, but also "most exclusive" — which is the elegant way of saying most expensive. — *The Fashionable Adventures of Joshua Craig*, David Graham Phillips, 1909.

3079 The children of the place had their own name for the severely grey brick house that stood at the top of the hill overlooking the town. They called it "The Giant's Castle." — *Mary Midthorne*, George Barr McCutcheon, 1911.

3080 The house of the Emery family was a singularly good example of the capacity of wood and plaster and brick to acquire personality. — *The Squirrel-Cage*, Dorothy Canfield Fisher, 1912.

3081 Mary Makebelieve lived with her mother in a small room at the very top of a big, dingy house in a Dublin back street. — "The Charwoman's Daughter," James Stephens, 1912.

3082 The Brangwens had lived for generations on the Marsh Farm, in the meadows where the Erewash twisted sluggishly through alder trees, separating Derbyshire from Nottinghamshire. — *The Rainbow*, D. H. Lawrence, 1915.

3083 "Peace and plenty, peace and plenty" — that was the phrase M. Jean Jacques Barbille, miller and money-master, applied to his home-scene, when he was at the height of his career. Both winter and summer the place had a look of content and comfort, even a kind of opulence. — *The Money Master*, Gilbert Parker, 1915.

3084 Sir Oliver Tressilian sat at his ease in the lofty dining-room of the handsome house of Penarrow, which he owed to the enterprise of his father of lamented and lamentable memory and to the skill and invention of an Italian engineer named Bagnolo who had come to England half

a century ago as one of the assistants of the famous Torrigiani. — *The Sea-Hawk*, Rafael Sabatini, 1915.

3085 About thirty years ago there was at the top of the right-hand side of Orange Street, in Polchester, a large stone house. I say "was"; the shell of it is still there, and the people who now live in it are quite unaware, I suppose, that anything has happened to the inside of it, except that they are certainly assured that their furniture is vastly superior to the furniture of their predecessors. — *Jeremy*, Hugh Walpole, 1919.

3086 To-night I am in a little cabin in the heart of a great wilderness. — *God's Country — The Trail to Happiness*, James Oliver Curwood, 1921.

3087 Thirty or forty years ago, in one of those grey towns along the Burlington railroad, which are so much greyer to-day than they were then, there was a house well known from Omaha to Denver for its hospitality and for a certain charm of atmosphere. — *A Lost Lady*, Willa Cather, 1923.

3088 Gissing lived alone (except for his Japanese butler) in a little house in the country, in that woodland suburb region called the Canine Estates. — *Where the Blue Begins*, Christopher Morley, 1923.

3089 We lived on the coast of California, on the Spanish grant my grandfather had purchased from the mission which still stands, deserted and crumbling, in the Santa Brigida Valley. — *The Pearl Lagoon*, Charles Nordhoff, 1924.

3090 The cool spring dusk fell drowsy and soft over Sandy Island, all but blotting out a log cabin that nestled under great moss-hung oaks close to the river's edge. — *Black April*, Julia Peterkin, 1927.

3091 In the house, in which they could not afford to live, it was unpleasantly quiet. — *Armed with Madness*, Mary Butts, 1928.

3092 He lay staring at the withy binders of his thatch shelter; the grass was infinitely green; his view embraced four counties; the roof was supported by six small oak sapling-trunks, roughly trimmed and brushed from above by apple boughs. — *The Last Post*, Ford Madox Ford, 1928.

3093 In the late summer of that year we lived in a house in a village that looked across the river and the plain to the mountains. — *A Farewell to Arms*, Ernest Hemingway, 1929.

3094 The house was very small. There was a narrow hall, a frigid parlour, a dining room and kitchen on the first floor. On the second there was a front bedroom, behind it the one the little girls used, and a rear room, a sort of storeroom, which in times of affluence was used by a maid of all work, called the hired girl, and in all times, good and bad, housed the trunks, the broken

chairs, the oil lamps in case the gas company turned off the gas — which was not infrequently — and all the other flotsam and jetsam of that curious heterogeneous group which was the Colfax family. — *This Strange Adventure*, Mary Roberts Rinehart, 1929.

3095 The old house, forgotten by the townspeople, stood behind padlocked gates and iron fences, buried in a wilderness of maple trees, and lost in encircling acres of knee-deep, billowing grass. Once, for its immensity, its magnificence, it had been the pride of the town. — *The Fierce Dispute*, Helen Hooven Santmyer, 1929.

3096 The Warwicke Armes was almost exactly like the other apartment houses that stood in a row at the suburban end of the new Lincoln Boulevard. All of them were great flat-faced cubes rigidly honeycombed into cells; the cells were all of about the same size, all subdivided in the same manner, all decorated (if the leasing agents' enticement was true authority) in the same "Olde Englysshe Style"; and they were all called by the same name, "kitchenette apartments." — *Young Mrs. Greeley*, Booth Tarkington, 1929.

3097 There were twenty-seven log houses in Hill Town, North Carolina, counting the jail and the shack where Major Tyrell kept his niggers. — *Long Hunt*, James Boyd, 1930.

3098 Old man Jimmie Vaiden's home was half a house and half a fort. — *The Forge*, T. S. Stribling, 1931.

3099 The old woman and the new-born child were the only living things in the house. — *Judith Paris*, Hugh Walpole, 1931.

3100 The house was quiet but awake. — *Precious Jeopardy*, Lloyd C. Douglas, 1933.

3101 She lived in a small house between the Cherokee Garage and the delicatessen shop of Mr. Petersen, whose daughter was an actress in New York. — "Miss Mehaffy," Louis Bromfield, 1934.

3102 The house at No. 55 could be at once distinguished from the others in the same street because of its size and because it had a fine wrought-iron grill with the initials D.F.H. in fading gilt. — "No. 55," Louis Bromfield, 1934.

3103 In a not distant past there stood on a street of the lower West Side of Manhattan a row of houses that were survivals of an earlier and friendlier age. Each house stood at the end of its small narrow garden; the gardens were fenced from the street by rusty fences of cast-iron; each house consisted of a basement and of four stories with wooden verandahs fastened to the long unpainted geranium-coloured bricks. — *An Altar in the Fields*, Ludwig Lewisohn, 1934.

3104 The home of Mrs. Sarah Pitkin, a widow well on in years, was situated on an

eminence overlooking the Rat River, near the town of Ottsville in the state of Vermont. — *A Cool Million*, Nathanael West, 1934.

3105 There was a run-down old tollbridge station in the Shoestring Valley of Southern Oregon where Uncle Preston Shiveley had lived for fifty years, outlasting a wife, two sons, several plagues of grasshoppers, wheat-rust and caterpillars, a couple or three invasions of land-hunting settlers and real-estate speculators, and everybody else except the scattering of old pioneers who had cockleburred themselves onto the country at about the same time he did. — *Honey in the Horn*, H. L. Davis, 1935.

3106 In a hole in the ground there lived a hobbit. — *The Hobbit*, J.R.R. Tolkien, 1937.

3107 The street was darkened by a smoky sunset, and light had not yet come on in the lamps near the empty house. Under a troubled sky the old house looked deserted but charged with reality. It was a place, Asa Timberlake thought, where everything had happened and nothing would ever happen again. — *In This Our Life*, Ellen Glasgow, 1938.

3108 Three years now, and three months more than that, the Chippman place had stood there and no smoke had come from the chimney, no light had said night was falling and a family would gather within for supper, to read or talk a little, then sleep. — *The Morning Is Near Us*, Susan Glaspell, 1940.

3109 Nothing could have been simpler, nothing more forthright, than the pattern made by the red roof of the Old Manor against the blue summer sky. — *The Stone of Chastity*, Margery Sharp, 1940.

3110 When Captain Roger Angmering built himself a house in the year 1782 on the island off Leathercombe Bay, it was thought the height of eccentricity on his part. — *Evil Under the Sun*, Agatha Christie, 1941.

3111 The cellars of this farm in north-eastern France were the oldest part of the house, since in 1919 they had only needed to be cleared of rubbish, and there they were, almost intact. An admirable foundation for the new house which, so far as looks go, had nothing to commend it. — *The Fort*, Storm Jameson, 1941.

3112 The villa stood on the top of a hill. — *Up at the Villa*, W. Somerset Maugham, 1941.

3113 The house was on Dresden Avenue in the Oak Knoll section of Pasadena, a big solid cool-looking house with burgundy brick walls, a terra-cotta tile roof, and a white stone trim. — *The High Window*, Raymond Chandler, 1942.

3114 Marling Hall stands on a little eminence among what would in more golden days have been called well-wooded parkland. — *Marling Hall*, Angela Thirkell, 1942.

3115 "A charming place," said Count Wolfgang von Bernstrom, as he looked about him. — *The Final Hour*, Taylor Caldwell, 1944.

3116 The rambling Elizabethan cottage stood at the dead end of Meg's Lane in the old city of Bristol, a few blocks from the docks and well within sight of the tall masts of the ships that lay at anchor off Kingroad. — *Lusty Wind for Carolina*, Inglis Fletcher, 1944.

3117 The house, it seems, is more important than the characters. "In me you exist," says the house. — *Take Three Senses*, Rumer Godden, 1945.

3118 The sweet old farmhouse burrowed into the upward slope of the land so deeply that you could enter either its bottom or middle floor at ground level. — *Mr. Blandings Builds His Dream House*, Eric Hodgins, 1946.

3119 On a country road near Brussels stood one of those small family estates so dear to Belgian hearts: a large vegetable garden; an orchard; a white table and chairs in the shade of an apple tree; a couple of meadows; a little duckpond; a formal French garden; and the house itself thrusting its tiled gable through a bower of trees. — *The Bridge of Years*, May Sarton, 1946.

3120 Britannia Mews was built in 1865 to accommodate the carriage-horses, coachmen, and other respectable dependents of the ten houses in Albion Place. — *Britannia Mews*, Margery Sharp, 1946.

3121 It was as quiet in my daughter's house that early December afternoon as it had been all summer and fall in my own home in the country. — *While the Angels Sing*, Gladys Hasty Carroll, 1947.

3122 Chipping Lodge is the oldest house on Chipping Hill, and the least typical: for being so high and airy, and only eight miles from Charing Cross, the district early attracted commercial or professional wealth, and the resulting villa-residences (each a monument to Victorian success) are as remarkable for exuberance of design as solidity of construction. — *The Foolish Gentlewoman*, Margery Sharp, 1948.

3123 Beliers Priory, as all East Barsetshire knows, is a very large and unmitigatedly hideous house, the property of Sir Harry Waring. — *Love Among the Ruins*, Angela Thirkell, 1948.

3124 "This is a quiet little hole," said the cook. She was telephoning to a friend in the market town of Swirrelsford, eight miles away. — *The Boat*, L. P. Hartley, 1949.

3125 The villa, facing south, stood above the little town and port, on the slope between the sea and the Forêt de Sorède. — *The World My Wilderness*, Rose Macaulay, 1950.

3126 The sunshine which is such an agreeable feature of life in and around Hollywood, when the weather is not unusual, blazed down

from a sky of turquoise blue on the spacious grounds of what, though that tempestuous Mexican star had ceased for nearly a year to be its owner and it was now the property of Mrs. Adela Shannon Cork, was still known locally as the Carmen Flores place. — *The Old Reliable*, P. G. Wodehouse, 1950.

3127 The room could scarcely have been more snug for two very old men. — *Renny's Daughter*, Mazo de la Roche, 1951.

3128 A one-room log cabin, with an indolently smoking chimney, squatted in sullen destitution a hundred yards away. — *When the Tree Flowered*, John G. Neihardt, 1951.

3129 The log cabin of Danny McGinnis and the boys stands on the side of a birch-covered slope where the Mulligan Plateau abruptly sheers off into the valley of the Big Dead River. — *Danny and the Boys*, Robert Traver, 1951.

3130 Although it was eventually to reach a point where there was no longer a great deal upon which they were able to agree, none of them ever denied, either silently to themselves or aloud to one another, the extraordinary summer beauty of the place. — *The Seasons' Difference*, Frederick Buechner, 1952.

3131 The armoured cat's face of the house withheld itself entirely from the afternoon — the house was high and square, built of stone blocks, rough cut like fish scales, but cut stone round all the windows fine as skin. — *Treasure Hunt*, Molly Keane *as* M. J. Farrell, 1952.

3132 In Nero Wolfe's old brownstone house on West Thirty-fifth Street that Monday afternoon in June, the atmosphere was sparky. — *Prisoner's Base*, Rex Stout, 1952.

3133 Our house is old, and noisy, and full. — *Life Among the Savages*, Shirley Jackson, 1953.

3134 Mrs. Appleyard owns the old Templeton house on Woodbrook Green. — *". . . With Kitchen Privileges"*, Louise Andrews Kent, 1953.

3135 The house had not been lived in for many years. Since last summer there had not been a footfall on its bare floors until just now. — *One White Star*, Gladys Hasty Carroll, 1954.

3136 Mrs. Merton, she who was once Lydia Keith, and her husband, Noel Merton, K.C. since 1946 and Q.C. since England had a Queen, had lived since the end of the war in her late parents' house near Northbridge. — *What Did It Mean?*, Angela Thirkell, 1954.

3137 All that summer, as no white people came to rent the empty, upstairs suites of the Valenti house or the Golden house, tension had mounted in the street. Only Negroes came. — *The Changelings*, Jo Sinclair, 1955.

3138 "Nobody lives at Malin now," said the man who was driving./ "I believe it's falling down," added the girl. "Houses do when they're left empty too long." — *A Haunted Land*, Randolph Stow, 1956.

3139 One winter before the Six Weeks War my tomcat, Petronius the Arbiter, and I lived in an old farmhouse in Connecticut. — *The Door Into Summer*, Robert A. Heinlein, 1957.

3140 Number One Avenue de Marigny in Paris is a large, square house of dark and venerable appearance. — *The Short Reign of Pippin IV*, John Steinbeck, 1957.

3141 The first morning in Madrid I went to Manuel's address off the Calle de Goya, and it was exactly as his sister had told me it would be. — *"Decision,"* Kay Boyle, 1958.

3142 I am always drawn back to places where I have lived, the houses and their neighborhoods. — *Breakfast at Tiffany's*, Truman Capote, 1958.

3143 When I saw the house I said, "The lines are good. It is in bad repair, but it will suit my purpose all the better." — *A Name for Evil*, Andrew Lytle, 1958.

3144 Palaces were built for elegance, not comfort, and the Tuileries was no exception. — *The Emperor's Ladies*, Noel B. Gerson, 1959.

3145 In the somnolent July afternoon the unbroken line of brownstone houses down the long Brooklyn street resembled an army massed at attention. — *Brown Girl, Brownstones*, Paule Marshall, 1959.

3146 The house stood upon a gentle slope, from which you might look down a broad, sun-flecked avenue into the forests which lined the creek. — *Theirs Be the Guilt*, Upton Sinclair, 1959.

3147 Jadewood, the house itself, as opposed to the plantation — since the name is used by the Jarretts to refer to both — sits in a liveoak grove on the outskirts of Atlanta. — *Jarrett's Jade*, Frank Yerby, 1959.

3148 Every New Yorker who knows Fifth Avenue knows Grandpa Millinder's houses, or rather what is left of them. — *The House of Five Talents*, Louis Auchincloss, 1960.

3149 There wasn't much to be said for the place, really, but it had a roof over it and a door which locked from the inside, which was all I cared about just then. — *The L-Shaped Room*, Lynne Reid Banks, 1960.

3150 When the American Civil War broke out, this house Jalna, in Ontario, had been completed not many years before. — *Morning at Jalna*, Mazo de la Roche, 1960.

3151 It is known that in every neighborhood in the United States there is at least one house that is special. — *All Fall Down*, James Leo Herlihy, 1960.

3152 Half way up the forested hill that lends its name to the town of Bukit Kallang the ground flattens into a grassy ledge one hundred yards

wide and two hundred yards deep and on this ledge a Chinese merchant, who had sought and found his fortune in Malaya, built himself a house. — *The Love Pavilion*, Paul Scott, 1960.

3153 West Ealing is a suburb to the west of London, and Keith Stewart lives there in the lower part of No. 56 Somerset Road. No. 56 is an unusual house and a peculiarly ugly one, a detached house standing in a row but in a fairly spacious garden, four storeys high if you include the basement, a tall, thin slip of a house. — *Trustee from the Toolroom*, Nevil Shute, 1960.

3154 Have you ever let lodgings in the winter? — *The Lime Twig*, John Hawkes, 1961.

3155 The great house of Marriott was shuttered against death; its noble façade, of palest cotswold stone, stared blindly across parkland towards the long silver serpent of the River Wye, and the distant Welsh Marches beyond. — *The White Rajah*, Nicholas Monsarrat, 1961.

3156 The house was at the corner of Harvard Road and Bucknell Street, set back on two sides from the unpaved sidewalks, and with a garage at the rear. — *Elizabeth Appleton*, John O'Hara, 1963.

3157 The Patterson house was not on the Patterson place. Few houses were on plantations in the Mississippi Delta now; planters liked to live in nearby towns. — *A Passage of Hawks*, Wirt Williams, 1963.

3158 The house was in waiting; low, and still, and grey, with clean curtains in the long windows, and a fresh line of white across the edge of the steps. — *Shadow of a Sun*, A. S. Byatt, 1964.

3159 On a barely wooded and sparsely settled hill in the town of Barnett, Long Island, there stood a tall narrow house whose encasing shingles had not yet attained the soft greyness of weatherbeaten wood. — *First Papers*, Laura Z. Hobson, 1964.

3160 The manor house at Slane St. Mary's is one of those ancient but nondescript country seats which eventually become private mental homes or preparatory schools after they have been offered to, and refused by, the National Trust. — *Not in the Calendar*, Margaret Kennedy, 1964.

3161 Whoever came to the Hornburys' house on Long Island was immediately intimidated by it, or charmed. — *A House on the Sound*, Kathrin Perutz, 1964.

3162 They are tearing down the little house at Parc Fasseville. — *The Dancer from the Dance*, Janet Burroway, 1965.

3163 The house was too quiet. — *A Drop of Patience*, William Melvin Kelley, 1965.

3164 I have a small white house here, with a courtyard. — *The Cat and Shakespeare*, Raja Rao, 1965.

3165 Their new house stood on a cliff top in Suffolk, its front windows looked out to the disordered garden with a lily pond beneath a poplar tree, and its name was Eastwold Vicarage. — *The Flag*, Robert Shaw, 1965.

3166 He lived in a grey shadowy street in Vienna two flights up behind four dirt stained never opened windows. — *The Saddest Summer of Samuel S*, J. P. Donleavy, 1966.

3167 In the spring of 1961 I was living in a furnished room with miniscule kitchenette and stunted bathtub in New York City. — *A Circle of Friends*, Julian Mitchell, 1966.

3168 I had never thought of the bungalow as lonely. — *The Courtesy of Death*, Geoffrey Household, 1967.

3169 Someone, thought Mitchell Pierce, is having his apartment painted. — *Dem*, William Melvin Kelley, 1967.

3170 Rosemary and Guy Woodhouse had signed a lease on a five-room apartment in a geometric white house on First Avenue when they received word, from a woman named Mrs. Cortez, that a four-room apartment in the Bramford had become available. — *Rosemary's Baby*, Ira Levin, 1967.

3171 When I first came to London, shortly after the end of the war, I found myself after a few days in a boarding-house, called a private hotel, in the Kensington High Street area. — *The Mimic Men*, V. S. Naipaul, 1967.

3172 I live in HARRY SAM. — *The Free-Lance Pallbearers*, Ishmael Reed, 1967.

3173 A house with white columns and a lawn descending to the water is always handsome, always aristocratic. — *A World of Profit*, Louis Auchincloss, 1968.

3174 "God," said Kit, "what a horrible house you live in!" — *The Survival of the Fittest*, Pamela Hansford Johnson, 1968.

3175 *Dypaloh*. There was a house made of dawn. — *House Made of Dawn*, N. Scott Momaday, 1968.

3176 At first, there was a beginning House, small, trim, and smelling of clean wood. — *Under the Boardwalk*, Norman Rosten, 1968.

3177 Passersby often remembered the house. Even on such a good street, where new young trees, carefully wired against dogs, wind and anarchy, are regularly set out to spindle, a house still occupied by a single family is a fireside glory to all. — *The New Yorkers*, Hortense Calisher, 1969.

3178 She glanced at the house, high on the green slope, as they turned off Great Road, and she knew at once that something was amiss. — *Trespass*, Fletcher Knebel, 1969.

3179 *Imagine a deserted estate in northern New England. Five hundred rolling acres, mainly forested*

with hemlock and white pine. Imposing stone gateposts; long sloping velvet lawns brocaded with the moving shadows of clouds; a thirty-five-room stone mansion in Victorian-baronial style; picturesque old stables and outbuildings; two Italian marble fountains, one indoors; three large artificial ponds stocked with fish and water lilies; and a once-famous rose garden. — *Real People*, Alison Lurie, 1969.

3180 Allan's father, thinking it a "country place," had bought a house in Rupert, Vermont, in 1951. They could not spend one summer there, and found it, as his mother said, "terrifyingly authentic." — *News*, Nicholas Delbanco, 1970.

3181 The house was built on the highest part of the narrow tongue of land between the harbor and the open sea. — *Islands in the Stream*, Ernest Hemingway, 1970.

3182 Here is the house. It is green and white. It has a red door. It is very pretty. — *The Bluest Eye*, Toni Morrison, 1970.

3183 The house across the street always did hold me, fascinated, even before we made the discovery about it, even before the Welches — Tom, Royal, Jinny, and May — had come to live there. — *Secrets*, Nancy Hale, 1971.

3184 The house had outlived its usefulness. It sat hooded and silent, a brown shingleboard monstrosity close to the road but backed by woods, far enough from downtown Baltimore to escape the ashy smell of the factories. — *The Clock Winder*, Anne Tyler, 1972.

3185 "It doesn't look any worse than most of the other houses in the neighborhood," George Clarke said. "Not as bad as some." — *Apostles of Light*, Ellen Douglas, 1973.

3186 The Merriwether House — as it was known in the neighborhood for most of its ninety years — is a three-minute walk from Harvard Square. — *Other Men's Daughters*, Richard G. Stern, 1973.

3187 "Howard four, four," the porter in the bowler said, consulting a typewritten list. — *Mungo's Dream*, J. I. M. Stewart, 1973.

3188 Number five Steadman Street was a little larger than any of the other houses. — *Twilight of the Day*, Mervyn Jones, 1974.

3189 When young Charles was seven he lived in his own suite of apartments at the Hotel Barbette in the capital. — *Blood Red, Sister Rose*, Thomas Keneally, 1974.

3190 "And there through the trees," said the guide in the blue uniform and scarlet armband, "there, ladies and gentlemen, is Woodiscombe Manor, the last country house." — *The Last of the Country House Murders*, Emma Tennant, 1974.

3191 In 1902 Father built a house at the crest of the Broadview Avenue hill in New Rochelle, New York. — *Ragtime*, E. L. Doctorow, 1975.

3192 This room of Charlie's and mine wasn't really a room, it was a small section of an abandoned warehouse near the South Hudson docks. — *Moise and the World of Reason*, Tennessee Williams, 1975.

3193 There were five bedrooms. — *Dead Babies*, Martin Amis, 1976.

3194 In early 1965, Edmund K. Holgate of East Bridgewater, Massachusetts, purchased two homes for himself and his wife, Judith. — *The Judgment of Deke Hunter*, George V. Higgins, 1976.

3195 Raman's was the last house in Ellaman Street; a little door on the back wall opened, beyond a stretch of sand, to the river. — *The Painter of Signs*, R. K. Narayan, 1976.

3196 At Nemi, that previous summer, there were three new houses of importance to the surrounding district. — *The Takeover*, Muriel Spark, 1976.

3197 Ivy Trask could never make up her mind which of the Irving Steins' dwellings she preferred: the rather huddled but comfortable Beaux-Arts town house on East 68th Street or the great gray two story Parisian *hôtel*, a rectangle enclosing a glass-covered courtyard, which they had erected and surrounded by flat, rich green lawns for their summers and weekends in Rye. — *The Dark Lady*, Louis Auchincloss, 1977.

3198 I was sent to stay with her two years after the war had ended, but in her house it seemed to be war-time. — *Great Granny Webster*, Caroline Blackwood, 1977.

3199 The palace's summer bedrooms gave on to a balustraded balcony shaded by a sloping terrace roof which overlooked the town. — *Warrior in Bronze*, George Shipway, 1977.

3200 In the summer of 1955 I was living with my wife and two children at St. Jean-Cap Ferrat in a decaying old villa called "L'Escapade." — *Goodbye Un-America*, James Aldridge, 1979.

3201 The Bronx has many mansions; many more than are probably supposed, and mansions, relatively speaking. — *A Glorious Third*, Cynthia Propper Seton, 1979.

3202 My family lived for fifteen years in a castle built more than a century ago by an eccentric man who wanted his Rhine-born wife to feel at home when he brought her to live in California. — *Hard Laughter*, Anne Lamott, 1980.

3203 The house on Clifton Avenue was a duplex. — *American Rose*, Julia Markus, 1980.

3204 The Wisewoman lived in the last soft fold of earth before the sea. — *Amanda/Miranda*, Richard Peck, 1980.

3205 A house on the northern coast of Maine. One story high, its rectangular sections extend in three directions, fitting through the abrupt rise and fall of the promontory rock: prosthetic

limbs, mechanical fingers, angle-jointed, clinging there against the wind like the roots of a scrub pine. —"The Death of Descartes," David Bosworth, 1981.

3206 So, when she and I walked into the house after we had been in the street so long, I knew that another time was coming when we would have to be in the street again. — *To Every Birth Its Blood*, Mongane Serote, 1981.

3207 On the main gravel road a quarter of a mile north of where the schoolhouse stood before the Fire was the home of an old man whose grandchildren were fellow pupils of Jay Alderson and his sister. — *Deepwood*, Walter S. J. Swanson, 1981.

3208 Pleasant Acres Rest Home. Burnaby, British Columbia. L-shaped, ranch-style, surrounded by the split-level houses of a subdivision. — *Trapper*, Thomas York, 1981.

3209 It wasn't Bridgeport, and it wasn't Horatio House, where Christina lived with nine other girls. This was a brick shed with copper bulbs on the roof. Cornices seemed to drop from a brown sky. The windows were little fists of bluish light. It was a dark castle on Thirty-seventh Street, a castle filled with Poles. — *Panna Maria*, Jerome Charyn, 1982.

3210 The Governor's residence stood majestic in its Georgian elegance. — *Destination Biafra*, Buchi Emecheta, 1982.

3211 They lived in a house in Santa Rosa that was always darkest in summertime. — *White Horses*, Alice Hoffman, 1982.

3212 Stainforth estate succeeded to Spinney Moor. — *A Prodigal Child*, David Storey, 1982.

3213 I lived in a bedsit in Chepstow Road. — *The Slipstream*, Ian Cochrane, 1983.

3214 He was growing into middle age and was living then in a bungalow on Woodland Avenue. — *The Assassination of Jesse James*, Ron Hansen, 1983.

3215 It is 1983. In Dorset the great house at Woodcombe Park bustles with life. In Ireland the more modest Kilneagh is as quiet as a grave. — *Fools of Fortune*, William Trevor, 1983.

3216 In a comfortably proportioned, but lately very empty-feeling, flat behind the Finchley Road lives a middle-aged woman called Maggie Langham. — *The Warning Bell*, Lynne Reid Banks, 1984.

3217 There were two beds and a wardrobe in the room. — *Blow Your House Down*, Pat Barker, 1984.

3218 The house on Palm Avenue was one we had noticed but never been inside—a bungalow, built in the forties, smaller than the others on its block, gray, with a screen porch and carpenter-Gothic trim. — *Second Marriage*, Frederick Barthelme, 1984.

3219 How did the settlers on the American prairies decide where to put their homes? — *No Other Place*, John Gould, 1984.

3220 When I was little, we had River Bend. — *Group Therapy*, Shelby Hearon, 1984.

3221 My uncle Zen's house was up next to the hills in the midst of his scraggly lemon grove. — *The State of Stony Lonesome*, Jessamyn West, 1984.

3222 Right now, here in Paris, we have seven different nests. — *Scumbler*, William Wharton, 1984.

3223 *Then there was one brief time when we didn't live in the big brick house with my grandmother but in a neat two-storey green-shingled white house in the holler below.* — *I Am One of You Forever*, Fred Chappell, 1985.

3224 We've got a ranch house. Daddy built it. — *The Beans of Egypt, Maine*, Carolyn Chute, 1985.

3225 On the paved road that went by the colored folks' church stood the Aycock place, a two-story white frame house that would have looked Greek Revival except for the four Doric columns that had been connected with Victorian latticework sometime last century. — *Where She Was*, Anderson Ferrell, 1985.

3226 In June of 1963, when I arrived in Florence, the Pensione Bardolini was in its ninth decade. — *The Blue Star*, Robert Ferro, 1985.

3227 The house was set back from the noisy main road in what seemed to be a rubbish tip. — *The Good Terrorist*, Doris Lessing, 1985.

3228 Frances Girard lived in somebody else's house. — *Group Sex*, Ann Arensberg, 1986.

3229 I am at a table in the living room of Léonie's apartment. — *Nadine*, Matt Cohen, 1986.

3230 Anyone can tell when they are passing the Ridolfi villa, the Ricordanza, because of the stone statues of what are known as "the Dwarfs" on the highest part of the surrounding walls. — *Innocence*, Penelope Fitzgerald, 1986.

3231 I had been living and writing in Paris for five months, staying with my friend Anna at her flat in the rue Jacob. — *Burning Houses*, Andrew Harvey, 1986.

3232 If on a sunny day you climb the steep path leading up from the little wooden bridge still referred to around here as "the Bridge of Hesitation," you will not have to walk far before the roof of my house becomes visible between the tops of two gingko trees. — *An Artist of the Floating World*, Kazuo Ishiguro, 1986.

3233 During the whole war and for some years after it had ended, my uncle Bolek and I lived at the Buckingham Hotel. — *My Life with Goya*, Andrew Potok, 1986.

3234 I'd always dreamed of Camelot, of having a place all my own. — *Magnolia Gardens*, Caroline Bridgwood, 1987.

3235 The old writer lived in a boxcar by the river. — *The Western Lands*, William S. Burroughs, 1987.

3236 124 was spiteful. — *Beloved*, Toni Morrison, 1987.

3237 It was an ordinary house: the type quite common among the better-off poor; the type that mockingly stands shoulder to shoulder with grotesque architectural blunders committed at enormous expense and in wondrously appalling taste; the type that is always springing up somewhere in the numerous potpourrious suburbs of Karachi since its continual expansion after the fateful birth of Pakistan. — *The 13th House*, Adam Zameenzad, 1987.

3238 Peter Chitepo paced across the hard concrete floor and peered through a dirty window at sun-baked pink clay and dusty rows of whitewashed shanties. — *Quimby*, Arthur Adams, 1988.

3239 Jackie Jeminovski lived in a fine home, in an old development north of Manzanita Canyon, just a few blocks from downtown Lincoln's Grove, in Marin County. — *From a Distant Place*, Don Carpenter, 1988.

3240 We lived in Brooklyn, just a block from Prospect Park. — *Say You Want Me*, Richard Cohen, 1988.

3241 New York stories are about homes: renting them, buying them, renovating them, being evicted from them. — *Real Estate*, Jane DeLynn, 1988.

3242 A gray wooden house with diamond window-panes in some places stands amid an endless array of suburban dwellings, each unique in its way but conforming to certain common principles: porches, back-yards, front-yards, attics, basements, buttercups. — *Sweet Desserts*, Lucy Ellmann, 1988.

3243 After some time he realized the house was speaking to whomever might be listening: this was Mark. — *Second Son*, Robert Ferro, 1988.

3244 At the Manfred, on Manhattan's seamy West 69th Street, all the lights and tenants have gone out, but one. — *The Hermit of 69th Street*, Jerzy Kosinski, 1988.

3245 Jennifer ran around and made one final check of the farmhouse. — *The Other Woman*, Ellen Lesser, 1988.

3246 "Remote," I said. I was at the window, the glass dirty with rain-spattered dust. — *A Stranger's House*, Bret Lott, 1988.

3247 Willie and Liberty broke into a house on Crab Key and lived there for a week. — *Breaking and Entering*, Joy Williams, 1988.

3248 Selbury Quade, that perfect country house set amid green wooded combes in the pleasant county of Somerset, seemed to every stranger's eye a serene and comfortable dwelling place, one that had surely sheltered generations of tranquil family life. — *The Quade Inheritance*, Barbara Ker Wilson, 1988.

3249 Let us first begin with the place in which Celia lived, and the house within which Celia lived within the place. — *Parlor Games*, Mavis Cheek, 1989.

3250 We didn't always live on Mango Street. — *The House on Mango Street*, Sandra Cisneros, 1989.

3251 Mr. Squalatush lived in a place of great beauty, tucked high among the folds of the Cordillera Entre Rios. — *Dollarville*, Pete Davies, 1989.

3252 The house is isolated, at the end of a long drive. — *Secret Lives*, Max Egremont, 1989.

3253 When Joe Starling was ten years old, his father's bank foreclosed on a fieldstone mansion which was by then a depressing ruin standing by itself in the middle of a fourteen-section cattle pasture. — *Keep the Change*, Thomas McGuane, 1989.

3254 Malcolm DeWitt lived exactly two miles from the house where he grew up. — *Limited Partnerships*, Lisa Zeidner, 1989.

3255 Weeks passed sometimes when Sugrue did nothing for the house. — *Crossing Borders*, Thomas E. Kennedy, 1990.

3256 Houses collect things: old newspapers, junk mail — Her. — *Her*, Cherry Muhanji, 1990.

3257 Just before midnight they went to the flat. It was dark and the blinds were down. — *The Dwarfs*, Harold Pinter, 1990.

3258 Afterward I lived in Paris, in the same apartment where I had painted the *Brooklyn Crucifixion*. — *The Gift of Asher Lev*, Chaim Potok, 1990.

3259 When you top the rise over the River Bridge, the first thing you see is the Birdsong house down at the end of Claxton Avenue, three blocks away, where the street makes a right angle with Birdsong Boulevard. — *Old Dogs and Children*, Robert Inman, 1991.

3260 The house fooled everyone. — *Chapel Street*, Sam North, 1991.

3261 After graduating from Smith in 1971, magna cum laude, Emily found herself a studio on East 92nd Street, just off Park, for $180 a month. — *Polite Sex*, James Wilcox, 1991.

3262 We live about as close to French Town as you can get and still be a white person. — *Crossing Blood*, Nanci Kincaid, 1992.

3263 The house in which the fourteen sisters of Emilio Montez O'Brien lived radiated femininity. — *The Fourteen Sisters of Emilio Montez O'Brien*, Oscar Hijuelos, 1993.

3264 Say there is a very fortunate young newlywed, a theoretical physicist named Mark Perdue, who has just purchased a deluxe semi-

detached unit in the Cobblestone Hearth Village Estates development — across from the Paradise Mall in Terra Linda — at the edge of the new-built Phase III section where the lawns and driveways aren't installed yet but where all the foundations meet new seismic code requirements and everybody is guaranteed a Mount Tamalpais view. — *Particles and Luck*, Louis B. Jones, 1993.

3265 La Rumorosa, for that was the name of the Joyce villa on the promontory just below Bellagio, where Lake Como divides to form a pair of clown's pantaloons, blue and green, gold speckled and shimmering, was one of those places where, sooner or later, everyone stayed. — *As Max Saw It*, Louis Begley, 1994.

Education

3266 In the year 1878 I took my degree of Doctor of Medicine of the University of London, and proceeded to Netley to go through the course prescribed for surgeons in the army. — *A Study in Scarlet*, Arthur Conan Doyle, 1887.

3267 The Time Traveller (for so it will be convenient to speak of him) was expounding a recondite matter to us. — *The Time Machine*, H. G. Wells, 1895.

3268 "I won't study another word to-day!" Helena tipped the table, spilling the books to the floor. *The Californians*, Gertrude Atherton, 1898.

3269 "Cum er long hunny an' let yer mammy fix yer 'spectabul, so yer ken go to skule. Yer mammy is 'tarmined ter gib yer all de book larning dar is ter be had eben ef she has ter lib on bred an' herrin's, an' die en de a'ms house." — *Imperium in Imperio*, Sutton E. Griggs, 1899.

3270 Toward the close of a May afternoon in the year 1884, Miss Priscilla Batte, having learned by heart the lesson in physical geography she would teach her senior class on the morrow, stood feeding her canary on the little square porch of the Dinwiddie Academy for Young Ladies. — *Virginia*, Ellen Glasgow, 1913.

3271 I wonder if there isn't a lot of bunkum in higher education? — *Parnassus on Wheels*, Christopher Morley, 1917.

3272 The education of Griffith Adams was begun, as far as he, himself, could remember, by his sharp-featured nurse, Carrie, seating him firmly upon a high straight-backed chair, after he had been tubbed, combed and arrayed in one of his stiff, starched piqué dresses, and given a long nail file and told from between firm lips, to

clean his nails, and that if he rumpled his dress, he would be locked in the closet. — *Salt*, Charles G. Norris, 1918.

3273 The education bestowed on Flora Poste by her parents had been expensive, athletic and prolonged; and when they died within a few weeks of one another during the annual epidemic of the influenza or Spanish Plague which occurred in her twentieth year, she was discovered to possess every art and grace save that of earning her own living. — *Cold Comfort Farm*, Stella Gibbons, 1932.

3274 It was thanks to Mr. Kandinsky that Joe knew a unicorn when he saw one. — *A Kid for Two Farthings*, Wolf Mankowitz, 1953.

3275 It was just past my sixteenth birthday that I first learned about the world; and this from my uncle Zachary, molasses chandler in the port of Mortar which, to we lads in Ayrshire then, seemed like some Babylon or Rome. — *Westward to Laughter*, Colin MacInnes, 1969.

3276 Reverting to the university at forty, one immediately recaptured all the crushing melancholy of the undergraduate condition. — *Books Do Furnish a Room*, Anthony Powell, 1971.

3277 My wife, Utchka (whose name I some time ago shortened to Utch), could teach patience to a time bomb. — *The 158-Pound Marriage*, John Irving, 1974.

3278 It was the third of June, 1947. This evening, the Viceroy was to make an important announcement. That's what Lala Kanshi Ram told his wife Prabha Rani, whose education had become his task. — *Azadi*, Chaman Nahal, 1975.

3279 His mother taught him numbers before he went to school. — *Wrinkles*, Charles Simmons, 1978.

3280 Barefoot conducts his seminars on his houseboat in Sausalito. It costs a hundred dollars to find out why we are on this Earth. You also get a sandwich, but I wasn't hungry that day. — *The Transmigration of Timothy Archer*, Philip K. Dick, 1982.

3281 I never did learn to speak Apache properly. — *Flashman and the Redskins*, George Mac Donald Fraser, 1982.

3282 One quiet morning, a Saturday, in the spring, when I was three, while Dudley Beaker was sitting on his porch drinking a cup of coffee and reading the morning paper, the thought struck him that it was time I learned to read. — "The Fox and the Clam," Eric Kraft, 1983.

3283 There we were, scattered around the Arts Quad, the proud men and women of Simon Straight College, Class of '71: a thousand gowns casually smoking joints and playing Frisbee with their mortarboards as the parents shook hands under the trees. — *The Breaks*, Richard Price, 1983.

3284 I'm back at school again. I have to teach the great works again — those aesthetic phenomena which alone, according to Nietzsche, make existence still bearable for us. — *Modus Vivendi*, Deirdre Levinson, 1984.

3285 As long as Helen was attending her adult education classes twice a week, everything worked out fine: Edgar could have a completely quiet house for his work, or his thinking, or whatever it was. — "In the Act," Rachel Ingalls, 1987.

3286 Six months ago a friend of mine and I left doctoral programs in chemistry under certain different circumstances. — *A Woman Named Drown*, Padgett Powell, 1987.

3287 It was her sister who taught her how to hyperventilate. — *This Is Your Life*, Meg Wolitzer, 1988.

3288 The moment one learns English, complications set in. — *Chromos*, Felipe Alfau, 1990.

3289 "*Now*, my dear Sir Harry, I must tell you," says her majesty, with that stubborn little duck of her head that always made Palmerston think she was going to butt him in the guts, "I am *quite* determined to learn *Hindoostanee*." — *Flashman and the Mountain of Light*, George MacDonald Fraser, 1990.

3290 From my father I learned astrology and medicine. — *The Alchymist's Journal*, Evan S. Connell, 1991.

3291 No shock. No tears./ I was taught that first and I learned fast, and most of the time, I think I've got it. — *Deadline*, Marcy Heidish, 1991.

3292 Actually, I was sitting on my bed in my apartment in Culver City, watching the Lakers game with the sound turned off, while I tried to study vocabulary for my introductory Japanese class. — *Rising Sun*, Michael Crichton, 1992.

3293 It was Mum who kept trying to make a lady of me through all my growing-up years but it was Grams who taught me her magic tricks and how to be a pickpocket, and of the two of them I have to say that Grams' lesson certainly proved the more valuable to me in my life. — *Caravan*, Dorothy Gilman, 1992.

3294 I can't say I've had much education. — *Bailey's Cafe*, Gloria Naylor, 1992.

Elevators

3295 Eileen Delaney heard the door of the noisy old elevator close behind her, and the diminuendo of its bang and rattle as its ascent progressed up the shaft. — *Red Threads*, Rex Stout, 1939.

3296 The law offices of Wellesley and Sable were over a savings bank on the main street of Santa Teresa. Their private elevator lifted you from a bare little lobby into an atmosphere of elegant simplicity. It created the impression that after years of struggle you were rising effortlessly to your natural level, one of the chosen. — *The Galton Case*, Ross Macdonald, 1959.

3297 The meeting was late in starting because Mr. Turtle had trouble with the lift. — *The Old Boys*, William Trevor, 1964.

3298 Brown quickened his steps down the corridor in order to enter the elevator with Schwarzlose. Watch Brown! Brown is our man. We will remain with Brown all evening and far into the night. He is the engine of our story. — *Killing Everybody*, Mark Harris, 1973.

3299 When the power supply failed in the old Pera quarter of Istanbul, the celebrated ironwork lift of the Palas Hotel clamped firmly on its central pole just below the fourth floor. There Paul Nathan found himself sitting on a narrow bench pleasantly close to the "Golden Wonder Holidays" girl, while from the stairs around them the sounds of opening doors and indignation mingled with higher pitched noises from suddenly blackened rooms. — *The Shadow Master*, Elaine Feinstein, 1978.

3300 He rose into the sky. You didn't notice the speed of ascent, the rapid movement up from the ground. — *The King's Evil*, David Helwig, 1984.

Emotions

3301 Elfride Swancourt was a girl whose emotions lay very near the surface. Their nature more precisely, and as modified by the creeping hours of time, was known only to those who watched the circumstances of her history. — *A Pair of Blue Eyes*, Thomas Hardy, 1873.

3302 Between herself and all that was waiting to flow in and settle upon this window-lit end of the long empty room, was the sense of missing Lionel Cholmley. — *Clear Horizon*, Dorothy M. Richardson, 1935.

3303 Outside the station, people settled down again to being emotionally commonplace. — *The Living and the Dead*, Patrick White, 1941.

3304 He had this ache in him again — this new ache that rose in him and tore like wild and savage hunger. — *The Treasure of Pleasant Valley*, Frank Yerby, 1955.

3305 Stubbornly Elijah Baley fought panic. — *The Naked Sun*, Isaac Asimov, 1957.

3306 Shame forbade Jacob, when he passed through Washington toward home, from calling or seeing Joleen. — *Something About a Soldier*, Mark Harris, 1957.

3307 On the first of April, 1900, Lance Falks rode out from Fairoaks in a driving rain. He was in a thoroughly bad humor, which, under the circumstances, was understandable. — *Fairoaks*, Frank Yerby, 1957.

3308 Eventually, people are willing to admit most of their flaws — greed, jealousy, pride, hostility — but the feeling they're most ashamed to admit is loneliness. — *Mr. Right Is Dead*, Rona Jaffe, 1960.

3309 "But Jack," she said, "I don't know if I want to go. I'm nervous." — *Diamond*, Brian Glanville, 1962.

3310 After a pause to phone a few numbers, Ben Pringle cut through on 83rd toward Amsterdam Avenue, getting more cheerful and calm. — *The Peacock's Tail*, Edward Hoagland, 1965.

3311 He felt giddy and foolish and awkward, and he also felt like a thief. — *The Paper Dragon*, Evan Hunter, 1966.

3312 Sometimes Big Track Bascomb felt good. — *The Klansman*, William Bradford Huie, 1967.

3313 I felt like a spectator and a participant both. — *Sons*, Evan Hunter, 1969.

3314 Against the season, which was spring, and against the day, iris limp and azaleas sodden in rain, Amelia Larson was in a burning mood. — *Against the Season*, Jane Rule, 1971.

3315 Commander Victor Henry rode a taxicab home from the Navy Building on Constitution Avenue, in a gusty gray March rainstorm that matched his mood. — *The Winds of War*, Herman Wouk, 1971.

3316 Because I guess I was kind of embarrassed. — *Tornado Pratt*, Paul Ableman, 1977.

3317 There's nothing like being ignored to make you feel every eye is on you. — *Love Bites*, Freda Garmaise, 1981.

3318 You would have to care about the country. — *Nobody's Angel*, Thomas McGuane, 1982.

3319 Everyone everywhere has always felt trapped in one way or another, and I was no exception. — *Alexandra Freed*, Lisa Zeidner, 1983.

3320 Blanche Vernon occupied her time most usefully in keeping feelings at bay. — *The Misalliance*, Anita Brookner, 1986.

3321 Dinnertime is when I miss Eddie the most. — *The Girl Who Loved Garbo*, Rachel Gallagher, 1990.

3322 I still miss Uncle Percy. — *Coming to Terms*, Anna Murdoch, 1991.

3323 At times I felt like the bear in the penny arcade game who scurried back and forth and spun around when you hit the target. — *The Big*

Hype, Avery Corman, 1992.

3324 Nne-nne was in a state that night before I left home. — *I Saw the Sky Catch Fire*, T. Obinkaram Echewa, 1992.

Employers and Employees

3325 It was characteristic of Mr. Philip Quentin that he first lectured his servant on the superiority of mind over matter and then took him cheerfully by the throat and threw him into a far corner of the room. — *Castle Craneycrow*, George Barr McCutcheon, 1902.

3326 In the pupils' room of the offices of Lucas & Enwright, architects, Russell Square, Bloomsbury, George Edwin Cannon, an articled pupil, leaned over a large drawing-board and looked up at Mr. Enwright, the head of the firm, who with cigarette and stick was on his way out after what he called a good day's work. — *The Roll-Call*, Arnold Bennett, 1918.

3327 "And by the way," said Mr. Hankin, arresting Miss Rossiter as she rose to go, "there is a new copy-writer coming in today." — *Murder Must Advertise*, Dorothy L. Sayers, 1933.

3328 The hired girl with a loud impatience told Mrs. Wigton not to bother her. — *The Foolscap Rose*, Joseph Hergesheimer, 1934.

3329 *There are alive today hundreds of men who saw Samuel Eaton, who accepted wages from him, envied him, hated him, laughed at him behind his back, worked hard for him, cheated him, and never addressed him except as Mr. Eaton or Mr. Samuel.* — *From the Terrace*, John O'Hara, 1958.

3330 In the summer of 1912, when I was fifteen years old, Schlifka the pimp offered me ten bucks to tell him when Hannah Isaacs showed up on Orchard Street in the building where I lived. — *My Own Ground*, Hugh Nissenson, 1972.

3331 Neville came with the house. — *Spreading Fires*, John Knowles, 1974.

3332 My mission had been made clear to me by the terrifying Man in Charge as I sat in his office on the 101st floor of the World Trade Center in New York. — *Moviola*, Garson Kanin, 1979.

3333 Everyone behind the mossy walls of Harvard University — as well as several hundred scholars beyond this academic pale — knew that if you wanted to communicate with Professor Jacob Barker the most efficient path was across the desk or into the telephone of his secretary, Miss Emily Compton. — *Professor Romeo*, Anne Bernays, 1989.

3334 Myra Wells stood in the mine office

after her shift and forfeited a week's pay in lieu of notice. — *Relative Distances*, Victoria Jenkins, 1990.

3335 In the morning Cathy McPherson put three soft-boiled eggs outside Benny Catchprice's door and in the afternoon she fired him from the Spare Parts Department. — *The Tax Inspector*, Peter Carey, 1991.

Endings

3336 The time of my end approaches. — "The Lifted Veil," George Eliot, 1878.

3337 *Nothing ever ends.* — *Compulsion*, Meyer Levin, 1956.

3338 Hiram Clegg, together with his wife Emma and four friends of the faith from Randolph Junction, were summoned by the Spirit and Mrs. Clara Collins, widow of the beloved Nazarene preacher Ely Collins, to West Condon on the weekend of the eighteenth and nineteenth of April, there to await the End of the World. — *The Origin of the Brunists*, Robert Coover, 1966.

3339 It had seemed like a message sent direct to him./ *If you are desperate*, the poster said. *If you are at the end of your rope*. Well, if it could be the end of something that had never properly begun, that's me. — *The End of the Line*, Monica Dickens, 1970.

3340 If it were only true that all's well that ends well, if only it were true. — *The Hothouse by the East River*, Muriel Spark, 1973.

3341 After the thing was all over, when peril had ceased to loom and happy endings had been distributed in heaping handfuls and we were driving home with our hats on the side of our heads, having shaken the dust of Steeple Bumpleigh from our tyres, I confessed to Jeeves that there had been moments during the recent proceedings when Bertram Wooster, though no weakling, had come very near to despair. — *Jeeves in the Morning*, P. G. Wodehouse, 1974.

3342 "In every show," my friend Sidney used to say, "there's a payoff scene. You don't have to kill them along the way if you bring off your finish, and it doesn't matter how great you are up to then if you don't. The end is everything." — *The Understudy*, Elia Kazan, 1975.

3343 End and beginning. The Ray Charles concert was over though it had been — and still was to be — a strange, bizarre evening. — *Night Studies*, Cyrus Colter, 1980.

3344 At the restaurant Jack wanted to tell Bernie about Harriet Post, a girl he had once been in love with. He wanted to put his head

down on the table and moan aloud with rage. Instead he placed his fork into a square of ravioli and said in a moderate tone, "History consists of endings." — *Happenstance*, Carol Shields, 1980.

3345 "In the end." "In the end"? What did she mean — in the *end* he would see? — *The Sweet-Shop Owner*, Graham Swift, 1980.

3346 "Then I guess that's that." — *A Lovely Time Was Had by All*, Ruth Doan MacDougall, 1982.

3347 You didn't really start noticing things again until the very end. — *Fragments*, Jack Fuller, 1984.

3348 I am near the end now. — *Season for War*, P. F. Kluge, 1984.

3349 It is, I suppose, the beginning of the end. — *The Arrowing of the Cane*, John Conyngham, 1986.

3350 New Year's Eve, and the end of a decade. — *The Radiant Way*, Margaret Drabble, 1987.

3351 Is this the promised end? — *I, Eve*, Edward Le Comte, 1988.

3352 When this happened, Vincent MacNamara thought it was the end of everything. — *The Other Side*, Mary Gordon, 1989.

3353 They always said I would hang, finish my life at the end of a rope swinging from some scaffold. — *The Serpent Amongst the Lilies*, P. C. Doherty, 1990.

3354 It was the beginning of the end of the world but not everyone noticed right away. — *People in Trouble*, Sarah Schulman, 1990.

3355 Not even a good two hours and it's all over. — *Daughters*, Paule Marshall, 1991.

Environment

3356 Bred up in luxurious indolence, I was surrounded by friends who seemed to have no business in this world but to save me the trouble of thinking or acting for myself; and I was confirmed in the pride of helplessness by being continually reminded that I was the only son and heir of the Earl of Glenthorn. — *Ennui*, Maria Edgeworth, 1804.

3357 Those two girls, Constance and Sophia Baines, paid no heed to the manifold interest of their situation, of which, indeed, they had never been conscious. — *The Old Wives' Tale*, Arnold Bennett, 1908.

3358 To Baree, for many days after he was born, the world was a vast gloomy cavern. — *Baree, Son of Kazan*, James Oliver Curwood, 1917.

3359 All of this universe known to me in the year 1864 was bounded by the wooded hills of a little Wisconsin coulee, and its center was the cottage in which my mother was living alone — my father was in the war. — *A Son of the Middle Border*, Hamlin Garland, 1917.

3360 "Well, so this is the background from which we are to face the world!" said Clara Bell, bending towards her two companions. "I hope it will prove an advantageous setting for us." — *Elders and Betters*, Ivy Compton-Burnett, 1944.

3361 Each generation sees and hears a different world. — *The Wilderness-Stone*, Robert Nathan, 1961.

3362 I know a place where there is no smog and no parking problem and no population explosion . . . no Cold War and no H-bombs and no television commercials . . . no Summit Conferences, no Foreign Aid, no hidden taxes — no income tax. The climate is the sort that Florida and California claim (and neither has), the land is lovely, the people are friendly and hospitable to strangers, the women are beautiful and amazingly anxious to please. — *Glory Road*, Robert A. Heinlein, 1963.

3363 No one knows how the arteries and nerves of the man next to you make him see you and the world that surrounds you both. — *Cabot Wright Begins*, James Purdy, 1964

3364 "In this country charity covers no sins!" — *The Sowers*, Henry Seton Merriman, 1967.

3365 The child's sombre eyes viewed three worlds. — *Eleanora Duse*, Jean Stubbs, 1970.

3366 Suddenly I was sick of the savagery of the world. — *Summer of the Red Wolf*, Morris West, 1971.

3367 He found it all around. It opened and was close. He felt it was himself, but felt it was more. — *Plus*, Joseph McElroy, 1977.

3368 It was dark and warm, and the world was small. — *Squeak*, John Bowen, 1983.

3369 I lived in a different country once. Nothing there was the same as now. All that happened then, if it happened here, would be strange and fresh. — *In the Mood*, Keith Waterhouse, 1983.

3370 It was the summer of 1986, and everywhere there were cuts. — *Cuts*, Malcolm Bradbury, 1987.

3371 The man they called Bao Dai lived in a three-colored world. Brown was the color of leeches. Orange was the color of Corporal Trinh's decayed boots. Green was the color of the jungle and of misfortune. — *Hard Rain*, Peter Abrahams, 1988.

3372 If we are to survive in the environment we have made for ourselves, may we have to be monstrous enough to greet our predicament? — *Hopeful Monsters*, Nicholas Mosley, 1990.

3373 My world is compressed. — *Cracking India*, Bapsi Sidhwa, 1991.

3374 — used to it — although sometimes the very fact of my having grown used to it strikes me as the oddest thing of all! — *In the Eye of the Sun*, Ahdaf Soueif, 1992.

Eras

3375 The days of the Stuarts, kings of Scotland, were the days of chivalry and romance. — *The Three Perils of Man*, James Hogg, 1822.

3376 At that famous period of history, when the seventeenth century (after a deal of quarrelling, king-killing, reforming, republicanizing, restoring, re-restoring, play-writing, sermon-writing, Oliver-Cromwellizing, Stuartizing, and Orangizing, to be sure) had sunk into its grave, giving place to the lusty eighteenth; when Mr. Isaac Newton was a tutor of Trinity, and Mr. Joseph Addison Commissioner of Appeals; when the presiding genius that watched over the destinies of the French nation had played out all the best cards in his hand, and his adversaries began to pour in their trumps; when there were two kings in Spain employed perpetually in running away from one another; when there was a queen in England, with such rogues for Ministers as have never been seen, no, not in our own day; and a General, of whom it may be severely argued, whether he was the meanest miser or the greatest hero in the world: when Mrs. Masham had not yet put Madam Marlborough's nose out of joint; when people had their ears cut off for writing very meek political pamphlets; and very large full-bottomed wigs were just beginning to be worn with powder; and the face of Louis the Great, as his was handed in to him behind the bed-curtains, was, when issuing thence, observed to look longer, older, and more dismal daily. . . .

About the year One thousand seven hundred and five, that is, in the glorious reign of Queen Anne, there existed certain characters, and befell a series of adventures, which, since they are strictly in accordance with the present fashionable style and taste; since they have been already partly described in the "Newgate Calendar;" since they are (as shall be seen anon) agreeably low, delightfully disgusting, and at the same time eminently pleasing and pathetic, may properly be set down here. — *Catherine*, William Makepeace Thackeray *as* Ikey Solomons, jun., 1839-1840.

3377 It was the best of times, it was the worst of times, it was the age of wisdom, it was the age

of foolishness, it was the epoch of belief, it was the epoch of incredulity, it was the season of Light, it was the season of Darkness, it was the spring of hope, it was the winter of despair, we had everything before us, we had nothing before us, we were all going direct to Heaven, we were all going direct the other way—in short, the period was so far like the present period, that some of its noisiest authorities insisted on its being received, for good or for evil, in the superlative degree of comparison only. —*A Tale of Two Cities*, Charles Dickens, 1859.

3378 At a very remote period, when editorials were mostly devoted to discussion as to whether the Democratic Convention (shortly to be held in Chicago) would or would not declare in favor of bi-metallism; when golf was a novel form of recreation in America, and people disputed how to pronounce its name, and pedestrians still turned to stare after an automobile; when, according to the fashion notes, "the godet skirts and huge sleeves of the present modes" were already doomed to extinction; when the baseball season had just begun, and some of our people were discussing the national game, and others the spectacular burning of the old Pennsylvania Railway depot at Thirty-third and Market Street in Philadelphia, and yet others the significance of General Fitzhugh Lee's recent appointment as consul-general to Habana:—at this remote time, Lichfield talked of nothing except the Pendomer divorce case. — *The Rivet in Grandfather's Neck*, James Branch Cabell, 1915.

3379 Porgy lived in a Golden Age. —*Porgy*, Du Bose Heyward, 1925.

3380 Ours is essentially a tragic age, so we refuse to take it tragically. —*Lady Chatterly's Lover*, D. H. Lawrence, 1928.

3381 Kinraddie lands had been won by a Norman childe, Cospatric de Gondeshil, in the days of William the Lyon, when gryphons and such-like beasts still roamed the Scots countryside and folk would waken in their beds to hear the children screaming, with a great wolf-beast, come through the hide window, tearing at their throats. —*Sunset Song*, Lewis Grassic Gibbon, 1932.

3382 People who were born a little before 1900 belong to no age. —"The Single Heart," Storm Jameson, 1932.

3383 It was in London in June of 1937—a London none of us will ever see again, a London in which the nineteenth century and sometimes even the eighteenth was just around the corner, for in London historical time has always lagged and one era overlapped another. — *What Became of Anna Bolton*, Louis Bromfield, 1944.

3384 Later, thinking back, Skinner would remember it as a time when neither of them had spoken. — *The End of My Life*, Vance Bourjaily, 1947.

3385 This was a Golden Age, a time of high adventure, rich living, and hard dying . . . but nobody thought so. — *The Stars My Destination*, Alfred Bester, 1957.

3386 It was with the advent of the Laurie London era that I realized the whole teenage epic was tottering to doom. —*Absolute Beginners*, Colin MacInnes, 1959.

3387 In those days, heaven was closer to earth, much of which still lay in darkness. — *The Fair*, Robert Nathan, 1964.

3388 There was a time when it was out of sight out of mind. —*Love Feast*, Frederick Buechner, 1974.

3389 Here we all were in that time when love and money solved everything. —*Swiftie the Magician*, Herbert Gold, 1974.

3390 We all remember that time. It was no different for me than for others. — *The Memoirs of a Survivor*, Doris Lessing, 1974.

3391 It was a bad time in many ways, some of them comprehensible, others not. —*September September*, Shelby Foote, 1977.

3392 *When did the twentieth-century nightmare begin?*/ In 1945, when, for many people, it seemed to have ended. —*1985*, Anthony Burgess, 1978.

3393 It was a period of my life I am not particularly proud of. It happened before the era of accomplishment. I had not yet become the hero of my life, nor was I even its villain. —*Confessions of Summer*, Phillip Lopate, 1979.

3394 When William McKinley was president and Russia had occupied Port Arthur in China, and there was a rush to the Klondike for gold, and people yelled "get a horse" at the first motor cars, it was then the old men in lazy contemplation and with some jocosity would gather on their piazzas to drink hot toddies. — *The Pembroke Colors*, Stephen Longstreet, 1981.

3395 For a long time I stayed away from the Acropolis. — *The Names*, Don DeLillo, 1982.

3396 It began in the old and golden days of England, in a time when all the hedgerows were green and the roads dusty, when hawthorn and wild roses bloomed, when big-bellied landlords brewed rich October ale at a penny a pint for rakish high-booted cavaliers with jingling spurs and long rapiers, when squires ate roast beef and belched and damned the Dutch over their claret while their faithful hounds slumbered on the rushes by the hearth, when summers were long and warm and drowsy, with honeysuckle and hollyhocks by cottage walls, when winter nights were clear and sharp with frost-rimmed moons shining on the silent snow, and Claud Duval and Swift Nick Nevison lurked in the bosky thickets, teeth gleaming beneath their masks as they

heard the rumble of coaches bearing paunchy well-lined nabobs and bright-eyed ladies with powdered hair who would gladly tread a measure by the wayside with the gallant tobyman, and bestow a kiss to save their husbands' guineas; an England where good King Charles lounged amiably on his throne, and scandalised Mr. Pepys (or was it Mr. Evelyn?) by climbing walls to ogle Pretty Nell; where gallants roistered and diced away their fathers' fortunes; where beaming yokels in spotless smocks made hay in the sunshine and ate bread and cheese and quaffed foaming tankards fit to do G. K. Chesterton's heart good; where threadbare pedlars with sharp eyes and long noses shared their morning bacon with weary travellers in dew-pearled woods and discoursed endlessly of "Hudibras" and the glories of nature; where burly earringed smugglers brought their stealthy sloops into midnight coves, and stowed their hard-run cargoes of Hollands and Brussels and fragrant Virginia in clammy caverns; where the poachers of Lincolnshire lifted hare and pheasants by the bushel and buffeted gamekeepers and jumped o'er everywhere... — *The Pyrates*, George MacDonald Fraser, 1984.

3397 "Days of wine and roses," said Wilt to himself. — *Wilt on High*, Tom Sharpe, 1984.

3398 In those days people still went on holiday by train and bus. Spain was where the onions came from. Abroad was for the privileged few. — *B-Movie*, Stan Barstow, 1987.

3399 I used to think cowboys lived forever, and maybe I would too, that the prairies would never be plowed and that the great trail rides up the Chisholm would roll on and on. — *Keeping Warm*, Mary Gardner, 1987.

3400 First, before the beginning of Sarum, came a time when the world was a colder and darker place. — *Sarum*, Edward Rutherfurd, 1987.

3401 It was a period when the future seemed more present than the present itself. — *After the War*, Frederic Raphael, 1988.

3402 Imagine./ Not the dark avenues of cities, the long files of traffic lights going green in unison, the throb of the all-night bus at its terminal stop, the lonely cruising taxi; but the moon-shadows of the maple leaves on quiet sidewalks, the sounds of birds that never sleep, sending their liquid keening into a honeysuckle midnight, and a time, only yesterday, but before television, before jet planes or astronauts, before civil rights, transistors, Xerox, AIDS, the Pill, or the Bomb. — *Apes and Angels*, Philip Appleman, 1989.

3403 Early in the last decade of the century, the earth began to die in earnest, though few of us noticed, and as in all times of unperceived cataclysm, the very air shuddered with myths, legends, and wondrous occurrences. — *King's Oak*, Anne Rivers Siddons, 1990.

3404 They were not long, the days of wine and yuppies. — *Fun with Dirk and Bree*, Alice Kahn, 1991.

Escape

3405 One moment he was a cool man who viewed his chances for escape and found them full of risk; and then a night wind moved over the river with its odors of dark soil warmed by summer rain and the resin scent of firs and the acrid taint of brush fires, and when these rank flavors came to him he knew at once he was done with caution. — *Alder Gulch*, Ernest Haycox, 1942.

3406 Martha Ingram had come to Rome to escape something: George Hartwell had been certain of it from the first. — *Knights & Dragons*, Elizabeth Spencer, 1965.

3407 In the early summer of 1902 John Barrington Ashley of Coaltown, a small mining center in southern Illinois, was tried for the murder of Breckenridge Lansing, also of Coaltown. He was found guilty and sentenced to death. Five days later, at one in the morning of Tuesday, July 22, he escaped from his guards on the train that was carrying him to his execution. — *The Eighth Day*, Thornton Wilder, 1967.

3408 The police came and found arsenic in the glass, but I was gone by then. — *Eva's Man*, Gayl Jones, 1976.

3409 I had been making the rounds of the Sacrifice Poles the day we heard my brother had escaped. — *The Wasp Factory*, Iain Banks, 1984.

3410 "Why didn't you run after her?" — *About Tilly Beamis*, Sumner Locke Elliott, 1984.

3411 This was the second day of their escape and when the light began to fade Lewis Mac-kenna drove the truck up the rise of the ground to where the camphor trees grew. — *The Wings of the Wind*, Ronald Hardy, 1987.

3412 The seed of desire to escape from his identity was planted in Stephen Cooper's heart on the evening of April 26, 1984, although he was not aware of it at the time. — *Somebody Else's Life*, Morris Philipson, 1987.

3413 Just because they found Martin Bormann's skull doesn't mean he's dead, my best beloved; for everyone knows that competent observers from every neutral country have reported sighting an old man in Argentina whose head is wrapped in bandages, and only the hunted eyes show, winking and blinking beneath the thousands of cranial splints; — and Anastasia

Romanoff, I know her: when Yurovsky and his Cheka men were murdering her family she fainted and they took her for dead; they piled her into a truck with the others, and while they were getting the hatchets and caustic acids ready she came to herself, ran into the deep dark taiga, and flung herself into the arms of the Whites just in time, where she was treated as befitted her nobility; and that's how the leopard got his spots. — *You Bright and Risen Angels*, William T. Vollmann, 1987.

3414 The news that Josef Virek had escaped from Czechoslovakia reached London at the end of April. — *A Season in the West*, Piers Paul Read, 1988.

3415 Markin wondered if he was running out of places to escape to, if the world was backing him into a corner. — *Leaving Losapas*, Roland Merullo, 1991.

3416 During the last retreat, when the Chinese and the army of the North swept down into the South, an old man and his wife fled from their village in the hills and embarked upon a panicky trek along the main road to Seoul and at one point scrambled with other refugees into a roadside ditch to avoid an approaching column of American tanks and jeeps. — *I Am the Clay*, Chaim Potok, 1992.

Establishments

3417 It was the opening of the season of eighteen hundred and thirty-two, at the Baths of WILDBAD. — *Armadale*, Wilkie Collins, 1866.

3418 The post-office in the middle Georgia village of Hillsborough used to be a queer little place, whatever it is now. — *On the Plantation*, Joel Chandler Harris, 1892.

3419 Yellow Jacket's post office was a rack of pigeonholes in the front corner of Badey's Emporium. — *Hardcase*, Luke Short, 1942.

3420 Bernard Clare looked around vaguely in the large reading room of the New York Public Library. — *Bernard Clare*, James T. Farrell, 1946.

3421 The inn lay in a hollow, the low hill, wooded with leafless beech trees, rising behind it in a gentle round just high enough to break the good draft from the inn chimneys, so that on this chill day the smoke rose a little and then fell downward. — *The Trial of Sören Qvist*, Janet Lewis, 1947.

3422 Beyond the edge of town, past tar-covered poor houses and a low hill bare except for fallen electric poles, was the institution, and

it sent its delicate and isolated buildings trembling over the gravel and cinder floor of the valley. — *The Cannibal*, John Hawkes, 1949.

3423 Blucher's *Annals of the North* (Grand Rapids, Michigan, 1919) which perforce omits the human element and which minces the few words at its disposal, has this to say:

> Centennial Club (formely the Shiawasee Rod and Gun Club): Grandest of the original sporting clubs of the Northern Lower Peninsula, founded by the barons of lumbering who logged off the white pine stands of the Saginaw Country.

— *The Sporting Club*, Thomas McGuane, 1968.

3424 The welfare center is housed in an armory, along with a police precinct. — *The Bag*, Sol Yurick, 1968.

3425 This is a beautiful library, timed perfectly, lush and American. — *The Abortion*, Richard Brautigan, 1971.

3426 That day the four of them went to the library, though at different times. — *Quartet in Autumn*, Barbara Pym, 1977.

3427 A public library, like a railway station, gets all kinds. — *Criminal Trespass*, Helen Hudson, 1985.

3428 "I hear the Museum'll be closing up shop," the cabbie says. — *Heartbreak Hotel*, Gabrielle Burton, 1986.

3429 The ramparts of the General Theological Seminary ring the block at Ninth Avenue and Twenty-first Street, just below Manhattan's waist, making an evangelical stronghold in the midst of the city's vast urgencies and agonies. — *Making Believe*, John Leggett, 1986.

3430 The post office in East Shelton reminded me of the one in the little town near my grandparents' summer home in Maine. — *The Good Mother*, Sue Miller, 1986.

3431 The Indian Cove boatyard takes up almost the whole wharf, with its floating dock and boat slips, its lobster shack, its chandlery and sail loft, the boat brokerage office around the back. — *Sailing*, Susan Kenney, 1988.

Events

3432 The course of four centuries has well-nigh elapsed since the series of events which are related in the following chapters took place on the Continent. — *Anne of Geierstein*, Sir Walter Scott, 1829.

3433 On the human imagination, events produce the effects of time. — *The Deerslayer*, James Fenimore Cooper, 1841.

3434 The events we are about to relate occurred near the middle of the last century, previously even to that struggle which it is the fashion of America to call "the old French War." — *The Two Admirals*, James Fenimore Cooper, 1842.

3435 It is difficult at all times to write or speak of circumstances which though perfectly at one with Nature appear to be removed from natural occurrences. — *The Life Everlasting*, Marie Corelli, 1911.

3436 Events happened very rapidly with Francis Morgan that late spring morning. — *Hearts of Three*, Jack London, 1920.

3437 All this happened a good many years ago. — *The Narrow Corner*, W. Somerset Maugham, 1932.

3438 An awkward incident took place at Rimi races. — *The African Witch*, Joyce Cary, 1936.

3439 It was the day of Gandhi's assassination; but on Calvary the sightseers were more interested in the contents of their picnic baskets than in the possible significance of the, after all, rather commonplace event they had turned out to witness. — *Ape and Essence*, Aldous Huxley, 1948.

3440 Something remarkable happened that cold Tuesday in January. — *Murder by the Book*, Rex Stout, 1951.

3441 The hostler, standing in the runway of Harmony's only livery stable, saw almost simultaneously two happenings that interested him this windy May morning. — *First Claim*, Luke Short, 1960.

3442 "It all seemed so faraway," Celia Harrodsen said. — *Once an Eagle*, Anton Myrer, 1968.

3443 Later, as he sat on his balcony eating the dog, Dr. Robert Laing reflected on the unusual events that had taken place within this huge apartment building during the previous three months. — *High-Rise*, J. G. Ballard, 1975.

3444 Two seemingly unconnected events heralded the summons of Mr. George Smiley from his dubious retirement. — *Smiley's People*, John Le Carré, 1980.

3445 Seven years came and went. But then we seem always in a state of getting ready for something that never quite occurs. — *Warlock*, Jim Harrison, 1981.

3446 It happened this way. — *Monsignor Quixote*, Graham Greene, 1982.

3447 Something funny was going on in Fontaine's Department Store. — *Christmas at Fontaine's*, William Kotzwinkle, 1982.

3448 Two things don't happen very often in Hillston, North Carolina. — *Uncivil Seasons*, Michael Malone, 1983.

3449 In a small Polish farm community, during the fall planting season of 1981, events occurred which electrified the world, sending reverberations of magnitude to capitals as diverse as Washington, Peking and especially Moscow. — *Poland*, James A. Michener, 1983.

3450 Two events were to mark that day in Tanniford. They were not connected with one another and each in its way was unique. — *Georgina and Georgette*, Malcolm Hutton, 1984.

3451 Brook was down in Denver when it happened, running an errand for his uncle Caleb. — *Beyond the Mountain*, William Dieter, 1985.

3452 This is what happened. — *Staring at the Sun*, Julian Barnes, 1986.

3453 This is what happened. — *The Power of One*, Bryce Courtenay, 1989.

3454 Now what's happening? — *I Hear Voices*, Paul Ableman, 1990.

3455 It had happened a little less than a year ago in the library on the high side. — *The Indian Lawyer*, James Welch, 1990.

Evidence

3456 The philosopher who broaches a new theory is bound to furnish, at least, some elementary proofs of the reasonableness of his positions, and the historian, who ventures to record marvels that have hitherto been hid from human knowledge, owes it to a decent regard to the opinions of others, to produce some credible testimony in favor of his veracity. — *The Monikins*, James Fenimore Cooper, 1835.

3457 I often like to think that the entire sequence of events of the afternoon and evening which I am now trying to set down tends to prove a theory to which I used to be partial. — *Thank You, Mr. Moto*, John P. Marquand, 1936.

3458 A single footprint lay alone. It seemed dropped from nowhere onto the underbrush between the black, muscular roots of the high tree which dominated the ragged, lonesome hollow. — *O Beulah Land*, Mary Lee Settle, 1956.

3459 "Now you," the policeman said. "Documents!" — *Speak Now*, Frank Yerby, 1969.

3460 "It is like this," said the Centurion Rosianus Geminus. — *The Antagonists*, Ernest K. Gann, 1970.

3461 Aaron Benham sits at his desk hearing the wrong voices. The human race he has been doomed to celebrate seems to be trying to prove to him that nothing is worthwhile, nothing at all. — *The Hair of Harold Roux*, Thomas Williams, 1974.

3462 I will be her witness. — *A Book of Common Prayer*, Joan Didion, 1977.

3463 I realize that my three hundred rabbits are the most serious piece of material evidence against me. — *Faultline*, Sheila Ortiz Taylor, 1982.

3464 It was the Bad Godesberg incident that gave the proof, though the German authorities had no earthly means of knowing this. — *The Little Drummer Girl*, John Le Carré, 1983.

3465 Noises out behind the barn during the day, at night the flicker of a campfire in the woods north of the house, one rainy morning the indistinct trace of someone who'd been wandering around the yard during the night — Webster noted them all, husbanding the evidence like a wavering believer fashioning an argument for the existence of God. — *Easeful Death*, Ralph McInerny, 1991.

3466 Christopher Columbus saw a blue light in the west, but "it was such an uncertain thing," he wrote in his journal to the crown, "that I did not feel it was adequate proof of land." — *The Heirs of Columbus*, Gerald Vizenor, 1991.

Excitement

3467 The usually quiet old town of Dijon was in a state of excitement. — *The Young Franc-Tireurs*, G. A. Henty, 1872.

3468 LESS BREAD! MORE TAXES! — and then all the people cheered again, and one man, who was more excited than the rest, flung his hat high into the air, and shouted (as well as I could make out) "Who roar for the Sub-Warden?" — *Sylvie and Bruno*, Lewis Carroll, 1889.

3469 Mr. and Mrs. Haddock were very excited about going abroad. — *Mr. and Mrs. Haddock Abroad*, Donald Ogden Stewart, 1924.

3470 When I was a child of about eleven, a new excitement suddenly flared up in my life. — *The Search*, C. P. Snow, 1934.

3471 With a journey before him, Charley Mason's mother was anxious that he should make a good breakfast, but he was too excited to eat. — *Christmas Holiday*, W. Somerset Maugham, 1939.

3472 Dear Sister:/ This will be the most exciting letter I ever wrote to anyone. I have a job! — *Another Pamela*, Upton Sinclair, 1950.

3473 Ever since she had come home, Shakuntala had felt happy and excited all day long. — *Esmond in India*, Ruth Prawer Jhabvala, 1958.

3474 I was excited. Stourton didn't usually send for me so late. — *The Divided Lady*, Bruce Marshall, 1960.

3475 "Take it easy, Dewberry," I said. — *Daughter of the Legend*, Jesse Stuart, 1965.

3476 TO THE PUBLIC/ *The late insurrection in Southampton has greatly excited the public mind and led to a thousand idle, exaggerated and mischievous reports.* — *The Confessions of Nat Turner*, William Styron, 1967.

3477 I have never been so moved by the beauty of our earth. Excitement of course sharpens the senses. — *Hostage: London*, Geoffrey Household, 1977.

3478 As often as he comes to the Rushes, Endore still feels a clash of excitement and dread in anticipation of the sights, sounds, odors that he knows will assault him. — *Rushes*, John Rechy, 1979.

3479 Many important people were expected at Mother's party on that particular February evening, I was excited. — *October Blood*, Francine du Plessix Gray, 1985.

3480 I've never felt less like a woman — it's terribly exciting. This absolute *no*. — *Her Own Terms*, Judith Grossman, 1988.

3481 "The most exciting thing that's happened during the last fifteen months," said Gaius Marius, "is the elephant Gaius Claudius showed at the *ludi Romani*." — *The Grass Crown*, Colleen McCullough, 1991.

Exercise

3482 Captain Hornblower was walking up and down along that sector of the ramparts of Rosas, delimited by two sentries with loaded muskets, which the commandant had granted to him for exercise. — *Captain Horatio Hornblower*, C. S. Forester, 1939.

3483 They could be seen together almost every evening of that spring on the high-fell road, and people would look out for them making their way back in the dusk, Cedric "the trainer" leading on his motor-bike, the bright blob of his headlight a shifting beacon on the hillside, and behind him Josh, heavy boots tugging on the slim bare legs, intent on being trained. — *Josh Lawton*, Melvyn Bragg, 1972.

3484 The jogger came around the bend in the mountain road shortly after nine, as he had almost every morning since work on the plant had entered its final stages. — *Decision*, Allen Drury, 1983.

3485 I don't know how I feel till I hold that steel. — *The Pretty Girl*, Andre Dubus, 1983.

3486 David Fleming and the Army lawyer who would defend him bent, and together they laced their jogging shoes, a gesture that felt vaguely fraternal to David and made him feel uncomfortable. — *On Distant Ground*, Robert Olen Butler, 1985.

3487 "Philip, where are my ankle weights? I have to work off that fruit cake I ate on the plane." — *Private Accounts*, Ursula Bentley, 1986.

Experiences

3488 In the long and intricately inwrought chain of circumstance which renders worthy of record some experiences of Cytherea Graye, Edward Springrove, and others, the first event directly influencing the issue was a Christmas visit. — *Desperate Remedies*, Thomas Hardy, 1871.

3489 There are some events of which each circumstance and surrounding detail seem to be graven on the memory in such fashion that we cannot forget them. — *She*, H. Rider Haggard, 1887.

3490 It may be, my dear grandchildren, that at one time or another I have told you nearly all the incidents which have occurred during my adventurous life. To your father and to your mother, at least, I know that none of them are unfamiliar. Yet when I consider that time wears on, and that a gray head is apt to contain a failing memory, I am prompted to use these long winter evenings in putting it all before you from the beginning, that you may have it as one clear story in your minds and pass it on as such to those who come after you. — *Micah Clarke*, Arthur Conan Doyle, 1888.

3491 There are some things and faces which, when felt or seen for the first time, project themselves upon the mind like a sun image on a sensitive plate and there remain unalterably fixed. — *Colonel Quaritch, V.C.*, H. Rider Haggard, 1888.

3492 Do you reckon Tom Sawyer was satisfied after all them adventures? — *Tom Sawyer Abroad*, Mark Twain, 1894.

3493 I am going to attempt a narrative of strange things which have happened within my experience, and which it is as well, perhaps, that my children and their children after them should know in the coming time, when the manners and customs of my country will — I hope — have greatly changed for the better. — *In the Days of Good Queen Bess*, Robert Haynes Cave, 1897.

3494 About eight o'clock on the morning of the 5th of November, 1900, those of the passengers and crew of the American liner *St. Louis* who happened, whether from causes of duty or of their own pleasure, to be on deck, had a very strange — in fact a quite unprecedented experience. — *A Honeymoon in Space*, George Griffith, 1901.

3495 I want very much to set down my thoughts and my experiences of life. I want to do so now that I have come to middle age and now that my attitudes are all defined and my personal drama worked out. — *The Passionate Friends*, H. G. Wells, 1913.

3496 I have decided to relate with Presision what occurred during my recent Christmas holaday. Although I was away from this school only four days, returning unexpectedly the day after Christmas, a number of Incidents occurred which I beleive I should narate. — *Bab*, Mary Roberts Rinehart, 1917.

3497 Now I, Allan Quatermain, come to the very weirdest (with one exception perhaps) of all the experiences which it has amused me to employ my idle hours in recording here in a strange land, for after all, England is strange to me. — *The Ancient Allan*, H. Rider Haggard, 1920.

3498 This is the story of a certain Mr. Preemby, a retired laundryman and widower, who abandoned his active interest in the Limpid Stream Laundry, in the parish of Saint Simon Unawares, near Woodford Wells, upon the death of his wife in the year of grace 1920. Some very remarkable experiences came to him. — *Christina Alberta's Father*, H. G. Wells, 1925.

3499 For one of those minutes that are not reckoned as time, but rather as a curious vessel to hold experience, she had stood still on the station platform, rapt and breathless and unmindful of the inquisitive glances that rested on her taut figure. — *Prologue to Love*, Martha Ostenso, 1932.

3500 All this happened to a Greek family named Helianos. — *Apartment in Athens*, Glenway Wescott, 1945.

3501 It happened that green and crazy summer when Frankie was twelve years old. — *The Member of the Wedding*, Carson McCullers, 1946.

3502 It's not you, is it? and it's not them; it's *when*, when it happens, and when it has happened then you're trapped, you can't escape. — *A Second Home*, Brian Glanville, 1965.

3503 This is what happened to me in Germany. — *The Junkers*, Piers Paul Read, 1968.

3504 Something happened to François when he was barely thirteen, without which the story that follows would not have been possible. — *A Story Like the Wind*, Laurens van der Post, 1972.

3505 Sometimes George felt that nothing real had ever happened to him. — *George Beneath a Paper Moon*, Nina Bawden, 1974.

3506 The hour is late, the hour rings with confusion, the voices and laughter of strangers, and something is happening to Albert St. Dennis. — *Unholy Loves*, Joyce Carol Oates, 1979.

3507 In the valley of Induspur, one of the smallest of the Indian states, curious things began

to occur among the few Europeans left there after the end of British rule. — *Noble Descents*, Gerald Hanley, 1982.

3508 The veteran journalist had covered sixteen wars or revolutions, he sometimes admitted. — *Mr. White Eyes*, Herbert Gold, 1984.

3509 I may sound cruel and hard-hearted, but in the long run I'm not sorry any of it happened. — *The Two of Us*, Nora Johnson, 1984.

3510 This is what happened to a man named Billy in the days before the end of the world. — *Shelter*, Marty Asher, 1986.

3511 Having retired, or rather having *been* retired, Burbank was on his way to some fishing off the Keys when a series of odd events came his way. — *A Visit to Yazoo*, Charles Neider, 1991.

3512 Fluke./ Nightmare, coincidence. — *The Torching*, Marcy Heidish, 1992.

3513 What happened to me on the bus wasn't unusual. The person sitting next to me was surprised and even outraged and that made me wonder for a moment at my own lack of outrage and surprise. — "Immaculate Man," Mary Gordon, 1993.

Failure

3514 As the little ship that had three times raced with death sailed past the majestic headlands and into the straits of San Francisco on that brilliant April morning of 1806, Rezánov forgot the bitter humiliations, the mental and physical torments, the deprivations and dangers of the past three years; forgot those harrowing months in the harbor of Nagasaki when the Russian bear had caged his tail in the presence of eyes aslant; his dismay at Kamchatka when he had been forced to send home another to vindicate his failure, and to remain in the Tsar's incontiguous and barbarous northeastern possessions as representative of his Imperial Majesty, and plenipotentiary of the Company his own genius had created; forgot the year of loneliness and hardship — and peril in whose jaws the bravest was impotent; forgot even his pitiable crew, diseased when he left Sitka, who had filled the *Juno* with their groans and laments; and the bells of youth, long still, rang in his soul once more. — *Rezánov*, Gertrude Atherton, 1906.

3515 DEAREST MOTHER,/ I'm sorry the Engadine isn't being a success, but I'm not surprised. Why on earth did you trust the Gordon's to choose a hotel? — *Together and Apart*, Margaret Kennedy, 1936.

3516 In hidden vainglory he had vowed that he would stay awake straight through the night, for he had wondered, and not without scorn, how they, grown men, could give way to sleep on this night of all the nights in their life, leaving Him without one friend in His worst hour; but some while before midnight, still unaware that he was so much as drowsy, he had fallen asleep; and now this listening sleep was broken and instantly Richard lay sharp awake, aware of his failure and of the night. — *The Morning Watch*, James Agee, 1951.

3517 "He can't have been a great man because he achieved nothing," said Ruth. — *A Man of Power*, Isabel Colegate, 1960.

3518 Dr. Paul Steiner, consulting psychiatrist at the Steen Clinic, sat in the front ground floor consulting-room and listened to his patient's highly rationalized explanation of the failure of his third marriage. — *A Mind to Murder*, P. D. James, 1963.

3519 "He's killed himself again. The bastard."/ "Dead, is he?"/ "That'll be the day. Here, gimme a hand." — *Mother Is a Country*, Kathrin Perutz, 1968.

3520 "No good!" said Lamont, sharply. "I didn't get anywhere." — *The Gods Themselves*, Isaac Asimov, 1972.

3521 Mary Margaret Redmond died on an April day when rain was misting across the lawn and condensing in crystal beads on the green snouts of the crocuses. She was alone, her mother having left the room a moment before; and her mind was filled with the certainty of failure. — *Song of the Pearl*, Ruth Nichols, 1976.

3522 I've always been a quitter. — *Budding Prospects*, T. Coraghessan Boyle, 1984.

3523 What do you say, after ten years of absence, to someone you have loved and failed? — *The Flame Bearers*, Kim Chernin, 1986.

3524 On Sunday evenings in San Francisco, one realizes that opportunities have come and gone. — *Longing*, Paul Reed, 1988.

3525 About halfway along in the meeting, Harry Towns could tell it was not going to work out. — *The Current Climate*, Bruce Jay Friedman, 1989.

3526 My sister did poorly at Stanford. — *Mexico Days*, Robert Roper, 1989.

Fame

3527 My True Name is so well known in the Records, or Registers at *Newgate*, and in the *Old-Baily*, and there are some things of such Consequence still depending there, relating to my

particular Conduct, that it is not to be expected I should set my Name, or the Account of my Family to this Work; perhaps, after my Death it may be better known, at present it would not be proper, no, not tho' a general Pardon should be issued, even without Exceptions and reserve of Persons or Crimes. — *Moll Flanders*, Daniel Defoe, 1722.

3528 The Browns have become illustrious by the pen of Thackeray and the pencil of Doyle, within the memory of the young gentlemen who are now matriculating at the Universities. — *Tom Brown's School Days*, Thomas Hughes, 1857.

3529 In the year 1860, the reputation of Doctor Wybrow as a London physician reached its highest point. It was reported on good authority that he was in receipt of one of the largest incomes derived from the practice of medicine in modern times. — *The Haunted Hotel*, Wilkie Collins, 1879.

3530 I was about to say that I had known the Celebrity from the time he wore kilts. — *The Celebrity*, Winston Churchill, 1898.

3531 Lionel Carvel, Esq., of Carvel Hall, in the county of Queen Anne, was no inconsiderable man in his Lordship's province of Maryland, and indeed he was not unknown in the colonial capitals from Williamsburg to Boston. — *Richard Carvel*, Winston Churchill, 1899.

3532 In Haverford on the Platte the towns people still talk of Lucy Gayheart. — *Lucy Gayheart*, Willa Cather, 1935.

3533 His mother was the daughter of William Baring, proprietor of the White Horse Inn at Caerlyn Sands. Baring, from all I ever heard, must have been a grand, boasting, foolish character, famous locally and known even in distant parts of Glebeshire. — *John Cornelius*, Hugh Walpole, 1937.

3534 When the *Lord Elgin* set Carney ashore at Packet Harbor he was already a legend on the coast. He was one of the small group of telegraphers who had manned the first Canadian wireless stations in the days when Marconi's invention was brand-new and regarded by most people as a species of black magic. — *The Nymph and the Lamp*, Thomas H. Raddall, 1950.

3535 Okonkwo was well known throughout the nine villages and even beyond. — *Things Fall Apart*, Chinua Achebe, 1959.

3536 Have you ever known a famous man before he became famous? — *Youngblood Hawke*, Herman Wouk, 1962.

3537 I have the distinction of having become a legend in my lifetime, but not a very nice one. — *The Embezzler*, Louis Auchincloss, 1966.

3538 At age eighteen, Shawn was officially loved by sixty thousand four hundred and eleven girls registered in his fan clubs. His parents

found this bizarre and in questionable taste, along with the change in spelling of his name from Sean. — *Dance the Eagle to Sleep*, Marge Piercy, 1970.

3539 Fame requires every kind of excess. — *Great Jones Street*, Don DeLillo, 1973.

3540 I had heard of Hatter Fox, but I had never seen her. — *Hatter Fox*, Marilyn Harris, 1973.

3541 During the wet autumn of 1974 I heard a lot about another American girl who was living in Paris. — *Sarah Phillips*, Andrea Lee, 1984.

3542 Philip Decker was mildly famous. — *Philip's Girl*, Lucy Ferriss, 1985.

3543 Gustav Ellingen was a legend in his day. — *The Afternoon Sun*, David Pryce-Jones, 1986.

3544 Finally, of course, Little Egypt made a great reputation for himself, and for a few weeks in the summer of 1922 everyone knew his name. — *Loving Little Egypt*, Thomas McMahon, 1987.

3545 I'm the Vampire Lestat. Remember me? The vampire who became a super rock star, the one who wrote the autobiography? The one with the blond hair and the gray eyes, and the insatiable desire for visibility and fame? You remember. — *The Queen of the Damned*, Anne Rice, 1988.

3546 There were so many things I didn't know when we were at Los Alamos: that memory cannot be controlled and has a will of its own; that a chain of events has continuous consequences; and that fame, even limited or dubious fame, is a second skin. — *Beginning the World Again*, Roberta Silman, 1990.

3547 A word of advice: Don't appear on the cover of *Sports Illustrated* when you're twenty-one. — *Season's End*, Tom Grimes, 1992.

Families

3548 In an old family mansion, situated on an estate in Gloucestershire known by the name of Rosevalley, resided Mrs. Mowbray, and Adeline her only child. — *Adeline Mowbray*, Amelia Opie *as* Mrs. Opie, 1804.

3549 The family of Dashwood had been long settled in Sussex. — *Sense and Sensibility*, Jane Austen, 1811.

3550 Claud Walkinshaw was the sole surviving male heir of the Walkinshaws of Kittlestonheugh. His grandfather, the last laird of the line, deluded by the golden visions that allured so many of the Scottish gentry to embark their fortunes in the Darien Expedition, sent his only son, the father of Claud, in one of the ships fitted

out at Cartsdyke, and with him an adventure in which he had staked more than the whole value of his estate. — *The Entail*, John Galt, 1822.

3551 It appears from tradition, as well as some parish registers still extant, that the lands of Dalcastle (or Dalchastel, as it is often spelled) were possessed by a family of the name of Colwan, about one hundred and fifty years ago, and for at least a century previous to that period. — *The Private Memoirs and Confessions of a Justified Sinner*, James Hogg, 1824.

3552 In a snowy villa, with a sloping lawn, just outside the great commercial seaport, Barkington, there lived a few years ago a happy family. A lady, middle-aged, but still charming, two young friends of hers, and a periodical visitor./ The lady was Mrs. Dodd; her occasional visitor was her husband; her friends were her son Edward, aged twenty, and her daughter Julia, nineteen; the fruit of a misalliance. — *Hard Cash*, Charles Reade, 1863.

3553 Perhaps it was more the fault of Daniel Caldigate the father than of his son John Caldigate, that they two could not live together in comfort in the days of the young man's early youth. And yet it would have been much for both of them that such comfortable association should have been possible to them. — *John Caldigate*, Anthony Trollope, 1879.

3554 A long time ago, in a town with which I used to be familiarly acquainted, there dwelt an elderly person of grim aspect, known by the name and title of Doctor Grimshawe, whose household consisted of a remarkably pretty and vivacious boy, and a perfect rosebud of a girl, two or three years younger than he, and an old maid of all work, of strangely mixed breed, crusty in temper and wonderfully sluttish in attire. — *Doctor Grimshawe's Secret*, Nathaniel Hawthorne, 1882.

3555 "Ef ther' ain't a flare-up in *this* haouse 'fore long, I miss *my* guess," said Alvira, as she kneaded the pie-crust, and pulled it out between her floury fingers to measure its consistency. — *Seth's Brother's Wife*, Harold Frederic, 1887.

3556 The relation of two step-sisters is unusual. — *Pietro Ghisleri*, F. Marion Crawford, 1892.

3557 The fortunes of the House of Egremont had their first great bloom through the agency of a platter of beans; and through a platter of beans more than a hundred years later the elder branch was ousted from one of the greatest estates in England, became wanderers and gentlemen adventurers throughout Europe, fought in quarrels not their own, served sovereigns of foreign countries, knew the dazzling heights of glory, and fell into the mire of penury and disrepute. — *The House of Egremont*, Molly Elliot Seawell, 1901.

3558 Those privileged to be present at a fam-

ily festival of the Forsytes have seen that charming and instructive sight — an upper-middle-class family in full plumage. — *The Man of Property*, John Galsworthy, 1906.

3559 The tobacco-roller and his son pitched their camp beneath a gum tree upon the edge of the wood. — *Lewis Rand*, Mary Johnston, 1908.

3560 The possessive instinct never stands still. Through florescence and feud, frosts and fires, it followed the laws of progression even in the Forsyte family which had believed it fixed for ever. — *In Chancery*, John Galsworthy, 1920.

3561 In the old New York of the 'fifties a few families ruled, in simplicity and affluence. Of these were the Ralstons. — "The Old Maid (The 'Fifties)," Edith Wharton, 1924.

3562 All he knew was this: that after listening to his paunchy, bearded, shrewd father for a time, after looking at his mother troubled in her wisdom, after feeling in his sister's eyes a keen hostility, he would arise and leave the house, knowing they were all wrong. — *Brother Saul*, Donn Byrne, 1927.

3563 The Blettsworthys, my family, have always been a very scrupulous family and gentle, the Wiltshire Blettsworthys perhaps even more so than the Sussex branch. — *Mr. Blettsworthy on Rampole Island*, H. G. Wells, 1928.

3564 All the Broomes have charm: it is their epithet. — *Broome Stages*, Winifred Ashton *as* Clemence Dane, 1929.

3565 All the Venables sat at Sunday dinner. — *Cimarron*, Edna Ferber, 1930.

3566 *The baby bawled. Lee heard a final sob from his wife. He slammed the door.* — *The Young Manhood of Studs Lonigan*, James T. Farrell, 1934.

3567 In this way Wang Yuan, son of Wang the Tiger, entered for the first time in his life the earthen house of his grandfather, Wang Lung. — *A House Divided*, Pearl S. Buck, 1935.

3568 Climbing up the dirt track to the house, he could hear them: his father and his sister, Clara. — "Jim," Martha Gellhorn, 1936.

3569 There lived in the city of Shanghai in the fifteenth year of the Chinese Republic and in the western year nineteen hundred and twenty-six, a rich banker whose surname was Wu, who had two sons. — *The Patriot*, Pearl S. Buck, 1939.

3570 In the remote hills of northern Scotland dwelt the clan of Murdock. — *Wild Geese Calling*, Stewart Edward White, 1940.

3571 When King Edward the Good had reigned nine years in England, his Norman favourites overthrew Earl Godwin, the King's father-in-law. — *The Golden Warrior*, Hope Muntz, 1949.

3572 Mr. Arnold Waite — husband, parent, man of his word — invariably leaned back in his chair after his second cup of breakfast coffee and

looked with some disbelief at his wife and two children. — *Hangsaman*, Shirley Jackson, 1951.

3573 Walter Price was talking about himself again, discoursing in detail on the distinguished and ancient history of the Price family. — *Women and Thomas Harrow*, John P. Marquand, 1958.

3574 "It is a pity you have not my charm, Simon," said Walter Challoner./ "Well, we hardly want a double share in a family." — *A Heritage and Its History*, Ivy Compton-Burnett, 1959.

3575 The trouble with family relationships is conscience, which is nearly always guilty. — *Set on Edge*, Bernice Rubens, 1960.

3576 On the day before Thanksgiving the Spencer clan began to gather. — *Spencer's Mountain*, Earl Hamner, 1961.

3577 All the rest of us in our family are dark, but Savata my sister is fair. — *The Fair Sister*, William Goyen, 1963.

3578 One morning in early spring a man and his daughter made their way along the country lane that led back from their house. — *With Shuddering Fall*, Joyce Carol Oates, 1964.

3579 I meant to begin this account of the summer of 1937-1938 with the problem which my wife Eileen and I face now with our seventeen-year-old son. — *My Brother Tom*, James Aldridge, 1966.

3580 Packed in among the blankets, linens, and Loco Poco's dolls, the three girls and their mother sat upright like bankers. — *Entering Ephesus*, Daphne Athas, 1971.

3581 One autumn evening in 1940, when she was four years old, Annie-May Gates passed within a yard of her future husband, her future mother-in-law, and neither of them noticed her. — *Anna Apparent*, Nina Bawden, 1972.

3582 Dressed in various shades of light brown, the Iron Orchid and her son sat upon a cream-coloured beach of crushed stone. — *An Alien Heat*, Michael Moorcock, 1972.

3583 After forty years as their family physician, Dr. Metcalf — "Doc" to all the world — knows the Renshaws better than anybody else. Which means only that Doc knows even less than anybody what ever to expect of them. Expect the worst: everybody who knows the Renshaws knows that. — *Proud Flesh*, William Humphrey, 1973.

3584 Nick Thirkield once told Keifetz that being in the same family with his father and his brother Tim was like living in the back leg of an all-glass piano. It was uncomfortable, it was noisy, and everyone could watch whatever he did; not that he could do much. — *Winter Kills*, Richard Condon, 1974.

3585 Guido Morris and Vincent Cardworthy were third cousins. No one remembered which Morris had married which Cardworthy, and no

one cared except at large family gatherings when this topic was introduced and subjected to the benign opinions of all. — *Happy All the Time*, Laurie Colwin, 1978.

3586 In 1909 three families stood at the center of the great Middleburg, West Virginia, coal boom: the Cliftons, the Hayeses, and the Catherwoods. — *A Vein of Riches*, John Knowles, 1978.

3587 I am beginning, once again, to have an urge to salute my Uncle Oswald. — *My Uncle Oswald*, Roald Dahl, 1979.

3588 The family of Francisco Manoel da Silva had assembled at Ouidah to honour his memory with a Requiem Mass and dinner. — *The Viceroy of Ouidah*, Bruce Chatwin, 1980.

3589 The principal approach to Felton House was through tall wrought-iron gates which turned, or had once turned, upon two heavily rusticated stone pillars. Perched on each of these was a rearing stone hippogriff ambiguously cavorting behind a bulbous and curly stone shield. When first ensconced, these composite monsters had witnessed to the respectability, indeed to the consequence, of the Feltons; now, lingering on in a markedly abraded state, they might be taken to testify to the antiquity of the family as well. — *Andrew and Tobias*, J. I. M. Stewart, 1980.

3590 Every family has relatives they don't talk about and others about whom they rarely stop talking. — *The Patriarch*, Chaim Bermant, 1981.

3591 After the big Sunday family picnic in Uncle Matt's grove, the men now having their pipes, and the women cleaning up with the girls helping, leaving only cider jugs on the spread blanket, Andrew Lane knew that the solemn family powwow over his mother's sudden situation was about to take place. — *The Architect*, Meyer Levin, 1981.

3592 All families, I thought as a child, should be like mine: two sets of grown-ups for one little girl at dead center of the universe. — *Higher Ground*, Meredith Sue Willis, 1981.

3593 Dawn Mueller pulled the baby closer to her breast, gripped the ship's railing with her free hand, and looked around for her daughter. — *War Brides*, Lois Battle, 1982.

3594 Polly Solo-Miller Demarest was the perfect flower of the Solo-Miller family. — *Family Happiness*, Laurie Colwin, 1982.

3595 Come, meet the family. — *Old World, New World*, Mark Dintenfass, 1982.

3596 Father wanted a small family, but he also wanted an heir, and he had four daughters and two wives before he eventually had a son. — *The House of Women*, Chaim Bermant, 1983.

3597 Family gatherings in rural Mississippi

are sober to a fault in the absence of anyone who will come forward and risk changing iced tea to wine. — *Blue Rise*, Rebecca Hill, 1983.

3598 Never had a family. — *Bluebird Canyon*, Dan McCall, 1983.

3599 There was a good turn-out from the village of Brinthorpe to watch Wally Carless take his daughter, Evelyn, to church to marry Terry Blackmore, but the women who gathered round the gate were nearly as interested in Evelyn's sister, Anne, newly returned from Canada, widowed and with a two-year-old daughter. — *Paths of Peace*, Kate Alexander, 1984.

3600 Different members of the Spiegelglass family had different opinions of the Brick. — *The Forever Street*, Frederic Morton, 1984.

3601 August. This was the time when the entire Winderman family, all sixteen of them, assembled at the Island. — *August People*, Ralph Graves, 1985.

3602 These were Rob Jay's last safe and secure moments of blessed innocence, but in his ignorance he considered it hardship to be forced to remain near his father's house with his brothers and his sister. — *The Physician*, Noah Gordon, 1986.

3603 After three hundred years as gentleman farmers, the Tancreds became accident-prone. — *Where the Rainbow Ends*, Christopher Hudson, 1986.

3604 That was the summer we lost the bald Jeeter who was not even mostly Jeeter anymore but was probably mostly Throckmorton or anyway was probably considered mostly Throckmorton which was an appreciable step up from being considered mostly Jeeter since Jeeters hadn't ever been anything much while Throckmortons had in fact been something once previously before the money got gone and the prestige fell away leaving merely the bluster and the taint and the general Throckmorton aroma all of which taken together hardly made for a legacy worth getting stirred up over but any one of which taken singly still outstripped the entire bulk of advancements ever attempted and realized by Jeeters who had scratched around in the dirt but were not much accomplished at farming and who had speculated in herds of cattle but were not much accomplished at speculating either and who at last had turned their energies to the construction of a henhouse which commenced ramshackle and got worse but became nonetheless the chief Jeeter advancement along with the hens and the little speckled brown eggs and the localized ammonia cloud which was itself most probably the primary Jeeter success though no particular Jeeter or group of Jeeters together actually contributed to it or could prevent it either and so when the bald Jeeter, with

the fat Jeeter as her maid of honor, exchanged vows with Braxton Porter Throckmorton III in the sanctuary of the Methodist church on Saturday June the twelfth, 1942, and afterwards set up house in Neely proper she got away from the hens and the henhouse and out from under the ammonia cloud which was most likely beginning to expand in June of 1942 since it set in to expanding most every June and swelled straight through August and on into September, especially this past August and especially this past September when it was bearing down on the town limits and posing some threat to the icehouse which was regular and ordinary for the season, particularly in August and particularly in September, so we were having what had come to be our usual summer straight up to the moment Mr. Derwood Bridger laid his ladder against the Throckmorton clapboard and climbed to the upper story where he pressed his nose to the bedroom windowscreen and shaded his eyes and called and hollered and shrieked at the bald Jeeter until he was satisfied that she was gone from us for good. — *Off for the Sweet Hereafter*, T. R. Pearson, 1986.

3605 It is not merely because of the horizon — mountains on one side, a city on the other — that for generations certain families of Lewiston have thought themselves very close to the center of the universe. — *Years from Now*, Gary Glickman, 1987.

3606 In the Fifties, Nick still had family. — *Family*, Caroline Leavitt, 1987.

3607 My family had everything anyone could want. — *The Butterfly Chair*, Marion Quednau, 1987.

3608 They were a close, conventional family in many ways, the five Brewster boys from Cape Cod, but when they got together with their various wives and children, somebody always broke, somebody drank too much, and then there was trouble. — *Missing Children*, Harry H. Taylor, 1987.

3609 This is what they will do, she and her mother. — *The Beginner's Book of Dreams*, Elizabeth Benedict, 1988.

3610 Mackenzie kept telling herself that if the family had stuck together after Alexander died, it would be different. Easier somehow. — *Waiting to Vanish*, Ann Hood, 1988.

3611 We didn't know we were an odd family. — *Trespasses*, Caroline Bridgwood, 1989.

3612 The story of my family's no different, really, than the story of yours. — *Long Distance Life*, Marita Golden, 1989.

3613 In my family we are all disposable. — *When We Get Home*, Maud Carol Markson, 1989.

3614 When I was a boy growing up on the

Kingdom gool, my father and my older brother Charlie couldn't say two words to each other without getting into an argument. — *A Stranger in the Kingdom*, Howard Frank Mosher, 1989.

3615 Pooler color was yellow. Everyone knew that. The farmhouse, the barns, the storage houses, the trucks — even the farm's mailbox was painted yellow. — *The Potato Baron*, John Thorndike, 1989.

3616 Max Lakeman, ever the alien, sat in his lawn chair in the thin shade of a dying peach tree, watching his family. — *Max Lakeman and the Beautiful Stranger*, Jon Cohen, 1990.

3617 "You know where we are?" said Jonas Torbett to his father. He didn't wait for an answer. "We're on the crust," he said. — *Dry Bones*, Hope Norman Coulter, 1990.

3618 There's a breed of whale that has a heart the size of a Volkswagen. That's not so hard to imagine. Not for me. We've got people walking around in this family with hearts big enough to kill them. — *The Picture Makers*, Emily Ellison, 1990.

3619 In the fall of 1960, when I was sixteen and my father was for a time not working, my mother met a man named Warren Miller and fell in love with him. — *Wildlife*, Richard Ford, 1990.

3620 All three girls are in the front seat, the fat girl with the glasses is driving. In the back seat their father is asleep sitting up. — *Falling Angels*, Barbara Gowdy, 1990.

3621 One day in our tiny rented winter cottage in Florida my brother Speed and I were in the kitchen and my mother and Babe Ruth were in the other room when from that other room came a terrible, frightening, awful commotion, as of persons fighting, and Babe Ruth shouted above it all, "I'll bust his chops." — *Speed*, Mark Harris, 1990.

3622 It occurred to Min that thinking about your family is like gardening. The mood hits you, the sun is beaming down, the smell of wet black earth coming in strong through an open window, and you say to yourself, Why not? I've got a few minutes. So you go out that door. — *Springs of Living Water*, Karen Lawrence, 1990.

3623 I was driving to Las Vegas to tell my sister that I'd had Mother's respirator unplugged. — *My Cousin, My Gastroenterologist*, Mark Leyner, 1990.

3624 "The Caswells of Hereford. Weren't they clients of yours, Geoffrey?" — *Debt of Dishonour*, Robert Goddard, 1991.

3625 The pull of the family is irresistible. — *The Dark Sister*, Rebecca Goldstein, 1991.

3626 My family has practiced the end of the world more than most, because of the five members of my family, three have top-security clear-

ance. — *Duck and Cover*, Brenda Peterson, 1991.

3627 The downfall of the Fleishman family began deceptively, without augury, as is common in our times. — *Saving Grace*, Barbara Rogan, 1991.

3628 A man told me about a woman who married her own son. — "Storyville," Charles Smith, 1991.

3629 In the late afternoon Dinah retreated to her bedroom in that deadly time before the family had dinner. — *Fortunate Lives*, Robb Forman Dew, 1992.

3630 The first time Ray Gollancz and his father, Dean, burned down a building, they drove from Bakersfield, California, to Chinatown in Los Angeles. — *Trombone*, Craig Nova, 1992.

3631 Lisa, her mother and her brother Max were dogsitting for a woman called Bunny, who owned a house in the Archway. — *Peerless Flats*, Esther Freud, 1993.

3632 We were a family of three girls. By Chinese standards, that wasn't lucky. *Bone*, Fae Myenne Ng, 1993.

3633 It is said that we kill each other in my family, and it may be true. — *Wildcatting*, Shann Nix, 1993.

Farming

3634 If you take the turn to the left after you pass the lyke-gate at Combehurst Church, you will come to the wooden bridge over the brook; keep along the field-path, which mounts higher and higher, and, in half a mile or so, you will be in a breezy upland field, almost large enough to be called a down, where sheep pasture on the short, fine elastic turf. — *The Moorland Cottage*, Elizabeth Gaskell, 1850.

3635 George Fielding cultivated a small farm in Berkshire./ This position is not so enviable as it was; years ago, the farmers of England, had they been as intelligent as other traders, could have purchased the English soil by means of the huge percentage it offered them. — *It Is Never Too Late to Mend*, Charles Reade, 1856.

3636 It was sheep-shearing time in Southern California, but sheep-shearing was late at the Señora Moreno's. — *Ramona*, Helen Hunt Jackson, 1884.

3637 The "Two Little Confederates" lived at Oakland. It was not a handsome place, as modern ideas go, but down in Old Virginia, where the standard was different from the later one, it passed in old times as one of the best

plantations in all that region. — "Two Little Confederates," Thomas Nelson Page, 1888.

3638 The old Gray plantation, "Red Rock," lay at the highest part of the rich rolling country, before it rose too abruptly in the wooded foothills of the blue mountains away to the westward. — *Red Rock*, Thomas Nelson Page, 1898.

3639 The Anglo-Saxon farmers had scarce conquered foothold, stronghold, freehold in the Western wilderness before they became sowers of hemp — with remembrance of Virginia, with remembrance of dear ancestral Britain. — *The Reign of Law*, James Allen Lane, 1900.

3640 One early April afternoon, in a Worcestershire field, the only field in that immediate landscape which was not down in grass, a man moved slowly athwart the furrows, sowing — a big man of heavy build, swinging his hairy brown arm with the grace of strength. — *The Freelands*, John Galsworthy, 1915.

3641 Already, in the third decade of the nineteenth century, the settlers in the valley of Leatherwood Creek had opened the primeval forest to their fields of corn and tobacco on the fertile slopes and rich bottom-lands. — *The Leatherwood God*, William Dean Howells, 1916.

3642 Some of the best land in the country, people said, was right here in Richland Township. — *Country People*, Ruth Suckow, 1924.

3643 The JC was a good ranch in a country of good ranches, although they were pretty well scattered because the available water supply controlled their location. — *Corson of the JC*, Clarence E. Mulford, 1927.

3644 They had obtained the cattle from the ranches within a day's ride of the old Bar 20. Most of them were in their own brand, but to fill a herd of that size and specifications it had been necessary to call on their neighbors. — *Trail Dust*, Clarence E. Mulford, 1934.

3645 The Alf Jefferys were turning their hay in the sunless heat of a June afternoon, the first rows of the first crop, the whole family stretched out like a line of dark and white washing across the river-meadow. — *A House of Women*, H. E. Bates, 1936.

3646 A man, with brown cheeks smoothly shaven and wearing a clean denim shirt because it was Monday morning, chaperoning his herd of Jerseys across the paved road from the barn side to the pasture side, saw a car coming and cussed. — *Double for Death*, Rex Stout, 1939.

3647 Rion and Archy had been in the west field all morning, gathering corn. — *Green Centuries*, Caroline Gordon, 1941.

3648 The Williamsons' farm lay on a hillside so that when it rained the water ran down and away from it. In fifty years it had worn out and starved out the three families who had tried to

work it. The Williamsons were the fourth. — *A Woman Called Fancy*, Frank Yerby, 1951.

3649 "What outfit, gents?" Hugh Kingmead leaned across the observation car rail, reading the brands on the cattle through the slats of the car on the siding at Ogallala. — *Return of a Fighter*, Ernest Haycox, 1952.

3650 The oranges were more plentiful than usual that year. — *Clea*, Lawrence Durrell, 1960.

3651 Scrub Fincher farms six miles out on State 21, or rather, back off it on the swamp edge. — *The Wandering of Desire*, Marion Montgomery, 1962.

3652 Ellen Creighton and her nine-year-old son, Jethro, were planting potatoes in the half-acre just south of their cabin that morning in mid-April, 1861; they were out in the field as soon as breakfast was over, and southern Illinois at that hour was pink with sunrise and swelling redbud and clusters of bloom over the apple orchard across the road. — *Across Five Aprils*, Irene Hunt, 1964.

3653 Everywhere the clayey soil was baked as hard as rock, even in the farmyard and the pigsties where normally the least shower of rain kept the usual thick seas of mud churning. — *Late Call*, Angus Wilson, 1964.

3654 The Danford pony breeding and schooling farm where Shetlands had been raised by father and son during the past forty years was several hundred acres of gently rolling foothills and fertile bottomland close to what people in the region for many generations had called the western rim of the bluegrass plateau. — *The Weather Shelter*, Erskine Caldwell, 1969.

3655 My Uncle Hezron's farm near Nazareth in Galilee is part of my childhood, in spite of the fact that I was born in Judea. — *Judas, My Brother*, Frank Yerby, 1969.

3656 It had been firm in my mind from the beginning that I ought to see the farm for the first time early in the morning. — *Bluegrass*, Borden Deal, 1976.

3657 My father bought the cow-in-calf at Low Crags cattle fair on a wet and soggy Tuesday in July. — *Captain of the Sands*, Keith Dewhurst, 1981.

3658 The plantation is called Aurora, nobody remembers why. — *The Stones of Bau*, Nicholas Wollaston, 1987.

3659 In 1966, when Allie McCain was six years old, her Great-Aunt Amalie asked her family to move back to Louisiana and help manage her plantation. — *The Errand of the Eye*, Hope Norman Coulter, 1988.

3660 They married them young back then and always with an eye on adjoining acreage, so it was hardly surprising that Lizzard Patout knew, even before knowing who the female was

to be, that he would impregnate her four times with four males in eight years — allowing a fallow year in between, which was sound, modern practice according to his agricultural course that came through the mail — one son for each farm bordering The Oaks, thus restoring the plantation to its original size. — *Precious in His Sight*, M. E. Hughes, 1988.

3661 Asgeir Gunnarsson farmed at Gunnars Stead near Undir Hofdi church in Austfjord. His homefield was nearly as large as the homefield at Gardar, where the absent bishop had his seat, and he had another large field as well. — *The Greenlanders*, Jane Smiley, 1988.

3662 During the years before the war broke out, Mose Johnson was known as a local expert on raising turkeys. — *The Turkey War*, Douglas Unger, 1988.

3663 We were such tiny people in the Quisenberrys' pecan orchard. — *Boomerang*, Barry Hannah, 1989.

3664 There is so much I would like to tell you, for example about the rice paddies and how beautiful they are under the wide sky, and how different they look depending on where you are standing when you look at them. — *Buffalo Afternoon*, Susan Fromberg Schaeffer, 1989.

3665 In the evening, along Route 7 south of Washington, the farm — still called John Spencer's place in spite of what had happened — filled the sky. It had been built by the Spencers before the Civil War on a high rise above the Potomac, white and colossal, inappropriate to the gentle watercolor landscape of the Virginia hills. — *A Country of Strangers*, Susan Richards Shreve, 1989.

3666 At sixty miles per hour, you could pass our farm in a minute, on County Road 686, which ran due north into the T intersection at Cabot Street Road. — *A Thousand Acres*, Jane Smiley, 1991.

3667 The lochs on the Black Moor of Lewis flashed blue sky, sun and scudding fluffs of cloud on this bright August afternoon as Mairi MacLeod and Catriona Nicolson came from the shieling, the beehive-shaped stone hut where the cousins had made cheese and butter while the township's cattle and sheep grazed in the summer pastures. — *The Island Harp*, Jeanne Williams, 1991.

3668 Against that panorama of wasteland you imagine them marching, one by one, pigtails framing thousand-year-old faces, driving what remains of their gaunt cattle before them. — *Next of Kin*, Marianne Langner Zeitlin, 1991.

3669 Two o'clock in the morning, a Thursday morning, the first bit of water broke through the ground of George Clatterbuck's back pasture

in Habit, Kentucky, and not a living soul saw it. — *The Patron Saint of Liars*, Ann Patchett, 1992.

Fate

3670 I suppose that I, Humphrey Arbuthnot, should begin this history in which Destiny has caused me to play so prominent a part, with some short account of myself and my circumstances. — *When the World Shook*, H. Rider Haggard, 1919.

3671 Young men in our country are brought up to believe that they have a destiny, a guiding idea shaped like a star; most of them pass their lives in unawareness that this destiny is gradually becoming the sum of everything that has happened to them, and need not have been represented by a star in the first place, being perhaps more like the false beacon set up by smugglers to direct a vessel toward a convenient disaster. Disaster, *dés*, from, *astre*, a star. — *Federigo*, Howard Nemerov, 1954.

3672 It was the fashion in those haunted days for a moneyless young male student to regard himself, publicly and privately, as doomed. — *Onionhead*, Weldon Hill, 1957.

3673 Much of his life John Donner had pondered that which secretly governed man and determined his destiny. — *A Simple Honorable Man*, Conrad Richter, 1962.

3674 If I were drowning I couldn't reach out a hand to save myself, so unwilling am I to set myself up against fate. — *The Waterfall*, Margaret Drabble, 1969.

3675 Folk said, before anything at all extraordinary had happened, that Fenella Phizackerley had never had a chance. — *Fenella Phizackerley*, Margaret Forster, 1970.

3676 When destiny came for Calvin Whitten, no one realized that his fate was the first skirmish in the war for the Two River Valley. — *Catch the Wind*, James Grady, 1980.

3677 By what thread of fate was I, despite myself, drawn into the web of imperial affairs, court intrigue, and ecclesiastical rivalries in which personages of greater rank were enmeshed, including Augustus Arcadius, the empress Eudoxia, the grand chamberlain Eutropius, and that pious and innocent man from Antioch, John Chrysostom? — *Olympia*, Elgin Groseclose, 1980.

3678 In darker moods Harriet felt she had been placed by fate under a leak in the world. — *Last Resorts*, Clare Boylan, 1984.

3679 The Duchess of Windsor begins *her*

memoirs with the question "Is our fate in our stars or does it lie within ourselves?" and I don't think there is any better way I could phrase it myself. — *Love Junkie*, Robert Plunket, 1992.

Fatigue

3680 In those west-country parishes where but a few years back the feast of Christmas Eve was usually prolonged with cake and cider, "crowding," and "geese dancing," till the ancient carols ushered in the day, a certain languor not seldom pervaded the services of the Church a few hours later. — *I Saw Three Ships*, Arthur Quiller-Couch, 1892.

3681 At four o'clock in the morning everybody in the tent was still asleep, exhausted by the terrible march of the previous day. — *A Man's Woman*, Frank Norris, 1900.

3682 Lily, the caretaker's daughter, was literally run off her feet. — *The Dead*, James Joyce, 1914.

3683 In mind he was tired, worn out, by years of hope deferred, of loneliness, of unrewarded toil. In body he was almost prostrate by the pain of an arm on the tenth day of vaccination. — *Hadrian the Seventh*, Frederick William Rolfe *as* Frederick Baron Corvo, 1925.

3684 The thing was, we had gone fishing that day and Pa had wore himself out with it the way he usually did when he went fishing. — *No Time for Sergeants*, Mac Hyman, 1954.

3685 Isabel lay on her bed in a fog of fatigue, too tired even to undress. — *Faithful Are the Wounds*, May Sarton, 1955.

3686 I was tired and very cold; a little scared, too. — *The Wreck of the Mary Deare*, Hammond Innes, 1956.

3687 The plan had been to cross the river at first light, but it was well into the morning before the head of the column reached the bank and dropped exhausted. — *The Mark of the Warrior*, Paul Scott, 1958.

3688 Coming to the top of the hill they flung down their bicycles in a heap and collapsed on the grass. — *The Kindling*, Janice Elliott, 1970.

3689 She pushed the balls of her thumbs into her eye-sockets, hard. Yellow streaks and whorls shot across the blue film. She pushed almost hard enough to hurt herself. She thought she might scream or faint or kill someone. — *The Languages of Love*, Sara Maitland, 1980.

3690 Julian Coates sat in his chair with the two merciless slavemasters looming over him, forbidding any respite and urging him monoton-

ously on in spite of his fatigue and his boredom. — *Tenth*, MacDonald Harris, 1984.

3691 There were crowds of people puffing and panting up that grassy hill, many seeming already to be in various stages of exhaustion. — *Unicorn Rampant*, Nigel Tranter, 1984.

3692 Reaching the place where the cliff path broadened out into a wide bracken-free spread of close-cropped turf, Ruth Winslade sat down thankfully on the long seat which stood close to the National Trust collecting box set up to receive the offerings of tourists and walkers on their way up to and down from nearby Hurlstone Point. — *Birds of a Feather*, Victor Canning, 1985.

3693 Sixteen hours after the *Niome* went down I was drooping with fatigue, still dressed in the same clothes, smelling of oily sea water and on a plane for London. — *Survivor*, Tom Gallacher, 1985.

3694 "At last I could row no further. . . ." — *Foe*, J. M. Coetzee, 1986.

3695 Late one afternoon when Jasper Whiting entered the cramped vestibule of 39 Charter Street, tired to the roots of his eyes, he found a woman huddled over the row of battered metal mailboxes, talking to herself. — *Face Value*, Don Bloch, 1987.

3696 He remembered that by then he was worn out from fighting the wind. — *Disappearing Moon Cafe*, Sky Lee, 1990.

3697 The curator had had a tiring day. — *Three Times Table*, Sara Maitland, 1990.

Fear

3698 It was the morning of the day on which I was slated to pop down to my Aunt Agatha's place at Woollam Chersey in the county of Herts for a visit of three solid weeks; and, as I seated myself at the breakfast table, I don't mind confessing that the heart was singularly heavy. We Woosters are men of iron, but beneath my intrepid exterior at that moment there lurked a nameless dread. — *Very Good, Jeeves!*, P. G. Wodehouse, 1930.

3699 Supported against the stair rail, Mr. Lecky might have been sick; but his stomach was empty. When he retched, all that rose was a bloodwarm lump — perhaps his heart bounced on the firm spurt of his terror. — *Castaway*, James Gould Cozzens, 1934.

3700 Master Awsten was lying in a great bed with painted hangings. He did not hear me steal into the room. His eyes were open, but the light

had gone from them; there was neither repose nor gaiety in his face, only fear. — *The Player's Boy*, Bryher, 1953.

3701 When I awoke I imagined that I was in my old room in my father's house, and looked in vain for the familiar crack of light at the top of the door opposite the foot of the bed. One of the terrors of my childhood seized me: I thought that during the night I had gone blind. — *Fantasy and Fugue*, Roy Fuller, 1954.

3702 Amanda had not been really frightened until she found the bottle. — *Death Walked in Cyprus*, M. M. Kaye, 1956.

3703 She hurried through the market, afraid she would miss him. — *The Voodoo Queen*, Robert Tallant, 1956.

3704 "It seems to me," Roger said, "that you're not as afraid of me as you were." — *Lovers and Strangers*, Joyce Marshall, 1957.

3705 He felt seized by a whirlpool of despair as his mother tucked the bedcovers about his shoulders, and his voice rose in a protesting wail:/ "Leave the light on!" *The Long Dream*, Richard Wright, 1958.

3706 Woof! Woof Woof! *Woof! Woof!/* Barking in the night. Barking, barking. I shriek but no one answers. I scream but there's not even an echo. — *Nexus*, Henry Miller, 1960.

3707 All her life, Mrs. Crominski had taken anxiety like a pep-pill. — *Madame Sousatzka*, Bernice Rubens, 1962.

3708 I must compose my face and push the fear and doubt beneath the skin. — *White Lotus*, John Hersey, 1965.

3709 The vaporetto to the Giudecca which Edward usually caught at night left the San Zaccaria pier at 11:59, an odd time which magnified his fear of missing it and having to hang around the Riva for another hour. — *Stitch*, Richard G. Stern, 1965.

3710 As the aeroplane slanted and began to come down, I suddenly felt frightened. Not frightened *of* anything in particular, but full of strange tension and insecurity. — *The Young Visitors*, John Wain, 1965.

3711 Settling himself in his seat in the aeroplane, a long narrow hand on each bony knee in the posture of an Egyptian priest-king, Chatteney closed his eyes. — *The Early Life of Stephen Hind*, Storm Jameson, 1966.

3712 *Over the fear, the foolishness . . . Feeds?* Too many "f"s. Foolishness! — *Anagrams*, David R. Slavitt, 1970.

3713 He was afraid of going to sleep. For three weeks, he had been afraid of going to sleep. — *Strange Meeting*, Susan Hill, 1971.

3714 The scorching sun drying, prickling his scalp, wet from swimming in Crazy Creek, Lucius reached out both hands, a sudden fear of snakes chilling him, to part thickly hanging vines that hung over the narrow path he never walked alone without fear, but he thirsted for the jungle shade, reeling off images of Sam Gulliver waking up in a secret cave, his neck across the boots of a half-breed Indian, staring into the eyes of a black panther. — *Bijou*, David Madden, 1974.

3715 The fears have moved in for the first time. — *Before My Time*, Maureen Howard, 1975.

3716 I took the cats and flew up to the island. All the time I was getting ready to go, packing, neatly, like a lady, I felt frozen. As if the trembling had frozen into a single shrieking note, high-pitched on a violin, so high that no one could hear, only the mad dogs of the universe. — *Bring Down the Sun*, Betty Lambert, 1979.

3717 I was afraid again this morning. — *False Match*, Henry Bean, 1982.

3718 I've put it off, sometimes easily, without even thinking, sometimes painfully, sometimes believing I was not putting it off at all, for — how long? Six months? Six years? Thirty years? — *A Lifetime Burning*, Ellen Douglas, 1982.

3719 When the year one thousand came, Thorkel Amundason was five years old, and hardly noticed how frightened everyone was. — *King Hereafter*, Dorothy Dunnett, 1982.

3720 Richard did not become frightened until darkness began to settle over the woods. — *The Sunne in Splendour*, Sharon Kay Penman, 1982.

3721 By that summer, the last of his long and blood-stained reign, Abdul Hamid's fears had become so great that they threatened to paralyse him altogether. — *The Rage of the Vulture*, Barry Unsworth, 1982.

3722 When report cards were handed out at the Babbington Grammar School, some of my classmates fell into a whimpering terror, instinctively cowering and covering their vulnerable spots, as skittish and apprehensive as squirrels. — "The Girl with the White Fur Muff," Eric Kraft, 1984.

3723 People are afraid to merge on freeways in Los Angeles. — *Less Than Zero*, Bret Easton Ellis, 1985.

3724 She had nothing to fear. — *Men and Angels*, Mary Gordon, 1985.

3725 Aurora on in to Lake Michigan, from Half Day to Flossmoor, King Panic reigns in fast forward. — *Chin Music*, James McManus, 1985.

3726 Fear is the surrogate for pain. It comes first. — *The Storyteller*, Harold Robbins, 1985.

3727 At first, I don't want to talk about the fear to anybody. — *The Chronicles of Doodah*, George Lee Walker, 1985.

3728 The boy stared down at his clean sheet of paper, afraid to begin, afraid to sully its perfect whiteness. — *Breaker Boys*, Jan Kubicki, 1986.

3729 "I think you might be frightening them," said Marleen. — *Wet Paint*, Gwynn Popovac, 1986.

3730 As they followed the Mississippi out of the Twin Cities on U.S. 61, Brendan wondered why his parents and his grandfather seemed not to share his dread. — *Grand Opening*, Jon Hassler, 1987.

3731 Where there is fear, everything is fearful. — *The Rape of the Rose*, Glyn Hughes, 1987.

3732 *Even before she opened her eyes, the child was afraid.* — *Homeplace*, Anne Rivers Siddons, 1987.

3733 I have been afraid of putting air in a tire ever since I saw a tractor tire blow up and throw Newt Hardbine's father over the top of the Standard Oil sign. — *The Bean Trees*, Barbara Kingsolver, 1988.

3734 Joe Reckler was dreading the whole idea. — *I'll Take It*, Paul Rudnick, 1989.

3735 Charlie Gallagher's biggest fear was that someone she knew would see her entering the church. — *Hearts of Glass*, Nicole Jeffords, 1992.

Finance

3736 "Bills, Harry? — Yes. — Dear me, where are they? — There! — No. Here? — O, look! — What do you think of this scarf? Isn't it lovely?" — *Dred*, Harriet Beecher Stowe, 1856.

3737 The 25th day of August, 1751, about two in the afternoon, I, David Balfour, came forth of the British Linen Company, a porter attending me with a bag of money, and some of the chief of these merchants bowing me from their doors. — *David Balfour*, Robert Louis Stevenson, 1893.

3738 Seated in his giant's chair behind his desk in his office, leaning back with his eyes half closed, Nero Wolfe muttered at me:/ "It is an interesting fact that the members of the National Industrial Association who were at that dinner last evening represent, in the aggregate, assets of something like thirty billion dollars." — *The Silent Speaker*, Rex Stout, 1946.

3739 For the third time I went over the final additions and subtractions on the first page of Form 1040, to make good and sure. — *And Be a Villain*, Rex Stout, 1948.

3740 Captain Crosbie came out of the bank with the pleased air of one who has cashed a cheque and has discovered that there is just a little more in his account than he thought there was. — *They Came to Baghdad*, Agatha Christie, 1951.

3741 Of all the communications that Bernard

Sands received on the day of his triumph the one which gave him the greatest satisfaction was the Treasury's final confirmation of official financial backing. — *Hemlock and After*, Angus Wilson, 1952.

3742 "The Bevan ticket," I said, "has expired, and will have to be renewed." — *That Uncertain Feeling*, Kingsley Amis, 1955.

3743 Hank counted the stack of money. — *A Rage in Harlem*, Chester Himes, 1957.

3744 "Five hundred guineas!" said Mor's wife. "Well I never!" — *The Sandcastle*, Iris Murdoch, 1957.

3745 In 1933 the thirty-first of December fell on a Sunday, and so the cash count at the Bank had to be done on the Saturday. — *The Accounting*, Bruce Marshall, 1958.

3746 "That's all very well, my dear," said Donald Salinger; "but we should need money. At least seventy thousand, I'd say." — *The Rich Pay Late*, Simon Raven, 1964.

3747 A sum of money is a leading character in this tale about people, just as a sum of honey might properly be a leading character in a tale about bees. — *God Bless You, Mr. Rosewater*, Kurt Vonnegut, 1965.

3748 There was a ten-dollar bill in Joseph Champlin's pocket on an evening in early March in 1933. — *Five Smooth Stones*, Ann Fairbairn, 1966.

3749 "What charge?" cried Agathon, rolling his eyes up, clinging to his crutch, "what charge?" — *Wreckage of Agathon*, John Gardner, 1970.

3750 Oh, sure, potatoes were cheaper all right, and so were tomatoes, just like Eddie Cantor kept singing on the radio, but who the hell had money to buy any except maybe Eddie Cantor? — *Potatoes Are Cheaper*, Max Shulman, 1971.

3751 In the spring of 1971, when it became apparent to Howard W. Amberson that neither he nor his wife had much time remaining, he walked to Woolworth's and purchased a large ledger, bound in red and gray. — *Praise the Human Season*, Don Robertson, 1974.

3752 "Jörg, expect seven million dollars from Crédit Parisien in the Number Two account by six o'clock tonight, Central European time, and place it overnight with first-class banks and triple 'A' commercial names. Otherwise, invest it in the overnight Euro dollar market. Understood?" — *Not a Penny More, Not a Penny Less*, Jeffrey Archer, 1976.

3753 We all agreed that it was very clever of Jimbo Ryder to hold his fundraiser at the Sons of Italy in America Hall. — *A Dime to Dance By*, Walter Walker, 1983.

3754 Artie was low on cash. — *Time Sharing*, Richard Krawiec, 1986.

3755 Jimmy McVay was still alive when the man kicked his hand away from the envelope

filled with hundred-dollar bills. — *Spirit of the Hills*, Dan O'Brien, 1988.

3756 In September, to raise cash for the estate, my brother and I sold off the last of our mother's houses. — *Boy, Girl, Boy, Girl*, David Michaelis, 1989.

3757 During the first part of the interview, when we are sitting on the porch looking down the valley, I try for exactitude more than anything — $343.67. — "Good Will," Jane Smiley, 1989.

3758 Like most farm workers in those days my mother distrusted banks. — *Poor Things*, Alasdair Gray, 1992.

Fire and Smoke

3759 She sat at the base of the big tree — her little sunbonnet pushed back, her arms locked about her knees, her bare feet gathered under her crimson gown and her deep eyes fixed on the smoke in the valley below. — *The Trail of the Lonesome Pine*, John Fox, Jr., 1908.

3760 A fire blazed in the deep, clay-plastered fireplace; logs of North Carolina pine dripped turpentine in the wave of flame and sent up scrolls of clotted smoke to join the night. — *Drums*, James Boyd, 1925.

3761 Fire in the night! — *At the South Gate*, Grace S. Richmond, 1928.

3762 In the kitchen of the small thatched farmhouse the mother sat on a low bamboo stool behind the earthen stove and fed grass deftly into the hole where a fire burned beneath the iron cauldron. — *The Mother*, Pearl S. Buck, 1934.

3763 A column of smoke rose thin and straight from the cabin chimney. — *The Yearling*, Marjorie Kinnan Rawlings, 1938.

3764 The fire in our habitual public-house spurted and fell. — *Strangers and Brothers*, C. P. Snow, 1940.

3765 The last piñon knot crumpled in the small conical fireplace. — *The Man Who Killed the Deer*, Frank Waters, 1942.

3766 It began on the night we thought all was ended — the night we left Hispaniola for home, with the town of Cap François burning red behind us and the smoke alive with the flicker of the fires, and the darkness wild with shots and cries. — *Pride's Fancy*, Thomas H. Raddall, 1946.

3767 "Is that fire smoking?" said Horace Lamb. — *Manservant and Maidservant*, Ivy Compton-Burnett, 1947.

3768 He had seen the smoke below an hour ago, a lifting pennant, gray against the mottled brass-bright desert. — *Ambush*, Luke Short, 1950.

3769 It was a pleasure to burn. — *Fahrenheit 451*, Ray Bradbury, 1953.

3770 In August of 1927 the Meridian papers carried a story about the Elbow Lake fire, with pictures on the back page, of "Fashionables Fighting Flames." — *The Golden Moment*, Isabella Holt, 1959.

3771 They were burning British garments. The fire that raged in the market square was just one of hundreds of thousands of similar fires all over the country. — *A Bend in the Ganges*, Manohar Malgonkar, 1964.

3772 The grass continued to burn for several days. — *The Kings of Vain Intent*, Graham Shelby, 1970.

3773 Far smoke furled; I studied it, was glad. — *In the Middle Distance*, Nicholas Delbanco, 1971.

3774 Doctor Eduardo Plarr stood in the small port on the Paraná, among the rails and yellow cranes, watching where a horizontal plume of smoke stretched over the Chaco. — *The Honorary Consul*, Graham Greene, 1973.

3775 At midday men were sent out with flaming torches to fire the suburbs. — *The Devil Is Loose*, Graham Shelby, 1973.

3776 Smoke was drifting through my high window, obscuring the light. — *The Malacia Tapestry*, Brian W. Aldiss, 1976.

3777 In the Detroit Riot of '43, Moseley had said that the city was burning. But that had not been true, Yasha reflected. — *The Long Hot Summers of Yasha K.*, Natalie L. M. Petesch, 1978.

3778 Claytor tongued the barn match and lifted the five-gallon can of gasoline with a gloved hand. — *The Land That Drank the Rain*, William Hoffman, 1982.

3779 That night the fields were on fire. — *My Old Sweetheart*, Susanna Moore, 1982.

3780 Mrs. Cronin was about to enter the area door of Mrs. Gallagher's boarding house in Great Britain Street when she stepped back, alarmed at the smell of smoke. — *Watson's Apology*, Beryl Bainbridge, 1984.

3781 The fire pit was about twenty-five feet long by ten feet wide, and perhaps two feet deep. The fire had been burning for hours. — *Job*, Robert A. Heinlein, 1984.

3782 It had been so hot that day in December, the day that Josie and her son arrived, that a fire had started in a bale of fermenting hay in the stable below BB's house. — *In Her Own Image*, Anna Murdoch, 1985.

3783 A swirling, ominous cloud of acrid black smoke rose from behind the ornate spire of St. Enoch's Church. — *The Killing of Yesterday's Children*, M. S. Power, 1985.

3784 The Jessop fire-raiser had been quiet for almost three months. — *The Fire-Raiser*, Maurice Gee, 1986.

3785 My mother was in the backyard, starting the fire. —*Memory of Departure*, Abdulrazak Gurnah, 1987.

3786 My father is on fire. — *Watching the Body Burn*, Thomas Glynn, 1989.

3787 At night, in my room, I saw from my window the dark shapes of people fluttering around the fires in those oil drums and trash cans. — *Tornado Alley*, Craig Nova, 1989.

3788 They needed firewood, and so they smashed the tables and the chairs in an abandoned cotton warehouse. —*Prisoners of Twilight*, Don Robertson, 1989.

3789 I was living alone again—had been for nearly a year—when I learned that my kid had set himself on fire. —*Alone*, David Small, 1991.

3790 The candleflame and the image of the candleflame caught in the pierglass twisted and righted when he entered the hall and again when he shut the door. —*All the Pretty Horses*, Cormac McCarthy, 1992.

3791 Ships were burning in the harbor. — *The Promise of Light*, Paul Watkins, 1992.

3792 The house glowed in the darkness. Thick smoke billowed from broken windows and jagged holes in the roof, forming black smudges against the eerie, orange-tinted sky. —*Fire and Rain*, Diane Chamberlain, 1993.

Flowers

3793 One morning as little "Sir" Bevis (such was his pet name) was digging in the farmhouse garden, he saw a daisy, and throwing aside his spade, he sat down on the grass to pick the flower to pieces. — *Wood Magic*, Richard Jefferies, 1881.

3794 The studio was filled with the rich odour of roses, and when the light summer wind stirred amidst the trees of the garden, there came through the open door the heavy scent of the lilac, or the more delicate perfume of the pink-flowering thorn. — *The Picture of Dorian Gray*, Oscar Wilde, 1891.

3795 I do not suppose that anyone who knows the name of Allan Quatermain would be likely to associate it with flowers, and especially with orchids. —*Allan and the Holy Flower*, H. Rider Haggard, 1915.

3796 The room was vital with air and fresh with the scent of many flowers. —*Flaming Youth*, Samuel Hopkins Adams *as* Warner Fabian, 1923.

3797 Mrs. Dalloway said she would buy the flowers herself. —*Mrs. Dalloway*, Virginia Woolf, 1925.

3798 There were crimson roses on the bench; they looked like splashes of blood. —*Strong Poison*, Dorothy L. Sayers, 1930.

3799 . . .*of wandering forever and the earth again . . . of seed-time, bloom, and the mellow-dropping harvest. And of the big flowers, the rich flowers, the strange unknown flowers.* —"No Door," Thomas Wolfe, 1933.

3800 I smelt blossom everywhere as I walked through the town that afternoon. — *The Light and the Dark*, C. P. Snow, 1947.

3801 Spring was in the air. The bright morning sunshine had dried the dew and warmed the ground, and crocuses, bordering the front brick walk, bloomed in yellow flame. — *The Third Generation*, Chester Himes, 1954.

3802 Dandelions were in yellow circles. —*Let No Man Write My Epitaph*, Willard Motley, 1958.

3803 The azaleas were dying. —*A Matter of Conviction*, Evan Hunter, 1959.

3804 Dearest Girl:/ The sadly macerated and decomposed specimen you sent me for identification is without doubt *Endymion nutans* or *Endymion non-scriptus*, or *Scilla nutans* or *non-scriptus*. Also called wood hyacinth, wood bell, wild hyacinth./ It is, in short, the common European bluebell. —*A Fairly Good Time*, Mavis Gallant, 1970.

3805 May 1971. After the coldest spring in memory, the shoots, the shrubs, and the flowers were burgeoning again at last. — *The Rivers of Eros*, Cyrus Colter, 1972.

3806 It was August and the warm day seemed as exultant as a mother who has a family of children to show for her labors. For here in all the garden beds was a rich profusion of late asters and early chrysanthemums, of roses and zinnias and snapdragons. — *The Flowering*, Agnes Sligh Turnbull, 1972.

3807 A warm morning in June, not a cloud in the sky, another winter and a long cold spring gone over at last and the lilac was in bloom again. — *Voices in Time*, Hugh MacLennan, 1980.

3808 All over the Gloucestershire countryside the poppies that summer were delicate on sunny banks, cowparsley and campion profuse. —*Other People's Worlds*, William Trevor, 1980.

3809 The room was filled with the heady scent of roses past their prime. — *The Two Mrs. Grenvilles*, Dominick Dunne, 1985.

3810 It is spring at last—after rain, and wet snow, and God-knows-what through April—and the window that looks on the street shows me a gay yellow flash of forsythia. —*Adele at the End of the Day*, Tom Marshall, 1987.

3811 It was almost roses, roses, all the way. —*Forgotten Life*, Brian W. Aldiss, 1989.

Food

3812 "Ho, Diomed, well met! Do you sup with Glaucus to-night?" said a young man of small stature, who wore his tunic in those loose and effeminate folds which proved him to be a gentleman and a coxcomb.

"Alas, no! dear Clodius; he has not invited me," replied Diomed, a man of portly frame and of middle age. "By Pollux, a scurvy trick! for they say his suppers are the best in Pompeii." — *The Last Days of Pompeii*, Edward Bulwer Lytton, 1834.

3813 One fine morning in the full London season, Major Arthur Pendennis came over from his lodgings, according to his custom, to breakfast at a certain Club in Pall Mall, of which he was a chief ornament. — *The History of Pendennis*, William Makepeace Thackeray, 1849–1850.

3814 Sixteen-year old Flora Hazeley stood by the table in the dingy little dining room, looking down earnestly and thoughtfully at a shapely, yellow sweet potato. — *The Hazeley Family*, Mrs. A. E. Johnson, 1894.

3815 It had just struck nine from the cuckoo clock that hung over the mantelpiece in the dining-room, when Victorine brought in the halved watermelon and set it in front of Mr. Bessemer's plate. — *Blix*, Frank Norris, 1899.

3816 It was Sunday, and, according to his custom on that day, McTeague took his dinner at two in the afternoon at the car conductors' coffee-joint on Polk Street. — *McTeague*, Frank Norris, 1899.

3817 "The Signorino will take coffee?" old Marietta asked, as she set the fruit before him. — *The Cardinal's Snuff-Box*, Henry Harland, 1900.

3818 Mr. Sherlock Holmes, who was usually very late in the mornings, save upon those not infrequent occasions when he was up all night, was seated at the breakfast table. — *The Hound of the Baskervilles*, Arthur Conan Doyle, 1902.

3819 Brock was breakfasting out-of-doors in the cheerful little garden of the Hôtel Chatham. — *The Husbands of Edith*, George Barr McCutcheon, 1908.

3820 I dined with Hartley Wiggins at the Hare and Tortoise on an evening in October, not very long ago. — *The Siege of the Seven Suitors*, Meredith Nicholson, 1910.

3821 Francesca Bassington sat in the drawing-room of her house in Blue Street, W., regaling herself and her estimable brother Henry with China tea and small cress sandwiches. The meal was of that elegant proportion which, while ministering sympathetically to the desires of the moment, is happily reminiscent of a satisfactory luncheon and blessedly expectant of an elaborate dinner to come. — *The Unbearable Bassington*, H. H. Munro *as* Saki, 1912.

3822 Once upon a time I owned a watermelon. — *The Light in the Clearing*, Irving Bacheller, 1917.

3823 The Cutter family was eating dinner. — *The Cutters*, Bess Streeter Aldrich, 1926.

3824 Little Jane Ward sat at her father's left hand at the family breakfast table, her sleek, brown pigtailed head bent discreetly over her plate. She was washing down great mouthfuls of bacon and eggs with gulps of too hot cocoa. — *Years of Grace*, Margaret Ayer Barnes, 1930.

3825 On a late Sunday afternoon in the spring of 1915 Miss Florence Seddon was crossing the hall of her home in Hampstead to give an order in the kitchen about supper. — *We That Were Young*, Irene Rathbone, 1932.

3826 Down the stairway of his house came Barney Glasgow on his way to breakfast. — *Come and Get It*, Edna Ferber, 1935.

3827 Breakfast in the Sylvester house was supposedly served at eight o'clock. — *You Can't Have Everything*, Kathleen Norris, 1937.

3828 Henry Colbert, the miller, always breakfasted with his wife — beyond that he appeared irregularly at the family table. — *Sapphira and the Slave Girl*, Willa Cather, 1940.

3829 In the mornings when they were in the city, they had breakfast on a card table in Jeffrey's study. — *So Little Time*, John P. Marquand, 1943.

3830 The house officers of Mercy Hospital ate dinner when and where they could. — *Mountain Time*, Bernard DeVoto, 1947.

3831 On a Sunday afternoon in nineteen-forty-eight John Pomfret, a widower of forty-five, sat over lunch with Miss Liz Jennings at one of the round tables set by a great window that opened on the park, a view which had made this hotel loved by the favoured of Europe when they visited London. — *Nothing*, Henry Green, 1950.

3832 "Will you be back for lunch?" asked Miss Paradise, clipping each word like a bean. "I am not going to walk miles in fog to get you sausages, to find you have preferred sandwiches in a pub." — *Cards of Identity*, Nigel Dennis, 1955.

3833 This, then, was the situation. Eight people were to dine that evening in the house at Campden Hill Square. — *The Long View*, Elizabeth Jane Howard, 1956.

3834 On and off, all that hot French August, we made ourselves ill from eating the greengages. — *The Greengage Summer*, Rumer Godden, 1958.

3835 Mark Darr was alone on the farm —

alone except for Mrs. Jensen, the neighbor woman who had come over to prepare the supper. — *A Man Had Tall Sons*, Martha Ostenso, 1958.

3836 Luke began breakfast alone to the drip of the rain from the creepers on the old house. — *Victors and Vanquished*, Francis Stuart, 1958.

3837 Jean Larcher, bookbinder, was at supper with his wife and son. The day was Easter Sunday, which in that year of Grace, 1694, the fifty-first year of the reign of Louis XIV, fell upon the eleventh of April. — *The Ghost of Monsieur Scarron*, Janet Lewis, 1959.

3838 Henry Lamb earnestly studied the dinner-table, wondering what he had forgotten. — *A Number of Things*, Honor Tracy, 1960.

3839 Jeeves placed the sizzling eggs and b. on the breakfast table, and Reginald (Kipper) Herring and I, licking the lips, squared our elbows and got down to it. — *How Right You Are, Jeeves*, P. G. Wodehouse, 1960.

3840 This morning I got a note from my aunt asking me to come for lunch. I know what this means. — *The Moviegoer*, Walker Percy, 1961.

3841 Etta was propped up on pillows in her bed. She was having an elegant breakfast from a tray. — *A Backward Place*, Ruth Prawer Jhabvala, 1965.

3842 The Slades sat down to their breakfast more asleep than awake. — *Up Above the World*, Paul Bowles, 1966.

3843 Fred Carlson had had an excellent lunch with his prospective employers. — *No One Hears But Him*, Taylor Caldwell, 1966.

3844 Hercule Poirot was sitting at the breakfast table. At his right hand was a steaming cup of chocolate. He had always had a sweet tooth. To accompany the chocolate was a brioche. It went agreeably with chocolate. He nodded his approval. This was from the fourth shop he had tried. — *Third Girl*, Agatha Christie, 1966.

3845 "Conquer taste, and you will have conquered the self," said Jagan to his listener, who asked, "Why conquer the self?" Jagan said, "I do not know, but all our sages advise us so." — *The Vendor of Sweets*, R. K. Narayan, 1967.

3846 On the Friday of the week following his mother's funeral, Tom Adamson had dinner with the Wentworths, Andrew and Madge. — *It's an Old Country*, J. B. Priestley, 1967.

3847 We were using the old blue china and the stainless steel cutlery, with place mats on the big oval table and odd-sized jelly glasses for the wine. — *Red Sky at Morning*, Richard Bradford, 1968.

3848 I could find him every noon, sitting on a bench in the Rathaus Park with a small, fat bag of hothouse radishes in his lap and a bottle of beer in one hand. — *Setting Free the Bears*, John Irving, 1969.

3849 Cecil crushed in his hands the empty Carnation evaporated milk can. — *Hurry Home*, John Edgar Wideman, 1970.

3850 As I slid into my chair at the breakfast table and started to deal with the toothsome eggs and bacon which Jeeves had given of his plenty, I was conscious of a strange exhilaration, if I've got the word right. — *Jeeves and the Tie That Binds*, P. G. Wodehouse, 1971.

3851 It was a fine feast. No one, not even the Praelector who was so old he could remember the Feast of '09, could recall its equal — and Porterhouse is famous for its food. — *Porterhouse Blue*, Tom Sharpe, 1974.

3852 George Bullay finished his soft-boiled egg and one slice of buttered wholewheat toast. After masticating his food thoroughly he washed the last bite down with a gulp of his tea, which had cooled. — *Death in Don Mills*, Hugh Garner, 1975.

3853 "I really do think, Mr. Carnelian, that we should at least *try* them raw, don't you?" — *The End of All Songs*, Michael Moorcock, 1976.

3854 It was the Sunday before Christmas, 1909. The Alfred Englekings were having supper. It was a simple meal: rice with milk and brown sugar, black rye bread with butter, and green tea. — *Green Earth*, Frederick Manfred, 1977.

3855 Castle, ever since he had joined the firm as a young recruit more than thirty years ago, had taken his lunch in a public house behind St. James's Street, not far from the office. — *The Human Factor*, Graham Greene, 1978.

3856 They had pork chops and butter beans for dinner. — *A Few Days in Weasel Creek*, Joanna Brent, 1979.

3857 One morning, in the middle of the year 1990, in a two-room shack in Charleston, South Carolina, Bill James has a comforting breakfast of mackerel and hominy grits. — *A Short Walk*, Alice Childress, 1979.

3858 He ate dinner first — some kind of greasy ham, "baked ham," the old lady who served the food told him when he asked her what it was, "with honey glaze. It's very nice," she added hopelessly. — *Wild Oats*, Jacob Epstein, 1979.

3859 Everywhere he went that summer, he saw Brie. — *Third Parties*, Laura Cunningham, 1980.

3860 Thoughtfully, Kate cut up Hugo's steak and spread each piece with a dab of mustard, then started to turn over her own spinach with her fork, as though inspecting it. — *The Middle Ground*, Margaret Drabble, 1980.

3861 Dr. Hugh Welchman put down his knife and fork and removed a kipper bone from his teeth. — *Sleeping Dogs Lie*, Julian Gloag, 1980.

3862 They are, I thought sadly, what they eat. — *General Ludd*, John Metcalf, 1980.

3863 The meal had the ill-subdued restlessness of a headquarters' mess on the eve of the battle. — *A Question of Guilt*, Richard Gordon, 1981.

3864 It is difficult to love the human race when you have watched a roomful of people eating as often as I have, but given the price that most of them are prepared to pay others for providing their food I've learned to tolerate their hoggish ways. — *The Sinner's Congregation*, Guy Bellamy, 1982.

3865 Sasha Greenberg Flynn looked down at the spilled Cheerios on the floor. — *Soon to Be Immortal*, Ellen Alexander Conley, 1982.

3866 The day began with a late breakfast at Mosby's Drugstore on Forty-ninth Street. — *The Follower*, Henry Bromell, 1983.

3867 The soft strong pull of the mouth at her breast was like the deep stroke of the mantel clock that pulled the sun toward midafternoon. — *Cajun*, Elizabeth Nell Dubus, 1983.

3868 Across the damask-covered, candle-lit table, Sir George Seaton watched his guest apply knife and fork to the thick slice of fresh-killed, perfectly roasted, pinkish-brown beef that the servant had lain before him — watched as he raised a morsel to his mouth, chewed slowly, swallowed, and lifted his small blue eyes to heaven. — *Red Barbarian*, Margaret Gaan, 1984.

3869 Dear Dr. Youngdahl:/ I want to thank you so much for the glorious lunch at Monti's La Casa Vieja and for giving me Mr. Klang's address. — *Lying in Bed*, Mark Harris, 1984.

3870 I do paradiddles with my digits while Dottie skims the Post-Dispatch and sculptures wedges from her Howard Johnson hotcakes with a fork. — *The Vestal Virgin Room*, C. W. Smith, 1984.

3871 "One egg sunny-side, toast 'n' coffee!" — *Blue North*, Kenneth White, 1984.

3872 Granpa McGregor was having his dinner when the crystal chandelier fell down just behind his chair. — *Annie Magdalene*, Barbara Hanrahan, 1985.

3873 I come in early and sit by the door. In the back a pair of tourists are having lunch. — *A Small Town*, Shelby Hearon, 1985.

3874 Joshie's all distracted at breakfast. — *Queen of Hearts*, Dan McCall, 1985.

3875 "What is this supposed to be?" demanded Sir Nitin Basu, poking at the lumpy cutlet on his plate. — *Plans for Departure*, Nayantara Sahgal, 1985.

3876 Enter the Sunset Mall from the south side, where the parking lot is always less crowded, and you find yourself in the "patio" section, surrounded by food: kosher hot dogs, stuffed potato skins, spareribs, gyro sandwiches, eggrolls, soft ice cream, Coney Island fries — the usual multi-ethnic array. — *A Loving Place*, Mark Dintenfass, 1986.

3877 We lunched late, on partridge and port, followed by Stilton and coffee: how I have always imagined a judge would dine. — *A Woman of Judah*, Ronald Frame, 1987.

3878 On the night before Bill Rau's fortieth birthday, his wife is having dinner with a man on their front porch in Iowa. — *The Second Bridge*, Gary Gildner, 1987.

3879 On Monte Paradiso, the family of the Duke of Granbörg, the Danish nobleman, was eating breakfast on the terrace of the Villa Paradiso. — *Cassata*, Rosemary Kingsland, 1987.

3880 Pursued by threat of war and violence in the streets, we came to a friend's house for dinner. — *The Two Deaths of Señora Puccini*, Stephen Dobyns, 1988.

3881 Halina had crisp rolls and coffee set out for a late breakfast. — *Mother's Girl*, Elaine Feinstein, 1988.

3882 The woman walked round the corner of the house and saw a snake consuming a large Tuscan toad. — *Summer's Lease*, John Mortimer, 1988.

3883 Then it was fall again and Harry was coming home for Sunday dinners and nobody could get a word in edgewise, my father would groan. — *Men in Trouble*, Sarah Payne Stuart, 1988.

3884 "Will you be eating with us?" — *Incline Our Hearts*, A. N. Wilson, 1988.

3885 She hasn't been dead four months and already I've eaten to the bottom of the deep freeze. — *A Virtuous Woman*, Kaye Gibbons, 1989.

3886 On New Year's Day Quinn served dinner at ten-fifteen. — *The Lie of the Land*, Haydn Middleton, 1989.

3887 Aden's fetters shaken off at last, I begin my journal in good heart this Christmas Day, 1910, having dined like a queen on boiled sheep's brains and a plum pudding raided from my stores. — *The Long Lost Journey*, Jennifer Potter, 1989.

3888 I was in the rocking chair giving our six-month-old Bug her late afternoon bottle. — *Room Temperature*, Nicholson Baker, 1990.

3889 Cameron and I were having a bite at Elephant & Castle one Tuesday night in early January. — *Spontaneous Combustion*, David B. Feinberg, 1991.

3890 At eight in the morning Samuel Taylor was eating eggs. — *All-Bright Court*, Connie Porter, 1991.

3891 A woman, not yet fifty-seven, slight and seeming frail, eats carefully at a table in a corner. — *Reading Turgenev*, William Trevor, 1991.

3892 Do you know what you had for breakfast today? — *Till the Fat Lady Sings*, Alisa Kwitney, 1992.

Forests

3893 In that pleasant district of merry England which is watered by the river Don, there extended in ancient times a large forest, covering the greater part of the beautiful hills and valleys which lie between Sheffield and the pleasant town of Doncaster. — *Ivanhoe*, Sir Walter Scott, 1819.

3894 A fine evening — six centuries ago — shed a bright parting light over Alton Wood, illuminating the gray lichens that clung to the rugged trunks of the old oak trees, and shining on the smoother bark of the graceful beech, with that sidelong light that, towards evening, gives an especial charm to woodland scenery. — *The Prince and the Page*, Charlotte Mary Yonge, 1866.

3895 It is close upon daybreak. The great wall of pines and hemlocks that keep off the east wind from Stillwater stretches black and indeterminate against the sky. — *The Stillwater Tragedy*, Thomas Bailey Aldrich, 1880.

3896 Dark spruce forest frowned on either side the frozen waterway. — *White Fang*, Jack London, 1906.

3897 The deep hush of noon hovered over the vast solitude of Canadian forest. — *The Gold Hunters*, James Oliver Curwood, 1909.

3898 Probably Florian would never have gone into the Forest of Acaire had he not been told, over and over again, to keep out of it. — *The High Place*, James Branch Cabell, 1923.

3899 Down to the left swirled the shining river, its steep green banks overhung with wide-branched limbs of trees which fringed the immeasurable forest, a tangle of great trunks, saplings, underbrush, and vines that spread illimitably. — *Shadow of the Long Knives*, Thomas Boyd, 1928.

3900 In the beginning was the forest. God made it and no man knew the end of it. — *The Forest and the Fort*, Hervey Allen, 1943.

3901 The first Frenchmen to penetrate the forests of Upper Varva were missionaries. — *The Decline of the West*, David Caute, 1966.

3902 Thomas dreamed he walked a familiar forest, following a timeworn path of the Tuscaroras. — *The House of Dies Drear*, Virginia Hamilton, 1968.

3903 Nature, creating the clearing in the Forest of Lions, had covered the rocky crust with a thin blanket of poor soil. — *The Knight*, George Shipway, 1969.

3904 Even in the dry heat of summer's end, the great forest was never silent. — *Shardik*, Richard Adams, 1974.

3905 Dawn came to the Congo rain forest. — *Congo*, Michael Crichton, 1980.

3906 The forest, the place of wild growth, was touohkomuk to the Massachusetts Indians, an uncultivated space, the haunt of many different kinds of wood. — *Torn Covenants*, Lois Swann, 1981.

3907 The clearing in the scrub oak woods lay silent in the sullen noonday heat. — *All Manner of Riches*, Mary Elmblad, 1987.

3908 At the moment, it's raining in the forest. — *The Hour of Blue*, Robert Froese, 1990.

3909 From far north, a breeze rushed and the forest creaked in a wave. — *The Ascent*, Jeff Long, 1992.

Friends

3910 I was a resident in this city in the year 1793. Many motives contributed to detain me, though departure was easy and commodious, and my friends were generally solicitous for me to go. — *Arthur Mervyn*, Charles Brockden Brown, 1799-1800.

3911 "Is it possible," exclaimed Vivian, "that you, Russell, my friend, my best friend, can tell me that this line is the motto of my character! — 'To see the best, and yet the worse pursue.' — Then you must think me either a villain or a madman." — "Vivian," Maria Edgeworth, 1812.

3912 From the club where the farewell dinner was given him, Ray went to the depot of the East & West Railroad with a friend of his own age, and they walked up and down the platform talking of their lives and their loves, as young men will do, till they both at once found themselves suddenly very drowsy. — *The World of Chance*, William Dean Howells, 1893.

3913 Strether's first question, when he reached the hotel, was about his friend; yet on his learning that Waymarsh was apparently not to arrive till evening he was not wholly disconcerted. — *The Ambassadors*, Henry James, 1903.

3914 Many men were in debt to the trader at Flambeau and many counted him as a friend. — *The Barrier*, Rex Beach, 1908.

3915 Several years ago circumstances thrust me into a position in which it became possible for the friend who figures in these pages as Godfrey Loring to do me a favor. — *The Husband's Story*, David Graham Phillips, 1910.

3916 The great doctor stood on the hearth-rug looking down at his friend who sprawled before him in an easy-chair. — *John Macnab*, John Buchan, 1925.

3917 In the town there were two mutes, and they were always together. — *The Heart Is a Lonely Hunter*, Carson McCullers, 1940.

3918 The voice was quiet, smiling. "Is that Miss Clarvoe?"/ "Yes."/ "You know who this is?"/ "No."/ "A friend."/ "I have a great many friends," Miss Clarvoe lied. — *Beast in View*, Margaret Millar, 1955.

3919 *My beloved Daisy: It has been so many years since I have seen you. . . .* — *A Stranger in My Grave*, Margaret Millar, 1960.

3920 Manning's old friend Proctor-Gould was in Moscow, and anxious to get in touch with him. Or so Manning was informed. — *The Russian Interpreter*, Michael Frayn, 1966.

3921 "You're my friend, ain't you?" the giant asked. — *The Heat's On*, Chester Himes, 1966.

3922 On the eve of Christmas and of his departure for Ceylon, Christopher Progoff stood in Notre Dame with the best of his remaining friends, Raoul. — *Man of Earth*, Maggi Lidchi, 1967.

3923 Once there were three patients who met in the hospital and decided to live together. — *Tell Me That You Love Me, Junie Moon*, Marjorie Kellogg, 1968.

3924 Friend (I may call you friend?), these are also our friends. — *House Mother Normal*, B. S. Johnson, 1971.

3925 George Harlequin and I have been friends for twenty years; yet I have to confess he is the one man I have ever truly envied. — *Harlequin*, Morris West, 1974.

3926 Five friends I had, and two of them snakes. — *Godric*, Frederick Buechner, 1980.

3927 The Five had always known they were special. — *Original Sins*, Lisa Alther, 1981.

3928 Hannah was my best friend until her father killed her mother with the bread knife when we were eight. — *Matters of Chance*, Gail Albert, 1982.

3929 Kate adjusted the bag on her shoulder. "I don't understand you. I thought you would be pleased. Jun is your friend, you introduced us." — *The Bonsai Tree*, Meira Chand, 1983.

3930 Raskolnikov and I had become good friends in a short time. — "Life on the Bolotomy," Eric Kraft, 1983.

3931 At the Convent of the Sacred Heart in Valenciennes in 1890 there were two pupils called Alice Ravanel and Françoise Bart, each ten years old, who had become locked together in one of those absorbing friendships formed by girls of that age. — *The Free Frenchman*, Piers Paul Read, 1986.

3932 My friend Matt is a real smart-ass. — *My Friend Matt and Hena the Whore*, Adam Zameenzad, 1988.

3933 On a Saturday in spring when Ramona was sixteen, she stood with her friends in the bright new heat and watched Ed King move away from her toward Luther Sherrill's pickup truck, sitting fueled and ready in the gas station's driveway. — *Dexterity*, Douglas Bauer, 1989.

3934 Jem was a joyful mystery to Alice. — *Temples of Delight*, Barbara Trapido, 1990.

Funerals

3935 Axiochus of Miletus was dead and in the dark hour before dawn the doors of his house were thrown open, the flute boy gave signal, the professional dirge-singers raised their voices in lamentation and issued into the street beating their breasts. — *The Immortal Marriage*, Gertrude Atherton, 1927.

3936 Freddi himself wouldn't have wanted an elaborate funeral or any fuss made over his broken body; but funerals are not for the dead, only for the living. — *Wide Is the Gate*, Upton Sinclair, 1943.

3937 "There's Vinny going in with the wreaths," Isabella had once said. — *The Sleeping Beauty*, Elizabeth Taylor, 1953.

3938 It was appropriate that Mrs. Bridgetower's funeral fell on a Thursday, for that had always been her At Home day. — *A Mixture of Frailties*, Robertson Davies, 1958.

3939 After the funeral they came back to the house, now indisputably Mrs. Halloran's. — *The Sundial*, Shirley Jackson, 1958.

3940 We buried my grandfather the second week before Christmas. It wasn't cold, but there was a light drizzle and all of us had come in thick clothes. My mother and I shared an umbrella. — *Flight into Camden*, David Storey, 1960.

3941 *I am the resurrection and the life, saith the Lord: he that believeth in me, though he were dead, yet shall he live./* Fanny Peronett was dead. That much her husband Hugh Peronett was certain of as he stood in the rain beside the grave which was shortly to receive his wife's mortal remains. — *An Unofficial Rose*, Iris Murdoch, 1962.

3942 To explain how my Uncle Nick asked me to join him, I have to go back to my mother's funeral. — *Lost Empires*, J. B. Priestley, 1965.

3943 After the funeral James came straight home, to look after his brother. — *The Tin Can Tree*, Anne Tyler, 1965.

3944 The man with the spade bent down and

shovelled some earth on to Geoffrey's coffin. He seemed to be in a hurry to get the grave filled in and move on to the next. People were dying all the time; you couldn't hang about. — *A Winter in the Hills*, John Wain, 1970.

3945 "She would have loved the funeral," said Anna. "The whole town was there. I've never seen anything like it since Churchill died." — *The Last Supper*, Chaim Bermant, 1973.

3946 "I thought Arlene did very well," said Boo. — *The Summer After the Funeral*, Jane Gardam, 1973.

3947 They had put out whiskey and cakes, as was the custom, and had left the cabin door wide for mourners to come and go with their condolences. — *The Chisholms*, Evan Hunter, 1976.

3948 My father's funeral was full of priests. — *Final Payments*, Mary Gordon, 1978.

3949 I saw him for the first time at the funeral. — *A Ring of Endless Light*, Madeleine L'Engle, 1980.

3950 A man approaches Harry Waltz at his father's wake and places an envelope full of cash in his hand. — *Waltz in Marathon*, Charles Dickinson, 1983.

3951 The services for Grandma Sophie, I learned from a placard on a wooden easel, would be held in Parlor One. — *The Great Pretender*, James Atlas, 1986.

3952 Emma Coen stood in a circlet of sunlight and listened as her brothers chanted the Kaddish prayer beside their father's newly dug grave. — *West to Eden*, Gloria Goldreich, 1987.

3953 All in all it was a pretty good funeral. — *Baby Todd and the Rattlesnake Stradivarius*, Teresa Kennedy, 1987.

3954 Whenever they held services for the dead at Dong Xuyen, the rifle reports caught Aaron off guard. — *Higher Ground*, Perry Oldham, 1987.

3955 Trover Kleeve had never gone to a wake in his life. As a lawyer he knew the value of precedent. You don't *go* to funerals, he reminded himself like a lifelong friend. And to his wife, asleep beside him, he said, "It feels like snow." — *A Wrestling Season*, Sharon Sheehe Stark, 1987.

3956 It was a hot day to be wearing black. The coffin-bearers counted themselves fortunate. The coffin resting on their shoulders measured less than four feet in length. It was also empty. The child's body had never been found. — *Dreams of Leaving*, Rupert Thomson, 1988.

3957 Maggie and Ira Moran had to go to a funeral in Deer Lick, Pennsylvania. — *Breathing Lessons*, Anne Tyler, 1988.

3958 The day her father dropped dead of a heart attack...("Suddenly and unexpectedly," her Aunt Kay would tell everyone at the funeral service, enunciating every syllable, tapping each captive auditor on the forearm with her folded-up, made-in-Japan lacquered paper fan. "And you *know* the man was as healthy as a horse. As a *horse*. And only forty-two years old! I don't know, but it's just criminal!")... Lynn Ann got her first inkling that something was wrong from halfway up the road. — *Risks*, Margaret Wander Bonanno, 1989.

3959 The American woman got out of the taxi and walked across the still-soggy ground to where the members of the family were clustered at the gravesite. — *Only Yesterday*, Syrell Rogovin Leahy, 1989.

3960 The coffin stuck fast at the angle of the garden path and the gateway out into the road. — *Passing On*, Penelope Lively, 1989.

3961 The friends and business acquaintances of the dead man, gathered in a perfectly appointed town house for a hastily arranged memorial service, are dressed as if for a costume party. — *Under the Shadow*, Gilbert Sorrentino, 1991.

3962 The Great Man lay dead while the little men watched and mourned and the rats in the walls perked up sniffing. — *Peter Doyle*, John Vernon, 1991.

3963 The narrow double doors opened at the back of the church, and in marched Beulah Marsh, the deceased woman's niece, dressed not for a funeral but as if she were attending the opera. — *The Road to Zena*, Joel Redon, 1992.

Gambling

3964 "I'll take the odds against Caravan."/ "In ponies?"/ "Done." — *Sybil*, Benjamin Disraeli, 1845.

3965 Everyone has heard of the three beautiful Miss Gunnings, who struck white flames in the hearts of the young bloods in the days of George II, the youngest of whom caused my noble Duke of Hamilton to lose a thousand pounds one night at faro because forsooth his eyes wandered to her beautiful face instead of to his game. — *Rosalie*, Charles Major, 1925.

3966 Green dice rolled across the green table, struck the rim together, and bounced back. One stopped short holding six white spots in two equal rows uppermost. The other tumbled out to the center of the table and came to rest with a single spot on top. — *The Glass Key*, Dashiell Hammett, 1931.

3967 We were playing poker in Kate Drummond's parlor and it was a pretty good game although no one could get badly hurt with a

twenty-five cent limit and four bits after the first raise or on the last card in case of stud. — *Temper the Wind*, Clyde Brion Davis, 1948.

3968 At the Morning Star it was rumoured that Dunlavin had won it. But at the Mendicity that morning, the queue waiting for breakfast were told by a fellow from Navan that Tralee Trembles owned the ticket. — *The Scarperer*, Brendan Behan, 1964.

3969 On the green, beneath the white overhang of faces, red dice clicked and caromed and bounced and stopped. "Seven crap!" pronounced Slade direly, and with his long stick-scepter he gathered and drew in a spilling tribute of chips. — *The Far Side*, Wirt Williams, 1972.

3970 It happened by the grace of God that Joseph Santangelo won his wife in a card game. — *Household Saints*, Francine Prose, 1981.

3971 The night it all began, he lost a wad on successive hands, suckered by miscalculation and his own aggressive style of play. — *Poker Game*, Fletcher Knebel, 1983.

Gardens

3972 The gardens of Clavering Park were removed some three hundred yards from the large, square, sombre-looking stone mansion which was the country-house of Sir Hugh Clavering, the eleventh baronet of that name; and in these gardens, which had but little of beauty to recommend them, I will introduce my readers to two of the personages with whom I wish to make them acquainted in the following story. — *The Claverings*, Anthony Trollope, 1867.

3973 I was happily at work this morning among my butter beans — a vegetable of solid merit and of a far greater suitableness to my palate than such bovine watery growths as the squash and the beet. — *Aftermath*, James Lane Allen, 1896.

3974 *November 7th.* — Plant the indoor bulbs. Just as I am in the middle of them, Lady Boxe calls. — *Diary of a Provincial Lady*, E. M. Delafield, 1931.

3975 Mr. Papenmeyer was ashamed of his celery! — *The Unpossessed*, Tess Slesinger, 1934.

3976 Mary Perrault sat at the top of the short steep flight of steps which led to the small platform which was the front porch of her house, and looked down into the dusty tangle of her flower garden. — *Against a Darkening Sky*, Janet Lewis, 1943.

3977 The Garden Committee had met to discuss the earth; not the whole earth, the terres-

trial globe, but the bit of it that had been stolen from the Gardens in the Square. — *An Episode of Sparrows*, Rumer Godden, 1955.

3978 Miss Jane Marple was sitting by her window. The window looked over her garden, once a source of pride to her. That was no longer so. Nowadays she looked out of the window and winced. — *The Mirror Crack'd*, Agatha Christie, 1962.

3979 Gardening is all of my pleasure. It was ever more of a joy than a duty, to watch the tender shoots burst forth in spring, and to know that I had a part of them, in the cold season. — *We Speak No Treason*, Rosemary Hawley Jarman, 1971.

3980 Ganesh, the old gardener at Shiraz Road was showing Ravi, the young gardener, how to sow the summer seeds. — *The Peacock Spring*, Rumer Godden, 1975.

3981 The warm effulgence of the late June day fell upon the Bishop's garden with a pleasing variance of light and shadow here and there. — *The Two Bishops*, Agnes Sligh Turnbull, 1980.

3982 Rosie Mortimer's garden, the one that has been seen and admired on television by millions, was as bleak as anyone else's in the middle of January. — *The Garden Path*, Kitty Burns Florey, 1983.

3983 The septic tank is in the shrubbery at the bottom of the garden. — *The Girls*, John Bowen, 1986.

Gatherings

3984 Within a sepulchral vault, and at midnight, two persons were seated. — *Rookwood*, William Harrison Ainsworth, 1834.

3985 A throng of bearded men in sad-colored garments and gray, steeple-crowned hats, intermixed with women, some wearing hoods, and others bareheaded, was assembled in front of a wooden edifice, the door of which was heavily timbered with oak, and studded with iron spikes. — *The Scarlet Letter*, Nathaniel Hawthorne, 1850.

3986 Four individuals, in whose fortunes we should be glad to interest the reader, happened to be standing in one of the saloons of the sculpture-gallery in the Capitol at Rome. — *The Marble Faun*, Nathaniel Hawthorne, 1860.

3987 In the best room of a farm-house on the skirts of a village in the hills of Northern Massachusetts, there sat one morning in August three people who were not strangers to the house, but who had apparently assembled in the parlor as

the place most in accord with an unaccustomed finery in their dress. — *The Lady of the Aroostook*, William Dean Howells, 1879.

3988 In the latter part of the afternoon of a summer day in the year 1863, a little crowd gathered near the door of the military hospital on Filbert Street, in the city of Philadelphia. — *In War Time*, S. Weir Mitchell, 1884.

3989 There were three at the breakfast-table — Mr. Newthorpe, his daughter Annabel, and their visitor (Annabel's cousin), Miss Paula Tyrrell. — *Thyrza*, George Gissing, 1887.

3990 There were four of us — George, and William Samuel Harris, and myself, and Montmorency. We were sitting in my room, smoking, and talking about how bad we were — bad from a medical point of view I mean, of course. — *Three Men in a Boat*, Jerome K. Jerome, 1889.

3991 No such throng had ever before been seen in the building during all its eight years of existence. — *The Damnation of Theron Ware*, Harold Frederic, 1896.

3992 The last day of October in 1777, Colonel Jonathan Hamilton came out of his high house on the river bank with a handsome, impatient company of guests, all Berwick gentlemen. — *The Tory Lover*, Sarah Orne Jewett, 1901.

3993 They were all at Charing Cross to see Lilia off — Philip, Harriet, Irma, Mrs. Herriton herself. — *Where Angels Fear to Tread*, E. M. Forster, 1905.

3994 Considering the state of the imperial city of Frankfort, one would not expect to find such a gathering as was assembled in the Kaiser cellar of the Rheingold drinking tavern. — *The Sword Maker*, Robert Barr, 1910.

3995 Four cowboys inclined their bodies over the barbed-wire fence which marked the dividing-line between the Centipede Ranch and their own, staring mournfully into a summer night such as only the far southwestern country knows. — *Going Some*, Rex Beach, 1910.

3996 On the opening day of the fall session of 1871 the court room was packed and the corridors jammed with a perspiring crowd struggling to get in. — *The Black Hood*, Thomas Dixon, Jr., 1924.

3997 In the time before steamships, or then more frequently than now, a stroller along the docks of any considerable seaport would occasionally have his attention arrested by a group of bronzed mariners, man-of-war's men or merchant sailors in holiday attire, ashore on liberty. — *Billy Budd*, Herman Melville, 1924.

3998 It was Sir Richard who asked me to stay at Pullinstown for the Springwell Harriers' point-to-point meeting. — *Conversation Piece*, Molly Keane *as* M. J. Farrell, 1932.

3999 Cigars had burned low, and we were

beginning to sample the disillusionment that usually afflicts old school friends who have met again as men and found themselves with less in common than they had believed they had. — *Lost Horizon*, James Hilton, 1933.

4000 As she laid down the last card and took in the final trick of the rubber it seemed to Mona that something strange had happened to the smoking-room and to all the people sitting about her. — "Fourteen Years After," Louis Bromfield, 1934.

4001 Bourke Prine went into the Palace, looked around the crowd a moment, and saw the door of the back room standing ajar. — *Man in the Saddle*, Ernest Haycox, 1938.

4002 The bonfire we built on Shrubsole High was blazing furiously a good half-hour before John Ward arrived. Everyone was there, even Sheriff Cropper, who seemed at a loss as to what he should do under such circumstances. — *For My Great Folly*, Thomas B. Costain, 1942.

4003 The three Americans standing in front of Shigo Kuyoshi drew a little more closely together. — *China Flight*, Pearl S. Buck, 1945.

4004 From the dusty windows of a small room over Black Ally's Café it could be seen that McGrath's ballroom was filling fast. — *A Ripple from the Storm*, Doris Lessing, 1958.

4005 In the summer of 1959, outside the hotel that would house the Tenth Anniversary Dinner for the Friends of Miss Friendship, in its halls and lobbies and arcades, on its wide staircase leading to the Grand Ballroom, in its elevators and bars, the human manifestations of holy eagerness made things seem more frenetic and crowded still, as though most of the population of the densely packed city had crowded into that area. — *Some Angry Angel*, Richard Condon, 1960.

4006 The two women were alone in the London flat. — *The Golden Notebook*, Doris Lessing, 1962.

4007 The gathering in the main building of the winter quarters of the Marvel Circus at Chippenham was an unusual one. Summoned by Sam Marvel, the recently arrived contract artistes and staff stood around in uneasy groups, murmuring and waiting. — *Love, Let Me Not Hunger*, Paul Gallico, 1963.

4008 Patrick Norval was forty-one years old and a nobody when the BBC, ITV, CBS, NBC, ABC, *Time, Newsweek, Life, Look, Queen, Nova, Paris-Match, Stern, Oggi*, Reuters, *The Times, Daily Telegraph, Daily Express, Daily Mail, Daily Mirror, Sun, Guardian, Church Times*, Tass, and a dozen other representatives of the world's communication media came to tea. — *Remember Jack Hoxie*, Jon Cleary, 1969.

4009 "Look at the people," Susie said. — *The Winner*, Borden Deal, 1973.

4010 Already a noble day, young summer soaring, vivid with promise, drenched blue and green, had divided them, on the terrace beside the mill, into sun and shadow. — "The Cloud," John Fowles, 1974.

4011 On the old docks of Jaffa, exactly where the Chaimovitch family had arrived twenty years back — the extent of Mati's lifetime, since he was already felt in the womb during the drawn-out voyage from Odessa — they were all gathered at summer's end in 1927 to see the lad off to America. — *The Harvest*, Meyer Levin, 1978.

4012 They had come by the thousands on that sunny June day, drawn by the mystique of their own past, or for some, the celebration of the future. — *Class Reunion*, Rona Jaffe, 1979.

4013 The union meeting, thought Al Veasy, had gone as well as could be expected, all things considered. — *The Butcher's Boy*, Thomas Perry, 1982.

4014 It was a quiet, sultry afternoon in Auburn. People were gathering at Sanders' store for news and the latest gossip. — *Joshua*, Joseph F. Girzone, 1983.

4015 At mid-morning, under a sky charged with metallic frost, they began to gather. — *Karpov's Brain*, Gerald Green, 1983.

4016 The room was crowded. Many of its occupants were scurrying from place to place in organized chaos. — *Long Voyage Back*, Luke Rhinehart, 1983.

4017 On a gray wintry day in November 1944, a welcoming party of French fascist collaborators stood on the railway platform at Sigmaringen, an ancient Hohenzollern town on the Danube that had become the last haven of the fallen Vichy government. — *The Exile of Céline*, Tom Clark, 1986.

4018 Finally after dinner they sat around the fire in the living room with the last of the wineglasses balanced on knees and end tables. — *Among Birches*, Rebecca Hill, 1986.

4019 Herb, Dave, Sherman and Joe sat around the table in Herb's hotel room. — "People to People," Rachel Ingalls, 1986.

4020 Arthur, who had a masterly way with meetings, was gathering this one together for a conclusion. — *The Lyre of Orpheus*, Robertson Davies, 1988.

4021 The children crossed into the heart of the swamp and huddled like tadpoles hiding from the great blue heron. — *Secret Harmonies*, Andrea Barrett, 1989.

4022 Each time, the faces are different but the group itself looks familiar. — *A Generation of Leaves*, Robert S. Bloom, 1991.

4023 Eight guests had been invited; seven had come. — *Parnell and the Englishwoman*, Hugh Leonard, 1991.

4024 The six hundred men are gathered in ten rows fronting Block 14A. — *Orbit of Darkness*, Ian MacMillan, 1991.

4025 There was a large crowd in the auditorium. — *Portrait of the Artist's Wife*, Barbara Anderson, 1993.

4026 After the children were taken away, we were seated outside on white folding chairs under a large blue tarpaulin. "To keep the pigeon poop off our heads," I heard another parent murmur as the crowd streamed past. — *Saving St. Germ*, Carol Muske Dukes, 1993.

Geography

4027 Near the centre of the State of New-York lies an extensive district of country, whose surface is a succession of hills and dales, or, to speak with greater deference to geographical definitions, of mountains and valleys. — *The Pioneers*, James Fenimore Cooper, 1823.

4028 A single glance at the map will make the reader acquainted with the position of the eastern coast of the island of Great Britain, as connected with the shores of the opposite continent. — *The Pilot*, James Fenimore Cooper, 1824.

4029 No one, who is familiar with the bustle and activity of an American commercial town, would recognise, in the repose which now reigns in the ancient mart of Rhode Island, a place that, in its day, has been ranked amongst the most important ports along the whole line of our extended coast. — *The Red Rover*, James Fenimore Cooper, 1827.

4030 The district of Beaufort, lying along the Atlantic coast in the State of South Carolina, is especially commended to the regards of the antiquarian as the region first distinguished in the history of the United States by an European settlement. — *The Yemassee*, William Gilmore Simms, 1835.

4031 The coast of England, though infinitely finer than our own, is more remarkable for its verdure, and for a general appearance of civilization, than for its natural beauties. — *Homeward Bound*, James Fenimore Cooper, 1838.

4032 The sublimity connected with vastness, is familiar to every eye. — *The Pathfinder*, James Fenimore Cooper, 1840.

4033 There are some fields near Manchester, well known to the inhabitants as "Green Heys Fields," through which runs a public footpath to a little village about two miles distant. — *Mary Barton*, Elizabeth Gaskell, 1848.

4034 More than three centuries and a half

ago, in the mid-springtime of 1492, we are sure that the angel of the dawn, as he travelled with broad slow wing from the Levant to the Pillars of Hercules, and from the summits of the Caucasus across all the snowy Alpine ridges to the dark nakedness of the Western Isles, saw nearly the same outline of firm land and unstable sea — saw the same great mountain shadows on the same valleys as he has seen to-day — saw olive mounts, and pine forests, and the broad plains green with young corn or rain-freshened grass — saw the domes and spires of cities rising by the riversides or mingled with the sedge-like masts on the many-curved seacoast, in the same spots where they rise to-day. — *Romola*, George Eliot, 1863.

4035 Sixty years since, a large part of central and western New York was a wilderness in which civilization had only gained an occasional foothold. — *Mabel Parker*, Horatio Alger, 1878.

4036 Bayou Teche is the dividing line. On its left is the land of bayous, lakes, and swamps; on its right, the beautiful short-turfed prairies of Western Louisiana. — *Bonaventure*, George W. Cable, 1888.

4037 The southern shore of the Sorrentine peninsula offers a striking contrast to the northern side. — *With the Immortals*, F. Marion Crawford, 1888.

4038 The place of the beginning of this story was a country neighborhood on a shore, if one may call it so, that divided a forest and a prairie in Central Illinois. — *The Graysons*, Edward Eggleston, 1888.

4039 Between the former site of old Fort Dearborn and the present site of our newest Board of Trade there lies a restricted yet tumultuous territory through which, during the course of the last fifty years, the rushing streams of commerce have worn many a deep and rugged chasm. — *The Cliff-Dwellers*, Henry B. Fuller, 1893.

4040 Subiaco lies beyond Tivoli, southeast from Rome, at the upper end of a wild gorge in the Samnite mountains. — *Casa Braccio*, F. Marion Crawford, 1894.

4041 To hear people talking about North Devon, and the savage part called Exmoor, you might almost think that there never was any place in the world so beautiful, or any living men so wonderful. — "Slain By the Doones," R. D. Blackmore, 1895.

4042 Our camp was in the heart of Copiah County, Mississippi, a mile or so west of Gallatin and about six miles east of that once robber-haunted road, the Natchez Trace. — *The Cavalier*, George W. Cable, 1901.

4043 Crossing the Niagara river in a direct line, the Canadian shore lies not more than eight miles from Buffalo, New York, and in the early 50's small bands of Indians were still familiar figures on both the American and Canadian borders. — *Winona*, Pauline Hopkins, 1902.

4044 Far off in the mountain lands, somewhere to the east of the setting sun, lies the principality of Graustark, serene relic of rare old feudal days. — *Beverly of Graustark*, George Barr McCutcheon, 1904.

4045 For the scene of this narrative please take into mind a wide quarter-circle of country, such as any of the pretty women we are to know in it might have covered on the map with her half-opened fan. — *Kincaid's Battery*, George W. Cable, 1908.

4046 The raw and mighty West, the greatest stage in all the history of the world for so many deeds of daring which verged on the insane, was seared and cross-barred with grave-lined trails and dotted with presumptuous, mushroom towns of brief stay, whose inhabitants flung their primal passions in the face of humanity and laughed in condescending contempt at what humanity had to say about it. — *Hopalong Cassidy*, Clarence E. Mulford, 1910.

4047 Before the railroad's thin lines of steel bit their way up through the wilderness, Athabasca Landing was the picturesque threshold over which one must step who would enter into the mystery and adventure of the great white North. — *The Valley of Silent Men*, James Oliver Curwood, 1920.

4048 Three marshes spread across the triangle made by the Royal Military Canal and the coasts of Sussex and Kent. — *Joanna Godden*, Sheila Kaye-Smith, 1921.

4049 Not far from the rugged and storm-whipped north shore of Lake Superior, and south of the Kaministiqua, yet not as far south as the Rainy River waterway, there lay a paradise lost in the heart of a wilderness world — and in that paradise "a little corner of hell." — *The Country Beyond*, James Oliver Curwood, 1922.

4050 Santa Barbara lies far to leeward, with a coast facing to the north and east. It is the richest of the sugar countries. — *Sard Harker*, John Masefield, 1924.

4051 Santa Barbara, being the most leeward of the Sugar States, is at the angle of the Continent, with two coasts, one facing north, the other east. The city of Santa Barbara is in a bay at the angle where these two coasts trend from each other. — *Odtaa*, John Masefield, 1926.

4052 Frenchman's Bend was a section of rich river-bottom country lying twenty miles southeast of Jefferson. — *The Hamlet*, William Faulkner, 1931.

4053 The borough of Segget stands under the Mounth, on the southern side, in the Mearns Howe, Fordoun lies near and Drumlithie nearer,

you can see the Laurencekirk lights of a night glimmer and glow as the mists come down. — *Cloud Howe*, Lewis Grassic Gibbon, 1933.

4054 There was no sign to indicate the point at which country ended and town began. — *Old Home Town*, Rose Wilder Lane, 1935.

4055 My strange life began on August 2, 1889, in Zagreb, the capital city of Croatia, which then still had near upon three decades to remain a province of the Hapsburg realm — before becoming a part of the new state of Serbians, Croatians and Slovenians: Yugoslavia. — *Cradle of Life*, Louis Adamic, 1936.

4056 St. David's Head is that part of what once was Roman Britain which juts furthest out into "our sea," as the biographer of St. Patrick calls St. George's Channel. This promontory is made a peninsula by an inlet from the northwest, which forms a deep division of sea-water, one hundred and fifty feet below, as crystal clear as Ogof Crystal itself — another but less-indenting inlet, some furlongs to the east. — *I Follow Saint Patrick*, Oliver St. John Gogarty, 1938.

4057 I remember Irish Parish. It was Ward Four in the old days before the Irish began coming in. — *The Parish and the Hill*, Mary Doyle Curran, 1948.

4058 Some of the oldest country in England is to be found in the parish of Leasan, in the district known as the Moat. — *The Happy Tree*, Sheila Kaye-Smith, 1949.

4059 Rockbottom, Pa., a village of 352 souls, is in lower Macungie County about equidistant from Allentown and Bethlehem. — *The Farmers Hotel*, John O'Hara, 1951.

4060 Into the length of San Diego Bay the downtown area of San Diego protrudes like a bent elbow; the forearm then follows a gradually rising ridge northward to end in a promontory called Mission Hills, which, broken up into canyons and ridges, resembles very much a hand with the fingers clenched to hold it tightly there, above the mud-flats and Old Town. — *Corpus of Joe Bailey*, Oakley Hall, 1953.

4061 In the cactus wild of Southern California, a distance of two hundred miles from the capital of cinema as I choose to call it, is the town of Desert D'Or. — *The Deer Park*, Norman Mailer, 1955.

4062 The Duchy of Grand Fenwick lies in a precipitous fold of the northern Alps and embraces in its tumbling landscape portions of three valleys, a river, one complete mountain with an elevation of two thousand feet and a castle. — *The Mouse That Roared*, Leonard Wibberley, 1955.

4063 From the most central point of London to the suburb of Manor Green is a distance of about six miles. — *The Crossing Point*, Gerda Charles, 1960.

4064 South of Santa Monica along the shore stretch the ocean beaches, from Venice and Ocean Park to Palos Verdes, from Huntington and Long Beach to Newport and San Diego. — *The Color of Evening*, Robert Nathan, 1960.

4065 Brightest New Mexico. — *Fire on the Mountain*, Edward Abbey, 1962.

4066 An excerpt from THE THUMB-NAIL ALMANAC, 1961 . . . Page 643:/ *An East South Central state in the Deep South, it is bounded on the north by Tennessee; east by Alabama; south by the Gulf of Mexico; west by Mississippi. — A Different Drummer*, William Melvin Kelley, 1962.

4067 When I first heard about Big Sur I didn't know that it was a member of the Confederate States of America. — *A Confederate General from Big Sur*, Richard Brautigan, 1964.

4068 Druid City lies upon the exact geological line that divides the northern half of the state from the southern. — *The Loser*, Borden Deal, 1964.

4069 Little Burgelstatham is in that part of East Suffolk which provokes little comment from the traveler when his train stops briefly, and will soon not stop at all, at the clay-colored veranda-petticoated little station with its prize-winning beds of wallflowers and rock plants, and its stationmaster, shirt-sleeved, high-stooled in his office, surrounded by bicycles taken under his care and protection for the day while their owners travel north in the train to Tydd, the largest town within seven miles, owning a Woolworth's, two ironmongers, several seed shops, auction mart, a museum, a park, a square containing a statue of a maid who dared to say no to Charles the Second, emphasizing her refusal with the present to him of a poisoned boiled rotten egg. — *The Adaptable Man*, Janet Frame, 1965.

4070 Across the road was Hampstead Heath. Well, not exactly; it was really the Heath Extension. They lived in Golders Green no matter how much they tried to kid themselves that it was Hampstead. — *The Dissent of Dominick Shapiro*, Bernard Kops, 1966.

4071 It humps northward five hundred miles from the precipitous, rock-cragged shores of Lake Superior to the flat and muddy seacoast of Hudson Bay — a big and lonely land of bog and forest, as diversified within as the constrasting coasts that mark its extremes. — *The Sparrow's Fall*, Fred Bodsworth, 1967.

4072 The land defied everyone's idea of what a land ought to be; just the land by being where it was, what it was and how it was. — *Return of the Sphinx*, Hugh MacLennan, 1967.

4073 You could travel west out of Reed City, a small county seat in an unfertile valley with a small yellow brick courthouse and a plugged cannon on its lawn next to a marble slab with the

names of the World War One and Two dead inscribed in gold and the not dead plainly inscribed with the suspicious neatness of cemetery script, *those who served*, further west through fifty miles of pine barrens dotted with small farm settlements often of less than thirty people, or merely a grocery store and gas station adjoined by a shabby aluminum trailer or a basement house with the first and perhaps second stories awaiting more prosperous times, the stores themselves with little and aged stock—lunch meat, bologna pickled in a jar, Polish sausage, tinned foods covered with dust, plaquettes of fish lures, mosquito repellent in aerosol cans, live bait and a pop cooler outside the door—but not many of these—a narrow road through mixed conifers, cedar and jack pine, some stunted scrub oak, birch, and the short-lived poplar, a pulp tree usually living less than twenty years and clotting the woods floor with its rotting trunks and branches, and west through the low pelvic mysteries of swamps divided invisibly from the air by interlocking creeks and small rivers, made unbearable in spring and summer by mosquitoes and black flies, swamps dank with brackish water and pools of green slime, small knolls of fern, bog marshes of sphagnum, spongelike and tortuous to the human foot and bordered by impenetrable tamarack thickets: in short a land with no appreciable history and a continuously vile climate, lumbered off for a hundred years with few traces of the grand white pine which once covered it, an occasional charred almost petrified stump four feet in diameter, evidence of trees which rose nearly two hundred feet and covered the northern half of the state and the Upper Peninsula, razed with truly insolent completeness by the lumber barons after the Civil War with all the money going to the cities of the south—Saginaw, Lansing, Detroit—and east to Boston and New York; and the houses, even the large farmhouses on reasonably good land, sloppily built, ramshackle and craftless compared to Massachusetts or Vermont; west to Lake Michigan then to turn north along its coast to the Straits of Mackinac, cross the mammoth bridge, travel west another three hundred miles through the sparsely populated Upper Peninsula and then north again into the comparatively vast, the peopleless Huron Mountains. — *Wolf*, Jim Harrison, 1971.

4074 Do you know where Moscow is? Moscow is never. — *All Heaven in a Rage*, Maureen Duffy, 1973.

4075 Anyone who has never before visited Krishnapur, and who approaches from the east, is likely to think he has reached the end of his journey a few miles sooner than he expected. — *The Siege of Krishnapur*, J. G. Farrell, 1973.

4076 Hendrick says,/ "On the same latitude as what?"/ "Omsk," I tell him./ "Anywhere else?" he says./ "A place I can't pronounce," I add, "in Khabarovsk." I pause./ "In North America, of course," I tell him, "Queen Charlotte's Island . . . Goose Bay."/ "And longitude?" he says./ "Saragossa. Cartegena. Oran in North Africa. Timbuctoo." — *A Temporary Life*, David Storey, 1973.

4077 His geography. — *Coming Through Slaughter*, Michael Ondaatje, 1976.

4078 Fielding's Corner was a couple of miles west of town, the intersection where Lone Rock traffic turned north across the Indian Reserve. — *Turn Again Home*, Herbert Harker, 1977.

4079 There was an area east of the Isle of Dogs in London which was an unusual mixture even for those surroundings. — *Darkness Visible*, William Golding, 1979.

4080 The place: a walled city called Zion, perched on fifteen-acre, finger-shaped, 750-foot-high limestone ridge pointing due south, five miles from the Dead Sea, ninety-three miles from the Sinai desert, thirty-five miles from the Mediterranean. — *King of Kings*, Malachi Martin, 1980.

4081 The small town of Santa Margarita del Banana stands on a desert coastline near some mountains. It is so far from other places that no one bothers to think about what country it is in. — *The Bunch from Bananas*, David Pownall, 1980.

4082 From the open window of the bedroom Jason fixed his eyes on the thin peninsula extending toward Taenarus, the entrance into Hades. — *Birds of Winter*, Theodore Vrettos, 1980.

4083 The Riviera coastline was cleaner in the late 1930s. — *The Night Fishers of Antibes*, Christopher Leopold, 1981.

4084 Between the windshorn Booradeela Range and the low-flung foothills of Mount Kaiser there is a mild sweep of earth. — *My Blue-Checker Corker and Me*, Paul John Radley, 1982.

4085 To Dicken Quinney, the junction of the Rhine and the Mosel at Koblenz had always seemed a point of separation in Germany. — *Once More the Hawks*, John Harris *as* Max Hennessy, 1984.

4086 Named like so much else in Australia for a place on the far side of the globe that its finders meant to honour and were piously homesick for, Killarney bears no resemblance to its Irish original. — *Harland's Half Acre*, David Malouf, 1984.

4087 Here—it is 1831 on the southernmost tip of the newest and oldest continent, the bottom of the world. — *Shallows*, Tim Winton, 1984.

4088 There had been a dispute for years over the exact location of Linden Hills. — *Linden Hills*, Gloria Naylor, 1985.

4089 The beginning of the end of the violin

lessons went back to the small hours of the night in a small railroad town (pop. 5,000) in a small country (pop. 14,000,000) in Central Europe which, like all the other countries crowded into this area, fancies itself the heart of the continent when, in fact, its geographical position is not at all eccentric like that of a heart, but if anything corresponds to the location of a gut. — *The Willys Dream Kit*, Jan Novak, 1985.

4090 My wound is geography. It is also my anchorage, my port of call. — *The Prince of Tides*, Pat Conroy, 1986.

4091 Captain Hendrik's property extended to the bay. — "Captain Hendrik's Story," Rachel Ingalls, 1986.

4092 Howard Beach is a white finger sticking into Jamaica Bay alongside Kennedy Airport, which is the reason Howard Beach first became famous, and everybody now wishes that nobody had ever heard of the place at all, but it certainly is too late for that. — *He Got Hungry and Forgot His Manners*, Jimmy Breslin, 1988.

4093 It is a long way from London to Los Angeles. — *Faulty Ground*, Gabrielle Donnelly, 1988.

4094 The village of Chiang Saen in northern Thailand lies along the Mekong River near the apex of the Golden Triangle where Laos, Burma and Thailand meet. — *Mrs. Pollifax and the Golden Triangle*, Dorothy Gilman, 1988.

4095 About a billion years ago, long before the continents had separated to define the ancient oceans, or their own outlines had been determined, a small protuberance jutted out from the northwest corner of what would later become North America. — *Alaska*, James A. Michener, 1988.

4096 August 1, 1899./ 64° 30′ north latitude. 165° 24′ west longitude. Nome blisters the lower lip of Seward Peninsula. A shallow land shelf extends into the Bering Sea. Breakers wash the flat beach. — *Fools' Gold*, Richard Wiley, 1988.

4097 Beaver County, Pennsylvania, lies on the Ohio border to the north and west of Pittsburgh. — *Fulton County*, James Goldman, 1989.

4098 The chief character in this narrative is the Caribbean Sea, one of the world's most alluring bodies of water, a rare gem among the oceans, defined by the islands that form a chain of lovely jewels to the north and east. — *Caribbean*, James A. Michener, 1989.

4099 Christopher Park, a small triangle of benches and trees enclosed by an iron fence with three gates, is, oddly enough for Greenwich Village, bordered by four streets: West Fourth, along with a sliver of Seventh Avenue South, Christopher Street, and Grove Street. — *The Christopher Park Regulars*, Edward Swift, 1989.

4100 Jamaica is shaped like a nice, big, fat Negro yam. — *The Last Room*, Elean Thomas, 1991.

Ghosts

4101 Abodes of horror have frequently been described, and castles, filled with spectres and chimeras, conjured up by the magic spell of genius to harrow the soul, and absorb the wondering mind. — *The Wrongs of Woman*, Mary Wollstonecraft Shelley, 1798.

4102 For some moments after he had materialized, and had become perceivable by human senses, the Sylan waited. — *Something About Eve*, James Branch Cabell, 1927.

4103 "If a female figure in a white shroud enters your bedchamber at midnight on the thirteenth day of this month, answer this letter; otherwise, do not." — *Pirates of Venus*, Edgar Rice Burroughs, 1941.

4104 The fact that the grim and extraordinary haunting of Paradine Hall, East Walsham, Norfolk, seat of the Lords Paradine since the year 1523, did not reach the ears of the scandalous press was not only fortunate but little less than a miracle. — *Too Many Ghosts*, Paul Gallico, 1959.

4105 The mist in the morning that covers the cool, unruffled coves, the autumn leaves burning and the lapping among the reeds, the musk of rotting woods and the coppery rush of the pheasant: these are the ghosts that haunt the Chesapeake and they haunt it still today just as they haunted it a hundred or a thousand years ago. — *The Seven Sisters*, Frederic Prokosch, 1962.

4106 He doesn't know what I am, but he knows I'm in him and behind him. — *A Smuggler's Bible*, Joseph McElroy, 1966.

4107 We all knew the same thing about the Linquists. Said the same thing, too. "One thing for sure," Maurice Dube said, "it had something to do with the ghosts." — *The Moon Lamp*, Mark Smith, 1976.

4108 The boy, who was dead, who had died eleven months ago, was standing on the corner of Christopher Street and Seventh Avenue in Sheridan Square, and when she saw her son, Mrs. Harrington-Smith Evans knew the truth of it and the illusion simultaneously. — *Bereavements*, Richard Lortz, 1980.

4109 It was twilight in the rain forest of Sarawak, and the girl stood very still and very quiet, knowing that any moment the spirits of her ancestors would be with her. — *Still Waters*, James Vance Marshall, 1982.

4110 The problem was not that I believed in ghosts. — *Angels All Over Town*, Luanne Rice, 1985.

4111 In Rome Frobisch had a vision on the Spanish Steps. — *Frobisch's Angel*, Doris Rochlin, 1987.

4112 She'd been having the visions of Joe for a week or so. — *Ringer*, Marshall Terry, 1987.

4113 In my early thirties, at a time when I am especially frightened of death, I will have a dream of my maternal grandfather; he will appear before me one night as a skeleton draped in a theatrically flowing grave shroud. — *An American Memory*, Eric Larsen, 1988.

4114 Ghosts and vampires were knocking at the wide front door of the old stone house in Cambridge. — *Spirit Lost*, Nancy Thayer, 1988.

4115 Now she is a light flitting through the halls of the Old Carnegie Library. — *Thereafter Johnnie*, Carolivia Herron, 1991.

4116 In the thirty-fourth year of my life, tragedy having turned my basic languor to indolence, my skepticism to sorrow, I came to be haunted by the ghost of a woman almost twice my age. — *The Girl Who Trod on a Loaf*, Kathryn Davis, 1993.

Gifts

4117 Wellingborough, as you are going to sea, suppose you take this shooting-jacket of mine along; it's just the thing — take it, it will save the expense of another. — *Redburn*, Herman Melville, 1849.

4118 "I wonder what he meant by it," said Sylvia, turning again in her chair, so that the summer light, softened and tinted by the drawn blinds, might fall upon the etching she held. — *A Rose of Yesterday*, F. Marion Crawford, 1896.

4119 We have had supper and my wife and I are sitting on our porch. It will not be dark for an hour yet and my wife has brought out some sewing. It is pink and full of lace and it is something she is making for a friend of hers who is going to be married soon. — *Company K*, William March, 1933.

4120 Long afterwards — "Not so long," said Toby, "it's only two years"; "Ages afterwards," said Sophie — Toby gave Sophie another lamp with kingfishers on it; he sent for it all the way to Profit David, of whom he disapproved. "And I am a fool," he said. "You will only lose it or give it away to someone else, or leave it behind somewhere." — *Kingfishers Catch Fire*, Rumer Godden, 1953.

4121 He sent her a music box which played an aria from *Trovatore* while simultaneously emitting Chanel's wonderful new scent. — *An Infinity of Mirrors*, Richard Condon, 1964.

4122 When Ben Joe Hawkes left home he gave his sister Susannah one used guitar, six shelves of *National Geographic*, a battered microscope, and a foot-high hourglass. — *If Morning Ever Comes*, Anne Tyler, 1964.

4123 The errand was out of his way and he was afraid he was running terribly late but he had the airport taxi take him to Asprey's to be able to bring along a small surprise for Bitsy. — *Arigato*, Richard Condon, 1972.

4124 It was not that Omri didn't appreciate Patrick's birthday present to him. Far from it. He was really very grateful — sort of. — *The Indian in the Cupboard*, Lynne Reid Banks, 1980.

4125 In 1967, to celebrate Canada's hundredth birthday and to give the woman something to do, a broker named Morgan Wickwire bought his wife a street in Toronto. — *The Year of the Child*, Marian Engel, 1981.

4126 The day of the bestowing was, he was told, in October 1927. — *Old Tom, Young Tom*, Thomas Adams, 1984.

4127 "What have you brought me Hester? What have you brought me from the shop?" — *The Well*, Elizabeth Jolley, 1986.

4128 The first snake I saw was dead and so were those of a long time after, but that first snake my father brought home and threw at my feet saying, "A dead snake." — *God's Snake*, Irini Spanidou, 1986.

4129 Even now, six years after the generals loosened their hold on Argentina, after their manicured hands were pried away from the delicate white throats of the disappeareds and the doors of certain buildings were closed and locked, even now Carlos Rueda's gift retains its mystery. — *Imagining Argentina*, Lawrence Thornton, 1987.

4130 A gift has come for you, said Henry. It is from your sister. — *Subject to Change*, Lois Gould, 1988.

4131 I saw an article in the newspaper last December about something called the Christmas Train that's been going through mining country for over forty years, delivering gifts to folks who don't have much at Christmas, or at any other time for that matter. — *A Blue Moon in Poorwater*, Cathryn Hankla, 1988.

4132 Madame Doche, with an air of appreciation no less generous for being regularly at her command, took the camembert from Lewis Percy, prodded it with an expert thumb, pronounced it to be good, and ushered him into the salon. — *Lewis Percy*, Anita Brookner, 1989.

4133 The western lands — the pale sun which

warms my face, the soft blue sky, the wind and the shining water, these are the gifts of their openhanded, childlike gods. — *The Blood Star*, Nicholas Guild, 1989.

4134 In the old days they would have given me a gold watch. — *No Other Life*, Brian Moore, 1993.

Girls

4135 Like two night-birds who had strayed into the wrong season, a pair of girls flopped about on the snowy walk or huddled together outside of the Hill house. — *Craque-o'-Doom*, Mary Hatwell Catherwood, 1881.

4136 The two young girls sat in a high though very narrow room of the old Moorish palace to which King Philip the Second had brought his court when he finally made Madrid his capital. — *In the Palace of the King*, F. Marion Crawford, 1900.

4137 Toward the close of an early summer afternoon, a little girl came running along the turnpike to where a boy stood wriggling his feet in the dust. — *The Battle-Ground*, Ellen Glasgow, 1902.

4138 "She's like Margaret; she's really one of us," remarked Mrs. Forrest to her brother. "She carries herself as Margaret did in her girlhood, and she's dark, as we all are." — *Zelda Dameron*, Meredith Nicholson, 1904.

4139 An extremely pretty girl occupied a second-class compartment in one of those trains which percolate through the rural tranquillities of middle England from Ganford in Oxfordshire to Rumbold Junction in Kent. — *Marriage*, H. G. Wells, 1912.

4140 On a hill by the Mississippi where Chippewas camped two generations ago, a girl stood in relief against the cornflower blue of Northern sky. — *Main Street*, Sinclair Lewis, 1920.

4141 The girl came into the room with a darting movement like a swallow, looked round her with the same birdlike quickness, and then ran across the polished floor to where a young man sat on a sofa with one leg laid along it. — *Huntingtower*, John Buchan, 1922.

4142 Since memory itself is but a picture-book, we can, if we turn back among the chronicles of the Rakonitz family, catch and loop into a frame, that sudden vision of Babette at fifteen, walking demurely with two of Napoleon's officers on her right, and three on her left. — *The Matriarch*, G. B. Stern, 1924.

4143 A girl in an orange-coloured shawl stood at the window of Pedlar's store and looked, through the falling snow, at the deserted road. Though she watched there without moving, her attitude, in its stillness, gave an impression of arrested flight, as if she were running toward life. — *Barren Ground*, Ellen Glasgow, 1925.

4144 The driver of the wagon swaying through forest and swamp of the Ohio wilderness was a ragged girl of fourteen. — *Arrowsmith*, Sinclair Lewis, 1925.

4145 Behind the girl who walked so swiftly along the stretch of muddy road lay the village like a cross, the church steeple and a dark nucleus of houses where the two roads met. — *Islanders*, Helen R. Hull, 1927.

4146 "Amaryllis," said Nurse Benson, "without exception, you are the naughtiest child that God ever made." — *The Magic Garden*, Gene Stratton-Porter, 1927.

4147 Erif Der was sitting on a bank of shingle and throwing pebbles into the Black Sea; for a girl, she threw very straight. — *The Corn King and the Spring Queen*, Naomi Mitchison, 1931.

4148 "Well, gapy-face," said Mrs. Ponsonby./ A girl of eleven responded to this morning greeting./ "I wasn't yawning, Grandma." — *Daughters and Sons*, Ivy Compton-Burnett, 1937.

4149 At nine o'clock on the morning of September nineteenth, in the year 1873, a young girl walked slowly up Western Avenue in Allegheny City, across the river from Pittsburgh. — *The Valley of Decision*, Marcia Davenport, 1942.

4150 On a Saturday morning late in April a fifteen-year-old girl named Leda March stood at the bend in Stony Road and looked back across the orchard and the swamp to her house. — *The Prodigal Women*, Nancy Hale, 1942.

4151 She had been allowed to come out to the royal flagship, and had been eating cherries and strawberries dipped in wine. — *Young Bess*, Margaret Irwin, 1945.

4152 The child moved warily outside the iron fence. She tried to peer through the harsh leafless mass of barberry and bitter orange, but the bushy branches were tangled and dark together. — *Wildwood*, Josephine W. Johnson, 1946.

4153 Maria was ten years old. She had dark hair in two pigtails, and brown eyes the color of marmite, but more shiny. She wore spectacles for the time being, though she would not have to wear them always, and her nature was a loving one. She was one of those tough and friendly people who do things first and think about them afterward. When she met cows, however, she did not like to be alone with them, and there were other dangers, such as her governess, from which she would have liked to have had a protector. — *Mistress Masham's Repose*, T. H. White, 1946.

4154 The girls are in the attic; they are young, giggling girls, still flat-bosomed, still rumply-haired, their noses shining, their voices hoarse; the girls are chattering noisily, they wear the rough woolen socks, the scuffed brown moccasins, the plaid skirts and fuzzy sweaters of their kind; the girls are exploring the attic, carrying their Coke bottles amid garret dust, amid mousy memories; they have opened a closet, they have opened trunks and boxes; the moppet with wild yellow hair—she is lifting a peculiar hat from a shelf, from the paper and silence which have wrapped it; she places the hat jauntily on her head; she is standing with legs wide apart, nose in air and hands on hips, as she cries amid yowls of the others, "Look what Grandma used to wear!"—*Midnight Lace*, MacKinlay Kantor, 1948.

4155 One fog-lidded dawn in summertime a city girl, whose name was Hester, stood near the whipping post on the Tunxis village green with half a hundred strangers waiting to round up woodchucks. — *The Marmot Drive*, John Hersey, 1953.

4156 "I, Cress," said the girl, "in the October day, in the dying October day."—*Cress Delahanty*, Jessamyn West, 1953.

4157 The first thing he noticed about her was her whiteness; she was a very white girl, as white in the face as the snowberries which grew under the elms at the foot of the Vicarage drive, and the skin of her delicate arms and legs was so pure in its pallor that it was almost indistinguishable from the tennis frock she was wearing. — *In the Time of Greenbloom*, Gabriel Fielding, 1956.

4158 This little Mary was eight years old, rather small and tender for her age, more puzzled than pleased by what she discovered around her, yet, at times, swept on the wings of a wild joy. — *Centenary at Jalna*, Mazo de la Roche, 1958.

4159 If it was trouble you were after, Miss Akst was your girl. — *The Enemy Camp*, Jerome Weidman, 1958.

4160 The girl, who was very beautiful, turned away from the window. — *Nylon Pirates*, Nicholas Monsarrat, 1960.

4161 With hard young strength ebbing, but still serving her, the girl set the pirogue against a downed log and one last shove of her paddle sent it wedging into the mud of the riverbank. — *Savanna*, Janice Holt Giles, 1961.

4162 Abbie's father called from a distance, urging her to hasten, but the girl kept hovering above the hen and chicks she loved. — *Spirit Lake*, MacKinlay Kantor, 1961.

4163 "Lily, Lily!" called the old man, the Clochard who was known as King Dagobert. "Look, child, how beautiful!"—*The Street Where the Heart Lies*, Ludwig Bemelmans, 1963.

4164 Carter saw the girl from a long way away, as one always could on a clear evening, with the sun behind one's head slanting down the highway. Even at a distance, she was a forlorn figure, picking her way painfully along the grass edge, turning her head briefly as the car ahead of his whipped past, then turning back again to plod onwards; and as his own car drew near, he saw that she was indeed forlorn. — *Something to Hide*, Nicholas Monsarrat, 1966.

4165 The girl in gray deerskins was fifteen, perhaps older, she wasn't exactly sure. — *A Country of Strangers*, Conrad Richter, 1966.

4166 One afternoon, in an early summer of this century, when Laura Rowan was just eighteen, she sat, embroidering a handkerchief, on the steps leading down from the terrace of her father's house to the gardens communally owned by the residents in Radnage Square. — *The Birds Fall Down*, Rebecca West, 1966.

4167 Once upon a time there will be a little girl called Uncumber.—*A Very Private Life*, Michael Frayn, 1968.

4168 A black convertible pulled up even with us. A little girl sat alone on the back seat, her blond hair streaming behind from beneath a green bandanna.—*Bishop's Progress*, D. Keith Mano, 1968.

4169 People do not give it credence that a fourteen-year-old girl could leave home and go off in the wintertime to avenge her father's blood but it did not seem so strange then, although I will say it did not happen every day. — *True Grit*, Charles Portis, 1968.

4170 A new century was beginning, and it was the best of all possible times for a girl to be approaching womanhood. — *The Crusader*, Noel B. Gerson, 1970.

4171 "That girl is perfect."—*Mirror, Mirror*, Noel B. Gerson, 1970.

4172 Not to every young girl is it given to enter the harem of the Sultan of Turkey and return to her homeland a virgin. — *The Ringed Castle*, Dorothy Dunnett, 1971.

4173 It began badly. Grandaunts were coming to tea and nobody wanted Lucy. — *A Few Fair Days*, Jane Gardam, 1971.

4174 In the autumn of 1967 a girl was to be seen following an older man across Boston Common. — *The Professor's Daughter*, Piers Paul Read, 1971.

4175 I was that little girl we had been talking about. And the details of her life meant everything to me. — *The Halt During the Chase*, Rosemary Tonks, 1972.

4176 I will call her Rose. On a broiling August afternoon in 1935 when I was close to thirteen years of age, a big towhaired country girl came to our house with dusty shoes, runs in

her stockings and a twinkle in her cornflower eyes. — *Rambling Rose*, Calder Willingham, 1972.

4177 On the morning after her birthday — she had got to be eight years old yesterday; "A real big girl," Poppa said — Fanny felt the warm wetness and woke up. — *The Girl from Storyville*, Frank Yerby, 1972.

4178 She was a bony slow-moving girl from a small bombed baroque German city, where all that was worthwhile keeping had been rebuilt and which now looked as pink and golden as a pretty child and as new as morning. — "The Pegnitz Junction," Mavis Gallant, 1973.

4179 Kate, no longer the roly-poly Kitty, but with the new adaptation of the venerable name fitting her like a glove, returned from school and entered the house. — *The Killing of the King*, David R. Slavitt, 1974.

4180 Perched on her trapeze, flaxen-haired, eight-year-old Anna Pulaski floated high in the hazy blue afternoon air. — *American Gold*, Ernest Seeman, 1978.

4181 Praxis Duveen, at the age of five, sitting on the beach at Brighton, made a pretty picture for the photographer. Round angel face, yellow curls, puffed sleeves, white socks and little white shoes — one on, one off, while she tried to take a pebble from between her tiny pink toes — delightful! — *Praxis*, Fay Weldon, 1978.

4182 Everything starts with little girls. — *Selena*, Ernest Brawley, 1979.

4183 Among the group of people waiting at the fortress was a schoolgirl in a brown and yellow uniform holding a green eiderdown quilt and, by the loop at its neck, a red hot-water bottle. — *Burger's Daughter*, Nadine Gordimer, 1979.

4184 I am a tall girl. — *The Playhouse*, Elaine Ford, 1980.

4185 I don't play with girls much, but Catlin's different. She was born a girl but ever since she was born she's wanted to be a boy. — *Catlin*, Don Higgins, 1980.

4186 This is the story of Emmeline Mosher, who, before her fourteenth birthday, was sent from her home on a farm in Maine to support her family by working in a cotton mill in Massachusetts. — *Emmeline*, Judith Rossner, 1980.

4187 Four girls sit on the steps outside the Laundromat. — *Baby Love*, Joyce Maynard, 1981.

4188 Two boys wanted her but her true lover, whose steady gaze gave growth and warmth, was the sun. — *Changing States*, Barbara Rogan, 1981.

4189 The small girl sat on the sand under a thorn tree. — *Dreams of the Kalahari*, Carolyn Slaughter, 1981.

4190 It wasn't until after Ethan Lovejoy had changed both boats and rivers in St. Louis that he noticed the girl. — *Western*, Frank Yerby, 1982.

4191 "Stand still, child! How can Miss Nancy fit your gown if you prance around like a skittish horse?" — *Lady Washington*, Dorothy Clarke Wilson, 1984.

4192 If you turn to page 266 of the Kerrybrook Academy for Girls 1967 yearbook, in the second row of seniors you will see a blonde girl in a poor-boy sweater and Yardley slicker lipstick. — *Bloom*, Margaret Mitchell Dukore, 1985.

4193 "Wipe your feet, lassie." — *Muckle Annie*, Jan Webster, 1985.

4194 The girl was a real pest. "I think it's terrible," she said. — *High Adventure*, Donald E. Westlake, 1985.

4195 From street level, high above the skating rink, his arms braced against the brass railing, he watched as the girl glided beneath the golden statue of Prometheus. — *Tuxedo Park*, Laura Furman, 1986.

4196 Lucinda Fragosi — even her name was gawky. She was a born victim, a mournful sparrow-faced little man of a girl who lurched when she walked and hunched when she sat and wiped her nose with the back of her skinny hand. — *The Conduct of the Game*, John Hough, Jr., 1986.

4197 When Theresa was small, she thought that the saddest thing she had ever seen was a Bavarian barometer with a little weather man and a little weather woman. — *Hidden Symptoms*, Deirdre Madden, 1986.

4198 Lily saw the enemy the moment she reached the top of the tree. — *Certain Kinds of Loving*, Nancy Zaroulis, 1986.

4199 Sarah was small, smaller than Nurse, smaller even than the happy children in the market square. — *Sarah*, Joel Gross, 1987.

4200 I was eleven years, three months, and four days old when I moved out of the world of the breasts and into the world of the tits. — *I Remember Valentine*, Liz Hamlin, 1987.

4201 Charlotte was a very emotional girl. Disturbed, some said. Unreliable. A colossal temper, her aunt complained. Too serious, cautioned Uncle Buck. — *The Powers of Charlotte*, Jane Lazarre, 1987.

4202 What was it Ralph Schwartz said to her, all those years ago? "What is it with you Catholic girls?" — *Catholic Girls*, Kit Reed, 1987.

4203 She strides down the path from the coast road, lithe with youth — a tall, slender girl in short shorts and a blue tee shirt, mirrored sunglasses and heavy hiking boots, with a bulging backpack rising behind her head. — *Moon Passage*, Jane LeCompte, 1989.

4204 One evening in the autumn nub of the year a girl appeared out of a clump of trees by the side of a gravelly mountain road and steered along the wet mud bank toward the black car that was waiting. — *A Good Baby*, Leon Rooke, 1989.

4205 The lights go out all at once. Twenty thousands girls leap to their feet, screaming. — *Tender*, Mark Childress, 1990.

4206 A girl in a striped bathing suit sits at the water's edge. — *The Art Lover*, Carole Maso, 1990.

4207 The girl is about seven years old and is wearing a blue velvet dress with a white lace collar. — *Prized Possessions*, Avery Corman, 1991.

4208 "A man," I said when Miss Nolan asked me what I wanted to be when I grew up. — *Not the End of the World*, Rebecca Stowe, 1991.

4209 Many years later, when there was little doubt left, people still marveled how Ana Magdalena as a young girl at least had possessed all the qualities you would expect in a young girl of good but impoverished family. — *The Love Queen of the Amazon*, Cecile Pineda, 1992.

4210 Strike spotted her: baby fat, baby face, Shanelle or Shanette, fourteen years old maybe, standing there with that queasy smile, trying to work up the nerve. — *Clockers*, Richard Price, 1992.

Greetings

4211 "Good mornin', Bob; how's butter dis mornin'?" — *Iola Leroy*, Frances E. W. Harper, 1892.

4212 "Men —" Taisie meant to say "Good morning, men," as usually she did if she came to the cook house door before they had finished breakfast. But this morning she hesitated, halted. — *North of 36*, Emerson Hough, 1923.

4213 "Morning, Jeeves," I said./ "Good morning, sir," said Jeeves. — *The Inimitable Jeeves*, P. G. Wodehouse, 1924.

4214 "Viva Santa Fe! Viva Santa Fe! Salud! Salud, amigos!" the stowaway child heard the men shout from all the oxcarts ahead of hers. — *The Wind Leaves No Shadow*, Ruth Laughlin, 1948.

4215 Hi, teach! — *Up the Down Staircase*, Bel Kaufman, 1964.

4216 Annick did not really, as some persons suggested, put out his tongue at new parents: he only seemed to do so. — *The Honours Board*, Pamela Hansford Johnson, 1970.

4217 "Good afternoon, your worship," said Frances to the Mayor. — *Half the Gladness*, Carol Bruggen, 1985.

4218 Reader, I do greet thee heartily! — *The Later Adventures of Tom Jones*, Bob Coleman, 1985.

4219 *To Nero Claudius Caesar Drusus Germanicus, The Glorious Father of Our Country, Prince of Youth, and Best of Men, from Polyclitus, Special Commissioner for the Investigation into the Recent Disturbances in the Province of Britain, Greetings!* — *Druid Time*, Jack Holland, 1986.

4220 *"Welcome to The Drinker's Hour!"/ That's how they introduced their 3:00 A.M. show, those doom jockeys.* — *The Golden Orange*, Joseph Wambaugh, 1990.

Grief

4221 *Dear Father and Mother,/ I have great Trouble, and some Comfort, to acquaint you with. The Trouble is, that my good Lady died of the Illness I mention'd to you, and left us all much griev'd for the Loss of her; for she was a dear good Lady, and kind to all us her Servants.* — *Pamela*, Samuel Richardson, 1740–1741.

4222 A lady in deep mourning was sitting crying bitterly by a fire in small lodgings in the town of Yarmouth. — *With Clive in India*, G. A. Henty, 1884.

4223 "I have just buried my boy, my handsome boy of whom I was so proud, and my heart is broken.... — *Allan Quatermain*, H. Rider Haggard, 1887.

4224 When the doctor had gone, and the two women from the village he had been waiting for were upstairs shut in with her dead father, Lucy went out into the garden and stood leaning on the gate staring at the sea. — *Vera*, Elizabeth von Arnim, 1921.

4225 Considering that Philip Lucas's aunt who died early in April was no less than eighty-three years old, and had spent the last seven of them bedridden in a private lunatic asylum, it had been generally and perhaps reasonably hoped among his friends and those of his wife that the bereavement would not be regarded by either of them as an intolerable tragedy. — *Lucia in London*, E. F. Benson, 1927.

4226 Though it was nearly a year since her husband's death, Emmeline Lucas (universally known to her friends as Lucia) still wore the deepest and most uncompromising mourning. Black certainly suited her very well, but that had nothing to do with this continued use of it, whatever anybody said. — *Mapp and Lucia*, E. F. Benson, 1931.

4227 My father passes. I am sinking in some gelatinous substance. — *What Comes Next*, Jonathan Baumbach, 1968.

4228 The first severity of mourning was over. — *Laura*, G. M. T. Parsons, 1978.

4229 Where is that grief for which I've sought in vain, I heard myself say for no particular

reason. — *Dyad*, Michael Brodsky, 1989.

4230 For three months after the funeral she refused to go back into the mainstream of laughing, talking, loving, hating people. — *The Bubble Reputation*, Cathie Pelletier, 1993.

Growing Up

4231 "Aunt Betsey, there's going to be a new Declaration of Independence." — *Work*, Louisa May Alcott, 1873.

4232 All children, except one, grow up. — *Peter Pan*, James M. Barrie, 1911.

4233 Because she was only fifteen and busy with her growing up, Lucia's periods of reflection were brief and infrequent; but this morning she felt weighted with responsibility. — *The Robe*, Lloyd C. Douglas, 1942.

4234 Reese Parmelee had always promised himself that when he grew up and married, he would never live at Parmelee Cove. — *Pursuit of the Prodigal*, Louis Auchincloss, 1959.

4235 I remember childhood as an intense and wonderful love-affair that was stamped out by the wilful circumstance of growing up. So you can be sure I won't spend long on it. — *A Start in Life*, Alan Sillitoe, 1970.

4236 For twelve straight years I had been on this earth when, for no apparent reason, God decided to stick me by allowing me to become a teen-ager. — *Do Black Patent Leather Shoes Really Reflect Up?*, John R. Powers, 1975.

4237 That Summer was a first growing up. — *The Gossamer Fly*, Meira Chand, 1980.

4238 "Go wid ya muddar," she told him. "Go and grow to a man. And when you a man, you'll get a sign to come and hear de most hurtful part." — *Clara's Heart*, Joseph Olshan, 1985.

4239 It seemed that when I was growing up, all the wild roads led to Charley Bland. — *Charley Bland*, Mary Lee Settle, 1989.

4240 I grew up in Beverly Hills where beauty was particularly esteemed while its old partner, truth, was held in about the same esteem as anyone's old partner was held. — *His Little Women*, Judith Rossner, 1990.

4241 I grew up in a small town. — *Small Town Girls*, Pamela Wallace, 1990.

4242 It's an American story: Before he was a thinker, or a doer, or an engineer, much less an imagineer like his self-made-millionaire friend Grover Ding, Ralph Chang was just a small boy in China, struggling to grow up his father's son. — *Typical American*, Gish Jen, 1991.

4243 Contrary to popular belief, I did grow up. — *For the Love of Robert E. Lee*, M. A. Harper, 1992.

Guns

4244 "What do you think she'd do if she caught us? We oughtn't to have it, you know," said Maisie./ "Beat me, and lock you up in your bedroom," Dick answered, without hesitation. "Have you got the cartridges?" — *The Light That Failed*, Rudyard Kipling, 1890.

4245 My father kept a little firearm shop in St. Louis. — *With the Indians in the Rockies*, James Willard Schultz, 1912.

4246 The master gunner said, 'All's well the guns, sir.'/ The mate answered, "Very well," and stood for a moment to watch the man go forward. — *Long Pennant*, Oliver La Farge, 1933.

4247 "Tarvin, you aint takin that gun out agin," says Fronnie. — *Trees of Heaven*, Jesse Stuart, 1940.

4248 Peter Dekatha, the cunning old hunter, would permit no sound — indeed no movement beyond the cautious repriming of our muskets. — *Son of the Hawk*, Thomas H. Raddall, 1950.

4249 One day a young man in an almost brimless fedora burst into the office where Feldman was dictating a letter to his secretary. He pointed a gun and said, "Reach, the jig is up, Feldman." — *A Bad Man*, Stanley Elkin, 1967.

4250 Years ago, a child in a tree with a small caliber rifle bushwhacked a piano through the open summer windows of a neighbor's living room. — *The Bushwhacked Piano*, Thomas McGuane, 1971.

4251 Jackie Brown at twenty-six, with no expression on his face, said that he could get some guns. — *The Friends of Eddie Coyle*, George V. Higgins, 1972.

4252 The AK-47s were chewing up everything. — *Captain Blackman*, John A. Williams, 1972.

4253 The men carried deer rifles, .30-caliber carbines mainly, and they approached the Park Service Museum building as if it were a deer, ready to spook. — *So Far from Heaven*, Richard Bradford, 1973.

4254 They crouched with their rifles in the pineapple field, watching a man teach his son how to ride a horse. — *The Hawkline Monster*, Richard Brautigan, 1974.

4255 Thomas Greenwood stood at the door of the chapel with a pistol in his hand. — *Jade*, Pat Barr, 1981.

4256 It was six inches long. He stroked it lightly, but he could not conjure an appropriate response: eroticism, revulsion, fascination, *terror.* — *The Glitter Dome*, Joseph Wambaugh, 1981.

4257 On a two-masted brig nearing the Port of Aden a cluster of English gentlemen stood watching a handsome young Army officer shoot the gulls which had begun to trail the ship's wake. — *Burton and Speke*, William Harrison, 1982.

4258 I may as well say at the outset that this is a story of guns and trouble. — *Winds of Blame*, Jane Gilmore Rushing, 1983.

4259 The gun was easy to make. — *Good Luck on Your Downward Journey*, Bob Williams, 1984.

4260 The rifle was real; it was the triggerman who looked like a toy. — *The International Garage Sale*, Stefan Kanfer, 1985.

4261 The boy shot Wild Bill's horse at dusk, while Bill was off in the bushes to relieve himself. — *Deadwood*, Pete Dexter, 1986.

4262 Karl kept one cannon on the front porch one on the back. — *Loop's Progress*, Chuck Rosenthal, 1986.

4263 Standing in front of his dresser mirror, the young man pointed the revolver at his reflection. — *Under Cover of Daylight*, James W. Hall, 1987.

4264 Gunfire in the woods all morning. — *Strickland*, Hilary Masters, 1989.

4265 I bought the gun on a Wednesday, that much I can be certain of. — *Small Game*, John Blades, 1992.

4266 Five men, clean-shaven, armed. — *Mad Dog*, Jack Kelly, 1992.

4267 "Gordon! GUN!" screamed Curtis, diving off his skateboard onto trash-covered concrete. — *Way Past Cool*, Jess Mowry, 1992.

4268 Karl kept one cannon on the front porch, one on the back. — *Loop's End*, Chuck Rosenthal, 1992.

Habits

4269 It was Mr. Ricardo's habit as soon as the second week of August came round to travel to Aix-les-Bains, in Savoy, where for five or six weeks he lived pleasantly. — *At the Villa Rose*, A. E. W. Mason, 1910.

4270 Ever since the age of six Troy Belknap of New York had embarked for Europe every June on the fastest steamer of one of the most expensive lines. — *The Marne*, Edith Wharton, 1918.

4271 It was the same old rigmarole. Sometimes I found it amusing; sometimes it only bored me; sometimes it gave me a pronounced pain, especially when I had had more of Wolfe than was good for either of us. — *Too Many Women*, Rex Stout, 1947.

4272 There was only one thing about Phyllis which annoyed Charles: she invariably served him sherry when he called on Sunday afternoons. — *The Balance Wheel*, Taylor Caldwell, 1951.

4273 They tell me that my father, a Latin teacher, would place his silver watch, with the Phi Beta key dangling, on the right-hand corner of the desk in his Vergil class. — *The Huge Season*, Wright Morris, 1954.

4274 Shortly after two a sandy-haired gentleman in the middle years hurried into the Café Julien, sat down at Alexander's table as he always did, ordered coffee and cognac as he always did, asked for stationery as he always did, shook out a fountain pen and proceeded to write. — *The Wicked Pavilion*, Dawn Powell, 1954.

4275 Colonel Baker, taking his usual solitary afternoon walk, was caught in a summer cloudburst. — *The Center of the Green*, John Bowen, 1959.

4276 My name is George Smith. I get up on the right side of the bed every morning because I pushed the left to the wall. — *A Singular Man*, J. P. Donleavy, 1963.

4277 I still have their picture, taken at the Falls, and one of the bright red Italian-style beach sandals, encrusted with rhinestones, that Elizavetta was affecting that summer — the right one, that she always allowed to slide down and dangle off her big toe when she crossed her legs, lit a cigarette and leaned forward to plunge into some heated bit of politics or gossip. — *That Summer*, Allen Drury, 1965.

4278 *I trip every time I pass the house on St. Marks Place.* — *To the Precipice*, Judith Rossner, 1966.

4279 I began it "NW" and signed it "AG" not to be different, but from habit. — *Death of a Dude*, Rex Stout, 1969.·

4280 In the afternoons it was the custom of Miss Jane Marple to unfold her second newspaper. — *Nemesis*, Agatha Christie, 1971.

4281 At six o'clock on the evening of the last Friday in the past July, Dr. Berners tells us, he reentered his office here in the hospital after reattaching the severed hand of an accident victim, and stood before the window, as is his habit when recovering his nonsurgery self. — *Standard Dreaming*, Hortense Calisher, 1972.

4282 Mr. Virgil Jones, a man devoid of friends and with a tongue rather too large for his mouth, was fond of descending this cliff-path on Tiusday mornings. (Mr. Jones, something of a pedant and interested in the origins of things, referred to the days of his week as Sunday, Moonday, Tiusday, Wodensday, Thorsday,

Freyday and Saturnday; it was affectations like this, among other things, that had left him friendless.)—*Grimus*, Salman Rushdie, 1975.

4283 In the old brown house on the corner, a mile from the middle of the city, we ate bacon for breakfast every morning of our lives. —*Monkey Grip*, Helen Garner, 1977.

4284 When he was a schoolboy, George Levanter had learned a convenient routine: a four-hour sleep in the afternoon enabled him to remain mentally and physically active until the early dawn, when he would again go to sleep for four hours and wake ready for the day. —*Blind Date*, Jerzy Kosinski, 1977.

4285 On weekdays, if Giorgio was there, he'd get up early and go down to the *fornaio* for hard little rolls, and to the coffee bar on the corner for a small carton of milk.—*A Feast of Ashes*, Sally Rosenbluth, 1980.

4286 Jorge Rojas Jiménez ascended the stone steps and emerged on the rooftop terrace for the habitual stroll he took before lunch, walking unhurriedly among the rows of rosebushes growing with a profusion of flowers in large wooden tubs. —*A New History of Torments*, Zulfikar Ghose, 1982.

4287 *For a long time I used to go to bed early.* — *The Arabian Nightmare*, Robert Irwin, 1983.

4288 Every weekday morning after Weber left for school Tom Larkin would set up the practice board; that was the first thing he did when he got out of bed. — *The Year of Silence*, Madison Smartt Bell, 1987.

4289 She walked down River Street every afternoon to buy the paper and her father's cigarettes. —*Due East*, Valerie Sayers, 1987.

4290 I never really warmed to Clovis—he was far too stupid to inspire real affection—but he always claimed a corner of my heart, largely, I suppose, because of the way he instinctively and unconsciously cupped his genitals whenever he was alarmed or nervous. —*Brazzaville Beach*, William Boyd, 1990.

4291 Earl Dean lost a good deal of hair quickly in his early twenties and the experience had left him in the habit of rubbing his head. —*Pomona Queen*, Kem Nunn, 1992.

Hair

4292 "'Hair almost silver—incredibly fair: a startling pallor.'" Otherwise, unmistakably, there was a close resemblance. —*Inclinations*, Ronald Firbank, 1916.

4293 Frank MacPherson was a big fellow with red hair just beginning to be touched with grey. —"Retread," Louis Bromfield, 1945.

4294 My father's hair must have been ruddy gold long ago; I can recollect the pinkish bloom of it, like reflected glow on spun silk. — *The Garretson Chronicle*, Gerald Warner Brace, 1947.

4295 "One seldom sees hair like that nowadays," said David Byfield. —*An Ordinary Lunacy*, Jessica Anderson, 1963.

4296 Morwenna's face floated in the single beam of light, lovely and framed in hair dark as my cloak; blood from her neck pattered to the stones. — *The Claw of the Conciliator*, Gene Wolfe, 1981.

4297 She was wise about her hair, Bethany was; how the corn-silk bangs over the forehead made both the most and the least of her long straight nose. — *True Love*, Herbert Gold, 1982.

4298 I saw him standing there, this young man with hair the color of Wise potato chips. —*Maiden Rites*, Sonia Pilcer, 1982.

4299 "It was in my hair, Severian," Dorcas said. — *The Sword of the Lictor*, Gene Wolfe, 1982.

4300 The midwife was a portly Frenchwoman whose thick ebony hair was braided into a glossy cable that normally fell below her almost nonexistent waistline. —*Gateway to Empire*, Allan W. Eckert, 1983.

4301 At eighteen, Carolyn Tanner was as thin as a stick, with lank no-colour hair which filled her mother with despair. —*Her Living Image*, Jane Rogers, 1986.

4302 Clara Velde, to begin with what was conspicuous about her, had short blonde hair, fashionably cut, growing upon a head unusually big. —*A Theft*, Saul Bellow, 1989.

Hangouts

4303 In the year 1775, there stood upon the borders of Epping Forest, at a distance of about twelve miles from London—measuring from the Standard in Cornhill, or rather from the spot on or near to which the Standard used to be in days of yore—a house of public entertainment called the Maypole; which fact was demonstrated to all such travellers as could neither read nor write (and sixty years ago a vast number both of travellers and stay-at-homes were in this condition) by the emblem reared on the roadside over against the house, which, if not of those goodly proportions that Maypoles were wont to present in olden times, was a fair young ash, thirty feet in height, and straight as any arrow that ever English yeoman drew.—*Barnaby Rudge*, Charles Dickens, 1841.

4304 In a certain quiet and sequestered nook of the retired village of London — perhaps in the neighbourhood of Berkeley Square, or at any rate somewhere near Burlington Gardens — there was once a house of entertainment called the "Bootjack Hotel." — "The Ravenswing," William Makepeace Thackeray, 1852.

4305 "Yes, sir?"/ Jules, the celebrated head waiter of the Grand Babylon, was bending formally towards the alert, middle-aged man who had just entered the smoking-room and dropped into a basket-chair in the corner by the conservatory. — *The Grand Babylon Hotel*, Arnold Bennett, 1902.

4306 A cold, thick drizzle, blown by a biting wind that sent chills to the marrow, marred the early spring night, and kept indoors the few hardy members who had haunted the clubhouse since the season's opening a week before. — *The Flyers*, George Barr McCutcheon, 1907.

4307 A shrieking wind, thick with the sleety snow that knows no mercy nor feels remorse, beat vainly and with savage insolence against the staid windows in the lounging room of one of New York's most desirable clubs — one of those characteristic homes for college men who were up for membership on the day they were born, if one may speak so broadly of the virtue that links the early eighteenth-century graduate with his great-grandson of the class of 1908. — *The Alternative*, George Barr McCutcheon, 1909.

4308 As he sat there in the withdrawing-room of Patrick Lynch's inn, all the life, all the spirit of Galway was evident to him. — *Blind Raftery and His Wife, Hilaria*, Donn Byrne, 1924.

4309 The Light of Day Club: midnight. The gilded and glazed Grand Hall (whose walls were mirrors), with its dancing-floor bordered on every side by a triple row of white-draped tables, nearly every one of them occupied by more or less beautiful women and more or less possessive men — attired in the extremity of correctness. — *"Piccadilly,"* Arnold Bennett, 1930.

4310 I was leaning against the bar in a speakeasy on Fifty-second Street, waiting for Nora to finish her Christmas shopping, when a girl got up from the table where she had been sitting with three other people and came over to me. — *The Thin Man*, Dashiell Hammett, 1934.

4311 The Yellow Bud Tavern had a long porch fronting on the canal with a rail about hip-high. — *Chad Hanna*, Walter D. Edmonds, 1940.

4312 It was quiet in the Saloon Bar of the Crown, that afternoon. — *Three Men in New Suits*, J. B. Priestley, 1945.

4313 At five minutes to six, Lieutenant Jerry Wright fidgeted at the bar of the officers' club of Gedsborough Airbase, near Kenwoulton, Hunt-ingdon, some ninety miles north of London. — *The Lonely*, Paul Gallico, 1947.

4314 Drinks were being served before the broad fireplace of the National Press Club where the news that nobody prints is privately circulated. — *Plunder*, Samuel Hopkins Adams, 1948.

4315 Halfway between the docks and the Darlinghurst tramway the "Sword of Fortune," an unpretentious public house, offered to the sailor, the coal-lumper and the dock worker a glittering array of pictures advertising beer. — *The Joyful Condemned*, Kylie Tennant, 1953.

4316 The Channel Club lay on a shelf of rock overlooking the sea, toward the southern end of the beach called Malibu. Above its long brown buildings, terraced gardens climbed like a richly carpeted stairway to the highway. The grounds were surrounded by a high wire fence topped with three barbed strands and masked with oleanders. — *The Barbarous Coast*, Ross Macdonald, 1956.

4317 Though Methuen usually lived at his Club whenever he was in London it was seldom that he was seen in the bar or the gaunt smoking-rooms. — *White Eagles Over Serbia*, Lawrence Durrell, 1957.

4318 When the young man started shouting, I was standing at the end of the long bar, talking to a couple of construction men and to the bush pilot who had flown me in that morning. — *The Time Before This*, Nicholas Monsarrat, 1962.

4319 There is a sort of coal hole in the heart of Soho that is open every afternoon: a dark, dank, dead-ended subterranean tunnel. It is a drinking club called the Crypt and the only light to penetrate it is the shaft of golden sunlight slipping through the doorway from time to time glancing off someone's nose or hair or glass of gin, all the more poignant for its sudden revelations, in an atmosphere almost solid with failure, of pure wind-swept nostalgia, of clean airy summer houses, of the beach, of windy reefs; of the sun radiating through the clouds the instant before the clouds race back over it again — leaving the day as sad and desperate as before. — *The Old Man and Me*, Elaine Dundy, 1964.

4320 The moment was strange. There was no reality in the bar: there was no longer solidity: all things merged, one into the other. Time had stopped. — *The City and the Pillar (revised)*, Gore Vidal, 1965.

4321 I'd been hearing about the Tennis Club for years, but I'd never been inside of it. — *Black Money*, Ross Macdonald, 1966.

4322 *My loves, Switzerland's most social snow heap will open for business again this week. Again Mount Griff will grow a few chic feet higher this winter and again nobody will have any idea why: the Peak Club chalet high on the slopes up there is ever so exclusive but*

doesn't know beans about pathology. — *Snow Gods*, Frederic Morton, 1968.

4323 Bartholomew Kedar Enos knew that the man he wanted could always be found downtown at the Blue Note Bar on his night off from work; and from his vantage point across the street in the diner he could easily keep an eye on the front of the bar. — *To Reach a Dream*, Nathan C. Heard, 1972.

4324 I had just been through hell and must have looked like death warmed over walking into the saloon, because when I asked the bartender whether they served zombies he said, "Sure, what'll you have?" — *I Hear America Swinging*, Peter De Vries, 1976.

4325 They were in a bar at Los Angeles International Airport, sitting at a small Formica table. — *Good Riddance*, Barbara Abercrombie, 1979.

4326 It was late afternoon, and the speakeasy was almost deserted. — *Speakeasy*, Nathaniel Benchley, 1982.

4327 Passing by the place, a casual observer wouldn't have been able to tell that it was one of those bars. — *Ringer*, David R. Slavitt, 1982.

4328 In the middle of the last century, at a crossroads junction called Radich, east of Melon Village and sixty kilometers south of Warsaw, flourished an inn called the Flying Goose, with a gabled roof, shuttered windows, and a yard walled in against thieves. — *Fathers and Children*, Judah Stampfer, 1983.

4329 You are not the kind of guy who would be at a place like this at this time of the morning. — *Bright Lights, Big City*, Jay McInerney, 1984.

4330 The Hope Club in D'Arblay Street, London W1 is unlike any other club. — *Hannie Richards*, Hilary Bailey, 1985.

4331 Then a young man in a three-piece suit came in — which was odd, for this was not, to Arleen's knowledge, a bar where that kind of thing was usually worn. — *Air*, Michael Upchurch, 1986.

4332 It was always night in the Hillcrest Club, one of those Southern California cocktail lounges with the red vinyl booths, artificial plants, Formica bar and no windows. — *Wirecutter*, John Brizzolara, 1987.

4333 Friday was the day of rest, and since it was a Friday, and not long before lunch, Gran Jones drifted into the bar-room of the Darwish Hotel with his unopened mail and copies of the *Morning Post* in their blue airmail wrappers, and settled his spent and lofty frame into one of the deep chairs by the long window. — *Deadline*, Tom Stacey, 1988.

4334 The place was called Café Exotica, and looked like a gigantic greenhouse. — *The Kentish*

Manor Murders, Julian Symons, 1988.

4335 Laughing out loud, he turned away from laughing faces and the noise of voices, all of them talking again all at once, with one or two over in the chimney corner trying to join together to sing out the familiar melody of some old round or common country song, but from the first note so out of tune as to be beyond recognition and repair; in a few quick strides left behind him, as if tossed over his shoulder, the sweet and heavy, yeasty odors of beer and ale, these good things commingled with the undeniable and inimitable stink of a close crowd of freely sweating men and, too, the small white pungent clouds made by the smokers of pipes and the acrid grease-laden scents of the rushlights and the cheap tallow candles offering as much smoke as light; left behind, then, above all, the light and shadow, sway and dance of it, of the well-stacked, high-blazing fireplace. — *Entered from the Sun*, George Garrett, 1990.

4336 Lula and her friend Beany Thorn sat at a table in the Raindrop Club drinking rum Co-Colas while watching and listening to a white blues band called The Bleach Boys. — *Wild at Heart*, Barry Gifford, 1990.

4337 Crab-like, Olivio scuttled up the ladder behind the broad leadwood bar. — *The White Rhino Hotel*, Bartle Bull, 1992.

Happiness

4338 Seldom has the earth held a couple of human beings so happy in each other as were Mr. Adam Blair and his wife. — *Adam Blair*, J. G. Lockhart, 1822.

4339 The world considered Eugene Lane a very fortunate young man; and if youth, health, social reputation, a seat in Parliament, a large income, and finally the promised hand of an acknowledged beauty can make a man happy, the world was right. — *Father Stafford*, Anthony Hope, 1891.

4340 Mr. Gabriel Bearse was happy. The prominence given to this statement is not meant to imply that Gabriel was, as a general rule, unhappy. — *"Shavings"*, Joseph C. Lincoln, 1918.

4341 An hour ago, under the marvelous canopy of the blue northern sky, David Carrigan, Sergeant in His Most Excellent Majesty's Royal Northwest Mounted Police, had hummed softly to himself, and had thanked God that he was alive. — *The Flaming Forest*, James Oliver Curwood, 1921.

4342 That evening, I remember, as I came

up through the Mill Meadow, I was feeling peculiarly happy and contented. — *The Three Hostages*, John Buchan, 1924.

4343 I find myself happy and I have an impression that I have been quite happy for two days. And further I believe against the critical protests of my intelligence, that I have been generally happy throughout my life. — *Apropos of Dolores*, H. G. Wells, 1938.

4344 Miss Ella Venn, aged seventy-four, coming downstairs just before dinner, saw her niece Amanda in the arms of a young farmer called Harry Dawbarn, who had just entered the house by way of the garden. The sight gave her such pleasure that she ran back to her room. "Oh, thank God!" she said to herself. She was tearful with joy. — *The Moonlight*, Joyce Cary, 1946.

4345 Lee Gordon was the happiest man in the world that afternoon. — *Lonely Crusade*, Chester Himes, 1947.

4346 Once there was a bright and spirited young man named Andrew Reale, who came into the world in the second decade of the twentieth century and grew up in the third and fourth, and was thus convinced that the road to happiness lay in becoming very rich very quickly. — *Aurora Dawn*, Herman Wouk, 1947.

4347 We are happy in our hut on the mountaintop for here we call no man Baas and Fanie hunts with a rifle like a white man. — *Mittee*, Daphne Rooke, 1951.

4348 "Darling," pleaded Mrs. Frieman, "all we want is that you should be happy!" — *The Bankrupts*, Brian Glanville, 1958.

4349 I marmaladed a slice of toast with something of a flourish, and I don't suppose I have ever come much closer to saying "Tra-la-la" as I did the lathering, for I was feeling in mid-season form this morning. — *Stiff Upper Lip, Jeeves*, P. G. Wodehouse, 1963.

4350 A June morning, the sky blue. If anybody had asked Gilbert Welton *Are you happy?* and if he could have been persuaded to answer (which is unlikely, because the question would not have seemed to him meaningful), he would have said *Yes.* — *The Man Who Lost His Wife*, Julian Symons, 1970.

4351 We've been pretty happy, Susan and I said George settling down into his sofa and smiling. — *Riches and Fame and the Pleasures of Sense*, Kathy Black, 1971.

4352 Mister sat at the top of the car-crusher as close to joy as he'd been in a long time. — *Car*, Harry Crews, 1972.

4353 It was going to be the happiest of times. — *Nightshade*, Derek Marlowe, 1976.

4354 Daisy read what her mother, Margaret Wallace, had written:/ "Dearest Daisy,/ "I am happier than I have ever been in my life. Oh, darling, of course I was very happy — ecstatic — when you were born, and when Dale was born, but that was such a tired, hot, muddled happiness. This happiness is an energetic sort, completely selfish, clear and pure. If you could see me, how I look now, and my house, this dear house with its windows full of ocean, you would understand. You *should* see me now, my goodness, you should — ..." — *Three Women at the Waters' Edge*, Nancy Thayer, 1981.

4355 Laura felt inappropriately happy. — *Occasion of Sin*, Rachel Billington, 1982.

4356 This was Happy Valley. — *Fiddle and Bow*, Robert Taylor, Jr., 1985.

4357 I have been happy at the Divinity School. — *Roger's Version*, John Updike, 1986.

Hatred

4358 F.Y. Grimsley hated Indians, full-blood, half-blood, quarter-blood and any with a known fraction of taint. — *The Genuine Article*, A. B. Guthrie, Jr., 1977.

4359 I think that I used to detest Doctor Fischer more than any other man I have known just as I loved his daughter more than any other woman. — *Doctor Fischer of Geneva*, Graham Greene, 1980.

4360 As a young child, in the small town of Visoka where she was born, Malka early learned to despise her contemporaries. — *Hand-Me-Downs*, Rhea Kohan, 1980.

4361 I hate. — *Darling Daughters*, Elizabeth Troop, 1981.

4362 "I don't want to be you! I don't want to be like you! I should hate to be like you. You show me what it is to be naked, to be barren, to be dispossessed. I hate everything I see in you! ..." — *Waiting to Live*, Mewa Ramgobin, 1986.

4363 "She's going to hate this. She's going to hate us," said Moira, her damp eyes on the faces of the two friends beside her as she steered down Borden Street. — *All Good Women*, Valerie Miner, 1987.

4364 *We are so jealous of their hatred.* — *The Pérez Family*, Christine Bell, 1990.

4365 It was Lucinda Fortune (to her friend Katie) who had first made the statement "I hate art students." — *Divine Concepts of Physical Beauty*, Michael Bracewell, 1990.

4366 We Athenians despise optimists, but we occasionally perpetrate unintentional optimism in the sacred name of shrewdness. — *The Walled Orchard*, Tom Holt, 1990.

Heat

4367 Thirty years ago, Marseilles lay burning in the sun, one day. — *Little Dorrit*, Charles Dickens, 1857.

4368 The day had been very oppressive, and at half-past five in the afternoon, the heat had scarcely abated, to the perception of Mr. Joshua Harkness, as he walked heavily up the Park Street mall in Boston Common. — *A Woman's Reason*, William Dean Howells, 1883.

4369 It is afternoon, but the sun's rays still pour down with great power upon rock and sand. How great the heat has been at midday may be seen by the quivering of the air as it rises from the ground and blurs all distant objects. — *The Young Carthaginian*, G. A. Henty, 1887.

4370 A long sultry Syrian day was drawing near its close./ The heavy heat was almost insupportable, and a poisonous stench oozed up from the damp earth-floors of the Jewish prison, charging what little air there was with a deadly sense of suffocation. — *Barabbas*, Marie Corelli, 1893.

4371 The day had been very hot under the tall trees which everywhere embower and stifle Saratoga, for they shut out the air as well as the sun; and after tea (they still have an early dinner at all the hotels in Saratoga, and tea is the last meal of the day) I strolled over to the pretty Congress Park, in the hope of getting a breath of coolness there. — *An Open-Eyed Conspiracy*, William Dean Howells, 1897.

4372 It was the first Saturday afternoon in August; it had been broiling hot all day, with a cloudless sky, and the sun had been beating down on the houses so that the top rooms were like ovens; but now with the approach of evening it was cooler, and everyone in Vere Street was out-of-doors. — *Liza of Lambeth*, W. Somerset Maugham, 1897.

4373 The afternoon was intensely, terribly hot. — *The Lady of the Heavens*, H. Rider Haggard, 1908.

4374 The hot summer sun beat down mercilessly upon the little town of Vacaville. It was late June heat, when the ranchers raced with the steadily ripening fruit, and the days became an hour-to-hour struggle against the fast maturing burden of trees and vines. The heat lay quivering over the flat floor of the valley and upon the sides of the distant, hazy hills. — *Brass*, Charles G. Norris, 1921.

4375 Prickly heat jabbed its claw into Ralph's sweaty neck as he staggered under the load. — *Mantrap*, Sinclair Lewis, 1926.

4376 It was a broiling afternoon of mid-August in Brinoë and everybody who was anybody had long ago quit its burning pavements and chilly palaces for the mountains or the sea. — *The Strange Case of Miss Annie Spragg*, Louis Bromfield, 1928.

4377 It was the first Tuesday in August. The Nebraska heat rolled in upon one like the engulfing waves of a dry sea, — a thick material substance against which one seemed to push when moving about. — *A White Bird Flying*, Bess Streeter Aldrich, 1931.

4378 U Po Kyin, Subdivisional Magistrate of Kyauktada, in Upper Burma, was sitting in his veranda. It was only half-past eight, but the month was April, and there was a closeness in the air, a threat of the long, stifling midday hours. — *Burmese Days*, George Orwell, 1934.

4379 Mr. Tench went out to look for his ether cylinder: out into the blazing Mexican sun and the bleaching dust. — *The Power and the Glory*, Graham Greene, 1940.

4380 It was hot, the grama grass was burnt to cinders on the pebbly soil. — *The American Cowboy*, Will James, 1942.

4381 On some nights New York is as hot as Bangkok. — *The Victim*, Saul Bellow, 1947.

4382 Spring came that year with the sudden fury of summer. The maddening heat blazed over fields and vineyards, drying up streams and springs, and withering the young crops, while flocks grew lean and died in the scorched pastures. — *The Robber*, Bertram Brooker, 1949.

4383 Generally the first week in September brings the hottest weather of the year, and this was no exception. — *Follow Me Down*, Shelby Foote, 1950.

4384 The night was sultry for square dancing. The Florida summer hesitated sullenly between continued heat and the equinoctial need of change. — *Jacob's Ladder*, Marjorie Kinnan Rawlings, 1950.

4385 All the heat of that summer's day seemed to burn on Doleham Valley station. The unshaded platform breathed like a stove, the flowers glared against the wall of the stationmaster's garden, the blue sky leaned and ached upon the roof. — *Mrs. Gailey*, Sheila Kaye-Smith, 1951.

4386 It was late September, and the summer had not yet gone. All day, the normally temperate city had sweltered, and now, as darkness approached, the heat remained: a sullen, humid blanket of air, so unfairly blown north from subtropic muck.... — *The Oracle*, Edwin O'Connor, 1951.

4387 In the hot weather there was little fighting. — *Yorktown*, Burke Davis, 1952.

4388 The summer of 1947 was not like other

Indian summers. Even the weather had a different feel in India that year. It was hotter than usual, and drier and dustier. — *Mano Majra*, Khushwant Singh, 1956.

4389 It was Monday, the first day of a heat wave, and the sun was just beginning to shine down on the shabbiest suburb in Bonn. — *The Hiding Place*, Robert Shaw, 1959.

4390 Already, an hour short of noon, the town was oven hot. — *The Governor's Lady*, Thomas H. Raddall, 1960.

4391 Heat increased steadily on this first October morning. — *The Crimson Gate*, Henry Gibbs, 1961.

4392 Soon it would be too hot. — *The Drowned World*, J. G. Ballard, 1962.

4393 The car was air-conditioned and the windows were up, sealing the two occupants against the hot world of Georgia outside. — *The Spangled Road*, Borden Deal, 1962.

4394 It had been a sweltering Friday afternoon in the latter part of August and now it was only a few minutes until five o'clock. — *The Last Night of Summer*, Erskine Caldwell, 1963.

4395 Morning, but the plaza blinding hot. — *Many Slippery Errors*, Alfred Grossman, 1963.

4396 It was that hot — steaming, stinking, sewer-vaporous, New York-humid, solid, soul-smiting hot. — *The Honey Badger*, Robert Ruark, 1965.

4397 A hot midsummer sun beat down without mercy, cracking the parched earth of plantations and homesteads scattered along the South Carolina seacoast. — *The Swamp Fox*, Noel B. Gerson, 1967.

4398 It is nine-fifteen on this hot September morn, hotter than any summer day we had. — *Diary of a Mad Housewife*, Sue Kaufman, 1967.

4399 It was a late afternoon of savage bottomlands heat in the April of 1935. — *Fools' Parade*, Davis Grubb, 1969.

4400 In the best years the summers in Eastern Tennessee are always hot. — *The Coming of Rain*, Richard Marius, 1969.

4401 The midsummer night, for Yorkshire, was so almost hot, old Lady Ramillies had come out to take the air. — *Rosa*, Margery Sharp, 1969.

4402 The heat in September in Los Angeles turns everything brown except where people love and water their gardens at great expense. — *Burning*, Diane Johnson, 1971.

4403 The summer of 1960 was hot and dry in Cocke County, Georgia. — *The Trapper's Last Shot*, John Yount, 1973.

4404 It had been a hot day and a lot of it. From the sun's first stretching right up till dinner time, the hours had steamed the ground until going barefoot was jumpy even for lizards. Sweating came easy, calling for nothing more than

showing up. Anyone could do it. — *Ode to Billy Joe*, Herman Raucher, 1976.

4405 It was the summer of 1968. It was Boston, and, even at six-fifteen in the morning, it was hot. — *King of Hearts*, David R. Slavitt, 1976.

4406 Laura went out into the sunlight, too hot even in her linen frock. — *Barren Corn*, Georgette Heyer, 1977.

4407 In August, on the Gulf coast of Florida, the heat doesn't ease when the sun goes down. It becomes more punishing; there is no shade. People go to bed with their windows closed. — *Acts of Love*, Elia Kazan, 1978.

4408 It was hot inside and hot outside. — *Leanna*, Doris Schwerin, 1978.

4409 A hot afternoon. Not a cloud; not even a wisp of it crosses the sky. — *Master and Servant*, David Mulwa, 1979.

4410 The New Year of 1944 was only two weeks old but already it looked as if it might be one of the hottest on record. The sun which blazed down across His Majesty's Australian Naval Dockyard at Williamstown was so fierce that it had stripped the sky of colour, and the crowded berths and wharves twisted and danced in an ever-changing mirage. — *A Ship Must Die*, Douglas Reeman, 1979.

4411 About half past eight on a July evening, Humphrey Leigh was walking along the side of the Square. It was very hot for London and hot enough for most other places. — *A Coat of Varnish*, C. P. Snow, 1979.

4412 Almost winter and the air like July; sunlight at a December slant, what came through the smoke, and the day hot as midsummer. — *The Affair at Honey Hill*, Berry Fleming, 1981.

4413 It was hot. The brown dry earth seared the feet and the large granite boulders scattered over the hillside burned the palms of hands. — *Field of Honor*, Timeri Murari, 1981.

4414 The postman took off his cap and wiped his forehead with the back of his pudgy hand. — *Goosefoot*, Patrick McGinley, 1982.

4415 It was said that the August of 1850 was one of the hottest and finest anyone could remember. — *Badge of Glory*, Douglas Reeman, 1982.

4416 Elijah Baley found himself in the shade of the tree and muttered to himself, "I knew it. I'm sweating." — *The Robots of Dawn*, Isaac Asimov, 1983.

4417 He watched from the quarterdeck as the chain fed through the whitecaps of the bay, its staccato clatter muffled, hollow in the midday heat. — *The Moghul*, Thomas Hoover, 1983.

4418 *Summer in the Gulf of Eilat. Beastly hot was an understatement.* — *Snow*, Jenifer Levin, 1983.

4419 The heat was something Ruth Reed could hold in her mouth and roll around on her

tongue like a hard candy. — *Pearl*, Anne Leaton, 1985.

4420 The August sun had already heated the seat of the concrete bench to an uncomfortable temperature when the old woman found her way across the courthouse square and wearily sat down. — *The Vigil*, Clay Reynolds, 1986.

4421 It was a hot afternoon after a day of solid heavy rain. — *No Telephone to Heaven*, Michelle Cliff, 1987.

4422 The sun was setting behind the First Methodist Church on Texas Avenue as we walked out of the federal courthouse and felt the hot late summer air on our faces. — "The Risi's Wife," John William Corrington, 1987.

4423 They were moving through rivers of heat westward across Algeria. — *Age of Consent*, Joanne Greenberg, 1987.

4424 Close to ninety degrees, today is typical of June in St. Louis. — *Snap*, Abby Frucht, 1988.

4425 I'm writing this in Westchester County, New York. Outside, the sky is such a solid blue I could touch it. In here it's sweltering; my hair feels heavy as a helmet. — *The Stand-In*, Deborah Moggach, 1991.

4426 It was over a hundred degrees in the mill. — *Patchwork*, Karen Osborn, 1991.

4427 The summer of 1846 was so hot that the Avon steamed and Stratford stank of drains and suffered a troublesome plague of flies. — *The Rise of Mr. Warde*, Duncan Sprott, 1991.

4428 A blazing sun beat upon the desert sands, painting strange images across an overheated horizon. — *Joshua in the Holy Land*, Joseph F. Girzone, 1992.

4429 Jessie Foster stood on the side of Highway 82, just outside Columbus, the Mississippi sun blistering her neck, tiny rivulets of perspiration huddled in her armpits. — *And Do Remember Me*, Marita Golden, 1992.

4430 I was standing in a locker in the Purlieu Street School on an August night, when a locker was a hot place to be. — *Where Do You Stop?*, Eric Kraft, 1992.

4431 It was an afternoon in late August, when people who could stay indoors did so, while others sought shade along the edges of buildings or other structures where they were obligated to be. — *Walking Dunes*, Sandra Scofield, 1992.

Heredity

4432 Remains of our good yeomanry blood will be found in Kent, developing stiff, solid, unobtrusive men, and very personable women. — *Rhoda Fleming*, George Meredith, 1865.

4433 So it was in him, then — an inherited fighting instinct, a driving intensity to kill. — *The Lone Star Ranger*, Zane Grey, 1915.

4434 Amory Blaine inherited from his mother every trait, except the stray inexpressible few, that made him worth while. — *This Side of Paradise*, F. Scott Fitzgerald, 1920.

4435 We were talking about the persistence of race qualities — how you might bury a strain for generations under fresh graftings, but the aboriginal sap would some day stir. — *The Runagates Club*, John Buchan, 1928.

4436 Sam Berman was taller than his father Ben by at least half a foot, and his father had been — he remembered this clearly — taller than *his* father; and yet — it was crazy — when he thought of them, things were always reversed: he saw his grandfather as tallest of all, with Ben next, and himself last — like the painted wooden dolls he'd seen in souvenir shops (from Russia, he thought, or Poland), in which, when you opened the largest one, there was one smaller, and when you opened the smaller one, there was one even smaller. — *The Rummage Shop*, Jay Neugeboren, 1974.

4437 She said it was a blood thing, Aunt Sister did, and not even from Great-granddaddy really but likely Great-uncle Jack that would be Great-uncle Cyrus Barnard Yount who got called Jack everywhere but the front of the Bible, and Aunt Sister insisted it was down from him with Great-granddaddy just a conduit to Granddaddy himself who got the whole of it, and Momma asked her the whole of what like she always asked her the whole of what and Aunt Sister waved her hand in the air like usual and like usual told her back, "You know," which Momma said did not tell her anything so she got waved at and You knowed all over again and Daddy suggested Temperament? and Daddy suggested Passion? but Aunt Sister stuck with foolishness like always, just plain foolishness she guessed with maybe some passion to it somewhere but foolishness mostly. — *The Last of How It Was*, T. R. Pearson, 1987.

4438 Eddie Socket had his mother's sharp, slightly prominent Anglican nose, and his father's deep-set, sentimental blue eyes and pale Irish complexion — standard white American features, neatly arranged but lacking authority, he felt, because of his chin. — *The Irreversible Decline of Eddie Socket*, John Weir, 1989.

Heritage

4439 Sir Walter Elliot, of Kellynch Hall, in Somersetshire, was a man who, for his own amusement, never took up any book but the Baronetage; there he found occupation for an idle hour, and consolation in a distressed one; there his faculties were roused into admiration and respect, by contemplating the limited remnant of the earliest patents; there any unwelcome sensations, arising from domestic affairs, changed naturally into pity and contempt, as he turned over the almost endless creations of the last century—and there, if every other leaf were powerless, he could read his own history with an interest which never failed—this was the page at which the favourite volume always opened:
ELLIOT OF KELLYNCH HALL
Walter Elliot, born March 1, 1760, married, July 15, 1784, Elizabeth, daughter of James Stevenson, Esq. of South Park, in the county of Gloucester; by which lady (who died 1800) he has issue Elizabeth, born June 1, 1785; Anne, born August 9, 1787; a stillborn son, Nov. 5, 1789; Mary, born Nov. 20, 1791.—*Persuasion*, Jane Austen, 1818.

4440 I am a Cockney among Cockneys.—*Alton Locke*, Charles Kingsley, 1850.

4441 There is nothing in New England corresponding at all to the feudal aristocracies of the Old World.—*Elsie Venner*, Oliver Wendell Holmes, Sr., 1859.

4442 It was admitted that Ferdinand Lopez was a "gentleman." It was not generally believed that Ferdinand Lopez was well born.—*The Prime Minister*, Anthony Trollope, 1876.

4443 In spite of Jean-Jacques and his school, men are not everywhere born free, any more than they are everywhere in chains, unless these be of their own individual making.—*Mr. Isaacs*, F. Marion Crawford, 1882.

4444 The Nestons, of Tottlebury Grange in the county of Suffolk, were an ancient and honourable family, never very distinguished or very rich, but yet for many generations back always richer and more distinguished than the common run of mankind.—*Mr. Witt's Widow*, Anthony Hope, 1892.

4445 I say we have a bitter heritage, but that is not to run it down.—*Tourmaline*, Randolph Stow, 1963.

4446 My old eighth-grade teacher, Miss Maggie Doubloon, said she was half Spanish, half French, and half Irish, a plethora of halves not entirely unnoticed by some of the brighter pupils.—*Slouching Towards Kalamazoo*, Peter De

Vries, 1983.

4447 "I am always puzzled," said Dr. Goebbels, "which part of you is Irish and which is American. Are you sure there is no German in you? You speak our language so well."—*City of Fading Light*, Jon Cleary, 1985.

4448 My name is Gideon Clarke, and, like my father before me, I have on more than one occasion been physically ejected from the corporate offices of the Chicago Cubs Baseball Club, which are located at Wrigley Field, 1060 West Addison, in Chicago.—*The Iowa Baseball Confederacy*, W. P. Kinsella, 1986.

4449 I am a boomer.—*Veteran's Day*, Rod Kane, 1990.

4450 Freak accidents ran in the family.—*The Diamond Lane*, Karen Karbo, 1991.

Heroes and Heroines

4451 No one who had ever seen Catherine Morland in her infancy, would have supposed her born to be an heroine.—*Northanger Abbey*, Jane Austen, 1818.

4452 Whether I shall turn out to be the hero of my own life, or whether that station will be held by anybody else, these pages must show.—*David Copperfield*, Charles Dickens, 1850.

4453 Who shall be the hero of this tale? Not I who write it. I am but the Chorus of the Play. I make remarks on the conduct of the characters: I narrate their simple story.—*Lovel the Widower*, William Makepeace Thackeray, 1860.

4454 Not a day passes over the earth, but men and women of no note do great deeds, speak great words, and suffer noble sorrows. Of these obscure heroes, philosophers, and martyrs, the greater part will never be known till that hour, when many that are great shall be small, and the small great; but of others the world's knowledge may be said to sleep: their lives and characters lie hidden from nations in the annals that record them.—*The Cloister and the Hearth*, Charles Reade, 1861.

4455 The heroic deeds of highlanders, both in these islands and elsewhere, have been told in verse and prose, and not more often, nor more loudly, than they deserve. But we must remember, now and then, that there have been heroes likewise in the lowland and in the fen.—*Hereward the Wake*, Charles Kingsley, 1866.

4456 There lived a man in the south, before Thangbrand, Wilibald's son, preached the White Christ in Iceland. He was named Eric Brighteyes, Thorgrimur's son, and in those days there

was no man like him for strength, beauty and daring, for in all these things he was the first. — *Eric Brighteyes*, H. Rider Haggard, 1891.

4457 A hundred years had passed since Natas, the Master of the Terror, had given into the hands of Richard Arnold his charge to the future generations of the Aerians—as the descendants of the Terrorists who had colonised the mountain-walled valley of Aeria, in Central Africa, were now called; since the man, who had planned and accomplished the greatest revolution in the history of the world, had given his last blessing to his companions-in-arms and their children, and had "turned his face to the wall and died." — *Olga Romanoff*, George Griffith, 1894.

4458 You do very well, my friends, to treat me with some little reverence, for in honouring me you are honouring both France and yourselves. — *The Exploits of Brigadier Gerard*, Arthur Conan Doyle, 1896.

4459 Like the Israelites of old, mankind is prone to worship false gods, and persistently sets up the brazen image of a sham hero, as its idol. — *Yolanda*, Charles Major, 1905.

4460 At the time when the celebrated Doc Macnooder, that amateur practitioner, but most professional financier, first dawned upon the school, he found the Tennessee Shad the admiration and the envy of the multitude. — *The Tennessee Shad*, Owen Johnson, 1911.

4461 When this story begins, Elizabeth Ann, who is the heroine of it, was a little girl of nine, who lived with her Great-aunt Harriet in a medium-sized city in a medium-sized State in the middle of this country; and that's all you need to know about the place, for it's not the important thing in the story; and anyhow you know all about it because it was probably very much like the place you live in yourself. — *Understood Betsy*, Dorothy Canfield Fisher, 1917.

4462 I first heard of Ántonia on what seemed to me an interminable journey across the great midland plain of North America. — *My Ántonia*, Willa Cather, 1918.

4463 Odysseus was ten years getting home from Troy. Homer made a hero out of him, the type of those who, though tossed about by waves of ocean or of fate, are resourceful and patient. Homer was his best friend. — *Penelope's Man*, John Erskine, 1928.

4464 Paul Bunyan is the unequaled hero of American outdoor history. — *The Saginaw Paul Bunyan*, James Stevens, 1932.

4465 "Aunt Bee," said Jane, breathing heavily into her soup, "was Noah a cleverer back-room boy than Ulysses, or was Ulysses a cleverer back-room boy than Noah?" — *Brat Farrar*, Elizabeth Mackintosh *as* Josephine Tey, 1949.

4466 Later he was to be famous and hon-oured throughout the South Caribbean; he was to be a hero of the people and after that, a British representative at Lake Success. — *The Mystic Masseur*, V. S. Naipaul, 1957.

4467 When I think of all the grey memorials erected in London to equestrian generals, the heroes of old colonial wars, and to frock-coated politicians who are even more deeply forgotten, I can find no reason to mock the modest stone that commemorates Jones on the far side of the international road which he failed to cross in a country far from home, though I am not to this day absolutely sure of where, geographically speaking, Jones's home lay. — *The Comedians*, Graham Greene, 1966.

4468 If I had been the hero everyone thought I was, or even a half-decent soldier, Lee would have won the battle of Gettysburg and probably captured Washington. That is another story, which I shall set down in its proper place if brandy and old age don't carry me off first, but I mention the fact here because it shows how great events are decided by trifles — *Royal Flash*, George MacDonald Fraser, 1970.

4469 . . . I was with him at Actium, when the sword struck fire from metal, and the blood of soldiers was awash on deck and stained the blue Ionian Sea, and the javelin whistled in the air, and the burning hulls hissed upon the water, and the day was loud with the screams of men whose flesh roasted in the armor they could not fling off; and earlier I was with him at Mutina, where that same Marcus Antonius overran our camp and the sword was thrust into the empty bed where Caesar Augustus had lain, and where we persevered and earned the first power that was to give us the world; and at Philippi, where he traveled so ill he could not stand and yet made himself to be carried among his troops in a litter, and came near death again by the murderer of his father, and where he fought until the murderers of the mortal Julius, who became a god, were destroyed by their own hands. — *Augustus*, John Williams, 1972.

4470 *Beginning A/* Captain Jarvis was a popular hero about the middle of 1902, on account of his celebrated march to Daji./ *Beginning B/* Jarvis, called on account of his beak and of something a little bantam-like in his character, Cock Jarvis, was Resident of Daji Province in Nigeria from the time when it was conquered and organised, by himself, in 1907, until 1921 when Daji was one of the provinces scheduled for abolition. — *Cock Jarvis (Unfinished)*, Joyce Cary, 1975.

4471 Afraid to go, afraid not to go, was that characteristic of a man who believes himself to be a hero in the making? — *The Common Wilderness*, Michael Seide, 1982.

4472 The hero came into the kitchen with a lurch. — *Under the Apple Tree*, Dan Wakefield, 1982.

4473 I was barely adolescent when I first encountered Larry Peters, the eponymous hero of a series of books called, collectively, The Adventures of Larry Peters. — "Call Me Larry," Eric Kraft, 1985.

4474 If Homer had been a woman she would have struck her lyre, stamped her feet to the cadence of the verse and sung of the deathless exploits of Alice Morell. — *Sweet Alice*, Coral Lansbury, 1986.

Hiding

4475 One morning in early May, when the wind was cold and the sun hot, and Jerome about twelve years old, he was in a favorite lurking-place of his, which nobody but himself knew. —*Jerome, A Poor Man*, Mary E. Wilkins Freeman, 1897.

4476 "Hannele!"/ "Ja--a."/ "Wo bist du?"/ "Hier."/ "Wo dann?" — *The Captain's Doll*, D. H. Lawrence, 1923.

4477 Many years passed. Hidden in a room on the river front Fantazius Mallare became a myth to his friends. — *The Kingdom of Evil*, Ben Hecht, 1924.

4478 From the summit, the searchlight spread upon the Constitutionalists as they sought shelter among the rocks on the extended promontory. — *The Fifth Horseman*, José Antonio Villarreal, 1974.

4479 Can a human being hide? — *Gala*, Paul West, 1976.

4480 Mira was hiding in the ladies' room. — *The Women's Room*, Marilyn French, 1977.

4481 After the death of General Franco, the Spanish dictator, a secret people emerged from hiding; after forty years of self-imposed imprisonment, they came from cellars and attics, caves in the mountains. — *To Slay the Dreamer*, Alexander Cordell, 1980.

4482 Voss lay on his back in the rowboat, not in the center, where he would have been visible from the hilltop, but braced with elbow and knee far to the high side as possible. — *Perimeters*, Helena Harlow Worthen, 1980.

4483 The men were hiding in the hills. — *The Flowers of the Forest*, Ruth Doan MacDougall, 1981.

4484 Papa visited me last night. I am thinking that I may have to hide now. — *The Journal of Nicholas the American*, Leigh Kennedy, 1986.

4485 Again, as in a recurring dream, Mason opened the closet door and stepped hesitantly into its huge darkness, its nonlineal shape: he pulled the door shut then crouched there on the floor — which seemed to be moving — with the breathing of The Impostor. — *My Amputations*, Clarence Major, 1986.

4486 We rode across the hillocks and vales of Missouri, hiding in uniforms of Yankee blue. — *Woe to Live On*, Daniel Woodrell, 1987.

4487 As a boy my brother Lawrence was always hiding. — *Blue River*, Ethan Canin, 1991.

4488 We waited just on the other side of the hedge where Grammy couldn't see us until he came out. — *Words of My Roaring*, Ernest J. Finney, 1993.

History

4489 As it is necessary that all great and surprising events, the designs of which are laid, conducted, and brought to perfection by the utmost force of human invention and art, should be produced by great and eminent men, so the lives of such may be justly and properly styled the quintessence of history. —*Jonathan Wild*, Henry Fielding, 1743.

4490 Cardinal de Retz very judiciously observes, that all historians must of necessity be subject to mistakes, in explaining the motives of those actions they record, unless they derive their intelligence from the candid confession of the person whose character they represent; and that, of consequence, every man of importance ought to write his own memoirs, provided he has honesty enough to tell the truth, without suppressing any circumstance that may tend to the information of the reader. — *Ferdinand Count Fathom*, Tobias Smollett, 1753.

4491 All true histories contain instruction; though, in some, the treasure may be hard to find, and, when found, so trivial in quantity, that the dry, shrivelled kernel scarcely compensates for the trouble of cracking the nut. — *Agnes Grey*, Anne Brontë, 1847.

4492 With a single drop of ink for a mirror, the Egyptian sorcerer undertakes to reveal to any chance comer far-reaching visions of the past. This is what I undertake to do for you, reader. — *Adam Bede*, George Eliot, 1859.

4493 It is a curious thing that at my age — I shall never see sixty again — I should find myself taking up a pen to try to write a history. I wonder what sort of a history it will be when I have finished it, if ever I come to the end of the trip! — *King Solomon's Mines*, H. Rider Haggard, 1885.

4494 The recesses of the desolate Libyan mountains that lie behind the temple and city of Abydus, the supposed burying place of the Holy Osiris, a tomb was recently discovered, among the contents of which were the papyrus rolls whereon this history is written. — *Cleopatra*, H. Rider Haggard, 1889.

4495 All my life I have had an awareness of other times and places. — *The Star Rover*, Jack London, 1915.

4496 Observe now your own epoch of history as it appears to the Last Men./ Long before the human spirit awoke to clear cognizance of the world and itself, it sometimes stirred in its sleep, opened bewildered eyes, and slept again. — *Last and First Men*, Olaf Stapledon, 1931.

4497 Great events, says the philosophic historian, spring only from great causes, though the immediate occasion may be small; but I think his law must have exceptions. — *The House of the Four Winds*, John Buchan, 1935.

4498 What don't we know about the Early Nineteen Hundreds. — *The Rising Tide*, Molly Keane *as* M. J. Farrell, 1937.

4499 I, Agabus the Decapolitan, began this work at Alexandria in the ninth year of the Emperor Domitian and completed it at Rome in the thirteenth year of the same. — *King Jesus*, Robert Graves, 1946.

4500 A story as complex as this has no obvious starting point; neither am I able to follow Colonel Spencer's suggestion of "beginning at the beginning and going on to the end," since history has a habit of meandering. — *The Mind Parasites*, Colin Wilson, 1967.

4501 *History has the relation to truth that theology has to religion — i.e., none to speak of.* — *Time Enough for Love*, Robert A. Heinlein, 1973.

4502 That we may be better acquainted with our colony of New Spain, of its peculiarities, its riches, the people who possessed it, and the beliefs, rites, and ceremonies which they heretofore held, we wish to be informed of all matters appertaining to the Indians during their existence in that land before the coming of our liberating forces, ambassadors, evangels, and colonizers. — *Aztec*, Gary Jennings, 1980.

4503 I am blind. But I am not deaf. Because of the incompleteness of my misfortune, I was obliged yesterday to listen for nearly six hours to a self-styled historian whose account of what the Athenians like to call "the Persian Wars" was nonsense of a sort that were I less old and more privileged, I would have risen in my seat at the Odeon and scandalized all Athens by answering him. — *Creation*, Gore Vidal, 1981.

4504 "The forces of history wrestle with each other like drunken strangers in a Turkish bath." From memory. Like a man talking in his sleep.

— *Quitting Time*, Leonard Kriegel, 1982.

4505 Two Virgins dominate the history of Mexico. — *The Children of the Sun*, Oakley Hall, 1983.

4506 The first part is a summing-up of about four years. — *The Diary of a Good Neighbour*, Doris Lessing *as* Jane Somers, 1983.

4507 I had thought that the technical means of preserving sight and sound would preserve the record of evil, and it has, but only for the victims. The evildoers seem to have been flattened against the curving wall of history. — *A Special Destiny*, Seymour Epstein, 1986.

4508 "I'm writing a history of the world," she says. And the hands of the nurse are arrested for a moment; she looks down at this old woman, this old ill woman. — *Moon Tiger*, Penelope Lively, 1987.

4509 It was Doctor Kaiserstiege who said that the world would perish because the accumulating traumas of human history were poisoning the human soul, just as morphine saturates the lungs and lunar caustic collects in deposits of metallic silver beneath the skin. — *The Fountains of Neptune*, Rikki Ducornet, 1989.

4510 History. Lived, not written, is such a thing not to understand always, but to marvel over. Time is so forever that life has many instances when you can say "Once upon a time" thousands of times in one life. — *Family*, J. California Cooper, 1991.

4511 "Shortest damned commission in naval history, I'll be bound," Alan Lewrie commented to his dining companions at Gloster's Hotel and Chop-House in Piccadilly. — *The King's Privateer*, Dewey Lambdin, 1992.

Holidays

4512 "Christmas won't be Christmas without any presents," grumbled Jo, lying on the rug. — *Little Women*, Louisa May Alcott, 1868.

4513 The Little King, destined to become the great King, Louis Le Grand, of France, had always found Christmas a dull day. — *The Little King*, Charles Major, 1910.

4514 The city was getting ready for Easter. Karl Erlich saw rows of white candles tipped with yellow flames in many windows. — *Time No Longer*, Taylor Caldwell, 1941.

4515 Yes, sir, here's the Glorious Fourth again. — *Raintree County*, Ross Lockridge, Jr., 1948.

4516 *New Orleans, La., New Year's Day:/* Playtime is over, and I am damned glad that is so. — *Playtime Is Over*, Clyde Brion Davis, 1949.

4517 It was noon on Easter Monday 1916 in the city of Dublin. O'Connell Street was crowded with people on holiday. — *Insurrection*, Liam O'Flaherty, 1950.

4518 It was Heroes Day in Piemburg and as usual the little capital of Zululand was quite unwarrantably gay. — *Indecent Exposure*, Tom Sharpe, 1973.

4519 By one o'clock on Christmas Day we were full up with food and fed up with visiting relatives. — *No More into the Garden*, David Watmough, 1978.

4520 It was always a great day when the Christmas tree was brought into the house. The fresh smell of pine needles in the winter rooms; the excitement of unwrapping the sparkling glass ornaments from the tissue paper in which they had been so carefully packed eleven months before; the warm waxy smell as the tiny red corkscrew candles flicker for the first time in their scalloped holders. — *The Christmas Tree*, Jennifer Johnston, 1981.

4521 It all came to a head in a couple of months, really, those two months ten years ago now when the town prepared for and then dismissed its barbaric Christmas. — *An Item from the Late News*, Thea Astley, 1982.

4522 At the very top of the tree — which is full, and thick, and green, and artificial — an old and fragile angel perches. — *Victim of Love*, Dyan Sheldon, 1982.

4523 It was Mother's Day and they were all watching The Bad Czech. — *The Delta Star*, Joseph Wambaugh, 1983.

4524 It was the first day of the new year according to the Jewish calendar, an ordinary Thursday for all the world. — *Vertical Hold*, Laurel Bauer, 1986.

4525 Holiday time. The image of perfection, once a year. — *A Fragile Peace*, Jonellen Heckler, 1986.

4526 On the Fourth of July, Hugh agrees to drive out to Mrs. LaMonte's house to get "the explosives," as he likes to call them. — *First Light*, Charles Baxter, 1987.

4527 If Holy Week and Passover hadn't fallen at the same time the year I was born, none of this would have happened. — *The Memoirs of Christopher Columbus*, Stephen Marlowe, 1987.

4528 It was Christmas Eve in Paris. — *Redemption*, Tariz Ali, 1990.

4529 "Promise me, Kate, that you won't let this ruin Christmas." — *Home Free*, Elizabeth Forsythe Hailey, 1991.

4530 All through June Daisy had been looking forward to the holidays when she would have Will and Tom and Janey and Essie and Beth and Weenie to herself. — *11 Edward Street*, Clare Boylan, 1992.

4531 *It's Christmastime at the Opryland Hotel, and you never saw anything like it!* — *The Devil's Dream*, Lee Smith, 1992.

4532 I am standing on Shultz Hill at six o'clock in the morning: Labor Day. — *Upstate*, Sallie Bingham, 1993.

Home

4533 I am the native of a sea-surrounded nook, a cloud-enshadowed land, which, when the surface of the globe, with its shoreless ocean and trackless continents, presents itself to my mind, appears only as an inconsiderable speck in the immense whole; and yet, when balanced in the scale of mental power, far outweighed countries of larger extent and more numerous population. — *The Last Man*, Mary Wollstonecraft Shelley, 1826.

4534 Ours was the prairie district, out West, where we had gone to grow up with the country. — *The Story of a Country Town*, Edgar Watson Howe, 1883.

4535 I stood on board the liner halted in midstream and looked upon Japan, my native land. But let me say at once that I am not a Japanese. I am very much a European. — *The Polyglots*, William Gerhardie, 1925.

4536 All the time you've been away from a town where you lived when you were a kid, you think about it and talk about it as if the air there were sweeter in the nostrils than other air. — *Blue City*, Kenneth Millar, 1947.

4537 It was four o'clock of a spring evening; and Robert Blair was thinking of going home. — *The Franchise Affair*, Elizabeth Mackintosh *as* Josephine Tey, 1948.

4538 Jessie Stillwell had purposely lost her way home, but sometimes she found herself there, innocent of the fact that she had taken to her heels long ago and was still running. — *Occasion for Loving*, Nadine Gordimer, 1963.

4539 That afternoon I had been walking with my son in what for me were familiar streets, streets of the town where I was born. — *The Sleep of Reason*, C. P. Snow, 1968.

4540 "Do you never want to go back?" — *A Card from Morocco*, Robert Shaw, 1969.

4541 They say you can never go home again, and I suppose in a sense that's true. — *Bright Candles*, Nathaniel Benchley, 1974.

4542 Dear Octavio,/ I am writing this letter on the theory that someday you will return to Primevera to explore your background. — *Birthplace*, William S. Wilson, 1982.

4543 Jacey Burdette was born in Hawaii, but he was a southerner nonetheless. — *Canaan*, Charlie Smith, 1984.

4544 For Manon, Louisiana was the end of the world, France's Siberia, and so, on some days, did it also seem to Mrs. Coco, who fancied herself an exile of sorts, even though Brookhaven, Mississippi, where she was born and where her brother and sister still lived, was only an hour's drive north. — *North Gladiola*, James Wilcox, 1985.

4545 Henderson's people lived in London. — *Mrs. Henderson*, Francis Wyndham, 1985.

4546 Our teacher Miss Turner was from Hugo, Texas, the home of Rogers "The Rajah" Hornsby. — *The Patch Boys*, Jay Parini, 1986.

4547 It was twenty years since Bertram Francis had last seen the island of his birth. — *A State of Independence*, Caryl Phillips, 1986.

4548 Learning the other ways into Nodd's Ridge, the back roads, takes a lifetime of living there. — *Pearl*, Tabitha King, 1988.

4549 Seeing Colorado from space was like looking back with new uncertainty on a place you've known forever but have never understood. — *Beautiful Islands*, Russell Martin, 1988.

4550 It is 1971, and the home that has been provided for Sarah Pollexfen for so long is still a provision that is necessary — *The Silence in the Garden*, William Trevor, 1988.

4551 Mamie Beaver, she had to come from the moon. — *The Book of Mamie*, Duff Brenna, 1989.

4552 Home is where you go for Christmas, Catherine thought, but she wondered what "home" meant. — *Everlasting*, Nancy Thayer, 1991.

4553 I come from Tokyo, I do. — *Salaryman*, Meg Pei, 1992.

Homecoming

4554 In the minority of Henry the Sixth, King of England, when the renowned John, Duke of Bedford, was Regent of France, and Humphry, the good Duke of Gloucester, was Protector of England, a worthy knight, called Sir Philip Harclay, returned from his travels to England, his native country. — *The Old English Baron*, Clara Reeve, 1778.

4555 When Mr. Effingham determined to return home, he sent orders to his agent to prepare his town-house in New York for his reception, intending to pass a month or two in it, then to repair to Washington for a few weeks, at the close of its season, and to visit his country resi-

dence when the spring should fairly open. — *Home as Found*, James Fenimore Cooper, 1838.

4556 Mr. Horatio Pulcifer was on his way home. — *Galusha the Magnificent*, Joseph C. Lincoln, 1921.

4557 For Jocelyn, on this June evening, the road she loved so much, the road around the great friendly lake toward their own friendly house, Derrymore Manor, was a tragedy more than a delight. — *Field of Honor*, Donn Byrne, 1929.

4558 It was in June of 1935 that I came home from my ranch in South America for a stay of about six months. — *The A.B.C. Murders*, Agatha Christie, 1936.

4559 New York had fetched out of the sunlit blue one of those gilded mornings that cause people disembarking from a southern cruise to wonder why they had ever dreaded their return home on March first. — *Love Passed This Way*, Martha Ostenso, 1942.

4560 It was the close of day when a boat touched Rodney's Landing on the Mississippi River and Clement Musgrove, an innocent planter, with a bag of gold and many presents, disembarked. — *The Robber Bridegroom*, Eudora Welty, 1942.

4561 It was not the home-coming of his dreams; but then so many dreams had come to nothing in the past three years. — *Roger Sudden*, Thomas H. Raddall, 1944.

4562 It was more than four years since Maurice Whiteoak had left his native land and now he was once again within its borders. — *Return to Jalna*, Mazo de la Roche, 1946.

4563 Through the late afternoon they flew southeast, going home to Ocanara at about two hundred miles an hour. — *Guard of Honor*, James Gould Cozzens, 1948.

4564 Elizabeth got out of the limousine and spoke to the chauffeur./ "Pick up Mr. Wayne at the office as usual, Walter," she said. "I don't think we'll be going out tonight. With my son coming home so soon..." — *A Light in the Window*, Mary Roberts Rinehart, 1948.

4565 Looking back to that summer day, when they had landed in England — like Pilgrims in reverse, he had pointed out to Perdita and Sonia, but they had been too excited to reply — he made no bones about admitting that at first he had felt no sensation of coming home. — *Family Trouble*, William McFee, 1949.

4566 William Felice was nineteen when he came back from Dunkirk. — "Novelette," A. L. Barker, 1951.

4567 When Charles Blagden Lillywhite, born in Somerset, 1873, resident in France since 1900, finally returned to England in 1946, the news of his repatriation did not arouse any strong family

enthusiasm. — *Lise Lillywhite*, Margery Sharp, 1951.

4568 Stephen Worth was going home for Christmas. — *Bright Procession*, Pearl S. Buck *as* John Sedges, 1952.

4569 At long last in early June the Gordons were expected home at Dene's Court, the house in Ireland which Violet Dene Gordon had inherited. — *A Shower of Summer Days*, May Sarton, 1952.

4570 Walter Mosca felt a sense of excitement and the last overwhelming loneliness before a homecoming. — *The Dark Arena*, Mario Puzo, 1955.

4571 It was a February afternoon of smoky sunshine, as I walked home along the Embankment to my wife. — *Homecomings*, C. P. Snow, 1956.

4572 For seven days the man who lived by the Western Sea had driven eastward toward the place where he was born, and every day he asked himself the same question. Why had he come? — *The Waters of Kronos*, Conrad Richter, 1960.

4573 To come home again is strange. And the truth of the matter is — you can't. — *Gillian*, Frank Yerby, 1960.

4574 I had to come home for my sister's wedding. Home is a house in Warwickshire, and where I was coming from was Paris. — *A Summer Bird-Cage*, Margaret Drabble, 1962.

4575 Benjamin Braddock graduated from a small Eastern college on a day in June. Then he flew home. — *The Graduate*, Charles Webb, 1963.

4576 The day after I met her I flew back to London. I'd promised Harriet to be home for the Friday evening. — *After the Act*, Winston Graham, 1965.

4577 To Athené then./ Young Gnossos Pappadopoulis, furry Pooh Bear, keeper of the flame, voyaged back from the asphalt seas of the great wasted land: oh highways U.S. 40 and unyielding 66, I am home to the glacier-gnawed gorges, the fingers of lakes, the golden girls of Westchester and Shaker Heights. See me loud with lies, big boots stomping, mind awash with schemes. — *Been Down So Long It Looks Like Up to Me*, Richard Fariña, 1966.

4578 Coming back to London was like waking out of a dream; at the time, it had all been real, but opening your eyes, it had gone; Rome, Claudio, everything. — *A Roman Marriage*, Brian Glanville, 1966.

4579 All the way home on the train my hands were shaking a lot but I pulled out the book I had bought at the station and opened it anyway, and tried to pretend that this was any other vacation and I was just going home. — *Something in the Wind*, Lee Smith, 1971.

4580 I flew home from Mazatlán on a Wednesday afternoon. As we approached Los Angeles, the Mexicana plane dropped low over the sea and I caught my first glimpse of the oil spill. — *Sleeping Beauty*, Ross Macdonald, 1973.

4581 Now it is the autumn again; the people are all coming back. — *The History Man*, Malcolm Bradbury, 1975.

4582 I suppose if something big is to be felt when you leave a place you love, then something bigger it should be when you go back, though standing here, all I feel is a drift of wonder beyond words or any telling. — *Green, Green My Valley Now*, Richard Llewellyn, 1975.

4583 His Royal and Religious Highness Crown Prince Ulrich of Evarchia returned to the Winter Palace unrepentant. — *Palace Without Chairs*, Brigid Brophy, 1978.

4584 When Ian returns to the Big House, it is for the first time in years. — *Sherbrookes*, Nicholas Delbanco, 1978.

4585 I lost an arm on my last trip home. — *Kindred*, Octavia E. Butler, 1979.

4586 Dewey got out of the penitentiary on a Friday, but it took him until the following Monday to get home. — *Mean Time*, Christopher T. Leland, 1982.

4587 Aberlady Bay./ The ship rounding the harbor and coming into full view of the cone-shaped hill of North Berwick Law, her mother and father waving to her from the shore, the cool fresh breeze of Archerfield on her face, peaceful Scottish woods, fields of autumn grass frolicking along the golden sand, endless ribbons of tern and gull zooming quietly over the sky. — *Lord Elgin's Lady*, Theodore Vrettos, 1982.

4588 John Washington was flying home to see his father and the woman his father loved. — *On Common Ground*, Deena Linett, 1983.

4589 There was, for Lizzie, a sense of discovery — no, of homecoming. — *Lizzie*, Evan Hunter, 1984.

4590 It wasn't that David Larson returned home from Vietnam to find that his girl had taken up with another man; he didn't have a girl when he left. — *Walk Me to the Distance*, Percival Everett, 1985.

4591 My dear boy,/ I write to you not with a renewed request that you return to your native land, for when you comprehend the matter I am about to relate, you will want to fly at the earliest moment; however, I must prepare you for what awaits you here. — *Palais-Royal*, Richard Sennett, 1986.

4592 Yesterday noon at the end of the Watch of the Fifth Ruler of the Day my lord the Captain came home to this his city — if the arrival of a box of dry bones from Spain can be called a homecoming. — *Death of the Fifth Sun*, Robert Somerlott, 1987.

4593 The somewhat veiled look of that portion of his daughter's face Ben Morrison could see as she embraced her mother, and the way her one visible eye searched his face, suggested at once that he and Lucky hadn't come home to simple continuity. — *Statutes of Limitations*, Monroe Engel, 1988.

4594 I came home on the last train. — *The Swimming-Pool Library*, Alan Hollinghurst, 1988.

4595 When I came back to Sunbury, toward the end of May, one of the first people I met uptown was Cousin Tune. — "Farewell, Summer," Helen Hooven Santmyer, 1988.

4596 A fine Saturday morning in late September 1940, and Ella was playing the half-shift from the mill because her husband was coming home on a weekend pass. — *Give Us This Day*, Stan Barstow, 1989.

4597 In July 1939 I arrived home from boarding school to find that Veronica had come to live with us. — *Veronica*, David Caute, 1989.

4598 I am living once again in the town where I grew up, having returned here several weeks ago in a state of dull torment for which the Germans probably have a word. — *All New People*, Anne Lamott, 1989.

4599 When Jimmy Hong got into the backseat of the taxi at Beijing Airport, he reached for his wife's hand. "Welcome home, Do Do," he said, holding her hand tightly with both of his. — *Gate of Rage*, C. Y. Lee, 1991.

4600 There is probably no greater anxiety in life than going home to visit your mother for Christmas. — *Doin' the Box Step*, Suzanne Falter-Barns, 1992.

4601 Last night I returned to Forest County from a two-year stint in the Army. — *Divine Days*, Leon Forrest, 1992.

4602 Zareen Ginwalla hurried into the hall when the bell rang, waved the cook who had popped out back into the kitchen, and opened the portals of their home to her husband. — *An American Brat*, Bapsi Sidhwa, 1993.

Hope

4603 Ye who listen with credulity to the whispers of fancy, and persue with eagerness the phantoms of hope; who expect that age will perform the promises of youth, and that the deficiencies of the present day will be supplied by the morrow; attend to the history of Rasselas prince of Abissinia. — *Rasselas*, Samuel Johnson, 1759.

4604 In the autumn of 1816, John Melmoth, a student in Trinity College, Dublin, quitted it to attend a dying uncle on whom his hopes for independence chiefly rested. — *Melmoth the Wanderer*, Charles Robert Maturin, 1820.

4605 "Then you offer me no hope, Doctor?" — *54-40 or Fight*, Emerson Hough, 1909.

4606 The sight of a third porter, this time a gentle-looking man carrying a pile of pillows and coming slowly, filled her with hope. But he passed on his way as heedless as the others. — *Oberland*, Dorothy M. Richardson, 1927.

4607 In their despair men must hope, when a promise is given, though it be only a promise. — *The Promise*, Pearl S. Buck, 1943.

4608 Pardon me for interrupting whatever it is that you might better be doing just now. Having got this far, I hope to grow on you. — *Tenement of Clay*, Paul West, 1965.

4609 This morning I have some hope of reaching the petition windows. — *My Petition for More Space*, John Hersey, 1974.

4610 At first there had been the breath of hot new life across the land, blowing like a summer wind from the Black Hills to the Missouri, making the People alive again, even when their bellies were only half-filled with corn and flour gravy. — *A Creek Called Wounded Knee*, Douglas C. Jones, 1978.

4611 In her mid-forties, Adrienne Ziegler believed she would find a man. — *Female Complaints*, Leslie Tonner, 1982.

4612 There are times when the word *hope* is but a synonym for *illusion*: it is the most virile of perils. — *A Casual Brutality*, Neil Bissoondath, 1988.

4613 I had hoped to remain unturned, but it was not to be. — *The Comforts of Madness*, Paul Sayer, 1988.

Hospitals

4614 The patient, an old-fashioned man, thought the nurse made a mistake in keeping both of the windows open, and her sprightly disregard of his protests added something to his hatred of her. — *Alice Adams*, Booth Tarkington, 1921.

4615 It was beginning to drizzle again as he walked out of the hospital grounds past the large illuminated face of the clock which said — he could not believe it was the same day — that it was not even seven. What had been the hurry? — *Of Mortal Love*, William Gerhardie, 1925.

4616 To be arriving at a shell-shock hospital in a state of unmilitant defiance of military

authority was an experience peculiar enough to stimulate my speculations about the immediate future. — *Sherston's Progress*, Siegfried Sassoon, 1936.

4617 Approaching the smart Hauptman Clinic off Wilshire Boulevard, one is sure to be struck by the estate's breadth and purity of line. — *Flash and Filigree*, Terry Southern, 1958.

4618 The hospital of Rhodes squats on the hill that rises to be Monte Smith. — *The Martlet's Tale*, Nicholas Delbanco, 1966.

4619 There were two waiting rooms for the visitors, so at least we weren't cluttering up their nice clean corridor outside the Intensive Care Unit. — *Such Good Friends*, Lois Gould, 1970.

4620 I was sitting up in bed, sipping hot coffee, when the nurse came into the room. The English girl with the big tits. — *The Betsy*, Harold Robbins, 1971.

4621 They came down to the emergency ward at noon and sat on the bench just behind the swinging doors that led in from the ambulance parking slot. — *The Terminal Man*, Michael Crichton, 1972.

4622 The important thing to remember when first confronted by the solid wall of the Leprosarium is that it was built, not to prevent our D & D (Deviation and Dismemberment Policies) clients from being seen, but from seeing others. — *The Leprosarium*, Natalie L. M. Petesch, 1978.

4623 It had been a quiet night in the emergency room except for the battle with the three-hundred-pound man. — *The Healers*, Gerald Green, 1979.

4624 Oliver Thompson entered the doctors' lounge of Mount Zion Hospital. — *The Scheme of Things*, Allen Wheelis, 1980.

4625 Despite the pains in her chest, Catherine walked through the hospital Emergency doors under her own power, and saw first, to her left, a man kneeling before a small girl. — *The Last Great Love*, Marilyn Harris, 1981.

4626 They brought her into the middle of our ward by the hand, like a child, and left her standing in the hallway, staring around like somebody's smart little dog. — *Bird-Eyes*, Madelyn Arnold, 1988.

4627 Alta Buena Hospital occupies one square block in the center of a residential neighborhood, convenient for the rest of the city but inconvenient for its neighbors, with the parking problems it brings, and its fortresslike shape of reinforced concrete casting shadows on neighboring gardens of privet and struggling geranium. — *Health and Happiness*, Diane Johnson, 1990.

4628 Before slipping him into his hospital gown, the nurses arranged his Arthur Murray

jewelry on the stainless steel night-stand. — *The Magic Step*, John Dranow, 1991.

4629 Pearly and I were half of the Red Cross Unit at Cu Chi. — *Flower Shadows*, Terry Farish, 1992.

Hotels and Motels

4630 The "Golden Star," Homburg, was a humble hotel, not used by gay gamblers, but by modest travellers. — *A Woman-Hater*, Charles Reade, 1877.

4631 On the pleasant shore of the French Riviera, about half way between Marseilles and the Italian border, stands a large, proud, rose-colored hotel. — *Tender Is the Night*, F. Scott Fitzgerald, 1934.

4632 The flat roof of the American House, the most spacious and important hotel in Black Thread Center, Connecticut, was lined with sheets of red-painted tin, each embossed with "Phoenix, the Tin of Kings." — *Work of Art*, Sinclair Lewis, 1934.

4633 They were in the Hotel Lotti in the Rue de Castiglione, but not in Léon's usual suite. — *House of All Nations*, Christina Stead, 1938.

4634 It's all wrong, Frances thought, looking around the fairly comfortable hotel room. A luxury hotel, on the intimate side — canaries singing, rock-garden in the lobby, complete with waterfall, some such charming nonsense would have been in the pattern of her life; a dump would be the unpredictable in Cousin Adah; but this middle ground — the commonplace — this run-of-the-mill was out — or should have been. — *Judd Rankin's Daughter*, Susan Glaspell, 1945.

4635 Djuna is lying down in a cell-shaped room of the tallest hotel in the City, in a building shooting upward like a railroad track set for the moon. — *The Voice*, Anaïs Nin, 1948.

4636 Lanny Budd, arriving in Paris in the middle of November 1944, was driven through pelting rain to the Crillon, a sumptuous hotel which was history to him, and also biography from his earliest days. — *O Shepherd, Speak!*, Upton Sinclair, 1949.

4637 On the thirty-first of October, which is to say on All Hallows' Eve, in the year 1949, Lucifer checked into the Hotel Pierre, in New York. — *The Innocent Eye*, Robert Nathan, 1951.

4638 The desk at the Grand Hotel in Bombay was crowded with incoming guests. — *Come, My Beloved*, Pearl S. Buck, 1953.

4639 It was a small hotel with eight or nine bedrooms and loch and sea fishing, the kind of

place that had the same guests season after season. — *The Other Landscape*, Neil M. Gunn, 1954.

4640 The hotel was freezing cold. I told Piney tell somebody send up some heat when he went for the mail, but he either never told anybody or else nobody listened. — *A Ticket for a Seamstitch*, Mark Harris, 1957.

4641 One evening last spring Scotty Bowman, the bank manager, was on Peel Street, standing at the lighted entrance of the Mount Royal Hotel. — *The Many Colored Coat*, Morley Callaghan, 1960.

4642 The hotel stationery was Wedgwood blue like the wallpaper, delicately embossed with a gold crest and a motto, *In virtu vinci*, a nice thought, whatever it meant, for a hotel. — *The Golden Spur*, Dawn Powell, 1962.

4643 On a hot February day, in the port town of Ganado Bay in the island of Jamaica in the Caribbean Sea, two white Americans stood by the side of an old, dilapidated hotel's deserted and dilapidated saltwater swimming pool. — *Go to the Widow-Maker*, James Jones, 1967.

4644 It was the end of a wet Monday afternoon in autumn. Professor Cosmo Saltana and Dr. Owen Tuby were sitting in the Small Lounge of Robinson's Hotel, Bayswater, London W.2. Robinson's is one of the city's few remaining good old-fashioned hotels, known to several generations of visitors for its quaint inconveniences and quiet discomfort. — *Out of Town*, J. B. Priestley, 1968.

4645 In those days the Majestic was still standing in Kilnalough at the very end of a slim peninsula covered with dead pines leaning here and there at odd angles. — *Troubles*, J. G. Farrell, 1970.

4646 The Catelli-Continental Hotel on Chowringhee Avenue, Calcutta, is the navel of the universe. — *The Tiger's Daughter*, Bharati Mukherjee, 1972.

4647 Every evening, before the hour of sunset, Princess, the young maidservant, starts to light the lamps in the hotel: oil lamps, long glass funnels enclosed in brass containers with handles. — *A Sea-Grape Tree*, Rosamond Lehmann, 1976.

4648 Someone says: "Motels. I like motels. I wish I owned a chain, worldwide. I'd like to go from one to another to another. There's something self-realizing about that." — *Players*, Don DeLillo, 1977.

4649 He watched my hand slide across the page as I signed a false name and address in the hotel register. — *Nelly's Version*, Eva Figes, 1977.

4650 Any number of uniformed flunkies at the Ritz Hotel might have gone from table to table in the bar to make the discreet announcements in those hushed tones reserved for the departure of an international aircraft from Lisbon. — *The Valkyrie Encounter*, Stephen Marlowe, 1978.

4651 The telephone in his bedroom purred discreetly: it was that kind of an hotel. — *West of Sunset*, Dirk Bogarde, 1984.

4652 The Rivoli Hotel backed into the boardwalk like a huge, white paddle-wheel steamer that was trying desperately to return to the ocean and instead had hit a bridge. — *The Golden Age Hotel*, David Lewis Stein, 1984.

4653 They were living at le Grau du Roi then and the hotel was on a canal that ran from the walled city of Aigues Mortes straight down to the sea. — *The Garden of Eden*, Ernest Hemingway, 1986.

4654 Besides the Empire State Building and the Statue of Liberty, the only other place in New York that she knew anything about was the Waldorf-Astoria. — *Love Affair*, Syrell Rogovin Leahy, 1986.

4655 Leaner turned on the air conditioner in the motel room before carrying in his suitcase and golf clubs. — *The Greening of Thurmond Leaner*, Michael Zagst, 1986.

4656 1: I write this on the first day of the last summer I — or anyone — will spend at the Aurora Sands Hotel. — *The Telling of Lies*, Timothy Findley, 1988.

4657 I am on this bed in a cheap motel listening to the growl of the Gulf. — *Loving Women*, Pete Hamill, 1989.

4658 Chapel checked into the usual hotel just after dark. — *For Love of the Game*, Michael Shaara, 1991.

4659 On a snow-swept January evening of 1991, Jonathan Pine, the English night manager of the Hotel Meister Palace in Zurich, forsook his office behind the reception desk and, in the grip of feelings he had not known before, took up his position in the lobby as a prelude to extending his hotel's welcome to a distinguished late arrival. — *The Night Manager*, John Le Carré, 1993.

Humor

4660 Ernest Verdun Mott thought it was dead funny, how a blanket over bent knees, with the sun on it, gets like a lot of little grey trees growing over a couple of smooth mountains, with hundreds of camp fires all along the top burning curly hairs of light. Beyond where the sun had took a clip of his shears along the shadows, thousands of them there little flashing white bits fell out of the dark part and rolled

about in the light, just floating round, they was, turning over and over, regardless as a shower of millionaires. — *None But the Lonely Heart*, Richard Llewellyn, 1943.

4661 When matters, events, or people bored or exhausted or troubled Dr. Francis Stevens, he would retire mentally to a pleasant place where he could reflect on the fact that he so closely resembled Francis Cardinal Spellman that it had become an affectionate joke between him and his friend. — *Tender Victory*, Taylor Caldwell, 1956.

4662 "The last rowers of summer." The younger man looked pointedly towards the lake, flirtatious eyes slanting the joke. — *The Humbler Creation*, Pamela Hansford Johnson, 1959.

4663 "What you've always got to remember about those chaps," Gunter said, "is that they've got no sense of humor. Absolutely none. . . ." — *Making Good Again*, Lionel Davidson, 1968.

4664 It was one of those nights./ One of life's little jokes./ Life's jokes are hardly ever funny, because you're usually the punch line. — *Someplace Safe*, Greg Herriges, 1984.

4665 Last year while he was passing through a crisis in his life my Uncle Benn (B. Crader, the well-known botanist) showed me a cartoon by Charles Addams. — *More Die of Heartbreak*, Saul Bellow, 1987.

4666 Let me tell you a joke. — *A Woman's Guide to Adultery*, Carol Clewlow, 1989.

4667 It had all started as something completely innocuous, a joke in a bar and some tough talk, and now the three men sat in the truck overlooking the school, a knee-deep pile of ducks and three shotguns in back. — *The Snake Game*, Wayne Johnson, 1990.

Hunger and Thirst

4668 Magister Nicholas Udal, the Lady Mary's pedagogue, was very hungry and very cold. — *The Fifth Queen*, Ford Madox Ford, 1906.

4669 Nureddin was hungry. — *The Sea of the Ravens*, Harold Lamb, 1927.

4670 On a Friday in April, Penrod Schofield, having returned from school at noon promptly, on account of an earnest appetite, found lunch considerably delayed and himself (after a bit of simple technique) alone in the pantry with a large, open, metal receptacle containing about two-thirds of a peck of perfect doughnuts just come into the world. — *Penrod Jashber*, Booth Tarkington, 1929.

4671 There is such a thing as hunger for more than food, and that was the hunger I fed on. — *Portrait of Jennie*, Robert Nathan, 1940.

4672 "I want a drink," the boy said./ "Me, too," the girl said./ "Well, we're almost there," the man said. "When we get there you can drink all you want." — *The Laughing Matter*, William Saroyan, 1953.

4673 Two young Indians paused at the edge of the Rio del Norte and bellied down to drink. — *Taos*, Irwin R. Blacker, 1959.

4674 The Royal Canadian Air Force North Star was forty-five minutes out of Dorval when its captain, a young flight looey with a boyish face and a middle-aged paunch, began having visions of steak again. — *The Atonement of Ashley Morden*, Fred Bodsworth, 1964.

4675 The year was 1872, the town was Manchester, North Carolina, and the boy was fourteen years old. His name was Oren Knox. He was hungry. — *The Tobacco Men*, Borden Deal, 1965.

4676 It is afterall a way of beginning. To have never quite enough so hunger grows faster than appetites and satisfaction never comes. — *A Glance Away*, John Edgar Wideman, 1967.

4677 Ye Lui himself met Psin at the door and walked behind him into the anteroom. Psin looked around at the shimmer of the silk hangings and the gold filigree and sat down. "I'm hungry." — *Until the Sun Falls*, Cecelia Holland, 1969.

4678 He stood at the back gateway of the abattoir, his hands thrust into his pockets, his stomach rigid with the ache of want. — *Cal*, Bernard MacLaverty, 1983.

4679 Like an army of ten thousand ghostly spears, smoke from the cooking fires of Toledo rose in the dark evening air; and from his perch on the stone wall Avram Halevi could feel his belly respond to this chorus of roasting food. — *The Spanish Doctor*, Matt Cohen, 1984.

4680 All day we'd been roaming the flooded fields for food. — *The Heroic Age*, Stratis Haviaras, 1984.

4681 "How soon will lunch be ready?" my father would ask. — *The Other Garden*, Francis Wyndham, 1987.

4682 Once again the People were fleeing on a road of hunger. — *Panther in the Sky*, James Alexander Thom, 1989.

Hunting and Fishing

4683 What true-bred city sportsman has not in his day put off the most urgent business — perhaps his marriage, or even the interment of

his rib—that he might "brave the morn" with that renowned pack, the Surrey subscription foxhounds?—*Jorrocks' Jaunts and Jollities*, Robert Smith Surtees, 1838.

4684 The cave had been their hiding-place as children; it was a secret refuge now against hunger or darkness when they were hunting in the woods.—*A Cumberland Vendetta*, John Fox, Jr., 1895.

4685 Though a score of Indians, Nazis, pythons, Zulus and midget Japanese aircraft had been shattered by Tom's index and middle finger, his grandfather had shot nothing.—*For Want of a Nail*, Melvyn Bragg, 1965.

4686 Olumba was in his reception hall mending some fish-traps.—*The Great Ponds*, Elechi Amadi, 1969.

4687 We spent days along the Wawanash River, helping Uncle Benny fish.—*Lives of Girls and Women*, Alice Munro, 1971.

4688 He stands at the rear of the rowboat casting toward a green rubbery beach of lily pads thirty feet away.—*Lunar Attractions*, Clark Blaise, 1979.

4689 "What do you think would happen," Colonel Theodore Roosevelt asked his son Kermit, "if I shot an elephant in the balls?"—*An Ice-Cream War*, William Boyd, 1982.

4690 Thomas Dunn, the head ghillie at the Castle, wasn't telling Father Declan anything he didn't already know: the river too high and wild from all the rains, and the salmon, therefore, not moving, just lying on the bottom, not showing themselves at all, and the midges terrible, and only the two days left to the season so of course all but the least desirable of the river-beats, number Four, was let already; "and Frank and Peter'll be ghillieing of the Americans stayin' at the Castle, Father, so I'll have to give you Seamus O'Conner and he's hardly worth the pay and that on top of the twenty pounds for the beat and you know yourself, Father, how beat Four is after a rainfall such as we've been having, the piers awash and the banks slippery as grease...."—*The All of It*, Jeannette Haien, 1986.

4691 The ice was still going off the river in bobbing tiles and platters when Cecil Roop hooked a snapping turtle as big as a saddle, using a rabbit's foot for bait.—*Seven Rivers West*, Edward Hoagland, 1986.

4692 I'm fishing.—*The Getbacks of Mother Superior*, Dennis Lehman, 1987.

4693 Dick Pierce swung the bait barrel off his wharf into his work skiff.—*Spartina*, John Casey, 1989.

4694 Texas summer morning, the softly bleak hour after dawn, the boy Harold and his father slowly hunted across a vast scrub-brush tumbleweed field, toward a mist-seeping river-bottom grove in the middle distance—Harold, at twelve, carrying his old single-shot twenty, and his father the twelve-gauge double with the Magnum-load.—*Texas Summer*, Terry Southern, 1991.

4695 The hunters burst silently out of the trees and ran along the narrow trail that led beside the shore of the small mountain spring.—*Daughter of the Red Deer*, Joan Wolf, 1991.

Ideas

4696 I had taken Mrs. Prest into my confidence; without her in truth I should have made but little advance, for the fruitful idea in the whole business dropped from her friendly lips.—"The Aspern Papers," Henry James, 1888.

4697 It all came to me one election day.—*John Barleycorn*, Jack London, 1913.

4698 A young man who had arrived uninvited from France lay under the green slate roof of the verandah perfecting the idea he had suggested to his hosts, that, if he had not come, they would have sent for him.—*Death of Felicity Taverner*, Mary Butts, 1932.

4699 The idea really came to me the day I got my new false teeth.—*Coming Up for Air*, George Orwell, 1939.

4700 "What *are* ideers?" said Mr. Edward Albert Tewler. "What *good* are they? What *good* do they do you?"/ Young Tewler had no answer.—*You Can't Be Too Careful*, H. G. Wells, 1942.

4701 Some voyages have their inception in the blueprint of a dream, some in the urgency of contradicting a dream.—*Seduction of the Minotaur*, Anaïs Nin, 1961.

4702 The idea for the six-day bike race came out of a meeting held in November, in Brooklyn, in the offices of Anthony Pastrumo, Sr.—*The Gang That Couldn't Shoot Straight*, Jimmy Breslin, 1969.

4703 It was seeing Jack Pryden that afternoon, after so many years, that gave me the idea of going to see old Baldur Blake, the sculptor.—*Baldur's Gate*, Eleanor Clark, 1970.

4704 Paul Denis remembered, though long after, while he talked to Bilara, that he thought he saw the idea in form and substance, opening behind his eyes almost as a blossom of light, standing that noon in hot Israeli sunshine, sniffing pinescent, watching a sunray flinging miles of diamonds in the Mediterranean's blue, praying for strength to do as he dreamed, sure in his soul that he could and in gentlest way ready to laugh aloud up at an eagle flashing gold burnish in black wings.—*A Hill of Many Dreams*, Richard Llewellyn, 1974.

4705 *Brewster Place was the bastard child of several clandestine meetings between the alderman of the sixth district and the managing director of Unico Realty Company.* — *The Women of Brewster Place*, Gloria Naylor, 1982.

4706 A few minutes before his brainstorm, or whatever it was, took place, George McCaffrey was having a quarrel with his wife. — *The Philosopher's Pupil*, Iris Murdoch, 1983.

4707 I have to admit it was Mrs. Biersdorf's — Eve's — idea. — *My Search for Warren Harding*, Robert Plunket, 1983.

4708 At Christmas-time in my sixth year, 1958, a revelation occurred to me on the third floor of Harrods, in the toy department. — *Winter Journey*, Ronald Frame, 1984.

4709 Eddy Bale took his idea to the Empire Children's Fund, to Children's Relief, to the Youth Emergency Committee. — *The Magic Kingdom*, Stanley Elkin, 1985.

4710 When she was finally crazy because she was about to have an abortion, she conceived of the most insane idea that any woman can think of. — *Don Quixote*, Kathy Acker, 1986.

4711 In retrospect, perhaps, getting into his half sister's mutton was not the brightest idea that Alan Lewrie had ever had. — *The King's Coat*, Dewey Lambdin, 1989.

4712 I've noticed over the years that Truly Bad Ideas, like flu strains named for Asian capitals, insidiously time their visits to occur during those periods when our defenses, reeling from some previous blow, are at their most tattered and flimsy. — *Putting on the Ritz*, Joe Keenan, 1991.

Identity

4713 Call me Ishmael. — *Moby Dick*, Herman Melville, 1851.

4714 My father's family name being Pirrip, and my christian name Philip, my infant tongue could make of both names nothing longer or more explicit than Pip. So I called myself Pip, and came to be called Pip. — *Great Expectations*, Charles Dickens, 1861.

4715 "TOM!" — *Tom Sawyer*, Mark Twain, 1876.

4716 "Wal, I 'clar, now, jes de quarest ting ob 'bout all dis matter o' freedom is de way dat it sloshes roun' de names 'mong us cullud folks...." — *Bricks Without Straw*, Albion W. Tourgée, 1880.

4717 "Where shall I sign my name?" — *Taquisara*, F. Marion Crawford, 1895.

4718 "My name is Eagle," said the little girl. — *Lazarre*, Mary Hartwell Catherwood, 1901.

4719 My uncle's name was Thomas Andrew William Addison. His father and mother had three girls and only one boy, so they said they would give him as many names as a boy could stand, to make up, in a manner, for his deficiency in number. — *Uncle Tom Andy Bill*, Charles Major, 1908.

4720 Honora Leffingwell is the original name of our heroine. — *A Modern Chronicle*, Winston Churchill, 1910.

4721 In the beginning he was Christopher Bellew. By the time he was at college he had become Chris Bellew. Later, in the Bohemian crowd of San Francisco, he was called Kit Bellew. And in the end he was known by no other name than Smoke Bellew. — *Smoke Bellew*, Jack London, 1912.

4722 Father calls me Mary. Mother calls me Marie. Everybody else calls me Mary Marie. The rest of my name is Anderson. — *Mary Marie*, Eleanor H. Porter, 1920.

4723 My name is J. Poindexter. But the full name is Jefferson Exodus Poindexter, Colored. But most always in general I has been known as Jeff, for short. — *J. Poindexter, Colored*, Irvin S. Cobb, 1922.

4724 The two girls were usually known by their surnames, Banford and March. — "The Fox," D. H. Lawrence, 1923.

4725 Until he was almost ten the name stuck to him. — *So Big*, Edna Ferber, 1924.

4726 "JAMES LEWIS MACFARLANE."/ The bearer of this name swung his feet to the floor and sat up suddenly, cupping his big hands over his knees to steady himself. — *The Keeper of the Bees*, Gene Stratton-Porter, 1925.

4727 Bizarre as was the name she bore, Kim Ravenal always said she was thankful it had been no worse. — *Show Boat*, Edna Ferber, 1926.

4728 His name wasn't Barnacle at all, nor was his Christian name Barnaby. But that is what his intimates called him, in college and out, — and not, it must be said, without some measure of glorification. — *Blades*, George Barr McCutcheon, 1928.

4729 "What is your name?"/ "Dana Hilliot, ordinary seaman." — *Ultramarine*, Malcolm Lowry, 1933.

4730 One of the stewards of the big Atlantic liner pushed his way among the passengers to a young lady who was leaning alone against the taffrail. "Mrs. Vance Weston?" — *The Gods Arrive*, Edith Wharton, 1933.

4731 By the third day out they were asking aboard the gigantic *Britannique*, Europe bound: "Who is Hiram Holliday?" or "Has anyone seen this M'sieu Holliday?" — *Adventures of Hiram Holliday*, Paul Gallico, 1939.

4732 The American boy's name was Lanning Budd; people called him Lanny, an agreeable name, easy to say. — *World's End*, Upton Sinclair, 1940.

4733 His name is John Sidney Howard, and he is a member of my club in London. — *Pied Piper*, Nevil Shute, 1942.

4734 His real name was Henry Dellicker, but for fifty years Pennsylvania knew him as Henry Free — or Frey, as he was called in the dialect. — *The Free Man*, Conrad Richter, 1943.

4735 "Mr. Isherwood?"/ "Speaking."/ "Mr. Christopher Isherwood?"/ "That's me." — *Prater Violet*, Christopher Isherwood, 1945.

4736 My name is Wesley Jackson, I'm nineteen years old, and my favorite song is *Valencia*. — *The Adventures of Wesley Jackson*, William Saroyan, 1946.

4737 He was to be known in his lifetime by at least seven different names, four of them within his first four years. — *Diamond Wedding*, Wilbur Daniel Steele, 1950.

4738 His name was Gaal Dornick and he was just a country boy who had never seen Trantor before. — *Foundation*, Isaac Asimov, 1951.

4739 "Mrs. Silverthrone, Miss Peabody, Mrs. Longstreet, Miss Whiteleather, Dr. Goodnight, Miss Vile, Colonel Birdwhistle, Captain Rainbird," Heeralal droned on, reading from his collection of odd English names, "Miss Wardrobe, Mrs. Stammers, Major Kneebone, Dr. Death, Dr. Blood, Dr. Slaughter, Mr. Still, Miss Stiff, Mrs. Quickly." — *Music for Mohini*, Bhabani Bhattacharya, 1952.

4740 There was a boy called Eustace Clarence Scrubb, and he almost deserved it. — *The Voyage of the* Dawn Treader, C. S. Lewis, 1952.

4741 From time immemorial people seemed to have been calling him "Margayya." No one knew, except his father and mother, who were only dimly recollected by a few cronies in his ancestral village, that he had been named after the enchanting god Krishna. — *The Financial Expert*, R. K. Narayan, 1952.

4742 They called him Roshan because his first cry was heard just as the light of a new day stretched long, pale fingers over the thatched roofs of The Village. — *House of Earth*, Dorothy Clarke Wilson, 1952.

4743 Fond parents often name their timid shrimp of a boy Warrior King or Brave in Battle. Hefty, pitch-dark girls go through life with the label Lightning Streak or Lotus Wreath. — *He Who Rides a Tiger*, Bhabani Bhattacharya, 1954.

4744 Grandfather did not like to be called "Grandfather," he liked to be called "Pall Mall"; but his elder grandchildren had shortened the name to the one word Pall, and consequently this was the syllable which came most readily to John Blaydon's mind at the sight of him or of anything connected with him. — *Brotherly Love*, Gabriel Fielding, 1954.

4745 My name is Edward G. Richardson and I am a commander in the Navy, skipper of the submarine Eel. — *Run Silent, Run Deep*, Edward L. Beach, 1955.

4746 Oh, who am I? — *Band of Angels*, Robert Penn Warren, 1955.

4747 We called him Old Yeller. — *Old Yeller*, Fred Gipson, 1956.

4748 My name was Rebecca Fowler. — *The Believers*, Janice Holt Giles, 1957.

4749 Abe Fielding/ Abraham Fielding/ Abraham K. Fielding/ What is the K for?/ Why? — *A Winter's Love*, Madeleine L'Engle, 1957.

4750 "Who is John Galt?" — *Atlas Shrugged*, Ayn Rand, 1957.

4751 In a sense, I am Jacob Horner. — *The End of the Road*, John Barth, 1958.

4752 It is, or would be if one bothered to think about it, a well-known fact that there are far more surnames than Christian names. — *Close Quarters*, Angela Thirkell, 1958.

4753 Little Oscar, Ma Larkin's seventh, to whom she hoped in due course to give a real proper ribbon of names, probably calling him after some famous explorer, admiral, or Roman Emperor, or even the whole lot, lay in his lavish silvery pram in the kitchen, looking remarkably like a very soft, very large apple dumpling that has been slightly overboiled. — *A Breath of French Air*, H. E. Bates, 1959.

4754 Her first name was India — she was never able to get used to it. — *Mrs. Bridge*, Evan S. Connell, 1959.

4755 "Your name Ian Ferguson?" — *The Land God Gave to Cain*, Hammond Innes, 1959.

4756 In babyhood and boyhood I was called Ambrose. — *The Pagan King*, Edison Marshall, 1959.

4757 "The name's Mekles," Jerry Wilton said. "Nicholas Mekles. You must have heard of him." — *The Pipe Dream*, Julian Symons, 1959.

4758 Who knows Miss Rosamond Lacey? — *Come with Me Home*, Gladys Hasty Carroll, 1960.

4759 Once upon a time there was a Martian named Valentine Michael Smith. — *Stranger in a Strange Land*, Robert A. Heinlein, 1961.

4760 When the miller Harmen Gerritszoon added "van Rijn" to his name, it was not to make himself sound like a person of consequence. He began to use the name of the river because there were so many Harmens and Gerrits, and with new mills springing up in the windy city of Leyden, it became advisable for him to indicate on his sacks that brewers who wanted more of his finely ground malt could depend on getting it from that particular Harmen, son of Gerrit,

whose mill was on the bank of the Rhine. — *Rembrandt*, Gladys Schmitt, 1961.

4761 "Your name, please?" — *The Final Deduction*, Rex Stout, 1961.

4762 My name is Howard W. Campbell, Jr./ I am an American by birth, a Nazi by reputation, and a nationless person by inclination. — *Mother Night*, Kurt Vonnegut, 1962.

4763 His name was Edward Arthur Ryan, and in July of 1926, he was twenty-two years old. — *The Silence of History*, James T. Farrell, 1963.

4764 My nickname in the Foreign Service is "the Drill-Pig." — *Smith and Jones*, Nicholas Monsarrat, 1963.

4765 Call me Jonah. My parents did, or nearly did. They called me John. — *Cat's Cradle*, Kurt Vonnegut, 1963.

4766 My name is Martyn Sutton. — *The Lost Colony*, Edison Marshall, 1964.

4767 "And it's Miss Smith, isn't it? Christine Smith. Do forgive me, but we've had so many replies, and quite a lot of them were Smiths. Your letter is on that table somewhere, but—" — *The Charmers*, Stella Gibbons, 1965.

4768 George is my name; my deeds have been heard of in Tower Hall, and my childhood has been chronicled in the *Journal of Experimental Psychology*. — *Giles Goat-Boy*, John Barth, 1966.

4769 Let me introduce myself./ My name is Rose Bavistock. I am a spinster, now in my middle fifties; but this story begins five years ago. — *Omar*, Wilfrid Blunt, 1966.

4770 My name is Wendy. — *I Want What I Want*, Geoff Brown, 1966.

4771 Catherine Tekakwitha, who are you? Are you (1656–1680)? Is that enough? Are you the Iroquois Virgin? Are you the Lily of the Shores of the Mohawk River? Can I love you in my own way? — *Beautiful Losers*, Leonard Cohen, 1966.

4772 Her name, apparently, was Mary. Apparently, I said to myself, because nobody is compelled to give her real name—or his real name. I lay in bed, looked at her, and wondered who she was. — *John and Mary*, Mervyn Jones, 1966.

4773 She had been christened Jane Pickthorn, and the name suited her. She was built on large lines, her features rough, her character prickly, and the whole effect that of a melancholy prehistoric animal. — *Miss Pickthorn and Mr. Hare*, May Sarton, 1966.

4774 My name is Rose. I was called after a distant cousin of my mother's whom she admired because she had married well. — *A Logical Girl*, Gerda Charles, 1967.

4775 Clara never failed to be astonished by the extraordinary felicity of her own name. — *Jerusalem the Golden*, Margaret Drabble, 1967.

4776 Some days my name is Mrs. Blood; some days it's Mrs. Thing. — *Mrs. Blood*, Audrey Thomas, 1967.

4777 My name is Gerda Shaffer./ My name is Mrs. Alec Shaffer, née Osborn./ Giddy Osborn. Giddy Gerda, sister of Judy the Prudy. (I am not sure any longer what I am called. Those names belong to someone who existed before I was born.) — *Children at the Gate*, Lynne Reid Banks, 1968.

4778 Pibble thought, I am the chosen vulture spiraling down onto a dying lion. — *The Old English Peep Show*, Peter Dickinson, 1969.

4779 HORN it said. Someone had scrawled it in black marker on the back of my seat. — *Horn*, D. Keith Mano, 1969.

4780 Once there was a brother and sister, and their names were Tobit and Judith. Their mother had named them after two books in the Bible, and their father, who was quiet, amused, and who rarely said anything, had not objected. — *A Walk Out of the World*, Ruth Nichols, 1969.

4781 "I'm Ivy Eckdorf," said Mrs. Eckdorf as the aeroplane rose from the ground. "How d'you do?" — *Mrs. Eckdorf in O'Neill's Hotel*, William Trevor, 1969.

4782 "Julius King."/ "You speak his name as if you were meditating upon it." — *A Fairly Honourable Defeat*, Iris Murdoch, 1970.

4783 It was I who christened my mother's lover. — *Love Child*, Maureen Duffy, 1971.

4784 VITA; DICK'S LOG:/ When Dick Gibson was a little boy he was not Dick Gibson. — *The Dick Gibson Show*, Stanley Elkin, 1971.

4785 Miss Nora O'Neill, usually called Tiddyboo for good and sufficient reasons, was carrying the silver cage with the big yellow cat in it. — *The View from Chivo*, H. Allen Smith, 1971.

4786 I am Turnlung. — *Daughter Buffalo*, Janet Frame, 1972.

4787 "What is your name?"/ "Clemence Dumas."/ "French?"/ "Half French."/ "You must call me m'lady, when you reply."/ "I'm sorry, m'lady." — *Upstairs, Downstairs*, John Hawkesworth, 1972.

4788 My name is Asher Lev, *the* Asher Lev, about whom you have read in newspapers and magazines, about whom you talk so much at your dinner affairs and cocktail parties, the notorious and legendary Lev of the *Brooklyn Crucifixion*. — *My Name Is Asher Lev*, Chaim Potok, 1972.

4789 I have white skin. Light brown hair. Blue eyes. I am tall: five feet, eleven inches. My mode of dress tends to the conservative: sports jacket, corduroy trousers, knitted ties. I wear spectacles for reading, though they are more an affectation than a necessity. I smoke cigarettes to

a moderate amount. Sometimes I drink alcohol. I do not believe in God; I do not go to church; I do not have any objections to other people doing so. When I married my wife, I was in love with her. I am very fond of my daughter Sally. I have no political ambitions. My name is Alan Whitman. — *Darkening Island*, Christopher Priest, 1972.

4790 "Sadie! Sadie Jackson!" — *Across the Barricades*, Joan Lingard, 1973.

4791 Call me Smitty. — *The Great American Novel*, Philip Roth, 1973.

4792 I look at myself in the mirror. I know that I was christened Clementine, and so it would make sense if people called me Clem, or even, come to think of it, Clementine, since that's my name: but they don't. People call me Tish. — *If Beale Street Could Talk*, James Baldwin, 1974.

4793 For the record, call me Marvin Molar. I said to call me Marvin Molar because that's not my real name. It's only what I call myself. I don't know my real name. — *The Gypsy's Curse*, Harry Crews, 1974.

4794 "Shotgun Coen." — *Blue Eyes*, Jerome Charyn, 1975.

4795 "*Permettez-moi de vous présénter Sam McGuire*," Charles says. — *Chilly Scenes of Winter*, Ann Beattie, 1976.

1796 *Who were they?* The names are known — Adam Mantoor and Elisabeth Larsson — and something of their history has been recorded. — *An Instant in the Wind*, André Brink, 1976.

4797 The American girl who called herself Victoria and no longer answered to a last name followed two armed men down a shale slope in the Guerrero mountains. — *Hoyt's Child*, R. V. Cassill, 1976.

4798 Call me Russel Wren. — *Who Is Teddy Villanova?*, Thomas Berger, 1977.

4799 "Isaac," he said. "Marmaduke. Which of the two do you more seem to yourself to be?" — *Abba Abba*, Anthony Burgess, 1977.

4800 Mother of myself, myself I sing: lord of loners, duke of dreams, king of the clowns. Youth and death I sing, sunbeams and moonbeams, laws and breakers of laws. I, Arthur Grumm, lover and killer. — *Portrait of a Romantic*, Steven Millhauser, 1977.

4801 Her name was not really Fanny Cornforth. — *Willowwood*, Elizabeth Savage, 1978.

4802 Jacaranda's name was pronounced "Jack-ah-*ran*-dah," as in jack-o'-*lan*-tern, the same rhythm. — *Sex and Rage*, Eve Babitz, 1979.

4803 "It was bleeding Adolf, wasn't it?" the private said. — *Fools Paradise*, Christopher Leopold, 1979.

4804 Out of all the futile activity of her day, only these moments made sense, when behind the discretion of a small white lace mask, she could forget the muddle of who she was and what she was. — *The Women of Eden*, Marilyn Harris, 1980.

4805 Lesser men had invented the name the world knew them by: *Comanche*. — *The Wolf and the Buffalo*, Elmer Kelton, 1980.

4806 Jackie never did like his real name — Andre Ezekiel Preston Montgomery. — *Gnawing at My Soul*, Kip Branch, 1981.

4807 I'm Bell Teesdale. I'm a lad. I'm eight. — *The Hollow Land*, Jane Gardam, 1981.

4808 Felicitas Maria Taylor was called after the one virgin martyr whose name contained some hope for ordinary human happiness. — *The Company of Women*, Mary Gordon, 1981.

4809 This much I know for sure:/ My name is Peter Sinclair, I am English and I am, or I was, twenty-nine years old. Already there is an uncertainty, and my sureness recedes. Age is a variable; I am no longer twenty-nine. — *The Affirmation*, Christopher Priest, 1981.

4810 — You./ The very old man chewed his lip./ — You. Is it really? *Shema. In God's Name.* Look at you. Look at you now. You. The one out of hell. — *The Portage to San Cristóbal of A. H.*, George Steiner, 1981.

4811 *Who was she?/* As she grew out of childhood into girlhood, the question became increasingly perplexing, baffling, disturbing. — *Lincoln's Mothers*, Dorothy Clarke Wilson, 1981.

4812 Kitty Maul was difficult to place. — *Providence*, Anita Brookner, 1982.

4813 Last time we were in here together, Jesús Rivera decided I was Jesse James. — *Sounding the Territory*, Laurel Goldman, 1982.

4814 Niki, the name we finally gave my younger daughter, is not an abbreviation; it was a compromise I reached with her father. — *A Pale View of Hills*, Kazuo Ishiguro, 1982.

4815 Call me Isabel. — *When Sisterhood Was in Flower*, Florence King, 1982.

4816 Groundhog Day was his birthday, Venus his star, and though he was called a number of names not his own, he always answered to the call of Jesse. — *Hero Jesse*, Lawrence Millman, 1982.

4817 His name was Presley Bivens. — *Summer Crossing*, Steve Tesich, 1982.

4818 I am Grim Fiddle. — *The Birth of the People's Republic of Antarctica*, John Calvin Batchelor, 1983.

4819 Pilgermann here. I call myself Pilgermann, it's a convenience. — *Pilgermann*, Russell Hoban, 1983.

4820 The documentation of Augustus Walmer is slight. — *The Proprietor*, Ann Schlee, 1983.

4821 Bernadette Woolley was aware that her name was professionally inappropriate. — *Scandal*, A. N. Wilson, 1983.

4822 When See-ho-kee was a small girl, she asked her grandmother a question. "Who am I?" — *Say These Names (Remember Them)*, Betty Sue Cummings, 1984.

4823 My name is Karl Russell and I'm an optimist. — *Mysterious Ways*, Terry Davis, 1984.

4824 He was named after a prominent Virginia family. — *Last One Home*, John Ehle, 1984.

4825 *I am Ann Rogers Clark. My blood's flowed across this land like rivers, from sea to sea.* — *From Sea to Shining Sea*, James Alexander Thom, 1984.

4826 My name has always been Russel Wren. — *Nowhere*, Thomas Berger, 1985.

4827 My name is Herbert Badgery. — *Illywhacker*, Peter Carey, 1985.

4828 Andrew Mavis here, goddamn. — *Dogwood Afternoons*, Kim Chapin, 1985.

4829 Hello Diary,/ My name is Niall Bruce and I am seven years and seven days old. — *What Niall Saw*, Brian Cullen, 1985.

4830 "Who's the broad?" asked Mumford. He had never told me he was a Bogart fan. — *Beef Wellington Blue*, Max Davidson, 1985.

4831 "Speke," I said, "Ivor Speke." And I spelled it. — *Blood for Blood*, Julian Gloag, 1985.

4832 That was the first time she heard the name of Michael Taverner. — *Ringarra*, Coral Lansbury, 1985.

4833 My name is Luke Wakefield, and I am a failure. — *Mr. Wakefield's Crusade*, Bernice Rubens, 1985.

4834 *Who was I before all this happened? I am trying to remember.* — *Almost Japanese*, Sarah Sheard, 1985.

4835 "Mr. Masterson?"/ Bat cocks an eye. — *The Old Colts*, Glendon Swarthout, 1985.

4836 I am what I remember. Nothing else. — *Star Turn*, Nigel Williams, 1985.

4837 My name is Frank Bascombe. I am a sportswriter. — *The Sportswriter*, Richard Ford, 1986.

4838 I am Polly Flint. — *Crusoe's Daughter*, Jane Gardam, 1986.

4839 They call me Talkative Man. — *Talkative Man*, R. K. Narayan, 1986.

4840 I am the widow called Baby. — *Baby Houston*, June Arnold, 1987.

4841 Somewhere in this world there exists an exceptional philosopher named Florie Rotondo. — *Answered Prayers*, Truman Capote, 1987.

4842 Somewhere along the journey the girl shed one name and emerged under the other. — *A Sport of Nature*, Nadine Gordimer, 1987.

4843 They called him "Lucky." — "Black Swan," Christopher Hope, 1987.

4844 I am a fifty-eight-year-old provincial. — "Nights at the Alexandra," William Trevor, 1987.

4845 *Henry . . . ?, The Fool's Progress*, Edward Abbey, 1988.

4846 Dear Sunny:/ I love your name. — *The Last of the True Believers*, Ann Birstein, 1988.

4847 You can call me Holder. — *Saigon, Illinois*, Paul Hoover, 1988.

4848 I have always used my maiden name. — *Midnight Sweets*, Bette Pesetsky, 1988.

4849 The girl I meet at the dance club Spit, across from Fenway Park, won't tell me her name. — *The Illustrator*, James Robison, 1988.

4850 My dear Hanneke,/ Your name is not much common here, I think it is so pretty too. I say it now and agin it tastes sweet in my mouth like honey or cane or how I picture the fotched-on candy from Mrs. Browns book about France, candy which mimicks roses. — *Fair and Tender Ladies*, Lee Smith, 1988.

4851 I wish it was simple just to say who I am, just to say my name is so-and-so and that makes you think of a certain kind of person and that would be me. — *The Deuce*, Robert Olen Butler, 1989.

4852 My name is Elizabeth Cole. — *Elizabeth Cole*, Susan Cheever, 1989.

4853 Imagine naming a kid Adonis, Heaven, or Solomon, Misha, Jethro, Huatlán, Wolfgang, Chamunda, Gaia, singling the kid out like that in a world of Jims, Johns and Jennifers. — *Green Bananas*, Michael Drinkard, 1989.

4854 Recently I think I became someone else. — *Self-Portrait of Someone Else*, Vincent Eaton, 1989.

4855 She was christened Gwendolen. — *The Family*, Buchi Emecheta, 1989.

4856 I am Rachel Levin. — *A Place at the Table*, Edith Konecky, 1989.

4857 *My name is Dinah. It is a desert name.* — *What Dinah Thought*, Deena Metzger, 1989.

4858 It was not 1959. It was not a cold November. It was not a small college town in New York, and he was not twenty-one. In fact, he was not even David Bennett. — *Bennett's Angel*, Barton A. Midwood, 1989.

4859 He was born Zeev Zali — that is the name on his birth-registration papers and it is written clearly, without smudge or error. — *Middlepost*, Antony Sher, 1989.

4860 My name is Jordan. — *Sexing the Cherry*, Jeanette Winterson, 1989.

4861 "See there! It's Launcelot!" — *The King*, Donald Barthelme, 1990.

4862 My name is Andrea. — *Mercy*, Andrea Dworkin, 1990.

4863 *A is for Achitophel.* — *Zulus*, Percival Everett, 1990.

4864 My name is Karim Amir, and I am an Englishman born and bred, almost. — *The Buddha of Suburbia*, Hanif Kureishi, 1990.

4865 My name is Eugene Debs Hartke, and

I was born in 1940. — *Hocus Pocus*, Kurt Vonnegut, 1990.

4866 Let us just think for a moment then who I am. — *The Summer of the Royal Visit*, Isabel Colegate, 1991.

4867 To Whom It May Concern — / I was The Green Ray. — *Further Adventures*, Jon Stephen Fink, 1991.

4868 I must face the fact that you will have forgotten who I am. — *The Second Bridegroom*, Rodney Hall, 1991.

4869 Before diving right into Alan Lewrie's latest naval adventure (if one may do so without besmirching one's own fine sense of honor by exposing it to such a rogue), it might be a good idea to discover just exactly who in the hell this Alan Lewrie character was. — *The King's Commission*, Dewey Lambdin, 1991.

4870 It is not easy to introduce myself. — *My House in Umbria*, William Trevor, 1991.

4871 Born from a pelvis that was blue with cold, and later swept southward to the darker green pastures of the Midlands, Annie Elizabeth Crook had sometimes heard her name pronounced as Cook, she knew not why, but concluded it all had to do with a change in the wind from up to down. — *The Women of Whitechapel and Jack the Ripper*, Paul West, 1991.

4872 My name is Rhoda Manning and I am a writer. — *Net of Jewels*, Ellen Gilchrist, 1992.

4873 Testing. Testing. Emily Shaw here. Caseworker 1766. — *Graced Land*, Laura Kalpakian, 1992.

4874 My name is Michael Householder. I'm an ordinary, average kind of guy. — *My Life as a Whale*, Dyan Sheldon, 1992.

4875 My name is Jordan Lerner. — *Wonders of the West*, Kate Braverman, 1993.

4876 Elizabeth Bean Mastracola: Head Mother, as one of the always-embattled guidance people called her; The Bitch to several generations of high school boys whom she drove with all but spurs, whip and electric prod through to their implausible graduation; also named Sweetie by the fifteen-year-old mothers whom she counseled, calling them that as they dropped out of school to raise their babies proudly for a while in rural-slum mobile home or sweat- and tinderbox apartment three blocks and all of their lives from school. — *Long Way from Home*, Frederick Busch, 1993.

4877 I am Flowers of the delta clan Flowers and the line of O Killens — I am hoodoo, I am griot, I am a man of power. — *Another Good Loving Blues*, Arthur Flowers, 1993.

4878 Ekaterina you were, and you were not at all. — *Ekaterina*, Donald Harington, 1993.

4879 *Killian*, he said aloud./ This hurt when he did it. He tried it again: *Killian, Killian, Kil-*

lian. — *A Portrait of My Desire*, MacDonald Harris, 1993.

4880 We are all Giulias, the girls in our family, named, as a sign of respect and according to tradition, after our grandmother Nonna Giulia. — *The Courtyard of Dreams*, Anna Monardo, 1993.

Ignorance

4881 "East? They wouldn't know the bloody East if they saw it. . . ." *Time for a Tiger*, Anthony Burgess, 1956.

4882 You never know, that's all, there's no way of knowing. — *The Shadow Knows*, Diane Johnson, 1974.

4883 The immigrants were without any deep consciousness of the role they were playing. — *The Immigrants*, Howard Fast, 1977.

4884 It is hard to tell what something you are part of is really like; it is the way you cannot see a picture if you are in it looking out. — *Painted Dresses*, Shelby Hearon, 1981.

4885 Because he knew nothing about horses. — *George Mills*, Stanley Elkin, 1982.

4886 I have no idea of the extent of this zoo. — *A Tiger for Malgudi*, R. K. Narayan, 1983.

4887 People drown in San Francisco Bay every year because of their ignorance of the ocean. — *The Sea Within*, Louise Murphy, 1985.

Imagination

4888 To a great majority of persons having the good fortune to possess an imagination, princesses as a class are exceedingly attractive. — *A Gentle Knight of Old Brandenburg*, Charles Major, 1909.

4889 MY BELOVED BOY:/ Your last brought great comfort to an anxious mother's heart. When your usual Sunday letter did not arrive I began to imagine all sorts of foolish things. — *Bricks Without Straw*, Charles G. Norris, 1938.

4890 In the dry places, men begin to dream. — *The Works of Love*, Wright Morris, 1952.

4891 Willis Wayde, before he went to sleep, could shut his eyes and see every detail of the Harcourt place. — *Sincerely, Willis Wayde*, John P. Marquand, 1955.

4892 John Foraday had always been quiet and imaginative, and this was the only fault his grandmother had found in him. — *Below the Salt*, Thomas B. Costain, 1957.

4893 Accept the illusion. Night. Mexico. The immense, rife stillness of a village in the Mictlán hills... — *Going Down*, David Markson, 1970.

4894 I keep thinking that I have a tunnel in my chest. — *After the First Death*, Robert Cormier, 1979.

4895 Standing in the middle of the vast Hall, surrounded by the huge, smooth, yet twisting black marble pillars, he thought now I am a beetle, the tiniest of beetles, finding his way through the towering trees of the jungle. — *Setting the World on Fire*, Angus Wilson, 1980.

4896 His hand creates an imaginary visor to complement his imaginary hat. He continues to squint. — *Higher Ground*, Caryl Phillips, 1986.

4897 McEvoy pauses, in mid-turn the lapels of his jacket fly apart and for a stalled instant of inappropriate whimsy he sees himself spatchcocked, pinned like a specimen to the blackboard. — *Zeno Was Here*, Jan Mark, 1987.

4898 Dear Abby-/ I see things when I close my eyes. — *The Organ Builder*, Robert Cohen, 1988.

4899 *She imagines it as a novelist might imagine it.* — *The Woman Who Was God*, Francis King, 1988.

4900 Before she falls asleep, Amelia allows herself a fantasy. — *Other Women's Children*, Perri Klass, 1990.

4901 On a certain day in Southern California, beneath a sky that held nothing of emergency or love, a lilac-eyed woman in the middle of life's youth dragged a garden hose across the lawn by its sprinkler; dropped it, without breaking stride, squarely in front of her house; and as she threw the spigot open, shaking her hair impatiently back from her face to see the trajectory of the teeming droplets, she cleared her throat, grimaced, and helplessly reinvented, while the whole shimmering world revolved, *everything*. — *Traffic and Laughter*, Ted Mooney, 1990.

4902 Eden Swift Riley was good at pretending. — *Secret Lives*, Diane Chamberlain, 1991.

4903 Lilias Papagay was of imagination all compact. — "The Conjugial Angel," A. S. Byatt, 1992.

4904 Sometimes even now I think I see him in the street or standing in a window or bent over a book in a coffee shop. — *The Blindfold*, Siri Hustvedt, 1992.

4905 I would like, in this book, to imagine a place in which humans can live. — *The Idea of Home*, Curtis White, 1992.

Impatience

4906 Three young men stood together on a wharf one bright October day, awaiting the arrival of an ocean steamer with an impatience which found a vent in lively skirmishes with a small lad, who pervaded the premises like a will-o'-the-wisp, and afforded much amusement to the other groups assembled there. — *Rose in Bloom*, Louisa May Alcott, 1876.

4907 When old Mr. Marshall finally took to his bed, the household viewed this action with more surprise than sympathy, and with more impatience than surprise. — *With the Procession*, Henry B. Fuller, 1895.

4908 "Stephen! Stephen! Stephen!"/ The impatient cry was heard through all the narrow gloomy street, where the old richly-carved house-fronts bowed to meet one another and left for the eye's comfort only a bare glimpse of blue. — *The Heart of Princess Osra*, Anthony Hope, 1896.

4909 Mrs. Gereth had said she would go with the rest to church, but suddenly it seemed to her that she should not be able to wait even till church-time for relief: breakfast, at Waterbath, was a punctual meal, and she had still nearly an hour on her hands. — *The Spoils of Poynton*, Henry James, 1897.

4910 Nearly the entire boat-load of passengers was jammed along the forward gates, ready to spring out upon the Jersey wharf, restive to reach the waiting trains. — *Hesper*, Hamlin Garland, 1903.

4911 After the appointment with Miss Merival reached him (through the hand of her manager), young Douglass grew feverishly impatient of the long days which lay between. — *The Light of the Star*, Hamlin Garland, 1904.

4912 Why be in such a hurry, old fool? — *Great Circle*, Conrad Aiken, 1933.

4913 David Harper could scarcely sit still. — *The Fires of Spring*, James A. Michener, 1949.

4914 "How long is it 'til Christmas?" Johnny asked in a low voice. — *Christmas Without Johnny*, Gladys Hasty Carroll, 1950.

4915 "The foreign gentleman seems to be in a terrible hurry, dear." — *The Blessing*, Nancy Mitford, 1951.

4916 An hour after announcing sailing time the shore gangs still worked cargo aboard the *Jennie North* and the little groups of well-wishers on the dock, having exhausted their stock of pleasantries, began to grow restive. — *The Adventurers*, Ernest Haycox, 1954.

4917 Fanny De Haven thumped the tip of her long-staffed parasol against the concrete in

impatience. — *The Life and Times of Buckshot South*, Frank Davis Adams, 1959.

4918 One August evening in 1942 a small, dapper man about fifty years old whose name was Jacob Isaacs came briskly walking into the lobby of the Union Station at Kansas City, paused, looked over his shoulder with an expression of impatience, and beckoned urgently. — *The Patriot*, Evan S. Connell, 1960.

4919 Cohen, a large, heavyset man of forty-three, was gradually losing his patience, and that would be a prelude to losing his temper and taking it out on everyone around him, and that had been happening too often. — *The Establishment*, Howard Fast, 1979.

4920 He was a man who travelled much and always in singular comfort, so that he had little of the curiosity of the tourist and much of the impatience of the executive who must dispatch his business and be gone again. — *Proteus*, Morris West, 1979.

4921 On a blustery February evening in 1905, Reanna Lovell stood before a pier glass in the guest room of her cousin Lucy Marr's house in Washington, D.C., waiting impatiently for her mother to finish adjusting the skirt of her new green, watered-silk gown. — *Women in the Wind*, Margaret Ritter, 1985.

4922 In the Fifties, in England, on a war-torn planet so weary it was a wonder, thought the woman who called herself Ilse Lamprey, it could still turn at all, in the northern reaches of the university city, sallow Ilse Lamprey sat in her wheelchair at her window and tapped the sill with a long varnished fingernail, chipped. Where was Babakov with the Bovril? — *Dr. Gruber's Daughter*, Janice Elliott, 1986.

4923 "You're wasting everybody's time, Mr. Commissioner for Information." — *Anthills of the Savannah*, Chinua Achebe, 1987.

4924 She was eager to get off the ferry. — *Tempting Fate*, Laurie Alberts, 1987.

4925 Tenny's mother honks. — *Domestic Life*, Paula Webb, 1992.

Inheritance

4926 John Courtenay was the son of Richard Courtenay. Richard was the younger son of a good Devonshire family: his elder brother inherited four thousand a year — he, fifteen hundred pounds from the same relative, his father — *vive l'Angleterre!* — *The Bloomer*, Charles Reade, 1855.

4927 "To my nephew, Waldo Yorke, of Beacon Street, Boston, Massachusetts, all such properties of mine as are vested in shipping, timber, or lumber, in the town of Sherman, in this State." — *Doctor Zay*, Elizabeth Stuart Phelps, 1882.

4928 When Fessenden Abbott heard that he was to inherit four hundred millions of dollars he experienced the profoundest discouragement he was ever to know, except on that midnight ten years later when he stood on a moonlit balcony in Hungary, alone with the daughter of an Emperor, and opened his contemptuous American mind to the deeper problems of Europe. — *Rulers of Kings*, Gertrude Atherton, 1904.

4929 I consider it at least useful — perhaps necessary — to have a complete and accurate record of all pertaining to the will of my late grand-uncle Roger Melton. — *The Lady of the Shroud*, Bram Stoker, 1909.

4930 By the bequest of an elder brother, I was left enough money to see me through a small college in Ohio, and to secure me four years in a medical school in the East. — *The After House*, Mary Roberts Rinehart, 1914.

4931 When James Brien inherited his father's estate near Moycullen, a few miles west of Galway, he went at once to Paris to look for a wife. — *Wild Geese*, Eilis Dillon, 1980.

4932 "If I were to die now, it would be years before you would be able to lay your hands on what I shall leave you," Grandfather told me when I first met him. — *My First Naked Lady*, Brian de Breffny, 1981.

4933 Consider your inheritances, fellow students. — *Continent*, Jim Crace, 1986.

4934 It was a damned silly will to have left, Joanna Lawson thought, as she sat listening to the executor, Mr. Pemberton, going through its contents after the funeral was over. — *The Beneficiaries*, Pamela Street, 1989.

Insanity

4935 Fantazius Mallare considered himself mad because he was unable to behold in the meaningless gesturings of time, space and evolution a dramatic little pantomime adroitly centered about the routine of his existence. — *Fantazius Mallare*, Ben Hecht, 1922.

4936 Quaintly he came raiking out of Molesworth Street into Kildare Street, an odd figure moldered by memories, and driven mad by dreams which had overflowed into life, making him turn himself into a merry mockery of all he had once held dear. — *As I Was Going Down Sackville Street*, Oliver St. John Gogarty, 1937.

4937 "Mom," said little Abner, "there's a feller down the street says he's goin' to make a wagon that'll run without a hoss."/ "He's crazy," said Mom. — *The Flivver King*, Upton Sinclair, 1937.

4938 Olson was cracking up. — *The Power*, Frank M. Robinson, 1956.

4939 If I am out of my mind, it's all right with me, thought Moses Herzog. — *Herzog*, Saul Bellow, 1964.

4940 Inside I meet the eyes of pure madness. — *The Buzzards*, Janet Burroway, 1969.

4941 There was this lunatic, see, he was working in the garden of the asylum. — *The Comic*, Brian Glanville, 1974.

4942 Joseph Rabinowitz was puzzled about going crazy. — *Contract with the World*, Jane Rule, 1980.

4943 On Thursday, the 25th October, 1810, a windy day with the first autumnal leaves floating down over the parks and commons of England, the old King went mad. — *The Stranger from the Sea*, Winston Graham, 1981.

4944 Am I crazy? — *The Nuclear Age*, Tim O'Brien, 1981.

4945 Rosa Lublin, a madwoman and a scavenger, gave up her store — she smashed it up herself — and moved to Miami. — "Rosa," Cynthia Ozick, 1984.

4946 "Of course we have to do with two madmen now, not with one." — *The Message to the Planet*, Iris Murdoch, 1989.

4947 He lived in a large brick house in an expensive suburb with his older brother and sister, and the neighbors suspected, though they could not be sure, that he was mad. — *The Investigator*, Richard Moore, 1991.

4948 I am not mad; I never was. — *After the War*, Richard Marius, 1992.

4949 "Margaret Hunter Bridges! Have you gone and lost your *mind*?" — *Looking for Atlanta*, Marilyn Dorn Staats, 1992.

Insects

4950 In 1860, an ant on its spring marching came upon the mountain of his cowhide boot. — *The Big Barn*, Walter D. Edmonds, 1930.

4951 The moth, which had been clattering frantically inside his lampshade for the last ten minutes, suddenly dropped onto the open page of his book and lay there stunned, only a slight questing of the antennae showing that it was still alive. — *The Happy Prisoner*, Monica Dickens, 1946.

4952 The midges were dancing over the water. — *Time of Hope*, C. P. Snow, 1949.

4953 General Kempton had just killed a mosquito. — *The Winston Affair*, Howard Fast, 1959.

4954 A moth had somehow gained entrance to Henry's mosquito net. Henry lay on his back and watched with resentment as it gyrated clumsily about the apex of his little muslin tent. — *Henry's War*, Jeremy Brooks, 1962.

4955 Newt Winger lay belly-flat at the edge of the cornfield, his brown chin close to the ground, his eyes glued to a hill of busy ants. — *The Learning Tree*, Gordon Parks, 1963.

4956 In the jungle, during one night in each month, the moths did not come to lanterns; through the black reaches of the outer night, so it was said, they flew toward the full moon. — *At Play in the Fields of the Lord*, Peter Matthiessen, 1965.

4957 A pair of sulphur butterflies emerged from the leaves of a single cottonwood. — *Eden Prairie*, Frederick Manfred, 1968.

4958 Above, in the dried aromatic scrub, an early cicada churred. — *The Wooden Shepherdess*, Richard Hughes, 1973.

4959 It was July. The midges were out, swarming under the trees, zinging like crazy, and scudding round my body looking for juicy spots. — *The Clearance*, Joan Lingard, 1974.

4960 Grasshoppers were bad that summer. — *Grasshopper Summer*, Jamie Lee Cooper, 1975.

4961 Gnats. A whole swarm of gnats plastered on the windscreen and the wipers out of order. — *Rumours of Rain*, André Brink, 1978.

4962 Now the lightning bugs come up from the mossy ground along the river bank, first one, then two together, more, hesitant at first, from the darkness gathered there already in the brush beneath the trees. — *Black Mountain Breakdown*, Lee Smith, 1980.

4963 Each ant emerged from the skull bearing an infinitesimal portion of brain. — *Kahawa*, Donald E. Westlake, 1982.

4964 The cicadas screamed. — *The Miniature Man*, R. Muir, 1987.

4965 There is a wasp in the kitchen. — *At Risk*, Alice Hoffman, 1988.

4966 *Collected in a small stagnant pool. Active swimmers. One swimmer fed on leaf hoppers.*/ *Drumheller, Alberta. September 29, 1945.* — *Still Life with Insects*, Brian Kiteley, 1989.

4967 Three butterflies rise from the field like white ash above a fire. — *Lilac and Flag*, John Berger, 1990.

4968 The cockroach paused on the corner of the table, twitched its feelers and front legs over the edge, turned, and crawled back under the lip of the plate. — *Easter Weekend*, David Bottoms, 1990.

4969 *The night before he leaves to kill a man, Daniel Hawthorn stands in front of his bedroom window watching fireflies.* — *The Gypsy Storyteller*, Thomas William Simpson, 1993.

Insults

4970 "Get out o' Mr. Fletcher's road, ye idle, lounging, little —"/ "Vagabond," I think the woman (Sally Watkins, once my nurse,) was going to say, but she changed her mind. — *John Halifax, Gentleman*, Dinah Maria Mulock *as* Mrs. Craik, 1856.

4971 "He is an idle vagabond!" the mayor of the good town of Southampton said, in high wrath — "a ne'er-do-well, and an insolent puppy; and as to you, Mistress Alice, if I catch you exchanging words with him again, ay, or nodding to him, or looking as if in any way you were conscious of his presence, I will put you on bread and water, and will send you away for six months to the care of my sister Deborah, who will, I warrant me, bring you to your senses." — *The Bravest of the Brave*, G. A. Henty, 1887.

4972 "I wonder when in the world you're going to do anything, Rudolf?" said my brother's wife. — *The Prisoner of Zenda*, Anthony Hope, 1894.

4973 "All Englishmen are pigs!" observed a young man who stood swaying in the doorway of the Café Cardinal. — *The Red Republic*, Robert W. Chambers, 1895.

4974 "He's just an infernal dude, your lordship, and I'll throw him in the river if he says a word too much." — *Cowardice Court*, George Barr McCutcheon, 1906.

4975 I am quite sure it was my Uncle Rilas who said that I was a fool. — *A Fool and His Money*, George Barr McCutcheon, 1913.

4976 "You idiot!" said his wife, and threw down her cards. — "The Spark (The 'Sixties)," Edith Wharton, 1924.

4977 "I think, Clara, that your cousin Andrew is a damned young fool. You must excuse the language, but on the whole I consider him the damnedest young fool with whom I ever had to do." — *Mary of Marion Isle*, H. Rider Haggard, 1929.

4978 It was Charles who called us the parasites. — *The Parasites*, Daphne du Maurier, 1949.

4979 "Get away from here, you dirty swine," she said./ "There's a dirty swine in every man," he said. — *The Ballad of Peckham Rye*, Muriel Spark, 1960.

4980 "He was always a little snotnose, that Harry Bandon," Vincent's grandmother said. — *The Jealous God*, John Braine, 1964.

4981 "John Hancock, you're a jackass!" — *Yankee Doodle Dandy*, Noel B. Gerson, 1965.

4982 Write it on the walls./ *H. Carter Gavin, Her Britannic Majesty's vice-consul in Athens, is a shit.* — *Dirty Story*, Eric Ambler, 1967.

4983 "You're going downhill," she said with vehemence and, he knew, turned from the stove to face him. — *An Exile*, Madison Jones, 1967.

4984 In a somewhat easygoing way, the two lookalike Greek detectives began to rib each other with familiar nationalistic-style insults. — *The Dick*, Bruce Jay Friedman, 1970.

4985 "What an unbecoming light this is!" said Eliza Heriot, looking from the globe above the table to the faces round it. — *The Last and the First*, Ivy Compton-Burnett, 1971.

4986 "But, my dear, it's so provincial of them," Mrs. Delmore said with a pleading gesture that caused the silver bracelets on her wrist to click. — *A Cry of Absence*, Madison Jones, 1971.

4987 "Diddakoi."/ "Tinker."/ "Tinkety-tink."/ "Gypsy gypsy joker/get a red-hot poker."/ "Rags an' tags."/ "Clothes-pegs. Who'll buy my clothespegs?" — only they said "cloes-pegs."/ "Who'll buy my flowers?" — only they said "flahrs"/ "Diddakoi." — *The Diddakoi*, Rumer Godden, 1972.

4988 If Otis Wasum had done the proper thing by crying out, "Defend yourself!" instead of just mumbling at me, "You little Fairchild sonofabitch," I maintain that I would have known instantly how to deal with him, and the whole thing would have ended right there. — *Hard on the Road*, Barbara Moore, 1974.

4989 *The thousand injuries of Fortunato I had borne as I best could, but when he ventured upon insult, I vowed revenge.* — *Matter of Paradise*, Brown Meggs, 1975.

4990 "Skivvy! Silly little skivvy!" jeered the new boots boy in the back scullery. — *Annie Parsons*, Sarah Shears, 1979.

4991 "Beggars!" exclaimed Count Horn. "They called us *beggars* for requiring what is ours by right of law and custom!" — *The Sea Beggars*, Cecelia Holland, 1982.

4992 The taxi driver thought he had offended me. — *The House of Stairs*, Ruth Rendell *as* Barbara Vine, 1988.

4993 "Bret Rensselaer, you are a ruthless bastard." — *Spy Sinker*, Len Deighton, 1990.

4994 In a whisper: "Who's that ghoul?" — *Rumor Has It*, Charles Dickinson, 1991.

4995 "I only met Lincoln Hayes once, but as far as I could tell he was an absolute prick...." — *Back in the Blue House*, Jeff Giles, 1992.

Intelligence

4996 Young Mrs. Petherwin stepped from the door of an old and well-appointed inn in a Wessex town to take a country walk. By her look and carriage she appeared to belong to that gentle order of society which has no worldly sorrow except when its jewellery gets stolen; but, as a fact not generally known, her claim to distinction was rather one of brains than of blood. — *The Hand of Ethelberta*, Thomas Hardy, 1876.

4997 Helen de l'Abbaye was allowed intelligence as a French habit. — *The Clash*, Storm Jameson, 1922.

4998 "Ladies and Gentlemen, our next number will prove conclusively that the gifts of reason and intelligence are not confined entirely to the human race...." — *Hepatica Hawks*, Rachel Field, 1932.

4999 Edward Haslatt was a young man both intelligent and cautious. — *The Long Love*, Pearl S. Buck *as* John Sedges, 1949.

5000 Were they truly intelligent? By themselves, that is? — *The Puppet Masters*, Robert A. Heinlein, 1951.

5001 It was the openness of the face that struck me most, more even than its intelligence. — *The Rise of Gerry Logan*, Brian Glanville, 1963.

5002 He was a clever one. He understood this world and this life. — "The Clever One," Martha Gellhorn, 1965.

5003 The new night Sister from Guadaloupe appears to be intelligent and to know her job. — *Doctor Frigo*, Eric Ambler, 1974.

5004 During the partners' lunch, old Gifford talked indistinctly about the Rawlinson account: something to do with the new man on the board not having a first-class brain — he didn't come up to scratch. — *Injury Time*, Beryl Bainbridge, 1977.

5005 Calvin Hart had an extemely high IQ, and his innocence, if anything, merely accented it. — *The Divorce Sonnets*, Harry H. Taylor, 1984.

5006 Let me say this: bein a idiot is no box of chocolates. — *Forrest Gump*, Winston Groom, 1986.

5007 I am more intelligent than my father. — *Works of Genius*, Richard Marek, 1987.

5008 "Freddy's *smaht*, but he ain't as *smaht* as he thinks he is," the dream father spoke from a pit he dug out in the barn to repair cars. — *Live Free or Die*, Ernest Hebert, 1990.

5009 No one ever said I was very bright. — *Making History*, Carolyn See, 1991.

5010 The rap on Jesse — one of the raps on Jesse — was that he wasn't very smart. — *Ricochet River*, Robin Cody, 1992.

Islands

5011 That long, narrow, and irregular island, usually called the Mainland of Zetland, because it is by far the largest of that Archipelago, terminates, as is well known to the mariners who navigate the stormy seas which surround the Thule of the ancients, in a cliff of immense height, entitled Sumburgh Head, which presents its bare scalp and naked sides to the weight of a tremendous surge, forming the extreme point of the isle to the south-east. — *The Pirate*, Sir Walter Scott, 1821.

5012 Squire Trelawney, Dr. Livesey, and the rest of these gentlemen having asked me to write down the whole particulars about Treasure Island, from the beginning to the end, keeping nothing back but the bearings of the island, and that only because there is still treasure not yet lifted, I take up my pen in the year of grace 17 —, and go back to the time when my father kept the "Admiral Benbow" inn, and the brown old seaman, with the sabre cut, first took up his lodging under our roof. — *Treasure Island*, Robert Louis Stevenson, 1883.

5013 "Quot homines tot sententiæ;" so many men, so many fancies. My fancy was for an island. — *Phroso*, Anthony Hope, 1897.

5014 Nevis gave of her bounty to none more generously than to John and Mary Fawcett. — *The Conqueror*, Gertrude Atherton, 1902.

5015 A cluster of islands, lying off the cape, made the shelter of our harbour. They were but great rocks, gray, ragged, wet with fog and surf, rising bleak and barren out of a sea that forever fretted a thousand miles of rocky coast as barren and as sombre and as desolate as they; but they broke wave and wind unfailingly and with vast unconcern — they were of old time, mighty, steadfast, remote from the rage of weather and the changing mood of the sea, surely providing safe shelter for us folk of the coast — and we loved them, as true men, everywhere, love home. — *Doctor Luke of the Labrador*, Norman Duncan, 1904.

5016 Every one who has been to school and still remembers what he was taught there, knows that Rügen is the biggest island Germany possesses, and that it lies in the Baltic Sea off the coast of Pomerania. — *The Adventures of Elizabeth in Rügen*, Elizabeth von Arnim, 1904.

5017 When Serenus Gowdey got back last fall from Brooklyn, where his twin brother, Sylvester, lives, he couldn't talk about anything but Coney Island. — *Samantha at Coney Island and a Thousand Other Islands*, Marietta Holley *as* Josiah Allen's Wife, 1911.

5018 The shallow sea that foams and murmurs on the shores of the thousand islands, big and little, which make up the Malay Archipelago has been for centuries the scene of adventurous undertakings. — *The Rescue*, Joseph Conrad, 1920.

5019 None of the men sitting in deck chairs under the awning were surprised to hear the Chief say that he had known Ipsilon in peacetime. — *Captain Macedoine's Daughter*, William McFee, 1920.

5020 Round them, and under their feet, the island pressed up warmly against itself, rock and earth and sweet turf covering it, trees and bushes, all summer through drying and crumbling in the sun, ringed about for ever with sea: Poieëssa, their island, their State. — *Cloud Cuckoo Land*, Naomi Mitchison, 1925.

5021 When Robert Bolles tried to put all the events in order, his mind would keep going back to Mercator Island, although he knew that Mercator Island was nearer the end than the beginning. — *Last Laugh, Mr. Moto*, John P. Marquand, 1942.

5022 Most of the islands in the Hawaiian group have a region called Kona, which means south or south-west. — *Kona*, Marjorie Sinclair, 1947

5023 It was a day of nervous shift and bustle overhead, the clouds going southwest very fast. They grayed out the islands below and suddenly lit them up again; they re-mapped the Caribbean with continents, purple and green; they raised new archipelagoes, tore them apart, and sent them scudding off to sink far out in the broken water. — *My Son and Foe*, Josephine Pinckney, 1952.

5024 Where am I? Francis thought, opening her eyes to the faded flowered wallpaper, and then she remembered, smiled, closed her eyes again to let pleasure soak in, the sense of holiday; they were really here on the island, the long summer opening ahead, lazy and timeless. — *The Birth of a Grandfather*, May Sarton, 1957.

5025 *Always the land was there — the rising mound between the great river on the west and the long, sluggish water on the east — sometimes an island; sometimes, in high water, when the thaws came down, only the mass of treetops above the flood.* — *The House on the Mound*, August Derleth, 1958.

5026 The island of Sicily./ Sicily — in July, 1943./ Sicily — sun-drenched, war-sick, huddling in her misery./ Sicily, a ripe fruit, fat for plucking. Sicily, the soft underbelly of Europe, pregnant with the peril of invasion. — *Execution*, Colin McDougall, 1958.

5027 If you ask me how I remember the island, what it was like to be stranded there by misadventure for nearly three months, I would

answer that it was a time and landscape of the mind if I did not have the visible signs to summon its materiality: my journal, the cat, the newspaper cuttings, the curiosity of my friends; and my sisters — how they always look at me, I think, as one returned from the dead. — *Robinson*, Muriel Spark, 1958.

5028 Pine Island, Maine, thrust itself out of the sea like a huge medieval castle. — *A Summer Place*, Sloan Wilson, 1958.

5029 The Marquis de Las Cases, who professed a leaning to letters, hunched his thick shoulders over the rail and stared at the rocky islet. "Have we been crossing the Styx all these months?" he asked his companions. "Surely this is hell which now faces us!" — *The Last Love*, Thomas B. Costain, 1963.

5030 Eldey Island loomed ahead of them like a gigantic red iceberg jutting from the frigid gray waters of the North Atlantic. — *The Great Auk*, Allan W. Eckert, 1963.

5031 The island was of stone, lying low in the sea, hidden from passing ships by mist and breakers. — *A World Elsewhere*, John Bowen, 1965.

5032 Kinja was the name of the island when it was British. — *Don't Stop the Carnival*, Herman Wouk, 1965.

5033 A south Pacific paradise. An island where storms were stormier, rain was rainier, sun was sunnier, where figs, bananas, passion fruit, pawpaws, fijoas, custard apples, guavas, grew and ripened; where the cold pale narcissi opened their buds at the official beginning of winter, and violets bloomed all year; where the only enemies of man, apart from man, were wasps as big as flying tigers, a few mosquitoes breeding a giant island strain, too many colonies of ants; and perhaps, though one does not explain why, the sullen gray mangroves standing in their beds of mud in the tidal inlets facing the mainland. — *A State of Siege*, Janet Frame, 1966.

5034 When Peter McNab — Peter the First, as some called him afterwards — came to Halifax, the island lay in the harbor entrance like a green cork in the neck of a green bottle; a cork twisted in a crude 8 and somewhat shrunken in width, so that it did not pretend to stop the mouth of the bottle but left passage for a stream of salt water on both sides. — *Hangman's Beach*, Thomas H. Raddall, 1966.

5035 We spent last summer, when I was just sixteen, on an island mistakenly named Greensward, its shores only thinly vegetated with beach grass and plum, its single forest destroyed by fire more than twenty years before. — *Last Summer*, Evan Hunter, 1968.

5036 This island made her feel exposed. — *The Perfectionists*, Gail Godwin, 1970.

5037 He had always intended to come back,

to see the island again. — *Summer of '42*, Herman Raucher, 1971.

5038 Even today Key West hides none of its flat terrain from those who approach it from the sea. — *The Truth About Them*, Jose Yglesias, 1971.

5039 The fog lifted. The island was there. The visitor walked to the end of the disused pier and saw it across three miles of ocean, riding the sea like an overturned fishing boat. — *Catholics*, Brian Moore, 1972.

5040 It was a beautiful evening in May on Inishnamona, an island off the west Irish coast that has been famous, now and then, throughout the world. — *The Quiet End of Evening*, Honor Tracy, 1972.

5041 The island was overcrowded; that much was clear. — *Capital*, Maureen Duffy, 1975.

5042 I am sitting in an apartment in Kulosaari, a suburb of Helsinki, the capital of Finland. "Kulosaari" means burned island; long ago they burned the trees here to fertilize the land. — *Stepping*, Nancy Thayer, 1980.

5043 At the uppermonst rim of the sea, on the imaginary line where the waters of the Indian and Pacific Oceans meet and merge, lies the island of Zenkali, a green and pleasant place, so remote that you would think that it could neither affect the outside world nor be influenced by it. — *The Mockery Bird*, Gerald Durrell, 1981.

5044 The island rose and sank. Twice. During periods in which history was recorded by indentations on rock and shell. — *Abeng*, Michelle Cliff, 1984.

5045 On that island where rivers run deep, where the sea sparkling in the sun earns it the name Jewel of the Antilles, the tops of the mountains are bare. — *My Love, My Love*, Rosa Guy, 1985.

5046 The building sits by the river./ The island sits in the sun./ They are very far from one another./ They will come together, soon enough. — *Pentagon*, Allen Drury, 1986.

5047 First there is the island. — *Hatteras Light*, Philip Gerard, 1986.

5048 Solomons Island is a tendril of land two miles long and half a mile wide that curls with a strangely languid and voluptuous look of tension, like a finger arched in ecstasy or death, into the estuary of the Patuxent River. — *Southern Light*, J. R. Salamanca, 1986.

5049 We live on St. Petin, a tiny island in the blue Caribbean. — *Uncharted Places*, Nora Johnson, 1988.

5050 There was always a moment, sailing between the boathouse on shore and Davenhall Island, when neither was in sight. — *Tours of the Black Clock*, Steve Erickson, 1989.

5051 The winds blew high over Jersey, clearing the sky for the stars to glimmer down on the island below. — *Lemprière's Dictionary*, Lawrence Norfolk, 1991.

5052 On the northern end of the Caribbean island of St. Catherine, there is an active volcano, Mount Soufrière. Dormant since its last eruption in 1902, its massive crater had collected a brown hot lake of tropical rains, and magma formed a fiery island within the lake in a gradual reawakening not many years ago. — *Swimming in the Volcano*, Bob Shacochis, 1993.

5053 Sophie,/ Just returned from Sardinia, where we'd planned to stay two weeks but ended up driving away after only five days because it is one HIDEOUS island, dahling, let me tell you. — *From the Teeth of Angels*, Jonathan Carroll, 1994.

Knowledge

5054 "Now, what I want is, Facts." — *Hard Times for These Times*, Charles Dickens, 1854.

5055 We white people think that we know everything. — *Child of Storm*, H. Rider Haggard, 1913.

5056 Unlike the old woman who lived in the shoe, Mrs. Spaine knew perfectly well what to do. — *The Merivales*, George Barr McCutcheon, 1929.

5057 "Do you know?" Matthew Carlton Hazard used to say in happier times, "the earliest chief thing I knew in my life?" — *A Distant Trumpet*, Paul Horgan, 1960.

5058 "Is that the best way to reach perception, then?" — *Whitewater*, Paul Horgan, 1970.

5059 I've been blind since birth. This means that much of what I am about to tell you is based upon the subjective descriptions or faulty memories of others, blended with an empirical knowledge of my own — forty-eight years of touching, hearing, and smelling. — *Streets of Gold*, Evan Hunter, 1974.

5060 To know is not enough. One must try to understand too. — *A Chain of Voices*, André Brink, 1982.

5061 Once a thing is known it can never be unknown. — *Look at Me*, Anita Brookner, 1983.

5062 It did not take long to find out. — *The Roads of Earth*, Allen Drury, 1984.

5063 No matter who you are, whether you're a moon lover or not, I think you ought to know one or two things. — *Why We Never Danced the Charleston*, Harlan Greene, 1984.

5064 Let me start by making this clear. I ate the fruit of the forbidden tree, the tree of knowledge, because I chose to. — *Eve*, Penelope Farmer, 1988.

5065 How did I find out? — *My Son's Story*, Nadine Gordimer, 1990.

Lakes

5066 At the little town of Vevey, in Switzerland, there is a particularly comfortable hotel; there are indeed many hotels, since the entertainment of tourists is the business of the place, which, as many travellers will remember, is seated upon the edge of a remarkably blue lake — a lake that it behoves every tourist to visit. — *Daisy Miller*, Henry James, 1879.

5067 Not very far from Upton-on-Severn — between it, in fact, and the Malvern Hills — stands the country seat of the Gordons of Bramley; well-timbered, well-cottaged, well-fenced and well-watered, having, in this latter respect, a stream that forks in exactly the right position to feed two large lakes in the grounds. — *The Well of Loneliness*, Radclyffe Hall, 1928.

5068 The lake was still with the dying away of wind at dusk, and the air was calm, a little sultry after daylong heat. — *Bright Journey*, August Derleth, 1940.

5069 There are ponds in the woods at Wood Ibis that appear perfect mirrors of a patch of sky fenced in by moss-hung trees, their glass unscratched and unmarred since the world began. — *Castle in the Swamp*, Edison Marshall, 1948.

5070 There's a strange little lake just below Helvellyn between Swirral Edge and Striding Edge. — *This Animal Is Mischievous*, David Benedictus, 1965.

5071 The bleak waters of the Gareloch were speckled with countless tiny whitecaps as the stiff south-westerly wind bore up from the Firth of Clyde and flattened the gorse of the distant hills like wet fur. — *The Deep Silence*, Douglas Reeman, 1967.

5072 He looked down over the roofs of the village to the blue steel gleam of the lake trapped between steep green hills. — *The Cawthorn Journals*, Stephen Marlowe, 1975.

5073 It was the silent time before dawn, along the shores of what had been one of the most beautiful lakes in southern Africa. — *The Covenant*, James A. Michener, 1980.

5074 The still green waters of the alkalche glittered brightly in the sunlight, producing a glare as intense and powerful as the shrilling of the locusts in the distant trees. — *Tikal*, Daniel Peters, 1983.

5075 Robert could see Oblong Lake from the roof of Ben's house. — *Crows*, Charles Dickinson, 1985.

5076 Like a great cat, the lake lay purring in the May sun. — *The Enchantress*, Han Suyin, 1985.

5077 The real world goes like this: The Neversummer Mountains like a jumble of broken glass. Snowfields weep slowly down. Chambers Lake, ringed by trees, gratefully catches the drip in its tin cup, and gives the mountains their own reflection in return. This is the real world, indifferent, unburdened. — *The Meadow*, James Galvin, 1992.

Landmarks

5078 On an evening of July, in the year 18 — , at East D — , a beautiful little town in a certain district of East Anglia, I first saw the light. — *Lavengro*, George Borrow, 1851.

5079 It is a great thing for a lad when he is first turned into the independence of lodgings. I do not think I ever was so satisfied and proud in my life as when, at seventeen, I sat down in a little three-cornered room above a pastry-cook's shop in the county town of Eltham. — *Cousin Phillis*, Elizabeth Gaskell, 1863.

5080 One of the most fateful days of John Vane's life was the day on which he took board with that genteel though decayed lady, the widow of a wholesale New York grocer who had come out at the little end of the horn of plenty, and the mother of two of the prettiest girls in Slowburgh, Mrs. Renssaclacr Smiles. — *Honest John Vane*, John W. De Forest, 1875.

5081 All things considered, I rate October 10th, 1920, as the most momentous day of my life. — *Hartmann the Anarchist*, E. Douglas Fawcett, 1893.

5082 A man who has lived in the world, marking how every act, although in itself perhaps light and insignificant, may become the source of consequences that spread far and wide, and flow for years or centuries, could scarcely feel secure in reckoning that with the death of the Duke of Strelsau and the restoration of King Rudolf to liberty and his throne, there would end, for good and all, the troubles born of Black Michael's daring conspiracy. — *Rupert of Hentzau*, Anthony Hope, 1898.

5083 The changeful April morning that she watched from the window of her flat looking over the river began a day of significance in the career of Trix Trevalla — of feminine significance, almost milliner's, perhaps, but of significance all the same. — *The Intrusions of Peggy*, Anthony Hope, 1902.

5084 I mind as if it were yesterday my first sight of the man. Little I knew at the time how big the moment was with destiny, or how often that face seen in the fitful moonlight would haunt my sleep and disturb my waking hours. But I mind yet the cold grue of terror I got from it, a terror which was surely more than the due of a few truant lads breaking the Sabbath with their play. — *Prester John*, John Buchan, 1910.

5085 They occurred very much at the same hour and together, the two main things that — exclusive of the death of his mother, recent and deeply felt by him — had yet befallen Ralph Pendrel, who, at thirty, had known fewer turns of fortune than many men of his age. — *The Sense of the Past*, Henry James, 1917.

5086 In 1913, when Anthony Patch was twenty-five, two years were already gone since irony, the Holy Ghost of this later day, had, theoretically at least, descended upon him. — *The Beautiful and Damned*, F. Scott Fitzgerald, 1922.

5087 May 12 – June 2, 1906. I remember hearing once about a child that was playing in a garden and a butterfly came along and brushed his cheek and how that incident changed the whole course of the boy's life. — *"The Great American Novel — ,"* Clyde Brion Davis, 1938.

5088 On a damp evening in December, the fifth of that month, in the year 1919 – a date which marked the beginning of a great change in my life — six o'clock had struck from the University tower and the soft mist from the Eldon River was creeping round the Experimental Pathology buildings at the foot of Fenner Hill, invading our long work-room that smelled faintly of formalin, and was lit only by low, green-shaded lamps. — *Shannon's Way*, A. J. Cronin, 1948.

5089 When "the crisis," as he always called it afterwards, occurred in the life of David Alexander Michaeljohn, I believe I was the only person who might have been of help to him — and I was far away in Africa. — *The Face Beside the Fire*, Laurens van der Post, 1953.

5090 Marvel was in no mood to talk or even think about a fortieth anniversary. — *Through the Fields of Clover*, Peter De Vries, 1961.

5091 Exactly three months before the killing at Martingale Mrs. Maxie gave a dinner party. Years later, when the trial was a half-forgotten scandal and the headlines were yellowing on the newspaper lining of cupboard drawers, Eleanor Maxie looked back on that spring evening as the opening scene of tragedy. — *Cover Her Face*, P. D. James, 1962.

5092 It is not given to many of us to pinpoint the actual moment of our entry into a world of new beginnings. — *Mr. Sermon*, R. F. Delderfield, 1963.

5093 The first real day of my life was when I banged the front door. That was when I made a decision for myself. — *Winds of the Day*, Howard Spring, 1964.

5094 That was the day Sweet Mary from Boston almost burned down The Place, not once but twice. The day it all started, I mean, and how I got the money. — *Take Me Where the Good Times Are*, Robert Cormier, 1965.

5095 It was in 1958, thought Morcar, looking back at it ruefully, that for him things had begun to change. — *A Man of His Time*, Phyllis Bentley, 1966.

5096 After the exercises I stood in the muddy field (it had rained at dawn) and felt the dark wool of my gown lap up the heat and din of noon, and at that instant, while the graduates ran with cries toward asterisks of waiting parents and the sun hung like an animal's tongue from a sickened blue maw, I heard the last stray call of a bugle — single, lost, unconnected — and in one moment I grew suddenly old. — *Trust*, Cynthia Ozick, 1966.

5097 It was one of those moments all over the world when time caught up with history. — *'Sippi*, John Oliver Killens, 1967.

5098 My new life began when my cousin Adam Keelby came into the Salisbury one muggy September evening. — *The Crying Game*, John Braine, 1968.

5099 Often he thought: My life did not begin until I knew her. — *Mr. Bridge*, Evan S. Connell, 1969.

5100 My lifelong involvement with Mrs. Dempster began at 5:58 o'clock P.M. on the 27th of December, 1908, at which time I was ten years and seven months old. — *Fifth Business*, Robertson Davies, 1970.

5101 The moment was to stand out forever in her memory. — *The Tenth Month*, Laura Z. Hobson, 1970.

5102 Taft Robinson was the first black student to be enrolled at Logos College in West Texas. They got him for his speed. — *End Zone*, Don DeLillo, 1972.

5103 We made our first gold on March 1st, 1972, two months before my thirty-fifth birthday. — *The Golden Virgin*, Alan Dipper, 1972.

5104 June 5th. Gilde left the house at Andilly and went to the Paris flat. A casual diary entry about a domestic arrangement made to obviate the long drive in to work?/ No. The beginning of a report on the end of one part of my life and the start of another. — *A Hole in the Head*, Francis Stuart, 1977.

5105 If one had to pinpoint the event that sent the Bagthorpes plunging into the madness that was to possess them for a whole season, then that event would be the burglary. — *Bagthorpes Unlimited*, Helen Cresswell, 1978.

5106 I thought at the time it was one of those unexplained and unexplainable coincidences that change lives. — *Tower Abbey*, Isabelle Holland, 1978.

5107 This is the first time I've worked without a net. — *Panama*, Thomas McGuane, 1978.

5108 A year ago today, the fifteenth of October, 1749, was the most important day of my now stretched-out life, even more so than the day of my wedding, or that of my sainted father's death, when I became the second duc de Saint-Simon. — *The Cat and the King*, Louis Auchincloss, 1981.

5109 Was it I wonder when I turned round, there in the car, and found him gazing straight at me. — *A Difference of Design*, W. M. Spackman, 1983.

5110 On the day that I found that Penny was not my sister, I knew that my life would change forever. — *The Best Is Yet to Be*, Philip D. Wheaton, 1983.

5111 All, or almost all, of the events of Megan Greene's life, its violent dislocations, geographic and otherwise, are set in motion in the instant in which she first sees a young man named George Wharton, an unremarkable person, and later not a crucial figure in her life, but at that moment, to Megan, he is compellingly exotic. — *Superior Women*, Alice Adams, 1984.

5112 It was the greatest moment of Andy Farmer's life, but he didn't want to get *too* excited and drop dead. — *Funny Farm*, Jay Cronley, 1985.

5113 It was Donald Rolandson brought the Sword of the Spirit into our house and it would have been about 1968. — *Tongues of Flame*, Tim Parks, 1985.

5114 The course of my life was changed by a religious experience. — *Mother's Little Helper*, Gina Cascone, 1986.

5115 MOST SECRET/ From Titus — Praetorian Prefect/ To Flavius Silva — Commanding Tenth Legion Frentensis Judea/ We must prepare even now for the day when we shall see a momentous and most difficult transition in state affairs. — *The Triumph*, Ernest K. Gann, 1986.

5116 Life began to change for George "Doc" Ella on Saturday the fourteenth of July, 1979. — *Doc's Legacy*, Leonard Wise, 1986.

5117 Lord, I remember. For me it started on the eighth of April, 1968, at about three thirty in the afternoon. — *The Hangman's Children*, Donald Hays, 1989.

5118 He remembered seeing it later, as though he were watching a movie, reviewing the event in slow motion. The girl, a blonde, wearing a wrinkled sort of colorless jumpsuit, reached and lifted a quart soft drink bottle from the shelf, gripping it by the top, and then dropped it before she realized what had happened./ An explosion,

the release of violent force as a result of pressure within. An extreme upheaval. An event that changes things. — *A Fine Time to Leave Me*, Terry Pringle, 1989.

5119 When Lilly Duke came to live with us here in Harmony, it was then that this place where I was born and brought up was for me forever and for all time changed. — *Harmony*, Susan Taylor Chehak, 1990.

5120 Although I did not know it then, my life of unpremeditated childhood ended on Wednesday, September 13, 1972. — *Father Melancholy's Daughter*, Gail Godwin, 1991.

5121 The instant Sugar Mecklin opened his eyes on that Sunday morning, he believed that this was a special day and that something new and completely different from anything he had ever known before was about to jump out at him from somewhere unexpected, a willow shade, a beehive, a bird's nest, the bream beds in Roebuck Lake, a watermelon patch, the bray of the iceman's mule, the cry of herons in the swamp, he did not know from where, but wherever it came from he believed it would be transforming, it would open up worlds to him that before today had been closed. — *Music of the Swamp*, Lewis Nordan, 1991.

5122 We lived in a Low Country. Both before and after that summer, but it was never the same. — *Southern Exposure*, Linda Lightsey Rice, 1991.

5123 When he looked back and tried to understand how it happened, for surely a man should be able to explain the things that altered the course of his life, he could say only that he had felt pierced by the sight of her, on that street corner, in the dawn. — *A Tale of the Wind*, Kay Nolte Smith, 1991.

5124 Between the time that was before and the time that came afterwards there hung a brutal moment: a moment that was simple, brief, that changed what had been and altered everything that was to come. — *This Day and Age*, Mike Nicol, 1992.

Landscape

5125 On the pleasant banks of the Garonne, in the province of Gascony, stood, in the year 1584, the chateau of Monsieur St. Aubert. From its windows were seen the pastoral landscapes of Guienne and Gascony, stretching along the river, gay with luxuriant woods and vines, and plantations of olives. To the south, the view was

bounded by the majestic Pyrenées, whose summits, veiled in clouds, or exhibiting awful forms, seen, and lost again, as the partial vapours rolled along, were sometimes barren, and gleamed through the blue tinge of air, and sometimes frowned with forests of gloomy pine, that swept downward to their base. — *The Mysteries of Udolpho*, Ann Radcliffe, 1794.

5126 Westward, beyond the still pleasant, but, even then, no longer solitary, hamlet of Charing, a broad space, broken here and there by scattered houses and venerable pollards, in the early spring of 1467, presented the rural scene for the sports and pastimes of the inhabitants of Westminster and London. — *The Last of the Barons*, Edward Bulwer Lytton, 1843.

5127 From Monte Motterone you survey the Lombard plain. It is a towering dome of green among a hundred pinnacles of grey and rust-red crags. — *Vittoria*, George Meredith, 1867.

5128 A long level of dull gray that further away became a faint blue, with here and there darker patches that looked like water. — *A Waif of the Plains*, Bret Harte, 1890.

5129 There is a fertile stretch of flat lands in Indiana where unagrarian Eastern travellers, glancing from car-windows, shudder and return their eyes to interior upholstery, preferring even the swaying caparisons of a Pullman to the monotony without. — *The Gentleman from Indiana*, Booth Tarkington, 1899.

5130 There was no Burlingame in the Sixties, the Western Addition was a desert of sand dunes and the goats gambolled through the rocky gulches of Nob Hill. — *Sleeping Fires*, Gertrude Atherton, 1922.

5131 The two large fields lay on a hillside facing south. Being newly cleared of hay, they were golden green, and they shone almost blindingly in the sunlight. — "Love Among the Haystacks," D. H. Lawrence, 1923.

5132 The prairie lay that afternoon as it had lain for centuries of September afternoons, vast as an ocean; motionless as an ocean coaxed into very little ripples by languid breezes; silent as an ocean where only very little waves slip back into their element. — *The Able McLaughlins*, Margaret Wilson, 1923.

5133 Bruce Dudley stood near a window that was covered with flecks of paint and through which could be faintly seen, first a pile of empty boxes, then a more or less littered factory yard running down to a steep bluff, and beyond the brown waters of the Ohio River. — *Dark Laughter*, Sherwood Anderson, 1925.

5134 Several yards of undermined sand and clay broke loose up near the top, and the land slid down to the floor of the crater. — *God's Little Acre*, Erskine Caldwell, 1933.

5135 Unearthly humps of land curved into the darkening sky like the backs of browsing pigs, like the rumps of elephants. — "*National Velvet*," Enid Bagnold, 1935.

5136 Gray mists overhung the stream called Mud Creek, and the sun stood clear above the earthy thimble known as Winter Green Knob. — *Canal Town*, Samuel Hopkins Adams, 1944.

5137 The June landscape of Pennsylvania was full of pictures. — *Portrait of a Marriage*, Pearl S. Buck, 1945.

5138 No gangs of yellow men carrying earth and rubble in baskets, no human chains of men and women, and even children, carrying stones in their lacerated arms, built these Walls of China. No Emperor Ch'in Shih Huang Ti directed over a million men to raise this extraordinary barrier lying athwart the bushlands in the southwest corner of the state of New South Wales, Australia. The colour of the country is reddish-brown, and upon this reddish-brown land the soft fingers of the wind built a wall of snow-white sand some twelve miles long, three quarters of a mile wide, and several hundred feet high. No one knows when the wind laboured so mightily to build the barrier, and no one knows who named it the Walls of China. — *Death of a Swagman*, Arthur W. Upfield, 1945.

5139 Ordinarily the high hills came right down to the banks of the Calumet River in dark green folds, but at Dawn's Mill, by direction of Providence, the hills receded to form a site for the hamlet. — *Jeremy Bell*, Clyde Brion Davis, 1947.

5140 About the beginning of this century, in the city of Dublin, there was upon the bank of the Grand Canal a small stretch of vacant ground. — *Mary O'Grady*, Mary Lavin, 1950.

5141 The fallow land was the scar most visible to the eye, since it was spring and since the paddy fields, divided by the narrow dyke paths, should have been brightly green and twinkling with water. — *The Storm Cloud*, Lettie Rogers, 1951.

5142 Riding down to Port Warwick from Richmond, the train begins to pick up speed on the outskirts of the city, past the tobacco factories with their ever-present haze of acrid, sweetish dust and past the rows of uniformly brown clapboard houses which stretch down the hilly streets for miles, it seems, the hundreds of rooftops all reflecting the pale light of dawn; past the suburban roads still sluggish and sleepy with early morning traffic, and rattling swiftly now over the bridge which separates the last two hills where in the valley below you can see the James River winding beneath its acid-green crust of scum out beside the chemical plants and more rows of clapboard houses and into the woods beyond. — *Lie Down in Darkness*, William Styron, 1951.

5143 The sun rose on a landscape still pale with the heat of the day before. There was no haze, but a sort of coppery burnish out of the air lit on flowing fields, rocks, the face of the one house, and the cliff of limestone overhanging the river. — *A World of Love*, Elizabeth Bowen, 1955.

5144 St. Michael Pendeverel is a hamlet standing a mile inland. North of it, across a few miles of intervening fields, you can see the clay hills. When the sky is gray, they are gray, too. When the sun shines, they blaze like a miniature range of snow-capped Sierras, cut out sharply on heaven's blue. — *These Lovers Fled Away*, Howard Spring, 1955.

5145 Seen from eye level, (as the child Martha, flat on her stomach, saw it), the patch of pebbly grass in the back garden of 5, Alcock Road had all the charm, mysteriousness and authority of a classic Chinese landscape. — *The Eye of Love*, Margery Sharp, 1957.

5146 Landscape-tones: brown to bronze, steep skyline, low cloud, pearl ground with shadowed oyster and violet reflections. — *Balthazar*, Lawrence Durrell, 1958.

5147 The house stood on a shelf above the sea; the empty moorlands, the desert-colored, California hills, already brown in July, rose up behind it toward the sky that was clear and pale like a mountain sky and blue as a cornflower. — *So Love Returns*, Robert Nathan, 1958.

5148 The country is a huge dead beast, lion-colored. — *They Came to Cordura*, Glendon Swarthout, 1958.

5149 Crete was the world, his father said. A yellow sun tinged with flame over mountains and precipices compounding sites of ambush with sagas of courage. Cemeteries of massive boulders above earth fecundated by the corpses of more than sixty centuries of dead. Great pillars of neolithic stone casting their shadow across a hard earth under a savage violet twilight. — *The Odyssey of Kostas Volakis*, Harry Mark Petrakis, 1963.

5150 Several miles, almost flat, greyish-brown, stretches the top of the moor, crossed by a few dry walls, parish boundaries, which are tumbled, in places, into mere black heaps of stone. — *A Place of Stone*, Jim Hunter, 1964.

5151 Come up towards the Rhondda from Llantrisant. The hills grow less gentle. The fields lose grace and lushness. The first coal tips sit fatly on torn slopes. — *A Welsh Eye*, Gwyn Thomas, 1964.

5152 Imagine, then, a flat landscape, dark for the moment, but even so conveying to a girl running in the still deeper shadow cast by the wall of the Bibighar Gardens an idea of immensity, of distance, such as years before Miss Crane had been conscious of standing where a lane ended and cultivation began: a different landscape but also in the alluvial plain between the mountains of the north and the plateau of the south. — *The Jewel in the Crown*, Paul Scott, 1966.

5153 Picture the ground rising on the east side of the pasture with scrub trees thick on the slope and pines higher up. — *Valdez Is Coming*, Elmore Leonard, 1969.

5154 Paradise Point extends for about half a mile from the eastern shore of Lake George, New York, just south of the narrows. The base of the point is two hundred feet high with steep granite cliffs in the crevices of which dwarfed white birches grow. The smooth gray rock at the end of the point tapers down to the edge of the clear water, and beyond, where it looks yellow on sunny days. — *All the Best People*, Sloan Wilson, 1970.

5155 His window looked onto a derelict mill half-hidden by a small wood above the three ponds, each on a slightly lower level. — *Black List, Section H*, Francis Stuart, 1971.

5156 Ultima came to stay with us the summer I was almost seven. When she came the beauty of the llano unfolded before my eyes, and the gurgling waters of the river sang to the hum of the turning earth. — *Bless Me, Ultima*, Rudolfo A. Anaya, 1972.

5157 From the front of the house and its big sweep of gravelled forecourt the land sloped away gently to the distant sea. — *The Finger of Saturn*, Victor Canning, 1973.

5158 There was the big lagoon just up the bay from Trangloek, what was its name? ...Dha-something Sap, ah yes, Dhaphut, named from the village half hidden where the white sand beach gave way to the dark mangroves. — *Thunder at Sunset*, John Masters, 1974.

5159 Stripped by the season, the countryside was bleak and desolate. — *The Cannaways*, Graham Shelby, 1978.

5160 The Montana landscape is always startling when one comes there straight from the East. — *Creek Mary's Blood*, Dee Brown, 1980.

5161 The land, looking from its highest point, stretched westward and south, rolling fields of broom grass and blackjack oak that glistened in the autumn dew, and a few scrubby pines and thistle bushes, and except in the draws where narrow swampy streams gurgled and tall hardwoods rose from the thickets, it was a harsh, unyielding place, long since timbered out and farmed out — aside from some truck vegetable patches that had been kept by the Negro families. — *As Summers Die*, Winston Groom, 1980.

5162 The lawn, green and smooth as a length of baize, sloped gently down through tall pines to the far end of the point where it ended in a neat curve, a crumbling stone urn of geraniums,

a low stone wall and the end of the land. — *Voices in the Garden*, Dirk Bogarde, 1981.

5163 April 1733 in the West Riding of Yorkshire. The wastes of peat on the hills have a grey clammy look of the cooled and sodden ashes of the forests that had been burnt there. — *Where I Used to Play on the Green*, Glyn Hughes, 1982.

5164 Landscape with figures. The landscape is the contrived and ordered landscape of around 1740: a terrace dropping down to a prospect which itself is discreetly separated by a ha-ha from the view it contemplates. — *Next to Nature, Art*, Penelope Lively, 1982.

5165 The Minervois was a desert. It hung under the sky as if it had been thrown up there, scorned by earth and spurned by Heaven. — *The Knight on the Bridge*, William Watson, 1982.

5166 In northern Ohio there is a county of some hundred thousand arable acres which breaks with the lake region flatland and begins to roll and climb, and to change into rural settings: roadside clusters of houses, small settlements that repose on the edge of nowhere, single lane bridges, backwater country stores with a single rusting gas pump, barns advertising Mail Pouch in frayed and faded postings. — *During the Reign of the Queen of Persia*, Joan Chase, 1983.

5167 It was morning, and the running tide flowed east towards the sun, towards the misty land that lay shadowed by the dark and brooding hills. — *The Wake of the Storm*, Ewan Clarkson, 1983.

5168 The bare hills encircling the Sussex village of Littledean grew greener each minute as the sun rose. — *Stand We at Last*, Zoë Fairbairns, 1983.

5169 He made a wide arc round the hill, until he came to a likely camp site; a place where there was a natural clearing among the skinny gums, just beneath several huge faulted sandstone blocks, and a shallow watercourse that would brim with brown water after heavy rain but in summer would empty to nourish maidenhair ferns in its gutter. — *Tooth and Claw*, Gabrielle Lord, 1983.

5170 Twenty-five years before, the land had been a swamp, a black, oozy mire, crisscrossed with stilting and archlike mangrove roots under which shrimp and snapper spawned and thrived, until it was rescued from its primordial state by an entrepreneur in plus fours. — *No Enemy But Time*, Evelyn Wilde Mayerson, 1983.

5171 The lush, green, horse-studded landscape was taken over by trees as he climbed. — *A Bowl of Cherries*, Shena Mackay, 1984.

5172 The Hampshire countryside gleamed dully after a heavy overnight mist. — *The First to Land*, Douglas Reeman, 1984.

5173 Lucien lived in a landscape of fear, on the dry lands known as los Llanos, "the flatlands," whose name stretched over the plains with a resigned echo of their flatness and that only. — *The Tiger*, Lisa St. Aubin de Terán, 1984.

5174 Here, and also south of us, the beaches have a yellow tint, but along the Keys of Florida the sand is like shattered ivory. — *Fiskadoro*, Denis Johnson, 1985.

5175 The land for miles around is a level spot, flat ground. — *A Flat-Land Fable*, Joe Coomer, 1986.

5176 The country was a wash of pale colours: pale yellow, pale green, pale blue of the foliage on the horizon. — *Swansong*, Richard Francis, 1986.

5177 This is a green and gentle country where I write . . . Sometimes my father drives me to a little beach beside a lake; the narrow strip of sand is white and pure, the water of a blue more deep than any I have ever known. — *Also Georgiana*, Alison Harding, 1986.

5178 They say it's flat as sea level and, so far as the eye can tell, it sure looks like it — some great, blunt stub of the earth, level as a table, as if the Creator had meant to mimic in dirt and pure planes of real estate the dark ascensions and black declinations of space, all His monotonous deep celestials. — *The Rabbi of Lud*, Stanley Elkin, 1987.

5179 On the west side of Paris, by the Sixteenth Arrondissement, where live the elite of the haute bourgeoisie, there is a park of pine, fir, and chestnut trees, landscaped at the turn of the century by le Baron Haussmann. — *Mercedes & the House of Rainbows*, Alan Jolis, 1988.

5180 From where he sat on the terrace outside Laforgue's escape hatch, he noted how the uphill sweep of paddock became a rough wedge of unslashed grass between eucalypt hedgings and moved to an unnatural vanishing point as if landscape had taken over and exaggerated the principles of perspective. — *The Genteel Poverty Bus Company*, Thea Astley, 1992.

5181 Outside the club car window, flat desert nothing as far as the eye could see; endless stubble in level light. — *Cutting Stone*, Janet Burroway, 1992.

Laughter

5182 A light laugh came floating into the sunshine through the green shutters of a room in the Hôtel Milano. — *Jocelyn*, John Galsworthy *as* John Sinjohn, 1898.

5183 He was born with a gift of laughter and a sense that the world was mad. — *Scaramouche*, Rafael Sabatini, 1921.

5184 After distributing the eight ice creams — they were the largest vanilla, chocolate, and raspberry super-bumpers, each in yellow, brown, and almost purple stripes — Pop Larkin climbed up into the cab of the gentian blue, home-painted thirty-hundredweight truck, laughing happily. — *The Darling Buds of May*, H. E. Bates, 1958.

5185 He was laughing, chin up, and shaking his head. — *The Spire*, William Golding, 1964.

5186 Jim MacVeagh's burst of laughter came so unexpectedly, his hand jiggled the stem of the wineglass, and a splash of champagne spotted the linen tablecloth. — *Night of Camp David*, Fletcher Knebel, 1965.

5187 "Why, Barry Day!"/ He had just said something designed to shock her, but Irene only laughed instead, and a minute later could not remember it, for she was half-asleep. — *No Place for an Angel*, Elizabeth Spencer, 1967.

5188 Ayasko stood up and clapped his hands; eyes turned. What was it he was about to say now, this restless man, the dancer whose mouth was always as busy as his feet? They waited in silence, their lips slightly open in readiness for the inevitable laughter. — *A Dancer of Fortune*, John Munonye, 1974.

5189 There were raised fists at the end of Seth's lecture. Laughter followed almost immediately. — *Double Double*, Jose Yglesias, 1974.

5190 Following his Apache trackers up the swale through the jumbles of paddle cactus and ocotillo whips, Cutler saw them gathered on the ridge, pointing, laughing: six of them, dirty brown legs under their filthy shirts astride brown ponies, long black hair in turbans. — *Apaches*, Oakley Hall, 1986.

5191 She is laughing, something to do with the hands, Henry is unsure what, but perhaps it doesn't matter. — *The Bishop*, David Helwig, 1986.

5192 On the twenty-third of April, in 1905, Luther Mathias's mother came into their house and sat down at the table and began to laugh hysterically. — *The Very Air*, Douglas Bauer, 1993.

Law

5193 I was born in the northern part of this united kingdom, in the house of my grandfather; a gentleman of considerable fortune and influence, who had, on many occasions, signalised himself in behalf of his country; and was remarkable for his abilities in the law, which he exercised with great success, in the station of a judge, particularly against beggars, for whom he had a singular aversion. — *The Adventures of Roderick Random*, Tobias Smollett, 1748.

5194 During the first two months of the year 1844, the greatest possible excitement existed in Dublin respecting the State Trials, in which Mr. O'Connell, his son, the Editors of three different repeal newspapers, Tom Steele, the Rev. Mr. Tierney — a priest who had taken a somewhat prominent part in the Repeal Movement — and Mr. Ray, the Secretary to the Repeal Association, were indicted for conspiracy. — *The Kellys and the O'Kellys*, Anthony Trollope, 1848.

5195 "Mamma, what was that I heard papa saying to you this morning about his lawsuit?" — *The Wide, Wide World*, Susan Warner, 1850.

5196 The gentlemen of the jury retired to consider their verdict. — *The Evil Genius*, Wilkie Collins, 1886.

5197 The last day of Circuit Court was over at Kingsborough. — *The Voice of the People*, Ellen Glasgow, 1900.

5198 "*Not guilty, your honor!*" — *The Right of Way*, Gilbert Parker, 1901.

5199 "That's the last case, your Honor," said the young prosecutor, bowing deferentially to the judge. "The calendar stands clear." — *The Cavalier of Tennessee*, Meredith Nicholson, 1928.

5200 The case of the Commonwealth against Stanley Howell and Robert Basso was the county's first trial of men charged with murder in more than a decade, and the district attorney's office, which had a good record for convictions, was anxious to win. — *The Just and the Unjust*, James Gould Cozzens, 1942.

5201 Until Jinny Marshland was called to the stand, the Judge was deplorably sleepy. — *Cass Timberlane*, Sinclair Lewis, 1945.

5202 It was a summer afternoon, the last day of the Bar final examinations. — *The Conscience of the Rich*, C. P. Snow, 1958.

5203 In the not very distant future, after the Third World War, Justice had made great strides. Legal Justice, Economic Justice, Social Justice, and many other forms of justice, of which we do not even know the names, had been attained; but there still remained spheres of human relationship and activity in which Justice did not reign. — *Facial Justice*, L. P. Hartley, 1960.

5204 In the stifling June day court-room the Judge, distaste in his gaunt, exhausted face, addressed the all male jury. — *Paper Sheriff*, Luke Short, 1966.

5205 Amerigo Bonasera sat in New York Criminal Court Number 3 and waited for justice; vengeance on the men who had so cruelly

hurt his daughter, who had tried to dishonor her. — *The Godfather*, Mario Puzo, 1969.

5206 When my lawyer-father was given Juli (Julian) Christo's case to defend, I don't think he realised the sort of moral puzzle he was getting into. — *The Untouchable Juli*, James Aldridge, 1975.

5207 I was with the President at his news conference that Wednesday morning when the maverick Supreme Court Justice William Douglas dropped his bombshell in the Rosenberg case. — *The Public Burning*, Robert Coover, 1977.

5208 On Friday 3 August 1973, three men sat in conference at one of the Inner London Crown Courts — one a fidgeting youth with a lean face; the second a plump, bespectacled man in a crumpled blue suit; and the third a tall, middle-aged barrister wearing a wig and gown. — *A Married Man*, Piers Paul Read, 1979.

5209 On the morning of the first day of Jean Dussault's trial on charges of extortion, Joe Gillis used his "State House Viewpoint" column in the Boston *Commoner* to "put the matter in political perspective." — *A Choice of Enemies*, George V. Higgins, 1984.

5210 "All rise./ "Superior Court of the state of California, in and for the county of Santa Felicia, is now in session, Judge George Hazeltine presiding." — *Spider Webs*, Margaret Millar, 1986.

5211 The law. If Colin Draggett's life was about anything it was about the law. — *The Stanton Succession*, Warren Kiefer, 1992.

Legends

5212 Countless are the stories told of the sayings that Count Antonio spoke and of the deeds that he did when he dwelt an outlaw in the hills. For tales and legends gather round his name thick as the berries hang on a bush, and with the passage of every succeeding year it grows harder to discern where truth lies and where the love of wonder, working together with the sway of a great man's memory, has wrought the embroidery of its fancy on the plain robe of fact. — *The Chronicles of Count Antonio*, Anthony Hope, 1895.

5213 They of Poictesme narrate that in the old days when miracles were as common as fruit pies, young Manuel was a swineherd, living modestly in attendance upon the miller's pigs. — *Figures of Earth*, James Branch Cabell, 1921.

5214 It is time now, I think, to tell the true story of Michael Martin, better known to the people of Ireland generally — though not to his home town — as Captain Lightfoot. I have heard about him all my life, and he has become, after all these years, in a sense, a familiar of mine. — *Captain Lightfoot*, W. R. Burnett, 1954.

5215 Tom Benton, the man, himself, came into Louisiana in 1842, riding out of Texas, out of the sunset, out, in fact, of the myths and legends already enshrouding his past; becoming, by that simple act of appearing at the end of the San Antonio Trace, for the space of years, a man living, breathing, thinking like other men, differing from them only in the minor peculiarities by which each man differs from his fellows. — *Benton's Row*, Frank Yerby, 1954.

5216 There is a young legend developing on the west side of the mountains. It will, inevitably, grow with the years. Like all legends, it is composed of falsehood and fact. In this case, the truth is more compelling than the trappings of imagination with which it has been invested. — *The Lilies of the Field*, William E. Barrett, 1962.

5217 There is the Legend, and there is the Myth. Nor is one to be confused with the other. — *All the Gods and Goddesses*, Kay Martin, 1963.

5218 They say my mom, Miss Essie Mae Loggins, was the wildest girl in Marengo County, Alabama. — *Addie Pray* (later retitled *Paper Moon*), Joe David Brown, 1971.

5219 - Once upon a time, Mary Ann tells herself, there was a beautiful princess named Miranda who had a wish-box. — *Only Children*, Alison Lurie, 1979.

5220 There is a legend of Maharawhenua or Memory Land with its town of Puamahara or Memory Flower. — *The Carpathians*, Janet Frame, 1988.

5221 "By means of certain myths which cannot easily be damaged or debased the majority of us survive. All old great cities possess their special myths. Amongst London's in recent years is the story of the Blitz, of our endurance." — *Mother London*, Michael Moorcock, 1988.

5222 Willow Springs. Everybody knows but nobody talks about the legend of Sapphira Wade. — *Mama Day*, Gloria Naylor, 1988.

5223 The legend in our family is that on the very day Columbus left Spain for the west, the Pintos, with thousands of other Jews, were forced to sail eastward from the port of Cadiz. — *Pinto and Sons*, Leslie Epstein, 1990.

5224 This is one of the German legends. — *The Translator*, Ward Just, 1991.

Lies and Liars

5225 "You lie; you always were a liar, and you always will be a liar. You told my father how I spent the money." — *Dawn*, H. Rider Haggard, 1884.

5226 Wherefore ... during '39–'45, these warring years, an appalling thing happened to me. I acquired a major Fault. I became secretive, told lies, at any rate, rarely the whole truth. Life seemed so many clashes and contests, sorry! and, well, Invention helps. — *All About H. Hatterr*, G. V. Desani, 1948.

5227 In the opinion of the late Queen Elizabeth, Captain John Smith was the most accomplished and versatile liar in England. — *Daughter of Eve*, Noel B. Gerson, 1958.

5228 People know when you are trying to be something that you are not. — *The Big Laugh*, John O'Hara, 1962.

5229 The man in the bar of the Phoenicia Hotel, by the main gate of Valletta, gave me more misinformation, in the space of two hours, than even six gin-and-tonics could really justify. — *The Kappillan of Malta*, Nicholas Monsarrat, 1973.

5230 Once, sometime in the 1930s, when journalists pressed me about the Henneker rumors, I cried out, "We were the great New British South Polar Expedition." We were the apogee, I was implying, of old-fashioned Britannic endeavor. If we lied, then all institutions were liars. — *Victim of the Aurora*, Thomas Keneally, 1977.

5231 Gynecologists lie. — *The Best Laid Plans*, Gail Parent, 1980.

5232 As I often tell the young ones, you must lie to survive. — *The Frog Who Dared to Croak*, Richard Sennett, 1982.

5233 Mary Fisher lives in a High Tower, on the edge of the sea: she writes a great deal about the nature of love. She tells lies. — *The Life and Loves of a She-Devil*, Fay Weldon, 1983.

5234 Caleb Sparrow lied to his father: he had for years. — *The Real World*, Christopher Knowlton, 1984.

5235 There are people who take themselves too seriously and say this David Ingram was a liar. — *The Wines of Pentagoët*, John Gould, 1986.

5236 My mother lied to me about everything. — *Collaborators*, Janet Kauffman, 1986.

5237 I've always been a liar — it runs in my family. — *Utrillo's Mother*, Sarah Baylis, 1987.

5238 At this most significant of moments, preparing for bed in their jointly leased apartment on the seventh floor of the handsome new glass-and-poured-concrete Greenwood Towers, after a year, or has it been more, of passion, and indecision, and speculation, and hesitation, and — much, much more: the intricacies of romantic love resist transcription — at this most delicate and intimate of moments Molly Marks, to her distress, finds herself in the awkward position of having caught her lover Jonathan McEwan in a lie. — *Lives of the Twins*, Joyce Carol Oates *as* Rosamond Smith, 1987.

5239 Marjorie's husband, Byron Coffin, had misled her for so long that she learned to lean away from life to keep from falling over, like a woman walking a large dog. — *The Woman Who Was Not All There*, Paula Sharp, 1988.

5240 No matter what lies they may tell about me in Philadelphia, I am a true American patriot. — *Jeremiah Martin*, Robert H. Fowler, 1989.

5241 *We are all masters of self-deception.* — *The Late-Summer Passion of a Woman of Mind*, Rebecca Goldstein, 1989.

5242 A lie: the three of us together on the water, me and two people I'm tied to for life. — *The War Zone*, Alexander Stuart, 1989.

5243 Every time I try to talk about Kate I find myself falling into oblique and deceptive descriptions. — *The Ouroboros*, Howard Coale, 1991.

5244 Hugo was a liar. — *A Matter of Life and Sex*, Oscar Moore, 1991.

5245 I used to lie to my father about Little League. — *Past the Bleachers*, Christopher A. Bohjalian, 1992.

5246 Someone must have been telling lies about Sitko Ghost Horse, because without having done anything wrong he was arrested. — *Kill Hole*, Jamake Highwater, 1992.

Life

5247 "The whole of this modern fabric of existence is a living lie!" cried Marzio Pandolfi, striking his little hammer upon the heavy table with an impatient rap. — *Marzio's Crucifix*, F. Marion Crawford, 1887.

5248 "'Tisn't life that matters! 'Tis the courage you bring to it" ... this from old Frosted Moses in the warm corner by the door. — *Fortitude*, Hugh Walpole, 1913.

5249 I returned from the city about three o'clock on that May afternoon pretty well disgusted with life. — *The Thirty-nine Steps*, John Buchan, 1915.

5250 To Emeline, wife of George Page, there came slowly, in her thirtieth year, a sullen

conviction that life was monstrously unfair. — *The Story of Julia Page*, Kathleen Norris, 1915.

5251 At five o'clock life seemed extinct up at the Villa Byrsa. — *The Labyrinth*, Cecil Roberts, 1944.

5252 I think I first began to come back to life when I decided to withdraw from it, or at least to cut my commitments. — *False Coin*, Harvey Swados, 1959.

5253 Everyone now knows how to find the meaning of life within himself. — *The Sirens of Titan*, Kurt Vonnegut, 1959.

5254 Life is like a long blind date. — *Where the Boys Are*, Glendon Swarthout, 1960.

5255 The hallelujah bum is what we're all on. And there's no end to it till we rate a pair of wings. — *The Paradise Bum*, Andrew Sinclair, 1963.

5256 "Oh, what a life, what a worthless, lousy, dirty life," one of them cursed beneath his breath, staring at the tick that was sucking the life from the hoary grey ear of the donkey that pulled the cart. — *The Children of Sisyphus*, Orlando Patterson, 1964.

5257 In his new boots, Joe Buck was six-foot-one and life was different. — *Midnight Cowboy*, James Leo Herlihy, 1965.

5258 "There's more life up this end," Mrs. Poulter said. — *The Solid Mandala*, Patrick White, 1966.

5259 ...maybe, Myra decides. Maybe the biggest problem in life is how to spend it. — *Maybe*, Burt Blechman, 1967.

5260 The first fresh minute of anno domini one thousand nine hundred and thirty-nine: sirens from the tarry tidal Thames, bells horns faint cheers all shredding the common watchful silence and rising into one hysterical disembodied note that was as ominous as joyous: folk glad to be alive or afraid to be alive. — *As Towns with Fire*, Anthony C. West, 1968.

5261 After death has passed by, the trappings of life that remain are not tragic, not even sad. — *My Friend Sashie*, Jane Duncan, 1972.

5262 When Man was still very young he had already become aware that certain elemental forces dominated the world womb. — *The Snow Walker*, Farley Mowat, 1975.

5263 Stop: The doorway of life. — *Emergency Exit*, Clarence Major, 1979.

5264 "There is a pattern," Blanche Dean was apt to sigh tiresomely, often. — *The Peach Groves*, Barbara Hanrahan, 1980.

5265 It seemed to Nellie that life was as deforming as an ill-fitting shoe, and that by a series of small, forced adjustments — the slow, worldwise business of surrendering natural edges and boundaries — she had become a strangely shaped creature. — *Nellie Without Hugo*, Janet Hobhouse, 1982.

5266 To the as-yet-unborn, to all innocent wisps of undifferentiated nothingness: Watch out for life. — *Deadeye Dick*, Kurt Vonnegut, 1982.

5267 Living things prefer to go on living. — *The Coffin Tree*, Wendy Law-Yone, 1983.

5268 The day was so delightful that I wished one could live slowly as one can play music slowly. — *This Real Night*, Rebecca West, 1984.

5269 Some threescore years have passed since I emerged from the vast Indifference; I expect that less than threescore days remain before I am swallowed up again. — *Between Eternities*, Robert H. Pilpel, 1985.

5270 To be alive is to have an open mind. — *Fine*, Samuel Shem, 1985.

5271 It was today — rather yesterday I think — that he told me it was important not to accept life as a brutal approximation. — *Dalva*, Jim Harrison, 1988.

5272 How many species? Surely as many as there are stars in the heavens, from lice glued onto a strand of hair to powerful gnats that can pierce a man's boot, from aphid cows enslaved by ants to weevils napping comfortably inside curled poplar leaves. — *The Closest Possible Union*, Joanna Scott, 1988.

5273 *If all life is change, I Hannah Brody must really be living!* — *A Woman of Spirit*, Herbert Tarr, 1989.

5274 Hazard rules our lives, or so it has seemed to me. — *Fire Along the Sky*, Robert Moss, 1990.

Lifestyles

5275 During the next month or two my solitary town-life seemed, by contrast, unusually dull and tedious. — *Sylvie and Bruno Concluded*, Lewis Carroll, 1893.

5276 It had occurred to her early that in her position — that of a young person spending, in framed and wired confinement, the life of a guineapig or a magpie — she should know a great many persons without their recognising the acquaintance. — *In the Cage*, Henry James, 1898.

5277 A wallaby would have done just as well as a human being to endure the nothingness of existence as it has been known to me. — *The End of My Career*, Miles Franklin, 1902.

5278 If I spoke with Altrurian breadth of the way New-Yorkers live, my dear Cyril, I should begin by saying that the New-Yorkers did not live at all. — *Through the Eye of the Needle*, William Dean Howells, 1907.

5279 There is no more joyous couple in all Mayfair than Sir Louis Marigold, Bart, M.P., and Lady Mary Marigold, and whether they are at Marigold Park, Bucks, or at Homburg, or in their spacious residence in Berkley Square, their lives form one unbroken round of pomp and successful achievement. — *The Freaks of Mayfair*, E. F. Benson, 1916.

5280 Until the other day we Americans lived as though we had no past. — *The Island Within*, Ludwig Lewisohn, 1928.

5281 I was a palm-wine drinkard since I was a boy of ten years of age. I had no other work more than to drink palm-wine in my life. — *The Palm-Wine Drinkard*, Amos Tutuola, 1952.

5282 I got no kicks coming, though. I live okay. — *Big Man*, Jay Neugeboren, 1966.

5283 There was this very old woman living last year in a way you could hardly have believed if you had known of it; not many did, and those few only superficially and in part. — *The Light Here Kindled*, Gladys Hasty Carroll, 1967.

5284 I'm only telling you this to let you know what a silly thing it is to live like I do. — *The Chantic Bird*, David Ireland, 1968.

5285 Freedom: by definition, what has not been attained. — "A Truth Lover," John Herdman, 1973.

5286 The land's fertile peace lulled, the warm Negev breeze held a lull, and the sky, a blue of the first firmament, of bluest delphiniums, glowed a wondrous lull, and working a seventy-two-hour week and sometimes more, Israeli-style, made its own lull, and day by day I felt myself returning to a commons of good life, saner, kindlier than I had known, remote from the lunatic strut I left with such relief. — *Bride of Israel, My Love*, Richard Llewellyn, 1973.

5287 In the winter, she lived like a mole, buried deep in her office, digging among maps and manuscripts. — *Bear*, Marian Engel, 1976.

5288 The wild life in Medan was something neither night nor DDT could stop. — *A Rude Awakening*, Brian W Aldiss, 1978.

5289 I've got this feeling that real life, by which I mean life as lived in London NW4 in the 1920s, which is of course just too soon for me really to remember it, must sooner or later return or even be rediscovered, going on perfectly normally (I use the word advisedly) in Basingstoke or Lincolnshire or Leeds. — *Lady on the Burning Deck*, Catherine Heath, 1978.

5290 I don't know how I should live. — *Life Before Man*, Margaret Atwood, 1979.

5291 Katherine Walden was not unaware of the alienation of modern life in general or the impersonal indifference of New York City in particular. — *a.k.a. Katherine Walden*, Ellen Feldman, 1982.

5292 Sometimes the sordidness of his present existence, not to mention the stifling, clammy heat of the apartment his finances had forced him to take, on the third floor of an ugly old house on Binghamton's West Side — "the nice part of town," everybody said (God have mercy on those who had to live in the bad parts) — made Peter Mickelsson clench his square yellow teeth in anger and once, in a moment of rage and frustration greater than usual, bring down the heel of his fist on the heavy old Goodwill oak table where his typewriter, papers, and books were laid out, or rather strewn. — *Mickelsson's Ghosts*, John Gardner, 1982.

5293 We were running flat out. — *Pitch Dark*, Renata Adler, 1983.

5294 During the last few years, since 1832, life in England has become settled, comfortable and prosperous. — *Havannah*, Hugh Thomas, 1984.

5295 The Beast destroyed my brief peace. Before him I could live without guilt, unwatched; for the first time in my life I found myself in the unfamiliar situation of having no one to disappoint. — *My Present Age*, Guy Vanderhaeghe, 1984.

5296 I promised Lily I was going to quit complaining about things, about my job, about the people I worked with, about the way things were at home with her, about our son Charles and the way he sometimes didn't seem to be coming along, about the country, about *Nightline* and *Crossfire*, about the mess we live in, the mess we make of our lives every day, about everybody lying all the time, smug and self-satisfied and just close enough to the facts to get by. — *Natural Selection*, Frederick Barthelme, 1986.

5297 The way we live now, jetting from palmy LaLa Land to gray and frenzied New York City, to azure Venice, the Serenissima of all Serenissime — the most serene republic of our dreams — we might as well be time traveling. And we are. — *Serenissima*, Erica Jong, 1987.

5298 Nothing sounded more inviting to her than settling down. — *To the Birdhouse*, Cathleen Schine, 1990.

5299 *Take a man with a nice face and sad eyes, fifty or more winters on his back, living a moderately pleasant life in a tranquil country.* — *Wartime Lies*, Louis Begley, 1991.

5300 *They lived happily ever after.* — *Hug Dancing*, Shelby Hearon, 1991.

5301 Put on plaid flannel shirts, sport a well-defined mustache, grow apprehensive, solvent: Young Gay Manhood at last. — *The Death of Donna-May Dean*, Joey Manley, 1991.

5302 We no longer see anyone anymore. — *City of Childhood*, Valerie Townsend Bayer, 1992.

5303 In October things settled down. — *Walking into the River*, Lorian Hemingway, 1992.

5304 I live a life of deceit. — *Divorcing Daddy*, Susan Trott, 1992.

Light and Lights

5305 The level light of a summer sunset, over a broad heath, is brightening its brown undulations with a melancholy flush, and turning all the stalks of heather in the foreground into twisted sticks of gold. — *The Rose and the Key*, J. Sheridan LeFanu, 1871.

5306 "Do you see any light yet, Joe?" — *Wild Western Scenes*, J. B. Jones, 1880.

5307 Light, entering the vast room — a room so high that its carved ceiling refused itself to exact scrutiny — travelled, with the wistful, cold curiosity of the dawn, over a fantastic storehouse of Time. Light, unaccompanied by the prejudice of human eyes, made strange revelation of incongruities, as though illuminating the dispassionate march of history. — *The Patrician*, John Galsworthy, 1911.

5308 The sunshine of a fair Spring morning fell graciously on London town. Out in Piccadilly its heartening warmth seemed to infuse into traffic and pedestrians alike a novel jauntiness, so that bus drivers jested and even the lips of chauffeurs uncurled into not unkindly smiles. — *Something New*, P. G. Wodehouse, 1915.

5309 Through the curtained windows of the furnished flat which Mrs. Horace Hignett had rented for her stay in New York, rays of golden sunlight peeped in like the foremost spies of some advancing army. — *The Girl on the Boat*, P. G. Wodehouse, 1922.

5310 Ghosts of centuries of sunlight crowded this August afternoon. — *The Mad Carews*, Martha Ostenso, 1927.

5311 Sunshine pierced the haze that enveloped London. It came down Fleet Street, turned to the right, stopped at the premises of the Mammoth Publishing Company, and, entering through an upper window, beamed pleasantly upon Lord Tilbury, founder and proprietor of that vast factory of popular literature as he sat reading the batch of weekly papers which his secretary had placed on the desk for his inspection. — *Heavy Weather*, P. G. Wodehouse, 1933.

5312 An invisible needle of light pried its way into the minute cavities of an uncut diamond. — *Before the Dawn*, Eric Temple Bell *as* John Taine, 1934.

5313 By eight o'clock the last day of October was about as well lighted as it would be. — *The Ante-Room*, Kate O'Brien, 1934.

5314 Though it was still far off sundown, the sun had hidden behind the tops of the tall elm-trees which overshadowed the deep garden. Long shafts of light, rich and golden as a tapestry, spread downwards through the foliage, and leaned across the garden; and in them the midges began their last dance of the day. — *King Richard's Land*, L. A. G. Strong, 1934.

5315 Down on the shore I saw the fishermen lighting their oil lamps. — *Storm and Echo*, Frederic Prokosch, 1948.

5316 It was very bright in the schoolroom. Fresh May sunshine washed down through the clear air and patterned the high windows across the desks and on the floor. — *On the Highest Hill*, Roderick L. Haig-Brown, 1949.

5317 The canvas walls of the dressing tent were discolored with brown water spots, with green grass stains and grey streaks of mildew, and the prickles of sun glittering came through. — *Burning Bright*, John Steinbeck, 1950.

5318 Occasional breaks in the foliage let shafts and freshets of sunlight fall on the hoof-scarred road. — *Forest of the Night*, Madison Jones, 1960.

5319 Everything sparkled. — *The Sun in Scorpio*, Margery Sharp, 1965.

5320 The lights in the bus burned dim, orange-hued behind opaque bevelled glass; ranged below the luggage racks they lit up the advertisement panels with repeated circles of bilious light. — *Langrishe, Go Down*, Aidan Higgins, 1966.

5321 *As Abrams and his children turned the corner and entered Longview Avenue, the street lights went on. The sudden discharge of light seemed to him overdramatic, a display he had staged, a trick prearranged with Consolidated Edison.* — *To Brooklyn with Love*, Gerald Green, 1967.

5322 It was the middle of Friday morning. The sun shone gold-brown on the expanse of parquet floor, in room after room. — *The Public Image*, Muriel Spark, 1968.

5323 Slanting between the red-brick ranks of apartment houses and business buildings of Upper Manhattan, the sun struck Norman on his bared head, finding its way also to the wooden platform from which he addressed the street-corner meeting. — *Standing Fast*, Harvey Swados, 1970.

5324 The little flame burned beneath a gilt-headed statue of the Virgin. It quivered in the draught that crept in the corners of the great chamber; it burned up and down, shining upon worn tapestries. At times its radiance stung the eyes of the woman in bed. — *The King's Grey Mare*, Rosemary Hawley Jarman, 1973.

5325 The water in the metal tank slopped sideways and a treacly ripple ran along the edge,

reached the corner and died away. Under the electric lights the broken surface was faceted as a cracked mirror, a watery harlequin's coat of tilting planes and lozenges in movement, one moment dull as stone and the next glittering like scalpels. — *The Plague Dogs*, Richard Adams, 1978.

5326 Light. Glowing yellow. It spills into the room of wavering shadows and forms a pool on the floor. — *Waking*, Eva Figes, 1981.

5327 Before they wake, sunlight is on the house, moving on the high east wall and windows through old glass wavy as broken water, onto the hard bright floor of waxed pine. — *Dreams of Sleep*, Josephine Humphreys, 1984.

5328 A moment before the sun appeared, its rays struck the top of the television antenna that poked through the center of the island like a spindle. — *Nerve Endings*, William Martin, 1984.

5329 When the boy Vanya awoke to the dappled light, filtering through swaying birches and the leaded glass windows pervading every room of the house, each window so multifaceted, so prismatic, that in later years mere sunlight would be invisible to him, a mysterious force burning the bridge of his nose during rugby matches, his shoulders as he lay on the beach at Nice, laziness always mixed with frustration. — *Inventing Ivanov*, Roberta Smoodin, 1985.

5330 Sun came through today. The kitchen filled up first, with pale orange stripes on red walls and Moura's blue-and-green porcelain cups going suddenly the colour of the sea outside. — *The Half-Mother*, Emma Tennant, 1985.

5331 Sifting through a thin screen of fog, the afternoon light gilded the domes and steeples rising over Russell Square, making the city seem to tremble with some secret illumination from within. — *The God of Mirrors*, Robert Reilly, 1986.

5332 He watched the lights fade one by one, smothered quick as kittens, as they turned the wicks down. — *Mrs. Randall*, Christopher T. Leland, 1987.

5333 The morning sun glittered on the bathroom tiles. — *The Other Hand Clapping*, Marco Vassi, 1987.

5334 The sun came in at a slant and hit all the rings and marks on the bar counter. — *Firefly Summer*, Maeve Binchy, 1988.

5335 The vision began at a quarter to six; around me the room was suffused with light, not the pellucid light of a fine midsummer morning but the dim light of a wet dawn in May. — *Glamorous Powers*, Susan Howatch, 1988.

5336 Rosa reached out and switched off the last light. — *Good Hearts*, Reynolds Price, 1988.

5337 The two women sit beneath the oak tree, and the sunlight that filters through the young leaves filigrees their upturned faces with a lacy radiance. — *Mothers*, Gloria Goldreich, 1989.

5338 Night. Lights on. The lights that glide in jewelled columns, red and white, that make glowing caverns of the windows opposite, that rake the bedroom ceiling in long yellow shafts. — *City of the Mind*, Penelope Lively, 1991.

5339 He looked down from the dark room at the streetlamp. Specks of dust danced in its orange glow like tiny flickering moths, appearing and disappearing as they turned over. — *The Sensationist*, Charles Palliser, 1991.

5340 The August sun was up, pouring through the open window, shimmering in visible waves again. — *His Master's Voice*, Robert Kotlowitz, 1992.

5341 The word *Patchogue* without the capital *P*, in Old Finnish, is the adjective used to describe the quality of light given off by the setting sun when seen through a stand of white birch trees. — *Going to Patchogue*, Thomas McGonigle, 1992.

5342 Sunlight begins to fill the town square. — *Blue Crystal*, Philip Lee Williams, 1993.

Likes and Dislikes

5343 For some months after our marriage, Euphemia and I boarded. But we did not like it; indeed, there was no reason why we should. — *Rudder Grange*, Frank R. Stockton, 1879.

5344 "I prefer the dark style, myself — like my cousin," said John Ralston, thoughtfully./ "And you will therefore naturally marry a fair woman," answered his companion, Hamilton Bright, stopping to look at the display in a florist's window. — *Katharine Lauderdale*, F. Marion Crawford, 1893.

5345 The Prince had always liked his London, when it had come to him; he was one of the modern Romans who find by the Thames a more convincing image of the truth of the ancient state than any they have left by the Tiber. — *The Golden Bowl*, Henry James, 1904.

5346 Young Rossiter did not like the task. — *The Purple Parasol*, George Barr McCutcheon, 1905.

5347 As the car mounted the hump of the canal bridge, Norby was talking to himself. "Well," he said, "if you don't like it you'll just have to lump it. That's all." — *Square Peg*, Walter Allen, 1951.

5348 What she liked was candy buttons, and books, and painted music (deep blue, or delicate silver) and the west sky, so altering, viewed from the steps of the back porch; and dandelions. — *Maud Martha*, Gwendolyn Brooks, 1953.

5349 Two men faced each other across the club table, the one cheerfully insensitive to the other's well-restrained dislike. — *Like Men Betrayed*, John Mortimer, 1953.

5350 "Can't you tell me, Mr. Lumley, just what it is that you don't like about the rooms?" — *Hurry On Down*, John Wain, 1953.

5351 In hot weather Hazel liked to sit in the dental chair. Its leather arms and back were cool and there was a fan in the ceiling above it. — *Wives and Lovers*, Margaret Millar, 1954.

5352 By the time they had lived seven years in the little house on Greentree Avenue in Westport, Connecticut, they both detested it. — *The Man in the Gray Flannel Suit*, Sloan Wilson, 1955.

5353 I hate the faces of peasants. — *A World of Strangers*, Nadine Gordimer, 1958.

5354 Louisa Mary Datchett was very fond of men. — *Something Light*, Margery Sharp, 1960.

5355 I will tell you in a few words who I am: lover of the hummingbird that darts to the flower beyond the rotted sill where my feet are propped; lover of bright needlepoint and the bright stitching fingers of humorless old ladies bent to their sweet and infamous designs; lover of parasols made from the same puffy stuff as a young girl's underdrawers; still lover of that small naval boat which somehow survived the distressing years of my life between her decks or in her pilothouse; and also lover of poor dear black Sonny, my mess boy, fellow victim and confidant, and of my wife and child. But most of all, lover of my harmless and sanguine self. — *Second Skin*, John Hawkes, 1964.

5356 What Esther Wells liked about Earls Court was that she didn't know anyone who lived there. — *...And the Wife Ran Away*, Fay Weldon, 1968.

5357 I sit with a whiskey on the terrace, contemplating the view. The view I detest. The view I once adored. No, I must be fair to myself; I never adored it. I saw its aesthetic qualities; that steep torrent of olive trees, pouring down the hill in a cascade of pale green. — *A Cry of Crickets*, Brian Glanville, 1970.

5358 Yes, everybody loves a parade. Don't you? All kinds, too. — *Proceedings of the Rabble*, Mark Mirsky, 1970.

5359 *No one hated more dearly my home town of Boutflour, planked down far south in this "Yankee state," than my Uncle Matt Lacey.* — *Jeremy's Version*, James Purdy, 1970.

5360 Lee spent a good deal of time on buses and trains. She liked traveling thought she wasn't much of a sightseer. — *Travelers*, Ruth Prawer Jhabvala, 1973.

5361 I don't want to go to the Zoo any more. — *Turtle Diary*, Russell Hoban, 1975.

5362 I love GOOD and hate EVIL. — *Skeletons*, Glendon Swarthout, 1979.

5363 "Hey, Faust," I said./ He didn't answer me./ He doesn't like it when I talk like that. — *Faust*, Robert Nye, 1980.

5364 He dreaded the summer. — *Lost and Found*, Julian Gloag, 1981.

5365 I used to dislike shopping, the rushing here and there, and all the details to remember. Now it's almost pleasant. — *A Season of Delight*, Joanne Greenberg, 1981.

5366 "Did you ever see a boy likes ice cream so much?" — *Mourners Below*, James Purdy, 1981.

5367 He hates that she came along. — *Only Shorter*, Ross Feld, 1982.

5368 As much as Martin Lalor loved India, there were times when he hated her. — *A Soldier of India*, Tom Gibson, 1982.

5369 "I thought you liked Tom," Martin said. He looked puzzled, not hurt. — *Poor Tom*, Mary Hobson, 1982.

5370 In the days of his youth, in the summertime, when school didn't interfere, Harry Eastep liked to spend a certain portion of his afternoons hanging around Marvin Conklin's drugstore, to catch the arrival of the Cincinnati-Lexington Greyhound. — *The Natural Man*, Ed McClanahan, 1983.

5371 I detest coronations. England has seen two such spectacles in my lifetime, and it has been my misfortune to attend both. — *Good King Harry*, Denise Giardina, 1984.

5372 Miss Pennyquick hated washdays. Up to her scant eyebrows in filthy water she reassessed her foot-square view of the yard and found it as depressing as ever; and the sodden curtains in the tub looked still, in spite of her frenzied ministrations, like old dishcloths. — *A Season of Mists*, Sarah Woodhouse, 1984.

5373 Amy loves rain. — *Rainy Day Man*, Rita Garitano, 1985.

5374 The only thing I disliked about having the paper route that summer was actually waking up. — *Second Brother*, David Guy, 1985.

5375 I've heard some pretty fancy explanations for why I hate helicopters. — *Hollaran's World War*, Tim Mahoney, 1985.

5376 I always liked this bathroom wallpaper, though I never expected to lie here staring up at it. — *Pay the Piper*, Joan Williams, 1988.

5377 John, 18, hated his face. — *Closer*, Dennis Cooper, 1989.

5378 Winnette has always been attracted to danger. — *The Widow's Trial*, John Ehle, 1989.

5379 No one could really like Jimmy Jamison, but that should come as no surprise. No one did. — *The Toothache Tree*, Jack Galloway, 1989.

5380 "Do you think Henry would like to feed the catfish?" — *Sort of Rich*, James Wilcox, 1989.

5381 If I contemplate the desires of my life, wise and foolish, if I ponder on their value and their strength, the absolute and most intricate attraction I have ever known concerns cats. — *The Drowning of a Goldfish*, Lidmila Sováková, 1990.

5382 The girls were fat and sassy and we guys liked them that way. We were tough and horny and they liked us that way. — *A Time for Wedding Cake*, Salvatore La Puma, 1991.

5383 Adrian John Northwood loved the snow almost as much as he disliked the modern world on which it fell. — *Innocent Darkness*, Edward R. F. Sheehan, 1993.

Literature

5384 You may be sure I received with resentment enough the account that a most ridiculous book, entitled, "My Life and Adventures," had been published in England, being fully assured nothing of truth could be contained in such a work; and though it may be true that my extravagant story may be the proper foundation of a romance, yet as no man has a title to publish it better than I have to expose and contradict it, I send you this by one of my particular friends, who, having an opportunity of returning into England, has promised to convey it faithfully to you, by which at least two things shall be made good to the world: first, that they shall be satisfied in the scandalous and unjust manner in which others have already treated me, and it shall give, in the meantime, a larger account of what may at present be fit to be made public of my unhappy though successful adventures. — *The King of Pirates*, Daniel Defoe, 1719.

5385 An author ought to consider himself, not as a gentleman who gives a private or eleemosynary treat, but rather as one who keeps a public ordinary, at which all persons are welcome for their money. — *Tom Jones*, Henry Fielding, 1749.

5386 As the reader is not to consider this performance in the light of a novel or a romance, but the real adventures of a person who has made some noise in the gay world, so he must not be surprised if he meets with nothing in these sheets bordering upon the marvellous or surprising. — *Memoirs of Maria Brown*, John Cleland, 1766.

5387 RESPECTED SIR,/ I have received your esteemed favour of the 13th ultimo, whereby it appeareth, that you have perused those same Letters, the which were delivered unto you by my friend the reverend Mr. Hugo Behn; and I am pleased to find you think they may be printed with a good prospect of success; in as much as the objections you mention, I humbly conceive, are such as may be redargued, if not entirely removed — And, first, in the first place, as touching what prosecutions may arise from printing the private correspondence of persons still living, give me leave, with all due submission, to observe, that the Letters in question were not written and sent under the seal of secrecy; that they have no tendency to the *mala fama*, or prejudice of any person whatsoever; but rather to the information and edification of mankind: so that it becometh a sort of duty to promulgate them *in usum publicum.* — *The Expedition of Humphry Clinker*, Tobias Smollett, 1771.

5388 I feel little reluctance in complying with your request. — *Wieland*, Charles Brockden Brown, 1798.

5389 I sit down, my friend, to comply with thy request. — *Edgar Huntly*, Charles Brockden Brown, 1799.

5390 As this my story will probably run counter to more than one fashion of the day, literary and other, it is prudent to bow to those fashions wherever I honestly can; and therefore to begin with a scrap of description. — *Yeast*, Charles Kingsley, 1851.

5391 What am I now about to write? — *Basil*, Wilkie Collins, 1852.

5392 Some years ago was printed, and published anonymously, dedicated to the author's enemies, a small book of original Aphorisms, under the heading, THE PILGRIM'S SCRIP. The book was noticeable for its quaint earnestness, and a perversity of view regarding Women, whom the writer seldom extolled, and appeared with all conscience to rank as creatures still doing service to the Serpent: bound to their instincts, and happily subordinate in public affairs, though but too powerful in their own walk. — *The Ordeal of Richard Feverel*, George Meredith, 1859.

5393 I wonder whether the novel-reading world — that part of it, at least, which may honour my pages — will be offended if I lay the plot of this story in Ireland! — *Castle Richmond*, Anthony Trollope, 1860.

5394 It will be observed by the literary and commercial world that, in this transaction, the name of the really responsible party does not show on the title-page. — *The Struggles of Brown, Jones, and Robinson*, Anthony Trollope, 1862.

5395 Let the reader be introduced to Lady Carbury, upon whose character and doings much will depend of whatever interest these pages may have, as she sits at her writing-table in her own room in her own house in Welbeck Street. — *The Way We Live Now*, Anthony Trollope, 1874-1875.

5396 A pretty little anthology might be made of poems by distinguished writers who have never for a moment professed to be poets, and who only "swept, with hurried hand, the strings" when they thought nobody was listening. — *Prince Otto*, Robert Louis Stevenson, 1885.

5397 He that has jilted the Muse, forsaking her gentle pipe to follow the drum and trumpet, shall fruitlessly besiege her again when the time comes to sit at home and write down his adventures. 'Tis her revenge, as I am extremely sensible: and methinks she is the harder to me, upon reflection how near I came to being her life-long servant, as you are to hear. — *The Splendid Spur*, Arthur Quiller-Couch *as* Q, 1889.

5398 The inner room of a tobacconist's shop is not perhaps the spot which a writer of fiction would naturally choose as the theatre of his play, nor does the inventor of pleasant romances, of stirring incident, or moving love-tales, feel himself instinctively inclined to turn to Munich as to the city of his dreams. — *A Cigarette-Maker's Romance*, F. Marion Crawford, 1890.

5399 The writer of this singular autobiography was my cousin, who died at the ——— Criminal Lunatic Asylum, of which he had been an inmate three years. — *Peter Ibbetson*, George du Maurier, 1892.

5400 The circumstances under which the following pages come to be printed are somewhat curious and worthy of record. — *Heart of the World*, H. Rider Haggard, 1895.

5401 Any one who hopes to find in what is here written a work of literature had better lay it aside unread. — *The Great K. & A. Robbery*, Paul Leicester Ford, 1897.

5402 It is a strange thing that I, an old Boer *vrouw*, should even think of beginning to write a book when there are such numbers already in the world, most of them worthless, and many of the rest a scandal and offence in the face of the Lord. — *Swallow*, H. Rider Haggard, 1899.

5403 For more than a week my pen has lain untouched. I have written nothing for seven whole days, not even a letter. Except during one or two bouts of illness such a thing has never happened in my life before. — *Henry Ryecroft*, George Gissing, 1903.

5404 First I am to write a love-story of long ago, of a time some little while after General Jackson had got into the White House and had shown the world what a real democracy was. — *Coniston*, Winston Churchill, 1906.

5405 *I saw a gray-haired man a figure of hale age, sitting at a desk and writing.* — *In the Days of the Comet*, H. G. Wells, 1906.

5406 To begin with I wish to disclaim the possession of those high gifts of imagination and expression which would have enabled my pen to create for the reader the personality of the man who called himself, after the Russian custom, Cyril son of Isidor — Kirylo Sidorovitch — Razumov. — *Under Western Eyes*, Joseph Conrad, 1911.

5407 The Scorpions were to meet at eight o'clock and before that hour Kenneth Forbes had to finish the first chapter of a serial story. — *Kathleen*, Christopher Morley, 1920.

5408 At the very beginning of the tale there comes a moment of puzzled hesitation. One way of approach is set beside another for choice, and a third contrived for better choice. Still the puzzle persists, all because the one precisely right way might seem — shall we say intense, high keyed, clamorous? Yet if one way is the only right way, why pause? Courage! Slightly dazed, though certain, let us be on, into the shrill thick of it. So, then — *Merton of the Movies*, Harry Leon Wilson, 1922.

5409 If there is progress then there is a novel. — *The Great American Novel*, William Carlos Williams, 1923.

5410 The great Professor Challenger has been — very improperly and imperfectly — used in fiction. A daring author placed him in impossible and romantic situations in order to see how he would react to them. — *The Land of Mist*, Arthur Conan Doyle, 1926.

5411 I am Doris of Colossæ, known by many as "The Woman of the Great Memories," and in this twelfth year of the reign of Domitian I have sworn, by the most high God, that I will write them down so that my readers shall be as they who have been wont to sit before me and listen, and this I do with no fear of the fate they shall bring upon me. — *Dawn*, Irving Bacheller, 1927.

5412 Had I the slightest qualifications for the task, I, Allan Quatermain, would like to write an essay on Temptation. — *Allan and the Ice-Gods*, H. Rider Haggard, 1927.

5413 By the time he was nineteen Vance Weston had graduated from the College of Euphoria, Illinois, where his parents then lived, had spent a week in Chicago, invented a new religion, and edited for a few months a college magazine called *Getting There*, to which he had contributed several love poems and a series of iconoclastic essays. — *Hudson River Bracketed*, Edith Wharton, 1929.

5414 Among the many problems which beset the novelist, not the least weighty is the choice of the moment at which to begin his novel. It is necessary, it is indeed unavoidable, that he should intersect the lives of his dramatis personae at a given hour; all that remains is to decide which hour it shall be, and in what situation they shall be discovered. — *The Edwardians*, V. Sackville-West, 1930.

5415 Lushington collected the pieces of type-written foolscap and shook them together so that the edges were level. — *Venusberg*, Anthony Powell, 1932.

5416 *June 9th.* — Life takes on entirely new aspect, owing to astonishing and unprecedented success of minute and unpretentious literary effort, published last December, and — incredibly — written by myself. — *The Provincial Lady in London*, E. M. Delafield, 1933.

5417 Commander James Driscoll, attached to the Intelligence branch of the United States Navy, has asked me to write this, in order that my version may be placed in the files with his own account of certain peculiar transactions which took place in Japan and China some months ago. — *No Hero*, John P. Marquand, 1935.

5418 What is not in the open street is false, derived, that is to say, *literature.* — *Black Spring*, Henry Miller, 1936.

5419 It was in the incongruous setting of an expensive London restaurant that an American publisher was moved to exclaim to an astonished dinner-guest whose novels he had published for years:/ "I wish to Heavens you'd go and live on a Collective Farm in Russia for six months, and write a funny book about it." — *I Visit the Soviets*, E. M. Delafield, 1937.

5420 If I were not perfectly sure of my power to write and of my marvelous ability to express ideas with the utmost grace and vividness . . . So, more or less, I had thought of beginning my tale. — *Despair*, Vladimir Nabokov, 1937.

5421 This book has not been written to prove a case. — *Northwest Passage*, Kenneth Roberts, 1937.

5422 It is a sin to write this. — *Anthem*, Ayn Rand, 1938.

5423 While still a young man, John Courteney Boot had, as his publisher proclaimed, "achieved an assured and enviable position in contemporary letters." — *Scoop*, Evelyn Waugh, 1938.

5424 Having placed in my mouth sufficient bread for three minutes' chewing, I withdrew my powers of sensual perception and retired into the privacy of my mind, my eyes and face assuming a vacant and preoccupied expression. I reflected on the subject of my spare-time literary activities. One beginning and one ending for a book was a thing I did not agree with. — *At Swim Two Birds*, Flann O'Brien, 1939.

5425 I have never begun a novel with more misgiving. — *The Razor's Edge*, W. Somerset Maugham, 1944.

5426 I have always believed that, when a man writes a record of a series of events, he should begin by giving certain information about himself: his age, where he was born, whether he be short or tall or fat or thin. — *Country Place*, Ann Petry, 1947.

5427 I'm not over-enthusiastic about books that teach or preach, but I may as well admit in the beginning that my primary reason for writing this book was to teach as many as possible of those who come after me how much hell and ruin are inevitably brought on innocent people and innocent countries by men who make a virtue of consistency. — *Lydia Bailey*, Kenneth Roberts, 1947.

5428 Sabra Stanton extended slim hands to the fire and over her shoulder watched her uncle's goosequill pen drive deliberately, precisely, over a new sheet of foolscap on his desk. — *Eagle in the Sky*, F. van Wyck Mason, 1948.

5429 The large room rented by the Australian Society of Creative Writers for its bi-monthly meetings was comfortably filled on the afternoon of 7th November. — *An Author Bites the Dust*, Arthur W. Upfield, 1948.

5430 I can show you what is left. After the pride, passion, agony, and bemused aspiration, what is left is in our hands. — *World Enough and Time*, Robert Penn Warren, 1950.

5431 Once, very long ago, before ever the flowers were named which struggled and fluttered below the rain-swept walls, there sat at an upper window a princess and a slave reading a story which even then was old: or, rather, to be entirely prosaic, on the wet afternoon of the Nones of May in the year (as it was computed later) of Our Lord 273, in the city of Colchester, Helena, red-haired, youngest daughter of Coel, Paramount Chief of the Trinovantes, gazed into the rain while her tutor read the *Iliad* of Homer in a Latin paraphrase. — *Helena*, Evelyn Waugh, 1950.

5432 I am writing this book because I understand that "revelations" are soon to appear about that great man who was once my husband, attacking his character, and my own. And I am afraid that they will be believed simply because nowadays everyone believes the worst of a famous man. The greater his name, the worse the stories. — *Prisoner of Grace*, Joyce Cary, 1952.

5433 I have never before sat down to write anything so long as this may be, though I have written plenty of sermons and articles for parish magazines. — *In the Wet*, Nevil Shute, 1953.

5434 We have at times been accused of putting so many people into our books that no one can remember who they are, in which stricture we entirely concur, as we often cannot remember who they are ourself (or selves). — *Jutland Cottage*, Angela Thirkell, 1953.

5435 This book is largely concerned with Hobbits, and from its pages a reader may discover much of their character and a little of their

history. — *The Fellowship of the Ring*, J. R. R. Tolkien, 1954.

5436 "The trouble with fiction," said John Rivers, "is that it makes too much sense. Reality never makes sense." — *The Genius and the Goddess*, Aldous Huxley, 1955.

5437 To someone like myself, whose literary activities have been confined since 1920 mainly to legal briefs and *Inquiry*-writing, the hardest thing about the task at hand — *viz.*, the explanation of a day in 1937 when I changed my mind — is getting into it. — *The Floating Opera*, John Barth, 1956.

5438 "But what on earth am I to write about?" asked Dr. Andrew Butler. — *The Straight and Narrow Path*, Honor Tracy, 1956.

5439 I have yarn to spin, colors to blend, a pattern to weave, and edges to bind securely for the preservation of the whole. I cannot promise that the yarn will not be loose, the colors too pale or too strong or ill-matched; please be tolerant of the workmanship. — *Sing Out the Glory*, Gladys Hasty Carroll, 1957.

5440 It may happen in the next hundred years that the English novelists of the present day will come to be valued as we now value the artists and craftsmen of the late eighteenth century. — *The Ordeal of Gilbert Pinfold*, Evelyn Waugh, 1957.

5441 "This is the opening sentence which I lost." — *The Sycamore Tree*, Christine Brooke-Rose, 1958.

5442 Why does Indiana produce so many writers? — *The Riddle of Genesis County*, Lynne Doyle, 1958.

5443 On the evening of March 14, 44 B.C., Caesar was dining in Rome at the house of Lepidus. After dinner he withdrew to a side table and began to write. — *The Young Caesar*, Rex Warner, 1958.

5444 *Dear Abner,/* This morning I sent off to you air-mail a four-pound play in one marathon act, which I call *Boswell's Manhattan Journal.* Notify me of its arrival. — *Wake Up, Stupid*, Mark Harris, 1959.

5445 The other night I had a dream that I was sitting on the sidewalk on Moody Street, Pawtucketville, Lowell, Mass., with a pencil and paper in my hand saying to myself "Describe the wrinkly tar of this sidewalk, also the iron pickets of Textile Institute, or the doorway where Lousy and you and G.J.'s always sittin and dont stop to think of words when you do stop, just stop to think of the picture better — and let your mind off yourself in this work." — *Doctor Sax*, Jack Kerouac, 1959.

5446 My friend Sarah Pearson helped me to write this book. I am an Indian and though I speak English, I think in Hindustani; therefore Sarah guided me through many difficulties. — *Beti*, Daphne Rooke, 1959.

5447 Dame Lettie Colston refilled her fountain pen and continued her letter:
One of these days I hope you will write as brilliantly on a happier theme. In these days of cold war I *do* feel we should soar above the murk & smog & get into the clear crystal.
— *Memento Mori*, Muriel Spark, 1959.

5448 In the last years of the seventeenth century there was to be found among the fops and fools of the London coffee-houses one rangy, gangling flitch called Ebenezer Cooke, more ambitious than talented, and yet more talented than prudent, who, like his friends-in-folly, all of whom were supposed to be educating at Oxford or Cambridge, had found the sound of Mother English more fun to game with than her sense to labor over, and so rather than applying himself to the pains of scholarship, had learned the knack of versifying, and ground out quires of couplets after the fashion of the day, afroth with *Joves* and *Jupiters*, aclang with jarring rhymes, and string-taut with similes stretched to the snapping-point. — *The Sot-Weed Factor*, John Barth, 1960.

5449 I set out to write this story of my friend Annie and I gave it the title "My Friend Annie" in all good faith and for what are, I think, three good reasons. — *My Friend Annie*, Jane Duncan, 1961.

5450 DEAR SIR,/ With reference to her legs encased in sheerest nylon, she turned the left one over, knees together, parting the flow of shimmering buti-silk boudoir coat in three colours, angel-blue, love-grey, and mutation, to expose a cream smooth thigh to Gerald's pulsating gaze. — *The Last Hours of Sandra Lee*, William Sansom, 1961.

5451 I, Alexander, son and heir of Philip of Macedon and of Olympias, daughter of Pirote's king, wrote this first chapter of my secret history, little more than its preface, with my own hand. — *The Conqueror*, Edison Marshall, 1962.

5452 *Pale Fire*, a poem in heroic couplets, of nine hundred ninety-nine lines, divided into four cantos, was composed by John Francis Shade (born July 5, 1898, died July 21, 1959) during the last twenty days of his life, at his residence in New Wye, Appalachia, U.S.A. — *Pale Fire*, Vladimir Nabokov, 1962.

5453 "*Chatterley of the Apes, Lady Tarzan's Lover*, sex and adventure, they're the money spinners — Harold." The Christian name slid through the tubby literary agent's whipcord lips discreetly, like a prune stone he was ashamed to be seen discarding. "There's no future in philosophy." — *The Month of the Falling Leaves*, Bruce Marshall, 1963.

5454 When Samson Shillitoe stepped off the subway the beginning of the poem brushed against his brain. — *A Fine Madness*, Elliott Baker, 1964.

5455 Parker Peterson had read *Ferdinand the Bull* as a child and Ernest Hemingway as a young man, but he found himself poorly prepared for a genuine bullfight. — *Fair Game*, Diane Johnson, 1965.

5456 I shall write two books. One, the memoirs of Sir Emmanuel Bernstein, is for my wife and all the world to read. This other is for myself alone, for Mannie Bernstein the kopje walloper who used to trudge from claim to claim buying diamonds; for an earlier Mannie who was a pedlar travelling to the diamond diggings of the Vaal. — *Diamond Jo*, Daphne Rooke, 1965.

5457 Sometimes, instead of a letter to thank his hostess, Freddy Hamilton would compose a set of formal verses — rondeaux redoubles, villanelles, rondels, or Sicilian octaves — to express his thanks neatly. It was part of his modest nature to do this. He always felt he had perhaps been boring during his stay, and it was one's duty in life to be agreeable. — *The Mandelbaum Gate*, Muriel Spark, 1965.

5458 I write in the time of the Ram, when the time of the Bull is passed, and I address you across more than three thousand years, you who live at the conjunction of the Fish and the Watercarrier. — *The Maze Maker*, Michael Ayrton, 1967.

5459 Solomon Alexei Sorge sat in bed, writing, waiting for his wife to join him. — *The Past and Present of Solomon Sorge*, Judith Barnard, 1967.

5460 Picking up the pen he began to write, the ink characters stalking away from him irrevocably across the paper wastes, burdens of intention laid across their slanting backs, and suddenly he wanted to call them back, to cry stop, that wasn't what I meant, how it was at all; remembering. — *The Paradox Players*, Maureen Duffy, 1967.

5461 It is time that I told this story. I do not know if I shall ever bring myself to publish it: not because of hurting the people involved — those it could have hurt most are dead; but because it is a sort of confession, and I dislike confessional writing. — *The Private Wound*, Cecil Day-Lewis *as* Nicholas Blake, 1968.

5462 To begin with, I feel it important to state certain policies and standards which have been brought to the writing of this book which you, the reader, have every right to expect stated beforehand to guard against the possibility of plunging recklessly into a rather longish piece of writing only to find that there was not contained in it the sorts of things you'd sought therein, that the time spent curled up within its pages, so to speak, was wasted or would have been better spent lollygagging at the local "watering hole."

— *Chewsday*, Dan Greenburg, 1968.

5463 Morrison was dead, Peterson wrote, at work on his third novel. — *High*, Thomas Hinde, 1968.

5464 *Ladybird, ladybird,/ Fly away home,/ Your house is on fire,/ Your children are gone./* -Crazy rhyme. Got it on the brain this morning. That's from trying to teach Jen a few human words yesterday. — *The Fire-Dwellers*, Margaret Laurence, 1969.

5465 Fidelman, a self-confessed failure as a painter, came to Italy to prepare a critical study of Giotto, the opening chapter of which he had carried across the ocean in a new pigskin leather brief case, now gripped in his perspiring hand. — *Pictures of Fidelman*, Bernard Malamud, 1969.

5466 "All happy families are more or less dissimilar; all unhappy ones are more or less alike," says a great Russian writer in the beginning of a famous novel (*Anna Arkadievitch Karenina*, transfigured into English by R. G. Stonelower, Mount Tabor Ltd., 1880). — *Ada*, Vladimir Nabokov, 1969.

5467 Ever wake up one fine morning to find yourself a character in a novel? — *Mrs. Wallop*, Peter De Vries, 1970.

5468 Students (not unlike yourselves) compelled to buy paperback copies of his novels — notably the first, *Travel Light*, though there has lately been some academic interest in his more surreal and "existential" and perhaps even "anarchist" second novel, *Brother Pig* — or encountering some essay from *When the Saints* in a shiny heavy anthology of mid-century literature costing $12.50, imagine that Henry Bech, like thousands less famous than he, is rich. He is not. — *Bech: A Book*, John Updike, 1970.

5469 Walter slowed and stopped and permitted himself a temporary delay at a section marked SPECIAL FICTION. — *Blue Dreams*, William Hanley, 1971.

5470 Just because I'm writing a book doesn't make me a writer. Let's get that straight from the start. — *Sunday Best*, Bernice Rubens, 1971.

5471 What if this young woman, who writes such bad poems, in competition with her husband, whose poems are equally bad, should stretch her remarkably long and well-made legs out before you, so that her skirt slips up to the tops of her stockings? It is an old story. — *Imaginative Qualities of Actual Things*, Gilbert Sorrentino, 1971.

5472 Nine years later Ransom would write a book analyzing the emotions of this day. — *Tight White Collar*, John L'Heureux, 1972.

5473 "Damnation," said Stanley Dinkle./ It had taken him half an hour to compose the sentence, and he had just read it aloud. — *The Tin Lizzie Troop*, Glendon Swarthout, 1972.

5474 I am in more than one way responsible for the work that follows. — *The Black Prince*, Iris Murdoch, 1973.

5475 Because I am an officer and a gentleman they have given me my notebooks, pen, ink and paper. So I write and wait. — *How Many Miles to Babylon?*, Jennifer Johnston, 1974.

5476 Only another writer, someone who had worked his heart out on a good book which sold three thousand copies, could appreciate the thrill that overcame me one April morning in 1973 when Dean Rivers of our small college in Georgia appeared at my classroom door. — *Centennial*, James A. Michener, 1974.

5477 If I were ever to write a book of travel, no matter how queer the events it described, I am sure I would never have the same trouble placing it with a publisher as I had when I tried to get into print Oswald Bastable's strange tale of his visit to the future in the year 1973. — *The Land Leviathan*, Michael Moorcock, 1974.

5478 Before the colors fade I must get this down. — *My Son the Jock*, Gerald Green, 1975.

5479 O let me open as though there were a beginning, though all there can be is the Great Round, uroboros, container of opposites, within which we war, laugh, and are silent. — *See the Old Lady Decently*, B. S. Johnson, 1975.

5480 *Little did I know when I wrote the poem "Flight to Canada" that there were so many secrets locked inside its world.* — *Flight to Canada*, Ishmael Reed, 1976.

5481 I write these lines in the fifty-fourth year of my life. They begin a tale I might long ago have tried to tell, but an intuition stayed my pen. — *The Melodeon*, Glendon Swarthout, 1977.

5482 It didn't occur to me to write a novel with A. as the prototype for its hero, Hamilton Stark, until fairly recently, a year ago this spring, when I drove forty miles from my home in Northwood across New Hampshire to his home outside the town of B. — *Hamilton Stark*, Russell Banks, 1978.

5483 I must say I am somewhat at a loss to present myself here and perform this task, since I have not willingly chosen it, and since writing an introduction is something I know little about. — *Shrinking*, Alan Lelchuk, 1978.

5484 To Marcus Polybius — my son in affection, though not in blood — and to my daughter Paula, I write in fulfilment of a promise. — *The Left-Handed Spirit*, Ruth Nichols, 1978.

5485 It was February 1922, the year Georgetown witnessed the rise of a brilliant young newspaper columnist writing under the name of Uncle Stapie. — *From the Heat of the Day*, Roy A. K. Heath, 1979.

5486 Gold had been asked many times to write about the Jewish exerience in America.

This was not strictly true. He'd been asked only twice, most recently by a woman in Wilmington, Delaware, where he had gone to read, for a fee, from his essays and books, and, when requested, from his poems and short stories. — *Good as Gold*, Joseph Heller, 1979.

5487 Three days after I finished this book, I rewarded myself with an afternoon of golf. — *A Year or So with Edgar*, George V. Higgins, 1979.

5488 I am writing this for myself. — *And Again?*, Sean O'Faolain, 1979.

5489 "Silky!" gasped the Gasper./ *That's* the way to open a story. A story it just busts with thrills, chills, laughs and Sex. — *Silky!*, Leo Rosten, 1979.

5490 My name is Brown. I am not in the book-writing business, a fact for which I make no apology. — *Spring Sonata*, Bernice Rubens, 1979.

5491 I make lists. — *Chez Cordelia*, Kitty Burns Florey, 1980.

5492 I, Fanny Hackabout-Jones, having been blest with long Life, which makes e'en the Harshest Events of Youth pale to Insignificance or, i'faith, appear as Comedies, do write this History of my Life and Adventures as a Testament for my only Daughter, Belinda. — *Fanny*, Erica Jong, 1980.

5493 Dr. Weiss, at forty, knew that her life had been ruined by literature. — *The Debut*, Anita Brookner, 1981.

5494 The following short story was first published in *An Argosy of Mystery Tales*, Christmas 1917.

A Strange Disappearance

This is a true story which is why, unlike so many fictional confections, it offers no definitive conclusion to its mystery. — *An Easter Egg Hunt*, Gillian Freeman, 1981.

5495 Megan Stone was walking along the deserted beach. You will probably ask, Why another book about another woman walking along another beach? — *Intrusions*, Ursula Hegi, 1981.

5496 I hesitate to put down some of the details in this story because they are so intensely personal, they are bound to be misunderstood by friends who know me for my objectivity and detachment, qualities that have made me quite successful in a field crowded by charlatans. — "Obsession," F. Sionil José, 1981.

5497 This is Ambien II, of the Five./ I have undertaken to write an account of our experiments on Rohanda, known to Canopus in this epoch as Shikasta. — *The Sirian Experiments*, Doris Lessing, 1981.

5498 Fanny Williams would have been much better off in an opera than a novel. — *Who Was Oswald Fish?*, A. N. Wilson, 1981.

5499 Now I guess I'll never write my mother's autobiography. — *Muldoon*, Don Bredes, 1982.

5500 The spider writing is there on the mirror. — *Living in Ether*, Patricia Geary, 1982.

5501 I am going to write it down. I wonder if I can? — *Cordelia?*, Garson Kanin, 1982.

5502 Since I have no other, I use as preface Jacob's preface which I read, sneakily, fifteen years ago, when it lay on the Goldmans' breakfast table, amid the cornflakes: — *Brother of the More Famous Jack*, Barbara Trapido, 1982.

5503 Though Henry Bech, the author, in his middle years had all but ceased to write, his books continued, as if ironically, to live, to cast shuddering shadows toward the center of his life, where that thing called his reputation cowered. — *Bech Is Back*, John Updike, 1982.

5504 The nights belonged to the novelist. — *Miss Peabody's Inheritance*, Elizabeth Jolley, 1983.

5505 These words I am writing should have been written by Russell Atha. — *In a Far Country*, Adam Kennedy, 1983.

5506 There was another book I writ before this one which give the story about how me and Jim went down the river on a raft, him looking for freedom on account of he's a nigger slave and me looking to get away from the Widow Douglas who's trying to sivilize me, and you could say we both wanted the same thing. — *The Further Adventures of Huckleberry Finn*, Greg Matthews, 1983.

5507 In one or other of G.F.H. Shadbold's two published notebooks, *Beyond Narcissus* and *Reticences of Thersites*, a short entry appears as to the likelihood of Ophelia's enigmatic cry: "O, how the wheel becomes it!" referring to the chorus or burden "a-down, a-down" in the ballad quoted by her a moment before, the aptness she sees in the refrain. — *O, How the Wheel Becomes It!*, Anthony Powell, 1983.

5508 I never expected anything from my Venice book; it was written in a hurry and would not have been written at all if my publisher had given me any encouragement when I told him about my novel. — *Johnnie Cross*, Terence de Vere White, 1983.

5509 A little while ago, some of those friends who were accusing me of writing books less well than I write rock and roll songs were also kind enough to tell me there was not much rock and roll in this one. — *Beloved Gravely*, Christian Gehman, 1984.

5510 I am writing about them because I saw myself in her. — *Paro, Dreams of Passion*, Namita Gokhale, 1984.

5511 Blood is not the easiest medium with which to write, especially with a split bamboo pen. — *Lama*, Fredrick R. Hyde-Chambers, 1984.

5512 When he talked about his craft, Graeme Baldwin liked to say that he and other important novelists were holding a dialogue with their own subconscious minds while allowing the rest of humanity the privilege of eavesdropping on their private thoughts. — *The Life and Death of Liam Faulds*, Hugh McLeave, 1984.

5513 "Never write a novel in the first person," Jack told me. — *A Likely Story*, Donald E. Westlake, 1984.

5514 And so let us beginne; and, as the Fabrick takes its Shape in front of you, alwaies keep the Structure intirely in Mind as you inscribe it. — *Hawksmoor*, Peter Ackroyd, 1985.

5515 I take to pad and pencil, I suppose, because I don't really know what else to do. — *Honorable Men*, Louis Auchincloss, 1985.

5516 I take my title from the name the Jews have traditionally given to the Roman Empire. — *The Kingdom of the Wicked*, Anthony Burgess, 1985.

5517 . . . *For two days have I sat holding this enormous ship's log, pondering how best to use its wealth of empty, ruled pages.* — *The Spoils of Eden*, Robert H. Fowler, 1985.

5518 What follows in Parts I and II consists of some firsthand facts and of diverse opinions, not all of which are soundly based or well-verified; there are also some asides and some commentary as well as other assorted data, dates, and events which (on the one hand) are well-known or which (on the other hand) are not and thus must be deduced. — *Dear Rafe*, Rolando Hinojosa-Smith, 1985.

5519 What *is* this? — *Private Papers*, Margaret Forster, 1986.

5520 I am reading aloud to my mother from Shakespeare's sonnets, trying to find one that would be appropriate to recite at her funeral. — *Enchantment*, Daphne Merkin, 1986.

5521 *Lines upon lines, they flow like food for the tail-eating snake. They love the void and they grow in death, they rise and become part of it like murals on a cracking wall that become the cracks themselves.* — *Daughters of Memory*, Peter Najarian, 1986.

5522 In the subway going to work, Vera decides to write about Bigfoot. — *Bigfoot Dreams*, Francine Prose, 1986.

5523 To make a start more swift than weighty,/ Hail Muse. Dear Reader, once upon/ A time, say, circa 1980,/ There lived a man. His name was John. — *The Golden Gate*, Vikram Seth, 1986.

5524 These are the last things, she wrote. — *In the Country of Last Things*, Paul Auster, 1987.

5525 The key is the torturer's horse; the apparent irrelevance to what is, in fact, the main theme. — *Circles of Deceit*, Nina Bawden, 1987.

5526 I shall forgo a fetching first line. — *Hubble Time*, Tom Bezzi, 1987.

5527 "Remember, Danny, how you used to write all those beautiful poems in Italian," his mother said. — *A Warmer Season*, Joseph Olshan, 1987.

5528 I have come back to Baltimore, and to the house on Ashby Street where I was raised, in order to write a full account of the events which led up to the mysterious death of my sister Mathilde, whose body was found in the Gobi Desert last summer. — *Second Sight*, Anne Redmon, 1987.

5529 The winter writers are spread out like pieces in a game; the rule seems to be: no two writers on the same block, and no more than three to a township. — *The Boys of Winter*, Wilfrid Sheed, 1987.

5530 This introductory chapter is a condensed version of an undergraduate paper I wrote in 1982 on the history of the literary weekly Belles Lettres. — *The Belles Lettres Papers*, Charles Simmons, 1987.

5531 Peter says I should write everything down./ He says it will save me. — *The Body's Memory*, Jean Stewart, 1989.

5532 This scroll is in poor condition and contains various lacunae. — *Soldier of Arete*, Gene Wolfe, 1989.

5533 *Photography, Art, Biography A–L, Biography M–Z, Travel.* — *Chapters and Verse*, Joel Barr, 1990.

5534 *This is a manuscript that the deceased poet and novelist Anna Hand left in a suitcase in a rented cottage in Beddiford, Maine.* — "Winter," Ellen Gilchrist, 1990.

5535 Jason Sams, in danger of losing his job (not ready to admit it was already lost), deemed it high time to return to the literary wars. — *Sams in a Dry Season*, Ivan Gold, 1990.

5536 *How I came to edit this curious manuscript — and how indeed Isadora Wing came to write it — are two of the many bizarre stories the ensuing pages have to tell.* — *Any Woman's Blues*, Erica Jong, 1990.

5537 Beginning the second day after his discharge from the United States Navy on Pine Street in March of 1946, John Sirovich made the rounds of book publishing houses in Manhattan bearing a stiff red folder with a black tie string which he had pinched from the supply base in Norfolk. — *The World's Last Night*, William Jovanovich, 1990.

5538 "I'll write them down. You begin." — *Deception*, Philip Roth, 1990.

5539 The narrative that follows is not mine but Geoffrey Elder's. I have, however, shaped and tinkered with it in a way that calls for some explanation. — *Death's Darkest Face*, Julian Symons, 1990.

5540 This is a novel — if novel it be — about Good Time and Bad Time. — *The Gates of Ivory*, Margaret Drabble, 1991.

5541 This Tuesday morning, 3 October 1990, at half after ten, I typed the last sentence of the novel that will complete what the critics have taken to calling "The Grenzler Octet," as if I had planned from the beginning to write eight interrelated books on the same theme. — *The Novel*, James A. Michener, 1991.

5542 Reader: Over the oceans, up and down the ladders, proud or ashamed, lucky or unlucky, smart or stupid, blundering or swift, giving their hearts away too quickly or not quickly enough, these characters are doing their part to keep the wolf from the door, the earth from returning to water, to keep evolution on an upward swing. — *The Pursuit of Happiness*, Anne Roiphe, 1991.

5543 He arrived in London on the same day that *Amelia* appeared in the bookstalls. Grim and realistic, this last of Henry Fielding's novels was to prove both a critical and commercial failure, although Nathaniel Carleton wouldn't know it had even been written. — *The Vast Memory of Love*, Malcolm Bosse, 1992.

5544 I don't yet know what this is going to be — a report or a journal or just a few notes — but this is the beginning, and the beginning is the Wall. — *A Journal of the Flood Year*, David Ely, 1992.

5545 Read these runes! They were inscribed by Thorn the Mannamavi, and at no master's dictation, but in Thorn's own words. — *Raptor*, Gary Jennings, 1992.

5546 In 1960, after two years of graduate school at Berkeley, I returned to New York without a Ph.D. or any idea what I'd do, only a desire to write stories. — *Sylvia*, Leonard Michaels, 1992.

5547 Today is Friday, December 14, 1979./ I write at my wife's behest. — "The Girls," Hollis Summers, 1992.

5548 The boy bears down on his goose quill, splattering dribbles of thin homemade ink on the coiling birch bark. — *The Life and Times of Captain N.*, Douglas Glover, 1993.

5549 I, Devorah Bat-David, write in the third year of Rehoboam's reign. — *The Lost Book of Paradise*, David Rosenberg, 1993.

5550 She wants to write a book about the wind, about the weather. — *Changing Heaven*, Jane Urquhart, 1993.

5551 This goes back to the letter Susan Morrow's first husband Edward sent her last September. He had written a book, a novel, and would she like to read it? — *Tony and Susan*, Austin Wright, 1993.

Lives

5552 Seeing my Life has been such a Chequer Work of Nature, and that I am able now to look back upon it from a safer Distance, than is ordinarily the Fate of the Clan to which I once belong'd; I think my History may find a place in the World, as well as some, who I see are every Day read with pleasure, tho' they have nothing in them so Diverting, or Instructing, as I believe mine will appear to be. — *Colonel Jack*, Daniel Defoe, 1722.

5553 MADAM, I sit down to give you an undeniable proof of my considering your desires as indispensible orders: ungracious then as the task may be, I shall recall to view those scandalous stages of my life, out of which I emerged at length, to the enjoyment of every blessing in the power of love, health, and fortune to bestow, whilst yet in the flower of youth, and not too late to employ the leisure afforded me by great ease and affluence, to cultivate an understanding naturally not a despicable one, and which had, even amidst the whirl of loose pleasures I had been tossed in, exerted more observation on the characters and manners of the world than what is common to those of my unhappy profession, who, looking on all thought or reflexion as their capital enemy, keep it at as great a distance as they can, or destroy it without mercy. — *Fanny Hill*, John Cleland, 1750.

5554 My life has for several years been a theatre of calamity. I have been a mark for the vigilance of tyranny, and I could not escape. — *Caleb Williams*, William Godwin, 1794.

5555 Emma Woodhouse, handsome, clever, and rich, with a comfortable home and happy disposition seemed to unite some of the best blessings of existence; and had lived nearly twenty-one years in the world with very little to distress or vex her. — *Emma*, Jane Austen, 1816.

5556 You have requested me, my dear friend, to bestow some of that leisure, with which Providence has blessed the decline of my life, in registering the hazards and difficulties which attended its commencement. — *Rob Roy*, Sir Walter Scott, 1817.

5557 The first ray of light which illumines the gloom, and converts into a dazzling brilliancy that obscurity in which the earlier history of the public career of the immortal Pickwick would appear to be involved, is derived from the perusal of the following entry in the Transactions of the Pickwick Club, which the editor of these papers feels the highest pleasure in laying before his readers, as a proof of the careful atten-

tion, indefatigable assiduity, and nice discrimination, with which his search among the multifarious documents confided to him has been conducted. — *The Pickwick Papers*, Charles Dickens, 1837.

5558 It has always been a favorite idea of mine, that there is so much of the human in every man, that the life of any one individual, however obscure, if really and vividly perceived in all its aspirations, struggles, failures, and successes, would command the interest of all others. — *Oldtown Folks*, Harriet Beecher Stowe, 1868.

5559 The resistless influences which are one day to reign supreme over our poor hearts, and to shape the sad short course of our lives, are sometimes of mysteriously remote origin, and find their devious ways to us through the hearts and the lives of strangers. — *The Fallen Leaves*, Wilkie Collins, 1879.

5560 There came an episode in the life of Cecilia Holt which it is essential should first be told. — *Kept in the Dark*, Anthony Trollope, 1882.

5561 Three chapters in the story of my life — three periods, distinct and well defined, yet consecutive — beginning when I had not completed twenty-five years and finishing before thirty, will probably prove the most eventful of all. — *The Purple Land*, W. H. Hudson, 1885.

5562 On who was in his day a person of great place and consideration, and has left a name which future generations shall surely repeat so long as the world may last, found no better rule for a man's life than that he should incline his mind to move in Charity, rest in Providence, and turn upon the poles of Truth. — *Simon Dale*, Anthony Hope, 1898.

5563 Before telling the story of my father's second visit to the remarkable country which he discovered now some thirty years since, I should perhaps say a few words about his career between the publication of his book in 1872, and his death in the early summer of 1891. — *Erewhon Revisited*, Samuel Butler, 1901.

5564 When Frank Algernon Cowperwood emerged from the Eastern District Penitentiary in Philadelphia he realized that the old life he had lived in that city since boyhood was ended. — *The Titan*, Theodore Dreiser, 1914.

5565 Much has been written critically about Felix Kennaston since the disappearance of his singular personality from the field of contemporary writers; and Mr. Froser's *Biography* contains all it is necessary to know as to the facts of Kennaston's life. — *The Cream of the Jest*, James Branch Cabell, 1917.

5566 The stage on which we play our little dramas of life and love has for most of us but one setting. — *The Amazing Interlude*, Mary Roberts Rinehart, 1918.

5567 I, Tiberius Claudius Drusus Nero Germanicus This-that-and-the-other (for I shall not trouble you yet with all my titles) who was once, and not so long ago either, known to my friends and relatives and associates as "Claudius the Idiot," or "That Claudius," or "Claudius the Stammerer," or "Clau-Clau-Claudius" or at best as "Poor Uncle Claudius," am now about to write this strange history of my life; starting from my earliest childhood and continuing year by year until I reach the fateful point of change where, some eight years ago, at the age of fifty-one, I suddenly found myself caught in what I may call the "golden predicament" from which I have never since become disentangled. — *I, Claudius*, Robert Graves, 1934.

5568 Now in November I can see our years as a whole. This autumn is like both an end and a beginning to our lives, and those days which seemed confused with the blur of all things too near and too familiar are clear and strange now. — *Now in November*, Josephine W. Johnson, 1934.

5569 I have spent my life in the attic rooms of requisitioned hotels. — *Night Journey*, Albert J. Guerard, 1950.

5570 Eloise Dilworth, without going so far as to attribute the various personal events that altered her life in the fall and early winter of 1949 to her mother's visit in the preceding August, was quite sure that she was right in dating them from that time. — *A Law for the Lion*, Louis Auchincloss, 1953.

5571 The bartender behind the length of mahogany of Whaley's Café near the corner of Potrero and Clybourn in Burbank, not far from Warner Brothers Studios, jerked his head in the direction of the afternoon paper lying on the bar with its page-one photo of the fiercely ruffled, angry-eyed old woman with the hawk's beak and imperious mien, and quoted the headline above it: "To Live Forever, says Multimillionairess Hannah Bascombe," and then added, "That's one she ain't gonna win, eh, brother?" — *The Foolish Immortals*, Paul Gallico, 1953.

5572 I suppose that every man, consciously or not, sees his own life as a path that has traversed gently rising slopes, then long, easy plateaus followed by sudden steep ascents, with always somewhere a saw-toothed passage of great contrasts and strange violence, a course filled with sharp, bottomless drops and terrible, towering chimeras that resemble his hopes and desires. And as more of this ribbon of his life unfolds, giving him greater perspective, somewhere in that topography which has otherwise become a jungle now forever closed behind him, he comes to know that a certain interval, marking a definite span of time, has become a peak; in fact, it will always remain, for him, the true apex of his life. — *The Crozart Story*, Kenneth Fearing, 1960.

5573 My career has always been marked by a strange mixture of confidence and cowardice: almost, one might say, made by it. — *The Millstone*, Margaret Drabble, 1965.

5574 *I will speak of a man. I will speak of a man in the winter of his soul. As there is a longitude and a latitude of the soul, there are also seasons and the season is also a co-ordinate.* — *The Advocate*, Borden Deal, 1968.

5575 There are "moments when the tide of man's life on earth pauses and begins slowly to shift — in which direction neither a man coming in nor a man going out can tell for the life of him, though always later it will be found to have been obvious." — *The Cloud Chamber*, Dexter Masters, 1971.

5576 If the explanation which dawned on me like a stroke of inspiration while listening to Lúcio's excited account of the discussions among my men in Goiânia is to be credited, then, it now occurs to me, it would have been a wonderful gesture of the gods if the first body in which my soul had resided had been that of Pedro Alvarez Cabral, the Portuguese commander who led the first expedition which discovered Brazil in 1500, that blessed year of which, rather than of mortal humans, I can truly claim to be the offspring. — *The Incredible Brazilian*, Zulfikar Ghose, 1972.

5577 In December, 1954, Henry Soames would hardly have said his life was just beginning. — *Nickel Mountain*, John Gardner, 1973.

5578 I planned my death carefully; unlike my life, which meandered along from one thing to another, despite my feeble attempts to control it. — *Lady Oracle*, Margaret Atwood, 1976.

5579 It has all been worth while. I regret nothing. — *Waiting for Sheila*, John Braine, 1976.

5580 "In every life, Richard, there is something, great or small, to be ashamed of," said my father with more force than necessary, and with reference to a concern unknown to me then; for we were simply conversing in general. — *The Thin Mountain Air*, Paul Horgan, 1977.

5581 There's Springer, sauntering through the wilderness of this world. — *Springer's Progress*, David Markson, 1977.

5582 It is June. This is what I have decided to do with my life just now. I will do this work of transformed and even distorted memory and lead this life, the one I am leading today. — *Sleepless Nights*, Elizabeth Hardwick, 1979.

5583 "Man that is born of a woman hath but a short time to live, and is full of misery," said the curate. — *A Short Time to Live*, Mervyn Jones, 1980.

5584 I think that all the great moments of my life have been played out to music in an

atmosphere reminiscent of Rosine's, redolent of spices, Bohemian, theatrical. —*Albion Walk*, Gwendoline Butler, 1982.

5585 Everything in the life of a famous man is supposed to matter but whether it does is doubtful. —*Slipstream*, Roger McDonald, 1982.

5586 Lately I have had the feeling that not only have I lived my life the only way I could have lived it, I have also lived my life all wrong. —*Doctor Blues*, Mark Smith, 1983.

5587 For a great many years, I made my way through this life dragging accolades behind me like tin cans on a newlywed's jalopy. —*Hoopla*, Harry Stein, 1983.

5588 At midnight yesterday, my whole life became a fiction: a dark Teutonic fairy tale of trolls and hobgoblins and star-crossed lovers in ruined castles full of creaks and cobwebs. — *The World Is Made of Glass*, Morris West, 1983.

5589 I had never done a reckless thing in my whole life. —*Looking for Bobby*, Gloria Norris, 1985.

5590 *I am looking at the towers and battlements of Toledo, the ancient capital of Spain, which stands on top of the hill across the ravine, and I have decided to make a note of all the important events of my life so that people will know what I have been through.* —*An Innocent Millionaire*, Stephen Vizinczey, 1985.

5591 The best thing about my life up to here is, nobody believes it. —*Kate Vaiden*, Reynolds Price, 1986.

5592 In these pages I have put down what I know for certain about Minna Grant's placid and only occasionally traumatic early life, her edenic college years, the cool ellipsis between the beginning of her marriage and its curiously uneventful end, and the sweet conclusion to the few climactic months she spent in the heartland. —*The Magician's Girl*, Doris Grumbach, 1987.

5593 On an afternoon two years ago my life veered from its day-in day-out course and became for a short while the kind of life that can be told as a story—that is, one in which events appear to have meaning. —*Rich in Love*, Josephine Humphreys, 1987.

5594 The many turns, twists, and circumstances that led Bruce Bacon down the curious path his life took probably threaded back through all his years on earth. — *The Pledge*, Howard Fast, 1988.

5595 It's no understatement, only sad truth, that Raymondo Cruz's life did not begin until he died. — *The Cruz Chronicle*, Henry H. Roth, 1989.

5596 How rarely is it possible for anyone to begin a new life at sixty! — *The Education of Harriet Hatfield*, May Sarton, 1989.

5597 Polly, he called me, from the first, as if I had had no life at all until then and was to have

no other thenceforth. —*Lord Byron's Daughter*, Paul West, 1989.

5598 The creation and first sixteen years of life of Olivia de Havilland Hand, only child of Daniel DeBardeleben Hand and Summer Deer Wagoner, of Tahlequah, Oklahoma. — "De Havilland Hand," Ellen Gilchrist, 1990.

5599 *The two strongest foundations of Julia's life are changing so dramatically she fears a structural collapse.* —*Worlds Beyond My Control*, Jane Lazarre, 1991.

5600 We believed. All our lives we believed, all our separate lives. —*The Lost Father*, Mona Simpson, 1992.

5601 His name was Kobus the Bookbinder. His whole life, aside from the period of his apprenticeship and early manhood, had been spent in a small town called Niedering. —*The God-Fearer*, Dan Jacobson, 1993.

5602 *In the name of Allah, the Merciful, the Compassionate:/ What can a man say of his life?* —*Turkish Delights*, David R. Slavitt, 1993.

Lost

5603 He was lost. This he realized with fear that burned in his skin like the heat of his home fire; that twitched in his muscles, grasping with little spasms at his cheeks and eyelids and lips, or running in shudders down his frame as if hordes of insects were feeding on his nerves. —*Intimations of Eve*, Vardis Fisher, 1946.

5604 To north, south, east or west, turning at will, it was not long before his landmarks fled him. — *Titus Alone*, Mervyn Peake, 1959.

5605 There wasn't any of that stuff about wondering where he was when he woke up: Popsy Meadows *knew* he didn't know. —*Baby, Come On Inside*, David Wagoner, 1968.

5606 I don't know where I am but wherever it is that I am I have to get out of here pronto! —*Myron*, Gore Vidal, 1974.

5607 from his apartment on Ferrell Anderson Place he liked to walk down to the quai which the local inhabitants referred to as The Reiser for reasons Carl was not able to determine but he somehow always lost his way on the way and found himself in a puzzle of winding and oblique streets complicated intersections which were not in themselves unpleasant in fact he would invariably find a series of book stalls an area of shops a neighborhood of fascinating if unpretentious architecture so that he would soon forget his original destination while absorbed in browsing through a collection of early Rhodesian medical texts or a group of mementos from the

1923 World Cup or speculating on the origins of a variation in the style of dormer windows in regional balloon frame houses — *Long Talking Bad Conditions Blues*, Ronald Sukenick, 1979.

5608 The roads in Connecticut all look alike and never go the same way twice and I was lost. — *Dr. Rocksinger and the Age of Longing*, Jill Robinson, 1982.

5609 Here they are, two North Americans, a man and a woman just over and just under forty, come to spend their lives in Mexico and already lost as they travel cross-country over the central plateau. — *Stones for Ibarra*, Harriet Doerr, 1984.

5610 I am one of those people who have no sense of direction. — *A Narrow Time*, Michael Downing, 1987.

5611 It is dark. He does not know where he is. — *Remembering*, Wendell Berry, 1988.

5612 "Where are we?" Alexander asked his mother. — *The Theory of Everything*, Lisa Grunwald, 1991.

Lounging

5613 On a brilliant day in May, in the year 1868, a gentleman was reclining at his ease on the great circular divan which at that period occupied the centre of the Salon Carré, in the Museum of the Louvre. — *The American*, Henry James, 1877.

5614 Midway of the Ponte Vecchio at Florence, where three arches break the line of the little jewellers' booths glittering on either hand, and open an approach to the parapet, Colville lounged against the corner of a shop and stared out upon the river. — *Indian Summer*, William Dean Howells, 1886.

5615 The work of the day being over, I sat down upon my doorstep, pipe in hand, to rest awhile in the cool of the evening. — *To Have and to Hold*, Mary Johnston, 1900.

5616 For an hour at least Emmeline lay quietly curled up on the rear seat of the Willing surrey. — *Emmeline*, Elsie Singmaster, 1916.

5617 Lounging idly in the deserted little waiting-room was the usual shabby, bored, lonely ticket-seller, prodigiously indifferent to the grave beauty of the scene before him and to the throng of ancient memories jostling him where he stood. — *The Brimming Cup*, Dorothy Canfield Fisher, 1921.

5618 A bunch of workmen were lying on the grass of the park beside Macquarie Street, in the dinner hour. — *Kangaroo*, D. H. Lawrence, 1923.

5619 Our story opens in the mind of Luther L. (L for LeRoy) Fliegler, who is lying in his bed, not thinking of anything, but just aware of sounds, conscious of his own breathing, and sensitive to his own heartbeats. — *Appointment in Samarra*, John O'Hara, 1934.

5620 "Hee-yah!"/ The sharp guttural cry roused Rogier from his reverie in the shadows of the porch where his heavy square-built body lounged motionless in a chair, his gaze enmeshed in the vast web of twilight translucent between the row of cottonwoods before him and the imponderable barrier of mountains rising farther west to cut off his world of thought. — *The Wild Earth's Nobility*, Frank Waters, 1935.

5621 The clock struck half past two. In the little office at the back of Mr. McKechnie's bookshop, Gordon — Gordon Comstock, last member of the Comstock family, aged twenty-nine and rather moth-eaten already — lounged across the table, pushing a fourpenny packet of Player's Weights open and shut with his thumb. — *Keep the Aspidistra Flying*, George Orwell, 1936.

5622 "Peaceful," said Gil Saunders, stretching his full length in the lawn chair. — *Through a Glass Darkly*, Kathleen Norris, 1957.

5623 The old man, propped against a high mound of pillows on the huge, canopied bed, kept his eyes closed. — *The Sun Is My Shadow*, Robert Wilder, 1960.

5624 Window blurred by out of season spray. Above the sea, overlooking the town, a body rolls upon a creaking bed: fish without fins, flat-headed, white-scaled, bound by a corridor room — dimensions rarely touched by the sun — Alistair Berg, hair-restorer, curled webbed toes, strung between heart and clock, nibbles in the half light, and laughter from the dance hall opposite. — *Berg*, Ann Quin, 1964.

5625 They sprawled along the counter and on the chairs. — *Last Exit to Brooklyn*, Hubert Selby, Jr., 1964.

5626 Louise Talbot chose to spend the last afternoon of her life lounging in the shade of a leafy sycamore at the split-rail fence before her home. — *A Covenant with Death*, Stephen Becker, 1965.

5627 The warm sun of late afternoon slanted across the balcony's corner where he lay on a padded deck chair and watched the golf carts as they traced a pattern of erratic beetles over the shining fairways. — *The Sea and the Stars*, Robert Wilder, 1967.

5628 On the second storey of the handsome brick dwelling he recently had had built on New Dollar Lane, Captain Micajah Paddock lay on that same narrow, gimbal-mounted sea bed he'd occupied a generation earlier aboard his first command, the whaling brig *Bountiful*. — *Harpoon in Eden*, F. van Wyck Mason, 1969.

5629 Eyes for once closed upon his new world, he lay unquietly toasting in the sand, in his thin flannel trousers and gossamer-thin vest, testimony to his still dominant feelings of self-exposure, toasting himself unmercifully in the broad bewildered noon, his rather anemic, traditionally indoor skin almost crinkling in the heat, which seemed to bounce off the sand and quiver, hovering almost visibly, in the air. — *A Shadow on Summer*, Christy Brown, 1974.

5630 At the time Apollo 11 took off for the moon, Harry Towns was in a reclining chair beside the pool at a Beverly Hills hotel, taking advantage of the first stretch of absolutely perfect weather he had run into in Los Angeles. — *About Harry Towns*, Bruce Jay Friedman, 1974.

5631 It was the second day of term, in Toby's third year at Cambridge. The weather was mild and sunny, and the young men were able to sit along the Backs enjoying the October warmth. — *The Good Listener*, Pamela Hansford Johnson, 1975.

5632 There had been a silence, as always happened at about the same time, a long silence when none of them moved except maybe to lift up a glass and hold it high over their heads for the dregs to drip into their open mouths, or to yawn and stretch and then slump back into their chairs, when one of them might scratch himself, another consider the voice of the woman in the backyard, the old woman who was scolding, rattling her words like stones in a tin, and all of them in their own time looking at the street outside, and the shadows, wondering if they were not yet long enough. — *Tsotsi*, Athol Fugard, 1979.

5633 She lay on the shore of Lemminjärvi, in the white night of midsummer. — *Swallow*, D. M. Thomas, 1984.

5634 Roger lay on my new blue rug in the corner by the television and the lamp that seemed like it always had the funny orange bubbles rising in it that he hated. — *Loving Roger*, Tim Parks, 1986.

5635 The old aunts lounge in the white wicker armchairs, flipping open their fans, snapping them shut. — *How the García Girls Lost Their Accents*, Julia Alvarez, 1991.

5636 Lounging in bed in the middle of a steamy summer afternoon, watching, mesmerized, as his wife nursed their three-week-old son, Spike Goldman felt utterly at peace, content to stay forever just as he was. — *The Way We Live Now*, Marian Thurm, 1991.

5637 All day Sunday I lay around in my dirty sweatpants and shirt until finally I decided to go to the store. — *The Male Cross-Dresser Support Group*, Tama Janowitz, 1992.

Love

5638 When Louis Trevelyan was twenty-four years old, he had all the world before him where to choose; and, among other things, he chose to go to the Mandarin Islands, and there fell in love with Emily Rowley, the daughter of Sir Marmaduke, the governor. — *He Knew He Was Right*, Anthony Trollope, 1868-1869.

5639 The opening chapter does not concern itself with Love — indeed that antagonist does not certainly appear until the third — and Mr. Lewisham is seen at his studies. — *Love and Mr. Lewisham*, H. G. Wells, 1900.

5640 Dare I say it? Dare I say that I, a plain, prosaic lieutenant in the Republican service have done the incredible things here set out for the love of a woman — for a chimera in female shape; for a pale, vapid ghost of woman-loveliness? — *Lieut. Gullivar Jones*, Edwin Lester Linden Arnold *as* Edwin L. Arnold, 1905.

5641 John Ordham had been in Munich several months before he met Margarethe Styr. Like all the young men, native and foreign, he chose to fancy himself in love with her, and although both too dignified and too shy to applaud with the vehemence of the Germans, he never failed to attend a performance at the "Hof" when the greatest *Hochdramatische* the new music had developed sang Iseult or Brynhild. — *Tower of Ivory*, Gertrude Atherton, 1910.

5642 For years I had been preoccupied with thoughts of love and by love I mean a noble and sensuous passion, absorbing the energies of the soul, fulfilling destiny, and reducing all that has gone before it to the level of a mere prelude. — *The Book of Carlotta*, Arnold Bennett, 1911.

5643 John and Jane were in love and they were deeply happy. — *Forgive Us Our Virtues*, Vardis Fisher, 1938.

5644 Neither love nor the lack of it kept Lucy Markle from marriage. — *Always Young and Fair*, Conrad Richter, 1947.

5645 *Poised in space, held between nothing and nothing, there floats a golden ball. Not only is it golden. It is blue as well, and red, and green, and brown, and gray. Touch gold and blue and red and green and brown and gray — touch them with love and there is poetry.* — *Wild Conquest*, Peter Abrahams, 1950.

5646 Love is mostly a willingness to perceive. — *A Flame for Doubting Thomas*, Richard Llewellyn, 1953.

5647 Love conquers all — *omnia vincit amor*, said the gold scroll in a curve beneath the dial of the old French gilt clock. — *By Love Possessed*, James Gould Cozzens, 1957.

5648 Throughout our youth in Llandudno, Gregory was ever the nasty prophet of our loves. — *Jampot Smith*, Jeremy Brooks, 1960.

5649 In spring a fancy young man turns to light thoughts of love and other promises. — *Therefore Be Bold*, Herbert Gold, 1960.

5650 Dearly touched a heart can be with proof of love from an absent one. — *Down Where the Moon Is Small*, Richard Llewellyn, 1960.

5651 It was love at first sight./ The first time Yossarian saw the chaplain he fell madly in love with him. — *Catch-22*, Joseph Heller, 1961.

5652 *I'm moving on. No more games! I'm different now.*/ With these three ideas (really one), Peter Hatten floated out of the tunnel of love. — *Salt*, Herbert Gold, 1963.

5653 Edward knew nothing about love as he sat in the back garden of St. Gregory's playing draughts with Brother Toby. — *The Love Department*, William Trevor, 1966.

5654 You know how love flourishes in time of war, women standing on station platforms and waiting for the lines of faces to pull out, men's heads three deep in the carriage windows and arms raised like the front legs of horses on the Parthenon. — *Impossible Object*, Nicholas Mosley, 1968.

5655 "For love, for love," the gold-toothed girl was murmuring. — *In the Twelfth Year of the War*, Philip Appleman, 1970.

5656 Love weaves its own tapestry, spins its own golden thread, with its own sweet breath breathes into being its mysteries — bucolic, lusty, gentle as the eyes of daisies or thick with pain. — *The Blood Oranges*, John Hawkes, 1971.

5657 Ain't never nobody loved me like I love myself, cept my mother and she's dead. — *Pic*, Jack Kerouac, 1971.

5658 I think I fell in love with Sally while she was eating breakfast, the first morning we were together. — *All My Friends Are Going to Be Strangers*, Larry McMurtry, 1972.

5659 Millicent De Frayne, who was young in 1913, the sole possessor of an immense oil fortune, languished of an incurable ailment, her willful, hopeless love for Elijah Thrush, "the mime, poet, painter of art nouveau," who, after ruining the lives of countless men and women, was finally himself in love, "incorrectly, if not indecently," with his great-grandson. — *I Am Elijah Thrush*, James Purdy, 1972.

5660 We must love one another, yes, yes, that's all true enough, but nothing says we have to like each other. — *The Glory of the Hummingbird*, Peter De Vries, 1974.

5661 CERTAINTY: the death of love, and so of poetry, since it is the death of the possible or probable. Certainty destroys wonder, desire, joy, sorrow — those inclinations swayed from love by love. — *Fugitive*, Marion Montgomery, 1974.

5662 Now Uther Pendragon, king of all Britain, conceived an inordinate passion for the fair Ygraine, duchess of Cornwall, and having otherwise no access to her, he proceeded to wage war upon her husband, Gorlois the duke. — *Arthur Rex*, Thomas Berger, 1978.

5663 Love and death are absolutes, this time of year, not merely tendencies. — *Limits of the Land*, Curtis Harnack, 1979.

5664 *Saint Peter loved Jesus,/ said the Basque Country Spaniard,/ but he didn't always understand him.* — *Jesus Tales*, Romulus Linney, 1980.

5665 "Love?" — *Poppa John*, Larry Woiwode, 1981.

5666 On the last day of summer Mrs. Bohannon fell in love. — *The Other Side of the Fire*, Alice Thomas Ellis, 1983.

5667 Nicholas Dicken Quinney always considered that his career sprang from the fact that he fell in love twice in the same day — once with a girl and once with flying. — *The Bright Blue Sky*, John Harris *as* Max Hennessy, 1983.

5668 I love him in full knowledge now. — *How He Saved Her*, Ellen Schwamm, 1983.

5669 First of all you have to see Vivien Canvey, the great love of my life. — *These Golden Days*, John Braine, 1985.

5670 *"Hello, darling. I am returned from Rome now. I miss you and want to fuck with you. I love you so much still. Call me. Ciao."* — *Hazzard's Head*, Scott Summer, 1985.

5671 All the sorrows of Evan Shepard's loutish adolescence were redeemed at seventeen, in 1935, when he fell in love with automobiles. — *Cold Spring Harbor*, Richard Yates, 1986.

5672 My mother adored my father. — *Sightings*, Susan Trott, 1987.

5673 The last time she saw Paris when last the sweet birds sang was from a fast train heading south in 1968 at the time of the student revolution, and it was almost the last train to get out, but that is getting ahead of the story, which began late one evening at the Coupole in Montparnasse when someone introduced her to Julian Mendes, and thereby hangs a tale of love in those days of rage. — *Love in the Days of Rage*, Lawrence Ferlinghetti, 1988.

5674 In June of my twenty-eighth year, in a heat ennobled by devotion, I hurdled the lowered bars of conscience, and landed in the arms of my student Sarah Rengert, and Sarah, who had admired me for months from the distance of her desk, responded with the soft energies of accomplished love. — *In the Heart of the Whole World*, John Rolfe Gardiner, 1988.

5675 What Paul loved about Marston was his self-evident (so he passionately believed) innocence. — *The Temple*, Stephen Spender, 1988.

5676 Julia understood the price that sometimes had to be paid for love. — *A Place for Outlaws*, Allen Wier, 1989.

5677 A: Well now, you ask, what is this thing called love? To give you a simple answer — love is enough to make you believe in God. — *Darcy's Utopia*, Fay Weldon, 1990.

5678 She was a romantic about love, a cynic about everything else. — *The Dylanist*, Brian Morton, 1991.

5679 Love was in the air. — *Daughters of Albion*, A. N. Wilson, 1991.

5680 My mother began to love at the same moment in her life that she began to search for who she was. — *My Mother*, Kathy Acker, 1993.

Machinery

5681 It was at a love-spinning that I saw Kester first. And if, in these new-fangled days, when strange inventions crowd upon us, when I hear tell there is even a machine coming into use in some parts of the country for reaping and mowing, if those that may happen will read this don't know what a love-spinning was, they shall hear in good time. — *Precious Bane*, Mary Webb, 1924.

5682 Walter said, "Well, I bet I could all right if we had a ball-bearing one like Chuck Rasmussen's." — *The Big Pink Kite*, Clyde Brion Davis, 1960.

5683 I was trying to fix the damn mimeograph machine when the doorbell rang. — *The Spy in the Ointment*, Donald E. Westlake, 1966.

5684 None of the merry-go-rounds seem to work anymore. — *True Confessions*, John Gregory Dunne, 1977.

5685 This is the story of a machine and of the people who made a story of its movements and of what happened to the machine and its people. — *The Powwow Highway*, David Seals, 1979.

5686 He felt the vibration in the soles of his feet, through the deep scarlet pile that covered the floor. — *The Ledger*, Joan Hurling, 1981.

5687 Look! It goes, and without the least heave-ho from me. — *A Totally Free Man*, John Krich, 1981.

5688 Somewhere deep inside the cemetery a bulldozer worked, its drone rising and falling, riding the air like an eagle aboard a thermal. — *Gardens of Stone*, Nicholas Proffitt, 1983.

5689 Heaving out of the muddy pond, a large gray cylinder comes slowly up the bank. — *Fire in Heaven*, Malcolm Bosse, 1985.

5690 She could never understand machinery. — *Sunflower*, Rebecca West, 1986.

5691 Her answering machine is on. — *Exes*, Robert Miner, 1987.

5692 A crane with a ball and chain came up over the cobblestones and got into position. — "Out of the Whirlpool," Alan Sillitoe, 1987.

Mankind

5693 The human race, to which so many of my readers belong, has been playing at children's games from the beginning, and will probably do it till the end, which is a nuisance for the few people who grow up. — *The Napoleon of Notting Hill*, G. K. Chesterton, 1904.

5694 Most people in this world seem to live "in character"; they have a beginning, a middle and an end, and the three are congruous one with another and true to the rules of their type. — *Tono-Bungay*, H. G. Wells, 1909.

5695 In the Five Towns human nature is reported to be so hard that you can break stones on it. — *Helen with the High Hand*, Arnold Bennett, 1911.

5696 Man is not naturally a gregarious animal, though he has become so under the compulsion of circumstances and civilisation. — *The Wise Virgins*, Leonard Woolf, 1914.

5697 God made man, like Himself, lonely. — *Adam and Eve*, John Erskine, 1927.

5698 *Every man is a good man in a bad world.* — *Rock Wagram*, William Saroyan, 1951.

5699 "Is it not a marvellous thing that amid all the miracles of modern science, incredible though they be, no one has succeeded in imitating the miracle of reproduction, that no matter who we may be, rich or poor, large or small, San Roquean or *extranjero*, each and every one of us is able to honour his father and his mother and to look forward, in pride and humility, to the day when we ourselves shall be partners in the still unique mystery of replenishing the earth? Without doubt, we are all made in the image of God, for it is surely God who has reserved this singular Grace for Man, thus ensuring each's brotherhood with all." — *A Wild Surmise*, Frederic Raphael, 1961.

5700 Man is the only species for whom the disposal of waste is a burden, a task often ill judged, costly, criminal — especially when he learns to include himself, living and dead, in the list of waste products. — *The Edge of the Alphabet*, Janet Frame, 1962.

5701 Man is vile, I know, but people are

wonderful. — *Let Me Count the Ways*, Peter De Vries, 1965.

5702 *Let us now turn to the old problem of human will power.* — "The Magic Striptease," George Garrett, 1973.

5703 It seemed almost incidental that he was African. So vast had his inner perceptions grown over the years that he preferred an identification with mankind to an identification with a particular environment. — *A Question of Power*, Bessie Head, 1973.

5704 Such a time it is now, as it was then, the first summer of the year, when in the brittle heat of the day the ber trees and the cactus sucked up their own shadows; when the sheep and the goats foraged not for the meager briars and shrubs but for whatever meager shadows not sucked up by the midday sun: and when mortal nights blew cold and brought frost to the earth and *only* the spirits of the desert, bedraggled creatures, knew the folly of human beings and the folly of their gods. — *Saraswattee*, Kit Puran Singh, 1982.

5705 The trouble with treating people as equals is that the first thing you know they may be doing the same thing to you. — *The Prick of Noon*, Peter De Vries, 1985.

5706 There is an internal landscape, a geography of the soul; we search for its outlines all our lives. — *Damage*, Josephine Hart, 1991.

Maps

5707 Every one who has looked at the map of Norway must have been struck with the singular character of its coast. On the map it looks so jagged; a strange mixture of land and sea. On the spot, however, this coast is very sublime. — *Feats on the Fjord*, Harriet Martineau, 1841.

5708 Among the many peculiarities which contribute to make New York unlike other cities is the construction of what may be called its social map. As in the puzzles used in teaching children geography, all the pieces are of different shapes, different sizes and different colours; but they fit neatly together in the compact whole though the lines which define each bit are distinctly visible, especially when the map has been long used by the industrious child. — *Marion Darche*, F. Marion Crawford, 1893.

5709 Chicago!/ Felix Fay saw with his mind's eye the map on the wall of the railway station— the map with a picture of iron roads from all over the middle west centering in a dark blotch in the corner. — *The Briary-Bush*, Floyd Dell, 1921.

5710 Behind the smokehouse that summer,

Ringo and I had a living map. — *The Unvanquished*, William Faulkner, 1938.

5711 The last drops of the thundershower had hardly ceased falling when the Pedestrian stuffed his map into his pocket, settled his pack more comfortably on his tired shoulders, and stepped out from the shelter of a large chestnut-tree into the middle of the road. — *Out of the Silent Planet*, C. S. Lewis, 1938.

5712 The forecaster caressed his bald head and then swept his bony fingers across the course from Honolulu to San Francisco. — *The High and the Mighty*, Ernest K. Gann, 1953.

5713 Trace on a map the high border country, the land of high plains and high mountains that is the vast northern boundary of the western United States. — "The Canyon," Jack Schaefer, 1953.

5714 The map of France had gone from the window of the German Propaganda Bureau and a map of the British Isles had taken its place. — *The Spoilt City*, Olivia Manning, 1962.

5715 The map was red and yellow. The red was for British India; the yellow for the India of the princes: the Rajas and the Maharajas, the Ranis and the Maharanis, the Nawabs, the Rawals, the Jams. — *The Princes*, Manohar Malgonkar, 1963.

5716 The watcher on the hilltop settled himself against the gnarled bole of an olive tree, tested his radio, opened his map case on his knees, focused his field glasses and began a slow meticulous survey from the southern tip of the Lake of Tiberias to the spur of Sha'ar Hagolan, where the Yarmuk River turned southwestward to join the Jordan. — *The Tower of Babel*, Morris West, 1968.

5717 It unrolled slowly, forced to show its colors, curling and snapping back whenever one of us turned loose. — *Deliverance*, James Dickey, 1970.

5718 She moves from room to room in the semi-dark of the house. Torn maps direct her journey. — *The Mirror of the Giant*, Penelope Shuttle, 1980.

5719 In the idealized vision of mapmakers, New Jersey is tinted a delicate pink that has nothing to do with the industrial darkness of its larger cities. — *Hearts*, Hilma Wolitzer, 1980.

5720 On the map it was about 160 miles from the aerodrome at Shoreham, across the English Channel and down through France to Pepriac, a scruffy little crossroads village some way south of Arras. — *War Story*, Derek Robinson, 1988.

5721 Let's begin with the map, shall we? — *The Magic We Do Here*, Lawrence Rudner, 1988.

5722 The map under glass made no sense. — *Avenue of Eternal Peace*, Nicholas Jose, 1989.

5723 From above, start with the privileged

view. Lay on the page a neat grid of neighbor-hoods, the quirky crosscuts of routes that followed secondary streams or an Indian footpath, what was decreed by nature or habit and is long forgotten, long a dead end or confusing turn in the city — the lost logic of a marsh or a stubborn farmer's lawsuit that will not let you pass. — *Natural History*, Maureen Howard, 1992.

5724 He parked the truck in front of a bull-dozed mound closing off the old timber road, folded the topo map and fit it in his back pocket, dropped an apple and a few shells into the knap-sack, placed three extra shells in his right front pocket, fitted a cap on his head, and began walking. — *An Elegy for September*, John Nichols, 1992.

Marriage

5725 I was ever of opinion, that the honest man who married and brought up a large family, did more service than he who continued single and only talked of population. — *The Vicar of Wakefield*, Oliver Goldsmith, 1766.

5726 It is a truth universally acknowledged, that a single man in possession of a good fortune must be in want of a wife. — *Pride and Prejudice*, Jane Austen, 1813.

5727 About thirty years ago, Miss Maria Ward of Huntingdon, with only seven thousand pounds, had the good luck to captivate Sir Thomas Bertram, of Mansfield Park, in the county of Northampton, and to be thereby raised to the rank of a baronet's lady, with all the comforts and conse-quences of an handsome house and large income. — *Mansfield Park*, Jane Austen, 1814.

5728 There once lived, in a sequestered part of the county of Devonshire, one Mr. Godfrey Nickleby: a worthy gentleman, who, taking it into his head rather late in life that he must get married, and not being young enough or rich enough to aspire to the hand of a lady of fortune, had wedded an old flame out of mere attach-ment, who in her turn had taken him for the same reason. — *Nicholas Nickleby*, Charles Dick-ens, 1839.

5729 "I don't believe that you'd care a cent if she did marry a Dutchman! She might as well as to marry some white folks I know." — *The End of the World*, Edward Eggleston, 1872.

5730 "If you never mean to marry, you might as well turn priest, too," said Ippolito Sara-cinesca to his elder brother, Orsino, with a laugh. — *Corleone*, F. Marion Crawford, 1896.

5731 "We're neither of us young people, I know, and I can very well believe that you had not thought of marrying again. I can account for your surprise at my offer, even your disgust —" Dr. Anther hesitated. — *The Son of Royal Lang-brith*, William Dean Howells, 1904.

5732 "And, then, oh yes! Atalanta is getting too pronounced." She spoke lightly, leaning back a little in her deep arm-chair. It was the end of a somewhat lively review. — *Vainglory*, Ronald Firbank, 1915.

5733 Splash! . . . That's me, Matilda Anne! That's me falling plump into the pool of matri-mony before I've had time to fall in love! — *The Prairie Wife*, Arthur Stringer, 1915.

5734 Mr. Templeton Thorpe was soon to be married for the second time. — *From the House-tops*, George Barr McCutcheon, 1916.

5735 It headed the list of marriages in *The Times*, a single unobtrusive little notice, couched in the customary bald form of words wherewith two human souls announce to the world at large that they have embarked together on the biggest adventure of life. — *Red Ashes*, Margaret Pedler, 1925.

5736 For thirty-six years Judge Gamaliel Bland Honeywell had endured the double-edged bliss of a perfect marriage; but it seemed to him, on this sparkling Easter Sunday, that he had lived those years with a stranger. — *The Romantic Comedians*, Ellen Glasgow, 1926.

5737 "I am asking you again to marry me as I did a fortnight ago." — *Wintersmoon*, Hugh Wal-pole, 1927.

5738 The last thing that Alcibiades had wanted was to marry, but one day on a wager he slapped the face of the father of his friend Cal-lias, and the wealthy and genial Hipponicus was so charmed with the grace of his apology that he offered him his daughter and ten talents as a marriage portion. — *The Jealous Gods*, Gertrude Atherton, 1928.

5739 While they were children playing to-gether, they said they would be married as soon as they were old enough, and when they were old enough they married. — *Let the Hurricane Roar*, Rose Wilder Lane, 1933.

5740 My Dear Honoria,/ So Peter is really married: I have ordered willow-wreaths for half my acquaintance. I understand that it is a decidu-ous tree; if nothing is available but the bare rods, I shall distribute them all the same, for the better beating of breasts. — *Busman's Honeymoon*, Dorothy L. Sayers, 1937.

5741 "Susan Gaylord is going to be married." — *This Proud Heart*, Pearl S. Buck, 1938.

5742 "Matrimony was ordained, thirdly," said Jane Studdock to herself, "for the mutual society, help, and comfort that the one ought to have of the other." — *That Hideous Strength*, C. S. Lewis, 1945.

5743 Unpleasant, not to say ominous, news from every part of the world was for a time almost entirely forgotten, or ignored, by much of Barsetshire, owing to the overriding interest in a marriage arranged, as *The Thunderer* puts it (though who arranges the marriages we do not know), between the Reverend Herbert Choyce, M.A., Vicar of Hatch End, and Dorothea Frances Merriman, whose Christian names had long been almost forgotten, buried in the affectionate "Merry" which all her friends and employers used. — *A Double Affair*, Angela Thirkell, 1957.

5744 Charlotte Anderson, by her own and her family's standards, made a good marriage. — *A Family's Affair*, Ellen Douglas, 1962.

5745 Husband, she thought, and would have left it there, comforted. — *Voyage to Sante Fe*, Janice Holt Giles, 1962.

5746 One evening, in bed, she said they had been friendly long enough now to think of getting married and then thought he might not have heard (though her lips brushed his left ear) because he lay on his back in silence. — *The Barbary Light*, P. H. Newby, 1962.

5747 When Judith Arneth Pedlock was past eighty and on a visit to the Mandersons on St. James's Square in London, she wrote a postcard to her daughter Gertrude (Mrs. Saul Lazar-Wolf) stating that the weather was rainy — *où sont les neiges d'antan?* — that the stiffness had left her right knee, and that she was bringing back to the old house at Norton-on-Hudson a Mr. Jacob Ellenbogan, whom she intended to marry. — *Pedlock & Sons*, Stephen Longstreet, 1966.

5748 To discover, after 7 years, that he doesn't know her, his wife. And money available, to leave with, to go to Mexico? And why not, to face her there, break out of that cocoon that he has carefully wrapped himself in, the mummy. — *The Sky Changes*, Gilbert Sorrentino, 1966.

5749 With much talk about teenage marriages, I feel, for whatever it may be worth to some young people on the brink of same, that I should tell about mine. — *Mr. and Mrs. Bo Jo Jones*, Ann Head, 1967.

5750 After some thirty years of marriage Mrs. Prelude's sole manifestation of independence was always, when travelling by plane, to sit in the tail. — *In Pious Memory*, Margery Sharp, 1967.

5751 When Medora Earnshaw, at the age of forty-six, married Beejay Leffaway only seven weeks after the sudden death of her husband of twenty-four years, many of the residents along Upper Greenwood Avenue had been harshly critical of Medora. — *The Earnshaw Neighborhood*, Erskine Caldwell, 1971.

5752 "Gracie darling, will you marry me?"/ "Yes."— *An Accidental Man*, Iris Murdoch, 1971.

5753 In June of 1900 Jimmie Blacksmith's maternal uncle Tabidgi — Jackie Smolders to the white world — was disturbed to get news that Jimmie had married a white girl in the Methodist church at Wallah. — *The Chant of Jimmie Blacksmith*, Thomas Keneally, 1972.

5754 During the recent months of Annette's marriage to Doan Thurmond, while living with him in the large and imposing graystone house on a high terrace in the rolling green hills of Zephyrfield, a quiet residential suburb of costly homes and estates several miles from Doan's law offices in the busy industrial city of Melbourne, there were numerous times when Annette was on the verge of leaving home. — *Annette*, Erskine Caldwell, 1973.

5755 It was a time of inexplicably happy marriages. — *Falling*, Susan Fromberg Schaeffer, 1973.

5756 We were married three times if you count the machine. — *The Marriage Machine*, Gillian Freeman, 1975.

5757 It was 1947 when Mutt and I was married. I was singing in Happy's Café around on Delaware Street. He didn't like for me to sing after we were married because he said that's why he married me so he could support me. — *Corregidora*, Gayl Jones, 1975.

5758 Dimple Dasgupta had set her heart on marrying a neurosurgeon, but her father was looking for engineers in the matrimonial ads. — *Wife*, Bharati Mukherjee, 1975.

5759 *"Him?/ Think not of him for your daughter, Signore, nor for her sister either. There will be none for him. Not him. He has taken his gallows, the noose and knot, to marry."*— "The Owl," John Hawkes, 1977.

5760 We were married in 1957, in those dark ages before legalized abortion. I know that's no excuse. There were always illegal abortions. — *In the Flesh*, Hilma Wolitzer, 1977.

5761 In the early 1950s Michael Dalzell was a young man. He owned estates in the Borders of Scotland and a small house in central London, and when he decided to marry, as we can see from this photograph, he chose as his bride a fair-haired girl of the same class as himself. — *The Bad Sister*, Emma Tennant, 1978.

5762 My grandmother, a woman of eighty-one, divorced, widowed, transplanted in her time, will be married again next month. — *The Old Girl*, Joshua Gidding, 1980.

5763 Marriages are funny things. — *New York Time*, Richard Peck, 1981.

5764 Of course, if Cynthia said she'd marry him, he would insist upon a prenuptial agreement. — *A Mere Formality*, Barbara Howell, 1982.

5765 Ned Fraser was forty and thought of himself as a "confirmed bachelor" when an unex-

pected event catapulted him into marriage. —*Anger*, May Sarton, 1982.

5766 "Marry me," said Louise Agar. — *Wise Virgin*, A. N. Wilson, 1982.

5767 I'm often asked what it's like to be married to a genius. — *The Mind-Body Problem*, Rebecca Goldstein, 1983.

5768 "Craig Towle's married a bobby-soxer," my father said, the evening before my mother left him. — *The Bobby-Soxer*, Hortense Calisher, 1986.

5769 A year after my father shot himself my mother married a two-faced hardware salesman named Roger Trewly — *The Burning Women of Far Cry*, Rick DeMarinis, 1986.

5770 Lily had married first when she was eighteen. — "Third Time Lucky," Rachel Ingalls, 1986.

5771 What could be more hopeless than a madwoman marrying a drunk? — *Curranne Trueheart*, Donald Newlove, 1986.

5772 He stood in the doorway to their bedroom, looked at his wife, and thought, I am married to a stone, a drift of snow. — *The Injured Party*, Susan Fromberg Schaeffer, 1986.

5773 William Faulkner, himself a writer, once offered some advice on the subject of wives. — *The Marriage Hearse*, Larry Duberstein, 1987.

5774 For the second time in a week the couple stood in church asking to be married. — *Summertime*, Maureen McCoy, 1987.

5775 If Sandro wasn't married, as he had let her know, casually (too casually perhaps? or rather, promisingly casually), then Julia might quite like to marry him. — *Home Thoughts*, Tim Parks, 1987.

5776 In every woman's life a time must come to think about marriage. — *In Every Woman's Life . . .*, Alix Kates Shulman, 1987.

5777 Looking back, I should have realized something was up as soon as I opened the bedroom door and found my wife asleep on top of the sheets with a strange man curled up like a foetus beside her. — *The South Will Rise at Noon*, Douglas Glover, 1988.

5778 Only the March rain, cold and relentlessly pervasive, was there to watch on the day that Michelle Paparo inadvertently detonated her marriage. — *Love in the Temperate Zone*, L. R. Wright, 1988.

5779 In the autumn of 1986 our youngest son Martinus, a KLM pilot with a lethal taste for girls that were too young for him and sports cars that were too expensive, finally married his latest airline stewardess, a Canadian blonde. — *The Centurion*, Jan de Hartog, 1989.

5780 Perhaps John Felton had got married too young, but he really did love Joanie and, besides, she was pregnant and came from a family which, though believing abortion was wrong, would have been disgraced by an illegitimate birth, with several of its members active in local church affairs and one in the politics of the county. — *Meeting Evil*, Thomas Berger, 1992.

5781 Everything was fine until my sister Caroline graduated from Barnard last May and announced she was going to marry Jonathan. — *Plain Jane*, Eve Horowitz, 1992.

5782 Morgan Riley announced he'd take a wife, a woman to help dear Annie. — *A Country Divorce*, Ann T. Jones, 1992.

5783 If anyone had told me that one day I'd marry, I wouldn't have believed it, and that's because people like me don't. — *Stella Landry*, Robin McCorquodale, 1992.

Meetings

5784 The evening before my departure for Blithedale, I was returning to my bachelor-apartments, after attending the wonderful exhibition of the Veiled Lady, when an elderly man of rather shabby appearance met me in an obscure part of the street. — *The Blithedale Romance*, Nathaniel Hawthorne, 1852.

5785 It was shortly after the capitulation of loyal Fort Sumter to rebellious South Carolina that Mr. Edward Colburne of New Boston made the acquaintance of Miss Lillie Ravenel of New Orleans. — *Miss Ravenel's Conversion from Secession to Loyalty*, John W. De Forest, 1867.

5786 When Bartley Hubbard went to interview Silas Lapham for the "Solid Men of Boston" series, which he undertook to finish up in *The Events*, after he replaced their original projector on that newspaper, Lapham received him in his private office by previous appointment. — *The Rise of Silas Lapham*, William Dean Howells, 1885.

5787 I was on my way from San Francisco to Yokohama, when in a very desultory and gradual manner I became acquainted with Mrs. Lecks and Mrs. Aleshine. — *The Casting Away of Mrs. Lecks and Mrs. Aleshine*, Frank R. Stockton, 1886.

5788 A procession of schoolboys having to meet a procession of schoolgirls on the Sunday's dead march, called a walk, round the park, could hardly go by without dropping to a hum in its chatter, and the shot of incurious half-eyes at the petticoated creatures — all so much of a swarm unless you stare at them like lanterns. — *Lord Ormont and His Aminta*, George Meredith, 1894.

5789 He happened into the place one afternoon in late autumn. They met by chance—the usual way. If he had shaved himself that morning, as he should have done, he never would have met Pink. Perhaps Fate issued a sub-decree. — *Pink Marsh*, George Ade, 1897.

5790 He was one of my first acquaintances when I came up to town to live; for I met him almost immediately after I gave up my country identity and melted into the sea of the city, though I did not learn his name for some time afterwards, and therefore knew him, as I found many others did, simply as, "the Old Gentleman of the Black Stock." — *The Old Gentleman of the Black Stock*, Thomas Nelson Page, 1897.

5791 "Allow me to present to you my friend, Filippo Brandolini, a gentleman of Citta di Castello." — *The Making of a Saint*, W. Somerset Maugham, 1898.

5792 Everyone has seen a hare, either crouched or running in the fields, or hanging dead in a poulterer's shop, or lastly pathetic, even dreadful-looking and in this form almost indistinguishable from a skinned cat, on the domestic table. But not many people have met a Mahatma, at least to their knowledge. — *The Mahatma and the Hare*, H. Rider Haggard, 1911.

5793 Next morning he saw her again. — *The Flower of the Chapdelaines*, George W. Cable, 1918.

5794 I confess that when I first made acquaintance with Charles Strickland I never for a moment discerned that there was in him anything out of the ordinary. — *The Moon and Sixpence*, W. Somerset Maugham, 1919.

5795 I remember as well as though it were yesterday the first time I met Auntie Sue. — *The Re-Creation of Brian Kent*, Harold Bell Wright, 1919.

5796 "The first time I saw the boy, Jack Irons, he was about nine years old. . . ." — *In the Days of Poor Richard*, Irving Bacheller, 1922.

5797 I first met Myra Henshawe when I was fifteen, but I had known her about ever since I could remember anything at all. — *My Mortal Enemy*, Willa Cather, 1926.

5798 The Assistant Commissioner was careful of his appearance before meeting men younger than himself. — *It's a Battlefield*, Graham Greene, 1934.

5799 One evening a year or two before the war, when most people still took it for granted that the overwhelming tragedies of life related to the private affairs of individuals, a very pale young man crossed the lawn of a large house in Montarac City and stopped dead when he came near enough to see that on the porch was standing a young woman who was far from pale. — "Life Sentence," Rebecca West, 1935.

5800 It was on 46th Street, between Madison and Fifth, that I caught sight of him, a short and rotund figure passing by me on the crowded sidewalk. "Littlejohn —" I muttered, scarcely crediting my eyes, turning my head to look: the extraordinary coat with its capacious pockets, designed to carry ducks; the funny looking cap with the ear flaps tied on top, like the one Gillette had worn in the play of Sherlock Holmes. — *Mr. Littlejohn*, Martin Flavin, 1940.

5801 It had all been arranged by telegram; Jeremy Pordage was to look out for a coloured chauffeur in a grey uniform with a carnation in his button-hole; and the coloured chauffeur was to look out for a middle-aged Englishman carrying the Poetical Works of Wordsworth. In spite of the crowds at the station, they found one another without difficulty. — *After Many a Summer Dies the Swan*, Aldous Huxley, 1940.

5802 The Cullens were Irish; but it was in France that I met them and was able to form an impression of their love and their trouble. — *The Pilgrim Hawk*, Glenway Wescott, 1940.

5803 I first met her, this girl you'll find soon enough, when she fished me out of the Sacramento River on an occasion when I was showing more originality than sense. — *Past All Dishonor*, James M. Cain, 1946.

5804 I saw Mr. John Turner first on June the 25th that year. — *The Chequer Board*, Nevil Shute, 1947.

5805 It must have been a Thursday night when I met her for the first time—at the dance hall. — *Sexus*, Henry Miller, 1949.

5806 Sybil met Philip Hilliard on the night of her twenty-first birthday and at a dance, too, just as Aunt Jo had always told her that those things happened. — *Sybil*, Louis Auchincloss, 1952.

5807 You might think that that first time I met her hadn't really a lot of significance. — *Fortune Is a Woman*, Winston Graham, 1953.

5808 I met the boy on the morning of the kidnapping. — *Meet Me at the Morgue*, Kenneth Millar *as* John Ross Macdonald, 1953.

5809 It was almost quitting time when Toddy met the man with no chin and the talking dog. — *The Golden Gizmo*, Jim Thompson, 1954.

5810 The first time the children saw the Devil, he was sitting next to them in the second row of deck chairs in the bandstand. — *Devil by the Sea*, Nina Bawden, 1957.

5811 I first met Dean not long after my wife and I split up. — *On the Road*, Jack Kerouac, 1957.

5812 Gouraud caught them as they crossed the hall of the hotel, between the dining room and the courtyard. He laid his nervous bony hand on the young man's arm. — *Last Score*, Storm Jameson, 1961.

5813 They met for the first time under the

gaslight of the tiny booking hall. — *The Wind Off the Sea*, David Beaty, 1962.

5814 As Lloyd and Jim negotiated the steepest part of 3rd Street, panting a little from the climb, they saw Hoxie coming toward them from the harbor, with his blue cotton workshirt heavily sweated and his longshoreman's hook hanging from his shoulder. — *The Goldseekers*, W. R. Burnett, 1962.

5815 The whim, yet not entirely a whim, that brought Manuel Andrada blundering into my life... — *The Exiles*, Albert J. Guerard, 1962.

5816 In 1935, when I first met Rose, I was twenty-five years old and I was quite certain that I knew right from wrong, but I do not blame myself entirely for this youthful conceit. — *My Friend Rose*, Jane Duncan, 1964.

5817 Jack had agreed to go to Victoria Station to meet her. He'd agreed, but all the same it gave him a grudge against her from the start. — *The Bogeyman*, Margaret Forster, 1965.

5818 I met Jack Kennedy in November, 1946. — *An American Dream*, Norman Mailer, 1965.

5819 If only I hadn't started pretending in front of my wife-to-be as well as to my friends. But I did so and very soon after we met. She was still someone else's wife at the time. — *In Pursuit of Evil*, Hugh Mills, 1967.

5820 When Tillie Shilepsky first laid eyes on her husband-to-be she thought, "No. Uh-uh. He's out." — *Witch's Milk*, Peter De Vries, 1968.

5821 Charles and I met for the first time in January 1944 when we were new boys together at a prep-school in the midlands. — *The Undiscovered Country*, Julian Mitchell, 1968.

5822 The writer encountered a Muslim woman once in a narrow street of a predominantly Hindu town, in the quarter inhabited by moneylenders. — *The Day of the Scorpion*, Paul Scott, 1968.

5823 The first time I met him, I thought he was a nut case, just a nutty old man hanging around the recreation grounds, leaning over the rails, shouting at people as they come by. — *The Olympian*, Brian Glanville, 1969.

5824 They had been retreating all day along mountain paths in brilliant cold when they saw the shepherd up ahead, crouched like an Indian, in an orange goatskin coat. — *Like Men Betrayed*, Frederic Raphael, 1970.

5825 "Mr. Marchant?" he said./ Jimmy, slightly taken aback — he had not expected quite so distinctive a presence — nodded. — *The Destiny Waltz*, Gerda Charles, 1971.

5826 MARCH/ Count Dracula meets Bonnie Parker. What will they do together? — *The Players and the Game*, Julian Symons, 1972.

5827 This is a tale of a meeting of two lonesome, skinny, fairly old white men on a planet which was dying fast. — *Breakfast of Champions*, Kurt Vonnegut, 1973.

5828 The chalice sat between them, gleaming on the table. Neither man was looking at it. — *The Man from Greek and Roman*, James Goldman, 1974.

5829 I met the first of my three or four successive wives in somewhat odd circumstances, the development of which resembled a clumsy conspiracy, with nonsensical details and a main plotter who not only knew nothing of its real object but insisted on making inept moves that seemed to preclude the slightest possibility of success. — *Look at the Harlequins!*, Vladimir Nabokov, 1974.

5830 They first saw each other, like Dante and Beatrice, on the Ponte Vecchio. — *A Painted Devil*, Rachel Billington, 1975.

5831 I knew the man, but only from the morning he caught me looking for copper in the Wilderness of Zin. — *Moses the Lawgiver*, Thomas Keneally, 1975.

5832 The interview seemed over. The Principal of the college sat looking at the candidate. — *Bilgewater*, Jane Gardam, 1976.

5833 Here is the first time I saw them:/ 1956./ Their home in Beverly Hills. — *Attachments*, Judith Rossner, 1977.

5834 There had been a nasty incident, halfway between France and England, when young Adolf, turning in a moment of weakness to take a last look at the hills of Boulogne, had come face to face with a man wearing a beard and thick spectacles. — *Young Adolf*, Beryl Bainbridge, 1978.

5835 There is no way, unless you have unusual self-control, of disguising the expression on your face when you first meet a dwarf. — *The Year of Living Dangerously*, C. J. Koch, 1978.

5836 They sometimes met on country roads when there were flowers or snow. — *Dubin's Lives*, Bernard Malamud, 1979.

5837 It was the last daylight hour of a December afternoon more than twenty years ago — I was twenty-three, writing and publishing my first short stories, and like many a *Bildungsroman* hero before me, already contemplating my own massive *Bildungsroman* — when I arrived at his hideaway to meet the great man. — *The Ghost Writer*, Philip Roth, 1979.

5838 I was in Madison, Wisconsin, on a lecture tour, when I first met Professor Agaard and his son. — *Freddy's Book*, John Gardner, 1980.

5839 We met in London, briefly, our paths crossing for an hour or two, as they had done at intervals over the past twenty years. — *The File on Fraulein Berg*, Joan Lingard, 1980.

5840 Philip Weber met Hermann Goering for the first time in the small elevator on the Ven-

dôme side of the Ritz. — *The Man Who Lived at the Ritz*, A. E. Hotchner, 1981.

5841 Hector's mother met Alejo Santinio, his Pop, in 1939 when she was twenty-seven years old and working as a ticket girl in the Neptuna movie theater in Holguín, Cuba. — *Our House in the Last World*, Oscar Hijuelos, 1983.

5842 The first time I met Byron Jaynes was in a series of three interview sessions at his home outside the Catskill village of Tamberlane, New York, in the autumn of 1968. — *The Life of Byron Jaynes*, James Howard Kunstler, 1983.

5843 The very first time Emma ever saw Duncan, he was trying to kill Zooey. — *Jealousies*, Caroline Leavitt, 1983.

5844 Nel Thompson introduces Mr. Gamal, the young salesman, and he opens his sample case. — *Now for the Turbulence*, Alma Stone, 1983.

5845 I first met her, this girl that I married a few days later, and that the papers have crucified under the pretense of glorification, on a Friday morning in June, on the parking lot by the Patuxent Building, that my office is in. — *Cloud Nine*, James M. Cain, 1984.

5846 His first feeling on turning around at the tap on his shoulder while he was buying cigarettes at the college canteen and seeing his old friend Murad was one of joy so that he gasped "Murad? You?" and the cigarettes fell from his hand in amazement, but this rapidly turned to anxiety when Murad gave a laugh, showing the betel-stained teeth beneath the small bristling moustache he still wore on his upper lip. — *In Custody*, Anita Desai, 1984.

5847 They met in a beachside bar on one of the Greek Islands. — *Tantalus*, Amanda Hemingway, 1984.

5848 Lee turned his attention to a Jewish boy named Carl Steinberg, whom he had known casually for about a year. The first time he saw Carl, Lee thought, "I could use that, if the family jewels weren't in pawn to Uncle Junk." — *Queer*, William S. Burroughs, 1985.

5849 Yesterday I ran into Paul Schneider. — *Goodbye, Karl Erich*, Sam Dann, 1985.

5850 I meet her at a party. It's a large room I first see her in. — *Fall & Rise*, Stephen Dixon, 1985.

5851 A man and a woman are about to pass each other in an empty corridor of Boston's Symphony Hall. — *Winter Concert*, Margaret Howe Freydberg, 1985.

5852 Flora had met James when she was going out with his younger brother, Edward. — "I See a Long Journey," Rachel Ingalls, 1985.

5853 I first saw Alice Blanders Russo at the American Center in Rome. — *Friends Along the Way*, Julia Markus, 1985.

5854 It was on a mild, fragrant evening in late September, several weeks after she had moved to Glenkill, Pennsylvania, to begin teaching at the Glenkill Academy for Boys, that Monica Jensen was introduced to Sheila Trask at a crowded reception in the headmaster's residence. — *Solstice*, Joyce Carol Oates, 1985.

5855 The first time I saw him, I didn't really see him. — *Mrs. Demming and the Mythical Beast*, Faith Sullivan, 1985.

5856 The first time we came across Xorandor we were sitting on him. — *Xorandor*, Christine Brooke-Rose, 1986.

5857 My parents met at a college mixer in 1942. — *The Fantasy*, Thomas Hauser, 1986.

5858 It was my ex-wife, on one of the rare meetings she fixed to see for herself how much I had deteriorated, who told me that Billy Bunter was still alive. — *The Joke of the Century*, David Hughes, 1986.

5859 He met her at twilight at the outdoor bar of the Royal Hawaiian Hotel, the old pink palace of the Pacific now imprisoned by the concrete towers of Waikiki like a lone rosebush in a canyon. — *Sabotage*, Fletcher Knebel, 1986.

5860 I first laid eyes on Mel Dworkin during the winter of . . . the Supremes. — *The Bachelors' Bride*, Stephen Koch, 1986.

5861 Elaine Mueller had been every bit a tomboy when, in the spring of 1936, she met Foley Menutis. — *Dansville*, Robin McCorquodale, 1986.

5862 "You look familiar," said the interviewer as he flexed a rubber band between his thumb and forefinger. — *The Mother Load*, Cindy Packard, 1986.

5863 I first got to know Oscar Livingstone in fairly humdrum circumstances. — *A Friend from England*, Anita Brookner, 1987.

5864 Axel and Eino met only because one morning Axel turned his head; he'd heard the cry of a bird — a seabird of some kind. — "An Artist's Life," Rachel Ingalls, 1987.

5865 When we met twenty-five years ago, I was an airplane pilot entranced by flight, looking for meanings behind instruments and airspeeds. — *One*, Richard Bach, 1988.

5866 So we're finally going to meet, Doctor. — *Mascara*, Ariel Dorfman, 1988.

5867 The first time I saw Billy he came walking out of a cloud. — *Anything for Billy*, Larry McMurtry, 1988.

5868 I met her in a bar and knew I was in trouble. — *Los Angeles Without a Map*, Richard Rayner, 1988.

5869 I met Maria during my next-to-last year in prep school. — *The Beautiful Room Is Empty*, Edmund White, 1988.

5870 I have had much leisure in the past months to reflect on my first encounter with

Fledge, and why he formed such an immediate and intense antipathy toward me. — *The Grotesque*, Patrick McGrath, 1989.

5871 It must have been late autumn of that year, and probably it was towards dusk for the sake of being less conspicuous. And yet a meeting between two professional gentlemen representing the chief branches of the law should surely not need to be concealed. — *The Quincunx*, Charles Palliser, 1989.

5872 When I was the fish baby. That's when I first met them. — *When the Parrot Boy Sings*, John Champagne, 1990.

5873 Chloe liked Olivia the moment she saw her. — *Chloe and Olivia*, Bell Gale Chevigny, 1990.

5874 *There was a glance, then a gesture of kindness which ended in blood.* — *Trumpets of Silver*, Norma Harris, 1990.

5875 Frank first laid eyes on Libby Girard at the Sunday matinee a minute before the lights went down. — *North of Hope*, Jon Hassler, 1990.

5876 "Eminenze, you wished to see me?" — *The Neon Madonna*, Dan Binchy, 1991.

5877 As it happened (and most of this did more or less happen), I first met her at the Booker Prize for Fiction. — *Doctor Criminale*, Malcolm Bradbury, 1992.

5878 She saw him and he saw her. — *Listen to the Nightingale*, Rumer Godden, 1992.

5879 We met outside an abortion clinic. — *She Needed Me*, Walter Kirn, 1992.

5880 In July 1965, wearing new sandals, blind to life's possibilities, I met the boy who would immediately become my husband, while we were standing at 54th and Sixth talking to Moondog. — *After Moondog*, Jane Shapiro, 1992.

5881 It was unbearably thrilling. — *Fugitive Nights*, Joseph Wambaugh, 1992.

5882 How in a village free of fog could the boy and the girl have never met? — *Love's Mansion*, Paul West, 1992.

Men

5883 The Marquis of — —, for a long Series of Years, was the first and most distinguished Favourite at Court: He held the most honourable Employments under the Crown, disposed of all Places of Profit as he pleased, presided at the Council, and in a manner governed the whole Kingdom. — *The Female Quixote*, Charlotte Lennox, 1752.

5884 John Farrago, was a man of about fifty-three years of age, of good natural sense, and considerable reading; but in some things whim-sical, owing perhaps to his greater knowledge of books than of the world; but, in some degree, also, to his having never married, being what they call an old bachelor, a characteristic of which is, usually, singularity and whim. — *Modern Chivalry*, Hugh Henry Brackenridge, 1792–1815.

5885 In consenting to lay before the world the experience of a common seaman, and, I may add, of one who has been such a sinner as the calling is only too apt to produce, I trust that no feeling of vanity has had an undue influence. — *Ned Myers*, James Fenimore Cooper, 1843.

5886 In the days when the spinning wheels hummed busily in the farmhouses — and even great ladies, clothed in silk and thread lace, had their toy spinning wheels of polished oak — there might be seen, in districts far away among the lanes, or deep in the bosom of the hills, certain pallid undersized men who, by the side of the brawny country-folk, looked like the remnants of a disinherited race. — *Silas Marner*, George Eliot, 1861.

5887 In the spring of 1849, old Lord Cheyne, the noted philanthropist, was, it will be remembered by all those interested in social reform, still alive and energetic. — *Love's Cross-Currents*, A. C. Swinburne, 1877.

5888 When I was a small boy at the beginning of the century I remember an old man who wore knee-breeches and worsted stockings, and who used to hobble about the street of our village with the help of a stick. — *The Way of All Flesh*, Samuel Butler, 1884.

5889 Mr. Utterson the lawyer was a man of a rugged countenance, that was never lighted by a smile; cold, scanty and embarrassed in discourse; backward in sentiment; lean, long, dusty, dreary and yet somehow lovable. — *The Strange Case of Dr. Jekyll and Mr. Hyde*, Robert Louis Stevenson, 1886.

5890 It was the opinion of a good many people that Charles Millard was "something of a dude." — *The Faith Doctor*, Edward Eggleston, 1891.

5891 "Oh, Mr. Fargeon! why are men so foolish?" — *The Captain of Company K*, Joseph Kirkland, 1891.

5892 As Clarence Brant, President of the Robles Land Company, and husband of the rich widow of John Peyton, of the Robles Ranche, mingled with the outgoing audience of the Cosmopolitan Theatre, at San Francisco, he elicited the usual smiling nods and recognition due to his good looks and good fortune. — *Clarence*, Bret Harte, 1895.

5893 He was an inch, perhaps two, under six feet, powerfully built, and he advanced straight at you with a slight stoop of the shoulders, head forward, and a fixed from-under stare which

made you think of a charging bull. — *Lord Jim*, Joseph Conrad, 1900.

5894 Mr. Jenkinson Neeld was an elderly man of comfortable private means; he had chambers in Pall Mall, close to the Imperium Club, and his short stoutish figure, topped by a chubby spectacled face, might be seen entering that dignified establishment every day at lunch time, and also at the hour of dinner on the evenings when he had no invitation elsewhere. — *Tristram of Blent*, Anthony Hope, 1901.

5895 A quiet, well-dressed man named Shelton, with a brown face and a short, fair beard, stood by the book-stall at Dover Station. — *The Island Pharisees*, John Galsworthy *as* John Sinjohn, 1904.

5896 He was imposing, even in his pensiveness. — *The Daughter of Anderson Crow*, George Barr McCutcheon, 1907.

5897 He was a tall, rawboned, rangy young fellow with a face so tanned by wind and sun you had the impression that his skin would feel like leather if you could affect the impertinence to test it by the sense of touch. — *Truxton King*, George Barr McCutcheon, 1909.

5898 Edwin Clayhanger stood on the steep-sloping, red-bricked canal bridge, in the valley between Bursley and its suburb Hillport. — *Clayhanger*, Arnold Bennett, 1910.

5899 Sun and wind of thirty-six out-of-door years had tanned Mr. Jeff Bransford's cheek to a rosy-brown, contrasting sharply with the whiteness of the upper part of his forehead, when exposed — as now — by the pushing up of his sombrero. — *Good Men and True*, Eugene Manlove Rhodes, 1910.

5900 Mr. Hungerton, her father, really was the most tactless person on earth, — a fluffy, feathery, untidy cockatoo of a man, perfectly good-natured, but absolutely centered upon his own silly self. — *The Lost World*, Arthur Conan Doyle, 1912.

5901 His was the first figure to catch my eye that evening in Petrograd; he stood under the dusky lamp in the vast gloomy Warsaw station, with exactly the expression that I was afterwards to know so well, impressed not only upon his face but also upon the baggy looseness of his trousers at the knees, the unfastened straps of his long black military boots. — *The Dark Forest*, Hugh Walpole, 1916.

5902 Bram Johnson was an unusual man, even for the northland. — *The Golden Snare*, James Oliver Curwood, 1918.

5903 With his long white beard and with his white hair, with his hook nose and his black eyes, with his little gold ear-rings, he was, as he sat back in his chair, his stick leaning against the arm of it, the coal fire playing on his face, a pic-

ture an Italian painter might have made. — *The Strangers' Banquet*, Donn Byrne, 1919.

5904 Between Conniston, of His Majesty's Royal Northwest Mounted Police, and Keith, the outlaw, there was a striking physical and facial resemblance. — *The River's End*, James Oliver Curwood, 1919.

5905 At the time of his death the name of Albert Sanger was barely known to the musical public of Great Britain. Among the very few who had heard of him there were even some who called him Sanjé, in the French manner, being disinclined to suppose that great men are occasionally born in Hammersmith. — *The Constant Nymph*, Margaret Kennedy, 1924.

5906 In any city you would have noticed that fierce old man, but in Dublin he called for no more than a passing glance, so many are there who seem exiled kings. — *O'Malley of Shanganagh*, Donn Byrne, 1925.

5907 Dave Green finished mopping off the bar and waddled sideways along it toward the big chair at its open end. Dave, to his utter disgust, was fat; he was very fat, and growing fatter. — *The Bar 20 Rides Again*, Clarence E. Mulford, 1926.

5908 Sam Vettori sat staring down into Halsted Street. He was a big man, fat as a hog, with a dark oily complexion, kinky black hair and a fat aquiline face. — *Little Caesar*, W. R. Burnett, 1929.

5909 James Forrester, the father of Anna-Marie, was a peculiar man. — *Let Me Alone*, Anna Kavan, 1930.

5910 A man tall, slender, enveloped in a mackintosh, stood on a little wooden pier, jutting out some fifty yards from a ledge of rock, glistening black, which formed a sea wall for the little harbor. — *The Arm of Gold*, Ralph Connor, 1932.

5911 Not a bad face, flat and white, broad and weighty: in the daylight, the worse for much wear — stained, a grim surface, rained upon and stared at by the sun at its haughtiest, yet pallid still: with a cropped blondish moustache of dirty lemon, of toothbrush texture: the left eye somewhat closed up — this was a sullen eye. The right eye was more open and looked bright; it sat undisturbed under its rolled-up wide-awake rounded lid. — *Snooty Baronet*, Wyndham Lewis, 1932.

5912 To look at, Mr. Holmes was a short, stout, middle-aged man with reddish hair just beginning to get thin on the crown. He had closely folded, rather prim clergyman's lips and a long astute pointed nose which was slightly crooked. His glance was cold, friendly and shrewd. — *Lions and Shadows*, Christopher Isherwood, 1938.

5913 Chancellor Schultz leaned confortably back in his cushioned chair and crossed his fat little legs. He laid his fat little hands side by side and palms downwards on the big mahogany table in front of him. — *Köningsmark*, A. E. W. Mason, 1938.

5914 Up to the time George Webber's father died, there were some unforgiving souls in the town of Libya Hill who spoke of him as a man who not only had deserted his wife and child, but had consummated his iniquity by going off to live with another woman. — *The Web and the Rock*, Thomas Wolfe, 1939.

5915 Ray Cooper was the kind of man nobody ever looks at twice. — *Tomorrow's Another Day*, W. R. Burnett, 1945.

5916 Fred Derry, twenty-one, and killer of a hundred men,/ Walked on the width of Welburn Field. The cargo ship/ Had set him down in noontime haze of early spring./ He smelled the onion farms:/ He heard the trucks in Highway 52,/ He saw the signboards, and the ugliness/ That was a beauty he had dreamed. — *Glory for Me*, MacKinlay Kantor, 1945.

5917 The father was a hard man; he was like flint. — *The American*, Howard Fast, 1946.

5918 If you searched every old folks' home in the country, you couldn't find anyone who looked more like Santa Claus. — *Miracle on 34th Street*, Valentine Davies, 1947.

5919 "It's not that there is anything wrong with Turnbull," said Colonel Casey. "It's just — how can I describe it — well, he's not quite one of *us*, if you know what I mean...." — *The Consul at Sunset*, Gerald Hanley, 1951.

5920 When he finished packing, he walked out on to the third-floor porch of the barracks brushing the dust from his hands, a very neat and deceptively slim young man in the summer khakis that were still early morning fresh. — *From Here to Eternity*, James Jones, 1951.

5921 He was of medium height, somewhat chubby, and good looking, with curly red hair and an innocent, gay face, more remarkable for a humorous air about the eyes and large mouth than for any strength of chin or nobility of nose. — *The Caine Mutiny*, Herman Wouk, 1951.

5922 I am an invisible man. — *Invisible Man*, Ralph Ellison, 1952.

5923 Fox was rather like a fox. — *The Second Curtain*, Roy Fuller, 1953.

5924 Until Hamilton Sacks was lifted off the C. & O. Pullman by his mother and one of the porters, nobody in Canona had any idea he was a chair-bound cripple. — *The Love Eaters*, Mary Lee Settle, 1954.

5925 My Uncle Daniel's just like your uncle, if you've got one — only he has one weakness. — "The Ponder Heart," Eudora Welty, 1954.

5926 The coach captain was young, smart in the grey uniform of the company, and a facile talker. — *The Battling Prophet*, Arthur W. Upfield, 1956.

5927 The man in the belted raincoat stands hesitant at the top of the gangway. — *The Great Days*, John Dos Passos, 1958.

5928 Daylight was approaching over London, the great city of bachelors. Half-pint bottles of milk began to be stood on the doorsteps of houses containing single apartments from Hampstead Heath to Greenwich Park, and from Wanstead Flats to Putney Heath; but especially in Hampstead, especially in Kensington. — *The Bachelors*, Muriel Spark, 1960.

5929 Stripped down to nothing but a suit of long underwear and gray cotton socks the tough bulk of the big man on the little hotel bed seemed bigger than if it had been dressed. — *The Watchman*, Davis Grubb, 1961.

5930 When Lady Ann Sercomb married George Smiley towards the end of the war she described him to her astonished Mayfair friends as breathtakingly ordinary. — *Call for the Dead*, John Le Carré, 1961.

5931 GRANDFATHER SAID:/ This is the kind of a man Boon Hogganbeck was. — *The Reivers*, William Faulkner, 1962.

5932 "What's he like?" — *One Fat Englishman*, Kingsley Amis, 1963.

5933 "Good God," I said. "He does look black." — *Under the Skin*, Nina Bawden, 1964.

5934 Given a little money, education and social standing, plus of course the necessary leisure, any man with any style at all can make a mess of his love life. — *Reuben, Reuben*, Peter De Vries, 1964.

5935 Mason Jarrett, a large man with bright black hair, brown eyes which had a tendency to become bloodshot, and a clement disposition, approached the spiked iron gates at the entrance of the Döbling villa. — *The Lost City*, John Gunther, 1964.

5936 Coles was a watcher. His friend Bernard Presage was always telling him so, accusing him of joylessness, saying: "The good times come and they pass you by." — *Gentlemen in Their Season*, Gabriel Fielding, 1966.

5937 He was restless, curiously remote. — *Vanished*, Fletcher Knebel, 1968.

5938 A skilled clerical worker, European of British birth, twenty, single, not a convicted criminal, not suffering from physical or mental illness, politically placid, beardless, Godfrey Rainbird was well qualified to be accepted as an assisted immigrant to New Zealand. — *Yellow Flowers in the Antipodean Room*, Janet Frame, 1969.

5939 Clive Lendrick was five feet eleven, at

forty-six was only slightly overweight, and hadn't had to consult a doctor for over twenty years. — *The View from Tower Hill*, John Braine, 1971.

5940 Wendover stood shivering in the grey dawn, gazing mournfully over the parapet of the flyover—a small, bony man wearing a thin inadequate raincoat. — *The Committed Men*, M. John Harrison, 1971.

5941 John Edward Scott Armitage: fifty-five years old, five feet eleven inches tall, weight thirteen stone three ounces. — *Mr. Armitage Isn't Back Yet*, Mervyn Jones, 1971.

5942 A man in late middle age, a crack in the center of his brow, as if it has been stamped on, split in two, stares at me. — *Blue Hill Avenue*, Mark Mirsky, 1972.

5943 Whose was that imposing bust, worthy of Spy (button-holed and adipose-lined from Georgian state-banquets), making its lordly way down the Paddington platform? Whose majestic profiled upholstered *embonpoint* was it that blocked for a spell the Pullman corridor—whose hand could it be that had flung the rich travelling rug upon the first-class corner seat with that gesture—whose mass that then returned arrogantly to obstruct the corridor? Whose but Shodbutt's? — *The Roaring Queen*, Wyndham Lewis, 1973.

5944 From the highway to the east, where his car is parked to the left of a mailbox propped in a milk can, we can see him standing in the knee-high grass at the edge of a field of grain stubble. —*A Life*, Wright Morris, 1973.

5945 Since before sunup Old Jack has been standing at the edge of the hotel porch, gazing out into the empty street of the town of Port William, and now the sun has risen and covered him from head to foot with light. — *The Memory of Old Jack*, Wendell Berry, 1974.

5946 A man's past is a landscape of erection. —*Mortal Flesh*, Gilbert Phelps, 1974.

5947 My brother Jeremy is a thirty-eight-year-old bachelor who never did leave home. Long ago we gave up expecting very much of him, but still he is the last man in our family and you would think that in time of tragedy he might pull himself together and take over a few of the responsibilities. Well, he didn't. — *Celestial Navigation*, Anne Tyler, 1974.

5948 "Of course he was a charming man. A delightful person. Who has ever questioned it? But not a great magician."— *World of Wonders*, Robertson Davies, 1975.

5949 There are 2,556,596 faggots in the New York City area. —*Faggots*, Larry Kramer, 1978.

5950 "Listen to me. I will tell you the truth about a man's life. I will tell you the truth about his love for women. That he never hates them. Already you think I'm on the wrong track. Stay with me. Really—I'm a master of magic...." —*Fools Die*, Mario Puzo, 1978.

5951 It had been five years, or nearly six, since I'd seen Gerry Berger. He looked a little older, his eyes particularly. —*Jo Stern*, David R. Slavitt, 1978.

5952 A young man leans with one shoulder against the wall, and his slender body remains motionless against the huge open slab of night sky and night water behind him. —*Nocturnes for the King of Naples*, Edmund White, 1978.

5953 I used to think of him as an ordinary, good-natured, harmless, unremarkable man. —*A Dry White Season*, André Brink, 1979.

5954 Unlike most people, Konrad Vost had a personality that was clearly defined: above all he was precise in what he did and correct in what he said. — *The Passion Artist*, John Hawkes, 1979.

5955 He was thick-chested and light-haired, with sloping shoulders joined so smoothly to his neck he seemed not to have any neck at all, and a head whose size made his shoulders look narrower than they were, a wide round head which he cocked slightly forward when he walked, swinging his arms as if he meant to smash through whatever stood in his way. —*Horn of Africa*, Philip Caputo, 1980.

5956 A smallish man, Mr. Martin B. Chain, but not at all dainty. — *The Chains*, Gerald Green, 1980.

5957 The man on the bicycle ahead of hers slowed down to a stop and looked back, waiting. —*Circle of Love*, Syrell Rogovin Leahy, 1980.

5958 *May 3* I am a dandy who can no longer be troubled to dress. — *The Death of Men*, Allan Massie, 1981.

5959 Mr. Bodasingh stood in front of the big picture window in the big sitting-room of his big house in Reservoir Hills. —*Ah, But Your Land Is Beautiful*, Alan Paton, 1981.

5960 Moran's first impression of Nolen Tyner: He looked like a high risk, the kind of guy who falls asleep smoking in bed. —*Cat Chaser*, Elmore Leonard, 1982.

5961 "He was a gaunt, handsome man," the woman said. —*So Long, Daddy*, H. B. Gilmour, 1983.

5962 Everyone always knew that Leo Kellermann had something, was something, special. —*In Search of Love and Beauty*, Ruth Prawer Jhabvala, 1983.

5963 Jasper Swift, owner although not sole possessor of Durraghglass, was back in the kitchen where he belonged. —*Time After Time*, Molly Keane, 1983.

5964 The man stood on a rooftop and faced the rising sun. — *The Illusionist*, Anita Mason, 1983.

5965 The Principal of the Edmond Fleg Pri-

mary School was originally (in a manner of speaking) a Frenchman, Paris-born—but whenever he quoted his long-dead father and mother, he quoted them in Yiddish. — *The Cannibal Galaxy*, Cynthia Ozick, 1983.

5966 Little Luther Wade just sits out there in the porch swing, swaying back and forth with his new suspenders on, a little bitty old shriveled-up man so short that his feet in the cowboy boots can't even touch the floor. — *Oral History*, Lee Smith, 1983.

5967 Donald Applebee was easily recognized on any downtown street in Fort Worth, Texas. — *Principia Martindale*, Edward Swift, 1983.

5968 He was an old man, clinging fiercely to the tattered garment that had once been his dignity. — *Amos*, Stanley Gordon West, 1983.

5969 Who is he, where is he? Handsome, brave, blond, kind? Was he, is he? — *Safe Houses*, Lynne Alexander, 1985.

5970 My husband was a vain man with a thick orange moustache who loved to look at his beautiful wife, slim like a model and striking on the streets. — *Dreamhouse*, Kate Grenville, 1986.

5971 *Gizeh. The sphinx. A pyramid. The image yields to:/ Red Square, Moscow. Lenin's Mausoleum. A queue. Soldiers. Then:/ Shaven head, gaunt face, staring eyes, in close-up. The man speaks, through broken teeth, as if remembering how he once lectured . . .* — *Sphinx*, D. M. Thomas, 1986.

5972 "If you want my opinion," said Gwen Cellan-Davies, "the old boy's a terrifically distinguished citizen of Wales." — *The Old Devils*, Kingsley Amis, 1987.

5973 "Men," wrote Eva Eichler, "cannot relate to other people without hiding behind a mask of Purpose. . . ." — *Coming First*, Paul Bryers, 1987.

5974 Asa enters a room with his arms crossed. He slides in sideways and takes a pose against the wall. — *Asa, as I Knew Him*, Susanna Kaysen, 1987.

5975 With his long black cloak swirling about him and his fedora set at a rakish angle, the Marquis de St. Lyre stops before the Place St. Sulpice and surveys its windswept acreage. — *Cuisine Novella*, Antoine Laurent, 1987.

5976 The premature lines cut deep into Sam's cheeks, sharp and clean. — *Variations in the Night*, Emily Listfield, 1987.

5977 There's this theory I've got about Neil Armstrong. — *Little Red Rooster*, Greg Matthews, 1987.

5978 Reuben was a small man. — *Reuben*, John Edgar Wideman, 1987.

5979 He stood in the cold outside and to the hinge side of the door so other people could move past him. — *Of Such Small Differences*, Joanne Greenberg, 1988.

5980 "A true knight," said Isobel de Vaumartin, "is as innocent as an angel, as fierce as a lion. . . ." — *The Lords of Vaumartin*, Cecelia Holland, 1988.

5981 From where I stood he seemed enormous, a great Viking warrior, ruddy and intense, his pale blue eyes scanning a wilderness for Celts or maybe wild boars. — *Defending Civilization*, Philip F. O'Connor, 1988.

5982 At sundown, on the bleak warehouse fringes of the old soot-and-sweat factory towns where things are Made in America, sinewy tattooed men in cowboy boots and grease-stained windbreakers and baseball caps crunch across gravel lots, past heaps of discarded tires and engine blocks and the sad rusted carcasses of cannibalized trucks; the men clean-shaven, rested and ready to roll now as they approach the line of hulking behemoths silhouetted against the magenta sky. — *King of the Road*, Paul Hemphill, 1989.

5983 Tadeusz Kaminski was the life of every party. — *In Three Minds*, Lara Marlowe, 1989.

5984 The bachelor owner of Mauley Hall, Charles Alistair Wentworth Woodley, Fifth Baron Pelham, Seventh Viscount Mauley, would not be considered an American film director's idea of a British peer. With his protruding eyes, thick lips, and bald head, over which were halfheartedly brushed a few strands of yellowish-white hair, Lord Mauley was rather a dismal subject. — *Cherton*, David Telfair, 1989.

5985 I am, I discover, a very untidy man. — *Restoration*, Rose Tremain, 1989.

5986 The man who had once been enormous sat up against the headboard of a bed that still was. — *Tables*, John Lucas, 1990.

5987 He was a high man and a hard one. — *Lazarus*, Morris West, 1990.

5988 Ben Gavilan was not a reckless man, or one ordinarily given to extravagant gestures; in all of his inclinations he was conservative and cautious. — *Glad Rags*, MacDonald Harris, 1991.

5989 The story of Mark Petrie begins with a man he never met, a small-time grifter, a man who took an enormous leap but didn't land. — *A Slow Suicide*, William Jovanovich, 1991.

5990 Two seats down from me in the pub in Folkestone where I wait for the ferry, a man has a vicious gash on his face that's sewn together with thick black thread whose ends knot in blackened stubble. — *Going for Broke*, Paul Lyons, 1991.

5991 If Franz was English, Nell thought, I would be charmed and reassured, even though he looks more like a best friend than a husband. — *The Sins of the Father*, Allan Massie, 1991.

5992 Her Carl. He'd been in life a man of proclivities and she was meaning to speak of one

of them, had even already discharged her customary wistful breath and was just before embarking upon her "Ah" and upon her "Carl," which served evermore as preamble to a proclivity, when she noticed how her grandbaby Delmon over by the doorscreen had assumed an unsavory posture which she elected to speak of instead and so apprised him of the perils of slouching like induced Delmon her grandbaby to elevate straightaway his lowslung parts as he laid once more his lips upon his Lorna Doone. — *Gospel Hour*, T. R. Pearson, 1991.

5993 The slave who came to fetch me on that unseasonably warm spring morning was a young man, hardly more than twenty. — *Roman Blood*, Steven Saylor, 1991.

5994 At thirty-eight Thomas Randall was looked upon as a rising young man, one who would go far. — *Gabrielle*, Albert J. Guerard, 1992.

5995 At seven in the evening on a Saturday in May near the center of Philadelphia, Pete Flowers, thirty-nine for several weeks yet, single for several years now, stretches out as much as he is able in his old, oil-needy swivel chair. — *Closing Distance*, Jim Oliver, 1992.

5996 I think of Alex always as I first saw him, darting across the corridor that separated our private inner quarters from the reception rooms, his long red silk scarf dancing about his gracefully modeled limbs. — *Antiquity Street*, Sonia Rami, 1992.

5997 For all his fine qualities — his honesty and devotion, his cleverness, his uncanny agility — Eco was not well suited for answering the door. Eco was mute. — *Arms of Nemesis*, Steven Saylor, 1992.

5998 Faredoon Junglewalla, Freddy for short, was a strikingly handsome, dulcet-voiced adventurer with so few scruples that he not only succeeded in carving a comfortable niche in the world for himself but he also earned the respect and gratitude of his entire community. — *The Crow Eaters*, Bapsi Sidhwa, 1992.

Messages

5999 I had just finished breakfast and was filling my pipe when I got Bullivant's telegram. — *Greenmantle*, John Buchan, 1916.

6000 The message came to me, at the second check of the hunt, that a countryman and a clansman needed me. — *Messer Marco Polo*, Donn Byrne, 1921.

6001 At the striking of noon on a certain fifth of March, there occurred within a causal radius

of Brandon railway-station and yet beyond the deepest pools of emptiness between the uttermost stellar systems one of those infinitesimal ripples in the creative silence of the First Cause which always occur when an exceptional stir of heightened consciousness agitates any living organism in this astronomical universe. Something passed at that moment, a wave, a motion, a vibration, too tenuous to be called magnetic, too subliminal to be called spiritual, between the soul of a particular human being who was emerging from a third-class carriage of the twelve-nineteen train from London and the divine-diabolic soul of the First Cause of all life. — *A Glastonbury Romance*, John Cowper Powys, 1932.

6002 Houlun sent the old serving-woman, Yasai, to the yurt of her half-brother, the crippled Kurelen. — *The Earth Is the Lord's*, Taylor Caldwell, 1940.

6003 At the fag end of the two restless days and nights in Sarasota, I sent Harvey Farthing a telegram urging him to try to arrange to leave New York for the week end and spend a few days in Florida. — *Love and Money*, Erskine Caldwell, 1954.

6004 In Fort Repose, a river town in Central Florida, it was said that sending a message by Western Union was the same as broadcasting it over the combined networks. — *Alas, Babylon*, Pat Frank, 1959.

6005 They came through on the hot line at about half past two in the afternoon. — *The Ipcress File*, Len Deighton, 1962.

6006 I opened the telegram and said, "He's dead—" and as I looked up into Graham Mill's gaze I saw that he knew who, before I could say. — *The Late Bourgeois World*, Nadine Gordimer, 1966.

6007 "I had a cable from Emmie this morning," said Lawrence in the taxi on our way to London airport. — *Lilacs Out of the Dead Land*, Rachel Billington, 1971.

6008 "A note from Robert to welcome us home. He really has, Robert, a high sense of occasion, don't you agree?" — *Private Worlds*, Sarah Gainham, 1971.

6009 The moment after Lew Nolan wheeled his horse away and disappeared over the edge of the escarpment with Raglan's message tucked in his gauntlet, I knew I was for it. — *Flashman at the Charge*, George MacDonald Fraser, 1973.

6010 He was sitting on the verandah drinking lime juice when the message came through, and he was alone. — *The Leopard and the Cliff*, Wallace Breem, 1978.

6011 That's what popped in my brain ("What the *hell* is going on?!") the minute I got the message from Jesus. — *King Silky!*, Leo Rosten, 1980.

6012 "I have an important message for you, Dr. Beckwith." — *Man, Woman and Child*, Erich Segal, 1980.

6013 By Christmas, 1980, the earth had had enough and was beginning to send out hints. — *The Terrible Twos*, Ishmael Reed, 1982.

6014 Three nights before he went to Ghaleh Bagh, my Khan Papa Doctor sent a message for me to come see him later in the library. — *The Book of Absent People*, Taghi Modarressi, 1986.

6015 In the beginning, sometimes I left messages in the street. — *Wittgenstein's Mistress*, David Markson, 1988.

6016 In her mind, the taxi's tires are beating out a message. — *Pretty Girls*, Garret Weyr, 1988.

6017 I entered the strange world of Justine Shade via a message on the bulletin board in a laundromat filled with bitterness and the hot breath of dryers. — *Two Girls, Fat and Thin*, Mary Gaitskill, 1991.

Mistakes

6018 Andy Rooney was a fellow who had the most singularly ingenious knack of doing everything the wrong way; disappointment waited on all affairs in which he bore a part, and destruction was at his fingers' ends; so the nickname the neighbours stuck upon him was Handy Andy, and the jeering jingle pleased them. — *Handy Andy*, Samuel Lover, 1842.

6019 When the widow of Martino Consalvi married young Corbario, people shook their heads and said that she was making a great mistake. — *Whosoever Shall Offend*, F. Marion Crawford, 1904.

6020 "Perez," observed Captain Eri cheerfully, "I'm tryin' to average up with the mistakes of Providence." — *Cap'n Eri*, Joseph C. Lincoln, 1904.

6021 There is good evidence for believing that an American gentleman staying at Beverley Court once so far forgot himself as to clean his own shoes: what is probably not true is that the head boot-boy subsequently borrowed the chef's carvers and committed *hara-kiri*. — *The Flowering Thorn*, Margery Sharp, 1933.

6022 "They made a silly mistake, though," the professor of history said, and his smile, as Dixon watched, gradually sank beneath the surface of his features at the memory. — *Lucky Jim*, Kingsley Amis, 1954.

6023 Hercule Poirot frowned./ "Miss Lemon," he said./ "Yes, M. Poirot?"/ "There are three mistakes in this letter." — *Hickory Dickory Death*, Agatha Christie, 1955.

6024 Yank Lucas fell asleep late one night and left the gas burning on the kitchen range. — *The Instrument*, John O'Hara, 1967.

6025 It began as a mistake. — *Post Office*, Charles Bukowski, 1971.

6026 It was a troublesome summer for George McIver. First there was Nadia, his mistress of three years' standing, and their little five-month-old mistake — which he had failed to prevent her naming Thorn. — *Our Father*, Thomas Hinde, 1975.

6027 "You had your chance," says Enid, "and you blew it." — *Incandescence*, Craig Nova, 1979.

6028 There could be no doubt about it; the new nameplate was crooked. — *The Skull Beneath the Skin*, P. D. James, 1982.

6029 Going back was a mistake but it was one of those mistakes I had to make. — *Wanderer Springs*, Robert Flynn, 1987.

6030 No way, he told himself. He wasn't going to end up making Daniel's mistake, he thought as he made the turn onto Park Presidio, the long line of streetlights stepping off into the black distance ahead, the avenue bordered by the darker blackness of the trees, the traffic lights at the intersections holding and changing in that rhythm that held you to a steady thirty miles an hour. — *Where All the Ladders Start*, Ron Loewinsohn, 1987.

6031 Don't write Jack Straw — They called me that but they were wrong. — *The Confession of Jack Straw*, Simone Zelitch, 1991.

6032 A woman I was introduced to at a dinner party told me how she buried the wrong dead cat. — *Begin to Exit Here*, John Welter, 1992.

Motives

6033 Hard is the Task you have imposed on me; not only to recount with Impartiality and Faithfulness the History of my own Life, but likewise to reveal those secret Motives of my Actions, which were once so little known to myself, that I was almost as much the Object of my own Deceit, as were either of my powerful Lovers. — *The Lives of Cleopatra and Octavia*, Sarah Fielding, 1757.

6034 Young Dr. Rider lived in the new quarter of Carlingford: had he aimed at a reputation in society, he could not possibly have done a more foolish thing; but such was not his leading motive. — *The Doctor's Family*, Margaret Oliphant as Mrs. Oliphant, 1863.

6035 I address these lines — written in India — to my relatives in England. My object is

to explain the motive which has induced me to refuse the right hand of friendship to my cousin, John Herncastle. — *The Moonstone*, Wilkie Collins, 1868.

6036 Roger Lawrence had come to town for the express purpose of doing a certain act, but as the hour for action approached he felt his ardor rapidly ebbing away. — *Watch and Ward*, Henry James, 1871.

6037 For reasons which many persons thought ridiculous, Mrs. Lightfoot Lee decided to pass the winter in Washington. — *Democracy*, Henry Adams, 1880.

6038 "But the thing I can't understand, Dinky-Dunk, is how you ever *could*."/ "Could what?" my husband asked in an aerated tone of voice./ I had to gulp before I got it out./ "Could kiss a woman like that," I managed to explain./ Duncan Argyll McKail looked at me with a much cooler eye than I had expected. If he saw my shudder, he paid no attention to it./ "On much the same principle," he quietly announced, "that the Chinese eat birds' nests." — *The Prairie Child*, Arthur Stringer, 1922.

6039 "And what," asked (loudly because of the music) this patrician parrot of a Tiresias from its wheelchair, skirt or trousers hidden by tartan rugs, "might be your purpose in going to St. Petersburg?" — *Honey for the Bears*, Anthony Burgess, 1963.

6040 Many people in the Miracle Valley had theories about why Joe Mondragón did it. — *The Milagro Beanfield War*, John Nichols, 1974.

6041 To have a reason to get up in the morning, it is necessary to possess a guiding principle. — *Ordinary People*, Judith Guest, 1976.

6042 Maybe it was on accounta it was a full moon. I dont know. — *Sitting Pretty*, Al Young, 1976.

6043 When anyone asked Frensic why he took snuff he replied that it was because by rights he should have lived in the eighteenth century. — *The Great Pursuit*, Tom Sharpe, 1977.

6044 Tomorrow I shall have to tell them. I shall have to stand in that court and tell them why I did it. — *I Hardly Knew You*, Edna O'Brien, 1978.

6045 You will want to know why I am writing this. — *Hers the Kingdom*, Shirley Streshinsky, 1981.

6046 The earth had moved under them: that's why they were there. — *The Weather Tomorrow*, John Sacret Young, 1981.

6047 We went there, each of us for our own reasons, though reasons never turn out to be quite as private or original as we hope they will be. — *Goodbye Europe*, Richard de Combray, 1983.

6048 What brought David Rayborne to Rome nobody ever learned. — *Year of the Gun*, Michael Mewshaw, 1984.

6049 I didn't have an abortion for two reasons — both people. — *The Book of Phoebe*, Mary-Ann Tirone Smith, 1985.

6050 "What's he mean, 'I suppose you want an explanation'? He doesn't explain anything." — *Cigarettes*, Harry Mathews, 1987.

6051 Robert Staples kept trying to explain why he'd thrown Heidi in the alligator pit. — *A Choice of Nightmares*, Lynn Kostoff, 1991.

Mountains

6052 The mountains forming the range of Alps which border on the northeastern confines of Italy were, in the autumn of the year 408, already furrowed in numerous directions by the tracks of the invading forces of those Northern nations generally comprised under the appellation of Goths. — *Antonina*, Wilkie Collins, 1850.

6053 The belt of mountains which traverses the state of Virginia diagonally, from north-east to south-west, it will be seen by an inspection of the map, is composed of a series of parallel ranges, presenting a conformation somewhat similar to that which may be observed in miniature on the sea-beach, amongst the minute lines of sand hillocks left by the retreating tide. — *Horse-Shoe Robinson*, John P. Kennedy, 1852.

6054 The Jebel es Zubleh is a mountain fifty miles and more in length, and so narrow that its tracery on the map gives it a likeness to a caterpillar crawling from the south to the north. — *Ben-Hur*, Lew Wallace, 1880.

6055 If you looked at the mountain from the west, the line of the summit was wandering and uncertain, like that of most mountain-tops; but, seen from the east, the mass of granite showing above the dense forests of the lower slopes had the form of a sleeping lion. — *The Landlord at Lion's Head*, William Dean Howells, 1897.

6056 Beyond the great prairies and in the shadow of the Rockies lie the Foothills. For nine hundred miles the prairies spread themselves out in vast level reaches, and then begin to climb over softly rounded mounds that ever grow higher and sharper till, here and there, they break into jagged points and at last rest upon the great bases of the mighty mountains. These rounded hills that join the prairies to the mountains form the Foothill Country. — *The Sky Pilot*, Ralph Connor, 1899.

6057 *Dear Polly,*/ I am on top of a mountain by a lake, with other mountains towering irregularly in all directions; a primeval wilderness, in fact, for every mountain is covered with

a dense forest, and we reached our lake by an ascent up an almost perpendicular "corduroy" road—made of logs.—*The Aristocrats*, Gertrude Atherton, 1901.

6058 From every street and corner in Tucson we see the mountains.—*The Mine with the Iron Door*, Harold Bell Wright, 1923.

6059 A deep red glow flushed the fronts of marble palaces piled up on the slope of an arid mountain whose barren ridge traced high on the darkening sky a ghostly and glimmering outline.—*Suspense*, Joseph Conrad, 1925.

6060 There, far below, is the knobbly backbone of England, the Pennine Range.—*The Good Companions*, J. B. Priestley, 1929.

6061 Union Square is surrounded on all sides by mountains. To the north are the Alps, to the east the Caucasus, to the west lie the Urals, while southward stand the Ozarks, with the plains of Texas just beyond. And south, further still, lies the heavy sea, which heaves and rolls like oil.—*Union Square*, Albert Halper, 1933.

6062 The gray dump of the Echo Mine clung desperately to a red hill in a tangle of wild red hills, lost between tangled ranges; the enormous black crest of the Continental Divide overhung and dwarfed them; and all the world was hills. So, in midocean, all the world is sea.—*The Proud Sheriff*, Eugene Manlove Rhodes, 1935.

6063 Southward, two mighty ranges of the Appalachians shouldered their way into the blue distance like tremendous caravans marching across eternity.—*Action at Aquila*, Hervey Allen, 1938.

6064 Far to the west, the mountain was shining like glass in colour and mystery upon the horizon.—*Far from Cibola*, Paul Horgan, 1938.

6065 *The mountains stood up from the plains. Straight up, from shoulders of dark pines and spruces until their naked tawny sides were lost in mist.*—*Bitter Creek*, James Boyd, 1939.

6066 Among the ranges of the Himalayan mountains there stands a certain lofty peak well known to mountain climbers but long unexplored.—*Other Gods*, Pearl S. Buck, 1940.

6067 Sometimes the Alps lying below in the moonlight had the appearance of crisp folds of crumpled cloth.—*Fair Stood the Wind for France*, H. E. Bates, 1944.

6068 Two mountain chains traverse the republic roughly from north to south, forming between them a number of valleys and plateaus.—*Under the Volcano*, Malcolm Lowry, 1947.

6069 Facing me was the last mountain I would have to cross before reaching the valley at the head of which was the township which I sought, Moonlea.—*Leaves in the Wind*, Gwyn Thomas, 1949.

6070 Ages ago, some unseen hand had carved the face of China in a contour of endless mountains.—*The Mountain Road*, Theodore H. White, 1958.

6071 Night. With about twelve other people he was climbing a mountain, scaling cliffs by means of ropes and spikes.—*The Hero Continues*, Donald Windham, 1960.

6072 If the mountain had not gleamed so white.—*Wilderness*, Robert Penn Warren, 1961.

6073 Mount Aergius is seen from a great distance, beautifully shaped, perfectly proportioned, its peak and sides covered with snow.—*America America*, Elia Kazan, 1962.

6074 When the helicopter had gone and its sound was no more than a minute concussion of the air on his eardrums Forbush stood in the centre of the ring of stones to look up at the smoking mountain, Erebus, and ask for a safe conduct through the summer.—*Forbush and the Penguins*, Graham Billing, 1965.

6075 Those afternoons, those lazy afternoons, when I used to sit, or lie down, on Desolation Peak, sometimes on the alpine grass, hundreds of miles of snowcovered rock all around, looming Mount Hozomeen on my north, vast snowy Jack to the south, the encharmed picture of the lake below to the west and the snowy hump of Mt. Baker beyond, and to the east the rilled and ridged monstrosities humping to the Cascade Ridge, and after that first time suddenly realizing "It's me that's changed and done all this and come and gone and complained and hurt and joyed and yelled, not the Void" and so that every time I thought of the void I'd be looking at Mt. Hozomeen (because chair and bed and meadowgrass faced north) until I realized "Hozomeen is the Void—at least Hozomeen means the void to my eyes"—Stark naked rock, pinnacles and thousand feet high protruding from hunchmuscles another thousand feet high protruding from immense timbered shoulders, and the green pointy-fir snake of my own (Starvation) ridge wriggling to it, to its awful vaulty blue smokebody rock, and the "clouds of hope" lazing in Canada beyond with their tittlefaces and parallel lumps and sneers and grins and lamby blanks and puffs of snout and mews of crack saying "Hoi! hoil earth!"—the very top tittermost peak abominables of Hozomeen made of black rock and only when storms blow I dont see them and all they do is return tooth for tooth to storm an imperturbable surl for cloudburst mist—Hozomeen that does not crack like cabin rigging in the winds, that when seen from upsidedown (when I'd do my headstand in the yard) is just a hanging bubble in the illimitable ocean of space—*Desolation Angels*, Jack Kerouac, 1965.

6076 We are at Base Camp No. 2 at the foot of the Superstition Mountains.—*The Mallot*

Diaries, Robert Nathan, 1965.

6077 All day the cold Virginia sky had hung low over Spencer's Mountain. — *The Homecoming*, Earl Hamner, 1970.

6078 There was just himself and one other, and the high mountain in front of them. — *Stringer*, Ward Just, 1974.

6079 It was the last afternoon of the year, and in the sunlight the distant peaks of the mountains shone dazzling white. — *The Coal War*, Upton Sinclair, 1976.

6080 Mount Latmos, now called Annadağ, had drawn nearer to the town. — *Blood Tie*, Mary Lee Settle, 1977.

6081 I live on a mountain. — *A Couple of Comedians*, Don Carpenter, 1979.

6082 It was not a pretty mountain. — *The Trick of the Ga Bolga*, Patrick McGinley, 1985.

6083 To get here you have to ford two creeks and go halfway up a mountain. — *Simple Gifts*, Joanne Greenberg, 1986.

6084 Along the Tennessee-North Carolina border they range and fall away shoulder to shoulder like great woolly bison, their bowed and humped backs heavy with Frazer fir, red spruce, and from a distance only barely visible, lost in the cool high winds and wide northeastern sky like a faded photograph. — *McCampbell's War*, Robert Herring, 1986.

6085 From time immemorial they have stood there proud and regally cloaked in pine and piñon, dark blue against the turquoise sky until sunset when they take on the blood-color of their name: the Sangre de Cristo. — *Flight from Fiesta*, Frank Waters, 1986.

6086 The first time Charlie Stuart took me up to the top of his mountain, he told me it was sacred and it was haunted. — *Dance Down the Mountain*, Richard Hammer, 1988.

6087 Could there be water in a haunch of the crouching mountains that ringed this plain like massive beasts, slate gray, purple, and ash, the more distant a blue only a hint more solid than the sky? — *Home Mountain*, Jeanne Williams, 1990.

6088 We didn't see the seven mountains ahead of us. We didn't see how they are always ahead, always calling us, always reminding us that there are more things to be done, dreams to be realised, joys to be re-discovered, promises made before birth to be fulfilled, beauty to be incarnated, and love embodied. — *Songs of Enchantment*, Ben Okri, 1993.

Moving

6089 I WAS BORN, *as my Friends told me*, at the City of POICTIERS, in the Province, or County of POICTOU, in *France*, from whence I was brought to *England* by my Parents, who fled for their Religion about the Year 1683, when the Protestants were Banish'd from *France* by the Cruelty of their Prosecutors. — *Roxana*, Daniel Defoe, 1724.

6090 The family of Armine entered England with William the Norman. — *Henrietta Temple*, Benjamin Disraeli, 1837.

6091 In the year 1691, Lois Barclay stood on a little wooden pier, steadying herself on the stable land, in much the same manner as, eight or nine weeks ago, she had tried to steady herself on the deck of the rocking ship which had carried her across from Old to New England. — *Lois the Witch*, Elizabeth Gaskell, 1861.

6092 The schoolmaster was leaving the village, and everybody seemed sorry. — *Jude the Obscure*, Thomas Hardy, 1896.

6093 Of all the people that ever went west that expedition was the most remarkable. — *Eben Holden*, Irving Bacheller, 1900.

6094 "My dear," said the Idiot one morning, as he and his good wife and the two little ones, Mollie and Tommy, sat down at the breakfast-table, "now that we are finally settled in our new house I move we celebrate. Let's give a dinner to my old friends of Mrs. Smithers's; they were nice old people, and I should like to get them together again. I saw Dr. Pedagog in the city yesterday, and he inquired most affectionately, not to say anxiously, about the children." — *The Idiot at Home*, John Kendrick Bangs, 1900.

6095 Early in the summer, five years after my marriage with Alice Leigh, my friend Clayborne moved into the country. — *Dr. North and His Friends*, S. Weir Mitchell, 1900.

6096 Faithfully to relate how Eliphalet Hopper came to St. Louis is to betray no secret. — *The Crisis*, Winston Churchill, 1901.

6097 Just why my father moved, at the close of the civil war, from Georgia to Texas, is to this good hour a mystery to me. — *The Log of a Cowboy*, Andy Adams, 1903.

6098 "But you can't do it, you know," friends said, to whom I applied for assistance in the matter of sinking myself down into the East End of London. — *The People of the Abyss*, Jack London, 1903.

6099 Early in the gray and red dawn of a March morning in 1883, two wagons moved slowly out of Boomtown, the two-year-old "giant

of the plains." — *The Moccasin Ranch*, Hamlin Garland, 1909.

6100 The first Penhallow crossed the Alleghanies long before the War for Independence and on the frontier of civilisation took up land where the axe was needed for the forest and the rifle for the Indian. — *Westways*, S. Weir Mitchell, 1913.

6101 In the early summer of 1831 Samson Traylor and his wife, Sarah, and two children left their old home near the village of Vergennes, Vermont, and began their travels toward the setting sun with four chairs, a bread board and rolling-pin, a feather bed and blankets, a small looking-glass, a skillet, an axe, a pack basket with a pad of sole leather on the same, a water pail, a box of dishes, a tub of salt pork, a rifle, a tea-pot, a sack of meal, sundry small provisions and a violin, in a double wagon drawn by oxen. — *A Man for the Ages*, Irving Bacheller, 1919.

6102 Miriam paused with her heavy bag dragging at her arm. It was a disaster. But it was the last of Mornington Road. — *The Tunnel*, Dorothy M. Richardson, 1919.

6103 "Look at 'em come, Jesse! More and more! Must be forty or fifty families." — *The Covered Wagon*, Emerson Hough, 1922.

6104 Miss Charlotte Smith, a kind-hearted lady of thirty or so, set forth in the year 1855 to conduct some fifty orphans, of various nationalities and all of them under ten years of age, from East London to San Francisco, where an orphanage had been provided for them by a wealthy philanthropist, who was so right-minded as to desire to use in this manner some of the riches he had obtained in the Californian gold rush of six years before. — *Orphan Island*, Rose Macaulay, 1924.

6105 The moving was over and done. — *The Professor's House*, Willa Cather, 1925.

6106 When her father died, Laura Willowes went to live in London with her elder brother and his family. — *Lolly Willowes*, Sylvia Townsend Warner, 1926.

6107 She moved from town to town, selling hair switches, giving osteopathic treatments, going on again when she felt the place had been played out. — *Bottom Dogs*, Edward Dahlberg, 1929.

6108 After she had parted from Mr. Mackenzie, Julia Martin went to live in a cheap hotel on the Quai des Grands Augustins. — *After Leaving Mr. Mackenzie*, Jean Rhys, 1930.

6109 The Jews were going into exile. Eastward across Europe the great columns moved slowly and with difficulty toward the deserts of Asia, where these unhappy people, driven from all the countries of the world, and for the last time in retreat, had been offered a haven by the Mongols. — *Road of Ages*, Robert Nathan, 1935.

6110 When he was seven years old, Belisarius was told by his widowed mother that it was now time for him to leave her for a while, and her retainers of the household and estate at Thracian Tchermen, and go to school at Adrianople, a city some miles away, where he would be under the guardianship of her brother, the Distinguished Modestus. — *Count Belisarius*, Robert Graves, 1938.

6111 The sisters left Darjeeling in the last week of October. They had come to settle in the General's Palace at Mopu, which was now to be known as the Convent of Saint Faith. — *Black Narcissus*, Rumer Godden, 1939.

6112 The boy had gathered his treasures together. On one side he put what he meant to take with him; and on the other, the things he must leave behind. — *They Went on Together*, Robert Nathan, 1941.

6113 Janie Driscoll Cauder, in the later years of her life, would often say, with that simper and arching of her head that her daughter, Laurie, could not endure without pressing her nails into the palms of her hands: "I landed here, a young widow, with twenty trunks and bags, three lads and a little lass, with none to care and only the help of God to sustain me. Ah, if it hadn't been for the good Lord, what would have become of me, a young widow, landing alone in a strange country, with nae hoose nor kinfolk to comfort me?" — *The Wide House*, Taylor Caldwell, 1945.

6114 In the second year of the war Miss Elsie Herkimer of Colvin, California, persuaded her mother to leave Omaha and come live with her. — *The Man Who Was There*, Wright Morris, 1945.

6115 In the last days of autumn, we had moved into a house overlooking the junction of a main road and a canal. — *To the Victors the Spoils*, Colin MacInnes, 1950.

6116 The first thing Miss Judith Hearne unpacked in her new lodgings was the silver-framed photograph of her aunt. — *The Lonely Passion of Judith Hearne*, Brian Moore, 1955.

6117 I spent the first nine years of my life in Germany, bundled to and fro between two houses. — *A Legacy*, Sybille Bedford, 1956.

6118 The deportation order arrived one clear, bright morning early in April. — *I Like It Here*, Kingsley Amis, 1958.

6119 I came to live in Paris when I was eighteen because my sister had married a Frenchman and our parents were dead. — *When We Had Other Names*, Gillian Tindall, 1960.

6120 My father was not an immigrant in the usual sense of the term, not having emigrated from Holland, so to speak, on purpose. — *The Blood of the Lamb*, Peter De Vries, 1961.

6121 "I don't want to go to the New World!"

Dorothy Bradford crouched dispiritedly on her pallet in the first hold of the *Mayflower*, directly below the main deck, and plucking at her thin coverlet of dirty gray wool, leaned against the bulkhead. — *The Land Is Bright*, Noel B. Gerson, 1961.

6122 Mamma formed a bad opinion of Zululand the moment she saw the railhead at Somkele where Pappie was waiting for us: he had come on ahead with my eldest brother Alwyn to make some preparations for our living quarters. — *A Lover for Estelle*, Daphne Rooke, 1961.

6123 A few weeks after my tenth birthday I was sent to stay with some very horsy relations in Leicestershire. — *The Skin Chairs*, Barbara Comyns, 1962.

6124 One day in early summer it seemed, miraculously, that Stern would not have to sell his house and move away. — *Stern*, Bruce Jay Friedman, 1962.

6125 One autumn in the late nineteen-twenties for no particular reason at all, as it would seem, we began to live in France. — *A Favourite of the Gods*, Sybille Bedford, 1963.

6126 The voice from the sound truck said:/ "Each family, no matter how big it is, will be asked to put up one thousand dollars. You will get your transportation free, five acres of fertile land in Africa, a mule and a plow and all the seed you need, free. Cows, pigs and chickens cost extra, but at the minimum. No profit on this deal." — *Cotton Comes to Harlem*, Chester Himes, 1965.

6127 Frank Wynn never spoke much of his early life but could have told you in detail of the vivid afternoon it was decided they would move to Mill's Landing. — *Old Powder Man*, Joan Williams, 1966.

6128 The Admiral's moved upstairs. — *Going to Jerusalem*, Jerome Charyn, 1967.

6129 It was in the January of the year when we come to that place. — *The Least One*, Borden Deal, 1967.

6130 Three months ago, his grandmother died, and then they had moved to this house. — *I'm the King of the Castle*, Susan Hill, 1970.

6131 When Eleanor and her son Philip moved out they took almost everything with them, leaving Graham only the kingsize bed in which his father had died, a black leather sofa suitable for his consulting room (already lined with black leather sofas), his record player and a few odd cups and plastic plates stained with old picnics. — *The Home*, Penelope Mortimer, 1971.

6132 Who was Benno Waxman-Weissman? Had that brilliant, tortured little man who juggled whole dictionaries in his head not left Vienna abruptly in 1934 and found his way to Sonoma County, there would be nothing to say about Anatole or any of the Waxman-Weissmans. — *The Tar Baby*, Jerome Charyn, 1973.

6133 *After I died they moved from Massachusetts and they bought a house and acres of land in New Hampshire where they rose early and worked all day at projects with their hands.* — *Manual Labor*, Frederick Busch, 1974.

6134 After Crazy Eights moved out I lost my wind. — *Are We There Yet?*, Diane Vreuls, 1975.

6135 That Mistress Anne Hutchinson should have desired to transport her large family across a wilderness of ocean waves to settle in Massachusetts in what was called the "Bay Colony" occasioned little enough surprise in Alford. — *The Winthrop Covenant*, Louis Auchincloss, 1976.

6136 I hadn't much wanted to go to California — the land of Milk and Molasses — because I was just barely getting used to Clay County, Missouri — the Land of Muck and Chitlings — but if I'd known how far that Unpromised Land was and what was laying and running and crouching inbetween, I wouldn't of let Ma and Pa start me and the hogs walking in that direction at all but would of dug in my heels like a hauled mule or maybe run off. — *Whole Hog*, David Wagoner, 1976.

6137 In 1929, when I was nineteen years old, I arrived in Paris on a bright September day almost straight from the dusty pavements and dirt roads of my birthplace — St. Helen, which is a pastoral country town in Victoria, Australia. — *One Last Glimpse*, James Aldridge, 1977.

6138 Movers carried in her things on the seventh of May. — *The Walnut Door*, John Hersey, 1977.

6139 "That's it then," I said when the removal van pulled up. — *Now Newman Was Old*, Chaim Bermant, 1978.

6140 Three years after Frederick Wursup moved across Lexington Avenue and turned his office into his home as well, he discovered that he could see the old apartment — where his ex-wife, Susannah, still lived with their two sons — from the roof. — *Natural Shocks*, Richard G. Stern, 1978.

6141 In the early nineteen sixties I joined one of the most gratuitous and contemptible migrations in history: the middle class deserting the cities for the suburbs. — *The Game Player*, Rafael Yglesias, 1978.

6142 In those days cheap apartments were almost impossible to find in Manhattan, so I had to move to Brooklyn. — *Sophie's Choice*, William Styron, 1979.

6143 Anne N. Fletcher sat cross-legged on the floor, unwrapping glassware from cocoons of newspaper. — *The Other Anne Fletcher*, Susanne Jaffe, 1980.

6144 "This is Laura. She has come from

Abroad," said Miss Trott. — *Secret Places*, Janice Elliott, 1981.

6145 Max Fried stepped over the threshold. He set down his navy-blue beret on a gleaming Formica surface and surveyed his new residence. His last, was it not? Its kitchen glistened whitely; every fixture ready and waiting, deceptively virginal. Neatness he liked, but this was antiseptic, reeking already of the purity of the beyond. — *Balancing Acts*, Lynne Sharon Schwartz, 1981.

6146 This is how Yuli, son of Alehaw, came to a place called Oldorando, where his descendants flourished in the better days that were to come. — *Helliconia Spring*, Brian W. Aldiss, 1982.

6147 The Chens had been living in the UK for four years, which was long enough to have lost their place in the society from which they had emigrated but not long enough to feel comfortable in the new. — *Sour Sweet*, Timothy Mo, 1982.

6148 When F.X. got out of jail, he went to live with his half brother, Mr. Pickens, who lived right next door to Dr. Henry's, the all-night store that sold beer and ice cubes and gas. — *Modern Baptists*, James Wilcox, 1983.

6149 For reasons that I'm ashamed of now, I was living in Montreal in the spring of 1967 when Hugh Gillespie decided that he must find cheaper digs and arrived at Madame Girard's in the east end. — *Journeyman*, Tom Gallacher, 1984.

6150 The houseplants were spread on the sidewalk like a flower show, along with a mounting collection of unessentials that wouldn't fit in the truck — picture frames, floor lamps, kitchen table, wok, and his armchair. — *Love, Infidelity and Drinking to Forget*, Elizabeth Gundy, 1984.

6151 Beverley moved to Munich during the late summer. — "On Ice," Rachel Ingalls, 1985.

6152 "We shall have to move," Gideon said. — *Heaven and Earth*, Frederic Raphael, 1985.

6153 I had never been out of the city before I moved there, nor, come to mention it, since. — *No News Is Good*, Julie Edelson, 1986.

6154 When it became obvious that Dorothea's nephew Hugo was going to be moving in with her, she rummaged through the boxes of junk on her closet shelf and under her bed and finally found what she was looking for: the newspaper clipping about Iris's death. — *Real Life*, Kitty Burns Florey, 1986.

6155 In 1833 a small band of illogical men and women left New Brunswick, Canada, in a pirogue to battle the upstream waters of the Mattagash River for one hundred and fifty miles until they came to shore at what is now Mattagash, Maine, where the river creates a natural boundary between the United States and Canada. — *The Funeral Makers*, Cathie Pelletier, 1986.

6156 They settled in with less difficulty than Dan had anticipated. — *September Faces*, Seymour Epstein, 1987.

6157 "Right, on your way, brother. Out. I'm not having you in my house. Go on, hop it." — *Difficulties with Girls*, Kingsley Amis, 1988.

6158 The camp circle was on the move again. — *Waterlily*, Ella Cara Deloria, 1988.

6159 In 1939, thirteen years before I was born, my father's aunt, Mayadebi, went to England with her husband and her son, Tridib. — *The Shadow Lines*, Amitav Ghosh, 1988.

6160 Grace was packing. From out here in the backyard, I could look in through the windows and see her walking from room to room — appearing in the bedroom, disappearing, reappearing in the kitchen. — *My Father in Dreams*, C. E. Poverman, 1988.

6161 It is almost a year since Hodge went to prison and Daley went into St. Bride's. A year, too, since Ann died and I moved here. — *One Is One*, Lucy Irvine, 1989.

6162 No Soviet emigrates for any real reason. — *Trespassers Welcome Here*, Karen Karbo, 1989.

6163 Most of my contemporaries, those of seventy summers or more, would find me absurdly oversimplifying the situation in dating the origin of my niece Natica's troubles to the day her family decamped from the large florid red-brick Georgian mansion in Smithport, Long Island, which my brother-in-law Harry had so rashly built in a palmy year before 1929, to the modest superintendent's cottage huddled at its gate. — *The Lady of Situations*, Louis Auchincloss, 1990.

6164 When I was three I moved in with my Cousin Ruth Davis. — *Cousin It*, Lynn Caraganis, 1991.

6165 It was 1948 and everyone watching the truck pull the house trailer across the front walk, breaking flagstones and crushing plantings, was unhappy. — *Thief of Dreams*, John Yount, 1991.

6166 It took William Badger some time to understand that he was going to be left behind, deliberately abandoned, what seemed like a thousand miles from home. — *Longleg*, Glenda Adams, 1992.

6167 The way I hear it, when nomads move on from one of their weathered, disassembled villages, the animals often return to forage where there was once food, and to curl up on the hot barren land right where they once slept in the sun outside the dwelling of a human being. — *1959*, Thulani Davis, 1992.

6168 In November 1980, I, Murray "Muz" Orloff, abandoned my father, Charles Justice Orloff, in the Sahara Desert because he'd turned from a simple pest into a dangerous man. — *A Good, Protected Life*, Joseph Kaufman, 1992.

6169 After my father died, my mother hired a U-Haul trailer and parked it outside our house, which was in Kingston. — *Sun Dial Street*, Marti Leimbach, 1992.

6170 When I was eight, I was sent to live on the melon farm of an uncle — a sixth-grade dropout who attributed his IQ of 70 to sniffing gasoline and glue from the age of five, and whose manner of compulsively clawing at the skin behind his neck was a characteristic sign of amphetamine toxicity. — *Et Tu, Babe*, Mark Leyner, 1992.

6171 In April, Tracy moved in with Margaret. — *Family Night*, Maria Flook, 1993.

6172 When Libby Holliday finally left her family, she went to Los Angeles, to Hollywood. — *Places to Stay the Night*, Ann Hood, 1993.

Murder

6173 "But if he thought the woman was being murdered — —"/ "My dear Charles," said the young man with the monocle, "it doesn't do for people, especially doctors, to go about 'thinking' things. They may get into frightful trouble...." — *Unnatural Death*, Dorothy L. Sayers, 1927.

6174 There are, fortunately, very few people who can say that they have actually attended a murder. — *Death of a Ghost*, Margery Allingham, 1934.

6175 Murder didn't mean much to Raven. It was just a new job. — *This Gun for Hire*, Graham Greene, 1936.

6176 Hale knew, before he had been in Brighton three hours, that they meant to murder him. — *Brighton Rock*, Graham Greene, 1938.

6177 MURDER MYSTERY
by Special Correspondent
Mary Turner, wife of Richard Turner, a farmer at Ngesi, was found murdered on the front veranda of their homestead yesterday morning. The houseboy, who has been arrested, has confessed to the crime. No motive has been discovered. It is thought he was in search of valuables.
— *The Grass Is Singing*, Doris Lessing, 1950.

6178 It was shortly after entering the bar of the Nelson Arms on a Saturday in August, 1955, that Stuart Hammer first perceived how he might commit the perfect murder. — *A Penknife in My Heart*, Cecil Day-Lewis *as* Nicholas Blake, 1958.

6179 Thirty were in the band that hit the Loman farm before daybreak. They slew all in the household and looted it of food, guns, and ammunition and vanished into the bush again, and nobody shouted *There they go!* because it was a sweet time for them to strike, when the morning ebb had drained the vigilance from the beleaguered settlers. — *The Leopard*, Victor Stafford Reid, 1958.

6180 Bat Dongin was a professional gunthrower the Moore boys brought in to kill Maurice Hanline. — *A Talent for Loving*, Richard Condon, 1961.

6181 Berenice was sixteen years old when she witnessed her father's murder, and she watched the sequence of events that led to it with curious indifference. — *Agrippa's Daughter*, Howard Fast, 1964.

6182 Not everybody knows how I killed old Phillip Mathers, smashing his jaw in with my spade; but first it is better to speak of my friendship with John Divney because it was he who first knocked old Mathers down by giving him a great blow in the neck with a special bicycle-pump which he manufactured himself out of a hollow iron bar. — *The Third Policeman*, Flann O'Brien, 1967.

6183 I am here to perform a delicate piece of surgery. I am here to commit a murder. Take your choice. — *Nobody Knew They Were There*, Evan Hunter, 1971.

6184 I was squeezing a baseball when a shirttail character named Lancaster banged into the sheriff's office to report what he said was a murder. — *Wild Pitch*, A. B. Guthrie, Jr., 1973.

6185 I thought of Mother and Dad when I heard about Conrad. Conrad was murdered and beheaded, with no money taken from his pants, in 1969. Mother and Dad were slain and thrown in a ditch in 1944. — *Nightwatchmen*, Barry Hannah, 1973.

6186 "Who told Thad she was dead?" Rena asked./ "Thad killed her," Eva said. "He already knew." — *The Surface of Earth*, Reynolds Price, 1975.

6187 When I arrived home from work I found my wife had killed our two sons and taken her own life. The cat was only sleeping. — *Mom Kills Kids and Self*, Alan Saperstein, 1979.

6188 Has it been said that killing a man can start up new life? — *Not Working*, George Szanto, 1982.

6189 I swear to God I didn't kill that black woman. — *The Lives of Riley Chance*, Robert Bausch, 1984.

6190 My gentle Michael would rather not kill. — *Hob's Daughter*, T. Alan Broughton, 1984.

6191 *A man was shot dead in East Belfast earlier this evening.* — *Sisters by Rite*, Joan Lingard, 1984.

6192 Joan stood in the kitchen, contemplating a murder. — *Family Myths and Legends*, Patricia Ferguson, 1985.

6193 "We need you to kill a man." — *The Cat Who Walks Through Walls*, Robert A. Heinlein, 1985.

6194 When he killed his father they sent him to a psychiatrist called Meiss in Wimpole Street. — *A Green Flesh*, Winston Graham, 1986.

6195 It wasn't the kind of homicide they're used to seeing around here. — *Blood Solstice*, James Howard Kunstler, 1986.

6196 It never occurred to me that Joseph Alexander Karnovsky had been murdered by the great painter Yevgeny Mikhailovich Malenov. — *Malenov's Revenge*, Arthur A. Cohen, 1987.

6197 When I was little I would think of ways to kill my daddy. — *Ellen Foster*, Kaye Gibbons, 1987.

6198 When Astra Rainbow was five, two years younger than what is considered to be the age of reason, she pushed an eight-year-old boy off a cliff to his death. — *A Sign of the Eighties*, Gail Parent, 1987.

6199 Murder stopping at a small town may have the effect of a nail dropped into the mechanism of town life. — *The True Detective*, Theodore Weesner, 1987.

6200 The process that led to the decision to kill Chuck Burgoyne, who for the first week of his visit had proved the perfect houseguest, began on the Sunday when, though he had promised to prepare breakfast for all (he was a superb cook), he had not yet appeared in the kitchen by half past noon. — *The Houseguest*, Thomas Berger, 1988.

6201 Humming a song on a Saturday morning was not the kind of aggressive act that could easily be explained in a court of law as an understandable reason for murder, but it struck Ervin Neal that he might finally have to kill his wife, or get rid of her in some way. — *The Night of the Weeping Women*, Lawrence Naumoff, 1988.

6202 Miliana Bartha always believed her life would end in murder. — *Pursued by the Crooked Man*, Susan Trott, 1988.

6203 The Whistler's fourth victim was his youngest, Valerie Mitchell, aged fifteen years, eight months and four days, and she died because she missed the 9.40 bus from Easthaven to Cobb's Marsh. — *Devices and Desires*, P. D. James, 1989.

6204 Only later, I began to dream of murder. — *She Drove Without Stopping*, Jaimy Gordon, 1990.

6205 The assassination happens in their sleep. — *Tokens of Grace*, Sheila O'Connor, 1990.

6206 Before the murder I was grateful to live where I live, to work where I work — for all the happy facts. — *The Murderer Next Door*, Rafael Yglesias, 1990.

6207 I was never so amazed in my life as when the Sniffer drew his concealed weapon from its case and struck me to the ground, stone dead. — *Murther & Walking Spirits*, Robertson Davies, 1991.

6208 The murder is seldom discussed without someone recalling that warm autumn night years before when Martha Horgan was only seventeen and Bob Hobart, a classmate, offered her a ride home from the library. — *A Dangerous Woman*, Mary McGarry Morris, 1991.

6209 My first contact with those cockamamy murders came on the night of September 29, a Sunday, when I was having dinner at Mom's house. — *Mom Doth Murder Sleep*, James Yaffe, 1991.

6210 I had been sent to Mexico to cover a murder, one of a remarkable kind. — *Mexico*, James A. Michener, 1992.

6211 On an April night almost midpoint in the Eighteenth Century, in the county of Orange and the colony of Virginia, Jacob Pollroot tasted his death a moment before swallowing it. He had, then, a moment to spit it out and save himself. — *Arc d'X*, Steve Erickson, 1993.

Music

6212 "Oh, how enchanting are those notes! surely some being from a happier world — some spirit, or some heavenly chorister, visits these woods, to charm us with celestial minstrelsy! Listen, Winifred, but do not speak: Oh, what a swell was there, and what a cadence!" — *The Nocturnal Minstrel*, Eleanor Sleath, 1810.

6213 At Naples, in the latter half of the last century, a worthy artist, named Gaetano Pisani, lived and flourished. He was a musician of great genius, but not of popular reputation; there was in all his compositions something capricious and fantastic, which did not please the taste of the Dilettanti of Naples. — *Zanoni*, Edward Bulwer Lytton, 1842.

6214 "Listen, John — I hear music —" — *The Honor of the Big Snows*, James Oliver Curwood, 1911.

6215 "Take off that mute, do!" cried Louisa, snatching her fingers from the piano keys, and turning abruptly to the violinist. — *The Trespasser*, D. H. Lawrence, 1912.

6216 In the huge shed of the wharf, piled with crates and baggage, broken by gang-planks leading up to ships on either side, a band plays a tinselly Hawaiian tune; people are dancing in and out among the piles of trunks and boxes. — *One Man's Initiation*, John Dos Passos, 1920.

6217 "*One* and two and three and four and — *one* and two and three and four and . . ."/ Mrs. Sturgis had a way of tapping the ivory keys of the piano with her pencil when she was counting the beat during a music lesson. — *Bread*, Charles G. Norris, 1923.

6218 1774, and Diony, in the spring, hearing Sam, her brother, scratching at a tune on the fiddle, hearing him break a song over the taut wires and fling out with his voice to supply all that the tune lacked, placed herself momentarily in life, calling mentally her name, Diony Hall. — *The Great Meadow*, Elizabeth Madox Roberts, 1930.

6219 Ordinarily, when the Heron River Band — an eight-man institution which included a twelve-year-old snare-drummer and a bass-drummer of sixty — played, of a summer night, *Hail, Hail, The Gang's All Here*, and proceeded with proper solemnity into *My Country, 'Tis of Thee*, old Shad Finney looked at old Nils Ulevik and said, "Wa-al, she's finished, mate. We better get along." And Nils, sucking on his pipe, would nod his head in grave accord. — *There's Always Another Year*, Martha Ostenso, 1933.

6220 That Sunday, from six o'clock in the evening, it was a Viennese orchestra that played. The season was late for an outdoor concert; already leaves were drifting on to the grass stage — here and there one turned over, crepitating as though in the act of dying, and during the music some more fell. — *The Heat of the Day*, Elizabeth Bowen, 1949.

6221 The guitar distilled its music. — *The Four-Chambered Heart*, Anaïs Nin, 1950.

6222 Doctor Ocie Pentecost heard a band playing "The Saint Louis Blues." — *Mountains of Gilead*, Jesse Hill Ford, 1961.

6223 To hell with jazz, Red said that morning as he ran through the dark quiet streets, pushing his zippered bass ahead of him on its rubber wheel. — *Big as Life*, E. L. Doctorow, 1966.

6224 I had been invited to compose a piece for the Festival of Contemporary Music, Cologne, 1966. My intention was a set of variations in serial form. I chose the serial formula, partly as a technical exercise, partly because I had a fancy to end each variation with the sound of a farmyard animal. — *October the First Is Too Late*, Fred Hoyle, 1966.

6225 At the beginning of August a band in scarlet uniforms began to play in the municipal gardens. To Boris, watching them through binoculars from the top of a tree, they appeared like bloodstained weevils that were shortly to bring about the collapse of summer. — *A Girl in the Head*, J. G. Farrell, 1967.

6226 The music-room in the Governor's House at Port Mahon, a tall, handsome, pillared octagon, was filled with the triumphant first movement of Locatelli's C major Quartet. — *Master and Commander*, Patrick O'Brian, 1969.

6227 I was reading a book on music by Ralph Vaughan Williams the other day, while listening to a gramophone record of his remarkable Fifth Symphony, when I came across the following remark: "I have struggled all my life to conquer amateurish technique, and now that perhaps I have mastered it, it seems too late to make any use of it." I found myself moved almost to tears by the poignancy of those words of a great musician. — *The Philosopher's Stone*, Colin Wilson, 1969.

6228 In 1950 I'm eight years old and gravely beholding, from my vantage slot under the bleachers, the Dream of Pines Colored High School band. — *Geronimo Rex*, Barry Hannah, 1972.

6229 I had a few spare moments before confessions that Saturday evening, so I headed for the church loft to play the organ a little. — *The Fancy Dancer*, Patricia Nell Warren, 1976.

6230 Inspirational music played as they moved from the terminal buildings into the ferry. — *Enemies of the System*, Brian W. Aldiss, 1978.

6231 Ron Starr's mother interrupted her own forceful murmurings from the mouth of his father's cave-like study to shout, "One-and-two-and-three-and-a-four-uneven!" while clapping her hands to emphasize the beat. — *Ron*, Carl Tiktin, 1979.

6232 LENINGRAD, October 9, 1973 — *An audience of 2,000 Soviet citizens, including high-ranking Communist party officials, sat in stunned disbelief tonight as renowned violinist Leonid Rabinovitz ended a concert at the Philharmonic Society here with an encore by an Israeli composer — an unpardonable gesture, by Soviet standards*. — *Simple Truths*, Sheila Levin, 1982.

6233 The fifth Brandenburg. Somewhere, some place, every moment, an orchestra is playing the fifth Brandenburg concerto. — *Perfect Happiness*, Penelope Lively, 1983.

6234 I certainly want to thank you for coming around to the club here to listen to my music. — *Jelly Roll Morton's Last Night at The Jungle Inn*, Samuel Charters, 1984.

6235 "I'm sorry to stop you so soon, but the opening is the most important part of the piece." — *An Evening of Brahms*, Richard Sennett, 1984.

6236 Good evening, my name is L. Goldkorn and my specialty is woodwind instruments, with emphasis on the flute. — "The Steinway Quintet," Leslie Epstein, 1985.

6237 Five nights a week Jerzy Wozzeck played the piano at a quiet little bistro on the

Boulevard Saint Michel. — *Body and Soul*, J. P. Smith, 1987.

6238 Claud Bannister sat beside his mother, enduring the concert. — *Second Fiddle*, Mary Wesley, 1988.

6239 The summer Laidlaw came back he spent all his time learning to drop-thumb on the banjo. — *Soldier's Joy*, Madison Smartt Bell, 1989.

6240 For Abby, it was not the applause that she loved. Or the way that audiences seemed to focus on her whenever she played her violin. In fact, those things embarrassed her. The thing she loved was the playing. The feel of the wood under her chin, the instant when the bow first touched the strings and the music began. — *Three-Legged Horse*, Ann Hood, 1989.

6241 I am looking for a one-storey town/ with trees/ river/ hills/ and a population of under two thousand/ one of whom must be called Gaden Lockyer./ Or/ Mother was a drummer in her own all-women's group,/ a throbber of a lady with midlife zest and an off-center/ smile./ Or/ I have decided to make up a list of all the convent girls/ who/ learnt to play "The Rustle of Spring" by Christian Sin-/ding between 1945 and 1960. — *Reaching Tin River*, Thea Astley, 1990.

6242 Dearest Father, listen to *this*!/ There's a society here in Vienna that gives benefit concerts to help musicians' widows. The orchestra, including the choir, is 180 strong. No virtuoso with any neighborly love declines to sing or play for free if the society invites him. — *Mozart and the Archbooby*, Charles Neider, 1991.

6243 The music was as much a gift as sunshine, as rain, as any blessing ever prayed for. — *Your Blues Ain't Like Mine*, Bebe Moore Campbell, 1992.

Nations of the World

6244 The latter part of the fifteenth century prepared a train of future events that ended by raising France to that state of formidable power which has ever since been, from time to time, the principal object of jealousy to the other European nations. — *Quentin Durward*, Sir Walter Scott, 1823.

6245 Although few, if any, of the countries of Europe have increased so rapidly in wealth and cultivation as Scotland during the last half-century, Sultan Mahmoud's owls might nevertheless have found in Caledonia, at any term within that flourishing period, their dowery of ruined villages. — *St. Ronan's Well*, Sir Walter Scott, 1823.

6246 Whether we take the pictures of the inimitable Cervantes, or of that scarcely less meritorious author from whom Le Sage has borrowed his immortal tale, for our guides; whether we confide in the graver legends of history, or put our trust in the accounts of modern travellers, the time has scarcely ever existed when the inns of Spain were good, or the roads safe. — *Mercedes of Castile*, James Fenimore Cooper, 1840.

6247 Siam is called by its people "Muang Thai" (the kingdom of the free). The appellation which we employ is derived from a Malay word *sagûm* (the brown race), and is never used by the natives themselves; nor is the country ever so named in the ancient or modern annals of the kingdom. — *Siamese Harem Life*, Anna Leonowens, 1873.

6248 In the year 1884 the Republic of Aureataland was certainly not in a flourishing condition. — *A Man of Mark*, Anthony Hope, 1890.

6249 Despite its long stretch of winter, in which May might wed December in no incompatible union, 'twas a happy soil, this Acadia, a country of good air and great spaces; two-thirds of the size of Scotland, with a population that could be packed away in a corner of Glasgow; a land of green forests and rosy cheeks; a land of milk and molasses; a land of little hills and great harbors, of rich valleys and lovely lakes, of overflowing rivers and oversurging tides that, with all their menace, did but fertilize the meadows with red silt and alluvial mud; a land over which France and England might well bicker when first they met oversea; a land which, if it never reached the restless energy of the States, never retained the Old World atmosphere that long lingered over New England villages; save here and there in some rare Acadian settlement that dreamed out its life in peace and prayer among its willow-trees and in the shadows of its orchards. — *The Master*, Israel Zangwill, 1895.

6250 I have just returned from Italy — the land of love and song. — *The Marryers*, Irving Bacheller, 1914.

6251 It was the sixth day of Mr. Direck's first visit to England, and he was at his acutest perception of differences. He found England in every way gratifying and satisfactory, and more of a contrast with things American than he had ever dared to hope. — *Mr. Britling Sees It Through*, H. G. Wells, 1916.

6252 ENGLAND! — *Easy to Kill*, Agatha Christie, 1938.

6253 He knew everything there was to know about Belgium. — *The Unspeakable Skipton*, Pamela Hansford Johnson, 1959.

6254 "Take all this business about Kenya,"

said Major Palgrave. "Lots of chaps grabbing away who know nothing about the place! Now *I* spent fourteen years of my life there. Some of the best years of my life, too—"—*A Caribbean Mystery*, Agatha Christie, 1964.

6255 It was absurd, grotesque. Here he was, a Minister of State in a sovereign power like the Irish Republic, a power brought into being by the heroism of countless generations, and he was afraid to walk out of his own office door.—*In a Year of Grace*, Honor Tracy, 1975.

6256 My country of Kush, landlocked between the mongrelized, neo-capitalist puppet states of Zanj and Sahel, is small for Africa, though larger than any two nations of Europe.—*The Coup*, John Updike, 1978.

6257 "Northern Ireland is perfectly simple really," said Edward Lumley, the company commander. "There are no two ways about it."—*A Breed of Heroes*, Alan Judd, 1981.

6258 Theirs was a land of awesome grandeur, a land of mountains and moorlands and cherished myths.—*Here Be Dragons*, Sharon Kay Penman, 1985.

6259 The thing was:/ One million years ago, back in 1986 A.D., Guayaquil was the chief seaport of the little South American democracy of Ecuador, whose capital was Quito, high in the Andes Mountains.—*Galápagos*, Kurt Vonnegut, 1985.

6260 Much later, when he had become a Member of Congress, Benjamin Tallmadge would look back on that particular time as that in which his country's fortunes were at their most precarious point of balance, ready to be pushed fatefully one way or the other.—*Major André*, Anthony Bailey, 1987.

6261 "The Old Country!" Buffy said.—*The Sugar Mother*, Elizabeth Jolley, 1988.

6262 They tell me India is an underdeveloped country.—*The Great Indian Novel*, Shashi Tharoor, 1989.

6263 Russia in winter is the time of gambling and treason.—*Gordon Liddy Is My Muse*, John Calvin Batchelor, 1990.

6264 We are in Cuba, of course.—*The Greatest Performance*, Elías Miguel Muñoz, 1991.

6265 I looked out from the deck of the Dún Laoghaire ferry and saw Ireland.—*Green Shadows, White Whale*, Ray Bradbury, 1992.

Neighborhoods

6266 Of all situations for a constant residence, that which appears to me most delightful is a little village far in the country; a small neighbourhood, not of fine mansions finely peopled, but of cottages and cottage-like houses, "messuages or tenements," as a friend of mine calls such ignoble and nondescript dwellings, with inhabitants whose faces are as familiar to us as the flowers in our garden; a little world of our own, close-packed and insulated like ants in an ant-hill, or bees in a hive, or sheep in a fold, or nuns in a convent, or sailors in a ship; where we know every one, are known to every one, interested in every one, and authorized to hope that every one feels an interest in us.—*Our Village*, Mary Russell Mitford, 1824.

6267 In that part of the celebrated parish of St. George, which is bounded on one side by Piccadilly and on the other by Curzon Street, is a district of a peculiar character. 'Tis a cluster of small streets of little houses, frequently intersected by mews, which here are numerous, and sometimes gradually, rather than abruptly, terminating in a ramification of those mysterious regions.—*Tancred*, Benjamin Disraeli, 1847.

6268 A row of brick-built houses with slate roofs, at the edge of a large mining village in Staffordshire. The houses are dingy and colorless, and without relief of any kind. So are those in the next row, so in the street beyond, and throughout the whole village.—*Facing Death*, G. A. Henty, 1882.

6269 "The Bottoms" succeeded to "Hell Row." Hell Row was a block of thatched, bulging cottages that stood by the brook-side on Greenhill Lane.—*Sons and Lovers*, D. H. Lawrence, 1913.

6270 A short by-street paved from side to side. Narrow house-fronts, and the endmost houses, hiding the passage that curved around into the furthest street, high enough to keep out of sight the neighbouring cubes of model dwellings and to leave, as principal feature in the upper air, the tower of St. Pancras church.—*The Trap*, Dorothy M. Richardson, 1925.

6271 It was one of the mixed blocks over on Central Avenue, the blocks that are not yet all Negro.—*Farewell, My Lovely*, Raymond Chandler, 1940.

6272 Cannery Row in Monterey in California is a poem, a stink, a grating noise, a quality of light, a tone, a habit, a nostalgia, a dream.—*Cannery Row*, John Steinbeck, 1945.

6273 In that place, where they tore the nightshade and blackberry patches from their roots to make room for the Medallion City Golf Course, there was once a neighborhood.—*Sula*, Toni Morrison, 1974.

6274 The small circle of Midtown New York surrounding the Port Authority Bus Terminal for a radius of half a dozen blocks goes by many

names. Tour guides call it the Crossroads of the World. The hookers who work it know it as the stroll. Pimps call it the fast track. Three-card monte players speak of Forty-Deuce. Maps show the neighborhood as Clinton. But to the stage-struck and starstruck it is still Broadway, to tourists it is Times Square, to the old people and derelicts who live off discards from the teeming Ninth Avenue food stalls of Paddy's Market it is more aptly Hell's Kitchen, and to the New York City Police, Vice Squad, and Mayor's Special Task Force on Crime it is simply the Midtown Enforcement Area. — *On the Stroll*, Alix Kates Shulman, 1981.

6275 The square belonged to the city of Savannah, but Eunnonia Grace Hampton had lived beside it for so long that she had come to think of it as her own property. — *Southern Women*, Lois Battle, 1984.

6276 Avenues A, B, C, and D form a dirty appendage to Manhattan's Lower East Side: these Alphabet Blocks have become Indian country, the land of murder and cocaine. — *War Cries Over Avenue C*, Jerome Charyn, 1985.

6277 Where I live, in Stonehurst Hills, there are rows of houses with alleys between them. — *Pride*, William Wharton, 1985.

6278 Whoever tells you he knows everything about his own neighborhood you can be sure is fooling himself. — *Florry of Washington Heights*, Steve Katz, 1988.

6279 The Israeli archaeologist Michal Dagan, once a professor at the Hebrew University on Mount Scopus, later director of the Staedtler Institute of Archaeology in West Jerusalem, lived with his wife in that leafy quarter of the city called Rehavya. — *On the Third Day*, Piers Paul Read, 1990.

6280 Rooney's Lot was a comma in a run-on sentence of brownstones, brick row houses, and small apartment buildings. — *This Is Next Year*, Philip Goldberg, 1991.

6281 This is a neighborhood of people who aren't quite making it. — "The Quick," Agnes Rossi, 1992.

Neighbors

6282 I have just returned from a visit to my landlord—the solitary neighbour that I shall be troubled with. — *Wuthering Heights*, Emily Brontë, 1847.

6283 Now, to tell my story—if not as it ought to be told, at least as I can tell it, — I must go back sixteen years, to the days when Whitbury boasted

of forty coaches per diem, instead of one railway, and set forth how in its southern suburb, there stood two pleasant houses side by side, with their gardens sloping down to the Whit, and parted from each other only by the high brick fruit-wall, through which there used to be a door of communication; for the two occupiers were fast friends. — *Two Years Ago*, Charles Kingsley, 1857.

6284 "Who can have taken the Ferguses' house, sister?" said a brisk little old lady, peeping through the window blinds. — *We and Our Neighbors*, Harriet Beecher Stowe, 1875.

6285 "If you please, mum," said the voice of a domestic from somewhere round the angle of the door, "number three is moving in." — *Beyond the City*, Arthur Conan Doyle, 1892.

6286 Mrs. Beever of Eastmead, and of "Beever and Bream," was a close, though not a cruel observer of what went on, as she always said, at the other house. — *The Other House*, Henry James, 1896.

6287 When Judith was eighteen, she saw that the house next door, empty for years, was getting ready again. — *Dusty Answer*, Rosamond Lehmann, 1927.

6288 We had lived together so long, the five families in Crescent Place, that it never occurred to any of us that in our own way we were rather unique. — *The Album*, Mary Roberts Rinehart, 1933.

6289 *In the first years after the war Mario Van de Weyer was almost my neighbour in Paris, for he lived just where the Left Bank ceases to be the Latin Quarter and I where it's not yet the Faubourg Saint Germain.* — *The Last Puritan*, George Santayana, 1936.

6290 Every morning when he got up Hat would sit on the banister of his back veranda and shout across, "What happening there, Bogart?" — *Miguel Street*, V. S. Naipaul, 1959.

6291 When she was home from her boarding-school I used to see her almost every day sometimes, because their house was right opposite the Town Hall Annexe. — *The Collector*, John Fowles, 1963.

6292 I am on the stoop these spring nights. The whoring, thieving gypsies, my next door neighbors, are out also. — *The Messenger*, Charles Wright, 1963.

6293 For the first fifteen years of our lives, Danny and I lived within five blocks of each other and neither of us knew of the other's existence. — *The Chosen*, Chaim Potok, 1967.

6294 Flaking distemper fell from the ceiling and lay like snow, a greyish slush, on the damp linoleum that had buckled and perished here and there, by the door that would not close, under the draining-board, around the dinted and seldom disinfected bucket that had no handle, before the stove with its coating of thick grease, as

Sharpe the taximan moved in the room above.
— *Balcony of Europe*, Aidan Higgins, 1972.

6295 She was seven years old. She was in love with Janie, who lived twelve houses away. — *Preparing for Sabbath*, Nessa Rapoport, 1981.

6296 Neighbours. That's what they were, Ellen Walsh and Alice Pickering, with a thin wall between their sitting-rooms and an even thinner one between their bedrooms on the first floor. — *Birds of Passage*, Bernice Rubens, 1981.

6297 Mr. Breaker lived alone in a stucco house next door to Gumma and Guppa, my mother's parents, on No Bridge Road. — "My Mother Takes a Tumble," Eric Kraft, 1982.

6298 I'll never forget the episode of *Ozzie & Harriet* where a beautiful single woman moves in next door. — *Uncoupling*, Ira Sadoff, 1982.

6299 When I got back to New York from Leningrad, I found that my newly rented apartment was gone — burned out by the fool on the floor below me, who had fallen asleep while puffing on his hookah. — *Old Devotions*, Ursula Perrin, 1983.

6300 For six months in the flat immediately above mine lived the recluse who believed himself to be the Man in the Iron Mask. — *The Man in the Iron Mask*, Peter Hoyle, 1984.

6301 "And oh yes," Jane Smart said in her hasty yet purposeful way; each *s* seemed the black tip of a just-extinguished match held in playful hurt, as children do, against the skin. "Sukie said a man has bought the Lenox mansion." — *The Witches of Eastwick*, John Updike, 1984.

6302 Gerard Maines lived across the hall from a woman named Benna, who four minutes into any conversation always managed to say the word *penis*. — *Anagrams*, Lorrie Moore, 1986.

6303 Simon looks out his window and sees something white moving in the window of the house next door. — *Illumination Night*, Alice Hoffman, 1987.

6304 I am still here on the twenty-fourth floor and when I sit in front of my mirror I can see, in the mirror, someone on the twenty-fourth floor across the street. — *Cabin Fever*, Elizabeth Jolley, 1990.

6305 Our neighborhood was never the same after Misty Rhodes and her family moved in across the street. — *Ferris Beach*, Jill McCorkle, 1990.

6306 On Waverly Street, everybody knew everybody else. — *Saint Maybe*, Anne Tyler, 1991.

News

6307 Can any thing, my good Sir, be more painful to a friendly mind than a necessity of communicating disagreeable intelligence? Indeed, it is sometimes difficult to determine, whether the relater or the receiver of evil tidings is most to be pitied. — *Evelina*, Fanny Burney, 1778.

6308 "Any news to-night?" asked Admiral Buzza, leading a trump./ "Hush, my love," interposed his wife timidly, with a glance at the Vicar. She liked to sit at her husband's left, and laid her small cards before him as so many tributes to his greatness. — *The Astonishing History of Troy Town*, Arthur Quiller-Couch, 1888.

6309 "Have you heard the news, Meg?" — *Megda*, Emma Dunham Kelley, 1891.

6310 "Fools and fanatics!"/ Colonel Worth crumpled the morning paper with a gesture of rage and walked to the window. — *Comrades*, Thomas Dixon, Jr., 1909.

6311 After two years we are turning once more to the morning's news with a sense of appetite and glad expectation. — *The Terror*, Arthur Machen, 1917.

6312 Some few years ago a brief account of me found its way into one or two country newspapers. — *Memoirs of a Midget*, Walter de la Mare, 1921.

6313 The news of Lee's surrender at Appomattox reached the little Massachusetts town of Mendon almost at the very hour of Sam Smith's birth. — *Pig Iron*, Charles G. Norris, 1925.

6314 They were interviewing Clint Maroon. — *Saratoga Trunk*, Edna Ferber, 1941.

6315 It seemed to Jerome Lindsey that disagreeable news invariably arrived when he and New York weather were in execrable moods. — *This Side of Innocence*, Taylor Caldwell, 1946.

6316 When Father Pavart climbed the uncarpeted stairs to the veteran's room overlooking the river he found the old man sitting in the window-seat, looking down on the crowd surrounding Peltier, the postillion. Peltier had just galloped across the bridge with the news. — *Seven Men of Gascony*, R. F. Delderfield, 1949.

6317 It was the big story — the biggest of his life. — *The Big Story*, Morris West, 1957.

6318 The weekly news magazine *World Reporter* goes to press at eleven o'clock on Friday night. — *A Kind of Anger*, Eric Ambler, 1964.

6319 As Adam Quince approached the newspaper building where he worked, a news item took place under the windows of Fleet Street. A

badger appeared from nowhere, and was run over by a double-decker bus. — *The Raker*, Andrew Sinclair, 1964.

6320 It wasn't even in the stop press. — *A Sentence of Life*, Julian Gloag, 1966.

6321 *A man fell to his death from a sixth-floor window of Peskett House, an office-block in Sellway Square today. He was a messenger employed by a soap manufacturing firm.* / Ruth startled from the newspaper by Leonard framed in the doorway. Against the white-washed wall. — *Three*, Ann Quin, 1966.

6322 Tattersall's most embarrassing moment was one for which any newspaper running such a feature would probably have paid the standard fee, but which he himself would gladly have given his life's savings to have been spared. — *The Cat's Pajamas*, Peter De Vries, 1968.

6323 As the car passed the first houses away from London Airport (the September night had closed down, lights shone from windows, in the back seat one heard the grinding of the wind-screen-wiper) Margaret said:/ "Is there anything waiting for us?"/ "I hope not."/ She meant bad news. — *Last Things*, C. P. Snow, 1970.

6324 The Kambani papers were full of reports about the Washona killings that week. — *The Wanderers*, Es'kia Mphahlele, 1971.

6325 If you were living in Chicago in the spring of 1948, and if you read one of the city's newspapers on the Monday following Easter, you may have seen the story. — *The Flight of Peter Fromm*, Martin Gardner, 1973.

6326 January 2, 1942 had some good news and some bad news. — *Dreaming of Babylon*, Richard Brautigan, 1977.

6327 When the news of Tu's death reached Blanford he was actually living in her house in Sussex, watching the first winter snow fall out of a dark sky, amidst darker woods, which had long since engulfed an ochre sunset. — *Livia*, Lawrence Durrell, 1978.

6328 By nightfall the headlines would be reporting devastation. — *The Transit of Venus*, Shirley Hazzard, 1980.

6329 Word spread quickly through the ghetto. — *The Prisoner's Wife*, Jack Holland, 1981.

6330 "Will he take it very badly?" Young Robinson looked with some trepidation in the direction of the elderly gentleman who had stationed himself near the door, flanked by two young ladies, to welcome the guests who were just beginning to arrive. — *Farewell to Europe*, Walter Laqueur, 1981.

6331 ". . . homeless by fires which . . . warning to countries in . . ."/ Tave switched stations and, finding none, twisted the dial back. — *Octavia's Hill*, Margaret Dickson, 1983.

6332 I was hurrying to the lunch shift when I heard that Jack Kennedy was dead. — *Cutting Through*, Keith Maillard, 1983.

6333 Faster than a man could ride, the news swept out of the West, blowing like the eddies that turn the autumn leaves. — *This Family of Women*, Richard Peck, 1983.

6334 News of the messenger's arrival spread like wildfire. — *Not Wanted on the Voyage*, Timothy Findley, 1984.

6335 Prentiss Granger was featured on the *CBS Evening News* tonight for the eighth time. — *Convictions*, Taffy Cannon, 1985.

6336 "Have you heard the news?" — *The Naylors*, J. I. M. Stewart, 1985.

6337 *Dear Shilda, / By now you've heard it, and I want you to call me collect as soon as possible.* — *Bobby Rex's Greatest Hit*, Marianne Gingher, 1986.

6338 I am your reporter, the best, the last, laying it out on the live wire. Current events, pole to pole. You've got ears. Hear me. This story of mine is loud enough to wake the dead, and cure warts. Say it over in your sleep. — *New Jerusalem*, Len Jenkin, 1986.

6339 When Lancelot came with the news of the accident, Claire was at home in her apartment in Rue François-Villon. — *Glowstone*, MacDonald Harris, 1987.

6340 It was Geoffrey who brought the news, and Nell didn't believe him. — *All You Need*, Elaine Feinstein, 1989.

6341 The news took days to circle the globe from Naples. — *Discovery*, Thomas Hoving, 1989.

6342 One of my duties as lieutenant governor of Oklahoma was to watch the news on national television. — *Crown Oklahoma*, Jim Lehrer, 1989.

6343 The bust made front page news in all the New York dailies. — *Smack Goodness*, Richard Stratton, 1990.

6344 As soon as the news came out of Aguascalientes in October, 1914, that Pancho Villa and Emiliano Zapata were ready to be friends, and had agreed to meet in the capital, I came running down out of California, back into Mexico for the first time in ten years, knowing this would be my last chance to stop the Revolution from coming unglued. — *The Prison Notebooks of Ricardo Flores Magón*, Douglas Day, 1991.

6345 To those who remembered him, it was typical that Nicholas should sail into Venice just as the latest news reached the Rialto, causing the ducat to fall below fifty groats and dip against the écu. — *Scales of Gold*, Dorothy Dunnett, 1992.

6346 When news of Gulliver Quick's death first reached the newspapers, there were curious rumors of five women attempting to take equal responsibility. — *Gulliver Quick*, Maureen Earl, 1992.

6347 Since Roosevelt died we haven't the heart for the news. — *When They Took Away the Man in the Moon*, Kate Lehrer, 1993.

Newspapers

6348 "On your college paper, I suppose?"/ "No, I never even wrote a letter to the editor." — *The Great God Success*, David Graham Phillips *as* John Graham, 1901.

6349 A few weeks ago, at a dinner, a discussion arose as to the unfinished dramas recorded in the daily press. The argument was, if I remember correctly, that they give us the beginning of many stories, and the endings of as many more. — *The Red Lamp*, Mary Roberts Rinehart, 1925.

6350 Mr. Dickson McCunn laid down the newspaper, took his spectacles from his nose, and polished them with a blue-and-white spotted handkerchief. — *Castle Gay*, John Buchan, 1930.

6351 I threw down the magazine section of the Sunday *Times* and yawned. — *The Rubber Band*, Rex Stout, 1936.

6352 In those days the weekly *Penarth Times* ran a curious column. — *Coming In with the Tide*, P. H. Newby, 1941.

6353 Between 7.30 and 8.30 every morning except Sundays, Johnnie Butt made the round of the village of Chipping Cleghorn on his bicycle, whistling vociferously through his teeth, and alighting at each house or cottage to shove through the letter-box such morning papers as had been ordered by the occupants of the house in question from Mr. Totman, stationer, of the High Street. — *A Murder Is Announced*, Agatha Christie, 1950.

6354 The open newspaper entered Rogerson's study like a kite and stopped before his desk. — *Jolly Rogerson*, Ralph McInerny, 1967.

6355 It was in Tuesday's paper. — *The Penny Wars*, Elliott Baker, 1968.

6356 Helena Cuthbertson picked up the crumpled *Times* by her sleeping husband and went to the flower room to iron it. — *The Camomile Lawn*, Mary Wesley, 1984.

6357 This is a book about newspapers and the stories they tell. I think that is quite a satisfactory opening sentence. — *Goebbels & Gladys*, Keith Colquhoun, 1985.

6358 *Dear Anne Francis,/ I am responding to the article printed in the* Examiner *about you and your husband.* — *Four Ways of Computing Midnight*, Francis Phelan, 1985.

6359 I never saw my father with a newspaper in his hands. — *Shepherd Avenue*, Charles Carillo, 1986.

6360 I usually don't read the *New York Times* so closely, but the *Times* was lying there, open, right where I couldn't miss it. — *Lament for a Silver-Eyed Woman*, Mary-Ann Tirone Smith, 1987.

Nights

6361 Walk with me, reader, into Whitecross Street. It is Saturday night, the market-night of the poor; also the one evening in the week which the weary toilers of our great city can devote to ease and recreation in the sweet assurance of a morrow unenslaved. Let us see how they spend this "Truce of God;" our opportunities will be of the best in the district we are entering. — *Workers in the Dawn*, George Gissing, 1880.

6362 Outside the bedroom the night was black and still. — *"I Say No,"* Wilkie Collins, 1884.

6363 It was nearly full moon on Long Island Sound — a night so faultless that almost all of the few passengers on the steamer were out upon deck. — *Circumstance*, S. Weir Mitchell, 1901.

6364 Beautiful, beautiful was that night! — *The Spirit of Bombatse*, H. Rider Haggard, 1906.

6365 It began on a villainously cold and sleety and tempest-twisted night in mid-December, one of those nights nobody wants. — *Gray Dawn*, Albert Payson Terhune, 1927.

6366 It was the night, remembered long after by the old hands, of the greatest flood ever seen up the country. — *Up the Country*, Miles Franklin, 1928.

6367 OH DEAR MABEL!/ *A cat like a beadle goose-stepped with eerie convulsions out of the night cast by a cluster of statuary, from the recesses of the entrance hall. A maid with matchless decorum left a door silently, she removed a massive copper candlestick. She reintegrated the gloom that the cat had left.* — *The Apes of God*, Wyndham Lewis, 1930.

6368 It was a shocking night, down where the Hamilton Avenue car used to reach the end of its journey in Erie Basin. — *The Beachcomber*, William McFee, 1935.

6369 The night was young, and so was he. But the night was sweet, and he was sour. — *Phantom Lady*, Cornell Woolrich *as* William Irish, 1942.

6370 One noon in mid-December when Tom had been called suddenly to Washington, Polly took the train from New York to spend the night at their country place in Pyefield. — *B. F.'s Daughter*, John P. Marquand, 1946.

6371 I stand at the window of this great house in the south of France as night falls, the night which is leading me to the most terrible morning of my life. — *Giovanni's Room*, James Baldwin, 1956.

6372 Oh Saturday night is the loneliest night in the week, Weissburg thought and hummed as he balanced against the sway of the General and then continued to tightrope his way back to the dining car. — *The Steagle*, Irvin Faust, 1966.

6373 In times long after that night there were those among them who swore that a single bolt of lightning had slashed the cloudless, starlit sky: lighting the faces of the just and the unjust, of sleepers and the watchers of the night, and of the slain and the slayers. — *Shadow of My Brother*, Davis Grubb, 1966.

6374 Let me reconstruct my first whole memory: the night my father lost himself and I lost him. — *Prince Elmo's Fire*, Ernest Lockridge, 1974.

6375 On this particular night in January the leaning tower of Pisa fell down. — *Brain 2000*, Ernest K. Gann, 1980.

6376 The black of night is never really black. — *Going to California*, David Littlejohn, 1981.

6377 It was the night Israel died. — *Tongues of Fire*, Peter Abrahams, 1982.

6378 I knew at once that it was one of those nights. — *The Paper Men*, William Golding, 1984.

6379 It was a night of patchy dreams, strangers' voices, rain hammering on the tarpaper roof close overhead. — *Marya*, Joyce Carol Oates, 1986.

6380 It was the black starry June night we had been waiting for. — *The Flood*, Carol Ascher, 1987.

6381 Running through the jungle of southern nights, running hard and fast over crumbling highways, arms out to catch a freshet of wind because the night is so goddamned long and hot and cloying and if you slow down and give in, oh Lord, how it will weasel up under your skin like hookworm and crawl around until it finds your brain. — *Smokehouse Jam*, Loyd Little, 1989.

6382 I was seven years old the night my father chased Red Elk out of the valley. — *Meteors in August*, Melanie Rae Thon, 1990.

6383 In the deepest part of the night, when all the candles save one had been put out and everyone lay quiet, the woman crossed silently to her desk and sat down. — *Mary Queen of Scotland and the Isles*, Margaret George, 1992.

6384 I was very, very young on the starry night it all began. It was a white night, June of 1968, so the stars above me were blurred by a flush of midnight sunlight that lit up the talcum veil of the last quarter moon low to the west. — *Peter Nevsky and the True Story of the Russian Moon Landing*, John Calvin Batchelor, 1993.

Nudity

6385 I remember, when I was a boy, meeting somewhere with the quaintly-written travels of *Moryson* through Ireland, and being particularly struck with his assertion, that so late as the days of Elizabeth, an Irish chieftain and his family were frequently seen round their domestic fire in a state of perfect nudity. — *The Wild Irish Girl*, Lady Morgan, 1806.

6386 From the back of the old four-poster bed, where blue flowers and white butterflies melted together in the faded chintz hangings, Darien watched Sally undressing just outside the pale pool of candle-light. — *Promenade*, G. B. Lancaster, 1938.

6387 Howard Roark laughed./ He stood naked at the edge of a cliff. — *The Fountainhead*, Ayn Rand, 1943.

6388 The woman and the girl began undressing in the bushes near the water, modestly taking their garments off at a little distance from each other and with their backs turned so as not to surprise each other's abashed flesh. — "The Crazy Hunter," Kay Boyle, 1958.

6389 The bitch! Both of them naked, the bitch! — *Castle Keep*, William Eastlake, 1965.

6390 *The naked man lies on the sand spit between the two legs of sea.* — *Gog*, Andrew Sinclair, 1967.

6391 I'm lying in bed, see, on my side, left side, leaving my right hand free, and just in front of me is Ethel, my landlady. We're both naked, of course, but we're not hutched up close to one another or nothing like that, because to be quite frank I find if I get a woman's bare backside pressed up against my stomach for any length of time I seem to get as I can't draw my breath or something. — *Alfie Darling*, Bill Naughton, 1970.

6392 Despite my protests, Marietta revealed her breasts. — *Two Sisters*, Gore Vidal, 1970.

6393 —Totally naked, for God's sake? — *MF*, Anthony Burgess, 1971.

6394 On the wide edge of a large kidney-shaped swimming pool sit two naked fourteen-year-old girls, Louisa Calloway and Kate Flickinger. — *Families and Survivors*, Alice Adams, 1974.

6395 Although the morning sun blazed across the fields, turning the newly blossoming wheat a dull gold, it was cool in the attic and the tall girl who stood naked beneath the beams shivered. — *Leah's Journey*, Gloria Goldreich, 1978.

6396 Except for her sunglasses, Berry is naked. — *The House of God*, Samuel Shem, 1978.

6397 AUSTRALIAN ACTRESS IN NUDE ROMP. JESS SCORES AGAIN. Black

and foreboding, the headlines sprang out at Elissa Campbell. — *Women of a Certain Age*, Colleen Klein, 1979.

6398 At an age when most young Scotsmen were lifting skirts, plowing furrows and spreading seed, Mungo Park was displaying his bare buttocks to al-haj' Ali Ibn Fatoudi, Emir of Ludamar. — *Water Music*, T. Coraghessan Boyle, 1981.

6399 *Mrs. Annie Simmons strutted down her front porch steps one May day butt-naked except for a pair of high-heeled pink satin bedroom slippers and a short strand of coral-colored pop beads.* — *Fish Tales*, Nettie Jones, 1983.

6400 Rebecca Harris backed into my life, naked, her buttocks red with the waffle pattern of the Volkswagen's upholstery. — "Peep Show," David Black, 1986.

6401 The naked fisherman flung his net, and posed, one arm aloft. His blackness, silhouetted against the light reflected from the silky river surface, seemed featureless, flat, incomprehensible. — *Tefuga*, Peter Dickinson, 1986.

6402 Katherine dreamed that she was walking through the dark tunnel of the library into the cold sea, naked. — *Katherine's House*, Margaret Howe Freydberg, 1986.

6403 ...dusk settling over the Caribbean ... the giant emerged from the smooth waters, stood, walked to the beach ... "giant" was the wrong word, he lacked the prerequisite size ... but it came to mind because his naked body, tanned so deeply by the sun, gave off such power ... and he was big ... big in the shoulders especially ... from somewhere on the small deserted island, the birds were doing their night vocalizing ... they had been his chief companions for so many years ... how many years...? — *Brothers*, William Goldman, 1986.

Occupations

6404 Stephen Dudley was a native of New York. He was educated to the profession of a painter. His father's trade was that of an apothecary. But, his son manifesting an attachment to the pencil, he was resolved that it should be gratified. — *Ormond*, Charles Brockden Brown, 1799.

6405 My father, Kerbelai Hassan, was one of the most celebrated barbers of Ispahan. — *The Adventures of Hajji Baba of Ispahan*, James Morier, 1824.

6406 In the county town of a certain shire there lived (about forty years ago) one Mr. Wilkins, a conveyancing attorney of considerable standing. — *A Dark Night's Work*, Elizabeth Gaskell, 1863.

6407 During a portion of the first half of the present century, and more particularly during the latter part of it, there flourished and practised in the city of New York a physician who enjoyed perhaps an exceptional share of the consideration which, in the United States, has always been bestowed upon members of the medical profession. — *Washington Square*, Henry James, 1881.

6408 As the master of the Indian Spring school emerged from the pine woods into the little clearing before the school-house, he stopped whistling, put his hat less jauntily on his head, threw away some wild flowers he had gathered on his way, and otherwise assumed the severe demeanor of his profession and his mature age — which was at least twenty. — *Cressy*, Bret Harte, 1889.

6409 In the middle years of the nineteenth century there first became abundant in this strange world of ours a class of men, men tending for the most part to become elderly, who are called, and who are very properly called, but who dislike extremely to be called — "Scientists." — *The Food of the Gods*, H. G. Wells, 1904.

6410 November 29. At half-past one to-day — half-past one exactly — I began my "career." — *The Social Secretary*, David Graham Phillips, 1905.

6411 McKnight is gradually taking over the criminal end of the business. — *The Man in Lower Ten*, Mary Roberts Rinehart, 1909.

6412 One morning, in the fall of 1880, a middle-aged woman, accompanied by a young girl of eighteen, presented herself at the clerk's desk of the principal hotel in Columbus, Ohio, and made inquiry as to whether there was anything about the place that she could do. — *Jennie Gerhardt*, Theodore Dreiser, 1911.

6413 The cat is the offspring of a cat and the dog of a dog, but butlers and lady's maids do not reproduce their kind. They have other duties. — *Bealby*, H. G. Wells, 1915.

6414 There was a man named Webster lived in a town of twenty-five thousand people in the state of Wisconsin. He had a wife named Mary and a daughter named Jane and he was himself a fairly prosperous manufacturer of washing machines. — *Many Marriages*, Sherwood Anderson, 1923.

6415 "Well, this is a nice thing! A nice thing this school-mastering!" — *Pastors and Masters*, Ivy Compton-Burnett, 1925.

6416 If one lives in Galloway, one either fishes or paints. "Either" is perhaps misleading, for most of the painters are fishers also in their spare time. — *The Five Red Herrings*, Dorothy L. Sayers, 1931.

6417 Before she was seven, Ishma, the youngest child of Marshall and Laviny Waycaster, had joined the class of burden-bearers. — *Call Home the Heart*, Olive Tilford Dargan *as* Fielding Burke, 1932.

6418 The Lazy S had been a good ranch to work for, and he had left it in much better condition than he had found it. — *Mesquite Jenkins, Tumbleweed*, Clarence E. Mulford, 1932.

6419 My present occupation is that of a book reviewer, but I live in the country. — *Yesterday's Burdens*, Robert M. Coates, 1933.

6420 When Sam Whistle was not the undertaker, he was the auctioneer at Haven's End. — *Haven's End*, John P. Marquand, 1933.

6421 The Miss Lonelyhearts of the New York *Post-Dispatch* (Are you in trouble? — Do-you-need-advice? — Write-to-Miss-Lonelyhearts-and-she-will-help-you) sat at his desk and stared at a piece of white cardboard. — *Miss Lonelyhearts*, Nathanael West, 1933.

6422 Jocelyn Britton was always the last to leave the office. — *The World Is Like That*, Kathleen Norris, 1940.

6423 My father, Seaton Wiswell of Milton and Boston, was an attorney. — *Oliver Wiswell*, Kenneth Roberts, 1940.

6424 Ever since Bo jo Brown and I had gone to one of those country day schools for little boys, Bo-jo had possessed what are known as "qualities of leadership"; that is to say, he had what it takes to be the Head Boy of the School. — *H. M. Pulham, Esquire*, John P. Marquand, 1941.

6425 Young Ames was listed as a junior clerk on the payroll of the famous commercial house of Chevalier, Deming & Post. — *Young Ames*, Walter D. Edmonds, 1942.

6426 Mr. Blingham, and may he fry in his own cooking-oil, was assistant treasurer of the Flaver-Saver Company. — *Kingsblood Royal*, Sinclair Lewis, 1947.

6427 In 1946 Scott-King had been classical master at Granchester for twenty-one years. He was himself a Granchesterian and had returned straight from the University after failing for a fellowship. There he had remained, growing slightly bald and slightly corpulent, known to generations of boys first as "Scottie," then of late years, while barely middle-aged, as "old Scottie"; a school "institution," whose precise and slightly nasal lamentations of modern decadence were widely parodied. — *Scott-King's Modern Europe*, Evelyn Waugh, 1947.

6428 He was an old man who fished alone in a skiff in the Gulf Stream and he had gone eighty-four days now without taking a fish. — *The Old Man and the Sea*, Ernest Hemingway, 1952.

6429 "So there we are, gentlemen," Hathon concluded in his best chairman manner. "Mr.

Selby will be Managing Director, with Mr. Torr as deputy." — *The Magicians*, J. B. Priestley, 1954.

6430 I became an engineer. — *A Single Pebble*, John Hersey, 1956.

6431 Everybody thought Arp was just a rubbish-picker, but that's all they knew, the dustman who tipped the rubbish on to the dump, so untidy you didn't know where to start picking, and the Old Cock who looked after the dump, and Rambam the dealer who bought Arp's rubbish from him (what he didn't decide to keep for a rainy day, that was). — *Old Soldiers Never Die*, Wolf Mankowitz, 1956.

6432 As a junior of exceptional promise, he had been sent to Egypt for a year in order to improve his Arabic and found himself attached to the High Commission as a sort of scribe to await his first diplomatic posting; but he was already conducting himself as a young secretary of legation, fully aware of the responsibilities of future office. — *Mountolive*, Lawrence Durrell, 1958.

6433 Perhaps a sense of being part of the highest human traffic of the day was the greatest satisfaction Charles Montfior enjoyed on his first anniversary as Master of the Restaurant Chez Pavan. — *Chez Pavan*, Richard Llewellyn, 1958.

6434 We were walking past the Sharanpur Club one morning when Sanad said he wanted to give up his job with Selkirk and Lowe. — *A Time to Be Happy*, Nayantara Sahgal, 1958.

6435 Ten weeks before he died, Mr. Mohun Biswas, a journalist of Sikkim Street, St. James, Port of Spain, was sacked. — *A House for Mr. Biswas*, V. S. Naipaul, 1961.

6436 When Paul Gate was seventy he retired, without heartbreak, from the post he had held for more than fifty years — fifty-four — in an obscure private school living on with the obstinacy of an old half-rotted tree in an equally obscure little town on the northeast coast: Danesacre. — *The Road from the Monument*, Storm Jameson, 1962.

6437 It was a wet afternoon in October, as I copied out the September accounts from the big gray ledger. I worked in a grocery shop in the north of Dublin and had been there for two years. — *The Lonely Girl*, Edna O'Brien, 1962.

6438 I call myself personal assistant to Arno Borian, but the only place I get credit is on the letters I dictate in his absence. — *Cockatrice*, Wolf Mankowitz, 1963.

6439 As a diplomat I have a good record. In his valedictory letter the President called it "a distinguished and meritorious career, the sum of whose service represents a great profit to the United States of America." — *The Ambassador*, Morris West, 1965.

6440 When Bernice Leach got the job, thirty-two months ago, as a domestic for the Burrmann

family, she was expected to cook three meals a day. — *The Meeting Point*, Austin Clarke, 1967.

6441 When Radar O'Reilly, just out of high school, left Ottumwa, Iowa, and enlisted in the United States Army it was with the express purpose of making a career of the Signal Corps. — *M*A*S*H*, Richard Hooker, 1968.

6442 On a Friday morning I went to apply for a job as a fortuneteller at Pacific Ocean Park. — *Loving Hands at Home*, Diane Johnson, 1968.

6443 Owen Tuby, Doctor of Literature and now Deputy Director of the *Institute of Social Imagistics*, 4 Half Moon House, Half Moon Street, W.1, walked back to the office after lunch. — *London End*, J. B. Priestley, 1968.

6444 By the time Spurgeon Robinson had been riding the ambulances thirty-six hours on and thirty-six hours off for three weeks, the driver, Meyerson, had long since gotten on his nerves and he was shaken by the gore and troubled by the traumas and didn't like the duty even a little bit. — *The Death Committee*, Noah Gordon, 1969.

6445 Burt Claris was a grifter. — *West of the Rockies*, Daniel Fuchs, 1971.

6446 In September 1939, when the war had just begun, Miss Batchelor retired from her post as superintendent of the Protestant mission schools in the city of Ranpur. — *The Towers of Silence*, Paul Scott, 1971.

6447 In the spring of 1926 I resigned from my job. — *Theophilus North*, Thornton Wilder, 1973.

6448 In the April of 1893 I was staying in the course of my business at the Devonshire Arms in Skipton, Yorkshire. I was then twenty-three years of age, and enjoying a modest and not unsuccessful career as commercial representative of the firm of Josiah Westerman & Sons, Purveyors of Leather Fancy Goods. — *The Space Machine*, Christopher Priest, 1976.

6449 Lee and I caddy at the Crescent Club. — *Hard Feelings*, Don Bredes, 1977.

6450 I am the apprentice of His Majesty, I have been taught by the King; and now that I come to die — for I am dying, they cannot fool me however much they attempt it — I feel that I have served well him whose creation I have been . . . as he has been mine, for it is as fellow artisans, almost more than as ruler and subject, that Nefer-Kheperu-Ra Akhenaten, tenth King and Pharaoh of the Eighteenth Dynasty to rule over the Two Lands of Kemet, and Bek, his chief sculptor, have labored all these years. — *Return to Thebes*, Allen Drury, 1977.

6451 For as long as I can remember my father has been the Regius Professor of Comparative Literature at Columbia, and his connection with the University goes back even

further than that. — *Looking for Work*, Susan Cheever, 1979.

6452 Sophie Glicksman was seventeen when Billy James came to work for the YW-YMHA. — *Everything in the Window*, Shirley Faessler, 1979.

6453 I have a client named Teddy Franklin. Teddy Franklin is a car thief. — *Kennedy for the Defense*, George V. Higgins, 1980.

6454 For one small chapter in the twentieth-century American epic, Mary Maguire, movie gossip columnist for the *Los Angeles Star*, served as bard and meistersinger, recorder, reporter, and, on occasion, inventor. — *The Missing Person*, Doris Grumbach, 1981.

6455 The day before I met Mildred Howell I quit my job. — *Customs*, Lisa Zeidner, 1981.

6456 Corde, who led the life of an executive in America — wasn't a college dean a kind of executive? — found himself six or seven thousand miles from his base, in Bucharest, in winter, shut up in an old-fashioned apartment. — *The Dean's December*, Saul Bellow, 1982.

6457 Long ago my father and I were servants at Cripplegate, a cottage plantation in South Carolina. — *Oxherding Tale*, Charles Johnson, 1982.

6458 My father was a carpenter (measure twice, cut once, that was Joe Durgin) and when he said his first and only house wouldn't collapse, it didn't. — *Lusts*, Clark Blaise, 1983.

6459 The woman peddler, who sold cabbages and radishes from the basket she carried on her head, was making her early morning round of the neighborhood, hawking. — *White Badge*, Ahn Junghyo, 1983.

6460 That is, I used to be the editor of a magazine, quit in anger when my boss was fired, and am now on my own. — *The Ticket Out*, Lucy Rosenthal, 1983.

6461 A listener from birth should not be surprised if his first occupation turns out to be that of wireless operator. — *The Lost Flying Boat*, Alan Sillitoe, 1983.

6462 "A caddy, hmm?" — *Last Dance*, Lee Grove, 1984.

6463 I had spent eight months in America, most of them teaching on an exchange basis at a preparatory school in Vermont. — *An Open Prison*, J. I. M. Stewart, 1984.

6464 Charley is in the habit when short of cash of remarking over her oatmeal, "I run a ranch half the size of a township and I do it for room and board." — *Charleyhorse*, Cecil Dawkins, 1985.

6465 Richard Tripp is the agent of Singer Sewing Machines in some Baltic capital similar to Tallinn. — *The Tenth Man*, Graham Greene, 1985.

6466 I've got to admit I'm more than a little concerned about my son, and about this awful new job of his. — *The Great Equalizer*, Rich Borsten, 1986.

6467 "Many readers may be completely unaware that, following his disastrous sojourn in Hollywood, John Towne somehow managed to resume his long-interrupted academic career during the tag end, the doggy days of the 1960s. It may come as a surprise to some, even among the best informed. . . ." — *Poison Pen*, George Garrett, 1986.

6468 Call me an agent. — *Blackballed*, Michael Mewshaw, 1986.

6469 She was a reporter, had been around the block a time or two, thought she'd seen it all, but she was wrong. — *Providence*, Geoffrey Wolff, 1986.

6470 Fred Wagner began his career of public invisibility in a large midtown post office. — *Being Invisible*, Thomas Berger, 1987.

6471 George Clifton ran a data-processing office of a large utility company in Chicago, where he got hired fresh out of the navy as a customer representative. — *The Grand Life*, Jan Novak, 1987.

6472 Emmanuel Yehoshua Sternholz, son of Rebecca and Samuel Sternholz, father of Jacob, R.I.P., and grandfather of innumerable unborn Sternholzes, was a waiter. — *Café Nevo*, Barbara Rogan, 1987.

6473 Way back in 1975, Sprayberry wouldn't have gone so far to say that he loved Parkland Life and Casualty. — *The Sanity Matinee*, Michael Zagst, 1987.

6474 Before departing, I had worked for a year in a tiny art gallery. — *The Whore of Tjampuan*, Harry Kondoleon, 1988.

6475 The last time I tried to quit my job I was turned down — on the grounds that I was incompetent. — *Falling Up the Stairs*, James Lileks, 1988.

6476 I suppose that my mother could have been a witch if she had chosen to. — *Thornyhold*, Mary Stewart, 1988.

6477 My father organized restaurant workers in New York City during the Great Depression. — *Tallien*, Frederic Tuten, 1988.

6478 I, Starlady Sandra, professional searcher after truth, rejector of fantasy, organiser of eternal laws into numerical form, confiner of cosmic events and swirling next-to-nothingness into detail not only comprehensible but communicable to a TV audience, was in flight from my own life, my own past, and the revenge of my friends. — *Leader of the Band*, Fay Weldon, 1988.

6479 I've just about always cleaned houses for a livin'. — *Same Blood*, Mermer Blakeslee, 1989.

6480 "Amy Doll, are you telling me that all those old girls upstairs are tarts?" — *The House of Dolls*, Barbara Comyns, 1989.

6481 Patrick Doyle was a teacher. Gradually he had become sickened by it. — *A Disaffection*, James Kelman, 1989.

6482 The Rabbi's only son, Yussel, sold insurance, mostly life. — *God's Ear*, Rhoda Lerman, 1989.

6483 On the fifth anniversary of his arrival in Timbali, Dr. Humphrey Lord was informed that his second promotion had finally been approved. — *The Music Programme*, Paul Micou, 1989.

6484 In the old country in South America, Carlotta's grandmother, Zedé, had been a seamstress, but really more of a sewing magician. — *The Temple of My Familiar*, Alice Walker, 1989.

6485 During my career as a backup singer with Vernon and Ruby Shakely and the Shakettes, it often occurred to me that this was not a lifetime occupation and that someday I would have to figure out my rightful place in society. — *Goodbye Without Leaving*, Laurie Colwin, 1990.

6486 Alchemy is what's really needed, yet we who eke a livelihood from these flimsy, modern conceptual endeavors usually persist in a feverish panning for gold. — *Hot Air*, Bob Katz, 1990.

6487 I first heard of Queen Heliokleia when I was eighteen: my father returned from Eskati that spring and told me that he had proposed me as one of her attendants. — *Horses of Heaven*, Gillian Bradshaw, 1991.

6488 I haul things. — *In Memory of Junior*, Clyde Edgerton, 1992.

6489 I'm usually out early, try to beat the freeway buildup and get to school by seven, even though I don't teach until eight; so when I go through the pool area in the middle of the apartment complex, there's nobody there, just the empty wire-backed chairs from Yardbirds and maybe a leftover towel or Coke can next to an ashtray filled with cigarette butts. — *Lucy Boomer*, Russell Hill, 1992.

6490 He wasn't just a taxi driver, he told himself. He was a student of human nature. — *Storyville*, Lois Battle, 1993.

6491 Somewhere in the middle of life's journey, Martin Weinstock lost his way and found himself Burke-Howland Lecturer in Poetry at Harvard University. — *Weinstock Among the Dying*, Michael Blumenthal, 1993.

6492 Already by her twentieth birthday, my grandmother was an excellent midwife, in great demand. — *Charms for the Easy Life*, Kaye Gibbons, 1993.

6493 Howard Beamish became a palaeontologist because of a rise in the interest rate when he was six years old. — *Cleopatra's Sister*, Penelope Lively, 1993.

6494 The Government still pays my wages but I no longer think of myself as a bureaucrat. Bureaucrats belong too much to the world, and I have fulfilled my worldly obligations. I am now a vanaprasthi, someone who has retired to the forest to reflect. — *A River Sutra*, Gita Mehta, 1993.

Offices

6495 Lilian, in dark blue office frock with an embroidered red line round the neck and detachable black wristlets that preserved the ends of the sleeves from dust and friction, sat idle at her flat desk in what was called "the small room" at Felix Grig's establishment in Clifford Street, off Bond Street. — *Lilian*, Arnold Bennett, 1922.

6496 During the first twenty-five years of this century, business people who had their offices in or near State Street, Boston, no doubt grew very familiar with the cadaverous and extraordinary figure of my uncle, Bascom Hawke. — "A Portrait of Bascom Hawke," Thomas Wolfe, 1932.

6497 "It's all yours, Pew, from now," he said, adding softly, "thank God," and waving round the office a mildly revolted hand. — *City of Spades*, Colin MacInnes, 1957.

6498 Unless you had an expert knowledge of the locality you would not reach the offices of *The Banner*. — *The Printer of Malgudi*, R. K. Narayan, 1957.

6499 I opened the large central window of my office room to its full on that fine early May morning. Then I stood for a few moments, breathing in the soft, warm air that was charged with the scent of white lilacs below. — *The Old Men at the Zoo*, Angus Wilson, 1961.

6500 Boy Kirton spent the most important part of his life in a box nine feet long by seven feet wide by eight feet high. — *The Plain Man*, Julian Symons, 1962.

6501 Rumbold had taken to sitting in the office all day. It was in a corner of the pump bay, a two-by-four place with glass-topped walls like the wheelhouse of a ship. — "The Joy-Ride," A. L. Barker, 1963.

6502 On a bleak wintry morning some years ago I was summoned to the office of our naval attaché at the American embassy in Kabul. — *Caravans*, James A. Michener, 1963.

6503 The lawyer, whose name was John Truttwell, kept me waiting in the outer room of his offices. It gave the room a chance to work me over gently. — *The Goodbye Look*, Ross Macdonald, 1969.

6504 I called Buckholz and Cripps into my office at about two-thirty. — *The Charisma Campaigns*, Jack Matthews, 1972.

6505 There was a lull in the late afternoon. The office was hushed; the intercommunications box was still. — *Mr. Nicholas*, David Ely, 1974.

6506 When the receptionist — not half bad, Jim Rush decided, as Washington receptionists go — ushered him into the Assistant Secretary's office, after a wait calculated to the second to put on record the Assistant Secretary's importance, Jim realized at once that he was in for trouble. — *Hail the Conquering Hero*, Frank Yerby, 1977.

6507 The office was stripped. — *Sun Dogs*, Robert Olen Butler, 1982.

6508 I never fell in love in my father's office, though I wanted to and tried. — *Crossroads*, Mary Morris, 1983.

6509 I was surprised when shortly after New Year's Day of 1983, the Governor of Texas summoned me to his office, because I hadn't been aware that he knew I was in town. — *Texas*, James A. Michener, 1985.

6510 All hell has been breaking loose around here, and my peaceful retreat in the Executive Office Building may be coming to a sudden rude end. — *Inside, Outside*, Herman Wouk, 1985.

6511 After the eye examination Doug Gardner sat across from Dr. Jeffrey Weiss in an office so dark with its heavy leather furniture, murky brown wallpaper and dim lighting, the only good light a desk lamp on the doctor's desk, he thought it might have been a psychological ploy. — *50*, Avery Corman, 1987.

6512 Anita Vogel's office in the Museum of North America, like those of other curators in the porticoed marble edifice on Central Park West, seemed designed to make its occupant feel that she was usurping the space of a more important functionary. — *The Golden Calves*, Louis Auchincloss, 1988.

6513 At the top of the Wandstar Building, high above Manhattan, dwarfing the towers of Chrysler and Pan Am, are the offices of SISTERHOOD magazine, commonly known as SIS. — *Dear Digby*, Carol Muske Dukes, 1989.

6514 Precisely at eight a.m. the Friday before Yom Kippur 1955, the Hebrew year 5716, Hyman Schwartz entered the offices of Teitlebaum & Sharfenstein, Accountants, in New York City. — *A Dissenter in the House of God*, Alvin Rosenfeld, 1990.

Offspring

6515 Manfred, Prince of Otranto, had one son and one daughter: the latter, a most beautiful virgin, aged eighteen, was called Matilda. Conrad, the son, was three years younger, a homely youth, sickly, and of no promising disposition; yet he was the darling of his father, who never showed any symptoms of affection to Matilda. — *The Castle of Otranto*, Horace Walpole, 1765.

6516 Richard Annesly was the only child of a wealthy tradesman in London, who, from the experience of that profit which his business afforded himself, was anxious to have it descend to his son. Unfortunately the young man had acquired a certain train of ideas which were totally averse to that line of life his father had marked out for him. — *The Man of the World*, Henry Mackenzie, 1773.

6517 Dreadful conflict! — whether to acknowledge to a son, who reveres me, the melancholy errors of an unfortunate mother, or by suffering him to remain in ignorance of those sad truths it is my duty to inform him of, retain, only by an effort of duplicity, his unmerited respect and love! — *Confessions of the Nun of St. Omer*, Rosa Matilda, 1805.

6518 William, the Conqueror of England, was, or supposed himself to be, the father of a certain William Peveril, who attended him to the battle of Hastings, and there distinguished himself. — *Peveril of the Peak*, Sir Walter Scott, 1823.

6519 Dombey sat in the corner of the darkened room in the great arm-chair by the bedside, and Son lay tucked up warm in a little basket bedstead, carefully disposed on a low settee immediately in front of the fire and close to it, as if his constitution were analogous to that of a muffin, and it was essential to toast him brown while he was very new. — *Dombey and Son*, Charles Dickens, 1848.

6520 "Sir — sir, it is a boy!"/ "A boy," said my father, looking up from his book, and evidently much puzzled; "what is a boy?" — *The Caxtons*, Edward Bulwer Lytton, 1849.

6521 When young Mark Robarts was leaving college, his father might well declare that all men began to say all good things to him, and to extol his fortune in that he had a son blessed with so excellent a disposition. — *Framley Parsonage*, Anthony Trollope, 1861.

6522 "I guess my daughter's in here," the old man said, leading the way into the little *salon de lecture*. — *The Reverberator*, Henry James, 1888.

6523 Alexander Lauderdale Junior was very much exercised in spirit concerning the welfare of his two daughters, of whom the elder was Charlotte and the younger was Katharine. — *The Ralstons*, F. Marion Crawford, 1893.

6524 When Colonel Wyatt died, all Weymouth agreed that it was a most unfortunate thing for his sons Julian and Frank. — *Through Russian Snows*, G. A. Henty, 1895.

6525 Mr. and Mrs. Wayne lived down the road a little way. They had three children. Two of them were boys. The other, at that time, did not matter. — *Kindling and Ashes*, George Barr McCutcheon, 1926.

6526 "So the children are not down yet?" said Ellen Edgeworth. — *A House and Its Head*, Ivy Compton-Burnett, 1935.

6527 Everybody agreed with Mrs. Baskett that her baby was a most remarkable child. They delighted to hear how, exploring the cellar, she ate coal to see how it tasted; how, investigating matches, she set the nursery curtains on fire and nearly burnt down the house. — *A Fearful Joy*, Joyce Cary, 1949.

6528 "My dear, good girls!" said Miles Mowbray. "My three dear daughters! To think I have ever felt dissatisfied with you and wished I had a son! I blush for the lack in me, that led me to such a feeling...." — *A Father and His Fate*, Ivy Compton-Burnett, 1957.

6529 "My God, what giants!" From her four-feet-ten mother looked up at five-feet-three of Horace and five-feet-two of me, and oh, the awe and astonishment in her voice. — *All in a Lifetime*, Walter Allen, 1959.

6530 You should have a son like I have a son! And then you would know. — *Once Upon a Droshky*, Jerome Charyn, 1964.

6531 *In the first weeks of World War II, in the fall of 1939, a six-year-old boy from a large city in Eastern Europe was sent by his parents, like thousands of other children, to the shelter of a distant village.* — *The Painted Bird*, Jerzy Kosinski, 1965.

6532 "You can be serious," Mother insisted, and so I could. It was very serious when I saw that parents *have* to like their children, and from that time on I pulled myself together, awaiting, a little stiffly perhaps, but amiably, my inevitable son. — *New Axis*, Charles Newman, 1966.

6533 Marianne had sharp, cold eyes and she was spiteful but her father loved her. — *Heroes and Villains*, Angela Carter, 1969.

6534 "He is very ugly," said his mother. — *Great Lion of God*, Taylor Caldwell, 1970.

6535 The son of a judge is worse off than the son of a preacher, and I thought I was the living proof. — *Where Is My Wandering Boy Tonight?*, David Wagoner, 1970.

6536 "Me wear a collar?" said Mason Ross, sitting up in bed and fingering the hard thing his

mother had put into his hands. — *The Incline*, William Mayne, 1972.

6537 This morning I abandoned my only child. — *Raw Silk*, Janet Burroway, 1977.

6538 She wanted a child. — *Walter*, David Cook, 1978.

6539 "Jack Cornock's daughter is coming back," said Keith Burtenshaw. — *The Only Daughter*, Jessica Anderson, 1980.

6540 "You're Sylvester Spearfield's daughter, aren't you?"/ "Occasionally." — *Spearfield's Daughter*, Jon Cleary, 1982.

6541 "Are they yours?"/ He looked startled. "Yes." — *Wives and Other Women*, Norma Klein, 1982.

6542 Everyone said that Rachaeli would never have declared him a bastard if it had not been for the pressures put upon her as a result of the mixup of her baby and another baby boy in Tel Aviv hospital, but that is not true. She had never intended for him to have a father. — *To the Tenth Generation*, Rita Kashner, 1984.

6543 When his boys were young, Guy Bishop formed the habit of stopping in their room each night on his way to bed. He would look down at them where they slept, and then he would sit in the rocking chair and listen to them breathe. — *The Barracks Thief*, Tobias Wolff, 1984.

6544 Phoebe Martin chose a bad time to tell her ex-husband Rusty that she was taking their son Andrew back East for two weeks. — *Her Native Colors*, Elisabeth Hyde, 1986.

6545 The courtship and remarriage of an old widower is always made more difficult when middle-aged children are involved — especially when there are unmarried daughters. — *A Summons to Memphis*, Peter Taylor, 1986.

6546 How would you feel if you raised up a son and he was handsome, successful, and then, overnight, starts fasting and wearing orange clothes and looking like Mahatma Gandhi? — *A Bliss Case*, Michael Aaron Rockland, 1989.

6547 I don't want Joe to find me on my knees, buffing the kitchen floor with an old cotton turtleneck, but he does, and says, "Mom! What are you doing? Relax!" — "Ordinary Love," Jane Smiley, 1989.

6548 Her son was studying Catherine as she stood at their kitchen window. She felt him. He'd been doing it more and more often, idly and with no special intensity, she thought, but with a kind of dreamy stare. — *Harry and Catherine*, Frederick Busch, 1990.

6549 As he weakened, Moran became afraid of his daughters. — *Amongst Women*, John McGahern, 1990.

6550 That August afternoon Ed Reece dreamed that his older son, Larry, had already returned and stood on the front lawn taking

practice swings with his father's driver. — *The Lies Boys Tell*, Lamar Herrin, 1991.

6551 Had my father been a Roman aristocrat, or a philosopher, he might have abandoned me to the wolves at my birth, for I was from the first dwarfed and odd-shapen, of little use to a poor Gallic goatherder. — *Dominic*, Kathleen Robinson, 1991.

6552 "Chollie!"/ I stretched my mouth open as wide as I could and called my son's name. — *Children of Men*, Jeanne Schinto, 1991.

6553 I suppose a man who has been the indisputable favorite of his mother keeps for life the feeling of a conqueror. — *Psyche*, Peter Michalos, 1993.

6554 I know I have to stop sleeping with my sons. — *One Way Home*, Susan Pepper Robbins, 1993.

Outings

6555 It was on a still evening in June, that Laura Montreville left her father's cottage, in the little village of Glenalbert, to begin a solitary ramble. — *Self-Control*, Mary Brunton, 1810.

6556 Contrary to a long-established usage, a summer had been passed within the walls of a large town: but, the moment of liberation arrived, the bird does not quit its cage with greater pleasure, than that with which post-horses were commanded. — *The Heidenmauer*, James Fenimore Cooper, 1832.

6557 It was a day in early spring; and as that sweet, genial time of year and atmosphere calls out tender greenness from the ground, — beautiful flowers, or leaves that look beautiful because so long unseen under the snow and decay, — so the pleasant air and warmth had called out three young people, who sat on a sunny hill-side enjoying the warm day and one another. — *Septimius Felton*, Nathaniel Hawthorne, 1871.

6558 An excursion beyond the immediate suburbs of London, projected long before his pony-carriage was hired to conduct him, in fact ever since his retirement from active service, led General Ople across a famous common, with which he fell in love at once, to a lofty highway along the borders of a park, for which he promptly exchanged his heart, and so gradually within a stone's-throw or so of the river-side, where he determined not solely to bestow his affections but to settle for life. — *The Case of General Ople and Lady Camper*, George Meredith, 1890.

6559 I took a walk on Spaulding's Farm the

other afternoon. — *Lilith*, George MacDonald, 1895.

6560 It was with a light heart and a pleasing consciousness of holiday that I set out from the inn at Allermuir to tramp my fifteen miles into the unknown. — "No-Man's-Land," John Buchan, 1898.

6561 It befel upon a very joyous season in the month of May that Queen Guinevere was of a mind to take gentle sport as folk do at that time of the year; wherefore on a day she ordained it in a court of pleasure that on the next morning certain knights and ladies of the court at Camelot should ride with her a-maying into the woods and fields, there to disport themselves amid the flowers and blossoms that grew in great multitudes beside the river. — *The Story of Sir Launcelot and His Companions*, Howard Pyle, 1907.

6562 The sea was a pale elfin green and the afternoon had already felt the fairy touch of evening as a young woman with dark hair, dressed in a crinkly copper-coloured sort of dress of the artistic order, was walking rather listlessly along the parade of Pebblewick-on-Sea, trailing a parasol and looking out upon the sea's horizon. — *The Flying Inn*, G. K. Chesterton, 1914.

6563 Once a term the whole school went for a walk — that is to say the three masters took part as well as all the boys. *Maurice*, E. M. Forster, 1914 (pub. 1971).

6564 The pines thinned as she neared Rainbow Rim, the turfy glades grew wider; she had glimpses of open country beyond — until, at last, crossing a little spit of high ground, she came to the fairest spot in all her voyage of exploration and discovery. — *Bransford of Rainbow Range*, Eugene Manlove Rhodes, 1914.

6565 "Yes, of course, if it's fine tomorrow," said Mrs. Ramsay. "But you'll have to be up with the lark," she added. — *To the Lighthouse*, Virginia Woolf, 1927.

6566 "Come the summer, we'll borrow old Polly and the spring cart from the 'Wagon and Horses' and all go over to Candleford," their father said, for the ten-millionth time, thought Laura. — *Over to Candleford*, Flora Thompson, 1941.

6567 . . . and then I walked and walked in the rain that turned half into snow and I was drenched and frozen; and walked upon a park that seemed like the very pasture of Hell where there were couples whispering in the shadows, all in some plot to warm the world tonight, and I went into a public place and saw annunciations drawn and written on the walls. — *The House of Breath*, William Goyen, 1950.

6568 One Whitsun holiday, when I was an art student in London, I got on my bicycle and left my room on Croom's Hill for my uncle's

vicarage in Surrey. — *A Voice Through a Cloud*, Denton Welch, 1950.

6569 Sometimes there was a compulsion which drew Ira Claffey from his plantation and sent him to walk the forest. — *Andersonville*, MacKinlay Kantor, 1955.

6570 When Pedlar Pascoe — the youngest, heaviest, and by general reckoning the most stupid of the Pinehollow Pascoes — drifted into Exeter in his mother's 1924 bull-nosed Morris that cheerless January morning in 1941, he had no intention of remaining in the city longer than it would take him to dispose of the car, drink several pints of beer, and make his way back to the Pascoe shanties by the quickest and cheapest means available. — *Stop at a Winner*, R. F. Delderfield, 1961.

6571 One day in the June of 1844 Madame Sophie Duval, née Busson, eighty years of age and mother of the mayor of Vibraye, a small commune in the département of Sarthe, rose from her chair in the salon of her property at le Gué de Launay, chose her favourite walking-stick from a stand in the hall, and calling to her dog made her way, as was her custom at this hour of the afternoon every Tuesday, down the short approach drive to the entrance gate. — *The Glass-Blowers*, Daphne du Maurier, 1963.

6572 My mother called and informed me we were going on a picnic. — *The Autobiography of My Mother*, Rosellen Brown, 1976.

6573 "Look," I said, "I'm going with you." — *Property Of*, Alice Hoffman, 1977.

6574 The pools from the night's rainfall were already steaming in the potholed road when Dr. Harry Lynd took his walking stick and began the trudge that would take him from the compound of the Hermitage to the crest of the scarp. — *Rivers of Darkness*, Ronald Hardy, 1979.

6575 It was early October when they drove out there from Brooklyn to see the model homes. — *The Ladies of Levittown*, Gene Horowitz, 1980.

6576 On the eve of the 4th of July we put our shoulders to it and pushed off into the river — four boys, each dressed in his own version of a pirate costume, and a dog. — *The Bohemians*, Alan Cheuse, 1982.

6577 Our history of the remarkable Zinn family, to end upon the final bold stroke of midnight, December 31, 1899, begins some twenty years earlier, on that beauteous September afternoon, in the golden haze of autumn, 1879 — ah, now so long past! — when, to the confus'd shame and horror of her loving family and the consternation of all of Bloodsmoor, Miss Deirdre Louisa Zinn, the adopted daughter of Mr. and Mrs. John Quincy Zinn, betook herself on an impetuous walk, with no companion, and was, by daylight, *abducted from the grounds belonging to the*

stately home of her grandparents, historic old Kidde-master Hall. — *A Bloodsmoor Romance*, Joyce Carol Oates, 1982.

6578 We're going for a midnight boat ride. — *A Boy's Own Story*, Edmund White, 1982.

6579 Stick said he wasn't going if they had to pick up anything. — *Stick*, Elmore Leonard, 1983.

6580 One bright day in October three poets set out to keep an appointment in the dismaying heart of London. — *A Fine Excess*, Jane Ellison, 1985.

6581 Usually for picnics we took a small brake seating about eight people. — *A Storm from Paradise*, Stuart Hood, 1985.

6582 Whatever it was was still behind him. — *That Day in Gordon*, Raymond H. Abbott, 1986.

6583 Today I took my daughter, Christine, for a ride on the streetcar. — *A Recent Martyr*, Valerie Martin, 1987.

6584 He had three seats to rest across while he wandered through the dream city of London and reduced it and his memories to ash. — "Going Home," John Sligo, 1987.

6585 When my mother told me I was going to Paradise that afternoon, I had no idea what she meant. — *Paradise*, Elena Castedo, 1990.

6586 Sunday morning, Ordell took Louis to watch the white-power demonstration in downtown Palm Beach. — *Rum Punch*, Elmore Leonard, 1992.

6587 Twice a week in every week of summer except the last in July and the first in August, their mother shut the front door, the white, eight-panel door that served as backdrop for every Easter, First Holy Communion, confirmation, and graduation photo in the family album, and with the flimsy screen leaning against her shoulder turned the key in the black lock, gripped the curve of the elaborate wrought-iron handle that had been sculpted to resemble a black vine curled into a question mark, and in what seemed a brief but accurate imitation of a desperate housebreaker, wrung the door on its hinges until, well satisfied, she turned, slipped away from the screen as if she were throwing a cloak from her shoulders, and said, "Let's go." — *At Weddings and Wakes*, Alice McDermott, 1992.

Pain

6588 "Boo, hoo! Ow, ow; Oh! oh! Me'll die. Boo, hoo. The pain, the pain! Boo, hoo!" — *My Brilliant Career*, Miles Franklin, 1901.

6589 The dentist was holding Henry Adams around the neck with one hand while the other hand held the medicine dropper. — *Runner Mack*, Barry Beckham, 1972.

6590 "Joey, Joey? O God! Joey?" his mother cried out of her extremity and pain. — *Captains and the Kings*, Taylor Caldwell, 1972.

6591 There it was again, like a signal along a wire. A clear brilliant flash of pain from *A* to *B*. — *Kleinzeit*, Russell Hoban, 1974.

6592 The man dying on the crude cross groaned in agony. — *Phantom of the Sacred Well*, Phyllis G. Leonard, 1975.

6593 The man in Bed 3 awoke to a familiar clutch of pain beneath his shoulder blades. — *The Protocol*, Sarah Allan Borisch, 1981.

6594 The youth lay sprawled on his back in the crisp snow; his oval face, furrowed with pain, faded to an ugly creamy colour accentuated by the pure white bed of snow. — *The Sword of Hachiman*, Lynn Guest, 1981.

6595 What surprised him was how little actual pain there was. — *The Far Side of Victory*, Joanne Greenberg, 1983.

6596 My left thumb is stiff, not particularly swollen although the veins at the base are prominent and I can't move it backward or pick up something without pain. — *Lives of the Poets*, E. L. Doctorow, 1984.

6597 The excruciating pain was gone now. — *The Nanny*, Dan Greenburg, 1987.

6598 Phil Doucet awoke in the darkened room, jolted by sudden pains and the feeling he could no longer breathe. — *Set for Life*, Judith Freeman, 1991.

6599 Paddy McEvilly was bursting for a piss, but he was too comfortable to leave the warm cocoon of blankets to relieve himself. — *Lovers*, Pádraig Standún, 1991.

6600 Now the burn seemed to smart behind his eyes. — "Proofs," George Steiner, 1992.

Parents

6601 I Was born in the Year 1632, in the City of *York*, of a good Family, tho' not of that Country, my Father being a Foreigner of *Bremen*, who settled first at *Hull*: He got a good Estate by Merchandise, and leaving off his Trade, lived afterward at *York*, from whence he had married my Mother, whose Relations were named *Robinson*, a very good Family in that Country, and from whom I was called *Robinson Kreutznaer*; but by the usual Corruption of Words in *England*, we are now called, nay we call our selves, and write our

Name *Crusoe*, and so my Companions always call'd me. — *Robinson Crusoe*, Daniel Defoe, 1719.

6602 My father had a small Estate in *Nottinghamshire*; I was the Third of five Sons. — *Gulliver's Travels*, Jonathan Swift, 1726.

6603 In a certain county of England, bounded on one side by the sea, and at the distance of one hundred miles from the metropolis, lived Gamaliel Pickle Esq; the father of that hero whose adventures we propose to record. — *Peregrine Pickle*, Tobias Smollett, 1751.

6604 I wish either my father or my mother, or indeed both of them, as they were in duty both equally bound to it, had minded what they were about when they begot me; had they duly considered how much depended upon what they were then doing; — that not only the production of a rational Being was concerned in it, but that possibly the happy formation and temperature of his body, perhaps his genius and the very cast of his mind; — and, for aught they knew to the contrary, even the fortunes of his whole house might take their turn from the humours and dispositions which were then uppermost; — Had they duly weighed and considered all this, and proceeded accordingly, — I am verily persuaded that I should have made a quite different figure in the world, from that in which the reader is likely to see me. — *Tristram Shandy*, Laurence Sterne, 1759–1767.

6605 Mary, the heroine of this fiction, was the daughter of Edward, who married Eliza, a gentle, fashionable girl, with a kind of indolence in her temper, which might be termed negative good-nature: her virtues, indeed, were all of that stamp. — *Mary*, Mary Wollstonecraft Shelley, 1788.

6606 I was the only son of my father. I was very young at the period of the death of my mother, and have retained scarcely any recollection of her. My father was so much affected by the loss of the amiable and affectionate partner of his days, that he resolved to withdraw for ever from those scenes where every object he saw was associated with the ideas of her kindness, her accomplishments, and her virtues: and, being habitually a lover of the sublime and romantic features of nature, he fixed upon a spot in Merionethshire, near the foot of Cader Idris, for the habitation of his declining life. — *Fleetwood*, William Godwin, 1805.

6607 I am an only child. My father was the younger son of one of our oldest earls, my mother the dowerless daughter of a Scotch peer. Mr. Pelham was a moderate whig, and gave sumptuous dinners; — Lady Frances was a woman of taste, and particularly fond of diamonds and old china. — *Pelham*, Edward Bulwer Lytton, 1828.

6608 My father was Cornelius Littlepage, of Satanstoe, in the county of Westchester, and state of New York; and my mother was Anneke Mordaunt, of Lilacsbush, a place long known by that name, which still stands near Kingsbridge, but on the Island of Manhattan, and consequently in one of the wards of New York, though quite eleven miles from town. — *The Chainbearer*, James Fenimore Cooper, 1845.

6609 Charles Reding was the only son of a clergyman, who was in possession of a valuable benefice in a midland county. — *Loss and Gain*, John Henry Newman, 1848.

6610 "Not attend her own son when he is ill!" said my mother. "She does not deserve to have a son!" And Mrs. Pendennis looked towards her own only darling whilst uttering this indignant exclamation. — *The Adventures of Philip*, William Makepeace Thackeray, 1862.

6611 My father belonged to the widespread family of the Campbells, and possessed a small landed property in the north of Argyll. But although of long descent and high connection, he was no richer than many a farmer of a few hundred acres. — *The Portent*, George MacDonald, 1864.

6612 Mrs. Amedroz, the wife of Bernard Amedroz, Esq., of Belton Castle, and mother of Charles and Clara Amedroz, died when those two children were only eight and six years old, thereby subjecting them to the greatest misfortune which children born in that sphere of life can be made to suffer. And, in the case of this boy and girl, the misfortune was aggravated greatly by the peculiarities of the father's character. — *The Belton Estate*, Anthony Trollope, 1866.

6613 There was an ominously anxious watch of eyes visible and invisible over the infancy of Willoughby, fifth in descent from Simon Patterne, of Patterne Hall, premier of this family, a lawyer, a man of solid acquirements and stout ambition, who well understood the foundation-work of a House, and was endowed with the power of saying No to those first agents of destruction, besieging relatives. — *The Egoist*, George Meredith, 1879.

6614 "How do you and your Pa get along now," asked the grocery-man of the bad boy, as he leaned against the counter instead of sitting down on a stool, while he bought a bottle of liniment. — *Peck's Bad Boy*, George W. Peck, 1883.

6615 "You heard what he said, George?"/ "Oh, mother, mother!" — *Sturdy and Strong*, G. A. Henty, 1888.

6616 "So to-morrow, Alice," said Dr. Madden, as he walked with his eldest daughter on the coast-downs by Clevedon, "I shall take steps for insuring my life for a thousand pounds." — *The Odd Women*, George Gissing, 1893.

6617 A poet may be a good companion, but, so far as I know, he is ever the worst of fathers. —*D'ri and I*, Irving Bacheller, 1901.

6618 My father was a blacksmith, and he and my mother came out of Clonmel, where I myself was born. — *The Boss*, Alfred Henry Lewis, 1903.

6619 "Elnora Comstock, have you lost your senses?" demanded the angry voice of Katharine Comstock as she glared at her daughter. —*A Girl of the Limberlost*, Gene Stratton-Porter, 1909.

6620 One Wednesday afternoon in late September, Ann Veronica Stanley came down from London in a state of solemn excitement and quite resolved to have things out with her father that very evening. —*Ann Veronica*, H. G. Wells, 1909.

6621 My father was killed in battle with the Sioux and three months later my birth cost my mother an illness which, during my third year, ended her life. — *John Sherwood*, S. Weir Mitchell, 1911.

6622 At the door of St. George's registry office, Charles Clare Winton strolled forward in the wake of the taxi-cab that was bearing his daughter away with "the fiddler fellow" she had married. —*Beyond*, John Galsworthy, 1917.

6623 Kenneth Gwynne was five years old when his father ran away with Rachel Carter, a widow. —*Viola Gwyn*, George Barr McCutcheon, 1922.

6624 A wet autumn night, a low lighted house, wheels on the soaked gravel, the open door, and Leda Perrin in her father's arms. —*Faint Perfume*, Zona Gale, 1923.

6625 In my younger and more vulnerable years my father gave me some advice that I've been turning over in my mind ever since. — *The Great Gatsby*, F. Scott Fitzgerald, 1925.

6626 When the crops were under cover on the Wayne farm near Pittsford in Vermont, when the winter wood was cut and the first light snow lay on the ground, Joseph Wayne went to the wing-back chair by the fireplace late one afternoon and stood before his father. — *To a God Unknown*, John Steinbeck, 1933.

6627 Kit didn't speak much or often of her father. — *Kit Brandon*, Sherwood Anderson, 1936.

6628 Christina Goering's father was an American industrialist of German parentage and her mother was a New York lady of a very distinguished family. — *Two Serious Ladies*, Jane Bowles, 1943.

6629 Sam Braden never talked about his father. If he spoke of his family it was always of his mother, and always with affection and respect. —*Journey in the Dark*, Martin Flavin, 1943.

6630 On Wednesday evenings Paul's mother took the tram from her work in the City Hall to the mid-week service at Merrion Chapel and he usually walked over from the university, after his five o'clock philosophy class, to meet her as she came out. But on this particular Wednesday, his interview with Professor Slade kept him late and, with a glance at his watch, he decided to go straight home. —*Beyond This Place*, A. J. Cronin, 1950.

6631 I was born in Kensington. My father was a composer. My mother came from a rich home, and was, I believe, incurably romantic. — *The Beautiful Visit*, Elizabeth Jane Howard, 1950.

6632 Mother wheeled me out on to the verandah this afternoon because I was having one of my "good days." She spread a rug over the place where my legs used to be and told me to behave and not make noise else she would bring me in. —*A Grove of Fever Trees*, Daphne Rooke, 1950.

6633 "Look, Father, horses. . ."/ "Ah, be still, you little divil." — *The Face of Time*, James T. Farrell, 1953.

6634 I don't know whether you've ever been interviewed by an adoption agency on behalf of friends bent on acquiring a child, or if you have, whether any doubts were in order concerning the qualifications of either of the prospective parents, or of yourself to judge, for that matter, and whether in that case you were realistic with the agency or romantic. — *The Tunnel of Love*, Peter De Vries, 1954.

6635 I was seven years old before I understood the meaning of "bad" and "good," because it was at that time I noticed carefully that my father married three wives as they were doing in those days, if it is not common nowadays. —*My Life in the Bush of Ghosts*, Amos Tutuola, 1954.

6636 His mother who died delivering him, and his father who was killed in Mesopotamia, might have been figures in a legend as far as Sriram was concerned. — *Waiting for the Mahatma*, R. K. Narayan, 1955.

6637 My father was a stuffy man. — *The Temple of Gold*, William Goldman, 1957.

6638 My mother poured herself a second cup of coffee, which she had never taken at breakfast until the doctor suggested she give up coffee altogether, and frowned as she saw me fold my napkin. — *The Ring of Truth*, Josephine Lawrence, 1958.

6639 Two hours ago he had handed up his theological exam papers and here he was in the compartment of an almost empty train, hurrying home to see his mother who was ill. — *The Choice*, Michael McLaverty, 1958.

6640 They went off for the day and left him, in the slyest, sneakiest way you could imagine. —*Green Water, Green Sky*, Mavis Gallant, 1959.

6641 "Perhaps you will be the one to live," my mother said. — *Eva*, Meyer Levin, 1959.

6642 When I turned back to the house, my father called after me and asked me did I figure that I was finished. — *April Morning*, Howard Fast, 1961.

6643 I was a terrible father to my son, at least until it was too late for him to know otherwise. — *In Any Case*, Richard G. Stern, 1962.

6644 The father of the infant was a French peasant from Normandy. — *Naked Came I*, David Weiss, 1963.

6645 These two very old people are the father and mother of Mr. Bucket. Their names are Grandpa Joe and Grandma Josephine. — *Charlie and the Chocolate Factory*, Roald Dahl, 1964.

6646 Above the town, on the hill brow, the stone angel used to stand. I wonder if she stands there yet, in memory of her who relinquished her feeble ghost as I gained my stubborn one, my mother's angel that my father bought in pride to mark her bones and proclaim his dynasty, as he fancied, forever and a day. — *The Stone Angel*, Margaret Laurence, 1964.

6647 I was born in 1927, the only child of middle-class parents, both English, and themselves born in the grotesquely elongated shadow, which they never rose sufficiently above history to leave, of that monstrous dwarf Queen Victoria. — *The Magus*, John Fowles, 1965.

6648 Coming back along the forsaken shore, his feet crunching in the limpet shells, the stones still damp from the outgoing tide, and the gulls gone inland to forage in the reaped fields, he thought once again of his father and mother and resolved to write to them before the evening light had withdrawn from the sky. — *The Brightening Day*, Michael McLaverty, 1965.

6649 *When a son's blood is finally spilled, which mother weeps most? The old mother Europa? The new mother America? Katherine? Erden?* — *King of Spades*, Frederick Manfred, 1966.

6650 I was born in a cold city to a beautiful warm mother and a handsome father whose life began again every time he met a beautiful woman. — *Above Ground*, Jack Ludwig, 1968.

6651 She was so deeply imbedded in my consciousness that for the first year of school I seem to have believed that each of my teachers was my mother in disguise. — *Portnoy's Complaint*, Philip Roth, 1969.

6652 Then in June, 1932, on the second Saturday, a year exactly till Teitlebaum would start in with his signs ("President Roosevelt had a hundred days but you got only till this Monday to enjoy such savings on our Farm Girl pot cheese"), not long after the Workmen's Circle took out space in the *Coney Island Bulletin* urging total membership to stay away from French wines and perfumes until Léon Blum was restored to his parliament; also the same week Luna Park finished off a lousy season with a nice fire; a day after Ringelman, the Dentist, got his glasses broken by Mrs. Weigholtz for proposing certain advanced oral-hygiene treatments; around the time Harry the Fish Man's daughter, Fat Rosalie, gave away her father's beautiful little Schaeffer pen for a Suchard, the semi-sweet; not too long after Margoshes of the *Forvitz* ran this little item at the foot of his column: "Which hotsy-totsy Mexican actress should be called Amhoretz Del Rio for denying her Jewish blood?"; around the time Mrs. Faygelees kept calling and calling the *News* to find out when Elinor Ames would be using her question ("Should the son of a sick mother whose husband was put on a piecework basis have to pay for the Gravesend Avenue line transfer of a girl not from his faith?"); nine days since Block and Sully and Belle Baker were on the Rudy Vallee show; this also happening to be the day Gromajinski the Super, in a fit of drunken Polish rage, snipped every radio aerial on the roof of 2094 Brighton Beach Avenue; while Mrs. Aranow's Stanley was still telling the story of how he had been hailed at Grand Central Station by this fellow in a racoon coat and a straw skimmer; how this fellow finished off a whole hip flask during the thirty-five cent ride; how he put three dimes and five pennies into Stanley's palm; how Stanley had extended his arm, saying "Mister, we work for tips" or "Mister, we depend on tips"; how talking and talking of the cabbie's plight he kept this arm extended; how this fellow had smashed at the arm with a cruel-looking cane and said through his fat nose, "Godfrey Daniel, if there's one thing I can't stand it's a one-armed cabdriver!;" while Mary Mixup still had her share, and more than her share, from Bicep the Wrestler; even as Benny still could not get himself to drown his kittens; right after Smitty tried out for a job with Mr. Bailey;/ Simon Sloan, all rosy and redolent of matzo and milk, waited till his father, whiffing and chuffing and grumbling away in some old argument, fell into a fuddled snooze. Then with both hands busy Simon came rolling over on top of his mother, going "Lemme lemme!" — *Teitlebaum's Window*, Wallace Markfield, 1970.

6653 Sometimes I think Mother hits it right on the nose when she calls me a cold cookie. — *The Season of the Witch*, James Leo Herlihy, 1971.

6654 My father was a connoisseur of wine; but times and incomes change and we with them, and now I am a connoisseur of weather. — *The Innocents*, Margery Sharp, 1971.

6655 The father of the principal protagonist

of this book was called Umberto. — *G.*, John Berger, 1972.

6656 When I was but a mere youth my father instructed me, "Son, I don't care what you choose to do in life, but do it right." — *The Trials and Tribulations of Aaron Amsted*, Kenneth A. Lapatine, 1974.

6657 They are two lights. My mother and father. — *Anya*, Susan Fromberg Schaeffer, 1974.

6658 "Where's Mummy?" — *American Made*, Shylah Boyd, 1975.

6659 My father was one of the fittest men I have ever known. — *Johnno*, David Malouf, 1975.

6660 Ma lasted a year after Pa was gone. — *The Education of Little Tree*, Forrest Carter, 1976.

6661 So do I sign myself, remembering the small, wizened, modest man who gave me life, thinking thereby to give him in return a fame of which he never dreamed in all his sixty humble years as a farmer:/ *Amon-ho-tep, Son of Hapu*, risen very high and destined, as we all declare so stoutly on our tombs and monuments, to live forever and ever. . . . — *A God Against the Gods*, Allen Drury, 1976.

6662 "Edgar!" His father was calling again. — *Founder's Praise*, Joanne Greenberg, 1976.

6663 Neither of the Grimes sisters would have a happy life, and looking back it always seemed that the trouble began with their parents' divorce. — *The Easter Parade*, Richard Yates, 1976.

6664 Today my father brought home his new bride. They came clip-clop across the flats in a dog-cart drawn by a horse with an ostrich-plume waving on its forehead, dusty after the long haul. Or perhaps they were drawn by two plumed donkeys, that is also possible. — *From the Heart of the Country*, J. M. Coetzee, 1977.

6665 *"Tanaquil summo loco nata,"* her father liked to say to her. — *Tanaquil*, Donald Windham, 1977.

6666 Never having known a mother, her mother had died when Janey was a year old, Janey depended on her father for everything and regarded her father as boyfriend, brother, sister, money, amusement, and father. — *Blood and Guts in High School*, Kathy Acker, 1978.

6667 I had only one parent. — *A Heavy Feather*, A. L. Barker, 1978.

6668 I did not kill my father, but I sometimes felt I had helped him on his way. — *The Cement Garden*, Ian McEwan, 1978.

6669 My mother snatched the hat off her thick coils of dark hair and threw it triumphantly across the lawn. — *A Woman's Age*, Rachel Billington, 1979.

6670 So we got my mother back. — *The Ballad of T. Rantula*, Kit Reed, 1979.

6671 For as long as I can remember, my father hibernated. — *Consenting Adults*, Peter De Vries, 1980.

6672 They were hateful presences in me. — *Loon Lake*, E. L. Doctorow, 1980.

6673 Ray is thirty-three and he was born of decent religious parents, I say. — *Ray*, Barry Hannah, 1980.

6674 "He's a Mad Scientist and I'm his Beautiful Daughter." — *The Number of the Beast*, Robert A. Heinlein, 1980.

6675 "Have you cleaned your teeth and been to the lavatory?" — *Living Arrows*, Gillian Martin, 1980.

6676 Let them. Just let them investigate until they're blue in the face, and bring it all up again and embarrass my papa. — *The Scapegoat*, Mary Lee Settle, 1980.

6677 He never really knew his mother. — *Gor Saga*, Maureen Duffy, 1981.

6678 When Mauberley was twelve years old, his father took him onto the roof of the Arlington Hotel in Boston and said to him; "I've always loved the view from here. Cambridge across the river. The red bricks of Harvard. . . . The Swan Boats in the public garden. The gilded dome on Beacon Hill and all the people walking on the grass. . . ." — *Famous Last Words*, Timothy Findley, 1981.

6679 "So he didn't cut his nails, didn't he, well well! That's an odd father. Here's your cake," Thomas said. — *Against the Stream*, James Hanley, 1981.

6680 Hutchins Mayfield had stripped and faced the water, intending to enter before his father and stage the drowned-man act to greet him. — *The Source of Light*, Reynolds Price, 1981.

6681 Every other Friday, right after supper, Dad cocks his head at me and says, "It seems to me you're getting a bit shaggy, Marvin." — *One Smart Kid*, Edwin Moses, 1982.

6682 When Bentley's father threw him out, on discovering Bentley's leaning towards homosexuality, Bentley's father threw an ornament at him. — *Ancient Enemies*, Elizabeth North, 1982.

6683 My father is a coarse, charming man, a lawyer, and a good one, and when I was flying over the desert and the German pursuit pilot began pouring round after round into my plane (a P-40), I was thinking of how I learned to drive, and how it affected my father. — *The Good Son*, Craig Nova, 1982.

6684 At night here I often dream of my parents. — *Voice of Our Shadow*, Jonathan Carroll, 1983.

6685 In 1924, the year I was born, my parents purchased six hundred acres of land near Wolcott, Rhode Island. — *The Interloper*, Frank Milburn, 1983.

6686 When he is sick, every man wants his

mother; if she's not around, other women must do. — *The Anatomy Lesson*, Philip Roth, 1983.

6687 For four weeks she had been living in her parents' big bed—a king-size bed, extra long because her father was tall and had big feet. —*Alice in Bed*, Cathleen Schine, 1983.

6688 During the night my mother called to see me. — *Walg*, B. Wongar, 1983.

6689 I was my father yesterday. —*Almost Innocent*, Sheila Bosworth, 1984.

6690 Like many women, Daria both loved her mother and prayed not to become her. — *Fly Away Home*, Marge Piercy, 1984.

6691 From a corner Maddy Dow watched her father. —*Maddy's Song*, Margaret Dickson, 1985.

6692 Mercy Betters sat in a squat-legged position on the kitchen floor, scratching the underbelly of an almost-grown bassett puppy and staring up at the back side of her mother. —*First Light*, Emily Ellison, 1985.

6693 Dad?/ Where are you, dad? —*Adventures in the Alaskan Skin Trade*, John Hawkes, 1985.

6694 All the men were trying to kiss my mother, so I kept pulling at her dress for us to get away. —*Before My Life Began*, Jay Neugeboren, 1985.

6695 My mother came from a small town in Poland, my father from a small town in Maine. —*Davita's Harp*, Chaim Potok, 1985.

6696 "Not," says her mother, "how one thing leads to another. No, in your case, it's how one scheme leads to another." —*Mainland*, Susan Fromberg Schaeffer, 1985.

6697 I am Tarcisius Tandihetsi. You must have known Eustace, my father, he was the bravest chief in the two valleys. — *Mangled Hands*, Johnny Stanton, 1985.

6698 Gabriel's father—a silent, stubborn man, so wary that when asked to go for a walk he would avert his eyes and say, "I'll tell you my answer in a minute"—insisted that in the morning the boy conjugate verbs from the household's sole book, an unglued and incomplete sheaf of pages stuffed between boards the rain had warped, an animal had chewed, the sun had bleached from red to pink. — *Caracole*, Edmund White, 1985.

6699 "Merritt, did they say? Any relation to Alec Merritt?"/ "He's my father. I don't see him. They split when I was a child." —*Loyalties*, Raymond Williams, 1985.

6700 Like most people I lived for a long time with my mother and father. — *Oranges Are Not the Only Fruit*, Jeanette Winterson, 1985.

6701 When I was nine and already toughened to carry the burden of expectation people had of me in a life made precarious by my parents' incompetence to manage it, I lay in my bed one night listening to them damage each other down-

stairs, waiting for my little sister Portia to break down. — *Life Drawing*, Emily Arnold, 1986.

6702 *You do not want to see this but you do: a woman in a tight green skirt, in nylons and shoe boots, a woman who looks very tired and worn for twenty-nine, is kissing her newborn child good-bye.* —*A Period of Confinement*, Moira Crone, 1986.

6703 Sudie's mama told her to stay off the tracks. —*Sudie*, Sara Flanigan, 1986.

6704 Once, when he was still a small boy, his mother showed him the Guardians. —*Singletusk*, Björn Kurtén, 1986.

6705 Our father doesn't go to church with us but we're all downstairs in the hall at the same time, bumbling, getting ready to go. —*Monkeys*, Susan Minot, 1986.

6706 My name is Max Darrigan./ My mother died in the first year of my life. I killed her, I'm sure, though no one has ever accused me of it. — *New Jersey*, Joseph Monninger, 1986.

6707 Krippendorf sat on the edge of his daughter's bed, sniffing through a pile of her multicoloured knickers. *Krippendorf's Tribe*, Frank Parkin, 1986.

6708 "One night, just as we left the cemetery gate, my mother, dressed all in black for one of those family funerals, gave me a strong push from behind...." —*Stalin's Shoe*, Zdena Tomin, 1986.

6709 "Where's Dad?" Charles, eleven, tugged at his mom's sleeve. —*Five Hundred Scorpions*, Shelby Hearon, 1987.

6710 "Go entertain Daddy," she said, leaning back against the glass doors in her cross-strapped sundress. —*Baby Teeth*, Blythe Holbrooke, 1987.

6711 Irreversible coma. Elaina—my mother—will tell you, I've never been anything but trouble. —*Extraordinary Means*, Donna Levin, 1987.

6712 On the eve of his seventy-seventh birthday Gulban told his four sons that he wished to see them in his room at eleven the following morning. — *The Red Men*, Patrick McGinley, 1987.

6713 Tamsen stopped inscribing the initials *R.W.* in the dust and instead watched her father descend the hillside into the Valley. —*Flowering Mimosa*, Natalie L. M. Petesch, 1987.

6714 Rumor was her mother was in California. —*Home Movie*, Ellen Akins, 1988.

6715 At the beginning of the summer I had lunch with my father, the gangster, who was in town for the weekend to transact some of his vague business. — *The Mysteries of Pittsburgh*, Michael Chabon, 1988.

6716 Dildo, that's what my old man called me. —*Outside Providence*, Peter Farrelly, 1988.

6717 Some weeks after he left the paper, where he had mostly been doing obits the last year, he found himself bringing the dead back to

life. His father, dead almost fifty years, was first. — *The Age of Wonder*, Michael Grieg, 1988.

6718 Perhaps I should describe Bert, my father, first. — *The White Cutter*, David Pownall, 1988.

6719 Michael Page stands at the window of the parsonage, watching his father. — *The Preacher's Boy*, Terry Pringle, 1988.

6720 This mania for finding your real parents, I've never bought it. I mean, once you're over eighteen, your family is who you decide it should be. — *White Horse Cafe*, Roberta Smoodin, 1988.

6721 "Ah, mother," Alida cried, "you never understand me!" — *On Her Own*, Naomi Bliven, 1989.

6722 Alice, a sturdy, steely haired woman of fifty-one, stood on the pavement waving good-bye to the last of her three children to leave home. — *Alice Alone*, Amanda Brookfield, 1989.

6723 Busy said that after Jennifer was born, she was taken in to see Daddy every morning. — *Daddy Boy*, Carey Cameron, 1989.

6724 Emily recognized the woman's brocade purse before she recognized her face. She knew this wasn't much of an accomplishment; the owner of the purse was her mother, Francine. — *Red Whiskey Blues*, Denise Gess, 1989.

6725 "Why can't the father, the father of your — what I mean is why can't he do something?"/ "I've told you, he's dead." — *My Father's Moon*, Elizabeth Jolley, 1989.

6726 My father was forty-seven when I was born. — *Quite the Other Way*, Kaylie Jones, 1989.

6727 "Mister Deck, are you my stinkin' Daddy?" a youthful, female, furious voice said into the phone. — *Some Can Whistle*, Larry McMurtry, 1989.

6728 I had often heard it said that Aunt Letty broke her father's heart when she married a heathen she'd met at the All India Medical Arts Institute. — *In the Forest at Midnight*, Rita Pratt Smith, 1989.

6729 "Get real," Cora says when I ask her how long she thinks Daddy will stay in the BOQ. — *My Father's Geisha*, James Gordon Bennett, 1990.

6730 When Rollin Thompkins was born on the third of December 1955 in New York City, her father tapped on the viewing window with a quarter and waved wildly until the nurse hurried out and told him to please put out the cigarette. — *Swallow Hard*, Sarah Gaddis, 1990.

6731 My father was not like most other fathers I knew. — *Hardscrub*, Lionel G. Garcia, 1990.

6732 My biological mother was seventeen when she had me in 1952, and even that was more than I wanted to know about her. — *Then She Found Me*, Elinor Lipman, 1990.

6733 My mother was bragging about having children, all by herself and at the age of twenty-four, from Maine to Florida, where my father was stationed in the army. — *Extraordinary People*, Paul Gervais, 1991.

6734 When I was seven years old, my mother decided I should have piano lessons. — *Skating in the Dark*, David Michael Kaplan, 1991.

6735 My father was a missionary murdered in Burundi in 1956. It was very much his own fault. — *Goodness*, Tim Parks, 1991.

6736 Whenever my mother talks to me, she begins the conversation as if we were already in the middle of an argument. — *The Kitchen God's Wife*, Amy Tan, 1991.

6737 Her first memory of pain was an image of her mother. — *Women of the Silk*, Gail Tsukiyama, 1991.

6738 "Now Papa..." my mother began, looking directly at me, and I waited for her to reach my name as she called the roll of the men in her life. — *Winter Return*, John Espey, 1992.

6739 By the time he was four, Burl knew his father was a little bad, and his mother very good. — *The Storm Season*, William Hauptman, 1992.

6740 I am taller than my mother, although not very much so, perhaps an inch, certainly not more. — *I Am Zoë Handke*, Eric Larsen, 1992.

6741 Mothers, like elephants, must always remember. — *The Names of the Mountains*, Reeve Lindbergh, 1992.

6742 Ever since I lost mine in a road accident when I was eight, I have had my eye on other people's parents. — *Black Dogs*, Ian McEwan, 1992.

6743 As a baby, Tom Avery had twenty-seven mothers. — *The Republic of Love*, Carol Shields, 1992.

6744 She was supposed to sit quietly with her mother in the slatted shadows of the wooden stand, learning to make better baskets than the clumsy-started circle that could still fit into her palm. — *I Been in Sorrow's Kitchen and Licked Out All the Pots*, Susan Straight, 1992.

6745 Mothers don't hurt children, then who does? — *Secret Words*, Jonathan Strong, 1992.

6746 I never knew my mother had a lover. — *Merry-Go-Round*, Joyce Thompson, 1992.

6747 I remember thinking that the last thing on my mind ought to be my mother. — *Replacing Dad*, Shelley Fraser Mickle, 1993.

6748 "You will marry a boy I choose," said Mrs. Rupa Mehra firmly to her younger daughter. — *A Suitable Boy*, Vikram Seth, 1993.

6749 I was born to Eastern European parents who never quite mastered the curious language Americans spoke. — *Temptations*, Paul Wilkes, 1993.

6750 "I pray every night that you do not go to law school," her mother said, as Lizzie perused the help-wanted section upon her somewhat inglorious return to Westchester County the February of 1974.— *The Year Roger Wasn't Well*, Sarah Payne Stuart, 1994.

Parties

6751 "Are you to be at Lady Clonbrony's gala next week?" said Lady Langdale to Mrs. Dareville, whilst they were waiting for their carriages in the crush-room of the opera-house./ "Oh, yes! every body's to be there, I hear," replied Mrs. Dareville. "Your ladyship, of course?"—"The Absentee," Maria Edgeworth, 1812.

6752 The hall of the banquets was made ready for the feast in the palace of Babylon. That night Belshazzar the king would drink wine with a thousand of his lords, and be merry before them; and everything was made ready.— *Zoroaster*, F. Marion Crawford, 1885.

6753 From his place on the floor of the Hemenway Gymnasium Mr. Elbridge Mavering looked on at the Class Day gayety with the advantage which his stature gave him over most people there.— *April Hopes*, William Dean Howells, 1887.

6754 It was an occasion, I felt—the prospect of a large party—to look out at the station for others, possible friends and even possible enemies, who might be going.— *The Sacred Fount*, Henry James, 1901.

6755 Sally looked contentedly down the long table. She felt happy at last. Everybody was talking and laughing now, and her party, rallying after an uncertain start, was plainly the success she had hoped it would be.— *The Adventures of Sally*, P. G. Wodehouse, 1922.

6756 If you can picture a little park, bright for the moment with the flush of early summer flowers and peopled with men and women in the costumes of the late nineties—If you can picture such a park set down in the midst of an inferno of fire, steel and smoke, there is no need to describe Cypress Hill on the afternoon of the garden party for the Governor.— *The Green Bay Tree*, Louis Bromfield, 1924.

6757/6758 There was a ball in the old Pentland house because for the first time in nearly forty years there was a young girl in the family to be introduced to the polite world of Boston and to the elect who had been asked to come on from New York and Philadelphia.— *Early*

Autumn, Louis Bromfield, 1926.

6759 Sylvester was giving a party./ His guests toiled up flight upon flight of dark stairs.— *Devoted Ladies*, Molly Keane *as* M. J. Farrell, 1934.

6760 In the year 1901, it was the custom at Harvard for seniors to entertain the incoming freshmen at "beer nights," where crackers and cheese and beer, to those who drank, and ginger ale, to those who did not drink, were served.— *Islandia*, Austin Tappan Wright, 1942.

6761 There was something about a fête which drew Arthur Rowe irresistibly, bound him a helpless victim to the distant blare of a band and the knock-knock of wooden balls against coconuts.— *The Ministry of Fear*, Graham Greene, 1943.

6762 I went to the Rankes' party because I hoped Diana would be there.— *The Immaterial Murder Case*, Julian Symons, 1945.

6763 I first met Pauline Delos at one of those substantial parties Earl Janoth liked to give every two or three months, attended by members of the staff, his personal friends, private moguls, and public nobodies, all in haphazard rotation.— *The Big Clock*, Kenneth Fearing, 1946.

6764 The party, that evening, was at the Novotnys'.— *The World in the Evening*, Christopher Isherwood, 1954.

6765 Even Camilla had enjoyed masquerades, of the safe sort where the mask may be dropped at that critical moment it presumes itself as reality.— *The Recognitions*, William Gaddis, 1955.

6766 Everyone knew the party was for someone, but no one quite knew for whom.— *Get Ready for Battle*, Ruth Prawer Jhabvala, 1962.

6767 A dozen years ago, before the Fifties were as fat and foolish as they would eventually become, and people still believed the new decade was going to be a continuation of the wild postwar years, there was an autumn of bad parties in New York, most of which May and Verger attended.— *Get Home Free*, John Clellon Holmes, 1964.

6768 "The Secret of a Successful At Home is Precise and Particular Preparation. There are three things which must be Prepared (1) The Food and Drink, (2) The Surroundings, (3) The People...."— *Miss Owen-Owen*, Margaret Forster, 1969.

6769 In the early summer of 1939 the American Jewish Defense Agency—known as AJDA—celebrated its fortieth anniversary. A gala dinner was held in the second-floor banquet room of the Plaza Hotel.— *The Voyage of the Franz Joseph*, James Yaffe, 1970.

6770 As the last party-guests were groping their way into the blackout, I belted upstairs and

shut myself in my bedroom. — *A Soldier Erect*, Brian W. Aldiss, 1971.

6771 It had been the most wonderful party, all the better because nobody expected it to happen — no party at all had been planned or intended. — *The Snare*, Elizabeth Spencer, 1972.

6772 What the celebration at the castle had been, Austin Grey never discovered. — *Checkmate*, Dorothy Dunnett, 1975.

6773 In the Cordova Hotel, near the docks of Barcelona, fourteen Marine Corps fighter pilots from the aircraft carrier *Forrestal* were throwing an obstreperously spirited going away party for Lieutenant Colonel Bull Meecham, the executive officer of their carrier based squadron. — *The Great Santini*, Pat Conroy, 1976.

6774 The people on Fieldstone Road in Wellesley, Massachusetts, celebrated the bombing of Pearl Harbor with an enormous party. — *Ice Brothers*, Sloan Wilson, 1979.

6775 Here we all are again, thought Nell Strickland, entering the party on the arm of her husband. — *A Mother and Two Daughters*, Gail Godwin, 1982.

6776 "The last place to have a ball, my dear Mrs. DelBelly, is at a formal dance. Or such I myself have found to be the case." — *Peckham's Marbles*, Peter De Vries, 1986.

6777 Fred Tatter's dinner party was about to begin. — *Hot Properties*, Rafael Yglesias, 1986.

6778 You were at a party when your father died — and immediately you were told, a miracle happened. — *The Sound of My Voice*, Ron Butlin, 1987.

6779 The Fiores were giving a ball, a celebration of the liberation of Paris from the Germans. — *Sons and Daughters*, Stephen Longstreet, 1987.

6780 The difference between American and English cocktail parties was the aroma of the cigarette smoke. — *A Time to Sing*, Sally Mandel, 1989.

6781 At a cocktail party in a downtown complex — it's chock full of folks as far as the eye can see, in the atrium (where I'm on duty as guest) and up on peripheral floor overhead with Urban Professnulls poised at porticos that pockmark the balcony. — *Muse-Echo Blues*, Xam Cartiér, 1991.

6782 Right now I'm supposed to be all geeked up because I'm getting ready for a New Year's Eve party that some guy named Lionel invited me to. — *Waiting to Exhale*, Terry McMillan, 1992.

6783 So here she was, on Wednesday, October 9, 1957, about to strip off her Pig-Pen costume consisting of dried-muddy sweatshirt and Levi's, in a bathroom in a sleazy motel across the Vermont line in New York, with a little party going on outside the bathroom door whose lock didn't work, her roommate and her roommate's date and her own impromptu date lolling around watching loud TV and imbibing rum-and-Cokes out of paper cups. — *Snowy*, Ruth Doan MacDougall, 1993.

The Past

6784 "I sometimes think that one's past life is written in a foreign language," said Mrs. Bowring, shutting the book she held, but keeping the place with one smooth, thin forefinger, while her still, blue eyes turned from her daughter's face towards the hazy hills that hemmed the sea thirty miles to the southward. — *Adam Johnstone's Son*, F. Marion Crawford, 1895.

6785 It was many years ago. — *The Man That Corrupted Hadleyburg*, Mark Twain, 1900.

6786 The past is a scene from which the light is slowly fading. — *A Richer Dust*, Storm Jameson, 1931.

6787 I was never one to begrudge people their memories. From a child I would listen when they spoke of the past. — *Time Out of Mind*, Rachel Field, 1935.

6788 "Yes, I knew him," I said, "but it was years ago — in England..." — *Nothing So Strange*, James Hilton, 1947.

6789 The past is a foreign country: they do things differently there. — *The Go-Between*, L. P. Hartley, 1953.

6790 I made up my mind that I would not see Iris Allbright again, not after so many years. I do not like looking back down the chasm of the past and seeing, in a moment of vertigo, some terror that looks like a joy, some joy crouched like a terror. — *An Impossible Marriage*, Pamela Hansford Johnson, 1954.

6791 Night is the time to escape from the past, for then all illusions of safety are most easily created, most easily believed, and a secure future beckons as it does not in the harsh light of day. — *The Fourth Horseman of Miami Beach*, Albert Halper, 1966.

6792 How can you tell the legend from the fact on these worlds that lie so many years away? — planets without names, called by their people simply The World, planets without history, where the past is a matter of myth, and a returning explorer finds his own doings of a few years back have become the gestures of a god. — *Rocannon's World*, Ursula K. Le Guin, 1966.

6793 At forty-one, Elizabeth Aidallbery had a way of dwelling on her past, and when memories

were doubtful there were photographs to help her. — *Elizabeth Alone*, William Trevor, 1973.

6794 I have never been one to return much to my own past. — *A Stolen Past*, John Knowles, 1983.

6795 Severance from the past was handled with a little pay. — *The Woman Who Escaped from Shame*, Toby Olson, 1986.

6796 On the day he lost his right foot, Walter Van Brunt had been haunted, however haphazardly, by ghosts of the past. — *World's End*, T. Coraghessan Boyle, 1987.

6797 It had been my intention to tell the story of Nicholas. But, unbidden, my own past intruded and in searching out my brother, I, also, discover myself. — *The Birthmark*, Dorothea Straus, 1987.

6798 "Not even God can change the past," Walter Hunsicker had once read somewhere, and after living almost six decades in which virtually every other supposedly unassailable truth had been successfully challenged (how soon would the techniques of cloning make death obsolete?; tax evaders were legion; often it was better *not* to have loved . . . etc.), he assumed this adage was sound as ever and would surely persist in being so unto infinity. — *Changing the Past*, Thomas Berger, 1989.

6799 Yes. I have returned to the past. — *English Music*, Peter Ackroyd, 1992.

6800 Leila Aluja had never been curious about her own past because the present was always so exciting. — *The Venerable Bead*, Richard Condon, 1992.

6804 We learned in childhood that appearances are deceitful, and our subsequent scrambling about upon this whirling globe has convinced many of us that the most deceptive of all appearances are those of peace. — *Women*, Booth Tarkington, 1925.

6805 An army post in peacetime is a dull place. — *Reflections in a Golden Eye*, Carson McCullers, 1941.

6806 Jashimpur had been invaded so often in the past that a long period of peaceful semi-slavery, even in steadily increasing poverty, had been welcomed by the Jashimpuri people, until the cold winds of reason began to blow into the valleys after the first world war. — *The Journey Homeward*, Gerald Hanley, 1961.

6807 "The Mass in English, *Lolita* in Latin, that's the recipe for peace in our time," Father Guardian said — the Superior had a bee in his bonnet about liturgy. — *Father Hilary's Holiday*, Bruce Marshall, 1965.

6808 The motto was "Pax," but the word was set in a circle of thorns. — *In This House of Brede*, Rumer Godden, 1969.

6809 "Peace," said Mrs. Armitage. She raised her glass of water. She, if anyone, could transform it to wine. — *A State of Peace*, Janice Elliott, 1971.

6810 "On this day of real peace in our time . . ."/ Magog put the raw steak on his left eye and winced. — *Magog*, Andrew Sinclair, 1972.

6811 The years immediately following the war were fertile for weeds. — *Leaving the Land*, Douglas Unger, 1984.

Peace

6801 Bright was the summer of 1296. The war which had desolated Scotland was then at an end. — *The Scottish Chiefs*, Jane Porter, 1810.

6802 The Chronicles, from which this narrative is extracted, assure us, that during the long period when the Welsh princes maintained their independence, the year 1187 was peculiarly marked as favorable to peace betwixt them and their warlike neighbors, the Lords Marchers, who inhabited those formidable castles on the frontiers of the ancient British, on the ruins of which the traveller gazes with wonder. — *The Betrothed*, Sir Walter Scott, 1825.

6803 The provisional articles of peace, between the King of Great Britain, and the revolted colonies of America, were signed at Paris, on the 13th November, 1782. — *Woodcraft*, William Gilmore Simms, 1854.

People

6812 A strenuous sense of justice is the most disturbing of all virtues, and those persons in whom it predominates are usually as disagreeable as they are good. — *A Forest Hearth*, Charles Major, 1903.

6813 The French, who hunted and traded on the western waters long before the first Virginian pioneers forced their way through the dense laurel and rhododendron of the Appalachian Mountains to the sylvan and perilous region beyond the Ouasioto Gap, called those later adventurous settlers Les Kaintocks. — *The Limestone Tree*, Joseph Hergesheimer, 1931.

6814 That lusty pioneer blood is tamed now, broken and gelded like the wild horse and the frontier settlement. — *The Sea of Grass*, Conrad Richter, 1937.

6815 Well, they are all gone now, all but me:

all those clear-eyed, clear-thinking people — people with their heads in the clouds and their feet firmly on the ground — who comprise the editorial staff of the Pacific City *Courier*. — *The Nothing Man*, Jim Thompson, 1954.

6816 Not human. Forget about human. It's too restricting. Think of something else. — *The Outer Mongolian*, David R. Slavitt, 1973.

6817 Cripples, one-eyed people, pregnant women: we are all the children of eggs, Miss Miller, we are all the children of eggs. — *Blown Figures*, Audrey Thomas, 1974.

6818 You won't find ordinary people here. — *Running Dog*, Don DeLillo, 1978.

6819 People like us don't appear in *People* Magazine. — *The House Next Door*, Anne Rivers Siddons, 1978.

6820 The Tame Wa are like pye-dogs, they will slink and snarl and grin for a bone. But the Wild Wa dwell high upon the mountain and smile for no man. — *The Blue-Eyed Shan*, Stephen Becker, 1982.

6821 Everyone knows three boring facts about Eskimos. I'll tell you another. — *Dolly and the Nanny Bird*, Dorothy Dunnett, 1982.

6822 "What you think is so different 'bout them?" — *Almost Family*, Roy Hoffman, 1983.

6823 "And don't forget," my father would say, as if he expected me at any moment to up and leave to seek my fortune in the wide world, "whatever you learn about people, however bad they turn out, each one of them has a heart, and each one of them was once a tiny baby sucking his mother's milk..." — *Waterland*, Graham Swift, 1983.

6824 On a Monday morning in October, Arnie Carrington went into a drugstore in Gulfport, Mississippi, and saw the one person he least wanted to see. — *The Salt Line*, Elizabeth Spencer, 1984.

6825 First of all there is Blue. — *Ghosts*, Paul Auster, 1986.

6826 Sometimes, when I see people like Rose, I imagine them as babies, as young children. — "Rose," Andre Dubus, 1986.

6827 At first the faces were a blur, but then he was able to identify the people who owned them. — *Reckless Eyeballing*, Ishmael Reed, 1986.

6828 There are, according to the latest census, two hundred thirty-seven million people in this country. — *White Light*, Patricia Volk, 1987.

6829 There is a heart in Chicago the size of a small house, a cottage and a fairy tale, with a door and six steps — one way in, no exit. — *Recent History*, Annette Williams Jaffee, 1988.

6830 With a single exception they were all white. And with five exceptions all male. — *Doctors*, Erich Segal, 1988.

6831 Some people came here on purpose, but for most it was by chance. — *Small Tales of a Town*, Susan Webster, 1988.

6832 Nobody was in a hurry here. — *The Consequences of Loving Syra*, Margaret Howe Freydberg, 1990.

6833 Mother Ann:/ I am a member of the world's people. — *The Divine Comedy of John Venner*, Gregory Blake Smith, 1992.

6834 According to Charles Townsend Mather, the mulatto was dark amber in colour and grey-haired and nearly blind. — *Sacred Hunger*, Barry Unsworth, 1992.

Philosophy

6835 "I am a realist," said Mr. Edmund Lushington, as if that explained everything. — *Fair Margaret*, F. Marion Crawford, 1905.

6836 "The cow is there," said Ansell, lighting a match and holding it out over the carpet. — *The Longest Journey*, E. M. Forster, 1907.

6837 Clifton Brant believed himself to be only one of innumerable flying grains of human dust in a world gone mad. — *The Ancient Highway*, James Oliver Curwood, 1925.

6838 A philosopher stood at the microphone of a radio station, a place to which philosophers are not often enough invited. — *The Return of Lanny Budd*, Upton Sinclair, 1953.

6839 I first discovered solipsism on a winter night just before Christmas, and it nearly scared me to death. — *Shadow of a Tiger*, Clyde Brion Davis, 1963.

6840 Me? What am I? Nothing. — *The Condor Passes*, Shirley Ann Grau, 1971.

6841 I am, therefore I think. — *Birchwood*, John Banville, 1973.

6842 This world is the unreality, he thinks between smiles and frowns over the letter. — *A Kindness Cup*, Thea Astley, 1974.

6843 The world is what it is; men who are nothing, who allow themselves to become nothing, have no place in it. — *A Bend in the River*, V. S. Naipaul, 1979.

6844 "Wittgenstein — —"/ "Yes?" said the Count. — *Nuns and Soldiers*, Iris Murdoch, 1980.

6845 "Mother," the kid once said, "has revised and updated Descartes. She despairs, therefore she is." — *Almost Famous*, David Small, 1982.

6846 You are all you have. — *Payofski's Dyscovery*, Hal Marden, 1986.

6847 Nothing is new, only freshly painted. — *Excelsior*, Randall Silvis, 1988.

6848 I don't know about Will Rogers, but I

grew up deciding the world was nothing but a sad, dangerous junk pile heaped with shabby geegaws, the bullies who peddled them, and the broken-up human beings who worked the line. — *Time's Witness*, Michael Malone, 1989.

Photographs

6849 The snapshots had become almost as dim as memories. — *Eyeless in Gaza*, Aldous Huxley, 1936.

6850 There is a photograph in existence of Aunt Sadie and her six children sitting around the tea-table at Alconleigh. — *The Pursuit of Love*, Nancy Mitford, 1945.

6851 Bill Martin gazed at the framed photographs of his wife Ethel and his five-year-old son, Jackie, which he kept on the right-hand corner of his desk. — *Invisible Swords*, James T. Farrell, 1971.

6852 The photograph definitely had never been there before. — *Mrs. 'Arris Goes to Moscow*, Paul Gallico, 1975.

6853 There was a photograph of Frank in an ad that ran in the *Detroit Free Press* and showed all the friendly salesmen at Red Bowers Chevrolet. — *Swag*, Elmore Leonard, 1976.

6854 The photograph album on the table beside the window lay on a brown velvet cloth and was the inseparable companion of the geranium. — *Farewell Companions*, James Plunkett, 1977.

6855 There is a photograph of the boy that shows him at age ten. — *Aberration of Starlight*, Gilbert Sorrentino, 1980.

6856 Jamie was still working at midnight, hanging the matted enlargements on every available inch of wall space, using double-faced Scotch tape for the plaster surfaces and pushpins for the old wooden beams. — *Love, Dad*, Evan Hunter, 1981.

6857 Here is the picture that haunts me the most: the two of them sitting in her garden, with me between them. — *Imaginary Crimes*, Sheila Ballantyne, 1982.

6858 "He's been taking pictures three years, look at the work," Maurice said. — *LaBrava*, Elmore Leonard, 1983.

6859 Page Garrity found his grandmother in the attic, slumped and skewed like an oversize rag doll, in an old rattan rocker; yellowed, scalloped-edged photographs scattered at her feet, spilling from her lap, clutched in her hands. — *Gideon's House*, Jean Brody, 1984.

6860 Dexter found, in a magazine, a photograph of the poet Tennyson, his wife and their two sons walking in the garden of their house on the Isle of Wight. — *The Children's Bach*, Helen Garner, 1984.

6861 There is a picture of my mother that she keeps tucked away in her old scrapbook, yellowed pages pressing crumbled corsages, letters, gum wrappers. — *The Cheer Leader*, Jill McCorkle, 1984.

6862 My first exposure to him was through a photograph, one the monks found tucked in with the wadding of the pillow I lay on when I came to them. — *Confessions of a Taoist on Wall Street*, David Payne, 1984.

6863 Elizabeth Waters, standing on the front porch of her father's house, opened the Halloween issue of the *Lakeview Daily Citizen* to a picture that looked exactly like her husband, who, according to a telegram from President Roosevelt, had died at the invasion of Normandy. — *Dreaming of Heroes*, Susan Richards Shreve, 1984.

6864 Ali Glazer was stitching up her husband's trouser hems, but had paused to glance up at the kitchen pinboard in some fascination. The photograph of a man, bearing a disconcerting resemblance to Thomas Adderley, had been torn from a Sunday magazine advertisement and pinned there by Ali's older daughter Camilla. — *Noah's Ark*, Barbara Trapido, 1984.

6865 Here is Sofka, in a wedding photograph; at least, I assume it is a wedding, although the bride and groom are absent. — *Family and Friends*, Anita Brookner, 1985.

6866 Three men against three tanks with only a bridge between them and Madrid. She brought the Leica into focus on the men and she left the tanks out of focus, finding an image that seemed as hopeless as the struggle. — *Comrades*, Clive Irving, 1986.

6867 Once, I remember, in an entirely different world, I interviewed that East Coast photographer who made a good living taking pictures of people as they jumped. — *Golden Days*, Carolyn See, 1987.

6868 At first glance, the picture looked like any other in a family album of that time, the sepia shade and tone, the formal poses, the men in solemn Sunday suits and the women, severely coiffed, in long skirts and billowing blouses. — *Fade*, Robert Cormier, 1988.

6869 Beauty is not in the eye of the beholder, as they say, but in the lens of the camera. — *Whistlejacket*, John Hawkes, 1988.

6870 The beano always ends with the photograph on the station. — *The Beano*, Rony Robinson, 1988.

6871 I found a photograph of Marshall inside one of his shoes in the closet. — *Elysian Fields*, Sally Savic, 1988.

6872 Check out the mug shot. — *Making It*, Oliver Lange, 1989.

6873 Tonio said, "Remember I was going to show you some pictures?" — *Gringa*, Sandra Scofield, 1989.

6874 This is a picture which I took of him myself. — *Ready to Catch Him Should He Fall*, Neil Bartlett, 1990.

6875 Click. From where I was sitting on the bumper of the Winnebago I was doing my utmost to outstare that camera of hers, but as usual, no such luck. — *Ride with Me, Mariah Montana*, Ivan Doig, 1990.

6876 We are a photograph, the same photograph of every year with me a summer older, so a summer taller: lanky Joan, outgrowing the world around her. — *Joanna*, Lisa St. Aubin de Terán, 1990.

6877 I always found having my picture taken with members of the public a frankly grim and, in the end, even a distressing experience. — *Alma*, Gordon Burn, 1991.

6878 One particular photograph best shows the difference between Victor and myself. — *First Confession*, Montserrat Fontes, 1991.

6879 My grandfather is belly down in the meadow with his camera, taking a close-up of a cow pie. — *Journey*, Patricia MacLachlan, 1991.

6880 One morning years ago, near Socorro, New Mexico, I photographed a Peregrine Falcon in midair. — *Language in the Blood*, Kent Nelson, 1991.

6881 On the wall in his private study at home there was an old black-and-white photograph of his father. The picture was taken on the outskirts of Seoul, Korea, in September 1950, just after the Inchŏn landing. — *Something to Die For*, James Webb, 1991.

6882 In the upper right hand corner of the photo is a miniature airplane that looks as if it is flying right into my forehead. — *Songs of the Humpback Whale*, Jodi Picoult, 1992.

6883 PHOTOGRAPHS ARE NOT MEMORIES. . . / For a long time my mother and I lived such a solitary life, city-trapped and economically precarious, so isolated from anything resembling family or stability, so utterly dependent on one another to provide a lovable human universe, that the existence of forebears, documented in hundreds of photographs — brown as leaves and dog-eared, but vivid, stylized, ornate, above all theatrical — seems to me even now a kind of fairy tale, not only in relation to what then seemed plausible but even in the terms in which it was cast. — *The Furies*, Janet Hobhouse, 1993.

Physicians

6884 The exquisitely beautiful portrait which the Rambler has painted of his friend Levett, well describes Gideon Gray, and many other village doctors, from whom Scotland reaps more benefit, and to whom she is perhaps more ungrateful than to any other class of men, excepting her schoolmasters. — *The Surgeon's Daughter*, Sir Walter Scott, 1827.

6885 Before the reader is introduced to the modest country medical practitioner who is to be the chief personage of the following tale, it will be well that he should be made acquainted with some particulars as to the locality in which, and the neighbours among whom, our doctor followed his profession. — *Doctor Thorne*, Anthony Trollope, 1858.

6886 In the year 18— I settled as a physician at one of the wealthiest of our great English towns, which I will designate by the initial L— —. — *A Strange Story*, Edward Bulwer Lytton, 1862.

6887 Dr. Malachi Finn had obtained a wide reputation as a country practitioner in the west of Ireland. — *Phineas Finn*, Anthony Trollope, 1869.

6888 The men from the *Marblehead* looked up from their cots and wondered what the doctor would be like. — *The Story of Dr. Wassell*, James Hilton, 1943.

6889 Doctor Stevens was leaning back in his desk chair and looking at his patient through his spectacles. — *The Bradshaws of Harniss*, Joseph C. Lincoln, 1943.

6890 That an able-minded man in his late forties could be made morally bilious by a dear innocent child of four or five, and that for years such a man, a family doctor, would return to that condition whenever he thought of that child, overtaxes credulity; but the thing has happened. — *The Show-Piece (Unfinished)*, Booth Tarkington, 1947.

6891 "All right, you can get dressed now," Matthews said. — *Angell, Pearl and Little God*, Winston Graham, 1970.

6892 Her gynecologist recommended him to me. Ironic: the best urologist in New York is French. Dr. Jean Claude Vigneron: ONLY BY APPOINTMENT. So I made one. — *The Water-Method Man*, John Irving, 1972.

6893 A nurse held the door open for them. Judge McKelva going first, then his daughter Laurel, then his wife Fay, they walked into the windowless room where the doctor would make his examination. — *The Optimist's Daughter*, Eudora Welty, 1972.

6894 Daniel Behenna, physician and surgeon, was forty years old and lived in a square, detached, untidy house in Goodwives Lane, Truro. He was himself square in build and detached in manner, but not at all unkempt, since the citizens of the town and district paid well for the benefit of his modern physical knowledge. — *The Four Swans*, Winston Graham, 1976.

6895 "When that breast comes up, get a bit for me, please." — *The Greatest Breakthrough Since Lunchtime*, Colin Douglas, 1979.

6896 Every three weeks, Grosbeck went to his doctor, less the valetudinarian than an English tripper on a low-fare excursion to the Delphic Oracle: sweating; half determined to sneer, half to believe; adding up the expense in his head (the brain so many bits of torn paper with figures on them that didn't add up); looking intently in the waiting room at a huge nineteenth-century German lithograph. — *God and Harvey Grosbeck*, Gilbert Millstein, 1983.

6897 Dr. Lulu Shinefeld opened the door to her waiting room and said hello to the girl who was scheduled for a consultation. — *August*, Judith Rossner, 1983.

6898 Dr. Hendrik Richters could best be described as a radiantly bad physician. — *Star of Peace*, Jan de Hartog, 1984.

6899 He waited for the innocent moment when it would hurt least. Because in nine cases out of ten it was going to hurt. — *August Break*, Edith Heal, 1984.

6900 The tiny doctor, hidden by tinted European eyeglasses, rose from her desk to face the windows. — *Descent from Xanadu*, Harold Robbins, 1984.

6901 For several years a Scottish physician named Kenneth Ayres, popularly known as "Honeydew" Ayres, had made his living from British expatriates in the International Settlement and, more particularly, from travellers stopping at the Astor House Hotel. — *Julia Paradise*, Rod Jones, 1986.

6902 Maybe you wouldn't believe it to look at me, but my grandad was a doctor. — *The River in Winter*, David Small, 1987.

Physics

6903 Oh, let us leave metaphysical conjectures for a time! It may be indeed that Time is one of the dimensions in space. — *Sixty Seconds*, Maxwell Bodenheim, 1929.

6904 Johannes Kepler, asleep in his ruff, has dreamed the solution to the cosmic mystery. — *Kepler*, John Banville, 1981.

6905 In a year, light travels six million million miles. — *Light Years*, Maggie Gee, 1985.

6906 There is a metaphysical law, and you can depend on metaphysical laws, that unity is a figment of the imagination. — *The Final Opus of Leon Solomon*, Jerome Badanes, 1988.

6907 *The grand unified theories*, Koenig writes, *are difficult to verify experimentally*. — *Charades*, Janette Turner Hospital, 1988.

Places

6908 Among all the provinces in Scotland, if an intelligent stranger were asked to describe the most varied and the most beautiful, it is probable he would name the county of Perth. — *The Fair Maid of Perth*, Sir Walter Scott, 1828.

6909 If places could speak, they would describe people far better than people can describe places. — *Paul Patoff*, F. Marion Crawford, 1887.

6910 There is a land where a man, to live, must be a man. — *When a Man's a Man*, Harold Bell Wright, 1916.

6911 This was where I used to come, as a child, for holidays. — *Charade*, John Mortimer, 1948.

6912 It had to be the place. There was the limestone bluff jutting abruptly up, crowned by cedars. It was bound to be the place. — *Flood*, Robert Penn Warren, 1964.

6913 "This is where we were to have spent the honeymoon," Eva Trout said, suddenly, pointing across the water. — *Eva Trout*, Elizabeth Bowen, 1968.

6914 In that place the wind prevailed. — *Bless the Beasts and Children*, Glendon Swarthout, 1970.

6915 The date (Old Calendar) was June 6, 2023, and the place, Faraway, New York, again in the Old Geography. — *The End of the Dream*, Philip Wylie, 1972.

6916 First of all, the place. — *Judgment Day*, Penelope Lively, 1980.

6917 "Years ago," the old man was speaking, his voice as soft as the river's easy breeze, "some folks allowed as how they's a kindly curious spot somewhere off down this here island. . . ." — *Hub*, Robert Herring, 1981.

6918 It is an actual place, although there is not much to market now except a mountain crossroads. — *Weedy Rough*, Douglas C. Jones, 1981.

6919 There is a special place behind the potting shed. — *To Have and to Hold*, Deborah Moggach, 1986.

6920 They call it the two-faced place in Genovese, and they are wary of its people. — *The Bay of Silence*, Lisa St. Aubin de Terán, 1986.

6921 Think of a place in the heart of nowhere. — *V for Victor*, Mark Childress, 1989.

6922 There are other places like it; our ancestors divined them. — *King of the Mountain*, Don Metz, 1990.

6923 About a mile to the north of the village of Rapstone there was an area of mixed woodland and uncultivated chalk downs. — *Titmuss Regained*, John Mortimer, 1990.

6924 The idea of the place was one thing. — *Memorial Bridge*, James Carroll, 1991.

6925 Orient Point, Long Island. It is very pleasant here. — *Sportsman's Paradise*, Nancy Lemann, 1992.

6926 First of all we need a place to stand. — *The Wrestler's Cruel Study*, Stephen Dobyns, 1993.

6927 Lou had a hard time finding this place. — "Game of Spirit," Jonathan Strong, 1993.

Plans

6928 In the month of June, 1872, Mr. Edward Lynde, the assistant cashier and bookkeeper of the Nautilus Bank at Rivermouth, found himself in a position to execute a plan which he had long meditated in secret. — *The Queen of Sheba*, Thomas Bailey Aldrich, 1877.

6929 "Well, mother, one thing is certain — something has got to be done. It is no use crying over spilled milk, that I can see. It is a horribly bad business, but grieving over it won't make it any better. What one has got to do is to decide on some plan or other, and then set to work to carry it out." — *Maori and Settler*, G. A. Henty, 1891.

6930 The young Frenchman did very well what he had planned to do. — *Monsieur Beaucaire*, Booth Tarkington, 1900.

6931 His plans had been running so beautifully, so goddamned beautifully, and now *she* was going to smash them all. — *A Kiss Before Dying*, Ira Levin, 1953.

6932 "Toulouse," says Vincent. "What are you going to do with your life?" — *The Adult Life of Toulouse Lautrec*, Kathy Acker, 1975.

6933 On the white beach of Hiva Oa, which looked toward the moonrise and the breakers on the outer reef, Kaloni Kienga the Navigator squatted under a palm tree and drew pictures in the sand. — *The Navigator*, Morris West, 1976.

6934 "All right," Nancy said. "What's everyone going to do today? First you, young lady." — *The Last Convertible*, Anton Myrer, 1978.

6935 Gordon McKay based his plan for a new city in the West on bees because of their energy. — *McKay's Bees*, Thomas McMahon, 1979.

6936 Quite how to go about doing it Clare could still not see, but the impression was strong with him that the doing would be important, might even be the rebeginning of his health. — *The Girl Green as Elderflower*, Randolph Stow, 1980.

6937 Some mornings my old man would sit on the edge of the bed with so many plans and so much energy he'd pick up the phone and dial seven numbers. Any numbers. — *Dixiana Moon*, William Price Fox, 1981.

6938 "Later we speak, O'Malley," Mister Dryden confided to me, climbing into the car that morning; I sat shotgun next to Jimmy, the driver. "I've a plan." — *Ambient*, Jack Womack, 1987.

6939 My uncle Oscar Carnovsky, my mother's brother, died last July even though we had planned a trip to Saratoga Springs in August, he and I, to see some racing. — *Carnovsky's Retreat*, Larry Duberstein, 1988.

6940 Looking back on the whole ghastly affair, what surprises me most is that when news of Gilbert's plan first reached me I felt no sense of foreboding whatsoever. — *Blue Heaven*, Joe Keenan, 1988.

6941 "Next year at this time, I want carpenters working on *our* house," Mama said. — *The Cape Ann*, Faith Sullivan, 1988.

6942 He had to have planned it because when we drove onto the dock the boat was there and the engine was running and you could see the water churning up phosphorescence in the river, which was the only light there was because there was no moon, nor no electric light either in the shack where the dockmaster should have been sitting, nor on the boat itself, and certainly not from the car, yet everyone knew where everything was, and when the big Packard came down the ramp Mickey the driver braked it so that the wheels hardly rattled the boards, and when he pulled up alongside the gangway the doors were already open and they hustled Bo and the girl upside before they even made a shadow in all that darkness. — *Billy Bathgate*, E. L. Doctorow, 1989.

6943 "Whadda you wanna do, young blood?" Table Legs says, leaning against the house counter, picking his gold front teeth with a toothpick. — *Table Legs*, Paul Lyons, 1991.

6944 Katie had already made plans to go to Texas with the baby. — *Beyond Deserving*, Sandra Scofield, 1991.

6945 I'm afraid there's been a change of plan, Mr. Eliot said. — *Folly*, Susan Minot, 1992.

6946 *Before we get started I just wanted to let you know I plan to stay out of this mess as much as possible.* — *This Way Madness Lies*, Thomas William Simpson, 1992.

Police

6947 "You've *got* to get him, boys — get him or bust!" said a tired police-chief, pounding a heavy fist on a table. — *The Bat*, Mary Roberts Rinehart, 1926.

6948 Bob Corson, owner of the JC ranch, and sheriff of Cactus County, had been over near Bentley, on the Old California Trail, serving a writ. — *The Round-Up*, Clarence E. Mulford, 1933.

6949 I arrived in St. Gatien from Nice on Tuesday, the 14th of August. I was arrested at 11.45 A.M. on Thursday, the 16th, by an *agent de police* and an inspector in plain clothes and taken to the Commissariat. — *Epitaph for a Spy*, Eric Ambler, 1930.

6950 The police official in his shoddy gray suit of European clothes looked up from his notebook and papers with expressionless dark eyes and sucked in his breath politely. — *Mr. Moto Is So Sorry*, John P. Marquand, 1938.

6951 Wearing the star, Dan Mitchell was a man whose tenure on living expired and was renewed from hour to hour, and since certainty was a thing he could never have in the major run of his life he prized it greatly and made the small details of his day into a pattern that seldom varied. — *Trail Town*, Ernest Haycox, 1941.

6952 Hopalong Cassidy, sheriff of Twin River County, opened the morning's mail, acquired a few more wanted posters, and hunted through a desk drawer for hammer and tacks. — *Hopalong Cassidy Serves a Writ*, Clarence E. Mulford, 1941.

6953 "Mr. Pugh, I came to ask you some questions about your life in Cwm Bugail and about Mrs. Vaughan of Gelli, Bronwen Vaughan. But now I think it would be better if you were to let me have a written account." — *Testimonies*, Patrick O'Brian, 1952.

6954 Deputy Canning had been Warlock's hope. — *Warlock*, Oakley Hall, 1958.

6955 It came down to this: if I had not been arrested by the Turkish police, I would have been arrested by the Greek police. — *The Light of Day*, Eric Ambler, 1962.

6956 The old girl kept writing and complaining about the police. — *Something to Answer For*, P. H. Newby, 1968.

6957 *To TIGELLINUS, Co-Commander, Praetorian Guard, from/ PAENUS, Tribune of Secret Police/* I have information. When can I see you?/ *To PAENUS, Tribune of Secret Police, from TIGELLINUS/* Come to me after the baths. — *The Conspiracy*, John Hersey, 1972.

6958 The wheel hummed and Rollow mumbled Yiddish curses as he put rouge on the glistening bronze surface. — *The Blue Knight*, Joseph Wambaugh, 1972.

6959 There were fifteen people seated in the patrol wagon that had not yet begun to move, and one young man sitting in the lotus position in the center of the aisle. — *The Underground Woman*, Kay Boyle, 1975.

6960 They came for him that Sunday. He had just returned from a night's vigil on the mountain. He was resting on his bed, Bible open at the Book of Revelation, when two police constables, one tall, the other short, knocked at the door. — *Petals of Blood*, Ngugi wa Thiong'o, 1977.

6961 "Dead cows," Sheriff Chick Charleston said. — *No Second Wind*, A. B. Guthrie, Jr., 1980.

6962 There was only one policeman, very young, his hands already on the steering wheel, by the time Merry got down to the police car. — *O My America!*, Johanna Kaplan, 1980.

6963 One day in the middle of the twentieth century I sat in an old graveyard which had not yet been demolished, in the Kensington area of London, when a young policeman stepped off the path and came over to me. — *Loitering with Intent*, Muriel Spark, 1981.

6964 August 21 — Called to Bayley Farm House on Oglethorpe Road, now occupied by W. and S. Simon, because of flashlights, and noise in yard behind house. — *Digs*, Bette Pesetsky, 1984.

6965 Following my arrest at the airport, I asked whether Mexico still retained the death penalty, and if so, what particular form it assumed, whether hanging, shooting or garotting. — *Tourists*, Richard B. Wright, 1984.

6966 POLICE RAID MALE STRIP JOINT, the headline said. — *Other Plans*, Constance C. Greene, 1985.

6967 Pezulu Pasha, the Chief of Police, was fiddling with his uniform hat, a tall shako made of white fur and lined with red silk, folding it with an air of regret and once jabbing a blunt forefinger through two holes just below the crown. — *Arrows of Desire*, Geoffrey Household, 1985.

6968 With malice, Paz ignored the flat voice of the dispatcher from the radio under the pickup's dash and let his eyes follow Ethelbert Quivari, the Papago patrol officer, toward the

mesquites of Mexico. — *The Fourth Codex*, Robert Houston, 1988.

6969 The word around town was that John "Pork" Meeker, the sheriff's new deputy, had blown up the hot springs pools at the river. — *All Around Me Peaceful*, Kent Nelson, 1989.

6970 Report from patrol car Tango India delta one four zero four for Sergeant McEvoy Donegall Pass Station Belfast timed at twenty two thirty November twenty one. — *Death Grows on You*, Niki Hill, 1990.

6971 When I finally arrived at the police station, Wren was standing on the front steps under a bright light, a pair of blue panties balled up in her right fist. — *Borrowed Lives*, Laramie Dunaway, 1992.

Politics

6972 Under the reign of the last Stuarts, there was an anxious wish on the part of Government to counteract, by every means in their power, the strict or puritanical spirit which had been the chief characteristic of the republican government, and to revive those feudal institutions which united the vassal to the liege lord, and both to the crown. — *Old Mortality*, Sir Walter Scott, 1817.

6973 The district of Orangeburg, in South Carolina, constitutes one of the *second tier* (from the seaboard) of the political and judicial divisions or districts of that state. — *The Forayers*, William Gilmore Simms, 1855.

6974 All the English world knows, or knows of, that branch of the Civil Service which is popularly called the Weights and Measures. Every inhabitant of London, and every casual visitor there, has admired the handsome edifice which generally goes by that name, and which stands so conspicuously confronting the Treasury Chambers. — *The Three Clerks*, Anthony Trollope, 1858.

6975 The general election of 18 — will be well remembered by all who take an interest in the political matters of the country. — *Phineas Redux*, Anthony Trollope, 1874.

6976 The experience of great officials who have laid down their dignities before death, or have had the philosophic mind to review themselves while still wielding the deputy sceptre, teaches them that in the exercise of authority over men an eccentric behaviour in trifles has most exposed them to hostile criticism and gone farthest to jeopardize their popularity. — "The House on the Beach," George Meredith, 1890.

6977 In the garden the question was settled without serious difference of opinion. If Sir Robert Perry really could not go on — and Lady Eynesford was by no means prepared to concede even that — then Mr. Puttock, *bourgeois* as he was, or Mr. Coxon, conceited and priggish though he might be, must come in. — *Half a Hero*, Anthony Hope, 1893.

6978 The men who govern India — more power to them and her! — are few. — *King — of the Khyber Rifles*, Talbot Mundy, 1916.

6979 In response to his wife's uncertain inquiry about the political speaking, Colonel Miltiades Vaiden called back from his gate that he did not think there would be any ladies at the courthouse that evening. — *The Store*, T. S. Stribling, 1932.

6980 Lou Farbstein, middle-aged but still referred to as the bright boy of the *World* (and bright boy he had actually been twenty years back), neither liked nor disliked Police Commissioner Theo. J. Hardy, the new power in the city. — *The Asphalt Jungle*, W. R. Burnett, 1949.

6981 Tomorrow I will go with Garth to the city to hear King George's man proclaim from the square that now Jamaica-men will begin to govern themselves. — *New Day*, Victor Stafford Reid, 1949.

6982 . . . *and the government of the United States of America is herewith suspended, except in the District of Columbia, as of the emergency.* — *Earth Abides*, George R. Stewart, 1949.

6983 Where treason to the state is defined simply as opposition to the government in power, the political leader convicted of it will not necessarily lose credit with the people. — *Judgment on Deltchev*, Eric Ambler, 1951.

6984 "They say that after two years I have lost touch," Ansel Gibbs said, looking not at the reporters who questioned him, but beyond them to the huge pane of blue sky where from time to time a plane climbed, slow and silver, into the bright day. — *The Return of Ansel Gibbs*, Frederick Buechner, 1958.

6985 (The committee met, pursuant to call, at 4:20 P.M., in Room 429, Capitol Offices, Senator Aaron Mansfield presiding. Present: Senators Mansfield, Skypack, and Voyolko; also present, Mr. Donald R. Broadbent, committee counsel.) — *The Child Buyer*, John Hersey, 1960.

6986 In the great pearl-gray slab of a room that is the North Delegates' Lounge of the United Nations in New York the late-September sun slanted down through the massive east windows and fell across the green carpets, the crowded chairs and sofas, the little knots of delegates standing or sitting or milling about in the midmorning hours before the General Assembly's seven committees began. — *A Shade of Difference*, Allen Drury, 1962.

6987 No one can deny that Chief the Honourable M. A. Nanga, M.P., was the most approachable politician in the country. — *A Man of the People*, Chinua Achebe, 1966.

6988 "Now if I may bring the two of you to a final point," said Ronnie Appleyard, with an air of genuinely asking permission, "what about the more long-term future? Wouldn't you agree that the present Government proposals" — he turned suddenly to the junior Minister on his left — "do no more than nibble at this vital human —" — *I Want It Now*, Kingsley Amis, 1968.

6989 Now is the time for all good men to come to the aid of their country. — *Adios, Scheherazade*, Donald E. Westlake, 1970.

6990 Major Bill McKinley was the greatest president I ever lived through. — *Willy Remembers*, Irvin Faust, 1971.

6991 CITIZEN: Sir, I want to congratulate you for coming out on April 3 for the sanctity of human life, including the life of the yet unborn. That required a lot of courage, especially in light of the November election results. — *Our Gang*, Philip Roth, 1971.

6992 Lee Lowder had hoped, after Tony's defeat in the State Senate election, that their life might be given back to them. — *I Come as a Thief*, Louis Auchincloss, 1972.

6993 I believe it was the sight of that old fool Gladstone, standing in the pouring rain holding his special constable's truncheon as though it were a bunch of lilies, and looking even more like an unemployed undertaker's mute than usual, that made me think seriously about going into politics. — *Flash for Freedom!*, George MacDonald Fraser, 1972.

6994 *Houston, Oct. 13* (AP) — The national committee recessed tonight after failing in five ballots to nominate a successor to the late Senator Walter Hudson, the presidential candidate who died just twenty-two days before the election. — *Dark Horse*, Fletcher Knebel, 1972.

6995 Now the August day has come when he and Secretary of State Orrin Knox are to go to the Washington Monument Grounds and there before their countrymen pledge their lives, their fortunes and their sacred honor — and as much cooperation with each other as they can manage. — *Come Nineveh, Come Tyre*, Allen Drury, 1973.

6996 Count Viktor von Preissendorf, who had profited from the advice of Adam Cassebeer respecting a splendid mare he had recommended for the count's purchase some years before, repaid the modest debt by suggesting his son, Hans, for the appointment. — *Hans Cassebeer and the Virgin's Rose*, Arthur A. Cohen, 1975.

6997 Now the August day has come when he and Governor Edward Montoya Jason of California are to go to the Washington Monument Grounds and there before their countrymen pledge their lives, their fortunes and their sacred honor — and as much cooperation with each other as they can manage. — *The Promise of Joy*, Allen Drury, 1975.

6998 The British have chosen the Maharajah. In fact they have had two stabs at it, choosing a merchant first, a victualling *bania*. — *The Golden Honeycomb*, Kamala Markandaya, 1977.

6999 In May 1979, only days after Britain's new Conservative government came to power, the yellow box that contains the daily report from M16 to the Prime Minister was delivered to her by a deputy secretary in the Cabinet Office. — *XPD*, Len Deighton, 1981.

7000 The Vietnam War was "over." Richard Nixon, ex-President of the United States, had been greatly ostracized for making a mockery of his high office. All other archcriminals of the Watergate scandal had spent a few months in prison and then become millionaires from publishing their bad novels and self-seeking memoirs. — *The Nirvana Blues*, John Nichols, 1981.

7001 In the later years of the last century, an avalanche began in Russia. — *Rivington Street*, Meredith Tax, 1982.

7002 Charles Parnell Cassidy — God rest his soul! — was the perfect specimen of an Irish politician. — *Cassidy*, Morris West, 1986.

7003 Subsidizing public transport had long been associated in the minds of both government and the majority of its public with the denial of individual liberty. — *The Child in Time*, Ian McEwan, 1987.

7004 "Glasnost is trying to escape over the Wall, and getting shot with a *silenced* machine gun!" said Kleindorf. — *Spy Line*, Len Deighton, 1989.

7005 Today the computers would tell Senator Gilbert Hennington about his impending campaign for reelection. — *The Spook Who Sat by the Door*, Sam Greenlee, 1990.

7006 Having no personal commitment to either of the new consuls, Gaius Julius Caesar and his son simply tacked themselves onto the procession which started nearest to their own house, the procession of the senior consul, Marcus Minucius Rufus. — *The First Man in Rome*, Colleen McCullough, 1990.

7007 I'd like to tell you about the time I was on the Short List — the Short List to be the Democrat nominee for vice-president of the United States. — *Short List*, Jim Lehrer, 1992.

Portent

7008 You will rejoice to hear that no disaster has accompanied the commencement of an enterprise which you have regarded with such evil forebodings. — *Frankenstein*, Mary Wollstonecraft Shelley, 1818.

7009 I have never believed, as some people, in omens and forewarnings, for the dramatic things in my life have generally come upon me as suddenly as a tropical thunder-storm. But I have observed that in a queer way I have been sometimes prepared for them by my mind drifting into an unexpected mood. — *The Island of Sheep*, John Buchan, 1936.

7010 "Ommernous, that's what it is, ommernous, every bit of it is ommernous." — *A Heart for the Gods of Mexico*, Conrad Aiken, 1939.

7011 "As a class," Helena said, "we are doomed" — indicating consciousness of her absurdity only by a bright flash in my direction from her Tiberian eye. — *An Avenue of Stone*, Pamela Hansford Johnson, 1947.

7012 If an oracle told you you would be a shirtsleeve philosopher by the time you were thirty, that you would be caught in bed with a woman named Mrs. Thicknesse, have your letters used for blackmail and your wife threaten to bring suit for sixty-five dollars because that was all you were worth, you would tell him he was out of his mind. — *Comfort Me with Apples*, Peter De Vries, 1956.

7013 When Bob Munson awoke in his apartment at the Sheraton-Park Hotel at seven thirty-one in the morning he had the feeling it would be a bad day. — *Advise and Consent*, Allen Drury, 1959.

7014 "Here's an explosion of some kind!" said Isa McKillop rubbing her nose with the back of her hand./ She gazed into the cup again./ "Oh gracious, no, it's not an explosion after all. I see now, it's a mansion house with an awful lot of chimney-pots!" — *Summer in the Greenhouse*, Elizabeth Mavor, 1959.

7015 At nine thirty, on the first Monday in June, Sheldon Friberg drank coffee in his office on the eleventh floor, and pronounced revelation of impending catastrophe. — *Marie Beginning*, Alfred Grossman, 1964.

7016 The night began badly. William felt, later, that he ought to have realized how significant this was. — *Mr. Bone's Retreat*, Margaret Forster, 1971.

7017 It is possible I already had some presentiment of my future. — *The Shadow of the Torturer*, Gene Wolfe, 1980.

7018 Now the pilot glanced down at the terrain and knew again a momentary sense of foreboding. — *The Aviator*, Ernest K. Gann, 1981.

7019 It was the end of a cold, blustery day. Storm clouds curled darkly over the East River and a foreboding hung like smoke in O'Farrell's tool shop. — *Shannon*, Gordon Parks, 1981.

7020 When Blanche Melanson upset a dish of crab-apple jelly on Mother Superior's pristine white tablecloth, Sister Agatha proclaimed it a sign. — *Felice*, Angela Davis-Gardner, 1982.

7021 The blessed gift of inner light possesses me and I see a vision of the future. — *The Winds of Sinhala*, Colin de Silva, 1982.

7022 There were no omens. — *Queen of Swords*, William Kotzwinkle, 1983.

7023 Once, on a lark, I consulted a palmist. — *Hell's Bells*, Cindy Packard, 1983.

7024 The night Vincent was shot he saw it coming. — *Glitz*, Elmore Leonard, 1985.

7025 From the moment he opened his cabin door and found a coiled blacksnake asleep on the stoop and heard warblers singing, out of season, in the sycamores by the creek, Ely Jackson knew in his bones that today was no day for stirring abroad. — *Bad Man Ballad*, Scott R. Sanders, 1986.

7026 "This is an ill-fated trip," said Heather Noakes. — *Poor Dear Charlotte*, Anabel Donald, 1988.

7027 Foreboding overcame Eaton Striker well before The Derailleurs began to play. — *Checker and the Derailleurs*, Lionel Shriver, 1988.

7028 There had been omens. — *Incident at Badamyâ*, Dorothy Gilman, 1989.

7029 By evening, it will all be over. This old earth will be no more for one of us, me or the Frenchman, d'Anthes. — *Great Black Russian*, John Oliver Killens, 1989.

7030 Lifetimes ago, under a banyan tree in the village of Hasnapur, an astrologer cupped his ears — his satellite dish to the stars — and foretold my widowhood and exile. — *Jasmine*, Bharati Mukherjee, 1989.

7031 Oklahoma, 1922/ That summer a water diviner named Michael Horse forecast a two-week dry spell. — *Mean Spirit*, Linda Hogan, 1990.

Poverty

7032 A dark Christmas!/ No bread on the table, no fire on the hearth; only a miserable candle inserted in an old bottle, shining dimly over the details of a cold, cheerless room, and lighting

up with its feeble glow, the care-worn faces of Poverty and Hunger. — *The Empire City*, George Lippard, 1850.

7033 Do you know what it is to be poor? Not poor with the arrogant poverty complained of by certain people who have five or six thousand a year to live upon, and who yet swear they can hardly manage to make both ends meet, but really poor, — downright, cruelly, hideously poor, with a poverty that is graceless, sordid and miserable? — *The Sorrows of Satan*, Marie Corelli, 1895.

7034 Poor people have children without much feeling of exaltation. — *Tar*, Sherwood Anderson, 1926.

7035 Because we were very poor and could not buy another bed, I used to sleep on a pallet made of old coats and comforters in the same room with my mother and father. — *Boston Adventure*, Jean Stafford, 1944.

7036 When the white beggars—the poor whites—came to the office, their faces were dusty from veld roads, their skins were bronzed, tanned, hardened by exposure to a sun from which there had been no buildings to flee into, and their palms were open. — *The Price of Diamonds*, Dan Jacobson, 1958.

7037 Long ago in 1945 all the nice people in England were poor, allowing for exceptions. — *The Girls of Slender Means*, Muriel Spark, 1963.

7038 You could see them in the courthouse square of every little Southern town, then, in the spring of 1932 — the dispossessed. — *Look Away, Look Away*, Ben Haas, 1964.

7039 Joseph was very poor at this time as he was giving all his money to beggars. — *Several Perceptions*, Angela Carter, 1968.

7040 In the dream, they were all in the living room. I knew they were poor; everything in the room said they were poor, but everything in the room was so clean, and the sunlight poured in as if the sun intended to set right in that room. — *Love*, Susan Fromberg Schaeffer, 1981.

7041 No husband, no children, no home, no money, no job./ But no pity, please. Choice was involved. — *Among Friends*, Irene Tiersten, 1982.

7042 In the beginning the four of us, with my little sister who was born a year after me, lived in a grey housing project for poor families in New York City. — *Anne's Youth*, Frances Gladstone, 1984.

7043 I was born poor in rich America, yet my secret instincts were better than money and were for me a source of power. — *My Secret History*, Paul Theroux, 1989.

7044 When my brother Claude was tiny he would run out barefoot in the sandy street and teach the island children how to beg. — *The Scissor Man*, Jean Arnold, 1990.

Pranks and Tricks

7045 The man in the green summer suit was cutting the girl's hand off at the wrist, but he wasn't doing it right. — *The Escape Artist*, David Wagoner, 1965.

7046 Once, during a summer we spent at Kerneham, Francis locked himself in the church for the whole of a night. — *The Bird of Night*, Susan Hill, 1972.

7047 Shooting snooker and pissing in the shuffleboard machine. — *Harvesting Ballads*, Philip Kimball, 1984.

7048 "This'll make them jump," Clive said as he rammed the gunpowder even harder into the copper pipe. — *For They Shall Inherit*, Malcolm Macdonald, 1984.

7049 Omri emerged cautiously from the station into Hove Road./ Someone with a sense of humor and a black spray can had recently added an *L* to the word "Hove" on the street sign on the corner, making it "Hovel Road." — *The Return of the Indian*, Lynne Reid Banks, 1986.

7050 Once upon a time in Hollywood, people got pushed into swimming pools and Errol Flynn let loose a bunch of white mice at a party and an actress shot a producer in the worst possible place. — *Unhealthful Air*, Elliott Baker, 1988.

7051 Dearest Michael,/ Today Judson sucked so hard on a Dixie cup his mouth turned purple. — *Long Distances*, Fabienne Marsh, 1988.

7052 The dipping tank was empty. The dip mixture lay green, drying in trickles and splashes on the grey clay soil. — *And They Didn't Die*, Lauretta Ngcobo, 1990.

7053 Ever since they proved the world was round it has played a cruel trick. — *Sea Level*, Roger King, 1992.

7054 Years ago, down in the Amazon, Santiago set me up. — *Santiago and the Drinking Party*, Clay Morgan, 1992.

Pregnancy and Childbirth

7055 Once upon a Time, there was a Man who had Three Sons by one Wife, and all at a Birth, neither could the Mid-Wife tell certainly which was the Eldest. — *A Tale of a Tub*, Jonathan Swift, 1704.

7056 Early in 1880, in spite of a well-founded

suspicion as to the advisability of perpetuating that race which has the sanction of the Lord and the disapproval of the people, Hedvig Volkbein — a Viennese woman of great strength and military beauty, lying upon a canopied bed of a rich spectacular crimson, the valance stamped with the bifurcated wings of the House of Hapsburg, the feather coverlet an envelope of satin on which, in massive and tarnished gold threads, stood the Volkbein arms — gave birth, at the age of forty-five, to an only child, a son, seven days after her physician predicted that she would be taken. — *Nightwood*, Djuna Barnes, 1936.

7057 "Have mercy! Lord, have mercy on my poor soul!" Women gave birth and whispered cries like this in caves and out-of-the-way places that humans didn't usually use for birthplaces. — *Moses, Man of the Mountain*, Zora Neale Hurston, 1939.

7058 There was a baby born named Ida. Its mother held it with her hands to keep Ida from being born but when the time came Ida came. And as Ida came, with her came her twin, so there she was Ida-Ida. — *Ida*, Gertrude Stein, 1941.

7059 It was in the middle of a snowstorm I was born, Palmer's brother's wedding night, Palmer went to the wedding and got snowbound, and when he arrived very late in the morning he had to bury my packing under the walnut tree, he always had to do this when we were born — six times in all, and none of us died, Mary said Granny used to give us manna to eat and that's why we didn't, but manna is stuff in the bible, perhaps they have it in places like Fortnham & Mason, but I've never seen it, or maybe Jews shops. — *Sisters by a River*, Barbara Comyns, 1947.

7060 It will not, we hope, surprise our readers to hear that Lady Cora Waring, formerly Lady Cora Palliser, only daughter of the Duke of Omnium, wife of Sir Cecil Waring of Beliers Priory, was expecting what used to be called an interesting event. — *Happy Return*, Angela Thirkell, 1952.

7061 Every third woman you passed on Gold Street in Baranof was young, pretty, and pregnant. The men, too, were young, virile, and pregnant with purpose. — *Ice Palace*, Edna Ferber, 1958.

7062 Shirl was nineteen years old, four months gone and just starting to show, bumping through Newtown on the back of a second-hand Norton. — *Bobbin Up*, Dorothy Hewett, 1959.

7063 I was born May 23, 1931, in the house of my grandmother. No doctor could be found to attend, only a midwife from three miles away in the country. My birth was loud and troublesome; the midwife, who was but a young girl, fainted away and my father, who was assisting,

had to force her again to consciousness. — *It Is Time, Lord*, Fred Chappell, 1963.

7064 Aaron would not come out. — *Boys and Girls Together*, William Goldman, 1964.

7065 "And if it's a boy," said Phyllida cheerfully, "we'll call him Prospero." — *This Rough Magic*, Mary Stewart, 1964.

7066 "Arnold, I can feel it moving! It's really there!" — *Nobody Does You Any Favors*, James Yaffe, 1966.

7067 A woman's cry. A sunlight flash and into it dipped a squalling newborn baby to ensure good luck. This was my beginning. My head touched the floor after the ancient fashion and I was here, I existed, a prince and citizen of Rome. — *Nero*, Mary Teresa Ronalds, 1969.

7068 A girl named Cedar Branches Waving lived in the country of sliding stones where the years are longer, and it came to her as it comes to women. — "'A Story'," Gene Wolfe, 1972.

7069 Elizabeth Warleggan was delivered of the first child of her new marriage at Trenwith House in the middle of February, 1794. It was an occasion of some tension and anxiety. — *The Black Moon*, Winston Graham, 1973.

7070 A. "I'm pregnant, mother."/ "Have a girl."/ "Why?"/ "A girl should have a girl."

B. "Mother, I'm pregnant with a girl."/ "How old is she?"/ "Seventeen years old."/ "Then you're pregnant with me." — *Her Mothers*, E. M. Broner, 1975.

7071 At the start of the summer when the child first moved within her, Mary had prayed for a son. She wanted to provide an heir for Albert as a way to make up to him for giving less of herself than conscience prompted. — *Now and Another Time*, Shelby Hearon, 1976.

7072 Mother's stomach bellied out like a sail. — *A Woman of the Future*, David Ireland, 1979.

7073 It is a curse in this family that the women bear only daughters, if anything at all. — *Plains Song, for Female Voices*, Wright Morris, 1980.

7074 Becca met Ulli in an Adult Education course in Pre-Columbian Art. They were both pregnant with their first children and sat like two Marimekko pumpkins in a field of withering vines, a group of professor's widows. — *Adult Education*, Annette Williams Jaffee, 1981.

7075 It had not been an easy birth, but then for Abel and Zaphia Rosnovski nothing had ever been easy, and in their own ways they had both become philosophical about that. — *The Prodigal Daughter*, Jeffrey Archer, 1982.

7076 Today is the day I will know for certain if my life is changed, if the tiles underfoot seem cool simply because of the August heat. — *Expecting*, Christine Lehner, 1982.

7077 The first thing the midwife noticed

about Michael K when she helped him out of his mother into the world was that he had a hare lip. — *Life & Times of Michael K*, J. M. Coetzee, 1983.

7078 Having harbored two sons in the waters of her womb, my mother considers herself something of an authority on human foetuses. — *The River Why*, David James Duncan, 1983.

7079 In November 1901, at the Tulip Tree, a whorehouse on Stockton Street in San Francisco, where she worked, the nineteen-year-old Opal Chong gave birth to Jacob. — *Suspects*, David Thomson, 1985.

7080 It was a wild night in the year of Federation that the birth took place. — *Lilian's Story*, Kate Grenville, 1986.

7081 It was Meditation Time in Painless Birth, and her eyes were supposed to be closed. — *Maud Gone*, Kathleen Rockwell Lawrence, 1986.

7082 *In late autumn, 1905, a woman arrived by train in Bethany, Massachusetts, with one satchel held together by ship rope and a belly large enough for a grown man to sit on.* — *Queen of Hearts*, Susan Richards Shreve, 1986.

7083 "Don't be ridiculous," Victoria said as she sauntered through the rain, umbrella held high. "How could anyone have a baby without being married?" — *Rag Woman, Rich Woman*, Margaret Thomson Davis, 1987.

7084 One late February night, at forty-one, leaning against the back door of the house that for the last four years she has shared with her mother who will die in less than a month, Coriola tilts her head towards the icy, star-ridden sky, her belly arched like a dome with a daughter being knit into flesh by her flesh, and her heart suddenly hammers with recognition of the grain-of-sand world, hammers with the full strangeness of being creature and human, beats with awe and fear that on this grain, smaller than the smallest speck of sand on any seashore, there could be, there should be, one creature, human, perched, wandering through years briefer than the blink of an eyelid, wondering in a time through which the blink of an eyelid lasts a thousand years. — *Concertina*, M. J. Fitzgerald, 1987.

7085 Nina and I had been living together in Brooklyn for over a year when she came home one afternoon, announced she was pregnant, tossed her briefcase to the floor and flopped down on the green vinyl sofa. — *The Object of My Affection*, Stephen McCauley, 1987.

7086 Feeling the tremor for the third time, she rises from the bed, certain that it is no mistake, neither nerves nor indigestion but a contraction; down low, an ache, growing sharp and then receding. Flow and ebb. — *The Surprise of Burning*, Michael Doane, 1988.

7087 Eleanor, Lady Eden, went up to the parapet alone in the chill early morning drizzle to escape Eve's cries of labor and to catch the first sight of the sorrowful procession of carriages coming toward Eden Castle. — *Eden and Honor*, Marilyn Harris, 1988.

7088 In late summer Line told him she was two months along. — *The Homesman*, Glendon Swarthout, 1988.

7089 At last, she felt the pain. — *Only Children*, Rafael Yglesias, 1988.

7090 A hush swallowed the hot little room as the mother shuddered one last time, pushed down hard, and bore her third child, her baby girl, into the world. — *Baby of the Family*, Tina McElroy Ansa, 1989.

7091 They say Guzmán had been a difficult pregnancy for Mamá Cielo, who had little patience for the bouncing ball in her belly. — *The Line of the Sun*, Judith Ortiz Cofer, 1989.

7092 My indecisive mother tried to abort me, but too late, and I danced out from under the knife in a splash of amniotic fluid, with something of rue but little of reproach. — *A Slight Lapse*, Robert Chibka, 1990.

7093 She was called Shereel Dupont, which was not her real name, and she had missed her period for the last three months running, but she was not pregnant and she knew it. — *Body*, Harry Crews, 1990.

7094 — You're wha'? said Jimmy Rabbitte Sr. — *The Snapper*, Roddy Doyle, 1990.

7095 When my mother entered her tenth month of carrying me, I stopped moving inside her womb. — *Floating in My Mother's Palm*, Ursula Hegi, 1990.

7096 I was soaring, sailing high above the waxed corridors of St. Peter's, the hospital where, exactly two hours earlier, at 5:56 A.M., Kate had given birth to a big bald baby who weighed in at just under nine pounds. — *Henry in Love*, Marian Thurm, 1990.

7097 It was a tight squeeze./ And though the safety, comfort, warmth, and humidity of her mother's womb seemed preferable to the glare and rubber gloves that now surrounded her, it was checkout time. And checkout time was as unavoidable as lunch was bland. — *The Second Greatest Story Ever Told*, Gorman Bechard, 1991.

7098 Nearly all of the seven dwarfs of pregnancy have shown up by now: Sleepy, Queasy, Spacey, Weepy, Gassy, and Moody. The only one who hasn't checked in is Happy. — *The Mommy Club*, Sarah Bird, 1991.

7099 On a warm afternoon in the late spring of 1959, pregnant women are strolling around the babywear department of Taylor & Haddon, Hemingford's principal department store. — *Too Much, Too Young*, Caroline Bridgwood, 1991.

7100 When the baby was born, the mother asked the midwife to take the afterbirth outside. — *Joey Dee Gets Wise*, Louisa Ermelino, 1991.

7101 Someone told her to squat for as long as she could and let her legs absorb the pain. — *Lost and Found*, Marilyn Harris, 1991.

7102 It was a breech birth; and so, right up to the very last moment of innocent ignorance, I remained aware of the midwife's boisterous, bawdy encouragement. — *Phantom*, Susan Kay, 1991.

7103 I was born in 1904, so that when I was pregnant in 1943 I was near enough to be past the rightful age to bear children. — *Jewel*, Bret Lott, 1991.

7104 "Massage the soft parts." — *Duchess of Milan*, Michael Ennis, 1992.

7105 Soon after she was born her father entered the hut. — *Ghost Woman*, Lawrence Thornton, 1992.

7106 In the house at 61 Allen Street, Sapphire Hayes was birthing the baby who would grow up to look into the eyes of the King. — *A Big Life*, Susan Johnson, 1993.

Presence

7107 "What in the world, Wimsey, are you doing in this Morgue?" demanded Captain Fentiman, flinging aside the "Evening Banner" with the air of a man released from an irksome duty. — *The Unpleasantness at the Bellona Club*, Dorothy L. Sayers, 1928.

7108 Back of Superintendent Russell's shoulder Court House Square lay, dusty yellow in the July sunshine, deserted on this week day morning save for one tall man dressed in faded blue shirt and overalls. — *Mountain Path*, Harriette Simpson Arnow, 1936.

7109 Feeding his rabbits in the garden of his residence, The Nook, his humane practice at the start of each new day, Mr. Cornelius, the house agent of Valley Fields, seemed to sense a presence. — *The Ice in the Bedroom*, P. G. Wodehouse, 1961.

7110 "Redcoats and Tories are everywhere. I swear to you, Rob, I look down that path toward the road, and I can see them coming up out of the swamp by the hundreds." — *Old Hickory*, Noel B. Gerson, 1964.

7111 "There's a mutie! Look out!" — *Orphans of the Sky*, Robert A. Heinlein, 1964.

7112 It was Sunday. Chance was in the garden. — *Being There*, Jerzy Kosinski, 1971.

7113 There he was in Big Playground. — *The Wanderers*, Richard Price, 1974.

7114 "Mr. Aaron Blattberg."/ "Here."/ "Miss Carmen Caravello."/ "Ina place!"/ "Mr. Karl Finsterwald."/ "Ratty!"/ "Mrs. R.R. Rodriguez."/ "*Sí.*"/ "Mr. Wolfgang Schmitt."/ "*Ja!*"/ "Yussel Spitz."/ No answer. — *O K*A*P*L*A*N! MY K*A*P*L*A*N!*, Leo Rosten, 1976.

7115 He was there because he had promised. — *Home Free*, Dan Wakefield, 1977.

7116 The professor was in the next room. — *The Flower of the Republic*, Raymond Kennedy, 1983.

7117 Because I was there; had been there. — *The Wall of the Plague*, André Brink, 1984.

7118 It seems to me now that Fanshawe was always there. — *The Locked Room*, Paul Auster, 1986.

7119 There they were. — *Waiting for Childhood*, Sumner Locke Elliott, 1987.

7120 "There was a time, and I was there." — *The Exile*, William Kotzwinkle, 1987.

7121 If only you could see me now. You can't and couldn't, but I'm here. — *Memoirs of an Invisible Man*, H. F. Saint, 1987.

7122 There Issa is. There, faltering on the top of the front stoop, wearing a red plaid dress with a white lace collar. — *The Kingdom of Brooklyn*, Merrill Joan Gerber, 1992.

7123 It seemed that Fanny was there from the beginning. — *Vindication*, Frances Sherwood, 1993.

Pride

7124 Superciliousness is not safe after all, because a person who forms the habit of wearing it may some day find his lower lip grown permanently projected beyond the upper, so that he can't get it back, and must go through life looking like the King of Spain. — *Gentle Julia*, Booth Tarkington, 1922.

7125 Young Cole, quivering with pride, surveyed the room./ So, at last, was one of his deepest ambitions realized. — *Jeremy at Crale*, Hugh Walpole, 1927.

7126 The black people who live in the Quarters at Blue Brook Plantation believe they are far the best black people living on the whole "Neck," as they call that long, narrow, rich strip of land lying between the sea on one side and the river with its swamps and deserted rice-fields on the other. — *Scarlet Sister Mary*, Julia Peterkin, 1928.

7127 "Boasting's the vulgarest thing there is," the fair young girl, Josephine, informed her three guests as they came out of the big brick

Oaklin house after lunch. — *Image of Josephine*, Booth Tarkington, 1945.

7128 Mr. Wellington Kee was very proud of his status as one of the senior controllers at Taipei International Airport. — *Band of Brothers*, Ernest K. Gann, 1973.

7129 "Don't ever forget you come from a harbor city!" the father would say, walking his brood of brother and sister down to the end of the pier, early of a spring evening, and standing there with his eyes as satisfied and his hands as pat on his stomach as if he'd just fished this out of the water, like a dirty pedigree. The self-congratulation of city-dwellers is endless, they say, and never worse than when the city is New York. — *On Keeping Women*, Hortense Calisher, 1977.

7130 Those of them who in that fateful year decided to winter were (except for Jessie) very proud and very thoughtful. — *Toward the End*, Elizabeth Savage, 1980.

Prison

7131 Though it was six days since Daniel Ordway had come out of prison, he was aware, when he reached the brow of the hill, and stopped to look back over the sunny Virginia road, that he drank in the wind as if it were his first breath of freedom. — *The Ancient Law*, Ellen Glasgow, 1908.

7132 "Claro," said the warder. "Claro, hombre!" It was the condescension of one caballero to another. His husky voice was modulated upon the principle of an omniscient rationality. — *The Revenge for Love*, Wyndham Lewis, 1937.

7133 Two men in gray cotton uniforms were standing in the shadow of the tower, one old and one young. They were prisoners. — *The Conspirators*, Frederic Prokosch, 1943.

7134 The cell was small, its walls were stained and grimy, its furnishings were scanty. — *Woman in Ambush*, Rex Beach, 1951.

7135 There was no sound of traffic in the room, the prisoner's exhausted mind told him. — *The Devil's Advocate*, Taylor Caldwell, 1952.

7136 Few of the other convicts at Jupiter could get a look or a word out of Joe Mundy. — *The Way to the Gold*, Wilbur Daniel Steele, 1955.

7137 Clinch did not get to know Big Dan until they were put into the infirmary together. He'd heard all about him, of course, as Dan was the talk of the prison. — *Underdog*, W. R. Burnett, 1957.

7138 Brother Andrés was on night duty, checking the cells. — *The Work of Saint Francis*, MacKinlay Kantor, 1958.

7139 "From this hook," said the guide, "was suspended the iron cage, two and a half meters square, in which Cardinal Balue was imprisoned for eleven years by Louis XI. He had, however, little ground for complaint, as the cage was his own invention." — *Come Out to Play*, Alex Comfort, 1961.

7140 Of the two young men sharing a cell in one of New York's popular police stations Tipton Plimsoll, the tall thin one, was the first to recover, if only gradually, from the effect of the potations which had led to his sojourn in the coop. — *The Brinkmanship of Galahad Threepwood*, P. G. Wodehouse, 1964.

7141 On that day everyone in the camp was painted. — *An Estate of Memory*, Ilona Karmel, 1969.

7142 Half Scotland sniggered, and the other half scowled, when in letters to the *Scotsman* and the *Glasgow Herald*, I put forward my suggestion that prisoners in Scottish jails be allowed to wear kilts as their national birthright, if such was their wish. — *Fergus Lamont*, Robin Jenkins, 1979.

7143 "Next time you scream like that in bed I'll turn the hose on you, you hear me!..." — *Chirundu*, Es'kia Mphahlele, 1979.

7144 Boethius, Walter Raleigh, Wilde, Sade — names that were going through my mind of those who had turned a prison cell into a work chamber. — *Memoir of a Gambler*, Jack Richardson, 1979.

7145 Yes — Kilgore Trout is back again. He could not make it on the outside. That is no disgrace. A lot of good people can't make it on the outside. — *Jailbird*, Kurt Vonnegut, 1979.

7146 The limestone walls of the underground prison were partially covered with a brown-and-green fungus, and in some of the seams that lay between the carved stones, streams of water ran slowly but constantly from somewhere up above. — *Dumachas and Sheba*, Leonard Wise, 1979.

7147 The "Big Yard" in reality wasn't big at all. — *House of Slammers*, Nathan C. Heard, 1983.

7148 I was in my cell packing my shit in a cardboard box. — *The Dixie Association*, Donald Hays, 1984.

7149 It was built as a bedlam more than a century ago, and became a prison, then a lunatic asylum long after that. The older inmates still call the central block "the madhouse," and sometimes, when the mist pours off the Black Mountains, you might think the whole institution a Gothic fantasy. — *A Cruel Madness*, Colin Thubron, 1984.

7150 Now that most of us have been pardoned and released from prison, the newspaper scribblers keep pestering me for personal stories

about the Chicago Conspiracy. — *Conspiracy of Knaves*, Dee Brown, 1986.

7151 At ten minutes to six on the morning of 12 May 1916, James Connolly was lying in a cell in Kilmainham gaol, Dublin, when the door opened and a small crowd of people trooped suddenly in. — *Saints and Scholars*, Terry Eagleton, 1987.

7152 In the women's prison where the Guards had taken Peacock, six people slept in a cell designed for one. — *Cry of the Peacock*, Gina Barkhordar Nahai, 1991.

7153 "I like escorting prisoners," said Captain Albert Cutler, settling back and stretching out his legs along the empty seats. — *City of Gold*, Len Deighton, 1992.

Problems

7154 There were two most disturbing problems confronting Frank Cowperwood at the time of his Chicago defeat, when, so reducingly and after so long a struggle, he lost his fight for a fifty-year franchise renewal. — *The Stoic*, Theodore Dreiser, 1947.

7155 *Their problems were solved: the poor they no longer had with them; the sick, the lame, the halt, and the blind were historic memories; the ancient causes of war no longer obtained; they had more freedom than Man has ever enjoyed. All of them should have been happy* — *Beyond This Horizon*, Robert A. Heinlein, 1948.

7156 When I saw Finn waiting for me at the corner of the street I knew at once that something had gone wrong. — *Under the Net*, Iris Murdoch, 1954.

7157 Ashley was the first one to notice that something was wrong. — *A Long Way to Go*, Borden Deal, 1966.

7158 The light switch did not work. The grumbling old janitor had had to be woken up to turn on the water and the heating; she dare not disturb him again. — *The Flute-Player*, D. M. Thomas, 1979.

7159 The first sign that something had gone wrong manifested itself while he was playing golf. — *The Second Coming*, Walker Percy, 1980.

7160 "Holy God, Mother! What's the matter?" — *A Midnight Clear*, William Wharton, 1982.

7161 The nail-biting should have been the first sign to Nora Beeme that something was wrong. — *Somebody's Baby*, Claire Harrison, 1989.

7162 *It isn't working very well anymore.* — *How to Leave a Country*, Cris Mazza, 1992.

Psychology

7163 It is a trite but true Observation, that Examples work more forcibly on the Mind than Precepts: and if this be just in what is odious and blameable, it is more strongly so in what is amiable and praiseworthy. — *Joseph Andrews*, Henry Fielding, 1742.

7164 In human affairs cause and effect often behave not like the inseparable twins science says they are but like two harebrains never even acquainted. — *Rumbin Galleries*, Booth Tarkington, 1937.

7165 It may take time to get over an obsession, even after the roots have been pulled out. — *Hilda's Letter*, L. P. Hartley, 1945.

7166 "Now, Sir Ransom, we shall have to have sunshine in ourselves today. There is none outside for us. But that should not be difficult for fortunate people like ourselves." — *Darkness and Day*, Ivy Compton-Burnett, 1951.

7167 "Well, as I keep saying," said Janet Links, "I think psycho-analysis would help you." — *A Travelling Woman*, John Wain, 1959.

7168 Even for a film star, not to mention the greatest film star of his generation—which he was—Tynan Bryson had an extremely weak grasp of reality. — *The Ecstasy Business*, Richard Condon, 1967.

7169 What makes Iago evil? some people ask. — *Play It as It Lays*, Joan Didion, 1970.

7170 Or look at it this way. Psychoanalysis is a permanent fad. — *Forever Panting*, Peter De Vries, 1973.

7171 There were 117 psychoanalysts on the Pan Am flight to Vienna and I'd been treated by at least six of them. — *Fear of Flying*, Erica Jong, 1973.

7172 "A fugue," Dr. Josko explained to her, "is a pathological amnesiac condition during which the patient is apparently conscious of his actions but on return to normal life has no recollection of them. . . ." — *Madder Music*, Peter De Vries, 1977.

7173 The first thing you should know about Mr. Fox is that he was not a psychopath. — *Love-Act*, Michael Austen, 1982.

7174 George remarked that he has trouble working with patients who complain of overbearing mothers. — *Disturbances in the Field*, Lynne Sharon Schwartz, 1983.

7175 "You must let go," I said. — *Phaedra*, June Rachuy Brindel, 1985.

7176 "Oh, I don't know, Dan. The men are all mousey. The women are all kittens or cats. They all survive by keeping a wall between

them. They seem to relate only through a rat hole chewed in the baseboard." — *Merely Players*, Gregory Mcdonald, 1988.

7177 As a psychoanalyst, I am a profound believer in middles, in the life itself. — *Separate Hours*, Jonathan Baumbach, 1990.

7178 Some years ago I became involved in the psycho-evolutionary work of Dr. Hugo Manarr. — *Poet and Dancer*, Ruth Prawer Jhabvala, 1993.

Punishment

7179 In former times, England had her Tyburn, to which the devoted victims of justice were conducted in solemn procession up what is now called Oxford Street. — *The Heart of Mid-Lothian*, Sir Walter Scott, 1818.

7180 As the Milvains sat down to breakfast the clock of Wattleborough parish church struck eight; it was two miles away, but the strokes were borne very distinctly on the west wind this autumn morning. Jasper, listening before he cracked an egg, remarked with cheerfulness:/ "There's a man being hanged in London at this moment." — *New Grub Street*, George Gissing, 1891.

7181 They used to hang men at Four Turnings in the old days. — *My Cousin Rachel*, Daphne du Maurier, 1951.

7182 Tomorrow the man I love is to die; horribly, and in public. — *The House at Old Vine*, Norah Lofts, 1961.

7183 The rawhide harness strap cut viciously through the air. The children half-concealed in the pine grove beyond the barn and tobacco storage silos winced when they heard it strike its target, and Anne Henry chewed on the ends of her cotton bonnet ties to keep from crying aloud. — *Give Me Liberty*, Noel B. Gerson, 1966.

7184 After the unsuccessful rebellion of 1863, many Polish noblemen were hanged; others — Count Wladislaw Jampolski among them — were banished to Siberia. — *The Manor*, Isaac Bashevis Singer, 1967.

7185 They didn't hang people anymore. — *Charlie, Come Home*, R. F. Delderfield, 1969.

7186 The Public Whipping of Miss Emma Marianne Locke, age sixteen, was scheduled to take place at seven in the morning on Friday, August the third, 1790, in the inner courtyard of Eden Castle, situated on the North Devon coast at the exact point where the Bristol Channel prepares to join the turbulence of the Atlantic Ocean. — *This Other Eden*, Marilyn Harris, 1977.

7187 Because she'd been forest bred, half Mohawk and half French-Canadian, Nellie Noisy Bluejay squeaked only softly when Jake Razors' palm smacked against the smoothness of her pale-brown buttocks. — *Guns for Rebellion*, F. van Wyck Mason, 1977.

7188 So I am to receive a hundred and eight strokes of the bastinado. I should have thought a hundred more than sufficient. — *Legend of the Yellow River*, Somerset de Chair, 1979.

7189 They hanged the five men that afternoon in a clearing on the bank of the big river. — *The Fate of O'Loughlin*, Dudley McCarthy, 1979.

7190 The gibbet stood at the head of the pass, under the vast, precipitous slope of Helvellyn. — *Hand of Glory*, Glen Petrie, 1980.

7191 Exile is the wound of kingship. — *The Fisher King*, Anthony Powell, 1986.

7192 Oh, the wages of sin! — *The Heart of the Country*, Fay Weldon, 1987.

7193 It wasn't the first time I'd been shut up in the closet, if closet isn't too grand a word for the little cupboard under the stairs. — *Mary Reilly*, Valerie Martin, 1990.

7194 At sundown, when they led him to the chair, Nail Chism began to understand the meaning of the name of his hometown, Stay More. — *The Choiring of the Trees*, Donald Harington, 1991.

Questions

7195 One summer afternoon a tall, good-looking stripling stopped in the midst of the town of New York, and asked his way to the governor's house. — *The Trail of the Sword*, Gilbert Parker, 1894.

7196 *Oh the infantree the infantree/ With the dirt behind their ears/* ARMIES CLASH AT VERDUN IN GLOBE'S GREATEST BATTLE/ 150,000 MEN AND WOMEN PARADE/ but another question and a very important one is raised. — *1919*, John Dos Passos, 1932.

7197 Phoebe Runnels left her written question unanswered. — *Lights Across the Delaware*, David Taylor, 1954.

7198 Where now? Who now? When now? Unquestioning. — *The Unnamable*, Samuel Beckett, 1958.

7199 Don't ask me why. Never ask me why. I mean if I knew *all* the answers I wouldn't be where I am now — down again, one more time, but not out. — *Which Ones Are the Enemy?*, George Garrett, 1961.

7200 Except for an occasional dry question, he left the talking to her, waiting while she fought out the difficult words. — *A Shooting Star*, Wallace Stegner, 1961.

7201 "I will ask you once more. It is the last time. Will you or will you not?" — *A God and His Gifts*, Ivy Compton-Burnett, 1963.

7202 The young man driving the car interrupted a question about mathematics to whistle. — *Triumph*, Philip Wylie, 1963.

7203 The relevant questions, as it happened, came by chance. — *A Compass Error*, Sybille Bedford, 1968.

7204 It happens once or twice a week. Lily Rowan and I, returning from a show or party or hockey game, leave the elevator and approach the door of her penthouse on top of the apartment building on Sixty-third Street between Madison and Park, and there is the key question. — *The Father Hunt*, Rex Stout, 1968.

7205 Now in these dread latter days of the old violent beloved U.S.A. and of the Christ-forgetting Christ-haunted death-dealing Western world I came to myself in a grove of young pines and the question came to me: has it happened at last? — *Love in the Ruins*, Walker Percy, 1971.

7206 "*Answer me!*" — *Song of the Wild*, Allan W. Eckert, 1980.

7207 I don't remember the first question I asked my mother, or the last answer she gave me. — *Summer*, Lisa Grunwald, 1985.

7208 The first thing these people always asked, whenever they went out, was where were "they"? — *O-Zone*, Paul Theroux, 1986.

7209 —We'll ask Jimmy, said Outspan. —Jimmy'll know. — *The Commitments*, Roddy Doyle, 1987.

7210 "Is this something?" — *M31*, Stephen Wright, 1988.

7211 People always ask me the same question. — *Dixie Riggs*, Sarah Gilbert, 1991.

7212 There is some question here. — *Photographing Fairies*, Steve Szilagyi, 1992.

7213 "Mommy, may I go over to Noorna's house?" As she often did, Lily started her question in the hall, concluding it only after she'd opened the door and run into her mother's bedroom, usually without knocking. — *The Diplomat's Daughter*, William Kinsolving, 1993.

Quests

7214 A young lady, just returned from college, was making a still-hunt in the house for old things — old furniture, old china, and old books.

— *A Little Union Scout*, Joel Chandler Harris, 1904.

7215 Freckles came down the corduroy that crosses the lower end of the Limberlost. At a glance he might have been mistaken for a tramp, but he was truly seeking work. — *Freckles*, Gene Stratton-Porter, 1904.

7216 Hard on twenty years have gone by since that night of Leo's vision — the most awful years, perhaps, which were ever endured by men — twenty years of search and hardship ending in soul-shaking wonder and amazement. — *Ayesha*, H. Rider Haggard, 1905.

7217 It was at the end of a summer evening, long after his usual bedtime, that Joseph, sitting on his grandmother's knee, heard her tell that Kish having lost his asses sent Saul, his son, to seek them in the land of the Benjamites and the land of Shalisha, whither they might have strayed. — *The Brook Kerith*, George Moore, 1916.

7218 Four o'clock on the First of November, a dark and foggy day. Sixteen characters in search of an author. — *Christmas Pudding*, Nancy Mitford, 1932.

7219 The day before his mother died, in the winter of 1873, Bruno Shadbolt made three journeys to Spella Ho, hunting for coal. — *Spella Ho*, H. E. Bates, 1938.

7220 All the June Saturday afternoon Sam Pollit's children were on the lookout for him as they skated round the dirt sidewalks and seamed old asphalt of R Street and Reservoir Road that bounded the deep-grassed acres of Tohoga House, their home. — *The Man Who Loved Children*, Christina Stead, 1940.

7221 Young Elk slipped along just under the crest of the ridges. He moved as the wolf travels, where he would not be silhouetted against the sky and yet where he could search the wide slopes of prairie on both sides, and vanish quickly in either direction if need be. — *The Horsecatcher*, Mari Sandoz, 1951.

7222 A month after he came to the village for quite another purpose, Smith set out to look for a place he only knew from the description an old woman had given him, many times, when he was a child. — *A Month Soon Goes*, Storm Jameson, 1963.

7223 I tethered my horse and buggy in front of the Breitung House on the east end of Iron Street and started on my quest. — *Laughing Whitefish*, Robert Traver, 1965.

7224 It's taken me long enough to find you. — *The Pious Agent*, John Braine, 1975.

7225 Here we go. The quest is on again. There's lots to do, many voices to hear and some to heed. — *Now Playing at Canterbury*, Vance Bourjaily, 1976.

7226 Everybody in New York City is looking

for something. — *Dancing Aztecs*, Donald E. Westlake, 1976.

7227 Only kneelers find wild strawberries. — *The Very Rich Hours of Count von Stauffenberg*, Paul West, 1980.

7228 In his long search, he already had most of his facts. What he quested after now, he told himself, in the wilderness of sea and shore where he hoped to be alone in that early spring, was the sense of men in a particular place, soldiers, who had struggled and died there a century ago. — *Mexico Bay*, Paul Horgan, 1982.

7229 Rodeo Drive in Beverly Hills, the buildings polished to the gleam of newly minted money by the whipping of silk skirts, fine wool trousers, and movie stars' fragrant bluish auras in an afternoon zephyr so light and caressing it seems man made, like the sound-stage breezes designed to tousle the hairdos of actresses: Alan Alexander carefully peruses the windows of the small, perfect, glittering stores, obviously involved in a quest separate from the questing after dollars, after long hard fingernails lacquered to Oriental symmetry, after designer labels on handbags, after the ideal table at lunch from which you can see everyone who enters and leaves the restaurant while pretending to be cool, unconcerned, interested only in the skirts whipping in the warm wind. — *Presto!*, Roberta Smoodin, 1982.

7230 Arriving at the edge of the Forest shortly after sunrise, he finds the scanty wooden house he was looking for without too much difficulty. — *Circles in a Forest*, Dalene Matthee, 1984.

7231 Except for that wild old doctor in the other bed who raves some and wanders up and down the hall looking for his family, it's peaceful here at Landis Homes. — *I Hear the Reaper's Song*, Sara Stambaugh, 1984.

7232 In the spring of 1803, I, Samuel Walker, and my Uncle William were sent by President Jefferson into the wilderness between the Ohio River and the Gulf of Mexico to find specimens of the animal called the giant sloth. — *An Embarrassment of Riches*, James Howard Kunstler, 1985.

7233 As soon as he turned the corner, he looked for the House above the Arch. — *Chatterton*, Peter Ackroyd, 1987.

7234 It seems increasingly likely that I really will undertake the expedition that has been preoccupying my imagination now for some days. — *The Remains of the Day*, Kazuo Ishiguro, 1989.

7235 Old man turtle ambles along the deerpath, seeking breakfast. — *Hayduke Lives!*, Edward Abbey, 1990.

7236 Nacho usually found the first five or six cans in the English classrooms at the far end of the hall. — *Aquaboogie*, Susan Straight, 1990.

7237 Eve moved hesitantly down the unfamiliar street looking for number 27, Big Dan's Tattoo Parlor. — *Eve's Tattoo*, Emily Prager, 1991.

Railroads

7238 Morning was breaking on the highroad to San José. The long lines of dusty, level track were beginning to extend their vanishing point in the growing light; on either side the awakening fields of wheat and oats were stretching out and broadening to the sky. — "Maruja," Bret Harte, 1885.

7239 That old bell, presage of a train, had just sounded through Oxford station; and the undergraduates who were waiting there, gay figures in tweed or flannels, moved to the margin of the platform and gazed idly up the line. — *Zuleika Dobson*, Max Beerbohm, 1911.

7240 A single car-track ran through Payton Street, and over it, once in a while, a small car jogged along, drawn by two mules. — *The Rising Tide*, Margaret Deland, 1916.

7241 Along this particular stretch of line no express had ever passed. All the trains — the few that there were — stopped at all the stations. — *Crome Yellow*, Aldous Huxley, 1921.

7242 The Sunday morning accommodation train puffed slowly up the river valley. — *Herbs and Apples*, Helen Hooven Santmyer, 1925.

7243 The train that first carried me into Rome was late, overcrowded and cold. — *The Cabala*, Thornton Wilder, 1926.

7244 Condicote is linked to Tatchester by a branch line, nine and a half miles long, upon which the Condicote-Tatchester expresses run to and fro four times daily, Sundays excepted, taking usually fifty-five minutes for the single journey. — *The Hawbucks*, John Masefield, 1929.

7245 He had said *the* train, as if there were no other. It must be the one great train of the night, the Paris train, that was to be an hour late. — *Dawn's Left Hand*, Dorothy M. Richardson, 1931.

7246 On an afternoon of January 1915, a small train dragged itself across the flat Dutch countryside in the neighbourhood of Bodegraven, carrying a group of English officers under guard. — *The Fountain*, Charles Morgan, 1932.

7247 This was April, 1868, with the combination work-passenger train running up the valley of the Lodgepole toward Cheyenne. — *Trouble Shooter*, Ernest Haycox, 1937.

7248 Toward the end of a Saturday afternoon, February 12, 1848, the train from Baltimore puffed and panted into Cumberland, the

end of the line. — *The Start of the Road*, John Erskine, 1938.

7249 When the train slowed at the first jarring application of the brakes, the crowd packed in the aisle of the coach swayed crushingly forward, with the grinding, heavy momentum of the start of a landslip. — *Night Rider*, Robert Penn Warren, 1939.

7250 The train passed the stock-pens, and when it was even with the station Will Ballard slung his saddle out into the night. — *Ride the Man Down*, Luke Short, 1942.

7251 The nickname of the train was the Yellow Dog. Its real name was the Yazoo-Delta. — *Delta Wedding*, Eudora Welty, 1946.

7252 The train moved across the vast sea of burgeoning grass like a stub-tailed and languorous snake. — *Colorado*, Louis Bromfield, 1947.

7253 Such a railway, thought Martin, should not be allowed to exist in the present stage of our civilization. — *The Lardners and the Laurelwoods*, Sheila Kaye-Smith, 1947.

7254 On the little branch line which starts at Wockley Junction and conveys passengers to Eggmarsh St. John, Ashenden Oakshott, Bishop's Ickenham and other small and somnolent hamlets of the south of England the early afternoon train had just begun its leisurely journey. — *Uncle Dynamite*, P. G. Wodehouse, 1948.

7255 It was six o'clock of a March morning, and still dark. The long train came sidling through the scattered lights of the yard, clicking gently over the points. — *The Singing Sands*, Elizabeth Mackintosh *as* Josephine Tey, 1952.

7256 The train drew up in the meadow, and stopped. — *The Train in the Meadow*, Robert Nathan, 1953.

7257 If they'd ever had a schedule for this narrow-gauge train, they'd lost it, Tully thought. — *Silver Rock*, Luke Short, 1953.

7258 Wisps of smoke from the bell-funneled locomotives of the New York Central Railroad drifted into the busy waiting room at Forty-second Street and Vanderbilt Avenue. — *Tenderloin*, Samuel Hopkins Adams, 1959.

7259 A light snow was falling as the train from Mexico City pulled into Ciudad Juárez. — *Pocho*, José Antonio Villarreal, 1959.

7260 The train was carried slowly through the night on rhythmically beating pistons, its centipede-brown belly sending the same morse-code symbol for hour after hour into black woods or arable rolling plain. — *The General*, Alan Sillitoe, 1960.

7261 The wheels of the Coronation Special from Sheffield, due at St. Pancras Station at six o'clock in the morning of Coronation Day, sang the steady, lulling *dickety-clax, dickety-clax* of the British Railways. — *Coronation*, Paul Gallico, 1962.

7262 Olyphant is the name of the tiny jerkwater town in Jackson County, northeast Arkansas, where the Missouri Pacific train I was riding to Little Rock stalled for thirty minutes in the late hours of a Sunday in late April, leaving me with nothing to do but read the paper and wait impatiently for the (as near as I could make out by expressing my anxiety to the conductor) triple-thierce camming pin on the glaring-rod of the fifth car's starboard glomhefter to be replaced. — *The Cherry Pit*, Donald Harington, 1965.

7263 Paint me a small railroad station then, ten minutes before dark. — *Bullet Park*, John Cheever, 1969.

7264 Visitors to Belgium will know the tram that runs, with a few inland incursions, along the coast from Ostend to Knokke near the Dutch border. It clangs along, past resort after resort: it is very convenient, and always crowded. — *The Holiday Friend*, Pamela Hansford Johnson, 1972.

7265 The special train from upstate pulled slowly up to the Granite Forks depot platform, gave a last sigh and stopped in the bright early-morning sunlight. — *The Outrider*, Luke Short, 1972.

7266 The southbound train from Paris was the one we had always taken from time immemorial — the same long slow-coach of a train, stringing out its bluish lights across the twilight landscapes like some super-glowworm. — *Monsieur*, Lawrence Durrell, 1974.

7267 The train pulled endlessly across flat stretches of deserted corn and wheat fields lying dank and dreary under a sullen November sky. — *The Devil's Hand*, Edith Summers Kelley, 1974.

7268 I boarded a first-class compartment on the midday train from Paddington to Hereford. The route was as familiar to me as the London street where I lived. — *An Older Love*, Charlotte Wolff, 1976.

7269 The train clacked slowly through the Southern Pacific switching yards, and finally came to a stop at Oakland Pier. — *All Over Again*, Nathaniel Benchley, 1981.

7270 When I was a small boy growing up in Nebraska, my father used to take me down to the railroad tracks to watch the trains roll by. — *Ashworth & Palmer*, Thomas Hauser, 1981.

7271 From midnight until five in the morning most country railway stations in Italy are shunned by people and trains alike. — *Any Four Women Could Rob the Bank of Italy*, Ann Cornelisen, 1983.

7272 It was All Hallow's Eve, 1864, and the afternoon train out of Toronto and limited to the border was running late as it rolled slowly out onto the Suspension Bridge that joined the United Provinces of Canada to the United States

of America. — *American Falls*, John Calvin Batchelor, 1985.

7273 Long before they planted beets in Argus and built the highways, there was a railroad. — *The Beet Queen*, Louise Erdrich, 1986.

7274 Pauline had forgotten about the straw seats on the train. — *In the City*, Joan Silber, 1987.

7275 The track stretched away in a flat line down past the signal box and on to the embankment, that looked in the heat as if it would fall onto them, as soon as the train's hooter shattered the deceptive quiet. — "Burnham Camp," John Sligo, 1987.

7276 The village train route is an odd voyage. — *Speaking in Tongues*, Linda Ashour, 1988.

7277 In 1913 the journey from Moscow to Charing Cross, changing at Warsaw, cost fourteen pounds, six shillings and threepence and took two and a half days. — *The Beginning of Spring*, Penelope Fitzgerald, 1988.

7278 A giant cyclops eye pierced the night./ Behind it, a locomotive, coal tender and sixty-one freight cars steadily increased speed, leaving Jacksonville. Five hundred wheels of solid steel screamed and scraped along the rails. — *Hallapoosa*, Robert Newton Peck, 1988.

7279 A train was travelling northwards from London through the grey squalls of a winter's afternoon. From a corner seat in one of its carriages a man watched his country with the scurried perspective of a railway traveller: crossing fields at a bias, chipping off the corner of a hill, barked at by sudden brick walls and engulfed in tunnels. — *Gerontius*, James Hamilton-Paterson, 1989.

7280 This is the first time I've been on a train. — *The Neon Bible*, John Kennedy Toole, 1989.

7281 The *Spirit of Des Moines* had sent signals ahead as it approached the Cincinnati depot in the coolness of dawn, detected by Shaman first as a delicate trembling barely perceived in the wooden station platform, then a pronounced shivering that he felt clearly, then a shaking. — *Shaman*, Noah Gordon, 1992.

7282 After it leaves Manhattan, the number seven train becomes an elevated, and crosses a landscape of abandoned railroad tracks, dilapidated buildings and, later, a conglomerate of ugly factories that blow serpentine plumes of gaudy poisonous smoke. — *Latin Moon in Manhattan*, Jaime Manrique, 1992.

7283 While her daughter, Zoe Mae, investigated some overgrown phlox at the edge of the platform, Kay Pinny waited for the rumble in the air, the wheeze of the black engine car to signal the arrival of the New York-Montreal passenger train. — *York Ferry*, Annie Dawid, 1993.

Rain

7284 It was on the great northern road from York to London, about the beginning of the month of October, and the hour of eight in the evening, that four travellers were, by a violent shower of rain, driven for shelter into a little public-house on the side of the highway, distinguished by a sign which was said to exhibit the figure of a black lion. — *The Adventures of Sir Launcelot Greaves*, Tobias Smollett, 1762.

7285 It was a cold November night. Holborn was noisy, murky, and sloppy. A drizzling rain descended through the haze: the chilling haze of a London winter night. — *Ranthorpe*, George Henry Lewes, 1847.

7286 The rainiest nights, like the rainiest lives, are by no means the saddest. — *The Silent Partner*, Elizabeth Stuart Phelps, 1871.

7287 In San Francisco the "rainy season" had been making itself a reality to the wondering Eastern immigrant. — *A Ward of the Golden Gate*, Bret Harte, 1890.

7288 In the swirling rain that came at dusk the broad avenue glistened with that deep bluish tint which is so widely condemned when it is put into pictures. — *George's Mother*, Stephen Crane, 1896.

7289 The days of that April had been days of mist and rain. Sometimes, for hours, there would come a miracle of blue sky, white cloud, and yellow light, but always between dark and dark the rain would fall and the mist creep up the mountains and steam from the tops — only to roll together from either range, drip back into the valleys, and lift, straightway, as mist again. — *The Little Shepherd of Kingdom Come*, John Fox, Jr., 1903.

7290 The gaunt man led the way. At his heels, doggedly, came the two short ones, fagged, yet uncomplaining; all of them drenched to the skin by the chill rain that swirled through the Gap, down into the night-ridden valley below. — *The Rose in the Ring*, George Barr McCutcheon, 1910.

7291 We have just had another flood, bad enough, but only a foot or two of water on the first floor. — *The Case of Jennie Brice*, Mary Roberts Rinehart, 1913.

7292 It was late afternoon — half an hour before sundown — and the earth, the air, the sky, had that cool, quickened freshness which preceded a spring shower. — *Samuel Drummond*, Thomas Boyd, 1925.

7293 It was midnight and still drizzling after hours of vain and sickly endeavor on the part of

Nature to bring about a full-sized, respectable downpour that might have rid the sky of its pall, permitting the moon of another and more conspicuous Romeo to look down in concern upon the heretofore unnoticed hero of this tale. — *Romeo in Moon Village*, George Barr McCutcheon, 1925.

7294 The thunderstorm broke very suddenly. With the first drops excited women's voices were heard, windows opened and wash was hastily taken off the clotheslines. It was one of those hard, mad rains that come down as if with deliberate fury. — *Summer in Williamsburg*, Daniel Fuchs, 1934.

7295 It was drizzling, and all the storekeepers of Neptune Beach stood at their doorsteps regarding the gloom reproachfully, as though they were being deliberately persecuted. — *Low Company*, Daniel Fuchs, 1937.

7296 It was about eleven o'clock in the morning, mid October, with the sun not shining and a look of hard wet rain in the clearness of the foothills. — *The Big Sleep*, Raymond Chandler, 1939.

7297 To the red country and part of the gray country of Oklahoma, the last rains came gently, and they did not cut the scarred earth. — *The Grapes of Wrath*, John Steinbeck, 1939.

7298 The day dawned clear, but it had rained the night before, the sudden squally rain of middle March. — *The Way West*, A. B. Guthrie, Jr., 1949.

7299 After a while it began to sprinkle and Thurs looked around for shelter. — *The Brother*, Frederick Manfred *as* Feike Feikema, 1950.

7300 A slanted, slashing rain saturated his wool coat while he rigged the pack animals, and coldness searched his bones. — *The Earthbreakers*, Ernest Haycox, 1952.

7301 In the early 1880's one August Sunday noon there was a rain storm up the Yocona River. — *This Crooked Way*, Elizabeth Spencer, 1952.

7302 It has rained all day. — *Auntie Mame*, Patrick Dennis, 1955.

7303 After dinner it rained so heavily that nobody went out. — *The Last Resort*, Pamela Hansford Johnson, 1956.

7304 The whole of the naval anchorage seemed subdued and cowed by the relentless, sleety rain which drove across the estuary, whipping the grey waves into a turbulent, white-capped frenzy. — *A Prayer for the Ship*, Douglas Reeman, 1958.

7305 Michael Duff lay in his creaking four-poster bed and harkened drowsily to the rain as it drove with vehemence against the windows. — *The First Day of Friday*, Honor Tracy, 1963.

7306 It was raining and it was going to rain.

— *And Wait for the Night*, John William Corrington, 1964.

7307 The view through the porthole was not encouraging. On a rainy day, Liverpool Docks were never at their best; on this rainy day, with the stuff coming down in sheets, spouting and sluicing off grimy warehouse roofs, then turning grimy itself and lying about in filthy pools and puddles the whole length of Liverpool Landing Stage — on this rainy day, Liverpool looked its depressing worst. — *A Fair Day's Work*, Nicholas Monsarrat, 1964.

7308 There had been rain in the afternoon, lightening the burden of the heat. There was a smell of wet grass and a misty sheen hung over the ricefields. — *The Dark Dancer*, Frederic Prokosch, 1964.

7309 It was August, and it shouldn't have been raining. — *The Far Side of the Dollar*, Ross Macdonald, 1965.

7310 Mud along the Thames, mud in the Chancery.... Mud in the Jersey flats. — *Square's Progress*, Wilfrid Sheed, 1965.

7311 — God Almighty, the bus driver groans./ This is no ordinary summer rain. — *The Upper Hand*, John William Corrington, 1967.

7312 It was really summer, but the rain had fallen all day and was still falling. The weather can best be described by saying it was the kind reserved for church fetes. — *The Pyramid*, William Golding, 1967.

7313 A half hour after I came down here, the rains began. — *All the Little Live Things*, Wallace Stegner, 1967.

7314 No rain had fallen in more than a month, and the brown soil of Texas was parched and cracked. — *Sam Houston*, Noel B. Gerson, 1968.

7315 A cold misty rain descends streaking the windows down an empty shopping street. — *The Onion Eaters*, J. P. Donleavy, 1971.

7316 Far off, up yonder, the mist and drizzle of rain made the road and the woods, and the sky too, what you could see of it above the heave of the bluff, all one splotchy, sliding-down grayness, as though everything, the sky and the world, was being washed away with old dishwater. — *Meet Me in the Green Glen*, Robert Penn Warren, 1971.

7317 London's purply-green morning behind silver raindarts splashing white against a jog of umbrellas and blocks of buses flushing scarlet in puddles almost painted what I felt, though looking back, I'm not sure I was capable of any feeling at all. What I saw seemed to smear vision for the moment and wisp off, and anything I heard merely impinged, and no more. — *The Night Is a Child*, Richard Llewellyn, 1972.

7318 March 20. A cold spring morning. It

rained last night, perforating the crusted snow of the Tates' front lawn, and everything is wet and glitters: the fine gravel of the drive, the ice in the ditch beside it, the bare elm twigs outside the bathroom window. — *The War Between the Tates*, Alison Lurie, 1974.

7319 It was raining. All over Manhattan and over as many of the other boroughs as attorney John Dalton Farrow could see from the windows of his ebony and teak paneled office on the fifty-first floor of the Dwight-Richardson Tower, the rain came down. — *The Voyage Unplanned*, Frank Yerby, 1974.

7320 Today I see the rain coming over the river again, swirling round and round in long columns, twisting and turning like sheets that are squeezed and wrung out, pumping, whirling in a violent wrestle with the wind, which butts it and drives it. — *Jonoah and the Green Stone*, Henry Dumas, 1976.

7321 In the evening the winds came and the rain swept and paused, swept again in a sheet of muddy drops, slowed and stopped. — *O Master Caliban!*, Phyllis Gotlieb, 1976.

7322 The flagstones of the Manhattan Battery are slick and black, varnished by the cold November rain coming across the harbor in swirls and clouds of mist. — *The Court-Martial of George Armstrong Custer*, Douglas C. Jones, 1976.

7323 The rains came unexpectedly that August, drenching the cotton lands and turning the dirt streets of the river towns into stinking quagmires. — *Flickers*, Phillip Rock, 1977.

7324 It was a Sunday morning. The rain was falling. Idemudia raised his head on his hands and looked out through the window. He was so disgusted by what he saw that he fell back on their eight-spring iron bed with a groan. — *Violence*, Festus Iyayi, 1979.

7325 Last night there was a storm. It rained torrentially, drumming with steel fingers on the slate roof of this cottage, but this morning all was blue and calm. — *The Bride of Lowther Fell*, Margaret Forster, 1980.

7326 September. A great gray storm swept its pelting rain up the pastures of Duncton Hill and then on into the depths of the oaks and beeches of Duncton Wood itself. — *Duncton Wood*, William Horwood, 1980.

7327 Rain fell across September's highways and carried the first taste of autumn from the fields and towns and outskirts of small cities just west of Boston into the Impala wagon's front seat. — *Running*, George Bower, 1982.

7328 Weeks of rain had so distorted visibility that the Glen seemed to be under water and the mail van, nosing in, had the look of a bathyscaphe sent to probe its depths. — *The Obedient Wife*, Julia O'Faolain, 1982.

7329 It's raining over the city, raining down steadily over all of us who live in the mountain's rain-shadow. — *A State of Fear*, Menán du Plessis, 1983.

7330 It was raining again. — *A Joke Goes a Long Way in the Country*, Alannah Hopkin, 1983.

7331 It had been raining daily for almost two weeks, and so he had put off slaughtering the cow. — *The Madness of a Seduced Woman*, Susan Fromberg Schaeffer, 1983.

7332 It had rained in the night. — *The Superintendent*, Blair T. Birmelin, 1984.

7333 The winter rains are over. — *Joe Jones*, Anne Lamott, 1985.

7334 In Vermont that fall it rained for weeks. — *Staying Afloat*, Muriel Spanier, 1985.

7335 Rain fell with that scrupulous attention unique to Cambridge as Miles Tattershall gazed through his obscure college window. — *Lost Time*, Catharine Arnold, 1986.

7336 It was the first day of Michaelmas term and acid rain was falling on the campus. — *The Mind and Body Shop*, Frank Parkin, 1986.

7337 The rain had been coming and going all afternoon, but I paid it no mind. — "Decoration Day," John William Corrington, 1987.

7338 For the first four days it rained. — *The Enigma of Arrival*, V. S. Naipaul, 1987.

7339 High noon over the Amazon. Tropical rainstorm skirting the Andes, greasing the alleys and filling the cafés of cities far beyond the jungle. — *A Guest in the Jungle*, James Polster, 1987.

7340 Herman Marshall squinted at the rain. — *The Ideal, Genuine Man*, Don Robertson, 1987.

7341 A chilly spring rain had been falling for two days when the clouds finally broke in the west. — *Woodrow's Trumpet*, Tim McLaurin, 1989.

7342 . . . Some things are not womenrain, as the Caribbeans refer to their lighter showers quickly absorbed by the sun. — *A Stone Gone Mad*, Jacquelyn Holt Park, 1991.

7343 It was pissing rain at eleven o'clock in the morning in front of St. Patrick's Cathedral. — *The Piranhas*, Harold Robbins, 1991.

7344 *Christmas 1990!* It rained the entire day. — *Keeper of the Light*, Diane Chamberlain, 1992.

7345 Drizzle coated Haledon, N.J., with a sad, ruinous sheen. — *Garden State*, Rick Moody, 1992.

Reading

7346 *"Alonzo now once more found himself upon an element that had twice proved destructive to his happiness, but Neptune was propitious, and with gentle*

breezes wafted him toward his haven of bliss, toward Amaryllis. Alas, when but one day from happiness, a Moorish zebec"—/ "Janice!" called a voice.—*Janice Meredith*, Paul Leicester Ford, 1899.

7347 Colonel Parsons sat by the window in the dining-room to catch the last glimmer of the fading day, looking through his *Standard* to make sure that he had overlooked no part of it.—*The Hero*, W. Somerset Maugham, 1901.

7348 By the open French window of the dining-room Jenny Blair Archbald was reading *Little Women* for the assured reward of a penny a page.—*The Sheltered Life*, Ellen Glasgow, 1932.

7349 Captain Horatio Hornblower was reading a smudgy proof which the printers had just sent round to his lodgings.—*Ship of the Line*, C. S. Forester, 1938.

7350 Nunnely Ballew rolled his quid of tobacco from one thin cheek to the other and read slowly, following each word with a knotty brown finger, the printing on the can of dog food in his hand.—*Hunter's Horn*, Harriette Simpson Arnow, 1949.

7351 A great many magazines come to our house and there are books too, but I don't think anybody even pretends to read them all and I know I don't or I wouldn't have time for anything else, I mean really *read* them, but I do like to look through them all, especially those with pictures, so I have got a pretty good idea of what people are writing about and talking about.—*The Newcomer*, Clyde Brion Davis, 1954.

7352 They sat there, crossword puzzles completed, quietly reading their newspapers, the elderly man of sixty-six and the young man of twenty.—*Committal Chamber*, Russell Braddon, 1966.

7353 I used to read a lot when I was a kid. I'd be telling myself a lie if I pretended not to understand why I don't much any more.—*The Man Who Knew Kennedy*, Vance Bourjaily, 1967.

7354 Sometimes he read.—*Preserve and Protect*, Allen Drury, 1968.

7355 "Here you are," said Lawrence./ George took the sheet of paper, closely covered with typing, and began to read.—*Joseph*, Mervyn Jones, 1970.

7356 She had been reading too long and by a light too dim.—*The Goddess Abides*, Pearl S. Buck, 1972.

7357 The order of these "reports" is arbitrary although their accuracy is strict. They can be read at any hour of the day and there is no time limit.—*Saw*, Steve Katz, 1972.

7358 "For goodness' sake, Peter, stop ruining your eyes and get out into the fresh air. The first spot of sun we've had for weeks, and you have to sit there poring over that tripe."—*The Riverside Villas Murder*, Kingsley Amis, 1973.

7359 Admiral of the Fleet Lord Fisher of Kilverstone, seventy-five years old and sick at heart, sat reading his Bible.—*To the Honor of the Fleet*, Robert H. Pilpel, 1979.

7360 "You are *not reading*, daddy."—*Labors of Love*, R. V. Cassill, 1980.

7361 Sitting on a rock on the Jebel Surgham overlooking the Nile at Omdurman, Lieutenant Dabney Augustus Rollo Goff studied the book he had taken from his saddle bag.—*Blunted Lance*, John Harris *as* Max Hennessy, 1981.

7362 Violet finished the library book and closed it with a snap.—*Light a Penny Candle*, Maeve Binchy, 1983.

7363 Eddie Ryan read the obituary again.—*Sam Holman*, James T. Farrell, 1983.

7364 A man named Lawrence Hux sat reading within a cone of yellow light that fell from the only decent lamp in the room.—*The Summoning*, Robert Towers, 1983.

7365 So she was reading the want ads.—*Sins of Omission*, Candace Flynt, 1984.

7366 The eyes lift from the paper.—*The Water Is Wide*, Elizabeth Gibson, 1984.

7367 George Martin, a banker, was sitting in his living room in a well-to-do suburb of Boston reading a local story in the newspaper headlined "Barking Dog Saves Family of Five."—*Only*, Winston Groom, 1984.

7368 Necessary and inexcusable, that is how murder appeared to them. Mediocre minds, confronted by this terrible problem, can take refuge by ignoring one or other of the terms of the dilemma. They are content, in the name of formal principles, to find all direct violence inexcusable and then to sanction that diffuse form of violence which takes place on the scale of world history . . .

Mercier was pretending to read Camus.—*The Mysteries of Algiers*, Robert Irwin, 1988.

7369 Papa is in his easy chair, reading the Sunday sports page.—*The Brothers K*, David James Duncan, 1992.

Recollection

7370 *It was in the time* that the earth begins to put on her new aparrel against the approch of her lover, and that the Sun rūning a most evē course becums an indifferent arbiter betweene the night and the day; when the hopelesse shepheard *Strephon* was come to the sandes, which lie against the Island of Cithera; where viewing the place with a heavy kinde of delight, and sometimes casting his eyes to the Ileward, he

called his friendly rivall, the pastor *Claius* unto him, and setting first downe in his darkened countenance a dolefull copie of what he would speake: O my *Claius*, said he, hether we are now come to pay the rent, for which we are so called unto by over-busie Remembrance, Remembrance, restlesse Remembrance, which claymes not only this dutie of us, but for it will have us forget our selves. — *Arcadia*, Philip Sidney, 1590.

7371 Metropolisville is nothing but a memory now. — *The Mystery of Metropolisville*, Edward Eggleston, 1873.

7372 It all seemed so real that I could hardly imagine that it had ever occurred before; and yet each episode came, not as a fresh step in the logic of things, but as something expected. It is in such wise that memory plays its pranks for good or ill; for pleasure or pain; for weal or woe. It is thus that life is bitter-sweet, and that which has been done becomes eternal. — *The Jewel of Seven Stars*, Bram Stoker, 1903.

7373 Across the most vital precincts of the mind a flippant sprite of memory will sometimes skip, to the dismay of all philosophy. — *Cherry*, Booth Tarkington, 1903.

7374 It was always a matter of wonder to Vandover that he was able to recall so little of his past life. — *Vandover and the Brute*, Frank Norris, 1914.

7375 This is written from memory, unfortunately. — *Herland*, Charlotte Perkins Gilman, 1915 (pub. 1979).

7376 "Oh, damn!" said Lord Peter Wimsey at Piccadilly Circus. "Hi, driver!" — *Whose Body?*, Dorothy L. Sayers, 1923.

7377 The fortunes of her family, her mother's life and her own earlier years were among the things about which Mrs. Crump liked to talk. — *The Case of Mr. Crump*, Ludwig Lewisohn, 1926.

7378 In modern Society, one thing after another, this spice on that, ensures a kind of memoristic vacuum, and Fleur Mont's passage of arms with Majorie Ferrar was, by the spring of 1926, well-nigh forgotten. — *Swan Song*, John Galsworthy, 1928.

7379 When people talked about things they could remember Matey always wondered what kind of remembering they meant — the kind that was just a sort of knowing how something in the past had happened or the other kind when suddenly everything seemed to be happening all over again. — *The Deepening Stream*, Dorothy Canfield Fisher, 1930.

7380 Johnny's earliest memory of the Farm was filled with snow and the sound of sleighbells. — *The Farm*, Louis Bromfield, 1933.

7381 The memory of the public is short. — *Thirteen at Dinner*, Agatha Christie, 1933.

7382 Of his boyhood Leo Foxe-Donnel remembered only three things — his father's death, the day of the burial, and how, after that, he went for the first time to Limerick. — *A Nest of Simple Folk*, Sean O'Faolain, 1933.

7383 It was as if a curtain had fallen, hiding everything I had ever known. — *Voyage in the Dark*, Jean Rhys, 1934.

7384 Amongst the people I have met, one of those who stand out the most vividly in my memory is a certain Mr. Ramsay MacDonald. — *In Hazard*, Richard Hughes, 1938.

7385 Often I heard my mother say that the dearest memory of her life was of her blue-eyed, blond, small boy touching her face with his hand as he said, "Mother, it's tomorrow mornin'." — *The Winds of God*, Irving Bacheller, 1941.

7386 It was years since I had set foot in the ell storeroom. But yesterday Aunt Em sent me there on an errand, and the souvenirs I came upon have disturbed me ever since, teasing my mind with memories that persist like fragments of old tunes. — *And Now Tomorrow*, Rachel Field, 1942.

7387 Do you know the feeling you have when you know something quite well and yet for the life of you can't recollect it? — *Unfinished Portrait*, Agatha Christie *as* Mary Westmacott, 1944.

7388 It is an uncertain thing when an old man sits down to write a tale of his youth, in the long ago; for even if he remembers well, his memory will be cold with time; and no matter how well he remembers, he is making a drama in which the players are dead and the scenes have been shifted . . . — *The Proud and the Free*, Howard Fast, 1950.

7389 In the middle of luncheon, Henry Peverel remembered that he had promised to hear Mostyn's niece recite. — *Catherine Carter*, Pamela Hansford Johnson, 1952.

7390 Jane and Prudence were walking in the college garden before dinner. Their conversation came in excited little bursts, for Oxford is very lovely in midsummer, and the glimpses of grey towers through the trees and the river at their side moved them to reminiscences of earlier days. — *Jane and Prudence*, Barbara Pym, 1953.

7391 My earliest recollections are of being pinched. — *Bad Boy*, Jim Thompson, 1953.

7392 When Adam Cryall thought he was never going to see Palster Manor again, the view of it that he remembered with acutest longing was, he told me, from the field behind the Parsonage. — *The View from the Parsonage*, Sheila Kaye-Smith, 1954.

7393 Even in my earliest memory of him, my Uncle Dan is waving his arms and yelling at the top of his voice. — *What's the Big Hurry?*, James Yaffe, 1954.

7394 I wasn't born yet so it was Cousin Gowan who was there and big enough to see and remember and tell me afterward when I was big enough for it to make sense. — *The Town*, William Faulkner, 1957.

7395 "That nigger going down the street," said Dr. Hasselbacher, standing in the Wonder Bar, "he reminds me of you, Mr. Wormold." — *Our Man in Havana*, Graham Greene, 1958.

7396 I look back on my course of action as lunacy; and yet at the time it seemed the only way out. — *Watcher in the Shadows*, Geoffrey Household, 1960.

7397 *LONNIE:/ I remember how green the early oat fields were, that year, and how the plains looked in April, after the mesquite leafed out.* — *Horseman, Pass By*, Larry McMurtry, 1961.

7398 While I was watching the advertisements on television last night I saw Sophy Brent. I have not set eyes on her for some months, and the sight of her filled me with a curious warm mixture of nostalgia and amusement. — *The Garrick Year*, Margaret Drabble, 1964.

7399 The bridge was just the way he remembered it. — *Hurry Sundown*, K. B. Gilden, 1964.

7400 I am trying to understand what has happened to us; in particular, I am trying to remember to keep on remembering and so to avoid the tracks in which my mind used to run. — *The Youngest*, Gillian Tindall, 1967.

7401 *Cogito ergo sum.* I close my eyes and go back seventeen years. — *I Am Mary Dunne*, Brian Moore, 1968.

7402 Almost the first thing he could remember was his mother standing on a stool in the kitchen, piling tins of food into the top cupboard. — *Out of the Shelter*, David Lodge, 1970.

7403 I have lived long. So long, it takes me days to remember even parts of it, and some I can't remember at all until I've been thinking over it a little now and then for weeks, and little Johann or Friedl ask, "Urgrossmuttchi, what is that, so cold in Canada the ground is stiff?" — *The Blue Mountains of China*, Rudy Wiebe, 1970.

7404 I remember everything. — *The War of Dreams*, Angela Carter, 1974.

7405 Who is there who has not felt a sudden startled pang at reliving an old experience or feeling an old emotion? — *Curtain*, Agatha Christie, 1975.

7406 I remember, I remember, 'tis a joy to recall. — *Valley Forge*, MacKinlay Kantor, 1975.

7407 Two pieces of yesterday were in Captain Davidson's mind when he woke, and he lay looking at them in the darkness for a while. — *The Word for World Is Forest*, Ursula K. Le Guin, 1976.

7408 That morning had come back to him many times. — *One Hundred Times to China*, Lloyd

Kropp, 1979.

7409 I can remember so much: the blood and screams of the settlers at Cherry Valley as we cut scalps through to hard skull bone, and cut much else; the scent of pomade and fresh linen as I walked down Berners Street in London on my first visit with Guy Johnson; the wet, warm smell of spring livening the woodlands around Johnson Hall and wrestling with Walter Butler, his bare torso as brown as my own, and Ganundagwa watching, her brown belly beneath the British shirting so soft to touch, and London again with my Lady Frances's body glaring white in the shrouded dark stillness of the inn... — *Brother Owl*, Al Hine, 1980.

7410 Once, after class, when the dancers were standing in little groups, gossiping and stretching their muscles, the girls idly chattered about first memories. — *Louisa Brancusi*, Darrell Husted, 1980.

7411 Later, when he had the loneliness to worry the events in his mind, Strange remembered the blind man rapping through the fog toward him. — *In the Secret State*, Robert McCrum, 1980.

7412 Anna Osgood remembered what she had said very well. Nobody would need to remind her, should they be so cruel. — *Marital Rites*, Margaret Forster, 1981.

7413 I find my earliest recollection is of two huge, gleaming eyes staring at me from utter darkness. — *Confessions of a Homing Pigeon*, Nicholas Meyer, 1981.

7414 Like their father, Anna Robison's three daughters loved to remember. — *At Paradise Gate*, Jane Smiley, 1981.

7415 My great-aunt in middle age became almost a recluse and when she died I remembered very little of her, because the last time I'd visited that stuffy basement flat in St. John's Wood had been thirty-seven years before, when I was only ten. — *Wish Her Safe at Home*, Stephen Benatar, 1982.

7416 By the time Abraham Gottenberg reached Galilee, Nebraska, on September 16, 1909, he had already forgotten what Sigmund Freud looked like. — *Minds*, David Black, 1982.

7417 The first thing I remember is being under something. — *Ham on Rye*, Charles Bukowski, 1982.

7418 The summer of 1969 was one that the people of Okaloosa, Alabama (pop. 38,400) are not likely to forget. — *Season of the Strangler*, Madison Jones, 1982.

7419 It was a night for memories. — *Richard A.*, Sol Yurick, 1982.

7420 *"Amand McCamey? Sure, I remember her...."* — *The Annunciation*, Ellen Gilchrist, 1983.

7421 Fred forgot three things in a row before

he reached the front door on his way to work. — *Mrs. Caliban*, Rachel Ingalls, 1983.

7422 I even remember the weather, that morning when my bad angel asked me to go to Bart's Fair with him. — *The Courts of Illusion*, Rosemary Hawley Jarman, 1983.

7423 Why do some events linger in the memory while others fade? — *Dancing Bear*, Chaim Bermant, 1984.

7424 How seductive are the memories of one's youth! — *The Wheel of Fortune*, Susan Howatch, 1984.

7425 *As I looked back, it seemed simple and concise.* — *Gone the Dreams and Dancing*, Douglas C. Jones, 1984.

7426 It's strange what you don't forget. — *Machine Dreams*, Jayne Anne Phillips, 1984.

7427 I cannot explain it, but one of my strongest, most persistent memories of those final days at the Cable Point is of the gull. — *A Season of Peace*, G. E. Armitage, 1985.

7428 *I've forgotten his name but I can see his face as clearly as if he left the room a moment ago.* — *The Fence Walker*, William Holinger, 1985.

7429 She would always remember the night before he died, because of the eclipse. — *Natural Selections*, Gloria Nagy, 1985.

7430 When Alfred let his memories sink down to their lowest, most watery, most childish point, he came up against a green cloth. — *A Secret Life*, Gillian Nelson, 1985.

7431 I have two first memories. — *Ice and Fire*, Andrea Dworkin, 1986.

7432 All right, now as far back as I can remember — *The Seductions of Natalie Bach*, William Luvaas, 1986.

7433 I go back to Korea. — *Hey Jack!*, Barry Hannah, 1987.

7434 I could hardly have been further from Shiuli in mind or body, but a chance encounter brought her back, the memories overwhelming me like a storm. — *The Last Armenian*, Francis Rolt, 1987.

7435 One thing I remember about that afternoon, almost as vividly as I remember the aristocratic old white woman we would encounter, was something as quixotic as the scorching rays of the sun. — *A Chocolate Soldier*, Cyrus Colter, 1988.

7436 I can remember when I was young, not very young, not an infant as some people claim to remember, but still young, when my body was weak and small. — *Valley of the Shadow*, Christopher Davis, 1988.

7437 Into my eye, Willie. A fleck of you flew in there, making a tear well up — that little shining star you saw and swept onto the tip of your finger to suck. — *Labrador*, Kathryn Davis, 1988.

7438 Oh, my lost ones. — *Ghosts*, Eva Figes, 1988.

7439 Whenever I touch cold tile, I remember praying for a bathroom lock. — *Flash*, Carole Mallory, 1988.

7440 For a long time the names and faces of my past had begun to appear to me in fabulously fractured versions, rearing into sleep and onto the blank sheets of canvas I still propped against an easel, into the face of the woman I sported with, and now as I came up the steps of the farmhouse under its scrawl of gingerbread filigree and its tin roof that I could see in starlight Frank still kept painted bright as a silver bullet, onto the porch where Hazel had set out swamp flowers — dazzle fern and sweetspire and bullace — in planters and buckets, where their old red mongrel Spin nosed up out of the shadows to greet me — voiceless, snuffling — I thought I saw Frank in a slouch hat and greatcoat standing among the fallen flowers beside the althea bush at the far end of the porch, grinning at me, holding his arms out to me. — *Shine Hawk*, Charlie Smith, 1988.

7441 "'Like the needle her mother would burnish in a candle flame before probing for a splinter under her skin, memories of those days pierced her with sudden clarity: a sister's footfall on the scoured stairs, the nursery smell of clothes boiling in the copper caldron on the stove, the angle of another sister's head, intent on the pattern she was cutting on the table. For long stretches she preferred to live in deliberate forgetfulness. . . .'" — *The Lost Father*, Marina Warner, 1988.

7442 "Scraps," said Juliet McCracken. "Debris from the day before." — *Taking Shelter*, Jessica Anderson, 1989.

7443 A first coherent memory is being wheeled through leafy streets in a pram that felt too small for me (I was well able to walk). I knew it was Copenhagen. — *Jigsaw*, Sybille Bedford, 1989.

7444 As founder of the Mnemosyne Institute in Philadelphia, forty years in the trade, I trained many executives, politicians, and members of the defense establishment, and now that I am retired, with the Institute in the capable hands of my son, I would like to forget about remembering. — *The Bellarosa Connection*, Saul Bellow, 1989.

7445 "You said you would never go back," Cressida reminded me. — *A Walk in the Wood*, Anna Gilbert, 1989.

7446 *Why, with his face wrapped up in a wet towel and the barbershop chair cranked back so that only the souls of his shoes are showing, should the men of the town seek him out? That is one of my earliest memories of my father.* — *The Unwritten Chronicles of Robert E. Lee*, Lamar Herrin, 1989.

7447 "Victory is certain! Trust in God and fear not! And remember the Alamo! Remember the Alamo!" — *No Resting Place*, William Humphrey, 1989.

7448 *Barbara*: Do you remember when we were seven?/ *Claire*: No. — *The Looking-Glass Lover*, Ursula Perrin, 1989.

7449 There is an alley down the side of the garage, you may remember it, you and your friends would sometimes play there. — *Age of Iron*, J. M. Coetzee, 1990.

7450 They found the guitar he remembered. — *Dog Horse Rat*, Christopher Davis, 1990.

7451 I've always found it odd that I can recall incidents from my boyhood with clarity and precision, and yet events that happened yesterday are blurred, and I have no confidence in my ability to remember them accurately at all. — *Spider*, Patrick McGrath, 1990.

7452 "Remember me?" — *Tycoon*, Terry Pringle, 1990.

7453 By a strange quirk of fate, I was brought back by a memory. — *Through the Arc of the Rain Forest*, Karen Tei Yamashita, 1990.

7454 Toward the end of his life, Dan's earliest memory came back clearer than ever. — *The Land Was Ours*, Charles W. Bailey, 1991.

7455 My name is Stuart, and I remember everything. — *Talking It Over*, Julian Barnes, 1991.

7456 Though he was probably about the right age for it — fifty-eight — Druff didn't suppose — not even when he was most fitfully struggling to bring forth a name like something caught in his throat, or spit out the word momentarily stuck on the tip of his tongue — that what he was experiencing was aphasia, or Alzheimer's, or the beginnings of senility, or anything importantly neurological at all. — *The MacGuffin*, Stanley Elkin, 1991.

7457 On a late-winter evening in 1983, while driving through fog along the Maine coast, recollections of old campfires began to drift into the March mist, and I thought of the Abnaki Indians of the Algonquin tribe who dwelt near Bangor a thousand years ago. — *Harlot's Ghost*, Norman Mailer, 1991.

7458 How can I remember her all at once when what I want is to forget? — *Darling*, William Tester, 1991.

7459 I have a sure memory of what Magda Sevillas looked like when she arrived by taxi at my home on the outskirts of Salonika for our first tutorial session that March afternoon in 1938. — *School for Pagan Lovers*, Edmund Keeley, 1993.

7460 From the summer of my twelfth year I carry a series of images more vivid and lasting than any others of my boyhood and indelible beyond all attempts the years make to erase or fade them.... — *Montana 1948*, Larry Watson, 1993.

Recovery

7461 There are various ways of mending a broken heart, but perhaps going to a learned conference is one of the more unusual. — *No Fond Return of Love*, Barbara Pym, 1961.

7462 I have had, now, time to recover; a smooth week in the womb. — *No Clouds of Glory*, Marian Engel, 1968.

7463 I am now at last able to move my right hand for extended periods of time. — *The Brothel in Rosenstrasse*, Michael Moorcock, 1982.

7464 Luterin had recovered. He was free of the mysterious illness. He was allowed out again. — *Helliconia Winter*, Brian W. Aldiss, 1985.

7465 Most of her friends thought Honey had recovered very quickly. — *Smile, Honey*, Anabel Donald, 1989.

7466 Jasper believes that eating turkey cures jet lag. — *Something Blue*, Ann Hood, 1991.

7467 In his lawn chair under the Carolina sun, Rob Wyatt sat recuperating, keeping an eye on what was out there — his ruined island town, the blue yonder — as if recovery could be gained by the old southern method of sitting, mulling one's fate, watching things that don't move much. — *The Fireman's Fair*, Josephine Humphreys, 1991.

Reflections

7468 Cicely Yeovil sat in a low swing chair, alternately looking at herself in a mirror and at the other occupant of the room in the flesh. Both prospects gave her undisguised satisfaction. — *When William Came*, H. H. Munro *as* Saki, 1913.

7469 Mother sat in front of her Circassian walnut dressing table, her f——, no, *plump* form enveloped in a lavender and green, chrysanthemum-covered, stork-bordered kimono, and surveyed herself in the glass. — *Mother Mason*, Bess Streeter Aldrich, 1916.

7470 Mrs. Maddison stood before the mirror and tried tipping her hat first over the right eye and then over the left. — "Mrs. Maddison," Martha Gellhorn, 1936.

7471 An oblong puddle inset in the coarse asphalt; like a fancy footprint filled to the brim with quicksilver; like a spatulate full through which you can see the nether sky. — *Bend Sinister*, Vladimir Nabokov, 1947.

7472 The mirror reflected what seemed at first a priest. A white robe, which fell from his thick shoulders in crescent folds, circumscribed with diminishing accuracy the ponderous art of his great head, and gave to his obesity the suggestion of vulnerability rather than strength as he sat face to face with the fact of himself. — *A Long Day's Dying*, Frederick Buechner, 1950.

7473 Mrs. Van Rydock moved a little back from the mirror and sighed./ "Well, that'll have to do," she murmured. — *Murder with Mirrors*, Agatha Christie, 1952.

7474 Roy Hobbs pawed at the glass before thinking to prick a match with his thumbnail and hold the spurting flame in his cupped palm close to the lower berth window, but by then he had figured it was a tunnel they were passing through and was no longer surprised at the bright sight of himself holding a yellow light over his head, peering back in. — *The Natural*, Bernard Malamud, 1952.

7475 Alayne turned from the mirror to Renny. "Do I look all right?" she asked, with an odd little smile, as though she deprecated her interest in her appearance at this moment. — *Variable Winds at Jalna*, Mazo de la Roche, 1954.

7476 She leaned across her dressing table and gazed into the gilt-framed mirror on the wall. — *Love Is Eternal*, Irving Stone, 1954.

7477 One evening — it was early in the spring — Stanley Margolies stood in front of the full-length mirror in his bathroom and looked himself up and down. — *Mister Margolies*, James Yaffe, 1962.

7478 Unaware that doom was overtaking him, Adrian Rookwhistle, in his shirt sleeves, was occupied in making faces at himself in his looking-glass. — *Rosy Is My Relative*, Gerald Durrell, 1968.

7479 One warm evening in August 1937 a girl in love stood before a mirror. — *them*, Joyce Carol Oates, 1969.

7480 Reinhart unwrapped himself from the terry-cloth robe and hung it on the back of the bathroom door by means of the embroidered label (BIGGIE'S, FOR A LOT O' GUY, trademark of a mail-order house specializing in the needs of the outsized), so obliterating the funhouse image of his gross nudity in the full-length mirror thereupon. — *Vital Parts*, Thomas Berger, 1970.

7481 The huge mirrors of the Zodiac Room at the Intercontinental, festooned in carved gilt, reflected everyone of consequence in the Ministry of Petroleum, and a lot of other officials besides. And their wives. And some of their daughters — the supple, flat-stomached young, with their saris tied low showing their navels, their hair swinging long and loose, or piled high in glossy architecture. — *The Day in Shadow*, Nayantara Sahgal, 1971.

7482 Beth was looking in the mirror of her mother's vanity. — *Small Changes*, Marge Piercy, 1973.

7483 Caroline, wearing a yellow dress, sits in her boudoir in her father's palace at Brunswick, staring into her mirror. — *The Abandoned Woman*, Richard Condon, 1977.

7484 The mirrors were wonderful. You could really see yourself. — *Afternoon of a Faun*, Shelby Hearon, 1983.

7485 Minou stood in front of the partly fogged up mirror in the public baths, looking at herself, smiling at her own reflection — brown hair, now black from being wet, brown eyes, an olive skin. — *Married to a Stranger*, Nahid Rachlin, 1983.

7486 I never tire of looking at myself. — *Goldenrod*, Peter Gault, 1984.

7487 Mireille sat in the dressing room she shared with the six other "pretty waiter girls" at the Dirty Spoon and stared at her reflection in the mirror. — *Devilseed*, Frank Yerby, 1984.

7488 I rose and went to the mirror. My name is Marcia. As to what I look like and how old I am, it's all in the mirror. — *The Limits of Vision*, Robert Irwin, 1986.

7489 Suppose you came across an antique Chinese mirror, a silvery disk of tin-rich bronze. Suppose you picked it up. — *Bronze Mirror*, Jeanne Larsen, 1991.

7490 At a quarter to three, my daughter, Kitty Montgomery, locked her register at the cosmetics counter in Pearson's Drugstore, tilted up one end of the round customer mirrors so she could see her face, and began preparing herself to go upstairs for her time with Frank Birdsong. — *Birdsong Ascending*, Sam Harrison, 1992.

Regret

7491 "I am more grieved than I can express, my dearest Miss Walsingham, by a cruel *contretemps*, which must prevent my indulging myself in the long-promised and long-expected pleasure of being at your *fête de famille* on Tuesday, to celebrate your dear father's birthday...." — *Manœuvring*, Maria Edgeworth, 1809.

7492 Perhaps I could have saved him, with only a word, two words, out of my mouth.

Perhaps I could have saved us all. But I never spoke them. — *Too Late the Phalarope*, Alan Paton, 1953.

7493 "I'm sorry," said Molly in her brisk way, "about the bag, Mr. Wragg." — *The Visitors*, Mary McMinnies, 1958.

7494 If you will tie a little blue cloth about such everyday things as socks and shirts and some handkerchiefs and a suit, then I suppose a bit of the dust from where you have been and even a smell of the soap you have used will go in there as well, and while I was shaping the knot I looked up as if a hand had been put steady on my shoulder, and I was seeing where they had been with me, and trying to think what else I might have done, or perhaps should have said at those times to put me in a better place, with more to show for my years and less, much less, to be sorry for. — *Up, into the Singing Mountain*, Richard Llewellyn, 1960.

7495 I should of been in school that April day. — *A Day No Pigs Would Die*, Robert Newton Peck, 1973.

7496 Abel regretted everything he had done. — *The Olive of Minerva*, Edward Dahlberg, 1976.

7497 "Jesus," Eddie said, "what a shame." — *Western Motel*, Polly Gross, 1985.

7498 A few months before he died, my father's father asked me to forgive him for not being able to climb the ramps at Tiger Stadium and watch me play football for Louisiana State University. — *Tupelo Nights*, John Ed Bradley, 1988.

7499 Regret can wash over you like water over stone. Regret can just wear you away. — *No Regrets*, Fern Kupfer, 1989.

Religion

7500 It is a thing past all contesting, that, in the Reformation, there was a spirit of far greater carnality among the champions of the cause, than among those who in later times so courageously, under the Lord, upheld the unspotted banners of the Covenant. — *Ringan Gilhaize*, John Galt, 1823.

7501 One night, at the latter end of April 1665, the family of a citizen of London carrying on an extensive business as a grocer in Wood Street, Cheapside, were assembled, according to custom, at prayer. — *Old Saint Paul's*, William Harrison Ainsworth, 1841.

7502 The Spanish Calendar is simpler than the Aztecan. In fact, Christian methods, of whatever nature, are better than heathen. — *The Fair God*, Lew Wallace, 1873.

7503 As, in the triumph of Christianity, the old religion lingered latest in the country, and died out at last as but paganism — the religion of the villagers, before the advance of the Christian Church; so, in an earlier century, it was in places remote from town-life that the older and purer forms of paganism itself had survived the longest. — *Marius the Epicurean*, Walter Pater, 1885.

7504 Khaled stood in the third heaven, which is the heaven of precious stones, and of Asrael, the angel of Death. — *Khaled*, F. Marion Crawford, 1891.

7505 In the days when Lord George Gordon became a Jew, and was suspected of insanity; when, out of respect for the prophecies, England denied her Jews every civic right except that of paying taxes; when the *Gentleman's Magazine* had ill words for the infidel alien; when Jewish marriages were invalid and bequests for Hebrew colleges void; when a prophet prophesying Primrose Day would have been set in the stocks, though Pitt inclined his private ear to Benjamin Goldsmid's views on the foreign loans — in those days, when Tevele Schiff was Rabbi in Israel, and Dr. de Falk, the Master of the Tetragrammaton, saint and Cabbalistic conjuror, flourished in Wellclose Square, and the composer of *The Death of Nelson* was a choir-boy in the Great Synagogue; Joseph Grobstock, pillar of the same, emerged one afternoon into the spring sunshine at the fag-end of the departing stream of worshippers. In his hand was a large canvas bag, and in his eye a twinkle. — *The King of Schnorrers*, Israel Zangwill, 1894.

7506 Has the age of miracle gone by, or is it still possible to the Voice of Faith calling aloud upon the earth to wring from the dumb heavens an audible answer to its prayer? — *The Wizard*, H. Rider Haggard, 1896.

7507 Go not with fanatics who see beyond thee and thine, and beyond the coming and the going of thee and thine, and yet beyond the ending thereof, — thy life and the lives that thou begettest, and the lives that shall spring from them, world without end, — for such need thee not, nor see thee, nor know thy lamenting, so confounded are they with thy damnation and the damnation of thy offspring, and the multiple damnation of those multitudes that shall be of thy race begotten, unto the number of fishes in thin waters, and unto the number of fishes in great waters. — *Ryder*, Djuna Barnes, 1928.

7508 When the Carmelo Mission of Alta California was being built, some time around 1776, a group of twenty converted Indians abandoned religion during a night, and in the morning they were gone from their huts. — *The Pastures of Heaven*, John Steinbeck, 1932.

7509 One morning in the late summer of 1930 the proprietor and several guests at the Union Hotel at Crestcrego, Texas, were annoyed to discover Biblical texts freshly written across the blotter on the public writing-desk. — *Heaven's My Destination*, Thornton Wilder, 1934.

7510 They recount how Charlemagne, the Franks' Emperor, combined religion with his family squabbles by setting forth to relieve the Pope at Rome. — *Smith*, James Branch Cabell, 1935.

7511 They had all told him that it was a sin to miss mass on Sunday, and God didn't like it if you did, because when you missed mass on Sunday, you hurt God's feelings, and when you hurt God's feelings and He was disappointed in you, you didn't know what He mightn't do to you, almost anything. — *A World I Never Made*, James T. Farrell, 1936.

7512 "And now to God the Father..." Old Mr. John Corner's voice rose as usual upon the phrase and paused there. — *Castle Corner*, Joyce Cary, 1938.

7513 The chapel stall of carved oak on which Sir Horatio Hornblower was sitting was most uncomfortable, and the sermon which the Dean of Westminster was preaching was deadly dull. — *Lord Hornblower*, C. S. Forester, 1946.

7514 The Master of the College of Augurs to Caius Julius Caesar, Supreme Pontiff and Dictator of the Roman People./ (Copies to the Priest of Capitoline Jupiter, etc.; to Madam President of the College of the Vestal Virgins, etc., etc.)/ [*September 1, 45* B.C.]/ To the most reverend Supreme Pontiff:/ Sixth report of this date./ Readings of the noon sacrifice:/ A goose: matriculations of the heart and liver. Herniation of the diaphragm./ Second goose and a cock: Nothing to remark./ A Pigeon: ominous condition, kidney displaced, liver enlarged and yellow in color. Pink quartz in crop. Further detailed study has been ordered./ Second pigeon: Nothing to remark./ Observed flights: an eagle from three miles north of Mt. Soracte to limit of vision over Tivoli. The bird showed some uncertainty as to direction in its approach toward the city./ Thunder: No thunder has been heard since that last reported twelve days ago./ Health and long life to the Supreme Pontiff. — *The Ides of March*, Thornton Wilder, 1948.

7515 The six rooms that they rented were built around a courtyard, a square of about eight feet with an uneven cement floor in the middle of which stood the divine tulasi that his wife worshiped. — *A Silence of Desire*, Kamala Markandaya, 1960.

7516 They have said that we owe allegiance to Safety, that he is our Red Cross who will provide us with ointment and bandages for our wounds and remove the foreign ideas the glass beads of fantasy the bent hairpins of unreason embedded in our minds. — *Faces in the Water*, Janet Frame, 1961.

7517 "Emily, pass the marmalade."/ But Emily, who was praying, did not hear. — *The Prince of Darkness & Co.*, Daryl Hine, 1961.

7518 *Libanius to Priscus/ Antioch, March [A.D.] 380/* Yesterday morning as I was about to enter the lecture hall, I was stopped by a Christian student who asked me in a voice eager with malice, "Have you heard about the Emperor Theodosius?"/ I cleared my throat ready to investigate the nature of this question, but he was too quick for me. "He has been baptized a Christian." — *Julian*, Gore Vidal, 1964.

7519 *"Ecumenism,"* Bishop Charles de Montauban said, tugging at the sash of his cassock and stretching his thin fingers toward the logs burning in the hearth, *"is undoubtedly the most overworked word in every tongue on earth. Pope John said it so much more simply and directly, you know. He had a real genius for that sort of thing. 'All men are brothers and have one Father, no matter what the different names we may call Him.'"* — *The Anthem*, Noel B. Gerson, 1967.

7520 In my life I've never given much attention to religion, but if I'd had a bent that way, I believe Cassius Marcellus Clay would have made a Calvinist out of me — *Hacey Miller*, James Sherburne, 1971.

7521 Praise be to God, the Merciful, the Compassionate, the Lord of the Two Worlds, and blessing and peace upon the Prince of Prophets, our Lord and Master Muhammad, whom God bless and preserve with abiding and continuing peace and blessings until the Day of the Faith! — *Eaters of the Dead*, Michael Crichton, 1976.

7522 *Nos miseri homines et egeni...* / For the first time since becoming a fellow of the college, I was listening to grace in hall. — *A Memorial Service*, J. I. M. Stewart, 1976.

7523 His name was Jud, Judson Rivers. When he was growing up, in the Bethel hills ten or twelve miles from town, the religion still had a great deal of the old starch left in it. — *Passage Through Gehenna*, Madison Jones, 1978.

7524 Whisper unto my soul, *I am thy salvation.* — *Son of the Morning*, Joyce Carol Oates, 1978.

7525 Religion, Amy thought, of all things for anybody in this family to break up about. Anything else, everything else, but religion? — *Over and Above*, Laura Z. Hobson, 1979.

7526 "Bless, o Lord, thy gifts to our use and us to thy service; for Christ's sake. Amen." — *Cannibals and Missionaries*, Mary McCarthy, 1979.

7527 The Greeks on the beautiful island of Cyprus worship Aphrodite, the goddess of love.

They pretend that they don't, that she is only a myth among the shards, a legend to beguile the tourists. But when they speak of her, their eyes have archaic shadows in them, and they recede a little, toward some private mischief. — *Aphrodite's Cave*, N. Richard Nash, 1980.

7528 "Is it *always* a mortal sin to eat meat on Friday?" demanded Father Francis X. Lyon, S.J., from his high perch atop the platform desk. — *A Catholic Education*, Robert Benard, 1982.

7529 And to think they once had a Chinese joss-house right on this plot my child, she said, standing in her shop expecting customers. — *Just Relations*, Rodney Hall, 1982.

7530 "Thank you, God, for Rita Manning." — *The Diviner*, Marilyn Harris, 1982.

7531 There was a time when religion was the overpowering concern of all the world, or at least the world as it appeared to the people who first settled on America's northeast coast. — *Covenant of Grace*, Jane Gilmore Rushing, 1982.

7532 When I think of all the names of cardinals lettered across the facades of churches in this city as testimony to their restorative ardor, I wonder if Connolly is content now with the more fleeting immortality he won for his efforts to bring the Holy Roman Catholic Church into the mainstream of the twentieth century. — *Connolly's Life*, Ralph McInerny, 1983.

7533 In the beginning I suppose there was a God, but he must be too bored by now to care about anyone or anything and certainly too preoccupied to take any note of the chipped plaster saints, the multicolored candles, the fragrance of incense, the dishes of mangoes and bananas and pennies, the gilt prayer cards: in short, all the elaborate equipment of Santeria which my mother assembled. — *Saul's Book*, Paul T. Rogers, 1983.

7534 Mrs. Flax was happiest when she was leaving a place, but I wanted to stay put long enough to fall down crazy and hear the Word of God. — *Mermaids*, Patty Dann, 1986.

7535 Damnation and forgiveness; we can't do without them. — *Family Laundry*, Dorie Friend, 1986.

7536 As long as he sought the Lord. In the twinkling of an eye before we heard Mother scream, my father said, "And as long as he sought the Lord, God made him to prosper." — *The Quick and the Dead*, Z. Vance Wilson, 1986.

7537 I knew that Mamta would never become a Christian. — *The Godchild*, Stephen Alter, 1987.

7538 She was wearing a picture of Christ giving sight to the blind when the supervisor came to fetch her. — *Imperial Purple*, Gillian Bradshaw, 1988.

7539 Edmund, a surgeon on the hospital staff, is thinking about the wisdom of the Church, which canonized St. Martin of Tours: "...met a beggar almost naked and frozen with cold ... cut his cloak in two and gave him half. That night he saw Our Lord clothed in the half cloak and heard him say to the angels, 'Martin, yet a catechumen, hath wrapped me in this garment.'" — *American Earthquakes*, Constance Urdang, 1988.

7540 At 3:00 A.M. Georgie sat on the bare tiles in her nightgown, poised over the toilet bowl in earnest prayer. — *Laugh Lines*, Ann Berk, 1989.

7541 *The priests of Pop and Zam in a time of deep grievances walked twice around the cave and stopped at the altar and at the altar each of the priests ran his hands over the stone where it was written — Justice Exists! Heaven Exists! At which point the great priest Chilam declared: Perhaps so. Perhaps not. Of what can we be certain? When were we ever certain?* — *Maya Red*, J. R. Humphreys, 1989.

7542 I am doomed to remember a boy with a wrecked voice — not because of his voice, or because he was the smallest person I ever knew, or even because he was the instrument of my mother's death, but because he is the reason I believe in God; I am a Christian because of Owen Meany. — *A Prayer for Owen Meany*, John Irving, 1989.

7543 I used to be proud that there is no sainthood in Judaism. — *Lives of the Saints*, David R. Slavitt, 1989.

7544 That was the summer the city filled with religious recruiters. — *Moments of Favor*, Daniel Bergner, 1991.

7545 The remote Australian tribe called the Barramatjara had two early brushes with Christianity, both of them so different as to make the tribespeople question whether Christianity was one entity or a series of intrusions from remote space. — *Flying Hero Class*, Thomas Keneally, 1991.

7546 Before finally, if not formally, renouncing her religion, Claire Mackey found herself wishing that Catholics had been encouraged to read the King James Version. — *Approaching Priests*, Mary Leland, 1991.

7547 The first light of morning barely illumined the sky as Gustad Noble faced eastward to offer his orisons to Ahura Mazda. — *Such a Long Journey*, Rohinton Mistry, 1991.

7548 Holy Father,/ I write to inform Your Excellency of the results of my investigation into the merits for possible Beatification of Frederich Loebus. — *The Viper Tree*, Joseph Monninger, 1991.

7549 Midway through the morning prayer, Edwin rubbed a patch in the pinestraw with his boot toe, shredded his cigarette into the sand. — *Hello Down There*, Michael Parker, 1993.

Reproach

7550 The kettle did it! Don't tell me what Mrs. Peerybingle said. I know better. — *The Cricket on the Hearth*, Charles Dickens, 1845.

7551 One thing was certain, that the *white* kitten had had nothing to do with it — it was the black kitten's fault entirely. — *Through the Looking-Glass and What Alice Found There*, Lewis Carroll, 1872.

7552 On their way back to the farm-house where they were boarding, Sewell's wife reproached him for what she called his recklessness. — *The Minister's Charge*, William Dean Howells, 1887.

7553 "I won't have it, Pearson; so it's no use your talking. If I had my way you shouldn't touch any of the field hands. And when I get my way — that won't be so very long — I will take good care you sha'n't. But you sha'n't hit Dan." — *With Lee in Virginia*, G. A. Henty, 1890.

7554 Like Adam, our first conspicuous ancestor, I must begin, and lay the blame upon a woman; I am glad to recognize that I differ from the father of my sex in no important particular, being as manlike as most of his sons. — *Lady Baltimore*, Owen Wister, 1906.

7555 "Undine Spragg — how *can* you?" her mother wailed, raising a prematurely-wrinkled hand heavy with rings to defend the note which a languid "bell-boy" had just brought in. — *The Custom of the Country*, Edith Wharton, 1913.

7556 "Justine, I have told you that I do not like the coffee touched until I come down. . . ." — *A Family and a Fortune*, Ivy Compton-Burnett, 1939.

7557 She had, Hannah decided, no one to blame but herself. — *Girls Turn Wives*, Norma Klein, 1976.

7558 "Blame is not important," my father used to say. — *Betrayed by F. Scott Fitzgerald*, Ron Carlson, 1977.

7559 I was Harry's fault. — *Adventure*, Borden Deal, 1978.

7560 "You could have been more gentle, Frank. That's all." — *Winter Journey*, T. Alan Broughton, 1980.

7561 "Waste of good water!" Miss Plimsoll cried, coming into the kitchen where Emma had been allowed to draw a glass of water but had not immediately turned the tap off. "Waste not, want not." — *A Bonfire*, Pamela Hansford Johnson, 1981.

7562 He no longer wondered where to lay down blame or whose was the responsibility or what the responsibility was. — *Seaview*, Toby Ol-son, 1982.

7563 Ellie said, "David, you have called the world down upon us."/ "Not to worry. They won't accept." — *A World Too Wide*, Gregory McdonaId, 1987.

7564 I don't know it yet but I'm getting yelled at for walking under the wing. — *Under Heat*, Michael David Brown, 1989.

7565 People made false estimates of her, how she was to blame. — *The Rise of Life on Earth*, Joyce Carol Oates, 1991.

7566 This is what his father always called him whenever he'd done something bad: "Where were *you* when this happened, *Boy*? What did you think you were doing, *Boy*?" — *Lost Boys*, Orson Scott Card, 1992.

Restaurants

7567 "Was you cal'latin' to buy one of them turnovers, bub?" casually inquired Mr. Clark, ceasing to gaze at his steaming boots, which were planted against the bulging center of the station stove, and turning toward the boy at the lunch counter. — *Partners of the Tide*, Joseph C. Lincoln, 1905.

7568 It was about half-past five on an October afternoon when Marya Zelli came out of the Café Lavenue, which is a dignified and comparatively expensive establishment on the Boulevard du Montparnasse. — *Quartet*, Jean Rhys, 1928.

7569 It was close to 2:00 A.M. and drizzling outside, and every time anyone entered to have a quick cup of coffee at the dirty counter or get a pack of cigarettes from the clanking machine near the door, there would beat on the consciousness of the four people inside the sudden coldness of the instreaming air and the rhythmic hum of the city as it pulsed through midtown, still undiminished. — *The Little Stockade*, Natalie Anderson Scott, 1954.

7570 The small hotel on Calle de Marengo stood back-to-back with a German restaurant whose cooks and kitchens had been flown from Berlin to Madrid by the late Luftwaffe. — *The Oldest Confession*, Richard Condon, 1958.

7571 Hugh Bennett had lunch that day as usual in Giuseppe's, which was the only good place to eat near the office. Good, that is, and cheap. — *The Progress of a Crime*, Julian Symons, 1960.

7572 "Kaffee, bitte. Schwarz," said Daniel Mond. — *The Sabre Squadron*, Simon Raven, 1966.

7573 No sooner has one gone over one's surprise at finding a genuine coaching inn less than 40 miles from London—and 8 from the M1—than one is marvelling at the quality of the equally genuine English fare (the occasional disaster apart!). — *The Green Man*, Kingsley Amis, 1969.

7574 The long-distance waitress sniffs the counter, she keeps glancing at the sandwiches two miles away. — *Babel*, Alan Burns, 1969.

7575 This is an old diner like the ones Cody and his father ate in, long ago, with that oldfashioned railroad car ceiling and sliding doors—the board where bread is cut is worn down fine as if with bread dust and a plane; the icebox ("Say I got some nice homefries tonight Cody!") is a huge brownwood thing with oldfashioned pull-out handles, windows, tile walls, full of lovely pans of eggs, butter pats, piles of bacon—old lunchcarts always have a dish of sliced raw onions ready to go on hamburgs. — *Visions of Cody*, Jack Kerouac, 1972.

7576 Eugene Quebaro, homeowner and husband, sat with the wife of another man in a restaurant on East 60th Street run by a canny Filipino who carried a $127,000 retirement policy sold him by Gene. — *Money Is Love*, Richard Condon, 1975.

7577 The Elite Café was entered by a staircase from the foyer of a cinema. — *Lanark*, Alasdair Gray, 1981.

7578 The cash register in the Greek's diner was an army-green NCR model that had been there when the Greek bought the place. — *Rules of the Knife Fight*, Walter Walker, 1986.

7579 Time was of the essence to the owners of L'Etoile de West, a restaurant slated to open in October. — *Desert Fabuloso*, Lisa Lovenheim, 1987.

7580 Nicholas Thornby peered needle-eyed into the delicatessen. — *Not That Sort of Girl*, Mary Wesley, 1987.

7581 *There was a crowd at the Rotonde but they found a table inside looking out through the windows at the* terrasse *and the boulevard.* — *Hemingway's Suitcase*, MacDonald Harris, 1990.

7582 You tend to notice the strawberry tart in Kranzler's Café a lot more when your diet forbids you to have any. — *The Pale Criminal*, Philip Kerr, 1990.

7583 Matthew never takes notes in a restaurant. — *Reservations Recommended*, Eric Kraft, 1990.

Reticence

7584 There is some rust about every man at the beginning. — It is so every where; though in some nations (among the French, for instance) the ideas of the inhabitants, from climate, or what other cause you will, are so vivacious, so eternally on the wing, that they must, even in small societies, have a frequent collision; the rust therefore will wear off sooner: but in Britain, it often goes with a man to his grave; nay, he dares not even pen a *hic jacet* to speak out for him after his death. — *The Man of Feeling*, Henry Mackenzie, 1771.

7585 Old Sergei walked in front. All the conversation Seryozha had, for the space of fifteen miles, was the expression of his father's neck. — *The Far-Away Bride*, Stella Benson, 1930.

7586 Alianor de Retteville lay on her bed and looked at Giles who was her lover. She did not speak. She had nothing to say. He did not speak either. — *The Corner That Held Them*, Sylvia Townsend Warner, 1948.

7587 As his train from London approached Kemble, only the impassivity of his English fellow-passengers kept Sturgess silent. — *The River Line*, Charles Morgan, 1949.

7588 It would not be strictly true to say that Wolfe and I were not speaking that Monday morning in May. — *If Death Ever Slept*, Rex Stout, 1957.

7589 There was such a long pause that I wondered whether my Mamma and my Papa were ever going to speak to each other again. — *The Fountain Overflows*, Rebecca West, 1957.

7590 Neither of them had spoken for a while and the silence was beginning to weigh on the younger woman. — "The Narrow Boat," A. L. Barker, 1963.

7591 As we walked across the fields we hardly spoke. I, myself, no longer had the heart to try and make conversation. — *The Seed and the Sower*, Laurens van der Post, 1963.

7592 Karl said, "Tussy?"/ She heard him, but she did not answer. — *Tussy Is Me*, Michael Hastings, 1970.

7593 There were two subjects I never discussed: my dead wife and Cashelmara. — *Cashelmara*, Susan Howatch, 1974.

7594 The man at the edge of the tide-mark stood a little apart from his fellows, not choosing to join the talk of the ship-boat's crew, wanting only to enjoy the hot July sun and the brief peace of the Plymouth shore. — *Running Proud*, Nicholas Monsarrat, 1978.

7595 —another Wednesday and I can't talk any more to anyone. — *The Duchess's Diary*, Robin Chapman, 1980.

7596 He couldn't tell her he was desperate. — *The Hanging Garden*, David Wagoner, 1980.

7597 Words fail me, Clio. — *The Newton Letter*, John Banville, 1982.

7598 I want to tell you these things because you have said to me this afternoon and before that you do not know certain things about me and that I have closed some things inside of me that I never speak of circus, he added imitating her accent. — *Quintesse*, Kevin Kiely, 1982.

7599 Both women in the wegiwa were silent now, each lost in her own thoughts, each feeling the resurgence of pain that their conversation had inspired. — *Johnny Logan*, Allan W. Eckert, 1983.

7600 *February 4* Baby so silent after the train pulled out of Chicago, I finally asked what was on her mind. — *Running Time*, Gavin Lambert, 1983.

7601 When I was five I began to have moments of sudden silence. — *Cobwebwalking*, Sara Banerji, 1987.

7602 "You know, we don't talk much anymore," Kate said. — *Doctors & Women*, Susan Cheever, 1987.

7603 Pete Butcher had not meant to speak to her. — *Scar Lover*, Harry Crews, 1992.

7604 It was I that saw most and have said least in the matter of the firedrake and the nightcrow, the soldier of God and the hunting of that fair white hind, the Queen of England. — *Firedrake's Eye*, Patricia Finney, 1992.

7605 It wasn't until we were halfway through France that we noticed Maretta wasn't talking. — *Hideous Kinky*, Esther Freud, 1992.

Riding

7606 It was a fine April morning (excepting that it had snowed hard the night before, and the ground remained covered with a dazzling mantle of six inches in depth) when two horsemen rode up to the Wallace Inn. — *The Black Dwarf*, Sir Walter Scott, 1817.

7607 Myles Falworth was but eight years of age at that time, and it was only afterwards, and when he grew old enough to know more of the ins and outs of the matter, that he could remember by bits and pieces the things that afterwards happened; how one evening a knight came clattering into the court-yard upon a horse, red-nostrilled and smeared with the sweat and foam of a desperate ride — Sir John Dale, a dear friend of the blind Lord. — *Men of Iron*, Howard Pyle, 1891.

7608 Upon a broad highway, straight and smooth, between ample farms, where the cheerful activities of spring sent forth a medley of noises very pleasant to hear, a young man rode his bicycle with leisurely strokes. — *Rosalynde's Lovers*, Maurice Thompson, 1901.

7609 The road which had begun as a rutted cart-track sank presently to a grassy footpath among scrub oaks, and as the boughs whipped his face the young man cried out impatiently and pulled up his horse to consider. — *Midwinter*, John Buchan, 1923.

7610 May fifth, 1587, Christopher Guest came into Plymouth from Exeter way, he and his man Anthony Little; both were well mounted, and a led horse carried effects of Guest's. — *Croatan*, Mary Johnston, 1923.

7611 Sitting sidewise on the mule, young James Fraser swung his tired, heavy legs. — *Marching On*, James Boyd, 1927.

7612 He was riding the hundred miles from T'o Tlakai to Tsé Lani to attend a dance, or rather, for the horse-racing that would come afterwards. — *Laughing Boy*, Oliver La Farge, 1929.

7613 The sky is overcast. A day in early July, 1634, is near its end. Two young men are riding at breakneck speed on a country road between hedgerows in the east of England. — *A Candle in the Wilderness*, Irving Bacheller, 1930.

7614 Hugh Tracy passed Indian Flat around seven of the morning, traveling fast and feeling only a slight pucker in his right flank where the bullet hole had been three months healing. — *Starlight Rider*, Ernest Haycox, 1933.

7615 Forty hours of steady riding brought Buck Surratt across the wide desert to these foothills. — *Trail Smoke*, Ernest Haycox, 1936.

7616 Two things, among countless thousands of others, were occurring simultaneously: Hopalong Cassidy, leaving a deputy to hold down the sheriff's office, was on his way to the Double Y, the ranch which he and Buck Peters jointly owned; and a considerable distance south of the town he had just left, another man was riding, bound for this town and for the Double Y beyond it. — *Hopalong Cassidy Takes Cards*, Clarence E. Mulford, 1937.

7617 On the grey afternoon of December 22nd, 1569, Nicholas Herries sat his lovely mare Juno on the moor inland from Silloth in Cumberland, every nerve alert because of the event that any instant might bring. — *The Bright Pavilions*, Hugh Walpole, 1940.

7618 Through the fresh, springtide morning of the Helderberg Hills, a lone horseman rode.

—Sunrise to Sunset, Samuel Hopkins Adams, 1950.

7619 They emerged from the dark woods and were suddenly in the hot September sunshine. At the bottom of the hill their horses stopped to drink from the shallow stream. — *The President's Lady*, Irving Stone, 1951.

7620 Instead of riding on to Relief's main four corners and beyond it to the Revenue Bar, his destination, Sam Holley put his horse into the deep night of the side alley by Poague's Emporium and tied him at its barred side door. —*Saddle by Starlight*, Luke Short, 1952.

7621 Crip Diels broke camp and started in across the Pass just as the sky was changing from a slate gray to dull blue.—*Pale Moon*, W. R. Burnett, 1956.

7622 Cain came riding down through a cloud. —*Riders of Judgment*, Frederick Manfred, 1957.

7623 The three men rode in through narrow East Canyon, then turned, at a sharp angle, toward the faraway cluster of long, low wooden buildings they could see, through a thin, mirage-like haze of blowing dust, stretching irregularly across the gently rolling floor of the tableland. —*Bitter Ground*, W. R. Burnett, 1958.

7624 Of all the myriad dawns which had broken over the dark Wald this one was the most beautiful, because never before had nature been afforded so much assistance. Three mounted figures occupied the crest of the hill: Macio of the Roymarcks, who had been the handsomest man on the plateau in his day, and his two daughters, both of whom were lovely enough to aid the sun in achieving a moment of transcendence. — *The Darkness and the Dawn*, Thomas B. Costain, 1959.

7625 Coming across the flat valley floor, Lin Ballou, riding a paint horse and leading a pack animal, struck the Snake River Road at a point where Hank Colqueen's homestead made a last forlorn stand against the vast stretch of sand and sage that swept eastward mile after mile until checked by the distant high mesa. —"A Rider of the High Mesa," Ernest Haycox, 1960.

7626 Among those competent to judge, Don Vito Cantú was the best horseman ever seen in Spain. — *The Hands of Cantú*, Tom Lea, 1964.

7627 Larry Angeluzzi spurred his jet black horse proudly through a canyon formed by two great walls of tenements, and at the foot of each wall, marooned on their separate blue-slate sidewalks, little children stopped their games to watch him with silent admiration. — *The Fortunate Pilgrim*, Mario Puzo, 1965.

7628 Coasting home fed-up, a spluttering engine below his knees, Alley Jaggers falls out of love with his motor-bike. Revving, he shuts out the engine noise and tunes in to himself with both ears, as he always does when he is miser-able. —*Alley Jaggers*, Paul West, 1966.

7629 This boy comes riding with his arms high and wide, his head dipped low, his ass light in the saddle, as if about to be shot into orbit from a forked sling. —*In Orbit*, Wright Morris, 1967.

7630 Mules, everybody agreed, were more sure-footed, so Isabella of Spain rode on a mule, her heavily pregnant body wrapped in a rain-repellent leather cloak, on her head a hood of the same material, her feet encased in a pair of boots similar to those worn by foot soldiers. — *The King's Pleasure*, Norah Lofts, 1969.

7631 Riding horses in a back pasture, gone wild. — *The Sunlight Dialogues*, John Gardner, 1972.

7632 In the time of a strange withered spring, a lone cowboy rode through country where scattered little flat-topped hills rose sharply above a rolling terrain watered by narrow running streams.—*Mary Dove*, Jane Gilmore Rushing, 1974.

7633 He rode into the dark of the woods and dismounted. — *The Killer Angels*, Michael Shaara, 1974.

7634 The elderly, rawboned, grizzled trail boss rode a circuit around the herd, quietly cursing to himself. — *Terrible Teague Bunch*, Gary Jennings, 1975.

7635 He thought: When I get there nobody will believe I could have managed a ride like this and neither by God will I. — *The Shootist*, Glendon Swarthout, 1975.

7636 Sam Dana reined up his bay on the foothill bench above the Bar D spread that he hadn't seen for more than a year. — *Trouble Country*, Luke Short, 1976.

7637 It was late in the afternoon of a torrid day in July, 1836, that Carter Blair arrived on the banks of the Ohio. He had been in the saddle since early morning, except for an hour at midday when he had stopped to eat, and in the sultry heat that lay on Kentucky he was beginning to find the way somewhat long. — *The Buckeyes*, Brand Whitlock, 1977.

7638 He saw them coming along Wire Road, could almost hear the steel-shod hooves on the frozen ground, although they were at least a mile away and all he could actually hear was the wind in the black locusts around him. —*Elkhorn Tavern*, Douglas C. Jones, 1980.

7639 The woman rode like fury, a column of yellow dust rising behind her and her mare's hooves rattling dully against the dried and rutted mud of the lower swamp trail.—*Swamp Angel*, Dorothy Langley, 1982.

7640 The single horseman was motionless at the crown of a small hill under a moon coming full. —*Season of Yellow Leaf*, Douglas C. Jones, 1983.

7641 She had kept silent until now, but when they brought a horse to her, saddled and bridled, the stirrups tied up neatly over the seat, Theophano said, "Shimon, I cannot ride." — *The Belt of Gold*, Cecelia Holland, 1984.

7642 Danny Kachiah pulled his hat tight, kicked his left foot free of the stirrup, and hunched forward in the saddle. — *Winterkill*, Craig Lesley, 1984.

7643 When the raiders emerged from the canyon, the boy could see that they had grown old and fat on their horses. — *The Great Thirst*, William Duggan, 1985.

7644 As he came riding back into the courtyard, his stableman came out to greet him, holding a lantern above his head. — *The Fourth King*, Glen Petrie, 1986.

7645 At a swift signal from one of their number the five young women swung their horses in a semicircle and came galloping across the meadow, toward where a brightly painted green and red and blue wagon stood. — *Robert and Arabella*, Kathleen Winsor, 1986.

7646 Moses Franklin stopped his bay atop a short rise of ground along the upper edge of a deep arroyo, lifted his hat, and scratched his head as he surveyed the rolling carpet of grass that lay before him. — *Franklin's Crossing*, Clay Reynolds, 1992.

Rivers

7647 The fine estuary which penetrates the American coast between the fortieth and the forty-first degrees of latitude, is formed by the confluence of the Hudson, the Hackensack, the Passaic, the Raritan, and a multitude of smaller streams, all of which pour their tribute into the ocean within the space named. — *The Water-Witch*, James Fenimore Cooper, 1830.

7648 Wandering in those deserts of Africa that border the Erythræan Sea, I came to the river Nile, to that ancient, and mighty, and famous stream, whose waters yielded us our earliest civilisation, and which, after having witnessed the formation of so many states and the invention of so many creeds, still flow on with the same serene beneficence, like all that we can conceive of Deity; in form sublime, in action systematic; in nature bountiful, in source unknown. — *Contarini Fleming*, Benjamin Disraeli, 1832.

7649 A wide plain, where the broadening Floss hurries on between its green banks to the sea, and the loving tide, rushing to meet it, checks its passage with an impetuous embrace. — *The Mill on the Floss*, George Eliot, 1860.

7650 On the 1st of May, 1774, the anchor-ice, which for so many months had silver-plated the river's bed with frosted crusts, was ripped off and dashed into a million gushing flakes by the amber outrush of the springtide flood. — *Cardigan*, Robert W. Chambers, 1901.

7651 The winter had broken early and the Scotch River was running ice-free and full from bank to bank. — *The Man from Glengarry*, Ralph Connor, 1901.

7652 Mrs. Rachel Lynde lived just where the Avonlea main road dipped down into a little hollow, fringed with alders and ladies' eardrops, and traversed by a brook that had its source away back in the woods of the old Cuthbert place; it was reputed to be an intricate, headlong brook in its earlier course through those woods, with dark secrets of pool and cascade; but by the time it reached Lynde's Hollow it was a quiet, well-conducted little stream, for not even a brook could run past Mrs. Rachel Lynde's door without due regard for decency and decorum; it probably was conscious that Mrs. Rachel was sitting at her window, keeping a sharp eye on everything that passed, from brooks and children up, and that if she noticed anything odd or out of place she would never rest until she had ferreted out the whys and wherefores thereof. — *Anne of Green Gables*, L. M. Montgomery, 1908.

7653 The time was the year 1872, and the place a bend in the river above a long pond terminating in a dam. — *The Riverman*, Stewart Edward White, 1908.

7654 Adam Larey gazed with hard and wondering eyes down the silent current of the red river upon which he meant to drift away into the desert. — *Wanderer of the Wasteland*, Zane Grey, 1923.

7655 High above the St. Lawrence stood Louis, Count Frontenac alone, soon after his arrival at Quebec as Governor. From a window of the Château St. Louis he was looking across the vast stream which is more renowned than any other in that hemisphere. — *The Power and the Glory*, Gilbert Parker, 1925.

7656 The Styx lay silent. — *There Is Another Heaven*, Robert Nathan, 1929.

7657 Northeastward of the heart of New England there is a broad river that runs widening to the sea, and all along its lower reaches, where it lets in the ocean salt and the tides, it is a boundary marking more than a division between two States of the Union. — *Mirthful Haven*, Booth Tarkington, 1930.

7658 One afternoon late in October of the year 1697, Euclide Auclair, the philosopher apothecary of Quebec, stood on the top of Cap

Diamant gazing down the broad, empty river far beneath him. — *Shadows on the Rock*, Willa Cather, 1931.

7659 A few miles south of Soledad, the Salinas River drops in close to the hillside bank and runs deep and green. — *Of Mice and Men*, John Steinbeck, 1937.

7660 From this height the Rhine looked narrow, sluggish, and unimportant. — *A Stricken Field*, Martha Gellhorn, 1940.

7661 When the east wind blows up Helford river the shining waters become troubled and disturbed, and the little waves beat angrily upon the sandy shores. — *Frenchman's Creek*, Daphne du Maurier, 1941.

7662 Goodnight crossed the river at a ford whose bottom sands were scarcely covered by water and made noon camp under the shade of a lonely willow. — *The Wild Bunch*, Ernest Haycox, 1943.

7663 The river was in Bengal, India, but for the purpose of this book, these thoughts, it might as easily have been a river in America, in Europe, in England, France, New Zealand, or Timbuctoo, though they do not of course have rivers in Timbuctoo. — *The River*, Rumer Godden, 1946.

7664 About fifteen miles above New Orleans the river goes very slowly. It has broadened out there until it is almost a sea and the water is yellow with the mud of half a continent. Where the sun strikes it, it is golden. — *The Foxes of Harrow*, Frank Yerby, 1946.

7665 In the spring sun, the Ohio lay like a gleaming sickle against the wooded hills above Cincinnati. — *The Tom-Walker*, Mari Sandoz, 1947.

7666 The little town of Steubenville lay by the Missouri, whose green-gray waters, occasionally dappled with mustard-colored foam, flowed slowly southward to the sea. — *The River Journey*, Robert Nathan, 1949.

7667 It was up above in the mountain meadows and the aspens that Roan Creek found and spent its first vigor. — *Fiddlefoot*, Luke Short, 1949.

7668 The town is Galloway. The Merrimac River, broad and placid, flows down to it from the New Hampshire hills, broken at the falls to make frothy havoc on the rocks, foaming on over ancient stone towards a place where the river suddenly swings about in a wide and peaceful basin, moving on now around the flank of the town, on to places known as Lawrence and Haverhill, through a wooded valley, and on to the sea at Plum Island, where the river enters an infinity of waters and is gone. — *The Town and the City*, Jack Kerouac, 1950.

7669 When the pioneers came across the plains to the place where the Little Bird River flowed into the Abanakas, they halted. — *Tomorrow!*, Philip Wylie, 1954.

7670 This is the river. It is an Indian of a river, drunk sometimes on flood water the way only an Indian becomes drunk. It can be quiet, too, though not peaceful for the violence lies always beneath the quietness. It is not a blue river, not yet, but it will become so for this river is to be tamed and civilized as no other river in the history of civilization has been tamed and civilized. This is the Tennessee. — *Dunbar's Cove*, Borden Deal, 1957.

7671 The water was slack at the inner bank. — *Where the High Winds Blow*, David Walker, 1960.

7672 The late afternoon sun sent shadows over the water sprinkling it with glistening lights as the current passed under the East River Bridge to her left, sharp and clear. — *Love Is Where You Find It*, Paula Christian, 1961.

7673 It was over twelve years since Gilligan had camped in this spot beside the Waso Larok River, and nothing had changed. — *Gilligan's Last Elephant*, Gerald Hanley, 1962.

7674 *Along the western slopes of the Oregon Coastal Range . . . come look; the hysterical crashing of tributaries as they merge into the Wakonda Auga River . . .* — *Sometimes a Great Notion*, Ken Kesey, 1964.

7675 We were approaching the river. — *Europe After the Rain*, Alan Burns, 1965.

7676 The first time I ever saw Karl Anthony he was floating down past our house in the river. — *The Island of Apples*, Glyn Jones, 1965.

7677 It was a hot day in late July when I sat with Uncle Miles at Belting beside the strippling ream. The deliberate Spoonerism was Uncle Miles's, and it did seem to express something about the stream that rippled beside us as we sat on the spongy grass. To say strippled rather than rippled conveyed something subtle about the movement of the water, and ream instead of stream suggested that large bream waited in it ready to be caught. — *The Belting Inheritance*, Julian Symons, 1965.

7678 A number of people jumped from bridges into the Tiber yesterday. — *Two People*, Donald Windham, 1965.

7679 Above all, the darkness of the river was what impressed Dr. Sanders as he looked out for the first time across the open mouth of the Matarre estuary. — *The Crystal World*, J. G. Ballard, 1966.

7680 I emptied my pipe into the/ brook and watched the current/ sweep the ashes seaward, tire of the/ task, and, after surreptitiously collecting them/ in the palm of a rock, tuck them under a rug of/ white foam. — *Rochelle*, David R. Slavitt, 1966.

7681 The Nile splits at Cairo, Egypt. The Damietta branch goes east, and the Rosetta west. — *Brill Among the Ruins*, Vance Bourjaily, 1970.

7682 Beyond the quaking rim of mud and grass where they are standing, the spumy falls are falling. — *The Gold Tip Pfitzer*, Irene Handl, 1973.

7683 He leaned against the steel balustrade at the end of the street, looking down at the East River. — *The Devil Tree*, Jerzy Kosinski, 1973.

7684 The river flowed both ways. The current moved from north to south, but the wind usually came from the south, rippling the bronze-green water in the opposite direction. This apparently impossible contradiction, made apparent and possible, still fascinated Morag, even after the years of river-watching. — *The Diviners*, Margaret Laurence, 1974.

7685 We dash the black river, its flats smooth as stone. Not a ship, not a dinghy, not one cry of white. The water lies broken, cracked from the wind. — *Light Years*, James Salter, 1975.

7686 *From the platform under the gallows beam, where the ropes were placed on execution day, you could stand and look out beyond the confluence of the Poteau and Arkansas rivers.* — *Winding Stair*, Douglas C. Jones, 1979.

7687 In a starless May night the town slept and the river flowed quietly through shadow. — *Malafrena*, Ursula K. Le Guin, 1979.

7688 The Bronx River is a wormy little stream famous for its catfish and the color of its mud; the Bronx catfish can swallow a tin can and slap a child off a mudbank with their long whiskers and bands of powerful teeth. — *The Catfish Man*, Jerome Charyn, 1980.

7689 It began at the waterfall, over the hill, beyond sight of the little croft. — *Goldeneye*, Malcolm Macdonald, 1981.

7690 The Floe last froze over fifteen years ago. — *The Skating Party*, Marina Warner, 1982.

7691 Around the headland that is called Algiers the Mississippi describes the majestic curve that gave to New Orleans its ekename of The Crescent City. — *The Great Steamboat Race*, John Brunner, 1983.

7692 Ferns covered the banks of the river that flowed in a dark, narrow channel, with the arching limbs of the tall trees forming a canopy above it. — *Don Bueno*, Zulfikar Ghose, 1983.

7693 The streams are frozen, and ice has formed shelves nearly to the center of the Big Horn River. — *Ammahabas*, Bill Hotchkiss, 1983.

7694 Over the rise there you can see Bright River. — *Bright River Trilogy*, Annie Greene, 1984.

7695 The first water for a civilization moves slowly, perhaps a couple of inches a second, as it moves through the woods in the night, the brook widening at the end of the woods and the water now moving at a foot per second and then much faster as it runs downhill on land that drops one foot in each ten thousand over the 115 miles to the city. — *Table Money*, Jimmy Breslin, 1986.

7696 Looking down from the window of the hospital cafeteria, which was on the third floor, Dr. Larimer could see that the river had been trapped in the trees and turned to silver. — *The Cactus Garden*, William Dieter, 1986.

7697 *The river in spring: gentle, invisible, constant activity.* — *The Life of Helen Alone*, Karen Lawrence, 1986.

7698 The river succours and impedes native and foreigner alike; it limits and it enables, it isolates and it joins. — *An Insular Possession*, Timothy Mo, 1986.

7699 The Heat stood at the window overlooking the Palisades, the Hudson running dark and deep in the twilight and the blocky figures of Manhattan's buildings beyond his shadowed profile. — *Utah*, Toby Olson, 1987.

7700 The Nile was falling. — *The Last Hero*, Peter Forbath, 1988.

7701 The echo of lions rumbled across the cold, humpback mountains, and the black winter sky was luminous with constellations reflecting undiluted in the quick, nervous river that ran by the compound. — *Echo of Lions*, Barbara Chase-Riboud, 1989.

7702 There was no way Daniel Shires could have known that the river which cut so conveniently through the eighty acres of Nebraska farmland that he chose to homestead back in 1859 was only running so high and wide that spring because it was flooded. — *The Story of Annie D.*, Susan Taylor Chehak, 1989.

7703 Consider a long and famous river, it teems with salmon and story. — *McX*, Todd McEwen, 1990.

7704 I will miss the seven rivers most. — *The Minus Man*, Lew McCreary, 1991.

7705 Will you look at us by the river! — *Cloudstreet*, Tim Winton, 1991.

7706 Eamon Redmond stood at the window looking down at the river which was deep brown after days of rain. — *The Heather Blazing*, Colm Tóibín, 1992.

7707 Tonight, I, Clover Adams, pulled the mauve velvet curtains aside, jingling their brass rings and shaking their ball trim. I stood close to the window and watched as the miasma rose from the swamps of the Potomac. — *Refinements of Love*, Sarah Booth Conroy, 1993.

Romance

7708 A proper tenderness for the Peerage will continue to pass current the illustrious gentleman who was inflamed by Cupid's darts to espouse the milkmaid, or dairymaid, under his ballad title of Duke of Dewlap: nor was it the smallest of the services rendered him by Beau Beamish, that he clapped the name upon her rustic Grace, the young duchess, the very first day of her arrival at the Wells. — "The Tale of Chloe," George Meredith, 1890.

7709 It was long ago in the days when men sighed when they fell in love; when people danced by candle and lamp, and did dance, too, instead of solemnly gliding about; in that mellow time so long ago, when the young were romantic and summer was roses and wine, old Carewe brought his lovely daughter home from the convent to wreck the hearts of the youth of Rouen. — *The Two Vanrevels*, Booth Tarkington, 1902.

7710 "Climb up in this tree, and play house!" Elizabeth Ferguson commanded. — *The Iron Woman*, Margaret Deland, 1911.

7711 Romance (he said) is a word I am shy of using. It has been so staled and pawed by fools that the bloom is gone from it, and to most people it stands for a sugary world as flat as an eighteenth-century Arcadia. — *The Dancing Floor*, John Buchan, 1926.

7712 Their feet, running down the wooden staircase from her room, made a sound like the scurrying of mice on midnight adventures; and when they paused on the landing to kiss, it was still in whispers that they told each other how much they were in love, as if they feared to awaken sleepers. — *Harriet Hume*, Rebecca West, 1929.

7713 Chipchase, judging it prudent from an increasingly set expression on Maltravers's face, to bring the story of his emotional life to an end, said:/ "I don't pretend that my love affairs are not sordid. They are. They always have been. I like sordid love affairs. What I object to is the assumption that just because one's love affairs are sordid it doesn't matter whether or not they go wrong." — *Agents and Patients*, Anthony Powell, 1936.

7714 Once upon a time there lived in Berlin, Germany, a man called Albinus. He was rich, respectable, happy; one day he abandoned his wife for the sake of a youthful mistress; he loved; was not loved; and his life ended in disaster. — *Laughter in the Dark*, Vladimir Nabokov, 1938.

7715 In the hot afternoon, Beric, who was no longer a child, had been with Flavia, who was no longer a child either. She had amused herself, but it was beginning to be dangerous. — *Blood of the Martyrs*, Naomi Mitchison, 1939.

7716 I heard Old Virgil say, "Henry's brung himself home a chippy." — *The Wild Country*, Louis Bromfield, 1948.

7717 He was Philemon, a Hellene, looking for a girl named Judith, a daughter of Israel, and he felt pretty absurd for having come down from Antioch because of an infatuation more than a year old. — *The Island of the Innocent*, Vardis Fisher, 1952.

7718 Customs of courtship vary greatly in different times and places, but the way the thing happens to be done here and now always seems the only natural way to do it. — *Marjorie Morningstar*, Herman Wouk, 1955.

7719 My love affair with Christiane Mondor did not begin yesterday. — *The Bystander*, Albert J. Guerard, 1958.

7720 In the summer of 1949, when he was twenty-seven, Houston found himself having an affair with a married woman. — *The Rose of Tibet*, Lionel Davidson, 1962.

7721 Simpkins, alderman, ex-mayor of this town, engineer by trade, longtime widower in public, longtime lover of a married woman in private. — *The Hidden Part*, Stan Barstow, 1969.

7722 It wasn't until I had become engaged to Miss Piano that I began avoiding her. — *Into Your Tent I'll Creep*, Peter De Vries, 1971.

7723 Shell lies on the resurrected grass of Memorial Park. His legs straddling her, Cob's body grinds over hers. — *The Fourth Angel*, John Rechy, 1972.

7724 A man with a woman on his hands, runs the proverb, is a man with his hands full. If this is so, what shall we say of a man with several women on his hands, say more than two or three? — *American Mischief*, Alan Lelchuk, 1973.

7725 He could not get used to going to the girl's apartment. — *Fifty-Two Pickup*, Elmore Leonard, 1974.

7726 I must undoubtedly have seen some of poor Doris Biddle's several previous lovers but Mr. Gogarty was the first one that I can recall at all well. — *The Lover Next Door*, Keith Alldritt, 1977.

7727 Temptation comes to me first in the conspicuous personage of Herbie Bratasky, social director, bandleader, crooner, comic, and m.c. of my family's mountainside resort hotel. — *The Professor of Desire*, Philip Roth, 1977.

7728 Conrad Jessup, foxy mustache, sly melancholy eyes, sat over his beer and brooded: "Loves me, loves me not, loves me, loves me not." — *Hunt*, A. Alvarez, 1978.

7729 Amy Hunt always associated the long cold winter of 1936 with her passion for Herman

Fidler. — *The Country Cousin*, Louis Auchincloss, 1978.

7730 If all's fair in love and war, label the Class of '70 Exhibit Aleph. — *So Help Me God!*, Herbert Tarr, 1979.

7731 One summer morning while I was still a virgin though my virginity was on its last legs, I woke up and didn't want to go to New Jersey; I didn't want to go — I was seventeen and no seventeen-year-old L.A. woman would go to New Jersey if she could get out of it, especially a seventeen-year-old with a boyfriend like mine — a dreamboat who was twenty-five, was under contract to Fox as a leading man, black wavy hair and blue eyes, his father a French leading man who'd once starred in a tearjerker with my Great Aunt Golda and made a million dollars which he lost on a misadventure. — *L.A. Woman*, Eve Babitz, 1982.

7732 I was always getting crushes on my teachers. — *In Thrall*, Jane DeLynn, 1982.

7733 When I was fourteen, I began what turned out to be a lifelong love affair with Felicity Annabel Arlington Jones. — *The Crying Heart Tattoo*, David Martin, 1982.

7734 There are many ways a love affair can begin. — *Anna's Book*, George MacBeth, 1983.

7735 What is it that drives men into the arms of women, and women to the arms of men? — "Music of the Spheres," Leslie Epstein, 1985.

7736 "I know he's seeing a woman he's got three children older than, Mrs. Kunsman. . . ." — *The Ditto List*, Stephen Greenleaf, 1985.

7737 Venables first saw the woman he wanted to marry on the day after his wedding. — *The Nudists*, Guy Bellamy, 1986.

7738 I liked this plumber. — *The Man Who Owned Vermont*, Bret Lott, 1987.

7739 That night when he came to claim her, he stood on the short lawn before her house, his knees bent, his fists driven into his thighs, and bellowed her name with such passion that even the friends who surrounded him, who had come to support him, to drag her from the house, to murder her family if they had to, let the chains they carried go limp in their hands. — *That Night*, Alice McDermott, 1987.

7740 The world was in a frenzy of mating. — "A New Eden?," John Sligo, 1987.

7741 In 1863, shortly after the Battle of the Sabine Pass, a woman by the name of Roberta Hightower set a trap, not for the man she loved but for the man she wanted. — *A Place with Promise*, Edward Swift, 1987.

7742 Harriet and David met each other at an office party neither had particularly wanted to go to, and both knew at once that this was what they had been waiting for. — *The Fifth Child*, Doris Lessing, 1988.

7743 I like this one whore on the lower East Side, her name is Goldie because of her teeth, and she's really sweet. — *I Pass Like Night*, Jonathan Ames, 1989.

7744 Joy has found a new man she says will save her. — *Joy Ride*, Barbara Howell, 1989.

7745 It was first love — there had been no time for earlier romance because Nicandra was only eight on April 8th, 1904. — *Queen Lear*, Molly Keane, 1989.

7746 Small men have never been indifferent to me. — *Little Woman*, Ellen Akins, 1990.

7747 In her dreams were many lovers, in her life but few. — *Last Loves*, Alan Sillitoe, 1990.

7748 She knew and she knew it well that there was nothing but shame waiting for a girl of her class who even thought about romance with one of the river people. — *Secret Anniversaries*, Scott Spencer, 1990.

7749 My father had four wives, but still he looked at women. — *The Animal Wife*, Elizabeth Marshall Thomas, 1990.

7750 Johnny said we couldn't miss. — *Striking Out*, Robert Lamb, 1991.

7751 There was no one listening the first time we made love, no one keeping track of our movements the morning we met, or any of the nights we spent that first summer in Mac's apartment off Dupont Circle or my cabin a few miles north of Washington, no one watching except Otis, sixty-five pounds of shedding, effusive yellow Labrador who slept at the foot of the bed, who had belonged to Sam, and now that Sam was gone, Mac took him everywhere except to work. — *Safe Conduct*, Elizabeth Benedict, 1993.

Rooms

7752 It was Christmas Eve in the year of grace 1858. Manuel Hunter sat in his private room, half office and half library, connected with his spacious mansion by a covered way, latticed at the sides and overgrown with vines. — *A Royal Gentleman*, Albion W. Tourgée, 1874.

7753 A misty evening in mid-October; a top room in one of the small dingy houses on the north side of Moon Street, its floor partially covered with pieces of drugget carpet trodden into rags; for furniture, an iron bed placed against the wall, a deal cupboard or wardrobe, a broken iron cot in a corner, a wooden box and three or four chairs, and a small square deal table; on the table one candle in a tin candlestick gave light to the two occupants of the room. — *Fan*, W. H. Hudson *as* Henry Harford, 1892.

7754 The glass-domed "palm-room" of the Grand Continental Hotel Magnifique in Rome is of vasty heights and distances, filled with a mellow green light which filters down languidly through the upper foliage of tall palms, so that the two hundred people who may be refreshing or displaying themselves there at the tea-hour have something the look of under-water creatures playing upon the sea-bed. — *His Own People*, Booth Tarkington, 1907.

7755 "The Signora had no business to do it," said Miss Bartlett, "no business at all. She promised us south rooms with a view close together, instead of which here are north rooms, looking into a courtyard, and a long way apart. Oh, Lucy!"— *A Room with a View*, E. M. Forster, 1908.

7756 A coal fire crackled cheerily in the little open grate that supplied warmth to the steam-heated living-room in the modest apartment of Mr. Thomas S. Bingle, lower New York, somewhere to the west of Fifth Avenue and not far removed from Washington Square — in the wrong direction, however, if one must be precise in the matter of emphasising the social independence of the Bingle family — and be it here recorded that without the genial aid of that grate of coals the living-room would have been a cheerless place indeed. — *Mr. Bingle*, George Barr McCutcheon, 1915.

7757 After a day of rain the sun came out suddenly at five o'clock and threw a golden bar into the deep Victorian gloom of the front parlour. — *Life and Gabriella*, Ellen Glasgow, 1916.

7758 When you came in the space was desultory, rectangular, warm after the drip of the winter night, and transfused with a brown-orange dust that was light. — *No More Parades*, Ford Madox Ford, 1925.

7759 Now that the children were getting big, it wasn't to be called the Nursery any longer. — *Thunder on the Left*, Christopher Morley, 1925.

7760 This was the library of the Townsend mansion in Harniss. Mrs. Townsend had so christened it when the mansion was built; or, to be more explicit, the Boston architect who drew the plans had lettered the word "Library" inside the rectangle indicating the big room, just as he had lettered "Drawing-Room" in the adjoining, and still larger, rectangle, and, Mrs. Townsend had approved both plans and lettering. — *The Big Mogul*, Joseph C. Lincoln, 1926.

7761 The room was long and lofty, a room of scarlet hangings and pale brown stone, unilluminated as yet by any of its red-shaded electric lights. — *Meanwhile*, H. G. Wells, 1927.

7762 The handsome dining room of the Hotel Wessex, with its gilded plaster shields and the mural depicting the Green Mountains, had been reserved for the Ladies' Night Dinner of the Fort Beulah Rotary Club. — *It Can't Happen Here*, Sinclair Lewis, 1935.

7763 From a little after two o'clock until almost sundown of the long still hot weary dead September afternoon they sat in what Miss Coldfield still called the office because her father had called it that — a dim hot airless room with the blinds all closed and fastened for forty-three summers because when she was a girl someone had believed that light and moving air carried heat and that dark was always cooler, and which (as the sun shone fuller and fuller on that side of the house) became latticed with yellow slashes full of dust motes which Quentin thought of as being flecks of the dead old dried paint itself blown inward from the scaling blinds as wind might have blown them. — *Absalom, Absalom!*, William Faulkner, 1936.

7764 For the first time, the living room of his father's house seemed to Jonathan Chance small and stuffy. — *Rope of Gold*, Josephine Herbst, 1939.

7765 "Quite like old times," the room says. "Yes? No?" — *Good Morning, Midnight*, Jean Rhys, 1939.

7766 Very quietly and carefully, hardly moving her thin young neck and round shoulders, Elsie looked round the room, first at the french windows into the garden, then at the door, measuring distances. — *The Friendly Young Ladies*, Mary Renault, 1944.

7767 "I didn't mind it at all," our visitor said gruffly but affably. "It's a pleasure." He glanced around. "I like rooms that men work in. This is a good one." — *The Second Confession*, Rex Stout, 1949.

7768 It was quiet and airy in the drawing-room of Suite A. — *Most Likely to Succeed*, John Dos Passos, 1954.

7769 The room was long and furnished with anonymity, a carbon copy of every other furnished room in New York City. — *Second Ending*, Evan Hunter, 1956.

7770 I am sitting at my desk in a little room on the Avenue Gabriel which a kindly old lady has lent me for three months. — *A Ballad of Love*, Frederic Prokosch, 1960.

7771 I could have profitably rented out the little room in front of my press. On Market Road, with a view of the fountain, it was coveted by every would-be shopkeeper in our town; I was considered a fool for not getting my money's worth out of it, while all the space I needed for my press and its personnel was at the back, beyond the blue curtain. — *The Man-Eater of Malgudi*, R. K. Narayan, 1961.

7772 Three reputations cling closely to the Radcliffe Camera in Oxford. To the clever people

it is the Reading Room of the famous Bodleian Library and, as such, entitled to the utmost veneration. To tourists and sightseers it is a quaint old circular building, from the roof of which a fine view of the colleges can be obtained. But to the young undergraduates it has more unusual associations, for that same circular roof is one of the very few places in the city of Oxford where they can meet in intimate conversation unchaperoned. — *Stephen Morris*, Nevil Shute, 1961.

7773 The drawing-room was entirely English. — *The Ice Saints*, Frank Tuohy, 1964.

7774 Maudie inspected the room and kitchen for the last time. — *The Travels of Maudie Tipstaff*, Margaret Forster, 1967.

7775 About 9:30 the next morning he entered the downstairs room which faced the almost painfully blue west and the tall ridge across the little valley, the room which his grandparents had used to call the "sun parlor." — *Dagon*, Fred Chappell, 1968.

7776 The room was practically dark, with all the blinds down, but the way the sun was blazing away out there the room was like a furnace anyway, even with the cooler going. — *Among Thieves*, George Cuomo, 1968.

7777 There were no curtains up. The window was a hard edged block the colour of the night sky. Inside the bedroom the darkness was of a gritty texture. — *KES (A Kestral for a Knave)*, Barry Hines, 1968.

7778 The room was old-fashioned, 1980 baroque, but it was wide, long, high, and luxurious. — *I Will Fear No Evil*, Robert A. Heinlein, 1970.

7779 Wisps of fog had collected high up against the ceiling of the hall. You could see them interweaving, swirling like smoke rings, grey and brown, around the electric light bulbs that hung so nakedly over the heads, the something too few heads of the audience. — *As If by Magic*, Angus Wilson, 1973.

7780 Come into my cell. — *Lancelot*, Walker Percy, 1977.

7781 Commander Robert Ainslie sat very still in a cane-backed chair and surveyed the waiting-room without enthusiasm. It was painted white and almost completely bare but for a couple of chairs and a portrait of the King on the opposite wall. — *Strike from the Sea*, Douglas Reeman, 1978.

7782 There was a lighted candle in the attic room, and a pewter pap-boat half filled with gruel. — *Call the Darkness Light*, Nancy Zaroulis, 1979.

7783 Ease down the hall to Jessie's room. — *Departing as Air*, Allen Wier, 1983.

7784 This is a good room. — *1982, Janine*, Alasdair Gray, 1984.

7785 *I've come to see the room:/* This hospital room with the two beds and the big window and the television on the wall. The place where they say the miracle happened; the place where the child lay dying, where the novena started and the cure, they say, began. — *Miracles*, Marcy Heidish, 1984.

7786 For seven years the concierge hadn't been inside the room on the third floor. — *The Gypsy Man*, Ronald Florence, 1985.

7787 Dr. Elizabeth Grant stepped into the white-walled loft, dazzled by the summer sun. — *Spirit in the Flesh*, Joel Gross, 1986.

7788 The room made a curious headquarters for a pioneer experiment in Artificial Intelligence. — *Conversations with Lord Byron on Perversion*, Amanda Prantera, 1987.

7789 The room was very quiet. — *An American Love Story*, Rona Jaffe, 1990.

7790 This is the room of the wolfmother wallpaper. — *Skinny Legs and All*, Tom Robbins, 1990.

7791 Studio B was the snakebite studio at WLT, the tomb of the radio mummy, and bad things happened to people who went in there. — *WLT: A Radio Romance*, Garrison Keillor, 1991.

7792 "And this is the attic," Mrs. Porter said, "where supposedly my husband's ancestors hid out during the Civil War ." — *Primitive People*, Francine Prose, 1992.

7793 When the Foundation sent him there, Miller had absolutely no idea that he was to be put up in Van Gogh's room in the small yellow house at Arles. — "Van Gogh's Room at Arles," Stanley Elkin, 1993.

Rulers

7794 The long-continued hostilities which had for centuries separated the south and the north divisions of the Island of Britain, had been happily terminated by the succession of the pacific James I. to the English Crown. — *Fortunes of Nigel*, Sir Walter Scott, 1822.

7795 In the beginning of the sixth century, when Uther Pendragon held the nominal sovereignty of Britain over a number of petty kings, Gwythno Garanhir was king of Caredigion. — *The Misfortunes of Elphin*, Thomas Love Peacock, 1829.

7796 Long ago there was a little land, over which ruled a regulus or kinglet, who was called King Peter, though his kingdom was but little. — *The Well at the World's End*, William Morris, 1896.

7797 It was but two hours after midnight, yet many were wakeful in Cæsarea on the Syrian coast. Herod Agrippa, King of all Palestine — by grace of the Romans — now at the very apex of his power, celebrated a festival in honour of the Emperor Claudius, to which had flocked all the mightiest in the land and tens of thousands of the people. — *Pearl-Maiden*, H. Rider Haggard, 1903.

7798 Salah-ed-din, Commander of the Faithful, the king Strong to Aid, Sovereign of the East, sat at night in his palace at Damascus and brooded on the wonderful ways of God, by Whom he had been lifted to his high estate. — *The Brethren*, H. Rider Haggard, 1904.

7799 It was evening in Egypt, thousands of years ago, when the Prince Abi, governor of Memphis and of great territories in the Delta, made fast his ship of state to a quay beneath the outermost walls of the mighty city of Uast or Thebes, which we moderns know as Luxor and Karnac on the Nile. — *Morning Star*, H. Rider Haggard, 1910.

7800 The brilliant young ruler of Spain, Charles V, had just extended his empire over the half of Europe, and his *Conquistadores* were planting the flag in Mexico and Darien. — *The Sun Virgin*, Thomas Dixon, Jr., 1929.

7801 *"We, Seth, Emperor of Azania, Chief of the Chiefs of Sakuyu, Lord of Wanda and Tyrant of the Seas, Bachelor of the Arts of Oxford University, being in this the twenty-fourth year of our life, summoned by the wisdom of Almighty God and the unanimous voice of our people to the throne of our ancestors, do hereby proclaim . . ."* Seth paused in his dictation and gazed out across the harbour where in the fresh breeze of early morning the last dhow was setting sail for the open sea. "Rats," he said; "stinking curs. They are all running away." — *Black Mischief*, Evelyn Waugh, 1932.

7802 Two years have gone by since I finished writing the long story of how I, Tiberius Claudius Drusus Nero Germanicus, the cripple, the stammerer, the fool of the family, whom none of his ambitious and bloody-minded relatives considered worth the trouble of executing, poisoning, forcing to suicide, banishing to a desert island or starving to death — which was how they one by one got rid of each other — how I survived them all, even my insane nephew Gaius Caligula, and was one day unexpectedly acclaimed Emperor by the corporals and sergeants of the Palace Guard. — *Claudius the God*, Robert Graves, 1936.

7803 In 1806 Napoleon set out to chastise the King of Prussia. — *The Schirmer Inheritance*, Eric Ambler, 1953.

7804 There is much more that the Encyclopedia has to say on the subject of the Mule and his Empire but almost all of it is not germane to the issue at immediate hand, and most of it is considerably too dry for our purposes in any case. — *Second Foundation*, Isaac Asimov, 1953.

7805 The High and Mighty Prince Albert Frederick George was dead, and the heralds and officers-at-arms had proclaimed the High and Mighty Princess Elizabeth Mary Alexandra our new Liege Lady. — *Only Fade Away*, Bruce Marshall, 1954.

7806 It was almost noon. The emperor's parasol cast a precise pool at the hem of his robe. The attendants who surrounded him did not move. — *In a Dark Wood*, Marina Warner, 1977.

7807 Lord of the world. Shadow of God on earth. God bring you increase. — *The Idol Hunter*, Barry Unsworth, 1980.

7808 When Alexander the Great came to the edge of the world of his time, and pitched his camp on the banks of the river Indus, he told his builders to build gigantic pavilions there and to fill each pavilion with a giant's furniture. — *The Voyage of the Destiny*, Robert Nye, 1982.

7809 Mouley Ali Aben Hassan, Caliph of Granada, the Arab kingdom on the Spanish border in Western Europe, twisted in his saddle to watch his men lumber up the mountain pass. — *1492*, Newton Frohlich, 1990.

7810 In the beginning, long before the sacred walls of Ilium rose high above the Plain, Dardanos came into the land, gathered his clans, and shaped them into a people. — *Fires in the Sky*, Phillip Parotti, 1990.

7811 On this day Huayna Capac, the eleventh Sapa Inca, Sole Lord of the Four Quarters, was departing from Cuzco. — *The Incas*, Daniel Peters, 1991.

7812 Can it be history's senseless happenstance that but a single king of England has borne the name of John? — *The Sheriff of Nottingham*, Richard Kluger, 1992.

7813 From all the corners of the earth the mad magician bade them come and from all the corners of the earth they came to offer themselves up as sacrifices on his monstrous bloody altar. — *Into What Far Harbor?*, Allen Drury, 1993.

Rules

7814 No American can be ignorant of the principal events that induced the Parliament of Great Britain, in 1774, to lay those impolitic restrictions on the port of Boston, which so effectually destroyed the trade of the chief town in her western colonies. — *Lionel Lincoln*, James Fenimore Cooper, 1825.

7815 Exceptions are so inevitable that no rule is without them—except the one just stated. —*Pasó por Aquí*, Eugene Manlove Rhodes, 1926.

7816 Obedient to the social law that makes the moot guest the early bird at a tea party, Mr. and Mrs. Joseph Lockman were the first to arrive in Utopia. —*The Oasis*, Mary McCarthy, 1949.

7817 Meg Eliot was well aware that in taking her place as chairman of the committee for the third time in succession she was acting in an unconstitutional way. —*The Middle Age of Mrs. Eliot*, Angus Wilson, 1958.

7818 Obeying an inalienable law, things grew, spreading riotous and strange in their instinct for growth. —*The Long Afternoon of Earth*, Brian W. Aldiss, 1962.

7819 Conventions, like clichés, have a way of surviving their own usefulness. —*Desert of the Heart*, Jane Rule, 1964.

7820 I see in *Lunaya Pravda* that Luna City Council has passed on first reading a bill to examine, license, inspect—and tax—public food vendors operating inside municipal pressure. —*The Moon Is a Harsh Mistress*, Robert A. Heinlein, 1966.

7821 So they're talking about amending the leg-before-wicket rule again. —*Flashman's Lady*, George MacDonald Fraser, 1977.

7822 Page had only one rule about his house: Telephone before stopping by. —*Jambeaux*, Laurence Gonzales, 1979.

7823 There is no rule against carrying binoculars in the National Gallery. —*Metroland*, Julian Barnes, 1980.

7824 At borders, as at death and in dreams, no amount of prior planning will necessarily avail. The law of boundaries applies. —*Borderline*, Janette Turner Hospital, 1985.

Rumors

7825 I am extremely concerned, my dearest friend, for the disturbances that have happened in your family. I know how it must hurt you to become the subject of the public talk; and yet upon an occasion so generally known, it is impossible but that whatever relates to a young lady, whose distinguished merits have made her the public care, should engage everybody's attention. —*Clarissa*, Samuel Richardson, 1747-1748.

7826 "Well, sir, they say I'm crooked!" —*The Main Chance*, Meredith Nicholson, 1903.

7827 I heard about the pair first from Emeline Eldredge, "Emmie T." we always call her. —*Mr. Pratt*, Joseph C. Lincoln, 1906.

7828 I had the story, bit by bit, from various people, and, as generally happens in such cases, each time it was a different story. —*Ethan Frome*, Edith Wharton, 1911.

7829 It had lately become common chatter at Brightwood Hospital—better known for three hundred miles around Detroit as Hudson's Clinic—that the chief was all but dead on his feet. —*Magnificent Obsession*, Lloyd C. Douglas, 1929.

7830 I heard the first rumour in the middle of an argument with my brother, when I was trying to persuade him not to marry, but it did not seem much more than a distraction. —*The New Men*, C. P. Snow, 1954.

7831 "The latest wacky rumor in this wacky city [reported one of the Washington *Evening Star*'s many lady columnists in Monday's paper] is that Patsy Jason Labaiya, sister of Presidential Likely Gov. Ted Jason of California and wife of Panamanian Ambassador Felix Labaiya, will run for the U.S. Senate...." —*Capable of Honor*, Allen Drury, 1966.

7832 There was much talk when Jane and Mary Ann Jenkins came home to Mount Kilimanjaro. —"On the Mountain," Martha Gellhorn, 1978.

7833 Rumours are the begetters of gossip. Even more they are the begetters of song. —*The Marriages Between Zones Three, Four, and Five*, Doris Lessing, 1980.

7834 Trout looked out his window at the dark offices and wondered, as they waited for a red light to change, if there was any truth to the rumor that there was no way they could screw this up. —*Cheap Shot*, Jay Cronley, 1984.

7835 The yellow police barriers had been set up in front of the Ellenberg Institute early that spring morning, but it was not until late afternoon, when the television crews arrived, that small crowds formed and the wondering whispering began. —*Leah's Children*, Gloria Goldreich, 1985.

7836 Hutch had heard a rumor that the meek might someday inherit the earth. Therefore he knew he'd really have to hustle to get his first. —*Dreaming*, Herbert Gold, 1988.

7837 What goes around, comes around, baseball players like to say. —*What Happened Was This*, Josh Greenfeld, 1990.

7838 Somebody in Hamburg is telling stories about me. —*Richard's Feet*, Carey Harrison, 1990.

7839 All of Beijing was blanketed with smoke and rumors. —*The Middle Kingdom*, Andrea Barrett, 1991.

7840 There has been too much stupid talk about what went on in the Manor in those last

days of Beltane's premiership; there was melodrama enough without the idiocies propounded by the channels and the amateur psychologists. I can tell you exactly what happened. I was there. — *The Destiny Makers*, George Turner, 1993.

Running

7841 It was three minutes to six o'clock in the evening of the fifteenth of March 192-./ Francis Joseph McPhillip ran up the concrete steps leading to the glass-panelled swing door that acted as street entrance to the Dunboy Lodging House. — *The Informer*, Liam O'Flaherty, 1925.

7842 Wakefield Whiteoak ran on and on, faster and faster, till he could run no farther. — *Jalna*, Mazo de la Roche, 1927.

7843 The shipowner's small daughter raced upstairs, but her eager run stopped at her father's study door. That was shut. — *Morning Light*, H. M. Tomlinson, 1946.

7844 Roy MacNair knew exactly where he was breaking clear of the bush, so he did not stop when he saw the old lumber road. He burst out of the undergrowth like a barrel that was hard to interrupt — a stocky figure, all muscle and all motion. — *The Hunter*, James Aldridge, 1950.

7845 Lok was running as fast as he could. — *The Inheritors*, William Golding, 1955.

7846 Aragorn sped on up the hill. — *The Two Towers*, J. R. R. Tolkien, 1955.

7847 As he ran for the bus he was glad: not only because he was going home, after a difficult day, but mainly because the run in itself was pleasant, as a break from the contained indifference that was still his dominant feeling of London. — *Border Country*, Raymond Williams, 1960.

7848 Valerie Schreiber ran across the gravel road yelling "Bucci, Bucci, get over here." — *Europe*, Richard G. Stern, 1961.

7849 From the small crossed window of his room above the stable in the brickyard, Yakov Bok saw people in their long overcoats running somewhere early that morning, everybody in the same direction. — *The Fixer*, Bernard Malamud, 1966.

7850 He had been running a long time, so now there was a sickness in him. The sickness came up from his belly in waves, and it tasted vile. — *Goat Song*, Frank Yerby, 1967.

7851 Lying prostrate, Serge Duran gaped at Augustus Plebesly who was racing inexorably around the track. That's a ridiculous name, thought Serge — Augustus Plebesly. It's a ridiculous name for a puny runt who can run like a goddamn antelope. — *The New Centurions*, Joseph Wambaugh, 1970.

7852 Arthur Rupp jogged with the joyless determination of a man working off the temporal punishment due to sin and thus was not disposed to feel indulgent one May morning when a yapping terrier began to pursue him with the tenacity of the Hound of Heaven. — *The Priest*, Ralph McInerny, 1973.

7853 A runner was seen coming through the Hole-in-the-Hills. He was coming very fast. He was carrying a war pipe. — *The Manly-Hearted Woman*, Frederick Manfred, 1975.

7854 Odell Mothersill was flying home, speeding through Washington Square Park, the first dried leaves of autumn, carried on a slightly chilling wind, swirling and scraping on the walk beneath his feet. — *Mothersill and the Foxes*, John A. Williams, 1975.

7855 Running was a strange thing. The sound was your feet slapping the pavement. The lights of passing cars batted your eyeballs. Your arms came up unevenly in front of you, reaching from nowhere, separate from you and from each other. It was like the hands of a lot of people drowning. And it was useless to notice these things. It was as if a car had crashed, the driver was dead, and this was the radio still playing to him. — *Laidlaw*, William McIlvanney, 1977.

7856 She was running through a brilliant light whose walls billowed like the hull of a ship. — *The Shadow Line*, Laura Furman, 1982.

7857 It was Raunchy Kauff who ran for a towel first. — *The Seventh Game*, Roger Kahn, 1982.

7858 Hugh McPhail dropped his trousers, stuffed them into his knapsack and started to run. — *Flanagan's Run*, Tom McNab, 1982.

7859 Roscoe Americus, Jr., slipped easily into the morning's rhythm. — *Mr. America's Last Season Blues*, John McCluskey, Jr., 1983.

7860 The woman ran out after him so fast she completely forgot herself. — *Cooling Off*, J. M. McCool, 1984.

7861 I'd gotten out of my car and was running for the porch when I saw her. — *A Hell of a Woman*, Jim Thompson, 1984.

7862 Matthew and Justin race alongside the late afternoon traffic of Eleventh Avenue, no more than a handspan between their shoulders. — *Waterboys*, Eric Gabriel, 1989.

7863 I am running toward my mother. — *Surviving the Wreck*, Susan Osborn, 1992.

Scandal

7864 When the vicar's wife went off with a young and penniless man the scandal knew no bounds. — *The Virgin and the Gypsy*, D. H. Lawrence, 1930.

7865 The manner of Hercules Flood's death made a scandal which eclipsed every other scandal that, during the long, candlelit evenings of Bristol winter, disturbed drawing-rooms and kept business lively in taverns. — *The Sun Is My Undoing*, Marguerite Steen, 1942.

7866 It was generally agreed, and with indignation by a few, that it had been a great scandal. — *Never Victorious, Never Defeated*, Taylor Caldwell, 1954.

7867 Mostly, she was a woman who loved scandal — and lived by it. — *The Kill-Off*, Jim Thompson, 1957.

7868 Yes, I admit that the whole affair does have the look of a charade or costume drama of some kind. — *The Rape of Tamar*, Dan Jacobson, 1970.

7869 The scandal, a typhoon in a thimble, broke one windy autumn morning and caused, at the beginning, and before anyone connected it with that sad, unexplained death, far more ribald and raucous amusement than it did concern. — *Grenelle*, Isabelle Holland, 1976.

7870 "Are we to gather that *Dreadnought* is asking us all to do something dishonest?" Richard asked. — *Offshore*, Penelope Fitzgerald, 1979.

7871 The gentleman from *Harper's Weekly*, who didn't know mesquite beans from goat shit, looked up from his reference collection of back issues and said, "I've got it!" Very pleased with himself. "We'll call this affair . . . are you ready? The Early-Moon Feud." — *Gunsights*, Elmore Leonard, 1979.

7872 It caused a mild scandal at the time, but in most people's memories it was quite outshone by what succeeded it. — *The Shooting Party*, Isabel Colegate, 1980.

7873 There is no family so secure that scandal cannot touch it. — *The Last Waltz*, Nancy Zaroulis, 1984.

7874 It was a good Monday morning to begin with — the Hoffmans slugging it out again, Dr. Palme on the phone with a suicidal ex-patient, the Coles' maid getting it off with one of their vibrators, Lesley and Phil meeting in the laundry room — and then it got even better. — *Sliver*, Ira Levin, 1991.

Schools

7875 In an ancient though not very populous settlement, in a retired corner of one of the New England States, arise the walls of a seminary of learning, which, for the convenience of a name, shall be entitled "Harley College." — *Fanshawe*, Nathaniel Hawthorne, 1828.

7876 St. Ambrose's College was a moderate-sized one. There might have been some seventy or eighty undergraduates in residence, when our hero appeared there as a freshman. Of these, unfortunately for the college, there were a very large proportion of the gentleman-commoners; enough, in fact, with the other men whom they drew round them, and who lived pretty much as they did, to form the largest and leading set in the college. So the college was decidedly fast; in fact, it was *the* fast college of the day. — *Tom Brown at Oxford*, Thomas Hughes, 1861.

7877 There was strange disorder in Miss Rutherford's school-room, wont to be the abode of decorum. — *The Unclassed*, George Gissing, 1884.

7878 Moncrief House, Panley Common. Scholastic establishment for the sons of gentlemen, etc./ Panley Common, viewed from the back windows of Moncrief House, is a tract of grass, furze, and rushes, stretching away to the western horizon. — *Cashel Byron's Profession*, George Bernard Shaw, 1885.

7879 On Mondays, Wednesdays and Fridays it was Court Hand and Summulae Logicales, while the rest of the week it was the Organon, Repetition and Astrology. — *The Sword in the Stone*, T. H. White, 1939.

7880 The school at which I was science-master was desirably situated, right in the centre of the town. — *Scenes from Provincial Life*, William Cooper, 1950.

7881 Centennial State University did not quite know how to take Cabot Cunningham when he appeared for matriculation as a Junior in 1895. — *Their Town*, Wilbur Daniel Steele, 1952.

7882 Half the campus was designed by Bottom the Weaver, half by Ludwig Mies van der Rohe; Benton had been endowed with one to begin with, and had smiled and sweated and spoken for the other. — *Pictures from an Institution*, Randall Jarrell, 1954.

7883 I went back to the Devon School not long ago, and found it looking oddly newer than when I was a student there fifteen years before. — *A Separate Peace*, John Knowles, 1959.

7884 At the time of which this true life ex-

perience takes place, there were many droll and amusing things at John Marshall Junior High School, of which I am a student. — *I Was a Teen-Age Dwarf*, Max Shulman, 1959.

7885 Prem sat at the only table they had and corrected his students' essay papers. — *The Householder*, Ruth Prawer Jhabvala, 1960.

7886 The greatness of Carne School has been ascribed by common consent to Edward VI, whose educational zeal is ascribed by history to the Duke of Somerset. — *A Murder of Quality*, John Le Carré, 1962.

7887 *The school stood at the crossroads in the valley, its loggish face southward. Flanked by teacherage and sagging barn, it waited with its doors yawning in the spring morning as the children neared on four roads cut like slashes through the bush.* — *Peace Shall Destroy Man*, Rudy Wiebe, 1962.

7888 Acting on mistaken principles of piety and snobbery, my parents sent me to a boarding-school in the English countryside which was run by Benedictine monks. — *Monk Dawson*, Piers Paul Read, 1969.

7889 The students were settling into their rooms for the new academic year. — *The Paragon*, John Knowles, 1971.

7890 William Stoner entered the University of Missouri as a freshman in the year 1910, at the age of nineteen. — *Stoner*, John Williams, 1972.

7891 The school Carmela attended for much of six years was founded by Dr. Barnes, a foreigner who had no better use for his money. — "The Four Seasons," Mavis Gallant, 1973.

7892 On a windy March day early in the century, I was seated in the office of the prefect of studies, awaiting admission to the Jesuit Day School of Saint Ignatius and, after seven rough years in the free Council schools of the city of Winton, rather glad to be there. — *Desmonde*, A. J. Cronin, 1975.

7893 John Muir High School is an imaginary institution in an imaginary neighborhood, in the imaginary County of Los Angeles. — *The Quartzsite Trip*, William Hogan, 1980.

7894 The Devon School had endured in the mind of Pete Hallam throughout his combat years in Italy as a close-held memory of peacetime. — *Peace Breaks Out*, John Knowles, 1981.

7895 One time, when Butch Miller was in grade school, there was an outbreak of flu and they arrived to find that they had a substitute teacher for their enriched reading class. — *Exotic*, Albert Haley, 1982.

7896 I went to teach at Brandeis University in 1949; since the institution was but a year old — founded the same year that Israel became a state — there were as yet no alumni to establish chairs, to construct halls, theaters and ornamental concrete benches where the weary might sit

and ponder the awful passage of time. — *For Mary, with Love*, Thomas Savage, 1983.

7897 Plato drove my elder brother mad and I spent two years at Highbury School — an establishment for recalcitrant and educationally subnormal boys. — *Real Illusions*, Russell Haley, 1984.

7898 I'm in Bluffton on a truancy spree, cutting, we call it, but all you do is walk off the unfenced yard during recess, where three hundred hunched-over kids are shooting marbles. — *Edisto*, Padgett Powell, 1984.

7899 Winthrop University. Momma said she liked the sound of the name. — *A Woman's Place*, Marita Golden, 1986.

7900 Before Christmas, I was living with my sister Lucy and going to this private school in North Hollywood, California. — *Highlights of the Off-Season*, Peter J. Smith, 1986.

7901 The Shrapnel Academy is an institution dedicated to the memory of that great military genius Henry Shrapnel — he who in 1804 invented the exploding cannonball. — *The Shrapnel Academy*, Fay Weldon, 1986.

7902 Martin Luther King High School was built with the best of intentions and without windows. — *The White Bus*, Ken Alder, 1987.

7903 One afternoon in March of 1855, in his college office, whose austerity reflected his own lack of pretense and an honesty bordering at times on the severe, C. Thomas Ridgeley, the Dean of Men, considered the request of the stocky auburn-haired sophomore who stood formally at attention, as was required of a student appearing before an officer of the college. — *A Different Kind of Christmas*, Alex Haley, 1988.

7904 In a broad Moscow street not two hundred yards from the Leningrad station, on the upper floor of an ornate and hideous hotel built by Stalin in the style known to Muscovites as Empire During the Plague, the British Council's first ever audio fair for the teaching of the English language and the spread of British culture was grinding to its excruciating end. — *The Russia House*, John Le Carré, 1989.

7905 Harvard Yard, the ancient center of college and university instruction, is an enclosure of a bit more than twenty acres in extent that is now the site only of libraries, a few classrooms, the handsome administration building, a number of dormitories for the entering class, a church and the stretch of greensward on which the annual commencement ceremonies are held. — *A Tenured Professor*, John Kenneth Galbraith, 1990.

7906 I could hardly wait to get back in from recess because Mrs. McMahon had promised to dismiss me just as soon as she finished calling the roll. — *Pledge of Allegiance*, Mark Lapin, 1991.

7907 That many years later, the clock tower

chimes you woke up hearing every morning were that many miles north by east from the sawmill whistles along Mobile River and Chickasabogue Creek, and the main thing each day was the also and also of the campus as it was when I arrived with my scholarship voucher and no return ticket that first September. — *The Spyglass Tree*, Albert Murray, 1991.

7908 In the middle of the last century, on a high bluff overlooking the ocean and the fishing hamlet of Yokohama, stood a family house attached to a seignorial school which for several hundred years had been run according to the despotic shogunate laws that prevailed in the land. — *Kagami*, Elizabeth Kata, 1992.

The Sea

7909 The charms of the Tyrrhenian Sea have been sung since the days of Homer. — *The Wing-and-Wing*, James Fenimore Cooper, 1842.

7910 Six months at sea! — *Typee*, Herman Melville, 1846.

7911 The Atlantic rushed across a mile or two of misty beach, boring into all its channels in the neck of Acadia. — *The Lady of Fort St. John*, Mary Hartwell Catherwood, 1891.

7912 The sea was very calm. — *The Explorer*, W. Somerset Maugham, 1907.

7913 It was so quiet in Charleston Harbour, that Dickie Ross, working his row-boat out to sea, felt as if half drowned in the tides that he could hear, while they moved invisibly. — *The Wave*, Evelyn Scott, 1929.

7914 Before me stretches a Danish sea. Cold, gray, limitless. There is no horizon. The sea and gray sky blend and become one. — *Daughter of Earth*, Agnes Smedley, 1929.

7915 The boy's eyes opened in wonder at the quantity of sea-tangle, at the breadth of the swath which curved with the curving beach on either hand. — *Morning Tide*, Neil M. Gunn, 1931.

7916 The Sea lost nothing of the swallowing identity of its great outer mass of waters in the emphatic, individual character of each particular wave. Each wave, as it rolled in upon the high-pebbled beach, was an epitome of the whole body of the sea, and carried with it all the vast mysterious quality of the earth's ancient antagonist. — *Weymouth Sands*, John Cowper Powys, 1934.

7917 My first vision of earth was water veiled. I am of the race of men and women who see all things through this curtain of sea, and my eyes are the color of water. — *House of Incest*, Anaïs Nin, 1936.

7918 On a summer day in the year 1804, Big

Angus, a middle-aged Scot, stood in the *guérite*, or watchtower, of York Factory, chief establishment of the Hudson's Bay Company, staring out over the wrinkled expanse of sea. — *The Fur Masters*, Alan Sullivan, 1938.

7919 His luggage was all ready to be taken ashore, his cabin in order and now he stood on the upper deck just beneath the bridge watching the flying fish scud out of each jade green land swell of the Arabian Gulf like swift pencils of silver and disappear again in glittering jets of spray. — *Night in Bombay*, Louis Bromfield, 1940.

7920 The sea was bitter cold. — "The Bridges at Toko-Ri," James A. Michener, 1953.

7921 Far below lay the Indian Ocean, unfurling its million waves. — *Nine Days to Mukalla*, Frederic Prokosch, 1953.

7922 The sea is high again today, with a thrilling flush of wind. — *Justine*, Lawrence Durrell, 1957.

7923 Back in the wide deep curve of the coast to the west of the three mouths of the Mississippi, the Gulf is brown and muddy. Always. — *The Hard Blue Sky*, Shirley Ann Grau, 1958.

7924 Millions upon millions of years ago, when the continents were already formed and the principal features of the earth had been decided, there existed, then as now, one aspect of the world that dwarfed all others. *Hawaii*, James A. Michener, 1959.

7925 Frankie Love came from the sea, and was greatly ill at ease elsewhere. — *Mr. Love and Justice*, Colin MacInnes, 1960.

7926 When the tide went out, the bay's black bottom would spring to life. — *The War of Camp Omongo*, Burt Blechman, 1963.

7927 After the spring rains when the first hot days of summer begin, the inland waters of the Gulf of Mexico turn smoky-green from the floating seaweed, fading to dark blue beyond the sandbars where the great white pelicans dive for fish. — *Half of Paradise*, James Lee Burke, 1965.

7928 The sea level had been slowly sinking for the last few thousand years. It lay so motionless that one could hardly tell whether its small waves broke from it against the shore or were in some way formed at the shoreline and cast back into the deep. — *Cryptozoic!*, Brian W. Aldiss, 1967.

7929 It was morning, and the new sun sparkled gold across the ripples of a gentle sea. — *Jonathan Livingston Seagull*, Richard Bach, 1970.

7930 Absolute calm, though not absolute stillness. The sea shifted lazily against the sandy beach, its motion indexed not by the white crests of ripples — the water was too oily for waves to break — but by the pale spots of imperishable plastic rubbish. — *The Wrong End of Time*, John Brunner, 1971.

7931 We search for signs of the sea, my daughter and I. — *The Second Dune*, Shelby Hearon, 1973.

7932 Behind my mother I see the ocean, the only one I knew when I was little, the Coney Island Ocean. — *Family Feeling*, Helen Yglesias, 1976.

7933 The sea which lies before me as I write glows rather than sparkles in the bland May sunshine. — *The Sea, the Sea*, Iris Murdoch, 1978.

7934 The castaway would have been dead before sundown but for the sharp eyes of an Italian seaman called Mario. — *The Devil's Alternative*, Frederick Forsyth, 1979.

7935 Hannah Bart looked out through the double thickness of plastic at dawn over the Atlantic. — *A Handsome Man*, Susan Cheever, 1981.

7936 Waves climbed the slope of the beach, fell back, and came again. — *Helliconia Summer*, Brian W. Aldiss, 1983.

7937 From his hotel room he could see the ocean on the east and the bay on the west. — *Far from the Sea*, Evan Hunter, 1983.

7938 Some insist it is best to live within sight of salt water. — *A Survey of the Atlantic Beaches*, Don Hendrie, Jr., 1987.

7939 Out beyond, the ocean heaved in a deep, unhurried rhythm, unleashing waves in long, powerful, frothing blue-green assaults upon the beach except where it struggled through a neck, suffering a constriction; there the water boiled and roared in a hissing fury. — *Jacob's Ladder*, John A. Williams, 1987.

7940 Five hundred miles to the west was Rio de Janeiro and five thousand feet down was the towering Trinidad Rise. — *The Last Whales*, Lloyd Abbey, 1989.

7941 It is about water. It was about water in the beginning, it will be in the end. The ocean mothered us all. — *Mile Zero*, Thomas Sanchez, 1989.

7942 My Dearest Wave,/ I cannot tell you what the Aegean looks like in the morning sun, but I'll try. — *Dorit in Lesbos*, Toby Olson, 1990.

7943 There was no wind; sea flat as a plate met sky the same colour as the water. — *A Sensible Life*, Mary Wesley, 1990.

7944 It began that summer I first saw the sea. — *What the Dead Remember*, Harlan Greene, 1991.

7945 The foam women are billowy, rolling, tumbling, white and dirty white and yellowish and dun, scudding, heaving, flying, broken. They lie at the longest reach of the waves, rounded and curded, shaking and trembling, shivering hips and quivering buttocks, torn by the stiff, piercing wind, dispersed to nothing, gone. The long wave breaks again and they lie white and dirty white, yellowish and dun, bil-lowing, trembling under the wind, flying, gone, till the long wave breaks again. — *Searoad*, Ursula K. Le Guin, 1991.

7946 At the bottom of the Pumpkin Patch Channel of Jamaica Bay, a burnt piece of seat belt decomposes. — *Aurora 7*, Thomas Mallon, 1991.

7947 And I half dreamed and half remembered Mom's never-ending passion for the sea. — *Impossible Vacation*, Spalding Gray, 1992.

Secrets

7948 Few have been in my secret while I was compiling these narratives, nor is it probable that they will ever become public during the life of their author. — *The Bride of Lammermoor*, Sir Walter Scott, 1819.

7949 "Tell him yourself, Pris."/ "No, no, Bab, I know too much for that! These men love not to be taught by a woman, although, if all were known, full many a whisper in the bedchamber comes out next day at the council board, and one grave master says to another, "Now look you, tell it not to the women lest they blab it!" never mistrusting in his owl-head that a woman set the whole matter afloat." — *Betty Alden*, Jane Goodwin Austin, 1891.

7950 There is a ruby mine hidden in the heart of the mountains near a remote little city of Central Asia, unknown to European travellers; and the secret of the treasure belongs to the two chief families of the place, and has been carefully guarded for many generations, handed down through the men from father to son; and often the children of these two families have married, yet none of the women ever learned the way to the mine from their fathers, or their brothers, or their husbands, none excepting one only, and her name was Baraka, which may perhaps mean "Blessed"; but no blessing came to her when she was born. — *Diva's Ruby*, F. Marion Crawford, 1907.

7951 I know that in writing the following pages I am divulging the great secret of my life, the secret which for some years I have guarded far more carefully than any of my earthly possessions; and it is a curious study to me to analyse the motives which prompt me to do it. — *The Autobiography of an Ex-Coloured Man*, James Weldon Johnson, 1912.

7952 Wherever he went that night people insisted on confiding in him. — *The Locusts Have No King*, Dawn Powell, 1948.

7953 On a fine evening in September Melissa Hallam sat in Kensington Gardens with a young man to whom she had been engaged for three days. They had begun to think of the future and she was trying to explain her reasons for keeping the engagement a secret as long as possible. — *Lucy Carmichael*, Margaret Kennedy, 1951.

7954 "You're sure she doesn't know?" said Georgie./ "Antonia? About us? Certain." — *A Severed Head*, Iris Murdoch, 1961.

7955 If you have to get to Philadelphia for a reason you don't want your wife to know about, the best way is to attend law school about thirty years before the time you have to be in the City of Brotherly Love. — *Tiffany Street*, Jerome Weidman, 1974.

7956 He called them the Dark Years. And pictured them thus: he would vomit out his intimate feelings to each person he met (imagining it was his soul he revealed), was quickly humiliated by having done so, and then spat where his vomit lay. — *The Work Is Innocent*, Rafael Yglesias, 1976.

7957 Women tell me things they don't normally tell men. — *Zoë*, Dirk Wittenborn, 1983.

7958 Moll Cutpurse was never one for keeping secrets. — *Moll Cutpurse, Her True History*, Ellen Galford, 1985.

7959 I know more secrets than any man I have ever met. — *The Congressman's Daughter*, Craig Nova, 1986.

7960 This is the day and this is the place where a dream turns a corner and a secret is told. — *In Pale Battalions*, Robert Goddard, 1988.

7961 *To start with . . . /* All families got secrets, but Joy's had more than their fair share. — *Joy*, Marsha Hunt, 1990.

7962 Tunis had a secret. — *Of Lizards and Angels*, Frederick Manfred, 1992.

7963 One evening, it was toward the end of October, Harry Arno said to the woman he'd been seeing on and off the past few years, "I've made a decision. I'm going to tell you something I've never told anyone before in my life." — *Pronto*, Elmore Leonard, 1993.

Self-Knowledge

7964 I am very far from being a wise girl. So conscience whispers me, and though vanity is eager to refute the charge, I must acknowledge that she is seldom successful. — *Jane Talbot*, Charles Brockden Brown, 1801.

7965 The world takes people very willingly at the estimate in which they hold themselves. — *The Bishop's Apron*, W. Somerset Maugham, 1906.

7966 Mr. Sorrell, just landed from New York after an almost too pleasant voyage, was accustomed to regard himself as the typical Homo Sapiens Europaeus. — *Ladies Whose Bright Eyes*, Ford Madox Ford, 1911.

7967 Andrew Stace was accustomed to say, that no man had ever despised him, and no man had ever broken him in. — *Brothers and Sisters*, Ivy Compton-Burnett, 1929.

7968 "Last week I got the idea that the one aim of my intercourse with other people is to prevent them from noticing how brittle and will-less I have become," Paul Hobbes was writing. — *Go*, John Clellon Holmes, 1952.

7969 The summer she was fifteen, Melanie discovered she was made of flesh and blood. — *The Magic Toyshop*, Angela Carter, 1967.

7970 To know who I am. To define myself through the why and the how of her death. — *Looking on Darkness*, André Brink, 1974.

7971 More and more I have come to credit first impressions. — *Rich Rewards*, Alice Adams, 1980.

7972 I never said I was easy to get along with. I never said I was easy to get along with. I never, never said I was easy to get along with. — *Rhine Maidens*, Carolyn See, 1981.

7973 I am not wholly admirable. — *An Admirable Woman*, Arthur A. Cohen, 1983.

7974 Know yourself is the old rule that people talk about, and who in his right mind would ever argue that it's not important? — *Sassafras*, Jack Matthews, 1983.

7975 I shall soon be quite redundant at last despite of all, as redundant as you after queue and as totally predictable, information-content zero. — *Amalgamemnon*, Christine Brooke-Rose, 1984.

7976 I am one of the great inventors of my age. — *The Laughter of Carthage*, Michael Moorcock, 1984.

7977 I have gingery hair and no money, and had habits like eating cold baked beans out of the tin. — *Fire Child*, Sally Emerson, 1987.

7978 At thirty-five, Maxwell Mather counted himself a fortunate man. — *Masterclass*, Morris West, 1988.

7979 Ever since his young wife had given birth to a cat as an unexpected consequence of his experiments in sexual alchemy, and ever since his accidental invention of a novel explosive that confounded Newtonian physics by loosing its force at the precise distance of 6.56 feet from the source of its blast, President Veracruz had thought of himself not only as an adept but also as an intellectual. — *Señor Vivo and the Coca Lord*, Louis de Bernières, 1991.

7980 Anne Rhodes had always thought of herself as self-confident and secure. — *The Hawthorne Group*, Thomas Hauser, 1991.

7981 No one sat me down and told me I was a Negro. That was something I figured out on the sly, late in my childhood career as a snoop, like discovering that babies didn't come from an exchange of spinach during a kiss. — *High Cotton*, Darryl Pinckney, 1992.

Sex

7982 "The sex instinct," repeated Mr. Talliaferro in his careful cockney, with that smug complacence with which you plead guilty to a characteristic which you privately consider a virtue, "is quite strong in me. Frankness, without which there can be no friendship, without which two people cannot really ever 'get' each other, as you artists say; frankness, as I was saying, I believe—"—*Mosquitoes*, William Faulkner, 1927.

7983 "It's been a long time," Lucienne Talbot said. — *The Devil's Laughter*, Frank Yerby, 1953.

7984 They're out there./ Black boys in white suits up before me to commit sex acts in the hall and get it mopped up before I can catch them. — *One Flew Over the Cuckoo's Nest*, Ken Keasey, 1962.

7985 Gently this time he came into her from behind, climbing up through the yielding reaches of soft flesh that drew him in until he lay full length over the undulations of buttock and along the straight back, his mouth against the line of her hair and the heaviness of the cheek turned away from the pillow. — *Wounds*, Maureen Duffy, 1969.

7986 "Then *she* says, now dig this, *she* says..." and he broke up laughing, a strange, rasping laugh, for maybe the fourth time since he started what was shaping up as an interminable story, "...*she* says: 'Listen, who do I have to fuck to get *off* this picture?!?'"—*Blue Movie*, Terry Southern, 1970.

7987 "I'm thirty, and I'm stuck." — *The Way Out of Berkeley Square*, Rosemary Tonks, 1970.

7988 No doubt about it, this was the end. She had complained of fatigue, sunstroke, a bad period, it didn't matter, when it comes to evading sex a woman's mendacity is limitless. With Eva it could mean only one thing: she was through with him. — *The Occupation*, David Caute, 1971.

7989 He waited over her. It was a full pushup. She heard the tension thrill of his toe and finger joints in the mattress springing. With

hisses, some exact hydraulic stamp, his torso dipped. — *The Proselytizer*, D. Keith Mano, 1972.

7990 "Upchuck," yells AJ. "What speed I couldn't tell, except it's like how Satan would be after two thousand million years of going without his greens, misering his sperms, and then one day out with his weapon big as a spaceship with a pearly warhead and working himself off both-handed. Floom, swoosh, it pours out, red-white-hot big flying rocks of come from out his balls underground and up the chute with a roar like that bomb at Hiroshima...." — *Bela Lugosi's White Christmas*, Paul West, 1972.

7991 The annunciation. On the night Timothy Fogel was conceived, his mother yelled out so loudly she was heard in distant rooms. — *The Wonder-Worker*, Dan Jacobson, 1973.

7992 I absolutely love to fuck. — *I Dreamt I Was a Nymphomaniac*, Kathy Acker, 1974.

7993 Sybil Davison has a genius I.Q. and has been laid by at least six different guys. — *Forever...*, Judy Blume, 1975.

7994 It all began innocently enough; I wanted to get laid. — *Two Much*, Donald E. Westlake, 1975.

7995 His friends called him Harry the Lover. But Harry would not screw just anyone. It had to be a woman ... a married woman. — *The Demon*, Hubert Selby, Jr., 1976.

7996 The last night I spent in London, I took some girl or other to the movies and, through her mediation, I paid you a little tribute of spermatazoa, Tristessa. — *The Passion of New Eve*, Angela Carter, 1977.

7997 I was 50 years old and hadn't been to bed with a woman for four years. — *Women*, Charles Bukowski, 1978.

7998 She woke, felt his finger in her. — *The Suicide's Wife*, David Madden, 1978.

7999 An Eden? Well, not exactly, I think, and sleepily reach for a cigarette. — *Heart Failures*, Ursula Perrin, 1978.

8000 Hugh was making love to a girl when the telephone rang. — *The Long-Haired Boy*, Christopher Matthew, 1980.

8001 In the week of April 7, 1969, I made love to five different women. — *The Kleber Flight*, Hans Koning, 1981.

8002 Lindsay knew when it was over that it was not over for her. Like a woman in love, she was convinced conception had taken place. — *Life Sentences*, Elizabeth Forsythe Hailey, 1982.

8003 This morning I watched my niece and her cousin making love in the river. — *Sole Survivor*, Maurice Gee, 1983.

8004 Sergei Rozanov had made an unnecessary journey from Moscow to Gorky, simply in order to sleep with a young blind woman. — *Ararat*, D. M. Thomas, 1983.

8005 The first time Teddy made love to her—hunkered at the edge of a cotton field near Winona, Mississippi, in an ancient borrowed car twice as big as his own, on a seat that smelled of goats and hay although she trusted it had been occupied by neither—he gave Jessie his working definition of politics. — *Civil Wars*, Rosellen Brown, 1984.

8006 Abishag the Shunammite washes her hands, powders her arms, removes her robe, and approaches my bed to lie down on top of me. — *God Knows*, Joseph Heller, 1984.

8007 As Lexi Steiner walked down the hallway of the federal court building in San Diego, she decided that sleeping with men you didn't care about was an acquired taste and that she had acquired it. — *Slow Dancing*, Elizabeth Benedict, 1985.

8008 "Why does everybody talk about the Virgin Mary?" Suki asked me. "What about the Virgin Joseph? If Mary never got around to doing it, neither did Joseph, did he?" — *A Girl of Forty*, Herbert Gold, 1986.

8009 When he finally did make love to Greta Garbo, she wore a glove. — *Time Loves a Hero*, Ben Greer, 1986.

8010 Every time the Good Time Gospel Boys came to town, Lucille Byrd got laid. — *The Good Time Gospel Boys*, Billy Bittinger, 1987.

8011 I suppose most couples the age of Rupert and me are not expected to be still compelled by sex. — *Age*, Hortense Calisher, 1987.

8012 and it's a story that might bore you but you don't have to listen, she told me, because she always knew it was going to be like that, and it was, she thinks, her first year, or, actually weekend, really a Friday, in September, at Camden, and this was three or four years ago, and she got so drunk that she ended up in bed, lost her virginity (late, she was eighteen) in Lorna Slavin's room, because she was a Freshman and had a roommate and Lorna was, she remembers, a Senior or a Junior and usually sometimes at her boyfriend's place off-campus, to who she thought was a Sophomore Ceramics major but who was actually either some guy from N.Y.U., a film student, and up in New Hampshire just for The Dressed To Get Screwed party, or a townie. — *The Rules of Attraction*, Bret Easton Ellis, 1987.

8013 "Try not to take this personally, okay, darling?" she begins, his first evening home. Jane has just had orgasm 2A and is tacking delicately toward 2B when she catches her breath, bites her lip, and blinks vaguely up at her husband. "But would you mind screwing elsewhere, please? At least for the time being. I need space." — *Flipping for It*, Daniel Asa Rose, 1987.

8014 Hot summer night. Nipples erect, hard, hard, under palms then fingertips working, in-

tense. — *Love Me Tender*, Catherine Texier, 1987.

8015 When she awoke, his hand was already under her nightgown, on her breast. — *Morning*, Nancy Thayer, 1987.

8016 Sex with Teo did not involve any major activity. — *Men*, Margaret Diehl, 1988.

8017 The air from his nostrils scorched the flesh between her cheekbone and her right ear. — *Mischief Makers*, Nettie Jones, 1989.

8018 In appearance, at least, she was so dramatically, so extravagantly concupiscent that for his first six months in the city William ignored her. — *Tango*, Alan Judd, 1989.

8019 I have been in love with Evelyn Cotton for twenty-four years and four months less eight days. We have made love twice. — *The Men Who Loved Evelyn Cotton*, Frank Ronan, 1989.

8020 While it was happening I watched the moon. — *The House Tibet*, Georgia Savage, 1989.

8021 "Why didn't I have a scorpion? Why'd I give birth to a human homosexual? Cause heterosexual fucking, which You gave the world, cursed me. Heterosexual fucking gives women pain. . . ." — *In Memoriam to Identity*, Kathy Acker, 1990.

8022 Dinah Kaufman lost her virginity a total of three times. — *Surrender the Pink*, Carrie Fisher, 1990.

8023 There's more to love than fucking — *The Grown-Ups*, Victoria Glendinning, 1990.

8024 That afternoon was the first time in her bustout life Rings'n'Things had met a man who wanted to know her real name before banging her silly. — *Homeboy*, Seth Morgan, 1990.

8025 For the record?/ I never slept with the President. — *Medusa's Gift*, Lois Gould, 1991.

8026 Looking back, Mrs. Fitzgibbons could not recall which of the major changes in her life had come about first, the discovery that she possessed a gift for persuasive speech, or the sudden quickening of her libido. — *Ride a Cockhorse*, Raymond Kennedy, 1991.

8027 Yesterday I met a woman, very beautiful, it was in one of those modern art galleries, you know the kind of place, all grey paint and grey steel chairs with big holes where you're supposed to sit and a grey-jacketed assistant whose haircut is presumably part of the exhibit, and I looked her up and down, thought I'd give it a try, so after I had smiled and introduced myself, noting—casually—that her eyes were those of Leonardo's *Madonna*, her grace was that of a Degas, and her cool allure would have left Renoir gasping, while her intellect, her intellect shamed the Tate Gallery's entire twentieth-century collection, after I told her that my one remaining desire, the only thing of any consequence to me now, was to beach my life, wreck it for ever if she should only wish, so I could

spend a few moments, an hour, perhaps a night, even a *lifetime* in her company (oh God, I exclaimed, I'm out of control, I don't believe I'm saying this, I adore you, it's everything, from your thick dark eyebrows which don't quite meet to your slim legs tucked into blue socks and Doc Martens, I have a pair also, no, not legs, though obviously I do, no Long John Silver me, but shoes like that, cue: cheesy chuckle), and after I had produced the yellow carnation bud kept behind my back until this moment, she smiled in return and asked me to repeat my name which was the cue for further wordplay—it was like fencing, I swear: lunge and thrust, party, thrust again with one hand and with the other beat death aside, *rinverso tondo ELA!*—and then off to a hotel, it was easier than her flat, she lived in Baron's Court or somewhere beyond the back of beyond, where we drank cool wine from tall glasses, slowly, undressed, slowly, kissed slowly but with a growing and eager passion, and whispered and laughed and licked and bit, then fucked each other into oblivion./ Didn't happen. — *The Elephant*, Richard Rayner, 1991.

8028 Was it sex, or love, that mysterious thing they seemed to have more of than anyone else? — *Christopher and Alexandra*, Maggie Gee, 1992.

8029 Eustina was watching the night Tendai was conceived. — *The Children Who Sleep by the River*, Debbie Taylor, 1992.

8030 Once, Douglas nearly told Estaban about the woman who died of a heart attack when she and Douglas were in bed. — *Are You Mine?*, Abby Frucht, 1993.

Shadows

8031 The night of summer comes late in this north land. Although it was nearly nine o'clock, the shadows, long gathering in the valleys and the woods, had but just now overflowed onto the broad levels of the river. — *When All the Woods Are Green*, S. Weir Mitchell, 1894.

8032 The dim shadow of the thing was but a blur against the dim shadows of the wood behind it. — *The Cave Girl*, Edgar Rice Burroughs, 1913.

8033 A shadow fell; there was a sense of catastrophe. A sudden rustle sprang through the park, and the deep green air began to quiver. — *The Idols of the Cave*, Frederic Prokosch, 1946.

8034 The shadow of a promontory lay forward on the sea like that of a giant resting on his elbows with the back of his neck to the late afternoon sun. — *Each Man's Son*, Hugh MacLennan, 1951.

8035 The waterman was now only a shadow. At last he had gone behind the moonlight. He had passed through a veil of transparent steel. — *Monstre Gai*, Wyndham Lewis, 1955.

8036 Slowly the night shadow passed from the island and the Sound. — *Greenvoe*, George Mackay Brown, 1972.

8037 7/14 a shadow solidifies in the mist. The cobbled seawall. — *98.6*, Ronald Sukenick, 1975.

8038 We finished supper and sat on the front steps in the cool shade, watching shadows stretch over the patch of grass my father was trying against all odds to grow in the adobe soil. — "Geronimo's Ponies," Harold Burton Meyers, 1989.

8039 No noise. Just a shadow. In a fraction of a second, I'm scared. — *Licorice*, Abby Frucht, 1990.

Shaving

8040 It was ordained that Shibli Bagarag, nephew to the renowned Baba Mustapha, chief barber to the Court of Persia, should shave Shagpat, the son of Shimpoor, the son of Shoolpi, the son of Shullum; and they had been clothiers for generations, even to the time of Shagpat, the illustrious. — *The Shaving of Shagpat*, George Meredith, 1855.

8041 Buck Mulligan came from the stairhead, bearing a bowl of lather on which a mirror and a razor lay crossed. — *Ulysses*, James Joyce, 1922.

8042 Dave Flynn stretched his boots over the footrest and his body eased lower into the barber chair. — *The Bounty Hunters*, Elmore Leonard, 1953.

8043 Nelson pushed out his jaw and drew the long cut-throat razor down his hard cheek. — *The Second Inheritance*, Melvyn Bragg, 1966.

8044 He stood before his mahogany shaving stand, stirred his brush in the white shaving bowl with blue flowers which sat on a circular shelf, added hot water from a copper jug, lathered his light-complected face and then opened his finely honed steel razor with its ebony handle. — *The Origin*, Irving Stone, 1980.

8045 Earlier, long before the sun had come up, he had methodically shaved himself for the new year. — *Temple*, Robert Greenfield, 1982.

8046 Every morning for the three years he terrorised the village, Captain Sylvester Nunes had his daughter, Frieda, shave him on the verandah. — *The Powers That Be*, Mike Nicol, 1989.

Ships and Boats

8047 "D'ye hear there, Mr. Mulford!" called out Captain Stephen Spike, of the half-rigged brigantine, Swash, or Molly Swash, as was her registered name, to his mate. "We shall be dropping out as soon as the tide makes, and I intend to get through the Gate, at least, on the next flood. Waiting for a wind in port is lubberly seamanship, for he that wants one should go outside and look for it." — *Jack Tier*, James Fenimore Cooper, 1848.

8048 In the year 1799, Captain Amasa Delano, of Duxbury, in Massachusetts, commanding a large sealer and general trader, lay at anchor with a valuable cargo, in the harbour of St. Maria — a small, desert, uninhabited island towards the southern extremity of the long coast of Chili. — *Benito Cereno*, Herman Melville, 1855.

8049 The great Pacific is the scene of our story. On a beautiful morning, many years ago, a little schooner might have been seen floating, light and graceful as a seamew, on the breast of the slumbering ocean. — *Gascoyne, the Sandal Wood Trader*, R. M. Ballantyne, 1863.

8050 In these times of ours, though concerning the exact year there is no need to be precise, a boat of dirty and disreputable appearance, with two figures in it, floated on the Thames, between Southwark Bridge which is of iron, and London Bridge which is of stone, as an autumn evening was closing in. — *Our Mutual Friend*, Charles Dickens, 1865.

8051 The magnificent ocean-steamer the *Australasian* was bound for England, on her homeward voyage from Melbourne, carrying Her Majesty's mails and ninety-eight first-class passengers. — *The New Paul and Virginia*, William H. Mallock, 1878.

8052 The ark of the mining interests, which had drifted about unsteadily after the break in bonanza stocks in the summer of 1877, had rested, a year or two later, in a lofty valley of Colorado, not far from the summit of that great "divide" which parts the waters of the Continent. — *The Led-Horse Claim*, Mary Hallock Foote, 1883.

8053 Lay your course south-east half east from the Campanella. If the weather is what it should be in late summer you will have a fresh breeze on the starboard quarter from ten in the morning till four or five o'clock in the afternoon. — *Children of the King*, F. Marion Crawford, 1885.

8054 It was the 4th of August, 1854, off Cape Corrientes. Morning was breaking over a heavy

sea, and the closely-reefed topsails of a barque that ran before it bearing down upon the faint outline of the Mexican coast. — *The Crusade of the Excelsior*, Bret Harte, 1887.

8055 The *Laughing Mary* was a light ship, as sailors term a vessel that stands high upon the water, having discharged her cargo at Callao, from which port we were proceeding in ballast to Cape Town, South Africa, there to call for orders. — *The Frozen Pirate*, William Clark Russell, 1887.

8056 On March 3, 1516, the trading vessel, the Swan, dropped anchor at Plymouth. She would in our days be considered a tiny craft indeed, but she was then looked upon as a large vessel, and one of which her owner, Master Diggory Beggs, had good reason to be proud. — *By Right of Conquest*, G. A. Henty, 1891.

8057 In the noon of a September day in the year of our dear Lord 1395, a merchant vessel nodded sleepily upon the gentle swells of warm water flowing in upon the Syrian coast. — *The Prince of India*, Lew Wallace, 1893.

8058 Early in the spring of the year 1884 the three-masted schooner *Castor*, from San Francisco to Valparaiso, was struck by a tornado off the coast of Peru. — *The Adventures of Captain Horn*, Frank R. Stockton, 1895.

8059 On February the 1st, 1887, the *Lady Vain* was lost by collision with a derelict when about the latitude 1° S. and longitude 107° W. — *The Island of Dr. Moreau*, H. G. Wells, 1896.

8060 Mr. Baker, chief mate of the ship *Narcissus*, stepped in one stride out of his lighted cabin into the darkness of the quarter-deck. — *The Nigger of the "Narcissus,"* Joseph Conrad, 1897.

8061 The public may possibly wonder why it is that they have never heard in the papers of the fate of the passengers of the *Korosko*. — *A Desert Drama*, Arthur Conan Doyle, 1897.

8062 The weather door of the smoking-room had been left open to the North Atlantic fog, as the big liner rolled and lifted, whistling to warn the fishing-fleet. — *Captains Courageous*, Rudyard Kipling, 1897.

8063 *Nellie*, a cruising yawl, swung to her anchor without a flutter of sails, and was at rest. — "Heart of Darkness," Joseph Conrad, 1902.

8064 About five in the afternoon on the 23d of May, 1792, the brig *Morning Star* of Bristol, John Maynard, master, with a topgallant breeze after her, ran into Delaware Bay in mid-channel between Cape May and Cape Henlopen. — *The Red City*, S. Weir Mitchell, 1908.

8065 I believe he had seen us out of the window coming off to dine in an overloaded dinghy of a fourteen-ton yawl belonging to Marlow, my host and skipper. — *Chance*, Joseph Conrad, 1914.

8066 After entering at break of day the inner

roadstead of the Port of Toulon, exchanging several loud hails with one of the guardboats of the Fleet, which directed him where he was to take up his berth, Master-Gunner Peyrol let go the anchor of the sea-worn and battered ship in his charge, between the arsenal and the town, in full view of the principal quay. — *The Rover*, Joseph Conrad, 1923.

8067 Sweeping about the thrust of Ware Neck Richard Bale lost sight of the wooded shore of Balisand. — *Balisand*, Joseph Hergesheimer, 1924.

8068 *Three gulls wheel above the broken boxes, orange rinds, spoiled cabbage heads that heave between the splintered plank walls, the green waves spume under the round bow as the ferry, skidding on the tide, crashes, gulps the broken water, slides, settles slowly into the slip.* — *Manhattan Transfer*, John Dos Passos, 1925.

8069 On the eighth of July, 1822, at half past six in the evening, the American clipper-built brig *Witch of the West* was beating out of Leghorn Harbour, close-hauled upon the increasing wind. — *The Orphan Angel*, Elinor Wylie, 1926.

8070 The steamer moved upriver at half-speed, and the sounds of life fell with the sun. — *Gallions Reach*, H. M. Tomlinson, 1927.

8071 All that Jake knew about the freighter on which he stoked was that it stank between sea and sky. — *Home to Harlem*, Claude McKay, 1928.

8072 As the big liner hung over the tugs swarming about her in the bay of Algiers, Martin Boyne looked down from the promenade deck on the troop of first-class passengers struggling up the gangway, their faces all unconsciously lifted ·to his inspection. — *The Children*, Edith Wharton, 1928.

8073 She came gliding along London's broadest street, and then halted, swaying gently. —*Angel Pavement*, J. B. Priestley, 1930.

8074 June 7, Friday, in the morning, the twin-screw turbine liner *San Pedro*, seventeen thousand tons, lay at her Hoboken pier. —*S.S. San Pedro*, James Gould Cozzens, 1931.

8075 It was Mr. Spenlove's custom to entertain the passengers at his table with yarns drawn from his thirty years in many ships, under several flags, on most of the waters of the globe. — *The Harbourmaster*, William McFee, 1931.

8076 When the sun had gone, I saw that the water was streaked with great patches of crimson and gold. They formed a ripple under the bridge that was part of the wake belonging to the barge. —*I'll Never Be Young Again*, Daphne du Maurier, 1932.

8077 An April morning in 1817, two passengers stood on the bows of the Greenbush Ferry. — *Erie Water*, Walter D. Edmonds, 1933.

8078 Clare, who for seventeen months had been the wife of Sir Gerald Corven of the Colonial Service, stood on the boat deck of an Orient liner in the river Thames, waiting for it to dock. — *One More River*, John Galsworthy, 1933.

8079 Capt. Oliver Dorman, of the armed merchant barque *Olive Branch*, of Arundel, ten guns and twenty-five men, stared calculatingly upward, quadrant in hand, his gray fringe of chin whisker seeming to point accusingly at the towering spread of canvas that half filled itself in the faint, hot air currents of the doldrums, only to go slack once more, as though every sail, from the vast courses to the small and distant royals, had sickened beneath the violent glare of the August sun. — *Captain Caution*, Kenneth Roberts, 1934.

8080 The small white steamer, Peter Stuyvesant, that delivered the immigrants from the stench and throb of the steerage to the stench and throb of New York tenements, rolled slightly on the water beside the stone quay in the lee of the weathered barracks and new brick buildings of Ellis Island. — *Call It Sleep*, Henry Roth, 1934.

8081 Mr. Hector Pecket had a boat. — *The Enchanted Voyage*, Robert Nathan, 1936.

8082 The Atlantic liner moved grandly down the St. Lawrence River, shaking out a proud white train on the glittering floor of the water. — *The Very House*, Mazo de la Roche, 1937.

8083 Ships at a distance have every man's wish on board. — *Their Eyes Were Watching God*, Zora Neale Hurston, 1937.

8084 Two weeks from San Francisco the *Newbern* dropped anchor in the tangle of sandbars and willow banks at the mouth of the Colorado, transferring its freight and its sole passenger, Eleanor Warren, to the steamer *Cocopah*, Captain Jack Mellon commanding. — *The Border Trumpet*, Ernest Haycox, 1939.

8085 The steamer, *Sestri Levante*, stood high above the dock side, and the watery sleet, carried on the wind blustering down from the Black Sea, had drenched even the small shelter deck. — *Journey into Fear*, Eric Ambler, 1940.

8086 Although it was midafternoon it was nearly as dark as a summer night. The ship swayed uneasily at her anchor as the wind howled round her, the rigging giving out musical tones, from the deep bass of the shrouds to the high treble of the running rigging. — *The Captain from Connecticut*, C. S. Forester, 1941.

8087 She was very slim and light. — *Delilah*, Marcus Goodrich, 1941.

8088 "We're foul of something." — *Pathfinders*, Cecil Lewis, 1944.

8089 The *Brigantes*, eighteen thousand tons, with seven hundred passengers, was proceeding at twenty knots toward Gibraltar, where she was due early next morning. — *Ship to Shore*, William McFee, 1944.

8090 From the window of his room in the attic Jonathan Goodliffe could see, if the day were fair, the white sails of ships upon the Irish Sea. — *The Townsman*, Pearl S. Buck *as* John Sedges, 1945.

8091 William Briggs was sorry that the press boat was alongside to take him off the support carrier where he had spent the last three weeks. — *Repent in Haste*, John P. Marquand, 1945.

8092 The small catboat slapped the waves of the gulf, and the salt-laden spray flew over the man and the woman; they were clad only in bathing suits and smiles, and it was the same as an early morning swim. — *One Clear Call*, Upton Sinclair, 1948.

8093 On a clear August evening, borne upon the light breath of a fair wind, the fleet was entering Torbay. The sight was so lovely that the men and women in the fishing villages grouped about the bay gazed in wonder and stilled the busyness of their lives for a moment to stand and watch, shielding their eyes with their hands, trying in their own way, consciously or unconsciously, to imprint this picture upon their memory so deeply that it should be for them a treasure while life should last. — *Gentian Hill*, Elizabeth Goudge, 1949.

8094 There were many little boats like the *Caledonian*, the *John Bosco*, the *Wayfarer*, the *Fred Holmes*, the *Ginger*, the *Capella*, the *Alert*, and the *Taage*. — *Fiddler's Green*, Ernest K. Gann, 1950.

8095 They started two hours before daylight, and at first, it was not necessary to break the ice across the canal as other boats had gone on ahead. — *Across the River and into the Trees*, Ernest Hemingway, 1950.

8096 Ross Pary stood on the deck of the steamboat *Crescent City*, staring out over the Mississippi. — *Floodtide*, Frank Yerby, 1950.

8097 It was night by the time the little ferry drew up alongside the dock. — *Let It Come Down*, Paul Bowles, 1952.

8098 Lieutenant William Bush came on board H.M.S. *Renown* as she lay at anchor in the Hamoaze and reported himself to the officer of the watch, who was a tall and rather gangling individual with hollow cheeks and a melancholy cast of countenance, whose uniform looked as if it had been put on in the dark and not readjusted since. — *Lieutenant Hornblower*, C. S. Forester, 1952.

8099 At the upper deck's railing Hugh Rawson watched the *Annie Conser's* bow swing shoreward to search for Klickitat's landing stage. — "Head of the Mountain," Ernest Haycox, 1952.

8100 Having climbed up through the locks, the canal boat was now winding over the pleasant Cotswold country. — *Hornblower and the Atropos*, C. S. Forester, 1953.

8101 *Barquentine* Cannibal *14 days out of Papeete — at anchorage — Suva./ October 12, 1927./ Begins calm. Middle part the same./ Last of copra loaded today. Battened down and ready to sail. Took water and stores aboard. Water sour. Port fees one pound three shillings./ Continues through the day very hot.* — *Twilight for the Gods*, Ernest K. Gann, 1956.

8102 Rear Admiral Lord Hornblower, for all his proud appointment as commander-in-chief of His Majesty's ships and vessels in the West Indies, paid his official visit to New Orleans in H.M. schooner *Crab*, mounting only two six-pounders and with a crew of no more than sixteen men, not counting supernumeraries. — *Admiral Hornblower in the West Indies*, C. S. Forester, 1958.

8103 The ship came into the bay in the early morning. — *Mrs. Panopoulis*, Jon Godden, 1959.

8104 In San Francisco, late on an October afternoon of 1944, the U.S.S. *General Pendleton* was warped out of her berth by a black tug. — *Raditzer*, Peter Matthiessen, 1961.

8105 The big ocean liner, snow white, with two red and black slanting funnels, lay at anchor, attracting sea gulls. — *The Château*, William Maxwell, 1961.

8106 A tall man, with a red-gold beard, stood at his study window high above the Adriatic and focussed his glass on the vessels lying at anchor between Trieste harbor and his castle of Miramar. — *The Cactus and the Crown*, Catherine Gavin, 1962.

8107 The two transports had sneaked up from the south in the first graying flush of dawn, their cumbersome mass cutting smoothly through the water whose still greater mass bore them silently, themselves as gray as the dawn which camouflaged them. — *The Thin Red Line*, James Jones, 1962.

8108 "Hello, ship," Jake Holman said under his breath. — *The Sand Pebbles*, Richard McKenna, 1962.

8109 The steamer sat in a bath of grey water. — *Lindmann*, Frederic Raphael, 1963.

8110 Half of the men who lived in Perquimans Precinct, of the new community of North Carolina, stood on the rough landing platform at the point of Durants Neck, watching a little ketch beat its way into port against a strong north wind. — *Rogue's Harbor*, Inglis Fletcher, 1964.

8111 The underwater craft surfaced, breaking the black water with a loud whoosh that disturbed only this particular minute section of the world. — *A Night of Their Own*, Peter Abrahams, 1965.

8112 On Tuesday the freighter steamed through the Straits of Gibraltar and for five days plowed eastward through the Mediterranean,

past islands and peninsulas rich in history, so that on Saturday night the steward advised Dr. Cullinane, "If you wish an early sight of the Holy Land you must be up at dawn." — *The Source*, James A. Michener, 1965.

8113 It was 5 A.M. and the fields of ice lay grey and silent under the stars as the whale-catcher S.S. *Petrel* stood out from the coast of Graham Land. — *My Boy John That Went to Sea*, James Vance Marshall, 1966.

8114 She ghosted in on the evening inshore breeze, wing-and-wing with her two lateen sails set port and starboard, and she looked like a huge bat, black against the dying glow to the west. — *The Gold of Malabar*, Berkely Mather, 1967.

8115 With four-week-old Mark wrapped in his woollen shawl she went out to the upper deck. Early morning, and the liner was landlocked, grappled in stoneland near the beginning of March, white frost painted on the customs sheds under a smoky pink sky, brilliant and sharply cold, more beautiful than she'd expected, a trace of cirrus cloud, as if just scratched there by a cry from the baby and an unthinking motion of his hand. — *A Tree on Fire*, Alan Sillitoe, 1967.

8116 There was no one in the *Kurt Hansen* when I boarded her that Saturday evening for my fourth season as a spotter with the Norwegian whaling fleet based on Port Natal. — *The Hunter and the Whale*, Laurens van der Post, 1967.

8117 The midday sun blazed relentlessly across Singapore's wide naval anchorage so that the lines of moored warships and auxiliaries seemed pinned to the sea's flat, glittering surface like models. — *The Pride and the Anguish*, Douglas Reeman, 1968.

8118 At seven o'clock, the morning of the 26th day of December, the S.S. *Poseidon*, 81,000 tons, homeward bound for Lisbon after a month-long Christmas cruise to African and South American ports, suddenly found herself in the midst of an unaccountable swell, 400 miles south-west of the Azores, and began to roll like a pig. — *The Poseidon Adventure*, Paul Gallico, 1969.

8119 At 3:15 A.M., with spectral quiet, His Majesty's yacht *Victoria and Albert* approached the harbor mouth and lay to. — *Strumpet City*, James Plunkett, 1969.

8120 The good ship *Cynthia* was on her way to California. — *Calico Palace*, Gwen Bristow, 1970.

8121 The towering sides of the fleet supply ship shone in the blazing sunlight like polished granite, and while her derricks swung busily above two frigates moored alongside the seamen employed on deck moved with equal vigour, if only to end the work and escape to the shade of

their messes. — *The Greatest Enemy*, Douglas Reeman, 1970.

8122 By the pale and watery light of a winter's sun a Third Rate ship-of-the-line sighted around noontime remained a towering black outline on the oil-smooth sea. — *Brimstone Club*, F. van Wyck Mason, 1971.

8123 It was only a two-day crossing from Piraeus to Alexandria, but as soon as I saw the dingy little Greek steamer I felt I ought to have made other arrangements. — *In a Free State*, V. S. Naipaul, 1971.

8124 *Prince Street, New York. December 21, 1842.* Only a week ago we reached New York on a clear, cold, moon-flooded night; I remember Matt Perry calling orders to the boys in the tops and at the ropes, the Commander, watchful, his face grim, scored with exhaustion, standing behind the quartermaster at the wheel as we threaded among the vessels in East River to our anchorage off the Navy Yard. — *Voyage to the First of December*, Henry Carlisle, 1972.

8125 Eight of us sat in the lounge of the S.S. *Kyle* as she creased her way over the oil-smooth water, her bow seeming steady as a rock beneath the bright point of the North Star. — *White Eskimo*, Harold Horwood, 1972.

8126 The wind was rising again. It rode up the main mast, and a sail struggled lazily into action. — *Natives of My Person*, George Lamming, 1972.

8127 At first dawn the swathes of rain drifting eastwards across the Channel parted long enough to show that the chase had altered course. — *Post Captain*, Patrick O'Brian, 1972.

8128 It was just nine o'clock on a February morning when His Majesty's Submarine *Tristram* edged against the greasy piles at Fort Blockhouse, Portsmouth and her lines were taken by the waiting shore-party. — *His Majesty's U-Boat*, Douglas Reeman, 1973.

8129 It was March, the wind cold from the north-east and the *Fisher Maid* plunging down the waves with a wicked twist to her tail. — *North Star*, Hammond Innes, 1974.

8130 I tore down the Continental Shelf off the Bogue Bank while the pogo made periscope hops trying to track me. — *The Computer Connection*, Alfred Bester, 1975.

8131 Lieutenant Tim Rowan stood on the side of Gladstone Dock and studied the overhanging bulk of the aircraft carrier with something like apprehension. — *Winged Escort*, Douglas Reeman, 1975.

8132 The merchant ship *The Glasgow Lass* left the Firth of Clyde behind and made for the open sea. Tossing about like a tiny cockleshell in the wide expanse of water, it sometimes disappeared completely from sight as waves swelled high to

engulf it. — *Roots of Bondage*, Margaret Thomson Davis, 1977.

8133 From his bedroom high up on Mount Carmel, the ailing Ezra Shultish could see the blue bay of Haifa, its toylike boats bobbing in the water; and, when the humidity broke, the entire curve of land up to Acco and the full length of the Lebanon range to the north. — *The Yemenite Girl*, Curt Leviant, 1977.

8134 The oars lifted and fell with a desolate splashing. — *The God in the Mountain*, Colin Thubron, 1977.

8135 Pete Lomas' mackerel drifter was an old, converted, coal-fired steam tug of a hundred and twenty-two tons, purchased as war surplus in 1919. — *Second Generation*, Howard Fast, 1978.

8136 As the destroyer drove westwards across the waters of Lyme Bay, the two officers standing by the Carley float lashed to the side of the bridge huddled deeper into the high collars of their khaki coats against the wind that bit sharply at their flesh. — *The Fox from His Lair*, John Harris, 1978.

8137 A liberty boat full of sleepy hung-over sailors came clanging alongside the U.S.S. *Northampton*, and a stocky captain in dress whites jumped out to the accommodation ladder. — *War and Remembrance*, Herman Wouk, 1978.

8138 "The *Groningen?* Impossible!" — *The White Sea Bird*, David Beaty, 1979.

8139 Inspector Griffin came down to the landing stage on a raw autumn morning to see the *Mauretania* berthing. — *Mr. American*, George MacDonald Fraser, 1980.

8140 There were no gestures of tenderness, no soft words of love when she was conceived. Those would come later when men lived with her, rode her, cursed her and finally came to love her. — *Final Harbor*, Harry Homewood, 1980.

8141 By the tenth day, the barque was ringed by the unbroken crust of its own garbage. — *The Sure Salvation*, John Hearne, 1981.

8142 That country is best approached from the sea, the ship ghosting shoreward through a fogbank, her deck and hull beaded, fresh water dripping from sheets and halyards. — *Slade's Glacier*, Robert F. Jones, 1981.

8143 My aunt will not come to the boat with us. — *The Same River Twice*, Corinne Demas Bliss, 1982.

8144 She was his. — *Lusitania*, David Butler, 1982.

8145 A high-nosed cedar canoe, nimble as a seabird, atop a tumbling white ridge of ocean. — *The Sea Runners*, Ivan Doig, 1982.

8146 On a grey day early in February, 1812, a convoy was anchored off Hendrawna Beach on the north-west coast of Cornwall. One of the vessels was a brig called *Henry*, and another a sloop *Elizabeth*. — *The Miller's Dance*, Winston Graham, 1982.

8147 Crinkled quiffs of white foam spurted from the steel bows of the five-thousand-ton French passenger freighter *Avignon* as they parted the warm, tropic-blue waters of the South China Sea. — *Saigon*, Anthony Grey, 1982.

8148 The boats went out before it was light, the nets were down before the sun came up. — *Shalimar*, Kamala Markandaya, 1982.

8149 They are pulling the pleasure boats up out of the water. — *Autumn*, A. G. Mojtabai, 1982.

8150 The wooden seats of the little pedal boat were angled so that Marie looked up at the sky. — *Cold Heaven*, Brian Moore, 1983.

8151 I first saw the vessel when I was seventeen. — *The Jonah Man*, Henry Carlisle, 1984.

8152 On an evening in late June 1813, His Majesty's Packet Ship *Queen Charlotte*, Captain Kirkness, master, slid into Falmouth harbour, the long hull scarcely disturbing the water, the evening sun making angular haloes about her lower topsails as they were lifted and furled. — *The Loving Cup*, Winston Graham, 1984.

8153 Michael Corleone stood on a long wooden dock in Palermo and watched the great ocean liner set sail for America. — *The Sicilian*, Mario Puzo, 1984.

8154 When the lighthouse on Duncansby Head came in sight, Captain Dougall left his cabin and went on the bridge. — *Standing into Danger*, Desmond Briggs, 1985.

8155 As my companion, Simon Baron, murmured his prayers behind me, I watched the last of the Huron canoes disappearing behind an adjacent island, its paddles leaving a trail of whirlpools in the quiet water. — *In the Land of the People Apart*, Stephen Duff, 1985.

8156 The men had six canoes in all, wide tree trunks hollowed out by burning away the heart, Indian style. — *Caribbee*, Thomas Hoover, 1985.

8157 The last cable was off, the green lane between ship and dock widened. — *I'm Dying Laughing*, Christina Stead, 1986.

8158 The castaways were lying together in the bilges of a cockboat when Sam Gristy and Harry Pascoe came alongside. — *Armada*, Charles Gidley, 1987.

8159 The fisherman swings his boat alongside the dock. — *Blues*, John Hersey, 1987.

8160 From Nagasaki, it took two days to sail down the western coast of Kyushu and around Cape Sata, its southern tip. — *Butterfly*, Paul Loewen, 1988.

8161 As soon as the *Conte Rosso* docked at Bombay's Ballard Pier, the usual bunch of port officials in white drill came on board. — *Mistaken Identity*, Nayantara Sahgal, 1988.

8162 The French were out. — *The French Admiral*, Dewey Lambdin, 1990.

8163 On July 25 Andrew Marsh sailed his sloop past the starting-line buoys and swept beneath the Golden Gate Bridge and out of the bay. — *A Gentleman's Guide to the Frontier*, Joanne Meschery, 1990.

8164 . . . there on the river, the Chautauqua, in a sepia sun, the rowboat bucking the choppy waves with a look almost of gaiety, defiance. — *I Lock My Door Upon Myself*, Joyce Carol Oates, 1990.

8165 Indians in Texas used oil for medicinal purposes centuries before a Spaniard named Luís de Moscoso, in 1543, took seepage from oil springs near Sabine Pass to calk his ships. — *Honor at Daybreak*, Elmer Kelton, 1991.

8166 England./ The ship was ready to sail. She remembered. — *Cambridge*, Caryl Phillips, 1991.

8167 The sailor put down the helm and Ada Fishburn felt the boat round up towards the forest. — *The Living*, Annie Dillard, 1992.

8168 The *Portia*, a shabbily comfortable fifty-foot boat, was tied up at the dock of a Haida Indian village a day's sail out of Prince Rupert. — *Certain Women*, Madeleine L'Engle, 1992.

8169 The cacique and his high priest had never seen anything like it. The three caravels had stood all morning in the ultramarine bay like great seaworthy beasts, while petrels swarmed their riggings. — *Bay of Arrows*, Jay Parini, 1992.

8170 The rain stopped as the *Inverness* rode into Dunedin harbour on the high tide under an escort of albatrosses. — *Dunedin*, Shena Mackay, 1993.

Shock and Surprise

8171 Dear Zack:/ I can imagine your surprise upon the receipt of this, when you first discover that I have really reached the Old Dominion. To requite you for my stealing off so quietly, I hold myself bound to an explanation, and, in revenge for your past friendship, to inflict upon you a full, true, and particular account of all my doings, or rather my seeings and thinkings, up to this present writing. — *Swallow Barn*, John Pendleton Kennedy, 1832.

8172 When Monsieur Doltaire entered the salon, and, dropping lazily into a chair beside Madame Duvarney and her daughter, drawled out, "England's Braddock — fool and general — has gone to heaven, Captain Moray, and your papers send you there also," I did not shift a jot,

but looked over at him gravely — for, God knows, I was startled — and I said,/ "The general is dead?" — *The Seats of the Mighty*, Gilbert Parker, 1896.

8173 Selden paused in surprise. In the afternoon rush of the Grand Central Station his eyes had been refreshed by the sight of Miss Lily Bart. — *The House of Mirth*, Edith Wharton, 1905.

8174 Audrey had just closed the safe in her father's study when she was startled by a slight noise. She turned like a defensive animal to face danger. — *The Lion's Share*, Arnold Bennett, 1916.

8175 She gave a startled cry. — *The Painted Veil*, W. Somerset Maugham, 1925.

8176 That sunny September day was full of surprises. — *Some Buried Caesar*, Rex Stout, 1939.

8177 Jack Rhyce had not expected to see the Russians in San Francisco. — *Stopover: Tokyo*, John P. Marquand, 1957.

8178 It was a night of early summer, and in one of the years of war when the Islanders, after a fine night, were grateful for daylight again, and now and then were rather surprised to find they were there to see it. — *The Trumpet Shall Sound*, H. M. Tomlinson, 1957.

8179 It was Thursday, Miss Millington's afternoon off, and Mr. Stone had to let himself in. Before he could switch on the hall light, the depthless green eyes held him, and in an instant the creature, eyes alone, leapt down the steps. Mr. Stone cowered against the dusty wall and shielded his head with his briefcase. The cat brushed against his legs and was out through the still open door. — *Mr. Stone and the Knights Companion*, V. S. Naipaul, 1963.

8180 For some moments after the girl came his mind stuck. She arrived so unexpectedly. — *One of the Founders*, P. H. Newby, 1965.

8181 Dear Patrick,/ I suppose you'll be surprised to hear from me after this long silence — almost as surprised as I should be to hear from you. — *A Meeting by the River*, Christopher Isherwood, 1967.

8182 "Jesus!" said the old man. "The Pope has forgiven the Jews." — *The Man in the Glass Booth*, Robert Shaw, 1967.

8183 The metal rail was cold. It pressed into the slack flesh of her belly and surprised her, it was so cold. — *Salvage*, Jacqueline Gillott, 1968.

8184 "Dear God!" cried Mr. Justice Routh. The words were as torn from his lips: he was not given to profanity. — *Settled in Chambers*, Honor Tracy, 1968.

8185 Ce qui m'étonnait c'était qu' it was my French that disintegrated first. — *In Transit*, Brigid Brophy, 1969.

8186 Hind surprised a tall old woman in his vestibule one morning shortly before the mailman came. — *Hind's Kidnap*, Joseph McElroy, 1969.

8187 Big Ben struck eleven, and I watched a patrol of police cars back smartly into line, admiring expert wheelwork, but suddenly I couldn't see, couldn't hear, could only stand there, as our villagers say, mazed and a-wonder. — *White Horse to Banbury Cross*, Richard Llewellyn, 1970.

8188 The real surprise — to me anyway — was not really what I did, but how I felt afterwards. Shocked, of course. But not guilty. — *The Book of Eve*, Constance Beresford-Howe, 1973.

8189 He did not expect to see blood. — *Kramer versus Kramer*, Avery Corman, 1977.

8190 Suprised? No. — *Casing the Promised Land*, Caleb Carr, 1980.

8191 If there was one place in this world Edith never expected trouble, it was Bloomingdale's. — *Control*, William Goldman, 1982.

8192 Silas Wicklowe stepped off the airplane steps after the five-hour flight from Honolulu and glanced with some surprise at the volcanic mountains covered with verdure. — *Black Coconuts, Brown Magic*, Joseph Theroux, 1983.

8193 He stood with his eyes shut tight and covered by his hand, holding his breath while the icy insect repellent dried on his skin. — *Hostages to Fortune*, William Humphrey, 1984.

8194 People who still believe in good surprises are always young; the ones who have come to believe surprises can only be bad, or that there will no longer be any surprises at all, are old — no matter what their real age is. — *After the Reunion*, Rona Jaffe, 1985.

8195 I had not expected to see you ever again. — *Contre-Jour*, Gabriel Josipovici, 1986.

8196 I was shocked but I can't honestly say I was surprised when Istvan Fallok told me about Gösta Kraken. — *The Medusa Frequency*, Russell Hoban, 1987.

8197 Dear Jack,/ I was appalled when Carol told me of your telephone conversation. — *Working for Love*, Tessa Dahl, 1989.

8198 The most appalling feature of the morning after I nearly committed adultery was my lack of surprise. — *Ultimate Prizes*, Susan Howatch, 1989.

8199 This is nothing like I was told. — *Falling*, Colin Thubron, 1989.

8200 *Dear God,/ All right, You're probably surprised to see me here. I know I'm not the type that spends a lot of time in this place.* — *Mom Meets Her Maker*, James Yaffe, 1990.

8201 The second coming of Camille Malone was a shock to me. — *Perfect Timing*, Philip Lee Williams, 1991.

8202 One warm blue night toward the middle of July, in the year 1920, John Franklin Payne, a newspaper cartoonist by trade, looked up from his desk in the third-floor study of his home in Mount Hebron, New York, and saw with surprise that it was three o'clock in the morning. — "The Little Kingdom of J. Franklin Payne," Steven Millhauser, 1993.

Siblings

8203 They sat close together — a rather isolated little pair, boy and girl, apparently brother and sister — at the merry tea-table of a children's party. — *His Little Mother*, Dinah Maria Mulock Craik, 1881.

8204 As Mrs. John McCandless Blair entered the house her brother, Wayne Craighill, met her in the hall. — *The Lords of High Decision*, Meredith Nicholson, 1909.

8205 "Have I got a Little Sister anywhere in this house?" inquired Laddie at the door, in his most coaxing voice. — *Laddie*, Gene Stratton-Porter, 1913.

8206 Ursula and Gudrun Brangwen sat one morning in the window-bay of their father's house in Beldover, working and talking. — *Women in Love*, D. H. Lawrence, 1920.

8207 Johnny and Jane Potter, being twins, went through Oxford together. — *Potterism*, Rose Macaulay, 1920.

8208 People used to say of the two Oliphant brothers that Harlan Oliphant looked as if he lived in the Oliphants' house, but Dan didn't. — *The Midlander*, Booth Tarkington, 1924.

8209 A day in May, and in the shade of the great white pines, remnants of the forest primeval decking the sloping side of the great headland that wandered gently down to the *Fleuve*, lay supine, at ease in the languorous aromatic air, a girl of nineteen and her brother, two years her junior. — *The Rock and the River*, Ralph Connor, 1931.

8210 Bill and Danny O'Neill idled in front of the small confectionery store on Prairie Avenue, their pockets full of money and their bellies full of ice cream. — *No Star Is Lost*, James T. Farrell, 1938.

8211 "I didn't know you had a sister, Eustace."/ "Oh, didn't you? Well, as a matter of fact, I have two."/ "Tell me about them." — *The Sixth Heaven*, L. P. Hartley, 1946.

8212 Two girls, sisters of seventeen and fifteen, turned from one steep muddy lane to another, descended a sharp grade under redwoods, and pushed open a little-used gate that gave on the terraces of a forest garden. — *High Holiday*, Kathleen Norris, 1949.

8213 David MacDonald stretched forth an arm to help his twin, Dougald, from the boat. — *The Scotswoman*, Inglis Fletcher, 1954.

8214 In the mid-summer evenings when they had tidied away the tea-things in the kitchen the two old sisters retired to the sitting-room, and there, with the two windows open to the long-legged sun, they sat in front of the pansy-leaf firescreen that hid the empty grate. — *School for Hope*, Michael McLaverty, 1954.

8215 "Agnes first, Hengist second, Leah third!" said Lavinia Middleton, as her sisters and brother contested the access to the cloak-room in the hall. — *The Mighty and Their Fall*, Ivy Compton-Burnett, 1961.

8216 Dolores got up from the glider as soon as she saw her two sisters on the sidewalk. "My tongue has been stuck to the roof of my mouth all day," she called out, "for lack of any-one to talk to!" — *A Wake in Ybor City*, Jose Yglesias, 1963.

8217 They were brothers, eight years old and nearly ten, one dark and hefty, the elder fair, very fair, and thin. — *The Flame*, Jim Hunter, 1965.

8218 "Tancredi," Gabriella said to her brother, "you must show them the fountain." — *The Evening of the Holiday*, Shirley Hazzard, 1966.

8219 We were seventeen when our parents died. — *The Shrouded Walls*, Susan Howatch, 1968.

8220 Mann Parker was a botanist, out in all weathers, lived with his sister that ran the sweet-shop, they ate meat Fridays, they were Protes-tants. — *A Pagan Place*, Edna O'Brien, 1970.

8221 When I was a boy my brother David and I had to go to bed early whether we were sleepy or not. — "The Fifth Head of Cerberus," Gene Wolfe, 1972.

8222 If I tell you that Mildred, my eldest sister, is married to an eldest brother, and that they are achievers, and that Dorothy, my young-est sister, is the baby of the family and married to a man who wants to keep her that way, and that I am the middle child of the same sex, you must not, in your social-scientist way, make judgments about us and miss the story I am tell-ing. — *Hannah's House*, Shelby Hearon, 1975.

8223 Like strangers thrown together for-tuitously at the same table in an overcrowded café and determined not to be invaded by each other's indentities, brother and sister breakfasted in the dark, high-ceilinged, old-fashioned kitchen above the surgery. — *The Needle*, Francis King, 1975.

8224 Because the baby had come, special at-tention had to be given to Margaret, who was eight. — *God on the Rocks*, Jane Gardam, 1978.

8225 Galton had been as a boy tall for his age, unlike his elder brother. — *The Murderer*, Roy A. K. Heath, 1978.

8226 One spring day Irv Bender gave up his

chances in life for his younger brother. — *Uncle*, Julia Markus, 1978.

8227 Did I ever tell you about the time I tried to get my little brother off the chain gang?... Oh, I did?... Okay, I *will* tell it again. — *Plea-sure-Dome*, David Madden, 1979.

8228 Alan Ross hadn't known he was a twin until he was in high school. — *Sons of Adam*, Frederick Manfred, 1980.

8229 Genetha was left to brood in the house when her brother Rohan went away, driven by the fear of incest after their father's death. — *Genetha*, Roy A. K. Heath, 1981.

8230 The summer my father bought the bear, none of us was born — we weren't even con-ceived: not Frank, the oldest; not Franny, the loudest; not me, the next; and not the youngest of us, Lilly and Egg. — *The Hotel New Hampshire*, John Irving, 1981.

8231 For forty-two years, Lewis and Ben-jamin Jones slept side by side, in their parents' bed, at their farm which was known as "The Vi-sion." — *On the Black Hill*, Bruce Chatwin, 1982.

8232 In the remote border town of Q., which when seen from the air resembles nothing so much as an ill-proportioned dumbbell, there once lived three lovely, and loving, sisters. — *Shame*, Salman Rushdie, 1983.

8233 As youngsters, Lyman Gene and Murana Bill had often been mistaken for twins, though she was the older by nearly three years. — *No Earthly Notion*, Susan Dodd, 1986.

8234 Rose Ann McKenzie looked at her brother Jeff, sitting — or rather lolling, with boneless and presumably aristocratic grace — on the seat opposite hers in the all but empty railroad car. — *McKenzie's Hundred*, Frank Yerby, 1986.

8235 I want to tell you about my brother, Bobby. — *No Ceiling but Heaven*, Mykal Mayfield Banto, 1987.

8236 My sister and I have always been a bit in love, though you couldn't call it incest. — *The Lay of the Land*, Dean Crawford, 1987.

8237 It was obvious that they were brothers in spite of the differences in their ages. They shared the same square shape of head with an ag-gressive thrusting jaw; the same prominent, thinly arched nose; the same green-flecked amber eyes and the same broad, sloping fore-head and sun-bleached light brown hair. But here the similarities ended. — *The Rising of the Moon*, Peter Berresford Ellis, 1987.

8238 "What the fuck are you doing in there?" his sister is screaming, pounding on the bath-room door. — *American Dreams*, Norma Klein, 1987.

8239 Kwame Atta was the bad twin, and his chin was strong enough to box with, even with

the sun on his tongue. — *Woman of the Aeroplanes*, Kojo Laing, 1988.

8240 It won't make a difference to write down here that I was the reason my younger brother, Matthew, died. — *The Fifth Station*, Kevin McIlvoy, 1988.

8241 The elderly McAlister sisters, Pearl in khaki pants and Wanda Gay in an organdy dress, sat on the wedding porch of their family house swinging and arguing over the placement of the new rose bushes that had arrived in the afternoon mail. — *Mother of Pearl*, Edward Swift, 1989.

8242 Elinor Fane collected prizes as easily as her sister's clothes collected dabs of paint. — *The Three Graces*, Elizabeth Wix, 1989.

8243 The world didn't begin with my sister, although I have sometimes thought that it could hardly go on without her. — *The Light Possessed*, Alan Cheuse, 1990.

8244 The women of her mother's village say that if one twin dies by water, the other will die by fire. — *The Journey*, Indira Ganesan, 1990.

8245 I remember the day my brother was brought to our house from the children's home, and everything is tinted a lemony yellow. — *A Soldier's Daughter Never Cries*, Kaylie Jones, 1990.

8246 Standing with my brother Arnie on the edge of town has become a yearly ritual. — *What's Eating Gilbert Grape*, Peter Hedges, 1991.

8247 My brother used to tell me I was the devil. — *Halfway Home*, Paul Monette, 1991.

8248 The three brothers used to sleep together in the room at the back of the house by the kitchen, Big Dan and Sam on the bunks and Peter in a cot by the windows, where he could see the trees sway in the breeze that came off the ocean. — *Like China*, Varley O'Connor, 1991.

8249 Sometimes when people asked Eileen Holland if she had any brothers or sisters, she had to think for a moment. — *Strong Motion*, Jonathan Franzen, 1992.

8250 Alma and Bruce were adopted. — "Sis and Bud," Rachel Ingalls, 1992.

8251 Let's say I have visited my sister, underwater. — *The Body in Four Parts*, Janet Kauffman, 1993.

Sight

8252 As Don Ippolito passed down the long narrow *calle* or footway leading from the Campo San Stefano to the Grand Canal in Venice, he peered anxiously about him: now turning for a backward look up the calle where there was no living thing in sight but a cat on a garden gate, now running a quick eye along the palace walls that rose vast on either hand, and notched the slender strip of blue sky visible overhead with the lines of their jutting balconies, chimneys and cornices, and now glancing towards the canal where he could see the noiseless black boats meeting and passing. — *A Foregone Conclusion*, William Dean Howells, 1875.

8253 "I'm so blind," said Miss Ferrars plaintively. "Where are my glasses?" — *The God in the Car*, Anthony Hope, 1894.

8254 At Surat, by a window of his private office in the East India Company's factory, a middle-aged man stared out upon the broad river and the wharves below. — *Hetty Wesley*, Arthur Quiller-Couch, 1903.

8255 Late one brilliant April afternoon Professor Lucius Wilson stood at the head of Chestnut Street, looking about him with the pleased air of a man of taste who does not very often get to Boston. — *Alexander's Bridge*, Willa Cather, 1912.

8256 Blake, the Second Deputy, raised his gloomy hound's eyes as the door opened and a woman stepped in. Then he dropped them again. — *Never-Fail Blake*, Arthur Stringer, 1913.

8257 At the open window of the great library of Blandings Castle, drooping like a wet sock, as was his habit when he had nothing to prop his spine against, the Earl of Emsworth, that amiable and boneheaded peer, stood gazing out over his domain. — *Leave It to Psmith*, P. G. Wodehouse, 1923.

8258 Jane Coombe stood on the hill above Plyn, looking down upon the harbour. — *The Loving Spirit*, Daphne du Maurier, 1931.

8259 Harriet Vane sat at her writing-table and stared out into Mecklenburg Square. The late tulips made a brave show in the Square garden, and a quartet of early tennis-players were energetically calling the score of a rather erratic and unpractised game. — *Gaudy Night*, Dorothy L. Sayers, 1935.

8260 Celia Marston was standing on a wooden stool and looking out of the high-set window. — *Celia*, E. H. Young, 1937.

8261 "I wonder who this is from," said Mrs. Brandon, picking a letter out of the heap that lay by her plate and holding it at arm's length upside down. "It is quite extraordinary how I can't see without my spectacles. It makes me laugh sometimes because it is so ridiculous." — *The Brandons*, Angela Thirkell, 1939.

8262 The owner of Laverings looked out of his bedroom window on a dewy June morning. — *Before Lunch*, Angela Thirkell, 1940.

8263 It was the hour of twilight on a soft spring day toward the end of April in the year of Our Lord 1929, and George Webber leaned his

elbows on the sill of his back window and looked out at what he could see of New York. — *You Can't Go Home Again*, Thomas Wolfe, 1940.

8264 I sat with young François, Peter Dekatha's son, in the huckleberry bushes, peering into the morning mist. — *His Majesty's Yankees*, Thomas H. Raddall, 1942.

8265 Joan Scudamore screwed up her eyes as she peered across the dimness of the Rest House dining room. She was slightly shortsighted. —*Absent in the Spring*, Agatha Christie *as* Mary Westmacott, 1944.

8266 Squatting, with the hams of his rump against his heels, his forearms resting at ease across his thighs and his big hands hanging limply as if broken at their wrists, Harg was gazing at a grove of trees. — *The Golden Rooms*, Vardis Fisher, 1944.

8267 Mr. Hackett turned the corner and saw, in the failing light, at some little distance, his seat. It seemed to be occupied. — *Watt*, Samuel Beckett, 1953.

8268 Lije Baley had just reached his desk when he became aware of R. Sammy watching him expectantly. — *The Caves of Steel*, Isaac Asimov, 1954.

8269 Pippin looked out from under the shelter of Gandalf's cloak. — *The Return of the King*, J. R. R. Tolkien, 1956.

8270 Paul Cable sat hunched forward at the edge of the pine shade, his boots crossed and his elbows supported on his knees. He put the field glasses to his eyes again and, four hundred yards down the slope, the two-story adobe was brought suddenly, silently before him. — *Last Stand at Saber River*, Elmore Leonard, 1959.

8271 With eyes wet and huge the deer watched; the young man watched back. — *Portrait of an Artist with Twenty-six Horses*, William Eastlake, 1963.

8272 I stood and sent my eyes around. — *Death of a Doxy*, Rex Stout, 1966.

8273 Old Jake Hanlon sits on the edge of the mesa and looks out over miles of southwestern plain. — *Mavericks*, Jack Schaefer, 1967.

8274 Rear-Admiral Percival Oldenshaw stood with his arms folded and stared pensively through his office window at the rambling expanse of Portsmouth Dockyard. — *To Risks Unknown*, Douglas Reeman, 1969.

8275 A man called Motke Bartov, then engaged in a count of animals in the Wadi Parek of southern Israel (this was February 1957), made the first sighting. —*Smith's Gazelle*, Lionel Davidson, 1971.

8276 What the boy sees where the children are crossing makes his eyes squint. — *Fire Sermon*, Wright Morris, 1971.

8277 The lady lay in a little glen — if bananas and coconuts and catstails and fire-of-the-forest and heat can make a cool-sounding thing like a glen — and from under thick lids examined Mrs. Filling who stood on the sand at the glen's edge with the sharp, green Caribbean sea behind her. — *The Pineapple Bay Hotel*, Jane Gardam, 1976.

8278 Connie got up from her kitchen table and walked slowly to the door. Either I saw him or I didn't and I'm crazy for real this time, she thought. — *Woman on the Edge of Time*, Marge Piercy, 1976.

8279 Whole sight; or all the rest is desolation. — *Daniel Martin*, John Fowles, 1977.

8280 Lieutenant-Commander John Devane sat on a plain wooden bench seat and regarded the opposite wall. Grey rough concrete. You could even see where the first layer had been tamped home. — *Torpedo Run*, Douglas Reeman, 1981.

8281 It's Saturday night and I'm coming into the park from the foot of Fifth and what do I see? — *The Washington Square Ensemble*, Madison Smartt Bell, 1983.

8282 Caroline switched off the ignition of her red Subaru, gripped the steering wheel with both gloved hands, and gazed across the parking lot down to Lake Glass. — *Other Women*, Lisa Alther, 1984.

8283 A woman stood by her window looking out at the garden with the gaze of someone surveying the sea or a long sweep of hills and fields. —*A Perfect Woman*, Carolyn Slaughter, 1984.

8284 He noticed it immediately. — *The Spoilers*, David Hooks, 1985.

8285 Fogel polishes the lenses for her, even though she's not going to be able to see out of them. — *Ivory Bright*, Elaine Ford, 1986.

8286 On the improvised dais — an upturned fruit box — Kevin Moorhouse stood with his eyes fixed well above the level of the observers' faces. —*Painting Classes*, Carol Jones, 1986.

8287 The view, or vista, that the squinting eye now beheld at leisure was, if one cared for that sort of thing, rather spectacular. — *The Devil at Home*, Oliver Lange, 1986.

8288 It was Kirsti who first noticed. — *Frozen Music*, Francis King, 1987.

8289 "Because our eyes are blue, most Chinese believe we can see into the ground to a depth of three feet." — *Peking*, Anthony Grey, 1988.

8290 Ina asks me what I see and I have to be honest: I see nothing. — *The Widows' Adventures*, Charles Dickinson, 1989.

8291 Frankie had seen enough. — *Still Lives*, Scott Sommer, 1989.

8292 Sometimes, when Reardon walked down the wing, she could see Brandy's fingers poking out of the spyhole. — *A World Like This*, Helen Benedict, 1990.

8293 It's just junk down this way in Florida, you have to make yourself look to see, you have to bring yourself to bear on things. — *The Lives of the Dead*, Charlie Smith, 1990.

8294 The Eleventh Earl of Gallerick sighed deeply and looked hard at the large man in the blue mohair suit seated opposite him. — *The Last Resort*, Dan Binchy, 1992.

8295 The black, unblinking eyes were fixed on his face. — *All I Have Is Blue*, James Colbert, 1992.

8296 As he kept telling them later, he had passed within two feet of the figure without really seeing it. — *Breach of Immunity*, Molly Hite, 1992.

8297 Vicky Clay could still see. Not well, not clearly, but in a vague and hazy way, as she might recall a dream. — *The Last Virginia Gentleman*, Michael Kilian, 1992.

8298 Dr. John Harvey Kellogg, inventor of the corn flake and peanut butter, not to mention caramel-cereal coffee, Bromose, Nuttolene and some seventy-five other gastrically correct foods, paused to level his gaze on the heavyset woman in the front row. — *The Road to Wellville*, T. Coraghessan Boyle, 1993.

Signs

8299 Nothing could have been more painful to my sensitiveness than to occupy myself, confused with blushes, at the centre of the whole world as a living advertisement of the least amusing ballet in Paris. — *The Beautiful Lady*, Booth Tarkington, 1905.

8300 A squat grey building of only thirty-four stories. Over the main entrance the words, Central London Hatchery and Conditioning Centre, and, in a shield, the World State's motto, Community, Identity, Stability. — *Brave New World*, Aldous Huxley, 1932.

8301 The sign above the drugstore windows had been there a long time — gold and black letters, a scabby gilt mortar-and-pestle.... It said simply, "Marsh's," and that meant a great deal to everybody in Hartfield. — *Happy Land*, MacKinlay Kantor, 1943.

8302 The board in the hall said Central Liaison Organization, 3rd floor. — *The Broken Penny*, Julian Symons, 1952.

8303 JESUS IS COMING — ARE YOU READY?/ When you've seen this sign, whitewashed high on the blasted cliff-face above the hairpin curve of the mountain pass, you will know you've reached the Holy Roller country. — *The Kiss of Kin*, Mary Lee Settle, 1955.

8304 "P.S.A.," said Sybil, in a tone of amiable comment. She was looking through the window of the bus and I had my arm around her. — *Scenes from Married Life*, William Cooper, 1961.

8305 On Monday a man came out to the house and took down the sign that said *FOR SALE*: A. C. BRADLEY, REALTOR and put up one that said *SOLD*: A. C. BRADLEY, REALTOR. — *Darrell*, Marion Montgomery, 1964.

8306 "A.V.C.C.", said the big blonde Wren. "I don't think I've ever seen them letters before." — *A Vision of Battlements*, Anthony Burgess, 1965.

8307 "What on earth is a 'No Station'?" asked Nigel, reading a huge overhead sign as they drove into the city. — *The Morning After Death*, Cecil Day-Lewis as Nicholas Blake, 1966.

8308 The Grove Chill Tonic sign thermometer on the drugstore door read 81 degrees when Doc Daniels opened up. — *Moonshine Light, Moonshine Bright*, William Price Fox, 1967.

8309 On 119th Street there had been a sign for years in the front window of an old dilapidated three-story brick house, announcing: FUNERALS PERFORMED. — *Blind Man with a Pistol*, Chester Himes, 1969.

8310 God is great/ God is good/ Let's clean up/ the neighborhood/ the shadow/ Frankie twisted the plastic cap over the wet end of his white marker and stepped back to gain perspective on his verse. — *Walls*, Jay Daly, 1980.

8311 Joshua Loftus Colby Goff stared at the flat oblong of stone and the sharply-cut roman lettering of the short inscription. — *The Iron Stallions*, John Harris as Max Hennessy, 1982.

8312 Ricn à Declarer declared the sign under which she entered Athens, trundling her bags efficiently on their aluminum dolly, freewheeling. — *The Diver's Tomb*, Ann Deagon, 1984.

8313 Sybil goes into her study, then comes out of it again and hangs over the door handle a printed notice which says DO NOT DISTURB. — *Voices in an Empty Room*, Francis King, 1984.

8314 TIME: *11:58 PM/* DATE: *1/9/* TEMP: *34 F–1 C/* This information I obtain not from my Bulova watch, long ago exchanged for a pawnshop ticket, but from the illuminated sign upon the shores of the nearby state of New Jersey. — "The Magic Flute," Leslie Epstein, 1985.

8315 IS THERE LIFE AFTER DEATH?/ TRESPASS AND FIND OUT./ The poster on the fence rail was commercially printed in vermillion ink with a veneer that made it look wet. — *Big Fish*, Thomas Perry, 1985.

8316 AVERAGE WAIT 4 HOURS 45 MINUTES, said a monitor strung up over the museum entrance, blinking incessantly, as if trying to knock something from its eye. — *The Magic Moment*, Gregg Easterbrook, 1986.

8317 "Welcome to Mt. Hope," the old sign read: "The World's Most Beautiful Racetrack, Playground of Millionaires, Sport of Kings." — *A Temporary Residence*, Helen Hudson, 1987.

8318 Someone had scrawled "Happy Reentry Jesus" in fat, uneven letters across the steel door. — *The Splintered Eye*, Beth S. Patric, 1987.

8319 On the way to the hospital in Paducah, Spence notices the row of signs along the highway: WHERE WILL YOU BE IN ETERNITY? — *Spence + Lila*, Bobbie Ann Mason, 1988.

8320 ABANDON ALL HOPE YE WHO ENTER HERE is scrawled in blood red lettering on the side of the Chemical Bank near the corner of Eleventh and First and is in print large enough to be seen from the backseat of the cab as it lurches forward in the traffic leaving Wall Street and just as Timothy Price notices the words a bus pulls up, the advertisement for *Les Misérables* on its side blocking his view, but Price who is with Pierce & Pierce and twenty-six doesn't seem to care because he tells the driver he will give him five dollars to turn up the radio, "Be My Baby" on WYNN, and the driver, black, not American, does so. — *American Psycho*, Bret Easton Ellis, 1991.

8321 There is a giant oak in front of World Headquarters with a sign on it. — *The Plagiarist*, Benjamin Cheever, 1992.

8322 On August 14 at three in the afternoon, Michael Schaeffer noticed a small poster on a board inside the front window of a small teahouse. — *Sleeping Dogs*, Thomas Perry, 1992.

8323 A Texaco star glows above the gas pumps, tinted purple by the steely glare of mercury vapor lights. — *Stones of the Dalai Lama*, Ken Mitchell, 1993.

Silence

8324 Silence, — silence! It is the hour of the deepest hush of night; the invisible intangible clouds of sleep brood over the brilliant city. — *Wormwood: A Drama of Paris*, Marie Corelli, 1890.

8325 The tumultuous storm had passed over Paris, and behind it there came a hollow silence, in which there were no echoes. — *The Arm and the Darkness*, Taylor Caldwell, 1943.

8326 The farmhouse was quiet, the soggy patch of field and the near forest were quiet under the flannel sky. — *The Wine of Astonishment*, Martha Gellhorn, 1948.

8327 At three o'clock in the afternoon the house became so quiet that you imagined that you could hear the river lapping softly at the foot of the green hill. — *The Strange Children*, Caroline Gordon, 1951.

8328 The garden was quiet. — *The Hidden Flower*, Pearl S. Buck, 1952.

8329 "Nennius!"/ There was no reply. Everything was still. — *Roman Wall*, Bryher, 1954.

8330 Not a leaf stirred in the July heat. There was no sound, neither the thump of a staff nor the tapping of a messenger's sandals. — *Ruan*, Bryher, 1960.

8331 I know of no quiet quite like that of a men's club at about half past nine on a summer Sunday evening. — "We're Friends Again," John O'Hara, 1960.

8332 Berman sat alone now on his sofa. For just a minute or two he felt relief at the silence. But then the quiet became dark and threatening like a vessel filling with a strange liquid. — *The Human Season*, Edward Lewis Wallant, 1960.

8333 At ten minutes to nine o'clock, silence everywhere; the instrument-room of the observatory interpenetrated by it as by the motionless mountain air, as by the soundlessness of outer space where only the hydrogen atoms "speak," cheeping like chicks in a limitless incubator: the crepuscular buzz of the universe seeping down through the ionised layer whose depths it was the observatory's purpose to measure. — *The Birthday King*, Gabriel Fielding, 1962.

8334 As so often, late in the evening, in the house in the quiet square, the stillness was so absolute that it distracted her. — *Cousin Henrietta*, Emma Cave, 1981.

8335 I can hear the silence, and through it individual sounds. — *The Seven Ages*, Eva Figes, 1986.

8336 The yard in front of Paren Comesee's house was full of restless silence. — *Angel*, Merle Collins, 1988.

8337 Quiet lay upon the meadow like a soft, green blanket. — *Joshua and the Children*, Joseph F. Girzone, 1989.

8338 Someone had turned off the wireless and, in spite of the room being full of people, there was a complete silence — in which Polly could feel, and almost hear, her own heart thudding. — *Marking Time*, Elizabeth Jane Howard, 1991.

Sitting

8339 London. Michaelmas Term lately over, and the Lord Chancellor sitting in Lincoln's Inn Hall. — *Bleak House*, Charles Dickens, 1853.

8340 In an easy chair of the spacious and handsome library of his town-house, sat William, Earl of Mount Severn. — *East Lynne*, Mrs. Henry Wood, 1861.

8341 On a certain Monday evening late in January, 1881, Paul Bultitude, Esq. (of Mincing Lane, Colonial Produce Merchant), was sitting alone in his dining-room at Westbourne Terrace after dinner. — *Vice Versa*, F. Anstey, 1882.

8342 On a spring day, in the year 1568, Mistress Talbot sat in her lodging at Hull, an upper chamber, with a large latticed window, glazed with the circle and diamond leading perpetuated in Dutch pictures, and opening on a carved balcony, whence, had she been so minded, she could have shaken hands with her opposite neighbour. — *Unknown to History*, Charlotte Mary Yonge, 1882.

8343 The child sat upon the roadside. — *The Descendant*, Ellen Glasgow *as* Anonymous, 1897.

8344 Two men were sitting side by side on a stone bench in the forgotten garden of the Arcadian Society, in Rome; and it was in early spring, not long ago. — *Cecilia*, F. Marion Crawford, 1902.

8345 She sat in her superb private drawing-room at the Hotel Cecil. She was facing the large window which overlooked the Embankment and the Thames and the bridges and the pageant of moving life by road and river. — *The Gates of Wrath*, Arnold Bennett, 1903.

8346 The Magister Udal sat in the room of his inn in Paris, where customarily the King of France lodged such envoys as came at his expense. — *Privy Seal*, Ford Madox Ford, 1907.

8347 On an evening in 1866 (exactly eight hundred years after the battle of Hastings) Mr. Henry Knight, a draper's manager, aged forty, dark, clean-shaven, short, but not stout, sat in his sitting-room on the second-floor over the shop which he managed in Oxford Street, London. — *A Great Man*, Arnold Bennett, 1911.

8348 The Crown Prince sat in the royal box and swung his legs. This was hardly princely, but the royal legs did not quite reach the floor from the high crimson-velvet seat of his chair. — *Long Live the King!*, Mary Roberts Rinehart, 1917.

8349 Sitting on the doorstep, Elizabeth Scott leaned her head against the stone wall of the old house. — *John Baring's House*, Elsie Singmaster, 1920.

8350 A young man and an old one sat in the shade of the willows beside the wide, still river. — *Quill's Window*, George Barr McCutcheon, 1921.

8351 The two young men — they were of the English public official class — sat in the perfectly appointed railway carriage. — *Some Do Not...*, Ford Madox Ford, 1924.

8352 The Bonneys were sitting out in the back yard of the parsonage. — *The Bonney Family*, Ruth Suckow, 1926.

8353 Helga Crane sat alone in her room, which at that hour, eight in the evening, was in soft gloom. — *Quicksand*, Nella Larsen, 1928.

8354 Mr. Sniggs, the Junior Dean, and Mr. Postlethwaite, the Domestic Bursar, sat alone in Mr. Sniggs's room overlooking the garden quad at Scone College. — *Decline and Fall*, Evelyn Waugh, 1928.

8355 There were as many chairs there and there were two a chair that can be found everywhere a rocking chair that is to say a rocking chair can be found everywhere. Two there one at one end and the other at the other end. They were in front of the building and in sitting and rocking there was a very slight declivity in front of the building. — *Lucy Church Amiably*, Gertrude Stein, 1930.

8356 In Philadelphia Mrs. Mark Baldwin sat on her grandmother's porch enjoying the height of the spring of 1813. The horrid winter of her discontent was practically over. — *The Valiant Wife*, Margaret Wilson, 1933.

8357 She had no favorite corner where, like most solitary old ladies, she chose to sit. — "The Listener," Louis Bromfield, 1934.

8358 Wilson sat on the balcony of the Bedford Hotel with his bald pink knees thrust against the ironwork. — *The Heart of the Matter*, Graham Greene, 1948.

8359 Here Martha Barden sat once more. Here she was, back in Dr. Fray's office. — *The Good Family*, MacKinlay Kantor, 1949.

8360 Theopolis Akers, six feet tall and broad-shouldered, sat on the sty where he had rested so many times after climbing the winding path from Fidis Artner's with a coffee-sack load of supplies. — *The Good Spirit of Laurel Ridge*, Jesse Stuart, 1953.

8361 The woman hunched by the ashes of the dead fire, her big shoulders squared forward. — *Hannah Fowler*, Janice Holt Giles, 1956.

8362 When I first saw them, they were sitting on the sea wall by the old cannon, near to where the river runs out across the beach. — *Autumn Equinox*, John Hearne, 1959.

8363 In front of one of the most palatial hotels in the world, a very young man was accustomed to sit on a bench which, when the light fell in a certain way, shone like gold. — *Malcolm*, James Purdy, 1959.

8364 Erlene is in the next room. She sits, like a blind person, in the dark. — *Scented Gardens for the Blind*, Janet Frame, 1963.

8365 They were sitting in the parlor they both hated so much but somehow liked, too, and

there wasn't a thing doing. — *Boys and Girls Together*, William Saroyan, 1963.

8366 A young man, sixteen years old, was sitting hunkered on his heels in a stretch of tall yellow sagegrass. — *The Inkling*, Fred Chappell, 1965.

8367 It was morning and Mrs. Pollifax was seated on the floor of her living room, legs crossed beneath her as she tried to sustain the lotus position. — *A Palm for Mrs. Pollifax*, Dorothy Gilman, 1973.

8368 It began that day at the café on the Place G., in the rain, as he sat alone in the squash of patrons under the awning. — "Dr. Heart," Eleanor Clark, 1974.

8369 There was only one bench in the shade and Converse went for it, although it was already occupied. — *Dog Soldiers*, Robert Stone, 1974.

8370 Leslie was balanced on the hard cushion of an antique chair designed for someone with a three-cornered behind. — *The High Cost of Living*, Marge Piercy, 1978.

8371 Once, when Esther the Black was eighteen, she sat on the porch of her grandmother's house and dragged her feet in the dust until her toes were coated and dark. — *The Drowning Season*, Alice Hoffman, 1979.

8372 Three caddies sat on the steps under the portico at the front entrance of the Nipmunk Country Club in Weston, Massachusetts, and watched the long, curving driveway bake in the late morning sun. — *The Patriot Game*, George V. Higgins, 1982.

8373 "How long have we been sitting here?" I said. — *Berlin Game*, Len Deighton, 1983.

8374 In the sunlight in the center of a ring of trees Lev sat cross-legged, his head bent above his hands. — *The Eye of the Heron*, Ursula K. Le Guin, 1983.

8375 Susan looked around her and saw that she was sitting in the middle of a sandpile. — *The Lucky Piece*, Francelia Butler, 1984.

8376 The fire chief sits in his special chair in the parlor, a paisley shawl with hand-knotted fringes tucked snugly around him. — *Descending Order*, Helen Faye Rosenblum, 1984.

8377 You can see me any afternoon during the summer months, sitting at one of the tables in the square under the chestnut trees and taking a vanilla ice with a small whisky poured over it. — *Pianoplayers*, Anthony Burgess, 1986.

8378 Mrs. Emmeline Pillson, "Lucia" to friends — and all the inhabitants of Tilling were her dear and devoted friends — sat in the window of the picturesque garden-room that was such an outstanding feature of Mallards, her elegant Queen Anne house. — *Lucia Triumphant*, Tom Holt, 1986.

8379 In the bush just beyond Accra, the bush that handfuls of wild guinea fowl raised with their cries, sat Beni Baidoo. — *Search Sweet Country*, Kojo Laing, 1986.

8380 I sit on the bed at a crooked angle, one foot on the floor, my hip against the tent of Mom's legs, my elbows on the hospital table. — *A Yellow Raft in Blue Water*, Michael Dorris, 1987.

8381 The two women are sitting at right angles to each other at the kitchen table on a sunny July morning in the nineteen-sixties. — *Can't Quit You, Baby*, Ellen Douglas, 1988.

8382 He sits in the woods holding her hand. — *Lie to Me*, David Martin, 1990.

8383 Slowly, William Randolph Hearst lowered his vast bear-like body into a handsome Biedermeier chair, all scrolls and lyres and marquetry. — *Hollywood*, Gore Vidal, 1990.

8384 Vernon Jackson sits on the side of his bed in his white Jockey undershorts — which have mostly separated from their waistband. — *Killer Diller*, Clyde Edgerton, 1991.

8385 Celia del Pino, equipped with binoculars and wearing her best housedress and drop pearl earrings, sits in her wicker swing guarding the north coast of Cuba. — *Dreaming in Cuban*, Cristina Garcia, 1992.

8386 On the rolling lawn of Barnaderg Bay Hospital, the long-term patient known as Miss Lucia Joyce sat in a position of slack repose, in a patch of weak sunlight. — *Clairvoyant*, Alison Leslie Gold, 1992.

8387 Chagak sat at the roof hole entrance of the ulaq, on the thick sod that was the ulaq roof. — *My Sister the Moon*, Sue Harrison, 1992.

8388 *Fade in: a medium shot of Tzu, sitting rigidly in a black director's chair, black background. — Watching TV with the Red Chinese*, Luke Whisnant, 1992.

The Sky

8389 The sun had disappeared behind the summits of the Tyrolean Alps, and the moon was already risen above the low barrier of the Lido. — *The Bravo*, James Fenimore Cooper, 1831.

8390 The room fronted the west, but a black cloud, barred with red, robbed the hour of twilight's tranquil charm. — *Moods*, Louisa May Alcott, 1864.

8391 The full African moon poured down its light from the blue sky into the wide, lonely plain. — *The Story of an African Farm*, Olive Schreiner, 1883.

8392 Midnight, — without darkness, without stars! Midnight, — and the unwearied sun stood, yet visible in the heavens, like a victorious king throned on a dais of royale purple bordered with gold. The sky above him, — his canopy, — gleamed with a cold yet lustrious blue, while across it slowly flitted a few wandering clouds of palest amber, deepening, as they sailed along, to a tawny orange. — *Thelma*, Marie Corelli, 1887.

8393 It was about six o'clock of a winter's morning. In the eastern sky faint streaks of grey had come and were succeeded by flashes of red, crimson-cloaked heralds of the coming day. — *The Uncalled*, Paul Laurence Dunbar, 1898.

8394 Above, the sky seemed one vast arc of solemn blue, set here and there with points of tremulous fire; below, to the shadowy horizon, stretched the plain of the soft grey sea, while from the fragrances of night and earth floated a breath of sleep and flowers. — *Stella Fregelius*, H. Rider Haggard, 1904.

8395 In the month of July of the year 1348, between the feasts of St. Benedict and of St. Swithin, a strange thing came upon England, for out of the east there drifted a monstrous cloud, purple and piled, heavy with evil, climbing slowly up the hushed heaven. — *Sir Nigel*, Arthur Conan Doyle, 1906.

8396 There was a glow in the sky as if great furnace doors were opened. — *The Hill of Dreams*, Arthur Machen, 1907.

8397 On the afternoon of the last day of April, 190-, a billowy sea of little broken clouds crowned the thin air above High Street, Kensington. — *Fraternity*, John Galsworthy, 1909.

8398 Saturday, April, 1852. There was a fervor in the sky as of an August noon, although the clocks of the city would presently strike five. — *Gideon's Band*, George W. Cable, 1914.

8399 The sun, which shone upon a day that was gathered to the past some three thousand years ago, was setting in full glory over the expanses of south-eastern Africa — the Libya of the ancients. — *Elissa*, H. Rider Haggard, 1917.

8400 Small feckless clouds were hurried across the vast untroubled sky — shepherdless, futile, imponderable — and were torn to fragments on the fangs of the mountains, so ending their ephemeral adventures with nothing of their fugitive existence left but a few tears. — *Gone to Earth*, Mary Webb, 1917.

8401 Overhead the clouds cloaked the sky; a ragged cloak it was, and, here and there, a star shone through a hole, to be obscured almost instantly as more cloud tatters were hurled across the rent. — *The Portygee*, Joseph C. Lincoln, 1920.

8402 The sun settled into the tawny marshes. — *The Apple of the Eye*, Glenway Wescott, 1924.

8403 Aunt Hager Williams stood in her doorway and looked out at the sun. The western sky was a sulphurous yellow and the sun a red ball dropping slowly behind the trees and housetops. Its setting left the rest of the heavens grey with clouds. — *Not Without Laughter*, Langston Hughes, 1930.

8404 The sun, dark and red, settled behind a bank of spear-shaped clouds which bisected it and diffused its inadequate light. — *The Murderer Invisible*, Philip Wylie, 1931.

8405 The thin papery sky of the early autumn afternoon was torn, and the eye of the sun, pale but piercing, looked through and down. — *The Inquisitor*, Hugh Walpole, 1935.

8406 After the night of rain, a smallish, wan sun was struggling through wool tatters of cloud. — *The Stone Field*, Martha Ostenso, 1937.

8407 The sun shone, having no alternative, on the nothing new. — *Murphy*, Samuel Beckett, 1938.

8408 It was the brilliant, high, windless sky of early autumn. — *At Heaven's Gate*, Robert Penn Warren, 1943.

8409 The sun rose with an upward push of colour toward the zenith. — *Toil of the Brave*, Inglis Fletcher, 1946.

8410 This March day the vast and brassy sky, always spangled with the silver glint of airplanes, roared and glittered with celestial traffic. — *Giant*, Edna Ferber, 1952.

8411 Today a rare sun of spring. — *The Ginger Man*, J. P. Donleavy, 1955.

8412 In that hour after dawn the horizon did not seem far away. The line where the watery sky met the gray sea was not well defined; it was as if the cheerless clouds grew denser out towards that circle until at the final meeting, all the way round, there was not an abrupt transition, but a simple mingling of twin elements. — *The Good Shepherd*, C. S. Forester, 1955.

8413 Over the rancho of Our Lady of the Little Columns a California sun shone hazily through a September day. — *Miss Harriet Townshend*, Kathleen Norris, 1955.

8414 If I hear a person say, "Man! That's a blue sky — for sure," I know exactly how the sky looks. — *A Patch of Blue*, Elizabeth Kata, 1961.

8415 Whitely bright the great moon of Maa showed a rim above the crater, moving up into a starred sky. — *A Man in a Mirror*, Richard Llewellyn, 1961.

8416 There was a glaring white haze over the sky that July afternoon. — *The Last Campaign*, Glen Ross, 1962.

8417 It was a Saturday afternoon in mid-July, and the sun was a burning yellow fire high up in the sharpened glare of a dry blue sky. — *What Time Collects*, James T. Farrell, 1964.

8418 It was an old moon, late in rising, and lopsided, shining wetly through the gathering clouds. — *The Love Letters*, Madeleine L'Engle, 1966.

8419 The sun turned black as sackcloth, the moon red as blood and the sky rolled together like a scroll curling shut. — *The Man with the Chocolate Egg*, John Noone, 1966.

8420 Though the stars hold, the moon is gone. The black of sky already thins. — *The Trojans*, Wirt Williams, 1966.

8421 Lying in bed, Beatrice Burns saw, through her unwashed window, the darkening day and the floating dark clouds in the somber sky. — *New Year's Eve/1929*, James T. Farrell, 1967.

8422 It was a bomber's sky: dry air, wind enough to clear the smoke, cloud broken enough to recognize a few stars. — *Bomber*, Len Deighton, 1970.

8423 When the rooster crowed, the moon had still not left the world but was going down on flushed cheek, one day short of the full. — *Losing Battles*, Eudora Welty, 1970.

8424 There was not a crack in the sky, not a blemish on the dense blue enamel. — *The Scorpion God*, William Golding, 1971.

8425 The Hunter's Moon rises as the sun is setting, and for several nights in late autumn it brightens the landscape with cold light. — *The Hunter's Moon*, Nathaniel Benchley, 1972.

8426 Three o'clock in February. All the sky was blue and high. — *A Fairy Tale of New York*, J. P. Donleavy, 1973.

8427 On Wednesday and Thursday, April 11 and 12, the sky closed in. — *A Lion's Share*, Mark Steadman, 1975.

8428 Low in the east spread an ivory fan, and the moon's bleached skull peeked from the rim of the sea. — *Voyage*, Sterling Hayden, 1976.

8429 I ran into the fields one April morning, thinking to climb to the benchland where Uncle Jolly was breaking new ground. The sky was as blue as a bottle. — *Sporty Creek*, James Still, 1977.

8430 Grey clouds streamed high over the headland. — *Bitter Orange*, Desmond Hamill, 1979.

8431 The sun hung low in the west, sending shafts of rose-colored light slanting through the pines. — *The Many-Forked Branch*, Ewan Clarkson, 1980.

8432 One afternoon, in early November, the sky slowly began to change color. — *Angel Landing*, Alice Hoffman, 1980.

8433 At midnight the sky had a sunrise glow that came not from the east but from the centre, near Chinatown, as people still called it. — *Turtle Beach*, Blanche d'Alpuget, 1981.

8434 All day north. She could hardly breathe under that leaden sky with the fir trees pointing upwards like dark fingers, the landscape one that had figured in many of her dreams. — *The Clearing*, Mary Elsie Robertson, 1982.

8435 This morning the sky opened again. — *The Winter Tree*, Georgina Lewis, 1983.

8436 The moon lofted off the horizon to drift low over the prairie, white and imperious as a commodore. — *Something to Be Desired*, Thomas McGuane, 1984.

8437 A willful April sun was preparing to break out from an iron-gray straitjacket of cloud. — *Jadis*, Ken Chowder, 1985.

8438 The sun was rising. Mother of all things, she sent her foreguard on first, to light the sky, and make the earth ready, and at her first warm touch, all life awoke. — *Pillar of the Sky*, Cecelia Holland, 1985.

8439 It was late August. The moon shone bright over a brisk seascape. — *Our Father's House*, Stephen Longstreet, 1985.

8440 The sky sat on top of their hill. — *Sometimes I Live in the Country*, Frederick Busch, 1986.

8441 Puffs of cloud coalesced out of nothing in the enormous sky and then evaporated. — *Heart's Desire*, Gwyneth Cravens, 1986.

8442 Now that the weather had changed, the moon of the falling leaves turned white in the blackening sky and White Man's Dog was restless. — *Fools Crow*, James Welch, 1986.

8443 It had been raining earlier in the day, a chill spring rain, but with the twilight the skies began to clear. — *The Road to Avalon*, Joan Wolf, 1988.

8444 In that part of the world the sky is everywhere, and the entire landscape seems to lie in abasement under its exacting light. — *The Chymical Wedding*, Lindsay Clarke, 1989.

8445 A low pale lemon grey sun hung over the winter moor. — *A Natural Curiosity*, Margaret Drabble, 1989.

8446 The sky came first, like clear blue glass behind the clouds. — *Theo and Matilda*, Rachel Billington, 1990.

8447 The horizon slanted, a bold slash across the bluest sky Alf had ever seen. — *And the Desert Shall Blossom*, Phyllis Barber, 1991.

8448 It is a warm summer's evening in Belfast, the full moon hangs low in the cloudless sky, seemingly about to touch the maze of slate roofs which radiate out from the shipyard. — *All Our Fault*, Daniel Mornin, 1991.

8449 There were no stars. — *The Reckoning*, Sharon Kay Penman, 1991.

8450 Sarah was sitting on her bed watching the moon sail high above the treetops, when a cloud, blowing suddenly out of the sky, crossed its path and threw the night into darkness. — *At the Sign of the Naked Waiter*, Amy Herrick, 1992.

8451 A chorus line of bright, white young-

lady ghosts pirouetted across the sky, swathed in moonlight. — *Looking for Leo*, Gloria Nagy, 1992.

8452 Snake Ripley stood at the fence, watching the thick red moon swing up slowly over the pines. — *Final Heat*, Philip Lee Williams, 1992.

Sleep

8453 About the middle of the last century, at eight o'clock in the evening, in a large but poor apartment, a man was slumbering on a rough couch. His rusty and worn suit of black was of a piece with his uncarpeted room, the deal table of home manufacture, and its slim unsnuffed candle. — *Peg Woffington*, Charles Reade, 1852.

8454 "Edith!" said Margaret gently, "Edith!"/ But as Margaret half suspected, Edith had fallen asleep. — *North and South*, Elizabeth Gaskell, 1855.

8455 We have just wakened from our first decent sleep for weeks — eight glorious dreamless hours of utter exhaustion. — *Not So Quiet...*, Helen Zenna Smith, 1930.

8456 Towards dawn Peter Corbett got up from the garage floor and, treading softly, moved into the driving seat of the car. Presently he fell into a doze, his head bowed forward on his arms, upon the steering wheel. — *Ordeal*, Nevil Shute, 1939.

8457 He never knew nowadays whether he was asleep or not, but he fancied he must have dozed in the train that trundled west from Hereford, lulling its passengers between the modest hills. — *Man Off Beat*, David Hughes, 1957.

8458 In a cabin on the treeless side of Phosphate Mountain, Jester was asleep in the saddle. He lay in the legs of his high-yellow woman and dreamed of the Kentucky Derby. — *Naked in Garden Hills*, Harry Crews, 1969.

8459 Asleep or awake — what difference? Or rather, if there were a difference, how would you recognize it? — *Nunquam*, Lawrence Durrell, 1970.

8460 Sometimes Jake wondered if the *Doktor*, given his declining years, slept with his mouth open, slack, or was it (more characteristically, perhaps) always clamped shut? — *St. Urbain's Horseman*, Mordecai Richler, 1971.

8461 It was late afternoon. As Marco dozed in his wheelchair the long lazy rays of the sun touched the top of his head and stroked the sparse gray hairs of his good arm and fell among the folds of his lap robe. — *Ask for Me Tomorrow*, Margaret Millar, 1976.

8462 Monday morning, six o'clock. Who's asleep? — *Remember Me*, Fay Weldon, 1976.

8463 Agent Willemse of the Dutch Customs Brigade and *Feldwebel* Krautschneider, "Kraut" for short, his German opposite number, had been lying all night in the wet grass underneath the hawthorn bush by the roadside. — *The Lamb's War*, Jan de Hartog, 1979.

8464 Little Arthur is asleep, with the same expression he has had for forty years. — *The Great Fire of London*, Peter Ackroyd, 1982.

8465 All the children were up the hall in pairs and threes, asleep. — *A World Made of Fire*, Mark Childress, 1984.

8466 In his sleep his hands, which were small, curled into fists. — *Elbowing the Seducer*, T. Gertler, 1984.

8467 Someone murmured "Mr. Herman" twice, three times, but Manny sank back into the rock of sleep. — *Manny and Rose*, Joan K. Peters, 1985.

8468 We slept in what had once been the gymnasium. — *The Handmaid's Tale*, Margaret Atwood, 1986.

8469 Shelly would never admit it to anybody, but she snores. — *Secondary Attachments*, Greg Herriges, 1986.

8470 At three in the afternoon — the hour when, all over the world, the literary stewpot boils over, when gossip in the book-reviewing departments of newspapers is most untamed and swarming, and when the autumn sky over Stockholm begins to draw down a translucent dusk (an eggshell shielding a blue-black yolk) across the spired and watery town — at this lachrymose yet exalted hour, Lars Andemening could be found in bed, napping. — *The Messiah of Stockholm*, Cynthia Ozick, 1987.

8471 The rain pattered on the rooftop of the house in which Emma and Jesse Tree lay sleeping. — *Keeping Secrets*, Sarah Shankman, 1988.

8472 This warm spring night, the second Friday in Lent, 1982, Maddie Cameron took deep breaths to keep herself awake. — *The Blue Nature*, Suzanne Hamilton Free, 1989.

8473 He is dozing, sitting in a wicker chair on a balcony of the Paradise Motel. — *The Paradise Motel*, Eric McCormack, 1989.

8474 When nothing else demanded her attention, Kendall slept. — *The Lover of History*, Jonathan Dee, 1990.

8475 The Girl slept restlessly, feeling the prickly straw as if it were teasing pinches from her mother. — *The Gilda Stories*, Jewelle Gomez, 1991.

Sleeplessness

8476 "Sawners M'Auslan," said the mistress, as soon as she had stretched herself in the bed beside him, "Sawners M'Auslan, are ye sound already?"/ "I'm no sleeping," replied the skipper, a little gruffly, still remaining with his face towards the wall. — *The Gathering of the West*, John Galt, 1823.

8477 In the winter of 188-, I was afflicted by a series of nervous ailments, brought on by over-work and over-worry. Chief among these was a protracted and terrible *insomnia*, accompanied by the utmost depression of spirits and anxiety of mind. — *A Romance of Two Worlds*, Marie Corelli, 1886.

8478 Nobody could sleep. — *The Naked and the Dead*, Norman Mailer, 1948.

8479 Claiborne had promised his wife to rise early on the morning of the *fête*, but he had not slept well the night before. — *The Malefactors*, Caroline Gordon, 1956.

8480 Hours before the nightbell had commenced its furious buzzing he had been awake, neither mildly awake nor half asleep, but wide-eyed and alert, his mind crammed with the photographic clarity of insomnia. — *The Last Angry Man*, Gerald Green, 1956.

8481 Malcolm Harmsworth—who, though the handsomest man in Redcliffe, had not been able to get soundly to sleep all night for frustration—stood at the bathroom window with the cord of its Venetian blind in the fingers of one hand and a Book of Common Prayer in the other. — *Black Summer*, Nancy Hale, 1963.

8482 All night long, Hooker Winslow's eyes were open. — *The Last of the Crazy People*, Timothy Findley, 1967.

8483 Sir Henry Yelverton lies warm in a great curtained bed, half awake, hearing the sound of breathing, the rustling of his servant, Peter, who, just or unjust, can sleep like a dog at any time, content in the trundle bed set at the foot of his own. — *Death of the Fox*, George Garrett, 1971.

8484 "Are you awake, my lord?"/ "Yes," Fulk said. "Light a candle, will you?" — *The Earl*, Cecelia Holland, 1971.

8485 On a mid-January morning in the early nineteen-seventies, at 2 A.M., Central Standard Time, Jane Clifford lay awake in a Midwestern university town, thinking about insomnia: traditions of insomnia, all the people she knew who had it, the poets and artists and saints who had left written testimonies of their sleeplessness. — *The Odd Woman*, Gail Godwin, 1974.

8486 As usual, Ezra Lipschitz had been unable to sleep, and in the morning he staggered out of bed and made his way to the bathroom where he showered and shaved. — *Fire Sale*, Robert Klane, 1975.

8487 Wide awake and restless, Paul Milton Perry clawed away the sheets and swung out of bed, blood weak, his fists clenching and closing like a pulse. He hadn't slept. — *Northern Lights*, Tim O'Brien, 1975.

8488 Every night when I'm not able to sleep, when scrolls of words and formulas unfurl in my mind and faces of those I love, both living and dead, rise from the dark, accusing me of apathy, ambition, self-indulgence, neglect—all of their accusations just—and there's no hope of rest, I try again to retrace the street. — *Beyond the Bedroom Wall*, Larry Woiwode, 1975.

8489 Past midnight so we are really 1 December. Useless trying to sleep with Löwe snoring and grunting like a blackman. — *Kolonialagent*, Robert Brain, 1977.

8490 The Prince's agent, Dr. Rainer, could hardly bear the tension. His body stiff with it for days, at night, sleepless, he had swung between optimism and despair. — *The House of Christina*, Ben Haas, 1977.

8491 It took Melissa nearly the full three weeks to grow used to sleeping in the bed that hung suspended from the ceiling of the flooded house, and even then, even after she had surrounded the bed with shower curtains to protect herself from water splashed or slapped, she would find herself awake in the night's stillest hour, listening to the pump's dull pulse as it circulated fresh seawater through the rooms, listening beyond that to the sea's slow suck as it entered the cove on which the house was built, and from the center of her insomnia she would gaze up through the skylight above her at the meteor showers that streaked the Caribbean sky, and she would think: I am going to die from the strangeness of this. By morning I will be dead of the aloneness and the strangeness. — *Easy Travel to Other Planets*, Ted Mooney, 1981.

8492 Would it ever get light, the old professor wondered. — *Night Thoughts of a Classical Physicist*, Russell McCormmach, 1982.

8493 The man at the desk looked as if he didn't sleep very much. — *Resistance*, Mary Jones, 1985.

8494 For the second time in my life—and I am now seventy—I am embarking on an effort which may well come to nothing but which has possessed my mind, haunts, and will not let me sleep. — *The Magnificent Spinster*, May Sarton, 1985.

8495 Insomnia is my inheritance, though I would have preferred amnesia. — *Blood Libels*, Clive Sinclair, 1985.

8496 You sit, in contemplative posture, your features agonized and your expressions pained; you sit for hours and hours and hours, sleepless, looking into darkness, hearing a small snore coming from the room next to yours. — *Maps*, Nuruddin Farah, 1986.

8497 Christopher Marlowe had slept poorly. — *The Shadow of the Earth*, Lee Wichelns, 1987.

8498 Monday January 13th, 1986. Victor Wilcox lies awake, in the dark bedroom, waiting for his quartz alarm clock to bleep. — *Nice Work*, David Lodge, 1988.

8499 At night, when Jody had trouble sleeping, Wayne seemed, in his sneaky way, always to be there in the shadows, his smooth voice still a whispered undertone of the breeze. — *Picturing Will*, Ann Beattie, 1989.

8500 It's not yet dawn. I feel the mended place in my shirtwaist where it molds over my breast. — *John and Anzia*, Norma Rosen, 1989.

8501 Oh Lord my God, Creator of the Universe, once again you caused me to remain awake the whole night through. — *Doctor Sleep*, Madison Smartt Bell, 1991.

8502 I had been kept awake by the tree limbs scratching on my window at night; the sound made my heart race. — *Forms of Shelter*, Angela Davis-Gardner, 1991.

8503 On the day I left for the war I woke at six, long before the alarm clock was set to ring, and couldn't go back to sleep. — *Afghanistan*, Alex Ullmann, 1991.

8504 All night he had lain awake, feeling the roll of the sea, listening to the creak of the ship, the snap of the sails, the sounds of his fellow passengers as they coughed and muttered and moaned, children crying, now and then a few words of prayer: "Save us, O Lord, and lead us to safe harbor!" — *Massachusetts*, Nancy Zaroulis, 1991.

8505 Louise had been awake since five, waiting for the alarm to go off. — *Small Victories*, Sallie Bingham, 1992.

8506 Last night again I couldn't sleep. I tossed my body, this venerable lump, about in the bed as if it belonged to someone else. — *Boat of Stone*, Maureen Earl, 1993.

Smells

8507 When Miriam got out of the train into the darkness she knew that there were woods all about her. The moist air was rich with the smell of trees — wet bark and branches — moss and lichen, damp dead leaves. — *Honeycomb*, Dorothy M. Richardson, 1917.

8508 Hay, verbena and mignonette scented the languid July day. — "False Dawn (The 'Forties)" — Edith Wharton, 1924.

8509 Petrograd smelt of carbolic acid. — *We the Living*, Ayn Rand, 1936.

8510 *Soft-Walker, the quiet one, paused on the trail and smelled the air. The east wind blew gently, not enough to dispel the cloying odor of locust blooms and the thick sweet fragrance of wild crab-apple that grew in the lowlands like pink clouds over all the prairie. There was something more, and the Sac's nostrils isolated it from the fragrance all around him: it was the smell of smoke.* — *Wind Over Wisconsin*, August Derleth, 1938.

8511 There was no lonelier smell in all the world, Lydie Clarence thought, than that of old, matted straw on a rainy November afternoon. — *The Mandrake Root*, Martha Ostenso, 1938.

8512 It was only today as I was walking down Fayette Street towards the river that I got a whiff of salt fish, and I remembered the day I stood at Pleasant Hill, under the dogwood tree. — *The Fathers*, Allen Tate, 1938.

8513 The cumulus cloud had ladled a sprinkle of rain on the fairgrounds a little while before and the grass smelled sweet and strong and full of clover. — *Blaze of Noon*, Ernest K. Gann, 1946.

8514 Everyone in the hills knows that when the snow has melted and the flowers are in their first glory, the scent in the high pastures is so strong that it makes a man drunk and he is likely to do strange things and wake with a headache. — *The Wild Sweet Witch*, Philip Mason, 1947.

8515 When Ben Start first began working for the Mayflower Dairy in the suburban village of Wahwahnissa Creek, he had made haste, morning and afternoon, to escape the mingled, smothering smells of the place. — *Mild Route*, Martha Ostenso, 1948.

8516 On this hot night, with the wind from the east, they already got the stink from the East River, even though it was still more than a block away. — *North of Welfare*, William Krasner, 1954.

8517 He was sure for a moment that he smelled the thing but after looking round him he decided that he had imagined it and stretched out on his back in the berry thicket, a late-summer sun full in his face, his hand on either side reaching out to break twigs off and bring the luscious fruit to his lips, each berry a deep blue skinful of juice. — *Pemmican*, Vardis Fisher, 1956.

8518 "And what is *this* smell?" asked Dr. Railton. He thrust a sort of ink-well under Edwin's nose. — *The Doctor Is Sick*, Anthony Burgess, 1960.

8519 It had been bright and clear as he left Keswick; but as he crossed the Styhead Pass two hours later, the air smelled of rain. — *The Glass Cage*, Colin Wilson, 1966.

8520 The night watchman at Sea Life Park pedaled his bike from the Oceanic Institute, which was part of his beat, to the park office area. There he smelled trouble. — *The Spy Who Spoke Porpoise*, Philip Wylie, 1969.

8521 Halfway down the subway stairs, he turned. There was a smell of stale urine. — *Lion Country*, Frederick Buechner, 1971.

8522 The river smelled like hair. — *Margins*, David Kranes, 1972.

8523 The smell of Venice suffused the night, lacustrine essences richly distilled. — *Temporary Kings*, Anthony Powell, 1973.

8524 I came in quietly, dabbing at the chill spots of rain on my forehead, and took my coat off and began sniffing. — *The Sun Chemist*, Lionel Davidson, 1976.

8525 A warm sour cloud wafted across to Tommy's side of the bed as his wife rolled over in her sleep. — *Bloodbrothers*, Richard Price, 1976.

8526 Nanda Kaul paused under the pine trees to take in their scented sibilance and listen to the cicadas fiddling invisibly under the mesh of pine needles when she saw the postman slowly winding his way along the Upper Mall. — *Fire on the Mountain*, Anita Desai, 1977.

8527 Sara loved the smells of her childhood best of all. — *The Bidders*, John Baxter, 1979.

8528 At eleven fifteen Dolores wearily retyped the first three pages, fourth draft, of Chapter IV of *High Styling Your Face*, breathed a thread of semipure air, curling chilly and thin beneath the cracked window of the room she called her "office," and believed she detected the last whiff of fall, the final leaf of a nonexistent tree, in this stale draft. — *Outlaw Games*, Vicki Lindner, 1982.

8529 "What smells like that?" — *In the Palomar Arms*, Hilma Wolitzer, 1983.

8530 In the young man's earliest memories, whenever they visited Great-Momma Sweetie Red — as Nathaniel and his father Arthur Witherspoon did that morning on June 5, 1944, after Grandfather Witherspoon's death — the boy Nathaniel sat there in the ancient rocking chair and opened himself up to the aroma of steaming-hot rolls, biscuits, lightbread, cornbread or muffins that his grandmother always kept bound up snugly in a series of interwoven Sante Fe bar towels, fashioned into sleeves that Great-Momma Sweetie Red called warming sleeves; but they in turn were bound about by ancient, faded rainbow-colored, Mississippi-spun bathing towels that she brought with her from the Reed plantation, and which she pronounced as warm-up jackets. — *Two Wings to Veil My Face*, Leon Forrest, 1984.

8531 He could smell the muscadines which, weeks earlier, had cracked at the skin and oozed freely and had been sucked dry in the hulls by bees. — *Dark Thirty*, Terry Kay, 1984.

8532 You filled your nose with all you could. — *The Lion of Pescara*, George MacBeth, 1984.

8533 In March a damp wind blows in Trenton, and it smells of cats. — *Unbalanced Accounts*, Kate Gallison, 1986.

8534 At dawn, I discovered Manila. I learned that Manila air was fog and sweat and steam, that it smelled of garbage fires and cooking and diesel fumes and, just possibly, the sea. — *MacArthur's Ghost*, P. F. Kluge, 1987.

8535 "You've got to get close enough without him smelling you — and he's got a sense of smell that is out of this world...." — *Private Woods*, Sandra Crockett Moore, 1988.

8536 The evening air lay heavy with the drifting fragrances of new leaf incense, which sent shivers of expectant pleasure through the inhabitants of Yellow Copse. — *The Cold Moons*, Aeron Clement, 1989.

8537 My mother's rooms smelled of the jungle and of death. — *Motherland*, Timothy O'Grady, 1989.

8538 1956. The air-conditioned darkness of the Avenue Theater smells of flowery pomade, sugary chocolates, cigarette smoke, and sweat. — *Dogeaters*, Jessica Hagedorn, 1990.

8539 Whatever it was, it had been dead for some time. — *Edge of Eden*, Nicholas Proffitt, 1990.

8540 The kitchen was full of the smells of baking. — *Circle of Friends*, Maeve Binchy, 1991.

8541 The smell of the rain forest came on the offshore breeze, long before they were in sight of land. It was a sour smell of putrefaction. — *MAMista*, Len Deighton, 1991.

8542 "You can't work in shit all day long and expect to walk away smelling like a rose." My Uncle Hooter Cooter gave me that advice when I was ten years old. — *The Cooter Farm*, Matthew F. Jones, 1991.

8543 Ever after, whenever she smelled the peculiar odor of new construction, of pine planking and plastic plumbing pipes, she would think of that summer, think of it as the time of changes. — *Object Lessons*, Anna Quindlen, 1991.

8544 As he stalked in the darkness past the tiny scurrying forms of the Chinese, through pockets of their mindless squealing chatter, he inhaled the stench of old fish and of human excrement, the reek of rotting fruit, the stink of the unnamable herbs and spices with which these people cooked their wretched food. — *Wilde West*, Walter Satterthwait, 1991.

Smiles

8545 When Farmer Oak smiled, the corners of his mouth spread till they were within an unimportant distance of his ears, his eyes were reduced to chinks, and diverging wrinkles appeared round them, extending upon his countenance like the rays in a rudimentary sketch of the rising sun. — *Far from the Madding Crowd*, Thomas Hardy, 1874.

8546 She had walked with her friend to the top of the wide steps of the Museum, those that descended from the galleries of painting, and then, after the young man had left her, smiling, looking back, waving all gayly and expressively his hat and stick, had watched him, smiling too, but with a different intensity — had kept him in sight till he passed out of the great door. — *Julia Bride*, Henry James, 1909.

8547 Renny Whiteoak stood with his brows drawn together but a smile softening his lips while a wire-haired terrier belonging to his brother Piers strove with controlled energy to dig her way into the burrow of some small animal. — *The Master of Jalna*, Mazo de la Roche, 1933.

8548 At the sight of her son Judith's eyes and mouth broke into the loveliest smile that any member of the Herries family, there present, had ever seen. It was Judith Paris' hundredth birthday. — *Vanessa*, Hugh Walpole, 1933.

8549 Nueces pushed the door marked CATTLEMEN'S ASSOCIATION — ENTER and grinned down at the young man at the desk. — *On the Trail of the Tumbling T*, Clarence E. Mulford, 1935.

8550 Lanny kept thinking: This must be the only man in France who can smile. — *A World to Win*, Upton Sinclair, 1946.

8551 Years later, when she had gone and was no longer part of their lives, the thing they remembered about her was her smile. — *Mary Anne*, Daphne du Maurier, 1954.

8552 On the terrace of the Café des Deux Magots, people raised their faces from breakfast coffee and newspapers and smiled to feel the April sun. — *His Own Man*, Martha Gellhorn, 1961.

8553 The Jodler Room was crowded. The glass eyes of mounted hawks and owls reflected the insolent flash of smiling teeth. — *Alp*, William Hjortsberg, 1969.

8554 Palm listened to the Bee Women, her smile like applause so that they were happy as she intended. — *Clonk Clonk*, William Golding, 1971.

8555 He noticed the girl in the green and gold dress standing at the edge of the lecture platform; when he caught her eye over the shoulder of an old lady who was asking him about electronic music, she smiled, then looked away. — *The Black Room*, Colin Wilson, 1971.

8556 The square-faced young man with the darkly humorous eyes nudged with his elbow his companion standing beside him, and jerked his head half-right, grinning, towards where Mirren Livingstone, the King's newest young lady, was intently inspecting herself inside her notably low-necked gown and scratching comprehensively at the same time — activity calculated to engender interesting speculation in any male worthy of the name. — *The Riven Realm*, Nigel Tranter, 1984.

8557 Hector smiled at the young woman. — *Stumbling on Melons*, Carol Bruggen, 1986.

8558 My brother would not smile for a photograph. — *I Look Divine*, Christopher Coe, 1987.

8559 Frank Sinatra, Jr., was saying, "I don't have to take this," getting up out of the guest chair, walking out. Howard Hart was grinning at him with his capped teeth. — *Touch*, Elmore Leonard, 1987.

8560 Some people look like idiots when they smile — they have that petrified daze, as if struck by a bolt of lightning. — *My Life in Action Painting*, J. B. Miller, 1990.

8561 The old woman stands at the stove stirring the simmering brown liquid with great concentration. Occasionally Zeta smiles as she stares into the big blue enamel pot. — *Almanac of the Dead*, Leslie Marmon Silko, 1991.

8562 The little boy's smile is so wide, sun in his eyes, that he seems to be crying. — *Before and After*, Rosellen Brown, 1992.

Smoking

8563 On an afternoon in the early summer of 1856 Captain Nathaniel Plum, master and owner of the sloop *Typhoon* was engaged in nothing more important than the smoking of an enormous pipe. — *The Courage of Captain Plum*, James Oliver Curwood, 1908.

8564 On Thursday, June 17, 1897, in the women's toilet-room at one end of a parlour-car on the Overland Limited, speeding westward from Chicago, a lady sat smoking a cigarette. — *The Tattooed Countess*, Carl Van Vechten, 1924.

8565 Walking up and down the platform alongside the train in the Pennsylvania Station, having wiped the sweat from my brow, I lit a cigarette with the feeling that after it had calmed my nerves a little I would be prepared to submit

bids for a contract to move the Pyramid of Cheops from Egypt to the top of the Empire State Building with my bare hands, in a swimming-suit; after what I had just gone through. — *Too Many Cooks*, Rex Stout, 1938.

8566 Lord Essex sat in the Douglas aeroplane and smoked his pipe and waited for another conveyance to come and take him away. — *The Diplomat*, James Aldridge, 1949.

8567 Maxwell Fleury rarely smoked. — *Island in the Sun*, Alec Waugh, 1955.

8568 The cold nicotine taste suddenly sour in his mouth, Marlowe flung the remains of his tattered cigar through the open window. The gesture was vaguely savage, a physical reflection of his current state of mind. — *The Horse Soldiers*, Harold Sinclair, 1956.

8569 It's all very fine to say smoking in the lobby only, but have you seen the lobby lately? — *Max Jamison*, Wilfrid Sheed, 1970.

8570 Two critics of the art sat by the window of a dank, ill-lit place and ordered cigars. — *Toro! Toro! Toro!*, William Hjortsberg, 1974.

8571 Benjie carefully finished rolling his cigarette, then he leaned back and admired it. — *Heart of Aztlán*, Rudolfo A. Anaya, 1976.

8572 This summer morning, Ivybridge was sitting behind his desk and smoking a pipe, which he kept taking out to give it a disgusted look. — *Found, Lost, Found*, J. B. Priestley, 1976.

8573 From the porch of his apartment he looks out at the meadowgreen Mediterranean and keeps exhaling through his slightly parted lips the smoke from his meerschaum. — *The Wanton Summer Air*, Samuel Hazo, 1982.

8574 *"Bitte."* The elderly, bearded passenger offers a pack of Capstan cigarettes to a blond young man sitting opposite him in the train compartment. — *The Warlord*, Malcolm Bosse, 1983.

8575 I took a last futile drag at my sodden cigarette and threw it inaccurately at the dustbin standing on guard outside the mortuary. — *The Room Upstairs*, Norma Levinson, 1984.

8576 Once when I was eleven years old, my father asked me not to buy him cigarettes, even if he begged. — *Crooked Hearts*, Robert Boswell, 1987.

8577 Hartmann, a voluptuary, lowered a spoonful of brown sugar crystals into his coffee cup, then placed a square of bitter chocolate on his tongue, and, while it was dissolving, lit his first cigarette. — *Latecomers*, Anita Brookner, 1988.

8578 Whitney was beside the pool. The woman in the chaise lounge next to her had been chain-smoking, using a fancy holder. — *Gathering Home*, Vicki Covington, 1988.

8579 Wick Longstreet was sitting in the bell tower smoking a cigarette and looking at the stars. — *The Loss of Heaven*, Ben Greer, 1988.

8580 At Kilmainham, in a palatial building on the western edge of Dublin, fifty-six-year-old General Sir John Grenfell Maxwell, Knight of the Order of the Bath, Companion of the Order of St. Michael and St. George, Commander of the Victorian Order and Distinguished Service Order, the new General Officer Commanding in His Majesty's armed forces in Ireland, was coughing like a donkey on his first cigarette of the day. — *Rebels*, Peter de Rosa, 1990.

8581 *Uncle Luther, back from the war, stares through the smoke that rises from his cigarette.* — *Unheard Melodies*, Warren Leamon, 1990.

8582 Alone in the corridor he scraped a wood match against the wall, lighting up another cigarette. — *Destiny Express*, Howard A. Rodman, 1990.

8583 *For a long time after his lover had dressed and gone, Raymond Cooper lay in the disordered bed under the windows that opened onto Ridgeway Avenue and smoked one cigarette after another.* — *The Victim's Daughter*, Robley Wilson, 1991.

Snow

8584 Without, a midwinter twilight, where wandering snowflakes eddied in the bitter wind between a leaden sky and frost-bound earth. — *A Modern Mephistopheles*, Louisa May Alcott, 1877.

8585 The snows of a grim February evening were falling in the fine flakes which predict a long storm. — *Far in the Forest*, S. Weir Mitchell, 1889.

8586 A dry snow had fallen steadily throughout the still night, so that when a cold, upper wind cleared the sky gloriously in the morning the incongruous Indiana town shone in a white harmony — roof, ledge, and earth as evenly covered as by moonlight. — *The Conquest of Canaan*, Booth Tarkington, 1905.

8587 About twenty years ago, late in January, snow was falling over North London. It fell for some hours continuously; "without intermission" the *Evening Star* said, whose sub-editor lived in the neighbourhood; and the said sub-editor sent his nephew, who was learning the business, to the British Museum, to look up heavy snowfalls from 1792 downwards. And by teatime the whole of North London, from the Manor House to High Barnet Church, from Hampstead Heath to Enfield Highway, was very white indeed. — *Casuals of the Sea*, William McFee, 1916.

8588 Outside the house it was storming, a busy downfall of flakes that the wind blew lightly across acres of old snow left from December. — *As the Earth Turns*, Gladys Hasty Carroll, 1933.

8589 The snow storm, which began at dawn on Tuesday, February 17th, and did not stop when darkness came, extended over all New England. — *The Last Adam*, James Gould Cozzens, 1933.

8590 March whistled stinging snow against the brick walls and up the gaunt girders. — *Christ in Concrete*, Pietro di Donato, 1939.

8591 The clouds darkening Boston Harbor looked so low and ghostlike Sergeant Timothy Bennett guessed snow would soon begin falling. In fact, the jumbled dark roofs and church spires of distant Cambridge were already graying out of sight. — *Stars on the Sea*, F. van Wyck Mason, 1940.

8592 That fall of 1777, winter had set in early in the Back Country. A hard frost had dropped upon the corn crop before September was gone; the first good hunting snow had come the last of October and now, since mid-November, the world had been buried deep in white. — *The Day Must Dawn*, Agnes Sligh Turnbull, 1942.

8593 It had been snowing steadily for three days. Now, all night, the snow had been drifted by the wind that lashed and whirled about the house like a giant beating with a thousand cat-o'-nine-tails. — *The Horses of the Sun*, Dr. Kathryn M. Whitten, 1942.

8594 Detroit is usually hot and sticky in the summer, and in the winter the snow in the streets is like a dirty, worn-out blanket. — *The Dark Tunnel*, Kenneth Millar, 1944.

8595 Snow clung wetly to the high-gabled roofs of that thriving city, New York. — *Banner by the Wayside*, Samuel Hopkins Adams, 1947.

8596 The town shone in the snowy twilight like a Christmas window, with the electric railway's lights tiny and festive at the foot of the white slope, among the muffled winter hills of the Tyrol. — *The Young Lions*, Irwin Shaw, 1948.

8597 From an invisible February sky a shimmering curtain of snowflakes fluttered down upon Chicago. — *The Outsider*, Richard Wright, 1953.

8598 The snow began quietly this time, like an after-thought to the gray Sunday night. — "Winter Thunder," Mari Sandoz, 1954.

8599 The snow began to fall in the afternoon. The flakes were large and swept lazily across the window of Rothstein's Discount Liquor Store, where I stood leaning on the handle of a broom. — *Lion at My Heart*, Harry Mark Petrakis, 1959.

8600 Snow had fallen all night and the house in the woods was already cut off from the road and the village by a four-foot drift at the bottom of the lane. — *A Winter's Tale*, Jon Godden, 1961.

8601 Snow./ She heard the shovels scraping on the campus walks when it was still dark, and she sat bolt upright in bed and thought *Snow!* and then almost called out in excitement to the bed across the dormitory room until she remembered Diane had changed rooms and the bed was empty. — *Mothers and Daughters*, Evan Hunter, 1961.

8602 The snow fell early in Germany in 1959 and lay almost as deep in the towns as in the fields. — *A Girl from Lübeck*, Bruce Marshall, 1962.

8603 Winter came late that year and there were still patches of snow in the park at the end of March. — *Jericho Sleep Alone*, Chaim Bermant, 1964.

8604 The snow began to fall into St. Botolphs at four-fifteen on Christmas Eve. — *The Wapshot Scandal*, John Cheever, 1964.

8605 Snow covered the airfield. — *The Looking Glass War*, John Le Carré, 1965.

8606 One evening in November of 1942, in the town of Leah, New Hampshire, the first real snow was falling. In the Town Square, at five o'clock, the big flakes fell slowly out of the darkness into the light from the store windows. They fell silently upon the bandstand, upon the long limbs of the elms, upon the few parked cars. Everything became bundled up and soft, and the snow still fell. — *Whipple's Castle*, Thomas Williams, 1968.

8607 The Cambridge sidewalks had not yet been shoveled. Julian and Charlotte walked in the street, following the bank of snow thrown up by the plough, Charles and Claud close behind, their faces bright with cold. — *The Ghost of Henry James*, David Plante, 1970.

8608 The high Arctic had more snow that year than anyone remembered. — *Night of the White Bear*, Alexander Knox, 1971.

8609 It is Sunday afternoon and it is going to snow. — *The Clam Shell*, Mary Lee Settle, 1971.

8610 Out in the early morning, a gentle snow brushed his face, the blacktop was white. — *Ya!*, Douglas Woolf, 1971.

8611 This was early May, and already the streams were grayed with melted snow. — *The Face of Jalanath*, Ronald Hardy, 1973.

8612 Snow fell again yesterday, blanketing everything, weighing down the branches of the pines and turning the stream that runs past my cabin into a dark, wavering line. — *A Winter's Reckoning*, Ellen Bromfield Geld, 1976.

8613 "It's going to snow for Christmas," called Mrs. Marsh from the kitchen, raising her voice — unnecessarily since the house was so small. — *The Birds of the Air*, Alice Thomas Ellis, 1980.

8614 It must have been snowing. — *Brothers*, Bernice Rubens, 1983.

8615 "April is the cruellest month," Persse McGarrigle quoted silently to himself, gazing through grimy windowpanes at the unseasonable

snow crusting the lawns and flowerbeds of the Rummidge campus. — *Small World*, David Lodge, 1984.

8616 Snow lay thick on the moorlands./ Snow drifted in mean-lipped skeins through the city streets. — *Call It a Canary*, Peter Tinniswood, 1985.

8617 The London sky darkening over the western reaches of Knightsbridge and the falling snow thickening as it began to whiten the streets and sidewalks. — *Are You Listening Rabbi Löw*, J. P. Donleavy, 1987.

8618 It was snowing when Brennan McCalmont carried the Christmas tree from his station wagon and propped it against the side of the house. — *Second Season*, Joseph Monninger, 1987.

8619 The moon was full and it was the February that it didn't snow. — *Faraway Places*, Tom Spanbauer, 1988.

8620 That November, God sent snow north to Italy, to the inconvenience of all who had to travel on horseback. — *Race of Scorpions*, Dorothy Dunnett, 1989.

8621 In my part of Connecticut — the northeast corner of Fairfield County — you shouldn't get an inch of snow in an April night. — *Natural Order*, Jonathan Penner, 1990.

8622 There are nights in the New England country when snow falls like the thick fur of cottonwoods along the water courses of a prairie. — *Here Lies the Water*, Meredith Steinbach, 1990.

8623 January, in East Anglia under a mantle of snow. — *Isvik*, Hammond Innes, 1991.

8624 As Amy Joy Lawler waited by her mailbox, several fat flakes of snow winged softly out of the gray sky. — *The Weight of Winter*, Cathie Pelletier, 1991.

8625 An iridescent confetti of snow tarnished by sodium arc light sifts from the void over the glowing horizontal bulk of Greenspark Academy. — *One on One*, Tabitha King, 1993.

Socializing

8626 A hush fell over the dinner-table, and every ear was open and inclined as Cameron, the host, continued: "No, I wouldn't say that. There are some things that are pretty well established — telepathy, for instance." — *The Shadow World*, Hamlin Garland, 1908.

8627 The dinner was being given by Mrs. Cortlandt Trend; that, in itself, was sufficient proof of its smartness if not entirely establishing its excellence along another line. — *The Butterfly Man*, George Barr McCutcheon, 1910.

8628 It was three o'clock, but the luncheon the Kinneys were giving at the Country Club had survived the passing of less leisurely patrons and now dominated the house. — *The Proof of the Pudding*, Meredith Nicholson, 1916.

8629 Natalie Spencer was giving a dinner. She was not an easy hostess. — *Dangerous Days*, Mary Roberts Rinehart, 1919.

8630 "But I don't think I want to, Cham."/ "Come along, Fanshaw, you've got to."/ "But I wouldn't know what to say to them."/ "They'll do the talking.... Look, you've got to come, date's all made an' everything." — *Streets of Night*, John Dos Passos, 1923.

8631 She was dressing for dinner. — *A Note in Music*, Rosamond Lehmann, 1930.

8632 In that coastal triangle of Cornwall lying between Truro, St. Ann's, and St. Michael, social life did not extend far in the 1790's. — *Warleggan*, Winston Graham, 1955.

8633 When Tom Orbell invited me to dinner at his club, I imagined that we should be alone. — *The Affair*, C. P. Snow, 1960.

8634 Peter Ash and Norah Palmer sat together at a table at Quadri's in the Piazza San Marco, drinking black coffee with ice-cream in it. — *The Birdcage*, John Bowen, 1962.

8635 My friend and I are very grand these days. We meet at the Ritz. — *The Last Night at the Ritz*, Elizabeth Savage, 1973.

8636 When Lord Nectarine of Walham Green resigned his mastership of foxhounds, got rid of his wife and shut of his children and happily set up as a bachelor again, installing an attractive erudite housekeeper, and a male secretary hard of hearing, in his new commodious town house, Schultz enjoyed to consult, lunch and dine with his Lordship with as much frequency as his Lordship's tight schedule of social events allowed. — *Schultz*, J. P. Donleavy, 1979.

8637 In her youth, such evenings alone with her three cherished contemporaries had been a rare indulgence; now that she approached her prime they formed the limping heart of her lame social round. — *Ease*, Patrick Gale, 1986.

8638 The liquor was flowing, everyone had a plate, folks had visited all the way back to the kitchen.... — *Be-Bop, Re-Bop*, Xam Cartiér, 1987.

8639 Mamie joined Sal at Luigi's after the Friday evening performance. — "The End of Tragedy," Rachel Ingalls, 1987.

8640 It was half past one, as Ezzie Fenwick always called it, in his rococo manner of speaking, on the Tuesday noon following Black Monday, and the midday social frenzy at Clarence's was at its peak, with every table filled to capacity, as if a financial catastrophe had not taken place. — *People Like Us*, Dominick Dunne, 1988.

Soldiers and Sailors

8641 On the library wall of one of the most famous writers of America, there hang two crossed swords, which his relatives wore in the great War of Independence. The one sword was gallantly drawn in the service of the King, the other was the weapon of a brave and honoured Republican soldier. — *The Virginians*, William Makepeace Thackeray, 1858-1859.

8642 When young Nevil Beauchamp was throwing off his midshipman's jacket for a holiday in the garb of peace, we had across Channel a host of dreadful military officers flashing swords at us for some critical observations of ours upon their sovereign, threatening Afric's fires and savagery. — *Beauchamp's Career*, George Meredith, 1875.

8643 "And we beseech Thee, O Lord, to give help and succor to thy servants the people of Holland, and to deliver them from the cruelties and persecutions of their wicked oppressors; and grant Thy blessing, we pray Thee, upon the arms of our soldiers now embarking to aid them in their extremity." — *By England's Aid*, G. A. Henty, 1891.

8644 A number of soldiers were standing in the road near the bungalow of Brigadier-General Mathieson, the officer in command of the force in the cantonments of Benares, and the surrounding district. — *The Lost Heir*, G. A. Henty, 1899.

8645 The company stood at attention, each man looking straight before him at the empty parade ground, where the cinder piles showed purple with evening. — *Three Soldiers*, John Dos Passos, 1921.

8646 Philippe, the Canon's brother, was among the first to enlist in the army that Raymond assembled to rescue the Holy Sepulchre from the Infidel. — *Héloïse and Abélard*, George Moore, 1921.

8647 "We are only soldiers three," said Hallock, bending toward the camp fire in order more easily to read the letter he held in his hand. "Ought to be soldiers four, all present or accounted for. Wonder what's the matter with Allison, anyhow?" — *Mother of Gold*, Emerson Hough, 1924.

8648 A farmer stood watching a battalion of infantry filing into his pasture. A queerer mixture of humanity could not have been imagined. — *The Spanish Farm*, R. H. Mottram, 1924.

8649 Lowe, Julian, number —, late a Flying Cadet, Umptieth Squadron, Air Service, known as "One Wing" by the other embryonic aces of his flight, regarded the world with a yellow and disgruntled eye. — *Soldier's Pay*, William Faulkner, 1926.

8650 *It was that emancipated race/ That was chargin up the hill/ Up to where them insurrectos/ Was afightin fit to kill./* CAPITAL CITY'S CENTURY CLOSED/ General Miles with his gaudy uniform and spirited charger was the center for all eyes especially as his steed was extremely restless. — *The 42nd Parallel*, John Dos Passos, 1930.

8651 We stop, and the word comes down the line to bivouac. — *Conceived in Liberty*, Howard Fast, 1939.

8652 When I reached C Company lines, which were at the top of the hill, I paused and looked back at the camp, just coming into full view below me through the grey mist of early morning. — *Brideshead Revisited*, Evelyn Waugh, 1945.

8653 Randall was asleep on his chicken-wire bed in the company headquarters dugout. He was sleeping dreamlessly and without any jerky movements, for he was young and had not as yet been worn down by war. — *Randall and the River of Time*, C. S. Forester, 1950.

8654 Often when the platoon turned out, no matter what the tour, Joseph Shetland sat waiting for the formation, leaning against a window near the washroom, sitting on a battered table, swinging his legs from a sill near the cell block, or sometimes ensconced on the shoe-shine throne at the farthest side of the room. — *Signal Thirty-Two*, MacKinlay Kantor, 1950.

8655 Wolf was the last member of his crew to leave Interrogation. — *Don't Touch Me*, MacKinlay Kantor, 1951.

8656 On April 4, 1952, I shot down my sixth and seventh MIGs. — *Sayonara*, James A. Michener, 1954.

8657 In nineteen forty-two, when I was twenty-six, I went to India as an officer-cadet on the troopship Athlone Castle, and although it would be untrue to say it was on the ship I first met Alan Hurst, that is how I look upon it. — *A Male Child*, Paul Scott, 1956.

8658 The car-hire driver was tall and dark and handsome; he looked the regular soldier he had been when the War broke out. — *The Hireling*, L. P. Hartley, 1957.

8659 *They came running through the fog across the snow, lumbering, the long rifles held up awkwardly high, the pot helmets they were all so proud of and never seemed to camouflage gleaming dully, running fast, but appearing to come slowly, lifting their feet high in the big thick boots, foreign, alien, brain-chilling.* — *Some Came Running*, James Jones, 1957.

8660 In dead silence the Bombardier paced along the mole of Dun Laoghaire Harbor, looking neither to right nor to left. — *The Prospects Are Pleasing*, Honor Tracy, 1958.

8661 And I don't care who your bleeding fathers are, or how much bleeding money they've got, or what bleeding school you went to—as long as you're here, I'm your bleeding father, and your bleeding mother, and your bleeding school, and you get twenty-eight bleeding bob a bleeding week, just like the bleeding rest of the bleeding bleeders. Bleed it.... —*The Breaking of Bumbo*, Andrew Sinclair, 1959.

8662 It was four o'clock and things at last were quiet in the Transient Company, so Sergeant Clay decided to pay a visit on Master Sergeant Slaughter. —*Soldier in the Rain*, William Goldman, 1960.

8663 Of the day and hour nothing can be known. Only the year as it was marked by some Spanish soldier in the boredom of his watch. On a broad parapet of the squat fort he had taken a knife or short sword and cut the date into the side of one of the four towers which studded the corners./ *1588*. He had dug the numerals out in the spongy stone and then added one word. *Cristo!* —*Plough the Sea*, Robert Wilder, 1961.

8664 When I was thrown out of the RAF, I received (for some reason I have now forgotten) two months' discharge pay. —*Adrift in Soho*, Colin Wilson, 1961.

8665 In a shed of unpainted boards, a kind of swollen privy, on a compound of like structures in a field of dirty snow somewhere in Indiana, an anonymous major after an eleventh-hour pitch for the Regular Army or at least the Reserve, bade goodbye to thirty-odd soldiers—among whom was Corporal Carlo Reinhart, 15302320, the oddest of the lot, take it as you would: clinically: his last six months' service had been as patient in the neuropsychiatric wards of sundry military hospitals abroad and at home; emotionally: as near as he could tell, he was the only man ever released from the U.S. Army who was sorry to go; legally: the official typist had printed an error on his discharge certificate. —*Reinhart in Love*, Thomas Berger, 1962.

8666 When Guy Crouchback returned to his regiment in the autumn of 1941 his position was in many ways anomalous. — *The End of the Battle*, Evelyn Waugh, 1962.

8667 Major Royce Morgan came out of the Army in 1945 expecting soon to be the twelfth president of Wellford College. —*The President*, R. V. Cassill, 1964.

8668 We didn't stay to do battle with the Me 109s. —*The Gun Garden*, David Beaty *as* Paul Stanton, 1965.

8669 "Sergeant Chamay, I have asked you to come here directly so that I may have your version of what happened this morning." —*In the Company of Eagles*, Ernest K. Gann, 1966.

8670 Norwood had to get a hardship discharge when Mr. Pratt died because there wasn't anyone else at home to look after Vernell. —*Norwood*, Charles Portis, 1966.

8671 Muirtagh reined in. One of his outriders was galloping down, waving one arm over his head in the signal that meant a large armed force was moving toward them. —*The Kings in Winter*, Cecelia Holland, 1968.

8672 Once upon a time, God save us all, there was an orphan boy called Marius Catto who grew up to be a lieutenant of infantry in the Army of the United States. —*When the War Is Over*, Stephen Becker, 1969.

8673 On Saturdays, when inspection was over and passes were issued in the Orderly Rooms, there was a stampede of escape down every company street in Camp Pickett, Virginia. —*A Special Providence*, Richard Yates, 1969.

8674 Red dust. Corpsman Andrew Jones, a Negro, scuffed the earth with his heavy boot. It was a surly act, a typical act. He regretted it at once: sweat formed along his spine where the unfamiliar black and green uniform shirt adhered to his back. —*War Is Heaven!*, D. Keith Mano, 1970.

8675 Mr. Donnelly, the track coach, ended the day's practice early because Henry Fuller's father came down to the high-school field to tell Henry that they had just got a telegram from Washington announcing that Henry's brother had been killed in action in Germany. —*Rich Man, Poor Man*, Irwin Shaw, 1970.

8676 When the two soldiers boarded the train at St. Louis they caught one another's eyes for a moment in a mutually questioning gaze that broke off teasingly short of recognition, like a dream not quite recalled. —*Going All the Way*, Dan Wakefield, 1970.

8677 Late in November 1945, as His Majesty's Troop-Ship *Georgic* was approaching Port Said, the O.C. Troops said to the Captain:/ "No shore leave for the Cadets, I think. They'd only go and get clap."—*Sound the Retreat*, Simon Raven, 1971.

8678 January 15, 1918, was a cold, sparkling, sunny day. Not much happened in the Great War that day. As usual, about two thousand men (of the millions along the Western Front) died, some because they stuck their heads up too high and got shot, some because they got their feet wet too often and caught pneumonia, many by accident, and a steady few by their own hand. —*Goshawk Squadron*, Derek Robinson, 1971.

8679 "44th Bengal Lancers ... will march past! Regiment will advance in squadron column from the right ... Walk march!" — *The Ravi Lancers*, John Masters, 1972.

8680 Forty-three days without a night: six pale-blue fluorescent weeks without a sniff of air,

sky, or a view of the stars. — *Spy Story*, Len Deighton, 1974.

8681 The Third Marines were bleeding and dying for three nameless hills north of Khe Sanh in 1967. — *The Choirboys*, Joseph Wambaugh, 1975.

8682 On a training exercise in mountain warfare, a section of Indian soldiers, a corporal and six men, walked in single file along the ridge. They were several miles behind the cease-fire line between Kashmir and Pakistan and were on their way back through bleak, uninhabited country to the base camp far below in the valley. — *Ahmed and the Old Lady*, Jon Godden, 1976.

8683 After his best friend had been killed by his side at the pitface Charlie Scorton decided to join the army. — *The Widower's Son*, Alan Sillitoe, 1976.

8684 I stood stiffly with my feet well apart, parade-rest fashion, at the break in the barbed-wire fence between the officers' country tents and the battalion motor pool. — *Close Quarters*, Larry Heinemann, 1977.

8685 Simon Boulderstone, aged twenty, came to Egypt with the draft. — *The Danger Tree*, Olivia Manning, 1977.

8686 Many years later he would sometimes think of them as beautiful young men who'd saved the world. But by the end of the war, Donald Upton hated his squad almost as much as the enemy. — *And We Were Young*, Elliott Baker, 1979.

8687 The Marines are looking for a few good men.... — *The Short-Timers*, Gustav Hasford, 1979.

8688 For generations, centuries indeed, the Barracloughs of Castle Reef had been soldiers. — *The Ballad of Castle Reef*, Honor Tracy, 1979.

8689 Dawson felt the two grenades on his chest bobbing like breasts. — *Savage*, Paul Boorstin, 1980.

8690 The soldiers marched toward them three abreast. — *Four Days*, Gloria Goldreich, 1980.

8691 We lay in ambush on the Laguna Madre, just below the lip of the great open basin of Corpus Christi Bay. — *Aransas*, Stephen Harrigan, 1980.

8692 The young soldier stood looking doubtfully up at the unlabelled entrance to ward X, his kit bag lowered to the ground while he assessed the possibility that this was indeed his ultimate destination. — *An Indecent Obsession*, Colleen McCullough, 1981.

8693 Shrapnel cut into Spencer Abbot's thigh. — *Buddies*, James Whitfield Ellison, 1983.

8694 On a wet March morning in the early months of the War Between the States, General Chester Arthur, in charge of the defenses of the city, sets out down lower Broadway on urgent domestic business. — *The Chester A. Arthur Conspiracy*, William Wiegand, 1983.

8695 Young Lamar Jimmerson went to France in 1917 with the American Expeditionary Forces, serving first with the Balloon Section, stumbling about in open fields holding one end of a long rope, and then later as a telephone switchboard operator at AEF headquarters in Chaumont. — *Masters of Atlantis*, Charles Portis, 1985.

8696 The captain was silhouetted on horseback like a piece of burnt iron against the sun. — *The Lost Get-Back Boogie*, James Lee Burke, 1986.

8697 That first day at Fort Dix all the recruits had been marched down to the post barbershop for haircuts. — *Sheltered Lives*, Frank Milburn, 1986.

8698 There was once a man called George Fairweather, who might have been many things, but was most singly a soldier. — *Season of the Jew*, Maurice Shadbolt, 1986.

8699 On a parade ground in Flanders two thousand survivors doggedly obeyed bawled orders: boots and rifle butts clashed like iron on the frozen ground. They were two British battalions and one colonial, and their field was bordered by rows of tents, wooden sheds and low ramshackle barracks. — *A Rendezvous in Haiti*, Stephen Becker, 1987.

8700 On his way to Heavenly Bridge outside Peking's Chien Men Gate, Fong Tai stopped to watch the Imperial troops drilling in the nearby wheatfield. — *China Saga*, C. Y. Lee, 1987.

8701 In the low wood, his head bowed so that his line of vision to the long column of infantry is blocked by the lightly fluttering leaves in the foreground: Vyuko, thighs embracing the horse, his lance point on the ground to his right. — *Proud Monster*, Ian MacMillan, 1987.

8702 Soldiers from England sang a song in the estaminets of northern France in 1916, and they had sung it too in the public houses, I have no doubt, of the Wiltshire I came to invade. — *War Babies*, Frederick Busch, 1988.

8703 *At night in the war I listened to monkeys in the jungle all around me.* — *Fatal Light*, Richard Currey, 1988.

8704 Then it was the day McDay's brothers left for the front by bus to the county seat, train to San Francisco, troop transfer ship to the Hawaiian Islands, and from there, catapulted into what was known as the Pacific theater, as if war had a proscenium, McKay thought, as if its horrors could be contained. — *Heart Mountain*, Gretel Ehrlich, 1988.

8705 OUR HEROES. WELCOME HOME. 369TH FIRST TO REACH THE RHINE. — *No Easy Place to Be*, Steven Corbin, 1989.

8706 German soldiers came once in the middle of the night in that little house where we lived that winter four of us in one room, the old couple sleeping in the kitchen next to the stove. —"Shadow Partisan," Nadja Tesich, 1989.

8707 It was Lieutenant Lofting who dominated the meeting. — *The Innocent*, Ian McEwan, 1990.

8708 First Lieutenant Jimmy Cross carried letters from a girl named Martha, a junior at Mount Sebastian College in New Jersey. They were not love letters, but Lieutenant Cross was hoping, so he kept them folded in plastic at the bottom of his rucksack. — *The Things They Carried*, Tim O'Brien, 1990.

8709 Finished with the War/ *A Soldier's Declaration*/ I am making this statement as an act of wilful defiance of military authority, because I believe the war is being deliberately prolonged by those who have the power to end it. — *Regeneration*, Pat Barker, 1991.

8710 He could see the soldiers coming, hear their shouts, and he saw the sunlight breaking silver on his father's cap-badge. — *The Run of the Country*, Shane Connaughton, 1991.

8711 Lieutenant Starret lay with his face in the dirt, pretending he was dead. — *Rising Like the Tucson*, Jeff Danziger, 1991.

8712 Imagine him in his prime. A fairly rich and large-eared farm boy newly cured of being a farm boy by what he called Th' War, meaning the second one. — *White People*, Allan Gurganus, 1991.

8713 "We are going to bring it to him," the Colonel said with satisfaction. A lot, more than usual. — *To the White Sea*, James Dickey, 1993.

Solitude

8714 No one, probably, ever felt himself to be more alone in the world than the Duke of Omnium when the Duchess died. — *The Duke's Children*, Anthony Trollope, 1880.

8715 Olney got back to Boston about the middle of July, and found himself in the social solitude which the summer makes more noticeable in that city than in any other. — *An Imperative Duty*, William Dean Howells, 1892.

8716 Billy Neilson was eighteen years old when the aunt, who had brought her up from babyhood, died. Miss Benton's death left Billy quite alone in the world — alone, and peculiarly forlorn. — *Miss Billy*, Eleanor H. Porter, 1911.

8717 Mary sometimes heard people say: "I can't bear to be alone." She could never under-

stand this. — *Mariana*, Monica Dickens, 1940.

8718 Grania Fox was eighteen. She was alone in a wood she knew very well, far beyond the house and above the river. — *Two Days in Aragon*, Molly Keane *as* M. J. Farrell, 1941.

8719 Lanny Budd was the only occupant of a small-sized reception-room. — *Dragon's Teeth*, Upton Sinclair, 1942.

8720 Edith Chapin was alone in her sewing room on the third floor of the house at Number 10 in Frederick Street. — *Ten North Frederick*, John O'Hara, 1955.

8721 It all begins on the Statue of Liberty because we're worried about my sick old grandmother who is living alone and shouldn't. — *How Much?*, Burt Blechman, 1961.

8722 The child sat on a large black boulder and looked at the sea, and she was all alone under a sky the color of smoke and beside waters as angry as an intemperate man and grayer than death. — *A Prologue to Love*, Taylor Caldwell, 1961.

8723 Sometimes Sonny felt like he was the only human creature in the town. — *The Last Picture Show*, Larry McMurtry, 1966.

8724 He stood alone in the centre of the white living room, as if waiting. — *Maundy*, Julian Gloag, 1969.

8725 Patsy sat by herself at the beginning of the evening, eating a melted Hershey bar. — *Moving On*, Larry McMurtry, 1970.

8726 I am alone in my room. — *Beyond the Bridge*, Jack Matthews, 1970.

8727 I am all alone in my pad, man, my piled-up-to-the-ceiling-with-junk pad. — *The Fan Man*, William Kotzwinkle, 1974.

8728 It was night and I was alone, behind the locked door, the bulletproof glass. — *Nightwork*, Irwin Shaw, 1975.

8729 *My name is Jodi. I live alone now on the western slope of the Carson Range, five miles up the mountain from the highway between Incline and South Tahoe.* — *Midheaven*, Ken Kuhlken, 1980.

8730 On the outskirts of a great northern city there lived an old man who kept a small apartment, alone, because that was the way his life had gone. — *The Last Good Time*, Richard Bausch, 1984.

8731 Jake is in Tijuana and I'm alone in the apartment. — *An Unfortunate Woman*, Barry Gifford, 1984.

8732 Solitude is limitless, especially for the lonely. — *The Antarctica Cookbook*, Crispin Kitto, 1984.

8733 Every other person in Veracruz was gone. — *Veracruz*, Rosalind Wright, 1986.

8734 I will tell you exactly how it was one day I said to my companion Gibble, "I am alone here, I need a wife," and he sent on the order without an adequate forewarning, he just

breathed with a panting effort, those pockets beneath his jowls throbbing like the gills of a river bass laid out in a pail. — *Fading, My Parmacheene Belle*, Joanna Scott, 1987.

8735 Nance Saturday agreed with Genesis, where it said that man should not be alone. — *The Terrible Threes*, Ishmael Reed, 1989.

8736 There were hills behind him (smoke coming off the summits) and fields of a yellowness that made him moan out loud — so must have felt the first man, seeing he was alone upon the world. — *Lee*, Tito Perdue, 1991.

Song

8737 The congregation in Tollamore Church were singing the evening hymn, the people gently swaying backwards and forwards like trees in a soft breeze. *An Indiscretion in the Life of an Heiress*, Thomas Hardy, 1878.

8738 When the accident happened, Cordova was singing the mad scene in *Lucia* for the last time in that season, and she had never sung it better. — *The Primadonna*, F. Marion Crawford, 1907.

8739 The old man and the little boy, his grandson, sat together in the shade of the big walnut tree in the front yard, watching the "Decoration Day Parade," as it passed up the long street; and when the last of the veterans was out of sight the grandfather murmured the words of the tune that came drifting back from the now distant band at the head of the procession. — *Ramsey Milholland*, Booth Tarkington, 1918.

8740 On a January evening of the early seventies, Christine Nilsson was singing in Faust at the Academy of Music in New York. — *The Age of Innocence*, Edith Wharton, 1920.

8741 My aunt Jenepher, who is so beautiful, and is blind, was sitting on a marble bench in the herb garden, whistling, and I was standing by her. — *Destiny Bay*, Donn Byrne, 1928.

8742 "Temps s'en va,/ Et rien n'ai fait" . . ./ Abelard raised his head. It was a pleasant voice, though a little drunken, and the words came clearly enough, a trifle blurred about the consonants, to the high window of the Maison du Poirier. — *Peter Abelard*, Helen Waddell, 1933.

8743 "Tirra-lirra, tirra-loo, tirra-lirra, tirra-lee — "/ "That doesn't make sense, daddy." — *Conversation*, Conrad Aiken, 1940.

8744 Big Joe Turner was singing a rock-and-roll adaptation of *Dink's Blues*. — *The Real Cool Killers*, Chester Himes, 1959.

8745 UNCLE SAM AIN'T NO WOMAN/ BUT HE SURE CAN TAKE YOUR MAN —/ That was the very very funny song some guitar-playing joker sang like Ledbelly at Solly's wedding reception just a few days ago when he was a newly wed civilian. — *And Then We Heard the Thunder*, John Oliver Killens, 1963.

8746 He had paused to listen to the exquisite madrigal of a Western meadow lark, and had offered to sing with it, choosing as his own, "Give Me the Sweet Delights of Love"; but he had found no bird that would sing with him, though now and then one, like the chat, would try to entice him into mimicry. — *Mountain Man*, Vardis Fisher, 1965.

8747 *The wind blows low, the wind blows high/ The snow comes falling from the sky,/ Rachel Cameron says she'll die/ For the want of the golden city./ She is handsome, she is pretty,/ She is the queen of the golden city —* / They are not actually chanting my name, of course. I only hear it that way from where I am watching at the classroom window, because I remember myself skipping rope to that song when I was about the age of the little girls out there now. — *A Jest of God*, Margaret Laurence, 1966.

8748 Somewhere he was singing. Pure, effortless tenor rising to the mellowest, highest note possible a sweet tenor ever sang. — *The Lynchers*, John Edgar Wideman, 1973.

8749 Becker, the first time you see him, is at the mainland terminus waving your car down the ramp onto the government ferry and singing to your headlights and to the salt air and to the long line of traffic behind you that he'd rather be a sparrow than a snail. Yes he would if he could, he loudly sings, he surely would. — *The Invention of the World*, Jack Hodgins, 1977.

8750 *Who's the lad that barks at us and bites our cheeks? Tiger John, Tiger John.* They sang that in the hall when he wasn't around, those Irishers from the Commissioner's office. — *Secret Isaac*, Jerome Charyn, 1978.

8751 A good song, I think. The end's good — that came to me in one piece — and the rest will do. — *The Praise Singer*, Mary Renault, 1978.

8752 As a young man, in upstate New York, my father studied to be a concert tenor. — *A Good School*, Richard Yates, 1978.

8753 "I want, I want, *o-o-oh*, I want you, baby." He sings it low and scratchy, crackling voice splitting the quiet hum of late night. — *Good Deeds*, Denise Gess, 1984.

8754 Everyone knows that the gondoliers of Venice are the greatest — correction, sorry — everyone *used to know* that the gondoliers of Venice are the greatest singers in the world. — *The Silent Gondoliers*, William Goldman *as* S. Morgenstern, 1984.

8755 The music was appropriate, although Hildon thought this particular version of the song was a downer: Barbra Streisand, singing "Happy Days." — *Love Always*, Ann Beattie, 1985.

8756 When I was sent upstairs after singing a sudden brilliant chorus of "God Shave The Queen," Colette knew what to do. — *A Certain Mr. Takahashi*, Ann Ireland, 1985.

8757 There was singing in his dream. — *Almost Midnight*, Don Belton, 1986.

8758 Anne always sang at the Friday-evening Mass, her pure voice rising from her dumpy form as effortlessly as the soul of a saint rising to heaven, her gooseberry-coloured eyes shining behind their plastic-rimmed spectacles. — *Holy Mother*, Gabrielle Donnelly, 1987.

8759 Listen, Master, while I sing to you. — *Resonating Bodies*, Lynne Alexander, 1988.

8760 *Loren held the sewing needle under hot running water. Twirling the eye end between his fingers, he hummed a song to himself — an old song written by a former governor of Louisiana. It was called "You Are My Sunshine" and Loren liked the words because he understood them.* — *Western Swing*, Tim Sandlin, 1988.

8761 Early evenings, the short woman with the bunned hair and smell of linens would lift him into her arms, and sing in a lulling voice, *Oyfen pripetshok brent a fayerl,/ Un in shtub iz heys./ Un der rebe lernt kleyned kinderlech/ Dem alef-beys./ Dem alef-boys./* And by the middle of the Yiddish song he'd be set back down in his crib, adrift with sleep. — *Brooklyn Boy*, Alan Lelchuk, 1989.

8762 The harper was singing a song about the death of Arthur. — *Born of the Sun*, Joan Wolf, 1989.

8763 The dull ache was not helped by the hymns. — *Guest of a Sinner*, James Wilcox, 1993.

Sounds

8764 "It *was* the horn I heard," said Scott, as the old mare again cocked her ears to the wind. — *Hawbuck Grange*, Robert Smith Surtees, 1847.

8765 Just after passing Caraher's saloon, on the County Road that ran south from Bonneville, and that divided the Broderson ranch from that of Los Muertos, Presley was suddenly aware of the faint and prolonged blowing of a steam whistle that he knew must come from the railroad shops near the depot at Bonneville. — *The Octopus*, Frank Norris, 1901.

8766 Through the soft summer night came the sounds of the silence that is heard only when nature sleeps, imperceptible except as one feels it behind the breath he draws or perhaps realizes it in the touch of an unexpected branch or flower. — *The Sherrods*, George Barr McCutcheon, 1903.

8767 The fair girl who was playing a banjo and singing to the wounded soldiers suddenly stopped, and, turning to the surgeon, whispered:/ "What's that?"/ "It sounds like a mob —" — *The Clansman*, Thomas Dixon, Jr., 1905.

8768 A sharp clip-clop of iron-shod hoofs deadened and died away, and clouds of yellow dust drifted from under the cottonwoods out over the sage. — *Riders of the Purple Sage*, Zane Grey, 1912.

8769 An appalling crash, piercing shrieks, a loud, unequal quarrel on a staircase, the sharp bang of a door.... — *Love at Second Sight*, Ada Leverson, 1916.

8770 About six o'clock the sound of a motor, collected out of the wide country and narrowed under the tree of the avenue, brought the household out in excitement on to the steps. — *The Last September*, Elizabeth Bowen, 1929.

8771 When the music stopped there was always a sound of the sea falling, remotely and eternally, on the shingles below the pier. It divided all time into a gentle boom, a pause, a shrieking drag of pebbles, and another gentle boom. — *The Fool of the Family*, Margaret Kennedy, 1930.

8772 It was Geraint's dog who heard the sound. — *The Man on the White Horse*, Warwick Deeping, 1934.

8773 Amid the din of traffic in the great American city of Megapolis a number of the shrillest, most raucous and disagreeable of the street sounds were superadded by deliberate intent to the general uproar for the paradoxical purpose of gaining a widespread, favorable and profitable publicity. — *The Sound Wagon*, T. S. Stribling, 1935.

8774 The first sound in the mornings was the clumping of the mill-girls' clogs down the cobbled street. Earlier than that, I suppose, there were factory whistles which I was never awake to hear. — *The Road to Wigan Pier*, George Orwell, 1937.

8775 There was a tattoo of hammers on the packing floor of Davenant's warehouse, Cheapside. — *The Day Before*, H. M. Tomlinson, 1939.

8776 Around quitting time, Tod Hackett heard a great din on the road outside his office. The groan of leather mingled with the jangle of iron and over all beat the tattoo of a thousand hooves. — *The Day of the Locust*, Nathanael West, 1939.

8777 Once he turned the corner out of Dauphine Street, the noise of the rioting faded until at last there was only dark silence broken

faintly by a distant pistol shot or the scream of a brawling harlot. — *Wild Is the River*, Louis Bromfield, 1941.

8778 He stood at his tall desk in this brown room, half parlor, half counting-house, and heard the sudden rattle of cartwheels on the sharp stones of the narrow street. — *Renegade*, Ludwig Lewisohn, 1942.

8779 Outside the snow was falling, thickly in great wet flakes, so that the sound of the traffic on Park Avenue coming through the drawn curtains was muted and distant. — *Mrs. Parkington*, Louis Bromfield, 1943.

8780 Grandpa's brogan shoes made a noise like whettin two rocks together as he shuffled back and forth on the witherin school-yard grass. — *Taps for Private Tussie*, Jesse Stuart, 1943.

8781 Serena Caudill heard a step outside and then the squeak of the cabin door and knew that John was coming in. — *The Big Sky*, A. B. Guthrie, Jr., 1947.

8782 The noise of the windshield wipers over the glass was a labored, asthmatic complaint. — *The Golden Salamander*, Victor Canning, 1948.

8783 The noise that the Water Star made as she came down out to sea sounded on the island like the humming of an insect, but it was in the very early morning when most insects are asleep. — *A Breath of Air*, Rumer Godden, 1950.

8784 The bedroom murmured to itself gently. It was almost below the limits of hearing — an irregular little sound, yet quite unmistakable, and quite deadly. — *The Stars, Like Dust*, Isaac Asimov, 1951.

8785 When was it that I first heard of the grass harp? — *The Grass Harp*, Truman Capote, 1951.

8786 Because it was raining the girl stood sheltered by the doorway, looking down across the hills, her ears straining to the sound of approaching riders; but she could see nobody in the wet morning nor any sign of life anywhere. — *The Valley of Vision*, Vardis Fisher, 1951.

8787 The snow had only just stopped, and in the court below my rooms all sounds were dulled. — *The Masters*, C. P. Snow, 1951.

8788 The liquid note of the thrush entered the house through the flowering privet, through the clumps of rhododendron, from where he whistled in the bed of pachysandra, but the Grandmother, eavesdropping on the stairs, wished he would shut up. — *The Deep Sleep*, Robert Nathan, 1953.

8789 My story has its manifest beginning in that moment when I came out on the stoep of my house in the turbulent twilight and heard on the steep slope below me the sound of desperate running, followed almost immediately by the exultant war-cry of the Amangtakwena: "Mattalahta Buka!" "At last we kill!" — *Flamingo Feather*, Laurens van der Post, 1955.

8790 Karla hesitated in the doorway of the adobe, then pushed open the screen door and came out into the sunlight as she heard again the faint, faraway sound of the wagon; and now she looked off toward the stand of willows that formed a windbreak along the north side of the yard, her eyes half closed in the sun glare and not moving from the motionless line of trees. — *Escape from Five Shadows*, Elmore Leonard, 1956.

8791 A movement in the reeds, a river pebble rolling on the stones ... the people stop to listen. — *Wizards' Country*, Daphne Rooke, 1957.

8792 For a moment, as he stood there in the prow, the sound of the sea against the vessel's sides sank so low that he could hear quite clearly the singing of the harp behind him. — *Harp into Battle*, Cecil Maiden, 1959.

8793 The sound began suddenly. It went high and keening through the mid-morning lethargy of Duncan's Bottom, desperate and lonesome, sounding almost terrified as though a knife offered at her throat. It went through the men on the store porch, jerking them around on a tight string, and somebody said, — Homer's coming. — *Dragon's Wine*, Borden Deal, 1960.

8794 Jim Reno, riding along the bottom of a considerable arroyo, heard the shot smash out of the right forward distance with that thinning flatness made only by a rifle. — "The Feudists," Ernest Haycox, 1960.

8795 In the quiet of the early morning, the buzzer sounded sharp and sudden, cutting the silence like the shrill notes of ten thousand cicadas. — *Eat a Bowl of Tea*, Louis Chu, 1961.

8796 Lily heard the shot at seventeen minutes to one. — *Run River*, Joan Didion, 1963.

8797 "Metal on concrete jars my drink lobes." — *The Interpreters*, Wole Soyinka, 1965.

8798 The sound of cars coming off the Williamsburg Bridge was deafening in the late, icy December night, even though Jay lived several streets away from the main arterial road. — *Seventh Avenue*, Norman Bogner, 1966.

8799 The woman at Otowi Crossing heard it now for the last time as she had heard it day after day for years on end: that long-drawn, half-screech, half-wail of No. 425 whistling round the bend — to her the most mysteriously exciting, excessively romantic, and poignantly haunting sound in the world. — *The Woman at Otowi Crossing*, Frank Waters, 1966.

8800 The whirr of grass-mowers droned in the hot afternoon. — *The Man Next Door*, Emanuel Litvinoff, 1968.

8801 A head of department, working quietly in his room in Whitehall on a summer afternoon, is not accustomed to being disturbed by the

near-by and indubitable sound of a revolver shot. — *The Nice and the Good*, Iris Murdoch, 1968.

8802 After he had gone, she lay very still./ She listened to the sound of his feet touching the steps./ She held the breath that a little while ago had sounded wild as a storm. — *The Day After Sunday*, Hollis Summers, 1968.

8803 From this distance it sounded like the barking of a dog. — *Karate Is a Thing of the Spirit*, Harry Crews, 1971.

8804 The heavy blue notepaper crackled as the man signed his name. — *Close-Up*, Len Deighton, 1972.

8805 The first loud thudding noise from the adjoining house shivered the kitchen. The second — or so it seemed to David Loomis — made the tea he was pouring leap from the china cup. — *Blockbuster*, Gerald Green, 1972.

8806 The door to the parlor of Francis Franklin's hotel suite was open a few inches, and we heard clucking noises inside. It was not uncommon for Franklin to have chickens in his suite. We heard a flopping sound, as though a great fish had been tossed onto the carpet, and Franklin's voice cried, "Oh, get down in it, baby!" — *Strange Peaches*, Edwin Shrake, 1972.

8807 A screaming comes across the sky. It has happened before, but there is nothing to compare it to now. — *Gravity's Rainbow*, Thomas Pynchon, 1973.

8808 I will soothe with the sound of names. — *Queen Emma of the South Seas*, Geoffrey Dutton, 1976.

8809 She heard the sound in the great green ferns. A soft sound, it might have been any animal, a wild goat or a blacktail deer. — *East Wind, Rain*, N. Richard Nash, 1977.

8810 Wes brought the sole of his boot down on the foot pedal of the bellows. The air made a hissing sound over the coals. — *A Darkness at Ingraham's Crest*, Frank Yerby, 1979.

8811 The engines had stopped half an hour ago while he was strapping up his bed-roll, and the ending of the comforting throb and shudder had brought a sudden astonishing silence. — *A Gentle Occupation*, Dirk Bogarde, 1980.

8812 The steel door to the caboose clanged open like a great church bell, scaring Cassie half to death. — *The War Train*, Brown Meggs, 1981.

8813 The disturbed silence of night was shedding its trust in darkness as its muted shafts of sound became one mobile daytime song: milkmen, paper boys, miners, cement workers, bike riders, motorists, shopkeepers, and early old amblers who could not sleep, all in their rising turns gave awakening power to the riddled morning. — *Jack Rivers and Me*, Paul John Radley, 1981.

8814 *The drums begin. You can hear them, like a million heartbeats from the deepest corner of your own*

insides. — *A Sense of Honor*, James Webb, 1981.

8815 Lying back on the park seat, her eyes closed, feet sprawled out in front of her, she heard the noise of children playing, clustered round the pond close by, sailing their model boats or flying kites fluttering in the hazy air; from time to time there came the noise of wheels on gravel as young wives passed, their infants invisible in the depths of prams; the roar of traffic from Bayswater Road came distantly, pleasantly muffled. — *A Promising Career*, Christy Brown, 1982.

8816 Jas had been scribbling spasmodically for some time in an untidy manuscript bound in black which she referred to as her Suicide Notebook, when a sound outdoors arrested her attention. — *Other Lips and Other Hearts*, Joan Sanders, 1982.

8817 He was composing a shot of O'Brien casting into the pool below the falls when he heard, above the water's rush and hiss, a sound like nothing he had ever heard before. — *DelCorso's Gallery*, Philip Caputo, 1983.

8818 Judy Greer thought she heard a noise. It was a rustling or a scraping or both, coming to her down the long, vertical cylinder of sleep. Echoing. — *Safekeeping*, Jonellen Heckler, 1983.

8819 Chinese Gordon was fully awake. He'd heard the clinking noise again, and now there was no question the cat was listening too. — *Metzger's Dog*, Thomas Perry, 1983.

8820 Three hundred yards downstream the noise of the falls, muffled by intervening trees and undergrowth in the crook of the bend, was reduced to a quiet murmur of pouring water, a natural sound more smoothly continuous than any other — than wind, insects or even night frogs in the marshes. — *Maia*, Richard Adams, 1984.

8821 A sudden crack. — *The Killing Fields*, Christopher Hudson, 1984.

8822 I didn't hear her until she was actually inside the room, locking the door shut behind her. — *The Ripoff*, Jim Thompson, 1985.

8823 Here, at dawn, the first sound is the calling of Gervaise to her cows. — *The Swimming Pool Season*, Rose Tremain, 1985.

8824 Frieda heard the sound and ignored it. — *In the Shadow of the Peacock*, Grace Edwards-Yearwood, 1988.

8825 There was a crackle, like air tearing. — *Come Sunday*, Bradford Morrow, 1988.

8826 So great was the noise during the day that I used to lie awake at night listening to the silence. — *A Far Cry from Kensington*, Muriel Spark, 1988.

8827 She was looking at him in the half-light from the window, at the way his chest rose and fell beneath his carefully crossed hands, and at

his face, and especially his nose, which stuck up into the morning air emitting a noise like a broken exhaust pipe. — *The Men's Room*, Ann Oakley, 1989.

8828 The noise from outside broke loud and sudden, as if somebody had begun cutting a superhighway through the woods. — *Summer People*, Marge Piercy, 1989.

8829 There goes Aggie again. Bang and crash and scrape all night. — *Honour Thy Father*, Lesley Glaister, 1990.

8830 Night is coming down and there is a hum of noise from the street. — *The South*, Colm Tóibín, 1990.

8831 *tic tic tic tic* . . . Tiny noises of compression, sounding through her skull. — *Canal Dreams*, Iain Banks, 1991.

8832 That airless night in early August, a persistent buzzing noise ripped through the rumpled fabric of my sleep. — *True Crime*, Michael Mewshaw, 1991.

8833 There it was: The same sound again. — *Hand in Glove*, Robert Goddard, 1992.

8834 I'm lying here, just occupying space, drifting in and out of a dream, when I hear something clattering and rumbling down the hall. — *Life-Size*, Jenefer Shute, 1992.

8835 Sound is queer here by the water, especially when the fog has come off Penobscot Bay, as it has now. — *Colony*, Anne Rivers Siddons, 1992.

8836 Wherever she went she heard it. — *Blood Dance*, James William Brown, 1993.

Speech

8837 Early in the last century two young women were talking together in a large apartment, richly furnished. One of these was Susan, cousin and dependent of Mrs. Anne Oldfield; the other was a flower-girl, whom that lady had fascinated by her scenic talent. — *Art*, Charles Reade, 1855.

8838 Miss Marjoribanks lost her mother when she was only fifteen, and when, to add to the misfortune, she was absent at school, and could not have it in her power to soothe her dear mamma's last moments, as she herself said. Words are sometimes very poor exponents of such an event: but it happens now and then, on the other hand, that a plain intimation expresses too much, and suggests emotion and suffering which, in reality, have but little, if any, existence. — *Miss Marjoribanks*, Margaret Oliphant *as* Mrs. Oliphant, 1865-1866.

8839 The morning-room of a large house in Portman Square, London./ A gentleman in the prime of life stood with his elbow on the broad mantel-piece, and made himself agreeable to a young lady, seated a little way off, playing at work. — *A Terrible Temptation*, Charles Reade, 1871.

8840 "I don't know what to say, my dear." — *In the Reign of Terror*, G. A. Henty, 1887.

8841 The people of France have made it no secret that those of England, as a general thing, are, to their perception, an inexpressive and speechless race, perpendicular and unsociable, unaddicted to enriching any bareness of contact with verbal or other embroidery. — *The Tragic Muse*, Henry James, 1890.

8842 Mr. Pierce was talking. Mr. Pierce was generally talking. — *The Honorable Peter Stirling*, Paul Leicester Ford, 1894.

8843 Rose was an unaccountable child from the start. She learned to speak early, and while she did not use "baby-talk" she had strange words of her own. — *Rose of Dutcher's Coolly*, Hamlin Garland, 1895.

8844 The recitations were over for the day. — *Of One Blood*, Pauline Hopkins, 1902-1903.

8845 She was walking, with her customary air of haughty and rapt leisure, across the market-place of Bursley, when she observed in front of her, at the top of Oldcastle Street, two men conversing and gesticulating vehemently, each seated alone in a dog-cart. — *Leonora*, Arnold Bennett, 1903.

8846 It was the old Brigadier who was talking in the café. — *Adventures of Gerard*, Arthur Conan Doyle, 1903.

8847 What determined the speech that startled him in the course of their encounter scarcely matters, being probably but some words spoken by himself quite without intention — spoken as they lingered and slowly moved together after their renewal of acquaintance. — *The Beast in the Jungle*, Henry James, 1903.

8848 "The Bishop of Rome — "/ Thomas Cranmer began a hesitating speech. — *The Fifth Queen Crowned*, Ford Madox Ford, 1908.

8849 Two men were standing in front of the Empire Theatre on Broadway, at the outer edge of the sidewalk, amiably discussing themselves in the first person singular. — *What's-His-Name*, George Barr McCutcheon, 1911.

8850 A swarthy turbaned face shone at Miriam from a tapestry screen standing between her and the ferns rising from a basket framework in the bow of the window. Consulting it at intervals as the afternoon wore on, she found that it made very light of the quiet propositions that were being elaborated within hearing of her inattentive ears. — *Backwater*, Dorothy M. Richardson, 1916.

8851 The three of us in that winter camp in the Selkirks were talking the slow aimless talk of wearied men. — *The Path of the King*, John Buchan, 1921.

8852 The tall, lanky Missourian leaning against the corner of a ramshackle saloon on Locust Street, St. Louis, Missouri — the St. Louis of the early forties — turned his whiskey-marked face toward his companion, a short and slender Mexican trader, sullenly listening to the latter's torrent of words, which was accompanied by many and excitable gesticulations. — *"Bring Me His Ears,"* Clarence E. Mulford, 1922.

8853 Hopalong Cassidy sat on the edge of the table in the sunny dining room of the Double-Y ranchhouse and listened to what his old-time foreman, and present partner, was saying. — *Hopalong Cassidy's Protégé*, Clarence E. Mulford, 1926.

8854 Daisy Simpson, having retired to bed at one o'clock in febrile and semi-intoxicated gaiety, woke in the dark yet glimmering grey of some later hour, and lay listening to the conversations that occurred in the streets of that town throughout the night and day; for Daisy was abroad, among those whom her mother in East Sheen called "the foreigners," and the foreigners, as is well known, rest not day nor night from speech. — *Keeping Up Appearances*, Rose Macaulay, 1928.

8855 There is no such thing as conversation. It is an illusion. There are intersecting monologues, that is all. — *"There Is No Conversation,"* Rebecca West, 1935.

8856 I have been talking to two very queer individuals and they have produced a peculiar disturbance of my mind. — *The Croquet Player*, H. G. Wells, 1937.

8857 It was a summer's night and they were talking, in the big room with the windows open to the garden, about the cesspool. — *Between the Acts*, Virginia Woolf, 1941.

8858 In the house in the rue Washington she sat watching d'Abrizzi, and listening with only half her mind to what he was saying. — *Until the Day Break*, Louis Bromfield, 1942.

8859 Andreas Ordy, Minister of Affairs in the Cabinet of the Communist Government of Hungary, sat in his office in the Barascy Palace in Budapest, facing a battery of still and newsreel cameramen and microphones, prepared to make an important speech. — *Trial by Terror*, Paul Gallico, 1952.

8860 Not that our small talk that Tuesday evening in April had any important bearing on the matter, but it will do for an overture, and it will help to explain a couple of reactions Nero Wolfe had later. — *Before Midnight*, Rex Stout, 1955.

8861 There he is on the midway, Grack the Frenchie, talking for his countstore or his zoo while the loudspeaker clamored under his come-on with a *hee hee hee* and a *ho ho ho*. — *The Man Who Was Not with It*, Herbert Gold, 1956.

8862 These three old men would sit and smoke and let a word fall and pause to hear the echoes of it as if they owned all time to speak their little pieces in. — *These Thousand Hills*, A. B. Guthrie, Jr., 1956.

8863 Mr. Charles Osman, speaking in his customary abstracted and precise manner, which came through to the young ladies and gentlemen of his class as a parody of the pedantic style, something sarcastically or hopelessly conscious of itself and of everything else in the world, began to gather together his books and papers while still talking, a sign that he had reached his peroration. — *The Homecoming Game*, Howard Nemerov, 1957.

8864 The Senator had just begun to speak. He bowed to the Mayor who had introduced him, and he stepped forward on the flag-draped platform, leaned, long-armed, smiling and relaxed on the speaker's podium, and he looked out into the clotted shirtsleeves and summer dresses, the little field of faces, black and white, that were close-pressed and tilted up and toward him like wild flowers in a light breeze. — *The Finished Man*, George Garrett, 1959.

8865 Somewhere near Venice, Guy began talking with a heavy, elderly man, a refugee from Germany on his way to Trieste. — *The Great Fortune*, Olivia Manning, 1960.

8866 His Excellency the Count of Mountjoy, Prime Minister of the Duchy of Grand Fenwick, the world's smallest sovereign nation, located on the northern slopes of the Alps between Switzerland and France, was preparing his annual budget speech which was to be given to a meeting of the Council of Freemen, the parliament of the Duchy, on the following week. — *The Mouse on the Moon*, Leonard Wibberley, 1962.

8867 "Your old man's really tuned up tonight," the big man said. — *The Some-Day Country*, Luke Short, 1964.

8868 "Say what you said because I know." — *The Dark*, John McGahern, 1965.

8869 Mrs. Quorn's dining room was not a place where the men were encouraged to hold general discussion groups after breakfast. A certain amount of genteel conversation was allowed as they waited their turns on the lavatory. — *Who Are the Violets Now?*, Auberon Waugh, 1965.

8870 "The aim of the Organization," Mr. Bekkus dictated, leaning back in his chair and casting up his eyes to the perforations of the sound-proof ceiling; "The *aim* of the Organization," he repeated with emphasis, as though he were directing a firing-squad — and then, "the

long-range aim," narrowing his eyes to this more distant target, "is to fully utilize the resources of the staff and hopefully by the end of the fiscal year to have laid stress—"/ Mr. Bekkus frequently misused the word "hopefully." He also made a point of saying locate instead of find, utilize instead of use, and never lost an opportunity to indicate or communicate; and would slip in a "basically" when he felt unsure of his ground./ "—to have laid greater stress upon the capacities of certain members of the staff at present in junior positions. Since this bears heavily"—Mr. Bekkus now leant forward and rested his elbows firmly on his frayed blue blotter—"on the nature of our future work force, attention is drawn to the Director-General's directive set out in (give the document symbol here, Germaine), asking that Personnel Officers communicate the names of staff members having—what was the wording there?" He reached for a mimeographed paper in his tray./ "Imagination," Germaine replied./ "—imagination and abilities which could be utilized in more responsible posts." Mr. Bekkus stopped again. "Where's Swoboda?"—*People in Glass Houses*, Shirley Hazzard, 1967.

8871 Someone listen to me. *She* never did. —*The Grain of Truth*, Nina Bawden, 1968.

8872 The royal personage, a hesitant cousin not yet forged into the mould of greatness, cleared his throat, shuffled the pages of his speech, and began timidly:/ "I *am* conscious—" —*Richer Than All His Tribe*, Nicholas Monsarrat, 1968.

8873 On the black-and-white television screen, the President was speaking, his brow furrowed in seriousness. —*Vector*, David R. Slavitt *as* Henry Sutton, 1970.

8874 Shockproof's mother was talking in code again. —*Shockproof Sydney Skate*, Marijane Meaker, 1972.

8875 When a new bridge between two sovereign states of the United States has been completed, it is time for speech. —*The Monkey Wrench Gang*, Edward Abbey, 1975.

8876 Although we have known each other for a long time and have spoken often, we have never spoken intimately. —*Cockpit*, Jerzy Kosinski, 1975.

8877 All they talked about for weeks when they were alone was the weather. —*Chez Charlotte and Emily*, Jonathan Baumbach, 1979.

8878 She knew she would have to tell Andy before he headed back east, and she was eager to get it over and done with. —*Walk Proud*, Evan Hunter, 1979.

8879 The speech she had just delivered was the one in which Phoebe dispensed traditional values as if they were free samples of her fudge, the one for which she was already known at Har-

vard and, because of a profile in *Fortune*, to specialized readers everywhere. —*Tender Offer*, Alexandra Marshall, 1981.

8880 The new lecturer was very eloquent in her talk of reform—in what she would like to see done and in what she would like to see undone in the university in particular and in Nigeria in general. —*Double Yoke*, Buchi Emecheta, 1982.

8881 When they weren't talking permanent community there around the fireplace in the big dining room, they were talking Makar. —*Music for a Broken Piano*, James Baker Hall, 1982.

8882 Old Man Dorne gathered the phlegm in his throat and spat it into a handkerchief, and that was how the storekeeper knew he was getting ready to launch into a speech. —*A Little More Than Kin*, Ernest Hebert, 1982.

8883 *Yat, yat yot.*/ Her words were pinched through a throat decomposing to fat, cooled by sips from a spritzer. —*!Click Song*, John A. Williams, 1982.

8884 Conversation was suspended while the maids cleared the lunch dishes and set platters of fruit on the table. —*Little Sister*, Margaret Gaan, 1983.

8885 Now there is no one for her to listen to. —*The Succession*, George Garrett, 1983.

8886 And now, ladies and gentlemen, honored guests, hangers-on, vagrants, idlers, and good-for-nothings, a brief talk by Dr. Vince Dubuque of The University on the hero of this tale, the tale itself, and sundry matters. —*Blue Pastoral*, Gilbert Sorrentino, 1983.

8887 "You speak Spanish, don't you, Marquis?"—*The Crimson Wind*, John Harris *as* Max Hennessy, 1985.

8888 Inside the house they were whispering. —*As Soon as It Rains*, Kaylie Jones, 1986.

8889 Humpety hump. Thems were my very words, No point in spittin, I said. —*The Engine of Owl-Light*, Sebastian Barry, 1987.

8890 Claire's first words to me I'll never forget. —*Unusual Company*, Margaret Erhart, 1987.

8891 "They're talking about you," said Abbas Mowlavi, noticing Chloe Fowler's glance behind him along the road, where the shrouded women peered at her, the whites of their eyes gleaming balefully out of the shadows of their veils. —*Persian Nights*, Diane Johnson, 1987.

8892 It's a pity that what Shanks Caulder says had to be saved for our grandchildren on the plastic ribbon of a tape recorder, because Shanks Caulder does not belong to the era of plastic ribbons and tape recorders. —*Hickory Cured*, Douglas C. Jones, 1987.

8893 All about the courthouse square were little groups of men. I saw them when I went to town with my mother to sell eggs and cream on this Saturday in August, 1932. They were stand-

ing around in the summer heat talking about Ace Ruggles. — *Cradle of the Copperheads*, Jesse Stuart, 1988.

8894 I understand that whenever Demosthenes got a little tongue-tied he'd leave Athens to camp out on the Mediterranean coast where, with pebbles in his mouth, he'd rehearse his oration against the sound of the Aegean Sea until his father unGreek diffidence ceased and words became waves within him. — *Dead Languages*, David Shields, 1989.

8895 "Have you talked to her?" Nat spoke in the garbled mumble which meant he was lighting his pipe. — *A Cooler Climate*, Zena Collier, 1990.

8896 Towards the end of the party, they began to talk about house prices again. — *Family Money*, Nina Bawden, 1991.

8897 They spoke in light, when they felt like speaking. — *Almanac Branch*, Bradford Morrow, 1991.

8898 "Do you believe her?" she said. Once said, it cannot be unsaid. That is the thing with words. — *Time and Tide*, Edna O'Brien, 1992.

Spies

8899 He had stealthily parted the branches and was spying on the dark and secret place where he had found his most precious magic, when he saw a movement downstream, and at once, with the instinctive shrinking of all hunted things, he drew back into the shadows. — *Adam and the Serpent*, Vardis Fisher, 1947.

8900 Stephen paused outside the door to listen. — *The Chameleons*, John Broderick, 1961.

8901 Lord Melamine is right about one thing, at least. I was never a spy. — *Doctor Cobb's Game*, R. V. Cassill, 1969.

8902 No, like you, I cannot claim ever to have caught a spy. Not officially anyway. And it depends on what you mean by caught. — *Doom's Caravan*, Geoffrey Household, 1971.

8903 "What is wrong, Sister Winifrede," says the Abbess, clear and loud to the receptive air, "with the traditional keyhole method?" — *The Abbess of Crewe*, Muriel Spark, 1974.

8904 I am a spy at the elbow of the powerful, a fly on their wall. — *The Kitchen Man*, Ira Wood, 1985.

8905 A detective was following Linda. — *Ghost Waves*, James McManus, 1988.

8906 I discovered Serge by listening at my parents' door. — *Starting with Serge*, Laurie Stone, 1990.

Sports

8907 Saturday had been a strenuous day for the baseball team of Winona University, and Victor Ollnee, its redoubtable catcher, slept late. — *Victor Ollnee's Discipline*, Hamlin Garland, 1911.

8908 Dr. Howard Archie had just come up from a game of pool with the Jewish clothier and two traveling men who happened to be staying overnight in Moonstone. — *The Song of the Lark*, Willa Cather, 1915.

8909 It was, probably, Lee Randon realized, the last time he would play golf that year. — *Cytherea*, Joseph Hergesheimer, 1922.

8910 Robert Cohn was once middleweight boxing champion of Princeton. Do not think that I am very much impressed by that as a boxing title, but it meant a lot to Cohn. — *The Sun Also Rises*, Ernest Hemingway, 1926.

8911 It was the Sunday after Easter, and the last bull-fight of the season in Mexico City. — *The Plumed Serpent*, D. H. Lawrence, 1926.

8912 It was the height of the racing-season at Saratoga. — *The Buccaneers*, Edith Wharton, 1938.

8913 Boys are playing basketball around a telephone pole with a backboard bolted to it. — *Rabbit, Run*, John Updike, 1960.

8914 The Southern Games were coming. — *The Games Were Coming*, Michael Anthony, 1963.

8915 Bottom half of the seventh, Brock's boy had made it through another inning unscratched, one! two! three! — *The Universal Baseball Association, Inc., J. Henry Waugh, Prop.*, Robert Coover, 1968.

8916 Sandy was in the lead. — *Come Winter*, Evan Hunter, 1973.

8917 They murdered him. — *The Chocolate War*, Robert Cormier, 1974.

8918 Martin Daugherty, age fifty and now the scorekeeper, observed it all as Billy Phelan, working on a perfect game, walked with the arrogance of a young, untried eagle toward the ball return, scooped up his black, two-finger ball, tossed it like a juggler from right to left hand, then held it in his left palm, weightlessly. — *Billy Phelan's Greatest Game*, William Kennedy, 1978.

8919 They were the laughing boys of the American League. Footloose imbeciles, they couldn't hit, they couldn't field, they couldn't run. — *The Seventh Babe*, Jerome Charyn, 1979.

8920 When Allie Brandon stepped through the narrow doorway into the press box he paused for a moment to watch the game over the heads of the shirt-sleeved sportswriters and telegraphers. — *The Last Great Season*, Donald Honig, 1979.

8921 Loney watched the muddy boys bang against each other and he thought of a passage from the Bible: "Turn away from man in whose nostrils is breath, for of what account is he?" — *The Death of Jim Loney*, James Welch, 1979.

8922 When I was a kid I always had dreams of playing football. — *Football Dreams*, David Guy, 1980.

8923 My father said he saw him years later playing in a tenth-rate commercial league in a textile town in Carolina, wearing shoes and an assumed name. — *Shoeless Joe*, W. P. Kinsella, 1982.

8924 They flowed out of the ancient square like multicolored grains of sand from an hourglass, out of the center of Addis Ababa, the three-thousand-year-old capital of Ethiopia and the start of the first annual Abebe Bikila Memorial Marathon, 26 miles and 385 yards of cruelest torture, even for a world-class marathon. — *Miles to Go*, Mark Kram, 1982.

8925 "This time," Coach Dodge said out loud as he drove the purple and white station wagon into Cooper Leaping Deer's yard, "this time, by doggies, that ornery flathead'll play." — *Indian Giver*, Gerald Duff, 1983.

8926 Our family came to New York in the winter of '89, and in the spring I saw my first game of baseball. — *The Celebrant*, Eric Rolfe Greenberg, 1983.

8927 That summer morning, in the distance, Daisy Meyer bent her blond head over her club, a short iron for the short sixth hole, in effortless concentration on her practice swing. — *Testing the Current*, William McPherson, 1984.

8928 In my day I was quite a ballplayer. — *Heart of the Order*, Tony Ardizzone, 1986.

8929 One fine day toward the middle of August, in the year 19____, in the city of B_____, I was seated at two o'clock in the afternoon on a wooden bench in a public park, watching a baseball game through half-closed eyes. — *From the Realm of Morpheus*, Steven Millhauser, 1986.

8930 At first golf was only a green shade protecting me from the gathering white heat of my mother's death. — *The Rub of the Green*, William Hallberg, 1988.

8931 "When it comes time to run through those goalposts," Harold Gravely said almost thirty years ago, "I want your butthole so wide damn open you'll need a pair of tenpenny nails stuck up it to keep your foul business from spilling out." — *The Best There Ever Was*, John Ed Bradley, 1990.

8932 When I was ten and Donny was twelve, I hit a ball that really sailed. — *A Short History of the Long Ball*, Justin Cronin, 1990.

8933 In May, when the grass turns green, and the lilacs fill the air with purple perfumes, and the orioles tell of orchards bursting with pink blossoms, then the boys, old and young, get out their bats and balls and run to the pastures and play the wonderful game of baseball. — *No Fun on Sunday*, Frederick Manfred, 1990.

8934 This is the story of how Truckbox Al McClintock almost got a tryout with the genuine St. Louis Cardinals of the National Baseball League, but instead ended up batting against Bob Feller, of Cleveland Indian fame, in Renfrew Park, down on the river flats, in Edmonton, Alberta, summer of 1945 or '46, no one can remember which, though the date in question has brought on more than one disagreement, which turned first to a shoving match, then to an altercation, and finally a fist fight, though not a brouhaha, the general consensus in the Six Towns area being that it takes more than two people to staff a brouhaha, the fist fight though, usually resulting in bent cartilage of someone's proboscis, and blood spots on a Sunday shirt. — *Box Socials*, W. P. Kinsella, 1991.

8935 From his classroom window Miles could see the football team scrimmaging down on the field. — *An Honorable Profession*, John L'Heureux, 1991.

8936 O. B. Brewster, in his winter daydreams, escaped into baseball. — *A Walk Through Fire*, William Cobb, 1992.

Statues

8937 The setting sunbeams slant over the antique gateway of Sorrento, fusing into a golden bronze freestone vestments of old Saint Antonio, who with his heavy stone mitre and upraised hands has for centuries kept watch thereupon. — *Agnes of Sorrento*, Harriet Beecher Stowe, 1862.

8938 Shortly after the appearance of the Budget in 1930, the eighth wonder of the world might have been observed in the neighbourhood of Victoria Station — three English people, of wholly different type, engaged in contemplating simultaneously a London statue. — *Flowering Wilderness*, John Galsworthy, 1932.

8939 I suppose the small greenish statue of a man in a wig on a horse is one of the famous statues of the world. I said to Cary, "Do you see how shiny the right knee is? It's been touched so often for luck, like St. Peter's foot in Rome." — *Loser Takes All*, Graham Greene, 1955.

8940 In the twilight, the bust appeared to be that of some cocked-hat Revolutionary War hero of not the very first rank, that is, not G. Wash-

ington but perhaps one of those excellent Europeans noted in fact and apocrypha for throwing their weight on our side, Lafayette, say, or von Steuben. — *Crazy in Berlin*, Thomas Berger, 1958.

8941 A large uncouth artifact stands in a little garden outside the Museum of Antiquities on the island of Thassos. It has the head of a seal, a body like a horizontal sausage roll, rudimentary wings, and human legs plunged into heavy boots. Few visitors think it beautiful. — *The Forgotten Smile*, Margaret Kennedy, 1961.

8942 In all the hosts of effigies that throng the aisles of Westminster Abbey one man only, and he a sailor, strikes a martial attitude. — *Unconditional Surrender*, Evelyn Waugh, 1961.

8943 Sweeney tipped his olive-green linen cap to the statue on the quay. "Old Rabelais," he said. "One of the all-time greats." — *The Legion of Noble Christians*, Gerald Green, 1965.

8944 The Divine Infant of Prague was only eleven inches tall yet heavy enough to break someone's toes if he fell off the dresser. — *The Emperor of Ice-Cream*, Brian Moore, 1965.

8945 The cover for <u>Trout Fishing in America</u> is a photograph taken late in the afternoon, a photograph of the Benjamin Franklin statue in San Francisco's Washington Square. — *Trout Fishing in America*, Richard Brautigan, 1967.

8946 Unspeakable dignity isolates the diminutive nobleman. — *The Connoisseur*, Evan S. Connell, 1974.

8947 "My weary head to rest upon a pillow/ next my favourite girl in Lala's bordello."/ Half singing, half muttering the words under his breath Luke, stood at the base of the slender obelisk, squinting querulous and famished up at the emblazoned head of Charles Stewart Parnell, which glinted wanly under the watery January sunlight; the eternal flame of revolution above the head that never wore a crown, and the graven words proclaiming the folly of putting boundaries to the forward march of a nation, a little tarnished with the droppings of generations of heedless unpatriotic pigeons. — *Wild Grow the Lilies*, Christy Brown, 1976.

8948 Day of portents, day when the skin crawls suddenly, day of soundless thunder enough to deafen you, the day when Caesar's statue in the forum begins to bleed mysteriously. — *A Secret History of Time to Come*, Robie Macauley, 1979.

8949 ZAMBO!! Suddenly I'm on my hands and knees down on the asphalt next to a bench near the statue of Diderot in the small Place beside the boulevard Saint-Germain, across from the Church of Saint-Germain-des-Prés. — *Last Lovers*, William Wharton, 1991.

8950 They all had names, but I have forgotten them. — *The Son of Laughter*, Frederick Buechner, 1993.

Stories

8951 It is the privilege of tale-tellers to open their story in an inn, the free rendezvous of all travellers, and where the humour of each displays itself, without ceremony or restraint. — *Kenilworth*, Sir Walter Scott, 1821.

8952 It was the day after Doune Fair when my story commences. — "The Two Drovers," Sir Walter Scott, 1827.

8953 The celebrated name which forms the title to this work will sufficently apprise the reader that it is in the earlier half of the fourteenth century that my story opens. — *Rienzi*, Edward Bulwer Lytton, 1835.

8954 This is the story of what a Woman's patience can endure, and what a Man's resolution can achieve. — *The Woman in White*, Wilkie Collins, 1860.

8955 It is not true that a rose by any other name will smell as sweet. Were it true, I should call this story "The Great Orley Farm Case." But who would ask for the ninth number of a serial work burthened with so very uncouth an appellation? Thence, and therefore, — Orley Farm. — *Orley Farm*, Anthony Trollope, 1861-1862.

8956 On Saturday, the 18th day of June, 1859, the "State Banner and Delphian Oracle," published weekly at Oxbow Village, one of the principal centres in a thriving river-town of New England, contained an advertisement which involved the story of a young life, and startled the emotions of a small community. — *The Guardian Angel*, Oliver Wendell Holmes, Sr., 1867.

8957 If anybody cares to read a simple tale told simply, I, John Ridd, of the parish of Oare, in the county of Somerset, yeoman and churchwarden, have seen and had a share in some doings of this neighborhood, which I will try to set down in order, God sparing my life and memory. — *Lorna Doone*, R. D. Blackmore, 1869.

8958 This is the Story of a Bad Boy. Well, not such a very bad, but a pretty bad boy; and I ought to know, for I am, or rather I was, that boy himself. — *The Story of a Bad Boy*, Thomas Bailey Aldrich, 1870.

8959 You are here invited to read the story of an Event which occurred some years since in an out-of-the-way corner of England./ The persons principally concerned in the Event are — a blind girl, two (twin) brothers, a skilled surgeon, and a curious foreign woman. I am the curious

foreign woman. And I take it on myself—for reasons which will presently appear—to tell the story. —*Poor Miss Finch*, Wilkie Collins, 1872.

8960 Every one remembers the severity of the Christmas of 187-. I will not designate the year more closely, lest I should enable those who are too curious to investigate the circumstances of this story, and inquire into details which I do not intend to make known. —*Christmas at Thompson Hall*, Anthony Trollope, 1877.

8961 I would that it were possible so to tell a story that a reader should beforehand know every detail of it up to a certain point, or be so circumstanced that he might be supposed to know. —*Is He Popenjoy?*, Anthony Trollope, 1878.

8962 It will be necessary, for the purpose of my story, that I shall go back more than once from the point at which it begins, so that I may explain with the least amount of awkwardness the things as they occurred which led up to the incidents that I am about to tell; and I may as well say that these first four chapters of the book—though they may be thought to be the most interesting of them all by those who look to incidents for their interest in a tale—are in this way only preliminary. —*Mr. Scarborough's Family*, Anthony Trollope, 1882-1883.

8963 I, Cornelio Grandi, who tell you these things, have a story of my own, of which some of you are not ignorant. —*A Roman Singer*, F. Marion Crawford, 1883.

8964 It is impossible to begin a story which must of necessity tax the powers of belief of readers unacquainted with the class of facts to which its central point of interest belongs without some words in the nature of preparation. —*A Mortal Antipathy*, Oliver Wendell Holmes, Sr., 1885.

8965 This is the year 1492. I am eighty-two years of age. The things I am going to tell you are things which I saw myself as a child and as a youth. —*Personal Recollections of Joan of Arc*, Mark Twain, 1896.

8966 With many expressions of sympathy and interest Edith listened to the story of my dream. —*Equality*, Edward Bellamy, 1897.

8967 The story had held us, round the fire, sufficiently breathless, but except the obvious remark that it was gruesome, as, on Christmas Eve in an old house, a strange tale should essentially be, I remember no comment uttered till somebody happened to say that it was the only case he had met in which such a visitation had fallen on a child. —*The Turn of the Screw*, Henry James, 1898.

8968 I have told this story to many audiences with diverse results, and once again I take my reputation in my hands and brave the perils. —"The Watcher by the Threshold," John Buchan, 1900.

8969 This, my story, is a very old story. —*The Shepherd of the Hills*, Harold Bell Wright, 1907.

8970 I may as well begin this story with Mr. Hilary Vane, more frequently addressed as the Honourable Hilary Vane, although it was the gentleman's proud boast that he had never held an office in his life. —*Mr. Crewe's Career*, Winston Churchill, 1908.

8971 This story began in the Ozark Mountains. It follows the trail that is nobody knows how old. But mostly this story happened in Corinth, a town of the middle class in a Middle Western state. —*The Calling of Dan Matthews*, Harold Bell Wright, 1909.

8972 I had this story from one who had no business to tell it to me, or to any other. —*Tarzan of the Apes*, Edgar Rice Burroughs, 1914.

8973 This is the saddest story I have ever heard. —*The Good Soldier*, Ford Madox Ford, 1915.

8974 This is the story of me, Ana the scribe, son of Meri, and of certain of the days that I have spent upon the earth. —*Moon of Israel*, H. Rider Haggard, 1918.

8975 This story began at a church party in the village of Pointview, Connecticut. —*The Scudders*, Irving Bacheller, 1923.

8976 On idle nights in Cambridge or later in Paris, when there foregathered in George Weatherby's rooms young people with an infinite zest for life and an infinite curiosity about it—some laughing yet passionately serious group, sitting up until all hours with pipes and cigarettes beside a dying fire in the grate and telling strange and sardonic stories of things that had happened in the towns they had come from—then George always thought of Michael Shenstone. —*Runaway*, Floyd Dell, 1925.

8977 This story is going to start like a lesson in geography. —*The Crippled Lady of Peribonka*, James Oliver Curwood, 1927.

8978 Every man and every woman, it is said, has one story. —*Exit*, Harold Bell Wright, 1930.

8979 I cannot pretend that the world is waiting for this story, for the world knows nothing about it. But I want to tell it. No one knows it better than I do except Michael Crowther, and he nowadays has time for nothing but his soul. —*The Sapphire*, A. E. W. Mason, 1933.

8980 *In the telling of a story the narrator takes a bit from life as definitely and completely as one would cut out a paper doll, trimming away all of the flimsy sheet excepting the figure.* —*Spring Came on Forever*, Bess Streeter Aldrich, 1935.

8981 This is the story of Danny and of Danny's friends and of Danny's house. —*Tortilla Flat*, John Steinbeck, 1935.

8982 In writing this story, I am fulfilling a

promise to my poor friend Fulano. — *Locos: A Comedy of Gestures*, Felipe Alfau, 1936.

8983 Maybe I am not the man to tell this story, but if I don't tell it no one else will, so here goes. — *Hope of Heaven*, John O'Hara, 1938.

8984 "Long, long into the night I lay—"/ (One!)/ "Long, long into the night I lay awake—"/ (Two!)/ "Long, long into the night I lay awake, thinking how I should tell my story!" — *The Good Child's River*, Thomas Wolfe, 1938 (pub. 1991).

8985 There are more ways than one of telling a story. — *Sergeant Lamb's America*, Robert Graves, 1940.

8986 The story was as old as the desert watch fires which had flickered for generations on the still, rapt faces of his forebears. — *The Herdsman*, Dorothy Clarke Wilson, 1946.

8987 The story of the *Trikkala* is a strange one. — *Maddon's Rock*, Hammond Innes, 1948.

8988 There was so much happening on this cold, clear New Year's Day that it is difficult to decide where the story should begin. — *Son of a Hundred Kings*, Thomas B. Costain, 1949.

8989 A story has no beginning or end; arbitrarily one chooses that moment of experience from which to look back or from which to look ahead. — *The End of the Affair*, Graham Greene, 1951.

8990 This is the story—the long and true story—of one ocean, two ships, and about a hundred and fifty men. — *The Cruel Sea*, Nicholas Monsarrat, 1951.

8991 This is the story of an adventure that happened in Narnia and Calormen and the lands between, in the Golden Age when Peter was High King in Narnia and his brother and his two sisters were King and Queens under him. — *The Horse and His Boy*, C. S. Lewis, 1954.

8992 This is a story about something that happened long ago when your grandfather was a child. — *The Magician's Nephew*, C. S. Lewis, 1955.

8993 Here begins a tale of action and passion, a guts-and-glory story of men with untamed hearts, of women with raging juices. — *Rally Round the Flag, Boys!*, Max Shulman, 1957.

8994 This is the story of two men, Robert Lamb and Ned Roper. I know them both and I'm going to tell the story as I watched it happen, straight through from the beginning to—well, I can't quite say "the end," because it hasn't ended yet, but at any rate as far as it's gone. — *The Contenders*, John Wain, 1958.

8995 There are some stories into which the reader should be led gently, and I think this may be one of them. — *The Watch That Ends the Night*, Hugh MacLennan, 1959.

8996 I'm telling this story mainly for my own benefit. — *The Right to an Answer*, Anthony Burgess, 1960.

8997 Will Aldrich would say that the story began at the Scholarship Bazaar which was held the first of May. — *Not a Word About Nightingales*, Maureen Howard, 1960.

8998 This story at no point becomes my own. — *The Edge of Sadness*, Edwin O'Connor, 1961.

8999 I am David Parr. The story is about my great-uncle, Colonel John Parr, V.C. I am introducing the story for him: he is telling it by means of a journal. And the journal is interspersed with observations of my own, written down when I first read it, together with a few others added at a later date. So in a sense you could say it is also my story, or rather bits and pieces of it that break like patches of sunlight through tangled branches to dapple the road beneath. — *The Winter People*, Gilbert Phelps, 1963.

9000 There's nothing I like better than a yarn, so I might as well get down to business. —*Among the Cinders*, Maurice Shadbolt, 1965.

9001 The hour this story begins is known. The minute is known; the exact moment is recorded. Even the state of the weather is known. To some this might not appear to be remarkable, but when it is considered that there are entire generations in the history of Santa Vittoria about which nothing at all is known, the statement becomes remarkable. — *The Secret of Santa Vittoria*, Robert Crichton, 1966.

9002 This is the story of Lovey Childs, of Philadelphia. — *Lovey Childs*, John O'Hara, 1969.

9003 "Look here, any more of that and there'll be no Mumpkin story tonight." — *Everything Must Go*, Keith Waterhouse, 1969.

9004 My name is Munchmeyer and this is my story. I have to put it down like that, cigarette dangling, words coming out obliquely from the corner of my mouth, or I'm not going to put it down at all. — *Munchmeyer and Prospero on The Island*, Audrey Thomas, 1971.

9005 This is Michael Howell's story and he tells most of it himself. I think that he should have told all of it. — *The Levanter*, Eric Ambler, 1972.

9006 It is not easy to tell the story of what happened to Scott Pirie and his pony that summer, because it was always more than the story of what happened to the boy and his horse. —*A Sporting Proposition*, James Aldridge, 1973.

9007 I am going to give you the full story of a very old Celtic tale, at least as I've been able to understand the truth of it. —"Eliduc," John Fowles, 1974.

9008 Although this story is as complete as anything can ever be in an human awareness bound to its miniscule ration of life in the here and now, I still have only to think of it to find it as

mysterious as some midnight visitation. — *A Mantis Carol*, Laurens van der Post, 1975.

9009 I am going to put my story down in black and white, just as it happened, hoping once it is finished to find even one little thread of sense in it, one little pointer as to why Cruise should have acted as he did. — *The Man from Next Door*, Honor Tracy, 1977.

9010 This is a fairy tale for children between the ages of six and ninety-six, and adults between the ages of three and six. It is the story of how the sun fell in love with the moon. Or was it the moon with the sun? — *The Sun and the Moon*, Niccolò Tucci, 1977.

9011 Once my mother phoned me and said, "Oh, why did the mother in your story have to be so slangy?" — *The Life I Really Lived*, Jessamyn West, 1979.

9012 This part of my story begins one evening early in January 1976 in Anchovy, Jamaica, a country village clinging to the hills of St. James Parish about twelve miles south and west of Montego Bay. — *The Book of Jamaica*, Russell Banks, 1980.

9013 This is a strange story. — *The Leaves on Grey*, Desmond Hogan, 1980.

9014 She reconstructed the story from the beginning. — *Sardines*, Nuruddin Farah, 1981.

9015 In the Choctaw language, Oklahoma means red people. But this is a story about white people. — *The Silver Spooner*, Darcy O'Brien, 1981.

9016 This is a story to be read in bed in an old house on a rainy night. — *Oh What a Paradise It Seems*, John Cheever, 1982.

9017 Hey you guys wake up, wake up, it's starting all over again, but this time it's going to be serious, the real story, no more evasions, procrastinations, and you won't believe this, it begins in the future, no I'm not kidding, well the near future, can't stray too far from the present, and besides there is a certain logic to keep in mind, a certain urgency too — *The Twofold Vibration*, Raymond Federman, 1982.

9018 Mine is an impossible story. — *Virginie*, John Hawkes, 1982.

9019 What can I tell you? The tale is chaotic, persons and paths crossing like the wiring of some, you should pardon the expression, diabolical brain, its function and purpose not to be deciphered from any simple separation of the jumbled connections. — *Satan*, Jeremy Leven, 1982.

9020 This is the story of Aletheia, the daughter of Grace-and-Glory and Fearless Witness, about whom you may have read in *Hinds' Feet on High Places* and *Mountains of Spices*. — *Eagles' Wings to the Higher Places*, Hannah Hurnard, 1983.

9021 This is a story that no one wanted told and, perhaps, it might have served a better purpose, both public and private, to have kept it buried in the archives. — *Valedictory*, W. S. Kuniczak, 1983.

9022 This is not a story of the war, except insofar as everything in my unsettled middle age seems to wind back to it. — *The American Blues*, Ward Just, 1984.

9023 Now you may think this story is crazy, but it really happened. — *Around the World in Eight Days*, Ron Kovic, 1984.

9024 This is the story of two contests in which I competed in the fifth grade. — "Take the Long Way Home," Eric Kraft, 1984.

9025 This is a tale of a book, the story of my friend, Christopher Iles. — *The Fabulous Englishman*, Robert McCrum, 1984.

9026 This story is about A.J. Poole and his friends to whom he was known as the Watermelon Kid, and it took place on the old roadhouse circuit, mainly in Arkansas, back in the 1950s along the river roads that ran into U.S. Highway 70 when it was fast and narrow and dangerous. — *The Watermelon Kid*, Bill Terry, 1984.

9027 *It's not memory you need for telling this story, the sad story of Robert Raymond Dubois, the story that ends along the back streets and alleys of Miami, Florida, on a February morning in 1981, that begins way to the north in Catamount, New Hampshire, on a cold, snowflecked afternoon in December 1979, the story that tells what happened to young Bob Dubois in the months between the wintry afternoon in New Hampshire and the dark, wet morning in Florida and tells what happened to the several people who loved him and to some Haitian people and a Jamaican and to Bob's older brother Teddy Dubois who loved him but thought he did not and to Bob's best friend Avery Boone who did not love him but thought he did and to the women who were loved by Bob Dubois nearly as much as and differently from the way that he loved his wife Elaine.* — *Continental Drift*, Russell Banks, 1985.

9028 I will tell you a tale I have not told before. — *They Were Also Strangers*, Borden Deal, 1985.

9029 The story of Moinous & Sucette. — *Smiles on Washington Square*, Raymond Federman, 1985.

9030 You said to put the story on tape the first chance I got, so here it is. — "The Bindlestiff," William Herrick, 1985.

9031 This is the story of a man. — *The Coconut Book*, Richard Maynard, 1985.

9032 It's an old story, darling, so don't get offended. — *The Grandmothers' Club*, Alan Cheuse, 1986.

9033 Let's begin with the first clean fact, James: This ain't no war story. — *Paco's Story*, Larry Heinemann, 1986.

9034 A story I heard years ago, when stories still had power to charm me: — *Redback*, Howard Jacobson, 1986.

9035 This is the story of my cousin, the actress Alexandra Reed, as I remember it myself, and as I have been able to reconstruct it from the recollections of others. — *The Private Life of Axie Reed*, John Knowles, 1986.

9036 I would not be in a position to tell Annie Jeynor's story were it not for the fact that my wife, too, is an actress. — *The Wind on the Heath*, Tom Gallacher, 1987.

9037 Over and over again I tell myself the story of Sarah. — *Best Intentions*, Kate Lehrer, 1987.

9038 Reader, I am going to tell you the story of Clifford, Helen and little Nell. — *The Hearts and Lives of Men*, Fay Weldon, 1987.

9039 Notes towards a love story. — *States of Emergency*, André Brink, 1988.

9040 There are thousands of stories: Moses and the dead angels, Hitler and the birdcage, Theodor Herzl's trip to the moon. — *Learning About God*, Norman Kotker, 1988.

9041 This is the true story. — *Vanished*, Mary McGarry Morris, 1988.

9042 The story begins — when? — *The King of the Fields*, Isaac Bashevis Singer, 1988.

9043 This is a true story but I can't believe it's really happening. — *London Fields*, Martin Amis, 1989.

9044 This is where your story starts. — *Memory of Snow and of Dust*, Breyten Breytenbach, 1989.

9045 It was a favorite story my father used to tell of a gun hidden in a cave, an evil witchdoctor, an educated Spaniard seeking a Rousseauan society of "natural men and women" here on our California coast — love, murder, martyrdom — you never heard such a tale! — *Power and Glory*, Robert Easton, 1989.

9046 Mine is a story that must be told. And a story that must be heard, because those who presume to tell it do not know it. — *The Moon Under Her Feet*, Clysta Kinstler, 1989.

9047 My beloved lord,/ Two days before I was murdered you laid on me a penance, to be fulfilled at your pleasure when I was well enough to bear it. Your Grace has a long memory; that night is now seven years ago. *The story as I lived it*: That is all you asked. — *The Burning of the Rose*, Ruth Nichols, 1989.

9048 This is the story of an eye, and how it came into its own. — *Leaving Brooklyn*, Lynne Sharon Schwartz, 1989.

9049 This is a story about Teddy Schroeder and his sister, Bean, and about some things that happened to them when they were children. — *The Wizard's Tide*, Frederick Buechner, 1990.

9050 Perhaps she had heard the story before. — *Coyote*, Peter Gadol, 1990.

9051 Twenty years ago at the dinner table, my father told us a story. — *17 Morton Street*, Catherine Hiller, 1990.

9052 The One True Story of the World — that's what he called it: the story my father told me every night, from the time I was three or maybe even before, until my mother and he got divorced when I was ten, and he went off to live on a sailboat christened *Ketch-22* that took him around the world twice but never home again. — *The One True Story of the World*, Lynne McFall, 1990.

9053 The story of the demon Blue-Shirt (known in His native land as AMORTOR-TAK) is hinted at in a variety of codices, being revealed nowhere and everywhere, like cabalistic doctrine. — *The Ice-Shirt*, William T. Vollmann, 1990.

9054 Let's say I'm telling you the story of the upstate lawyer, the post-traumatic combat stress, the splendid wife, their solitudes and infidelities, their children, his client with her awkward affinities, the sense of impending recognition by which he is haunted. — *Closing Arguments*, Frederick Busch, 1991.

9055 If you're the devil, then it's not me telling this story. — *The Man Who Fell in Love with the Moon*, Tom Spanbauer, 1991.

9056 This is an old story. — *Strange Business*, Rilla Askew, 1992.

9057 Prologue or epilogue. And keep the story simple. — *The Dream Life*, Bo Huston, 1992.

9058 *The Vampire Lestat here. I have a story to tell you. It's about something that happened to me.* — *The Tale of the Body Thief*, Anne Rice, 1992.

9059 You won't know about this story unless you've already read *The Powwow Highway*, or you've seen the movie, but that doesn't matter. — *Sweet Medicine*, David Seals, 1992.

9060 The story of Zenia ought to begin when Zenia began. It must have been someplace long ago and distant in space, thinks Tony; someplace bruised, and very tangled. — *The Robber Bride*, Margaret Atwood, 1993.

9061 The setting of a story my parents liked to tell on themselves when I was small is rather exotic in an ends-of-the-earth kind of way. — *Rebel Powers*, Richard Bausch, 1993.

9062 I have come to tell the story of changes, bodies and beings, mortal and immortal, who make up this world and to tell how the world itself came to be. I measure my words against those of the deities; I honor the earth, our mother; the sun, our father; their children; and all holy people that make up the world. — *Tunkashila*, Gerald Hausman, 1993.

Storms

9063 As the storm broke and a shower of hail rattled like a handful of pebbles against our little window, I choked back a sob and edged my small green-painted stool a trifle nearer the hearth. — *The Romance of a Plain Man*, Ellen Glasgow, 1909.

9064 On a December night in the year 1906 a ferocious storm swept across our town. — *Harmer John*, Hugh Walpole, 1926.

9065 Out of the north Atlantic a January storm came down in the night, sweeping the American coast with wind and snow and sleet upon a great oblique front from Nova Scotia to the Delaware capes. — *The Plutocrat*, Booth Tarkington, 1927.

9066 God was grumbling his thunder and playing the zig-zag lightning thru his fingers. —*Jonah's Gourd Vine*, Zora Neale Hurston, 1934.

9067 The cocks had just heralded the break of day when the first clap of thunder burst above Black Valley. — *Famine*, Liam O'Flaherty, 1937.

9068 It was, as they were always afterwards to remember, a stormy day of early spring. — *For Ever Wilt Thou Love*, Ludwig Lewisohn, 1939.

9069 All day the sea had boomed in the rocks from the storm outside in the ocean. — *The Key of the Chest*, Neil M. Gunn, 1945.

9070 Suddenly ablaze with lightnings, the piled-up thundercloud swept northward across the tops of the mountains. — *Fire*, George R. Stewart, 1948.

9071 A storm was bearing down on our Cumberlands, sudden and ravenous. — *Daughter of the Hills*, Myra Page, 1950.

9072 The newspapers all said that heavy thunderstorms were general over the whole Midwest, from the Great Lakes on the north to the Ohio River on the south, and from the Pennsylvania border on the east to the Kansas steppes on the west. — *Vanity Row*, W. R. Burnett, 1952.

9073 A hurricane in the Caribbean Sea, nicknamed Felicity after the whimsical manner of meteorological officers, had made a brief and spectacular appearance as a series of closely packed concentric circles on all the weather charts of the world. — *The Four Winds*, David Beaty, 1955.

9074 The thunderstorm frightened a great many people in East Head. — *The Oracles*, Margaret Kennedy, 1955.

9075 As he breathed he tasted salt. — *The Sun Doctor*, Robert Shaw, 1959.

9076 By the brief unearthly glare of lightning flashes which steadily were becoming more vivid, Peter Vesey—Doctor of Medicine by virtue of degrees hard-earned at Oxford and Edinburgh Universities—could glimpse through a ragged pattern of trees a faint sheen created by the Upper Thames. — *Manila Galleon*, F. van Wyck Mason, 1961.

9077 When I went to bed, the sky was clouded over, lightning fluttered on and off, very nervous and jumpy, gusts of wind swirled up strong and then died, and thunder grumbled along steady on the horizon toward the river, where most of our storms come from. — *Two Roads to Guadalupé*, Robert Lewis Taylor, 1964.

9078 The storm, which for three days had spun in great, looping gusts from the Hatteras Cape, had worn itself out in the Carolina Low Country. — *Wind from the Carolinas*, Robert Wilder, 1964.

9079 The storm broke over the house. — *Washington, D.C.*, Gore Vidal, 1967.

9080 The summer storm that swept the meadows and set the peasants grumbling and shaking their heads, ceased as suddenly as it had begun. — *The Colors of Vaud*, Bryher, 1969.

9081 North-west over Squallacombe and Ricksey Ball the low sky, a sheet of beaten lead, was scored suddenly by a snake's tongue of lightning that struck eastwards towards the cloud-darkened heart of Exmoor. — *The Kingsford Mark*, Victor Canning, 1975.

9082 The night's storm had almost blown itself out, but ragged banners of black cloud were still flying on the dawn wind. — *The Heights of Rimring*, Duff Hart-Davis, 1980.

9083 After a warm thunderstorm, the old French Quarter was steaming like a Cajun bayou. — *Jazz, Jazz, Jazz*, Patrick Skene Catling, 1981.

9084 Doops was sitting on a dead cypress tree, uprooted years before by one of the hurricanes that periodically blow in from the gulf and wear themselves out as they seek to accomplish the same wrack in the thickets and timberlands as they inflict upon the towns and villages along the shoreline. — *The Glad River*, Will D. Campbell, 1982.

9085 Sam Bentinck remembered the day after the great storm, even better than the storm itself. — *Don Juan's New World*, Robin Hardy, 1985.

9086 Down in Georgia in the summer-fall the hurricane girls go by as if competing in a talent show for Miss Tropical Disturbance—Delia, Ethel, Flora that year, and then Gilda; all of us at the box in our Kustom-Kitchen watching her "slashing and clawing" at South Florida (after "casting her roving eye all over the Caribbean, making passes at every land mass from the Leeward Islands to Cuba," the anchor trying to

modernize the Weather Bulletin with some lubricity). — *Captain Bennett's Folly*, Berry Fleming, 1989.

9087 Munday lay still on the bed, harking to the storm's cold anger, its stern ecclesiastical wrath speaking out in fury against man. — *Gentlemen, I Address You Privately*, Kay Boyle, 1991.

9088 July in Mainsfield brought so many storms that grown men and women were counting *mississippis* between the flashes of lightning and the cracks of thunder. — *The Moralist of the Alphabet Streets*, Fabienne Marsh, 1991.

9089 On the Outer Banks of North Carolina there is a legend about the ships that have come to grief in the great autumn storms off those hungry shoals. — *Outer Banks*, Anne Rivers Siddons, 1991.

Strangers

9090 The Lord Justice-Clerk was a stranger in that part of the country; but his lady wife was known there from a child, as her race had been before her. — *Weir of Hermiston*, Robert Louis Stevenson, 1896.

9091 A person who differed from the local wayfarers was climbing the steep road which leads through the sea-skirted townlet definable as the Street of Wells, and forms a pass into that Gibraltar of Wessex, the singular peninsula once an island, and still called such, that stretches out like the head of a bird into the English Channel. — *The Well-Beloved*, Thomas Hardy, 1897.

9092 The stranger came early in February one wintry day, through a biting wind and a driving snow, the last snowfall of the year, over the down, walking as it seemed from Bramblehurst railway station and carrying a little black portmanteau in his thickly gloved hand. — *The Invisible Man*, H. G. Wells, 1897.

9093 It was past four o'clock on a sunny October day, when a stranger, who had ridden over the "corduroy" road between Applegate and Old Church, dismounted near the cross-roads before the small public house known to its frequenters as Bottom's Ordinary. — *The Miller of Old Church*, Ellen Glasgow, 1911.

9094 "No, my lord," Banks had replied, "no stranger has yet arrived. But I'll see if any one has come in — or who has." — *The Outcry*, Henry James, 1911.

9095 There were several outsiders in the club on this particular night. — *East of the Setting Sun*, George Barr McCutcheon, 1924.

9096 The middle-aged stranger whom I met by chance upon the lower rocks at Mary's Neck, that salt-washed promontory of the New England coast, was at first taciturn but became voluble when a little conversation developed the fact that we were both from the Midland country. — *Mary's Neck*, Booth Tarkington, 1932.

9097 My first impression was that the stranger's eyes were of an unusually light blue. — *The Last of Mr. Norris*, Christopher Isherwood, 1935.

9098 It was good corn-growing weather that July night when the stranger first came along, making his music through the hollow all the way up to Rosy Ridge. — *The Romance of Rosy Ridge*, MacKinlay Kantor, 1937.

9099 From the stairwell I could see the strangers in the kitchen while they could not see me. — *A Dream of Kings*, Davis Grubb, 1955.

9100 Strangers who arrived during the week supposed they had come to a large city, recently deserted. — *Wanderers Eastward, Wanderers West*, Kathleen Winsor, 1965.

9101 The horsemen were first seen crossing the quicksands of Morecambe Bay by Harry Martin and Boniface Baker, stableboys of Swarthmoor Hall. — *The Peaceable Kingdom*, Jan de Hartog, 1971.

9102 The people in the village left them alone. It was a remote part of Provence, the villagers were untravelled, unsophisticated, suspicious of strangers. — *The Silken Net*, Melvyn Bragg, 1974.

9103 Come a restorer to us, out of the Panhandle, in those days. Come back! — *Come, the Restorer*, William Goyen, 1974.

9104 I awoke in the middle of the night of January 17 and heard all fifty of our camp dogs howling their warning that strange men and dogs were coming toward us in the dark. — *Spirit Wrestler*, James Houston, 1980.

9105 They did not quite know what to make of each other, Juliet and the boy. They were very strange to each other. — *The Ivory Swing*, Janette Turner Hospital, 1982.

9106 Ike Tucker was adjusting the Knuckle's chain the day the stranger came asking for him. — *Tapping the Source*, Kem Nunn, 1984.

9107 There's a stranger in the street. — *The Fringe of Heaven*, Margaret Sutherland, 1984.

9108 At first Lauren had liked being new to London and not knowing a soul. — *Doctor Slaughter*, Paul Theroux, 1984.

9109 Long after the Fenian rising in Kilpeder in 1867, after both Robert Delaney and Ned Nolan were dead, after Ardmor had settled in Italy, at a time when only Hugh MacMahon was alive who knew one part of the story, and old Lionel Forrester who knew another part, a stranger to Kilpeder found himself given over, at

first without realising it, to fitting the pieces together. — *The Tenants of Time*, Thomas Flanagan, 1988.

9110 Staś had to admit that he felt out of place. — *Lone Stars*, Sophia Healy, 1989.

9111 They came from another country, it was clear, considering the way they entered the General Store. — *Indian Affairs*, Larry Woiwode, 1991.

Streets and Roads

9112 Early in October, 1832, a travelling-carriage stopped on the summit of that long descent where the road pitches from the elevated plain of Moudon, in Switzerland, to the level of the lake of Geneva, immediately above the little city of Vévey. — *The Headsman*, James Fenimore Cooper, 1833.

9113 Five-and-thirty years ago the glory had not yet departed from the old coach-roads: the great roadside inns were still brilliant with well-polished tankards, the smiling glances of pretty barmaids, and the repartees of jocose ostlers; the mail still announced itself by the merry notes of the horn; the hedge-cutter or the rick-thatcher might still know the exact hour by the unfailing yet otherwise meteoric apparition of the pea-green Tally-ho or the yellow Independent; and elderly gentlemen in pony-chaises, quartering nervously to make way for the rolling swinging swiftness, had not ceased to remark that times were finely changed since they used to see the pack-horses and hear the tinkling of their bells on this very highway. — *Felix Holt, the Radical*, George Eliot, 1866.

9114 Some years ago, at a time when the rapid growth of the city was changing the character of many localities, two young men were sitting, one afternoon early in April, in the parlor of a house on one of those streets which, without having yet accomplished their destiny as business thoroughfares, were no longer the homes of the decorous ease that once inhabited them. — *The Undiscovered Country*, William Dean Howells, 1880.

9115 Where the great highway of the Sierras nears the summit, and the pines begin to show sterile reaches of rock and waste in their drawn-up files, there are signs of occasional departures from the main road, as if the weary traveler had at times succumbed to the long ascent, and turned aside for rest and breath again. — "A Phyllis of the Sierras," Bret Harte, 1888.

9116 Where the San Leandro turnpike stretches its dusty, hot, and interminable length along the valley, at a point where the heat and dust have become intolerable, the monotonous expanse of wild oats on either side illimitable, and the distant horizon apparently remoter than ever, it suddenly slips between a stunted thicket or hedge of scrub oaks, which until that moment had been undistinguishable above the long, misty, quivering level of the grain. — *Susy*, Bret Harte, 1893.

9117 The old street, keeping its New England Sabbath afternoon so decently under its majestic elms, was as goodly an example of its sort as the late seventies of the century just gone could show. — *Bylow Hill*, George W. Cable, 1902.

9118 When I was young the road leading out of the heart of the Five Towns up to Toft End was nothing to me save a steep path toward fresh air and far horizons; but now that I have lived a little it seems the very avenue to a loving comprehension of human nature, and I climb it with a strange, overpowering, mystical sense of the wonder of existence. — *Whom God Hath Joined*, Arnold Bennett, 1906.

9119 There are old Parisians who will tell you pompously that the boulevards, like the political cafés, have ceased to exist, but this means only that the boulevards no longer gossip of Louis Napoleon, the Return of the Bourbons, or of General Boulanger, for these highways are always too busily stirring with present movements not to be forgetful of their yesterdays. — *The Guest of Quesnay*, Booth Tarkington, 1908.

9120 The maple-bordered street was as still as a country Sunday; so quiet that there seemed an echo to my footsteps. — *Beasley's Christmas Party*, Booth Tarkington, 1909.

9121 The way led along upon what had once been the embankment of a railroad. — *The Scarlet Plague*, Jack London, 1915.

9122 The Street stretched away north and south in two lines of ancient houses that seemed to meet in the distance. *K.*, Mary Roberts Rinehart, 1915.

9123 As the streets that lead from the Strand to the Embankment are very narrow, it it better not to walk down them arm-in-arm. — *The Voyage Out*, Virginia Woolf, 1915.

9124 Certain streets have an atmosphere of their own, a sort of universal fame and the particular affection of their citizens. — *The Arrow of Gold*, Joseph Conrad, 1919.

9125 The hot, bright street looked almost deserted. — *The Narrow House*, Evelyn Scott, 1921.

9126 Cedartown sits beside a great highway which was once a buffalo trail. — *A Lantern in Her Hand*, Bess Streeter Aldrich, 1928.

9127 The rider slowed and stopped as he topped the little rise, and looked through close-lidded eyes along the desert track, following it as it meandered over the straighter, more direct openings through sage, cactus, and greasewood, at times wavering and thinning in the quivering iridescence of heat waves streaming up from the hot desert floor. — *Mesquite Jenkins*, Clarence E. Mulford, 1928.

9128 In 1850, the road to Boonville wound out of the Tug Hill country through long stretches of soft wood. — *Rome Haul*, Walter D. Edmonds, 1929.

9129 Opal Street, as streets go, is no jewel of the first water. — *Plum Bun*, Jessie Redmon Fauset, 1929.

9130 The traffic of Dockland, where my omnibus stopped, loosened into a broadway. There the vans and lorries, released from the congestion of narrow streets, opened out and made speed in an uproar of iron-shod wheels and hooves on granite blocks. — *All Our Yesterdays*, H. M. Tomlinson, 1930.

9131 Peter Pentecost, from his eyrie among the hazels, looked down on the King's highway as it dipped from Stowood through the narrow pass to the Wood Eaton meadows. — *The Blanket of the Dark*, John Buchan, 1931.

9132 The road from the village, after keeping low by the white sands of the river, climbed a steep ridge, and ran for some distance on the top of it. — *The Brothers*, L. A. G. Strong, 1932.

9133 Between the villages of Aubière and Romagnat in the ancient Province of Auvergne there is an old road that comes suddenly over the top of a high hill. — *Anthony Adverse*, Hervey Allen, 1933.

9134 The road from Vinehall meets the road from Leasan at Superstition Corner. A few yards farther on, the London road runs off westward through Harlot's Wood, while the road to Hastings winds southward down the hill, past Newhouse and Doucegrove, deep into the valley of the River Tillingham. — *Superstition Corner*, Sheila Kaye-Smith, 1934.

9135 The street led from the Friday mosque down to the park. — *Omar Khayyam*, Harold Lamb, 1934.

9136 In 1870 York Road ran rich with life, the whole nine miles of it teeming, from the salt marsh up Grou'nut Hill and along the flats to Claypit, down into the sands past the school building, over Dockham's bridge and by the Selden Hill Dam, up Rolling Rock Hill and around the turn past Captain's eddy and the blind lane leading only to Mount Assabenbeduc, then on to the Nubble Point where the meeting-house stood. — *A Few Foolish Ones*, Gladys Hasty Carroll, 1935.

9137 From my window, the deep solemn massive street. — *Goodbye to Berlin*, Christopher Isherwood, 1939.

9138 In days gone by the only way from Woodhorn to Potcommon was down Ember Lane as far as Four Legged Crouch and then up the hill past Egypt Farm to what is now the crossroads by the market place. — *Ember Lane*, Sheila Kaye-Smith, 1940.

9139 The sun having set, the streets of the little city were bright but shadowless. — *Come Back to Erin*, Sean O'Faolain, 1940.

9140 Twisting its way among fat bluffs, the Highway reaches the Sioux River, crosses it, and enters eastern South Dakota. — *The Golden Bowl*, Frederick Manfred *as* Feike Feikema, 1944.

9141 From the top of the hill where the boy lay, his thin, vibrant body half hidden by an overhanging shelf of rock, there was a long, clear view of the road from Jerusalem. Unthreading itself from the knotted mass of gray-green mountains on the south, it coiled downward in a thin, white ribbon out of the distant foothills; then, passing over the broad, flat triangle of the great Plain of Esdraelon, it suddenly straightened itself like a curtain cord drawn taut, baring the stage for its ceaseless pageant of the centuries. — *The Brother*, Dorothy Clarke Wilson, 1944.

9142 As soon as he entered Portland, Logan Stuart stabled his horse at the Fashion Livery on Oak and retraced his way along Front Street toward the express office. — *Canyon Passage*, Ernest Haycox, 1945.

9143 To get there you follow Highway 58, going northeast out of the city, and it is a good highway and new. Or was new, that day we went up it. — *All the King's Men*, Robert Penn Warren, 1946.

9144 Edward Burgess came out of the narrow side street and picked his way through a scattered litter of paving blocks where the street menders had been at work. — *The Chasm*, Victor Canning, 1947.

9145 Forty-two miles below San Ysidro, on a great north-south highway in California, there is a crossroad which for eighty-odd years has been called Rebel Corners. — *The Wayward Bus*, John Steinbeck, 1947.

9146 There is a lovely road that runs from Ixopo into the hills. — *Cry, the Beloved Country*, Alan Paton, 1948.

9147 There couldn't be a colder — a lonelier place in the whole world, thought Margy Shannon, than a deserted Brooklyn street on a Saturday night. — *Tomorrow Will Be Better*, Betty Smith, 1948.

9148 Until 1929 the road between Douro and Castalia remained unpaved. — *The Sign of Jonah*, Nancy Hale, 1950.

9149 The sunlight of late September filled the pale, formal streets between Portland Place and Manchester Square. — *The Tortoise and the Hare*, Elizabeth Jenkins, 1954.

9150 Abraham's Path, which ran east from the old Common Pasture and through the woods, then doubled north around the inner reaches of the salt marsh and made its way eastward again out of the trees and onto the open headland of Shipman's Point, is nearly forgotten in the village. — *Race Rock*, Peter Matthiessen, 1954.

9151 Franc watched the tiny head and shoulders of a man jogging toward the towngate along the path in the wheat, and at the same time he tried not to take his eye off the dust cloud, south, where the road went down toward Rome. — *Warden of the Smoke and Bells*, Richard Llewellyn, 1956.

9152 The path which led from the village of Hillsborough to the farms of Sandy Creek was seldom travelled; on the vaguely marked trail the grass was high and wet with rain. — *The Wind in the Forest*, Inglis Fletcher, 1957.

9153 The tangled path across the wasteyard behind old St. Barnabas serpentined beneath high clumps of gorse and splintered branches. It stopped abruptly in front of the iron railings which marked the Church's boundary. — *The Game*, Michael Hastings, 1957.

9154 The road mounted straight ahead of him. It topped the horizon against a brassy noonday sky. — *The Innocent*, Madison Jones, 1957.

9155 Sambuco./ Of the drive from Salerno to Sambuco, Nagel's *Italy* has this to say: "The road is hewn nearly the whole way in the cliffs of the coast...." — *Set This House on Fire*, William Styron, 1960.

9156 The path was rough and narrow but well defined. It climbed a gentle slope, the trees pressing in on either side, leaning over it, dangling feathery creepers and broken, dead branches above it, endlessly carpeting it with leaves. — *An Affair of Men*, Errol Brathwaite, 1961.

9157 He was facing Seventh Avenue, at Times Square. — *Another Country*, James Baldwin, 1962.

9158 The road was a thin streak through the rain jungle. It looked like a lancet wound which went deep and ran even. — *The 480*, Eugene Burdick, 1964.

9159 They rode through the lush farm country in the middle of autumn, through quaint old towns whose streets showed the brilliant colors of turning trees. — *I Never Promised You a Rose Garden*, Joanne Greenberg *as* Hannah Green, 1964.

9160 If you stand, today, in Between Towns Road, you can see either way: west to the spires and towers of the cathedral and colleges; east to

the yards and sheds of the motor works. You see different worlds, but there is no frontier between them; there is only the movement and traffic of a single city. — *Second Generation*, Raymond Williams, 1964.

9161 In the heart of the West End, there are many quiet pockets, unknown to almost all but taxi drivers who traverse them with expert knowledge, and arrive triumphantly thereby at Park Lane, Berkeley Square, or South Audley Street. — *At Bertram's Hotel*, Agatha Christie, 1965.

9162 First I will write:/ When I go home I walk through all the dim two-family-house streets where the colors are brown and gray with what they call cream trim. — *Bridgeport Bus*, Maureen Howard, 1965.

9163 For some time now the road had been deserted, white and scorching yet, though the sun was already reddening the western sky. — *The Orchard Keeper*, Cormac McCarthy, 1965.

9164 As they turned into Upshot Rise where his parents lived, Jack let go of Ruth's hand. Upshot Rise was not a hand-holding street. — *Mate in Three*, Bernice Rubens, 1965.

9165 The road from Boston to Cape Cod is long and straight and ruthless. — *The Room Upstairs*, Monica Dickens, 1966.

9166 Eustace Chisholm's street, with the Home for the Incurables to the south and the streetcar line to the west, extended east up to blue immense choppy Lake Michigan. — *Eustace Chisholm and the Works*, James Purdy, 1967.

9167 The road lay like a length of black tape across the desert. — *Welcome to Xanadu*, Nathaniel Benchley, 1968.

9168 The lower section of the road the woman was traveling, the winding stretch that lay at the very bottom of the old, soaring cathedral of a hill, had washed away as usual in the heavy, unseasonable rain that had fallen the night before. — *The Chosen Place, the Timeless People*, Paule Marshall, 1969.

9169 All summer long the Cape roads are busy with cars going up and down, taking mothers and aunts to market and children to the shore. — *Mia*, Robert Nathan, 1970.

9170 It was Sunday, the street empty, the canal black under a louring sky. — *Levkas Man*, Hammond Innes, 1971.

9171 I can't believe I'm on this road again, twisting along past the lake where the white birches are dying, the disease is spreading up from the south, and I notice they now have seaplanes for hire. — *Surfacing*, Margaret Atwood, 1972.

9172 The street lay like a snake sleeping; dull-dusty, gray-black in the dingy darkness. — *South Street*, David Bradley, 1975.

9173 The only place where you can get a vodka martini in Shepford is just by the M. 1 slip

road, ambitiously described in the official guide-book as the Highway to Europe. — *Billy Liar on the Moon*, Keith Waterhouse, 1975.

9174 Along this overused coast of Connecticut, the beach was a relatively obscure one, reached by a narrow asphalt road kept in only fair repair and full of unexplained forks and windings and turnings-off. — *Marry Me*, John Updike, 1976.

9175 Daemon Wente Waye you could see from the Whitechapel Road, going over the rise between the bombed streets never rebuilt after the war, turning down Cinnamon Alley, and along King David's Lane, toward dear pale-tea Thames, bubbling all the way across to the South Bank, sometimes with a coaster steaming west for the Pool, often with a string of barges under brown sails, east to the Estuary, and ever, thankfully, with a wonderful sense of going home. — *Tell Me Now, and Again*, Richard Llewellyn, 1977.

9176 *As soon as you cross the town line from Afton to Stonecrop there's no need of a sign to tell you so: the road gets bumpy and narrow.* — *Stonecrop*, Teo Savory, 1977.

9177 Olumati reached the main road and turned right. That way the road led to Isiali, half a day's journey away. — *The Slave*, Elechi Amadi, 1978.

9178 The back streets of Stepney was where it all began. — *Maggie*, Lena Kennedy, 1979.

9179 At the end of Trinity Street, the path grew old and crooked, like cobblestones, with grass and frilled weeds and clover and dandelions springing out between the cracks. — *The Skaters' Waltz*, Philip Norman, 1979.

9180 The highroad between Los Angeles, City of the Angels, and Las Vegas, City Without Clocks, cuts through the mountains and across the desert for a distance of three hundred miles. — *Nick the Greek*, Harry Mark Petrakis, 1979.

9181 The highway entering Salt Lake City from the west curves around the southern end of Great Salt Lake past Black Rock and the ratty beaches, swings north away from the smoke of the smelter towns, veers toward the dry lake bed where a long time ago the domes of the Saltair Pavilion used to rise like an Arabic exhalation, and straightens out eastward again. — *Recapitulation*, Wallace Stegner, 1979.

9182 "Which road this afternoon, madam?"/ "The same, Teakle — the one we took yesterday." — *The Twyborn Affair*, Patrick White, 1979.

9183 Then came a long gentle curve in the highway, like the bottom of an arabic letter. — *The Family of Max Desir*, Robert Ferro, 1983.

9184 Down a long road all sun and shadowy with trees overhead and a slow look from cows across a fence and you're there. — *The Treatment and the Cure*, Peter Kocan, 1983.

9185 In all Christendom I have seen no highway to compare with this, the great highway in the heart of Akbar's Mogul Empire — four hundred miles of broad tree-lined avenue running from Lahore to Agra. — *Lord of the Dance*, Robin Lloyd-Jones, 1983.

9186 From Heaven it has a certain symmetry, this synapse, where the Cloverleaf appears as two pair of perfect buttocks, a cluster of genes which coyly holds the history of our future within its simple fastness. Here in four respective swales, grow four groves of twice-planted pin oak, the curious inflorescent leaves of which at improbable maturity, will photosynthesize all the emissions we can manage. — *White Jazz*, Charles Newman, 1984.

9187 Quite soon after I left Richmond station I turned into a quiet street where the snow was almost undisturbed and, climbing higher, I came to a road that appeared to be deserted. — *The Juniper Tree*, Barbara Comyns, 1985.

9188 As it neared Odawara the highway from Yedo sloped up through the riverside marshes to cross the plain rolling away towards jagged mountains and on to the far-distant Imperial Capital. — *Yedo*, Lynn Guest, 1985.

9189 For what seem to him not very good reasons, he lives on the Street of the Cat Who Fishes, reputed to be the shortest, narrowest street in the world. — *Rat Man of Paris*, Paul West, 1986.

9190 Didi recognized the street as soon as he stepped into it, though now he saw it from a different angle. — *Blue Mountain*, Margaret Gaan, 1987.

9191 Telegraph Avenue shone and clattered like a street fair in the afternoon sun. — *Out of Danger*, Suzanne Lipsett, 1987.

9192 On the first lap of the march, the demonstrators took over the southbound lanes of Highway 95, twenty miles north of Boston. — *The Saviors*, Helen Yglesias, 1987.

9193 The road was dry, dusty, and pock-marked with potholes. — *A Border Station*, Shane Connaughton, 1989.

9194 The house was half a mile east of town on a two-lane road that clung to the contours of the land, rising and falling with the peaks and valleys, a continuous double yellow line down its center because there was never enough view of the road ahead to make passing safe. — *Frigor Mortis*, Ralph McInerny, 1989.

9195 Frost and thin mist afflicted the street outside. — *Vacant Places*, Stanley Middleton, 1989.

9196 She wasn't sure she had the right street. — *A Lot to Make Up For*, John Buell, 1990.

9197 Fliegelman walked the granite canyons that held his city. — *Fliegelman's Desire*, Lewis Buzbee, 1990.

9198 Along the trade route that linked the towns of the Chickasaw nation with the river called Father of Waters there lay a wild and dark swamp that was sacred to the Chickasaw people. — *A Story of Deep Delight*, Thomas McNamee, 1990.

9199 The highway is called by some, Route 27, and by others, the Montauk Highway, but by most, just "the Highway," because it is the only way in or out of the Hamptons. — *A House in the Hamptons*, Gloria Nagy, 1990.

9200 In the beginning there was a river. The river became a road and the road branched out to the whole world. And because the road was once a river it was always hungry. — *The Famished Road*, Ben Okri, 1991.

9201 How many times have I followed the road down the mountain we call Big Top, steep and curved enough to make the gravel trucks shift groaning into first, and twist past Middleman, which is hardly bigger than five houses set back in the woods. — *Revelations*, Sophy Burnham, 1992.

9202 Warrior Road led to the river or to town, depending on which way you were going. — *Night Ride Home*, Vicki Covington, 1992.

9203 Upper Main Street in the village of North Bath, just above the town's two-block-long business district, was quietly residential for three more blocks, then became even more quietly rural along old Route 27A, a serpentine two-lane blacktop that snaked its way through the Adirondacks of northern New York, with their tiny, down-at-the-heels resort towns, all the way to Montreal and prosperity. — *Nobody's Fool*, Richard Russo, 1993.

9204 *South of Lupine, the highway ascended rapidly, curving in broad swaths along the rim of the valley.* — *More Than Allies*, Sandra Scofield, 1993.

Structures

9205 At the northern extremity of the small town which bears its name, situated at the head of Lake Erie, stands, or rather stood — for the fortifications then existing were subsequently destroyed — the small fortress of Amherstburg. — *The Canadian Brothers*, John Richardson, 1840.

9206 Towards the west end of Grove Street, in Carlingford, on the shabby side of the street, stood a red brick building, presenting a pinched gable terminated by a curious little belfry, not intended for any bell, and looking not unlike a handle to lift up the edifice by to the public obser-

vation. — *Salem Chapel*, Margaret Oliphant *as* Mrs. Oliphant, 1863.

9207 An ancient English Cathedral Tower? How can the ancient English Cathedral Tower be here! — *The Mystery of Edwin Drood (unfinished)*, Charles Dickens, 1870.

9208 Alone and desolate, within hearing of the thunder of the waters of the North Sea, but not upon them, stand the ruins of Ramborough Abbey. — *Joan Haste*, H. Rider Haggard, 1895.

9209 On one corner stood the house of Monsieur Garon the avocat; on another, the shop of the Little Chemist; on another, the office of Medallion the auctioneer; and on the last, the Hotel Louis Quinze. — *When Valmond Came to Pontiac*, Gilbert Parker, 1895.

9210 The people of the little Kentucky capital do not often honor the gray walls of their state-house. — *The Kentuckians*, John Fox, Jr., 1897.

9211 The lonely station of Manzanita stood out, sharp and unsightly, in the keen February sunlight. — *Success*, Samuel Hopkins Adams, 1921.

9212 The towers of Zenith aspired above the morning mist; austere towers of steel and cement and limestone, sturdy as cliffs and delicate as silver rods. — *Babbitt*, Sinclair Lewis, 1922.

9213 The building of the large hall had been brought about by people who gave no thought to the wonder of moving from one space to another and up and down stairs. — *Revolving Lights*, Dorothy M. Richardson, 1923.

9214 Quite a number of years ago there was an old rickety building on the rock above Seatown in Polchester, and it was one of a number in an old grass-grown square known as Pontippy Square. — *The Old Ladies*, Hugh Walpole, 1924.

9215 From the turnstile where the tickets were taken, a passage covered by striped red and white awning led to the hall of the Coliseum. The cement floor of this passage was wet from many muddy footprints, and an icy draft raced through it with a speed greater than that of the swift horses within. — *Whiteoaks of Jalna*, Mazo de la Roche, 1929.

9216 One of the fruits of Emancipation in the West Indian islands is the number of the ruins, either attached to the houses that remain or within a stone's throw of them: ruined slaves' quarters, ruined sugar-grinding houses, ruined boiling houses; often ruined mansions that were too expensive to maintain. — *A High Wind in Jamaica*, Richard Hughes, 1929.

9217 Shibi Rest Camp on the Niger was built by Bradgate, then assistant resident, about 1912. He wanted to make his station there, but the doctors refused to pass the site on account of the swamps close behind which fill it with mosquitoes. — *Aissa Saved*, Joyce Cary, 1932.

9218 The proud skyline of The Wall was slowly drawn across the darkness, at first faintly in gray on gray, and then in transparent blue on gold. — *Bonfire*, Dorothy Canfield Fisher, 1933.

9219 The Schoolhouse was not a schoolhouse, and the Valley was not a valley. — *The Valley*, Nathan Asch, 1935.

9220 Wind and rain and summer's sun had turned the log stage station a silver gray. — *Sundown Jim*, Ernest Haycox, 1938.

9221 From the outside the building was — just a building. It was not beautiful, but it impressed one by its sheer massivity. — "The Party at Jack's," Thomas Wolfe, 1939.

9222 The Treloar Building was, and is, on Olive Street, near Sixth, on the west side. — *The Lady in the Lake*, Raymond Chandler, 1943.

9223 Gormenghast, that is, the main massing of the original stone, taken by itself would have displayed a certain ponderous architectural quality were it possible to have ignored the circumfusion of those mean dwellings that swarmed like an epidemic around its Outer Walls. — *Titus Groan*, Mervyn Peake, 1946.

9224 The thin streak of silver along the water line to the east touched the tops of the great swells rolling into the cove and outlined the roof of the only building on the shore, a fishhouse. — *West of the Hill*, Gladys Hasty Carroll, 1949.

9225 The building presented a not unpleasant architectural scheme, the banks of wide windows reflecting golden sunlight, the browned weathered brick façade, the ivy clinging to the brick and framing the windows. — *The Blackboard Jungle*, Evan Hunter, 1954.

9226 Early on a cold morning in February Joseph Parks arrived at the county courthouse, an adequate stone structure he had hardly noticed before but which now interested him enormously. — *The Simple Truth*, Elizabeth Hardwick, 1955.

9227 The Citadel of Troizen, where the Palace stands, was built by giants before anyone remembers. — *The King Must Die*, Mary Renault, 1958.

9228 The tower. Driving 61, up from New Orleans, you could see it ten miles out: straight and sharp and converging to spearpoint, flagpole spurting out of the point and into the sky, the sky maybe flame-blue with sun or maybe tomb-gray with rain clouds hung low and dark over the the low dark country. — *Ada Dallas*, Wirt Williams, 1959.

9229 There's no use pretending that Government House architecturally has anything to recommend it at all because it hasn't; it is quite agreeable inside with nice airy rooms and deep-set verandahs, but outside it is unequivocally hideous. Viewed from any aspect it looks like a gargantuan mauve blancmange. — *Pomp and Circumstance*, Noël Coward, 1960.

9230 A few stones still lie in the heather at a crossroads on the long southern slopes of Exmoor. They are all that is left of a hut which once stood there, offering shelter for poor people on the roads. — *A Night in Cold Harbor*, Margaret Kennedy, 1960.

9231 Crossing the road by the bombed-out public house on the corner and pondering the mystery which dominates vistas framed by a ruined door, I felt for some reason glad the place had not yet been rebuilt. — *Casanova's Chinese Restaurant*, Anthony Powell, 1960.

9232 The Madison-Mayfair Agency was in a new building, just off Curzon Street, that Sterndale had never seen before. It looked like all the others, he decided sourly. — *The Shapes of Sleep*, J. B. Priestley, 1962.

9233 It was an out-of-date town hall in an up-to-date progressive college town in a midwestern state. The corridor was long and dark with narrow benches at intervals against the wall, and a brass cuspidor by each bench. — *Joy in the Morning*, Betty Smith, 1963.

9234 It is still called Papa John's. — *The Feast of Saint Barnabas*, Jesse Hill Ford, 1969.

9235 I come into the red wooden showerhouse. It is up on piles to keep snakes — cobras, vipers — from crawling up the drains. — *Coming Home*, George Davis, 1971.

9236 In Parliament Square at night there is the building like a battleship and the Abbey like a toad and the starred sky unseen as if security or long grass were hiding it. — *Natalie Natalia*, Nicholas Mosley, 1971.

9237 The stone skeleton of the old Wheal Garth engine housing came at me out of the dark, its chimney pointing a gaunt finger at the night. — *The Golden Soak*, Hammond Innes, 1973.

9238 The wall is straight at that point, although later he would always think of it as curved. — *People Will Always Be Kind*, Wilfrid Sheed, 1973.

9239 Cold wind swirled the fallen snow in the avenue where their hired cab passed. The sky to the east was black, to the west the sun blazed between lowering clouds and the gentle hills they had traveled that afternoon, casting brilliant light on the white government buildings, some still fire-blackened above the windows, others under construction with scaffolding and piles of numbered stones before them; enough, it seemed to the girl, for the Pyramids. — *The Land Where the Sun Dies*, Henry Carlisle, 1975.

9240 "I call this a pretty fair plant," Ben Tate said, knowing he exaggerated. — *The Last Valley*, A. B. Guthrie, Jr., 1975.

9241 In those days we used to have a red-and-white garden swing set up in the back-yard

beside the garage, a noisy outbuilding of rusty corrugated metal stamped in shivering, wave-like sheets, which rumbled with theatrical thunder when the wind blew hard. — *The Swing in the Garden*, Hugh Hood, 1975.

9242 Walls./ Only there weren't any tops to them now. — *Tobias and the Angel*, Frank Yerby, 1975.

9243 The rot began when they removed the railings. — *The Second Mrs. Whitberg*, Chaim Bermant, 1976.

9244 The enormous building waited as though braced to defend itself, standing back resolutely from its great courtyard under a frozen January sky, colourless, cloudless, leafless and pigeonless. — *The Golden Child*, Penelope Fitzgerald, 1977.

9245 To most of the outside world, the Pentagon is a huge five-sided pile of cement, looming squat and commanding on the Virginia bank of the Potomac River across from Washington, D.C. — *Cold Is the Sea*, Edward L. Beach, 1978.

9246 Richie Flynn went up to look at the synagogue the day after Fowler had spoken to him about it. — *Made in America*, Peter Maas, 1979.

9247 At precisely five minutes after five o'clock, on a certain sun-dappled June day in our time, the Montauk Lighthouse, which had sent forth the first reassuring signals of candlepower to thousands of hoodeyed sea captains following their stars and compasses along the North Atlantic bridgeways to America, quite suddenly developed a crack at the base of its red-and-white, candy-striped tower. — *The Montauk Fault*, Herbert Mitgang, 1981.

9248 In the beginning the two tall gate-towers of medieval Avignon, the Gog and Magog of its civic life, were called *Quiquenparle* and *Quiquengrogne*. — *Constance*, Lawrence Durrell, 1982.

9249 The building was broad and squat and thick, designed to house a substance that was heavy and unwieldy and potentially hazardous, as dense and inert as the granite blocks that had been quarried to contain it. — *State's Evidence*, Stephen Greenleaf, 1982.

9250 The Waynesboro Female College in the eighteen fifties and sixties was a fitting subject, along with the Court House, the churches, the "gentlemen's mansions," for a steel engraving of the sort then fashionable. — *"...And Ladies of the Club,"* Helen Hooven Santmyer, 1982.

9251 In 1969 I had my first opportunity to catch a glimpse of the Wailing Wall, about which I had heard so much. — *The Penitent*, Isaac Bashevis Singer, 1983.

9252 The Magistrates' Court in Port Morris is down a side street, in a converted swimming baths; the façade of the building has no pretensions to legal grandeur. — *Banana Cat*, Christopher Hood, 1985.

9253 The tenement was over a hundred years old. It faced the street with its grey granite stone, and its old windows which in order to be cleaned had to be manoeuvred on ropes like glassy sails, and its greenish door on which passing boys and men had scrawled graffiti. — *The Tenement*, Iain Crichton Smith, 1985.

9254 The Building is huge, a grotesque magnificence. — *The Building*, Thomas Glynn, 1986.

9255 At the turn of the eighteenth century, there stood on a side-road three quarters of a mile outside the old gates of Düsseldorf the ruins of an Abbey built in the perpendicular Gothic style. — *The Abbey in the Wood*, Antony Lambton, 1986.

9256 The massive skeleton of the empty Greenhouse stood alone on a cold November night. — *The Greenhouse*, Susan Hillmore, 1988.

9257 The building is pink, bright pink. — *The Boys and Their Baby*, Larry Wolff, 1988.

9258 The medical buildings in Richmond were packed together like components on a circuit board. — *Wilderness*, Dennis Danvers, 1991.

9259 Or look at *that* bugger, then. — *Now You Know*, Michael Frayn, 1992.

Success

9260 It must be allowed in the world, that a man who has thrice reached the highest station of life, in his line, has a good right to set forth the particulars of the discretion and prudence by which he lifted himself so far above the ordinaries of his day and generation; indeed, the generality of mankind may claim this as a duty; for the conduct of public men, as it has been often wisely said, is a species of public property, and their rules and observances have in all ages been considered things of a national concernment. — *The Provost*, John Galt, 1822.

9261 It was admitted by all her friends, and also by her enemies — who were in truth the more numerous and active body of the two — that Lizzie Greystock had done very well with herself. — *The Eustace Diamonds*, Anthony Trollope, 1872.

9262 I knew nothing about what General Melville A. Goodwin had done in Berlin until I read of his feat in my own script shortly before going on the air one evening in October 1949. — *Melville Goodwin, USA*, John P. Marquand, 1951.

9263 I was on the whole very pleased with my day — not many conflicts and worries, above all

not too much self-criticism. I had done almost all the things I wanted to do, and as a result I felt heroic and satisfied. — *Grateful to Life and Death*, R. K. Narayan, 1953.

9264 Well, sir, I should have been sitting pretty, just about as pretty as a man could sit. — *Pop. 1280*, Jim Thompson, 1964.

9265 All right, wifey, maybe I'm a big pain in the you-know-what but after I've given you a recitation of the troubles I had to go through to make good in America between 1935 and more or less now, 1967, and although I also know everybody in the world's had his own troubles, you'll understand that my particular form of anguish came from being too sensitive to all the lunkheads I had to deal with just so I could get to be a high school football star, a college student pouring coffee and washing dishes and scrimmaging till dark and reading Homer's *Iliad* in three days all at the same time, and God help me, a W R I T E R whose very "success," far from being a happy triumph as of old, was the sign of doom Himself. (Insofar as nobody loves my dashes anyway, I'll use regular punctuation for the new illiterate generation.) — *Vanity of Duluoz*, Jack Kerouac, 1968.

9266 Teresa wrote saying that Judith had been a sensational success in London, that she was very happy, and that she had bought a house in Kensington. — *Judith*, James T. Farrell, 1969.

9267 "Thata boy, come on now, thata boy . . . thata boy . . . thata boy . . . *there* we go . . . thata Boy!" — *The Promisekeeper*, Charles Newman, 1971.

9268 Now I believe they will leave me alone. — *Angle of Repose*, Wallace Stegner, 1971.

9269 "That's eet, that's eet! Yo'm found eet, yo' bugger! Yis, that's eet!" — *Coming from Behind*, Howard Jacobson, 1983.

9270 It had been one of Susan's most successful evenings. — *Stanley and the Women*, Kingsley Amis, 1984.

9271 By God, he had done it! — *Masterpiece*, Thomas Hoving, 1986.

9272 "Congratulations." — *The World as It Is*, Norma Klein, 1989.

9273 It had been an auspicious week for Capitan Rodrigo José Figueras. — *The War of Don Emmanuel's Nether Parts*, Louis de Bernières, 1990.

9274 Billy Brand distinguished himself on the very first day. — *Billy Brazil*, Emilio DeGrazia, 1992.

Suffering

9275 Painfully hungry, achingly sleepy, hot, uncomfortable, ignored, Esteban had given up even crying. — *Sparks Fly Upward*, Oliver La Farge, 1931.

9276 It was cold and the sun was a pale blaze hurting his eyes and all the morning was loud with birds. — *An Odor of Sanctity*, Frank Yerby, 1965.

9277 Do we always return to the place where we have suffered the most? — *Beyond Defeat*, Ellen Glasgow, 1966.

9278 We have not far to look for suffering. — *The Desert*, Allen Wheelis, 1970.

9279 When I was seventeen and in full obedience to my heart's most urgent commands, I stepped far from the pathway of normal life and in a moment's time ruined everything I loved — I loved so deeply, and when the love was interrupted, when the incorporeal body of love shrank back in terror and my own body was locked away, it was hard for others to believe that a life so new could suffer so irrevocably. — *Endless Love*, Scott Spencer, 1979.

9280 For almost a year Dexter Fairchild had been suffering from a growing discrepancy between the turbulence of his private state of mind and the continued placidity of his outward demeanor. — *Watchfires*, Louis Auchincloss, 1982.

9281 I'm suffocating. — *Catherine, Her Book*, John Wheatcroft, 1983.

9282 Suffering puts a gloss on certain women. — *Foreign Bodies*, Barbara Grizzuti Harrison, 1984.

9283 The dog was suffering, mainly from old age. — *Straight Cut*, Madison Smartt Bell, 1986.

9284 These days, if you are a German you spend your time in Purgatory before you die, in earthly suffering for all your country's unpunished and unrepented sins, until the day when, with the aid of the prayers of the Powers — or three of them, anyway — Germany is finally purified. — *A German Requiem*, Philip Kerr, 1991.

Suicide

9285 "Thrust from the bloody bowels of woman and driven into the black, perpetual hiding place called death — with little between but blood and women and solitude —" said Finnley Wren, drawing a line of the tablecloth with

his knife—"sometimes I am so terrified of life that I come near putting an end to it as a boon to my dreadful little nerves...."—*Finnley Wren*, Philip Wylie, 1934.

9286 In Paris, in the spring of our times, a young girl was about to throw herself into the Seine.—"Love of Seven Dolls," Paul Gallico, 1954.

9287 It might have happened anywhere, at any time, and it could certainly have been a good deal worse.—*The Sea Change*, Elizabeth Jane Howard, 1959.

9288 The moment he decided to commit suicide, Edgar began to live in the present. It was, for him, a novel sensation.—*Living in the Present*, John Wain, 1960.

9289 I had even reached the point of wondering if Geraldine Brevoort's suicide, so long dreaded, might not prove in the event a relief, but like everything else about Geraldine, when it came, it came with a nasty twist.—*Portrait in Brownstone*, Louis Auchincloss, 1962.

9290 Several years ago, during the spring semester of my junior year in college, as an alternative to either deserting or marrying a girl, I signed a suicide pact with her.—*The Sterile Cuckoo*, John Nichols, 1965.

9291 Madame Dieudonné arose, stark and stripped, in her underground villa at 0600 as was her wont, turned on the shortwave radio and heard the report from Laos that Captain Clancy was dead, then she walked, still naked, to her jewel box, removed a small, black, heavy object, raised it to her head and blew her pretty French brains out. Pas vrai. Not true.—*The Bamboo Bed*, William Eastlake, 1969.

9292 Harold Chasen stepped up on the chair and placed the noose about his neck.—*Harold and Maude*, Colin Higgins, 1971.

9293 When you consider what Nadia eventually became it is extraordinary anyone ever thought she had once tried to throw herself off the Great Pyramid.—*Kith*, P. H. Newby, 1977.

9294 Miss Hawkins looked at her watch. It was two-thirty. If everything went according to schedule, she could safely reckon to be dead by six o'clock.—*Favours*, Bernice Rubens, 1979.

9295 At the age of eighty-seven, Erica March died in a cupboard. She wrapped her body in a chenille tablecloth, laid it out neatly under the few skirts and dresses that still hung on the clothes rail and put it to death very quietly, pill by pill.—*The Cupboard*, Rose Tremain, 1981.

9296 Sebastian Holiday read the note in his hand for the twentieth time with pride in his hollow senses when he came to the three phrases—"Wish I were like you. Love you. You and Mary please take care of John."—*The Angel at the Gate*, Wilson Harris, 1982.

9297 You're not going to like this, but some years ago, in the family room of the house where I grew up in Lake Success, New York, my mother cancelled an unrelenting life by plunging her head through the twenty-six-inch screen of a Motorola color television.—*Inner Tube*, Hob Brown, 1985.

9298 *She had been waiting for a sign to release her into death, now the sign was granted.*—*You Must Remember This*, Joyce Carol Oates, 1987.

9299 Maybe it comes from living in San Francisco, city of clammy humors and foghorns that warn and warn—omen, o-o-men, o dolorous omen, o dolors of omens—and not enough sun, but Wittman Ah Sing considered suicide every day.—*Tripmaster Monkey*, Maxine Hong Kingston, 1989.

9300 "*CRAZY!* Good God, Turner, this is *CRAZY*—absolutely *CRAZY*—finally having my life come down to me parked across these railroad tracks by a stormy, surging Irish Sea, lightning bolts streaking the sky, in the green Jaguar sedan with the canoe still atop it—Bach's 'Sleepers Awake' booming out over my tapedeck (E. Power Biggs on the organ)—gargling down this last bottle of Irish wine, drunk blissfully out of my mind, and waiting for the train from Kilcoole to come roaring round the bend and end it all with a bang!..."—*Irish Wine*, Dick Wimmer, 1989.

9301 An hour before he shot himself, my best friend Philip Strayhorn called to talk about thumbs.—*A Child Across the Sky*, Jonathan Carroll, 1990.

Suspicion

9302 Very little was known about George, the Dalmatian, and the servants in the house of Angelo Beroviero, as well as the workmen of the latter's glass furnace, called him Zorzi, distrusted him, suggested that he was probably a heretic, and did not hide their suspicion that he was in love with the master's only daughter, Marietta.—*Marietta*, F. Marion Crawford, 1901.

9303 In the Pennsylvania Station two M.P.'s looked suspiciously at Barnett Morgan. Then they saw the green patch on his shoulder and didn't say anything.—*The Stars Incline*, Clyde Brion Davis, 1946.

9304 Bishop Rodrigo Tenorio, with his escort of four horsemen, swung around the last bend of the rising road that brought them into view of the palace of Governor Pacheco. The palace was a squat dark fist of stone. Its windows

and embrasures were few and narrow. The Bishop's eyes as he stared up at it were tight with loathing and suspicion. — *A Wolf at Dusk*, Gwyn Thomas, 1959.

9305 I am the last man to be suspicious of a colleague, but on thinking it over I have the distinct feeling that the Vice-Chancellor's motives, in button-holing me as he did this afternoon, were at least partly feigned. — *Strike the Father Dead*, John Wain, 1962.

9306 For some time now they had been suspicious of him. — *Chesapeake*, James A. Michener, 1978.

9307 Bess Lytle suspicioned something might happen. — *In the Hollow of His Hand*, James Purdy, 1986.

9308 Ryland Guthrie had the perpetual feeling that he was getting gypped. — *Casting the Circle*, Elizabeth Arthur, 1988.

Swearing

9309 Many men swore that The Orphan was bad, and many swore profanely and with wonderful command of epithets because he was bad, but for obvious reasons that was as far as the majority went to show their displeasure. — *The Orphan*, Clarence E. Mulford, 1908.

9310 The trail boss shook his fist after the department puncher and swore softly. — *The Coming of Cassidy—and the Others*, Clarence E. Mulford, 1913.

9311 The horse stopped suddenly and her rider came to his senses with a jerk, his hand streaking to a six-gun, while he muttered a profane inquiry as he swiftly scrutinized his surroundings. — *Johnny Nelson*, Clarence E. Mulford, 1920.

9312 The T Bar trail-boss swore steadily, monotonously, his rain-drenched face ghastly in the incessant play of the lightning. — *Black Buttes*, Clarence E. Mulford, 1923.

9313 "Clusterfist. Slipshop demisemiwit." Sir Benjamin Drayton's swearing was always too literary to be really offensive. — *The Eve of Saint Venus*, Anthony Burgess, 1964.

9314 "Bifocal spectacles!" shouted my mother, coughing heavily over her daisy-wheel printer. — *Send a Fax to the Kasbah*, Dorothy Dunnett, 1991.

9315 I'll be go to hell. — *Shadow Catcher*, Charles Fergus, 1991.

9316 "Edward," the old woman calls./ "Fuck you," I answer. — *Her Monster*, Jeff Collignon, 1992.

Swimming

9317 Bruce Storrs stood up tall and straight on a prostrate sycamore, the sunlight gleaming upon his lithe, vigorous body, and with a quick, assured lifting of the arms plunged into the cool depths of the river. — *The Hope of Happiness*, Meredith Nicholson, 1923.

9318 The boy, white and tense as a soldier going into battle, let himself into the water. — *The Narrowing Stream*, John Mortimer, 1954.

9319 He was struggling in every direction, he was the centre of the writhing and kicking knot of his own body. There was no up or down, no light and no air. — *Pincher Martin*, William Golding, 1956.

9320 It was a cold evening for July, not quite 55°, and it had been raining since noon, but the man climbing out of the gray Mercedes parked in front of the Saratoga Springs YMCA intended to go swimming. — *Saratoga Swimmer*, Stephen Dobyns, 1981.

9321 In the summer of 1955, when I was seven, Mavis and her male friend Uncle Alex decided between dry martinis on a cloudy day that they could teach me how to dive into a swimming pool. — *Separate Checks*, Marianne Wiggins, 1984.

9322 He was swimming, rotating from front to back, thrashing his arms and legs and puffing out his cheeks, and it seemed as if he'd been swimming forever. — *East Is East*, T. Coraghessan Boyle, 1990.

9323 *Girls always like to go swimming at night.* — *The Names of the Lost*, Liza Wieland, 1992.

9324 Now that really was a sight to behold. From the sea, from the nesting place of the sun, we could see two objects swimming toward us, looking for all the world like two enormous seabirds with white feathers fluttering in a breeze that had newly sprung up. — *Cape of Storms*, André Brink, 1993.

Tardiness

9325 She waited, Kate Croy, for her father to come in, but he kept her unconscionably, and there were moments at which she showed herself, in the glass over the mantel, a face positively pale with the irritation that had brought her to the point of going away without sight of him. — *The Wings of the Dove*, Henry James, 1902.

9326 "He ought to be here," said Lady Tranmore, as she turned away from the window. — *The Marriage of William Ashe*, Mary Augusta Ward *as* Mrs. Humphry Ward, 1905.

9327 "There's only one thing I must really implore you, Edith," said Bruce anxiously. "*Don't make me late at the office!*" — *Love's Shadow*, Ada Leverson, 1908.

9328 On the second Friday in September the evening passenger train from the East pulled into the Maple City station, a little late as usual, like an old man with a chronic complaint which he accepts stoically. — *The Rim of the Prairie*, Bess Streeter Aldrich, 1932.

9329 It was growing late, and still there was no sign of Engaine. Could Ninian have been mistaken? — *The Black Rose*, Thomas B. Costain, 1945.

9330 After dinner I sat and waited for Pyle in my room over the rue Catinat: he had said, "I'll be with you at latest by ten," and when midnight had struck I couldn't stay quiet any longer and went down into the street. — *The Quiet American*, Graham Greene, 1955.

9331 "They're late," said Belle Nash, and glanced up at the station clock. "If that clock is right." — *The Country of Marriage*, Jon Cleary, 1962.

9332 We'd been eight and a half minutes earlier on the dress rehearsal. This time we were held up in a traffic jam at Lexington and Fiftieth Street. — *Only When I Laugh*, Len Deighton, 1968.

9333 The train was late and didn't get into Yuma until after dark. — *Forty Lashes Less One*, Elmore Leonard, 1972.

9334 Alan was waiting in the Lyceum cafe for his sister Madge. He hadn't seen her for fifteen years and she was already three-quarters of an hour late. — *A Quiet Life*, Beryl Bainbridge, 1976.

9335 The new dean of humanities allowed each full professor one hour. Klynt, determined to be prompt, arrived by bicycle twenty minutes late. — *Klynt's Law*, Elliott Baker, 1976.

9336 Billie is late — of course, she is always late — but the crowd in this small packed room is not resigned: people are restless, and tense. — *Listening to Billie*, Alice Adams, 1978.

9337 Her intention is to arrive early to avoid confusion, but a detail detains her at home. — *Adjacent Lives*, Ellen Schwamm, 1978.

9338 He was already late. — *The Cage*, Susan Cheever, 1982.

9339 "Mamma." Edna Earle waited, then stuck her head in through the open door. Over the sound of chicken frying and pots banging she shouted again, "Mam-ma! Isn't it time Elmo was home?" — *A Family Likeness*, Janis Stout, 1982.

9340 Six-twenty. He was late. Some last-minute emergency at the office — a sick dog or a mauled cat. — *Watch Dog*, Faith Sullivan, 1982.

9341 She supposed the new snow slowed him down. — *Winter Wife*, Jessica Auerbach, 1983.

9342 Without checking the rhinestone-studded Felix the Cat clock that hangs on the kitchen wall, its tail wagging, or the wristwatch that is jammed unwisely into the back pocket of her pants, Laura knows she is late. — *Walking Distance*, Marian Thurm, 1987.

9343 Eleanor Linnane arrived fifteen minutes late for her appointment at Lincoln's Inn Fields. — *Trust*, Mary Flanagan, 1988.

9344 Lowell came late to the war. — *One True Thing*, Greg Matthews, 1989.

9345 So help me, I am an hour too late. — *The Great Letter E*, Sandra Schor, 1990.

9346 I pulled much too quickly into the parking lot because I was going to be late again. — *The Sun Maiden*, Erika Taylor, 1991.

9347 It was a paradox, of which Ben over the years became fond, that he, ostensibly the most punctual and reliable of men, should have been late in the major matters of existence, that he always somehow missed his train. — *The Man Who Was Late*, Louis Begley, 1993.

Teatime

9348 Mrs. Katy Scudder had invited Mrs. Brown, and Mrs. Jones, and Deacon Twitchel's wife to take tea with her on the afternoon of June second, A.D. 17 — . — *The Minister's Wooing*, Harriet Beecher Stowe, 1859.

9349 Under certain circumstances there are few hours in life more agreeable than the hour dedicated to the ceremony known as afternoon tea. — *The Portrait of a Lady*, Henry James, 1881.

9350 It was a Sunday evening in October, and in common with many other young ladies of her class, Katharine Hilbery was pouring out tea. — *Night and Day*, Virginia Woolf, 1919.

9351 The saucepan cover lay wrong side up on the saucepan, so that its concave surface might give secure lodgment for the teapot which was perched upon it. — *Stroke of Luck*, Arnold Bennett, 1932.

9352 One day my mother told me that Mrs. Jardine had asked us to pick primroses on her hill, and then, when we had picked as many as we wanted, to come in and have tea with her. — *The Ballad and the Source*, Rosamond Lehmann, 1944.

9353 A confused impression of English tourists shuffling round a church in Ravenna, peer-

ing at mosaics, came to Catherine Oliphant as she sat brooding over her pot of tea. — *Less Than Angels*, Barbara Pym, 1955.

9354 It was cold outside, and the winter afternoon was dropping darkly down to tea-time. — *The Angel in the Corner*, Monica Dickens, 1956.

9355 She lay naked on his bed, a crumpled sheet bunched at her feet. It did not seem incongruous to them that he was preparing tea, setting out cups and saucers, lacing the table with a cloth. — *My Son Africa*, Froma Sand, 1965.

9356 You like to have some cup of tea? — *July's People*, Nadine Gordimer, 1981.

9357 That summer Saturday in 1951, Daisy Brown aged fifteen, going to tea with Ruth Perkin, also aged fifteen, had an unusual sense of adventure. — *The Ice House*, Nina Bawden, 1983.

9358 An hour out of Bagdad, Rosamund Coleridge considered the two and a half days of heat and dust that lay ahead of them and decided it was time she made tea for everyone. — *Rosamund's Vision*, Stuart Mitchner, 1983.

9359 Cup of tea: it was New Orleans hot but she was cold. — *Rainbow Roun Mah Shoulder*, Linda Brown Bragg, 1984.

9360 They'd called me for tea but they couldn't find me. — *Birds of the Air*, Ray Salisbury, 1988.

Television and Radio

9361 "I want to be. I want to be."/ The radio crackled wheezily. "I want to be back home in Dixie. Where the children play in the..." — *The Golden Ripple*, Alec Waugh, 1933.

9362 "It's not a hearing aid," Hubert Farnham explained. "It's a radio, tuned to the emergency frequency." — *Farnham's Freehold*, Robert A. Heinlein, 1964.

9363 On a shelf above the club car's bar the small radio stuttered and crackled, clearing abruptly as the outside interference faded. One of the white-jacketed attendants reached up to make a tuning adjustment as a couple of the Los Angeles stations tried to creep onto the same wavelength. — *The Sound of Drums and Cymbals*, Robert Wilder, 1974.

9364 The machines chatter, the big boards blink, the arrows dart, the markers move. — *Mark Coffin, U.S.S.*, Allen Drury, 1979.

9365 "This is WMFT, your music, news, and sports station in Nashville, Tennessee, the country-music capital of the world, 1240 on your dial... You in the mood for the finest female vocalist in the nation? Then, honey, *who* you're in the mood for is Loretta Lynn, singing number

three on the chart, 'Your Squaw Is on the Warpath' — on the Big Bob Travis Night Owl Show. Where else?" — *On the Big Wind*, David Madden, 1980.

9366 At home in my parents' house in Babbington Heights, in the corner of the attic that was my bedroom, I had, on a table beside my bed, a small Philco radio. — "The Static of the Spheres," Eric Kraft, 1983.

9367 "They want you to do it on television," was what Jenny Roo's agent had said on the telephone. — *In a Certain Light*, Karen Brownstein, 1985.

9368 I said, "But it was only just on." I said, "It was only just an instant ago when it was on." I said, "Come on, can't you tell me what it was?" — *Peru*, Gordon Lish, 1986.

9369 My father brought home a radio. — *The Northern Lights*, Howard Norman, 1987.

9370 It was a Saturday afternoon on La Salle Street, years and years ago when I was a little kid, and around three o'clock Mrs. Shannon, the heavy Irish woman in her perpetually soup-stained dress, opened her back window and shouted out into the courtyard, "Hey, Cesar, yoo-hoo, I think you're on television, I swear it's you!" — *The Mambo Kings Play Songs of Love*, Oscar Hijuelos, 1989.

9371 I suppose my connection with the Eritreans, brave and starved creatures of the Horn, began not with my first visit to Africa but a little later, with something I and half the world saw on television. — *To Asmara*, Thomas Keneally, 1989.

9372 Now Momma, you got to understand I didn't have no idea what all those camera people were doing when the show went out over the air. — *Elvis Presley Calls His Mother After The Ed Sullivan Show*, Samuel Charters, 1992.

9373 In one of my earliest memories, my mother and I are on the front porch of our rented Carter Avenue house watching two delivery men carry our brand-new television set up the steps. — *She's Come Undone*, Wally Lamb, 1992.

9374 Anna sat in the dark as the radio crackled like one emotion too many. — *Empathy*, Sarah Schulman, 1992.

9375 I remember I was sitting among my abandoned children watching television when Nixon resigned. — *Memories of the Ford Administration*, John Updike, 1992.

Theater

9376 It must be admitted that a London theatre abounds with fascination; indeed, it

operates as a kind of spell or enchantment: the glare of the lights, the embellishments of the house, the splendour of the scenery, the elegance of the dresses, the enlivening sounds issuing from the orchestra, the brilliancy of the audience, and the applause so liberally bestowed upon the actors, all united, tend in a great degree to add fuel to fire upon the feelings of "theatrically bitten youths," by alienating their minds from business, and impelling them to try their fortunes upon the stage; but nineteen out of twenty persons (who make the boards their profession) find out by woful experience, after walking from country villages to towns year after year, that such fascination or enthusiasm is paid for dearly indeed! — *The Life of an Actor*, Pierce Egan, 1825.

9377 It was in the Théatre St. Philippe (they had laid a temporary floor over the parquette seats) in the city we now call New Orleans, in the month of September, and in the year 1803. — *The Grandissimes*, George W. Cable, 1880.

9378 The piece was a West End success so brilliant that even if you belonged to the intellectual despisers of the British theatre you could not hold up your head in the world unless you had seen it; even for such as you it was undeniably a success of curiosity at least. — *The Pretty Lady*, Arnold Bennett, 1918.

9379 "Talk. Talk. Talk.... Good lines and no action ... said all ... not even promising first act ... eighth failure and season more than half over ... rather be a playwright and fail than a critic compelled to listen to has-beens and would-bes trying to put over bad plays...." — *Black Oxen*, Gertrude Atherton, 1923.

9380 It was the opening night of London's new National Opera House and consequently an occasion. Royalty was there. The Press were there. The fashionable were there in large quantities. — *Giants' Bread*, Agatha Christie *as* Mary Westmacott, 1930.

9381 Roland Lane Smith was swung up out of the Tube railway — full, glittering, cool carriages, with homing theatregoers, intoxicated males arguing lovingly arm in arm, amorous couples, inscrutable and silent men, inscrutable and silent women, newspaper scanners, book readers, smokers, indifferent and courteous guards apparently insensible to fatigue and monotony and ennui, all unwealthy — into the hot July night at South Kensington. — *Dream of Destiny*, Arnold Bennett, 1932.

9382 People who have read "The Lost Theatre" by Owen Gilbert may recall his printed opinion that the heyday of the theatre and the best time to be young were in the days when the dépôt hack still struggled against the station taxicab and extinction. — *Presenting Lily Mars*, Booth Tarkington, 1933.

9383 Adeline thought that never, never in her life had she seen anything so beautiful as *The Bohemian Girl*. — *The Building of Jalna*, Mazo de la Roche, 1944.

9384 "Pretty squalid play all round, I thought!" — *Doting*, Henry Green, 1952.

9385 The train call for the Number One Company of *A Clerical Error* was for nine o'clock. — *The Sugar House*, Antonia White, 1952.

9386 Look. In a condemned house in Brooklyn, some children are performing *Hamlet*. — *The Violated*, Vance Bourjaily, 1958.

9387 The final dying sounds of their dress rehearsal left the Laurel Players with nothing to do but stand there, silent and helpless, blinking out over the footlights of an empty auditorium. — *Revolutionary Road*, Richard Yates, 1961.

9388 It was just before tea, on Maundy Thursday, when I decided to become an actress. — *Simon Says*, Margaret Ritter, 1966.

9389 The unlit auditorium of the huge theatre was a constant presence of authority and grandeur, containing in its looming interior the promise and threat of the evening lights and chatter, of the public who were its loving judges. — *Night Falls on the City*, Sarah Gainham, 1967.

9390 Well, it's all over. The Odéon has fallen! — *The Merry Month of May*, James Jones, 1971

9391 She had invited Alexander, whether on the spur of the moment or with malice aforethought he did not know, to come and hear Flora Robson do Queen Elizabeth at the National Portrait Gallery. — *The Virgin in the Garden*, A. S. Byatt, 1978.

9392 They were up on the stage with the lights shining in their faces. — *The Bonner Boys*, Campbell Geeslin, 1981.

9393 In July Regina received a phone call from Andrew, who asked her to appear in a revival of *The Sea Gull*. — *Regina*, Leslie Epstein, 1982.

9394 It must have been 1963, because the musical of *Dombey and Son* was running at the Alexandra, and it must have been the autumn, because it was surely some time in October that a performance was seriously delayed because two of the cast had slipped and hurt themselves in B dressing-room corridor, and the reason for that was that the floor appeared to be flooded with something sticky and glutinous. — *At Freddie's*, Penelope Fitzgerald, 1982.

9395 I have always felt blessed to have had the chance to play Leah in the Leon Dalashinsky production of *The Dybbuk*. — *Hungry Hearts*, Francine Prose, 1983.

9396 It was a gala night at the Royal Theatre, London. — *Thursday's Children*, Rumer Godden, 1984.

9397 When Sophie was eleven and the world much older, her brother played a too-delicate Shark in his junior high school production of *West Side Story*. — *Footstool in Heaven*, Brett Singer, 1986.

9398 He stood there alone on the edge of the stage, looking out over a sea of seventy thousand faces. — *The Rest of Our Lives*, Hall Bartlett, 1988.

9399 It was the Saracen! Even when he dropped us, he was with us. — *Garments the Living Wear*, James Purdy, 1989.

9400 In the West End of London, at eight o'clock on a cold starry evening, the red velvet curtain trembled and lifted a few inches off the floor of the great stage, letting out a shimmer of soft amber light. — *Foolscap*, Michael Malone, 1991.

9401 Back in the days when Shakespeare still meant something to a lot of people, I wanted to be a great dramatic actress. — *Margaret in Hollywood*, Darcy O'Brien, 1991.

Thoughts

9402 Rosalina, for some time lost in thought, rested her head on her white arm, till the increasing gloom of her chamber made her look to her expiring lamp; hastily she arose to trim it, for she feared to be left in the shades of darkness, as her thoughts were sorrowful, and sleep seemed not inclined to "steep her senses in forgetfulness." — *Manfroné*, Mary-Anne Radcliffe, 1828.

9403 "Now, you think this thing over, March, and let me know the last of next week," said Fulkerson. — *A Hazard of New Fortunes*, William Dean Howells, 1890.

9404 In the small hours of a bitter January morning I sat in my room gazing into the fire, and thinking over many things. — *A Girl Among the Anarchists*, Isabel Meredith, 1903.

9405 "You must give me a moment," said the old man, leaning back./ Percy resettled himself in his chair and waited, chin on hand. — *Lord of the World*, Robert Hugh Benson, 1907.

9406 Miriam left the gaslit hall and went slowly upstairs. The March twilight lay upon the landings, but the staircase was almost dark. The top landing was quite dark and silent. There was no one about. It would be quiet in her room. She could sit by the fire and be quiet and think things over until Eve and Harriet came back with the parcels. — *Pointed Roofs*, Dorothy M. Richardson, 1915.

9407 William Sylvanus Baxter paused for a moment of thought in front of the drug-store at the corner of Washington Street and Central Avenue. — *Seventeen*, Booth Tarkington, 1916.

9408 Very late indeed in May, but early in the morning, Laurel Ammidon lay in bed considering two widely different aspects of chairs. — *Java Head*, Joseph Hergesheimer, 1919.

9409 Miriam ran upstairs narrowly ahead of her thoughts. In the small enclosure of her room they surged about her, gathering power from the familiar objects silently waiting to share her astounded contemplation of the fresh material. — *Deadlock*, Dorothy M. Richardson, 1921.

9410 When Howard Gage had gone, his mother's brother sat with his head bowed in frowning thought. — *The Bright Shawl*, Joseph Hergesheimer, 1922.

9411 Gumbril, Theodore Gumbril Junior, B. A. Oxon, sat in his oaken stall on the north side of the School Chapel and wondered, as he listened through the uneasy silence of half a thousand schoolboys to the First Lesson, pondered, as he looked up at the vast window opposite, all blue and jaundiced and bloody with nineteenth century glass, speculated in his rapid and rambling way about the existence and nature of God. — *Antic Hay*, Aldous Huxley, 1923.

9412 From Waterloo Station to the small country town of Ramsgard in Dorset is a journey of not more than three or four hours, but having by good luck found a compartment to himself, Wolf Solent was able to indulge in such an orgy of concentrated thought, that these three or four hours lengthened themselves out into something beyond all human measurement. — *Wolf Solent*, John Cowper Powys, 1929.

9413 Reclining in her steamer chair, her pretty eyes fixed pensively on the blue horizon line just visible over the Atlanta's rail, Olivia was thinking of Harry. — *Westward Passage*, Margaret Ayer Barnes, 1931.

9414 Sitting beside the road, watching the wagon mount the hill toward her, Lena thinks, "I have come from Alabama: a fur piece. All the way from Alabama a-walking. A fur piece." — *Light in August*, William Faulkner, 1932.

9415 It was night when the thought first came to him. — *Roll River*, James Boyd, 1935.

9416 "Whiteness and strength"—the words popped into Mr. Melton's mind again as he looked forward and saw Judith Hingham come on deck. — *East of the Giants*, George R. Stewart, 1938.

9417 Kit Anderson crossed the landing from his wife's room to his own, and, too much occupied with his thoughts to switch on the light, walked through the dark with the accuracy of habit to his bed. — *Kind Are Her Answers*, Mary Renault, 1940.

9418 Leithen had been too busy all day to

concern himself with the thoughts which hung heavily at the back of his mind. — *Mountain Meadow*, John Buchan, 1941.

9419 "I suppose my thoughts are nothing to be proud of," said Eleanor Sullivan./ "Then they are different from the rest of you, I am sure, dear." — *Parents and Children*, Ivy Compton-Burnett, 1941.

9420 In the week which preceded the outbreak of the Second World War — days of surmise and apprehension which cannot, without irony, be called the last days of peace — and on the Sunday morning when all doubts were finally resolved and misconceptions corrected, three rich women thought first and mainly of Basil Seal. They were his sister, his mother and his mistress. — *Put Out More Flags*, Evelyn Waugh, 1942.

9421 Tyler Spotswood was racking his brains. — *Number One*, John Dos Passos, 1943.

9422 There was a time when people were in the habit of addressing themselves frequently and felt no shame at making a record of their inward transactions. — *Dangling Man*, Saul Bellow, 1944.

9423 Thinking of Cluny Brown, Mr. Porritt, a successful plumber, allowed himself to be carried past his 'bus stop and in consequence missed the Sunday dinner awaiting him at his sister's. — *Cluny Brown*, Margery Sharp, 1944.

9424 Charles Gray had not thought for a long time, consciously at least, about Clyde, Massachusetts, and he sometimes wondered later what caused him to do so one morning in mid-April, 1947. — *Point of No Return*, John P. Marquand, 1949.

9425 Abbie Crunch began to walk slowly as she turned into Dumble Street, market basket over her arm, trying not to look at the river; because she knew that once she saw it with the sun shining on it she would begin to think about Link, to worry about Link, to remember Link as a little boy. — *The Narrows*, Ann Petry, 1953.

9126 Ten twenty fifty brown birds flew past the window and then a few stragglers, out of sight. A fringe of Mrs. Vardoe's mind flew after them (what were they — birds returning in migration of course) and then was drawn back into the close fabric of her preoccupations. — *Swamp Angel*, Ethel Wilson, 1954.

9427 At times during the morning, he would think of the man named Kirby Frye. — *The Law at Randado*, Elmore Leonard, 1955.

9428 My body sat in the back seat, but my mind was up front with the driver. — *Call Me Captain*, David Beaty *as* Paul Stanton, 1959.

9429 Lying in bed, I abandoned the facts again and was back in Ambrosia. — *Billy Liar*, Keith Waterhouse, 1959.

9430 The things that went through his mind were thought in English as he walked up the lane that mounted between gardens, and tidy little orchards, and neatly spaced vegetable rows. — *Generation Without Farewell*, Kay Boyle, 1960.

9431 It was December of 1951 and a dull, sullen southwest-of-England morning when I stood by the ship's rail while all the last-minute bustle of sailing went on about me and discovered in my mind the thought — the thought as complete, concrete, clearly delineated and unexpected as a newly minted silver sixpence found lying on the ground at one's feet — that I was about to sail back to St. Jago and that this was something that I did not want to do. — *My Friend, Cousin Emmie*, Jane Duncan, 1964.

9432 It was Adam Appleby's misfortune that at the moment of awakening from sleep his consciousness was immediately flooded with everything he least wanted to think about. — *The British Museum Is Falling Down*, David Lodge, 1965.

9433 There were still times when Rachel thought of Daniel. — *The Waiting Sands*, Susan Howatch, 1966.

9434 One fine day in early summer a young man lay thinking in Central Park. — *The Last Gentleman*, Walker Percy, 1966.

9435 I've spent a lot of time over the past months thinking about what happened to Tom McMann and me last winter in Sophis: asking myself exactly what it was the Truth Seekers did to us there, and how. — *Imaginary Friends*, Alison Lurie, 1967.

9436 Riding in low, tail tucked in, cuffs thick with grease, past tinseled mailboxes, mahogany ducks floating on the lawn, trees stocked with impossible fruit — lemons and figs swelling from branch tips like overgrown Christmas bulbs, I dreamed of Matty Zalushioon, dead in that dark lemonless city where I was born. — *Eisenhower, My Eisenhower*, Jerome Charyn, 1971.

9437 As the soft feminine sound of singing splashed out at him from behind the bathroom door, Amos lay back in bed, squinted out the window at the morning sun, and thought, as dispassionately as he could, about Lila. — *Father's Day*, William Goldman, 1971.

9438 Sometimes I think: if only time could have stopped there. — *Money Is Love*, Brian Glanville, 1972.

9439 Morning flight. Cross-country from New York with but one thought in mind: to sell a few million paper cups to a lavatory firm in Los Angeles. — *The Last Catholic in America*, John R. Powers, 1973.

9440 Marney had not thought about the Conway twins for a long time. — *April's Grave*, Susan Howatch, 1974.

9441 He always thought of her in the midst of pure and delicate colours: white, green and grey. — *Lord Richard's Passion*, Mervyn Jones, 1974.

9442 I watch a gull's shadow float among feet on the concrete as I walk in a day of my life with a bell, its brass tongue in my hand, and think after all that the first constant was water. — *The Leavetaking*, John McGahern, 1974.

9443 Muhlbach, having locked his front door and tested it, stands for a moment on the horsehair welcome mat to consider the neighborhood. — *Double Honeymoon*, Evan S. Connell, 1976.

9444 "I see..." said the vampire thoughtfully, and slowly he walked across the room towards the window. — *Interview with the Vampire*, Anne Rice, 1976.

9445 Ts'its'tsi'nako, Thought-Woman,/ is sitting in her room/ and whatever she thinks about/ appears. — *Ceremony*, Leslie Marmon Silko, 1977.

9446 This is the third attempt to put my thoughts down on paper; in my mind they chafe mercilessly. — *Relations*, Carolyn Slaughter, 1977.

9447 All day long I had been thinking that I had grounds for believing I was an original. — *Picture Palace*, Paul Theroux, 1978.

9448 *Teeth, straight teeth.* The thought surfaced, but he pushed it back into the depths, for this was early morning, when the mind could do such things. — *The Dogs of March*, Ernest Hebert, 1979.

9449 Look at me now, Joshua thought. — *Joshua Then and Now*, Mordecai Richler, 1980.

9450 After several efforts to apply himself to his work, Jason Knowles gave up and allowed the distracting current that was running in his head to have its way. — *Leave of Absence*, Theodore Morrison, 1981.

9451 Running out of gas, Rabbit Angstrom thinks as he stands behind the summer-dusty windows of the Springer Motors display room watching the traffic go by on Route 111, traffic somehow thin and scared compared to what it used to be. — *Rabbit Is Rich*, John Updike, 1981.

9452 The Count of Mountjoy, deep in thought, was lying on a huge couch in his bedroom in the castle of Grand Fenwick examining the ceiling. — *The Mouse That Saved the West*, Leonard Wibberley, 1981.

9453 Paul Michael Martin was, you might say, single-minded. He wondered about women's breasts all the time. — *Queen Bee*, Eugene Kennedy, 1982.

9454 Later, in February of that memorable winter, when the numbness of his mind receded and Sutherland wondered if he would ever have a reason to laugh again in his life, he began to think about Manfredi. — *Dear Friends*, Tom McHale, 1982.

9455 They are watching me, thought Rupert Stonebird, as he saw the two women walking rather too slowly down the road. — *An Unsuitable Attachment*, Barbara Pym, 1982.

9456 While Pearl Tull was dying, a funny thought occurred to her. — *Dinner at the Homesick Restaurant*, Anne Tyler, 1982.

9457 Crude thoughts and fierce forces are my state. — *Ancient Evenings*, Norman Mailer, 1983.

9458 "Not to be thought of," Sir Arthur Detling said. "I tell you it is not to be thought of, and there's an end of it." — *The Detling Secret*, Julian Symons, 1983.

9459 He was thinking of Treblinka. He had already finished with Dachau and Auschwitz. — *All We Need of Hell*, Harry Crews, 1987.

9460 Martha Price sat at her window. She considered the blank pane. As she watched, the glass cleared. She raised her hand and there was the harbour. Two fishing boats steaming in. A yacht. On the other side of the water a small village climbed the steep hill to the cliff-top. A scattering of gulls in the mid-air./ She might have been a painter. Or a writer./ She pondered, considered the coastguard cottages crouched against the sky./ There was movement. A figure, then two or three. She nodded./ Let it begin. — *The Sadness of Witches*, Janice Elliott, 1987.

9461 "What do you imagine they could be thinking?" my mother would ask us. — *The Murderous McLaughlins*, Jack Dunphy, 1988.

9462 Anna knew that he was doing his best to be interested. — *Silver Wedding*, Maeve Binchy, 1989.

9463 Fabio was running./ In his mind he ran. It flickered like a cinema screen with images which he never allowed to linger more than a fraction of a second lest they fix themselves and take on life. He ran from words, ideas, certain sights. — *The Racket*, Anita Mason, 1990.

9464 Lydie McBride occupied a café table in the Jardin du Palais Royal and thought how fine it was to be an American woman in Paris at the end of the twentieth century. — *Secrets of Paris*, Luanne Rice, 1991.

Time

9465 The time which passes over our heads so imperceptibly, makes the same gradual change in habits, manners, and character, as in personal appearance. — *The Abbot*, Sir Walter Scott, 1820.

9466 The hands on the hall-clock pointed to half-past six in the morning. The house was a country residence in West Somersetshire, called

Combe-Raven. The day was the fourth of March, and the year was eighteen hundred and forty-six. — *No Name*, Wilkie Collins, 1862.

9467 A French clock on the mantel-piece, framed of brass and crystal, which betrayed its inner structure as the transparent sides of some insects betray their vital processes, struck ten with the mellow and lingering clangor of a distant cathedral bell. — *The Bread-Winners*, John Hay, 1883.

9468 Time touches all things with destroying hand; and if he seem now and then to bestow the bloom of youth, the sap of spring, it is but a brief mockery, to be surely and swiftly followed by the wrinkles of old age, the dry leaves and bare branches of winter. — *The House Behind the Cedars*, Charles Waddell Chesnutt, 1900.

9469 Six o'clock was striking. — *Nocturne*, Frank Swinnerton, 1917.

9470 Arthur Charles Prohack came downstairs at eight thirty, as usual, and found breakfast ready in the empty dining-room. This pleased him, because there was nothing in life he hated more than to be hurried. For him, hell was a place of which the inhabitants always had an eye on the clock and the clock was always further advanced than they had hoped. — *Mr. Prohack*, Arnold Bennett, 1922.

9471 When Mark Worth left Tony undressing and came downstairs, he saw that the tall clock on the landing had stopped. — *Time of Peace*, Ben Ames Williams, 1942.

9472 Somewhere in the distance a clock chimed. — *Mine Boy*, Peter Abrahams, 1946.

9473 It was a bright cold day in April, and the clocks were striking thirteen. — *Nineteen Eighty-four*, George Orwell, 1949.

9474 The clock on the acoustically perfect wall moved toward nine-thirty, nibbling at Thursday night. — *The Troubled Air*, Irwin Shaw, 1951.

9475 Once upon a time there was time. — *Go in Beauty*, William Eastlake, 1956.

9476 "If you call five *six*, you embarrass five, seeing that people then are going to expect of him the refulgence of six." — *Self Condemned*, Wyndham Lewis, 1957.

9477 It was the first time he had ever heard the clock strike ten at night. — *The Charioteer*, Mary Renault, 1959.

9478 It was six o'clock. Will Harris knew without looking at the clock. — *If We Must Die*, Junius Edwards, 1963.

9479 Time and a windless noon, the leaves on the full-fledged trees limp in a simmering sun. Time: time's temptations and terrors, patience and impatience. — *The Ferret Fancier*, Anthony C. West, 1963.

9480 We were right on time. — *The Flight of the Falcon*, Daphne du Maurier, 1965.

9481 Forever is such a very great while. — *A Tree Full of Stars*, Davis Grubb, 1965.

9482 November opened its eye. — *Hammer on the Sea*, Theodore Vrettos, 1965.

9483 The chief commodity of San Ignacio del Tule is time, and the people of Tule passionately enjoy wasting it. — *The Lowest Trees Have Tops*, Martha Gellhorn, 1967.

9484 Her nearby Mickey Mouse pointed its glowing arms at 3. — *It's All Zoo*, Gerald A. Browne, 1968.

9485 So it's almost time. — *My Main Mother*, Barry Beckham, 1969.

9486 It is eight thirty in the morning, eastern time — five thirty for me, since I flew in from Portland, Oregon, yesterday. — *The God of the Labyrinth*, Colin Wilson, 1970.

9487 There will be a short interval. — *There Will Be a Short Interval*, Storm Jameson, 1973.

9488 Tallien pressed his old royal watch and it chimed a new republican nine. — *Napoleon Symphony*, Anthony Burgess, 1974.

9489 The minutes swam by like sharks. — *The Entwining*, Richard Condon, 1980.

9490 Big Ben stands at six o'clock. — *A Woman Called Scylla*, David Gurr, 1981.

9491 It is five o'clock in the morning, Daylight Saving Time. — *The Killing Ground*, Mary Lee Settle, 1982.

9492 I glanced at my left arm to see what time it was, only to discover that in my hurry, I'd forgotten my watch. — *Nana's Ark*, Michael Borich, 1984.

9493 Charles./ So far, as even such a phrase implies, the course has been forward in time so that it is now later than when I began to write. — *Anticipation*, Frederick Ted Castle, 1984.

9494 That month of June swam into the Two Medicine country. — *English Creek*, Ivan Doig, 1984.

9495 At one minute to six on the morning of 14 June, 1936, the black chicken on Kate Kingsley's alarm clock nodded up and down, in time with the ticking of the second hand, as it had done for the past fifteen years with only brief intervals for running repairs. — *A Flower That's Free*, Sarah Harrison, 1984.

9496 At last — fifteen months after the death of his mother, eight months after the marriage of his son — Martin found that he was no longer oppressed by the clock. — *Astonishment of Heart*, Edwin Moses, 1984.

9497 Elihu B. Washburne opened his gold watch. — *Lincoln*, Gore Vidal, 1984.

9498 Maude Mason was losing her place./ Time was starting to melt and mix like a thick liquid. — *Under the House*, Leslie Hall Pinder, 1986.

9499 The clock on the kitchen wall had not

reached seven, but the headless bird predicted the hour. — *Cooper*, Hilary Masters, 1987.

9500 Time is not a line but a dimension, like the dimensions of space. — *Cat's Eye*, Margaret Atwood, 1988.

9501 "This won't take long, sir." — *Sacred Monster*, Donald E. Westlake, 1989.

9502 Killing Time. One spends more and more time doing it, I find. — *A Bottle in the Smoke*, A. N. Wilson, 1989.

9503 *Underneath the earth's crust there are layers and layers pressed tight, flat as ribbons, weighed down by millenniums and the force of human breathing. Compressed by physics, dark and wounded, time lies coiled there, measured in heat and gasses.* — *Flying Lessons*, Susan Johnson, 1990.

9504 "All right, Pearse. It's time." — *My Father in the Night*, Terence Clarke, 1991.

9505 It's been almost thirty-five years. I can scarcely believe it, niño. Time trusts no one and so it disappears before us like the smoke, the smoke from my cigarette. — *Valentino's Hair*, Yvonne V. Sapia, 1991.

9506 These things take time. — *Out of Time*, Helen Schulman, 1991.

9507 In some distant arcade, a clock tower calls out six times and then stops. — *Einstein's Dreams*, Alan Lightman, 1993.

Travel

9508 It has for some ages been thought so wonderful a thing to sail the tour or circle of the globe, that when a man has done this mighty feat he presently thinks it deserves to be recorded, like Sir Francis Drake's. — *A New Voyage Round the World*, Daniel Defoe, 1724.

9509 Your resolution to accompany Mrs. Reeves to London, has greatly alarmed your three Lovers. And two of them, at least, will let you know that it has. Such a lovely girl as my Harriet, must expect to be more accountable for her steps than one less excellent and less attractive. — *The History of Sir Charles Grandison*, Samuel Richardson, 1753-1754.

9510 They order, said I, this matter better in France — / You have been in France? said my gentleman, turning quick upon me with the most civil triumph in the world. — *Sentimental Journey*, Laurence Sterne, 1768.

9511 It was early on a fine summer's day, near the end of the eighteenth century, when a young man, of genteel appearance, journeying towards the north-east of Scotland, provided himself with a ticket in one of those public car-

riages which travel between Edinburgh and the Queensferry, at which place, as the name implies, and as is well known to all my northern readers, there is a passage-boat for crossing the Firth of Forth. — *The Antiquary*, Sir Walter Scott, 1816.

9512 It was near the close of the year 1780 that a solitary traveler was seen pursuing his way through one of the numerous little valleys of Westchester.* / [*As each state of the American Union has its own counties, it often happens that there are several which bear the same name. The scene of this tale is in New York, whose county of Westchester is the nearest adjoining to the city.] — *The Spy*, James Fenimore Cooper, 1821.

9513 Mrs. Bethune Baliol's Memorandum begins thus:/ It is five-and-thirty, or perhaps nearer forty years ago, since, to relieve the dejection of spirits occasioned by a great family loss sustained two or three months before, I undertook what was called the short Highland tour. — "The Highland Widow," Sir Walter Scott, 1827.

9514 My uncle Ro and myself had been travelling together in the East, and had been absent from home fully five years when we reached Paris. — *The Redskins*, James Fenimore Cooper, 1846.

9515 The traveller who at the present day is content to travel in the good old Asiatic style, neither rushed along by a locomotive, nor dragged by a stage-coach; who is willing to enjoy hospitalities at far-scattered farmhouses, instead of paying his bill at an inn; who is not to be frightened by any amount of loneliness, or to be deterred by the roughest roads or the highest hills; such a traveller in the eastern part of Berkshire, Mass., will find ample food for poetic reflection in the singular scenery of a country, which, owing to the ruggedness of the soil and its lying out of the track of all public conveyances, remains almost as unknown to the general tourist as the interior of Bohemia. — *Israel Potter*, Herman Melville, 1855.

9516 "It's time to go to the station, Tom." — *An Old-Fashioned Girl*, Louisa May Alcott, 1870.

9517 Many years have passed since my wife and I left the United States to pay our first visit to England. — *The Two Destinies*, Wilkie Collins, 1876.

9518 Four years ago — in 1874 — two young Englishmen had occasion to go to the United States. — *An International Episode*, Henry James, 1879.

9519 The rambler who, for old association's sake, should trace the forsaken coach-road running almost in a meridional line from Bristol to the south shore of England, would find himself during the latter half of his journey in the vicinity

of some extensive woodlands, interspersed with apple-orchards. — *The Woodlanders*, Thomas Hardy, 1887.

9520 There was a king travelling through the country, and he and those with him were so far away from home that darkness caught them by the heels, and they had to stop at a stone mill for the night, because there was no other place handy. — *The Wonder Clock*, Howard Pyle, 1887.

9521 Travelling south from New Orleans to the Islands, you pass through a strange land into a strange sea, by various winding waterways. — *Chita: A Memory of Last Island*, Lafcadio Hearn, 1889.

9522 Some years since — it was during the winter before the Zulu War — a White Man was travelling through Natal. His name does not matter, for he plays no part in this story. — *Nada the Lily*, H. Rider Haggard, 1892.

9523 When the train slowed before drawing into the station at Fitchburg, Sister Althea took up her bag from the floor, and began to collect her paper parcels into her lap, as if she were going to leave the car. — *The Day of Their Wedding*, William Dean Howells, 1896.

9524 *3 May. Bistritz.* — Left Munich at 8:35 P.M., on 1st May, arriving at Vienna early next morning; should have arrived at 6:46, but train was an hour late. Buda-Pesth seems a wonderful place, from the glimpse which I got of it from the train and the little I could walk through the streets. — *Dracula*, Bram Stoker, 1897.

9525 When Caroline Meeber boarded the afternoon train for Chicago, her total outfit consisted of a small trunk, a cheap imitation alligator-skin satchel, a small lunch in a paper box, and a yellow leather snap purse, containing her ticket, a scrap of paper with her sister's address in Van Buren Street, and four dollars in money. — *Sister Carrie*, Theodore Dreiser, 1900.

9526 Some notable sight was drawing the passengers, both men and women, to the window; and therefore I rose and crossed the car to see what it was. — *The Virginian*, Owen Wister, 1902.

9527 High noon of a crisp October day, sunshine flooding the earth with the warmth and light of old wine and, going single-file up through the jagged gap that the dripping of water has worn down through the Cumberland Mountains from crest to valley-level, a gray horse and two big mules, a man and two young girls. — *A Knight of the Cumberland*, John Fox, Jr., 1906.

9528 The long train from the North rolled into the Grand Central Station and came to a jerky stop, while out the doors and down the steps surged a hurrying throng of men and women who seemed intent on reaching a given point in the shortest possible time. — *Cross Currents*, Eleanor H. Porter, 1907.

9529 When young Stover disembarked at the Trenton station on the fourth day after the opening of the spring term he had acquired in his brief journey so much of the Pennsylvania rolling stock as could be detached and concealed. Inserted between his nether and outer shirts were two gilt "Directions to Travelers" which clung like mustard plasters to his back, while a jagged tin sign, wrenched from the home terminal, embraced his stomach with the painful tenacity of the historic Spartan fox. In his pockets were objects — small objects but precious and dangerous to unscrew and acquire. — *The Varmint*, Owen Johnson, 1910.

9530 I could not say at which station the woman and her baby entered the train. — *The Hampdenshire Wonder*, J. D. Beresford, 1911.

9531 Dink Stover, freshman, chose his seat in the afternoon express that would soon be rushing him to New Haven and his first glimpse of Yale University. — *Stover at Yale*, Owen Johnson, 1912.

9532 The train, which had roared through a withering gale of sleet all the way up from New York, came to a standstill, with many an ear-splitting sigh, alongside the little station, and a reluctant porter opened his vestibule door to descend to the snow-swept platform: a solitary passenger had reached the journey's end. — *The Hollow of Her Hand*, George Barr McCutcheon, 1912.

9533 I spent one-third of my journey looking out of the window of a first-class carriage, the next in a local motor-car following the course of a trout stream in a shallow valley, and the last tramping over a ridge of down and through great beech woods to my quarters for the night. — *Mr. Standfast*, John Buchan, 1919.

9534 France. France swirled under her feet for now that the boat was static it seemed, inappositely, that the earth must roll, revolve and whirl. — *Asphodel*, Hilda Doolittle *as* H. D., 1922.

9535 Once on a time Conachúr mac Nessa was on a journey, and had to pass the night at the house of Felimid mac Dall, his story-teller. — *Deirdre*, James Stephens, 1923.

9536 Sorrell was trying to fasten the straps of the little brown portmanteau, but since the portmanteau was old and also very full, he had to deal with it tenderly. — *Sorrell and Son*, Warwick Deeping, 1926.

9537 The young man who, at the end of September, 1924, dismounted from a taxicab in South Square, Westminster, was so unobtrusively American that his driver had some hesitation in asking for double his fare. The young man had no hesitation in refusing it. — *The Silver Spoon*, John Galsworthy, 1926.

9538 When Mr. Hazard was forty years old, he decided to revisit England. — *Mr. Hodge and Mr. Hazard*, Elinor Wylie, 1928.

9539 The purser took the last landing card in his hand and watched the passengers pass the grey wet quay, over a wilderness of rails and points, round the corners of abandoned trucks. — *Stamboul Train*, Graham Greene, 1932.

9540 Nanda was on her way to the Convent of the Five Wounds. She sat very upright on the slippery seat of the one-horse bus, her tightly-gaitered legs dangling in the straw, and her cold hands squeezed into an opossum muff. A fog screened every window, clouding the yellow light that shone on the faces of the three passengers as they jolted slowly along invisible streets. — *Frost in May*, Antonia White, 1933.

9541 They threw me off the hay truck about noon. — *The Postman Always Rings Twice*, James M. Cain, 1934.

9542 "You take the white omnibus in the Platz," murmured the Princess, "but do not forget to change into an ultramarine on reaching the Flower Market, or you will find yourself in the 'Abattoirs.'..." — *The Artificial Princess*, Ronald Firbank, 1934.

9543 At Hanover Junction it was necessary for him to change trains. — *Long Remember*, Mac-Kinlay Kantor, 1934.

9544 It was the second day of their journey to their first home. — *Drums Along the Mohawk*, Walter D. Edmonds, 1936.

9545 Late one October afternoon in the year 1921, a shabby young man gazed with fixed intensity through the window of a third-class compartment in the almost empty train labouring up the Penowell valley from Swansea. — *The Citadel*, A. J. Cronin, 1937.

9546 Very late one windless September night twenty-two men and a beautiful woman were crossing a dried river bed on the caravan road that led from Kashgar eastward toward Aqsu. — *The Seven Who Fled*, Frederic Prokosch, 1937.

9547 Gil and I crossed the eastern divide about two by the sun. — *The Ox-Bow Incident*, Walter Van Tilburg Clark, 1940.

9548 The train was nearing its destination and the three men lighted cigarettes and fixed their eyes on the swiftly passing fields, expectant of the first glimpse of the town. — *Whiteoak Heritage*, Mazo de la Roche, 1940.

9549 He traveled steadily northward over a land of grass that ran ever onward and faded at last into a farther flatness his eyes could not see; and distance and openness and emptiness were all around him. — *Action by Night*, Ernest Haycox, 1943.

9550 The porter said he'd mind her bag./ "To be sure, miss. Look, I'll put it inside here, the way the sun won't boil it on you." — *The Last of Summer*, Kate O'Brien, 1943.

9551 In one compartment, set directly over the loud concussion of the wheels, there were three people traveling. — *Avalanche*, Kay Boyle, 1944.

9552 The young man in the taxi leaned forward. — *The Bishop's Mantle*, Agnes Sligh Turnbull, 1947.

9553 Now a traveler must make his way to Noon City by the best means he can, for there are no buses or trains heading in that direction, though six days a week a truck from the Chuberry Turpentine Company collects mail and supplies in the next-door town of Paradise Chapel: occasionally a person bound for Noon City can catch a ride with the driver of the truck, Sam Radclif. — *Other Voices, Other Rooms*, Truman Capote, 1948.

9554 Stubby red-faced Elof Lofblom stood thumbing a ride on an Iowa highway corner. — *The Chokeberry Tree*, Frederick Manfred *as* Feike Feikema, 1948.

9555 After a while other hitch-hikers joined Thurs along the New Jersey highway. — *The Giant*, Frederick Manfred *as* Feike Feikema, 1951.

9556 Walter Jackson climbed up onto the bus top and found a seat on the left-hand side of the upper deck, so that he could look down onto the pavements and watch the people as he rode along. — *Another Kind*, Anthony P. West, 1951.

9557 Bel Riose traveled without escort, which is not what court etiquette prescribes for the head of a fleet stationed in a yet-sullen stellar system on the Marches of the Galactic Empire. — *Foundation and Empire*, Isaac Asimov, 1952.

9558 Hazel Motes sat at a forward angle on the green plush train seat, looking one minute at the window as if he might want to jump out of it, and the next down the aisle at the other end of the car. — *Wise Blood*, Flannery O'Connor, 1952.

9559 When Guy Crouchback's grandparents, Gervase and Hermione, came to Italy on their honeymoon, French troops manned the defenses of Rome, the Sovereign Pontiff drove out in an open carriage and Cardinals took their exercise side-saddle on the Pincian Hill. — *Men at Arms*, Evelyn Waugh, 1952.

9560 Sarah knew in a magic of singing voices outside that the coach had crossed the border from England into Wales. The air was full of the same smell of wood smoke, lamps gave the same dull candlelight, and clogs made the same clatter on the cobbles, but the ostlers changing the horses no longer had an English shape to their mouths. — *The Witch of Merthyn*, Richard Llewellyn, 1954.

9561 Sir Henry rested his horse, Ponderer, by Indal Water, where it rounded in clear green pools among the boulders beneath Hart's Hill. — *Sir Henry*, Robert Nathan, 1955.

9562 The train was beginning to slow down again, and Abraham noticed lights in the distance. — *The Sacrifice*, Adele Wiseman, 1956.

9563 The sprawling, haze-dimmed outline of Angels, Casabella County's official seat and only town, had been in front of Clint Charterhouse all during the last five miles riding across the undulating prairie. — "Dead Man Range," Ernest Haycox, 1957.

9564 The elderly passenger sitting on the north-window side of that inexorably moving railway coach, next to an empty seat and facing two empty ones, was none other than Professor Timofey Pnin. — *Pnin*, Vladimir Nabokov, 1957.

9565 During the early part of June, 1947, a small party of sightseers found itself trapped in what was then the newly-discovered labyrinth of Cefalû, in the island of Crete. — *The Dark Labyrinth*, Lawrence Durrell, 1958.

9566 What made me take this trip to Africa? — *Henderson the Rain King*, Saul Bellow, 1959.

9567 When not tending New York holdings, Guy Grand was generally, as he expressed it, "*on the go.*" — *The Magic Christian*, Terry Southern, 1959.

9568 "Man, you're so good-looking!" said the Welsh steward. "You take my breath away." — *Through Streets Broad and Narrow*, Gabriel Fielding, 1960.

9569 *The summer term at Oxford was only half over (four wet and wintry weeks old) but already the tourists had begun to appear like crocuses.* — *A Middle Class Education*, Wilfrid Sheed, 1960.

9570 Anna Teller was the only refugee on the plane from Munich to New York. — *Anna Teller*, Jo Sinclair, 1960.

9571 S. Levin, formerly a drunkard, after a long and tiring transcontinental journey, got off the train at Marathon, Cascadia, toward evening of the last Sunday in August, 1950. — *A New Life*, Bernard Malamud, 1961.

9572 Lucy Winter sat in the train, swaying and rocking its way north from New York City, with a sense of achievement; the journey set a seal on the depressing limbo of the last months, the stifling summer in New York with her mother; already she sensed the change of air, the lift of autumn. — *The Small Room*, May Sarton, 1961.

9573 "How far away is it?"/ "Fifteen miles."/ "Is there a bus?"/ "There is not."/ "Is there a taxi or a car I can hire in the village?"/ "There is not." — *The Uniform*, Iris Murdoch, 1963.

9574 Rakesh stood at one end of the dusty verandah of Palam airport in the crowd that had just got off the plane, while luggage clattered noisily past him along the moving belt. — *This Time of Morning*, Nayantara Sahgal, 1965.

9575 The position at the moment is as follows. I joined the gastronomic cruise at Venice, as planned, and the *Polyolbion* is now throbbing south-east in glorious summer Adriatic weather. — *Tremor of Intent*, Anthony Burgess, 1966.

9576 *I came out by the north, it has to be understood, and turned north, myself, ten men and twenty pack animals, with thirty days' rations.* — *The Menorah Men*, Lionel Davidson, 1966.

9577 The tour had begun. The excursion bus was cruising along the pocked, narrow highway that ran from the capital city eighty miles northwest to the town of Santomaso. — *The Tour*, David Ely, 1967.

9578 Kakia Grabowska, aged twenty-three, cartoonist and citizen of Warsaw, travelled to Moscow in 1949 with an electric light bulb in case the hotel lamps were too dim for her to draw by, and a bathplug saved from her own house after it was destroyed. — *A State of Change*, Penelope Gilliatt, 1967.

9579 The blond stewardess was demonstrating the use of a life jacket. She touched the lungs, the nipples of the jacket with delicate fingers, no more than indicating the nozzle and tapes. — *My Friend Says It's Bulletproof*, Penelope Mortimer, 1967.

9580 Diddy the Good was taking a business trip. — *Death Kit*, Susan Sontag, 1967.

9581 I was traveling farther south. The villages were small and poor; each time I stopped in one, a crowd gathered around my car and the children followed my every move. — *Steps*, Jerzy Kosinski, 1968.

9582 Rome welcomed me with lit fountains, a melon-slice of moon, the Company's Rolls-Royce, and the comfort of a suite at our Head Office, just above the Piazza di Spagna. — *But We Didn't Get the Fox*, Richard Llewellyn, 1969.

9583 Carlita Rojas Mundez walked out of the men's restroom of the Gulf Oil station in Cumseh, Georgia, and saw the Greyhound Bus leaving her. — *This Thing Don't Lead to Heaven*, Harry Crews, 1970.

9584 On Memorial Day in 1967 Daniel Lewin thumbed his way from New York to Worcester, Mass., in just under five hours. — *The Book of Daniel*, E. L. Doctorow, 1971.

9585 The creature onto whose head Gombold had strayed was some hundreds of miles high; it was impossible not to think this unique. — *Head to Toe*, Joe Orton, 1971.

9586 The guard at Exeter warned him he would have to change at Dulverton to pick up the westbound train to Bamfylde Bridge Halt, the nearest railhead to the school, but did not add

that the wait between trains was an hour. — *To Serve Them All My Days*, R. F. Delderfield, 1972.

9587 Instinct told Murontzeff he was being followed. — *A Death Out of Season*, Emanuel Litvinoff, 1973.

9588 The journey of Mercier and Camier is one I can tell, if I will, for I was with them all the time. — *Mercier and Camier*, Samuel Beckett, 1974.

9589 David arrived at Coëtminais the afternoon after the one he had landed at Cherbourg and driven down to Avranches, where he had spent the intervening Tuesday night. — "The Ebony Tower," John Fowles, 1974.

9590 An hour after you leave New York City everything is green; even though you are still on the highway you know you are in a different place. — *Family Secrets*, Rona Jaffe, 1974.

9591 In the main entrance of the air terminal a young man stood beside a cigarette machine, searching in the breast pocket of his blue suit for his passport. — *Sweet William*, Beryl Bainbridge, 1975.

9592 Anthony unpacked. He brought little on such journeys, since the house sufficed. — *Small Rain*, Nicholas Delbanco, 1975.

9593 In the rainy March of 196-, he had, an hour or so before being driven to the airport, cast his remaining metal lire into the Trevi fountain, daring Rome to call him back again. — *Beard's Roman Women*, Anthony Burgess, 1976.

9594 Little Billy Twillig stepped aboard a Sony 747 bound for a distant land. This much is known for certain. He boarded the plane. — *Ratner's Star*, Don DeLillo, 1976.

9595 The plane from Belfast arrived on time, but when the passengers disembarked there was a long wait for baggage. — *The Doctor's Wife*, Brian Moore, 1976.

9596 Cato Forbes had already crossed Hungerford railway bridge three times, once from north to south, then from south to north, and again from north to south. — *Henry and Cato*, Iris Murdoch, 1976.

9597 The fortune teller and her grandfather went to New York City on an Amtrak train, racketing along with their identical, peaky white faces set due north. — *Searching for Caleb*, Anne Tyler, 1976.

9598 Dear Berthold,/ Well, here we are. I can't quite believe it myself, but there's the sun outside to prove it, and the blue skies, and the palm-trees. — *The Squire of Bor Shachor*, Chaim Bermant, 1977.

9599 Six days ago, when the workhouse cart left Wrexham, there had been eight of us, but the Crowther lads had hopped off at Denbigh and the Rhubarb Twins left us in Conway. — *This Sweet and Bitter Earth*, Alexander Cordell, 1977.

9600 I am riding the bicycle and I am on Route 31 in Monument, Massachusetts, on my way to Rutterburg, Vermont, and I'm pedaling furiously because this is an old-fashioned bike, no speeds, no fenders, only the warped tires and the brakes that don't always work and the handlebars with cracked rubber grips to steer with. — *I Am the Cheese*, Robert Cormier, 1977.

9601 In the late afternoon of the first Wednesday in September, two years ago, we were about three miles due east of Oak Bluffs, under power, heading home. — *Dreamland*, George V. Higgins, 1977.

9602 The North Carolina Mutual Life Insurance agent promised to fly from Mercy to the other side of Lake Superior at three o'clock. — *Song of Solomon*, Toni Morrison, 1977.

9603 Most of the passengers, including me, hurried up to the boat deck where the announcement was to be made, already prepared for the worst. — *Quarantine*, Nicholas Hasluck, 1978.

9604 One day Mandragon toured a personal future. — *Mandragon*, R. M. Koster, 1979.

9605 I watched the sun cross and recross the carriages as the train came in between the pillars, lighting the grey roofs; and then hands began to draw down windows, doors flew open, and the first figures met the platform with a jolt, and started to run. — *The Pornographer*, John McGahern, 1979.

9606 What are the first words a visitor from France can expect to hear upon his arrival at a German airport? — *How German Is It?*, Walter Abish, 1980.

9607 His deck chair was a bale of hay. — *A Game Men Play*, Vance Bourjaily, 1980.

9608 It was important, Dolan thought, to approach as though nothing was wrong. — *Fault Lines*, James Carroll, 1980.

9609 There were things at the bottom of Brother Sebastian's bag that he didn't know were there. — *Lamb*, Bernard MacLaverty, 1980.

9610 Visitors to Rhenish Prussia, in the summer of 1851, found much to charm them. — *Rhine Journey*, Ann Schlee, 1980.

9611 A visitor to San Francisco in the late 'fifties might well have been advised that along with the cable cars, the Coit Tower, and the Golden Gate Bridge, he should look for Big Dan Lavette. — *The Legacy*, Howard Fast, 1981.

9612 On the train from New York I sat next to a young man with a blue shirt and long black hair. — *The Country*, David Plante, 1981.

9613 *Dearest Gisela,/ I give you a warm bear-hug from the new world!* — *The White Hotel*, D. M. Thomas, 1981.

9614 Graybeard Fenn would be happy to give it another go; we* have fiddled with our tale through this whole sabbatical voyage: down the Intracoastal in the fall in our cruising sailboat,

Pokey, Wye I., from Chesapeake Bay to the Gulf of Mexico and across to Yucatán; all about the Caribbean, island-hopping through the mild winter of 1980; and in May through our first long open-ocean passage, from St. John in the U.S. Virgins direct for the Virginia Capes, Chesapeake Bay, Wye Island, the closing of the circle, sabbatical's end./ [*This *we*, those verses, Susan's tears, these notes at the feet of certain pages—all shall be made clear, in time.]—*Sabbatical*, John Barth, 1982.

9615 Constance looked out of the small circular window of the plane and tingled with a wonderful sense of freedom. Soaring through crystal skies, separated from the past and the future, from home and destination, in limbo, almost in a place of disorientation, she felt quite buoyant. —*Heart of the River*, Carolyn Slaughter, 1982.

9616 The scene: Florida, St. Petersburg and the outlying beaches, in late June when heat rises shimmering from the highways and sidewalks and all native life moves at a slow pace, while the tourists hurry, scarlet, feverish with sunburn, anxious not to miss anything, darting from air-conditioned shop to shop, speeding to the beaches, cursing the stop-and-start traffic, in which eight out of ten cars bear out-of-state license plates.—*Oh, Susannah!*, Kate Wilhelm, 1982.

9617 I swung myself down from the seat of the canvas-covered freight wagon, the steady rain streaking my face when I looked up to take my leather bag from the driver's hand.—*Kildeer Mountain*, Dee Brown, 1983.

9618 Taking the train, this empty lonely Dublin day of Sunday.—*Leila*, J. P. Donleavy, 1983.

9619 "Land ... Land..."/ The cry beat against the wind then floated gently to the decks. —*And the Wild Birds Sing*, Lola Irish, 1983.

9620 In the Oakland Greyhound all the people were dwarfs, and they pushed and shoved to get on the bus, even cutting in ahead of the two nuns, who were there first.—*Angels*, Denis Johnson, 1983.

9621 He began by visiting Arlington Cemetery.—*A Country Such as This*, James Webb, 1983.

9622 So I moved slowly north, passing through dozens of springs, virtually traveling north with greening spring herself overhead and below, pausing here and there to wait for her and for my own courage to gather.—*Sundog*, Jim Harrison, 1984.

9623 There was always too much to pack. —*Family Truths*, Syrell Rogovin Leahy, 1984.

9624 I changed airplanes at Tampa, nodded when the flight attendant, a guy with stiff hair and freckles, told me the DC-3 was the safest thing in the air, and took a seat in the back.

—*Tracer*, Frederick Barthelme, 1985.

9625 I looked right and left, up and down, though less danger there, bought the ticket. —*Circuits*, Michael Brodsky, 1985.

9626 I have travelled by various conveyances, over the years—womb, baby carriage, family shoulders, slaves' shoulders, toy wagon, hobbyhorse (with no real progress to speak of,) raft, canoe, keelboat, flatboat, steamboat, gondola, ark, toboggan, sled, sleigh, horse, mule, ass, camel, elephant, donkey-cart, stagecoach, European diligence, horse-drawn carriages of all descriptions, train, Australian cable-car, jinrikisha, bicycle, automobile, and, at long journey's end, coffin—airborne, thanks to loving hands. —*I Been There Before*, David Carkeet, 1985.

9627 The train bore them onwards and downwards through the sluices and barrages which contained the exuberance of the Rhône, across the drowsy plain, towards the City of the Popes, where now in a frail spring sunshine the pigeons fluttered like confetti and the belfries purged their guilt in the twanging of holy bells. —*Quinx*, Lawrence Durrell, 1985.

9628 In the late and last afternoon of an April long ago, a forlorn little group of travellers cross a remote upland in the far south-west of England.—*A Maggot*, John Fowles, 1985.

9629 Ten minutes out from Kennedy Airport he discovers that the man sitting beside him has no legs.—*Nothing Happens in Carmincross*, Benedict Kiely, 1985.

9630 On the flight home she sat across the aisle from an Israeli couple and their four-year-old son, coming to the States for a year.—*Miriam in Her Forties*, Alan Lelchuk, 1985.

9631 It took him only a few moments to put his two leather-strapped bags through the *octroi*, customs, and carry them along the quai to the Boulogne railroad station.—*Depths of Glory*, Irving Stone, 1985.

9632 ...I see a young man on the hot straight road to Paris, travelling from Calais. —*Mr. Thistlewood*, Nicholas Wollaston, 1985.

9633 She said, "To Jerusalem." Then, to herself, "Yer-ush-al-ay-im," and felt her lips burn on the name, as if from a seraph's kiss. —*Winter in Jerusalem*, Blanche d'Alpuget, 1986.

9634 Heading the long straggle of pilgrims, the hardy and the dogged paused to look out over the flat of the Bendigo Valley. —*The Place of the Swan*, Lola Irish, 1986.

9635 In 1673, Louis Jolliet and Père Jacques Marquette traveled by canoe down the Mississippi River as far as the Arkansas River, then turned back.—*La Salle*, John Vernon, 1986.

9636 It gives me pleasure to hinder American tourists occasionally.—*Soldiers in Hiding*, Richard Wiley, 1986.

9637 Leonard Penlynne called up to his coachman. — *Seeds of Anger*, James Ambrose Brown, 1987.

9638 The first trainload of men arrived from South Africa. — *Lovers of the African Night*, William Duggan, 1987.

9639 *And now, after much time, Greece is where I am.* — *American Beauty*, C. J. Hribal, 1987.

9640 We stopped. We had to. — *Upon This Rock*, Walter F. Murphy, 1987.

9641 James Drayton was making his way along Platform Three at Paddington Station. He edged past trunks and suitcases, stepped round a traveling cage containing a black rabbit, pushed through a mob of squealing gray-uniformed schoolgirls. "Excuse me," he said to a sturdy young woman whom he had identified by her clipboard as being in charge. "I'm looking for the Morehaven train." — *Chasing Shadows*, Louisa Dawkins, 1988.

9642 This was the year he rode the subway to the ends of the city, two hundred miles of track. — *Libra*, Don DeLillo, 1988.

9643 They crossed the border into Brittany at noon, soon afterward found themselves in an eerily silent landscape, shrouded in dense, spectral fog. — *Falls the Shadow*, Sharon Kay Penman, 1988.

9644 Dearest Charles-/ The distance between us grows, even as my pen hesitates. — *S.*, John Updike, 1988.

9645 This the trip I took that day, day they brought Walter in. — *Dirty Work*, Larry Brown, 1989.

9646 Yesterday I took a miniature trip with M., back and forth on the Staten Island Ferry. — *Horse Crazy*, Gary Indiana, 1989.

9647 Shackled to his seat by ten pounds of steel leg braces and the dead weight of his own legs, the president struggled to point out the road. — *Another Time*, Sidney Jacobson, 1989.

9648 *That year we rode so far south in Mexico we came upon little men who jumped around in trees.* — *Buffalo Nickel*, C. W. Smith, 1989.

9649 It's one of my favorite parts of being out here . . . when the headlights keep streaming past my thumb, and I'm weary from the cold and the dust and the stares, I wait until between cars to slip away from the roadside. — *Finding Signs*, Sharlene Baker, 1990.

9650 The steward is a stand-up comic. "If you are on the wrong flight," he says as they shut the door, "now would be an excellent time to deplane." — *My Life and Dr. Joyce Brothers*, Kelly Cherry, 1990.

9651 When the ship left Buenos Aires, most of the Italian-speaking passengers were gone. — *A Cloud on Sand*, Gabriella De Ferrari, 1990.

9652 TRACELEEN   So it was summer and Miss Crystal had decided we should all go up to Maine and get to know that part of the country. — "A Summer in Maine," Ellen Gilchrist, 1990.

9653 Jonathan was in the Reykjavík Airport with his passport and travelers' checks in his jacket pocket, his Icelandair ticket with baggage claim checks attached in his shirt pocket, and no baggage at all. — *Far Afield*, Susanna Kaysen, 1990.

9654 On a fall afternoon, several years before he was to be drafted to fight in the Second World War, a young man named William Clay sat in the day coach of a train that traveled between Chicago and Kansas City. — *Fall Quarter*, Weldon Kees, 1990.

9655 Change at Maryborough, change at Ballybrophy, change at Roscrea. — *Hell Hath No Fury*, Malcolm Macdonald, 1990.

9656 Maria Dark flew north, from one America to the other, with a bag of treasures between her feet. — *Stone Heart*, Luanne Rice, 1990.

9657 On a winter evening of the year 19—, after arduous travels across two continents and as many centuries, pursued by harsh weather and threatened with worse, an aging emeritus professor from an American university, burdened with illness, jet lag, great misgivings, and an excess of luggage, eases himself and his encumbrances down from his carriage onto a railway platform in what many hold to be the most magical city in the world, experiencing not so much that hot terror which initiates are said to suffer when their eyes first light on an image of eternal beauty, as rather that cold chill that strikes lonely travelers who find themselves in the wrong place at the wrong time. — *Pinocchio in Venice*, Robert Coover, 1991.

9658 Lord Orcis was on one of his tours of inspection. — *Carmichael's Dog*, R. M. Koster, 1992.

9659 Three people are in a first-class compartment on a train traveling from Milan to Turin. An old woman, a young woman, a young man. The young man is the old woman's son; the young woman will marry the young man when they return to America in two weeks. — "The Rest of Life," Mary Gordon, 1993.

Trees and Plants

9660 The close observers of vegetable nature have remarked, that when a new graft is taken from an aged tree, it possesses indeed in exterior form the appearance of a youthful shoot, but has in fact attained to the same state of maturity, or

even decay, which has been reached by the parent stem. — *Count Robert of Paris*, Sir Walter Scott, 1832.

9661 To dwellers in a wood almost every species of tree has its voice as well as its feature. — *Under the Greenwood Tree*, Thomas Hardy, 1872.

9662 Up to the days of Indiana's early statehood, probably as late as 1825, there stood, in what is now the beautiful little city of Vincennes on the Wabash, the decaying remnant of an old and curiously gnarled cherry tree, known as the Roussillon tree, *le cerisier de Monsieur Roussillon*, as the French inhabitants called it, which as long as it lived bore fruit remarkable for richness of flavor and peculiar dark ruby depth of color. — *Alice of Old Vincennes*, Maurice Thompson, 1900.

9663 On the west side of Ellen's father's house was a file of Norway spruce-trees, standing with a sharp pointing of dark boughs towards the north, which gave them an air of expectancy of progress. — *The Portion of Labor*, Mary E. Wilkins Freeman, 1901.

9664 The Deacons were at supper. In the middle of the table was a small, appealing tulip plant, looking as anything would look whose sun was a gas jet. — *Miss Lulu Bett*, Zona Gale, 1920.

9665 Thirty years ago Madame Holbein had seen the wisteria and taken the house. "I didn't look at anything else," she said. "I didn't need to." — *A Candle for St. Jude*, Rumer Godden, 1948.

9666 Waist-high ferns in the narrow glade of the deep woods bore silvery webs of dawn light. — *The Sunset Tree*, Martha Ostenso, 1949.

9667 It was October. The leaves were gold above my head; single ones fluttered from a bough as if waiting for some archer to shoot them down to their fellows. — *The Fourteenth of October*, Bryher, 1952.

9668 Two elderly women sat knitting on that part of the verandah which was screened from the sun by a golden shower creeper; the tough stems were so thick with flower it was as if the glaring afternoon was dammed against them in a surf of its own light made visible in the dripping, orange-coloured clusters. — *Martha Quest*, Doris Lessing, 1952.

9669 It was a good tree by the sea-loch, with many cones and much sunshine; it was homely too, with rests among its topmost branches as comfortable as chairs. — *The Cone-Gatherers*, Robin Jenkins, 1955.

9670 Black and bristling, the long patch of brushwood waited in the blossoming hedge, firm as a new toothbrush. — *Cobbler's Dream*, Monica Dickens, 1963.

9671 The hedges of scented whitethorn on either side of the villa gates had the longest fiercest thorns they had ever seen. — *The Battle of the Villa Fiorita*, Rumer Godden, 1963.

9672 The flame trees enclosed the hockey field in a high leafy wall of bulging green; rotting orangey-red blossoms littered the moist grass. — *Girls at Play*, Paul Theroux, 1969.

9673 The primroses were over. Toward the edge of the wood, where the ground became open and sloped down to an old fence and a brambly ditch beyond, only a few fading patches of pale yellow still showed among the dog's mercury and oak-tree roots. — *Watership Down*, Richard Adams, 1972.

9674 The crab-apple tree leaned from a gap in Evreux's ancient rampart where the palisade had rotted behind Dean Fulk's timbered house. The roots clutched the earthen bank and sucked life to a gnarled trunk clothed in mildewed bark, and a branched canopy which spread a sun-dappled shade in summer. By September the tree always bore a few wrinkled, black-spotted apples; we harvested them greedily and pretended to enjoy their bitterness. — *The Paladin*, George Shipway, 1972.

9675 The elm tree planted by Eleanor Bold, the judge's daughter, fell last night. — *Peace*, Gene Wolfe, 1975.

9676 I stopped the car and got out and examined the vegetation. — *The Pardoner's Tale*, John Wain, 1978.

9677 John Joel was high up in the tree, the one tall tree in the backyard. — *Falling in Place*, Ann Beattie, 1980.

9678 Here I am up in the window, that indistinguishable head you see listing toward the sun and waiting to be watered. — *Meditations in Green*, Stephen Wright, 1983.

9679 The beet is the most intense of vegetables. — *Jitterbug Perfume*, Tom Robbins, 1984.

9680 There were twenty objects hidden in the tree. — *Hidden Pictures*, Meg Wolitzer, 1986.

9681 There aren't many holly berries this year; the leaves are dark viridian green, deeply dented, sharp-pointed; but virtually no berries. — *Tidings*, William Wharton, 1987.

9682 The paths were matted with leaves. Long black seedpods from the monkeypod trees lay on the rotten garden benches and Clio thought at first that the seedpods were centipedes. — *Sleeping Beauties*, Susanna Moore, 1993.

9683 April warmth had opened the buds of the little cherry tree to lovely pink blossoms and its smooth bark was a deep wine color. — *The Longest Road*, Jeanne Williams, 1993.

Trust

9684 "And *consequently*," the old man said, "I don't trust a one of them to cure calf, mule or pig, and for another thing they charge too much. — *Fire in the Morning*, Elizabeth Spencer, 1948.

9685 *If we didn't believe each other, if we didn't trust each other, our life together would become quite impossible.* — *Evidence of Love*, Dan Jacobson, 1960.

9686 Trust me for a while. — *Magic*, William Goldman, 1976.

9687 Sunny Shannon sat on the hilltop and tried to decide whether to take him back again, whether to forgive and forget, whether she should or would dare trust that man — and herself — again. — *Saudi*, Laurie Devine, 1984.

9688 By the time he was twenty-three, Michael Davenport had learned to trust his own skepticism. — *Young Hearts Crying*, Richard Yates, 1984.

9689 In this City of the Angels, you can trust nothing, not even the dense and erratic air. — *Palm Latitudes*, Kate Braverman, 1988.

9690 Polly Alter used to like men, but she didn't trust them anymore, or have very much to do with them. — *The Truth About Lorin Jones*, Alison Lurie, 1988.

9691 I trust water. — *Three Children*, Lori Toppel, 1992.

Truth

9692 The full truth of this odd matter is what the world has long been looking for and public curiosity is sure to welcome. — *The Master of Ballantrae*, Robert Louis Stevenson, 1889.

9693 *"Aw kid, come on! Be square!"* — *Michael O'Halloran*, Gene Stratton-Porter, 1915.

9694 Having no wish to pose as a man of letters, but earnestly desiring to see justice done, I, Steven Nason, of the town of Arundel, in the county of York and the province of Maine, herein set down the truth, as I saw it, of certain occurrences connected in various ways with this neighborhood. — *Arundel*, Kenneth Roberts, 1930.

9695 This is my statement, so help me God, as I hope to be hung. — *Not Honour More*, Joyce Cary, 1955.

9696 Truth. In these days of so many trials by association, where a man A can show, with an infinity of fine brush strokes, how he once was an intimate of the man B, and the man B assert, with what only God might see to be craft or virtue, that he never knew the man A, I see truth as an old, hobbled unicorn limping through the forests of allegation and denial, pausing here and there to try to warm itself at some sun-foil of proof that shines for a moment through the trees. — *False Entry*, Hortense Calisher, 1961.

9697 "Well," I said, "I will try. I honestly will try to be honest with you, although I suppose really what you're more interested in is not my being honest, if you see what I mean." — *The Pumpkin Eater*, Penelope Mortimer, 1962.

9698 I'll make my report as if I told a story, for I was taught as a child on my homeworld that Truth is a matter of the imagination. — *The Left Hand of Darkness*, Ursula K. Le Guin, 1969.

9699 When everything is at best debatable and always doubtful, I can't see any sense whatsoever in choosing to ignore the facts. — "The Satyr Shall Cry," George Garrett, 1973.

9700 There once was a man who tried to find out the truth about Hector Cabot. — *The Life of the Party*, Maureen Freely, 1984.

9701 "If I am not mistaken," and when President Garland used that particular phrase to the Board of Governors of Pequod College everyone knew the truth stood tall on battlements of commonsense and right reason, "If I am not mistaken, these alleged rapes were pure fantasy in one case and an attempted mugging in the other." — *Felicity*, Coral Lansbury, 1987.

9702 *so when i saw his hand go under the seat i reached out the boot laying in the bed behind the spare tire and hit him before he could get the gun up and thats the way it has to be because thats the way it happened and cops lawyers judges all of them are interested only in the facts they say so if its truth enough for one family its truth enough for everyone else because wheres the point in scattering truth around like pennies so some appleass can find it and hammer it into a bigger badge for himself* — *The Homestead*, Chilton Williamson, Jr., 1990.

Upbringing

9703 Sir Andrew Wylie, like the generality of great geniuses, was born and bred in very humble circumstances. — *Sir Andrew Wylie*, John Galt, 1822.

9704 A child's early life is such as those who rule over him make it; but they can only modify what he is. Yet, as all know, after their influence has ceased, the man himself has to deal with the effects of blood and breed, and, too, with the consequences of the mistakes of his elders in the way of education. — *Hugh Wynne*, S. Weir Mitchell, 1897.

9705 Andy Thomas would of most likely been a plain average and just a hard-riding cowboy if he'd been brought up where such kind of men rode. — *The Three Mustangeers*, Will James, 1933.

9706 If you really want to hear about it, the first thing you'll probably want to know is where I was born, and what my lousy childhood was like, and how my parents were occupied and all before they had me, and all that David Copperfield kind of crap, but I don't feel like going into it, if you want to know the truth. — *The Catcher in the Rye*, J. D. Salinger, 1951.

9707 I am a white man and never forgot it, but I was brought up by the Cheyenne Indians from the age of ten. — *Little Big Man*, Thomas Berger, 1964.

9708 First, foremost, the puppyish, protected upbringing above his father's shoe store in Camden. — *My Life As a Man*, Philip Roth, 1974.

9709 I was brought up on three dead languages — Hebrew, Aramaic, and Yiddish (some consider the last not a language at all) — and in a culture that developed in Babylon: the Talmud. — *Shosha*, Isaac Bashevis Singer, 1978.

9710 My name is Ruth. I grew up with my younger sister, Lucille, under the care of my grandmother, Mrs. Sylvia Foster, and when she died, of her sisters-in-law, Misses Lily and Nona Foster, and when they fled, of her daughter, Mrs. Sylvia Fisher. — *Housekeeping*, Marilynne Robinson, 1980.

9711 Reader, I was born in Kingston Hospital (Alight at Norbiton) and brought up in Worcester Park. — *The Natural Order*, Ursula Bentley, 1982.

9712 I was brought up in two countries. — *The Foreigner*, David Plante, 1984.

9713 I was raised by decent hypocrites to respect truth. — *A Father's Words*, Richard G. Stern, 1986.

9714 I am not the kind of snob that I was raised to be. — *Lifestyle*, Peter Warner, 1986.

9715 I was born in Poland in 1921 and moved with my family to Manchester in 1925 and have no recollection of my birthplace whatever. By the time I started school a year or so later, I had picked up sufficient English to pass as a native, at least in my own eyes, and thought I was accepted as such by others. It was not that I was ashamed of being Polish, but that I had an aversion to being different. — *Titch*, Chaim Bermant, 1987.

9716 In their mother's eyes, Josie Salazar knew, she and her sister Serena were more like the Indians than the Spanish ladies they were brought up to be. — *Migrant Souls*, Arturo Islas, 1990.

9717 He stopped the car at the side of the road on a rise that overlooked the town where he was born and bred. — *Saint Hiroshima*, Leigh Kennedy, 1990.

9718 The trouble with an Orphanage upbringing is that when the College discharges you at age eighteen you are burstingly healthy, educated to the edge of intellectual indigestion and as innocent of day-to-day reality as a blind dummy. — *Brain Child*, George Turner, 1991.

9719 Here is an account of a few years in the life of Quoyle, born in Brooklyn and raised in a shuffle of dreary upstate towns. — *The Shipping News*, E. Annie Proulx, 1993.

Vacations

9720 It was in the early days of April; Bernard Longueville had been spending the winter in Rome. — *Confidence*, Henry James, 1879.

9721 The Schoessels — Ed and Etta and the three children, Rich, Marjorie, and Buddie — went sometimes in the summer to visit Grandma and Grandpa Schoessel in the country near Germantown. — *The Odyssey of a Nice Girl*, Ruth Suckow, 1925.

9722 One summer, several years before the war began, a young boy of fifteen was staying with his father and two elder brothers at a hotel near the Thames in Surrey. — *In Youth Is Pleasure*, Denton Welch, 1944.

9723 It was Brent, the film producer, who suggested that I should go down to Tralorna and stay at the Royal Ocean Hotel. — *Bright Day*, J. B. Priestley, 1946.

9724 Usually, Claude Batchelor was so eager to get down to Sussex for his annual three weeks holiday that, the moment the prize-giving was over, he changed hurriedly into tweeds and was on his way within an hour. This year, for the first time, he had decided to take things more easily and go down the following day. — *Beyond the Glass*, Antonia White, 1954.

9725 Rio. At this hour the beach was not usually so deserted. — *Away from Home*, Rona Jaffe, 1960.

9726 As a boy and until I was sixteen I spent a large part of every summer at my grandfather's house in Lyons, Pennsylvania. — *Ourselves to Know*, John O'Hara, 1960.

9727 It always takes me a while to get used to New York after I've been to Virginia for the summer. — *You Can't Get There from Here*, Earl Hamner, 1965.

9728 Ten more glorious days without horses! — *The Red and the Green*, Iris Murdoch, 1965.

9729 Before Maggie Deloach went back for

her senior year at college there had been a Benevolent Order of Elks parade, a water ballet at the municipal swimming pool in which she had starred with a flimsy backstroke and a water-lily face, a rhinestone tiara loaned from a gift and jewelry chain store in Atlanta, a speech by the governor, and a tattered monkey on the end of a leash held by a Jaycee. — *Heartbreak Hotel*, Anne Rivers Siddons, 1976.

9730 Dr. Linda Mack had brought the five girls down to her Devon cottage in the car: it was June and the weather was fair. — *Miss Herbert*, Christina Stead, 1976.

9731 They were supposed to stay at the beach a week, but neither of them had the heart for it and they decided to come back early. — *The Accidental Tourist*, Anne Tyler, 1985.

9732 Although they had been married nearly a dozen years, when Andrew and his wife went to Bermuda in early May it was almost as if they had embarked on another honeymoon — a honeymoon in Bermuda, of all places. — *To the Sargasso Sea*, William McPherson, 1987.

9733 I remember, in '69, three years before he died, when I was home for a brief while in the summer, how we sat up together all night watching those first moon-men take their first, shy steps on the moon. — *Out of This World*, Graham Swift, 1988.

9734 From my twelfth to my fifteenth year, in the early 1930s, my parents used to rent a cottage for the summer in Bar Harbor, on beautiful Mount Desert Island just off the Maine coast. — *Fellow Passengers*, Louis Auchincloss, 1989.

9735 Vacations were automatic and followed a pattern. — *Jack Gance*, Ward Just, 1989.

9736 On the third day of their honeymoon, Andrea and John ran out of milk. — *Brokenhearted*, Nancy Weber, 1989.

9737 "You should take a week's leave and come out here," said Lisa. "It's so restful, just what you need." — *Pride's Harvest*, Jon Cleary, 1991.

Valleys

9738 In one of those beautiful valleys, through which the Thames (not yet polluted by the tide, the scouring of cities, or even the minor defilement of the sandy streams of Surrey), rolls a clear flood through flowery meadows, under the shade of old beech woods, and the smooth glossy greensward of the chalk hills (which pour into it their tributary rivulets, as pure and pellucid as the fountain of Bandusium, or the wells of

Scamander, by which the wives and daughters of the Trojans washed their splendid garments in the days of peace, before the coming of the Greeks); in one of those beautiful valleys, on a bold round-surfaced lawn, spotted with junipers, that opened itself in the bosom of an old wood, which rose with a steep, but not precipitous ascent, from the river to the summit of the hill, stood the castellated villa of a retired citizen. — *Crotchet Castle*, Thomas Love Peacock, 1831.

9739 I awoke at the first break of day, and, leaving the postillion fast asleep, stepped out of the tent. The dingle was dank and dripping. — *The Romany Rye*, George Borrow, 1857.

9740 The first beams of the sun of August 17, 1777, were glancing down the long valley, which opening to the East, lets in the early rays of morning, upon the village of Stockbridge. Then, as now, the Housatonic crept still and darkling around the beetling base of Fisher's Nest, and in the meadows laughed above its pebbly shoals, embracing the verdant fields with many a loving curve. Then, as now, the mountains cradled the valley in their eternal arms, all round, from the Hill of the Wolves, on the north, to the peaks that guard the Ice Glen, away to the far southeast. Then, as now, many a lake and pond gemmed the landscape, and many a brook hung like a burnished silver chain upon the verdant slopes. — *The Duke of Stockbridge*, Edward Bellamy, 1879.

9741 The village of Glen Cairn was situated in a valley in the broken country lying to the west of the Pentland Hills, some fifteen miles north of the town of Lanark, and the country around it was wild and picturesque. — *In Freedom's Cause*, G. A. Henty, 1885.

9742 It was a brilliant afternoon towards the end of May. The spring had been unusually cold and late, and it was evident from the general aspect of the lonely Westmoreland valley of Long Whindale that warmth and sunshine had only just penetrated to its bare green recesses, where the few scattered trees were fast rushing into their full summer dress, while at their feet, and along the bank of the stream, the flowers of March and April still lingered, as though they found it impossible to believe that their rough brother, the east wind, had at last deserted them. — *Robert Elsmere*, Mary Augusta Ward *as* Mrs. Humphry Ward, 1888.

9743 The village lay in a valley which had been the bed of a great river in the far-off days when Ireland, Wales and Brittany were joined together, and the Thames flowed into the Seine. — *The Weavers*, Gilbert Parker, 1907.

9744 The little valley, like many others, had lain unnoticed, almost unknown, since the fur-trade days, when it had yielded up its beaver and

straightway joined the ranks of the unimportant. — *Cottonwood Gulch*, Clarence E. Mulford, 1925.

9745 In all our lovely land there is no valley fairer than the Fairy Glen. Deep, deep, like a hollow bowl, it lies among the mountains, so high above the plains and the sea that no man ever saw it but from the mountain tops or sailing the sky in ships. — *The Wilderness*, Liam O'Flaherty, 1927.

9746 The Valley of the Red Cedar is in eastern Iowa — a long strip of fertile land sprawling out beside the river whose name it bears. — *Song of Years*, Bess Streeter Aldrich, 1939.

9747 The time of this in its beginning, in men's time, is 1880 in the summer, and its place is the Athabaska valley, near its head in the mountains, and along the other waters falling into it, and beyond them a bit, over Yellowhead Pass to the westward, where the Fraser, rising in a lake, flows through wilderness and canyon down to the Pacific. — *Tay John*, Howard O'Hagan, 1939.

9748 To three races and four generations, through all its many names, it has been known simply as the beautiful blue valley. — *People of the Valley*, Frank Waters, 1941.

9749 A massively-built man between thirty and forty years of age stood for a few minutes looking around him with keen, appraising blue eyes, as he surveyed the wide saucer-shaped valley, the steaming low country four thousand feet below him, and the towering peak of Ratnagalla. — *Elephant Walk*, Robert Standish, 1948.

9750 He rode into our valley in the summer of '89. — *Shane*, Jack Schaefer, 1949.

9751 The Salinas Valley is in Northern California. It is a long narrow swale between two ranges of mountains, and the Salinas River winds and twists up the center until it falls at last into Monterey Bay. — *East of Eden*, John Steinbeck, 1952.

9752 Tiger went to see the valley the day after his father talked to him. — *Turn Again Tiger*, Samuel Selvon, 1958.

9753 After parking the Rolls-Royce between the pigsties and the muck heap where the twenty young turkeys were lazily stretching in the hot mid-morning air, Pop Larkin, looking spruce and perky in a biscuit-colored summer suit, paused to look back across his beloved little valley. — *When the Green Woods Laugh*, H. E. Bates, 1960.

9754 Coming over the pass you can see the whole valley spread out below. On a clear morning, when it lies broad and colored under a white sky, with the mountains standing far back on either side, you can imagine it's the promised land. — *The Wycherly Woman*, Ross Macdonald, 1961.

9755 Long before the soldiers arrived the life forms of the valley had established a stable symbiotic balance. — *The 13th Valley*, John M. Del Vecchio, 1982.

9756 Now dawn began to fringe the prickly leaves of the hemlock and tamarack trees, rising over the scarred mountains that formed a natural, radio-quiet shield in the protected valley at Earth Station One in Andover, Maine. — *Kings in the Countinghouse*, Herbert Mitgang, 1983.

Vehicles

9757 While the present century was in its teens, and on one sunshiny morning in June, there drove up to the great iron gate of Miss Pinkerton's academy for young ladies, on Chiswick Mall, a large family coach, with two fat horses in blazing harness, driven by a fat coachman in a three-cornered hat and wig, at the rate of four miles an hour. — *Vanity Fair*, William Makepeace Thackeray, 1848.

9758 On the road to the Kennebec, below the town of Bath, in the State of Maine, might have been seen, on a certain autumnal afternoon, a one-horse wagon, in which two persons were sitting. — *The Pearl of Orr's Island*, Harriet Beecher Stowe, 1862.

9759 Early in the cool hush of a June morning in the seventies, a curious vehicle left Farmer Councill's door, loaded with a merry group of young people. It was a huge omnibus, constructed out of a heavy farm wagon and a hay rack, and was drawn by six horses. — *A Spoil of Office*, Hamlin Garland, 1892.

9760 It was four o'clock when the ceremony was over and the carriages began to arrive. — *The Jungle*, Upton Sinclair, 1906.

9761 The year was 1891, the month October, the day Monday. In the dark outside the railway-station at Worsted Skeynes Mr. Horace Pendyce's omnibus, his brougham, his luggage-cart, monopolised space. — *The Country House*, John Galsworthy, 1907.

9762 Jefferson Worth's outfit of four mules and a big wagon pulled out of San Felipe at daybreak, headed for Rubio City. — *The Winning of Barbara Worth*, Harold Bell Wright, 1911.

9763 Mr. William B. Aikins, *alias* "Softy" Hubbard, *alias* Billy The Hopper, paused for breath behind a hedge that bordered a quiet lane and peered out into the highway at a roadster whose tail light advertised its presence to his felonious gaze. — *A Reversible Santa Claus*, Meredith Nicholson, 1917.

9764 One sunny morning in July, Mr. Joseph Balterghen's blue Rolls Royce oozed silently away from the pavement in Berkeley Square, slid across Piccadilly into St. James's, and sped softly eastward towards the City of London. — *Uncommon Danger*, Eric Ambler, 1937.

9765 Fontaine Allard watched the three vehicles move down the drive. — *None Shall Look Back*, Caroline Gordon, 1937.

9766 Across these two miles of sun-blasted desert the small black line faded and reappeared and faded again, but big Dave Wallace knew it was only the heat and that the stage was really coming. — *Sunset Graze*, Luke Short, 1942.

9767 Dave Nash reined up and let the buggy pass ahead of him on the narrow road entering the switchbacks that finally let down into Signal's street. — *Ramrod*, Luke Short, 1943.

9768 Francis Ellery leaned against the side of a bus which apparently had abandoned the idea of going any further in the fog. — *Ride with Me*, Thomas B. Costain, 1944.

9769 "If I get killed to-day, it won't be by falling off the top of a truck," Joseph thought, digging his fingers into the tarred canvas cover of the swaying and lurching vehicle. — *Thieves in the Night*, Arthur Koestler, 1946.

9770 I first saw the *Nancy Flyer* in about 1835, at a time when stagecoaches like her were speeding up all the life of folks in these New Hampshire mountains. — *The Nancy Flyer*, Ernest Poole, 1949.

9771 On a gusty March afternoon in the year eighteen and eighty-one, a battered black hack drawn by two gray horses appeared on the top of Haldeman's Hill, swayed for a moment as the wind from the high ground struck it, and then lurched forward in the hub-deep mud almost upon the horses' haunches as the down grade sharply began. — *The Gown of Glory*, Agnes Sligh Turnbull, 1952.

9772 The wheels of the stagecoach stirred up a long trail of dust, to sift away eastward like a plume of smoke sprouting from the wide spring prairie. — *Miss Morissa*, Mari Sandoz, 1955.

9773 A cart drove between the two big stringybarks and stopped. — *The Tree of Man*, Patrick White, 1955.

9774 On a winter afternoon, unseasonably warm, a car was racing over country roads toward town. — *The Voice at the Back Door*, Elizabeth Spencer, 1956.

9775 Early one morning last September the men squatting on the northeast corner of the town square looked up from their whittling to see, already halfway down the west side and passing under the shadow of the Confederate monument, a dusty long black hearse with a Dallas County license plate. — *Home from the Hill*, William Humphrey, 1958.

9776 When the sun teetered in the sky and began the long, spring solstice slide toward afternoon, he came out from under the hood of a wrecked Plymouth where he was stripping parts for Jeffcoat's A-1. — *Racers to the Sun*, James B. Hall, 1960.

9777 The coach from Ellsworth to Butcher's Crossing was a dougherty that had been converted to carry passengers and small freight. — *Butcher's Crossing*, John Williams, 1960.

9778 As the taxi turned the corner at Shepherd's Bush, the first flakes of snow drifted against the window. — *Necessary Doubt*, Colin Wilson, 1964.

9779 Mother jumped into the taxi as it was beginning to move. — *Ben Preserve Us*, Chaim Bermant, 1965.

9780 Somewhere between Meknes and Fez, the bus came to a sudden halt. — *A Woman of My Age*, Nina Bawden, 1967.

9781 The light from the bus moved uncertainly down the road until finally the two vague circles caught some indistinct object on the side of the road where it curved out in front. — *The Beautiful One Are Not Yet Born*, Ayi Kwei Armah, 1968.

9782 Three men and a boy sat in the dark in a battered 1958 Ford on a shale road that wound along the base of the mountain. — *To the Bright and Shining Sun*, James Lee Burke, 1970.

9783 The ancient Rolls-Royce moved majestically and incongruously along the beach at the ocean's edge. — *The Other Side of the Sun*, Madeleine L'Engle, 1971.

9784 "What is it?"/ "What?"/ "The job."/ "It's a Porsche." — *The Pedlock Inheritance*, Stephen Longstreet, 1972.

9785 The camouflaged Humber staff car ground to a halt, its front bumper within feet of the jetty's edge, and stood vibrating noisily as if eager to be off again. — *Rendezvous — South Atlantic*, Douglas Reeman, 1972.

9786 Again today Alex Housman drove the Buick Riviera. The Buick, coppertone, white sidewalls, was the model of the year, a '59, although the 1960 models were already out. — *The Car Thief*, Theodore Weesner, 1972.

9787 There were three keys on the transmission hump of the XK-E. — *The Digger's Game*, George V. Higgins, 1973.

9788 "He ought to sound his horn," Professor Burch remarked nervously as the bus rounded a hairpin bend and without further ado was swallowed up by a tunnel, vanishing into the belly of a petrified whale lined with jagged basalt. — *The Call Girls*, Arthur Koestler, 1973.

9789 Once upon a winter's night when the wind blew its guts out and a fishy piece of moon

scuttled among the clouds, a coach came thundering down the long hill outside of Dorking. — *The Sound of Coaches*, Leon Garfield, 1974.

9790 "That's torn it!" said Lord Peter Wimsey./ The car lay, helpless and ridiculous, her nose deep in the ditch, her back wheels cocked absurdly up on the bank, as though she were doing her best to bolt to earth and were scraping herself a burrow beneath the drifted snow. — *The Nine Tailors*, Dorothy L. Sayers, 1975.

9791 The camouflaged three-ton Bedford slewed round on the narrow track, its wheels churning in a mixture of dirty snow and loose stones, and came to a shuddering halt. — *Surface with Daring*, Douglas Reeman, 1976.

9792 Its flaking red paint almost obscured by dust, an old swayback gray horse between the shafts, the caravan stood out even among the bizarre lines of transport that filled the last free roads of France that bright June morning in 1940. — *Bel Ria*, Sheila Burnford, 1977.

9793 Regal Pettibone, who once upon a time owned a repossessed, especially designed silver Packard, now drove a gold and white Lincoln chariot. — *The Bloodworth Orphans*, Leon Forrest, 1977.

9794 A long black limousine, California license MK-1, pulls off the path and onto the lawn, crushing only a few daisies. — *Waiting for Cordelia*, Herbert Gold, 1977.

9795 Towards the end of the third decade of the present century a coal haulier's cart, pulled by a large, dirt-grey horse, came into the narrow streets of the village of Saxton, a small mining community in the low hill-land of south Yorkshire. — *Saville*, David Storey, 1977.

9796 The bus, because of the unevenness of the road, lurched and swayed so that the old man sitting across the way from Sister Luiza had trouble with his eating. — *Birdcage*, Victor Canning, 1978.

9797 For two weeks there have been no buses to catch and scarcely any taxis. — *Sweet Country*, Caroline Richards, 1979.

9798 The pickup, carrying a homemade camper knocked together out of painted plywood and sheet metal, moved down Interstate 40 at a steady fifty-five. — *Next of Kin*, Oliver Lange, 1980.

9799 Shifty as a shortstop, the Stingray swung in for gas at the outskirts of town. — *Shame the Devil*, Philip Appleman, 1981.

9800 It was just dawn as the black Porsche stopped with a sputter at the intersection of Mulholland and Laurel Canyon Boulevard. — *Turnaround*, Don Carpenter, 1981.

9801 On my last night but one as a taxi driver in Manhattan, the dispatcher gave me a cab that wanted desperately to die. — *Not a Through Street*,

Ernest Larsen, 1981.

9802 Sophie drove up in a borrowed Mercedes one afternoon early in July. — *A Craving*, Emily Arnold, 1982.

9803 The truck missed us by two feet or less, Jimmie Dee says, and tries to hold his hands steady that much apart. — *Joyride*, Gordon Chaplin, 1982.

9804 Three buses moved with almost funereal slowness through the narrow winding country lanes. — *Goodbye, Mickey Mouse*, Len Deighton, 1982.

9805 When Patrick Domostroy turned the ignition key of his car, no sound came from the engine and no lights showed on the dashboard. — *Pinball*, Jerzy Kosinski, 1982.

9806 A taxi drove through a part of north London. — *The Ladies' Man*, Max Egremont, 1983.

9807 As my cab curled off FDR Drive, somewhere in the early Hundreds, a low-slung Tomahawk full of black guys came sharking out of lane and sloped in fast right across our bows. — *Money*, Martin Amis, 1984.

9808 Valenti's Chrysler nosed past McHale's sere yellow midsummer front lawn and Henna felt safe. — *Men with Debts*, Anthony Giardina, 1984.

9809 Both headlights had been smashed out of the Chevrolet years before when Dillard had tried to park it himself one night in the car shed. — *Square Dance*, Alan Hines, 1984.

9810 Dawn was beginning to soften the edge of the night as the Buick convertible cruised through the Essex countryside. — *Piece of Cake*, Derek Robinson, 1984.

9811 The silver Rolls-Royce glided off Key Biscayne as smoothly as a dolphin cutting the green water of the bay. — *A Land Remembered*, Patrick D. Smith, 1984.

9812 At quarter to eight on a Tuesday morning, a highway patrol car appeared on the vast desert surface of Interstate 81, about ten miles out of Roanoke and southbound for that city. — *Waiting for the End of the World*, Madison Smartt Bell, 1985.

9813 A United States Army truck jolted and jarred its way along a rutted road in France. — *The Gentle Infantryman*, William Young Boyd, 1985.

9814 The station wagons arrived at noon, a long shining line that coursed through the west campus. — *White Noise*, Don DeLillo, 1985.

9815 A bird, hovering high above the Quantock hills, would not have been alarmed by the car's progress. — *The Anderson Question*, Bel Mooney, 1985.

9816 North of Tokyo in Toshima Ward the bus halted to allow a troop of schoolboys to cross the street. — *East and West*, Gerald Green, 1986.

9817 The van, glistening like opal in a rare day of summer sunshine, turned in off Praed Street, picked its way among the standing taxis, and came to a stop in front of Paddington Station. — *The Little People*, MacDonald Harris, 1986.

9818 Dad has the ute going outside. — *That Eye, The Sky*, Tim Winton, 1986.

9819 From the outside it looked like any new 1964 Cadillac limousine. — *The Propheteers*, Max Apple, 1987.

9820 The car taking him back to the Residence entered Proclamation Square sometime between nine and nine-fifteen. — *The Color of Blood*, Brian Moore, 1987.

9821 Of course I'd been thinking about Coyote when it happened: when I'd put my car into forward instead of reverse; when I'd plowed my silver-gray Mercedes 450SL up and over the hood of the metallic-gold Porsche Targa that had been parked head-to-head with me in the parking garage of the Beverly Hills Neiman-Marcus. — *Coyote*, Lynn Vannucci, 1987.

9822 A Somerville-bodied Rolls-Royce was to be seen waiting at the door of number 32 Connaught Square, every weekday morning, at precisely ten o'clock. — *Honour and Obey*, Malcolm Macdonald, 1988.

9823 It came down the hill sideways, this giant orange garbage truck sliding on the ice. — *The Gold Flake Hydrant*, Greg Matthews, 1988.

9824 Electric gates draw back, and a silver-blue Mercedes — a 300SEL roadster model — enters an underground car park in Geneva. — *Penelope's Hat*, Ronald Frame, 1989.

9825 It's a Lincoln Trader. The name seems odd, so I look twice to make sure there's no mistake. — *Sister Hollywood*, C. K. Stead, 1989.

9826 An ivory BMW with two pairs of skis on the roof descended a long hill, granite cliffs spiked with fir trees rising up on either side of the road. — *Bedrock*, Lisa Alther, 1990.

9827 Once our father bought a convertible. Don't ask me. I was five. — *A Home at the End of the World*, Michael Cunningham, 1990.

9828 The big Leyland double-decked bus spun its way up the darkened street, past shuttered shops, a few late restaurants and a darkened cinema: other traffic was sparse and only solitary walkers braved the rain. — *The Final Glass*, Laurence Henderson, 1990.

9829 They swung onto the gravel shoulder behind me just outside of Rawlins — a '66 Impala rusted halfway up the doors. — *Sirens*, Stephen Pett, 1990.

9830 The manure cart had big heavy wooden wheels with wooden spokes and iron rims. — *Ben*, Max Schott, 1990.

9831 Black cars were passing through the smaller streets. — *Lights Out in the Reptile House*, Jim Shepard, 1990.

9832 Buckboard was a fitting name for this — this vehicle! — *No Roof but Heaven*, Jeanne Williams, 1990.

9833 Shortly after nightfall on the last Friday of February 1953, a blue Volga limousine, its windows showing black, entered the west gate of the Kremlin, cut sharply left, slowed, passed between the two watchtowers, and swept with sudden speed into the cold, stale darkness of a tunnel. — *Radical Surgery*, Wallace Markfield, 1991.

9834 In the summer of 1949, in eastern Colorado, far from the nearest metric wrench, our car died and sank into a sea of sheep. — *Now You See It*, Cornelia Nixon, 1991.

9835 At a quarter to five a car could be heard coming down the dirt road from the direction of the quarry, and Catherine Mansure and her young son, Ben, went out to meet it. — *The Trespassers*, Robert Roper, 1992.

9836 "I thought you said you had a car?" — *A Dubious Legacy*, Mary Wesley, 1992.

9837 All night the image recurred: he could see the car dangling from a chain, spotlighted above the black lake, water cascading as if from some jagged rupture. — *Trial by Water*, George Cuomo, 1993.

9838 There's something sad about a prison bus. — *Six Out Seven*, Jess Mowry, 1993.

Violence

9839 He — for there could be no doubt of his sex, though the fashion of the time did something to disguise it — was in the act of slicing at the head of a Moor which swung from the rafters. — *Orlando*, Virginia Woolf, 1928.

9840 Through the fence, between the curling flower spaces, I could see them hitting. — *The Sound and the Fury*, William Faulkner, 1929.

9841 They struggled with the deceptive fury of strong young cats at play. Clawing and snarling, their bodies spinning in a threshing tangle, the two boys beat a whirling course across the sandy hillock. Flying knees tore into the soft earth. Browning clumps of springy grass and the delicately green and pleated fans of young palmetto shoots were flattened by their rolling weight. Then, abruptly, and as though by prearranged signal, the contest ended in a series of sharp, whistling sighs and the heavy, panting gasps of labored breathing. — *Bright Feather*, Robert Wilder, 1948.

9842 The two quiet Indians, resting in Z shapes, could watch and hear the shots going back and forth, back and forth, as in a Western movie. But suddenly someone was hurt and it wasn't like a Western movie now. — *The Bronc People*, William Eastlake, 1958.

9843 He lurched at her from the doorway. — *Three Women*, March Hastings, 1958.

9844 Caldwell turned and as he turned his ankle received an arrow. — *The Centaur*, John Updike, 1963.

9845 When he heard the shot in Mr. Hibbert's office, Francis Vollmer saw his future flash before his eyes. — *Any God Will Do*, Richard Condon, 1964.

9846 It was ten years after the violence in which he died. And his time on this earth was over. — *The Adventurers*, Harold Robbins, 1966.

9847 "Violence lies very close to the surface in the Punjab." — *Storm in Chandigarh*, Nayantara Sahgal, 1969.

9848 Agatha Teel's left shoulder had been shattered by a bullet fifty-one seconds ago. — *The Whisper of the Axe*, Richard Condon, 1976.

9849 The damn'd blood burst, first through his nostrils, then pounded through the veins in his neck, the scarlet torrent exploded through his mouth, it reached his eyes and blinded him, and brought Arthur down, down, down, down. — *Just Above My Head*, James Baldwin, 1979.

9850 In the winter of 1981 a multimillionaire by the name of Robinson Daniels shot a Haitian refugee who had broken into his home in Palm Beach. — *Split Images*, Elmore Leonard, 1982.

9851 Lily. Dan looked at the blonde coat stiffened with blood. — *We Can't All Be Heroes, You Know*, Linda Anderson, 1985.

9852 At least nothing was broken. — *Heat*, William Goldman, 1985.

9853 A young nun told us one morning during catechism class how missionaries from France had been captured and tortured by the Indians in America. — *The Catholic*, David Plante, 1985.

9854 When they shot that boy in both legs up against my wall I was in the house sitting at the fire by myself. — *Give Them Stones*, Mary Beckett, 1987.

Visitors

9855 D'abord, madame, c'est impossible! — Madame ne descendra pas ici?" said François, the footman of Mad. de Fleury, with a half ex-
postulatory, half indignant look, as he let down the step of her carriage at the entrance of a dirty passage, that led to one of the most miserable-looking houses in Paris. — "Madame de Fleury," Maria Edgeworth, 1809.

9856 "There is Helen in the lime-walk," said Mrs. Collingwood to her husband, as she looked out of the window. — *Helen*, Maria Edgeworth, 1834.

9857 Mallet had made his arrangements to sail for Europe on the first of September, and having in the interval a fortnight to spare, he determined to spend it with his cousin Cecilia, the widow of a nephew of his father. — *Roderick Hudson*, Henry James, 1876.

9858 Towards the close of last July, when the London season was fast dying of the dust, Otho Laurence had invited what the *Morning Post* called a "select circle of friends," to spend a quiet Sunday with him at his cool villa by the sea. — *The New Republic*, William H. Mallock, 1877.

9859 Mrs. Sam Wyndham was generally at home after five o'clock. The established custom whereby the ladies who live in Beacon Street all receive their friends on Monday afternoon did not seem to her satisfactory. She was willing to conform to the practice, but she reserved the right of seeing people on other days as well. — *An American Politician*, F. Marion Crawford, 1884.

9860 CONCORD, March 1, 1774./ "MY DEAR COUSIN: I am leaving next week with my husband for England, where we intend to pass some time visiting friends. John and I have determined to accept the invitation you gave us last summer for Harold to come and spend a few months with you. His father thinks that a great future will ere many years open in the West, and that it is therefore well the boy should learn something of frontier life. For myself, I would rather that he stayed quietly at home, for he is at present over-fond of adventure; but as my husband is meditating selling his estate here and moving west, it is perhaps better for him. . . ." — *True to the Old Flag*, G. A. Henty, 1885.

9861 "Oh yes, I daresay I can find the child, if you would like to see him," Miss Pynsent said; she had a fluttering wish to assent to every suggestion made by her visitor, whom she regarded as a high and rather terrible personage. — *The Princess Casamassima*, Henry James, 1886.

9862 "I have written to ask Ralph Conway to come and stay for a time with me." — *One of the 28th*, G. A. Henty, 1889.

9863 "I'm going to stay with the three Miss Miners at the Trehearnes' place," said Louis Lawrence, looking down into the blue water as he leaned over the rail of the *Sappho*, on the sunny side of the steamer. — *Love in Idleness*, F. Marion Crawford, 1894.

9864 I confess that with all my curiosity to meet an Altrurian, I was in no hospitable mood towards the traveler when he finally presented himself, pursuant to the letter of advice sent me by the friend who introduced him. — *A Traveler from Altruria*, William Dean Howells, 1894.

9865 "I am glad you came, Clarke; very glad indeed. I was not sure you could spare the time." — "The Great God Pan," Arthur Machen, 1894.

9866 "Father," said Dora, "I am going upstairs for a little, to see Mrs. Hesketh, if you have no objection."/ "And who is Mrs. Hesketh, if I might make so bold as to ask?" Mr. Mannering said, lifting his eyes from his evening paper. — *A House in Bloomsbury*, Margaret Oliphant *as* Mrs. Oliphant, 1894.

9867 "It is so good of you to come early," said Mrs. Porter, as Alice Langham entered the drawing-room. — *Soldiers of Fortune*, Richard Harding Davis, 1897.

9868 "If we receive this Lady Mary Montgomery, we shall also have to receive her dreadful husband." — *Senator North*, Gertrude Atherton, 1900.

9869 Walking along the river wall at Botzen, Edmund Dawney said to Alois Harz:/ "There's a family at Villa Rubein, the pink house — would you care to know them?"/ Harz answered with a smile:/ "Perhaps." — *Villa Rubein*, John Galsworthy *as* John Sinjohn, 1900.

9870 The Baroness Volterra drove to the Palazzo Conti in the heart of Rome at nine o'clock in the morning, to be sure of finding Donna Clementina at home. — *The Heart of Rome*, F. Marion Crawford, 1903.

9871 "Mr. Hood will see you in the library, sir." — *Constance Trescot*, S. Weir Mitchell, 1905.

9872 Dr. Lavendar and Goliath had toiled up the hill to call on old Mr. Benjamin Wright; when they jogged back in the late afternoon it was with the peculiar complacency which follows the doing of a disagreeable duty. — *The Awakening of Helena Richie*, Margaret Deland, 1906.

9873 The tall young lady who arrived fifteen minutes before the Freddy Tunbridges' dinner-hour, was not taken into the great empty drawing-room, but, as though she were not to be of the party expected that night, straight upstairs she went behind the footman, and then up more stairs behind a maid. — *The Convert*, Elizabeth Robins, 1907.

9874 A young Irish gentleman of the numerous clan O'Donnells, and a Patrick, hardly a distinction of him until we know him, had bound himself, by purchase of a railway-ticket, to travel direct to the borders of North Wales, on a visit to a notable landowner of those marches, the Squire Adister, whose family-seat was where the hills begin to lift and spy into the heart of black mountains. — *Celt and Saxon*, George Meredith, 1910.

9875 Della Wetherby tripped up the somewhat imposing steps of her sister's Commonwealth Avenue home and pressed an energetic finger against the electic-bell button. — *Pollyanna Grows Up*, Eleanor H. Porter, 1915.

9876 Uncle Charlie Wheeler stamped on the steps before Nance McGregor's bake shop on the Main Street of the town of Coal Creek Pennsylvania and then went quickly inside. — *Marching Men*, Sherwood Anderson, 1917.

9877 Mr. Salteena was an elderly man of 42 and was fond of asking peaple to stay with him. — *The Young Visiters*, Daisy Ashford, 1919.

9878 Miriam thumped her Gladstone bag down on to the doorstep. — *Interim*, Dorothy M. Richardson, 1919.

9879 In Caracas, Thomas Strawbridge called at the American Consulate, from a sense of duty. — *Fombombo*, T. S. Stribling, 1923.

9880 Miss Bruss, the perfect secretary, received Nona Manford at the door of her mother's boudoir ("the office," Mrs. Manford's children called it) with a gesture of the kindliest denial. — *Twilight Sleep*, Edith Wharton, 1927.

9881 It was on this very day — the thirteenth of July — and in just such weather that Sophia Willoughby had been taken to see the Duke of Wellington. — *Summer Will Show*, Sylvia Townsend Warner, 1931.

9882 Monsieur de Grammont, most lighthearted of all Seventeenth Century young gentlemen, and more light-hearted than ever in exile, was delighted one March morning, after too merry a night with King Charles at Whitehall, to receive a compatriot who was, like himself, youthful, a fine flower from the garden of Versailles, and bore gayly another resemblance even more striking. — *Wanton Mally*, Booth Tarkington, 1932.

9883 Raymond opened the door with a flourish, pushed the electric switch and preceded his two guests into the dimly illuminated room. — *Infants of the Spring*, Wallace Thurman, 1932.

9884 "It is with an especial feeling that I welcome you back to-day," said Josephine Napier, rising from her desk and advancing across her study to greet the woman who had entered it. — *More Women Than Men*, Ivy Compton-Burnett, 1933.

9885 The knocking on the door did not wake Isabelle because she had started up from sleep very early that morning. — *The Thinking Reed*, Rebecca West, 1936.

9886 Wolfe looked at our visitor with his eyes wide open — a sign, with him, either of indifference or of irritation. — *The Red Box*, Rex Stout, 1937.

9887 The knocking sounded again, at once discreet and peremptory, while the doctor was descending the stairs, the flashlight's beam lancing on before him down the brown-stained stairwell and into the brown-stained tongue-and-groove box of the lower hall. — *The Wild Palms*, William Faulkner, 1939.

9888 The bell rang and I went to the front and opened the door and there she was. — *Over My Dead Body*, Rex Stout, 1940.

9889 On a cool, pleasant early fall morning, in the year 1774, Dr. Benjamin Franklin was told that Thomas Paine had been waiting to see him for almost an hour. — *Citizen Tom Paine*, Howard Fast, 1943.

9890 As I left the railway station at Worchester and set out on the three-mile walk to Ransom's cottage, I reflected that no one on that platform could possibly guess the truth about the man I was going to visit. — *Perelandra*, C. S. Lewis, 1943.

9891 I was in Paris when Parfitt, my man, came to me and said that a lady had called to see me. — *The Rose and the Yew Tree*, Agatha Christie as Mary Westmacott, 1947.

9892 The Royal Standard of France waved above the towers of the Louvre. It was an unusual sight, for the King bore Paris no love and seldom came there. — *The Moneyman*, Thomas B. Costain, 1947.

9893 The nearest Jennie ever came to being untrue to Jennie was the night all four of them were staying with her. — *Not Now but Now*, M. F. K. Fisher, 1947.

9894 From the window of his room in a two-roomed hut, the Commandant of the camp watched his visitor approaching him from the gate. — *The Black Laurel*, Storm Jameson, 1947.

9895 It was nothing out of the ordinary that Mrs. Barry Rackham had made the appointment with her finger pressed to her lips. — *In the Best Families*, Rex Stout, 1950.

9896 Mrs. Desmond Cottrell was spending the week-end with a friend who lived at Barnet, an ancient village situated in the northern outskirts of London, and on the second day of her visit it was proposed that they should call upon a certain Lady Dagleish, who was very old and who liked to see a new face. — *The Swiss Summer*, Stella Gibbons, 1951.

9897 Christie Fraser first visited Cate Conboy on December 24, 1899. — *The Witch Diggers*, Jessamyn West, 1951.

9898 As the collie whined again, the old man quietened her and listened, wondering if some of the lads had turned up for a night's poaching. — *Bloodhunt*, Neil M. Gunn, 1952.

9899 Directly Madeleine came to the door, Dinah said, without looking at her:/ "You've got

the blue tubs." — *The Echoing Grove*, Rosamond Lehmann, 1953.

9900 When the doorbell rings while Nero Wolfe and I are at dinner, in the old brownstone house on West Thirty-fifth Street, ordinarily it is left to Fritz to answer it. — *The Golden Spiders*, Rex Stout, 1953.

9901 "The person has arrived, ma'am."/ "What person?" said Mrs. Hume./ "The person who was expected, ma'am."/ "And who was expecting her?" — *Mother and Son*, Ivy Compton-Burnett, 1955.

9902 Most of the people who come to see Nero Wolfe by appointment, especially from as far away as Nebraska, show some sign of being in trouble, but that one didn't. — *Might as Well Be Dead*, Rex Stout, 1956.

9903 "There is a man here, miss, asking for your uncle," said Rose./ And stood breathing. — *Voss*, Patrick White, 1957.

9904 Friday, in the evening, the landlady shouted up the stairs:/ "Oh God, oh Jesus, oh Sacred Heart. Boy, there's two gentlemen to see you." — *Borstal Boy*, Brendan Behan, 1958.

9905 She had been waiting for him. The door opened gently. There were no sudden movements, no unexpected noise, in this house. She held out her arms and he came across the room and kissed her forehead — "In Sickness and in Health," Martha Gellhorn, 1958.

9906 Raju welcomed the intrusion — something to relieve the loneliness of the place. — *The Guide*, R. K. Narayan, 1958.

9907 "Hallo, Miss Bunn," Dick Thompson said on a note of celebration. "Do come in, that's right. Here, let me take that for you. I expect you'd like to go straight up, wouldn't you?" — *Take a Girl Like You*, Kingsley Amis, 1960.

9908 The Little Swine had his head well down in the books when I went in, so it was clear Miss Vosper had forestalled me after all. — *Night of Wenceslas*, Lionel Davidson, 1960.

9909 When he had got deposited in the red leather chair I went to my desk, whirled my chair to face him, sat, and regarded him politely but without enthusiasm. — *Too Many Clients*, Rex Stout, 1960.

9910 "I've come," announced Mr. Joyce, "to talk about Martha." — *Martha in Paris*, Margery Sharp, 1962.

9911 At twenty-seven minutes past eleven that Monday morning in February, Lincoln's Birthday, I opened the door between the office and the front room, entered, shut the door, and said, "Miss Blount is here." — *Gambit*, Rex Stout, 1962.

9912 When the doorbell rang a little after eleven that Tuesday morning in early June and I went to the hall and took a look through the

one-way glass panel in the front door, I saw what, or whom, I expected to see: a face a little too narrow, gray eyes a little too big, and a figure a little too thin for the best curves. — *The Mother Hunt*, Rex Stout, 1963.

9913 He had no appointment and, looking at him across the doorsill, it didn't seem likely that he would be bringing the first big fee of 1964. — *A Right to Die*, Rex Stout, 1964.

9914 Norman Crocker was mixing a short drink for himself when the doorbell rang. — *A Firm Word or Two*, Nathaniel Benchley, 1965.

9915 One evening I was sitting down to my favourite dish — rice-pudding with a blob of jam — when there was a knock on the door, and in came Mrs. Kamenetz-Podolsk. — *Berl Make Tea*, Chaim Bermant, 1965.

9916 When the hotel porter rang to say a gentleman awaited her in the hall, Harriet Pringle dropped the receiver and ran from the room without putting on her shoes. — *Friends and Heroes*, Olivia Manning, 1965.

9917 I heard the dogs barking and I knew that old man Gidharee was coming up the road. — *Green Days by the River*, Michael Anthony, 1967.

9918 In the spring of 1966 my father and mother came to visit me in San Francisco. He was eighty years old and thought he ought to see Hawaii too, why not? while he was out there on the West Coast. — *Fathers*, Herbert Gold, 1967.

9919 Charlie Yost, the Chicago gunman, called on Horace Appleby one morning in June as he chatted with Basher Evans before going off to the Wallingford races. — *Do Butlers Burgle Banks?*, P. G. Wodehouse, 1968.

9920 The thundering knock on the door of his room in the bachelor officers' quarters caught First Lieutenant Pete Brisbin as he was finishing shaving. — *The Deserters*, Luke Short, 1969.

9921 It was a fine evening in early May when she drove up in one of the station taxis to the gate of the house. — *Mrs. Starr Lives Alone*, Jon Godden, 1971.

9922 My luck you're not here. — *Ancient History*, Joseph McElroy, 1971.

9923 "Of *course* I don't mind, my darling. Of *course* I don't." She wore the top half of his pyjamas and was putting cherry jam on a piece of toast. She thought for a moment, and then added, "It will be lovely for me to have someone to talk to while you're in London." — *Odd Girl Out*, Elizabeth Jane Howard, 1972.

9924 Dots was sweating when she arrived at Bernice's apartment. — *Storm of Fortune*, Austin Clarke, 1973.

9925 Billy Bob Mavis had been in twice that morning — talking to George with his mouth full of tacks — about Volkswagen headliners. — *The Hawk Is Dying*, Harry Crews, 1973.

9926 Mrs. April opens the door (a side door, one can always recognise them) in the same moment that she says, "I am Mrs. April." We smile, ask each other how we are doing, how we are. — *Long Distance*, Penelope Mortimer, 1974.

9927 The boy was there again this evening, and the dogs were not barking. — *The Sacred and Profane Love Machine*, Iris Murdoch, 1974.

9928 It was to be the consultant physician's last visit and Dalgliesh suspected that neither of them regretted it, arrogance and patronage on one side and weakness, gratitude and dependence on the other being no foundation for a satisfactory adult relationship however transitory. — *The Black Tower*, P. D. James, 1975.

9929 On Wednesday afternoon, at his headquarters in Senlis, the Marshal had a visit from the Premier of France. — *Gossip from the Forest*, Thomas Keneally, 1975.

9930 "I say, an absolutely stunning coloured girl was here looking for you." — *A Word Child*, Iris Murdoch, 1975.

9931 A few months ago the spirited Yugoslav widow Mrs. Moja Javich visited her son, a wine importer, in London. — *Season in Purgatory*, Thomas Keneally, 1976.

9932 Every year, just before the World Series began, Sol would leave his apartment in Brooklyn and go around the country by train to visit his old boys. — *An Orphan's Tale*, Jay Neugeboren, 1976.

9933 "Hullo," Adam said, when the girl opened the door, "it's only me. Anyone at home?" — *The Glittering Prizes*, Frederic Raphael, 1976.

9934 As the carriage drew away from the Circular Wharf Mr. Stafford Merivale tapped the back of his wife's hand and remarked that they had done their duty. — *A Fringe of Leaves*, Patrick White, 1976.

9935 In October, Charlotte went to Brookroyd to visit Ellen Nussey, her childhood friend. — *Path to the Silent Country*, Lynne Reid Banks, 1977.

9936 Groff, the producer, smelled the visitors before he saw them. — "Girl," Gerald Green, 1977.

9937 I arrive at the house wearing a suit — greyish, it doesn't matter. — *Tirra Lirra by the River*, Jessica Anderson, 1978.

9938 They left half an hour ago. Since then I've been sitting in an exhausted reverie. — *The Glassy Sea*, Marian Engel, 1978.

9939 There was a white man coming up her road, as if God had ordained it and as if he owned the road. — *Sally Hemings*, Barbara Chase-Riboud, 1979.

9940 "Monsieur Alberto Santos-Dumont, sir," Mme. Dufresne said, opening the door

wide. "The balloonist. His letter and your reply are in the blue cover." — *A Night of Bright Stars*, Richard Llewellyn, 1979.

9941 On June 26th, 1959, at Boianai in Papua, visitants appeared to the Reverend William Booth Gill, himself a visitant of thirteen years standing, and to thirty-seven witnesses of another colour. — *Visitants*, Randolph Stow, 1979.

9942 Aw, come on, Birdy! This is Al here, all the way from Dix. Stop it, huh! — *Birdy*, William Wharton, 1979.

9943 When Mrs. Hines came into the cottage sitting room she knew he would be there for his shabby old motor car was parked on the concrete outside her garage alongside the orchard. — *Fall from Grace*, Victor Canning, 1980.

9944 Uncle Red showed up at our farm one day during a dust storm. — *Honkytonk Man*, Clancy Carlile, 1980.

9945 Algar the Prior was in his lodging, listening to the complaints of his bursar about the cellarer's extravagance, when they were disturbed by a cautious opening of the door. — *Flambard's Confession*, Marilyn Durham, 1982.

9946 About an hour before sundown, she saw a man moving through her deadened woods, coming toward her house. — *The Winter People*, John Ehle, 1982.

9947 The G came around again to Frankie Coolin on Thursday, just when he was taking the last of the radiators out of the six-flat he had bought in June. — *Time for Frankie Coolin*, Bill Griffith, 1982.

9948 "Mr. Gavin! Mrs. Whittington's ready to come out." — *Getting It Right*, Elizabeth Jane Howard, 1982.

9949 From time to time, my parents would take me to stay for a weekend with my father's large and sturdy parents, whom I called Big Grandfather and Big Grandmother, or simply Grandfather and Grandmother. — *"Do Clams Bite?"*, Eric Kraft, 1982.

9950 One afternoon at the end of autumn, during my last time at home with my father—a farewell visit is how I thought of it, though with any luck it might not be—I walked alone to an abandoned farmhouse on the other side of the stream that was up for sale at last and which I thought I might make a bid for; a way perhaps of ensuring the future would exist by setting my hand to an official document, a ninety-nine year lease. — *"Child's Play,"* David Malouf, 1982.

9951 On Sunday afternoons, when the world pauses and waits for the next great event, when the streets are empty and unnaturally still and the weight of obligation hangs over the land, the residents of Wincaster Row come calling on me. — *The President's Child*, Fay Weldon, 1982.

9952 "There's a crippled gentleman at the door. And he wants to see you!" — *Corrigan*, Caroline Blackwood, 1984.

9953 — A glass of tea? Or maybe a little schnapps? — *The Border*, Elaine Feinstein, 1984.

9954 They have said that twelve thousand people are dead because William Walker came to Central America. — *The Nation Thief*, Robert Houston, 1984.

9955 Scarcely was it dawn of a remarkably chill morning in May, — indeed, large damp clumps of snow were being blown about like blossoms — when, seemingly out of nowhere, Miss Georgina Kilgarvan, the eldest daughter of the late Judge, appeared, accompanied by her Negro servant Pride, to ring the bell of a tradesman named Phineas Cutter (of Cutter Brothers Mills, on the Temperance Vale Road), and to make a most unusual request. — *Mysteries of Winterthurn*, Joyce Carol Oates, 1984.

9956 I could hardly wait for Leo Hermann to arrive in order to get rid of him. — *Hope Diamond Refuses*, Iris Owens, 1984.

9957 Out of nowhere, and after years of silence, George showed up one July day and put his face against the screen door and said, "Remember me?" — *Doctor De Marr*, Paul Theroux, 1984.

9958 Rob said he'd promised Linc we'd come by Sunday afternoon to see him, Taffy, and the baby. — *Give and Take*, Norma Klein, 1985.

9959 His host was Wm. Tiny. — *Kite*, Ed Minus, 1985.

9960 Here's the plan:/ On the 15th you arrive in L.A. i'll pick you up at the airport and head for San Fernando, to my tíos Fermín and Filomena's house. — *The Mixquiahuala Letters*, Ana Castillo, 1986.

9961 "Come in."/ Chief Detective Inspector Corby pushed away from him the two piles of typescript, reports read and unread. — *Unusual Behaviour*, Lettice Cooper, 1986.

9962 When the visitor walked into the coffeehouse on the central square of Pamplona, he saw with some pleasure that nothing had changed. — *Acts of Faith*, Hans Koning, 1986.

9963 The woman searched for the bell, and failing to find it in the patchy darkness knocked hard on the door. — *An After-Dinner's Sleep*, Stanley Middleton, 1986.

9964 One June morning in 1948, in the town of Leah, New Hampshire, Doris Perkins watched John Hearne cross his backyard and her backyard, which met his, and lightly climb the woodshed roof to her bedroom window. — *The Moon Pinnace*, Thomas Williams, 1986.

9965 If he was flying up to "chew a few things over" with her on a freezing winter Wednesday afternoon, that had to mean something major, something probably quite unpleasant, was

heading into her fan. — *First Ladies*, Catherine Breslin, 1987.

9966 Going to see Clare's family on the isolated hilltop where Ralph Quick had built his domestic fortress was an ordeal for Julia. — *A Southern Family*, Gail Godwin, 1987.

9967 The midnight-blue pickup stopped at the curb in front of Gus and Jewel Lafleur's house. — *Broken Ground*, John Keeble, 1987.

9968 He's coming at seven. He promised. Handle it. Act normal. — *Girls' Night Out*, Kathy Lette, 1987.

9969 The old man came to see me today, journeying out from Verona with only one slave, as dignified and ancient as he is, to drive him. — *The Key*, Benita Kane Jaro, 1988.

9970 She's coming. — *The Trick of It*, Michael Frayn, 1989.

9971 Amos Watson was getting ready for what would surely be his most unpleasant visit to Malacañan Palace. — *Share of Honor*, Ralph Graves, 1989.

9972 *"¿Quién es?"* — *The Ancient Child*, N. Scott Momaday, 1989.

9973 Nancy Meade's grandmother, Leellen-Kay Phillips, was a portrait of health and independence when she came to St. Augustine in August, 1902, on the Florida East Coast Special. — *American Girl*, Page Edwards, 1990.

9974 Pray be seated, sir, and pardon such humble surroundings. — *The Tree of Knowledge*, Eva Figes, 1990.

9975 It had been raining without a stop for four days when Demelza Poldark saw a horseman riding down the valley. — *The Twisted Sword*, Winston Graham, 1990.

9976 I quietly ask myself, "Who is it?" before entering even my own home. — *Little Peg*, Kevin McIlvoy, 1990.

9977 An out-of-town visitor from Dragoon, Arizona, dangled from a window ledge on the thirty-eighth floor of the Empire State Building one cold and dreary day in New York City. — *Waiting for Rain*, Indiana Nelson, 1990.

9978 In 1908, when my father was ten, three Polish peasants, drunk and celebrating, came to the shtetl and banged on the door to his father's house. — *The Tree Still Stands*, Mae Briskin, 1991.

9979 The lawyer came out to Tatekeya's place along the river that day. — *From the River's Edge*, Elizabeth Cook-Lynn, 1991.

9980 "Look, Mommy, someone's here." — *Heat Storm*, Linda Chandler Munson, 1991.

9981 The day after Christmas, they set out for Chicago to visit his mother. — *Violence*, Richard Bausch, 1992.

9982 The assignment editor, a woman named Jennifer Eugene, had walked over from Lifestyle. — *Love & Obits*, John Ed Bradley, 1992.

9983 It began to seem to Haskell that every time he came to the house something else was being taken away. — *The Empty Lot*, Mary Gray Hughes, 1992.

9984 When Susan Sternfeld was three, she went downstairs to visit her grandparents, who lived in the apartment below. — *Field of Stars*, Alice Mattison, 1992.

9985 Every day during haying Grandma came around from her house and looked in at them through the screen door. — *Dreams Like Thunder*, Diane Simmons, 1992.

9986 Leslie Beck came to see me the other day. — *Life Force*, Fay Weldon, 1992.

9987 I was in Elgin, upstairs in my study, gazing at the sea and reflecting, I remember, on a line of Goethe when Mrs. Gregor tapped at the door that Saturday and said there was a young man to see me in the surgery, a pilot. — *Dr. Haggard's Disease*, Patrick McGrath, 1993.

9988 "Who was that knocking at your front door?" asked Annette, as Spicer got back into bed and entwined his legs through hers. — *Trouble*, Fay Weldon, 1993.

Voices

9989 I Nathaniel Peacock, of the parish of St. Giles, haberdasher and author, solemnly declare, That on the third of last August, sitting alone in my study, up three pair of stairs, between the hours of eleven and twelve at night, meditating upon the uncertainty of sublunary enjoyment, I heard a shrill, small voice, seemingly proceeding from a chink or crevice in my own pericranium, call distinctly three times, "Nathaniel Peacock, Nathaniel Peacock, Nathaniel Peacock." Astonished, yea, even affrighted, at this citation, I replied in a faultering tone, "In the name of the Lord, what art thou?" Thus adjured, the voice answered and said, "I am an atom." — *The History and Adventures of an Atom*, Tobias Smollett, 1769.

9990 *Cur me exanimas querelis tuis?* — In plain English, Why do you deafen me with your croaking? — *Redgauntlet*, Sir Walter Scott, 1824.

9991 "Kaspar! Makan!"/ The well-known shrill voice startled Almayer from his dream of splendid future into the unpleasant realities of the present hour. — *Almayer's Folly*, Joseph Conrad, 1895.

9992 "You won't be late?" There was anxiety in Marjorie Carling's voice, there was something like entreaty. — *Point Counter Point*, Aldous Huxley, 1928.

9993 ...In the year that the locusts came, something that happened in the year the locusts came, two voices that I heard there in that year.... Child! Child! — "The Web of Earth," Thomas Wolfe, 1932.

9994 Her voice was something to dream about, on any night when she was running through the hills. — *The Voice of Bugle Ann*, MacKinlay Kantor, 1935.

9995 The February sun slipped down behind the tiger-colored hills across the tawny Jabalón valley and they became solid and disturbing; the cliffs above the olive slopes ceased to glow, and of the three voices singing among the dark multitude of olive trees two were suddenly quiet. — *The Olive Field*, Ralph Bates, 1936.

9996 Every few hours the captain took the launch in towards the bank and the monotonous voice of the man with the sounding chain quickened. — *Dead Man Leading*, V. S. Pritchett, 1937.

9997 Ling Tan lifted his head. Over the rice field in which he stood to his knees in water he heard his wife's high loud voice. — *Dragon Seed*, Pearl S. Buck, 1942.

9998 "Eustace! Eustace!" Hilda's tones were always urgent; it might not be anything very serious. — *The Shrimp and the Anemone*, L. P. Hartley, 1944.

9999 The blue lines down the floor of the swimming pool wavered and shivered incessantly, and something about the shape of the place — the fact that it was long and narrow, perhaps, and lined with tile to the ceiling — made their voices ring. — *The Folded Leaf*, William Maxwell, 1945.

10000 "Do you hear voices?" he asked. — *The Snake Pit*, Mary Jane Ward, 1946.

10001 The curtains between the loggia and the rest of the villa were no defence against the eunuch's voice. — *Envoy Extraordinary*, William Golding, 1956.

10002 Epsom's white paint glimmered against scintillant grass as he had always remembered, and the bookmakers' shouts came on lulls of the wind, exactly like listening to a sea shell. — *Mr. Hamish Gleave*, Richard Llewellyn, 1956.

10003 The voice on the telephone seemed to be sharp and peremptory, but I didn't hear too well what it said — partly because I was only half awake and partly because I was holding the receiver upside down. — *Playback*, Raymond Chandler, 1958.

10004 "Terrifying," Ninian La Touche said to Miss Fellowe in a voice that made all but his sister Violet turn and look. — *A Season of Mists*, Honor Tracy, 1961.

10005 "Attention," a voice began to call, and it was as though an oboe had suddenly become articulate. "Attention," it repeated in the same high, nasal monotone. "Attention." — *Island*, Aldous Huxley, 1962.

10006 On an evening in late November, in the year 1962, the voice of the announcer boomed across the airport waiting room at New York's Idlewild. — *The Mule on the Minaret*, Alec Waugh, 1965.

10007 Hip hole and hupmobile, Braunschweiger, you didn't invite Geiger and his counter for nothing, here is D.J. the friendLee voice at your service — hold tight young America — introductions come. — *Why Are We in Vietnam?*, Norman Mailer, 1967.

10008 I was still sitting benumbed in the bedroom when the outer door opened and closed and I heard Marie's voice. — *The Do-Gooders*, Alfred Grossman, 1968.

10009 *"Jeremiah! Miah!"/ He heard the shots ring out/ It was 8:20 and he ran fast/ The woods collided, the dense growth clashed/ And then he heard the darkhunt: the voice distending raw and clear and black as christened snow:/ Jeremiah! Miah!* — *Jeremiah 8:20*, Carol Hill, 1970.

10010 He grunted — the low brief rumble that isn't meant to be heard — turned his head to dart a glance at me, and turned back to Dr. Vollmer, who was in the red leather chair facing the end of Wolfe's desk. — *Please Pass the Guilt*, Rex Stout, 1973.

10011 — Money...? in a voice that rustled. — *J R*, William Gaddis, 1975.

10012 Hubert Anvil's voice rose above the sound of the choir and full orchestra, reaching the vertex of the loftiest dome in the Old World and the western doors of the longest nave in Christendom. — *The Alteration*, Kingsley Amis, 1977.

10013 Gertrude Conover turned on her cassette player, and over it came the unmistakable voice of my father-in-law Leo Bebb. — *Treasure Hunt*, Frederick Buechner, 1977.

10014 Thinned and distorted by the sea breeze came the voice: "Duncan — Duncan!" — "A Sentimental Education," Joyce Carol Oates, 1979.

10015 A voice comes to one in the dark. Imagine. — "Company," Samuel Beckett, 1980.

10016 "Yoh! Ivan ... Ivanhoe yoh!" Without pausing in her work in the open kitchen, Miss 'Mando listened to the echoes of her whoop bouncing back and forth against the hillsides and away down the valley, growing fainter as they went. — *The Harder They Come*, Michael Thelwell, 1980.

10017 Somewhere from the depths of the city there came a brutish cry. — *The Magistrate*, Ernest K. Gann, 1982.

10018 *To whom do I owe the power behind my voice, what strength I have become, yeasting up like*

sudden blood from under the bruised skin's blister?
— *Zami: A New Spelling of My Name*, Audre Lorde, 1982.

10019 I heard Candy out in the front yard calling Gram Mon. — *A Gathering of Old Men*, Ernest J. Gaines, 1983.

10020 A voice was calling me, lifting me up from the covers that were heavy because it was only May and nights were still cool. — *The Empty Meadow*, Ben Logan, 1983.

10021 We could hear our children's voices in the darkness on the sweet-smelling hill by my friend's house, and could hear the barking of Angus, his dog. — *Shawno*, George Dennison, 1984.

10022 Ah, Luigi, Luigi! In the worn and wrinkled fustian of those old pages I hear your very voice again. — *The Journeyer*, Gary Jennings, 1984.

10023 Voices trickled insistent but subdued in the open air. — *Valley of Decision*, Stanley Middleton, 1985.

10024 She's still at the top end of the gangway when she hears Mickey scream. — *Then Again*, Sue McCauley, 1986.

10025 Captain Anderson turned away from me, cupped his hands round his mouth and roared. — *Fire Down Below*, William Golding, 1989.

10026 I turn the pages of the transcript and hear the singsong voice of an old Indian woman. — *Desierto*, Charles Bowden, 1991.

10027 You could have paved your driveway with Willy's voice, which was smoother than dirt, but not as even as asphalt. The gravel in it made him sound naturally surly, even when he said hello. — *The Last Studebaker*, Robin Hemley, 1992.

10028 In the beginning was the voice of Father. — *Lasher*, Anne Rice, 1993.

Waiting

10029 "Has she come?"/ "No, Mamma, not yet." — *Behind a Mask*, Louisa May Alcott *as* A. M. Barnard, 1866.

10030 On the forward promenade of the Saguenay boat which had been advertised to leave Quebec at seven o'clock on Tuesday morning, Miss Kitty Ellison sat tranquilly expectant of the joys which its departure should bring, and tolerantly patient of its delay; for if all the Saguenay had not been in promise, she would have thought it the greatest happiness just to have that prospect of the St. Lawrence and Quebec. — *A*

Chance Acquaintance, William Dean Howells, 1873.

10031 "Olive will come down in about ten minutes; she told me to tell you that." — *The Bostonians*, Henry James, 1886.

10032 Northwick's man met him at the station with the cutter. The train was a little late, and Elbridge was a little early; after a few moments of formal waiting, he began to walk the clipped horses up and down the street. — *The Quality of Mercy*, William Dean Howells, 1892.

10033 When the Great King, that mirror of a majesty whereof modern times have robbed the world, recoiled aghast from the threatened indignity of having to wait, he laid his finger with a true touch on a characteristic incident of the lot of common men, from which it was seemly that the state of God's Vicegerents should be free. — *A Change of Air*, Anthony Hope, 1893.

10034 On the field of Appomattox General Lee was waiting the return of a courier. — *The Leopard's Spots*, Thomas Dixon, Jr., 1902.

10035 At eight o'clock in the inner vestibule of the Auditorium Theatre by the window of the box office, Laura Dearborn, her younger sister Page, and their aunt — Aunt Wess' — were still waiting for the rest of the theatre-party to appear. — *The Pit*, Frank Norris, 1903.

10036 It was a bright, clear afternoon in the late fall that pretty Miss Cable drove up in her trap and waited at the curb for her father to come forth from his office in one of Chicago's tallest buildings. — *Jane Cable*, George Barr McCutcheon, 1906.

10037 John Durham, while he waited for Madame de Malrive to draw on her gloves, stood in the hotel doorway looking out across the Rue de Rivoli at the afternoon brightness of the Tuileries gardens. — "Madame de Treymes," Edith Wharton, 1907.

10038 A woman, tall, somewhat angular, dark of hair and eye, strong of features — a woman now approaching middle age — sat looking out over the long, tree-clad slopes that ran down from the gallery front of the mansion house to the gate at the distant roadway. She had sat thus for some moments, many moments, her gaze intently fixed, as though waiting for something — something or someone that she did not now see, but expected soon to see. — *The Magnificent Adventure*, Emerson Hough, 1916.

10039 It was not openly spoken of, but the family was waiting for Caleb Gare. — *Wild Geese*, Martha Ostenso, 1925.

10040 Henry Martin, on his terrace, lay in his deck chair waiting for his secretary, an ill-humoured, spectacled, young Englishman of the name of Macdonald who, not unusually, failed to keep his engagements. — *Henry for Hugh*, Ford Madox Ford, 1934.

10041 She might have been waiting for her lover. For half an hour she had sat on the same high stool, half turned from the counter, watching the swing door. — *England Made Me*, Graham Greene, 1935.

10042 About fifteen years ago, at the end of the second decade of this century, four people were standing together on the platform of the railway station of a town in the hills of western Catawba. — *Of Time and the River*, Thomas Wolfe, 1935.

10043 On a late Sunday afternoon in April 1866, Thomas Linthorne waited behind the thick Osage orange hedgerow on the lip of Chilton's upper pasture field as was his wont for the two Sundays past. — *The Earth Abideth*, George Dell, 1938.

10044 She is waiting for him. She was waiting for him for twenty years. He is coming today. — *Winter of Artifice*, Anaïs Nin, 1939.

10045 They stood in the chilling April rain under a street light on the corner, and waited for the bus. Once in a while they exchanged fretful glances, as if each thought the other might hurry the bus along somehow. — *O River, Remember!*, Martha Ostenso, 1943.

10046 I seemed to be standing in a bus queue by the side of a long, mean street. — *The Great Divorce*, C. S. Lewis, 1945.

10047 While I was waiting for you in the foyer of that superb hotel, I started talking with the head porter. — *Leave Cancelled*, Nicholas Monsarrat, 1945.

10048 Renn sat down, to wait for his friend, at a table outside the café. — *Before the Crossing*, Storm Jameson, 1947.

10049 It's the waiting, Shep was thinking. You wait to get inside the gate, you wait outside the great man's office, you wait for your agent to make the deal, you wait for the assignment, you wait for instructions on how to write what they want you to write, and then, when you finish your treatment and turn it in, you wait for that unique contribution to art, the story conference. — *The Disenchanted*, Budd Schulberg, 1950.

10050 I found her waiting at the door of my office. — *The Ivory Grin*, Kenneth Millar *as* John Ross Macdonald, 1952.

10051 Between the marriage elms at the foot of the broad lawn, there hung a scarlet canvas hammock where Andrew Shipley squandered the changeless afternoons of early June. Books lay in heaps beneath him on the grass, but he seldom read; he had lost the craft of losing himself and threads of adventure snarled in his mind; the simplest words looked strange. His kite was stuck in the top of a tree and black ants moved militantly over his pole and tackle box. He was waiting. — *The Catherine Wheel*, Jean Stafford, 1952.

10052 Away back somewhere there must have been a man who had a dog, and one time something happened to her, and she didn't come home, although the man kept the fire up all night long. — *The Daughter of Bugle Ann*, MacKinlay Kantor, 1953.

10053 In the heat of a spacious August noon, in the heart of the great summer of 1870, the three famous Sylvester women waited in their parlour to receive and make welcome the fourth. — *The Gipsy in the Parlour*, Margery Sharp, 1953.

10054 She came through the turnstile and joined the crowd waiting for the ferry: the women in cotton pyjama suits, the men with felt slippers and gold teeth. — *The World of Suzie Wong*, Richard Mason, 1957.

10055 Eager and tensely expectant, chin resting on knees and her arms locked tightly around her legs, Claudelle had been sitting on the steps of the front porch for nearly half an hour and waiting for Archer Gunnson, the mail carrier, to come around the bend in the road. — *Claudelle Inglish*, Erskine Caldwell, 1958.

10056 No Name waited until it was dark. — *Conquering Horse*, Frederick Manfred, 1959.

10057 For five hours now, the man had waited. — *Village of Stars*, David Beaty *as* Paul Stanton, 1960.

10058 She was waiting at the office door when I got back from my morning coffee break. — *The Zebra-Striped Hearse*, Ross Macdonald, 1962.

10059 The American handed Leamas another cup of coffee and said, "Why don't you go back and sleep? We can ring you if he shows up." — *The Spy Who Came in from the Cold*, John Le Carré, 1963.

10060 Every evening at six o'clock a sense of expectancy filled the house, brightening the long, vague and dreamy afternoon. — *A Song of Sixpence*, A. J. Cronin, 1964.

10061 Seems like that bus just don't want to get here today, and me with my feet hurtin' to beat the band. — *God Bless the Child*, Kristin Hunter, 1964.

10062 The bus-driver was whistling, perhaps in anticipation of his wife, who would be a woman with ample breasts, those of a realized maturity. — *Miss MacIntosh, My Darling*, Marguerite Young, 1965.

10063 John T. sat easy on his motorcycle, and he wondered if his nephew, soon to arrive on the afternoon train, was really as big a pain in the neck as certain relatives had painted him up to be. — *The Wizard of Loneliness*, John Nichols, 1966.

10064 Balfour, unbearably shy, was waiting for them. — *Another Part of the Wood*, Beryl Bainbridge, 1968.

10065 Now that I am here, waiting, I try to remember. — *Sanctuary V*, Budd Schulberg, 1969.

10066 "Stand right here," they had said. "It's the safest spot. The place looks deserted, but there's a cook in the kitchen. The back door is open; if someone tries to bother you, scream and run in." — *The Weedkiller's Daughter*, Harriette Simpson Arnow, 1970.

10067 In a dingy office in a ratty building where in New York Broadway and Seventh Avenue unite briefly for a block in the middle forties, three men sat at three desks, strenuously doing nothing except eyeing three silent telephones reposing in front of them. — *Matilda*, Paul Gallico, 1970.

10068 They sat on the bench and waited. — *In This Sign*, Joanne Greenberg, 1970.

10069 On that Monday night, the heat of the Arizona day was gone, and a dozen people were gathered on El Cuervo's station platform. — *Three for the Money*, Luke Short, 1970.

10070 All that summer the boy watched the road. — *The Chandler Heritage*, Ben Haas, 1971.

10071 The other Aer Lingus passengers had left and Sally was alone in the Invalides. — *Three Lovers*, Julia O'Faolain, 1971.

10072 He stood there and waited. He was good at that. — *The Needle's Eye*, Margaret Drabble, 1972.

10073 A woman stood on her back step, arms folded, waiting. — *The Summer Before the Dark*, Doris Lessing, 1973.

10074 We waited for Poppie to return from Ohio where he had gone to find fame and fortune. — *The Land Beyond the River*, Jesse Stuart, 1973.

10075 Cold./ He stood in the dense cold of the mountain snow waiting to see her. — *Let's Fall in Love*, Carol Hill, 1974.

10076 This morning they were here for the melons: about sixty of them waiting patiently by the two stake trucks and the old blue-painted school bus. — *Mr. Majestyk*, Elmore Leonard, 1974.

10077 Always in Jerusalem there is this sense of expectancy, this feeling that some new spark of meaning will appear and glow for an instant, and that it must be caught before it fades. — *The Spell of Time*, Meyer Levin, 1974.

10078 "Little Man, would you come on? You keep it up and you're gonna make us late." — *Roll of Thunder, Hear My Cry*, Mildred D. Taylor, 1976.

10079 Captain Colin Huntington, R.N. (ret.) stood at the arched entrance to the office building in St. Martin's-le-Grand, waiting for his solicitor to appear, as the dome of St. Paul's bloomed at his left. — *Bandicoot*, Richard Condon, 1978.

10080 As soon as Ben got off the plane in Albany, he saw Ephram waiting for him. — *Small Town*, Sloan Wilson, 1978.

10081 Dixie was daydreaming over coffee waiting for Mr. Balducci to arrive. — *Tinsel*, William Goldman, 1979.

10082 I see her dimly as I enter our front door, waiting for me on the far side of the room in a chair I've never seen. — *Chasing Dad*, Candace Flynt, 1980.

10083 In the last quarter of the twentieth century, at a time when Western civilization was declining too rapidly for comfort and yet too slowly to be very exciting, much of the world sat on the edge of an increasingly expensive theater seat, waiting — with various combinations of dread, hope, and ennui — for something momentous to occur. — *Still Life with Woodpecker*, Tom Robbins, 1980.

10084 They had said between noon and nightfall. So any time now. — *The Cannaway Concern*, Graham Shelby, 1980.

10085 The cab driver sits in his car in the rain, half dozing, listening to McCoy Tyner on the radio. — *The Hard Rain*, Dinitia Smith, 1980.

10086 Wolsey Lowell sat very upright on a carved oak settle in the great hall of the archbishop's palace at Scrooby, waiting. — *Thanksgiving*, Terry Coleman, 1981.

10087 For two days the Irishman had watched the house and waited. — *After Eli*, Terry Kay, 1981.

10088 In the early morning hours of the first day of January 1956, three men waited in the cold dark of Forrest Langley's barn in Enoch, New Hampshire. — *Plowing Up a Snake*, Merle Drown, 1982.

10089 She hoped they weren't waiting for her. — *Silver Rose*, David A. Kaufelt, 1982.

10090 Clara has been waiting for Ambrose all day, without really believing that he will come. — *In the Clear Light*, Fiona Kidman, 1983.

10091 I am waiting for them to come. I'm not frightened at all. Their coming for me is the only certainty, so I hold to it. I even want them to come. — *The Banquet*, Carolyn Slaughter, 1983.

10092 The morning before Easter Sunday, June Kashpaw was walking down the clogged main street of oil boomtown Williston, North Dakota, killing time before the noon bus arrived that would take her home. — *Love Medicine*, Louise Erdrich, 1984.

10093 The watcher crouched behind the wet bushes at the top of the low hill above the road, knowing the car would soon be along because the driver was always punctual. — *A Death at St. Anselm's*, Isabelle Holland, 1984.

10094 The Drowning Kid and I crouched in the darkness beyond the yard lights waiting for

the train to move out toward us. — *Poor Boy and a Long Way from Home*, James Sherburne, 1984.

10095 The bench by the duck pond was icy, but I preferred waiting there. — *Confessions of a Prodigal Daughter*, Mary Rose Callaghan, 1985.

10096 *April 13*. The city is waiting now. — *A Wilderness Called Peace*, Edmund Keeley, 1985.

10097 Laforgue felt his body tremble. What can be keeping them? — *Black Robe*, Brian Moore, 1985.

10098 He lay on the cold sand on the top of the dune in the waving marram grass with the rifle across his forearm wrapped in a towel to protect it from the blowing sand and waited for Skaggs to come down the beach, and he thought about what he was going to do. — *Staying Out of Hell*, James Alexander Thom, 1985.

10099 Spike was waiting patiently for the train. — *Bad Guys*, Elizabeth Arthur, 1986.

10100 On a cool May morning in the year 1928, Irma Shrewsbury sat in her huge Crane Simplex on Pier 84 waiting for the *Aquitania* to dock, not at all sure why she had taken the trouble to greet Emily, whom she had never liked. — *The Last Blossom on the Plum Tree*, Brooke Astor, 1986.

10101 "Girl, my fingernails could grow an inch just waiting for you." — *High Hearts*, Rita Mae Brown, 1986.

10102 Although every minute made my need more urgent, I paused outside my father's classroom. — *Scarlett Greene*, Barbara Ucko, 1987.

10103 I was out waiting by the mailbox and I heard James coming. — *Winterchill*, Ernest J. Finney, 1989.

10104 I can stand just as still as he can, for just as long as he can. I can outwait anybody. — *Waltzing in the Attic*, P. B. Parris, 1990.

10105 Marta sits by the Virgin of Charity, waiting for the men to decide. — *Los Gusanos*, John Sayles, 1991.

10106 I was laying on my belly in a loblolly deadfall, a great tangle of sand clods and hair roots and gnarly tap roots as big around as my thigh. — *Hot Water*, Don Wallace, 1991.

10107 The students were assembled in the courtyard and the principal was waiting for the artist to arrive so that he could begin his speech. — *Indigo*, Richard Wiley, 1992.

Waking

10108 The ambiguous light of a December morning, peeping through the windows of the Holyhead mail, dispelled the soft visions of the four insides, who had slept, or seemed to sleep, through the first seventy miles of the road, with as much comfort as may be supposed consistent with the jolting of the vehicle, and an occasional admonition to *remember the coachman*, thundered through the open door, accompanied by the gentle breath of Boreas, into the ears of the drowsy traveller. — *Headlong Hall*, Thomas Love Peacock, 1816.

10109 Merry was the month of May in the year of our Lord 1052. Few were the boys, and few the lasses, who overslept themselves on the first of that buxom month. — *Harold*, Edward Bulwer Lytton, 1848.

10110 I awoke one morning with the usual perplexity of mind which accompanies the return of consciousness. — *Phantastes*, George Mac-Donald, 1858.

10111 Dr. Dolliver, a worthy personage of extreme antiquity, was aroused rather prematurely, one summer morning, by the shouts of the child Pansie, in an adjoining chamber, summoning old Martha (who performed the duties of nurse, housekeeper, and kitchen-maid, in the Doctor's establishment) to take up her little ladyship and dress her. — *The Dolliver Romance (unfinished)*, Nathaniel Hawthorne, 1864.

10112 "Wake up there, youngster," said a rough voice. — *Ragged Dick*, Horatio Alger, 1868.

10113 One midnight of a winter month the sleepers in Riversley Grange were awakened by a ringing of the outer bell and blows upon the great hall-doors. — *The Adventures of Harry Richmond*, George Meredith, 1871.

10114 I opened my eyes and saw a pea-green world all around me. Then I heard the doctor say: "Give 'er another whiff or two." — *The Prairie Mother*, Arthur Stringer, 1920.

10115 Claude Wheeler opened his eyes before the sun was up and vigorously shook his younger brother, who lay in the other half of the same bed. — *One of Ours*, Willa Cather, 1922.

10116 Meromic turned over and blinked at the light; the sea-mist was streaming away, thinner and thinner, whitely luminous already with the sun behind. He stretched out his arms and threw back the blanket: it was going to be a fine day and he could do anything he liked with it. — *The Conquered*, Naomi Mitchison, 1923.

10117 Elizabeth Spellman opened her eyes, turned on her pillow, and minutely studied the face of her sleeping husband. — *The White Flag*, Gene Stratton-Porter, 1923.

10118 Kate Clephane was wakened, as usual, by the slant of Riviera sun across her bed. — *The Mother's Recompense*, Edith Wharton, 1925.

10119 Lord Peter Wimsey stretched himself luxuriously between the sheets provided by the

Hôtel Meurice. — *Clouds of Witness*, Dorothy L. Sayers, 1926.

10120 I afterwards found that it was six o'clock in the morning when first I opened my eyes. — *Adèle and Co.*, Dornford Yates, 1931.

10121 Sleep drifted across her mind, tattered edges of fog vanishing in the strong light. She stirred, trying to escape, pursuing anxiously the shapes of her dream. Voices died away. The substantial dream became insubstantial. She grew confused, afraid, as the uncertainty touched one and then another of her friends. Let me stay, she said, with doubt and growing fear. But now she was conscious of the room and of a half-seen whiteness on its wall. Slowly, with a sour heavy reluctance, she awoke to herself lying between coarse sheets in the tumbled bed. The whiteness resolved itself into a shape of sunlight on a level with her eyes. — "A Day Off," Storm Jameson, 1932.

10122 Blue was roused from sound sleep before dawn that morning. His father's voice called him, his father's hand shook his shoulder. — *Bright Skin*, Julia Peterkin, 1932.

10123 David Markand opened his eyes. He knew what he was going to see; he closed them. "Sunday," he assured himself and waited for more sleep. — *The Death and Birth of David Markand*, Waldo Frank, 1934.

10124 "Monsieur Van Gogh! It's time to wake up!" — *Lust for Life*, Irving Stone, 1934.

10125 When Martha awoke it was still dark and bitter cold. — *The Stars Look Down*, A. J. Cronin, 1935.

10126 On this Sunday morning in May, this girl who later was to be the cause of a sensation in New York, awoke much too early for her night before. — *Butterfield 8*, John O'Hara, 1935.

10127 As the alarm clock on the chest of drawers exploded like a horrid little bomb of bell metal, Dorothy, wrenched from the depths of some complex, troubling dream, awoke with a start and lay on her back looking into the darkness in extreme exhaustion. — *A Clergyman's Daughter*, George Orwell, 1935.

10128 Turning over in bed, she was aware of a summons: Rouse yourself. — *The Weather in the Streets*, Rosamond Lehmann, 1936.

10129 Young Doctor Arden was going through the process of reorienting himself after a night's sleep. — *The Doctor*, Mary Roberts Rinehart, 1936.

10130 Bunny did not waken all at once. A sound (what, he did not know) struck the surface of his sleep and sank like a stone. His dream subsided, leaving him awake, stranded, on his bed. — *They Came Like Swallows*, William Maxwell, 1937.

10131 Mr. Rowland Palace woke up abruptly at seventeen minutes past three in the morning. A minute ago he had been in that uncharted region beyond dreamland where indeed the mind has its motions but their issue is stillborn and no trace survives, and now he was wide-awake in a world of cheerless realities, persistent and inexorable. — *Brynhild*, H. G. Wells, 1937.

10132 At seven o'clock the phone beside my bed rang quietly. I stirred, then roused sharply, from that fitful and uneasy sleep which a man experiences when he has gone to bed late knowing he has got to get up early. — "'I Have a Thing to Tell You'," Thomas Wolfe, 1937.

10133 "Happy New Year!" Fred Delaney said, standing in the doorway and smiling at the in-no-way beautiful person of Mr. Munden. — *The Joyful Delaneys*, Hugh Walpole, 1938.

10134 The young woman sat up in bed, like one raised from drowning. — *The Captain's Wife*, Storm Jameson, 1939.

10135 Sheriff Jeff McCurtain was sound asleep in bed with his wife on the top floor of the jailhouse in Andrewjones, the county seat, when the noise of somebody pounding on the door woke him up. — *Trouble in July*, Erskine Caldwell, 1940.

10136 Jim O'Neill sat up in bed and yawned. — *Father and Son*, James T. Farrell, 1940.

10137 *Brrrrrrriiiiiiiiiiiiiiiiiinng!/* An alarm clock clanged in the dark and silent room. A bed spring creaked. A woman's voice sang out impatiently:/ "Bigger, shut that thing off!" — *Native Son*, Richard Wright, 1940.

10138 Hyacinth Martyn-Lynch roused himself to fuller consciousness. The bride who had fallen asleep on his arm the night before was gone. — *Mad Grandeur*, Oliver St. John Gogarty, 1941.

10139 With the heat running like warm water from the sides of the room, backed by three closed windows and a closed door, he slept badly and restlessly, waking up, closing his eyes firmly, dozing, prodded into consciousness, fighting consciousness because he was a man who slept well most of the time, rolling over from a wet spot on the pillow, dreaming, recalling, forgetting, finding a painful ache in all the packed, broad, slab-like pictures that went to make up his memory. — *The Unvanquished*, Howard Fast, 1942.

10140 Trembling with fright, twelve-year-old Grass Woman awoke. — *Sacajawea of the Shoshones*, Della Gould Emmons, 1943.

10141 When Charles Stanton awoke he was cold, and he realized he had been cold all night. — *The Mothers*, Vardis Fisher, 1943.

10142 Peter Marshall stirred in the broad light of day and woke up slowly. The pale sun of February streamed into his narrow room, a gold

streak crossing the foot of his bed and lighting on the deal washstand. — *Pastoral*, Nevil Shute, 1944.

10143 That day so well remembered — a day, indeed, impossible to forget — was the first of September, 1921; on the morning of which George Boswell — then only Councillor Boswell, then sandy-brown-haired with not a trace of gray — woke before dawn, looked at his watch, and promptly slept again till Annie brought in the morning paper, a cup of tea, and some letters that had just arrived. — *So Well Remembered*, James Hilton, 1945.

10144 Judith Redcliff floated up from the timeless and bottomless world of sleep, feeling its monstrous landscape swing away and fall before the yellow ray that pierced the eastern shutters. — *Three O'Clock Dinner*, Josephine Pinckney, 1945.

10145 Leslie March stirred, and sighed, and felt the hot bright sunlight on her eyelids, and sat up. — *Give Me the Stars*, Gladys Taber, 1945.

10146 September 1653. The last of summer. The first chill winds of autumn. The sun no longer strikes my eastern window as I wake, but, turning laggard, does not top the hill before eight o'clock. — *The King's General*, Daphne du Maurier, 1946.

10147 Someone turned on the radio in the wheelhouse. A loud and sentimental song awakened him. — *Williwaw*, Gore Vidal, 1946.

10148 Jessie Bourne liked to wake very slowly in the morning, gradually feeling the coming to life of each of her senses. — *East Side, West Side*, Marcia Davenport, 1947.

10149 Kino awakened in the near dark. The stars still shone and the day had drawn only a pale wash of light in the lower sky to the east. — *The Pearl*, John Steinbeck, 1947.

10150 Mr. Rock rose with a groan. — *Concluding*, Henry Green, 1948.

10151 Sometimes we wake in the night and know why we have become what we are. — *The Precipice*, Hugh MacLennan, 1948.

10152 At seven o'clock on Saturday morning the golden hours began. As soon as she opened her eyes Priscilla could feel in her bones that it was Saturday. — *It's All in the Family*, Margaret Millar, 1948.

10153 He awoke, opened his eyes. — *The Sheltering Sky*, Paul Bowles, 1949.

10154 This was like no awakening she had ever had. — *Mary Wakefield*, Mazo de la Roche, 1949.

10155 Sayward awoke this day with the feeling that something had happened to her. — *The Town*, Conrad Richter, 1950.

10156 Thoughts and dreams jostled in disorder about the inward eye of the man with the head wound as he returned, slowly, laboriously,

and painfully from oblivion to consciousness. — *The Vintage*, Anthony P. West, 1950.

10157 The spear, a thin shaft of shadow above the glow of the fire, hit the tree trunk just above Bayard's head. He jerked up straight, banging his head against the tree, and was instantly wide awake. — *Justin Bayard*, Jon Cleary, 1955.

10158 Faintly, through the mist of sleep, he heard someone calling, "Look, a smoke!" — *The Years of the City*, George R. Stewart, 1955.

10159 Those wretched people had turned on the radio again. Horatio shifted the bedclothes with great caution and felt for the switch. — *Beowulf*, Bryher, 1956.

10160 Waking in the morning was the worst time: the first thing he saw was always the *campanile*, pink and white and green, lurid against a grey winter sky, or stark against a sky of summer blue. — *Along the Arno*, Brian Glanville, 1956.

10161 Lieutenant Commander Peter Holmes of the Royal Australian Navy woke soon after dawn. — *On the Beach*, Nevil Shute, 1957.

10162 On the first day of his holiday Laurence Manders woke to hear his grandmother's voice below. — *The Comforters*, Muriel Spark, 1957.

10163 Barry Morris was nine. He didn't much like getting up in the morning. For as long as he could, after the maid knocked on his door, he would lie back on the pillow with his eyes shut tight, trying to go on with his dream. But it never did any good. Pretty soon he would start to worry about dinnertime. And as soon as he did that, he just couldn't sleep any more. — *Nothing but the Night*, James Yaffe, 1957.

10164 A child dragged a stick along the corrugated-iron wall of a hut, and Heriot woke. — *To the Islands*, Randolph Stow, 1958.

10165 The alarm clock shrilled hideously. Duncan put out his hand to shut it off. His groping fingers touched cold metal, strayed along it to the catch, then halted. No. Let it ring. If he shut the alarm off now, he would surely go back to sleep. And he couldn't go back to sleep. He couldn't. — *The Serpent and the Staff*, Frank Yerby, 1958.

10166 Either side of the bed was the wrong side. — *Beds in the East*, Anthony Burgess, 1959.

10167 I woke up hearing a word break like a wave on the shells of my ears: *Mission*. — *The War Lover*, John Hersey, 1959.

10168 Philip Sidney Wood got up on a bright May morning. — *The John Wood Case*, Ruth Suckow, 1959.

10169 Mr. Twombly was awake before Cynthia. Usually they slept only until the sun entered their room, and usually Cynthia woke first, woke him. Not today. — *Fade Out*, Douglas Woolf, 1959.

10170 He lay in the darkness of the lodge, warily alert, and tried to think what had awakened him. — *Johnny Osage*, Janice Holt Giles, 1960.

10171 The alarm clock went off. It was meant for both of them. Kelly shut his mind to this and grimaced. — *The Circle Home*, Edward Hoagland, 1960.

10172 I wakened quickly and sat up in bed abruptly. It is only when I am anxious that I waken easily, and for a minute I did not know why my heart was beating faster than usual. — *The Country Girls*, Edna O'Brien, 1960.

10173 That Saturday morning in October I woke up with the curious sense of unreality that had plagued me for three months. — *A Sense of Values*, Sloan Wilson, 1960.

10174 When the fair gold morning of April stirred Mary Hawley awake, she turned over to her husband and saw him, little fingers pulling a frog mouth at her. — *The Winter of Our Discontent*, John Steinbeck, 1961.

10175 She woke me up by lifting my eyelids; then she slipped under the bedclothes beside me and lay there smiling, her arms around my neck. — *Life at the Top*, John Braine, 1962.

10176 The next morning — moist, shining, and still — I awoke in the shadowy bedroom. — *Morning in Antibes*, John Knowles, 1962.

10177 A donkey brayed./ The noise startled a figure huddled on the floor and woke it from an uneasy sleep. — *The Coin of Carthage*, Bryher, 1963.

10178 When he came awake he didn't know whether it was day or night. — *A Hero for Regis*, Jack Hoffenberg, 1963.

10179 When I woke up Dad was standing by the bed shaking my foot. — *Leaving Cheyenne*, Larry McMurtry, 1963.

10180 From watering his roses he came back into the twilight of his house, which was open front and back to benefit from whatever cool movement there might be of hot July evening air, and called to his wife, calling her Ma, and found her dozing over her knitting in a room that smelled of honeysuckle, and waking her, said: "Where's that boy?" — *The Bender*, Paul Scott, 1963.

10181 The sheet of paper clutched in the hand of a backward-twisting arm was being jiggled in front of the face of Alexander Hero, investigator for the Society of Psychical Research of Great Britain, and roused him from the doze into which he had fallen. — *The Hand of Mary Constable*, Paul Gallico, 1964.

10182 The telephone wakened him from a sleep so sound that he reached out a hand and groped to switch if off, thinking it must be his alarm clock. — *Second Time Round*, Clifford Hanley, 1964.

10183 He awoke./ He could not have been asleep for more than a few hours, and yet he felt curiously refreshed, coming instantly awake without passing through that fuzzy borderland he usually associated with rising. — *Buddwing*, Evan Hunter, 1964.

10184 Waking up begins with saying *am* and *now*. That which has awoken then lies for a while staring up at the ceiling and down into itself until it has recognized *I*, and therefrom deduced *I am, I am now. Here* comes next, and is at least negatively reassuring; because *here*, this morning, is where it has expected to find itself: what's called *at home.* — *A Single Man*, Christopher Isherwood, 1964.

10185 It was Tuesday morning, it was early September. Seven o'clock: outside, the first morning haze of late summer, a slight trembling of the air that was not quite a breeze, silence except for starlings. Old Daniel Considine woke. He woke, simply, by opening his eyes wide. — *I Was Dancing*, Edwin O'Connor, 1964.

10186 The sun shone brightly. Its rays struck me dead center as I arose from a deep, peaceful sleep after having made love to a white woman the night before. I felt totally content outwardly but boiling with hate within. — *Cornered*, William West, 1964.

10187 He woke to the sound of the sea. — *Visa for Avalon*, Bryher, 1965.

10188 On the winter morning of Rabbi Michael Kind's forty-fifth birthday he lay alone in the oversized brass bed that had once belonged to his grandfather, clinging to the numbness of sleep but listening against his will to the noises made by the woman in the kitchen below. — *The Rabbi*, Noah Gordon, 1965.

10189 Now it is a Friday morning in November./ She woke at exactly quarter past seven in a back bedroom on the top floor of a house in Lansdowne Road. — *After Julius*, Elizabeth Jane Howard, 1965.

10190 First of all, a way to be tunnelled carefully through the blankets until the outside air and a triangular view of our chest of drawers and its mushroom knobs. Then, one arm, well covered with pyjama sleeve, down the tunnel and out into the cold on to the floor groping for the alarm. Up with the alarm (that hadn't alarmed) until, by squinting, I can just make out that it's — twenty past nine. *Twenty past nine!* And that's how the beginning of the best day of my week could have been ruined for me, for I was just about to fling off the bed-clothes and out on to the arctic wastes of our linoleum when it came to me. *Saturday.* Saturday? I lay as still as any wrapped old mummy, considering.... — *The Liberty Lad*, Maurice Leitch, 1965.

10191 Hilary Stevens half opened her eyes, then closed them again. — *Mrs. Stevens Hears the Mermaids Singing*, May Sarton, 1965.

10192 She stirred in the cozy depths of her inclined seat, opening sleep-rimmed eyes, and the air hostess paused in her hurried flight down the passageway, leaned over and said, "An extra blanket, Madam?" — *Shadow from Ladakh*, Bhabani Bhattacharya, 1966.

10193 It was Sunday morning. The year was 1920, the place was Middlehope in eastern Pennsylvania, in the United States of America. Joan Richards, lying softly relaxed and asleep in her bed, opened her eyes quietly and fully to see the sunshine of June streaming into her window. — *The Time Is Noon*, Pearl S. Buck, 1966.

10194 Last night Bianca shook me awake and told me to stop grinding my teeth. Nothing gives her more satisfaction than to humiliate me. — *The Diary of a Rapist*, Evan S. Connell, 1966.

10195 He woke at first light: up instantly out of sleep and totally awake without effort, the way he woke each morning before day came. — *The Thousand Hour Day*, W. S. Kuniczak, 1966.

10196 In the darkness of the predawn, the cold was intense and the centurion, sitting hunched on the side of his pallet bed, was glad of the bowl of hot wine, sweetened with wild honey, that his servant, Ruafocus, had brought him on awakening. — *The Centurion*, Leonard Wibberley, 1966.

10197 When I woke up there she was, lying beside me, and I thought, watching her, Jesus, if only she wouldn't talk. — *The Artist Type*, Brian Glanville, 1967.

10198 A high lozenge of light told Medlar's one cracked and sleep-blurred eye that dawn had come. — *Under the Eye of the Storm*, John Hersey, 1967.

10199 In deep sleep the traveller heard — did he hear? — a broken sound, a phrase, the same phrase, repeated, without intelligible words, less speech than an animal whimper with human undertones. Struggling to attend, he opened his eyes in not quite complete darkness. — *The White Crow*, Storm Jameson, 1968.

10200 When the alarm bell rang Anthony Scott-Williams lay quite still and let the warm sun of Siena seep through his eyelids. — *The Man Whose Dreams Came True*, Julian Symons, 1968.

10201 I know I was all right on Friday when I got up; if anything I was feeling more stolid than usual. — *The Edible Woman*, Margaret Atwood, 1969.

10202 As he woke, the word "wife" raced up from the fathoms of his dream and broke the surface of his mind as gently as the moonlight met his eyes. And the word basked under the light, rubbed itself against his unnerved flesh, tumbled slowly about the lapping waves of sense before plunging once more down, taking its news back to the dying dream. — *The Hired Man*, Melvyn Bragg, 1969.

10203 The backfiring of a motorcycle as it roared over the loose planks of the swinging bridge opened Lone's eyes. — *Cassandra Singing*, David Madden, 1969.

10204 Bruno was waking up. — *Bruno's Dream*, Iris Murdoch, 1969.

10205 The child was wakened by the knotting of the snake's coils about his waist. — *Fire from Heaven*, Mary Renault, 1969.

10206 Norman Zweck dared not open his eyes. He turned over on his stomach, raised his knee high, stiffening straight the other leg. He slipped his toe into the division of the two mattresses, savouring the chill of the other side, the inherited side. — *Chosen People*, Bernice Rubens, 1969.

10207 It was the lousy blue jays that woke me up. — *The Lost Skiff*, Donald Wetzel, 1969.

10208 Eugene Browning woke and groaned softly. — *Sons of Darkness, Sons of Light*, John A. Williams, 1969.

10209 Joseph's eyes opened with a blink of fright. Only the first bird in the garden: a thrush. The nightmare slid out of his mind. — *A Place in England*, Melvyn Bragg, 1970.

10210 Jagat, the Maharana of Amarpur, India, was wakened as usual on this summer morning by the flutter of pigeons outside the window of his bedroom. — *Mandala*, Pearl S. Buck, 1970.

10211 A bird cried out on the roof, and he woke up. — *A Guest of Honour*, Nadine Gordimer, 1970.

10212 The child awoke with the sun, as was her custom, and shot up instantly out of the nest of blankets, her brown feet reaching for the uneven floor almost before she had rubbed the sleep out of her eyes. — *The Child from the Sea*, Elizabeth Goudge, 1970.

10213 "Boy! Chig! Wake up and mover over. Please." — *Dunfords Travels Everywheres*, William Melvin Kelley, 1970.

10214 It happened like this. We were in the house. It was early morning, about six, I heard the central heating start up like the engine of a small pleasure boat. Jonny started to cry. Ricci got out of bed and fell over on the yellow carpet. "Fuck," he said. — *The Incurable*, Nell Dunn, 1971.

10215 The American journalist awoke with a start. The room was dark; it still seemed very much the depths of the cool summer night. He remained on his back, puzzled, not stirring, only shifting his eyes across the darkness, listening in the silence, trying to locate the disturbance that had reached into his sleep. — *Seven Seasons*, Peter Forbath, 1971.

10216 On the morning of the first murder Miss Muriel Beale, Inspector of Nurse Training Schools to the General Nursing Council, stirred

into wakefulness soon after 6 o'clock and into a sluggish early morning awareness that it was Monday, 12th January, and the day of the John Carpendar Hospital inspection. — *Shroud for a Nightingale*, P. D. James, 1971.

10217 The alarm rang and he sleepily turned and snapped it shut and the little clock fell to the floor. — *The Moonlighter*, Henry Kane, 1971.

10218 A rattle of leaves woke me some time before dawn. — *The Underground Man*, Ross Macdonald, 1971.

10219 Lesser catching sight of himself in his lonely glass wakes to finish his book. — *The Tenants*, Bernard Malamud, 1971.

10220 She was awake./ Sound asleep one moment, her eyes wide open the next, staring up into the blackness of the ceiling. She didn't like the night, but she had forced her mind to wake her in the deepest part of it. — *The Camerons*, Robert Crichton, 1972.

10221 I woke up backwards, a breech delivery, yanked out of sleep like a weed. — *Brides of Price*, Dan Davin, 1972.

10222 Emma awoke to the sound of planes passing overhead, but she was not fully conscious, and the sound merged with her dream. — *Rule Brittania*, Daphne du Maurier, 1972.

10223 There was a crik, and a crack, then another crik, then crack, crack, cra.... Adah pulled herself up with a start and sat in the hollow of the large double bed. — *In the Ditch*, Buchi Emecheta, 1972.

10224 Herman Broder turned over and opened one eye. — *Enemies*, Isaac Bashevis Singer, 1972.

10225 He woke to find the room full of sunlight. — *Pasmore*, David Storey, 1972.

10226 She had waked first. At home, in Athens, Ohio, Tom would have waked first. — *The Garden*, Hollis Summers, 1972.

10227 I was thrown out of bed. The mirror fell off the wall and shattered over the dresser. The floor moved again and the ceiling sagged towards me. — *Quake*, Rudolph Wurlitzer, 1972.

10228 Beyond my bed, opposite me, a contraption of weights, raised heaps, ropes (they had figured in my nightmares) materialized into a traction device. — *How She Died*, Helen Yglesias, 1972.

10229 The dentist's drill of the alarm probed viciously into the diseased pulp of his dream, and Georgie Cornell awakened. — *Regiment of Women*, Thomas Berger, 1973.

10230 John Perrell awoke slowly at daybreak under the railroad trestle near Gaviota, on the coast of California, hearing the cry of gulls and the thunder of ocean surf. — *Escape from Sonora*, Will Bryant, 1973.

10231 I woke to hear my sister calling from the window. — *Images of Rose*, Anna Gilbert, 1973.

10232 Double-anchored off Cudjoe Key: barely dawn and she's still asleep but I was awakened by water birds. — *A Good Day to Die*, Jim Harrison, 1973.

10233 I am the first person in the house to awaken, but I am unsure of the implications. — *Forgetting Elena*, Edmund White, 1973.

10234 It had been an awful night and I came to in the morning, with the deepest physical reluctance, to find the alarm clock hatefully clamoring and my head and mouth and limbs giving me unmistakable messages of woe and protest as if I'd been on the worst sort of binge. — *Two Is Lonely*, Lynne Reid Banks, 1974.

10235 The first thing he saw on waking was his lower denture on the floor, its groove encrusted with dried Dentisement, or it might be Orastik, Mouthficks, Gripdent, or Bite (called *Bait* in Tangier, where he could be said to have a sort of permanent, that is to say, if you could talk of permanency these days in anything, so to speak, address); the fully teethed in my audience will hardly conceive of the variety of denture adhesives on the market. — *The Clockwork Testament*, Anthony Burgess, 1974.

10236 Matthew woke up in the dark. He was lying on his back under a single sheet: heavy, naked and uncomfortably hot. — *The Crystal Garden*, Elaine Feinstein, 1974.

10237 So how does it feel to wake up for the twenty-sixth consecutive New Year's Day of your life alone in bed? — *A Book of Ruth*, Syrell Rogovin Leahy, 1974.

10238 The whistles always woke Mazie. — *Yonnondio*, Tillie Olsen, 1974.

10239 Saltfleet woke up in the middle of the night and thought about the dead girl. — *The Schoolgirl Murder Case*, Colin Wilson, 1974.

10240 She woke up crying. The devil moon had turned into a devil sun and the light was hurting her eyes. — *Who Is Angelina?*, Al Young, 1975.

10241 His holidays began at 5 A.M. He awoke a few minutes ahead of time, turned the alarm button off, and got up quietly not to disturb his wife in the other bed. — *Playground*, John Buell, 1976.

10242 They both woke simultaneously when the light came, via a rationed sky, and the brick forest. — *A Dream Journey*, James Hanley, 1976.

10243 "Well, if it ain't Moses, hey you!"/ I begin to come back to myself and where I am. — *A Woman Called Moses*, Marcy Heidish, 1976.

10244 Jack Sadler woke up in what had once been the Colonel's room. — *Sadler's Birthday*, Rose Tremain, 1976.

10245 "Sah ... *sah!*"/ The twin sounds punctured Bill Rutherford's consciousness through a

thin veil of uneasy sleep. — *Excellency*, David Beaty, 1977.

10246 Sandy sat up in bed and looked at the clock. — *Wifey*, Judy Blume, 1978.

10247 When his right arm went to sleep Colman Brady woke up. — *Mortal Friends*, James Carroll, 1978.

10248 I awoke from a restless sleep. — *Tortuga*, Rudolfo A. Anaya, 1979.

10249 *Baruch awoke each morning expecting arrest.* — *The Jerusalem Diamond*, Noah Gordon, 1979.

10250 It was almost dawn when Imamu opened his eyes and lay staring through the darkness. — *The Disappearance*, Rosa Guy, 1979.

10251 The alarm went. He resisted it, burrowing against Kate's warm back. He felt her reach out, bang the clock, lie in disquieting wakefulness. She said, "Tom?" He burrowed again. — *Treasures of Time*, Penelope Lively, 1979.

10252 When the dream ended, she awoke. — *The Bleeding Heart*, Marilyn French, 1980.

10253 She opened her eyes, and was surprised to know that she had slept. — *Sweet Adelaide*, Julian Symons, 1980.

10254 "HYMIE, HYMIE HYMIE HYMIE, IT'S TIME HYMIE —" — *My America!*, Eliot Wagner, 1980.

10255 Her first feeling, as she smelled the air, was one of intense and helpless gratitude. — *Other People*, Martin Amis, 1981.

10256 He rose with the fog. It always came dripping from the sea to announce itself in sunlight which it captured on the rise and magnified. When he was at home, as he had been for some days now, he felt it lying on his window and, he would have sworn, against the clapboard and plaster and lath of the walls themselves, and on his pillow and on his face. — *Take This Man*, Frederick Busch, 1981.

10257 Each afternoon, when the whole city beyond the dark green shutters of their hotel windows began to stir, Colin and Mary were woken by the methodical chipping of steel tools against the iron barges which moored by the hotel café pontoon. — *The Comfort of Strangers*, Ian McEwan, 1981.

10258 A thunderous noise shook the ground and jolted Maureen from her dream. — *Oh!*, Mary Robison, 1981.

10259 *He was in a strange bed.* — *Bread Upon the Waters*, Irwin Shaw, 1981.

10260 It was conscious of a luminous and infinite haze, as if it were floating, godlike, alpha and omega, over a sea of vapor and looking down; then less happily, after an interval of obscure duration, of murmured sounds and peripheral shadows, which reduced the impression of boundless space and empire to something much more contracted and unaccommodating.

— *Mantissa*, John Fowles, 1982.

10261 The smallest movement woke her every time. — *Doctor Love*, Gael Greene, 1982.

10262 Sarge woke up the way he did every morning, thinking about the kid. — *Water Dancer*, Jenifer Levin, 1982.

10263 Often even now when I wake up I think I'm there. — *Green Island*, Michael Schmidt, 1982.

10264 The city woke, wrenching John Moore out of the sweaty torpor which was sleep in Chungking's sweltering summer. — *Till Morning Comes*, Han Suyin, 1982.

10265 Sarah had fallen asleep on top of the covers, fully dressed, expectant, and in the middle of the night she was awakened. — *The Favorite*, L. R. Wright, 1982.

10266 Riada woke and lay with her eyes closed, her body lax in the aftermath of love and sleep. — *Raving Wind*, Victor Canning, 1983.

10267 *The Great Light came into the cave and woke him and he opened his eyes.* — *Hunter's Orange*, William Dieter, 1983.

10268 He was up earlier than usual. — *Close Sesame*, Nuruddin Farah, 1983.

10269 The sky was still dark when he opened his eyes and saw it through the uncurtained window. — *Light*, Eva Figes, 1983.

10270 Diana woke slowly. — *This Year in Jerusalem*, Joel Gross, 1983.

10271 She woke with a terrible taste in her mouth and a queasy, seasick feeling in her stomach. It was as if she had been eating ashes. — *Souvenir*, David A. Kaufelt, 1983.

10272 A clattering rumble shattered my sleep. — *Shield of Three Lions*, Pamela Kaufman, 1983.

10273 He was awake at the first dim waver of light, watching the gray night shapes become slowly infused with color. — *Jacob's Well*, Stephen Harrigan, 1984.

10274 The night before Ernst Kestner left Lübeck to start his journey, he was awoken in the small hours by the next-door dog. — *The Pork Butcher*, David Hughes, 1984.

10275 On the morning of the girls' departure, Alfred Baxter woke two hours earlier than usual and dressed himself hurriedly. — *Wanting*, Angela Huth, 1984.

10276 Afterwards Sarah could never be quite sure whether it was the moonlight or that soft, furtive sound that had awakened her. — *Death in Kashmir*, M. M. Kaye, 1984.

10277 At dawn, if it was low tide on the flats, I would awaken to the chatter of gulls. — *Tough Guys Don't Dance*, Norman Mailer, 1984.

10278 When the young sailor awoke, he could do no more than stare blankly into the nighttime of his empty cabin. — *Smoke Street*, Mark Smith, 1984.

10279 Consider Charlotte Simson as she wakes. — *Only the Best*, Toby Stein, 1984.

10280 When Aggie wakens, it's to an impression that something has happened to alter the ordinary sensations of coming alert for the day, something not nice. — *Duet for Three*, Joan Barfoot, 1985.

10281 I always wake up remembering. — *Kentucky Love*, Joe Coomer, 1985.

10282 Mike Halsey woke up a little earlier than usual, probably in response to the harsh cackle of a nearby possum. — *Tokyo Woes*, Bruce Jay Friedman, 1985.

10283 She woke. Her body tingled — an electric shock. — *Mirror Images*, Linda Gray Sexton, 1985.

10284 This fine Saturday morning in April, Nell woke up alone. — *Nell*, Nancy Thayer, 1985.

10285 He must have spent quite a turbulent night, though when he woke, the Reverend Anawari Mallee remembered little except for a few dark tribal faces still lingering in his mind. — *Karan*, B. Wongar, 1985.

10286 I opened my eyes, waking from a state of unconsciousness. — *Judge, Jury and Executioner*, Huey Freeman, 1986.

10287 Oliver Darley opened his eyes and blinked slowly as the last wisps of dream dissolved in the dim light of the March afternoon. — *Only Yesterday*, Julian Gloag, 1986.

10288 The King woke up, his heart pounding. — *All the King's Ladies*, Janice Law, 1986.

10289 When he woke, it was dark except for a dim red light down the corridor. — *The Man Who Made the Devil Glad*, Donald McCaig, 1986.

10290 I remember the dots of the digital clock scrambling and forming into 6:00 as though one moment is followed by another — I remember the first bird. — *Dr. Excitement's Elixir of Longevity*, William Ryan, 1986.

10291 On April Fools' Day, 1969, a woman woke at daybreak from a pitch of familiar dreams released by her first night without pain or drugs. — *Celebration*, Mary Lee Settle, 1986.

10292 Waking, he saw aqueous light on the blue-white ceiling — the morning sun reflected from the swimming pool just outside the window. — *Children of Light*, Robert Stone, 1986.

10293 Most of the seven o'clock women woke with the first ting of the alarm beside the bed, and smothered it with a moist hand before sitting up and dragging their feet out of the deep tunnel of the blankets, but there were others who rose slowly out of the buried night and lingered for a while in the warm and murmuring depths. — *The Flood*, John Broderick, 1987.

10294 Senator Richard Cromwell awakened, and with a sigh of resignation accepted the fact that it was five o'clock in the morning. — *The Dinner Party*, Howard Fast, 1987.

10295 "Who is it?"/ Henry had just woken to thin sunlight and the sound of someone knocking on her surgery door. — *Kansas in August*, Patrick Gale, 1987.

10296 Clapperton woke agreeably one December morning in a bed warmed down the middle by the heat of his extended body, and stretched out his feet towards the cool peripheries. — *Clapperton*, John Herdman, 1987.

10297 *On Rafi's first day of basic training he woke at 3:45 A.M. to the sounds of boots stomping, wood crashing, and a large object hurtling past him to smash against the barracks' concrete wall.* — *Shimoni's Lover*, Jenifer Levin, 1987.

10298 Virginia wakes to the gentle pressure of Mark's hand, there, the baby, distended abdomen like a moonlit mountain in the pale glare of a streetlight. — *Tending to Virginia*, Jill McCorkle, 1987.

10299 Floating upward through a confusion of dreams and memory, curving like a trout through the rings of previous risings, I surface. My eyes open. I am awake. — *Crossing to Safety*, Wallace Stegner, 1987.

10300 Henry Melville struggles up from sleep as if from under water, lifting, stretching, comes awake sitting up, arm extended, reaching. — *The Doctor of Desire*, Allen Wheelis, 1987.

10301 At four-thirty on Sunday morning Mag came up from sleep with her heart thumping and sweat pouring from her, the way she'd awakened years ago when her son Izzy was out delivering newspapers and she found him two blocks away lying on the street with a broken ankle. — *Safe Passage*, Ellyn Bache, 1988.

10302 When the telephone woke Anna, she saw Grace Nettinger standing beside the bed, holding a pair of hair-cutting scissors. — *Anna L·M·N·O*, Sarah Glasscock, 1988.

10303 Clumsily./ Todd gets up. The leftover smoke from last night's cigarettes stuffed in his throat like cotton. — *Scary Kisses*, Brad Gooch, 1988.

10304 When I woke up, I sensed the presence of the child in the room. — *Foreign Matter*, Robert MacLean, 1988.

10305 He woke up in their new bedroom. — *The Romantic*, Aram Saroyan, 1988.

10306 Behind her eyes, Merelene Durham was searching for something. — *Blind Tongues*, Sterling Watson, 1989.

10307 A squirrel chattered in the oak tree and awakened Cassie Steele from her doze. — *Changes and Chances*, Mary Elmblad, 1990.

10308 Waking beneath the vine, Laki would leave his hutch on the roof and go out into the turquoise dawn. — *That Time in Malomba*, James Hamilton-Paterson, 1990.

10309 The day began at five to seven when the alarm clock (given to Phyllis by her mother when she started service) went off and on and on and on until she quenched it. — *The Light Years*, Elizabeth Jane Howard, 1990.

10310 Later than usual one summer morning in 1984, Zoyd Wheeler drifted awake in sunlight through a creeping fig that hung in the window, with a squadron of blue jays stomping around on the roof. — *Vineland*, Thomas Pynchon, 1990.

10311 Coyote woke up one morning earlier than he wanted; he squinted at Sun and said, "Go away and come back later." — *Cambio Bay*, Kate Wilhelm, 1990.

10312 Winter term of Nathaniel's eleventh-grade year, sometime between midnight and dawn, his mother woke him from untroubled sleep. — *The Final Club*, Geoffrey Wolff, 1990.

10313 I moved forward, out of the blackest sleep, to find myself surrounded by *doctors* . . . American doctors: I sensed their vigor, scarcely held in check, like the profusion of their body hair; and the forbidding touch of their forbidding hands — doctor's hands, so strong, so clean, so aromatic. — *Time's Arrow*, Martin Amis, 1991.

10314 Sometimes waking feels *priggish*: you know? — *The Runaway Soul*, Harold Brodkey, 1991.

10315 I awake to the violent scent of roses. — *The Blessed*, Nona Caspers, 1991.

10316 She rises celestially, thought Zeljko. — *Bloody Marko*, J. Madison Davis, 1991.

10317 The child woke, her face hot from a stab of sunshine arrowed through the window to her face. — *The Playroom*, Frances Hegarty, 1991.

10318 I wake suddenly from a doze on the couch and there is my mother's taste in furniture all around me again, and outside the window day or night it is still Sioux City, and if it weren't for the television flickering in front of me, I'd think I'd never left home. — *She and I*, Eileen Lottman, 1991.

10319 I woke up with a head like a rodeo. — *Strange Loyalties*, William McIlvanney, 1991.

10320 When Amalia Gómez woke up, a half hour later than on other Saturdays because last night she had had three beers instead of her usual weekend two, she looked out, startled by God knows what, past the screenless iron-barred window of her stucco bungalow unit in one of the many decaying neighborhoods that sprout off the shabbiest part of Hollywood Boulevard; and she saw a large silver cross in the otherwise clear sky. — *The Miraculous Day of Amalia Gómez*, John Rechy, 1991.

10321 Listen, I've only got a sec. Only a sec left. I know it for absolute sure as I wake today, panting. — *The Indoor Boy*, Antony Sher, 1991.

10322 When Freddy Bascomb wakes up, sometime late in the 1980s, she has two children, no husband, and a moderate level of debt. — *Bones*, Joyce Thompson, 1991.

10323 This is the story of Bella, who woke up one morning and realised she'd had enough. — *The Weekend*, Helen Zahavi, 1991.

10324 The Long Island Railroad ran through our backyard crossed into my window over my black oval rug ran into my mirror crossing back out again circling round my black oval rug out through my window, in and out like the E train as Ma would say, waking me up in time to see the cows milked. — *Nissequott*, Margaret Dawe, 1992.

10325 Eve opens her eyes and sits up in bed, clutching the bed sheets up around her neck with one hand, while she leans over and opens the window with the other hand. — *Eve's Longing*, Deborah McKay, 1992.

10326 For young Lemuel the day began with the buzzing of a fly. — *Hearsay*, Peter Spielberg, 1992.

10327 - When he wakes up, the fat man finds he's been tied hand and foot, and something powerful's smelling all around him. — *Indigo*, Marina Warner, 1992.

10328 When Matussem Ramoud opened his eyes each morning, his wife would still not be there. He was amazed by this. — *Arabian Jazz*, Diana Abu-Jaber, 1993.

Walking

10329 The burning sun of Syria had not yet attained its highest point in the horizon, when a knight of the Red Cross, who had left his distant northern home and joined the host of the Crusaders in Palestine, was pacing slowly along the sandy deserts which lie in the vicinity of the Dead Sea, or, as it is called the Lake Asphaltites, where the waves of the Jordan pour themselves into an inland sea, from which there is no discharge of waters. — *The Talisman*, Sir Walter Scott, 1825.

10330 There was no possibility of taking a walk that day. — *Jane Eyre*, Charlotte Brontë, 1847.

10331 One evening of late summer, before the present century had reached its thirtieth year, a young man and woman, the latter carrying a child, were approaching the large village of Weydon-Priors, in Upper Wessex, on foot. — *The Mayor of Casterbridge*, Thomas Hardy, 1886.

10332 One day—it was about a week after Allan Quatermain told me his story of the "Three Lions," and of the moving death of Jim-Jim—he and I were walking home together on the termination of a day's shooting. — *Maiwa's Revenge*, H. Rider Haggard, 1888.

10333 On an evening in the latter part of May a middle-aged man was walking homeward from Shaston to the village of Marlott, in the adjoining Vale of Blakemore or Blackmoor. — *Tess of the D'Urbervilles*, Thomas Hardy, 1891.

10334 Arthur Burdon and Dr. Porhoët walked in silence. They had lunched at a restaurant in the Boulevard Saint Michel, and were sauntering now in the gardens of the Luxembourg. — *The Magician*, W. Somerset Maugham, 1908.

10335 He walked along Holywell that afternoon of early June with his short gown drooping down in his arms, and no cap on his thick dark hair. — *The Dark Flower*, John Galsworthy, 1913.

10336 Valentine Corliss walked up Corliss Street the hottest afternoon of that hot August, a year ago, wearing a suit of white serge which attracted a little attention from those observers who were able to observe anything except the heat. — *The Flirt*, Booth Tarkington, 1913.

10337 Though the sun was hot on this July morning, Mrs. Lucas preferred to cover the half mile that lay between the station and her house on her own brisk feet, and sent on her maid and her luggage in the fly that her husband had ordered to meet her. — *Queen Lucia*, E. F. Benson, 1920.

10338 On an autumn afternoon of 1919 a hatless man, with a slight limp, might have been observed ascending the gentle, broad acclivity of Riceyman Steps, which lead from King's Cross Road up to Riceyman Square, in the great metropolitan industrial district of Clerkenwell. — *Riceyman Steps*, Arnold Bennett, 1923.

10339 Coming down the steps of Snooks' Club, so well worn by the apostles of things as they were, on that momentous mid-October afternoon of 1922, Sir Lawrence Mont, ninth baronet, set his fine nose toward the east wind, and moved his thin legs with speed. — *The White Monkey*, John Galsworthy, 1924.

10340 Nu, the son of Nu, his mighty muscles rolling beneath his smooth bronzed skin, moved silently through the jungle primeval. — *The Eternal Lover*, Edgar Rice Burroughs, 1925.

10341 The real story of Lucian Dorrit is not that of his boyish worship and sorrow for the mighty and ineffectual William Dorrit, his father, nor is it that of the passion and tragedy and beauty of his mature life. It has to do rather with two weeks in the autumn of his twenty-first year when he traveled on foot through the sprawl-ing prairie towns and past the rich new farms of that very new northern land which the great William Dorrit had chosen for his own. — *The Dark Dawn*, Martha Ostenso, 1926.

10342 Anatole Longfellow, alias the Scarlet Creeper, strutted aimfully down the east side of Seventh Avenue. — *Nigger Heaven*, Carl Van Vechten, 1926.

10343 On a sunny afternoon in May, 1749, a dog, a boy, a man, and a woman had crossed the oak opens of Tonteur's Hill and were trailing toward the deeper wilderness of the French frontier westward of the Richelieu and Lake Champlain—the dog first, the boy following, the man next, and the woman last. — *The Plains of Abraham*, James Oliver Curwood, 1928.

10344 He came over the top of the down as the last light failed and could almost have cried with relief at sight of the wood below. — *The Man Within*, Graham Greene, 1929.

10345 The lady El Isa Beth el Ain paced the grim stone cell that was her boudoir, like a caged tigress. — *Soldiers of Misfortune*, Percival Christopher Wren, 1929.

10346 Jewel and I come up from the field, following the path in single file. — *As I Lay Dying*, William Faulkner, 1930.

10347 Lov Bensey trudged homeward through the deep white sand of the gully-washed tobacco road with a sack of winter turnips on his back. — *Tobacco Road*, Erskine Caldwell, 1932.

10348 "But what is Hasluck doing with the miners? What does she want if she isn't a miner or a trader or a teacher or a missionary?"/ "Just walking." — *An American Visitor*, Joyce Cary, 1933.

10349 All around her the street walls were dripping in fog as Chris Colquohoun made her way up the Gallowgate, yellow fog that hung tiny veils on her eyelashes, curled wet, and had in her throat the acrid taste of an ancient smoke. — *Grey Granite*, Lewis Grassic Gibbon, 1934.

10350 Bill walked round and round the Red Square. — *Winter in Moscow*, Malcolm Muggeridge, 1934.

10351 Mrs. Emmeline Lucas was walking briskly and elegantly up and down the cinder path which traversed her kitchen garden and was so conveniently dry underfoot even after heavy rain. — *The Worshipful Lucia*, E. F. Benson, 1935.

10352 Balkan strode through the heavy morning mist that tenderly covered the dirty streets of Williamsburg feeling mysteriously enveloped by unreality, like one who walks in dreams. This conception was occupying his mind with its pleasant strangeness, but it was possible only because at the same time he was overlooking the character of his gait. — *Homage to Blenholt*, Daniel Fuchs, 1936.

10353 A woman walking a narrow roadway in the hour of the dawn. She went forward slowly in a steady pace, as if she had walked for an hour or more, and as if she had in mind some distant place where she wanted to be. — *Black Is My Truelove's Hair*, Elizabeth Madox Roberts, 1938.

10354 They moved along in the bobbing, springy gait of a family that followed the woods as some families follow the sea. — *The Trees*, Conrad Richter, 1940.

10355 She walked across the wide stretch of lawn, with its fine cedars, through a wrought-iron gate in a brick wall mellow with age, and out into the formal garden. — *The Hour Before the Dawn*, W. Somerset Maugham, 1942.

10356 I was walking by the Thames. — *The Horse's Mouth*, Joyce Cary, 1944.

10357 She moved up the trace, a strong young figure, "cam" and on the deliberate side in her red-brown shawl, with her "willer" basket on her arm. — *The Fields*, Conrad Richter, 1946.

10358 "Walk up," hissed Cleo, somewhat fiercely. — *The Living Is Easy*, Dorothy West, 1948.

10359 From the curved and wooded privacies of an upland suburb, commuters come striding down toward the train. — *The Man Who Made Friends with Himself*, Christopher Morley, 1949.

10360 He was in plenty of time, even a little early, but he walked rapidly along Piccadilly and turned into Berkeley Street as though the devil were after him. — *The Green Man*, Storm Jameson, 1952.

10361 On the last day of September in 1933, up a tree-lined street in furthest Brooklyn, Nina Bishop was walking home from the subway. — *Leaving Home*, Elizabeth Janeway, 1953.

10362 Dock's shoes on the rocks up the hill and his heavy breathing had shut out all sound so that it seemed a long while she had heard nothing, and Amos lay too still, not clawing at the blanket as when they had started. — *The Dollmaker*, Harriette Simpson Arnow, 1954.

10363 The boy with fair hair lowered himself down the last few feet of rock and began to pick his way toward the lagoon. — *Lord of the Flies*, William Golding, 1954.

10364 It was half past four in the afternoon./ Two young women were loitering down the pavement in the shade of the sunblinds that screened the shopwindows. — *A Proper Marriage*, Doris Lessing, 1954.

10365 Andrew walked slowly down the road, the evening sun hot on the back of his neck, dust on his shoes, one strap of his brief case flapping open and his bowler hat heavy as lead. — *A Villa in Summer*, Penelope Mortimer, 1954.

10366 As Thomas Welles approached the newspaper kiosk, he slowed down to a saunter. He was not buying a paper today, but he would walk slowly enough to read the headlines as he passed by. — *Castle Garac*, Nicholas Monsarrat, 1955.

10367 I rode a streetcar to the edge of the city limits, then I started to walk, swinging the old thumb whenever I saw a car coming. — *After Dark, My Sweet*, Jim Thompson, 1955.

10368 The great curving stairway hung delicately between the floors like an unsupported cloud as though designed only for light, happy, unladen feet; but the two men, with no thought of the beauty of its architecture, descended it now heavily and without speaking. — *The Golden Journey*, Agnes Sligh Turnbull, 1955.

10369 Mrs. McGillicuddy panted along the platform in the wake of the porter carrying her suitcase. Mrs. McGillicuddy was short and stout, the porter was tall and free-striding. In addition, Mrs. McGillicuddy was burdened with a large quantity of parcels; the result of a day's Christmas shopping. The race was, therefore, an uneven one, and the porter turned the corner at the end of the platform while Mrs. McGillicuddy was still coming up the straight. — *What Mrs. McGillicuddy Saw!*, Agatha Christie, 1957.

10370 I left the car by the side of the cathedral, and then walked down the steps into the Place des Jacobins. — *The Scapegoat*, Daphne du Maurier, 1957.

10371 His heels drummed a quick, descending tattoo on the bare boards of the tavern stairway. — *The Land Beyond the Mountains*, Janice Holt Giles, 1958.

10372 I walked along the evening avenue. The elms flanked me as regular as railings. I was behind eighty-foot bars with bushy tops. — *My Friend Judas*, Andrew Sinclair, 1959.

10373 The sun beat down on the frock coat and tall silk hat of the man striding westward across the prairie. It glinted on the gold head of the cane he carried as jauntily as though he were moving through a thousand watching people. — *Son of the Gamblin' Man*, Mari Sandoz, 1960.

10374 On a June afternoon at sunset, an American woman and her daughter fended their way along a crowded street in Florence and entered with relief the spacious Piazza della Signoria. — "The Light in the Piazza," Elizabeth Spencer, 1960.

10375 He came out of the Underground at Hyde Park Corner with his head lowered, ignoring the people who pressed around him and leaving it to them to steer out of his way. — *Ritual in the Dark*, Colin Wilson, 1960.

10376 Nigel Strangeways and Clare were strolling down the hill past the Park. — *The Worm of Death*, Cecil Day-Lewis *as* Nicholas Blake, 1961.

10377 *Walking the earth under the stars,/ musing midnight in midcentury,/ a man treads the road with his dog;/ the dog, less timebound in her universe of stench and/ shrill, trots eager ahead.* — *Midcentury*, John Dos Passos, 1961.

10378 Alvin walked through deep snow over a mesh of railroad tracks. — *The Beautiful Greed*, David Madden, 1961.

10379 His feet crunched on the hard-packed sand. — *The Pawnbroker*, Edward Lewis Wallant, 1961.

10380 Although he smiled, and stepped readily enough aside for the busy walkers, Claude Squires did not enjoy this stroll to work nearly so much as they no doubt thought he did. — *Wall to Wall*, Douglas Woolf, 1962.

10381 Bernard walking in the suburbs with his dog. — *You're a Big Boy Now*, David Benedictus, 1963.

10382 A man came down the steps cut in the rock. By nature agile, he made the descent with unusual caution, placing each foot first tentatively then extra firmly. — *The Little Girls*, Elizabeth Bowen, 1963.

10383 Under the maples, burning like bonfires, pure yellow and pure red, walked Dr. Dominick Maudlin Parke, his hands clasped behind his back. — *Night and Silence, Who Is Here?*, Pamela Hansford Johnson, 1963.

10384 Dazed by the daylight, the three of them padded back and forth across the cool floor like penned animals. — *The Children at the Gate*, Edward Lewis Wallant, 1964.

10385 "Someone walked over my grave." The old man shuddered as he talked to himself. — *Yes from No-Man's Land*, Bernard Kops, 1965.

10386 All afternoon Frank Dawley walked across the Lincolnshire uplands. — *The Death of William Posters*, Alan Sillitoe, 1965.

10387 A girl and an older woman were walking along a metaled pathway. — *The Anti-Death League*, Kingsley Amis, 1966.

10388 In the year 1483 a tall, lean man in the black habit of a Dominican friar walked along a street in Segovia. — *Torquemada*, Howard Fast, 1966.

10389 From the roof of a long stone house with battlements a man in a brown mackintosh looked down at a yard with stables; a girl in riding clothes walking across it. — *Assassins*, Nicholas Mosley, 1966.

10390 It was late at night, all the houses were in darkness and all the people in all the houses fast asleep. Willa came hurrying along a road that was not the one she inhabited but that led there. — *Casualties of Peace*, Edna O'Brien, 1966.

10391 A procession moved up the valleys on to the moorlands of Yorkshire, the Highlands of Scotland, the Chilterns, the Cotswolds, the Cheviots, the Pennines and the Southern Uplands. It was led by a little-rich-girl. — *Game in Heaven with Tussy Marx*, Piers Paul Read, 1966.

10392 He had been walking along Portage Avenue for more than an hour, glance searching out first a store window, then a car gliding by under throttled power, looking intensely though come the evening's end and dropping into bed he would remember not one detail of the mass, couples chatting as they passed oblivious, when looking down into a restaurant below street level Abe Ross saw the girl seated alone at a table. — *First and Vital Candle*, Rudy Wiebe, 1966.

10393 Then there was a dazzle of green and white, white and green. Then the colours separated, became clear: the white was above, the green below. — *At the Jerusalem*, Paul Bailey, 1967.

10394 John Morann slowly pushed himself erect from where he leaned over the parapet of London Bridge, gave one final glance at the river and began to walk toward Tooley Street. — *The Horses of Winter*, A. A. T. Davies, 1967.

10395 She walked down Fulham Broadway past a shop hung about with cheap underwear, the week-old baby clutched in her arms, his face brick red against his new white bonnet. — *Poor Cow*, Nell Dunn, 1967.

10396 One January morning Thomas Rapidan was walking down the windy side of the street. — *Wolf at the Door*, John Yount, 1967.

10397 His legs gobbled up the placid country road, his eyes foraged all around it greedily, spotting loot in the quite ordinary ditches and hedges and fields, even his arms were swinging too energetically, seeming to plunder the air, grabbing handfuls of light before they could be darkened and lost in the evening. — *Without a City Wall*, Melvyn Bragg, 1968.

10398 I walked a far piece. I'm sure of that. — *Flats*, Rudolph Wurlitzer, 1970.

10399 Colonel Pierre Roquebrun emerged from his villa at nine o'clock on a certain bright, sunshine-filled Riviera morning, and walked down the path to his antique shop which was located one kilometre before the village of La Tourette on the road between Vence and Grasse. — *The Zoo Gang*, Paul Gallico, 1971.

10400 Following the footpath along the high bank, stumbling on roots and rocks, they could see the gray still pond below them through the dark trees. — *Slides*, David Plante, 1971.

10401 They moved up the trail vigorously, their slim young figures in rhythmic cadence. — *The Passions of the Mind*, Irving Stone, 1971.

10402 On the day before Christmas — this was just a few years ago — in a dusty little dorp in up-country Malawi, which is in Central Africa, a young man sloped down the main road, alone. — *Jungle Lovers*, Paul Theroux, 1971.

10403 Harriet said: "No you don't, you keep walking." — *Harriet Said*, Beryl Bainbridge, 1972.

10404 Val followed the old tumbled-down wall, its lichen-covered boulders and slabs of granite half sunk in the soft ground; it led him across the field to the edge of the autumn woods. — *Relatives*, David Plante, 1972.

10405 The man interrupted his slow, shuffling progress along the forest track and stood, stooped over, listening to the distant thud of hoofbeats. — *The Oath and the Sword*, Graham Shelby, 1972.

10406 We had been walking in the rose garden, my wife Cordelia and I. — *The Summer Meadows*, Robert Nathan, 1973.

10407 Lieutenant-Commander Keith Drummond kept his head lowered as he walked around the deep puddles left by overnight rain. — *The Destroyers*, Douglas Reeman, 1974.

10408 I saw him walking./ He had the lean-to walk of a tall person who doesn't want to knock over the world with his tallness, who's leaning over a bit to see you. — *Bed/Time/Story*, Jill Robinson, 1974.

10409 Three creatures in the woodland rain. A man walking, looking about. A horse, browsing as he goes, hitched to the man by a long rawhide lead strap. A young dog, following of his own free will. — *The Raider*, Jesse Hill Ford, 1975.

10410 He left the lonely warmth of the car, pulling his hat tighter, and squeezed between the other cars, side by side and still warm, too, in the darkness. — *Slammer*, Ben Greer, 1975.

10411 The September morning was so fine that Philip decided to walk the half mile to the Whitelaws for their ritual game of tennis and Sunday dinner. — *Crucial Conversations*, May Sarton, 1975.

10412 The pony stepped carefully down the rock-strewn path, the pony boy walking ten paces behind, his long hillman's stride effortlessly keeping pace. — *The Himalayan Concerto*, John Masters, 1976.

10413 Customs Special Agent Charlie Holloway walked toward his apartment on New York's East Side, his gait shambling and his head lowered as he cursed under his breath. — *The Smugglers*, Noel B. Gerson, 1977.

10414 Walking down Marlboro Street in Boston, Laura Spelman saw the low brick houses, the strong blue sky, the delicate shape of the leafless trees, even the dirty lumps of snow along the curb as so piercing in their beauty that she felt a little drunk. — *A Reckoning*, May Sarton, 1978.

10415 I got off the bus at the intersection, wearing my old army surplus trench coat, carrying my backpack, my portable typewriter, and a suitcase full of books and papers, and walked two blocks to the overpass through which the road ran out toward Chickasaw Ridge. — *The Rock Cried Out*, Ellen Douglas, 1979.

10416 *Dear friend now in the dusty clockless hours of the town when the streets lie black and steaming in the wake of the watertrucks and now when the drunk and the homeless have washed up in the lee of walls in alleys or abandoned lots and cats go forth highshouldered and lean in the grim perimeters about, now in these sootblacked brick or cobbled corridors where lightwire shadows make a gothic harp of cellar doors no soul shall walk save you.* — *Suttree*, Cormac McCarthy, 1979.

10417 Two men were walking in Mediterranean sunlight only four blocks from their hotel. — *Life in the West*, Brian W. Aldiss, 1980.

10418 To stretch his legs between consultations, Maclean escorted his last patient to Baker Street station. — *No Face in the Mirror*, Hugh McLeave, 1980.

10419 On the Sunday after Easter — Low Sunday, Emma believed it was called — the villagers were permitted to walk in the park and woods surrounding the manor. — *A Few Green Leaves*, Barbara Pym, 1980.

10420 On a certain day in June, 19—, a young man was making his way on foot northward from the great City to a town or place called Edgewood, that he had been told of but had never visited. — *Little, Big*, John Crowley, 1981.

10421 He walked through the cool October night, his shoes sinking in the sand at the water's edge; he looked out of place in the gray business suit and white shirt, the carefully knotted tie. His pace was purposeful, but it was the purposefulness of long habit — anyone watching would have said he had lost his way, or was searching for something. — *A Green Desire*, Anton Myrer, 1981.

10422 On the day that his brother Nachman died, Nathan Malkin, a wealthy sixty-four-year-old American, was walking along the beach of a nature sanctuary in Israel. — *The Stolen Jew*, Jay Neugeboren, 1981.

10423 As I left the Kenya Beanstalk capsule he was right on my heels. — *Friday*, Robert A. Heinlein, 1982.

10424 The children were walking. — *Holy Pictures*, Clare Boylan, 1983.

10425 Old tail-wagging weather-beaten dog out in the dry road dust of an August dusk, sparrows strung on barbed wire going hum-flutter, and little puffs of red dirt at the toe of each shoe. — *The Decatur Road*, Joe Coomer, 1983.

10426 Sirola watched as his uncle walked heavily toward the rear of the store, rocking from side to side, his eyes harsh. — *Family Honor*, George Cuomo, 1983.

10427 The three novices walked fast down the margin of the hay field. — *Flying to Nowhere*, John Fuller, 1983.

10428 He moved barefoot across the bright geometries of the turkey carpet as though they concealed thorns. — *Tamsen*, David Galloway, 1983.

10429 He walks down the street. The asphalt reels by him. — *The Bone People*, Keri Hulme, 1983.

10430 The princess skipped down the garden path accompanied by her court. — *Banshee*, Margaret Millar, 1983.

10431 In the spring of 1899 six families set out on foot through lower French Canada. — *Marie Blythe*, Howard Frank Mosher, 1983.

10432 Look at Henderson Dores walking up Park Avenue in New York City. — *Stars and Bars*, William Boyd, 1984.

10433 September: I am walking across the campus toward my office where (although I do not yet know it) my second wife, Ada, is waiting for me. — *The Only Son*, David Helwig, 1984.

10434 In the dream John Everett was back in Prospect, walking slowly down Troy Street with a woman he thought must be his wife, although he could not see her face. — *At the Border*, Robert Hemenway, 1984.

10435 Sara Will came down the road, quick steps deep in shadows, her head lifted to the autumn air. — *Sara Will*, Sue Ellen Bridgers, 1985.

10436 Emma Rowena Riley presently walks to South Station lugging a dead dog in a Samsonite suitcase. — *Woman Wanted*, Joanna McClelland Glass, 1985.

10437 Lance walked on his own around Cambridge on the eve of his leaving. — *In These Promiscuous Parts*, Menna Gallie, 1986.

10438 Early on a rainy Sunday afternoon in November a man was hurrying down Third Avenue, past closed and barred florist shops and newsstands, his hands stuffed in his pockets and his head bent against the wind. — *The Lost Language of Cranes*, David Leavitt, 1986.

10439 Sixteen years to the day after she married Edward — she no longer thought of it as an anniversary — Vera came out of the Hotel Columbus on the Via della Conciliazione, turned to her left, and walked toward St. Peter's. — *Leave of Absence*, Ralph McInerny, 1986.

10440 The two young men walked down the street in silence. — *Family Skeletons*, Henrietta Garnett, 1987.

10441 Cambridge, 1914. The woman in the white silk dress, her face shaded by the wide brim of her hat, walked slowly in long strides from the hip, conscious of herself and of the glances of black-gowned undergraduates as they passed on the narrow stone bridge that led from King's College to the tow-path on the far side of the river. — *Once a Gentleman*, Donald James, 1987.

10442 Like an African, the white doctor came to work on foot, along a road that lined the port of Dar es Salaam. — *Antonia Saw the Oryx First*, Maria Thomas, 1987.

10443 His satchel bouncing against his fat bottom in time to his stride, Benson walked home from school through the park. — *Brothers in Arms*, Michael Carson, 1988.

10444 Sarah Broderhouse walked toward her twin sister and the river with the feeling that she was walking toward the woman in her dream. — *The Women in Her Dreams*, Candace Denning, 1988.

10445 Although she had fled the blood-spattered scene and fled the collected crowd of identical individuals — one-legged, nose-picking, vigilant-eyed — and hurried down the street at a speed uncommon for her, a speed no one would have thought possible on those high red heels that were no longer firm but wobbled drunkenly under the weight of her thick, purple-veined legs, Lotte slowed as she neared her door. — *Baumgartner's Bombay*, Anita Desai, 1988.

10446 Bill Lemmen walks the dirtier streets of San Francisco, looking only at Asian faces. — *We're Not Here*, Tim Mahoney, 1988.

10447 In moonlight, Leon Woodard limps to his barn. — *Catamount Bridge*, Don Metz, 1988.

10448 He took the side path, over the bridge where several of the gleaming red fish scurried underneath in the pale green water of a pool. — *Bloodstream*, Joel Redon, 1988.

10449 She said it was like walking deep in the ocean. — *The Foreign Husband*, Clive Collins, 1989.

10450 One time not too long ago on a beginning of night in the latter part of May, a middle-aged gent was walking homeward along the forest path from Roamin Road to the village of Carlott, behind Holy House in the valley of Stainmoor or Stay More. — *The Cockroaches of Stay More*, Donald Harington, 1989.

10451 Bahía de Santa Maria (Chesapeake Bay) 1571./ On a sun-washed September morning on the north bank of the Pamunkey River, four men tramped toward the Indian village of Uttamussack, their heavy shoes disturbing the primeval carpet of pine needles and dry leaves. — *A Durable Fire*, Virginia Bernhard, 1990.

10452 Coming through the Escalante Desert, at least ten more hard miles to Paragonah, in southwest Utah, he catches himself walking eyes up, forgetting to survey the ground around his boots for scorpions. — *Six Miles to Roadside Business*, Michael Doane, 1990.

10453 The whalebone digging stick was cold in Shuganan's hand, but he leaned against it as

he walked, and the end of the stick marked his path with a line of small holes in the dark beach gravel. — *Mother Earth, Father Sky*, Sue Harrison, 1990.

10454 Beneath a sky as clear as Eden's, Catharine Reilly walked up the dun slope of the South Pass. — *The Bear Flag*, Cecelia Holland, 1990.

10455 Morris walked across the square faster than he would have liked. — *Juggling the Stars*, Tim Parks, 1990.

10456 On West Adams, just inside the Loop, he was almost killed. — *Chicago Loop*, Paul Theroux, 1990.

10457 The road lay long and black ahead of them and the heat was coming now through the thin soles of their shoes. — *Joe*, Larry Brown, 1991.

10458 The railway workers were traveling from Seattle to Tenino on foot and had stopped, midday, to rest. — *Sarah Canary*, Karen Joy Fowler, 1991.

10459 At 7.15 A.M. Bertha Sommer walked down the road from the main German garrison towards the town of Laun. — *The Last Shot*, Hugo Hamilton, 1991.

10460 What a difficulty it must be for us all that it was destined to be such a long and, as you can now hear, applauseless walk for me to make it up here to here at the lectern from where I had been sitting next to Jim Salter. — *My Romance*, Gordon Lish, 1991.

10461 Angela and Stephen Landis followed the winding creek to one end of the property, tramped across the shallow water, and walked back on the other side, meandering through a narrow grove of trees. — *Mystery Ride*, Robert Boswell, 1992.

10462 After walking three hundred feet into the earth, three hundred feet along a descending stone passageway — naturally formed but resembling a miniature subway tunnel — he stops in total darkness to unbutton his overcoat. — *Bring Me Children*, David Martin, 1992.

10463 Dion Moloch walked with the dreamy stride of a noctambulo among the apparitions on the bowery. — *Moloch*, Henry Miller, 1992.

War

10464 It Cannot be unknown to any that have travell'd into the Dominions of the Czar of *Muscovy*, that this famous rising Monarch, having studied all Methods for the Encrease of his Power, and the Enriching as well as Polishing his Subjects, has travell'd through most part of *Europe*, and visited the Courts of the greatest Princes; from whence, by his own Observation, as well as by carrying with him Artists in most useful Knowledge, he has transmitted most of our General Practice, especially in War and Trade, to his own Unpolite People; and the Effects of this Curiosity of his are exceeding visible in his present Proceedings; for by the Improvements he obtained in his *European* Travels, he has Modell'd his Armies, form'd new Fleets, settled Foreign Negoce in several remote Parts of the World; and we now see his Forces besieging strong Towns, with regular Approaches; and his Engineers raising Batteries, throwing Bombs, &c. like other Nations; whereas before, they had nothing of Order among them, but carried all by *Onslaught* and *Scalado*, wherein they either prevailed by the Force of Irresistible Multitude, or were Slaughter'd by heaps, and left the Ditches of their Enemies fill'd with their Dead Bodies. — *The Consolidator*, Daniel Defoe, 1705.

10465 I was not above Seventeen Years of Age when the Battle of *Gillycranky* was fought between the Two Highland Generals, the Lord Viscount *Dundee* and *Mackay*. And being then a Stripling at the University of *Aberdeen* and understanding that several Clans were gathering into a Body in defence of King *James* II I sold my Books and Furniture of my Lodgings, and equipp'd my self to observe the Martial Call, I found my self prompted with. — *The Memoirs of Major Alexander Ramkins, a Highland Officer*, Daniel Defoe, 1718.

10466 In the Year one Thousand six Hundred seventy two, War being proclaimed with *Holland*, it was looked upon among Nobility and Gentry, as a Blemish, not to attend the Duke of *York* aboard the Fleet, who was then declared Admiral. — *The Memoirs of an English Officer*, Daniel Defoe *as* Captain George Carleton, 1728.

10467 It was during the period of that great and bloody Civil War which agitated Britain during the seventeenth century, that our tale has its commencement. — *A Legend of Montrose*, Sir Walter Scott, 1819.

10468 It was a feature peculiar to the colonial wars of North America, that the toils and dangers of the wilderness were to be encountered, before the adverse hosts could meet. — *The Last of the Mohicans*, James Fenimore Cooper, 1826.

10469 Our narrative begins in South Carolina, during the summer of 1780. The arms of the British were at that time triumphant throughout the colony. — *The Partisan*, William Gilmore Simms, 1835.

10470 At the period when our story opens, the colonies of North America united in resistance to the mother-country, had closed the fifth

year of their war of independence. — *The Scout*, William Gilmore Simms, 1854.

10471 Now glory be to God who has given us the victory! It is true, the strength of Spain is shattered, her ships are sunk or fled, the sea has swallowed her soldiers and her sailors by hundreds and by thousands, and England breathes again. — *Montezuma's Daughter*, H. Rider Haggard, 1893.

10472 The cold passed reluctantly from the earth, and the retiring fogs revealed an army stretched out on the hills, resting. — *The Red Badge of Courage*, Stephen Crane, 1895.

10473 It was a spring afternoon in the sixth year of the reign of King Henry VII of England. There had been a great show in London, for that day his Grace opened the newly convened Parliament, and announced to his faithful people — who received the news with much cheering, since war is ever popular at first — his intention of invading France, and of leading the English armies in person. — *Margaret*, H. Rider Haggard, 1907.

10474 They knew nothing of it in England or all the Western countries in those days before Crecy was fought, when the third Edward sat upon the throne. There was none to tell them of the doom that the East, whence come light and life, death and the decrees of God, had loosed upon the world. — *Red Eve*, H. Rider Haggard, 1911.

10475 The casualty lists went on appearing for a long time after the Armistice — last spasms of Europe's severed arteries. — *Death of a Hero*, Richard Aldington, 1929.

10476 Now when by the favour of the most high God, Him whom I worship, to whom every man is gathered at last, now, I say, when I am old, many have urged upon me that I, Ramosé, should set down certain of those things that I have seen in the days of my life, and particularly the tale of the fall of Babylon the mighty city, before Cyrus the Persian, which chanced when he whom the Greeks called Nabonidus being newly dead, Belshazzar his son was king. — *Belshazzar*, H. Rider Haggard, 1930.

10477 That September day the English appeared so suddenly that they seemed to have dropped from the sky; appeared, and fired. — *The Invasion*, Janet Lewis, 1932.

10478 It was Cap Huff who said that no business or profession, not even the managing of a distillery, can provide the profusion of delights to be encountered in a good war. — *Rabble in Arms*, Kenneth Roberts, 1933.

10479 Sophia Garfield had a clear mental picture of what the outbreak of war was going to be like. — *Pigeon Pie*, Nancy Mitford, 1940.

10480 When spring was almost done the war began in earnest. — *This Above All*, Eric Knight, 1941.

10481 By ten-forty-five it was all over. The town was occupied, the defenders defeated, and the war finished. — *The Moon Is Down*, John Steinbeck, 1942.

10482 When war broke out in September we were told to expect air raids. — *Caught*, Henry Green, 1943.

10483 The war was done — the long and bloody struggle that was, at the time, the greatest people's war the world had ever known — and the men in blue marched home. — *Freedom Road*, Howard Fast, 1944.

10484 Invasion had come to the town of Adano. — *A Bell for Adano*, John Hersey, 1944.

10485 When Wolfe was in Spain, issues were clear because they were simplified by the war. — *Of Many Men*, James Aldridge, 1946.

10486 Brigadier Catlock had signalled for Colonel Nicobar to come up to Vienna at once and help him to rehabilitate Austria, and, deep in the panting heart of Rome, the colonel was having one last read through the papers in his in-tray just in case somebody from a higher level than the brigadier should have ordered him to go to Athens instead. — *Vespers in Vienna*, Bruce Marshall, 1947.

10487 When it was over, it was not really over, and that was the trouble. — *The Vixens*, Frank Yerby, 1947.

10488 "What the hell goes on here?" Whitey Ardmore demanded. — *Sixth Column*, Robert A. Heinlein, 1949.

10489 The war is over, and for all one can see in the streets or newspapers, or hear around the cracker barrel or campus or bartop, it is forgotten. — *Call It Treason*, George Howe, 1949.

10490 Probably I was in the war. — *Barbary Shore*, Norman Mailer, 1951.

10491 Long before the first bugles sounded from the barracks within the city and the cantonments surrounding it, most of the people in the city were already awake. — *A Fable*, William Faulkner, 1954.

10492 When the war came to Monterey and to Cannery Row everybody fought it more or less, in one way or another. — *Sweet Thursday*, John Steinbeck, 1954.

10493 It was in the year 1815 and the people of England were suffering from strange and unpredictable humors. The war against the French had been going on too long. — *The Tontine*, Thomas B. Costain, 1955.

10494 The sky over London was glorious, ochre and madder, as though a dozen tropic suns were simultaneously setting round the horizon; everywhere the searchlights clustered and hovered, then swept apart; here and there pitchy

clouds drifted and billowed; now and then a huge flash momentarily froze the serene fireside glow. — *Officers and Gentlemen*, Evelyn Waugh, 1955.

10495 Both David Alexander Bonbright and Agatha Winlake belonged to the race of the golden Californians in the period between the wars — that first one which President Wilson called the war to end wars, and that second one which the people of the United States in their honest distaste for it always spoke of as This Thing: "When we go into This Thing. . ." "As long as This Thing lasts. . ." "When This Thing is over. . ." — *Give Me Possession*, Paul Horgan, 1957.

10496 The year was 1940. In September of 1939 England had declared war against Germany but it was spring again, and Americans were still safe. — *Command the Morning*, Pearl S. Buck, 1959.

10497 "There should be a baptism in blood. We have had enough of target practice." — *I Shall Not Hear the Nightingale*, Khushwant Singh, 1959.

10498 The General was tired of war, yet war had made him what he was, and in its absence he wandered in labyrinths of uncertainty. — *Comrade Jacob*, David Caute, 1961.

10499 This is war, he thought. The damp grass hissed and parted, the cat paused. This is war, thought Major Kane. — *The Major*, David Hughes, 1964.

10500 The war came early one morning in June of 1950, and by the time the North Koreans occupied our capital city, Seoul, we had already left our university, where we were instructors in the History of Human Civilization. — *The Martyred*, Richard E. Kim, 1964.

10501 It was October, 1944. The war was everywhere and nowhere. — *Justin Moyan*, David Weiss, 1965.

10502 Demobilization sounded like the best word in the language in 1946. — *Indian Summer*, John Knowles, 1966.

10503 They listened. The camp was a clock. Ticking, it told the time of the war. When it stopped the war would end. Over the clock, the silence was like glass. Whistles shattered it. — *The Eagle and the Iron Cross*, Glendon Swarthout, 1966.

10504 Racing clouds in Confederate gray had been taking up their positions above the enemy since daybreak. — *The National Standard*, Gerald Jay Goldberg, 1968.

10505 The sky was on fire. Shells leaped and crackled round the aircraft: sometimes above, sometimes below, sometimes close alongside. — *A Survivor*, Mervyn Jones, 1968.

10506 The war came to an end late one evening in the summer of 1953, and before we could grow accustomed to the eerie stillness in the trenches and bunkers along the front line, I had

already been relieved of my rifle company and was in Pusan, on my way to the United States, where I was to attend the Officers' Advanced Course at Fort Benning in Georgia. — *The Innocent*, Richard E. Kim, 1968.

10507 After the battle of Singapore Kyoga never felt the same again about war. — *See You in Yasukuni*, Gerald Hanley, 1969.

10508 All this happened, more or less. The war parts, anyway, are pretty much true. — *Slaughterhouse-Five*, Kurt Vonnegut, 1969.

10509 They stormed out of the dustcloud in a solid, scurrying mass, horse and foot in about equal proportions, but in no sort of formation; a mob of armed fugitives, with nothing in mind but to escape the hangman, or the bayonets of the Highlanders who had rushed the town at first light and had now fought their way as far as the Ranee's palace. — *God Is an Englishman*, R. F. Delderfield, 1970.

10510 Letter from Joseph Bodenland to his wife, Mina:/ *August 20th, 2020/ New Houston/* My dearest Mina,/ I will entrust this to good old mail services, since I learn that CompC, being much more sophisticated, has been entirely disorganized by the recent impact-raids. What has not? — *Frankenstein Unbound*, Brian W. Aldiss, 1973.

10511 Ages ago, Alex, Allen and Alva arrived at Antibes, and Alva allowing all, allowing anyone, against Alex's admonition, against Allen's angry assertion: another African amusement . . . anyhow, as all argued, an awesome African army assembled and arduously advanced against an African anthill, assiduously annihilating ant after ant, and afterward, Alex astonishingly accuses Albert as also accepting Africa's antipotal ant annexation. — *Alphabetical Africa*, Walter Abish, 1974.

10512 Four things one particularly notices after wars of any respectable size: preparations for the next one, confidence that armed conflict is finished for ever, starvation, and feasting. — *The Eighty-Minute Hour*, Brian W. Aldiss, 1974.

10513 The last great battle was being fought: Armageddon had arrived, as prophesied. — *Heaven and Hell and the Megas Factor*, Robert Nathan, 1975.

10514 Hitler was dead, the peace in Europe almost a month old; only the Japanese remained to be dealt with. — *A Division of the Spoils*, Paul Scott, 1975.

10515 There was a hush in the broad Glasgow street on the day the French soldiers hauled down their flag. — *Traitor's Gate*, Catherine Gavin, 1976.

10516 "The Revolution has started and it looks like a long war, Your Worship."/ "You can say that again," George Washington said. — *The*

Long Naked Descent into Boston, William Eastlake, 1977.

10517 To be ten years old in 1944 was to know one's place in the war effort, to collect scrap paper for the scrap paper drive, save Minuteman war stamps, and memorize the silhouettes of enemy aircraft, then crouch on the roof of a building at twilight hoping to spot a Stuka before it could strafe the neighborhood. — *The Old Neighborhood*, Avery Corman, 1980.

10518 As the arc of noon passes over the Urals its high sun pours down on a continent aflame from end to end with a war that has been raging out of control for seventeen months. — *Heart of War*, John Masters, 1980.

10519 The dogs had fled. The alleys were quiet because the rockets had fallen on Saigon until the dogs had stopped barking at them and felt the terror of the people and joined the refugees rushing out of the city into nowhere. — *The Alleys of Eden*, Robert Olen Butler, 1981.

10520 Between 1963 and 1966 a state of undeclared war existed between Indonesia and the newly established Federation of Malaysia. — *The Villa Golitsyn*, Piers Paul Read, 1981.

10521 What he actually said—his exact words, I have been told; in his own thunderous language—the blood-fouled old general, seven times consul, Gaius Marius the Mule-driver, staggering in the last malodorous days of his last term of office, from his bed to the latrine on swollen septic feet to heave out his bowels—his life indeed, the undigested indigestible gobbets of his failed ambition—from both ends at the same time (and most of it spattered on his sheets or his nightshirt before he could get there, according to his doctor—who ever heard these days of a discreet doctor? they tell everything to everyone these days in case someone accuses them of poisoning people)—his exact words were as follows: "*Inter Arma Silent Leges*": "Once the weapons are out, the laws fall silent." And by god so they do. — *Vox Pop*, John Arden, 1982.

10522 The weak seemed always to outnumber the strong; always the weak came in droves and the strong in platoons. — *Promise the Earth*, Clive Irving, 1982.

10523 War came to the Dutch East Indies in late 1941. — *The Trail of the Serpent*, Jan de Hartog, 1983.

10524 Wars came early to Shanghai, overtaking each other like the tides that raced up the Yangtze and returned to this gaudy city all the coffins cast adrift from the funeral piers of the Chinese Bund. — *Empire of the Sun*, J. G. Ballard, 1984.

10525 It might have been supposed that the outbreak of war would have broken the spirit of Mrs. Emmeline Pillson, formerly Lucas, *née*

Smythe, always Lucia, three times Mayor of Tilling. — *Lucia in Wartime*, Tom Holt, 1985.

10526 In that late, cheerless spring of 1945, blood still stained the great rivers of Europe. — *Vatican*, Malachi Martin, 1986.

10527 No doubt, some men and women truly believe in the "beautiful madness of war." — *American Blood*, John Nichols, 1987.

10528 "The war ended last night, Caroline. Help me with these flowers." — *Empire*, Gore Vidal, 1987.

10529 What it all hung upon really was a dash through the darkness many years ago, a wartime drive to the north whose destination was not known and might never be known because the driver was now dead; and upon that came to hang a number of theories, and with those theories certain people identified themselves so closely that they felt threatened when the correctness of the theories was questioned and their behaviour became in some cases distinctly odd. — *Deceits of Time*, Isabel Colegate, 1988.

10530 Steel, as you probably don't have to be reminded, is an alloy based on iron. It contains anything from 0.1 to 1.7 percent of carbon, as well as traces of sulphur, phosphorous, manganese, nickel and chromium. It is tough and yet malleable, so you can make swords out of it. It is Mars's own alloy. — *Any Old Iron*, Anthony Burgess, 1989.

10531 I was born in a war, I grew up in a war, and there was war all along. — *Flawless Jade*, Barbara Hanrahan, 1989.

10532 A rotted cardboard suitcase, open like a book, haunted the front gate of the refugee camp. — *The Extras*, Wayne Karlin, 1989.

10533 Somewhere out behind a black wall of monsoon rain and beyond our wire, the Phantom Blooper laughs. — *The Phantom Blooper*, Gustav Hasford, 1990.

10534 Thirty years ago during the cold October of 1956, my friends and I on Damjanich Street hoarded fallen chestnuts, the missiles for our battles in the park. — *Broken Places*, László Petrovics-Ofner, 1990.

10535 It was the year that a distinguished British general, seldom menaced by more than a hundred warriors, took ten embittering weeks to march four regiments just sixty New Zealand miles, and at last found a war worth leaving unwon. — *Monday's Warriors*, Maurice Shadbolt, 1990.

10536 Every afternoon in Shanghai during the summer of 1937 I rode down to the Bund to see if the war had begun. — *The Kindness of Women*, J. G. Ballard, 1991.

10537 Below, at the zigzag patchwork of trenches, the front was quiet. — *Touch the Sky*, Harold Livingston, 1991.

Warnings

10538 "Carpentaria!"/ One of the three richly-uniformed officials who were in charge of the captive balloon, destined to be a leading attraction of the City of Pleasure, murmured this name warningly to his companions, as if to advise them that the moment had arrived for them to mind their p's and q's. — *The City of Pleasure*, Arnold Bennett, 1907.

10539 The long wail of the first air-raid warning of the night shrieked through the unlighted Chinese city and rebounded from the darkening hills outside its walls. — *China Sky*, Pearl S. Buck, 1942.

10540 "Hei-ee! Hold your fretful feet away from the well—" Lakshmi peered out of the cowhouse door, calling to her son, Nago, as he flew a red-and-green kite and his three-foot figure hopped past in the sunlit yard, the reel gripped in his small hands, eyes fixed skyward. — *A Goddess Named Gold*, Bhabani Bhattacharya, 1960.

10541 For the fourth time that morning the lookout unsheathed his knife and turned the blade until it caught the sun. The warning flash was acknowledged by the horsemen clustered below him on the plateau, and they urged their mounts into the forest. — *The Wolf at the Door*, Graham Shelby, 1975.

10542 That summer they hanged a fat man at the Western Gate as a warning and example to all. — *The Chinese Bandit*, Stephen Becker, 1976.

10543 Sheridan put a restraining hand on the younger man's arm./ "Careful, the Prince might hear you." — *The Prince and the Tobacco Lords*, Margaret Thomson Davis, 1976.

10544 Boog warned me about Washington, but until I saw the rich lady set her pugs on the dinner table, I didn't take him seriously. — *Cadillac Jack*, Larry McMurtry, 1982.

10545 NOTICE/ Do not use my Good Blankets And/ Pillows In Room Three/ Signed Matron H. Price — *Mr. Scobie's Riddle*, Elizabeth Jolley, 1983.

10546 I look through the eyes of a rattler, tail up and rattles going like hail on a roof but Pa goes right on, never heeding my warning. — *Refugio, They Named You Wrong*, Susan Clark Schofield, 1991.

10547 All the children, but especially the girl children, were warned away from Uncle Billy's shed; warned the same way you tell a child not to fool with matches, or flirt with November ice. — *Women of Granite*, Dana Andrew Jennings, 1992.

10548 These are, I should warn you, the words of a dead man. — *Ever After*, Graham Swift, 1992.

Wealth

10549 The main road to wealth in New Orleans has long been Carondelet street. — *Dr. Sevier*, George W. Cable, 1884.

10550 I cannot remember the time when I was not absolutely certain that I would be a millionaire. — *The Master-Rogue*, David Graham Phillips, 1903.

10551 There is, as every schoolboy knows in this scientific age, a very close chemical relation between coal and diamonds. It is the reason, I believe, why some people allude to coal as "black diamonds." Both these commodities represent wealth; but coal is a much less portable form of property. — *Victory*, Joseph Conrad, 1915.

10552 There was a thoughtful frown on the face of the man who was the possessor of twenty million dollars. — *Oh, Money! Money!*, Eleanor H. Porter, 1918.

10553 Major Amberson had "made a fortune" in 1873, when other people were losing fortunes, and the magnificence of the Ambersons began then. — *The Magnificent Ambersons*, Booth Tarkington, 1918.

10554 "The Little Sons of the Rich" were gathered about the long table in Pettingill's studio. — *Brewster's Millions*, George Barr McCutcheon, 1925.

10555 The best remedy for a bruised heart is not, as so many people seem to think, repose upon a manly bosom. Much more efficacious are honest work, physical activity, and the sudden acquisition of wealth. — *Have His Carcase*, Dorothy L. Sayers, 1932.

10556 I am obliged to begin this story with a brief account of the Hampton family, because it is necessary to emphasise the fact once and for all that the Hamptons were very grand as well as very rich. — *Love in a Cold Climate*, Nancy Mitford, 1949.

10557 The richest man in Antioch, by common report, was Ignatius, the dealer in olive oil. — *The Silver Chalice*, Thomas B. Costain, 1952.

10558 So you think it undemocratic that I — Apple County's wealthiest man — should be first chosen to speak about the woman, Marcy Cresap. — *The Voices of Glory*, Davis Grubb, 1962.

10559 One summer afternoon Mrs. Oedipa Maas came home from a Tupperware party whose hostess had put perhaps too much kirsch

in the fondue to find that she, Oedipa, had been named executor, or she supposed executrix, of the estate of one Pierce Inverarity, a California real estate mogul who had once lost two million dollars in his spare time but still had assets numerous and tangled enough to make the job of sorting it all out more than honorary. — *The Crying of Lot 49*, Thomas Pynchon, 1966.

10560 We all have friends who are richer than ourselves, and they, you may be sure, have richer friends of their own. We are most of us within spitting distance of millionaires./ Spit away, if that's what you feel like. — *Words of Advice*, Fay Weldon, 1977.

10561 Mr. Van Eyck had a great deal of money which he didn't want to spend, and a great deal of time which he didn't know how to spend. — *The Murder of Miranda*, Margaret Millar, 1979.

10562 Ivo Bilic, a wealthy Zagreb banker, bought the Villa Ribar in the late 1920s. — *Leap in the Dark*, Anthony McCandless, 1980.

10563 "What the hell are you doing on a bus, with your dough?" — *Zuckerman Unbound*, Philip Roth, 1981.

10564 Standing there among the trees in the old Ricklehouse family plot in Westchester, among the other Ricklehouse graves, it began to creep over me. I'm rich. — *Tender Offer*, Nora Johnson, 1985.

10565 The richer the host, the later dinner was served. — *Rich Like Us*, Nayantara Sahgal, 1985.

Weather and Seasons

10566 There are some strange summer mornings in the country, when he who is but a sojourner from the city shall early walk forth into the fields, and be wonder-smitten with the trance-like aspect of the green and golden world. — *Pierre*, Herman Melville, 1852.

10567 It had been one of the warm and almost sultry days which sometimes come in November; a maligned month, which is really an epitome of the other eleven, or a sort of index to the whole year's changes of storm and sunshine. — *A Country Doctor*, Sarah Orne Jewett, 1884.

10568 "I'm afraid that he won't come," said Laura McIntyre, in a disconsolate voice./ "Why not?"/ "Oh, look at the weather; it is something too awful." — *The Doings of Raffles Haw*, Arthur Conan Doyle, 1891.

10569 All this New-year's Day of 1850 the sun shone cloudless but wrought no thaw. — *A Kentucky Cardinal*, James Lane Allen, 1895.

10570 Winter in the upper heights of the Bear Tooth Range is a glittering desolation of snow with a flaming blue sky above. — *The Captain of the Gray-Horse Troop*, Hamlin Garland, 1901.

10571 The peculiar angle of the earth's axis to the plane of the ecliptic — that angle which is chiefly responsible for our geography and therefore for our history — had caused the phenomenon known in London as summer. — *Buried Alive*, Arnold Bennett, 1908.

10572 It was winter — cold and snow and ice and naked trees and leaden clouds and stinging wind. — *The Eyes of the World*, Harold Bell Wright, 1914.

10573 Harvest-time was almost come, and the great new land was resting under coverlets of gold. — *The World for Sale*, Gilbert Parker, 1916.

10574 All afternoon the wind sifted out of the black Welsh glens, crying notice that Winter was come sliding down over the world from the Pole; and riverward there was the faint moaning of new ice. — *Cup of Gold*, John Steinbeck, 1929.

10575 All along the road from the river the frost made patterns on the ground, and how beautifully the air smelt.... — *Saraband*, Eliot Bliss, 1931.

10576 It was dry that summer. — *Siesta*, Berry Fleming, 1935.

10577 It was a cold grey day in late November. The weather had changed overnight, when a backing wind brought a granite sky and a mizzling rain with it, and although it was now only a little after two o'clock in the afternoon the pallor of a winter evening seemed to have closed upon the hills, cloaking them in mist. — *The Jamaica Inn*, Daphne du Maurier, 1936.

10578 It was an uncertain spring. The weather, perpetually changing, sent clouds of blue and of purple flying over the land. — *The Years*, Virginia Woolf, 1937.

10579 Renny Whiteoak had done well to provide himself against the weather for, though it was now March, the wind was as icy as in winter and it needed his rubber boots to keep out the icy slush of the road. — *Wakefield's Course*, Mazo de la Roche, 1941.

10580 Dark fog came in from the ocean during the autumn afternoon and made mysterious the steep San Francisco street and the rooms of the brick house. — *The Venables*, Kathleen Norris, 1941.

10581 All summer had been filled with dust. — *Signed with Their Honour*, James Aldridge, 1942.

10582 A lowering fog hung menacingly over San Francisco. On this bleak December day in 1933, it looked like a giant's hand with claw-

shaped fingers poised above the town as if to clutch it in a strangling grip. — *Flint*, Charles G. Norris, 1944.

10583 That summer in Montreal was cool and dry, the June days cloudlessly blue and sunny. — *The Unreasoning Heart*, Constance Beresford-Howe, 1946.

10584 It was spring in the city of K'aifeng, a late spring in the northern Chinese province of Honan. — *Peony*, Pearl S. Buck, 1948.

10585 The sky had cleared, the clouds raveled to tatters, and at four oclock the sun broke through, silver on the bright green of grass and leaves and golden on the puddles in the road; all down the column men quickened the step, smiling in the sudden burst of gold and silver weather. — *Shiloh*, Shelby Foote, 1952.

10586 The sun was shining, and a small breeze was spicing along Piccadilly when Christine came out for her lunch. — *The Nightingales Are Singing*, Monica Dickens, 1953.

10587 The year was 1450 and the day the twentieth of May; May the month of Mary, the Mother of God; the month of summer's promise; the month of the May dance and revels; the month when vineyards were painted with fresh green and hedgerows were bright with flowers; a month of laughter among people and of song among birds. — *Beware of the Mouse*, Leonard Wibberley, 1958.

10588 It was sunny in San Francisco; a fabulous condition. — *The Manchurian Candidate*, Richard Condon, 1959.

10589 Sometimes, winter comes gradually to northern New England so that there is an element of order and sequence to time and season. — *Return to Peyton Place*, Grace Metalious, 1959.

10590 Valour was in the spring wind. Winter's white shabby screens had been leaning anciently together across the Duchy; to-day however the screens had toppled, revealing green fields lost but now found, and trees already scattered hard with bud, and a blue prodigal sky into which the spires, towers, belfries soared more strongly than ever. — *The Tournament*, Peter Vansittart, 1959.

10591 *The great brown harvest-hand of autumn lying on the long road, painting her colors on undone summer's green.* — *The Native Moment*, Anthony C. West, 1959.

10592 The autumn morning was so brilliant that Moray, judiciously consulting the rheostat thermometer outside his window, decided to breakfast on the balcony of his bedroom. — *The Judas Tree*, A. J. Cronin, 1961.

10593 Another summer has passed. — *With Gall and Honey*, R. Leslie Gourse, 1961.

10594 It was dolphin weather, when I sailed into Piraeus with my comrades of the Cretan bull ring. — *The Bull from the Sea*, Mary Renault, 1962.

10595 In Australia it is winter that comes in June and not summer. — *Flight to Landfall*, G. M. Glaskin, 1963.

10596 The sun shone all summer. Everybody knows that. — *Statues in a Garden*, Isabel Colegate, 1964.

10597 It was one of those artificially hot days that they used to call Indian summer. — *Funeral in Berlin*, Len Deighton, 1964.

10598 Much cruelty was abroad that winter. Groans sounded in the wind, and sky and earth faltered. — *The Lost Lands*, Peter Vansittart, 1964.

10599 The weather bureau forecast sun. — *August Is a Wicked Month*, Edna O'Brien, 1965.

10600 It was a warm, moist morning in the last week of April, with a feel of early summer in the southerly breeze. — *Miss Mamma Aimee*, Erskine Caldwell, 1967.

10601 *The Report begins:/* One afternoon early in a certain January, the weather showed a lack of character. There was no frost or wind; the trees in the garden did not stir. — *Report on Probability A*, Brian W. Aldiss, 1969.

10602 It is May and the sun is shining. It is warm. — *Trespasses*, Paul Bailey, 1970.

10603 It had been a thunderous spring. — *A Dutiful Daughter*, Thomas Keneally, 1971.

10604 The fog was breaking up. A moment ago he had marvelled at the huge edifice of blue air which occupied the street, obliterating houses and the telegraph poles. — *Water with Berries*, George Lamming, 1971.

10605 Did weather exist, when nobody looked at it? — *Eagle Eye*, Hortense Calisher, 1973.

10606 On a February morning, when a weather front is moving in off the Pacific but has not quite arrived, and the winds are changeable and gusty and clouds drive over and an occasional flurry of fine rain darkens the terrace bricks, this place conforms to none of the clichés about California with which they advertise the Sunshine Cities for the Sunset Years. — *The Spectator Bird*, Wallace Stegner, 1976.

10607 Blue strips of sky between bleak clouds this chill day before Christmas as winter entrenched across the remote midlands of Ireland. — *The Destinies of Darcy Dancer, Gentleman*, J. P. Donleavy, 1977.

10608 Overnight, spring came down from the seven hills and fell on him like a curse. — *The Last Magic*, N. Richard Nash, 1978.

10609 Winter had come in early that year. One night while the boys slept, it had come in like a black dog howling down from the northeast, wandering over the hills, licking the ringing fence wires with frost. — *How Jerem Came Home*, Paul Kaser, 1980.

10610 The coulee is so still right now that if

a match were to be lit, the flame would not waver. — *Obasan*, Joy Kogawa, 1981.

10611 She was hot and blind. The sunlight poured over her, the energy impelling her body as it impelled the whole earth, the northern hemisphere now in its favorable inclination, the passionate seasonal shape of the Canadian year, brooding dark and sudden light, unfolding its summer in her body as it did on the whole island. — *It Is Always Summer*, David Helwig, 1982.

10612 It is just after eight o'clock in the morning of a dark February day, in this year of grace nineteen hundred and fifty-two. An atmospheric depression has combined with the coal smoke from a million chimneys to cast a pall over London. — *Souls and Bodies*, David Lodge, 1982.

10613 It gets cold on this coast in September. — *Prince Ombra*, Roderick MacLeish, 1982.

10614 This is that story/ The heaving high seas were laden with scum/ The dull sky glowed red/ Dust and ashes drifted in the wind circling the earth/ The burdened seas slanted this way, and that, flooding the scorched land under a daylight moon/ A black oily rain rained/ No one was there — *God's Grace*, Bernard Malamud, 1982.

10615 It was a Sunday in the Bois de Boulogne and the fine weather which had arrived so late in July had flushed out the Parisians and the wild bouillabaisse of nationalities now temporarily inhabiting the capital. — *Gentlemen of Adventure*, Ernest K. Gann, 1983.

10616 The harbor was cool and damp, not yet warmed by the sun breaking through the clouds rolling in the trade winds above the Waianae and Koolau mountain ranges. — *O God of Battles*, Harry Homewood, 1983.

10617 The January day was cold with a grey sky that seemed to rest on the hedge at the end of the unploughed field. — *Foggage*, Patrick McGinley, 1983.

10618 The winter had been fierce and relentless, but it loosed its grip some as it surged into mid-March. — *The Silence of Snakes*, Lewis W. Green, 1984.

10619 It was earthquake weather and everyone knew it. — *Fortune's Daughter*, Alice Hoffman, 1985.

10620 The summers at Cold Spring Harbor were as close to heaven on earth as anything Jeremy Singer had known in his young life. — *All for Love*, Ring Lardner, Jr., 1985.

10621 The sun hovered behind a pink haze that engulfed all of St. Louis that Indian summer of 1959. — *Betsey Brown*, Ntozake Shange, 1985.

10622 Summer that year held into September, golden and hot, surfacing a wave of unexpected optimism that took most people by surprise; but like summer itself, like the long baking days that hung on precariously for a few weeks more, it didn't last. — *Sea Changes*, Robert Kotlowitz, 1986.

10623 School was out, and the long green summer days fastened themselves on the hills of Walden Valley and browsed, slowly and gently as cows graze, throughout the low swales between the hills. — *A Summer Ago*, George Scarbrough, 1986.

10624 It is June and winter is memory. — *The Beginning of Sorrows*, David Martin, 1987.

10625 They said it was August, and that's about right. — *Zions Cause*, Jim Peyton, 1987.

10626 Spring is good in this land. — *Blessed McGill*, Edwin Shrake, 1987.

10627 Often January brings a strange false spring to much of northern California. — *Second Chances*, Alice Adams, 1988.

10628 You are aware of the weather first of all, and the limits of the known world, the sign of the Army and Navy Store on the Avenue, or from the fifteenth story the line of mist out toward Staten Island. — *This Coffin Has No Handles*, Thomas McGrath, 1988.

10629 Yesterday the overcast flowed over the front range like an aerial ocean. — *Light*, Seymour Epstein, 1989.

10630 A rime of frost lay thick on the puddles in Old Common Lane that February morning. — *His Father's Son*, Malcolm Macdonald, 1989.

10631 Winters are long in Mattagash, Maine. — *Once Upon a Time on the Banks*, Cathie Pelletier, 1989.

10632 It was the Saturday before Easter and all day the weather had been seesawing between winter and spring. — *Homework*, Margot Livesey, 1990.

10633 Autumn of the year 1974. — *Ghost of the Sun*, Harry Mark Petrakis, 1990.

10634 Spring in southern New Mexico is a dirty time. — *Airman Mortensen*, Michael Blake, 1991.

10635 *The fog pulsated with each breath that she exhaled.* — *If Not on Earth, Then in Heaven*, Joel Redon, 1991.

10636 It was winter now. — *The Loop*, Joe Coomer, 1992.

10637 Thick cloud had pressed down on Berlin all night, and now it was lingering into what passed for the morning. — *Fatherland*, Robert Harris, 1992.

10638 Spring. The wrong time of year again. — *Del-Del*, Victor Kelleher, 1992.

10639 On the mainland it was the beginning of spring, but here it might have been the dead of winter. — *Mainland*, Robert McCrum, 1992.

10640 That winter was the warmest in a hundred years. — *Outerbridge Reach*, Robert Stone, 1992.

Weddings

10641 "The abbot, in his alb arrayed," stood at the altar in the abbey-chapel of Rubygill, with all his plump, sleek, rosy friars, in goodly lines disposed, to solemnize the nuptials of the beautiful Matilda Fitzwater, daughter of the Baron of Arlingford, with the noble Robert Fitz-Ooth, Earl of Locksley and Huntingdon. — *Maid Marian*, Thomas Love Peacock, 1822.

10642 Setting aside the consideration of the risk, the baby-weddings of the Middle Ages must have been very pretty sights. — *The Chaplet of Pearls*, Charlotte Mary Yonge, 1868.

10643 The evening before Helen Jeffrey's wedding day, the whole household at the rectory came out into the garden. — *John Ward, Preacher*, Margaret Deland, 1888.

10644 She stood before the minister who was to marry them, very tall and straight. With lips slightly parted she looked at him steadfastly, not at the man beside her who was about to become her husband. — *Together*, Robert Herrick, 1908.

10645 The air in the house, Carlotta thought when she stuck out her tongue, tasted of a wedding—just as it had done four years ago when her big brother David was married to Seena Nordstrom. — *The Waters Under the Earth*, Martha Ostenso, 1930.

10646 The morning of the Tilney-Studdart wedding rain fell steadily from before daylight, veiling trees and garden and darkening the canvas of the marquee that should have caught the earliest sun in happy augury. — *Friends and Relations*, Elizabeth Bowen, 1931.

10647 It was Wang Lung's marriage day. — *The Good Earth*, Pearl S. Buck, 1931.

10648 The year before Jennie Middleton's marriage Lexington was a town of thirty thousand people. Twelve months later the population was increased by thirty thousand souls. — *The Wedding*, Grace Lumpkin, 1939.

10649 I was sitting in the Guards' Chapel under the terra-cotta lunette which contains the Centurion saying to one, Go, and he goeth; and to another, Come, and he cometh; and to his servant, Do this, and he doeth it. The occasion was the wedding of a girl called Fitzgibbon who was marrying a young man in the Coldstream. — *What's Become of Waring*, Anthony Powell, 1939.

10650 The organ blared, piped, and pealed, coaxing the bride to come into the aisle. — *The Devil Loves Me*, Margaret Millar, 1942.

10651 "In the presence of our Lord and of this assembly, I, Solon Barnes, take Benecia Wallin to be my wife, promising, with divine assistance, to be unto her a loving and faithful husband until death shall separate us." — *The Bulwark*, Theodore Dreiser, 1946.

10652 Lilian's wedding went without a hitch. This is an unusual fact to set down of any wedding. — *The Flower of May*, Kate O'Brien, 1953.

10653 After all there were no carriages for her wedding. The distance between the church porch and the house on the corner of the square was so short, everyone said, that it was simply not worth while. — *The Sleepless Moon*, H. E. Bates, 1956.

10654 "Isn't that the place where you attended your father's wedding?" Colin's voice was indistinct on the telephone. It was impossible to be certain that he was laughing. — *The Italian Wife*, Emyr Humphreys, 1957.

10655 "Repeat after me," said the parson. "I, Horatio, take thee, Maria Ellen—" — *Hornblower and the Hotspur*, C. S. Forester, 1962.

10656 It was June, 1933, one week after Commencement, when Kay Leiland Strong, Vassar '33, the first of her class to run around the table at the Class Day dinner, was married to Harald Petersen, Reed '27, in the chapel of St. George's Church, P.E., Karl F. Reiland, Rector. — *The Group*, Mary McCarthy, 1963.

10657 Towards the end of the bridegroom's speech, the bride turned aside and began to throw crumbs of wedding cake through an opening in the marquee to the doves outside. She did so with gentle absorption, and more doves came down from their wooden house above the stables. — *The Soul of Kindness*, Elizabeth Taylor, 1964.

10658 On the day that his grannie was killed by the English, Sir William Scott the Younger of Buccleuch was at Melrose Abbey, marrying his aunt. — *The Disorderly Knights*, Dorothy Dunnett, 1966.

10659 The Quayne ladies, adjusting their mantillas, hurried across the courtyard to the chapel. — *The Wedding Group*, Elizabeth Taylor, 1968.

10660 When Oliver saw his sister in her bridesmaid's dress he laughed so much he could hardly stand. — *Something in Disguise*, Elizabeth Jane Howard, 1969.

10661 On the fifteenth day of January, 1913, in the presence of both families and about two hundred invited guests, William Bloodgood Ewing and Edna Everett became man and wife. — *The Ewings*, John O'Hara, 1972.

10662 Shortly before midnight, July 1, 1833, Colonel Aaron Burr, aged seventy-seven, married Eliza Jumel, born Bowen fifty-eight years ago (more likely sixty-five but remember: she is prone to litigation!). — *Burr*, Gore Vidal, 1973.

10663 We never missed a wedding. — *Where the Cherries End Up*, Gail Henley, 1978.

10664 Corrado Prizzi's granddaughter was being married before the baroque altar of Santa Grazia de Traghetto, the lucky church of the Prizzi family. — *Prizzi's Honor*, Richard Condon, 1982.

10665 The day before Aunt Leela got married, Mr. Patel took Sumitra to Kampala to buy fireworks. — *Sumitra's Story*, Rukshana Smith, 1982.

10666 It was a strange wedding. — *The Long Shadow*, Anna Gilbert, 1984.

10667 All in all, Henry Laines' wedding was one of the worst events in my experience, tragic in society. — *Lives of the Saints*, Nancy Lemann, 1985.

10668 Julia Murphy knew that the bride ironed her hair. — *Adventures with Julia*, Candace Denning, 1986.

10669 It's the Duke of Windsor's wedding day. — *Whatever Happened to Gloomy Gus of the Chicago Bears?*, Robert Coover, 1987.

10670 I never doubted the Bridegroom would be back. — *Keeping the Faith*, Carol Clewlow, 1988.

10671 Ruby Levy's wedding to Ben Berliner was one of the social events of 1919, despite the fact that the bride was a nobody. — *Union Square*, Meredith Tax, 1988.

10672 "Dearly beloved, we are gathered together..." began the singsong holier-than-thou voice of the Very Reverend Peachy. — *A Cast of Smiles*, Amanda Brookfield, 1990.

10673 True was married yesterday, in a bower by the beach at Ainahau. — *The Shores of Paradise*, Shirley Streshinsky, 1991.

10674 Michael Ruane — Indianapolis born, Indianapolis bred — had planned to climb Vesuvio that morning and look down into the volcanic crater, but he was persuaded instead to go to a wedding in the basilica of Santa Chiara and present himself as the "uncle from Rome." — *The Uncle from Rome*, Joseph Caldwell, 1992.

10675 The best wedding I ever went to was Louise Crane's. — *On Mermaid Avenue*, Binnie Kirshenbaum, 1992.

10676 The only time my mother took me to Heyton Hall was Easter of '74. We were there for Aunt Helen's garden wedding — a small one, her third, a Mr. Bolini. — *Gatherings*, Marina Rust, 1993.

Wind

10677 "How the wind is rising!" said Rosamond. — "God help the poor people at sea to night!" — *Patronage*, Maria Edgeworth, 1814.

10678 It was winter — that is, about the second week in November — and great gusts were rattling at the windows, and wailing and thundering among our tall trees and ivied chimneys — a very dark night, and a very cheerful fire blazing, a pleasant mixture of good round coal and spluttering dry wood, in a genuine old fireplace, in a sombre old room. — *Uncle Silas*, J. Sheridan LeFanu, 1864.

10679 It was late in the afternoon in the spring of the year 1630; the hilltops of the south of Scotland were covered with masses of cloud, and a fierce wind swept the driving rain before it with such force that it was not easy to make way against it. — *The Lion of the North*, G. A. Henty, 1886.

10680 "It blows," said Joe Wingate. — *A First Family of Tasajara*, Bret Harte, 1891.

10681 It was very dark, and the wind was increasing. The last gust had been preceded by an ominous roaring down the whole mountainside, which continued for some time after the trees in the little valley had lapsed into silence. — *In a Hollow of the Hills*, Bret Harte, 1895.

10682 The masterful wind was up and out, shouting and chasing, the lord of the morning. — *The Golden Age*, Kenneth Grahame, 1898.

10683 The soft summer wind stirs the redwoods, and Wild-Water ripples sweet cadences over its mossy stones. — *The Iron Heel*, Jack London, 1908.

10684 A wind sprang high in the west like a wave of unreasonable happiness and tore eastward across England, trailing with it the frosty scent of forests and the cold intoxication of the sea. In a million holes and corners it refreshed a man like a flagon, and astonished him like a blow. — *Manalive*, G. K. Chesterton, 1912.

10685 One January day, thirty years ago, the little town of Hanover, anchored on a windy Nebraska tableland, was trying not to be blown away. — *O Pioneers!*, Willa Cather, 1913.

10686 A fitful breeze played among the mesquite bushes. — *Heart of the Sunset*, Rex Beach, 1915.

10687 Beyond the outskirts of the Village, Wentworth, the wind blew, if not more boisterously than in the city proper, with a sweep uninterrupted by dwelling houses or other obstacles. — *Village*, Robert McAlmon, 1924.

10688 All day it had rained and all day the wind had blown savagely from the northeast. — *The Aristocratic Miss Brewster*, Joseph C. Lincoln, 1927.

10689 "All the time the wind was south-west you were deadly keen on seals." — *All the Conspirators*, Christopher Isherwood, 1928.

10690 Wind blows flat and strong across the

city and carries the rain with it. —"Joe and Pete," Martha Gellhorn, 1936.

10691 Ruby let the wind push her head back. —"Ruby," Martha Gellhorn, 1936.

10692 A cold November wind was blowing as a cowboy rode down the point of a low ridge to where little of that sharp wind could reach him. —*Flint Spears*, Will James, 1938.

10693 Back and forth in the rocky valley of Polvosa a lazy dry wind shuttled. —*Bold Rider*, Luke Short, 1938.

10694 From the high edge of Mogul to the floor of Powder Desert was a sheer drop of fourteen hundred and sixty feet; and even on the quietest day a stream of warm air from the desert boiled up the face of the rim, so that if a man stood at the breakoff and tossed his hat outward it invariably sailed back to him. —*Saddle and Ride*, Ernest Haycox, 1940.

10695 He lay flat on the brown, pine-needled floor of the forest, his chin on his folded arms, and high overhead the wind blew in the tops of the pine trees. —*For Whom the Bell Tolls*, Ernest Hemingway, 1940.

10696 The other day, in an inland town, I saw through an open window, a branch of fuschia waving stiffly up and down in the breeze; and at once I smelt the breeze salty, and had a picture of a bright curtain flapping inwards and, beyond the curtain, dazzling sunlight on miles of crinkling water. —*The House of Children*, Joyce Cary, 1941.

10697 A southerly breeze from the low country, languid and moist, was drifting over the newly plowed fields of the upland slope and rustling the leaves of the tall red oaks that surrounded the aging house. —*A House in the Uplands*, Erskine Caldwell, 1946.

10698 The raw southwester—bearing up the spongy odors of spring—came hard aginst Lily Barnes when she stepped from the house, plucking at the falls of her dark hair and winding her coat about her in sudden twists. —*Long Storm*, Ernest Haycox, 1946.

10699 There was a cold November wind blowing through 116th Street. It rattled the tops of garbage cans, sucked window shades out through the top of opened windows and set them flapping back against the windows; and it drove most of the people off the street in the block between Seventh and Eighth Avenues except for a few hurried pedestrians who bent double in an effort to offer the least possible exposure to its violent assault. —*The Street*, Ann Petry, 1946.

10700 So brightly blazed the sun upon the dunes and down the curving beach, so tranquilly dozed the village under its ragged palms, that only the rising wind marked September's ominous departure. —*The Yogi of Cockroach Court*, Frank Waters, 1947.

10701 All day the heat had been barely supportable but at evening a breeze arose in the West, blowing from the heart of the setting sun and from the ocean, which lay unseen, unheard behind the scrubby foothills. It shook the rusty fringes of palm-leaf and swelled the dry sounds of summer, the frog-voices, the grating cicadas, and the ever present pulse of music from the neighbouring native huts. —*The Loved One*, Evelyn Waugh, 1948.

10702 There was no wind in all that sweep of sky. —*The Golden Hawk*, Frank Yerby, 1948.

10703 For the time of year it was chilly inside the large, two-storied, white, colonnaded house, but a balmy spring breeze, smelling of dew-damp jasmine, was blowing intermittently through the open windows, and rustling the Sunday paper on the kitchen table. —*Place Called Estherville*, Erskine Caldwell, 1949.

10704 A January gale was roaring up the Channel, blustering loudly, and bearing on its bosom rain squalls whose big drops rattled loudly on the tarpaulin clothing of those among the officers and men whose duties kept them on deck. —*Mr. Midshipman Hornblower*, C. S. Forester, 1950.

10705 The failing whirlwind skipped toward him, brushing leaves from its path, spinning first a long thin column and then with the dying wind squatting, showering its dust to both sides of the road, finally becoming nothing, leaving only the running dust on the yellow road. —*The Season of the Stranger*, Stephen Becker, 1951.

10706 A March morning in the year of our Lord, 1950, and the wind so high that on the top floor of a skyscraper in the city of New York William Lane felt a tremor under his feet. —*God's Men*, Pearl S. Buck, 1951.

10707 An hour before daylight the wind came up and swept along the floor of the desert, moving the sand, changing the shapes of the hummocks under the dark mesquite. —*The Wonderful Country*, Tom Lea, 1952.

10708 The early November street was dark though night had ended, but the wind, to the grocer's surprise, already clawed. —*The Assistant*, Bernard Malamud, 1957.

10709 There were deserts to the north, and at the time of the Harmattan, winds, cold at the source, crossed the watershed to the plain of Ukari. —*The Men from the Bush*, Ronald Hardy, 1959.

10710 When the winds blew strongly from the North, bringing an icy reminder that the great ice-cap was still advancing, we used to pile all our stores of brushwood and broken trees in front of the cave, make a really roaring fire, and tell ourselves that however far south it came this

time, even in Africa, we could meet it and beat it. — *The Evolution Man*, Roy Lewis, 1960.

10711 It was a day of spindrift and blowing sea-foam, with black clouds presaging rain driven over the mountains from the sea by a wild March wind. — *Hear Us O Lord from Heaven Thy Dwelling Place*, Malcolm Lowry, 1961.

10712 The dust came first. — *The Wind from Nowhere*, J. G. Ballard, 1962.

10713 Despite the car heater, the cold wind sneaked into the convertible attacking Val's wrists, throat and face. — *This Side of Love*, Paula Christian, 1963.

10714 A brisk little wind sprang out of the east. — *Trot*, David Ely, 1963.

10715 It was a wild late February evening, cold and gusty, and the elm branches beat against the old, blue glass of the panes. — *The Dark Traveler*, Josephine W. Johnson, 1963.

10716 Joanna stood in the prow of the boat that wends its way with mail and passengers from island to island in the Aegean sea, and let the wind blow her hair wild. — *Joanna and Ulysses*, May Sarton, 1963.

10717 In the whole wide promenade less than a dozen people were pretending that the March sun was stronger than the cruel north wind sharpening its razor on exposed skin, trying to strip the flesh from the bones, rattling the dry palm trees, fracturing the sea into glassy splinters falling like hailstones on the bare shingle. — *The Blind Heart*, Storm Jameson, 1964.

10718 The wind came in from the sea so that the plume of smoke that had not left the top of Zopocomapetl for five years now bent inland above the tropical rainforest, and Peter could see the town. — *The Old Gods Laugh*, Frank Yerby, 1964.

10719 In fierce short gusts the bitter north wind swept across the wide confines of Portsmouth harbour, the ranks of wavelets made by the incoming tide crumbling into white confusion at each successive blast. — *H.M.S. Saracen*, Douglas Reeman, 1965.

10720 In the last days of the last moonphase of Autumn a wind blew from the northern ranges through the dying forests of Askatevar, a cold wind that smelled of smoke and snow. — *Planet of Exile*, Ursula K. Le Guin, 1966.

10721 The scraps of paper blew against the chain-link, rust-proof fence and were trapped, vibrating in the wind angrily, struggling against the unbendable alloy mesh in their efforts to break away. — *Angel Loves Nobody*, Richard Miles, 1967.

10722 The wind had quickened to a fury that night. — *The Golden Sickle*, Davis Grubb, 1968.

10723 I am carried away by the same wind that blows all these people down the street, like pieces of paper and dead leaves, in all directions. — *My Argument with the Gestapo*, Thomas Merton, 1968.

10724 An easterly is the most disagreeable wind in Lyme Bay — Lyme Bay being that largest bite from the underside of England's outstretched southwestern leg — and a person of curiosity could at once have deduced several strong probabilities about the pair who began to walk down the quay at Lyme Regis, the small but ancient eponym of the inbite, one incisively sharp and blustery morning in the late March of 1867. — *The French Lieutenant's Woman*, John Fowles, 1969.

10725 Violent, like the furious breath of an ice-dragon, the gale howled across the frozen plateau. — *Indoctrinaire*, Christopher Priest, 1970.

10726 Last night the wind blew across empty miles of Texas desert, and gathering dust into slashing gray clouds it thrust them against the city. — *This Day's Death*, John Rechy, 1970.

10727 When I awoke, the first sound I heard was the south wind whispering and moaning, forcing its foul warmth against the front of the snowhouse. — *The White Dawn*, James Houston, 1971.

10728 I need a wind. A good strong wind. — *Briefing for a Descent into Hell*, Doris Lessing, 1971.

10729 "We're in for a bit of a blow. What about a nightcap? We may need a spot of fortification." Kenny pushed the flop of blond hair from his forehead and stared at the curtained porthole. — *A Woman of Character*, Julian Gloag, 1973.

10730 *The storm broke and thrashed along the river in the summer darkness, with water slanting, leaves flying, trees bent and writhing in the wind.* — *A Cry of Angels*, Jeff Fields, 1974.

10731 There's always a breeze from Central Park, Jack was used to saying about his apartment in summer; at night I even turn off the air-conditioners — after all, Manhattan must once have been a breezy little island. — *The Kill Price*, Jose Yglesias, 1976.

10732 It was windy. The pale afternoon sky was shredded with clouds, the road, grown dustier and more uneven in the last hour, was scattered with blown and rustling leaves. — *The Angry Tide*, Winston Graham, 1977.

10733 All day it had been windy — strange weather for late July — the wind swirling through the hedges like an invisible flood-tide among seaweed; tugging, compelling them in its own direction, dragging them one way until the patches of elder and privet sagged outward from the tougher stretches of blackthorn on either side. — *The Girl in a Swing*, Richard Adams, 1980.

10734 He huddled in his sheepskin coat,

shelter from the night wind that whipped across the Platz der Republik and whistled with icy tongues through columns of the cavernous railroad station. — *Crossing in Berlin*, Fletcher Knebel, 1981.

10735 Jessica stood alone at the curb, her long white gown and black velvet evening coat little protection from a harsh, late March wind. — *Defects of the Heart*, Barbara Gordon, 1983.

10736 There was no wind and in the damp stillness of the winter day the trees were motionless. — *The Challenging Heights*, John Harris *as* Max Hennessy, 1983.

10737 Spring came blowing gently to us from the southern ocean. We could smell it, warm and salty on the breeze. — *Eagle Song*, James Houston, 1983.

10738 What I remember about that spring in the city is how the wind used to blow at night, a real wind too, like in the country, bending the spindly little trees and making the old windows rattle. — *Say Goodbye to Sam*, Michael J. Arlen, 1984.

10739 A wind blew through Europe. — *Milk and Honey*, Elizabeth Jolley, 1984.

10740 All through the black Appalachian night the wind, messenger of death, howls and shrieks and circles like some giant mythical Ulsterian vulture, raging against the ageless log house, hurling hickory limbs and pine cones at the skittery tin roof, rattling frail windows, cartwheeling loose pails across the yard, tearing gates from rusty hinges, throwing icicle darts at the creaking barn, blowing its hoary breath at terrified animals cowering in the naked orchard, demanding a word with the survivors. — *The Six-killer Chronicles*, Paul Hemphill, 1985.

10741 Sometimes the winds reverse, and instead of blowing eastward from the Pacific, they come up off the yellow back of the desert and whistle westward down through the mountains. — *These Latter Days*, Laura Kalpakian, 1985.

10742 The wind was particularly bitter, even for January in Holloman, Connecticut. — *A Creed for the Third Millenium*, Colleen McCullough, 1985.

10743 The wind has risen early tonight. It catches the outhouse door which bangs open and shut, while urgent voices in the trees betoken rain. Thank God the time for hurricanes is past. — *The Taking of Agnès*, Jennifer Potter, 1985.

10744 "Why does the wind in New Mexico always blow from west to east?" Nat says./ "I don't know," Tara says. "I give up."/ "Because Texas sucks," Nat says. — *Museum Pieces*, Elizabeth Tallent, 1985.

10745 The chill in the breeze was a relief from the stewpot of summer. — *El Yanqui*, Douglas Unger, 1986.

10746 The wind pulled back, the sound of a huge, emotionless suction outside the head, and then, at a distance fairly far off in day or night, caused itself to be circling and milling, a strange tilt to it. — *Alnilam*, James Dickey, 1987.

10747 At night outside my sleeping chamber the wind moans in the trees. — *The Assyrian*, Nicholas Guild, 1987.

10748 Wind worried a confusion of bunting and *REFERENDUM* signs. — *Kisses of the Enemy*, Rodney Hall, 1987.

10749 Waiting on the curb for the driver to take her bicycle from the luggage compartment, Chrissy heard wind — the breeze that comes near dawn when the darkness thins. — *Family Life*, Mary Elsie Robertson, 1987.

10750 Caroline Cutler shivered in the wind knifing down Third Avenue and glared at the Doberman hovering indecisively over the gutter. — *A Truce with Time*, Parke Godwin, 1988.

10751 From the east where time began, the wind blew hard through the canyons and cold off the snowy mountains as Rosendo Guerrero waited in the early grey morning for Joseph Simons to emerge from his office. — *The Brick People*, Alejandro Morales, 1988.

10752 What I remember about growing up is mostly the wind. — *The Real Life Diary of a Boom-town Girl*, David Breskin, 1989.

10753 From where he stood at the window of his familiar room in the west wing of the ancient Széchy Manor, General Wulf could see the huge trees shiver on the hillside in the late October wind. — *The Hunt*, Tamas Aczel, 1990.

10754 How could the wind be so strong, so far inland, that cyclists coming into the town in the late afternoon looked more like sailors in peril? — *The Gate of Angels*, Penelope Fitzgerald, 1990.

10755 It was a moaning wind, inarticulate, meaningless — but a distraction nonetheless. — *The Limits of Glory*, James McDonough, 1991.

Wisdom

10756 In the centre of the pine wood called Coilla Doraca there lived not long ago two Philosophers. They were wiser than anything else in the world except the Salmon who lies in the pool of Glyn Cagny into which the nuts of knowledge fall from the hazel bush on its bank. — *The Crock of Gold*, James Stephens, 1912.

10757 I believe it was the old Egyptians, a very wise people, probably indeed much wiser than we know, for in the leisure of their ample

centuries they had time to think out things, who declared that each individual personality is made up of six or seven different elements, although the Bible only allows us three, namely, body, soul, and spirit. — *She and Allan*, H. Rider Haggard, 1921.

10758 Between what matters and what seems to matter, how should the world we know judge wisely? — *Trent's Last Case*, E. C. Bentley, 1930.

10759 In the prime assurance of his youth, in the fresh arrogance of his wisdom, and power in wisdom, with a sense of his extreme handsomeness, if not indeed beauty (for Gerta had said more than once that he was beautiful, and his own mirror had pleasantly corroborated this) Jasper Ammen leaned from the sixth floor window and projected his own image upon the world. — *King Coffin*, Conrad Aiken, 1935.

10760 My father was no different from other men; he had the wisdom of hindsight. — *Your Sins and Mine*, Taylor Caldwell, 1959.

10761 "Richard, Richard," they said to me in my childhood, "when will you begin to see things as they are?" — *Things as They Are*, Paul Horgan, 1964.

10762 Understand, and forgive. — *Female Friends*, Fay Weldon, 1975.

10763 Dinny Long, TD, was too wise to get married and too young to recognise the pain of loneliness. — *The Atheist*, Seán MacMathúna, 1987.

Women

10764 The late Accident, which gives Birth to the ensuing Pages, is an unhappy Instance of what Mr. *Addison* has so judiciously observ'd, *That Women talk*, and *move*, and *smile* with *a Design upon Us*. That though their *Thoughts* are ever turn'd upon appearing *Amiable*, yet every *Feature* of their *Faces* and every *Part* of their *Dress* is fill'd with *Snares* and *Allurements*. There would be no such *Animals* as *Prudes* or *Coquets* in the World, were there not such an *Animal* as *Man*. — *Authentick Memoirs of the Life, Intrigues, and Adventures of the Celebrated Sally Salisbury*, Charles Walker, 1723.

10765 It was always my opinion, that fewer women were undone by love than vanity; and that those mistakes the sex are sometimes guilty of, proceed, for the most part, rather from inadvertency, than a vicious inclination. — *The History of Miss Betsy Thoughtless*, Eliza Haywood, 1751.

10766 What a misfortune it is to be born a woman! In vain, dear Leonora, would you recon-cile me to my doom. Condemned to incessant hypocrisy, or everlasting misery, woman is the slave or the outcast of society. — *Leonora*, Maria Edgeworth, 1806.

10767 Anthelia Melincourt, at the age of twenty-one, was mistress of herself and of ten thousand a year, and of a very ancient and venerable castle in one of the wildest valleys in Westmoreland. It follows of course, without reference to her personal qualifications, that she had a very numerous list of admirers, and equally of course that there were both Irishmen and clergymen among them. — *Melincourt*, Thomas Love Peacock, 1817.

10768 At that remarkable period when Louis XVIII. was restored a second time to the throne of his fathers, and all the English who had money or leisure rushed over to the Continent, there lived in a certain boarding-house at Brussels a genteel young widow, who bore the elegant name of Mrs. Wellesley Macarty. — *A Shabby Genteel Story*, William Makepeace Thackeray, 1852.

10769 In the first place, Cranford is in possession of the Amazons; all the holders of houses above a certain rent are women. — *Cranford*, Elizabeth Gaskell *as* Mrs. Gaskell, 1853.

10770 Since the days of Adam, there has been hardly a mischief done in this world but a woman has been at the bottom of it. — *Barry Lyndon*, William Makepeace Thackeray, 1856.

10771 Nearly a quarter of a century ago, Lucy Fountain, a young lady of beauty and distinction, was, by the death of her mother, her sole surviving parent, left in the hands of her two trustees, Edward Fountain, Esq., of Font Abbey, and Mr. Bazalgette, a merchant whose wife was Mrs. Fountain's half-sister. — *Love Me Little, Love Me Long*, Charles Reade, 1859.

10772 There are women who cannot grow alone as standard trees; — for whom the support and warmth of some wall, some paling, some post, is absolutely necessary; — who, in their growth, will blend and incline themselves towards some such prop for their life, creeping with their tendrils along the ground till they reach it when the circumstances of life have brought no such prop within their natural and immediate reach. — *Rachel Ray*, Anthony Trollope, 1863.

10773 We are to make acquaintance with some serious damsels, as this English generation knows them, and at a season verging upon May. — *Emilia in England*, George Meredith, 1864.

10774 Her eyes had an outer ring of seeming black, but in effect of deep blue and dark grey mixed; this soft and broad circle of colour sharply divided the subtle and tender white, pale as pure milk, from an iris which should have been hazel or grey, blue or green, but was instead a more

delicate and significant shade of the colour more common with beast or bird; pure gold, without alloy or allay, like the yellowest part of a clear flame; such eyes as the greatest analyst of spirit and flesh that ever lived and spoke has noticed as proper to certain rare women, and has given for a perpetual and terrible memory to his Georgian girl. — *Lesbia Brandon*, A. C. Swinburne, 1864 (pub. 1952).

10775 Old Lady Macleod was a good woman, though subject to two most serious drawbacks. — *Can You Forgive Her?*, Anthony Trollope, 1864.

10776 Miss Brooke had that kind of beauty which seems to be thrown into relief by poor dress. — *Middlemarch*, George Eliot, 1872.

10777 Josephine Murray was one of those young women whom every body likes very much on a first acquaintance. — *Playing the Mischief*, John W. De Forest, 1875.

10778 Was she beautiful or not beautiful? and what was the secret of form or expression which gave the dynamic quality to her glance? Was the good or the evil genius dominant in those beams? Probably the evil; else why was the effect that of unrest rather than of undisturbed charm? Why was the wish to look again felt as coercion, and not as a longing in which the whole being consents? — *Daniel Deronda*, George Eliot, 1876.

10779 In the days of high-waisted and muslin-gowned women, when the vast amount of soldiering going on in the country was a cause of much trembling to the sex, there lived in a village near the Wessex coast two ladies of good report, though unfortunately of limited means. — *The Trumpet-Major*, Thomas Hardy, 1880.

10780 In the dusk of an October evening, a sensible-looking woman of forty came out through an oaken door to a broad landing on the first floor of an old English country-house. — *An Unsocial Socialist*, George Bernard Shaw, 1884.

10781 Among the Diaries beginning with the second quarter of our century, there is frequent mention of a lady then becoming famous for her beauty and her wit: "an unusual combination," in the deliberate syllables of one of the writers, who is, however, not disposed to personal irony when speaking of her. — *Diana of the Crossways*, George Meredith, 1885.

10782 On a beautiful September afternoon, in a handsome room of one of the grand, uptown hotels in New York, sat Mrs. Cliff, widow and millionaire. — *Mrs. Cliff's Yacht*, Frank R. Stockton, 1896.

10783 Maria Montalto was dressed as a Neapolitan Acquaiola and kept the lemonade stall at the Kermess in Villa Borghese. — *A Lady of Rome*, F. Marion Crawford, 1906.

10784 The four children were lying on the grass./ "... and the Prince went further and further into the forest," said the elder girl, "till he came to a beautiful glade — a glade, you know, is a place in the forest that is open and green and lovely. And there he saw a lady, a beautiful lady, in a long white dress that hung down to her ankles, with a golden belt and a golden crown. She was lying on the sward — a sward, you know, is grass as smooth as velvet, just like green velvet — and the Prince saw the marks of travel on her garments. The bottom of the lovely silk dress was all dirty —" — *The Getting of Wisdom*, Ethel Florence Lindesay Richardson *as* Henry Handel Richardson, 1910.

10785 Miss Polly Harrington entered her kitchen a little hurriedly this June morning. Miss Polly did not usually make hurried movements; she specially prided herself on her repose of manner. But to-day she was hurrying — actually hurrying. — *Pollyanna*, Eleanor H. Porter, 1913.

10786 In the evening dimness of old Mrs. Maldon's sitting-room stood the beautiful virgin, Rachel Louisa Fleckring. — *The Price of Love*, Arnold Bennett, 1914.

10787 You could not have lived a week in Winnebago without being aware of Mrs. Brandeis. — *Fanny Herself*, Edna Ferber, 1917.

10788 She was one of those girls who have become much more common of late years among the upper-middle classes, the comfortably fixed classes, than they have ever been since the aristocracy left off marrying Italian *primedonne*. You know the type of English beauty, so often insisted on, say, twenty years ago — placid, fair, gentle, blue-eyed, fining into distinction in Lady Clara Vere de Vere? — *Command*, William McFee, 1922.

10789 "So like Prudence!" the tennis party said. — *Young Entry*, Molly Keane *as* M. J. Farrell, 1928.

10790 Some women give birth to murderers, some go to bed with them, and some marry them. — *Before the Fact*, Francis Iles, 1932.

10791 My mother was a proud, angry woman, who had married a man less than herself in birth and intellect. — *Delicate Monster*, Storm Jameson, 1933.

10792 The Rue du Coq d'Or, Paris, seven in the morning. A succession of furious, choking yells from the street. Madame Monce, who kept the little hotel opposite mine, had come out on to the pavement to address a lodger on the third floor. Her bare feet were stuck into sabots and her grey hair was streaming down. — *Down and Out in Paris and London*, George Orwell, 1933.

10793 Scarlett O'Hara was not beautiful, but men seldom realized it when caught by her charm as the Tarleton twins were. — *Gone with the Wind*, Margaret Mitchell, 1936.

10794 It was not surprising that Sylvia Raffray, on that Saturday in September, had occasion for discourse with various men, none of them utterly ordinary, and with one remarkable young woman; it was not surprising that all this happened without any special effort on Sylvia's part, for she was rich, personable to an extreme, an orphan, and six months short of twenty-one years. — *The Hand in the Glove*, Rex Stout, 1937.

10795 The young women of Fada, in Nigeria, are well known for beauty. — *Mister Johnson*, Joyce Cary, 1939.

10796 In Jutland at this time lived dozens of women who were no less beautiful than the wife of Earl Sigmund of Lökken, but none who had a more superb complexion. — *Hamlet Had an Uncle*, James Branch Cabell, 1940.

10797 Mrs. Appleyard is about as tall as the Venus de Milo and weighs a little more. — *Mrs. Appleyard's Year*, Louise Andrews Kent, 1941.

10798 A stranger in that still enlarging city might see Kate Fennigate at any of its selective social gatherings without particularly noticing her; or, even if he were properly sensitive to the looks of people, he'd probably fail to recognize her as the most remarkable person present. — *Kate Fennigate*, Booth Tarkington, 1943.

10799 Mrs. Muir was a little woman. — *The Ghost and Mrs. Muir*, R. A. Dick, 1945.

10800 As she sat in the train that June morning Carol Spencer did not look like a young woman facing anything unusual. — *The Yellow Room*, Mary Roberts Rinehart, 1945.

10801 Lillian was always in a state of fermentation. Her eyes rent the air and left phosphorescent streaks. Her large teeth were lustful. — *Ladders to Fire*, Anaïs Nin, 1946.

10802 It is not easy to describe my mother. — *Sleep Has His House*, Anna Kavan, 1948.

10803 She was standing on Westminster Bridge. — *All Hallows' Eve*, Charles Williams, 1948.

10804 If you didn't look at her face she was less than thirty, quick-bodied and slim as a girl. — *The Drowning Pool*, Ross Macdonald, 1950.

10805 "Ah, you ladies! Always on the spot when there's something happening!" — *Excellent Women*, Barbara Pym, 1952.

10806 One afternoon in late June a young woman none of the passengers had ever seen before got on the bus, and the bus-driver behind the wheel set his soiled white sea-captain's beaked cap at a jauntier angle as she mounted the step and put her suitcase down. — *The Seagull on the Step*, Kay Boyle, 1955.

10807 Lolita, light of my life, fire of my loin. My sin, my soul. — *Lolita*, Vladimir Nabokov, 1955.

10808 Indian summer is like a woman. Ripe, hotly passionate, but fickle, she comes and goes as she pleases so that one is never sure whether she will come at all, nor for how long she will stay. — *Peyton Place*, Grace Metalious, 1956.

10809 May Turner was a retired school teacher. — *The Wild Swan*, Margaret Kennedy, 1957.

10810 This chick, with her sun-tan oil, her beach towel, her rubber volleyball, and her radio, came along the beach at the edge of the water where the sand was firm. — *Love Among the Cannibals*, Wright Morris, 1957.

10811 Uncle Telemachus told about water and women, how they sank a man, weak soft, tears and water, rot and win. — *Know Nothing*, Mary Lee Settle, 1960.

10812 "Who was that woman?" asked Mrs. Colquhoun, a rich lady who had come recently to live at Sarsaparilla./ "Ah," Mrs. Sugden said, and laughed, "that was Miss Hare." — *Riders in the Chariot*, Patrick White, 1961.

10813 "Anybody ever tell you you're a mighty pretty woman — I mean lady, Mrs. Trevor?" Hector Griffin said. — *Griffin's Way*, Frank Yerby, 1962.

10814 In view of the far-reaching effects that a few words mumbled by a disreputable old Irishwoman were to have on the life of Hero Athena Hollis, only child of Barclay Hollis of Boston, Massachusetts, it would be interesting to know to what degree, if any, pre-natal influence was responsible for her character and opinions. — *Trade Wind*, M. M. Kaye, 1963.

10815 Nyokabi called him. She was a small, black woman, with a bold but grave face. One could tell by her small eyes full of life and warmth that she had once been beautiful. But time and bad conditions do not favour beauty. — *Weep Not, Child*, Ngugi wa Thiong'o, 1964.

10816 One day in late summer a blond young woman in a sky-blue smock strode briskly into the lounge of the Repulse Bay Hotel. She was carrying a butterfly net and a flat, misty killing jar; she wore dusty white sneakers and a floppy straw hat. — *The Wreck of the Cassandra*, Frederic Prokosch, 1966.

10817 She is a tall dark beauty containing a great many beauty spots: one above the breast, one above the belly, one above the knee, one above the ankle, one above the buttock, one on the back of the neck. — *Snow White*, Donald Barthelme, 1967.

10818 Hester sat knitting upon the beach, hemmed in by towels, the tumbled clothes of the children, an empty carpet bag and a thermos flask. — *The Tyranny of Love*, Colin Spencer, 1967.

10819 One April evening, four years ago, at a cocktail party in Via Sistina, I found myself on a sofa beside the Marchesa del Rosso, a lady in

her sixties, who was dressed in a suit of black garbardine. — *The Missolonghi Manuscript*, Frederic Prokosch, 1968.

10820 I am Myra Breckinridge whom no man will ever possess. — *Myra Breckinridge*, Gore Vidal, 1968.

10821 Evie Decker was not musical. You could tell that just from the way she looked — short and wide, heavy-footed. — *A Slipping-Down Life*, Anne Tyler, 1970.

10822 Down among the women. What a place to be! Yet here we all are by accident of birth, sprouted breasts and bellies, as cyclical of nature as our timekeeper the moon — and down here among the women we have no option but to stay. — *Down Among the Women*, Fay Weldon, 1971.

10823 She never could sit on the sidelines. — *The Way We Were*, Arthur Laurents, 1972.

10824 Under God's stars, with the younger children lying close on one side and the other side of her, the girls curled against each other on the left and the boys on her right, Feigel truly felt herself like a great mother bird with her brood nestling under her wings. — *The Settlers*, Meyer Levin, 1972.

10825 Her yellow teeth are hard. — *Turkey Hash*, Craig Nova, 1972.

10826 She had enough irony to nourish an entire block of underprivileged children; on herself it had a less than helpful effect since she generally used it to saw at her own head instead of at the bars surrounding her life. — *Any Minute I Can Split*, Judith Rossner, 1972.

10827 Christie Malry was a simple person. — *Christie Malry's Own Double-Entry*, B. S. Johnson, 1973.

10828 Lucy was beautiful. People said it to her constantly. They also said it to each other though then jealousy made them try to criticize. — *Beautiful*, Rachel Billington, 1974.

10829 "The success of a marriage invariably depends on the woman," Mrs. Greenway said. — *Terms of Endearment*, Larry McMurtry, 1975.

10830 Cora is putting on a dress. It's blue with white flowers. Her lips are pressed tightly together. — *Reflex and Bone Structure*, Clarence Major, 1975.

10831 When she was a child, Amy Evans would steal into the sweet shop on the way home from school and buy a stick of rock. It was forbidden, strictly forbidden, murderous to the teeth that the good Lord gave you, her Mam would say, and as it turned out her Mam was right, for by thirty they were gone from the upper deck, and by forty from the lower, and by fifty, unlike her clothes, they were too big for her, clamped with crude fixative on to her gums, and seasoning each morsel of food with the taste of glue. — *I Sent a Letter to My Love*, Bernice Rubens, 1975.

10832 In a wheel chair with her skin stretched tight across her sharp bones and beaked nose, Grace Hogan Dunne looked birdlike. — *The Dunne Family*, James T. Farrell, 1976.

10833 In the darkened street, Ruth Wheeler might have been mistaken for a boy of middle growth, spare-bodied, light on her feet. She nearly always wore trousers, and the empty right sleeve of her windbreaker could seem a boy's quirk of style. — *The Young in One Another's Arms*, Jane Rule, 1977.

10834 Kathy is a middle-class, though she has no money, American white girl, twenty-nine years of age, no lovers and no prospects of money, who doesn't believe in anyone or anything. — *Kathy Goes to Haiti*, Kathy Acker, 1978.

10835 "All I've learned about women is that whatever it is they want it's what I don't have," I said, to see what kind of rise it would get. — *Somebody's Darling*, Larry McMurtry, 1978.

10836 "The sale room is no place for a woman," declared Humphrey Boyce, as he and his nephew James sat having lunch with the attractive stranger they had picked up at a Bond Street sale room half an hour ago. — *The Sweet Dove Died*, Barbara Pym, 1978.

10837 With joy and envy I read the lives of those great revolutionary women of the past — the "Moscow Amazons" of the eighteen sixties, seventies, and eighties who helped assassinate the Tsar, the "Pétroleuses" who mounted the barricades of Paris to defend the Commune, and all the other brave, single-minded women who devoted their lives to the revolution: Rosa Luxemburg, Emma Goldman, Louise Michel, La Pasionaria. — *Burning Questions*, Alix Kates Shulman, 1978.

10838 "You are on strike against God" — said by a nineteenth-century American judge to a group of women workers from a textile mill. He was right, too, and I don't wonder at him. What I do wonder is where did they get the nerve to defy God? — *On Strike Against God*, Joanna Russ, 1980.

10839 From this angle, with her foot resting lightly on the surface of the water, you might take her for some pale ornamental giant-killer, gracefully poised on the neck of her prey. — *La Presidenta*, Lois Gould, 1981.

10840 Maura Dooley was seventeen, Irish, and Catholic. — *Maura's Dream*, Joel Gross, 1981.

10841 She was there again. He saw the black circle of her eye, inside the brown circle, as it appeared to widen and narrow, widen and narrow. — *White Rising*, Zane Kotker, 1981.

10842 Women wanted to talk about anger, identity, politics, etc. — *The Men's Club*, Leonard Michaels, 1981.

10843 They leave, they go abroad, they

marry, go about their husbands' businesses and thrive. They thrive with exclamation marks. — *Dames*, Elizabeth North, 1981.

10844 Like innumerable other mid-life women who suffer from insecurity, paranoia, grave misgivings, vague longings, and obvious shortcomings, I'm basically a happy person. — *Repent, Lanny Merkel*, Faith Sullivan, 1981.

10845 Maude visits two old women — her mother, who is strong in body, dispirited in mind; the mother's nurse, who is ailing but spirited and bright. — *Grace Abounding*, Maureen Howard, 1982.

10846 The girl was conspicuous even before she entered the office. It was a windy day and everything was in motion except her face. — *Mermaid*, Margaret Millar, 1982.

10847 Where there is a woman there is magic. — *Sassafrass, Cypress & Indigo*, Ntozake Shange, 1982.

10848 The girls in Australia were just as beautiful as American women, but much more loving, or so the young sailors told each other. — *Pacific Interlude*, Sloan Wilson, 1982.

10849 I used to think I understood women; that I could get along with them reasonably well. — *Beautiful Women; Ugly Scenes*, C. D. B. Bryan, 1983.

10850 A young woman, dressed in black, stood on the corner of the rue de Rivoli and the rue Cambon. — *Natural Victims*, Isabel Eberstadt, 1983.

10851 It is difficult for me to relate this story because it concerns a woman for whom I have always had the deepest affection. — "Platinum," F. Sionil José, 1983.

10852 There were many things about Elizabeth Ferguson that the people of Bayview disliked. They thought her too tall, too thin, too aloof. Her neck was too long and her breasts were too big. The men, who could have lived with the size of her breasts, found her unwilling to flirt and labeled her cold. The women were jealous of how well her clothes hung on her, and that she managed to look elegant in outfits that would have made them look like the bag ladies of late autumn. — *Rosie*, Anne Lamott, 1983.

10853 "All women feel guilty in not being born sons," said the old grandmother Timo to the boy on the stone floor stringing mushrooms by her side. — *All or Nothing*, Stephen Longstreet, 1983.

10854 By the end few could remember any longer, but in fact she had once been beautiful. — *Mindspell*, Kay Nolte Smith, 1983.

10855 Women, women, women! I am the slave of women, when I am not their buffoon. — *The Book Class*, Louis Auchincloss, 1984.

10856 I became convinced that the second woman was not a woman at all. — *The McGuffin*, John Bowen, 1984.

10857 Isadora, separated from Josh, is like a kid in her twenties. — *Parachutes & Kisses*, Erica Jong, 1984.

10858 Old Professor Flashy's first law of economics is that the time to beware of a pretty woman is not when you're flush of cash (well, you know what she's after, and what's a bankroll more or less?), but when you're *short* of the scratch, and she offers to set you right. — *Flashman and the Dragon*, George MacDonald Fraser, 1985.

10859 Sr. Thomas Aquinas rocked forward and backwards on her sturdily-shod feet. — *The Killeen*, Mary Leland, 1985.

10860 Daddy said it was a bedsheet, a fitted bedsheet, and he said she was wearing it up on her shoulders like a cape with two of the corners knotted around her neck. She was standing barefoot on an oak stump, he said, standing on the one nearest the front walk where there was ordinarily a clay pot of geraniums, and he said her hair was mostly braided and bunned up in the back but for some few squirrel-colored strands of it that had worked their way loose and hung kind of wild and scraggly down across her forehead and almost to her nose. She was talking, he said. — *A Short History of a Small Place*, T. R. Pearson, 1985.

10861 Among the people who knew Helen Bradshaw best there were few who imagined they knew her well. — *No Place to Cry*, Adam Kennedy, 1986.

10862 Once upon a time, some twenty years ago, there were three nice young women, who lived together at 73b Oakmoor Road, London N.W.2. — *Love Unknown*, A. N. Wilson, 1986.

10863 The woman at the open window looked like any other of her class and vintage, clad to meet a conclave of like-minded, well-heeled matrons. — *Crescendo*, Laura Kalpakian, 1987.

10864 The five women were dead. — *Breaking the Rules*, Caroline Lassalle, 1987.

10865 "Dear Cassandra," smiled Mrs. Gower, "you are always so punctual." — *Civil to Strangers*, Barbara Pym, 1987.

10866 Dana was the only woman in our freshman dental class, one of two that year in the whole dental school. — "The Age of Grief," Jane Smiley, 1987.

10867 All women are mortal. I wonder if I believed it that autumn day I walked into the art gallery in St. Ives, New Hampshire — I paint — and saw her for the first time. — *An Adultery*, Alexander Theroux, 1987.

10868 Eleanor had two faces. — *Complicity*, Elizabeth Cooke, 1988.

10869 The first thing he noticed was the

women. — *Cold Feet*, Patricia Weaver Francisco, 1988.

10870 There was, after all, the mystery of Lulu. — *Lulu Incognito*, Raymond Kennedy, 1988.

10871 I, Daniel Quinn, neither the first nor the last of a line of such Quinns, set eyes on Maud the wondrous on a late December day in 1849 on the banks of the river of the aristocrats and paupers, just as the great courtesan, Magdalena Colón, also known as La Última, a woman whose presence turned men into spittling, masturbating pigs, boarded a skiff to carry her across the river's icy water from Albany to Greenbush, her first stop en route to the city of Troy, a community of iron, where later that evening she was scheduled to enact, yet again, her role as the lascivious Lais, that fabled prostitute who spurned Demosthenes' gold and yielded without fee to Diogenes, the virtuous, impecunious tub-dweller. — *Quinn's Book*, William Kennedy, 1988.

10872 When she became a woman, and Tom Lockhart saw her standing there, serene on the doorstep of her father's house, he partly understood. — *Imago*, James McClure, 1988.

10873 Mom was a world of her own, filled with secret thoughts and motions nobody else could see. — *The History of Luminous Motion*, Scott Bradfield, 1989.

10874 My grandmother has always been my tormentor. — *The Floating World*, Cynthia Kadohata, 1989.

10875 All down the winding length of River Street, the invisible women are hanging out the wash, filling the sweet morning with the *skreek-skreek* of their clothesline pulleys and the high faint smell of bleach. — *August Heat*, Beth Lordan, 1989.

10876 *All I can say is this. I'm tired of women. Black women in particular, 'cause that's about all I ever deal with. Maybe a fine Puerto Rican here and there, but not much. They're all the same, that's for damn sure. Want all your time and energy. Want the world to revolve around them.* — *Disappearing Acts*, Terry McMillan, 1989.

10877 "The beast changes to a woman or the woman changes to a beast," the doctor says. — *Carmen Dog*, Carol Emshwiller, 1990.

10878 People are not always kind, but the kind thing to say of Jenny was that she was simple. — *The Great World*, David Malouf, 1990.

10879 I once knew this girl who thought she was God. — *Sati*, Christopher Pike, 1990.

10880 In the neighborhood where I grew up, women didn't work. — *What Waiting Really Means*, June Akers Seese, 1990.

10881 In the black of the night, three o'clock in the morning, the night from Saturday to Sunday (why does it always happen on Saturday night?), the cervix opens up, the cunt flushes out blood clots. — *Panic Blood*, Catherine Texier, 1990.

10882 In truth, my mother was not a beautiful woman. — *Thicker Than Water*, Kathryn Harrison, 1991.

10883 The slim woman lying beneath the hotel umbrella in the brutal Mexican sun looked deceptively healthy and completely at rest. — *Remember Me*, Suzanne Lipsett, 1991.

10884 Stefan Nagy stopped short in front of the sidewalk cafe on Rakoczy Street. Before him, at a little table in the front row, sat the most beautiful girl in Budapest. No — in the world. — *Stefan in Love*, Joseph Machlis, 1991.

10885 Eleanor is tall, taller than most men, and her face is long, her thin nose long as a lake-edging highway, her long face and her eyes like almonds, almost, a very strange long woman. — *Fox*, Margaret Sweatman, 1991.

10886 I had been earmarked as scholar bait and spinster material as far back as the second grade. — "The Jiru Road," Maria Thomas, 1991.

10887 A frail, elderly Japanese woman in traditional kimono looked up from the papers she was sorting. — *The Seventh Stone*, Nancy Freedman, 1992.

10888 I never knew her really. *Sin*, Josephine Hart, 1992.

10889 Sth, I know that woman. — *Jazz*, Toni Morrison, 1992.

10890 She stands up in the garden where she has been working and looks into the distance. — *The English Patient*, Michael Ondaatje, 1992.

10891 I am sitting across from the largest woman I have ever seen: six-and-a-half feet tall and easily as wide. — *The Junk-Drawer Corner-Store Front-Porch Blues*, John R. Powers, 1992.

10892 When women get together they are always complimenting each other — oh what a pretty blouse, I *love* those earrings, how did you do that with your hair? — sickening. — *The Right Bitch*, Anna Shapiro, 1992.

10893 I stand by the window and watch the woman running./ Is it Laura?/ I wonder that, as I watch her flickering like blown leaves through the trees./ I am Laura. — *The Invisible Worm*, Jennifer Johnston, 1993.

10894 A woman in her early thirties, our traveler, the handsome but slightly frowning Kate Gaffney-Kozinski, running across the rain-glossed pavement in Potts Point, saw from a poster in front of the closed newsagent's that her defrocked uncle had given another interview to one of those smooth-paged magazines. — *Woman of the Inner Sea*, Thomas Keneally, 1993.

10895 Women on their own run in Alice's family. — *Pigs in Heaven*, Barbara Kingsolver, 1993.

10896 I went to college with a woman named Carla, who had majored in religious studies and was now a cook and worked at a small café on the University's West Bank. — *Blue Bel Air*, Brett Laidlaw, 1993.

10897 She was so beautiful. You have no idea. So Beautiful. — *First Nights*, Susan Fromberg Schaeffer, 1993.

Words

10898 The village described in the Benedictine's manuscript by the name of Kennaquhair, bears the same Celtic termination which occurs in Traquhair, Caquhair, and other compounds. — *The Monastery*, Sir Walter Scott, 1820.

10899 "Palestine soup!" said the Reverend Doctor Opimian, dining with his friend Squire Gryll, "a curiously complicated misnomer. We have an excellent old vegetable, the artichoke, of which we eat the head; we have another of subsequent introduction, of which we eat the root, and which we also call artichoke, because it resembles the first in flavour, although, *me judice*, a very inferior affair. This last is a species of the helianthus, or sunflower genus of the *Syngenesia frustranea* class of plants. It is therefore a girasol, or turn-to-the-sun. From this girasol we have made Jerusalem, and from the Jerusalem artichoke we make Palestine soup." — *Gryll Grange*, Thomas Love Peacock, 1861.

10900 The word "fantastical" is accentuated in our tongue to so scornful an utterance that the constant good service it does would make it seem an appointed instrument for reviewers of books of imaginative matter distasteful to those expository pens. — *The Tragic Comedians*, George Meredith, 1880.

10901 I first heard Personville called Poisonville by a red-haired mucker named Hickey Dewey in the Big Ship in Butte. He also called his shirt a shoit. — *Red Harvest*, Dashiell Hammett, 1929.

10902 " — My dear and beloved Children — "/ The words had a grave resonance, like the opening of the funeral Mass, like the organ sound of limitless mourning and the last murmur of futile tragedy. — *Let Love Come Last*, Taylor Caldwell, 1949.

10903 "'into the vast vacuity of the empyrean,'" Miss Dawson read. "And can you tell me what 'empyrean' means?" — *Angel*, Elizabeth Taylor, 1957.

10904 Well, here it is, the whole thing, about ninety thousand words, I imagine. — *Saturn Over the Water*, J. B. Priestley, 1961.

10905 The satchel gave him a *bias*. That was the word. His father's bowls had them. It meant a weight on one side. — *Sandel*, Angus Stewart, 1968.

10906 KoKo. What did that mean? — *Steelwork*, Gilbert Sorrentino, 1970.

10907 The words — what were the words? — *Miss Seeton Sings*, Heron Carvic, 1973.

10908 "I." "I" is the first word that comes to me. — *Lost & Found*, Sheldon Greene, 1980.

10909 Guernsey, Guernesey, Garnsai, Sarnia: so they say. — *The Book of Ebenezer Le Page*, G. B. Edwards, 1981.

10910 I have only recently begun to use words, but my tuition has been such that, while I make perhaps too much use of the first thousand selected by the wise ones at Oxford who compiled "Basic English," as being adequate for communication, my teacher has been a person given not only to Victorianisms but also to a robust manner. — *The Textures of Silence*, Gordon Vorster, 1982.

10911 Isolation./ Such a grandiose word./ Insulation./ There was the connection in the dictionary staring me in the eye. — *The Railway Station Man*, Jennifer Johnston, 1984.

10912 Now this kid with the shaved head has been saying the words to this song for the past 450 miles, over and over, ever since the trucker picked him up just outside of the Holland Tunnel. — *July 7th*, Jill McCorkle, 1984.

10913 Here the masculine is universal. The pronoun *he* and its possessive *him* connote not sexual identity but simple sentient being. — *Conscience Place*, Joyce Thompson, 1984.

10914 She carried a word to her father. *Chicago*. — *Voices from Home*, Neil Caudle, 1989.

Work

10915 The Lessways household, consisting of Hilda and her widowed mother, was temporarily without a servant. Hilda hated domestic work, and because she hated it she often did it passionately and thoroughly. — *Hilda Lessways*, Arnold Bennett, 1911.

10916 The Marchioness carefully draped the dust-cloth over the head of an andiron and, before putting the question to the parlour-maid, consulted, with the intensity of a near-sighted person, the ornate French clock in the centre of the mantelpiece. — *The City of Masks*, George Barr McCutcheon, 1918.

10917 Three-four of us older ones were down winding up Red Cross, and eight-ten of our daughters were helping; not my daughter—I ain't connect'—but Friendship Village daughters in general. Or I don't know but it was us older ones that were helping them. — *Peace in Friendship Village*, Zona Gale, 1919.

10918 Sarnac had worked almost continuously for the better part of a year upon some very subtle chemical reactions of the nervous cells of the sympathetic system. — *The Dream*, H. G. Wells, 1924.

10919 The servants at the vicarage had gone to bed. Edith had just locked the back door, and Alice had taken the master the hot milk that he drank every evening at ten o'clock. — *Mr. Tasker's Gods*, T. F. Powys, 1925.

10920 The hotel clerk, deftly twirling the register with one hand, offered the freshly dipped pen with the other. — *Hopalong Cassidy and the Eagle's Brood*, Clarence E. Mulford, 1931.

10921 There was no reason why I shouldn't have been sent for the beer that day, for the last ends of the Fairmont National Bank case had been gathered in the week before and there was nothing for me to do but errands, and Wolfe never hesitated about running me down to Murray Street for a can of shoe-polish if he happened to need one. — *Fer-de-Lance*, Rex Stout, 1934.

10922 The learned Narciso Rich was washing his shirt. — *To the Indies*, C. S. Forester, 1940.

10923 In the spring of 1931, on a lawn in Glendale, California, a man was bracing trees. — *Mildred Pierce*, James M. Cain, 1941.

10924 Eighty-odd years ago, two brothers were toiling in a deep ravine which wandering Mormons had called Gold Canyon. — *City of Illusion*, Vardis Fisher, 1941.

10925 All morning I had been wrestling with the tractor on the Ferguson Place, a long way from the barns and the repair shop. — "Kenny," Louis Bromfield, 1944.

10926 It was shortly before noon of a day in March, 1879, at the village of Manister on the coast of County Mayo. Elizabeth Henry St. George was sitting at her desk, in a corner of the living room at Manister Lodge, drawing up the household weekly accounts. — *Land*, Liam O'Flaherty, 1946.

10927 Lucy Hanks, pulling corn, hating the weary task, moved slowly up the clearing. She wrenched off the full ears with a resentful vehemence, tossing them in little piles behind her. — *House Divided*, Ben Ames Williams, 1947.

10928 "What's the old man doing?" I said, and I looked down the trail, beyond the ragged box elder, where the old man stood in the door of the barn, fooling with an inner tube. — *The Home Place*, Wright Morris, 1948.

10929 Two workmen, one average-sized, the other tall, were cutting down a colossus of a cottonwood tree along an east-west country lane. — *The Primitive*, Frederick Manfred *as* Feike Feikema, 1949.

10930 The men at work at the corner of the street had made a kind of camp for themselves, where, marked out by tripods hung with red hurricane-lamps, an abyss in the road led down to a network of subterranean drain-pipes. — *A Question of Upbringing*, Anthony Powell, 1951.

10931 Toward midnight Charles Anderson finished some notes on a talk he had had with a newspaper editor at lunch—nothing very important, but he thought he ought to keep Bingay decently informed. — *Time and Time Again*, James Hilton, 1953.

10932 "But, Mama," Polly Knowles said, "why must we do this? Nobody else sprinkles sand on the parlor floor. And they certainly don't sweep it into curlicues, and then lock up the room..." — *Bride of Liberty*, Frank Yerby, 1954.

10933 Albert, fleshy, sallow, blue chinned, breathing hard, sweating a little, fitted an iron bar into sockets on either side of the wooden shutters he had just closed across the final window of the stable-block. — *The Kindly Ones*, Anthony Powell, 1962.

10934 Mrs. Reegan darned an old woollen sock as the February night came on, her head bent, catching the threads on the needle by the light of the fire, the daylight gone without her noticing. — *The Barracks*, John McGahern, 1963.

10935 Twentyman's dreadful equipment was unloaded at a dock in Montreal on a cold wet Wednesday. — *Stick Your Neck Out*, Mordecai Richler, 1963.

10936 "I always say," Mr. Barr always said, "if you want a job done decently, do it yourself." — *The Butterflies of the Province*, Honor Tracy, 1970.

10937 It was Sunday, and Mumma had gone next door with Lena and the little ones. Under the pepper tree in the yard Pa was sorting, counting, the empty bottles he would sell back: the bottles going clink clink as Pa stuck them on the stack. — *The Vivisector*, Patrick White, 1970.

10938 He had worked all night on the engines and when he was finished he wanted to make a test. — *The Hot Blue Sea*, Richard Jessup, 1974.

10939 Mama came in off the back porch, and her hands were wringing wet with blood. She pushed the door open with her behind and made straight for the sink. "Turn those taps on for me, Verna, I'm drenched." — *Representing Super Doll*, Richard Peck, 1974.

10940 Jud Clasby, hidden in the yet unleafed sassafras clump, watched the work going on in

the camp. — *The Massacre at Fall Creek*, Jessamyn West, 1975.

10941 I have been sent on errands to our Colonies on many planets. — *Shikasta*, Doris Lessing, 1979.

10942 Consider the thin, crackly, wrapping paper skin of the onion, as I did this morning while cleaning out the refrigerator. — *Cleaning House*, Nancy Hayfield, 1980.

10943 On the second Wednesday in January of the year 1637, Virginia Taylor lowered a large wooden bucket into the icy water of the brook behind the house in which she'd lived for the past three years. — *Home of the Brave*, Joel Gross, 1982.

10944 To tell a patient they are about to die is never the easiest of tasks. — *The Flower Garden*, Margaret Pemberton, 1982.

10945 Early Christmas morning, like every other winter morning, Lewis Burkholder and Nop went out to feed the livestock. — *Nop's Trials*, Donald McCaig, 1984.

10946 Half-a-dozen men were working at the hay on the slantwise, south-facing field on the lower slopes of Lindifferon Hill that June afternoon, the horseman noted; but whilst five were toiling near to each other towards the bottom end, one was by himself towards the top. — *James, by the Grace of God*, Nigel Tranter, 1985.

10947 Maybe it had been rash to say he would do this job himself. — *In the Dark*, R. M. Lamming, 1986.

10948 Slant the chisel just so, so that the hammer, tapping lightly on the shaft, lifts up the layers, flakes them off like skin. — *Frieze*, Cecile Pineda, 1986.

10949 Anna Delaney jammed the claw end of a hammer under the two-by-four nailed across the doorway to her son's room. She pried but she couldn't budge it, not even by propping her feet against the door and hanging all her weight from the hammer. — *Anna Delaney's Child*, John Thorndike, 1986.

10950 I did their dirty work. — *Bread and Circus*, Morris Renek, 1987.

10951 Evan was working at seat G16 at one of the long desks that radiated from the heart of the reading room. — *Facing the Tank*, Patrick Gale, 1988.

10952 Adjiba Yazzie, also known as La Tejedora, was setting up her loom. — *"Ganado Red,"* Susan Lowell, 1988.

10953 Translating forty lines of Greek is hard work in the most tranquil circumstances, but Artie Dunne's task became impossible when, for the third time that evening, the Hedgehog hurled his body against the wall. — *Arts and Sciences*, Thomas Mallon, 1988.

10954 For Baker it was simple, nice and simple. — *Hazard and the Five Delights*, Christopher Noël, 1988.

10955 "When your mama was the geek, my dreamlets," Papa would say, "she made the nipping off of noggins such a crystal mystery that the hens themselves yearned toward her, waltzing around her, hypnotized with longing. 'Spread your lips, sweet Lil,' they'd cluck, 'and show us your choppers!'" — *Geek Love*, Katherine Dunn, 1989.

10956 When she comes home from work she finds him laying the carpet in the loft, finally. — *Monkey Bay*, Elaine Ford, 1989.

10957 It is still said, in those small towns on the island of Kaua'i that have remained unchanged for years, that if the legendary *menehune* do not finish a task in one night's work, they abandon it forever at dawn. — *The Whiteness of Bones*, Susanna Moore, 1989.

10958 At a quarter to nine, just before going off work, Dillon went down to reception to check the staff roster for tomorrow. — *Lies of Silence*, Brian Moore, 1990.

10959 From my window I can see Denis as he mows the lawn. — *Drowning*, Lee Grove, 1991.

10960 I was on the back porch washing greens when Harold drove around the side of the house with a stolen canoe on top of the truck and a bushel of oysters in back. — *"Crystal River,"* Charles Smith, 1991.

10961 The bottle was big and obzockee. I was having a hard time toting it. — *Divina Trace*, Robert Antoni, 1992.

10962 My grandmother accomplished her chief female functions by knife. — *The Waking Spell*, Carol Dawson, 1992.

10963 I had just returned from an exorcism and was flinging some shirts into the washing-machine when my colleague entered the kitchen. — *Mystical Paths*, Susan Howatch, 1992.

10964 The girl with the brick-red lips tapped Daniel on the shoulder. "Excuse me, can I just snake this in here?" — *A Visit Home*, Will Aitken, 1993.

Worry

10965 I was a shade perturbed. Nothing to signify, really, but still just a spot concerned. — *Thank You, Jeeves*, P. G. Wodehouse, 1934.

10966 In the days when the King of Spain's only concern was that no one should clip a second off his record run from San Sebastian to Biarritz.... — *Now I Lay Me Down to Sleep*, Ludwig Bemelmans, 1944.

10967 Nothing was wrong. The phrase spoke in Ann's mind. Nothing was wrong. — *Night Unto Night*, Philip Wylie, 1944.

10968 A few days before the end of October last year, George Winthrop awoke at dawn, his worries rested enough by five hours of sleep to start bothering him again. — *Georgie Winthrop*, Sloan Wilson, 1963.

10969 It troubled me when my father told me that from now on Miss Alexandria wanted me to sleep in her house. — *The Aristocrat*, Conrad Richter, 1968.

10970 On Monday morning, Miss Lena Ricks was in a great hurry to get to her shop and make sure nothing had happened to it over the weekend. — *The Survivors*, Kristin Hunter, 1975.

10971 When, after an hour, Farris's twelve-year-old son did not return to the apartment, the man began to worry. — *Final Things*, Richard B. Wright, 1980.

10972 He was nervous. She could see that in the way he paced around the room, occasionally going to the window and lifting the lace curtain to look out at the rain-swept Geneva street. — *Goodbye, Janette*, Harold Robbins, 1981.

10973 The year we moved to Elsome Street I was due to go up into the Big Girls, so that was something extra to worry about. — *The Coconut Kiss*, Dee Phillips, 1982.

10974 The Prince was in a vexation. — *Sebastian*, Lawrence Durrell, 1983.

10975 Sarah Galbraeth had never had to worry about schoolwork, or getting dates for basketball games, or where her next meal was coming from, or whether her mom and dad loved each other. — *Splendor and Misery*, Faye Levine, 1983.

10976 *A few things to clear up before we get started here: this great worry that everyone has that Biddy will go all to pieces at the drop of a hat does more harm than good.* — *Flights*, Jim Shepard, 1983.

10977 Of course I was desperate about Dwayne, wondering if he was dead or alive, or I wouldn't ever have gone to a psychic, the one whose card I found on the corner of the bulletin board in the laundrymat — a little card smudged like a cat with muddy feet had slid across it — half-hidden behind a notice for Tai Chi lessons. — *What I Have to Tell You*, Mary Elsie Robertson, 1989.

10978 On the night before the first official meeting of the Babbington Flotilla of the Young Tars, I paced the floor of my attic bedroom, certain that, the next day, as the first official piece of business at the first official meeting, I would be demoted from the rank of Commodore, probably all the way down to Swabby. — "The Young Tars," Eric Kraft, 1992.

10979 I worry a good deal. — *Dunster*, John Mortimer, 1993.

Years

10980 Here, then, we are — arrived at another spin of the wheel. Another January; another New Year; presently another quickening of the sap in the trees, of green in the undergrowth, of the blood in man's veins, of activity among publishers and birds; in brief, another year. — *A Casual Commentary*, Rose Macaulay, 1925.

10981 *The year begins in silence, the shrill midnight shoutings and dinners over.* — *Jordanstown*, Josephine W. Johnson, 1937.

10982 The New Year had begun inauspiciously, there was no doubt of it. — *The Great Blizzard*, Albert E. Idell, 1948.

10983 It was April in the city of Peking, the fifth month of the solar year of 1852, the third month of the moon year, the two hundred and eighth year of the Manchu, the great Ch'ing dynasty. — *Imperial Woman*, Pearl S. Buck, 1956.

10984 The year was 4214 after Tangun of Korea, and 1881 after Jesus of Judea. — *The Living Reed*, Pearl S. Buck, 1963.

10985 Then we came to the end of another dull and lurid year. — *Americana*, Don DeLillo, 1971.

10986 1933/ *January 1st*/ Heil Hitler!/ What a year it's going to be. It can't fail. Heil New Year! Heil New Baby! — *The Confessions of Elisabeth Von S.*, Gillian Freeman, 1978.

10987 That singular year began not in January but in summer, at Barbara Finnegan's party honoring the new Head of the Tigris School, Valerie Green. — *The School Book*, Anne Bernays, 1980.

10988 It was a vintage year. — *Rituals*, Linda Gray Sexton, 1982.

10989 It's been a hell of a year. — *Almost Dark*, Charlie McDade, 1983.

10990 Already, this has been a year for dying. — *Dreams of an Average Man*, Dyan Sheldon, 1985.

10991 That strange and crazy year began in the last hot days of August. — *The Queen of October*, Shelley Fraser Mickle, 1989.

10992 This has been a year of strange events: some wonderful, some terrible. — *The Cloning of Joanna May*, Fay Weldon, 1989.

10993 The year has turned again, bringing us to the end of the first decade of the new century. — *The Last Station*, Jay Parini, 1990.

10994 Christmas again in Yucatán. Another year gone and I was still scratching around on

this limestone peninsula. — *Gringos*, Charles Portis, 1991.

Youth

10995 It is not often that youth allows itself to feel individedly happy: the sensation is too much the result of selection and elimination to be within reach of the awakening clutch on life. — "Sanctuary," Edith Wharton, 1903.

10996 Only the young have such moments. — *The Shadow Line*, Joseph Conrad, 1917.

10997 "There is something amiss with the younger people here in Corfu, though I find it hard to explain what. You'll discover that for yourself soon enough," Mrs. Nicolidou said, continuing to address her son-in-law, as she had done throughout their entire drive, and to disregard her daughter. — *The Dark Glasses*, Francis King, 1954.

10998 I am very young, indeed only twenty-one years old, and it is quite certain that many of my observations are inexact, many of my views mistaken. — *The Converts*, Rex Warner, 1967.

10999 Youth is truth. — *The Drifters*, James A. Michener, 1971.

11000 He spoke tenderly of the youth he had been as if there were no connection through the navel string of the years, as if age had come upon him in a sudden access. This painstaking description of a former self grew night by night from the hotel terrace like some lusty shrub forcing up the paving slab laid over its roots. — *The Lives and Times of Bernardo Brown*, Geoffrey Household, 1973.

11001 It is a hard thing for the young in body to face the fact that up the road a piece old age waits for everyone, and once it joins us will not leave us and we never again be free of it on this lovely earth. For what can the young in body know of age beyond that which they see and hear and read of it? — *Unless You Die Young*, Gladys Hasty Carroll, 1977.

11002 Everything has had youth. — *Mount's Mistake*, Lew McCreary, 1987.

11003 How stupid the young are. — *Theory of War*, Joan Brady, 1993.

11004 Queer thing — but yes — we do mourn for the England we lost — maybe because the darkness of the tragedy awaiting us in New South Wales has left the memories of our youth bathed by contrast in clear simple light — and after so many years of exile one's gentler adventures tend to rise to the surface more and more appealingly — *The Grisly Wife*, Rodney Hall, 1993.

Index of Subjects, Key Words, and Key Phrases

In this index, key words and phrases are contained in quote marks. In phrases, the key word is listed first, followed by significant trailing words, then by a comma, then by words preceding the key word in the text. Fictional character and real person names are listed without quote marks, with last names first. Those character names appearing in text either as single first names, single last names, or nicknames are indexed as they appear. Subject headings appear in bold type.

Since text appears here in both American and British forms, it will be necessary to search for certain words, such as jail/gaol and harbor/harbour, under both forms. The first section of this index is a listing of years appearing in the text. Those years in word form have been converted to numerical form for inclusion in this index, and the years are listed in numerical order.

45 B.C. 7514	1608 778	1773 1
44 B.C. 5443	1626 2887	1774 6218, 7650, 7814, 9860, 9889
273 5431	1630 356, 10679	1775 655, 4303
380 7518	1632 6601	1776 7508
408 6052	1634 7613	1777 3992, 8592, 9740
1000 3719	1637 10943	1779 1339
1052 10109	1641 841	1780 9512, 10469
1090 2554	1653 10146	1782 3110, 6803
1145 2133	1656–1680 4771	1784 4439
1187 6802	1663 120	1785 4439
1296 6801	1664 120	1787 4439
1348 8395	1665 7501	1789 4439
1349 169	1672 10466	1790 7186
1395 8057	1673 9635	1790s 8632
1450 10587	1683 6089	1791 4439
1467 5126	1684 473	1792 8064, 8587
1483 10388	1691 950, 6091	1793 3910
1492 4034, 8965	1694 3837	1794 7069
1500 5576	1697 7658	1795 2194
1516 8056	17 2087, 5012, 9318	1799 8040
1523 4104	1702 355	18 — 5078, 6886, 6975
1529 948	1705 3376	1800 4439
1543 8165	1714 15	1803 7232, 9377
1544 1352	1728 1007	1804 7901, 7918
1553 1196	1733 5163	1806 2385, 3514, 7803
1568 8342	1740 5164	1809 1188
1569 7617	1741 2286	1810 4943
1571 10451	1743 1598	1810s 9757
1572 1346	1749 5108, 10343	1812 832, 8146
1577 1852	1750 804	1813 1161, 8152, 8356
1584 5125	1751 1570, 3737	1815 10493
1587 7610	1760 4439	1816 4604
1588 8663	1764 1293	1817 2411, 2600, 8077
1589 2185	1767 1756	1818 2702

1820 1615
1820s 3074
1822 8069
1823 586
1825 9662
1827 239
1830 1349
1831 4087, 6101
1832 3417, 5294, 9112
1833 6155, 10662
1835 1491, 9770
1836 7637
1837 1294
1839 787
1840 1518
1842 994, 5215, 8124
1843 43
1844 5194, 6571
1845 798
1846 1377, 4427, 9466
1848 1494, 7248
1849 5887, 10871
185- 1487
1850 1614, 4415, 9128, 10569
1850s 1180, 4043
1851 772, 800, 1181, 2383, 9610
1852 8398, 10983
1854 8054
1855 6104, 7903
1856 8563
1857 782, 3067
1858 7752
1859 82, 7702, 8956
1860 269, 3529, 4950
1861 3652
1862 2188
1863 3988, 7184, 7741
1864 3359, 7272
1865 1343, 3120
1866 790, 1465, 8347, 10043
1867 784, 9109, 10724
1868 5613, 7247
187- 8960
1870 135, 2486, 9136, 10053
1870s 2023, 9117
1871 3996
1872 4675, 5563, 6928, 7653
1873 4149, 4567, 7219, 10553
1874 9518
1875 2383
1877 8052
1878 821, 1596, 3266
1879 1402, 2357, 6577, 10926
188- 8477
1880 807, 1295, 5466, 6412, 7056,
   9747
1880s 2023, 7301
1881 8341, 9771, 10984
1883 808, 6099
1884 1363, 3270, 6248, 8058
1886 2019
1887 8059
1889 1363, 8926, 9750
1890 788, 1375, 1468, 2516, 3931
1890s 2023, 2041

1891 5563, 9761
1892 1362
1893 962, 6448
1895 7881
1897 847, 8564
1898 5452
1899 791, 2375, 4096, 6577, 9897,
   10431
19— 32, 9657, 8929, 10420
190- 8397
1900 1531, 2137, 3307, 3382, 3494,
   4567, 5753
1901 6760, 7079
1902 3191, 3407, 4470, 5052, 9973
1903 1373
1904 7103, 7745
1905 4921, 5192, 7082
1906 1312, 5087, 9064
1907 4470
1908 4307, 5100, 9978
1909 3586, 3854, 7416
1910 3887, 7890
1912 2491, 3330, 9217
1913 5086, 5659, 7277, 10661
1914 6344, 10441
1915 331, 851, 3825, 7246
1916 2024, 2305, 4517, 7151, 8702
1917 2336, 2469, 5494, 8695
1918 1285, 8678
1918-1919 1698
1919 818, 3111, 3423, 5088, 8135,
   10338, 10671
192- 7841
1920 1586, 3498, 5081, 5437, 8202,
   10193
1920s 1611, 2957, 5289, 10562
1921 251, 3015, 4470, 9545, 9715,
   10143
1922 826, 840, 2386, 3544, 5485,
   7031, 10339
1923 5607
1924 2592, 6570, 6685, 9537
1925 2592, 9715
1926 2336, 3569, 4763, 6447, 7378
1927 3770, 4011, 4126, 6647, 8101
1928 2153, 10100
1929 1541, 2161, 6137, 6163, 8263,
   9148
1930 1533, 7509, 8938
1930s 4083, 5230, 9734
1931 30, 1415, 7063, 10923
1932 6652, 7038, 8893
1933 3745, 3748, 10361, 10582,
   10656, 10986
1934 1934, 2451, 6132
1935 1456, 4176, 4399, 4558, 5671,
   5816, 9265
1936 5861, 7729, 9495
1937 1201, 1519, 3383, 5437, 7479,
   10536
1937-1938 3579
1938 1498, 7459
1938-39 900
1939 819, 2056, 2532, 2537, 4597,
   5260, 5841, 6159, 6446, 6531,

6769, 10496
1940 3581, 4596, 4865, 9792, 10496
1941 873, 975, 2441, 6570, 8666,
   10523
1942 889, 2040, 3604, 4918, 5857,
   6326, 8606, 8657
1943 829, 2360, 2540, 2883, 3777,
   5026, 7103
1944 532, 3049, 4017, 4410, 4636,
   5821, 6185, 8104, 8530, 10501,
   10517
1945 2560, 3049, 3392, 4966,
   7037, 8667, 8677, 8934, 10526
1946 1529, 2155, 2175, 3136, 4567,
   5537, 5818, 6427, 8934, 10502
1947 1500, 3278, 4388, 5757,
   9424, 9565
1948 63, 3831, 6165, 6325, 9964
1949 4637, 5570, 7720, 7896,
   9262, 9578, 9834
1950 814, 2143, 6228, 6881, 9571,
   10500, 10706
1950s 1892, 5761, 9026
1951 3180, 9357, 9431
1952 6732, 8656, 10612
1953 9833, 10506
1954 2360, 2881, 5577
1955 1653, 2839, 3200, 6178, 6514,
   6730, 9321
1956 159, 561, 5833, 6735, 8538,
   10088, 10534
1957 2012, 2432, 3023, 5760,
   6783, 8275
1958 2069, 2149, 2183, 4708, 5095,
   9782
1959 505, 4005, 4858, 5452, 7099,
   8602, 9941, 10621
196- 9593
1960 64, 633, 3619, 4403, 5546,
   9786
1960s 6141, 6467, 8381
1961 3167, 4066
1962 208, 2339, 10006
1963 2538, 3226, 9394, 10520
1964 2280, 9913
1965 1787, 3194, 5880
1966 830, 1758, 2539, 3659, 6224,
   9918, 10520
1967 2518, 4125, 4174, 4192, 6149,
   8681, 9265, 9584
1968 1214, 4405, 5113, 5117, 5673,
   5842, 6384
1969 216, 6185, 7418, 8001, 9251,
   9733, 10291
197- 1676
1970s 8485
1971 3261, 3283, 3751, 3805, 4550
1972 2373, 5103, 5120
1973 2998, 5208, 5476, 5477, 6232
1974 217, 2424, 2567, 3541, 6750,
   10633, 10676
1975 6473
1976 2934, 9012
1978 2616
1979 228, 5116, 5547, 6999, 9027

1980 917, 2568, 5523, 6013, 6168, 7778
1980s 1064, 10322
1981 3449, 9027, 9850
1982 5530, 8472
1983 1087, 1889, 3215, 6509, 7457
1984 1757, 2576, 3412, 10310
1985 1073, 1240
1986 3370, 5779, 6259, 8498
1987 2443
1988 1159
1990 3857, 5541, 7344
1991 4659
2020 10510
2023 6915
4214 10984

"A & P supermarket" 921
"a cappella choirs" 1305
Aaron 3954, 7064
"aback, slightly taken" 5825
"Abanakas, the" 7669
"abandon it forever at dawn" 10957
"abandon once and for all" 2479
"abandoned, deliberately" 6166
"abandoned his active interest" 3498
"abandoned his wife, one day he" 7714
"abandoned me to the wolves, he might have" 6551
"abandoned my father" 6160
"abandoned my only child" 6537
"abandoned religion during a night" 7508
"abandoned the facts again" 9429
Abandonment 1682, 1733, 2662, 2664, 2677, 2683, 2735, 5914, 6166, 6168, 6537, 6623, 6640, 7508, 7714, 8188
"abasement, lie in" 8444
"abattoir, back gateway of the" 4678
"Abattoirs" 9542
"Abbess, the" 8903
Abbey, Stephen 2096
"Abbey, Cleeve" 666
"Abbey, Font" 10771
"Abbey, Nightmare" 3058
"Abbey, Ramborough" 9208
"Abbey, Westminster" 8942
"Abbey built in the perpendicular Gothic style" 9255
"Abbey like a toad" 9236
"Abbey of Clair-Marais" 1691
Abbie 4162
Abbot, Spencer 8693
"abbot in his alb arrayed" 10641
Abbott, Billy 2542
Abbott, Fessenden 4928
"abbreviation, not an" 4814
Abby 4898, 6240
"ABC" 4008
Abdication 1525
"abdication, signed an instrument

of" 1525
"abdomen, distended" 10298
"abducted from my house" 2576
"abducted from the grounds" 6577
Abduction 2576, 6577
Abel 1925, 7496
Abelard 8742
"*Aberdeen*, University of" 10465
Abhor 369
Abi, Prince 7799
"abilities in the law, remarkable for his" 5193
"abilities . . . were so peculiarly marked" 1
Ability 94, 490, 518, 2008, 2112, 5501, 6930, 7626, 10954
"ability to express ideas, my marvelous" 5420
"ability to paint, before I lost my" 518
Abishag the Shunammite 8006
"Abissinia, prince of" 4603
"ablaze with lightnings" 9070
"able-minded man" 6890
"Abnaki Indians" 7457
Abner 4937, 5444
"abnormality on his EKG" 166
"aboard his first command" 5628
"abode" 1968
"abode of Ometeotl" 2635
"abodes of horror" 4101
"abominables of Horomeon, very top tittermost peak" 6075
"Aboriginal" 984
"aboriginal sap would some day stir" 4435
"abort me, tried to" 7092
Abortion 4710, 5760, 5780, 6049
"abortion, I didn't have an" 6049
"abortion, in those dark ages before legalized" 5760
"abortion, she was about to have an" 4710
"abortion clinic" 5879
"abortion was wrong, believing" 5780
"abortions, there were always illegal" 5760
"abraded state, markedly" 3589
Abraham 9562
Abrahams, Aaron 2486
"Abraham's Path" 9150
Abrams 5321
"abroad, Daisy was" 8854
"abroad, going" 3469
"Abroad, she has come from" 6144
"abroad, they go" 10843
"abroad, two monotonous years" 2089
"abroad at the outbreak of the war" 1590
"abroad was for the privileged few" 3398
"abruptly, stopped so" 1619
"abruptly than I would have

wished, more" 2381
"*Absalom! Absalom!*" 921
"abscesses, producing magnificent" 3057
Absence 2541, 2654, 3302, 3321, 3322
"absence, Duckling's" 2574
"absence, ten years of" 3523
"absence was opaque, her" 2654
"absent, bride and groom are" 6865
"absent at school, she was" 8838
"absent one, an" 5650
"absolute calm" 7930
"absorb the wondering mind" 4101
"absorption, gentle" 10657
"abstinence from alcohol" 2926
"absurd, he felt pretty" 7717
"absurd, it was" 6255
"absurd, it was he who made the place" 1180
"absurd as he knew it to be" 2308
"absurdity, consciousness of her" 7011
"abundance, unimaginable" 455
"abundant in this strange world of ours" 6409
"abused us, our guards greatly" 1162
"Abydus, city of" 4494
"abyss, I fell into the" 2520
"abyss, tidal" 435
"abyss in the road" 10930
"acacia tree" 475
"academic interest, lately been some" 5468
"academic wife" 2332
"Academy, Greenspark" 8625
"Academy, Miss English's" 376
"Academy, Shrapnel" 7901
"Academy for Boys, Glenkill" 5854
"Academy for Girls, Kerrybrook" 4192
"academy for young ladies, Miss Pinkerton's" 9757
"Academy of Design, National" 1012
"Academy of Music" 1012, 8740
"Acadia" 6249
"Acadia, neck of" 7911
"Acadian settlement" 6249
"Acaire, Forest of" 3898
"accent, imitating her" 7598
"accented it, merely" 5005
"accept, they won't" 7563
"accepted as a candidate" 1514
"accepted his change" 2044
"accepting, gratefully" 2922
"accepts stoically" 9328
"accident?" 2354
"accident, by" 8678
"accident, hurt in the" 18
"accident, I lost mine in a road" 6742
"accident, news of the" 6339
"accident, several days after the" 42
"accident, still haven't figured out my" 678

"Accident, the late" 10764
"accident, the purest" 1219
"accident happened" 30
"accident happened, when the" 8738
"accident of birth" 10822
"accident-prone, became" 3603
Accidents 678, 877, 1964, 2325, 2353, 2354, 2361, 2374, 2450, 2798, 2901, 2943, 3056, 3603, 3733, 3865, 4450, 4585, 4887, 6321, 6339, 6588, 6742, 7020, 8059, 8738, 9319, 9790, 9821, 10456
"accidents, freak" 4450
"accidents ran in the family" 4450
"accidents which befell a very worthy couple" 1964
"acclivity, gentle broad" 10338
"Acco" 8133
"accolades behind me, dragging" 5587
"accommodate them, he would not" 985
"accompanied by her court" 10430
"accompanied by her Negro servant Pride" 9955
"accompany Mrs. Reeves to London" 9509
"accomplish, undoing everything he had tried to" 2934
"accomplished at farming, were not much" 3604
Accomplishment 192, 1852, 1859, 4457, 7362, 8875, 9271, 9508
"accomplishment, era of" 3393
"accomplishment, wasn't much of an" 6724
"accomplishments, her" 6606
Accompong 2642
"accord, nod his head in grave" 6219
"according to Charles Townsend Mather" 6834
"according to the Poet" 289
"account, a little more in his" 3740
"account, full true and particular" 8171
"account, here is an" 9719
"account, his own" 5417
"account, I meant to begin this" 3579
"account is he, of what" 8921
"account of his Gallic Wars, my father's" 920
"account of me, brief" 6312
"account of the Hampton family, brief" 10556
"accountable for her steps, expect to be more" 9509
"Accountants" 6514
"accounts, household weekly" 10926
"accounts, September" 6437
"Accra" 8379
"accuracy is strict, their" 7357

"accuracy of habit" 9417
Accusations 8488, 10511
"accusations just, all of their" 8488
"accused, we have at times been" 5434
"accused me of it, no one has ever" 6706
"accuses, astonishingly" 10511
"accusing me" 8488
"aces of his flight, embryonic" 8649
"ache, dull" 8763
"ache, finding a painful" 10139
"ache growing sharp and then receding" 7086
"ache in him again, he had this" 3304
"ache of want" 4678
"ache that rose in him" 3304
"achieved an assured and enviable position" 5423
"achieved nothing, he" 3517
Achievement 5227, 8954, 9272, 9274
"achievement, sense of" 9572
"achievement of modern America, that incomparable" 1390
"achievers, they are" 8222
Achitophel 4863
"Achitophel, A is for" 4863
"acid, carbolic" 8509
"acid rain" 7336
"acids, caustic" 3413
"acknowledge to a son" 6517
"acknowledged by the horsemen" 10541
"acne on his back" 2846
"acoustically, no butterfly" 218
"acoustically perfect wall" 9474
Acquaintance 582, 2321, 3530, 4758, 5100, 8876, 10861
"acquaintance, disturbed uncomfortable and mutually disparaging" 582
"acquaintance, made the" 5785
"acquaintance, old school-" 1903
"acquaintance, renewal of" 8847
"acquaintance, we are to make" 10773
"acquaintance which lasted for the rest of their lives" 582
"acquaintance with Charles Strickland, when I first made" 5794
"acquaintances, business" 3961
"acquaintances, he was one of my first" 5790
"acquainted, never even" 7164
"acquainted with Mrs. Lecks and Mrs. Aleshine" 5787
"Acquaiola, Neapolitan" 10783
"acquired a certain train of ideas" 6516
"acquired in his brief journey" 9529
"acquirements, solid" 6613
"acquires rot" 275
"acquires sadness and wrinkles" 275

"acreage, an eye on adjoining" 3660
"acreage, windswept" 5975
"acres, deep-grassed" 7220
"acres, encircling" 3095
"acres, five hundred rolling" 3179
"acres, hundred thousand arable" 5166
"acres, nine hundred and fifty" 3069
"acres which formed the farm of Midbranch" 3069
"acrid black smoke" 3783
"acrid taint of brush fires" 3405
Acrimony 374, 375, 377, 381, 385, 389, 392, 395, 1823, 6315
"Acropolis, the" 3395
"across the English Channel" 5720
"act, doing a certain" 6036
"act, drowned-man" 6680
"act, her last" 2335
"act, it was a surly" 8674
"act, my first" 828
"act, not even promising first" 9379
"act, that simple" 5215
"act, typical" 8674
"act, vanishing" 2579
"act normal" 9968
"act of wilful defiance" 8709
"act that could easily be explained in a court of law" 6201
"act was half over, the first" 130
"acted as he did, why Cruise should have" 9009
Acting 1317, 6680
"acting in an unconstitutional way" 7817
"acting on mistaken principles" 7888
"acting on orders from his superiors" 1167
"acting on the screen" 1317
"action, course of" 7396
"action, energy and" 638
"action, hour for" 6036
"action, no" 9379
"action, not a part of the main" 583
"action and passion, tale of" 8993
Actions 5954, 6033, 7172, 7396
"actions, great" 357
"actions, seldom doubted her" 2738
"actions they record, motives of those" 4490
"Actium, I was with him at" 4469
"active, remain mentally and physically" 4284
"active body" 9261
"activities of spring, cheerful" 7608
"activity, futile" 4804
"activity, major" 8016
"activity, physical" 10555
"activity, unusual" 641
"activity among publishers and birds" 10980
"activity calculated to engender interesting speculation" 8556

Actors 1318, 1332, 7168, 9376, 9387, 9397
"actors" 9376
"actor's secret vice" 1332
"actress" 9036
"actress, anyone ever called her an" 840
"actress, hotsy-totsy Mexican" 6652
"actress, I decided to become an" 9388
"actress, I wanted to be a great dramatic" 9401
"actress, whose daughter was an" 3101
"actress Alexandra Reed" 9035
"ACTRESS IN NUDE ROMP" 6397
Actresses 130, 840, 1329, 6397, 7986, 9035, 9036, 9388, 9393, 9395, 9401
"actresses" 243
"actresses, hairdos of" 7229
"acutely than ever before, more" 46
"ad that ran in the *Detroit Free Press*" 6853
Ada 10433
"adage was sound as ever, assumed this" 6798
Adah 10223
Adah, Cousin 4634
Adam 359, 601, 1175, 2633, 2930, 7554, 9933, 10770
"Adam, the days of" 10770
"Adam and Eve" 359
Adams, Clover 7707
Adams, Ezra 2301
Adams, Griffith 3272
Adams, Henry 6589
Adams, Hilda 564
"Adam's apple, huge" 344
Adamson, Mr. 2117
Adamson, Tom 3846
"Adano, town of" 10484
"adaptation, the new" 4179
Addams, Charles 4665
"added at a later date" 8999
Adderley, Thomas 6864
"addict centers, storefront" 1515
"Addicts, the" 2013
"adding with a sigh" 1239
"Addis Ababa" 8924
Addison, Mr. 10764
Addison, Mr. Joseph 3376
Addison, Thomas Andrew William 4719
"Addison, West" 4448
"additions and subtractions, I went over the final" 3739
"address, I wasn't sure of your" 1956
"address, Manuel's" 3141
"address, Mr. Klang's" 3869
"address a lodger on the third floor" 10792
"address her son-in-law" 10997

"addressed him except as Mr. Eaton or Mr. Samuel, never" 3329
"addressed the all male jury" 5204
"addressed the street-corner meeting" 5323
"addressing themselves frequently" 9422
"Addu Atoll" 2538
Adeline 3548, 9383
"Adelphi" 2964
"Adelphi, the" 1196
"Aden's fetters shaken off at last" 3887
"adept, an" 7979
"adhesives, denture" 10235
"adipose-lined" 5943
"Adirondacks of northern New York" 9203
Adister, Squire 9874
"adjective used to describe the quality of light" 5341
"adjectives, protected by mild" 1284
"adjured, thus" 9989
"adjusted to the Great Depression by the time I arrived" 815
"adjusting the Knuckle's chain" 9106
"adjusting the skirt" 4921
"adjusting their mantillas" 10659
"adjustments, series of small forced" 5265
"Adler limousine" 1714
"admirable, not wholly" 7973
Admiral, The 6128
"Admiral of the Fleet" 7359
"Admiralty, First Lord of the" 2491
Admiration 251, 1981, 4774, 7627
"admiration, excited so much" 1293
"admiration, silent" 7627
"admiration and the envy of the multitude" 4460
"admire him" 2462
"admired because she had married well" 4774
"admired by sportsmen everywhere" 2835
"admired it" 8571
"admired the handsome edifice" 6971
"admirers, she had a very numerous list of" 10767
"admires everything he's done" 1981
"admiring expert wheelwork" 8187
"admit, I have to" 4707
"admit I kissed her" 1800
"admit in the beginning, I may as well" 5427
"admit it to anybody, never" 8469
"admit most of their flaws" 3308
"admittance free" 1089
"admitted by all her friends" 9261
"admonition" 10511
"admonition to *remember the coachman*, an occasional" 10108

"ado, without further" 9788
"adobe, two-story" 8270
Adolescence 1277, 5648
"adolescence, loutish" 5671
"adolescence, vivid painful" 2539
"adolescent, I was barely" 4473
"adolescent girl" 2565
Adolescents 4200, 8366
Adolf 4803, 5834
Adonis 4853
"adopted, Alma and Bruce were" 8250
"adopted adults" 87
Adoption 6634, 8250
"adore you, I" 8027
"adored my father, my mother" 5672
"Adrianople" 6110
"Adriatic, high above the" 8106
"Adriatic weather" 9575
"adrift with sleep" 8761
"ads, matrimonial" 5758
"ads, want" 7365
Adultery 1988, 7012, 7720, 8198
"adultery, nearly committed" 8198
"adultery, watched his wife commit" 1988
"adults, adopted" 87
"adults between the ages of three and six" 9010
"advance, should have made but little" 4696
"advanced, arduously" 10511
"advancement, became nonetheless the chief Jeeter" 3604
"advancements ever attempted and realized by Jeeters, outstripped the entire bulk of" 3604
"advancing in life and experience" 675
"advancing on Tripoli" 155
"advent of the Laurie London era" 3386
Adventure 588, 1219, 1283, 3376, 3490, 3492, 3550, 4457, 4869, 5018, 5384, 5386, 5397, 5492, 5735, 6603, 6813, 8991, 9357, 9860, 10051
"adventure, an" 3550
"adventure, intellectual" 588
"adventure, latest naval" 4869
"adventure, modern romantic" 1354
"adventure, over-fond of" 9860
"adventure, they had a remarkable" 1283
"adventure, time of high" 3385
"adventure, unusual sense of" 9357
"adventure began with a legacy, my" 588
"adventure of life, the biggest" 5735
"adventure snarled in his mind, threads of" 10051
"adventure that happened in Narnia and Calormen" 8991
"adventurer, dulcet-voiced" 5998

"adventurers, gentlemen" 3557
"adventures, series of" 3376
"adventures, all them" 3492
"adventures, ephemeral" 8400
"adventures, midnight" 7712
"adventures, my" 1570
"adventures, my unhappy though successful" 5384
"adventures, one's gentler" 11004
"adventures, write down his" 5397
"adventures of a person, real" 5386
"Adventures of Larry Peters, The" 4473
"adventures of Mr. Cavor, these amazing" 1219
"adventures we propose to record" 6603
"Adventures of Tom Sawyer, The" 896
"adventurous life, my" 3490
"adventurous undertakings" 5018
"adversaries began to pour in their trumps" 3376
Adversity 115, 273, 279, 631, 1256, 1490, 1578, 2142, 2177, 2500, 2953, 4509, 6026, 6163, 6612, 6929, 7154, 7462
"advertise the Sunshine Cities for the Sunset Years" 10606
"advertised him as the German" 2518
"advertisement, living" 8299
"advertisement, Sunday magazine" 6864
"advertisement panels" 5320
"advertisement which involved the story of a young life" 8956
Advertising 4315, 6853, 8299, 8301, 8309, 8323
"advertising beer" 4315
Advice 377, 714, 2672, 3547, 3845, 5232, 5271, 5773, 6625, 6656, 6996, 7101, 7104, 7175, 8542
"advice" 2672
"advice, do-you-need-" 6421
"advice, gave me some" 6625
"advice, gave me that" 8542
"advice, gave valuable" 714
"advice, offered some" 5773
"advice, profited from the" 6996
"advice, word of" 3547
"advice on the subject of wives" 5773
"advise us so, all our sages" 3845
"Aegean, the" 7942
"Aegean Sea" 8894
"Aegean sea" 10716
"aegis of Saint Swithin, under the" 2150
"Aer Lingus passengers" 10071
"Aergius, Mount" 6073
"Aeria, mountain-walled valley of" 4457
"Aerians" 4457
"aerodrome at Shoreham" 5720
"aerodrome on our starboard wing"

197
"aeroplane" 3711
"aeroplane, body of the" 220
"aeroplane, Douglas" 8566
"aeroplane rose from the ground" 4781
"aeroplane slanted and began to come down" 3710
"aeroplanes were wheeling and darting like bright-coloured insects" 193
"aesthetic phenomena" 3284
"aesthetic qualities" 5357
"affair, at the very least to have an" 254
"affair, details of the" 675
"affair, love" 7733, 7734
"affair, the whole" 7868
"affair, the whole ghastly" 6940
"affair, this" 7871
"affair with a married woman, having an" 7720
Affairs 254, 3619, 4576, 5777, 7713, 7719, 7720, 7864
"affairs, human" 7164
"affairs, imperial" 3677
"affairs, my love" 7713
"affairs of individuals, private" 5799
"affectation than a necessity, more an" 4789
"affectations like this" 4282
"affected my father, how it" 6683
Affection 1990, 4290, 4599, 7743, 10851
"affection" 6629
"affection, deepest" 10851
"affection, inspire real" 4290
"affection, never showed any symptoms of" 6515
"affection of their citizens" 9124
"affections, determined not solely to bestow his" 6558
"affinities, awkward" 9054
Afflictions 306, 2405, 3990, 5403, 10271, 10883
"afflictions, various" 2287
"affluence, in times of" 3094
"affluence, simplicity and" 3561
"affrighted at this citation" 9989
"aflame from end to end with a war" 10518
"afraid, the child was" 3732
"afraid, woke up" 2804
"afraid again, I was" 3717
"afraid not to go" 4471
"afraid of dying, it is not that I'm" 2399
"afraid of going to sleep" 3713
"afraid of him, she was" 2652
"afraid of his daughters, became" 6549
"afraid of me as you were, you're not as" 3704
"afraid of putting air in a tire" 3733
"afraid she would miss him" 3703

"afraid to be alive" 5260
"afraid to begin" 3728
"afraid to go" 4471
"afraid to merge" 3723
"afraid to sully its perfect whiteness" 3728
"afraid to walk out of his own office door" 6255
"Africa" 2530, 6126, 6256, 9371, 9566, 10511, 10710
"Africa, Central" 4457, 10402
"Africa, Gold Coast of" 1069
"Africa, I was far away in" 5089
"Africa, North" 4076
"Africa, South" 9638
"Africa, south-eastern" 8399
"Africa, southern" 5073
"Africa, those deserts of" 7648
"Africa, West" 804
"African" 8118, 10511
"African, incidental that he was" 5703
"African, like an" 10442
"African, South" 1420
"African girl" 2106
"African hunter" 1610
"African moon" 8391
"Africans, didn't like" 2106
"Africans, six North" 315
"afterbirth" 7100
"afterglow . . . faded and was swallowed up in the dusk" 2199
"afterglow illuminating the summits of the range" 2199
Afternoon 1115, 2190, 2192, 2194, 2225, 2234, 2238, 2253, 2254, 2263, 2272, 2280, 2284, 4373, 4399, 9354, 10287
"afternoon, and any other" 1223
"afternoon, August" 485, 5310
"afternoon, autumn" 2192, 10580
"afternoon, beauteous September" 6577
"afternoon, beautiful September" 10782
"afternoon, bleak and gusty Saturday" 1629
"afternoon, bright August" 3667
"afternoon, bright clear" 10036
"afternoon, bright December" 292
"afternoon, bright tropical" 1566
"afternoon, brilliant" 9742
"afternoon, brilliant April" 8255
"afternoon, broiling" 4376
"afternoon, broiling August" 4176
"afternoon, cold snow-flecked" 9027
"afternoon, depressing" 2501
"afternoon, dismal Autumn" 310
"afternoon, drizzling February" 829
"afternoon, early December" 3121
"afternoon, early summer" 4137
"afternoon, early winter" 2190
"afternoon, end of a summer" 491
"afternoon, exactly like any other" 2238

"afternoon, five o'clock in the" 2187, 2225
"afternoon, fragrant" 2194
"afternoon, freezing winter Wednesday" 9965
"afternoon, glaring" 9668
"afternoon, grey" 7617
"afternoon, gusty March" 9771
"afternoon, hot" 4409, 4421, 7715, 8800
"afternoon, hottest" 10336
"afternoon, humid July" 2263
"afternoon, it can only be late" 2284
"afternoon, it is Sunday" 8609
"afternoon, June" 10946
"afternoon, late" 2253, 4399, 8461
"afternoon, late and last" 9628
"afternoon, late on a late autumn" 1373
"afternoon, late Sunday" 3825
"afternoon, latter part of the" 3988
"afternoon, long still hot weary dead September" 7763
"afternoon, long vague and dreamy" 10060
"afternoon, mid-" 2254
"afternoon, mild Friday" 2616
"afternoon, momentous mid–October" 10339
"afternoon, New England Sabbath" 9117
"afternoon, October" 7568
"afternoon, quiet sultry" 4014
"afternoon, rainy November" 8511
"afternoon, rainy Sunday" 10438
"afternoon, somnolent July" 3145
"afternoon, steamy summer" 5636
"afternoon, sticky June Chesapeake" 1998
"afternoon, summer" 7195, 10559
"afternoon, sweltering Friday" 4394
"afternoon, that" 7435
"afternoon, three in the" 8322, 8470
"afternoon, two in the" 3816
"afternoon, vivid" 6127
"afternoon, wet" 5431
"afternoon, wet Sunday" 1294, 2272
"afternoon, winter's" 7279
"afternoon, wintry" 9027
"afternoon, withheld itself entirely from the" 3131
"afternoon as hot as they come" 3032
"afternoon brightness" 10037
"afternoon early in a certain January" 10601
"afternoon had turned to evening" 2228
"afternoon in autumn, wet Monday" 4644
"afternoon in late August" 4431
"afternoon in late autumn" 5789
"afternoon in October, it was a wet" 6437

"afternoon in the weeds, satisfactory" 662
"afternoon of April 22nd 1973" 2998
"afternoon of her life, the last" 5626
"afternoon of smoky sunshine" 4571
"afternoon off" 8179
"afternoon was dammed against them in a surf of its own light" 9668
"afternoon was dropping darkly down" 9354
"afternoon wore on" 8850
"afternoons, centuries of September" 5132
"afternoons, long shimmering" 1115
"afternoons, on Sunday" 1853, 9951
"afternoons, spend a certain portion of his" 5370
"afternoons, those lazy" 6075
"afternoons of early June, changeless" 10051
"afternoons of high summer" 1115
"after-thought to the gray Sunday night, like an" 8598
"Afton" 9176
Agaard, Professor 5838
Agabus the Decapolitan 4499
Agar, Louise 5766
Agatha, Aunt 3698
Agatha, Sister 7020
Agathon 3749
"Agatite Texas" 1460
Age 526, 834, 846, 871, 974, 1002, 1275, 2319, 2337, 2936, 3214, 4236, 4603, 4763, 4809, 4844, 5596, 6452, 6726, 7103, 7488, 7997, 8194, 8233, 8965, 9022, 10804, 11000
"age" 526
"age, approach of" 2199
"age, at almost exactly the same" 2319
"age, at an" 6398
"age, at my" 4493
"age, belong to no" 3382
"age, earlier and friendlier" 3103
"age, eighty years of" 6571
"age, figure of hale" 5405
"Age, Golden" 3379, 8991
"age, his" 5426
"age, in spite of his" 85
"age, late middle" 5942
"age, mellow with" 10355
"age, men of his" 5085
"age, middle" 3214, 3495, 10038
"age, my" 7976
"age, my unsettled middle" 9022
"age, old" 101, 108, 11001
"age, ours is essentially a tragic" 3380
"age, prayer" 83
"age, she had reached the" 84
"age, the younger" 3071
"age, thirteen years of" 4176
"age, this scientific" 10551

"age eighteen" 9718
"age eighteen, at" 3538
"age for it, the right" 7456
"age had come upon him" 11000
"age is, no matter what their real" 8194
"age is a variable" 4809
"age of eighty-seven" 9295
"age of five, at the" 4181
"age of foolishness" 3377
"age of nineteen" 7890
"age of reason, what is considered to be the" 6198
"age of six, ever since the" 4270
"age of the little girls out there now" 8747
"age of twenty-one" 10767
"age of wisdom" 3377
"age ten" 6855
"age thirty-eight, by" 91
"age to bear children, rightful" 7103
"age will perform the promises of youth" 4603
"aged eighteen" 6515
"aged forty" 8347
"aged man would you take me to be, what" 82
"aged seventy-seven" 10662
"aged tree" 9660
"aged twenty" 3552
"aged twenty-nine" 5621
Agedness 84, 89, 111, 306, 477, 1275, 1812, 1977, 4493, 4508, 5283, 5968, 6409, 6645, 8194, 8357, 8460, 8494, 8721, 9283, 9468, 11001
"agency, adoption" 6634
"Agency, Madison-Mayfair" 9232
"agent, call me an" 6468
"Agent, Customs Special" 10413
"agent, house" 7109
"agent, Insurance" 9602
"agent, Prince's" 8490
"agent, your" 10049
"agent de police" 6949
"agents of the Crown" 2386
"ages, future" 707
"Ages, Middle" 10642
"ages ago" 6070
Aggie 8829, 10280
"aggressive act, not the kind of" 6201
"aghast, recoiled" 10033
"agile, by nature" 10382
"agility, his uncanny" 5997
Aging 84, 91, 5951, 7456, 7643, 10831, 11000, 11001
Agios 1136
"agitates any living organism in this astronomical universe" 6001
Agnes 8215
"agon, the" 1825
"agonies, urgencies and" 3429
Agony 2397, 5430, 6592
"agony" 5430

"agony, days and nights of" 2397
"agony, groaned in" 6592
"agony, incredible" 143
"Agra" 9185
"agree with you" 2567
"agreeable, duty in life to be" 5457
"agreeable inside, it is quite" 9229
"agreeable name" 4732
"agreeable to a young lady, made himself" 8839
"agreed, it was generally" 7866
"agreed and thought no more about it" 541
"agreed with Genesis" 8735
"agreement, prenuptial" 5764
"agricultural and ranching center" 1460
"agricultural course that came through the mail" 3660
"agricultural interest" 359
"Agricultural Society, Pymantoning County" 293
Agriculture 293, 359, 415, 420, 751, 1042, 1269, 1385, 1568, 2592, 3075, 3603, 3604, 3635, 3636, 3639, 3640, 3641, 3642, 3643, 3645, 3647, 3649, 3650, 3651, 3652, 3653, 3660, 3661, 3662, 3663, 3664, 3667, 3668, 4374, 4382, 5042, 5131, 5681, 6418, 6464, 7273, 7331, 8429, 10927, 10945, 10946
"Aguascalientes" 6344
"agulp with ambitions" 260
"ahead of me" 1619
"aid of their country, come to the" 6989
Aidallbery, Elizabeth 6793
"AIDS" 3402
"Aigues Mortes, walled city of" 4653
Aikins, Mr. William B. 9763
"ailing but spirited and bright" 10845
"ailment, incurable" 5659
Ailments 34, 468, 642, 853, 1519, 2449, 2508, 3051, 3055, 4625, 5659, 6593, 6596, 6610, 6632, 6639, 6686, 6896, 7463, 7464, 8477
"ailments, nervous" 8477
"aim, long-range" 8870
"aim of the Organization" 8870
"aimed at vacancy" 215
"aimless talk" 8851
Ainslie, Commander Robert 7781
"Ainur, he made first the" 2632
Air 1437, 4369, 4386, 5679, 7569, 7768, 8033, 8422, 8507, 8534, 9689, 10023, 10575, 10645
"air, autumn" 10435
"air, blue tinge of" 5125
"air, change of" 9572
"air, clarity of the" 179
"air, clear" 5316

"air, cold and brilliant" 661
"air, Coldmouth" 1633
"air, coldness of the instreaming" 7569
"air, come out to take the" 4401
"air, cool" 188
"air, coppery burnish out of the" 5143
"air, courtly in your" 2101
"air, customary" 8845
"air, dark evening" 4679
"air, deep green" 8033
"air, dense and erratic" 9689
"air, dying spring" 2198
"air, evening" 8536
"air, fresh" 7358
"air, frozen" 187
"air, going on the" 9262
"air, good" 6249
"air, hazy" 2114, 8815
"air, hazy blue afternoon" 4180
"air, hot July evening" 10180
"air, hot mid-morning" 9753
"air, huge edifice of blue" 10604
"air, in the open" 10023
"air, languorous aromatic" 8209
"air, love was in the" 5679
"air, mass of humid" 182
"air, moist" 8507
"air, morning" 8827
"air, motionless mountain" 8333
"air, night" 181
"air, no" 9319
"air, outside" 10190
"air, pleased" 3740
"air, plunder the" 10397
"air, quivering of the" 4369
"air, receptive" 8903
"air, safest thing in the" 9624
"air, salt" 8749
"air, shadowed humid jungle" 1526
"air, shut out the" 4371
"air, slight trembling of the" 10185
"air, smell that" 180
"air, soft warm" 6499
"air, still" 176
"air, stream of warm" 10694
"air, sullen humid blanket of" 4386
"air, the" 7292
"air, the very" 3403
"air, thin" 8397
"air, thread of semipure" 8528
"air, vital with" 3796
"air, what was that cold rush of" 184
"air, when seen from the" 8232
"air, without a sniff of" 8680
"air above nine thousand feet was black and cold and very smooth" 181
"air and warmth, pleasant" 6557
"air began leaking so conspicuously from my life" 2450
"air began to quiver" 8033
"Air Cavalry, First" 230

"air conditioned, car was" 4393
"air conditioner, newly repaired" 1992
"air conditioner, turned on the" 4655
"air conditioner clanking in the background" 1992
"air curled with its distortion" 189
"air curling chilly and thin beneath the cracked window" 8528
"air currents of the doldrums, faint hot" 8079
"air from his nostrils" 8017
"air from the desert boiled up the face of the rim" 10694
"air gets the first sting of salt" 186
"air hardening the deep insides of your nostrils, feel the freezing" 761
"air in the cave was quiet" 191
"air in the house" 10645
"air is still" 2183
"air is thick" 175
"air lay as heavy as water" 185
"air like July" 4412
"air made a hissing sound" 8810
"air of a man of taste, pleased" 8255
"air of a man released from an irksome duty" 7107
"air of a martyr" 1577
"air of expectancy" 9663
"air on our faces, hot late summer" 4422
"air raid warning" 10539
"air raids" 1282
"air raids, told to expect" 10482
"Air Service" 8649
"air shuddered with myths legends and wondrous occurrences" 3403
"air smelled of rain" 8519
"air smelt, how beautifully the" 10575
"air so unfairly blown north from subtropic muck" 4386
"air tearing, like" 8825
"air that was charged with the scent of white lilacs" 6499
"air there was, what little" 4370
"air there were sweeter in the nostrils than other air, as if the" 4536
"air was auspicious" 1437
"air was calm" 5068
"air was fog and sweat and steam" 8534
"air was getting thick" 183
"air was glacial, morning" 178
"air was rich with the smell of trees" 8507
"air was slashed by modish dresses and fierce make-up" 1302
"air was still saturated with moisture" 177
"air which occupied the street" 10604

"Airbase, Gedsborough" 4313
Aircraft 192, 194, 198, 200, 201, 203, 207, 210, 212, 213, 214, 216, 223, 228, 235, 1030, 1409, 2042, 4580, 5750, 6984, 7018, 7564, 8656, 8668, 8783, 9594, 9624, 10505
"aircraft" 10505
"aircraft, an" 1409
"aircraft, international" 4650
"aircraft, memorize the silhouettes of enemy" 10517
"aircraft, midget Japanese" 4685
"aircraft, your" 213
"aircraft carrier, overhanging bulk of the" 8131
"aircraft named the *Thin Man*, huge big-bellied" 221
"aircraft of the Third Reich" 223
"airfield, snow covered the" 8605
"airliner had lifted itself like a cripple grown used to his crutches" 201
"airmail wrappers, blue" 4333
"airplane, death shaped vaguely like an" 2447
"airplane, little paper" 1854
"airplane, miniature" 6882
"airplane, sitting here in the" 1957
"airplane, stepped off the" 8192
"airplane that looks as if it is flying right into my forehead" 6882
Airplanes 193, 195, 197, 199, 202, 204, 205, 206, 208, 209, 217, 218, 219, 220, 221, 222, 224, 225, 227, 231, 686, 1640, 1854, 1957, 2447, 3710, 3711, 4674, 4781, 6882, 8192, 8410, 8566, 9570, 9594, 9595, 9615, 9650, 10080, 10222
"airplanes, I changed" 9624
"airplanes, spangled with the silver glint of" 8410
"Airport, Beijing" 4599
"Airport, Congonhas" 217
"airport, Essendon" 197
"airport, Geneva's Cointrin" 2563
"airport, German" 9606
"Airport, Idlewild" 208
"Airport, Kennedy" 1699, 4092, 9629
"airport, London" 6007
"Airport, London" 6323
"airport, Los Angeles" 1687
"Airport, Los Angeles International" 1725, 4325
"airport, municipal" 2337
"airport, my arrest at the" 6965
"airport, Palam" 9574
"airport, past the" 883
"airport, pick you up at the" 9960
"Airport, Reykjavík" 9653
"Airport, Southwest Florida Regional" 2447
"Airport, Taipei International" 7128

"airport is not yet New York U.S.A." 276
"airport waiting room" 10006
Airports 197, 208, 227, 232, 276, 883, 890, 1687, 1699, 2447, 4325, 8605, 9574, 9653, 10006
"airs, tepid August" 299
"airship, great" 194
"airstrip, valley" 198
"Airways, AusCan" 202
"Airways, Kiwi" 228
"airy, high and" 3122
"aisles, narrow" 921
"Aix-les-Bains" 4269
AJ 7990
"Ajaib-Gher, the old" 2017
Akers, Theopolis 8360
"AK-47s were chewing up everything" 4252
Akhenaten, Nefer-Khcperu-Ra 6450
Akst, Miss 4159
Aku-nna 2708
Al 9942
"Al Kahira" 1351
"Alabama" 582, 2374, 2967, 4066, 5218, 7418
"Alabama, I have come from" 9414
Alabaster, Lady 2117
"Alamo, remember the" 7447
Alan 837, 9334
Alard 2300
"alarm, dentist's drill of the" 10229
"alarm, distant burglar" 2721
"alarm, groping for the" 10190
"alarm, unwelcome" 1155
"alarm, up with the" 10190
"alarm, waiting for the" 8505
"alarm bell rang" 10200
"alarm clock" 10127, 10165
"alarm clock clanged" 10137
"alarm clock was set to ring, long before the" 8503
"alarm rang" 10217
"alarm (that hadn't alarmed)" 10190
"alarm went, the" 10251
"alarm went CLANG*angangangangang*" 2721
"alarm went off" 862
"alarmed at the smell of smoke" 3780
"alarmed by the car's progress, would not have been" 9815
"alarmed your three Lovers" 9509
Alarms 1155, 2721, 8498, 8505, 8795, 8807, 10137, 10165, 10171, 10182, 10217, 10229, 10251, 10309, 10539
Alayne 7475
"alb, abbot in his" 10641
"Albany" 10080, 10871
"Albany, fifty miles or so northwest of" 370
"albatrosses, escort of" 8170
Albert 7071, 10511, 10933

Albert Frederick George, Prince 7805
"Alberta" 4966, 8934
Albinus 7714
"Albuquerque, town of" 2957
"alchemy, experiments in sexual" 7979
"alchemy is what's really needed" 6486
Alcibiades 5738
"alcohol, day's abstinence from" 2926
"alcohol, sometimes I drink" 4789
"alcohol coiled from the turned-back lid" 189
"Alconleigh" 6850
"Aldebaran" 534
"alderman" 7721
"alderman at the Lord Mayor's show, like an" 2639
"alderman of the sixth district" 4705
"alders" 7652
Alderson, Jay 3207
Aldrich, Will 8997
Aldridge, Dunky 1233
"ale, rich October" 3396
Alec 2091
Alchaw 6146
Alejo 1164
Aleko 2165
"alert" 2997
"alert, coming" 10280
Alert, the" 8094
"alert, warily" 10170
"alert, wide-eyed and" 8480
"alert to the threat of disaster" 2599
Aleshine, Mrs. 5787
Aletheia 9020
Alex 717, 5996, 10511
Alex, Uncle 9321
Alexander 3610, 5451, 5612, 9391
Alexander, Alan 7229
Alexander the Great 7808
"Alexandra, the" 9394
Alexandria, Miss 10969
"Alexandria" 4499, 8123
"Alexandria Illinois" 1363
"Alexandria, three hundred miles above" 1485
Alf 8447
"Alford" 6135
Alfred 7430
Algar the Prior 9945
"Algeria" 4423
"Algiers" 8072
"Algiers, headland that is called" 7691
"Algonquin tribe" 7457
Ali 856
"Ali! Ali! Ali!" 3006
"alias the Scarlet Creeper" 10342
Alice 894, 2004, 2388, 2940, 3934, 6616, 6722, 10895, 10919
Alice, Mistress 4971
"*Alice*, the cards in" 2855

Alida 6721
"alien, ever the" 3616
"alien, infidel" 7505
"alienation of modern life" 5291
"alighted from a green gig" 1572
"alive, afraid to be" 5260
"alive, glad to be" 5260
"alive, he may be" 2442
"alive, it was still" 4951
"alive, make sure they are still" 1149
"alive, still" 5858
"alive, thanked God that he was"
    4341
"alive, therefore I am" 2535
"alive, to be" 5270
"alive again, making the People"
    4610
"alive and energetic" 5887
"alive today, there are" 3329
"alive tonight, if Bart were" 2154
"alive when the man kicked his
    hand away" 3755
"alkalche, waters of the" 5074
"all but me" 6815
"All Hallows' Eve" 4637
"All Hallow's Eve" 7272
"all over, after the thing was" 3341
"all right, are you sure you're go-
    ing to be" 1793
"all right, it's" 1792
"all right, sure that you'll be" 1795
"all right, that's" 722
"all right with me" 4939
"Allah, in the name of" 1955, 5602
Allan 3180
Allard, Fontaine 9765
Allbright 6790
"allegation and denial, forests of"
    9696
"Alleghanies, crossed the" 6100
"Alleghany City" 4149
Allen 10511
Allen, Josiah 637
"Allentown" 4059
"Allermuir, inn at" 6560
"Alley, Cinnamon" 9175
"alley, side" 7620
"alley, there is an" 7449
"alley it shares with the junior high"
    2724
"alleys, greasing the" 7339
"alleys were quiet" 10519
"allez vous-en" 722
"alligator, that awful stuffed" 2614
"alligator pit" 6051
"Allington" 3063
Allison 8647
"allowed herself" 2915
"allowed him a day off from school"
    837
"allowed to exist, should not be"
    7253
"allowing for exceptions" 7037
"all's well that ends well" 3340
"allude to coal as 'black diamonds'"

10551
"allure, her cool" 8027
"allure would have left Renoir
    gasping" 8027
"*Allurements, Snares* and" 10764
"alluvial mud" 6249
"alluvial plain" 5152
Alma 2971, 8250
"Almagated Television" 1032
"Almanac, The Thumb-Nail" 4066
Almayer 9991
"Almighty God" 7801
"almighty secret and desperate
    society" 2837
"almonds, eyes like" 10885
"almost there, we're" 4672
"aloft, borne" 650
"alone" 8730
"alone, can't bear to be" 8717
"alone, he sat" 8368
"alone, he stood there" 9398
"alone, he was" 6010
"alone, hoped to be" 7228
"alone, I was" 8728
"alone, imagined that we should be"
    8633
"alone, left them" 9102
"alone, man should not be" 8735
"alone, sat" 8332
"alone, sat all" 2070
"alone, she lived all" 430
"alone, she was" 3521, 8718
"alone, she was all" 8722
"alone, sitting" 8341
"alone, woke up" 10284
"alone and desolate" 9208
"alone and peculiarly forlorn" 8716
"alone and undisturbed for six
    weeks" 2906
"alone at a table, girl seated" 10392
"alone by the sea" 2769
"alone except for Mrs. Jensen" 3835
"alone here, I am" 8734
"alone here, we are all" 935
"alone in bed" 2002, 10237
"alone in her room" 8353
"alone in her sewing room" 8720
"alone in her silent house" 869
"alone in my pad, I am all" 8727
"alone in my room, I am" 8726
"alone in the apartment" 8731
"alone in the back of his brother-
    in-law's car" 2965
"alone in the corridor" 8582
"alone in the Invalides" 10071
"alone in the kitchen" 2712
"alone in the London flat" 4006
"alone in the pantry" 4670
"alone in the world" 2278, 8714
"alone in the world, quite" 8716
"alone on the farm" 3835
"alone upon the world" 8736
"alone with them, she did not like
    to be" 4153
"aloneness, the" 8491

"along, two months" 7088
Alonzo 7346
"aloof, too" 10852
"aloofly" 2107
"aloud, he said" 4879
"aloud, read it" 5473
"alpha and omega" 10260
"alpine grass" 6075
"Alpine ridges" 4034
"Alps, northern slopes of the" 8866
"Alps, precipitous fold of the
    northern" 4062
"Alps, range of" 6052
"Alps, the" 6061, 6067
"Alps, Tyrolean" 8389
"also and also of the campus" 7907
Alston, Mr. Isaac 2973
"Alta California" 7508
"Altamont" 1221
"altar, monstrous bloody" 7813
"altar, stopped at the" 7541
"altar in the abbey-chapel of Ruby-
    gill" 10641
"altar of the Virgin" 1210
Alter 1155
Alter, Polly 9690
"altercation" 8934
"altered everything that was to
    come, moment that..." 5124
"altered the course of his life" 5123
"alternative, having no" 8407
"alternative to either deserting or
    marrying a girl" 9290
Althea, Sister 9523
"althea bush" 7440
"altitude of some four thousand
    feet above the sea" 1357
"Altrurian, an" 9864
"Altrurian breadth, if I spoke with"
    5278
Aluja, Leila 6800
"alumni, there were as yet no" 7896
Alva 10511
Alvin 10378
Alvira 3555
Alwyn 6122
"Alzheimer's" 7456
Amalie, Great-Aunt 3659
Amanda 3702, 4344
"Amangtakwena, the" 8789
"Amarpur India" 10210
Amaryllis 4146
"Amaryllis" 7346
"amateur practitioner" 4460
"amateur psychologists" 7840
Amato 2848
"amazed by this" 10328
"amazed in my life, never so" 6207
Amazement 6207, 10328
"amazement" 7216
"Amazon, down in the" 7054
"Amazon, high noon over the" 7339
"Amazon, the" 473
"Amazonia" 473
"Amazons, Moscow" 10837

"Amazons, the" 10769
"Ambassador, Panamanian" 7831
"Ambassador, the" 2475
"ambassadors" 4502
"amber and gold" 2188
Amberson, Howard W. 3751
Amberson, Major 10553
Ambien II of the Five 5497
"ambiguities that a person feels but cannot readily comprehend" 1209
"ambiguously cavorting" 3589
Ambition 1496, 3234, 4208, 5994, 6088, 6486, 6932, 7125, 8494, 8922, 9388, 9401, 10521, 10550
"ambition" 8488
"ambition, folly of all human" 1496
"ambition, my main" 248
"ambition, stout" 6613
"ambition, undigested indigestible gobbets of his failed" 10521
"ambition urged me to higher aims" 239
"ambitions, political" 4789
"ambitions enormous, agulp with" 260
"ambitions realized, one of his deepest" 7125
"ambitious than talented, more" 5448
"ambitiously described in the official guidebook" 9173
"amblers who could not sleep, early old" 8813
"ambling across the Oberlin campus" 2083
Ambrose 4756, 10090
Ambrose, The Reverend Augustin 99
"Ambrosia, back in" 9429
"ambulance driver" 131
"ambulance parking lot" 4621
"ambulances, riding the" 6444
"ambush, day for an" 2160
"ambush, fell into an" 1934
"ambush, lay in" 8691
"ambush, sites of" 5149
"ambushed a band of terrorists" 2026
Ambushes 1934, 2026, 2160, 8691
Amedroz, Bernard 6612
Amedroz, Charles 6612
Amedroz, Clara 6612
Amedroz, Mrs. 6612
Amelia 1897, 4900
"Amelia" 5543
"amen" 7526
America 2360, 3425, 4066, 4464, 4544, 5719, 6251, 6454, 7531, 8875, 9512
"America" 1494, 2446, 5486, 7663
"America, achievement of modern" 1390
"America, arrived from" 1613
"America, awfulness of" 286
"America, back and forth across" 3037

"America, bridgeways to" 9247
"America, brought his future to" 2383
"America, came back to" 1571
"America, Central" 9954
"America, colonies of" 6803
"America, Confederate States of" 4067
"America, corner of" 291
"America, deprived" 2360
"America, flat outland countries of" 584
"America, in" 284
"America, Indians in" 9853
"America, less of that high polish in" 267
"America, Made in" 5982
"America, make good in" 9265
"America, new mother" 6649
"America, North" 4076, 4095, 4462, 10468, 10470
"America, one of the most famous writers of" 8641
"America, publishers in" 1914
"America, remote period of the annals of" 263
"America, return to" 9659
"America, rich" 7043
"America, see the lad off to" 4011
"America, set sail for" 8153
"America, Sons of Italy in" 3753
"America, South" 4558, 6484
"America, spent eight months in" 6463
"America, stepping off toward" 288
"America, streets of" 283
"America, United States of" 268, 361, 1360, 2310, 6439, 6982, 7272, 10193
"America, you can not understand" 271
"America, young" 10007
"America and God had gone into business together" 285
"America to the other, from one" 9656
"American, an" 1520
"American, contrast with things" 6251
"American, discovered her first" 2615
"American, I am an" 245
"American, I want to be an" 244
"American, lush and" 3425
"American, so unobtrusively" 9537
"American, South" 740, 6259
"American, the" 10059
"American, ubiquitous" 1351
"American, wealthy sixty-four-year-old" 10422
"American, which [part of you] is" 4447
"American, you are not an" 271
"American and Canadian borders"

4043
"American ax" 271
"American barber shop" 1838
"American base" 228
"American boy's name" 4732
"American by birth" 4762
"American can be ignorant, no" 7814
"American Center in Rome" 5853
"American cities, most large" 1054
"AMERICAN CITIZEN LATEST MARTYR TO IRISH CAUSE" 2386
"American citizenship" 829
"American city, great" 8773
"American Civil War" 3150
"American clipper-built brig" 8069
"American coast" 7647, 9065
"American cocktail parties" 6780
"American colonies, revolt of our" 3059
"American commercial town" 4029
"American Consciousness, The" 899
"American Consulate" 9879
"American county seat town" 1425
"American doctors" 10313
"American eating" 508
"American Embassy" 939
"American embassy" 6502
"American epic" 6454
"American Expeditionary Forces" 8695
"American features, standard white" 4438
"American film director" 5984
"American forces" 219
"American gentleman" 1090, 6021
"American girl" 3541, 4797
"American heartland, lies in the" 278
"American House" 4632
"American journalist" 10215
"American judge" 10838
"American king, the first" 1442
"American ladies" 1828
"American lady" 1090
"American League" 8919
"American liberty" 266
"American liner" 3494
"American masses" 2681
"American mind, his" 4928
"American outdoor history" 4464
"American patriot" 5240
"American People" 273
"American Pioneer" 270
"American portrait-painter" 491
"American prairies" 3219
"American publisher" 5419
"American scenery" 264
"American soil" 277
"American story" 4242
"American sunlight" 290
"American thing, peculiarly" 282
"American tourists" 9636
"American Union" 9512

"American university" 9657
"American way, the" 289
"American woman" 3959, 9464, 10374
"American women" 10848
Americans 245, 508, 2615, 4003, 4643, 5280, 6021, 9464, 9537, 9636, 10374, 10496
Americans (Native) 752, 959, 1720, 1735, 2606, 3714, 3906, 4043, 4140, 4358, 4502, 4682, 5190, 6100, 7457, 7508, 7599, 7612, 8155, 8165, 8510, 9015, 9198, 9707, 9842, 9853, 10940
"Americans" 1396
"Americans, three" 4003
"Americans, two North" 5609
"Americans, two white" 4643
"Americans, we" 5280
"Americans called a K-bar" 1166
"Americans spoke, the curious language" 6749
"Americans stayin' at the Castle" 4690
"Americans were still safe" 10496
"America's northeast coast" 7531
"America's shallowness of background in human history" 274
Americus, Roscoe Jr. 7859
"Amerindians would come into Charlestown" 1720
Ames, Elinor 6652
Ames, Young 6425
"Amherstburg" 9205
"amiability, he was a pattern of" 2342
"amiable" 7163
Amiable, appearing" 10764
"amiable and boneheaded peer" 8257
"amiably" 6532
"amid the cornflakes" 5502
"amidst its town" 1298
Amir, Karim 4864
"amiss, something was" 3178
"amiss, will surely not be" 698
Ammen, Jasper 10759
Ammidon, Laurel 9408
Amnesia 7172, 8495
"amnesia, I would have preferred" 8495
"amnesiac condition, pathological" 7172
"amniotic fluid, splash of" 7092
"amoebae leave no fossils" 2372
"among the living, his last night" 2456
Amon-ho-tep 6661
"amor, omnia vincit" 5647
"amorous couples" 9381
"amorphous" 2803
"Amorra" 1385
AMORTORTAK 9053
Amos 9437, 10362
"amount to much, it didn't" 2837

"amphetamine toxicity" 6170
"amphora, black sculptured" 2805
Amrita 2963
"Amsterdam" 120
"Amtrak train" 9597
"amulet he called his Medicine" 2854
Amundason, Thorkel 3719
"amused, crying out for charity's sake to be" 927
"amused herself, she had" 7715
Amusement 2131, 4886, 4906, 4998, 7869
"amusement" 4906, 6666
"amusement, for his own" 4439
"amusement, nostalgia and" 7398
"amusement, ribald and raucous" 7869
"amusing, sometimes I found it" 4271
"amusing ballet, the least" 8299
"amusing things" 7884
Amy 5373, 7525
Amy Doll 6480
Ana 8974
"analyse the motives" 7951
"analyst, intelligence" 2251
"analyst of spirit and flesh, the greatest" 10774
"analyzing the emotions of this day" 5472
"anarchist" 5468
"Anarchist, bearded" 876
Anarchy 7050
Anatole 6132
"Anatolian, the" 2398
Anatomy 549, 4295, 4297, 4894, 5712, 5912, 8237, 10340, 10443, 10817, 10832
"ancestor, my" 713
"ancestor, our first conspicuous" 7554
Ancestors 4109, 6883, 6922, 8986
"Ancestors, Histories of their" 353
"ancestors, my" 360
"ancestors, spirits of her" 4109
"ancestors, throne of our" 7801
"ancestors divined them" 6922
"ancestors hid out during the Civil War, my husband's" 7792
"ancestors migrated from England" 361
"ancestors of whom to be proud, have no" 362
"ancestral Britain" 3639
"ancestral estate" 1090
Ancestry 409, 831, 1090, 3356, 3533, 3573, 3598, 3605, 4432, 4434, 4446, 5223, 6146, 6611, 6628, 6631, 6650, 6695, 7187, 7981
"ancestry, take great pride in our" 362
"anchor, dropped" 8056, 8084
"anchor, lay at" 3116, 8048, 8098,

8105
"anchor, let go the" 8066
"anchor, swung to her" 8063
"anchorage, my" 4090
"anchorage, naval" 7304
"anchorage, our" 8124
"anchored, finally" 1111
"Anchovy Jamaica" 9012
"ancient" 10753
"ancient antagonist, earth's" 7916
"ancient as he is" 9969
"ancient battlements" 1178
"ancient British" 6802
"ancient capital of Spain" 5590
"ancient churches" 2225
"ancient city of London" 781
"ancient communities" 1384
"ancient fashion, after the" 7067
"ancient heir-looms" 358
"ancient houses" 9122
"ancient memories" 5617
"Ancient of Days" 2633
"ancient rampart" 9674
"ancient state" 5345
"ancient thing, woman was an" 118
"ancient times" 3893
"anciently together, leaning" 10590
"ancients, Thule of the" 5011
Andemening, Lars 8470
Anderson 4722
Anderson, Captain 10025
Anderson, Carrie 1031
Anderson, Charles 10931
Anderson, Charley 2891
Anderson, Charlotte 5744
Anderson, Kit 9417
"Andes, in the" 1715
"Andes, the" 7339
"Andilly" 5104
"Andover Maine" 9756
Andrada, Manuel 5815
Andrea 4862, 9736
Andrés, Brother 7138
Andrew 2860, 4977, 6544, 9393, 9732, 10365
"Andrewjones" 10135
"Andriff" 1615
"Andromeda lies far off" 528
Andy 2869, 8878
"angel, my bad" 7422
"angel, my mother's" 6646
"angel, soft stone smile of an" 1221
"angel again, saw the" 2647
"angel of Death" 7504
"angel of the dawn" 4034
"angel perches, an old and fragile" 4522
"angel said, the" 2634
"angel used to stand, stone" 6646
"angelic messengers" 2623
Angels 2634, 2639, 2647, 2731, 4034, 4522
"Angels" 9563
"angels, dead" 9040
"angels, heard him say to the" 7539

"angels in the glass" 2639
"angels sounding trumpets" 2731
"Angelus, bells were ringing the" 649
"Angelus bell" 650, 665
Angeluzzi, Larry 7627
Anger 104, 543, 813, 1691, 1820, 2503, 2593, 2633, 2714, 3749, 4919, 5292, 6310, 6460, 8568, 10358, 10842
"anger" 10842
"anger, abrupt as" 2503
"anger, clench his square yellow teeth in" 5292
"anger, departed from it in" 1691
"anger, eyes bright with" 376
"anger, quit in" 6460
"anger, storm's cold" 9087
"anger, talk about" 10842
"anger and lust, tuba blast of" 391
"anger and resentment, screamed out his" 813
"anger of gods" 104
"Anger's my meat" 390
"angle, saw it from a different" 9190
"angle, the peculiar" 10571
"angle of another sister's head" 7441
"Angles, the" 1837
"Angleterre, vive l" 4926
"Anglia, East" 1180, 5078, 8623
"Anglican churchyard" 807
"Anglican nose" 4438
"Anglo-Saxon" 1444
"Anglo-Saxon farmers" 3639
Angmering, Captain Roger 3110
"angrily" 1706
"angry, got" 384
"angry because he is ill" 734
"angry plays, the" 390
"angry voice" 6619
"angry with me, clearly" 398
"angry-eyed old woman" 5571
Angstrom, Rabbit 2447, 9451
"anguish, my particular form of" 9265
"angular, somewhat" 10038
Angus 10021
Anika 276
"animal, burrow of some small" 8547
"animal, climbed down from this" 1643
"animal, gregarious" 5696
"animal, it might have been any" 8809
"animal, leading a pack" 7625
"animal, like a defensive" 8174
"animal, melancholy prehistoric" 4773
"animal, sound of a farmyard" 6224
"animal called the giant sloth" 7232
"animal had chewed" 6698
"animal whimper" 10199
Animals 961, 1178, 1271, 1537, 1643, 2458, 3045, 3274, 3463, 4155,

4747, 4998, 5135, 6167, 6224, 6961, 7232, 7848, 8230, 8275, 8809, 9684, 9728, 9753, 9994, 10282, 10307, 10499
"animals, engaged in a count of" 8275
"animals, killing the" 451
"animals, like penned" 10384
"animals, like young" 985
"animals, pack" 7300
"animals, terrified" 10740
"animals, twenty pack" 9576
"animals cowering in the naked orchard" 10740
"animals often return to forage" 6167
"ankle, broken" 10301
"ankle, the" 10817
"ankle received an arrow" 9844
"ankle turned under her" 16
"ankles, bare brown" 980
"ankles, copper-colored" 980
"ankles lashed at the corners" 1166
"ankles secured to the corners" 1170
Ann 1869, 2884, 6161, 10967
"Ann, S." 652
Anna 44, 3231, 3945, 9374, 9462, 10302
"Anna Arkadievitch Karenina" 5466
Anna Marie 5909
Annabel 2009, 3989
"Annadag had drawn nearer to the town" 6080
"annals of the kingdom, ancient or modern" 6247
"annals that record them" 4454
"Annals of the North, Blucher's" 3423
Anne 135, 3599, 4439, 8758
Anne, Queen 3376
Annesly, Richard 6516
Annette 2471, 5754, 9988
"annexation, antipotal ant" 10511
Annick 4216
Annie 2486, 5449, 5782, 10143
"Annie Conser" 8099
"annihilating, assiduously" 10511
Anniversaries 228, 5090, 6433, 6483, 6769, 10439
"anniversary, celebrated its fortieth" 6769
"anniversary, fiftieth" 228
"anniversary, fortieth" 5090
"anniversary, no longer thought of it as an" 10439
"anniversary as Master of the Restaurant Chez Pavan" 6433
"anniversary of his arrival, on the fifth" 6483
"anno domini" 5260
"announce his return" 1761
"announce to the world at large" 5735
"announced he'd take a wife" 5782
"announced himself unequivocally as himself" 559

"announced his decision" 2472
"announced over ordinary coffee that he felt like God" 1994
"announced she was going to marry" 5781
"announced she was pregnant" 7085
"announced to his faithful people" 10473
"announcement, black-bordered" 2348
"announcement, make an important" 3278
"announcement was to be made" 9603
Announcements 559, 856, 2348, 3278, 4650, 5735, 5781, 5782, 7085, 9603
"announcements, make the discreet" 4650
"announcer, voice of the" 10006
"annoy her husband" 2008
Annoyance 641, 2008, 4272
"annoyed Charles, one thing about Phyllis which" 4272
"annoyed to discover Biblical texts" 7509
"annunciation, the" 7991
"annunciations drawn and written on the walls" 6567
"anomalous, his position was in many ways" 8666
"anonymity, furnished with" 7769
"Anschluss, wholly beneficent ends of the" 223
Ansell 6836
Anselm, Brother 1534
"answer, give you a simple" 5677
"answer, had no" 4700
"answer, he didn't wait for an" 3617
"answer, no" 7114
"answer, she did not" 7592
"answer, the last" 7207
"answer in a minute, I'll tell you my" 6698
"answer it, left to Fritz to" 9900
"answer me" 7206
"answer me, he didn't" 5363
"answer to which he was wholly indifferent" 1493
"answered by the lame butler" 1098
"answered every hour in various ways" 1487
"answered to the call of Jesse, he always" 4816
"answering him, scandalized all Athens by" 4503
"answering machine is on" 5691
"answering the door, not well suited for" 5997
Answers 1487, 7199, 7206, 7207, 9316
"answers, if I knew *all* the" 7199
"answers, no one" 3706
"answers, outraged at the" 2593
"ant" 10511

"ant emerged from the skull" 4963
"Ant Farm" 230
"ant on its spring marching" 4950
"antacid tablets" 2057
"antagonist, earth's ancient" 7916
"antagonist does not certainly appear until the third" 5639
"antarctic" 2218
"Antarctica" 228
"antecedents, say nothing of my" 1568
"antelope, run like a goddamn" 7851
"antenna that poked through the center of the island like a spindle" 5328
"antennae, slight questing of the" 4951
Anther, Dr. 5731
"anthology, pretty little" 5396
"anthology might be made of poems" 5396
"anthology of mid-century literature, shiny heavy" 5468
Anthony 9592
Anthony, Karl 7676
"anthropologists" 1209
Anthropology 1209
"Antibes" 10511
"anticipated, worse than Martin Stone had" 1644
"anticipating his death with good taste" 139
Anticipation 460, 530, 1953, 3037, 4530, 4906, 6701, 8268, 8536, 9336, 9341, 10077, 10536
"anticipation, ears quivering in" 460
"anticipation of his wife" 10062
"anticipation of the sights" 3478
"Antilles, Jewel of the" 5045
"Antioch" 7518, 7717
"Antioch, man from" 3677
"Antioch, richest man in" 10557
"antipathy toward me, why he formed such an immediate and intense" 5870
"antiquarian" 4030
"antiquaries, learned" 357
"antique chair" 8370
"antique customs" 1342
"antique shop" 1017
Antiques 7214
"Antiquities, Museum of" 8941
"antiquity, bears witness to its" 1355
"antiquity, dream from" 1464
"antiquity, personage of extreme" 10111
"antiquity, proud of their" 358
"antiquity, venerable from its" 1171
"antiquity of the family" 3589
"antiseptic, but this was" 6145
Antonia 4462, 7954
Antonio, Count 5212
Antonio, Saint 8937

Antonius, Marcus 4469
Ants 4950, 4955, 10051
"ants, enslaved by" 5272
"ants, hill of busy" 4955
"ants, too many colonies of" 5033
"ants moved militantly over his pole and tackle box" 10051
Anvil, Hubert 10012
Anwari, Tor 460
Anxiety 2814, 3707, 8477, 9992, 10301
"anxiety" 5846
"anxiety, my" 7262
"anxiety, salt trace of" 2814
"anxiety in life, no greater" 4600
"anxiety in Marjorie Carling's voice" 9992
"anxiety like a pep-pill, had taken" 3707
"anxiety of mind" 8477
"anxious, only when I am" 10172
"anxious for the world" 2623
"anxious mother's heart" 4889
"anxious not to miss anything" 9616
"anxious that he should make a good breakfast" 3471
"anxious to get in touch with him" 3920
"anxious to have it descend to his son" 6516
"anxious to please, amazingly" 3362
"anyone else at home, there wasn't" 8670
"anywhere, didn't get" 3520
"Apache, speak" 3281
"Apache trackers" 5190
"aparrel, her new" 7370
"apartment, alone in the" 8731
"apartment, Bernice's" 9924
"apartment, cheap one-room bachelor" 2758
"apartment, five-room" 3170
"apartment, four-room" 3170
"apartment, girl's" 7725
"apartment, her" 1951, 6339
"apartment, his" 2424, 5607, 10731
"apartment, his small two-room" 1787
"apartment, in a large but poor" 8453
"apartment, in my" 1932
"apartment, Léonie's" 3229
"apartment, lived in the" 9984
"apartment, Mac's" 7751
"apartment, modest" 7756
"apartment, my" 3292
"apartment, on the way to his" 2999
"apartment, our Paris" 2823
"apartment, porch of his" 8573
"apartment, Ruby's" 1154
"apartment, see the old" 6140
"apartment, shut up in an old-fashioned" 6456
"apartment, small" 8730

"apartment, sweat- and tinderbox" 4876
"apartment, their jointly leased" 5238
"apartment, their new" 2073
"apartment, very pleasant" 3064
"apartment building" 1774, 2773
"apartment building on Sixty-third Street" 7204
"apartment buildings" 6280
"apartment complex" 6489
"apartment his finances had forced him to take" 5292
"apartment hotels" 3078
"apartment houses" 5323
"apartment houses, almost exactly like the other" 3096
"apartment houses that stood in a row" 3096
"apartment in Brooklyn" 9932
"apartment in Kulosaari" 5042
"apartment in the Bramford had become available" 3170
"apartment on the seventh floor" 5238
"apartment painted, having his" 3169
"apartment richly furnished" 8837
"apartment was gone, my newly rented" 6299
"apartment where I had painted the *Brooklyn Crucifixion*" 3258
Apartments 1665, 1787, 2073, 2758, 3064, 3078, 3096, 3169, 3170, 3187, 3189, 3229, 3257, 3258, 3261, 5104, 5309, 5350, 6140, 6142, 6299, 7204, 7756
"apartments, bachelor-" 5784
"apartments, cheap" 6142
"apartments, high-rise" 1931
"apartments, his own suite of" 3189
"apartments, kitchenette" 3096
"apartments, single" 5928
"apathy" 8488
"Ape, there lived an" 424
"ape who lived in a cage by himself" 426
Apes 424, 426
"apex of his life" 5572
"aphasia" 7456
"aphid cows enslaved by ants" 5272
"Aphorisms, book of original" 5392
Aphrodite 7527
Apley, George William 790
"apogee, we were the" 5230
"Apollo 11" 5630
Apologies 341, 2550, 2714, 4608, 5490, 5738
"apologize, call her from work later and" 2714
"apology, fact for which I make no" 5490
"apology, charmed with the grace of his" 5738
"apology to arriving guests" 2550

"apostles of things as they were" 10339

"Apostolic Church of the Children of Sinai" 1309

"apothecary, an" 6404

"apothecary, philosopher" 7658

"Appalachia" 5452

"Appalachian night, black" 10740

"Appalachians" 6063

"appalled, I was" 8197

"appalling feature, most" 8198

"appalling taste, wondrously" 3237

"appalling thing happened to me" 5226

"apparent, it became" 3751

"apparition, meteoric" 9113

"apparitions on the bowery" 10463

"appeal to Lord Hardinge, copy of Maharaja Pratap's" 1930

"appear before me one night" 4113

"appear to me in fabulously fractured versions" 7440

Appearance 597, 1517, 1567, 1647, 1672, 1786, 2733, 4204, 5476, 5798

"appearance, brief and spectacular" 9073

"appearance, careful of his" 5798

"appearance, her" 7475

"appearance, his" 597

"appearance, in" 8018

"appearance, outward" 1395

"appearance, personal" 9465

"appearance, rather shabby" 5784

"appearance of a youthful shoot" 9660

"appearances are deceitful" 6804

"appeared, had not yet" 6200

"appeared and fired" 10477

"appeared at my classroom door" 5476

"appeared on the hill at first light" 1786

"appeared on the top of Haldeman's Hill" 9771

"appeared out of a clump of trees" 4204

"appeared out of the darkness" 1732

"appeared suddenly as Manco Capac at the lake Titicaca" 1567

"appeared with the sun at their backs" 1764

"appeareth, it" 5387

"appearing at the end of the San Antonio Trace" 5215

"appearing in the bedroom" 6160

"appearing to come slowly" 8659

"appears, a figure" 1672

"appears, whatever she thinks about" 9445

"appellation, so very uncouth an" 8955

"appellation which we employ" 6247

"appendage, form a dirty" 6276

"appetite, an earnest" 4670

"appetite, mental" 2089

"appetite, sense of" 6311

"appetites, hunger grows faster than" 4676

"applause" 2103

"applause, not the" 6240

"applause so liberally bestowed upon the actors" 9376

"apple orchards" 9519

"apple tree" 3119

"appleass, some" 9702

Applebee, Donald 5967

Appleby, Adam 9432

Appleby, Horace 9919

"Applegate" 9093

"apples, a few wrinkled black-spotted" 9674

"apples, Granny Smith" 921

Appleton, Miss 6

Appleyard, Mrs. 3134, 10797

Appleyard, Ronnie 6988

"application of the brakes, the first jarring" 7249

"applied for assistance" 6098

"apply for a job" 6442

"applying himself" 5448

"appointment, by" 9902

"appointment, he had no" 9913

"appointment, keep an" 6580

"appointment, late for her" 9343

"appointment, made the" 9895

"appointment, previous" 5786

"appointment with Miss Merival" 4911

Appointments 4911, 5786, 6580, 6892, 9343, 9895, 9902, 10040

"Appomattox, on the field of" 10034

"appraisal, inspection and" 1373

"appreciate" 4124

"appreciated the beauties" 2147

Appreciation 2147, 4124

"appreciation, air of" 4132

"appreciation, cultivated" 1314

"apprehension, days of surmise and" 9420

"apprehension, with something like" 8131

"apprehensive, grow" 5301

"apprehensive, skittish and" 3722

"apprentice of His Majesty" 6450

"apprentices had closed and barred the shutters" 1007

"apprenticeship, his" 5601

"apprise the reader" 8953

"apprised him of the perils of slouching" 5992

"approach, one way of" 5408

"approach as though nothing was wrong" 9608

"approach it from the sea" 5038

"approach to Felton House" 3589

"approached each other at a combined velocity of 1200 miles per hour" 216

"approached from the sea" 8142

"approached his own dwelling" 2496

"approached Kemble" 7587

"approached Stonehenge, when I" 1671

"approached the newspaper building" 6319

"approached the newspaper kiosk" 10366

"approved both plans and lettering" 7760

"approximation, brutal" 5271

"apricots, dried" 1874

April 2435

April, Mrs. 9926

"April" 14, 157, 905, 948, 1567, 1606, 1623, 1892, 2132, 2244, 2281, 2373, 2491, 2516, 2561, 2678, 2775, 2998, 3307, 3338, 3412, 3414, 3521, 3640, 3652, 3810, 3837, 4150, 4378, 4399, 4670, 5083, 5117, 5163, 5192, 5476, 6171, 6211, 6448, 7247, 7262, 7289, 7397, 7495, 7606, 7745, 8001, 8077, 8263, 8398, 8427, 8429, 8621, 8656, 8860, 9114, 9424, 9473, 9720, 9742, 10043, 10096, 10174, 10284, 10819

"April, early in" 4225, 6118

"April, end of" 7501

"April, it was" 10983

"April, last day of" 8397

"April, last week of" 10600

"April afternoon" 8255

"April Fools' Day" 10291

"April is the cruellest month" 8615

"April long ago" 9628

"April morning" 254, 3514

"April sun" 8437

"April Sunday" 2005

"April sunlight" 421

"April warmth" 9683

"apse, the" 1296

Apter 1159

"aptness she sees in the refrain" 5507

"Aqsu" 9546

"aqueous light" 10292

"Aquitania" 10100

"Arab kingdom" 7809

"arabesques in faded gilt" 717

"Arabia, southern mountains of" 2221

"Arabian Gulf" 7919

"Arabic, improve his" 6432

"arabic letter" 9183

"Arabic exhalation, rise like an" 9181

"arable rolling plain" 7260

"arable surface" 3069

Aragorn 7846

"Aramaic" 9709

Aranow, Mrs. 6652

Aranow, Stanley 6652

"Arawaks, the" 1192

"arbiter betweene the night and the

day" 7370
"arbitrarily one chooses" 8989
"arbour in the thicket, wild-grape" 959
Arbuthnot, Humphrey 3670
"arc of dawn" 2257
"arc of night" 2262
"arc of noon" 10518
"arc round the hill, he made a wide" 5169
"arcade, in some distant" 9507
"Arcadia, eighteenth-century" 7711
"Arcadian Society" 8344
Arcadius, Augustus 3677
"arcane ritual" 1214
"Arch, St. Louis" 3038
"arch, through an" 1596
"archaeologist" 6279
"archaeologists, work of our" 2605
Archaeology 1384, 2605, 4494, 5532, 6279
"Archaeology, Staedtler Institute of" 6279
"*Archangel*, wing of" 686
"archangels, His" 2638
Archbald, Jenny Blair 7348
"archbishop had come to see me" 856
"Archbishop of Canterbury" 1145, 1691
"Archbishop was leaving for Paris" 1506
"archbishop's palace" 10086
"archcriminals of the Watergate scandal" 7000
"Archdeacon of Oxford" 1527
Archer, Tim 2961
"Archerfield" 4587
"arches, golden" 3001
Archie, Dr. Howard 8908
"Archipelago" 5011
"Archipelago, Malay" 5018
"archipelagoes, raised new" 5023
"architect, celebrated" 2443
"architect, 35-year-old" 2998
"architect who drew the plans" 7760
Architects 2443
"architects" 3326
"architectural blunders, grotesque" 3237
"architectural quality, displayed a certain ponderous" 9223
"architectural scheme, a not unpleasant" 9225
"architecturally has anything to recommend it" 9229
Architecture 1334, 3084, 7882, 9213, 9223, 9225, 9229, 10368
"architecture" 1334
"architecture, beauty of its" 10368
"architecture, domestic" 1390
"architecture, fascinating if unpretentious" 5607
"architecture, glossy" 7481
"Archive, Levinson" 2604

"archives, buried in the" 9021
"Archway, house in the" 3631
Archy 3647
"arcs, moving" 3044
"arctic" 2218
"Arctic, the high" 8608
"arctic dark" 1213
"Arctic night" 2227
"Arctic season, like an" 2229
"arctic wastes of our linoleum" 10190
"Arda" 2632
Arden, Doctor 10129
Ardmore 930
Ardmore, Whitey 10488
"ardor, restorative" 7532
"ardor rapidly ebbing away" 6036
"area of grey, receding" 2718
"area of mixed woodland and uncultivated chalk downs" 6923
"areas, isolated rural" 115
"Argentina" 3413, 4129
"*Argosy of Mystery Tales, An*" 5494
"argue that it's not important" 7974
"argued, it may be severely" 3376
"arguing, as usual they were" 1836
"arguing, two American ladies in 404" 1828
"arguing lovingly" 9381
"arguing over the placement of the new rose bushes" 8241
"argument, in the middle of an" 6736
"argument, some old" 6652
"argument, the" 6349
"argument, without getting into an" 3614
"argument about where the Dolphin case history should really begin" 1834
"argument about whether or not they wanted to go" 1832
"argument for the existence of God, fashioning an" 3465
"argument over a Chevy Nomad" 2069
"argument with my brother" 7830
Arguments 1142, 1489, 1512, 1706, 1822, 1823, 1824, 1828, 1830, 1834, 1835, 1836, 1838, 1841, 1843, 1845, 1846, 1848, 2069, 3555, 3568, 3614, 3621, 4706, 6349, 6701, 7830, 7874, 8241, 8769
"arguments, didn't really mind these" 1848
"Argus" 7273
"Argyll, house of" 354
"Argyll, in the north of" 6611
Ari 311, 2682
"aria soaring out of the car's tape deck" 3026
"arid gullies" 2949
"Aries" 535
"arise, I will" 1806

"aristocracies of the Old World, feudal" 4441
Aristocracy 4439, 4441
"aristocracy, commercial" 1021
"aristocracy left off marrying Italian *primedonne*" 10788
"aristocracy of England" 834
"aristocracy of Zenith" 2104
"aristocrat, Roman" 6551
"aristocratic" 3173
"aristocratic and rich, make her feel" 2590
"aristocratic grace" 8234
"aristocratic origin" 358
"aristocratic prejudices" 1342
Aristotle 509
"Arizona" 140, 9977, 10069
"Arizona, wild part of" 869
"Arizona pioneer" 2340
"Arizona town, small" 596
"ark" 9626
"ark of the mining interests" 8052
"Arkansas" 25, 2436, 9026
"Arkansas, northeast" 7262
"Arkansas rivers, Poteau and" 7686
"Arkansaw" 1160
Arkie 1791
Arkwright, Rachel 2008
"Arlberg, the" 1396
Arleen 4331
Arlene 3946
"Arles" 7793
"Arlington Cemetery" 9621
"arm, backward-twisting" 10181
"arm, extend your" 2107
"arm, her strong" 1792
"arm, her tennis" 1792
"arm, his good" 8461
"arm, his hairy brown" 3640
"arm, his woolly" 2985
"arm, I lost an" 4585
"arm, my father's right" 348
"arm, stretched forth an" 8213
"arm, young man's" 5812
"arm around her, I had my" 8304
"arm badly broken at the elbow, got his" 22
"arm ended not in a hand but at the elbow" 348
"arm extended" 10300
"arm in arm" 9123, 9381
"arm over the edge of the chair" 901
"arm well covered with pyjama sleeve" 10190
"Armageddon had arrived as prophesied" 10513
"armband, scarlet" 3190
"armchair, carved" 1199
"armchairs, white wicker" 5635
"armed" 4266
Armies 1172, 4042, 6052, 8646, 10472, 10474, 10511
"armies, English" 10473
"Armies, his" 10464
Armine, family of 6090

"Armistice, the" 10475

Armitage, John Edward Scott 5941

Armitage, Mrs. 6809

"armor they could not fling off, flesh roasted in the" 4469

"armory, housed in an" 3424

Armour, Colonel 1901

"armour, ship's" 1005

"armpits, perspiration huddled in her" 4429

"arms, folded his" 1980

"arms, held out her" 9905

"arms, lacerated" 5138

"arms, landed in the" 5674

"arms, quick assured lifting of the" 9317

"arms, swinging his" 5955

"arms about each other" 2529

"arms and back were cool, its leather" 5351

"arms and legs, thrashing his" 9322

"arms around my neck, her" 10175

"arms came up unevenly in front of you" 7855

"arms folded" 10073

"arms folded across his chest" 2398

"arms like wings, spread his" 1521

"arms of a young farmer, in the" 1344

"arms of the British" 10469

"arms out to catch a freshet of wind" 6381

"arms out to me, holding his" 7440

"arms raised like the front legs of horses on the Parthenon" 5654

"arms were folded over his chest" 2876

"arms were spread like a dancer's" 983

Armstrong 1838

Armstrong, Neil 5977

"army, awesome African" 10511

"Army, came out of the" 8667

"Army, Continental" 713

"Army, Indian" 1757

"army, join the" 8683

"Army, Regular" 8665

"army, service in the" 940

"army, some advancing" 5309

"army, stationed in the" 6733

"Army, stint in the" 4601

"Army, The Tartan" 883

"Army, U. S." 8665

"Army, United States" 1529, 6441

"army greatcoat" 2841

"Army installation, inconspicuous" 2560

"Army lawyer" 3486

"army massed at attention, resembled an" 3145

"army of ten thousand ghostly spears, like an" 4679

"army of the North" 3416

"Army of the United States" 8672

"Army officer, handsome young"

4257

"Army officer, Indian" 987

"army patrol" 2026

"army post in peacetime" 6805

"army stretched out on the hills" 10472

"army that Raymond assembled" 8646

Arnie 8246

Arno, Harry 7963

Arnold 2442, 7066

Arnold, Richard 4457

"aroma, the general Throckmorton" 3604

"aroma of gardenias" 1194

"aroma of steaming-hot rolls" 8530

"aroma of the cigarette smoke" 6780

"aromatic air" 8209

"arose from a deep peaceful sleep" 10186

"arose on her trim hind hoofs" 410

"arose stark and stripped" 9291

"arose to trim it, hastily she" 9402

Arouet, F. M. 2629

"around, if she's not" 6686

"around the block a time or two" 6469

"arouse any strong family enthusiasm, did not" 4567

"aroused rather prematurely" 10111

Arp 6431

"arranged, neatly" 4438

"arranged by telegram" 5801

"arrangement, domestic" 5104

"arrangements, I ought to have made other" 8123

"arrangements, made his" 9857

"arrangements to send Sister home, making" 1158

"arranges drive-aways, this outfit" 1054

"Arras" 5720

"arrest at the airport, following my" 6965

"arrest, expecting" 10249

"arrested" 6955

"arrested, he was" 5246

"arrested, houseboy who has been" 6177

"arrested, I was" 6949

"arrested, my father was" 2179

"arrested her attention" 8816

"arrested in Boston" 2040

"arresting Miss Rossiter as she rose to go" 3327

Arrests 2040, 2179, 5246, 6343, 6949, 6955, 6960, 6965, 7246, 10249

Arrival 35, 179, 198, 213, 217, 218, 221, 225, 232, 277, 288, 316, 320, 382, 759, 829, 884, 950, 991, 1047, 1055, 1126, 1135, 1250, 1257, 1450, 1488, 1504, 1529, 1534, 1561, 1564, 1565, 1567, 1572,

1576, 1580, 1582, 1584, 1591, 1593, 1594, 1595, 1596, 1605, 1606, 1608, 1609, 1612, 1613, 1614, 1618, 1620, 1624, 1625, 1629, 1631, 1632, 1638, 1639, 1640, 1641, 1642, 1645, 1647, 1648, 1649, 1651, 1652, 1653, 1655, 1657, 1659, 1660, 1667, 1671, 1672, 1673, 1674, 1675, 1678, 1680, 1685, 1688, 1691, 1692, 1694, 1698, 1701, 1703, 1704, 1706, 1707, 1708, 1709, 1711, 1715, 1716, 1721, 1722, 1723, 1725, 1726, 1727, 1729, 1730, 1732, 1736, 1738, 1742, 1748, 1751, 1757, 1759, 1764, 1766, 1767, 1768, 1775, 1776, 1778, 1779, 1784, 1786, 1908, 1976, 1991, 1996, 2012, 2688, 2842, 2903, 2948, 2964, 2967, 2981, 2987, 3257, 3303, 3692, 3695, 3782, 3913, 3959, 4002, 4102, 4141, 4253, 4305, 4560, 4562, 4565, 4584, 4587, 4602, 4616, 4636, 4637, 4655, 4658, 4659, 5034, 5098, 5156, 5370, 5543, 5817, 5837, 5924, 5927, 5935, 5974, 6048, 6096, 6113, 6118, 6129, 6137, 6144, 6149, 6164, 6187, 6319, 6330, 6334, 6345, 6403, 6514, 6550, 6664, 6775, 6949, 6971, 7082, 7110, 7204, 7250, 7265, 7269, 7283, 7416, 7459, 7606, 7610, 7622, 7623, 7637, 7638, 7644, 7675, 7816, 7853, 7895, 7966, 8010, 8066, 8068, 8073, 8078, 8084, 8097, 8099, 8103, 8110, 8119, 8124, 8128, 8152, 8171, 8180, 8192, 8204, 8213, 8245, 8268, 8281, 8312, 8507, 8524, 8549, 8651, 8685, 8692, 8770, 8781, 8793, 9092, 9094, 9098, 9111, 9142, 9161, 9184, 9226, 9328, 9335, 9337, 9343, 9480, 9486, 9514, 9528, 9532, 9537, 9539, 9541, 9571, 9582, 9589, 9592, 9595, 9598, 9605, 9606, 9617, 9638, 9645, 9657, 9750, 9794, 9814, 9835, 9855, 9867, 9875, 9876, 9878, 9894, 9901, 9905, 9907, 9915, 9917, 9921, 9924, 9937, 9939, 9944, 9960, 9973, 9982, 10080, 10082, 10084, 10337, 10511, 10594, 10810, 10956

"arrival, day of her" 950

"arrival, distinguished late" 4659

"arrival, messenger's" 6334

"arrival, this moment of" 1639

"arrival, upon his" 9606

"arrival at Quebec as Governor, soon after his" 7655

"arrival at the Wells" 7708

"arrival in Timbali" 6483

"arrival of a box of dry bones" 4592

"arrival of the Cincinnati-Lexington Greyhound" 5370

"arrival of the new Rector" 1488
"arrival of the waiter, expected the prompt" 654
"arrivals, three new" 1738
"arrive" 198
"arrive, first person to" 1766
"arrive, first to" 1976
"arrive, just beginning to" 6330
"arrive, wait for Leo Hermann to" 9956
"arrive at the house, I" 9937
"arrive early, intention is to" 9337
"arrive in Utopia, the first to" 7816
"arrive on the afternoon train, soon to" 10063
"arrive till evening, not to" 3913
"arrived" 6118, 6949
"arrived, before John Ward" 4002
"arrived, by the time I" 815
"arrived, Josie and her son" 3782
"arrived, month before they" 1693
"arrived, no sooner" 991
"arrived, no stranger has yet" 9094
"arrived, person has" 9901
"arrived, they" 1631
"arrived at Agatha McGee's house" 1727
"arrived at another spin of the wheel" 10980
"arrived at Bernice's apartment" 9924
"arrived at his hideaway" 5837
"arrived at Los Angeles International" 1725
"arrived at the corner of Mayton Park Avenue" 1629
"arrived at the county courthouse" 9226
"arrived at the King's camp in Normandy" 1779
"arrived by bicycle" 9335
"arrived by taxi at my home" 7459
"arrived by train" 7082
"arrived fifteen minutes before" 9873
"arrived fifteen minutes late" 9343
"arrived from America" 1613
"arrived from South Africa" 9638
"arrived home from work" 1701
"arrived home from work, when I" 6187
"arrived in England with his beloved Moura" 2012
"arrived in Jerusalem" 1722
"arrived in Korea in a snowstorm" 221
"arrived in London" 5543
"arrived in New Orleans, I" 1688
"arrived in our town" 1698
"arrived in the center of the ambulant Fair" 1250
"arrived in town with his pajamas" 1675
"arrived on earth, officially" 829
"arrived on her husband's estate" 1715
"arrived on the banks of the Ohio" 7637
"arrived on time" 9595
"arrived so unexpectedly" 8180
"arrived twenty years back, family had" 4011
"arrived uninvited from France" 4698
"arrived with my scholarship voucher, as it was when I" 7907
"arriving at a shell-shock hospital" 4616
"arriving at his cottage" 1591
"arriving at the edge of the Forest" 7230
"arriving at Vienna" 9524
"arriving in Paris" 4636
"arriving in Pickett, within one hour of" 35
"arriving in Venice" 1126
"arriving to pick up Eddie" 1660
"arrogance" 9928
"arrogance of a young untried eagle" 8918
"arrogance of his wisdom" 10759
"arrogantly, whose mass that then returned" 5943
"Arrondissement, the Sixteenth" 5179
"arrow, his ankle received an" 9844
"arrow, straight as an" 4303
"arrow, thick shaft of the yellow" 3001
"arrow piercing the royal-blue field" 3001
"arrows dart" 9364
"arroyo, considerable" 8794
"arroyo, upper edge of a deep" 7646
"arsenals of scenes and images" 1449
"arsenic in the glass, found" 3408
Art 484, 489, 492, 494, 495, 496, 497, 498, 503, 504, 505, 507, 508, 509, 510, 511, 512, 513, 514, 515, 517, 518, 962, 1314, 2731, 3258, 3744, 4365, 4671, 5465, 7823, 8546, 8570, 8941, 10049
"art" 5533
"art, critics of the" 8570
"Art, Pre-Columbian" 7074
"art, thought I would study" 517
"art, unique contribution to" 10049
"art, work of" 10
"art galleries, in one of those modern" 8027
"art gallery" 6474, 10867
"Art Gallery, Rede" 489
"art nouveau, painter of" 5659
"art student" 6568
"arteries and nerves of the man next to you" 3363
Arthur 2075, 2901, 4020, 8762, 9849
Arthur, General Chester 8694
Arthur, Little 8464
"artichoke" 10899
"artichoke, Jerusalem" 10899
"artichoke, which we also call" 10899
"article printed in the *Examiner* about you and your husband" 6358
"articled pupil" 3326
"articles, variety of" 712
"articles for parish magazines" 5433
"articles of daily use, small" 1045
"articulation, mute" 879
Artie 3754
"artifact, large uncouth" 8941
"Artificial Intelligence" 7788
"artificially hot days" 10597
"artisans, fellow" 6450
"artist, some severe" 484
"artist, waiting for the" 10107
"artist, worthy" 6213
"artist in the system" 506
"artist of Goss's stature" 500
"artistes, contract" 4007
Artists 484, 485, 486, 488, 491, 494, 495, 497, 498, 499, 500, 501, 502, 503, 506, 508, 509, 510, 511, 512, 514, 518, 3258, 4703, 5465, 5659, 6196, 6416, 6884, 8242, 10107, 10867
"artists" 499, 8485
"artists and craftsmen of the late eighteenth century" 5440
"Artists in most useful Knowledge" 10464
"artists say, as you" 7982
Artner, Fidis 8360
"arts" 499
"Arts Quad" 3283
"Arundel" 8079
"Arundel, our town of" 1374
"Arundel, town of" 9694
Asa 5974
"ascended the marble steps that led to it" 1293
"ascended the stone steps" 4286
"ascended to the highest peak" 2628
"ascending a hillside" 994
"ascensions, dark" 5178
"ascent, speed of" 3300
"ascent progressed up the shaft" 3295
"ascents, sudden steep" 5572
"ascribed by common consent to Edward VI" 7886
"ascribed by history to the Duke of Somerset" 7886
Asel 321
Ash, Peter 8634
"ash, fair young" 4303
"ash, reduced it and his memories to" 6584
"ashamed, proud or" 5542

"ashamed of, something great or small to be" 5580
"ashamed of his celery" 3975
"ashamed of now" 6149
"ashamed to admit" 3308
"ashamed to be seen discarding, like a prune stone he was" 5453
Ashburner 1702
Ashenden, R. 1590
"Ashenden Oakshott" 7254
"Ashersham market-place" 1027
"ashes, cooled and sodden" 5163
"ashes, his mother's" 2422
"ashes came today, Randy's" 2457
"ashes seaward, sweep the" 7680
Ashley 7157
Ashley, John Barrington 3407
"ashore, circumstances in which I came" 817
"ashore, ready to be taken" 7919
"ashore on liberty" 3997
Ashton, Rob 242
"Asia" 6109
"Asia, body of" 1405
"Asia, Central" 7950
"Asia, Russian" 2257
"Asia, Southeast" 2577
"Asia was left in darkness" 2202
"Asian alpine sunshine" 247
"Asian faces" 10446
"Asiatic style, good old" 9515
"asides, some" 5518
"ask, if I might make so bold as to" 9866
"ask, you will probably" 5495
"ask each other how we are doing" 9926
"ask Jimmy, we'll" 7209
"ask me, don't" 9827
"ask me why, never" 7199
"ask myself, I quietly" 9976
"ask no one else, they would" 705
"ask you once more, I will" 7201
"Askatevar" 10720
"asked, I'm often" 5767
"asked, that is all you" 9047
"asked, these people always" 7208
"asked by her daughter Hilda" 717
"asked for stationery as he always did" 4274
"asked for the third time" 1795
"asked Frensic why he took snuff" 6043
"asked her, like she always" 4437
"asked her the whole of what" 4437
"asked himself the same question" 4572
"asked himself what had brought him back here" 1633
"asked his way to the governor's house" 7195
"asked me in a voice eager with malice" 7518
"asked me to repeat my name" 8027

"asked me to stay at Pullinstown" 3998
"asked what was on her mind" 7600
"asking, Charlotte was" 2100
"asking for your uncle" 9903
"asking him about electronic music" 8555
"asking me to come for lunch" 3840
"asking myself exactly what it was" 9435
"asking them how they did" 1493
"asking to be married" 5774
"asking you again to marry me" 5737
"asks herself" 2483
"asleep" 8465
"asleep, before she falls" 4900
"asleep, fallen" 10265
"asleep, fast" 9739, 10390
"asleep, fell" 6024
"asleep, had fallen" 3516, 6299, 8454
"asleep, half" 5187, 8480
"asleep, Little Arthur is" 8464
"asleep, she's still" 10232
"asleep, still" 3681
"asleep, Thankful is" 848
"asleep, while you were still" 1656
"asleep, who's" 8462
"asleep beside her, half" 3025
"asleep beside him" 3955
"asleep for more than a few hours, could not have been" 10183
"asleep in bed, sound" 10135
"asleep in her high wind-rocked moon-haunted bed" 2776
"asleep in his bed" 2801
"asleep in his ruff" 6904
"asleep in the saddle" 8458
"asleep on his chicken-wire bed" 8653
"asleep one moment, sound" 10220
"asleep or awake—what difference?" 8459
"asleep or not, never knew nowadays whether he was" 8457
"asleep sitting up" 3620
"asleep than awake, more" 3842
"asleep when he heard the telephone ringing" 1102
"asleep when it began" 2810
Aspasia 2079
"aspect, its dreariest" 1368
"aspect of the world that dwarfed all others" 7924
"Aspen Colorado" 1396
"Aspen in Tyrol, village of" 1396
"Aspen sisters" 2960
"aspens" 7667
"asphalt, coarse" 7471
"asphalt, not as even as" 10027
"asphalt of R Street, seamed old" 7220
"asphalt reels by him" 10429
"asphalt springy like turf" 1280

"Asphaltites, Lake" 10329
"aspiration, bemused" 5430
"aspirations, in all its" 5558
"Asprey's" 4123
Asrael 7504
"ass" 9626
"ass, real smart-" 3932
"ass is better, when an" 433
"ass light in the saddle" 7629
"Assabenbeduc, Mount" 9136
"assassinate the Tsar" 10837
"assassination, Gandhi's" 3439
"assassination, Kennedy's" 2815
"assassination happens in their sleep" 6205
Assassinations 2028, 2815, 6332
Assassins 6180
"assault, its violent" 10699
"assault him, he knows will" 3478
"assaults upon the beach, long powerful frothing blue-green" 7939
"assemblage of stores and saloons, straggling" 1365
"assembled at the Island" 3601
"assembled in the parlor" 3987
"Assembly, General" 6986
"assent to every suggestion" 9861
"assertion, angry" 10511
"asses, lost his" 7217
"assessed the possibility" 8692
"assets numerous and tangled" 10559
"assets of something like thirty billion dollars" 3738
"assiduity, indefatigable" 5557
"assignment, wait for the" 10049
"assistant, grey-jacketed" 8027
"assistant, I call myself personal" 6438
"assistant to Arno Borian" 6438
"assistants of the famous Torrigiani" 3084
"associates, among his" 1
"Association, National Industrial" 3738
"Association, Repeal" 5194
"assurance, sweet" 6361
Astaire, Fred 2115
"asterisks of waiting parents" 5096
"asters, late" 3806
"astonished" 2083, 9989
"astonished, never failed to be" 4775
"astonished dinner-guest" 5419
"astonished him like a blow" 10684
"astonishing" 5416
Astonishment 1914, 4775, 6529
"astonishment, certain quality of" 1219
"astonishment, incredulous" 1914
"astonishment in her voice" 6529
"astounded, I am" 1081
"astounded contemplation" 9409
"astrologer cupped his ears" 7030

"Astrologer enough to examine, I was never" 778
Astrology 3290, 3679, 7030
"astrology" 3290
"Astrology" 7879
"astronaut in space, like a weightless" 1690
"astronauts" 3402
"astronomical universe, this" 6001
Astronomy 2591, 8333
"astronomy, greatest advance in lunar" 539
"Asylum, Criminal Lunatic" 5399
"asylum, garden of the" 4941
"asylum, lunatic" 7149
"asylum, orphan" 1250
"asylum, private lunatic" 4225
Atalanta 5732
"Atalanta is getting too pronounced" 5732
"ate coal to see how it tasted" 6527
"ate dinner when and where they could" 3830
"ate meat Fridays" 8220
"ate roast beef and belched" 3396
"ate the fruit of the forbidden tree" 5064
Atha, Russell 5505
"Athabasca Landing" 4047
"Athené" 4577
"Athene, full-grown as" 794
"Athenian" 707
"Athenians" 4503
"Athenians, we" 4366
"Athens" 1034, 1471, 4503, 4982, 8894, 10486
"Athens, she entered" 8312
"Athens Hilton" 2995
"Athens Ohio" 10226
Athletes 10, 160, 342, 8918, 8919, 8923, 8925
"athletic" 349
"Athlone Castle, troopship" 8657
"athwart the furrows" 3640
"Atlanta" 214, 930, 3147, 9729
"Atlantic, dawn over the" 7935
"Atlantic, north" 9065
"Atlantic, North" 5030, 8062, 9247
"Atlantic, the" 1360
"Atlantic City" 1073
"Atlantic coast" 1640, 4030
"Atlantic liner, big" 4730
"Atlantic Ocean" 7186
"Atlantic [Ocean]" 7911
"atmosphere, a certain charm of" 3087
"atmosphere, gaseous film of the" 525
"atmosphere, gray smoke-laden" 1368
"atmosphere, Old World" 6249
"atmosphere almost solid with failure" 4319
"atmosphere in the sickroom" 190
"atmosphere of elegant simplicity"

3296
"atmosphere of their own, certain streets have an" 9124
"atmosphere reminiscent of Rosine's" 5584
"atmosphere than form, more" 1376
"atmosphere was sparky" 3132
"atmospheric depression" 10612
"Atoll, Addu" 2538
"atom, I am an" 9989
"atoms, hydrogen" 8333
"atoms of the eternal Energy" 785
"atrophied, functions and powers" 309
Atta, Kwame 8239
"attaché, naval" 6502
"attachments, discussing disastrous" 2596
"attack, take part in a bomb" 2006
Attacks 873, 957, 1735, 2006, 8807, 9848, 9852, 10157, 10505
"attained, what has not been" 5285
"attempt, this is the third" 9446
"attempt, would be a fruitless" 1292
"attempt to decipher what is written" 987
"attempt to put my thoughts down on paper" 9446
"attempts, half a dozen futile" 2549
"attempts the years make to erase or fade them" 7460
"attempts to control it, feeble" 5578
"attend her own son" 6610
"attend law school" 7955
"attendants, one of her" 6487
"attendants, valet parking" 1705
"attendants, white-jacketed" 9363
"attendants who surrounded him did not move" 7806
"Attention" 10005
"attention, arrested her" 8816
"attention, company stood at" 8645
"attention, divert public" 125
"attention, I didn't pay much" 1875
"attention, my full" 2450
"attention, nothing else demanded her" 8474
"attention, scrupulous" 7335
"attention, should engage everybody's" 7825
"attention, special" 8224
"attention arrested" 3997
"attic, cool in the" 6395
"attic, corner of the" 9366
"attic, in the" 4154
"attic, this is the" 7792
"attic bedroom" 10978
"attic room" 7782
"Attica" 1439
Attics 4154, 7792
"attics" 4481
"attire, wonderfully sluttish in" 3554
"attired in the extremity of correctness" 4309
"attitude gave an impression of ar-

rested flight" 4143
"attitudes are all defined" 3495
"attorney" 2732, 6423
"attorney, conveyancing" 6406
"attorney John Dalton Farrow" 7319
"attracted a little attention" 10336
"attracted by him, not" 1318
"attracted to danger" 5378
"attracting sea gulls" 8105
Attraction 1318, 1970, 5378, 5848, 5873, 7746, 10777
"attraction, absolute and most intricate" 5381
"attractive" 9509
"attractive, made it seem more" 1350
"attributed his IQ of 70 to sniffing gasoline and glue" 6170
Atwater 3048
"Aubière" 9133
"Auburn" 4014
Aubyn, Mrs. 696
Auclair, Euclide 7658
"auction, Paris" 1087
"auction off Missus Pimber's things" 1037
"auctioneer, Medallion the" 9209
"auctioneer at Haven's End" 6420
"auctioneer was waiting" 1775
Auctions 1037, 1087
Auctor, Bim 2061
"audience, brilliancy of the" 9376
"audience, faced their" 331
"audience, heads of the" 7779
"audience, outgoing" 5892
"audience, TV" 6478
"audience of 2,000 Soviet citizens" 6232
"audiences, many" 8968
Audiences 331, 630, 1317, 1532, 5810, 6234, 7779, 8286, 8864, 10460
"audiences seemed to focus on her" 6240
"audio fair" 7904
"auditorium" 4025
"auditorium, empty" 9387
"auditorium, unlit" 9389
"auditors, thronged with" 1292
Audrey 8174
Augie, Little 1269
"Augurs, College of" 7514
"augury, happy" 10646
"augury, without" 3627
August 152
"August" 159, 299, 485, 775, 938, 1100, 1172, 1312, 1415, 1562, 1569, 1603, 1787, 2152, 2158, 2280, 2330, 2343, 2472, 2560, 2675, 3601, 3667, 3737, 3770, 3806, 3987, 4055, 4096, 4176, 4269, 4372, 4377, 4407, 4420, 4431, 4439, 4918, 5208, 5310, 6178, 6225, 6550, 6587, 6939, 6949, 6964, 7076, 7186, 7301, 7309,

7323, 7479, 8054, 8079, 8093, 8322, 8398, 8439, 8832, 8893, 8929, 9571, 9740, 9973, 9989, 10053, 10510, 10991
"August, hot French" 3834
"August, late in" 2275
"August, latter part of" 4394
"August, preceding" 5570
"August, they said it was" 10625
"August day half of hot sun half of rain" 1090
"August dusk" 10425
"August night" 559, 4430
"August of 1850" 4415
"August Thursday" 2177
Augustus 459
"aunt, her" 4201
"aunt, his" 951, 2807
"aunt, marrying his" 10658
"aunt, my" 1257, 1643, 2870, 3840, 8143, 8741
"aunt, my father's" 6159
"aunt, my great-" 7415
"aunt, photograph of her" 6116
"aunt, the Baltic" 2025
"aunt, their" 10035
"aunt and uncle, my" 824
"aunt and uncle, our" 2573
"aunt who had brought her up from babyhood" 8716
Aunts 248, 951, 2312, 2019, 2411, 4225, 8143, 8741, 10658
"aunts, old" 5635
"auras, fragrant bluish" 7229
"Aureataland, Republic of" 6248
"aureoled with flaming hues of orange" 2188
Aurora 3043
"Aurora, the plantation is called" 3658
"Aurora on in to Lake Michigan" 3725
"AusCan Airways" 202
"Auschwitz" 9459
"auspicious week, it had been an" 9273
"Auster, small" 203
"austere antique civility" 2865
"austerity reflected his own lack of pretense" 7903
"Austfjord" 3661
"Austin Minimoke, my" 3006
"Australasian, the" 8051
"Australia" 1466, 4086, 5138, 6137, 10595
"Australia, girls in" 10848
"Australia, the deep south-west of Western" 105
"AUSTRALIAN ACTRESS IN NUDE ROMP" 6397
"Australian cable-car" 9626
"Australian Naval Dockyard" 4410
"Australian Navy, Royal" 10161
"Australian Security Intelligence Organization" 1758

"Australian Society of Creative Writers" 5429
"Australian tribe called the Barramatjara" 7545
"Austria" 10486
"authentic, terrifyingly" 3180
"author, daring" 5410
"author, decided to be a famous" 257
"author, during the life of their" 7948
"author, haberdasher and" 9989
"author, scarcely less meritorious" 6246
"author, sixteen characters in search of an" 7218
"author, the" 5503
"author ought to consider himself" 5385
"author's enemies" 5392
"authorities, German" 3464
"authorities, noisiest" 3377
"authority, considers herself something of an" 7078
"authority, constant presence of" 9389
"authority, lacking" 4438
"authority, military" 4616, 8709
"authority of a classic Chinese landscape" 5145
"authority on male shortcomings" 982
"authority over men, exercise of" 6976
Authors 257, 4463, 5385, 5410, 7218
Autobiography 695, 699, 700, 703, 711, 715, 717, 2550, 3545, 3679, 4490, 5399, 5590
"autobiography, my mother's" 5499
"autobiography, promised you an" 2550
"autobiography, singular" 5399
"autobiography, wrote the" 3545
"automobile" 9626
"automobile, imported closed" 1315
"automobile, receding" 1670
"automobiles, fell in love with" 5671
Autumn 310, 1558, 1696, 4581, 6220, 7327, 8408, 9667, 10146, 10567, 10573, 10591, 10592, 10613, 10633, 10720
"autumn" 1696
"autumn, at the end of" 9950
"autumn, day in" 2165
"autumn, early" 1849
"autumn, first taste of" 7327
"autumn, golden haze of" 6577
"autumn, great brown harvest-hand of" 10591
"autumn, in late" 5789
"autumn, in the last days of" 6115
"autumn, last" 1609
"Autumn, last moonphase of" 10720
"autumn, late" 7082, 8425

"autumn, late in the" 2944
"autumn, leaves of" 7854
"autumn, lift of" 9572
"autumn, must have been the" 9394
"autumn, sky of early" 8408
"autumn, winds of" 10146
"autumn afternoon" 331, 10338
"Autumn afternoon, dismal" 310
"autumn afternoon, early" 8405
"autumn again, it is the" 4581
"autumn air, the" 10435
"autumn dusk" 2119
"autumn is like both an end and a beginning" 5568
"autumn leaves" 4105, 6333
"autumn morning" 10592
"autumn nub of the year" 4204
"autumn of bad parties" 6767
"autumn of his twenty-first year" 10341
"autumn of 1941" 8666
"autumn of 1974, during the wet" 3541
"autumn of 1967" 4174
"autumn of that year, it must have been late" 5871
"autumn of the year 1974" 10633
"autumn Saturdays, several" 296
"autumn storms" 9089
"autumn woods" 10404
"autumnal afternoon" 9758
"Auvergne, Province of" 9133
"avalanche began in Russia" 7001
"avalanche of rock and boulder" 38
"avant-garde in New York" 77
"avant-garde of losing money" 77
"Ave, an" 1499
"avenge her father's blood" 4169
"Avenida Atlántica" 1762
"Avenue, Amsterdam" 3310
"Avenue, Brighton Beach" 6652
"avenue, broad sun-flecked" 3146
"Avenue, Broadview" 3191
"Avenue, Carter" 9373
"Avenue, Central" 962, 2327, 6271, 9407
"Avenue, Chowringhee" 4646
"Avenue, Claxton" 3259
"Avenue, Clifton" 3203
"Avenue, Commonwealth" 9875
"Avenue, Constitution" 3315
"avenue, distant reaches of the" 1115
"Avenue, Dresden" 3113
"Avenue, Eighth" 2896
"Avenue, Eleventh" 7862
"avenue, elm-tree" 3065
"avenue, evening" 10372
"Avenue, Fifth" 1233, 1295, 1767, 1967, 2864, 3148, 7756
"Avenue, First" 3170
"Avenue, Fitzjohn's" 1665
"avenue, four hundred miles of broad tree-lined" 9185
"Avenue, Gravesend" 6652
"Avenue, Greentree" 5352

"Avenue, Hamilton" 6368
"Avenue, Lexington" 6140
"Avenue, Longview" 5321
"Avenue, Madison" 2511
"Avenue, Mayton Park" 1629
"Avenue, Ninth" 3429, 6274
"Avenue, Palm" 3218
"Avenue, Park" 2073, 2846, 8779, 10432
"Avenue, Portage" 10392
"Avenue, Prairie" 8210
"Avenue, Ridgeway" 8583
"Avenue, Santa Clara" 968
"Avenue, Seventh" 1379, 3031, 4108, 9157, 10067, 10342
"Avenue, Shaftesbury" 2841
"Avenue, Telegraph" 9191
"Avenue, Texas" 4422
"Avenue, Third" 10438, 10750
"Avenue, Uhuru" 1040
"Avenue, Upper Greenwood" 5751
"Avenue, Vanderbilt" 7258
"Avenue, Western" 4149
"Avenue, Woodland" 3214
"avenue bordered by the darker blackness of the trees" 6030
"Avenue de Marigny" 3140
"Avenue Foch" 797
"Avenue Gabriel" 7770
"avenue glistened with that deep bluish tint" 7288
"avenue running from Lahore to Agra" 9185
"Avenue South, Seventh" 4099
"avenue that led to the house" 2951
"avenue to a loving comprehension of human nature" 9118
"avenues, flat and green semi-suburban" 1390
"avenues, one of Chicago's most fashionable" 1580
"Avenues, Seventh and Eighth" 10699
"Avenues A, B, C, and D" 6276
"average kind of guy" 4874
"average up with the mistakes of Providence" 6020
"aversion, singular" 5193
"aversion to being different" 9715
"avert his eyes" 6698
Avery, Tom 6743
Aviation 196, 202, 226, 228, 5779
"aviation, civil" 202
"aviation the hard way, I came into" 196
Aviators 2178
"aviators" 2178
"avidly stalking a dame" 2045
"Avignon" 487
"*Avignon*, freighter" 8147
"Avignon, medieval" 9248
"avocat, the" 9209
Avocations 847, 1149, 2034, 4090
"avoid an approaching column of American tanks and jeeps" 3416

Avoidance 1990, 3395, 3629, 7722
"avoided intimate dealings with the Chinese" 1053
"avoiding her" 7722
"Avon steamed" 4427
"Avonlea main road" 7652
"Avranches" 9589
"await the End of the World" 3338
"awaited her in the hall, gentleman" 9916
"awaited the end" 2363
"awaited the results of his sudden taking off" 2295
"awaiting a little stiffly perhaps" 6532
"awaiting the arrival" 4906
"awaiting the verdict" 2682
"awake, all night he had lain" 8504
"awake, already" 10491
"awake, are you" 8484
"awake, asleep or" 8459
"awake, Bianca shook me" 10194
"awake, coming instantly" 10183
"awake, deep breaths to keep herself" 8472
"awake, drifted" 10310
"awake, fully" 8819
"awake, half" 8483
"awake, he had been" 8480
"awake, I am" 10299
"awake, I lay" 8984
"awake, I was only half" 10003
"awake, instantly" 737
"awake, instantly wide" 10157
"awake, lay sharp" 3516
"awake, mildly" 8480
"awake, remain" 8501
"awake, she was" 10220
"awake, stirred Mary Hawley" 10174
"awake, when he came" 10178
"awake all night" 2549
"awake and restless, wide" 8487
"awake at night, lie" 8826
"awake at the first dim waver of light" 10273
"awake before Cynthia" 10169
"awake by the tree limbs, I had been kept" 8502
"awake early enough, if he is" 995
"awake enough, wide" 1132
"awake in the dark bedroom" 8498
"awake in the night's stillest hour" 8491
"awake now" 2782
"awake since five" 8505
"awake sitting up, comes" 10300
"awake to hear, never" 8774
"awake to the violent scent of roses" 10315
"awake without effort" 10195
"awaken, I am the first person in the house to" 10233
"awaken sleepers, feared to" 7712
"awaken to the chatter of gulls"

10277
"awakened" 10229, 10294
"awakened, she was" 10265
"awakened by a ringing of the outer bell" 10113
"awakened by water birds" 10232
"awakened Cassie Steele" 10307
"awakened from a dream about his daughter" 2773
"awakened from medieval obscurity" 1464
"awakened her" 2784, 10276
"awakened him" 10170
"awakened him, loud and sentimental song" 10147
"awakened in the near dark" 10149
"awakened rudely" 670
"awakening, on" 10196
"awakening clutch on life, within reach of the" 10995
"awakening from sleep, at the moment of" 9432
"awakening power to the riddled morning" 8813
"awakening she had ever had, like no" 10154
Awards 1950, 8242
"aware, he had already become" 5262
"aware, our readers are doubtless" 696
"aware, she is perfectly well" 110
"aware, was suddenly" 8765
"aware of a summons" 10128
"aware of it, not very many people were" 838
"aware of it at the time, he was not" 3412
"aware of its contents, became" 1920
"aware of sounds" 5619
"aware of the weather, you are" 10628
"awareness, human" 9008
"awareness, sluggish early morning" 10216
"awareness of other times and places" 4495
"awash in clay" 2808
"awash with a sense of history and continuity" 2681
"awe" 6529
"awful, something" 2782
"Awful Alley" 988
"awful forms, exhibiting" 5125
"awfulness of America" 286
"awkward" 3311
"awkward position" 5238
"awkward time, at a very" 2451
"awkwardness, least amount of" 8962
"awning, striped red and white" 9215
"awoke, all life" 8438
"awoke, Grass Woman" 10140

"awoke, he" 10153, 10183
"awoke, she" 10252
"awoke, when I" 3701, 10727
"awoke, when Martha" 10125
"awoke, when she" 8015
"awoke, young sailor" 10278
"awoke a few minutes ahead of time" 10241
"awoke at dawn" 10968
"awoke at the first break of day" 9739
"awoke each morning" 10249
"awoke from a dream of an ancient wood" 2754
"awoke from a restless sleep" 10248
"awoke he was cold" 10141
"awoke him, telephone extension" 2785
"awoke in his apartment" 7013
"awoke in some confusion" 2762
"awoke in the darkened room" 6598
"awoke in the middle of the night" 9104
"awoke in the shadowy bedroom" 10176
"awoke much too early for her night before" 10126
"awoke one morning" 10110
"awoke slowly at daybreak" 10230
"awoke this day" 10155
"awoke to a familiar clutch of pain" 6593
"awoke to clear cognizance of the world and itself" 4496
"awoke to herself lying between coarse sheets" 10121
"awoke to the dappled light" 5329
"awoke to the sound of planes" 10222
"awoke with a start" 10127, 10215
"awoke with the sun, child" 10212
"awoken, that which has" 10184
"awoken in the small hours" 10274
Awsten, Master 3700
"ax, American" 271
"axe was needed for the forest" 6100
Axel 5864
Axiochus of Miletus 3935
Ayasko 5188
Ayres, Honeydew 6901
Ayres, Kenneth 6901
"Ayrshire" 3275
"azaleas are in bloom" 2377
"azaleas sodden in rain" 3314
"azaleas were dying" 3803
"Azania, Emperor of" 7801
"Azores" 8118
"Aztecan, simpler than the" 7502

Baal 467
"Baas, we call no man" 4347
Bab 7949
Babakov 4922
"Babbington Heights" 9366

Babe Ruth 3621
Babette 4142
Babies 813, 832, 1893, 2081, 2086, 2919, 3099, 3566, 3593, 3867, 3888, 5872, 6026, 6519, 6520, 6527, 6542, 6702, 6723, 6743, 6823, 6826, 6944, 7058, 7064, 7067, 7083, 7090, 7096, 7100, 7106, 8115, 8224, 10298, 10395
"babies, do with these" 551
"babies, I imagine them as" 6826
"babies, new" 556
"babies, raise their" 4876
"babies come from, where do" 552
"babies didn't come from an exchange of spinach during a kiss" 7981
"babies ugly, thought all" 554
Baby 4840, 7600
"baby, as a" 6743
"baby, big bald" 7096
"baby, cry from the" 8115
"baby, dead" 1893
"baby, go to Texas with the" 6944
"baby, her" 6542, 9530
"baby, here is this" 2086
"baby, I never heard such a" 540
"baby, I was an extremely interesting" 553
"baby, many a way to mark a" 558
"baby, once a tiny" 6823
"baby, squalling newborn" 7067
"baby, the" 547, 9958, 10298
"baby, week-old" 10395
"baby, when I was the fish" 5872
"baby arrived, the" 559
"baby bawled" 3566
"baby born named Ida" 7058
"baby boy even closer to her body, pulled the" 557
"baby carriages, husband-propelled" 1013
"baby closer to her breast, pulled the" 3593
"baby clutched in her arms" 10395
"baby crying" 2081
"baby crying in my arms" 2086
"baby daughter, old Queen's" 541
"baby face" 4210
"baby fat" 4210
"baby girl" 542, 7090
"baby girl, end of that" 541
"baby had come" 8224
"baby of the family" 8222
"baby shouted, the" 555
"baby sucking his mother's milk" 6823
"baby turned up, acted mad every time a new" 543
"baby was a most remarkable child, her" 6527
"baby was born" 7100
"baby was two months old" 560
"baby who was forty-four" 547

"baby who weighed in at just under nine pounds" 7096
"baby who would grow up to look into the eyes of the King" 7106
"baby with a meatless bone in his mouth" 550
"baby with bowlegs" 546
"baby without being married, have a" 7083
"baby-talk" 8843
"baby-weddings of the Middle Ages" 10642
"babyhood" 4756
"babyhood, brought her up from" 8716
"Babylon" 2636, 6752, 9709
"Babylon or Rome, seemed like some" 3275
"Babylon the mighty city" 10476
"babywear department" 7099
Bach 1746, 9300
"bachelor, confirmed" 5765
"bachelor, old" 5884
"bachelor again, happily set up as a" 8636
"bachelor apartments" 5784
"bachelor officers' quarters" 9920
"bachelor owner of Mauley Hall" 5984
"bachelor who never did leave home" 5947
"Bachelor of the Arts of Oxford University" 7801
Bachelors 5765, 5884, 5928, 5947, 8636
"bachelors, great city of" 5928
"Bach's 'Sleepers Awake'" 9300
"Bach's Saint Matthew Passion" 1746
"back, broad green-sweatered" 2940
"back, I am" 1690
"back, I shan't be" 1646
"back, Kate's warm" 10251
"back, Parlabane is" 1708
"back and forth" 9646, 10693
"Back Country" 8592
"back from the war" 8581
"back in Ambrosia" 9429
"back now, she was" 1776
"back seat, in the" 6323
"backboard bolted to it" 8913
"backbone of England, knobbly" 6060
"backed a long-priced winner" 1101
"backed by woods" 3184
"backed out of the room" 1697
"backfiring of a motorcycle" 10203
"background, black" 8388
"background, explore your" 4542
"background, this is the" 3360
"background of kitchen, against a" 964
"backpack, bulging" 4203
"backpack, carrying my" 10415
"backpack rising behind her head"

4203
"backs, bowed and humped" 6084
"Backs, the" 5631
"backs, their slanting" 5460
"backside, bare" 6391
"backslidings" 274
"backstretch, along the" 246
"backstroke, flimsy" 9729
"backward in sentiment" 5889
"backwater of Angel Street, distinguished" 2964
"backyard, from out here in the" 6160
"backyard, her" 9964
"backyard, his" 9964
"backyard of his house" 968
Bacon, Bruce 5594
"bacon, piles of" 7575
"bacon for breakfast" 4283
"bad, because he was" 9309
"bad, good and" 1342
"bad, good or" 638
"bad, he'd done something" 7566
"bad, it is too" 721
"bad, not half" 6506
"bad, poems are equally" 5471
"*bad*, she was" 1967
"bad, The Orphan was" 9309
"'bad' and 'good'" 6635
"bad and good, there be" 978
"bad as some, not as" 3185
"bad crossing, clearly going to be a" 47
Bad Czech, The 4523
"bad enough" 7291
"bad from a medical point of view" 3990
"bad humor, in a thoroughly" 3307
"bad news" 6323
"bad plays" 9379
"bad they turn out, however" 6823
"bad thing, become a" 1259
"bad things happened to people who went in there" 7791
"bad time" 3391
"Bad Time" 5540
"bad time, it was a" 66
"bad world" 5698
"bade them come" 7813
"Baden" 569
"badge for himself, bigger" 9702
Badger, William 6166
"badger appeared from nowhere" 6319
Badgery, Herbert 4827
"badly, the day started" 2170
Baer, Lonnie 1725
"baffled" 1226
"baffled Carlsen, what" 683
"baffling" 4811
"bag, about the" 7493
"bag, ancient brown" 1496
"bag, beaded" 2846
"bag, Brother Sebastian's" 9609
"bag, her Gladstone" 9878

"bag, her heavy" 6102
"bag, his black" 2351
"bag, his kit" 8692
"bag, in Lou's" 2893
"bag, large canvas" 7505
"bag, mind her" 9550
"bag, my leather" 9617
"bag, saddle" 7361
"bag, small fat" 3848
"bag, small white CVS" 1748
"bag ladies" 10852
"bag of gold" 4560
"bag of money" 3737
"bag of treasures between her feet" 9656
Bagarag, Shibli 8040
"Bagdad, an hour out of" 9358
Bagese 1264
"baggage at all, no" 9653
Bagnolo 3084
"bags, trundling her" 8312
"bags, two battered brown leather" 1604
"bags, two leather-strapped" 9631
Bagthorpes, the 5105
"*Bahía de Santa Maria*" 10451
Baidoo, Beni 8379
Bailey 2766
Bailey, Mr. 6652
Baines, Constance 3357
Baines, Sophia 3357
Baird, Dr. 1516
"bait, live" 4073
"bait, rabbit's foot for" 4691
"bait, scholar" 10886
"baitfish, work the" 439
"baked a chocolate cake" 860
Baker 10954
Baker, Belle 6652
Baker, Boniface 9101
Baker, Colonel 4275
Baker, Judson 1061
Baker, Kathy 2065
Baker, Mr. 8060
"Bakersfield California" 3630
"bakery products" 921
"baking, smells of" 8540
"balance, lost his" 34
"balance, most precarious point of" 6260
"balance, recovers her" 475
"balance, stable symbiotic" 9755
"balanced in the scale of mental power" 4533
"balanced on the hard cushion of an antique chair" 8370
"balancing on the bars of the fire escape" 483
Balaram 991
"balconies, jutting" 8252
"balcony, balustraded" 3199
"balcony, carved" 8342
"balcony of the Paradise Motel" 8473
"balcony's corner where he lay"

5627
"bald, growing slightly" 6427
"bald head" 5984
"bald Jeeter, we lost the" 3604
Balderson, Dick 928
Baldness 73, 4291
Baldo, Don Hipólito 473
Balducci, Mr. 10081
Baldwin, Graeme 5512
Baldwin, Mr. 1761
Baldwin, Mrs. Mark 8356
Baldwin, Old True 2950
Bale, Eddy 4709
Bale, Richard 8067
Baley, Elijah 3305, 4416
Baley, Lije 8268
Balfour 10064
Balfour, David 3737
Baliol, Mrs. Bethune 9513
"Balisand, wooded shore of" 8067
Balkan 10352
"ball, black two-finger" 8918
"ball, formal" 2118
"ball, giving a" 6779
"ball, have a" 6776
"ball, kicking a" 311
"ball, like a grotesque grey" 1895
"ball, playing" 2638
"ball, there floats a golden" 5645
"ball, there was a" 6757
"ball he found at the hospital" 302
"ball in her belly, the bouncing" 7091
"ball of mirrors spinning on its axis" 2118
"ball that really sailed, I hit a" 8932
"ballad quoted by her a moment before" 5507
"ballads, book of" 915
Ballard, Will 7250
"ball-bearing one" 5682
Ballet 2105, 2113
"ballet, decided to go to the" 2113
"ballet, something like a scene in a" 2105
"ballet, water" 9729
"ballet in Paris, the least amusing" 8299
Ballew, Nunnely 7350
Balloon, Mickey 981
"balloon, the captive" 10538
"balloon of a head" 2859
"Balloon Section" 8695
"balloonist, the" 9940
Ballou, Lin 7625
"ballplayer, I was quite a" 8928
"ballroom" 1651
"Ballroom, Grand" 4005
"ballroom, McGrath's" 4004
"ballroom was filling fast" 4004
Balls 302, 311, 313, 2118, 6779, 8918
"balls, backhand snags of ground" 160
"balls, come from out his" 7990
"balls, in the" 4689

"balls, knock-knock of wooden" 6761

"balls against coconuts" 6761

"Bally C" 684

"Ballybrophy, change at" 9655

"Balmoral" 1179

"balmy sunshine" 2264

Balterghen, Mr. Joseph 9764

Balthus, Jacob 2806

"Baltic aunt" 2025

"Baltic capital" 6465

"Baltimore" 1442, 3184, 5528, 7248

Balue, Cardinal 7139

"balustrade, steel" 7683

"balustrade, went flat into a" 733

"balustraded balcony" 3199

"bamboo pen, split" 5511

"Bamfylde Bridge Halt" 9586

Banana Mac 1840

"bananas" 5033, 7533, 8277

"bananas, eat" 328

"bananas and stew, squashed" 852

"Banbury Feed and General Supply Pty. Ltd." 2961

"band, beat the" 10061

"band, distant blare of a" 6761

"band, Dream of Pines Colored High School" 6228

"Band, Heron River" 6219

"band, now distant" 8739

"band, thirty were in the" 6179

"band, wandering fluid" 433

"band, white blues" 4336

"band in scarlet uniforms" 6225

"band of illogical men and women" 6155

"band playing" 6222

"band plays a tinselly Hawaiian tune" 6216

"band that hit the Loman farm before daybreak" 6179

"band-aids" 1067

"bandanna, green" 4168

"Bandidos" 2052

"bandit, little black" 2014

"bandleader" 7727

"band'll be along" 2102

Bandon, Harry 4980

Bands 2102, 2106, 4336, 6216, 6219, 6222, 6225, 6228, 7027, 8739

"bands of spectral birds" 745

"bandstand, second row of deck chairs in the" 5810

"bandstand, the" 8606

"Bandusium, fountain of" 9738

"bane of her existence" 951

Banford 4724

"bang and crash and scrape" 8829

"bang and rattle, its" 3295

"bang, end it all with a" 9300

"bang, there was a little" 2406

"bang of a door, sharp" 8769

"bang the clock" 10251

"banged into the sheriff's office" 6184

"banged the front door" 5093

"banging down the phone" 1132

"banging her silly" 8024

"Bangkok" 1832

"Bangkok, as hot as" 4381

"Bangor" 7457

"bangs, corn-silk" 4297

"bania, victualling" 6998

"banished to Siberia" 7184

"banishing to a desert island" 7802

"banjo, learning to drop-thumb on the" 6239

"banjo, playing a" 8767

"bank, along the high" 10400

"bank, came out of the" 3740

"Bank, Chemical" 8320

"Bank, City of London (Paris branch)" 1654

"Bank, Fairmont National" 10921

"bank, his father's" 3253

"bank, inner" 7671

"Bank, Nautilus" 6928

"Bank, South" 9175

"bank blew up" 882

"bank of the big river" 7189

"bank of the Grand Canal" 5140

"bank of the stream, along the" 9742

"banker, a" 7367

"banker, pauper and" 2303

"banker, rich" 3569

"banker, wealthy Zagreb" 10562

Bankers 3569, 10562

"bankruptcy, moral" 2023

Banks 882, 3740, 3742, 3745, 3758

"banks" 309, 3752

"banks, distrusted" 3758

"banks, its green" 7649

"banks, pleasant" 5125

"banks, steep green" 3899

"banks, sunny" 3808

"banks of the River of Time" 2638

"banks slippery as grease" 4690

"Banner, The" 6498

"banner in defeat" 2973

"banners of the Covenant, unspotted" 7500

Bannister, Claud 6238

Bannister, Ray 1858

"banquets, Georgian state-" 5943

"bantam-like in his character" 4470

Bantry, Mrs. 2757

"banyan tree, under a" 7030

Bao Dai 3371

"baptise illegitimate infants" 1493

Baptism 1218

"baptism in blood" 10497

"Baptist Chapel" 1518

"baptized a Christian" 7518

"baptized in blood" 1218

"Bar, Beachcomber" 1003

"bar, beachside" 5847

"Bar, Blue Note" 4323

"bar, broad leadwood" 4337

"bar, club car's" 9363

"bar, I met her in a" 5868

"bar, in a" 4325

"bar, mopping off the" 5907

"bar, no reality in the" 4320

"Bar, Revenue" 7620

"Bar, Saloon" 4312

"bar, seldom he was seen in the" 4317

"bar, shiny surface of the" 2888

"bar, sitting in the" 2919

"bar, standing at the end of the long" 4318

"bar, warm Burke House" 1548

"Bar, Wonder" 7395

"bar counter" 5334

"Bar final examinations" 5202

"Bar Harbor" 9734

"bar in a speakeasy" 4310

"bar in the desert" 2615

"bar of the Nelson Arms" 6178

"bar of the officers' club" 4313

"bar of the Phoenicia Hotel" 5229

"bar of the Royal Hawaiian Hotel" 5859

"bar where that kind of thing was usually worn" 4331

Baraka 7950

"Baralong village" 1427

"Baranof" 7061

Barbara 7448

"barbaric yawp over the roofs" 281

"barbecue grill, lurking charcoal-soiled freewheeling easy-cook superchef" 1866

"barber shop, American" 1838

"barber to the Court of Persia" 8040

"barberry and bitter orange" 4152

Barbers 1838, 6405

"barbers of Ispahan, one of the most celebrated" 6405

"barbershop, the post" 8697

"barbershop chair" 7446

Barbille, M. Jean Jacques 3083

"Barcelona" 2341

"Barcelona, docks of" 6773

"Barchester" 1406, 1407

Barclay, Lois 6091

Barcroft, Major Malcolm 2320

"bard" 6454

Barden, Martha 8359

"bare, almost completely" 7781

"bare backside pressed up against my stomach, if I get a woman's" 6391

Baree 3358

Barefoot 3280

"barefoot" 7044

"barefoot, he moved" 10428

"barefoot was jumpy, going" 4404

"bare-legged" 246

"barely, but only" 1418

Barette, Jean Marie 1525

"barge, the" 8076
"barges, iron" 10257
"barges under brown sails" 9175
"barges which moored by the hotel café pontoon" 10257
Baring, William 3533
"baring the stage" 9141
"bark, coiling birch" 5548
"bark, mildewed" 9674
"bark and branches, wet" 8507
"bark of the graceful beech" 3894
"bark was a deep wine color" 9683
"barked at by sudden brick walls" 7279
"barked at the pigeons" 421
Barker, Professor Jacob 3333
"barking, could hear the" 10021
"barking, dogs were not" 9927
"Barking Dog Saves Family of Five" 7367
"barking in the night" 3706
"barking of a dog, sounded like the" 8803
"Barkington" 3552
"barmaids, pretty" 9113
"barn, creaking" 10740
"barn, Forrest Langley's" 10088
"barn, sagging" 7887
"barn, that" 512
"barn side" 3646
Barnabas 1573
Barnaby 4728
Barnack, Sebastian 969
Barnacle 4728
Barnacle, Betsy 540
"Barnard, graduated from" 5781
Barnes, Dr. 7891
Barnes, Lily 10698
Barnes, Solon 10651
"Barnet" 9896
"Barnett Long Island" 3159
"Barnoldswick" 1518
"barns, the" 3615
"barns advertising Mail Pouch" 5166
Barnstaple, Mr. 932
"barometer of his emotional nature" 901
"barometer with a little weather man and a little weather woman" 4197
Baron, Simon 8155
"Baron of Arlingford" 10641
"Baron Pelham, Fifth" 5984
"baroness, old" 79
"baronet, ninth" 10339
"baronet of that name, the eleventh" 3972
"barons, lumber" 4073
"baroque, 1980" 7778
"baroque German city" 4178
"barouche, brown" 2945
"barque, armed merchant" 8079
"barque, the" 8141
"barque that ran before it" 8054

"Barquentine" 8101
Barr, Mr. 10936
"barracks" 5920
"barracks, in the lee of the weathered" 8080
"barracks, low ramshackle" 8699
"barracks within the city" 10491
Barraclough 1225
"Barracloughs, the" 8688
"barrages" 9627
"Barramatjara, tribe called the" 7545
"barred by a broad green-sweatered back" 2940
"barrel, bait" 4693
"barrel, cracker" 10489
"barrel, like a" 7844
"barren" 4362
"barren, sometimes" 5125
"Barricades, the" 2232
"barricades of Paris, mounted the" 10837
"barrier, raise this extraordinary" 5138
"barrier lying athwart the bush-lands" 5138
"barrier of mountains, imponder-able" 5620
"barriers, yellow police" 7835
"barrister, tall middle-aged" 5208
"barrister wearing a wig and gown" 5208
"bar-room of the Darwish Hotel" 4333
Barry 1996
Bars 1759, 2615, 2888, 2919, 2935, 4310, 4312, 4317, 4318, 4320, 4323, 4325, 4327, 4331, 4333, 5847, 5859, 5868, 5907, 7395
"bars, ice for the" 2210
"bars, it was one of those" 4327
"bars surrounding her life" 10826
"bars with bushy tops, I was behind eighty-foot" 10372
"Barsetshire" 5743
"Barsetshire, East" 3123
Bart 2154
Bart, Françoise 3931
Bart, Hannah 7935
Bart, Miss Lily 8173
"bartender" 4324, 5571
"bartender, Charles the" 2896
"bartender slid the glass and the bottle in front of him" 2888
Bartenders 4324
Bartha, Miliana 6202
Bartlett, Miss 7755
Bartov, Motke 8275
Baruch 10249
Bascomb, Big Track 3312
Bascomb, Freddy 10322
Bascombe, Frank 4837
Bascombe, Hannah 5571
"base on Ross Island" 228
Baseball 160, 2179, 3378, 4546,

6184, 7837, 8907, 8915, 8918, 8919, 8923, 8926, 8928, 8929, 8932, 8933, 8934, 8936, 9932
"baseball, escaped into" 8936
"baseball, saw my first game of" 8926
"baseball, squeezing a" 6184
"baseball, wonderful game of" 8933
"baseball cap, imaginary" 302
"Baseball Club, Chicage Cubs" 4448
"baseball game, watching a" 8929
"Baseball League, National" 8934
"baseball players" 7837
"baseball season had just begun" 3378
"baseball team" 8907
"basement house" 4073
"basement of his own house" 2419
"basement shops" 1477
"baserunner, like a scared" 2995
"basic training, first day of" 10297
"Basin, Erie" 6368
"basin, great open" 8691
"Basingstoke" 5289
"basked in the sunsets of the Hudson River School" 1012
"basket on her arm, her 'willer'" 10357
"basket over her arm, market" 9425
"basket she carried on her head" 6459
"basket tied with rosy ribbons" 2826
Basketball 8913
"basketball, playing" 8913
"basketball games, dates for" 10975
"baskets, make better" 6744
Baskett, Mrs. 6527
"Basque Country Spaniard" 5664
"bass, pushing his zippered" 6223
"bass, river" 8734
"bass, the deep" 8086
Bassington, Francesca 3821
Basso, Robert 5200
Bastable, Adela 148
Bastable, Oswald 5477
"bastard, snow blowing around like a" 1153
"Bastard, the" 207
"bastard, the" 3519
"bastard, would never have declared him a" 6542
"bastard, you are a ruthless" 4993
"bastard child" 4705
Bastards 4993, 6542
"bastards, smug" 2527
"bastinado, receive a hundred and eight strokes of the" 7188
Basu, Sir Nitin 3875
Bat 4835
"bat, like a huge" 8114
Batchelor, Claude 1626, 9724
Batchelor, Miss 6446
Bat-David, Devorah 5549

"bath, lay in her" 563
"bath, lay in the" 574
"bath, liked her" 562
"bath, sat in his" 565
"bath, she had taken a long" 564
"bath, taking a" 568
"bath, took a" 572
"Bath, town of" 9758
"bath, Turkish" 4504
"bath, when I was in my" 571
"bath of grey water, steamer sat in a" 8109
"bath salts, using plenty of" 564
"bathed in gold light" 2225
"bathed in pearly light" 2228
"bathers in Baden" 569
Bathing 6388, 9437
"bathing suit" 2757
"bathing suit, striped" 4206
"bathing suits and smiles" 8092
"bathroom, downstairs" 20
"bathroom, his" 7477
"bathroom, made his way to the" 8486
"bathroom, postage-stamp" 2079
"bathroom door" 8238
"bathroom in a sleazy motel" 6783
"bathroom lock, praying for a" 7439
"bathroom tiles" 5333
"bathroom wallpaper" 5376
"baths, converted swimming" 9252
"baths, in the public" 7485
"Baths of WILDBAD" 3417
"bath-tub, sat in the" 567
"bathtub, stunted" 3167
"bathyscaphe sent to probe its depths" 7328
"Batoro" 1833
"bats and balls, get out their" 8933
"battalion motor pool" 8684
"battalion of infantry filing into his pasture" 8648
"battalions, British" 8699
Batte, Miss Priscilla 3270
"battened down" 8101
"Battery, Manhattan" 7322
"batting against Bob Feller" 8934
"battle, dying" 786
"battle, eve of the" 3863
"battle, globe's greatest" 7196
"battle of Gettysburg" 4468
"Battle of *Gillycranky*" 10465
"battle of Hastings" 6518, 8347
"Battle of Newport" 713
"Battle of Rhode Island" 713
"battle of Singapore" 10507
"Battle of the Sabine Pass" 7741
"battle the upstream waters of the Mattagash River" 6155
"battle was being fought, the last great" 10513
"battle with the Me 109s" 8668
"battle with the Sioux" 6621
"battle with the three-hundred-

pound man" 4623
"battlements, ancient" 1178
"battlements, towers and" 5590
Battles 786, 2026, 4468, 4623, 6518, 6683, 7196, 8650, 8656, 8668, 9842, 10477, 10505, 10507, 10513, 10534
"battles in the park" 10534
"Bavaria" 2019
"Bavarian barometer" 4197
Bavistock, Rose 4769
"bawling of the thirsty trail herd, the uneasy" 2215
Baxter, Alfred 10275
Baxter, Oliver 788
Baxter, William Sylvanus 9407
"Bay, Aberlady" 4587
"bay, bend of" 1175
"Bay, Camp's" 2006
"bay, city faced the" 1404
"Bay, Corpus Christi" 8691
"Bay, Delaware" 8064
"Bay, Dublin" 1173
"Bay, Ganado" 4643
"Bay, Goose" 4076
"bay, great" 480, 1421
"Bay, Hirado" 1851
"Bay, Hudson" 4071
"Bay, Jamaica" 4092, 7946
"Bay, Leathercombe" 3110
"Bay, Lyme" 8136, 10724
"Bay, Monterey" 9751
"bay, out of the" 8163
"Bay, Penobscot" 8835
"Bay, Redcliffe" 2982
"bay, reigned up his" 7636
"Bay, Repulse" 10816
"Bay, San Diego" 4060
"Bay, San Francisco" 4887
"Bay, Sitka" 1052
"bay, stopped his" 7646
"bay, the" 4091
"bay, ultramarine" 8169
"bay, water of the" 9811
"bay, whitecaps of the" 4417
"bay at the angle, in a" 4051
"Bay Colony" 6135
"bay of Algiers" 8072
"Bay of Biscay" 853
"bay of Haifa, blue" 8133
"bay on the west" 7937
"Bay St. Louis Mississippi" 1481
Bayard 10157
Baylor 230
"bayonets of the Highlanders" 10509
"bayou, steaming like a Cajun" 9083
"Bayou Teche" 4036
Bays 1404, 7937, 8133
"bay's black bottom" 7926
"Bayswater" 4644
"Bayview, people of" 10852
"Bazaar, Scholarship" 8997
Bazalgette, Mr. 10771
BB 3782

"BBC" 4008
"be, asked me what I wanted to" 4208
"be, but it was not to" 4613
"be, what's it going to" 2473
"Be My Baby" 8320
"be on, let us" 5408
"be something that you are not, when you are trying to" 5228
"be you, I don't want to" 4362
"beach, assaults upon the" 7939
"beach, came along the" 10810
"beach, curled up on the" 1895
"beach, curving" 7915
"beach, deserted" 5495
"beach, down the curving" 10700
"beach, flat" 4096
"beach, get to the" 1762
"beach, green rubbery" 4688
"Beach, Hendrawna" 8146
"beach, high-pebbled" 7916
"Beach, Howard" 3020, 4092
"beach, knitting upon the" 10818
"beach, mile or two of misty" 7911
"Beach, Neptune" 7295
"Beach, North" 2906
"beach, on the" 598
"beach, sandy" 7930
"beach, sea-" 6053
"beach, see the" 2730
"beach, slope of the" 7936
"beach, the" 4319
"beach, walking along the" 10422
"beach, white sand" 5158
"beach, yellow-gold" 980
"beach a week, stay at the" 9731
"beach at Ainahau" 10673
"beach at Brighton" 4181
"beach at Nice, as he lay on the" 5329
"beach beside a lake, little" 5177
"beach gave way to the dark mangroves" 5158
"beach just south of Ensenada" 1216
"beach my life" 8027
"beach of crushed stone, cream-coloured" 3582
"beach of Hiva Oa, on the white" 6933
"beach towel, her" 10810
"beach was a relatively obscure one" 9174
"beach was not usually so deserted" 9725
Beaches 598, 980, 1762, 1895, 2730, 2769, 3582, 4064, 4181, 5174, 6390, 6933, 7915, 7916, 7936, 9174, 9725, 10421, 10700, 10810, 10818
"beaches, his native" 2242
"beaches, outlying" 9616
"beaches, ratty" 9181
"beaches, speeding to the" 9616
"beaches, stretch the ocean" 4064
"beaches have a yellow tint" 5174

"beacon, shifting" 3483
"Beacon Hill" 6678
"beacon set up by smugglers" 3671
"beads, crystal" 3521
"beads, first see the" 2856
"beads, short strand of coral-colored pop" 6399
"beads . . . were missing" 2060
"beak, bird-of-prey's" 474
"beak, glint of a" 1812
"beak, hawk's" 5571
"beak, on account of his" 4470
Beaker, Dudley 3282
Beale, Miss Muriel 10216
"beamed pleasantly upon Lord Tilbury" 5311
Beamish, Beau 7708
Beamish, Howard 6493
"beams, old wooden" 6856
"beams, those" 10778
Bean 9049
Bean, Bunker 241
"bean, clipping each word like a" 3832
"beano always ends with the photograph" 6870
"beans, butter" 3856, 3973
"beans, doesn't know" 4322
"beans, platter of" 3557
"bear, became a" 1264
"bear, bought the" 8230
"bear, more than you can" 69
"bear children, age to" 7103
"bear cub, black" 407
"bear hug, I give you a warm" 9613
"bear in the penny arcade game, I felt like the" 3323
"bear it no longer, able to" 1743
"bear on things, you have to bring yourself to" 8293
"bear was huge" 466
"beard, dark yellow" 365
"beard, dirty cotton-white" 1524
"beard, long white" 5903
"beard, red-gold" 8106
"beard, short fair" 5895
"beard, streaked" 365
"beard from the Colonel's face, burned the" 877
"bearded Anarchist" 876
"bearded faces" 336
"beardless" 5938
"bearer of bad news" 2419
"bearing an infinitesimal portion of brain" 4963
"bearing down on the town limits" 3604
"bearing on its bosom" 10704
"bearing on the matter, any important" 8860
"bearings of the island" 5012
Bears 404, 407, 466, 8230
"bear-like body" 8383
Bearse, Mr. Gabriel 4340
"beast, great wolf-" 3381

"beast, huge dead" 5148
"Beast, The" 5295
"beast changes to a woman" 10877
"beast or bird" 10774
"beastly hot was an understatement" 4418
Beasts 3381, 10877
"beasts, like great seaworthy" 8169
"beasts, like massive" 6087
"beat, emphasize the" 6231
"beat, part of his" 8520
"beat death aside" 8027
"beat Galileo at marbles" 326
"beat it, we could meet it and" 10710
"beat me and lock you up in your bedroom" 4244
"beat the band" 10061
"beat the tattoo of a thousand hooves" 8776
"beat up the Mexican crew leader" 1321
"beat urgent as love" 2106
"beaten at school" 57
"Beatification of Frederich Loebus" 7548
"beating lights" 2997
"beating of breasts" 5740
"beating out a message, the taxi's tires are" 6016
"beating out of Leghorn Harbour" 8069
"beating with a thousand cat-o'-nine-tails, like a giant" 8593
Beatrice 1935, 5830
"beats with awe and fear" 7084
Beauchamp, Lucas 2022
Beauchamp, Nevil 8642
"Beaufort, district of" 4030
"Beaulieu, great bell of" 648
"beauties, its natural" 4031
"beauties of such a fine warm and crystal-clear September day" 2147
"beautiful, every city should be so" 1470
"beautiful, few visitors think it" 8941
"beautiful, girl who was very" 4160
"beautiful, had she seen anything so" 9383
"beautiful, how" 4163
"beautiful, it was not" 9221
"beautiful, it's" 2844
"beautiful, Lucy was" 10828
"beautiful, most" 6908
"beautiful, not" 10793
"beautiful, she had once been" 10815, 10854
"beautiful, she was" 408
"beautiful, she was so" 10897
"Beautiful, so" 10897
"beautiful, very" 8027
"beautiful, women who were no less" 10796
"beautiful as American women, just

as" 10848
"beautiful beautiful" 6364
"beautiful Countess of Cressett" 927
"beautiful evening" 2206, 5040
"beautiful hills and valleys" 3893
"beautiful in your honour, made themselves" 2117
"beautiful June day, it was going to be a" 2157
"beautiful Matilda Fitzwater" 10641
"beautiful Miss Gunnings, the three" 3965
"beautiful or not beautiful, was she" 10778
"beautiful person, the in-no-way" 10133
"beautiful portrait" 6884
"beautiful than she'd expected, more" 8115
"beautiful they are, how" 3664
"beautiful things" 1084
"beautiful to eat, it is too" 773
"beautiful virgin" 10786
"beautiful virgin, a most" 6515
"beautiful Wilma Filmer" 2756
"beautiful women, more or less" 4309
"beautifully, so goddamned" 6931
"beautifully shaped" 6073
Beauty 636, 1260, 1368, 1470, 1981, 2117, 2147, 2206, 2844, 3130, 3251, 3477, 3965, 4041, 4160, 4163, 4240, 5156, 5617, 5640, 5916, 6364, 6674, 6869, 6908, 8741, 9383, 9568, 10368, 10414, 10759, 10771, 10776, 10778, 10788, 10795, 10813, 10815, 10817, 10828, 10848, 10854, 10882, 10884, 10897
"beauty" 1368, 4456
"beauty, acknowledged" 4339
"beauty, begin with" 636
"beauty, English" 10788
"beauty, her" 10781
"beauty, image of eternal" 9657
"beauty, military" 7056
"beauty, most exquisite and rare" 455
"beauty, she is a tall dark" 10817
"beauty, so piercing in their" 10414
"beauty, that kind of" 10776
"beauty, time and bad conditions do not favor" 10815
"beauty, well known for" 10795
"beauty and distinction, lady of" 10771
"beauty he had dreamed" 5916
"beauty is not in the eye of the beholder" 6869
"beauty of his mature life" 10341
"beauty of its architecture" 10368
"beauty of our earth" 3477
"beauty of the place, extraordinary summer" 3130
"beauty of the scene, grave" 5617
"beauty spots, great many" 10817

"beauty to be incarnated" 6088
"beauty to recommend them, had but little of" 3972
"beauty was particularly esteemed" 4240
Beaver, Mamie 4551
Beaver, Mrs. 17
"beaver, yielded up its" 9744
Beavers, Wesley 2973
Bebb, Leo 2358, 10013
"became, what Nadia eventually" 9293
"became man and wife" 10661
Becca 7074
Bech, Henry 5468, 5503
Beck, Leslie 9986
Becker 8749
Becker, David 2416
Becker, Joe 2936
Becker, Reverend 1516
"beckoned urgently" 4918
Beckwith, Dr. 6012
Becky 2677
"become nothing, allow themselves to" 6843
"become of him, what's to" 477
"become what I am, made me" 1276
"bed, alone in" 2002, 10237
"bed, approaches my" 8006
"bed, canopied" 7056
"bed, caught in" 7012
"bed, chicken-wire" 8653
"bed, could not buy another" 7035
"bed, creaking" 5624
"bed, creaking four-poster" 7305
"bed, disordered" 8583
"bed, eight-spring iron" 7324
"bed, empty" 4469
"bed, ended up in" 8012
"bed, go to" 4407
"bed, gone to" 10919
"bed, got out of" 10214
"bed, great curtained" 8483
"bed, headboard of a" 5986
"bed, her" 2463
"bed, her parents' big" 6687
"bed, high old" 673
"bed, high wind-rocked moon-haunted" 2776
"bed, his" 8384
"bed, his daughter's" 6707
"bed, huge canopied" 5623
"bed, I had just gone to" 1095
"bed, I was thrown out of" 10227
"bed, in" 8030
"bed, in a strange" 10259
"bed, in her" 3841
"bed, in the" 8476
"bed, in their enormous" 1706
"bed, iron" 7753
"bed, king-size" 6687
"bed, large double" 10223
"bed, little hotel" 5929
"bed, lying in" 6391, 8421

"bed, my" 10228
"bed, narrow gimbal-mounted sea" 5628
"bed, narrow walnut" 2352
"bed, old four-poster" 6386
"bed, on this" 4657
"bed, one evening in" 5746
"bed, oversized brass" 10188
"bed, preparing for" 5238
"bed, rickety wall-" 2758
"bed, sat in" 5459
"bed, sat up in" 10246
"bed, smoking in" 5960
"bed, staggered out of" 8486
"bed, swung out of" 8487
"bed, their parents'" 8231
"bed, Tommy's side of the" 8525
"bed, took to his" 4907
"bed, trundle" 8483
"bed, tumbled" 10121
"bed, turning over in" 10128
"bed, when I went to" 9077
"bed early, had to go to" 8221
"bed early, used to go to" 4287
"bed in which his father had died" 6131
"bed late, when he has gone to" 10132
"bed placed against the wall" 7753
"bed she shared with her old sister" 1923
"bed spring creaked" 10137
"bed that had once belonged to his grandfather" 10188
"bed that hung suspended from the ceiling" 8491
"bed warmed down the middle" 10296
"bed was cold and silent" 2420
"bed was empty" 8601
"bed was the wrong side, either side of the" 10166
"bed with a woman for four years, hadn't been to" 7997
"bed with painted hangings, great" 3700
"bed with shower curtains, surrounded the" 8491
"bed with them, go to" 10790
"bedchamber, enters your" 4103
"bedchamber, whisper in the" 7949
"bedclothes, shifted the" 10159
"Beddiford Maine" 5534
Bedford, Malcolm 2310
"Bedford, camouflaged three-ton" 9791
"bedlam, it was built as a" 7149
"bedraggled creatures" 5704
"bedroom, corner of the attic that was my" 9366
"bedroom, dark" 1752, 8498
"bedroom, front" 808, 3094
"bedroom, her mother's" 7213
"bedroom, his" 325, 1573
"bedroom, in a back" 10189

"bedroom, in his" 9452
"bedroom, in my" 767
"bedroom, inside the" 7777
"bedroom, Mrs. Little's" 2756
"bedroom, my attic" 10978
"bedroom, shadowy" 10176
"bedroom, the" 8784
"bedroom, their new" 10305
"bedroom ceiling" 5338
"bedroom high up on Mount Carmel" 8133
"bedroom window" 9964
"bedrooms, eight or nine" 4639
"bedrooms, five" 3193
"bedrooms, their" 6296
Beds 161, 1923, 2002, 2420, 2776, 2891, 4276, 4657, 5628, 5929, 5986, 6687, 7324, 8006, 8384, 8421, 8476, 8483, 8653, 9437, 10119, 10166, 10259, 10296
"beds, two" 3217
"bedsheet, Daddy said it was a" 10860
"bedside, by the" 6519
"bedside, quarreling at his" 1841
"bedsit, I lived in a" 3213
"bed-sitter" 1557
"bedstead, a little basket" 6519
Bedtime 1095, 4287, 6543, 6675, 8221, 9417, 10919
"bedtime, long after his usual" 7217
Bedworth, Johnnie 852
Bee, Aunt 4465
"bee in his bonnet about liturgy" 6807
Bee Women 8554
"beech, the graceful" 3894
"beeches, oaks and" 7326
"beef, thick slice of fresh-killed perfectly roasted pinkish-brown" 3868
"beehive" 5121
Beeler, Dolf 1057
Beeme, Nora 7161
"been through, what I have" 5590
"beer, advertising" 4315
"beer, bottle of" 3848
"beer, crackers and cheese and" 6760
"beer, drink several pints of" 6570
"beer, eleven pints of" 2901
"beer, sent for the" 10921
"beer, swig of the" 2351
"beer, was having its" 2887
"beer and ale, yeasty odors of" 4335
"beer from a bottle, drinking" 2351
"beer nights" 6760
"beers, she had had three" 10320
"bees" 8531
"bees, honey" 864
"bees, tale about" 3747
"bees because of their energy" 6935
"bees in a hive" 6266
"beet, the" 3973

"beet is the most intense of vegetables" 9679
"beetle, now I am a" 4895
"beetles, pattern of erratic" 5627
"beetles, the tiniest of" 4895
"beets, long before they planted" 7273
Beever, Mrs. 6286
"Beever and Bream" 6286
"before Pim with Pim after Pim" 708
"beg, how to" 7044
"began, how it" 596
"began, however it" 600
"began, I suppose it all" 595, 2674
"began, it all" 586, 6384
"began, so it" 801
"began, the day it" 604
"began, the night it all" 3971
"began, the whole thing" 1517
"began, where it all" 9178
"began as such an ordinary day" 2167
"began at the waterfall" 7689
"began badly, it" 4173
"began by visiting Arlington Cemetery" 9621
"began deceptively" 3627
"began for them" 582
"began her return journey" 1581
"began in a corridor of the Park View Hotel" 2616
"began innocently enough, it all" 7994
"began it 'NW'" 4279
"began long before I died, all this" 627
"began much like other days" 2146
"began no differently from any other" 1893
"began oddly, it" 600
"began on the night we thought all was ended" 3766
"began one day, it all" 905
"began one day in May, it" 850
"began one New Year's Eve" 2037
"began quickly, the case" 589
"began so quietly" 615
"began that afternoon" 614
"began that morning in 1948" 63
"began that summer, it" 7944
"began the second day of the Moon of Fattening" 586
"began timidly" 8872
"begetters of gossip" 7833
"begetters of song" 7833
"beggar almost naked and frozen with cold" 7539
"beggars, giving all his money to" 7039
"*beggars*, they called us" 4991
"beggars, white" 7036
"beggars for whom he had a singular aversion" 5193
"begged, if he" 8576

Begging 7036, 8576
"begging you to call him up" 1094
Beggs, Master Diggory 8056
"begin, about ready to" 583
"begin, about to" 6777
"begin, hard to know where to" 626
"begin, how did it all" 591
"begin, I might" 580
"begin, I must" 7554
"begin, I scarcely know where to" 581
"begin, let it" 9460
"begin, let us first" 3249
"begin, let's" 9033
"begin, no earthly reason to" 616
"begin, wasn't sure at all where to" 592
"begin, where to" 611
"begin, who knows how things" 619
"begin, you" 5538
"begin a new life at sixty" 5596
"begin again" 609
"begin at the beginning" 597, 608
"begin by describing it" 594
"begin by giving certain information about himself" 5426
"begin his novel, moment at which to" 5414
"begin this account" 2538
"begin this personal history" 2543
"begin to dream" 4890
"begin to look at our situation, we can" 76
"begin with, to" 616, 2288
"begin with a scrap of description" 5390
"begin with beauty" 636
"begin with the map, let's" 5721
"begin with who I am" 609
"begin yesterday, did not" 7719
"beginne, let us" 5514
"beginning, at the" 687, 7584, 7869
"beginning, before the" 514, 618, 2550
"beginning, dark of the" 2119
"beginning, end and" 3343
"beginning, end and a" 5568
"beginning, from the" 7123, 8994, 9014
"beginning, I was there at the" 610
"beginning, if this story has a" 633
"beginning, in its" 9747
"beginning, in the" 601, 612, 629, 1230, 1238, 2642, 2817, 3900, 4721, 5427, 6015, 7042, 7533, 7810, 9200, 9248, 10028
"beginning, it is afterall a way of" 4676
"beginning, it was about water in the" 7941
"beginning, its manifest" 8789
"beginning, life was just" 5577
"beginning, make a" 593
"beginning, my" 2347
"beginning, nearer the end than the" 5021
"beginning, one" 5424
"beginning, open as though there were a" 5479
"beginning, tell you at the" 1801
"beginning, there was no" 612
"beginning, they have a" 5694
"beginning, this is the" 5544
"beginning, this was my" 7067
"beginning at the beginning and going on to the end" 4500
"beginning House, there was a" 3176
"beginning is the Wall" 5544
"beginning my tale, I had thought of" 5420
"beginning occurred on a hot July day in the year 1960" 633
"beginning of his sixty-third decisive summer" 2988
"beginning of it" 157
"beginning of many stories" 6349
"beginning of Sarum, before the" 3400
"beginning of the end" 3349, 4089
"beginning of the end of the world" 3354
"beginning of the tale" 5408
"beginning or end, story has no" 8989
"beginning to the end" 5012
"beginning with them, how to make a" 590

Beginnings 63, 67, 157, 395, 688, 782, 799, 801, 850, 905, 1145, 1230, 1238, 1240, 1266, 1276, 1289, 1363, 1468, 1517, 1825, 1906, 2119, 2130, 2131, 2146, 2148, 2155, 2167, 2168, 2170, 2180, 2242, 2288, 2347, 2396, 2538, 2545, 2550, 2642, 2655, 2674, 2774, 2817, 3049, 3176, 3343, 3349, 3354, 3392, 3396, 3579, 3627, 3669, 3670, 3728, 3766, 3866, 3900, 3971, 4038, 4170, 4173, 4182, 4279, 4461, 4500, 4667, 4676, 5021, 5083, 5088, 5091, 5092, 5094, 5098, 5099, 5100, 5109, 5111, 5117, 5390, 5402, 5408, 5414, 5420, 5424, 5425, 5441, 5454, 5479, 5489, 5514, 5544, 5568, 5577, 5595, 5596, 5673, 5694, 5721, 5989, 6025, 6235, 6240, 6349, 6365, 6384, 6410, 6650, 6916, 7016, 7042, 7067, 7123, 7601, 7689, 7733, 7734, 7810, 7869, 7941, 7944, 7994, 8368, 8721, 8789, 8848, 8952, 8964, 8970, 8975, 8977, 8988, 8989, 8994, 8997, 9000, 9001, 9012, 9014, 9017, 9033, 9042, 9044, 9057, 9060, 9178, 9371, 9460, 9621, 10028, 10309, 10467, 10536, 10981, 10982, 10987, 10991

"beginnings, he liked the clear" 2242

"beginnings, her" 799

"beginnings, world of new" 5092

"beginnings are hard" 605

"beginnings of itself, first gray" 3029

"begins, it" 1825

"begins, so it" 623

"begins, the story" 9042

"begins, you know how it" 632

"begins and ends" 2130

"begins her memoirs with the question" 3679

"begins in darkness, tale" 2119

"begins in silence, year" 10981

"begins in the future" 9017

"begins on a June afternoon" 598

"begins some twenty years earlier" 6577

"begins way to the north in Catamount New Hampshire" 9027

"begins with, what it" 395

"begins with a man he never met" 5989

"begins with the *rigodón de honor*" 2118

"begot me, when they" 6604

"begotten on the giant of Cerne Abbas, I was" 805

"begrudge people their memories" 6787

"begs us to say" 696

"begun, never properly" 3339

"begun, when had it all" 617

"begun another fashion, you have" 603

"begun inauspiciously" 10982

"begun otherwise, could it have" 600

"behave, told me to" 6632

"behave not like the inseparable twins" 7164

"behaving herself" 207

"behaving that way" 640

Behavior 111, 207, 2020, 2038, 2578, 4919, 9280, 10529

"behavior, normal" 642

"behavior, strange criminal" 2578

"behavior of knaves and fools, erratic" 2997

"behavior slipped, my" 644

"behaviour became in some cases distinctly odd" 10529

"behaviour in trifles, eccentric" 6976

"beheaded, murdered and" 6185

"behemoths, line of hulking" 5982

"behemoths, they put the" 472

Behenna, Daniel 6894

"behest, my wife's" 5547

"behind, close" 8607

"behind, his small red" 813

"behind, pushed the door open with her" 10939

"behind, someone with a three-cornered" 8370

"behind her eyes" 10306

"behind him, still" 6582

"behind his back" 3329

"behind the locked door" 8728

Behn, Mr. Hugo 5387

"beholder, eye of the" 6869

"beholding, gravely" 6228

"Beijing" 7839

"Beijing Airport" 4599

"Being, rational" 6604

"being, simple sentient" 10913

"being from a happier world, some" 6212

"being of infinite goodness" 2642

"beings, two eternal" 2620

Bek 6450

Bekkus, Mr. 8870

Bel 1583

"Bel-Marduk" 2636

"belched" 3396

"belched and lifted free" 215

"Beldover" 8206

"beleaguered settlers" 6179

"Belfast" 8448, 9595

"Belfast, East" 6191

"belfries" 10590

"belfries purged their guilt in the twanging of holy bells" 9627

"belfry, curious little" 9206

"belfry, sits in the" 2937

"belfry not intended for any bell" 9206

"Belgian hearts, so dear to" 3119

"Belgium" 6253, 7264

Belief 2746, 5600, 8898, 9685

"belief, contrary to popular" 4243

"belief, it was the epoch of" 3377

"belief, powers of" 8964

Beliefs 117, 1247, 1711, 2308, 9447

"Beliers Priory" 3123, 7060

"believe, hard for others to" 9279

"believe, hard to" 2744

"believe, I can't" 9043

"believe, I no longer" 117

"believe, I would never" 2735

"believe, nobody will" 7635

"believe, they did not" 1236

"believe against the critical protests of my intelligence" 4343

"believe anything, never" 2743

"believe each other" 9685

"believe everything, don't" 2742

"believe her, do you" 8898

"believe him, didn't" 6340

"believe him, she is almost beginning to" 2746

"believe I'm doing this, I can't" 2750

"believe in, doesn't" 10834

"believe in God" 1516, 7542

"believe in God, I do not" 4789

"believe in God, make you" 5677

"believe in good surprises" 8194

"believe in the 'beautiful madness of war'" 10527

"believe it, can't quite" 9598

"believe it, couldn't" 2747

"believe it, I can never bring myself to" 2732

"believe it, I can scarcely" 9505

"believe it, I don't" 62, 2745

"*believe* it, I simply can't" 2748

"believe it, you won't" 2737

"believe it to look at me, maybe you wouldn't" 6902

"believe that they have a destiny" 3671

"believe they are far the best black people living on the whole 'Neck'" 7126

"believe this shit, I don't" 2749

"believed, all our lives we" 5600

"believed, he passionately" 5675

"believed, I have always" 5426

"believed, it was not generally" 4442

"believed, no one would have" 519

"believed he was safe" 1711

"believed it, I wonder if I" 10867

"believed it, I wouldn't have" 5783

"believed she would find a man" 4611

"believer, dedicated" 1178

"believer, like a wavering" 3465

"believer in middles, profound" 7177

"believes himself to be a hero in the making" 4471

"believes it, nobody" 5591

"believes only in horses" 2967

"believeth in me, he that" 3941

"believing I was an original, grounds for" 9447

"believing that he will come, without really" 10090

Belinda 5492

Belisarius 6110

Belknap, the Reverend Jeremy 356

Belknap, Troy 4270

Bell 2032

Bell, Clara 3360

"bell, Angelus" 650, 665

"bell, dismissal" 659

"bell, distant cathedral" 9467

"Bell Foundry, Kay's" 662

"bell, great church" 8812

"bell, rang the" 654, 656

"bell, ringing of the outer" 10113

"bell, searched for the" 9963

"bell, that old" 7239

"bell, there goes the" 657

"bell clanged" 658

"bell clanged somewhere" 669

"bell from far up on Cade's Ridge could be dimly heard" 664

"bell in the rusty tower of the courthouse" 663

"bell of Beaulieu, the great" 648
"bell of Cleeve Abbey, the great" 666
"bell of the North Liberty Second Presbyterian Church" 646
"bell rang" 4602, 9888
"bell rang, a single" 667
"bell rang, alarm" 10200
"bell rang, the nine o'clock" 672
"bell ringers" 661
"bell sounded, teleprinter's" 1118
"bell tinkled" 651
"bell tower" 8579
"bell upon Tunstall Moat House" 647
Bella 10323
"Bellagio" 3265
"Bellatrix" 534
"bell-boy" 7555
Belle 1105
Bellefleur, Gideon 1706
Bellefleur, Leah 1706
"Belles Lettres" 5530
Bellew, Chris 4721
Bellew, Christopher 4721
Bellew, Kit 4721
Bellew, Smoke 4721
"bellied down to drink" 4673
"bellies full of ice cream" 8210
"bellies were only half-filled with corn and flour gravy" 4610
"Bellingham Washington" 1787
"bellow, hearty" 660
"bellowed her name with such passion" 7739
"bellowing 'Decadent' at his contemporaries" 962
"bellows, the" 8810
Bells 1118, 2906, 5260, 9467, 9627, 9888, 9900, 9914, 10113, 10200
"bells, chiming on two" 660
"bells, church" 653, 673
"bells, clangour of" 652
"bells, new" 662
"bells, resounded" 652
"bells, sweet" 645
"bells, tape-recorded" 671
"bells, twanging of holy" 9627
"bells horns faint cheers" 5260
"bells in the skid row slums" 2906
"bells of Boston" 655
"bells of the little church" 670
"bells ring in four places" 668
"bells . . . rang out across the ripening fields" 653
"bells were ringing the Angelus" 649
"belly, came up from his" 7850
"belly, her brown" 7409
"belly, its centipede-brown" 7260
"belly, laying on my" 10106
"belly, slack flesh of her" 8183
"belly, the" 10817
"belly arched like a dome" 7084
"belly down in the meadow" 6879

"belly large enough for a grown man to sit on" 7082
"belly of a petrified whale" 9788
"belly respond, feel his" 4679
"belong to no age" 3382
"belonged anywhere, she had never felt that she" 1715
"belonged there, felt that she" 1715
"belonged to him, decided that I" 997
"belonged to someone else, as if it" 8506
"belonged to Thomas Jefferson" 371
"belongs to everybody and to all times at once" 1380
"beloved, dearly" 10672
"beloved, my best" 3413
"beloved Daisy, my" 3919
"beloved friend" 2310
"beloved Moura, his" 2012
Belshazzar 1512, 6752, 10476
"belt, golden" 10784
Beltane 7840
"belted upstairs" 6770
"Belting" 7677
"bemoaning the fact that nothing would ever improve" 2509
"bemused aspiration" 5430
Ben 542, 4436, 5075, 9347, 9835, 10080
"Benares, cantonments of" 8644
Benbow, Admiral 5012
"bench, plain wooden" 8280
"bench, stone" 8344
"bench by the duck pond was icy" 10095
"bench in the shade, only one" 8369
"bench of alabaster" 2644
"bench which . . . shone like gold" 8363
"benches, ornamental concrete" 7896
"benches, rotten garden" 9682
"benches where the weary might sit" 7896
"benchland" 8429
"bend, round the" 8799, 9300
"bend in the river" 7653
"bend of bay" 1175
Bender, Irv 8226
"bending as though craving for a further supply of materials" 1849
"beneath another, one" 1384
"beneath my intrepid exterior" 3698
"Benedictine monks" 7888
"Benedictine's manuscript" 10898
"benefice, in possession of a valuable" 6609
"beneficence, serene" 7648
"benefit, mainly for my own" 8996
"benefit, reaps more" 6884
Beneker, Mrs. 1511
"Bengal, East" 1385
"Bengal India" 7663
Benham, Aaron 3461

"Benjamites, land of the" 7217
Benjie 8571
Benn, Uncle 4665
Benna 6302
Bennet, Abigail 1860
Bennett, David 4858
Bennett, Hugh 7571
Bennett, Sergeant Timothy 8591
Benny 6652
Benny, Uncle 4687
Bensey, Lov 10347
Benson 10443
Benson, Nurse 4146
"bent down to find a clean collar" 2299
"bent down towards the second long drawer" 2299
"bent over a book" 4904
"bent that way, if I'd had a" 7520
Bentinck, Sam 9085
Bentley 6682
"Bentley" 6948
Benton 7882
Benton, Miss 8716
Benton, Tome 5215
"bequest of an elder brother" 4930
"bequests for Hebrew colleges void" 7505
"ber trees" 5704
"Berea" 1679
Bereavement 2385, 4225
"bereavement" 4225
"bereavement, shared" 2385
Berenice 6181
Berenson, Max 159
Beresford, Mr. and Mrs. 1978
"beret, his navy-blue" 6145
Berg, Alistair 5624
Berger, Gerry 5951
Beric 7715
"Berkeley" 5546
"Berkeley Square" 5279, 9161, 9764
"Berkshire" 3635
"Berkshire Hills, highest corner of the" 2258
"Berkshire Mass." 9515
"Berkshire sow" 1178
Berlin, Larry 2994
"Berlin" 1442, 2237, 7570, 9262, 10637
"Berlin Germany" 7714
Berliner, Ben 10671
Berman 8332
Berman, Sam 4436
"Bermuda" 9732
Bernard 148, 1938, 10381
Berners, Dr. 4281
Bernhardt, Dr. Josef 2518
Bernice 9924
Bernie 2351, 3344
Bernstein, Mannie 5456
Bernstein, Sir Emmanuel 5456
Bernstrom, Count Wolfgang von 3115
Beroviero, Angelo 9302

"berries, holly" 9681
"berries, virtually no" 9681
Berringer, Marshall 1139
Berry 6396
"berry a deep blue skinful of juice" 8517
Bert 2011, 6718
Berthold 9598
"berths and wharves, the crowded" 4410
Bertram, Sir Thomas 5727
"Berwick gentlemen" 3992
Besharat, Hadi 1958
"besiege her again, fruitlessly" 5397
"besieged the whole countryside" 2341
"besmirching one's own fine sense of honor" 4869
"bespectacled" 1048
Bessemer, Mr. 3815
Bessie 858
"best, see the" 3911
"best, the" 6338
"best, work out for the" 1234
"best at breakfast, such men are not at their" 2507
"best black people living on the whole 'Neck'" 7126
"best day" 2184
"best for both of us" 2681
"Best Friend, her" 982
"best man he ever knew" 2310
"best of all" 8527
"Best of Men" 4219
"best of times" 3377
"best place" 827
"best thing about my life up to here" 5591
"best time" 827
"best way, the" 7955
"bestowing, day of the" 4126
"bestowing such illustrious names on places" 1431
"bestseller was *Greed*, last season's" 2525
Bet 116
"bet I could" 5682
Betaut 1125
"Betelgeuse" 534
Beth 4530, 7482
Bethany 4297
"Bethany Massachusetts" 7082
Bethel 840
"Bethlehem" 4059
"Bethnal Green" 1557
Betrayal 7054
"betrayed its inner structure" 9467
"bets were off" 1778
Betsey, Aunt 4231
"better, could have done it all much" 12
"better, for want of anything" 2536
"better, then it got even" 7874
"better if you were to let me have a written account" 6953

"better in France" 9510
"better off in an opera than a novel" 5498
"better times" 1675
Betters, Mercy 6692
Betty 219, 1848
"between the sheets" 10119
Beverages 3817, 9356, 9953
Beveridge, Lady 45
Beverley 6151
"Beverly Hills" 4240, 5833, 7229
"Beverly Hills hotel" 5630
"Beverly Hills Neiman-Marcus" 9821
Bevis, Sir 3793
"bewildered eyes" 4496
Bewilderment 611, 1633, 4496, 4746, 4942, 9435, 10110, 10178
"beyond, purity of the" 6145
"beyond sight of the little croft" 7689
"beyond the back of beyond" 8027
"Beyond Narcissus" 5507
Bhengu, Sam 2391
Bianca 10194
"Biarritz" 10966
"bias, the satchel gave him a" 10905
"Bibighar Gardens" 5152
Bible 2622, 4780, 7359, 7546, 8735
"Bible" 2622
"Bible, front of the" 4437
"bible, manna is stuff in the" 7059
"Bible, passage from the" 8921
"Bible, reading his" 7359
"Bible, the" 10757
"Bible, two books in the" 4780
"Bible open at the Book of Revelation" 6960
"bibles, boy who sold" 2911
"Biblical texts freshly written" 7509
Bicep the Wrestler 6652
"bicker, might well" 6249
"bicycle" 9626
"bicycle, arrived by" 9335
"bicycle, I am riding the" 9600
"bicycle, I got on my" 6568
"bicycle, knocked her gently off her" 41
"bicycle, man on the" 5957
"bicycle, on his" 6353
"bicycle, rode his" 7608
"bicycle between the sexes, fence of" 977
"bicycle from the luggage compartment, take her" 10749
"bicycle pump, special" 6182
"bicycle swerved with a flourish" 1000
Bicycles 977, 1000, 3688, 5957, 7608, 9600
"bicycles, flung down their" 3688
"bicycles, their" 977
"bicycles taken under his care" 4069
Bicycling 41, 6353, 6568, 8520,

9436, 9600, 10754
"bid, no" 318
"bid for, thought I might make a" 9950
Biddle, Doris 7726
Biddy 10976
"Bideford, little white town of" 1336
"Biedermeier chair" 8383
Biersdorf, Mrs. 4707
"bifocal spectacles" 9314
"big, getting" 7759
Big Angus 7918
"big as a spaceship" 7990
"big at all, wasn't" 7147
"Big Ben" 9490
"Big Ben struck eleven" 8187
Big Dan 7237
"big enough for it to make sense" 7394
"big enough to see and remember" 7394
"big for her, they were too" 10831
"Big Freeze" 2443
"Big Girls" 10973
Big Grandfather 9949
Big Grandmother 9949
"big in the shoulders" 6403
"big one, pull off a" 2036
"Big Playground, there he was in" 7113
"big pricks" 346
"Big Ship" 10901
"big story" 6317
"Big Sur" 4067
"Big Sur woods" 2906
"Big Top" 9201
Bigfoot 5522
Bigger 10137
"biggest of his life" 6317
Biggs, E. Power 9300
Biggs, Eugene Talmadge 2874
"bike, motor-" 7628
"bike, old-fashioned" 9600
"bike, pedaled his" 8520
"bike race, six-day" 4702
"bike riders" 8813
Bikila, Abebe 8924
Bilara 4704
"Bildungsroman hero" 5837
Bilic, Ivo 10562
"bilious, morally" 6890
Bill 10350
Bill, Wild 4261
"bill, ten-dollar" 3748
"Billarooby" 1466
Billie 9336
"billings, credit card" 2664
"billowing" 7945
"billowing grass" 3095
"bills" 3736
"bills, hundred-dollar" 3755
Billy 2010, 2798, 2933, 3510, 5867
Billy, Uncle 10547
Billy The Hopper 9763
"bi-metallism" 3378

"bin, I'll fill your" 446
"binding, dull and distressed leather" 926
Bingay 10931
"binge, the worst sort of" 10234
"Binghamton's West Side" 5292
Bingle, Mr. Thomas S. 7756
"binoculars, carrying" 7823
"binoculars, equipped with" 8385
"binoculars, man with" 596
"binoculars, watching them through" 6225
Binstead, Stan 1991
"biochemists, fairly young" 1065
"biographer, his most recent" 2516
"biographer of St. Patrick" 4056
Biography 3545, 4636
"biography" 5533
"Biography, An Experiment in" 716
"biography, speaks of this story as a" 701
"biography, token" 704
"biography, write his" 702, 705
"biography from his earliest days" 4636
"biography of the novelist Edward Granville" 710
"biologists, molecular" 1065
Biology 5272, 6817, 10881
"bioscope, go to the" 1100
"birch" 4073
"birch, fir and" 3024
"birches, dwarfed white" 5154
"birches, swaying" 5329
"birches are dying, white" 9171
"Birchester" 1609
Bird, Elsdon 1893
Bird, William Wagner 2343
"bird, big menacing black" 772
"bird, cry of a" 5864
"bird, early" 7816
"bird, headless" 9499
"bird, I remember the first" 10290
"bird, like a great mother" 10824
"bird, like a little" 489
"bird, night" 766
"bird, the" 763
"bird, this" 773
"bird, young" 416
"bird cried out" 10211
"bird does not quit its cage with greater pleasure" 6556
"bird had died, the" 764
"bird hovering high above the Quantock hills" 9815
"bird in the garden, the first" 10209
"bird showed some uncertainty as to direction" 7514
"bird that had been disturbed" 733
"bird that would sing with him, found no" 8746
"bird watchers" 2178
"bird winging back to one of the islands" 766
"bird with her brood nestling under

her wings" 10824
"birdcage, Hitler and the" 9040
"birdlike, looked" 10832
Birds 186, 421, 442, 836, 1186, 1554, 1812, 2178, 2183, 2230, 2790, 3270, 4021, 4026, 4105, 4162, 4257, 4704, 4778, 5355, 5864, 6334, 6403, 6880, 7427, 7927, 8068, 8170, 8746, 8788, 9067, 9276, 9426, 9499, 9815, 10185, 10207, 10209, 10210, 10211, 10232, 10277, 10290, 10310, 10425, 10657
"birds, bands of spectral" 745
"birds, like two night-" 4135
"birds, loud with" 9276
"birds, publishers and" 10980
"birds, size of" 303
"birds, song among" 10587
"birds, ten twenty fifty brown" 9426
"birds, water" 10232
"birds, world full of" 836
"birds are aloft again" 774
"birds are not yet awake" 2183
"birds beginning" 2230
"birds bobbed like clothespins on the telephone line" 1554
"birds clustered on the pavement searching for God knows what" 745
"birds flew around" 744
"birds flew past the window" 9426
"birds returning in migration" 9426
"birds that never sleep" 3402
"birds were doing their night vocalizing" 6403
Birdsong, Frank 7490
Birdwhistle, Colonel 4739
Birdy 9942
"Birmingham" 1006, 1592
Birth 57, 337, 355, 358, 370, 447, 471, 543, 760, 958, 1228, 1359, 1421, 1531, 2360, 2408, 2427, 2428, 2631, 3358, 3382, 3655, 4055, 4354, 4360, 4527, 4543, 4547, 4742, 4859, 4865, 4871, 5183, 5193, 5269, 5583, 5598, 6089, 6313, 6520, 6551, 6601, 6618, 6621, 6631, 6646, 6647, 6650, 6673, 6685, 6723, 6726, 6730, 6732, 6749, 7056, 7059, 7063, 7073, 7075, 7079, 7080, 7090, 7096, 7103, 7105, 8021, 9703, 9706, 9711, 9715, 9717, 9719, 10531, 10822
"birth, accident of" 10822
"Birth, all at a" 7055
"birth, American by" 4762
"birth, at my" 6551
"birth, died giving" 807
"birth, disgraced by an illegitimate" 5780
"birth, gave" 7056
"birth, give" 8021, 10790
"birth, had given" 7096

"birth, I derive my" 356
"birth, island of his" 4547
"birth, it had not been an easy" 7075
"birth, it was a breech" 7102
"birth, less than herself in" 10791
"birth, my" 786, 6621
"birth, my place of" 817
"birth, nearly twelve months before her" 1706
"Birth, Painless" 7081
"birth, resisting his" 471
"birth, right of" 361
"birth, Sam Smith's" 6313
"Birth, some extraordinary Influence affected my" 778
"birth, women gave" 7057
"birth cost my mother an illness" 6621
"birth to a cat, wife had given" 7979
"birth to a son, gave" 561
"birth to Jacob, gave" 7079
"Birth to the ensuing Pages, gives" 10764
"birth took place" 7080
"birth was loud and troublesome, my" 7063
"birth was unpropitious" 358
"birthday, before her fourteenth" 4186
"birthday, Bethel's sixth" 840
"birthday, eve of his seventy-seventh" 6712
"birthday, fortieth" 3878
"birthday, fortnight after her thirty-second" 2153
"birthday, forty-fifth" 10188
"birthday, Groundhog Day was his" 4816
"birthday, happy" 845, 849, 852, 858
"birthday, her eighteenth" 869
"birthday, her fortieth" 2583
"birthday, her fourth" 851
"birthday, his forty-first" 867
"birthday, his seventieth" 847
"birthday, his sixtieth" 2678
"birthday, his sixty-fifth" 1525
"birthday, his thirtieth" 854
"birthday, hundredth" 8548
"birthday, it was Gerane's" 838
"birthday, it was her fortieth" 842
"birthday, it was his fourteenth" 837
"birthday, it was on his fourteenth" 898
"birthday, it's my brother Mack's" 868
"birthday, just past my sixteenth" 3275
"Birthday, Lincoln's" 9911
"birthday, morning after her" 4177
"birthday, morning of my hundredth" 846

"birthday, my" 844, 860, 862
"birthday, my eighty-first" 856
"birthday, my fifteenth" 841
"birthday, my fiftieth" 850
"birthday, my tenth" 859, 6123
"birthday, my thirteenth" 839
"birthday, ninth" 866
"birthday, on the morning of her" 836
"birthday, sick yesterday on my" 853
"birthday, signalized my" 863
"birthday, sixth" 870
"birthday, sixty-fifth" 864
"birthday, the only" 865
"birthday, thirteenth" 835
"birthday, today is my" 855
"birthday, twenty-first" 5806
"birthday, twenty-fourth" 843
"birthday, twenty-sixth" 135
"birthday, two months before my thirty-fifth" 5103
"birthday, your father's" 7491
"birthday had brought showers of blessing" 844
"birthday party" 861
"birthday present" 898
"birthday presents this year, no" 866
Birthdays 135, 898, 975, 2072, 2583, 2678, 4124, 4125, 4177, 5806, 6712, 7491, 8548, 9911
"birthing the baby" 7106
"birthplace, my" 6137
"birthplace, no recollection of my" 9715
"birthplaces" 7057
"birth-registration papers" 4859
"birthright, national" 7142
"biscuits" 8530
"bisected it" 8404
Bishop, Guy 6543
Bishop, Nina 10361
"bishop, absent" 3661
"Bishop, bloody funny" 1508
"bishop, if there was a" 1535
"Bishop, missionary" 1494
"bishop, the" 126
"Bishop, who was to be the new" 1487
"Bishop always shaved on holy days" 1503
"Bishop of Porthminster" 2307
"Bishop of Rochester, it was not the" 1522
"Bishop of Rome" 8848
"Bishop's garden" 3981
"Bishop's Ickenham" 7254
"Bishop's secretary" 1928
"bison, great woolly" 6084
"Bistritz" 9524
"bistro, quiet little" 6237
Biswas, Mr. Mohun 6435
"bit by bit" 7828
"bit each bird off at the knee" 770

"bitch, black" 21
"Bitch, The" 4876
"bitch, the" 6389
"bite, having a" 3889
"bite, last" 3852
"bites her lip" 8013
"Bithoor" 1930
"biting the polish off her nails" 1323
"bits, thousands of them there little flashing white" 4660
"bits and pieces, remember by" 7607
"bits and pieces of it" 8999
Bitsy 4123
"bitten by a snake" 633
"bitten off a big mouthful, he had recently" 242
"bitter, you mustn't get" 377
"bitter cold" 10125
"bitter disputation" 1823
"bitter heritage" 4445
"bitter hurt" 2953
"bitter orange, barberry and" 4152
"bitterly disappointed" 2584
"bitterness" 6017
"bitterness, enjoy their" 9674
"bitterness, tasted" 374
"bitterness in the air, cold" 375
"bitter-sweet, life is" 7372
Bivens, Presley 4817
"bivouac, word comes down the line to" 8651
"bizarre, his parents found this" 3538
"bizarre as was the name she bore" 4727
"bizarre lines of transport" 9792
"blab it" 7949
Black, Wendell 682
"black" 181
"black, always wore" 2862
"black, dressed in rusty ill-shaped" 2822
"black, glistening" 5910
"black, he does look" 5933
"black, it'd gone" 2269
"black, never really" 6376
"black, part" 369
"black, they're entirely in" 2855
"black, wearing" 3956
"black against the dying glow to the west" 8114
"black and bristling" 9670
"black and silent, fell suddenly" 2205
"black and white" 9009
"black as sackcloth, sun turned" 8419
"black background" 8388
"black bitch" 21
"black boy dressed in all he could borrow" 2973
"black certainly suited her very well" 4226
"black complexion, her luscious" 46

"black figures" 1764
"Black Friday" 815
"Black Hills" 4610
"Black Lace" 2111
"black lover, her" 2815
"black magic, species of" 3534
"black men, two" 3007
Black Michael 5082
"Black Monday" 8640
"black of night" 6376
"black of sky" 8420
"black people, the" 7126
"Black Rock" 9181
"Black Sea" 4147
"black Sonny, poor dear" 5355
"black student, the first" 5102
"Black Thread Center Connecticut" 4632
"black woman" 10815
"black women in particular" 10876
"blackberry patches" 6273
Blackbird, The 2935
"Black-Gowns, the" 2555
"Blackladies, gallery of" 487
Blackmail 7012
"blackmail" 7012
"blackman, like a" 8489
"Blackmoor" 10333
Blackmore, Terry 3599
"blackness, his" 6401
"blackness, native" 1356
"Blacknose Point" 1375
"blackout" 236
"blackout, the" 6770
Blacks 681, 5102, 8674
Blacksmith, Jimmie 5753
"blacksmith, my father was a" 6618
"blacksnake, coiled" 7025
"blacktop, serpentine two-lane" 9203
"blacktop that snaked its way through the Adirondacks" 9203
"blacktop was white" 8610
"Blackwell" 3044
Blackwood, Mary Katherine 337
"bladder, removal of a stone from his" 1519
"blade until it caught the sun, turned the" 10541
Blaine, Amory 4434
Blaine, Marcia 977
Blainey 59
Blair, Carter 7637
Blair, Mr. Adam 4338
Blair, Mrs. John McCandless 8204
Blair, Robert 4537
Blake 8256
Blake, Baldur 4703
"Blakemore" 10333
"Blakesburg" 1393
Blame 581, 5816, 6735, 7550, 7551, 7554, 7557, 7558, 7559, 7562, 7565
"blame, how she was to" 7565
"blame, lay down" 7562

"blame but herself, no one to" 7557
"blame is not important" 7558
"blame myself entirely, I do not" 5816
"blame upon a woman, lay the" 7554
"blameable" 7163
"blancmange, gargantuan mauve" 9229
Bland, Charley 4239
"blandness on his strong features, an unaccustomed" 1887
Blanford 6327
"blanker than all the hungry word-less pages" 514
"blanker than an eggshell" 514
"blanker than the blankest scroll" 514
"blanket, like a dirty worn-out" 8594
"blanket, soft green" 8337
"blanket over bent knees" 4660
"blanket that put the fire out, charred" 1217
"blankets, bundle of" 1738
"blankets, deep tunnel of the" 10293
"blankets, nest of" 10212
"Blankets and Pillows, my Good" 10545
Blankhard, Mr. 2967
"blast, chemical" 877
"blast, each successive" 10719
"blast burned the beard from the Colonel's face" 877
"blast finally came" 874
Blattberg, Mr. Aaron 7114
"blaze, pale" 9276
"blaze like a miniature range of snow-capped Sierras" 5144
"blaze of a cloudless Carolina summer" 1879
"blazed down from a sky of tur-quoise blue" 3126
"blazed the sun, brightly" 10700
"blazing furiously" 4002
"bleach, smell of" 10875
"Bleach Boys, The" 4336
"bleachers, under the" 6228
"bleak and desolate" 5159
"bleak as anyone else's" 3982
"bleak hour, softly" 4694
"Bleakridge" 1362, 2496
"bled and purged the boy" 2363
"bleed mysteriously, statue in the forum begins to" 8948
"bleeders, bleeding" 8661
"bleeding, head still" 3056
"bleeding Adolf, it was" 4803
"bleeding and dying" 8681
"bleeding bob" 8661
"bleeding father" 8661
"bleeding fathers" 8661
"bleeding money" 8661
"bleeding mother" 8661
"bleeding school" 8661

"bleeding week" 8661
"Blemish, a" 10466
"Blenheim, the magnificence of" 2088
"bless me Father" 1803, 1808, 1811
"bless o Lord thy gifts" 7526
"blessed, I have always felt" 9395
"'Blessed', may perhaps mean" 7950
"blessed to have had the chance to play Leah" 9395
"blessedly expectant" 3821
"blessing, a" 1179
"blessing, given his last" 4457
"blessing, showers of" 844
"blessing came to her when she was born, no" 7950
"blessing ever prayed for, any" 6243
"blessings of existence" 5555
Blettsworthys, the 3563
"blew against the chain-link rust-proof fence" 10721
"blew it, and you" 6027
"blew the fountain out" 1606
"blew up, when the bank" 882
"blighted heart" 2492
"blind, giving sight to the" 7538
"blind, had gone" 3701
"blind, I am" 4503
"blind, I'm so" 8253
"blind, nearly" 6834
"blind, the" 7155
"blind, Venetian" 8481
"blind date, long" 5254
"blind dummy" 9718
"blind Lord" 7607
"blind men looking on" 1831
"blind person, like a" 8364
"blind since birth" 5059
"blind to life's possibilities" 5880
"blind woman, young" 8004
"blinded him" 9849
Blindness 3701, 5059, 8741
"blinds, pulling up the" 2693
"blinds all closed and fastened" 7763
"blinds were down" 3257
"blinds which screened the win-dows" 1020
Blingham, Mr. 6426
"blink, big boards" 9364
"blink, on the" 2046
"blink of an eyelid lasts a thousand years" 7084
"blinked at the light" 10116
"blinked slowly" 10287
"blinking" 1041
"blinking, winking and" 3413
"blinking incessantly" 8316
"blinking out over the footlights" 9387
"blinks vaguely up at her husband" 8013
"blip on the radar screen, tiny" 227
"bliss, endured the double-edged"

5736
"bliss, haven of" 7346
"blissfully out of my mind, drunk" 9300
"blister, the bruised skin's" 10018
"blisterer in the taxi" 1830
"Blithedale" 5784
Blithers, Mr. 1822
"Blitz, the story of the" 5221
Blix 1924
Block 6652
"block, around the" 6469
"block, central" 7149
"block, bombed-out" 2811
"block, uncarved" 514
"block between Seventh and Eighth Avenues" 10699
"blocked for a spell the Pullman corridor" 5943
"blocked her" 1990
"blocks, granite" 9249
"blocks, huge faulted sandstone" 5169
"blocks, one of the mixed" 6271
"blocks, paving" 9144
"blocks rough cut like fish scales" 3131
"blonde, a" 5118
"blonde, Canadian" 5779
"blonde girl in a poor-boy sweater" 4192
Blood, Dr. 4739
Blood, Mrs. 4776
Blood 1218, 4825, 6649, 8189, 10526, 10939
"blood, avenge her father's" 4169
"blood, baptism in" 10497
"blood, baptized in" 1218
"blood, cool hasty" 756
"blood, ended in" 5874
"blood, hands were wringing wet with" 10939
"blood, he did not expect to see" 8189
"blood, looked like splashes of" 3798
"blood, lusty pioneer" 6814
"blood, moon red as" 8419
"blood, my" 4825
"blood, Saxon" 357
"blood, stains of old" 2463
"blood, stiffened with" 9851
"blood, yeasting up like sudden" 10018
"blood, yeomanry" 4432
"blood, young" 6943
"blood and breed, deal with the effects of" 9704
"blood and screams of the settlers" 7409
"blood and women and solitude" 9285
"blood burst, damn'd" 9849
"blood clots, cunt flushes out" 10881

"blood from her neck pattered to the stones" 4296

"blood in man's veins" 10980

"blood is finally spilled, son's" 6649

"blood is not the easiest medium with which to write" 5511

"blood is tamed now" 6814

"blood of her veins" 2799

"blood of soldiers was awash on deck" 4469

"blood spots on a Sunday shirt" 8934

"blood . . . stained the blue Ionian Sea" 4469

"blood still stained the great rivers of Europe" 10526

"blood thing, she said it was a" 4437

"blood weak" 8487

"blood-color of their name" 6085

"bloodhound, the big half-bred" 429

"bloods, young" 3965

"blood's flowed across this land like rivers" 4825

"Bloodsmoor" 6577

"blood-spattered scene" 10445

"bloodstained weevils" 6225

"bloody" 9411

"bloody altar, monstrous" 7813

"bloody bowels of woman" 9285

"bloody juju medicine stalls" 1064

Bloom, Dr. Liat 163

"bloom" 3799

"bloom, clusters of" 3652

"bloom, their first great" 3557

"bloom again, lilac was in" 3807

"bloom is gone from it" 7711

"bloomed, dome of St. Paul's" 10079

"bloomed in yellow flame" 3801

"Bloomingdale's" 8191

"Bloomsbury" 3326

"blossom everywhere, I smelt" 3800

"blossom of light" 4704

"blossoming hedge" 9670

"blossoms, lovely pink" 9683

"blossoms, rotting orangey-red" 9672

"blot upon a beautiful picture, like a" 3070

"blotter on the public writing-desk" 7509

"blotting out a log cabin, all but" 3090

Blount, Miss 9911

"blouse, black" 2658

"blouse, oh what a pretty" 10892

"blouse blown out behind her like a banner in defeat" 2973

"blouse of a young woman, unbuttoned" 2529

"blouses, billowing" 6868

"blow, in for a bit of a" 10729

"blow, some previous" 4712

"blow from west to east" 10744

"blow in the neck, giving him a great" 6182

"blow up, I saw a tractor tire" 3733

"blow you down too" 2337

"blowing, raining and" 1106

"blowing eastward from the Pacific" 10741

"blowing from the heart of the setting sun" 10701

"blowing gently, spring came" 10737

"blowing like a summer wind" 4610

"blowing like a wind" 1496

"blowing like the eddies that turn the autumn leaves" 6333

"blowing of a steam whistle, the faint and prolonged" 8765

"blowing too hard" 882

"blown about like blossoms" 9955

"blown away, trying not to be" 10685

"blown up the hot springs pools at the river" 6969

"blows, it" 10680

"blows upon the great hall-doors" 10113

Blue 6825, 10122

"blue, angel-" 5450

"blue, cornflower" 4140

"blue, dark" 6085

"blue, deep" 10774

"blue, flame-" 9228

"blue, Mr. Robert Pagebrook was" 2494

"blue, the sunlit" 4559

"blue as a bottle" 8429

"blue as a cornflower" 5147

"blue as veronica flowers" 2072

"blue chinned" 10933

Blue Dandy 246

Blue Eyes 339

"Blue Flame" 1078

"Blue Grass Ohio" 2702

"blue in the face" 6676

"blue jays" 10310

"blue jays that woke me up, the lousy" 10207

"blue jeans, trousers of" 954

"blue more deep" 5177

"Blue Note Bar" 4323

"blue on gold, transparent" 9218

"blue only a hint more solid than the sky" 6087

"Blue Ridge" 783

"blue with cold" 4871

"blue with white flowers" 10830

"blue yonder" 7467

Bluebeard 1656

"bluebell, European" 3804

"blue-eyed" 10788

"blueprint of a dream" 4701

Blue-Shirt 9053

"bluff, heave of the" 7316

"bluff, limestone" 6912

"bluff, steep" 5133

"bluff jutting abruptly up" 6912

"bluff overlooking the ocean" 7908

"bluff overlooking the Ohio" 2513

"bluffs, fat" 9140

"Bluffton, I'm in" 7898

Blum, Léon 6652

"blundering into my life" 5815

"blundering or swift" 5542

"blunders, grotesque architectural" 3237

"blurred about the consonants, a trifle" 8742

"blush for the lack in me" 6528

"blushes, confused with" 8299

"bluster and the taint, leaving merely the" 3604

"blustering loudly" 10704

"blustery morning" 10724

"BMW, ivory" 9826

Bo 6942

"boar, kilt a wyld" 857

"Board, Milk Marketing" 73

"board, off the high" 10

"board in the hall" 8302

"board rooms" 309

"board where bread is cut is worn down fine" 7575

"Board of Governors" 9701

"Board of Health, O" 1337

"Board of Trade" 4039

"boarded, Euphemia and I" 5313

"boarded a first-class compartment" 7268

"boarded a skiff" 10871

"boarded her that Saturday evening" 8116

"boarded the east-bound express" 1577

"boarded the train" 8676

"boarding, where they were" 7552

"boarding the ten A.M. flight to London" 1724

"boarding-house" 3171, 10768

"boarding-school" 6291, 7888

"boardwalk" 4652

"boars, wild" 5981

"boast, gentleman's proud" 8970

"boasted the market vendor" 773

"boasting's the vulgarest thing there is" 7127

"boat, canal" 8100

"boat, engine of a small pleasure" 10214

"boat, Father would give me a" 839

"boat, fisherman swings his" 8159

"boat, gun-" 928

"boat, her makeshift" 1824

"boat, House-" 2016

"boat, liberty" 8137

"boat, like an overturned fishing" 5039

"boat, little pedal" 8150

"boat, Mr. Hector Pecket had a" 8081

"boat, passage-" 9511
"boat, press" 8091
"boat, row-" 7913
"boat, Saguenay" 10030
"boat, shabbily comfortable fifty-foot" 8168
"boat, small" 1751
"boat, small naval" 5355
"boat, twelve hours by" 1465
"boat, will not come to the" 8143
"boat deck" 9603
"boat full of sleepy hung-over sailors" 8137
"boat of dirty and disreputable appearance" 8050
"boat ride, midnight" 6578
"boat round up towards the forest" 8167
"boat slips" 3431
"boat that wends its way with mail and passengers" 10716
"boat touched Rodney's Landing" 4560
"boat was static" 9534
"boat was there" 6942
"boathouse" 5050
Boats 472, 732, 839, 1009, 1052, 1479, 1751, 1824, 1883, 1998, 2016, 2285, 3694, 3709, 4161, 4190, 4482, 4560, 4688, 4693, 4924, 5050, 5355, 6155, 6428, 6578, 6942, 7676, 7913, 8050, 8052, 8053, 8065, 8067, 8076, 8081, 8091, 8092, 8094, 8095, 8096, 8099, 8100, 8110, 8111, 8119, 8126, 8128, 8133, 8134, 8143, 8144, 8145, 8148, 8149, 8150, 8156, 8158, 8159, 8160, 8163, 8164, 8167, 8168, 8213, 9511, 9601, 9996, 10030, 10594, 10716
"boats, little" 732
"boats, many little" 8094
"boats, noiseless black" 8252
"boats, pleasure" 8149
"boats, toylike" 8133
"boats, two fishing" 9460
"boats and rivers" 4190
"boats bobbing in the water" 8133
"boats had gone on ahead" 8095
"boats went out before it was light" 8148
"boatyard, Indian Cove" 3431
Bob 4211
"bob a bleeding week, you get twenty-eight bleeding" 8661
"bobbing into view" 1775
Bobby 305, 1214, 8235
"bobby-soxer, married a" 5768
Bodasingh, Mr. 5959
"Bodegraven, in the neighbourhood of" 7246
Bodenland, Joseph 10510
Bodies 1886, 1889, 1890, 8506, 9428, 10817
"bodies, inclined their" 3995

"bodies, their mere mortal" 1706
"bodies forward, threw their" 1632
"bodies in the street, many" 1886
"bodies of children, mangled" 29
"bodies of water, one of the world's most alluring" 4098
"bodies spinning in a threshing tangle" 9841
"bodies were discovered" 1891
"bodies were found" 1889
"Bodleian Library" 7772
"body" 10757
"body, a" 1888
"body, allowing the swirling water to surround her" 573
"body, closer to her" 557
"body, drag the" 2329
"body, energy impelling her" 10611
"body, heat of his extended" 10296
"body, her" 1250, 9295
"body, his broken" 3936
"body, his heavy square-built" 5620
"body, his lithe vigorous" 9317
"body, his long" 131
"body, his own" 9319
"body, his slender" 5952
"body, his thin vibrant" 9141
"body, his vast bear-like" 8383
"body, I say it was a" 1899
"body, I tossed my" 8506
"body, in her" 2449
"body, just with his" 2973
"body, Maria's" 2426
"body, metallic" 193
"Body, my" 2286
"body, my" 4959, 9428
"body, not one of us noticed the" 1890
"body, pick up a" 164
"body, strong in" 10845
"body, temperature of his" 6604
"body against the wall, hurled his" 10953
"body disappeared, my mother's" 1884
"body dumped into the Cassadaga River" 1896
"body eased lower into the barber chair" 8042
"body glaring white in the shrouded dark" 7409
"body grinds over hers" 7723
"body had never been found" 3956
"body is found, when my" 2354
"body lax, her" 10266
"body lay in the next room" 1880
"body like a horizontal sausage roll" 8941
"body of love" 9279
"body of Rebecca Carpenter was found" 1894
"body of the man" 1892
"body rolls upon a creaking bed" 5624
"body stiff, his" 8490

"body tingled, her" 10283
"body tremble, felt his" 10097
"body was found in the Gobi Desert last summer" 5528
"body was locked away, my own" 9279
"body was weak and small, when my" 7436
"body which was about twelve inches long" 416
"bodyguard" 1528
"Boer *vrouw*" 5402
Boethius 7144
"bog marshes of sphagnum" 4073
Bogart 6290
"Bogart fan, never told me he was a" 4830
"Bogue Bank" 8130
Bohannon, Mrs. 5666
"Bohegan, town of" 1407
"Bohemia" 9515
"Bohemian" 5584
"Bohemian crowd of San Francisco" 4721
"Bohemian Girl, The" 9383
"Boianai in Papua" 9941
"boiled two lobsters in seawater" 860
"boiling with hate within" 10186
"Bois de Boulogne" 10615
"boisterous bawdy encouragement" 7102
"boisterously than in the city proper, more" 10687
Bok, Yakov 7849
Bold, Eleanor 9675
"bolder than most" 458
Boldesca, Carlo 421
"bole of an olive tree, gnarled" 5716
Bolek 3233
Bolini, Mr. 10676
Bolles, Robert 5021
"bologna pickled in a jar" 4073
"bolster, old-country" 2398
"bolt to earth" 9790
"bomb, dispose of a" 892
"bomb, holding a homemade" 876
"bomb, I threw the" 2019
"bomb, the" 884
"Bomb, the" 3402
"bomb, time" 3277
"bomb at Heathrow, planted a" 883
"bomb at Hiroshima, like that" 7990
"bomb goes off, the first" 890
"bomb of bell metal, horrid little" 10127
"bomb went off, when the" 886
"Bombardier paced along the mole" 8660
"Bombay" 811, 4638
"Bombay's Ballard Pier" 8161
"Bombay's Victoria Station" 1757
"bombed baroque German city" 4178

"bombed-out block" 2811
"bomber, twin-engined Mitsubishi Zero-1 medium" 219
"bombing of Pearl Harbor" 6774
Bombs 873, 875, 876, 878, 879, 882, 883, 884, 886, 888, 889, 890, 892, 2006, 2019, 3277, 3362, 7901, 8689, 8693
"bombs?" 875
"Bombs, throwing" 10464
"bombs falling, he heard the" 888
"bombs lit, when the first" 873
"bombshell, dropped his" 5207
Bon, Peter Innocent 2072
Bonasera, Amerigo 5205
Bonbright, David Alexander 10495
"bond, brewery company" 1023
"bond, forms a" 879
Bone 1050
"bone, all long" 979
"bone, hard skull" 7409
"bone, ill-mended" 2607
"bone ridges, high" 498
"boneheaded peer" 8257
"bones about admitting, he made no" 4565
"bones, box of dry" 4592
"bones, could feel in her" 10152
"bones, knew in his" 7025
"bones, mark her" 6646
"bones, never laughed over her" 2376
"bones, sharp" 10832
"bones, strip the flesh from the" 10717
"bonfire we built" 4002
"Bonn" 247, 4389
"Bonneville" 8765
Bonneys, the 8352
Bonthorn 1597
Boo 3946
"boo hoo" 6588
Boog 10544
"book, a most ridiculous" 5384
"book, after I finished this" 5487
"book, bent over a" 4904
"book, black-bound" 924
"book, chapters of the" 8962
"Book, Friend's" 917
"Book, Good" 2622
"book, he had written a" 5551
"book, household's sole" 6698
"book, I am writing this" 5432
"book, in this" 4905
"book, last page of my" 710
"book, library" 899, 905, 7362
"book, looking up from his" 6520
"book, my favorite" 914
"book, my Venice" 5508
"book, one beginning and one ending for a" 5424
"book, open page of his" 4951
"book, purpose of this" 7663
"book, seep out slowly through a" 1801

"book, small yellow-paged" 926
"book, somewhere in this" 700
"book, studied the" 7361
"book, tale of a" 9025
"book, this" 6655
"book, told in another" 1283
"book, wakes to finish his" 10219
"book, write a" 5402
"book, write a funny" 5419
"book, write this" 5446
"book, writing a" 5470
"book, writing of this" 5462
"book, writing this" 5427
"book about another woman walking" 5495
"book about France, Mrs. Browns" 4850
"book about newspapers, this is a" 6357
"book about the Washington correspondents" 794
"book about the wind, write a" 5550
"book by the name of *The Adventures of Tom Sawyer*" 896
"book called *The Lion the Witch and the Wardrobe*" 1283
"book concealed inside it" 926
"book has not been written to prove a case" 5421
"book her sister was reading" 894
"book I had bought at the station" 1570
"book I writ before this one" 5506
"Book in his hand" 2751
"book in its dull and distressed leather binding" 926
"book is addressed to young men" 1977
"book is largely concerned with Hobbits" 5435
"book larning" 3269
"book might be called also *The Triumph of Love*" 897
"book must be dropped" 918
"book of ballads" 915
"Book of Common Prayer" 8481
"book of original Aphorisms" 5392
"Book of Revelation" 6960
"book of travel" 5477
"book on music" 6227
"book out of his coat pocket, he brought a" 845
"book publishing houses" 5537
"book readers" 9381
"book reviewer" 6419
"book she held, shutting the" 6784
"book somewhere inside him, every man has a" 916
"book somewhere near the floor" 901
"book stalls" 5607
"book still untitled" 710
"book that I had not opened for years" 1940
"book tours, on my" 2067

"book was noticeable for its quaint earnestness" 5392
"book was thick and black" 922
"book which sold three thousand copies" 5476
"bookbag, clasped her" 1765
Bookbinder, Herbert 970
"bookbinder" 3837
"Bookbinder" 5601
"Booker Prize for Fiction" 5877
"bookkeeper" 6928
Bookless, Sean 1050
"book-lice" 2555
"bookmakers' shouts" 10002
"bookmark, I slipped a" 923
"book-reviewing departments of newspapers" 8470
Books 694, 700, 710, 712, 794, 1013, 1283, 1408, 1801, 1940, 1977, 2014, 2551, 2555, 2751, 3034, 3268, 4473, 4491, 4951, 5348, 5384, 5392, 5400, 5402, 5416, 5421, 5424, 5427, 5432, 5434, 5435, 5446, 5453, 5455, 5456, 5462, 5468, 5469, 5470, 5472, 5476, 5477, 5486, 5487, 5490, 5494, 5495, 5503, 5506, 5508, 5509, 5533, 5543, 5550, 5551, 5607, 5884, 6227, 6357, 6385, 6419, 6655, 6698, 7348, 7349, 7351, 7361, 7362, 8481, 8962, 9025, 9050, 9382, 10051, 10219, 10900
"books" 377, 913, 5348, 5486
"books, four new crisp rent" 1033
"books, greater knowledge of" 5884
"books, his head well down in the" 9908
"books, I shall write two" 5456
"books, old" 7214
"books, paperback" 1067
"books, probably read some of my" 908
"books, putting so many people into our" 5434
"books, series of" 4473
"Books, sold my" 10465
"books, spilling the" 3268
"books, steal for the" 2014
"books, the wrong" 911
"books, three full-length" 712
"books, turning from his" 98
"books, writing" 5509
"books and papers" 902, 911
"books and papers, gather together his" 8863
"books are so nice, says our" 1408
"books checked out" 909
"books continued . . . to live" 5503
"books dog-eared and faded from their purple" 906
"books ever written, among the dullest" 920
"books lay in heaps beneath him on the grass" 10051

"books Nero Wolfe reads" 907

"books on the car seat beside him shoot forward onto the floor" 3034

"books on the same theme, eight interrelated" 5541

"books that teach or preach" 5427

"books too, there are" 7351

"books used to begin, the way all the" 904

"books were arranged in a tall pyramid" 919

"books were laid out" 5292

"books with titles for chapters" 904

"bookshop, a very remarkable" 1013

"bookshop, Mr. McKechnie's" 5621

"book-worms" 2555

"book-writing business, I am not in the" 5490

"boom, another gentle" 8771

"boom, gentle" 8771

"boom, coal" 3586

"boom of delight" 444

"boomed out over the dank cold fields" 666

"boomer, I am a" 4449

"boomerang, handle shaped like a" 2697

Boomfell 1086

"booming out over my tapedeck" 9300

"booming strokes" 1606

"boomps-a-daisy" 567

"Boomtown" 6099

"boomtown, oil" 10092

"boon to my dreadful little nerves" 9285

Boone, Avery 9027

"Boonton Vermont" 218

"Boonville" 9128

"Booradeela Range" 4084

"boosts itself with homemade miracles" 1429

Boot, John Courteney 5423

"boot, cowhide" 4950

"boot, his heavy" 8674

"boot, sole of his" 8810

"boot scuffed it, General's" 2571

"boot toe" 7549

Booth, Vincent 508

Boots 2690, 8042

"boots, big thick" 8659

"boots, cowboy" 5966, 5982

"boots, decayed" 3371

"boots, heavy hiking" 4203

"boots, his" 8042, 10452

"boots, his long black military" 5901

"boots, in his new" 5257

"boots, looking at the" 2690

"boots, rubber" 10579

"boots, steaming" 7567

"boots crossed, his" 8270

"boots of a half-breed Indian" 3714

"boots on, he had big" 2909

"boots similar to those worn by foot

soldiers" 7630

"boots stomping, big" 4577

"booze, stream of friendly" 1804

"bordello, Lala's" 8947

"bordered by four streets" 4099

"borderland, fuzzy" 10183

"borders, at" 7824

"bore her third child" 7090

"bore them silently" 8107

"Boreas, gentle breath of" 10108

"bored, gloriously" 933

"bored, sick of being" 940

"bored, who gets" 514

"bored by now, he must be too" 7533

"bored me, sometimes it only" 4271

"bored with being bored" 940

"bored with their summer freedom" 938

Boredom 99, 514, 894, 1374, 2539, 3690, 4271, 5457, 6351, 6821, 6943, 7987, 8365, 10083

"boredom, his" 3690

"boredom of his watch" 8663

Borian, Arno 6438

"boring, can be" 941

"boring during his stay" 5457

Boris 2575, 6225

Bormann, Martin 3413

"born, a baby" 7058

"born, a was" 822

"born, after he was" 2408

"born, after Jennifer was" 6723

"born, before Breck Hord was" 436

"born, before I was" 4777

"born, Eli was" 1421

"born, for many days after he was" 3358

"born, I was" 43, 801, 814, 6089, 6631, 6647, 7063, 9711

"born, in the middle of a snow-storm I was" 7059

"born, it was" 801

"born, know when I was" 823

"born, manchild was" 804

"born, none of us was" 8230

"born, on the day I was" 57

"born, on the day she was" 2428

"born, on the day they were" 4307

"born, Paris-" 5965

"born, place where he was" 4572

"born, soon after she was" 7105

"born, the night the boy was" 825

"born, the year I was" 4527, 6685

"born, thirteen years before I was" 6159

"born, to keep Ida from being" 7058

"born, town where I was" 4539

"born, was" 760, 808, 818, 821, 1359

"born, well" 4442

"born, when Challenge was" 789

"born, when Dale was" 4354

"born, when I was" 6726

"born, when she was" 7950

"born, when the baby was" 7100

"born, when you were" 4354

"born, where he was" 5426

"born, where I myself was" 6618

"born, where I was" 793, 9706

"born, where she was" 4360, 4544

"born a girl" 4185

"born a little before 1900" 3382

"born a werewolf" 337

"born a woman, misfortune it is to be" 10766

"born again, to be" 2427

"born and bred" 4864, 9703, 9717

"born at all, lucky for me I was" 795

"born at Little Empton" 787

"born at 1:06 A.M. on August 1 1943" 2360

"born at Restwell, I was" 786

"born at twenty after six, was not" 812

"born before my time" 796

"born Bowen fifty-eight years ago" 10662

"born free, not everywhere" 4443

"born from a pelvis that was blue with cold" 4871

"born ill-favoured" 1228

"born in 1845" 798

"born in 1940" 4865

"born in 1904, I was" 7103

"born in 1917" 2336

"born in a camp near the crest of a pass in the Himalayas" 810

"born in a cold city, I was" 6650

"born in a place called Georgia" 806

"born in a two-room sharecropper's cabin" 826

"born in a valley, I was" 780

"born in a war" 10531

"born in Brooklyn" 9719

"born in Chacallit New York" 370

"born in *Cumbria*, I was" 824

"born in Hammersmith, great men are occasionally" 5905

"born in Hawaii" 4543

"born in Ireland" 447

"born in Jersey City New Jersey" 802

"born in Judea" 3655

"born in Paris, he was" 797

"born in Somerset" 4567

"born in that sphere of life" 6612

"born in the city of Bombay, I was" 811

"born in the County of *SALOP*, I was" 778

"born in the house of his maternal grandfather" 790

"born in the land of Puritania" 963

"born in the northern part of this united kingdom" 5193

"Born in the Parish of *Stepney* near

London" 355
"born in the town of Vliss" 809
"born in the year of victories" 792
"born in the Year 1632, I Was"
6601
"born July 5 1898" 5452
"born November 5 1900" 1531
"born of a woman, man that is"
5583
"born of decent religious parents"
6673
"born on a farm on Whileaway"
803
"born on a vile October day in
1890" 788
"born on Clinton Street, I was" 820
"born on January 6 1939, I was"
819
"born on July 1 1880" 807
"born on the Nunnery Grounds"
816
"born on the rainy dawn" 830
"born on the third of December"
6730
"born on the thirty-first of December" 791
"born one Sunday night" 794
"born poor in rich America" 7043
"born the illegitimate son of a
Palestinian mother and a French
father" 831
"born the year of the Crash" 815
"born to a poor family" 781
"born to be a Londoner" 958
"born to Eastern European parents"
6749
"born under the Blue Ridge, I was"
783
"born victim, a" 4196
"born with a gift of laughter" 5183
"born yet, I wasn't" 7394
"born Zeev Zali, he was" 4859
"borne aloft on the wings of the
evening breeze" 650
"borne as I best could, I had" 4989
"borne on the breezy sweep of sunlight" 1762
"borne the name of John" 7812
"borne upon the light breath of a
fair wind" 8093
"borough, New York's unknown"
1515
"Borough of Queens" 1884
"borough of superb sunsets" 1013
"boroughs, many of the other" 7319
"borrow old Polly" 6566
"borrow pit" 437
"borrowed the chef's carvers and
committed *hara-kiri*" 6021
Borthen, Dave 1638
"bosky thickets" 3396
"bosom, bearing on its" 10704
"bosom, manly" 10555
"bosom of an old wood" 9738
"bosomed, still flat-" 4154

"boss, elderly rawboned grizzled
trail" 7634
"Boss, Substantial" 2633
"boss, T Bar trail-" 9312
"boss, trail" 9310
"boss came in" 1048
"boss was fired, my" 6460
Boston 6678, 8715
"Boston" 206, 2040, 2319, 3041,
3531, 4073, 5094, 6423, 6496,
6678, 7327, 7367, 9165, 9192,
10414
"Boston, bells of" 655
"Boston, does not very often get to"
8255
"Boston, first met in" 2648
"Boston, got back to" 8715
"Boston, in the city of" 782
"Boston, it was" 4405
"Boston, polite world of" 6757
"Boston, port of" 7814
"Boston, Solid Men of" 5786
"Boston architect" 7760
"Boston Common" 4174, 4368
"Boston Common, sitting on a
bench in" 2828
"Boston Harbor" 8591
"Boston Massachusetts" 4927, 10814
"Boston's Symphony Hall" 5851
Boswell, George 10143
"Boswell's Manhattan Journal" 5444
"botanist" 8220
"botanist, the well-known" 4665
"bother her, not to" 3328
"bothering him again" 10968
Bott, the Reverend Samuel 1500
"bottle, blue as a" 8429
"bottle, found the" 3702
"bottle, in the neck of a green"
5034
"bottle, late afternoon" 3888
"bottle, opened the" 2911
"bottle, red hot-water" 4183
"bottle, took to the" 2918
"bottle of Flor de Cana" 2924
"bottle of Irish wine, this last" 9300
"bottle of Old Taylor" 2896
"bottle of Robinson's B.E.B. right
in Lou's bag" 2893
Bottles 3702, 10961
"bottles, counting the empty" 10937
"bottles going clink clink" 10937
"bottles stood beside the telephone"
3052
"bottom, his fat" 10443
"bottom, in the" 1361
"bottom of it, at the" 10770
"bottom of the world" 4087
Bottom the Weaver 7882
"bottomland, fertile" 3654
"bottom-lands, rich" 3641
"Bottoms, The" 6269
"Bottom's Ordinary" 9093
"Botzen" 9869
Bouchard, Honore 2315

Bouchard, Jules 2315
"boudoir, her" 10345
"boudoir, her mother's" 9880
"boudoir, sits in her" 7483
"boudoir coat" 5450
"bough, fluttered from a" 9667
"boughs, apple" 3092
"boughs, dark" 9663
"boughs, interstices of broken" 2195
"boughs whipped his face" 7609
"bought a bottle of liniment" 6614
"bought a pint of whiskey" 2911
"bought an army greatcoat" 2841
"bought hers, where her mother
had" 2864
"bought his wife a street" 4125
"bought in pride" 6646
"bought in the same fine store on
Fifth Avenue" 2864
"bought it, I've never" 6720
"bought it from the last of the line
in the 1850s" 1180
"bought the bear" 8230
"bought the Lenox mansion, a man
has" 6301
"bought the place, when the Greek"
7578
"bought the Villa Ribar in the late
1920s" 10562
"bought this here nigger, I don't
know why you" 681
"bought together on time" 2069
"bouillabaisse of nationalities, wild"
10615
Boulanger, General 9119
"boulders, cemeteries of massive"
5149
"boulders, large granite" 4413
"boulders, lichen-covered" 10404
"boulders beneath Hart's Hill" 9561
"boulders scattered over the hillside"
4413
Boulderstone, Simon 155, 1694,
8685
"boules, playing" 315
"Boulevard, Birdsong" 3259
"Boulevard, Hollywood" 10320
"Boulevard, Laurel Canyon Boulevard" 9800
"Boulevard, Lincoln" 3096
"Boulevard, Mission" 3017
"Boulevard, Wilshire" 4617
"Boulevard du Montparnasse" 7568
"boulevard Saint-Germain" 8949
"Boulevard Saint Michel" 6237,
10334
"boulevards, the" 9119
"boulevards no longer gossip of
Louis Napoleon" 9119
Boulez 1143
"Boulogne" 9631
"Boulogne, the hills of" 5834
"bounced it in the library" 302
"bouncing it off the sidewalks and
off walls" 302

"bound, I'll be" 4511
"bound, wrists" 1170
"bound by a corridor room" 5624
"bound for England" 8051
"bound for this town and for the
    Double Y beyond it" 7616
Boundaries 4036, 4054, 5150
"boundaries, Civil War" 1445
"boundaries, law of" 7824
"boundaries, parish" 5150
"boundaries where all is infinite, no"
    526
"boundary, a" 7657
"boundary, glittering" 2218
"boundary, natural" 6155
"boundary, the Church's" 9153
"boundary between the United
    States and Canada" 6155
"boundary of the western United
    States, the vast northern" 5713
"bounded on the north by Tennes-
    see" 4066
"boundless space and empire" 10260
"bountiful, in nature" 7648
"Bountiful, the whaling brig" 5628
"bounty, gave of her" 5014
"bourbon, was it the" 2941
"Bourbons, Return of the" 9119
"bourgeois as he was" 6977
"bourgeoisie, haute" 5179
Bourne, Jessie 10148
"Boutflour" 5359
"Bovril" 4922
"bow, a deep" 2101
"bow, take a" 2877
"bow first touched the strings" 6240
"bow her head" 1216
"bow swing shoreward" 8099
"bow to the corners of the world"
    1211
Bowan, Billy 2772
"bowed and bowed again" 2103
"bowed to the Mayor" 8864
"bowels, bloody" 9285
"bowels, loose" 2926
"bower by the beach at Ainahau"
    10673
"bower of trees" 3119
Bowers, Red 6853
"bowers, tapestried" 2088
"bowery, apparitions on the" 10463
"bowing deferentially to the judge"
    5199
"bowing me, merchants" 3737
"bowl, her mixing-" 1860
"bowl, like a hollow" 9745
"bowl of hot wine" 10196
"bowl of lather, bearing a" 8041
"bowl of ocher mud" 2833
"bowler, porter in the" 3187
"bowling ball goes thundering down
    the alley" 313
"bowls had them, his father's" 10905
Bowman, Scotty 4641
"Bowport" 1375

Bowring, Mrs. 6784
"box, dispatch" 2610
"box, I built the" 1857
"box, it was a brown" 2610
"box, mechanical" 1250
"box, press" 8920
"box, upturned fruit" 8286
"box, wooden" 7753
"box, yellow" 6999
"box elder, the ragged" 10928
"box nine feet long by seven feet
    wide by eight feet high" 6500
"box office" 10035
"box with, strong enough to" 8239
"boxcar, lived in a" 3235
Boxe, Lady 3974
Boxes 2604, 2610, 2614, 7148
"boxes, dusty" 2614
"boxes, seventeen iron" 2604
"boxing champion, middleweight"
    8910
"boy, a" 997, 4137
"boy, active" 994
"boy, as a" 4487, 8225, 9726
"boy, baby" 557
"boy, back-room" 4465
"boy, bad" 6614
"boy, black" 2973
"boy, bled and purged the" 2363
"boy, blond gangling country" 2911
"boy, blue-eyed blond small" 7385
"boy, Brock's" 8915
"boy, buried my" 4223
"boy, eight-year-old" 6198
"boy, fairly rich and large-eared
    farm" 8712
"boy, fifteen-year-old" 980
"boy, flute" 3935
"boy, happy" 2956
"boy, heat boot-" 6021
"boy, I was the only" 2374
"boy, idiot" 965
"boy, if it's a" 7065
"boy, it is a" 6520
"boy, Jewish" 5848
"boy, just a country" 4738
"boy, large-headed partly toothless
    little" 964
"boy, little" 952, 968, 981, 4784,
    8739
"boy, lonely" 983
"boy, lonely temperamental impul-
    sive" 497
"boy, met the" 5808
"Boy, My Beloved" 4889
"boy, my dear" 4591
"boy, my handsome" 4223
"boy, my mess" 5355
"boy, never saw such a" 956
"boy, new boots" 4990
"boy, nicens little" 961
"boy, old" 5972
"boy, orphan" 8672
"boy, photograph of the" 6855
"boy, pony" 10412

"boy, pretty bad" 8958
"boy, pretty little" 952
"boy, ragged" 953
"boy, remarkably pretty and
    vivacious" 3554
"boy, remember Link as a little"
    9425
"boy, six-year-old" 987, 6531
"boy, small" 984, 7270
"boy, stout little dark-haired" 970
"boy, strange" 955
"boy, strange small" 988
"boy, tall big-boned" 960
"boy, teen-age" 2565
"boy, that" 9854
"boy, thata" 9267
"boy, the" 151, 973, 991, 992, 1421,
    2874, 3728, 4261, 4672, 4675,
    5548, 5796, 6698, 7643, 7915,
    8530, 9006, 9105, 9318, 10070
"boy, thin knobby" 979
"boy, timid shrimp of a" 4743
"boy, undersized" 966
"boy, very bad" 951
"boy, very dangerous" 1004
"boy, very little" 957
"boy, wanted to be a" 4185
"boy, what is a" 6520
"boy, when he was still a small"
    6704
"boy, when I was a" 285, 2510,
    6385, 8221
"boy, when I was a little" 947
"boy, when I was a small" 5888
"boy, when I was a young" 57
"boy, where's that" 10180
"boy, woke the" 243
"boy, you silly" 2432
"boy and a horse" 979
"boy and girl" 8203
"boy and girl, this" 6612
"boy and the dog" 973
"boy and the girl have never met"
    5882
"boy at the lunch counter" 7567
"boy called Eustace Clarence
    Scrubb" 4740
"boy came over a ridge of a hill"
    1576
"boy comes riding" 7629
"boy could see that, even a" 2837
"boy cried, the" 993
"boy from a large city in Eastern
    Europe" 6531
"boy got too drunk to finish digging
    his grave" 2329
"boy growing up, when I was a"
    3614
"boy growing up in Nebraska" 7270
"boy had gathered his treasures to-
    gether" 6112
"boy Harold" 4694
"boy I choose, marry a" 6748
"boy in a glen plaid suit" 2111
"boy in China, small" 4242

"boy in the river" 998
"boy lay, where the" 9141
"boy likes ice cream so much, did you ever see a" 5366
"boy named Ulysses Macauley" 968
"boy of fifteen, young" 9722
"boy of middle growth, mistaken for a" 10833
"boy of ten years of age, since I was a" 5281
"boy of the *World*, bright" 6980
"boy of twelve" 246
"boy on a bicycle" 1000
"boy on the stone floor" 10853
"boy on Venice Blvd." 505
"boy sees, what the" 8276
"boy sees the men walk past the farmhouse" 995
"boy should learn something" 9860
"boy sits" 1001
"boy Vanya, the" 5329
"boy was about fifteen years old" 974
"boy was born to a poor family" 781
"boy was there again" 9927
"boy who sold bibles" 2911
"boy who was born in the land of Puritania" 963
"boy who was dead" 4108
"boy who would immediately become my husband" 5880
"boy with a wrecked voice" 7542
"boy with fair hair" 10363
Boyce, Humphrey 10836
"boyfriend" 6666
"boyfriend, her" 2011
"boyfriend like mine" 7731
"boyfriend's place" 8012
"boyhood" 4756
"boyhood, his" 7382
"boyhood, my" 7451, 7460
"boyhood, since" 5564
"boyish worship and sorrow" 10341
Boyne, Martin 8072
Boys 57, 243, 246, 260, 296, 505, 781, 837, 1172, 1453, 1510, 1576, 2111, 2329, 2363, 2510, 2565, 2787, 2827, 2837, 3272, 3504, 3554, 3728, 4108, 4137, 4185, 4188, 4238, 4261, 4284, 4475, 4487, 4670, 4672, 4675, 4694, 4715, 4719, 4732, 4738, 4740, 4784, 4807, 4895, 4906, 4970, 4990, 5079, 5087, 5329, 5366, 5370, 5788, 5796, 5808, 5821, 5880, 6110, 6112, 6170, 6424, 6520, 6525, 6531, 6563, 6576, 6614, 6704, 6855, 7270, 7542, 7566, 7567, 7629, 7915, 8221, 8225, 8276, 8562, 8672, 8913, 8921, 8933, 8958, 9006, 9267, 9318, 9425, 9722, 9841, 9854, 9927, 10078, 10109, 10180, 10213, 10363, 10412, 10833, 10853
"boys" 292

"boys, black" 7984
"boys, Catholic" 1510
"boys, dead" 1879
"boys, few were the" 10109
"boys, five Brewster" 3608
"boys, four" 6576
"boys, frat" 1453
"boys, generations of" 6427
"boys, larger" 955
"boys, laughing" 8919
"boys, little" 6424
"boys, muddy" 8921
"boys, party of country" 954
"boys, rare month for" 978
"boys, recalcitrant and educationally sub-normal" 7897
"boys, several generations of high school" 4876
"boys, six eight-year-old" 990
"boys, the" 977, 3129, 6563
"Boys, The Six" 2106
"boys, these little" 959
"boys, three" 2056
"boys, two" 989
"boys, two of them were" 6525
"boys, two teenage Filipino" 1003
"boys, white" 959
"boys and men, passing" 9253
"boys are playing basketball" 8913
"boys bang against each other" 8921
"boys beat a whirling course across the sandy hillock" 9841
"boys between seven and fourteen" 959
"boys herded a seventh, six" 999
"boys in the tops" 8124
"boys in white suits" 7984
"boy's name" 4732
"boys of Camperlea" 982
"boys old and young" 8933
"boys on her right" 10824
"boy's quirk of style" 10833
"boys scurrying to get dressed" 990
"boys shuffled along" 986
"boys slept, while the" 10609
"boys together, new" 5821
"boys wanted her, two" 4188
"boys were likely to be away" 977
"boys were young, when his" 6543
"boys who were playing there" 959
Boysie 1931
"braced with elbow and knee" 4482
"bracelet, touched the" 2844
"bracelets on her wrist, silver" 4986
"braces, steel leg" 9647
Braddock 8172
Braddock, Benjamin 4575
Braden, Sam 6629
Bradford, Dorothy 6121
Bradford, Persis 2319
Bradgate 9217
Bradley, A. C. 8305
Bradley, William 2185
Bradshaw, Helen 10861
Brady, Colman 10247

Brady, Kate 2509
Bragging 6733, 7127, 8970
"bragging about having children" 6733
"brain, brushed against his" 5454
"brain, crawl around until it finds your" 6381
"brain, diabolical" 9019
"brain, got it on the" 5464
"brain, infinitesimal portion of" 4963
"brain, not having a first-class" 5004
"brain, quicksilver of the" 2766
"brain, they cut out my" 627
"brain, what popped in my" 6011
"brain cancer, dying of" 2454
"brain damage" 642
"brain so many bits of torn paper" 6896
"brain-chilling" 8659
"brain-reactions of a fox" 1016
Brains 627, 642, 4963
"brains" 4996
"brains, boiled sheep's" 3887
"brains, racking his" 9421
"brains out, blew her pretty French" 9291
"brainstorm, a few minutes before his" 4706
Braithwaite, John Henry 1180
"brake, took a small" 6581
"brake, went for the" 2989
"braked before the high familiar gates" 2987
"braked without knowing why" 2982
"brakes, hits the" 3034
"brakes that don't always work" 9600
"Bramblehurst railway station" 9092
"brambly ditch" 9673
"Bramford, the" 3170
"Bramley" 5067
Bramstone, Will 3009
"branch, the Sussex" 3563
"branch of Poor Fork, a nameless" 436
"branches, broken dead" 9156
"branches, bushy" 4152
"branches, splintered" 9153
"branches, topmost" 9669
Brand, Billy 9274
"brand, in their own" 3644
"branded and denounced as a vagrant" 358
Brandeis, Mrs. 10787
"Brandenburg, the fifth" 6233
"brandishing his shinny stick" 962
Brandolini, Filippo 5791
"Brandon" 6001
Brandon, Adam 787
Brandon, Allie 8920
Brandon, Mrs. 8261

"brands on the cattle" 3649
Brandt, Emily 2671
Brandy 8292
"brandy, drinking" 2209, 2929
"brandy, golden" 2927
"brandy and old age" 4468
"brandy trickle over his tongue" 2939
Brangwen, Gudrun 8206
Brangwen, Ursula 8206
Brangwens, the 3082
Bransford, Mr. Jeff 5899
Branson, Lise Hurwitz 2573
Brant, Clarence 5892
Brant, Clifton 6837
Branting 1098
"bras in 1954, we all wore" 2881
"brass-bright desert" 3768
"brass reinforced corners" 2610
"brat must be got rid of at once" 541
Bratasky, Herbie 7727
"Bratslav" 2278
"Braunschweiger" 10007
"brave" 5969
"Brave in Battle" 4743
"brave single-minded women" 10837
"brave the morn" 4683
Bravery 6697
"bravest chief in the two valleys" 6697
"brawny country-folk" 5886
"bray of the iceman's mule" 5121
"brazen" 658
"Brazil" 5576
"Brazilian father" 800
"bread" 1876
"bread dust" 7575
"bread for three minutes' chewing, sufficient" 5424
"bread on the table, no" 7032
"bread with butter, black rye" 3854
"break, nice pleasant" 940
"break a song" 6218
"break down" 6701
"break from the contained indifference" 7847
"break of day" 9067
"break stones on it, you can" 5695
"break up about" 7525
"breakdown, might have been nearing a" 2516
Breaker, Mr. 6297
"breakers on the outer reef" 6933
"breakers wash the flat beach" 4096
Breakfast 386, 595, 873, 1874, 1978, 2333, 2507, 3471, 3572, 3818, 3819, 3824, 3826, 3827, 3828, 3829, 3839, 3841, 3842, 3844, 3850, 3852, 3857, 3865, 3866, 3874, 3881, 3890, 3892, 3989, 4212, 4283, 4285, 4349, 4909, 5999, 6200, 6638, 7180, 7235, 8223, 8552, 9470, 10592
"breakfast" 6638

"breakfast, after" 8869
"breakfast, bacon for" 4283
"breakfast, before they had finished" 4212
"breakfast, comforting" 3857
"breakfast, distracted at" 3874
"breakfast, eating" 873, 3879
"breakfast, I had just finished" 5999
"breakfast, late" 3866, 3881
"breakfast, livid at" 386
"breakfast, make a good" 3471
"breakfast, not their best at" 2507
"breakfast, on his way to" 3826
"breakfast, promised to prepare" 6200
"breakfast, sat down to" 7180
"breakfast, sat down to their" 3842
"breakfast, seeking" 7235
"breakfast, slugs for his" 723
"breakfast, toast at" 2333
"breakfast, tomorrow's" 1874
"breakfast, while she was eating" 5658
"breakfast alone" 3836
"breakfast at a certain Club" 3813
"breakfast at Waterbath was a punctual meal" 4909
"breakfast coffee" 3572, 8552
"breakfast dishes were put away" 851
"breakfast from a tray, elegant" 3841
"breakfast in the Sylvester house" 3827
"breakfast on a card table in Jeffrey's study" 3829
"breakfast on the balcony" 10592
"breakfast ready in the empty dining-room" 9470
"breakfast table" 1587, 1947, 3698, 3839, 3844, 3850
"breakfast table, drag the body from the" 2329
"breakfast table, family" 3824
"breakfast table, Goldmans'" 5502
"breakfast table, seated at the" 3818
"breakfast table, sitting at the" 1978
"breakfast table, their royal" 1902
"breakfast table, three at the" 3989
"breakfast today, what you had for" 3892
"breakfast tray in front of me, put a" 595
"breakfast . . . was supposedly served at eight o'clock" 3827
"breakfasted, brother and sister" 8223
"breakfasted with his wife" 3828
"breakfasting out-of-doors" 3819
"breaking and entering" 2059
"breaking clear" 7844
"breaking for lunch" 3007
"breaking new ground" 8429
"breaking of the cup, it was the" 2476

"breaking sky" 222
"bream beds in Roebuck Lake" 5121
"bream waited in it ready to be caught" 7677
"breast, holding her" 2529
"breast, mouth at her" 3867
"breast, my" 8500
"breast, on her" 8015
"breast, the" 10817
"breast comes up, when that" 6895
Breasts 1792, 3867, 4620, 6392, 6895, 9453, 10062
"breasts, ample" 10062
"breasts, beating of" 5740
"breasts, beating their" 3935
"breasts, bobbing like" 8689
"breasts, felt the snake between her" 2851
"breasts, guide his head to between her" 1792
"breasts, men who could have lived with the size of her" 10852
"breasts, revealed her" 6392
"breasts, wondered about women's" 9453
"breasts, world of the" 4200
"breasts and bellies, sprouted" 10822
"breasts . . . of a realized maturity" 10062
"breasts of recumbent giant women" 2225
"breasts were too big" 10852
Breath 1524, 2727, 7131, 8017
"breath, blowing its hoary" 10740
"breath, discharged her customary wistful" 5992
"breath, holding his" 8193
"breath, human" 1356
"breath, paused for" 9763
"breath, said under his" 8108
"breath, when she catches her" 8013
"breath, with its own sweet" 5656
"breath after long harsh breath" 2352
"breath away, you take my" 9568
"breath clouding the glass" 482
"breath he draws" 8766
"breath he drew was an incredible agony" 143
"breath might fog the blue-moon window, your" 2727
"breath of an ice-dragon, like the furious" 10725
"breath of Boreas, the gentle" 10108
"breath of Coldmouth air, had scarcely drawn a" 1633
"breath of coolness" 4371
"breath of crowded human beings" 175
"breath of hot new life across the land" 4610
"breath of sleep and flowers" 8394
"breath or something, I can't draw my" 6391

"breath politely, sucked in his" 6950
"breath still coming rapidly" 2782
"breath stunk to high heaven" 1524
"breath that a little while ago had sounded wild as a storm" 8802
"breath that she exhaled, each" 10635
"breathe, dreamed that Billy couldn't" 2798
"breathe, he could no longer" 6598
"breathe, listen to them" 6543
"breathe, she could hardly" 8434
"breathed, as he" 9075
"breathed a sigh of relief" 1663
"breathed a thread of semipure air" 8528
"breathed with a panting effort" 8734
Breathing 151, 469, 2352, 2798, 4485, 5619, 6499, 8472, 9075, 9503, 10635
"breathing" 5215
"breathing, conscious of his own" 5619
"breathing, heavy" 10362
"breathing, human" 9503
"breathing, lying there in her narrow walnut bed" 2352
"breathing, stood" 9903
"breathing a stream of friendly booze" 1804
"breathing an ominous death rattle" 2405
"breathing hard" 10933
"breathing heavily into her soup" 4465
"breathing in the soft warm air" 6499
"breathing of The Impostor" 4485 •
"breathing through it wasn't [easy]" 151
"breathless, rapt and" 3499
"breathless, sufficiently" 8967
"breaths, took deep" 8472
Breckinridge, Myra 10820
"bred, she'd been forest" 7187
"bred up in luxurious indolence" 3356
"breeches, gray knee" 970
"breeches, knee-" 5888
"breed, light-skinned" 984
"breed, strangely mixed" 3554
"breeding, claims to polite" 359
"breeze, balmy spring" 10703
"breeze, chill in the" 10745
"breeze, chilly" 1554
"breeze, cool fresh" 4587
"breeze, evening inshore" 8114
"breeze, fitful" 10686
"breeze, in the" 10696
"breeze, it would be a" 2668
"breeze, light" 8864
"breeze, not quite a" 10185
"breeze, offshore" 8541
"breeze, river's easy" 6917

"breeze, sea" 10014
"breeze, southerly" 10600, 10697
"breeze, warm and salty on the" 10737
"breeze, warm Negev" 5286
"breeze, wings of the evening" 650
"breeze, you will have a fresh" 8053
"breeze after her, a topgallant" 8064
"breeze arose in the West" 10701
"breeze from Central Park" 10731
"breeze held a lull" 5286
"breeze of early morning, the fresh" 7801
"breeze . . . on her face" 4587
"breeze rushed" 3909
"breeze that came off the ocean" 8248
"breeze that comes near dawn when the darkness thins" 10749
"breeze was spicing along, a small" 10586
"breezes, clean" 1447
"breezes, gentle" 7346
"breezes, languid" 5132
"breezes, like the sound-stage" 7229
"breezes designed to tousle the hairdos of actresses" 7229
"breezy little island" 10731
"breezy sweep of sunlight" 1762
"Bremen, Foreigner of" 6601
Brenda 27
Brendan 3730
Brent 9723
Brent, Sophy 7398
"Bretton, clean and ancient town of" 3061
Breuer, Josef 674
Brevoort, Geraldine 9289
"brewers who wanted more of his finely ground malt" 4760
Brewster, O. B. 8936
"Brewster boys" 3608
"Brewster Place" 4705
Brian 976
"briars and shrubs" 5704
"brick, shapes of soft red" 1376
"brick façade" 9225
"brick forest" 10242
"Brickfield Terrace" 3073
"Bricklayers', what if it is the" 2102
"bricks, long unpainted geranium-coloured" 3103
"bricks by the million, make" 1005
"bride, coaxing the" 10650
"bride, his" 5761
"bride, his new" 6664
"bride and groom are absent" 6865
"bride ironed her hair" 10668
"bride turned aside" 10657
"bride was a nobody" 10671
"bride who had fallen asleep" 10138
"Bridegroom would be back" 10670
"bridegroom's speech" 10657
Brides 1996, 5732, 6664, 10138,

10650, 10668, 10671
"Bridesley Birmingham" 1592
"bridesmaids, she was one of my" 952
"Bridewell" 1196
"bridge, at this" 768
"bridge, canal" 5347
"Bridge, cross the" 1208
"bridge, Dockham's" 9136
"Bridge, East River" 7672
"Bridge, Golden Gate" 8163, 9611
"bridge, had hit a" 4652
"Bridge, Heavenly" 8700
"bridge, Hungerford railway" 9596
"bridge, little wooden" 3232
"Bridge, London" 14, 1196, 8050, 10394
"bridge, mammoth" 4073
"bridge, many-arched old" 1336
"bridge, narrow stone" 10441
"bridge, new" 8875
"bridge, over the" 5142, 10448
"Bridge, River" 3259
"Bridge, Southwark" 8050
"bridge, steep-sloping red-bricked canal" 5898
"Bridge, Suspension" 1029
"bridge, suspension" 7272
"bridge, swinging" 10203
"bridge, the" 7399, 8076
"bridge, went out on the" 8154
"Bridge, Westminster" 10803
"Bridge, Williamsburg" 8798
"bridge, wooden" 3634
"bridge in all Peru, the finest" 15
"bridge fell away" 1668
"bridge between them, only a" 6866
"bridge . . . broke" 15
"Bridge of Hesitation" 3232
"Bridgeport, it wasn't" 3209
Bridger, Mr. Derwood 3604
Bridges, Isabel 2650
Bridges, Margaret Hunter 4949
Bridges 15, 768, 1208, 2339, 5898, 7272, 7399, 7672, 7678, 8875, 9596, 10203, 10394, 10448, 10803
"bridges, jumped from" 7678
"bridges, single lane" 5166
"bridges, the" 8345
Bridgetower, Mrs. 3938
"bridgeways to America" 9247
"bridle all the disorders by and by" 1337
"Brie, he saw" 3859
"brief case flapping open" 10365
"briefcase, shielded his head with his" 8179
"briefs, legal" 5437
Brien, James 4931
"brig, American clipper-built" 8069
"brig, two-masted" 4257
"brig *Bountiful*, whaling" 5628
"brig called *Henry*" 8146
"brig *Morning Star* of Bristol" 8064
"brig *Witch of the West*" 8069

Brigadier, the old 8846
"brigandage, polite" 294
"*Brigantes*, the" 8089
"brigantine Swash or Molly Swash, the half-rigged" 8047
Briggs 1908
Briggs, William 8091
Bright, Hamilton 5344
"bright, it was very" 5316
"bright, no one ever said I was very" 5009
"bright, whitely" 8415
"bright and clear" 8519
"bright and pretty" 3067
"bright and spirited young man" 4346
"bright as a silver bullet" 7440
"bright parting light" 3894
"bright pink" 9257
"bright was the summer of 1296" 6801
"bright with flowers" 10587
"brighten them whenever he will" 1489
"brightening, sunshine" 2756
"brightening its brown undulations with a melancholy flush" 5305
"brightening the long vague and dreamy afternoon" 10060
"brightest idea, not the" 4711
Brighteyes, Eric 4456
"brightly blazed the sun" 10700
"brightness, heat and" 2119
"brightness of the Tuileries gardens, the afternoon" 10037
"Brighton" 6176
"Brighton, beach at" 4181
"brilliance, in all its" 2281
"brilliance, its harsh" 2118
"brilliance, unusual" 533
"brilliancy, converts into dazzling" 5557
"brilliant, so" 9378
"brilliant and enviable" 237
"brilliant high windless sky" 8408
"brilliantly, write as" 5447
"brim with brown water" 5169
Brimstone, Old 3009
"bring it all up again" 6676
"bring it to him, we are going to" 8713
"bring me in, else she would" 6632
"Brinöe" 4376
"Brinthorpe, village of" 3599
"brioche" 3844
"Brisbane" 1562
Brisbin, First Lieutenant Pete 9920
"brisk way" 7493
"briskly, walked" 2842
"bristles that grew in the ears" 2859
"bristling, black and" 9670
"bristling, hair" 475
"Bristol" 8064, 9519
"Bristol, old city of" 3116
"Bristol winter" 7865

"Britain" 10467
"Britain, dear ancestral" 3639
"Britain, Great" 4028
"Britain, in" 7584
"Britain, Island of" 7794
"Britain, king of all" 5662
"Britain, Province of" 4219
"Britain, Roman" 4056
"Britain, sovereignty of" 7795
"Britain's new Conservative government" 6999
"Britannia Mews" 3120
"Britannic endeavor, old-fashioned" 5230
"*Britannique*, aboard the gigantic" 4731
"British, ancient" 6802
"British, arms of the" 10469
"British, coming of the" 1464
"British, when it was" 5032
"British battalions" 8699
"British birth" 5938
"British cantonments" 3067
"British Columbia" 3208
"British Council" 7904
"British culture" 7904
"British expatriates" 6901
"British garments, burning" 3771
"British general, distinguished" 10535
"British have chosen the Maharajah" 6998
"British India" 5715
"British Isles, map of the" 5714
"British Linen Company" 3737
"British Museum" 8587
"British Museum Reading Room" 1658
"British peer" 5984
"British Railways" 7261
"British representative" 4466
"British rule, end of" 3507
"British ships of war" 2491
"British shirting" 7409
"British South Polar Expedition" 5230
"British theatre" 9378
"Britisher, the ubiquitous" 1351
Britsky, Max 813
"Brittany" 9643, 9743
"brittle and will-less I have become" 7968
"brittle heat of the day" 5704
Britton, Jocelyn 6422
"broad, who's the" 4830
Broadbent, Mr. Donald R. 6985
"Broadcasting House" 1051
"Broadway" 1379, 3031
"Broadway, it is still" 6274
"broadway, loosened into a" 9130
"Broadway, lower" 8694
"Broadway, on" 8849
"Broadway and Seventh Avenue" 10067
Brock 3819, 8915

Broder, Herman 10224
Broderhouse, Sarah 10444
Broderson 8765
Brodrick, John 1615
Brody, Hannah 5273
"broke, somebody always" 3608
"broke down and cried" 2073
"broke her father's heart" 6728
"broke into a house" 3247
"broke my heart, you" 397
"broke out of it at two thousand" 197
"broke out with one of his private and peculiar idioms" 931
"broke the mother's heart" 28
"broke up laughing" 7986
"broken, nothing was" 9852
"broken and exhausted, rendering him" 1706
"broken and gelded like the wild horse" 6814
"broken as an enemy" 1
"broken body" 3936
"broken heart" 970
"broken him in, no man had ever" 7967
"broken into his home in Palm Beach" 9850
"Bronx" 970
"Bronx, the" 3201
"Bronx River" 7688
"bronze, in thronging" 1606
"bronze, tin-rich" 7489
"bronze surface, glistening" 6958
"brood, her" 10824
"brood in the house" 8229
"brood of brother and sister" 7129
"brooded on the wonderful ways of God" 7798
Brooding 7728, 7798
"brooding over her pot of tea" 9353
Brook 3451
"brook, intricate headlong" 7652
"brook, the" 3634, 7695
"brook, toward the" 2095
"brook hung like a burnished silver chain, many a" 9740
"brook that had its source away back in the woods" 7652
Brooke, Miss 10776
"Brookhaven Mississippi" 4544
"Brooklyn" 1388, 3145, 4702, 5017, 6142, 6575, 7085, 9147, 9386, 9932
"Brooklyn, born in" 9719
"Brooklyn, central" 1073
"Brooklyn, furthest" 10361
"Brooklyn, if you are ever in" 1013
"Brooklyn, we lived in" 3240
"*Brooklyn Crucifixion*" 4788
"Brookroyd" 9935
Brooks, Tom 2313
Broomes 3564
"brothels, penny" 1886
Brother 1652

"brother" 6666
"brother, elder" 4930
"brother, Henry's" 8675
"brother, her" 129, 3631, 4138, 6110, 6218, 8204, 8209, 8218, 8229, 8234, 9397
"brother, her big" 10645
"brother, her elder" 6106
"brother, her estimable" 3821
"brother, his" 681, 867, 2069, 3584, 3943, 8547, 8991, 10422
"brother, his elder" 4926, 5730
"brother, his half-" 6148
"brother, his mother's" 9410
"brother, his older" 4947
"brother, his twin" 5017
"brother, his younger" 5852, 8226, 10115
"brother, my" 22, 868, 1271, 2116, 2573, 2660, 3409, 3621, 3756, 4487, 5947, 6797, 7044, 7830, 8221, 8235, 8245, 8246, 8247, 8558
"brother, my elder" 7897
"brother, my eldest" 6122
"brother, my little" 8227
"brother, my older" 2578, 3614
"brother, my twin" 255
"brother, my younger" 1157, 8240
"brother, no" 162
"brother, older" 9027
"brother, the Canon's" 8646
"brother, their elder" 2960
"brother, their rough" 9742
"brother, unlike his elder" 8225
"brother and sister breakfasted" 8223
"brother and sister, her" 4544
"brother and sister, once there was a" 4780
Brother Andrés 7138
Brother Anselm 1534
"brother of the deceased" 2310
"Brother Pig" 5468
"brother was brought to our house from the children's home" 8245
"brotherhood with all, ensuring each's" 5699
"brother-in-law, his" 1010
"Brotherly Love, City of" 7955
Brothers 129, 867, 1311, 2116, 2578, 2660, 2960, 3409, 3584, 4487, 7044, 7897, 8203, 8210, 8213, 8217, 8225, 8229, 8231, 8235, 8237, 8246, 8704, 10115, 10924
"brothers, her" 3952
"brothers, his" 3602
"brothers, obvious that they were" 8237
"brothers, their" 7950
"brothers, they were" 8217
"brothers, three" 8248
"brothers, two" 10924
"brothers, two elder" 9722
"brothers, two Oliphant" 8208

"brothers, two (twin)" 8959
"brothers left for the front" 8704
"brothers left the chapel" 1311
"brothers Moon, the" 1756
"brothers or sisters" 8249
"brothers used to sleep together" 8248
"brougham" 9761
"brought back by a memory" 7453
"brought David Rayborne to Rome, what" 6048
"brought her back" 7434
"brought her up from babyhood" 8716
"brought him back here, what had" 1633
"brought me, what have you" 4127
"brought the Sword of the Spirit into our house" 5113
"brought up by the Cheyenne Indians" 9707
"brought up in two countries, I was" 9712
"brought up on three dead languages" 9709
"brought up to be" 9716
"brought up to believe that they have a destiny" 3671
"brought up where such kind of men rode" 9705
"brought Walter in, day they" 9645
"brouhaha, it takes more than two people to staff a" 8934
"brouhaha, not a" 8934
"brow, crack in the center of his" 5942
"brow and nose, solid line of" 347
"brow furrowed in seriousness" 8873
Brown 3298, 5490
Brown, Bo-jo 6424
Brown, Cluny 9423
Brown, Daisy 9357
Brown, Jackie 4251
Brown, Mrs. 4850, 9348
"brown as leaves" 6883
Brownfield 1670
Browning, Eugene 10208
"Browns, the" 3528
"brownstone, the dark" 2554
"brownstone, the old" 668
"brownstones" 6280
"brows, thickish" 333
"brows drawn together" 8547
"browsed slowly and gently as cows graze" 10623
"browsing" 5607
Bruce 125, 8250, 9327
Bruce, David Spencer 1757
Bruce, Lenny 1254
Bruce, Niall 4829
Bruce, Robert 383
Brucie 1739
"Bruges" 839
"Bruh, hey" 2788

"bruised heart" 10555
Brun, Felix 489
"brunch, preparing" 1865
Bruno 10204
"Brunswick, palace at" 7483
"brushed, neatly" 1887
"brushing his suit carefully" 2831
"brushing the dust from his hands" 5920
"brushwood, long patch of" 9670
Bruss, Miss 9880
"Brussels" 3119, 3396, 10768
"brutish cry" 10017
Bryson, Tynan 7168
"bub" 7567
"bubble, tiny silver" 531
"bubble in the illimitable ocean of space" 6075
"bubbles, funny orange" 5634
"bubbles rising in it that he hated" 5634
Bucci 7848
"Buccleuch" 10658
"Bucharest" 6456
Buck 100
Buck, Billy 2220
Buck, Joe 5257
Buck, Uncle 4201
"buckboard was a fitting name" 9832
Bucket, Mr. 6645
"bucket, dinted and seldom disinfected" 6294
"bucket, large wooden" 10943
"bucket, patent canvas" 810
"bucket, red and white longitudes of the enormous" 3001
Buckholz 6504
"bucking the choppy waves, rowboat" 8164
"buckle, brass" 2835
"buckled at the knees" 152
"bucks, offered me ten" 3330
"Bucks" 5279
"Budapest" 8859, 10884
"Budapest, why is London like" 1476
"Buda-Pesth seems a wonderful place" 9524
Budd, Lanning 4732
Budd, Lanny 2958, 4636, 8719
"Buddha" 1523
Buddie 9721
"budge it, she couldn't" 10949
"buds of the little cherry tree" 9683
"Buenos Aires" 9651
"Buffalo" 2112
"Buffalo New York" 4043
"buffing the kitchen floor" 6547
"buffoon, I am not their" 10855
Buffy 6261
Bug 3888
"bugged everybody" 302
"bugger, *that*" 9259
"bugger, yo'" 9269

"buggy, horse and" 2967, 7223
"buggy pass ahead of him, let the"
    9767
"bugle, last stray call of a" 5096
"bugles sounded from the barracks"
    10491
"bugs, lightning" 4962
"Buick" 2971
"Buick convertible" 9810
"Buick Electra" 9786
"build gigantic pavilions" 7808
"builder, jerry" 1856
"building, Air Terminal" 1699
"building, apartment" 1774, 2773
"building, burned down a" 3630
"Building, Empire State" 4654,
    8565, 9977
"building, enormous" 9244
"Building, Executive Office" 6510
"building, façade of the" 9252
"building, fashionable apartment"
    1714
"building, handsome administra-
    tion" 7905
"building, huge apartment" 3443
"building, in front of the" 8355
"building, large low triangular"
    1068
"building, long low wooden" 7623
"building, low buff" 3001
"Building, Navy" 3315
"building, new" 9232
"building, newspaper" 6319
"building, old rickety" 9214
"building, on the second floor of a"
    1029
"building, palatial" 8580
"Building, Patuxent" 5845
"building, quaint old circular" 7772
"building, ratty" 10067
"building, red brick" 9206
"building, rustic" 847
"building, squat grey" 8300
"building, three-storeyed tenement"
    1419
"Building, Treloar" 9222
"Building, Wandstar" 6513
"Building is huge" 9254
"building is pink" 9257
"building like a battleship" 9236
"building of the large hall" 9213
"building of Tom Rowhedge's new
    house" 1852
"building presented a not unpleas-
    ant architectural scheme" 9225
"building shooting upward like a
    railroad track set for the moon"
    4635
"building sits by the river" 5046
"building up of a frontier farm"
    1850
"building waited as though braced
    to defend itself" 9244
"building was broad and squat and
    thick" 9249

"building was - just a building"
    9221
"building where I lived" 3330
"building where I worked" 1748
Buildings 779, 1008, 1026, 1028,
    1029, 1044, 1293, 1299, 1304,
    1306, 1310, 1345, 1368, 1400, 1420,
    1425, 1596, 1774, 1849, 1851, 2161,
    2401, 2636, 2715, 3001, 3059,
    3064, 3089, 3096, 3097, 3120,
    3144, 3160, 3208, 3226, 3422,
    3424, 3425, 3429, 3430, 3431,
    3630, 3985, 3986, 3991, 4311,
    4316, 4328, 4385, 4618, 4627,
    4631, 4635, 4645, 4652, 4654,
    5046, 6059, 6280, 6375, 6513,
    6924, 6974, 7108, 7229, 7263,
    7282, 7529, 7699, 7772, 7808,
    7875, 7887, 7902, 7908, 8300,
    8321, 8355, 8590, 8625, 9205,
    9206, 9208, 9209, 9210, 9211,
    9212, 9213, 9214, 9215, 9216,
    9218, 9220, 9221, 9222, 9223,
    9224, 9225, 9226, 9227, 9228,
    9229, 9231, 9232, 9233, 9234,
    9235, 9236, 9237, 9239, 9240,
    9241, 9243, 9244, 9245, 9246,
    9247, 9249, 9250, 9252, 9253,
    9254, 9255, 9256, 9257, 9258,
    9259, 10036, 10706
"buildings, business" 5323
"buildings, delicate and isolated"
    3422
"buildings, dilapidated" 7282
"Buildings, Dodd's" 1596
"buildings, doors of certain" 4129
"buildings, Experimental Pathology"
    5088
"buildings, grazing the tops of the
    tall" 1399
"buildings, long brown" 4316
"buildings, Manhattan's" 7699
"buildings, medical" 9258
"buildings, modestly tall" 1420
"buildings, new brick" 8080
"buildings, one of Chicago's tallest"
    10036
"buildings, tall" 1115
"buildings, vast aggregation of"
    1345
"buildings, white government" 9239
"buildings polished to the gleam of
    newly minted money" 7229
"buildings to flee into, no" 7036
"built, country was being" 272
"built, powerfully" 5893
"built, rashly" 6163
"built, was being" 7508
"built a fragment of Holland on the
    north arm of Hirado Bay" 1851
"built by giants before anyone re-
    members" 9227
"built by the Spencers before the
    Civil War" 3665
"built himself a house" 3110, 3152

"built in 1865" 3120
"built in the forties" 3218
"built line upon line and tower
    upon tower" 1356
"built of stone blocks" 3131
"built of uncut rocks roughly mor-
    tared" 1855
"built on large lines, she was" 4773
"built the box real careful" 1857
"built upon the ruins" 1384
"Bukit Kallang, town of" 3152
Bulbo, Prince 1902
"bulbs, plant the indoor" 3974
"Bulinga" 1631
"bulk, glowing horizontal" 8625
Bulkley, Dave 1538
"bull, made you think of a charg-
    ing" 5893
"Bull, the time of the" 5458
"bull ring, Cretan" 10594
"bullace" 7440
Bullard, Avery 134
Bullay, George 3852
"bulldozer worked" 5688
"bullet, sharp splat of the" 410
"bullet, shoulder had been shat-
    tered by a" 9848
"bullet, silver" 7440
"bullet hole" 7614
"bulletin board" 10977
"bulletproof glass" 8728
"bullfight, genuine" 5455
"bull-fight of the season, the last"
    8911
Bullfights 8911
"bullies who peddled them" 6848
Bullivant 5999
"bullring" 1549
Bulow, Arthur 2736
Bultitude, Paul 8341
"bum, hallelujah" 5255
"bum is what we're all on" 5255
"Bumblebee for the first time, saw
    the" 2162
"bumbling" 6705
Bumpass, Mrs. Ephephtha 1985
"bumped into him, I nearly" 1619
"bumped twice in the noon-day
    heat" 199
"bumper to bumper" 3041
"bumper within feet of the jetty's
    edge" 9785
"bumping through Newtown" 7062
"bums still asleep" 2210
"bun, hot dog" 1259
"Bund" 10536
"bundled to and fro between two
    houses" 6117
"bundled up and soft, everything
    became" 8606
"bungalow" 3218, 8644
"bungalow, his" 2026
"bungalow, living then in a" 3214
"bungalow as lonely, never thought
    of the" 3168

"bungalow unit, her stucco" 10320
"bungalows, silhouetted" 537
"bunk, lay in his" 2891
"bunks" 8248
"bunkum in higher education" 3271
Bunn, Miss 9907
Bunny 78, 3631, 10130
Bunter, Billy 5858
"bunting and *REFERENDUM* signs" 10748
Bunyan, Paul 4464
"buoyant, she felt quite" 9615
"buoys, starting-line" 8163
Burbank 3511
"Burbank" 5571
Burch, Miss Agatha 2316
Burch, Professor 9788
"burden" 5507
"burden of the heat, lightening the" 7308
"burden of trees and vines, fast maturing" 4374
"Burden upon his back" 2751
"burden-bearers" 6417
"burdened with a large quantity of parcels" 10369
Burdens 4853, 5700, 10369
"burdens of intention" 5460
Burdette, Jacey 4543
Burdette, Jack 1768
Burdon, Arthur 10334
"bureaucrat, I no longer think of myself as a" 6494
"bureaucrats belong too much to the world" 6494
"burgeoning, the shoots the shrubs and the flowers were" 3805
Burgess, Edward 9144
"burglars could wear over their faces" 2066
Burglary 872, 2059
"burglary, that event would be the" 5105
Burgoyne, Chuck 6200
Burial 1190, 1192, 2300, 2329, 2344, 2443, 3940, 4223, 4683, 7382
"burial, day of the" 7382
"buried, Daniel was to be" 2456
"buried alive, I'm being" 944
"buried at a church" 2443
"buried deep in white" 8592
"buried her two days later" 807
"buried here, Kafka is not" 1195
"buried in a wilderness of maple trees" 3095
"buried in the archives" 9021
"buried in the cemetery" 1190
"buried in Winchelsea church" 2300
"buried my boy" 4223
"buried my grandfather" 3940
"buried old Harry, they" 2344
"buried the wrong dead cat" 6032
"buried towns" 1384
"buried two husbands" 2379

Burke, Sergeant 1099
Burkholder, Lewis 10945
Burl 6739
"Burlingame" 5130
"Burlington Gardens" 4304
"Burlington railroad" 3087
"burly bespectacled white cashier" 1048
"Burma" 1757, 4094
"Burma, Upper" 4378
"burn, it was a pleasure to" 3769
"burn, the grass continued to" 3772
"burn seemed to smart behind his eyes" 6600
"Burnaby British Columbia" 3208
"burned down a building" 3630
"burned down The Place, almost" 5094
"burned island" 5042
"burned out by the fool on the floor below me" 6299
"burned over our heads" 835
"burned the palms of hands, boulders..." 4413
"burned the trees" 5042
"burned up and down" 5324
Burnes 990
"burning, city was" 3777
"burning, Venice is" 505
"burning British garments" 3771
"burning hulls hissed upon the water" 4469
"burning in the harbor, ships were" 3791
"burning in the sun" 4367
"burning red behind us" 3766
"burning the bridge of his nose during rugby matches" 5329
"burnish in a candle flame" 7411
Burns, Beatrice 8421
"burnt to cinders" 4380
Burr, Colonel Aaron 10662
"burrow, scraping herself a" 9790
"burrowed again, he" 10251
"burrowed into the upward slope of the land" 3118
"burrowing against Kate's warm back" 10251
"bursar, complaints of his" 9945
"Bursar, Domestic" 8354
"Bursley" 784, 1362, 5898
"Bursley, the market-place of" 8845
"burst and dispersed" 893
"burst forth in spring" 3979
"burst into flaming gold and red" 2150
"burst of laughter" 5186
"burst silently out of the trees" 4695
"bursting for a piss" 6599
"burstingly healthy" 9718
"bursts, conversation came in excited little" 7390
Burtenshaw, Keith 6539
"burthened with so very uncouth an appellation" 8955

Burton, Keith 898
"Burundi" 6735
"bury dissenters, he did not care to" 1493
"bury it in a decent and Christian way" 2329
"burying place" 4494
"burying-ground" 726
"burying-ground, Linden" 1186
"bus, a" 9768
"bus, all-night" 3402
"bus, big Leyland double-decked" 9828
"bus, country" 1620
"bus, double-decker" 6319
"bus, excursion" 9577
"bus, fell off the" 2353
"bus, got on the" 10806
"Bus, Greyhound" 9583
"bus, I got off the" 10415
"bus, is there a" 9573
"bus, leave the" 2588
"bus, lights in the" 5320
"bus, looking through the window of the" 8304
"bus, old blue-painted school" 10076
"bus, on the" 3513
"bus, one-horse" 9540
"bus, prison" 9838
"bus, pushed and shoved to get on the" 9620
"bus, stepping off the" 1250
"bus, the" 9781, 9796
"bus, waited for the" 10045
"bus, what the hell are you doing on a" 10563
"bus arrived that would take her home" 10092
"bus came to a sudden halt" 9780
"bus coursed down through red clay and pine hills" 2911
"bus driver, the" 7311
"bus drivers jested" 5308
"bus from Market Square" 1629
"bus had to stop" 136
"bus halted" 9816
"bus just don't want to get here" 10061
"bus queue, standing in a" 10046
"bus rounded a hairpin bend" 9788
"bus she should take, which" 1158
"bus stop" 9423
"bus stopping at East and Market streets" 1608
"bus stops, the" 1771
"Bus Terminal, Port Authority" 6274
"bus top" 9556
"bus was pulling away" 1671
"bus-driver behind the wheel" 10806
"bus-driver was whistling" 10062
Buses 136, 1158, 1608, 1620, 1629, 1671, 1726, 1771, 2353, 2588, 2911, 3513, 5320, 5360, 5370, 6319,

7311, 8304, 9130, 9423, 9540,
9556, 9577, 9583, 9620, 9768,
9780, 9781, 9788, 9796, 9797,
9804, 9816, 9828, 9838, 10045,
10046, 10061, 10092, 10415, 10563,
10806
"buses and trains" 5360
"buses flushing scarlet in puddles"
7317
"buses moved with almost funereal
slowness" 9804
"buses plying" 1726
"buses to catch, there have been no"
9797
Bush, Lieutenant William 8098
"bush, hazel" 10756
"bush, in the" 8379
"bush, slick shiny green of gum and
sassafras" 973
"bush that handfuls of wild guinea
fowl raised with their cries" 8379
"bushes, among the mesquite"
10686
"bushes, laurel" 3036
"bushes, thistle" 5161
"bushes which surrounded the
spring" 2890
"bushlands" 5138
"bushwhacked a piano" 4250
Business 285, 1355, 1401, 1443,
1455, 1460, 1992, 2491, 2538,
2548, 2592, 2845, 3054, 3154,
3194, 3586, 3657, 3738, 3914,
4029, 4039, 4265, 4683, 4760,
5004, 5170, 5844, 5963, 6353,
6411, 6414, 6425, 6459, 6465,
6516, 6715, 6918, 7099, 7154,
7295, 7814, 8052, 8870, 8893,
8896, 9567, 9580, 9665, 9827,
10478, 10557, 10836
"business, book-writing" 5490
"business, criminal end of the" 6411
"business, dispatch his" 4920
"business, first official piece of"
10978
"business, he had a" 1033
"business, his" 6516
"business, horribly bad" 6929
"business, I might as well get down
to" 9000
"business, in the course of my"
6448
"business, in the habit of commencing" 2290
"Business, inventory of my" 1066
"business, lack of profitable" 583
"business, learning the" 8587
"business, minding her own" 2640
"business, no" 7755
"business, put off the most urgent"
4683
"business, this branch of its" 1015
"business, this little" 1050
"business, transact some of his
vague" 6715

"business, urgent domestic" 8694
"business, very little" 1010
"business, world-wise" 5265
"business acquaintances" 3961
"business buildings" 5323
"business district, two-block-long"
9203
"business failed, that was the year"
1019
"business from spilling out, your
foul" 8931
"business houses were ruined" 1019
"business lively in taverns, kept"
7865
"business of the place" 5066
"business or profession" 10478
"business people" 6496
"business people of Carson City"
1082
"business section, noisy haphazard
but to the inhabitants very homelike" 1390
"business to tell it to me, no" 8972
"business together, had gone into"
285
"business trip" 9580
"businesses, their husbands'" 10843
"bust, get him or" 6947
"bust, the" 8940
"bust, whose was that imposing"
5943
"bust made front page news" 6343
"bust of Homer" 509
"busted my eardrums, I thought I'd"
882
"bustles with life" 3215
"bustling indifferent city" 1183
"busts with thrills chills laughs and
Sex" 5489
Busy 6723
"busy, tired of being so" 1493
"busy all day, too" 9418
"busybody, well-meaning" 1201
"busyness of their lives" 8093
Butcher, Pete 7603
"Butcher's Crossing" 9777
Butchery 10955
Butler, Dr. Andrew 5438
Butler, Walter 7409
"butler, Japanese" 3088
"butler, lame" 1098
"butler, old" 2316
"butler whom Lanny had hired in
Spain" 1098
"butlers and lady's maids do not
reproduce their kind" 6413
Butt, Johnnie 6353
"butt him in the guts" 3289
"butt-naked" 6399
"Butte" 1474, 10901
"butter, how's" 4211
"butter pats" 7575
Butterflies 303, 4957, 4967, 5087
"butterflies, pair of sulphur" 4957
"butterflies, plastic" 303

"butterflies, white" 6386
"butterflies emerged from the leaves
of a single cottonwood" 4957
"butterflies rise from the field" 4967
"butterfly accoustically, no" 218
"butterfly came along and brushed
his cheek" 5087
"butterfly collection, vivid" 2156
"butterfly net" 10816
Buttermere 82
"butternuts, cracked" 2312
"butthole so damn wide, I want
your" 8931
"buttock, the" 10817
"buttock, undulations of" 7985
Buttocks 6398, 6400, 8370
"buttocks, displaying his bare" 6398
"buttocks, quivering" 7945
"buttocks, smoothness of her pale-
brown" 7187
"buttocks, two pair of perfect" 9186
"buttocks red, her" 6400
"button, electic-bell" 9875
"button at the front door" 668
"buttoned into a black overcoat,
tightly" 1702
"button-holed" 5943
"button-holing me as he did this
afternoon" 9305
"buttons, lapels of his coat were
covered with celluloid" 2828
"buttons, long-gone" 1548
"buttons, numerous brass" 1313
"buttons, three bone" 2787
"buy, trying to" 1024
"buy a desk" 1035
"buy a stick of rock" 10831
"buy a transistor radio" 1046
"buy fireworks" 10665
"buy the flowers herself" 3797
"buy the paper and her father's
cigarettes" 4289
"buying a paper today, he was not"
10366
"buying diamonds" 5456
"buying [homes]" 3241
"buzz, crepuscular" 8333
"buzz, glary red" 2891
"buzz of the universe" 8333
Buzza, Admiral 6308
"buzzard lazed" 729
"buzzed and clicked the deck of
cards" 308
"buzzer sounded sharp and sudden"
8795
"buzzing, furious" 8480
"buzzing of a fly" 10326
"Bwamba" 1833
Byfield, David 4295
Byne, Austin 1106
Bynum, Lincoln 2441
Byrd, Lucille 8010
Byrd, Richard E. 228
"byre, dunghill behind the" 1863
"Byzantine eyes" 1305

"C. & O. Pullman" 5924
"cab, I got out of a" 1625
"cab, their hired" 9239
"cab, turned his" 2970
"cab as it lurches forward" 8320
"cab curled off, my" 9807
"cab driver" 10085
"cab dropped him at the Place
   Pigalle" 1678
"cab sixteen" 1003
"cab that wanted desperately to die"
   9801
"cabalistic doctrine, like" 9053
"caballero" 7132
"cabbage" 1085
"cabbage heads, spoiled" 8068
"Cabbalistic conjuror" 7505
"cabbie, the" 3428
"cabbie's plight" 6652
"cabdriver, if there's one thing I
   can't stand it's a one-armed" 6652
"cabin, his empty" 10278
"cabin, his lighted" 8060
"cabin, Judy Conlon's" 1700
"cabin, little" 3086
"cabin, log" 3129
"cabin, log-and-mud" 437
"cabin, my" 7751, 8612
"cabin, one-room log" 3128
"cabin, their" 3652
"cabin, two-room sharecropper's"
   826
"cabin chimney" 3763
"cabin door" 1556, 7025
"cabin in order, his" 7919
"cabin of two rooms, cozy log"
   3074
"cabin that nestled under great
   moss-hung oaks" 3090
"Cabinet Office" 6999
"cabinets, moldy green filing" 2700
Cabins 437, 826, 3074, 3086,
   3090, 3128, 3129, 3763
Cable, Miss 10036
Cable, Paul 8270
"cable cars" 9611
"cable from Emmie, I had a" 6007
"Cable Point" 7427
"cable was off, the last" 8157
"cable-car, Australian" 9626
"caboose, door to the" 8812
Cabot, Hector 9700
Cabral, Pedro Alvarez 5576
"cacique, the" 8169
"cackle, harsh" 10282
"cactus" 9127
"cactus, paddle" 5190
"cactus sucked up their own
   shadows" 5704
"cactus wild" 4061
"cadaverous and extraordinary
   figure of my uncle" 6496
"caddies, three" 8372
"Caddos, capture a few" 1076
"caddy, a" 6462

"caddy at the Crescent Club" 6449
"cadence of the verse" 4474
"cadence, rhythmic" 10401
"cadence, what a" 6212
"cadences over its mossy stones,
   ripples sweet" 10683
"Cader Idris" 6606
"Cadet, Flying" 8649
"Cadets, the" 8677
"Cadillac" 3030
"Cadillac, new 1964" 9819
"Cadiz, port of" 5223
"Caerlyn Sands" 3533
Caesar 5443, 8948
Caesar, Caius Julius 7514
Caesar, Gaius Julius 7006
Caesar Augustus 4469
"Caesar's statue in the forum" 8948
"Café, Black Ally's" 4004
"café, cheapest kind of" 2856
"Café, Elite" 7577
"cafe, garage and" 1080
"café, in an overcrowded" 8223
"Café, Happy's" 5757
"Café, Kranzler's" 7582
"cafe, outdoor" 2912
"café, outside the" 10048
"cafe, sidewalk" 10884
"café, small" 10896
"café, talking in the" 8846
"Café, Whaley's" 5571
"Café Cardinal" 4973
"Café des Deux Magots" 8552
"Café Exotica" 4334
"Café Julien" 4274
"Café Lavenue" 7568
"Café Stieckus" 2806
"cafés, political" 9119
"cafés of cities far beyond the
   jungle" 7339
"cage, silver" 4785
"cage, wire netting of her" 740
"cage in which Cardinal Balue was
   imprisoned, the iron" 7139
"cage was too small" 762
"caged tigress, like a" 10345
Cain 7622
"Cairo" 1351, 1694
"Cairo Egypt" 7681
"Cairo slum" 889
"Cajun bayou" 9083
"Cajuns, two" 1652
"cake, here's your" 6679
"cake, wedding" 10657
"cake and cider" 3680
"cake for the party later" 860
Cal 2704
"Calais" 9632
"calamity, theatre of" 5554
"Calcutta" 4646
Caldigate, Daniel 3553
Caldigate, John 3553
"caldron on the stove, copper" 7441
Caldwell 9844
Caleb, uncle 3451

"Caledonia" 6245
"Caledonian, the" 8094
"calefactory, in the" 139
"calendar, battered" 491
"calendar, Jewish" 4524
"calendar, like last year's" 2685
"Calendar, Newgate" 3376
"Calendar, Old" 6915
"Calendar, Spanish" 7502
"calendar devised by man,
   measured on any" 2628
"calendar on his desk" 2155
"calendar stands clear" 5199
"calendar that hung against the
   wall" 491
Calendars 491, 7502
"calf" 9684
"calf, stillborn" 453
Califia, Queen 280
California 287, 7309
"California" 280, 287, 968, 1454,
   2956, 3362, 3630, 5210, 6114,
   6272, 6344, 6997, 7508, 7831,
   7900, 9145, 10230, 10559, 10923
"California, cactus wild of
   Southern" 4061
"California, clichés about" 10606
"California, coast of" 3089
"California, her mother was in"
   6714
"California, I hadn't much wanted
   to go to" 6136
"California, live in" 3202
"California, northern" 2441, 10627
"California, Northern" 9751
"California, on her way to" 8120
"California, Southern" 309, 470,
   3636, 4332, 4901
"California coast" 9045
"California hills" 5147
"California license MK-1" 9794
"California sun" 8413
"California Trail, Old" 6948
"Californian gold rush" 6104
"Californian sun" 1324
"Californians, race of the golden"
   10495
Caligula, Gaius 7802
"Caliph of Granada" 7809
"calk his ships" 8165
"call, make a quick telephone" 1101
"call, my first middle-of-the-night
   crisis" 1146
"call, one day I get a" 1152
"call, phone" 1120
"call, received a phone" 1139
"call, would he accept a collect" 1141
"call Agios, forced myself to" 1136
"call Aubrey George Grant" 1108
"call came, the" 1142
"call come, when the" 1103
"call distinctly three times" 9989
"call five *six*, if you" 9476
"call from a father" 1153
"call from Daisy" 1141

"call from God" 1518
"call from the leper hospital" 164
"call had come at 6:12 precisely" 1123
"call her from work later and apologize" 2714
"call her Rose, I will" 4176
"call him on the phone using a code name" 2906
"call him Prospero, we'll" 7065
"call him up, begging you to" 1094
"call me" 1114
"call me an agent" 6468
"call me collect" 6337
"call me Holder, you can" 4847
"call me Isabel" 4815
"call me Ishmael" 4713
"call me Jonah" 4765
"call me Russel Wren" 4798
"call me Smitty" 4791
"call me Talkative Man, they" 4839
"call me the minute you get there" 1135
"call myself Pilgermann, I" 4819
"call myself, what I" 4793
"call of a bugle" 5096
"call to dispose of a bomb, got a" 892
Callaghan, Isobel 866
Callant, John 246
"Callao" 8055
"cal'latin' to buy one of them turnovers" 7567
calle, long narrow" 8252
"Calle de Goya" 3141
"Calle de Marengo" 7570
"called, Betaut" 1125
"called Ambrose, I was" 4756
"called and hollered and shrieked at the bald Jeeter" 3604
"called and told Tristan's mom" 1151
"called at the American Consulate" 9879
"called away to Miami" 159
"called back from his gate" 6979
"called Buckholz and Cripps into my office" 6504
"called by their people simply The World" 6792
"called for two cards" 295
"called from a distance, father" 4162
"called from the Home" 1158
"called her down in mid-afternoon, never" 2254
"called her the old baroness" 79
"called him" 10815
"called him, what his intimates" 4728
"called him, what his wife" 1966
"called him 'Lucky'" 4843
"called him afterwards, as some" 5034
"called him Harry the Lover" 7995
"called him Lanny, people" 4732
"called him Roshan" 4742

"called him Sanjé in the French manner" 5905
"called in the dialect, as he was" 4734
"called it afterwards, as he always" 5089
"called Jack everywhere but the front of the Bible" 4437
"called John Spencer's place, still" 3665
"called me for tea" 9360
"called me from Chicago at one in the morning" 1157
"called me from the first" 5597
"called me John, they" 4765
"called me that, they" 6031
"called my son's name" 6552
"called myself Pip" 4714
"called on Horace Appleby" 9919
"called suddenly to Washington" 6370
"called Tiddyboo for good and sufficient reasons" 4785
"called to Bayley Farm House" 6964
"called to him" 1784
"called to his wife" 10180
"called to see me" 6688
"called to the stand" 5201
Callias 5738
"calling, heard someone" 10158
"calling, somebody was" 2764
"calling again" 6662
"calling and calling the *News*" 6652
"calling and testing in the small hours" 1118
"calling Gram Mon" 10019
"calling her Ma" 10180
"calling him 'Margayya', people seemed to have been" 4741
"calling mentally her name" 6218
"calling of a world full of birds, multitudinous silver" 836
"calling of Gervaise to her cows" 8823
"calling on me" 9951
"calling or seeing Joleen" 3306
"calling the roll" 7906
"calling the score, energetically" 8259
"calling us, always" 6088
"Calling-Together, a" 2623
Calloway, Louisa 6394
Calls 164, 892, 2254, 2392, 2785, 3310, 3918, 5691, 6727, 6937, 6964, 7874, 8000, 8197, 9011, 9301, 10132, 10182, 10302, 10654
"calls, Lady Boxe" 3974
"calls me Marie, Mother" 4722
"calls me Mary, Father" 4722
"calls me Mary Marie, everybody else" 4722
"calm" 3310
"calm, absolute" 7930
"calm, the curtained and velvety"

1011
"calm her down by tickling her stomach" 740
"Calormen" 8991
"caltrops gules upon a field argent, three" 2686
"Calumet" 1612
"Calvary" 3439
"Calvinist out of me, would have made a" 7520
"'cam' and on the deliberate side" 10357
"Cambridge" 4114, 5448, 8607, 8976, 10437, 10441
"Cambridge, distant" 8591
"Cambridge, third year at" 5631
"Cambridge, unique to" 7335
"Cambridge across the river" 6678
"Camden" 8012, 9708
"came, Ida" 7058
"came, when my aunt Zita" 1257
"came along, she" 5367
"came along the beach" 10810
"came around from her house" 9985
"came at me out of the dark" 9237
"came back" 1768
"came back, when he" 4566
"came back into the twilight of his house" 10180
"came back on a new track" 1948
"came back to America" 1571
"came back to Evensford" 2960
"came back to Sunbury, when I" 4595
"came back to the house" 3939
"came back to the river" 1640
"came back with the parcels" 9406
"came down, a man" 10382
"came down by the lift" 1595
"came down from London" 6620
"came down here" 7313
"came down the corduroy" 7215
"came down the hill sideways" 9823
"came down the steps" 1610
"came down to sea" 8783
"came down to the high-school field" 8675
"came downstairs" 9471
"came downstairs at eight thirty" 9470
"came for him that Sunday" 6960
"came from, wherever it" 5121
"came from another country" 9111
"came from the dark bedroom into the morning light" 1752
"came from the sea" 7925
"came from the shieling" 3667
"came from the stairhead" 8041
"came here on purpose" 6831
"came home from a Tupperware party" 10559
"came home to this his city" 4592
"came in, Julia" 1605
"came in off the back porch" 10939

"came into her from behind" 7985
"came into its own" 9048
"came into Louisiana in 1842" 5215
"came into Plymouth from Exeter way" 7610
"came into the land" 7810
"came into the stable" 460
"came into the world" 4346
"came late to the war" 9344
"came like a caravan of carnival folk" 1680
"came on board" 8161
"came once in the middle of the night" 8706
"came out into the sunlight" 8790
"came out of his bedroom" 1573
"came out of his high house" 3992
"came out of the Army" 8667
"came out of the big brick Oaklin house" 7127
"came out of the Café Lavenue" 7568
"came out of the Hotel Columbus" 10439
"came out of the house" 1604
"came out of the Underground" 10375
"came out on the porch" 459
"came out to the house" 8305
"came over to me" 6963
"came straight home" 3943
"came there in the off-season" 1770
"came through the turnstile" 10054
"came to, I" 10234
"came to a beautiful glade" 10784
"came to a head, it all" 4521
"came to a likely camp site" 5169
"came to a stop" 7269
"came to Bellefleur Manor" 1706
"came to Bruges, we" 839
"came to Central America" 9954
"came to Egypt with the draft" 8685
"came to Essendon airport" 197
"came to Halifax" 5034
"came to her as it comes to women" 7068
"came to herself, she" 3413
"came to Italy" 5465
"came to Italy on their honeymoon" 9559
"came to live with us" 5119
"came to London, when I first" 3171
"came to me, it all" 4697
"came to me, when it" 10190
"came to me from the sea" 154
"came to me in one piece" 8751
"came to myself in a grove of young pines" 7205
"came to our house with dusty shoes" 4176
"came to see me the other day" 9986
"came to see me today" 9969
"came to shore at what is now

Mattagash Maine" 6155
"came to stay with us" 5156
"came to the Claremont Hotel" 1674
"came to the edge of the world of his time" 7808
"came to the fairest spot" 6564
"came to the Hornburys' house, whoever" 3161
"came to the house, every time he" 9983
"came to this town, I" 1478
"came to town" 8010
"came to us, Aunt Hat" 248
"came to work on foot" 10442
"came up against a green cloth" 7430
"came up the steps of the farmhouse" 7440
"came up to town to live" 5790
"came with the house, Neville" 3331
"came yesterday" 1692
"camel" 9626
"camel, drat that" 445
"camel, take my" 1643
"camel caravan, unreachable by" 1429
"Camelot, court at" 6561
"Camelot, dreamed of" 3234
"camembert" 4132
"camera, in the meadow with his" 6879
"camera, lens of the" 6869
"Camera, Radcliffe" 7772
"camera of hers, outstare that" 6875
"camera people, all those" 9372
"cameramen, still and newsreel" 8859
Camerlengo, Cardinal 1525
Cameron 3889, 8626
Cameron, Maddie 8472
Cameron, Rachel 8747
Camier 9588
Camilla 6765, 6864
Camille 1733
"camouflage" 8659
"camouflaged Humber staff car" 9785
"camouflaged them, gray as the dawn which" 8107
"camouflaged three-ton Bedford" 9791
"camp, base" 8682
"camp, broke" 7621
"camp, everyone in the" 7141
"camp, King's" 1779
"camp, looked back at the" 8652
"camp, made noon" 7662
"camp, our" 4042
"camp, overran our" 4469
"camp, refugee" 10532
"Camp, Shibi Rest" 9217
"camp, the" 10940
"camp, train starts pulling out of the" 1738

"camp circle" 6158
"camp for themselves, made a kind of" 10930
"camp in the Selkirks, that winter" 8851
"Camp No. 2, Base" 6076
"camp of fear" 1310
"camp on the banks of the river Indus" 7808
"camp out on the Mediterranean coast" 8894
"Camp Pickett Virginia" 8673
"camp site, likely" 5169
"camp was a clock" 10503
"campaign for reelection" 7005
"Campanella, the" 8053
"campanile" 10160
Campbell 354, 6611
Campbell, Elissa 6397
Campbell, Howard W. Jr. 4762
"camped in this spot" 7673
"camper, homemade" 9798
"camper knocked together out of painted plywood and sheet metal" 9798
"Camperlea" 982
"campfire in the woods, flicker of a" 3465
"campfires, old" 7457
"camp-fires faded" 2191
"camphor trees" 3411
Camping 1560, 7673
"camping" 1560
"campion, cowparsley and" 3808
"Campo San Stefano" 8252
Camps 3067, 3559, 4042, 5169, 6076, 6158, 7141, 7662, 7808, 8652, 9217, 10503, 10532, 10930
"camps, coal-" 1365
Campton, John 491
"campus, acid rain was falling on the" 7336
"campus, also and also of the" 7907
"campus, Oberlin" 2083
"campus, Rummidge" 8615
"campus, west" 9814
"campus walks" 8601
"campus was designed, half the" 7882
Campuses 5088, 7336, 7882, 7907
Camus 7368
"can, the empty Carnation evaporated milk" 3849
"can of Beef and Potatoes, stirred a" 1864
can you, how" 7555
Canada 1543, 3897, 4125
"Canada" 807, 1139, 3599, 5480, 6075, 6155, 7403
"Canada, lower French" 10431
"Canada, United Provinces of" 7272
"Canada's hundredth birthday" 4125
"Canadian, French-" 7187

"Canadian blonde" 5779
"Canadian forest" 3897
"Canadian shore" 4043
"Canadian wilderness" 1543
"Canadian wireless stations" 3534
"Canadian year, passionate seasonal shape of the" 10611
"canal, across the" 8095
"canal, fronting on the" 4311
"Canal, Grand" 5140, 8252
"Canal, Kanawha" 1465
"Canal, Royal Military" 4048
"canal black, the" 9170
"canals filled with Rhine water" 1352
"canaries singing" 4634
"canary, feeding her" 3270
"cancer, brain" 2454
"cancer, everyone is dying of" 2377
Candace 2950
"Candia" 120
"candid confession" 4490
"candidate" 5832
"candidate, presidential" 6994
"candidate, to be accepted as a" 1514
"candle, allowed me to carry the" 1210
"candle, light a" 8484
"candle, lighted" 7782
"candle, miserable" 7032
"candle, slim unsnuffed" 8453
"candle flame" 7441
"candle in a tin candlestick" 7753
"candle inserted in an old bottle" 7032
"candleflame, the" 3790
"Candleford, go over to" 6566
"candlelight" 1305
"candle-light, pale pool of" 6386
"Candlemasday" 2887
"candles" 6383
"candles, cheap tallow" 4335
"candles, multicolored" 7533
"candles, tiny red corkscrew" 4520
"candles, wax" 1342
"candles flicker for the first time in their scalloped holders" 4520
"candles in the cellar rooms" 2129
"candle's light, half-gloom of a solitary" 458
"candles tipped with yellow flames, rows of white" 4514
"candlestick, removed a massive copper" 6367
"candlestick, tin" 7753
Candy 10019
"candy, hard" 4419
"candy, the fotched-on" 4850
"candy buttons" 5348
"candy which mimicks roses" 4850
"candy-counter" 1448
"cane, cruel-looking" 6652
"cane he carried" 10373
"canned goods, house-brand" 921

"Cannery Row" 6272, 10492
Canning, Deputy 6954
Cannon, George Edwin 3326
"cannon, plugged" 4073
"cannon on the front porch" 4262, 4268
"cannonball, exploding" 7901
"canoe" 9626
"canoe, high-nosed cedar" 8145
"canoe, stolen" 10960
"canoe, traveled by" 9635
"canoe on top of the truck" 10960
"canoe still atop it" 9300
Canoes 4161, 8145, 8155, 8156
"canoes, Huron" 8155
"canoes in all, six" 8156
"Canona" 5924
"canonized St. Martin of Tours" 7539
"Canopus" 5497
"canopy, forming a" 7692
"canopy, under a wooden" 1080
"canopy which spread a sun-dappled shade" 9674
"cans, the first five or six" 7236
"can't and couldn't, you" 7121
"Cantata, Christmas" 2869
"Canterbury" 1691
"Canterbury, Archbishop of" 1145
"Canterbury bells" 1376
"Canterbury Cathedral" 2461
"cantonments" 10491
"cantonments, British" 3067
"cantonments of Benares" 8644
Cantor, Eddie 3750
"cantos, four" 5452
Cantú, Don Vito 7626
Canty 781
"canvas, blank sheets of" 7440
"canvas, oils onto" 518
"canvas, pricking a framed" 484
"canvas, towering spread of" 8079
"canvas that half filled itself" 8079
"canvas walls" 5317
"canvassed the apartments" 1510
Canvey, Vivien 5669
"Canyon, East" 7623
"Canyon, Gold" 10924
"Canyon, Manzanita" 3239
"canyon, wilderness and" 9747
"canyon formed by two great walls of tenements" 7627
"canyons, granite" 9197
"canyons, railroads ran up into the" 1365
"canyons, wind blew hard through the" 10751
"cap, awkwardly removed his" 2688
"cap, baseball" 302
"cap, chap did *not* touch his" 2044
"cap, funny looking" 5800
"cap, gauze" 2826
"cap, green hunting" 2859
"cap, soiled white sea-captain's beaked" 10806

"cap, tipped his olive-green linen" 8943
"cap, took off his" 4414
"Cap Diamant" 7658
"Cap François, town of" 3766
"cap on his head, fitted a" 5724
"cap squeezed the top of the fleshy balloon of a head" 2859
"cap with the ear flaps tied on top" 5800
"capable of it, never have thought herself" 2059
"caparisons of a Pullman, swaying" 5129
"Cape, Hatteras" 9078
"cape, lying off the" 5015
"Cape, on the" 2807
"Cape, the" 2006
"cape, wearing it up on her shoulders like a" 10860
"Cape Cod" 3041, 3608, 9165
"Cape Corrientes" 8054
"Cape Henlopen" 8064
"Cape May" 8064
"Cape roads are busy" 9169
"Cape Sata" 8160
"Cape Town" 8055
"*Capella*, the" 8094
"capes, Delaware" 9065
"capital, comfortable working" 1016
"Capital, Imperial" 9188
"capital, it was the" 1387
"capital, some war-torn Middle Eastern" 2811
"capital, the" 10615
"capital of cinema" 4061
"capital of commerce and art" 1308
"capital of Ethiopia, three-thousand-year-old" 8924
"capital of Finland" 5042
"capital of my country, the former" 791
"capital of Spain, the ancient" 5590
"capital of Zululand" 4518
"capital was Quito" 6259
"capitalism, a little" 1042
"capitalist, neo-" 6256
"capitals, colonial" 3531
"Capitol at Rome" 3986
"Capitol Offices" 6985
"Capitoline Jupiter, Priest of" 7514
"capitulation of loyal Fort Sumter" 5785
"Caplin Bight, village of" 1421
"capricious and fantastic, something" 6213
"caps, baseball" 5982
"capsule, Kenya Beanstalk" 10423
"captain, as a senior" 202
"captain, Chinese" 200
"captain, old" 2328
"captain, stocky" 8137
"captain, the" 2897, 8696, 9996
"Captain, the" 865, 4592, 8677
"captain and highwayman" 360

"captain in dress whites" 8137

"captain was young" 5926

"captivate" 5727

"captivated by its movement" 976

Captivity 3407, 3414, 6148, 7133, 7139, 7140, 7141, 7145, 7153, 10327

"captivity at the hands of King Philip" 2051

"capture a few Caddos to sell to the French" 1076

"captured and tortured by the Indians in America" 9853

"Capuchins, church of the" 1292

"Caquhair" 10898

"car, ancient borrowed" 8005

"car, black" 4204

"car, bouncing headlights of his" 3011

"car, brother-in-law's" 2965

"car, camouflaged Humber staff" 9785

"car, climbing into the" 6938

"car, collided with a" 25

"car, dispose of the" 6570

"car, driving seat of the" 8456

"car, driving the" 7202

"car, drowned" 2946

"car, every sad" 2973

"car, examined the tracks of the" 19

"car, gets out of his" 2243

"car, got out of the" 1654

"car, he crawled into the" 2974

"car, highway patrol" 9812

"car, I left the" 10370

"car, I stopped the" 2982, 9676

"car, I'd gotten out of my" 7861

"car, ignition key of his" 9805

"car, in the" 9730

"car, in the stolen" 1845

"car, left his" 1046

"car, little Italian" 59

"car, lonely warmth of the" 10410

"car, my" 9581

"car, parlour-" 8564

"car, patrol" 6970

"car, police" 6962

"car, shabby old motor" 9943

"car, sits in his" 2993, 10085

"car, small curtained touring" 1604

"car, spots the" 2994

"car, stop the" 3033

"car, stopped his" 1112

"car, stopped the" 1378, 3008, 9717

"car, the" 2985

"car, there in the" 5109

"car, touring" 1970

"car, wanted a new" 2526

"car, what I'm doing in this" 2656

"car, without getting out of the" 1730

"car, you said you had a" 9836

"car ahead of his whipped past" 4164

"car coming" 3646

"car coming, whenever I saw a" 10367

"car could be heard coming down the dirt road" 9835

"car dangling from a chain" 9837

"car died and sank into a sea of sheep" 9834

"car drew near, as his own" 4164

"car drift down the road" 476

"car gliding by under throttled power" 10392

"car had crashed, as if a" 7855

"car had gone off the road and had overturned" 40

"car he was driving was carried away with the bridge" 2339

"car hoods, beneath their" 1477

"car into forward instead of reverse, put my" 9821

"car is parked to the left of a mailbox" 5944

"car jogged along, small" 7240

"car lay helpless and ridiculous" 9790

"car passed, when a" 1056

"car passed the first houses" 6323

"car seat, books on the" 3034

"car taking him back to the Residence" 9820

"car that was waiting" 4204

"car thief" 6453

"car up" 7947

"car used to reach the end of its journey" 6368

"car was air-conditioned" 4393

"car was beginning to act skittish" 2972

"car was racing over country roads" 9774

"car was speeding" 2955

"car would soon be along" 10093

"Caracas" 9879

Caraher 8765

Caravan 3964

"caravan, camel" 1429

"caravan of carnival folk" 1680

"caravan road" 9546

"caravan stood out" 9792

Caravello, Miss Carmen 7114

"caravels had stood all morning in the ultramarine bay" 8169

"carbines, .30-caliber" 4253

"carbolic acid" 8509

"carbon copy" 7769

"carbuncle south of Baltimore" 1442

"car-crusher, the" 4352

"card, as she laid down the last" 4000

"card game, won his wife in a" 3970

"card I found on the corner of the bulletin board" 10977

"card smudged like a cat with muddy feet had slid across it" 10977

Cardgames 295, 301, 308, 309, 318, 3970, 4976, 6308

"cardiac disease" 141

"Cardin" 309

Cardinal, the Rev. Charles 2299

Cardinal Balue 7139

"cardinals, names of" 7532

"Cardinals, full consistory of" 1525

"Cardinals, St. Louis" 8934

"Cardinals, three" 1494

"Cardinals took their exercise side-saddle" 9559

"cards, called for two" 295

"cards, dealt and received" 309

"cards, deck of" 308

"cards, play" 2057

"cards, played" 2332

"cards, prayer" 7533

"cards, shuffling the" 301

"cards, the two" 869

"cards, threw down her" 4976

"cards before him, laid her small" 6308

"cards in *Alice*, make them look like the" 2855

"cards in his hand, played out all the best" 3376

Cardworthy, Vincent 3585

"care, loving" 2840

"care, the public" 7825

"care, you would think I" 1789

"care about, men you didn't" 8007

"care about anyone or anything" 7533

"care about the country, you would have to" 3318

"care of my grandmother, under the" 9710

"cared for that sort of thing, if one" 8287

"Caredigion, king of" 7795

"career, began his" 6470

"career, distinguished and meritorious" 6439

"career, enjoying a modest and not unsuccessful" 6448

"'career', I began my" 6410

"career, height of his" 3083

"career, his" 5667

"career, long-interrupted academic" 6467

"career, stayed with her" 1329

"career as a backup singer, my" 6485

"career as a snoop, late in my childhood" 7981

"career as commercial representative" 6448

"career has always been marked, my" 5573

"career of the Signal Corps" 6441

Careers 1329, 6410, 6439, 6441, 6467, 6470, 6485

"careful, habitually" 2997

"careful, if you're not" 1881

"careful, real" 1857
"careful about money, we have to be very" 866
"carelessness, abortive attempt at" 295
"caress the famous names" 903
"caressing, light and" 7229
Carew, Alexander 2939
Carew, Poppy 2673
Carewe 7709
"cargo, valuable" 8048
"cargo, worked" 4916
"cargo at Callao, discharged her" 8055
"Caribbean" 6403, 9086
"Caribbean, blue" 5049
"Caribbean, re-mapped the" 5023
"Caribbean, South" 4466
"Caribbean, the" 9614
"Caribbean island" 5052
"Caribbean sea" 8277
"Caribbean Sea" 4098, 4643, 9073
"Caribbean sky" 8491
"Caribbeans refer to their lighter showers" 7342
"carillon, subdued" 652
Carl 5607, 5992
Carla 2672, 10896
Carless, Wally 3599
Carleton, Nathaniel 5543
Carling, Marjorie 9992
"Carlingford" 1488, 6034, 9206
Carlisle, Fanny 2206
Carlo, Tommy 2062
"Carlott, village of" 10450
Carlotta 6484, 10645
Carlsen 683
Carlson, Fred 3843
Carmela 7891
Carmelita Banditita 2014
"Carmen, the opera" 571
Carnac 297
"carnal desires of the flesh" 1205
"carnality, spirit of far greater" 7500
"carnation bud, yellow" 8027
"Carnation evaporated milk can" 3849
"carnation in his button-hole" 5801
"Carnegie Hall" 1746
Carnelian, Mr. 3853
Carney 3534
"Carnival, celebrating the end of" 2364
"Carnival, first day of" 2131
"carnival folk" 1680
Carnovsky, Oscar 6939
Carol 8197
"Carolina" 8923
"Carolina Low Country" 9078
"Carolina summer" 1879
"Carolina sun" 7467
Caroline 2777, 3040, 5781, 7483, 8282, 10528
"Carolingian princes" 1444

"carols ushered in the day, the ancient" 3680
Carpenter, Rebecca 1894
"Carpenter, a" 355
"carpenter, my father was a" 6458
"carpenters working on our house, I want" 6941
"carpet bag, empty" 10818
"carpet, bright geometries of the turkey" 10428
"carpet, pieces of drugget" 7753
"carpet, primeval" 10451
"carpets, damned tartan" 1179
"carpets, green" 6986
"carpets, Oriental" 1305
"carriage, baby" 9626
"carriage, first-class" 9533
"carriage, left the" 2842
"carriage, open" 9559
"carriage, travelling-" 9112
"carriage drew away" 9934
"carriage of the twelve-nineteen train" 6001
"carriage passes, as the last" 1738
"carriage rattled over the street" 2963
"carriage-horses" 3120
Carriages 2190, 2963, 7087, 9113, 9511, 9757, 9760, 9761, 9771, 9777, 9789, 9855, 10108, 10653
"carriages, full glittering cool" 9381
"carriages, horse-drawn" 9626
"carriages, no" 10653
"carriages, public" 9511
"carriages, sorrowful procession of" 7087
"carriages began to arrive" 9760
Carrie 3073, 3272
"carried across the ocean" 5465
"carried among his troops in a litter" 4469
"carried past his 'bus stop, allowed himself to be" 9423
"carried the Christmas tree" 8618
"carrier, aircraft" 6773
"carrier, mail" 10055
"carrier, support" 8091
"carries herself as Margaret did, she" 4138
Carrigan, David 4341
Carrington, Arnie 6824
"carry me over the threshold" 1996
"carry them along the quai" 9631
"carrying a butterfly net" 10816
"carrying a little black port-manteau" 9092
"carrying a pile of pillows" 4606
"carrying a portable typewriter" 1629
"carrying a war pipe" 7853
"carrying earth and rubble in baskets" 5138
"carrying me, tenth month of" 7095
"carrying stones in their lacerated arms" 5138

"carrying the silver cage" 4785
Cars 19, 25, 40, 59, 235, 755, 1039, 1046, 1047, 1071, 1315, 1599, 1604, 1670, 1678, 1714, 1769, 1783, 1970, 2069, 2243, 2339, 2526, 2590, 2656, 2899, 2946, 2947, 2955, 2960, 2961, 2965, 2972, 2974, 2982, 2984, 2985, 2993, 2994, 2999, 3002, 3006, 3008, 3011, 3018, 3030, 3033, 3036, 3038, 3378, 3646, 4168, 4204, 4393, 4937, 5671, 5944, 6323, 6570, 7327, 7855, 8005, 8187, 8282, 8770, 8782, 8798, 9169, 9320, 9581, 9582, 9649, 9676, 9753, 9763, 9764, 9765, 9774, 9775, 9776, 9778, 9779, 9782, 9783, 9784, 9785, 9786, 9787, 9790, 9793, 9794, 9799, 9800, 9801, 9802, 9805, 9806, 9807, 9808, 9809, 9810, 9811, 9812, 9814, 9815, 9819, 9820, 9821, 9822, 9824, 9825, 9826, 9827, 9829, 9831, 9833, 9834, 9835, 9836, 9837, 9925, 9943, 9947, 10085, 10093, 10370, 10410, 10713
"cars, eight out of ten" 9616
"cars, repair" 5008
"cars, sixty-one freight" 7278
"cars, slow line of" 2973
"cars, sound of" 8798
"cars, the few parked" 8606
"cars, used" 1992
"cars back smartly into line" 8187
"cars for delivery, drive" 1054
"cars going up and down" 9169
"car's progress" 9815
"car's tape deck" 3026
"cars were passing through the smaller streets" 9831
"Carson" 2952
"Carson City" 1082
"cart, a" 9773
"cart, coal haulier's" 9795
"cart, ox-" 1602
"cart, spring" 1617, 6566
"cart, two-wheeled timber" 1632
"cart, workhouse" 9599
"Cartegena" 4076
Carter 4164
Carter, Caroline 2005
Carter, Rachel 6623
Carteret, Mrs. 101
"cartoon by Charles Addams" 4665
"cartoonist" 9578
"cartoonist by trade, newspaper" 8202
"cartoons from Double Bubble gum" 634
"cartridges, have you got the" 4244
Carts 9773, 9795, 9830
"Cartsdyke" 3550
"carved in marble" 168
"carved the face of China" 6070
Carvel, Lionel 3531

Carver, George Abraham 806
"carving a comfortable niche in the world" 5998
Cary 2800, 8939
"Casa Vieja, La" 3869
"cascade, pool and" 7652
"cascade of pale green" 5357
"Cascade Ridge" 6075
"Cascadia" 9571
"case, after coming off a" 564
"case, Fairmont National Bank" 10921
"case, neat morocco" 3047
"case, new pigskin leather brief" 5465
"case, prove a" 5421
"case, Rosenberg" 5207
"Case, Sherlock Holmes's Last" 2037
"case, that's the last" 5199
"case, the" 5200
"case began quickly, the" 589
"case history, Dolphin" 1834
"caseworker 1766" 4873
Casey, Colonel 5919
"cash, envelope full of" 3950
"cash, flush of" 10858
"cash, low on" 3754
"cash, short of" 6464
"cash count at the Bank" 3745
"cash for the estate, raise" 3756
"cash register in the Greek's diner" 7578
"Cashelmara" 7593
"cashier, assistant" 6928
"cashier, burly bespectacled white" 1048
"casinos, three Prizzi" 1073
Caskoden 362
"Caspian, the" 1345
Cassandra 446, 10865
Cassebeer, Adam 6996
Cassidy 2991
Cassidy, Charles Parnell 7002
Cassidy, Hopalong 6952, 7616, 8853
Cassie 2551, 8812
Cassilis 418
"cast a precise pool at the hem of his robe" 7806
"cast its shelter and its spell" 1298
"Castalia" 9148
"castaway would have been dead before sundown" 7934
"castaways, the" 8158
"Castel Rodriguez, city of" 2140
"casting a red pulsing glow" 1212
"casting into the pool" 8817
"casting toward a green rubbery beach" 4688
Castle 3855
"Castle" 4690
"castle" 1177
"castle, a" 4062
"Castle, Baynard's" 1196

"Castle, Belton" 6612
"Castle, Blandings" 1178, 8257
"castle, celebration at the" 6772
"Castle, Eden" 1181, 7087, 7186
"Castle, Howth" 1175
"castle, is the dungeon part of the" 1182
"castle, it was a dark" 3209
"castle, like a huge medieval" 5028
"castle, mediaeval" 1180
"Castle, the" 2006
"Castle, The Giant's" 3079
"castle, they could see the" 1176
"castle, very ancient and venerable" 10767
"Castle, Windsor" 948, 971
"castle built more than a century ago" 3202
"Castle Davenant" 1173
"castle filled with Poles" 3209
"Castle Hermitage" 2885
"castle of Athlin" 1171
"Castle of Dover, the grand" 1174
"castle of Grand Fenwick" 9452
"castle of Miramar" 8106
"castle of the Earl of Evesham" 1172
"Castle Reef" 8688
"Castlerampart, town of" 1299
Castles 948, 971, 3202, 3209, 4101, 4690, 6772, 6802, 7087, 7186, 8106, 8257, 10767
"Castles, English" 300
"castles, ruined" 5588
"castles, surrounded by sand" 1420
"castles, those formidable" 6802
"castles filled with spectres and chimeras" 4101
"castles full of creaks and cobwebs" 5588
Castleton 2094
"Castlewood, house of" 950
Castor, schooner" 8058
Castro 2052
"casually, promisingly" 5775
"casually perhaps, too" 5775
"casualty lists" 10475
Caswells 3624
"cat, Baal the" 467
"cat, big yellow" 4785
"cat, blue" 483
"cat, like a great" 5076
"cat, mauled" 9340
"cat, skinned" 5792
"cat, the" 5027
"cat, white" 450
"cat, wrong dead" 6032
"Cat About Town" 425
"cat brushed against his legs" 8179
"cat got into the milk" 1613
"cat is the offspring of a cat" 6413
"cat like a beadle" 6367
"cat on a garden gate" 8252
"cat paused" 10499
"cat peered in through the French window" 483

"cat saw what it had come to see" 483
"cat was listening too" 8819
"cat was only sleeping" 6187
"cat with muddy feet" 10977
"cataclysm, times of unperceived" 3403
"catafalque, carved in marble on a" 168
"catalogue, Monkey-Ward" 2835
"Catalonia" 2339
"catamite, in bed with my" 856
"Catamount New Hampshire" 9027
"cat-o'-nine-tails, a thousand" 8593
"catapult, like a missile from a" 410
"catapulted" 8704
"catapulted him into marriage" 5765
"cataract of Niagara, celebrated" 2619
Catastrophe 1019, 8640
"catastrophe, financial" 8640
"catastrophe, pronounced revelation of impending" 7015
"catastrophe, there was a sense of" 8033
"Catawba, western" 10042
"catboat, small" 8092
"catch and loop into a frame" 4142
"catch me, come and" 297
"catch the last glimmer of the fading day" 7347
"catcher, redoubtable" 8907
Catchprice, Benny 3335
"catechism class" 9853
"catechumen, yet a" 7539
"caterpillar crawling from the south to the north" 6054
"caterpillars" 3105
"catfish, Bronx" 7688
"catfish, feed the" 5380
"catfish, great white" 473
"Cathay" 1069
"Cathedral, Canterbury" 2461
"Cathedral, Helstonleigh" 645
"Cathedral, St. Patrick's" 7343
"Cathedral, size of the" 1306
"cathedral, the" 10370
"cathedral, why pounce upon the" 1298
"cathedral and colleges" 9160
"cathedral bell" 9467
"cathedral city of Barchester" 1487
"cathedral dignitaries" 1486
"cathedral tower" 667
"Cathedral Tower, ancient English" 9207
"cathedral town of _____" 1486
"Cathedral of Saint Valdopin" 1308
Catherine 2412, 4552, 4625, 6548
Catherwoods, the 3586
"Catholic" 10840
"Catholic boys" 1510
"Catholic Church, Holy Roman" 7532

"Catholic girls, what is it with you"
    4202
"Catholics" 7546
Catlin 4185
Catlin, the Reverend Jerry 582
Catlock, Brigadier 10486
Cats 425, 450, 467, 476, 481, 483,
    1613, 3139, 4785, 5381, 6032,
    6187, 6367, 7551, 7848, 8179,
    8533, 8819, 10499
"cats" 5381
"cats, I took the" 3716
"cats, smells of" 8533
"cats, strong young" 9841
"cats go forth highshouldered and
    lean" 10416
"Catskill village" 5842
"catstails" 8277
Cattle 415, 453, 961, 2215, 3644,
    3646, 3649, 3657, 3668, 6836,
    6961, 7331, 8823
"cattle, brands on the" 3649
"cattle, head of" 415
"cattle, herds of" 3604
"cattle, they had obtained the" 3644
"cattle, what remains of their
    gaunt" 3668
"cattle and sheep grazed in the
    summer pastures" 3667
"cattle fair" 3657
Cattleman, Paul 2120
"CATTLEMEN'S ASSOCIA-
    TION" 8549
Catto, Marius 8672
"Caucasian, tanned" 984
"Caucasus, summits of the" 4034
"Caucasus, the" 6061
Cauder, Janie Driscoll 6113
Caudill, Serena 8781
"caught, depends on what you
    mean by" 8902
"caught before it fades, it must be"
    10077
"caught his balance upon the dim
    whiteness" 1648
"caught in the body trap-line" 1213
"caught me looking for copper in
    the Wilderness of Zin" 5831
"caught my first glimpse" 4580
"caught one another's eyes for a
    moment" 8676
"caught them" 5812
"caught us, if she" 4244
"caught us off our guard" 2326
"caul for muscles" 2066
Caulder, Shanks 8892
"cause and effect" 7164
"cause of a sensation" 10126
"cause of it all, place the" 581
"caused, a death I may have" 2446
"caused her final decision" 2476
"caused him to do so" 9424
"caused my noble Duke of Hamil-
    ton to lose a thousand pounds"
    3965

"causes, spring only from great"
    4497
Caution 319, 2997, 4999, 5589,
    10382
"caution, done with" 3405
"caution, unusual" 10382
"caution, with great" 10159
"cautious" 4999
"cautious, conservative and" 5988
"cautious man" 2997
"cavaliers, rakish high-booted" 3396
"Cavalry, First Air" 230
"cavalry, severe outbreaks of" 296
"cavalryman, one-time" 847
"cave, air in the" 191
"cave, came into the" 10267
"cave, in front of the" 10710
"cave, Plato's" 220
"cave, secret" 3714
"cave, so great and deep a" 2124
"cave, the" 4684
"cave-like study" 6231
"cavern, world was a vast gloomy"
    3358
"caverns, clammy" 3396
"caverns of the windows, glowing"
    5338
Caves 191, 1369, 2124, 4684, 7057
"Caves, Marabar" 1369
"caves and out-of-the way places"
    7057
"caves in the mountains" 4481
"cavities, minute" 5312
Cavor, Mr. 1219
"cavorting behind a bulbous and
    curly stone shield" 3589
"Caxton Iowa" 960
"Cæsarea" 7797
"CBS" 4008
Cean 1602
"ceased as suddenly as it had be-
    gun" 9080
"ceased to exist" 9119
"Cebu" 235
Cecil 3849
Cecil, Hon. Bertie 2820
Cecilia 9857
"cedar" 4073
Cedar Branches Waving 7068
"cedars, crowned by" 6912
"cedars, its fine" 10355
"Cedartown" 9126
Cedric 3483
"Cefalû, labyrinth of" 9565
"ceiling, blue-white" 10292
"ceiling, condition of the" 909
"ceiling, examining the" 9452
"ceiling, oldfashioned railroad car"
    7575
"ceiling of the hall" 7779
"ceiling refused itself to exact
    scrutiny" 5307
"ceiling sagged towards me" 10227
"celebrate" 6094
"celebrate, doomed to" 3461

"celebrate your father's birthday"
    7491
"celebrated Doc Macnooder, the"
    4460
"celebrated its fortieth anniversary"
    6769
"celebrated Saturday morning" 1987
"celebrated the bombing of Pearl
    Harbor" 6774
"celebrating the end of Carnival"
    2364
"celebration, note of" 9907
"celebration, small" 1468
"celebration at the castle" 6772
"celebration of the future" 4012
"celebration of the liberation of
    Paris from the Germans" 6779
Celebrations 857, 864, 1086, 1468,
    1987, 2910, 2931, 4005, 4125,
    4516, 4518, 5260, 6094, 6694,
    6753, 6761, 6769, 6772, 6774,
    6779, 7678, 7797, 8479, 8745,
    9978, 10981
"celebrative, I imagined the Ameri-
    can masses" 2681
"Celebrity, the" 3530
"celery, ashamed of his" 3975
"celestial minstrelsy" 6212
"celestial traffic" 8410
"celestials, monotonous deep" 5178
Celia 684, 3249
"cell, come into my" 7780
"cell, grim stone" 10345
"cell, in my" 7148
"cell, lying in a" 7151
"cell block" 8654
"cell designed for one" 7152
"cell in one of New York's popular
    police stations" 7140
"cell was small, the" 7134
Cellan-Davies, Gwen 5972
"cellar, Kaiser" 3994
"cellar rooms" 2129
"cellarer's extravagance" 9945
"cellars" 4481
"cellars of this farm" 3111
"cells, checking the" 7138
"cells, rigidly honeycombed into"
    3096
"cells of the sympathetic system"
    10918
"cells were all of about the same
    size" 3096
"Celtic origin" 357
"Celtic tale" 9007
"Celtic termination, bears the same"
    10898
"Celts, scanning a wilderness for"
    5981
"cement, huge five-sided pile of"
    9245
"cement workers" 8813
Cemeteries 725, 726, 807, 3984,
    5149, 5688, 6708, 6963, 9621,
    10564

"cemeteries of massive boulders" 5149

"Cemetery, Arlington" 9621

"cemetery, blighted gate of the" 1193

"cemetery, buried in the" 1190

"cemetery, country" 1187

"Cemetery, Mount Pleasant" 1189

"Cemetery, Old Jewish" 2424

"Cemetery, Saint Agnes" 1191

"cemetery, somewhere deep inside the" 5688

"cemetery gate, as we left the" 6708

"cemetery script" 4073

"census, according to the latest" 6828

"Center, American" 5853

"Center, World Trade" 3332

"centipedes, thought at first that the seedpods were" 9682

"centre of interest, no reason why she should be the" 125

"centre of the whole world" 8299

"centuries, as it had lain for" 5132

"centuries, for" 7794, 8937

"centuries, for six" 1027

"centuries, in the course of the" 3071

"centuries, in the leisure of their ample" 10757

"centuries, the course of four" 3432

"centuries ago, six" 3894

"centuries indeed" 8688

"centuries of dead, more than sixty" 5149

"centuries of sunlight" 5310

"Centurion" 3460

"centurion, graying" 1757

"centurion, the" 10196

"Centurion saying to one Go and he goeth" 10649

"century, about the middle of the last" 8453

"century, as old as the" 89

"century, at the end of the twentieth" 9464

"century, beginning of the sixth" 7795

"century, beginning of this" 5140

"century, during the last half-" 6245

"century, during the past half-" 1314

"century, earlier half of the fourteenth" 8953

"century, early decades of this" 268

"century, early in the" 7892

"century, early in the last" 8837

"century, early in the last decade of the" 3403

"century, early twentieth" 1464

"century, eighteenth" 6043, 2558, 9255

"Century, Eighteenth" 6211

"century, end of the eighteenth" 9511

"century, end of the seventeenth" 2686

"century, fifteenth" 6244

"century, first twenty-five years of this" 6496

"century, for a third of a" 1458

"century, for nearly half a" 2041

"century, in an earlier" 7503

"century, in an early summer of this" 4166

"century, in the latter half of the last" 6213

"century, in the middle of the last" 4328

"century, in the middle of the twentieth" 6963

"century, last quarter of the twentieth" 10083

"century, late eighteenth" 5440

"[century], lusty eighteenth" 3376

"century, middle of the last" 3434

"century, my" 89

"century, new" 1593, 10993

"century, nineteenth" 519, 1443, 3641, 6409

"century, our benighted" 2786

"century, second decade of this" 10042

"century, seventeenth" 1397, 3376, 5448

"Century, Seventeenth" 9882

"century, sixteenth" 781

"century, the present" 6407, 9795, 10331

"century, toward the end of the last" 1025

"century, twentieth" 273, 4346, 7532

"century, under the turn of the" 1400

"century ago, half a" 3084

"century ago, more than a" 7149

"century ago, nearly a quarter of a" 10771

"century and a half" 2636

"century was beginning, new" 4170

"century was in its teens, the present" 9757

"CEO of the Prizzi family" 1073

Cephas 1904

"cerebral hemorrhage" 134

Ceremonies 1196, 1197, 1200, 1201, 1202, 1203, 1204, 1207, 1208, 1211, 1213, 1216, 1217, 1767, 3912, 3935, 5371, 7541, 9349, 9760, 10652

"ceremonies" 4502

"ceremony known as afternoon tea" 9349

"ceremony or restraint, without" 8951

"ceremony was over" 9760

"Ceres" 3044

"cerisier de Monsieur Roussillon, le" 9662

"Cerne Abbas, giant of" 805

"certain, of what can we be" 7541

"certain, one thing was" 7551

"certain, when were we ever" 7541

"certain of, that much I can be" 4265

"certain of it from the first" 3406

"certain that I would be a millionaire" 10550

Certainty 5661, 6951, 10091

"certainty, everything follows with dead" 2314

"certainty, the only" 10091

"certainty destroys wonder" 5661

"certainty was a thing he could never have" 6951

"certificate, his discharge" 8665

Cervantes 6246

"Cervantes, inimitable" 6246

"cervix opens up" 10881

Cesar 9370

"Cessna 172, single-engine" 227

"cesspool" 8857

"Ceylon" 3922

"C-47, bucket-seat" 204

"Chaco, the" 3774

Chadwick, Davy 2576

"chafe mercilessly" 9446

Chagak 8387

Chaimovitch family 4011

Chain, Mr. Martin B. 5956

"chain, sliding back the" 2770

"chain, sounding" 9996

"chain, the Knuckle's" 9106

"chain gang" 8227

"chain of circumstance, long and intricately inwrought" 3488

"chained up for a runaway slave" 1160

"chains, everywhere in" 4443

"chains, human" 5138

"chains they carried go limp in their hands" 7739

"chair, ancient rocking" 8530

"chair, antique" 8370

"chair, barber" 8042

"chair, big" 5907

"chair, black director's" 8388

"chair, cane-backed" 7781

"chair, deck" 9607

"chair, dental" 5351

"chair, easy" 8340

"chair, handsome Biedermeier" 8383

"chair, high straight-backed" 3272

"chair, his cushioned" 5913

"chair, his easy" 7369

"chair, his giant's" 3738

"chair, his old oil-needy swivel" 5995

"chair, his straight-backed wooden" 98

"chair, in his lawn" 7467

"chair, lawn" 5622

"chair, led him to the" 7194

"chair, low swing" 7468

"chair, my" 9909
"chair, padded deck" 5627
"chair, reclining" 5630
"chair, red leather" 9909, 10010
"chair, resettled himself in his" 9405
"chair, rocking" 3888, 6543, 8355
"chair, sat back in his" 5903
"chair, set up in a ladder-back" 2973
"chair, slid into my" 3850
"chair, stately oak" 2495
"chair, the" 93
"chair, there were two a" 8355
"chair, wicker" 8473
"chair, wing-back" 6626
"chair can be found everywhere, rocking" 8355
"chair designed for someone with a three-cornered behind" 8370
"chair I've never seen" 10082
"chair in the parlor, special" 8376
"chair misplaced, nor a" 935
"chair that can be found every-where" 8355
"chair-cover" 484
"chairman manner, his best" 6429
"chairman of the committee" 7817
Chairs 93, 8355, 8370, 8383, 9607
"chairs, broken" 3094
"chairs, empty wire-backed" 6489
"chairs, grey steel" 8027
"chairs, one of the deep" 4333
"chairs, three or four" 7753
"chairs, two widely different aspects of" 9408
"chairs, white folding" 4026
"chairs and sofas, crowded" 6986
"chairs there, there were as many" 8355
"Chakrata, village of" 1446
Chakravarty, Mrs. Radha 2963
"chalet high on the slopes up there" 4322
"chalice sat between them" 5828
"chalk, piece of" 495
"chalk downs, uncultivated" 6923
Challenge 789
"challenged, successfully" 6798
Challenger, Professor 5410
Challoner, Walter 3574
Cham 8630
Chamay, Sergeant 8669
"chamber, adjoining" 10111
"chamber, gloom of her" 9402
"chamber, my sleeping" 10747
"chamber, upper" 8342
"chamber, work" 7144
Chamberlain, Ralph 2773
"chamberlain" 1528
Chambers 1182, 7144, 9389
"chambers in Pall Mall" 5894
"chambers of the castle, lowest sub-terranean" 1182
"chameleon, like the eyes of the"

457
Chamfort 1222
"champagne, splash of" 5186
"champagne glass" 1199
"champagne glasses, throwing their" 1203
Champie, Mrs. Jeanette 2340
Champion 2820
Champion, Steve 2916
"champions of the cause" 7500
Champlin, Joseph 3748
Chamunda 4853
Chance 7112
Chance, Jonathan 7764
Chance 1219, 1220, 1221, 1222, 1223, 1230, 1232, 1233, 1238, 1243, 1460, 3675, 3970, 5789, 5829, 6027, 6831, 7203, 7434
"chance" 1222
"chance, came by" 7203
"chance, desperate" 1220
"chance, for most it was by" 6831
"chance, it was by" 1233
"chance, met by" 5789, 9096
"chance, never had a" 3675
"chance, that dark miracle of" 1221
"chance, words scattered by" 1230
"chance, you had your" 6027
"chance encounter" 7434
"chance of say one to one hundred" 1220
"chance was in the beginning" 1238
"Chancery, Head of" 247
"Chancery, mud in the" 7310
"chances he could or would take" 1460
"chances in life, gave up his" 8226
"chandelier, crystal" 3872
"chandler, molasses" 3275
"chandlery" 3431
"Chandrapore, city of" 1369
"Chanel's wonderful new scent" 4121
Chang, Ralph 4242
Change 97, 265, 549, 929, 1168, 1242, 1251, 1344, 1937, 4384, 5088, 5106, 5116, 5119, 5124, 5273, 5599, 5652, 6075, 6654, 6945, 7076, 7673, 8026, 8543, 9062, 9465
"change, a" 929
"change, accepted his" 2044
"change, all life is" 5273
"change, and then for a" 931
"change, as if nothing would ever" 1069
"change, equinoctial need of" 4384
"change, fateful point of" 5567
"change, it'll" 549
"change, life began to" 5116
"change, must suffer a sea" 1254
"change, one's ideas can" 1247
"change, service in the Zouaves had wrought a" 486
"change, suffered a radical" 1344
"change, things had begun to" 5095

"change, time is the only measure of" 526
"change, traumatic" 2679
"change, unprepared for the" 1168
"change a library book" 905
"change began to be visible" 1244
"change for the better, no" 549
"change forever, my life would" 5110
"change in habits manners and character" 9465
"change in my life, great" 5088
"change in the wind from up to down" 4871
"change of air, already she sensed the" 9572
"change of plan, I'm afraid there's been a" 6945
"change relentless and imperceptible as the approach of age" 2199
"change within the changeless" 526
"changed, beautifully" 1260
"changed, forever and for all time" 5119
"changed, me that's" 6075
"changed, my life is" 7076
"changed, nothing had" 7673, 9962
"changed, staircase had" 1255
"changed both boats and rivers" 4190
"changed hurriedly into tweeds" 9724
"changed I am, how" 1252
"changed little in outward appear-ance" 1395
"changed what had been, moment that..." 5124
"changeless afternoons" 10051
"changeover day" 2181
"changes, destined to undergo great and rapid" 265
"changes, story of" 9062
"changes, time of" 8543
"changes, whole year's" 10567
"changes, wonderful" 1245
"changes everywhere" 1257
"changes in her life, major" 8026
"changing, weather perpetually" 10578
"changing iced tea to wine, risk" 3597
"changing in the order of things we had fashioned for ourselves" 1253
"changing lanes" 2997
"changing so dramatically" 5599
"changing so fast, everything's" 1258
"changing the shapes of the hum-mocks under the dark mesquite" 10707
"Channel, across" 8642
"Channel, Bristol" 7186
"Channel, English" 5720, 9091
"Channel, Pumpkin Patch" 7946
"Channel, St. George's" 4056

"Channel, the" 8127
"channels, idiocies propounded by the" 7840
"chant, Gregorian" 1312
"chanted the Kaddish prayer" 3952
"chanting my name, not actually" 8747
"chanting voices" 1305
Chaos 618, 2314, 4016, 6510, 7877
"chaos, even in the midst of" 2314
"chaos, organized" 4016
"chaos, there was" 618
"chap" 3
"chap did *not* touch his cap" 2044
Chapel 4658
"chapel, abbey-" 10641
"Chapel, Guards'" 10649
"chapel, had come into the" 1534
"Chapel, Merrion" 6630
"chapel, school" 1206
"Chapel, School" 9411
"Chapel, Sistine" 515
"chapel, small neglected" 1297
"chapel, stood at the door of the" 4255
"chapel, the" 10659
"chapel of St. George's Church" 10656
"chapel stall of carved oak" 7513
"chaperoning his herd of Jerseys" 3646
Chapin, Edith 8720
Chapin, Paul 583
"chaplain, his" 1503
"chaplain, the" 5651
"chaplain in the infantry" 1529
"Chapman's Yankee Trader" 1067
"chaps, remember about those" 4663
"chaps grabbing away, lots of" 6254
"chapter, opening" 5465
"chapter, the head of this" 779
"chapter, the opening" 5639
"chapter, this first" 5451
"chapter, this introductory" 5530
"Chapter IV of *High Styling Your Face*" 8528
"chapter of a serial story, finish the first" 5407
"chapters, the following" 3432
"chapters in the story of my life" 5561
"chapters of the book, these first four" 8962
Char 2423
Character 261, 497, 945, 1682, 2446, 2976, 2997, 4437, 4471, 4543, 4663, 4773, 4823, 4874, 4980, 4986, 5086, 5301, 5379, 5435, 5457, 5496, 5510, 5573, 5617, 5675, 5694, 5701, 5759, 5983, 6424, 6533, 6605, 7958, 7980, 7982, 8842, 9302, 9457, 9465, 9714, 10525, 10868, 10878
"character" 9465

"character, attacking his" 5432
"character, emphatic individual" 7916
"character, father's" 6612
"character, grand boasting foolish" 3533
"character, in" 5694
"character, manly" 2885
"character, motto of my" 3911
"character, no very ambitious" 949
"character, shirttail" 6184
"character, their" 5435
"character, tired of being a" 945
"character and doings much will depend" 5395
"character and opinions, her" 10814
"character in this narrative, the chief" 4098
"character in this tale" 3747
"character of many localities" 9114
"character prickly, her" 4773
"characteristic, plead guilty to a" 7982
"characteristic of a man" 4471
"characteristic of Mr. Philip Quentin" 3325
"characteristic of the republican government" 6972
"characteristic which you privately consider a virtue" 7982
"characteristically" 8460
Characters 3117, 3298, 5406, 5414, 5434, 5450, 5498, 5542, 7218
"characters, conduct of the" 4453
"characters, the" 3117
"characters are doing their part" 5542
"characters in search of an author, sixteen" 7218
"charade, the look of a" 7868
"Charbury" 316
"charge, in" 8694
"charge, no" 1089
"charge, refute the" 7964
"charge, what" 3749
"charge splitting at the last moment to pass on either side" 1735
"charge too much, they" 9684
"charger, spirited" 8650
"Charing, no longer solitary hamlet of" 5126
"Charing Cross" 3122, 3993, 7277
"Charing Cross Hospital" 1519
"chariot, Lincoln" 9793
"charitable people" 1149
Charity 294, 3364, 5562
"Charity, move in" 5562
"charity covers no sins" 3364
"charlatans, field crowded by" 5496
Charlemagne 7510
Charles 1956, 1995, 2896, 3189, 4272, 4795, 5296, 5821, 6173, 6709, 8607, 9493, 9644
Charles, King 3396, 9882
Charles, Ray 3343

Charles I 2887
Charles II 360, 361
Charles III, King 2485
Charles the Second 4069
Charleston, Sheriff Chick 6961
"Charleston" 331
"Charleston Harbour" 7913
"Charleston South Carolina" 3857
"Charlestown" 1720
Charlev V, Emperor 1352
Charley 6464
Charlie 2714, 3192, 3614
Charlotte 2100, 4201, 6523, 8607, 9935
Charm 3564, 3574, 10778, 10793
"charm, all the" 5145
"charm, all the Broomes have" 3564
"charm, caught by her" 10793
"charm, twilight's tranquil" 8390
"charm, undisturbed" 10778
"charm, you have not my" 3574
"charm me, stories still had power to" 9034
"charm them, found much to" 9610
"charm to woodland scenery, gives an especial" 3894
"charm us with celestial minstrelsy" 6212
"charmed, immediately intimidated by it or" 3161
"charmed and reassured, I would be" 5991
Charmian 843
"charming, middle-aged but still" 3552
"charming dream" 2752
"charms of the Tyrrhenian Sea" 7909
Charon 1009
"Charon the Ferryman" 1009
Charterhouse, Clint 9563
"chase had altered course" 8127
"chased by a Russian choir" 2756
"chased Red Elk out of the valley" 6382
Chasen, Harold 9292
"chasing an idiot boy" 965
"chasm, worn many a deep and rugged" 4039
"chastise, set out to" 7803
"chateau of Monsieur St. Aubert" 5125
"Château St. Louis" 7655
"chateaux" 309
"Chattahoochee, the" 2377
"chatted with Basher Evans" 9919
Chatteney 3711
"chatter" 9389
"chatter, lately become common" 7829
"chatter, machines" 9364
"chatter, their mindless squealing" 8544
"chatter of gulls" 10277
"chattered, idly" 7410

"chattering noisily" 4154
"Chatterley of the Apes" 5453
"chatting, couples" 10392
Chatworth 1804
"chauffeur, colored" 1315
"chauffeur, coloured" 5801
"chauffeur, spoke to the" 4564
"chauffeur waiting with fuming
    breath" 1714
"chauffeurs, lips of" 5308
"Chaumont" 8695
"Chautauqua, the" 8164
"cheap, didn't mean anything" 11
"cheap, good that is and" 7571
"cheap apartments" 6142
"cheaper, potatoes were" 3750
"cheaper digs" 6149
"Cheapside" 2286, 7501, 8775
"cheated him" 3329
Cheating 3329
"check for a little over three thou-
    sand" 1071
"check of the farmhouse, one final"
    3245
"check out the mug shot" 6872
"check the staff roster for tomor-
    row" 10958
"checked into the Hotel Pierre"
    4637
"checked into the usual hotel" 4658
"check-list, worked stolidly through
    the" 200
"checkout time was as unavoidable
    as lunch was bland" 7097
"checkpoints, army" 883
"checks, couple of" 1106
"checkup, during a routine" 166
"Checquer Work of Nature" 5552
"cheek, down his hard" 8043
"cheek, flushed" 8423
"cheek, heaviness of the" 7985
"cheeks" 5603
"cheeks, his lean" 498
"cheeks, hollow" 8098
"cheeks, rosy" 6249
"cheeks, Sam's" 5976
"cheeks smoothly shaven" 3646
"cheeks that could blunt a scary
    color" 339
"cheeping like chicks" 8333
"cheer, good" 1301
"cheer up" 2517
"cheerful" 3310
"cheerful activities of spring" 7608
"cheerful occasion, cannot be con-
    sidered a" 579
"cheerfully" 6020, 7065
"cheerfully said" 2129
"cheerfulness, remarked with" 7180
"cheering, much" 10473
"Cheerios on the floor, the spilled"
    3865
"cheers, bells horns faint" 5260
Cheese 3859, 4132
"cheese, Farm Girl pot" 6652

"cheese from a dairy window" 719
"cheesy chuckle" 8027
"chefs working around the clock"
    1872
"Cheka men" 3413
"chemical plants" 5142
"chemical reactions, very subtle"
    10918
"chemical relation between coal
    and diamonds" 10551
"Chemist, the Little" 9209
Chemistry 7979, 10551, 10918
"chemistry, left doctoral programs
    in" 3286
"chenille tablecloth" 9295
Chens, the 6147
"Cheops, Pyramid of" 8565
"Cherbourg" 9589
"cherries, eating" 4151
Cherry 1281
"cherry tree" 28
"cherry tree, the little" 9683
"Chesapeake" 1998
"Chesapeake Bay" 9614, 10451
"Chesapeake, ghosts that haunt the"
    4105
"chess, two people playing" 310
"chest, his deep little" 305
"chest, spots on my" 571
"chest, tunnel in my" 4894
"chest of drawers and its mushroom
    knobs" 10190
"chest rose and fell" 8827
Chesterton, G. K. 3396
"chestnut posts" 3069
"chestnuts, hoarded fallen" 10534
"Chevalier Deming & Post" 6425
"Cheviots, the" 10391
"Chevrolet" 9809
"Chevrolet, Red Bowers" 6853
"Chevy Nomad" 2069
"chew a few things over" 9965
"chew of tobacco" 246
"chewed at his lip" 383
"chewed his lip" 4810
"chewed on the ends of her cotton
    bonnet" 7183
"chewed slowly" 3868
"chewed the end of his pen" 2541
"chewing, three minutes'" 5424
"chewing gum" 2111
"chewing the rag" 1840
"chewing up everything, the
    AK-47s" 4252
"Cheyenne" 7247
"Cheyenne, the" 1735
"Cheyenne Indians" 9707
Cheyne, Lord 5887
Chhuon, Cahuom 2803
Chi, Aunt 1886
"Chiang Saen, village of" 4094
Chicago 245, 1060, 5709, 10914
"Chicago" 1157, 1579, 1580, 1587,
    1685, 2019, 2653, 3378, 4448,
    5413, 6325, 6471, 6829, 7600,

8564, 8597, 9525, 9654, 10036,
    10914
"Chicago!" 5709
"Chicago, they set out for" 9981
"Chicago born" 245
"Chicago business, this" 1060
"Chicago Conspiracy" 7150
"Chicago Cubs Baseball Club" 4448
"Chicago defeat, his" 7154
"Chicago gunman" 9919
"Chicago that somber city" 245
"chick, this" 10810
"Chickasaw Agency" 1400
"Chickasaw nation" 9198
"Chickasaw Ridge" 10415
"chicken, such a passion for" 1872
"chicken frying" 9339
Chickens 734, 10955
"chickens, dressed as" 2867
"chickens cost extra" 6126
"chickens in his suite" 8806
"Chicokema, small town of" 3007
"chief, bravest" 6697
"Chief, the" 5019
"Chief of Police" 6967
"Chief of the Chiefs of Sakuyu"
    7801
"Chief of the Trinovantes, Para-
    mount" 5431
"chief was all but dead on his feet"
    7829
"chieftain, Irish" 6385
Chig 10213
Chilam 7541
"child!" 9993
"child, a" 304, 10164
"child, an only" 7056
"child, as a" 1269, 1275, 6911
"child, as a young" 4360
"child, assignment of the" 2649
"child, bastard" 4705
"child, bent on acquiring a" 6634
"child, carrying a" 10331
"child, dear innocent" 6890
"child, disguised to myself as a"
    1270
"child, first" 7069
"child, her" 2079
"child, her newborn" 6702
"child, her only" 3548
"child, I am an only" 6607
"child, I can find the" 9861
"child, I thought as a" 3592
"child, illegitimate" 1765
"Child, in the name of this" 1205
"child, industrious" 5708
"child, like a" 4626
"child, my" 2054
"child, my only" 6537
"child, new-born" 3099
"child, only" 1902, 5598, 10814
"child, presence of the" 10304
"child, pretty" 4178
"child, prostitute's dead" 1538
"child, remember hearing once

about a" 5087
"child, see the" 1287
"child, she wanted a" 6538
"child, stowaway" 4214
"child, that" 672
"child, that's the" 1281
"child, the" 5145, 8722, 10212
"child, the only" 6516, 6647
"child, to a" 1288
"child, unaccountable" 8843
"child, was no longer a" 7715
"child, when he was a" 7222
"child, when I first saw the" 1286
"child, when I was a" 6699
"child, when she was a" 10831
"child, when your grandfather was a" 8992
"child crying" 2085
"child disappeared" 2572
"child either, was no longer a" 7715
"child first moved within her" 7071
"child in a tree with a small caliber rifle" 4250
"child is standing on a chair" 1870
"child lay dying" 7785
"child looking, eyes of the" 1289
"child moved warily" 4152
"child murderer, I was a" 2031
"child of a great love" 1290
"child of a wealthy tradesman in London" 6516
"child of about eleven, when I was a" 3470
"child of eight" 1285
"child of four or five" 6890
"child of my century, I am a" 89
"child of the same sex, middle" 8222
"child played a poem" 1284
"child sat upon the roadside" 8343
"child that God ever made, the naughtiest" 4146
"child was afraid" 3732
"child was wakened" 10205
"child woke" 10317
Childbirth 559, 561, 807, 813, 2419, 6636, 7055, 7056, 7057, 7058, 7059, 7063, 7064, 7067, 7069, 7075, 7077, 7079, 7001, 7086, 7087, 7089, 7090, 7092, 7096, 7097, 7100, 7101, 7102, 7104, 7106, 8021, 10790
"childbirth, our father died in" 2419
"childe, Norman" 3381
Childhood 132, 548, 587, 639, 1197, 1285, 1801, 2031, 2312, 2512, 2956, 3189, 3220, 3253, 3501, 3614, 3655, 3701, 4235, 4236, 4242, 4360, 4536, 4756, 4768, 5120, 5556, 5739, 6117, 6164, 6293, 6613, 6734, 6739, 6742, 6911, 7270, 7353, 7377, 7382, 7436, 7443, 7448, 7449, 7460, 8221, 8527, 8922, 8932, 8965, 9049, 9704, 9706, 9707, 9827,

10341, 10517, 10531, 10752, 10761, 10831
"childhood, grew out of" 4811
"childhood, I remember" 4235
"childhood, in her" 1250
"childhood, learned in" 6804
"childhood, my" 1267, 1274, 3701, 4768, 10761
"childhood, my earliest" 5567
"childhood, my early" 1276
"childhood, my lousy" 9706
"childhood, no event in" 1197
"childhood, old rigmarole of" 1266
"childhood, part of my" 3655
"childhood, the smells of her" 8527
"childhood, unpremeditated" 5120
"childhood can't be cured, a happy" 1273
"childhood career as a snoop" 7981
"childhood had slipped by" 2323
"childhood has been chronicled" 4768
"childhood lies behind me muted" 1274
"childhood like the one he had" 1278
"childhood was a queer and not altogether happy one" 1268
"childish point, most" 7430
Children 23, 27, 29, 292, 299, 304, 305, 307, 311, 380, 653, 672, 938, 962, 965, 969, 981, 1210, 1271, 1538, 1870, 2031, 2079, 2085, 2298, 2336, 2410, 2572, 2613, 2649, 3079, 3365, 3381, 3470, 3572, 3719, 3732, 3927, 4021, 4026, 4146, 4152, 4162, 4167, 4173, 4197, 4199, 4214, 4232, 4250, 4753, 4807, 4987, 4994, 5598, 5739, 5810, 6104, 6228, 6417, 6526, 6538, 6551, 6623, 6634, 6644, 6647, 6692, 6703, 6733, 6826, 6876, 6890, 7034, 7044, 7051, 7183, 7213, 7220, 7627, 7745, 7759, 7785, 7843, 8215, 8217, 8224, 8233, 8276, 8343, 8465, 8722, 8843, 9275, 9386, 9581, 9861, 9984, 10021, 10111, 10205, 10212, 10304, 10317, 10424, 10547, 10784, 10824
"children, all the" 8465, 10547
"children, and even" 5138
"children, bear" 7103
"children, happy" 4199
"children, have" 7034
"children, he's got three" 7736
"children, her" 2712
"children, her six" 6850
"children, his" 319, 5321
"children, his only" 2393
"children, his other" 1761
"children, hurt" 6745
"children, island" 7044
"children, like their" 6532
"children, like thousands of other"

6531
"children, mangled bodies of" 29
"children, middle-aged" 6545
"children, Mrs. Manford's" 9880
"children, my abandoned" 9375
"Children, my dear and beloved" 10902
"children, no" 7041
"children, once there were four" 1282, 1283
"children, one of his" 2026
"children, our last summer as" 1277
"children, she has two" 10322
"children, shut of his" 8636
"children, teaching" 5708
"children, the" 1662, 2613, 4021, 7183
"children, the three" 9721
"children, their" 4457, 9054, 9062
"children, their two" 2447
"children, they had three" 6525
"children, those two" 6612
"children, tumbled clothes of the" 10818
"children, two" 3572
"children, two hundred young" 307
"children, underprivileged" 10826
"children, when they were" 9049
"children, wives and" 3608
"children, young" 6826
"children are crossing" 8276
"children are fighting in the back seat" 1291
"children are not down yet" 6526
"children are performing *Hamlet*" 9386
"children between the ages of six and ninety-six" 9010
"children born in that sphere of life" 6612
"children crying" 8504
"children do, as" 6301
"children followed my every move" 9581
"children grow up, all" 4232
"children half-concealed in the pine grove" 7183
"children lying close on one side" 10824
"children neared on four roads cut like slashes through the bush" 7887
"children of eggs, we are all the" 6817
"children of the place" 3079
"children of these two families have married" 7950
"children playing at greatness, four" 299
"children playing together, while they were" 5739
"children screaming" 3381
"children stopped their games to watch him" 7627
"children to leave home, last of her

three" 6722
"children to show for her labors" 3806
"children to the shore, taking..." 9169
"children watched for the first star" 653
"children were chasing an idiot boy" 965
"children were getting big, now that the" 7759
"children were getting bored" 938
"children were lying on the grass" 10784
"children were on the lookout for him" 7220
"children were taken away" 4026
"children were walking" 10424
"Children's Relief" 4709
Childs, Lovey 9002
"child's body" 3956
"child's dead, the" 2298
"child's early life" 9704
"child's hand" 495
"child's sombre eyes" 3365
"Chile" 2341
"Chile, military coup in" 1139
"Chilean refugee" 1139
Chili 2062
"Chili, the long coast of" 8048
"chill, that cold" 9657
"chill about it, a suspicion of" 177
"chill day" 3421
"chill in the breeze" 10745
"chill in the house, early-morning" 2233
"chill of fall, the first" 1558
"chill of the high country spring" 1548
"chill of the other side, savouring the" 10206
"chillness, late October" 1546
"chills" 5489
"chilly, it was" 10703
"chilly day" 2886
"Chilterns, the" 10391
"chimed a new republican nine" 9488
"chimera in female shape" 5640
"chimeras, spectres and" 4101
"chimeras, terrible towering" 5572
"chimes, clock tower" 7907
"chimes ... broke into Josef Breuer's reverie" 674
"chimes of San Salvatore" 674
"chimes you woke up hearing every morning" 7907
"chimney, an indolently smoking" 3128
"chimney, cabin" 3763
"chimney, huge clustered" 3060
"chimney of the corner house" 775
"chimney pointing a gaunt finger" 9237
Chimneys 3128, 3763, 9237

"chimneys, a million" 10612
"chimneys, four broad" 3077
"chimneys, ivied" 10678
"chin, because of his" 4438
"chin, his brown" 4955
"chin, man with no" 5809
"chin, red juice on his" 28
"chin, settled her" 1916
"chin, strength of" 5921
"chin a jutting v" 333
"chin close to the ground" 4955
"chin on his folded arms" 10695
"chin propped on hands" 987
"chin was strong enough to box with" 8239
"China" 93, 3394, 5417
"China, carved the face of" 6070
"china, old" 7214
"china, old blue" 3847
"China, People's Republic of" 561
"China, small boy in" 4242
"China, Walls of" 5138
"China had retained a respect for mercantile tradition" 1021
"China tea" 3821
"China white" 3057
"Chinatown" 300, 3041, 3630, 8433
"Chinese, dealings with the" 1053
"Chinese, the" 3416
"Chinese, tiny scurrying forms of the" 8544
"Chinese believe, most" 8289
"Chinese Bund" 10524
"Chinese captain" 200
"Chinese city" 10539
"Chinese eat birds' nests" 6038
"Chinese immigrant" 1040
"Chinese joss-house" 7529
"Chinese landscape, classic" 5145
"Chinese merchant" 3152
"Chinese mirror, antique" 7489
"Chinese province of Honan" 10584
"Chinese Republic" 3569
"Chinese standards, by" 3632
"Ch'ing dynasty, the great" 10983
"chinned, blue" 10933
Chipchase 7713
"Chippenham" 4007
"Chippewas camped two generations ago" 4140
"Chipping Cleghorn, village of" 6353
"chippy, brung himself home a" 7716
"chips, a spilling tribute of" 3969
"chips of several generations of sturdy wood-choppers" 3069
"chisel, slant the" 10948
Chisholm, Eustace 9166
Chisholm, Father Francis 1498
"Chisholm, the" 3399
Chism, Nail 7194
"Chiswick Mall" 9757
Chitepo, Peter 3238
"Chitlings, Land of Muck and"

6136
"chivalric love" 260
"chivalry and romance" 3375
Chloe 5873
"chocolate" 5184
"chocolate, square of bitter" 8577
"chocolate, steaming cup of" 3844
"chocolate kisses" 634
"chocolates, no box of" 5006
"chocolates, sugary" 8538
"Choctaw language" 9015
"choice, take your" 6183
"choice, you couldn't have made a better" 1432
"choice of the moment" 5414
"choice was involved" 7041
"choir, Russian" 2756
"choir, the" 6242
"choir-boy in the Great Synagogue" 7505
"choirs, a cappella" 1305
"choke with envy" 2527
Chollie 6552
Cholmley, Lionel 3302
Chong, Opal 7079
"choosing, of my own" 1729
"choosing a merchant first" 6998
"Chop-House, Hotel and" 4511
"choppers, show us your" 10955
"chopping wood" 2906
"chopping wood beside his shack" 2095
"chops, I'll bust his" 3621
"chops onions in a wooden bowl" 1870
Chores 401, 1082, 1701, 3652, 7138, 10875, 10922, 10945, 10946, 10959, 10963
"chorister, some heavenly" 6212
"chorus" 5507
"chorus, sudden brilliant" 8756
"chorus line of bright white young-lady ghosts" 8451
"Chorus of the Play" 4453
"choruses of the night" 2790
"chose as his bride" 5761
"chose his seat in the afternoon express" 9531
"chosen, one of the" 3296
"chosen without the grave and solid deliberation, has not been" 2466
"Chow Phya, steamer" 2188
Choyce, the Reverend Herbert 5743
Chrissy 10749
Christ 1302, 7538
Christ, White 4456
"Christ, wearing a picture of" 7538
"Christ walking on waves in an off-hand way" 1302
"Christ-forgetting" 7205
"Christ-haunted" 7205
"Christ's sake, for" 7526
"Christendom" 10012
"Christendom, in all" 9185

"christened, she was" 4855
"christened Clementine, I was" 4792
"christened her" 1216
"christened in a patent canvas bucket" 810
"christened it when the mansion was built" 7760
"christened Jane Pickthorn" 4773
"christened my mother's lover" 4783
"christening — and not a child's" 1198
Christenings 810, 1198, 1205, 1216, 4855
Christian, Frank 2215
"Christian, baptized a" 7518
"Christian, I am a" 7542
"Christian, would never become a" 7537
"Christian Church, before the advance of the" 7503
"Christian city" 2794
"Christian era" 1485
"Christian methods" 7502
"Christian minister, I am a" 1520
"Christian name" 4728
"Christian names" 4752, 5743
"Christian student" 7518
"Christian way, bury it in a decent and" 2329
Christianity 7503, 7537, 7545
"Christianity, triumph of" 7503
"Christianity, two early brushes with" 7545
"Christianity was one entity or a series of intrusions from remote space" 7545
Christine 6589, 10586
Christine, Aunt 2313
Christmas 521, 661, 1061, 1158, 1679, 1937, 2504, 2507, 2514, 2517, 2586, 3017, 3488, 3496, 3680, 3887, 4131, 4310, 4512, 4513, 4519, 4520, 4521, 4522, 4528, 4529, 4531, 4552, 4568, 4600, 4914, 7032, 7344, 7752, 8604, 8613, 8618, 8960, 10607, 10945, 10994
"Christmas" 841, 1142, 1158, 1240, 2514, 2586, 3940, 4600, 5494, 6013, 7344
"Christmas, barbaric" 4521
"Christmas, before" 7900
"Christmas, celebrating" 661
"Christmas, dark" 7032
"Christmas, day before" 10607
"Christmas, died a few days before" 2319
"Christmas, home is where you go for" 4552
"Christmas, how long is it 'til" 4914
"Christmas, it will soon be" 2517
"Christmas, just before" 6839

"Christmas, let this ruin" 4529
"Christmas, night before" 1727
"Christmas, on the day before" 10402
"Christmas, on the eve of" 3922
"Christmas, post-" 2447
"Christmas, snow for" 8613
"Christmas, the day after" 9981
"Christmas, the Sunday before" 3854
"Christmas, the week before" 2507
"Christmas, two days after" 1679
"Christmas a dull day, always found" 4513
"Christmas again in Yucatán" 10994
"Christmas bulbs, like overgrown" 9436
"Christmas Cantata" 2869
"Christmas cruise" 8118
"Christmas Day" 3887, 4519
"Christmas Eve" 521, 1541, 2839, 3680, 4528, 7752, 8604
"Christmas Eve in an old house" 8967
"Christmas holaday, my recent" 3496
"Christmas is always like this" 3017
"Christmas letter" 1937
"Christmas morning" 10945
"Christmas of 107-" 0960
"Christmas shopping" 4310, 10369
"Christmas should ever come to be sad" 2504
"Christmas Train" 4131
"Christmas tree, carried the" 8618
"Christmas tree was brought into the house" 4520
"Christmas trees, sold" 1061
"Christmas visit" 3488
"Christmas window" 8596
"Christmas won't be Christmas" 4512
"Christmas-time" 4708
"Christmastime at the Opryland Hotel" 4531
Christo, Juli (Julian) 5206
Christopher, Paul 2787
"chromium" 10530
"chronicle, events of this" 698
"chronicle, this" 1349
"Chronicles, The" 6802
"chronicles of the Rakonitz family" 4142
"chrysanthemums, early" 3806
"chrysanthemums, explosion of" 1305
"Chrysler" 6513
"Chrysler, Valenti's" 9808
Chrysostom, John 3677
Chub 2083
"chubby, somewhat" 5921
Chuck 74
"chuckle, cheesy" 8027
"chuckled mildly to himself" 1009

"chuffing" 6652
"chum, his" 928
"Chungking's sweltering summer" 10264
"church" 3599
"church, apparently in the" 1104
"church, at the back of the" 3963
"church, colored folks'" 3225
"Church, Combehurst" 3634
"church, entering the" 3735
"Church, First" 1492
"Church, First Methodist" 4422
"church, go with the rest to" 4909
"church, handsome parish" 2088
"church, headed for the" 6229
"Church, High Barnet" 8587
"Church, Holy Apostles" 2869
"church, I do not go to" 4789
"church, Jack is the" 2003
"church, little" 1307
"church, locked himself in the" 7046
"church, Lutheran" 1190
"church, Methodist" 3604
"Church, North Liberty Second Presbyterian" 646
"church, people filled the" 1296
"church, Presbyterian" 314
"Church, St. Enoch's" 3783
"Church, St. George's" 10656
"Church, St. James's" 1184
"Church, St. John the Baptist" 670
"church, St. Pancras" 6270
"Church, services of the" 3680
"church, spire of the" 1299
"church, stood in" 5774
"church, suburban" 1303
"church, the" 1202
"Church, Tollamore" 8737
"church, ugly" 1304
"church, Undir Hofdi" 3661
"church, Wattleborough parish" 7180
"church, Winchelsea" 2300
"Church, wisdom of the" 7539
"church at Wallah, Methodist" 5753
"church bells" 673
"church bells of Hillsboro" 653
"church belonging to a very ancient convent" 1293
"church fetes" 7312
"church in Ravenna" 9353
"church is blowing a sad windblown 'Kathleen'" 2906
"church monstrous and vulgar" 1304
"church of his own design" 2443
"church of St. Columba" 1498
"Church of Saint-Germain-des-Prés" 8949
"church of St. John's, the new" 1295
"Church of the Believer, Tabernacle of the Eternal" 1532
"church of the Capuchins" 1292

"Church of the Children of Sinai, Apostolic" 1309
"church of the Prizzi family, the lucky" 10664
"church party" 8975
"church spires" 8591
"church steeple" 4145
"*Church Times*" 4008
"church tower, from the" 661
"church was cold" 1301
"church windows" 1312
"church with loudspeakers in its steeple" 671
"church with two colored windows" 1386
"church with us, doesn't go to" 6705
"church without ceremony, he is a" 2003
Churches 314, 645, 646, 652, 653, 666, 670, 671, 673, 1104, 1202, 1206, 1210, 1521, 1532, 1534, 1541, 2003, 2088, 2225, 2443, 2906, 3680, 3735, 3783, 3922, 4255, 4909, 5774, 6229, 6270, 7046, 7343, 7511, 7513, 7532, 8737, 8758, 8942, 8975, 9153, 9207, 9353, 10012, 10079, 10641, 10649, 10653, 10664
"churches" 9250
"churches, domes of ancient" 2225
"churches, facades of" 7532
"churches, interiors of parish" 503
"churches and mosques, a few desolate" 2006
Churchill 3945
Churchill, Winston 2491
"Churchill died, since" 3945
"Church's boundary" 9153
"churchwarden" 8957
"churchyard" 965
"churchyard, Anglican" 807
"churchyard, pretty" 1304
"churchyard, St. David's" 1188
"churchyard on the corner" 725
"churred, cicada" 4958
"chute with a roar, up the" 7990
Chuzzlewit Family 359
"ciao" 5670
"cicada churred, an early" 4958
"cicadas, grating" 10701
"cicadas, like the shrill notes of ten thousand" 8795
"cicadas fiddling invisibly" 8526
"cicadas screamed" 4964
"cider, cake and" 3680
"cider jugs" 3591
Cielo, Mamá 7091
"cigar, remains of his tattered" 8568
"cigarette" 3053
"cigarette, he searched for a" 1096
"cigarette, his" 8581
"cigarette, I lit a" 8565
"cigarette, lighting up another"

8582
"cigarette, lit a" 4277
"cigarette, lit his first" 8577
"cigarette, my sodden" 8575
"cigarette, please put out the" 6730
"cigarette, rolling his" 8571
"cigarette, shredded his" 7549
"cigarette, sleepily reach for a" 7999
"cigarette, smoke from my" 9505
"cigarette, smoking a" 8564, 8579
"cigarette, stub of his" 298
"cigarette after another, smoked one" 8583
"cigarette and stick" 3326
"cigarette at his mouth, aimed a" 2974
"cigarette behind his ear" 2111
"cigarette butts, ashtray filled with" 6489
"cigarette dangling" 9004
"cigarette of the day, his first" 8580
"cigarette smoke" 6780, 8538
Cigarettes 4289, 7549, 8571, 8574, 8576, 9505
"cigarettes" 8976
"cigarettes, asked me not to buy him" 8576
"cigarettes, buying" 5846
"cigarettes, get a pack of" 7569
"cigarettes, her father's" 4289
"cigarettes, I smoke" 4789
"cigarettes, last night's" 10303
"cigarettes, pack of Capstan" 8574
"cigarettes, three men lighted" 9548
"cigarettes fell from his hand in amazement" 5846
"cigarettes from the clanking machine near the door" 7569
"cigars, ordered" 8570
"cigars had burned low" 3999
"cigar-puffing" 2045
"Cincinnati" 1029, 5370, 7665
"Cincinnati depot" 7281
"Cincinnatus" 1431
Cinema 2351, 3342, 4061, 5875, 8538, 9463
"cinema" 1325
"cinema, capital of" 4061
"cinema, darkened" 9828
"cinema, foyer of a" 7577
"cinema screen, flickered like a" 9463
"circle, cutting a" 771
"circle of colour, this soft and broad" 10774
"circled prettily" 218
"circles, series of closely packed concentric" 9073
"circles, two vague" 9781
"circles across the dull sky, a lot of perfect" 3044
"circles if they could, would make" 3044
"circling and milling, caused itself

to be" 10746
"circling from nowhere to nowhere" 211
"circling madly about the heap" 957
"circuit, the old roadhouse" 9026
"circuit board, like components on a" 9258
"Circuit Court" 5197
"circuit downwind, we were on the" 197
"circuits of the air, making slow" 224
"circulated, privately" 4314
"circumcised and uncircumcised" 349
"circumcision, obligatory" 556
"circumcision was a Jewish notion" 2817
"circumfusion of those mean dwellings" 9223
"circumstance, apparently comfortable" 2581
"circumstance, that vicious" 1844
"circumstances, compulsion of" 5696
"circumstances, fairly humdrum" 5863
"circumstances, my" 3670
"circumstances, pleasant established" 562
"circumstances, somewhat odd" 5829
"circumstances, turns twists and" 5594
"circumstances, under certain" 9349
"circumstances, under certain different" 3286
"circumstances, under such" 4002
"circumstances, under the" 3307
"circumstances, very humble" 9703
"circumstances of life" 10772
"circumstances that encompassed her" 2506
"circumstances thrust me into a position" 3915
"Circus, Marvel" 4007
"Circus, Piccadilly" 7376
"circus celebrating death" 2327
"cirrus cloud" 8115
"Citadel of Troizen" 9227
"Cithera, Island of" 7370
Cities 245, 272, 307, 1005, 1013, 1014, 1060, 1183, 1262, 1562, 1668, 2140, 2149, 2186, 2210, 2280, 2710, 2745, 2811, 3383, 3402, 3429, 3777, 3994, 4051, 4055, 4060, 4074, 4080, 4178, 4367, 4386, 4389, 4405, 4461, 4514, 4517, 5042, 5221, 5331, 5345, 5398, 5590, 5708, 5709, 6058, 6153, 6259, 6274, 6275, 6584, 6935, 7129, 7319, 7345, 7443, 7544, 7569, 7665, 7691, 7695, 7839, 8263, 8324, 8398, 8448, 8523, 8534, 8594, 8595, 8597,

8730, 8773, 9100, 9114, 9157,
9160, 9180, 9197, 9210, 9212,
9248, 9524, 9611, 9627, 9657,
9689, 10017, 10096, 10476, 10491,
10524, 10544, 10582, 10584, 10621,
10637, 10690, 10726, 10738, 10914,
10983
"cities, dark avenues of" 3402
"cities, deserting the" 6141
"cities, domes and spires of" 4034
"cities, far from the soundness of"
    1452
"cities, fine flower of middle Euro-
    pean" 1308
"cities, in the" 272
"cities, its larger" 5719
"cities, most large American" 1054
"cities, old great" 5221
"cities, outskirts of small" 7327
"Cities, Sunshine" 10606
"cities, the most romantic of" 1354
"cities, the scouring of" 9738
"cities, unlike other" 5708
"cities divided by a river" 1476
"cities possess their special myths,
    all old great" 5221
"cities within a city, two" 1469
"citizen, retired" 9738
"citizen of Rome" 7067
"citizens, affection of their" 9124
"Citta di Castello" 5791
"city, a" 1359, 3605
"city, ancient" 781
"city, ancient walled" 1417
"city, approached a" 2966
"city, canyons that held his" 9197
"city, capital" 2965, 9577
"city, defenses of the" 8694
"city, densely packed" 4005
"city, depths of the" 10017
"city, dirty and wonderful" 1364
"city, dream" 6584
"city, ends of the" 9642
"city, great American" 8773
"city, growing dark in the" 2186
"city, had never been out of the"
    6153
"city, harbor" 7129
"city, heart of a bustling indifferent"
    1183
"city, here in the" 2213
"city, his first six months in the"
    8018
"city, his little manufacturing" 1014
"city, huge sprawling Midwestern"
    1399
"city, imperial" 3994
"city, in any" 5906
"city, in the" 1264
"city, large" 1471, 9100
"city, looking out over the" 2745
"city, medium-sized" 4461
"city, Midwestern industrial" 1390
"city, on the outskirts of a great
    northern" 8730

"city, our capital" 10500
"city, our great" 6361
"city, out of the" 9143
"city, outskirts of the" 5142
"city, power in the" 6980
"city, primitive" 1345
"city, raining over the" 7329
"city, rapid growth of the" 9114
"city, sea of the" 5790
"city, silent dead" 1433
"city, single" 9160
"city, small bombed baroque
    German" 4178
"city, small weightless" 1433
"city, that still enlarging" 10798
"city, the" 1426
"city, the brilliant" 8324
"city, the capital" 1382
"City, the great" 10420
"city, the little" 9139
"city, the normally temperate" 4386
"city, the sleeping" 745
"city, there is a midland" 1364
"city, this gaudy" 10524
"city, this wacky" 7831
"city, thriving" 8595
"city, thrust them against the"
    10726
"city, university" 4922
"city, unlighted Chinese" 10539
"city, vibrant little" 1464
"city, when they were in the" 3829
"city . . . began to stir" 10257
"city beyond the dark green shutters
    of their hotel windows" 10257
"city built of magnet" 1437
"city built on top of a hill" 1473
"city by the river looked dirty
    bleak and ugly" 1399
"city by the sea, great and godly"
    1348
"City Council, Luna" 7820
"city faced the bay" 1404
"city floating near the surface of a
    bottomless pool of clouds" 1433
"city had sweltered" 4386
"City Hall" 6630
"city has changed" 1262
"city in the heart of fair open
    country" 1364
"city in the West, plan for a new"
    6935
"city in the world, most magical"
    9657
"city is nothing more than a por-
    trait of itself" 1449
"city is particularly and peculiarly
    associated with the name Thud-
    bury" 1401
"city is waiting" 10096
"city lay along the bed of the Little
    Grand River" 1382
"city lies in a plain" 1372
"city limits" 10367
"city nesting dingily in the fog of its

own smoke" 1364
"city of antique customs" 1342
"city of B_____, in the" 8929
"city of bachelors" 5928
"City of Brotherly Love" 7955
"city of Central Asia, remote little"
    7950
"city of clammy humors and fog-
    horns" 9299
"city of Colchester" 5431
"city of his dreams" 5398
"city of Leyden, the windy" 4760
"City of Limitless Options" 1448
"City of London" 1354
"City of Mexico" 2731
"City of Pleasure" 10538
"city of Seattle" 1391
"city of that kind" 1390
"City of the Angels" 9180, 9689
"City of the Popes" 9627
"city of Troy" 2603
"city on the western shore of the
    Caspian" 1345
"city once conservative and pro-
    vincial" 1360
"city seem to tremble, making the"
    5331
"city should be so beautiful, every"
    1470
"city streets" 8616
"city turned its dreariest aspect
    toward the railway station" 1368
"city was burning, said that the"
    3777
"city was renowned for its clean
    breezes" 1447
"city was unlike any other" 1392
"city were mine, as if the" 1441
"city where I was born, that dark
    lemonless" 9436
"city which was to be the scene"
    1390
"City Without Clocks" 9180
"city woke, the" 10264
"city-dwellers" 7129
"city's blank white concrete slabs"
    307
"city's vast urgencies and agonies"
    3429
"Ciudad Juárez" 7259
"civic life" 9248
"civic right" 7505
"civil, be" 1847
"civil aviation" 202
"civil rights, before" 3402
"Civil Service" 6974
Civil War 786, 6313
"Civil War" 1445, 4073, 6097, 7792
"Civil War, American" 3150
"Civil War, back during the" 1279
"Civil War, before the" 3665
"Civil War, that great and bloody"
    10467
"Civil War memorial" 2828
"civilian, newly wed" 8745

"civilisation" 5696
"civilisation, our earliest" 7648
"civility, austere antique" 2865
Civilization 263, 271, 516, 4031,
    4035, 5696, 7253, 7648
"civilization" 4035
"civilization, general appearance of"
    4031
"civilization, history of" 7670
"civilization, instrument of" 271
"civilization, present stage of our"
    7253
"civilization, sorry state of" 2057
"civilization was declining, Western"
    10083
"civilized" 7670
"civilized, it becomes" 275
"civilized, to be" 250
"civilized than a capital city, more"
    2965
"clad only in bathing suits and
    smiles" 8092
"clad to meet a conclave of like-
    minded well-heeled matrons"
    10863
Claffey, Ira 6569
Claiborne 8479
"claim her, when he came to" 7739
"claiming the sympathy due" 580
Claire 1795, 2670, 2685, 2946,
    6339, 7448, 8890
Claius 7370
"clammy caverns" 3396
"clammy look, grey" 5163
"clammy with the breath of crowded
    human beings" 175
"clamor of the 5:30-A.M. bells" 670
"clamoring, shrill" 659
"clamorous" 5408
"clamour and movement, full of"
    1280
"clamoured down the soft wind of
    mid June" 673
"clamped with crude fixative on to
    her gums" 10831
"clan, delta" 4877
"clan, Spencer" 3576
"clan, the whole Murdoch" 543
"clan O'Donnells, of the numerous"
    9874
"clan of Murdoch" 3570
"Clan to which I once belong'd"
    5552
Clancy, Captain 9291
"clandestine meetings" 4705
"clanged open like a great church
    bell" 8812
"clanging alongside the U.S.S.
    Northampton" 8137
"clangor, mellow and lingering"
    9467
"clangor and swell, musical" 648
"clangor of a distant cathedral bell"
    9467
"clangour of bells grew insistent"

652
"clangs along, it" 7264
"clans, gathered his" 7810
"clap, the" 172
"clap, they'd only go and get" 8677
"clapboard, the Throckmorton"
    3604
Clapp, Sanford 1950
Clapperton 10296
"clapping her hands to emphasize
    the beat" 6231
Clara 2422, 3568, 4775, 4977,
    10090
Clare 6936, 8078, 9966, 10376
Clare, Bernard 3420
Clare, Henry 734
Clarence, Lydie 8511
"Clarence's" 8640
"claret, swallowing a certain
    number of bottles of" 2885
Claris, Burt 6445
Clarise 1561
"clarity, pierced her with sudden"
    7441
"clarity and precision" 7451
"clarity of the air" 179
Clark, Ann Rogers 4825
Clark, Mr. 7567
Clark, William 336
Clarke 9865
Clarke, George 3185
Clarke, Gideon 4448
"Clarksville is in Texas" 1418
Clarvoe, Miss 3918
Clasby, Jud 10940
"class, as a" 7011
"class, catechism" 9853
"class, English public official" 8351
"class, five o'clock philosophy" 6630
"class, freshman dental" 10866
"class, girl of her" 7748
"class, her" 9350
"class, her senior" 3270
"class, introductory Japanese" 3292
"class, middle" 6141
"class, my passing-out" 1816
"class, Vergil" 4273
"class, young ladies and gentlemen
    of his" 8863
"class and vintage, looked like any
    other of her" 10863
"class as himself, the same" 5761
"class filed into the hall" 986
"class of men" 6409
"class of 1908" 4307
"Class of '70" 7730
"Class of '71" 3283
"classes, adult education" 3285
"classes, among the upper-middle"
    10788
"classes, comfortably fixed" 10788
"classical master at Granchester"
    6427
"classmate, a" 6208
"classmates, some of my" 3722

"classmates fell into a whimpering
    terror" 3722
"classroom, my father's" 10102
"classroom window" 8747
"classrooms, English" 7236
"clatter, staccato" 4417
Clatterbuck, George 3669
"clattered, shone and" 9191
"clattering and rumbling" 8834
"clattering frantically" 4951
"clattering into the court-yard"
    7607
Clau-Clau-Claudius 5567
Claud 8607
Claude 2657, 7044
Claudelle 10055
Claudia 1261
Claudio 4578
Claudius, Emperor 7797
Claudius, Poor Uncle 5567
Claudius, That 5567
Claudius the Idiot 5567
Claudius the Stammerer 5567
Clavering, Sir Hugh 3972
"clawed away the sheets" 8487
"clawing and snarling" 9841
"clawing at the blanket" 10362
"clawing at the skin behind his
    neck, compulsively" 6170
"Claws, look for the" 991
Clay, Cassius Marcellus 7520
Clay, Sergeant 8662
Clay, Vicky 8297
Clay, William 9654
"clay, awash in" 2808
"clay, sun-baked pink" 3238
"clay hills" 5144
Clayborne 6095
"clayey soil" 3653
Clayhanger, Edwin 5898
"Claypit" 9136
Clayton 176
Claytor 3778
"clean, everything in the room was
    so" 7040
"clean, he was still looking" 1503
"clean, see that it was kept" 2436
"clean his nails" 3272
"clean his own shoes" 6021
"clean their own houses" 1477
"cleaned your teeth" 6675
"cleaner in the late 1930s" 4083
"cleaner rose from her knees" 1621
"cleaning, spring" 401
"clean-shaven" 5982, 8347
"clear and loud" 8903
"clear and pure" 4354
"clear as a bell, his mind was as"
    119
"clear but not cold" 2190
"clear crystal, get into the" 5447
"clear up before we get started here"
    10976
"cleared his bearded throat" 1199
"cleared his throat" 8872

"cleared my throat, I" 7518
"cleared the sky gloriously" 8586
"clear-eyed" 6815
"clearing among the skinny gums, natural" 5169
"clearing in the Forest of Lions" 3903
"clearing in the scrub oak woods" 3907
"clearing the sky for the stars" 5051
"clear-thinking" 6815
Cleary, Meggie 851
"cleats bared" 2995
"Cleeve Abbey" 666
Clegg, Emma 3338
Clegg, Hiram 3338
Clem 2903, 4792
Clemenceau, Georges 2491
Clementine 4792
Cleo 10358
Cleopatra 934
Clephane, Kate 10118
"clergyman, a" 1493
"clergyman, beneficed" 1486
"clergyman, little old" 1496
"clergyman, only son of a" 6609
Clergymen 49, 99, 126, 129, 139, 856, 1145, 1309, 1691, 1803, 1807, 2299, 2307, 2392, 2555, 2757, 3338, 3948, 5433, 5651, 6229, 6308, 6482, 6535, 6609, 6807, 7513, 7519, 7528, 7541, 7864, 8848, 9559, 10388, 10641, 10644, 10655, 10672, 10767
"clergymen" 10767
Clerical Error, A 9385
"clerk, bureau" 1126
"clerk, hotel" 10920
"clerk, junior" 6425
"clerk at Keith Prowse's" 675
"Clerkenwell" 1968
"Clerkenwell, great metropolitan industrial district of" 10338
"Clerkenwell Green" 1184
Clery, Hank 1579
"Clevedon" 6616
Cleveland, Tiny 331
"Cleveland Indian fame" 8934
"clever" 5555
"clever of Jimbo Ryder, it was very" 3753
"clever one, he was a" 5002
"clever people" 7772
"cleverer back-room boy" 4465
Cleverness 3753, 4465, 5002
"cleverness" 5997
"clichés, conventions like" 7819
"clichés about California" 10606
"clicking gently over the points" 7255
"client, I have a" 6453
"client, my" 2045
Clients 3624, 6453
"clients, counted amongst their" 1015

"clients from being seen, prevent our . . ." 4622
"clients in hand" 1047
"clients of yours" 3624
Cliff, Jack Dempsey 1003
Cliff, Mrs. 10782
"cliff, at the edge of a" 6387
"cliff, upon its own" 1174
"cliff of immense height" 5011
"cliff of limestone" 5143
Clifford 9038
Clifford, Jane 8485
"cliffs, granite" 9826
"cliffs, inland" 1485
"cliffs, scaling" 6071
"cliffs, steep granite" 5154
"cliffs, sturdy as" 9212
"cliffs above the olive slopes" 9995
"cliffs of Park Avenue, white" 2073
"cliffs of the coast" 9155
Clifton, George 6471
Cliftons, the 3586
"climate, continuously vile" 4073
"climate or what other cause you will" 7584
"climb, the" 5814
"climb into the freezer" 2097
"climb it" 9118
"climb the cherry tree" 28
"climb the steep path" 3232
"climb the woodshed roof to her bedroom window" 9964
"climb to the benchland" 8429
"climbed, as he" 5171
"climbed down from this animal" 1643
"climbed out stiffly" 3008
"climbed the ridge" 1713
"climbed the stairs" 1609
"climbed the sunny flank" 1367
"climbed to the upper story" 3604
"climbed up onto the bus top" 9556
Climbing 1609, 1713, 4337, 5171, 6071
"climbing a mountain" 6071
"climbing into the car" 6938
"climbing steadily on the narrow road" 2969
"climbing the steep road" 9091
"climbing the winding path" 8360
Clinch 7137
"clinging fiercely to the tattered garment" 5968
"clinging there against the wind" 3205
"clinging to them, the look of constant indoor light" 1041
"clinic, abortion" 5879
"Clinic, Family Planning" 2480
"Clinic, Hudson's" 7829
"Clinic, Steen" 3518
"clink clink" 10937
"Clinton" 6274

Clio 7597, 9682
"clip-clop, they came" 6664
Clive 7048
"cloak, Gandalf's" 8269
"cloak, his long black" 5975
"cloak, rain-repellent leather" 7630
"cloak in two, cut his" 7539
"cloak it was, ragged" 8401
"cloak swirling about him" 5975
"cloaked in pine and piñon" 6085
"cloakroom" 8215
"clock" 9472
"clock, alarm" 9495, 10165, 10137, 10309
"clock, bang the" 10251
"clock, cuckoo" 1017, 3815
"clock, digital" 10290
"clock, electric bedside" 1123
"clock, eye on the" 9470
"clock, French" 9467
"clock, knew without looking at the" 9478
"clock, large illuminated face of the" 4615
"clock, looked at the" 10246
"clock, mantel" 3867
"clock, old French gilt" 5647
"clock, oppressed by the" 9496
"clock, ornate French" 10916
"clock, quartz alarm" 8498
"clock, rhinestone-studded Felix the Cat" 9342
"clock, synchronous with the movements of the" 2274
"clock, the camp was a" 10503
"clock, thinking it must be his alarm" 10182
"clock . . . exploded like a horrid little bomb of bell metal" 10127
"clock fell to the floor" 10217
"clock . . . framed of brass and crystal" 9467
"clock hatefully clamoring, alarm" 10234
"clock is right, if that" 9331
"clock of Wattleborough parish church" 7180
"clock on the acoustically perfect wall" 9474
"clock on the kitchen wall" 9499
"clock on the landing had stopped" 9471
"clock on the mantel-piece" 9467
"clock on the small night-table" 1131
"clock shrilled hideously" 10165
"clock strike ten at night, heard the" 9477
"clock struck half past two" 5621
"clock that hangs on the kitchen wall" 9342
"clock that hung over the mantel-piece" 3815
"clock tower calls out six times and then stops" 9507
"clock tower chimes" 7907

"clock was always further advanced than they had hoped" 9470
"clock went off, alarm" 10171
"clocked off at exactly half past three" 1753
Clocks 163, 660, 1017, 1123, 1131, 2064, 2274, 2335, 3815, 4615, 5647, 7180, 8398, 8498, 9331, 9342, 9466, 9467, 9469, 9470, 9471, 9472, 9473, 9474, 9477, 9478, 9484, 9488, 9490, 9492, 9495, 9496, 9497, 9499, 9507, 10127, 10137, 10165, 10171, 10217, 10229, 10246, 10251, 10290, 10309, 10503, 10916
"clocks in her house, set the" 2064
"clocks of the city would presently strike five" 8398
"clocks were striking thirteen" 9473
Clodius 3812
"clods, sand" 10106
"clogs, clumping of the mill-girls'" 8774
"clogs made the same clatter on the cobbles" 9560
Clonbrony, Lady 6751
"Cloncraig, small village called" 2024
"cloning, the techniques of" 6798
"clonk from the side of its mouth, a little" 660
"Clonmel where I myself was born" 6618
"close behind" 8607
"close enough, you've got to get" 8535
"close ranks" 61
"close to the road" 3184
"closed, remained significantly" 2290
"closed it with a snap" 7362
"closed the door of the surgery" 2707
"closed the front door" 2726
"closed the pantry door" 1777
"closed the safe" 8174
"closed them again" 10191
"close-hauled" 8069
"closeness in the air, there was a" 4378
"close-packed" 6266
"closet, Jack's" 2614
"closet isn't too grand a word, if" 7193
"close-up" 5971
"close-up of a cow pie, taking a" 6879
"closing up shop" 3428
"cloth, brown velvet" 6854
"cloth, came up against a green" 7430
"cloth, the appearance of crisp folds of crumpled" 6067
"cloth, tie a little blue" 7494
"cloth my mother used to tie round

her hair, little blue" 1607
"clothed in mildewed bark" 9674
"clothes, dark well-cut" 2842
"clothes, new" 2863
"clothes, riding" 10389
"clothes, thick" 3940
"clothes, unlike her" 10831
"clothes, wearing orange" 6546
"clothes, work" 1952, 2852
"clothes boiling in the copper caldron" 7441
"clothes collected dabs of paint" 8242
"clothes hung on her, how well her" 10852
"clothes of the children, tumbled" 10818
"clothes piled inside" 2484
"clothes-horse" 122
"clotheslines" 7294
"clothes-pegs" 4987
"clothespins on the telephone line" 1554
"clothier, Jewish" 8908
"clothiers for generations" 8040
"clothing on the beds, odd pieces of" 990
"cloud, black" 8390
"cloud, covered with masses of" 10679
"cloud, cumulus" 8513
"cloud, heavy" 522
"cloud, iron-gray straitjacket of" 8437
"cloud, like an unsupported" 10368
"cloud, localized ammonia" 3604
"cloud, low" 5146
"cloud, monstrous" 8395
"cloud, not a" 4409
"cloud, puffs of" 8441
"cloud, ragged banners of black" 9082
"cloud, scudding fluffs of" 3667
"cloud, slow-spreading white" 757
"cloud, thick" 10637
"cloud, thick white" 2572
"cloud, trace of cirrus" 8115
"cloud, walking out of a" 5867
"cloud, warm sour" 8525
"cloud, white" 7289
"cloud, wool tatters of" 8406
"cloud blowing suddenly out of the sky" 8450
Cloud boys 663
"cloud coalesced out of nothing" 8441
"cloud had pressed down on Berlin" 10637
"cloud in the sky, not a" 3807
"cloud no bigger'n a man's hand" 584
"cloud of acrid black smoke, swirling ominous" 3783
"cloud of reserve and despond" 2502

"cloud passed swiftly away before the wind" 522
"cloud purple and piled heavy with evil" 8395
"cloud tatters were hurled across the rent" 8401
"cloud wafted across to Tommy's side of the bed" 8525
"cloudburst, caught in a summer" 4275
"cloud-enshadowed land" 4533
"clouding the yellow light" 9540
"cloudless" 2277
"cloudless sky" 2255, 4372
Clouds 197, 522, 584, 1312, 1399, 1757, 2176, 2211, 5023, 5867, 7019, 7341, 8115, 8390, 8392, 8395, 8397, 8400, 8401, 8403, 8404, 8406, 8412, 8418, 8421, 8422, 8430, 8437, 8441, 8446, 8450, 8451, 8513, 8525, 8591, 9070, 9082, 9789, 10504, 10578, 10637, 10679, 10711
"clouds, bank of spear-shaped" 8404
"clouds, behind the" 8446
"clouds, billowy sea of little broken" 8397
"clouds, bottomless pool of" 1433
"clouds, cheerless" 8412
"clouds, dark rain-" 1399
"clouds, distant" 1299
"clouds, fleecy" 2211
"clouds, floating dark" 8421
"clouds, gathering" 8418
"clouds, grey with" 8403
"clouds, high scudding dizzy" 2393
"clouds, leaden" 10572
"clouds, lowering" 9239
"clouds, moving shadows of" 3179
"clouds, racing" 10504
"clouds, shredded with" 10732
"clouds, slashing gray" 10726
"clouds, small feckless" 8400
"clouds, small white pungent" 4335
"clouds, summits veiled in" 5125
"clouds, wrack of gray" 1312
"clouds cloaked the sky" 8401
"clouds curled darkly over the East River" 7019
"clouds darkening Boston Harbor" 8591
"clouds drifted and billowed, pitchy" 10494
"clouds drive over" 10606
"clouds finally broke in the west" 7341
"clouds going southwest very fast" 5023
"clouds . . . grayed out the islands below" 5023
"clouds grew denser" 8412
"clouds hung low and dark" 9228
"clouds in Confederate gray" 10504
"clouds . . . looked so low and

ghostlike" 8591

"clouds of blue and of purple flying over the land" 10578

"clouds of hope" 6075

"clouds of mist" 7322

"clouds of palest amber, a few wandering" 8392

"clouds of sleep, invisible intangible" 8324

"clouds of yellow dust" 8768

"clouds presaging rain, black" 10711

"clouds raveled to tatters" 10585

"clouds rolling in the trade winds" 10616

"clouds scudded across a half moon" 2176

"clouds streamed high, grey" 8430

"clouds were hurried across the vast untroubled sky" 8400

"cloudy day" 175, 9321

"clover, full of" 8513

"cloverleaf appears as two pair of perfect buttocks" 9186

"cloverleaf of new road" 2995

Clovis 4290

"clown portraits" 504

"clowns, king of the" 4800

"clown's pantaloons, pair of" 3265

"cloying odor" 8510

"Club, Centennial" 3423

"club, coming around to the" 6234

"Club, Country" 8628

"Club, Crescent" 6449

"club, dinner at his" 8633

"club, drinking" 4319

"Club, Drones" 1610

"Club, Exeter Country" 1603

"Club, Fort Beulah Rotary" 7762

"Club, Hillcrest" 4332

"Club, Hope" 4330

"Club, Imperium" 5894

"Club, Kenneepoose Canoe" 2104

"club, member of my" 4733

"club, men's" 8331

"Club, National Press" 4314

"Club, Nipmunk Country" 8372

"club, officers'" 4313

"Club, Peak" 4322

"Club, Pickwick" 5557

"Club, Pinnacle Rock" 10

"Club, Raindrop" 4336

"club, several outsiders in the" 9095

"Club, Sharanpur" 6434

"Club, Shiawasee Rod and Gun" 3423

"Club, Snooks'" 10339

"Club, Tennis" 4321

"club, the" 3912

"Club, The Channel" 4316

"Club, The Light of Day" 4309

"club, unlike any other" 4330

"Club, usually lived at his" 4317

"club car's bar" 9363

"Club in Pall Mall" 3813

"club Spit, dance" 4849

"club-house, emerged from a" 1569

"clubhouse, haunted the" 4306

Clubs 1603, 1610, 2104, 3423, 3478, 3813, 4306, 4307, 4309, 4313, 4314, 4316, 4317, 4319, 4321, 4330, 4334, 4336, 4733, 5894, 6449, 6966, 8331, 8633, 9095, 10339

"clubs, fan" 3538

"clubs, one of New York's most desirable" 4307

"clubs, original sporting" 3423

"clucking noises inside" 8806

"clumping of the mill-girls' clogs" 8774

"clumsily" 10303

"clumsily, drops" 475

"clung desperately to a red hill" 6062

"clung like mustard plasters to his back" 9529

"clung to it now" 2765

"cluster of houses" 1413

"clusterfist" 9313

"clusters, dripping orange-coloured" 9668

"clutch it in a strangling grip, as if to" 10582

"clutch on life, awakening" 10995

"clutched a mouth-organ" 976

"clutching miserably at their hats and hair" 55

"clutching the bed sheets up around her neck" 10325

"clutter of memories, her head a" 3019

"cluttered with stalls and people striving to sell things" 1045

"Clybourn, corner of Potrero and" 5571

"Clyde Massachusetts" 9424

"coach, aisle of the" 7249

"coach, large family" 9757

"coach, track" 8675

"coach came thundering down the long hill" 9789

"coach captain" 5926

"coach from Ellsworth to Butcher's Crossing" 9777

"coach had crossed the border from England into Wales" 9560

"coaches, rumble of" 3396

"coaches per diem, forty" 6283

"coachman, called up to his" 9637

"coachman, fat" 9757

"coachmen" 3120

Coal 1018, 7219, 10551

"coal, good round" 10678

"coal and diamonds" 10551

"coal as 'black diamonds'" 10551

"coal boom, the great Middleburg West Virginia" 3586

"Coal Creek Pennsylvania" 9876

"coal hole in the heart of Soho" 4319

"coal is a much less portable form of property" 10551

"coal miner" 497

"coal tender" 7278

"coal tips sit fatly on torn slopes" 5151

"coal-camps" 1365

"coal-lumper" 4315

"coals, merry but unnoticed bed of" 1907

"coals, over the" 8810

"coals crackled fiercely" 1907

"Coaltown" 3407

"coast, American" 7647, 9065

"coast, America's northeast" 7531

"coast, Atlantic" 1640, 4030

"coast, cliffs of the" 9155

"coast, cold on this" 10613

"coast, Dorset" 1440

"Coast, East" 6867

"coast, Gulf" 4407

"coast, Maine" 7457

"coast, Mediterranean" 8894

"coast, New England" 9096

"Coast, Pacific" 1392

"coast, paradisal" 1039

"coast, singular character of its" 5707

"coast, Syrian" 8057

"coast, the opposite" 1174

"coast, the whole of our extended" 4029

"Coast, West" 309

"coast, west Irish" 5040

"coast, wide deep curve of the" 7923

"coast as barren and as sombre and as desolate" 5015

"coast facing to the north and east" 4050

"coast is very sublime" 5707

"coast of Connecticut, this over-used" 9174

"coast of County Mayo" 10926

"coast of England" 4031

"coast of Graham Land" 8113

"coast of Maine" 3205

"coast of Peru, off the" 8058

"coast of Pomerania" 5016

"coast of Scotland, on the north-east" 1171

"coastal triangle" 8632

"coast-downs" 6616

"coaster steaming west for the Pool" 9175

"coasting home fed-up" 7628

"coastline, desert" 4081

"coastline, Riviera" 4083

Coasts 1440, 4028, 4031, 4048, 4050, 4051, 4083, 5707, 9174, 10613

"coasts of Sussex and Kent" 4048

"coasts of the Great West or Salt Continent" 2605

"coasts trend from each other, these two" 4051
"coat, black velvet evening" 10735
"coat, blonde" 9851
"coat, duffel" 909
"coat, extraordinary" 5800
"coat, frock" 10373
"coat, gorgeous light-blue" 1313
"coat, her sable" 1916
"coat, in an orange goatskin" 5824
"coat, my old army surplus trench" 10415
"coat, palomino mink car" 2846
"coat, shabby black" 1496
"coat, sheepskin" 10734
"coat, shimmering buti-silk boudoir" 5450
"coat, trench" 1759
"coat, watery harlequin's" 5325
"coat, winding her" 10698
"coat and boots, her" 1777
"coat hangers, new plastic" 2840
"coat of arms" 2686
"coat of arms, supporters on a" 381
"coat of tilting planes and lozenges in movement" 5325
"coat sodden across his shoulders" 1759
"coat three sizes too large" 876
"coated, rough-" 979
Coates, Julian 3690
"coats, khaki" 8136
"coats, old" 7035
"coaxing the bride to come into the aisle" 10650
"coaxing voice, his most" 8205
Cob 7723
"Cobargo was a terribly dull place in 1935" 1456
"cobbled seawall" 8037
"cobbler, the" 2025
"cobble-stones" 1250
"cobblestones, came up over the" 5692
"cobblestones, like" 9179
"Cobb's Marsh" 6203
"Cobbton" 2489
"cobra, dancing with a" 2108
"cobras" 9235
"cocaine" 6276
"cocaine still rampaging around his body" 3056
"cock, a" 7514
"cock, cry of the" 1221
"Cock, Old" 6431
"cockamamy murders" 6209
"cockatoo of a man" 5900
"cockboat, bilges of a" 8158
"Cocke County Georgia" 4403
"cockney, careful" 7982
"Cockney among Cockneys, I am a" 4440
"Cockney Venus" 817
"cockpit, from the noise-bound" 1409

"cockroach, the" 4968
"cocks an eye" 4835
"cocks had just heralded the break of day" 9067
"cocks were crowing" 731
"cocktail parties" 4788
"cocktail party" 10819
Coco, Mrs 4544
"cocoa needs cooking in a saucepan" 1862
"coconuts" 8277
"cocoon, break out of that" 5748
"cocoon of blankets, warm" 6599
"cocoon that he has carefully wrapped himself in" 5748
"cocoons of newspaper" 6143
Cocopah, steamer" 8084
"coddled and protected" 2590
"code again, talking in" 8874
"codices, variety of" 9053
Cody 3045, 7575
Cody, Amos "Pinky" 10
Coel 5431
Coen, Emma 3952
Coen, Shotgun 4794
"coercion, felt as" 10778
"Coëtminais" 9589
Coffee 6638, 7556, 7572, 10059
"coffee" 3881
"coffee, another cup of" 10059
"coffee, black" 8634
"coffee, breakfast" 8552
"coffee, cognac and" 4274
"coffee, cup of" 3282
"coffee, drank" 7015
"coffee, give up" 6638
"coffee, have a quick cup of" 7569
"coffee, my third cup of" 1120
"coffee, ordinary" 1994
"coffee, second cup of" 6638
"coffee, second cup of breakfast" 3572
"coffee, sipping hot" 4620
"coffee, Stilton and" 3877
"coffee, take" 3817
"coffee, toast 'n'" 3871
"coffee bar on the corner" 4285
"coffee break, my morning " 10058
"coffee came round" 2245
"coffee cup" 298, 8577
"coffee shop" 4904
"coffee touched, I do not like the" 7556
"coffeehouse on the central square of Pamplona" 9962
"coffee-joint, the car conductors'" 3816
"coffee-room of the Goose and Gherkin" 1101
Coffin, Byron 5239
"coffin" 9626
"coffin, Geoffrey's" 3944
"coffin, his son's" 2384
"coffin, in his" 1887
"coffin, laid out in the" 1878

"coffin resting on their shoulders" 3956
"coffin stuck fast" 3960
"coffin-bearers counted themselves fortunate" 3956
Coffins 1878, 1887, 3956, 3960, 10524
"coffins cast adrift" 10524
Cogitation 2070, 3443, 4710, 4928, 6841, 9413, 9421
"cogito ergo sum" 7401
"cognac and coffee" 4274
"cognizance of the world and itself" 4496
Cohen 4919
Cohn, Robert 8910
"coiffed, severely" 6868
"coiled downward in a thin white ribbon" 9141
"Coilla Doraca, wood called" 10756
"coin, deposited the" 2888
Coincidence 1232, 2291, 3512, 5106
"coincidence" 1232, 3512
"coincidences, unexplained and un-explainable" 5106
"Coit Tower" 9611
Coitus 7983, 7985, 7986, 7989, 7991, 7993, 7994, 7995, 7997, 7999, 8000, 8001, 8002, 8003, 8005, 8007, 8008, 8009, 8010, 8012, 8013, 8014, 8016, 8019, 8020, 8021, 8022, 8023, 8024, 8025, 8027, 8029, 8030
"Coke bottles" 4154
Colar, Virginia 2709
Colbert, Henry 3828
Colburne, Mr. Edward 5785
Colby, Peter 2997
"Colchester, city of" 5431
Cold 178, 181, 187, 375, 727, 765, 1002, 1301, 2250, 2440, 2784, 2809, 2932, 3686, 3788, 4640, 4668, 6365, 6395, 7243, 7285, 7300, 7403, 7569, 7693, 7920, 8129, 8136, 8183, 8607, 9147, 9239, 9276, 9354, 9359, 10075, 10095, 10125, 10141, 10196, 10472, 10569, 10572, 10575, 10613, 10692, 10710, 10713, 10715, 10717, 10734, 10750
"cold" 181
"cold, bitter" 10125
"cold, blue with" 4871
"cold, brilliant and sharply" 8115
"cold, but she was" 9359
"cold, dense" 10075
"cold, faces bright with" 8607
"cold, freezing" 4640
"cold, hated being" 1553
"cold, I caught the" 157
"cold, it was" 1551, 1557, 1564, 9276
"cold, it wasn't" 3940
"cold, it's so" 1552
"cold, labeled her" 10852
"cold, in brilliant" 5824

"cold, metal rail was" 8183
"cold, nights blew" 5704
"cold, realized she was" 2784
"cold, sea was bitter" 7920
"cold, shivering" 2250
"cold, so" 1547, 1559
"cold, the" 1002
"cold, unusually" 9742
"cold, very" 4668
"cold, villainously" 6365
"cold, worst thing is the" 1553
"cold all night, he had been" 10141
"cold and gusty" 10715
"cold and relentlessly pervasive" 5778
"cold and silent, his bed was" 2420
"cold and snow and ice" 10572
"cold as the beer, feeling suddenly as" 2351
"cold Brisbane can be, I'd forgotten how" 1562
"cold cookie, calls me a" 6653
"cold day" 1550
"cold in Canada" 7403
"cold like dog-nose" 1561
"cold night, it was a" 2932
"cold on this coast, it gets" 10613
"cold outside, it was" 9354
"cold passed reluctantly from the earth" 10472
"cold spell of 1851, the record" 772
"cold war, in these days of" 5447
"Cold War, no" 3362
"cold was intense" 10196
"cold weather, bitter" 765
"cold where he sits" 1555
"colder, there couldn't be a" 9147
Coldfield, Miss 7763
"Coldmouth" 1633
"coldness crept upon Morgana" 2809
"coldness of the instreaming air, the sudden" 7569
"coldness searched his bones" 7300
"Coldstream, young man in the" 10649
Cole 7125
Cole, Elizabeth 4852
Coleridge, Rosamund 9358
Coles 5936
Coles, the 7874
Coleses, the 1208
Colette 8756
Colfax 3094
"Colfax, headed for" 204
Colin 10257, 10654
"Coliseum" 9215
"collaborators, French fascist" 4017
"collapse, structural" 5599
"collapsed on the grass" 3688
"collar, me wear a" 6536
"collar, white lace" 4207, 7122
"colleague, my" 10963
"colleague, suspicious of a" 9305
"colleagues, my" 714

"collect call" 1141
"collect her paper parcels" 9523
"collect things, houses" 3256
"collected prizes" 8242
"collected the pieces of typewritten foolscap" 5415
"collecting dead people" 2414
"collecting them, after surreptitiously" 7680
"collection, entire twentieth-century" 8027
"collection, snug little" 1349
"collection, vivid butterfly" 2156
"collection of back issues" 7871
"collection of early Rhodesian medical texts" 5607
"collection of odd English names" 4739
"collection of pictures" 1586
Collections 634, 2414, 8242
"Collective Farm in Russia" 5419
College 3039, 4930, 8012, 10441, 10896, 10953
"college, by the time he was at" 4721
"College, Caraway" 2468
"college, driving my son to" 3039
"college, fellow of the" 7522
"College, Harley" 7875
"college, her senior year at" 9729
"College, Jocelyn" 1920
"college, just returned from" 7214
"College, King's" 10441
"college, leaving" 6521
"College, Logos" 5102
"College, Mount Sebastian" 8708
"college, my junior year in" 9290
"College, Pequod" 9701
"College, St. Ambrose's" 7076
"College, Scone" 8354
"College, Simon Straight" 3283
"college, small Eastern" 4575
"College, Trinity" 4604
"College, Waynesboro Female" 9250
"College, Wellford" 8667
"college, went to" 10896
"college canteen" 5846
"College discharges you at age eighteen" 9718
"College for Women, Ridgedale" 1214
"college garden" 7390
"college in Georgia, our small" 5476
"college in Ohio, small" 4930
"college lingered gently" 2489
"college magazine" 5413
"college men" 4307
"college mixer" 5857
"College of Augurs" 7514
"College of Euphoria Illinois" 5413
"College of the Vestal Virgins" 7514
"college office" 7903
"college student pouring coffee and

washing dishes" 9265
"college town" 9233
"college was decidedly fast" 7876
"college years, edenic" 5592
Colleges 1214, 1740, 2489, 2568, 3266, 3276, 3283, 3286, 3526, 4604, 5102, 5413, 5631, 5832, 6279, 6451, 6760, 7336, 7522, 7772, 7875, 7876, 7881, 7882, 7890, 7896, 7899, 7903, 7905, 7907, 8207, 8354, 8880, 9250, 9531, 9569, 9814, 10437, 10866
"colleges, cathedral and" 9160
"colleges, Hebrew" 7505
"colleges, view of the" 7772
"collide, where the various wests" 278
"collided with a car on a country highway" 25
"collie, huge mahogany-and-snow" 412
"collie whined again" 9898
Collingsworth, Benton 1667
Collingwood, Mrs. 9856
Collins, Ely 3338
Collins, Mrs. Clara 3338
"collision, have a frequent" 7584
"collision of two very different cultures" 1989
"collision with a derelict" 8059
"Cologne" 6224
"Colombia" 2341
Colón, Magdalena 10871
"Colonel, the" 10244
"Colonel, the old" 2357
"colonial wars of North America" 10468
"Colonial Service" 8078
"colonies, western" 7814
"colonies of America, the revolted" 6803
"colonies of North America" 10470
"Colonies on many planets" 10941
"colonizers" 4502
"colony, triumphant throughout the" 10469
"colony of New Spain" 4502
"colony of self-devoted and pious refugees" 263
"color, dark ruby depth of" 9662
"color, slowly infused with" 10273
"color, the blood-" 6085
"color is old-rose and pink" 548
"color of gruel" 1274
"color of water" 7917
"color variation, her marked" 46
"color was yellow" 3615
"Colorado" 1357, 1969, 8052
"Colorado, Aspen" 1396
"Colorado, eastern" 9834
"Colorado, mouth of the" 8084
"Colorado from space, seeing" 4549
"colored chauffeur" 1315
"colored folks' church" 3225
"Colored High School band,

Dream of Pines" 6228
"colored woman" 964
Colors 763, 1274, 3371, 3615, 5146, 5176, 5478, 5645, 7288, 9441, 10393, 10591
"colors, brilliant" 9159
"colors, forced to show its" 5717
"colors, painting her" 10591
"colors are brown and gray" 9162
"colors fade, before the" 5478
"colors to blend" 5439
"colors too pale or too strong or ill-matched" 5439
"colossal, white and" 3665
"Colossæ" 5411
"colossus of a cottonwood tree" 10929
"colour, circle of" 10774
"colour, dark amber in" 6834
"colour float wide through the sky, flossy webs of" 2188
"colour lost, its" 763
"colour more common with beast or bird" 10774
"colour of the country is reddish-brown" 5138
"colour of the sea outside" 5330
"coloured girl" 9930
"colours, bewildering extravagance of" 2620
"colours, obliterating discordant" 484
"colours, pale" 5176
"colours, pure and delicate" 9441
"colours separated" 10393
Colquhoun, Mrs. 10812
Colquohoun, Chris 10349
Colston, Dame Lettie 5447
"colt beside her" 437
Colter, Jeannie Laird 2157
"Columbia" 6451
Columbus 5223
Columbus, Christopher 3466
"Columbus" 4429
"Columbus left Spain for the west" 5223
"Columbus Ohio" 6412
"column, ran a curious" 6352
"column, squadron" 8679
"column in the Boston *Commoner*" 5209
"column reached the bank" 3687
"columnist, brilliant young newspaper" 5485
"columnist, movie gossip" 6454
"columnists, many lady" 7831
"columns, four Doric" 3225
"columns moved slowly and with difficulty, the great" 6109
"columns of the cavernous railroad station" 10734
Colville 5614
"Colvin California" 6114
Colwan 3551
"coma, irreversible" 6711

"Comanche" 4805
"combat stress" 9054
"combat years in Italy" 7894
"Combehurst Church" 3634
"Combe-Raven" 9466
"combes, set amid green wooded" 3248
"combination, an unusual" 10781
"combination, perfect" 352
"combination of dysentery and the clap, particularly pernicious" 172
"combinations showed, his" 1501
"come, did he think I wouldn't" 1728
"come, has she" 10029
"come, I'm afraid that he won't" 10568
"come, seven had" 4023
"come, why had he" 4572
"come again soon" 1661
"come and catch me" 297
"come and gone, opportunities have" 3524
"come and gone and complained and hurt and joyed and yelled" 6075
"Come and he cometh" 10649
"come as a child, this was where I used to" 6911
"come as most do, if you" 186
"come at all, one is never sure whether she will" 10808
"come back, he had always intended to" 5037
"come back, is he going to" 1763
"come back early" 9731
"come back later" 10311
"come back to Baltimore, I have" 5528
"come back to him many times, that morning had" 7408
"come back to myself" 10243
"come by, we'd" 9958
"come by the thousands, they had" 4012
"come close" 2727
"come down in about ten minutes" 10031
"come for lunch, asking me to" 3840
"come forth from his office" 10036
"come from out his balls, big flying rocks of" 7990
"come from Tokyo, I" 4553
"come here" 1583
"come home again" 4573
"come *in*" 2550
"come in like a black dog howling" 10609
"come into my cell" 7780
"come into the country" 1337
"come now, here they" 1657
"come on" 9693, 9942
"come on, would you" 10078
"come on along" 2102

"come on Elizabeth" 2528
"come on foot, he has" 1685
"come on now" 9267
"come out, would not" 7064
"come out on to the pavement" 10792
"come out to the royal flagship, allowed to" 4151
"come the summer" 6566
"come till thirtieth, please don't" 44
"come to Chicago, he has" 1685
"come to me" 6957
"come to meet" 2447
"come to the window" 2696
"come to Thursgood's, would never have" 1684
"come together soon enough, they will" 5046
"come twice already, had" 1735
"come up to Harlem" 74
"come up to scratch" 5004
"come up to Vienna at once" 10486
"come upstairs" 2317
"come where I was going, I have" 1729
"come with us after all" 1719
"Comedies, appear as" 5492
Comedy 9650
"come-on, his" 8861
"comer, any chance" 4492
"comes and goes as she pleases" 10808
"comes out of it again" 8313
"comes to women, as it" 7068
"comes together, it all" 879
Comesee, Paren 8336
"comet, Halley's" 2591
"comet flashed across the evening sky" 832
Comfort 6599
"comfort" 7097
"comfort, always in singular" 4920
"comfort, rather too thin for" 425
"Comfort, some" 4221
"comfort as may be supposed consistent with the jolting of the vehicle" 10108
"comfort of a suite at our Head Office" 9582
"comfort to an anxious mother's heart" 4889
"comfortable" 5294
"comfortable, he was too" 6599
"comfortable, serene and" 3248
"comfortable as chairs" 9669
"comfortable in the new, not long enough to feel" 6147
"comfortable niche in the world" 5998
"comforted" 5745
"comforters" 7035
"comforts" 5727
"comic" 7727
"comic, stand-up" 9650
"comics" 1254

Coming 44, 1504, 1583, 1590, 1605, 1643, 1644, 1680, 1694, 1720, 1728, 1742, 1770, 3406, 6048, 7622, 8201, 8685, 10044, 10091
"coming, he saw it" 7024
"coming, heard James" 10103
"coming, really" 9766
"coming, she's" 9970
"coming, the four of them were" 1693
"coming, the second" 8201
"coming, their" 10091
"coming at seven, he's" 9968
"coming at sunset, felt it" 2513
"coming back" 6539
"coming back, the people are all" 4581
"coming back along the forsaken shore" 6648
"coming back was worse" 1644
"coming down, after several years" 1690
"coming down along the road" 961
"coming down the Quarters" 1742
"coming down with the flu or something" 164
"coming gently through the mists" 1972
"coming home, he had felt no sensation of" 4565
"coming home so soon" 4564
"coming in, man" 5575
"coming into Cairo on leave" 1694
"coming into the kitchen" 7561
"coming into the living room" 996
"coming of the British" 1464
"coming out on April 3" 6991
"coming over the pass" 9754
"coming slowly" 4606
"coming through the Hole-in-the-Hills" 7853
"coming to a sudden rude end" 6510
"coming to the States for a year" 9630
"coming today, he is" 10044
"coming toward him, something awful" 2782
"coming up out of the swamp" 7110
"coming up the road" 9917
"coming very fast" 7853
"comma in a run-on sentence" 6280
"command, his first" 5628
"commandant" 3482
"Commandant of the camp" 9894
"commander, company" 6257
"commander, Portuguese" 5576
"commander in the Navy" 4745
"Commander of the Faithful" 7798
"Commander of the Victorian Order and Distinguished Service Order" 8580
"commander-in-chief" 8102
"commanding a large sealer and general trader" 8048

"commemorate the fiftieth anniversary" 228
"commemorate their moment of salvation" 1217
"commenced ramshackle and got worse" 3604
"commencement, hazards and difficulties which attended its" 5556
"Commencement, one week after" 10656
"commencement, our tale has its" 10467
"commencement ceremonies" 7905
"commencement exercises" 1204
"commencement of an enterprise" 7008
"commences, my story" 8952
"commend it, had nothing to" 3111
"commensense" 9701
"comment, tone of amiable" 8304
"comment uttered, no" 8967
"commentary, some" 5518
"commentator, flight" 228
"commented to his dining companions" 4511
"commerce, natural deposit of" 1443
"commerce, rushing streams of" 4039
"commercial, make her more" 1079
"commercial aristocracy of the East" 1021
"commercial enterprise, almost as a" 2341
"commercial house, famous" 6425
"commercial or professional wealth" 3122
"commercial representative" 6448
"commercial world" 5394
"Commissariat" 6949
"Commission, High" 6432
"commission in naval history, shortest damned" 4511
"Commissioner, Assistant" 5798
"Commissioner, Special" 4219
"Commissioner for Information, Mr." 4923
"Commissioner of Appeals" 3376
"Commissioners, District" 1833
"commit a crime" 2036
"commitment, no personal" 7006
"commitments, cut my" 5252
"committed *hara-kiri*" 6021
"committee, chairman of the" 7817
"Committee, Festival" 2469
"Committee, Youth Emergency" 4709
"committee met" 6985
"committee recessed tonight" 6994
Committees 2469, 3977, 7817
"committees, sitting on" 1493
"commodities represent wealth" 10551
"commodity, chief" 9483
"commodius vicus of recirculation" 1175

"Commodore, rank of" 10978
"Common, Boston" 4174
"common, famous" 6558
"common, less in" 3999
"Common, Panley" 7878
"common in our times" 3627
"common nowadays, if it is not" 6635
"common with which he fell in love at once" 6558
"commonplace" 4634
"commonplace, emotionally" 3303
"commonplaces, share its" 1025
"commotion, terrible frightening awful" 3621
"Commune, defend the" 10837
"commune, small" 6571
"communicable to a TV audience" 6478
"communicate their disturbing contents, did not" 1947
"communicating disagreeable intelligence" 6307
Communication 3333, 6001, 6307, 7968
"communication, adequate for" 10910
"communication, radio" 228
"communication media, the world's" 4008
"communications, of all the" 3741
"Communion, First Holy" 6587
"Communist Government" 8859
"Communist party officials, high-ranking" 6232
Communities 1384, 5166
"communities, ancient" 1384
"community, his entire" 5998
"community, permanent" 8881
"community, small" 1466, 8956
"community, small mining" 9795
"community, small Polish farm" 3449
"community of iron" 10871
"commuted to work in a seaplane" 231
"commuters come striding down toward the train" 10359
Commuting 231, 5104, 10359
Companies 1015, 1016, 1020, 1021, 1030, 1034, 1041, 1054, 1065, 1077, 2538, 3737, 6425, 6426, 6471, 6473
"companion" 1528
"companion, good" 6617
"companion, his" 5344, 8852
"companion, my" 8155, 8734
"companion, secret morning" 537
"companion, with no" 6577
"companion of the geranium, inseparable" 6854
"Companion of the Order of St. Michael and St. George" 8580
"companion standing beside him" 8556

Companions 537, 585, 708, 989, 999, 1999, 2080, 3483, 3486, 3917, 4003, 4135, 4511, 4796, 4797, 4813, 5337, 5710, 6557, 6573, 6617, 6854, 7352, 7623, 7862, 8155, 8158, 8209, 8350, 8570, 8852, 9357, 9514, 9782, 10343, 10364, 10376, 10427, 10440
"companions, dining" 4511
"companions, two" 662
"Companions always call'd me, so my" 6601
"companions-in-arms" 4457
"Company, Bird & Son's Old Blockhouse Distilling" 1912
"Company, British Linen" 3737
"Company, Chuberry Turpentine" 9553
"Company, East India" 1930
"Company, Flaver-Saver" 6426
"company, gas" 3094
"Company, Harnsworth Furniture" 1020
"Company, Hudson River Trust" 1028
"Company, Hudson's Bay" 7918
"company, kept him" 2456
"company, large utility" 6471
"Company, Mammoth Publishing" 5311
"company, new bioengineering" 1065
"Company, Number One" 9385
"company, prosperity of the" 2538
"Company, Robles Land" 5892
"Company, Transient" 8662
"Company, Unico Realty" 4705
"company, uniform of the" 5926
"company commander" 6257
"company is still talked about in the Peloponnese" 1034
"Company lines, C" 8652
"company president" 1925
"company stood at attention" 8645
"company whose brief I hold" 1030
"compare it to now, there is nothing to" 8807
"comparing the boys of Camperlea" 982
"comparison, superlative degree of" 3377
"compartment, first-class" 7268, 9659
"compartment, rear" 1315
"compartment, second-class" 4139
"compartment, third-class" 1496, 9545
"compass, points of the" 3060
"compasses, following their stars and" 9247
Compassion 580, 1929, 2076, 2918, 7160
"Compassionate, the" 5602
"compatriot, receive a" 9882
Competition 4702, 5471, 10104

"competition with her husband" 5471
"compiled 'Basic English'" 10910
"compiling these narratives" 7948
"complacence, smug" 7982
"complacency, peculiar" 9872
Complain, Roy 378
"complain, did nothing but" 652
"complain of overbearing mothers" 7174
"complained, her aunt" 4201
"complained to herself" 3017
"complaining, going to quit" 5296
"complaining about the police" 6956
"complaint, chronic" 9328
"complaint, labored asthmatic" 8782
"complaint, little ground for" 7139
Complaints 1869, 5296, 6956, 9945
"complaints, listening to the" 9945
"complement his imaginary hat" 4896
"complete as anything can ever be" 9008
"complex, in a downtown" 6781
Complexion 46, 984, 4157, 10796
"complexion, dark oily" 5908
"complexion, her luscious black" 46
"complexion, pale Irish" 4438
"complexion, superb" 10796
Compliance 5388, 5389
"complicated, had in fact been" 2649
"complicated intersections" 5607
"complications, there will be a pack of troublesome" 1578
"complications set in" 3288
"complimenting each other, they are always" 10892
Compliments 2, 9568, 10892
"comply with thy request" 5389
"compose a piece, invited to" 6224
"compose a set of formal verses" 5457
"compose the sentence, half an hour to" 5473
"composed an abusive letter, mentally" 1916
"composed by John Francis Shade" 5452
"composer, Israeli" 6232
"composer, my father was a" 6631
"composer of *The Death of Nelson*" 7505
"compositions, in all his" 6213
"comprehend, cannot readily" 1209
"comprehend the matter I am about to relate" 4591
"comprehensible" 3391, 6478
"comprehension of human nature" 9118
"compressed, my world is" 3373
"compressed by physics" 9503
"compromise I reached with her

father" 4814
Compton, Miss Emily 3333
"compulsion of circumstances and civilisation" 5696
"compulsion to tell about it, one fierce" 2036
"compulsion which drew Ira Claffey from his plantation" 6569
"computers would tell" 7005
"comrades, my" 10594
Comstock, Elnora 6619
Comstock, Gordon 5621
Comstock, Katharine 6619
Conboy, Cate 9897
"concealed from sight" 1349
"concealed on his person" 879
"conceit, self-" 239
"conceit, youthful" 5816
"conceited and priggish" 6977
"conceive, I humbly" 5387
"conceived, she was" 8140
"conceived, the day Don Juan was" 572
"conceived, the night Tendai was" 8029
"conceived, was" 7991
"conceived, we weren't even" 8230
"concentrate on the onion, forced herself to" 1871
"concentration, great" 8561
"concentration on her practice swing, in effortless" 8927
"concept, do you dig the" 1081
Conception 572, 5699, 7991, 8002, 8029, 8140
"conception had taken place" 8002
"concern, only" 10966
"concern, overpowering" 7531
"concerned, I am extremely" 7825
"concerned, just a spot" 10965
"concerned about his twelve-year-old son" 1153
"concerned about my son" 6466
"concert, enduring the" 6238
"concert, outdoor" 6220
"concert, Ray Charles" 3343
"concert at the Philharmonic Society" 6232
"concert tenor" 8752
"concerto, fifth Brandenburg" 6233
Concerts 1746, 3343, 6220, 6232, 6233, 6238, 6242
"concerts, gives benefit" 6242
"concierge, the" 7786
"concierge's lodge" 1654
"concise, simple and" 7425
"conclave of like-minded well-heeled matrons" 10863
"conclusion, sweet" 5592
"Concord" 9860
"concrete, fortresslike shape of reinforced" 4627
"concrete, grey rough" 8280
"concrete, prying great chunks of" 29

"concrete, trash-covered" 4267
"concrete slabs, blank white" 307
"concupiscent, she was so dramatically so extravagantly" 8018
"concur, we entirely" 5434
"concussion" 872
"condemnation, singling a particular person out for" 1533
"condemned to incessant hypocrisy" 10766
"condensed version" 5530
"condescending contempt" 4046
"condescension of one caballero to another" 7132
"Condicote" 7244
"condition, fabulous" 10588
"condition, much better" 6418
"condition, poor" 5532
"condition, that" 6890
"condition had been successfully treated with drugs" 166
"conditions we live in today" 879
"condolences, come and go with their" 3947
"Conduct, my particular" 3527
"conduct of public men" 9260
"conduct of the characters" 4453
"conducted in solemn procession" 7179
"conduit of the markets" 14
"conduit to Granddaddy himself" 4437
Coney Island Bulletin, took out space in the" 6652
"Coney Island fries" 3876
"Coney Island Ocean" 7932
"Confederate gray, clouds in" 10504
"Confederate monument" 9775
"Confederate States of America" 4067
"Confederates, Two Little" 3637
"conference, learned" 7461
"conference, story" 10049
"conference at one of the Inner London Crown Courts" 5208
Conferences 5208, 7461, 8707
"confess, I" 5794, 9864
"confess, I promised to" 1815
"confess, yet I have to" 3925
"confess to you at once, let me" 1816
"confessed to Jeeves" 3341
"confessed to the crime" 6177
"confessing, I don't mind" 3698
"confessing that he had been the murderer" 1812
Confession 916, 1539, 3308, 4490, 5461, 6229, 7952
"confession" 916
"confession, four days since my last" 1803
"confession, it is a sort of" 5461
"confession, masturbated during" 1539
"confession, you want to hear a

good" 1804
"confession of the person whose character they represent" 4490
"confessions that Saturday evening" 6229
"confetti, light spatter of last night's" 2690
"confidant, fellow victim and" 5355
"confided to me" 6938
Confidence 87, 4704, 5573, 7980, 10512, 10550, 10759
"confidence" 10512
"confidence, into my" 4696
"confidence, might induce" 87
"confidence and cowardice, strange mixture of" 5573
"confidence in my ability to remember them, I have no" 7451
"confiding in him, people insisted on" 7952
"confinement, framed and wired" 5276
"confiner of cosmic events" 6478
"confines Gormenghast, his" 972
"confirmation" 6587
"confirmation of official financial backing" 3741
"conflict, armed" 10512
"conflict, dreadful" 6517
"conflict between the Bwamba and Batoro peoples" 1833
"conflict with the gale, almost magically detached from his" 14
"conflicts and worries, not many" 9263
"confluence" 7647
"confluence of the Poteau and Arkansas rivers" 7686
"conform to the practice" 9859
"conforms to none of the clichés about California" 10606
"confrontation of Dorothy Merlin and her new doctor" 381
"confronted by the solid wall of the Leprosarium" 4622
"confused, I've been" 679
"confused, she grew" 10121
"confused observations" 1833
"confused with blushes" 8299
"confused with the other, nor is one to be" 5217
Confusion 116, 675, 679, 3506, 10121, 10178, 10263
"confusion, awoke in some" 2762
"confusion, crumbling into white" 10719
"confusion, mist of pleasant" 116
"confusion, my timid" 675
"confusion, the hour rings with" 3506
"confusion, to avoid" 9337
"confusion of dreams and memory" 10299
"congestion of narrow streets" 9130
"congestion on the approach-roads,

avoid the usual" 883
"conglomerate of ugly factories" 7282
"Congo rain forest" 3905
"congratulate you, I want to" 6991
Congratulations 1859, 6991, 9272
"congratulations" 9272
"congregation" 1533
"congregation, murmur and rustle of the enormous" 1532
"congregation in Tollamore Church" 8737
"Congress, Member of" 6260
"congruous one with another, the three are" 5694
"conic sections" 99
"conifers, mixed" 4073
"conjectures, metaphysical" 6903
"conjugate verbs" 6698
"conjunction of the Fish and the Water-carrier" 5458
"conjure an appropriate response, he could not" 4256
"conjured up by the magic spell of genius" 4101
"conjuror, Cabbalistic" 7505
Conklin, Marvin 5370
Conlon, Judy 1700
"Connecticut" 1242, 2360, 2554, 3139, 4632, 5352, 5608, 8975, 9174, 10742
"Connecticut, in my part of" 8621
"Connecticut, spectacular part of" 2950
"connection, don't see the" 677
"connection, high" 6611
"connection between the two is my proposition" 1977
"connection with the Eritreans" 9371
"connections, jumbled" 9019
"connexion with my mother's parents, some long-forgotten" 364
Connie 2816, 8278
Conniston 5904
"connoisseur" 847
"connoisseur of weather, now I am a" 6651
"connoisseur of wine" 6654
Connolly 7532
Connolly, James 7151
Connolly, Paddy 1100
"connote not sexual identity but simple sentient being" 10913
Conover, Gertrude 10013
"conquer taste" 3845
"conquered and organised" 4470
"conquered foothold" 3639
"conquered the self, you will have" 3845
"conqueror, feeling of a" 6553
"conqueror, old-world" 1351
"Conqueror of England, William the" 6518

"Conquest, Norman" 834
"conquests, glorious in" 425
"Conquistadores" 7800
Conrad 6515
Consalvi, Martino 6019
Conscience 3575, 7071, 7964
"conscience, hurdled the lowered bars of" 5674
"conscience prompted" 7071
"conscience which is nearly always guilty" 3575
"conscience whispers me" 7964
"conscious, had never been" 3357
"conscious, I *am*" 8872
"conscious, it probably was" 7652
"conscious, not fully" 10222
"conscious of a strange exhilaration" 3850
"conscious of herself" 10441
"conscious of his actions" 7172
"conscious of his own breathing" 5619
"conscious of itself, sarcastically or hopelessly" 8863
"conscious of the dark stillness" 2122
"conscious of the room" 10121
"consciously at least" 9424
"consciously or unconsciously" 8093
Consciousness 6001, 10110, 10156, 10245, 10260
"consciousness, exceptional stir of heightened" 6001
"consciousness, fighting" 10139
"consciousness, from oblivion to" 10156
"consciousness, fuller" 10138
"consciousness, prodded into" 10139
"consciousness, punctured Bill Rutherford's" 10245
"consciousness, return of" 10110
"consciousness, she was so deeply imbedded in my" 6651
"consciousness, without any deep" 4883
"consciousness of her absurdity" 7011
"consciousness of the four people, beat on the" 7569
"consciousness was immediately flooded" 9432
"consensus, general" 8934
"consequence, everyone of" 7481
"consequence, like a person of" 4760
"consequence, the" 3589
"consequence to me now, the only thing of any" 8027
Consequences 619, 2314, 3546
"consequences" 5727
"consequences, continuous" 3546
"consequences, the source of" 5082
"consequences are what we have to live with" 619
"consequences of the mistakes of his elders" 9704

"consequences that spread far and wide and flow for years or centuries" 5082
"conservative, my mode of dress tends to the" 4789
"conservative and cautious" 5988
"Conservative government" 6999
"conservatory" 4305
"consider fascia" 2066
"consideration of the risk" 10642
"considered, all things" 4013, 5081
"considered the two and a half days of heat and dust" 9358
"considering two widely different aspects of chairs" 9408
"considering what she smelt" 385
"considering what to make" 1860
Considine, Old Daniel 10185
"consistency, make a virtue of" 5427
"consistency, measure its" 3555
"consistory of Cardinals, a full" 1525
"consolation" 844
"consolation in a distressed [hour]" 4439
"console, hi-fi" 34
"Consolidated Edison" 5321
"consonants, a trifle blurred about the" 8742
"conspicuous, for the sake of being less" 5871
"conspicuous about her, what was" 4302
"conspicuous ancestor, our first" 7554
"conspicuous even before she entered the office" 10846
"conspicuous part" 2752
Conspiracy 1330, 5082, 5194
"conspiracy, becomes suddenly aware of the" 1330
"Conspiracy, Chicago" 7150
"conspiracy, daring" 5082
"conspiracy, indicted for" 5194
"conspiracy, resembled a clumsy" 5829
"constables, police" 6960
Constance 337, 9615
"Constantinople" 717, 2411
"Constantinople was bigger than he had ever imagined" 1461
"constantly, said it to her" 10828
"constellations, teaching us the names of the" 536
"consternation of all of Bloodsmoor" 6577
"constitution were analagous to a muffin, as if his" 6519
"Constitutionalists" 4478
"constriction, suffering a" 7939
"construct halls" 7896
"constructed by a man" 1856
"constructed out of a heavy farm wagon and a hay rack" 9759

Construction 272, 1180, 2401, 3110, 3152, 3191, 3224, 3484, 4259, 6458, 7508, 7808, 7902, 8543, 8571, 8875, 9213, 9227, 10930, 10964
"construction, solidity of" 3122
"construction of a henhouse, turned their energies to the" 3604
"construction site" 2401
Consuela 1828
"Consulate, American" 9879
"consul-general" 3378
"consuls, new" 7006
"consultation, scheduled for a" 6897
"consultations, between" 10418
"consulting a typewritten list" 3187
"consulting it at intervals" 8850
"consulting the rheostat thermometer, judiciously" 10592
"consummated his iniquity" 5914
"consumption, dying of" 2019
"consumption, I am certainly in a" 121
"consumptive" 652
"contact, bareness of" 8841
"contact, my first" 6209
"contagious disease, some sort of" 545
"container of opposites" 5479
"*Conte Rosso*, the" 8161
"contemplate the desires of my life" 5381
"contemplating" 8938
"contemplating a battered calendar" 491
"contemplating a murder" 6192
"contemplating my own massive *Bildungsroman*" 5837
"contemplating the bust of Homer" 509
"contemplating the view" 5357
"contemplation, lazy" 3394
"contemplation of the fresh material, her astounded" 9409
"contemporaries, despise her" 4360
"contemporaries, hordes of my" 718
"contemporaries, most of my" 6163
"contemporaries, three cherished" 8637
"contemporary letters" 5423
"contempt at what humanity had to say about it" 4046
"contemptible migrations" 6141
"contemptuous leer" 1565
"contemptuously, toss your head" 399
"content and comfort, place had a look of" 3083
"content in the trundle bed" 8483
"content now, wonder if Connolly is" 7532
"content outwardly, I felt totally" 10186
"content to stay forever just as he was" 5636

"content with what I had" 337
"contentedly" 6755
Contentment 112, 337, 4342, 5282, 5555, 5579, 5636, 9263
"contentment, never since then had she known" 2506
"contest ended in a series of sharp whistling sighs" 9841
"contested the access to the cloak-room" 8215
"contests, two" 9024
"Continent, at the angle of the" 4051
"Continent, Great West or Salt" 2605
"continent, heart of the" 4089
"continent, mud of half a" 7664
"continent, newest and oldest" 4087
"Continent, on the" 2293
"Continent, parts the waters of the" 8052
"continent, royal and long-established" 2257
"Continent, the" 10768
"Continent, took place on the" 3432
"continent aflame from end to end with a war" 10518
"continent in ruins" 2262
"continent of Europe" 2264
"Continental Divide" 6062
"Continental Shelf" 0130
"continents, green" 2623
"continents, trackless" 4533
"continents had separated, long before the" 4095
"continents purple and green" 5023
"continents were already formed, when the" 7924
"continues, it" 801
"contract to move the Pyramid of Cheops" 8565
"contracted during a single debauch" 172
"contraction" 7086
"contradicting a dream" 4701
"contradiction, this apparently impossible" 7684
"contraption of weights" 10228
"contrary to the romantic myth" 2539
"contrast, offers a striking" 4037
"contrast, stark" 926
"contrast with things American" 6251
"contrasting clearly with the subdued carillon" 652
"contrasting sharply" 5899
"contrasts, great" 5572
"*contre-temps*, a cruel" 7491
"contributed several love poems" 5413
"contrived, a third" 5408
"contrived to live in the highest company" 238

"control, I'm out of" 8027
"control, impossible to" 2796
"control, raging out of" 10518
"control, simple act of" 512
"controllers, senior" 7128
"convalescence, atmosphere of fragile" 1452
"convenience, it's a" 4819
"convenient, it is very" 7264
"convent, home from the" 7709
"convent, very ancient" 1293
"Convent of Saint Faith" 6111
"Convent of the Five Wounds" 9540
"convent of the order of the *Black Penitents*" 1293
"Convent of the Sacred Heart" 3931
"Convention, Democratic" 3378
"Convention, Democratic National" 1214
"conventions . . . have a way of surviving their own usefulness" 7819
"conventions like clichés" 7819
"converging to a spearpoint" 9228
Conversation 286, 582, 716, 977, 1107, 1113, 1129, 1826, 2400, 2620, 2896, 3695, 3883, 3912, 3990, 4277, 4318, 5580, 6302, 6736, 7200, 7377, 7390, 7410, 7590, 7591, 7602, 7603, 7772, 8197, 8216, 8837, 8839, 8845, 8847, 8849, 8851, 8852, 8853, 8854, 8855, 8856, 8857, 8858, 8860, 8865, 8867, 8869, 8871, 8877, 8881, 8884, 8891, 8893, 8896, 9096, 9301, 9752, 9925, 10047, 10794, 10842, 10931
"conversation" 7585
"conversation, a little" 9096
"conversation, begins the" 6736
"conversation, certain amount of genteel" 8869
"conversation, fell into" 582
"conversation, four minutes into any" 6302
"conversation, having a quiet" 2896
"conversation, intimate" 7772
"conversation, someone else's" 1129
"conversation, telephone" 1113, 8197
"conversation, there is no such thing as" 8855
"conversation, try and make" 7591
"conversation came in excited little bursts" 7390
"conversation had inspired, pain that their" 7599
"conversation was suspended" 8884
"conversational, so" 1493
"conversations, shorthand notes of" 716
"conversations that occurred in the streets of that town throughout the night and day" 8854
"converse amidst stupendous sur-

roundings" 2620
Converse 8369
Converse, Prill 2702
"conversing, two men" 8845
"conversing in general" 5580
"conversion of Scotland" 1499
"convert, he had made but one" 1495
"converted Indians" 7508
"convertible, black" 4168
"convertible, Buick" 9810
"convertible, our father bought a" 9827
"convertible, the" 10713
"convertible pulled up even with us" 4168
"conveyances, lying out of the track of all public" 9515
"conveyed something subtle about the movement of the water" 7677
"convict, a pardoned ex-" 2956
"conviction, a sullen" 5250
"convictions, good record for" 5200
Convicts 2956, 5564, 7131, 7136
"convicts" 1165
"convicts at Jupiter" 7136
"convinced, I became" 10856
"convinced many of us" 6804
"convinced that a soft shoulder of the road had given way" 19
"convinced that the road to happiness lay in becoming very rich" 4346
"Convocation of the saints" 2623
"convoy was anchored" 8146
"convulsion of nature" 1174
"convulsions, eerie" 6367
Conway, Ralph 9862
"Conway" 9599
Conway twins 9440
Conyers, General 364
Cook, Jeremy 3038
"cook, he was a superb" 6200
"cook, now a" 10896
"cook, the" 3124
"cook three meals a day" 6440
"cook who had popped out back into the kitchen" 4602
Cooke, Ebenezer 5418
"cooked their wretched food" 8544
"cookie, cold" 6653
"cookies" 1876
Cooking 550, 860, 3555, 3853, 6440, 8540, 9339
"cooking in a saucepan, cocoa needs" 1862
Cooks 3124, 6440
"cool, now that we are" 1820
"cool, pretending to be" 7229
"cool and dry" 10583
"cool in the attic" 6395
"cool movement" 10180
"cool of the evening" 5615
"cooled by sips from a spritzer" 8883

"cooler, it was" 4372
Coolidge, Calvin 970
Coolin, Frankie 9947
Coombe, Jane 8258
"coon tails" 2973
"coop, his sojourn in the" 7140
Cooper, Ray 5915
Cooper, Raymond 8583
Cooper, Stephen 3412
"cooperation with each other" 6995, 6997
"co-ordinate" 5574
Cooter, Uncle Hooter 8542
"cop, some racist" 74
"cope of gold wrought silk" 1198
"cope with a situation" 1400
"Copenhagen, I knew it was" 7443
Copenhaver, Frank 1783
"Copiah County Mississippi" 4042
"copie of what he would speake, a dolefull" 7370
"copied out the September accounts" 6437
"copies, three thousand" 5476
"copper, looking for" 5831
Copperfield, David 9706
"Copperfield, Historic Museum Village of" 233
"coppertone" 9786
"copra loaded today" 8101
"cops lawyers judges all of them" 9702
"copy, carbon" 7769
"copy-writer coming in today, there is a new" 3327
"*Coquets*" 10764
Cora 6729, 10830
"coral cry of the cock" 1221
Corbario 6019
Corbena 964
Corbett, Mrs. 549
Corbett, Peter 8456
Corbett, Professor 549
Corby, Chief Detective Inspector 9961
Corde 6456
Cordelia 2359, 10406
"Cordillera Entre Rios" 3251
Cordova 8738
"corduroy that crosses the lower end of the Limberlost" 7215
"core, no" 1389
Corfe, Lady 2786
"Corfu" 10997
"*co-rhea*" 172
"Corinth" 8971
"Corinth, Gulf of" 1439
Coriola 7084
"*Coriolanus*" 390
Cork, Mrs. Adela Shannon 3126
"Cork" 1173
"cork, like a green" 5034
"cork twisted in a crude 8" 5034
Corleone, Michael 8153
Corliss, Valentine 10336

"corn, fields of" 3641
"corn, gathering" 3647
"corn, pulling" 10927
"corn, young" 4034
"corn and wheat fields" 7267
"corn crop" 8592
"corn flake, the" 8298
"cornbread" 8530
"corncob pipe" 899
Cornelius, Mr. 7109
Cornell, Georgie 10229
Corner, Mr. John 7512
"corner, backing him into a" 3415
"Corner, Fielding's" 4078
"Corner, Hyde Park" 10375
"corner, in the after starboard" 570
"corner, no favorite" 8357
"corner, on one" 9209
"Corner, Superstition" 9134
"corner by the door, the warm" 5248
"corner by the television, in the" 5634
"corner of America, remote and desolate" 291
"corner of Eleventh and First" 8320
"corner of Lord North Street" 1655
"corner of my mouth" 9004
"corner of the hi-fi console" 34
"corner of the living room" 10926
"corner of Washington Street and Central Avenue" 9407
"corner of your own insides, the deepest" 8814
"corners, brass reinforced" 2610
"corners, dusty little" 1834
"Corners, Rebel" 9145
"corners where London's secret servants drink together" 1834
"cornets sounded a final flourish" 1565
"cornfield, at the edge of a" 4955
"cornflakes, amid the" 5502
"cornflower, blue as a" 5147
"cornflower eyes" 4176
Cornforth, Fanny 4801
"Cornhill, Standard of" 4303
Cornock, Jack 6539
"Cornwall" 5662, 8632
"Cornwall, North" 1500
"Cornwall, north-west coast of" 8146
"coronary, massive" 2373
"coronary catheterization" 166
"coronation, my" 1197
"Coronation Day" 7261
"Coronation Special" 7261
Coronations 2887, 5371
"coronations, I detest" 5371
"corporate offices" 4448
"Corps, Signal" 6441
"corpse, horses had grown used to the" 1885
"corpse without hands" 1883
Corpses 164, 2286, 2333, 2346,

2351, 2354, 2367, 2398, 2426, 2456, 3956, 5149, 5528, 8539, 10548
"corpses of more than sixty centuries of dead" 5149
"corpulent, slightly" 6427
"corral, by the" 566
"correct in every particular" 1959
"correct in what he said" 5954
"corrected his students' essay papers" 7885
"correctness, extremity of" 4309
Correspondence 5458, 10055
"correspondence of persons still living" 5387
"correspondent, your" 1833
"correspondents, so few regular" 696
"correspondents, Washington" 794
"corridor, alone in the" 8582
"corridor, empty" 5851
"corridor, their nice clean" 4619
"corridor that separated our private inner quarters from the reception rooms" 5996
"corridor was long and dark" 9233
"corridors, sootblacked brick or cobbled" 10416
"corridors jammed with a perspiring crowd" 3996
"corridors where lightwire shadows make a gothic harp of cellar doors" 10416
Corrine 2013
"corrugated metal, rusty" 9241
"corrupt wisdoms, learns all the" 275
Corruption 1530, 2039, 2053
"corruption" 2039
"corruption, you asked me about their" 2053
"corsages, crumbled" 6861
Corson, Bob 6948
Corven, Sir Gerald 8078
Cosgrove, Mr. Billy 1303
"cosmic events" 6478
"Cosmic Link" 2633
"cosmos, God creating the" 2630
"cost, win it at any" 1839
"costume, hunting" 2878
"costume, Pig-Pen" 6783
"costume, theatrical" 2841
"costume party" 3961
"costume for the Ku Klux Klan" 2837
"costumes of the late nineties" 6756
"cot by the windows" 8248
"cot in a corner, a broken iron" 7753
"Cotswold country" 8100
"Cotswolds, the" 10391
"cottage" 1683
"cottage, her Devon" 9730
"cottage, his" 1591
"cottage, my little" 1444

"cottage, rambling Elizabethan" 3116
"cottage, Ransom's" 9890
"cottage, rented" 5534
"cottage, superintendent's" 6163
"cottage, this" 7325
"cottage, tiny rented winter" 3621
"cottage, weather-beaten tumble-down" 3070
"cottage door stood open" 2691
"cottage for the summer" 9734
"cottage in which my mother was living alone" 3359
"cottaged, well-" 5067
Cottages 1591, 2691, 2780, 3070, 3116, 3359, 6269, 9730
"cottages, coastguard" 9460
"cottages, country" 2780
"cottages, thatched bulging" 6269
"cottages and cottage-like houses" 6266
"cottages crouched against the sky" 9460
"cottages that stood by the brook-side" 6269
Cotton, Evelyn 8019
"cotton, chop" 1269
"cotton, I have interest still in" 1042
"cotton lands" 7323
"cotton mill" 1386
"cotton mill, working in a" 4186
"cottonwood, a single" 4957
"cottonwoods" 8768
"cottonwoods, row of" 5620
"cottonwoods, thick fur of" 8622
Cottrell, Mrs. Desmond 9896
"couch, huge" 9452
"couch, rough" 8453
"Cougar, 380-hp copper" 2999
"coughing heavily" 9314
"coughing like a donkey" 8580
"could, how you ever" 6038
"coulee, little Wisconsin" 3359
"coulee is so still right now" 10610
"Council, British" 7904
"Council, General Nursing" 10216
"Council of Freemen" 8866
Councill, Farmer 9759
"counseling, compulsory" 87
"counselor to a pope" 1528
Count, the 6844
Count of Mountjoy 8866, 9452
"counted himself a fortunate man" 7978
"counted the stack of money" 3743
"countenance, cast of" 984
"countenance, his" 8545
"countenance, his darkened" 7370
"countenance, lively" 14
"countenance, melancholy cast of" 8098
"countenance, rugged" 5889
"counter, at the dirty" 7569
"counteract by every means in their

power" 6972
Counterfeiting 2061
Countess of Cressett 927
"counting *mississippis* between the flashes of lightning and the cracks of thunder" 9088
"counting the beat during a music lesson" 6217
"counting the empty bottles" 10937
"counting-house, half" 8778
Countries 724, 3318, 3369, 4081, 4533, 8142, 9515, 9712
"countries, flat outland" 584
"countries, foreign" 3557
"countries, I was brought up in two" 9712
"countries, innocent" 5427
"countries, richest of the sugar" 4050
"countries crowded into this area, like all the other" 4089
"countries of Europe" 6245
"countries of larger extent, far out-weighed" 4533
"countries of the world" 6109
Country 4054, 4058, 10566
"Country, Back" 8592
"country, bleak uninhabited" 8682
"country, broken" 9741
"country, capital of my" 791
"country, care about the" 3310
"country, come into the" 1337
"country, come to the aid of their" 6989
"country, every European" 267
"country, extensive district of" 4027
"country, fair open" 1364
"country, far southwestern" 3995
"Country, Foothill" 6056
"country, gray" 7297
"country, green and gentle" 5177
"country, high border" 5713
"country, highest part of the rich rolling" 3638
"country, his native" 4554
"country, I live in the" 6419
"country, I lived in a different" 3369
"country, in a tranquil" 5299
"country, in our" 3671
"country, in the" 161, 310, 3121, 6987
"country, in this" 3364, 6828
"country, land in the" 3642
"country, landing alone in a strange" 6113
"Country, Low" 5122
"country, low dark" 9228
"country, lush farm" 9159
"country, manners and customs of my" 3493
"country, Midland" 9096
"country, mining" 4131
"country, my native" 1568
"country, New England" 8622

"Country, North" 958
"Country, Old" 6261
"country, over this" 724
"country, past is a foreign" 6789
"country, pleasant Cotswold" 8100
"country, red" 7297
"country, rich river-bottom" 4052
"country, sister" 2087
"country, small" 4089
"country, steaming low" 9749
"country, that" 8142
"country, that part of the" 9652
"country, they came from another" 9111
"country, this" 265
"country, three months in this" 2615
"country, Two Medicine" 9494
"country, underdeveloped" 6262
"country, virgin" 1912
"country, we left the" 1744
"country, wide" 8770
"country, wide open" 1616
"country, wide quarter-circle of" 4045
"country around it was wild and picturesque" 9741
"country cottages" 2780
"country ended" 4054
"country far from home" 4467
"country identity, my" 5790
"country in England, some of the oldest" 4058
"country in Europe, as if it were a" 2400
"country is a huge dead beast" 5148
"country it is in, what" 4081
"country looked alike, all the" 1244
"country music capital of the world" 9365
"country near Germantown" 9721
"country of good air and great spaces" 6249
"country of good ranches" 3643
"country of sliding stones" 7068
"country of the Elder Gods" 2236
"country seat" 5067
"country was a wash of pale colours" 5176
"country was being built" 272
"country which he discovered, re-markable" 5563
"country-house" 3972
"countryman and a clansman needed me" 6000
"countrymen, his" 971
"countryside, Essex" 9810
"countryside, flat Dutch" 7246
"countryside, Gloucestershire" 3808
"countryside, Javanese" 2480
"countryside, Scots" 3381
"countryside between Gerona and Barcelona" 2341
"countryside gleamed dully after a heavy overnight mist" 5172

"countryside seemingly empty" 2965
"countryside was bleak and deso-
late" 5159
"County, Apple" 10558
"County, Beaver" 4097
"County, Cactus" 6948
"County, Casabella" 9563
"County, Claxford" 2374
"County, Clay" 6136
"County, Dallas" 9775
"County, Ether" 167
"County, Fairfield" 8621
"County, Forest" 4601
"County, Jackson" 7262
"County, Lane" 2947
"County, Macungie" 4059
"county, midland" 6609
"County, Pymantoning" 293
"County, Sonoma" 6132
"County, Sussex" 485
"County, Twin River" 6952
"County, Westchester" 1908, 4425,
6750
"County Hants" 950
"County Kilkenny" 2834
"County Mayo" 10926
"county of Lincoln" 3058
"County of Los Angeles, imaginary"
7893
"county of Santa Felicia" 5210
"county of Somerset, the pleasant"
3248
"County Road 686" 3666
"county seat, small" 4073
"county seat town" 1425
"coup in Chile" 1139
"couple, guilt of the" 1967
"couple, happy" 1975
"couple, impressive even imposing"
2005
"couple, Israeli" 9630
"couple, old" 8706
"couple, teenage" 1992
"couple, there is no more joyous"
5279
"couple, they were an ordinary"
1978
"couple, very worthy" 1964
"couple, what did you make of the
new" 1979
"couple of human beings" 4338
"couple stood in church" 5774
Couples 515, 641, 1142, 1741, 1822,
1839, 1844, 1848, 2044, 2051,
2073, 2083, 2112, 2146, 2529,
2561, 2648, 2657, 2658, 2659,
2663, 2668, 2673, 2680, 2685,
2949, 2999, 3136, 3170, 3416,
3469, 3751, 3828, 3831, 3878,
4125, 4338, 4344, 4351, 4596,
4602, 4976, 5109, 5239, 5279,
5343, 5352, 5609, 5643, 5737,
5746, 5748, 5750, 5766, 5774,
5775, 5851, 5930, 6201, 6279,
6356, 6370, 6391, 6775, 6857,

7085, 7589, 7716, 7731, 7827,
7953, 7988, 7989, 8011, 8013,
8028, 8092, 8479, 8525, 8639,
8731, 9164, 9355, 9732, 9736,
9934, 9988, 10062, 10117, 10169,
10197, 10406, 10661, 10724, 10857,
10937
"couples, amorous" 9381
"couples, hundreds of elderly" 1978
"couples chatting as they passed
oblivious" 10392
"couples sitting at the edge with
their arms about each other"
2529
"couples the age of me and Rupert"
8011
"couples whispering in the shadows"
6567
"couplets, heroic" 5452
"couplets, quires of" 5448
"Coupole in Montparnasse" 5673
Courage 53, 5248, 6991, 9622
"courage!" 5408
"courage, sagas of" 5149
"courage, that required a lot of"
6991
"courage to be courageous, it takes"
53
"courage to gather, my own" 9622
"courage to tell the truth, I shall
never have the" 2734
"courage you bring to it" 5248
"courageously" 7500
"Courier, Pacific City" 6815
"courier, waiting the return of a"
10034
"course, Adult Education" 7074
"course, its steady" 199
"course, lay your" 8053
"course around the sun" 525
"courses, the vast" 8079
"Court, Baron's" 8027
"Court, Beverley" 6021
"Court, Circuit" 5197
"Court, Dene's" 4569
"court, divorce-" 2649
"Court, Earls" 5356
"Court, Hand and Ball" 2245
"court, her" 10430
"Court, King's-Hintock" 3072
"Court, Magistrates'" 9252
"court, marched into" 2045
"court, stand in that" 6044
"Court, Superior" 5210
"court below my rooms" 8787
"court building, federal" 8007
"Court Hand" 7879
"court house" 7108
"Court House" 9250
"Court Number 3, New York
Criminal" 5205
"court of law" 6201
"court of pleasure, in a" 6561
"court room was packed" 3996
Courtenay, John 4926

Courtenay, Richard 4926
"courteous guards" 9381
"courtesan, great" 10871
"courtesy Mrs. Macdermot, by"
563
"courthouse" 663
"courthouse, county" 9226
"courthouse, federal" 4422
"courthouse, he left the" 1712
"courthouse, small yellow brick"
4073
"courthouse, usually ornate stone"
1425
"courthouse is less old than the
town" 1400
"courthouse square" 4420, 7038,
8893
"court-room, the stifling June day"
5204
Courts 2027, 2045, 2649, 2682,
3798, 5197, 5198, 5199, 5201,
5204, 5205, 5208, 5210, 6044,
6201, 9226, 9252
"Courts, Inner London Crown"
5208
"courtship" 6545
"courtship, customs of" 7718
"courtyard, its great" 9244
"courtyard, with a" 3164
"cousin, distant" 4774
"cousin, her" 4921, 8003
"cousin, hesitant" 8872
"cousin, his" 1901, 9857
"cousin, his beloved" 2315
"cousin, my" 251, 716, 1159, 1277,
1925, 5098, 5344, 5399, 6035,
9035
"Cousin, my" 6164
"cousin, your" 4977
"cousin and dependent of Mrs.
Anne Oldfield" 8837
"cousins, one of those distant
Tampa" 1151
"cousins, third" 3585
"cousins had made cheese and
butter" 3667
"cove on which the house was built"
8491
"Cove, Parmelee" 4234
"cove, the" 9224
"Covenant, unspotted banners of
the" 7500
"covered as by moonlight, as
evenly" 8586
"covered his long body with a clean
white sheet" 131
"coverlet, feather" 7056
"coverlet of dirty gray wool" 6121
"coverlets of gold, land was resting
under" 10573
"covers, on top of the" 10265
"covers that were heavy" 10020
"coves, cool unruffled" 4105
"coveted by every would-be shopkeeper" 7771

"coveted, I" 2432
"covetous desires" 1205
"Covington Kentucky" 1029
"cow, put off slaughtering the" 7331
"Cow Brand Soda" 2828
"cow is there, the" 6836
"cow pie, close-up of a" 6879
"cowardice" 2481
"cowardice, confidence and" 5573
"cowboy, lone" 7632
"cowboy, plain average and just a hard-riding" 9705
"cowboy boots" 5966
"cowboy hat" 2839
"cowboy pictures" 634
"cowboy rode down the point of a low ridge" 10692
"cowboy rode through country" 7632
Cowboys 246, 1320, 1582, 2215, 3399, 3995, 6418, 7250, 7616, 7620, 7621, 7623, 7632, 7634, 7636, 8853, 9127, 9310, 9311, 9312, 9705, 9767, 9842, 10692
"cowboys" 1320
"cowboys, four" 3995
"cowboys lived forever" 3399
"cowed, subdued and" 7304
"cowered against the dusty wall" 8179
"cowering and covering their vulnerable spots" 3722
"cowhide, genuine" 2835
"cow-in-calf" 3657
"cowl, monk's" 142
"cowlicked" 462
"cowparsley and campion profuse" 3808
Cowperwood, Frank 7154
Cowperwood, Frank Algernon 1359, 5564
"cows" 6126
"cows, a slow look from" 9184
"cows, dead" 6961
"cows, her" 8823
"cows, mind the" 1269
"cows, when she met" 4153
"cows graze, as" 10623
"cowtown, it was a" 1442
"coxcomb, gentleman and a" 3812
Coxon, Mr. 6977
"coy, extremely" 2306
Coyote 9821, 10311
"coyotes were sneaking" 454
"cozy depths of her inclined seat" 10192
"cozy snug in his blanket cocoon" 2250
Crab, H. M. schooner 8102
"crab-apple, wild" 8510
"crab-apple tree" 9674
"crab-like" 4337
"crack, quite suddenly developed a" 9247
"crack, sudden" 8821

"crack at the base of its red-and-white candy-striped tower" 9247
"crack in the center of his brow" 5942
"cracked at the skin and oozed freely" 8531
"cracked from the wind" 7685
"cracked like an eggshell" 39
"crackers and cheese and beer" 6760
"cracking me on the noggin" 38
"cracking the back of his head" 34
"cracking up" 4938
"crackle, there was a" 8825
"crackled" 8804
"crackled, radio" 9374
"Cracow, edge of the ancient center of" 1714
Craddock 2926
Crader, B. 4665
"craft, talked about his" 5512
"craft, tiny" 8056
"craft, underwater" 8111
"craft of losing himself" 10051
Crafts 484, 6450
"craftsman, some Turkish" 717
"crags, grey and rust-red" 5127
Craighill, Wayne 8204
"Cramoisys" 2555
Crane, Helga 8353
Crane, Louise 10675
Crane, Miss 5152
"crane on the summit, a mason's" 1849
"Crane Simplex" 10100
"crane with a ball and chain" 5692
"craned his neck" 2764
"cranes, like ghostly" 730
"cranes, yellow" 3774
"Cranford" 10769
"cranial splints, thousands of" 3413
Cranmer, Thomas 8848
"crap, all that David Copperfield kind of" 9706
"crap, seven" 3969
"crash, appalling" 8769
"crash, his last car-" 2361
"Crash, year of the" 815
"crashing, wood" 10297
"crater, floor of the" 5134
"crater, its massive" 5052
"crater, rim above the" 8415
"crater, volcanic" 10674
"Craven Falls" 807
Crawford, Beth 1689
"crawl around until it finds your brain" 6381
"crawl out again" 1095
"crawled back under the lip of the plate" 4968
"crawled into the car" 2974
"crazied him, what" 2651
"*CRAZY!*" 9300
"crazy, am I" 4944
"crazy, fall down" 7534

"crazy, he's" 4937
"crazy, it was" 4436
"crazy, not" 109
"crazy, puzzled about going" 4942
"crazy, when she was finally" 4710
Crazy Eights 6134
"crazy for real this time, I'm" 8278
"crazy thing, like a" 993
"creaked, bed spring" 10137
"creaking, steady" 739
"creased her way over the oil-smooth water" 8125
"create for the reader" 5406
"created four sons" 2635
"created something like a record" 202
"created the impression" 3296
"creating the clearing" 3903
Creation 2630, 2632
"creation, awesome as" 2986
"creation and first sixteen years of life" 5598
"Creation of the World" 515
"creative silence" 6001
"Creative Writers, Australian Society of" 5429
Creativity 5445, 5454
"Creator, a signal instance of the hand of the" 2619
"Creator, the" 2310
"Creator had meant to mimic" 5178
"Creator of All Things" 2635
"Creator of Heaven and worlds and suns" 2626
"Creator of the Universe" 8501
"creature, she had become a strangely shaped" 5265
"creature, small and exquisite" 969
"creature, the" 428, 8179
"creature onto whose head Gombold had strayed" 9585
"creature ... was some hundreds of miles high" 9585
"creature was subdued and hushed, every" 2790
"creatures, bedraggled" 5704
"creatures, petticoated" 5788
"creatures, three" 10409
"creatures, under-water" 7754
"creatures of the Horn, brave and starved" 9371
"creatures still doing service to the Serpent" 5392
"creatures that swarm and multiply in a drop of water" 519
"Crecy was fought, days before" 10474
"credence, people do not give it" 4169
"credible" 2739
"credit, the only place I get" 6438
"credit card billings" 2664
"credo, a sort of" 916
"credulity, overtaxes" 6890
Cree, Captain Joe 2325

"creeds, invention of so many" 7648

"Creek, Chickasabogue" 7907

"Creek, Crazy" 3714

"creek, forests which lined the" 3146

"Creek, Leatherwood" 3641

"Creek, Mud" 5136

"Creek, Roan" 7667

"Creek, Sandy" 9152

"creek, sycamores by the" 7025

"Creek, Wahwahnissa" 8515

"creek, winding" 10461

"creek curving there, he saw the" 1413

"creeks, ford two" 6083

"creep over me, began to" 10564

"creeper, golden shower" 9668

"creeper, scarlet" 2209

"creepers, dangling feathery" 9156

"creepers on the old house" 3836

"creeping out among the glory still afloat" 660

"creeping with their tendrils along the ground" 10772

"creeps, he crouches and he" 2030

Creighton, Ellen 3652

"crenellating the roof" 1180

"crepitating as though in the act of dying" 6220

"crepuscular buzz of the universe" 8333

"crepuscular frames of an old newsreel" 876

Cresap, Marcy 10558

Crescent, Alma 2795

"*Crescent City*, steamboat" 8096

"Crescent City, The" 7691

Cress 4156

Cressida 7445

"crest, at the" 878

"crest, enormous black" 6062

"crest, serried" 2195

"crest of the hill" 1764, 2989

"Crestcrego Texas" 7509

"crested with drifting sand" 1485

"Cretan bull ring" 10594

"Crete, island of" 9565

"Crete was the world" 5149

"crew, last member of his" 8655

"crew, ship-boat's" 7594

"crew cut" 3050

"crew leader" 1321

Crewe, Jacinth 1646

"crib, set back down in his" 8761

"cried, she broke down and" 2073

"cried, she went home and" 2076

"cried out" 5230

"cried out impatiently, the young man" 7609

"cried with relief" 10344

"cries, raised with their" 8379

"cries, shots and" 3766

"cries, whispered" 7057

"cries amid yowls of the others" 4154

"cries of labor" 7087

"crik and a crack, there was a" 10223

"Crillon, the" 4636

"Crim Tartary" 1902

Crime 872, 1812, 2014, 2015, 2017, 2018, 2019, 2020, 2021, 2022, 2023, 2025, 2026, 2027, 2028, 2029, 2030, 2031, 2032, 2034, 2035, 2036, 2037, 2038, 2039, 2040, 2041, 2042, 2043, 2046, 2047, 2048, 2049, 2051, 2053, 2054, 2055, 2056, 2057, 2058, 2059, 2060, 2061, 2062, 2065, 2066, 2067, 2068, 2069, 2461, 2576, 2869, 3407, 3408, 3630, 3977, 5105, 5200, 5205, 5759, 6177, 6179, 6183, 6185, 6203, 6276, 6343, 6453, 7850, 9701, 9702, 9850

"crime, as if in evidence of some" 2335

"crime, commit a" 2036

"crime, confessed to the" 6177

"crime, last major" 2069

"crime, premeditated" 2035

"Crime, Task Force on" 6274

"Crimes" 3527

"crimes, extraordinary series of" 2041

"crimes, one of those mysterious" 2018

"crimes known to the press" 2037

"crimes that keep our newspapers and detective agencies happy and prosperous" 2018

"criminal" 5700

"criminal, manner of executing a" 2043

"criminal, master" 2044

"criminal, not a convicted" 5938

"criminal end of the business" 6411

"criminal I ever met, the most dangerous" 2033

"Criminal Lunatic Asylum" 5399

"criminal millionaires" 286

Criminals 367, 1505, 2014, 2016, 2017, 2019, 2020, 2021, 2027, 2029, 2033, 2034, 2038, 2040, 2042, 2043, 2044, 2050, 2052, 2065, 2068, 2304, 2578, 3311, 3407, 4507, 4586, 5209, 5759, 6161, 6177, 6947, 7000, 7145, 7186, 7194, 9702, 10790

Crimond, David 2871

"crimson, rich spectacular" 7056

"crimson and gold, great patches of" 8076

"cripple, he was a chair-bound" 5924

"cripple, the" 7802

"cripple grown used to his crutches, like a" 201

"Cripplegate, servants at" 6457

"cripples" 6817

"cripples running for the priest" 1831

Cripps 6504

"crises" 274

Crisis 1146, 4665, 5089, 6260, 6989

"crisis, the" 5089

"crisis call" 1146

"crisis in his life" 4665

"crisscrossed with stilting and arch-like mangrove roots" 5170

"Cristo!" 8663

"critic compelled to listen to has-beens and would-bes" 9379

"critical, harshly" 5751

Criticism 5751, 6976, 10828

"criticism, exposed them to hostile" 6976

"criticism and disparagement, unspoken" 385

"criticize, jealousy made them try to" 10828

"critics have taken to calling 'The Grenzler Octet'" 5541

"critics of the art" 8570

Crittendon, Neale 962

"croaking, deafen me with your" 9990

"Croatia" 4055

"Croatians" 4055

Crocker, Norman 9914

Crockett, Davy 368

Crockett, Jason 368

"crocuses, appear like" 9569

"crocuses, green snouts of the" 3521

"crocuses bordering the front walk" 3801

"croft, the little" 7689

Crominski, Mrs. 3707

Cromwell, Senator Richard 10294

"cronies in his ancestral village" 4741

Cronin, Mrs. 3780

Crook, Annie Elizabeth 4871

"crook, mildly incompetent mostly harmless petty" 2068

"crooked, nameplate was" 6028

"crooked, they say I'm" 7826

"croon, funeral" 2084

"crooner" 7727

"crooning over my spoon and dropper" 3050

"crop, corn" 8592

"crop, first rows of the first" 3645

"crop from his estates, halved the" 2592

Cropper, Sheriff 4002

"crops were under cover" 6626

Crosbie, Captain 3740

Cross, Faith 253

Cross, First Lieutenant Jimmy 8708

"cross, dying on the crude" 6592

"cross, large silver" 10320

"cross his backyard and her backyard" 9964

"cross the river" 3687
"cross the town line" 9176
"cross-country from New York" 9439
"crossed his fat little legs" 5913
"crossed Hungerford railway bridge" 9596
"crossed silently to her desk" 6383
"crossed state lines in the stolen car" 1845
"crossed the Alleghanies" 6100
"crossed the border into Brittany at noon" 9643
"crossed the eastern divide" 9547
"crossed the hall of the hotel" 5812
"crossed the landing" 9417
"crossed the lawn" 5799
"*Crossfire*" 5296
"crossing, bad" 47
"crossing, it was only a two-day" 8123
"Crossing, Otowi" 8799
"crossing a dried river bed" 9546
"crossing a little spit of high ground" 6564
"crossing from Piraeus to Alexandria" 8123
"crossing London Bridge" 14
"crossing the Bay of Biscay" 853
"crossing the Firth of Forth" 9511
"crossing the hall of her home" 3825
"crossing the road" 9231
"crossing the Sahara desert" 2640
"cross-legged, sat" 6143
"crossroad, there is a" 9145
"crossroads, mountain" 6918
"crossroads, school stood at the" 7887
"cross-roads by the market place" 9138
"crossroads junction" 4328
"Crossroads of the World" 6274
"crossroads on the long southern slopes of Exmoor" 9230
"crossword puzzles completed" 7352
"crouch on the roof of a building" 10517
Crouchback, Guy 8666, 9559
"crouched at the low railing" 1598
"crouched behind the wet bushes" 10093
"crouched dispiritedly" 6121
"crouched in the darkness" 10094
"crouched like an Indian" 5824
"crouched there on the floor" 4485
"crouches and he creeps" 2030
"crouching mountains" 6087
"crow, the scout" 769
"crow cawed irritably" 777
"crow who had flown away with a cheese" 719
"crowd, Bohemian" 4721
"crowd, joined the" 10054
"crowd, large" 4025

"crowd, morning" 1091
"crowd, perspiring" 3996
"crowd, surging" 3006
"crowd, tan excited post–Christmas" 2447
"crowd, the" 6316, 9336
"crowd, with the" 1746
"crowd at the Rotonde" 7581
"crowd gathered, a little" 3988
"crowd gathered around my car" 9581
"crowd of identical individuals" 10445
"crowd of people" 2940
"crowd of people, small" 7151
"crowd packed in the aisle" 7249
"crowd streamed past" 4026
"crowd . . . swayed crushingly forward" 7249
"crowd that had just got off the plane" 9574
"crowd waiting for the ferry" 10054
"crowd was assembled either from motives of piety or thirst of information" 1292
"crowd was thickest" 330
"crowd watching, a" 2461
"crowd-cutter, make a" 2107
"crowded, always" 7264
"crowded, room was" 4016
"crowded, street that led to the hotel was" 1045
"crowded, the Jodler Room was" 8553
"crowded human beings" 175
"crowded to the doors" 300
"crowded with incoming guests" 4638
"crowded with people on holiday" 4517
"crowding" 3680
Crowds 300, 1045, 1089, 1091, 1746, 2447, 2940, 3006, 3468, 3691, 3988, 3996, 4001, 4009, 4016, 4025, 4517, 4638, 5041, 6316, 7581, 9336, 9390, 9574, 10054, 10445
"crowds, sloppy" 1089
"crowds, small" 7835
"crowds at the station" 5801
"crowds of people" 3691
Crowe, Dale 2065
"crowed, the rooster" 8423
"crowing of roosters" 2790
Crown, David 2419
"Crown, agents of the" 2386
"Crown, Employments under the" 5883
"Crown, English" 7794
"crown, golden" 10784
"crown, the" 3466
"*Crown*, the" 4312
"crown a German as Emperor" 1444
"crown and kingdom" 1483
"crown himself, Napoleon was

about to" 363
"crowned by cedars" 6912
"crowned heads were running over Europe" 927
"crowned her with a broken starfish" 1216
"crowned with due rejoicings" 2887
"Crownflights, when I reached" 1055
"crows, three" 775
"crows, three greasy brother" 771
"crows cawing in the stableyard" 750
"crows flew low over the fresh mound" 1186
"crows in his eyes" 1812
"crows took up residence" 775
Crowther, Michael 8979
Crowther lads 9599
Croy, Kate 9325
"crucified, papers have" 5845
"cruel, should they be so" 7412
"cruel and hard-hearted, I may sound" 3509
"cruellest month, April is the" 8615
"cruelly, more" 2381
Cruelty 1166, 1170, 3509, 4689, 6051, 7188, 7412, 9853, 10598
"Cruelty of their Prosecutors" 6089
"cruelty was abroad that winter" 10598
Cruise 9009
"cruise, gastronomic" 9575
"cruise, southern" 4559
"cruised on a westerly course" 219
"cruised through the Essex countryside" 9810
"cruiser anchored well to the south of the channel" 766
"cruising along" 9577
"cruising slowly along the Styx" 1009
"crumbling into white confusion at each successive blast" 10719
Crump, Mrs. 7377
"crumpled, last piñon knot" 3765
"crumpled the morning paper" 6310
"crumpled the parchment" 363
"crumpled the single sheet" 396
"crumpled *Times*" 6356
Crunch, Abbie 9425
"crunched, his feet" 10379
"Crusaders in Palestine" 10329
"crushed" 33
"crushed in his hands" 3849
"crushes on my teachers, always getting" 7732
"crushing me to the pavement" 38
"crushing only a few daisies" 9794
"crushing plantings" 6165
"crushingly forward, swayed" 7249
Crusoe 399, 6601
"crust, we're on the" 3617
"crusts, frosted" 7650
"crutch, clinging to his" 3749

Cruyer, Dicky 3021
Cruz, Raymondo 5595
"cry, a" 376
"cry, brutish" 10017
"cry, harsh sobbing" 766
"cry, his first" 4742
"cry, impatient" 4908
"cry, inscrutable war" 2942
"cry, letting out his first" 832
"cry, Ophelia's enigmatic" 5507
"cry, sharp guttural" 5620
"cry, she gave a startled" 8175
"cry, started to" 10214
"cry, woman's" 7067
"cry beat against the wind" 9619
"cry down the shrieks of the bleak
    December wind, vain effort to"
    1907
"cry from the baby" 8115
"cry of a bird" 5864
"cry of impatience and irritation,
    gave a sudden sharp" 1920
"cry of protest, a hearty male" 555
"cry of the cock, the proud coral"
    1221
"cry of white, not one" 7685
"cry together, had a good long"
    2074
Cryall, Adam 7392
Crying 2406, 2751, 3291, 4222,
    4363, 4742, 6588, 6649, 9063,
    10240
"crying, baby" 2086
"crying, child" 2085
"crying, children" 8504
"crying, far-away" 2075
"crying, had given up even" 9275
"crying, he seems to be" 8562
"crying, she woke up" 10240
"crying, stop" 2078
"crying, the only one" 2082
"crying aloud, to keep from" 7183
"crying as she sat by the window"
    2071
"crying behind the gym" 2077
"crying bitterly" 4222
"crying from the cold" 1129
"crying like the spotted hawk" 281
"crying notice" 10574
"crying out" 4988
"crying out for charity's sake to be
    amused" 927
"crying over spilled milk" 6929
"Crypt, the" 4319
Crystal, Martin 705
Crystal, Miss 9652
"Crystal, Ogof" 4056
"crystal beads" 3521
"crystal clear" 4056
"crystals, spoonful of brown sugar"
    8577
"Cu Chi" 4629
"Cuba" 1925, 5841, 9086
"Cuba, guarding the north coast of"
    8385

"Cuba, we are in" 6264
"cubes, great flat-faced" 3096
"cucumber, rotted" 2656
"cue for further wordplay" 8027
"Cuenca, city of" 1398
"cuff, French" 2848
"cuffs thick with grease" 9436
Cullen, Joe 1759
Cullens, the 5802
Cullinane, Dr. 8112
"cullud folks, 'mong us" 4716
"cultivated a small farm in Berk-
    shire" 3635
"cultivated appreciation" 1314
"cultural renown, not without its"
    1401
Culture 267, 879, 1401, 1989, 7904,
    9709
"culture, a" 1209
"culture, British" 7904
"culture that developed in Babylon"
    9709
"cultures, collision of two very
    different" 1989
"Culver City" 3292
"Cumberland" 7248, 7617
"Cumberlands, our" 9071
"Cumbria" 824
"Cumseh Georgia" 9583
"cumulus, a layer of" 197
"cunning old hunter" 4248
Cunningham, Cabot 7881
"cunt flushes out blood clots"
    10881
"cup, breaking of the" 2476
"cup, coffee" 298
"cup, cracked porcelain" 1212
"cup of coffee" 10059
"cup of coffee, I was on my third"
    1120
"cup of coffee, second" 6638
"cupboard, deal" 7753
"cupboard under the stairs" 7193
"Cupid's darts" 7708
"cups, a few odd" 6131
"cups, blue-and-green porcelain"
    5330
"curandera, la" 1799
"curate, the" 5583
"curate seemed quite a nice young
    man" 1501
"curate was admitted to the Charing
    Cross Hospital" 1519
"Curate-in-charge" 1491
"curates, abundant shower of" 1484
"curator, the" 3697
"curators" 6512
"cure, the" 7785
"cure calf mule or pig" 9684
"cure warts" 6338
"cures jet lag, eating turkey" 7466
"curiosities, the case of" 1087
Curiosity 483, 552, 693, 3599,
    3875, 4152, 4822, 4920, 5612,
    5858, 6284, 6286, 6290, 6527,

    6800, 7023, 7207, 7211, 8211,
    8238, 8960, 9692, 9864, 10464,
    10488
"Curiosity, Effects of this" 10464
"curiosity, fresh food for" 2600
"curiosity, infinite" 8976
"curiosity, lively" 2095
"curiosity, my" 9864
"curiosity, person of" 10724
"curiosity, public" 9692
"curiosity, success of" 9378
"curiosity extended his tour" 2087
"curiosity interfere with his punc-
    tuality, if he lets his" 2088
"curiosity of my friends" 5027
"curiosity of the dawn, wistful cold"
    5307
"curiosity of the tourist, he had lit-
    tle of the" 4920
"curious, somewhat" 5400
"curious, those who are too" 8960
"curious about her own past, had
    never been" 6800
"curious path his life took" 5594
"curious sense of unreality" 10173
"curious thing" 4493
"curled at the feet by too hot an
    oven" 152
"curled behind him on the stone
    floor" 458
"curled up, lay quietly" 5616
"curled up like a foetus" 5777
"curled up on the beach" 1895
"curlews, long-tailed" 368
"curls, yellow" 4181
"curls with a strangely languid and
    voluptuous look of tension" 5048
"currency, first bill of Bim Auctor's"
    2061
"current, to be taken somewhere
    else on its" 2529
"current moved from north to
    south" 7684
"current sweep the ashes seaward"
    7680
"current that was running in his
    head, distracting" 9450
"current-borne" 435
"curs, stinking" 7801
"curse, a" 408
"curse, a decided" 46
"curse, spring . . . fell on him like
    a" 10608
"curse in this family, it is a" 7073
"curse on the child of a great love,
    a special" 1290
"cursed beneath his breath" 5256
"cursed her" 8140
"cursed it, God" 2637
"cursed under his breath" 10413
Curses 1290, 7073, 10608
"curses, mumbled Yiddish" 6958
"cursing as his skull collided" 24
"cursing the stop-and-start traffic"
    9616

"cursing to himself, quietly" 7634
"curt speech of farewell" 1525
"curtain, beyond the blue" 7771
"curtain, lace" 10972
"curtain, red velvet" 9400
"curtain flapping inwards, bright" 10696
"curtain had fallen, it was as if a" 7383
"curtain of sea" 7917
"curtain of snowflakes, a shimmering" 8597
"curtain trembled and lifted a few inches off the floor" 9400
"curtains" 10001
"curtains, mauve velvet" 7707
"curtains, my bedroom" 2269
"curtains, were no" 7777
"curtains in the tub, sodden" 5372
Curtis 4267
"curve, describes the majestic" 7691
"curve, ended in a neat" 5162
"curve, many a loving" 9740
"curve in the rutted Vermont dirt road" 3036
"curve of the mountain pass" 8303
"curve your right arm about her torso" 2107
"curves, sweet regular" 3044
"curves, the best" 9912
"curving in broad swaths" 9204
"curving like a trout" 10299
"cushion, hard" 8370
"cuspidor, brass" 9233
Cuss, Thomas 3042
"cussed" 3646
"cussing our farm" 1686
"custard, poured" 1868
"custard apples" 5033
"custody of Ari their son, verdict on the" 2682
"custom, according to his" 3813
"custom, as was her" 10212
"custom, as was his" 568
"custom, as was the" 3947
"custom, established" 9859
"custom, it was the" 4280
"custom, Mr. Spenlove's" 8075
"custom, Russian" 5406
"custom at Harvard" 6760
"custom at this hour of the afternoon, as was her" 6571
"custom in moments of stress, as was her" 1916
"custom on that day, according to his" 3816
"customer, pick up a" 1152
"customer, second" 1091
"customer representative" 6471
"customers, cut him off from his best" 2592
"customers, potential" 1047
"customers, waiting" 1048
"customers receipts, giving" 1048
Customs 2293, 7718

"customs" 9631
"customs, antique" 1342
"customs of courtship" 7718
"customs sheds" 8115
"Customs Special Agent" 10413
"cut, sabre" 5012
"cut his cloak in two" 7539
"cut his hand" 20
"cut my commitments" 5252
"cut off his world of thought" 5620
"cut off the motor" 2962
"cut out my brain" 627
"cut the date into the side" 8663
"cut the scarred earth, they did not" 7297
"cut the soldier's lung in half" 2933
"cut through on 83rd" 3310
Cuthbert 7652
Cuthbertson, Helena 6356
Cutler 5190
Cutler, Captain Albert 7153
Cutler, Caroline 10750
"cutlery, stainless steel" 3847
"cutlet, lumpy" 3875
Cutpurse, Moll 7958
"cuts, everywhere there were" 3370
Cutter, Phineas 9955
Cutter family 3823
"cutting a superhighway through the woods, as if somebody had begun" 8828
"cutting down a colossus of a cottonwood tree" 10929
"cutting in ahead of the two nuns" 9620
"cutting in and out of the slow line of cars" 2973
"cutting on the table, pattern she was" 7441
"cutting smoothly through the water" 8107
"cutting the girl's hand off" 7045
"cutting we call it" 7898
"Cuzco" 7811
"Cwm Bugail" 6953
"cyclical of nature" 10822
"cyclists coming into town" 10754
"cyclops eye, giant" 7278
"cylinder, large grey" 5689
"cynic about everything else, a" 5678
Cynicism 5678, 6848, 10834
Cynthia 635, 5764, 10169
"cypress grove" 1217
"Cyprus" 120, 2237, 7527
"Cyrano's" 1086
Cyril 5278
Cyril son of Isidor 5406
Cyrus, the Persian 10476
"Czar of Muscovy" 10464
"Czechoslovakia" 2383, 3414

d'Abrizzi 8858
"dabs of paint" 8242

"Dachau" 9459
Dad 6185, 6681, 6693, 6709, 9818, 10179
"dad, his" 1151
"dad, mom and" 10975
"dad, where are you" 6693
"Dad, where's" 6709
Daddy 386, 644, 2436, 6710, 10860
"daddy" 7360, 8743
"Daddy" 1900, 6729
"Daddy, are you my stinkin'" 6727
"daddy, my" 6197
"Daddy built it" 3224
"Daddy every morning, see" 6723
"Daemon Wente Waye" 9175
Dagan, Michal 6279
Dagleish, Lady 9896
Dagobert, King 4163
"dahling" 5053
"dailies, New York" 6343
"Daily Citizen" 6863
"Daily Express" 4008
"Daily Mail" 4008
"Daily Mirror" 4008
"Daily Telegraph" 4008
"Daimler, enormous brown coachwork" 2960
"Daimler, little" 2984
"Daimler buzzed out of its garage" 2984
"dainty, not at all" 5956
"daiquiris for us, he fixed" 2917
"Dairy, Mayflower" 8515
"dairy window" 719
"dairymaid" 7708
"dais, improvised" 8286
Daisy 1141, 3919, 4354, 4530
"daisy, saw a" 3793
"Daitch Shopwell" 1031
"Dakota, a" 205
"Dakota, shabby old" 199
"Dakota, weekly" 198
Dalashinsky, Leon 9395
"Dalcastle, lands of" 3551
Dale 4354
Dale, Shady 1904
Dale, Sir John 7607
Daley 6161
Daley, Jack 2112
"Dallas" 2815
"Dallas County" 9775
Dalloway, Mrs. 3797
"Dalmailing, minister of" 1483
"Dalmation, George the" 9302
Dalmire 2922
Dalzell, Michael 5761
"dam, doomed by the" 752
"Dam, Selden Hill" 9136
"dam, terminating in a" 7653
"damage, brain" 642
"damage each other" 6701
"Damascus" 7798
"dame, stalking a" 2045
"Damietta branch" 7681

"damn, oh" 7376
"damn it double" 1060
"damn it to hell" 1060
"damn mimeograph machine" 5683
"damn snaky feeling" 1878
"damn sure, that's for" 10876
"damnation" 5473, 7535
"damnation, multiple" 7507
"damnation, thy" 7507
"damnation of thy offspring" 7507
"damned, God-" 2479
"damned commission" 4511
"damned silly will to have left"
    4934
"damned tartan carpets" 1179
"damned the Dutch" 3396
"damned young fool" 4977
"damnedest young fool" 4977
"damsels, some serious" 10773
Dan 6156, 7176, 7454, 7553, 9851
Dan, Big 7137, 8248
Dan, Uncle 1613, 7393
Dana 10866
Dana, Sam 7636
"Danbury Connecticut" 1242
Dance 1250, 5188
"dance, at a" 5806
"dance, attend a" 7612
"dance, formal" 6776
"dance, menacing" 223
"dance, you must" 2117
"dance and revels, the May" 10587
"dance club Spit" 4849
"dance hall, at the" 5805
"dance . . . instead of solemnly
    gliding about" 7709
"dance of the day, their last" 5314
"dance scholarship" 1250
"dance without tripping on their
    feet" 2118
"danced, while the seniors" 2332
"danced awkwardly with a girl" 2111
"danced by candle and lamp" 7709
"danced out from under the knife"
    7092
"dancer, Russian" 2103
"dancer, the" 5188
"dancer who had taken Paris by
    storm" 2103
Dancers 2103, 2112, 2114, 2118, 7410
"dancer's, arms were spread like a"
    983
"dancers, Pi-Ume-Sha" 2114
"Dancers, The" 2899
"dancers circle through the hazy air"
    2114
"dancers in Buffalo, best" 2112
"dancers were standing in little
    groups" 7410
"dancers will have to be pulled in
    from the Women's School" 2118
Dances 2104, 2118, 4309, 5805,
    5806, 6776, 7612
"dances like Fred Astaire" 2115
"dancin', you just love" 2102

Dancing 2101, 2104, 2106, 2107,
    2108, 2110, 2111, 2114, 2115, 2116,
    2117, 2118, 2885, 2929, 6216
"dancing, geese" 3680
"dancing, had come back from"
    2929
"dancing, no" 2885
"dancing, square" 4384
"dancing, stayed out Saturday
    night" 2110
"dancing at the Kennepoose Canoe
    Club" 2104
"dancing in and out among the
    piles of trunks and boxes" 6216
"dancing over the water, midges
    were" 4952
"dancing pairs" 2118
"dancing the highlife with an Afri-
    can girl" 2106
"dancing with a cobra in Congo
    Square" 2108
"dancing with my brother" 2116
"dancing-floor" 4309
"dandelions" 5348
"dandelions springing out between
    the cracks" 9179
"dandelions were in yellow circles"
    3802
"dandy, I am a" 5958
"dandy who can no longer be
    troubled to dress" 5958
Danes, Geoffrey 394
"Danesacre" 6436
Danger 442, 1004, 2149, 5107,
    5274, 5378, 7715, 8174, 9625
"danger, always been attracted to"
    5378
"danger, to face" 8174
"danger he would soon be in" 2901
"danger signal" 442
"danger there, less" 9625
"danger zone, ulcerated" 286
"dangerous, fast and narrow and"
    9026
"dangerous, it was beginning to be"
    7715
"dangerous boy" 1004
"dangerous criminal" 2033
"dangerous man" 6168
"dangers such as her governess"
    4153
"dangled from a window ledge"
    9977
"dangling from a top branch" 360
Daniel 2456, 2569, 6030, 9433,
    10964
Daniel, Uncle 5925
Daniels 448
Daniels, Anne Duncan 2653
Daniels, Doc 8308
Daniels, Robinson 9850
Daniels, Zeke 2653
"Danish nobleman" 3879
"Danish sea" 7914
Danner, Abednego 1969

D'Annunzio 962
Danny 1981, 2435, 2811, 5527,
    6293, 8981
Dante 5830
d'Anthes 7029
"Danube, on the" 4017
"dapple the road beneath" 8999
"dappled in the early morning sun-
    fall" 1194
"dappled light" 5329
"dappled with mustard-colored
    foam, occasionally" 7666
"Dar es Salaam" 10442
Darconville 2862
Dardanos 7810
"dared to hope, he had ever" 6251
"dares not even pen a *hic jacet*" 7584
Dareville, Mrs. 6751
Daria 6690
Darien 6386
"Darien" 7800
"Darien Expedition" 3550
"daring" 4456
"daring, deeds of" 4046
"Darjeeling" 6111
Dark, Maria 9656
"dark, arctic" 1213
"dark, brooding" 10611
"dark, came out only at" 2123
"dark, cold" 10088
"dark, edges of the" 329
"dark, especially in the" 2125
"dark, had to be" 2124
"dark, in the" 2130, 9104, 10015
"dark, it is" 5611
"dark, it was" 2127, 3257
"dark, it was getting" 2266
"dark, it was not so" 2231
"dark, it was still" 10125
"dark, it was very" 10681
"dark, just after" 4658
"dark, near" 10149
"dark, quite" 2706
"dark, sat in the" 9374
"dark, still" 7255
"dark, ten minutes before" 7263
"dark, there was" 2282
"dark, trackless" 211
"dark, until after" 9333
"dark, waited until it was" 10056
"dark, walked through the" 9417
"dark ages, those" 5760
"dark and dark, between" 7289
"dark and hefty" 8217
"dark and silent room" 10137
"dark and the rain, in the" 41
"dark and threatening" 8332
"dark and warm, it was" 3368
"dark and wounded" 9503
"dark as a summer night" 8086
"dark as my cloak" 4296
"dark as the thoughts of the three
    unmourning mourners" 1186
"dark as we all are, she's" 4138
"dark except for a dim red light"

10289
"dark for an hour yet, it will not be" 4119
"dark for the moment" 5152
"dark had barely gathered the first gray beginnings of itself" 3029
"dark in here, it's so" 2120
"dark in the city, it was growing" 2186
"dark of hair and eye" 10038
"dark of the beginning is dawn" 2119
"dark of the end is an autumn dusk" 2119
"dark spaces" 523
"dark stillness" 2122
"dark style, I prefer the" 5344
"dark was always cooler" 7763
"dark wet day, it had been a" 2150
"dark wove threads like cool smoke, the" 329
"Dark Years, he called them the" 7956
"darken my doors" 1489
"darkening the canvas of the marquee" 10646
"darkest in summertime" 3211
"darkhunt" 10009
Darkness 236, 2706, 3029, 3368, 3387, 3720, 4485, 5611, 6376, 7407, 7413, 7777, 8364, 8450, 8484, 8492, 8538, 9172, 9374, 9402, 9417, 9520, 10015, 10056, 10125, 10127, 10170, 10250, 10289, 10708
"darkness, air-conditioned" 8538
"darkness, all that" 6942
"darkness, appeared out of the" 1732
"darkness, Asia was left in" 2202
"darkness, begins in" 2119
"darkness, cold stale" 9833
"darkness, cool glassy" 731
"darkness, dingy" 9172
"darkness, ends in" 2119
"darkness, imagine" 2121
"darkness, in the" 7407, 10410
"darkness, in the thick" 1601
"darkness, in total" 2790
"darkness, industrial" 5719
"darkness, into the" 8507
"Darkness, it was the season of" 3377
"darkness, its huge" 4485
"darkness, keep out the" 2128
"darkness, left the whole country-side in" 2209
"darkness, light of coming" 1216
"darkness, looking into the" 10127
"darkness, not quite complete" 10199
"darkness, patchy" 9963
"darkness, shades of" 9402
"darkness, shedding its trust in" 8813

"darkness, stalked in the" 8544
"darkness, staring through the" 10250
"darkness, still lay in" 3387
"darkness, sudden onrush of" 2235
"darkness, summer" 10730
"darkness, the" 2431, 9218, 10215
"darkness, total" 10462
"darkness, utter" 7413
"darkness, veil of" 2262
"darkness, voices in the" 10021
"darkness and light, between" 2781
"darkness approached" 4386
"darkness before the dawn" 731
"darkness began to settle over the woods" 3720
"darkness beyond the yard lights" 10094
"darkness came" 8589
"darkness caught them by the heels" 9520
"darkness gathered" 2126
"darkness gathered there" 4962
"darkness of the country road" 2955
"darkness of the lodge" 10170
"darkness of the predawn" 10196
"darkness of the underworld" 1593
"darkness thins" 10749
"darkness was of a gritty texture" 7777
"darkness wild with shots and cries" 3766
"darknesses, twilight between" 2273
Darley, Oliver 10287
"darling" 1719, 5752, 8013
"Darling" 2637
"darling, hello" 5670
"darling, her own her only her dead and vanished" 969
"darling, her own only" 6610
"darling, my" 9923
"Darling, My" 2683
"darling, oh" 4354
"darling of his father" 6515
"Darlinghurst tramway" 4315
"darned an old woollen sock" 10934
Darnell, Edward 2754
Darr, Mark 3835
Darrigan, Max 6706
"darted through the orange orchard" 723
"darting across the corridor" 5996
"darting from air-conditioned shop to shop" 9616
Dasgupta, Dimple 5758
"dash the black river, we" 7685
"dash through the darkness" 10529
"dashboard, no lights showed on the" 9805
"dashes, nobody loves my" 9265
Dashwood 3549
da Silva, Francisco Manoel 3588
"data-processing office" 6471
Datchett, Louisa Mary 5354
"date, cut the" 8663

"date, her own impromptu" 6783
"date, her roommate's" 6783
"date, long blind" 5254
"date, the" 6915
"date in question has brought on more than one disagreement" 8934
"date's all made" 8630
"dates for basketball games" 10975
Daugherty, Martin 8918
"daughter" 6540
"daughter, a" 6414
"daughter, adopted" 6577
"Daughter, Beautiful" 6674
"daughter, caretaker's" 3682
"daughter, Harry the Fish Man's" 6652
"daughter, her" 717, 2334, 2963, 3552, 5747, 6113, 6619, 6784, 8172, 9710, 10374, 10997
"daughter, her younger" 6748
"daughter, his" 1571, 1865, 2061, 2486, 2726, 2773, 3578, 3599, 3989, 4359, 5205, 6622, 6707, 6893, 8046
"daughter, his eldest" 6616
"daughter, his lovely" 7709
"daughter, his sixteen-year-old" 1199
"daughter, Jack Cornock's" 6539
"Daughter, Jezebel's" 2291
"daughter, judge's" 9675
"daughter, master's only" 9302
"daughter, my" 4789, 5484, 6522, 6583, 7490, 7931
"Daughter, my only" 5492
"daughter, my younger" 4814
"daughter, oldest" 6864
"daughter, one" 6515
"daughter, pretty" 2732
"daughter, red-haired youngest" 5431
"daughter, shipowner's small" 7843
"daughter, the" 9020
"daughter, their" 2670
"daughter, your" 5759
"daughter being knit into flesh by her flesh" 7084
"daughter of a Scotch peer, dower-less" 6607
"daughter of an Emperor" 4928
"daughter of Coel" 5431
"daughter of Edward" 6605
"daughter of Israel" 7717
"daughter of Pirote's king" 5451
"daughter of Sir Marmaduke" 5638
"daughter of the Baron of Arling-ford" 10641
"daughter of the Duke of Omnium" 7060
"daughter of the late Judge, the eldest" 9955
"daughter of William Baring" 3533
"daughter-in-law" 2447
Daughters 1199, 1571, 2486, 2934,

2950, 3593, 3594, 3599, 3682, 4593, 4743, 4814, 4971, 5205, 5492, 5759, 6522, 6528, 6539, 6540, 6616, 6622, 6624, 6674, 6691, 6692, 7070, 7073, 7090, 7283, 7490, 7624, 7931, 9020, 9325, 10175
"daughters, afraid of his" 6549
"daughters, four" 3596
"daughters, his two" 2292, 6523, 7624
"daughters, my three dear" 6528
"daughters, our" 10917
"daughters, some of their" 7481
"daughters, sons and" 640
"daughters, unmarried" 6545
"daughters, wives and" 9738
"daughters, women bear only" 7073
"daughter's face, his" 4593
"daughter's head go under water, saw his" 577
"daughters loved to remember" 7414
"Dauphin, Grand" 493
Dave 4019
Davenport, Michael 9688
David 1766, 7563, 7742, 8221, 9589, 10645
Davidson, Captain 7407
Davie 497, 1957
Davis, Cousin Ruth 6164
Davis, Pierce 1676
Davison, Sybil 7993
Dawbarn, Harry 4344
Dawley, Frank 10386
Dawn 731, 1433, 1732, 1786, 2119, 2141, 2163, 2188, 2191, 2197, 2214, 2217, 2218, 2226, 2231, 2237, 2251, 2252, 2255, 2257, 2267, 2269, 2278, 2283, 2986, 3175, 3895, 3905, 4034, 5073, 5328, 5342, 7298, 7624, 7935, 8036, 8127, 8178, 8412, 8420, 8823, 9082, 9224, 9666, 9756, 9800, 9810, 9955, 10198, 10232, 10277, 10308, 10749
"dawn, abandon it forever at" 10957
"dawn, almost" 10250
"dawn, an hour before" 2424
"dawn, angel of the" 4034
"dawn, at" 8534, 8823, 10277
"dawn, at first" 8127
"dawn, at the moment of" 1732
"dawn, awoke at" 10968
"dawn, barely" 10232
"dawn, before" 10122
"dawn, breeze that comes near" 10749
"dawn, bright streak of" 2218
"dawn, coolness of" 7281
"dawn, dark of the beginning is" 2119
"dawn, darkness before the" 731
"dawn, false" 2269
"dawn, first faint tremulous blush

of" 2188
"dawn, first graying flush of" 8107
"dawn, first light of" 1433
"dawn, gray and red" 6099
"dawn, grey" 5940
"dawn, hour after" 4694
"dawn, in the" 5123
"dawn, in the hour of the" 10353
"dawn, it was just" 9800
"dawn, it's not yet" 8500
"dawn, light at" 2267
"dawn, light of a wet" 5335
"dawn, one fog-lidded" 4155
"dawn, pale light of" 5142
"dawn, rainy" 830
"dawn, scarcely was it" 9955
"dawn, silent time before" 5073
"dawn, that hour after" 8412
"dawn, there was a house made of" 3175
"dawn, thin robin's-egg-blue" 2251
"dawn, towards" 8456
"dawn, turquoise" 10308
"dawn, until the early" 4284
"dawn, up at" 8112
"dawn, woke me some time before" 10218
"dawn, woke soon after" 10161
"dawn began to fringe the prickly leaves" 9756
"dawn broke somewhere up the line" 2226
"dawn came" 3905
"dawn came early" 2255
"dawn had come" 10198
"dawn had not yet begun" 2283
"dawn in a normal sky" 911
"dawn light, silvery webs of" 9666
"dawn of a remarkably chill morning in May" 9955
"dawn on the tenth day of summer" 1716
"dawn or dusk, might have been" 2278
"dawn over the Atlantic" 7935
"dawn passes over the steppes of Russian Asia" 2257
"dawn was beginning to soften the edge of the night" 9810
"dawn wind" 9082
"dawned bright and clear" 2217
"dawned clear" 2163
"dawned dark that year, March fourth" 2141
"dawned upon the school, first" 4460
Dawney, Edmund 9869
"dawning moments, in the early" 745
"dawns, of all the myriad" 7624
"dawns, summer" 836
"Dawn's Mill" 5139
Dawson 8689
Dawson, Miss 10903
"Dawson's Landing, town of" 1349

Day, Barry 5187
"day, afternoon of the October" 2234
"day, against the" 3314
"day, always a great" 4520
"day, April" 7495
"day, bad" 7013
"day, beautiful June" 2157
"day, beautiful spring" 2056
"day, beautifully clear" 2160
"day, before that" 512
"day, best time of the" 2232
"day, big" 2217
"day, bleak December" 10582
"day, break of" 9067
"day, bright October" 4906
"day, bright sunny" 2182
"day, certain autumn" 781
"day, changeover" 2181
"day, chill" 10607
"day, chilly" 2886
"Day, Class" 6753
"day, cloudy" 175, 9321
"day, cold and dreary" 9977
"day, cold blowy February" 1724
"day, cold blustery" 7019
"day, cold grey" 10577
"day, cold sparkling sunny" 8678
"day, crisp October" 9527
"day, damp and misty" 865
"day, damp stillness of the winter" 10736
"day, dark and foggy" 7218
"day, dark February" 10612
"day, dark wet" 2150
"day, darkening" 8421
"Day, Decoration" 8739
"day, difficult" 7847
"day, dull" 4513
"day, dull autumn" 2077
"day, dying October" 4156
"day, each new" 7109
"day, fading" 7347
"day, fine summer's" 9511
"day, fine sunny showery" 2132
"day, fine warm and crystal-clear September" 2147
"day, first" 2164, 4524
"Day, First Pasturing" 2154
"day, glorious" 2204
"day, going to be a fine" 10116
"day, good time of" 2249
"day, gray" 1399
"day, gray cold" 1550
"day, gray wintry" 4017
"day, great" 2140
"day, grey" 8146
"Day, Groundhog" 4816
"day, gusty April" 14
"day, harsh light of" 6791
"day, her At Home" 3938
"Day, Heroes" 4518
"day, his greatest" 2159
"day, hot" 900, 4404
"day, hot February" 4643

"day, hot July" 633
"day, hot peaceful optimistic sort of" 2144
"day, hour of the" 2209
"day, in his" 4683
"day, in my" 8928
"day, it began that" 8368
"day, it was the" 8704
"Day, Labor" 3041, 4532
"day, languid July" 8508
"day, last" 5197, 5202
"day, late June" 3981
"day, late summer's" 2006
"day, light of a new" 4742
"day, long sultry Syrian" 4370
"day, lucky" 1303
"day, March" 8410
"day, marriage" 10647
"day, May" 6399
"Day, Memorial" 2971
"day, mild October" 2213
"day, momentous" 2158
"day, most important" 5108
"day, most of the" 2972
"Day, Mother's" 4523
"day, my first" 2180
"day, naming" 857
"day, near enough our" 1025
"Day, New Year's" 3886, 6509, 10237
"Day, New-year's" 10569
"day, noble" 4010
"day, not Wolf's" 2135
"day, on a" 1698
"day, on that" 25
"day, on this" 7811
"day, perfect" 2178
"day, pleased with my" 9263
"Day, Primrose" 7505
"day, rainy" 1627, 7307
"day, rotten" 1073
"day, same" 4615
"day, Saturdays was the best" 2184
"day, September" 10477
"day, short winter's" 2196
"day, sixth" 6251
"day, soft spring" 8263
"day, spent the whole" 1024
"day, strenuous" 8907
"day, such a" 2134
"day, such an ordinary" 2167
"day, summer" 3988, 4565
"day, sunny" 3232
"day, sunny June" 4012
"day, sunny October" 9093
"day, sunny September" 8176
"day, Texas January" 2138
"day, that" 9645, 10921
"day, that was the" 5094
"day, that'll be the" 3519
"day, the" 572, 2148, 2153, 2162, 2448, 2659, 5110
"day, the coming" 8393
"day, this is the" 7960
"day, this was a special" 5121

"day, tiring" 3697
"day, torrid" 7637
"day, unhappy" 2500
"day, until the other" 5280
"day, very first" 9274
"day, wedding" 10643
"day, windy" 4943
"day, winter" 2957
"day, wintry" 9092
"day after day" 8799
"day after the great storm" 9085
"day as sad and desperate as before, leaving the" 4319
"day at Fort Dix, that first" 8697
"day before, the" 7442
"day before the night, this was the" 2587
"day began, the" 3866
"day began at five to seven" 10309
"day began with the buzzing of a fly" 10326
"day broke gray and dull" 2197
"day broke unlike any other" 2168
"day by day" 5286
"day dawned clear" 7290
"day . . . drenched blue and green" 4010
"day had been a hard one" 2142
"day had been very hot" 4371
"day had been very oppressive" 4368
"day had drawn only a pale wash of light" 10149
"day has come, the August" 6995, 6997
"day hot as midsummer" 4412
"day I left for the war" 8503
"day in April, bright cold" 9473
"day in autumn, that glowing" 2165
"day in December, that" 3782
"day in early spring" 6557
"day in early summer, one fine" 9434
"day in July, drowsy buzzing" 2156
"day in late summer" 10816
"day in May, brilliant" 5613
"day in October, one bright" 6580
"day in our time, on a certain sun-dappled June" 9247
"day in the middle of the night, one fine" 1831
"day in the year 1878, the shortest" 1596
"day indeed impossible to forget" 10143
"day is drawing to its close" 2213
"day is early" 2230
"day it all started, the" 5094
"day it began" 604
"day last fall, one" 2470
"day like this, on a" 350
"day long, all" 9447
"day nor night, it was neither" 2278
"day of calm weather" 2543
"day of early spring, stormy" 9068

"day of Gandhi's assassination" 3439
"day of her last happiness" 2506
"day of his life, the last" 2185
"day of his triumph" 3741
"day of my life, the first real" 5093
"day of my life, the most momentous" 5081
"day of my week, beginning of the best" 10190
"day of nervous shift and bustle overhead" 5023
"day of portents" 8948
"day of rest" 4333
"day of sacrifice" 2627
"day of significance" 5083
"day of soundless thunder enough to deafen you" 8948
"day of spindrift and blowing seafoam" 10711
"day of summer" 2172
"day of summer, the last" 5666
"day of summer sunshine, rare" 9817
"day of Sunday, this empty lonely Dublin" 9618
"day of the bestowing" 4126
"Day of the Faith" 7521
"day of the Fern Grammar School picnic" 2506
"day of their honeymoon, on the third" 9736
"day off from school" 837
"day on the great airship, that first" 194
"day on which Emily Stockwell Turner fell out of love" 2146
"day or night" 10178, 10318
"day passes over the earth, not a" 4454
"day promised to be hot" 2139
"day set in, before regular" 2986
"day short of the full, one" 8423
"day so well remembered" 10143
"day something like right now" 2151
"day started badly and then got worse" 2170
"day that his brother Nachman died" 10422
"day that is good to live and breathe in" 82
"day that Josie and her son arrived" 3782
"day that was gathered to the past" 8399
"day the child disappeared" 2572
"day the revolution started" 2902
"day they were born" 4307
"day toward the middle of August, one fine" 8929
"day Um Mona dreaded, the" 2163
"day very hot" 8101
"day . . . vivid with promise" 4010
"day was all blue and gold and barely crisp" 2138

"day was breaking" 1622
"day was cold with a grey sky" 10617
"day was drawing to a close" 1178
"day was drawing to its close" 2196
"day was drooping on a fine evening" 2945
"day was dying" 2222
"day was loud with the screams of men" 4469
"day was so delightful" 5268
"day when Caesar's statue in the forum begins to bleed mysteriously" 8948
"day when the skin crawls suddenly" 8948
"daybreak" 2252
"daybreak, after" 1764
"daybreak, at" 2220
"daybreak, close upon" 3895
"daybreak, just before" 463
Daybright, Owen 1548
"daydream" 2808
"daydream, wanting only to" 2771
"daydreaming over coffee" 10081
Daydreams 2771, 2808, 8936, 9991, 10081
"daydreams, winter" 8936
"daylight, an hour before" 10707
"daylight, before" 758, 10646
"daylight, dazed by the" 10384
"daylight, glimmer of" 2199
"daylight, grateful for" 8178
"daylight gone without her noticing" 10934
"daylight hour, it was the last" 5837
"daylight hours, during the" 296
"daylight lingers for an extra hour" 2239
"Daylight Saving Time" 9491
"daylight was approaching over London" 5928
Days 82, 194, 350, 572, 604, 655, 841, 865, 936, 1223, 1303, 1550, 1565, 1698, 1893, 2196, 2197, 2204, 2213, 2217, 2222, 2227, 2357, 2448, 2500, 2506, 2519, 2572, 2587, 2608, 2627, 2659, 2887, 2902, 3397, 3404, 3450, 3697, 3741, 3782, 3837, 3938, 3958, 4010, 4126, 4156, 4282, 4370, 4398, 4404, 4513, 4524, 4943, 5080, 5081, 5083, 5093, 5094, 5108, 5110, 5117, 5121, 5268, 5313, 5472, 5568, 5626, 5666, 5778, 6146, 6326, 6796, 6915, 7013, 7019, 7025, 7218, 7219, 7289, 7302, 7495, 7960, 8176, 8421, 8508, 8678, 8704, 8948, 8952, 8974, 9068, 9085, 9473, 9544, 9618, 9645, 9761, 9981, 10116, 10143, 10515, 10567, 10569, 10577, 10583, 10597, 10617, 10623, 10632, 10647, 10658, 10669
"days, another of those fine September" 2136
"days, back in the" 9401
"days, better" 6146
"days, dark" 253
"days, earlier" 7390
"days, fur-trade" 9744
"days, halcyon" 2173
"days, his earliest" 4636
"days, in more golden" 3114
"days, in the" 1012, 3510, 5886, 7505, 9382, 10966
"days, in the far-off" 9743
"days, in the last" 10720
"days, in the old" 1454, 1966, 4057, 4134, 5213, 7181
"days, in these dread latter" 7205
"days, in these new-fangled" 5681
"days, in those" 26, 2418, 2938, 3387, 3398, 3758, 4645, 6142, 6352, 6635, 9241
"days, last malodorous" 10521
"days, like the long baking" 10622
"days, memories of those" 7441
"days, my" 936
"days, old and golden" 3396
"days, old-fashioned" 3064
"days, one of the most fateful" 5080
"days, one of the warm and almost sultry" 10567
"days, one of those artificially hot" 10597
"days, only four" 3496
"days, rare old feudal" 4044
"days, sometime in the next few" 2000
"days, summer" 10623
"days, ten more glorious" 9728
"days, the first four" 7338
"days, the old" 3075
"days, those" 1252
"days, those final" 7427
"days, those haunted" 3672
"days, those last" 7840
"days after the accident, it isn't until several" 42
"days ahead of me, no new" 2519
"days along the Wawanash River, we spent" 4687
"days and nights, two restless" 6003
"days are numbered, once you know your" 2430
"days ... are pallid and dull me" 936
"days became an hour-to-hour struggle" 4374
"days cloudlessly blue and sunny" 10583
"days gone by, in" 9138
"days have consisted of three trays" 128
"days indeed, strange" 2174
"days no longer seemed eternal" 2323
"days of Adam, since the" 10770
"days of August, last hot" 10991
"days of chivalry and romance" 3375
"days of Christmas, the last of the twelve" 841
"days of Elizabeth" 6385
"days of George II" 3965
"days of heat and dust, two and a half" 9358
"days of his life, during the last twenty" 5452
"days of his week" 4282
"days of Indiana's early statehood" 9662
"days of mist and rain" 7289
"days of peace" 9738
"days of peace, the last" 9420
"days of rage" 5673
"days of surmise and apprehension" 9420
"days of that April" 7289
"days of the 1960s, doggy" 6467
"days of the Stuarts" 3375
"days of the young man's early youth" 3553
"days of wine and roses" 3397
"days of wine and yuppies" 3404
"days of yore" 4303
"days prior to the Revolution" 3064
"days remain before I am swallowed up again, less than threescore" 5269
"days that hung on precariously for a few weeks more" 10622
"days that I have spent upon the earth" 8974
"days when men sighed when they fell in love" 7709
"days when Whitbury boasted of forty coaches per diem" 6283
"days which lay between, the long" 4911
"days which seemed confused with the blur of all things" 5568
"days without a night, forty-three" 8680
"days without horses, ten more glorious" 9728
"daytime song, became one mobile" 8813
"day-to-day reality" 9718
"daze, they have that petrified" 8560
"dazed" 515
"dazed, slightly" 5408
"dazed by the daylight" 10384
"dazzle fern" 7440
"dazzle of green and white" 10393
"dazzle of the sun" 983
"dazzled by the summer sun" 7787
"dazzling freshness of new white stone" 1849
"dazzling heights of glory" 3557
"dazzling mantle" 7606
"dazzling white, shone" 6079
"DC-3, the" 9624

"DDT" 5288
Deacon, Mr. 494
Deacons 9664
"dead, being newly" 10476
"dead, Captain Clancy was" 9291
"dead, cept my mother and she's" 5657
"dead, child's" 2298
"dead, Disco was" 2109
"dead, doesn't mean he's" 3413
"dead, driver was" 7855
"dead, driver was now" 10529
"dead, drop" 5112
"dead, dropped" 1684
"dead, even" 2426
"dead, Fanny Peronett was" 3941
"dead, father is" 2413
"dead, felt closer to the" 2456
"dead, first snake I saw was" 4128
"dead, five women were" 10864
"dead, fourteen years" 1402
"dead, funerals are not for the" 3936
"dead, general is" 8172
"dead, Grandpa was" 1151
"dead, hanging" 5792
"dead, he may be" 2442
"dead, he was as sardonic" 2304
"dead, heard that Jack Kennedy was" 6332
"dead, he's" 6006, 6725
"dead, High and Mighty Prince Albert Frederick George was" 7805
"dead, Hitler was" 10514
"dead, I found her" 2333
"dead, I really don't think he's" 2369
"dead, I shall soon be quite" 2324
"dead, I think I am" 2409
"dead, I think I should drop" 930
"dead, I was" 2459
"dead, in memory of the" 1206
"dead, lay" 3962
"dead, lie" 2383
"dead, making much of their" 2293
"dead, man's almost" 124
"dead, Marley was" 2288
"dead, more than sixty centuries of" 5149
"dead, Morrison was" 5463
"dead, my Body had been some-time" 2286
"dead, Nero is" 2350
"dead, our parents were" 6119
"dead, Papa Francesco was" 2380
"dead, poisons us" 1337
"dead, Pope was" 1509
"dead, pretending he was" 8711
"dead, returned from the" 5027
"dead, she was" 2387
"dead, she would be much happier" 2313
"dead, shot" 6191
"dead, souls of the" 747

"dead, struck me to the ground stone" 6207
"dead, Sultane Valide is" 2411
"dead, Sutton was" 2392
"dead, the" 1191
"dead, their" 1192
"dead, they took her for" 3413
"dead, they were" 2415
"dead, though he were" 3941
"dead, told Thad she was" 6186
"dead, twelve thousand people are" 9954
"dead, wake the" 6338
"dead, we are" 935
"dead a year, Ned was" 2420
"dead and buried" 2294
"dead and vanished darling" 969
"dead at her feet" 733
"dead baby, found the" 1893
"dead back to life, bringing the" 6717
"dead before I was at liberty to quit it" 2286
"dead before sundown" 7934
"Dead Bodies, left the Ditches of their Enemies fill'd with their" 10464
"dead boys, what was left of eight" 1879
"dead by absolute proofs" 2294
"dead by six o'clock" 9294
"dead cat, the wrong" 6032
"dead cows" 6961
"dead doesn't settle anything" 2437
"dead drunk" 2901
"dead end" 1423, 3116, 5723
"dead father, her" 4224
"dead for a long time" 2409
"dead for only half a day" 2329
"dead for several weeks, Bunny had been" 78
"dead for some hundred-and-twenty-odd years" 1910
"dead for some time, it had been" 8539
"dead for up to a year" 1889
"dead four months" 3885
"dead girl" 10239
"dead had their rights" 2376
"dead in plastic wardrobe, man found" 1881
"dead is he?" 3519
"dead is the best high I've ever seen" 2437
"dead king, not a" 2398
"dead languages" 9709
"dead legally" 2294
"dead man" 1882, 2304, 3961
"dead man, he was that" 2351
"dead man, I who write this am a" 2294
"dead man, words of a" 10548
"dead man floating in our pool" 1900
"dead man's son" 2303

"dead men, two" 1831
"dead of the aloneness and the strangeness, I will be" 8491
"dead of winter" 10639
"dead on his feet, all but" 7829
"dead 101 days" 1897
"dead or alive, wondering if he was" 10977
"Dead Sea" 4080, 10329
"dead set against me going" 1747
"dead wife, my" 7593
"dead-ending into the curve" 1462
"deadfall, loblolly" 10106
"deadly, quite" 8784
"deaf, but I am not" 4503
"deafen me with your croaking, why do you" 9990
"deafening, sound was" 8798
"deal, make the" 10049
"deal, this" 6126
"deal cupboard" 7753
"deal table" 8453
"deal was off, the last" 1778
"deal with, 'cause that's about all I ever" 10876
"deal with him, I would have known instantly how to" 4988
"deal with the toothsome eggs and bacon" 3850
"dealer who bought Arp's rubbish from him" 6431
"dealings with the Chinese, inti mate" 1053
"dealt with, Japanese remained to be" 10514
Dean 3630, 5811
Dean, Blanche 5264
Dean, Earl 4291
"dean, college" 6456
"Dean, Junior" 8354
"dean of humanities, the new" 9335
"Dean of Men" 7903
"Dean of Westminster" 7513
"dear, my" 603, 3746
"Dear God!" 8184
Dearborn, Laura 10035
"Dearborn, Fort" 4039
Dearest 2259
"dearest Father" 6242
Death, Dr. 4739
Death 29, 113, 124, 139, 526, 644, 707, 747, 749, 754, 764, 807, 828, 889, 935, 943, 969, 1151, 1154, 1163, 1186, 1189, 1190, 1191, 1192, 1195, 1206, 1507, 1509, 1538, 1571, 1684, 1718, 1819, 1877, 1878, 1880, 1882, 1886, 1887, 1889, 1890, 1891, 1893, 1897, 1901, 1905, 2000, 2185, 2509, 2520, 2541, 2558, 2798, 2960, 3155, 3273, 3336, 3498, 3521, 3588, 3610, 3846, 3885, 3935, 3936, 3937, 3939, 3940, 3941, 3944, 3947, 3948, 3949, 3952, 3953, 3958, 3959, 3961, 3962, 3963, 4113,

Death, *cont.* 4221, 4223, 4224, 4225, 4226, 4227, 4228, 4230, 4457, 4481, 4592, 4800, 4882, 4887, 4932, 4934, 5082, 5085, 5108, 5255, 5261, 5269, 5463, 5528, 5534, 5571, 5578, 5595, 5657, 5663, 5751, 5905, 5914, 6006, 6106, 6130, 6133, 6154, 6161, 6169, 6185, 6186, 6196, 6202, 6203, 6321, 6327, 6332, 6346, 6347, 6435, 6524, 6606, 6612, 6621, 6636, 6646, 6660, 6668, 6706, 6717, 6725, 6735, 6742, 6778, 6863, 6939, 6961, 7029, 7084, 7182, 7219, 7363, 7382, 7415, 7429, 7498, 7504, 7542, 7805, 7865, 7869, 7970, 8030, 8172, 8219, 8229, 8240, 8244, 8315, 8491, 8537, 8539, 8670, 8675, 8678, 8683, 8714, 8716, 8762, 8838, 8930, 9285, 9291, 9294, 9295, 9298, 9436, 9496, 9513, 9846, 9954, 10239, 10332, 10422, 10533, 10559, 10658, 10771, 10864, 10944, 10990
"death" 526
"death, after his" 7584
"death, after Mrs Gray's" 717
"Death, after my" 3527
"death, after the" 2960
"death, always been into" 2366
"Death, angel of" 7504
"death, anticipating his" 139
"death, as at" 7824
"death, at" 2378
"death, at the time of his" 5905
"death, Bernie Pryde's" 2359
"death, black perpetual hiding place called" 9285
"death, circus celebrating" 2327
"death, deal with" 2449
"death, doesn't seem to be afraid of" 2462
"death, done to" 1325
"death, ecstacy or" 5048
"death, escape from" 1217
"death, fell to his" 6321
"death, fought grimly with" 2463
"death, frightened of" 4113
"death, grayer than" 8722
"death, half to" 8812
"death, he was so near to" 154
"death, her husband's" 4226
"death, him who had passed beyond" 2303
"death, his father's" 7382
"death, his first" 2389
"death, his own" 1718, 2447
"death, his wife's" 2971
"death, husband will have put me to" 2000
"death, I planned my" 5578
"death, idea of" 2341
"death, instrument of my mother's" 7542

"death, Iris's" 6154
"death, laid down their dignities before" 6976
"death, love and" 5663
"death, manner of Hercules Flood's" 7865
"death, many years after his" 494
"death, more protracted" 2397
"death, my grandfather's" 1905
"death, my mother's" 8930
"death, news of Gulliver Quick's" 6346
"death, news of whose" 707
"death, our mother's" 2418
"death, prepare other men for" 1507
"death, pushed an eight-year-old boy off a cliff to his" 6198
"death, release her into" 9298
"death, revenge that" 2393
"death, sad unexplained" 7869
"death, sainted father's" 5108
"death, sentenced to" 3407
"death, shuttered against" 3155
"death, smelled of the jungle and of" 8537
"death, start it after his" 2304
"death, talked about" 2400
"death, tasted his" 6211
"death, the" 2558
"death, the why and the how of her" 7970
"death, their father's" 8229
"death, their father's ignoble" 2393
"death, they grow in" 5521
"death, think seriously about" 2323
"death, threat of" 1163
"death, Tu's" 6327
"death, waiting so long for" 2444
"death, youth and" 4800
"death again, came near" 4469
"death as represented by her person" 2341
"death aside, beat" 8027
"death at 1:06 A.M. on August 1 1954" 2360
"death claimed him before he could find one" 2299
"death had spared Arnold Soby" 2332
"death had taken Mr. Melchisedec Harrington" 2290
"death has passed by, after" 5261
"death I may have caused, this is about a" 2446
"Death if you tell any of Them" 1819
"death is always the same" 2331
"death is no answer" 2362
"death leapt upon the Rev. Charles Cardinal" 2299
"death left Billy quite alone in the world" 8716
"death may be all three, my" 2354
"death obsolete, make" 6798
"death of a friend, violent" 2370

"death of Arthur, song about the" 8762
"death of General Franco" 4481
"death of her mother" 10771
"death of his mother" 5085, 9496
"death of his wife" 3498
"death of Jim-Jim, moving" 10332
"death of Judge Kilburn" 1571
"death of love, the" 5661
"death of my mother" 6606
"death of my sister Mathilde, mysterious" 5528
Death of Nelson, The 7505
"death of one of their delegates to the Old Land" 2386
"death of sleep, little" 2767
"death of Taswell Skaggs was stimulating" 2297
"death of the Duke of Strelsau" 5082
"death of the possible or probable" 5661
"death of their elder brother" 2960
"death penalty" 6965
"death rattle, ominous" 2405
"death shall separate us, until" 10651
"death shaped vaguely like an airplane" 2447
"death sliced into her gums" 2463
"death to die, one" 2403
"death very quietly, put it to" 9295
"death warmed over, looked like" 4324
"death-dealing" 7205
"deaths, my parents'" 2417
"deaths of others" 1718
"deaths of two foreign gentlemen" 2291
"debatable, at best" 9699
"debate, the" 1826
"debating whether to buy one or two" 2478
"debauch, a single" 172
Debbie 1149
Deborah 4971
"debris from the day before" 7442
"debt, moderate level of" 10322
"debt, repaid the modest" 6996
"debt, were in" 3914
"debt that someone else had contracted" 50
"decade, new" 6767
"decade, prosperous" 1726
"decade, the end of a" 3350
"decadence, modern" 6427
"decadence of the Ottoman Empire, stupifying" 1464
"decay" 9660
"decaying neighborhoods" 10320
"decaying remnant" 9662
"deceased, the" 1190, 2310
"deceased woman's niece" 3963
"deceit, life of" 5304
"Deceit, Object of my own" 6033

"deceitful, appearances are" 6804
"deceiving my public" 567
"December" 155, 791, 818, 851, 873, 1073, 1398, 1614, 2149, 2286, 2539, 2576, 2908, 3745, 3782, 4131, 4412, 5088, 5100, 5416, 5547, 5577, 5837, 6365, 6370, 6577, 6730, 7617, 8118, 8124, 8489, 8588, 9027, 9064, 9431, 9897, 10108, 10296, 10582, 10871
"December, in early" 2383
"December afternoon" 292, 3121
"December night" 8798
"December nights" 1545
"December wind" 1907
"decency and decorum, due regard for" 7652
"decent, let alone" 150
Deception 1430, 5304, 6804
"deceptive, Piemburg is" 1430
"deceptive of all appearances, the most" 6804
"deceptive quiet" 7275
"deceptively, began" 3627
"deceptively virginal" 6145
"decide, tried to" 9687
"decide, waiting for the men to" 10105
"decide it should be, your family is who you" 6720
"decide to live in Kreiswald" 2490
"decide to take Grace with me" 2481
"decide where the story should begin, difficult to" 8988
"decide whether to postpone the Festival, met to" 2469
"decide which hour it shall be" 5414
"decided, finally" 2486
"decided between dry martinis" 9321
"decided it would be best for both of us" 2681
"decided not to bother, she could have" 795
"decided on, what you" 2489
"decided sourly" 9232
"decided that after all it didn't matter so much" 2467
"decided that I belonged to him" 997
"decided that it was time he settled down" 425
"decided that something had to be done" 2480
"decided that the world was coming to an end" 2468
"decided they would move to Mill's Landing" 6127
"decided to become an actress" 9388
"decided to come back early" 9731
"decided to commit suicide" 9288
"decided to do with my life" 5582
"decided to get a haircut" 2482

"decided to go straight home" 6630
"decided to go to the store" 5637
"decided to join the army" 8683
"decided to leave Howard" 2675
"decided to leave my husband" 2662
"decided to leave school" 2471
"decided to live together" 3923
"decided to make a note" 5590
"decided to marry" 5761
"decided to relate with Presision" 3496
"decided to report, I have" 2475
"decided to revisit England" 9538
"decided to take things more easily" 9724
"decided to walk the half mile" 10411
"decided to winter" 7130
"decided to withdraw from it" 5252
"decided today" 2479
"decides to write about Bigfoot" 5522
"deciding factor, it was the" 594
"deciduous tree" 5740
"decimal system" 2741
"decision, announced his" 2472
"decision, critical" 2491
"decision, final" 2185
"decision, her final" 2476
"decision, I've made a" 7963
"decision, process that led to the" 6200
"decision, the" 2649
"decision for myself, I made a" 5093
"decision that had just come to her in the middle of the night" 2484
"decision to withdraw the Unit" 2474
"decision which actually had been arrived at some months before" 2472
Decisions 1, 257, 795, 997, 1743, 2113, 2649, 2662, 2675, 2992, 3219, 5093, 5252, 5522, 5582, 5590, 5637, 6037, 6127, 6149, 6200, 6630, 7130, 7731, 7963, 8683, 9288, 9388, 9538, 9566, 9687, 9731, 10105, 10411, 10592
Deck, Mister 6727
"deck, come on" 9416
"deck, promenade" 8072
"deck, upper" 9556
"deck and hull beaded" 8142
Decker, Evie 10821
Decker, Philip 3542
Declan, Father 4690
"Declaration, A Soldier's" 8709
"Declaration of Independence" 269
"Declaration of Independence, going to be a new" 4231
"declare yourself" 1809
"declinations, black" 5178
"decline, the thirty years of his" 2513

"decline of my life" 5556
"declining too rapidly for comfort" 10083
"declining years" 8460
"declivity, a very slight" 8355
"decorated . . . in the same 'Olde Englysshe Style'" 3096
"Decoration Day Parade" 8739
"decorum, abode of" 7877
"decorum, decency and" 7652
"decorum, matchless" 6367
"decreed by nature or habit" 5723
"dedicated to older women" 1977
"dedicated to the author's enemies" 5392
"dedicated to the memory" 7901
"dedication service" 1202
"deduced *I am*" 10184
Dee, Jimmie 9803
"deed, rub his nose in her" 2684
"deeds, do great" 4454
"deeds, my" 4768
"deeds of daring which verged on the insane" 4046
"deeds that he did" 5212
"deep, the" 7928
"deep deep like a hollow bowl" 9745
"deep in thought" 9452
"deeply, very" 1516
"deeply dented" 9681
"deer, as if it were a" 4253
"deer, blacktail" 8809
"deer, mule" 368
"deer hunting, dreamed he was" 429
"Deer Lick Pennsylvania" 3957
"deer watched, the" 8271
Deering, Billy 1908
Deering, Chuck 1130
"deerskins, gray" 4165
de Falk, Dr. 7505
"defeat, his Chicago" 7154
"defeat, like a banner in" 2973
"defeat, Tony's" 6992
"defeated, defenders" 10481
Defects 2046, 7156, 7158, 7162, 9247, 9805, 10775
"defence, no" 10001
"defence, she had offered no" 2038
"defend the Commune" 10837
"defend yourself" 4988
"defenders defeated" 10481
"defense establishment" 7444
"defenses . . . are at their most tattered and flimsy" 4712
"defenses of Rome" 9559
"defenses of the city" 8694
"defenses reeling from some previous blow" 4712
"deferentially, bowing" 5199
Defiance 8709, 10838
"defiance" 8164
"defiance, act of wilful" 8709
"defiance of military authority" 4616
"defiance of municipal orders" 2017

"deficiencies of the present day will be supplied by the morrow" 4603

"deficiency in number, his" 4719

"defied everyone's idea" 4072

"defilement of the sandy streams of Surrey, the minor" 9738

de Fleury, Mad. 9855

De Frayne, Millicent 5659

"defy God" 10838

Degas 8027

"Degas, grace was that of a" 8027

de Gondeshil, Cospatric 3381

de Grammont, Monsieur 9882

"degree, I took my" 3266

"degrees, close to ninety" 4424

"degrees hard-earned, by virtue of" 9076

"degrees in the mill, it was over a hundred" 4426

De Haven, Fanny 4917

Deirdre 2655

"deities, the" 9062

"dejection of spirits" 9513

Dekatha, Peter 4248, 8264

de l'Abbaye, Helen 4997

de la Cueva, Antonio 2570

Delaney, Anna 10949

Delaney, Eileen 3295

Delaney, Fred 10133

Delaney, Jack 164

Delaney, Mrs. 1578

Delaney, Pierce 1224

Delaney, Robert 9109

Delaney, Terry 1064

Delano, Captain Amasa 8048

de Las Cases, Marquis 5029

"Delaware" 5486

"Delaware Bay" 8064

"Delaware capes" 9065

"delay, temporary" 5469

"delayed for two hours by police and army checkpoints" 883

DelBelly, Mrs. 6776

"delectable Lida" 2044

"delegates, little knots of" 6986

"Delhi" 1431

"Delhi, when I arrived in" 1564

Delia 9086

"deliberate forgetfulness" 7441

"deliberate side, on the" 10357

"deliberate Spoonerism" 7677

"deliberation, grave and solid" 2466

"delicacy, subtle cellolike" 1706

"delicate as silver rods" 9212

"delicatessen" 7580

"delicatessen shop" 3101

"delight, all people in the world existed for his" 1285

"delight, boom of" 444

"delight, heavy kinde of" 7370

"delighted one March morning" 9882

"delighted to receive your charming letter" 1945

"delightful!" 4181

"delightful, the day was so" 5268

"delightfully disgusting" 3376

"delights to be encountered in a good war, profusion of" 10478

"delimited by two sentries" 3482

"deliver his opinions with characteristic weight and vivacity" 2820

"delivered, have him" 1164

"delivered instead wilted lettuce" 2656

"delivered of the first child" 7069

"delivered the immigrants" 8080

"delivering him, mother who died" 6636

"delivery, breech" 10221

Dellicker, Henry 4734

Delmon 5992

Delmore, Mrs. 4986

Deloach, Maggie 9729

Deloraine, Tommy 585

Delos, Pauline 6763

"Delphic Oracle" 6896

"delphiniums, bluest" 5286

del Pino, Celia 8385

Del Rio, Amhoretz 6652

"Delta, Mississippi" 3157

"Delta, the" 7799

de Luci, Richard 1691

"deluded by the golden visions" 3550

de Malrive, Madame 10037

"demand, in great" 6492

"demanded Sir Nitin Basu" 3875

"demanded the angry voice" 6619

Demarest, Polly Solo-Miller 3594

Demarest, William 2948

"demeanor, assumed the severe" 6408

"demeanor, outward" 9280

De Medici, Julien 332

"Demera" 1445

"demisemiwit, slipshop" 9313

Demjanjuk, John 1159

"demobilization sounded like the best word" 10502

"democracy" 1444

"democracy, little South American" 6259

"democracy was, what a real" 5404

"Democrat nominee for vice-president of the United States" 7007

"Democratic Convention" 3378

"Democratic National Convention, 1968" 1214

"demolished, had not yet been" 6963

Demolition 3788, 5692

"demon Blue-Shirt" 9053

Demons 2799, 9053, 9658

"demonstrating the use of a life jacket" 9579

"demonstration, white-power" 6586

"demonstrators took over" 9192

de Montauban, Bishop Charles 7519

de Moscoso, Luís 8165

Demosthenes 8894, 10871

"demoted from the rank of Commodore" 10978

Dempster, Mrs. 5100

"demurely, walking" 4142

"Denbigh" 9599

"Denboro, village of" 1373

Dench, Eustace 2044

"denial, gesture of the kindliest" 9880

"denial of individual liberty" 7003

"denied, none of them ever" 3130

Denis 10959

Denis, Paul 4704

"denomination, my" 1520

"denounced as a vagrant" 358

"dental class" 10866

"dental school, in the whole" 10866

"dented, deeply" 9681

"Dentisement, dried" 10235

"dentist, the" 6589

"dentists drilling too deep" 2356

"denture, his lower" 10235

"Denver" 1577, 3087, 3451

"depart for good, decided to" 1743

"departed from it in anger" 1691

"departing, before" 6474

"departing from Cuzco" 7811

"Department, Spare Parts" 3335

"Department of Recorded Programmes" 1051

Departure 201, 204, 206, 254, 644, 745, 890, 1041, 1078, 1328, 1410, 1506, 1566, 1568, 1569, 1570, 1574, 1575, 1577, 1578, 1579, 1581, 1587, 1588, 1589, 1597, 1598, 1599, 1600, 1601, 1602, 1603, 1604, 1607, 1610, 1611, 1615, 1616, 1617, 1619, 1623, 1626, 1627, 1628, 1630, 1634, 1635, 1636, 1637, 1646, 1650, 1656, 1658, 1661, 1662, 1663, 1666, 1668, 1669, 1670, 1671, 1676, 1677, 1679, 1681, 1682, 1686, 1687, 1689, 1691, 1695, 1696, 1697, 1700, 1702, 1705, 1712, 1713, 1714, 1717, 1724, 1731, 1733, 1741, 1743, 1744, 1745, 1746, 1749, 1750, 1753, 1754, 1756, 1758, 1763, 1765, 1769, 1771, 1772, 1773, 1774, 1777, 1782, 1783, 1784, 1785, 1787, 2148, 2484, 2516, 2570, 2653, 2655, 2658, 2659, 2662, 2663, 2667, 2668, 2669, 2670, 2677, 2793, 2931, 2934, 2945, 2954, 3000, 3050, 3309, 3324, 3410, 3562, 3566, 3716, 3766, 3910, 3922, 3933, 3993, 4117, 4122, 4270, 4335, 4471, 4615, 4674, 4781, 4916, 4996, 5093, 5654, 5754, 5784, 5834, 6099, 6108, 6112, 6114, 6157, 6474, 6497, 6537, 6555, 6560, 6568, 6576, 6705, 6713, 6722, 6944, 7421,

7534, 7568, 7811, 7919, 8035,
8047, 8069, 8091, 8095, 8153,
8157, 8188, 8229, 8546, 8559,
8655, 8665, 8694, 8704, 8802,
9410, 9516, 9593, 9625, 9649,
9724, 9762, 9934, 9938, 9981,
10030, 10138, 10275, 10359, 10431,
10519
"departure, girls'" 10275
"departure, my" 5784
"departure, night before their" 890
"departure, September's ominous"
 10700
"departure, time of his" 2359
"departure for Ceylon" 3922
"departure of an international aircraft from Lisbon" 4650
"departure was easy and commodious" 3910
"depend on getting it from that
 particular Harmen" 4760
"depended upon what they were
 then doing, how much" 6604
"dependence" 9928
"dependent on one another" 6883
"dependents, other respectable" 3120
"dependents of the ten houses in
 Albion Place" 3120
"depending on where you are
 standing" 3664
"Depends, It" 2532
"deplane, excellent time to" 9650
"deposit, simply a ten-dollar" 1043
"deposit a couple of checks" 1106
"deposited in the red leather chair"
 9909
"deposited the coin with elaborate
 precision" 2888
"depository for its records" 1400
"depot, only a" 1436
"depot, Pennsylvania Railway" 3378
"depot, walked toward the" 1732
"depot at Bonneville" 8765
"dépôt hack" 9382
"depot platform" 7265
"deprecated" 7475
"depressed, I certainly was feeling"
 2499
"depressed, Mr. Godfrey was" 2515
"depressed on Sundays, I get" 2512
"depressed on Sundays, no valid
 reason for not getting" 2512
"depressing as ever" 5372
"depressing limbo of the last
 months" 9572
Depression 73, 567, 970, 1563,
 2444, 2673, 2675, 8477, 9454,
 9513
"Depression, Great" 815, 6477
"depression, realized he had been
 in a" 2518
"depression, undergoing a" 2516
"depression of spirits" 8477
"depression plunged through him"
 2503

"depressions, between two disastrous economic" 1726
"depressive temperament, mildy but
 persistently" 2507
"Depressives, the" 2013
"deprived America of her most
 gifted writer" 2360
"deprived him of the academic wife"
 2332
"depth, six inches in" 7606
"depths, warm and murmuring"
 10293
"deputy, Mr. Torr as" 6429
"Deputy, Second" 8256
"deputy, sheriff's new" 6969
"Deputy Director" 6443
"deputy to hold down the sheriff's
 office" 7616
Der, Erif 4147
"Derailleurs, The" 7027
"Derbyshire" 3082
"derelict, collision with a" 8059
"derelict mill" 5155
"derelicts who live off discards"
 6274
de Retteville, Alianor 7586
de Retz, Cardinal 4490
"derived" 5418
de Rochefauld, Catherine 1750
"derricks swung busily" 8121
Derry, Fred 5916
"Derry and Toms" 2740
de St. Lyre, Marquis 5975
Descartes 2535, 6845
"Descartes, revised and updated"
 6845
"descend the hillside into the
 Valley" 6713
"descendants flourished" 6146
"descended a sharp grade under
 redwoods" 8212
"descended from Captain John
 Underhill" 356
"descended from the fabulous Davy
 Crockett" 368
"descended from the house of
 Argyll, lineally" 354
"descended in a direct line from
 Adam and Eve" 359
"descended it now heavily and
 without speaking" 10368
"descended that celebrated eminence" 1569
"descending like doves to the green
 continents" 2623
"descending the stairs" 9887
"descent, fifth in" 6613
"descent, made the" 10382
"descent, of long" 6611
"descent, that long" 9112
Deschamps, Pierre 135
"describe Bert, perhaps I should"
 6718
"describe my mother, not easy to"
 10802

"describe people" 6909
"describe the most varied and the
 most beautiful" 6908
"described him to her astonished
 Mayfair friends" 5930
"described in the offical guidebook"
 9173
"describing it, begin by" 594
"description, begin with a scrap of"
 5390
"description, painstaking" 11000
"description an old woman had
 given him" 7222
"descriptions, oblique and deceptive" 5243
"descriptions, subjective" 5059
"desert, across the" 9167, 9180
"desert, across the wide" 7615
"desert, bar in the" 2615
"desert, drift away into the" 7654
"Desert, Escalante" 10452
"desert, flat and lonely waste of"
 2949
"desert, flew in from the" 234
"desert, floor of the" 10707
"Desert, Gobi" 5528
"desert, Minervois was a" 5165
"desert, mottled brass-bright" 3768
"desert, Nevada-California" 2956
"Desert, Powder" 10694
"desert, Sahara" 2640
"Desert, Sahara" 6168
"desert, Sinai" 4080
"desert, spirits of the" 5704
"desert, sun-blasted" 9766
"desert, Texas" 10726
"desert, yellow back of the" 10741
"desert coastline near some mountains" 4081
"Desert D'Or, town of" 4061
"desert floor, hot" 9127
"desert name" 4857
"desert nothing, flat" 5181
"desert sands" 4428
"desert track" 9127
"desert watch fires" 8986
"deserted, almost" 4326
"deserted, place looks" 10066
"deserted, recently" 9100
"deserted, street looked almost"
 9125
"deserted and crumbling" 3089
"deserted Brooklyn street" 9147
"deserted by its inhabitants" 1736
"deserted estate" 3179
"deserted her domestic gods in the
 city" 2018
"deserted his wife and child" 5914
"deserted them" 9742
"deserting or marrying a girl" 9290
"deserting the cities for the suburbs"
 6141
Deserts 888, 2640, 3768, 4428,
 5165, 5181, 9127, 9167, 10329,
 10694, 10709

"deserts, the interior" 2605
"deserts of Asia" 6109
"deserts to the north" 10709
"deserts which lie in the vicinity of the Dead Sea" 10329
"deserve to have a son, she does not" 6610
"deserved it, he almost" 4740
"deserves to be recorded, thinks it" 9508
"design, exuberance of" 3122
"Design, National Academy of" 1012
"designate the year more closely, I will not" 8960
"designed only for light happy unladen feet" 10368
"designer labels on handbags" 7229
"designs, bent to their sweet and infamous" 5355
"desirable, horribly" 2624
Desire 2624, 5381, 5661, 6538
"desire" 5661
"desire, express one's" 2464
"desire, I no longer have the" 2521
"desire, my one remaining" 8027
"desire, their heart's" 249
"desire . . . and its fulfillment" 2524
"desire for visibility, insatiable" 3545
"desire to escape from his identity" 3412
"desire to write stories" 5546
"desires, at the mercy of their own" 938
"desires, covetous" 1205
"desires of my life" 5381
"desires of the flesh, carnal" 1205
"desires of the moment" 3821
"desk, across the" 3333
"desk, from the distance of her" 5674
"desk, her" 2728, 6383, 9884, 10926
"desk, her flat" 6495
"desk, his" 1854, 2155, 2419, 2924, 3738, 6851, 8202
"desk, I was at my" 767
"desk, I went to my" 9909
"desk, kidney-shaped walnut veneer" 2848
"desk, let it lie on my" 1949
"desk, my" 710, 900, 1122, 2692
"desk, public writing-" 7509
"desk, right-hand corner of the" 4273
"desk, rose from her" 6900
"desk, sat at a" 970
"desk, sat at his" 6421
"desk, seated at his" 1877
"desk, sitting at a" 5405
"desk, sitting at my" 7770
"desk, sitting behind his" 8572
"desk, small front" 982
"desk, Wolfe's" 10010
"desk as shield between them" 381
Desks 351, 767, 1122, 1155, 2692,

5316, 5674, 6383, 6851, 7770, 8572, 10067, 10951
"desks, one of the long" 10951
"desolate, alone and" 9208
"desolate, bleak and" 5159
"desolate splashing" 8134
"desolated Scotland, war which had" 6801
"desolation, all the rest is" 8279
"desolation of snow, glittering" 10570
Despair 146, 2431, 2506, 3341, 3705, 4301, 4607, 6845, 8490
"despair, filled her mother with" 4301
"despair, had come very near to" 3341
"despair, in their" 4607
"despair, it was the winter of" 3377
"despair, optimism and" 8490
"despair, whirlpool of" 3705
"despair so deep, caught up in" 2506
"despairs therefore she is, she" 6845
"desperate, he was" 7596
"desperate, if you are" 3339
"desperate, sad and" 4319
"desperate about Dwayne, I was" 10977
"desperate ride" 7607
"desperate society" 2837
Desperation 3339, 7596
"desperation, in" 3057
"despise her contemporaries, early learned to" 4360
"despised him, no man had ever" 7967
"despisers of the British theatre, intellectual" 9378
"despite my protests" 6392
"despond, reserve and" 2502
"despotic sway" 1292
"destination, forget his original" 5607
"destination, he had come to his" 1624
"destination, his" 7620
"destination, home and" 9615
"destination, possibility that this was indeed his ultimate" 8692
"destination was not known" 10529
Destinations 1737, 3003, 8692
"destined" 1874
"destined to be" 10460
"destined to become the great King" 4513
"destined to undergo great and rapid changes" 265
"destinies of the French nation" 3376
Destiny 265, 829, 1093, 1221, 1460, 2956, 3670, 3671, 3673, 3676, 4451, 5084, 5642, 6020
"Destiny" 3670
"destiny, a" 829

"destiny, a man's" 1460
"destiny, ambiguous" 2956
"destiny, believe that they have a" 3671
"destiny, determined his" 3673
"destiny, fulfilling" 5642
"destiny, how big the moment was with" 5084
"Destiny, supernatural paraphernalia of inscrutable" 1093
"destiny came" 3676
"destiny is gradually becoming the sum of everything" 3671
"destiny that leads the English to the Dutch" 1221
"destiny was open to whatever chances he could or would take" 1460
"destitution, squatted in sullen" 3128
"destroy me, these things might" 92
"destroyed, subsequently" 9205
"destroyed, the swimming pool" 2470
"destroyed by their own hands" 4469
"destroyed my brief peace" 5295
"destroyer drove westwards" 8136
"destroying it, finally" 2630
"destroys, success that" 282
Destruction 282, 2470, 2630, 6018
"destruction, those first agents of" 6613
"destruction was at his fingers' ends" 6018
"desultory, space was" 7758
"desultory and gradual manner" 5787
"detached in manner" 6894
"detail, see every" 4891
"details, nonsensical" 5829
"details of her life meant everything to me" 4175
"details of the affair" 675
"details which I do not intend to make known" 8960
"detained by a dream" 2781
"detains her at home, a detail" 9337
"detective agencies" 2018
"detective story" 1325
"detective was following Linda" 8905
Detectives 4984, 8905
"detectives, two lookalike Greek" 4984
"detectives from the homicide squad" 19
de Tenorio, Don Juan 2558
"deteriorated, how much I had" 5858
"determination, comic" 755
"determination, joyless" 7852
"determined not to be invaded by each other's identities" 8223
"deterred by the roughest roads or

the highest hills" 9515
"detest Doctor Fischer" 4359
"detested it, they both" 5352
Detling, Sir Arthur 9458
"detonated her marriage" 5778
"Detroit" 4073, 7829
"Detroit, I got by nicely without"
 1458
"Detroit Free Press" 6853
"Detroit is usually hot and sticky in
 the summer" 8594
"Detroit Riot of '43" 3777
Devane, Lieutenant-Commander
 John 8280
DeVane, Ursula 2791
"devastated many parts of Cata
 lonia, floods that" 2339
"devastation, reporting" 6328
de Vaumartin, Isobel 5980
"development, Cobblestone Hearth
 Village Estates" 3264
"development, in an old" 3239
"development of rapid photography"
 1314
"Deviation and Dismemberment
 Policies" 4622
"device, traction" 10228
"device of infernal origin" 128
"Devil, children saw the" 5810
"devil, if you're the" 9055
"Devil, Printer's" 601
"devil, renounce the" 1205
"devil, such a" 372
"devil, tell me I was the" 8247
"devil moon" 10240
"devil sun" 10240
"devil were after him, as though
 the" 10360
"Devil's Row" 957
Devine, Chick 620
Devlin, Mrs. 2352
"devoid of friends" 4282
Devon 2564
"Devon, in the north of" 2887
"Devon, North" 1336, 4041, 7186
"Devon, south" 1736
"Devon cottage" 9730
"Devonshire, county of" 5728
"Devonshire Arms" 6448
"Devonshire family" 1926
"devote myself exclusively" 2488
"devoted their lives to the revolution" 10837
"devoted victims of justice" 7179
"devotion" 5997
"devotion, heat ennobled by" 5674
"devotion, true" 1292
"devour itself, it attempts to" 275
"dew, autumn" 5161
"dew, glistening" 1892
"dew, wet with diamonds of" 2275
Dewberry 3475
Dewey 4586
Dewey, Hickey 10901
DeWitt, Malcolm 3254

"dews, evening" 2279
"dewy June morning" 8262
Dexter 6860
"Dha-something Sap" 5158
"Dhaphut" 5158
"dhow was setting sail for the open
 sea" 7801
"diabolical brain" 9019
"diagnosed, subsequently" 134
"dial, illuminated" 1123
"dial, 1240 on your" 9365
"dial, twisted the" 6331
"dial tone, no" 1144
"dialect, in the" 4734
"dialogue with their own subconscious minds" 5512
"diamond, it was a" 2602
"diamond, like a" 2977
"diamond, uncut" 5312
"diamond diggings of the Vaal"
 5456
Diamonds 2602, 5312, 10551
"diamonds, black" 10551
"diamonds, buying" 5456
"diamonds, coal and" 10551
"diamonds, fond of" 6607
"diamonds, miles of" 4704
"diamonds of dew" 2275
Diana 1796, 6762, 10270
Diane 8601
Diaries 252, 4829, 5104, 10781; *see
 also* **Journals**
"diaries, both kept" 2539
"diaries, the girls kept" 2534
"Diaries beginning with the second
 quarter of our century" 10781
"diary" 2533
"Diary" 2543
"diary, hello" 4829
"diary, I have taken up this" 2536
"diary, informal" 2531
"diary, my" 2538
"diary, my sister's" 2544
"diary, start this" 2540
"diary, wrote in her" 252
"diary, wrote in his" 2535
"diary entry, casual" 5104
"diary of daily events" 2532
"Diary of John Haye" 2531
"diary of this past troubled summer"
 2550
"dice clicked and caromed and
 bounced and stopped" 3969
"dice rolled, green" 3966
"diced away their fathers' fortunes"
 3396
Dick 137, 2296, 4244
"dickety-clax" 7261
"dictation, no master's" 5545
"dictation, paused in his" 7801
"dictation, take" 1118
"dictator, Spanish" 4481
"Dictator of the Roman People"
 7514
"dictionaries in his head, juggled

whole" 6132
"dictionary, in the" 10911
"did the house, when she" 1607
"did to us there, what it was the
 Truth Seekers" 9435
"did very well" 3946
"diddakoi" 4987
Diddy the Good 9580
Diderot 8949
"Diderot, statue of" 8949
Didi 9190
"die, before I" 121
"die, before you" 9284
"die, cab that wanted desperately
 to" 9801
"die, did I ask to" 2404
"die, don't mean I'm in a hurry to"
 2434
"die, first you have to" 2427
"die, I am going to" 2399
"die, I come to" 6450
"die, If Joan Drake should" 2311
"die, it just took her until now to"
 2428
"die, made up my mind to" 2305
"die, me'll" 6588
"die, not to" 2529
"die, one death to" 2403
"die, the man I love is to" 7182
"die, they are about to" 10944
"die, thought he was about to"
 2416
"die, town that refused to" 1406
"Die, Watching Father" 2396
"die, went out to India to" 2421
"die at last, did" 2318
"die by fire, the other will" 8244
"die from the strangeness of this, I
 am going to" 8491
"die here, did the old man" 2317
"die horribly and in public" 7182
"die in earnest, earth began to"
 3403
"die in her own bed" 2449
"die instead, to" 2362
"die now, if I were to" 4932
"die of, what did Jewel's mother"
 2465
"die the way we were, we'd" 2509
"die three times, was to" 2389
"die together, how wonderful it
 would be if we could all" 2452
"die with a key" 2453
"die young" 113
"died" 2432
"died, a few months before he"
 7498
"died, a friend" 2337
"died, after Alexander" 3610
"died, after I" 6133
"died, after Mamma and Richard
 Quin" 943
"died, all this began long before I"
 627
"died, Ann" 6161

"died, at the end of this period she" 2353
"died, aunt..." 8716
"died, aunt who" 4225
"died, before he" 9733
"died, Char" 2423
"died, Colonel Wyatt" 6524
"died, father" 5914
"died, girl who" 2355
"died, good thing if my Aunt Christine" 2313
"died, had" 1901
"died, he had" 2308
"died, her mother had" 6666
"died, his brother Nachman" 10422
"died, his grandmother" 6130
"died, his mother" 7219
"died, Jim Watson had" 2304
"died, Julia" 2438
"died, kingsize bed in which his father had" 6131
"died, life did not begin until he" 5595
"died, my father" 6169
"died, my husband" 2368
"died, my younger brother Matthew" 8240
"died, none of us" 7059
"died, only people I did not know" 2410
"died, our parents" 8219
"died, poor Ezra Adams" 2301
"died, since Roosevelt" 6347
"died, soldiers who had struggled and" 7228
"died, stood on the fox until it" 2458
"died, ten weeks before he" 6435
"died, the bird had" 764
"died, the Great Horned Owl had" 749
"died, the morning Dinah" 2440
"died, the night before he" 7429
"died, the old Colonel" 2357
"died, to prove it she" 2394
"died, Tommy" 2448
"died, turned his face to the wall and" 4457
"died, two years after Robert E. Lee" 468
"died, violence in which he" 9846
"died, when Egbert Dormer" 2292
"died, when he" 2320, 2382
"died, when her father" 6106
"died, when Jérôme Lafirme" 2295
"died, when Mr. Pratt" 8670
"died, when she" 7415, 9710
"died, when the Duchess" 8714
"died, when the old captain" 2328
"died, who" 5399
"died, without even turning around" 2402
"died a few days before Christmas" 2319
"died and went to San Francisco"

644
"died at his own convenience" 2359
"died at the invasion of Normandy" 6863
"died at the same time, if everyone hadn't" 2445
"died because she missed the 9.40 bus" 6203
"died before her, her mother had" 2319
"died delivering him" 6636
"died eleven months ago" 4108
"died far away" 2441
"died from natural causes" 1889
"died giving birth to me" 807
"died hours after he was born" 2408
"died in a cupboard" 9295
"died in childbirth" 2419
"died in her sleep" 2330
"died in his bed" 2364
"died in the first year of my life, my mother" 6706
"died July 21 1959" 5452
"died last July" 6939
"died of a heart attack" 754
"died of a massive coronary" 2373
"died of a second and long-expected stroke" 2424
"died of lockjaw" 468
"died of the Illness I mention'd to you" 4221
"died on an April day" 3521
"died on me finally" 2433
"died on the night of October 20 1962" 2339
"died standing up, she" 2455
"died suddenly one morning" 2451
"died suddenly when he was forty, my father" 2407
"died ten minutes into lunch break" 2401
"died Tuesday in Phoenix" 2340
"died twice" 2403
"died when he was so very Young" 355
"died when those two children were only eight and six years old" 6612
"died within a few weeks of one another" 3273
"died yesterday" 2361
Diels, Crip 7621
"dies, everybody" 2338
"dies by water, if one twin" 8244
"dies in his own way, each man" 2331
"diesel, garotte of" 183
"diet forbids you to have any" 7582
Dieudonné, Madame 9291
"differ from the father of my sex in no important particular" 7554
"difference, a locked door wont make any" 2030
"difference, aint no" 2268
"difference, it won't make a" 8240
"difference, marked a sharp" 1821

"difference, with a" 1408
"difference between American and English cocktail parties" 6780
"difference between Victor and my-self" 6878
"differences, acutest perception of" 6251
"different, it would be" 3610
"different, not to be" 4279
"different, this one is" 544
"different, wishing he could be" 241
"different 'bout them, so" 6822
"different for me than for others, it was no" 3390
"different from anything he had ever known before" 5121
"different from the rest of you" 9419
"different now, I'm" 5652
"different they look, how" 3664
"different times and places" 7718
"differently there, do things" 6789
"differing from them only in the minor peculiarities" 5215
"differs from his fellows, each man" 5215
"difficult, made more" 6545
"difficult, some men would have found more" 4
"difficult day" 7847
"difficult of access" 1465
"difficult to overestimate" 2894
"difficult to verify" 6907
"difficult words" 7200
"difficulties, guided me through many" 5446
"difficulties, hazards and" 5556
"difficulty" 115
"difficulty, had some" 100
"difficulty, less" 6156
"difficulty, without too much" 7230
"difficulty it must be for us all" 10460
"diffidence, father unGreek" 8894
"diffused its inadequate light" 8404
DiFranco, Terri 1749
"dig the concept, do you" 1081
"dig this, now" 7986
"digging, scientific" 1384
"digging a moat" 1180
"digging his fingers into the tarred canvas cover" 9769
"digging his grave" 2329
"digging in the farmhouse garden" 3793
"digging into buried towns" 1384
"digging it up, keep the dogs from" 2329
"diggings, diamond" 5456
"digits, my" 3870
"dignified" 9969
"dignified, too" 5641
"dignified traditions" 1314
"dignitaries, cathedral" 1486
"dignities before death, laid down their" 6976

Dignity 5968, 8946
"dignity, tattered garment that had once been his" 5968
"dignity, unspeakable" 8946
"digs, cheaper" 6149
"Dijon, town of" 3467
"dike, wet grassy paddy" 1864
"dilapidation, highly picturesque state of semi-" 3058
Dildo 6716
"dilemma, terms of the" 7368
"Dilettanti of Naples" 6213
"diligence, European" 9626
Dillard 9809
Dillon 10958
Dillon, Roy 143
"Dillsborough" 1340
Dilworth, Eloise 5570
"dim as memories" 6849
"dime, that's my last" 2888
"dimensions, extraordinary" 500
"dimensions in space" 6903
"dimensions of space" 9500
"dimensions rarely touched by the sun" 5624
"diminuendo of its bang and rattle" 3295
"dimness, the evening" 10786
"din, heard a great" 8776
"din of noon" 5096
"din of traffic" 8773
Dinah 156, 2440, 3629, 4857, 9899
"dine, eight people were to" 3833
"dine in an overloaded dinghy" 8065
"dine in hall with my learned friend" 2088
"dined like a queen on boiled sheep's brains" 3887
"dined with Hartley Wiggins at the Hare and Tortoise" 3820
"dined with her and her black lover" 2815
"diner, the Greek's" 7578
"diner like the ones Cody and his father ate in" 7575
Ding, Grover 4242
"dinghy, an overloaded" 8065
"dinghy, not a" 7685
"dinghy, small sailing" 1883
"dingily, nesting" 1364
"dingle was dank and dripping" 9739
"dingy houses" 7753
Dining 1086, 1143, 1494, 1592, 2088, 2815, 3812, 3820, 3833, 3847, 3877, 3878, 3887, 3889, 4511, 5419, 5443, 5894, 6209, 6715, 8065, 8626, 8627, 8631, 8633, 8636, 10334, 10565
"dining car" 6372
"dining companions" 4511
"dining in Rome" 5443
"dining room, Mrs. Quorn's" 8869
"dining together" 1494

"dining with his friend" 10899
"dining-parlor, well-furnished" 2886
Dinkle, Stanley 5473
"Dink's Blues" 8744
Dinky-Dunk 6038
Dinner 3823, 3880, 6769, 6777, 7762, 8629
"dinner" 3856, 3880
"dinner, after" 4018, 5443, 8341
"dinner, at" 9900
"dinner, at a" 6349
"dinner, ate" 3830
"dinner, came back from" 1592
"dinner, Class Day" 10656
"dinner, deadly time before the family had" 3629
"dinner, dressing for" 8631
"dinner, eating" 3823
"dinner, farewell" 3912
"dinner, gala" 6769
"dinner, giving a" 8629
"dinner, go for a pleasant" 1143
"dinner, having his" 3872
"dinner, hour of" 5894
"Dinner, Ladies' Night" 7762
"dinner, Sunday" 10411
"Dinner, Tenth Anniversary" 4005
"dinner, took her out to" 2663
"dinner affairs" 4788
"dinner at his club" 8633
"dinner at Mom's house, having" 6209
"dinner at ten-fifteen, served" 3886
"dinner at two in the afternoon, took his" 3816
"dinner awaiting him at his sister's" 9423
"dinner first, he ate" 3858
"dinner hour" 5618
"dinner last evening" 3738
"dinner party" 6032
"dinner party was about to begin" 6777
"dinner time, right up till" 4404
"dinner to come, elaborate" 3821
"dinner was being given by Mrs. Cortlandt Trend" 8627
"dinner was served, the later" 10565
"dinner with a man" 3878
"dinner with the Wentworths" 3846
"dinner-hour" 9873
"dinner-table, studied the" 3838
"dinners, gave sumptuous" 6607
"dinners, Sunday" 3883
"dinnertime" 3321
"dinnertime, worry about" 10163
"dinosauric" 309
"Dinwiddie Academy for Young Ladies" 3270
"diocese of Canterbury" 1691
Diogenes 10871
Diomed 3812
Diony 6218
"diplomat, as a" 6439
"diplomatic posting, await his first"

6432
Diplomats 6432, 6439
"dipped a squalling newborn baby" 7067
Direck, Mr. 6251
"directed over a million men" 5138
"direction, everybody in the same" 7849
"direction, in the wrong" 7756
"direction, no sense of" 5610
"direction of the quarry, from the" 9835
Directions 529, 1361, 3232, 3634, 6083, 7195, 9184, 9542
"directions, in all" 528, 10723
"directions at once, indicating two" 2859
"Directions to Travelers" 9529
"directions upon the earth, rule over each of the" 2635
"director, deputy" 1621
"Director, Deputy" 6443
"director, film" 5984
"Director, its" 1051
"Director, Managing" 6429
"director of the Staedtler Institute of Archaeology" 6279
"director of Unico Realty Company" 4705
"Director-General" 1758
"direly, pronounced Slade" 3969
"Dirraleg, open countryside of" 3042
"dirt, greasy" 183
"dirt, little puffs of red" 10425
"dirt and debris of a table" 2856
"dirt anywhere, there is not a crumb of" 935
"Dirty Spoon" 7487
"dirty weather" 2607
"dirty work, I did their" 10950
"disagreeable" 8773
"disagreeable as they are good, usually as" 6812
"disagreeable duty" 9872
Disagreement 1636, 1747, 1802, 1820, 1821, 1827, 1840, 1842, 4088, 7510
"disappear, before anyone saw her" 1777
"disappear again in glittering jets of spray" 7919
Disappearance 1884, 2129, 4129, 5565, 9360
"disappearance, his" 2578
"disappearance of Don Juan de Tenorio" 2558
"disappearance of his singular personality" 5565
"disappeared, child" 2572
"disappeared, Daniel had" 2569
"disappeared, Lucy Bear and Rainbo Woman have" 2566
"disappeared, my nephew" 2567
"disappeared, mysteriously" 2568

"disappeared, quickly" 3040

"disappeared, the day after she" 2573

"disappeared from an inconspicuous Army installation" 2560

"disappeareds, the" 4129

"disappearing" 6160

"disappearing, she was" 2583

"disappearing below the trees" 224

"disappears before us like the smoke" 9505

"disappoint, having no one to" 5295

"disappointed, she was" 2590

"disappointed in his son, bitterly" 2584

"disappointed in you, He was" 7511

"disappointment" 2588

"disappointment, big" 2591

"disappointment, great" 2586

"disappointment struck, knives of official" 2587

"disappointment waited on all affairs in which he bore a part" 6018

"disapproved of" 2351

Disaster 2934, 3671, 6102, 6467, 7008, 7714

"disaster, a minute away from" 2595

"disaster, convenient" 3671

"disaster, feed on" 2593

"disaster, heading toward" 2934

"disaster, his life ended in" 7714

"disaster, it was a" 6102

"disaster, most common" 2598

"disaster, my great" 2597

"disaster, no" 7008

"disaster, threat of" 2599

"disaster finally arrived" 2599

"disasters, succession of national" 2592

"disastrous" 1984

"disastrous attachments, discussing" 2596

Disbelief 62, 2732, 2735, 2737, 2742, 2743, 2744, 2745, 2746, 2747, 2748, 2749, 2750, 3572, 5591, 5783, 6340, 7635, 8964

"disbelief, stunned" 6232

"discerned, never for a moment" 5794

"discharge, hardship" 8670

"discharge from the United States Army" 1529

"discharge from the United States Navy" 5537

"discharge pay" 8664

"discharges you, College" 9718

"Disco was dead" 2109

"discolored with brown water spots" 5317

Discomfort 411, 1544, 1549, 1553, 2535, 2907, 4668, 6598, 6599, 7300, 7513, 8475, 9275, 9276,

9359, 10234, 10236, 10365

"discomfort, I feel" 2535

"discomfort, quiet" 4644

"discomfort, this one final petty" 1553

"disconcerted, not wholly" 3913

"disconcerting resemblance" 6864

"disconsolate seekers in the desert" 1302

"discontent, winter of her" 8356

"discouragement" 1686

"discouragement, profoundest" 4928

"discourse, embarrassed in" 5889

"Discourse, ordinary" 120

"discourse with various men" 10794

"discoursing in detail" 3573

"discover, I" 5985

"discover after 7 years" 5748

"discover just exactly who in the hell this Alan Lewrie character was" 4869

"discover much of their character" 5435

"discover myself" 6797

"discover something underground, I was bound to" 2607

"discover that for yourself soon enough" 10997

"discover that I have really reached the Old Dominion" 8171

"discover the instigation of passion and doom" 2608

"discover what had been caught in the body trap-line overnight" 1213

"discovered, bodies were" 1891

"discovered an abnormality on his EKG" 166

"discovered Duckling's absence" 2574

"discovered he was being robbed" 2057

"discovered her first American" 2615

"discovered I can magnify objects" 2611

"discovered Manila" 8534

"discovered my wife was stealing from me" 2051

"discovered Serge, I" 8906

"discovered she was made of flesh and blood" 7969

"discovered that he could see the old apartment" 6140

"discovered the Great Terror" 898

"discovered traces of a lost people" 2605

"discoverers of our time, one of the most remarkable medical" 2616

Discoveries 1898, 1903, 1911, 2553, 3183, 5532, 6839, 6859, 6860, 7224, 7450, 7969, 7981

"discoveries set you free, some" 2612

"discovering Bentley's leaning

towards homosexuality" 6682

"discovers that the man sitting beside him has no legs" 9629

Discovery 461, 754, 898, 1384, 1877, 1891, 1893, 2010, 2051, 2370, 2574, 2583, 3702, 4494, 4589, 5435, 5557, 5748, 5985, 6564, 6797, 6871, 8906, 9629

"discovery, exploration and" 6564

"discovery, made the" 3183

"discovery, made the uncomfortable" 2583

"discovery, sense of" 4589

"discovery, voyage of" 2600

"discovery that she possessed a gift for persuasive speech" 8026

"discreet" 9887

"discreetly over her plate, bent" 3824

"discrepancy, a growing" 9280

"discretion" 9260

"discrimination, nice" 5557

"discuss the sorry state of civilization" 2057

"discussed, two subjects I never" 7593

"discussed with a certain restraint, illness was" 139

"discussing disastrous attachments" 2596

"discussing themselves, amiably" 8849

"discussion arose" 6349

"discussion groups, encouraged to hold general" 8869

Disease 120, 132, 146, 165, 167, 169, 171, 172, 173, 174, 545, 2019, 2375, 2377, 2408, 2425, 2454, 7895, 8677, 10883

"disease, cardiac" 141

"disease, contagious" 545

"disease, kidney" 2408

"disease, revealed the dimensions of the" 166

"disease is spreading up from the south" 9171

"disembarked" 4560

"disembarked at the Trenton station" 9529

"disembarking from a southern cruise" 4559

"disembodied eyes" 324

"disembodied note, hysterical" 5260

"disenchantment took shape" 2736

"disentangled, never since become" 5567

"disgrace, that is no" 7145

"disgraced by an illegitimate birth" 5780

"disguise, my mother in" 6651

"disguise it" 9839

"disguise the nose the mouth the eyes" 2066

"disguising the expression on your face" 5835

Disgust 5249, 7324, 8572
"disgust, to his utter" 5907
"disgust, your" 5731
"disgusted by what he saw" 7324
"disgusted look, give it a" 8572
"disgusted with life" 5249
"disgusting, delightfully" 3376
"dish, my favourite" 9915
"dishcloths, like old" 5372
"dishes of mangoes and bananas and pennies" 7533
"dishonest, do something" 7870
Dishonesty 2015, 5228, 5998, 7826, 7870, 9893
"dishonor her, tried to" 5205
"dishwater, old" 7316
"disillusionment, sample the" 3999
"disinherited race" 5886
"disk of tin-rich bronze, silvery" 7489
"dislike, well-restrained" 5349
"dislike extremely to be called 'Scientists'" 6409
"disliked about having the paper route" 5374
"disliked the modern world" 5383
Dislikes 3027, 5343, 5346, 5347, 5349, 5350, 5352, 5353, 5357, 5359, 5361, 5362, 5363, 5364, 5365, 5367, 5368, 5369, 5371, 5372, 5374, 5375, 5377, 5379, 5383, 5634, 5757, 5870, 6444, 8365, 9384, 10380, 10852
"dislocations, violent" 5111
"dismal Autumn afternoon" 310
"dismal daily, more" 3376
"dismay" 3514
"dismay of all philosophy, to the" 7373
"dismounted" 7633
"dismounted in front of the best hotel" 1582
Disobedience 3898
Disorder 2125, 7877
"disorder, strange" 7877
"disordered bed" 8583
"disorders, bridle all the" 1337
"disorganized, entirely" 10510
"disorientation, almost in a place of" 9615
"disparagement, criticism and" 385
"disparaging" 582
"dispassionate march of history" 5307
"dispensed traditional values" 8879
"dispersed to nothing" 7945
"display room" 9451
"displaying themselves" 7754
"displeasure, show their" 9309
"disport themselves amid the flowers and blossoms" 6561
"disposable, we are all" 3613
"disposal of waste is a burden" 5700
"disposed on a low settee, carefully" 6519

"disposition, clement" 5935
"disposition, happy" 5555
"disposition, of no promising" 6515
"disposition, so excellent a" 6521
"dispositions, humours and" 6604
"dispossessed" 4362
"dispossessed, the" 7038
"disputation, scene of bitter" 1823
"dispute, in loud" 652
"dispute for years, there had been a" 4088
"disregard her daughter" 10997
"disregard of his protests" 4614
"disrepute, penury and" 3557
Dissatisfaction 2509, 2849, 4754, 5377
"dissatisfaction, tiny" 2589
"dissatisfied" 2509
"dissatisfied with you" 6528
"dissemble" 2521
"dissuaded by the idea" 2537
"distance, dusty" 669
"Distance, from a safer" 5552
"distance, from this" 8803
"distance, in the" 8927
"distance, in the middle" 4694
"distance, into the blue" 6063
"distance, lights in the" 9562
"distance, looks into the" 10890
"distance, meet in the" 9122
"distance and openness and emptiness" 9549
"distance between us" 385
"distance between us grows" 9644
"distance fairly far off in day or night" 10746
"distances, measuring" 7766
"distaste, honest" 10495
"distaste, regarding with" 565
"distaste in his gaunt exhausted face" 5204
"distemper, flaking" 6294
"distemper fell from the ceiling" 6294
"distempered office" 247
"distilled, lacustrine essences richly" 8523
"distilled its music, the guitar" 6221
"distillery, the managing of a" 10478
"distinction, fining into" 10788
"distinction, her claim to" 4996
"distinction, I have the" 3537
"distinction, marked or singular" 1197
"distinction of him until we know him, hardly a" 9874
"distinguished, richer and more" 4444
"distinguished, terrifically" 5972
"distinguished and meritorious career" 6439
"distinguished British general" 10535
"distinguished himself" 6518, 9274

"distinguished it, three things" 1387
"Distinguished Modestus" 6110
"distinguished writers" 5396
"distortion, air curled with its" 189
"distracted at breakfast" 3874
"distraction, it did not seem much more than a" 7830
"distraction nonetheless, a" 10755
Distractions 3874, 10755
"distress, surprise and" 898
"distress, to her" 5238
"distresses me, not the rape that" 2048
"district, that pleasant" 3893
"district, the surrounding" 3196
"district known as the Moat" 4058
"district of a peculiar character" 6267
"district of Beaufort" 4030
"District of Columbia" 6982
"district of Orangeburg" 6973
"District Six" 2006
"districts of that state" 6973
Distrust 2277, 2741, 3758, 9302
"DISTURB, DO NOT" 8313
"disturb him again, she dare not" 7158
"disturb me, saw much to" 1530
"disturbance of my mind, peculiar" 8856
"disturbance that reached into his sleep" 10215
"disturbances that have happened in your family" 7825
"disturbed, not accustomed to being" 8801
"disturbed by a cautious opening of the door" 9945
"disturbed by the near-by and indubitable sound of a revolver shot" 8801
"disturbed drawing-rooms" 7865
"disturbed some said" 4201
"disturbed the sleeper" 673
"disturbing" 4811
"disturbing, solid and" 9995
"disturbing contents" 1947
"ditch, brambly" 9673
"ditch, deep in the" 9790
"ditch, roadside" 3416
"ditches, irrigating" 1357
"ditches, quite ordinary" 10397
"divan, great circular" 5613
"dive, the" 10
"dive a work of art" 10
"dive into a swimming pool" 9321
"divers, like breath-starved" 390
"divert public attention, as if to" 125
"Diverting, nothing in them so" 5552
"divide, eastern" 9547
"divide, great" 8052
"divided all time into a gentle boom" 8771

"divided by the narrow dyke paths"
5141
"divided into four cantos" 5452
"divided into old and new" 1362
"Divided Into Three Parts" 1403
"divided the Broderson ranch from
that of Los Muertos" 8765
"divided them, something" 1844
"divided them . . . into sun and
shadow" 4010
"dividing-line" 3995
"divil, you little" 6633
"divine assistance" 10651
"divined them, our ancestors" 6922
"divine-diabolic soul" 6001
"diviner, water" 7031
"diving off his skateboard" 4267
"diving right into Alan Lewrie's
latest naval adventure" 4869
Divinities 1496, 4808, 5664, 8008
"Divinity School" 4357
"division between great and small,
signalled a most curious" 2385
"division between two States of the
Union" 7657
Divney, John 6182
Divorce 3378, 3518, 5811, 6663,
7525, 8636, 9052
"divorce, after her" 2653
"divorce, best of friends during"
2671
"divorce, request for a" 2678
"divorce, talking about" 2660
"divorce, their parents'" 6663
"divorce case" 3378
"divorce that did it, it's" 2666
"divorce-court" 2649
"divorced" 5762
"divorced, mother and he got" 9052
"divorced, why we were" 2665
"divulging the great secret of my
life" 7951
"Dix, all the way from" 9942
Dixie 10081
"Dixie" 9361
"Dixie cup" 7051
"Dixie Cup lids" 634
Dixon 6022
Djuna 1250, 4635
"do, that'll have to" 7473
"do, this is what they will" 3609
"do, Whadda you wanna" 6943
"do, what do you" 2483
"do, what he was about to" 2402
"do, What shall I" 2751
"do anything, going to" 4972
"do anything at all, could not" 2060
"do anything he liked with it, he
could" 10116
Do Do 4599
"do her in, why I don't" 1999
"do in life, I don't care what you
choose to" 6656
"do it, anyone could" 4404
"do it, but you can't" 6098

"do it, did he really" 2067
"do it right" 6656
"do it yourself" 10936
"do something, why can't he" 6725
"do things first and think about
them afterward" 4153
"do this, why must we" 10932
"Do this and he doeth it" 10649
"do this to me, how *dare* he" 24
"do today, what's everyone going
to" 6934
"do together, what will they" 5826
"do under such circumstances, what
he should" 4002
"do with them, have very much to"
9690
"Doberman hovering indecisively
over the gutter" 10750
Dobie, Mr. 1493
"Doc Martens" 8027
Doche, Madame 4132
Dock 10362
"dock, drew up alongside the" 8097
"dock, floating" 3431
"Dock, Gladstone" 8131
"dock, long wooden" 8153
"dock, walked into the" 1829
"dock worker" 4315
"docked at Bombay's Ballard Pier"
8161
"Dockland" 9130
"dockmaster" 6942
"Docks, Liverpool" 7307
"docks, South Hudson" 3192
"docks, the" 4315
"docks of Jaffa, old" 4011
"Dockyard, Portsmouth" 8274
Doctor 5866
"doctor, family" 166, 6890
"doctor, great" 3916
"doctor, hadn't had to consult a"
5939
"doctor, his" 10521
"doctor, my" 141
"doctor, my grandad was a" 6902
"doctor, no" 7063
"doctor, our" 6885
"doctor, the" 140, 2449, 9887, 10114
"Doctor, the" 98, 2804
"doctor, tiny" 6900
"doctor, went to his" 6896
"doctor, white" 10442
"doctor had gone" 4224
"doctor in the other bed, that wild
old" 7231
"Doctor of Literature" 6443
"Doctor of Medicine" 3266, 9076
"doctor paused and had a quick
look at his notes" 162
"doctor pull the sheet up over the
face of the man on the bed" 2351
"doctor says" 10877
"doctor suggested she give up coffee
altogether" 6638
"doctor would be like, wondered

what the" 6888
"doctor would make his examination" 6893
"doctoral programs in chemistry,
left" 3286
"doctors, American" 10313
"doctors, especially" 6173
"doctors, surrounded by" 10313
"doctors, village" 6884
"Doctor's house" 121
"doctors' lounge" 4624
"doctor's orders, against" 2892
"doctrine, cabalistic" 9053
"doctrine of democracy and self-
emasculation" 1444
"document, setting my hand to an
official" 9950
"documentation of Augustus Walmer is slight" 4820
Documents 1930, 3459, 3742,
4859, 4929, 5430, 5557, 6118,
6803, 9591
"documents!" 3459
"documents, he will promptly return any" 696
"documents, multifarious" 5557
Dodd, Mrs. 3552
Dodge, Coach 8925
"doer, a" 4242
"dog, a" 478, 6576
"dog, big" 770
"dog, black" 10609
"dog, calling to her" 6571
"dog, dead" 10436
"dog, eating the" 3443
"dog, his" 10021
"dog, his wistful" 2497
"dog, I'd like to have a" 419
"dog, invisible" 1724
"dog, like somebody's smart little"
4626
"dog, little black" 419
"dog, man who had a" 10052
"dog, muzzled" 421
"dog, next-door" 10274
"dog, old tail-wagging weather-
beaten" 10425
"dog, rough-coated little" 994
"dog, sick" 9340
"dog, sleep like a" 8483
"dog, the" 399
"dog, the talking" 5809
"dog, tidewater" 400
"dog, walking a large" 5239
"dog, with his" 10377, 10381
"dog, yellow" 448
"dog, young" 10409
"dog appeared" 436
"dog coming from down the street"
1784
"dog crouched low on the ground"
442
"dog food, can of" 7350
"dog in the manger" 443
"dog named Daniels lay dreaming"

448
"dog of a dog" 6413
"dog sick" 151
"dog strong of muscle and with warm long hair" 400
"dog trainer" 470
"dog was a tan fice" 462
"dog was suffering" 9283
"dog who heard the sound" 8772
"dog-eared" 6883
"dogged, the" 9634
"doggedly" 7290
"doggies, by" 8925
"doggy days of the 1960s" 6467
"doghouse, shooting at his new" 576
"dogmas of superstition" 2492
Dogs 31, 379, 399, 400, 403, 405, 406, 408, 409, 412, 413, 416, 417, 419, 421, 429, 436, 442, 443, 448, 461, 462, 469, 470, 477, 478, 482, 671, 770, 973, 994, 1198, 1724, 1784, 2135, 2497, 2679, 2689, 2820, 3358, 3443, 3631, 3706, 4683, 4747, 5809, 6571, 6576, 6692, 7367, 7751, 7852, 8547, 8772, 9104, 9283, 9898, 9917, 9927, 9994, 10021, 10052, 10274, 10377, 10381, 10409, 10425, 10436, 10519, 10544, 10750
"dogs" 2679
"dogs, all fifty of our camp" 9104
"dogs, like pye-" 6820
"dogs barking" 9917
"dogs breathe in my face" 469
"dogs chased half-naked women" 516
"dogs from digging it up, keep the" 2329
"dogs had fled" 10519
"dogs in my dreams" 671
"dog's mercury" 9673
"dogs of the universe, mad" 3716
"dogs were not barking" 9927
"dogsitting" 3631
"dogwood seedlings, heavy veins of" 973
"dogwood tree, under the" 8512
Doherty, Annie 1944
"doing, how we are" 9926
"doing, supposed to be" 686
"doing, there wasn't a thing" 8365
"doing, what are you" 6547
"doing, what's the old man" 10928
"doing a certain act" 6036
"doing in there, what the fuck are you" 8238
"doing in those days, as they were" 6635
"doing it" 8008
"doing it, how to go about" 6936
"doing it right, he wasn't" 7045
"doing just now, you might better be" 4608
"doing the same thing they were doing" 1853

"doing the same thing to you" 5705
"doing this, I can't believe I'm" 2750
"doing what some men would have found more difficult" 4
"doing would be important, the" 6936
"doings, all my" 8171
"doings of a few years back, his own" 6792
"doings of this neighborhood" 8957
Doktor 8460
Dolan 9608
"doldrums, the" 8079
"dolefull copie" 7370
"doll, slumped and skewed like an oversize rag" 6859
"dollars, a hundred" 3280
"dollars, a million" 7731
"dollars, four hundred millions of" 4928
"dollars, put up one thousand" 6126
"dollars, questing after" 7229
"dollars, seven million" 3752
"dollars, thirty billion" 3738
"dollars, twenty million" 10552
"dollars, two million" 10559
Dolliver, Dr. 10111
"dolls, like the painted wooden" 4436
"dolls, Loco Poco's" 3580
"dolls he'd seen in souvenir shops" 4436
Dolores 8216, 8528
"Dolphin case" 1834
"dolphin cutting the green water" 9811
"dolphin weather, it was" 10594
Doltaire, Monsieur 8172
"domain, his" 8257
"domain, looking out over his" 404
"domaine, Toro y Plata" 455
Dombey 6519
"dome, gilded" 6678
"dome in the Old World, loftiest" 10012
"dome of green, towering" 5127
"domed, glass-" 7754
"domes, gilded" 2280
"domes and steeples rising over Russell Square" 5331
"domes of ancient churches" 2225
"domes of the Saltair Pavilion" 9181
"domestic, a" 6440
"domestic, voice of a" 6285
"domestic arrangement" 5104
"Domestic Bursar" 8354
"domestic gods" 2018
"Domestic Justice, Hall of" 2682
"domestics, the" 950
"dominant over the wild prairie" 789
"dominated the house, luncheon..." 8628
"dominated the meeting" 8707

"Dominican friar" 10388
"Dominion, Old" 8171
Domitian 5411
Domitian, Emperor 4499
"Domitian I" 5411
Domostroy, Patrick 9805
"Don, the river" 3893
Don Juan 572
Donald 1131
"Doncaster, the pleasant town of" 3893
"done, something must be" 2814
"done in Berlin, what General Melville A. Goodwin had" 9262
"done it, he had" 9271
"done to death" 1325
Donegall, Sergeant McEvoy 6970
"dong, hanging on to his" 2374
"dong, he was still holding on to his" 2374
"Dong Xuyen" 3954
Dongin, Bat 6180
"donkey brayed" 10177
"donkey that pulled the cart" 5256
"donkey-cart" 9626
"donkeys, two plumed" 6664
Donna Clementina 9870
Donnelly, Mr. 8675
Donner, John 3673
Donnington 1225
Donny 8932
Dooley, Al 910
Dooley, Maura 10840
Doom 112, 2608, 3386, 3672, 7011, 7478, 9265, 10474, 10766
"doom, none to tell them of the" 10474
"doom, passion and" 2608
"doom, reconcile me to my" 10766
"doom, sign of" 9265
"doom, tottering to" 3386
"doom jockeys" 4220
"doom was overtaking him, unaware that" 7478
"doomed, Mrs. Exley felt" 112
"doomed, regard himself publicly and privately as" 3672
"doomed, we are" 7011
"doomed by the dam" 752
"doomed to celebrate" 3461
"doomed to remember a boy" 7542
Doone 246
"Doonhaven" 1615
Doops 9084
"door, a fellow knows his own" 2711
"door, at the" 7766, 8205, 9952
"door, back" 2702, 2724
"door, banged the front" 5093
"door, barred side" 7620
"door, bathroom" 7480, 8238
"door, behind the locked" 8728
"door, black" 2727
"door, cabin" 1556
"door, came to the" 9899
"door, closed" 10139

"door, closed the" 2706
"door, closed the front" 2726
"door, closet" 4485
"door, cook house" 4212
"door, could tell by the" 2697
"door, cowhouse" 10540
"door, from behind the bathroom" 9437
"door, front" 668, 2720, 7421, 9912
"door, glass-panelled swing" 7841
"door, hinge side of the" 5979
"door, his cabin" 7025
"door, his study" 1119
"door, I opened the" 9911
"door, its greenish" 9253
"door, kicks open the" 1996
"door, knocked hard on the" 9963
"door, knocking on the" 9885
"door, locked" 2030
"door, locked his front" 9443
"door, locked the back" 10919
"door, my classroom" 5476
"door, my front" 2550
"door, my parents'" 8906
"door, oaken" 10780
"door, office" 10058
"door, open" 6624
"door, opened his vestibule" 9532
"door, opened the" 2688, 2721, 9888
"door, opened the bathroom" 577
"door, opened the bedroom" 5777
"door, opening of the" 9945
"door, opens the" 9926
"door, passed out of the great" 8546
"door, pounding sounded at the" 2784
"door, pushed open the white-washed" 2708
"door, red" 3182
"door, ruined" 9231
"door, screen" 2713, 8790, 9957, 9985
"door, sharp bang of a" 8769
"door, shut the" 2128, 3790, 9911
"door, slammed the" 1626, 3566
"door, so you go out that" 3622
"door, squeak of the cabin" 8781
"door, steel" 8318
"door, study" 7843
"door, surgery" 10295
"door, unlock his front" 1784
"door, unlocked his front" 1574
"door, weather" 8062
"door, white eight-panel" 6587
"door, wide front" 4114
"door carefully, closed the" 1594
"door for her, held the" 1783
"door gently, I pressed the" 2698
"door had been forced" 2725
"door marked CATTLEMEN'S ASSOCIATION—ENTER" 8549
"door marked FIRE EXIT" 2700
"door of a farm-house" 1572
"door of communication" 6283

"door of her mother's boudoir" 9880
"door of her penthouse" 7204
"door of his room" 9920
"door of my father's house" 1570
"door of my office" 10050
"door of the back room" 4001
"door of the Drones Club swung open" 1610
"door of the military hospital" 3988
"door of the noisy old elevator" 3295
"door of the smoking-room had been left open" 8062
"door of the surgery, closed the" 2707
"door of which was heavily timbered with oak" 3985
"door on the back wall, a little" 3195
"door on which passing boys and men had scrawled graffiti" 9253
"door opened" 8256
"door opened, the" 1605
"door opened and closed" 10008
"door opened gently" 9905
"door . . . opens on an alley" 2724
"door or a telephone pole" 2107
"door shut, pulled the" 4485
"door shut, slammed the" 1663
"door slammed shut, the screen" 1765
"door slammed shut at the back of the house" 2729
"door stood open, the cottage" 2691
"door swung open" 2694
"door that acted as street entrance" 7841
"door that served as backdrop for every Easter" 6587
"door that would not close" 6294
"door to admit me, opening the" 2770
"door to her waiting room" 6897
"door to his small two-room apartment" 1787
"door to the caboose, the steel" 8812
"door to the Mohawk Grill" 2724
"door to the parlor" 8806
"door which bangs open and shut" 10743
"door which locked from the inside" 3149
"door whose lock didn't work" 6783
"door wide, left the cabin" 3947
"door wide, opening the" 9940
"doorbell rang" 5683, 9912, 9914
"doorbell rings" 9900
"door-locking" 286
"doorman" 2720
Doors 872, 1008, 1091, 1119, 1293, 1556, 1574, 1605, 1635, 1651, 1749, 1784, 1787, 2030, 2128, 2687, 2688, 2691, 2694, 2697, 2698, 2700, 2701, 2702, 2705, 2706,

2707, 2708, 2709, 2711, 2713, 2714, 2720, 2721, 2724, 2725, 2726, 2727, 2729, 2731, 3118, 3195, 3566, 3985, 4001, 5263, 5979, 7577, 7843, 8062, 8318, 8549, 8769, 8790, 8812, 8822, 8900, 9253, 9920, 9945, 9963, 10041, 10295, 10780
"doors, cellar" 10416
"doors, closed" 2705
"doors, darken my" 1489
"doors, great hall-" 10113
"doors, out the" 9528
"doors, sliding" 7575
"doors, they are my" 1489
"doors burst open, vault" 872
"doors flew open" 9605
"doors of certain buildings were closed and locked" 4129
"doors opened, narrow double" 3963
"doors were opened, as if great furnace" 8396
"doors where children watched for the first star" 653
"doors yawning" 7887
"doorstep, on to the" 9878
"doorsteps of houses" 5928
"doorway, framed in the" 6321
"doorway, from the" 9843
"doorway, opulent baroque" 2731
"doorway of a mansion" 1580
"doorway of life" 5263
"doorway of the abode" 8790
"doorway of the royal palace" 2731
"doorway to her son's room" 10949
"doorway where Lousy and you and G.J.'s always sittin" 5445
"dope-taking" 286
Dora 9866
Dorcas 4299
Dores, Henderson 10432
Dorfman, Mrs. M. 505
"Doric columns" 3225
Doris of Colossæ 5411
"Dorking" 9789
Dorman, Capt. Oliver 8079
"dormant since its last eruption in 1902" 5052
Dormer, Egbert 2292
"dormitories for the entering class" 7905
"dormitory room" 8601
Dorne, Old Man 8882
Dornick, Gaal 4738
Dorothea 6154
Dorothy 8222, 10127
"dorp, dusty little" 10402
Dorrit, Lucian 10341
Dorrit, William 10341
"Dorset" 3022, 3215, 9412
"Dorset coast" 1440
"Dorsetshire" 3066
Dortmunder 1043, 2721
"Dorval" 4674

Dot 1643
Dots 9924
"dots of the digital clock" 10290
Dottie 3870
"double, twelve-gauge" 4694
"Double Bubble gum" 634
Doubloon, Miss Maggie 4446
Doubt 2736, 3708, 4169, 9699
"doubt, fear and" 3708
"doubt, flavour of" 2733
"doubt, I had no" 2397
"doubt, there can be no" 2187
"doubt, when in" 2740
"doubt about a doubt, dispelling of a" 2736
"doubt about it, no" 6028
"doubt left, when there was little" 4209
"doubt of his sex, there could be no" 9839
"doubt of it, there was no" 10982
"doubted that any man was capable of a love so profound" 1706
"doubted that any woman was capable of comprehending the nature of a man's passion" 1706
"doubtful, always" 9699
"doubtful, but whether it does is" 5585
"doubtful, memories were" 6793
"doubtfully" 837
"doubting His Own Self" 2625
"doubts were finally resolved" 9420
"Doucegrove" 9134
Doucet, Phil 6598
Dougall, Captain 8154
"dough, with your" 10563
"dougherty that had been converted to carry passengers" 9777
"doughnuts, two-thirds of a peck of perfect" 4670
"doughnuts just come into the world" 4670
Douglas 8030
Douglas, Supreme Court Justice William 5207
Douglass 4911
"Doune Fair, day after" 8952
"Douro" 9148
Douthit, Spence 1024
"dove" 763
"Dover" 728
Dover, Major 1684
"Dover, Castle of" 1174
"Dover Station" 5895
"doves, descending like" 2623
"doves came down from their wooden house" 10657
Dow, Maddy 6691
"dowery of ruined villages" 6245
Dowling, Lucius 2302
"down, almost large enough to be called a" 3634
"down, getting me" 937
"down, must get this" 5478

"down, over the" 9092
"down, top of the" 10344
"down . . . but not out" 7199
"down from him" 4437
"down on the asphalt" 8949
"down the stairway of his house" 3826
"down the tunnel and out into the cold" 10190
"downcast eyes" 2493
"downer, song was a" 8755
"downfall of Count Kornowski" 2592
"downfall of the Fleishman family" 3627
"downhill, no wonder everything had run" 2334
"downhill, you're going" 4983
"downpour, full-sized respectable" 7293
"Downs, Bundel" 857
"downs, chalk" 6923
"Downs, the" 2228
"downstairs in the hall, we're all" 6705
"downtown, the eight-block crescent of" 1481
"downtown Baltimore" 3184
"downtown renovation" 1453
"downwardly mobile" 77
Doyle 3528
Doyle, Patrick 6181
"doze, fell into a" 8456
"doze, her" 10307
"doze, roused him from the" 10181
"doze on the couch" 10318
"dozed in his wheelchair" 8461
"dozed in the train, must have" 8457
"dozed the village, so tranquilly" 10700
"dozing" 10139
"dozing, half" 10085
"dozing, he is" 8473
"dozing over her knitting" 10180
"drab in a ditch, not littered by a" 358
Dracula, Count 5826
"draft, came to Egypt with the" 8685
"draft, first" 1926
"draft, fourth" 8528
"draft, icy" 9215
"draft, in this stale" 8528
"draft from the inn chimneys" 3421
"drafted to fight, he was to be" 9654
"drag, took a last futile" 8575
"drag her from the house" 7739
"drag the body from the breakfast table" 2329
"dragged a garden hose across the lawn by its sprinkler" 4901
"dragged a stick" 10164
"dragged along" 994

"dragged back under the first of the stars" 420
"dragged by a stage-coach" 9515
Draggett, Colin 5211
"dragging, her heavy bag" 6102
"dragging accolades behind me" 5587
"dragging the pushchair" 672
"dragon, ice-" 10725
"Dragoon Arizona" 9977
"drain-pipes, subterranean" 10930
"drains, this opening of all the" 1337
Drake 295
Drake, Joan 2311
Drake, Sir Francis 9508
Drake, Stoner 2311
"drama, costume" 7868
"drama, making a" 7388
"drama, my personal" 3495
"dramas of life and love" 5566
"dramas recorded in the daily press, the unfinished" 6349
"dramatis personae" 5414
"drank, never" 2897
"drank, those who" 6760
"drank cool wine from tall glasses" 8027
"drank down a half bottle of the Silver Sun's best" 2904
"drank in the wind" 7131
"drank too much, somebody" 3600
"draped the dust-cloth over the head of an andiron" 10916
"draught that crept in the corners of the great chamber" 5324
"draughts, playing" 5653
"draw a glass of water" 7561
"drawbacks, two most serious" 10775
"drawing a line of the tablecloth with his knife" 9285
"drawing of an American" 508
"drawing of an envelope" 1918
"drawing up the household weekly accounts" 10926
"drawing water" 2906
"drawing-board, large" 3326
"drawing-room" 484
"drawingroom" 7768
"drawing-room was entirely English" 7773
"drawled out" 8172
"drawn back, I am always" 3142
"drawn by six horses" 9759
"drawn by the mystique of their own past" 4012
"drawn by two horses and two mules" 3069
Drayton, James 9641
Drayton, Sir Benjamin 9313
Dread 927, 1553, 2163, 3478, 3698, 3730, 3734, 10083
"dread" 1553, 10083
"dread, excitement and" 3478

"dread, far more" 2492
"dread, nameless" 3698
"dread, possessed with" 1112
"dread, seemed not to share his" 3730
"dread they have of moping, you know what a" 927
"dreaded, the day Um Mona" 2163
"dreaded the summer" 5364
"dreaded their return home" 4559
"dreadful little nerves, my" 9285
"dreading the whole idea" 3734
"_Dreadnought_" 7870
"dream, a" 6272
"dream, amorphous iridescent blue almost black" 2803
"Dream, as I slept I dreamed a" 2751
"dream, as in a recurring" 4485
"dream, as she might recall a" 8297
"dream, begin to" 4890
"dream, begun like a" 2774
"dream, blueprint of a" 4701
"dream, charming" 2752
"dream, complex troubling" 10127
"dream, contradicting a" 4701
"dream, drifting in and out of a" 8834
"dream, dying" 10202
"dream, enjoying her" 2757
"dream, fathoms of his" 10202
"dream, he was having a pleasant" 2785
"dream, her" 10222
"dream, his" 2811, 8757
"dream, I had a disagreeable" 2792
"dream, I had this" 2788
"dream, I was detained by a" 2781
"dream, in Devon's" 2564
"dream, in his" 2778, 2787
"dream, in the" 7040, 10434
"dream, in this" 2761
"dream, in your" 2463
"dream, it was a marvelous" 2767
"dream, it was a weird" 2773
"dream, jolted Maureen from her" 10258
"dream, last wisps of" 10287
"dream, like waking out of a" 4578
"dream, man in her" 2809
"dream, Nathan had the" 2807
"dream, probed viciously into the diseased pulp of his" 10229
"dream, pursuing anxiously the shapes of her" 10121
"dream, settler's" 1377
"dream, story of my" 8966
"dream, substantial" 10121
"dream, this real bad" 2788
"dream, this was his" 2801
"dream, trying to go on with his" 10163
"dream, uneasy breath of a" 2759
"dream, whenever I want to" 2816
"dream, woman in her" 10444

"dream about God, had a" 2783
"dream about his daughter" 2773
"dream about the Prison" 2762
"dream again, that" 2782
"dream city" 6584
"dream dissolved in the dim light" 10287
"dream ended, when the" 10252
"dream from antiquity suddenly stirring to life" 1464
"dream in the dream" 1284
"dream is incomplete, his" 2779
"dream many times before, he had seen the" 2789
"dream not quite recalled, like a" 8676
"dream of an ancient wood" 2754
"dream of country cottages, many people" 2780
"dream of his life" 250
"dream of murder" 6204
"dream of my maternal grandfather" 4113
"dream of my parents" 6684
"dream of splendid future" 9991
"dream remained, nothing of the" 2802
"dream she was having evaporates" 2814
"dream subsided leaving him awake" 10130
"dream that anything untoward was to happen to him" 405
"dream that I was sitting on the sidewalk on Moody Street" 5445
"dream that she was still beautiful Wilma Filmer" 2756
"dream turns a corner" 7960
"dream which seems to have originated from nowhere" 2774
"dreamboat, a" 7731
"dreamed" 6550
"dreamed, beauty he had" 5916
"dreamed, half" 7947
"dreamed, he so rarely" 2765
"dreamed, last night I" 2791
"dreamed, strength to do as he" 4704
"dreamed a fellow asked me if I wanted a dog" 419
"dreamed about Alma Crescent" 2795
"dreamed about fish last night" 2770
"dreamed again of the Café Stieckus" 2806
"dreamed he walked" 3902
"dreamed he was deer hunting" 429
"dreamed just before opening his eyes" 2766
"dreamed of, ever" 1444
"dreamed of a boy" 963
"dreamed of Camelot, I'd always" 3234
"dreamed of Evangeline, I often"

2776
"dreamed of him, sometimes I still" 2800
"dreamed of the Kentucky Derby" 8458
"dreamed out its life in peace and prayer" 6249
"dreamed someday of being old enough" 246
"dreamed that Billy couldn't breathe" 2798
"dreamed that she was walking" 6402
"dreamed the solution" 6904
"Dreaminess, her" 127
"dreaming" 956, 2758, 10139
"dreaming, dog named Daniels lay" 448
"dreaming, dreamt I was" 2775
"dreaming, Milo was" 2765
"dreaming, Mrs. Bantry was" 2757
"dreaming, Nicola was" 2769
"dreaming about a hairless ape" 426
"dreaming in the Asian alpine sunshine" 247
"dreaming in the heather, lay" 2797
"dreaming of men screaming and dying" 2784
"dreaming of soft-bodied women" 2772
"dreaming of the old house in New Orleans again" 2804
"dreaming that Alexander Pushkin was beside her" 2794
"dreaming with new intensity" 2793
"dreamland, uncharted region beyond" 10131
"dreamless hours, glorious" 8455
"dreamlets, my" 10955
Dreams 247, 250, 258, 419, 426, 429, 448, 956, 963, 1252, 1284, 1377, 2463, 2564, 3234, 3902, 4113, 4561, 4578, 4701, 4890, 4936, 5445, 5916, 6204, 6272, 6379, 6402, 6550, 6684, 6904, 7040, 7747, 7856, 7960, 8434, 8458, 8757, 8834, 8966, 10121, 10127, 10130, 10139, 10140, 10156, 10163, 10202, 10209, 10222, 10229, 10252, 10258, 10285, 10287, 10291, 10299, 10434, 10444, 10546
"dreams, as so many of his" 2767
"dreams, dogs in my" 671
"dreams, duke of" 4800
"dreams, familiar" 10291
"dreams, his heart was full of" 258
"dreams, I know her from my" 2812
"dreams, in" 7824
"dreams, in half-" 243
"dreams, in my" 2760
"dreams, it's often that way with bad" 2813
"dreams, like one who walks in" 10352

"dreams, liquid and vaporous" 2212

"dreams, many of her" 8434

"dreams, not the home-coming of his" 4561

"dreams, patchy" 6379

"dreams, pictures that thronged my" 2753

"dreams, remember my" 2816

"dreams, serene republic of our" 5297

"dreams, sleep without" 2771

"dreams, sometimes in my" 2796

"dreams, thoughts and" 10156

"dreams a night, ten thousand" 2815

"dreams and memory, confusion of" 10299

"dreams had come to nothing, so many" 4561

"dreams of playing football" 8922

"dreams of the sleeping, raked the" 2790

"dreams still take place here" 2818

"dreams stood around her cot again" 2799

"dreams that night, he entered her" 2805

"dreams to be realised" 6088

"dreams turn to mockery or abasement of spirit" 2767

"dreams were many lovers, in her" 7747

"dreams which had overflowed into life" 4936

"dreamt about Kennedy's assassination" 2815

"dreamt I was dreaming" 2775

"dreamt I went to Manderley" 2755

"dreamt of Caroline again, last night I" 2777

"dreariest aspect" 1368

"dreary" 5889

"dregs to drip into their open mouths" 5632

"drenched, I'm" 10939

"drenched to the skin by the chill rain" 7290

"drenching the cotton lands" 7323

Dress 954, 966, 1002, 1207, 1313, 1501, 1544, 1548, 1554, 1569, 1982, 2432, 2658, 2719, 2787, 2914, 3554, 3582, 3961, 3963, 3985, 3987, 4117, 4165, 4191, 4207, 4226, 4309, 4331, 4406, 4921, 5257, 5800, 5901, 5910, 5920, 5927, 5940, 5958, 5966, 6388, 6399, 6495, 6536, 6702, 6868, 7108, 7122, 7133, 7469, 7470, 7483, 7538, 8009, 8098, 8384, 8385, 8453, 8500, 8631, 9753, 9839, 9851, 9937, 10054, 10335, 10336, 10373, 10388, 10415, 10421, 10660, 10735, 10776, 10783, 10819, 10830, 10833, 10850, 10860, 10863, 10922

"dress, blue velvet" 4207

"dress, bridesmaid's" 10660

"dress, can no longer be troubled to" 5958

"dress, crinkly copper-coloured sort of" 6562

"dress, doesn't she have a nice" 2877

"*Dress*, every *Part* of their" 10764

"dress, her tight-fitting Persian" 2832

"dress, I kept pulling at her" 6694

"dress, if he rumpled his" 3272

"dress, in evening" 1569

"dress, long white" 10784

"dress, lovely silk" 10784

"dress, organdy" 8241

"dress, perpetually soup-stained" 9370

"dress, poor" 10776

"dress, putting on a" 10830

"dress, red plaid" 7122

"dress, sullen silk" 2658

"dress, sunshine-yellow" 1432

"dress, their full summer" 9742

"dress, white silk" 10441

"dress, yellow" 7483

"dress of the artistic order" 6562

"dress quivers, green sequined" 1982

"dress rehearsal" 9387

"dress she would wear, the" 2064

"dress tends to the conservative, my mode of" 4789

"dress that hung down to her ankles" 10784

"dress whites" 8137

"dressed, a man merely" 2823

"dressed, badly" 2843

"dressed, fully" 10265

"dressed all in black" 6708

"dressed as a Neapolitan Acquaiola" 10783

"dressed as chickens, two people" 2867

"dressed as if for a costume party" 3961

"dressed himself hurriedly" 10275

"dressed in a white shirt" 970

"dressed in all he could borrow" 2973

"dressed in black" 10850

"dressed in his best" 964

"dressed in ratty jeans" 2872

"dressed in slacks shirt and sweater" 2852

"dressed in sport shirts from Sulka and Cardin" 309

"dressed in the same clothes" 3693

"dressed in various shades of light brown" 3582

"dressed not for a funeral but as if she were attending the opera" 3963

"dressed now, get" 6891

"dressed up, get" 2863

"dresser, supposedly solid-walnut" 1057

"dresses, elegance of the" 9376

"dresses, modish" 1302

"dresses, one of his stiff starched piqué" 3272

"dresses, summer" 8864

Dressing 964, 1251, 2836, 8631, 10830

"dressing, Mrs. Sylvester Perkins was" 2836

"dressing for dinner" 8631

"dressing room" 7487

"dressing table" 7476

"dressing tent" 5317

"dressing that morning" 1251

"dressing up" 2883

"drew a fine family tree" 360

"drew a little more closely together" 4003

"drew pictures in the sand" 6933

"drier and dustier" 4388

"drift, four-foot" 8600

"drift away into the desert" 7654

"drift into the March mist" 7457

"drifted awake" 10310

"drifted from the overgrown graves" 1194

"drifted into Exeter" 6570

"drifted into the bar-room" 4333

"drifter, mackerel" 8135

"drifting in and out of a dream" 8834

"driftwood that bore them to shore" 1217

"drill, in white" 8161

Drill-Pig 4764

"drink, bellied down to" 4673

"drink, come for a" 1143

"drink, I want a" 4672

"drink, let us" 2931

"drink, lips still glistened with" 2925

"drink, mixing a short" 9914

"drink, this" 2923

"drink, this is my last" 2888

"drink, those who did not" 6760

"drink, to have asked them over for a" 2920

"drink alcohol, sometimes I" 4789

"drink all the wine in the world, decided to" 2933

"drink all you want, you can" 4672

"drink and play cards" 2057

"drink and whore and play the horses" 322

"drink hot toddies" 3394

"drink lobes, jars my" 8797

"drink palm-wine in my life" 5281

"drink several pints of beer" 6570

"drink together" 1834

"drink wine with a thousand of his lords" 6752

"drink your ginger ale" 2426

"drinkard, I was a palm-wine" 5281
"drinkers, beer" 2936
"Drinker's Hour, The" 4220
Drinking 295, 322, 574, 899, 1143, 1203, 1834, 2209, 2351, 2509, 2885, 2886, 2887, 2888, 2890, 2892, 2893, 2896, 2897, 2898, 2900, 2901, 2904, 2906, 2907, 2911, 2912, 2913, 2915, 2916, 2917, 2918, 2919, 2920, 2921, 2922, 2923, 2924, 2925, 2927, 2929, 2931, 2933, 2934, 2935, 2936, 2937, 2938, 2939, 2940, 2941, 2942, 3394, 3848, 4272, 4274, 4318, 4319, 4324, 4335, 4336, 5186, 5229, 5281, 5357, 6010, 6570, 6752, 6760, 6783, 7728, 9173, 9300, 9321, 9914, 10729
"drinking, began" 2934
"drinking, watched the man" 2890
"drinking a cup of coffee" 3282
"drinking a lot" 2938
"drinking beer from a bottle" 2351
"drinking black coffee with ice-cream in it" 8634
"drinking bout, another" 2906
"drinking brandy" 2209
"drinking brandy, still up" 2929
"drinking club called the Crypt" 4319
"drinking gin and tonics" 2919
"drinking lime juice" 6010
"drinking rum Co-Colas" 4336
"drinking tavern" 3994
"drinking too much, told himself he was" 2935
"drinks, put aside" 1201
"drinks table" 2940
"drinks were being served" 4314
"drip in its tin cup" 5077
"drip of the rain" 3836
Driscoll, Commander James 5417
Driscoll, John Chrysostom Spartacus (Sparky) 2386
"drive, did nothing but" 3037
"Drive, FDR" 9807
"drive, how I learned to" 6683
"drive, I'll" 3013
"Drive, Memorial" 2999
"drive, motor-" 2953
"Drive, Peninsula" 2971
"Drive, Rodeo" 7229
"drive, shadowy" 1000
"drive, throughout their entire" 10997
"drive, wartime" 10529
"drive cars for delivery" 1054
"drive from Salerno to Sambuco" 9155
"drive in to work, the long" 5104
"drive me to his cabin in the Big Sur woods" 2906
"drive north, only an hour's" 4544
"drive out, agrees to" 4526
"drive out to have a look at George

Lockwood's wall" 1853
"drive slowly down its slope" 2970
"drive through the town" 3014
"drive to Thrushcross Grange" 3000
"drive up to the Junction" 2967
"drive-aways" 1054
"drive-ins" 1039
"driven and romantic enough, if one was" 1448
"driven by a fat coachman" 9757
"driven by Sammy his man" 2973
"driven eastward toward the place where he was born" 4572
"driven from all the countries of the world" 6109
"driven in to the place about five in the afternoon" 2981
"driven onward by the wind" 2337
"driven through pelting rain" 4636
"driven with such impatient exuberance" 40
"driver, bulky ambulance-" 131
"driver, bus" 7311
"driver, cab" 10085
"driver, car-hire" 8658
"driver, hi" 7376
"driver, his father's" 6550
"driver, stage" 2900
"driver, taxi" 4992
"driver, the" 10749
"driver, truck" 3023
"driver, wasn't just a taxi" 6490
"driver of the truck" 9553
"driver of the wagon" 4144
"driver was always punctual" 10093
"driver was dead" 7855
"driver was getting irritable" 2972
"driver was tall and dark and handsome" 8658
Drivers 2900, 2942, 2972, 4992, 7311, 7376, 8658, 10093, 10529
"drivers, taxi" 9161
"drivers, three new truck" 1023
"driver's hand" 9617
"drives me to a little beach" 5177
"driveway, long curving" 8372
"driveway, winding and oak-shaded furlong of" 412
Driving 40, 41, 286, 382, 384, 485, 755, 878, 1191, 1193, 1242, 1378, 1668, 1730, 1845, 2337, 2339, 2361, 2656, 2884, 3138, 3178, 3411, 3620, 3623, 3630, 3723, 3730, 4144, 4164, 4168, 4363, 4393, 4572, 4961, 5347, 6030, 6323, 6381, 6575, 6624, 6683, 6942, 6970, 7202, 7327, 7457, 8282, 8307, 8319, 8782, 8925, 9143, 9161, 9183, 9201, 9228, 9346, 9361, 9428, 9589, 9717, 9786, 9802, 9807, 9817, 9821, 9828, 9829, 9870, 9921, 9969, 10036, 10093, 10960, 10997
"driving, attention was on her" 2990

"driving, fat girl with the glasses is" 3620
"driving, liked" 3027
"driving, man who was" 3138
"driving, Sam Hughes is" 3025
"driving, sister who is" 3028
"driving, the car he was" 2339
"driving, they had been" 2972
"driving alone" 2956
"driving along the broad federal highway" 2966
"driving along the road in France" 3024
"driving away after only five days" 5053
"driving carefully" 2957
"driving down the high-speed exit lane" 2998
"driving from Carson to Reno" 2952
"driving from London to Dorset" 3022
"driving home" 3019
"driving home with our hats on the side of our heads" 3341
"driving in the enormous brown coachwork Daimler" 2960
"driving like that" 2983
"driving my son to college" 3039
"driving north on Route 27" 2994
"driving out to Howard Beach" 3020
"driving 61" 9228
"driving the car" 7202
"driving through fog along the Maine coast" 7457
"driving through mountains and desert and now mountains again" 2972
"driving to Las Vegas" 3623
"driving what remains of their gaunt cattle before them" 3668
"drizzle, beginning to" 4615
"drizzle, chill early morning" 7087
"drizzle, cold thick" 4306
"drizzle, in this cold" 729
"drizzle, light" 3940
"drizzle, steady" 1399
"drizzle blown by a biting wind" 4306
"drizzle coated Haledon N.J." 7345
"drizzle falling on yellow leaves & damp ground" 310
"drizzle of rain" 7316
"drizzling" 7293
"drizzling, it was" 7295
"drizzling outside" 7569
"droll and amusing things" 7884
"drone rising and falling, its" 5688
"drooling, stop" 2528
"drooping horse-car" 1012
"drooping like a wet sock" 8257
"drooping on a fine evening, day was" 2945
"drooping with fatigue" 3693

"drop of a hat, at the" 10976
"drop thy pipe thy happy pipe" 2230
"droplets, trajectory of the teeming" 4901
"dropout, sixth-grade" 6170
"dropped dead at Taunton races" 1684
"dropped exhausted" 3687
"dropped from nowhere onto the underbrush" 3458
"dropped from the sky, they seemed to have" 10477
"dropped him, the cab" 1678
"dropped his trousers" 7858
"dropped into a basket-chair" 4305
"dropped it before she realized what had happened" 5118
"dropped off Leah at dawn" 1716
"dropped the receiver" 9916
"dropped the *Spectator*" 696
"dropped the stub of his cigarette" 298
"dropped us he was with us, even when he" 9399
"dropper, medicine" 6589
"dropping darkly down, afternoon was" 9354
"dropping into bed" 10392
"dropping lazily into a chair" 8172
"dropping the screen door against the frame" 1769
"droppings of generations of heedless unpatriotic pigeons" 8947
"drops, sharp bottomless" 5572
"drops, sheet of muddy" 7321
"drops clumsily out of an acacia tree" 475
"drops jabbed into her eyes and chilled her cheeks" 2946
"drops rattled loudly on the tarpauling clothing" 10704
"dross, yellow" 1420
"dross of a full half century's frenetic burrowing for gold" 1420
Drought 7031, 7314
"drought year" 366
"droughts of 1924 and 1925" 2592
"drove aimlessly" 2976
"drove along the east road" 485
"drove around the side of the house" 10960
"drove away" 1599
"drove between the two big stringy-barks" 9773
"drove contentedly through the evening sunlight" 2991
"drove down from his university town" 2988
"drove down Main Street hill" 2968
"drove from Bakersfield California to Chinatown" 3630
"drove going, Aurora" 3043
"drove his Buick back from a real-estate trip to Kentucky" 2971

"drove home, Rosie" 3043
"drove it . . . down the main street of the town" 2961
"drove most of the people off the street" 10699
"drove north along the South Dixie Highway" 2997
"drove north to Lichfield through the morning" 3010
"drove northward along the Palisades" 2958
"drove out in an open carriage" 9559
"drove out there from Brooklyn" 6575
"drove over the low pass" 2986
"drove past Tiny Polski's mansion house" 286
"drove slowly into the small town" 3007
"drove slowly through the open countryside of Dirrabeg" 3042
"drove the Buick Riviera" 9786
"drove the Lincoln" 3018
"drove there from Nestor or Wal mouth" 1894
"drove through the woods" 2989
"drove through Yorkville" 384
"drove to the Palazzo Conti" 9870
"drove uncertainly along the avenue" 2951
"drove up, when he" 1751
"drove up in a borrowed Mercedes" 9802
"drove up in her trap" 10036
"drove up in one of the station taxis" 9921
"drove up to Flanders" 3015
"drove up to the great iron gate" 9757
"drove up to the house" 382
"drove up to the house on a private road" 3005
"drove us out of Berea" 1679
"drove with his moist palms gripping the wheel" 2980
"drown his kittens, still could not get himself to" 6652
"drown in San Francisco Bay" 4887
"drowned car" 2946
"drowned in the tides, felt as if half" 7913
"drowned-man act, stage the" 6680
Drowning 2798, 3674
"drowning, if I were" 3674
"drowning, learned of the" 2798
"drowning, like one raised from" 10134
"drowning, rescuing someone from" 248
Drowning Kid, The 10094
"drowsily, harkened" 7305
"drowsy" 2794
"drowsy, found themselves suddenly very" 3912

"drowsy buzzing day in July" 2156
"drowsy traveller" 10108
Druff 7456
"drug store, the corner" 2948
"drugged eye, my" 1452
"drugget carpet" 7753
"druggist by the name of Timothy Partridge" 1025
Drugs 166, 1515, 4509, 5846, 6170, 6276, 10291
"drugs, successfully treated with" 166
"drugs, without pain or" 10291
"drugs help me bend my fingers around a pen" 3051
"drug-smuggling trade" 3054
"drugstore" 8308
"drug-store" 9407
"drugstore, headed for the nearest" 26
"drugstore, Marvin Conklin's" 5370
"Drugstore, Mosby's" 3866
"Drugstore, Pearson's" 7490
"Drugstore, Steadman's" 1772
"drugstore, went into a" 6894
"drugstore products" 1067
"Druid City" 4068
"drum and trumpet, follow the" 5397
"Drumheller Alberta" 4966
"Drumlithie" 4053
"drummer, twelve year old snare-" 6219
"drummer of sixty, bass-" 6219
Drummond, Kate 3967
Drummond, Lieutenant-Commander Keith 10407
"drums begin, the" 8814
"drunk, Aunt Natasha was" 2902
"drunk, being" 2374
"drunk, boy got too" 2329
"drunk, Clem was" 2903
"drunk, dead" 2901
"drunk, Elmer Gantry was" 2889
"drunk, eloquently" 2889
"drunk, getting silly" 2906
"drunk, I was" 2932
"drunk, lovingly and pugnaciously" 2889
"drunk, makes a man" 8514
"drunk, marrying a" 5771
"drunk, quite" 2930
"drunk, she felt a little" 10414
"drunk, she got so" 8012
"drunk, stone" 2914
"drunk, too" 2895
"drunk, watched the stage driver get" 2900
"drunk and celebrating" 9978
"drunk and the homeless have washed up in the lee of walls" 10416
"drunk blissfully out of my mind" 9300
"drunk but not blindly so" 2894

"drunk in a Rolls-Royce Silver Wraith" 2899

"drunk sometimes on flood" 7670

"drunkard, formerly a" 9571

"drunken, a little" 8742

"drunken strangers in a Turkish bath" 4504

"drunkenly, wobbled" 10445

Drunkenness 1804, 2329, 2374, 2687, 2885, 2888, 2889, 2891, 2894, 2895, 2898, 2899, 2900, 2901, 2902, 2903, 2905, 2906, 2907, 2908, 2909, 2910, 2913, 2914, 2918, 2926, 2928, 2930, 2932, 2935, 4973, 5281, 5771, 6372, 7140, 7670, 8012, 8137, 8514, 8742, 9300, 9978, 10445

"drunker than ever" 2908

"dry" 2151

"dry, considerably too" 7804

"dry that summer" 10576

Dryden, Mister 6938

"dryers, hot breath of" 6017

"drying himself in the wash house" 660

"Duality, the Place of" 2635

Duane 576

Dube, Maurice 4107

"Dublin" 1600, 2024, 3081, 4517, 4604, 5140, 5194, 5906, 7151, 8580

"Dublin, in the north of" 6437

"Dublin day of Sunday, this empty lonely" 9618

Dubois, Bob 9027

Dubois, Robert Raymond 9027

Dubois, Teddy 9027

Dubuque, Dr. Vince 8886

"ducat to fall below fifty groats and dip against the écu" 6345

"duchess, the" 572

"Duchess, the" 952, 8714

"duchess, young" 7708

"duchess of Cornwall" 5662

"Duchess of Windsor" 3679

"Duchess of Wrexe" 489

"Duchy, across the" 10590

"Duchy of Grand Fenwick" 4062, 8866

"duck flying in from the south" 753

"duck stumps, stubble of" 770

"duck that stretched its neck in hopes of becoming a goose" 773

Duckling 2574

"duckpond, a little" 3119

"ducks, knee-deep pile of" 4667

"ducks floating on the lawn, mahogany" 9436

"ducks swam" 735

"ducks were caught by their feet" 770

"dude, he's just an infernal" 4974

"dude, something of a" 5890

Dudley, Bruce 5133

Dudley, Stephen 6404

"due early next morning" 8089

"due to go up into the Big Girls, I was" 10973

Dufalette, Gloria 1100

Duff, Michael 7305

Dufore, Marie 2456

Dufresne, Mme. 9940

"dug in my heels like a hauled mule" 6136

"dug the numerals out in the spongy stone" 8663

"dugout, company headquarters" 8653

"dugout, paddled the" 1052

"Dugton, town of" 2374

Duk, Donald 2115

"duke of dreams" 4800

Duke, Lilly 5119

"Duke of Bedford" 4554

"Duke of Dewlap" 7708

"Duke of Gloucester" 4554

"Duke of Granbörg" 3879

"Duke of Greenwich" 354

"Duke of Northumberland" 1196

"Duke of Omnium" 7060, 8714

"Duke of Somerset" 7886

"Duke of St. James" 834

"Duke of Strelsau" 5082

"Duke of Wellington" 9881

"Duke of Windsor" 10669

"Duke of Windsor's wedding day" 10669

"Duke of York" 10466

"dulcet-voiced" 5998

"dull" 939

"dull, deadly" 7513

"dull, quite extraordinarily" 2539

"dull and tedious, unusually" 5275

"dull as stone" 5325

"dull day" 4513

"dull enough reading" 1910

"dull place" 6805

"dull place, terribly" 1456

"dull sky" 3044

"dulled, all sounds were" 8787

"dullest books ever written" 920

"dulling the silver surface of the lake" 1178

Duluoz, Gerard 2336

"Duluth" 1451

"Dulverton" 9586

Dumas, Clemence 4787

"dumbbell, ill-proportioned" 8232

"dummies shouting Hurry on" 1831

"dummy, blind" 9718

"dump, the" 6431

"dump of the Echo Mine, the gray" 6062

"dumpling, very soft very large apple" 4753

"dumpsters, gulls circle" 186

"Dun Laoghaire Harbor" 8660

Duncan 5843, 10014, 10165

"Duncan's Bottom" 8793

"Duncansby Head" 8154

Dundee, Lord Viscount 10465

"dune, on top of the" 10098

"Dunedin harbour" 8170

"dunes" 2285, 10700

"dunes, desert of sand" 5130

"dungeon" 1182

"dungeon part of the castle itself, is the" 1182

"dunghill behind the byre" 1863

"Dunkirk, came back from" 4566

Dunlavin 3968

Dunn, Thomas 4690

Dunne, Artie 10953

Dunne, Grace Hogan 10832

"Dunnet, coast town of" 1350

"dunnock, female" 765

"Dunwich" 1436

"duodecimal volumes" 2555

"duplicity, only by an effort of" 6517

Dupont, Shereel 7093

Dupree, Guy 2664

Duran, Serge 7851

Durand, Filmore 488

Durant, Grady 2869

Durant, Miss 2581

"Durants Neck" 8110

Durgin, Joe 6458

Durham, John 10037

Durham, Merelene 10306

Durland, Grace 2467

"Durraghglass" 5963

Dusk 869, 1407, 1437, 2126, 2186, 2195, 2196, 2198, 2199, 2200, 2205, 2209, 2215, 2219, 2222, 2223, 2235, 2265, 2266, 2276, 2278, 2282, 2405, 3090, 3720, 5068, 7263, 7292, 7347, 8050, 8389, 10425

"dusk, at" 4261, 7288

"dusk, autumn" 2119

"dusk, brief interval of grey" 2227

"dusk, cool spring" 3090

"dusk, dawn or" 2278

"dusk, dying away of wind at" 5068

"dusk, in the" 3483

"dusk, probably it was towards" 5871

"dusk, swallowed up in the" 2199

"dusk, translucent" 8470

"dusk, [twilight] was falling in throbs of gathered" 2196

"dusk dropped into the air" 2265

"dusk fell drowsy and soft" 3090

"dusk fell on her eighteenth birthday" 869

"dusk had fallen on Blandings Castle" 1178

"dusk in Washington, a summer's" 1437

"dusk like soft blue smoke" 2198

"dusk of a summer night" 2200

"dusk of an October evening" 10780

"dusk of the Indian Nations was settling swiftly" 2215

"dusk settling over the Caribbean" 6403
"dusk was cold" 2405
Dussault, Jean 5209
"Düsseldorf, outside the old gates of" 9255
Dust 1056, 2952, 8768, 9772, 10712, 10726
"dust, acrid sweetish" 5142
"dust, amid garret" 4154
"dust, billowing cloud of" 3009
"dust, bleaching" 4379
"dust, blowing" 7623
"dust, clouds of yellow" 8768
"dust, column of yellow" 7639
"dust, covered with" 922
"dust, dry road" 10425
"dust, filled with" 10581
"dust, flying grains of human" 6837
"dust, gathering" 1067, 10726
"dust, leaving only the running" 10705
"dust, long trail of" 9772
"dust, obscured by" 9792
"dust, rain-spattered" 3246
"dust, red" 8674
"dust, showering its" 10705
"dust, sullen banner of" 2952
"dust and ashes drifted in the wind" 10614
"dust and languor, season of" 2236
"dust boil up in the valley" 2952
"dust came first" 10712
"dust cloud" 9151
"dust coming down the quarter" 2983
"dust danced in its orange glow, specks of" 5339
"dust from his throat, cleared the" 2904
"dust from where you have been, a bit of the" 7494
"dust has settled, now that the" 76
"dust motes" 7763
"dust of Steeple Bumpleigh from our tyres, shaken the" 3341
"dust of the earth" 2641
"dust on his shoes" 10365
"dust rising behind her" 7639
"dust slid down the grooves in their tin roofs" 1056
"dust that was light, brown-orange" 7758
"dust was thick" 1056
"dust would fly into the open air" 2831
"dustbin standing on guard outside the mortuary" 8575
"dustier, drier and" 4388
"dustman who tipped the rubbish on to the dump" 6431
"dusty" 5889
"dusty, hot and" 1337
"dusty dusty" 2151
"dusty shoes" 4176

"dusty world" 1221
"Dutch, damned the" 3396
"Dutch, the" 1221
"Dutch, the careful" 1851
"Dutch border" 7264
"Dutch countryside, flat" 7246
"Dutch Customs Brigade" 8463
"Dutch East Indies" 10523
"Dutch pictures" 8342
"Dutchman, care a cent if she did marry a" 5729
"dutie of us, claymes not only this" 7370
Duties 1269, 6342, 6413, 9260, 9872, 9934, 10704
"duties, one of my" 6342
"duties, they have other" 6413
"duties kept them on deck" 10704
Duty 5387, 7370, 9879
"duty, became his" 1269
"duty, didn't like the" 6444
"duty, it becometh a sort of" 5387
"duty, on night" 7138
"duty, relieved from an irksome" 7107
"duty, sense of" 9879
"duty, the doing of a disagreeable" 9872
"duty, they had done their" 9934
"duty aboard" 941
"duty both equally bound to it" 6604
"duty in life to be agreeable" 5457
"duty to inform him" 6517
"duty to say a few words" 694
Duval, Claud 3396
Duval, Claude 360
Duval, Madame Sophie 6571
Duvarney, Madame 8172
Duveen, Praxis 4181
"Duxbury Massachusetts" 8048
"dwarf, that monstrous" 6647
"dwarf, there lived a" 340
"dwarf, when you first meet a" 5835
"dwarfed all others, one aspect of the world that" 7924
"dwarfed and odd-shapen" 6551
"dwarfed them" 6062
"dwarfing the towers of Chrysler and Pan Am" 6513
Dwarfs 340, 5835, 9620
"dwarfs, all the people were" 9620
Dwayne 10977
"dwell high upon the mountain" 6820
"dwell within, those who" 1347
"dwellers in a wood" 9661
"dwelling, handsome brick" 5628
"dwelling, his own" 2496
"dwelling he recently had had built" 5628
"dwelling in a great and goodly city by the sea" 1348
"dwelling of a human being" 6167
"dwelling on her past" 6793

"dwelling place, serene and comfortable" 3248
Dwellings 156, 438, 746, 937, 1179, 1557, 1600, 1749, 1772, 1774, 1859, 1932, 1956, 1983, 2001, 2161, 2327, 2691, 2711, 2758, 2822, 3443, 3621, 3695, 3762, 3780, 4006, 4347, 4477, 5079, 5292, 5784, 6111, 6117, 6145, 6163, 6165, 6167, 6266, 6280, 6294, 6339, 6456, 7042, 7134, 7415, 7515, 7725, 7753, 7769, 7770, 7771, 7775, 7841, 8270, 8387, 8573, 8727, 8730, 8869, 9223, 9243, 9253, 9443, 9466, 9738, 9966
"dwellings" 3197
"dwellings, circumfusion of those mean" 9223
"dwellings, endless array of suburban" 3242
"dwellings, model" 6270
"dwellings, modest one- and two-story frame" 1349
"dwellings, such ignoble and non-descript" 6266
"dwellings that swarmed like an epidemic around its Outer Walls" 9223
"dwelt the clan of Murdock" 3570
Dworkin, Mel 5860
"*Dybbuk, The*" 9395
"dybbukn, the" 2799
"dye fumes" 2941
Dying 101, 124, 150, 754, 1697, 2019, 2286, 2289, 2292, 2296, 2299, 2302, 2307, 2309, 2311, 2314, 2315, 2316, 2318, 2319, 2326, 2330, 2331, 2335, 2338, 2339, 2341, 2342, 2343, 2345, 2351, 2352, 2353, 2356, 2363, 2364, 2373, 2375, 2377, 2378, 2389, 2391, 2396, 2397, 2399, 2401, 2402, 2403, 2405, 2410, 2412, 2416, 2421, 2424, 2425, 2427, 2428, 2429, 2430, 2434, 2435, 2451, 2452, 2453, 2454, 2455, 2458, 2460, 2463, 3336, 3521, 4604, 6524, 6592, 7785, 7865, 8678, 8681, 9456, 10944, 10990
"dying" 2356
"dying, azaleas were" 3803
"dying, bleeding and" 8681
"dying, child lay" 7785
"dying, day was" 2222
"dying, enjoyed her" 2345
"dying, Hamnet was" 2363
"dying, hard" 3385
"dying, I am" 2343, 2412, 6450
"dying, I am a long time" 101
"dying, knew he was" 2315
"dying, knew that he was" 2391
"dying, this has been a year for" 10990
"dying, thought she was" 2435

"dying, Wang Lung lay" 2309
"dying, we started" 2425
"dying, when old Lucius Dowling lay" 2302
"dying, while Pearl Tull was" 9456
"dying all the time, people were" 3944
"dying fast, planet which was" 5827
"dying for a long time" 2315
"dying fresh as a blade of grass" 2463
"dying in his room" 2316
"dying in the night caught us off our guard" 2326
"dying October day, in the" 4156
"dying of brain cancer" 2454
"dying of cancer, everyone is" 2377
"dying of consumption" 2019
"dying of the dust" 9858
"dying on the crude cross" 6592
"dying sounds, the final" 9387
"dying uncle, attend a" 4604
"dying words, at his bedside to take down his" 2336
"dying-out of the Eagle Moon" 407
"dying's not so bad" 2460
"dyke paths, narrow" 5141
"dynamite, each of us carries a stick of" 879
"dynasties, hungry word-filled" 514
"dynasty, great Ch'ing" 10983
"dynasty, proclaim his" 6646
"Dynmouth nestled on the Dorset coast" 1440
"Dypaloh" 3175
"dysentery" 172
"dyspepsia, suffering from" 306

"eager, she was" 4924
"eager to get down to Sussex" 9724
"eager to get it over and done with" 8878
"eager with malice, voice" 7518
Eagerness 4924, 8878, 10055
"eagerness, human manifestations of holy" 4005
"eagerness, joining the hunt with" 428
Eagle 4718
"eagle, first sea" 760
"Eagle, giant" 724
"eagle, their final" 752
"eagle, young untried" 8918
"eagle aboard a thermal, like an" 5688
"eagle flashing gold burnish in black wings" 4704
"eagle from three miles north of Mt. Soracte to limit of vision over Tivoli" 7514
"eagle pair climbed the midmorning sky" 757
"eagle Sun, the" 752
"eagle to spread his wings" 762

Eales, Eamonn 1863
"Ealing, West" 3153
"ear, hoary grey" 5256
"ear, inclined his private" 7505
"ear, murmured in her" 1121
"ear flopped, one" 462
"ear was open and inclined, every" 8626
"earflaps full of large ears and uncut hair" 2859
"Earl of Emsworth" 8257
"Earl of Evesham" 1172
"Earl of Gallerick, Eleventh" 8294
"Earl of Glenthorn" 3356
"Earl of Locksley and Huntingdon" 10641
"Earl of Mount Severn" 8340
"Earl of Pembroke" 1196
"Earl of Scroope" 3066
"Earl of Slane" 102
"Earl of Wroxton" 306
Earle, Edna 9339
Earle, Roy 2956
"earlier than that" 8774
"earliest recollections" 7391
"earlobes, extraordinarily well developed" 561
"earls, one of our oldest" 6607
"early, a little" 10032
"early, even a little" 10360
"early, get up" 4285
"early, so good of you to come" 9867
"early bird" 7816
"early hour, it is surely an" 720
"Early Nineteen Hundreds" 4498
"early to bed" 1178
"early to rise" 1178
"earmarked as scholar bait and spinster material" 10886
"earned the first power" 4469
"earned the respect and gratitude" 5998
"earnestly studied the dinner-table" 3838
"earnestness, quaint" 5392
"earning her own living" 3273
Earnshaw, Medora 5751
"earrings, drop pearl" 8385
"earrings, I *love* those" 10892
"ear-rings, little gold" 5903
"ears, dirt behind their" 7196
"ears, her inattentive" 8850
"ears, large" 2859
"ears, shells of my" 10167
"ears, with both" 7628
"ears, wrenched off the full" 10927
"ears, you've got" 6338
"ears cut off for writing" 3376
"ears of the drowsy traveller" 10108
"ears of the scandalous press" 4104
"ears quivering in anticipation" 460
"ears straining to the sound" 8786
"ears to the wind, cocked her" 8764
"ears too far back on the head" 498

Earth 521, 525, 532, 2218, 2274, 2641, 3387, 3477, 5149, 5156, 5645, 6013, 9503, 9534, 10571, 10598, 10614
"Earth" 539
"earth, all his years on" 5594
"earth, all the corners of the" 7813
"earth, beauty of our" 3477
"earth, by now you must be" 2346
"earth, cracking the parched" 4397
"earth, dust of the" 2641
"earth, ends of the" 249
"Earth, find out why we are on this" 3280
"earth, frost-bound" 8584
"earth, God's" 2311
"earth, hard" 5149
"earth, heaven was closer to" 3387
"earth, his time on this" 9846
"earth, honor the" 9062
"earth, hum of the turning" 5156
"earth, I had been on this" 4236
"earth, impelled the whole" 10611
"earth, last soft fold of" 3204
"earth, mild sweep of" 4084
"earth, motion of the" 2274
"earth, mounds of moist" 1188
"earth, my first vision of" 7917
"Earth, Planet" 532
"earth, principal features of the" 7924
"earth, replenishing the" 5699
"earth, scorned by" 5165
"earth, some great blunt stub of the" 5178
"earth, the" 3977, 7292
"earth, the brown dry" 4413
"earth, the dark" 522
"earth, the great sphere of the" 525
"earth, the scarred" 7297
"earth, the soft" 9841
"earth, this" 2575
"earth, this lovely" 11001
"earth, wet black" 3622
"earth, what on" 5438, 8307
"earth, wind circling the" 10614
"earth again, I'm on" 1690
"earth again, the" 3799
"earth and sky" 1284
"earth began to die in earnest" 3403
"earth begins to put on her new apparel" 7370
"earth below a washout" 2606
"earth faltered" 10598
"earth fecundated by the corpses of more than sixty centuries of dead" 5149
"earth from returning to water" 5542
"earth had had enough" 6013
"earth had moved under them" 6046
"earth must roll revolve and whirl" 9534
"earth or slime" 2346

"earth rang like slag" 1547
"earth seared the feet" 4413
"earth sighed as it turned in its course" 2202
"earth spun upon its axis" 525
"Earth Station One" 9756
"earth was half frozen" 521
"earth will be no more, this old" 7029
"earthly scene, this" 2310
"earthquake" 1217, 2452
"earthquake weather" 10619
Earthquakes 2452, 6046, 10227, 10619
"earthquakes" 1288
"earth's ancient antagonist" 7916
"earth's axis" 10571
"earth's crust, underneath the" 9503
"Earth's most famous town" 1380
"ease down the hall to Jessie's room" 7783
"ease into very slowly" 624
"easel, propped against an" 7440
"easel, slender" 485
"easier somehow" 3610
"easier than her flat" 8027
"east of the setting sun, somewhere to the" 4044
"East, back" 6544
"East, comes there straight from the" 5160
"East, in the" 4930
"east, the" 10714
"East, the bloody" 4881
"East Belfast" 6191
"East Bridgewater Massachusetts" 3194
"East Head" 9074
"East India Company" 8254
"East London" 6104
"East Sheen" 8854
"East Shelton" 3430
"East Side, lower" 7743
"East Side, Lower" 820
"East Walsham Norfolk" 4104
"east where time began, from the" 10751
"east wind" 9742
"Eastbourne" 2943
Eastep, Harry 5370
Easter 2064, 4514
"Easter" 6325
"Easter, city was getting ready for" 4514
"Easter, every" 6587
"Easter, on the Sunday after" 10419
"Easter, Saturday before" 10632
"Easter, Sunday after" 8911
"Easter Fair, there used to be an" 314
"Easter Monday 1916, noon on" 4517
"Easter of '74" 10676
"Easter Rising, the bloody and abortive" 2024

"Easter Sunday" 2064, 3837, 10092
"Easter Sunday, sparkling" 5736
"easterly is the most disagreeable wind" 10724
"Eastern travellers" 5129
"Easthaven" 6203
"Eastmead" 6286
"easy, take it" 3475
"easy, wasn't" 151
"easy to get along with, I never said I was" 7972
"easy to make" 4259
"easy to say" 4732
"easygoing way" 4984
"eat, all the things he liked best to" 854
"eat, enough to" 2509
"eat, place to" 7571
"eat, some of the things he no longer cared to" 854
"eat, stopped to" 7637
"eat, they are . . . what they" 3862
"eat, too beautiful to" 773
"eat, too excited to" 3471
"eat birds' nests" 6038
"eat it in tissue-paper slices, so rich I wanted to" 860
"eat meat on Friday" 7528
"eat the head" 10899
"eat the root" 10899
"eaten to the bottom of the deep freeze" 3005
Eating 28, 248, 459, 508, 854, 3487, 3824, 3834, 3841, 3844, 3845, 3852, 3854, 3858, 3861, 3862, 3864, 3868, 3879, 3884, 3885, 3890, 3891, 4151, 4283, 5064, 5424, 5658, 6679, 7528, 7977, 8517, 8725, 9796
"eating, roomful of people" 3864
"eating, trouble with his" 9796
"eating a melted Hershey bar" 8725
"eating a rattlesnake" 459
"eating ashes, as if she had been" 10271
"eating breakfast" 873
"eating breakfast, while she was" 5658
"eating breakfast on the terrace of the Villa Paradiso" 3879
"eating cherries and strawberries dipped in wine" 4151
"eating cold beans out of the tin" 7977
"eating eggs" 3890
"eating the greengages" 3834
"eating turkey cures jet lag" 7466
"eating with us, will you be" 3884
Eaton, Mr. 3329
Eaton, Samuel 3329
"eats carefully at a table in a corner" 3891
Eavesdropping 8900, 8903, 8904, 8906
"eavesdropping on the stairs" 8788

"eavesdropping on their private thoughts" 5512
"ebb, the morning" 6179
"ebony handle" 8044
"eccentric behaviour" 6976
"eccentric like that of a heart, position is not at all" 4089
"eccentricity, the height of" 3110
"echo, like an" 378
"echo, there's not even an" 3706
"echo of their flatness, a resigned" 5173
"echo to my footsteps, there seemed an" 9120
"echoed through the hills" 391
Echoes 8862, 9120, 10016
"echoes, in which there were no" 8325
"echoes, pause to hear the" 8862
"echoes of her whoop" 10016
"echoing" 8818
Eckdorf, Ivy 4781
"eclipse, because of the" 7429
"eclipsed every other scandal" 7865
"ecliptic, plane of the" 10571
Eco 5997
"economically precarious" 6883
"economics, first law of" 10858
"economy, enter the" 2061
Ecstasy 2377
"ecstacy or death" 5018
"ecstatic" 4954
"Ecuador" 6259
"ecumenical services in the district" 1309
"ecumenism" 7519
Ed 9721
Eddie 1848, 3321, 7497
"eddies that turn the autumn leaves, blowing like the" 6333
"eddy, Captain's" 9136
Edelman, Misha 1992
"Eden, an" 7999
"Eden, myth about" 2633
"edenic college years" 5592
Edgar 2865, 3285, 6662, 9288
"edge of the clear water" 5154
"edge of the night" 9810
"edge of the world of his time" 7808
"edged against the greasy piles" 8128
"edges were level" 5415
"Edgewood, town or place called" 10420
Edgeworth, Ellen 6526
"edification of mankind" 5387
"edifice, handle to pick up the" 9206
"edifice, handsome" 6974
"edifice, porticoed marble" 6512
"edifice, wooden" 3985
"edifice built on the summit of a rock" 1171
"Edinburgh" 833, 9511
"Edinburgh, Oxford and" 9076

"edit the memoirs" 717
"edit this curious manuscript" 5536
"edited for a few months a college magazine" 5413
Edith 125, 8191, 8454, 8966, 9327, 10919
Editing 717, 5539
"editor, assignment" 9982
"editor, letter to the" 6348
"editor, newspaper" 10931
"editor of a magazine, I used to be the" 6460
"editor of these papers" 5557
"editorial staff" 6815
Editors 5536
"Editors of three different repeal newspapers" 5194
"Edmonton Alberta" 8934
Edmund 1282, 1283, 2673, 7539
Edna, Auntie 2353
"educated to the edge of intellectual indigestion" 9718
Education 99, 196, 245, 513, 536, 895, 1284, 2101, 3039, 3526, 3980, 4254, 4548, 4930, 5096, 5427, 6239, 6436, 6446, 6450, 6683, 6698, 6744, 6750, 7074, 7444, 7879, 7886, 7891, 7892, 7900, 7904, 7905, 7955, 8207, 9704, 9718, 10866
"education" 5934
"education, bunkum in higher" 3271
"education, I can't say I've had much" 3294
"education, in the way of" 9704
"education bestowed on Flora Poste" 3273
"education had become his task" 3278
"education . . . had been expensive athletic and prolonged" 3273
"education of Griffith Adams" 3272
"educational zeal" 7886
Educators 4876, 6451
Edward 3552, 3709, 5551, 5653, 5852, 6605, 9316, 10439
Edward, the third 10474
Edward VI 1196, 7886
Edwin 7549, 8518
"eee-thud eee-thud of the mortars" 878
"eerie convulsions" 6367
"effect, cause and" 7164
"effect, it had a less than helpful" 10826
"effect, produced the desired" 2015
"effect, unsettling" 901
"effects, far-reaching" 10814
"efficacious" 10555
"effigies that throng the aisles of Westminster Abbey" 8942
Effingham, Mr. 4555
"effort, literary" 5416
"effort, without any special" 10794
"effort which may well come to

nothing" 8494
"effortlessly as the soul of a saint rising to heaven" 8758
"efforts, after several" 9450
"efforts to break away" 10721
"effulgence, the warm" 3981
Egan, Father 2924
Egg 8230
"egg, cracked an" 7180
"egg, poisoned boiled rotten" 4069
"egg, quivered a black" 612
"egg, soft-boiled" 3852
"egg sunny-side, one" 3871
"Eggmarsh St. John" 7254
"eggrolls" 3876
"eggs, children of" 6817
"eggs, eating" 3890
"eggs, full of lovely pans of" 7575
"eggs, little speckled brown" 3604
"eggs, pale freckled" 751
"eggs, three soft-boiled" 3335
"eggs and b., the sizzling" 3839
"eggs and bacon, toothsome" 3850
"eggshell shielding a blue-black yolk" 8470
Egotism 239
Egremont 3557
Egress 1569, 1573, 1574, 1585, 1586, 1589, 1597, 1601, 1622, 1635, 1683, 1699, 1700, 1712, 1734, 1749, 1774, 2655, 2713, 4488, 6555, 10339, 10399, 10423
"egrets, a few white" 730
"Egypt" 1042, 6432, 7681, 8565, 8685
"Egypt, evening in" 7799
"Egyptian" 203
"Egyptian mummy" 1331
"Egyptian priest-king, posture of an" 3711
"Egyptian sorcerer" 4492
"Egyptians, the old" 10757
Eichler, Eva 5973
"eight, Molly was" 132
"Eight Bells" 1669
"eighteen, once you're over" 6720
"eighteen, when I was" 6119
"eighteen, when Judith was" 6287
"eighteen, when Laura Rowan was just" 4166
"eighty if she's a day" 114
"Eilat, Gulf of" 4418
Eileen 3579
Eino 5864
"ejected, physically" 4448
Ekaterina 4878
"ekename, its" 7691
"EKG, his" 166
"Ektachrome, 16mm Commercial" 1321
"elaborate dinner to come" 3821
"elaborate funeral" 3936
el Ain, El Isa Beth 10345
Elaina 6711
Elaine 1869, 9027

"elapsed, well-nigh" 3432
"elbow, like a bent" 4060
"elbows, squared our" 3839
"elbows supported on his knees" 8270
Elbridge 10032
"El Cajon New Mexico" 1584
"El Cuervo" 10069
Elder, Geoffrey 5539
"Elder Gods" 2236
"elderly, tending for the most part to become" 6409
"elderly relative" 2464
"elders, mistakes of his" 9704
"Eldest, which was the" 7055
Eldon 2316
Eldredge, Emeline 7827
Eleanor 6131, 7087, 10868, 10885
"election" 6994
"election, State Senate" 6992
"election day, one" 4697
"election of 18—" 6975
"election results" 6991
Elections 2472, 4697, 6429, 6975, 6991, 6994, 7005, 7007
"Electra, in the back of the" 1783
"electric, switch to" 1079
"electric light bulbs" 7779
"electric shock" 10283
"electric switch" 9883
"electrified the world" 3449
"electrocuted the Rosenbergs, the summer they" 680
"electronic music" 8555
"eleemosynary treat" 5385
"elegance, Georgian" 3210
"elegance, palaces were built for" 3144
"elegance of the dresses" 9376
"elegant and dignified traditions" 1314
"elegant name" 10768
"elegant simplicity" 3296
"elements, twin" 8412
"elephant" 9626
"elephant, if I shot an" 4689
"elephant, seen the last of the" 465
"Elephant & Castle" 3889
"elephant Gaius Claudius showed at the *ludi Romani*" 3481
"elephantine pillars and arches" 1302
"elephants, like" 6741
"elephants, rumps of" 5135
"elephants, the" 472
"elevate straightaway his lowslung parts" 5992
"elevator, enter the" 3298
"elevator, in the small" 5840
"elevator, leave the" 7204
"elevator, noisy old" 3295
"elevator lifted you from a bare little lobby into an atmosphere of elegant simplicity" 3296
"elevator operator" 1638

"eleven, when Sophie was" 9397
"Elgin, I was in" 9987
Eli 1421
"elimination, selection and" 10995
Eliot, Meg 7817
Eliot, Mr. 6945
Elise 1871, 2001
"elite of the haute bourgeoisie" 5179
"elixir from the Wandering Jew, I received the" 3055
Eliza 6605
Elizabeth 109, 1181, 2528, 4439, 4564, 6385
Elizabeth, Miss 1552
Elizabeth, Queen 5227, 9391
Elizabeth Ann 4461
"Elizabeth City" 186
Elizabeth Mary Alexandra, Princess 7805
"Elizabeth, S." 652
"Elizabethan cottage" 3116
"Elizabethan structure" 3066
Elizavetta 4277
"Elks, Benevolent Order of" 9729
Ella 4596
Ella, George "Doc" 5116
Ellen 9663
Ellenbogan, Mr. Jacob 5747
Ellera, Franco 1528
Ellery, Francis 1611, 9768
Ellie 7563
Ellingen, Gustav 3543
Elliot, Sir Walter 4439
"ellipsis, cool" 5592
"Ellis Island" 8080
Ellison, Miss Kitty 10030
"Ellsworth" 9777
"elm tree" 9675
"elm trees, tall" 5314
Elmo 9339
"elms, majestic" 9117
"elms, the long limbs of the" 8606
"elms, the marriage" 10051
"elms flanked me as regular as railings" 10372
"eloquent in her talk of reform" 8880
Elsa 1616
Elsie 1968, 7766
"Eltham, county town of" 5079
Elvira 2345
Em, Aunt 7386
"emanating from the bathtub" 578
"Emancipation, fruits of" 9216
"emasculation, self-" 1444
"embalming room" 2710
"Embankment, along the" 4571
"embankment, the" 7275
"Embankment, the" 8345, 9123
"embankment of a railroad" 9121
"embarked, Voyage on which we are" 2543
"embarked for Europe every June" 4270
"embarked on another honeymoon"

9732
"embarked together on the biggest adventure of life" 5735
"embarked upon a panicky trek" 3416
"embarking on an effort" 8494
"embarking upon her 'Ah' and upon her 'Carl'" 5992
"embarrass five, you" 9476
"embarrass my papa" 6676
"embarrassed, kind of" 3316
"embarrassed her, those things" 6240
"embarrassed in discourse" 5889
"embarrassed stares" 1201
"embarrassing moment, most" 6322
Embarrassment 1201, 3316, 6322, 6676, 8299, 9476
"Embassy, American" 939
"embassy, some great" 247
"embassy in Kabul, American" 6502
"embellishments of the house" 9376
"embittered him" 372
"embittering weeks, ten" 10535
"embonpoint, majestic profiled upholstered" 5943
"embossed with a gold crest and a motto, delicately" 4642
"embrace, impetuous" 7649
"embrace, they" 2080
"embraced her mother" 4593
"embraced his stomach with the painful tenacity of the historic Spartan fox" 9529
"embracing the horse, thighs" 8701
"embrasures" 9304
"embroidered red line" 6495
"embroidering a handkerchief" 4166
"embroidery, verbal or other" 8841
"embrowned itself moment by moment" 2189
Embry, Professor Hengist Morton 3046
"embryo is curled up in a ball, the human" 2378
"embryonic aces of his flight" 8649
Emeline 5250
"emerald, this" 338
"emerge from his office" 10751
"emerge pale, men" 1041
"emerged cautiously" 7049
"emerged from a fashionable apartment building" 1714
"emerged from his villa" 10399
"emerged from the bunkhouse" 2220
"emerged from the dark woods" 7619
"emerged from the vast Indifference" 5269
"emerged on the northwestern scene" 368
"emerged on the rooftop terrace" 4286

"emerged one afternoon into the spring sunshine" 7505
"emerged to the sidewalk" 1315
Emergencies 6982, 9340
"emergency, as of the" 6982
"emergency, some last-minute" 9340
"emergency room" 4623
"emerging from a third-class carriage" 6001
Emery family 3080
"emigrants to New England, one of the first" 356
"emigrated, society from which they had" 6147
"emigrates, no Soviet" 6162
Emigration 6147, 6162
Emilia 1814
Emily 3261, 7517, 10100
"eminence, a little" 3114
"eminence, that celebrated" 1569
"eminence of a friend, illustrious" 1
"eminence overlooking the Rat River" 3104
"eminent corporation lawyer" 2511
"eminently pleasing and pathetic" 3376
"emissions we can manage, all the" 9186
"emitting a noise" 8827
Emma 3030, 5843, 7561, 10222, 10419
Emma Lou 46
Emmeline 5616
Emmet 1263
Emmie 6007
Emmie T. 7827
"emotion, feeling an old" 7405
"emotion and suffering which in reality have but little if any existence" 8838
"emotion too many, like one" 9374
"emotional girl, very" 4201
"emotional life, story of his" 7713
"emotional nature, barometer of his" 901
"emotionally commonplace" 3303
"emotionless suction, a huge" 10746
Emotions 992, 1209, 1790, 1878, 2078, 2524, 3344, 3367, 3477, 4046, 4201, 4230, 5036, 5472, 7317, 7405, 8723, 8838, 8856, 8956, 9110, 9279, 9280, 9374, 9615, 10414, 10493
"emotions lay very near the surface" 3301
"emotions of a small community" 8956
"emotions of this day" 5472
"Emperor, acclaimed" 7802
"Emperor, Roman" 4753
"Emperor, the Franks'" 7510
Emperor Ch'in Shih Huang Ti 5138
"Emperor of Azania" 7801

"Emperor of the Holy Roman Empire" 1444
"emperor's parasol" 7806
"emphasis, with greatly increased" 931
"emphasize the beat" 6231
"emphasizing a figure already overdrawn" 189
"empire, extended his" 7800
"Empire, his" 7804
"Empire, Holy Roman" 1444
"Empire, Ottoman" 1464
"Empire State Building, the top of the" 8565
"employed by a soap manufacturing firm" 6321
"employed by Ivor Llewellyn" 1687
Employees 12, 1048, 1552, 3325, 3326, 3327, 3328, 3329, 3331, 3332, 3334, 3335, 3474, 4787, 7538, 9310
Employers 1048, 1552, 3325, 3326, 3328, 3329, 3332, 3335, 3474, 3843, 4787, 9310
"employers" 5743
"employers, prospective" 3843
Employment 1077, 6412
"Employments under the Crown, most honourable" 5883
"Emporium, Badey's" 3419
"Emporium, Poague's" 7620
"Empress of Blandings" 1178
Emptiness 1036, 1058
"emptiness, huge dark space of cool windy" 1584
"emptiness, only an" 612
"emptiness, pools of" 6001
"empty, dipping tank was" 7052
"empty, it was also" 3956
"empty, seed bins are" 1036, 1058
"empty for years" 6287
"empty himself, periodically needing to" 1333
"empty too long, when they're left" 3138
"empyrean, the vast vacuity of the" 10903
"en route to the city of Troy" 10871
"enabling him to work and to carry on his life" 166
"enact yet again her role as the lascivious Lais" 10871
"enamel, dense blue" 8424
"enchanting are those notes, how" 6212
"enclosed by an iron fence with three gates" 4099
"encore by an Israeli composer" 6232
"encounter, chance" 7434
"encounter, my first" 5870
"encounter, their" 8847
"encountered, when I first" 4473
"encountered a Muslim woman once" 5822

"encouragement, boisterous bawdy" 7102
"encouragement, had given me any" 5508
"encouragement to men, message of" 723
"encumbrances" 9657
"encyclical" 701
"encyclopædia, it is more in the nature of an" 701
"Encyclopedia" 7804
"end, an" 5694
"end, at the" 2352
"end, at the fag" 6003
"end, awaited the" 2363
"end, by the" 10854
"end, come the evening's" 10392
"end, curiously uneventful" 5592
"end, dead" 5723
"end, going on to the" 4500
"end, I am near the" 3348
"end, in the" 1768, 3345, 4721
"end, is this the promised" 3351
"end, its excruciating" 7904
"end, my" 3336
"end, nearer the" 5021
"end, nearing my" 1185
"end, refusing to" 1060
"end, sudden rude" 6510
"end, the beginning of the" 3349
"end, the very" 3347
"end, this was the" 7988
"end, this window-lit" 3302
"end, we came to the" 10985
"end, world was coming to an" 2468
"end and a beginning" 5568
"end and beginning" 3343
"end is everything, the" 3342
"end is my beginning, in my" 2347
"end it all with a bang" 9300
"end of a cold blustery day" 7019
"end of a somewhat lively review" 5732
"end of everything" 3352
"end of it, the" 3900
"end of it, there's an" 9458
"end of Seth's lecture" 5189
"end of that baby girl, that would have been the" 541
"end of the day, it was close to the" 2989
"end of the first decade of the new century" 10993
"end of the line" 7248
"end of the violin lessons" 4089
"end of the war, shortly after the" 3171
"end of the war, since the" 2518
"end of the world" 874, 3354, 3626, 4544
"end of things" 687
"end of Trinity Street, at the" 9179
"end of your rope" 3339
"end to it, I come near putting an"

9285
"end to it, there's no" 5255
"endeavor, old-fashioned Britannic" 5230
"endeavor on the part of Nature, hours of vain and sickly" 7293
"endeavors, flimsy modern conceptual" 6486
"ended, it seemed to have" 3392
"ended a concert at the Philharmonic Society" 6232
"ended her life" 6621
"ended right there, the whole thing would have" 4988
"ended yet, it hasn't" 8994
Enderby, Mr. 2910
Enders, Elgar 1033
"ending, one" 5424
"ending their ephemeral adventures" 8400
Endings 1060, 1225, 2119, 2130, 2171, 2381, 2429, 2468, 3392, 4089, 4279, 4500, 5021, 5082, 5120, 5424, 5568, 5694, 6232, 6349, 6510, 6870, 7941, 7988, 8751, 8994, 9057, 9390, 9760, 10487, 10985, 10993
"endings, happy" 3341
"endings, history consists of" 3344
"endings of as many more" 6349
Endore 3478
"endowed with one to begin with" 7882
"endowed with the power of saying No" 6613
"ends, begins and" 2130
"ends, nothing ever" 3337
"end's good, the" 8751
"ends in darkness" 2119
"ends meet, make both" 7033
"ends well, all's well that" 3340
"ends with me" 366
"ends with the photograph" 6870
Endurance 43, 5221
"endurance, our" 5221
"endure, the real thing was bound to" 2681
"enduring the concert" 6238
"Endymion non-scriptus" 3804
"Endymion nutans" 3804
Enemies 1, 1161, 4198, 6754, 8686, 8713, 9261, 10504
"enemies, her" 9261
"enemies, possible" 6754
"enemies, the author's" 5392
"Enemies, their" 10464
"enemies of man" 5033
"enemy, above the" 10504
"enemy, broken as an" 1
"enemy, hands of the" 1161
"enemy, saw the" 4198
"enemy, the" 8686
"enemy triumphantly straddling his chest, like an" 137
"energetic, alive and" 5887

"energetic sort" 4354
"energetically, arms were swinging too" 10397
Energy 526, 6935, 6937
"Energy, atoms of the eternal" 785
"energy, bees because of their" 6935
"energy, controlled" 8547
"energy, so much" 6937
"energy and action may be of two sorts" 638
"energy of the States, restless" 6249
"Enfield Highway" 8587
"Enforcement Area, Midtown" 6274
"Engadine isn't being a success" 3515
"engaged for three days" 7953
"engaged to Miss Piano" 7722
"engagement a secret, keeping the" 7953
"engagements, failed to keep his" 10040
Engaine 9329
"engine, no sound came from the" 9805
"engine below his knees, spluttering" 7628
"engine blocks" 5982
"engine coughed and missed" 229
"engine noise" 7628
"engine was running" 6942
"engineer, an" 4242
"engineer, an Italian" 3084
"engineer, I became an" 6430
"engineer by trade" 7721
"engineers, looking for" 5758
Engines 229, 10938
"engines, worked all night on the" 10938
"engines had stopped" 8811
England, Victor 1326
England 1978, 3396, 3497, 4031, 6251, 6252, 9517, 10471, 10493, 10496, 11004
"England" 696, 1568, 1691, 1761, 3084, 3376, 3557, 3571, 4058, 4922, 5227, 5294, 5371, 5834, 6089, 6249, 6251, 6252, 6601, 6788, 7037, 7663, 8051, 8166, 8395, 9538, 9560, 9860, 10473, 10684
"England, aristocracy of" 834
"England, arrived in" 2012
"England, backbone of" 6060
"England, Conqueror of" 6518
"England, duke of" 354
"England, entered" 6090
"England, far south-west of" 9628
"England, farmers of" 3635
"England, having breakfast all over" 1978
"England, in a certain county of" 6603
"England, in much of southern" 2385

"England, in the east of" 7613
"England, kicked out of" 1756
"England, king of" 7812
"England, King of" 4554
"England, knew nothing of it in" 10474
"England, landed in" 4565
"England, loveliest district in" 948
"England, managed to get back to" 1590
"England, merry" 3893
"England, migrated from" 361
"England, middle" 4139
"England, my relatives in" 6035
"England, north-eastern shores of" 1338
"England, old and golden days of" 3396
"England, Old to New" 6091
"England, our first visit to" 9517
"England, out-of-the-way corner of" 8959
"England, parks and commons of" 4943
"England, published in" 5384
"England, Queen of" 7604
"England, returned to" 4567
"England, rural" 2193
"England, soldiers from" 8702
"England, south shore of" 9519
"England, the coast of" 4031
"England, the north of" 1484, 2087
"England, the people of" 10493
"England, the south of" 7254
"England, the south-west of" 1936
"England, those of" 8841
"England, went to" 6159
"England breathes again" 10471
"England denied her Jews every civic right" 7505
"England had a Queen, since" 3136
"England had declared war against Germany" 10496
"England had her Tyburn" 7179
"England his native country" 4554
"England in every way gratifying and satisfactory, he found" 6251
"England is strange to me" 3497
"England we lost, mourn for the" 11004
"England's Braddock" 8172
"England's outstretched southwestern leg" 10724
Englekings, the Alfred 3854
English, Miss 376
English 3288, 9430, 9715
"English" 6647
"English, Basic" 10910
"English, entirely" 7773
"English, I am" 4809
"English, if Franz was" 5991
"English, in plain" 9990
"English, Mass in" 6807
"English, Mother" 5448
"English, one learns" 3288

"English, sufficient" 9715
"English, the" 1221, 10658
"English, though I speak" 5446
"English, thought in" 9430
"English, transfigured into" 5466
"English appeared so suddenly" 10477
"English armies" 10473
"English beauty, you know the type of" 10788
"English castles" 309
"English Cathedral Tower, an ancient" 9207
"English Channel" 5720, 9091
"English classrooms" 7236
"English cocktail parties" 6780
"English country-house" 10780
"English countryside" 7888
"English county, rich" 2944
"English Crown" 7794
"English fare" 7573
"English fellow-passengers" 7587
"English generation, this" 10773
"English gentleman, young" 2087
"English gentlemen" 4257
"English girl" 4620
"English language" 7904
"English Literature, professors of" 216
"English mother" 800
"English names, odd" 4739
"English night manager" 4659
"English novelists of the present day" 5440
"English officers" 7246
"English people, three" 8938
"English public official class" 8351
"English shape to their mouths" 9560
"English sincerity" 695
"English soil" 3635
"English spring, an" 1177
"English tourists" 9353
"English towns, great" 6886
"English travellers in Italy" 1293
"English tripper" 6896
"English visitor" 3046
"English who had money or leisure" 10768
"English world, all the" 6974
"English yeoman" 4303
"Englishman, ill-humoured spec-tacled young" 10040
"Englishman, middle-aged" 5801
"Englishman born and bred, I am an" 4864
Englishmen 4973
"Englishmen, two young" 9518
"Englishmen are pigs, all" 4973
"Englysshe Style, Olde" 3096
"engraved MARTIN HOUSE STUDY" 1915
"engraving, steel" 9250
"enhaloed, magnificently" 2620
Enid 6027

"Enigma Georgia" 1423
"enigmatic cry, Ophelia's" 5507
"enjoy the hot July sun, wanting only to" 7594
"enjoy the motor-drive home, had not expected to" 2953
"enjoy the newspaper credit of my generosity" 121
"enjoy their bitterness, pretended to" 9674
"enjoy this stroll to work, did not" 10380
"enjoyed her dying" 2345
"enjoyed on his first anniversary" 6433
"enjoying himself" 306
"enjoying the early October sunlight" 1923
"enjoying the height of the spring of 1813" 8356
"enjoying the October warmth" 5631
"enjoying the warm day and one another" 6557
Enjoyment 306, 2345
"enjoyment, additional means of" 2600
"enjoyment, sublunary" 9989
"enlargements, matted" 6856
Enlightenment 4067, 5078
"enlist in the army, among the first to" 8646
"enlistees were ordered down to the basement" 1215
"ennobles some people" 1163
"ennui" 10083
"ennui, fatigue and monotony and" 9381
"ennui, mask of" 332
"Enoch New Hampshire" 10088
"enormous, he seemed" 5981
"enormous, man who had once been" 5986
"enormously, interested him" 9226
Enos, Bartholomew Kedar 4323
"enough, I find that" 3048
"enough, realised she'd had" 10323
"enough, to have never quite" 4676
"enquired generally of the small room" 990
"ensconced, when first" 3589
"ensconced on the shoe-shine throne" 8654
"Ensenada" 1216
"ensure good luck" 7067
"ensuring the future would exist" 9950
"enter, about to" 1651
"enter, why" 1089
"enter before his father, intending to" 6680
"enter the lecture hall, as I was about to" 7518
"entered her kitchen a little hurriedly" 10785
"entered his office suite" 1934

"entered the doctors' lounge" 4624
"entered the General Store, the way they" 9111
"entered the hall" 3790
"entered the house" 4179, 8204
"entered the hut" 7105
"entered the offices of Teitlebaum & Sharfenstein" 6514
"entered the room quietly" 1641
"entered the sacristy of a suburban church" 1303
"entered the salon" 8172
"entered the train" 9530
"entered the University of Missouri" 7890
"entered the west gate of the Kremlin" 9833
"entered to have a quick cup of coffee" 7569
"entering even my own home, before" 9976
"entering the church" 3735
"entering through an upper window" 5311
"enterprise, commercial" 2341
"enterprise, the" 1016
"enterprise of his father" 3084
"enterprise of my fellow-citizens" 2600
"enterprise which you have regarded with such evil forebodings" 7008
"enters a room with his arms crossed" 5974
"enters the room" 1673
"entertain Daddy" 6710
"entertain the incoming freshmen" 6760
"entertain the passengers at his table" 8075
"entertainment, charity" 294
"entertainment, house of" 4304
"entertainment of tourists" 5066
"entertainment profession" 2758
Entertainments 293, 321, 2131, 2469, 3481, 4998, 6710, 8861
Enthusiasm 6036
"enthusiasm, family" 4567
"enthusiasm, without" 7781, 9909
"enthusiasm is paid for dearly indeed" 9376
"enthusiastic, I'm not over-" 5427
"entirely what it seems to be, nothing about it is" 1430
"entires" 433
"entitled to the utmost veneration" 7772
"entrance, main" 1165, 8300
"entrance into Hades" 4082
"entrance into history" 971
"entrance to a flea market" 1089
"entrance to his establishment" 1078
"entrance to ward X, unlabelled" 8692
"entreaty, something like" 9992

"entrepreneur in plus fours" 5170
"entries, two handwritten" 396
"entry, a short" 5507
"entwined his legs through hers" 9988
"envelope, unresponsive blue" 1907
"envelope, wobbled diagonally across the" 1948
"envelope embossed with the familiar OGPU emblem" 1934
"envelope filled with hundred-dollar bills" 3755
"envelope marked 'Clara'" 2422
"envelope of satin" 7056
"envelope that lay on the end of the long table" 1907
"enveloped in the gaseous film of the atmosphere" 525
"enviable, brilliant and" 237
"enviable as it was, position is not so" 3635
"enviable position in contemporary letters" 5423
"envied, the one man I have ever truly" 3925
"envied him" 3329
"envious" 1226
Environment 407, 500, 879, 947, 1253, 1288, 2125, 3132, 4158, 5703, 9974, 10815
"environment, identification with a particular" 5703
"environment, natural" 1209
"environment, the other people in her" 46
"environment we have made for ourselves" 3372
"Environs" 1175
"environs of Naples" 1293
"envoys, such" 8346
Envy 237, 251, 1226, 2497, 3329, 3925, 10837
"envy, choke with" 2527
"envy, gazed with" 2497
"envy, joy and" 10837
Enwright, Mr. 3326
"ephemeral adventures" 8400
Ephram 10080
"epic, teenage" 3386
"epic, twentieth-century American" 6454
"epic was tottering to doom" 3386
"epidemic, dwellings that swarmed like an" 9223
"epidemic of rabies" 167
"epidemic of the influenza" 3273
"epidemic spreads like spilt quicksilver" 171
Epidemics 120, 165, 167, 169, 171, 173, 2425
"epilogue, prologue or" 9057
"episode came, each" 7372
"episode in the life of Cecilia Holt" 5560
"episode of *Ozzie & Harriet*" 6298

"episode which already appears less horrible than grotesque" 2734

"epithet, it is their" 3564

"epithet, the" 962

Epithets 3932, 4970, 4971, 4973, 4974, 4978, 4979, 4980, 4981, 4982, 4987, 4988, 4990, 4991, 4993, 4994, 4995, 6310, 6389, 6633, 6653, 6716, 7634, 8925, 9309, 9314, 10214

"epithets, wonderful command of" 9309

"epitome, an" 10567

"epitome of the whole body of the sea" 7916

"epoch, in this" 5497

"epoch of belief" 3377

"epoch of history, your own" 4496

"epoch of incredulity" 3377

Epochs 7205, 10495

"eponym of the inbite, small but ancient" 10724

"eponymous hero" 4473

"Epping Forest" 4303

"Epsom" 1221

"Epsom's white paint" 10002

Equality 5705

"equals, treating people as" 5705

"equidistant from Allentown and Bethlehem" 4059

"equinoctial need of change" 4384

"equipment, Twentyman's dreadful" 10935

"equipment of Santeria, all the elaborate" 7533

"era, Laurie London" 3386

"era of accomplishment" 3393

"era of plastic ribbons and tape recorders" 8892

"era overlapped another, one" 3383

Eras 26, 66, 89, 1726, 2023, 2443, 2938, 4170, 4353, 4496, 4498, 5561, 5755, 5760, 7120, 7709, 7910, 7956, 7976, 8892, 8991, 9382, 10768, 10779

"erase from your memory" 1955

Erc 825

Erden 6649

"Erebus" 6074

"erect, unimpeachably" 215

"erection, a landscape of" 5946

"Erewash, the" 3082

Eri, Captain 6020

Eric 131, 1641

"Erie Basin" 6368

"Eritreans" 9371

Erlene 8364

Erlich, Karl 4514

Ernest 1096

Ernie 2334

"eroticism" 4256

"errand, running an" 3451

"errand, sent me there on an" 7386

"errand was out of his way" 4123

Errands 3451, 4123, 10665, 10921, 10941

"errands, I have been sent on" 10941

"errands, nothing for me to do but" 10921

"errands to our Colonies on many planets" 10941

"erratic behavior" 2997

Errol 945

"error, there is a widespread" 264

"errors of an unfortunate mother" 6517

Eru 2632

"eruption, its last" 5052

"escalators" 1748

Escape 885, 1160, 6770, 8673

"escape, I could not" 5554

"escape, second day of their" 3411

"escape, trying to" 10121

"escape, viewed his chances for" 3405

"escape, you can't" 3502

"escape both" 2972

"escape from death" 1217

"escape from his identity, desire to" 3412

"escape from the bay, we made good our" 1566

"escape something" 3406

"escape the ashy smell of the factories" 3184

"escape the mingled smothering smells of the place" 8515

"escape to, places to" 3415

"escape to the shade of their messes" 8121

"escaped, my brother had" 3409

"escaped from Czechoslovakia" 3414

"escaped from his guards" 3407

"escarpment, edge of the" 6009

"Escondido" 2241

"escort of albatrosses, under an" 8170

"escort of four horsemen" 9304

"escorted his last patient to Baker Street station" 10418

"escutcheon, crowned by an" 1165

"Esdraelon, Plain of" 9141

"Eskati" 6487

"Eskimos, three boring facts about" 6821

"essay, encountering some" 5468

"essay papers, students'" 7885

Essays 5412, 5413

"essays" 5486

"essays, series of iconoclastic" 5413

"essences richly distilled, lacustrine" 8523

"Essendon airport" 197

"essential, it is" 5560

Essex, Lord 8566

"Essex countryside" 9810

Essie 4530

Estaban 8030

"establishment, chief" 7918

"establishment, dignified" 5894

"establishment, dignified and comparatively expensive" 7568

"establishment, Doctor's" 10111

"establishment, his" 1078

"establishment, scholastic" 7878

"establishment on the Boulevard du Montparnasse" 7568

Establishments 1006, 1007, 1008, 1039, 1044, 1051, 1055, 1078, 1080, 1083, 1324, 1851, 4316, 4322, 6805, 7875, 7905, 7908, 8320, 8549

"estaminets of northern France" 8702

"estate, deserted" 3179

"estate, executor of his" 2310

"estate, her husband's" 1715

"estate, more than the whole value of his" 3550

"estate, sell his ancestral" 1090

"estate, Stainforth" 3212

"estate, the" 449

"estate at Thracian Tchermen" 6110

"estate in northern New England" 3179

"Estate in Nottinghamshire" 6602

"estate of one Pierce Inverarity" 10559

Estates 3119, 3126, 3130, 3179, 3212, 5067, 5157, 7392, 8257

"Estates, Canine" 3088

"estates, one of those small family" 3119

"estates and farms" 2489

"estate's breadth and purity of line" 4617

"estates in England, one of the greatest" 3557

"estates in the Borders of Scotland" 5761

Esteban 9275

"esteemed, beauty was particularly" 4240

Esther the Black 8371

"estimable brother, her" 3821

"estimate in which they hold themselves" 7965

"estimates of her, false" 7565

"estuary" 7304

"Estuary, east to the" 9175

"estuary, fine" 7647

"estuary, Matarre" 7679

"estuary of the Patuxent River" 5048

"etching she held" 4118

"eternal, days no longer seemed" 2323

"eternal, that which has been done becomes" 7372

"eternal beings, two" 2620

"Eternal City, olden Ghetto of" 1347

"eternal hell" 2492

"eternal laws, organiser of" 6478

"eternally on the wing" 7584

"eternity, tremendous caravans marching across" 6063
"ETERNITY, WHERE WILL YOU BE IN" 8319
Ethel 6391, 6851, 9086
"ether, clear bright many-tinted" 2188
"ether between the stars" 2790
"Ether County Georgia" 167
"ether cylinder" 4379
"Ethiopia" 8924
"etiquette, court" 9557
"Etoile de West, L'" 7579
Etta 3841, 9721
Eudoxia, empress 3677
Eugene, Jennifer 9982
"*Eugénie*, the" 406
"eunuch's voice" 10001
Euphemia 5343
"euphoria, special gift of a brisk" 316
"Euphoria Illinois" 5413
"Europa, old mother" 6649
Europe 169, 223, 267, 2257, 2262, 4928, 10475, 10526, 10739
"Europe" 927, 1006, 1115, 1779, 2257, 2262, 2481, 6256, 7663, 7800, 10739
"Europe, a country in" 2400
"Europe, Central" 4089
"Europe, continent of" 2264
"Europe, countries of" 6245
"Europe, Eastern" 6531
"Europe, eastward across" 6109
"Europe, embarked for" 4270
"Europe, favoured of" 3831
"Europe, Highway to" 9173
"Europe, peace in" 10514
"Europe, plague stalked" 169
"Europe, rivers of" 10526
"Europe, sail for" 9857
"Europe, soft underbelly of" 5026
"Europe, summer in" 515
"Europe, the deeper problems of" 4928
"Europe, travell'd through most part of" 10464
"Europe, war in" 1206
"Europe, Western" 7809
"Europe bound" 4731
"Europe where they afterwards saw each other" 2648
"European, Eastern" 6749
"European, I am very much a" 4535
"European bluebell" 3804
"European cities" 1308
"European clothes, suit of" 6950
"European country, every" 267
"European eyeglasses" 6900
"European Heaven, central" 223
"European nations" 6244
"European of British birth" 5938
"European settlement" 4030
"European travellers" 7950

"European Travels" 10464
"Europeans" 3507
"Europeans, one of those excellent" 8940
"Europe's severed arteries" 10475
Eustace 6697, 8211, 9998
Eustina 8029
Eutropius 3677
Eva 6186, 7988
Evan 10951
"evangelical stronghold" 3429
Evangeline 2776
"evangelists, itinerant" 1497
"evangels" 4502
Evans, Amy 10831
Evans, Basher 9919
Evans, Mrs. Harrington-Smith 4108
"evaporates, dream she was having" 2814
"Evarchia" 4583
"evasions, no more" 9017
Eve 359, 1175, 2633, 2805, 4707, 7087, 7237, 9406, 10325
"Eve, Adam and" 359
"Eve, All Hallows'" 4637
Evelyn 1595, 2408, 3599
Evelyn, Mr. 3396
Evening 1007, 2133, 2192, 2196, 2206, 2208, 2213, 2228, 2240, 2241, 2246, 2268, 2279, 3894, 4372, 4422, 5040, 6562, 8353, 8399, 8402, 8645, 8830, 9270
"evening, afternoon had turned to" 2228
"evening, at eight o'clock in the" 8453
"evening, at last it was" 2208
"evening, at the end of a summer" 7217
"evening, certain fine" 1572
"evening, cold" 9320
"evening, cold starry" 9400
"evening, cool of the" 5615
"evening, dull" 1007
"evening, early spring" 1409
"evening, fading into" 2192
"evening, fairy touch of" 6562
"evening, fine" 2945, 3894
"evening, grim February" 8585
"evening, it was already" 1671
"evening, late-winter" 7457
"evening, like a winter" 2245
"evening, lost in the" 10397
"evening, lovely late-March" 2846
"evening, on a blustery February" 4921
"evening, on a summer Sunday" 8331
"evening, one April" 10819
"evening, one muggy September" 5098
"evening, one summer" 1494
"evening, pious Friday" 2246
"evening, snow-swept January"

4659
"evening, strange bizarre" 3343
"evening, summer" 960
"evening, that fine cool" 2513
"evening, that very" 6620
"evening, this" 3278
"evening, this autumn" 2241
"evening, this first early summer" 2930
"evening, this morning like this" 2268
"evening, warm summer's" 8448
"evening, what a beautiful" 2206
"evening, wild late February" 10715
"evening, with the approach of" 4372
"'Evening Banner'" 7107
"evening dimness" 10786
"evening in August, one warm" 7479
"evening in December, a damp" 5088
"evening in June, on a still" 6555
"evening in late September, mild fragrant" 5854
"evening in May, beautiful" 5040
"evening in mid-October, misty" 7753
"evening . . . seems no different than countless others" 2241
"*Evening Star*, the" 8587
"*Evening Star*, Washington" 7831
"evening toward sunset, one" 983
"evening was closing in, an autumn" 8050
"evenings, long candlelit" 7865
"evenings, long winter" 3490
"evenings, mid-summer" 8214
"evenings, on Sunday" 3524
"evenings, one of the loveliest" 948
"evenings, summer" 1270
"evenings alone" 8637
"evening's end" 10392
"event, an" 834
"event, interesting" 7060
"event, pinpoint the" 5105
"event, rather commonplace" 3439
"event, rather exciting" 1488
"event, reviewing the" 5118
"event, such an" 8838
"event, the next great" 9951
"event, unexpected" 5765
"event catapulted him into marriage" 5765
"event directly influencing the issue" 3488
"event in childhood" 1197
"event that any instant might bring" 7617
"event that changes things" 5118
"Event which occurred some years since" 8959
"eventful of all, most" 5561
Events 688, 698, 834, 928, 946, 1197, 1223, 1265, 1276, 1338, 1488,

1613, 2162, 2445, 2616, 2737, 2894, 3107, 3457, 3464, 3488, 3489, 3493, 3497, 3506, 3511, 3546, 4468, 4489, 4497, 5021, 5082, 5087, 5105, 5111, 5118, 5426, 5492, 5518, 5528, 5590, 5593, 5594, 5765, 6181, 6244, 7060, 7205, 7394, 7411, 7423, 7451, 7616, 8959, 9307, 9694, 9729, 10667, 10992
"events" 5303
"events, all great and surprising" 4489
"events, chain of" 3546
"events, cosmic" 6478
"events, current" 6338
"events, entire sequence of" 3457
"events, great" 4468, 4497
"events, series of" 3432
"events, series of odd" 3511
"events, record of a series of" 5426
"events, sequence of" 2626, 6181
"events, series of" 709
"events, social" 10671
"events, some" 7423
"events, surface of" 633
"Events, The" 5786
"events, there are some" 3489
"events, tight schedule of social" 8636
"events, train of future" 6244
"events, two seemingly unconnected" 3444
"events, unusual" 3443
"events, various personal" 5570
"events, worry the" 7411
"events, year of strange" 10992
"events appear to have meaning" 5593
"events are decided by trifles" 4468
"events came his way" 3511
"events happened very rapidly" 3436
"events in my experience, one of the worst" 10667
"events in order, put all the" 5021
"events it described, no matter how queer the" 5477
"events narrated in the following pages" 1338
"events occurred which electrified the world" 3449
"events of my life, all the important" 5590
"events of this chronicle" 698
"Events of Youth, Harshest" 5492
"events produce the effects of time" 3433
"events that happened yesterday are blurred" 7451
"events we are about to relate" 3434
"events were to mark that day, two" 3450
"events which are related in the fol-

lowing chapters" 3432
"events which had taken place" 2894
"events which led up to the mysterious death" 5528
"ever after" 8543
Everett, Edna 10661
Everett, John 10434
"every body's to be there" 6751
"everybody in New York City" 7226
"everybody in the tent" 3681
"everybody who was anybody" 4376
"everyone everywhere has always felt trapped" 3319
"everyone in the hills" 8514
"everyone was older than he" 81
"everyone was there" 4002
"everything, helplessly reinvented..." 4901
"everything, too much of" 1391
"everything anyone could want, my family had" 3607
"everything began to go wrong" 64
"everything I wished I were" 251
"everything was changing, all around us" 1253
"everywhere he went" 3859
"evicted from [homes], being" 3241
"evidence, husbanding the" 3465
"evidence, there is good" 6021
"evidence against me" 3463
"evidence of a shared bereavement, gave ample" 2385
Evil 4507, 7169, 8395, 10778
"evil, good and" 2633
"EVIL, hate" 5362
"evil, preserve the record of" 4507
"evil, what makes Iago" 7169
"evil forebodings" 7008
"evil genius" 10778
"evildoers" 4507
Evolution 4935, 5542
"evolution" 4935
"evolution on an upward swing" 5542
Evreux 9674
Ewing, William Bloodgood 10661
"exact, to be" 788
"exactitude, I try for" 3757
"exactly, well not" 4070
"exaggerated and mischievous reports" 3476
"exaggerated, knowing he" 9240
Exaggeration 284, 9240
"exaltation, without much feeling of" 7034
"exalted hour" 8470
"exam, theological" 6639
"examination, doctor would make his" 6893
"examinations, Bar final" 5202
"examinations, post-mortem" 1889
"examined her feet" 564
"examined the vegetation" 9676

"Examiner, the" 6358
"examining the ceiling" 9452
"example, singularly good" 3080
"examples of Mr. Deacon's work" 494
"Examples work more forcibly in the Mind than Precepts" 7163
"excavations" 1342
Excell, The Rev. Mr. 1492
"excellence along another line, establishing its" 8627
"Excellency, His" 247, 8866
"excellent" 9509
"exception, I was no" 3319
"exception, with a single" 6830
"exceptions, allowing for" 7037
"exceptions, his law must have" 4497
"exceptions, with five" 6830
"exceptions are so inevitable" 7815
"excerpt from THE THUMB-NAIL ALMANAC" 4066
"excess, fame requires every kind of" 3539
"excessively romantic" 8799
"exchanged vows with Braxton Porter Throckmorton III" 3604
"excited, happy and" 3473
"excited, I was" 3474, 3479
"excited about going abroad" 3469
"excited and drop dead, get too" 5112
"excited the public mind" 3476
"excited to eat, he was too" 3471
"excited to reply, they had been too" 4565
Excitement 268, 1488, 4520, 4570, 5112, 6620, 8601, 9916
"excitement" 3477
"excitement, almost called out in" 8601
"excitement, felt a sense of" 4570
"excitement, greatest possible" 5194
"excitement, intense inner" 380
"excitement, out in" 8770
"excitement, state of" 3467
"excitement, state of solemn" 6620
"excitement, without" 732
"excitement and dread, clash of" 3478
"excitement of a religious sort, very widely spread" 268
"excitement of unwrapping the sparkling glass ornaments" 4520
"excitement suddenly flared up in my life" 3470
"exciting, mysteriously" 8799
"exciting, terribly" 3480
"exciting, the present was always so" 6800
"exciting, too slowly to be very" 10083
"exciting event for Carlingford, a rather" 1488
"exciting letter" 3472

"exclaimed sorrowfully" 721
"exclamation, indignant" 6610
"exclamation marks, thrive with"
    10843
"exclusive, ever so" 4322
"exclusive, most" 3078
"excrement, her own watery" 3057
"excrement, human" 8544
"excursion, low-fare" 6896
"excursion beyond the immediate
    suburbs of London" 6558
"excursions in the environs of
    Naples" 1293
"excuse, I know that's no" 5760
"Exec-Career" 1077
"execute a plan" 6928
"executing, worth the trouble of"
    7802
"executing a criminal, the manner
    of" 2043
"execution, the more triumphant
    the" 2035
"execution, train that was carrying
    him to his" 3407
"execution day" 7686
Executions 680, 2043, 2461, 3407,
    7179, 7180, 7194
"executive, a kind of" 6456
"executive who must dispatch his
    business and be gone again"
    4920
"executor" 10559
"executor, listening to the" 4934
"executor of his estate" 2310
"executrix" 10559
Exercise 8367
"exercise, for" 3482
"exercise, technical" 6224
"exercise, training" 8682
"exercise side-saddle" 9559
"exercised under the care of a dozen
    supervisors in white coveralls"
    307
"exercises, after the" 5096
"Exeter" 1486, 7610, 9586
"exhalation, an Arabic" 9181
"exhaled" 1147
"exhaling through his slightly parted
    lips" 8573
"exhaust of the automobile, per-
    manent" 1039
"exhausted, dropped" 3687
"exhausted by the terrible march of
    the previous day" 3681
"exhaustion, in extreme" 10127
"exhaustion, in various stages of"
    3691
"exhaustion, utter" 8455
"Exhibit Aleph" 7730
"Exhibition, Wild West" 1320
"exhibition, wonderful" 5784
"exhilaration, a strange" 3850
"ex-husband" 2682
"ex-husband, her" 6544
Exile 4481, 7191, 11004

"exile" 7030
"exile, in" 9882
"exile, Jews were going into" 6109
"exile is the wound of kingship"
    7191
"exile of sorts" 4544
"exist, ceased to" 9119
"exist, in me you" 3117
"existed, I" 7067
"existed for so long" 102
Existence 800, 1252, 2387, 3117,
    4878, 5277
"existence, adroitly centered about
    the routine of his" 4935
"existence, became aware of her"
    2387
"existence, blessings of" 5555
"existence, fugitive" 8400
"existence, his present" 5292
"existence, major matters of" 9347
"existence, neither of us knew of the
    other's" 6293
"existence, nothingness of" 5277
"existence, this modern fabric of"
    5247
"existence, wonder of" 9118
"existence of God, argument for
    the" 3465
"existence still bearable for us,
    make" 3284
"existences, many previous" 800
"existential" 5468
"exit, no" 6829
Exley, Mrs. 112
"Exmoor" 4041
"Exmoor, cloud-darkened heart of"
    9081
"Exmoor, long southern slopes of"
    9230
"exorcism, just returned from an"
    10963
"exotic, compellingly" 5111
"exotic in an ends-of-the-earth kind
    of way" 9061
"exotic or wicked" 1288
"expanse, rambling" 8274
"expansively" 2
"expatriates, British" 6901
"expect of him the refulgence of six"
    9476
"expect of them" 3583
"expect the worse" 3583
"expectancy, sense of" 10060, 10077
"expectancy of progress" 9663
"expectant" 10265
"expectant, eager and tensely"
    10055
"expectant, tranquilly" 10030
"expectant of an elaborate dinner to
    come" 3821
Expectation 1711, 1997, 2701, 5462,
    6311, 8667, 10030, 10060, 10070,
    10249
"expectation, burden of" 6701
"expectation, glad" 6311

"expectation, sweet" 1711
"expectations, against all my" 1816
"expected, a way she least" 252
"expected, had not" 5825
"expected, it was not how I" 288
"expected, something" 7372
"expected home at Dene's Court"
    4569
"expected it to happen, nobody"
    6771
"expected of him, nothing else
    could have been" 2292
"expected the back of the limousine
    to be luxurious" 2590
"expected to find someone there,
    always half" 1665
"expected to see the Russians, had
    not" 8177
"expected too much" 1997
"expecting her, who was" 9901
"expecting me by seven o'clock"
    1664
"expecting the knock" 2701
"expecting very much of him, we
    gave up" 5947
"expecting what used to be called
    an interesting event" 7060
"expedient, the simple" 2023
"Expedition, Darien" 3550
"expedition, that" 6093
"expedition, undertake the" 7234
"Expedition, we were the great
    New British South Polar" 5230
"expedition which discovered Brazil"
    5576
Expeditions 2600, 2605, 3466,
    3681, 5230, 5576, 5724, 6076,
    6093, 7232, 7234, 9635
"expeditions have recently dis-
    covered traces of a lost people"
    2605
"expenditure, a considerable" 1030
"expense, at great" 4402
"expense, enormous" 3237
"expense in his head, adding up
    the" 6896
"expense of another, it will save
    the" 4117
"expensive, the elegant way of say-
    ing most" 3078
"expensive lines, one of the most"
    4270
"experience, curious vessel to hold"
    3499
"experience, frankly grim and even
    a distressing" 6877
"experience, moment of" 8989
"experience, quite unprecedented"
    3494
"experience, religious" 5114
"experience, reliving an old" 7405
"experience, this true life" 7884
"experience, violent" 1801
"experience, within my" 3493
"experience, woful" 9376

"experience had left him in the habit" 4291
"experience of great officials" 6976
"experience peculiar enough" 4616
"experience with junk, my first" 3049
Experiences 640, 1276, 1964, 2445, 3352, 3671, 3675, 4527, 4616, 4834, 5021, 5085, 5553, 5560, 5561, 7372, 7451, 8669, 8989, 9058, 9287
"experiences, some" 3488
"experiences came to him, some very remarkable" 3498
"experiences of life, my" 3495
"experiences when he has gone to bed late" 10132
"experiment in Artificial Intelligence, a pioneer" 7788
"experimental prison" 2033
"experimentally, verify" 6907
Experiments 5497, 6907, 7788, 7979, 10918
"experiments on Rohanda" 5497
"expert on raising turkeys, local" 3662
"expertly tanned" 2835
"explain, it will help to" 8860
"explain, though I find it hard to" 10997
"explain anything, he doesn't" 6050
"explain how my Uncle Nick asked me to join him" 3942
"explain myself to someone" 1810
"explain the things that altered the course of his life" 5123
"explain to you, if only I could" 1252
"explain why he'd thrown Heidi in the alligator pit" 6051
"explain with the least amount of awkwardness" 8962
"explained everything, as if that" 6835
"explanation, bound to an" 8171
"explanation, calls for some" 5539
"explanation, highly rationalized" 3518
"explanation, I suppose you want an" 6050
"explanation, the" 5437
"explanation which dawned on me" 5576
Explanations 1810, 3518, 5375, 5437, 5539, 5576, 6044, 6050, 7953, 8171
"explanations, I've heard some pretty fancy" 5375
"explicit" 4714
"explicit, to be more" 7760
"exploded in a Cairo slum, hand grenade" 889
"exploded like a horrid little bomb" 10127

"exploding, the light was" 887
"exploding cannonball" 7901
"exploits, deathless" 4474
"exploration and discovery" 6564
"explore your background" 4542
"explored, its wonders of curiosity" 2600
"explorer, reflective Spanish" 473
"explorer, returning" 6792
Explorers 473, 6792
"exploring the attic" 4154
"explosion" 872, 5118
"explosion, sound of the" 891
"explosion, with the effect of a bad-tempered" 913
"explosion after all, it's not an" 7014
"explosion of chrysanthemums" 1305
"explosion of some kind" 7014
Explosions 753, 872, 874, 877, 878, 880, 882, 885, 886, 887, 889, 890, 891, 893, 5118, 6969, 7014, 7048, 7979
"explosions, four or five ponderous" 753
"explosive, accidental invention of a novel" 7979
"explosives, the" 4526
"exponents of such an event, words are sometimes very poor" 8838
"expose a cream smooth thigh" 5450
"exposed, made her feel" 5036
"exposed myself" 614
"expository pens" 10900
"expostulatory, half" 9855
"exposure to a sun, hardened by" 7036
"exposure to him, my first" 6862
"exposure to its violent assault, offer the least possible" 10699
"expounding a recondite matter to us" 3267
"express, afternoon" 9531
"express, east-bound" 1577
"Express, Simplon-Orient" 1750
"express had ever passed, no" 7241
"expresses run to and fro" 7244
"expression, imagination and" 5406
"expression, the same" 8464
"expression, vacant and preoccupied" 5424
"expression on Maltravers's face, an increasingly set" 7713
"expression on your face" 5835
"expression that I was afterwards to know so well" 5901
"expressions pained, your" 8496
"exterior, my intrepid" 3698
"exteriors, whitewashed" 1349
"extinct, life seemed" 5251
"extinction" 9382
"extinction, doomed to" 3378
"extortion, charges of" 5209
"*extranjero*" 5699

"extraordinary, anything at all" 3675
"extraordinary, it is" 9293
"extraordinary, it is quite" 8261
"extraordinary, nothing" 1369
"extraordinary figure" 6496
"extraordinary series of crimes" 2041
"extravagance, the cellarer's" 9945
"extremely coy" 2306
"extremes, always in" 956
"extremity, at the northern" 9205
"exuberance, impatient" 40
"exuberance of design" 3122
"exuberance of the Rhône" 9627
"exultant as a mother" 3806
"exultant war-cry" 8789
"exultation, with" 1581
"ex-wife, his" 6140
"ex-wife, my" 5858
"eye, as if trying to knock something from its" 8316
"eye, black circle of her" 10841
"eye, bright look in its" 2593
"eye, casting her roving" 9086
"eye, casual" 304
"eye, cocks an" 4835
"eye, dreamer's" 1356
"eye, even to my drugged" 1452
"eye, familiar to every" 4032
"eye, he caught her" 8555
"eye, her one visible" 4593
"eye, her Tiberian" 7011
"eye, his left" 151, 6810
"eye, if you got something in your" 26
"eye, in the twinkling of an" 7536
"eye, into my" 7437
"eye, inward" 10156
"eye, keep an" 4323
"eye, much cooler" 6038
"eye, November opened its" 9482
"eye, one cracked and sleep-blurred" 10198
"eye, opened one" 2432, 10224
"eye, quick" 8252
"eye, saw with his mind's" 5709
"eye, separating personal" 1284
"eye, squinting" 8287
"eye, story of an" 9048
"eye, this was a sullen" 5911
"eye, to every stranger's" 3248
"eye, with his bushy" 911
"eye, yellow and disgruntled" 8649
"eye a twinkle, in his" 7505
"eye caught the clock on the small night-table" 1131
"eye concentrated upon it" 304
"eye could see, as far as the" 5181
"eye cut by a broken bottle" 1505
"eye examination" 6511
"eye is on you, every" 3317
"eye level, seen from" 5145
"eye of the beholder" 6869
"eye of the sun" 8405

"eye off the dust cloud, tried not to take his" 9151
"eye on adjoining acreage" 3660
"eye on everything that passed, a sharp" 7652
"eye on other people's parents, I have had my" 6742
"eye on the clock" 9470
"eye on what was out there" 7467
"eye pale and pasty, cold" 537
"eye pierced the night, a giant cyclops" 7278
"eye . . . sat undisturbed under its rolled-up wide-awake rounded lid" 5911
"eye somewhat closed up" 5911
"eye was more open and looked bright" 5911
"eyebrows, heavy" 1887
"eyebrows, her scant" 5372
"eyebrows, knitting his pale" 909
"eyebrows, your thick dark" 8027
"eyebrows were hairy" 340
"eyebrows which don't quite meet" 8027
"eyed, clear-" 6815
"eyed, needle-" 7580
Eyeglasses 2857, 6350, 8285
"eyeglasses, tinted European" 6900
"eyeing me most of the way home" 2588
"eyeing the unresponsive blue envelope" 1907
"eyeing three silent telephones" 10067
"eyelashes curled wet" 10349
"eyelets, brass" 2835
"eyelids" 5603
"eyelids, her" 10145
"eyelids, lifting my" 10175
"eyelids, warm sun of Siena seep through his" 10200
"eye-rolling" 2045
Eyes 324, 333, 335, 336, 338, 344, 345, 457, 877, 1289, 1697, 1812, 1847, 2072, 2367, 2429, 2611, 2693, 3689, 3700, 3759, 4662, 4835, 4896, 4898, 4940, 5299, 5324, 5951, 6600, 6810, 7358, 7366, 7413, 7654, 7915, 7917, 8256, 8265, 8271, 8272, 8276, 8286, 8287, 8289, 8295, 8482, 8553, 8758, 9048, 9097, 10153, 10198, 10287, 10426, 10774, 10841, 10885
"eyes" 457
"eyes, amber-colored" 498
"eyes, behind her" 10306
"eyes, black" 336, 960, 5903
"eyes, black unblinking" 8295
"eyes, blue" 365, 4789
"eyes, blue serious" 2336
"eyes, brown" 482, 2804, 5935, 7485
"eyes, Byzantine" 1305

"eyes, caught one another's" 8676
"eyes, center for all" 8650
"eyes, child's sombre" 3365
"eyes, close-lidded" 9127
"eyes, close your" 602
"eyes, closed her" 5024
"eyes, closed his" 3711
"eyes, crows in his" 1812
"eyes, dared not open his" 10206
"eyes, darkly humorous" 8556
"eyes, deep" 3759
"eyes, deepset dark" 412
"eyes, depthless green" 8179
"eyes, downcast" 2493
"eyes, even before she opened her" 3732
"eyes, expressionless dark" 6950
"eyes, first laid" 5820, 5875
"eyes, glass" 8553
"eyes, glass suspended in front of his" 2857
"eyes, fixed their" 9548
"eyes, gooseberry-coloured" 8758
"eyes, Grandmother's" 338
"eyes, gray" 3545
"eyes, green-flecked amber" 8237
"eyes, half-" 5788
"eyes, half-closed" 8929
"eyes, half opened her" 10191
"eyes, hard and wondering" 7654
"eyes, her cornflower" 4176
"eyes, her damp" 4363
"eyes, her hazel" 376
"eyes, her still blue" 6784
"eyes, his" 335, 6968
"eyes, his father's deep-set sentimental blue" 4438
"eyes, his gloomy hound's" 8256
"eyes, his pale blue" 5981
"eyes, his protruding" 5984
"eyes, his sharp" 489
"eyes, his vacant blue" 976
"eyes, human" 5307
"eyes, humorous air about the" 5921
"eyes, hurting his" 9276
"eyes, I close my" 7401
"eyes, I first laid" 5860
"eyes, I opened my" 10114
"eyes, impudent blue" 246
"eyes, in their mother's" 9716
"eyes, keen appraising blue" 9749
"eyes, king's" 345
"eyes, lids of my" 2611
"eyes, lifting his" 9866
"eyes, light was hurting her" 10240
"eyes, moonlight met his" 10202
"eyes, my" 5800
"eyes, opened bewildered" 4496
"eyes, opened her" 10117, 10152, 10253
"eyes, opened his" 5121, 10115, 10123, 10153, 10199, 10199, 10250, 10267, 10269, 10287, 10328
"eyes, opened Lone's" 10203

"eyes, opened my" 10120, 10286
"eyes, opening behind his" 4704
"eyes, opening her" 5024
"eyes, opening sleep-rimmed" 10192
"eyes, opens her" 10325
"eyes, peered with screwed up rheumy" 2693
"eyes, pleaded with her" 1847
"eyes, reached his" 9849
"eyes, rubbed the sleep out of her" 10212
"eyes, sad" 419, 5299
"eyes, screwed up her" 8265
"eyes, shaded his" 3604
"eyes, sharp" 3396, 7934
"eyes, sharp cold" 6533
"eyes, sharp disembodied" 324
"eyes, shielding their" 8093
"eyes, shut his" 4891
"eyes, shut his tired old" 1496
"eyes, slate-gray" 336
"eyes, sly melancholy" 7728
"eyes, small blue" 3868
"eyes, smart behind his" 6600
"eyes, soft" 347
"eyes, squinted his" 2764
"eyes, staring" 5971
"eyes, stop ruining your" 7358
"eyes, sun in his" 8562
"eyes, sunlight on a level with her" 10121
"eyes, tired to the roots of his" 3695
"eyes, unfolded before my" 5156
"eyes, when I close my" 4898
"eyes, whites of their" 8891
"eyes, yellow-grey" 333
"eyes a little too big" 9912
"eyes alone" 8179
"eyes and mouth, Judith's" 8548
"eyes and teeth, twinkled her" 1432
"eyes are blue" 365
"eyes are open, his" 2367
"eyes are the color of water, my" 7917
"eyes around, sent my" 8272
"eyes as the greatest analyst of spirit and flesh that ever lived and spoke" 10774
"eyes aslant" 3514
"eyes blue as veronica flowers" 2072
"eyes bright with anger" 376
"eyes closed" 1887
"eyes closed, it did help some to keep his" 1213
"eyes closed, kept his" 5623
"eye's comfort" 4908
"eyes could not see" 9549
"eyes first light on an image" 9657
"eyes fixed pensively, her pretty" 9413
"eyes fixed skyward" 10540
"eyes fixed well above the level of the observers' faces" 8286
"eyes for once closed" 5629

"eyes foraged all around it greedily" 10397

"eyes full of life and warmth" 10815

"eyes gleeming balefully" 8891

"eyes glued to a hill of busy ants" 4955

"eyes had an outer ring of seeming black" 10774

"eyes had been refreshed by the sight" 8173

"eyes half closed" 403, 3738

"eyes half closed in the sun glare" 8790

"eyes harsh, his" 10426

"eyes have archaic shadows in them" 7527

"eyes held him" 8179

"eyes in the final spasm, her" 2429

"eyes in whose depths lurked a Soul" 412

"eyes lift from the paper" 7366

"eyes like almonds almost" 10885

"eyes like mine, the lust of" 1011

"eyes like two line drives, blue" 344

"eyes . . . mottled and devoid of vitality" 340

"eyes of a black panther" 3714

"eyes of a rattler" 10546

"eyes of pure madness" 4940

"eyes of the child looking" 1289

"eyes of the King, look into the" 7106

"eyes of the sick man" 122

"eyes of the woman in bed" 5324

"eyes off, not taking his" 1670

"eyes on her for some months, have not set" 7398

"eyes on Maud the wondrous, set" 10871

"eyes on Terry Lennox, I laid" 2899

"eyes on the driver" 2884

"eyes open, my" 10299

"eyes opened, as his" 2754

"eyes opened in wonder" 7915

"eyes opened with a blink of fright" 10209

"eyes particularly, his" 5951

"eyes quietly and fully, opened her" 10193

"eyes rested thoughtfully upon the sinewy forearm and wrist" 3047

"eyes scanning a wilderness" 5981

"eyes shining behind their plastic-rimmed spectacles" 8758

"eyes show, only the hunted" 3413

"eyes shut tight" 8193, 10163

"eyes slanting the joke, flirtatious" 4662

"eyes spied on him" 324

"eyes squint, makes his" 8276

"eyes staring as if with ecstasy" 1521

"eyes staring at me, two huge gleaming" 7413

"eyes taking in" 973

"eyes that peered out from the shadow of those eyebrows" 340

"eyes the color of marmite" 4153

"eyes their characteristic powdery blue, gave to his" 877

"eyes tight shut" 575

"eyes to heaven, lifted his small blue" 3868

"eyes to interior upholstery, return their" 5129

"eyes to the Ileward, casting his" 7370

"eyes turned" 5188

"eyes unfocused and glazed" 1697

"eyes up, rolling his" 3749

"eyes visible and invisible" 6613

"eyes wandered to her beautiful face instead of to his game" 3965

"eyes were of an unusually light blue" 9097

"eyes were open" 8482

"eyes were open, her" 1202

"eyes were open, his" 3700

"eyes were reduced to chinks" 8545

"eyes were sad" 1296

"eyes were supposed to be closed" 7081

"eyes were those of Leonardo's *Madonna*" 8027

"eyes . . . were tight with loathing and suspicion" 9304

"eyes wet and huge" 8271

"eyes which can no longer supply tears" 2287

"eyes which had a tendency to become bloodshot" 5935

"eyes wide, simply opening his" 10185

"eyes wide open" 9886, 10220

"eyes wide-set but heavy-lidded" 498

Eyesight 158, 898

"eyesight, weak" 158

"eye-sockets" 3689

Eynesford, Lady 6977

"eyrie among the hazels, from his" 9131

Ezra 476

F.X. 6148

Fabian 2482

Fabio 9463

"fables seem possible, make" 1025

"fabric of existence" 5247

"fabric of her preoccupations" 9426

"fabricate tales" 2521

"Fabrick, the" 5514

"fabulously fractured versions" 7440

"façade, browned weathered brick" 9225

"façade, its noble" 3155

"façade of palest cotswold stone" 3155

"façade of the building" 9252

"face, black" 475

"face, boyish" 4674

"face, baby" 4210

"face, blue in the" 6676

"face, bold but grave" 10815

"face, brown" 5895

"face, can see his" 7428

"face, chubby spectacled" 5894

"face, compose my" 3708

"face, could not see her" 10434

"face, dogs breathe in my" 469

"face, everything was in motion except her" 10846

"face, expression on your" 5835

"face, eyes were fixed on his" 8295

"face, fan George Gallion's" 2985

"face, fat aquiline" 5908

"face, feel its heat on his" 2778

"face, fire playing on his" 5903

"face, gapy-" 4148

"face, gash on his" 5990

"face, gaunt" 5971

"face, gaunt exhausted" 5204

"face, gentle snow brushed his" 8610

"face, hated his" 5377

"face, her beautiful" 3965

"face, her daughter's" 6784

"face, her long" 10885

"face, here is my" 855

"face, his" 891, 8827

"face, his daughter's" 4593

"face, his light-complected" 8044

"face, his oval" 6594

"face, his rain-drenched" 9312

"face, his square" 243

"face, I could not see his" 1641

"face, in everybody's" 2973

"face, in front of the" 10181

"face, innocent gay" 5921

"face, large sad" 1609

"face, liked to see a new" 9896

"face, look at her" 10804

"face, Maltravers's" 7713

"face, my" 73, 4133

"face, neither repose nor gaiety in his" 3700

"face, nice" 5299

"face, no expression on his" 4251

"face, not a bad" 5911

"face, not only upon his" 5901

"face, on his" 10256

"face, openness of the" 5001

"face, over his" 151

"face, painted his" 1076

"face, pointed little" 462

"face, priest's" 1524

"face, pure and tranquil" 2336

"face, recognized her" 6724

"face, round angel" 4181

"face, scanning his" 1610

"face, searched his" 4593

"face, see her" 7490

"face, seraphic" 969

"face, she was indebted to the gouges in his" 339

"face, smeared the mud over his" 2833
"face, soldier's" 59
"face, streaking my" 9617
"face, swarthy turbaned" 8850
"face, that" 512, 5084
"face, the Colonel's" 877
"face, touching her" 7385
"face, water-lily" 9729
"face, wee screwed up protestant" 822
"face, whiskey-marked" 8852
"face, wrinkled" 1680
"face a little too narrow" 9912
"face against the screen door" 9957
"face as close to the windshield as the safety belt allowed" 2991
"face brick red against his new white bonnet" 10395
"face . . . broad and weighty" 5911
"face danger" 8174
"face exalted, his old" 1521
"face flat and white" 5911
"face floated in the single beam of light" 4296
"face floating in the polished silver mirror" 855
"face from his own house" 2751
"face furrowed with pain" 6594
"face ghastly in the incessant play of the lightning" 9312
"face glowed in the light of the lamp beams" 2492
"face grim [and] scored with exhaustion" 8124
"face her there" 5748
"face him" 9909
"face hot from a stab of sunshine" 10317
"face in the mud, my" 2894
"face is long, her" 10885
"face is thinner than it was a week ago" 2399
"face looks a hundred years old" 73
"face . . . lovely and framed in hair" 4296
"face moved with smiling" 243
"face of China" 6070
"face of her sleeping husband" 10117
"face of humanity" 4046
"face of Julien De Medici" 332
"face of Louis the Great" 3376
"face of the man" 10552
"face of the man on the bed" 2351
"face of the woman I sported with" 7440
"face of trouble, he saw the grinning" 50
"face open to the ceiling" 2398
"face positively pale with the irritation" 9325
"face shaded by the wide brim of her hat" 10441
"face shines boldly out" 2188
"face shone at Miriam" 8850

"face so tanned by wind and sun" 5897
"face southward, its loggish" 7887
"face stretched longer and thinner" 189
"face the fact" 11001
"face the windows" 6900
"face to face" 5834
"face to face with the fact of himself" 7472
"face towards the wall" 8476
"face was a sickish green" 143
"face was red" 1202
"face wrapped up in a wet towel" 7446
"faced, red-" 9554
"faced each other across the club table" 5349
"faced eastward" 7547
"faced north, chair and bed and meadowgrass" 6075
"faced the rising sun" 5964
"faced the view screen" 2682
"faced the water, stripped and" 6680
"faced their audience" 331
"face-down in the glistening dew" 1892
Faces 73, 189, 332, 333, 335, 339, 347, 469, 498, 822, 855, 877, 891, 1296, 1521, 1524, 1609, 1610, 1641, 2399, 2963, 3700, 3708, 4022, 4148, 4251, 4296, 4438, 4593, 5001, 5084, 5299, 5337, 5353, 5377, 5897, 5899, 5901, 5904, 5908, 5911, 5921, 5976, 6373, 6594, 6724, 6827, 7428, 7490, 8295, 8464, 8488, 8607, 8850, 8986, 9312, 9325, 9392, 10181, 10285, 10317, 10446, 10552, 10804, 10868, 10885
"faces, a few dark tribal" 10285
"faces, Asian" 10446
"faces, bearded" 336
"faces, beneath the white overhang of" 3969
"faces, Eleanor had two" 10868
"*Faces*, every *Feature* of their" 10764
"faces, grave" 2963
"faces, laughing" 4335
"faces, lights shining in their" 9392
"faces, lines of" 5654
"faces, little field of" 8864
"faces, making" 28
"faces, observers'" 8286
"faces, raised their" 8552
"faces, sea of seventy thousand" 9398
"faces, specific" 2356
"faces, summer air on our" 4422
"faces, things and" 3491
"faces, thousand-year-old" 3668
"faces, upturned" 5337
"faces, upturned young" 330
"faces, wear over their" 2066

"faces all unconsciously lifted to his inspection" 8072
"faces are as familiar to us as the flowers in our garden" 6266
"faces are different, each time the" 4022
"faces at himself, making" 7478
"faces black and white" 8864
"faces bright with cold" 8607
"faces full of pride and pleasure" 1245
"faces lingering in his mind" 10285
"faces of his forebears, the still rapt" 8986
"faces of my past" 7440
"faces of peasants" 5353
"faces of Poverty and Hunger, the care-worn" 7032
"faces of the carved angels" 2731
"faces of the just and the unjust" 6373
"faces of the three passengers" 9540
"faces of the two friends beside her" 4363
"faces of those I love" 8488
"faces round it, the" 4985
"faces set due north, identical peaky white" 9597
"faces was written the history of their nation, in whose" 1296
"faces were a blur, at first the" 6827
"faces were dusty from veld roads" 7036
"faceted as a cracked mirror" 5325
"facetiously place the cause of it all" 581
"facile talker, a" 5926
"facing anything unusual" 10800
"facing Seventh Avenue" 9157
"facing the large window" 8345
"facing the way she had come, dropped down" 410
"facing two empty ones" 9564
"fact, as a matter of" 1984
"fact, face the" 4868
"fact, first clean" 9033
"fact, it is an interesting" 3738
"fact, plain robe of" 5212
"fact, well-known" 4752
"factor, the deciding" 594
Factories 189, 1007, 1014, 1070, 4426, 5133, 7282, 8254
"factories, conglomerate of ugly" 7282
"factories, smell of the" 3184
"factories, tobacco" 5142
"factory, East India Company's" 8254
"Factory, I haven't been able to stop the" 1072
"Factory, York" 7918
"factory areas, bleaker" 1390
"factory of popular literature" 5311
"factory whistles" 8774
"factory yard, littered" 5133

"factotum to the Hon. Bertie Cecil" 2820

Facts 5054, 5216, 5518, 6821, 7228, 8964, 9033, 9699, 9702

"facts, abandoned the" 9429

"facts, already had most of his" 7228

"facts, class of" 8964

"facts, firsthand" 5518

"facts, happy" 6206

"facts, ignore the" 9699

"facts, interested only in the" 9702

"facts, the" 2581

"Facts, what I want is" 5054

"facts about Eskimos" 6821

"faculties, exercise of their keenest" 1826

"faculties were aroused" 4439

"fad" 7170

"Fada" 10795

"fade, others" 7423

"fade in" 8388

"fades, caught before it" 10077

"fading but still visible" 2105

"fading into evening" 2192

Fads 7170

"fag-end, at the" 7505

"fagged yet uncomplaining" 7290

"faggots, there are 2,556,596" 5949

"faggots in the New York City area" 5949

"fail, it can't" 10986

"fail to recognize her" 10798

"failed him, the big toe of Zivanias had" 350

"failed to do this, I have" 711

"failing for a fellowship" 6427

"failing in five ballots to nominate a successor" 6994

Failure 1019, 1072, 2479, 4319, 4833, 5465, 5543, 6281, 6508, 9379, 10521

"failure, atmosphere almost solid with" 4319

"failure, aware of his" 3516

"failure, certainty of" 3521

"failure, critical and commercial" 5543

"failure, eighth" 9379

"failure, I am a" 4833

"failure, vindicate his" 3514

"failure as a painter, self-confessed" 5465

"failure of his third marriage" 3518

"failures" 5558

Fain, Billy 2863

"faint, scream or" 3689

"fainted and they took her for dead" 3413

"fainted away" 7063

"fainter as they went, growing" 10016

"faintly through the mist of sleep" 10158

"Fair, ambulant" 1250

"fair, audio" 7904

"Fair, Bart's" 7422

"Fair, Doune" 8952

"Fair, Easter" 314

"fair, forty-sixth annual" 293

"fair, like a street" 9191

"fair, seems only" 597

"fair and thin" 8217

"fair in love and war, all's" 7730

Fairchild, Dexter 9280

"fairgrounds, the" 8513

"Fairoaks" 3307

Fairs 293, 314, 1250, 7422, 7904

"fairways, the shining" 5627

Fairweather, George 8698

"fairy tale" 5588, 6829

"fairy tale, a kind of" 6883

"fairy tale, this is a" 9010

"Fairy Glen" 9745

Faith 7506

"faith, in all good" 5449

"faith, I've lost my" 2399

"Faith, Voice of" 7506

"faithful hounds" 3396

"Faithfulness" 6033

"fake, it's a" 507

"faked up for him, royal genealogy they had" 363

"Falcon, Peregrine" 6880

"Falconer" 1165

Falks, Lance 3307

"fall, don't" 870

"fall, first chill of" 1558

"fall, we continued to" 2425

"fall again, it was" 3883

"fall at last into the hands of the enemy" 1161

"fall from the footholds" 32

"fall in love" 5733

"fall . . . left him unconscious and terribly mutilated" 32

"fall of 1777" 8592

"fall onto them, as if it would" 7275

"fallen, the Odéon has" 9390

"fallen asleep" 10265

"falling down, it's" 3138

"falling leaves, moon of the" 8442

"falling off the top of a truck" 9769

"falling over, keep from" 5239

"falling plump into the pool of matrimony" 5733

Fallok, Istvan 8196

Fallon, Max 136

"fallow land" 5141

"fallow year" 3660

Falls, old man 2303

"falls are falling, spumy" 7682

"falls at last into Monterey Bay" 9751

"falls out of love with his motorbike" 7628

"Falmouth harbour" 8152

"false, what is not in the open street is" 5418

"false beacon, more like the" 3671

"false dawn" 2269

"False Divide" 415

"false estimates of her, people made" 7565

"false teeth" 4699

Falsehood 5216, 5235, 5241

"falsehood and fact, composed of" 5216

"faltered, sky and earth" 10598

"faltering on the top of the front stoop" 7122

Falworth, Myles 7607

Fame 108, 257, 927, 1329, 1332, 1380, 1447, 4092, 4321, 4466, 4788, 5040, 5212, 5214, 5215, 5423, 5432, 5562, 5585, 5797, 6405, 6661, 7137, 7168, 9124, 10781

"fame, a sort of universal" 9124

"fame, Cleveland Indian" 8934

"fame, limited or dubious" 3546

"fame, of no" 3066

"fame, visibility and" 3545

"fame and fortune, gone to find" 10074

"fame . . . is a second skin" 3546

"fame of which he never dreamed" 6661

"fame requires every kind of excess" 3539

"familiar, group itself looks" 4022

"familiar, no doubt grew very" 6496

"familiar, you look" 5862

"familiar in her world" 1288

"familiar of mine, a" 5214

"familiar streets" 4539

Families 353, 354, 357, 358, 359, 360, 361, 428, 493, 513, 694, 781, 808, 1180, 1602, 1667, 1775, 1865, 2061, 2300, 2320, 2328, 2334, 2366, 2398, 2441, 2452, 2510, 2660, 2670, 2672, 2712, 3025, 3059, 3071, 3080, 3082, 3094, 3108, 3177, 3200, 3202, 3490, 3500, 3528, 3615, 3648, 3659, 3823, 3837, 3842, 3854, 3942, 3959, 4011, 4107, 4186, 4209, 4437, 4444, 4450, 4545, 4567, 4593, 4714, 4824, 5192, 5223, 5355, 5466, 5636, 5725, 5744, 5780, 6089, 6090, 6094, 6101, 6103, 6122, 6131, 6135, 6159, 6172, 6187, 6288, 6305, 6385, 6414, 6577, 6601, 6611, 6628, 6629, 6720, 6850, 6851, 6860, 6868, 7042, 7073, 7129, 7377, 7441, 7501, 7510, 7756, 7802, 7825, 7873, 7950, 7961, 8352, 8548, 8688, 8926, 9054, 9410, 9527, 9630, 9659, 9664, 9721, 9869, 9958, 9966, 10039, 10331, 10354, 10553, 10556, 10895

"families, certain" 3605

"families, forty or fifty" 6103

"Families, full Accounts of their" 353
"families, in the presence of both" 10661
"families, many" 1019
"families, Negro" 5161
"families, our best" 640
"families, six" 10431
"families, the three" 3648
"[families] are more or less alike, unhappy" 5466
"families are more or less dissimilar, all happy" 5466
"families got secrets, all" 7961
"families in Crescent Place, the five" 6288
"families of the place, the two chief" 7950
"families ruled, a few" 3561
"families ... should be like mine" 3592
"families stood at the center" 3586
"family, accidents ran in the" 4450
"Family, Account of my" 3527
"family, ancient and honourable" 4444
"family, antiquity of the" 3589
"family, anybody in this" 7525
"family, being in the same" 3584
"family, Bingle" 7756
"family, close conventional" 3608
"family, Colfax" 3094
"family, Comstock" 5621
"family, Cutter" 3823
"family, divided" 2398
"family, entire Winderman" 3601
"family, finally left her" 6172
"family, Fleishman" 3627
"family, fortunes of her" 7377
"family, German-Jewish" 369
"Family, good" 6601
"family, good but impoverished" 4209
"family, good Devonshire" 4926
"family, Greek" 3500
"family, Hampton" 10556
"family, happy" 3552
"family, her" 3413, 6305
"family, her father's branch of the" 2672
"family, her loving" 6577
"family, her whole" 2341
"family, Herries" 8548
"family, his" 6106, 6385, 6629
"family, in a" 3574
"family, in my" 3613
"family, it runs in my" 5237
"family, large" 5725, 6135
"family, legend in our" 5223
"family, looking for his" 7231
"family, meet the" 3595
"family, murder her" 7739
"family, my" 361, 808, 2366, 3202, 3563, 3607, 3612, 3626, 3633, 7727

"family, never had a" 3598
"family, occupied by a single" 3177
"family, of a very distinguished" 6628
"family, our" 4880, 5947, 8926
"family, poor" 781
"family, possessed by a" 3551
"family, Price" 3573
"family, Prizzi" 1068, 10664
"family, prominent Virginia" 4824
"family, pull of the" 3625
"family, remarkable Zinn" 6577
"family, run in Alice's" 10895
"family, small" 3596
"family, Solo-Miller" 3594
"family, some Hindi in the" 365
"family, Spiegelglass" 3600
"family, still had" 3606
"family, support her" 4186
"family, the" 3069, 3588, 3629
"family, the whole" 3645
"family, thinking about your" 3622
"family, this" 6613, 7073
"family, upper-middle-class" 3558
"family, very scrupulous" 3563
"family, watching his" 3616
"family, we were an odd" 3611
"family, your" 1043, 7825
"family album" 6868
"family are dark, our" 3577
"family enthusiasm" 4567
"family estates" 3119
"family festival" 3558
"family gatherings" 3597
"family had stuck together, if the" 3610
"family has practiced the end of the world" 3626
"family has relatives, every" 3590
"family in full plumage" 3558
"Family in that Country, a very good" 6601
"family is who you decide it should be" 6720
"family life, tranquil" 3248
"family loss, a great" 9513
"family now awaited the end" 2363
"family of Armine" 6090
"family of Dashwood" 3549
"family of the Campbells, widespread" 6611
"family of the Duke of Granbörg" 3879
"family of three girls" 3632
"family of wild swans" 741
"Family Planning Clinic, the brand new" 2480
"family relationships, the trouble with" 3575
"family so proud of their antiquity" 358
"family so secure, there is no" 7873
"family status" 2679
"family that followed the woods as some families follow the sea"

10354
"family to move back to Louisiana, asked her" 3659
"family tragedy" 2510
"family tree, a fine" 360
"family was waiting for Caleb Gare" 10039
"family went strange and it wasn't with grief" 2328
"family were clustered at the grave-site" 3959
"family would gather within" 3108
"family-seat" 9874
"famous, before he became" 3536
"famous, first became" 4092
"famous, mildly" 3542
"famous, not to be" 250
"famous and honoured throughout the South Caribbean" 4466
"famous for her beauty and her wit" 10781
"famous for its food, Porterhouse is" 3851
"famous locally" 3533
"famous man" 5585
"famous man, have you ever known a" 3536
"famous novelist" 696
"famous now and then" 5040
"famous Sylvester women, the three" 10053
"famous than he, like thousands less" 5468
"famous Torrigiani, the" 3084
"famous wooden horse of the Greeks" 2603
"famous writers" 8641
"fan, folded-up made-in-Japan lacquered paper" 3958
"fan, heading into her" 9965
"fan, her half-opened" 4045
"fan, spread an ivory" 8428
"fan clubs, girls registered in his" 3538
"fan George Gallion's face" 2985
"fan in the ceiling above it" 5351
Fanaticism 7507
"fanatics, fools and" 6310
"fanatics, go not with" 7507
"fancied, those who" 2619
"fancied, would have" 1610
"fancied herself an exile of sorts" 4544
"fancied himself a man with a mission" 259
"fancied she was piloting a drowned car" 2946
"fancies itself the heart of the continent" 4089
"fancy, whispers of" 4603
"fancy, wrought the embroidery of its" 5212
"fancy holder, using a" 8578
"fancy was for an island" 5013
Fane, Elinor 8242

"fangs of the mountains" 8400
Fanie 4347
Fanny 2539, 4177, 7123
"fans, flipping open their" 5635
"fans of young palmetto shoots, delicately green and pleated" 9841
Fanshaw 8630
Fanshawe 7118
"fantastical" 10900
Fantasy 4900, 7516, 9701
"fantasy, allows herself a" 4900
"fantasy, glass beads of" 7516
"fantasy, Gothic" 7149
"fantasy, my" 2795
"fantasy, not even in an outrageous" 2006
"fantasy, pure" 9701
"fantasy, rejector of" 6478
"Fanua, island of" 1495
"far and wide" 2607
"far as the eye can see" 6781
"far away" 2966
"far away, not all that" 2810
"far away, not so" 806
"far away from home, so" 9520
"far away in Africa, I was" 5089
"far away is it, how" 9573
"far below" 6060
"far below lay the Indian Ocean" 7921
"far enough from downtown Baltimore" 3184
"far from other places, it is so" 4081
"far from the nearest metric wrench" 9834
"far off" 7316
"far piece, I walked a" 10398
"far to look, we have not" 9278
Faraday, Mr. William 703
"faraway, it all seemed so" 3442
"Faraway New York" 6915
"far-beyond-it-all and happy look" 2429
"Farbridge" 1629
Farbstein, Lou 6980
"fare, asking for double his" 9537
"fare, genuine English" 7573
"farewell, curt speech of" 1525
"farewell, gesture of" 2552
"farewell, lifted her hand briefly in" 1602
"farewell dinner" 3912
"Farewell Farewell Farewell" 1669
"farewell note" 2570
"farewell visit" 9950
"farewell word to say" 1677
Farewells 996, 1525, 1575, 1599, 1602, 1617, 1630, 1658, 1661, 1669, 1670, 1677, 1929, 2009, 2552, 2683, 3912, 4011, 6722, 6773
Fargeon, Mr. 5891
Farishta, Gibreel 2427
"farm, alone on the" 3835
"farm, born on a" 803
"farm, county poor" 2947

"farm, cussing our" 1686
"farm, Danford pony breeding and schooling" 3654
"Farm, Egypt" 9138
"farm, frontier" 1850
"Farm, Hardpan" 2695
"farm, Indiana" 2956
"farm, Loman" 6179
"Farm, Manor" 2895
"Farm, Marsh" 3082
"farm, melon" 6170
"Farm, memory of the" 7380
"farm, my Uncle Hezron's" 3655
"Farm, Orley" 8955
"farm, our" 9944
"farm, pass our" 3666
"Farm, Poor" 2303
"farm, see the" 3656
"Farm, Spaulding's" 6559
"farm, the" 3615, 3665
"farm, their" 8231
"Farm, Wayne" 6626
"farm boy" 8712
"Farm House, Bayley" 6964
"farm in Arkansaw, Tom's uncle Silas's" 1160
"farm in Berkshire, cultivated a small" 3635
"farm in Maine" 4186
"farm in north-eastern France" 3111
"farm lay on a hillside" 3648
"farm of Midbranch" 3069
"farm workers" 3758
"farmed at Gunnars Stead" 3661
"farmed out" 5161
Farmer, Andy 5112
"farmer, gentleman" 239
"farmer, his sixty humble years as a" 6661
"farmer, young" 4344
"farmer of a few hundred acres, no richer than many a" 6611
"farmer stood watching" 8648
Farmers 2895, 3603, 3635, 3639, 3640, 3646, 3651, 3652, 3668, 4560, 5213, 8648
"farmers, Anglo-Saxon" 3639
"farmers, gentleman" 3603
"farmers of England" 3635
"farmhouse" 989
"farm-house" 3987
"farmhouse, abandoned" 9950
"farmhouse, in a" 807
"farmhouse, men walk past the" 995
"farm-house, old" 835
"farmhouse, old" 3139
"farmhouse, one final check of the" 3245
"farmhouse, rooms of the" 185
"farmhouse, small thatched" 3762
"farmhouse, sweet old" 3118
"farmhouse, the" 3615, 7440
"farmhouse, the plain white" 2554
"farmhouse on the river, that rotting" 2776

"farmhouse was quiet" 8326
"farmhouses" 5886
"farmhouses, far-scattered" 9515
"farmhouses, gray" 3044
Farming 3758, 10927, 10946
"farming, cattle or sheep" 1568
"farming, were not much accomplished at" 3604
"farmland, Nebraska" 7702
"farmlands began" 224
Farms 803, 1686, 1850, 2275, 2895, 3069, 3082, 3157, 3615, 3634, 3635, 3637, 3638, 3643, 3644, 3648, 3651, 3652, 3653, 3654, 3655, 3656, 3661, 3664, 3665, 3666, 3669, 3835, 6418, 6559, 6626, 7126, 7380, 8231, 8429, 9753, 10925
"farms, ample" 7608
"farms, estates and" 2489
"farms, rich new" 10341
"farms of Sandy Creek" 9152
"farms six miles out on State 21" 3651
"farmyard" 966
"farmyard, in the" 3653
Farnham, Hubert 9362
"faro" 3965
Farr, Nancy 1061
Farrago, John 5884
Farris 10971
Farrow, John Dalton 7319
"farthin'" 1085
Farthing, Harvey 6003
"fascia, consider" 2066
"fascinated by her scenic talent" 8837
"fascinated by Rhoda" 1323
"fascinated by *The Maltese Falcon*" 1323
"fascinated Morag" 7684
"fascinating if unpretentious architecture" 5607
"fascinating place" 1410
Fascination 1323, 4256
"fascination" 4256
"fascination, in some" 6864
"fascist collaborators, French" 4017
Fashion 603, 3378
"fashion, it was the" 3672
"fashion, the ancient" 7067
"fashion, you have begun another" 603
"fashion across the water, they have a" 2293
"fashion of the time did something to disguise it" 9839
"fashionable girl" 6605
"fashionable style and taste" 3376
"fashionable were there in large quantities, the" 9380
"Fashionables Fighting Flames" 3770
"fashioned for ourselves, things we had" 1253

"fashions, bow to those" 5390
"fast, the man is" 9
"fast and narrow and dangerous" 9026
"fast college of the day, *the*" 7876
"fast forward" 3725
"fast I reckon, mighty" 2296
"fast track, the" 6274
"fastened themselves on the hills of Walden Valley" 10623
"faster and faster" 7842
"faster than a man could ride" 6333
"faster than he would have liked" 10455
"fastest fucker in town" 9
"fasting and wearing orange clothes" 6546
"fat, baby" 4210
"fat, few and" 569
"fat, he was very" 5907
"fat, old and" 7643
"fat, throat decomposing to" 8883
"fat, to his utter disgust was" 5907
"fat and foolish, Fifties were as" 6767
"fat and sassy" 5382
"fat as a hog" 5908
"fat coachman" 9757
"fat for plucking" 5026
"fat horses" 9757
"fat Jeeter as her maid of honor, the" 3604
"fat man" 10327
Fat Rosalie 6652
"fat stock" 1027
"fatal plunge" 2374
Fate 1221, 1235, 1243, 2286, 2683, 4613, 5080, 5411, 5562, 5789, 7026, 7106, 7453, 7478, 10766
"fate" 4463
"Fate, eternal Law of" 2286
"fate, his" 3676
"fate, mulling one's" 7467
"fate, no fear of the" 5411
"fate, placed by" 3678
"fate, strange quirk of" 7453
"fate, thread of" 3677
"fate, unwilling to set myself up against" 3674
"fate in our stars, is our" 3679
"Fate issued a sub-decree" 5789
"fate . . . lie within ourselves" 3679
"Fate of the Clan to which I once belong'd" 5552
"fate of the passengers" 8061
"fate says *Quit*, if" 2683
"fateful birth of Pakistan" 3237
"fateful year, in that" 7130
Father 286, 839, 1811, 2093, 2552, 3191, 4221, 4722, 6242, 9866, 10028
"father" 2014
"father, a" 365
"father, Allan's" 3180
"father, Bentley's" 6682

"Father, bless me" 1803
"father, Brazilian" 800
"father, call from a" 1153
"father, Christina Goering's" 6628
"father, French" 831
"father, Gabriel's" 6698
"father, handsome" 6650
"Father, have one" 7519
"Father, Heavenly" 2625
"father, Henry Fuller's" 8675
"father, her" 1602, 1617, 1947, 2672, 3928, 3958, 4166, 4169, 4289, 4587, 4814, 5758, 5900, 6106, 6620, 6627, 6665, 6687, 6713, 6728, 6730, 6863, 7105, 7763, 7843, 8174, 9325, 10036, 10872, 10914
"father, her dead" 4224
"father, his" 159, 898, 1492, 1908, 2666, 3071, 3084, 3253, 3568, 3584, 3602, 3617, 3630, 4242, 4436, 4438, 4469, 4588, 4694, 4719, 4741, 4926, 5149, 5234, 5699, 6131, 6194, 6231, 6515, 6516, 6521, 6550, 6623, 6626, 6629, 6636, 6652, 6662, 6678, 6680, 6717, 6719, 6739, 6881, 7382, 7575, 7764, 9708, 9722, 9752, 9857, 9860, 10122, 10341, 10905
"Father, his" 355
"father, his paunchy bearded shrewd" 3562
"father, his tipsy" 2942
"Father, Holy" 7548
"father, I was my" 6689
"father, I'm your bleeding" 8661
"father, Janey depended on her" 6666
"father, just like his" 1502
"father, killed his" 6194
"father, my" 57, 239, 322, 364, 536, 662, 845, 891, 920, 1540, 1570, 1752, 1806, 1846, 1887, 1897, 1930, 2175, 2179, 2407, 2441, 2450, 2489, 2510, 2667, 2735, 2967, 3290, 3359, 3614, 3619, 3657, 3786, 3883, 3948, 4128, 4245, 4273, 4448, 4681, 5007, 5012, 5177, 5225, 5245, 5563, 5580, 5672, 5768, 6097, 6120, 6159, 6168, 6169, 6359, 6374, 6382, 6405, 6423, 6451, 6457, 6477, 6508, 6520, 6551, 6602, 6604, 6606, 6607, 6608, 6611, 6618, 6621, 6625, 6631, 6635, 6637, 6642, 6646, 6654, 6656, 6657, 6659, 6668, 6671, 6683, 6695, 6697, 6699, 6700, 6715, 6718, 6726, 6731, 6733, 6735, 6823, 7035, 7063, 7270, 7446, 7536, 7558, 7749, 8038, 8230, 8576, 8752, 8923, 9045, 9051, 9052, 9369, 9918, 9949, 9950, 10102, 10969

"Father, my" 2626, 6601
"father, never intended for him to have a" 6542
"father, Newt Hardbine's" 3733
"father, our" 2419, 6705, 9062
"father, some peasant" 366
"father, that's an odd" 6679
"father, the" 3553, 5909, 5917, 6603, 6612, 6655, 6725, 7129
"father, their" 2393, 3620, 3952, 4780, 6566, 7414, 8206
"Father, voice of" 10028
"father, watched her" 6691
"father, your" 3490
"Father Almighty" 2626
"father always called him, what his" 7566
"father and mother, his" 6648
"father and mother, his long-dead" 5965
"father before me, my" 4448
"father bought a convertible" 9827
"father brought home his new bride" 6664
"Father built a house" 3191
"*Father Die, Watching*" 2396
"father died" 5914
"father died, after my" 6169
"father died, your" 6778
"father dropped dead" 3958
"father had ever got killed, whose" 2374
"father had wanted to kill me" 57
"father hanged, I saw my" 2461
"father is dead" 2413
"father is on fire" 3786
"father loved her, her" 6533
"father of a certain William Peveril" 6518
"Father of Gods and Men" 2628
"father of Jacob" 6472
"father of my sex" 7554
"Father of Our Country, Glorious" 4219
"father of the infant" 6644
"Father of Waters" 9198
"father often remarked" 1064
"father passes, my" 4227
"father quiet and rich" 797
"father returned, my" 6487
"father shot himself, my" 5769
"father spoke, dream" 5008
"father to come in" 9325
"father to my son, I was a terrible" 6643
"father to son, from" 7950
"father took me to Ireland" 2510
"father unGreek diffidence" 8894
"father wanted a small family" 3596
"father was a blacksmith" 6618
"father was a carpenter, my" 6458
"father was a little bad" 6739
"father was a Methodist minister" 1540

"father was a missionary murdered in Burundi" 6735

"father was arrested" 2179

"father was doing, what my" 2175

"father was no different from other men" 10760

"father was ten, when my" 9978

"father who was quiet amused and who rarely said anything" 4780

"Father you had to go away" 2541

"father-in-law, my" 2358, 10013

"father-in-law, the King's" 3571

Fathers 57, 159, 239, 322, 348, 355, 366, 369, 386, 536, 577, 644, 662, 667, 794, 797, 839, 845, 891, 920, 1153, 1492, 1570, 1571, 1686, 1752, 1806, 1846, 1887, 1908, 2014, 2175, 2179, 2367, 2374, 2407, 2413, 2419, 2441, 2450, 2461, 2489, 2510, 2541, 2552, 2584, 2666, 2667, 2672, 2726, 2735, 2771, 2950, 3084, 3191, 3224, 3290, 3553, 3559, 3562, 3568, 3578, 3584, 3596, 3602, 3614, 3617, 3619, 3630, 3657, 3684, 3786, 3950, 3952, 3958, 4128, 4162, 4169, 4227, 4242, 4245, 4273, 4289, 4294, 4448, 4484, 4588, 4681, 4694, 4714, 4722, 4741, 4780, 4926, 4931, 5007, 5008, 5012, 5108, 5177, 5234, 5245, 5563, 5580, 5758, 5768, 5841, 5900, 5909, 5914, 5917, 5965, 6097, 6106, 6120, 6122, 6168, 6169, 6181, 6194, 6197, 6359, 6374, 6382, 6405, 6423, 6451, 6457, 6458, 6477, 6487, 6508, 6515, 6516, 6518, 6519, 6520, 6521, 6523, 6524, 6528, 6533, 6535, 6541, 6542, 6543, 6549, 6550, 6551, 6602, 6603, 6604, 6605, 6606, 6607, 6612, 6613, 6614, 6616, 6617, 6620, 6621, 6623, 6624, 6625, 6626, 6628, 6629, 6633, 6635, 6636, 6637, 6642, 6643, 6644, 6646, 6652, 6654, 6655, 6656, 6657, 6659, 6660, 6661, 6662, 6664, 6665, 6668, 6671, 6674, 6676, 6678, 6679, 6680, 6681, 6682, 6683, 6687, 6689, 6691, 6693, 6697, 6698, 6699, 6705, 6707, 6709, 6710, 6712, 6713, 6715, 6716, 6717, 6718, 6719, 6723, 6725, 6726, 6727, 6728, 6729, 6730, 6731, 6733, 6735, 6739, 6778, 6881, 6937, 7035, 7105, 7129, 7183, 7270, 7360, 7369, 7414, 7446, 7536, 7558, 7566, 7585, 7624, 7749, 7764, 7843, 8038, 8229, 8230, 8576, 8661, 8675, 8710, 8752, 8867, 8894, 9051, 9052, 9325, 9369, 9708, 9752, 9818, 9827, 9866, 9918, 9950, 10028, 10036, 10102,

10122, 10179, 10341, 10546, 10760, 10791, 10914, 10969, 10971

"fathers, his" 10768

"fathers, the worst of" 6617

"fathers, their" 1244, 7950

"fathers are, I don't care who your bleeding" 8661

"father's arms, in her" 6624

"father's cap-badge, his" 8710

"father's cottage, her" 6555

"father's death" 8229

"father's estate, his" 4931

"father's family name" 4714

"father's father, my" 7498

"father's hair, my" 4294

"Father's head, the Dead" 2367

"father's house" 667, 3602, 9663

"father's house, my" 947, 3701

"father's inscrutable war cry" 2942

"father's large and sturdy parents" 9949

"father's left hand, sat at her" 3824

"father's murder, her" 6181

"father's neck, expression of his" 7585

"father's right arm, my" 348

"father's side, on his" 367

"father's voice, his" 10122

"father's wake, his" 3950

"father's wedding, your" 10654

Fatigue 557, 4375, 4420, 8360, 8455, 8851

"fatigue" 7988

"fatigue, drooping with" 3693

"fatigue, in a fog of" 3685

"fatigue, in spite of his" 3690

"fatigue and monotony and ennui" 9381

Fatoudi, Ali Ibn 6398

"fatter, growing" 5907

"Faubourg Saint Germain" 6289

Faulkner, William 5773

"Fault, I acquired a major" 5226

"fault, I was Harry's" 7559

"fault, it was very much his own" 6735

"fault entirely, black kitten's" 7551

"fault his grandmother had found in him, the only" 4892

"fault of Daniel Caldigate" 3553

"faults, for all its" 1410

"fauna, flora and" 455

Faust 5363

Faust, Tony 503

"Faust, singing in" 8740

"favor, do me a" 3915

"favorite of his mother, indisput-able" 6553

"favorite song" 4736

Favors 3915, 6996

"favour, I have received your esteemed" 5387

"favourably known" 1012

"favoured of Europe" 3831

"favourite, Hamlet's" 2689

"Favourite at Court, first and most distinguished" 5883

"favourites, his Norman" 3571

Fawcett, John 5014

Fawcett, Mary 5014

Fawn-Cochley, Major 1026

Fay 6893

Fay, Felix 5709

Faygelees, Mrs. 6652

Fear 104, 144, 387, 410, 885, 1112, 1763, 2362, 2462, 2599, 2652, 2705, 2804, 3686, 4113, 4256, 4471, 4600, 5173, 5260, 5599, 5603, 6255, 6549, 6790, 6839, 7084, 7447, 8039, 8179, 8229, 8491, 8502, 8812, 9063, 9074, 9285, 9318, 9402, 9992, 10004, 10121, 10140, 10209

"fear, biggest" 3735

"fear, camp of" 1310

"fear, growing" 10121

"fear, I don't want to talk about the" 3727

"fear, landscape of" 5173

"fear, never walked alone without" 3714

"fear, nothing to" 3724

"fear, only" 3700

"fear, over the" 3712

"fear, walks in" 2362

"fear, where there is" 3731

"fear and doubt beneath the skin, push the" 3708

"fear from the anger of gods, have not much to" 104

"fear is strange" 144

"fear is the surrogate for pain" 3726

"fear not" 7447

"fear of incest" 8229

"fear of missing it, magnified his" 3709

"fear of prosecution" 2567

"fear of ridicule, not from" 2734

"fear of saying something that would haunt me" 387

"fear of snakes chilling him" 3714

"fear that burned in his skin" 5603

"feared to awaken sleepers" 7712

"feared to be left in the shades of darkness" 9402

"fearful, everything is" 3731

"fearful of hurting it" 1140

Fearless Witness 9020

"fears a structural collapse" 5599

"fears had become so great that they threatened to paralyse him" 3721

"fears have moved in" 3715

"feast, it was a fine" 3851

"feast in the palace of Babylon" 6752

"feast of Christmas Eve" 3680

"Feast of '09" 3851

"feasting" 10512

Feasts 3851, 10512

"feat, I read of his" 9262
"feat, this mighty" 9508
"feathers fluttering in a breeze"
    9324
Feats 8001, 9262, 9268, 9508
"Feature of their *Faces"* 10764
"featured on the *CBS Evening News"*
    6335
"featureless" 6401
Features 332, 333, 334, 336, 340,
    343, 347, 352, 549, 984, 3577,
    4157, 4184, 4292, 4295, 4297,
    5001, 5712, 5894, 5895, 5912,
    5935, 5956, 5961, 6403, 7036,
    7488, 8098, 8237, 8361, 8545,
    8658, 9097, 10832, 10882
"features, delicate" 2731
"features, fineness of the" 334
"features, his strong" 1887
"features, standard white American"
    4438
"features, strong of" 10038
"features, surface of his" 6022
"features agonized, your" 8496
"features rough, her" 4773
"February" 829, 1724, 2559, 2886,
    3479, 4571, 4643, 4921, 5485,
    6750, 7069, 7084, 7248, 7600,
    8059, 8128, 8146, 8275, 8426,
    8585, 8589, 8597, 9027, 9092,
    9226, 9454, 9833, 9911, 10606,
    10612, 10630, 10715, 10934
"February, at the end of" 2960
"February morning" 2954
"February sun" 9995
"February sunlight" 9211
"February that it didn't snow" 8619
"fecundated by the corpses" 5149
"fed up with visiting relatives" 4519
"Federation, year of" 7080
"fedora, almost brimless" 4249
"fedora set at a rakish angle" 5975
"fed-up" 7628
"fee, the standard" 6322
"fee of 1964, the first big" 9913
"feebly shook" 652
"feed him here, she could not" 557
"feed on disaster, it goes off to"
    2593
"feed the catfish" 5380
"feed the livestock" 10945
"feeding his rabbits" 7109
"feel, began to" 46
"feel, don't know how I" 3485
"feel, how do I" 65
"feel, how would you" 6546
"feel, so how does it" 10237
"feel bad in the morning" 2907
"feel in his prime" 82
"feel individedly happy" 10995
"feel is a drift of wonder, all I" 4582
"feel it moving" 7066
"feel of the wood under her chin"
    6240
"feel the mended place in my shirt-

waist" 8500
"feel this way after so long" 2524
"feeling, damn snaky" 1878
"feeling, funny sudden" 2447
"feeling, her first" 10255
"feeling, human" 1790
"feeling, I have had the" 5586
"feeling, I have the distinct" 9305
"feeling, I've got this" 5289
"feeling, it is with an especial" 9884
"feeling, perpetual" 9308
"feeling, uneasy" 1675
"feeling at all, not sure I was cap-
    able of any" 7317
"feeling boomps-a-daisy" 567
"feeling both lonely and splendid"
    992
"feeling depressed" 2499
"feeling he could no longer breathe"
    6598
"feeling in her stomach, queasy
    seasick" 10271
"feeling in mid-season form this
    morning" 4349
"feeling it would be a bad day" 7013
"feeling more stolid than usual"
    10201
"feeling of a conqueror, keeps for
    life the" 6553
"feeling of London, his dominant"
    7847
"feeling quite themselves" 127
"feeling suddenly as cold as the
    beer" 2351
"feeling that some new spark of
    meaning will appear" 10077
"feeling that something had hap-
    pened to her" 10155
"feeling that something must be
    done" 2814
"feeling the prickly straw" 8475
"feeling very well, had not been"
    125
"feeling you have, do you know the"
    7387
Feelings 1675, 3323, 3850, 9308,
    10155, 10173, 10507
"feelings, hurt God's" 7511
"feelings, intimate" 7956
"feelings at bay, keeping her" 3320
"feelings he had not known before,
    in the grip of" 4659
"feelings of self-exposure, still
    dominant" 5629
"feels a clash of excitement and
    dread" 3478
Feet 158, 342, 352, 5686, 6796,
    8371, 10061
"feet, beneath his" 7854
"feet, big" 6687
"feet, examined her" 564
"feet, fretful" 10540
"feet, her bare" 3759, 10792
"feet, her brown" 10212
"feet, light happy unladen" 10368

"feet, my" 8684
"feet, on her own brisk" 10337
"feet, oversize" 979
"feet, poor" 158
"feet, run off her" 3682
"feet, shuffle of" 14
"feet, soles of his" 5686
"feet, stamped her" 4474
"feet, stamped his numb" 1544
"feet, sturdily-shod" 10859
"feet, swollen septic" 10521
"feet, their" 342
"feet, under their" 5020
"feet, wipe your" 4193
"feet are propped, my" 5355
"feet crunched on the hard-packed
    sand" 10379
"feet crunching in the limpet shells"
    6648
"feet encased in a pair of boots"
    7630
"feet felt the snow" 1648
"feet firmly on the ground" 6815
"feet hurtin', my" 10061
"feet in the cowboy boots can't even
    touch the floor" 5966
"feet in the dust, dragged her" 8371
"feet in the dust, wriggling his"
    4137
"feet slapping the pavement" 7855
"feet touching the steps" 8802
"feet upon American soil, as he set
    his" 277
"feet were stuck into sabots" 10792
"feet wet too often, they got their"
    8678
Feigel 10824
"feigned, at least partly" 9305
Feldman 4249
Felice, William 4566
"felicity of her own name, extraor-
    dinary" 4775
"Felix the Cat clock" 9342
"fell, she" 16
"fell, slowly" 733
"fell backwards" 34
"fell down, she" 23
"fell flat on the gravel" 2342
"fell from the top-most stair to the
    bottom" 2901
"fell in love" 7709, 9010
"fell in love with automobiles" 5671
"fell in love with Emily Rowley"
    5638
"fell in love with Sally" 5658
"fell in the grass" 1784
"fell into a doze" 8456
"fell into the abyss" 2520
"fell off the bus" 2353
"fell out of love with her husband"
    2146
"fell out of the apple tree" 27
"fell out of the dark part" 4660
"fell out of the window" 2520
"fell over on the yellow carpet" 10214

"fell over the edge" 1948
"fell to his death" 6321
Feller, Bob 8934
"feller, wife-left" 2651
"feller down the street" 4937
Fellow, Miss 10004
"fellow, big" 4293
"fellow, fiddler" 6622
"fellow, tall rawboned rangy young" 5897
"fellow, the next" 56
"fellow, young" 2688
"fellow in a racoon coat and a straw skimmer" 6652
"fellow of the college" 7522
"fellow of twenty-seven, young" 242
"fellow-citizens" 2600
"fellows, good" 2885
"fellows, his" 7594
"fellowship, failing for a" 6427
"fellow-townsmen, his" 1821
"felonious gaze" 9763
"felt, if something big is to be" 4582
"felt afterwards, how I" 8188
"felt better within herself" 2249
"felt by him, deeply" 5085
"felt good" 3312
"felt him, she" 6548
"felt his finger in her" 7998
"felt it coming at sunset" 2513
"felt it was himself" 3367
"felt it was more" 3367
"felt like God, he" 1994
"felt like he was the only human creature in the town" 8723
"felt out of place" 9110
"felt the dark wool of my gown lap up the heat and din of noon" 5096
"felt the hot bright sunlight" 10145
"felt the same, never" 10507
"felt to the touch like a squab or a young bird" 416
Felton, John 5780
Feltons, the 3589
"female figure in a white shroud" 4103
"female of the species vanished" 2559
"feminine population" 1012
"feminine significance" 5083
"femininity, radiated" 3263
"fen, in the" 4455
"fence, barbed-wire" 3995
"fence, chain-link rust-proof" 10721
"fence, high wire" 4316
"fence, old" 9673
"fence, outside the iron" 4152
"fence, split-rail" 5626
"fence, white-washed" 726
"fence of bicycle between the sexes" 977
"fence of the burying-ground" 726
"fence rail, poster on the" 8315
"fence topped with three barbed strands and masked with oleanders" 4316
"fence wires, ringing" 10609
"fence with three gates, iron" 4099
"fenced in by two rivers" 1393
"fenced, well-" 5067
"fences, iron" 3095
"fences of cast-iron" 3103
"fencing, it was like" 8027
"fencing, lesson in" 2101
"fended their way along a crowded street" 10374
"Fenian rising" 9109
Fenn, Graybeard 9614
Fennigate, Kate 10798
"fens, land between the sea and the" 3058
Fentiman, Captain 7107
"Fenway Park" 4849
Fenwick, Ezzie 8640
Ferguson, Elizabeth 7710, 10852
Ferguson, Ian 4755
"fermentation, always in a state of" 10801
Fermín 9960
Fernández, Diego 151
"ferns covered the banks of the river" 7692
"ferns, great green" 8809
"ferns, maidenhair" 5169
"ferns, waist-high" 9666
"ferns in the narrow glade of the deep woods" 9666
"ferns rising from a basket framework" 8850
Ferrar, Marjorie 7378
Ferrars, Miss 8253
"ferret of a kid, a little" 967
"ferreted out the whys and wherefores thereof" 7652
"ferriage, monopoly in" 1009
Ferries 1126, 5990, 6265, 8068, 8077, 8097, 8749, 9646, 10054
Ferriter, Francis 1600
"ferry" 6230
"ferry, at the" 1126
"ferry, Dún Laoghaire" 6265
"ferry, get off the" 4924
"ferry, government" 8749
"Ferry, Greenbush" 8077
"ferry, little" 8097
"Ferry, Staten Island" 9646
"ferry, wait for the" 5990
"ferry, waiting for the" 10054
"ferry dock, Piraeus" 2995
"ferry skidding on the tide crashes" 8068
"fertile for weeds" 6811
"fertile stretch of flat lands" 5129
"fertilize the land" 5042
"fertilize the meadows with red silt and alluvial mud" 6249
"fervor in the sky" 8398
"festival, celebrated a" 7797
"festival, family" 3558
"Festival Committee" 2469
"Festival of Contemporary Music" 6224
"festive" 8596
Festivity 5288, 8638
"festooned in carved gilt" 7481
"fetch me" 5993
"fetched out of the sunlit blue" 4559
"*fête*, morning of the" 8479
"*fête*, something about a" 6761
"*fête de famille*" 7491
"fetes, church" 7312
"Fêtes, Garden" 1914
"fetlocked, heavy-" 979
"fetters shaken off, Aden's" 3887
Fetuses 2378, 6991, 7066, 7078
"Feud, The Early-Moon" 7871
"feudal aristocracies" 4441
"feudal days, rare old" 4044
"feudal institutions which united the vassal to the liege lord" 6972
"fever, in her" 2129
"feverish with sunburn" 9616
"feverishly impatient" 4911
Fevvers 817
"few, a steady" 8678
"few, a tattered" 774
"few and fat" 569
"Fez" 9780
"fice, a tan" 462
"fickle" 10808
Fiction 3075, 5410, 5436, 5469
"fiction, improperly and imperfectly used in" 5410
"fiction, my whole life became a" 5588
"FICTION, SPECIAL" 5469
"fiction, the trouble with" 5436
"fiction, this" 6605
"fiction, writer of" 5398
"fiction has said so much in regret of the old days" 3075
"fictional confections" 5494
"fiddle, scratching at a tune on the" 6218
"fiddler who turned a fiddlepeg" 1680
"fiddling invisibly, cicadas" 8526
"fiddling with his uniform hat" 6967
Fidelman 5465
"fidgeted at the bar" 4313
Fidler, Herman 7729
Field, James 2934
"field, breezy upland" 3634
"field, end of the unploughed" 10617
"field, hay" 10427
"field, high-school" 8675
"field, hockey" 9672
"field, in the west" 3647
"Field, Kelly" 204
"Field, Lindbergh" 227
"field, pineapple" 4254
"field, rice" 9997
"field, slantwise south-facing" 10946
"field, soggy patch of" 8326

"field, they couldn't" 8919
"field, upper pasture" 10043
"field, vast scrub-brush tumbleweed" 4694
"Field, Welburn" 5916
"Field, Wheeler" 873
"Field, Wrigley" 4448
"field as well, he had another large"
  3661
"field behind the Parsonage" 7392
"field glasses" 5716
"field of dirty snow" 8665
"field of grain stubble" 5944
"field on the lower slopes of Lindifferon Hill" 10946
Fielding, Abe 4749
Fielding, Abraham 4749
Fielding, Abraham K. 4749
Fielding, George 3635
Fielding, Henry 5543
Fields, Jenny 2040
Fields, W. C. 1254
Fields 1244, 3634, 3641, 3652,
  3779, 4033, 4680, 5131, 5141,
  5944, 7397, 8326, 8429, 10590
"fields, across a few miles of intervening" 5144
"fields, dank cold" 666
"fields, early oat" 7397
"fields, flooded" 4680
"fields, flowing" 5143
"Fields, Green Heys" 4033
"fields, hills and" 8283
"fields, newly plowed" 10697
"fields, paddy" 5141
"fields, ran into the" 8429
"fields, reaped" 6648
"fields, rice" 730
"fields, ripening" 653
"fields, smiling" 263
"fields, swiftly passing" 9548
"fields, verdant" 9740
"fields, walk forth into the" 10566
"fields and woods and hills" 3064
"fields at a bias, crossing" 7279
"fields lay on a hillside facing
  south" 5131
"fields lose grace and lushness" 5151
"fields lost but now found, green"
  10590
"fields lying dank and dreary" 7267
"fields near Manchester" 4033
"fields of a yellowness that made
  him moan out loud" 8736
"fields of autumn grass" 4587
"fields of broom grass" 5161
"fields of corn and tobacco" 3641
"fields of ice lay grey and silent"
  8113
"fields of wheat and oats, awakening" 7238
"fields were left to themselves" 1244
"fields were on fire" 3779
"fierce as a lion" 5980
"fierce make-up" 1302

"fierce wind" 10679
"fiercely, somewhat" 10358
"fiery island" 5052
"fifteen-year-old, poised dumbfounded" 1954
"Fifth, the foot of" 8281
"fifties, in my middle" 4769
"Fifties, in the" 3606, 4922
"Fifties, the" 6767
"50th and Eighth Avenue" 2896
"fifty-eight-year-old provincial, I
  am a" 4844
"fifty-seven, not yet" 3891
"fig, creeping" 10310
"fig that hung in the window" 10310
"fight, each senseless" 1846
"fight, fist" 8934
"fight, lost his" 7154
"fight, two dead men got up to"
  1831
"fight, win this" 1839
"fighting, in the hot weather there
  was little" 4387
"fighting, persons" 3621
"fighting being fomented in Ulster,
  observe the" 2386
"fighting in the back seat" 1291
"fighting instinct" 4433
"fighting the wind" 3696
Fights 1291, 1512, 1831, 1839, 8934,
  9839, 9840, 9841
"figs" 5033
Figueras, Capitan Rodrigo José
  9273
"figure, cadaverous and extraordinary" 6496
"figure, crucial" 5111
"figure, her own" 1317
"figure, her taut" 3499
"figure, his three-foot" 10540
"figure, odd" 4936
"figure, short and rotund" 5800
"figure, short stoutish" 5894
"figure, stocky" 7844
"figure, strong young" 10357
"figure a little too thin for the best
  curves" 9912
"figure already overdrawn" 189
"figure appears, a" 1672
"figure in the world, I should have
  made a quite different" 6604
"figure of hale age" 5405
"figure out which one, she could
  never" 2050
"figure to catch my eye, the first"
  5901
"figured in many of her dreams"
  8434
"figured it was a tunnel they were
  passing through" 7474
"figured out my accident, still
  haven't" 678
"figured out on the sly, something I"
  7981
"figures, black" 1764

"figures, gay" 7239
"figures, their slim young" 10401
"figures, they were down to single"
  2996
"figures, three mounted" 7624
"figures carved in marble on a
  catafalque" 168
"figures in a legend, might have
  been" 6636
"figures met the platform with a
  jolt" 9605
"fijoas" 5033
"file of Norway spruce-trees" 9663
"files, placed in the" 5417
"filigree, gingerbread" 7440
"filigree, gold" 4677
"filigrees their upturned faces" 5337
"filing into his pasture" 8648
"Filipino, canny" 7576
"fill each pavilion with a giant's
  furniture" 7808
"filled the needle with her own
  watery excrement" 3057
"filled the sky" 3665
"filled to capacity, every table" 8640
"filled your nose with all you could"
  8532
Filling, Mrs. 8277
"filling fast, ballroom was" 4004
"filling the cafés of cities far beyond
  the jungle" 7339
"filling the gas tank" 663
"film, pivotal scene in the" 1330
"film director, American" 5984
"film producer" 9723
Filmer, Wilma 2756
"films, on the" 1318
Filomena 9960
"filthy water" 5372
"final spasm" 2429
Finance 77, 1106, 2592, 3624,
  5453, 6345, 6493, 7003, 8640,
  9908
"financial area" 1028
"financial backing, official" 3741
"financial catastrophe" 8640
"financier, professional" 4460
Fincher, Scrub 3651
"find, almost impossible to" 6142
"find a man, believed she would"
  4611
"find him every noon, I could" 3848
"find it in the patchy darkness, failing to" 9963
"find itself, where it has expected
  to" 10184
"find me, they couldn't" 9360
"find me on my knees" 6547
"find myself, to" 10313
"find out, did not take long to" 5062
"find out, how did I" 5065
"find out about Irma for me" 2091
"find the child, I can" 9861
"find you, it's taken me long
  enough to" 7224

"finders meant to honour" 4086
"finding a passage" 2600
"finding Donna Clementina at home" 9870
"finding his way" 4895
"finding this place" 6927
"finding your real parents" 6720
"finds previous foundations" 1384
"finds the scanty wooden house" 7230
"fine, everything was" 5781
"fine as skin" 3131
"finery in their dress, unaccustomed" 3987
"finger, an energetic" 9875
"finger, God puts his finger" 2641
"finger, her index" 925
"finger, her right index" 1873
"finger, index and middle" 4685
"finger, knotty brown" 7350
"finger, licked his index" 2422
"finger, moonstone on her" 2463
"finger, pointing a gaunt" 9237
"finger, shake her" 2426
"finger, turning a ring around on her" 338
"finger arched in ecstasy or death, like a" 5048
"finger in her, his" 7998
"finger of bone" 142
"finger pressed to her lips" 9095
"finger that has undergone a transformation" 1259
"finger with a true touch, laid his" 10033
"fingering the hard thing his mother had put into his hands" 6536
"fingernail, long varnished" 4922
"fingernails, long hard" 7229
"fingernails lacquered to Oriental symmetry" 7229
"fingernails would grow an inch" 10101
Fingers 575, 925, 1259, 1873, 2844, 2913, 6596, 7998, 8292
"fingers, bony" 5712
"fingers, bright stitching" 5355
"fingers, claw-shaped" 10582
"fingers, delicate" 9579
"fingers, floury" 3555
"fingers, her pointed" 2844
"fingers, his" 9769
"fingers, his groping" 10165
"fingers, his mother's" 575
"fingers, lightning thru his" 9066
"fingers, like dark" 8434
"fingers, little" 10174
"fingers, long pale" 4742
"fingers, long white nervous" 3047
"fingers, mechanical" 3205
"fingers, right between my" 910
"fingers, snatching her" 6215
"fingers, splayed her" 1760
"fingers, stretching his thin" 7519
"fingers, thin" 2335

"fingers, tips of her" 2101
"fingers, touch of her" 2463
"fingers are clenched around a sharp cleaver" 1870
"fingers around a pen, bend my" 3051
"fingers hundredfold, wound my" 2913
"fingers of lakes" 4577
"fingers of my outstretched hands" 2894
"fingers on both my hands, two middle" 337
"fingers poking out" 8292
"fingers pulling a frog mouth at her" 10174
"fingers still between the pages" 901
"fingers were like steel" 575
"fingertips working" 8014
"fining into distinction" 10788
"finish, bring off your" 3342
"finish up, that's the way you'll" 1881
"finished, carefully" 8571
"finished, did I figure that I was" 6642
"finished, once it is" 9009
"finished mate, she's" 6219
"finished off a whole hip flask" 6652
"finished the building" 1852
"finished the Honourable George" 2823
"finished the library book" 7362
"Finland" 5042
Finn 7156
Finn, Dr. Malachi 6887
Finnegan, Barbara 10987
Finney, Shad 6219
"Finnish, Old" 5341
Finnocchino, Father 1510
Finsterwald, Mr. Karl 7114
Fiores, the 6779
"fir, Frazer" 6084
"fir and birch, woods of" 3024
"fir trees" 8434
"fir trees, spiked with" 9826
Fire 92, 505, 825, 835, 1162, 1552, 1555, 2114, 2191, 2773, 3465, 3630, 3759, 3760, 3761, 3762, 3764, 3765, 3766, 3767, 3769, 3770, 3771, 3772, 3775, 3777, 3778, 3779, 3781, 3782, 3783, 3784, 3785, 3786, 3787, 3788, 3789, 3790, 3791, 3792, 4002, 5094, 5163, 5324, 6024, 6299, 6836, 7474, 8986, 9404, 10052, 10678, 10710
"fire" 1217
"fire, add fuel to" 9376
"fire, ashes of the dead" 8361
"Fire, before the" 3207
"fire, beside a dying" 8976
"fire, camp" 8647
"fire, Elbow Lake" 3770
"fire, fell into a pig-rendering" 2450

"fire, fields were on" 3779
"fire, forest destroyed by" 5035
"fire, frequently seen round their domestic" 6385
"fire, gazing into the" 9404
"fire, glow of the" 10157
"fire, have you lit a" 1552
"fire, heat of an intense" 92
"fire, in front of the" 6519
"fire, light of the" 10934
"fire, like white ash above a" 4967
"fire, make a really roaring" 10710
"fire, my father is on" 3786
"fire, never-ending" 2492
"fire, nice" 6652
"fire, points of tremulous" 8394
"fire, sat looking into the" 696
"fire, set himself on" 3789
"fire, set the nursery curtains on" 6527
"fire, sit by the" 9406
"fire, starting the" 3785
"fire, wood" 869
"fire, woods by the boy's house catch" 825
"fire alive in the grate, keep the" 1162
"fire blazed, a" 3760
"fire blazing, very cheerful" 10678
"fire burned beneath the iron cauldron" 3762
"fire chief" 8376
"fire crackled cheerily" 7756
"fire escape" 483
"fire had been burning for hours" 3781
"fire had started in a bale of fermenting hay" 3782
"fire in our habitual public-house" 3764
"fire in the night" 3761
"fire of my loin" 10807
"fire on the hearth, no" 7032
"fire pit" 3781
"fire playing on his face" 5903
"fire smoking, is that" 3767
"fire ... spurted and fell" 3764
"fire that raged in the market square" 3771
"fire the suburbs" 3775
"fire to his apartment building, set" 2773
"fire up all night long, man kept the" 10052
"firearm shop, kept a little" 4245
"fired, appeared and" 10477
"fired, my boss was" 6460
"fired him, she" 3335
"firedrake" 7604
"fireflies, watching" 4969
"firelight, in the" 332
"fire-of-the-forest" 8277
"fireplace" 6626
"fireplace, around the" 8881
"fireplace, deep clay-plastered" 3760

"fireplace, genuine old" 10678
"fireplace, small conical" 3765
"fireplace, well-stacked high-
blazing" 4335
Fireplaces 1907, 3765, 7756
"fire-raiser had been quiet" 3784
"fires, at least they can set" 1555
"fires, brush" 3405
"fires, burning" 2114
"fires, desert watch" 8986
"fires, flicker of the" 3766
"fires, garbage" 8534
"fires, hundreds of camp" 4660
"fires, just one of hundreds of
thousands of similar" 3771
"fires all along the top burning
curly hairs of light" 4660
"fires all over the country" 3771
"fires and savagery, Afric's" 8642
"fires in those oil drums and trash
cans" 3787
"fires which had flickered for generations" 8986
"firescreen that hid the empty
grate" 8214
"fireside glow, serene" 10494
"firewood, they needed" 3788
Fireworks 885, 10665
"fireworks, buy" 10665
"fireworks went off behind me" 885
"firm, head hunting" 1077
"firm, joined the" 3855
"firm, lavatory" 9439
"firm, soap manufacturing" 6321
"firm, worked for the same" 2011
"firm in question, the" 1008
"firm of Hitchings Brothers" 1021
"firm of Josiah Westerman & Sons"
6448
"firm was very proud of this
branch of its business" 1015
Firms 1008, 1015, 1021, 1077, 3326,
6448, 6514
"first, at" 517, 3727
"first, get there" 2973
"first, it comes" 3726
"First Cause" 6001
"first cry" 4742
"first day of Carnival, it was the"
2131
"first day of Michaelmas term" 7336
"first light" 3687
"first move, made the" 625
"first of all" 6825, 6916, 10190, 10628
"first of her class to run around the
table" 10656
"first on the block to reach widowhood" 77
"first person, in the" 5513
"first thing, the" 1792
"first thing about her" 2824
"first thing he noticed" 10869
"first time, it was the" 9477
"first time I saw Billy" 5867
"first time in months, for the" 59

"firth, shaft blew from the" 392
"Firth of Clyde" 5071, 8132
"Firth of Forth" 9511
Fischer, Doctor 4359
Fish 402, 439, 457, 473, 2770,
5380, 7688, 7703, 7919, 10756
"fish, a certain" 457
"fish, eighty-four days now without
taking a" 6428
"fish, gleaming red" 10448
"fish, helping Uncle Benny" 4687
"fish, like a nocturnal" 2123
"fish, salt" 8512
"fish, shadowy" 402
"fish, sunken world of" 1480
"fish baby" 5872
"fish had been tossed onto the carpet, as though a great" 8806
"fish scurried underneath" 10448
"fish without fins" 5624
Fishburn, Ada 8167
"fished alone in a skiff" 6428
"fished me out of the Sacramento
River, she" 5803
Fisher, Harry 319
Fisher, Mary 5233
Fisher, Miss 2954
Fisher, Mrs. Sylvia 9710
Fisher Maid, the" 8129
"fisherman, the naked" 6401
"fisherman swings his boat" 8159
"Fisherman's ring" 1525
Fishermen 5315, 6401, 6416, 8159
"fishermen lighting their oil lamps"
5315
"Fisher's Nest, the beetling base of"
9740
"fishes or paints, one either" 6416
"fishhouse" 9224
Fishing 998, 3423, 3511, 3684,
4686, 4687, 4688, 4690, 4691,
4692, 4693, 6401, 6416, 6428,
7677, 8148, 8817
"fishing, gone" 3684
"fishing, I'm" 4692
"fishing, loch and sea" 4639
"fishing harbour, a small" 1440
"fishing off the Keys" 3511
"fishing villages" 8093
"fishing-fleet" 8062
"fishy piece of moon" 9789
"fist, in her right" 6971
"fist, pounding a heavy" 6947
"fist, shook his" 9310
"fist fight" 8934
"fist of stone, a squat dark" 9304
"fistful of sulphur matches" 876
"fists, its little" 540
"fists, there were raised" 5189
"fists clenching and closing like a
pulse" 8487
"fists driven into his thighs" 7739
"fit, I was now" 796
"fit neatly together in the compact
whole" 5708

"fit your gown" 4191
"Fitchburg, station at" 9523
Fitness 6659
"fitted an iron bar into sockets"
10933
"fitted well" 1391
"fittest men I have ever known,
one of the" 6659
"fitting her like a glove, name" 4179
Fitzgerald, Miss 1589
Fitzgibbon 10649
Fitzgibbons, Mrs. 8026
Fitz-Ooth, Robert 10641
Fitzwater, Matilda 10641
"five, it was about half-past" 7568
"Five, The" 3927
"Five Towns" 784, 5695, 9118
"fix the damn mimeograph
machine" 5683
"fix themselves, lest they" 9463
"fixative, crude" 10831
"fixed, remain unalterably" 3491
"fixed daiquiris for us" 2917
"fixed his eyes on the thin peninsula" 4082
"fixed the old man to the table" 1166
"fixture ready and waiting, every"
6145
"fizgig, doo-wack-a-doo and voo-
do-dee-odo" 1982
"fizzling out like a planet still shining but dead" 260
"flag, hauled down their" 10515
"flag, planting the" 7800
"flag, red" 382
"flagpole spurting out of the point"
9228
Flags 9892, 10515
"flags, under several" 8075
"flags were out in front of the
houses and stores" 2971
"flagship, royal" 4151
"flagstones of the Manhattan Battery are slick and black" 7322
"flagstones that lay lemon-colored"
421
"flakes, a million gushing" 7650
"flakes, busy downfall of" 8588
"flakes, thickly in great wet" 8779
"flakes fell slowly out of the darkness, the big" 8606
"flakes them off like skin" 10948
"flakes were large and swept lazily
across the window" 8599
"Flambeau" 3914
"flame, candle" 7441
"flame, clear" 10774
"flame, hold the spurting" 7474
"flame, keeper of the" 4577
"flame, little" 5324
"flame, old" 5728
"flame, wave of" 3760
"flame in his cupped palm" 7474
"flame trees" 9672
"flame would not waver" 10610

"flame-blue" 9228
"Flames, Fashionables Fighting"
  3770
"flames, he roasted in the" 2773
"flames, white" 3965
"flames of a never-ending fire" 2492
"flaming blue sky" 10570
"flaming gold and red" 2150
"flaming hues of orange" 2188
"flaming torches" 3775
Flanders, Betty 1588
"Flanders" 1691, 3015, 8699
"flank, sunny" 1367
"flanked by teacherage and sagging
  barn" 7887
"flanked by two young ladies" 6330
"flapping back against the windows,
  set them" 10699
"flare-up in *this* haouse" 3555
"flash, huge" 10494
"flash, silent" 880
"flash, sunlight" 7067
"flash, warning" 10541
"flash in my direction, a bright" 7011
"flash momentarily froze the serene
  fireside glow" 10494
"flash there in the city's grid" 880
"flashed blue sky" 3667
"flashes of red" 8393
"flashing suddenly out again" 2195
"flashing swords at us" 8642
"flashlights and noise in yard
  behind house" 6964
"flashlight's beam lancing on before
  him" 9887
Flashy, Professor 10858
"flask, hip" 6652
"flask, thermos" 10818
"flask to his mouth" 2939
"flat, comfortably proportioned but
  lately very empty-feeling" 3216
"flat, coming to our" 2327
"flat, furnished" 5309
"flat, her" 2581, 5083
"Flat, Indian" 7614
"flat, it was easier than her" 8027
"flat, London" 4006
"flat, stuffy basement" 7415
"flat, the Fitzjohn's Avenue" 1665
"flat, the Paris" 5104
"flat, they went to the" 3257
"flat, tiny" 2822
"flat as a man of gingerbread" 152
"flat as a plate, sea" 7943
"flat as ribbons" 9503
"flat as sea level" 5178
"flat immediately above mine, the"
  6300
"flat in the rue Jacob, at her" 3231
"flat land" 3044
"flat lands" 5129
"flat on her stomach" 5145
"flat out, running" 5293
"flatboat" 9626
"Flatbush, central" 1068

"flathead, ornery" 8925
"flatland, lake region" 5166
"flatlands, the" 5173
"flatness, echo of their" 5173
"flatness, thinning" 8794
"flatness his eyes could not see"
  9549
"flats, block of" 2365
"flats, Jersey" 7310
"flats, one of the top-floor-rear"
  3078
"Flats, Wanstead" 5928
"flats smooth as stone" 7685
"flattened the gorse of the distant
  hills like wet fur" 5071
"flatter the lust of eyes like mine"
  1011
"flattered me" 844
"flattered myself" 2600
"flatteringly" 1856
Flaubert 315
"Flaubert's statue" 315
Flavia 7715
"flavor, richness of" 9662
"flavors, rank" 3405
"flaws, admit most of their" 3308
Flax, Mrs. 7534
"flax, stripped" 2236
"flaxen-haired" 4180
"flea market" 1063, 1089
Fleckring, Rachel Louisa 10786
"flecks of the dead old dried paint"
  7763
"fled, when they" 9710
"fled for their Religion" 6089
"fled from their village" 3416
"fled the South, I suppose we" 1733
Fledge 5870
"fleecy clouds" 2211
"fleeing on a road of hunger" 4682
"fleet, fishing-" 8062
"fleet, head of a" 9557
"fleet, Norwegian whaling" 8116
"Fleet, the" 8066, 10466
"fleet was entering Torbay" 8093
"Fleets, form'd new" 10464
Fleisher, Von Humboldt 915
Fleishman 3627
Fleming, David 3186
"Flemish sky" 193
"flesh, carnal desires of the" 1205
"flesh, his unnerved" 10202
"flesh, in the" 7468
"flesh, not to surprise each other's
  abashed" 6388
"flesh, scorched the" 8017
"flesh, sculpturing of" 10
"flesh, spirit and" 10774
"flesh, yielding reaches of soft"
  7985
"flesh and blood, she was made of"
  7969
"flesh from the bones, strip the"
  10717
"flesh had blackened" 2463

"flesh of her heart, gorge themselves on the" 2799
"flesh rise on one's arms and neck,
  making the" 1706
"flesh roasted in the armor they
  could not fling off" 4469
"flesh that drew him in" 7985
"fleshy" 10933
Fletcher, Anne N. 6143
Fletcher, Hugo 1633
Fletcher, Mr. 4970
Fleury, Maxwell 8567
Fleuve, the" 8209
"flew back to London" 4576
"flew home, then he" 4575
"flew home from Mazatlán" 4580
"flew in from Portland Oregon"
  9486
"flew in from the desert" 234
"flew in there, a fleck of you" 7437
"flew north from one America to
  the other" 9656
"flew southeast, they" 4563
"flew through the air" 763
"flew toward the full moon" 4956
"flew up to the island" 3716
"flexed a rubber band between his
  thumb and forefinger" 5862
"flick, skin" 1327
"flicker of the fires" 3766
"flickered for generations" 8986
"flickered like a cinema screen with
  images" 9463
"flickering like blown leaves through
  the trees" 10893
Flickinger, Kate 6394
"flicks, loved the" 1333
Fliegelman 9197
Fliegler, Luther L. (L for LeRoy)
  5619
"flies, black" 4073
"flies, it" 192
"flies sluggish" 177
"flight, day" 211
"flight, during his transatlantic"
  1326
"flight, entranced by" 5865
"flight, morning" 9439
"flight, one pause of the" 721
"flight, sleepless eleven-hour" 1722
"flight, soaring spiral" 757
"flight, wrong" 9650
"flight attendant" 9624
"flight commentator" 228
"Flight Five Zero" 228
"flight from Honolulu" 8192
"flight from my own life" 6478
"flight home, on the" 9630
"flight over the South Pole, Richard
  E. Byrd's" 228
"'Flight to Canada'" 5480
"flight to London" 1724
"flight to Vienna, Pan Am" 7171
"flights, observed" 7514
"flights, one of the last" 2577

"flights, Piedmont and Delta" 214
"flights up, two" 3166
"fling off the bed-clothes, just about to" 10190
"fling out with his voice" 6218
"flinging aside the 'Evening Banner'" 7107
"flinging some shirts into the washing machine" 10963
"flings the shadow of his wing" 724
Flint, Polly 4838
"Flint" 1390
"flint, he was like" 5917
"flippant sprite of memory" 7373
"flipped open the magazine" 926
"flirt, unwilling to" 10852
"flirt with November ice" 10547
"flirtatious eyes" 4662
Flirting 5450, 8555
"flitch, one rangy gangling" 5448
"floated as far, or" 1896
"floated gently to the decks" 9619
"floated high in the hazy blue afternoon air" 4180
"floated up from the timeless and bottomless world of sleep" 10144
"floating down past our house in the river" 7676
"floating godlike" 10260
"floating in a stagnant pond" 2609
"floating in segments" 727
"floating in unseen about to land" 2447
"floating light and graceful as a seamew" 8049
"floating round they was" 4660
"floating upward" 10299
"flock of his own kind" 748
"flocks grew lean" 4382
"Floe, the" 7690
Flood, Ambrose 325
Flood, Hercules 7865
Flood, Peter 1002
"flood" 7670
"flood, amber outrush of the springtide" 7650
"flood, greatest" 6366
"flood, on the next" 8047
"flood, treetops above the" 5025
"flood, we have just had another" 7291
"flood of reminiscence, a swirling" 2337
"flooded, it was" 7702
"flooded fields" 4680
"flooded with something sticky and glutinous" 9394
"flooding the scorched land under a daylight moon" 10614
Floods 735, 2339, 5025, 6366, 7291, 7650, 7670, 7702, 10614
"floods that devastated many parts of Catalonia" 2339
"flood-tide, invisible" 10733
"floom swoosh" 7990

"floor, cool" 10384
"floor, expanse of parquet" 5322
"floor, garage" 8456
"floor, hard concrete" 3238
"floor, on the fifty-first" 7319
"floor, on the thirty-eighth" 9977
"floor, uneven" 10212
"floor, uneven cement" 7515
"floor moved again" 10227
"floor of the forest, brown pine-needled" 10695
"floor of the great stage" 9400
"floor of the valley, flat" 4374
"floor of waxed pine, hard bright" 5327
"floor partially covered" 7753
"floor was bare" 2761
"floor which seemed to be moving" 4485
"floorboards of his bedroom, it was under the" 325
"floors, wooden" 921
"floozy, a slatternly" 1982
"flopped about on the snowy walk" 4135
"flopped down on the green vinyl sofa" 7085
"flopping sound, we heard a" 8806
"Flor de Cana, bottle of" 2924
"flora and fauna . . . flourish in unimaginable abundance" 455
"flora and fauna of a most exquisite and rare beauty" 455
Flora 5852, 9086
Flora 1480, 3811, 5180, 9673, 10753
Florence 2904
"Florence" 5614, 10374
"Florence, leaving" 1611
"Florence, when I arrived in" 3226
"Florence Alabama" 582
Flores, Carmen 3126
Flores, Master Sergeant Cesario 1677
"florescence and feud" 3560
Florian 3898
"florid and loud and innocent" 275
"Florida" 2447, 3362, 3621, 6733, 8293, 9027, 9616
"Florida, Central" 6004
"Florida, Gulf coast of" 4407
"Florida, Keys of" 5174
"Florida, South" 9086
"Florida, spend a few days in" 6003
"Florida, west" 1394
"Florida East Coast Special" 9973
"Florida summer" 4384
"Floss, broadening" 7649
"Flossmoor" 3725
"Flotilla of the Young Tars, Babbington" 10978
"flotsam and jetsam" 3094
"flotsam from a shipwreck, like" 1775
"flourish, a final" 1565

"flourish, opened the door with a" 9883
"flourish, with something of a" 4349
"flourished, lived and" 6213
"flourished an inn" 4328
"flourished in Wellclose Square" 7505
"flourishing condition, certainly not in a" 6248
"flourishing period, that" 6245
"flow and ebb" 7086
"flow of shimmering buti-silk boudoir coat" 5450
"flow on with the same serene beneficence" 7648
"flowed across this land, my blood's" 4825
"flowed out of the ancient square like multicolored grains of sand" 8924
"flowed slowly southward to the sea" 7666
"flowed through the minds of the War Gods" 2621
"flower, taking the form of a" 1496
"flower, that" 512
"flower, the perfect" 3594
"flower, thick with" 9668
"flower from the garden of Versailles" 9882
"flower garden, dusty tangle of her" 3976
"flower room" 6356
"flower show" 2757
"flower show, like a" 6150
"flower to pieces, pick the" 3793
"flower-garden, lovely" 3064
"flower-girl" 8837
Flowers 4877
Flowers, Pete 5995
Flowers 1194, 3314, 4385, 5033, 5836, 6499, 6557, 6561, 8259, 9352, 9683, 9742, 10528
"flowers, associate it with" 3795
"flowers, beautiful" 6557
"flowers, big" 3799
"flowers, blue" 6386
"flowers, bright with" 10587
"flowers, buy the" 3797
"flowers, flush of early summer" 6756
"flowers, help me with these" 10528
"flowers, like wild" 8864
"flowers, profusion of" 4286
"flowers, rich" 3799
"flowers, scent of many" 3796
"flowers, strange unknown" 3799
"flowers, swamp" 7440
"flowers, veronica" 2072
"flowers, who'll buy my" 4987
"flowers and blossoms that grew in great multitudes beside the river" 6561
"flowers are in their first glory" 8514
"flowers banked round him" 2973

"flowers glared against the wall of the stationmaster's garden" 4385

"flowers he had gathered, wild" 6408

"flowers of March and April still lingered" 9742

"Flowers of Summer" 2923

"flowers or snow, when there were" 5836

"flowers were burgeoning" 3805

"flowers were named, before ever the" 5431

"flowers . . . which struggled and fluttered" 5431

"flown so well, I had never" 207

"flows down to it from the New Hampshire hills" 7668

"flows through water-meadows" 1408

"flows through wilderness and canyon down to the Pacific" 9747

"flu, coming down with the" 164

"flu, outbreak of" 7895

"flu strains named for Asian capitals" 4712

"fluffs of cloud, scudding" 3667

"fluke" 3512

"fluke, all because of a" 2429

"flung herself into the arms of the Whites" 3413

"flung it in the face of the chief herald" 363

"flung the remains of his tattered cigar" 8568

"flung the rich travelling rug" 5943

"flung their primal passions in the face of humanity" 4046

"flunkies, any number of uniformed" 4650

"flush, melancholy" 5305

"flush of cash" 10858

"flute, emphasis on the" 6236

"fluttered down, snowflakes" 8597

"fly, buzzing of a" 10326

"fly at the earliest moment, you will want to" 4591

"fly at the moment, actually straining to" 761

"fly from Mercy to the other side of Lake Superior" 9602

"fly in an Army plane, I wouldn't" 210

"fly on their wall, a" 8904

"fly-catchers, quick nervous flutter of" 742

Flying 181, 192, 193, 194, 195, 197, 200, 203, 204, 205, 207, 209, 210, 211, 216, 224, 226, 229, 231, 232, 234, 235, 880, 1409, 1677, 1722, 1724, 1943, 1957, 2478, 2577, 2794, 3693, 3711, 4563, 4575, 4576, 4580, 4781, 5667, 5750, 6683, 7018, 7171, 7660, 7921, 8668, 9439, 9570, 9579,

9594, 9602, 9615, 9624, 9630, 9650, 9656, 9965, 10192

"flying, he goes" 2030

"flying, he was" 226

"flying, once with" 5667

"flying a DC-6B" 202

"flying at night, save time by" 211

"flying back to New York" 1957

"flying down these screaming highways" 2656

"flying east, seabird was" 756

"flying fish, watching the" 7919

"Flying Goose, inn called the" 4328

"flying home" 7854

"flying home to Leningrad" 2794

"flying home to see his father" 4588

"flying out the next morning" 1677

"flying over the desert, when I was" 6683

"flying right into my forehead" 6882

"flying rocks of come" 7990

"flying school" 196

"flying up, if he was" 9965

Flynn, Dave 8042

Flynn, Errol 7050

Flynn, Richie 9246

Flynn, Sasha Greenberg 3865

"flyover, parapet of the" 5940

"foal, big" 447

"foal was resisting his birth" 471

"foals, magpie" 433

"foam, crinkled quiffs of white" 8147

"foam, like spent dirty" 2690

"foam, mustard-colored" 7666

"foam, rug of white" 7680

"foam spurted from the steel bows" 8147

"foam women" 7945

"foaming on over ancient stone" 7668

"focus, Leica into" 6866

"focused his field glasses" 5716

"foetus, curled up like a" 5777

Fog 206, 733, 1364, 2572, 5331, 5882, 7779, 8534, 8835, 9643, 9768, 10256, 10349, 10472, 10580, 10582, 10604, 10635

"fog" 8534

"fog, dark" 10580

"fog, dense spectral" 9643

"fog, driving through" 7457

"fog, he rose with the" 10256

"fog, in the" 9768

"fog, lowering" 10582

"fog, North Atlantic" 8062

"fog, rapping through the" 7411

"fog, running through the" 8659

"fog, tattered edges of" 10121

"fog, thick Thames" 971

"fog, thin screen of" 5331

"fog, village free of" 5882

"fog, walk miles in" 3832

"fog, walls were dripping in" 10349

"fog, wisps of" 7779

"fog, without" 2182

"fog, yellow" 10349

"fog came in from the ocean" 10580

"fog came up early" 2572

"fog had collected high up against the ceiling of the hall" 7779

"fog has come off Penobscot Bay" 8835

"fog hung menacingly over San Francisco" 10582

"fog in New York" 206

"fog lifted" 5039

"fog of fatigue" 3685

"fog of its own smoke" 1364

"fog pulsated with each breath that she exhaled" 10635

"fog screened every window" 9540

"fog that hung tiny veils on her eyelashes" 10349

"fog vanishing in the strong light" 10121

"fog was breaking up" 10604

"fog was so dense" 733

Fogel 8285

Fogel, Timothy 7991

"fogged the distance between us" 385

"fogged up, everything so" 591

"foghorns that warn and warn" 9299

"fogs, the retiring" 10472

"folder, stiff red" 5537

"foliage, occasional breaks in the" 5318

"foliage, through the" 5314

"foliage of tall palms" 7754

"foliage on the horizon" 5176

"folios, sixth and subsequent" 703

"folk, brawny country-" 5886

"folk glad to be alive or afraid to be alive" 5260

"folk of the coast" 5015

"folk who lived among the mule deer" 368

"Folkestone" 5990

"folks" 8638

"folks, chock full of" 6781

"folks, cullud" 4716

"folks, my" 793

"folks, now" 1037

"folks, white" 5729

"folks in these New Hampshire mountains" 9770

"follow Highway 58" 9143

"follow the drum and trumpet" 5397

"follow you into smoky rooms" 2796

"followed, he was being" 9587

"followed by a young fellow" 2688

"followed by an invisible dog" 1724

"followed her, he" 2648

"followed the old tumbled-down wall" 10404

"followed the winding creek" 10461

"following an older man" 4174

"following Linda, a detective was"
8905
"following of his own free will"
10409
"following so closely behind his
prisoner" 2045
"following the bank of snow thrown
up by the plough" 8607
"following the footpath" 10400
"following the path in single file"
10346
"following their stars and compasses" 9247
"following us, are they still" 3030
"follows of course, it" 10767
"follows the trail" 8971
"folly of all human ambition" 1496
"folly of human beings" 5704
"folly of their gods" 5704
"fond, over the years became" 9347
"fond of descending this cliff-path"
4282
"fond of diamonds and old china,
particularly" 6607
"fond of men, very" 5354
"fond of my daughter Sally, I am
very" 4789
"fond of themselves" 1415
"fondue, kirsch in the" 10559
Fong, Sam 1040
Fong Tai 8700
"Font Abbey" 10771
"Fonthill" 1533
Food 776, 1003, 1085, 1872, 3557,
3973, 4519, 4671, 4674, 4679,
4680, 4711, 7573, 7574, 7582,
7782, 7820, 8530, 8544, 10347,
10899, 10960
"food, certainly not" 745
"food, chorus of roasting" 4679
"food, cooked their wretched" 8544
"food, famous for its" 3851
"food, full up with" 4519
"food, masticating his" 3852
"food, providing their" 3864
"food, put me off my" 1179
"food, roaming the flooded fields
for" 4680
"food, seasoning each morsel of"
10831
"food, served the" 3858
"food, surrounded by" 3876
"food, tins of" 7402
"Food and Drink, The" 6768
"food for curiosity, fresh" 2600
"food for poetic reflection, find
ample" 9515
"food for the tail-eating snake" 5521
"food stalls, the teeming Ninth
Avenue" 6274
"food to give them, no" 721
"foods, gastrically correct" 8298
"foods, tinned" 4073
"foodstuffs" 1067
"fool, damned young" 4977

"fool, I am a" 4120
"fool, I was considered a" 7771
"fool, old" 4912, 6993
"fool, said that I was a" 4975
"fool and general" 8172
"fool around, his own tendency
to" 1111
"fool for not getting my money's
worth out of it" 7771
"fool of a Reever, that" 687
"fool of the family" 7802
"fool on the floor below me" 6299
"fooled everyone, the house" 3260
"foolin around" 2430
"fooling himself" 6278
"fooling with an inner tube" 10928
"foolish" 3311
"foolish, why are men so" 5891
"foolish, wise and" 5381
"foolish or bold, he was" 1731
"foolish sum" 773
"foolish thing, he could not possibly
have done a more" 6034
"foolish things, imagine all sorts of"
4889
Foolishness 3712, 4437, 5891, 6034
"foolishness" 3712
"foolishness, it was the age of" 3377
"foolishness, just plain" 4437
"foolishness like always, Aunt Sister
stuck with" 4437
"foolishness she guessed with maybe
some passion to it" 4437
Fools 687, 2997, 4975, 4977, 6993,
7771
"fools" 5448
"fools, knaves and" 2997
"fools and fanatics" 6310
"'Fool's Confession, A'" 962
"foolscap, a new sheet of" 5428
"foolscaps, pieces of typewritten"
5415
"foot, come on" 1685
"foot, he lost his right" 6796
"foot, making his way on" 10420
"foot, Martin's right" 352
"foot, meditative" 567
"foot, my" 10179
"foot, on" 10331, 10442, 10458
"foot, placing each" 10382
"foot, St. Peter's" 8939
"foot alternating diffidently between
accelerator and brake" 2991
"foot of the Superstition Mountains" 6076
"foot on God's earth, he would
never set his" 2311
"foot on the box to steady it" 2973
"foot on the first step" 1594
"foot or a little one, which is not a
big" 2835
"foot resting lightly on the surface
of the water" 10839
Football 8917, 8921, 8922, 8931,
8935

"football, playing" 8922
"football, watch me play" 7498
"football star, so I could get to be a
high school" 9265
"football team scrimmaging down
on the field" 8935
"footbridge" 1983
"footed, heavy-" 10821
"footfall on its bare floors" 3135
"footfall on the scoured stairs" 7441
"foothill bench above the Bar D
spread" 7636
"Foothill Country" 6056
"foothills, distant" 9141
"foothills, dusty" 2949
"foothills, gently rolling" 3654
"foothills, in the clearness of the"
7296
"foothills, scrubby" 10701
"Foothills, the" 6056
"foothills, these" 7615
"foothills of Mount Kaiser, the
low-flung" 4084
"foothills of the blue mountains,
wooded" 3638
"foothold" 3639
"foothold, occasional" 4035
"footholds cut into the rock high
above the bay" 32
"footing, lost his" 32
"footlights of an empty auditorium"
9387
"footman, the" 9873
"footpath, grassy" 7609
"footpath, Indian" 5723
"footpath, public" 4033
"footpath along the high bank"
10400
"footprint, like a fancy" 7471
"footprint, single" 3458
"footprints, many muddy" 9215
"footsteps, my" 9120
"fops" 5448
Foraday, John 4892
"forage in the reaped fields" 6648
"foraged, sheep and the goats"
5704
Forbes, Cato 9596
Forbes, Kenneth 5407
"forbidden, it was" 10831
"forbidden, strictly" 10831
Forbush 6074
"force, large armed" 8671
"force, mysterious" 5329
"force of human breathing" 9503
"Force of Irresistible Multitude"
10464
"forced myself to call Agios" 1136
"forced to land, they had been" 206
"forces, American" 219
"Forces, American Expeditionary"
8695
"forces, fierce" 9457
"forces, liberating" 4502
"Forces, National Security" 2047

"Forces beseiging strong Towns" 10464

"forces dominated the world womb, certain elemental" 5262

"forces of history wrestle with each other" 4504

"Forchheim, village of" 1444

"forcing things, no sense" 624

"Ford, battered 1958" 9782

"Ford, driving the" 3002

"Ford, rattled like an old" 235

"Ford, the old" 2962

"Ford dealer" 1071

"ford whose bottom sands were scarcely covered by water" 7662

"Fordoun lies near" 4053

"forearms, his" 8266

"forebears, existence of" 6883

"forebears, the faces of his" 8986

Foreboding 6940, 7008, 7010, 7013, 7015, 7016, 7017, 7018, 7019, 7024, 7025, 7026, 7027, 7028, 7029, 8395, 8948

"foreboding" 6397

"foreboding, felt no sense of" 6940

"foreboding, momentary sense of" 7018

"foreboding hung like smoke in O'Farrell's tool shop" 7019

"foreboding overcame Eaton Striker" 7027

"forebodings, evil" 7008

"forecast a two-week dry spell" 7031

"forecaster, the" 5712

"foreclosed on a fieldstone mansion" 3253

"forecourt, big sweep of gravelled" 5157

"forefinger, blunt" 6967

"forefinger, one smooth thin" 6784

"foregathered in George Weatherby's rooms" 8976

"forehead, broad sloping" 8237

"forehead, Cahuom Chhuon's" 2803

"forehead, flat broad" 498

"forehead, flying right into my" 6882

"forehead, whiteness of the upper part of his" 5099

"Foreign Aid, no" 3362

"foreign gentleman" 4915

"foreign language" 6784

"Foreign Service" 4764

"foreigner, a" 7891

"foreigner, intelligent" 1342

"foreigners, the" 8854

"foreigners . . . rest not day nor night from speech" 8854

"foreman, burly beer-bellied" 1057

"foreman, his old-time" 8853

"foresee, easy to" 265

"foreseen, came" 874

"forest" 3900, 4038

"forest, axe was needed for the" 6100

"forest, brick" 10242

"forest, Congo rain" 3905

"forest, dark spruce" 3896

"forest, dense" 6057

"Forest, edge of the" 7230

"Forest, Epping" 4303

"forest, familiar" 3902

"forest, great" 3904

"forest, immeasurable" 3899

"forest, in the" 2126

"forest, large" 3893

"forest, near" 8326

"forest, on the borders of an extensive" 3059

"forest, primeval" 3641

"forest, rain" 4109

"forest, raining in the" 3908

"forest, the" 3906

"forest, vast solitude of Canadian" 3897

"forest, walk the" 6569

"forest, went further and further into the" 10784

"forest covering the greater part of the beautiful hills and valleys" 3893

"forest creaked in a wave" 3909

"forest destroyed by fire" 5035

"forest frowned on either side the frozen waterway" 3896

"forest garden" 8212

"Forest of Acaire" 3898

"Forest of Lions" 3903

"forest of Sarawak, rain" 4109

"forest of the West Coast, the rainfall" 309

"forest pond, silent like a" 1706

"forest primeval, remnants of the" 8209

"forest track" 10405

"forest was covered in a thick white cloud" 2572

"forestalled me, Miss Vosper had" 9908

"forested with hemlock and white pine" 3179

Forests 455, 825, 2126, 2195, 3076, 3146, 4073, 5125, 5163, 6057, 8167, 8209, 8326, 8541, 8718, 9128, 9519, 9663, 10784

"forests, dense" 6055

"forests, frosty scent of" 10684

"forests, green" 6249

"forests, pine" 4034

"forests of allegation and denial" 9696

"forests of Askatevar, dying" 10720

"forests of gloomy pine" 5125

"forests of tall trees and tangled underbrush" 3074

"forests of Upper Varva" 3901

"forests that had been burnt there" 5163

"forests which lined the creek" 3146

"Forêt de Sorède" 3125

"foretold my widowhood and exile" 7030

"forever, wandering" 3799

"forever and a day" 6646

"forever is such a very great while" 9481

"forewarning, without an adequate" 8734

"forfeited a week's pay" 3334

"forge in steel from the finest needle up to a ship's armour" 1005

"forget, and don't" 6823

"forget, I'll never" 6298, 8890

"forget, it's strange what you don't" 7426

"forget, not likely to" 7418

"forget, what I want is to" 7458

"forget about human" 6816

"forget his original destination" 5607

"forget our selves, it will have us" 7370

"forget them, cannot" 3489

"forget you got shot inna back" 74

"forget you're hungry" 74

"forgetful of their yesterdays" 9119

Forgetfulness 2495, 7381, 7387, 7416, 7456, 9492

"forgetfulness, deliberate" 7441

"forget-me-not on the wallpaper" 2343

Forgetting 2546, 4804, 4868, 7274, 7383, 7421, 7458, 10489

"forgetting" 10139

"forgive, understand and" 10762

"forgive and forget" 9687

"forgive him, asked me to" 7498

"forgive me" 4767

"forgive me my denomination and my town" 1520

"forgiven the Jews, the Pope has" 8182

Forgiveness 7498, 7535, 8182, 9687, 10762

"forgiveness" 7535

"forgot, he never" 81

"forgot, never" 2153

"forgot about the catch on the screen door" 2713

"forgot herself, she completely" 7860

"forgot himself" 6021

"forgot three things in a row" 7421

"forgot to bring my journal" 2546

"forgotten" 108

"forgotten, almost entirely" 5743

"forgotten, as if carelessly" 921

"forgotten, even more deeply" 4467

"forgotten, he had already" 7416

"forgotten, it is" 10489

"forgotten, long" 5723

"forgotten, Pauline had" 7274

"forgotten, well-nigh" 7378

"forgotten, wondering what he had" 3838

"forgotten by the townspeople" 3095

"forgotten how cold, I'd" 1562

"forgotten in the village, nearly" 9150

"forgotten my watch, I'd" 9492

"forgotten who I am" 4868

"fork into a square of ravioli" 3344

"Forks" 1223

"Forks, Granite" 7265

"forlorn, he saw that she was indeed" 4164

"forlorn, peculiarly" 8716

"forlorn figure, she was a" 4164

"form, conventional" 709

"form, her dumpy" 8758

"form, it is bad" 2464

"form, mid-season" 4349

"form, plump" 7469

"Form 1040" 3739

"formal verses" 5457

"formations, unlike the" 1118

"Formica surface, gleaming" 6145

"formidable castles" 6802

"formidable power" 6244

"*fornaio*, go down to the" 4285

Forrest, Mrs. 4138

Forrestal, aircraft carrier" 6773

Forrester, James 5909

Forrester, Lionel 9109

"forsaking her gentle pipe" 5397

"forsook his office behind the reception desk" 4659

Forsyte, Soames 1586

Forsyte family 3560

Forsytes 3558

"forsythia, gay yellow flash of" 3810

"fort, half a" 3098

"fort, squat" 8663

"Fort Bedford" 2959

"Fort Benning" 10506

"Fort Blockhouse" 8128

"Fort Dearborn" 4039

"Fort Dix" 8697

"Fort Klamath Oregon" 2383

"Fort Lauderdale" 3046

"Fort Lyttleton" 2959

"Fort Repose" 6004

"Fort Sumter" 5785

"Fort Wayne Indiana" 2631

"Fort Worth Texas" 5967

"Forth, Firth of" 9511

"forthright, nothing more" 3109

"forties, mid-" 4611

"fortification, spot of" 10729

"fortifications then existing were subsequently destroyed" 9205

"Fortnham & Mason" 7059

"fortnight to spare" 9857

"fortress, domestic" 9966

"Fortress, like some gigantic" 1356

"fortress, waiting at the" 4183

"fortress of Amherstburg, the small" 9205

Forts 3098, 9205

"fortunate, counted themselves" 3956

"fortunate, we are" 1224

"fortunate man, a" 7978

"fortunate people like ourselves" 7166

Fortunato 4989

Fortune, Lucinda 4365

Fortune, Reverend Timothy 1495

Fortune 1235, 5085

"fortune, extol his" 6521

"fortune, fame and" 10074

"Fortune, Goddess" 1220

"fortune, good" 4888, 5892

"fortune, immense oil" 5659

"fortune, in possession of a good" 5726

"fortune, it is an ill-" 1228

"fortune, made a" 10553

"*Fortune*, profile in" 8879

"fortune, seek my" 6823

"fortune, small" 238

"fortune, sought and found his" 3152

"fortune, turns of" 5085

"fortune and influence, gentleman of considerable" 5193

"fortune teller" 9597

"fortune teller's Tarot cards" 1329

"Fortune when not smiling on you" 1235

"fortunes, better my" 1568

"fortunes, embark on their" 3550

"fortunes, fathers'" 3396

"fortunes, his country's" 6260

"fortunes, losing" 10553

"fortunes of his whole house" 6604

"fortunes of the House of Egremont" 3557

"fortunes upon the stage, try their" 9376

"fortuneteller, job as a" 6442

"forty, at" 3276

"forty, might have been" 80

"Forty-Deuce" 6274

"forty-one, at" 6793

"*Forvitz*, the" 6652

"fossils, amoebae leave no" 2372

Foster, Jessie 4429

Foster, Lily 9710

Foster, Mrs. Sylvia 9710

Foster, Nona 9710

"foster home, my first night in the" 997

"fotched-on candy" 4850

"fought, last great battle was being" 10513

"fought, we" 1845

"fought, where he" 4469

"fought in quarrels not their own" 3557

"fought it more or less, everybody" 10492

"fought out the difficult words" 7200

"fought their way" 10509

"foul of something, we're" 8088

"found, waiting to be" 1169

"found a coiled blacksnake asleep on the stoop" 7025

"found a photograph of Marshall" 6871

"found a seat on the left-hand side" 9556

"found and spent its first vigor" 7667

"found eet, yo'm" 9269

"found guilty" 3407

"found her" 461

"found her dead" 2333

"found her waiting" 10050

"found herself a studio on East 92nd Street" 3261

"found him, when I" 154

"found him gazing straight at me" 5109

"found in a cardboard suitcase" 2609

"found it all around" 3367

"found late one October night" 1894

"found Martin Bormann's skull" 3413

"found me, when the girl" 2084

"found Old Josiah in the morning" 1877

"found one another without difficulty" 5801

"found out the next day" 34

"found Ruby, Billy" 2010

"found that Penny was not my sister" 5110

"found the bottle" 3702

"found the dead baby" 1893

"found the first five or six cans" 7236

"found the roll of film, she" 2618

"found themselves in an eerily silent landscape" 9643

"found tucked in with the wadding of the pillow" 6862

"found under a jerrycan" 2553

"foundation, admirable" 3111

"foundation, no" 9928

"foundations, previous" 1384

"foundations meet new seismic code requirements" 3264

"foundations of Julia's life, two strongest" 5599

"founded by the barons of lumbering" 3423

"founded on love" 1482

"founded on war" 1482

"founded the same year that Israel became a state" 7896

"founder and proprietor" 5311

"founder of the Mnemosyne Institute" 7444

Founders 7444, 7891

"fount of all modern romantic adventure" 1354

Fountain, Edward 10771
Fountain, Lucy 10771
Fountain, Mrs. 10771
"fountain, show them the" 8218
"fountain, Trevi" 9593
"fountain, view of the" 7771
"fountain, water" 2585
"fountain of Bandusium" 9738
"fountain out, blew the" 1606
"fountain pen" 5447
"fountains, Italian marble" 3179
"fountains, lit" 9582
"Four Legged Crouch" 9138
"four of them, the" 3426
"four of us, there were" 3990
"Four Seasons" 503
"Four Seasons, The" 2743
"Four Turnings" 7181
"fourteen, when I was" 7733
"Fourth again, here's the Glorious"
   4515
"Fourth of July" 2390, 4526
"fowl, wild guinea" 8379
Fowler 9246
Fowler, Chloe 8891
Fowler, Rebecca 4748
Fox 5923
Fox, Grania 8718
Fox, Hatter 3540
Fox, Montague 926
Fox, Mr. 7173
"fox, brain-reactions of a" 1016
"fox, historic Spartan" 9529
"fox, rather like a" 5923
"fox, stood on the" 2458
Foxe-Donnel, Leo 7382
"foxes, silver" 1016
"foxhounds, mastership of" 8636
"foxhounds, Surrey subscription"
   4683
"foyer of her apartment" 1951
"fractured versions, fabulously"
   7440
"fracturing the sea into glassy
   splinters" 10717
"fragments, torn to" 8400
Fragosi, Lucinda 4196
"fragrance, thick sweet" 8510
"fragrance all around him" 0510
"fragrance of incense" 7533
"fragrances, air lay heavy with the
   drifting" 8536
"fragrances of night and earth"
   8394
"fragrant" 2277
"fragrant Virginia" 3396
"frail, more" 2399
"frail, slight and seeming" 3891
"frail for hard labor, too" 1269
"frame, his ravaged" 2405
"frame, his spent and lofty" 4333
"framed in the doorway" 6321
Franc 9151
"France" 1015, 2555, 3024, 4458,
   4513, 4554, 4567, 5720, 5802,

   5834, 6089, 6244, 6249, 7663,
   8550, 8695, 8866, 9606, 9792
"France, arrived uninvited from"
   4698
"France, better in" 9510
"France, book about" 4850
"France, halfway through" 7605
"France, invading" 10473
"France, map of" 5714
"France, missionaries from" 9853
"France, north-eastern" 3111
"France, northern" 8702
"France, people of" 8841
"France, Premier of" 9929
"France, restaurant in" 508
"France, road in" 9813
"France, Royal Standard of" 9892
"France, the south of" 6371
"France, underground" 1917
"France, we began to live in" 6125
"France swirled under her feet"
   9534
Frances 4217, 4634
Frances, Aunt 450
Frances, Lady 6607, 7409
"France's Siberia" 4544
Francesco, Papa 2380
Francie 2770
Francine 6724
Francis 496, 950, 5024, 7046
Francis, Anne 6358
Francis, Bertram 4547
Francis, Uncle 1852
Francl, Joseph 2383
Franco, General 4481
François 3504, 8264, 9855
"frank, to be quite" 6391
Frank 8, 4690, 5875, 6524, 6853,
   7440, 7560, 8230
"Frankfort" 3994
Frankie 3501, 8291, 8310
"Frankish tribes" 1444
Franklin, Benjamin 8945
Franklin, Dr. Benjamin 9889
Franklin, Francis 8806
Franklin, Lydia 2554
Franklin, Moses 7646
Franklin, Teddy 6453
"frankness without which there can
   be no friendship" 7982
Franny 8230
"frantically, clattering" 4951
Franz 5991
Fraser, Christie 9897
Fraser, James 7611
Fraser, Ned 5765
Fraser, Ulysses Turner 1752
"Fraser, the" 9747
"frat boys push their sorority
   sisters" 1453
"fraternal, gesture that felt
   vaguely" 3486
"fray, without becoming part of
   the" 976
Fray, Dr. 8359

"freckle, tiny flowershaped" 343
Freckles 7215
Fred 7421
"Fred Holmes, the" 8094
Freddi 3936
Freddy 51, 5008
Freddy for short 5998
Frederick, George Augustus 834
Free, Henry 4734
"free, admittance" 1089
"free, born" 4443
"free his left eye" 151
"free of rot" 275
"free to you with my heart, making
   so" 1816
"free will" 10409
"Free Press, Detroit" 6853
Freedom 1616, 1765, 4443, 4716,
   5285, 5564, 7131, 7155, 9615
"Freedom" 5285
"freedom, all dis matter o'" 4716
"freedom, first breath of" 7131
"freedom, looking for" 5506
"freedom, more" 7155
"freedom, reach out for the" 1616
"freedom, summer" 938
"freedom, transformed from a
   heavy nightmare to" 1250
"freedom, wonderful sense of" 9615
"freedom and release" 1616
"freedom at last" 1765
"Freedom Bird" 225
"freehold" 3639
"freeway buildup, beat the" 6489
"freeways in Los Angeles" 3723
"freewheeled down the long hill"
   1499
"freewheeling" 8312
"Freeze, Big" 2443
"freezing, it's" 1560
"freighter, five-thousand-ton French
   passenger" 8147
"freighter on which he stoked" 8071
"freighter steamed through the
   Straits of Gibraltar" 8112
"French" 4787
"French, among the" 7584
"French, best urologist in New
   York is" 6892
"French, half" 4446, 4787
"French, the" 1076, 6813
"French, war against the" 10493
"French August" 3834
"French brains out, blew her
   pretty" 9291
"French Broad" 274
"French Canada, lower" 10431
"French clock" 9467
"French fascist collaborators" 4017
"French fashion, after the" 1654
"French father" 831
"French frontier" 10343
"French garden" 3119
"French habit" 4997
"French inhabitants" 9662

"French manner, in the" 5905
"French nation, destinies of the" 3376
"French peasant from Normandy" 6644
"French premier" 2491
"French Quarter, the old" 9083
"French rat, the" 2657
"French Riviera" 4631
"French settler" 503
"French soldiers" 10515
"French that disintegrated first, it was my" 8185
"French Town" 3262
"French troops" 9559
"French village" 2198
"French War, the old" 3434
"French were out, the" 8162
"French window" 7348
"French wines and perfumes, stay away from" 6652
"French-Canadian, half" 7187
"Frenchman" 1222
"Frenchman, married a" 6119
"Frenchman, originally (in a manner of speaking) a" 5965
"Frenchman, the" 7029
"Frenchman, young" 6930
"Frenchman's Bend" 4052
"Frenchmen" 3901
"Frenchmen who have to earn their living" 135
"Frenchwoman, portly" 4300
"frenetic, made things seem more" 4005
Frensic 6043
"frenzied ministrations" 5372
"frenzy, midday social" 8640
"frenzy, turbulent white-capped" 7304
"frenzy of mating" 7740
"frequency, emergency" 9362
"fresh, early morning" 5920
"fresh, strange and" 3369
"fresh and new and awesome as creation" 2986
"fresh material" 9409
"freshet of wind" 6381
"freshman" 9531
"freshman in the year 1910" 7890
"freshmen, incoming" 6760
"freshness, dazzling" 1849
"freshness, that cool quickened" 7292
"fretful" 652
"fretted, forever" 5015
"fretting against the pillow, barely" 147
"fretwork, exquisite open" 1849
Freud, Sigmund 7416
Frey 4734
"Freyday" 4282
"friar, Dominican" 10388
"friars, plump sleek rosy" 10641
Friberg, Sheldon 7015

"Friday, balmy May" 2175
"Friday was the day of rest" 4333
Fried, Max 6145
Frieda 8046, 8824
Friedl 7403
Frieman, Mrs. 4348
"friend, a" 3918, 9896
"Friend, Best" 982
"friend, Bob's best" 9027
"friend, death of a" 2370
"friend, dining with his" 10899
"friend, her" 4336, 8546
"friend, her childhood" 9935
"friend, her male" 9321
"friend, his" 1168, 3913, 4661, 5936, 6884, 10048
"friend, his best" 2304, 8683
"friend, his old" 5846
"friend, Homer was his best" 4463
"friend, less and less reliable a" 3057
"friend, like a lifelong" 3955
"friend, looking down at his" 3916
"friend, many counted him as a" 3914
"friend, may I call you" 3924
"friend, my" 152, 328, 1100, 1378, 2896, 3231, 3342, 3932, 5387, 5389, 5446, 5791, 6095, 8635, 9025
"friend, my best" 3911, 3928, 9301
"friend, my dear" 5556
"friend, my dearest" 7825
"friend, my learned" 2088
"friend, old" 3920
"friend, our" 1139
"friend, our beloved" 2310
"friend, poor" 8982
"friend, raised to the illustrious eminence of a" 1
"friend, self-made-millionaire" 4242
"friend, William's" 298
"friend, your" 3929
"friend, you're my" 3921
"friend Annie, my" 5449
"friend died, a" 2337
"friend in the government of Oklahoma, his best" 398
"friend like me, a good old" 24
"friend of hers who is going to be married soon" 4119
"friend of his own age" 3912
"friend of mine" 3286, 6266
"friend of mine, a dear" 952
"friend of the blind Lord, a dear" 7607
"friend perhaps, a close" 162
"friend Rich, our" 1527
"friend than a husband, he looks more like a best" 5991
"friend who figures in these pages" 3915
"friend who introduced him" 9864
"friendless, that had left him" 4282
"friendly, people are" 3362

"friendly lips, her" 4696
"friendly long enough now to think of getting married" 5746
"friendly people, one of those tough and" 4153
Friends 1, 24, 152, 298, 328, 694, 936, 952, 997, 1139, 1168, 2088, 2089, 2304, 2337, 2369, 2896, 3231, 3286, 3356, 3999, 4282, 4336, 4363, 4365, 4463, 4477, 4661, 4728, 5446, 5449, 5496, 5509, 5791, 5846, 5991, 6095, 6098, 6182, 6283, 6293, 6344, 6478, 6634, 6754, 6884, 7449, 7465, 8378, 8546, 8635, 8637, 8683, 8981, 8982, 9025, 9261, 9301, 9896, 9932, 9935, 10048, 10560
"friends, all her" 9261
"friends, astonished Mayfair" 5930
"friends, best of his remaining" 3922
"friends, Danny's" 8981
"friends, dear and devoted" 8378
"friends, devoid of" 4282
"friends, encircled by" 936
"friends, famous novelist's" 696
"friends, gentlemen" 2102
"friends, had become good" 3930
"friends, her" 3552, 5743, 7465, 10121
"friends, his" 4225, 4477, 7995, 9026
"friends, I have a great many" 3918
"friends, my" 707, 3910, 4458, 5027, 5819, 10534
"friends, my three very old" 2369
"friends, old school" 3999
"friends, one of my particular" 5384
"friends, personal" 6763
"friends, possible" 6754
"friends, ready to be" 6344
"friends, receive their" 9859
"friends, revenge of my" 6478
"friends, select circle of" 9858
"friends, she stood with her" 3933
"friends, so few intimate" 696
"friends, some of those" 5509
"friends, surrounded by" 3356
"friends, the" 3961
"friends, the two occupiers were fast" 6283
"friends, these are also our" 3924
"friends, you and your" 7449
"friends beside her, the two" 4363
"friends for twenty years" 3925
"friend's house, came to a" 3880
"friends I had, five" 3926
"friends of hers, two young" 3552
"Friends of Miss Friendship" 4005
"friends of the faith" 3338
"friends of their own, richer" 10560
"friends said" 6098
"friends who are richer than ourselves, we all have" 10560

"friends who surrounded him" 7739
Friendship 3322, 3931, 7378, 8171
"friendship" 7982
"friendship, refuse the right hand of" 6035
"friendship, your past" 8171
"friendship for the family" 694
"Friendship Village" 10917
"friendship with John Divney, my" 6182
"friendships formed by girls of that age" 3931
"friends-in-folly" 5448
"fries, Coney Island" 3876
"frigates moored alongside" 8121
"fright, a blink of" 10209
"fright, trembling with" 10140
"frightened, had not been really" 3702
"frightened, I suddenly felt" 3710
"frightened a great many people, the thunderstorm" 9074
"frightened at all, I'm not" 10091
"frightened by any amount of loneliness, not to be" 9515
"frightened everyone was, how" 3719
"frightened of anything in particular, not" 3710
"frightened of death, I am especially" 4113
"frightened of its thirteen constituent states" 1442
"frightened until darkness began to settle, did not become" 3720
"frightening them, I think you might be" 3729
"fringed with alders and ladies' eardrops" 7652
"fringed with amber and gold" 2188
"fringes, bleak warehouse" 5982
"fringes of palm-leaf, rusty" 10701
"Frisbee with their mortarboards, playing" 3283
Fritz 668, 9900
Frobisch 4111
Frobisher 1015
"frock, dark blue office" 6495
"frock, linen" 4406
"frock, tennis" 4157
"frog, great big" 719
"frog in a pool underneath him" 719
"frog mouth" 10174
"frog-voices" 10701
Fronnie 4247
"front, great oblique" 9065
"front, left for the" 8704
"Front, Western" 8678
"front line" 10506
"front was quiet, the" 10537
"frontier, somewhere on the" 2781
"frontier, the adjacent" 2087
"frontier between them, there is no" 9160
"frontier farm" 1850
"frontier life" 9860

"frontier of civilisation" 6100
"frontier settlement" 6814
"frontierland of western New York" 1497
"frontiers of the ancient British" 6802
"front-runner of the downwardly mobile" 77
Froser, Mr. 5565
"frost, hard" 8592
"frost, metallic" 4015
"frost, rime of" 10630
"frost, ringing fence wires with" 10609
"frost, windless" 2196
"frost and thin mist" 9195
"frost had dropped upon the corn crop" 8592
"frost had gone deep into the streets" 1545
"frost made patterns on the ground" 10575
"frost of the open field" 464
"frost on a plum, the delicate silver" 1550
"frost painted on the customs sheds" 8115
"frost to the earth, brought" 5704
Frosted Moses 5248
"frosts and fires" 3560
"frown, thoughtful" 10552
"frown on the face of the man" 10552
"frowned, forest" 3896
"frowned as she saw me fold my napkin" 6638
"frowned with forests of gloomy pine" 5125
"frowning, slightly" 10894
Frowns 6638, 10552, 10894
"frowns" 6842
"froze in the night" 770
"froze over fifteen years ago" 7690
"frozen, I felt" 3716
"frozen air, I spent my time in the" 187
"frozen plateau" 10725
"frozen with cold" 7539
Fruit 28, 3834, 5033, 5064, 8531, 9674
"fruit, advertising exec type" 3050
"fruit, gather" 2101
"fruit, platters of" 8884
"fruit, ripe" 5026
"fruit, rotting" 8544
"fruit, steadily ripening" 4374
"fruit before him, set the" 3817
"fruit is sucking away inside, her" 2080
"fruit of a misalliance" 3552
"fruit of the forbidden tree" 5064
"fruit remarkable for richness of flavor" 9662
"fruit to his lips, bring the luscious"

8517
"fruitcake, like a yummy" 2656
"fruitlessly besiege her again" 5397
Frustration 5329, 8481
"frustration" 8481
"frustration, laziness always mixed with" 5329
"frustration, rage and" 5292
"fry in his own cooking-oil, may he" 6426
Frye, Kirby 9427
"Fuck" 10214
"fuck, I absolutely love to" 7992
"fuck, what the" 8238
"fuck, who do I have to" 7986
"fuck with you, want to" 5670
"fuck you" 9316
"fucked each other into oblivion" 8027
"fucker in town, fastest" 9
"fucking, heterosexual" 8021
"fucking, more to love than" 8023
"fucking close-up pictures of the moon, four thousand" 539
"fucking wreck I am, what a" 73
"fudge, free samples of her" 8879
"fugitive Archbishop of Canterbury" 1691
"fugitive existence" 8400
"fugitives, armed" 10509
"fugue, a" 7172
Fulano 8982
"Fulham Broadway" 10395
Fulk 8484
Fulk, Dean 9674
Fulkerson 9403
"full up with food" 4519
"full-blood" 4358
Fuller, Burr 975
Fuller, Henry 8675
"full-grown as Athene" 794
"fumbled out of habit for the long-gone buttons of his sheepskin" 1548
"fumes, diesel" 8534
"fumes, dye" 2941
Fun 194, 302, 306, 307, 311, 317, 322, 330, 965, 6776, 10691
"fun, diary would be" 2531
"function and purpose not to be deciphered" 9019
"functionary, more important" 6512
"functioning, to keep it" 627
"functions, chief female" 10962
"Fund, Empire Children's" 4709
"fundraiser at the Sons of Italy in America Hall" 3753
"funeral, after the" 3939, 3943
"funeral, at the" 3949
"funeral, for three months after the" 4230
"funeral, go back to my mother's" 3942
"funeral, his mother's" 3846
"funeral, dressed not for a" 3963

"funeral, my father's" 3948
"funeral, pretty good" 3953
"funeral, recite at her" 5520
"funeral, she would have loved the" 3945
"funeral, something was wrong about this" 2371
"funeral, they had a" 2353
"funeral, went home after the" 2074
"funeral, wouldn't have wanted an elaborate" 3936
"funeral croon, moaning a tuneless" 2084
"funeral fell on a Thursday" 3938
"funeral in Deer Lick Pennsylvania" 3957
"funeral Mass, like the opening of the" 10902
"funeral service" 3958
"funeral umbrage" 1183
"funeral was full of priests" 3948
"funeral was over" 4934
Funerals 1538, 1878, 2074, 2084, 2344, 2353, 2358, 2371, 2384, 3846, 4230, 4934, 5520, 6708, 8309, 10902
"funerals, one of those family" 6708
"funerals, you don't *go* to" 3955
"funerals are not for the dead" 3936
"FUNERALS PERFORMED" 8309
"funereal slowness" 9804
"fungus, a brown-and-green" 7146
"funnels, two red and black slanting" 8105
"funny, dead" 4660
"funny, did not think it was" 2164
"funny, something" 3447
"funny things, marriages are" 5763
"funny thought" 9456
"Fur Person" 425
"fur that made our lives what they were" 1022
Furey, Donald 2805
"furnace, glass" 9302
"furnace, room was like a" 7776
"furnish him with information" 696
"furnishings were scanty" 7134
Furniture 1035, 3085, 3217
"furniture, giant's" 7808
"furniture, heavy leather" 6511
"furniture, new" 2754
"furniture, old" 7214
"furniture, taste in" 10318
"furniture is vastly superior" 3085
"furniture of their predecessors" 3085
"furrows, athwart the" 3640
"furrows, plowing" 6398
"furrows, worry" 2803
"further from Shiuli, I could hardly have been" 7434
"fur-trade days" 9744
Furuseth, Charley 581
"fury, deliberate" 7294

"fury, hissing" 7939
"fury, rode like" 7639
"fury of strong young cats at play, deceptive" 9841
"fury was a constant state of being" 388
"furze" 7878
"fuschia, a branch of" 10696
"fusing into a golden bronze" 8937
"fuss about it, couldn't you make a" 51
"fuss made over his broken body" 3936
"fussed by Matilda's unusual activity" 641
"fustian of those old pages, worn and wrinkled" 10022
"futile" 8400
"futility" 962
Futuransky, Lila 2050
Future 256, 1586, 2519, 3401, 4616, 5477, 6088, 6791, 6988, 7017, 7021, 7023, 9186, 9186, 9604, 9845, 9950
"future, a personal" 9604
"future, celebration of the" 4012
"future, dream of splendid" 9991
"future, great" 9860
"future, history of our" 9186
"future, in the" 2491
"future, long-term" 6988
"Future, looking into the" 1586
"future, only a short skip into the" 2810
"future, presentiment of my" 7017
"future, secure" 6791
"future, the" 9615
"future, the immediate" 4616
"future, the not very distant" 5203
"future, think of the" 7953
"future, vision of the" 7021
"future, visit to the" 5477
"future, wants to change the" 256
"future, what will someday be the" 514
"future ages" 707
"future events" 6244
"future flash before his eyes, saw his" 9845
"future generations" 5562
"future in philosophy, no" 5453
"future seemed more present than the present itself" 3401
"future would exist" 9950
"fuzzy borderland" 10183

"G came around again" 9947
G.J. 5445
Gabe 3051
"gaberdines, gates and" 1347
"gable, a pinched" 9206
"gable, its tiled" 3119
"gable terminated by a curious little belfry" 9206

"gables, seven acutely peaked" 3060
"gables facing towards various points of the compass" 3060
Gabriel 6698
Gabriella 8218
"*Gaelic American*, the" 2386
Gaffney-Kozinski, Kate 10894
Gage, Howard 9410
Gaia 4853
"gaiety, a look almost of" 8164
"gaiety, febrile and semi-intoxicated" 8854
"gaiety, transformed by its" 1250
"gainer, slow half" 10
"gait, bobbing springy" 10354
"gait, character of his" 10352
"gait, his predatory slightly uneven" 1731
"gait shambling" 10413
"gaiters, woolen" 1274
Gaither, Sally 1169
Gaius Claudius 3481
Gaius Marius 3481
Gaius Marius the Mule-driver 10521
"gala, Lady Clonbrony's" 6751
"gala dinner" 6769
"Galactic Empire, the Marches of the" 9557
"Galaxxy, red aluminum" 2810
Galbraeth, Sarah 10975
"gale, conflict with the" 14
"gale, January" 10704
"gale at South, strong" 2543
"gale force, building up to" 2337
"gale howled across the frozen plateau" 10725
"gale was roaring up the Channel" 10704
"Galilee" 3655
"Galilee Nebraska" 7416
Galileo 326, 539
Gallagher, Charlie 3735
Gallagher, Mrs. 3780
"gallant tobyman" 3396
"gallantly drawn, sword was" 8641
"gallants roistered" 3396
"Gallatin Mississippi" 4042
"galleries of painting" 8546
"Gallery" 1586
"gallery, art" 10867
"gallery, modest" 511
"gallery, my" 2983
"Gallery, National" 7823
"Gallery, National Portrait" 9391
"Gallery, Rede Art" 489
"gallery, sculpture-" 3986
"Gallery, Tate" 8027
"gallery, tiny art" 6474
"gallery of Blackladies, great" 487
"Gallic goatherder" 6551
"Gallic Wars" 920
Gallimore, Guts 1078
Gallion, George 2985
"galloped across the bridge" 6316

"galloping across the meadow" 7645
"galloping down" 8671
"galloping for all she might" 2786
Galloway, Ron 2561
"Galloway" 6416
"Galloway, the town is" 7668
"Gallowgate" 10349
"gallows, taken his" 5759
"gallows beam" 7686
"gallows tree" 495
Galt, John 4750
Galton 8225
"Galway" 4308, 4931
"Galway city" 1438
Gamal, Mr. 5844
"Gambia, The" 804
"gambler fashion, fancy river-boat"
   301
"gamblers, gay" 4630
Gambling 322, 1220, 6263, 10002
"gambling" 6263
"game, a rather erratic and unpractised" 8259
"game, perfect" 8918
"game, the" 312
"game, the national" 3378
"game, watch the" 8920
"game, watching the Lakers" 3292
"game, what about a" 298
"game between the Addicts and the
   Depressives" 2013
"game of anything, nobody ever
   won a" 319
"game of baseball, wonderful" 8933
"game of tennis, their ritual" 10411
"game of 'three old cat'" 955
"game was ended" 2304
"game was to start, no one believed
   that a new" 2304
Games 8, 295, 296, 297, 298, 301,
   308, 309, 310, 311, 312, 313, 315,
   318, 319, 320, 324, 326, 327,
   955, 959, 3283, 3323, 3966,
   3967, 3969, 4000, 5653, 5710,
   6669, 7047, 8747, 8908, 8920,
   9680, 10411
"games, children's" 5693
"games, make-believe of their" 959
"games, no more" 5652
"Games, Southern" 8914
"games, stopped their" 7627
"games, we played our" 327
"Ganado Bay, port town of" 4643
Gandalf 8269
Gandhi, Mahatma 6546
"Gandhi's assassination" 3439
Ganesh 3980
"Ganford" 4139
"gang, chain" 8227
"gang of singers, rowdy" 2901
"gang-planks leading to ships" 6216
"gangs, shore" 4916
"gangs of yellow men" 5138
"gangster, the" 6715
"gangster's money, stole the" 2684

"gangway, hesitant at the top of
   the" 5927
"gangway, still at the top end of
   the" 10024
Gannon, Will 2900
Gant, Old Man 989
Gantry, Elmer 2889
Ganundagwa 7409
"gaol, Kilmainham" 7151
"gaol, sentenced to six months in"
   1505
"gap, jagged" 9527
"Gap, Ouasioto" 6813
"gap below him, in the" 176
"gap between my bedroom
   curtains" 2269
"gape and forget, openly" 1333
"gaped at Augustus Plebesly" 7851
"gaped up into the boughs" 933
"gapy-face" 4148
"Garage, Cherokee" 3101
"garage, the" 9241
"garage and cafe, a sun-blistered"
   1080
"garage at the rear" 3156
"garage floor" 8456
Garanhir, Gwythno 7795
"garb of peace" 8642
"garbage, crust of its own" 8141
"garbage cans, rattled the tops of"
   10699
"garbage dump, world's largest"
   1083
"garbage of a life" 2656
"garbardine, black" 10819
Garbo, Greta 8009
"Gardar" 3661
"garden, Bishop's" 3981
"garden, came out into the" 10643
"garden, cheerful little" 3819
"garden, college" 7390
"garden, deep" 5314
"garden, disordered" 3165
"garden, fairly spacious" 3153
"garden, farmhouse" 3793
"garden, flower" 3976
"garden, forest" 8212
"garden, formal" 10355
"garden, formal French" 3119
"garden, her" 3978
"garden, her kitchen" 10351
"garden, herb" 8741
"garden, in the" 7112
"garden, kitchen" 2984
"garden, large vegetable" 3119
"garden, looking out at the" 8283
"garden, once-famous rose" 3179
"Garden, right across the street
   from the" 2896
"garden, rose" 10406
"garden, Rosie Mortimer's" 3982
"garden, sitting in her" 6857
"garden, small narrow" 3103
"garden, Square" 8259
"garden, stationmaster's" 4385

"garden, the" 3983
"garden, trees of the" 3794
"garden, went out into the" 4224
"garden beds" 3806
"Garden Committee" 3977
"garden in the square" 18
"garden of 5 Alcock Road" 5145
"garden of his residence" 7109
"garden of the Arcadian Society,
   the forgotten" 8344
"garden of the asylum" 4941
"garden of Versailles" 9882
"garden outside the Museum of
   Antiquities" 8941
"garden quad" 8354
"garden was quiet, the" 8328
"garden where she has been working" 10890
"gardener, the" 2025
"gardener, the old" 3980
"gardener, the young" 3980
"gardenias rich and pungent,
   aroma of" 1194
Gardening 3622, 3974, 3975,
   3977, 3979, 3980, 4941, 8241,
   10890
"gardening, thinking about your
   family is like" 3622
"gardening is all of my pleasure"
   3979
Gardens 431, 3165, 3793, 3806,
   4402, 7112, 8203, 8328, 8344,
   10037, 10334, 10355, 10643
"Gardens, Augusta" 696
"Gardens, Bibighar" 5152
"Gardens, Burlington" 4304
"Gardens, Kensington" 7953
"gardens, love and water their"
   4402
"gardens, luxuriant beauty of the
   orange" 1355
"gardens, municipal" 6225
"Gardens, the" 2006
"gardens, Tuileries" 10037
"gardens climbed like a richly
   carpeted stairway" 4316
"gardens communally owned" 4166
"Gardens in the Square" 3977
"gardens massed with sunflowers"
   1376
"gardens of Clavering Park" 3972
"gardens of the Luxembourg" 10334
"gardens sloping down to the
   Whit" 6283
"gardens were fenced from the
   street" 3103
Gardner, Doug 6511
Gare, Caleb 10039
"Gare de l'Est" 1750
"Gare du Nord" 2954
"Gareloch" 5071
Garfield, Roak 140
Garfield, Sophia 10479
"gargling down this last bottle of
   Irish wine" 9300

"gargoyles, grotesque" 2799
"gargoyles waiting for her to sleep"
    2799
Garland, Frances 2844
Garlock, "Little Red" 1896
Garland, President 9701
"garment, tattered" 5968
"garment, wrapped me in this"
    7539
"garment that had once been his
    dignity" 5968
"garments, sad-colored" 3985
"garments, splendid" 9738
"garments off, modestly taking
    their" 6388
"Garnsai" 10909
Garon, Monsieur 9209
"Garonne, the" 5125
"garotte of diesel and greasy dirt"
    183
"garotting" 6965
Garp 2040
"garrison, German" 10459
Garrity, Jason Aloysius 670
Garrity, Page 6859
Garth 6981
Garth, Susan 869
"Garth in Garthdale, village of"
    1361
"gas" 1067
"gas, running out of" 9451
"gas, stopped for" 3007
"gas burning on the kitchen range,
    left the" 6024
"gas company turned off the gas,
    in case the" 3094
"gas pumps" 8323
"gas pumps out front" 1080
"gas station, Pete's" 1083
"gas station's driveway" 3933
"gas tank, filling the" 663
"Gascony" 5125
"gash on his face" 5990
"gaslight, under the" 5813
"gasoline, five-gallon can of" 3778
"gasoline, fresh supply of" 1970
"gasped the Gasper" 5489
Gasper 5489
"gasping, left Renoir" 8027
"gasps of labored breathing, heavy
    panting" 9841
"Gassy" 7098
Gate, Paul 6436
"Gate, Chien Men" 8700
"gate, closed the" 1597
"gate, front" 1765, 10532
"gate, great" 953, 3065
"gate, great iron" 9757
"gate, little-used" 8212
"Gate, The Wicket" 1669
"Gate, Western" 10542
"gate, wide entrance" 3069
"gate, wrought-iron" 1659, 10355
"gate at the distant roadway" 10038
"gate of the cemetery, blighted" 1193

"gate of the house" 9921
"gate that gave on the terraces of a
    forest garden" 8212
"gateposts, imposing stone" 3179
Gates, Annie-May 3581
Gates 953, 1597, 1659, 2987, 3065,
    3069, 5935, 8937, 9248, 9671,
    10532
"gates, dock" 59
"gates, high familiar" 2987
"gates, old" 9255
"gates, padlocked" 3095
"gates, spike iron" 5935
"gates, tall wrought-iron" 3589
"gates, wrought-iron" 2945
"gates and gaberdines" 1347
"gates draw back, electric" 9824
"gates with the coupling snakes
    woven into the wrought iron"
    2987
"gate-towers, the two tall" 9248
"gateway of Sorrento, antique"
    8937
"gateway out into the road" 3960
"gather, began to" 3576, 4015
"gather on their piazzas to drink
    hot toddies" 3394
"gathered, many people had" 1302
"gathered about the long table"
    10554
"gathered and drew in a spilling
    tribute of chips" 3969
"gathered at summer's end in 1927"
    4011
"gathered his clans" 7810
"gathered in a perfectly appointed
    town house" 3961
"gathered in ten rows fronting
    Block 14A" 4024
"gathered in the dining hall" 1214
"gathered on El Cuervo's station
    platform" 10069
"gathered on the ridge" 5190
"gathering, people were" 4014
"gathering, such a" 3994
"gathering, the" 4007
"gathering corn" 3647
"gathering dust into slashing gray
    clouds" 10726
"gathering of pale men and women,
    a vast" 1296
"gathering power from the familiar
    objects" 9409
Gatherings 330, 1214, 1280, 1292,
    1296, 1302, 1532, 1565, 1634,
    2623, 2914, 2940, 3338, 3576,
    3591, 3597, 3599, 3601, 3833,
    3959, 3961, 4155, 4183, 4257,
    4335, 4478, 4530, 4985, 5190,
    5208, 5323, 5429, 5625, 5681,
    5854, 5892, 6586, 6755, 6775,
    6781, 6959, 6985, 6986, 7110,
    7151, 7501, 7594, 7762, 7797,
    8110, 8338, 8553, 8626, 8637,
    8638, 8737, 8857, 8893, 8938,

8976, 8997, 9581, 9858, 10035,
    10042, 10054, 10069, 10076,
    10088, 10554, 10643
"gatherings, family" 3597
"gatherings, large family" 3585
"gatherings, selective social" 10798
"*gauche, rive*" 1371
"Gaudiness, her" 127
"gaudy uniform" 8650
"Gaumont Graphic" 1320
"gaunt exhausted face" 5204
"gaunt face" 5971
"gaunt girders" 8590
"gaunt handsome man" 5961
"gaunt smoking-rooms" 4317
"gauntlet, message tucked in his"
    6009
"gave his sister Susannah" 4122
"gave the man a twenty pence tip"
    2044
"gave up" 5947, 9450
"gave up his chances in life" 8226
Gaver, Raymond 2453
Gavilan, Ben 5988
Gavin, H. Carter 4982
Gavin, Mr. 9948
"Gaviota California" 10230
"gawky, even her name was" 4196
"gay, quite unwarrantably" 4518
"Gay Manhood, Young" 5301
"gay with luxuriant woods and
    vines" 5125
"gayety, Class Day" 6753
Gayheart, Lucy 3532
Gaylord, Susan 5741
"gaze, a mutually questioning" 8676
"gaze, Gerald's pulsating" 5450
"gaze, his felonious" 9763
"gaze, inscrutable" 2486
"gaze, level his" 8298
"gaze at his steaming boots" 7567
"gaze enmeshed in the vast web of
    twilight" 5620
"gaze gave growth and warmth"
    4188
"gaze intently fixed" 10038
"gaze lingering" 336
"gaze of someone surveying the
    sea" 8283
"gaze that broke off teasingly short
    of recognition" 8676
"gaze up through the skylight above
    her" 8491
"gazebo, green painted" 301
"gazed" 7335
"gazed at the figure that seemed to
    hover over the yard" 2761
"gazed at the framed photographs"
    6851
"gazed idly up the line" 7239
"gazed in wonder" 8093
"gazed into the cup again" 7014
"gazed into the gilt-framed mirror
    on the wall" 7476
"gazed into the rain" 5431

"gazed out across the harbour" 7801
"gazed up and down Bond Street" 489
"gazed with envy at Duke" 2497
"gazed with fixed intensity" 9545
"gazed with hard and wondering eyes" 7654
"gazes with wonder" 6802
"gazing at a grove of trees" 8266
"gazing at the magnificent scene" 948
"gazing at the sea" 9987
"gazing down the broad empty river" 7658
"gazing into the fire" 9404
"gazing mournfully" 5940
"gazing out into the empty street" 5945
"gazing out over his domain" 8257
"gazing straight at me" 5109
"gazing through grimy window-panes" 8615
"Gedsborough Airbase" 4313
"geegaws, shabby" 6848
"geek, when your mama was the" 10955
"geeked up, I'm supposed to be all" 6782
Geese 737, 748, 761
"geese, earthbound" 748
"geese dancing" 3680
"Geiger and his counter" 10007
"geisha girls, the little" 1320
"gelded, broken and" 6814
"Gelli" 6953
"gem among the oceans, a rare" 4098
"gem-encrusted receptacle" 110
Geminus, Rosianus 3460
Gene 7576
"genealogical tree" 358
"genealogy they had faked up for him, the royal" 363
"General, a" 3376
"general, a distinguished British" 10535
"general, blood-fouled old" 10521
"general, fool and" 8172
"General, the" 2571, 6372
"General, the old" 2513
"General Assembly" 6986
"general is dead, the" 8172
"General of the Military Staff" 2364
"General Pendleton, the U.S.S." 8104
"general practitioner, an over-worked" 2616
"generals, equestrian" 4467
"generals, the" 4129
"Generals, Two Highland" 10465
"General's boot" 2571
"generation, each" 3361
"generation, English" 10773
"generation, new illiterate" 9265
"generation earlier, a" 5628
"generation of misfit District Com-

missioners" 1833
"generations back, for many" 4444
"generations back, many" 358
"generations, bury a strain for" 4435
"generations, entire" 9001
"generations, flickered for" 8986
"generations, for" 3605, 8688
"generations, four" 9748
"generations, future" 5562
"generations, heroism of countless" 6255
"generations, many" 7950
"generations, three" 3071
"generations of boys" 6427
"generations of tranquil family life" 3248
Generosity 121, 1798, 5014
"generosity, my" 121
"generously" 5014
"genes, a cluster of" 9186
"Genesis" 2622
"Genesis, agreed with" 8735
Genetha 8229
"geneticists" 1065
"Geneva" 2563, 9824, 10972
"Geneva, lake of" 9112
Genie 2723
"genitals, instinctively and uncon-sciously cupped his" 4290
Genius 237, 5767, 7901, 7993, 9703
"genius, good or the evil" 10778
"genius, his" 6604
"genius, his own" 3514
"genius, magic spell of" 4101
"genius, married to a" 5767
"genius, musician of great" 6213
"genius, that great military" 7901
"genius, the presiding" 3376
"genius and skill, human" 237
"genius for that sort of thing, a real" 7519
"genius I.Q." 7993
"geniuses, generality of great" 9703
"Genovese, in" 6920
"gent, middle-aged" 10450
"genteel appearance" 9511
"genteel conversation" 8869
"gentle, you could have been more" 7560
"gentle absorption" 10657
"gentle as the eyes of daisies" 5656
"gentle fashionable girl" 6605
"gentleman" 4442
"gentleman, a" 2943
"gentleman, American" 1090, 6021
"gentleman, country" 2825
"gentleman, crippled" 9952
"gentleman, elderly" 306, 6330
"gentleman, foreign" 4915
"gentleman, illustrious" 7708
"gentleman, my" 9510
"gentleman, not as a" 5385
"gentleman, worthy" 5728

"gentleman, young" 2223
"gentleman, young Irish" 9874
"gentleman and a coxcomb" 3812
"gentleman enveloped in a cloak" 1569
"gentleman from *Harper's Weekly*" 7871
"gentleman in the middle years, a sandy-haired" 4274
"gentleman in the prime of life" 8839
"gentleman noteworthy for a lively countenance" 14
"gentleman of Citta di Castello" 5791
"gentleman of considerable fortune and influence" 5193
"Gentleman of the Black Stock, the Old" 5790
"gentleman was reclining" 5613
"gentleman-commoners" 7876
"Gentleman's Magazine" 7505
Gentlemen 1569, 2825, 4442, 5475, 5728
"gentlemen, Berwick" 3992
"gentlemen, cluster of English" 4257
"gentlemen, elderly" 9113
"gentlemen, ladies and" 8886
"gentlemen, the rest of these" 5012
"gentlemen, two" 9904
"gentlemen, two professional" 5871
"gentlemen, young" 3528, 9882
"gentlemen adventurers" 3557
"gentlemen friends" 2102
"gentlemen of his class" 8863
"gentlemen were sitting alone" 2886
"gently this time" 7985
"Gentry" 10466
"gentry, Scottish" 3550
"genuine cowhide" 2835
Geoffrey 3624, 3944, 6340
"geographical definitions" 4027
"geographical position, its" 4089
"geographically speaking" 4467
Geography 291, 1173, 1335, 1341, 1352, 1372, 1374, 1375, 1381, 1383, 1394, 1398, 1404, 1405, 1418, 1421, 1427, 1439, 1471, 3082, 3181, 3270, 4534, 4881, 5016, 5022, 5023, 5026, 5043, 5046, 5048, 5126, 5140, 5158, 5706, 5707, 5708, 5713, 5714, 5715, 5719, 5720, 5721, 5723, 6053, 6056, 6060, 6061, 6066, 6068, 6155, 6254, 6256, 6257, 6258, 6261, 6264, 6269, 6608, 6918, 6921, 6923, 7186, 7647, 7657, 7668, 7923, 7924, 8048, 8399, 8632, 8691, 8977, 9203, 9519, 9741, 9743, 9744, 9746, 10571, 10724
"geography, his" 4077
"geography, lesson in" 8977
"geography, my wound is" 4090
"Geography, Old" 6915

"geography, our" 10571
"geography, physical" 3270
"geography, teaching children" 5708
"geography of space" 526
"geography of the soul" 5706
"geological line, exact" 4068
Geology 5044, 9503
George 2097, 3505, 3990, 4351, 4768, 6615, 7174, 7355, 9302, 9925, 9957
George, Honourable 2823
George, Sacred Majesty King 1483
George, Sir 2699
George II 3965
"Georgetown" 5485
"Georgia" 167, 826, 1423, 4403, 5476, 6097, 9583, 10506
"Georgia, born in a place called" 806
"Georgia, down in" 9086
"Georgia, hot world of" 4393
"Georgia, middle" 3418
"Georgian elegance" 3210
"Georgian girl" 10774
"Georgian state-banquets" 5943
"Georgian town houses" 309
"*Georgic*, His Majesty's Troop-Ship" 8677
Georgie 7540, 7954
Geraint 8772
Gerald 5450
Gerane 838
"geranium, inseparable companion of the" 6854
"geranium, struggling" 4627
"geraniums" 5162
"geraniums, clay pot of" 10860
Gereth, Mrs. 4909
Germaine 1706, 8870
"German" 369, 8463, 9606
"German, crown a" 1444
"German, if you are a" 9284
"German authorities" 3464
"German city" 4178
"German garrison" 10459
"German in you, are you sure there is no" 4447
"German legends" 5224
"German lithograph" 6896
"German parentage" 6628
"German Propaganda Bureau" 5714
"German pursuit pilot" 6683
"German restaurant" 7570
"German royalty, pictures of" 1179
"German soldiers" 8706
"German tariff war" 2592
"German who just came down from McGill" 2518
"germane to the issue" 7804
Germanicus, Nero Claudius Caesar Drusus 4219
Germanicus, Tiberius Claudius Drusus Nero 5567, 7802
"Germans" 2025, 6779

"Germans, applaud with the vehemence of the" 5641
"Germans probably have a word" 4598
"Germantown" 9721
Germany 223, 10496
"Germany" 3503, 4085, 5016, 6117, 7714, 8602
"Germany, killed in action in" 8675
"Germany, refugee from" 8865
"Germany, war against" 10496
"Germany is finally purified" 9284
"Gerona" 2341
Gerrit 4760
Gerritszoon, Harmen 4760
Gerta 10759
Gertrude 5747
Gervaise 8823
Gervase 9559
"gesticulating vehemently" 8845
"gesticulations, many and excitable" 8852
"gesture, pleading" 4986
"gesture, single" 633
"gesture, that" 5943
"gesture, unpardonable" 6232
"gesture broke the surface of events" 633
"gesture of farewell" 2552
"gesture of the gods, wonderful" 5576
"gesture of the kindliest denial" 9880
"gesture that felt vaguely fraternal" 3486
"gesture was vaguely savage" 8568
"gestures, extravagant" 5988
"gestures of a god" 6792
"gesturings, meaningless" 4935
"get along, we better" 6219
"get along now, how do you and your Pa" 6614
"get along with, easy to" 7972
"get along with them" 10849
"get away" 6694
"get away from the Widow Douglas" 5506
"get down in it baby, oh" 8806
"get him, Jaime will" 1164
"get him, you've *got* to" 6947
"get him or bust" 6947
"get in, I told Joyce we was gonna" 1739
"get in, people were always trying to" 426
"get in, we gotta" 1739
"get in touch" 3920
"get it back, he can't" 7124
"get on, I" 1771
"get out of here pronto, I have to" 5606
"get there, the minute you" 1135
"get there, when I" 7635
"get up" 2358
"get up early" 4285

"get up early, knowing he has got to" 10132
"get up on the right side of the bed" 4276
Getchel, Libby 1088
"gets up" 10303
"getting into his half sister's mutton" 4711
"getting my tail to Juarez" 2656
"getting ready" 9971
"getting ready for a New Year's Eve party" 6782
"getting ready for something" 3445
"*Getting There*" 5413
"getting up in the morning, he didn't much like" 10163
"getting up out of the guest chair" 8559
"Gettysburg, battle of" 4468
"Ghaleh Bagh" 6014
"Ghetto, London" 1347
"ghetto, the" 6329
"ghetto, Warsaw" 2604
"Ghetto of the Eternal City" 1347
"ghillie, head" 4690
"ghost, her feeble" 6646
"Ghost, Holy" 1496
"ghost, once you have given up the" 2314
Ghost Horse, Sitko 5246
"ghost of a woman, haunted by the" 4116
"ghost of woman-loveliness, pale vapid" 5640
"ghosted in on the evening inshore breeze" 8114
Ghosts 5310, 6086, 6796, 8967
"ghosts" 4114
"ghosts, bright white young-lady" 8451
"ghosts, it had something to do with the" 4107
"ghosts, not that I believed in" 4110
"ghosts for an instant" 1041
"ghosts of centuries of sunlight" 5310
"ghosts of the past" 6796
"ghosts that haunt the Chesapeake" 4105
"ghoul, who's that" 4994
"giant, the" 3921
"giant Eagle" 724
"giant emerged from the smooth waters" 6403
"giant of Cerne Abbas" 805
"giant resting on his elbows" 8034
"giant women, recumbent" 2225
"giantess, the" 1190
"giant-killer, pale ornamental" 10839
"giants" 6529
"giants, built by" 9227
"giant's furniture" 7808
"giant's hand, it looked like a" 10582

"gibbering" 169
"gibbet stood at the head of the pass" 7190
Gibble 8734
Gibbs, Ansel 6984
"Gibraltar" 8089
"Gibraltar, Straits of" 8112
"Gibraltar of Wessex" 9091
Gibson, Dick 4784
"giddy, felt" 3311
Giddy Gerda 4777
Gideon 6152
Gidharee 9917
Gifford 5004
"gift for my tenth birthday" 859
"gift for persuasive speech" 8026
"gift has come for you" 4130
"gift of inner light possesses me" 7021
"gift of laughter, born with a" 5183
"gift retains its mystery" 4129
"gifted writer, her most" 2360
Gifts 839, 845, 851, 859, 863, 866, 1258, 2846, 3950, 4512, 4560, 4930, 7526
"gifts, bless o Lord thy" 7526
"gifts, delivering" 4131
"gifts of imagination and expression, those high" 5406
"gifts of their openhanded childlike gods" 4133
"gig, a green" 1572
"gigantic greenhouse" 4334
Gil 2573, 9547
Gilbert 6940
Gilbert, Owen 9382
Gilbertson, Cole 2934
Gilbey 230
Gilda 9086
Gilde 5104
"gilded and glazed" 4309
"gilded like all the landscape with the slanting beams of sunset" 2944
Giles 7586
Giles, Uncle 1921
Gill, Reverend William Booth 9941
Gillespie, Hugh 6149
Gillette 5800
Gilligan 7673
Gillis, Joe 5209
"gills of a river bass, like the" 8734
"Gillycranky, Battle of" 10465
Gilman, Jeff 1604
"gilt, carved" 7481
"gilt, faded" 717
"gilt, fading" 3102
"gilt monograms" 2960
"gimcrackery, terra-cotta" 1362
"gimme a hand" 3519
Gin 1767
"gin, glass of" 4319
"gin, gratefully accepting the" 2922
"gin and tonics, drinking" 2919

"gin fizzes, having a few gloomy" 2509
"gin-and-tonics could really justify, than even six" 5229
"Ginger, the" 8094
"ginger ale" 6760
"gingerbread, flat as a man of" 152
"gingerbread filigree" 7440
"gingko trees" 3232
Ginny 1216
"gins, seven small" 2901
Ginwalla, Zareen 4602
Giorgio 4285
Giotto 5465
Girard, Frances 3228
Girard, Libby 5875
Girard, Madame 6149
"girasol" 10899
"girders, gaunt" 8590
"girdle, her" 2658
"Girdlestone and Co." 1008
"girl, a" 3301, 4204, 5152, 7068, 7717, 10387
"girl, absolutely stunning coloured" 9930
"girl, adolescent" 2565
"girl, African" 2106
"girl, American" 3541, 4797
"girl, as a young" 4209
"girl, baby" 542
"girl, big towhaired country" 4176
"girl, blind" 8959
"girl, blonde" 4192
"girl, bony slow-moving" 4178
"girl, born a" 4185
"girl, city" 4155
"girl, dead" 10239
"girl, elder" 10784
"girl, extremely pretty" 4139
"girl, fair" 8767
"girl, fair young" 7127
"girl, fair-haired" 5761
"girl, fat" 3620
"girl, fifteen-year-old" 4150
"girl, flower-" 8837
"girl, for a" 4147
"girl, fourteen-year-old" 4169
"girl, gentle fashionable" 6605
"girl, gold-toothed" 5655
"girl, he noticed the" 4190
"girl, hired" 3094, 3328
"girl, his Georgian" 10774
"girl, I am a tall" 4184
"girl, I am very far from being a wise" 7964
"girl, I once knew this" 10879
"girl, I was that little" 4175
"girl, little" 4137, 4167, 4168, 4461, 4718
"girl, little-rich-" 10391
"girl, making love to a" 8000
"girl, middle-class American white" 10834
"girl, Miss Akst was your" 4159

"girl, mournful sparrow-faced little man of a" 4196
"girl, not to every young" 4172
"girl, once with a" 5667
"girl, other" 1772
"girl, perfect rosebud of a" 3554
"girl, real big" 4177
"girl, saw the" 4164
"girl, small" 4189, 4625, 4822
"girl, still a little" 28
"girl, such a lovely" 9509
"girl, tall slender" 4203
"girl, that" 4171
"girl, the" 2084, 3138, 4109, 4156, 4161, 4195, 4672, 5118, 6388, 6942, 8786, 9933
"girl, ticket" 5841
"girl, very emotional" 4201
"girl, when I was a" 904
"girl, when she was a" 7763
"girl, white" 4157, 5753
"girl, who was maybe his" 2973
"girl, wildest" 5218
"girl, young" 4149, 7063, 9286
"girl at dead center of the universe, one little" 3592
"girl called Fitzgibbon" 10649
"girl came, after the" 8180
"girl came into the room" 4141
"girl came out of lawyer Royall's house" 1585
"girl children" 10547
"girl friend, his new" 1865
"girl got up from the table" 4310
"girl had taken up with another man, his" 4590
"girl he had once been in love with" 3344
"girl I meet" 4849
"girl in a striped bathing suit" 4206
"girl in an orange-coloured shawl" 4143
"girl in Budapest, most beautiful" 10884
"girl in gray deerskins" 4165
"girl in love" 7479
"girl in riding clothes walking across it" 10389
"girl in the family, a young" 6757
"girl in the green and gold dress" 8555
"girl in the picture, see the" 2877
"girl is about seven years old" 4207
"girl is an inanimate object, pretend the" 2107
"girl is perfect" 4171
"girl kept hovering above the hen and chicks she loved" 4162
"girl named Martha" 8708
"girl next door" 1784
"girl not from his faith" 6652
"girl of eighteen, a young" 6412
"girl of eleven" 4148
"girl of fourteen, ragged" 4144

"girl of good but impoverished family" 4209

"girl of her class" 7748

"girl of his dreams" 2083

"girl of nineteen" 8209

"girl of the same class as himself" 5761

"girl or other, some" 7996

"girl seated alone at a table" 10392

"girl shed one name" 4842

"Girl slept restlessly" 8475

"girl stood in relief" 4140

"girl that I married, this" 5845

"girl to be approaching woman-hood" 4170

"girl was a real pest" 4194

"girl was conspicuous" 10846

"girl was to be seen" 4174

"girl we had been talking about" 4175

"girl who died" 2355

"girl who later was to be the cause of a sensation" 10126

"girl who made his stomach buzz" 2111

"girl who stood naked" 6395

"girl who thought she was God" 10879

"girl who walked so swiftly" 4145

"girl who was scheduled for a con-sultation" 6897

"girl who was very beautiful" 4160

"girl with the big tits, the English" 4620

"girl with the brick-red lips" 10964

"girl you'll find soon enough, this" 5803

Girlfriends 4590, 7716

"girlhood" 4811

"girlhood, in her" 4138

Girls 207, 297, 840, 851, 977, 982, 1453, 1585, 1784, 1923, 2014, 2054, 2077, 2078, 2100, 2111, 2355, 2500, 2534, 2565, 2877, 3299, 3301, 3357, 3538, 3554, 3580, 3592, 3632, 3824, 3931, 4109, 4233, 4301, 4461, 4476, 4625, 4672, 4718, 4811, 4880, 5145, 5382, 5616, 5655, 5788, 6198, 6291, 6295, 6394, 6395, 6525, 6605, 6727, 6757, 7068, 7070, 7127, 7479, 7481, 7482, 7592, 7717, 7745, 7748, 8180, 8212, 8555, 8747, 8843, 9286, 9323, 9357, 9730, 9930, 10109, 10239, 10389, 10391, 10430, 10547, 10831, 10964

"girls" 292, 3209

"girls, all three" 3620

"Girls, Big" 10973

"girls, Catholic" 4202

"girls, convent" 6241

"girls, family of three" 3632

"girls, five" 9730

"girls, four" 4187

"girls, hefty pitch-dark" 4743

"girls, I don't play with" 4185

"girls, lethal taste for" 5779

"girls, little" 3094, 4182, 8747

"girls, my dear good" 6528

"girls, naked fourteen-year-old" 6394

"girls, pair of" 4135

"girls, pretty waiter" 7487

"girls, she was one of those" 10788

"girls, sixty thousand four hundred and eleven" 3538

"girls, those two" 3357

"girls, three" 3580

"girls, twenty thousand" 4205

"girls, two" 4724, 8212

"girls, two of the prettiest" 5080

"girls, two young" 4136, 9527

"girls, young giggling" 4154

"girls always like to go swimming at night" 9323

"girl's apartment" 7725

"girls are chattering noisily" 4154

"girls are exploring the attic" 4154

"girls are in the attic" 4154

"girls curled against each other" 10824

"girls from Marcia Blaine School" 977

"girl's hand off, cutting the" 7045

"girls idly chattered" 7410

"girls in Australia" 10848

"girls in our family" 4880

"girls kept diaries" 2534

"girls leap to their feet" 4205

"girls of that age" 3931

"girls registered in his fan clubs" 3538

"girls were fat and sassy" 5382

"girls who have become much more common of late years" 10788

Gisela 9613

Gissing 3088

"Giudecca, the" 3709

Giulia 4880

Giulia, Nonna 4880

"Giuseppe's" 7571

Giustina 244

"give in, if you slow down and" 6381

"'Give Me the Sweet Delights of Love'" 8746

"give up" 129

"give up coffee" 6638

"give up, I" 10744

"given me a gold watch, they would have" 4134

"given of his plenty" 3850

"giving a dinner" 8629

"giving their hearts away too quickly" 5542

"Giza" 1694

"Gizeh" 5971

"glacial, air was" 178

"glad, damned" 4516

"glad, he was" 7847

"glad, was" 3773

"glad enough" 1713

"glad it was over and done with for this lifetime" 2429

"glad of the bowl of hot wine" 10196

"glad the heart" 2134

"glad the place had not yet been rebuilt" 9231

"glad to be alive" 5260

"glad to be there, rather" 7892

"glad you came, I am" 9865

"glade, beautiful" 10784

"glade, narrow" 9666

"glades grew wider, the turfy" 6564

"gladly have given up taking pupils" 99

Gladstone 6993

"Gladstone bag" 9878

Gladys 2936

"glance, a passing" 5906

"glance, at a" 7215

"glance, at first" 6868

"glance, Eagle's proud" 724

"glance, her" 10778

"glance, there was a" 5874

"glance at his watch" 6630

"glance at me, dart a" 10010

"glance at the river, one final" 10394

"glance at the Vicar" 6308

"glance at this page" 593

"glance behind him along the road" 8891

"glance searching out first a store window" 10392

"glance up at the kitchen pinboard" 6864

"glance was cold friendly and shrewd" 5912

"glanced again toward the sunny rectangle" 1556

"glanced around" 7767

"glanced at the house" 3178

"glanced down" 7018

"glanced with some surprise" 8192

Glances 3499, 10045, 10778

"glances, inquisitive" 3499

"glances, they exchanged fretful" 10045

"glances of black-gowned under-graduates" 10441

"glances of pretty barmaids, smil-ing" 9113

"glances that rested on her taut figure" 3499

"glancing at the sandwiches two miles away" 7574

"glancing from car-windows" 5129

"glancing towards the canal" 8252

"glare and rubber gloves that now surrounded her" 7097

"glare as intense and powerful as the shrilling of the locusts" 5074

"glare of lightning flashes, brief unearthly" 9076
"glare of mercury vapor lights, the steely" 8323
"glare of the August sun" 8079
"glare of the lamp, shaded the" 122
"glared at each other" 381
"glared at her daughter" 6619
"glared at the Doberman" 10750
Glasgow, Barney 3826
"Glasgow" 1496, 6249
"Glasgow Herald" 7142
"Glasgow Lass, The" 8132
"Glasgow street" 10515
"Glasnost" 7004
"glass, bulletproof" 8728
"glass, diamond-paned" 2686
"glass, focussed his" 8106
"glass, grimed" 2703
"glass, his lonely" 10219
"glass, hold up a" 5632
"glass, holding up his" 2916
"glass, jumble of broken" 5077
"glass, lifted a cut crystal" 2927
"glass, like cedar blue" 8446
"glass, nineteenth century" 9411
"glass, one-way" 9912
"glass, opaque bevelled" 5320
"glass, pier" 4921
"glass, silence was like" 10503
"glass, the breaking" 891
"glass, the shattered" 1217
"glass, two little discs of" 2857
"glass dirty with rain-spattered dust" 3246
"glass had cooled, once the" 483
"glass of water" 7561
"glass of water, raised her" 6809
"glass over the mantel" 9325
"glass panes, old bubbly" 2692
"glass unscratched and unmarred since the world began" 5069
"glass wavy as broken water, old" 5327
"glass-domed" 7754
"glasses broken by Mrs. Weigholtz" 6652
"glasses, dark" 2739
"glasses, field" 5716, 8270
"glasses, odd-sized jelly" 3847
"glasses, where are my" 8253
Glaucus 3812
"glazed, gilded and" 4309
"glazed with the circle and diamond leading" 8342
Glazer, Ali 6864
"gleam of newly minted money" 7229
"gleamed dully, countryside" 5172
"gleamed so white" 6072
"gleamed through the blue tinge of air" 5125
"Glebeshire" 3533
"Glebeshire, South" 2299
"glen, a little" 8277

"glen, cool-sounding thing like a" 8277
"Glen, Fairy" 9745
"Glen Cairn, village of" 9741
"Glen seemed to be under water, the" 7328
"Glenalbert, little village of" 6555
"Glendale, I drove out to" 1023
"Glendale California" 10923
"Glenkill Pennsylvania" 5854
Glennard 696
"glens, black Welsh" 10574
"glen's edge, at the" 8277
Glickman, Avrom 85
Glicksman, Sophie 6452
"glide up and glide her up and down" 2107
"glided, girl" 4195
"glided off Key Biscayne" 9811
"glider, got up from the" 8216
"gliding about, solemnly" 7709
"gliding along" 3046
"gliding along London's broadest street, she came" 8073
"glimmer of daylight lingered in the sky" 2199
"glimmer of the fading day, the last" 7347
"glimmering over a waste of water" 1416
"glimpse, caught my first" 4580
"glimpse of blue, bare" 4908
"glimpse of the strange land, catch an early" 2188
"glimpse of Yale University, his first" 9531
"glimpse through a ragged pattern of trees" 9076
"glimpse which I got of it" 9524
"glimpses of grey towers through the trees" 7390
"glimpses of open country beyond" 6564
"glinted on the gold head of the cane" 10373
"glistened, broad avenue" 7288
"glistened in the autumn dew" 5161
"glistening bronze surface" 6958
"glistening like opal" 9817
"glittered brightly in the sunlight" 5074
"glittered in the road's blacktop" 2977
"glittered on the bathroom tiles" 5333
"glittering, sun" 5317
"glittering array of pictures" 4315
"glittering desolation of snow" 10570
"glittering in the bouncing headlights" 3011
"glittering in the headlights' beam" 3016
"glittering like scalpels" 5325
"glittering on either hand" 5614
"glittering stores" 7229

"globe, circle the" 6341
"globe, surface of the" 4533
"globe, terrestrial" 3977
"globe, the" 531, 9508
"globe, this whirling" 6804
"globe, waters of the" 8075
Glogauer, Karl 2740
"glomhefter, starboard" 7262
"gloom, deep Victorian" 7757
"gloom, regarding the" 7295
"gloom, soft" 8353
"gloom of her chamber, the increasing" 9402
"gloom of the millpond" 402
"gloom that the cat had left, she reintegrated the" 6367
"gloomy pine, forests of" 5125
"gloomy warehouses" 1368
Gloria 1942
"Gloria, a" 1499
"glories of nature" 3396
"glorification, some measure of" 4728
"glorification, under the pretense of" 5845
"glorious, sky over London was" 10494
"glorious dreamless hours" 8455
"Glorious Fourth" 4515
"glorious in conquests" 425
"glorious reign" 3376
"gloriously, cleared the sky" 8586
"gloriously bored" 933
"glory, dazzling heights of" 3557
"glory, flowers are in their first" 8514
"glory had not departed from the old coach-roads" 9113
"glory of his style, multi-colored" 962
"glory still afloat" 660
"glory to all, a fireside" 3177
"glossy architecture" 7481
"Gloucester" 1486
"Gloucester, county of" 4439
"Gloucestershire" 3548
"Gloucestershire countryside" 3808
Glourie, Lord 736
"glove, she wore a" 8009
"gloves, draw on her" 10037
"gloves, picking at the fingers of her" 1589
"gloves, took off his" 2974
"glow, ceased to" 9995
"glow, deep red" 6059
"glow, feeble" 7032
"glow, orange" 5339
"glow, red pulsing" 1212
"glow, serene fireside" 10494
"glow for an instant" 10077
"glow in the east, faint" 2214
"glow in the sky" 8396
"glow on spun silk, like reflected" 4294
"glow to the west, the dying" 8114

"glowing from a dark forest depth of pines" 3076

"glowing in gorgeous reds and yellows" 1496

"glowing yellow" 5326

Glowry, Christopher 3058

"glowworm, like some super-" 7266

"glue, encased in a thin layer of peach" 1867

"glue, taste of" 10831

"glum, felt unusually" 2508

"Glyn Cagny" 10756

"gnarled bole" 5716

"gnarled trunk" 9674

"gnarly tap roots" 10106

"gnashing his teeth" 962

"gnats, whole swarm of" 4961

"gnats that can pierce a man's boot" 5272

"go, don't know if I want to" 3309

"go, getting ready to" 3716, 6705

"go, here we" 7225

"go, let's" 6587

"go, nowhere to" 932

"go, on the" 9567

"go, so I will" 1664

"go, *there* we" 9267

"go, time to" 1650

"go, watching her" 1602

"go, where is there to" 1737

"Go and he goeth" 10649

"go around the country by train" 9932

"go away" 10311

"go back, do you never want to" 4540

"go back, something bigger it should be when you" 4582

"go back, you can never" 1781

"go back, you would never" 7445

"go back seventeen years" 7401

"go down the following day" 9724

"go down to Tralorna, suggested that I should" 9723

"go for good and all" 1682

"go nowhere, now I" 1729

"go on for hours yet" 1113

"go over to Noorna's house" 7213

"go past down the dirt road" 2095

"go to my father" 1806

"go up to Oxford" 1410

"go with, he had no one to" 932

"go with Garth to the city, I will" 6981

"goaded the horses on to greater effort" 3009

"goalposts, run through those" 8931

"goat, like a performing nanny" 1882

"goat, wild" 8809

"goat shit" 7871

"goatherder, poor Gallic" 6551

"goat-herd's hut" 650

"goats foraged" 5704

"goats gambolled" 5130

"*Gobble Gobbles* commenced" 882

"Gobi Desert" 5528

God 1763, 2783, 4146, 9066

God 36, 69, 285, 1496, 1516, 1518, 1763, 1805, 1994, 2619, 2622, 2625, 2626, 2629, 2630, 2633, 2637, 2640, 2641, 2643, 2645, 2646, 2783, 3900, 4146, 4236, 5178, 5677, 5697, 5699, 6113, 6798, 7447, 7506, 7511, 7512, 7519, 7521, 7530, 7533, 7534, 7536, 7542, 7798, 7807, 8200, 8501, 8620, 9066, 9411, 9695, 9939, 10838, 10879

"God" 52, 3174, 6798, 7530, 8310

"God, a dream about" 2783

"God, Almighty" 1496, 7801

"God, America and" 285

"God, believe in" 5677

"God, by" 7635, 9271

"God, by the grace of" 3970

"God, call from" 1518

"God, Dear" 8184, 8200

"God, death and the decrees of" 10474

"God, do you believe in" 1516

"God, existence and nature of" 9411

"God, existence of" 3465

"God, Eye of" 1396

"god, gestures of a" 6792

"God, girl who thought she was" 10879

"God, glory be to" 10471

"God, good" 5933, 9300

"God, he felt like" 1994

"God, hear the Word of" 7534

"God, Holy" 7160

"God, I believe in" 7542

"God, I do not believe in" 4789

"God, I suppose there was a" 7533

"God, I swear to" 6189

"God, image of" 5699

"god, Julius who became a" 4469

"God, Mary the Mother of" 10587

"God, most high" 10476

"God, my" 6529

"God, O" 2296

"God, oh" 8027, 9904

"God, oh thank" 4344

"God, praise be to" 7521

"God, prayed" 75

"God, shadow of" 7807

"God, she ran into" 2640

"God, so help me" 9695

"God, soldier of" 7604

"God, Son of" 2644

"God, strike against" 10838

"God, swear to" 681

"God, tell nobody but" 1805

"God, thank" 6497, 10743

"God, thanked" 4341

"God, Triune" 2626

"God, Truce of" 6361

"God, trust in" 7447

"God, where did they get the nerve to defy" 10838

"God, which we call" 785

"God, wonderful ways of" 7798

"God Almighty" 7311

"God bless and preserve with abiding and continuing peace and blessings" 7521

"god both male and female" 2635

"God bring you increase" 7807

"God called again" 2646

"God creating the cosmos, I have seen" 2630

"God cursed it, before" 2637

"God decided to stick me by allowing me to become a teen-ager" 4236

"God 'did'" 2622

"God did not exist, if" 2629

"God didn't like it" 7511

"God don't give you more than you can bear" 69

"God ever made, naughtiest child that" 4146

"God had ordained it, as if" 9939

"God have mercy" 5292

"God help me" 2737, 9265

"God help the poor people at sea" 10677

"God Himself" 2633

"God knows" 8172

"God knows what" 745, 10320

"god Krishna, the enchanting" 4741

"God love Him" 2625

"God made him to prosper" 7536

"God made it" 3900

"God made man" 5697

"God might see to be craft or virtue" 9696

"god of the great Osages" 789

"God only knows why" 2383

"God puts His finger" 2641

"God rest his soul" 7002

"God save us all" 8672

"God sent snow forth" 8620

"God Shave The Queen" 8756

"God sparing my life and memory" 8957

"god Tano, the great" 2627

"God the Father" 7512

"God the Merciful [and] the Compassionate" 7521

"God to sustain me, only the help of" 6113

"God was grumbling" 9066

"God who has reserved this singular Grace for Man" 5699

"goddamn" 4828

"goddamn antelope, run like a" 7851

"goddamned beautifully, so" 6931

"goddamned long, night is so" 6381

"God-damned Tumulty project" 2479

"goddess, a matter of a" 2624

"Goddess Fortune" 1220
"goddess of love" 7527
Goddesses 2624, 7527
"godfather, honoured" 2545
Godfrey, Mr. 2515
"Godfrey Daniel" 6652
"God-knows-what through April" 3810
"godlike" 10260
"godmother, my" 3061
Gods 104, 789, 2620, 2621, 2627, 2628, 2632, 2635, 2636, 2637, 2638, 2642, 2644, 4133, 4459, 4741, 5576, 5704, 10879
"gods, anger of" 104
"gods, domestic" 2018
"Gods, Elder" 2236
"gods, false" 4459
"gods, folly of their" 5704
"gods, openhanded childlike" 4133
"Gods, War" 2621
"gods, wonderful gesture of the" 5576
"God's earth" 2311
"God's feelings, you hurt" 7511
"God's heart is not easily swayed" 2645
"God's Name, in" 4810
"gods of rebellious Babylon, humbled the" 2636
"God's sake, for" 6393
"God's stars, under" 10824
"God's Vicegerents" 10033
"God's will" 36
Godwin, Earl 3571
Goebbels, Dr. 4447
Goering, Christina 6628
Goering, Hermann 5040
"goes, it" 5687
"goes, so here" 8983
"goes around, what" 7837
"goes away, each thing that" 1666
"goes into her study" 8313
"goes on here" 10488
Goessler, Eugene 2422
Goethe 9987
Goff, Joshua Loftus Colby 8311
Goff, Lieutenant Dabney Augustus Rollo 7361
"Gog and Magog of its civic life" 9248
Gogarty, Mr. 7726
"go-getter she was, what a" 261
"goggles, staring due-north through" 2973
"Goiânia" 5576
"goin', an' I'm er" 2296
Going 1078, 1566, 1578, 1602, 1607, 1623, 1627, 1628, 1646, 1664, 1695, 1737, 1746, 1747, 1753, 1754, 1771, 1782, 1783, 1785, 2484, 2654, 2657, 2668, 3426, 4117, 6587
"going, he was dead set against me" 1747

"going, I have come where I was" 1729
"going, said he wasn't" 6579
"going, where was he" 3003
"going, who might be" 6754
"going any further in the fog, abandoned the idea of" 9768
"going back was a mistake" 6029
"going down on flushed cheek" 8423
"going for a midnight boat ride" 6578
"going from the Valley, I am" 1607
"going home" 7847
"going home, with a wonderful sense of" 9175
"going into it, I don't feel like" 9706
"going none too well, things were" 49
"going northeast out of the city" 9143
"going off to live with another woman" 5914
"going off to the Wallingford races" 9919
"going off work, just before" 10958
"going on, something funny was" 3447
"going on here, what's" 1048
"going on leave tomorrow" 1646
"going out, a man" 5575
"going out of the harbour" 732
"going out tonight, I don't think we'll be" 4564
"going out with his younger brother" 5852
"going over the house" 950
"going to a learned conference" 7461
"going to stay with the three Miss Miners" 9863
"going to the county jail" 1579
"going to the girl's apartment, could not get used to" 7725
"going to the top of Lone Tree Hill" 786
"going to the window, occasionally" 10972
"going to work" 5522
"going with you, I'm" 6573
"going without his greens" 7990
Gold 5486
Gold 283, 2601
"gold, a full half century's frenetic burrowing for" 1420
"gold, bag of" 4560
"gold, bordered with" 8392
"gold, Demosthenes'" 10871
"gold, molten" 983
"gold, paved with" 283
"gold, persist in a feverish panning for" 6486
"gold, pure" 10774
"gold, rush to the Klondike for" 3394
"gold, taka the" 2014

"gold, twisted sticks of" 5305
"gold, we made our first" 5103
"gold and red, flaming" 2150
"gold at last, struck" 2601
"Gold Coast of Africa" 1069
"gold dust everywhere" 283
"gold filigree" 4677
"gold head of the cane" 10373
"gold light" 2225
"gold rush, Californian" 6104
"gold speckled" 3265
"gold teeth" 10054
"gold watch" 9497
"gold without alloy or allay" 10774
"gold wrought silk" 1198
Golda, Great Aunt 7731
"golden, it is" 7664
"golden arches" 3001
"golden girls of Westchester" 4577
"golden green" 5131
"golden in the evening light, they are turned" 2080
"Golden Age" 3379, 3385, 8991
"Golden Gate Bridge" 9611
"'Golden Star', the" 4630
"Golden Triangle" 4094
"Golden Wonder Holidays girl" 3299
"Golders Green" 4070
Goldie 7743
Goldkorn, L. 6236
Goldman 5502
Goldman, Emma 10837
Goldman, Spike 5636
Goldsmid, Benjamin 7505
"golems, the" 2799
Golf 3378, 5487, 6273, 6449, 6462, 7159, 8909, 8927, 8930
"golf, afternoon of" 5487
"golf, play" 8909
"golf, while he was playing" 7159
"golf carts" 5627
"golf clubs" 4655
"Golf Course, Medallion City" 6273
"golf was a novel form of recreation" 3378
"golf was only a green shade" 8930
Goliath 9872
Gollancz, Ray 3630
Gombold 9585
Gómez, Amalia 10320
"gondola" 9626
"gondoliers of Venice" 8754
"gone, after he had" 8802
"gone, after Pa was" 6660
"gone, every other person in Veracruz was" 8733
"gone, four months" 7062
"gone, he is" 2439
"gone, it was" 2055
"gone, she would be" 1754
"gone, we should a" 657
"gone, when she was" 8551
"gone by then, I was" 3408
"gone from their huts" 7508

"gone from us for good, she was" 3604

"gone next door" 10937

"gone now, they are all" 6815

"gone through, what I had just" 8565

"gone to heaven" 8172

"'good', 'bad' and" 6635

"good, being" 639

"good, felt" 3312

"good, he's really" 8

"GOOD, I love" 5362

"good, it could be for" 2683

"good, it never did any" 10163

"good, ought to be doing a great deal of" 1484

"good about it, she also felt" 112

"good and bad" 1342

"good and bad, in all times" 3094

"good and evil" 2633

"good and sure, to make" 3739

"*good* are they, what" 4700

"good at that, he was" 10072

"'good days', I was having one of my" 6632

"good day's work, what he called a" 3326

"*good* do they do you, what" 4700

"good enough, not because life was not" 2071

"good lines and no action" 9379

"good looking" 5921

"good luck" 7067

"good man in a bad world, every man is a" 5698

"good men, all" 6989

"good morning" 4213

"good night, say" 996

"good one, this is a" 7767

"good or bad" 638

"good or ill" 7372

"good taste, with" 139

"good that is and cheap" 7571

"Good Thing, the" 253

"good things of life, all the" 796

"Good Time" 5540

"Good Time Gospel Boys" 8010

"good-by, to say" 1929

"goodbye, bade" 8665

"goodbye, saying" 1604

"goodbye, waving" 6722

Goodbyes 1604, 1621, 1844, 6702, 8665

"good-bye to his wife" 2009

"good-for-nothings" 8886

Goodliffe, Jonathan 8090

"good-looking, you're so" 9568

Goodman, Mrs. 2318

"good-nature, negative" 6605

"good-natured, perfectly" 5900

"goodness, a being of infinite" 2642

Goodnight 7662

Goodnight, Dr. 4739

Goodnough, Edith 161

"Goodwill oak table" 5292

Goodwin, General Melville A. 9262

"gool, Kingdom" 3614

"goopy, woebegone and" 2906

"goose, a" 7514

"goose, barnacle" 737

"Goose and Gherkin" 1101

"goose seemingly hanging in front of a cloud is flying" 761

"goose up in the sky, when you see a" 761

"goose-stepped with eerie convulsions" 6367

"gopher hole, the new" 968

Gordon 1769, 3515, 4267

Gordon, Chinese 8819

Gordon, Lee 4345

Gordon, Lord George 7505

Gordon, Violet Dene 4569

Gordons of Bramley 5067

"gore, shaken by the" 6444

"gorge, at the upper end of a wild" 4040

"gorge themselves on the flesh of her heart" 2799

"gorgeous" 1391

"gorgeous gem-encrusted receptacle" 110

"gorgeous Wednesday in August" 2152

"gorges, glacier-gnawed" 4577

"gorges of the San Benito Hills" 2199

"gorges . . . were filled with a purplish haze" 2199

"Gorky" 8004

Gorlois the duke 5662

"Gormenghast" 972, 9223

"gorse, high clumps of" 9153

"gorse of the distant hills" 5071

"Goshen" 1465, 2505

"gospel, minister of the" 1533

Goss 500

Gosselyn, Michael 1605

Gossip 4014, 7833

"gossip" 4277

"gossip, begetters of" 7833

"gossip, casual disguises of philosophical" 2383

"gossip, latest" 4014

"gossip in the book-reviewing departments of newspapers" 8470

"gossip . . . is most untamed and swarming" 8470

"gossip of Louis Napoleon" 9119

"gossiping" 7410

"got back into bed" 9988

"got back last fall from Brooklyn" 5017

"got down to it" 3839

"got into the utility" 2961

"got it, I've" 7871

"got off the plane in Albany" 10080

"got out, I" 1734

"got out of a cab" 1625

"got out of the limousine" 4564

"got out of the train" 8507

"got together, when they" 3608

"got up, even before he" 1785

"got up, when I" 10201

"got up at a quarter to four" 1208

"got up from the garage floor" 8456

"got up from the glider" 8216

"got up on a bright May morning" 10168

"gothic harp" 10416

"Gothic fantasy" 7149

"Gothic structure" 1171

"Gothic style, perpendicular" 9255

"Goths, appellation of" 6052

Gottenberg, Abraham 7416

Gouache, Anastase 486

Gouraud 5812

"gout, particularly violent attack of" 306

"gout and mortgaged estates were traced" 358

"govern India, men who" 6978

"govern themselves, Jamaica-men will begin to " 6981

"governed man, that which secretly" 3673

"governed the whole Kingdom, in a manner" 5883

"governess, clever loving" 631

"governess, her" 4153

Government 247, 269, 368, 398, 1064, 1165, 1442, 3278, 4466, 4982, 5115, 5883, 6342, 6494, 6502, 6972, 6973, 6974, 6977, 6978, 6981, 6982, 6983, 6985, 6986, 6988, 6990, 6992, 6998, 6999, 7003, 7006, 7799, 7814, 7817, 7820, 7831, 8859, 8866, 10473

"government" 7003

"government, Britain's new Conservative" 6999

"government, fallen Vichy" 4017

"government, republican" 6972

"government, sovereign power of" 1165

"government, squalid little" 1442

"Government, wish on the part of" 6972

"government in power" 6983

"government . . . is herewith suspended" 6982

"government of Oklahoma" 398

"government of the United States of America" 6982

"Government still pays my wages" 6494

"government wharf" 2270

"Governor" 6997

"Governor, arrival at Quebec as" 7655

"governor, speech by the" 9729

"governor, the" 5638

"governor, young" 1912

"governor of Louisiana, a former"

8760
"Governor of Texas" 6509
"Governor of the Province" 1042
"Governor tore off his wig" 373
"Governor-General in India" 1930
"Governor-General of India" 1
"Governors, Board of" 9701
"governor's house" 7195
"Governor's Palace" 1387
"Governor's residence" 3210
Gowan, Cousin 7394
Gowdey, Serenus 5017
Gower, Mrs. 10865
"gown, a" 122
"gown, crimson" 3759
"gown, dark wool of my" 5096
"gown, fit your" 4191
"gown, her new green watered-silk"
   4921
"gown, her notably low-necked" 8556
"gown, her taffeta" 376
"gown, his hospital" 4628
"gown, long white" 10735
"gown, shell-pink organdie" 2826
"gown drooping down in his arms"
   10335
"gowns, a thousand" 3283
"gowns, one of her chiffon" 2863
"grab air and jump" 602
Grabowska, Kakia 9578
"grace, honeless and presumably
   aristocratic" 8234
"grace, with any" 2586
"grace and vividness, express ideas
   with the utmost" 5420
"grace in hall, listening to" 7522
"grace of God" 3970
"grace of strength" 3640
"grace was that of a Degas" 8027
Grace 2481, 6160
"Grace, this singular" 5699
"Grace, Your" 9047
Grace-and-Glory 9020
"graceful and gray" 903
"graceful beech" 3894
"gracefully but grumpily" 1629
Gracie 1783, 5752
Grack the Frenchie 8861
"graduate, early eighteenth-
   century" 4307
"graduate school, after two years
   of" 5546
"graduated from a small Eastern
   college" 4575
"graduated from Barnard" 5781
"graduated from the College of
   Euphoria Illinois" 5413
"graduates, guild of" 1513
"graduates ran with cries toward
   asterisks of waiting parents" 5096
"graduating from Smith in 1971"
   3261
Graduation 1204, 3261, 3283,
   4575, 5096, 6521
"graduation, their implausible" 4876

"graduation photo" 6587
Graffiti 4982
"graffiti, scrawled" 9253
"graft is taken from an aged tree"
   9660
"graftings, fresh" 4435
Graham 6131
"Graham Land" 8113
"grain, long misty quivering level
   of the" 9116
Grainger, Miss Winifred 2348
Gram Mon 10019
Grammy 4488
"gramophone record" 6227
Grams 3293
"Granada" 7809
"Granchester" 6427
"Granchesterian" 6427
Grand, Guy 9567
"grand, the Hamptons were very"
   10556
"Grand Babylon, the" 4305
"Grand Central Station" 8173
"Grand Rapids Michigan" 3423
"grand these days, my friend and I
   are very" 8635
"grandad, my" 6902
"Grandaunts" 4173
"grandbaby, her" 5992
Grandchildren 5992, 10664
"grandchildren" 3207
"grandchildren, his elder" 4744
"grandchildren, my dear" 3490
"grandchildren, our" 8892
"granddaughter, Corrado Prizzi's"
   10664
"grandeur" 9389
"grandeur, legal" 9252
Grandfather 4744, 4932
"grandfather, her" 651, 3022, 9597
"grandfather, his" 3567, 3730,
   4436, 10188
"grandfather, his maternal" 790
"grandfather, my" 361, 1905, 2570,
   3089, 3940, 5193, 6879
"grandfather, my maternal" 4113
"grandfather, the" 8739
"Grandfather did not like to be
   called 'Grandfather'" 4744
"grandfather had shot nothing, his"
   4685
"grandfather of innumerable unborn
   Sternholzes" 6472
"Grandfather told me" 4932
"grandfather was a child, when
   your" 8992
Grandfathers 367, 543, 790, 1076,
   1905, 2570, 3550, 3567, 4113,
   4685, 4744, 4932, 5193, 5931,
   6879, 6902, 7498, 8992, 9726
"grandfather's house, my" 9726
Grandi, Cornelio 8963
"grandiose word" 10911
Grandma 4148, 4154, 9985
"grandma" 3951

Grandmother 2129
"grandmother, Carlotta's" 6484
"grandmother, her" 1199, 1870,
   4822, 8356, 8371
"grandmother, his" 4892, 6130,
   7217, 8530, 10162
"grandmother, house of my" 7063
"grandmother, my" 369, 370, 371,
   1875, 2452, 2570, 3223, 5762,
   6492, 9710, 10874, 10962
"grandmother, my sick old" 8721
"grandmother, Nancy Meade's"
   9973
"grandmother, old" 10853
"grandmother, our" 4880
"Grandmother, the" 8788
"grandmother, Vincent's" 4980
"grandmother in the attic, found
   his" 6859
"grandmother says" 3025
Grandmothers 338, 369, 370, 371,
   1199, 1870, 1875, 2129, 2452,
   2570, 3223, 3951, 4488, 4880,
   4892, 4980, 5762, 6130, 6492,
   6859, 7217, 8530, 8721, 8788,
   9973, 10162, 10658, 10853, 10874,
   10962
"grandmothers, old gimped" 253
"Grandmother's eyes, color resembles" 338
Grandpa 1151, 8780
Grandparents 6297, 9949
"grandparents, Guy Crouchback's"
   9559
"grandparents, her" 6577, 9984
"grandparents, his" 7775
"grandparents, my" 3430
"grandson" 367
"Grandson" 355
"Grandson, great" 355
"grandson, his" 8739
"grandson, his visiting" 985
"grand-uncle, my late" 4929
"Grange, Riversley" 10113
"Grange, Thrushcross" 3000
"Grange, Trottlebury" 4444
Granger, Prentiss 6335
"granite, like polished" 8121
"granite, mass of" 6055
"granite, slabs of" 10404
"granite blocks" 9130
"granite canyons" 9197
"granite stone" 9253
"grannie was killed by the English"
   10658
"Granny Smith apples" 921
"granny woman, old Gullah" 118
"granpa, my" 1085
Granpap 543
Grant, Aubrey George 1108
Grant, Dr. Elizabeth 7787
Grant, Minna 5592
Grant, Simon 334
"grant, Spanish" 3089
"Grant Land" 205

"granted, took for" 1285
Granville, Edward 710
Grape, John 2113
"grapes, purpling" 1849
"grapes of a very special flavor"
    1059
"grappled in stoneland" 8115
"grasp, a better" 2249
"grasping with little spasms" 5603
Grass 3772, 5145
"grass, clumps of springy" 9841
"grass, grama" 4380
"grass, in the waving marram"
    10098
"grass, knee-deep billowing" 3095
"grass, moist" 9672
"grass, patch of" 8038
"grass, pebbly" 5145
"grass, rain-freshened" 4034
"grass, resurrected" 7723
"grass, rolling carpet of" 7646
"grass, rough edge of unslashed"
    5180
"grass, scintillant" 10002
"grass, smell of wet" 7308
"grass, spongy" 7677
"grass, vast sea of burgeoning" 7252
"grass, witherin school-yard" 8780
"grass and frilled weeds and clover
    and dandelions" 9179
"grass as smooth as velvet" 10784
"grass continued to burn" 3772
"grass frolicking along the golden
    sand" 4587
"grass hissed and parted" 10499
"grass smelled sweet and strong"
    8513
"grass still holding the sun's
    warmth" 449
"grass that has sprung up around
    the city of Troy" 2603
"grass turns green, when the" 8933
"grass was infinitely green" 3092
Grass Woman 10140
"Grasse" 10399
"grasshoppers, several plagues of"
    3105
"grasshoppers were bad that sum-
    mer" 4960
"grate, the little open" 7756
"grate of coals, genial aid of that"
    7756
"grateful, very" 4124
"grateful for daylight again" 8178
"grateful to live where I live" 6206
"gratified, it should be" 6404
"gratifying" 6251
"grating cicadas" 10701
Gratitude 1217, 1962, 2922, 3274,
    3869, 4124, 4341, 5457, 5998,
    6234, 7521, 8178, 9865, 10255
"gratitude" 9928
"gratitude, intense and helpless"
    10255
"gratitude, respect and" 5998

"gratuitous and contemptible
    migrations" 6141
"Graustark, principality of" 4044
"grave, at the head of the" 2329
"grave, digging his" 2329
"grave, father's newly dug" 3952
"grave, goes with a man to his"
    7584
"grave, ground was waiting to
    become another" 2395
"grave, quiet as a" 3215
"grave, someone walked over my"
    10385
"grave, stood by the" 1185
"grave, sunk into its" 3376
"grave and solid deliberation" 2466
"grave filled in" 3944
"grave misgivings" 10844
"grave on the verge of which I
    hover" 2287
"grave that had been dug at dawn"
    1188
"grave that was lost forever" 2383
"grave which was shortly to receive
    his wife's mortal remains" 3941
"gravel crackled" 2571
"gravel in it" 10027
"gravel of the drive" 7318
Gravely, Harold 8931
Graves 1578
Graves, Mrs. 1578
Graves 807, 1185, 1186, 1188, 1189,
    1194, 2287, 2329, 2395, 2436,
    3941, 3944, 3952, 3984, 4494,
    6646, 10385
"graves, among the other Rickle-
    house" 10564
"graves along the hill" 1194
"graves in a row, three new" 1189
"Gravesend, a mile from" 484
"gravesite, clustered at the" 3959
"graveyard" 2384
"grave-yard, narrow" 1183
"graveyard, old" 6963
"graveyard of St. James's Church"
    1184
"gravity of our situation" 78
Gray, Charles 9424
Gray, Gideon 6884
Gray, Grandfather 717
Gray, Mrs. 717
"gray, slate" 6087
"gray, tomb-" 9228
"gray on gray" 9218
Graye, Cytherea 3488
"graying out of sight" 8591
"Grayling Montana" 1468
"grayness, splotchy sliding-down"
    7316
"grays and blacks, twilight" 962
"graze, as cows" 10623
"grazed in the summer pastures"
    3667
"grazed over the False Divide" 415
"greasewood" 9127

"greasing the alleys" 7339
Great Britain 4028
"Great Britain" 1174, 5905, 10181
"Great Britain, independence from"
    2681
"Great Britain, island of" 4028
"Great Britain, King of" 6803
"Great Britain, Parliament of" 7814
"Great Depression" 815
"Great Depression, during the"
    6477
"great event, the next" 9951
"Great House" 3063
"Great Lakes" 9072
"great man, he can't have been a"
    3517
"great man, meet the" 5837
"Great Man, The" 3962
"great men themselves must play"
    299
"great musician" 6227
"'Great Orley Farm Case, The'"
    8955
"great shall be small, many that
    are" 4454
"Great War" 8678
"great you are, doesn't matter how"
    3342
"Great-Aunt Amalie, her" 3659
"greatcoat" 7440
"greatcoat, army" 2841
"greatest hero" 3376
"greatest natural talent" 5
"greatest president" 6990
Great-granddaddy 4437
"great-grandfather, my" 1076
"great-grandson, her" 2456
"great-grandson, his" 4307, 5659
"great-grandson of the holy Baal
    Shem Tov" 2278
"great-great-grandfather, my" 1518
Greatness 299, 7886, 7976
"greatness, children playing at" 299
"greatness, not yet forged into the
    mould of" 8872
"greatness, tributes to his" 6308
"greatness of Carne School" 7886
"greats, one of the all-time" 8943
"great-uncle, my" 8999
"Greece, country we call" 1471
"Greece is where I am" 9639
Greed 2522, 2525, 2527, 2530,
    3308
"greed" 3308
"*Greed*, last season's bestseller was"
    2525
"greedily, harvested them" 9674
Greek, the 7578
"Greek, forty lines of" 10953
"Greek detectives" 4984
"Greek family" 3500
"Greek Islands" 5847
"Greek police" 6955
"Greek Revival" 3225
"Greek steamer" 8123

"Greeks, before the coming of the" 9738
"Greeks, famous wooden horse of the" 2603
"Greeks, the" 10476
"Greeks on the beautiful island of Cyprus" 7527
Green, Dave 5907
Green, Valerie 10987
"green, a sickish" 143
"green, dark viridian" 9681
"green, everything is" 9590
"green, golden" 5131
"Green, Golders" 4070
"green, palest shade of" 2255
"green, should have been brightly" 5141
"green, undone summer's" 10591
"green, village" 4155
"Green, Woodbrook" 3134
"green and white, it is" 3182
"Green Hat, The" 2824
"green in the undergrowth" 10980
"green with young corn" 4034
"Green Ray, I was the" 4867
"Greenbank" 955
"Greenbush" 10871
Greene, Megan 5111
Greenfield, Dora 2652
"greengages, eating the" 3834
"greenhouse, gigantic" 4334
"Greenhouse, skeleton of the empty" 9256
Greenlaw 298
"greenness, tender" 6557
"greens, going without his" 7990
"greens, washing" 10960
"Greenspark Academy, glowing horizontal bulk of" 8625
"Greensward, island mistakenly named" 5035
"greensward, stretch of" 7905
"greensward of the chalk hills, smooth glossy" 9738
Greenway, Mrs. 10829
"Greenwich" 1410
"Greenwich, Duke of" 354
"Greenwich Park" 5928
"Greenwich Village" 4099
Greenwood, Thomas 4255
"Greenwood Towers, handsome new glass-and-poured-concrete" 5238
Greer, Judy 8818
"greet him" 6680
"greet him, his stableman came out to" 7644
"greet me" 7440
"greet our predicament" 3372
"greet the woman who had entered it" 9884
"greet thee heartily, I do" 4218
"greeting, responded to this morning" 4148
Greetings 849, 1124, 1658, 4017,

4599, 4781, 6008, 6680, 6897, 7644, 8108, 8110, 8317, 8705, 9884, 9907, 9933, 9974, 10027, 10100, 10133
"Greetings" 4219
"gregarious animal" 5696
Gregor, Mrs. 9987
"Gregorian chant" 1312
Gregory 5648
Gregory XVII, Pope 1525
"grenade, hand" 889
"grenades, the two" 8689
"grew out of childhood into girl-hood" 4811
"grew to manhood" 81
"grew up" 4234
"grew up, house where he" 3254
"grew up, I" 6848
"grew up, neighborhood where I" 10880
"grew up, town where I" 4598
"grew up, when I" 4208
"grew up in a small town" 4241
"grew up in a war" 10531
"grew up in Beverly Hills" 1240
"grew up in the third and fourth" 4346
"grew up with my younger sister" 9710
Grey, Austin 6772
Grey, Vivian 1265
"grey, dark" 1315, 10774
"grey, love-" 5450
"greyer to-day than they were then" 3087
"grey-haired" 6834
"Greyhound, Cincinnati-Lexington" 5370
"Greyhound, Oakland" 9620
"Greyhound Bus" 9583
Greystock, Lizzie 9261
"Gridiron" 415
Grief 969, 2074, 2082, 2084, 2337, 5740, 6929, 8838
"grief, came to" 2594
"grief, ships that have come to" 9089
"grief, where is that" 4229
"griev'd for the Loss of her" 4221
"grievances, time of deep" 7541
"grieved than I can express, more" 7491
"grieving over it" 6929
Griffin, Hector 10813
Griffin, Inspector 8139
"grifter" 6445
"grifter, small-time" 5989
Grig, Felix 6495
"grill, fine wrought-iron" 3102
"Grill, Mohawk" 2724
"grim and realistic" 5543
"grim aspect, person of" 3554
Grim Fiddle 4818
"grimaced" 4901, 10171
Grimes 6663

"grimly" 101
Grimshawe, Augustus 2326
Grimshawe, Doctor 3554
Grimsley, F. Y. 4358
"grimy, walls were stained and" 7134
"grimy itself, turning" 7307
"grin, understanding" 837
"grinding heavy momentum" 7249
"grinding of the windscreen-wiper" 6323
"grinding to its excruciating end" 7904
"grinds over hers, Cob's body" 7723
"grinned down at her" 2904
"grinned down at the young man at the desk" 8549
"grinning" 8556
"grinning and gesturing to others" 1680
"grinning at him with his capped teeth" 8559
"grinning at me" 7440
"grinning at you" 1235
"grinning face of trouble" 50
"griot, I am" 4877
"grip, clutch it in a strangling" 10582
"gripped in his perspiring hand" 5465
"gripped the curve of the elaborate wrought iron handle" 6587
"gripping it by the top" 5118
"grips, cracked rubber" 9600
Gristy, Sam 8158
Griswold 930
"groan, my father would" 3883
"groan, rose with a" 10150
"groan, with a" 7324
"groan of leather" 8776
"groaned in agony" 6592
"groaned softly" 10208
"groaning from another drinking bout" 2906
"groaning most of all because I'd ruined my 'secret return'" 2906
"groans, bus driver" 7311
"groans sounded in the wind" 10598
Grobstock, Joseph 7505
"groceries, unloaded her" 1031
"grocery shop, worked in a" 6437
"grocery store" 1040, 4073
"grocery-man" 6614
Groff 9936
Gromajinski the Super 6652
Grooming 115, 562, 563, 564, 566, 572, 575, 660, 1503, 2482, 2823, 2879, 3269, 3272, 5798, 6675, 6679, 6782, 7473, 7475, 7490, 8006, 8040, 8041, 8044, 8045, 8046, 8486, 8697, 10668
Grooters 2853
"groping fingers" 10165
"groping for the alarm" 10190
Grosbeck 6896

"grotesque" 6255
"grotesque, less horrible than" 2734
"grotesque gargoyles" 2799
"grotesque grey ball" 1895
"grotesque magnificence" 9254
Grouch 2045
"Groucho, an eye-rolling cigar-puffing" 2045
"ground, breaking new" 8429
"ground, felt unsure of his" 8870
"ground, flat" 5175
"ground, frozen" 7638, 8699
"ground, little spit of high" 6564
"ground, middle" 4634
"ground, pearl" 5146
"ground, short rise of" 7646
"ground, small stretch of vacant" 5140
"ground, soft" 10404
"ground along in low gear" 2947
"ground flattens into a grassy ledge" 3152
"ground is stiff" 7403
"ground remained covered with a dazzling mantle" 7606
"ground rising" 5153
"ground to a halt" 9785
"ground was waiting to become another grave" 2395
"Groundhog Day was his birthday" 4816
"grounds, spacious" 3126
"grounds belonging to the stately home of her grandparents" 6577
"grounds for believing I was an original" 9447
"grounds were surrounded by a high wire fence" 4316
"group, all-women's" 6241
"group, member of a" 1209
"group, that curious heterogeneous" 3094
"group itself looks familiar" 4022
"group of people" 4183
"group of young people, a merry" 9759
"group which was the Colfax family" 3094
"groups, uneasy" 4007
"grove, lemon" 3221
"grove, liveoak" 3147
"grove, mist-seeping river-bottom" 4694
"grove, pine" 7183
Grover 1606
"groves of twice-planted pin oak" 9186
"grow a few chic feet higher this winter, Mount Griff will" 4322
"grow accustomed" 10506
"grow alone, women who cannot" 10772
"grow in death, they" 5521
"grow in the adobe soil, trying against all odds to" 8038

"grow on you, I hope to" 4608
"grow to a man, go and" 4238
"grow up, I did" 4243
"grow up, the few people who" 5693
"grow up, when I" 244, 257
"grow up his father's son" 4242
"grow up with the country" 4534
"growing fatter" 5907
"growing into middle age" 3214
"growing old" 99
Growing Up 257, 3254, 4208, 4346, 4534, 5693, 7523, 7759, 8672
"growing up, a boy" 3614
"growing up, a first" 4237
"growing up, busy with her" 4233
"growing up, the wilful circumstance of" 4235
"growing up, what I remember about" 10752
"growing up, when he was" 7523
"growing up, when I was" 4239
"growing slightly bald" 6427
"growl of the Gulf" 4657
"grown much, Demera had never" 1445
"grown up to knuckly hands, not yet" 979
"grown-up world" 2593
"grown-ups, two sets of" 3592
"grows in the North Country" 958
Growth 1392, 1445, 7818
"growth, dense" 10009
"growth, hideous parasite" 324
"growth, in their" 10772
"growth, instinct for" 7818
"growth, low tangled" 2205
"growth, place of wild" 3906
"growth, watching its" 2630
"growth and warmth, steady gaze gave" 4188
"growth of the city" 9114
"growth of young oak and pine and palmetto" 2205
"growths, bovine watery" 3973
"grudge against her from the start" 5817
Grudges 5817
"gruel, half filled with" 7782
"gruesome, it was" 8967
"gruffly" 8476
"gruffly but affably, said" 7767
Grumbit, Mrs. Dorothy 951
"grumble over pie crust" 1869
"grumbled" 4512
"grumbling away in some old argument" 6652
Grumm, Arthur 4800
"Grummans" 210
"grumpily, gracefully but" 1629
"grumpily turning to shake her finger" 2426
Grundy 2975
"grunt on a mouth-harp" 882
"grunted, he" 10010

"grunting, snoring and" 8489
Gryll, Squire 10899
"gryphons and such-like beasts" 3381
"Guadaloupe" 5003
"guarded for many generations" 7950
Guardian, Father 6807
Guardian 4008
"Guardians, showed him the" 6704
"guardianship of her brother" 6110
"Guards, First Life" 2820
"guards, indifferent and courteous" 9381
"Guards, the" 7152
"guards greatly abused us" 1162
"Guatemala, Free Occupied" 230
"guavas" 5033
"Guayaquil" 6259
"Gué de Launay, le" 6571
"*guérite*, stood in the" 7918
"Guernesey" 10909
"Guernica network" 2916
"Guernsey" 10909
Guerrero, Rosendo 10751
"Guerrero mountains" 4797
Guerzon, M. D. 714
"guess, I miss *my*" 3555
Guest, Christopher 7610
"guest, half-expected" 94
"guest, moot" 7816
"guest, watched his" 3868
Guests 852, 3479, 3992, 4023, 6330, 6759, 7816, 9877, 9883, 10039
"guests, about two hundred invited" 10661
"guests, apology to arriving" 2550
"guests, handsome impatient company of" 3992
"guests, her three" 7127
"guests, his" 852
"guests, his two" 9883
"guests, honored" 8886
"guests, welcome the" 6330
"guests at a party, like unwanted" 454
"guests had been invited, eight" 4023
"guests season after season, the same" 4639
"guests toiled up flight upon flight of dark stairs" 6759
"guide in the blue uniform and scarlet armband" 3190
"guidebook, official" 9173
"guidebook to Nihilon" 912
"guide-books say, just what the" 1417
"guided me through many difficulties" 5446
"Guienne" 5125
"guild, little" 1530
"guillotine, build the" 1858
Guillotines 1858
Guilt 1967, 3575, 5295, 6668, 10853

"guilt, live without" 5295
"guilt of the couple, added to the" 1967
"guilty, but not" 8188
"guilty, found" 3407
"guilty, nearly always" 3575
"guilty, not" 5198
"guilty, plead" 7982
"Guilty', the jury said" 2027
"guilty, women feel" 10853
"guineapig" 5276
"guineas, five hundred" 3744
Guinevere, Queen 6561
"guitar, one used" 4122
"guitar distilled its music" 6221
"guitar he remembered, they found the" 7450
Guitars 6221, 7450
Gulban 6712
"Gulf, Arabian" 7919
"Gulf, growl of the" 4657
"Gulf, overlooking the" 301
"Gulf, the" 2911
"gulf, waves of the" 8092
"gulf below" 15
"Gulf coast of Florida" 4407
"Gulf is brown and muddy" 7923
"Gulf of Corinth" 1439
"Gulf of Eilat" 4418
"Gulf of Leyte" 219
"Gulf of Mexico" 4066, 7232, 7927, 9614
"Gulf of Siam" 2188
"Gulf Oil station" 9583
"Gulf Stream" 6428
"Gulfport Mississippi" 6824
"gull, tern and" 4587
"gull, the" 7427
"Gullah granny woman" 110
"gullies, arid" 2949
Gulliver, Sam 3714
Gulls 728, 8068
"gulls, a scattering of" 9460
"gulls, chatter of" 10277
"gulls, cry of" 10230
"gulls, handfuls of lost and disoriented" 186
"gulls, herring" 2623
"gulls, sea" 8105
"gulls, shoot the" 4257
"gulls, smooth swoop of the" 742
"gulls circle dumpsters" 186
"gulls escorted the trawlers, no" 732
"gulls gone inland" 6648
"gulls swept over Dover" 728
"gulls wheel above the broken boxes" 8068
"gulp before I got it out" 6038
"gulp of his tea" 3852
"gulps of air" 1711
"gulps of too hot cocoa" 3824
"gulps the broken water" 8068
"gum wrappers" 6861
Gumbril, Theodore Junior 9411
Gumma 6297

"gums, her" 10831
"gums, skinny" 5169
"GUN!" 4267
"gun, I bought the" 4265
"gun, machine" 7004
"gun, pointed a" 4249
"gun, six-" 9311
"gun hidden in a cave" 9045
"gun on his shoulder" 2223
"gun out agin, you aint takin that" 4247
"gun up, hit him before he could get the" 9702
"gun was easy to make" 4259
"gun Zam-Zammah, astride the" 2017
"gunfire in the woods all morning" 4264
"gunman, Chicago" 9919
Gunn, Father 12
Gunn, James Payton "Beau" II 829
Gunnarsson, Asgeir 3661
"gunner, master" 4246
Gunnings, Miss 3965
Gunnson, Archer 10055
"gunpowder, rammed the" 7048
Guns 576, 786, 2017, 4347, 4694, 9291, 9311, 10098
"guns, all's well the" 4246
"guns, he could get some" 4251
"guns, ten" 8079
"guns and trouble, a story of" 4250
"guns of North and South" 786
"gunships, one of the new Sikorsky" 230
"gunshot scared the hell out of him" 34
Gunshots 34, 410, 2406, 3766, 3954, 8794, 8801, 9845, 10009
Gunter 4663
"gunthrower, professional" 6180
Guppa 6297
"Guru had told him so" 1231
Gus 641
"gusts, fierce short" 10719
"gusts, great looping" 9078
"gusts of wind" 9077
"gusts were rattling at the windows, great" 10678
"gusty" 10606
"gusty, cold and" 10715
"gusty March afternoon" 9771
"gut, corresponds to the location of a" 4089
Guthrie, Ryland 9308
"Guthrie" 3044
"guts, butt him in the" 3289
"guts-and-glory story" 8993
"guttural cry, sharp" 5620
Guy 8865
"guy, ordinary average kind of" 4874
"guy, two seats away is a" 344
"guy, what a grand" 2892
"guy, you are not the kind of" 4329

"guy from N.Y.U., some" 8012
"guy named Lionel, some" 6782
"guy who falls asleep smoking in bed" 5960
"guy who would be at a place like this" 4329
"guys, black" 9807
"guys, six different" 7993
"guys, we" 5382
Guzmán 7091
Gwendolen 4855
Gwynne, Kenneth 6623
"Gymnasium, Hemenway" 6753
"gymnasium, what had once been the" 8468
"gynecologist, her" 6892
"gynecologists lie" 5231
"gypped, he was getting" 9308
"gypsies, the whoring thieving" 6292
"gypsy, scholar-" 1431
"gypsy gypsy joker" 4987
"gyrated clumsily" 4954
"gyro sandwiches" 3876

"H-bombs, no" 3362
"ha'penny" 1085
"Ha'penny Bit, the" 971
"Habana" 3378
"haberdasher and author" 9989
"habit, a" 6272
"habit, accuracy of" 9417
"habit, amusing little" 960
"habit, as was his" 8257
"habit, black" 10388
"habit, French" 4997
"habit, from" 4279
"habit, it was Mr. Ricardo's" 4269
"habit, out of" 1548
"habit, purposefulness of long" 10421
"Habit Kentucky" 3669
"habit of a Dominican friar" 10388
"habit of meandering, history has a" 4500
"habit of rubbing his head" 4291
"habit of stopping in their room" 6543
"habit of wearing it" 7124
Habits 321, 480, 568, 1326, 1500, 1548, 1626, 2154, 2997, 3047, 3484, 3813, 3816, 4647, 4956, 4997, 5264, 6043, 6272, 6290, 6543, 6571, 6630, 6681, 7109, 7124, 7977, 8046, 8363, 9417, 9465, 9822, 9932, 10169, 10195, 10262, 10421, 10919, 10945
"habits" 9465
"habits, bad" 7977
"habitually careful" 2997
"hack, battered black" 9771
"hack, dépôt" 9382
"hack drawn by two gray horses" 9771

"hack it, but can you" 1081
Hackabout-Jones, Fanny 5492
"Hackensack, the" 7647
Hackett, Mr. 8267
Hackett, Tod 8776
"had me, before they" 9706
"had to, we" 9640
"had to go up" 2764
Haddock, Mr. and Mrs. 3469
"Hades, entrance into" 4082
"Hades, ruffianly inhabitants of"
   2016
Haforn 760
Haggerty, Shrimp 1878
Haggin, Mister 405
"ha-ha, separated by a" 5164
"Haida Indian village" 8168
"Haifa, blue bay of" 8133
"hail, shower of" 9063
"Hail Hail The Gang's All Here" 6219
"Hail Muse" 5523
"hail on a roof, like" 10546
"hail rattled like a handful of
   pebbles" 9063
"hailed at Grand Central
   Station" 6652
"hails, several loud" 8066
Hair 1867, 2482, 2913, 7977,
   8522, 10335, 10668
"hair, blond" 3545
"hair, bride ironed her" 10668
"hair, bright black" 5935
"hair, brown" 960, 7485
"hair, covered with blue and silver"
   416
"hair, curly red" 5921
"hair, dark" 6562
"hair, evidently false 'front' of fair"
   2822
"hair, few strands of yellowish-
   white" 5984
"hair, fine dark" 2772
"hair, flop of blond" 10729
"hair, found" 2913
"hair, ginger" 1432
"hair, graying" 87
"hair, head of black" 822
"hair, her blond" 4168
"hair, his thick white" 1887
"hair, how did you do that with
   your" 10892
"hair, I have gingery" 7977
"hair, it was in my" 4299
"hair, kinky black" 5908
"hair, lank no-colour" 4301
"hair, light brown" 4789
"hair, little soft shroud of" 2336
"hair, long black" 5190, 9612
"hair, lost a good deal of" 4291
"hair, my" 73
"hair, pale brown" 333
"hair, pale curly" 969
"hair, plucking at the falls of her
   dark" 10698
"hair, profusion of their body" 10313

"hair, red" 4293
"hair, reddish" 5912
"hair, river smelled like" 8522
"hair, short blonde" 4302
"hair, short slightly graying" 564
"hair, stiff black gold-tipped" 419
"hair, sun-bleached light brown"
   8237
"hair, thick coils of dark" 6669
"hair, thick dark" 10335
"hair, thick ebony" 4300
"hair, uncut" 2859
"hair, white" 5903
"hair, wild yellow" 4154
"hair, wise about her" 4297
"hair almost silver" 4292
"hair blue-rinsed, having her
   white" 2373
"hair bristling" 475
"hair curling forward in thatches"
   498
"hair falling down his brow" 2336
"hair feels heavy as a helmet" 4425
"hair impatiently back from her
   face, shaking her" 4901
"hair in turbans" 5190
"hair in two pigtails, dark" 4153
"hair just beginning to be touched
   with grey" 4293
"hair just beginning to get thin on
   the crown" 5912
"hair like that, one seldom sees"
   4295
"hair must have been ruddy gold"
   4294
"hair now black from being wet"
   7485
"hair on my arms, every" 1867
"hair ... piled high in glossy architecture" 7481
"hair roots" 10106
"hair spray" 1067
"hair streaming behind from beneath a green bandanna" 4168
"hair style, Rudolph Valentino
   parted-down-the-middle" 1982
"hair swinging long and loose" 7481
"hair switches, selling" 6107
"hair the color of Wise potato
   chips" 4298
"hair was braided into a glossy
   cable" 4300
"hair was mostly braided and
   bunned up in the back" 10860
"hair was streaming down, her
   grey" 10792
"hair wild, wind blow her" 10716
"haircut, decided to get a" 2482
"haircut is presumably part of the
   exhibit" 8027
Haircuts 8697
"haircuts" 8697
"hairdos of actresses" 7229
"haired, flaxen-" 4180
"haired, grey-" 6834

"haired, rumply-" 4154
"haired, yellow-" 365
"hairpin curve" 8303
"hair-restorer" 5624
"hairs, sparse gray" 8461
"hair's all falling out, my" 73
"Haitian people, some" 9027
"Haitian refugee" 9850
"Hakenkreuz, large ornamental gold-
   on-black-enamel" 1714
"halcyon days, sequence of" 2173
Hale 1796, 6176
"hale age, a figure of" 5405
"Haledon N.J." 7345
Halevi, Avram 4679
"Half Day to Flossmoor" 3725
"half-asleep" 5187
"half-blood" 4358
"halfheartedly, only rather" 706
"halfheartedly brushed" 5984
Halifax 234
"Halifax" 5034
Halina 3881
Hall, Diony 6218
"hall, ancient" 3059
"hall, brown-stained tongue-and-
   groove box of the lower" 9887
"Hall, Carnegie" 1746
"Hall, Carvel" 3531
"hall, ceiling of the" 7779
"hall, dim" 1594
"hall, gaslit" 9406
"Hall, Grand" 4309
"hall, great front-" 1595
"Hall, Heyton" 10676
"hall, in the great" 10086
"Hall, Johnson" 7409
"Hall, Kellynch" 4439
"Hall, Kiddemaster" 6577
"hall, large" 9213
"hall, lecture" 7518
"Hall, Lincoln's Inn" 8339
"Hall, make a great" 1180
"Hall, Marling" 3114
"Hall, Mauley" 5984
"hall, narrow" 3094
"Hall, Paradise" 4104
"Hall, Patna" 2181
"Hall, Patterne" 6613
"Hall, Sedon" 2745
"Hall, Sons of Italy in America"
   3753
"Hall, Swarthmoor" 9101
"hall, tiny booking" 5813
"Hall, Tower" 4768
"hall, town" 9233
"Hall, Town" 2214
"Hall, vast" 4895
"hall complete with minstrels' gal-
   lery" 1180
"Hall of Domestic Justice" 2682
"hall of the banquets" 6752
Hallam, Melissa 7953
Hallam, Pete 7894
"hallelujah bum, the" 5255

"Halley's comet" 2591
Hallock 8647
Halloran, Mrs. 3939
"Hallowe'en costumes" 1876
"Halloween issue of the *Lakeview Daily Citizen*" 6863
"halls, its painted" 2088
"haloes, angular" 8152
Halpern, Roger 1997
Halsey, Mike 10282
"halt, came to a shuddering" 9791
"halt, ground to a" 9785
"halt, the" 7155
"halted" 8073
"halted, they" 7669
"ham, some kind of greasy" 3858
"Hamburg, somebody in" 7838
"hamburgs, onions ready to go on" 7575
Hamid, Abdul 3721
Hamilton, Colonel Jonathan 3992
Hamilton, Duke of 3965
Hamilton, Freddy 5457
Hamilton, Peter 2622
Hamlet 2689
Hamlet 9386
"hamlet, site for the" 5139
"hamlet of Charing" 5126
"hamlet of Yokohama, fishing" 7908
"hamlet standing a mile inland" 5144
"hamlet stood on a gentle rise" 1484
"hamlets, small and somnolent" 7254
"hamlets of the south of England" 7254
Hammer, Stuart 6178
"hammer, claw end of a" 10949
"hammer, his little" 5247
"hammer it into a bigger badge for himself" 9702
"hammer tapping lightly on the shaft" 10948
"hammers, a tattoo of" 8775
"Hammersmith" 5905
"hammock, a scarlet canvas" 10051
Hammond, Madeline 1584
Hamnet 2363
"Hamoaze" 8098
"Hampshire countryside" 5172
"Hampstead" 3825, 5928
"Hampstead Heath" 4070, 5928, 8587
Hampton, Eunnonia Grace 6275
"Hampton family" 10556
"Hamptons, the" 9199
"hams of his rump" 8266
"hamster, my pet" 859
Hanan 311
Hancock, John 4981
Hancock, William Leeds 790
Hand, Anna 5534
Hand, Daniel DeBardeleben 5598
Hand, Olivia de Havilland 5598
"hand, by their own" 8678

"hand, child's" 495
"Hand, Court" 7879
"hand, his perspiring" 5465
"hand, his pudgy" 4414
"hand, his thickly gloved" 9092
"hand, long narrow" 3711
"hand, prematurely-wrinkled" 7555
"hand, restraining" 10543
"hand, unthinking motion of his" 8115
"hand, his wife's" 4599, 9934
"hand, holding her" 8382
"hand, in his right" 2820
"hand, its brass tongue in my" 9442
"hand, let go of Ruth's" 9164
"hand, mildly revolted" 6497
"hand, move my right" 7463
"hand, nervous bony" 5812
"hand, pencil and paper in my" 5445
"hand, promised" 4339
"hand, reattaching the severed" 4281
"hand, skinny" 4196
"hand, some unseen" 6070
"hand, stretch out a large" 492
"hand, take her" 2101
"hand, the size of an open" 924
"hand, watched my" 4649
"hand, with my own" 5451
"hand, worked up by" 1824
"hand, your right" 2817
"Hand and Ball Court" 2245
"hand away, kicked his" 3755
"hand could it be, whose" 5943
"hand creates an imaginary visor" 4896
"hand free, leaving my right" 6391
"hand from under the blankets, I reached out a" 656
"hand go under the seat, saw his" 9702
"hand heavy with rings" 7555
"hand in hand" 515
"hand in hand, no longer" 515
"hand in the air, waved her" 4437
"hand inside the unbuttoned blouse of a young woman" 2529
"hand jiggled the stem of the wine-glass" 5186
"hand moved across the letter paper" 1923
"hand moved just then to start the windshield wipers" 1990
"hand off, cutting the girl's" 7045
"hand over the top, place her" 2921
"hand resting with casual vigilance" 2045
"hand shook his shoulder, his father's" 10122
"hand slide across the page" 4649
"hand streaking to a six-gun" 9311
"hand that fed me, I'd just bitten the" 2646
"hand tightly, holding Mama's" 1618

"hand to Hale's shoulder, dropping a" 1796
"hand tremble, had never seen her friend's" 2089
"hand was already under her night-gown" 8015
"hand was played out, the" 2304
"hand with claw-shaped fingers poised above the town" 10582
"handbags, designer labels on" 7229
"handcuffs of seawater" 980
"handed down through the men from father to son" 7950
"handed in to him behind the bed-curtains" 3376
"handed it to me" 845
"handed up his theological exam papers" 6639
"handfuls, heaping" 3341
"hand-holding street" 9164
Handicaps 58, 547, 5924, 5997, 6632, 7077, 9647
"handing over the letter" 1954
"handkerchief, blue-and-white spotted" 6350
"handkerchief, embroidering a" 4166
"handkerchief, little" 2070
"handle, elaborate wrought-iron" 6587
"handle it" 9960
"handle shaped like a boomerang, a copper" 2697
"handle to lift up the edifice by, looking not unlike a" 9206
"handlebars, holding the" 977
"handles, oldfashioned pull-out" 7575
Handley, Albert 1046
Hands 351, 1251, 1760, 1883, 4281, 5191, 8382, 8466
"hands, brushing the dust from his" 5920
"hands, clapped his" 5188
"hands, clutched in her" 6859
"hands, corpse without" 1883
"hands, destroyed by their own" 4469
"hands, doctor's" 10313
"hands, field" 7553
"hands, forbidding" 10313
"hands, gloved" 8282
"hands, Grundy's" 2975
"hands, her cold" 9540
"hands, her small but capable" 564
"hands, his carefully crossed" 8827
"hands, his fat little" 5913
"hands, holding" 2677
"hands, in our" 5430
"hands, knuckly" 979
"hands, loving" 9626
"hands, my outstretched" 2894
"hands, nearly an hour on her" 4909
"hands, noticed the change in his" 1251

"hands, old" 6366
"hands, palms of" 4413
"hands, parents shook" 3283
"hands, something to do with the" 5191
"hands, two human" 351
"hands, upraised" 8937
"hands, with my bare" 8565
"hands, worked all day at projects with their" 6133
"hands already on the steering wheel" 6962
"hands and knees, on my" 8949
"hands began to draw down windows" 9605
"hands busy, with both" 6652
"hands clasped behind his back" 10383
"hands . . . curled into fists" 8466
"hands hanging limply, his big" 8266
"hands large strong and hairy" 2975
"hands of a lot of people drowning, like the" 7855
"hands of a temporarily unemployed housepainter" 2061
"hands of the enemy" 1161
"hands of the nurse are arrested for a moment" 4508
"hands of the Tabors, in the" 1180
"hands off the wheel" 3004
"hands on hips" 4154
"hands on his hips for dear life" 2973
"hands on the wall-clock" 9466
"hands on what I shall leave you, lay your" 4932
"hands out, reaching his" 1207
"hands over his knees, cupping his big" 4726
"hands side by side and palms downwards" 5913
"hands squeezed into an opossum muff" 9540
"hands steady, tries to hold his" 9803
"hands stuffed in his pockets" 10438
"hands thrust into his pockets" 4678
"hands to the fire, extended slim" 5428
"hands together, clasp my" 1211
"hands were pried away from the delicate white throats" 4129
"hands were shaking a lot" 4579
"hands were wringing wet with blood" 10939
"hands which were small" 8466
"handsome" 3173, 5555, 5969, 6546
"handsome, strikingly" 5998
"handsome, tall and dark and" 8658
"handsome but slightly frowning" 10894
"handsome man" 5961
"handsome place, it was not a" 3637

"handsomeness, extreme" 10759
"handspan between their shoulders" 7862
"handwriting, elegant" 917
"handwriting, neat constricted" 1921
"handy, no other place" 9520
Handy Andy 6018
"hang, they always said I would" 3353
"hang about, you couldn't" 3944
"hang around my neck like a rainbow" 1273
"hang around the Riva for another hour" 3709
"hang men, they used to" 7181
"hang people, they didn't" 7185
"hang your right hand high" 2107
"hanged, he had been" 2304
"hanged, Polish noblemen were" 7184
"hanged a fat man, they" 10542
"hanged by his best friend" 2304
"hanged for a thief" 2461
"hanged in London" 7180
"hanged the five men" 7189
"hangers-on" 8886
"hanging" 6965
"hanging all her weight from the hammer" 10949
"hanging around Marvin Conklin's drugstore" 5370
"hanging on to his dong" 2374
Hangings 495, 2304, 2461, 3353, 7179, 7180, 7181, 7184, 7185, 7189, 9292, 10542
"hangings, faded chintz" 6386
"hangings, scarlet" 7761
"hangman, escape the" 10509
Hangovers 2891, 2926, 10319
"hangovers were trivially unpleasant" 2926
"hangs over the door handle a printed notice" 8313
Hank 3743
Hankin, Mr. 3327
Hanks, Lucy 10927
Hanline, Maurice 6180
Hanlon, Old Jake 8273
Hannah 2553, 3928, 7557
Hanneke 4850
Hannele 4476
"Hanover Nebraska" 10685
Hans 6996
"Hans Place" 2930
Hapgood, Mrs. 2976
"haphazard rotation" 6763
"happen, didn't" 8027
"happen, nobody expected it to" 6771
"happen, something would" 928
"happen, suspicioned something might" 9307
"happen, what do you think would" 4689
"happen every day, it did not" 4169

"happen on Saturday night, why does it always" 10881
"happen to me, if anything really interesting should" 930
"happen very often, two things don't" 3448
"happened, all this" 10508
"happened, as it" 5877
"happened, before all this" 4834
"happened, exactly what" 7840
"happened, fill in the first part of what" 1705
"happened, in spite of what had" 3665
"happened, it" 3501
"happened, it really" 9023
"happened, just as it" 9009
"happened, none of this would have" 2445, 4527
"happened, something remarkable" 3440
"happened, something that" 9993
"happened, that was the way it" 1223
"happened, the thing has" 6890
"happened, the things that afterwards" 7607
"happened, this is what" 3453
"happened, understand how it" 5123
"happened, what" 3513
"happened, what had" 688
"happened, when it" 3451, 9821
"happened, when this" 3352
"happened, where were you when this" 7566
"happened, why it" 640
"happened a good many years ago, all this" 3437
"happened a little less than a year ago" 3455
"happened anywhere, might have" 9287
"happened at last, has it" 7205
"happened before, it has" 8807
"happened before the era of accomplishment" 3393
"happened by the grace of God" 3970
"happened here, if it" 3369
"happened in the Great War that day, not much" 8678
"happened then, all that" 3369
"happened this way" 3446
"happened to a Greek family, all this" 3500
"happened to François, something" 3504
"happened to her, feeling that something had" 10155
"happened to her, something" 10052
"happened to him, nothing real had ever" 3505
"happened to it, make sure nothing had" 10970

"happened to me, it's about something that" 9058
"happened to me in Germany, this is what" 3503
"happened to the inside of it" 3085
"happened to the machine and its people, what" 5685
"happened to them, sum of everything that has" 3671
"happened to us, understand what has" 7400
"happened without any special effort" 10794
"happening, can't believe it's really" 9043
"happening, precious little was" 946
"happening, so much" 8988
"happening, when there's something" 10805
"happening, while it was" 8020
"happening all over again" 7379
"happening outside, guess what was" 2701
"happening there, what" 6290
"happening to Albert St. Dennis, something is" 3506
"happening too often, that had been" 4919
Happenings 2445, 3441, 3451, 3501, 3502, 3506, 7205, 9058, 10155, 10805
"happenings, daily" 2533
"happenings that interested him" 3441
"happens, nothing ever really" 1459
"happens, when it" 3502
"happens in it, nothing" 1374
"happens once or twice a week" 7204
"happens to millions, it" 133
"happenstance, history's senseless" 7812
"happier than I have ever been in my life" 4354
"happier theme" 5447
"happier times" 5057
"happier world" 6212
"happiest man in the world" 4345
"happiest of times" 4353
"happiest time, their" 2507
"happiest when she was leaving a place" 7534
"happily, lived" 5300
"happily for herself" 1174
"happily reminiscent of a satisfactory luncheon" 3821
Happiness 250, 444, 1273, 1904, 1975, 2134, 2506, 2958, 3473, 3773, 4158, 4808, 5184, 5300, 5643, 5755, 6755, 7096, 7155, 7166, 7534, 7714, 7847, 8554, 9266, 10030, 10844, 10995
"happiness, destructive to his" 7346
"happiness, her last" 2506
"happiness, ordinary human" 4808

"happiness, road to" 4346
"happiness, such a tired hot muddled" 4354
"happiness, the greatest" 10030
"happiness, wave of unreasonable" 10684
"happiness and unhappiness" 1342
"happy" 7714
"Happy" 7098
"happy, are you" 4350
"happy, deeply" 5643
"happy, I find myself" 4343
"happy, if not exactly" 2429
"happy, inappropriately" 4355
"happy, individedly" 10995
"happy, make a man" 4339
"happy, Mr. Gabriel Bearse was" 4340
"happy, never" 135
"happy, not even to be" 250
"happy, she was very" 9266
"happy, should have been" 7155
"happy, we've been pretty" 4351
"happy, you should be" 4348
"happy and contented, feeling peculiarly" 4342
"happy and excited, felt" 3473
"happy and prosperous" 2018
"happy as she intended" 8554
"happy at last" 6755
"happy at the Divinity School" 4357
"happy augury" 10646
"happy birthday" 845, 858
"happy birthday to you" 852
"happy Blue whales" 444
"Happy Days" 8755
"happy endings had been distributed in heaping handfuls" 3341
"happy facts, for all the" 6206
"happy for two days, I have been quite" 4343
"happy formation" 6604
"happy in each other" 4338
"happy in our hut" 4347
"happy life" 6663
"happy look" 2429
"happy marriages, inexplicably" 5755
"happy New Year" 10133
"happy now, you will be" 1904
"happy person, I'm basically a" 10844
"happy soil" 6249
"happy throughout my life, I have been generally" 4343
"happy unladen feet" 10368
"Happy Valley, this was" 4356
"happy ... when you were born" 4354
"Hapsburg" 4055
"Hapsburg, House of" 7056
Hapu 6661
"hara-kiri" 6021
Harbans, Mr. Surujpat 21
Harbingers 2204, 7016

"Harbor, Boston" 8591
"Harbor, Cold Spring" 10620
"Harbor, Dun Laoghaire" 8660
"Harbor, Packet" 3534
"Harbor, Pearl" 6774
"harbor, safe" 8504
"harbor, ship rounding the" 4587
"harbor, ships were burning in the" 3791
"harbor, the little" 5910
"harbor entrance" 5034
"harbor was cool and damp" 10616
"harbored two sons in the waters of her womb" 7078
Harbors 1440, 3791, 5015, 8258
"harbors, great" 6249
"Harbour, Charleston" 7913
"harbour, Dunedin" 8170
"harbour, Falmouth" 8152
"harbour, gazed out across the" 7801
"harbour, going out of the" 732
"Harbour, Leghorn" 8069
"harbour, looking down upon the" 8258
"harbour, our" 5015
"harbour, small fishing" 1440
"harbour, still waters of the" 1751
"harbour, there was the" 9460
"harbour, wide confines of Portsmouth" 10719
"harbour of St. Maria" 8040
Harclay, Sir Philip 4554
Harcourt 4891
"hard, so" 5695
"hard as rock" 3653
"hard at work" 485
"hard hard" 8014
"hard man, father was a" 5917
"hard one, a high man and a" 5987
"hard ones" 349
"hard part, killing the animals was the" 451
"hard time" 6927
"hard times of the 1980s" 1064
"hard to believe, find our voyage" 2744
"hard to know where to begin" 626
"hard under palms" 8014
"hard work in the most tranquil circumstances" 10953
Hardbine, Newt 3733
"harder to me, she is the" 5397
"hardest thing, the" 5437
"hard-hearted" 3509
Harding, the Rev. Septimus 1486
Hardinge, Lord 1930
Hardship 1850, 3602, 7216
"hardship" 1882
"hardship discharge, had to get a" 8670
"hardships, terrible the" 1850
"Hardware, Bud's" 1057
"hardwoods, tall" 5161
Hardy 962

Hardy, Luke 2918
Hardy, Theo. J. 6980
"hardy, the" 9634
Hare, Miss 10812
"hare, everyone has seen a" 5792
"Hare and Tortoise, the" 3820
"hare lip, he had a" 7077
"harebrains never even acquainted" 7164
"harem, enter the" 4172
Harg 8266
"harkened drowsily to the rain" 7305
Harker, Kay 2500
Harkness, Mr. Joshua 4368
Harlan, Andrew 1861
"Harlem" 74
Harlequin, George 3925
Harley, Mrs. 2695
"harlot, scream of a brawling" 8777
"harm than good, does more" 10976
"Harmattan, the time of the" 10709
Harmen 4760
Harmony 3019
"Harmony" 3441, 5119
"harmony, a white" 8586
"Harmony Village" 292
Harmsworth, Malcolm 8481
"Harniss" 7760
Harold 1492, 2091, 4694, 5453, 9860, 10960
"harp, gothic" 10416
"harp, grass" 8785
"harp, singing of the" 8792
Harper, David 4913
"harper was singing a song" 8762
"Harper's Weekly" 7871
"Harriers', Springwell" 3998
Harriet 3678, 3993, 4576, 6298, 7742, 9406, 9509, 10403
Harriet, Great-aunt 4461
Harriette 1599
Harrington, Miss Polly 10785
Harrington, Mr. Melchisedec 2290
Harris 929
Harris, Rebecca 6400
Harris, Will 9478
Harris, William Samuel 3990
"Harrods" 4708
Harrodsen, Celia 3442
"Harrow Massachusetts" 1088
"harrow the soul" 4101
"harrowing of hell" 609
Harry 2344, 2574, 3736, 3883, 6163, 7559, 9413
Harry, Sir 3289
"Harry Arno" 7963
Harry the Fish Man 6652
Harry the Goth 308
Harry the Lover 7995
Hart, Calvin 5005
Hart, Howard 8559
"Hartfield" 8301
Hartke, Eugene Debs 4865
Hartley, Sam 2073

Hartman, Rabbi David 1529
Hartmann 8577
Hartwell, George 3406
"Harvard" 6760
"Harvard, already known at" 8879
"Harvard, red bricks of" 6678
"Harvard University" 6491
"Harvard University, behind the mossy walls of" 3333
"Harvard Yard" 7905
"harvest, mellow-dropping" 3799
"harvest-hand of autumn" 10591
"harvest-time was almost come" 10573
"harvested them greedily" 9674
Harz, Alois 9869
Haskell 9983
Haslatt, Edward 4999
Haslitt 1015
Hasluck 10348
"Hasnapur, village of" 7030
Hassan, Kerbelai 6405
Hassan, Mouley Ali Aben 7809
Hasselbacher, Dr. 7395
"hassocks" 1311
Hassoon, Sam 203
"haste, he had made" 8515
"haste to get out, in her" 2713
"hastily arranged memorial service" 3961
Hastings, Warren 1
"Hastings" 2943, 9134
"Hastings, battle of" 6518, 8347
"hasty yet purposeful way" 6301
Hat 6290
Hat, Aunt 248
"hat, at the drop of a" 10976
"hat, big cowboy" 2839
"hat, dark top" 3001
"hat, floppy straw" 10816
"hat, flung his" 3468
"hat, gardening" 2658
"hat, green" 2824
"hat, his imaginary" 4896
"hat, I put on my" 121
"hat, lifted his" 7646
"hat, peculiar" 4154
"hat, slouch" 7440
"hat, tak your" 2821
"hat, tall silk" 10373
"hat, three-cornered" 9757
"hat, tossed his" 10694
"hat, tried tipping her" 7470
"hat, uniform" 6967
"hat, wide brim of her" 10441
"hat and coat, take his" 1908
"hat and wig" 9757
"hat had played a conspicuous part" 2752
"hat heavy as lead, his bowler" 10365
"hat jauntily on her head, places the" 4154
"hat less jauntily on his head" 6408
"hat soaked, his" 1759

"hat tight, pulled his" 7642
"hat tighter, pulling his" 10410
Hatch, Maggie 2880
"Hatch End" 1408
"hatched, like Helen of Troy was" 817
"hatchets and caustic acids" 3413
"hate, I" 4361
"hate, stress and" 760
"hate everything I see in you" 4362
"hate EVIL" 5362
"hate helicopters, why I" 5375
"hate this, she's going to" 4363
"hate to be like you, I should" 4362
"hate us, she's going to" 4363
"hate within, boiling with" 10186
"hated, bubbles rising in it that he" 5634
"hated being cold, I've always" 1553
"hated domestic work" 10915
"hated her, times when he" 5368
"hated him" 3329
"hated his face" 5377
"hated his squad" 8686
"hated more, nothing in life he" 9470
"hated more dearly my home town, no one" 5359
"hated so much, parlor they both" 8365
"hated washdays" 5372
"hateful presences in me" 6672
"hates that she came along" 5367
"hates them, he never" 5950
Hathon 6429
"hating people" 4230
"hating the weary task" 10927
Hatred 3329, 5368, 6672, 8686, 9304, 10186, 10915
"hatred, jealous of their" 4364
"hatred of her, added something to his" 4614
Hats 2824, 2850, 6967, 7470
"hats, gray steeple-crowned" 3985
"hats on the side of our heads" 3341
Hatten, Peter 5652
"Hatteras Cape" 9078
Hattersley, Father 1541
"haughty mien" 675
"haul, the long" 1329, 6664
"haul things, I" 6488
"haulier extraordinary" 847
"hauling one pine box and one black boy" 2973
"haunch of the crouching mountains" 6087
"haunches, the horses'" 9771
"haunt it still today just as they haunted it a hundred or a thousand years ago" 4105
"haunt me, saying something that would" 387
"haunt of many different kinds of wood" 3906

"haunt the Chesapeake, ghosts that" 4105
"haunted, had been" 6796
"haunted, he is" 9054
"haunted, it was" 6086
"haunted by the ghost of a woman" 4116
"haunted the clubhouse" 4306
"haunted the front gate of the refugee camp" 10532
"haunted the obituaries" 2569
"haunting, grim and extraordinary" 4104
"haunting sound, poignantly" 8799
"haunts" 8494
Haussmann, le Baron 5179
"Havana" 2210
"have, it's what I don't" 10835
"have it, we oughtn't to" 4244
"have things out" 6620
"haven, last" 4017
"haven, offered a" 6109
"Haverford" 3532
"Haverhill" 7668
"havoc on the rocks, make frothy" 7668
"Hawaii" 9918
"Hawaii, born in" 4543
"Hawaiian group, islands in the" 5022
"Hawaiian Islands" 8704
"Hawaiian tune, tinselly" 6216
"hawk, spotted" 281
Hawke, Bascom 6496
Hawkes, Ben Joe 4122
"hawking" 6459
Hawkins, Miss 9294
Hawkins, Parson Wibird 1490
"hawks and owls, mounted" 8553
Hawley, Mary 10174
Hawthorn, Daniel 4969
"hawthorn" 3396
"hawthorn, her accustomed" 720
"hay" 8508
"hay, bale of" 9607
"hay, bale of fermenting" 3782
"hay, newly cleared of" 5131
"hay, sweet clover" 463
"hay, turning their" 3645
"hay, working at the" 10946
"hay field" 10427
"hay in the sunshine, made" 3396
Haye, John 2531
Hayes, C. Harry 398
Hayes, Lincoln 4995
Hayes, Mr. Raleigh W. 70
Hayes, Sapphire 7106
Hayeses, the 3586
"haying, every day during" 9985
Haynes, Virgil 214
Hayworth, Cletus 367
Hazard 432
Hazard, Matthew Carlton 5057
Hazard, Mr. 9538
Hazard, Timothy 704

"hazard rules our lives" 5274
"hazardous, potentially" 9249
"hazards and difficulties" 5556
"hazards, unseen" 2991
"haze, chilling" 7285
"haze, dissolved into a haze" 1115
"haze, glaring white" 8416
"haze, industrial" 1032
"haze, luminous and infinite" 10260
"haze, pale lavender" 2284
"haze, pink" 10621
"haze, purplish" 2199
"haze, thin mirage-like" 7623
"haze, trace of saffron" 1854
"haze of a London winter night" 7285
"haze of acrid sweetish dust" 5142
"haze of autumn, in the golden" 6577
"haze of early spring, noontime" 5916
"haze of late summer, the first morning" 10185
"haze over the sky" 8416
"haze suspended in the air over Manhattan Island" 1854
"haze that engulfed all of St. Louis" 10621
"haze that enveloped London" 5311
"hazed over by mid-day heat" 1694
Hazel 770, 5351, 7440
"hazel bush" 10756
Hazeley, Flora 3814
Hazeltine, Judge George 5210
"head, another sister's" 7441
"head, Bayard's" 10157
"Head, Bray" 1173
"head, caressed his bald" 5712
"head, cocked her" 1799
"head, cracking the back of his" 34
"head, current that was running in his" 9450
"head, Dead Father's" 2367
"Head, Duncansby" 8154
"Head, East" 9074
"head, eat the" 10899
"head, fleshy balloon of a" 2859
"head, high over my" 305
"head, his bared" 5323
"head, in his owl-" 7949
"head, in my" 1932
"head, inside my" 1327
"head, jerked his" 5571
"head, lifted his" 9997
"head, my" 5800
"head, old woman's" 147
"head, pitching forward on his" 2374
"head, plunging her" 9297
"head, ponderous art of his great" 7472
"head, raised his" 8742
"head, ribbon on top of his" 416
"head, rubbing his" 4291
"head, shake his" 2351

"head, shaking his" 5185
"head, shape of the" 334
"head, shaven" 5971
"head, shielded his" 8179
"head, sleek brown pigtailed" 3824
"head, square shape of" 8237
"Head, Sumburgh" 5011
"head, taking it into his" 5728
"head, that stubborn little duck of her" 3289
"head, thick" 2926
"head, top of his" 8461
"head, turned his" 5864
"head, when you raise your" 761
"head, wide round" 5955
"head, with that simper and arching of her" 6113
"head, without moving his" 1110
"head against the tree, banging his" 10157
"head at me, cocks his" 6681
"head back, wind push her" 10691
"head bent, her" 10934
"head bent above his hands" 8374
"head bent against the wind" 10438
"head boot-boy" 6021
"head bowed" 8701
"head bowed, she kept her" 1202
"head bowed forward on his arms" 8456
"Head Boy of the School" 6424
"head dipped low" 7629
"head down on the table, put his" 3344
"head fallen forward upon his arms" 1877
"head go under water, saw his daughter's" 577
"head hunters" 1077
"head in the world, you could not hold up your" 9378
"head is apt to contain a failing memory, a gray" 3490
"head is wrapped in bandages" 3413
"head like a rodeo" 10319
"head lowered" 10375, 10413
"head lowered, kept his" 10407
"head of a Moor, slicing at the" 9839
"head of a seal" 8941
"head of cattle, around six hundred" 415
"head of department" 8801
"head of its mother" 453
"head of Lake Erie, situated at the" 9205
"head of the firm" 3326
"head of the procession" 8739
"head on her white arm, rested her" 9402
"head on his hands, raised his" 7324
"head out the window, stuck its" 3040
"head over heels" 24

"head over her club, bent her blond" 8927
"head still bleeding" 3056
"head supported by an old-country bolster" 2398
"head that never wore a crown" 8947
"head touched the floor after the ancient fashion" 7067
"head unusually big, a" 4302
"head was bowed" 440
"head was full of schemes" 258
"head whose size made his shoulders look narrower" 5955
"head wound" 10156
"head you see, that indistinguishable" 9678
"headache, each with a mild" 515
"headache, wake with a" 8514
"headed, flat-" 5624
"headed, small-" 903
"headed back east" 8878
"headed for Colfax" 204
"headed for Rubio City" 9762
"headed for the church" 6229
"heading for the gap in the rosy brick wall" 2984
"headland, onto the open" 9150
"headland, over the" 8430
"headland, the great" 8209
"headlands, majestic" 3514
"headlight, the bright blob of his" 3483
"headlights, I pulled on the" 3029
"headlights had been smashed out" 9809
"headlights keep streaming past my thumb" 9649
"headline said" 6966
"headlines" 6328
"headlines, read the" 10366
"headlines, spills into" 1332
"headlines sprang out" 6397
"headlines were yellowing on the newspaper lining of cupboard drawers" 5091
"Headmaster, Deputy" 986
"headmaster's residence" 5854
"headquarters, business" 1068
"headquarters, curious" 7788
"headquarters in Chaumont, AEF" 8695
"headquarters in Senlis" 9929
Heads 334, 2367, 4302, 9585
"heads, housemaids who lost their" 17
"heads, shaking their" 9080
"heads, shook their" 6019
"heads in the clouds" 6815
"heads of the audience, the something too few" 7779
"heads three deep in the carriage windows" 5654
"heads uncovered and bowed" 650

"heads up too high and got shot, stuck their" 8678
"headstand in the yard" 6075
"heady scent" 3809
"healer, old" 1799
"healing, three months" 7614
"healing from the obligatory circumcision" 556
Health 569, 936, 1337, 4339, 5939, 6896, 6936, 9973
"health" 9973
"health, in perfect" 936
"Health, O Board of" 1337
"health, rebeginning of his" 6936
"health and long life to the Supreme Pontiff" 7514
"healthy, burstingly" 9718
"healthy, looked deceptively" 10883
"heaping handfuls" 3341
"heaps, raised" 10228
"hear, couldn't" 8187
"hear, did he" 10199
"hear, so high that no one could" 3716
"hear a person" 8414
"hear about it, if you really want to" 9706
"hear around the crackel barrel" 10489
"hear from me, surprised to" 8181
"hear from you" 8181
"hear her, I didn't" 8822
"hear his grandmother's voice" 10162
"hear in diminuendo the guns of North and South" 786
"hear in good time, they shall" 5681
"hear it that way" 8747
"hear King George's man proclaim" 6981
"hear me" 6338
"hear Mostyn's niece recite" 7389
"hear of it, came to" 541
"hear quite clearly the singing of the harp behind him" 8792
"hear something clattering and rumbling" 8834
"hear the first eee-thud eee-thud of the mortars" 878
"hear the steel-shod hooves on the frozen ground" 7638
"hear the two American ladies in 404 arguing" 1828
"hear them, he could" 3568
"hear them, he didn't" 2027
"hear them, you can" 8814
"heard, dimly" 664
"heard, he might not have" 5746
"heard a great din" 8776
"heard a lot about another American girl" 3541
"heard about it, I don't think you have ever" 1381
"heard about that, nobody here has" 2855

"heard about the pair first from Emeline Eldredge" 7827
"heard again the faint faraway sound of the wagon" 8790
"heard by now, as you must have" 1264
"heard him, she" 7592
"heard his astonishing revelations" 2336
"heard in distant rooms" 7991
"heard it, by now you've" 6337
"heard it, wherever she went she" 8836
"heard it day after day for years on end" 8799
"heard it now for the last time" 8799
"heard James coming" 10103
"heard merely impinged, anything I" 7317
"heard nothing" 10362
"heard of Antonia, I first" 4462
"heard of him, very few who had" 5905
"heard of him, you must have" 4757
"heard of me, you've never" 908
"heard of the three beautiful Miss Gunnings" 3965
"heard on the steep slope below me" 8789
"heard only when nature sleeps" 8766
"heard so much, about which I had" 9251
"heard such a baby, I never" 540
"heard that Jack Kennedy was dead" 6332
"heard the clinking noise again" 8819
"heard the last stray call of a bugle" 5096
"heard the shot" 8794
"heard the sudden rattle of cartwheels" 8778
"heard the telephone ringing" 1095
"heard the tension thrill" 7989
"heard warblers singing" 7025
"heard what he said" 6615
"hearing" 5059
"hearing, hard of" 8636
"hearing a small snore" 8496
"hearing about the Tennis Club for years" 4321
"hearing aid, not a" 9362
"hearing aid turned off" 2419
"hearing Sam" 6218
"hearing the sound of breathing" 8483
"hearing the telephone ring, shock of" 1104
"hearing the wrong voices" 3461
Hearne, John 9964
Hearne, Miss Judith 6116
"hears Mickey scream" 10024

"hearse, dusty long black" 9775
"hearse, the" 2365
Hearst, William Randolph 8383
"heart, anxious mother's" 4889
"heart, beating" 378
"heart, blighted" 2492
"heart, breaks your" 1791
"heart, broke her father's" 6728
"heart, broke the mother's" 28
"heart, broken" 970
"heart, bruised" 10555
"heart, corner of my" 4290
"heart, each one of them has a" 6823
"heart, flesh of her" 2799
"heart, free to you with my" 1816
"heart, glad the" 2134
"heart, heavy" 2493
"heart, her pierced" 45
"heart, his pounding" 1648
"heart, in good" 3887
"heart, limping" 8637
"heart, mending a broken" 7461
"heart, my" 2541, 9279, 10172
"heart, no longer had the" 7591
"heart, promptly exchanged his" 6558
"heart, reappraised the recalcitrant" 163
"heart, rheumatic" 2336
"heart, sick at" 7359
"heart, Stephen Cooper's" 3412
"heart, sunshine in the" 2511
"heart, sword in her" 969
"heart, with a light" 6560
"heart, you broke my" 397
"heart and a soul, she had a" 408
"heart and clock, strung between" 5624
"heart attack" 159, 3958, 8030
"heart attack, died of a" 754
"heart attack was strange" 144
"heart bounced on the firm spurt of his terror, perhaps his" 3699
"heart can be, dearly touched a" 5650
"heart exhausted by various afflictions" 2287
"heart for it, neither of them had the" 9731
"heart, heavy, make her" 2504
"heart in Chicago" 6829
"heart is broken" 4223
"heart is not easily swayed, God's" 2645
"heart of New England" 7657
"heart of the continent" 4089
"heart of the setting sun" 10701
"heart pounding, his" 10288
"heart pounding in sweet expectation" 1711
"heart suddenly hammers with recognition" 7084
"heart the size of a Volkswagen" 3618

"heart thudding, her own" 8338
"heart thumping" 10301
"heart was beating faster than usual" 10172
"heart was full of dreams" 258
"heart was high" 2958
"heart was singularly heavy" 3698
"heartbeats, like a million" 8814
"heartbeats, sensitive to his own" 5619
"heartbreak, without" 6436
"hearth, logs burning in the" 7519
"hearth, nearer the" 9063
"hearth, sat by the" 2704
"heartland" 5592
"heartland, American" 278
Hearts 163, 2645, 3618, 6829, 8338
"hearts, Belgian" 3119
"hearts, our poor" 5559
"hearts, people's" 395
"hearts, untamed" 8993
"hearts away, giving their" 5542
"hearts big enough to kill them" 3618
"heart's most urgent commands" 9279
"hearts of the young bloods" 3965
"hearts of the youth, wreck the" 7709
Heat, The 7699
Heat 92, 327, 900, 1115, 1556, 1694, 2139, 2144, 2151, 2216, 3782, 3806, 3907, 3956, 5068, 5143, 5629, 5704, 7275, 7308, 7637, 7776, 8101, 8330, 9083, 9127, 9359, 9766, 10236, 10264, 10337, 10457, 10597, 10701, 10745
"heat, beneath a misty glimmering" 2754
"heat, burden of the" 7308
"heat, burning afternoon" 1280
"heat, continued" 4384
"heat, daylong" 5068
"heat, dry" 3904
"heat, gathering white" 8930
"heat, heavy" 4370
"heat, in the" 7275
"heat, in the sunless" 3645
"heat, July" 8330
"heat, knew it was only the" 9766
"heat, lap up the" 5096
"heat, late June" 4374
"heat, mid-day" 1694
"heat, midday" 4417
"heat, Nebraska" 4377
"heat, prickly" 4375
"heat, rivers of" 4423
"heat, savage bottomlands" 4399
"heat, send up some" 4640
"heat, simply because of the August" 7076
"heat, stifling clammy" 5292
"heat, sullen noonday" 3907
"heat, summer" 8893

"heat, the" 10336
"heat, tortured his eyebrows in the" 189
"heat and brightness, withering away of" 2119
"heat and dust have become intolerable" 9116
"heat blazed, maddening" 4382
"heat closing in, I can feel the" 3050
"heat doesn't ease when the sun goes down" 4407
"heat ennobled by devotion" 5674
"heat had been barely supportable" 10701
"heat had scarcely abated" 4368
"heat has been, how great the" 4369
"heat haze, in the" 730
"heat in September in Los Angeles" 4402
"heat increased steadily" 4391
"heat jabbed its claw into Ralph's sweaty neck" 4375
"heat lay quivering over the flat floor of the valley" 4374
"heat of a spacious August noon" 10053
"heat of an intense fire, the sustained" 92
"heat of his home fire" 5603
"heat of summer, in the" 327
"heat of that summer's day" 4385
"heat of the Arizona day was gone" 10069
"heat of the day, the brittle" 5704
"heat of the day before, the" 5143
"heat of the hearth, despite the" 1556
"heat on his face, feel its" 2778
"heat remained" 4386
"heat rises shimmering from the highways and sidewalks" 9616
"heat running like warm water" 10139
"heat that lay on Kentucky, sultry" 7637
"heat was almost insupportable, the heavy" 4370
"heat was coming now" 10457
"heat was locked into the streets" 1115
"heat was something Ruth Reed could hold in her mouth" 4419
"heat wave, the first day of a" 4389
"heat waves, quivering iridescence of" 9127
"heat which seemed to bounce off the sand and quiver" 5629
"heater, car" 10713
"heath, broad" 5305
"Heath, Egdon" 2189
"Heath, Hampstead" 4070, 5928, 8587
"Heath, Putney" 5928
"Heath Extension" 4070

"heathen, Christian methods . . . are better than" 7502
"heathen, married a" 6728
"heather" 1764
"heather, stalks of" 5305
"Heathrow" 232, 883, 890
"heating, central" 10214
"heave of the bluff" 7316
"heave out his bowels" 10521
"heave-ho from me, without the least" 5687
Heaven 4853
Heaven 2338, 2644, 3387, 7504, 7541, 9186
"Heaven, as though in self-defence against" 1356
"heaven, Central European" 223
"heaven, eyes to" 3868
"Heaven, from" 9186
"heaven, gone to" 8172
"heaven, halls of" 2644
"heaven, hushed" 8395
"heaven, in" 2623
"Heaven, praised be" 694
"heaven, revelations of" 2336
"Heaven, sinned against" 1806
"Heaven, spurned by" 5165
"heaven, third" 7504
"Heaven, we were all going direct to" 3377
"Heaven, winds of" 55
"Heaven Exists" 7541
"Heaven knows" 616
"heaven nor hell, there's neither" 2338
"heaven of precious stones" 7504
"heaven on earth, as close to" 10620
"heaven was closer to earth" 3387
"heavenly chorister" 6212
"Heavenly Father off in a corner, find the" 2625
"heavens, above the twelve" 2635
"heavens, tumbling from the" 2427
"Heavens, wish to" 5419
"heavens, wring from the dumb" 7506
"heaven's blue, cut out sharply on" 5144
"heavenward" 1305
"heaving out of the muddy pond" 5689
"heavy and oppressive" 177
"heavy enough to break someone's toes if he fell off the dresser" 8944
"heavy heart" 2493
"heavy of coat" 412
"heavy to hold, getting too" 900
"heavy-footed" 10821
Hebe 1946
"Hebrew" 9709
"Hebrew colleges" 7505
"Hebrew year 5716" 6514
Hector 5841, 8557
Hector, Old 2090
"hedge, blossoming" 9670

"hedge of thorn, behind a sparse" 414
"hedge-cutter" 9113
Hedgehog 10953
"hedgerows" 2944
"hedgerows were bright with flowers" 10587
"hedgerows were green" 3396
"hedges of scented whitethorn" 9671
"hedgings, eucalypt" 5180
"hee hee hee" 8861
"heed, paid no" 3357
"heed, some to" 7225
"heeding my warning, never" 10546
"heedless as the others" 4606
"heel caught as I stepped off the train" 1723
"heels, at his" 994, 7290
"heels, dug in my" 6136
"heels, high red" 10445
"heels, right on my" 10423
"heels, rocked back on his" 1980
"heels, taken to her" 4538
"heels drummed a quick descending tattoo" 10371
"heels rather deeper in the sand" 1588
Heeralal 4739
"hee-yah!" 5620
"hefty, dark and" 8217
Heidi 6051
"height, from this" 7660
"height, he was of medium" 5921
"height of his career, when he was at the" 3083
"height of the racing-season" 8912
"Heights, Babbington" 9366
"heights and distances, vasty" 7754
"Heil Hitler!" 10986
"Heil New Year!" 10986
"heir, he wanted an" 3596
"heir, provide an" 7071
"heir, sole surviving male" 3550
"heir of Padella" 1902
"heir of the Earl of Glenthorn" 3356
"heir-looms of aristocratic origin" 358
Heirs 3550, 3596, 3660, 7071
Held, Truman 3007
"held an infant in the crook of her right arm" 2919
"held back" 705
"held in playful hurt . . . against the skin" 6301
"held it in his left palm weightlessly" 8918
"held the sewing needle under hot running water" 8760
"held up at the dock gates" 59
Helen 1203, 1792, 1906, 2076, 3285, 9038, 9856
Helen, Aunt 10676
Helen of the High Wire 817
Helen of Troy 817
Helena 3268, 5431, 7011

"Helford river" 7661
Helianos 3500
"helianthus, species of the" 10899
"helicopter, hire a Fly-By-Nite" 233
"helicopter, old Westland" 2847
"helicopter, patrol" 236
"helicopter had gone, when the" 6074
Helicopters 209, 230, 233, 236, 2847, 5375, 6074
"helicopters, clumsy-looking" 209
"helicopters, why I hate" 5375
Heliokleia, Queen 6487
Hell 2338, 2492, 5029, 9315, 9470
"Hell" 2721
"hell" 9470
"hell, a little corner of" 4049
"hell, an eternal" 2492
"hell, damn it to" 1060
"hell, heaven nor" 2338
"hell, I had just been through" 4324
"hell, I'll be go to" 9315
"hell, sheer" 1984
"hell, the harrowing of" 609
"hell, the one out of" 4810
"Hell, the very pasture of" 6567
"hell, there is a" 2492
"hell, what the" 10488, 10563
"hell, where the" 2571
"hell, who in the" 4869
"hell, who the" 3750
"hell and ruin are inevitably brought on innocent people" 5427
"hell has been breaking loose around here" 6510
"hell is going on, what the" 6011
"Hell no!" 1516
"hell of a blighted heart" 2492
"hell of a sense of timing" 2685
"hell of a year, it's been a" 10989
"hell of it, for nothing but the" 744
"hell out of him, scared the" 34
"Hell Row" 6269
"hell they like, what the" 2589
"hell which now faces us, surely this is" 5029
"hell with jazz, to" 6223
"Hellene, a" 7717
"hello, even when he said" 10027
"hello darling" 5670
"hello diary" 4829
"hello ship" 8108
"hello to the girl, said" 6897
"Hell's Kitchen" 6274
"helm, put down the" 8167
"helmets they were all so proud of and never seemed to camouflage" 8659
"help dear Annie, a woman to" 5782
"help her, photographs to" 6793
"help her with the suitcases, wouldn't let me" 1716
"help it, I cannot" 488
"help me, so" 9345
"help me, wishes sincerely to" 1167

"help musicians' widows" 6242
"help, the" 2118
"help, without no extra" 1686
"help things much, it didn't really" 48
"help to him, I was the only person who might have been of" 5089
"help you, psycho-analysis would" 7167
"helped him on his way, I sometimes felt I had" 6668
"helped me to write this book" 5446
"helping them" 10917
"helping Uncle Benny fish" 4687
"helpless, silent and" 9387
"helpless and ridiculous" 9790
"helplessly, he watched" 2773
"helplessness, pride of" 3356
"help-wanted section" 6750
"Helsinki" 5042
"Helstonleigh Cathedral" 645
"Helvellyn" 5070
"Helvellyn, vast precipitous slope of" 7190
"Helwan" 155
"Hemingford" 7099
Hemingway, Ernest 5455
"hemisphere, in that" 7655
"hemisphere, northern" 10611
"hemlock" 3179
"hemlock, leaves of the" 9756
"hemmed in by towels" 10818
"hemorrhage, cerebral" 194
"hemp, sowers of" 3639
"hen-houses, locked the" 2895
Henderson 4545
Hendrick 4076
Hendrick, Graham 1988
Hendrik, Captain 4091
Hengist 8215
Henley, Edward Milton 808
Henna 9808
Hennington, Senator Gilbert 7005
Henri 3004
Henrietta 2954
Henrietta, Great-Aunt 2312
Henry 31, 166, 1701, 3821, 4130, 4845, 4954, 5191, 5380, 7716, 10295
Henry, Anne 7183
Henry, Commander Victor 3315
Henry, King 1691
Henry, Nina 562
Henry, Sir 9561
Henry the Eighth 948
Henry VII, King 10473
Henry the Sixth 4554
"hens, the" 3604
"hens themselves yearned toward her" 10955
Henshawe, Myra 5797
"herald, chief" 363
"herald a glorious day" 2204
"heralded the break of day" 9067
"heralded the summons" 3444

"heralds, the" 7805
"heralds of the coming day, crimson-cloaked" 8393
Herb 4019
Herbert of Bosham 1691
Herberts, the 3059
"herbs and spices, unnamable" 8544
"Hercules, Pillars of" 4034
"herd, small and scattered" 415
"herd, rode a circuit around the" 7634
"herd, thirsty trail" 2215
"herd of Jerseys" 3646
"herd of that size and specifications" 3644
Herds 415, 420, 2215, 3644, 3646
"herds of cattle" 3604
"here, bring him back" 1718
"here, but I'm" 7121
"here, how I got" 1707
"here, I was" 7067
"here, now he was" 1639
"here, now that I am" 10065
"here, someone's" 9980
"here, to get" 6083
"here, you're not" 9922
"here and now, in the" 9008
"here and there" 3981, 10494
"here in Paris" 3222
"here it is" 10904
"here no longer, shortly will be" 2375
"here she was" 9959
"here they are" 2855
"here we are" 9598
Heredity 346, 357, 365, 4138, 4358, 4444, 5237, 7073, 7917, 8495, 9186, 9704, 10895
"Hereford" 1486, 7268
"Hereford, the Caswells of" 3624
"Hereford, train that trundled west from" 8457
"heretic, he was probably a" 9302
Heriot 10164
Heriot, Eliza 4985
Heriot, Gina 3027
Heritage 958, 1502, 8688
"heritage, we have a bitter" 4445
Herkimer, Miss Elsie 6114
Herman, Mr. 8467
Hermann, Leo 9956
Hermione 9559
"Hermitage, the" 6574
"Hermitage, The" 847
"Hermosillo, all the way north from" 229
Herncastle, John 6035
"herniation of the diaphragm" 7514
Hero, Alexander 10181
"hero, *Bildungsroman*" 5837
"hero, brazen image of a sham" 4459
"hero, eponymous" 4473
"hero, its" 5482
"hero, our" 7876

"hero, popular" 4470
"hero, some cocked-hat Revolutionary War" 8940
"hero, the unequaled" 4464
"hero came into the kitchen" 4472
"hero everyone thought I was" 4468
"hero in the making" 4471
"hero in the world, the greatest" 3376
"hero of a series of books" 4473
"hero of American outdoor history" 4464
"hero of my life, I had not yet become the" 3393
"hero of my own life" 4452
"hero of the people, he was to be a" 4466
"hero of this tale" 8886
"hero of this tale, the heretofore unnoticed" 7293
"hero of this tale, who shall be the" 4453
"hero out of him, made a" 4463
"hero whose adventures we propose to record" 6603
Herod Agrippa 7797
Heroes 3393, 4452, 4453, 4454, 4455, 4456, 4457, 4458, 4459, 4460, 4463, 4464, 4465, 4466, 4467, 4468, 4469, 4470, 4471, 4472, 4473, 4518, 5482, 5837, 7293, 7010, 8940, 8943
"heroes, obscure" 4454
"heroes, our" 8705
"Heroes Day" 4518
"heroes likewise in the lowland and in the fen" 4455
"heroes of old colonial wars" 4467
"heroic and satisfied, I felt" 9263
"heroic deeds of highlanders" 4455
"heroic stature" 1391
"heroine, born an" 4451
"heroine, our" 4720
"heroine of it" 4461
"heroine of this fiction" 6605
"heroism of countless generations" 6255
"heron, great blue" 4021
"herons in the swamp, cry of" 5121
Herries 8548
Herries, Nicholas 7617
Herring, Reginald (Kipper) 3839
Herriton, Mrs. 3993
"Hershey bar, a melted" 8725
"Herts, the county of" 3698
Hervey, Lord 715
Herzl, Theodor 9040
Herzog, Moses 4939
"hesitantly, moved" 7237
"hesitate to put down some of the details" 5496
"hesitate to record an episode" 2734
"hesitated, never" 10921
"hesitated, she" 4212

"hesitated in the doorway of the adobe" 8790

"hesitated sullenly, summer" 4384

"hesitating before the closed front door" 2930

"hesitation" 5238

"hesitation, no" 9537

"hesitation, puzzled" 5408

"hesitation, without" 4244

Hesketh, Mrs. 9866

Hester 4127, 4155, 10818

"heyday of the theatre" 9382

Hezron, Uncle 3655

"hi teach" 4215

Hibbert, Mr. 9845

"hibernated, my father" 6671

"hic jacet" 168

"hic jacet" 7584

"hid out during the Civil War" 7792

"hidden by tinted European eye-glasses" 6900

"hidden from passing ships" 5031

"hidden in a room" 4477

"hidden in the heart of the mountains" 7950

"hidden in the tree" 9680

"hidden in the yet unleafed sassafras clump" 10940

"hide, can a human being" 4479

"hide now, I may have to" 4484

"hide-and-seek, used to play" 329

"hide-and-seek inside his stomach" 2901

"hide-and-seek with words and memories" 116

"hideaway, arrived at his" 5837

"hideous, unequivocally" 9229

"hideous house" 3123

"hideously, shrilled" 10165

Hiding 8899

"hiding, always" 4487

"hiding, emerged from" 4481

"hiding everything I had ever known" 7383

"hiding from the great blue heron" 4021

"hiding in the alleys with bums" 2906

"hiding in the hills" 4483

"hiding in the ladies' room" 4480

"hiding in uniforms of Yankee blue" 4486

"hiding it, as if security or long grass were" 9236

"hiding place, black perpetual" 9285

"hiding-place" 4684

"hi-fi console" 34

"high, hundreds of miles" 9585

"high, seven thousand feet" 1681

"high, several hundred feet" 5138

"High, Shrubsole" 4002

"high, ten inches" 2835

"high, two hundred feet" 5154

"high above the Plain" 7810

"high above the plains and the sea" 9745

"high and airy" 3122

"high and low and far and wide" 2607

"High and Mighty" 7805

"high connection" 6611

"high I've ever seen, the best" 2437

"high in the Andes Mountains" 6259

"high keyed" 5408

"high man and a hard one, he was a" 5987

"High Mightiness, her" 360

"high noon" 7339

"High School, John Marshall Junior" 7884

"High School, Martin Luther King" 7902

"high school, until he was in" 8228

"high society" 2118

"high summer" 2236

"High Tower" 5233

"high time" 5535

"highest company" 238

"Highland tour" 9513

"Highlanders, bayonets of the" 10509

"highlanders, heroic deeds of" 4455

"Highlands, the" 1171

"Highlands of Scotland" 10391

"Highness, his Serene" 360

"highroad between Los Angeles . . . and Las Vegas" 9180

"highroad . . . cuts through the mountains and across the desert" 9180

"high-stooled in his office" 4069

Hightower, Roberta 7741

"highway, along the" 1080

"highway, broad federal" 2966

"highway, country" 25

"Highway, Enfield" 8587

"highway, great" 9115, 9126

"highway, great north-south" 9145

"highway, it is a good" 9143

"highway, King's" 9131

"highway, lake-edging" 10885

"highway, long gentle curve in the" 9183

"highway, macadam" 2978

"Highway, Montauk" 9199

"highway, New Jersey" 9555

"highway, on the" 745

"highway, open" 2945

"highway, peninsular" 1778

"highway, pocked narrow" 9577

"highway, side of the" 7284

"Highway, South Dixie" 2997

"highway, still on the" 9590

"Highway, the" 9199

"highway, this very" 9113

"highway, upon a broad" 7608

"highway along the borders of a park" 6558

"highway ascended rapidly" 9204

"highway between Incline and South Tahoe" 8729

"Highway 82" 4429

"highway entering Salt Lake City" 9181

"Highway 58" 9143

"highway from Yedo" 9188

"highway in the heart of Akbar's Mogul Empire" 9185

"highway is called by some Route 27" 9199

"Highway 95" 9192

"Highway reaches the Sioux River" 9140

"Highway 70, U.S." 9026

"highway southwest of Milwaukee" 3023

"highway straight and smooth" 7608

"highway to compare with this, I have seen no" 9185

"Highway to Europe" 9173

"highway to the east" 5944

"highways, built the" 7273

"highways, crumbling" 6381

"highways, September's" 7327

"highways, these screaming" 2656

"highways are always too busily stirring" 9119

Hignett, Mrs. Horace 5309

"hiking" 2906

"hilarity, uncontrollable" 652

Hilbery, Katharine 9350

Hilda 142, 475, 717, 9998

Hildon 8755

"hill, barely wooded and sparsely settled" 3159

"Hill, Beacon" 790, 6678

"hill, bottom of the" 7619

"hill, brow of the" 7131

"Hill, Chipping" 3122

"hill, cone-shaped" 4587

"hill, corner of a" 7279

"hill, crest of the" 2989, 7624

"Hill, Croom's" 6568

"hill, crown of a small" 7640

"Hill, Cypress" 6756

"Hill, Duncton" 7326

"Hill, Fenner" 5088

"hill, foot of the green" 8327

"hill, forested" 3152

"hill, from the top of the" 9141

"Hill, Grou'nut" 9136

"Hill, Haldeman's" 9771

"Hill, Hart's" 9561

"hill, I went out on to the" 374

"Hill, Lindifferon" 10946

"Hill, Lone Tree" 786

"hill, low" 3421

"Hill, Needle" 214

"hill, old soaring cathedral of a" 9168

"hill, on the crest of the" 1764

"hill, on top of a" 1473

"hill, on top of the" 5590

"hill, over the" 7689
"Hill, Pincian" 9559
"Hill, Pleasant" 8512
"hill, red" 6062
"Hill, Rolling Rock" 9136
"Hill, Schultz" 4532
"hill, sped on up the" 7846
"hill, squats on the" 4618
"hill, sweet-smelling" 10021
"Hill, the" 2967
"Hill, Tonteur's" 10343
"hill, top of a" 3112
"hill, top of the" 3688, 8652
"Hill, Tug" 9128
"hill, up the" 9138
"hill above the road" 10093
"hill brow" 6646
"hill by the Mississippi" 4140
"hill falling sharply down to the
   sea" 1173
"hill fell away to the right" 1639
"hill of North Berwick Law" 4587
"Hill of the Wolves" 9740
"hill on which I stood" 29
"hill should have such a gleaming
   pinnacle, every" 1470
"hill that lends its name to the
   town of Bukit Kallang" 3152
"hill that overlooks the town" 954
"Hill Town North Carolina" 3097
Hillary, David 2905
Hilliard, Mrs. Eudora 2567
Hilliard, Philip 5806
Hilliot, Dana 4729
"hillock, diminutive" 1018
"hillock, sandy" 9841
"hillocks, sand" 6053
"hillocks and vales" 4486
"Hillport" 5898
Hills 374, 724, 1470, 1473, 2199,
   3112, 3152, 3191, 3665, 3691,
   4084, 4483, 4618, 5139, 5144,
   5147, 5153, 5163, 5167, 5168,
   6056, 6062, 8258, 8440, 8681
"hills, all the world was" 6062
"hills, bare" 5168
"Hills, Berkshire" 2258
"hills, Bethel" 7523
"Hills, Beverly" 4240, 5833
"Hills, Black" 4610
"hills, blackjack" 789
"hills, brisk little" 2950
"hills, chalk" 9738
"hills, clay" 5144
"hills, dark and brooding" 5167
"hills, dark New England" 2224
"hills, darkening" 10539
"hills, deep in the bosom of the"
   5886
"hills, desert-colored California"
   5147
"hills, distant" 5071
"hills, everyone in the" 8514
"hills, gentle" 9239
"hills, hazy" 6784

"Hills, Helderberg" 7618
"hills, hiding in the" 4483
"hills, high" 5139
"hills, highest" 9515
"hills, little" 6249
"Hills, Malvern" 5067
"Hills, Mictlán" 4893
"Hills, Mission" 4060
"hills, muffled winter" 8596
"hills, mystical" 2631
"hills, New Hampshire" 7668
"Hills, Nichols" 2009
"Hills, Pentland" 9741
"Hills, Quantock" 9815
"Hills, Radford" 1908
"Hills, Reservoir" 5959
"hills, rolling green" 5754
"hills, round-backed" 2949
"hills, rounded" 6056
"Hills, Sabine" 1494
"Hills, San Benito" 2199
"hills, scattered little flat-topped"
   7632
"hills, seven" 10608
"hills, sides of the distant hazy"
   4374
"hills, steep green" 5072
"Hills, Stonehurst" 6277
"hills, sunny" 3074
"hills, Surrey" 3076
"hills, tangle of wild red" 6062
"hills, the" 10577
"hills, three nameless" 8681
"hills, tiger-colored" 9995
"hills, Virginia" 3665
"hills, wooded" 3359
"hills above Cincinnati, the
   wooded" 7665
"hills and dales, surface is a succession of" 4027
"hills and fields, a long sweep of"
   8283
"hills and the sea, between the" 665
"hills and valleys, beautiful" 3893
"hills begin to lift and spy into the
   heart of black mountains" 9874
"hills behind him" 8736
"[hills] grew greener each minute"
   5168
"hills grow less gentle" 5151
"hills of Moab" 2237
"hills of northern Scotland, the remote" 3570
"hills of the Whale Back, the outlying" 32
"hills of Umbria, the rolling" 1473
"hills of Walden Valley" 10623
"hills of western Catawba" 10042
"hills rose sharply above a rolling
   terrain" 7632
"hills . . . rose up behind it toward
   the sky" 5147
"hills that are like rocks planted in
   green water" 724
"hills that hemmed the sea" 6784

"hills that shut in Altamont" 1221
"Hillsboro" 653
"Hillsborough, village of" 3418,
   9152
"Hillsborough and its outlying suburbs" 1005
"Hillston North Carolina" 3448
"hilltop, isolated" 9966
"hilltop, sat on the" 9687
"hilltop, visible from the" 4482
"Hilton, Athens" 2995
"Himalayan mountains" 6066
"Himalayas" 810
Himmelhoch, Samuel 2553
"himself, he was" 6427
"Himself, like" 5697
"himself, one was by" 10946
"himself, out of" 2635
"himself and one other, just"
   6078
Hind 8186
"hind, that fair white" 7604
"hinder American tourists" 9636
"Hindi in the family, there was
   some" 365
"Hindoostanee, learn" 3289
"Hinds' Feet on High Places" 9020
Hindsight 10760
"hindsight, he had the wisdom of"
   10760
"Hindu town" 5822
"Hindustani, I think in" 5446
Hines, Mrs. 9943
Hingham, Judith 9416
"hinted at in a variety of codices"
   9053
"hints, beginning to send out" 6013
"hip hole and hupmobile" 10007
"hippogriff, a rearing stone" 3589
Hipponicus 5738
"hippopotamus, stalking a" 1610
"hippos, the" 472
"hips, blue jeans low on her" 2875
"hips, shivering" 7945
"hire a licensed one" 1319
"hired fresh out of the navy" 6471
"hired girl" 3094, 3328
"hired in Spain" 1098
"hired to conduct him, pony-
   carriage was" 6558
"Hiroshima, like that bomb at"
   7990
"His Excellency" 247
"His Majesty's armed forces" 8580
"His Majesty's ships and vessels"
   8102
"Hispaniola" 3766
"hissed Cleo" 10358
"hisses, with" 7989
"hissing fury" 7939
"hissing sound" 8810
"historian, philosophic" 4497
"historian, self-styled" 4503
"historian, that elegant accurate
   and interesting" 356

"historian who ventures to record marvels" 3456

"historians must of necessity be subject to mistakes" 4490

"historic old Kiddemaster Hall" 6577

"historical value, ultimate" 2532

"histories contain instruction, all true" 4491

History 270, 356, 694, 698, 920, 2538, 3344, 3456, 3497, 3573, 3670, 4030, 4046, 4464, 4603, 4636, 5097, 5307, 5400, 5426, 5435, 5451, 5492, 5530, 5567, 6260, 6789, 7810, 7812, 8663, 9186, 10476, 10571

"history" 4501, 4510, 5044

"history, a little of their" 5435

"history, American outdoor" 4464

"history, begin this" 3670

"history, circumstances of her" 3301

"history, curving wall of" 4507

"history, entrance into" 971

"history, epoch of" 4496

"history, famous period of" 3376

"history, forces of" 4504

"history, he could read his own" 4439

"history, human" 274

"history, illuminating the dispassionate march of" 5307

"history, in" 6141

"history, legends of" 6246

"History, my" 5552

"history, my own" 698

"history, my secret" 5451

"history, naval" 4511

"history, never rose sufficiently above" 6647

"history, our" 10571

"history, planets without" 6792

"history, professor of" 6022

"History, Professor of" 2468

"history, quintessence of" 4489

"history, rich in" 8112

"history, subject of the following" 1964

"history, this personal" 2543

"history, this unimportant" 2824

"history, time caught up with" 5097

"history, world" 7368

"history, write a" 4493

"history and continuity, sense of" 2681

"history consists of endings" 3344

"history has a habit of meandering" 4500

"history has been recorded, something of their" 4796

"history has granted him the justice of perspective" 270

"history is written, this" 4494

"history of civilization" 7670

"History of Human Civilization" 10500

"history of Mexico" 4505

"History of my Life" 5492

"History of my own Life" 6033

"History of New Hampshire" 356

"history of our future, coyly holds the" 9186

"history of Rasselas prince of Abissinia" 4603

"history of the literary weekly Belles Lettres" 5530

"history of the Price family, distinguished and ancient" 3573

"history of the public career" 5557

"history of the remarkable Zinn family" 6577

"history of the United States" 4030

"history of the world" 4046, 4457

"history of the world, I'm writing a" 4508

"history of their nation" 1296

"history to him" 4636

"history's senseless happenstance" 7812

"hit, an immediate" 915

"hit, Henry got" 31

"hit, they couldn't" 8919

"hit Dan, you sha'n't" 7553

"hit hard down the line" 160

"hit him before he could get the gun up" 9702

"hit the Loman farm" 6179

"hitch, wedding went without a" 10652

"hitch-hikers joined Thurs, other" 9555

Hitchhiking 9554, 9555, 9584, 9649, 10367

Hitchings, Wilson 1021

Hitler 9040, 10514, 10986

"Hitler, Heil" 10986

"Hitler and the birdcage" 9040

"hits the brakes" 3034

"hitting, I could see them" 9840

"hitting the pike in such a position and condition" 2374

"Hiva Oa" 6933

"ho ho ho" 8861

"hoarded fallen chestnuts" 10534

Hobart, Bob 6208

"Hobart, South" 1310

Hobbes, Paul 7968

"hobbit" 3106

"Hobbits" 5435

"hobble about the street" 5888

"hobbles, pony broke its" 433

Hobbs, Roy 7474

"hobby-horse" 9626

"hobgoblins, trolls and" 5588

"Hoboken pier, lay at her" 8074

"Hochdramatische, the greatest" 5641

"hockey field" 9672

"hockey game" 7204

"hockshop" 2760

Hodge 6161

Hodges 1864

Hoffmans, the 7874

"hog, fat as a" 5908

Hogan, Biddy 2866

Hogg 2589

Hogganbeck, Boon 5931

"hogs, the" 6136

"Hohenzollern town" 4017

Holbein, Madame 9665

"Holborn was noisy murky and sloppy" 7285

"hold back, you cannot" 602

"hold back hot words" 383

"hold tight young America" 10007

"hold to it, so I" 10091

Holder 4847

"holding hands in the cold" 2677

"holding Henry Adams around the neck" 6589

"holding her breast" 2529

"holding her hand tightly with both of his" 4599

"holding in her hand" 2348

"holding it at arm's length upside down" 8261

"holding one end of a long rope" 8695

"holding the handlebars" 977

"holding up a gas station" 2869

"holdings, New York" 9567

"hole!" 931

"Hole, Beastly Silly Wheeze of a" 931

"hole, gopher" 968

"hole, quiet little" 3124

"hole, the sixth" 8927

"hole, when I get out of this" 1167

"hole in the ground" 3106

"Hole-in-the-Hills, the" 7853

Holgate, Edmund K. 3194

"Holguín Cuba" 5841

Holiday, Sebastian 9296

"holiday, first day of his" 10162

"holiday, his annual three weeks" 9724

"holiday, in urgent need of a" 932

"holiday, it was a" 954

"holiday, one Whitsun" 6568

"holiday, people on" 4517

"holiday, pleasing consciousness of" 6560

"holiday, the sense of" 5024

"holiday, went on" 3398

"holiday in the garb of peace" 8642

"holiday time" 4525

"holiday-making, the fashion of summer" 1344

Holidays 954, 1061, 1158, 2064, 2131, 2504, 2517, 2661, 2887, 2910, 2971, 3017, 3041, 3350, 3496, 3576, 3680, 3837, 3886, 4131, 4568, 4600, 6568, 8613, 8618, 8988, 10237, 10241, 10569, 10994

"holidays, the" 4530

"holidays, where I used to come as a child for" 6911
"holidays began at 5 a.m., his" 10241
Holland, Eileen 8249
Holland, Henry Lyulph 102
"Holland" 120, 3396, 10466
"Holland, a fragment of" 1851
"Holland, emigrated from" 6120
"Holland, thy servants the people of" 8643
"Holland Tunnel" 10912
Hollander, Margaret 2867
"holler below, in the" 3223
Holley, Sam 7620
Holliday, Hiram 4731
Holliday, Libby 6172
Hollis, Barclay 10814
Hollis, Hero Athena 10814
Hollister, Felix 1603
"Holloman Connecticut" 10742
"hollow, little" 7652
"Hollow, Lynde's" 7652
"hollow, ragged lonesome" 3458
"hollow, the" 9098
"hollow containing people staring at a blank wall" 220
Holloway, Charlie 10413
"Holloway" 3073
"holly berries, there aren't many" 9681
Holly 1103, 1701
"Hollywood" 1023, 1687, 3126, 6172, 6467, 7050
"Hollywood, North" 7900
Holman, Jake 8108
Holmes, Lieutenant Commander Peter 10161
Holmes, Mr. 5912
Holmes, Mr. Sherlock 3818
Holmes, Sherlock 2037, 3047, 5800
Holt, Cecilia 5560
"Holt" 1768
Holt brothers 2321
"holy days" 1503
"Holy Father" 7548
"Holy Ghost" 1496
"Holy Ghost of this later day" 5086
"Holy God" 7160
"Holy Land" 8112
"holy mountain Parnassus" 1439
"Holy of Holies" 2626
"Holy Ones" 2632
"holy people" 9062
"Holy Roller country, you've reached the " 8303
"Holy Roman Catholic Church" 7532
"Holy Roman Empire" 1444
"Holy Sepulchre" 8646
"Holy Terror, it's a" 540
"Holy Week" 4527
"Holy Writ" 1691
"Holyhead mail" 10108

"Holywell" 10335
"hombre" 7132
Homburg, Julia 597
"Homburg" 4630, 5279
Home 854, 3001, 4467, 4572, 4573, 5015, 5119, 5359, 7220, 7847, 7854, 7925, 9096, 9733, 10318
"home, a thousand miles from" 6166
"home, anyone at" 9933
"home, at" 6881, 10226
"home, at his" 5842
"home, broken into his" 9850
"home, came" 4592, 7832
"home, came from a rich" 6631
"home, came straight" 3943
"home, children's" 8245
"home, coasting" 7628
"home, comfortable" 5555
"home, coming" 4565
"home, decide where to put their" 3219
"home, decided to go straight" 6630
"home, detains her at" 9337
"home, driving" 3019
"home, ever since she had come" 3473
"home, expected" 4569
"home, far from" 4467
"home, feel at" 3202
"home, flying" 7854
"home, foster" 997
"home, go" 854
"home, going" 4600, 9175
"home, grandparents' summer" 3430
"home, he feels he is" 3001
"home, he flew" 4575
"home, he was going" 7847
"home, heading" 9601
"home, her" 2702, 3825
"home, her husband was coming" 4596
"home, her sister's Commonwealth Avenue" 9875
"home, his" 6140
"home, his distant northern" 10329
"home, his first evening" 8013
"home, his little" 401
"home, hurrying" 6639
"home, I arrived" 4597
"home, I came" 4558, 4594
"home, I had to come" 4574
"home, I left" 3324
"home, I return" 2128
"home, I was just going" 4579
"home, I'd think I'd never left" 10318
"home, leave" 4169
"home, left" 2441
"home, left his" 1758
"home, left their old" 6101
"home, lived in a fine" 3239
"home, lost her way" 4538
"home, love" 5015

"home, marched" 10483
"home, my" 7459
"home, my last trip" 4585
"home, my own" 3121, 9976
"home, never did leave" 5947
"home, no" 7041
"home, nursing" 549
"home, on his way" 4556
"home, on the verge of leaving" 5754
"home, on the way" 3040
"Home, Rest" 3208
"home, return" 4555, 4559
"home, returned" 4590
"home, send Sister" 1158
"home, sent from her" 4186
"home, she didn't come" 10052
"home, so far away from" 9520
"home, stately" 6577
"home, take her" 10092
"home, ten years getting" 4463
"Home, the" 1158
"home, the motor-drive" 2953
"home, the way" 2588
"home, their" 4602, 7220
"home, their first" 9544
"home, thinking of going" 4537
"home, took him until the following Monday to get" 4586
"home, uncles began to come" 1277
"home, walked" 4571
"home, welcome" 8705
"home, welcome us" 6008
"home, went" 1784
"home, when I go" 9162
"home, when I left" 1568
"home, when she comes" 10956
"home after five o'clock" 9859
"home again, but never" 9052
"home again, to come" 4573
"home again, you can never go" 4541
"home and destination" 9615
"home for a brief while" 9733
"home for Christmas" 1158
"home for Christmas, going" 4568
"home for Sunday dinners, coming" 3883
"home for the Friday evening" 4576
"Home for the Incurables" 9166
"home from her boarding-school" 6291
"home from school, on the way" 10831
"home from the convent" 7709
"home in Beverly Hills" 5833
"home in Mount Hebron New York" 8202
"home is a house in Warwickshire" 4574
"home is where you go for Christmas" 4552
"home manufacture" 8453
"home movie" 1331
"home of an old man" 3207

"home of Mrs. Sarah Pitkin" 3104
"home of Rogers 'The Rajah'
 Hornsby" 4546
"home of three generations at once"
 3071
"home on the train, all the way"
 4579
"home run, sixty-first" 2179
"home so soon, son coming" 4564
"home that has been provided" 4550
"home to Ocanara, going" 4563
"home to simple continuity, hadn't
 come" 4593
"home to the glacier-gnawed
 gorges" 4577
"home town, my" 5359
"home was half a house and half a
 fort" 3098
"home with my father, my last
 time at" 9950
Homecoming 1277, 1498, 1571,
 1708, 2072, 2089, 2128, 2467,
 2960, 3019, 3306, 3473, 4172,
 4463, 4541, 4542, 5249, 5528,
 6008, 6239, 6250, 6487, 6539,
 6624, 6639, 7832, 8013, 8705,
 9162, 10092, 10346, 10347, 10483
"homecoming" 4589, 4592
"homecoming, loneliness before a"
 4570
"home-coming of his dreams, it
 was not the" 4561
"homefield at Gardar" 3661
"homefield was nearly as large as
 the homefield at Gardar" 3661
"homefries, nice" 7575
"homeland, return to her" 4172
"homeless, the" 10416
"homely too, it was" 9669
"homely youth" 6515
"homemade miracles" 1429
"homeowner and husband" 7576
Homer 99, 509, 4463, 4474, 5431,
 7909, 8793, 9265
"Homer, *Iliad* of" 5431
"Homer, sung since the days of"
 7909
"Homer made a hero out of him"
 4463
Homes 3219, 3241, 9544
"homes, about" 3241
"Homes, Landis" 7231
"homes, model" 6575
"homes, neat vine-covered" 3070
"homes, purchased two" 3194
"homes for college men, one of
 those characteristic" 4307
"homes of the decorous ease" 9114
"home-scene, his" 3083
"homesick for, piously" 4086
"homestead" 7625
"homestead, he chose to" 7702
"homesteads" 4397
"hometown, name of his" 7194
"homeward, trudged" 10347

"homeward, walking" 10333
"homeward bound" 8118
"homeworld, my" 9698
"homicide squad" 19
"homicide they're used to seeing
 around here, the kind of" 6195
"homines tot sententiæ, quot" 5013
"homing theatregoers" 9381
"Homo Sapiens Europaeus" 7966
"homosexual, a human" 8021
Homosexuality 1802, 5301, 5949,
 6682, 8021
"homosexuality, Bentley's leaning
 toward" 6682
"Honan, the northern Chinese
 province of" 10584
"honest, I have to be" 8290
"honest with you, try to be" 9697
"honest work" 10555
Honesty 2015, 4490, 6634, 8290,
 9693, 9697
"honesty" 5997
"honesty, his peculiar" 2015
"honesty bordering at times on the
 severe" 7903
"honesty enough to tell the truth"
 4490
"honey might properly be a leading
 character" 3747
Honey 7465
"honey, sweetened with wild" 10196
"honeymoon, embarked on
 another" 9732
"honeymoon, on their" 9559
"honeymoon, their" 9736
"honeymoon, where we were to
 have spent the" 6913
"honeymoon in Bermuda of all
 places" 9732
Honeymoons 6913, 9559, 9732,
 9736
"honeysuckle, coral" 726
"honeysuckle, smelled of" 10180
"honeysuckle and hollyhocks" 3396
"honeysuckles" 1349
Honeywell, Judge Gamaliol Bland
 5736
Hong, Jimmy 4599
"Hong Kong is a pore" 1405
"honks, Tenny's mother" 4925
"Honolulu" 5712, 8192
Honor 4466, 9210
"honor, one's own fine sense of"
 4869
"honor, their sacred" 6995, 6997
"honor, you do me great" 707
"Honor, your" 5199
"honor of Rum Alley" 957
"honor the gray walls" 9210
"honorable mention" 356
"honored guests" 8886
Honoria 5740
"honour, old-fashioned" 1342
"honour his father and his mother"
 5699

"honour my pages" 5393
"honouring both France and yourselves" 4458
"honouring me, in" 4458
Hood 3053
Hood, Mr. 9871
"hood, came out from under the"
 9776
"hooded and silent, it sat" 3184
"hoodoo, I am" 4877
"hoof, right front" 440
"hoofs, sharp clip-clop of iron-
 shod" 8768
"hoofs, trim hind" 410
"hook, longshoreman's" 5814
"hookah, puffing on his" 6299
"hookers who work it know it as
 the stroll" 6274
"hooks, off the" 150
Hooper, Gilda 982
"hooter, train's" 7275
"hooves, small" 456
"hooves, steel-shod" 7638
"hooves, tattoo of a thousand" 8776
"hooves, wheels and" 9130
"hooves rattling dully against the
 dried and rutted mud" 7639
"hop it" 6157
Hope 2398, 3683, 5401, 6762,
 6954, 10083
"hope" 10083
"hope, clouds of" 6075
"hope, dared to" 6251
"hope, filled her with" 4606
"hope, green bindings expressed a"
 99
"hope, have some" 4609
"hope, in their despair men must"
 4607
"hope, it was the spring of" 3377
"hope, offer me no" 4605
"hope, phantoms of" 4603
"hope, Warlock's" 6954
"hope deferred, years of" 3683
"hope is but a synonym for illusion" 4612
"hope not, I" 6323
"hope of finding a passage" 2600
"hope of rest, there's no" 8488
"hope on earth" 2398
"hope still unrealised" 99
"hope that every one feels an interest in us" 6266
"hoped, generally and perhaps reasonably" 4225
"hoped Diana would be there" 6762
"hoped it would be, the success she
 had" 6755
"hoped they weren't waiting for
 her" 10089
"hoped to remain unturned, I had"
 4613
"hopeless, what could be more"
 5771
"hopeless as the struggle" 6866

"hopeless love" 5659
"hopelessly, she added" 3858
Hopelessness 5771
"hopes and desires" 5572
"hopes for independence" 4604
"hopes of becoming a goose" 773
"hopes of getting a breath of coolness" 4371
"hoping" 9009
Hopper, Eliphalet 6096
"hops, periscope" 8130
Horace 99, 6529
"Horace, his beloved" 99
Horatio 10159, 10655
"Horatio House, it wasn't" 3209
Hord, Breck 436
"horde had gone rampaging away" 1634
"hordes of insects" 5603
Horgan, Martha 6208
"horizon, because of the" 3605
"horizon, blue" 492, 9413
"horizon, distant" 9116
"horizon, foliage on the" 5176
"horizon, highest point in the" 10329
"horizon, it topped the" 9154
"horizon, mystery upon the" 6064
"horizon, on the" 9077
"horizon, overheated" 4428
"horizon, sea's" 6562
"horizon, shadowy" 8394
"horizon, the" 10494
"horizon, there is no" 7914
"horizon, western" 7878
"horizon did not seem far away" 8412
"horizon slanted, the" 8447
"horizon was cloudless that evening" 2199
Horizons 2199, 3605, 4428, 5176, 8394, 8412, 8447, 9154
Horn, Count 4991
"horn, he ought to sound his" 9788
"horn, merry notes of the" 9113
"Horn, the" 9371
"horn I heard, it *was* the" 8764
"HORN it said" 4779
"horn of plenty, the little end of the" 5080
"Hornbeck" 1057
Hornblower 2701
Hornblower, Captain 3482
Hornblower, Captain Horatio 7349
Hornblower, Captain Sir Horatio 565
Hornblower, Rear Admiral Lord 8102
Hornblower, Sir Horatio 7513
Hornbury 3161
Horner, Jacob 4751
"horns, like muted" 2075
Hornsby, Rogers "The Rajah" 4546
"horny, tough and" 5382
"horrible than grotesque, less" 2734

"horribly, die" 7182
"horribly impossible" 2734
"horrid winter of her discontent" 8356
"horror, abodes of" 4101
"horror, shame and" 6577
"horrors could be contained, as if its" 8704
Horse, Michael 7031
"horse" 9626
"horse, big gaunt old draft" 979
"horse, black" 464
"horse, boy and a" 979
"horse, boy shot Wild Bill's" 4261
"horse, drowned" 288
"horse, get a" 3394
"horse, gray" 9527
"horse, his" 7620
"horse, his jet black" 7627
"horse, his mighty" 1704
"horse, how to ride a" 4254
"horse, large dirt-grey" 9795
"horse, like a skittish" 4191
"horse, like the wild" 6814
"horse, old swayback gray" 9792
"horse, paint" 7625
"horse, pulled up his" 7609
"horse, rested his" 9561
"horse, stabled his" 9142
"horse, stolen a" 2025
"horse, the" 246
"horse, the torturer's" 5525
"horse, thighs embracing the" 8701
"horse, upon a" 7607
"horse and buggy" 2967, 7223
"horse and foot in about equal proportions" 10509
"horse away, wheeled his" 6009
"horse between the shafts" 9792
"horse browsing as he goes" 10409
"horse carried effects of Guest's" 7610
"horse of the Greeks, famous wooden" 2603
"horse pawed the floor" 460
"horse raising the dust in the road" 1704
"horse stopped suddenly" 9311
"horse to her, brought a" 7641
"horse was first to know" 464
"horse with an ostrich-plume" 6664
"horseback, silhouetted on" 8696
"horseback, travel on" 8620
"horse-car, drooping" 1012
"horseman, lone" 7618
"horseman, the single" 7640
"horseman ever seen in Spain, best" 7626
"horseman noted, the" 10946
"horseman riding down the valley" 9975
"horsemen" 9101
"horsemen, four" 9304
"horsemen clustered below him on the plateau" 10541

"horsemen rode up to the Wallace Inn" 7606
Horseracing 3964, 9215, 10002
"horse-racing that would come afterwards" 7612
Horses 246, 288, 410, 411, 427, 432, 433, 437, 440, 446, 447, 460, 464, 468, 471, 979, 1885, 2025, 3009, 3045, 3654, 3964, 4254, 4261, 4885, 5190, 5525, 6556, 6633, 6996, 7617, 7619, 7620, 7631, 7636, 7641, 7645, 8650, 8764, 8768, 9006, 9113, 9142, 9561, 9728, 9795, 10032, 10409, 10412
"horses" 6633
"horses, believes only in" 2967
"horses, carriage-" 3120
"horses, clipped" 10032
"horses, days without" 9728
"horses, drawn by six" 9759
"horses, he knew nothing about" 4885
"horses, play the" 322
"horses, post-" 6556
"horses, riding" 7631
"horses, six sweat-lathered black" 3009
"horses, lead the" 1269
"horses, sumpter" 1779
"horses, swift" 9215
"horses, swing their" 7645
"horses, two" 3069
"horses, two fat" 9757
"horses, two gray" 9771
"horses had grown used to the corpse" 1885
"horses' haunches" 9771
"horses in blazing harness" 9757
"horses in the trailer" 3045
"horses on the island, there had always been" 433
"horses' shoes ring upon the cobblestones" 1545
"horses stopped to drink" 7619
"horse-studded landscape" 5171
"Horsethief" 415
Horvath, Laszlo 2012
"hosanna, burst with a white" 906
"hose, garden" 4901
"hose on you, I'll turn the" 7143
"Hospital, Alta Buena" 4627
"hospital, ball he found at the" 302
"Hospital, Barnaderg Bay" 8386
"Hospital, Brightwood" 7829
"Hospital, Charing Cross" 1519
"hospital, formality of the" 2449
"hospital, he was in the" 34
"Hospital, Holy Redeemer" 2401
"hospital, in the" 161, 1151
"Hospital, John Carpendar" 10216
"Hospital, Kingston" 9711
"hospital, leper" 164
"Hospital, Mercy" 3830
"hospital, met in the" 3923

"hospital, military" 3988
"Hospital, Mount Zion" 4624
"hospital, on the way to the" 8319
"Hospital, Peretz Memorial" 1884
"hospital, psychiatric" 2001
"hospital, shell-shock" 4616
"hospital, Tel Aviv" 6542
"hospital, the" 7096
"Hospital, USVA" 682
"hospital at Helwan, sent to the" 155
"hospital bed, the side of her" 2435
"hospital cafeteria" 7696
"hospital gown" 4628
"hospital grounds" 4615
"hospital of Rhodes" 4618
"hospital of the orphanage" 556
"hospital room" 7785
"hospital ruins" 1751
"hospital staff" 7539
"hospital table" 8380
"hospitalities at far-scattered farm-houses, willing to enjoy" 9515
"hospitality, well known for its" 3087
Hospitals 34, 155, 161, 164, 190, 556, 1519, 1884, 2401, 2480, 3830, 3923, 3988, 7785, 7829, 8380, 8386, 10216
"hospitals, sundry military" 8665
"hoss, wagon that'll run without a" 4937
"host, the richer the" 10565
"host and skipper, my" 8065
"host was Wm. Tiny, his" 9959
"hostess, a letter to thank his" 5457
"hostess, beautiful Pan American" 595
"hostess, she was not an easy" 8629
"hostess had put perhaps too much kirsch in the fondue" 10559
"hostilities, long-continued" 7794
"hostilities . . . had been happily terminated" 7794
Hostility 3308, 6035, 7794
"hostility" 3308
"hostility, in his sister's eyes a keen" 3562
"hostler, the" 3441
"hosts of effigies" 8942
"hot" 2151, 9275
"hot, beastly" 4418
"hot, blinding" 4395
"hot, day had been very" 4371
"hot, day promised to be" 2139
"hot, intensely terribly" 4373
"hot, it had been so" 3782
"hot, it is" 1337
"hot, it was" 4380, 4405, 4413
"hot, it was that" 4396
"hot, New Orleans" 9359
"hot, red-white-" 7990
"hot, so" 4427
"hot, so almost" 4401
"hot, steaming stinking sewer-

vaporous New York-humid solid soul-smiting" 4396
"hot, too" 4392, 4406
"hot, town was oven" 4390
"hot, uncomfortably" 10236
"hot afternoon" 4409
"hot all day, it had been broiling" 4372
"hot and blind, she was" 10611
"hot and clear, morning shone" 2216
"hot and dry, summer of 1960 was" 4403
"hot and dusty" 1337
"hot and sticky in the summer" 8594
"hot as midsummer" 4412
"hot as they come, afternoon as" 3032
"hot August, that" 10336
"hot day, a" 900
"hot day, it had been a" 4404
"hot day, it was a" 3956, 7677
"hot days" 10597
"hot dog bun" 1259
"hot dogs, kosher" 3876
"hot enough for most other places" 4411
"hot for London, it was very" 4411
"hot inside and hot outside" 4408
"hot late summer air" 4422
"hot line, they came through on the" 6005
"hot on the back of his neck" 10365
"hot place to be, a locker was a" 4430
"hot summer night" 8014
"hot summer sun" 4374
"hot tub, Duane was in the" 576
"hot with the burden of two sheets and a blanket" 836
"hot words, hold back" 383
"hotcakes, Howard Johnson" 3870
"Hotel, Arlington" 6678
"Hotel, Astor House" 6901
"Hotel, Aurora Sands" 4656
"Hotel, Bedford" 8358
"hotel, best" 1582
"hotel, Beverly Hills" 5630
"Hotel, Beverly Hills" 2453
"Hotel, Bootjack" 4304
"Hotel, Buckingham" 3233
"Hotel, Catelli-Continental" 4646
"hotel, cheap" 6108
"hotel, checked into the usual" 4658
"Hotel, Claremont" 1674
"Hotel, Cordova" 6773
"Hotel, Darwish" 4333
"Hotel, Fifth Avenue" 1967
"Hotel, Grand" 316, 4638
"*hôtel*, great gray two story Parisian" 3197
"hotel, humble" 4630
"hotel, hurried out of the" 1589
"Hotel, Knightsbridge" 1586

"hotel, lamps in the" 4647
"hotel, large proud rose-colored" 4631
"hotel, lived in this" 2935
"Hotel, Lone Tree" 2696
"hotel, luxury" 4634
"hotel, most spacious and important" 4632
"Hotel, Mount Royal" 4641
"hotel, mountainside resort" 7727
"hotel, old" 1638
"hotel, old dilapidated" 4643
"Hotel, Opryland" 4531
"hotel, ornate and hideous" 7904
"Hotel, Palas" 3299
"hotel, Pankot's new five-storey glass and concrete" 2373
"Hotel, Park View" 2616
"hotel, particularly comfortable" 5066
"Hotel, Phoenicia" 5229
"Hotel, Plaza" 547, 6769
"hotel, principal" 6412
"hotel, private" 3171
"hotel, reached the" 3913
"Hotel, Repulse Bay" 10816
"Hotel, Ritz" 4650
"Hotel, Rivoli" 4652
"Hotel, Robinson's" 4644
"Hotel, Royal Hawaiian" 5859
"Hotel, Royal Ocean" 9723
"Hotel, Sheraton-Park" 7013
"hotel, small" 4639, 7570
"hotel, sumptuous" 4636
"hotel, that kind of an" 4651
"hotel, that superb" 10047
"hotel, the" 4005
"hotel, then off to a" 8027
"hotel, this" 3831
"hotel, trust the Gordon's to choose a" 3515
"Hotel, Union" 7509
"Hotel and Chop-House, Gloster's" 4511
"Hotel backed into the boardwalk" 4652
"Hotel Barbette" 3189
"hotel built by Stalin" 7904
"Hotel Cecil" 8345
"Hôtel Chatham" 3819
"hotel clerk" 10920
"Hotel Columbus" 10439
"hotel doorway" 10037
"hotel girls" 11
"hotel in New York" 1653
"hotel in the City, tallest" 4635
"Hotel Lotti" 4633
"Hotel Louis Quinze" 9209
"Hotel Magnifique, Grand Continental" 7754
"Hotel Meister Palace" 4659
"Hôtel Meurice" 10119
"Hôtel Milano" 5182
"hotel near the Thames in Surrey" 9722

"hotel opposite mine, the little" 10792

"Hotel Pierre" 4637

"hotel porter" 9916

"Hotel Prado" 598

"hotel register" 4649

"hotel room" 1116, 4019

"hotel room, fairly comfortable" 4634

"hotel room, from his" 7937

"Hotel Splendide" 654

"hotel stationery" 4642

"hotel suite" 8806

"hotel was freezing cold" 4640

"hotel was on a canal" 4653

"Hotel Wessex" 7762

"hotel windows" 10257

Hotels 598, 654, 1082, 1586, 1638, 1674, 1967, 2453, 2696, 2935, 3078, 3171, 3189, 3233, 3299, 3515, 3819, 3831, 3913, 4005, 4019, 4304, 4333, 4531, 4630, 4631, 4632, 4633, 4634, 4635, 4636, 4637, 4638, 4639, 4640, 4641, 4642, 4643, 4644, 4645, 4646, 4647, 4649, 4650, 4651, 4652, 4653, 4654, 4656, 4658, 4659, 5066, 5182, 5569, 5624, 5630, 5859, 6108, 6412, 6448, 7509, 7570, 7573, 7727, 7754, 7762, 7768, 7937, 8358, 8363, 8806, 9578, 9722, 9723, 10047, 10119, 10702, 10816, 10920

"hotels" 1342

"hotels, biggest of Washington's apartment" 3078

"hotels, good old-fashioned" 4644

"hotels, little" 1082

"hotels, one of the grand up-town" 10782

"hotels, requisitioned" 5569

"hotels in the world, one of the most palatial" 8363

"hotel's welcome, extending his" 4659

"hotter than any summer day we had" 4398

"hotter than usual" 4388

"hottest afternoon of that hot August" 10336

"hottest and finest anyone could remember" 4415

"hottest on record, might be one of the" 4410

"hottest weather of the year" 4383

Houlon 6002

"Hound of Heaven" 7852

"hounds, faithful" 3396

"hound's eyes" 8256

"hounds jump about him so" 2820

"hour, at this lachrymose yet exalted" 8470

"hour, his worst" 3516

"hour, loudly announced the" 1201

"hour, night's stillest" 8491

"hour, within a single" 2654

"hour after dawn, the softly bleak" 4694

"hour after hour" 7260

"hour for action approached" 6036

"hour is late, the" 3506

"hour rings with confusion" 3506

"hourglass" 8924

"hourglass, a foot-high" 4122

"hours, eight glorious dreamless" 8455

"hours, every few" 9996

"hours, in the dusty clockless" 10416

"hours, in the small" 9404

"hours, long stifling midday" 4378

"hours, my idle" 3497

"hours, not even a good two" 3355

"hours, these three or four" 3355

"hours began, the golden" 10152

"hours had steamed the ground" 4404

"hours lengthened themselves out into something beyond all human measurement" 9412

"hours now, for five" 10057

"hours of time, creeping" 3301

"hours seem to pass like lazy cattle" 103

"hours to go, two" 892

"Housatonic, the storied" 2950

"Housatonic crept still and darkling, the" 9740

"house, a" 949, 1702, 3205

"house, adjoining" 8805

"house, ageless log" 10740

"house, aging" 10697

"House, Amalgatel" 1032

"House, American" 4632

"house, apartment" 2720

"house, armoured cat's face of the" 3131

"house, at the back of the" 2729

"house, at the other" 6286

"house, back door of her" 1782

"house, basement" 4073

"house, BB's" 3782

"house, Ben's" 5075

"house, big" 1180, 1555

"House, Big" 4584

"house, big brick" 3223

"house, big brick Oaklin" 7127

"house, big dingy" 3081

"house, big solid cool-looking" 3113

"house, big white" 797

"house, Birdsong" 3259

"house, boarding" 2898, 3780

"house, bombed-out public" 9231

"house, bought a" 3180, 6133, 9266

"House, Breitung" 7223

"house, brick" 10580

"house, built himself a" 3110, 3152

"House, Burke" 1548

"house, came back to the" 3939

"house, came out of the" 1622

"house, coming toward her" 9946

"house, commodious town" 8636

"house, completely quiet" 3285

"house, condemned" 9386

"house, corner" 775

"house, country-" 3972

"house, Danny's" 8981

"house, did nothing for the" 3255

"house, drove up to the" 382

"House, Durham" 1196

"house, elegant Queen Anne" 8378

"house, empty" 3107

"house, empty old" 1148

"house, every time I pass the" 4278

"house, expectancy filled the" 10060

"house, face of one" 5143

"house, famous commercial" 6425

"house, father's" 9663

"House, Felton" 3589

"house, flooded" 8491

"House, foundation-work of a" 6613

"house, from the front of the" 5157

"house, geometric white" 3170

"house, going over the" 950

"House, Golden" 3137

"House, Government" 9229

"house, governor's" 7195

"House, Governor's" 6226

"house, gray wooden" 3242

"house, great" 6371

"House, Great" 3063

"house, Great-Grandfather's" 329

"house, Gus and Jewel Lafleur's" 9967

"house, half a" 3098

"house, handsome" 3061, 3084, 5727

"House, Hare-Hatch" 2945

"house, her" 3821, 4150, 10969

"house, her father's" 4166, 6863, 10872

"house, her grandmother's" 8371

"house, her late parents'" 3136

"house, her own" 9578

"house, her silent" 869

"house, here is the" 3182

"house, his" 950, 1619

"house, his aunt's" 2807

"house, his big" 5959

"house, his father's" 667, 1908, 7764

"house, his high" 3992

"house, his log" 2513

"house, his own" 2419

"house, his sister Alma's" 2971

"house, his town-" 4555

"House, Holy" 10450

"house, Hornburys'" 3161

"house, horrible" 3174

"house, I have a small white" 3164

"house, I was in the" 9854

"house, in an old" 9016

"house, in front of the" 2984

"house, in her own" 5395

"house, in the" 3091, 8858

"house, in the semi-dark of the" 5718

"house, in this" 9905
"house, large" 5799, 8839
"house, large and imposing graystone" 5754
"house, large brick" 4947
"house, large square" 3140
"house, large stone" 3085
"house, large two-storied white
  colonnaded" 10703
"house, last country" 3190
"house, lawyer Royall's" 1585
"house, leave the" 1636, 1745
"house, left to brood in the" 8229
"house, little" 3162, 5352
"house, little public-" 7284
"house, lived in a big" 1983
"house, long stone" 10389
"house, looked for the" 7233
"house, low and still and grey"
  3158
"house, low lighted" 6624
"house, Lucy Marr's" 4921
"house, manor" 3160
"House, Manor" 8587
"house, mansion" 286, 7014, 10038
"house, Mom's" 6209
"House, Moncrief" 7878
"house, moved to this" 6130
"house, moving the" 2786
"house, my" 82, 3232, 4354, 6157,
  8789
"house, my daughter's" 3121
"house, my father's" 1570
"house, my friend's" 10021
"house, my grandfather's" 9726
"house, nearly burnt down the"
  6527
"house, neat two-storey green-
  shingled white" 3223
"house, Neville came with the" 3331
"house, new" 1852, 3111
"house, Noorna's" 7213
"house, North London" 1889
"house, notary's" 317
"house, old" 3065, 3095, 3107,
  3836, 8349
"house, old brown" 4283
"house, old brownstone" 3132,
  9900
"house, old dilapidated three-story
  brick" 8309
"house, old English country-" 10780
"house, old Pentland" 6757
"house, old red-brick" 3076
"house, old stone" 4114
"house, old Templeton" 3134
"house, oldest" 3122
"house, oldest part of the" 3111
"house, Oliphant's" 8208
"house, on the third floor of the"
  8720
"house, one rule about his" 7822
"house, ordinary" 3237
"house, our" 859, 3133, 5113
"house, our new" 3073, 6094

"house, our rented Carter Avenue"
  9373
"house, our tiny" 311
"house, outside the" 1547
"house, Paren Comesee's" 8336
"house, parents'" 9366
"house, passersby often remembered the" 3177
"house, Patterson" 3157
"house, pervading every room of
  the" 5329
"House, Peskett" 6321
"house, pink" 9869
"house, plain brick" 3077
"house, play" 7710
"house, public" 3855
"house, rambling" 1787
"house, ranch" 2075
"house, rather huddled but comfortable Beaux-Arts town" 3197
"house, rented" 2001
"House, Rest" 8265
"house, rusty wooden" 3060
"house, scanty wooden" 7230
"house, severely grey brick" 3079
"house, slate-colored" 1911
"house, small" 3101, 5761
"House, Small" 3063
"house, small public" 9093
"house, sold his first" 1086
"house, somebody else's" 3228
"house, square detached untidy"
  6894
"house, squarely in front of her"
  4901
"house, stepped from his" 1681
"house, stepped out of his" 1626
"house, storm broke over the" 9079
"house, stucco" 6297
"house, suburban" 2557
"House, Sunnybank" 412
"house, Sylvester" 3827
"house, taken the" 9665
"house, tall" 3053
"house, tall narrow" 3159
"house, tall thin slip of a" 3153
"house, that little" 8706
"house, that perfect country" 3248
"house, the" 3099, 3117, 3147,
  3249, 3263, 8588, 10943
"House, The Merriwether" 3186
"house, their family" 8241
"house, their father's" 8206
"house, their new" 3165
"house, their own friendly" 4557
"House, there was a beginning"
  3176
"house, this" 8205
"house, this dear" 4354
"house, timbered" 9674
"House, Tohoga" 7220
"House, Trenwith" 7069
"House, Tunstall Moat" 647
"house, Valenti" 3137
"house, twilight of his" 10180

"house, two-story white frame" 3225
"house, ugly old" 5292
"house, unfinished" 1859
"house, unusual" 3153
"house, very large and unmitigatedly hideous" 3123
"house, walked into the" 3206
"house, we've got a ranch" 3224
"house, when I saw the" 3143
"House, White" 5404
"house, who can have taken the
  Ferguses'" 6284
"House, Wonder" 2017
"house, working on our" 6941
"house, yellow-gray" 2209
"House above the Arch" 7233
"house across the street" 3183
"house at Andilly" 5104
"house at Arles, small yellow" 7793
"house at Norton-on-Hudson" 5747
"house at No. 55" 3102
"house at Number 10 in Frederick
  Street" 8720
"house at 61 Allen Street" 7106
"house at Woodcombe Park, the
  great" 3215
"house attached to a seignorial
  school" 7908
"house became so quiet" 8327
"house consisted of a basement and
  of four stories" 3103
"house fooled everyone" 3260
"house for the summer, took a furnished" 2018
"house glowed in the darkness"
  3792
"house had not been lived in for
  many years" 3135
"house had outlived its usefulness"
  3184
"house he was looking for" 7230
"house high on the green slope"
  3178
"house in a Dublin back street" 3081
"house in East Anglia" 1180
"house in Ellaman Street, the last"
  3195
"house in Ireland which Violet Dene
  Gordon had inherited" 4569
"house in Landsdowne Road" 10189
"house in Neely proper" 3604
"house in New Orleans, the old"
  2804
"house in Reservoir Hills" 5959
"house in Santa Rosa" 3211
"house in Tangier" 2416
"house in the Archway" 3631
"house in the country, a little" 3088
"house in the Nichols Hills section
  of Oklahoma City" 2009
"house in the quiet square" 8334
"House in the Wheel" 535
"house in the woods" 8600
"house in which Emma and Jesse
  Tree lay sleeping" 8471

"house is isolated" 3252
"house is old and noisy and full" 3133
"house itself thrusting its tiled gable through a bower of trees" 3119
"house looked all right, the little" 1669
"house looked deserted" 3107
"house made of dawn" 3175
"house next door" 6287, 6303
"House of Commons" 585
"house of dark and venerable appearance" 3140
"House of Egremont" 3557
"house of entertainment" 4304
"house of Felimid mac Dall" 9535
"house of his grandfather, the earthen" 3567
"house of Lepidus" 5443
"house of Marriott, the great" 3155
"house of Monsieur Garon the avocat" 9209
"house of my grandfather" 5193
"house of Penarrow" 3084
"house of public entertainment" 4303
"House of Representatives" 2009
"house of the Emery family" 3080
"house on Ashby Street where I was raised" 5528
"house on Chipping Hill" 3122
"house on Clifton Avenue was a duplex" 3203
"house on Crab Key" 3247
"house on Mt. Vernon Street" 2319
"house on Palm Avenue, the" 3218
"house on Santa Clara Avenue" 968
"house on the corner" 9231
"house on the Ridge" 3000
"house overlooking the junction of a main road and a canal" 6115
"house prices" 8896
"house she rented" 156
"house . . . sits in a liveoak grove" 3147
"house standing in a row" 3153
"house stood at the end of its small narrow garden" 3103
"house stood on a cliff top in Suffolk" 3165
"house stood on a shelf above the sea" 5147
"house stood upon a gentle slope" 3146
"house sufficed" 9592
"house that is special" 3151
"house that stood at the top of the hill overlooking the town" 3079
"house too is cold" 1555
"house trailer" 6165
"house upon the hill, his" 1498
"house was a country residence" 9466
"house was a neat though a lowly one" 3062

"house was an Elizabethan structure of some pretensions" 3066
"house was at the corner" 3156
"house was built on the highest part" 3181
"house was half a mile east of town" 9194
"house was high and square" 3131
"house was in waiting" 3158
"house was on Dresden Avenue" 3113
"house was quiet but awake" 3100
"house was set back from the noisy main road" 3227
"house was so small" 8613
"house was speaking" 3243
"house was too quiet" 3163
"house was up next to the hills" 3221
"house was very small" 3094
"house well known from Omaha to Denver" 3087
"house where he grew up" 3254
"house where I grew up" 9297
"house where we lived that winter" 8706
"house which was in Kingston" 6169
"house with an awful lot of chimney-pots" 7014
"house with battlements" 10389
"house with white columns" 3173
"house wouldn't collapse, his first and only" 6458
"house you live in, what a horrible" 3174
"houseboat" 3280
"houseboy who has been arrested" 6177
"housebreaker, brief but accurate imitation of a desperate" 6587
"housedress, her best" 8385
"house-fronts, narrow" 6270
"house-fronts, old richly-carved" 4908
"houseguest, the perfect" 6200
"household" 3554
"household, an erupting" 847
"household, such a" 3075
"household, the" 4907
"household, the whole" 10613
"household out, brought the" 8770
"household weekly accounts" 10926
Householder, Michael 4874
"housekeeper" 2451
"housekeeper, attractive and erudite" 8636
"housekeeper, the" 950
"housekeeper, the loss of my" 2021
"housekeeper, their" 12
Housekeepers 2021, 2581
"housemaid, head" 2316
"housemaids who lost their heads" 17
"houseplants were spread on the sidewalk" 6150

Houses 156, 185, 329, 382, 775, 790, 808, 835, 949, 950, 989, 1148, 1180, 1349, 1555, 1619, 1669, 1745, 1787, 1852, 1859, 1983, 2001, 2233, 2317, 2319, 2416, 2702, 2729, 2776, 2804, 3005, 3058, 3059, 3060, 3061, 3062, 3063, 3065, 3066, 3069, 3070, 3072, 3073, 3075, 3076, 3077, 3079, 3080, 3081, 3083, 3084, 3085, 3087, 3088, 3090, 3091, 3093, 3094, 3095, 3097, 3098, 3099, 3100, 3101, 3102, 3103, 3104, 3107, 3108, 3109, 3110, 3111, 3113, 3114, 3117, 3118, 3119, 3121, 3122, 3123, 3128, 3130, 3131, 3132, 3133, 3134, 3135, 3136, 3138, 3139, 3140, 3142, 3143, 3145, 3146, 3147, 3148, 3150, 3151, 3152, 3153, 3155, 3156, 3157, 3158, 3159, 3160, 3161, 3162, 3163, 3164, 3165, 3168, 3173, 3174, 3175, 3176, 3177, 3178, 3179, 3180, 3181, 3182, 3183, 3184, 3185, 3186, 3188, 3190, 3191, 3194, 3195, 3196, 3197, 3198, 3203, 3205, 3206, 3207, 3209, 3210, 3211, 3214, 3215, 3218, 3219, 3220, 3221, 3223, 3224, 3225, 3227, 3228, 3232, 3236, 3237, 3238, 3239, 3241, 3242, 3243, 3245, 3246, 3247, 3248, 3249, 3252, 3253, 3254, 3255, 3256, 3259, 3260, 3263, 3264, 3285, 3331, 3567, 3631, 3756, 3763, 3792, 3836, 3939, 4114, 4150, 4262, 4268, 4278, 4283, 4555, 4569, 4891, 4947, 5075, 5104, 5143, 5147, 5157, 5251, 5327, 5352, 5528, 5628, 5718, 5959, 6115, 6124, 6130, 6163, 6226, 6266, 6268, 6277, 6283, 6284, 6287, 6291, 6297, 6327, 6371, 6458, 6479, 6575, 6941, 7014, 7195, 7214, 7230, 7233, 7440, 7760, 7763, 7764, 7822, 7908, 8206, 8229, 8305, 8326, 8327, 8334, 8336, 8349, 8471, 8491, 8593, 8600, 8706, 8720, 8805, 8896, 8981, 9079, 9122, 9162, 9194, 9266, 9386, 9466, 9592, 9663, 9665, 9738, 9855, 9905, 9950, 9967, 9983, 10060, 10087, 10189, 10414, 10580, 10697, 10703, 10769, 10780, 10943
"houses" 3148
"houses, a little larger than any of the other" 3188
"houses, always cleaned" 6479
"houses, apartment" 5323
"houses, brick row" 6280
"houses, came to the" 2207
"houses, clean airy summer" 4319
"houses, cottage-like" 6266

"houses, dark nucleus of" 4145
"houses, do not clean their own" 1477
"houses, endmost" 6270
"houses, friendly cluster of" 1413
"houses, little" 6267
"houses, low brick" 10414
"houses, obliterating" 10604
"houses, one of the small dingy" 7753
"houses, public" 8702
"houses, regional balloon frame" 5607
"houses, roadside clusters of" 5166
"houses, row of brick-built" 6268
"houses, ruined boiling" 9216
"houses, ruined sugar-grinding" 9216
"houses, scattered" 5126
"houses, split-level" 3208
"houses, storage" 3615
"houses, tar-covered poor" 3422
"houses, the last of our mother's" 3756
"houses, the ten" 3120
"houses, town" 309
"houses, twenty-seven log" 3097
"houses, two lines of ancient" 9122
"houses, two-room" 1386
"houses, unbroken line of brown-stone" 3145
"houses, uniformly brown clap-board" 5142
"houses above a certain rent" 10769
"houses and their neighborhoods" 3142
"houses are dingy and colorless" 6268
"houses collect things" 3256
"houses containing single apart-ments" 5928
"houses do when they're left empty too long" 3138
"houses in Paris, one of the most miserable-looking" 9855
"houses in the neighborhood" 3185
"houses of importance, three new" 3196
"houses side by side, two pleasant" 6283
"houses that remain" 9216
"houses that were survivals of an earlier and friendlier age" 3103
"houses were in darkness, all the" 10390
"houses where the workers live" 1386
"houses with alleys between them" 6277
"housing, old Wheal Garth engine" 9237
"housing project" 7042
"housing-place, its intended" 487
Housman, Alex 9786
Houston 7720

"Houston" 6994
"hovel" 7049
"hover over the yard, figure that seemed to" 2761
"how it is, that's" 1831
"how it was" 4072
"how to take Cabot Cunningham" 7881
Howard 2675
Howard, Clarence 2492
Howard, John Sidney 4733
"Howard Beach" 3020
"Howard Johnson hotcakes" 3870
"Howard Johnson's, they decided to pull in at the" 2992
Howe, Emma 1952
Howell, Michael 9005
Howell, Mildred 6455
Howell, Stanley 5200
"howling their warning" 9104
Hoxie 5814
"Hoxton" 1500
Hoyt 2883
"Hozomeen that does not crack like cabin rigging in the winds" 6075
Huatlán 4853
Huayna Capac 7811
Hubbard 701
Hubbard, Bartley 5786
Hubbard, Leon 2401
Hubbard, "Softy" 9763
Huber, Lorna 370
"huckleberry bushes" 8264
"huddled deeper into the high collars" 8136
"huddled in his sheepskin coat" 10734
"huddled like tadpoles" 4021
"huddled shapes of soft red brick" 1376
"huddled together" 4135
"huddled up" 1198
"huddling in her misery" 5026
Hudibras 3396
Hudson 3036
Hudson, Senator Walter 6994
"Hudson Bay" 4071
"Hudson River School" 1012
"Hudson running dark and deep" 7699
"Hudson, the" 7647
"Hudson's Bay Company" 7918
Huff, Cap 10478
"huge, bear was" 466
"hugging the little suitcase" 3030
Hugh 4526, 8000
Hughes, Sam 3025
Hugo 768, 1271, 3860, 5244, 6154
"Hugo Texas" 4546
"Hull" 8342
"Hull, settled first at" 6601
"hullo" 9933
"hulls, burning" 4469
"hum in its chatter, dropping to a" 5788

"hum of noise from the street" 8830
"hum of the city, rhythmic" 7569
"human, not" 6816
"human affairs" 638, 7164
"human awareness" 9008
"human being" 5277
"human being, certified a" 829
"human being hide, can a" 4479
Human Beings 2378, 4479, 5704, 6816
"human beings, broken-up" 6848
"human beings, couple of" 4338
"human beings, crowded" 175
"human beings, folly of" 5704
"human beings who worked the line" 6848
"human breathing" 9503
"human chains of men and women" 5138
"human condition, the" 879
"human creature in the town, the only" 8723
"human dust, flying grains of" 6837
"human element, omits the" 3423
"human embryo" 2378
"human excrement" 8544
"human feeling, it wasn't any lack of" 1790
"human foetuses, authority on" 7078
"human history, traumas of" 4509
"human imagination" 3433
"human in every man" 5558
"human life, sanctity of" 6991
"human measurement, beyond all" 9412
Human Nature 5695, 5705, 5706
"human nature" 9118
"human nature, student of" 6490
"human nature is reported to be so hard" 5695
Human Race 5693
"human race" 4998
"human race, difficult to love the" 3864
"human race, the" 5693
"human race he has been doomed to celebrate" 3461
"human shapes" 785
"human soul" 4509
"human souls, two" 5735
"human spirit" 4496
"human traffic of the day, being part of the highest" 6433
"human universe, lovable" 6883
"human will power" 5702
"humane practice" 7109
Humanity 3461, 4046, 7084
"humanity, in the face of" 4046
"humanity, queerer mixture of" 8648
"humanity, the rest of" 5512
"humanity had to say about, what" 4046
"humans, mortal" 5576

"humans can live, a place in which" 4905
"humble circumstances" 9703
"humble surroundings" 9974
"humbled the gods of rebellious Babylon, Xerxes had" 2636
Hume, Mrs. 9901
"hum-flutter, [sparrows] going" 10425
"humid, New York-" 4396
"humidity broke" 8133
"humidity of her mother's womb" 7097
"humiliate me" 10194
"humiliated by having done so" 7956
Humiliation 1553, 7956, 10194
"humiliation" 1553
"humiliation, rested in" 2973
"humiliations, bitter" 3514
"humility, pride and" 5699
"hummed" 6372
"hummed a little under her breath" 1860
"hummed a song to himself" 8760
"hummed along" 3026
"hummed softly to himself" 4341
"humming a song on a Saturday morning" 6201
"hummingbird that darts to the flower" 5355
"hummocks under the dark mesquite" 10707
Humor 2164, 2304, 4271, 4324, 5185, 5186, 5188, 5191, 7142, 7398, 7478, 7884, 8261, 8951, 9456, 10533, 10660
"humor, bad" 3307
"humor, no sense of" 4663
"humor, sense of" 7049
"humorous air about the eyes" 5921
"humorous eyes, darkly" 8556
"humors, clammy" 9299
"humors, strange and unpredictable" 10493
"humour, Irish" 695
"humour of each displays itself without ceremony or restraint" 8951
"humours and dispositions which were then uppermost" 6604
"hump, transmission" 9787
"humpbacked and ugly" 340
"humpety hump" 8889
Humphry 4554
"humps northward, it" 4071
"hunched by the ashes" 8361
"hunched forward in the saddle" 7642
"hunched over it in the *roka*" 2536
"hundredfold" 2913
"hung, I hope to be" 9695
"hung kind of wild and scraggly down across her forehead" 10860
"hung on by her teeth" 1842

"hung on precariously" 10622
"hung perilously in the balance" 410
"hung under the sky" 5165
"hung up by a nail" 453
"hung up instantly, she should have" 1134
Hung Shiu-Ch'uan 832
"Hungary" 4928, 8859
Hunger 74, 557, 3280, 4668, 4669, 4670, 4671, 4674, 4675, 4676, 4677, 4678, 4679, 4680, 4681, 4682, 7032, 9200, 9275
"Hunger" 7032
"hunger, like wild and savage" 3304
"hunger, road of" 4682
"hunger for more than food, there is such a thing as" 4671
"hunger grows faster than appetites" 4676
"hunger I fed on" 4671
"Hungerford" 9596
"Hungerford, bell ringers of" 661
Hungerton, Mr. 5900
"hung-over sailors" 8137
"hungry, forget you're" 74
"hungry, he was" 4675
"hungry, I'm" 4677
"hungry, Nureddin was" 4669
"hungry, painfully" 9275
"hungry, road ... was always" 9200
"hungry, very" 4668
"hungry and tired, he was" 557
"hungry shoals" 9089
"hungry that day, I wasn't" 3280
Hunnicutt, Native 1226
Hunsicker, Walter 6798
Hunt, Amy 7729
"hunt, a still-" 7214
"hunt, at the second check of the" 6000
"hunt, the" 428
"hunted across a vast scrub-brush tumbleweed field" 4694
"hunted and traded" 6813
"hunted eyes" 3413
"hunted through a desk drawer for hammer and tacks" 6952
Hunter, Dock 2949
Hunter, Manuel 7752
"hunter, cunning old" 4248
"hunter stalking a hippopotamus, an African" 1610
"hunters burst silently out of the trees" 4695
Hunting 428, 429, 476, 857, 2223, 2820, 2878, 3423, 4248, 4347, 4667, 4683, 4684, 4685, 4691, 4694, 4695, 6000, 8264, 8764, 10332, 10499
"hunting, deer" 429
"hunting costume" 2878
"hunting for coal" 7219
"hunting in the woods" 4684
"hunting snow, the first good" 8592

"hunting toggery, article of" 2820
"Huntingdon" 4313, 5727
Huntington, Captain Colin 10079
"Huntington" 4064
"hunts with a rifle like a white man" 4347
"hupmobile, hip hole and" 10007
"Huron canoes" 8155
"Huron Mountains" 4073
"hurricane, a" 9073
"hurricane girls" 9086
"hurricane of sound" 652
Hurricanes 9073, 9084, 9086, 10743
"hurricanes, time for" 10743
"hurricanes that periodically blow in from the gulf" 9084
"hurried, to be" 9470
"hurried across the courtyard to the chapel" 10659
"hurried down the steps" 1749
"hurried down the street" 10445
"hurried into the Café Julien" 4274
"hurried into the hall" 4602
"hurried movements, did not usually make" 10785
"hurried out of the Hotel" 1589
"hurried through the market" 3703
"hurriedly, a little" 10785
"hurries, no Latino villager ever" 1737
"hurry, in a" 3944
"hurry, in a great" 10970
"hurry, in a terrible" 4915
"hurry, in my" 9492
"hurry, nobody was in a" 6832
"hurry, what had been the" 4615
"hurry, why be in such a" 4912
"hurry the bus along somehow" 10045
Hurrying 1737, 4915, 10785
"hurrying, to-day she was" 10785
"hurrying along a road" 10390
"hurrying down Third Avenue" 10438
"hurrying home to see his mother who was ill" 6639
"hurrying to the lunch shift" 6332
Hurst, Alan 8657
"hurt, it was going to" 6899
"hurt, playful" 6301
"hurt, she had received a bitter" 2953
"hurt, someone was" 9842
"hurt, was anyone" 17
"hurt children, mothers don't" 6745
"hurt each other" 1820
"hurt God's feelings" 7511
"hurt herself" 3689
"hurt his daughter, cruelly" 5205
"hurt in the accident" 18
"hurt least, when it would" 6899
"hurt when he did it" 4879
"hurt you to become the subject of the public talk" 7825

"hurtful part, hear de most" 4238
"hurting her eyes" 10240
"hurting his eyes" 9276
"hurtling past him, large object" 10297
"husband" 3572
"husband, about to become her" 10644
"husband, annoy her" 2008
"husband, be unto her a loving and faithful" 10651
"husband, Elsie and her" 1968
"husband, first" 5551
"husband, Grady Durant's" 2869
"husband, her" 338, 1715, 1826, 1980, 1985, 1994, 2146, 2317, 2334, 2652, 2738, 2846, 3136, 3552, 3941, 4602, 5471, 5662, 6159, 6308, 6863, 6864, 8013, 9856, 10174, 10337
"husband, her dreadful" 9868
"husband, her future" 3581
"husband, her sleeping" 6356, 10117
"husband, leave her" 2659
"husband, looks more like a best friend than a" 5991
"husband, Marjorie's" 5239
"husband, my" 231, 902, 1843, 1972, 1973, 2000, 2661, 2662, 2676, 5880, 5970, 6038, 7792, 9860
"husband, no" 7041, 10322
"husband, on the arm of her" 6775
"husband, one" 2307
"husband, sudden death of her" 5751
"husband, who was once my" 5432
"husband, you and your" 6358
"husband die, watched her" 2388
"husband died, my" 2368
"husband is with me again, I think that my" 1972
"husband left her and their daughter" 2670
"husband left me, my" 2676
"husband of the rich widow" 5892
"husband she thought" 5745
"husband was a vain man" 5970
"husband was coming home, her" 4596
"husband was put on a piecework basis" 6652
"husband will have put me to death" 2000
"husbanding the evidence" 3465
Husbands 231, 1972, 1980, 1985, 1994, 1998, 2000, 2008, 2146, 2368, 2379, 2388, 2652, 2656, 2661, 2662, 2670, 2676, 2738, 2869, 3572, 3581, 3941, 4226, 4602, 5239, 5432, 5745, 5820, 5880, 5930, 5970, 5991, 5992, 6308, 6356, 6863, 9868, 10174, 10322, 10651

"husbands, buried two" 2379
"husbands, their" 7950
"husbands' businesses, go about their" 10843
"husbands' guineas, their" 3396
"husband-to-be" 5820
"hush fell over the dinner-table" 8626
"hush in the broad Glasgow street" 10515
"hush my love" 6308
"hush of night, the deepest" 8324
"hush swallowed the hot little room, a" 7090
"hushed, office was" 6505
"hushed them all" 652
"hushed tones, in those" 4650
Hussein, Ahmoud 502
"hustle to get his first" 7836
"hustled Bo and the girl upside" 6942
"hustling for money" 2068
"hut, all that is left of a" 9230
"hut, beehive-shaped stone" 3667
"hut, discrete" 3001
"hut, entered the" 7105
"hut, I leave the" 740
"hut, in a goat-herd's" 650
"hut, two-roomed" 9894
"hut, wall of a" 10164
"hut built of turf" 3068
"hut on the mountaintop" 4347
"hut which once stood there" 9230
Hutch 328, 7836
"hutch, leave his" 10308
"hutched up close to one another, we're not" 6391
Hutchinson, Mistress Anne 6135
Huts 650, 4347, 9230
"huts, gone from their" 7508
"huts, mere" 1345
"huts, neighbouring native" 10701
Hux, Lawrence 7364
"hyacinth, wild" 3804
"hyacinth, wood" 3804
"Hyannisport" 3041
"Hyde Park" 2822
"Hyde Park Corner" 10375
"Hyderabad" 1901
"hydrogen atoms" 8333
Hymie 10254
"hymn, evening" 8737
"hymns, the dull ache was not helped by the" 8763
"hyperventilate, taught her how to" 3287
"hypnotist's house" 1730
"hypnotized with longing" 10955
"hypocrisy, condemned to incessant" 10766
Hypocrites 9713
"hypocrites, decent" 9713
"hypodermic syringe" 3047
"hysterical disembodied note" 5260

Iago 7169
Ian 4584
Ice 727, 3016, 7650, 7693, 7696, 9823, 10574
"ice, anchor-" 7650
"ice, faint moaning of new" 10574
"ice, fields of" 8113
"ice, polar" 205
"ice, sun-soaked" 205
"ice, that morning's" 727
"ice, vanilla" 8377
"Ice Age" 2162
"ice cream" 5366
"ice cream, bellies full of" 8210
"ice cream, soft" 3876
"ice cream cones" 776
"ice creams, eight" 5184
"ice cubes of us all, would make" 1278
"ice for the bars" 2210
"Ice Glen, the peaks that guard the" 9740
"ice has formed shelves" 7693
"ice in the ditch" 7318
"ice lay grey and silent under the stars" 8113
"ice was still going off the river" 4691
"iceberg, like a gigantic red" 5030
"icebox ('Say I got some nice home-fries tonight Cody!') is a huge brownwood thing" 7575
"ice-cap was still advancing" 10710
"Icecream Parlor, Jock's" 248
"icehouse, threat to the" 3604
"Iceland" 4456
"Icelandair ticket" 9653
"iconoclastic essays" 5413
"icy patches glittering in the head-lights' beam" 3016
"icy reminder" 10710
Ida 7058
Ida-Ida 7058
"idea, absolutely no" 7793
"idea, always liked the" 904
"idea, American film director's" 5984
"idea, defied everyone's" 4072
"idea, do not encourage the" 1292
"idea, dreading the whole" 3734
"idea, faintest" 2723
"idea, fruitful" 4696
"idea, gave me the" 4703
"idea, guiding" 3671
"idea, had any" 5924
"idea, his" 4709
"idea, I didn't have no" 9372
"idea, I have no" 4886
"idea, insane" 4710
"idea, might be a good" 4869
"idea, Mrs. Biersdorf's - Eve's -" 4707
"idea, perfecting the" 4698
"idea, the" 4702
"idea, you have no" 10897

"idea in form and substance, thought he saw the" 4704
"idea of death" 2341
"idea of immensity" 5152
"*idea* of it that hurt so, it was the" 1166
"idea of mine, a favorite" 5558
"idea of Susie, just to give you an" 261
"idea really came to me" 4699
"idea shaped like a star" 3671
"idea what I'd do" 5546
"idea what she meant, I had no" 6585
"idea why, nobody will have any" 4322
"idealized vision of mapmakers" 5719
Ideas 1166, 1247, 3734, 5420, 6178, 6904, 9463
"ideas, a certain train of" 6516
"ideas, foreign" 7516
"ideas, marvelous ability to express" 5420
"ideas, three" 5652
"Ideas, Truly Bad" 4712
"ideas can change, one's" 1247
"ideas go, as modern" 3637
"ideas of the inhabitants" 7584
"ideas which were totally averse to that line of life" 6516
"ideers, what *are*" 4700
"identify the people who owned them" 6827
Identity 609, 908, 1815, 3412, 3918, 4440, 4449, 6031, 6132, 6689, 6837, 6840, 7969, 7970, 9707, 9972, 10842, 10893
"identity" 10842
"identity, desire to escape from his" 3412
"identity, gave up my country" 5790
"identity, sexual" 10913
"identity, the swallowing" 7916
"ideology, beyond the reach of" 1882
"Ides of March" 70
"idiocies propounded by the channels" 7840
"idiocy, metropolis of" 1378
"idioms, one of his private and peculiar" 931
"idiot, bein a" 5006
"Idiot, the" 6094
"idiot, you" 4976
Idiots 5006, 8560
"idiots when they smile, some people look like" 8560
"Idle Hour Bar & Grill" 2936
"idle hours" 3497
"idle lounging little —" 4970
Idlemudia 7324
Idleness 3255, 6495
"idlers" 8886

"Idlewild, New York's" 10006
"Idlewild Airport" 208
"idol" 4459
Ignatius 10557
"ignoble death" 2393
Ignorance 690, 3546, 3602, 3611, 5653, 6517, 7954, 9372, 9718
"ignorance, in his" 3602
"ignorance, very last moment of innocent" 7102
"ignorance of the brain-reactions of a fox" 1016
"ignorance of the ocean" 4887
"ignorance of those sad truths" 6517
"ignorant, some of you are not" 8963
"ignore the facts" 9699
"ignored" 5743, 9275
"ignored, nothing like being" 3317
"ignored four or five ponderous explosions" 753
"ignored her" 8018
"ignored it, heard the sound and" 8824
"ignored the circumfusion of those mean dwellings, were it possible to have" 9223
"ignored the flat voice" 6968
"ignoring the people who pressed around him" 10375
Iles, Christopher 9025
"Ileward, eyes to the" 7370
"*Iliad*, Homer's" 9265
"*Iliad* of Homer" 5431
"Ilium, sacred walls of" 7810
"Ilium New York" 1403
Ilka 2615
"ill, angry because he is" 734
"ill, far more" 129
"ill, good or" 7372
"ill, made ourselves" 3834
"ill, mother who was" 6639
"ill, suddenly taken" 145
"ill, traveled so" 4469
"ill, when he is" 6610
"ill, wife so" 2508
"ill at ease elsewhere, greatly" 7925
"ill enough to justify being in bed" 129
"ill for the most part of his life" 2336
"ill words" 7505
"illegal abortions" 5760
"illegitimate child" 1765
"illegitimate infants" 1493
"ill-fated trip" 7026
"illimitable, oats on either side" 9116
"Illinois" 1363, 1402, 3407, 5413
"Illinois, Central" 4038
"Illinois, southern" 3652
Illiteracy 4303
"illiterate generation, the new" 9265

Illness 139, 145, 734, 2424, 2508, 3834, 4221, 6621
"illness, birth cost my mother an" 6621
"illness, burdened with" 9657
"illness, felt the whole burden of his" 137
"illness, mysterious" 7464
"illness, not suffering from physical or mental" 5938
"illness, one or two bouts of" 5403
"Illness I mention'd to you, died of the" 4221
"illness was discussed with a certain restraint" 139
"illogical men and women" 6155
"illuminating the gray lichens" 3894
"illuminating with the uncompromising clarity of mid-morning" 1379
"illumination from within, some secret" 5331
Illusion 4108, 4612, 4893, 4897, 6791
"illusion, accept the" 4893
"illusion, hope is but a synonym for" 4612
"illusion, it is an" 8855
"illusion, the" 4108
"illusions of safety" 6791
"illustrating it in a vivid and memorable motto" 711
"illustrations, beautiful half-tone" 926
"illustrious, become" 3528
"illustrious eminence of a friend" 1
"illustrious names" 1431
Ilúvatar 2632
"image, living" 969
"image, obliterating the fun-house" 7480
"image, projected his own" 10759
"image of God, we are all made in the" 5699
"image of her mother" 6737
"image of perfection" 4525
"image of the candleflame" 3790
"image of the mind" 220
"image recurred, the" 9837
"image that seemed as hopeless as the struggle" 6866
"images, I carry a series of" 7460
"images, painting strange" 4428
"images, reflected" 2118
"images more vivid and lasting than any others" 7460
"images of Sam Gulliver" 3714
"images which he never allowed to linger" 9463
"imaginary hat" 4896
"imaginary visor" 4896
Imagination 220, 237, 324, 1972, 2121, 2263, 2454, 2766, 2795, 3433, 4709, 5406, 5445, 6826, 6906, 7234, 8327, 9698, 9754, 10479

"imagination" 8870
"imagination, figment of the" 6906
"imagination, human" 237, 3433
"imagination, possess an" 4888
"imagination, preoccupying my" 7234
"imagination, trappings of" 5216
"imagination, Truth is a matter of the" 9698
"imagination all compact" 4903
"imagination and expression" 5406
"imaginative, quiet and" 4892
"imaginative matter distasteful to those expository pens" 10900
"imagine" 10015
"imagine, I" 10904
"imagine, not so hard to" 3618
"imagine, one could" 1230
"imagine, you could" 6640
"imagine a deserted estate" 3179
"imagine a place in which humans can live" 4905
"imagine all sorts of foolish things, I began to" 4889
"imagine darkness" 2121
"imagine it's the promised land" 9754
"imagine that it had ever occurred before, I could hardly" 7372
"imagine them marching" 3668
"imagined, bigger than he had ever" 1461
"imagined, could not have been" 8648
"imagined, no one could have" 2006
"imagined, you" 8327
"imagined it, he had" 8517
"imagineer, an" 4242
"imagines it as a novelist might imagine it" 4899
"imagining it was his soul he revealed" 7956
Imamu 10250
"imbeciles, footloose" 8919
"imbibing rum-and-Cokes out of paper cups" 6783
"imitating her accent" 7598
"imitating the miracle of reproduction, no one has yet succeeded in" 5699
"immemorial, time" 6085
"immemorially" 364
"immense whole" 4533
"immensity, idea of" 5152
"immensity, its" 3095
"immensity, the" 2431
"immigrant, assisted" 5938
"immigrant, Chinese" 1040
"immigrant, wondering Eastern" 7287
"immigrant in the usual sense of the term, not an" 6120
Immigrants 1040, 4883, 5938, 6120, 7287
"immigrants" 4883

"immigrants, delivered the" 8080
Immigration 290
Immorality 2020, 7169
"immortal, I'm" 92
"immortal, mortal and" 9062
"immortal, public had begun to regard him as" 102
"immortal Pickwick" 5557
Immortality 92, 102, 7532
"immortality, fleeting" 7532
"immortality he won for his efforts" 7532
"immovable" 175
"immutable, perfect and" 2156
"impaired by time" 1293
"Impala, a '66" 9829
"Impala wagon's front seat" 7327
"Impartiality" 6033
"impassivity of his English fellow-passengers" 7587
Impatience 1920, 2464, 3328, 3992, 7091, 7262, 7906, 8238, 9325, 9327, 9479, 10029, 10097, 10101
"impatience" 1920, 4906
"impatience, expression of" 4918
"impatience, in" 4917
"impatience, loud" 3328
"impatience, patience and" 9479
"impatience of the executive" 4920
"impatience than surprise, more" 4907
"impatient, grew feverishly" 4911
"impatient cry" 4908
"impatient exuberance, driven with such" 40
"impatient rap, an" 5247
"impatiently, wait" 7262
"impatiently, waiting" 4921
"impatiently, woman's voice sang out" 10137
"impenetrable reaches" 455
"imperceptible as the approach of age" 2199
"imperceptible except as one feels it behind the breath he draws" 8766
"imperceptibly" 9465
Imperfection 7157, 7159
"imperious as a commodore" 8436
"imperious mien" 5571
Impertinence 1827
"impertinence to test it by the sense of touch" 5897
"impertinent, distressingly" 1827
"impetuous embrace" 7649
"impetuous streams" 1280
"impetuous walk, an" 6577
"implications, unsure of the" 10233
"implore you, one thing I must really" 9327
"imponderable" 8400
"imponderable barrier of mountains" 5620
"importance, Assistant Secretary's" 6506

"importance, degree of" 1335
"importance, every man of" 4490
"importance, matters of" 2466
"importance, objects of vast" 2600
"importance, place of no" 809
"importance of a thick black line around them" 2541
"importance to me of the events" 2894
"important, I am going to be" 252
"important, it did not look" 1855
"important part of the piece, the most" 6235
"important to him than to you" 1094
"imposing, he was" 5896
"impossible" 8138
"impossible, so horribly" 2734
"impossible, to reach it seemed" 2730
"impossible to begin a story" 8964
"impotent" 652
"impotent, the bravest was" 3514
"impoverished family" 4209
"impregnate her four times with four males in eight years" 3660
"impressed, very much" 8910
"impressed one by its sheer massivity" 9221
"impression, adequate" 1397
"impression, created the" 3296
"impression, first" 1584, 5960
"impression, I have an" 4343
"impression, my first" 9097
"impression, the" 977
"impression of English tourists, a confused" 9353
"impression of their love and their trouble" 5802
"impression that something has happened" 10280
"impression was strong with him" 6936
Impressions 1584, 7971, 10280
"impressions, first" 7971
"imprint this picture upon their memory" 8093
"imprisoned by the concrete towers of Waikiki" 5859
"imprisoned for eleven years" 7139
"imprisonment, self-imposed" 4481
"imprisonment, short period of" 1168
"improbable, it all seems so" 2734
"improve, nothing would ever" 2509
Improvement 1057, 1334, 3169, 4686, 6847
"improvement, a visible" 1334
"improvident, saucy and" 1162
"improving, you are" 2101
"improvised dais" 8286
"impudent, freeing Negroes made them" 1827
"impudent blue eyes" 246
"impulsive" 497

Ina 8290
Inability 7641
Inactivity 3784
"inactivity, blameless" 703
"inadequate light" 8404
"inadvertency" 10765
"inadvertently detonated her marriage" 5778
"inanimate object" 2107
"inapplicable though the expression may seem" 2297
"inappropriate, professionally" 4821
"inappropriate to the gentle watercolor landscape" 3665
"inarticulate longing, swollen with" 1706
"inauspiciously, begun" 10982
"Inca, the eleventh Sapa" 7811
Incarceration 1168, 1505, 2020, 2021, 2931, 2956, 3482, 7135, 7137, 7150
"incarnated themselves" 785
"incense" 1342
"incense, fragrance of" 7533
"incense, new leaf" 8536
"incense, plumes of" 1305
"inception in the blueprint of a dream" 4701
"incessant hypocrisy" 10766
Incest 3628, 8020, 8229, 8236
"incest, driven by the fear of" 8229
"incest, you couldn't call it" 8236
"inch, perhaps an" 6740
"Inchon landing, just after the" 6881
"incident, awkward" 3438
"incident, Bad Godesberg" 3464
"incident, extraordinary" 1265
"incident, nasty" 5834
"incident changed the whole course of the boy's life" 5087
"incidents for their interest in a tale, those who look to" 8962
"Incidents occurred which I beleive I should narate" 3496
"incidents recorded in these pages" 1360
"incidents that I am about to tell" 8962
"incipient power" 447
"incision, made the first" 607
"inclination, favorable" 10611
"inclination, nationless person by" 4762
"inclinations swayed from love by love" 5661
"Incline" 8729
"incline of the narrow clay road" 2989
"incline themselves towards some such prop" 10772
"include, how much to" 2556
Income 3529
"income, large" 4339, 5727
"incomes, one of the highest" 3529
"incomes change" 6654

Incompetence 2068, 6475
"incompetent, I was" 6475
"incompleteness of my misfortune" 4503
"incomprehensible" 6401
"incongruities, strange revelation of" 5307
"incongruous Indiana town" 8586
"incongruous setting" 5419
"incongruous to them, it did not seem" 9355
"inconspicuous shop" 1012
"inconvenience" 8620
"inconveniences, its quaint" 4644
"incorporated at a small celebration in 1890" 1468
"incorporeal body of love" 9279
"incorrectly if not indecently" 5659
"increase, God bring you" 7807
"incredible agony" 143
"incredible though they be" 5699
"incredibly" 5416
"incredulity, it was the epoch of" 3377
"incredulous astonishment" 1914
"incredulous smile" 2492
"incubator, limitless" 8333
"incurable ailment" 5659
"Incurables, Home for the" 9166
"incurious half-eyes" 5788
"Indal Water" 9561
"indebted, he will be greatly" 696
"indebted to my colleagues" 714
"indecently" 5659
Indecision 592, 1164, 2306, 2478, 2487, 2556, 2860, 3197, 3309, 4002, 5517, 6517, 6945, 7201, 9196, 10750
"indecision" 5238
"indefatigable assiduity" 5557
"indelible beyond all attempts the years make to erase or fade them" 7460
"identities, invaded by each other's" 8223
Independence 4231, 5750, 6802, 9973
"independence" 9973
"Independence, Declaration of" 4231
"independence, hopes for" 4604
"independence, maintained their" 6802
"independence, sole manifestation of" 5750
"independence, war of" 10470
"Independence, War of" 361, 8641
"independence from Great Britain" 2681
"Independent, yellow" 9113
India 4754
"India" 1, 1385, 1901, 1930, 2421, 4388, 5368, 6728, 6978, 7663, 10210
"India, British" 5715
"India, I went to" 8657
"India, written in" 6035

"India is an underdeveloped country" 6262
"India of the princes" 5715
"Indian, crouched like an" 5824
"Indian, half-breed" 3714
"Indian, I am an" 5446
"Indian, rifle [needed] for the" 6100
"Indian and Pacific Oceans meet and merge" 5043
"Indian Army" 1757
"Indian Army officer" 987
"Indian clerk" 2026
"Indian country" 6276
"Indian Flat" 7614
"Indian footpath" 5723
"Indian Nations" 2215
"Indian Ocean" 7921
"Indian of a river" 7670
"Indian Reserve" 4078
"Indian soldiers" 8682
"Indian states" 3507
"Indian style" 8156
"Indian summer" 10597
"Indian summer is like a woman" 10808
"Indian summer of 1959" 10621
"Indian summers, not like other" 4388
"Indian village" 8168
"Indian woman, old" 10026
Indiana 2631, 5442
"Indiana" 3074, 5129
"Indiana, holy land of" 2631
"Indiana, somewhere in" 8665
"Indiana farm, an" 2956
"Indiana produce so many writers, why does" 5442
"Indiana town" 8586
"Indianapolis born Indianapolis bred" 10674
"Indiana's early statehood" 9662
Indians *see* **Americans (Native)**
"Indians" 752
"Indians, Abnaki" 7457
"Indians, all matters appertaining to the" 4502
"Indians, Cheyenne" 9707
"Indians, group of twenty converted" 7508
"Indians, hated" 4358
"Indians, Massachusetts" 3906
"Indians, more like the" 9716
"Indians, Osage" 503
"Indians, score of" 4685
"Indians, small bands of" 4043
"Indians, the" 959
"Indians, two quiet" 9842
"Indians, two young" 4673
"Indians in America, captured and tortured by the" 9853
"Indians in Texas" 8165
"Indians moved out, as the" 959
"Indians' playgrounds" 959
"indicating the nozzle and tapes, no more than" 9579

"indication, gave no" 2402
"indicted for conspiracy" 5194
"Indies, West" 8102
Indifference 5617, 6181
"indifference" 9886
"indifference, curious" 6181
"indifference, the contained" 7847
"Indifference, the vast" 5269
"indifferent" 5077
"indifferent, prodigiously" 5617
"indifferent and courteous guards" 9381
"indifferent to me" 7746
"indigestion, intellectual" 9718
"indignant exclamation" 6610
"indignant look" 9855
"indignation" 3299
"indignity, threatened" 10033
"indigo" 1355
"indisposition of his own" 125
"indisputably" 3939
"indistinguishable from normal behavior" 642
"indistinguishable head" 9678
"individedly happy" 10995
"individual, himself as an" 1209
"individual, life of any one" 5558
"individual, tall and rather gangling" 8098
"individuals, four" 3986
"individuals, private affairs of" 5799
"individuals, two very queer" 8856
"indolence, luxurious" 3356
"indolence, tragedy having turned my basic languor to" 4116
"indolence in her temper" 6605
"indolent watchfulness" 2295
"Indonesia" 10520
"indoors, stay" 4431
"indulge in such an orgy of concentrated thought" 9412
"indulgence" 2865
"indulgence, early" 2903
"indulgence, rare" 8637
"indulgent, not disposed to feel" 7852
"indulgent colored woman" 964
"indulging myself, prevent my" 7491
"Indus, river" 7808
"Induspur, valley of" 3507
"industrial darkness of its larger cities" 5719
"industrial haze" 1032
"industrial importance" 1401
"industrialist, American" 6628
"industrious child" 5708
"industrious of late" 1017
Industry 1005, 1014, 1072
"industry, principal" 1014
"Ineffable One" 2626
"ineffectual, mighty and" 10341
"inept moves" 5829
"inevitable, exceptions are so" 7815
"inexorable, persistent and" 10131
"inexorably, racing" 7851

Inexperience 7964
"inexpressive and speechless race" 8841
"infancy, in her" 4451
"infancy of Vivian Grey" 1265
"infancy of Willoughby" 6613
"infant, father of the" 6644
"Infant of Prague, Divine" 8944
"infant was two months old" 2919
"infantree the infantree" 7196
"infantry, battalion of" 8648
"infantry, long column of" 8701
"infants, illegitimate" 1493
"infants visible in the depths of prams" 8815
Infatuation 7717
"infatuation, an" 7717
"inferior affair, a very" 10899
"inferno of fire steel and smoke" 6756
"Infidel, the" 8646
"infidel alien" 7505
"infidelities" 9054
"infinite, no boundaries where all is" 526
"infinite curiosity" 8976
"infinite haze" 10260
"infinite zest for life" 8976
"infinitude, the sky's" 531
Infinity 3337
"infinity, being so unto" 6798
"infirm the old rector was, realise how" 1536
"infirmary together, they were put into the" 7137
"inflamed by Cupid's darts" 7708
"inflict upon you a full true and particular account" 8171
"influence, pre-natal" 10814
"influence, undue" 5885
"influence has ceased, after their" 9704
"influences, restless" 5559
"influenza, epidemic of the" 3273
"information, furnish him with" 696
"information, I have" 6957
"information, thirst of" 1292
"information about himself, begin by giving certain" 5426
"information and edification of mankind" 5387
"information on, pass this" 554
"information-content zero" 7975
"informed, decently" 10931
"infuse into traffic and pedestrians alike" 5308
Ingles, Ned 2981
Ingram, David 5235
Ingram, Martha 3406
Ingratitude 2646, 6884
"inhabitant of London, every" 6974
"inhabitants" 6266
"inhabitants, deserted by its" 1736
"inhabitants, first" 1192
"inhabitants, French" 9662

"inhabitants, local" 5607
"inhabitants, ruffianly" 2016
"inhabitants of Westminster and London" 5126
"inhabited those formidable castles" 6802
"inhabiting the crepuscular frames of an old newsreel" 876
"inhaled the stench of old fish" 8544
"inherit, he was to" 4928
"inherit the earth" 7836
Inheritance 2292, 3660, 4434, 4604, 7836, 8495, 10559
"Inheritance, first saw the" 2522
"inheritance, insomnia is my" 8495
"inheritances, consider your" 4933
"inherited" 4569
"inherited four thousand a year" 4926
"inherited from his mother" 4434
"inherited his father's estate" 4931
"inherited side, the" 10206
"inimitable Cervantes" 6246
"iniquity, consummated his" 5914
"Inishnamona" 5040
"injected into her arm, no matter how much of it she" 3057
"Injunction imposed on all Souls" 2286
"injured so near their gate" 36
"injuries, unspeakable" 2450
"injuries of Fortunato, the thousand" 4989
Injury 14, 17, 18, 20, 22, 23, 24, 26, 28, 29, 31, 32, 33, 34, 35, 36, 38, 124, 877, 1505, 1537, 2353, 2450, 2784, 3056, 4281, 4296, 4585, 6588, 6594, 6796, 7614, 8189, 8693, 9844, 9848, 9849, 9851, 9852, 9854, 10156, 10301
"ink, splattering dribbles of thin homemade" 5548
"ink characters stalking away from him" 5460
"inkling, first" 3958
Inkpen 1079
"inmate, he had been an" 5399
"inmates, the older" 7149
"inn, genuine coaching" 7573
"inn, gloomy-looking" 1183
"inn, kept the 'Admiral Benbow'" 5012
"inn, old and well-appointed" 4996
"inn, open their story in an" 8951
"inn, Patrick Lynch's" 4308
"inn, paying his bill at an" 9515
"Inn, Wallace" 7606
"Inn, White Horse" 3533
"inn called the Flying Goose" 4328
"inn lay in a hollow" 3421
"inning unscratched, made it through another" 8915
Innocence 3602, 5005, 5675, 7551, 7994
"innocence, his" 5005

"innocence, his self-evident . . ."
5675
"innocence, loses its" 275
"innocence, safe and secure moments of blessed" 3602
"innocent, florid and loud and" 275
"innocent as an angel" 5980
"innocent countries" 5427
"innocent ignorance" 7102
"innocent of day-to-day reality as a blind dummy" 9718
"innocent of the fact" 4538
"innocent people" 5427
"innocent planter" 4560
"innocently enough, it all began" 7994
"innocuous, something completely" 4667
Inns 3421, 3764, 4303, 4304, 4308, 4315, 4328, 5012, 6246, 7284, 8339, 8951, 9113
"inns, great roadside" 9113
"inns of Spain" 6246
"inquest, an" 1889
"inquired, casually" 7567
"inquiry, uncertain" 6979
"ins and outs of the matter" 7607
"insane, deeds of daring which verged on the" 4046
"insane nephew" 7802
Insanity 107, 109, 875, 2018, 2593, 2651, 2828, 3012, 4710, 5183, 5399, 5771, 6300, 7396, 7813, 7897, 8278, 8665, 10527
"insanity, suspected of" 7505
"inscribed *Dodd's Buildings*" 1596
"inscribing the initials *R.W.* in the dust" 6713
"inscription, short" 8311
"inscrutable, motionless and" 1523
"inscrutable and silent men" 9381
"inscrutable and silent women" 9381
"insect repellent, icy" 8193
Insects 2211, 2227, 3032, 4427, 4895, 5033, 5074, 5256, 5314, 8526, 9993, 10326
"insects are asleep" 8783
"insects betray their vital processes" 9467
"insects droning in the sunshine" 2211
"insects were feeding on his nerves" 5603
"insecurity" 10844
"insecurity, tension and" 3710
"insensible to fatigue and monotony and ennui" 9381
"insensitive, cheerfully" 5349
"inseparable twins" 7164
"inserted between his nether and outer shirts" 9529
"inside of it, but I'd never been" 4321
"insides, the deepest corner of your own" 8814

"Insignificance, pale to" 5492
"insisted, Mother" 6532
"insisted it was down from him" 4437
"insisted on making inept moves" 5829
"insistence, raucous" 1123
"insistent" 658
"insolence, savage" 4307
"insolent flash of smiling teeth" 8553
"insomnia, from the center of her" 8491
"insomnia, photographic clarity of" 8480
"*insomnia*, protracted and terrible" 8477
"insomnia, thinking about" 8485
"insomnia is my inheritance" 8495
"inspect the weather" 2402
"inspected the room and kitchen" 7774
"inspecting herself, intently" 8556
"inspecting it, as though" 3860
Inspection 1373, 7774, 9658
"inspection, tours of" 9658
"inspection and appraisal, undergoing" 1373
"inspection was over" 8673
"inspector in plain clothes" 6949
"Inspector of Nurse Training Schools" 10216
Inspiration 4890
"inspiration" 1882
"inspiration, stroke of" 5576
"Instance, an unhappy" 10764
"instant, at that" 5096
"instant, in an" 8179
"instant of inappropriate whimsy, for a stalled" 4897
"instanter, stop" 84
"instigation of passion and doom" 2608
"instinct, inherited fighting" 4433
"instinct, possessive" 3560
"instinct, sex" 7982
"instinct for growth" 7818
"instinct told Murontzeff" 9587
"instinctively cowering" 3722
Instincts 3560, 4433, 7043, 7818, 7982, 9587
"instincts, bound to their" 5392
"instincts, my secret" 7043
"instincts for self-preservation" 1209
"instincts were better than money" 7043
"Institute, Ellenberg" 7835
"Institute, Oceanic" 8520
"Institute, Textile" 5445
"*Institute of Social Imagistics*" 6443
"'institution', a school" 6427
"institution, eight-man" 6219
"institution, imaginary" 7893
"institution, the" 3422
"institution, the whole" 7149

"institution dedicated to the memory of that great military genius" 7901
"institution of the sort, most remarkable" 1006
"institution was but a year old" 7896
Institutions 1006, 1337, 1515, 2585, 3160, 3226, 3418, 3419, 3420, 3422, 3428, 3429, 3430, 6974, 7149, 7823, 7893, 7902, 8302, 8333, 9252
"instructed me, my father" 6656
"Instructing" 5552
Instruction 4491, 7044, 7444, 9579
"instruction, college and university" 7905
Instructions 6768, 10066
"instructions on how to write what they want you to write" 10049
"instructor of literature, middle-aged" 1920
"instructors in the History of Human Civilization" 10500
"instrument of civilization" 271
"instrument of my mother's death" 7542
"instruments, tuning their" 1680
"instruments picked up the massive outline" 683
"insulated like ants in an ant-hill" 6266
"insulation" 10911
"insult, when he ventured upon" 4989
Insults 2685, 3174, 6310, 6716, 8247
"insults, familiar nationalistic-style" 4984
Insurance 2478, 6616
"Insurance, North Carolina Mutual Life" 9602
"insurance, sold" 6482
"insurance policies, air-flight" 2478
"insurrection in Southampton" 3476
"insurrectos" 8650
"intangible tensions" 2607
"intellect" 10791
"intellect shamed the Tate Gallery's entire twentieth-century collection" 8027
"intellectual" 7979
"intellectual adventure, an" 588
"intellectual despisers" 9378
"intellectual indigestion" 9718
Intellectuals 7979
Intelligence 1981, 3635, 5767, 7788, 7993
"intelligence" 4998, 5001
"Intelligence, Artificial" 7788
"intelligence, derive their" 4490
"intelligence, disagreeable" 6307
"intelligence, the critical protests of my" 4343

"intelligence analyst" 2251
"intelligence as a French habit" 4997
"Intelligence branch of the United States Navy" 5417
"intelligences greater than man's" 519
"intelligent" 4999
"intelligent, appears to be" 5003
"intelligent, she's" 1981
"intelligent, truly" 5000
"intelligent as other traders, had they been as" 3635
"intelligent foreigner" 1342
"intelligent stranger" 6908
"intelligent than my father, I am more" 5007
"intense" 8014
"intense, cold was" 10196
"intense, shall we say" 5408
"intensity, different" 8546
"intensity, dreaming with new" 2793
"intensity, no special" 6548
"intensity of a near-sighted person" 10916
"Intensive Care Unit" 4619
"intent, deliberate" 8773
"intention, burdens of" 5460
"intention, it had been my" 6797
"intention, my" 6224
"intention, quite without" 8847
"intention is to arrive early" 9337
"intentions, built with the best of" 7902
"Intercontinental, the" 7481
"intercourse with other people" 7968
"intercourse with the great world, long" 267
"interest, he lost" 2588
"interest, manifold" 3357
"interest rate, rise in the" 6493
"interest these pages may have, whatever" 5395
"interested, doing his best to be" 9462
"interested, wasn't" 2893
"interested him enormously" 9226
"interested in, what you're more" 9697
"interested in every one" 6266
"interested in the origins of things" 4282
"interested only in the facts" 9702
"interested only in the skirts" 7229
"interesting, anything really" 930
"interesting again, nothing was ever so" 943
"interesting baby, I was an extremely" 553
"interesting to watch, it has been" 1314
"interference faded" 9363
"interior, its looming" 9389

Interludes 1143, 3154, 6370, 6505, 9487, 9592, 9728
"interment of his rib" 4683
"interminable story" 7986
"International Settlement" 6901
"internees are given the minimum of supervision" 2033
"interpenetrated by it" 8333
"interposed his wife timidly" 6308
"Interrogation" 8655
"interrupted a question about mathematics" 7202
"interrupted her own forceful murmurings" 6231
"interrupted him" 1260
"interrupted his slow shuffling progress" 10405
"interrupted it" 1843
"interrupting, pardon me for" 4608
Interruptions 1260, 1843, 1920, 4608, 4078
"interruptions could positively be brooked no longer" 1920
"intersect the lives of his dramatis personae" 5414
"intersecting monologues" 8855
"intersection, slanting" 1379
"intersection, T" 3666
"intersection, the" 4078
"intersections, complicated" 5607
"Interstate 40" 9798
"interval, there will be a short" 9487
"interval of obscure duration" 10260
"intervals, at slow but regular" 1109
"intervals over the past twenty years" 5839
"interview, first part of the" 3757
"interview, going to his first" 2843
"interview, had given another" 10894
"interview, went to" 5786
"interview seemed over" 5832
"interview sessions, series of three" 5842
"interview with Professor Slade" 6630
"interview with the company president" 1925
"interviewed that East Coast photographer" 6867
"interviewer" 5862
"interviewer, told an" 1329
"interviewing Clint Maroon" 6314
Interviews 716, 1514, 1925, 2843, 3757, 5786, 5842, 5862, 6314, 6348, 6630, 6867, 10894
"interviews always make me nervous" 1514
"interweaving, you could see them" 7779
Intimacy 1053, 8876
"intimate conversation" 7772
"intimate dealings" 1053
"intimate feelings" 7956

"intimate friends, so few" 696
"intimately, never spoken" 8876
"intimately and favourably known" 1012
"intimately his, ominous and" 2447
"intimates called him, what his" 4728
"intimation expresses too much, a plain" 8838
"intimidated by it or charmed, immediately" 3161
"intoxicated males" 9381
"Intracoastal, the" 9614
"intrepid exterior, my" 3698
"intrigue, court" 3677
Intrigues 541, 1060, 1112, 3677, 4251, 4480, 5801, 6942, 6957, 7604, 7840, 7868, 7871, 7954, 8904, 8905, 9045
"intrigues" 1342
"intriguing in its transitions" 304
"introduce myself, it is not easy to" 4870
"introduce myself, let me" 4769
"introduced myself" 8027
"introduced their 3:00 A.M. show" 4220
"introduced to, a woman I was" 6032
"introduced to Sheila Trask" 5854
"introduces Mr. Gamal" 5844
"introducing the story for him, I am" 8999
"introduction, writing an" 5483
Introductions 4795, 4870
"introductions come" 10007
Introspection 9422
"intruded again, Poppa" 2771
"intrusion, welcomed the" 9906
"intrusions from remote space" 7545
Intuition 5481
"intuition stayed my pen" 5481
"invade, I came to" 8702
"invaded by each other's identities" 8223
"invaded so often in the past" 6806
"invading France" 10473
"invalid, privileges of the" 125
"invalid V.I.P., like an" 2903
"Invalides, alone in the" 10071
"invariably find a series of book stalls" 5607
Invasion 10484
"invasion, peril of" 5026
"invasion had come" 10484
"invasion of Normandy" 6863
"invent him, it would be necessary to" 2629
"invent them, hours to" 2417
"invented a new religion" 5413
"invented one morning" 1443
"invented the exploding cannon-ball" 7901
"invented the name the world knew them by" 4805

Invention 1443, 2417, 2629, 4901, 4937, 7139, 7976, 7979
"invention, the cage was his own" 7139
"invention and art, utmost force of human" 4489
"Invention helps" 5226
"invention was brand-new, Marconi's" 3534
"inventions crowd upon us, strange" 5681
"inventor" 6454
"inventor of pleasant romances" 5398
"inventor of the corn flake and peanut butter" 8298
Inventors 7901, 7976
"inventors of my age, I am one of the great" 7976
"inventory of my Business" 1066
"invents, what it sees from what it" 1429
Inverarity, Pierce 10559
Inverness, the" 8170
"investigate the circumstances of this story" 8960
"investigate the nature of this question" 7518
"investigate until they're blue in the face" 6676
"investigated and understood, every thing" 2600
"investigation, my" 7548
Investigations 6676, 7548
Investment 3752
"investors" 1019
Invisibility 683, 1724, 2129, 2582, 5922, 7121
"invisibility, public" 6470
"invisible, his first moment of feeling" 2562
"invisible, I had become" 2582
"invisible, it was still" 683
"Invisible, King of the" 467
"invisible, we're" 2129
"invisible dog" 1724
"invisible man, I am an" 5922
"invisible streets" 9540
"invisible to him, sunlight would be" 5329
"invisible waves" 5340
"invisibly, moved" 7913
"invitation, accept the" 9860
"invitation to assist at a séance" 2306
"invitation to Sunday afternoon tea" 1921
Invitations 1143, 1179, 1535, 1767, 1816, 1921, 1945, 2306, 2727, 2920, 3812, 3840, 3942, 3998, 4023, 8633, 8959, 9348, 9352, 9391, 9860, 9877
"invite Geiger and his counter" 10007
"invite me to Balmoral" 1179

"invited, eight guests had been" 4023
"invited Alexander, she had" 9391
"invited me, he has not" 3812
"invited me to dinner at his club" 8633
"invited Mrs. Brown" 9348
"invited to compose a piece" 6224
"invited to read the story" 8959
"invited what the *Morning Post* called a 'select circle of friends'" 9858
"inviting him to address my passing-out class" 1816
"inviting me to participate in your January School" 1945
"inviting to her, nothing sounded more" 5298
"involved, found herself" 2018
"involvement, my lifelong" 5100
"Ionian Sea" 4469
"Iowa" 960, 1676, 3878, 6441
"Iowa, eastern" 9746
"Iowa highway corner" 9554
Ippolito, Don 8252
"Ipsilon" 5019
"I.Q., a genius" 7993
"IQ, an extemely high" 5005
"IQ of 70" 6170
Irani, Cyrus 1746
Ireland 2885, 6265, 10607
"Ireland" 447, 2005, 3215, 1569, 5393, 6265, 6385, 8580, 9743
"Ireland, in southern" 2024
"Ireland, in the west of" 6887
"Ireland, my father took me to" 2510
"Ireland, Northern" 6257
"Ireland, people of" 5214
"Ireland, remote midlands of" 10607
Irene 5187
"Irene, S." 652
"iridescent blue" 2803
Iris 206, 6154, 6790
"iris limp" 3314
"iris which should have been hazel or grey" 10774
"Irish" 10840
"Irish, half" 4446
"Irish, the Cullens were" 5802
"Irish, which part of you is" 4447
"Irish began coming in" 4057
"IRISH CAUSE, LATEST MARTYR TO" 2386
"Irish chieftain" 6385
"Irish coast, west" 5040
"Irish complexion" 4438
"Irish Freedom, The Friends of" 2386
"Irish gentleman" 9874
"Irish humour" 695
"Irish original" 4086
"Irish Parish, I remember" 4057
"Irish politician" 7002
"Irish Republic" 6255
"Irish Sea" 8090

"Irish Sea, stormy surging" 9300
"Irish wine" 9300
"Irish woman, heavy" 9370
"Irishers from the Commissioner's office" 8750
"Irishman had watched the house and waited" 10087
"Irishmen" 10767
"Irishwoman, disreputable old" 10814
"irksome duty" 7107
Irma 2091, 3993
"iron, jangle of" 8776
"iron, like a piece of burnt" 8696
"iron, men of" 3698
"iron, steel is an alloy based on" 10530
"iron bar, a hollow" 6182
"iron for the short sixth hole, a short" 8927
"iron it" 6356
Iron Orchid 3582
"ironic" 6892
"ironically, as if" 5503
"ironically or sentimentally" 1302
"ironing a shirt" 2853
"ironmongers" 4069
Irons, Jack 5796
"iron-works" 175
Irony 5086, 10826
"irony, she had enough" 10826
"irony, without" 9420
"irony . . . descended upon him" 5086
"irony when speaking of her, not disposed to personal" 10781
"Iroquois Virgin, are you the" 4771
"irrelevance, apparent" 5525
"irresistible" 3625
"irresistibly, drew Arthur Rowe" 6761
"irrigating ditches" 1357
Irritability 379
"irritable, driver was getting" 2972
"irritable people" 379
Irritation 1920, 9325
"irritation" 1920, 9886
"irritation that had brought her to the point of going away" 9325
Isaac 4799
Isaacs, Hannah 3330
Isaacs, Jacob 4918
Isabel 3685, 4815
Isabella 3937
Isabella B." 1598
Isabella of Spain 7630
Isabelle 9885
Isadora 2569, 10857
"Isar" 274
Isherwood, Mr. Christopher 4735
Ishma 6417
Ishmael 1114, 4713
Isidor 5406
"island, adjacent" 8155
"Island, assembled at the" 3601

"island, bearings of the" 5012
"Island, Bloody" 1751
"island, breezy little" 10731
"island, burned" 5042
"island, Caribbean" 5052
"island, center of the" 5328
"Island, Coney" 5017, 7932
"Island, Davenhall" 5050
"Island, Eldey" 5030
"Island, Ellis" 8080
"island, fiery" 5052
"island, first there is the" 5047
"island, flew up to the" 3716
"island, how I remember the" 5027
"island, it is one HIDEOUS" 5053
"Island, Long" 6363
"island, long narrow and irregular" 5011
"Island, Manhattan" 1854
"Island, Mercator" 5021
"Island, Mount Desert" 9734
"island, my fancy was for an" 5013
"island, name of the" 5032
"island, once an" 9091
"Island, Pine" 5028
"Island, Plum" 7668
"Island, Queen Charlotte's" 4076
"Island, Ross" 228
"Island, Sandy" 3090
"island, small desert uninhabited" 8048
"island, small deserted" 6403
"Island, Solomons" 5048
"island, sometimes an" 5025
"Island, Staten" 9646, 10628
"Island, Tawabaw" 118
"island, the" 171, 5051, 8036
"island, their" 5020
"island, they were really here on the" 5024
"island, this here" 6917
"island, tiny" 5049
"island, toward the" 1735
"Island, Treasure" 5012
"island, twilight in the" 2239
"island again, see the" 5037
"island lay in the harbor entrance like a green cork in the neck of a green bottle" 5034
"island made her feel exposed" 5036
"island mistakenly named Greensward" 5035
"Island of Britain" 7794
"Island of Cithera" 7370
"island of Cyprus, beautiful" 7527
"island of Fanua" 1495
"island of his birth, had last seen the" 4547
"island of Jamaica in the Caribbean Sea" 4643
"island of Kaua'i" 10957
"island of St. Catherine" 5052
"island of Sakhalin" 2516
"island of Sicily" 5026
"island of Thassos" 8941

"island of Zenkali" 5043
"island off the west Irish coast" 5040
"island pressed up warmly against itself" 5020
"island rose and sank" 5044
"island sits in the sun" 5046
"island to island, from" 10716
"island towards the southern extremity of the long coast of Chili" 8048
"island was of stone" 5031
"island was overcrowded" 5041
"island was there" 5039
"island where rivers run deep" 5045
"island where storms were stormier" 5033
"Islanders" 8178
"island-hopping" 9614
Islands 1495, 3601, 4028, 4100, 4547, 4643, 5051, 5149, 6917, 6933, 8036, 8048, 10611, 10731
"islands" 457
"islands, chain of offshore" 1421
"islands, cluster of" 5015
"Islands, Hawaiian" 8704
"islands, in these" 4455
"Islands, Leeward" 9086
"Islands, Mandarin" 5638
"Islands, the" 9521
"islands, the thousand" 5018
"islands, West Indian" 9216
"islands and peninsulas rich in history" 8112
"islands below" 5023
"islands in the Hawaiian group" 5022
"islands that form a chain of lovely jewels" 4098
"Isle of Dogs" 4079
"Isle of Wight" 6860
"Isles, Western" 4034
"islet, the rocky" 5029
"Islington" 1596
"isolated" 108
"isolated, house is" 3252
"isolated from anything resembling family or stability" 6883
Isolation 108, 6883, 8946, 10911
"isolation" 10911
"Ispahan" 6405
Israel 2080
"Israel" 7717, 8275, 10422
"Israel, Rabbi in" 7505
"Israel became a state" 7896
"Israel died, the night" 6377
"Israeli archaeologist" 6279
"Israeli composer" 6232
"Israeli couple and their four-year-old son" 9630
"Israeli radio" 1159
"Israeli sunshine, hot" 4704
"Israeli-style" 5286
"Israelites of old, like the" 4459
Issa 7122
"issues, back" 7871

"issues were clear" 10485
"Istanbul" 3299
"Italian, beautiful poems in" 5527
"Italian border" 4631
"Italian car" 59
"Italian engineer" 3084
"Italian marble fountains" 3179
"Italian painter" 5903
"Italian *primedonne*" 10788
"Italian seaman" 7934
"Italian-speaking passengers" 9651
"Italian-style beach sandals" 4277
Italy 6250
"Italy" 120, 1293, 5465, 6250, 8620, 9109, 9559
"Italy, combat years in" 7894
"Italy, in the center of" 1473
"*Italy*, Nagel's" 9155
"Italy, northeastern confines of" 6052
"Italy, railway stations in" 7271
"Italy, Sons of" 3753
"Italy, southern" 1219, 2576
"item appeared, the following" 2386
"item at the foot of his column, ran this little" 6652
"iteration, monotony of tiresome" 3075
"Ithaca" 1431
"Ithaca California" 968
"itinerant evangelists" 1497
"ITV" 4008
Ivan the Terrible 1159
Ivanhoe 10016
"Ivanhoe yoh!" 10016
"Ivers" 1755
"ivory, shattered" 5174
"ivy clinging to the brick and framing the windows" 9225
"Ivy League" 3050
Ivybridge 8572
"Ixopo" 9146
Izzy 10301

"Jabalón valley" 9995
"jabbing a blunt forefinger" 6967
Jacaranda 4802
"*jacet, hic*" 7584
Jack 1047, 2003, 2614, 2674, 3309, 3344, 5513, 5817, 8197, 9164, 10731
Jack, Great-uncle 4437
Jack, Old 5945
Jack, Uncle 987
"Jack to the south, vast snowy" 6075
"jackass, you're a" 4981
"jacket, double-breasted dinner" 1714
"jacket, it was not a *very* white" 2819
"jacket, midshipman's" 8642
"jacket, sports" 4789
"jacket, straight" 2876
"jacket, suede" 2839

"jacket of mine, shooting-" 4117
"jacket ripped off, leather" 2062
"jacket that is too light" 1002
"jackets, embroidered silk" 2432
Jackie 4806, 6851
Jackson, Ely 7025
Jackson, General 5404
Jackson, Marylou 1772
Jackson, Sadie 4790
Jackson, Vernon 8384
Jackson, Walter 9556
Jackson, Wesley 4736
"Jacksonville" 7278
Jacob 1721, 3306, 5502, 6472, 7079
"Jacobins, Place des" 10370
"Jacuzzi" 573
"Jadewood the house" 3147
"Jaffa" 4011
Jaffar, Si 1635
Jagan 3845
Jagat the Maharana of Amarpur 10210
Jaggers, Alley 7628
"Jaguar sedan, green" 9300
Jail 589, 1505, 1579, 2022, 3097, 10135
"Jail, Durham" 2033
"jail, got out of" 6148
"jail, let out of" 2931
"jail, sheriff reached the" 2022
"jail, tho" 3007
"jail, the county" 1579
"jail, women's floor of the county" 589
"jailhouse" 10135
"jails, Scottish" 7142
Jaime 1164
Jake 2382, 8071, 8460, 8731
"Jalna, this house" 3150
"jalopy, newlywed's" 5587
"jam, cherry" 9923
"Jamaica" 4100, 4643, 9012
"Jamaica, the first inhabitants of" 1192
"Jamaica Bay" 4092, 7946
"Jamaica-men will begin to govern themselves" 6981
"Jamaican, a" 9027
James 1963, 2663, 3943, 5852, 10103, 10836
James, Bill 3857
James, Billy 6452
James, Jesse 4813
James I 7794
James II, King 10465
Jamie 2999, 6856
Jamison, Jimmy 5379
"jammed along the forward gates" 4910
"jammed the claw end of a hammer" 10949
"jammed together in the one seat" 2955
Jampolski, Count Wladislaw 7184

"Jams, the" 5715
Jane 123, 903, 2279, 3000, 4465, 5643, 6414, 7390, 8013
Janet 833, 2903
Janey 1414, 4530, 6666
"jangle of iron" 8776
Janice 63, 7346
Janie 6295
"janitor, grumbling old" 7158
Janoth, Earl 6763
"January" 67, 667, 765, 790, 819, 841, 917, 1159, 1674, 2155, 2161, 2357, 2385, 2443, 3440, 3889, 3982, 4659, 5821, 6129, 6326, 6375, 6570, 7246, 8485, 8498, 8587, 8623, 8678, 8740, 9104, 9244, 9404, 10216, 10396, 10617, 10627, 10661, 10742, 10943, 10986
"January, a certain" 10601
"January, another" 10980
"January, early in" 9012
"January, first day of" 10088
"January, late in" 8341
"January, not in" 10987
"January day, one" 10685
"January sunlight" 8947
"Japan" 5417
"Japan, since I came to" 2536
"Japan, since leaving" 2552
"Japan my native land" 4535
"Japanese, I am not a" 4535
"Japanese butler" 3088
"Japanese class" 3292
"Japanese remained to be dealt with" 10514
"Japanese woman" 10887
"jar, flat misty killing" 10816
"Jardin du Palais Royal" 9464
Jardine, Mrs. 9352
Jarrett, Mason 5935
Jarretts, the 3147
"jarring application of the brakes" 7249
"jars my drink lobes" 8797
Jarvis, Captain 4470
Jarvis, Cock 4470
Jas 8816
"Jashimpur" 6806
"Jashimpuri people" 6806
Jasmin 625
Jason 220, 4082
Jason, Gov. Ted 7831
Jason, Governor Edward Montoya 6997
Jasper 1602, 7466
"jaundiced" 9411
"jauntily as though he were moving through a thousand watching people" 10373
"jauntiness, a novel" 5308
"Javanese countryside, in the middle of the" 2480
"javelin whistled in the air" 4469
Javich, Mrs. Moja 9931
"jaw, aggressive thrusting" 8237

"jaw, pushed out his" 8043
"jaw, strong jutting" 336
"jaw in, smashing his" 6182
"jaw resolutely jutting" 2045
"jaw was long and bony" 333
Jay 8798
Jay, Rob 3602
"Jaycee, a" 9729
Jaynes, Byron 5842
Jazz 6223
"jazz, to hell with" 6223
"jealous, women were" 10852
"jealous of their hatred" 4364
Jealousy 125, 541, 3308, 4364, 6244, 10828
"jealousy" 3308
"jealousy, principal object of" 6244
"jealousy made them try to criticize" 10828
"jealousy of the privileges of the invalid" 125
Jean-Jacques 4443
"jeans, ratty" 2872
"jeans, tight blue" 2075
"Jebel es Zubleh" 6054
"Jebel Surgham" 7361
"jeep, front tire of the" 755
"jeep wagon" 2980
"jeeps, tanks and" 3416
"jeered the new boots boy" 1990
"jeering jingle pleased them" 6018
Jeeter 3604
Jeeves 656, 3341, 3839, 3850, 4213
Jeff 4723, 8234
Jeffcoat 9776
Jefferson, President 7232
Jefferson, Thomas 371
"Jefferson" 4052
Jefferys, the Alf 3645
Jeffrey 3829
Jeffrey, Helen 10643
"jelly, upset a dish of crab-apple" 7020
"jellyfish drifts in the tidal abyss" 435
Jem 22, 3934
Jeminovski, Jackie 3239
Jen 5464
Jencks, Mrs. 990
Jenepher 8741
Jenkins, Jane and Mary Ann 7832
Jennie 9893
"Jennie North" 4916
Jennifer 1788, 2712, 3245, 4853, 6723
Jennings, Miss Liz 3831
Jenny 10878
Jensen, Monica 5854
Jensen, Mrs. 3835
"jeopardize their popularity" 6976
Jeremiah 10009
Jeremy 2984, 5947
"jerked his head half-right" 8556
"jerking them around" 8793

"jerking up and down backward and forward" 2963
"jerkwater town" 7262
Jerome 4475
Jerry 405
"jerry builder" 1856
"jerrycan, found under a" 2553
"Jersey" 5051
"Jersey City New Jersey" 802
"Jersey flats" 7310
"Jersey wharf" 4910
"Jerseys, herd of" 3646
"Jerusalem" 1159, 1464, 1722, 9141, 9633, 10077
"Jerusalem, from this girasol we have made" 10899
"Jerusalem, West" 6279
"Jerusalem artichoke" 10899
"Jerusalem wall" 1059
Jess 6397
Jesse 4816, 5010, 6103
Jessica 10735
Jessie 870, 7130, 7783, 8005
"Jessop" 3784
Jessup, Conrad 7728
"jested, bus drivers" 5308
Jester 8458
"Jesuit Day School of Saint Ignatius" 7892
Jesuit Relations 2555
Jesus 5664, 6011, 7497, 8182, 8303, 8318, 10197
"Jesus!" 8182
"Jesus, Happy Reentry" 8318
"Jesus, I got the message from" 6011
Jesus Christ 73
"Jesus Christ, Our Lord" 1496
"Jesus, oh" 9904
Jesus of Judea 10984
"JESUS IS COMING" 8303
"jet lag" 7466, 9657
"jet planes, before" 3402
"jet sighed tiredly and fell silent" 208
Jethro 3652, 4853
"jetliner" 235
"jetsam, flotsam and" 3094
"jetting from palmy LaLa Land to gray and frenzied New York City" 5297
"jetty's edge" 9785
"Jew, became a" 7505
"Jew, Wandering" 3055
Jewel 2465, 10346
"jewel, warmth of a rare" 3076
"Jewel of the Antilles" 5045
"jewel of the first water, no" 9129
"jeweler's case" 2861
"jewellers' booths, little" 5614
"jewellery gets stolen" 4996
Jewelry 338, 2055, 2844, 2854, 2856, 2858, 2861, 2868, 4628, 4986
"jewelry, his Arthur Murray" 4628
"jewels, chain of lovely" 4098

"jewels, the family" 5848
"jewels will you be wearing tonight, what" 2868
"Jewish" 369
"Jewish affairs, state of" 910
"Jewish affairs right between my fingers" 910
"Jewish blood, denying her" 6652
"Jewish boy" 5848
"Jewish calendar" 4524
"Jewish clothier" 8908
"Jewish Defense Agency, American" 6769
"Jewish experience in America" 5486
"Jewish marriages were invalid" 7505
"Jewish notion, circumcision was a" 2817
"Jewish prison" 4370
Jews 1059, 5486, 5516
"Jews, forgiven the" 8182
"Jews, the" 5516
"Jews, with thousands of other" 5223
"Jews every civic right, England denied her" 7505
"Jews shops" 7059
"Jews were going into exile" 6109
"Jews were like these grapes" 1059
Jeynor, Annie 9036
Jezebel 2291
"Jezebel's Daughter, in the matter of" 2291
"Jezow" 2592
"jig is up" 4249
Jiggs 2690
"jilted the Muse, he that has" 5397
Jim 302, 1160, 1684, 4853, 5506, 5814
Jim, Uncle 2837
Jiménez, Jorge Rojas 4286
Jimmerson, Lamar 8695
Jimmy 5825, 6938, 7209
Jimson, Mrs. 2021
"jingle of brass rings" 1807
Jinny 3183
"jinrikisha" 9626
Jo 4512
Jo, Aunt 5806
Jo, Mrs. 1245
Joan 6192, 6876
Joanie 5780
Joanna 1432, 1665, 10716
"job, a" 2527
"job, apply for a" 6442
"job, awful new" 6466
"job, got the" 6440
"job, I have a" 3472
"job, I quit my" 6455
"job, I resigned from my" 6447
"job, interviewed for a teaching" 254
"job, just a new" 6175
"job, know her" 5003

"job, last day on the" 892
"job, losing his" 5535
"job, my" 5296
"job, no" 7041
"job, no one else could have done the" 7
"job, quit my" 6475
"job, routine" 615
"job, the" 9784
"job, wanted to give up his" 6434
"job, wearying of his" 1493
"job done decently, if you want a" 10936
"job himself, do this" 10947
"job of sorting it all out" 10559
"job that pays me back" 936
"job with Mr. Bailey, Smitty tried out for a" 6652
Jobs 7, 254, 615, 892, 936, 1753, 2487, 2527, 3330, 3332, 3472, 3697, 4596, 5206, 5286, 5374, 5535, 6175, 6193, 6348, 6410, 6418, 6434, 6440, 6442, 6447, 6455, 6466, 6475, 6487, 6497, 6750, 9784, 10559, 10936
"jobs, doing small fix-it" 1477
Jocelyn 4557
"Jocelyn Pennsylvania" 1920
"jockeys, doom" 4220
"jocose ostlers" 9113
"jocosity, with some" 3394
Jodi 8729
Jody 8499
Joe 996, 1202, 1968, 3274, 4019, 4112, 5306, 6547
Joe, Grandpa 6645
Joe Flushing Avenue 3020
Joe The Engineer 3020
Joey 1627, 6590
"jogged back in the late afternoon" 9872
"jogged with the joyless determination" 7852
"jogger, the" 3484
Jogging 7852
"jogging, man" 9151
Johann 7403
"Johannesburg" 2028
"Johannesburg from the air" 1420
John 702, 963, 1502, 2732, 4554, 4765, 4853, 5377, 5523, 5643, 6214, 7812, 8781, 9296, 9736, 9860
John, Tiger 8750
John Bosco, the" 8094
John Joel 9677
Johnny 465, 4914, 7380, 7750
Johnson, Avey 2484
Johnson, Bram 5902
Johnson, Guy 7409
Johnson, Mose 3662
"join him, asked me to" 3942
"join the army" 8683
"joined Sal, Mamie" 8639

"joined the host of the Crusaders" 10329
Joiner, Frank 160
"joints, casually smoking" 3283
"joints, his toe and finger" 7989
"joke, affectionate" 4661
"joke, flirtatious eyes slanting the" 4662
"joke, let me tell you a" 4666
"joke, my" 360
"joke in a bar" 4667
"joker, some guitar-playing" 8745
Jokes 4661, 4662, 4664, 4666, 4667
"jokes, one of life's little" 4664
Joleen 3306
Jolliet, Louis 9635
Jolly, Uncle 8429
"jolly after all, I don't feel so" 2496
"Jolly Chums Club, The" 2828
"jolt him face down into the gritty water" 976
"jolted and jarred its way" 9813
"jolted by sudden pains" 6598
"jolted Maureen from her dream" 10258
"jolted monotonously against his steering wheel" 2947
"jolted slowly along invisible streets" 9540
"jolting of the vehicle" 10108
Jonah 4765
Jonas 1909
Jonathan 5781, 9653
Jonathan, Professor 1762
Jones 4467
Jones, Benjamin 8231
Jones, Colonel 121
Jones, Corpsman Andrew 8674
Jones, Davy 2820
Jones, Felicity Annabel Arlington 7733
Jones, Gran 4333
Jones, Lewis 8231
Jones, Mr. 1939, 2895
Jones, Mr. Virgil 4282
Jones, Mrs. 9348
Jonny 10214
Jonson, Ben 2931
Jordan 4860
"Jordan" 2080
"Jordan, the" 5716, 10329
Jörg 3752
"Jornada del Muerto" 888
Joseph 1862, 7039, 7217, 8008, 9769, 10209
Joseph, Virgin 8008
Josephine 7127
Josephine, Grandma 6645
Josh 860, 2682, 3483, 10857
Joshie 3874
Joshua 9449
Josiah, Old 1877
Josie 3782
Josko, Dr. 7172

Joslin, Professor 696
"joss-house, Chinese" 7529
"journal" 5544
"journal, always wanted to keep a" 2537
"Journal, Boswell's Manhattan" 5444
"journal, entry in my" 2548
"journal, I begin my" 3887
"journal, I begin the" 2545
"journal, kept a" 2547
"journal, my" 2546
"journal, picked up her" 2551
"journal, the" 5027
"Journal, the" 2541
"journal, wrote in his" 3466
"journal is interspersed with observations of my own" 8999
"journal of Samuel Himmelhoch" 2553
"journal published in New York City" 2386
Journalism 4008, 6352
"journalist, American" 10215
"journalist, veteran" 3508
"journalist of Sikkim Street" 6435
"journalists pressed me about the Henneker rumors" 5230
Journals *(see also* **Diaries)** 2537, 2541, 2545, 2546, 2547, 2548, 2549, 2551, 2553, 2554, 2555, 3887, 8999
"journals, leave you these" 2549
"journals of the Black-Gowns" 2555
"journals with her, she took her" 2554
"journey, after a month's" 1779
"journey, along the" 4842
"journey, an interminable" 4462
"journey, during the latter half of his" 9519
"journey, end of his" 4075
"journey, end of its" 6368
"journey, half a day's" 1349, 9177
"journey, her return" 1581
"journey, his brief" 9529
"journey, leisurely" 7254
"journey, life's" 6491
"journey, long and tiring transcontinental" 9571
"journey, made an unnecessary" 8004
"journey, my" 9533
"journey, my father's" 662
"journey, on a" 9535
"journey, on the return" 732
"journey, return" 198
"journey, start his" 10274
"journey, the fifteen miles of his" 1615
"journey, the single" 7244
"journey, torn maps direct her" 5718
"journey, twenty-three-mile" 1465
"journey before him" 3471

"journey continued southwards" 762
"journey from Moscow to Charing Cross" 7277
"journey from Moscow to Gorky" 8004
"journey of Mercier and Camier, the" 9588
"journey of not more than three or four hours" 9412
"journey of over sixty-five hundred miles" 2516
"journey of the dead" 888
"journey set a seal on the depressing limbo" 9572
"journey thro' life, after a long and painful" 2287
"journey to their first home" 9544
"journeying out from Verona" 9969
"journeying towards the north east of Scotland" 9511
"journeying up *klongs*" 1832
Journeys 199, 662, 762, 1465, 1581, 1615, 1676, 1707, 1758, 1779, 2516, 2944, 2956, 2959, 2965, 2972, 2980, 2992, 3011, 3012, 3471, 4075, 4462, 4577, 4842, 5181, 5482, 5604, 5718, 5834, 6039, 6069, 6560, 7026, 7219, 7244, 7252, 7254, 7267, 7276, 7277, 7311, 7416, 7609, 7611, 7612, 7615, 7621, 7625, 7639, 8004, 9112, 9168, 9177, 9201, 9358, 9412, 9414, 9436, 9519, 9525, 9529, 9532, 9533, 9535, 9544, 9545, 9547, 9549, 9553, 9563, 9571, 9572, 9576, 9584, 9588, 9592, 9599, 9600, 9626, 9634, 9637, 9655, 9768, 9780, 9796, 9969, 10274, 10333, 10343, 10362, 10367, 10397, 10420, 10431, 10450, 10451, 10452, 10529, 10966
"journeys" 9592
"journeys, made three" 7219
"journey's end" 9532
"journey's end, long" 9626
Joy 7744, 7961
Joy, Harry 2389
Joy 661, 1581, 3979, 4344, 4352, 4355, 5260, 5279, 5661, 6790, 7406, 10837
"joy" 5661, 5846
"joy, clear exclamations of" 661
"joy, close to" 4352
"joy, swept on the wings of a wild" 4158
"joy, tearful with" 4344
"joy and envy" 10837
"joy crouched like a terror" 6790
"joy than a duty, more of a" 3979
"joy to recall, 'tis a" 7406
Joyce 1739
Joyce, Miss Lucia 8386
Joyce, Mr. 9910

"Joyce villa" 3265
"joyful mystery" 3934
"joylessness, accusing him of" 5936
"joyous, as ominous as" 5260
"joys to be re-discovered" 6088
"joys which its depature should
    bring" 10030
Juanita 173
"Juarez" 2656
"Juárez, Ciudad" 7259
"Jubilee month" 847
Jud 7523
Judaism 910, 2817, 5965, 7505,
    7543, 8182
"Judaism" 7543
Judd 2668
Jude 3028
"'Jude the Obscure'" 962
"Judea" 1059, 3655, 5115
"judge, among those competent to"
    7626
"judge, bowing deferentially to the"
    5199
"judge, nineteenth-century Ameri-
    can" 10838
"judge, son of a" 6535
"judge, the" 2020
"Judge, the" 5204
"Judge, the late" 9955
"judge, the station of a" 5193
"judge leaving, remember the" 1705
"Judge said 'Life'" 2027
"Judge was deplorably sleepy" 5201
"judge wisely" 10758
"judge would dine, imagined a"
    3877
"judgement of the divorce-court"
    2649
Judges 388, 2020, 3877, 5193,
    5199, 5201, 5204, 5207, 5210,
    6535, 10838
"judges, loving" 9389
"judging it prudent" 7713
Judgment 1436, 3946, 5207, 5820,
    7971, 9384, 10758
"judgments about us, make" 8222
"judice, me" 10899
"judicial, political and" 6973
"judiciously consulting" 10592
"judiciously observ'd" 10764
Judith 1788, 3194, 4780, 6287,
    7717, 8548, 9266
Judson 7051
Judy the Prudy 4777
"Juffure, village of" 804
"jug, copper" 8044
"jug filled, had come to get a" 2329
"juices, raging" 8993
Jules 4305
Julia 563, 1605, 1661, 2317, 2349,
    2438, 2549, 3552, 5599, 5676,
    5775, 9966
Julian 236, 6524, 8607
Julian the Apostate 1447
Juliet 9105

Julius 4469
"July" 15, 50, 135, 633, 807, 821,
    826, 1188, 1196, 1487, 1914, 1934,
    2137, 2156, 2183, 2263, 2336,
    2469, 2702, 2883, 2985, 3023,
    3032, 3145, 3407, 3657, 4411,
    4412, 4439, 4597, 4763, 4959,
    5026, 5116, 5147, 5452, 5880,
    6587, 6939, 7594, 7637, 7677,
    8069, 8163, 8202, 8395, 8416,
    8417, 8508, 8715, 9088, 9098,
    9320, 9381, 9393, 9802, 9858,
    9881, 9957, 10180, 10615, 10662
"July, early in" 7613
"July, evening of" 5078
"July, Fourth of" 2390, 4526
"July, 4th of" 6576
"July, late" 10733
"July, morning in" 9764
"July, the past" 4281
"July, third day of" 655
"July heat" 8330
"July morning" 10337
"July sunshine" 7108
"jumble of broken glass" 5077
Jumel, Eliza 10662
"jump, grab air and" 602
"jump, this'll make them" 7048
"jump out at him from somewhere
    unexpected, about to" 5121
"jump out of it, as if he might
    want to" 9558
"jumped, taking pictures of people
    as they" 6867
"jumped around in trees, little men
    who" 9648
"jumped back" 34
"jumped from bridges into the
    Tiber yesterday" 7678
"jumped into a construction ditch"
    885
"jumped out to the accommodation
    ladder" 8137
"jumped through a glass roof into
    the paved court" 17
"jumpsuit, a wrinkled sort of color-
    less" 5118
Jun 3929
"Junction, Hanover" 9543
"Junction, Sibley" 1357
"Junction, the" 2967
"Junction, Wockley" 7254
"June" 134, 586, 673, 840, 847,
    1570, 1598, 1600, 1757, 2145,
    2150, 2157, 2506, 2567, 2756,
    2967, 3132, 3226, 3278, 3604,
    3807, 3981, 4012, 4350, 4374,
    4424, 4439, 4558, 4569, 4575,
    5087, 5104, 5204, 5416, 5582,
    5674, 5753, 5804, 6384, 6571,
    6652, 6915, 6928, 7015, 7220,
    8074, 8152, 8262, 8530, 8564,
    8956, 9247, 9348, 9495, 9565,
    9616, 9757, 9759, 9792, 9912,
    9919, 9941, 9947, 9964, 10335,

10500, 10595, 10624, 10656,
    10785, 10800, 10946
"June, a night in" 1356
"June, all through" 4530
"June, certain day in" 10420
"June, evening in" 6555
"June, in early" 2934
"June, in late" 10806
"June, morning in" 5845
"June, second week of" 1422
"June, sunshine of" 10193
"June afternoon" 3645
"June Chesapeake afternoon" 1998
"June days" 10583
"June evening" 4557
"June had, only" 2242
"June landscape" 5137
"June night" 2258, 6380
"June swam, that month of" 9494
"jungle" 3371
"jungle, far beyond the" 7339
"jungle, get out of the" 1623
"jungle, in the" 4956
"jungle, pushed-back" 449
"jungle, rain" 9158
"jungle, smelled of the" 8537
"jungle, towering trees of the" 4895
"jungle air" 1526
"jungle edging the estate" 449
"jungle now forever closed behind
    him" 5572
"jungle of southern nights" 6381
"jungle primeval" 10340
"jungle shade" 3714
Jungles 449, 1526, 1623, 3371,
    4956, 8703, 9158, 10340
Junglewalla, Faredoon 5998
Junior 1260
"junior at Mount Sebastian Col-
    lege" 8708
"Junior Dean" 8354
"juniper was smoldering" 1212
"junipers, lawn spotted with" 9738
"junk, boxes of" 6154
"junk, my first experience with"
    3049
"junk, she rages against" 393
"junk down this way in Florida, it's
    just" 8293
"junk pile, sad dangerous" 6848
"Junk, Uncle" 5848
Juno 7617
"Jupiter" 7136
"Jupiter, Capitoline" 7514
Jurgen 1966
"jury, all male" 5204
"jury, gentlemen of the" 5196
"jury said 'Guilty'" 2027
"just people and unjust" 1342
Justice 5203, 5205, 6812, 7179,
    7541, 9694
"Justice" 1165
"justice, do him" 706
"Justice, Economic" 5203
"Justice, Legal" 5203

"Justice, Social" 5203
"justice, strenuous sense of" 6812
"Justice, Supreme Court" 5207
"justice, victims of" 7179
"justice, waited for" 5205
"Justice did not reign" 5203
"justice done, earnestly desiring to see" 9694
"Justice Exists" 7541
"Justice had made great strides" 5203
"justice of perspective" 270
"Justice-Clerk" 9090
"Justiciar, King Henry's" 1691
"justified, do I think that he was" 2067
Justin 7862
Justine 7556
"Jutland" 10796
"jutting abruptly up" 6912
"jutting from the frigid gray waters" 5030

K, Michael 7077
"K for, what is the" 4749
"Kabul" 6502
Kachiah, Danny 2114, 7642
"Kaddish prayer" 3952
"K'aifeng, the city of" 10584
"Kaffee bitte" 7572
Kafka 1195
"Kafka is not buried here" 1195
Kahan, Louise 1951
"Kaintocks, Les" 6813
Kaiserstiege, Doctor 4509
"Kalapur, town of" 1038
"Kambani" 6324
"Kamchatka" 3514
Kamenetz-Podolsk, Mrs. 9915
Kaminer, Daniel 145
"Kaministiqua, south of the" 4049
Kaminski, Tadeusz 5983
"Kampala" 10665
Kandinsky, Mr. 3274
Kane, Major 10499
Kane, Rachel 1722
"Kansas" 1457
"Kansas City" 4918, 9654
"Kansas steppes" 9072
"Kanthapura is its name" 1381
Kaplan, Mr. 794
"kapok tree, my favorite" 2084
"Kara, in the province of" 1381
"Karachi" 3237
"Karate Killings" 2037
Karenina, Anna Arkadievitch 5466
Karl 4262, 4268, 7592
Karla 8790
"Karnac" 7799
Karnovsky, Joseph Alexander 6196
"Kashgar" 9546
"Kashmir" 8682
Kashpaw, June 10092
Kaspar 9991

Kate 3860, 3929, 4179, 4529, 5243, 7096, 7602, 10251
Katharine 6523
Katherine 130, 6402, 6649
Katherine Elizabeth, Sister 2047
Kathleen 2906
Kathy 2847, 10834
Katie 4365, 6944
"katydids" 2763
"katydids saw and saw" 3032
"Kaua'i, island of" 10957
Kauff, Raunchy 7857
Kaufman, Dinah 8022
Kaul, Nanda 8526
Kay, Aunt 3958
Kazan 403
"K-bar" 1166
"K. C. since 1946" 3136
Keating, Anthony 754
Kee, Mr. Wellington 7128
"keelboat" 9626
Keelby, Adam 5098
Keene, Thomas 1066
"Keep Cool With Coolidge" 2828
"keep for a rainy day" 6431
"keep it, too happy to" 488
"keep it up" 10078
"keeper of the flame" 4577
"keeping nothing back" 5012
"keeping them, what can be" 10097
Keese, Earl 2920
Keifetz 3504
Keith 5904
Keith, Lydia 3136
Kellerman, Frank 864
Kellerman, Leo 5962
Kellogg, Dr. John Harvey 8298
Kelly 10171
Kelly, Red 1878
"Kelly Field" 204
"Kemble" 7587
"Kemet, Two Lands of" 6450
Kempton, General 4953
Kendall 8474
"Kennaquhair" 10898
Kennaston, Felix 5565
"Kennebec" 9758
Kennedy 2815
"Kennedy Airport" 1699, 4092
Kennedy, Jack 5818, 6332
Kennedy, Mrs. 12
"Kennedy's assassination" 2815
Kenny 10729
"Kensington" 696, 3171, 5928, 6631, 8397, 9266
"Kensington, South" 2581
"Kensington area of London" 6963
"Kensington Gardens" 7953
"Kent" 787, 4048, 4139, 4432
"Kenthill at last" 1608
Kentons, the 1965
Kentucky 2194
"Kentucky" 1029, 1422, 2886, 2971, 3669, 7637

"Kentucky, green wilderness of" 2194
"Kentucky capital, little" 9210
"Kentucky Derby, dreamed of the" 8458
"Kentucky mountaineers, a kind of well-to-do" 1396
"Kenwoulton Huntingdon" 4313
"Kenya" 2605
"Kenya, all this business about" 6254
"Kenya Beanstalk capsule" 10423
Keogh, Dunwoodie 2148
Kepler, Johannes 6904
"kept her, he" 9325
"ker o' Dick, take" 2296
Kerenyi, Georg 597
"Kermess, the" 10783
"Kerneham" 7046
"kernel, dry shrivelled" 4491
"kernel of meanness" 395
"Kerrybrook Academy for Girls" 4192
Kester 5681
Kestler, Mr. 162
Kestner, Ernst 10274
Kestoe, Johnnie 2106
"Keswick" 8519
"ketch, a little" 8110
Ketch-22 9052
"kettle, electric" 1874
"kettle, stopped into the" 1861
"kettle did it, the" 7550
"Key, Crab" 3247
"Key, Cudjoe" 10232
"key, ignition" 9805
"Key Biscayne" 9811
"key dangling, the Phi Beta" 4273
"key for the last time, took the" 1570
"key in the black lock, turned the" 6587
"key into the keyhole" 2708
"key is the torturer's horse, the" 5525
"key question, there is the" 7204
"key to his Mercury" 1769
"key to the Beverly Hills Hotel" 2453
"Key West" 5038
"keyed, high" 5408
"keyhole method, the traditional" 8903
"keynote, restraint is the" 1204
"Keys, fishing off the" 3511
"keys, three" 9787
"Keys of Florida" 5174
"keys of the piano, ivory" 6217
"Khabarovsk" 4076
"khaki pants" 8241
"khakis that were still early morning fresh" 5920
Khaled 7504
Khan, Elizabeth 2707
"Khe Sanh" 8681

"kicked his hand away from the en-velope" 3755
"kicked his left foot free of the stir-rup" 7642
"kicked out of England in 1767" 1756
"kicked viciously" 471
"kicking a ball" 311
"kicking the furniture" 986
"kicks coming, I got no" 5282
"kicks open the door" 1996
"kick-the-can, too old to play" 320
"kid, imagine naming a" 4853
"kid, little ferret of a" 967
"kid, my" 3789
"kid, sickly little" 2336
"kid, thinking about the" 10262
"kid, when I was a" 2512, 8922
"kid, when I was a little" 9370
"kid, when you were a" 4536
"kid in her twenties, like a" 10857
"kid themselves, no matter how much they tried to" 4070
"kid with a rheumatic heart and many other complications" 2336
"kid with the shaved head" 10912
Kidd, Captain 2016
"kidding, I'm not" 9017
Kidnapping 1164, 5808
"kidnapping, on the morning of the" 5808
"kidney displaced" 7514
"kids" 2435
"kids, flying bolts of screamed-up" 976
"kids are shooting marbles, three hundred hunched-over" 7898
"kids from the slums" 640
"kids were in bed" 2677
Kienga, Kaloni 6933
Kilburn, Judge 1571
"Kilcoole" 9300
Kilgarvan, Miss Georgina 9955
"Kiliminjaro, Mount" 7832
"kill, afightin fit to" 8650
"kill, at last we" 8789
"kill, decision to" 6200
"kill, driving intensity to" 4433
"kill, would rather not" 6190
"kill a man" 4969, 6193
"kill each other in my family, we" 3633
"kill his wife, he might finally have to" 6201
"kill Maurice Hanline" 6180
"kill me, my father had wanted to" 57
"kill me, trying to" 73
"kill my daddy" 6197
"kill my father, I did not" 6668
"kill my mother" 828
"kill someone" 3689
"kill that black woman, I didn't" 6189

"kill them along the way, don't have to" 3342
"kill your mammy, it'd" 1805
"kill Zooey, trying to" 5843
"Killala, Acres of" 1700
"Killarney bears no resemblance to its Irish original" 4086
"killed, got" 2374
"killed, he was almost" 10456
"killed, some of these people *want* to get" 3021
"killed a white man" 2022
"killed by his side at the pitface" 8683
"killed by the English, his grannie was" 10658
"killed Captain Joe Cree" 2325
"killed cleanly then and there" 2397
"killed eight policemen" 2019
"killed her, I" 6706
"killed her, Thad" 6186
"killed her mother" 3928
"killed himself again, he's" 3519
"killed his father" 6194
"killed holding up a gas station" 2869
"killed in action in Germany" 8675
"killed in battle with the Sioux" 6621
"killed in Mesopotamia" 6636
"killed Lucy Bondurant Chastain Venable on the day she was born" 2428
"killed old Phillip Mathers, how I" 6182
"killed our two sons" 6187
"killed the two white women and the black bitch, nearly" 21
"killed to-day, if I get" 9769
"killed while performing his mis-sion" 2386
"killer, lover and" 4800
"killer of a hundred men" 5916
"killer-diller, last week was a" 72
"killers, see the" 2704
Killian 4879
"killing, king-" 3376
"killing a man can start up new life" 6188
"killing at Martingale, the" 5091
"killing one man instantly" 889
"killing the animals was the hard part" 451
"killing time" 10092
"Killing Time" 9502
"Killings, Karate" 2037
"killings, Washona" 6324
"Kilmainham" 8580
"Kilmainham gaol" 7151
"Kilnalough" 4645
"Kilneagh" 3215
"Kilpeder" 9109
"kilt, here in a" 2871
"kilt, knock-kneed in a" 1179
"kilts, allowed to wear" 7142

"kilts, from the time he wore" 3530
"Kilverstone" 7359
"kimono, lavender and green chrysanthemum-covered stork-bordered" 7469
"kimono, traditional" 10887
Kincaid, Robert 1787
Kind, Rabbi Michael 10188
"kind" 5969
"kind, people are not always" 10878
"kind thing to say" 10878
"kind to all us her Servants" 4221
"kindliest denial, gesture of the" 9880
"kindling pile" 1857
"kindness, gesture of" 5874
"kindness, her" 6606
"kinds, gets all" 3427
"kinemas showed scenes from the Wild West Exhibition" 1320
King, Austin 50
King, Ed 3933
King, Julius 4782
King, Martin Luther 1214, 7902
"King, eyes of the" 7106
"king, first American king" 1442
"King, Great" 10033
"King, High" 8991
"king, his" 798
"king, his son was" 10476
"King, in the service of the" 8641
"King, Little" 4513
"king, not a dead" 2398
"King, old" 4943
"king, Pirote's" 5451
"King, portrait of the" 7781
"king, right high and puissant" 948
"King, she told the" 541
"King, taught by the" 6450
"King, the" 8556, 9892
"king, unwearied sun stood like a victorious" 8392
"King and Queens under him" 8991
"King bore Paris no love" 9892
King Charles 3396, 9882
King Charles III 2485
King Dagobert 4163
King Edward the Good 3571
King George 1483, 6981
King Henry 1691
king Henry the Eighth 948
King Henry VII 10473
King James II 10465
King Peter 7796
King Philip 2051
King Philip the Second 4136
King Rudolf 5082
"King James Version" 7546
"King of all Palestine" 7797
"king of Caredigion" 7795
"King of Crim Tartary" 1902
"king of England" 7812
"King of England" 4554
"King of France" 8346
"King of Great Britain" 6803

"King of Paflagonia" 1902
"King of Prussia" 7803
"King of Spain" 7124, 10966
"king of the clowns" 4800
"King of the Invisible" 467
"King Panic reigns in fast forward" 3725
"king Strong to Aid" 7798
"king throned on a dais of royale purple" 8392
"king travelling through the country" 9520
"king would drink wine with a thousand of his lords" 6752
"King went mad" 4943
"King who by now had almost forgotten the old Queen" 541
"King woke up, the" 10288
"King's camp" 1779
"King's College" 10441
"king's eyes, see her with the" 345
"kingdom, a certain" 340
"kingdom, annals of the" 6247
"kingdom, Arab" 7809
"Kingdom, governed the whole" 5883
"kingdom, this united" 5193
"Kingdom gool" 3614
"kingdom of the free" 6247
"kingdom was but little" 7796
Kingdoms 7796
"kingdom's wealth" 1005
"kingfisher, had seen a" 768
"king-killing" 3376
"kinglet who was called King Peter" 7796
Kingmead, Hugh 3649
"Kingroad" 3116
Kings 363, 541, 798, 1779, 2485, 3571, 4513, 4943, 5082, 6450, 6518, 6752, 7106, 7191, 7794, 7795, 7796, 7797, 7798, 7803, 7805, 7812, 7886, 8762, 8991, 9520, 10033, 10288, 10473, 10476
"kings, a number of petty" 7795
"kings, seem exiled" 5906
"Kings, Sport of" 8317
"kings in Spain" 3376
"kings of Scotland" 3375
"Kingsborough" 5197
"Kingsbridge" 6608
"kingship, exile is the wound of" 7191
Kingsley, Kate 9495
Kingston, Carolyn 812
"Kingston" 6169
"Kinja was the name of the island" 5032
"kinky, delightfully" 1214
Kinneys, the 8628
Kino 10149
"Kinraddie lands" 3381
Kinship 364, 3356, 4434, 4545
Kinte, Binta 804
Kinte, Omoro 804

"kiosk, newspaper" 10366
"kipper bone" 3861
Kirkness, Captain 8152
"kirsch in the fondue, too much" 10559
Kirsten 2393
"Kirstenbosch" 2006
Kirsti 8288
Kirton, Boy 6500
Kish 7217
"kiss, an exchange of spinach during a" 7981
"kiss, as if from a seraph's" 9633
"kiss, paused on the landing to" 7712
"kiss, their last" 1844
"kiss a woman like that" 6038
"kiss his wife good morning and good-bye" 1658
"kiss my mother, men were trying to" 6694
"kiss to save their husbands' guineas" 3396
"kissed her" 1800
"kissed her forehead" 9905
"kissed slowly but with a growing and eager passion" 8027
"kissed your eyes, he" 1656
Kisses 1656, 1658, 1800, 1844, 6038, 6694, 7712, 8017, 9905
"kisses, chocolate" 631
"kissing her newborn child good-bye" 6702
Kit 3174, 6627
"kit, officers'" 2841
"kitbag, nudging and kicking the" 1703
"kitchen, a background of" 964
"kitchen, came into the" 4472
"kitchen, dark high-ceilinged old-fashioned" 8223
"kitchen, in the" 668, 3762
"kitchen, in the open" 10016
"kitchen, shivered the" 8805
"kitchen, the" 8540
"kitchen, Wentworth's" 1593
"kitchen above the surgery" 8223
"kitchen counter" 1870
"kitchen filled up first" 5330
"kitchen glistened whitely" 6145
"kitchen on the first floor" 3094
"kitchen where he belonged, back in the" 5963
"kitchenette, miniscule" 3167
"kitchenette apartments" 3096
Kitchens 1593, 1869, 5963, 7570, 7774
"kite, flew a red-and-green" 10540
"kite was stuck in the top of a tree" 10051
"kites, flying" 8815
"Kitezh, sacred early Christian city of" 2794
"kitten, tabby striped" 18
"kitten, they had taken her" 481

"kitten, *white*" 7551
Kittering, James 1854
"Kittlestonheugh" 3550
Kitty 2520, 4179
Klang, Mr. 3869
"klaxon vs. cheap birch veneer" 1119
Kleeve, Trover 3955
Kleindorf 7004
"Klickitat" 8099
"Klondike" 3394
"*klongs*, journeying up" 1832
Klynt 9335
"knack of doing everything the wrong way, most singularly ingenious" 6018
"knackery in the sky, great" 1050
"knapsack, stuffed them into his" 7858
"knapsack, the" 5724
"knaves and fools" 2997
"kneaded the pie-crust" 3555
"knee, each bony" 3711
"knee, the" 10817
"knee, wrenched my" 128
"knee high, raised his" 10206
Kneebone, Major 4739
"kneelers find wild strawberries" 7227
"kneeling before a small girl" 4625
"knees, bald pink" 8358
"knees, nostrils placed between the two" 2378
"knees, on my" 6547
"knees bent, his" 7739
"knees together" 5450
"knees tore into the soft earth" 9841
"knelt beneath a cool oak" 1194
"knelt in the corner of his vestry" 1541
"knew, but that's all they" 6431
"knew, everyone always" 5962
"knew, he already" 6186
"knew, no one" 4741
"knew, no one quite" 6766
"knew about the freighter, all that Jake" 8071
"knew at once that something was amiss" 3178
"knew at once that something had gone wrong" 7156
"knew at once that this was what they had been waiting for" 7742
"knew before the first act was half over" 130
"knew everybody else, everybody" 6306
"knew everything there was to know about Belgium" 6253
"*knew* he didn't know" 5605
"knew he was on his way" 1785
"knew he would be there, she" 9943
"knew Helen Bradshaw best, people who" 10861
"knew her, never" 10888

"knew her well, few who imagined they" 10861
"knew him, I" 6788
"knew himself to be lucky" 1231
"knew I was in town, I hadn't been aware that he" 6509
"knew I was in trouble" 5868
"knew in his bones that today was no day for stirring abroad" 7025
"knew it, everyone in the boarding house" 2898
"knew it, I" 2607
"knew it was going to be like that" 8012
"knew it was only the heat" 9766
"knew it well, she" 7748
"knew just what he wanted to do" 322
"knew not why, she" 4871
"knew nothing about horses" 4885
"knew nothing about love" 5653
"knew nothing of its real object" 5829
"knew of him, it was all I" 154
"knew or cared, no one" 1710
"knew perfectly well what to do" 5056
"knew she was an outlaw, always" 2050
"knew she would, I" 1692
"knew that, everyone" 3615
"knew the man, I" 5831
"knew the same thing, we all" 4107
"knew the truth of it and the illusion simultaneously" 4108
"knew what he had been doing" 1112
"knew what to do" 8756
"Knickerbocker Glories, eat as many" 248
"knickers, multicoloured" 6707
"knife, by" 10962
"knife, morning ... like a" 2244
"knife, stabbed him with a" 70
"knife, unsheathed his" 10541
"knife and fork" 3861, 3868
"knife ... had been stuck through his scrotum" 1166
"knife or short sword, he had taken a" 8663
"knife was with Saint Paul" 2817
Knight, Mr. Henry 8347
Knight, Sebastian 791
"knight, true" 5980
"knight, worthy" 4554
"knight came clattering into the court-yard upon a horse" 7607
"Knight of the Order of the Bath" 8580
"knight of the realm" 2443
"knight of the Red Cross" 10329
"knighted" 247
Knights 4554, 5980, 7607, 10329
"knights and ladies of the court at Camelot" 6561

"Knightsbridge, western reaches of" 8617
"knitting, two elderly women sat" 9668
"knitting upon the beach" 10818
"Knob, Winter Green" 5136
"knob of the front door" 2720
"knobs, mushroom" 10190
"knock, innocent" 245
"knock on the door" 2701, 9915
"knock on the door, the thundering" 9920
"knock over the world, doesn't want to" 10408
"knocked at the door" 6960
"knocked faintly" 653
"knocked hard on the door" 9963
"knocked her gently off her bicycle" 41
"knocked old Mathers down" 6182
"knocked on his door" 10163
Knocker 2874
"knocking, ghosts and vampires were" 4114
"knocking, someone" 10295
"knocking, usually without" 7213
"knocking at the front door" 2709
"knocking at your front door, who was that" 9988
"knocking on the door" 9885
"knocking sounded again" 9887
Knockout 2874
"Knokke near the Dutch border" 7264
"knoll, a" 847
"Knoll, Oak" 3113
"knot, while I was shaping the" 7494
"knotted around her neck, two of the corners" 10860
"know, and then you would" 6530
"know, as far as I" 587
"know, because I" 8868
"know, do you" 3892
"know, first to" 464
"know, great satisfaction to" 359
"know, he might be supposed to" 8961
"know, I didn't" 690, 2395
"know, I do not" 3845
"know, I don't" 689, 10744
"know, I dont" 6042
"know, I just wanted to let you" 6946
"know, I plumb downright plain don't" 681
"know, Jimmy'll" 7209
"know, *knew* he didn't" 5605
"know, let me" 9403
"know, little did I" 5480
"know, people" 5228
"know, the first thing you'll probably want to" 9706
"know, things I didn't" 3546

"know, thought that I might ever" 154
"know, wanted to" 2097
"know, wants to" 173, 2094
"know, what we don't" 4498
"know, you never" 4882
"know, you want to" 693, 2487
"know, you will want to" 6045
"know, you're sure she doesn't" 7954
"know about her, more than I wanted to" 6732
"know about me, you don't" 896
"know anybody in Arizona" 140
"know anyone who lived there, she didn't" 5356
"know better, I" 7550
"know certain things about me, you do not" 7598
"know every detail" 8961
"know every one, where we" 6266
"know everything, think that we" 5055
"know exactly how the sky looks" 8414
"know for certain if my life is changed" 7076
"know for sure, this much I" 4809
"know from where, he did not" 5121
"know her, he doesn't" 5748
"know her from my dreams" 2812
"know how long Mama was sick" 149
"know how much to include, I don't" 2556
"know is not enough, to" 5060
"know it, do not" 9046
"know it, lucky enough to" 91
"know it for absolute sure" 10321
"know little about, something I" 5483
"know more of the ins and outs of the matter" 7607
"know one or two things, you ought to" 5063
"know Oscar Livingstone, first got to" 5863
"know otherwise, it was too late for him to" 6643
"know something quite well" 7387
"know that, maybe they" 1553
"know that woman, I" 10889
"know them both, I" 8994
"know too much" 7949
"know very little about it, we really" 427
"know what I am, he doesn't" 4106
"know what I was doing in New York, I didn't" 680
"know what this means, I" 3840
"know what to make of each other" 9105
"know what to say, I didn't" 1158
"know when I was born" 823
"know where he is, he does not" 5611

"know where I am, I don't" 5606
"know where to begin, it's hard to" 626
"know who I am, to" 7970
"know who this is" 3918
"know why, I don't" 1692
"know why, if you want to" 2328
"know why we have become what we are" 10151
"know yourself" 7974
"knowing, no way of" 2442
"knowing, there's no way of" 4882
"knowing a soul, not" 9108
"knowing that it would be for the last time" 3015
"knowing this, no earthly means of" 3464
Knowledge 823, 1112, 2094, 2442, 2612, 2812, 3274, 3456, 4498, 4882, 5019, 5228, 5668, 5816, 5884, 6253, 6278, 6498, 7199, 7209, 7550, 7742, 7954, 7959, 8071, 8868, 9046, 10464, 10888, 10889
"knowledge, at least to their" 5792
"knowledge, empirical" 5059
"knowledge, expert" 9161
"knowledge, full" 5668
"knowledge, human" 3456
"knowledge, modern physical" 6894
"knowledge, nuts of" 10756
"knowledge may be said to sleep, the world's" 4454
"knowledge of the locality, expert" 6498
"knowledge, that branch of" 238
"knowledge, to Arleen's" 4331
"knowledge, tree of" 5064
Knowles, Jason 9450
Knowles, Polly 10932
"known, had always" 3927
"known, hiding everything I had ever" 7383
"known, nothing can be" 2431
"known, once a thing is" 5061
"known, well" 3535
"known a famous man, have you ever" 3536
"known about George, very little was" 9302
"known as, I has been" 4723
"known at Harvard, she was already" 8879
"known before, anything he had ever" 5121
"known better, should have" 1222
"known by no other name than Smoke Bellew" 4721
"known by their surnames" 4724
"known each other for a long time" 8876
"known even in distant parts of Glebeshire" 3533
"known for certain, this much is" 9594

"known forever, a place you've" 4549
"known himself in better times" 1675
"known in His native land as AMORTORTAK" 9053
"known instantly how to deal with him, I would have" 4988
"known Ipsilon in peace-time, he had" 5019
"known simply as the beautiful blue valley" 9748
"known them so well, nobody else could have" 2321
"known there from a child" 9090
"known till that hour, will never be" 4454
"known to every one" 6266
"known to several generations of visitors" 4644
"knows but nobody talks, everybody" 5222
"knows everything about his own neighborhood" 6278
"knows how to find the meaning of life" 5253
"knows I'm in him and behind him" 4106
"knows it better than I do, no one" 8979
"knows, no one" 3363, 5138
"knows, not everybody" 6182
"knows that, everybody" 10596
Knox, Oren 4675
Knox, Orrin 6995
"Knoxville Tennessee" 1270
Knuckle 9106
"knucklebone of St. So-and-so" 110
"knuckle-duster" 976
"knuckles in his lap, his" 547
K.O. 2874
"Koblenz" 4085
Kobus the Bookbinder 5601
"koels began to call" 758
Koenig 6907
Kohler, Big Joe 2057
"KoKo" 10906
"Kona, region called" 5022
"Koolau mountain ranges" 10616
"kopje walloper" 5456
"Korea" 221, 6881
"Korea, I go back to" 7433
"Korean war" 1277
"Koreans, North" 10500
Kornowski, Count 2592
Korosko, the" 8061
"KORRHEA" 172
"kosher hot dogs" 3876
Kraken, Gösta 8196
Krautschneider, Feldwebel 8463
"Kravasaras, village of" 1439
"Kreiswald" 2490
"Kremlin, west gate of the" 9833
Kreutznaer, Robinson 6601
Krippendorf 6707

Krishna 4741
"Krishna, enchanting god" 4741
Krishnan, Girija 2026
"Krishnapur" 4075
"Ku Klux Klan" 2837
"'Kulosaari' means burned island" 5042
Kunsman, Mrs. 7736
Kuo Hsiao-mei 561
Kurelen 6002
Kurt Hansen, the" 8116
"Kush, my country of" 6256
"Kustom-Kitchen" 9086
Kuyoshi, Shigo 4003
Kyle, S.S." 8125
Kyoga 10507
"Kyushu" 8160

"L.A., you arrive in" 9960
Labaiya, Felix 7831
Labaiya, Patsy Jason 7831
"label the Class of '70 Exhibit Aleph" 7730
"labeled her cold" 10852
Labor 271, 1269, 3645, 3973, 6133, 6450, 10923, 10925
"labor, cries of" 7087
"labor, implement of" 271
"labor, too frail for hard" 1269
"Labor Day, Saturday after" 2176
"Labor Day traffic" 3041
"labor regulations" 1319
"laboriously" 10156
"labors, for her" 3806
"labouring low overhead" 739
"Labrador, sixty-five pounds of shedding effusive yellow" 7751
"La Brea apartments" 2061
"labyrinth of Cefalù" 9565
"lace, pink and full of" 4119
"lacerated from his scalp to his ankles" 1537
"lacework fabric of a half-built minster spire" 1849
Lacey, Miss Rosamond 4758
Lacey, Uncle Matt 5359
"lachrymose yet exalted hour" 8470
"lacing the table with a cloth" 9355
"lackeys of Marie Antoinette" 1011
"lacking authority" 4438
"lacunae, contains various" 5532
"lacustrine essences richly distilled" 8523
Lacy 625
"lad" 5079
"lad, I'm a" 4807
"lad, small" 4906
"lad, the" 4011
"lad of some fifteen years of age" 1172
"lad of twelve years of age" 950
"lad that barks at us and bites our cheeks" 8750

"ladder against the Throckmorton clapboard, laid his" 3604
"ladders, up and down the" 5542
Laddie 8205
"ladies, ah you" 10805
"ladies, bag" 10852
"ladies, bright-eyed" 3396
"ladies, knights and" 6561
"ladies, like most solitary old" 8357
"ladies, old" 5355
"ladies, our young" 2117
"ladies, society-page" 2118
"ladies, Spanish" 9716
"ladies, two American" 1828
"ladies, two young" 6330
"ladies, young" 8863, 9350, 9757
"ladies and gentlemen" 630, 3190, 8886
"ladies at the courthouse" 6979
"ladies clothed in silk and thread lace" 5886
"ladies' eardrops" 7652
"ladies of good report" 10779
"ladies' room" 4480
"ladies sitting in a formal circle" 2885
"ladies unmoving and passive" 2963
"ladies who live in Beacon Street" 9859
"lads, a few truant" 5084
"lads, the Crowther" 9599
"lads had turned up" 9898
"lads in Ayrshire, we" 3275
"lady, a" 2943, 3552
"lady, acted like a" 207
"lady, American" 1090
"lady, baronet's" 5727
"lady, beautiful" 10784
"lady, brisk little old" 6284
"lady, genteel though decayed" 5080
"lady, his old" 2651
"lady, kindly old" 7770
"lady, King's newest young" 8556
"lady, like a" 1717
"lady, little" 2206
"Lady, my good" 4221
"lady, New York" 6628
"lady, nice" 1371
"lady, old" 2365, 3858, 8555
"lady, rich" 10544, 10812
"Lady, she was a dear good" 4221
"lady, shrunken sallow old" 2822
"lady, tall young" 9873
"lady, the" 10345
"lady, throbber of a" 6241
"lady, turn to your" 2101
"Lady, Veiled" 5784
"lady, Welcome Wagon" 1432
"lady, young" 484, 4730, 6934, 7214, 7825, 8839
Lady Carbury 5395
Lady Eden 7087
"lady had called to see me" 9891
"lady he had dumbass married" 2678

"lady in deep mourning" 4222
"lady in her sixties" 10819
"lady lay in a little glen" 8277
Lady Mary 4668
"lady of beauty and distinction, young" 10771
"lady of fortune" 5728
"lady of me, make a" 3293
"lady of thirty or so, kind-hearted" 6104
"lady sat smoking a cigarette" 8564
"lady then becoming famous for her beauty and her wit" 10781
"*Lady Vain*, the" 8059
"lady was Mrs. Dodd" 3552
"ladyship, her little" 10111
"Laerg" 2474
Lafayette 8940
Lafirme, Jérôme 2295
Lafleur, Gus 9967
Lafleur, Jewel 9967
Laforgue 5180, 10097
"laggard, [sun] turning" 10146
"lagoon" 10363
"lagoon, in the" 736
"lagoon just up the bay from Trangloek" 5158
"Laguna Madre" 8691
"Lahore" 9185
"Lahore Museum" 2017
"laid, got" 8010
"laid, I wanted to get" 7994
"laid against his back like sleep" 2973
"laid by at least six different guys" 7993
"laid out in the coffin" 1878
"laid this one flat amid the shuffle of feet" 14
"laid-back" 349
Laidlaw 6239
"lain wanting only to daydream" 2771
Laine, Frankie 2111
Laines, Henry 10667
Laing, Dr. Robert 3443
Laird, Fate 1639
"laird of the line, the last" 3550
Lais 10871
"Lais, lascivious" 10871
"lake, black" 9837
"lake, blue steel gleam of the" 5072
"Lake, Chambers" 5077
"lake, encharmed picture of the" 6075
"lake, great friendly" 4557
"Lake, Great Salt" 9181
"Lake, Oblong" 5075
"lake, remarkably blue" 5066
"lake, rising in a" 9747
"Lake, Roebuck" 5121
"lake, silver surface of the" 1178
"lake, strange little" 5070
"lake and pond gemmed the landscape, many a" 9740

"Lake Asphaltites" 10329
"lake bed, dry" 9181
"Lake Champlain" 10343
"Lake Como" 3265
"Lake Erie" 9205
"Lake George New York" 5154
"Lake Glass" 8282
"lake lay purring in the May sun" 5076
"Lake Michigan" 3725, 4073
"Lake Michigan, blue immense choppy" 9166
"Lake Noir, the great" 1706
"Lake of Tiberias" 5716
"lake of tropical rains, a brown hot" 5052
"Lake Success" 4466
"Lake Success New York" 9297
"Lake Superior" 4049, 4071, 9602
"lake Titicaca" 1567
"lake trapped between steep green hills" 5072
"lake was still" 5068
Lakeman, Max 3616
"Lakers game" 3292
"lakes, lovely" 6249
"lakes in southern Africa, one of the most beautiful" 5073
"lakes in the grounds, two large" 5067
"Lakeview" 6863
Laki 10308
Lakshmi 10540
"LaLa Land" 5297
Lalor, Martin 5368
"La Luz, the town of" 1090
Lam Fan 2432
Lamb, Henry 3838
Lamb, Horace 3767
Lamb, Robert 8994
"Lambeth North" 2359
"lambs to sell" 1075
"lame, the" 7155
"lame butler" 1098
"lame social round" 8637
"lamentation, raised their voices in" 3935
"lamentations of modern decadence, precise and slightly nasal" 6427
"lamented and lamentable memory" 3084
"lamenting, know thy" 7507
Lamming, Mark 3022
Lamont 3520
LaMonte, Mrs. 4526
"lamp, dusky" 5901
"lamp, glare of the" 122
"lamp, her expiring" 9402
"lamp in the room, the only decent" 7364
"lamp that seemed like it always had the funny orange bubbles" 5634
"lamp with kingfishers on it" 4120
Lamprey, Ilse 4922
Lamprias 1034

"lamps, low green-shaded" 5088
"lamps, oil" 3094, 4647, 5315
"lamps, red hurricane-" 10930
"lamps gave the same dull candle-light" 9560
"lamps in the hotel" 4647
"Lanark, town of" 9741
Lancaster 6184
Lancaster, Mr. 706
Lance 10437
"lance point on the ground to his right" 8701
Lancelot 6339
"Lancers, 44th Bengal-" 8679
Land 179, 1038, 1090, 3089, 3466, 3551, 3642, 4072, 4133, 5025, 5140, 5141, 5157, 5167, 6685, 7126, 9619, 10573
"Land" 9619
"land, a big and lonely" 4071
"land, a certain" 340
"land, a cloud-enshadowed" 4533
"land, a little" 7796
"land, a strange" 9521
"land, a tendril of" 5048
"land, a wild" 783
"land, about to" 2447
"land, acres of" 6133
"land, an ice-bound" 2196
"land, began to buy" 1038
"land, bound for a distant" 9594
"land, came into the" 7810
"land, contours of the" 9194
"land, fertilize the" 5042
"land, firm" 4034
"land, five acres of fertile" 6126
"land, flat" 3044
"land, great wasted" 4577
"land, His native" 9053
"Land, Holy" 8112
"land, in all our lovely" 9745
"land, in sight of" 8541
"land, long strip of fertile" 9746
"land, misty" 5167
"land, narrow tongue of" 3181
"Land, Old" 2386
"Land, palmy LaLa" 5297
"land, promised" 9754
"land, proof of" 3466
"land, scorched" 10614
"land, sharp green colour of the" 179
"land, six hundred acres of" 6685
"land, spring is good in this" 10626
"land, strange" 3497
"land, strip of dry" 3058
"land, that long narrow rich strip of" 7126
"land, that very new northern" 10341
"land, the" 5161
"land, the end of the" 5162
"land, the fallow" 5141
"land, the great new" 10573
"land, there is a" 6910

"land, this north" 8031
"land, this reddish-brown" 5138
"land, unearthly humps of" 5135
"Land, Unpromised" 6136
"land, upward slope of the" 3118
"land, waste crown" 1568
"land and sea, strange mixture of" 5707
"land between the sea and the fens" 3058
"land defied everyone's idea of what a land ought to be" 4072
"land for miles around" 5175
"land had been a swamp" 5170
"land in the country, some of the best" 3642
"land is darkened" 724
"land is lovely" 3362
"land lying between the sea on one side and the river" 7126
"land of awesome grandeur" 6258
"land of game and forest and rushing waters" 783
"land of grass that ran ever onward" 9549
"land of green forests and rosy cheeks" 6249
"land of high plains" 5713
"land of little hills and great harbors" 6249
"land of love and song" 6250
"land of milk and molasses" 6249
"land of Milk and Molasses" 6136
"land of mountains and moorlands and cherished myths" 6258
"Land of Muck and Chitlings" 6136
"land of murder and cocaine" 6276
"land of the Undead" 324
"land over which France and England might well bicker" 6249
"Land Rover" 1662
"land shelf, a shallow" 4096
"land slid down" 5134
"land sloped away gently" 5157
"land up to Acco, entire curve of" 8133
"land was left behind" 1628
"land was no longer there, suddenly the" 201
"land was resting under coverlets of gold" 10573
"land was there, always the" 5025
"land where the axe was needed for the forest" 6100
"land with no appreciable history" 4073
"land's fertile peace lulled" 5286
"landau, gleaming" 2190
"landbirds, sudden inruption of" 742
"landed at Heathrow" 232
"landed here, I" 6113
"landed in England" 4565
"landed on her pate" 2353
"landed with a jarring shock" 225

"landing, Inchon" 6881
"Landing, Mill's" 6127
"Landing, Rodney's" 4560
"landing a small Auster" 203
"landing card" 9539
"landing in two hours' time, will be" 213
"landing stage" 8099, 8139
"Landing Stage, Liverpool" 7307
"landing was quite dark and silent" 9406
"landings of mermaids, previous" 2733
Landis, Angela 10461
Landis, Stephen 10461
"landlady, my" 6391
"landlady shouted up the stairs" 9904
"landlocked" 6256
"landlocked, liner was" 8115
"landlord, my" 6282
"landlords" 1038
"landlords, big-bellied" 3396
"landlords denying heat" 2356
"landmark, conspicuous" 1173
Landmarks 70, 86, 591, 850, 1210, 2162, 2185, 2506, 3412, 3502, 3719, 5572, 5575, 5584, 5604, 5652, 5781, 5807, 6127, 6163, 6371, 10154
"landmarks fled him, it was not long before his" 5604
Landon, Freddy 2773
"landowner, notable" 9874
Lands 4044, 4071, 4533, 5149, 5220, 6258, 6910, 9515, 9521, 10626
"lands, cotton" 7323
"lands, fertile stretch of flat" 5129
"lands, Kinraddie" 3381
"lands, the dry" 5173
"lands, western" 4133
"lands known as los Llanos" 5173
"lands of Dalcastle" 3551
Landscape 179, 783, 1244, 1367, 1398, 1413, 1421, 3074, 3129, 3251, 3421, 3654, 3665, 3903, 4027, 4048, 4071, 4084, 4133, 4428, 5011, 5020, 5038, 5045, 5077, 5155, 5173, 5305, 5357, 5706, 5707, 5946, 6055, 6062, 6064, 6068, 6070, 6073, 6075, 6084, 7238, 7266, 7279, 7282, 7625, 7632, 7649, 7668, 7674, 7682, 7692, 7694, 7775, 8133, 8389, 8444, 8736, 9116, 9170, 9549, 9643, 9738, 9740, 9745, 9747, 9754, 10573, 10694, 10697
"landscape, a classic Chinese" 5145
"landscape, a different" 5152
"landscape, brightens the" 8425
"landscape, contrived and ordered" 5164
"landscape, eerily silent" 9643
"landscape, entire" 8444

"landscape, gentle watercolor" 3665
"landscape, imagine then a flat"
    5152
"landscape, internal" 5706
"landscape, its tumbling" 4062
"landscape, lush green horse-
    studded" 5171
"landscape, strewn about the" 1879
"landscape, that immediate" 3640
"landscape had taken over" 5180
"landscape of abandoned railroad
    tracks" 7282
"landscape of erection" 5946
"landscape of fear" 5173
"landscape of Pennsylvania, the
    June" 5137
"landscape of the mind" 5027
"landscape one, the" 8434
"landscape still pale with the heat
    of the day before" 5143
"landscape swing away, feeling its
    monstrous" 10144
"landscape with figures" 5164
"landscaped at the turn of the
    century" 5179
"landscaper" 847
"landscapes, twilight" 7266
"landscapes of Guienne and Gas-
    cony, the pastoral" 5125
"landscapes . . . stretching along
    the river" 5125
"landscape-tones" 5146
"landslip, the start of a" 7249
Lane, Andrew 3591
Lane, Eugene 4339
Lane, William 10706
"lane, country" 3578, 10929
"Lane, Ember" 9138
"Lane, Goodwives" 6894
"Lane, Greenhill" 6269
"Lane, King David's" 9175
"Lane, Meg's" 3116
"Lane, Mincing" 8341
"lane, narrow" 2991
"Lane, New Dollar" 5628
"Lane, Old Common" 10630
"Lane, Park" 9161
"lane, private" 3036
"lane, quiet" 9763
"lane, steep muddy" 8212
"lane, very rough" 2943
"lane between ship and dock" 8157
"lane that led back from their
    house" 3578
"lanes, narrow winding country"
    9804
Langdale, Lady 6751
Langham, Alice 9867
Langham, Maggie 3216
Langley, Forrest 10088
"Langton on Holm" 1348
Language 3281, 3288, 3289, 3292,
    4447, 5446, 6749, 6784, 6807,
    7904, 8185, 8843, 8887, 9709,
    9715, 10901, 10910

"language, Choctaw" 9015
"language, excuse the" 4977
"language, thunderous" 10521
"language, written in a foreign"
    6784
"language Americans spoke, the
    curious" 6749
"language at all, not a" 9709
"language so well, you speak our"
    4447
"languages, brought up on three
    dead" 9709
"languid, strangely" 5048
"languid 'bell-boy'" 7555
"languid breezes" 5132
"languid July day" 8508
"languidly, filters down" 7754
"languished of an incurable ail-
    ment" 5659
"languor, a certain" 3680
"languor, dust and" 2236
"languorous aromatic air" 8209
"lanky Joan" 6876
Lanny 1098, 4732, 8550
Lanscombe, Old 2693
Lansing, Breckenridge 3407
"Lansing" 1390, 4073
"lantern above his head, holding a"
    7644
"Lantern Waste" 424
Lao Li 1782
"Laos" 4094, 9291
"lap, standing on my" 546
"lap up the heat and din of noon"
    5096
"lapels of his jacket fly apart" 4897
Lapham, Silas 5786
"lapping among the reeds" 4105
Larcher, Jean 3837
"Larchmont New York" 511
Larey, Adam 7654
"large or small" 5699
"larger than any two nations of
    Europe" 6256
"largest of that Archipelago" 5011
"largest woman I have ever seen"
    10891
"*largo* to express wide open spaces"
    1320
Larimer, Dr. 7696
"lark, on a" 7023
"lark, up with the" 6565
Larkin, Ma 4753
Larkin, Pop 5184, 9753
Larkin, Tom 4288
"larking" 1089
"larks" 2763
"larks in the wheat stubble" 2236
Larry 1847, 6550
Larson, Amelia 3314
Larson, David 4590
Larsson, Elisabeth 4796
LaRue, Romelle 2758
"La Rumorosa" 3265
"Las Vegas" 3623, 9180

"Las Vegas, eastward out of" 3019
Lasco, Edward 2001
"lashed in the twisted phone wire"
    1111
"lasses, few the" 10109
"lassie" 4193
"last, it didn't" 10622
"last, on our special" 2835
"last, the" 6338
"last days, in those" 7840
"Last Men" 4496
"last of Mornington Road" 6102
"last of the line" 1180
"last out the night, will she" 2289
"last the sweet birds sang, when"
    5673
"last thing about her" 2824
"last things" 5524
"last to leave the office, always the"
    6422
"last year" 10968
"lasted a year, Ma" 6660
"latch, the" 2687
Latchmer 2720
"late, a little" 9328, 10032
"late, always" 9336
"late, arrived fifteen minutes" 9343
"late, gone to bed" 10132
"late, half an hour" 2359
"late, he was" 9340
"late, he was already" 9338
"late, I am an hour too" 9345
"late, it is too" 3004
"late, it was growing" 9329
"late, kept him" 6630
"late, knows she is" 9342
"late, running" 7272
"late, running terribly" 4123
"late, they're" 9331
"late, three-quarters of an hour"
    9334
"late, to be an hour" 7245
"late, twenty minutes" 9335
"late, you won't be" 9992
"late, you're gonna make us" 10078
"late again, I was going to be"
    9346
"late at night, it was" 10390
"late at the office, *Don't* make me"
    9327
"late 'fifties" 9611
"late for that, too" 4092
"late in rising" 8418
"late in starting, the meeting was"
    3297
"late in the mornings, usually very"
    3818
"late of course, it is too" 1664
"late one night" 6024
"late one October night" 1894
"late to the war" 9344
"lateen sails" 8114
"later, a few hours" 3680
"later, nine years" 5472
"later than usual" 10310

"lathered his light-complected face" 8044
Latimer, Charles 2563
"Latin, *Lolita* in" 6807
"Latin paraphrase" 5431
"Latin Quarter" 6289
"Latin teacher" 4273
"Latino villager" 1737
"latitude" 5574
"latitude, 64 30' north" 4096
"latitude as what, on the same" 4076
"latitude, between the fortieth and the forty-first degrees of" 7647
"Latmos, Mount" 6080
"latrine" 10521
"latticed at the sides" 7752
"latticed with yellow slashes full of dust motes" 7763
"latticework, Victorian" 3225
La Touche, Ninian 10004
"La Tourette, village of" 10399
Lauderdale, Alexander 6523
"lauds" 1312
"laugh" 5479
"laugh, a light" 5182
"laugh, a strange rasping" 7986
"laugh, gave a" 5846
"laugh, with a" 5730
"laugh again, reason to" 9454
"laugh aloud up at an eagle" 4704
"laugh came floating into the sunshine" 5182
"laugh hysterically, began to" 5192
"laugh in my face" 2492
"laugh sometimes, it makes me" 8261
"laughed" 8027, 10812
"laughed, he" 702
"laughed, Howard Roark" 6387
"laughed at him" 2356
"laughed at him behind his back" 3329
"laughed in condescending contempt" 4046
"laughed instead, only" 5187
"laughed over her bones, never" 2376
"laughed so much he could hardly stand" 10660
"laughed wildly as he roasted in the flames" 2773
"laughing" 4230
"laughing, he broke up" 7986
"laughing, he was" 5185
"laughing, impossible to be certain that he was" 10654
"laughing, she is" 5191
"laughing faces" 4335
"laughing happily" 5184
"Laughing Mary, the" 8055
"laughing now" 6755
"laughing out loud" 4335
"laughing yet passionately serious" 8976

"laughs" 5489
"laughs, Phantom Blooper" 10533
Laughter 702, 2376, 2773, 3329, 3506, 4335, 5624, 6387, 10533, 10660
"laughter, a gift of" 5183
"laughter, burst of" 5186
"laughter, the inevitable" 5188
"laughter among people" 10587
"laughter came so unexpectedly" 5186
"laughter followed almost immediately" 5189
"laughter from the dance hall opposite" 5624
"laughter of strangers" 3506
"Laun, town of" 10459
Launcelot 4861
"launch in towards the bank, took the" 9996
"Laundromat" 4187
"laundromat filled with bitterness" 6017
"Laundry, Limpid Stream" 3498
"Laundry, St. Gabbione" 1073
"Laundry, St. Joseph's" 1068
"laundryman, retired" 3498
"laundrymat" 10977
Laura 672, 1617, 2426, 2728, 4355, 4406, 6144, 6566, 9342, 10899
Laurel 6893
"laurel, dense" 6813
"laurel bushes" 3036
"Laurels, The" 3073
Lauren 9108
Laurence, Otho 9858
"Laurencekirk lights of a night" 4053
Laurie 6113
Lauro 2462
"lavatory, been to the" 6675
"lavatory, waited their turns on the" 8869
"lavatory firm in Los Angeles" 9439
Laveau, Marie 2108
Lavendar, Dr. 9872
"Laverings, the owner of" 8262
Lavette, Big Dan 9611
"laving river of light" 1333
Law 2567, 2649, 2682, 3527, 4800, 5387, 5871, 6201, 7817, 7820, 7824, 9252
"law, abilities in the" 5193
"law, chief branches of the" 5871
"law, court of" 6201
"law, inalienable" 7818
"law, metaphysical" 6906
"Law, North Berwick" 4587
"law, social" 7816
"law, the" 5211
"law, they had announced the" 309
"law and order triumphant" 2045
"law of boundaries applies" 7824
"law of inverse probability" 1325

"law offices" 3296
"law school" 6750
"law school, attend" 7955
Lawler, Amy Joy 8624
"lawn, bold round-surfaced" 9738
"lawn, broad" 10051
"lawn, great-aunt's" 301
"lawn, mows the" 10959
"lawn, on the rolling" 8386
"lawn, sere yellow midsummer front" 9808
"lawn, sloping" 3552
"lawn, wide stretch of" 10355
"lawn descending to the water" 3173
"lawn green and smooth as a length of baize" 5162
"lawn spotted with junipers" 9738
"lawn ... that opened itself in the bosom of an old wood" 9738
"lawns, long sloping velvet" 3179
"lawns, snakes on Ruth's" 449
"lawns and driveways aren't installed yet" 3264
"lawns brocaded with the moving shadows of clouds" 3179
Lawrence 4487, 6007, 7355
Lawrence, Louis 9863
Lawrence, Roger 6036
"Lawrence" 7668
Laws 1817, 6906, 7814, 7816, 7818, 10521
"laws, despotic shogunate" 7908
"laws, eternal" 6478
"laws, musty old" 1817
"laws and annals of Scotland" 357
"laws and breakers of laws" 4800
"laws fall silent" 10521
"laws of progression" 3560
"laws that prevailed in the land" 7908
Lawson, Joanna 4934
"lawsuit, about his" 5195
"lawsuit, stubborn farmer's" 5723
Lawsuits 5195, 5723, 7012
"lawyer, a" 6613, 6683
"lawyer, as a" 3955
"lawyer, eminent corporation" 2511
"lawyer, the" 5889, 6503, 9979
"lawyer, upstate" 9054
"lawyer Royall's house" 1585
"lawyer who would defend him" 3486
"lawyer-father, my" 5206
Lawyers 1585, 2511, 3486, 3955, 5206, 5889, 6406, 6423, 6503, 9979
"lay alone" 10188
"lay around in my dirty sweatpants and shirt" 5637
"lay as still as any wrapped old mummy" 10190
"lay at anchor" 8105
"lay at anchor with a valuable cargo" 8048
"lay awake" 8485

"lay back in bed" 9437
"lay belly-flat at the edge of the cornfield" 4955
"lay dead" 3962
"lay dreaming" 2797
"lay dying in his room" 2316
"lay flat, he" 10695
"lay forward on the sea" 8034
"lay full length over the undulations of buttock" 7985
"lay in bed" 4772, 9408
"lay in her bath singing the Marseillaise" 563
"lay in his barrel kennel" 429
"lay in his creaking four-poster bed" 7305
"lay in state" 2398
"lay in the bottom of a small sailing dinghy" 1883
"lay in the darkness" 10170
"lay in the disordered bed" 8583
"lay like a gleaming sickle" 7665
"lay naked on his bed" 9355
"lay on a padded deck chair" 5627
"lay on a shelf of rock" 4316
"lay on her back looking into the darkness" 10127
"lay on her bed" 3685, 7586
"lay on his back in the rowboat" 4482
"lay on his back in silence" 5746
"lay on his bed trying to see . . . a body" 1888
"lay on my new blue rug" 5634
"lay on that same narrow gimbal-mounted sea bed" 5628
"lay on the cold sand" 10098
"lay on the hardstand" 686
"lay on the shore of Lemminjärvi" 5633
"lay quiet, everyone" 6383
"lay quietly curled up" 5616
"lay quite still" 10200
"lay rolled in his blanket" 527
"lay sprawled on his back" 6594
"lay staring" 3092
"lay still on the bed" 9087
"lay there smiling" 10175
"lay thinking in Central Park" 9434
"lay tucked up warm" 6519
"lay unquietly toasting" 5629
"lay very still, she" 8802
"layer had been tamped home, the first" 8280
"layers, lifts up the" 10948
"layers and layers pressed tight" 9503
"laying and running and crouching inbetween" 6136
"laying around in bed" 1103
"laying carpet in the loft" 10956
"laying on my belly" 10106
Lazar-Wolf, Mrs. Saul 5747
"lazily stirred a can of Beef and Potatoes" 1864

Laziness 3356
"laziness always mixed with frustration" 5329
"lazing in Canada beyond" 6075
"lazy and timeless" 5024
Leach, Bernice 6440
"lead, in the" 8916
"lead him back to his seat" 2901
"lead us to safe harbor" 8504
Leadbetter 1892
"leaden clouds" 10572
"leader, political" 6983
"leader, Russian" 507
Leaders 4457, 4469, 6424, 6976, 7810
"leadership, qualities of" 6424
"leading, the circle and diamond" 8342
"leading a trump" 6308
"leading the way" 6522
"leads to another, how one thing" 6696
"leaf, vein of a yellowing" 1382
"leaf of a nonexistent tree, final" 8528
"leaf stirred, not a" 8330
Leafy, Morgan 2922
"League, American" 8919
"league, tenth-rate commercial" 8923
"League of Saint Columba" 1499
Leah 1716, 2713, 8215, 9395
"Leah New Hampshire" 8606, 9964
"leak, I took a" 437
"leak, take a" 3023
Leamas 10059
"lean" 5889
"lean her head on his shoulder" 1990
"lean in winter" 769
"leaned across her dressing table" 7476
"leaned against the armrest" 1804
"leaned against the counter instead of sitting down" 6614
"leaned against the open shutter-door" 2917
"leaned against the side of a bus" 9768
"leaned against the steel balustrade" 7683
"leaned back" 8571
"leaned back in his chair" 942
"leaned back in his chair, invariably" 3572
"leaned confortably back in his cushioned chair" 5913
"leaned forward" 9552
"leaned from a gap in Evreux's ancient rampart" 9674
"leaned her head against the stone wall" 8349
"leaned his elbows on the sill" 8263
"leaned over a large drawing-board" 3326

"leaned over the parapet of London Bridge" 10394
"leaned over the rail" 9863
Leaner 4655
"leaning against a window near the washroom" 8654
"leaning against the corner of a ramshackle saloon" 8852
"leaning against the house counter" 6943
"leaning alone against the taffrail" 4730
"leaning anciently together across the Duchy" 10590
"leaning back" 9405
"leaning back a little" 5732
"leaning back against the glass doors" 6710
"leaning back in his desk chair" 6889
"leaning back with his eyes half closed" 3738
"leaning over a bit to see you" 10408
"leaning over a hot stove" 854
"leaning over the oaken table" 2492
"leaning over the terrace-wall" 948
"leaning that black motorcycle side to side" 2973
"leaning tower of Pisa" 6375
"leans over and opens the window" 10325
"leans with one shoulder against the wall" 5952
"leap, enormous" 5989
"leaped ahead like a missile from a catapult" 410
Leaping Deer, Cooper 8925
"leapt down the steps" 8179
"learn, I've come to" 2598
"learn about people, whatever you" 6823
"learn *Hindoostanee*" 3289
"learn his name for some time afterwards, I did not" 5790
"learn to speak Apache" 3281
"learned, nobody ever" 6048
"learned a convenient routine" 4284
"learned about the other Philip Roth" 1159
"learned about the world" 3275
"learned astrology and medicine, I" 3290
"learned by heart" 3270
"learned fast" 3291
"learned friend" 2088
"learned in childhood" 6804
"learned Narciso Rich, the" 10922
"learned that Manila air was fog and sweat and steam" 8534
"learned that this was the way to remember them" 2852
"learned to drive, how I" 6683
"learned to lean away from life" 5239

"learned to read" 3282
"learned to trust his own skepticism" 9688
"learning the business" 8587
"learning the other ways into Nodd's Ridge" 4548
"learning to make better baskets" 6744
"learning to pose" 513
"learns all the corrupt wisdoms" 275
"Leasan" 9134
"Leasan, parish of" 4058
"lease, ninety-nine year" 9950
"lease on a five-room apartment" 3170
"least, to say the" 2297
"leather, decayed dark brown" 2610
"leather, groan of" 8776
"leather, prime" 2835
"Leather Fancy Goods, Purveyors of" 6448
"leathers ain't as white as snow, if his" 2820
"leathers might just as well never have been cleaned" 2820
"leave, not a good time to" 1696
"leave, nothing for it but to" 1588
"leave, on" 1694
"leave, take a week's" 9737
"leave, taking" 1669
"leave, they" 10843
"leave, tried to" 1702
"leave, up and" 6823
"leave a place you love, when you" 4582
"leave behind, things he must" 6112
"leave for New York to-night" 1578
"leave for the Cadets, no shore" 8677
"leave her for a while, time for him to" 6110
"leave his apartment in Brooklyn" 9932
"leave home, never did" 5947
"leave home and go off in the wintertime" 4169
"leave Howard, I decided to" 2675
"leave it or lose it, you can never" 1451
"leave me, waited for Rambeau to" 2669
"leave me alone, they will" 9268
"leave my husband" 2662
"leave my poor remains to the surgeons" 121
"leave out, how much to" 2556
"leave the car, going to" 9523
"leave the house" 1745
"leave the house, I shall" 1636
"leave the office, always the last to" 6422
"leave you, I shall not" 1788
"leave you tonight, I have to" 2683
Leaver, Robert 1126
"leaves, autumn" 6333

"leaves, blown and rustling" 10732
"leaves, curious inflorescent" 9186
"leaves, damp dead" 8507
"leaves, dead" 10723
"leaves, endlessly carpeting it with" 9156
"leaves, falling" 8442
"leaves, first autumnal" 4943
"leaves, moon shadows of the maple" 3402
"leaves, rattle of" 10218
"leaves, rustling the" 10697
"leaves are dark viridian green" 9681
"leaves burning, autumn" 4105
"leaves flying" 10730
"leaves in the foreground, lightly fluttering" 8701
"leaves of autumn, the first dried" 7854
"leaves of the hemlock" 9756
"leaves on the full-fledged trees" 9479
"leaves . . . swirling and scraping on the walk" 7854
"leaves that look beautiful" 6557
"leaves were drifting on to the grass stage" 6220
"leaves were gold above my head" 9667
"leavin summat behind yer, yo're allus" 2821
"leaving, eve of his" 10437
"leaving, misery of" 1616
"leaving, so many were" 1637
"leaving, Ursula is" 2658
"leaving college" 6521
"leaving her, he was" 2663
"leaving her, saw the Greyhound Bus" 9583
"leaving her, when he said he was" 2677
"leaving Judd" 2668
"leaving me, she is" 2658
"leaving us, so you're" 1646
"leaving you, I'm" 2677
"Lebanon range to the north" 8133
Lebow, Aaron 1143
Lecks, Mrs. 5787
Lecky, Mr. 3699
"lecture, salon de" 6522
"lecture, Seth's" 5189
"lecture hall" 7518
"lecture tour" 5838
"lectured, remembering how he once" 5971
"lectured his servant" 3325
"lecturer, the new" 8880
Lectures 1587, 5189
"lectures to deliver" 1587
"led by a little-rich-girl" 10391
"led forth the Frankish tribes" 1444
"led gently, reader should be" 8995
"led him across the field to the edge of the autumn woods" 10404

"led the way" 7290
"led you just now, what" 593
Ledbelly 8745
"ledger, big gray" 6437
"ledger bound in red and gray" 3751
"ledgers, opened their" 1069
Ledoux, Marguerite 1598
Ledyard, Uncle 246
Lee 886, 3566, 5360, 5848, 6313, 6449
Lee, Angela 2483
Lee, Annabel 2403
Lee, General 10034
Lee, General Fitzhugh 3378
Lee, Mrs. Lightfoot 6037
Lee, Robert E. 468
Lee, [Robert E.] 4468
"leeches" 3371
"Leeds" 5289
Leela, Aunt 10665
"leer, contemptuous" 1565
Leffaway, Beejay 5751
Leffingwell, Honora 4720
"left, her husband's" 6308
"left, I can show you what is" 5430
"left, I got my things and" 1695
"left, they" 9938
"left a door silently" 6367
"Left Bank" 6289
"left behind" 6166
"left behind him" 4335
"left Carnegie Hall with the crowd" 1746
"left Claude, I" 2657
"left for Minneapolis" 1741
"left for the war, the day I" 8503
"left her family" 6172
"left her father's cottage" 6555
"left her husband" 2652
"left him" 6640
"left his distant northern home" 10329
"left his home in Moscow" 2516
"left Hispaniola for home" 3766
"left home, I'd think I'd never" 10318
"left home, when Ben Joe Hawkes" 4122
"left in the hands of her two trustees" 10771
"left is in our hands, what is" 5430
"left it in much better condition than he had found it" 6418
"left it with regret, I always" 1410
"left Kelly Field in a bucket-seat C-47" 204
"left me, when Jack" 2674
"left my husband, I" 2661
"left my room on Croom's Hill" 6568
"left New Brunswick Canada" 6155
"left Paradise" 1627
"left Phoenix in the morning" 745
"left Si Jaffar's door, when Stenham" 1635

"left the house at Andilly" 5104
"left the offices of the *Morning Star*" 1600
"left the railway station at Worchester" 9890
"left the room a moment before" 3521
"left the switch-yards" 1579
"left their house" 3000
"left Tony undressing" 9471
"leg, peg" 1620
"leg, you're pulling my" 1560
"leg, your" 148
Legacy 588, 3604
"legacy worth getting stirred up over, hardly made for a" 3604
"legal firms" 1687
"legal grandeur, no pretensions to" 9252
"legalized abortions" 5760
"legatee, residuary" 1901
"legation, young secretary of" 6432
"legend, figures in a" 6636
"Legend, there is the" 5217
"legend, young" 5216
"legend about the ships that have come to grief" 9089
"legend from the fact, how can you tell the" 6792
"legend in his day" 3543
"legend in my lifetime" 3537
"legend in our family" 5223
"legend of Maharawhenua" 5220
"legend of Sapphira Wade" 5222
"legend on the coast, he was already a" 3534
"legend to beguile the tourists" 7527
"legendary" 4788
"legendary, traffic was" 3041
Legends 3403, 3534, 3537, 3543, 6636, 6792, 7527, 9089, 10957
"legends" 3403
"legends, myths and" 5215
"legends, one of the German" 5224
"legends, tales and" 5212
"legends of history, graver" 6246
"legged, long-" 903
"legitimate five pound note" 2044
Legs 148, 565, 7611, 10445
"legs, bare slim" 3483
"legs, between my" 343
"legs, dead weight of his own" 9647
"legs, dirty brown" 5190
"legs, fat little" 5913
"legs, her tightly-gaitered" 9540
"legs, his" 9988
"legs, his thin" 10339
"legs, man sitting beside him has no" 9629
"legs, Mom's" 8380
"legs, remarkably long and well-made" 5471
"legs, spreading his" 2090
"legs, stretch his" 10418
"legs, stretching out his" 7153

"legs, swung his" 8348
"legs, thick purple-veined" 10445
"legs, thin pointed sticks for" 462
"legs, tired heavy" 7611
"legs, your slim" 8027
"legs absorb the pain" 7101
"legs crossed beneath her" 8367
"legs dangling in the straw" 9540
"legs dangling over the end" 565
"legs did not quite reach the floor, the royal" 8348
"legs encased in sheerest nylon" 5450
"legs gobbled up the placid country road" 10397
"legs of his high-yellow woman, he lay in the" 8458
"legs plunged into heavy boots" 8941
"legs splayed" 1170
"legs spread wide in a V, his scrawny" 1166
"legs straddling her" 7723
"legs that were slender but strong" 447
"legs tucked beneath her" 1923
"legs tucked into blue socks" 8027
"legs used to be, the place where my" 6632
"legs were crooked" 340
"Leica into focus, brought the" 6866
"Leicestershire" 6123
"Leidseplein" 2912
Leigh, Alice 6095
Leigh, Humphrey 4411
"Leighton Ridge" 1529
Leila 557
Leisure 10561
"leisure" 5934
"leisure, haughty and rapt" 8845
"leisure, money or" 10768
"leisure afforded me by great ease and affluence" 5553
"leisure in the past months, I have had much" 5870
"leisure of their ample centuries" 10757
"leisure with which Providence has blessed the decline of my life" 5556
"leisurely journey" 7254
"leisurely strokes" 7608
Leithen 9418
"lemme lemme" 6652
Lemmen, Bill 10446
"Lemminjärvi" 5633
Lemoine, Oscar 2528
Lemon, Miss 6023
"lemon grove, his scraggly" 3221
"lemonade, fetch glasses of" 2117
"lemonade stall" 10783
"lemons and figs swelling from branch tips" 9436
Lemuel 10326
"Lemuria, ancient continent of" 280

Lena 9414, 10937
Lendrick, Clive 5939
"length of River Street, all down the winding" 10875
"Lenin's Mausoleum" 5971
"Leningrad" 2794, 6232, 6299
"Leningrad station" 7904
Lennox, Terry 2899
Lenox 6301
"lens of the camera" 6869
"lenses, polishes the" 8285
"Lent" 8472
"lent me for three months" 7770
Leo 7216
Léon 4633
Leonard 2843, 6321
Leonardo 8027
Léonie 3229
Leonora 10766
"leopard got his spots, that's how the" 3413
"leopards, at least nine different" 1537
"leper hospital" 164
Lepidus 5443
"Leprosarium" 4622
Lerner, Jordan 4875
Le Sage 6246
"Les Misérables" 8320
Lesley 7874
Leslie 8370
Lesser 10219
"lesson, music" 6217
Lessons 3270, 3293, 4089, 6217, 6734, 10977
"lessons, Tai Chi" 10977
"lessons, violin" 4089
Lessways, Hilda 10915
Lestat 92, 3545, 9058
"let go, you must" 7175
"let go of the railing" 2909
"let himself in, had to" 8179
"lethargy, mid-morning" 8793
"Lethem" 3032
"letter, Allen Southby's" 1915
"letter, continued her" 5447
"letter, courteous and charming" 1914
"letter, dictating a" 4249
"letter, didn't you get my" 1938
"letter, express" 1927
"letter, extract of a" 2567
"letter, get his first" 1953
"letter, handing over the" 1954
"letter, his" 9940
"letter, I found in my desk the following copy of a" 1903
"letter, I found your" 1922
"letter, it was the last" 1913
"letter, like the bottom of an arabic" 9183
"letter, looking at the" 1919
"letter, mentally composed an abusive" 1916
"letter, most exciting" 3472

"letter, my usual Christmas" 1937
"letter, picking a" 8261
"letter, read the" 8647
"letter, received your" 1939
"letter, reread the" 1950
"letter, said in his" 1026
"letter, she found the" 1911
"letter, the" 6842
"letter, this is not a" 1929
"letter, three mistakes in this" 6023
"letter, today there arrived a" 1917
"letter, unfolded the President's" 1920
"letter, valedictory" 6439
"letter, write you a" 2549
"letter, writing this" 4542
"letter, writing to you this" 1957
"letter, wrote a" 1912
"letter, your charming" 1945
"letter also *hers*, is the" 1954
"letter arrived in early October" 1949
"letter bringing news of my grandfather's death" 1905
"letter came addressed to my maiden name" 1924
"letter came to his office" 1948
"letter did not arrive, your usual Sunday" 4889
"letter for you, here is a" 1904
"letter from Beatrice, I had a" 1935
"letter from India" 1901
"letter from my cousin" 1925
"letter I am sending, twelfth start of the" 1941
"letter is on that table" 4767
"letter makes dull enough reading" 1910
"letter of advice" 9864
"letter on onionskin paper, write the" 1958
"letter paper" 1923
"letter she had ever written in her life, first" 1959
"letter Susan Morrow's first husband Edward sent her" 5551
"letter to thank his hostess, instead of a" 5457
"letter to the editor, never even wrote a" 6348
"letter which announces to His Majesty a proposed visit" 1902
"lettered 'Drawing-Room'" 7760
"lettered the word 'Library'" 7760
"lettering, sharply-cut roman" 8311
Letters 869, 1026, 1901, 1902, 1903, 1904, 1905, 1906, 1907, 1908, 1910, 1911, 1912, 1913, 1914, 1915, 1916, 1917, 1919, 1920, 1921, 1922, 1923, 1924, 1925, 1926, 1927, 1929, 1931, 1932, 1934, 1935, 1936, 1937, 1938, 1939, 1940, 1941, 1943, 1945, 1946, 1947, 1948, 1949, 1950, 1952, 1953, 1954, 1955, 1956, 1957,

1958, 1959, 1961, 1962, 1963, 2549, 2567, 2684, 3472, 3515, 4219, 4354, 4767, 4889, 5387, 5447, 5457, 5551, 5747, 6023, 6355, 6648, 6842, 6956, 8171, 8181, 8261, 8647, 8708, 9862, 9864, 9940
"letters" 6861
"letters, contemporary" 5423
"letters, exchanged huge" 2906
"letters, gold and black" 8301
"letters, man of" 9694
"letters, professed a leaning to" 5029
"letters, thank you for your" 1962
"letters, they were not love" 8708
"letters, writing" 1931
"Letters, you have perused those same" 5387
"letters across the steel door, fat uneven" 8318
"letters before, don't think I've ever seen them" 8306
"letters from a girl named Martha" 8708
"letters I dictate in his absence" 6438
"letters in my head, writing" 1932
"Letters in question" 5387
"letters that day, two" 1947
"letters that had just arrived" 10143
"letters that lay on the table, turning over the" 1908
"letters to her sister" 1906
"letters to the post for me, take these" 1946
"letters were changing, shapes of my" 1937
"letters will be of special value" 696
"lettuce, wilted" 2656
Letty, Aunt 6728
Lev 8374
Lev, Asher 4788
"Levant, the" 120, 4034
Levanter, George 4284
Levaster, Dr. 3018
"level, somebody from a higher" 10486
"level as a table" 5178
"level of dull gray, long" 5128
Levett 6884
"leviathan, the" 473
Levin, Rachel 4856
Levin, S. 9571
"Levinson Archive" 2604
"Levi's" 6783
"levis, black" 2839
Levy, Ruby 10671
Lewin, Daniel 9584
Lewis, Meriwether 336
"Lewis, Black Moor of" 3667
Lewisham, Mr. 5639
"Lewiston" 3605
Lewrie, Alan 4511, 4711, 4869
"Lexington" 5370, 9332

"Lexington Virginia" 1465
"Lexington was a town of thirty thousand people" 10648
"Leyden, city of" 1352, 4760
"liability, somewhat of a" 46
"liar, Hugo was a" 5244
"liar, I've always been a" 5237
"liar, most accomplished and versatile" 5227
"liar, was a" 5235
"liar, you always were a" 5225
Liars 5225, 5227, 5229, 5230, 5231, 5233, 5234, 5235, 5237, 5238, 5244
"liars, then all institutions were" 5230
Lias 1602
Libanius 7518
"liberating forces" 4502
"liberation, the moment of" 6556
"liberation of Paris" 6779
Liberty 3247
"Liberty" 1165
"liberty, American" 266
"liberty, ashore on" 3997
"liberty, barefaced" 2589
"liberty, individual" 7003
"liberty afforded him" 2087
"libido, sudden quickening of her" 8026
Libraries 909, 3420, 3425, 3426, 3427, 3455, 4115, 5533, 6402, 7760, 7772
"library, a ride home from the" 6208
"Library, Bodleian" 7772
"library, bounced it in the" 302
"library, dark tunnel of the" 6402
"library, half" 7752
"library, her grandfather's" 651
"library, in my own" 2734
"Library, New York Public" 3420
"Library, Old Carnegie" 4115
"library, public" 969, 3427
"library, sat in the" 1907
"library, see you in the" 9871
"library, spacious and handsome" 8340
"Library, the" 1767
"library, this is a beautiful" 3425
"library, went to the" 3426
"library book" 905
"library closing time" 909
"library of Blandings Castle" 8257
"library of the Townsend mansion" 7760
"library on the high side" 3455
"library wall" 8641
"Libya Hill, town of" 5914
"Libya of the ancients" 8399
"Libyan mountains" 4494
"lice, like a cluster of" 1382
"lice glued onto a strand of hair" 5272
"license plates, out-of-state" 9616

"lichen, moss and" 8507
"lichen-covered boulders" 10404
"lichens, gray" 3894
"lichens that clung to the rugged trunks of the old oak trees" 3894
Lichfield 3378
"Lichfield" 3010
"licked and bit" 8027
"licking the lips" 3839
"licking the ringing fence wires with frost" 10609
"lid, rolled-up wide-awake rounded" 5911
Lida 2044
"Lido, low barrier of the" 8389
"lids, from under thick" 8277
"lids of my eyes, a slight pressure on the" 2611
"lie, a" 5242
"lie, a living" 5247
"lie, caught her lover Jonathan McEwan in a" 5238
"lie, gynecologists" 5231
"lie, I used to" 5245
"lie, telling myself a" 7353
"lie, you" 5225
"lie at the longest reach of the waves" 7945
"lie awake at night listening to the silence" 8826
"lie back on the pillow with his eyes shut tight" 10163
"lie detector" 1102
"lie down on top of me" 8006
"lie here staring up at it" 5376
"lie in disquieting wakefulness" 10251
"lie in the south aisle on their altar tombs" 2300
"lie to survive, you must" 5232
"lied, if we" 5230
"lied, Miss Clarvoe" 3918
"lied to his father" 5234
"lied to me about everything" 5236
"Liege Lady, our new" 7805
"liege lord" 6972
Lies 703, 3918, 5225, 5226, 5227, 5229, 5230, 5231, 5232, 5233, 5234, 5236, 5237, 5238, 5239, 5240, 5241, 5242, 5243, 5245, 5246, 5296
"lies, see me loud with" 4577
"lies, she tells" 5233
"lies, telling" 5246
"lies, told" 5226
"lies among the mountains" 9745
"lies awake in the dark bedroom" 8498
"lies broad and colored under a white sky" 9754
"lies for a while" 10184
"lies on the resurrected grass" 7723
"lies on the sand spit" 6390
"lies there, he" 168
"lies they may tell about me" 5240

"lies warm" 8483
"lieutenant, plain prosaic" 5640
"lieutenant governor of Oklahoma" 6342
"lieutenant of infantry" 8672
Life 417, 526, 796, 801, 2071, 2287, 2362, 2369, 2378, 2434, 2442, 3215, 3495, 4143, 4510, 4610, 4664, 5002, 5239, 5289, 5562, 5566, 5580, 5699, 5799, 5880, 6218, 6641, 6717, 6991, 7372, 8980, 9285, 9349, 9463, 10995
"*Life*" 4008
"life, a child's early" 9704
"life, a garbage of a" 2656
"life, a man's" 2383, 5950
"life, a symbol of his whole" 2299
"life, a young" 8956
"life, advancing in" 675
"life, agreeable feature of" 3126
"life, all her" 3707
"life, all my" 4495, 5214
"life, all the" 4308
"life, altered her" 5570
"life, altered the course of his" 5123
"life, anxiety in" 4600
"life, any account of my" 699
"life, at that time of" 251
"life, at the end of his" 716
"life, awakening clutch on" 10995
"life, backed into my" 6400
"life, bars surrounding her" 10826
"life, beach my" 8027
"life, best thing about my" 5591
"life, biggest adventure of" 5735
"life, biggest of his" 6317
"life, biggest problem in" 5259
"Life, blest with long" 5492
"life, blundering into my" 5815
"life, breath of hot new" 4610
"life, bustles with" 3215
"life, cancelled an unrelenting" 9297
"life, center of his" 5503
"life, chances in" 8226
"life, circumstances of" 10772
"life, come back to" 5252
"life, complicate your" 2612
"Life, Consequences of my" 778
"life, day of my" 5081
"life, days of my" 10476
"life, dead back to" 6717
"life, decline of my" 5556
"life, details of her" 4175
"life, distressing years of my" 5355
"life, do with your" 6932
"life, doorway of" 5263
"life, dream of his" 250
"life, dreams which had overflowed into" 4936
"life, duty in" 5457
"life, easy slide of his" 940
"life, emotional" 7713
"life, ended her" 6621
"life, evaluate his" 712

"life, events of my" 5590
"life, ever so satisfied and proud in my" 5079
"life, experiences of" 3495
"life, final year of my" 2776
"life, finish my" 3353
"life, First Cause of all" 6001
"life, first nine years of my" 6117
"life, first real day of my" 5093
"life, first sixteen years of" 5598
"life, for dear" 2973
"life, for their" 10772
"life, fourteen years of my" 6254
"life, frontier" 9860
"life, go through" 4743
"life, good things of" 796
"life, great love of my" 5669
"life, have a happy" 6663
"life, he'd been in" 5992
"life, her" 8026
"life, her bustout" 8024
"life, her mother's" 7377
"life, his" 4665, 5594, 10521
"life, his declining" 6606
"life, his early" 6127
"life, his past" 7374
"life, his whole" 5601
"life, history of his" 703
"Life, History of my own" 6033
"life, human" 6991
"Life, I departed this" 2286
"life, I made my way through this" 5587
"life, in" 584, 1882, 9349
"life, in every" 5580
"life, in every woman's" 5776
"life, in flight from my own" 6478
"life, in her" 1959, 5680, 7747
"life, in his" 8970, 9454
"life, in his young" 10620
"life, in its long" 1298
"life, in my" 5281, 7009, 7520
"life, in my daily" 2800
"life, in my whole" 5589
"life, in one" 4510
"life, in their" 3516
"life, infinite zest for" 8976
"life, insuring my" 6616
"life, journey thro'" 2287
"'Life', Judge said" 2027
"life, Julia's" 5599
"life, Kennaston's" 5565
"life, last afternoon of her" 5626
"life, last day of his" 2185
"life, last twenty days of his" 5452
"life, late in" 2594, 5728
"life, lead this" 5582
"life, learned to lean away from" 5239
"life, led the" 6456
"life, light of my" 10807
"life, line of" 6516
"life, living a moderately pleasant" 5299
"life, long-vanished boisterous" 2006

"life, major run of his" 6951
"life, man who gave me" 6661
"life, mature" 10341
"life, meaning of" 5253
"life, Megan Green's" 5111
"life, melancholy view of" 2501
"life, men in her" 6738
"life, modern" 5291
"life, most important part of his" 6500
"life, most of my" 679
"life, much of his" 3673
"life, must go through" 7124
"life, my" 597, 2450, 2550, 3293, 3393, 3470, 4343, 4354, 5057, 5088, 5099, 5104, 5120, 5381, 5481, 5554, 5561, 5569, 5578, 5582, 5584, 5586, 5593, 6706, 7951, 7963, 9442
"Life, my" 5492, 5552
"life, my adventurous" 3490
"life, my now stretched-out" 5108
"life, my own" 4452
"life, my solitary town-" 5275
"life, my strange" 4055
"life, my whole" 5588
"life, never happened in my" 5403
"life, never knew you in" 2312
"life, Nina Henry's" 562
"life, normal" 7172
"life, nothing in" 9470
"life, our" 7801
"life, overwhelming tragedies of" 5799
"life, pageant of moving" 8345
"life, past" 6784
"life, pathway of normal" 9279
"life, pattern of her" 4634
"life, period of my" 3393
"life, placed herself momentarily in" 6218
"life, placid and only occasionally traumatic early" 5592
"life, pretty well disgusted with" 5249
"life, prime of" 8839
"life, ran rich with" 9136
"life, ration of" 9008
"life, real" 5289
"life, real wake-a-day" 2753
"life, rest of her" 174
"Life, return to" 2286
"life, returning to a commons of good" 5286
"life, ribbon of his" 5572
"life, rule for a man's" 5562
"life, running toward" 4143
"life, say of his" 5602
"life, scandalous stages of my" 5553
"life, second time in my" 8494
"life, sees his own" 5572
"life, she had begun" 413
"life, sixteen years of Janet's" 833
"life, social" 8632
"life, solitary" 6883

"life, some of the best years of my" 6254
"life, sounds of" 8070
"life, spent nearly their whole married" 1965
"life, spring to" 7926
"life, start up a new" 6188
"life, stirring to" 1464
"life, strange history of my" 5567
"life, sucked" 9674
"life, suddenly obliged to examine his" 86
"life, take on" 9463
"life, taken her own" 6187
"life, takes a bit from" 8980
"life, terrified of" 9285
"life, that sphere of" 6612
"life, their own strong violent" 736
"life, this" 5002
"life, this Olaf" 1267
"life, thrice reached the highest station of" 9260
"life, throughout her" 2547
"life, tied to for" 5242
"life, time in his" 2515
"life, toward the end of his" 7454
"life, town" 6199
"life, tranquil family" 3248
"life, trappings of" 5261
"life, true apex of his" 5572
"life, viewer's real" 1325
"life, watch out for" 5266
"life, way of" 1396
"life, what a worthless lousy dirty" 5256
"life, wild" 5288
"life, worst week in my" 63
"life, wreckless with his" 2381
"*Life*, young person from" 1107
"LIFE AFTER DEATH, IS THERE" 8315
"life and love, dramas of" 5566
"life and the lives that thou begettest, thy" 7507
"life and warmth, eyes full of" 10815
"life anywhere, nor any sign of" 8786
"life as a brutal approximation" 5271
"life as a path" 5572
"life at all until then, as if I had had no" 5597
"life at home, carry on his" 166
"life at sixty, begin a new" 5596
"life awoke, all" 8438
"life became a fiction" 5588
"life began, my new" 5098
"life began again every time he met a beautiful woman" 6650
"life began in wartime" 833
"life began to change" 5116
"life come down to me, having my" 9300
"life did not begin until he died" 5595

"life did not begin until I knew her, my" 5099
"life did not seem the same to him any more" 417
"life ended in disaster" 7714
"life forms of the valley" 9755
"life from the hoary grey ear, sucking the" 5256
"life had been ruined by literature, her" 5493
"life had been smacked into his small red behind" 813
"life had gone, the way his" 8730
"life he had lived, the old" 5564
"life his father had marked out for him" 6516
"life in Cwm Bugail, your" 6953
"life in England has become settled comfortable and prosperous" 5294
"life in the orphan asylum" 1250
"life in which much had gone wrong" 2349
"life is a riddle" 2362
"life is bitter-sweet" 7372
"life is change" 5273
"life is changed, my" 7076
"life is diseased, my" 146
"life is like a long blind date" 5254
"life is the indestructible pulse of energy" 526
"life itself, in the" 7177
"life jacket, demonstrating the use of a" 9579
"life left, less than six months of" 2449
"life made precarious" 6701
"life might be given back to them, their" 6992
"life moves at a slow pace, all native" 9616
"life of a famous man, everything in the" 5585
"life of a guineapig or a magpie" 5276
"life of any one individual" 5558
"life of Cecilia Holt" 5560
"life of David Alexander Michaeljohn" 5089
"life of deceit, I live a" 5304
"life of every party" 5983
"life of folks" 9770
"life of Hero Athena Hollis" 10814
"life of him, can tell for the" 5575
"life of Mrs. Aubyn" 696
"life of the yet unborn" 6991
"life of their author" 7948
"life of unpremeditated childhood" 5120
"life of you, for the" 7387
"life on earth, man's" 5575
"life saner kindlier than I had known" 5286
"life seemed extinct up at the Villa Byrsa" 5251

"life seemed so many clashes and
  contests" 5226
"life so new could suffer so irrevocably" 9279
"life takes on an entirely new aspect" 5416
"life that can be told as a story, the
  kind of" 5593
"life that matters, 'tisn't" 5248
"life to live, each of us has only
  one" 2403
"life together, our" 1741
"life together was sheer hell, their"
  1984
"life together would become quite
  impossible" 9685
"life up this end, there's more" 5258
"life veered from its day-in day-out
  course" 5593
"life was about anything, if Colin
  Draggett's" 5211
"life was as deforming as an ill-
  fitting shoe" 5265
"life was changed, the course of
  my" 5114
"life was different" 5257
"life was just beginning" 5577
"life was monstrously unfair" 5250
"life was not good enough, not because" 2071
"life which ended in July 1926" 2336
"life which was soon taken from
  him" 2381
"life would change forever, my" 5110
"life would end in murder" 6202
"life's journey, in the middle of"
  6491
"life's little jokes" 4664
"life's possibilities, blind to" 5880
"lifesaver, Sandy The Sea Serpent
  rubber " 308
Lifestyles 1022, 4479, 4634, 9284
"lifetime, for this" 2429
"lifetime, his" 4737
"lifetime, in my" 5371
"lifetime, last a" 2177
"*lifetime* in her company" 8027
"lifetime of living there, takes a"
  4548
"lifetimes ago" 7030
"lift, celebrated ironwork" 3299
"lift, the" 1595
"lift, trouble with the" 3297
"lift him into her arms" 8761
"lift of autumn" 9572
"lifted free" 215
"lifted off the C. & O. Pullman"
  5924
"lifted the shadows from the ruins
  of Berlin and Nuremberg" 2237
"lifted the woman's stocking he was
  wearing" 151
"lifting" 10300
"lifting his eyes from his evening
  paper" 9866

"lifting itself out of an invisible
  paddock" 224
"lifting me up from the covers"
  10020
"lifting the lace curtain" 10972
"lifting their feet high in the big
  thick boots" 8659
"lifts up the layers" 10948
Light 332, 1036, 1593, 2228,
  2258, 2267, 2782, 2951, 3466,
  3894, 3981, 4296, 5306, 5307,
  5312, 5321, 5324, 5326, 5331,
  5335, 5339, 5341, 6272, 6786,
  6905, 7364, 8363, 8425, 8444,
  8897, 9400, 10108, 10116, 10198,
  10242, 10273
"light" 5326
"light, afternoon" 2280, 5331
"light, aqueous" 10292
"light, at first" 1786, 10509
"light, bathed in gold" 2225
"light, bathed in pearly" 2228
"light, between darkness and" 2781
"light, blossom of" 4704
"light, blue in the evening" 783
"light, brilliant" 7856
"light, casting brilliant" 9239
"light, clear simple" 11004
"light, cold" 8425
"light, cone of yellow" 7364
"light, constant indoor" 1041
"light, covered him from head to
  foot with" 5945
"light, dappled" 5329
"light, dawn" 9666
"light, diffused its inadequate" 8404
"light, dim" 10287
"light, dim red" 10289
"light, evening" 2080
"light, familiar crack of" 3701
"light, first" 3687
"light, first dim waver of" 10273
"light, first ray of" 5557
"light, full of" 2796
"light, glittery underwater" 2782
"light, grabbing handfuls of" 10397
"light, high lozenge of" 10198
"light, I first saw the" 782, 5078
"light, in the failing" 8267
"light, invisible needle of" 5312
"Light, it was the season of" 3377
"light, its exacting" 8444
"light, level" 5181
"light, little squares of" 1407
"light, long shafts of" 5314
"light, mellow green" 7754
"light, milk white no-" 2278
"light, moon poured down its" 8391
"light, morning" 1752
"light, no" 9319
"light, obscuring the" 3776
"light, only the wood fire for" 869
"light, outdoor" 1041
"light, pale first" 2285
"light, pale wash of" 10149

"light, pellucid" 5335
"light, private modest unblinking"
  537
"light, quality of" 6272
"light, queer" 2704
"light, reflected" 2118
"light, repeated circles of bilious"
  5320
"light, room was suffused with"
  5335
"light, scattered" 7255
"light, shafts of rose-colored" 8431
"light, shed a bright parting" 3894
"light, single beam of" 4296
"light, slanting rainy" 1036
"light, soft amber" 9400
"light, still some" 2258
"light, strong" 10121
"light, sudden" 10611
"light, sudden discharge of" 5321
"light, summer" 1754, 4118
"light, surf of its own" 9668
"light, switch on the" 9417
"light, switch on the hall" 8179
"light, switched off the last" 5336
"light, that laving river of" 1333
"light, that sidelong" 3894
"Light, the Great" 10267
"light, there was" 2282
"light, they spoke in" 8897
"light, top burning curly hair of"
  4660
"light, under a bright" 6971
"light, watching the golden" 2209
"light, what an unbecoming" 4985
"light, would it ever get" 8492
"light, yellow" 7289
"light and darkness, silver balance
  between" 2278
"light and moving air carried heat"
  7763
"light and shadow" 3981
"light at dawn" 2267
"light began to fade" 3411
"light bulb, electric" 9578
"light bulbs, electric" 7779
"light bulbs that hung so nakedly
  over the heads" 7779
"light came, when the" 10242
"light came and went and came
  again" 1606
"light . . . dispelled the soft visions
  of the four insides" 10108
"light entering the vast room" 5307
"light failed, the last" 10344
"light fell in a certain way, when
  the" 8363
"light filtering through swaying
  birches" 5329
"light flitting, she is a" 4115
"light from the bus" 9781
"light from the store windows"
  8606
"light gilded the domes and
  steeples" 5331

"light given off by the setting sun" 5341

"light had withdrawn from the sky" 6648

"light in the west, a blue" 3466

"light is slowly fading" 6786

"light of a December morning, ambiguous" 10108

"light of a new day" 4742

"light of a summer sunset" 5305

"light of a wet dawn in May" 5335

"light of a winter's sun, pale and watery" 8122

"light of coming darkness" 1216

"light of day, harsh" 6791

"light of day, the broad" 10142

"light of my life" 10807

"light of the fire, by the" 10934

"light of the lamp beams" 2492

"light of the sun" 92

"light of the swamp ended, where the" 224

"light of the Wentworth's kitchen" 1593

"light on, leave the" 3705

"light on her feet" 10833

"light on the corner, under a street" 10045

"light over his head, holding a yellow" 7474

"light over it, a red" 2700

"light reflected on glass, molten" 483

"light slanting through the pines" 8431

"light softened and tinted by the drawn blinds" 4118

"light switch did not work" 7158

"light that fell between the tree-trunks, bars of" 2951

"light that shone on the faces of the three passengers" 9540

"light the lamps in the hotel" 4647

"light the sky" 8438

"light thoughts of love" 5649

"light to dark, sudden shift from" 2239

"light to the two occupants of the room" 7753

"light too dim" 7356

"light travels" 6905

"light turned red" 3031

"light unaccompanied by the prejudice of human eyes" 5307

"light under a bushel, hiding my" 239

"light was exploding" 887

"light was hurting her eyes" 10240

"light was losing" 2282

"light which filters down languidly" 7754

"light which illumines the gloom" 5557

"light yet, do you see any" 5306

"lightbread" 8530

"lighted as it would be, about as well" 5313

"lighted by a smile, never" 5889

"lighted upon him" 950

"lightened and then it'd gone black" 2269

"lightening the burden of the heat" 7308

"lighter and more frail, I feel" 2399

Lightfoot, Captain 5214

"light-headed" 1700

"light-hearted" 9882

"lighthouse" 8154

"Lighthouse, Montauk" 9247

"lighting, dim" 6511

"lighting on the deal washstand" 10142

"lighting the faces" 6373

"lighting the grey roofs" 9605

"lighting up another cigarette" 8582

"lightning, bolt of" 8560

"lightning, flashes of" 9088

"lightning, incessant play of the" 9312

"lightning, playing the zig-zag" 9066

"lightning, single bolt of" 6373

"lightning, snake's tongue of" 9081

"lightning bolts streaking the sky" 9300

"lightning bugs" 4962

"lightning flashes, brief unearthly glare of" 9076

"lightning fluttered on and off" 9077

"lightning had slashed" 6373

"Lightning Streak" 4743

"Lightnings" 210

"lightnings, ablaze with" 9070

"lightpoised on the balls of his greasestained tennis shoes" 2690

Lights 122, 537, 887, 1078, 1407, 2219, 2245, 3029, 3244, 3705, 3872, 4053, 4205, 4478, 4647, 4985, 5315, 5320, 5321, 5324, 5325, 5332, 5336, 5338, 5339, 6511, 6657, 7672, 7779, 7782, 7856, 8154, 8323, 9247, 9392, 9402, 9562, 9578

"lights, a million twinkling" 1956

"lights, electric" 5325

"lights, evening" 9389

"lights, filled with ever-changing" 1469

"lights, glare of the" 9376

"lights, long files of traffic" 3402

"lights, mercury vapor" 8323

"lights, red-shaded electric" 7761

"lights, sprinkling it with glistening" 7672

"lights, stringing out its bluish" 7266

"lights, they are two" 6657

"lights and tenants have gone out, all the" 3244

"lights fade one by one" 5332

"lights gleaming sharp upon its native blackness" 1356

"lights go out all at once" 4205

"lights in the bus" 5320

"lights in the distance" 9562

"lights in the slate-gray eyes, changing" 336

"lights of a night glimmer and glow" 4053

"lights of passing cars batted your eyeballs" 7855

"lights of this country, one of the" 927

"lights on" 5338

"lights shining in their faces" 9392

"lights shone from windows" 6323

"lights showed on the dashboard, no" 9805

"lights that glide in jewelled columns" 5338

"lights tiny and festive" 8596

"lights went down" 5875

"lights went on" 5321

"lights went up, one by one the" 2219

"ligneous soil" 3069

"like, I'm" 2749

"like, no one could really" 5379

"like, what was it really" 2096

"like, what's he" 5932

"like about the rooms, you don't" 5350

"like better than a yarn, there's nothing I" 9000

"like each other, nothing says we have to" 5660

"like it, never seen anything" 2857

"like it, we did not" 5343

"like it here, you're really going to" 1432

"like it when I talk like that, he doesn't" 5363

"like Margaret, she's" 4138

"like men, used to" 9690

"like most people" 6700

"like Prudence, so" 10789

"like their children, parents have to" 6532

"like their father" 7414

"like them, which was" 1976

"like to, I'd really" 3013

"like to feed the catfish" 5380

"like you, I don't want to be" 4362

"like you, wish I were" 9296

"liked, do anything he" 10116

"liked, whom she had never" 10100

"liked about Earls Court" 5356

"liked being new to London" 9108

"liked her bath" 562

"liked his London, had always" 5345

"liked Olivia, Chloe" 5873

"liked the flat land" 3044

"liked the idea, I've always" 904

"liked the words because he understood them" 8760

"liked them that way, we guys" 5382

"liked this bathroom wallpaper, I always" 5376

"liked this plumber, I" 7738

"liked to say to her" 6665

"liked to sit at her husband's left" 6308

"liked to walk" 5607

"liked Tom, I thought you" 5369

"liked traveling" 5360

"liked us that way" 5382

"likelihood of Ophelia's enigmatic cry" 5507

"likely, seems increasingly" 7234

"likeness, not pleased with the" 488

Likes 562, 854, 904, 3013, 5013, 5344, 5345, 5351, 5354, 5355, 5356, 5358, 5360, 5362, 5365, 5366, 5368, 5370, 5373, 5376, 5378, 5380, 5381, 5382, 5383, 5660, 5873, 6240, 7153, 7738, 7867, 8365, 9000, 9690

"liking this, not" 3027

Lil 10955

Lila 9437

Lila Mae 1760

"lilac, heavy scent of the" 3794

"lilac was in bloom again" 3807

"lilacs, white" 6499

"lilacs fill the air with purple perfumes" 8933

"Lilacsbush" 6608

Lilia 3993

Lilian 312, 6495, 10652

"lilies" 1302

"lilies, as though it were a bunch of" 6993

Lilley, Reverend 1533

Lillian 1766, 10801

Lilly 8230

Lillywhite, Charles Blagden 4567

Lily 2074, 2814, 2990, 3682, 4163, 4198, 5296, 5770, 7213, 8796, 9851

"Lily of the Shores of the Mohawk River, are you the" 4771

"lily pads" 4688

"lily pond" 3165

"limb, broke a" 28

"limber up, let his mind" 1213

"Limberlost" 7215

"limbo, in" 9615

"limbo of the last months" 9572

"limbs, hickory" 10740

"limbs, his gracefully modeled" 5996

"limbs, his long" 152

"limbs, lost the use of my" 2894

"limbs, prosthetic" 3205

"limbs, stout" 1228

"limbs of the tall trees" 7692

"limbs were hurting him, as though his" 2595

"Limerick, he went for the first time to" 7382

"limestone peninsula" 10994

"lime-trees, shadow of the" 2951

"lime-walk" 9856

"Limited, Overland" 8564

"limitless" 7914

"limits, city" 10367

"limits and it enables" 7698

"limits of the known world" 10628

"limousine, blue Volga" 9833

"limousine, Cadillac" 9819

"limousine, enormous and even in this blackened world lustrous Adler" 1714

"limousine, got out of the" 1767, 4564

"limousine, long black" 9794

"limousine stood waiting" 217

"limousine to be luxurious, expected the back of the" 2590

"limp, with a slight" 10338

"limp in a simmering sun" 9479

"limped away" 28

"limped up the steep path" 1498

"limpet shells" 6648

Limping 1498, 10338, 10447

"limps to his barn" 10447

Linc 9958

Lincoln, Abraham 1402

"Lincoln, county of" 3058

"Lincoln, drove the" 3018

"Lincoln chariot, gold and white" 9793

"Lincoln Trader" 9825

"Lincoln's Birthday" 9911

"Lincoln's Grove" 3239

"Lincoln's Inn Fields" 9343

"Lincoln's Inn Hall" 8339

"Lincolnshire" 3396, 5289

"Lincolnshire uplands" 10386

Linda 2984, 8905

"Lindbergh Field" 227

"Linden Hills" 4088

Lindsay 8002

Lindsey, Jerome 6315

Line 7088

"Line, Bakerloo" 2359

"line, branch" 7244

"line, cease-fire" 8682

"line, continuous double yellow" 9194

"line, dark wavering" 8612

"line, dividing" 4036

"line, end of the" 7248

"line, front" 10506

"line, I shall forgo a fetching first" 5526

"line, little branch" 7254

"line, long shining" 9814

"line, purity of" 4617

"line, small black" 9766

"line, thick black" 2541

"line, this particular stretch of" 7241

"line, town" 9176

"line . . . dates from Montenotte, my" 363

"line down its center" 9194

"line faded and reappeared and faded again" 9766

"line is an old one, our" 366

"line transfer" 6652

"line which starts at Wockley Junction" 7254

"lined with tile to the ceiling" 9999

"liner, Atlantic" 8082

"liner, big" 8072

"liner, big Atlantic" 4730

"liner, Orient" 8078

"liner, the" 4535

"liner, twin-screw turbine" 8074

"liner hung over the tugs" 8072

"liner rolled and lifted" 8062

"liner was landlocked" 8115

"lines, C Company" 8652

"lines, good" 9379

"lines, I address these" 6035

"lines, nine hundred ninety-nine" 5452

"lines, one of the most expensive" 4270

"lines are good, the" 3143

"lines cut deep into Sam's cheeks, premature" 5976

"lines disposed, in goodly" 10641

"lines . . . flow like food for the tail-eating snake" 5521

"lines left by the skater shone like a tangle of red-hot wires" 983

"lines upon lines" 5521

"lines . . . wavered and shivered incessantly" 9999

"lines were taken by the waiting shore-party" 8128

Ling Tan 9997

Lingard, Andrew 1658

"lingered behind" 1311

"lingering in his mind, faces" 10285

"lingering on in a markedly abraded state" 3589

"liniment, bought a bottle of" 6614

Link 9425

"Link, Cosmic" 2633

Linkhorn, Fitz 2651

Links, Janet 7167

Linnane, Eleanor 9343

"linoleum, arctic wastes of our" 10190

"linoleum that had buckled and perished here and there" 6294

Linquists, the 4107

Linthorne, Thomas 10043

Linton, Anne 3010

"lion, black" 7284

"lion, dying" 4778

"lion, form of a sleeping" 6055

"lion-colored" 5148

Lionel 6782

"lioness, old" 463

"lioness stared at the Hertfordshire road" 414
Lions 414, 441, 463, 479
"lions, echo of" 7701
"Lions, Forest of" 3903
"Lions, Three" 10332
"lions any more, were no" 441
"lions at their feet" 2300
"lions roaring in the park" 479
"lip, bites her" 8013
"lip, chewed at his" 383
"lip, chewed his" 4810
"lip, curl your" 2492
"lip, his lower" 7124
"lip, long upper" 246
"lip grown permanently projected" 7124
"lips" 5603
"lips, brick-red" 10964
"lips, closely folded rather prim clergyman's" 5912
"lips, dropped from her friendly" 4696
"lips, finger pressed to her" 9895
"lips, firm" 3272
"lips, his moustachioed" 2927
"lips, licking the" 3839
"lips, red" 1432
"lips, thick" 5984
"lips, whipcord" 5453
"lips are pressed tightly together" 10030
"lips brushed his left ear, her" 5746
"lips drawn back" 475
"lips of chauffeurs uncurled into not unkindly smiles" 5308
"lips pucker" 891
"lips slightly open in readiness" 5188
"lips slightly parted" 10644
"lips upon his Lorna Doone, he laid once more his" 5992
Lipschitz, Ezra 8486
"lipstick, indelible veronica of" 2589
"lipstick, Yardley slicker" 4192
"liquid, simmering brown" 8561
"liquid, strange" 8332
"liquids congealed in a pot, like incompatible" 1362
"liquor was flowing" 8638
"lire, cast his remaining metal" 9593
Lisa 3631, 9737
"Lisbon" 4650, 8118
Lise 2856
"list, typewritten" 3187
"list of marriages in *The Times*, it headed the" 5735
"listen, paused outside the door to" 8900
"listen, people stop to" 8791
"listen, you don't have to" 8012
"listen for nearly six hours" 4503
"listen to, no one for her to" 8885
"listen to me" 5950
"listen to me, someone" 8871

"listen to them breathe" 6543
"listen to *this*" 6242
"listen with credulity to the whispers of fancy" 4603
"listened, nobody" 4640
"listened, they" 10503
"listened respectfully" 2589
"listened through the uneasy silence" 9411
"listened to Elaine grumble" 1869
"listened to his patient" 3518
"listened to the Bee Women" 8554
"listened to what his old-time foreman and present partner was saying" 8853
"listened with a wrinkled face" 1680
"listener, his" 3845
"listener from birth" 6461
Listening 1799, 6461, 8554, 8853, 8858, 8885, 8906, 9411
"listening, no one" 7751
"listening, when they thought nobody was" 5396
"listening, whomever might be" 3243
"listening against his will" 10188
"listening at my parents' door" 8906
"listening beyond that to the sea's slow suck" 8491
"listening to a gramophone record" 6227
"listening to a sea shell, exactly like" 10002
"listening to McCoy Tyner on the radio" 10085
"listening to the conversations" 8854
"listening to the creak of the ship" 8504
"listening to the distant thud of hoofbeats" 10405
"listening to the executor" 4934
"listening to the growl of the Gulf" 4657
"listening to the latter's torrent of words, sullenly" 8852
"listening to the murmur and rustle" 1532
"listening to the pump's dull pulse" 8491
"listening to the silence" 8826
"listening to them" 6701
"listening too, the cat was" 8819
"listening with only half her mind" 8858
Lister 1673
"listing to its passenger's side" 40
"listing toward the sun" 9678
"listless, look" 2107
"lists, casualty" 10475
"lists, I make" 5491
"lit a fire, have you" 1552
"lit them up again, suddenly" 5023
"literary activities" 5437
"literary activities, my spare-time" 5424

"literary agent, tubby" 5453
"literary and commercial world" 5394
"literary and other" 5390
"literary effort, minute and unpretentious" 5416
"literary stewpot boils over" 8470
"literary to be really offensive, too" 9313
"literary wars" 5535
"literary weekly" 5530
Literature 216, 257, 274, 390, 696, 700, 702, 705, 706, 707, 710, 712, 713, 714, 716, 717, 896, 897, 901, 902, 903, 904, 906, 910, 912, 914, 920, 921, 924, 926, 962, 1006, 1314, 1325, 1527, 2360, 2466, 2531, 2534, 2535, 2536, 2541, 2542, 2543, 2544, 2546, 2549, 2550, 2553, 2554, 2555, 3284, 3670, 4425, 4455, 4491, 4493, 4494, 4499, 4500, 4508, 5029, 5209, 5311, 5565, 6352, 6358, 6385, 6419, 6454, 6491, 6860, 7218, 7348, 7349, 7351, 7375, 7388, 8310, 8470, 8663, 9011, 9446, 9987, 10022, 10049, 10548, 10904
"literature, anthology of mid-century" 5468
"Literature, Doctor of" 6443
"Literature, English" 216
"literature, factory of popular" 5311
"literature, her life had been ruined by" 5493
"literature, instructor of" 1920
"Literature, Regius Professor of Comparative" 6451
"*literature*, that is to say" 5418
"literature, work of" 5401
"literature, world of" 1314
"lithe with youth" 4203
"lithograph, huge nineteenth-century German" 6896
"litigation, prone to" 10662
"litigation had seemed interminable" 2649
"litter, scattered" 9144
"littered the moist grass" 9672
Little, Anthony 7610
Little, Mrs. 2756
"little, when I was" 3220, 7932
"little, when we were very" 1271
Little Arthur 8464
Little Augie 1269
Little Brother 2436
"Little Burgelstatham" 4069
"little by little" 2199
"Little Empton" 787
Little Egypt 3544
"Little League" 5245
"Little Man" 10078
"little ones, the" 10937
"little ones, the two" 6094
"Little Rock" 7262

"*Little Women*, reading" 7348
"Littledean, village of" 5168
Littlejohn 5800
Littlepage, Cornelius 6608
Littlepage, Mr. Virginius Curle 2501
"liturgy, bee in his bonnet about" 6807
"live, but a short time to" 5583
"live, came up to town to" 5790
"live, how I should" 5290
"live, perhaps you will be the one to" 6641
"live, the way New-Yorkers" 5278
"live, to" 6910
"live, where I" 6277
"live, yet shall he" 3941
"live a life of deceit" 5304
"live about as close to French Town as you can get" 3262
"live alone" 1149
"live alone now" 8729
"live and breath in, a day that is good to" 82
"live at Dillsborough" 1340
"live at Sarsaparilla, had come recently to" 10812
"live forever and ever" 6661
"live in a cheap hotel, went to" 6108
"live in California" 3202
"live 'in character'" 5694
"live in deliberate forgetfulness" 7441
"live in HARRY SAM" 3172
"live in it, the people who now" 3085
"live in Kreiswald, decide to" 2490
"live in London" 6106
"live in nearby towns" 3157
"live in Paris, I came to" 6119
"live in the highest company" 238
"live in the present, began to" 9288
"live in the Quarters" 7126
"live in today, conditions we" 879
"live like I do" 5284
"live now, the way we" 5297
"live okay, I" 5282
"live on a mountain" 6081
"live on a sailboat, he went off to" 9052
"live on Mango Street, we didn't always" 3250
"live on St. Petin, we" 5049
"live on the melon farm of an uncle" 6170
"live on the *rive gauche*" 1371
"live slowly" 5268
"live the elite of the haute bourgeoisie" 5179
"live there, those who" 1374
"live to be seventy, never" 1275
"live together" 3923
"live together in comfort, could not" 3553
"live under the threat of death" 1163

"live where I live, grateful to" 6206
"live wire" 6338
"live with, consequences are what we have to" 619
"live with another woman" 5914
"live with her, come" 6114
"live with his half-brother" 6148
"live with my sister" 337
"live within sight of salt water" 7938
"live without guilt" 5295
"lived, building where I" 3330
"lived, I feel that I've not" 2399
"lived, places where I have" 3142
"lived, where his parents" 9164
"lived a few years ago" 3552
"lived a hobbit, there" 3106
"lived a little, now that I have" 9118
"lived a week in Winnebago" 10787
"lived across the hall from a woman named Benna" 6302
"lived all alone, she" 430
"lived alone (except for his Japanese butler)" 3088
"lived alone in a stucco house" 6297
"lived and flourished" 6213
"lived as though we had no past" 5280
"lived at Oakland" 3637
"lived at Scroope Manor" 3066
"lived at the Buckingham Hotel" 3233
"lived beside it" 6275
"lived by it" 7867
"lived by the Western Sea" 4572
"lived down the road a little way" 6525
"lived exactly two miles from the house where he grew up" 3254
"lived for a long time with my mother and father" 6700
"lived for fifteen years in a castle" 3202
"lived for generations on the Marsh Farm" 3082
"lived happily ever after" 1984, 5300
"lived in" 3228
"lived in a bedsit" 3213
"lived in a boxcar by the river" 3235
"lived in a certain boarding-house" 10768
"lived in a grey housing project" 7042
"lived in a house" 3093
"lived in a house in Santa Rosa" 3211
"lived in a landscape of fear" 5173
"lived in a large brick house" 4947
"lived in a Low Country" 5122
"lived in a place of great beauty" 3251
"lived in a small house, she" 3101
"lived in an old farmhouse" 3139
"lived in Baron's Court or some-

where beyond the back of beyond" 8027
"lived in Berlin Germany" 7714
"lived in Golders Green" 4070
"lived ... in her late parents' house" 3136
"lived in his own suite of apartments" 3189
"lived in London" 4545
"lived in Paris, afterward I" 3258
"lived in that suburb" 2041
"lived in the apartment below" 9984
"lived in the eighteenth century, by rights he should have" 6043
"lived in the last soft fold of earth before the sea" 3204
"lived in the neighbourhood" 8587
"lived in the new quarter of Carlingford" 6034
"lived in the Oliphant's house" 8208
"lived in this hotel" 2935
"lived just where the Left Bank ceases to be the Latin Quarter" 6289
"lived like a mole" 5287
"lived long, I have" 7403
"lived my life all wrong" 5586
"lived my life the only way I could have lived it" 5586
"lived not long ago two Philosophers" 10756
"lived on the coast of California" 3089
"lived pleasantly, for five or six weeks he" 4269
"lived rent-free" 694
"lived right next door to Dr. Henry's" 6148
"lived scared" 2599
"lived seven years in the little house" 5352
"lived since his wife's death, where he had" 2971
"lived there for a week" 3247
"lived together at 73b Oakmoor Road" 10862
"lived together so long" 6288
"lived twelve houses away" 6295
"lived when you were a kid, town where you" 4536
"lived with her mother" 3081
"lived with his sister" 8220
"lived with his wife and daughter in Santa Venetia" 2061
"lived with his wife in that leafy quarter of the city" 6279
"lived with Lauro" 2462
"lived with their two sons" 6140
"lived within five blocks of each other" 6293
"livelihood, we who eke a" 6486
"lively countenance and a waistcoat to match it" 14
"lively review" 5732

"liver enlarged and yellow in color" 7514
Livermore, Mrs. 493
"Liverpool Docks were never at their best" 7307
"Liverpool Landing Stage" 7307
"Liverpool looked its depressing worst" 7307
"livery, his" 566
"Livery, Fashion" 9142
"livery stable" 3441
"Livery Stable, Jander's" 495
"livery-stable, their stick-horse" 959
Lives 43, 86, 146, 166, 250, 353, 699, 703, 704, 707, 708, 712, 778, 833, 931, 940, 1163, 1234, 1246, 1250, 1267, 1741, 1984, 2130, 2185, 2299, 2381, 2383, 2399, 2403, 2450, 2509, 2515, 2539, 2550, 2594, 2612, 2656, 3353, 3379, 3393, 3470, 3488, 3490, 3493, 3537, 3670, 3707, 3912, 4055, 4175, 4283, 4343, 4452, 4454, 4489, 4665, 4935, 4936, 5057, 5081, 5087, 5089, 5098, 5099, 5106, 5108, 5110, 5111, 5112, 5114, 5116, 5120, 5211, 5226, 5255, 5257, 5265, 5275, 5276, 5278, 5279, 5283, 5284, 5290, 5293, 5295, 5296, 5299, 5304, 5416, 5492, 5493, 5503, 5626, 5694, 5706, 5736, 5776, 5815, 5950, 6033, 6117, 6188, 6202, 6254, 6293, 6317, 6400, 6456, 6467, 6478, 6491, 6500, 6606, 6616, 6650, 6660, 6663, 6701, 6784, 6883, 6932, 6951, 6953, 6992, 7076, 7177, 7199, 7286, 7403, 7454, 7507, 7714, 7747, 7951, 8026, 8226, 8494, 8730, 8974, 9047, 9279, 9288, 9300, 9685, 9719, 10476, 10814, 10826, 10837, 11004
"lives, all our" 5706
"lives, all our separate" 5600
"lives, busyness of their" 8093
"lives, change" 5106
"lives, devoted their" 10837
"lives, every morning of our" 4283
"lives, first fifteen years of our" 6293
"lives, hazard rules our" 5274
"lives, mess we make of our" 5296
"lives, no longer part of their" 8551
"lives, our" 1022, 5568
"lives, rainiest" 7286
"lives, rest of their" 582
"lives, sad short course of our" 5559
"lives, their" 3912
"lives and characters lie hidden" 4454
"lives and loves of Timothy Hazard" 704
"lives at Malin now, nobody" 3138
"lives form one unbroken round of

pomp and successful achievement" 5279
"Lives have been remarkable" 353
"lives in a High Tower" 5233
"lives in Galloway, if one" 6416
"lives in Mexico, spend their" 5609
"lives in the younger Rome" 3071
"lives in unawareness, pass their" 3671
"lives of countless men and women, ruining the" 5659
"lives of her children" 2712
"lives of his dramatis personae" 5414
"lives of those great revolutionary women of the past" 10837
"lives on the Street of the Cat Who Fishes" 9189
"lives there in the lower part of No. 56 Somerset Road" 3153
"lives this close to an artist, when one" 500
"lives were ... quite extraordinarily dull" 2539
Livesey, Dr. 5012
"livestock, feed the" 10945
"livid at breakfast" 386
"livin', for a" 6479
Living 5267, 5293
"living" 5215
"living, earn their" 135
"living, earning her own" 3273
"living, made a good" 6867
"living, made his" 6901
"living, must really be" 5273
"living, only for the" 3936
"living, prefer to go on" 5267
"living, rich" 3385
"living, tenure on" 6951
"living, the" 1191
"living almost six decades" 6798
"living alone" 3359
"living alone again, I was" 3789
"living alone and shouldn't" 8721
"living and dead, both" 8488
"living and writing in Paris" 3231
"living at le Grau du Roi" 4653
"living at the Villa Borghese" 935
"living in a furnished room" 3167
"living in her house in Sussex" 6327
"living in her parents' big bed" 6687
"living in London as we do" 427
"living in Paris" 3541
"living in the back leg of an all-glass piano, like" 3584
"living in the UK for four years" 6147
"living last year in a way you could hardly have believed" 5283
"living modestly" 5213
"living once again in the town where I grew up" 4598
"living organism, any" 6001
"living proof, I thought I was the" 6535
"living quarters" 6122

"living room, they were all in the" 7040
"living then in a bungalow" 3214
"living things in the house, the only" 3099
"living things prefer to go on living" 5267
"living together, Nina and I had been" 7085
"living with my sister" 7900
"living-room, steam-heated" 7756
"living-room would have been a cheerless place indeed" 7756
Livingstone, Mirren 8556
Livingstone, Oscar 5863
Liz 2082
Liza 111
"lizard, self-consuming bile-green" 474
"lizard again" 474
"lizard with the bird-of-prey's beak" 474
"lizards" 4404
Lizzie 1961, 4589, 6750
"Llandudno, our youth in" 5648
"llano, beauty of the" 5156
"Llanos, los" 5173
"Llantrisant" 5151
Llewellyn, Ivor 1687
"Llewellyn City" 1324, 1687
Lloyd 5814
"loaded with a merry group of young people" 9759
"loaned from a gift and jewelry chain store" 9729
"loathe it, love it or" 1451
"loathing and suspicion" 9304
"lobby, bare little" 3296
"lobby lately, have you seen the" 8569
"lobby of the old hotel" 1638
"lobes, drink" 8797
"loblolly deadfall" 10106
"loblolly saplings" 1879
"lobster shack" 3431
"lobsters, boiled two" 860
"locality" 6885
"locality, knowledge of the" 6498
"locate instead of find, saying" 8870
"Locatelli" 6226
"Locatelli's C major Quartet" 6226
"location of Linden Hills, the exact" 4088
"lochs on the Black Moor of Lewis" 3667
"lock into place, slid the" 2484
"lock up the room" 10932
"lock you up in your bedroom" 4244
Locke, Miss Emma Marianne 7186
"locked away, my own body was" 9279
"locked himself in the church" 7046
"locked in a morocco writing case" 717

"locked in the closet, he would be"
3272
"locked the back door" 10919
"locked the door" 1787
"locked the hen-houses for the
night" 2895
"locked together in one of those absorbing friendships" 3931
"locker was a hot place to be" 4430
Lockhart, Tom 10872
"locking the door shut behind her"
8822
"lockjaw, died of" 468
Lockman, Mr. and Mrs. Joseph
7816
Lockwood, George 1853
Lockyer, Gaden 6241
Loco Poco 3580
"locomotive" 7278
"locomotive, rushed along by a"
9515
"locomotives, bell-funneled" 7258
"locusts, black" 7638
"locusts, shrilling of the" 5074
"locusts came, the year that the"
9993
"Lodge, Chipping" 3122
"Lodge, Holly" 310
"Lodge, Manister" 10926
"lodge, the" 10170
"Lodgepole, valley of the" 7247
"lodger on the third floor" 10792
"lodging, her" 8342
"lodging, in his" 9945
"Lodging House, Dunboy" 7841
"lodging under our roof" 5012
"lodgings, her new" 6116
"lodgings, his" 3813, 7349
"lodgings, independence of" 5079
"lodgings, let" 3154
"lodgings, my" 487
"Lodgings, my" 2286, 10465
"lodgings, small" 4222
"lodgings, William Shakespeare's"
2931
"lodgings in Lower Gardiner
Street" 1600
Loebus, Frederich 7548
Lofblom, Elof 9554
"loft, church" 6229
"loft, white-walled" 7787
Lofting, Lieutenant 8707
"log, a downed" 4161
"log, enormous ship's" 5517
"log cabin" 3090, 3129
"logged off the white pine stands of
the Saginaw Country" 3423
"loggia" 10001
Loggins, Miss Essie Mae 5218
"loggish face southward" 7887
"logic of things" 7372
"logic to keep in mind, a certain"
9017
"Logicales, Summulae" 7879
"logs burning in the hearth" 7519

"loin, fire of my" 10807
"loins, a quick warm flooding about
his" 380
"Loire" 274
"Loire valley" 2976
Lois 335, 1105, 2334
Loisel, Régis 336
"loitering down the pavement"
10364
Lok 7845
Lolita 10807
"*Lolita* in Latin" 6807
"lolling around watching loud TV"
6783
"lolling with boneless and presumably aristocratic grace" 8234
"lollygagging at the local 'watering
hole'" 5462
Loman 6179
Lomas, Pete 8135
"Lombard plain" 5127
"Lombardy" 2281
London, Laurie 3386
London 947, 1347, 1356, 1358,
1409, 1476, 3383, 4063, 4093,
5289, 5345
"London" 355, 427, 947, 1181,
1196, 1294, 1320, 1354, 1442,
1519, 1654, 1724, 1726, 1834,
1891, 2041, 2273, 2509, 2616,
2865, 2930, 3022, 3153, 3171,
3414, 3529, 4079, 4093, 4303,
4304, 4313, 4330, 4411, 4467,
4545, 4576, 4644, 4733, 5126,
5208, 5221, 5308, 5311, 5747,
5761, 5839, 6001, 6106, 6516,
6568, 6620, 6963, 6974, 7180,
7268, 7279, 7284, 7317, 7409,
7573, 7587, 7847, 7996, 8300,
8339, 8347, 8839, 9108, 9266,
9380, 9396, 9509, 9858, 9931,
10494, 10571, 10612, 10862
"London, ancient city of" 781
"London, arrived in" 5543
"London, being hauled to" 2786
"London, Central" 1112
"London, citizen of" 7501
"London, City of" 9764
"London, coming back to" 4578
"London, dismaying heart of" 6580
"London, dream city of" 6584
"London, East" 6104
"London, East End of" 6098
"London, great show in" 10473
"London, Greater" 2557
"London, had always liked his"
5345
"London, in central" 2998
"London, most central point of"
4063
"London, north" 9806
"London, North" 1889, 8587
"London, northern outskirts of"
9896
"London, on a plane for" 3693

"London, reached" 1991
"London, smoky old" 817
"London, suburbs of" 6558
"London, sunset side of" 1358
"London, they had been safe in"
2149
"London, University of" 3266
"London, went back to" 2667
"London, West End of" 9400
"London, when they visited" 3831
"London, whenever he was in" 4317
"London, while you're in" 9923
"London, wide circle of" 1409
"London airport" 6007
"London Airport" 6323
"London Bridge" 14, 1196, 8050,
10394
"London coffee-houses" 5448
"London during the war" 1282
"London ended, after" 1244
"London flat" 4006
"London Ghetto" 1347
"London like Budapest, why is"
1476
"London none of us will ever see
again" 3383
"London NW4" 5289
"London restaurant" 5419
"London road" 9134
"London season" 1337, 3813
"London sky" 8617
"London statue" 8938
"London swart and grim" 1356
"London the great city of bache-
lors" 5928
"London theatre abounds with
fascination" 9376
"London when it had come to him"
5345
"London winter night" 7285
"Londoner, born to be a" 958
"London's broadest street" 8073
Lone 10203
"Lone Rock" 4078
"lonelier place" 9147
"loneliest night in the week" 6372
Loneliness 2493, 2651, 3168, 3216,
3308, 3683, 4164, 4570, 5697,
6372, 8491, 8717, 8723, 8732,
8763, 9906, 10763
"loneliness" 3308, 3683
"loneliness, frightened by any
amount of" 9515
"loneliness, pain of" 10763
"loneliness, when he had the" 7411
"loneliness before a homecoming,
the last overwhelming" 4570
"loneliness of the place, something
to relieve the" 9906
"lonely" 497, 5697
"lonely, the" 8732
"lonely, thought of the bungalow
as" 3168
"lonely and splendid" 992
"lonely boy, a" 983

"lonely Mag Smith" 2493
"lonely Westmoreland valley" 9742
Lonelyhearts, Miss 6421
"loners, lord of" 4800
"lonesome" 2651
Loney 8921
Long, Davy 1863
Long, Dinny 10763
"long, it was six inches" 4256
"long, night is so goddamned" 6381
"long, some twelve miles" 5138
"long afterwards" 4120
"long ago" 4294, 4538, 5042,
    5042, 5404, 5947, 6457, 7037,
    7575, 7709, 8314, 8992, 9060,
    9628
"long ago, in the" 7388
"long ago, long" 806
"long ago, not" 1009, 2509, 8344
"long ago, not so" 5567
"long ago, not too" 10450
"long ago, not very" 3820
"long ago, very" 5431
"long ago there was a little land"
    7796
"long as he can, for just as" 10104
"long as he could" 10163
"Long Beach" 4064
"long before" 7810
"Long Island" 3159, 3161, 6163,
    6925
"Long Island Sound" 6363
"long run, in the" 3509
"long time, it's been a" 7983
"long way, it is a" 4093
"long way round, gone the" 883
"Long Whindale" 9742
"long-ago summer" 2771
"longed for what I felt couldn't be
    fulfilled even by making love"
    2529
Longfellow, Anatole 10342
"longing, inarticulate" 1706
"longing in which the whole being
    consents" 10778
"longings, vague" 10844
"longitude" 4076, 5574
"longitude, 165 24' west" 4096
Longridge, Piers 1104
Longstreet, Mrs. 4739
Longstreet, Wick 8579
Longueville, Bernard 9720
Lonigan, Studs 2827
Lonnie 7397
Lonzo 1602
"looey, young flight" 4674
Look 4008
"look, began to" 530
"look, disgusted" 8572
"look, far-beyond-it-all and happy"
    2429
"look, had not let himself" 1639
"look, half expostulatory half indig-
    nant" 9855
"look, if you know where to" 1993

"look, keen tense" 1610
"look, last" 5834
"look, not far to" 9278
"look, somewhat veiled" 4593
"look, starry-eyed" 1101
"look, stopped for a last" 2982
"look, turn and" 10004
"look, turning for a backward"
    8252
"look after his brother" 3943
"look after Vernell" 8670
"look ahead" 8989
"look alike, roads in Connecticut"
    5608
"look all right, do I" 7475
"look and carriage, her" 4996
"look and tell" 1322
"look at, get a" 2432
"look at anything else, didn't" 9665
"look at 'em come" 6103
"look at her as they would look at
    a relic" 110
"look at her face, if you didn't"
    10804
"look at his notes, had a quick" 162
"look at me, how they always" 5027
"look at me now" 9449
"look at myself, I" 4792
"look at the river, trying not to"
    9425
"look at the shops" 1084
"look at the work" 6050
"look at them, when you" 3664
"look at us by the river, will you"
    7705
"look at you now" 4810
"look back" 8989
"look back upon it from a safer
    Distance" 5552
"look down at that precise point"
    880
"look down at them where they
    slept" 6543
"look down in concern" 7293
"look down onto the pavements"
    9556
"look for a place" 7222
"look from cows, a slow" 9184
"look here" 9003
"look in through the windows and
    see her, I could" 6160
"look into the eyes of the King"
    7106
"look it, he did not" 365
"look like, what I" 7488
"look like a young woman facing
    anything unusual, did not" 10800
"look now, how I" 4354
"look of tension, a strangely
    languid and voluptuous" 5048
"look or a word out of Joe Mundy,
    get a" 7136
"look out" 7111
"look out at the city of Port of
    Spain" 1419

"look out at the rain-swept Geneva
    street" 10972
"look out at the station" 6754
"look out at the yard" 1866
"look out beyond the confluence of
    the Poteau and Arkansas rivers"
    7686
"look out of his small window" 98
"look out through the old bubbly
    glass panes" 2692
"look through the eyes of a rattler"
    10546
"look through the one-way glass
    panel" 9912
"look to her expiring lamp" 9402
"look to see, you have to make
    yourself" 8293
"look twice to make sure there's no
    mistake" 9825
"look up heavy snowfalls from 1792
    downwards" 8587
"looked, the way she" 10821
"looked a little older" 5951
"looked across the river and the
    plain to the mountains" 3093
"looked after the dump" 6431
"looked around" 4677
"looked around and then quickly
    disappeared" 3040
"looked around for her daughter"
    3593
"looked around for shelter" 7299
"looked around her" 8375
"looked around the crowd" 4001
"looked around vaguely" 3420
"looked as if he lived in the Oli-
    phants' house" 8208
"looked at Giles" 7586
"looked at her" 4772
"looked at her brother Jeff" 8234
"looked at her watch" 9294
"looked at him steadfastly" 10644
"looked at his wife" 5772
"looked at me" 6038
"looked at old Nils Ulevik" 6219
"looked at our sister" 244
"looked at our visitor with his eyes
    wide open" 9886
"looked at the baby, had scarcely"
    541
"looked at the mountain" 6055
"looked at the stars" 520, 524
"looked at the vast window" 9411
"looked at women" 7749
"looked away" 8555
"looked back, as I" 7425
"looked back, when he" 5123
"looked back across the orchard"
    4150
"looked back and remembered"
    2506
"looked back at the camp" 8652
"looked back on that spring eve-
    ning" 5091
"looked back waiting" 5957

"looked contentedly down the long table" 6755

"looked down at a yard with stables" 10389

"looked down from the dark room at the streetlamp" 5339

"looked down from the promenade deck" 8072

"looked down into the dusty tangle of her flower garden" 3976

"looked down over the roofs of the village" 5072

"looked down the broad cleft to the sea" 2982

"looked down the trail" 10928

"looked forward to a ripe old senility" 116

"looked gloomily at the turbid steam" 928

"looked hard" 8294

"looked her up and down" 8027

"looked himself up and down" 7477

"looked in at them through the screen door" 9985

"looked in vain" 3701

"looked into the living room" 1591

"looked like, it" 9819

"looked like, what Magda Sevillas" 7459

"looked like a gigantic greenhouse" 4334

"looked like all the others" 9232

"looked off toward the stand of willows" 8790

"looked on at the Class Day gayety" 6753

"looked onto a derelict mill" 5155

"looked out" 10320

"looked out at the sun" 8403

"looked out at the teenage couple" 1992

"looked out at what he could see of New York" 8263

"looked out for the first time" 7679

"looked out from under the shelter of Gandalf's cloak" 8269

"looked out of his bedroom window" 8262

"looked out of place" 10421

"looked out of the small circular window" 9615

"looked out of the window and winced" 3978

"looked out the window" 2712

"looked out through the window" 7324

"looked out upon a depressing afternoon" 2501

"looked over at him gravely" 8172

"looked pointedly towards the lake" 4662

"looked quickly from side to side" 1110

"looked round the room" 7766

"looked through and down" 8405

"looked through close-lidded eyes" 9127

"looked toward the door" 2714

"looked toward the moonrise" 6933

"looked up, Michael Gosselyn" 1605

"looked up as if a hand had been put steady on my shoulder" 7494

"looked up at Mr. Enwright" 3326

"looked up at the sky" 8150

"looked up from his desk" 8202

"looked up from his notebook and papers" 6950

"looked up from their cots" 6888

"looked up from their whittling" 9775

"looked up into Graham Mill's gaze" 6006

"looked up to see" 1181

"looked upon Japan" 4535

"looked westward" 1438

"looked with some disbelief" 3572

"looked with some trepidation" 6330

"looked younger" 88

Looking 404, 520, 1993, 2220, 2719, 3420, 4143, 4150, 7486, 7683, 7686, 7696, 8258, 8786

"looking, good" 5921

"looking, the child" 1289

"looking about him" 1184

"looking across the vast stream" 7655

"looking around" 1659

"looking around him" 9749

"looking around the fairly comfortable hotel room" 4634

"looking at a hot dog bun" 1259

"looking at her, without" 9899

"looking at herself" 7485

"looking at herself in a mirror" 7468

"looking at him" 969

"looking at him across the doorsill" 9913

"looking at him in the half-light from the window" 8827

"looking at his patient through his spectacles" 6889

"looking at it, neither man was" 5828

"looking at Mt. Hozomeen" 6075

"looking at myself" 7486

"looking at the stars" 8579

"looking back" 2538, 5777, 6663, 7317, 8026, 8546

"looking back at it ruefully" 5095

"looking back down the chasm of the past" 6790

"looking back on the whole ghastly affair" 6940

"looking back to that summer day" 4565

"looking back with new uncertainty" 4549

"looking down across the hills" 8786

"looking down at a great big frog" 719

"looking down at the East River" 7683

"looking down at the river" 7706

"looking down earnestly and thoughtfully" 3814

"looking down from the window" 7696

"looking down into a restaurant below street level" 10392

"looking down into the blue water" 9863

"looking down on the crowd" 6316

"looking down the valley" 3757

"looking down upon the harbour" 8258

"looking for a certain dog" 470

"looking for a few good men" 8687

"looking for a girl" 7717

"looking for copper" 5831

"looking for engineers in the matrimonial ads" 5758

"looking for his family" 7231

"looking for juicy spots" 4959

"looking for number 27" 7237

"looking for something" 7226

"looking for you, girl was here" 9930

"looking forward" 4530

"looking in the mirror" 7482

"looking intensely though come the evening's end" 10392

"looking intently in the waiting room" 6896

"looking into darkness" 8496

"looking into the dark valley" 1353

"looking into the darkness" 10127

"looking into the fire" 696

"looking into the Future" 1586

"looking into the soldier's face" 59

"looking into the wind, had given up" 2973

"looking into vacancy" 1697

"looking like Mahatma Gandhi" 6546

"looking like the King of Spain" 7124

"looking neither to right nor to left" 8660

"looking on, two blind men" 1831

"looking one minute at the window" 9558

"looking only at Asian faces" 10446

"looking out, in it" 4884

"looking out across the Rue de Rivoli" 10037

"looking out at the garden" 8283

"looking out of the high-set window" 8260

"looking out of the window" 2709, 9533

"looking out over a sea of seventy thousand faces" 9398

"looking out over the still waters" 1751

"looking out the long window" 2719

"looking out through the windows" 7581

"looking purposefully up and down" 1589

"looking spruce and perky" 9753

"looking through his *Standard*" 7347

"looking up at the sky" 2220

"looking up from his book" 6520

"looking-glass, making faces at himself in his" 7478

"lookout, on the" 7220

"lookout, the" 10541

"looks, good" 5892

"looks at twice, nobody ever" 5915

"looks down at this old woman" 4508

"looks into the distance" 10890

"looks of people" 10798

"looks out at the meadowgreen Mediterranean" 8573

"looks out his window" 6303

"looks out over miles of southwestern plain" 8273

"looks so jagged" 5707

"loom, setting up her" 10952

"looming squat and commanding" 9245

Loomis, David 8805

Looney, Rose 1243

"Loop, just inside the" 10456

"loops of synthetic cord" 1166

"loose, turned" 5717

"loosened into a broadway" 9130

"loosened their hold on Argentina" 4129

"loot, spotting" 10397

"looted it of food guns and ammunition" 6179

Lopez, Ferdinand 4442

"lopsided" 8418

Lord, Dr. Humphrey 6483

"Lord" 10

"Lord, blind" 7607

"Lord, in the face of the" 5402

"Lord, in the name of the" 9989

"Lord, in the presence of our" 10651

"lord, liege" 6972

"lord, my" 4592, 9094

"lord, my beloved" 9047

"lord, noble" 1167

"Lord, o" 7526

"Lord, O" 8504

"Lord, oh" 6381

"Lord, saith the" 3941

"Lord, sanction of the" 7056

"Lord, sought the" 7536

"Lord, the good" 6113

"Lord, under the" 7500

"Lord, we beseech Thee O" 8643

"lord, young" 2492

"lord of loners" 4800

"lord of the world" 7807

"Lord and the Lady of the Duality" 2635

"Lord Chancellor" 8339

"Lord clothed in the half cloak, he saw Our" 7539

"Lord Elgin, the" 3534

Lord Emsworth 1178

Lord Essex 8566

Lord Fisher of Kilverstone 7359

"Lord gave you, the good" 10831

"Lord God of Hosts" 2626

"Lord have mercy on my soul" 7057

Lord Hervey 715

"Lord I remember" 5117

"Lord Lord Lord" 2643

"Lord my God, oh" 8501

"Lord of the Four Quarters, Sole" 7811

"Lord of the Two Worlds" 7521

"Lord of the Universe" 2638

"Lord of Wanda" 7801

"Lord's grace, year of our" 2133

"Lords Marchers" 6802

"lordship, your" 4974

Loren 8760

Loring, Godfrey 3915

"Lorna Doone" 5992

"lorries, vans and" 9130

Lorry, Mr. Grenfall 1577

"Los Alamos" 3546

Los Angeles 814, 3723, 4093, 9689

"Los Angeles" 505, 1039, 2836, 3630, 3723, 4093, 4402, 5630, 6172, 9180, 9439

"Los Angeles, as we approached" 4580

"Los Angeles, County of" 7893

"Los Angeles, rather odd part of" 814

"Los Angeles airport" 1687

"Los Angeles International" 1725

"Los Angeles International Airport" 4325

"Los Angeles Star" 6454

"Los Angeles stations" 9363

"Los Muertos" 8765

"lose a thousand pounds one night at faro" 3965

"lose it, leave it or" 1451

"lose people, I" 2580

"loser lost, the" 2304

"losing fortunes" 10553

"losing her place" 9498

"losing himself" 10051

"losing itself" 458

"losing money, avant-garde of" 77

"loss, I am somewhat at a" 5483

"loss sustained two or three months before" 9513

"loss was correspondingly greater" 2337

Lost 4538, 6374, 6498, 9498

"lost, already" 5609

"lost, he was" 5603

"lost, I was" 5608

"lost, nothing in the end is" 1666

"lost a good deal of hair quickly" 4291

"lost a wad on successive hands" 3971

"lost again" 5125

"lost between tangled ranges" 6062

"lost by collision with a derelict" 8059

"lost her mind" 2018

"lost her mother when she was only fifteen" 8838

"lost her way home" 4538

"lost him, I" 6374

"lost himself" 6374

"lost his asses" 7217

"lost his balance" 34

"lost his way" 10421

"lost his way on the way" 5607

"lost in encircling acres of knee-deep billowing grass" 3095

"lost in her own thoughts" 7599

"lost in solemn research" 794

"lost in thought, for some time" 9402

"lost it, they'd" 7257

"lost ones, oh my" 7438

"lost people" 2605

"lost the craft of losing himself" 10051

"lost the use of my limbs" 2894

"lost two million dollars, had once" 10550

"lost your *mind*, have you gone and" 4949

"lost your senses, have you" 6619

"Lot, Rooney's" 6280

"lots, abandoned" 10416

Lotte 10445

Lottie 42

"lotus position, sitting in the" 6959

"lotus position, tried to sustain the" 8367

"Lotus Wreath" 4743

Lou 2893, 6927

"loud, clear and" 8903

"loud and innocent, florid and" 275

"loud concussion of the wheels" 9551

"loud enough to wake the dead" 6338

"loud with birds" 9276

"loud with the screams of men" 4469

"loudest, the" 8230

"loudspeaker clamored" 8861

Louie 2821, 6586

Louis Count Frontenac 7655

Louis Le Grand 4513

Louis Napoleon 9119

Louis XVIII 10768

Louis XI 7139

Louis XIV 3837

Louis the Great 3376

Louisa 6215

"Louisana State University" 7498

Louise 2435, 8505

Louisiana 262, 4036
"Louisiana" 5215, 8760
"Louisiana, move back to" 3659
"Louisiana, vast regions of" 262
"Louisiana, Western" 4036
"Louisiana was the end of the
    world" 4544
"lounge, doctors'" 4624
"Lounge, North Delegates'" 6986
"Lounge, Small" 4644
"lounge of the Repulse Bay Hotel"
    10816
"lounged across the table" 5621
"lounged against the corner of a
    shop" 5614
"lounged motionless in a chair"
    5620
"lounges, one of the Southern Cal-
    ifornia cocktail" 4332
Lounging 956, 985, 1103, 2912,
    3616, 3916, 4635, 5376, 7305,
    7586, 8209, 8517, 8578, 8815,
    9408, 9413, 9429, 9434, 9452,
    10106, 10472
"lounging idly" 5617
"lounging in bed" 5636
"lounging in the shade" 5626
"lounging on the living room rug"
    985
"louring sky, under a" 9170
Lousy 5445
"lousy blue jays" 10207
"loutish adolescence" 5671
"Louvre, Museum of the" 5613
"Louvre, the" 9892
"lovable, yet somehow" 5889
Love, Frankie 7925
Love 281, 1278, 1290, 1482, 1669,
    1706, 1844, 2007, 2067, 2146,
    2529, 2677, 2680, 3344, 3389,
    3523, 3538, 3619, 4359, 4771,
    5099, 5233, 5238, 5566, 5733,
    5780, 5802, 5934, 5950, 5970,
    6295, 6473, 6508, 6517, 6533,
    7182, 7479, 7527, 7712, 7713,
    7714, 7719, 7728, 7730, 7733,
    7745, 8002, 8019, 8023, 8028,
    8140, 8236, 9010, 9027, 9039,
    9279, 9687, 10266, 10765, 10807
"love" 9045
"*love?*" 5665
"love, a girl in" 7479
"love, a great" 1290
"love, a romantic about" 5678
"love, always been a bit in" 8236
"love, be equal to his" 1706
"love, beat urgent as" 2106
"love, began to" 5680
"love, death of" 5661
"love, dramas of life and" 5566
"love, faces of those I" 8488
"love, fall in" 5733
"love, falls out of" 7628
"love, fell in" 5638, 5658, 5666,
    5671, 7709, 9010

"love, fell madly in" 5651
"love, fell out of" 2146
"love, first time we made" 7751
"love, floated out of the tunnel of"
    5652
"love, for" 5655
"love, founded on" 1482
"love, goddess of" 7527
"love, her willful hopeless" 5659
"love, how much they were in" 7712
"love, hush my" 6308
"love, in" 5643, 9302
"love, incorporeal body of" 9279
"love, it was first" 7745
"love, knew nothing about" 5653
"love, leave a place you" 4582
"love, made" 8001, 8019, 10186
"love, make" 8009
"love, making" 2529
"love, man I" 7182
"love, money or for" 2067
"love, nature of" 5233
"love, neighborly" 6242
"love, never fell in" 1278
"Love, opening chapter does not
    concern itself with" 5639
"love, price that sometimes had to
    be paid for" 5676
"love, proof of" 5650
"love, respect and" 6517
"love, romantic" 5238
"love, sex or" 8028
"love, soft energies of accom-
    plished" 5674
"love, soft words of" 8140
"love, swayed from love by" 5661
"love, tale of" 5673
"love, their" 5802
"love, there's more to" 8023
"love, thoughts of" 5642, 5649
"love, touch them with" 5645
"love, undone by" 10765
"love, was finally himself in" 5659
"love, what is this thing called"
    5677
"love, woman in" 8002
"love affair, my" 7719
"love affair, what turned out to be
    a lifelong" 7733
"love affair can begin, there are
    many ways a" 7734
"love affairs, my" 7713
"love and death are absolutes" 5663
"love and money solved everything"
    3389
"love and sleep, aftermath of" 10266
"love and war, all's fair in" 7730
"love at first sight" 5651
"love at once, common with which
    he fell in" 6558
"love conquers all" 5647
"love embodied" 6088
"love flourishes in time of war, you
    know how" 5654
"love for women, his" 5950

"love forever, so we" 1669
"love GOOD" 5362
"love her, came to" 8140
"love Him, God" 2625
"love him but thought he did, did
    not" 9027
"love him in full knowledge, I" 5668
"love in my father's office, I never
    fell in" 6508
"love in the river, making" 8003
"love is enough to make you believe
    in God" 5677
"love is mostly a willingness to per-
    ceive" 5646
"love it or loathe it" 1451
"love Joanie, he really did" 5780
"love letters" 8708
"love life, make a mess of his" 5934
"love myself, ain't never nobody
    loved me like I" 5657
"love nor the lack of it, neither"
    5644
"love of a woman" 5640
"love of a world, an almost chival-
    ric" 260
"love of my life, the great" 5669
"love of Our Lord Jesus Christ"
    1496
"love one another, we must" 5660
"love poems" 5413
"love so profound it could lie silent
    like a forest pond" 1706
"love song" 740
"love the void" 5521
"*love* those earrings" 10892
"love to a girl, making" 8000
"love to five different women,
    made" 8001
"love to fuck" 7992
"love to her, made" 8005
"love twice, fell in" 5667
"love was in the air" 5679
"love was interrupted" 9279
"love was too ravenous to be con-
    tained by their mere mortal
    bodies" 1706
"love weaves its own tapestry" 5656
"love with, in" 3344
"love with another woman, I'm in"
    2677
"love with Evelyn Cotton, I have
    been in" 8019
"love with her, I was in" 4789
"love with her, in" 5641
"love with him, fell in" 3619
"love . . . with his great-grandson"
    5659
"love with Janie, she was in" 6295
"love you" 9296
"love you anymore, I don't" 2007
"love you in my own way, can I"
    4771
"love you so much still" 5670
"love-affair, intense and wonderful"
    4235

"loved, he" 7714
"loved, hen and chicks she" 4162
"loved, ruined everything I" 9279
"loved, the man she" 7741
"loved, was not" 7714
"loved, woman his father" 4588
"loved, wouldn't have gone so far to say that he" 6473
"loved about Marston, what Paul" 5675
"loved and failed, someone you have" 3523
"loved by Bob Dubois, women who were" 9027
"loved by sixty thousand four hundred and eleven girls" 3538
"loved each other, whether her mom and dad" 10975
"loved her, her father" 6533
"loved her mother and prayed not to become her" 6690
"loved him, the several people who" 9027
"loved him but thought he did not" 9027
"loved his daughter" 4359
"loved his wife, the way that he" 9027
"loved India" 5368
"loved Jesus, Saint Peter" 5664
"loved scandal, a woman who" 7867
"loved so deeply" 9279
"loved the snow" 5383
"loved the way the snake looked" 2851
"loved them as true men everywhere love home" 5015
"loved to remember" 7414
Lovejoy, Ethan 4190
Lovell, Reanna 4921
"lovely, is n't it" 3736
"lover, her" 5238, 7586, 10041
"lover, her black" 2815
"lover, her true" 4188
"lover, moon" 5063
"lover, my mother had a" 6746
"lover, my mother's" 4783
"lovely and loving sisters" 8232
"lovely enough to aid the sun in achieving a moment of transcendence" 7624
"lovely in midsummer, Oxford is very" 7390
Lovemaking 572, 856, 5670, 5746, 6389, 6391, 7409, 7751, 7985, 7989, 7991, 7992, 7993, 7997, 7999, 8000, 8001, 8002, 8003, 8005, 8007, 8009, 8010, 8011, 8012, 8013, 8014, 8015, 8016, 8019, 8022, 8023, 8025, 8030, 8458, 8802, 10186, 10266, 10790
"lover, approch of her" 7370
"lover, was to become his" 798
"lover and killer" 4800

"lover had dressed and gone" 8583
"lover of a married woman in private, longtime" 7721
"lover of mine who worshipped me" 2381
"lover of the merry-go-round" 304
"lover of the sublime and romantic features of nature" 6606
Lovers 798, 2381, 4188, 4783, 5238, 6746, 7586, 7721, 7726, 7747, 7954, 8583, 10041, 10807
"Lovers, either of my powerful" 6033
"lovers, many" 7747
"lovers, no" 10834
"lovers, rather uneasy" 2502
"lovers, several previous" 7726
"lovers, star-crossed" 5588
"Lovers, your three" 9509
"lovers and married, they were young" 515
"loves, their" 3912
"loves a parade, everybody" 5358
"loves me loves me not" 7728
"love-spinning, it was at a" 5681
"love-story of long ago" 5404
"love-tales, moving" 5398
"loving" 4230
"loving, much more" 10848
"loving care" 2840
"loving one, her nature was a" 4153
"loving sisters" 8232
"lovingly, arguing" 9381
Low, Bob 138
"low, agreeably" 3376
"low country" 9749
"Low Country" 5122
"Low Crags" 3657
"Low Sunday" 10419
Lowder, Lee 6992
Lowe 6434
Löwe 8489
Lowe, Julian 8649
Lowell 9344
Lowell, Wolsey 10086
"Lowell Mass." 5445
"Lower East Side" 820
"lowered himself down" 10363
"lowered his vast bear-like body" 8383
"lowlands, the" 8510
"lowlands, they had left the" 2969
"loyal Fort Sumter" 5785
"loyalty, a" 2887
"lozenge, it was a metal" 2384
"lozenges in movement" 5325
"L-shaped" 3208
"Lübeck" 10274
"Lubianka, on the third floor of the" 1934
Lublin, Rosa 4945
"lubricity" 9086
Lucas 1813
Lucas, Emmeline 4226
Lucas, Mrs. 10337

Lucas, Mrs. Emmeline 10351
Lucas, Philip 4225
Lucas, Yank 6024
Lucia 4233, 8378, 10525
"Lucia, the mad scene in" 8738
Lucien 5173
Lucifer 4637
Lucille 9710
Lúcio 5576
Lucius 3714
Luck 337, 795, 1220, 1224, 1225, 1226, 1227, 1228, 1229, 1231, 1234, 1236, 1237, 1239, 1240, 1241, 1242, 1243, 1303, 3632, 5727, 8939, 9922
"luck, a change of" 1242
"luck, by good" 9412
"luck, couldn't believe our" 1237
"luck, good" 5727, 7067
"luck, it was" 1236
"luck, my" 9922
"luck, my bad" 1240
"luck, no such" 6875
"luck, touched so often for" 8939
"luck, with any" 9950
"luck at all, no" 975
"luck at all, with any" 337
"luck never seems to change for the better" 1239
"luck or providence" 1243
"luck would have it, as" 1241
"luckier" 1225
"luckiest" 1225
Lucky 4593, 4843
"lucky, knew himself to be" 1231
"lucky, Potter was" 1229
"lucky, that wasn't" 3632
"lucky, this was" 1227
"lucky day" 1303
"lucky enough to know it" 91
"lucky for all of us" 1225
"lucky for me I was born at all" 795
"lucky ones, the" 155
"lucky or unlucky" 5542
Lucy 138, 1282, 1283, 2373, 4173, 4224, 7755, 7900, 10828
Lucy Bear 2566
"ludi Romani" 3481
Ludwig 798
"Luftwaffe, the late" 7570
Luggage 9550, 10905
"luggage, an excess of" 9657
"luggage, poking at the" 1662
"luggage clattered noisily past him along the moving belt" 9574
"luggage on the sidewalk, arranged three pieces of" 1653
"lugging a dead dog" 10436
Luigi 10022
"Luigi's" 8639
Luiza, Sister 9796
Luke 1074, 1311, 3836
Lula 4336
Lulah 2073
"lull, made its own" 5286

"lull, warm Negev breeze held a" 5286
"lull, wondrous" 5286
"lull in the late afternoon" 6505
"lulled to sleep by the tolling of tape-recorded bells" 671
"lulling *dickety-clax*" 7261
"lulling its passengers" 8457
"lulls of the wind" 10002
Lulu 10870
"lumber barons" 4073
"lumbering, barons of" 3423
"lumbers towards the three new arrivals" 1738
"luminous already, whitely" 10116
Lumley, Edward 6257
Lumley, Mr. 5350
"lump, all that rose was a blood-warm" 3699
"lump, my body this venerable" 8506
"lump it, you'll just have to" 5347
"lumps, parallel" 6075
"lunacy, course of action as" 7396
"Lunaday" 2145
"lunar astronomy" 539
"lunatic, there was this" 4941
"lunatic asylum" 4225, 7149
"lunatic strut I left with such relief" 5286
Lunatics 2052, 4941
"lunatics" 2052
"*Lunaya Pravda*" 7820
"lunch, after" 3000, 7127
"lunch, an excellent" 3843
"lunch, breaking for" 3007
"lunch, came out for her" 10586
"lunch, come for" 3840
"lunch, glorious" 3869
"lunch, met Tommy Carlo for" 2062
"lunch, not long before" 4333
"lunch, partners'" 5004
"lunch, returning home to" 1654
"lunch, sat over" 3831
"lunch, will you be back for" 3832
"lunch be ready, how soon will" 4681
"lunch considerably delayed" 4670
"lunch in a paper box" 9525
"lunch in a public house" 3855
"lunch that day as usual" 7571
"lunch time" 5894
"lunch with my father" 6715
"lunch with the attractive stranger" 10836
"lunched at a restaurant in the Boulevard Saint Michel" 10334
"lunched late, we" 3877
"luncheon, in the middle of" 7389
"luncheon, satisfactory" 3821
"luncheon the Kinneys were giving" 8628
"lunette, terra-cotta" 10649
"lunge and thrust" 8027

"lungs, still-powerful" 2405
"lunkheads I had to deal with" 9265
"Lunsbury Missouri" 182
"Lupine" 9204
"lurch, came into the kitchen with a" 4472
"lurched at her" 9843
"lurched forward in the hub-deep mud" 9771
"lurid against a grey winter sky" 10160
"lurked a nameless dread" 3698
"lurked a Soul" 412
"lurked in the bosky thickets" 3396
"luscious black complexion" 46
"luscious fruit" 8517
"lush and American" 3425
"lush years" 309
Lushington 5415
Lushington, Mr. Edmund 6835
"lushness, grace and" 5151
"*Lusitania*, the" 2315
"lust, anger and" 391
"lust of eyes like mine" 1011
"luster, so singularly lacking in" 1431
"lustily, sang this as" 852
"lusty eighteenth" [century] 3376
"lusty pioneer blood" 6814
Luterin 7464
Luther, Uncle 8581
"Lutheran church" 1190
Lux the Poet 3056
"Luxembourg, gardens of the" 10334
Luxemburg, Rosa 10837
"Luxor" 7799
"luxuriant woods" 5125
"luxurious" 7778
"luxurious indolence" 3356
"luxuriously, stretched himself" 10119
"luxuriously soaping himself" 570
Luxury 2590, 3356
"Luzerne" 954
"lying, downright" 703
"lying all night in the wet grass" 8463
"lying all the time, everybody" 5296
"lying beneath the hotel umbrella" 10883
"lying beside me" 10197
"lying between coarse sheets" 10121
"lying down" 4635
"lying half-asleep" 956
"lying here, I'm" 8834
"lying in a great bed" 3700
"lying in bed" 9429
"lying in bed, I'm" 6391
"lying in his bed" 5619
"lying in the marsh" 2894
"lying in the rickety wall-bed" 2758
"lying on a huge couch" 9452
"lying on his back" 10236
"lying on the grass of the park" 5618

"lying on the sward" 10784
"lying prostrate" 7851
"lying quietly on his back in his coffin" 1887
"lying softly relaxed and asleep" 10193
"lying together in the bilges of a cockboat" 8158
"lying under the burnt-out truck" 3056
Lyman Gene 8233
"Lyme Bay" 10724
"Lyme Regis" 10724
"Lymport-on-the-Sea, town of" 2290
Lynch, Father 1530
"Lynchburg Virginia" 1465
Lynd, Dr. Harry 6574
Lynde, Mr. Edward 6928
Lynde, Mrs. Rachel 7652
Lynn, Loretta 9365
Lynn Ann 3958
Lyon, Father Francis X. 7528
"Lyons Pennsylvania" 9726
"lyre, struck her" 4474
Lytle, Bess 9307

M. 9646
Ma 6136, 6660, 10180
"Maa, great moon of" 8415
Maas, Mrs. Oedipa 10559
Mabel 6367
Mac 1804, 7751
"macadam highway" 2978
"McAlister sisters" 8241
Macarty, Mrs. Wellesley 10768
Macauley, Ulysses 968
"*Macbeth*" 390
McBride, Lydie 9464
McCaffrey, George 4706
McCain, Allie 3659
McCalmont, Brennan 8618
McCamey, Amand 7420
MacCarthy 1700
McClintock, Truckbox Al 8934
McConnell, Rose 338
McCoy, Agnes 214
McCracken, Juliet 7442
McCreary, Raymond 2937
McCunn, Mr. Dickson 6350
McCurtain, Sheriff Jeff 10135
mac Dall, Felimid 9535
McDay 8704
Macdermot, Mrs. 563
Macdonald 10040
MacDonald, David 8213
MacDonald, Dougald 8213
MacDonald, Mr. Ramsay 7384
"McDonald's, stepped into the" 183
"Macedon" 5451
"Macedonia" 1413
"macerated and decomposed specimen" 3804
McEvilly, Paddy 6599

McEvoy 4897
McEwan, Jonathan 5238
McFarlane, James Lewis 4726
McGarrigle, Persse 8615
McGee, Agatha 1727
McGehee, Edward 2310
McGehee, Hugh 2310
McGillicuddy, Mrs. 10369
McGinnis, Danny 3129
McGrath, B. J. 2879
MacGregor 2847
McGregor, Granpa 3872
McGregor, Nance 9876
McGuire, Brian 2722
McGuire, Sam 4795
McHale 9808
McHenry, Langston James 826
Machin, Edward Henry 784, 2496
"machine, answering" 5691
"machine, become one with the" 33
"machine, cigarette" 9591
"machine, clanking" 7569
"machine, great unnatural" 762
"machine, if you count the" 5756
"machine, story of a" 5685
"machine, damn mimeograph" 5683
"machine, washing" 10963
"machine coming into use in some
    parts of the country" 5681
"machine . . . for reaping and
    mowing" 5681
Machinery 94, 4352, 5756
"machinery, she could never
    understand" 5690
"machinery's rusty, the" 94
"machines, washing" 6414
"machines chatter" 9364
McInnes, Colum 1318
McIntyre, Laura 10568
Macio of the Roymarcks 7624
McIver, George 6026
Mack 868
Mack, Dr. Linda 9730
McKail, Duncan Argyll 6038
Mackay 10465
McKay, Gordon 6935
McKay, Jake 504
McKay, Joe 2678
McKay, Stub 372
McKechnie, Mr. 5621
McKee 1549
McKelva, Judge 6893
Mackenna, Lewis 3411
Mackenzie 3610
Mackenzie, Mr. 6108
McKenzie, Peter 2833
McKenzie, Rose Ann 8234
"mackerel and hominy grits, break-
    fast of" 3857
"mackerel drifter" 8135
"mackerels, two dead" 340
Mackey, Claire 7546
Mackey, Mrs. 2770
McKillop, Isa 7014
McKinley, Major Bill 6990

McKinley, William 3394
"mackintosh, brown" 10389
"mackintosh, enveloped in a" 5910
McKnight 6411
Maclean 10418
MacLeod, Mairi 3667
Macleod, Old Lady 10775
MacMahon, Hugh 9109
McMahon, Mrs. 7906
McMann, Tom 9435
McNab, Peter 5034
MacNair, Roy 7844
MacNamara, Vincent 3352
mac Nessa, Conachúr 9535
Macnooder, Doc 4460
McPhail, Hugh 7858
McPherson, Cathy 3335
MacPherson, Frank 4293
MacPherson, Mr. 2508
McPherson, Sam 960
McPhillip, Francis Joseph 7841
McShane, Molly 2936
McTeague 3816
McVay, Jimmy 3755
MacVeagh, Jim 5186
"mad, a world gone" 6837
"mad, considered himself" 4935
"mad, driven" 4936
"mad, he acted" 543
"mad, I am not" 107, 4948
"mad, old King went" 4943
"mad, Plato drove my elder
    brother" 7897
"mad, suspected . . . that he was"
    4947
"mad, thought the grown-up world
    to be" 2593
"mad, wasn't obviously" 394
"mad, world was" 5183
"mad every time a new baby turned
    up" 543
"mad scene" 8738
"Mad Scientist" 6674
"Madaket, shore at" 439
Madden, Dr. 6616
"maddening" 658
"madder, ochre and" 10494
Maddison, Mrs. 7470
Maddy-Monkey 1819
"made a fortune" 10553
"made a little paper airplane" 1854
"made cheese and butter" 3667
"made her way up the Gallowgate"
    10349
"Made in America" 5982
"made love" 10186
"made love twice, we have" 8019
"made straight for the sink" 10939
"made to our specifications" 2835
Madeleine 9899
Madge 9334
"madhouse" 7149
"Madison and Fifth, between" 5800
"Madison and Park, between" 7204
"Madison Wisconsin" 5838

"madman" 3911
"madmen now, we have to do with
    two" 4946
"madness, eyes of pure" 4940
"madness, it was" 3012
"madness, plunging into the" 5105
"madness I ever thought I would
    get mixed up in" 3054
"madness of war, beautiful" 10527
"madness that was to possess them
    for a whole season" 5105
"Madonna, Leonardo's" 8027
"madonnas" 503
"Madrid" 1292, 6866, 7570
"Madrid, first morning in" 3141
"Madrid his capital, made" 4136
"madrigal, exquisite" 8746
"madwoman and a scavenger" 4945
"madwoman marrying a drunk"
    5771
Mag 10301
"magazine, college" 5413
"magazine, editor of a" 6460
"magazine, flipped open the" 926
"magazine, glossy clay-and-glucose-
    sprayed" 926
"magazine, in a" 6860
"Magazine, *People*" 6819
"magazine, weekly news" 6318
"magazine section of the Sunday
    Times" 6351
Magazines 926, 1107, 3547, 5413,
    6318, 6460, 6513, 6819, 6860,
    7351, 7871, 8945, 10894
"magazines, one of those smooth-
    paged" 10894
"magazines, parish" 5433
"magazines come to our house"
    7351
Magdalena, Ana 4209
Magic 578, 2306, 2579, 3293,
    4101, 5950, 7045, 7813, 8899,
    10847
"magic, black" 3534
"magic, his most precious" 8899
"magic, I'm a master of" 5950
"magic, there is" 10847
"magic in a dusty world, makes
    new" 1221
"magic of singing voices" 9560
"magic spell of genius" 4101
"magic tricks" 3293
"magical churning, something" 578
"magician, a sewing" 6484
"magician, mad" 7813
"magician, not a great" 5948
"Magician says, the" 2923
Magicians 2923, 5948, 6484, 7813
"magician's underwear" 2609
"Magistrate of Kyauktada, Subdi-
    visional" 4378
"magma formed a fiery island" 5052
"magna cum laude" 3261
"magnetic, too tenuous to be
    called" 6001

"magnificence, grotesque" 9254
"magnificence, its" 3095
"magnificence of Blenheim" 2088
"magnificence of the Ambersons began then" 10553
"magnificence of this portico" 1293
"magnificent abscesses" 3057
"magnificent scene" 948
"magnificently enhaloed" 2620
"magnified his fear of missing it" 3709
"magnify objects" 2611
"Magnum, .44" 576
Magog 6810
"Magog" 772
"magpie" 5276
Maguire, Mary 6454
Mahalaleel 1706
"Maharajah, British have chosen the" 6998
"Maharajas, the" 5715
"Maharanis, the" 5715
"Maharawhenua, legend of" 5220
"Mahatma, met a" 5792
Mahmoud, Sultan 6245
"mahogany, length of" 5571
"mahogany shaving stand" 8044
"maid, her" 10337
"maid, it was the parlor-" 1877
"maid, parlour-" 10916
"maid getting it off with one of their vibrators" 7874
"maid knocked on his door" 10163
"maid of all work" 3094
"maid of all work, old" 3554
"maid of honor" 3604
"maid with matchless decorum" 6367
"maiden name, my" 1924, 4848
"maids cleared the lunch dishes" 8884
Maids 3554, 6367
"maids, lady's" 6413
"maid-servant, standing with a" 947
"maidservant, young" 4647
Mail 1909, 1913, 1928, 1944, 1951, 1960, 1925, 6952, 8624, 9113
"mail, anything important in the" 1928
"mail, arrived in the afternoon" 8241
"mail, day's incoming" 1925
"mail, getting the" 1944
"mail, his unopened" 4333
"mail, Holyhead" 10108
"mail, junk" 3256
"mail, little pile of morning" 1913
"mail, morning's" 6952
"mail, opening his" 1960
"mail, sorted her" 1951
"mail, the" 9113
"Mail Pouch" 5166
"mail pouch, old leather" 1909
"mail van" 7328
"mailbox, waited by her" 8624

"mailbox propped in a milk can" 5944
"mailbox was painted yellow" 3615
"mailboxes, tinseled" 9436
Mailings 357
"mailman came, shortly before the" 8186
"mail-order house" 7480
"mails, carrying Her Majesty's" 8051
"Maine" 556, 682, 1591, 3430, 4186, 5028, 5534, 6155, 6695, 6733, 9652, 9756, 9758, 10631
"Maine, eastern" 1350
"Maine, northern coast of" 3205
"Maine, province of" 9694
"Maine, Province of" 1374
"Maine, sailing off the coast of" 2368
"Maine coast" 7457, 9734
"Maine coast, down on the" 1375
Maines, Gerard 6302
"mainland, on the" 10639
"Mainsfield" 9088
"mainstream, refused to go back into the" 4230
"mainstream of the twentieth century" 7532
Maisie 4244
"Maison du Poirier" 8742
Maitland 1513
Maitland, Robert 2998
"majestic, residence stood" 3210
"Majestic, the" 4645
"majestic Pyrenées" 5125
"majesty, her" 3289
"Majesty, His" 1902, 6450
"Majesty, Imperial" 3514
"majesty, mirror of a" 10033
"major, an anonymous" 8665
"Majorca" 598
"majored in religious studies" 10896
"majority went, as far as the" 9309
Makan 9991
"make, gun was easy to" 4259
"make bricks by the million" 1005
"make it on the outside, he could not" 7145
"make room" 6273
"make up in time to have their party" 1837
Makebelieve, Mary 3081
"make-believe of their games" 959
"makeup, touching up her" 2879
"make-up at mouth and eye, fierce" 1302
"making, their own individual" 4443
"making an omelette" 1863
"making at a cost of time and tinted wool" 484
"making for a friend of hers" 4119
"making it, people who aren't quite" 6281

"making love, couldn't be fulfilled even by" 2529
"making love to a girl" 8000
"making the People alive again" 4610
"making the rounds" 3409
"*mala fama*, they have no tendency to the" 5387
"Malagita" 2570
"Malawi" 10402
"Malay Archipelago" 5018
"Malay Quarter" 2006
"Malay second pilot" 200
"Malay word *sagûm* (the brown race)" 6247
"Malaya" 3152
"Malaysia, newly established Federation of" 10520
"Maldives" 2538
Maldon, Mrs. 10786
"male, all" 6830
"male friend" 9321
"male of his line, the last" 2320
"male shortcomings, authority on" 982
"male worthy of the name" 8556
Malenov, Yevgeny Mikhailovich 6196
"males, intoxicated" 9381
"Malibu, southern end of the beach called" 4316
"malice, a voice eager with" 7518
"malice, with" 6968
"malice aforethought" 9391
"maligned month" 10567
"Malin" 3138
Malka 4360
Malkin, Nathan 10422
"Mall, Chiswick" 9757
"Mall, Paradise" 3264
"mall, Park Street" 4368
"mall, pedestrian" 1001
"Mall, Sunset" 3876
"Mall, Upper" 8526
"Mallards" 1826, 8378
Mallare, Fantazius 4477, 4935
"malleable, it is tough and yet" 10530
Mallee, Reverend Anawari 10285
Mallet 9857
Malone, Atlas 2647
Malone, Camille 8201
Malry, Christie 10827
"malt, his finely ground" 4760
"Malta" 853
Maltese Falcon, The 1323
Maltravers 7713
Mam 10831
Mama 149, 1121, 1802, 2436, 2660, 6941, 10932, 10939
"mama, Sudie's" 6703
"mama was the geek, when your" 10955
Mamba 1593
"Mametz" 2305

Mamie 8639
Mamma 943, 5195, 6122, 7589, 9339, 10029
"Mamma, my" 7589
"mamma's last moments, her dear" 8838
"mammy, yer" 3269
"mammy, your" 1805
Mamta 7537
"man, a" 28, 82, 86, 1653, 1702, 1856, 1969, 2002, 2507, 2993, 3578, 3628, 3646, 3878, 3950, 4208, 4254, 4282, 4471, 4625, 4969, 5609, 5851, 5914, 6321, 6414, 6864, 6910, 6951, 7279, 7364, 7714, 8024, 8305, 8453, 9260, 9527, 10132, 10382, 10389, 10438, 10811
"man, able-minded" 6890
"man, aged" 2644
"man, alert middle-aged" 4305
"man, another" 7616
"man, any" 1706
"man, beautiful" 2846
"man, big" 3640, 5908, 8867
"man, blind" 7411
"man, blond young" 8574
"man, bright and spirited young" 4346
"man, brilliant tortured little" 6132
"man, brown" 2
"man, Brown is our" 3298
"man, can't have been a great" 9517
"man, cautious" 2997
"man, charming" 5948
"man, clever nervy young" 260
"man, coarse charming" 6683
"man, cool" 3405
"man, crazy" 2828
"man, dangerous" 6168
"man, dead" 1882, 1900, 2294, 2303, 2304, 3961, 10548
"man, each" 2331
"man, earnest young" 794
"man, eccentric" 3202
"man, elderly" 5784, 5894, 7352, 9877
"man, enemies of" 5033
"man, every" 256, 5558, 5572, 5690, 8978
"man, famous" 5432, 5585
"man, fancy young" 5649
"man, fat" 1680, 10327
"man, fierce old" 5906
"man, find a" 4611
"man, fluffy feathery untidy cockatoo of a" 5900
"man, for a" 2835
"man, fortunate" 7978
"man, found a new" 7744
"man, gaunt" 7290
"man, gaunt handsome" 5961
"man, gentle-looking" 4606
"man, God made" 5697
"man, good" 2922, 5698

"man, gray-haired" 5405
"man, great" 2405, 5432, 5837
"man, handsomest" 8481
"man, hanged a fat" 10542
"man, hanging" 495
"man, happiest" 4345
"man, hard" 5917
"man, hatless" 10338
"man, heavy elderly" 8865
"man, high" 5987
"man, his" 7610
"man, holy" 1489
"man, honest" 5725
"man, I am a white" 9707
"man, I am an invisible" 5922
"man, I am an old" 96
"man, I knew the" 5831
"man, I will speak of a" 5574
"man, kill a" 6193
"man, killing one" 889
"man, King George's" 6981
"man, lank disjointed young" 909
"man, large" 5935, 8294
"man, large heavyset" 4919
"man, leading" 7731
"man, little" 1609, 2557
"Man, Little" 10078
"man, little bitty old shriveled-up" 5966
"man, little weather" 4197
"man, mangy-looking" 413
"man, massively built" 9749
"man, met a" 3619
"man, middle-aged" 8254, 10333
"man, must be a" 6910
"man, my" 9891
"man, my first sight of the" 5084
"man, my old" 1686, 6716, 6937
"man, naked" 6390
"man, neat and deceptively slim young" 5920
"man, new" 5004
"man, no inconsiderable" 3531
"man, Northwick's" 10032
"man, not a reckless" 5988
"man, nutty old" 5823
"man, old" 100, 520, 1166, 1184, 1185, 1946, 2317, 2792, 2801, 3207, 3413, 3416, 4163, 5623, 5888, 5968, 6316, 6428, 6522, 8182, 8730, 8739, 9328, 9405, 9684, 9796, 9898, 9917, 9969, 10385, 10928
"man, older" 4174
"man, old-fashioned" 4614
"man, one tall" 7108
"man, one young" 2529, 6959
"man, ordinary good-natured harmless unremarkable" 5953
"man, peculiar" 5909
"man, pious and innocent" 3677
"man, quiet well-dressed" 5895
"man, quite a nice young" 1501
"Man, reserved this singular Grace for" 5699

"man, restless" 5188
"man, Reuben was a small" 5978
"man, richest" 10557
"man, rising young" 5994
"man, shabby young" 9545
"man, short stout middle-aged" 5912
"man, sick" 122
"man, silent stubborn" 6698
"man, single" 5726
"man, small bony" 5940
"man, small dapper" 4918
"man, small neat" 2842
"man, small wizened modest" 6661
"man, smallish" 5956
"man, so must have felt the first" 8736
"man, soft-voiced" 2478
"man, square-faced young" 8556
"man, story of a" 9031
"man, strange" 5777
"man, stuffy" 6637
"Man, such an *Animal* as" 10764
"man, swine in every" 4979
"man, take a" 5299
"man, tall" 8106
"man, tall lean" 10388
"man, tall young" 1580, 1714
"man, the" 36, 953, 1895, 2044, 2588, 3138, 3371, 3755, 4572, 4672, 5215, 5406, 5964, 6592, 6593, 7594, 8092, 8804, 9320, 10057, 10156, 10373, 10405, 10971
"Man, The Great" 3962
"man, the kind of" 5915
"man, the kind of a" 5931
"man, the only" 8665
"man, there lived a" 4456, 5523
"man, there once was a" 9700
"man, thin young" 1726
"man, think of the" 9427
"man, three-hundred-pound" 4623
"man, tiny head and shoulders of a" 9151
"man, tough bulk of the big" 5929
"man, trust that" 9687
"man, unusual" 5902
"man, vain" 5970
"man, very fortunate young" 4339
"man, very old" 4810
"man, very pale young" 5799
"man, very untidy" 5985
"man, very young" 8363
"man, wealthiest" 10558
"man, when you a" 4238
"man, while still a young" 5423
"man, white" 2022, 4347, 9939
"Man, White" 9522
"man, young" 1, 88, 485, 566, 667, 1348, 1596, 1610, 1614, 1620, 1659, 1970, 2773, 2989, 3553, 4141, 4249, 4263, 4298, 4318, 4331, 4698, 4973, 4999, 5111, 5455, 5761, 5812, 5952, 5993, 6173, 6516, 7202, 7352, 7608, 7609, 7953, 8271, 8350, 8366,

8530, 8546, 8549, 8752, 9434, 9511, 9537, 9552, 9591, 9612, 9632, 9654, 9659, 9987, 10402, 10420, 10649

"man, young and penniless" 7864

"man, younger" 4662

"man alleged to be Ivan the Terrible" 1159

"man and wife, became" 10661

"man and woman, young" 10331

"man as myself, so young a" 697

"man at the desk" 8493

"man being hanged in London" 7180

"man beside her" 10644

"man called George Fairweather" 8698

"man drinking, watched the" 2890

"man fell dead" 2406

"man found dead in plastic wardrobe" 1881

"Man from Bodie, the" 2904

"man had lain unconscious" 2405

"man has a book somewhere inside him, every" 916

"man has a vicious gash on his face" 5990

"man he ever knew, the best" 2310

"man he never met" 5989

"man he wanted" 4323

"man here, there is a" 9903

"man himself, the" 9704

"man I have ever met, any" 7959

"man I have ever truly envied, he is the one" 3925

"man I love" 7182

"man I was going to visit" 9890

"man in a crumpled blue suit, a plump bespectacled" 5208

"man in an expensive overcoat" 1714

"Man in Charge, terrifying" 3332

"man in cream-colors" 1567

"man in France who can smile, the only" 8550

"man in her dream" 2809

"man in his late forties" 6890

"man in late middle age" 5942

"man in our family, the last" 5947

"man in the bar" 5229

"man in the belted raincoat" 5927

"man in the green summer suit" 7045

"Man in the Iron Mask" 6300

"man in town, luckiest" 1226

"man in whose nostrils is breath" 8921

"man is fast, the" 9

"man is not naturally a gregarious animal" 5696

"man is the only species" 5700

"man is vile" 5701

"man jogging toward the towngate" 9151

"man less than herself" 10791

"man like him, no" 4456

"man looking at a map" 1443

"man looking straight before him, each" 8645

"man lost his footing" 32

"man merely dressed" 2823

"man moved slowly" 3640

"man moving through her deadened woods" 9946

"man named Billy" 3510

"man next to you" 3363

"man of a rugged countenance" 5889

"man of comfortable private means" 5894

"man of genteel appearance" 9511

"man of heavy build" 3640

"man of his word" 3572

"man of importance, every" 4490

"man of letters" 9694

"man of portly frame and of middle age" 3812

"man of power, I am a" 4877

"man of proclivities" 5992

"man of small stature, young" 3812

"man of solid acquirements and stout ambition" 6613

"man of startling redness" 1738

"man of taste" 8255

"man on the bed" 2351

"man on the bicycle ahead of hers" 5957

"man on the plateau, the handsomest" 7624

"man only, one" 8942

"man say of his life, what can a" 5602

"man she loved" 7741

"man she wanted" 7741

"man should not be alone" 8735

"man sitting beside him has no legs" 9629

"man so short" 5966

"man speaks" 5971

"man standing guard" 161

"man standing in the shadow, the" 1544

"man tall [and] slender" 5910

"man that he is, old" 477

"man that is born of a woman" 5583

"man to his grave, often goes with a" 7584

"man to tell this story, maybe I am not the" 8983

"man treads the road with his dog" 10377

"man walking, a" 10409

"man wants his mother, every" 6686

"man was as healthy as a horse" 3958

"man was not there" 2835

"man was shot dead" 6191

"Man was still very young, when" 5262

"man watched his country" 7279

"man well turned out" 2823

"man who called himself, the" 2563

"man who gave me life" 6661

"man who had a dog" 10052

"man who had once been enormous" 5986

"Man who had Three Sons by one Wife" 7055

"man who risks his all" 1220

"man who took an enormous leap but didn't land" 5989

"man who travelled much" 4920

"man who wanted his Rhine-born wife to feel at home" 3202

"man who was the possessor of twenty million dollars" 10552

"man will ever possess, whom no" 10820

"man with a microscope" 519

"man with a mission" 259

"man with a woman on his hands" 7724

"man with any style at all" 5934

"man with binoculars" 596

"man with guitar" 1680

"man with his hands full" 7724

"man with no chin" 5809

"man with several women on his hands" 7724

"man with the brown eyes" 2804

"man with the monocle" 6173

"man with the sounding chain" 9996

"man with the spade" 3944

"manager, bank" 4641

"manager, draper's" 8347

"manager, English night" 4659

"manager, her" 4911

"manager, rubber-estate" 2026

Manarr, Dr. Hugo 7178

"Manchester" 4033, 9715

"Manchester North Carolina" 4675

"manchild was born" 804

"Manchu, two hundred and eighth year of the" 10983

Manco Capac 1567

"Mandarin Islands" 5638

"Manderley" 2755

Manders, Laurence 10162

Mandersons, the 5747

'Mando, Miss 10016

Mandragon 9604

"maneuver himself" 989

"maneuvering like a weightless astronaut in space" 1690

Manford, Mrs. 9880

Manfred 6515

"Manfred, at the" 3244

Manfredi 9454

"manganese" 10530

"manger, no dog in the" 443

"mango" 1480

"mangoes" 7533

"mangrove roots, stilting and arch-like" 5170
"mangroves, dark" 5158
"mangroves, sullen gray" 5033
"mangy-looking man" 413
Manhattan 1334, 6276
"Manhattan" 537, 1065, 2867, 5537, 6142, 6513, 7319, 9801
"Manhattan, after it leaves" 7282
"Manhattan, goodly town of" 1334
"Manhattan, Island of" 6608
"Manhattan, lower West Side of" 3103
"Manhattan, splendours and squalors of" 1932
"Manhattan, Upper" 5323
"Manhattan Battery" 7322
"Manhattan Flyer, the" 243
"Manhattan Island" 1854
"Manhattan Island, vaguely recall a stunted" 1420
"Manhattan Journal, Boswell's" 5444
"Manhattan must once have been a breezy little island" 10731
"Manhattan's buildings, blocky figures of" 7699
"Manhattan's Lower East Side" 6276
"Manhattan's seamy West 69th Street" 3244
"Manhattan's waist" 3429
"manhood, early" 5601
"manhood, grew to" 81
"Manhood, Young Gay" 5301
"mania for finding your real parents" 6720
"manicured hands" 4129
"manifested itself while he was playing golf" 7159
"Manila" 8534
"Manister, village of" 10926
Mankind 4443, 8978
"mankind, common run of" 4444
"mankind, generality of" 9260
"mankind, identification with" 5703
"mankind, information and edification of" 5387
"mankind, torment" 253
"mankind is prone to worship false gods" 1459
Mankowski, Chris 892
"manlike as most of his sons" 7554
"manly bosom, repose upon a" 10555
"manly character" 2885
Mann, Major 180
"manna is stuff in the bible" 7059
"manna to eat, Granny used to give us" 7059
"manned the defenses of Rome" 9559
"manner, a very desultory and casual" 5787
"manner, abstracted and precise" 8863

"manner, whimsical" 9073
"manner of speaking, rococo" 8640
Mannering, Mr. 9866
"manners" 9465
Manning 3920
Manning, Rhoda 4872
Manning, Rita 7530
Manny 8467
"man-of-war's men" 3997
Manolis 2165
Manon 4544
"Manor, Bellefleur" 1706
"Manor, Derrymore" 4557
"manor, half-" 1180
"Manor, Ley" 2887
"Manor, Old" 3109
"Manor, Palster" 7392
"manor, park and woods surrounding the" 10419
"Manor, Scroope" 3066
"Manor, what went on in the" 7840
"Manor, Woodiscombe" 3190
"Manor Green, suburb of" 4063
"man's almost dead" 124
"man's life, truth about a" 5950
"man's passion, nature of a" 1706
"man's wish, every" 8083
Mansfield, Senator Aaron 6985
"Mansfield Park" 5727
"Mansfield Park, straight out of" 1527
"mansion, bought the Lenox" 6301
"mansion, fieldstone" 3253
"mansion, his spacious" 7752
"mansion, large florid red-brick Georgian" 6163
"mansion, large square sombre-looking stone" 3972
"mansion, old family" 3069, 3548
"mansion, the" 3064
"mansion, thirty-five-room stone" 3179
"mansion, Townsend" 7760
"mansion, venerable family-" 3058
"mansion house" 286
"mansion in one of Chicago's most fashionable avenues" 1580
"mansion in Victorian-baronial style" 3179
"mansion situated on an estate in Gloucestershire" 3548
"mansion was built, when the" 7760
Mansions 1580, 2088, 3058, 3064, 3069, 3072, 3179, 3201, 3253, 3972, 6301, 7760
"mansions, Bronx has many" 3201
"mansions, gentlemen's" 9250
"mansions, Moorish" 309
"mansions, one of the most imposing of the" 3072
"mansions, ruined" 9216
"mansions finely peopled" 6266
"mansions relatively speaking" 3201
Mansure, Catherine 9835
"mantel-piece, broad" 8839
"mantelpiece, centre of the" 10916

"mantelpiece, clock that hung over the" 3815
"mantillas, adjusting their" 10659
"mantle, a dazzling" 7606
Mantoor, Adam 4796
Manuel 3141, 5213
"manufacture, of home" 8453
"manufactured himself out of a hollow iron bar" 6182
"manufacturer, fairly prosperous" 6414
"manufacturers, munitions" 2315
"manufacturing city" 1014
"manure cart" 9830
"manuscript, Benedictine's" 10898
"manuscript, this curious" 5536
"manuscript, this is a" 5534
"manuscript bound in black, untidy" 8816
Manuscripts 714, 5444, 5534, 5536, 5537, 10904
Manya 130
"Manzanita" 9211
"map, an inspection of the" 6053
"map, folded the topo" 5724
"map, his" 5711
"map, its tracery on the" 6054
"map, let's begin with the" 5721
"map, living" 5710
"map, man looking at a" 1443
"map, on the" 5720
"map, single glance at the" 4028
"map, social" 5708
"map, trace on a" 5713
"map case, opened his" 5716
"map has been long used by the industrious child" 5708
"map of France" 5714
"map of Norway, every one who has looked at the" 5707
"map of the British Isles" 5714
"map on the wall" 5709
"map under glass made no sense" 5722
"map was red and yellow" 5715
"Maple City" 9328
"maple saplings" 3036
"maple trees" 3095
"maples burning like bonfires" 10383
"mapmakers, idealized vision of" 5719
Mapp, Miss Elizabeth 80
Maps 230, 1443, 4028, 6053, 6054
"maps, on the latest" 230
"maps and manuscripts" 5287
"maps direct her journey, torn" 5718
"maps show the neighborhood as Clinton" 6274
"Marabar Caves" 1369
"Marathon" 9571
"Marathon, Abebe Bikila Memorial" 8924
"marathon, world-class" 8924

Marble, Sally 1798
"marble, figures carved in" 168
"Marblehead" 1598
"*Marblehead*, the" 6888
"marbles, beat Galileo at" 326
"marbles, shooting" 7898
March 4724, 9403
March, Erica 9295
March, Leda 4150
March, Leslie 10145
"March" 32, 195, 830, 1106, 1184,
    1309, 1615, 1629, 1676, 1758,
    1889, 1985, 2141, 2188, 2225,
    2386, 2393, 2405, 2424, 2538,
    2773, 2945, 3315, 3748, 4439,
    5103, 5443, 5537, 5778, 5826,
    6001, 6099, 7255, 7298, 7318,
    7459, 7518, 7841, 7903, 8056,
    8115, 8129, 8410, 8533, 8590,
    8694, 9466, 9742, 9771, 9860,
    9882, 10618, 10711, 10724, 10735,
    10926
"March, early" 1561
"March, end of" 8603
"march, first lap of the" 9192
"march, his celebrated" 4470
"March, Ides of" 70
"March, last week of" 316
"March, late-" 2846
"March, late in the month of" 407
"March, rainy" 9593
"march, Sunday's dead" 5788
"March, though it was now" 10579
"March afternoon" 10287
"March day, windy" 7892
"march four regiments just sixty
    New Zealand miles" 10535
"March mist" 7457
"March morning" 10706
"March noon" 223
"march of the previous day, terri-
    ble" 3681
"march past" 8679
"March twilight" 9406
Marchant, Mr. 5825
"marched Beulah Marsh, in" 3963
"marched into court" 2045
"Marchers, Lords" 6802
"Marches, Welsh" 3155
Marching 290, 3668, 8651, 8679,
    8690, 9192, 10535, 10585
"marching forth into North Beach"
    2906
"marching into American sunlight"
    290
"marching one by one" 3668
"Marchioness, the" 10916
Marcia 7488
Marco 8461
Marconi 3534
"Marconi's invention was brand-
    new" 3534
Marcus 1974
"mare, bay" 410, 411
"mare, get hold of a" 432

"mare, old" 8764
"mare, sorrel" 437
"mare, splendid" 6996
"mare again cocked her ears to the
    wind" 8764
"mare Juno, his lovely" 7617
"Marengo County Alabama" 5218
"mares" 433
"mare's hooves" 7639
Maretta 7605
Margaret 1824, 4138, 6171, 6323,
    8224, 8454
Margayya 4741
Margo 573
Margolies, Stanley 7477
Margoshes 6652
Maria 2426, 4153, 5869
Maria Ellen 10655
Marianne 6533
Marie 4722, 8150, 10008
Marie, aunt 2870
Marie Antoinette 1011
"Mariel harbor" 2052
Marietta 3817, 6392, 9302
Marigold, Lady Mary 5279
Marigold, Sir Louis 5279
"Marigold Park" 5279
Marilyn 1560
"Marimekko pumpkins, sat like
    two" 7074
"Marin County" 3239
"Marine Corps fighter pilots" 6773
"mariners, group of bronzed" 3997
"mariners skirting the coast" 1173
"mariners who navigate the stormy
    seas" 5011
"Marines" 8687
"Marines were bleeding and dying"
    8681
Mario 980, 7934
Maris, Roger 2179
"maritime villages" 1350
Marius 2795
Marius, Gaius 10521
Marjoribanks, Miss 8838
Marjorie 1994, 5239, 9721
Mark 3243, 8115, 10298
"Mark, S." 652
"mark her bones" 6646
"mark time on the traffic island"
    3031
Markand, David 10123
"marker that had a single word:
    BABY" 1194
"markers move" 9364
"Market, Eke" 1049
"market, flea" 1063, 1089
"Market, Flower" 9542
"market, hurried through the" 3703
"market, overnight Euro dollar"
    3752
"Market, Paddy's" 6274
"market, taking mothers and aunts
    to" 9169
"market, Washington is a" 1455

"market, world" 1016
"market now, not much to" 6918
"market of fat stock" 1027
"market-place" 906
"market-place, Ashersham" 1027
Markets 906, 1027, 1049, 1063,
    1089, 1455, 3703
Markin 3415
Markle, Lucy 5644
Marks, Molly 5238
Marlborough, Madam 3376
Marleen 3729
Marley 2288
"Marlott, village of" 10333
Marlow 8065
Marlowe 8568
Marlowe, Christopher 8497
Marmaduke 4799
Marmaduke, Sir 5638
"marmalade, pass the" 7517
"marmaladed a slice of toast" 4349
"marmite, eyes the color of" 4153
Marney 9440
Maroon, Clint 6314
"marooned on their separate blue-
    slate sidewalks" 7627
Marple, Miss Jane 3978, 4280
"marquee, an opening in the" 10657
"marquee, the" 10646
"marquetry, scrolls and lyres and"
    8383
Marquette, Père Jacques 9635
"Marquis" 8887
"Marquis of _____" 5883
Marr, Lucy 4921
"Marrakech is an ancient walled
    city" 1417
"marram grass" 10098
"marred by only a trace of saffron
    haze" 1854
"marred the early spring night"
    4306
Marriage 254, 1965, 1975, 1994,
    1995, 1996, 2146, 2509, 2554,
    2648, 2652, 2660, 2661, 2662,
    2671, 2672, 2678, 2681, 3073,
    3518, 3585, 3599, 3604, 3628,
    4234, 4683, 4931, 5343, 5344,
    5592, 5644, 5930, 5970, 6019,
    6095, 6119, 6545, 6622, 6635,
    6664, 6728, 6748, 7069, 7083,
    7737, 7830, 7995, 8222, 8734,
    9458, 9496, 9732, 10138, 10644,
    10648, 10651, 10658, 10661,
    10666, 10673, 10763, 10790,
    10791, 10829
"marriage" 5738
"marriage, after our" 5343
"marriage, Annette's" 5754
"marriage, by" 563
"marriage, catapulted him into"
    5765
"marriage, couldn't get along in"
    2671
"marriage, five years after my" 6095

"marriage, her" 5592
"marriage, his" 4683
"marriage, his third" 3518
"marriage, inadvertently detonated her" 5778
"marriage, Jennie Middleton's" 10648
"marriage, kept Lucy Markle from" 5644
"marriage, made a good" 5744
"marriage, new" 7069
"marriage, overriding interest in a" 5743
"marriage, perfect" 5736
"marriage, success of a" 10829
"marriage, think about" 5776
"marriage, thirty years of" 5750
"marriage broke up" 2672
"marriage day" 10647
"marriage elms" 10051
"marriage of his son" 9496
"marriage wasn't going well" 2662
"marriages, inexplicably happy" 5755
"marriages, list of" 5735
"marriages, teenage" 5749
"marriages, who arranges the" 5743
"marriages are funny things" 5763
"marriages were invalid, Jewish" 7505
"married" 2509, 4234
"married, asking to be" 5774
"married, Aunt Leela got" 10665
"married, going to be" 5741
"married, having never" 5884
"married, he must get" 5728
"married, dumbass" 2678
"married, if Sandro wasn't" 5775
"married, Mutt and I was" 5757
"married, Peter is really" 5740
"married, she had" 6622
"married, soon to be" 5734
"married, think of getting" 5746
"married, too wise to get" 10763
"married, when they were old enough they" 5739
"married, young lovers and" 515
"married a Frenchman" 6119
"married a heathen" 6720
"married a man less than herself" 10791
"married a two-faced hardware salesman, my mother" 5769
"married a white girl" 5753
"married again next month" 5762
"married and brought up a large family" 5725
"married as soon as they were old enough" 5739
"married before the baroque altar" 10664
"married Edward, after she" 10439
"married Eliza" 6605
"married Eliza Jumel" 10662

"married first when she was eighteen" 5770
"married for the second time" 5734
"married George Smiley" 5930
"married George Webster in 1909" 2554
"married her own son, woman who" 3628
"married his latest airline stewardess" 5779
"married in 1957" 5760
"married in two days, we get" 1995
"married life" 1965
"married me so he could support me" 5757
"married my wife, when I" 4789
"married nearly a dozen years" 9732
"married soon, going to be" 4119
"married them young back then, they" 3660
"married three times, we were" 5756
"married three wives" 6635
"married to a genius" 5767
"married to a man who wants to keep her that way" 8222
"married to a stone, I am" 5772
"married to an eldest brother" 8222
"married to Harald Petersen" 10656
"married to Seena Nordstrom" 10645
"married too young, got" 5780
"married well" 4774
"married woman, affair with a" 7720
"married yesterday" 10673
"married young Corbario" 6019
Marriott 3155
"marry" 3599
"marry, if you never mean to" 5730
"marry, noose and knot to" 5759
"marry, one day I'd" 5783
"marry, persuade him not to" 7830
"marry, they" 10843
"marry, when he decided to" 5761
"marry, whom she intended to" 5747
"marry, woman he wanted to" 7737
"marry a boy I choose, you will" 6748
"marry a Dutchman" 5729
"marry a fair woman" 5344
"marry him, might quite like to" 5775
"marry him, said she'd" 5764
"marry Jonathan" 5781
"marry me" 5766
"marry me, asking you again to" 5737
"marry me, will you" 5752
"marry some white folks" 5729
"marry somebody as promptly as possible" 254
"marry the young man" 9659

"marry them, some" 10790
"marrying a drunk, a madwoman" 5771
"marrying a girl" 9290
"marrying a neurosurgeon, set her heart on" 5758
"marrying a young man in the Coldstream" 10649
"marrying again, had not thought of" 5731
"marrying his aunt" 10658
"marrying Italian *primedonne*" 10788
"Marseillaise, singing the" 563
"Marseilles" 4631
"Marseilles lay burning in the sun" 4367
Marsh, Andrew 8163
Marsh, Beulah 3963
Marsh, Mrs. 8613
"marsh, inner reaches of the salt" 9150
"marsh, lost logic of a" 5723
"marsh, lying in the" 2894
"marsh, salt" 9136
"marsh pool" 1824
"Marsh's" 8301
"Marshal, the" 9929
Marshall 6871
Marshall, Herman 7340
Marshall, Mr. 4907
Marshall, Peter 10142
"marshes, riverside" 9188
"marshes, tawny" 8402
"marshes spread across the triangle" 4048
Marshland, Jinny 5201
"Mars's own alloy" 10530
Marston 5675
Marston, Celia 8260
Marta 10105
Martha 1113, 2703, 5145, 8708, 9910, 10111, 10125
"martial attitude, strikes a" 8942
"Martial Call, the" 10465
"Martian, there was a" 4759
Martin 352, 5369, 7253, 7539, 9496
Martin, Bill 6851
Martin, George 7367
Martin, Harry 9101
Martin, Henry 10040
Martin, Julia 6108
Martin, Michael 5214
Martin, Paul Michael 9453
Martin, Phoebe 6544
"Martingale" 5091
"martini, vodka" 9173
"martinis, beaker of" 2942
"martinis, dry" 9321
Martinus 5779
Martyn-Lynch, Hyacinth 10138
"martyr, the one virgin" 4808
"martyr, with all the air of a" 1577
"MARTYR TO IRISH CAUSE" 2386

"martyrdom" 9045
Martyrs 1577, 4454
"martyrs" 503, 4454
"marvel over" 4510
Marvel 5090
Marvel, Sam 4007
"marveled, people still" 4209
"marvelled at the huge edifice of
    blue air" 10604
"marvelling at the quality" 7573
"marvellous thing, is it not a"
    5699
Marvin 6681
Mary 48, 1873, 1923, 2486, 4158,
    4722, 4772, 6414, 6605, 7059,
    7071, 8717, 9296, 10257
Mary, Sweet 5094
Mary, Virgin 8008
Mary Ann 5219
Mary Jess 1667
Mary Marie 4722
Mary the Mother of God 10587
"Mary, S." 652
"Maryborough, change at" 9655
"Maryland, his Lordship's province
    of" 3531
"Maryland, Western" 543
"Mary's Neck" 9096
"masculine is universal" 10913
Masham, Mrs. 3376
"mask, small white lace" 4804
"mask, wearing a" 2869
"mask may be dropped" 6765
"mask of ennui, gray and scarlet"
    332
"mask of Purpose, hiding behind
    a" 5973
Masked Rider 1704
Masks 151, 2066, 2869, 6765
Mason 4485
Mason, Boyd 2971
Mason, Charley 3471
Mason, Maude 9498
"masquerades, enjoyed" 6765
"mass, cumbersome" 8107
"mass, he would remember not one
    detail of the" 10392
"mass on Sunday, sin to miss" 7511
"mass that then returned arrogantly
    to obstruct the corridor" 5943
"Mass" 1303
"Mass." 5445, 9515, 9584
"Mass, Friday-evening" 8758
"Mass, had to say" 1513
"Mass, High" 1643
"Mass, Midnight" 1541
"Mass, Requiem" 3588
"mass, solid scurrying" 10509
"Mass in English" 6807
"Mass on a headland for a guild of
    graduates" 1513
"Massachusetts" 356, 510, 1088,
    3194, 4073, 4186, 4927, 6133,
    6135, 6313, 6774, 7082, 8048,
    8372, 9424, 9600, 10814

"Massachusetts, Commonwealth
    of" 1373
"Massachusetts, Northern" 3987
"Massachusetts Indians" 3906
"massage the soft parts" 7104
"massing of the original stone, the
    main" 9223
"massive and noble" 1174
"massive beasts" 6087
"massive outline" 683
"massivity, its sheer" 9221
Mast, Pfc Richard 873
"mast, main" 8126
"master, classical" 6427
"master, my" 326
"master, the" 10919
"master and owner of the sloop"
    8563
"Master come unto the earth" 2631
"master criminal" 2044
"Master in the study of Holy Writ"
    1691
"master of the Indian Spring
    school" 6408
"Master of the Restaurant Chez
    Pavan" 6433
"Master of the Terror" 4457
"Master of the Tetragrammaton"
    7505
"master returning" 482
"mastered the curious language
    Americans spoke, never quite"
    6749
"masters" 3075
"mastership of foxhounds, resigned
    his" 8636
Masterson, Mr. 4835
"masticating his food thoroughly"
    3852
Mastracola, Elizabeth Bean 4876
"masts, sedge-like" 4034
"masts of the ships, tall" 3116
"masturbated, priest rarely" 1539
"masturbating pigs, spittling" 10871
Masturbation 1539, 7874
"mat, horsehair welcome" 9443
"Matarre estuary" 7679
"match, barn" 3778
"match, just-extinguished" 6301
"match, lighting a" 6836
"match, prick a" 7474
"match, wood" 8582
"match was also broken off" 2648
"match was made in Europe" 2648
"match were to be lit, if a" 10610
"matched his mood" 3315
"matches, fistful of sulphur" 876
"matches, fool with" 10547
"matches, spilled wine over our"
    2129
"matchless morning" 2193
"mate, chief" 8060
"mate, its" 428
"mate, the" 4246
"mate, took one of them as his" 748

"material doesn't stain" 2845
"materiality, summon its" 5027
"materialized, he had" 4102
"materialized into a traction de-
    vice" 10228
Matey 7379
Mathematics 895, 2100, 2741,
    2874, 3279, 3739, 3743, 3745,
    7202
"mathematics, a question about"
    7202
Mather, Charles Townsend 6834
Mather, Maxwell 7978
Mathers, Phillip 6182
Mathias, Luther 5192
Mathieson, Brigadier-General 8644
Mathilde 5528
Mati 4011
Matilda 450, 641, 1969, 6515
Matilda Anne 5733
"matinee, Sunday" 5875
"mating, frenzy of" 7740
"mating, skittish with" 420
"matins" 1312
"matriculating at the Universities"
    3528
"matriculation, appeared for" 7881
"matriculations of the heart and
    liver" 7514
"matrimonial ads" 5758
"matrimony, pool of" 5733
"matrimony, uniting in the state
    of" 1964
"matrimony was ordained" 5742
"matrons, like-minded well-heeled"
    10863
Matt 681, 3932
Matt, Uncle 3591
"Mattagash Maine" 6155, 10631
"Mattalahta Buka" 8789
"matter, but that ain't no" 896
"matter, it doesn't" 9937
"matter, perhaps it doesn't" 5191
"matter, supposed to" 5585
"matter, the other at that time did
    not" 6525
"matter, this odd" 9692
"matter, what seems to" 10758
"matter, what's the" 7160, 8647
"matter so much, it didn't" 2467
"mattered, centre of all that" 1049
Matthew 681, 7583, 7862, 8240,
    10236
Matthews 6891
"mattress springing" 7989
"mattresses, division of the two"
    10206
Matulli 541
Maturation 4170, 4200, 4232
"maturity, a realized" 10062
"maturity, at improbable" 9186
"maturity, attained to the same
    state of" 9660
Mauberley 6678
Maud 10871

Maude 10845
Maudie 7774
Maul, Kitty 4812
"mauled cat" 9340
Mauley, Lord 5984
"Maundy Thursday" 9388
Maureen 10258
Mauretania berthing" 8139
Maurice 6858
M'Auslan, Sawners 8476
"Mausoleum, Lenin's" 5971
"maverick Supreme Court Justice" 5207
Mavering, Mr. Elbridge 6753
Mavis 9321
Mavis, Andrew 4828
Mavis, Billy Bob 9925
Mavrozomes 524
"maw, sickened blue" 5096
"Maw Maw Maw!" 479
Max 251, 2599, 3631
Maxie, Eleanor 5091
Maxim, Gifford 1624
"maxim of early to bed and early to rise" 1170
Maxwell, General Sir John Gren fell 8580
May 1667, 2577, 3183, 6767
"May" 738, 784, 808, 850, 949, 964, 970, 975, 1161, 1181, 1517, 1586, 1623, 2056, 2133, 2216, 2250, 2401, 2451, 2468, 2486, 2563, 2912, 3441, 3805, 4475, 4595, 5040, 5076, 5087, 5316, 5335, 5431, 5613, 5781, 5958, 5995, 6138, 6399, 6499, 6561, 6999, 7151, 7588, 7610, 7650, 7687, 7852, 7933, 8064, 8611, 8933, 8997, 9408, 9524, 9614, 9732, 9742, 9921, 9955, 10020, 10109, 10126, 10168, 10333, 10450, 10773
May Liza 743
"May might wed December" 6249
"May the month of Mary" 10587
Mayadebi 6159
"Mayfair" 5279
Mayfield, Hutchins 6680
Mayflower" 6121
Maynard, Clarissa 2153
Maynard, John 8064
Mayor, Bridget 1309
"mayor, mother of the" 6571
"mayor, the" 2850
"Mayor, the" 4217, 8864
"mayor of the city" 2472
"mayor of the good town of Southampton" 4971
"mayor of this town, ex-" 7721
"Mayor of New Orleans" 1982
"Mayor of Tilling, three times" 10525
"Mayor's Special Task Force on Crime" 6274
"Maypole, the" 4303

"Mazatlán" 4580
Mazda, Ahura 7547
"maze of slate roofs" 8448
"mazed and a-wonder" 8187
Mazie 10238
Mazzo 2162
"m.c. of my family's mountainside resort hotel" 7727
"me, it's only" 9933
"me, that's" 4735
Meade, Mrs. 1909
Meade, Nancy 9973
"meadow, at the bottom of Gurney's" 2894
"Meadow, Mill" 4342
"meadow, river-" 3645
"meadow lark, Western" 8746
Meadows, Popsy 5605
Meadows, Reverend Doctor John Tinker 1532
"meadows, couple of" 3119
"meadows, flowery" 9738
"meadows, mountain" 7667
"meadows, water-" 1408
"meadows, wide flat" 1352
"meadows, Wood Eaton" 9131
"meadows laughed" 9740
"meadows where the Erewash twisted sluggishly" 3082
"meager briars and shrubs" 5704
"meager shadows" 5704
"meal, it was a simple" 3854
"meal, punctual" 4909
"meal, the" 3863
"meal of rubbery mutton" 2463
"meal was coming from, where her next" 10975
"meal was of that elegant proportion" 3821
Meals 386, 446, 723, 873, 1207, 1494, 1587, 1654, 1863, 1864, 1865, 1868, 1874, 1902, 1978, 2401, 2495, 2663, 3007, 3048, 3321, 3344, 3439, 3443, 3471, 3565, 3629, 3812, 3813, 3814, 3815, 3816, 3817, 3818, 3819, 3820, 3821, 3823, 3824, 3825, 3826, 3827, 3828, 3829, 3830, 3831, 3832, 3833, 3834, 3835, 3836, 3837, 3838, 3839, 3840, 3841, 3842, 3843, 3844, 3846, 3847, 3848, 3849, 3850, 3851, 3852, 3853, 3854, 3855, 3856, 3857, 3858, 3860, 3861, 3863, 3864, 3865, 3866, 3867, 3868, 3869, 3870, 3871, 3872, 3873, 3874, 3875, 3876, 3877, 3878, 3879, 3880, 3881, 3882, 3883, 3884, 3885, 3886, 3887, 3888, 3889, 3890, 3891, 3892, 3989, 4283, 4285, 4349, 4670, 4681, 4711, 4909, 5004, 5624, 5636, 5658, 6440, 6443, 6581, 6715, 7235, 7303, 7517, 7571, 7782, 8038, 8223, 8377, 8628, 8633,

8869, 8884, 9051, 9423, 9470, 9664, 9900, 9915, 10039, 10163, 10411, 10565, 10586, 10836, 10899
"meals a day, cook three" 6440
"mean, what did she" 3345
"mean, what did that" 10906
"mean, what does it really" 2347
"mean, what's he" 6050
"meandered over the straighter more direct openings" 9127
"meandering, history has a habit of" 4500
"meandering through" 10461
"meanest miser" 3376
"meaning, some new spark of" 10077
"meaning of a man's life, ultimate" 2383
"meaning of life" 5253
"meaning to, for years I have been" 706
"meanness, kernel of" 395
"means, comfortable private" 5894
"means, limited" 10779
"means available, quickest and cheapest" 6570
"means in their power" 6972
"meant, that wasn't what I" 5460
"meant, whatever it" 4642
"meant a great deal to everybody in Hartfield" 8301
"meant by it, I wonder what he" 4118
"meant everything to me" 4175
Meany, Owen 7542
"Mearns Howe" 4053
"measure, in a great" 1343
"measure, tape" 2915
"measure its consistency" 3555
"measured in heat and gasses" 9503
"measured less than four feet in length" 3956
"measurement, beyond all human" 9412
"measuring distances" 7766
"meat, lunch" 4073
"Meat Packing Company, Denny" 537
Mechanics 9776, 9947, 10925, 10938
"mechanism of town life" 6199
Mecklin, Sugar 5121
Medallion 9209
"Medan" 5288
"mediaeval castle, features of a" 1180
"mediation, through her" 7996
"Medical Arts Institute, All India" 6728
"medical discoverers" 2616
"medical opinion" 150
"medical point of view" 3990
"medical practitioner, modest country" 6885
"medical profession" 6407

"medical school, secure me four years in a" 4930
"medical texts, early Rhodesian" 5607
"medicinal purposes" 8165
Medicine 166, 1024, 1064, 3048, 3055, 3290, 3529, 8165, 9258
"medicine" 3290
"Medicine, Doctor of" 3266, 9076
"medicine, practice of" 3529
"medicine stalls, bloody juju" 1064
"medieval castle, like a huge" 5028
"medieval obscurity, awakened from" 1464
"meditate upon the folly of all human ambition" 1496
"meditated in secret" 6928
"meditating upon it" 4782
"meditating upon the uncertainty of sublunary enjoyment" 9989
"meditation, the longer the" 2035
"Meditation Time in Painless Birth" 7081
"meditative foot" 567
"Mediterranean" 4080, 10417
"Mediterranean, meadowgreen" 8573
"Mediterranean, the" 2202, 8112
"Mediterranean coast" 8894
"Mediterranean seaside village" 1481
"Mediterranean's blue" 4704
Medlar 10198
Meeber, Caroline 9525
Meecham, Lieutenant Colonel Bull 6773
"meek might someday inherit the earth" 7836
Meeker, John "Pork" 6969
Meers, Harold 3
"meerschaum, smoke from his" 8573
"Meeson's" 1006
"meet, we're finally going to" 5866
"meet at eight o'clock" 5407
"meet at the dance club Spit" 4849
"meet at the Fifth Avenue Hotel, they used to" 1967
"meet at the Ritz, we" 8635
"meet her" 5817
"meet her as she came out" 6630
"meet her at a party, I" 5850
"meet his master and mistress" 1294
"meet in intimate conversation un-chaperoned" 7772
"meet it, went out to" 9835
"meet Sonya on the way to school, didn't" 1241
"meet the great man" 5837
"meeting, dominated the" 8707
"meeting, first official" 10978
"meeting, first to arrive for the" 2716
"meeting, halfway along in the" 3525
"meeting, regular monthly" 1911

"meeting, Springwell Harriers' point-to-point" 3998
"meeting, street-corner" 5323
"meeting, union" 4013
"meeting between two professional gentlemen" 5871
"meeting . . . had gone as well as could be expected" 4013
"meeting in the laundry room" 7874
"meeting men younger than him-self" 5798
"meeting of the Babbington Flotilla of the Young Tars" 10978
"meeting of the Council of Free-men" 8866
"meeting of two lonesome skinny fairly old white men" 5827
"meeting people, I like" 1514
"meeting . . . should surely not need to be concealed" 5871
"meeting was late in starting" 3297
"meeting-house" 9136
Meetings 497, 865, 961, 997, 1233, 1241, 1286, 1294, 1634, 1911, 2010, 2478, 2648, 2716, 2826, 2899, 3008, 3297, 3525, 3595, 3695, 3923, 3949, 3977, 3998, 4013, 4020, 4310, 4473, 4576, 4595, 4702, 4703, 4849, 4932, 4940, 4995, 5080, 5084, 5111, 5651, 5681, 6017, 6400, 6455, 6504, 6763, 6985, 7074, 7434, 7676, 7742, 7751, 8024, 8027, 8294, 8657, 8676, 8749, 8847, 8857, 9096, 9335, 9864, 9926, 10043, 10243
"meetings, attending parish" 1493
"meetings, bi-monthly" 5429
"meetings, clandestine" 4705
"meetings, had a masterly way with" 4020
"meetings, one of the rare" 5858
"meets Bonnie Parker" 5826
Meg 6309
Meg, Mrs. 1245
"Megapolis" 8773
Mehra, Mrs. Rupa 6748
Meintjies, Mina 614
Meiss 6194
"meistersinger" 6454
Mekles, Nicholas 4757
"Meknes" 9780
"Mekong River" 4094
Melamine, Lord 8901
"melancholy, a greater" 2513
"melancholy cast of countenance" 8098
"melancholy errors" 6517
"melancholy flush" 5305
"melancholy of the undergraduate condition, crushing" 3276
"melancholy prehistoric animal" 4773
"melancholy view of life" 2501
Melanie 7969

Melanson, Blanche 7020
Melba 740
"Melbourne" 1758, 8051
"Melbourne, busy industrial city of" 5754
Melendez, Veronica 925
Melendy, Vaughan 1391
Melincourt, Anthelia 10767
Melissa 8491
Mellon, Captain Jack 8084
"mellow in the sunshine" 1398
"mellow time, that" 7709
"mellow with age" 10355
"mellowest highest note" 8748
Melmoth, John 4604
"melodrama enough without the idiocies" 7840
"melodramatic situations" 1325
"Melon Village" 4328
"melons, they were here for the" 10076
"Melrose Abbey" 10658
"melted into the sea of the city" 5790
Melton, Mr. 9416
Melton, Roger 4929
Melville, Ellen 2071
Melville, Henry 10300
"member of a group" 1209
"member of my club, he is a" 4733
"member of the Comstock family, last" 5621
"member of the world's people, I am a" 6833
"members, the few hardy" 4306
"members of my family, five" 3626
"members of the Spiegelglass family" 3600
"members who had haunted the clubhouse" 4306
"membership, up for" 4307
"membrane, a transparent" 2066
Mementos 6861
"mementos from the 1923 World Cup" 5607
"memo" 1942
"memoir, in any" 711
"memoir, write this" 718
Memoirs 697, 699, 703, 711, 713, 715, 717, 718, 3679, 4490
"memoirs, begins her" 3679
"memoirs, edit the" 717
"memoirs, embark on these" 715
"memoirs, make public his" 713
"memoirs, self-seeking" 7000
"memoirs, write his" 703
"memoirs, write his own" 4490
"memoirs of Sir Emmanuel Bern-stein" 5456
"MEMOIRS OF THE RACK-RENT FAMILY" 694
"memorable picture" 2045
"memoranda, his" 3072
"Memorandum begins thus" 9513

"memorial service, hastily arranged" 3961
"Memorial Day" 2971, 9584
"memorials erected in London"
  4467
Memories 116, 859, 867, 870,
  1270, 1538, 1840, 1843, 2116,
  2177, 2544, 3019, 3384, 3514,
  4057, 4235, 4342, 4536, 4836,
  4936, 5027, 5059, 5411, 5617,
  5795, 5888, 5996, 6022, 6374,
  6584, 6737, 6787, 6793, 6849,
  6857, 6883, 7155, 7371, 7373,
  7378, 7379, 7380, 7382, 7385,
  7386, 7388, 7391, 7393, 7394,
  7397, 7402, 7403, 7404, 7405,
  7409, 7410, 7413, 7415, 7417,
  7419, 7420, 7422, 7423, 7424,
  7426, 7427, 7429, 7430, 7431,
  7433, 7434, 7435, 7436, 7437,
  7438, 7439, 7440, 7441, 7442,
  7443, 7446, 7450, 7453, 7454,
  7455, 7459, 7460, 7607, 7765,
  7872, 7894, 7932, 7947, 8488,
  8512, 8551, 9353, 9373, 9425,
  9429, 9733, 9837, 10139, 10285,
  10290, 10624, 10738, 10752, 11004
"memories, amid mousy" 4154
"memories, chattered about first"
  7410
"memories, dim as" 6849
"memories, faulty" 5059
"memories, head a clutter of" 3019
"memories, his" 6584
"memories, historic" 7155
"memories, I have two first" 7431
"memories, in most people's" 7872
"memories, in one of my earliest"
  9373
"memories, moldered by" 4936
"memories, my earliest" 7446
"memories, never one to begrudge
  people their" 6787
"memories, night for" 7419
"memories, one of my strongest
  most persistent" 7427
"memories, photographs are not"
  6883
"memories, throng of ancient" 5617
"memories, words and" 116
"memories, young man's earliest"
  8530
"memories jostling him where he
  stood" 5617
"memories of one's youth" 7424
"memories of our youth" 11004
"memories of those days" 7441
"memories overwhelming me like a
  storm" 7434
"memories . . . pierced her with
  sudden clarity" 7441
"memories sink down, let his"
  7430
"memories that persist like fragments of old tunes" 7386

"memories were doubtful, when"
  6793
"memoristic vacuum" 7378
Memory 799, 800, 1197, 1955,
  2852, 3489, 3491, 3546, 4142,
  4504, 5101, 5582, 6741, 7372,
  7375, 7378, 7384, 7399, 7404,
  7407, 7421, 7425, 7432, 7444,
  7448, 7456, 8093, 9047, 10139,
  10281, 10299
"memory" 6022
"memory, brought back by a" 7453
"memory, dearest" 7385
"memory, dreams and" 10299
"memory, earliest" 7454
"memory, erase from your" 1955
"memory, failing" 3490
"memory, first coherent" 7443
"memory, flippant sprite of" 7373
"memory, from" 4504
"memory, graven on the" 3489
"memory, his" 10139
"memory, honour his" 3588
"memory, I have a sure" 7459
"memory, imprint this picture
  upon their" 8093
"memory, in" 2111
"memory, lamented and lamentable" 3084
"memory, linger in the" 7423
"memory, long" 9047
"memory, my" 1197, 7384
"memory, my first whole" 6374
"memory, perpetual and terrible"
  10774
"memory, stand out forever in her"
  5101
"memory, sway of a great man's"
  5212
"memory, transformed and even
  distorted" 5582
"memory, winter is" 10624
"memory, within the" 3528
"memory, written from" 7375
"memory cannot be controlled"
  3546
"Memory Flower" 5220
"memory . . . has a will of its own"
  3546
"memory itself is but a picture-
  book" 4142
"Memory Land" 5220
"memory now, nothing but a" 7371
"memory of her who relinquished
  her feeble ghost" 6646
"memory of him, my earliest" 7393
"memory of pain, her first" 6737
"memory of peacetime, close-held"
  7894
"memory of the dead, in" 1206
"memory of the Farm, earliest"
  7380
"memory of the public is short" 7381
"memory plays its pranks for good
  or ill" 7372

"memory will be cold with time"
  7388
"memory you need, it's not" 9027
"Memphis, governor of" 7799
Men 55, 88, 98, 105, 119, 150, 152,
  154, 242, 259, 336, 344, 355,
  368, 497, 498, 847, 916, 995,
  1391, 1477, 1501, 1524, 1569,
  1609, 1706, 1738, 1831, 1952,
  1977, 1982, 1994, 2328, 2405,
  2446, 2507, 2598, 2656, 2809,
  2828, 2834, 2839, 2842, 2889,
  2892, 2904, 2914, 3298, 3329,
  3517, 3536, 3543, 4041, 4174,
  4208, 4266, 4282, 4291, 4293,
  4298, 4329, 4339, 4340, 4345,
  4375, 4442, 4456, 4465, 4483,
  4489, 4789, 4874, 4892, 4979,
  5001, 5183, 5208, 5215, 5257,
  5299, 5349, 5354, 5523, 5581,
  5621, 5624, 5628, 5649, 5654,
  5726, 5728, 5759, 5790, 5814,
  5827, 6018, 6297, 6330, 6414,
  6426, 6427, 6496, 6553, 6592,
  6593, 6613, 6659, 6683, 6686,
  6694, 6738, 6910, 6978, 7061,
  7116, 7133, 7176, 7182, 7195,
  7384, 7554, 7626, 7683, 7714,
  7724, 7744, 7746, 7949, 7952,
  7959, 7978, 8007, 8024, 8254,
  8255, 8347, 8350, 8453, 8481,
  8493, 8550, 8556, 8658, 8698,
  8707, 8736, 8827, 8845, 8954,
  8993, 8994, 9031, 9317, 9347,
  9427, 9434, 9612, 9690, 9749,
  9877, 9913, 9946, 10105, 10389,
  10408, 10438, 10552, 10557,
  10561, 10764, 10811, 10928, 10933
"men, a class of" 6409
"men, a few good" 8687
"men, a group of" 331
"men, about a hundred and fifty"
  8990
"men, all good" 6989
"men, armed" 1172
"men, beautiful young" 8686
"Men, Best of" 4219
"men, boys and" 9253
"men, certain pallid undersized"
  5886
"men, class of" 6884
"men, college" 4307
"men, common" 10033
"men, conjure" 253
"men, delivery" 9373
"men, endured by" 7216
"men, first trainload of" 9638
"men, five" 4266
"men, four" 2024, 10451
"men, freely sweating" 4335
"men, great" 5905
"men, great and eminent" 4489
"men, grown" 3516
"men, half-a-dozen" 10946
"men, hang" 7181

"men, hundreds of" 3329
"men, inscrutable and silent" 9381
"men, lesser" 4805
"men, little" 3962, 9648
"men, little groups of" 8893
"men, man-of-war's" 3997
"men, many" 3914, 9309
"men, old" 1149, 1244, 3394
"men, over a million" 5138
"men, possessive" 4309
"men, public" 9260
"men, sinewy tattooed" 5982
"men, six" 650
"men, six hundred" 4024
"men, sleeping with" 8007
"men, small" 7746
"men, stiff solid unobtrusive" 4432
"men, strange" 9104
"men, the" 4214, 5019, 7061, 8110,
    8156, 8869, 10852
"Men, the Last" 4496
"men, ten" 9576
"men, they don't normally tell"
    7957
"men, three" 4667, 5208, 6866,
    7623, 10067, 10088
"men, three old" 8862
"men, three young" 2955
"men, throng of bearded" 3985
"men, twenty-five" 8079
"men, twenty-two" 9546
"men, two" 5349, 7133, 8344,
    8845, 8849, 8994, 10368, 10417
"men, two armed" 4797
"men, two black" 3007
"men, two blind" 1831
"men, two dead" 1831
"men, two lonesome skinny fairly
    old white" 5827
"men, two old" 1907
"men, two traveling" 8908
"men, two very old" 3127
"men, two young" 7140, 7613,
    8351, 9114, 10440
"men, unfamiliar" 464
"men, used to like" 9690
"men, various" 10794
"men, very fond of" 5354
"men, wearied" 8851
"men, young" 330, 1977, 3671,
    3912, 4906, 5631, 5641
"men and women, both" 9526
"men and women, countless" 5659
"men and women, illogical" 6155
"men and women, some" 10527
"men and women, the" 8093
"men and women of no note" 4454
"men and women of Simon Straight
    College, the proud" 3283
"men are all mousey" 7176
"men are brothers" 7519
"men are inclined to throw back
    their heads like horses" 55
"men are not everywhere born
    free" 4443

"men at the table, three" 2914
"men at work" 10930
"men below, the" 992
"men busied themselves" 519
"men cannot relate to other people"
    5973
"men . . . died, about two thou-
    sand" 8678
"men do not tinker beneath their
    car hoods" 1477
"men dressed like women" 2870
"men emerge pale" 1041
"men first walked on the moon" 538
"men for death, prepare other" 1507
"men from the *Marblehead*" 6888
"men got up to fight, two dead"
    1831
"men I have ever known, one of
    the fittest" 6659
"men in a particular place, sense
    of" 7228
"men in blue marched home" 10483
"men in her life" 6738
"men in lazy contemplation" 3394
"men in solemn Sunday suits" 6868
"men into the arms of women,
    drives" 7735
"men lived with her" 8140
"men love not to be taught by a
    woman" 7949
"men now having their pipes" 3591
"men of his age" 5085
"men of iron" 3698
"men of the town" 7446
"men quickened the step" 10585
"men screaming and dying" 2784
"men seldom realized it" 10793
"men so foolish, why are" 5891
"men so wonderful, any living" 4041
"men squatting" 9775
"men tending for the most part to
    become elderly" 6409
"men to sea, drive" 2598
"men were hiding in the hills" 4483
"men were sent out with flaming
    torches" 3775
"men were trying to kiss my
    mother" 6694
"men who are nothing" 6843
"men who govern India" 6978
"men who jumped around in trees"
    9648
"men who make a virtue of consis-
    tency" 5427
"men with guns" 476
"men with untamed hearts" 8993
"men you didn't care about" 8007
"men younger than himself" 5798
"menace, with all their" 6249
"menaced, seldom" 10535
"menders, street" 9144
Mendes, Julian 5673
"mending a broken heart, various
    ways of" 7461
"mending some fish-traps" 4686

"Mendon, town of" 6313
"*menehune*, the legendary" 10957
"menopausal plumpness" 87
Menstruation 7093
"mental homes, eventually become
    private" 3160
"mental picture, had a clear" 10479
"mental power, balanced in the
    scale of" 4533
"mentally, he would retire" 4661
"mention, honorable" 356
"mention it, come to" 6153
"mention of a lady, there is fre-
    quent" 10781
Menutis, Foley 5861
"mercantile tradition, respect for"
    1021
"Mercedes, a borrowed" 9802
"Mercedes, gray" 9320
"Mercedes, silver-blue" 9824
"Mercedes - a 300SEL roadster
    model" 9824
"Mercedes 450SL, my silver-gray"
    9821
"Merchandise, he got a good
    Estate by" 6601
"merchandise, stripped of" 1036
"merchandise for the Ice Age" 2162
"merchant, Chinese" 3152
"Merchant, Colonial Produce" 8341
"merchant, tea" 2557
"merchant designed" 1011
"merchant vessel" 8057
"merchant whose wife was Mrs.
    Fountain's half-sister" 10771
"merchants, cloth" 1304
"merchants bowing me from their
    doors" 3737
Mercier 7368, 9588
"Merciful, the" 5602
"mercilessly, chafe" 9446
"Mercury, key to his" 1769
"Mercy" 9602
"mercy, any" 2397
"mercy, have" 7057
"mercy of their own desires, too
    many hours at the" 938
Mereth 1140
"merge, afraid to" 3723
"merged one into the other, all
    things" 4320
Meri 8974
"Meridian" 3770
"meridional line" 9519
"Merionethshire" 6606
"meritorious author" 6246
"meritorious career" 6439
"merits, distinguished" 7825
"merits, eminent" 357
"merits for possible Beatification"
    7548
"merits have made her the public
    care" 7825
Merival, Miss 4911
Merivale, Mr. Stafford 9934

Merlin, Dorothy 381
"mermaids, landings of" 2733
Meromic 10116
"Merravay" 1852
Merriman, Dorothea Frances 5743
Merritt, Alec 6699
Merry 5743, 6962
"merry a night, too" 9882
"merry before them, be" 6752
"merry England" 3893
"merry group" 9759
"merry was the month of May" 10109
"merry-go-round" 304
"merry-go-round, music of the" 1250
"merry-go-rounds" 5684
Merton, Mrs. 3136
Merton, Noel 3136
"mesa, across the" 2957
"mesa, distant high" 7625
"mesa, sits on the edge of the" 8273
"mesh, unbendable alloy" 10721
"mesmerized" 5636
"Mesopotamia" 6636
"mesquite, dark" 10707
"mesquite, gray-dusty dry-scraggly" 1647
"mesquite beans from goat shit, didn't know" 7871
"mesquite leafed out, after the" 7397
"mesquite sucked deep into the desert soil" 888
"mesquites of Mexico" 6968
"mess, everything was a" 2125
"mess, headquarters'" 3863
"mess, plan to stay out of this" 6946
"mess we live in, the" 5296
"message, leaves a" 1094
"message, seemed the main" 2634
"message, sending a" 6004
"message, tires are beating out a" 6016
"message, warning" 884
"message came through, when the" 6010
"message came to me" 6000
"message for me to come see him later in the library" 6014
"message for you, I have an important" 6012
"message from Jesus, the minute I got the" 6011
"message of encouragement to men" 723
"message on the bulletin board" 6017
"message sent direct to him" 3339
"message tucked in his gauntlet" 6009
Messages 228, 884, 1094, 1118, 1122, 1761, 1942, 2570, 2634, 3339, 3741, 6970, 7555, 9296, 10034, 10541

"messages, telephone" 1122
"messages in the street, sometimes I left" 6015
"messages of woe and protest, unmistakable" 10234
"messenger, he was a" 6321
"messengers, angelic" 2623
"messenger's arrival" 6334
"messengers who traveled between heaven and earth" 2623
Messiahs 2631
"messuages" 6266
"met, boy and the girl have never" 5882
"met, each person he" 7956
"met, I first" 5797, 5838, 6763
"met, man he never" 5989
"met, people I have" 7384
"met, the morning we" 7751
"met, they" 5813, 5847
"met, they sometimes" 5836
"met, we" 5819
"met, well" 3812
"met, when we" 5865
"met a beautiful woman" 6650
"met a beggar" 7539
"met a Mahatma, not many people have" 5792
"met a man who wanted to know her real name" 8024
"met a nicens little boy named baby tuckoo" 961
"met a woman, I" 8027
"met again as men" 3999
"met Alan Hurst, I first" 8657
"met at the All India Medical Arts Institute" 6728
"met Auntie Sue, the first time I" 5795
"met by chance" 5789, 9096
"met Byron Jaynes, the first time I" 5842
"met cows, when she" 4153
"met Davie, I first" 497
"met Dean, first" 5811
"met Dunky Aldridge" 1233
"met each other at an office party" 7742
"met Foley Menutis, she" 5861
"met for the first time" 5821
"met her, I" 4576, 5807
"met her, I first" 5803, 5845, 5877
"met her at twilight" 5859
"met her for the first time" 5805
"met her in a bar, I" 5868
"met her in the hall" 8204
"met him" 5823
"met him almost immediately after I gave up my country identity" 5790
"met him at the station" 10032
"met in Boston" 2648
"met in London briefly" 5839
"met in the hospital" 3923
"met Jack Kennedy, I" 5818

"met James, Flora" 5852
"met Maria, I" 5869
"met Mildred Howell, the day before I" 6455
"met on country roads" 5836
"met only because" 5864
"met outside an abortion clinic" 5879
"met Psin at the door" 4677
"met Rose, when I first" 5816
"met the boy" 5808, 5880
"met the first of my three or four successive wives" 5829
"met the man with no chin" 5809
"met them, I" 5802
"met them, when I first" 5872
"met to discuss the earth" 3977
"met uptown, one of the first people I" 4595
"metal on concrete" 8797
"metal on metal, like" 1545
"metamorphosis I have gone through" 1246
"metaphysical conjectures" 6903
"metaphysical law" 6906
Metaphysics 6903, 6906
Metcalf, Dr. 3583
"meteor showers that streaked the Caribbean sky" 8491
"meteoric apparition" 9113
"meteorological officers" 9073
"methinks she is the harder to me" 5397
"method, traditional keyhole" 8903
"Methodism, Southern" 1540
"Methodist church" 3604, 5753
"Methodist minister" 1540
Methods 5058, 7502, 8903
"methods, Christian" 7502
Methuen 4317
"meticulous survey" 5716
"metropolis, all over the seaport" 1407
"metropolis, the" 6603
"metropolis of idiocy" 1378
"Metropolisville" 7371
"Meurthe, district of" 3024
"Mews, Britannia" 3120
"mews, intesected by" 6267
"Mexican actress" 6652
"Mexican coast" 8054
"Mexican crew leader" 1321
"Mexican December, sunshine of" 1398
"Mexican star, tempestuous" 3126
"Mexican sun, brutal" 10883
"Mexican trader, short and slender" 8852
"Mexicana plane" 4580
Mexico 4505
"Mexico" 4893, 6344, 6965, 6968, 7800, 9648
"Mexico, City of" 2731
"Mexico, go to" 5748
"Mexico, Gulf of" 7232, 7927

"Mexico, history of" 4505
"Mexico, I had been sent to" 6210
"Mexico, spend their lives in" 5609
"Mexico City" 7259, 8911
Meyer, Daisy 8927
Meyerson 6444
"Miami" 159, 2609, 4945
"Miami Beach" 2062
"Miami Florida" 9027
"miasma of their hideous parasite growth" 324
"miasma of unspoken criticism and disparagement" 385
"miasma rose from the swamps" 7707
Mice 418, 1017
"mice, no more" 1017
"mice, scurrying of" 7712
"mice, white" 7050
Michael 11, 255, 406, 1216, 6190, 7051
Michael, Black 5082
Michaeljohn, David Alexander 5089
"Michaelmas term" 7336
"Michaelmas Term" 8339
Michel, Louise 10837
"Michelangelo's 'Creation of the World'" 515
Michelson, Gabriel 1699
"Michigan" 1390, 3423
"Michigan road" 3074
Mick 986
Mickelsson, Peter 5292
Mickey 3013, 6942, 10024
Mickey Mouse 9484
"Mickey Mouse, her nearby" 9484
"Mickey Walker's" 2896
"microphone of a radio station" 6838
"microphones" 8859
"microscope, battered" 4122
"microscope, man with a" 519
"Mictlán hills" 4893
"Midbranch, farm of" 3069
"middle, a" 5694
"middle age" 3214
"middle age, not really much past" 79
"middle age, now that I have come to" 3495
"Middle Ages" 10642
"middle class" 6141
"middle class, town of the" 8971
"middle of the night" 10265
"Middle West" 1360, 1821, 1965
"middle-aged" 6980
"middle-aged, barely" 6427
"middle-aged but still charming" 3552
"middle-aged children" 6545
"middle-aged Scot" 7918
"middle-aged stranger" 9096
"Middleburg West Virginia" 3586
"Middlehope Pennsylvania" 10193

"Middleman" 9201
Middleton, Gerald 2507
Middleton, Jennie 10648
Middleton, Lavinia 8215
"mid-forties, in her" 4611
"midges began their last dance of the day" 5314
"midges terrible" 4690
"midges were dancing over the water" 4952
"midges were out" 4959
"Midland country, we were both from the" 9096
"Midlands, pastures of the" 4871
"mid-life women" 10844
Midnight 2248, 2259, 4103, 8392, 8433
"midnight" 655, 2377, 4309
"midnight, after" 2955
"midnight, at" 3984, 8433
"midnight, final bold stroke of" 6577
"midnight, honeysuckle" 3402
"midnight, it was" 7293
"midnight, it was just about" 1635
"midnight, it was past" 2248
"midnight, it's" 2259
"midnight, just before" 3257
"midnight, nearly" 1584
"midnight, on that" 4928
"midnight, past" 8489
"midnight, shortly after" 1600
"midnight, shortly before" 10662
"midnight, ten minutes to" 2246
"midnight, toward" 10931
"midnight, two hours after" 7797
"midnight, whistles were tooting" 2968
"midnight, working at" 6856
"midnight adventures" 7712
"midnight and dawn, between" 2364
"midnight and dawn, sometime between" 10312
"midnight boat ride" 6578
"midnight had struck" 9330
"Midnight Mass" 1541
"midnight of a winter month" 10113
"midnight on the thirteenth day of this month" 4103
"midnight shoutings, shrill" 10981
"midnight visitation" 9008
"midnight without darkness [and] without stars" 8392
"midnight yesterday" 5588
"midocean" 6062
"mid-season form" 4349
"midshipman" 928
"midshipman's jacket" 8642
"midst, in its" 1425
"midstream, halted in" 4535
"Midtown New York" 6274
"midway, on the" 8861
"Midwest, the whole" 9072
"midwife" 7077, 7100

"Mid-Wife" 7055
"midwife, excellent" 6492
"midwife from three miles away" 7063
"midwife was a portly Frenchwoman" 4300
"midwife's boisterous bawdy encouragement" 7102
"midwife's hands" 832
"mien, haughty" 675
"mien, imperious" 5571
"mighty" 5015
"mighty, not to be" 250
"mighty and ineffectual William Dorrit" 10341
"mighty of chest and shoulder" 412
Mignon 2101
"mignonette" 8508
"migrated from England" 361
"migration, birds returning in" 9426
"migrations, one of the most gratuitous and contemptible" 6141
"migratory workers" 25
"MIGs, shot down my sixth and seventh" 8656
Mike 211
"Milan" 9659
"Milan was an imperial capital" 1447
"mildew, grey streaks of" 5317
Mildred 8222
"mile after mile" 7625
Miles 8935
Miles, General 8650
Miles, Uncle 7677
"miles, fifteen" 9573
"miles, for the past 450" 10912
"miles, it was about 160" 5720
"miles, it's about thirty" 2967
"miles, New Zealand" 10535
"miles, one hundred" 6603
"miles, one hundred and fifty" 6155
"miles, six million million" 6905
"miles, ten more hard" 10452
"miles, three hundred" 9180
"miles an hour, cut their speed to seven hundred" 683
"miles an hour, two hundred" 4563
"miles away, when they were a thousand" 683
"miles high, hundreds of" 9585
"miles north by east, that many" 7907
"miles per hour, at sixty" 3666
"miles were draining away" 2996
Military 204, 210, 212, 219, 230, 364, 486, 713, 928, 940, 941, 1529, 1646, 1677, 1757, 2024, 2026, 2474, 2571, 2936, 3266, 3486, 3676, 4313, 4590, 4601, 4616, 4803, 5537, 6441, 6502, 6733, 6773, 6805, 6866, 6881, 7246, 7322, 7894, 8137, 8172, 8641, 8642, 8644, 8645, 8646, 8648, 8649, 8650, 8651, 8654,

8655, 8657, 8661, 8662, 8664, 8667, 8669, 8670, 8671, 8672, 8673, 8674, 8675, 8677, 8678, 8679, 8680, 8681, 8682, 8683, 8684, 8685, 8687, 8690, 8692, 8694, 8695, 8697, 8700, 8701, 8702, 8704, 8707, 8708, 8713, 8745, 9245, 9262, 9303, 9929, 10034, 10297, 10465, 10466, 10469, 10470, 10483, 10486, 10491, 10498, 10500, 10502, 10503, 10506, 10514, 10515, 10533, 10535, 10779
"military authority" 8709
"military authority, defiance of" 4616
"military genius" 7901
"military officers, a host of dreadful" 8642
"Military Staff, General of the" 2364
"milk, crying over spilled" 6929
"milk, half-pint bottles of" 5928
"milk, his mother's" 6823
"milk, pale as pure" 10774
"milk, ran out of" 9736
"milk, small carton of" 4285
"milk can, the empty Carnation evaporated" 3849
"milk that he drank every evening, the hot" 10919
"milkmaid, espouse the" 7708
"milkmen" 8813
"Milky Way" 529
Mill, Graham 6006
"mill, cotton" 1386
"Mill, Dawn's" 5139
"mill, derelict" 5155
"mill, over a hundred degrees in the" 4426
"mill, stone" 9520
"mill, textile" 10838
"Mill, the" 1014
"mill was on the bank of the Rhine" 4760
Millard, Charles 5890
"milleniums, weighed down by" 9503
Miller 7793
Miller, Butch 7895
Miller, Captain Bill 942
Miller, Max 691
Miller, Miss 6817
Miller, Warren 3619
"miller, the" 4760
"miller and money-master" 3083
Millie 1991
Millinder, Grandpa 3148
Millington, Miss 8179
"million heartbeats" 8814
"million men" 5138
"million waves" 7921
"millionaire, as brash nervous and noisy as its newest" 1420
"millionaire, certain that I would be a" 10550

"millionaire, self-made-" 4242
"millionaire, widow and" 10782
"millionaires" 243
"millionaires, become" 7000
"millionaires, criminal" 286
"Millionaires, Playground of" 8317
"millionaires, shower of" 4660
"millionaires, within spitting distance of" 10560
"millions, it happens to" 133
"millions, stole" 2023
"millions, the" 1298
"millions along the Western Front" 8678
"millpond, gloom of the" 402
Mills, Pauline 699
"Mills, Cutter Brothers" 9955
"mills, two textile" 1038
"mills springing up" 4760
"Millsburgh" 1014
"Millville" 1057
Milo 2765
Milos 1732
"Milton" 6423
Milvain, Jasper 7180
"Milwaukee" 3023
"mime" 5659
"mimeograph machine, the damn" 5683
"mimic, Creator had meant to" 5178
"mimicry, entice him into" 8746
Min 3622
Mina 10510
"mincemeat out of her, they could make" 389
"minces the few words at its disposal" 3423
Mind 220, 5270
"mind, Ann's" 10967
"mind, anxiety of" 8477
"mind, back of his" 9418
"mind, broke the surface of his" 10202
"mind, Captain Davidson's" 7407
"mind, changed my" 5437
"mind, dispirited in" 10845
"mind, don't" 9923
"mind, entirely of the" 1429
"mind, firm in my" 3656
"mind, friendly" 6307
"mind, fringe of Mrs. Vardoe's" 9426
"mind, have you gone and lost your" 4949
"mind, her" 10220
"mind, his current state of" 8568
"mind, I paid it no" 7337
"mind, if I am out of my" 4939
"mind, image of the" 220
"mind, in" 3683
"mind, in her" 6016
"mind, in his" 7411
"mind, in my" 9446
"mind, last thing on my" 6747
"mind, lingering in his" 10285

"mind, lost her" 2018
"mind, made up my" 2305, 6790
"mind, Mr. Melton's" 9416
"mind, most vital precincts of the" 7373
"mind, my" 685, 9431
"mind, numbness of his" 9454
"mind, occupying his" 10352
"mind, open" 5270
"mind, opened his contemptuous American" 4928
"mind, out of his" 7012
"mind, out of my" 9300
"mind, peculiar disturbance of my" 8856
"mind, perplexity of" 10110
"mind, possessed my" 8494
"mind, presents itself to my" 4533
"mind, privacy of my" 5424
"mind, private state of" 9280
"mind, project themselves upon the" 3491
"mind, public" 3476
"mind, restless in your" 743
"mind, seem also to be of the" 1429
"mind, she changed her" 4970
"mind, shut his" 10171
"mind, state of" 2673
"mind, surface in his" 390
"mind, teasing my" 7386
"mind, threads of adventure snarled in his" 10051
"mind, time and landscape of the" 5027
"mind, turning over in my" 6625
"mind, unfurl in my" 8488
"mind, very cast of his" 6604
"mind, went through his" 9430
"mind, what was on her" 7600
"mind, who in his right" 7974
"mind, wondering" 4101
"mind, you're out of your" 875
"mind at all, didn't" 1988
"mind awash with schemes" 4577
"mind cannot divide what it sees from what it invents" 1429
"mind could do such things" 9448
"mind crammed with the photographic clarity of insomnia" 8480
"mind didn't register" 685
"mind drifting into an unexpected mood" 7009
"mind has its motions" 10131
"mind he ran, in his" 9463
"mind it at all, I didn't" 7767
"mind limber up, let his" 1213
"mind of Luther L. (L for LeRoy) Fliegler" 5619
"mind of Pete Hallam, endured in the" 7894
"mind off yourself in this work, let your" 5445
"mind or body, in" 7434
"mind over matter" 3325
"mind stuck, his" 8180

"mind to the game, not giving her" 312
"mind used to run, tracks in which my" 7400
"mind was as clear as a bell" 119
"mind was filled with the certainty of failure" 3521
"mind was up front with the driver, my" 9428
"mind would keep going back to Mercator Island" 5021
"minded, had she been so" 8342
"minded, single-" 9453
"minded what they were about" 6604
"minding her own business" 2640
Minds 119, 1429, 5619, 7373, 9428, 9448
"minds, mediocre" 7368
"minds, our" 7516
"minds, their own subconscious" 5512
"mind's eye" 5709
"minds of both government and the majority of its public" 7003
"minds of the War Gods" 2621
"mind's reach, beyond the" 528
"Mine, Echo" 6062
"mine, ruby" 7950
"mine whistles" 2968
"mine-dumps, they are" 1420
Miner, Miss 9863
"miner, she isn't a" 10348
"miner, young coal" 497
"miners" 8813, 10348
"Minervois was a desert" 5165
"mingled but never mixed" 1362
"mingled with the jangle of iron" 8776
"mingling of twin elements" 8412
Mingolla 230
"miniature airplane" 6882
"miniature is a sugarplum, a good" 323
"Minimoke, Austin" 3006
Mining 1018, 2601, 8052
"mining center, small" 3407
"mining country" 4131
"mining interests" 8052
"minister, Christian" 1520
"minister, father was a Methodist" 1540
"Minister of Affairs" 8859
"minister of Dalmailing" 1483
"Minister of State" 6255
"minister of the Baptist Chapel" 1518
"minister of the gospel" 1533
"minister who was to marry them" 10644
"ministering sympathetically to the desires of the moment" 3821
"Ministers, rogues for" 3376
"ministrations, in spite of her frenzied" 5372

"Ministry of Petroleum" 7481
"Minneapolis" 1741
"Minnesota" 2594
Minou 7485
"Minstrels, Tiny Cleveland's" 331
"minstrels' gallery" 1180
"minute, first fresh" 5260
"minute, marking the precise" 2335
"minute is known, the" 9001
"Minuteman war stamps" 10517
"minutes, I've got a few" 3622
"minutes, one of those" 3499
"minutes swam by like sharks" 9489
"minutes that are not reckoned as time" 3499
Mira 4480
"miracle, age of" 7506
"miracle, little less than a" 4104
"miracle, nothing short of a" 269, 1246
"miracle happened" 6778, 7785
"miracle of blue sky" 7289
"miracle of chance, that dark" 1221
"miracle of reproduction" 5699
Miracles 1246, 1429, 4104, 5213, 5699, 6124, 6778, 7506, 7785
"miracles, homemade" 1429
"miracles, windows with their" 1302
"miracles of modern science" 5699
"miracles were as common as fruit pies" 5213
"miraculous, wasn't it" 2524
"miraculously" 6124
"mirage, ever-changing" 4410
"mirages of creeks and ditches" 2977
"Miramar, castle of" 8106
Miranda 5219
"mire, black oozy" 5170
"mire of penury and disrepute" 3557
Mireille 7487
Miriam 622, 8507, 8850, 9406, 9409, 9878
"mirror, antique Chinese" 7489
"mirror, before the" 7470
"mirror, cracked" 5325
"mirror, dresser" 4263
"mirror, drop of ink for a" 4492
"mirror, full-length" 7477, 7480
"mirror, gilt-framed" 7476
"mirror, herself in a" 7468
"mirror, it's all in the" 7488
"mirror, looking in the" 7482
"mirror, moved a little back from the" 7473
"mirror, my" 6304
"mirror, on the" 5500
"mirror, partly fogged up" 7485
"mirror, peered into the" 2399
"mirror, polished silver" 855
"mirror, rear-view" 1668
"mirror, reflection in the" 7487
"mirror, staring into her" 7483
"mirror, stood before a" 7479

"mirror, turned from the" 7475
"mirror, went to the" 7488
"mirror and a razor lay crossed" 8041
"mirror fell off the wall" 10227
"mirror of a majesty" 10033
"mirror of her mother's vanity" 7482
"mirror of the second-floor bedroom" 498
"mirror reflected, the" 7472
"mirror to the mouth, hold a" 2439
Mirrors 855, 2399, 2879, 4263, 4492, 4792, 4921, 5500, 6304, 7468, 7469, 7470, 7472, 7473, 7475, 7476, 7477, 7478, 7479, 7480, 7481, 7482, 7483, 7484, 7485, 7486, 7487, 7488, 7489, 7490, 8041, 9325
"mirrors, ball of" 2118
"mirrors, huge" 7481
"mirrors, round customer" 7490
"mirrors, walls were" 4309
"mirrors of a patch of sky fenced in by moss-hung trees" 5069
"mirrors of the Zodiac Room" 7481
"mirrors were wonderful" 7484
"misadventure" 7731
"misadventure, stranded there by" 5027
"misalliance, fruit of a" 3552
"miscalculation, suckered by" 3971
Mischief 445, 2175, 4244, 7527, 9003, 10770
"mischief, toward some private" 7527
"mischief done in this world" 10770
"mischievous reports" 3476
"mischievously, smiled" 2025
"misconceptions corrected" 9420
Miscreants 540, 640, 951, 1004, 2014, 2020, 2030, 2033, 2034, 2578, 4146, 4159, 4249, 6198, 6453, 6614, 7898, 7984, 8046, 9309
Misdeeds 1805, 1806, 1818, 1967, 2025, 3364, 4244, 4261, 5914, 6517, 7183, 7496, 7500
"miser, meanest" 3376
"miserable, as he always does when he is" 7628
"miserably" 1984
"miserably, clutching" 55
"misering his sperms" 7990
Misery 1616, 5583, 7033
"misery, everlasting" 10766
"misery, full of" 5583
"misery, huddling in her" 5026
"misery of leaving" 1616
"misfit District Commissioners" 1833
Misfortune 6612, 9432
"misfortune" 3371
"misfortune, Adam Appleby's" 9432
"misfortune, I suffered a great" 2021

"misfortune, incompleteness of my" 4503

"misfortune, my" 5371

"misfortune, subjecting them to the greatest" 6612

"misfortune, to add to the" 8838

"misfortune it is to be born a woman" 10766

"misfortune was aggravated greatly" 6612

"misgiving, never begun a novel with more" 5425

"misgivings, grave" 10844

"misgivings, great" 9657

Misha 4853

"misinformation, gave me more" 5229

"misleading, perhaps" 6416

"misled her for so long" 5239

"misnomer, curiously complicated" 10899

"miss, we couldn't" 7750

"miss anything, anxious not to" 9616

"miss Eddie the most" 3321

"miss him, afraid she would" 3703

"miss it, right where I couldn't" 6360

"miss the seven rivers, I will" 7704

"miss Uncle Percy, I still" 3322

"miss you, I" 5670

"miss you in my heart" 2541

"missed ever since" 2145

"missed him from two inches away" 34

"missed the Sunday dinner" 9423

"missed yet another day of summer" 2172

"missiles for our battles in the park" 10534

"missing, May is" 2577

"missing for some four months" 2581

"missing it, fear of" 3709

"missing Lionel Cholmley" 3302

"missing person, commonest kind of" 2565

"mission" 10167

"Mission, Carmelo" 7508

"mission, man with a" 259

"mission had been made clear to me" 3332

"mission to the Allies, a secret" 2315

"mission which still stands" 3089

"missionaries" 3901

"missionaries from France had been captured and tortured" 9853

"missionary" 10348

"missionary murdered in Burundi" 6735

Missions 259, 3332, 6002, 10167

"Mississippi" 1481, 1531, 3597, 4042, 4066, 4544, 6824, 8005

"Mississippi, followed the" 3730

"Mississippi, the" 4140, 8096

"Mississippi, the Missouri side of the" 1349

"Mississippi, three mouths of the" 7923

"Mississippi Delta" 3157

"Mississippi [River]" 7691

"Mississippi sun" 4429

"*mississippis*, counting" 9088

"Missouri" 182, 4486, 6136, 8852

"Missouri, the" 4610, 7666

"Missouri, University of" 7890

"Missouri side of the Mississippi" 1349

"Missourian, tall lanky" 8852

Mist 2105, 2223, 2246, 4053, 4105, 5172, 8037, 10628

"mist, autumnal" 2223

"mist, cloaking [the hills] in" 10577

"mist, clouds of" 7322

"mist, fine river" 2246

"mist, frigid" 2105

"mist, heavy morning" 10352

"mist, heavy overnight" 5172

"mist, in the" 8037

"mist, line of" 10628

"mist, lost in" 6065

"mist, March" 7457

"mist, morning" 8264

"mist, soft" 5088

"mist, thin" 9195

"mist, warm close" 1356

"mist and drizzle of rain" 7316

"mist and haze" 2188

"mist creep up the mountains" 7289

"mist in the morning" 4105

"mist lying in the market square" 2246

"mist of early morning, the grey" 8652

"mist of mingled human breath and acrid vapour" 1356

"mist of pleasant confusion" 116

"mist of sleep" 10158

"mist pours off the Black Mountains" 7149

"mist that tenderly covered the dirty streets" 10352

"mist was already creeping" 2223

"mist was creeping" 5088

"mistake, certain that it is no" 7086

"mistake, going back was a" 6029

"mistake, it began as a" 6025

"mistake, make sure there's no" 9825

"mistake, nurse made a" 4614

"mistake, she was making a great" 6019

"mistake, silly" 6022

"mistake, their little five-month old" 6026

"mistake, wasn't going to end up making Daniel's" 6030

"mistake this time, no" 2601

"mistaken, could Ninian have been" 9329

"mistaken, if I am not" 9701

"mistaken, my views" 10998

"mistaken for a boy of middle growth" 10833

"mistaken for a tramp" 7215

"mistaken for twins" 8233

Mistakes 264, 1138, 2895, 4490, 7565, 9329, 9704, 10765

"mistakes, subject to" 4490

"mistakes in this letter" 6023

"mistakes of his elders" 9704

"mistakes of Providence" 6020

"mistakes the sex are sometimes guilty of" 10765

Mister 4352

"mistress, for the sake of a youthful" 7714

"mistress, his" 9420

"mistress, the" 8476

"mistress dwelled, where his" 1668

"mistress of herself and of ten thousand a year" 10767

"Mistress of the Robes" 127

"mistress of three years' standing" 6026

"mistrust symmetry, I have learned to" 2741

"mists come down" 4053

"Mitsubishi Zero-1 medium bomber" 219

"misty sheen hung over the rice fields" 7908

Misunderstanding 6585, 6721

"misunderstood by friends who know me for my objectivity and detachment" 5496

Mitchell, Dan 6951

Mitchell, Daniel 1194

Mitchell, Joan 301

Mitchell, Valerie 6203

"mitre, heavy stone" 8937

"mixed up in, get" 3054

"mixer, college" 5857

"mixture, dip" 7052

"mixture, unusual" 4079

"mixture of good round coal and spluttering dry wood" 10678

"mixture of the unmixable, she was a" 409

Mixup, Mary 6652

"mixup of her baby and another baby boy" 6542

"m'lady, you must call me" 4787

"Moab" 2237

"moan aloud with rage" 3344

"moan out loud" 8736

"moaned slightly, she could have" 147

"moaning a tuneless funeral croon" 2084

"moaning of new ice" 10574

"moat, digging a" 1180

"Moat, the" 4058

"Moat House, Tunstall" 647

"mob, sounds like a" 8767

"mob of armed fugitives" 10509
"mobile, downwardly" 77
Mobs 8767, 10509
"moccasins, scuffed brown" 4154
"mockery" 2767
"mockery, brief" 9468
"mockery, merry" 4936
"mockery of his high office, making a" 7000
"mockingly" 3237
"model, slim like a" 5970
"model be handled carefully, may the" 1030
"model of the year" 9786
"model railway" 325
Models 325, 1030
"models, like" 8117
"models were already out, the 1960" 9786
"modern decadence" 6427
"modern life" 5291
"modern times" 10033
"modest Kilneagh" 3215
"modest nature, his" 5457
Modestus 6110
"modify what he is, they can only" 9704
"modish dresses" 1302
"modulated, his husky voice was" 7132
"mogul, California real estate" 10559
"Mogul, high edge of" 10694
"Mogul Empire, Akbar's" 9185
"moguls, private" 6763
"Mohammedan" 203
"Mohawk, half" 7187
"Mohawk, tributary of the" 370
"moiety I should say" 1042
Moinous 9029
Moira 4363
"moisture, saturated with" 177
Moke 2123
Molar, Marvin 4793
"moldered by memories" 4936
"molds over my breast, where it" 8500
Mole, The 401
"mole, lived like a" 5287
"mole of Dun Laoghaire Harbor" 8660
Mollie 6094
Molly 132, 211, 2007, 2074, 2455, 2670, 7493
Moloch, Dion 10463
Mom 634, 2100, 4937, 6209, 6547, 7947, 8380
"mom, they say my" 5218
"mom, Tristan's" 1151
"mom and dad" 10975
"Mom was a world of her own" 10873
"Mom's legs, the tent of" 8380
"mom's sleeve, tugged at his" 6709
"moment" 633

"moment, at any" 977
"moment, at that particular" 1978
"moment, at the same" 1613
"moment, at this very" 807
"moment, critical" 6765
"moment, for one brilliant" 2209
"moment, innocent" 6899
"moment, pinpoint the actual" 5092
"moment, the" 3288
"moment, there hung a brutal" 5124
"moment, there was always a" 5050
"moment, this" 1829
"moment, you must give me a" 9405
"moment at which to begin his novel" 5414
"moment by moment" 2189
"moment had come, the" 1108
"moment he opened his cabin door" 7025
"moment I grew suddenly old, in one" 5096
"moment is followed by another, as though one" 10290
"moment is recorded, the exact" 9001
"moment of Andy Farmer's life, the greatest" 5112
"moment of experience" 8989
"moment of puzzled hesitation" 5408
"moment of rage and frustration" 5292
"moment that . . . altered everything that was to come" 5124
"moment . . . that changed what had been" 5124
"moment that was simple" 5124
"moment was strange" 4320
"moment was to stand out forever" 5101
"moment when I came out" 8789
"moment when she set her right foot down, precisely at the" 1250
"moment you come in" 1094
"momentous, something" 10083
"momentous day" 2158
"momentous day of my life, the most" 5081
"momentous mid-October afternoon" 10339
Moments 685, 1108, 1250, 1829, 2562, 4320, 4804, 5050, 5092, 5096, 5097, 5101, 5111, 5112, 5124, 5238, 5575, 5584, 6322, 8989, 10996
"moments, a few spare" 6229
"moments, at this most delicate and intimate of" 5238
"moments, at this most significant of" 5238
"moments, her dear mamma's last" 8838
"moments, it was one of those" 5097

"moments, many" 10038
"moments, only a few" 9631
"moments, only the young have such" 10996
"moments, safe and secure" 3602
"moments, there are" 5575
"moments, there were" 9325
"moments after the girl came, for some" 8180
"moments during the recent proceedings" 3341
"moments made sense, only these" 4804
"moments of my life, all the great" 5584
"momentum, grinding heavy" 7249
Momma 4437, 7899
"Momma" 9372
Mommy 552, 7213, 9980
Mona 4000
Mona, Um 2163
Monahan, Silky 1130
"Monarch, this famous rising" 10464
Monce, Madame 10792
Mond, Daniel 7572
Mondor, Christiane 7719
Mondragón, Joe 6040
Money 238, 866, 872, 1052, 1084, 1354, 2023, 2067, 2068, 2527, 2684, 2735, 3037, 3389, 3737, 3738, 3740, 3743, 3745, 3746, 3747, 3748, 3749, 3750, 3752, 3754, 3755, 3757, 3950, 3971, 4928, 4930, 5094, 5225, 5453, 6464, 7039, 7348, 7891, 7977, 8210, 8661, 9593, 10011, 10858
"money" 6666, 10011
"money, a little" 5934
"money, a lot of" 2527
"money, all persons are welcome for their" 5385
"money, always hustling for" 2068
"money, bag of" 3737
"money, better than" 7043
"money, careful about" 866
"money, cost somebody some" 1400
"money, four dollars in" 9525
"money, great deal of" 10561
"money, how I got the" 5094
"money, how I spent the" 5225
"money, I was left enough" 4930
"money, insurance" 2863
"money, losing" 77
"money, love and" 3389
"money, newly minted" 7229
"money, no" 7041, 7977
"money, no better use for his" 7891
"money, pockets full of" 8210
"money, run away with the" 2735
"money, she has no" 10834
"money, stack of" 3743
"money, stole the gangster's" 2684
"money, time and" 1030
"money, we should need" 3746

"money, without asking for" 1167
"money available to leave with" 5748
"money got gone, before the" 3604
"money is, that is where the" 1084
"money is a leading character in this tale" 3747
"money is racked" 872
"money is the fount of all modern romantic adventure" 1354
"money or for love, did they do it for the" 2067
"money or leisure" 10768
"money smuggled into his head" 2765
"money spinners" 5453
"money they've got, how much bleeding" 8661
"money through the steel bars, receiving" 1048
"money to beggars, giving all his" 7039
"money to buy any" 3750
"money to run out" 3037
"money to see me through a small college in Ohio" 4930
"money to the square yard, more" 1354
"money was not replaced" 2581
"money which he didn't want to spend" 10561
"money's worth, not getting my" 7771
"moneylenders, in the quarter inhabited by" 5822
"money-master" 3083
"Mongols" 6109
"Mongols, who were the" 2093
"mongrel, old red" 7440
"mongrelized neo-capitalist puppet states" 6256
Monica 639
Monika 2542
"monitor strung up over the museum entrance" 8316
"monk, young" 1485
"monk's cowl" 142
"monkey, tattered" 9729
"monkey, you look like a" 852
"monkey on the end of a leash held by a Jaycee" 9729
"Monkey Nest coal mine" 1018
"monkeys in the jungle, listened to" 8703
"Monkey-Ward catalogue" 2835
"monks, Benedictine" 7888
"monks, the" 6862
"Monks Ford" 248
"Monkshaven, town called" 1338
"monocle, man with the" 6173
"monograms on the doors, gilt" 2960
"monologues, there are intersecting" 8855
"monopoly in ferriage" 1009

"monotone, the same high nasal" 10005
"monotony of tiresome iteration, relief from the" 3075
"monotony without, the" 5129
Monroe 1784
Monsanto, Lorenz 2906
"monsoon rain, black wall of" 10533
"monsters, these composite" 3589
"monstrosities, rilled and ridged" 6075
"monstrosity, a brown shingle-board" 3184
"monstrous dwarf" 6647
"monstrous enough to greet our predicament" 3372
Mont, Fleur 7378
Mont, Sir Lawrence 10339
Montalto, Maria 10783
Montana 5160
"Montana" 1468
"Montana landscape is always startling" 5160
"Montarac City" 5799
"Montauk Highway" 9199
"Montauk Lighthouse" 9247
"Monte Motterone" 5127
"Monte Paradiso" 3879
"Monte Smith" 4618
"Montego Bay" 9012
Montenotte 363
"Monterey" 6272, 10492
Monthor, Charles 6433
Montgomery, Andre Ezekiel Preston 4806
Montgomery, Kitty 7490
Montgomery, Lady Mary 9868
"month, April is the cruellest" 8615
"month, buxom" 10109
"month, maligned" 10567
"month for boys, a rare" 978
"month of laughter among people" 10587
"month of summer's promise" 10587
"month of the May dance and revels" 10587
Months 978, 9482, 9494, 10587, 10625, 10983
"months, few climactic" 5592
"months, for nearly three" 5027
"Montmartre" 491, 1250
Montmorency 3990
"Montparnasse" 5673
"Montreal" 9203, 10935
"Montréal" 2555
"Montreal, along the entire river front of" 2191
"Montreal, living in" 6149
"Montreal, that summer in" 10583
"Montreal, when I leave for" 254
Montreville, Laura 6555
"Monument" 1858
"monument, Confederate" 9775
"Monument Massachusetts" 9600
Monuments 6646, 8311

"monuments" 1342, 6661
"moocow coming down along the road" 961
"mood, an unexpected" 7009
"mood, her" 1250
"mood, in a burning" 3314
"mood, in a gray" 2498
"mood, in no" 5090
"mood, in the" 9365
"mood, in the grip of a prodigal" 1086
"mood, no hospitable" 9864
"mood, rainstorm that matched his" 3315
"mood for, *who* you're in the" 9365
"mood hits you" 3622
"mood of the sea, the changing" 5015
Moods 2498, 3315, 5090, 7009
"moods, execrable" 6315
"moods, in darker" 3678
"Moody" 7098
Moon, the brothers 1756
Moon 530, 538, 539, 2176, 2979, 4551, 5063, 6042, 7293, 7640, 8020, 8389, 8391, 8415, 8418, 8419, 8420, 8423, 8425, 8428, 8436, 8439, 8442, 8448, 8450, 8452, 8619, 9582, 9733, 9789
"moon, a half" 2176
"moon, daylight" 10614
"moon, devil" 10240
"Moon, Eagle" 407
"moon, fishy piece of" 9789
"moon, full" 4956, 8448
"moon, full African" 8391
"moon, I watched the" 8020
"moon, it was an old" 8418
"moon, it was nearly full" 6363
"moon, last quarter" 6384
"moon, melon-slice of" 9582
"moon, on accounta it was a full" 6042
"moon, our timekeeper the" 10822
"moon, pictures of the" 539
"moon, railroad track set for the" 4635
"moon, she had to come from the" 4551
"moon, signs of the new" 530
"moon, steps on the" 9733
"moon, sun fell in love with the" 9010
"Moon, the Hunter's" 8425
"moon, there was no" 6942
"moon, thick red" 8452
"moon, took off for the" 5630
"moon, trip to the" 9040
"moon, walked on the" 538
"moon, wet full" 2979
"moon coming full, under a" 7640
"moon had still not left the world" 8423
"moon hangs low in the cloudless sky" 8448

"moon is gone" 8420
"moon lofted off the horizon" 8436
"moon lover" 5063
"moon of another and more conspicuous Romeo" 7293
"Moon of Fattening" 586
"moon of Maa, great" 8415
"moon of the falling leaves" 8442
"moon poured down its light" 8391
"moon red as blood" 8419
"moon sail high above the treetops"
  8450
"moon scuttled among the clouds"
  9789
"moon shone bright over a brisk
  seascape" 8439
"moon swing up slowly over the
  pines" 8452
"moon ... turned white in the
  blackening sky" 8442
"moon was already risen" 8389
"moon was full" 8619
"moonbeams, sunbeams and" 4800
"Moonday" 4282
Moondog 5880
Mooney, Terry 68
"Moonlea" 6069
Moonlight 8035, 8451, 10276
"moonlight" 8035, 10276
"moonlight, covered as by" 8586
"moonlight, fitful" 5084
"moonlight, in" 10447
"moonlight, lying below in the"
  6067
"moonlight, swathed in" 8451
"moon-men, those first" 9733
"moonrise, looked toward the" 6933
"moons, frost-rimmed" 3396
"moon's bleached skull" 8428
"moonshine whisky" 899
"Moonstone" 8908
"moonstone on her finger" 2463
"Moor, Black" 3667
"Moor, High" 1361
"Moor, Spinney" 3212
"moor, top of the" 5150
"moor, winter" 8445
"moor inland from Silloth" 7617
"Moor which swung from the
  rafters" 9839
Moore, John 10264
Moore, Patrick Dennis 2834
Moore boys 6180
"moored alongside, frigates" 8121
Moorhouse, Kevin 8286
"moorings, torn from its" 2016
"Moorish mansions" 309
"Moorish palace" 4136
"Moorish zebec" 7346
"moorlands, empty" 5147
"moorlands, mountains and" 6258
"moorlands, snow lay thick on the"
  8616
"moorlands of Yorkshire" 10391
"moot guest" 7816

"moping, what a dread they have
  of" 927
"mopped up before I can catch
  them, get it" 7984
"moppet with wild yellow hair" 4154
"mopping off the bar" 5907
Mopsy 481
"Mopu" 6111
Mor 3744
Morag 7684
Moragoda, Devar 86
"moral bankruptcy" 2023
"moral sense, behaved like a
  woman without any" 2020
"moral sneaks" 286
Morality 2023, 2738
"morally bilious" 6890
Moran 5960, 6549
Moran, Ira 3957
Moran, Maggie 3957
Morann, John 10394
Moray 10592
Moray, Captain 8172
Morcar 5095
Mordaunt, Anneke 6608
"more for me, no" 2921
"more of than anyone else" 8028
"more of that, any" 9003
"more or less" 92, 10508
"Morecambe Bay" 9101
Morell, Alice 4474
Moreno, Señora 3636
Morgan, Barnett 9303
Morgan, Francis 3436
Morgan, Major Royce 8667
Morgan, Robert Sylvester 1926
Morgana 2809
"morgue, the inside of the" 2322
"Morgue, what ... are you doing
  in this" 7107
"moribund Amtrak sleeping car"
  691
Morland, Catherine 4451
Morley, Martin 1868
"Mormons, wandering" 10924
"morn, brave the" 4683
"morn, this hot September" 4398
"mornin', good" 4211
Morning 137, 177, 727, 770, 939,
  1379, 1622, 1949, 2137, 2145,
  2168, 2171, 2183, 2193, 2201,
  2203, 2204, 2207, 2210, 2211,
  2216, 2217, 2218, 2220, 2230,
  2232, 2233, 2237, 2242, 2243,
  2244, 2245, 2249, 2250, 2260,
  2264, 2268, 2270, 2271, 2273,
  2275, 2277, 2281, 2285, 2333,
  2440, 2625, 3656, 3717, 3801,
  3807, 3890, 4211, 4212, 4213,
  4378, 4391, 4395, 4398, 4559,
  5167, 5313, 5928, 6371, 7238,
  7296, 7606, 7929, 7942, 8054,
  8393, 8409, 8423, 8438, 8462,
  8774, 8795, 8813, 9067, 9408,
  9491, 10108, 10120, 10143, 10176,

  10185, 10196, 10214, 10290,
  10294, 10411, 10592, 10637, 10708
"morning, a certain bright sunshine-
  filled Riviera" 10399
"morning, beautiful" 8049
"morning, bitter cold" 2385
"morning, bitter January" 9404
"morning, bleak wintry" 6502
"morning, bright" 1172
"morning, bright fresh summer"
  1726
"morning, bright May" 949, 10168
"morning, brilliant April" 3514
"morning, changeful April" 5083
"morning, clear bright" 6118
"morning, cold" 9226
"morning, cold spring" 7318
"morning, cool May" 10100
"morning, cool pleasant early fall"
  9889
"morning, dark wet" 9027
"morning, dewy June" 8262
"morning, dull sullen southwest-of-
  England" 9431
"morning, during the" 9427
"morning, early" 2232, 8115, 8795
"morning, early grey" 10751
"morning, early in the" 1991, 2210,
  3656, 9408
"morning, early in the cool hush of
  a June" 9759
"morning, early rays of" 9740
"morning, eight in the" 3890
"morning, eight thirty in the" 9486
"morning, every" 8046
"morning, every weekday" 9822
"morning, fair gold" 10174
"morning, feel bad in the" 2907
"morning, fine June" 1598
"morning, fine midsummer" 5335
"morning, fine Saturday" 4596
"morning, fine spring" 1912
"morning, first light of" 7547
"morning, first October" 4391
"morning, four o'clock in the" 3681
"morning, fracture Hazel's" 770
"morning, fresh springtide" 7618
"morning, good" 1414, 4212, 4213
"morning, grey mist of early" 8652
"morning, in the" 2468, 4405
"morning, in the early" 980, 1433
"morning, in the small hours of a
  blustery October" 1736
"morning, it is" 2218
"morning, it is on a windy" 2393
"morning, it was" 5167, 7929, 8367
"morning, it was a fine April" 7606
"morning, it was a glorious" 2211
"morning, it was a golden" 1554
"morning, it was early" 543, 10214
"morning, it was one o'clock in
  the" 2176
"morning, it was Sunday" 10193
"morning, it was the" 2137
"morning, it was the sort of" 2625

"morning, it was Tuesday" 10185

"morning, it was very early in the" 2270

"morning, London's purply-green" 7317

"morning, lord of the" 10682

"morning, Monday" 2233, 8462

"morning, more night than" 2285

"morning, new as" 4178

"morning, not much different from any other" 2171

"morning, on a certain cold gray" 1614

"morning, on a clear" 9754

"morning, on a golden May" 970

"morning, on a recent clear September" 1854

"morning, on that Sunday" 5121

"morning, on this Sunday" 10126

"morning, one April" 5476

"morning, one dark greasy February" 2954

"morning, one fine" 3813

"morning, one incisively sharp and blustery" 10724

"morning, one quiet" 3282

"morning, one rainy" 3465

"morning, one summer" 7731, 10310

"morning, one windy autumn" 7869

"morning, out in the early" 8610

"morning, raw autumn" 8139

"morning, seven in the" 10792

"morning, seven o'clock on Saturday" 10152

"morning, shadowless London" 2273

"morning, spring" 7887

"morning, sun-washed September" 10451

"morning, sunny July" 8381

"morning, that" 2171, 8530

"morning, that cheerless January" 6570

"morning, that fine early May" 6499

"morning, that hot September" 2082

"morning, that late spring" 3436

"morning, that long-ago midsummer" 2216

"morning, that raw Tuesday" 1106

"morning, that summer" 8927

"morning, that Sunday" 2022

"morning, that unseasonably warm spring" 5993

"morning, the" 2204

"morning, the next" 10176

"morning, the riddled" 8813

"morning, the sweet" 10875

"morning, this" 148, 3717, 3973, 4609

"morning, this autumn" 7180

"morning, this June" 10785

"morning, this summer" 8572, 10210

"morning, this Sunday" 1558

"morning, this time of the" 4329

"morning, this windy May" 3441

"morning, three o'clock in the" 8202, 10881

"morning, two o'clock in the" 151, 3669

"morning, warm and bright Saturday" 964

"morning, warm moist" 10600

"morning, wet September" 1642

"morning, what passed for the" 10637

"morning, winter's" 8393

"morning after, the" 8198

"morning after her birthday" 4177

"morning air" 177

"morning barely illumined the sky" 7547

"morning behind silver raindarts" 7317

"morning - cold and fresh" 137

"morning Dinah died was cold, the" 2440

"morning drawing within itself" 2207

"morning early in October, one" 1702

"morning ebb, the" 6179

"morning grass" 2275

"morning had brought him out" 2242

"morning had come back to him many times, that" 7408

"morning hours, early" 10088

"morning I found her dead was gray" 2333

"morning in April, this fine Saturday" 10284

"morning in early April" 2244

"morning in early May" 4475

"morning in early spring" 3578

"morning in June, a warm" 3807

"morning in June, one sunshiny" 9757

"morning in Lombardy" 2281

"morning in May, remarkably chill" 9955

"morning in November, one foggy" 1496

"morning in October, that Saturday" 10173

"morning in rural England, a matchless" 2193

"morning in succession, for the second" 566

"morning is rising in silence" 2271

"morning . . . like a knife driven suddenly into the cold strong heart of winter" 2244

"morning like this evening" 2268

"morning mist" 8264

"morning moist shining and still" 10176

"morning . . . moved in sun and shadow over the Common" 2207

"morning not to be trusted" 2277

"morning of blue and gold" 2211

"morning of my life, most terrible" 6371

"morning of the big day" 2217

"morning of warm and balmy sunshine" 2264

"Morning Post, copies of the" 4333

"Morning Post, the" 9858

"morning rose above the hills of Moab" 2237

"morning so full and clear" 1949

"Morning Star, brig" 8064

"Morning Star, the" 1600

"morning tastes bitterly" 2243

"morning to begin with, a good Monday" 7874

"morning was all blue and calm" 7325

"morning was breaking" 7238, 8054

"morning was gray" 2498

"morning was loud with birds" 9276

"morning was Roxy's good time of day" 2249

"morning was so brilliant, the autumn" 10592

"morning was so fine, the September" 10111

"morning we all remember from years ago" 2145

"morning we were together, the first" 5658

"morning when all nature shouted 'Fore!'" 2201

"morning when he got up, every" 6290

"morning wore on" 2245

"morning-glories" 1349

"mornings, it was one of those May" 2277

"mornings, one of the few sunny" 30

"mornings, one of those gilded" 4559

"mornings, Sunday" 939

"mornings, Tiusday" 4282

"mornings, winter" 2250

"mornings in the country, strange summer" 10566

"mornings slice their way into being" 2260

"mornings were still shivering cold" 2250

"morocco writing case" 717

"morosely, sat" 2497

"morosely said" 1878

"morphine saturates the lungs" 4509

Morris 10455

Morris, Barry 10163

Morris, Guido 3585

"Morris, his mother's 1924 bull-nosed" 6570

Morrison 5463
Morrison, Ben 4593
"Morristown New Jersey" 1339
Morrow, Susan 5551
"morse-code symbol" 7260
"morsel to his mouth, raised a"
    3868
"mortal, all women are" 10867
"mortal and immortal" 9062
"mortal as his own" 519
"mortal Julius" 4469
"mortal nights" 5704
"mortality, the item of" 779
"Mortar, port of" 3275
"mortar-and-pestle, scabby gilt"
    8301
"mortarboards, playing Frisbee
    with their" 3283
"mortars, eee-thud eee-thud of the"
    878
"mortgaged estates" 358
Mortimer, Rosie 3982
"Mortimer family" 2041
Morton, Mrs. 294
"mortuary, outside the" 8575
Morwenna 4296
Moryson 6385
"mosaics, peering at" 9353
Mosca, Walter 4570
Moscow 4074
"Moscow" 2516, 3449, 3920, 5971,
    7277, 8004
"Moscow, travelled to" 9578
"Moscow Amazons" 10837
"Moscow is, do you know where"
    4074
"Moscow is never" 4074
"Moscow street" 7904
"Mosel, the" 4085
Moseley 3777
Moses 1763, 9040, 10243
"Moses and the dead angels" 9040
Mosher, Emmeline 4186
"Moslem bystanders" 1565
"Mosman" 1758
"mosque, the Friday" 9135
"mosquito, killed a" 4953
"mosquito repellent in aerosol
    cans" 4073
Mosquitoes 2227, 4953, 9217
"mosquitoes" 4073
"mosquitoes, fill it with" 9217
"mosquitoes breeding a giant island
    strain" 5033
"mosquitoes swarm up like clouds
    of smoke" 2227
"moss and lichen" 8507
"mossy ground" 4962
Mostyn 7389
"motel, cheap" 4657
"Motel, Paradise" 8473
"motel, sleazy" 6783
"motel room" 4655
Motels 4648, 4655, 4657, 8473
"motels" 1039

"motels, I like" 4648
Motes, Hazel 9558
"moth, the" 4951
"moth had somehow gained en-
    trance" 4954
"moth-eaten already, rather" 5621
Mother 431, 1202, 1587, 2335,
    2868, 3515, 3623, 4221, 4722,
    6185, 6532, 6632, 6653, 6845,
    7072, 7160, 7385, 7536
"mother" 7469
"Mother" 9779
"mother, ah" 6721
"mother, back side of her" 6692
"mother, beautiful warm" 6650
"mother, beautiful young" 2079
"mother, Charley Mason's" 3471
"mother, death of his" 5085
"mother, embraced her" 4593
"mother, English" 800
"mother, Garp's" 2040
"mother, having never known a"
    6666
"mother, he never really knew his"
    6677
"Mother, Head" 4876
"mother, Hector's" 5841
"mother, helped him out of his"
    7077
"mother, her" 851, 866, 1154, 1602,
    1827, 1947, 2319, 2681, 2864,
    3081, 3521, 3631, 4301, 4354,
    4587, 4921, 6114, 6690, 6696,
    6714, 6724, 6737, 6744, 6750,
    7084, 7097, 7213, 7377, 7441,
    7482, 7555, 8475, 8838, 8854,
    9572, 9880, 10309, 10771, 10845
"mother, her four-feet-ten" 6529
"mother, her widowed" 10915
"mother, his" 28, 550, 572, 575,
    837, 854, 976, 1670, 1769, 1926,
    2345, 2704, 3071, 3279, 3533,
    3591, 3705, 3846, 4434, 4438,
    4719, 4741, 5085, 5527, 5612,
    5699, 5924, 6238, 6534, 6536,
    6553, 6629, 6636, 6639, 6652,
    6686, 6704, 6739, 6823, 7402,
    7991, 9410, 9420, 9496, 10312
"mother, his widowed" 6110
"mother, I'm pregnant" 7070
"mother, kill my" 828
"mother, killed her" 3928
"mother, loved her" 6690
"mother, Michael's" 11
"mother, my" 90, 113, 364, 633,
    807, 844, 1185, 1210, 1607, 1763,
    1845, 1846, 1884, 1967, 2441,
    2573, 2667, 2878, 3359, 3619,
    3621, 3758, 3785, 3940, 3942,
    4774, 5236, 5520, 5657, 5672,
    5680, 5769, 6169, 6297, 6476,
    6604, 6606, 6607, 6608, 6610,
    6618, 6621, 6631, 6638, 6641,
    6646, 6651, 6657, 6669, 6670,
    6688, 6694, 6695, 6700, 6706,

    6708, 6711, 6733, 6734, 6736,
    6738, 6740, 6746, 6747, 6861,
    6883, 7035, 7078, 7095, 7207,
    7385, 7533, 7542, 7863, 7932,
    8537, 8893, 8930, 9011, 9052,
    9314, 9352, 9373, 9461, 9918,
    10318, 10676, 10791, 10802, 10882
"Mother, my" 6601
"mother, my biological" 6732
"mother, my father's" 369
"mother, my indecisive" 7092
"mother, oh" 6615
"mother, Olwen Taylor's" 1100
"mother, our" 2418, 3756, 9062
"mother, Palestinian" 831
"mother, Paul's" 6630
"mother, Ron Starr's" 6231
"mother, running toward my" 7863
"mother, she and her" 3609
"mother, Shockproof's" 8874
"mother, sick" 6652
"mother, Tenny's" 4925
"mother, the" 3762, 7100
"mother, the head of its" 453
"mother, their" 3580, 4780, 6587
"mother, unfortunate" 6517
"mother, visit his" 9981
"mother, visit your" 4600
"mother, well" 6929
"mother, your" 1075, 2014, 3490
"mother, your bleeding" 8661
"mother America" 6649
Mother Ann 6833
"mother back, so we got my" 6670
"mother blond and beautiful" 797
"mother called, my" 6572
"mother came into their house" 5192
"mother cancelled an unrelenting
    life, my" 9297
"mother cried, his" 6590
"mother die of, what did Jewel's"
    2465
"mother died, his" 7219
"mother died at five fifty-eight"
    2335
"mother Europa" 6649
"mother had a lover, I never knew
    my" 6746
"mother had died, her" 6666
"mother held it with her hands"
    7058
"mother in your story" 9011
"Mother insisted" 6532
"mother jumped into the taxi" 9779
"mother left him, my" 5768
"mother lived to be old" 113
"Mother of all things" 8438
"mother of Charles and Clara
    Amedroz" 6612
"Mother of God, Mary the" 10587
"mother of myself" 4800
"mother of Small Henry" 2408
"mother of the mayor" 6571
"mother showed him the Guardi-
    ans" 6704

"mother shuddered one last time" 7090
"Mother Superior" 7020
"mother told me, my" 2394, 6585
"mother troubled in her wisdom, his" 3562
"mother very good" 6739
"mother was a drummer" 6241
"mother was a New York lady" 6628
"mother was seventeen when she had me" 6732
"mother was talking in code again" 8874
"mother weeps most, which" 6649
"mother who has a family of children" 3806
"mother who was ill" 6639
"mother who will die in less than a month" 7084
"mother would have him to tea, my" 1535
"mother-country" 10470
"mothered us all, the ocean" 7941
"mother-in-law, her future" 3581
Mothers 90, 113, 149, 369, 431, 550, 552, 554, 561, 572, 575, 633, 797, 807, 828, 844, 851, 854, 943, 976, 1121, 1154, 1202, 1210, 1535, 1763, 1802, 1805, 1827, 1845, 1846, 1884, 1926, 2014, 2040, 2079, 2296, 2319, 2335, 2345, 2394, 2408, 2418, 2422, 2465, 2573, 2667, 2704, 2765, 2864, 2868, 2878, 2919, 3269, 3279, 3471, 3479, 3533, 3548, 3562, 3582, 3591, 3609, 3619, 3621, 3623, 3628, 3705, 3758, 3762, 3785, 3942, 4238, 4301, 4434, 4593, 4600, 4722, 4741, 4780, 4783, 4889, 4921, 4925, 4937, 5085, 5192, 5218, 5236, 5499, 5520, 5527, 5612, 5657, 5680, 5768, 5769, 5841, 5965, 6110, 6114, 6122, 6169, 6231, 6238, 6241, 6476, 6517, 6529, 6532, 6536, 6538, 6542, 6547, 6548, 6553, 6554, 6572, 6585, 6587, 6604, 6605, 6606, 6607, 6610, 6612, 6615, 6619, 6621, 6628, 6629, 6630, 6632, 6636, 6638, 6639, 6641, 6646, 6649, 6651, 6652, 6653, 6657, 6658, 6660, 6669, 6670, 6677, 6686, 6688, 6690, 6692, 6694, 6696, 6702, 6703, 6704, 6706, 6708, 6709, 6710, 6711, 6721, 6722, 6724, 6732, 6733, 6734, 6736, 6737, 6738, 6739, 6740, 6741, 6743, 6744, 6745, 6746, 6747, 6748, 6750, 6845, 6861, 7035, 7058, 7070, 7072, 7078, 7090, 7092, 7095, 7100, 7174, 7207, 7213, 7219, 7377, 7385, 7402, 7441, 7469, 7533, 7536,
7542, 7555, 7863, 7932, 7941, 7947, 8475, 8537, 8661, 8838, 8874, 8930, 9011, 9297, 9314, 9339, 9373, 9461, 9496, 9572, 9716, 9779, 9931, 9980, 10312, 10676, 10771, 10791, 10802, 10845, 10873, 10882, 10939, 10997
"mothers, fifteen-year-old" 4876
"mothers, overbearing" 7174
"mothers, their" 554
"mothers, twenty-seven" 6743
"mother's ashes, his" 2422
"mother's autobiography, my" 5499
"mother's brother, my" 6939
"Mother's Day" 4523
"mother's death, I had nothing to do with our" 2418
"mothers don't hurt children" 6745
"mother's eyes, in their" 9716
"mother's funeral, my" 3942
"mother's heart, an anxious" 4889
"mothers like elephants must always remember" 6711
"mother's lover, my" 4783
"mother's parents, my" 6297
"mother's stomach" 7072
"mother's village, her" 8244
"mother's visit" 5570
Mothersill, Odell 7851
Moths 4951, 4954, 4956
"moths, like tiny flickering" 5339
"moths appearing and disappearing as they turned over" 5339
"moths did not come to lanterns" 4956
"motion, a" 6001
"motion, everything was in" 10046
"motion, set in" 5111
"motion, slow" 5118
"motion is the opposite of stillness" 117
"motionless, body remains" 5952
"motionless, it lay so" 7928
"motionless and inscrutable" 1523
"motionless and transfixed, held everything" 2212
"motionless as an ocean" 5132
"motionless at the crown of a small hill" 7640
"motionless in a chair, lounged" 5620
"motion-picture studio" 1324
"motions nobody else could see" 10873
Motivation 10723
"motive, explain the" 6035
"motive, such was not his leading" 6034
"motive has been discovered, no" 6177
Motives 1167, 7951, 9305
"motives, analyse the" 7951
"motives, Vice-Chancellor's" 9305
"motives are, I cannot be sure what his" 1167
"motives contributed to detain me, many" 3910
"Motives of my Actions" 6033
"motives of piety" 1292
"motives of those actions they record" 4490
Motley, Shade 1413
"motonony and ennui" 9381
"motor, cut off the" 2962
"motor, sound of a" 8770
"motor cars, first" 3394
"motor pool, battalion" 8684
"motor works" 9160
"motor-bike" 7628
"motor-bike, on his" 3483
"motor-car, a local" 9533
"motorcycle, backfiring of a" 10203
"motorcycle, sat easy on his" 10063
"motorcycle, that black" 2973
Motorcycles 2973, 7628, 10203
"motorists" 8813
"Motors, Springer" 9451
Mott, Ernest Verdun 4660
"mottled brass-bright desert" 3768
"motto, gold crest and a" 4642
"motto, vivid and memorable" 711
"motto, World State's" 8300
"motto of my character" 3911
"motto was 'Tax'" 6808
"Moudon, elevated plain of" 9112
MouMou 461
"mound, a bulldozed" 5724
"mound, fresh" 1186
"mound in the Linden burying-ground" 1186
"mounds and tumuli of that unexplored waste" 2605
"mounds that ever grow higher and sharper, softly rounded" 6056
"Mount Aergius" 6073
"Mount Assabenbeduc" 9136
"Mt. Baker, snowy hump of" 6075
"Mount Carmel" 8133
"Mount Griff" 4322
"Mount Hebron New York" 8202
"Mount Hope" 1482
"Mt. Hope" 8317
"Mount Hozomeen" 6075
"Mount Kaiser" 4084
"Mount Kilimanjaro" 7832
"Mount Latmos" 6080
"Mount Moriah" 2973
"Mount Olympus" 2628
"Mount Scopus" 6279
"Mt. Soracte" 7514
"Mount Soufrière" 5052
"Mount Tabor Ltd." 5466
"Mount Tamalpais" 3264
"Mount Vernon" 1401
"Mount Vesuvius" 212
"mountain, a" 1393
"mountain, ancient holy" 1439
"mountain, arid" 6059

"mountain, base of the" 9782
"mountain, climbing a" 6071
"mountain, dwell high upon the" 6820
"mountain, five miles up the" 8729
"mountain, halfway up a" 6083
"mountain, height of a young" 1018
"mountain, high flank of the" 2969
"mountain, I live on a" 6081
"mountain, it was not a pretty" 6082
"mountain, like a moonlit" 10298
"mountain, looked at the" 6055
"mountain, on the" 1413
"mountain, on top of a" 6057
"mountain, one complete" 4062
"Mountain, Phosphate" 8458
"mountain, smoking" 6074
"Mountain, Spencer's" 6077
"Mountain, the" 2006
"mountain, the top of his" 6086
"mountain, the way over the" 529
"mountain, vigil on the" 6960
"mountain air, motionless" 8333
"mountain chains traverse the re-
    public" 6068
"mountain climbers" 6066
"mountain country" 1365
"mountain crossroads" 6918
"mountain fifty miles and more in
    length" 6054
"mountain had not gleamed so
    white, if the" 6072
"mountain I would have to cross,
    the last" 6069
"mountain in front of them" 6078
"mountain lands, far off in the"
    4044
"mountain meadows" 7667
"mountain of his cowhide boot"
    4950
"mountain pass" 7809, 8303
"mountain paths" 5824
"mountain ranges" 10616
"mountain shadows" 4034
"mountain sky, like a" 5147
"mountain snow" 10075
"mountain tops" 9745
"mountain was shining like glass"
    6064
"mountain we call Big Top" 9201
"mountain West" 1581
"mountain with an elevation of two
    thousand feet" 4062
Mountains 212, 1341, 1367, 1372,
    1396, 1398, 1439, 2221, 4027,
    4084, 4494, 5045, 5052, 5077,
    5125, 5149, 5620, 5713, 7190,
    7329, 7667, 7674, 7701, 8192,
    8389, 8400, 8729, 8971, 9070,
    9115, 9141, 9740, 9747, 9749,
    9751, 9754, 9756, 9782, 10616
"mountains" 4027, 4376, 5216
"mountains, a countour of endless"
    6070

"mountains, a couple of smooth"
    4660
"Mountains, Andes" 6259
"Mountains, Appalachian" 6813
"mountains, around it rose the" 1341
"mountains, belt of" 6053
"Mountains, Black" 7149
"mountains, blowing off the" 2957
"mountains, blue" 1398, 3638
"Mountains, Blue Ridge" 1465
"mountains, cold humpback" 7701
"Mountains, comparatively vast
    the peopleless Huron" 4073
"mountains, crouching" 6087
"Mountains, Cumberland" 9527
"mountains, cuts through the" 9180
"mountains, desolate Libyan" 4494
"mountains, fangs of the" 8400
"mountains, great bases of the
    mighty" 6056
"Mountains, Green" 7762
"mountains, Guerrero" 4797
"mountains, heart of black" 9874
"mountains, high" 5713
"mountains, Himalayan" 6066
"mountains, imponderable barrier
    of" 5620
"mountains, in the heart of the"
    7950
"mountains, jagged" 9188
"mountains, knotted mass of gray-
    green" 9141
"mountains, lies among the" 9745
"mountains, near its head in the"
    9747
"mountains, near some" 4081
"Mountains, Neversummer" 5077
"mountains, New Hampshire" 9770
"mountains, one of Vermont's
    green" 1367
"mountains, ornamented with" 1372
"Mountains, Ozark" 8971
"mountains, peaks of the" 6079
"mountains, rain driven over the"
    10711
"mountains, rising over the
    scarred" 9756
"mountains, Samnite" 4040
"mountains, snow in the" 78
"mountains, snowy" 10751
"Mountains, Superstition" 6076
"mountains, surrounded on all
    sides by" 6061
"mountains, tops of the" 9070
"mountains, two ranges of" 9751
"mountains, we see the" 6058
"mountains ahead of us, we didn't
    see the seven" 6088
"mountains and moorlands, land
    of" 6258
"mountains and precipices com-
    pounding sites of ambush with
    sagas of courage" 5149
"mountains are bare, tops of the"
    5045

"mountains covered with verdure"
    8192
"mountains cradled the valley in
    their eternal arms" 9740
"mountains forming the range of
    Alps" 6052
"mountains of Arabia" 2221
"Mountains of Spices" 9020
"mountains of the north" 5152
"mountains on one side" 3605
"mountain's rain-shadow" 7329
"mountains standing far back on
    either side" 9754
"mountains stood up from the
    plains" 6065
"mountains that formed a natural
    radio-quiet shield" 9756
"mountains that ringed this plain
    like massive beasts" 6087
"mountains towering irregularly"
    6057
"mountaintop, hut on the" 4347
"mounted, well" 7610
"Mounth, the" 4053
"mounts, olive" 4034
"mounts, urged their" 10541
Moura 2012, 5330
"mourn for the England we lost"
    11004
"mourned, watched and" 3962
"mourners" 3947
"mourners, three unmourning" 1186
"mournful look of him" 2336
Mourning 4222, 4226, 4228,
    4230, 10902
"mourning, deep" 4222
"mourning, deepest and most un-
    compromising" 4226
"mourning, organ sound of limit-
    less" 10902
"mourning purples" 962
"mourning was over, the first
    severity of" 4228
Mouse, Mickey 9484
"mouse last night, we had a" 418
"mousing in the meadow" 476
"moustache, small bristling" 5846
"moustache, thick orange" 5970
"moustache concealing his mouth,
    a shaggy" 1952
"moustache of dirty lemon, cropped
    blondish" 5911
"moustache . . . of toothbrush tex-
    ture" 5911
Mouth, Miss Miami 933
"mouth, clonk from the side of its"
    660
"mouth, corner of my" 9004
"mouth, corners of his" 8545
"mouth, cupped his hands round
    his" 10025
"mouth, exploded through his" 9849
"mouth, frog" 10174
"mouth, his" 3868
"mouth, hold in her" 4419

"mouth, in my" 5424
"mouth, John Callant's" 246
"mouth, large" 5921
"mouth, pebbles in his" 8894
"mouth, roof of my" 8216
"mouth, soft strong pull of the" 3867
"mouth, sour in his" 8568
"mouth, tongue rather too large for his" 4282
"mouth, towel in his" 2876
"mouth, two words out of my" 7492
"mouth, v of his" 333
"mouth a little soft" 347
"mouth against the line of her hair" 7985
"mouth at her breast" 3867
"mouth full of tacks" 9925
"mouth of his father's cave-like study" 6231
"mouth of the Arundel River" 1374
"mouth open, I stretched my" 6552
"mouth turned purple" 7051
"mouth was always as busy as his feet" 5188
"mouthful, bitten off a big" 242
"mouthfuls of bacon and eggs" 3824
"mouth-harp, grunt on a" 882
"mouth-organ" 976
"mouths, English shape to their" 9560
"mouths, their open" 5632
"move, first" 625
"move, they were easier to" 1846
"move, we shall have to" 6152
"move again, on the" 6158
"move around a little" 624
"move away" 6124
"move closer in one shadowy spring" 2205
"move into their room" 2415
"move my right hand, I am now at last able to" 7463
"move on to the next" 3944
"move to Brooklyn, I had to" 6142
"move to Mill's Landing" 6127
"moved, have never been so" 3477
"moved across Lexington Avenue" 6140
"moved almost to tears, I found myself" 6227
"moved along in the bobbing springy gait" 10354
"moved as the wolf travels" 7221
"moved down Interstate 40 at a steady fifty-five" 9798
"moved from Massachusetts" 6133
"moved from town to town" 6107
"moved here, I" 6161
"moved hesitantly down the unfamiliar street" 7237
"moved his thin legs with speed" 10339
"moved in" 6171
"moved in, I" 6164

"moved in, they had" 959
"moved in across the street" 6305
"moved in the room above" 6294
"moved in to live with me" 1986
"moved in with her mother for a while" 2681
"moved inflexibly in its course around the sun" 525
"moved into a house" 6115
"moved into it, when I" 82
"moved into the country" 6095
"moved invisibly, while they" 7913
"moved majestically and incongruously along the beach" 9783
"moved out" 6131
"moved out, after Crazy Eights" 6134
"moved out, Indians" 959
"moved restlessly all day" 1469
"moved silently" 10340
"moved slowly up the clearing" 10927
"moved there, before I" 6153
"moved to Elsome Street, the year we" 10973
"moved to Glenkill Pennsylvania" 5854
"moved to Miami" 4945
"moved to Munich" 6151
"moved to this house" 6130
"moved totteringly from room to room" 2692
"moved toward nine-thirty" 9474
"moved up the trace" 10357
"moved up the trail vigorously" 10401
"moved upstairs" 6128
"moved with equal vigour" 8121
"moved with my family" 9715
"movement, rapid" 3300
"Movement, Repeal" 5194
"movement, the only perceptible" 757
"movement, the smallest" 10261
"movement, the triumphant first" 6226
"movement in the reeds" 8791
"movement like a swallow, a darting" 4141
"movements, jerky" 8653
"movements, no sudden" 9905
"movements, stirring with present" 9119
"movements, story of its" 5685
"movements, vigor of her" 376
"movers carried in her things" 6138
"moves, making inept" 5829
"moves, making their" 3050
"moves from room to room" 5718
"moves in next door" 6298
"movie, her last" 1329
"movie, home" 1331
"movie, like being in a" 1237
"movie, seen the" 9059
"movie, watching a" 5118

"movie began to roll, the first" 1322
"movie house, pitch-dark" 1323
"movie stars' fragrant bluish auras" 7229
"movie theater" 2040
"movie was on television, maybe the" 2351
Movies 328, 1237, 1320, 1322, 1323, 1326, 1328, 1329, 1330, 1333, 7986, 7996, 9059, 9463
"movies, at the" 328
"movies, in the" 2351
"movies, one of his old" 2045
"movies, the" 7996
"movie's much too violent for me, this" 1328
Moving 289, 1518, 1529, 1733, 1986, 2018, 2415, 2554, 2573, 2677, 2681, 2786, 3198, 3261, 3659, 4534, 4871, 4945, 5223, 5790, 5854, 6285, 6298, 6305, 6558, 7191, 7704, 8504, 8636, 8926, 9414, 9715, 10973
"moving, I can feel it" 7066
"moving, something white" 6303
"moving from one space to another" 9213
"moving her thin young neck, hardly" 7766
"moving in" 6285
"moving in with her" 6154
"moving in with her, I'm" 2677
"moving life" 8345
"moving on" 289
"moving on, I'm" 5652
"moving the sand" 10707
"moving through a thousand watching people" 10373
"moving through rivers of heat" 4423
"moving up into a starred sky" 8415
"moving was over and done" 6105
"Moving-Picture Show, Nickelorion" 1313
Mowbray, Miles 6528
Mowbray, Mrs. 3548
"mowers, grass-" 8800
"mowing, reaping and" 5681
Mowlavi, Abbas 0091
"mows the lawn" 10959
"Moycullen" 4931
"M.P.'s looked suspiciously at Barnett Morgan" 9303
"M16" 6999
"M3, the" 883
"muck, subtropic" 4386
"Muck and Chitlings, Land of" 6136
"muck heap" 9753
"mucker, red-haired" 10901
"mud, alluvial" 6249
"mud, dried and rutted" 7639
"mud, hub-deep" 9771
"mud, yellow-brown" 742
"mud along the Thames" 7310
"mud beginning to ooze" 2894

"mud churning, the usual thick
    seas of" 3653
"mud in the Chancery" 7310
"mud in the Jersey flats" 7310
"mud of half a continent" 7664
"mud of the riverbank" 4161
"muddar, go wid ya" 4238
"muddled happiness" 4354
"muddleheaded" 687
"muddy flat" 175
"muddy here" 1337
Mueller, Dawn 3593
Mueller, Elaine 5861
Mueller, Karl 105
"muff, opossum" 9540
"muffin, analogous to a" 6519
"muffins" 8530
"muffled, pleasantly" 8815
"muffler danced in the wind, his"
    983
"muffler she was knitting" 1909
"mug, Sweet Caporal pasted in
    his" 2827
"mug shot" 6872
"mugging, an attempted" 9701
"mugging, the" 2058
Muhammad 7521
"Muhammad, our Lord and
    Master" 7521
Muhlbach 9443
Muir, Mrs. 10799
Muirtagh 8671
"mulatto was dark amber in
    colour" 6834
Mulcahy, Henry 1920
Mule 7804
"mule" 9626, 9684
"mule, a" 6126
"mule, bray of the iceman's" 5121
"mule, his white" 1565
"mule, like a hauled" 6136
"mule, rode on a" 7630
"mule, sitting sideways on the" 7611
"Mule, the" 7804
"mules, a span of" 2374
"mules, drawn by two" 7240
"mules, four" 9762
"mules, her fluffy" 2853
"mules, two" 3069
"mules, two big" 9527
"mules . . . were more sure-footed"
    7630
Mulford, Mr. 8047
"Mulhall" 3044
"Mulholland" 9800
Mullhouse, Edwin Abraham 2360
Mulligan, Buck 8041
"mulling one's fate" 7467
"mullioned" 2686
"multifaceted" 5329
"multifarious documents" 5557
"multimillionaire" 9850
"Multimillionairess" 5571
Mulvanney, Alan 818
Mum 3293

"mum, if you please" 6285
"Mum, it was" 3293
"mumble, garbled" 8895
"mumble of vague weekend music"
    2974
"mumbled Yiddish curses" 6958
"mumbling at me" 4988
Mumford 4830
Mumma 10937
"mummy, Egyptian" 1331
"mummy, radio" 7791
"mummy, the" 5748
"Mummy, where's" 6658
"mummy, wrapped old" 10190
"Mumpkin story" 9003
Munchmeyer 9004
Munday 9087
Munday, Dr. A.B.W. 1833
Munden, Mr. 10133
Mundez, Carlita Rojas 9583
Mundy, Joe 7136
"Munich" 5398, 5641, 9524, 9570
"Munich, moved to" 6151
"municipal pressure" 7820
Munson, Bob 7013
Munson, Buford 2329
Murad 5846
"mural depicting the Green Moun-
    tains" 7762
"mural labeled *Civilization Teeters*"
    516
"murals on a cracking wall that
    become the cracks themselves"
    5521
Murana Bill 8233
Murchison, Reverend Peter 2399
Murder 73, 828, 1164, 1812, 1883,
    1999, 2000, 2019, 2022, 2031,
    2034, 2041, 2354, 2406, 2418,
    2428, 3407, 3928, 4969, 5091,
    5200, 5843, 6044, 6276, 6324,
    6706, 6735, 7368, 9047, 10216
"murder" 6276, 9045
"murder?" 2354
"murder, actually attended a" 6174
"murder, before the" 6206
"murder, charged with" 5200
"murder, contemplating a" 6192
"murder, cover a" 6210
"murder, dream of" 6204
"murder, first perceived how he
    might commit the perfect" 6178
"murder, her life would end in"
    6202
"murder, here to commit a" 6183
"murder, morning of the first"
    10216
"murder, reason for" 6201
"murder, tried for the" 3407
"murder, what he said was a" 6184
"murder, witnessed her father's"
    6181
"murder appeared to them, how"
    7368
"murder didn't mean much" 6175

"murder her family if they had to"
    7739
"murder him, they meant to" 6176
"murder is seldom discussed" 6208
"Murder Mystery" 6177
"murder . . . of a remarkable kind"
    6210
"murder stopping at a small town"
    6199
"murdered, two days before I was"
    9047
"murdered, woman was being" 6173
"murdered and beheaded" 6185
"murdered by the great painter"
    6196
"murdered him, they" 8917
"murdered in Burundi, missionary"
    6735
"murdered on the front veranda"
    6177
"murderer, he had been the" 1812
"murderer, I was a child" 2031
"murderer of his father" 4469
Murderers 1812, 2031, 2052, 2178,
    6186, 10790
"murderers" 2052
"murderers, give birth to" 10790
"murderers, sniping" 2178
"murderers of the mortal Julius"
    4469
"murderess, I become a" 2034
"murdering her family" 3413
"murderous to the teeth" 10831
"murders, those cockamamy" 6209
Murdoch 543
Murdock 3570
Murfy, Malachi Desmond 713
"murk" 5447
"murmur, quiet" 8820
"murmured, she" 7473
"murmured in her ear" 1121
"murmured 'Mr. Herman' twice,
    someone" 8467
"murmured sounds" 10260
"murmured the nice lady" 1371
"murmured the Princess" 9542
"murmured the words of the tune"
    8739
"murmured to itself gently" 8784
"murmuring" 4007, 5655
"murmuring vibration, alive with
    the" 423
"murmurings, her own" 6231
Murontzeff 9587
Murphy, Julia 10668
Murphy, Tasmania 1924
Murray, Arthur 4628
Murray, Cass 566
Murray, Josephine 10777
"muscadines" 8531
"muscle, stringy" 979
"muscles, stretching their" 7410
"muscles rolling, his mighty" 10340
Musco 444
"Muscovites" 7904

"Muscovy, Czar of" 10464
"Muse, Hail" 5523
"Muse, jilted the" 5397
"museum" 4069
"Museum, British" 8587
"Museum, Lahore" 2017
"Museum, Norman Rockwell" 510
"Museum, Park Service" 4253
"Museum, the" 8546
"museum entrance" 8316
"Museum of Antiquities" 8941
"Museum of North America" 6512
"Museum of the Louvre" 5613
"Museum Reading Room, British" 1658
"Museum'll be closing up shop" 3428
Museums 3428, 5613, 8316, 8546, 8941
Musgrove, Clement 4560
"mushrooms, he had chosen the best" 1863
"mushrooms, stringing" 10853
"mushrooms, they were good" 1863
"mushrooms Eamonn Eales had collected" 1863
Music 3, 646, 648, 649, 652, 655, 882, 915, 962, 1250, 1320, 2102, 2106, 2111, 2885, 2974, 3026, 3386, 4089, 4121, 4336, 5268, 5348, 5509, 5584, 5641, 5905, 6405, 6791, 7027, 8739, 8743, 8755, 8759, 8767, 8771, 8792, 8814, 9098, 9300, 10012, 10085, 10650, 10701, 10906
"music, a book on" 6227
"Music, Academy of" 1012, 8740
"music, during the" 6220
"music, electronic" 8555
"music, ever present pulse of" 10701
"Music, Festival of Contemporary" 6224
"music, gipsy" 1308
"music, guitar distilled its" 6221
"music, I hear" 6214
"music, inspirational" 6230
"music, listen to my" 6234
"music, making his" 9098
"music, mumble of vague weekend" 2974
"music, new" 5641
"music, no" 2885
"music, painted" 5348
"music, played out to" 5584
"music began" 6240
"music box, he sent her a" 4121
"music from the neighbouring native huts" 10701
"music lesson" 6217
"music of the merry-go-round" 1250
"music slowly, play" 5268
"music stopped, when the" 8771
"music was appropriate, the" 8755
"music was as much a gift as sunshine" 6243

"music . . . was unleashed from its mechanical box" 1250
"musical, Evie Decker was not" 10821
"musical clangor and swell" 648
"musical of *Dombey and Son*" 9394
"musical public of Great Britain" 5905
"musical tones" 8086
"musician, a great" 6227
"musician of great genius" 6213
Musicians 3, 6213, 6215, 6219, 6223, 6224, 6227, 6229, 6232, 6234, 6235, 6236, 6237, 6240, 6242
"musicians on chairs in the truck-bed" 1680
"musicians' widows" 6242
"music-room" 6226
"musing midnight in midcentury" 10377
"musingly, said I" 121
"musk of rotting woods" 4105
"muskets, cautious repriming of our" 4248
"muskets, loaded" 3482
"Muslim woman" 5822
"muslin, covered with grimed" 2703
Muspratt, Gerald 2402
"mustache, foxy" 7728
"mustache, well-defined" 5301
"mustache, white" 100
Mustapha, Baba 8040
"mustard, dab of" 3860
Mustian, Emma 2765
Mustian, Rosacoke 2973
"musty old laws" 1817
"mutation" 5450
"mute, Eco was" 5997
"mute, take off that" 6215
"mute, unemployed undertaker's" 6993
"mute and motionless" 442
"mute and motionless, Kazan lay" 403
"mute articulation" 879
"mutes, in the town there were two" 3917
"mutic, there's a" 7111
"mutilated, terribly" 32
"Mutina, I was with him at" 4469
Mutt 5757
"muttered a profane inquiry" 9311
"muttered at me" 3738
"muttered to himself" 4416
"muttering, went around" 62
"muttering nonetheless" 62
"mutton, his half sister's" 4711
"mutton, rubbery" 2463
"My Country 'Tis of Thee" 6219
"Myddelton Square" 1968
Myra 5259
"myself, concerning" 694
"myself, kill" 75
"myself, looking at" 7486

"myself, paragraph exclusively about" 700
"myself, short account of" 3670
"myself, to define" 7970
"myself alone, for" 5456
"myself I sing" 4800
Mysteries 473, 4820, 6097
"mysteries, breathes into being its" 5656
"mysterious, made" 10580
"mysterious as some midnight visitation" 9008
"mysterious death of my sister Mathilde" 5528
"mysterious force" 5329
"mysterious quality, the vast" 7916
"mysterious thing" 8028
"mysteriously disappeared" 2568
"mysteriously enveloped by unreality" 10352
"mysteriously exciting" 8799
"mysteriousness" 5145
Mystery 1368, 2175, 3934, 4129, 10870
"mystery, cosmic" 6904
"mystery, crystal" 10955
"mystery, definitive conclusion to its" 5494
"mystery, gave it" 1368
"mystery, gift retains its" 4129
"mystery, joyful" 3934
"Mystery, Murder" 6177
"mystery, remained a" 473
"mystery of Lulu" 10870
"mystery of replenishing the earth, still unique" 5699
"mystery to me" 6097
"mystery which dominates vistas framed by a ruined door" 9231
"mystical sense of the wonder of existence" 9118
"mystified" 1226
"mystique of their own past" 4012
"myth, romantic" 2539
"myth, the past is a matter of" 6792
"Myth, there is the" 5217
"myth, you remember the old" 2633
"myth among the shards, she is only a" 7527
"myth to his friends, became a" 4477
Myths 2633, 3403, 5215, 5217, 5221, 6258, 6792, 7527
"myths" 3403
"myths, all old great cities possess their special" 5221
"myths, cherished" 6258
"myths and legends already enshrouding his past" 5215
"myths which cannot easily be damaged or debased" 5221

"nabobs, pauncy well-lined" 3396
Nabonidus 10476

Nachman 10422
Nachman of Bratslav 2278
Nacho 7236
Nadia 2794, 6026, 9293
Nadina 2103
Nagaraj 259
"Nagasaki" 8160
"Nagasaki, harbor of" 3514
Nago 10540
Nagy, Stefan 10884
"nail dropped into the mechanism of town life" 6199
"nail file, a long" 3272
"nail-biting" 7161
"nails, a pair of tenpenny" 8931
"nails, didn't cut his" 6679
"nails, do their own" 1477
"naked" 6400, 6402, 10236
"naked, Berry is" 6396
"naked, both of them" 6389
"naked, butt-" 6399
"naked, girl who stood" 6395
"naked, he was" 1166
"naked, sitting" 1169
"naked, totally" 6393
"naked, you show me what it is to be" 4362
"naked as babes, they were both" 2773
"naked at the edge of a cliff" 6387
"naked body" 6403
"naked man" 6390
"naked of course, we're both" 6391
"naked on a bed, he lies" 1170
"naked on his bed, she lay" 9355
"naked sides" 5011
"naked to the waist" 1681
"naked trees" 10572
"name, a fitting" 9832
"name, added 'van Rijn' to his" 4760
"name, agreeable" 4732
"name, American boy's" 4732
"name, asked me to repeat my" 8027
"name, assumed" 8923
"name, bearer of this" 4726
"name, blood-color of their" 6085
"name, bore the elegant" 10768
"name, called my son's" 6552
"name, celebrated" 8953
"name, change in spelling of his" 3538
"name, Christian" 5453
"name, clear his" 2567
"name, did not learn his" 5790
"name, don't know my real" 4793
"name, everyone knew his" 3544
"name, forgotten his" 7428
"name, George is my" 4768
"name, goodness and antiquity of the" 354
"name, heard the" 4832
"name, her" 2919, 4772, 4801, 4871, 6218, 7739, 7950

"name, her lips burn on the" 9633
"name, her own" 4775
"name, his" 365, 2919, 4675, 4733, 4763, 4782, 4817, 5523, 5601, 7523
"name, his Christian" 4728
"name, his real" 4734, 4772
"name, I have always used my maiden" 4848
"name, I love your" 4846
"name, I will assign no fictitious" 779
"name, it had no" 606
"name, it is a desert" 4857
"name, it's a good" 2579
"name, its real" 7251
"name, Jacaranda's" 4802
"name, knows the" 3795
"name, left a" 5562
"name, my" 337, 502, 2019, 4276, 4448, 4723, 4736, 4745, 4748, 4762, 4766, 4769, 4770, 4776, 4777, 4788, 4789, 4809, 4823, 4827, 4829, 4833, 4837, 4857, 4860, 4862, 4864, 4865, 4872, 4874, 4875, 5490, 6236, 6706, 7455, 7488, 8729, 8747, 9004, 9710
"Name, my" 778
"name, my christian" 4714
"name, my father's family" 4714
"name, my last" 1729
"name, my maiden" 1924
"name, my mother's" 2573
"Name, my True" 3527
"name, my uncle's" 4719
"name, never did like his real" 4806
"name, no longer answered to a last" 4797
"name, nobody is compelled to give her real" 4772
"name, not her real" 7093
"name, not my real" 4793
"name, pet" 3793
"name, shed one" 4842
"name, sign my" 4717
"name, signed a false" 4649
"name, signed his" 8804
"name, sound of the" 7899
"name, struggling to bring forth a" 7456
"name, that's a ridiculous" 7851
"name, under a false" 2019
"name, venerable" 4179
"name, waited for her to reach my" 6738
"name, wanted to know her real" 8024
"name, what is your" 4729, 4787
"name, what was its" 5158
"name, won't tell me her" 4849
"name, your" 4755
"name contained some hope" 4808
"Name Crusoe, write our" 6601
"name does not matter" 9522

"name fitting her like a glove" 4179
"name for the severely grey brick house" 3079
"name has always been, my" 4826
"name in the phone book, the first" 1054
"name is Anderson, rest of my" 4722
"name is Branting, he says his" 1098
"name is Eagle, my" 4718
"name is not much common here, your" 4850
"name is prefixed to the head of this chapter" 779
"name is Rose, my" 4774
"name is so-and-so, my" 4851
"name of Albert Sanger was barely known" 5905
"name of John, borne the" 7812
"name of our heroine, the original" 4720
"name of the really responsible party" 5394
"name of the river" 4760
"name on his birth-registration papers" 4859
"name please, your" 4761
"name seems odd" 9825
"name she bore" 4727
"name slid through the tubby literary agent's whipcord lips discreetly" 5453
"name stretched over the plains" 5173
"name stuck to him" 4725
"name suited her, the" 4773
"name the world knew them by" 4805
"name upon her rustic Grace, clapped the" 7708
"name was gawky" 4196
"name was India, her first" 4754
"name was Mopsy" 481
"name was not really Fanny Cornforth" 4801
"name was professionally inappropriate" 4821
"name wasn't Barnacle at all" 4728
"name we finally gave my younger daughter" 4814
Name-calling 4982, 6653
"named, he was" 4824
"named after the enchanting god Krishna" 4741
"named as a sign of respect and according to tradition" 4880
"named for the negro Queen Califia" 280
"named like so much else in Australia" 4086
"named them after two books in the Bible" 4780
"nameless dread, there lurked a" 3698
"nameplate was crooked" 6028

Names 71, 266, 354, 365, 481, 502, 536, 556, 606, 752, 903, 917, 1159, 1389, 1401, 1729, 1924, 2019, 2573, 2579, 2797, 3079, 3527, 3538, 3544, 3658, 3795, 4086, 4167, 4179, 4196, 4276, 4649, 4675, 4713, 4714, 4715, 4716, 4717, 4718, 4719, 4720, 4721, 4722, 4723, 4724, 4725, 4726, 4727, 4728, 4729, 4730, 4731, 4732, 4733, 4734, 4735, 4736, 4737, 4738, 4739, 4740, 4741, 4742, 4743, 4744, 4747, 4748, 4749, 4750, 4752, 4753, 4755, 4756, 4757, 4759, 4760, 4761, 4762, 4763, 4764, 4765, 4766, 4767, 4768, 4769, 4770, 4772, 4773, 4774, 4775, 4776, 4777, 4779, 4780, 4781, 4782, 4783, 4785, 4786, 4787, 4789, 4790, 4791, 4792, 4793, 4794, 4796, 4798, 4799, 4800, 4801, 4802, 4805, 4806, 4807, 4808, 4809, 4810, 4814, 4815, 4816, 4817, 4818, 4819, 4821, 4823, 4824, 4825, 4826, 4827, 4828, 4829, 4831, 4832, 4833, 4835, 4837, 4838, 4839, 4840, 4841, 4842, 4843, 4845, 4846, 4847, 4848, 4849, 4850, 4851, 4852, 4853, 4855, 4856, 4857, 4858, 4859, 4860, 4862, 4863, 4864, 4865, 4867, 4871, 4872, 4873, 4874, 4875, 4876, 4877, 4878, 4879, 4880, 4908, 5032, 5394, 5485, 5490, 5516, 5523, 5597, 5601, 5905, 6018, 6026, 6031, 6218, 6236, 6247, 6274, 6552, 6601, 6699, 6706, 6716, 6738, 6825, 6844, 7065, 7093, 7251, 7420, 7428, 7455, 7488, 7523, 7532, 7708, 7743, 7812, 7851, 7899, 7995, 8024, 8698, 8729, 8804, 8808, 8950, 8953, 9004, 9522, 9633, 9710, 9825, 9832, 9998, 10019, 10898, 10909
"names, at least seven different" 4737
"names, Christian" 4752
"names, collection of odd English" 4739
"names, famous" 903
"names, goes by many" 6274
"names, real proper ribbon of" 4753
"names, sloshes roun' de" 4716
"names, sound of" 8808
"names, the use of" 266
"names, their" 4780
"names, they all had" 8950
"names, they still used fathers'" 365
"names, through all its many" 9748
"names and faces of my past" 7440
"names as a boy could stand, give him as many" 4719

"names had long been almost for-gotten" 5743
"name's Mekles" 4757
"names not his own, he was called a number of" 4816
"names of cardinals lettered across the facades of churches" 7532
"names on places, such illustrious" 1431
"names that were going through my mind" 7144
"names we may call Him" 7519
"naming a kid" 4853
"naming day, on my" 857
Nan 3017
Nance 8735
Nancy 1974, 6934
Nancy, Miss 4191
"Nancy Flyer in about 1835, I first saw the" 9770
"Nancy [France]" 3024
Nanda 9540
Nanga, M. A. 6987
Napier, Josephine 9884
"napkin, damask" 1199
"Naples" 1293, 1905, 6213, 6341
Napoleon 363, 1872, 7803
"Napoleon's officers" 4142
"napping, found in bed" 8470
"napping comfortably inside curled poplar leaves" 5272
Naran, Prem 1231
"narcissi, cold pale" 5033
Narcissism 7486, 10759
"Narcissus, Beyond" 5507
"Narcissus, the ship" 8060
"Narnia" 8991
"Narnia, in the last days of" 424
"narrate their simple story" 4453
"narrative, I am going to attempt a" 3493
"narrative, my" 698
"narrative, this" 4098
"narrative begins, our" 10469
"narrative that follows" 5539
"narratives, compiling these" 7948
"narrator, the" 8980
"narrow, so" 6054
"narrowed to a private lane" 3036
"narrowed under the tree of the avenue" 8770
"narrows, just south of the" 5154
Nash, Belle 9331
Nash, Dave 9767
"Nashville Tennessee" 9365
Nason, Steven 9694
Nat 8895, 10744
"Natal" 9522
Natas 4457
Natasha, Aunt 2902
"Natchez Trace" 4042
Nathan 2807
Nathan, Paul 3299
Nathaniel 8530, 10312
Natica 6163

"nation, across the" 1424
"nation, Chickasaw" 9198
"nation, forward march of a" 8947
"nation, in whose faces was written the history of their" 1296
"nation, it is a young" 275
"nation, world's smallest sovereign" 8866
"National Geographic, six shelves of" 4122
"National Security Forces" 2047
"National Trust" 3160
"nationalistic-style insults" 4984
"nationalities, wild bouillabaise of" 10615
Nationality 244, 361, 1520, 4446, 4447, 4535, 4864, 5703, 10840
"nationality" 1882
"nationless person by inclination" 4762
Nations 272, 275, 279, 4050, 4051, 4062, 4089, 5020, 6377, 6989, 7648, 7796, 10520
"nations, European" 6244
"nations, in some" 7584
"Nations, Indian" 2215
"nations of Europe, larger than any two" 6256
"native, pass as a" 9715
"native country, his" 4554
"native huts" 10701
"native land" 4562
"native land, His" 9053
"native land, my" 4535
"native land, return to your" 4591
"native of a sea-surrounded nook" 4533
"natives, the" 2017
"natives themselves, never used by the" 6247
"natural occurrences, [circum-stances] appear to be removed from" 3435
"natural power" 2765
"natural way to do it" 7718
"naturally formed" 10462
Nature 3435, 3903, 7624
"Nature" 3903
"Nature, Checquer Work of" 5552
"nature, convulsion of" 1174
"nature, cyclical of" 10822
"Nature, endeavor on the part of" 7293
"nature, glories of" 3396
"nature, his modest" 5457
"Nature, obsessional neurosis of" 1452
"Nature, perfectly at one with" 3435
"nature, second" 1123
"nature, sublime and romantic fea-tures of" 6606
"nature, your subject's" 711
"nature been afforded so much assistance, never before had" 7624

"nature of love" 5233
"nature sanctuary" 10422
"nature shouted 'Fore!'" 2201
"nature sleeps" 8766
"nature was a loving one, her" 4153
"naughtiest child" 4146
"Navajo Nation" 752
"Navajos" 529
"naval adventure" 4869
"naval anchorage, the whole of the" 7304
"naval anchorage, wide" 8117
"naval attaché" 6502
"Naval Dockyard, His Majesty's Australian" 4410
"naval history" 4511
"Navan, a fellow from" 3968
"nave in Christendom, longest" 10012
"navel of the universe" 4646
"navel string of the years" 11000
"navels, showing their" 7481
"navigated the old road" 3026
"Navigator, the" 6933
"Navy, commander in the" 4745
"navy, hired fresh out of the" 6471
"Navy, Royal Australian" 10161
"Navy, United States" 5417, 5537
"Navy, U. S." 941
"Navy Building" 3315
"Navy Yard" 8124
"Nawab, the" 1689
"Nawabs, the" 5715
"Nazarene preacher" 3338
"Nazareth" 3655
"Nazi by reputation" 4762
"Nazis" 4685
"NBC" 4008
"NCR model, an army-green" 7578
Neal, Ervin 6201
"Neapolitan Acquaiola" 10783
"neared Rainbow Rim" 6564
"nearer the end than the beginning" 5021
"neat in dark grey" 1315
"neatly arranged" 4438
"neatness he liked" 6145
"Nebraska" 4377, 7270, 7416, 9902, 10685
"Nebraska farmland" 7702
Nebuchadnezzar 1512
"necessary, absolutely" 10772
"necessary, perhaps" 4929
"necessary, provision that is" 4550
"necessary, wouldn't go down there if it were not absolutely" 1578
"neck, almost broke his" 35
"neck, back of the" 10817
"neck, her thin young" 7766
"neck, his unconscious" 2374
"Neck, Mary's" 9096
"neck, pain in the" 10063
"neck, Ralph's sweaty" 4375
"Neck, Ware" 8067

"neck across the boots of a half-breed Indian" 3714
"neck was too long" 10852
"neckers, teenage" 1894
"necks, outstretched" 739
Nectarine, Lord 8636
Ned 2420
"need, just what you" 9737
"need, physical" 2673
"need and emotion ceased" 2673
"need has come to explain myself to someone" 1810
"need more urgent, every minute made my" 10102
"need of a holiday, in urgent" 932
"need you, I" 1143
"needed, exactly what she" 861
"needed firewood" 3788
"needing to be with me, in a phase of" 1692
"needle, delicate" 3047
"needle, filled the" 3057
"needle, finest" 1005
"needle, sewing" 8760
"needle her mother would burnish" 7441
"needle-eyed" 7580
"needlepoint, bright" 5355
Needs 1692, 1810, 3746, 3788, 10102, 10728
"needs of the outsized, the" 7480
Neelan, Gertie 2878
Neeld, Mr. Jenkinson 5894
"Neely" 3604
"ne'er-do-well" 4971
Neewa 407
"negative good-nature" 6605
"Negev" 5286
"neglect" 8488
"neglected chapel" 1297
"negligee, her" 2658
"Negoce, Foreign" 10464
"negotiated the steepest part of 3rd Street" 5814
"Negro, a" 8674
"Negro, not yet all" 6271
"Negro, told me I was a" 7981
"negro driver" 1909
"Negro families" 5161
"Negro named Buford Munson" 2329
"negro Queen Califia, named for the" 280
"Negro servant" 9955
"Negro woman" 1272
"Negro yam, nice big fat" 4100
"Negroes, freeing" 1827
"Negroes came, only" 3137
"neighbor woman" 3835
"neighborhood, country" 4038
"neighborhood, doings of this" 8957
"neighborhood, imaginary" 7893
"neighborhood, in every" 3151
"neighborhood, knows everything about his own" 6278

"neighborhood, other houses in the" 3185
"neighborhood, residential" 4627
"neighborhood, the" 3020, 3186, 6274, 6459, 9443
"neighborhood, there was once a" 6273
"neighborhood, this" 9694
"neighborhood of fascinating if unpretentious architecture" 5607
"neighborhood of people who aren't quite making it" 6281
"neighborhood was never the same" 6305
"neighborhood where I grew up" 10880
Neighborhoods 296, 454, 814, 820, 1191, 3103, 3122, 3142, 3145, 3151, 3185, 3240, 3242, 3262, 4038, 4057, 4627, 4705, 5356, 6288, 6305, 7893, 9114, 9122, 9162, 9443, 9694, 10880
"neighborhoods" 3142
"neighborhoods, in one of the many decaying" 10320
"neighborhoods, neat grid of" 5723
"neighborhoods, settled down in" 1191
"neighborhoods that sprout off the shabbiest part of Hollywood Boulevard" 10320
Neighbors 1617, 3644, 4947, 6802
"neighbors, call on their" 3644
"neighbors, his" 2295
"neighbors, inconvenient for its" 4627
"neighbors, my next door" 6292
"neighbors, their urban" 815
"neighbors, warlike" 6802
"neighbors suspected" 4947
"neighbour, her opposite" 8342
"neighbour in Paris, almost my" 6289
"neighbour know that I was nine, let the" 844
"neighbour that I shall be troubled with, the solitary" 6282
"neighbourhood, a small" 6266
"neighbourhood, Schofield" 296
"neighbourhood of Berkeley Square" 4304
"neighbouring cubes of model dwellings" 6270
"neighbouring native huts" 10701
"neighbours" 6296
"neighbours, waved to the" 1617
"neighbours among whom our doctor followed his profession" 6885
Neilsen 2739
Neilson, Billy 8716
"Neiman-Marcus" 9821
Nell 5991, 6340, 9038, 10284
Nell, Pretty 3396
Nellie 5265
"Nellie" 8063

Nellie Noisy Bluejay 7187
Nelly, Lady 1300
Nelson 2447, 8043
"Nemi" 3196
Nennius 8329
"neolithic stone, great pillars of"
  5149
"nephew, his" 8587, 10063, 10836
"nephew, Mr. Blankhard's" 2967
"nephew, my" 2567, 4927
"nephew, my insane" 7802
"nephew of his father" 9857
"nephew to the renowned Baba
  Mustapha" 8040
"nephews, four" 2307
"Neptune Beach" 7295
"Neptune was propitious" 7346
Nerds 10886
Nero 2350
"nerve, trying to work up the"
  4210
"nerve alert, every" 7617
"nerve to defy God, where did they
  get the" 10838
"nerves, after it had calmed my"
  8565
"nerves, arteries and" 3363
"nerves, insects were feeding on
  his" 5603
"nerves, my dreadful little" 9285
"nerves, on his" 6444
"nervous, he was" 10972
"nervous, I'm" 3309
"nervous, interviews always make
  me" 1514
"nervous, owl is making me" 743
"nervous ailments" 8477
"nervous and jumpy" 9077
"nervous tension, kept the ape in a
  state of" 426
Nervousness 426, 743, 1514, 3309,
  4313, 4579, 8565, 10972
"nest, bird's" 5121
"nest, crow's" 992
"nest, large" 746
"nestle against him, she tried to"
  1990
Nestons, the 4444
"Nestor" 1894
"nests, Chinese eat birds'" 6038
"nests, we have seven different"
  3222
"net, butterfly" 10816
Netherlands, Elaine 1242
"Netherlands" 1352
"Netley" 3266
"nets were down before the sun
  came up" 8148
Nettinger, Grace 10302
Nettleship, Maudie 1947
"network, at the" 1130
"network, Guernica" 2916
"network of subterranean drain-
  pipes" 10930
"networks, combined" 6004

"neurological, anything importantly" 7456
"neurosis of Nature, obsessional"
  1452
"neurosurgeon, marrying a" 5758
"Nevada" 704, 2956
"never go the same way twice"
  5608
Neville 836, 3331
"Nevis" 5014
Nevison, Swift Nick 3396
"new, nothing is" 6847
"new, on the nothing" 8407
"new, something" 5121
"new as morning" 4178
"New Boston" 5785
"New Brunswick Canada" 6155
"new comers" 1340
"New England" 356, 2224, 3060,
  3179, 4441, 6091, 7657, 8956
"New England, extended over all"
  8589
"New England, northern" 10589
"New England coast" 9096
"New England country" 8622
"New England profile" 347
"New England Sabbath afternoon"
  9117
"New England States, one of the"
  7875
"New England villages" 6249
"New Hampshire" 5402, 6133,
  7668, 8012, 8606, 9027, 9770,
  9964, 10088, 10867
"New Hampshire, History of" 356
"New Haven" 9531
New Jersey 8314
"New Jersey" 802, 1339, 7731,
  8314, 8708
"New Jersey highway" 9555
"New Jersey is tinted a delicate
  pink" 5719
New Mexico 10634
"New Mexico" 752, 1584, 6880,
  10744
"New Mexico, brightest" 4065
"New Mexico, southern" 10634
New Orleans 4516, 7691, 9083,
  9377, 10549
"New Orleans" 1688, 2804, 4516,
  5785, 7664, 7691, 8102, 9228,
  9377, 9521, 10549
"New Orleans, Mayor of" 1982
"New Orleans hot" 9359
"New Orleans ringed all around
  them" 1479
"New Rochelle New York" 3191
"New South Wales" 11004
"New South Wales Australia" 1466,
  5138
"new to London" 9108
"New World" 1518, 6121
"New Wye Appalachia" 5452
New Year 5260, 7678, 10569
"New Year" 10982

"New Year, a few days after the"
  1159
"New Year, and a very happy" 2910
"New Year, another" 10980
"New Year, happy" 10133
"New Year, Heil" 10986
"New Year, the" 4410
"New Year's Day" 1901, 3886,
  4516, 6509, 10237
"New Year's Day, this cold clear"
  8988
"New Year's Eve" 2037, 3350
"New Year's Eve party" 6782
New York 1434, 1561, 3148, 3241,
  4035, 4381, 5278, 5291, 7129,
  8595, 9590, 9727
"New York" 77, 206, 276, 370,
  511, 680, 821, 1139, 1159, 1214,
  1313, 1388, 1401, 1403, 1414, 1515,
  1545, 1561, 1578, 1653, 1722,
  1957, 2152, 2511, 2567, 3101,
  3191, 3332, 4043, 4073, 4270,
  4307, 4425, 4559, 4637, 4654,
  4858, 5154, 5205, 5309, 5546,
  5708, 5842, 6003, 6370, 6407,
  6757, 6767, 6783, 6892, 6915,
  6986, 7129, 7140, 7195, 7966,
  8202, 8263, 8595, 8740, 8926,
  9297, 9439, 9512, 9570, 9584,
  9612, 10067, 10126, 10782
"New York, all the way up from"
  9532
"New York, frontierland of western" 1497
"New York, get used to" 9727
"New York, his town-house in"
  4555
"New York, in the city of" 10706
"New York, lived in" 2110
"New York, lower" 7756
"New York, Midtown" 6274
"New York, native of" 6404
"New York, near the centre of the
  state of" 4027
"New York, northern" 9203
"New York, *not* like a miniature"
  1420
"New York, one of the wards of"
  6608
"New York, state of" 6608
"New York, that is" 1441
"New York, upstate" 1187, 8752
"New York, Upstate" 1312
"New York, we reached" 8124
"New York, when I got back to"
  6299
"New York Central Railroad" 7258
"New York City" 1774, 2386, 3167,
  5949, 6477, 6514, 6730, 7042,
  7226, 7769, 9572, 9597, 9977,
  10432
"New York City, after you leave"
  9590
"New York City, gray and fren-
  zied" 5297

"New York City, impersonal in-
  difference of" 5291
"New York City Police" 6274
"New York dailies" 6343
"New York grocer" 5080
"New York holdings" 9567
"New York is as hot as Bangkok"
  4381
"New York lady" 6628
"New York of the 'fifties" 3561
"New York *Post-Dispatch*" 6421
"New York Public Library" 3420
"New York stories" 3241
"New York tenements" 8080
"New York Times" 6360
"New York was a wilderness" 4035
"New York was almost still that
  night" 1370
"New York weather" 6315
"New Yorker, every" 3148
"New Yorkers did not live at all"
  5278
"New Yorkers live, the way" 5278
"New York-humid" 4396
"New York's East Side" 10413
"New York's Idlewild" 10006
"New York's traffic" 1012
"New Zealand" 228, 5938, 7663
"New Zealand miles" 10535
"Newbern" 8084
"newborn baby" 7067
"newborn child" 6702
"newer, looking oddly" 7883
"newer [community], a" 1384
"new-fangled days" 5681
"new-fashioned scandal" 1342
"Newfield Connecticut" 2360
"Newgate" 3527
"Newhouse" 9134
"newlywed, very fortunate young"
  3264
"newlywed's jalopy, like tin cans on
  a" 5587
"Newport" 4064
"Newport, Battle of" 713
News 400, 707, 1817, 1905, 1950,
  2419, 3414, 3770, 4014, 4591,
  5571, 5735, 5743, 5753, 6349,
  6397, 7831, 8859, 9291, 9364
"news" 4014
"news, bad" 6323
"news, bearer of bad" 2419
"news, brought the" 6340
"News, CBS Evening" 6335
"news, disagreeable" 6315
"news, disturbed to get" 5753
"news, front page" 6343
"news, have you heard the" 6309,
  6336
"News, Illustrated London" 987
"news, some bad" 6326
"news, some good" 6326
"news, the" 6316
"News, the" 6652
"news, the morning's" 6311

"news, unexpected" 1950
"news, watch the" 6342
"news, we haven't the heart for
  the" 6347
"news conference" 5207
"news from every part of the
  world" 5743
"news item took place" 6319
"news of Gilbert's plan" 6940
"news of his repatriation" 4567
"news of Lee's surrender" 6313
"news of my grandfather's death"
  1905
"news of the accident" 6339
"news of the messenger's arrival"
  6334
"news of Tu's death" 6327
"news of whose death we have just
  heard" 707
"news ... reached the little Massachusetts town of Mendon" 6313
"news reached the Rialto" 6345
"news swept out of the West" 6333
"news that Josef Virek had escaped" 3414
"news that nobody prints" 4314
"news to-night, any" 6308
"news took days" 6341
"newsboy" 3021
"newspaper" 6322
"newspaper, in the" 4131
"newspaper, laid down the" 6350
"newspaper, on that" 5786
"newspaper, startled from the" 6321
"newspaper, unfold her second"
  4280
"newspaper building" 6319
"newspaper clipping" 6154
"newspaper clipping, yellowed" 829
"newspaper columnist, brilliant
  young" 5485
"newspaper credit of my generosity"
  121
"newspaper cuttings" 5027
"newspaper editor" 10931
"newspaper entered Rogerson's
  study like a kite" 6354
"newspaper in his hands" 6359
"newspaper kiosk" 10366
"Newspaper of Claremont Street"
  1710
"newspaper scanners" 9381
"newspaper scribblers" 7150
"newspaperman" 2829
Newspapers 696, 847, 987, 1931,
  2018, 3770, 4280, 4289, 5209,
  5485, 5571, 5786, 6310, 6312,
  6319, 6320, 6321, 6322, 6324,
  6325, 6328, 6397, 6421, 6717,
  6815, 6853, 6863, 7107, 7352,
  7365, 7367, 7369, 7820, 7831,
  8061, 8470, 8956
"newspapers" 2018
"newspapers, book-reviewing
  departments of" 8470

"newspapers, country" 6312
"newspapers, first reached the" 6346
"newspapers, old" 3256
"newspapers, read the" 400
"newspapers, reading their" 7352
"newspapers, repeal" 5194
"newspapers all said" 9072
"newspapers and magazines" 4788
"newsreel, an old" 876
"newsstands" 10438
"Newsweek" 4008
Newthorpe, Mr. 3989
Newton, Mr. Isaac 3376
"Newtown" 7062
"next year at this time" 6941
"next-to-nothingness" 6478
"Ngesi" 6177
"Niagara, celebrated cataract of"
  2619
"Niagara river" 4043
"nibble, no more than" 6988
"nibbled cruelly up and down his
  long limbs and sides" 152
"nibbles in the half light" 5624
"nibbling at Thursday night" 9474
"Nicaise, S." 652
Nicandra 7745
"Nice" 5329, 6949
"nice, be" 2877
"nice, it would have been" 2920
"nice, something not" 10280
"nice and simple" 10954
"nice of you to come to the station"
  1504
"nice people" 7037
"niche in the world, a comfortable"
  5998
Nicholas 6345, 6797
Nick 684, 3606
Nick, Uncle 3942
"nicked me into facets" 2977
"nickel" 10530
Nickleby, Mr. Godfrey 5728
"nickname, my" 4764
"nickname for Providence" 1222
"nickname in the Foreign Service"
  4764
"nickname of the train" 7251
"nickname the neighbours stuck
  upon him" 6018
"nicknamed Felicity" 9073
Nicknames 4764, 6018
Nicky 2171
Nicobar, Colonel 10486
Nicola 2769
Nicolidou, Mrs. 10997
Nicolson, Catriona 3667
"nicotine taste, cold" 8568
"niece, deceased woman's" 3963
"niece, my" 8003
"niece Amanda, her" 4344
"nieces, three" 11
"nieces, two" 2307
"Niedering, small town called" 5601
Nietzsche 3284

"Nietzsche, according to" 3284
Nigel 8307
"Niger, river" 1429
"Niger, the" 9217
Nigeria 8880
"Nigeria" 4470, 8880, 10795
"nigger, bought this here" 681
"nigger going down the street"
  7395
"nigger Jim, our old" 1160
"nigger slave, on account of he's a"
  5506
"nigger-chaser on the *Eugénie*" 406
"niggers, shack where Major Tyrell
  kept his" 3097
Night 2202, 2247, 2256, 2261,
  2262
"night" 523, 2268, 5338
"night, after a fine" 8178
"night, all" 2972, 8593
"night, amphitheatre of" 2191
"night, Arctic" 2227
"night, at" 3787, 6684, 10747
"night, awful" 10234
"night, bad" 411
"night, beautiful was that" 6364
"night, black Appalachian" 10740
"night, black of" 6376
"night, black reaches of the outer"
  4956
"night, black starry June" 6380
"night, buried" 10743
"night, clear cold moon-flooded"
  8124
"night, cold" 2932
"night, cold November" 7285,
  9256
"night, cool October" 10421
"night, day or" 10178
"night, deepest part of the" 6383
"night, depths of the cool summer"
  10215
"night, descending" 2266
"night, during the" 6688
"night, each" 6543
"night, early spring" 4306
"night, edge of the" 9810
"night, every" 8488
"night, fire in the" 3761
"night, flying at" 211
"night, fogbound winter" 833
"night, forty-three days without a"
  8680
"night, gala" 9396
"night, giant cyclops eye pierced
  the" 7278
"night, gray Sunday" 8598
"night, hardly a" 1999
"night, hot July" 9381
"night, hot summer" 8014
"night, hour of the deepest hush
  of" 8324
"night, in the black of the" 10881
"night, in the company of" 1685
"night, in the dead of" 1138

"night, in the middle of the" 2374,
  10265
"night, into the" 1683
"night, it is always" 2247
"night, it must have been a Thursday" 5805
"night, it was" 8097, 8728
"night, it was a shocking" 6368
"night, it was a summer's" 8857
"night, it was always" 4332
"night, it was the" 6366
"night, last" 2783, 10726
"night, late icy December" 8798
"night, late one October" 1894
"night, lesser choruses of the" 2790
"night, London winter" 7285
"night, loneliest" 6372
"night, long long into the" 8984
"night, long winter" 2229
"night, middle of an August" 559
"night, middle of the" 8706
"night, midsummer" 4401
"night, mild January" 667
"night, now it was" 420
"night, on a June" 2258
"night, on a Saturday" 9147
"night, on a winter" 596
"night, on any" 9994
"night, on my last" 9801
"night, on that Monday" 10069
"night, on this hot" 8516
"night, on this particular" 9095
"night, once upon a winter's"
  9789
"night, one" 6708
"night, one cold March" 1985
"night, one late February" 7084
"night, one warm blue" 8202
"night, opening" 9380
"night, quiet" 4623
"night, quiet hum of late" 8753
"night, quite a turbulent" 10285
"night, rained in the" 7332
"night, rainy" 9016
"night, rich warm" 1569
"night, Saturday" 2863, 6372
"night, shadow of" 2202
"night, she didn't like the" 10220
"night, silence of" 8813
"night, small hours of the" 4089
"night, soft summer" 8766
"night, sometimes at" 1972
"night, starless May" 7687
"night, starry" 6384
"night, still" 8586
"night, suffused the" 8523
"night, sultry August" 1603
"night, summer" 520, 3995
"night, swimming at" 9323
"night, that" 2463, 3779, 6373,
  7739, 10722
"night, that July" 9098
"night, that Monday" 1095
"night, that warm autumn" 6208
"night, the" 3760, 6377

"night, this immense and silent
  winter's" 2521
"night, this particular" 6375
"night, this tumultuous rain-
  lashed" 1706
"night, this warm spring" 8472
"night, up all" 3818
"night, very dark" 10678
"night, very late one windless September" 9546
"night, villainously cold and sleety
  and tempest-twisted" 6365
"night, warm spring" 1601
"night, wet autumn" 6624
"night, what of the" 2942
"night, white" 6384
"night, wild" 7080
"night air" 181
"night and day" 1284
"night before, awoke much too early
  for her" 10126
"night before Christmas" 1727
"night before he died, remember
  the" 7429
"night before we learned of the
  drowning, the" 2798
"night began badly" 7016
"night Billy cut the soldier's lung in
  half" 2933
"night came on, as the February"
  10934
"night cast by a cluster of statuary"
  6367
"night comes as a surprise in the
  tropics" 2261
"night could pass without a summons of that sort, a whole" 1118
"night entered the clearing from
  the scrub" 2205
"night falls" 6371
"night filled with promise" 1437
"night for memories" 7419
"night from Saturday to Sunday"
  10881
"night gradually dissolved around
  them" 2191
"night . . . had already begun"
  2229
"night had closed down" 6323
"night had come" 2256
"night had ended" 10708
"night I spent in London, the last"
  7996
"night in August, one" 2675
"night in each month, during one"
  4956
"night in early August, that airless"
  8832
"night in late September" 1706
"night in 1942, a clear" 889
"night in November, one cold" 1960
"night in the dark New England
  hills" 2224
"night in the early spring of 1962"
  208

"night in the foster home, my first" 997

"night into darkness, threw the" 8450

"night is coming down" 8830

"night is generally my time for walking" 96

"night is now seven years ago, that" 9047

"night is so goddamned long and hot and cloying" 6381

"night is the time to escape" 6791

"night it all began" 3971

"night long, all" 375, 8482

"night my father chased Red Elk out of the valley" 6382

"night my father lost himself and I lost him" 6374

"night nor DDT could stop" 5288

"night of August 13th" 2343

"night of early summer" 8178

"night of midsummer, in the white" 5633

"night of my birth" 786

"night of my thirteenth birthday" 835

"night of patchy dreams" 6379

"night of rain, after the" 8406

"night of September 29" 6209

"night of summer comes late" 8031

"night of the side alley, the deep" 7620

"night off from work" 4323

"night passes westward over Europe" 2262

"night shadow passed, slowly the" 8036

"night shapes, gray" 10273

"night so faultless" 6363

"night so sulfurous so restless so swollen with inarticulate longing" 1706

"night Tendai was conceived" 8029

"night the boy was born" 825

"night through, the whole" 8501

"night was a torment to me, every" 75

"night was black and still" 6362

"night was falling" 3108

"night was mute and black" 2790

"night . . . was so almost hot" 4401

"night was sultry for square dancing" 4384

"night was sweet and he was sour" 6369

"night was young and so was he" 6369

"night watchman" 8520

"night water" 5952

"night we left Hispaniola for home" 3766

"night we thought all was ended" 3766

"night with King Charles, too merry a" 9882

"night with wind, snowy" 1727

"night without pain or drugs, her first" 10291

"nightbell" 8480

"nightcap, what about a" 10729

"nightcrow" 7604

"nightfall, before" 1615

"nightfall, by" 6328

"nightfall, shortly after" 9833

"nightfall, third" 530

"nightfall was coming" 2235

"nightgown, in a long flannel" 2831

"nightgown, in her" 7540

"nightgown, under her" 8015

"*Nightline*" 5296

"nightmare" 3512

"nightmare, a heavy" 1250

"nightmare, it was a" 2813

"nightmare, the" 2817

"nightmare, twentieth-century" 3392

"Nightmare Abbey" 3058

"nightmare is terrifying because it can never be undone" 2768

"nightmare slid out of his mind" 10209

Nightmares 2768, 2782, 2813, 2817, 3392, 10209, 10228

"nightmares, figured in my" 10228

Nights 75, 96, 181, 375, 411, 520, 523, 559, 560, 596, 621, 825, 835, 1370, 1437, 1545, 1569, 1584, 1603, 1683, 1685, 1706, 1960, 2105, 2200, 2205, 2224, 2227, 2229, 2258, 2275, 2283, 2521, 2790, 2856, 2863, 2932, 2933, 3343, 3516, 3760, 3761, 3766, 3779, 3787, 3995, 4332, 4381, 4384, 4401, 4664, 4956, 4969, 5288, 5338, 5504, 5633, 6684, 6688, 6791, 7016, 7080, 7216, 7271, 7285, 7286, 7332, 7419, 7429, 7687, 7996, 8031, 8036, 8097, 8324, 8392, 8449, 8450, 8463, 8472, 8482, 8492, 8499, 8500, 8501, 8523, 8598, 8703, 8728, 8766, 8813, 8829, 8830, 8832, 9016, 9095, 9396, 9415, 9789, 9893, 10020, 10069, 10220, 10234, 10285, 10291, 10390, 10416, 10678, 10722, 10747

"nights, mortal" 5704

"nights, on idle" 8976

"nights, on some" 4381

"nights, one of those" 4664, 6378

"nights, one of those December" 1545

"nights, rainiest" 7286

"nights, southern" 6381

"nights, these spring" 6292

"nights are long here" 621

"nights at the farm" 2275

"nights belonged to the novelist" 5504

"nights blew cold" 5704

"nights in the New England country" 8622

"nights nobody wants, one of those" 6365

"night's stillest hour" 8491

"nights were clear and sharp" 3396

"nights were still cool" 10020

"nightshade" 6273

"night-stand, stainless steel" 4628

Nighttime 2123, 2248

"nighttime of his empty cabin" 10278

"Nihilon, guidebook to" 912

Niki 4814

"Nile, river" 7648

"Nile, sandy soil watered by the" 1351

"Nile, the" 7361, 7681, 7799

"Nile was falling, the" 7700

Nilsson, Christine 1012, 8740

Nina 7085

"nineteen, by the time he was" 5413

"nineteen twice, later he was" 871

"ninety, she was over" 2456

"Nineveh" 1431

Ninian 9329

Nino 2426

"niño" 9505

"nipping off of noggins" 10955

"nipples erect" 8014

"nipples of the jacket" 9579

Nitburg, Kyle 1279

Nixon 9375

Nixon, Richard 7000

"Nixon resigned, when" 9375

"N.J." 7345

Nne-nne 3324

Nnu Ego 1697

"no!" 1842

"*no*, absolute" 3480

"no, knew that he ought to have said" 50

"No, power of saying" 6613

"no he don't" 256

"no longer twenty-nine, I am" 4809

No Name 10056

"no one" 799, 2578, 7751, 10966

"no one about, there was" 9406

"no one else will" 8983

"no one was there" 10614

"no one with him" 2362

"no other, since I have" 5502

"no thanks" 2921

Noah 2266, 4465

Noakes, Heather 7026

"Noat, Public School of" 2531

"Nob Hill, rocky gulches of" 5130

"Nobility" 10466

"nobility, treated as befitted her" 3413

"nobility of nose" 5921

Noble, Gustad 7547

"noble, tall massive and" 1174

"noble lord" 1167

"nobleman, Danish" 3879

"nobleman, diminutive" 8946
"noblemen were hanged" 7184
"nobodies, public" 6763
"nobody, a" 4008
"nobody, bride was a" 10671
"nobody, son of" 366
"nobody in Alabama" 2967
"nobody knows" 279
"nobody remembers why" 3658
"nobody thought so" 3385
"nobody was in a hurry" 6832
"noctambulo, dreamy stride of a" 10463
"nod at every sad car in the line, trying to" 2973
"nod his head in grave accord" 6219
"nod to Briggs, with a" 1908
"nodded and then replied solemnly" 298
"nodded his approval" 3844
"nodded sleepily upon the gentle swells of warm water" 8057
"nodding to him" 4971
"noggin, cracking me on the" 38
"noggins, nipping off of" 10955
"noise, clinking" 8819
"noise, first loud thudding" 8805
"noise, grating" 6272
"noise, he shuts out the engine" 7628
"noise, no" 8039
"noise, no unexpected" 9905
"noise, persistent buzzing" 8832
"noise, slight" 8174
"noise, thought she heard a" 8818
"noise, thunderous" 10258
"noise during the day, so great was the" 8826
"noise from outside broke loud and sudden" 8828
"noise from the street, a hum of" 8830
"noise in yard behind house" 6964
"noise like a broken exhaust pipe" 8827
"noise like whettin two rocks together" 8780
"noise of a patrol helicopter" 236
"noise of children playing" 8815
"noise of somebody pounding on the door" 10135
"noise of the falls" 8820
"noise of the rioting" 8777
"noise of the windshield wipers" 8782
"noise of wheels on gravel" 8815
"noise ripped through the rumpled fabric of my sleep" 8832
"noise shook the ground" 10258
"noise startled a figure" 10177
"noise that the Water Star made" 8783
"noises, amidst intolerable" 1093
"noises, clucking" 8806
"noises, higher pitched" 3299

"noises, medley of" 7608
"noises made by the woman" 10188
"noises muted and monotonous" 1274
"noises of compression, tiny" 8831
"noises out behind the barn" 3465
"noises very pleasant to hear" 7608
"noisy" 3584
"noisy woman" 2589
Nolan, Lew 6009
Nolan, Miss 4208
"nomad, the" 1426
"nomads" 6167
"Nome blisters the lower lip of Seward Peninsula" 4096
"nominate a successor" 6994
"nominee for vice-president" 7007
"none other than Professor Timofey Pnin" 9564
"none to speak of" 4501
"Nones of May" 5431
Nonsense 3271, 8743
"nonsense, some such charming" 4634
"nonsense about it, no" 660
"nonsense of a sort" 4503
"nook, a certain quiet and sequestered" 4304
"nook, a sea-surrounded" 4533
"Nook, The" 7109
"nook of the retired village of London" 4304
Noon 2221, 2236, 10518
"noon, at the striking of" 6001
"noon, August" 8398
"noon, broad bewildered" 5629
"noon, calm early summer" 2221
"noon, deep hush of" 3897
"noon, heat and din of" 5096
"noon, high" 9527
"noon, hour short of" 4390
"noon, it was" 1650
"noon, it was a bright" 2236
"noon, it was almost" 7806
"noon, just before" 2406
"noon, shortly before" 10926
"noon, spacious August" 10053
"noon, windless" 9479
"noon and nightfall, between" 10084
"noon chiming on two bells, listening to" 660
"Noon City" 9553
"noon of a September day" 8057
"noon over the Amazon, high" 7339
"noon passes over the Urals" 10518
"noose about his neck, placed the" 9292
Nop 10945
Nora 691, 2298, 4310
"Norbiton" 9711
Norby 5347
Nordau 962
Nordstrom, Seena 10645
"Norfolk" 4104, 5537
"Norfolk Virginia" 2839

Norma 2664
"normal, act" 9968
"normal, not quite" 1801
"normal behavior" 642
Normalyn 396
Norman 1111, 5323
"Norman childe" 3381
"Norman Conquest" 834
"Norman favourites, his" 3571
"Normandy" 1779, 6644
"Normandy, invasion of" 6863
"north, all day" 8434
"North, great white" 4047
"North America" 4076, 4462, 10468, 10470
"North America, what would later become" 4095
"North Americans, two" 5609
"North Bath, village of" 9203
"North Berwick Law" 4587
"North Carolina" 3097, 3448, 4675, 6084, 8110
"North Carolina, Outer Banks of" 9089
"North Carolina Mutual Life Insurance" 9602
"North Carolina pine, logs of" 3760
"North Cornwall" 1500
"North Dakota" 10092
"North Devon" 1336
"North Dormer" 1585
"North Koreans" 10500
"north of east" 1361
"North Oxford" 2272
"North Pole, high above the" 216
"north south east or west" 5604
"North Star" 527
"Northampton" 286, 5727
"Northampton, U.S.S." 8137
"Northbridge" 3136
"Northern Ireland" 6257
"Northington Connecticut" 2554
"northland, the" 5902
"Northumberland" 2786
Northwick 10032
Northwood, Adrian John 5383
"Northwood" 5482
"Norton, second-hand" 7062
"Norton-on-Hudson" 5747
Norval, Patrick 4008
"Norway" 5707
"Norway spruce-trees" 9663
"Norwegian whaling fleet" 8116
Norwood 8670
"nose, beaked" 10832
"nose, bridge of his" 5329
"nose, cut off my" 2394
"nose, Edwin's" 8518
"nose, especially his" 8827
"nose, filled your" 8532
"nose, his mother's sharp slightly prominent Anglican" 4438
"nose, hits it right on the" 6653
"nose, hold your" 602
"nose, hook" 5903

"nose, hooked" 333
"nose, long astute pointed" 5912
"nose, long straight" 4297
"nose, nobility of" 5921
"nose, not a" 549
"nose, prominent thinly arched" 8237
"nose, rubbing her" 7014
"nose, set his fine" 10339
"nose, wiped her" 4196
"nose between his forepaws, his gray" 403
"nose deep in the ditch" 9790
"nose in air" 4154
"nose long as a lake-edging highway" 10885
"nose or hair or glass of gin, glancing off someone's" 4319
"nose out of joint, put Madam Marlborough's" 3376
"nose to the bedroom window-screen, pressed his" 3604
"nose which stuck up into the morning air" 8827
"nose which was slightly crooked" 5912
"nosed up out of the shadows to greet me" 7440
"nose-picking" 10445
Noses 333, 549, 8532
"noses, sharp" 3396
"noses shining" 4154
Nostalgia 4319, 6272
"nostalgia, a" 6272
"nostalgia, pure wind-swept" 4319
"nostalgia and amusement, a curious warm mixture of" 7398
"nostrils, air from his" 8017
"nostrils, sweeter in the" 4536
"nostrils, the deep insides of your" 761
"nostrils, the Sac's" 8510
"nostrils, through his" 9849
"nostrils placed between the two knees" 2378
"not 1959, it was" 4858
"not a cold November, it was" 4858
"not a small college town in New York, it was" 4858
"not even David Bennett, he was" 4858
"not twenty-one, he was" 4858
"not yours" 1489
"notary's house" 317
"note, farewell" 2570
"note, legitimate five pound" 2044
"note, mellowest highest" 8748
"note, one hysterical disembodied" 5260
"note, scribbled a" 1816
"note, sent him a" 2684
"note, single shrieking" 3716
"note . . . entered the house" 8788
"note from my aunt, I got a" 3840
"note from Robert" 6008

"note high-pitched on a violin" 3716
"note in his hand" 9296
"note of the thrush, the liquid" 8788
"note to the fiddler, give a" 1680
"note which a languid 'bell-boy' had just brought in" 7555
"notebook, Billy Abbott's" 2542
"Notebook, Suicide" 8816
"notebooks, my" 5475
"notebooks, two published" 5507
"noted in fact and apocrypha" 8940
"noted them all" 3465
"noted with pleasure" 1263
"notepaper crackled, heavy blue" 8804
"notes, a quick look at his" 162
"notes, finished some" 10931
"notes, how enchanting are those" 6212
"notes, just a few" 5544
"notes, shorthand" 716
"notes in a restaurant, never takes" 7583
"nothing, become" 6843
"nothing, finally becoming" 10705
"nothing, men who are" 6843
"nothing, strenuously doing" 10067
"nothing at all" 3461
"nothing can be known, of the day and hour" 8663
"nothing ever ends" 3337
"nothing ever goes right" 60
"nothing ever really happens" 1459
"nothing for me to do but errands" 10921
"nothing happens in it" 1374
"nothing he could do, there was" 1747
"nothing in life he hated more" 9470
"nothing is new" 6847
"nothing is worthwhile" 3461
"nothing like I was told, this is" 8199
"nothing much" 629
"nothing of the sort for me" 1163
"nothing of their fugitive existence left" 8400
"nothing there was the same as now" 3369
"nothing to be done but wait" 2625
"nothing to do, having" 894
"nothing to do but stand there" 9387
"nothing to do with it" 7551
"nothing was ever so interesting again" 943
"nothing was the same now" 1248
"nothingness, innocent wisps of undifferentiated" 5266
"nothingness of existence" 5277
"notice, first" 1256
"notice, I take no" 740
"notice, printed" 8313

"notice, single unobtrusive little" 5735
"notice couched in the customary bald form of words" 5735
"notice that Winter was come" 10574
"notice these things, useless to" 7855
"noticed, few of us" 3403
"noticed, first" 8288
"noticed, first thing I" 179
"noticed for some time" 637
"noticed for the first time that I had become invisible" 2582
"noticed him" 335
"noticed it immediately" 8284
"noticed over the years" 4712
"noticed right away, not everyone" 3354
"noticed the girl" 4190
"noticed the small track" 2606
"notices it, first" 160
"noticing her" 10798
"noticing things again" 3347
"notions, his slick and thrifty" 583
Notoriety 500, 3537, 4768
"notorious" 4788
"Notre Dame" 3922
"Notre Dame des Doms, within the shadow of" 487
"no-trump, one" 318
"Nottinghamshire" 3082, 6602
"nourish an entire block of underprivileged children" 10826
"nourish maidenhair ferns" 5169
"nouveau, art" 5659
"*Nova*" 4008
"Nova Scotia" 9065
"novel, a" 5551
"novel, begin his" 5414
"novel, better off in an opera than a" 5498
"novel, character in a" 5467
"novel, his third" 5463
"novel, in the beginning of a famous" 5466
"novel, last sentence of the" 5541
"novel, second" 5468
"novel, then there is a" 5409
"novel, this is a" 5540
"novel, when I told him about my" 5508
"novel, write a" 5482
"novel in the first person, never write a" 5513
"novel or a romance, in the light of a" 5386
"novel that would make all those smug bastards at Williams choke with envy" 2527
"novel with more misgiving, I have never begun a" 5425
"novelist, nights belonged to the" 5504
"novelist, poet and" 5534

"novelist, problems which beset the" 5414

"novelist Edward Granville" 710

"novelist might imagine it, as a" 4899

"novelist's friends, any of the famous" 696

"novelists of the present day, English" 5440

"novelists were holding a dialogue with their own subconscious minds" 5512

Novelists 696, 710, 4899, 5414, 5423, 5440, 5504, 5512, 5534

"novel-reading world" 5393

Novels 921, 2527, 5386, 5393, 5409, 5414, 5419, 5425, 5441, 5463, 5466, 5467, 5468, 5482, 5498, 5508, 5513, 5518, 5540, 5541, 5543, 5551, 7348, 10904

"novels, Henry Fielding's" 5543

"novels, paperback copies of his" 5468

"novels, their bad" 7000

"novels he had published for years" 5419

"November" 228, 583, 754, 1201, 1294, 1496, 1611, 1960, 2087, 2189, 2501, 3494, 3974, 4017, 4636, 4702, 4858, 5429, 5568, 5818, 6168, 6410, 6003, 6970, 6991, 7079, 7218, 7285, 7322, 8432, 8511, 8592, 8606, 8620, 8677, 9256, 10006, 10189, 10438, 10567, 10577, 10678, 10692, 10699, 10708

"November evening" 971

"November evenings" 2240

"November opened its eye" 9482

"November sky" 7267

"novena started" 7785

"novices, three" 10427

Novotny 6764

"now and then" 10494

"now is the time" 6989

"now on, from" 10969

"nowhere, out of" 9957

"nowhere, seemingly out of" 9955

"nowhere, the heart of" 6921

"nowhere to go" 932

"nowhere to nowhere" 211

Nu 10340

Nu Wa 514

"NUDE ROMP" 6397

"nudged with his elbow" 8556

Nudity 568, 573, 1166, 1169, 2773, 6680, 6891, 7480, 9291, 9355, 10236

"nudity, his gross" 7480

"nudity, in a state of perfect" 6385

Nueces 8549

"nuisance, a" 5693

"nuisance for both of us, a great" 51

"number, wrong" 1138

"numbers, taught him" 3279

"numerical form" 6478

"numerous, the more" 9261

"nun, young" 9853

Nunes, Captain Sylvester 8046

"Nunnery Grounds" 816

Nuns 36, 1312, 2047, 5003, 6111, 10859

"nuns, thirty" 1312

"nuns, two" 9620

"nuns in a convent" 6266

"nuns lived, where the" 2047

"nuns of St. Louis de France Parochial School" 2336

"nuns said it was God's will" 36

"nuptials, solemnize the" 10641

Nureddin 4669

"Nuremberg" 2237

Nurse 4199

"nurse, hands of the" 4508

"nurse, her" 541

"nurse, his sharp-featured" 3272

"nurse, monthly" 540

"nurse, mother's" 10845

"nurse, night" 1770

"nurse, once my" 4970

"nurse, the" 2298

"nurse at ten o'clock each morning" 128

Nurse Benson 4146

"nurse came into the room" 4620

"nurse came stealing" 1770

"nurse held the door open" 6893

"nurse made a mistake" 4614

"nursed their three-week-old son" 5636

"Nursery any longer, it wasn't to be called the" 7759

"nursery smell of clothes boiling" 7441

Nurses 556, 1770, 2298, 4508, 4614, 4620, 4628, 10845

"nurses, the" 4628

"nurses were in charge of naming the new babies" 556

Nussey, Ellen 9935

"nut, the trouble of cracking the" 4491

"nut case, thought he was a" 5823

Nutmeg, Maximilian 2068

"nuts of knowledge fall from the hazel bush" 10756

Nye, Reverend Mr. Nathaniel 1518

"nylon, sheerest" 5450

Nyokabi 10815

O 1753

"O, You Kid" 2828

Oak, Farmer 8545

"oak, blackjack" 5161

"oak, cool" 1194

"oak, giant" 8321

"Oak, on" 9142

"oak, polished" 5886

"oak, scrub" 4073

"oak, twice-planted pin" 9186

"oak, young" 2205

"Oak Bluffs" 9601

"Oak River" 1377

"oak sapling-trunks" 3092

"oak tree" 10307

"oak trees" 3894

"Oakland" 3637

"Oakland Greyhound" 9620

"Oakland Pier" 7269

Oaklin 7127

"oaks, great moss-hung" 3090

"oaks, scrub" 1018, 7609, 9116

"oaks, tall red" 10697

"Oaks, The" 3660

"oaks and beeches, into the depths of the" 7326

"oaks close to the river's edge" 3090

"oak-tree roots" 9673

"Oare, parish of" 8957

"oars, little thick" 839

"oars lifted and fell with a desolate splashing" 8134

"oats, monotonous expanse of wild" 9116

"obedience to my heart's most urgent commands" 9279

"obedient to the social law" 7816

O'Beirne, Miss 1436

"obelisk, slender" 8947

"Oberlin campus" 2083

Obesity 5907, 5908, 5913, 5943, 6570, 7472, 7643, 10443

"obesity, his" 7472

"obeyed bawled orders, doggedly" 8699

"obeying its summons to evening prayer" 650

"obits, doing" 6717

Obituaries 2569, 6320, 6717, 7363

"obituaries, haunted the" 2569

"obituary, read the" 7363

"object, inanimate" 2107

"object, indistinct" 9781

"object, its real" 5829

"object, my" 2110

"object and show" 1284

"object hurtling past him" 10297

"Object of my own Deceit" 6033

"object to, what I" 7713

"objection, if you have no" 9866

"objections to other people doing so, I do not have any" 4789

"objections you mention" 5387

"objectives, I have two" 254

"Objects, Unidentified Frozen" 2618

"objects hidden in the tree" 9680

"objects of vast importance" 2600

"objects that were new to me, vast variety of" 947

"obligation hangs over the land, weight of" 9951

"obligations, I have fulfilled my worldly" 6494

"obliged to load her with so much pity and advice" 2672
"oblique streets" 5607
"obliquely, words coming out" 9004
"obliquely across the gravel, shadows of the lime-trees strike" 2951
"obliterating discordant colours, bent on" 484
"obliterating houses and the telegraph poles" 10604
"oblivion, fucked each other into" 8027
"oblivion to consciousness, from" 10156
"oblivious, passed" 10392
"oblivious to it, remaining" 2450
"oboe had suddenly become articulate" 10005
O'Brien 8817
O'Brien, Emilio Montez 3263
O'Brien, James 503
"obscure, however" 5558
"obscured almost instantly" 8401
"obscured by dust" 9792
"obscured the four small white stores" 1056
"obscurely, a sale held" 494
Obscurity 908, 4008, 5557
"obscurity" 5557
"obscurity, medieval" 1464
"observation on the characters and manners of the world" 5553
Observation 205, 948, 1859, 2613, 3363, 3864, 3995, 4955, 8268, 8282, 8288, 8845, 10998
"Observation, trite but true" 7163
"observations, confused" 1833
"observations are inexact, many of my" 10998
"observations of my own" 8999
"observations of ours, some critical" 8642
"observatory" 8333
"observed it all" 8918
"observer, casual" 4327
"observer, close but not cruel" 6286
"observer of what went on" 6286
"observers from every neutral country, competent" 3413
"observers of vegetable nature" 9660
"observers who were able to observe anything except the heat" 10336
"observes, very judiciously" 4490
"obsessed with waste" 1261
Obsession 1261, 7165, 7739, 8494, 9453
"obsession, take time to get over an" 7165
"obsolete" 309
"obstacle, unexpected" 44
"obstinacy of an old half-rotted tree" 6436
"obviate the long drive in to work" 5104

"obvious, it became" 6154
"obvious, later it will be found to have been" 5575
"obzockee, bottle was big and" 10961
"Ocanara" 4563
"occasion, an" 9380
"occasion, cannot be considered a cheerful" 579
"occasion, high sense of" 6008
"occasion, it was an" 6754
"occasion, the" 843
"occasion of some tension and anxiety" 7069
"occasion so generally known" 7825
"occasion was exceptional" 2738
"occasionally" 6540
Occasions 579, 843, 7069, 9380
"occasions, one of those" 2088
"Occidental world" 1021
"occupant, the only" 8719
"occupant of a small-sized reception-room" 8719
"occupant of the room, the other" 7468
"occupants, the two" 4393
"occupants of the room" 7753
"occupants were scurrying from place to place" 4016
"occupation, my present" 6419
"occupation, same quiet" 239
"occupation, this was not a life-time" 6485
"occupation for an idle hour" 4439
"occupation turns out to be that of wireless operator" 6461
Occupations 84, 87, 196, 231, 239, 240, 257, 349, 499, 501, 503, 506, 513, 847, 892, 1254, 1319, 1483, 1491, 1493, 1502, 1520, 1540, 1590, 1654, 1968, 2011, 2096, 2178, 3124, 3327, 3472, 3508, 3534, 3697, 3758, 3855, 4186, 4273, 4352, 4629, 4729, 4745, 4821, 4837, 4872, 5003, 5213, 5286, 5287, 5311, 5490, 5569, 5667, 5757, 5758, 5841, 5854, 5865, 5982, 6107, 6175, 6183, 6319, 6495, 6497, 6628, 6867, 6886, 6898, 6901, 6928, 6951, 6987, 7079, 7128, 7177, 7721, 7727, 7880, 7896, 8040, 8071, 8220, 8341, 8515, 8901, 9327, 9423, 9460, 9801, 10557, 10809, 10896, 10958
"occupied, it seemed to be" 8267
"occupied, it was already" 8369
"occupied, town was" 10481
"occupied a café table" 9464
"occupied a second-class compartment" 4139
"occupied by someone else" 796
"occupied by W. and S. Simon" 6964

"occupied for some public purpose" 949
"occupied our capital city" 10500
"occupy myself" 8299
"occupying space, just" 8834
"occur to me, it didn't" 5482
"occurred, things as they" 8962
"occurred before" 7372
"occurred during my recent Christmas holaday" 3496
"occurred the morning of the day before he ran away" 2562
"occurred to any of us, it never" 6288
"occurred to her, it had" 5276
"occurred to me, it had never" 675
"occurred to Min, it" 3622
"occurred to Rob Ashton, it had just" 242
"occurred very much at the same hour and together" 5085
"occurred within a causal radius of Brandon railway-station" 6001
Occurrences 165, 709, 887, 3403, 9006, 9049, 9694
"occurrences, removed from natural" 3435
"occurrences, wondrous" 3403
"occurrences connected in various ways with this neighborhood" 9694
"occurring in our region, something strange is" 165
"occurring simultaneously" 7616
"occurs, never quite" 3445
"ocean, all of which pour their tribute into the" 7647
"Ocean, Atlantic" 7186
"ocean, atop a tumbling white ridge of" 8145
"ocean, breeze that came off the" 8248
"Ocean, Coney Island" 7932
"ocean, from the" 10701
"ocean, I see the" 7932
"ocean, ignorance of the" 4887
"Ocean, Indian" 7921
"ocean, like an aerial" 10629
"ocean, motionless as an" 5132
"ocean, on the breast of the slumbering" 8049
"ocean, one" 8990
"ocean, over the" 2199
"ocean, return to the" 4652
"ocean, shoreless" 4533
"ocean, silent as an" 5132
"ocean, southern" 10737
"ocean, storm outside in the" 9069
"ocean, the whole might of" 435
"ocean, three miles of" 5039
"ocean, vast as an" 5132
"ocean, windows full of" 4354
"ocean beaches" 4064
"ocean coaxed into very little ripples" 5132

"ocean heaved in a deep unhurried rhythm" 7939
"ocean liner, big" 8105
"ocean liner, great" 8153
"ocean mothered us all" 7941
"ocean on the east" 7937
"Ocean Park" 4064
"ocean salt" 7657
"ocean surf, thunder of" 10230
"ocean waves, across a wilderness of" 6135
"ocean which lay unseen" 10701
"Oceanic Institute" 8520
Oceans 4098, 7921, 9747
"oceans, define the ancient" 4095
"oceans, glowing blue" 2623
"oceans, over the" 5542
"oceans, rare gem among the" 4098
"oceans, water forming the" 525
"ocean's edge, at the" 9783
"oceans ran wild with stress and hate" 760
"ocher mud, bowl of" 2833
"ochre and madder" 10494
Ockham, Mrs. 969
O'Connell, Mr. 5194
O'Connor, Seamus 4690
"ocotillo whips" 5190
"octagon, tall handsome pillared" 6226
"octaves, Sicilian" 5457
Octavia 1230
Octavio 4542
"Octet, The Grenzler" 5541
"October" 532, 635, 788, 1295, 1736, 1852, 1894, 1905, 1923, 1949, 2213, 2234, 2264, 2272, 2339, 2474, 2518, 3820, 3992, 4126, 4391, 4637, 4943, 5081, 5108, 5303, 5313, 5541, 5631, 6111, 6232, 6344, 6437, 6575, 6580, 6783, 6824, 7284, 7568, 7579, 7658, 7753, 7963, 8101, 8104, 8592, 9093, 9262, 9350, 9394, 9527, 9761, 9935, 10173, 10339, 10421, 10501, 10780, 10968
"October, early in" 1702, 9112
"October, gray" 2233
"October, it was" 970, 1301, 9667
"October, mid" 7296
"October, middle of" 1057
"October, that day in" 2235
"October afternoon" 1826, 9545
"October day" 4906
"October day, in the dying" 4156
"October of 1956, during the cold" 10534
"October sunlight" 1379
"October wind" 10753
"octopus lived in a square plastic box" 438
"*octroi*" 9631
"Odawara" 9188
"odd, I've always found it" 7451
"odd, it is" 1247

"odd, name seems" 9825
"odd, which was" 4331
"odd happened, something" 887
"odd matter, this" 9692
"odd or out of place" 7652
"odd to say it" 2544
"oddest thing of all" 3374
"oddly enough for Greenwich Village" 4099
"odds, at" 1302
"odds, I'll take the" 3964
"Odeon, the" 4503
"Odéon has fallen, the" 9390
"Odessa, voyage from" 4011
"odious" 7163
O'Donnells 9874
"odor of locust blooms, the cloying" 8510
"odor of new construction, peculiar" 8543
"odors" 3478
"odors, sweet and heavy yeasty" 4335
"odors of dark soil warmed by summer rain" 3405
"odors of spring, spongy" 10698
"odour of roses, the rich" 3794
Odysseus 4463
"Odyssey" 1086
O'Farrell 7019
"off, so much was" 1778
"off and on and on and on" 10309
"off guard, rifle in pants caught Aaron" 3954
"off the hooks, practically" 150
"offence, scene of the" 1967
"offended, don't get" 9032
"offended if I lay the plot of this story in Ireland" 5393
"offended me, thought he had" 4992
"offensive, too literary to be really" 9313
"offer, my" 5731
"offer the little understanding I had" 1929
"offered a haven by the Mongols" 6109
"offered her a ride home from the library" 6208
"offered some token" 1217
"offered the freshly dipped pen" 10920
"offered themselves, others who might with some justification have" 705
"offered to and refused by the National Trust" 3160
"offering of blood and milk" 1212
"offerings of tourists and walkers" 3692
"off-hand way, walking on waves in an" 1302
"office" 1772, 6501, 6512
"office, Assistant Secretary's" 6506
"office, at the" 4564, 9340
"office, back in Dr. Fray's" 8359

"office, boat brokerage" 3431
"office, buried deep in her" 5287
"office, burst into the" 4249
"Office, Cabinet" 6999
"office, data-processing" 6471
"office, dingy" 10067
"office, district attorney's" 5200
"office, door of my" 10050
"office, ebony and teak paneled" 7319
"office, entered the" 10846
"office, estate agent's" 615
"office, express" 9142
"office, from inside his" 1992
"office, from the back of the" 2870
"office, future" 6432
"office, great man's" 10049
"office, half" 7752
"office, he had never held an" 8970
"office, his" 1619, 3738, 6140, 6509, 8274, 10036, 10751
"office, his college" 7903
"office, his private" 8254
"office, in his" 7015
"office, in the" 668
"office, large" 1854
"office, last term of" 10521
"office, last to leave the" 6422
"office, letter came to his" 1948
"office, mine" 3334
"office, my" 6504, 10433
"office, my father's" 6508
"office, near the" 7571
"office, pale-blue distempered" 247
"office, private" 5786
"office, registry" 6622
"office, road outside his" 8776
"office, sat in his" 3332, 8859
"office, sits in his" 1982
"office, the" 583, 3855, 7763, 9880, 9911
"office, walked back to the" 6443
"office, windowless" 1942
"office at the back of Mr. McKechnie's bookshop" 5621
"office door" 10058
"office here in the hospital" 4281
"office of Conger & Way" 1029
"office of Medallion the auctioneer" 9209
"office of our naval attaché" 6502
"office of the manager of Guildenstern's Stores" 2511
"office of the prefect of studies" 7892
"office room, my" 6499
"office so dark, an" 6511
"office was hushed" 6505
"office was stripped" 6507
"officer, commanding" 570
"officer, executive" 6773
"officer, handsome young Army" 4257
"officer, patrol" 6968
"officer, probation" 2065

"officer and a gentleman, I am an" 5475
"Officer Commanding, General" 8580
"officer in command" 8644
"officer of the college" 7903
"officer of the watch" 8098
"officer-cadet" 8657
Officers 364, 570, 1646, 1757, 2560, 2571, 2897, 4257, 4313, 4511, 4745, 5475, 6128, 6429, 6773, 7153, 7246, 7361, 7903, 8047, 8060, 8066, 8084, 8098, 8102, 8136, 8563, 8580, 8642, 8644, 8650, 8657, 8672, 8694, 8696, 8711, 8713, 9273, 9929, 9961, 10025, 10161, 10498, 10499, 10535, 10978
"officers, Napoleon's" 4142
"officers, two" 8136
"Officers' Advanced Course" 10506
"officers in all, nineteen" 204
"officers' kit" 2841
"officers under guard, English" 7246
"officers-at-arms" 7805
Offices 247, 1008, 1029, 1619, 1854, 1992, 2501, 2511, 3296, 3326, 3332, 4249, 5287, 5621, 6443, 6471, 7903, 8859, 9880, 10050, 10058, 10067
"offices, corporate" 4448
"offices, dark" 7834
"offices, family's executive" 1073
"offices, law" 3296
"offices in or near State Street" 6496
"offices of Girdlestone and Co." 1008
"offices of Lucas & Enwright" 3326
"offices of *The Banner*" 6498
"official, nameless" 87
"official, richly-uniformed" 10538
"officially, not" 8902
Officials 373, 1042, 2390, 2475, 3210, 4466, 6255, 6509, 6950, 6976, 7000, 7481, 7655, 7817, 8161, 8354, 8859, 8866, 8873, 9929
"officials, a lot of other" 7481
"officials, great" 6976
"officials, the usual bunch of port" 8161
Offspring 319, 366, 561, 577, 640, 644, 1121, 1153, 1290, 1502, 1570, 1761, 1765, 1845, 2054, 2079, 2292, 2296, 2393, 2435, 2552, 2584, 2632, 2635, 2649, 2682, 2726, 2765, 2773, 3279, 3283, 3548, 3552, 3553, 3572, 3578, 3579, 3582, 3592, 3593, 3617, 3628, 3630, 3660, 3705, 3789, 4169, 4434, 4438, 4448, 4539, 4564, 4694, 4780, 4889, 4926, 5007, 5484, 5576, 5636, 5699, 5779, 6026, 6187, 6238, 6413, 6583, 6602, 6605, 6609, 6610,

6612, 6613, 6614, 6619, 6620, 6626, 6630, 6632, 6643, 6652, 6654, 6665, 6668, 6674, 6675, 6677, 6680, 6681, 6682, 6683, 6687, 6688, 6690, 6694, 6698, 6699, 6700, 6707, 6711, 6712, 6713, 6719, 6722, 6736, 6743, 6744, 6745, 6748, 6750, 7034, 7035, 7055, 7056, 7059, 7073, 7090, 7183, 7414, 7843, 7863, 8046, 8548, 9003, 9375, 9496, 9866, 10036, 10122, 10322, 10971
"offspring, I can truly claim to be the" 5576
"offspring of a cat" 6413
"offspring of his thought" 2632
O'Flynn, Father 1511
"often as every eighteen months, perhaps as" 1921
"Ogallala" 3649
"*Oggi*" 4008
"ogle Pretty Nell" 3396
"Ogof Crystal" 4056
O'Hara, Scarlett 10793
"Ohio" 533, 2702, 4930, 6412, 10074, 10226
"Ohio, banks of the" 7637
"Ohio, northern" 5166
"Ohio, the" 2513, 7665
"Ohio border" 4097
"Ohio River" 9072
"Ohio wilderness" 4144
Oil 2766, 8165
"oil, an essential" 2766
"oil, he who owns the" 2491
"oil, powered by" 2491
"oil boomtown" 10092
"oil drums" 3787
"oil for medicinal purposes" 8165
"oil fortune, an immense" 5659
"oil lamps" 5315
"oil pumps" 1039
"oil spill, caught my first glimpse of the" 4580
"oil springs" 8165
"oil that when massaged on eyelids became the quicksilver of the brain" 2766
"oils onto canvas, slamming and smudging colorful" 518
"*Oink Oink here and an Oink Oink there*" 882
"ointment and bandages for our wounds" 7516
"Okaloosa Alabama" 7418
"okay" 1135, 8013, 8227
"okay, I live" 5282
O Killens 4877
"Oklahoma" 398, 2009, 5598, 6342, 7031, 7297
"Oklahoma City" 2009
"Oklahoma means red people" 9015
Okonkwo 3535
Okonkwo, Obi 1829
Olaf 1267

"old, growing" 99
"old, I am certainly very" 98
"old, I believe I am" 98
"old, in one moment I grew suddenly" 5096
"old, lived to be" 113
"old, now am" 106
"old, one" 7133
"old, only" 107
"old, she was" 109
"old, so" 3851
"old, were I less" 4503
"old, when I am" 10476
"old, who was very" 9896
"old age" 4468, 9283
"old age, wrinkles of" 9468
"old age waits for everyone" 11001
"old age will be served" 101
"old and crooked, path grew" 9179
"old and fat on their horses, they had grown" 7643
"old and still, now that I am" 117
"old are you, how" 95
"old as the century" 89
"old baroness" 79
"old boys, visit his" 9932
"Old Church" 9093
"Old Cock, the" 6431
"Old Country" 6261
"old country, in the" 6484
"old couple" 8706
"old days" 7181
"Old Dominion" 8171
"old enough" 5739
"old enough to know more" 7607
"old folks' home in the country, every" 5918
"old girl, the" 6956
"old I am, how" 7488
"old I am, tell me how" 90
"old lady" 8555
"'Old MacDonald Had a Farm'" 882
"old man" 1166, 2317, 3207, 5623, 5968, 7388, 8739, 9405
"old man, my" 1686, 6716
"old man, your" 8867
Old Men 96, 100, 520, 1184, 1185, 1907, 3127, 3394, 5823, 5888, 5906, 6316, 6428, 6522, 6917, 7359, 7388, 8574, 8730, 8862, 9796, 10385
"old Mrs. Goodman" 2318
"old now, I am" 104
"old people" 6274
"old people, two" 1554
"Old Taylor, bottle of" 2896
"old times" 3637
"old times, quite like" 7765
"Old Town" 4060
"old when China was young" 93
"old woman" 147, 773, 3099, 5571, 8561
"old woman, I am an" 97
Old Women 113, 114, 5283, 5635

"Old World" 4441
"Old World atmosphere" 6249
"Old World writers" 274
Old Yeller 4747
"Old-Baily" 3527
Oldenshaw, Rear-Admiral Percival 8274
"older, looked a little" 5951
"older, me a summer" 6876
"older now, I am eight years" 675
"older ones, us" 10917
"older than he, everyone was" 81
"older than she had expected" 87
"older women" 1977
"oldest, the" 8230
"oldest house" 3122
"oldest part of the house" 3111
"old-fashioned honour" 1342
Oldfield, Mrs. Anne 8837
"Oldorando" 6146
"old-timer" 105
"oleanders, masked with" 4316
Olga 2049
Oliphant, Catherine 9353
Oliphant, Dan 8208
Oliphant, Harlan 8208
Oliphant, Oliver 119
"olive groves" 1417
"olive mounts" 4034
"olive oil, the dealer in" 10557
"olive tree" 5716
"olive trees, steep torrent of" 5357
Olive 10031
Olive Branch, armed merchant barque" 8079
Oliver 153, 10660
Oliver, Jay 2893
"Oliver-Cromwellizing" 3376
"olives, plantations of" 5125
Olivia 1689, 5873, 9413
Olivio 4337
Ollnee, Victor 8907
Olney 8715
Olson 4938
Olumati 9177
Olumba 4686
Olympias 5451
"Olyphant" 7262
"Omaha" 3087, 6114
O'Malley 6938
"Omburdam" 7361
Omecihuatl 2635
"omelette, just right for a special" 1863
"omelette surprise" 1863
"omelette with the mushrooms Eamonn Eales had collected" 1863
"omen, o dolorous" 9299
Omens 832, 7009, 7020, 7022, 7025, 7028, 9298, 9299
"omens, o dolors of" 9299
"omens, there had been" 7028
"omens, there were no" 7022
"omens and forewarnings" 7009

Ometecuhtli 2635
Ometeotl 2635
"Omeyocan" 2635
"ominous and intimately, something more" 2447
"ominous as joyous" 5260
"ominous cloud of acrid black smoke" 3783
"ominous condition" 7514
"ominous departure, September's" 10700
"ominous news" 5743
"ommernous, every bit of it is" 7010
omnia vincit amor" 5647
"omnibus" 953, 9761
"omnibus, huge" 9759
"omnibus, white" 9542
"omnibus stopped" 9130
"omniscient rationality" 7132
Omri 4124, 7049
"Omsk" 4076
"on, but it was only just" 9368
"on and on and on" 2721, 10309
"on foot, set out" 10431
"on her way" 9540
"on his way within an hour" 9724
"on my own, am now" 6460
"on the go" 9567
"on your way" 6157
"once again" 4682, 8501
"once in a way" 1921
"once on a time" 9535
"once there were three patients" 3923
"once upon a day" 2316
"once upon a time" 806, 811, 1469, 1576, 1969, 3822, 4167, 4510, 4759, 5219, 5523, 7050, 7055, 7714, 8672, 9475, 9793, 10862
"Once upon a time and a very good time it was" 961
"once upon a winter's night" 9789
"One, the" 2632
"*one* and two and three and four" 6217
"one of them, I think this may be" 8995
"one of *us*, not quite" 5919
"one of us, she's really" 4138
"one we took yesterday, the" 9182
"One Wing" 8649
"one-and-two-and-three-and-a-four-uneven" 6231
O'Neill, Bill and Danny 8210
O'Neill, Jim 10136
O'Neill, Miss Nora 4785
"one-legged" 10445
"onion, thin crackly wrapping paper skin of the" 10942
"onion she was cutting into small regular cubes" 1871
"onions, chops" 1870
"onions, dish of sliced raw" 7575
"onions came from, where the" 3398

"only for them" 2168
"Onslaught" 10464
"Ontario" 1640, 3150
"Ontario Canada" 807
"ooze through the spaces between the fingers" 2894
"oozed freely" 8531
"oozed silently away" 9764
"opal, glistening like" 9817
"Opelika" 2911
"open, O let me" 5479
"open a story, that's the way to" 5489
"open again, immediately jerked it" 2726
"open and shut with his thumb" 5621
"open as though there were a beginning" 5479
"open country" 6564
"open for business again this week" 4322
"open it, where you" 1408
"open like a book" 10532
"open mind, have an" 5270
"open the window, don't you want me to" 2120
"open up worlds to him, it would" 5121
"opened and was close, it" 3367
"opened her eyes, as soon as she" 10152
"opened his cabin door" 7025
"opened his gold watch" 9497
"opened his map case on his knees" 5716
"opened Lone's eyes" 10203
"opened my eyes, when first I" 10120
"opened the bathroom door" 577
"opened the bottle" 2911
"opened the closet door" 4485
"opened the door" 2721, 6897, 7213, 9933
"opened the door of the rear compartment" 1315
"opened the door with a latch-key" 2688
"opened the door with a flourish" 9883
"opened the large central window" 6499
"opened the largest one" 4436
"opened the morning's mail" 6952
"opened the portals of their home" 4602
"opened the smaller one" 4436
"opened up" 8308
Openers 711, 5408, 5420, 5425, 5441, 5479, 5489, 5523, 5526, 6241, 6357
"opening chapter" 5639
"opening is the most important part of the piece" 6235
"opening of Myrtle Wood's one-woman pottery show" 511

"opening of the spring term" 9529
"opening the door wide" 9940
Opera 571, 5498, 8738, 9380
"opera, as if she were attending
the" 3963
"opera, better off in an" 5498
"opera *Carmen*" 571
"Opera House, National" 9380
"opera-house, crush-room of the"
6751
"operator, wireless" 6461
Ophelia 5507
Opimian, Reverend Doctor 10899
"opinion, ever of" 5725
"opinion, formed a bad" 6122
"opinion, his printed" 9382
"opinion, if you want my" 5972
"opinion, it was always my" 10765
"opinion, medical" 150
"opinion, voice his" 1931
"opinion, without serious difference
of" 6977
"opinion here" 2310
"opinion of a good many people"
5890
"opinion of the late Queen Elizabeth" 5227
Opinions 699, 1821, 1827, 1931,
3585, 3600, 5227, 5518, 5890,
5972, 6122, 10814
"opinions, deliver his" 2820
"opinions, diverse" 5518
"opinions, subjected to the benign"
3585
"opinions of others" 3456
"opinions of Owen Powell" 1821
"opinions of the Brick" 3600
"opium mixture" 3053
Ople, General 6558
"opossum muff" 9540
"opportunities, our" 6361
"opportunities for a little capitalism" 1042
"opportunities have come and
gone" 3524
Opportunity 3524, 6027
"opportunity, have an" 2543
"opportunity, I had my first" 9251
"opportunity, taken advantage of
this" 80
"opportunity, we will take this" 1408
"opposite direction" 7684
"opposites, container of" 5479
"oppressed by the clock, he was no
longer" 9496
"oppressive, heavy and" 177
"oppressors, cruelties and persecutions of their wicked" 8643
"Opryland Hotel" 4531
Optimism 2144, 4366, 4823, 6088,
8490, 10622
"optimism, occasionally perpetrate
unintentional" 4366
"optimism, wave of unexpected"
10622

"optimism and despair, swung between" 8490
"optimism that took most people
by surprise" 10622
"optimist, I'm an" 4823
"optimistic" 2144
"optimists, despise" 4366
"option but to stay, we have no"
10822
"Options, City of Limitless" 1448
"opulence, even a kind of" 3083
"oracle" 7012
"Oracle, Delphic" 6896
"oral-hygiene treatments, proposing certain advanced" 6652
"Oran in North Africa" 4076
"Orange, county of" 6211
"orange, deepening to a tawny"
8392
"orange, flaming hues of" 2188
"orange, Osage" 10043
"orange orchard" 723
"orange rinds" 8068
"Orangeburg, district of" 6973
"oranges were more plentiful than
usual" 3650
"Orangizing" 3376
"oration, rehearse his" 8894
Orbell, Tom 8633
"orbit about the sun" 532
"orchard" 3119
"orchard, apple" 3652
"orchard, naked" 10740
"orchard, orange" 723
"orchard, pecan" 3663
"orchards, apple-" 9519
"orchards, shadows of its" 6249
"orchards, tiny little" 9430
"orchards bursting with pink blossoms" 8933
"orchestra" 9376
"orchestra, the" 6242
"orchestra, Viennese" 6220
"orchestra is playing the fifth Brandenburg concerto" 6233
Orchestras 6220, 6233, 6242
"orchids, especially with" 3795
Orcis, Lord 9658
"ordained, it was" 8040
"ordained it, on a day she" 6561
"ordeal, my" 1145
"ordeal for Julia" 9966
Ordell 6586
"order, deportation" 6118
"order, noted for her sense of" 2976
"order, sense of" 493
"order and sequence to time and
season" 10589
"order in the kitchen, give an" 3825
"Order of St. Clement" 1303
"order of the *Black Penitents*" 1293
"order of these 'reports' is arbitrary" 7357
"ordered coffee and cognac as he
always did" 4274

"ordered her outside" 851
"ordered him to go to Athens instead" 10486
"ordered the swimming pool destroyed" 2470
"ordered willow-wreaths for half
my acquaintance" 5740
"Orderly Rooms" 8673
Orders 6118, 8734, 10486
"orders, doctor's" 2892
"orders, municipal" 2017
"orders, obeyed bawled" 8699
"orders, there to call for" 8055
"orders from his superiors" 1167
Ordham, John 5641
"ordinaries of his day and generation" 9260
"ordinarily, so very" 615
"ordinary, breathtakingly" 5930
"ordinary, none of them utterly"
10794
"ordinary, nothing out of the"
9895
"ordinary, there was in him anything out of the" 5794
"ordinary average kind of guy, I'm
an" 4874
"ordinary day, began as such an"
2167
"ordinary people" 6818
"ordnance, loud discharge of" 1196
Ordway, Daniel 7131
Ordy, Andreas 8859
"Oregon" 2383, 9486
"Oregon, Southern" 3105
"Oregon behind him, leaving" 1713
"Oregon Coastal Range" 7674
O'Reilly, Radar 6441
"organ, on the" 9300
"organ a little, play the" 6229
"organ blared piped and pealed"
10650
"organdy dress" 8241
"organiser of eternal laws" 6478
"organism, any living" 6001
"organism, no live" 2763
"Organization, aim of the" 8870
"ORGANIZATION, CENTRAL
LIAISON" 8302
Organizations 1029, 1051, 1068,
2837, 3423, 3424, 5407, 5429,
6429, 6769, 6986, 8870, 9232
"organized restaurant workers" 6477
"Organon" 7879
"orgasm 2A, just had" 8013
"orgy of concentrated thought" 9412
"Orient liner" 8078
"Orient Point" 6925
"Oriental carpets" 1305
"Oriental symmetry" 7229
"origin, mysteriously remote" 5559
"original, believing I was an" 9447
"originality" 5803
"Originals, insist much upon their"
353

Origins 584, 631, 817, 1138, 1256, 2029, 4182, 5095, 5570, 6163, 9415
"origins" 584
"origins of a variation" 5607
"origins of things, interested in the" 4282
Orina, Alejo 714
"Orinoco" 274
"orioles tell of orchards bursting with pink blossoms" 8933
"Orion, the constellation" 529
"orisons to Ahura Mazda, offer his" 7547
"Orlando" 3044
Orloff, Charles Justice 6168
Orloff, Murray "Muz" 6168
Ormsby, Mr. 2761
"ornament, he was a chief" 3813
"ornamented with mountains" 1372
"ornaments, sparkling glass" 4520
"ornate stone courthouse" 1425
"ornateness, of a certain" 304
"orncry flathcad" 8925
Orphan, The 9309
"orphan, an" 10794
"orphan alone in the world" 580
"orphan asylum" 1250
"orphanage, hospital of the" 556
"orphanage had been provided for them by a wealthy philanthropist" 6104
"Orphanage upbringing" 9718
Orphans 580, 6104, 9718
"orphans, conduct some fifty" 6104
"orphans of various nationalities and all of them under ten years of age" 6104
Orsino 5730
Ortiz de León, Don Enrique 1090
"Osage Indians" 503
"Osages, the great" 789
Osborn, Giddy 4777
Oscar, Little 4753
Osgood, Anna 7412
O'Shane, Sir Ulick 2885
Osiris, Holy 4494
Osman, Mr. Charles 8863
"Ostend" 7264
"ostensibly on the grounds" 1493
"osteopathic treatments" 6107
"ostlers, jocose" 9113
"ostlers changing the horses" 9560
"ostracized for making a mockery of his high office" 7000
Oswald, Uncle 3587
Otis 7751
"Otowi Crossing" 8799
"Otranto, Prince of" 6515
"Ottoman Empire" 1464
"Ottsville, town of" 3104
"Ottumwa Iowa" 6441
"Ouichitta Mississippi" 1531
"Ouidah" 3588

"Our Lady of the Little Columns" 8413
"Our Lady of the Vapors" 1143
"our times" 3627
"ours, what is" 4991
"ousted from one of the greatest estates in England" 3557
"out, I would have been" 1106
"out, the French were" 8162
"out, the only way" 7396
"out beyond" 7939
"out loud, not necessarily" 62
"out of nowhere" 9957
"out of order, the wipers" 4961
"out of place" 7652
"out of place, felt" 9110
"out of place, he looked" 10421
"out of reach" 209
"out of sight" 9426
"out of sight out of mind" 3388
"out of the north Atlantic" 9065
"out of the sunset" 5215
"out of the way about the package, nothing" 2617
"out of thc woods" 65
"out of this world, sense of smell that is" 8535
"out of town" 2018
"out there, they're" 7984
"outbreak of the Second World War" 9420
"outbreak of war" 10525
"outbreak of war was going to be like" 10479
"outbreaks of cavalry, severe" 296
"outbuilding, noisy" 9241
"outcast of society" 10766
"outcome of the purest accident" 1219
"outdoor history, American" 4464
"outfit of four mules and a big wagon" 9762
"outfits for sport" 2841
"outfits that would have made them look like the bag ladies of late autumn" 10852
"outgrowing the world around her" 6876
"outhouse door" 10743
Outings 684, 847, 1100, 1213, 1597, 1601, 1683, 1710, 1719, 1830, 3617, 3688, 4368, 4371, 4379, 4996, 5724, 6153, 6640, 7208, 7213, 8212, 8718, 9169, 9658, 10354, 10377, 10386, 10409, 10411
"outlaw, always knew she was an" 2050
"outlaw, dwelt an" 5212
"outlaw, the" 5904
"outline, ghostly and glimmering" 6059
"outline, massive" 683
"outline, sprawling haze-dimmed" 9563

"outline on the oil-smooth sea, a towering black" 8122
"outlive me, it will" 801
"outlived its usefulness, the house had" 3184
"outlived practically everybody" 2434
"out-of-date town hall" 9233
"out-of-doors, everyone in Vere Street was" 4372
Outrage 1553, 3513
"outrage" 1553
"outrage and surprise, my own lack of" 3513
"outrage of a breaking sky" 222
"outraged at the answers" 2593
"outrageous, be a bit" 111
"outriders" 2959
"outriders was galloping down, one of his" 8671
"outset, say at the" 4258
"outshone by what succeeded it" 7872
"outsiders" 1910
"outsiders in the club" 9095
"outskirts of a small village called Cloncraig" 2024
"outskirts of Atlanta" 3147
"outskirts of Chicago" 1579
"outskirts of Miami" 2609
"outskirts of Salonika" 7459
"outskirts of the city" 5142
"outskirts of the pretty town of N_____" 3070
"outskirts of the Village" 10687
Outspan 7209
"outstare that camera of hers" 6875
"outwait anybody, I can" 10104
"oven, too hot an" 152
"ovens, thc top rooms wcrc likc" 4372
"over, it was all" 10481
"over, it was not really" 10487
"over, it will all be" 7029
"over, it's all" 3355, 9390
"over, when it was" 10487
"over and done with" 2429
"over and over" 10912
"over and over again" 9037
"over for her, not" 8002
"overabundance" 921
"overalls, faded" 2303
"overbearing mothers" 7174
"overboiled, slightly" 4753
"overcast flowed over the front range" 10629
"overcoat, expensive" 1714
"overcoat, shabby" 969
"overcoat, unbutton his" 10462
"overcrowded, the island was" 5041
"overdramatic" 5321
"overestimate, difficult to" 2894
"overflowing rivers" 6249
"overgrown with sumac" 3036
"overgrown with vines" 7752
"overhang of faces, the white" 3969

"overhung and dwarfed them" 6062

"overlook in Woodedge" 1894

"overlooked no part of it, make sure that he had" 7347

"overlooked the town" 3199

"overlooking Russell Square, windows" 2699

"overlooking the garden quad at Scone College" 8354

"overlooking the sea" 4316

"overlooking the town" 5624

"overnight, fresh from his" 1143

"overran our camp" 4469

"overseer of the county poor farm" 2947

"overseers" 3075

"overshadowed the deep garden" 5314

"oversimplifying, absurdly" 6163

"overslept themselves" 10109

"oversurging tides" 6249

"overtaxes credulity" 6890

"overthrew Earl Godwin" 3571

"overture, it will do for an" 8860

"overturned in black rushing water" 40

"overturned in toiling up its long ascent" 2943

"overweight, only slightly" 5939

"overwhelmed by a newer that built upon the ruins" 1384

"overwhelmed by the sense of being in the presence of an untamed thing" 2796

"overwhelming me like a storm, memories" 7434

"overwhelming tragedies of life" 5799

"overwork and over-worry" 8477

"overworked general practitioner" 2616

"owe, to whom do I" 10018

Owen 2393

"Owensville Vermont" 1462

"owing to & by me" 1066

"Owl, Great Horned" 749

"owl, that old screech" 743

"owls, Sultan Mahmoud's" 6245

"own the world" 2491

"owned a watermelon" 3822

"owned by Sam Fong" 1040

"owner although not sole possessor of Durraghglass" 5963

"owner of Laverings" 8262

"owner of the JC ranch" 6948

"owner-manager" 1319

"owners of L'Etoile de West" 7579

"owns the oil, he who" 2491

"owns the old Templeton house" 3134

"Oxbow Village" 8956

"ox-cart" 1602

"oxcarts" 4214

"oxen, drawn by" 6101

"Oxford" 1410, 1431, 1435, 1740, 5448, 7772, 9569

"Oxford, Archdeacon of" 1527

"Oxford, city of" 7772

"Oxford, North" 2272

"Oxford, scholarship to" 138

"Oxford, since he was at" 1121

"Oxford, university of" 2087

"Oxford, wise ones at" 10910

"Oxford and Edinburgh Universities" 9076

"Oxford is very lovely in midsummer" 7390

"Oxford station" 7239

"Oxford together, went through" 8207

"Oxford University" 7801

"Oxfordshire" 1395, 4139

"Oxfordshire, flat wheat-growing north-east corner of" 1383

"ox-hides" 1355

"Oxon" 9411

"oxygen tent, he'd be ready for an" 2514

"oyster and violet reflections, shadowed" 5146

"oysters in back, a bushel of" 10960

"Ozarks, the" 6061

Ozzie 6298

"*Ozzie & Harriet*, episode of" 6298

"P_____, town of" 2886

Pa 3684, 6136, 6660, 10546, 10937

"Pa, your" 6614

"pace, effortlessly keeping" 10412

"pace, furious" 1626

"pace, steady" 10353

"pace of the drooping horse-car" 1012

"pace was purposeful" 10421

"paced along the mole" 8660

"paced around the room" 10972

"paced the floor of my attic bedroom" 10978

"paced the grim stone cell" 10345

"paces in each direction, only twenty" 1272

"paces restlessly up an unwatched street" 876

Pacheco, Governor 9304

"pachysandra, bed of" 8788

"Pacific, across the" 202

"Pacific, blowing eastward from the" 10741

"Pacific, down to the" 9747

"Pacific, palace of the" 5859

"Pacific, the" 1360, 10606

"Pacific, the great" 8049

"Pacific City *Courier*" 6815

"Pacific Coast" 1392

"pacific James I, the" 7794

"Pacific Oceans, Indian and" 5043

"Pacific paradise" 5033

"Pacific tests, those" 2267

"Pacific theater" 8704

"pacing slowly along the sandy deserts" 10329

"pack, that renowned" 4683

"pack, there was always too much to" 9623

"pack come nigh him at Royallieu" 2820

"pack it in" 2464

"pack more comfortably on his tired shoulders, settled his" 5711

"pack my two shirts with my other socks and my best suit" 1607

"package, the" 2617

"package of freshly laundered work clothes" 2852

Packages 902, 2617

"Packard, big" 6942

"Packard, repossessed especially designed silver" 9793

"packet-boat stewardess" 1827

Packett, Mrs. 563

"pack-horses" 9113

Packing 1607, 2484, 6160, 7148, 9623

"packing, bury my" 7059

"packing, Grace was" 6160

"packing, when he finished" 5920

"packing my shit" 7148

"packing neatly like a lady" 3716

"pact, suicide" 9290

"pact to revenge that death, make a" 2393

"pad, my piled-up-to-the-ceiling-with-junk" 8727

"pad and pencil" 5515

"padded back and forth across the cool floor" 10384

"Paddington" 7268

"Paddington London" 1891

"Paddington platform" 5943

"Paddington Station" 9641

Paddock, Captain Micajah 5628

"paddock, invisible" 224

"paddock, uphill sweep of" 5180

"paddy dike" 1864

"paddy fields" 5141

"Padella, heir of" 1902

"padlocked gates" 3095

"Paducah" 8319

Paenus 6957

"Paflagonia" 1902

"paganism" 7503

"paganism, older and purer forms of" 7503

"paganism itself had survived the longest" 7503

Page 7822, 10035

Page, George 5250

Page, Michael 6719

"page, glance at this" 593

"page of my book, the last" 710

"pageant of moving life by road and river" 8345

"pageant of the centuries, its ceaseless" 9141

Pagebrook, Mr. Robert 2494

"pages, friend who figures in these" 3915

"pages, from its" 5435

"pages, honour my" 5393

"pages, hungry wordless" 514

"pages, in these" 2737

"pages, its wealth of empty ruled" 5517

"pages, the ensuing" 5536

"pages, the following" 1338, 5400, 7951

"pages, these" 5395

"pages, those old" 10022

"pages from the journal" 2553

"pages must show, these" 4452

"pages pressing crumbled corsages" 6861

"pagoda, the bombed" 730

"paid the cabby with a legitimate five pound note" 2044

"paid the driver" 1653, 1736

"paid well for the benefit" 6894

"pails, cartwheeling loose" 10740

Pain 128, 306, 1166, 3683, 3726, 4625, 4879, 6737, 6810, 7086, 7089, 7101, 8021, 10156, 10291

"pain, alleviation of his various" 306

"pain, can't move it backward or pick up something without" 6596

"pain, clear brilliant flash of" 6591

"pain, excruciating" 6597

"pain, face furrowed with" 6594

"pain, familiar clutch of" 6593

"pain, fear is the surrogate for" 3726

"pain, feeling the resurgence of" 7599

"pain, first memory of" 6737

"pain, gives women" 8021

"pain, he was almost prostrate by the" 3683

"pain, her extremity and" 6590

"pain, legs absorb the" 7101

"pain, little actual" 6595

"pain, pleasure or" 7372

"pain, she felt the" 7089

"pain, sometimes it gave me a pronounced" 4271

"pain, the" 6588

"pain, thick with" 5656

"pain in the neck" 10063

"pain in the you-know-what, I'm a big" 9265

"pain of a broken heart" 970

"pain of an arm on the tenth day of vaccination" 3683

"pain of loneliness" 10763

"pain or drugs, without" 10291

"pain out of my leg, supposed to bake the" 128

Paine, Thomas 9889

"pained at them for touching *that* tree of all those in the forest" 2633

"painful, beginning to be" 583

"painful adolescence" 2539

"painful as it looked, it was not as" 1166

"painful to a friendly mind" 6307

"painful to my sensitiveness" 8299

"painfully" 10156

"painfully, pedalling" 41

"painfully, sometimes" 3718

"pains, jolted by sudden" 6598

"pains in her chest" 4625

"paint, ability to" 518

"paint, all grey" 8027

"paint, carrying a box of" 1662

"paint, dabs of" 8242

"paint, flaking red" 9792

"paint, flecks of the dead old dried" 7763

"paint, I" 10867

"paint glimmered against scintillant grass" 10002

"paint today as you painted yesterday, you cannot" 490

"paint tomorrow as you paint today, you cannot" 490

"paint what I see, I" 488

"painted, apartment" 3169

"painted, everyone in the camp was" 7141

"painted, freshly" 6847

"painted bright as a silver bullet" 7440

"painted him up to be, as certain relatives had" 10063

"painted his face yellow and black" 1076

"painted of his friend Levett" 6884

"painted the *Brooklyn Crucifixion*" 3258

"painted what I felt" 7317

"painted white" 7781

"painted yellow" 3615

"painter, failure as a" 5465

"painter, I am a" 501

"painter, Italian" 5903

"painter, might have been a" 9460

"painter, murdered by the great" 6196

"painter, portrait-" 491

"painter, profession of a" 6404

"painter, the" 486

"painter of art nouveau" 5659

"painter of note" 499

"painter of saints" 503

Painters 485, 486, 488, 491, 494, 497, 501, 503, 512, 518, 5465, 5659, 6196, 6416, 6884, 8242, 10867

"painters are fishers also in their spare time" 6416

"painting, a" 490

"painting, galleries of" 8546

"painting, make a" 508

"painting, small exquisite" 507

"painting had always been a simple act of control for me" 512

"painting her colors on undone summer's green" 10591

Painting 488, 490, 501, 510, 512, 518

Paintings 487, 489, 492, 493, 496, 504, 507, 508, 516, 3258, 4207, 6884

"paints, fishes or" 6416

"paints under circumstances which shame me" 497

"pair, a rather isolated little" 8203

"pair, heard about the" 7827

"paisley shawl" 8376

"pajamas, his" 1675

"pajamas and slippers, in his" 996

"Pakistan" 8682

"Pakistan, fateful birth of" 3237

Palace, Mr. Rowland 10131

"palace, archbishop's" 10086

"Palace, Barascy" 8859

"Palace, General's" 6111

"Palace, Governor's" 1387

"palace, her father's" 7483

"palace, his" 7798

"Palace, Malacañan" 9971

"palace, old brick" 373

"palace, old Moorish" 4136

"palace, Ranee's" 10509

"palace, vast old" 3071

"Palace, went into the" 4001

"Palace, Winter" 4583

"Palace Guard" 7802

"palace in the City of Mexico" 2731

"palace of Babylon" 6752

"palace of Governor Pacheco" 9304

"palace of the Pacific, old pink" 5859

"Palace stands, where the" 9227

"palace walls" 8252

"palace was a squat dark fist of stone" 9304

Palaces 373, 1387, 2731, 3071, 3144, 3199, 4001, 4136, 6059, 6111, 9304, 9971

"palaces, chilly" 4376

"palaces, marble" 6059

"palaces piled up on the slope" 6059

"palace's summer bedrooms" 3199

"palaces were built for elegance" 3144

"palaeontologist, became a" 6493

"Palam airport" 9574

"Palas Hotel" 3299

"palate, suitableness to my" 3973

"palatial hotels, one of the most" 8363

"palazzo, cavernous seventeenth-century Roman" 1523

"Palazzo Conti" 9870

"pale, beyond this academic" 3333

"pale, young woman who was far from" 5799
"pale and thin, he is" 1287
"pale as pure milk" 10774
"pale blue" 5176
"Pale Fire" 5452
"pale green" 5176
"pale to Insignificance" 5492
"pale yellow" 5176
"pale young man" 5799
"Palermo" 8153
"Palestine" 10329
"Palestine, King of all" 7797
"Palestine soup" 10899
"Palestinian mother" 831
"palette, somberly mixing on his" 962
Palfrey, Mrs. 1674
Palgrave, Major 6254
"paling as they go" 2188
"palisade had rotted" 9674
"Palisades, the" 2958, 7699
Pall 4744
"pall, rid the sky of its" 7293
Pall Mall 4744
"Pall Mall" 5894
"Pall Mall, Club in" 3813
"pall over London, cast a" 10612
"pallid still" 5911
"pallid undersized men" 5886
Palliser, Lady Cora 7060
"pallor, pure in its" 4157
"pallor, startling" 4292
"pallor of a winter evening" 10577
Palm 8554
"palm, put three dimes and five pennies into Stanley's" 6652
"Palm Beach" 6586, 9850
"palm of a rock" 7680
"palm smacked" 7187
"palm to her right, apply your left" 2107
"palm tree" 6933
Palme, Dr. 7874
Palmer 7059
Palmer, Norah 8634
Palmerston 3289
"palmetto" 2205
"palmetto shoots, young" 9841
"palmist, I consulted a" 7023
"palm-room" 7754
"palms, his moist" 2980
"palms, nipples erect hard hard under" 8014
"palms, swaying" 1480
"palms, tall" 7754
"palms, under its ragged" 10700
"palms were open" 7036
"Palmyra" 1226, 1497
"Palos" 2498
"Palos Verdes" 4064
"pamphlets, political" 3376
"Pamplona" 9962
"Pan Am" 6513

"Pan American hostess, beautiful" 595
"Panamanian Ambassador" 7831
Pandolfi, Marzio 5247
"pane, blank" 9460
"panes, old blue glass of the" 10715
"pang, sudden startled" 7405
"Panhandle, out of the" 9103
Panic 3305, 3725
"panic, fought" 3305
"Panic, King" 3725
"panorama of wasteland" 3668
Pansie 10111
Pantaleone, Massimo Count 2364
"pantaloons, clown's" 3265
"panted along the platform" 10369
"panther, black" 422, 3714
"panties, pair of blue" 6971
"panting" 10321
"panting, puffing and" 3691
"panting a little from the climb" 5814
"panting at the distance" 1129
"pantomime, dramatic little" 4935
"pantomime of stars" 523
"pants, baggy brown" 2925
"pants, khaki" 8241
"pants, wore the tightest" 2834
"pants on, put my" 2873
papa 5195
Papa 2660, 4484, 6738, 7369, 7589, 10955
"papa, my" 6676
"Papa, my" 7589
"Papa Doctor, my Khan" 6014
Papagay, Lilias 4903
"Papago patrol officer" 6968
Paparo, Michelle 5778
"papaya" 1480
"pap-boat, pewter" 7782
"Papeete" 8101
Papenmeyer, Mr. 3975
"paper, afternoon" 5571
"paper, an undergraduate" 5530
"paper, buy the" 4289
"paper, buying a" 10366
"paper, clean sheet of" 3728
"paper, collect scrap" 10517
"paper, his evening" 9866
"paper, morning" 3282, 6310, 10143
"paper, on your college" 6348
"paper, onionskin" 1958
"paper, printing tons of worthless" 2023
"paper, sheet of" 10181
"paper, took the sheet of" 7355
"paper, Tuesday's" 6355
"paper boys" 8813
"paper cups, sell a few million" 9439
"paper I wrote in 1982" 5530
"paper route" 5374
"paper wastes, across the" 5460
"paperback" 925

"paperback, black Penguin" 1748
"paperback, seemingly well-read" 921
"paperback copies of his novels" 5468
"papers, batch of weekly" 5311
"papers, books and" 902
"papers, local" 1067
"papers, morning" 6353
"papers, my father's" 1930
"papers, never heard in the" 8061
"papers, students' essay" 7885
"papers, the" 5845
"papers, these" 5557
"papers, wrong" 911
"papers carried a story" 3770
"papers on his desk, neat stack of" 1934
"papers on my table, frightening the" 184
"papers were full of reports" 6324
Pappadopoulis, Gnossos 4577
Pappie 6122
"Papua" 9941
"papyrus rolls" 4494
"parachute she'd stolen" 2064
"parade, Benevolent Order of Elks" 9729
"Parade, Decoration Day" 8739
"parade, everybody loves a" 5358
"Parade, Lendrick Mills" 316
"parade, 150,000 men and women" 7196
"Parade, the" 2006
Parades 5358, 7196, 8739
"paradiddles with my digits" 3870
"Paradine, Lords" 4104
"paradisal coast" 1039
Paradise, Miss 3832
"Paradise" 1627
"Paradise, going to" 6585
"Paradise, in" 2638
"paradise, south Pacific" 5033
"Paradise Chapel" 9553
"paradise lost in the heart of a wilderness world" 4049
"paradox, it was a" 9347
"paradox of success that destroys" 282
"paradoxical purpose" 8773
"Paragonah" 10452
"Paraguay" 2341
"paralyse him, threatened to" 3721
"paralysed" 652
"Paraná" 3774
"paranoia" 10844
"parapet, broad" 8663
"parapet, went up to the" 7087
"parapet of the flyover" 5940
"paraphernalia of inscrutable Destiny, supernatural" 1093
"paraphrase, Latin" 5431
"parasite growth" 324
"parasites, called us the" 4978
"parasol, long-staffed" 4917

"parasol, the emperor's" 7806
"parasols" 5355
"parasols were once again in fashion" 330
"Parc Fasseville" 3162
"parcel, brown paper" 851
"parcel of books and papers, large" 902
"parcels, came back with the" 9406
"parcels, number of small" 2604
"parchment, crumpled the" 363
"pardon me for interrupting" 4608
"Pardon should be issued, tho' a general" 3527
"pardon the expression, you should" 9019
"pardoned and released from prison" 7150
"parent" 3572
"parent, her sole surviving" 10771
"parent, I had only one" 6667
"parent murmur, I heard another" 4026
"parent stem" 9660
"parentage, German" 6628
"parenthood, single" 2679
Parents 196, 793, 815, 831, 1846, 2417, 2660, 3273, 3283, 3359, 3538, 3592, 4438, 4587, 4743, 4765, 5096, 5195, 5672, 5699, 5857, 6185, 6525, 6531, 6532, 6537, 6546, 7589, 7888, 8219, 8906, 9003, 9052, 9061, 9572, 9706, 9734, 9918, 9949
"parents, asterisks of waiting" 5096
"parents, dream of my" 6684
"parents, Eastern European" 6749
"parents, finding your real" 6720
"parents, fond" 4743
"parents, her" 3273
"parents, her late" 3136
"parents, his" 963, 3538, 3730, 5413, 6531, 9164
"parents, large and sturdy" 9949
"parents, middle-class" 6647
"parents, my" 196, 4765, 5857, 6685, 7888, 8906, 9061, 9366, 9706, 9734, 9949
"Parents, my" 6089
"parents, my farmer" 815
"parents, my mother's" 364, 6297
"parents, new" 4216
"parents, other people's" 6742
"parents, prospective" 6634
"parents, religious" 6673
"parents' big bed" 6687
"parents' deaths" 2417
"parents died, our" 8219
"parents' divorce, their" 6663
"parents found this bizarre" 3538
"parents had done their crashing well" 815
"parents *have* to like their children" 6532

"parents' house, at home in my" 9366
"parents' incompetence" 6701
"parents met, my" 5857
"parents shook hands under the trees" 3283
"parents were dead, our" 6119
"parents would take me to stay for a weekend" 9949
Parfitt 9891
Parham, Mr. 2306
Paris, Judith 8548
Paris 5673, 9892
"Paris" 247, 1442, 1750, 2341, 2539, 2686, 2846, 3140, 3222, 3258, 3541, 4528, 4636, 4931, 5104, 6119, 6289, 6803, 7266, 8299, 8325, 8346, 8976, 9286, 9464, 9632, 9855, 10792
"Paris, arrived in" 6137
"Paris, barricades of" 10837
"Paris, born in" 797
"Paris, I was coming from" 4574
"Paris, I was in" 9891
"Paris, last time she saw" 5673
"Paris, leaving for" 1506
"Paris, liberation of" 6779
"Paris, living and writing in" 3231
"Paris, west side of" 5179
"Paris, when we reached" 9514
"*Paris*, you can't know" 1371
"Paris apartment" 2029
"Paris auction" 1087
"Paris branch" 1654
"Paris by storm" 2103
"Paris hints of sacrifice" 1366
"Paris morning so full and clear" 1949
"Paris night, rubbish of the" 2856
"Paris no love, the King bore" 9892
"Paris train" 7245
"Paris-born" 5965
"Parish, Irish" 4057
"parish, of no particular" 1891
"Parish, town of" 665
"parish boundaries" 5150
"parish magazines" 5433
"parish of Leasan" 4058
"parish of St. George, celebrated" 6267
"parish of St. Matthew's" 1891
"parish of Saint Simon Unawares" 3498
"parishes, in those west-country" 3680
"parishioners, calling on" 1493
"Parisian street" 151
"Parisians" 10615
"Parisians, old" 9119
"Parisians called *l'heure bleue*" 2276
"*Paris-Match*" 4008
Park, Mungo 2308, 6398
"park, battles in the" 10534
"Park, Central" 6512, 9434, 10731
"Park, Christopher" 4099

"Park, Clavering" 3972
"Park, Congress" 4371
"park, Davy Long's" 1863
"Park, Fenway" 4849
"Park, Greenwich" 5928
"Park, Hyde" 2822
"park, if you can picture a little" 6756
"park, in a public" 8929
"Park, Luna" 6652
"Park, Memorial" 7723
"Park, Pacific Ocean" 6442
"park, prettiest greenest" 2005
"Park, Prospect" 3240
"Park, Rathaus" 3848
"Park, Renfrew" 8934
"park, round the" 5788
"Park, Sea Life" 8520
"park, the" 8281
"Park, Washington Square" 1774, 7854
"Park, Woodcombe" 3215
"park of pine fir and chestnut trees" 5179
"Park Presidio" 6030
"Park was alive, the" 423
Parke, Dr. Dominick Maudlin 10383
"parked across these railroad tracks" 9300
"parked head-to-head with me" 9821
"parked on the east corner of Peninsula Drive and Crest Ridge Road" 2971
"parked on top of Needle Hill" 214
"parked the truck" 5724
Parker, Bonnie 5826
Parker, Mann 8220
Parkhurst, Harry 928
"parking garage" 9821
"parking lot" 9346
"parking problems" 4627
"parkland, well-wooded" 3114
"Parkland Life and Casualty" 6473
Parks, Joseph 9226
Parks, Monroe 681
Parks 423, 479, 2005, 4099, 5179, 6756, 10731
"parks carefully at the curb" 1730
Parlabane 1708
"Parliament, newly convened" 10473
"parliament, restored to his" 6652
"Parliament, seat in" 4339
"Parliament of Great Britain" 7814
"parliament of the Duchy" 8866
"Parliament Square" 2716, 9236
"parlor" 450
"parlor, assembled in the" 3987
"parlor, big best" 2070
"parlor, half" 8778
"parlor, in the" 8376
"parlor of a house" 9114
"parlor of Francis Franklin's hotel suite" 8806

"parlor they both hated so much but somehow liked" 8365
"parlour, frigid" 3094
"parlour, front" 7757
"parlour-car on the Overland Limited" 8564
Parmelee, Reese 4234
"Parnassus, ancient holy mountain" 1439
Parnell, Charles Stewart 8947
"parodied, widely" 6427
"parody of Descartes" 2535
"parody of the pedantic style" 8863
"parquet floor" 5322
Parr, Colonel John 8999
Parr, David 8999
"parrot, a green and yellow" 722
"parrots, six flocks of small banana-green" 730
Parsifal, Boulez" 1143
"parson, the" 10655
"parsonage" 8352
"Parsonage" 7392
"parsonage, window of the" 6719
Parsons, Colonel 7347
"part, a conspicuous" 2752
"part, since I play no mean" 698
"part in the events of this chronicle" 698
Partanna, Charley 1073
"parted from Mr. Mackenzie, after she had" 6108
"Parthenon" 5654
"participant" 3313
"participation, my" 1219
"particular about 'em, he is uncommon" 2820
"particulars, the" 9260
Parties 852, 860, 861, 996, 1578, 1766, 1837, 2942, 3479, 3558, 5091, 5850, 5983, 6216, 6870, 7491, 7742, 7797, 7816, 8203, 8628, 8896, 8975, 10559, 10789, 10819, 10987
"parties, autumn of bad" 6767
"parties, cocktail" 4788, 6780
"parties, one of those substantial" 6763
"parties, wall flowers at the" 2332
"Partigiani, hills to the" 2025
Parting 1997, 2007, 2486, 2648, 2652, 2654, 2655, 2656, 2657, 2658, 2659, 2661, 2662, 2663, 2664, 2667, 2668, 2670, 2673, 2675, 2676, 2677, 2680, 2681, 2683, 2684, 2685, 3566, 5811, 5914, 6699, 7714, 7988, 8013, 8188
"parting, the *idea* of" 2681
"parting with Edmund" 2673
"partner, amiable and affectionate" 6606
"partner, anyone's old" 4240
"partner, its old" 4240
"partner, present" 8853

"partners, its two" 1016
"partners in the still unique mystery of replenishing the earth" 5699
Partridge, Timothy 1025
"partridge and port" 3877
"parts, his lowslung" 5992
"party" 7050, 8027
"party, baked a chocolate cake for the" 860
"party, Barbara Finnegan's" 10987
"party, birthday" 861
"party, children's" 8203
"party, church" 8975
"party, cocktail" 6781, 10819
"party, costume" 3961
"party, dinner" 6032, 6777
"party, enormous" 6774
"party, entering the" 6775
"party, fun" 2942
"party, garden" 6756
"party, gave a dinner" 5091
"party, giving a" 6759
"party, have their" 1837
"party, her" 6755
"party, I meet her at a" 5850
"party, I went to the Rankes'" 6762
"party, it had been the most wonderful" 6771
"party, Lillian's spring cocktail" 1766
"party, Mother's" 3479
"party, New Year's Eve" 6782
"party, obstreperously spirited going away" 6773
"party, office" 7742
"party, prospect of a large" 6754
"Party, small town of" 278
"party, tea" 7816
"party, tennis" 10789
"party, the" 6764
"party, The Dressed To Get Screwed" 8012
"party, the life of every" 5983
"party, theatre-" 10035
"party, towards the end of the" 8896
"party, Tupperware" 10559
"party, welcoming" 4017
"party, you were at a" 6778
"party at all, no" 6771
"party expected that night" 9873
"party going on outside the bathroom door" 6783
"party in Via Sistina" 10819
"party neither had particularly wanted to go to" 7742
"party people" 996
"party that some guy named Lionel invited me to" 6782
"party to-night, count me in on the box" 1578
"party was for someone" 6766
"party-guests" 6770
Pary, Ross 8096

"Pasadena, Oak Knoll section of" 3113
Pascoe, Harry 8158
Pascoe, John 202
Pascoe, Pedlar 6570
"Pascoes, the Pinehollow" 6570
Pasha, Pezula 6967
Pasionaria, La 10837
"pass, head of the" 7190
"pass, mountain" 7809
"Pass, Sabine" 8165
"Pass, South" 10454
"Pass, Styhead" 8519
"Pass, the" 7621
"pass, weekend" 4596
"Pass, Yellowhead" 9747
"pass our farm in a minute, you could" 3666
"pass the night" 9535
"pass through a strange land" 9521
"pass through Norfolk Virginia" 2839
"passage, entrance of a dirty" 9855
"passage, our first long open-ocean" 9614
"passage, saw-toothed" 5572
"passage, some brief unidentifiable" 1118
"passage from the Bible" 8921
"passage of arms" 7378
"passage of on the whole undistinguished prose" 1118
"passage to a new and untried world" 2600
"passageway, a descending stone" 10462
"Passaic, the" 7647
"passed a pickup truck" 3040
"passed at that moment, something" 6001
"passed between the two watchtowers" 9833
"passed from the street" 1011
"passed oblivious" 10392
"passed on, since her mother had" 1154
"passed out" 2374
"passed up the long street" 8739
"passed within a yard" 3581
"passed within two feet of the figure" 8296
"passenger, elderly" 9564
"passenger, elderly bearded" 8574
"passenger, its sole" 8084
"passenger, solitary" 9532
"passenger had reached the journey's end" 9532
Passengers 1371, 2595, 4139, 4730, 4910, 6363, 6959, 7249, 7587, 8061, 8072, 8075, 8077, 8084, 8234, 8351, 8457, 9526, 9530, 9532, 9539, 9540, 9550, 9552, 9556, 9558, 9562, 9564, 9570, 9572, 9595, 9612, 9620, 9651, 10071, 10108, 10800, 10806, 10912

"passengers" 3494, 10806
"passengers, boat-load of" 4910
"passengers, conveys" 7254
"passengers, English fellow-" 7587
"passengers, first-class" 8072
"passengers, most of the" 9603
"passengers, ninety-eight first-class" 8051
"passengers, pushed his way among the" 4730
"passengers, seven hundred" 8089
"passengers, some notable sight was drawing the" 9526
"passengers, three" 9540
"passengers, two" 8077
"passengers as they coughed and muttered and moaned" 8504
"passengers at his table" 8075
"passengers disembarked" 9595
"passengers had left" 10071
"passengers on the steamer" 6363
"passengers pass the grey wet quay" 9539
"passer-by, observant" 1610
"passers-by" 2005
"passes were issued" 8673
"passing Caraher's saloon, just after" 8765
"passing in reckless ways" 2997
"passing safe, to make" 9194
Passion 1706, 1872, 2608, 2851, 4437, 5238, 5430, 5642, 5662, 7729, 7947, 8017, 8993, 10341, 10807
"passion" 5430
"Passion" 4437
"passion, a growing and eager" 8027
"passion, a noble and sensuous" 5642
"passion, action and" 8993
"passion, after a year … of" 5238
"passion, conceived an inordinate" 5662
"passion, nature of a man's" 1706
"passion, never-ending" 7947
"passion, with such" 7739
"passion and doom, instigation of" 2608
"passion and tragedy and beauty of his mature life" 10341
"passion for chicken" 1872
"passion for Herman Fidler" 7729
"passion for the sea" 7947
"passion fruit" 5033
"passion to it, maybe some" 4437
"passion which might tear through him" 1706
"passionate, hotly" 10808
"passionate words" 2311
"passionately" 10915
"passionately believed" 5675
"passionately serious" 8976
"passions, primal" 4046
"Passover" 4527

"passover song" 2278
"passport, his" 9591
"passport and travelers' checks in his jacket pocket" 9653
"password primeval" 281
Past 514, 1353, 1836, 2502, 3398, 3402, 3437, 5458, 5946, 6478, 7050, 7374, 7440, 8928, 9060, 9422, 9505
"past, a day that was gathered to the" 8399
"past, a man's" 5946
"past, chasm of the" 6790
"past, deprivations and dangers of the" 3514
"past, dim forgotten" 1836
"past, dwelling on her" 6793
"past, ghosts of the" 6796
"past, her" 2502
"past, her own" 6800
"past, in a not distant" 3103
"past, in the" 7379
"past, lived as though we had no" 5280
"past, my" 7440
"past, my own" 6478, 6794
"past, myths and legends enshrouding his" 5215
"past, not even God can change the" 6798
"past, now so long" 6577
"past, severance from the" 6795
"past, spoke of the" 6787
"past, the" 6791, 6799, 9615
"past, their own" 4012
"past, visions of the" 4492
"past, when I think of my" 1246
"past Eve and Adam's" 1175
"past intruded, my own" 6797
"past is a foreign country" 6789
"past is a landscape of erection, a man's" 5946
"past is a matter of myth" 6792
"past is a scene" 6786
"past life, his" 7374
"past life, one's" 6784
"past she was revealing" 1967
"past the rightful age to bear children" 7103
"paste, a pliant" 2833
"pastimes, sports and" 5126
"pastor, the" 1521
"pastor *Claius*" 7370
"pastoral landscapes" 5125
"pastorate of the First Church" 1492
Pastrumo, Anthony 4702
"pasture, fourteen-section cattle" 3253
"pasture, George Clatterbuck's back" 3669
"Pasture, old Common" 9150
"pasture side" 3646
"pasture with scrub trees thick on the slope and pines higher up" 5153

"pastures, scorched" 4382
"pastures, summer" 3667
"pastures of the Midlands, darker green" 4871
Patch, Anthony 5086
"patch of gray-dusty dry-scraggly mesquite" 1647
"patch of pebbly grass" 5145
"patches, truck vegetable" 5161
"patches that looked like water" 5128
"*Patchogue* without the capital *P*" 5341
"pate, landed on her" 2353
Patel, Mr. 10665
"patent leather, shining like" 2727
"Pater, a" 1499
"Path, Abraham's" 9150
"path, along the forest" 10450
"path, brushing leaves from its" 10705
"path, cinder" 10351
"path, cliff" 3692, 4282
"path, cow" 973
"path, field-" 3634
"path, following the" 10346
"path, garden" 3960, 10430
"path, gravel" 2984
"path, he took the side" 10448
"path, marked his" 10453
"path, raced down a" 32
"path, rock strewn" 10412
"path, sandy" 1659
"path, steep" 1498, 3232
"path, stepped off the straight and narrow" 2015
"path, tangled" 9153
"path, the" 9152
"path, timeworn" 3902
"path, winding" 8360
"path across the wasteyard" 9153
"path grew old and crooked" 9179
"path he never walked alone without fear" 3714
"path his life took, curious" 5594
"path in the wheat" 9151
"path toward fresh air and far horizons" 9118
"path was rough and narrow" 9156
"Pathé Pictorial" 1320
"pathetic, pleasing and" 3376
"pathological" 7172
"pathology, doesn't know beans about" 4322
Paths 3714, 3902, 5723, 5824, 9152, 9153, 9156, 9179, 9682, 10400, 10448, 10453
"paths, mountain" 5824
"paths, narrow dyke" 5141
"paths, their own erratic" 2989
"paths crossing for an hour or two" 5839
"paths were matted with leaves" 9682
"pathway, metaled" 10387

"pathway of normal life, I stepped far from the" 9279
Patience 2625, 3277, 4463, 6832, 8954, 9479, 10030, 10076, 10099
"patience, gradually losing his" 4919
"patience, little" 7091
"patience and impatience" 9479
"patience can endure, a Woman's" 8954
"patience save us all, His Own" 2625
"patience to a time bomb, could teach" 3277
"patient, his" 3518, 6889
"patient, his last" 10418
"patient, long-term" 8386
"patient, on the phone with a suicidal ex-" 7874
"patient, tell a" 10944
"patient, the" 4614
"patient, tolerantly" 10030
"patient in the neuropsychiatric wards" 8665
Patients 34, 131, 140, 153, 162, 166, 1519, 3518, 3923, 4614, 4620, 4626, 6589, 6889, 6891, 6893, 6897, 7174, 7355, 8359, 8386, 10114, 10418, 10944
"patients, three" 3923
"patients who complain of overbearing mothers" 7174
Patout, Lizzard 3660
"patrician parrot of a Tiresias" 6039
Patrick 1203, 1943, 4124, 8181, 9874
"patriot, I am a true American" 5240
"patriotic, I cannot be" 52
"patrol, army" 2026
"patrol of police cars" 8187
"patrol officer" 6968
"patronage" 9928
"patrons, less leisurely" 8628
"patrons, procession of" 1315
"patrons, squash of" 8368
Patsy 8725
"pattern, conscious of a" 1113
"pattern, followed a" 9735
"pattern, there is a" 5264
"pattern made by the red roof" 3109
"pattern she was cutting on the table" 7441
"pattern that seldom varied" 6951
Patterne, Simon 6613
"patterns that appealed to me" 518
Pattie 1552
Paul 574, 5675, 6630
Paul, Saint 2817
Paula 5484
Pauline 7274
"Paumanok, fish-shape" 281
"paunch, middle-aged" 4674
"pauper and banker" 2303
"pause, there was such a long" 7589
"pause, why" 5408

"pause of the flight, in one" 724
"paused and looked back at the camp" 8652
"paused as usual outside the concierge's lodge" 1654
"paused before going up stairs" 2820
"paused for a moment" 8920
"paused for a moment of thought" 9407
"paused for breath behind a hedge" 9763
"paused in his dictation" 7801
"paused in surprise" 8173
"paused on the landing to kiss" 7712
"paused outside my father's classroom" 10102
"paused to look out" 9634
"paused with her heavy bag dragging" 6102
Pavart, Father 6316
"paved from side to side" 6270
"paved with yellow sands" 1336
"pavement, narrow" 1045
"pavements, burning" 4376
"pavements, dusty" 6137
"Pavilion, Saltair" 9181
"pavilions, build gigantic" 7808
"pawed at the glass" 7474
"pawnbroker, a" 1966
"pawning some old trinkets" 2021
"pawnshop, stepped slowly into the" 2905
"pawnshop ticket" 8314
"pawpaws" 5033
"Pawtucketville Lowell Mass." 5445
"Pax, motto was" 6808
"pay, forfeited a week's" 3334
"pay, handled with a little" 6795
"pay, hardly worth the" 4690
"pay, two months' discharge" 8664
"pay for me, how much did you" 1052
"pay off an old debt" 50
"pay the rent, hether we are now come to" 7370
"paying for it, without" 583
"paying his bill at an inn" 9515
"paying taxes" 7505
Payne, John Franklin 8202
"pay-off, some highly idiosyncratic" 2589
"payroll, on the" 6425
Paz 6968
Peabody, Miss 4739
Peace 2144, 2527, 5019, 5295, 5622, 6510, 7521, 7894, 9420, 10514, 10528
"peace" 6804, 6809
"peace, a little" 2527
"peace, felt" 2506
"peace, felt utterly at" 5636
"peace, garb of" 8642
"peace, land's fertile" 5286
"peace, last days of" 9420

"peace, my brief" 5295
"peace, peculiarly marked as favorable to" 6802
"peace, provisional articles of" 6803
"peace and blessings" 7521
"peace and plenty" 3083
"peace and war" 3071
"peace at last, in" 2019
"peace in Europe almost a month old" 10514
"peace in our time, on this day of real" 6810
"peace in our time, recipe for" 6807
"peace of the Plymouth shore, the brief" 7594
"peaceful" 2144, 5622
"peaceful, not" 7670
"peaceful a man as you're likely to meet, I'm as" 2446
"peaceful for the moment" 14
"peaceful here at Landis Homes" 7231
"peaceful retreat" 6510
"peaceful Scottish woods" 4587
"peaceful semi-slavery" 6806
"peace-time" 5019
"peacetime, army post in" 6805
"peacetime, memory of" 7894
Peachey, Arthur 1574
Peachy, Very Reverend 10672
Peacock 7152
Peacock, Nathaniel 9989
"peacock comes out of his little house" 725
"peak, a certain lofty" 6066
"Peak, Desolation" 6075
"peak, highest" 2628
"peak and sides covered with snow" 6073
"peak of Ratnagalla, the towering" 9749
"peaks, distant" 6079
"peaks, towering" 1439
"peaks and valleys" 9194
"peaks of the mountains shone dazzling white" 6079
"peal on impatient peal" 1096
"peanut butter" 8298
"pear, prickly" 755
Pearl 2919, 8241
Pearl, Philip 35
"Pearl Harbor" 6774
Pearly 4629
"pearly light" 2228
Pearse 9504
Pearse, Daniel 830
Pearson 7553
Pearson, Sarah 5446
"peas, sweet" 2757
"peasant, French" 6644
"peasant father" 366
Peasants 5353, 9080, 9978
"peasants, faces of" 5353
"peasants, three Polish" 9978
"peasants grumbling" 9080

"peat on the hills, wastes of" 5163
"pebble from between her tiny pink toes, she tried to take a" 4181
"pebble rolling on the stones" 8791
"pebbles in his mouth" 8894
"Pebblewick-on-Sea" 6562
"pecan orchard" 3663
Pecket, Mr. Hector 8081
"pecking the sick one" 734
"peculiar complacency" 9872
"peculiar dark ruby depth of color" 9662
"peculiar disturbance of my mind" 8856
"peculiar enough, an experience" 4616
"peculiar man" 5909
"peculiarities, minor" 5215
"peculiarities of the father's character" 6612
"peculiarities which contribute to make New York unlike other cities" 5708
"peculiarity, a" 1032
"peculiarly American thing" 282
Pedagog, Dr. 6094
"pedagogue, Lady Mary's" 4668
"pedaled his bike" 8520
"pedaling furiously" 9600
"pedalling painfully along the gutter" 41
"pedant, something of a" 4282
"pedantic style, parody of the" 8863
"peddler, the woman" 6459
"Pedestrian, the" 5711
"pedestrian mall" 1001
Pedestrians 3021, 9816, 10699
"pedestrians, except for a few hurried" 10699
"pedestrians, traffic and" 5308
"pedestrians still turned to stare after an automobile" 3378
"pedestrians who bent double" 10699
"pedigree, like a dirty" 7129
"Pedigree, my" 353
"pedigree, the matter of" 360
"Pedigrees, the" 357
"pedlar travelling to the diamond diggings of the Vaal" 5456
"pedlars, threadbare" 3396
"pedlars with sharp eyes and long noses" 3396
Pedlock, Judith Arneth 5747
"Pedro, town of" 1365
"peeping through every crevice of the exquisite open fretwork" 1849
"peeping through the window blinds" 6284
"peeping through the windows" 10108
"peer, amiable and boneheaded" 8257
"peer, British" 5984

"peer through the harsh leafless mass" 4152
"Peerage, a proper tenderness for the" 7708
"peered across the dimness" 8265
"peered anxiously about him" 8252
"peered around, he" 1198
"peered at her, women" 8891
"peered eagerly" 2188
"peered into the mirror" 2399
"peered needle-eyed into the delicatessen" 7580
"peered out into the highway at a roadster" 9763
"peering at mosaics" 9353
"peering back in" 7474
"peering into the morning mist" 8264
Peerybingle, Mrs. 7550
"peg leg" 1620
Peggy 1144, 2547
"Peking" 3449
"Peking, April in the city of" 10983
"Peking's Chien Men Gate" 8700
Pelham, Mr. 6607
Pelham-Martyn, Ashton Hilary Akbar 810
"pelicans, great white" 7927
"pellucid, pure and" 9738
"pellucid light" 5335
"Peloponnese" 1034
"Peloponnesus, the" 1439
Peltier 6316
"pelting at him" 957
"pelting rain" 4636
"pelvis that was blue with cold" 4871
Pemberton 1508
Pemberton, Alice 2953
Pemberton, Mr. 4934
"pen, bend my fingers around a" 3051
"pen, chewed the end of his" 2541
"pen, freshly dipped" 10920
"pen, her father's beautiful little Schaeffer" 6652
"pen, her uncle's goosequill" 5428
"pen, I take up my" 5012
"pen, my" 1816, 5403, 5406, 5481
"pen, picking up the" 5460
"pen, shook out a fountain" 4274
"pen, split bamboo" 5511
"pen, stroke of the" 2023
"pen, taking up a" 4493
"pen a *hic jacet*" 7584
"pen drive deliberately" 5428
"pen has lain untouched" 5403
"pen hesitates, even as my" 9644
"pen of Thackeray" 3528
"penal colony" 2516
"penalty, death" 6965
"penance, you laid on me a" 9047
"penance to be fulfilled at your pleasure" 9047
"Penarrow, house of" 3084

"*Penarth Times*" 6352
"pencil, an attachment to the" 6404
"pencil, space" 215
"pencil and paper in my hand" 5445
"pencil of Doyle" 3528
"pencil that I managed to steal" 2049
"pencils of silver, like swift" 7919
Pencraft, Miss 1945
Pendennis, Major Arthur 3813
Pendennis, Mrs. 6610
Pendragon, Uther 5662, 7795
Pendrel, Ralph 5085
Pendyce, Mr. Horace 9761
Penelope 2659
"penetrate, nothing for them to" 3029
Penhallow 6100
"Peninsula, Northern Lower" 3423
"peninsula, promontory is made a" 4056
"Peninsula, Seward" 4096
"peninsula, singular" 9091
"peninsula, slim" 4645
"peninsula, Sorrentine" 4037
"peninsula, this limestone" 10994
"Peninsula, Upper" 4073
"peninsula extending toward Taenarus" 4082
"*penis*, always managed to say the word" 6302
Penises 346, 349, 556, 2374
"penises, their little" 556
"penises in my line of work, you see a lot of" 349
"Penitentiary, Eastern District" 5564
"penitentiary, got out of the" 4586
"*Penitents, Black*" 1293
Penlynne, Leonard 9637
Penmark, Mrs. 2506
"pennant, a lifting" 3768
"penned animals, like" 10384
Pennefather, Margaret 1318
"pennies" 7533
"penniless upon the world, utterly" 2292
Penniloe, Rev. Philip 1491
"Pennine Range" 6060
"Pennines, the" 10391
Pennington, First Lieutenant Allerd 2560
"Pa." 4059
"Pennsylvania" 1188, 1221, 1920, 2568, 3957, 4097, 4734, 5854, 9726, 9876
"Pennsylvania, eastern" 10193
"Pennsylvania, June landscape of" 5137
"Pennsylvania border" 9072
"Pennsylvania road" 2959
"Pennsylvania rolling stock" 9529
"Pennsylvania Station" 8565, 9303
Penny 5110
"penny" 1085

"penny a pint" 3396
Pennyquick, Miss 5372
"Penowell valley" 9545
"Penrith" 1064
Penrod 2497
"pens, those expository" 10900
"Pensione Bardolini" 3226
"Pensione Sofia" 1126
"pensiveness" 5896
"Pentagon, the" 9245
Pentecost, Doctor Ocie 6222
Pentecost, Peter 9131
"penthouse, her" 7204
"penthouse, suite in the" 1032
"penury and disrepute" 3557
People 1396, 2523, 3216, 3303, 4861, 5695, 5701, 5705, 6174, 6909, 6920, 7037, 7118, 9027, 10757
"people, a great multitude of" 1296
"people, a lost" 2605
"people, a lot of good" 7145
"people, a number of" 7678
"people, a secret" 4481
"people, a thousand watching" 10373
"people, about sixty" 1774
"people, always-embattled guidance" 4876
"people, business" 6496
"people, clear-eyed clear-thinking" 6815
"people, clever" 7772
"people, dark shapes of" 3787
"people, dead" 2414
"people, describe" 6909
"people, disapproval of the" 7056
"people, elderly" 115
"people, fifteen" 6959
"people, from various" 7828
"people, full of" 8338
"people, Henderson's" 4545
"People, his own Unpolite" 10464
"people, I lose" 2580
"people, innocent" 5427
"people, learn about" 6823
"people, less than a dozen" 10717
"people, look at the" 4009
"people, many important" 3479
"people, member of the world's" 6833
"people, nice" 1432
"people, of all the" 6093
"people, one-eyed" 6817
"people, poor" 7034
"people, river" 7748
"people, shaped them into a" 7810
"people, such tiny" 3663
"people, the" 6983
"People, the" 4682
"People, The" 6768
"people, their" 2621
"people, these" 8544
"people, these two very old" 6645
"people, these unhappy" 6109

"people, those wretched" 10159
"people, three little" 1298
"people, three young" 6557
"people, two hundred" 7754
"people, two hundred thirty-seven million" 6828
"people, unanimous voice of our" 7801
"people, very few" 6174
"people, wary of its" 6920
"people, watch the" 9556
"people, white" 61, 3137, 5055, 9015
"people, with about twelve other" 6071
"people, young" 5749, 8976, 9759
"people always ask me" 7211
"people are not always kind" 10878
"people are wonderful" 5701
"people at sea, the poor" 10677
"people came here on purpose, some" 6831
"people can describe places, far better than" 6909
"people cheered again, all the" 3468
"people dream of country cottages" 2780
"people everywhere" 330
"people fluttering around the fires" 3787
"people gently swaying" 8737
"people had gathered, many" 1302
"people here, won't find ordinary" 6818
"people I have met" 7384
"people I worked with" 5296
"people in all the houses fast asleep, all the" 10390
"people in England were poor, all the nice" 7037
"people in her environment" 46
"people in the town" 1790
"people in the village" 79
"people in the world, all" 1285
"people in their long overcoats" 7849
"people in this world, most" 5694
"people insisted on confiding in him" 7952
"people into our books, putting so many" 5434
"people like Rose, when I see" 6826
"people like us don't appear in *People* Magazine" 6819
"*People* Magazine" 6819
"people may wonder" 2354
"people of Okaloosa Alabama" 7418
"people off the street, drove most of the" 10699
"people on Fieldstone Road" 6774
"people raised their faces" 8552
"people said it to her constantly" 10828
"people seem to look familiar" 510
"people settled down again" 3303

"people shook their heads" 6019
"people sitting about her, all the" 4000
"people stop to listen" 8791
"people then are going to expect of him" 9476
"people to cross the Bridge, among the first" 1208
"people used to say" 8208
"people were always trying to get in" 426
"people were dying all the time" 3944
"people were gathered" 10069
"people who aren't quite making it" 6281
"people who come to see Nero Wolfe" 9902
"people who could stay indoors did so" 4431
"people who first settled on America's northeast coast" 7531
"people who live in the Quarters at Blue Brook Plantation" 7126
"people who live there are very fond of themselves" 1415
"people who loved him, the several" 9027
"people who made a story of its movements" 5685
"people who now live in it" 3085
"people who owned them, identify the" 6827
"people who pressed around him" 10375
"people will know what I have been through" 5590
"peopled with men and women" 6756
"People's Republic of China" 561
"pepper tree" 10937
"pep-pill, had taken anxiety like a" 3707
"Pepriac" 5720
Pepys, Mr. 3396
"Pequod Pennsylvania" 2568
"Pera quarter of Istanbul" 3299
"Peradore" 2145
"perceivable by human senses" 4102
"perceive, willingness to" 5646
"perceived, vividly" 5558
"percentage it offered them, the huge" 3635
"perception, reach" 5058
"perception, sensual" 5424
"perceptions, inner" 5703
"perched in my favorite kapok tree" 2084
"perched like a little bird" 489
"perched on a tree" 719
"perched on her trapeze" 4180
"perching along the sides of little boats" 732
"percolate through the rural tranquillities of middle England" 4139

Percy 9405
Percy, Lewis 4132
Percy, Uncle 3322
Perdita 4565
Perdue, Mark 3264
"Peregrine Falcon" 6880
"Perelkop" 2028
"peremptory" 9887
"peremptory, sharp and" 10003
Perez 6020
"perfect and immutable" 2156
"perfect specimen" 7002
Perfection 4171, 4525
"perfection, image of" 4525
"perforating the crusted snow" 7318
"performance, attend a" 5641
"performance, brilliant" 2
"performance, consider this" 5386
"performance, Friday evening" 8639
"performance was seriously delayed" 9394
Performances 2, 1317, 5188, 5228, 5641, 9367, 9383, 9386, 9392
Performers 5
"performing those final touches" 2823
"perfume of the pink-flowering thorn, the more delicate" 3794
"perfumes, purple" 8933
"perfumes, vases hold" 785
Pericles the Athenian 707
"pericranium, chink or crevice in my own" 9989
"peril had ceased to loom" 3341
"peril of invasion, pregnant with the" 5026
"perilous, sudden and" 2765
Perils 43, 4612
"perils, brave the" 8968
"perils, endured many" 43
"perils, the most virile of" 4612
"perils of slouching" 5992
"perimeters about, in the grim" 10416
"period, bad" 7988
"period, it was a" 3401
"period, like the present" 3377
"period, remote" 263
"period, she had missed her" 7093
"period, that remarkable" 10768
"period of history, that famous" 3376
"periods, three" 5561
"peripheries, cool" 10296
"perish, the world would" 4509
"perished, of his unspeakable injuries" 2450
"perked up sniffing, rats in the walls" 3962
Perkin, Ruth 9357
Perkins, Doris 9964
Perkins, Mrs. Sylvester 2836
Perkins, Thankful 848
Perlman, Lisa 71
"Perlycross" 1491

"permitted to pass into camp ground, before they are" 1254
"Pernod, toying with a" 2912
Peronett, Fanny 3941
Peronett, Hugh 3941
"peroration, reached his" 8863
"perpendicular and unsociable" 8841
"Perpetrator of men" 2626
"perpetual hiding place" 9285
"perpetuated in Dutch pictures" 8342
"perplexed, mildly" 682
"perplexed, you are" 693
"perplexing, increasingly" 4811
"perplexity of mind, the usual" 10110
"Perquimans Precinct" 8110
Perrault, Mary 3976
Perrell, John 10230
Perrin, Leda 6624
Perry, Lowell 2526
Perry, Matt 8124
Perry, Paul Milton 8487
Perry, Peter Manderson 1627
Perry, Sir Robert 6977
"Perry" 3044
"persecuted, deliberately" 7295
Persecution 6089
Persephone 2054
"persevered, where we" 4469
"Persia, Court of" 8040
"Persian, Cyrus the" 10476
"Persian Wars" 4503
"persistent and inexorable" 10131
"person, certain kind of" 4851
"person, delightful" 5948
"person, elderly" 3554
"person, first" 5513
"person, I was a normal" 1960
"person, in-no-way beautiful" 10133
"person, missing" 2565
"person, most remarkable" 10798
"person, simple" 10827
"person, unremarkable" 5111
"person, young" 1107, 5276
"person he least wanted to see, saw the one" 6824
"person I ever knew, smallest" 7542
"person I want, here's the" 2523
"person in Veracruz, every other" 8733
"person of curiosity" 10724
"person of great place and consideration" 5562
"person of grim aspect" 3554
"person on earth, the most tactless" 5900
"person out of work" 2850
"person singular, in the first" 8849
"person who forms the habit of wearing it" 7124
"personable to an extreme" 10794
"personage, conspicuous" 7727
"personage, high and rather terrible" 9861
"personage, public" 1313

"personage, royal" 8872
"personage, worthy" 10111
"personage of extreme antiquity" 10111
"personage of the following tale" 6885
Personages 8298, 9861
"personages, two of the" 3972
"personal, inescapably" 162
"personal, so intensely" 5496
"personal appearance" 9465
"personal drama worked out, my" 3495
"personal was intended, presumed that something" 1486
Personality 486, 3080, 5954, 10757, 10777, 10857
"personality, acquire" 3080
"personality, each individual" 10757
"personality, singular" 5565
"personality of the man" 5406
"personality that was clearly defined" 5954
"personally, try not to take this" 8013
"Personnel Officers" 8870
"Persons, great" 353
"persons, great majority of" 4888
"persons, the most famous" 108
"persons and paths crossing" 9019
"persons having the good fortune to possess an imagination" 4888
"persons in whom it predominates are usually as disagreeable as they are good" 6812
"Personville" 10901
"perspective, distorts" 114
"perspective, exaggerated the principles of" 5180
"perspective, greater" 5572
"perspective, justice of" 270
"perspective, scurried" 7279
"perspicacious" 6
"perspiration, tiny rivulets of" 4429
"persuade him not to marry" 7830
"persuaded her mother to leave Omaha" 6114
"persuaded me" 715
"persuaded to answer" 4350
Persuasion 684, 715
"persue with eagerness the phantoms of hope" 4603
"Perth, the county of" 6908
"perturbed, I was a shade" 10965
"Peru" 15, 2341, 8058
"perused the help-wanted section" 6750
"peruses the windows" 7229
Peruzzi, Dr. Charles 2616
"pervading every room of the house" 5329
"pervasive, relentlessly" 5778
"perversity of view regarding Women" 5392
"pest, girl was a real" 4194

"pest, simple" 6168
"pestering me, keep" 7150
"pet hamster, my" 859
"pet name" 3793
Pet 987
Petal 987
Pete 987, 1083
Pete, Old 2095
Peter 18, 798, 987, 1282, 1283,
	4690, 5531, 5740, 7358, 8248,
	8483, 8991, 10718
Peter, King 7796
Peter, Saint 5664
"Peter Stuyvesant, steamer" 8080
Peter the First 5034
Peterkin 987
Peters, Buck 7616
Peters, Larry 4473
Petersen, Harald 10656
Petersen, Mr. 3101
Peterson 5463
Peterson, Parker 5455
Petherwin, Mrs. 4996
"petrels swarmed their riggings"
	8169
Petrie, Mark 5989
Petrie, Professor J. Adlee 582
"petrifying into perfect statues"
	2885
"Petrograd" 5901
"Petrograd smelt of carbolic acid"
	8509
"Petroleum, Ministry of" 7481
"Pétroleuses" 10837
Petronius the Arbiter 3139
Petrov 676
Pets 422, 859, 1271
"pets, my poor" 721
Pettibone, Regal 9793
"petticoat, a red" 122
Pettingill 10554
Peverel, Henry 7389
Peveril, William 6518
Pew 6497
"pews, old black" 1296
"pewter pap-boat" 7782
Peyrol, Master-Gunner 8066
Peyton, John 5892
"P-40" 6683
Phantom Blooper 10533
"Phantom Blooper laughs" 10533
Phantoms 4102
"phantoms of hope" 4603
"Pharaoh of the Eighteenth
	Dynasty" 6450
"pharmacist, without a" 1067
"Ph.D., without a" 5546
"pheasant, coppery rush of the"
	4105
"pheasant flying over Anthony
	Keating's pond" 754
Phelan, Billy 8918
Phelan, Francis 1191
"phenomena, aesthetic" 3284
"phenomenon" 10571

"Phi Beta key" 4273
Phil 7874
"Philadelphia" 1359, 3378, 3988,
	5240, 5564, 6757, 7444, 7955,
	8356, 9002
"Philadelphia, near the center of"
	5995
"Philadelphia, South" 2401
"Philadelphia is a place where
	nothing ever really happens"
	1459
Philammon 1485
"philanthropist, noted" 5887
"philanthropist, wealthy" 6104
Philemon 7717
"Philharmonic Society" 6232
Philip 377, 3487, 3993, 4714, 6131,
	10411
Philip, King 2051
Philip of Macedon 5451
Philip the Second, King 4136
Philippa 1757
Philippe 8646
"Philippi" 4469
Phillips, Leellen-Kay 9973
"philosopher" 6551
"philosopher, exceptional" 4841
"philosopher, shirtsleeve" 7012
"philosopher apothecary" 7658
"philosopher loved the flicks" 1333
"philosopher stood at the micro-
	phone" 6838
"philosopher who broaches a new
	theory" 3456
Philosophers 509, 1333, 3456,
	4454, 4841, 6838, 7012, 10756
"philosophers" 4454
"Philosophers, two" 10756
"philosophers are not often enough
	invited" 6838
"philosophic mind to review them-
	selves" 6976
"philosophical" 7075
Philosophy 526, 2383, 3280,
	3284, 3456, 5264, 5271, 5698,
	6798, 7084, 7373, 7897, 8649
"philosophy, dismay of all" 7373
"philosophy, no future in" 5453
"philosophy class" 6630
Phizackerley, Fenella 3675
"phlegm in his throat, gathered
	the" 8882
"phlox, investigated some over-
	grown" 7283
Phoebe 8879
"Phoenix" 745, 2340
"phone, banging down the" 1132
"phone, reached for the" 1131
"phone, said into the" 6727
"phone a few numbers" 3310
"phone beside my bed rang
	quietly" 10132
"phone book" 1054
"phone call" 1843
"phone call, received a" 9393

"phone call, wait three years for a"
	1120
"phone call came" 1115
"phone rang" 1127
"phone rang for a long time" 1133
"phone receiver, replaced the" 1140
"phone was ringing" 1148
"phone wire, twisted" 1111
"phone woke him" 1137
"phone would stop ringing, he
	wished the" 1097
"phoned, Pinchot" 1150
"phoned, priest" 2392
"phoned me" 1106
"phoned me, my mother" 9011
"phone's first ring" 1119
"phosphorescence in the river,
	churning up" 6942
"phosphorous" 10530
"photo, in the upper right hand
	corner of the" 6882
"photo, one-page" 5571
"photo in the family album" 6587
"photograph, a" 6862, 8945
"photograph, like a faded" 6084
"photograph, one particular" 6878
"photograph, see from this" 5761
"photograph, the" 6852
"photograph, we are a" 6876
"photograph, wedding" 6865
"photograph, would not smile for
	a" 8558
"photograph album on the table"
	6854
"photograph in existence, there is
	a" 6850
"photograph of a man" 6864
"photograph of every year" 6876
"photograph of Frank" 6853
"photograph of her aunt, silver-
	framed" 6116
"photograph of his father, an old
	black-and-white" 6881
"photograph of Marshall" 6871
"photograph of the boy" 6855
"photograph of the Indian Army
	officer" 987
"photograph of the poet Tennyson"
	6860
"photograph on the station" 6870
"photographed a Peregrine Falcon
	in midair" 6880
"photographer" 4181
"photographer who made a good
	living" 6867
Photographers 2178, 6866, 6867
"photographers" 2178
Photographs 539, 987, 2618,
	2838, 2877, 3770, 4181, 4192,
	4277, 5571, 5761, 6116, 6793,
	6816, 8945
"photographs, framed" 6851
"photographs, hundreds of" 6883
"photographs, when he looked at
	the" 2838

"photographs, yellowed scalloped-edged" 6859

"photographs are not memories" 6883

"photographs to help her" 6793

Photography 4884, 6856, 6858, 6866, 6869, 6875, 6879, 6880, 8558, 8817

"photography" 5533

"photography, rapid" 1314

"photosynthesize all the emissions we can manage" 9186

"phrase, used that particular" 9701

"phrase spoke in Ann's mind" 10967

Phyllida 7065

Phyllis 4272, 10309

"physical activity" 10555

"physician" 6894

"physician, consultant" 9928

"physician, family" 3583

"physician, I settled as a" 6886

"physician, London" 3529

"physician, radiantly bad" 6898

"physician, Scottish" 6901

"physician, the" 2957

"physician had bled and purged the boy" 2363

"physician predicted" 7056

"physician who enjoyed perhaps an exceptional share of the consideration" 6407

Physicians 121, 123, 140, 141, 162, 163, 166, 381, 542, 682, 2351, 2363, 2449, 2518, 2616, 2892, 2957, 3266, 3529, 3583, 4281, 4605, 4624, 5231, 5939, 6173, 6407, 6511, 6638, 7104, 7231, 7539, 7829, 8359, 8767, 9076, 9872, 9887, 9928, 10114, 10313, 10442, 10944

"physicist, theoretical" 3264

Physics 526, 7824, 7979, 8333, 9500, 9503

"physics, compressed by" 9503

Piano, Miss 7722

"piano, back leg of an all-glass" 3584

"piano, keys of the" 6217

"piano, played the" 6237

"piano keys" 6215

"piano lessons, mother decided I should have" 6734

"piano sounded a touching staccato" 1320

Piatkov, Peter 1934

"piazza" 1245

"Piazza, the" 1300

"Piazza della Signoria" 10374

"Piazza di Spagna" 2225, 9582

"Piazza San Marco" 421, 8634

"piazzas, gather on their" 3394

Pibble 4778

"Piccadilly" 4511, 5308, 6267, 9764, 10360, 10586

"Piccadilly Circus" 7376

"pick the cherry tree" 28

"pick up a customer" 1152

"pick up anything, if they had to" 6579

"pick up Eddie" 1660

"pick up Mr. Wayne at the office as usual" 4564

"pick up Rodney" 2967

"picked as many as we wanted" 9352

"picked him up under one arm" 405

"picked it up, suppose you" 7489

"picked up, stranger they had" 10836

"picked up my pen and scribbled a note" 1816

"picked up the crumpled *Times*" 6356

Pickens, Mr. 6148

Pickering 1905

Pickering, Alice 6296

"pickets, iron" 5445

"Pickett" 35

"picking, you didn't know where to start" 6431

"picking a letter out of the heap" 8261

"picking her way painfully along the grass edge" 4164

"picking his gold front teeth with a toothpick" 6943

Pickle, Gamaliel 6603

"pickpocket, how to be a" 3293

"picks me up" 1996

Pickthorn, Jane 4773

"pickup, midnight-blue" 9967

"pickup carrying a homemade camper" 9798

"pickup's dash, radio under the" 6968

Pickwick 5557

"Pickwick Club" 5557

"picnic, big Sunday family" 3591

"picnic, Fern Grammar School" 2506

"picnic, we were going on a" 6572

"picnic baskets" 3439

Picnics 3439, 3591, 6572, 6581

"picnics" 6581

"picnics, plates stained with old" 6131

"picture, cannot see a" 4884

"picture, get off this" 7986

"picture, girl in the" 2877

"picture, I still have their" 4277

"picture, made a pretty" 4181

"picture, this is a" 6874

"picture an Italian painter might have made" 5903

"picture hangs at my lodgings" 487

"picture looked like any other" 6868

"picture of my mother" 6861

"picture postcard, sea and sand and rocks were part of a" 2730

"picture taken, having my" 6877

"picture that haunts me the most" 6857

"picture that looked exactly like her husband" 6863

"picture that was hung against the blue horizon" 492

"picture the ground rising" 5153

"picture upon their memory, imprint this" 8093

"picture was taken on the outskirts of Seoul" 6881

"picture-book" 4142

Pictures 2753, 6868, 7538

"pictures, collected" 492

"pictures, collection of" 1586

"pictures, Dutch" 8342

"pictures, He's been taking" 6858

"pictures, I was brought up in" 1316

"pictures, I was going to show you some" 6873

"pictures, landscape of Pennsylvania was full of" 5137

"pictures, multitudes of" 2753

"pictures, packed broad slab-like" 10139

"pictures, put into" 7288

"pictures advertising beer" 4315

"pictures in the sand, drew" 6933

"pictures of German royalty, endless" 1179

"pictures of people as they jumped, taking" 6867

"pictures of the inimitable Cervantes" 6246

"pictures of the moon, four thousand fucking close-up" 539

"pictures or conversations, without" 894

"Pictures! Pictures! Pictures!" 2753

"pictures that thronged my dreams" 2753

"pictures the like of which I had never seen in real wake-a-day life" 2753

"picturesque" 1376

"picturesque, one of the most" 270

"pie, bilberry" 1868

"pie, cow" 6879

"pie crust" 1869, 1876

"piebalds, tinker's" 433

"piece, far" 10398

"piece, fur" 9414

"piece, most important part of the" 6235

"piece, the" 9378

"pieces, Biddy will go all to" 10976

"pieces, play at the" 298

"pieces are of different shapes" 5708

"pieces of paper and dead leaves" 10723

"pieces together, fitting the" 9109

"Piedmont and Delta flights" 214

"Piemburg" 4518

"Piemburg is deceptive" 1430

"Pier, Ballard" 8161

"pier, little wooden" 6091
"Pier, Oakland" 7269
"pier, San Zaccaria" 3709
"pier glass" 4921
Pierce, Dick 4693
Pierce, Mitchell 3169
Pierce, Mr. 8842
"Pierce & Pierce" 8320
"pierced by the sight of her" 5123
"pierced her with sudden clarity" 7441
"piercing space" 2118
"pierglass, caught in the" 3790
Piers 8547
"piety" 7888
"piety, motives of" 1292
"pig" 9684
"pig, las wyld" 857
"pig, little" 609
"pig rose up out of nowhere" 3040
"pigeon, a" 7514
"pigeon poop" 4026
"pigeon was it?" 763
"pigeonholes, rack of" 3419
Pigeons 421, 776, 8947, 9627
"pigeons, feed the" 776
"pigeons, flutter of" 10210
"pigeons fluttered like confetti" 9627
"pigeons which strutted" 421
"pigeon-toed" 342
Pignatelli, Jim 792
"Pig-Pen costume" 6783
Pigs 459, 1178, 3040
"pigs" 6126
"pigs, backs of browsing" 5135
"pigs, miller's" 5213
"pigs, spittling masturbating" 10871
"pigs were eating a rattlesnake" 459
"pigsties" 3653, 9753
"pigtails framing thousand-year-old faces" 3668
"Pikes-Peak-or-Busting" 1686
"pile, deep scarlet" 5686
"pile was venerable from its antiquity" 1171
"piled her into a truck with the others" 3413
"piles, greasy" 8128
Pilgermann 4819
Pilgrims 263, 9634
"pilgrims, long straggle of" 9634
"Pilgrims in reverse" 4565
"PILGRIM'S SCRIP, THE" 5392
"piling tins of food into the top cupboard" 7402
"pill, pep-" 3707
"Pill, the" 3402
"pill by pill" 9295
"pillage" 872
"pillars, huge smooth yet twisting black marble" 4895
"pillars, two heavily rusticated stone" 3589
"pillars and arches, elephantine" 1302

"pillars glimmered smooth white, stone" 329
"Pillars of Hercules" 4034
"pillars of neolithic stone, great" 5149
"pillow, on his" 10256
"pillow, turned away from the" 7985
"pillow, turned on her" 10117
"pillow beneath Eric's head" 131
"pillow I lay on when I came to them" 6862
"pillows, a high mound of" 5623
"pills, three No Doz" 1675
Pillson, Georgie 1826
Pillson, Lucia 1826
Pillson, Mrs. Emmeline 8378, 10525
"pilot, a" 9987
"pilot, airplane" 5865
"pilot, bush" 4318
"pilot, German pursuit" 6683
"pilot, KLM" 5779
"pilot, the" 7018
"pilot began pouring round after round into my plane" 6683
"pilot in civil aviation" 202
"pilot training" 196
"pilot who had flown me in that morning" 4318
"piloting a drowned car" 2946
Pilots 200, 202, 5779, 7018, 8649
"pilots, fighter" 6773
Pim 708
Pimber, Missus 1037
"Pimm's Number One" 2589
"pimp offered me ten bucks" 3330
"pimps call it the fast track" 6274
"pin, triple-thierce cramming" 7262
"pin held an insect to a collector's board, as surely as a" 1166
"pinched, being" 2697, 7391
"pinched from the supply base" 5537
"pinches from her mother" 8475
Pinchot 1150
"Pincian Hill" 9559
Pine, Jonathan 4659
"pine" 2205
"pine, grand white" 4073
"pine, jack" 4073
"pine, like the roots of a scrub" 3205
"pine, North Carolina" 3760
"pine, white" 3179
"pine and piñon" 6085
"pine cones" 10740
"pine forests" 4034
"Pine Island Maine" 5028
"pine needles" 1879, 8526
"pine shade" 8270
"pines, a few scrubby" 5161
"pines, branches of the" 8612
"pines, dead" 4645
"pines, depth of" 3076

"pines, great white" 8209
"pines, grove of young" 7205
"pines, tall" 5162
"pines, the" 8431, 8452
"pines and hemlocks, great wall of" 3895
"pines and spruces, dark" 6065
"pines higher up" 5153
"pines leaning here and there at odd angles" 4645
"pines thinned, the" 6564
"pinescent, sniffing" 4704
Piney 4640
Pinfold 988
Pink 5789
"pink, stucco-" 1480
"pink and golden as a pretty child" 4178
"pink clouds over all the prairie, like" 8510
Pinkerton, Miss 9757
"pinkish bloom of it" 4294
"pinnacle, gleaming" 1470
"pinnacle of triangular shape" 1396
"pinnacles" 6075
"pinnacles of grey and rust-red crags, a hundred" 5127
"pinned like a specimen to the blackboard" 4897
"pinned to the sea's flat glittering surface like models" 8117
Pinny, Kay 7283
"pinpoint the actual moment" 5092
"pins, smashes the" 313
Pintos, the 5223
"piñon, pine and" 6085
"piñon knot crumpled, the last" 3765
"Pioneer, American" 270
"pioneer, Arizona" 2340
"pioneer blood, lusty" 6814
Pioneers 263, 270, 2340, 4030, 4046, 6100, 6103, 6813, 6814, 7669
"pioneers, Virginian" 6813
"pioneers came across the plains" 7669
"pioneers who had cockleburred themselves onto the country" 3105
"pious Smiths, the" 1497
"pious thousands" 2555
Pip 4714
"pipe, corncob" 899
"pipe, filling my" 5999
"pipe, her gentle" 5397
"pipe, lighting his" 8895
"pipe, smoked his" 8566
"pipe, smoking a" 8572
"pipe, smoking of an enormous" 8563
"pipe, sucking on his" 6219
"pipe, thickly shining" 284
"pipe in hand" 5615

"pipe into the brook, I emptied my" 7680

"pipe to carry the bad stuff away" 284

"pipe which he kept taking out to give it a disgusted look" 8572

"piped its danger signal" 442

"pipes" 8976

"pipes, now having their" 3591

"pipes, plastic plumbing" 8543

"pipes, smokers of" 4335

"piping like the child in the poem" 2230

Pippin 8269

"Piraeus" 8123, 10594

"Piraeus ferry dock" 2995

Piranesi, Miss 1273

"pirate, vengeful" 2016

"pirate costume" 6576

Pirie, Scott 9006

"pirogue" 4161, 6155

"Pirote's king" 5451

"pirouetted across the sky" 8451

Pirrip 4714

"Pisa, leaning tower of" 6375

Pisani, Gaetano 6213

"piss, bursting for a" 6599

"piss on the hindquarters of one of a span of mules" 2374

"pissed, now I'm" 397

"pissing in the shuffleboard machine" 7047

"pissing rain" 7149

"pistol, butt of his" 2045

"pistol in his hand" 4255

"piston, pressed down the tiny" 3047

"pistons, rhythmically beating" 7260

"pit, alligator" 6051

"pit, borrow" 437

"pit, fire" 3781

"pitch it had never reached before" 2063

"pitch of familiar dreams" 10291

"pitched his camp" 7808

"pitched their camp" 3559

"pitching forward on his head" 2374

"pitchy clouds" 10494

"piteousness of his little soft shroud of hair" 2336

"pitface, at the" 8683

"pitied, be" 6307

Pitkin, Mrs. Sarah 3104

"pits, gravel" 1416

Pitt 7505

"Pittsburgh" 4149

"Pittsburgh, west of" 4097

"Pittsford" 6626

Pity 2381, 2672, 6307, 7041

"pity" 2672

"pity, it is a" 3574

"pity, it's a" 8892

"pity, no" 7041

"pity him in the end, I came to" 2381

"pity it was that his combinations showed, what a" 1501

"Pi-Ume-Sha dancers" 2114

"pivotal scene" 1330

"pizzas, send out for" 2550

"Place, Albion" 3120

"place, Aycock" 3225

"place, best" 827

"Place, Brewster" 4705

"place, came to a" 6146

"place, Carmen Flores" 3126

"place, charming" 3115

"place, Chippman" 3108

"place, country" 3180, 6370

"Place, Crescent" 6288

"place, dank ill-lit" 8570

"place, dark and secret" 8899

"place, difficult to" 4812

"place, dull" 6805

"place, fascinating" 1410

"place, favorite lurking-" 4475

"Place, Ferguson" 10925

"Place, Ferrell Anderson" 5607

"place, finding this" 6927

"place, green and pleasant" 5043

"place, Harcourt" 4891

"place, harsh unyielding" 5161

"place, I know a" 3362

"place, I was at my" 2028

"place, idea of the" 6924

"place, in that" 6273, 6914

"place, in the first" 2042

"place, it had to be the" 6912

"place, it is an actual" 6918

"place, it was bound to be the" 6912

"place, know you are in a different" 9590

"place, lonelier" 9147

"place, lonely remote" 1465

"place, long occupied a distinguished" 357

"place, losing her" 9498

"place, lost their" 6147

"place, my Aunt Agatha's" 3698

"place, old" 1411

"place, old Cuthbert" 7652

"place, only" 9173

"place, Patterson" 3157

"Place, Portland" 9149

"place, put me in a better" 7494

"place, queer little" 3418

"Place, St. Marks" 4278

"place, small" 1374

"place, such a strange" 1961

"place, terribly dull" 1456

"place, the" 3149, 6915, 6916, 7653

"Place, The" 5094

"place, think of a" 6921

"place, this" 10606

"place, this is the" 7960

"place, this sluggish hot-smelling sprawl of a" 1478

"place, Trehearnes'" 9863

"place, two-faced" 6920

"place, wonderful" 9524

"place, when we come to that" 6129

"place, you know the kind of" 8027

"place all my own, having a" 3234

"place along the river, Tatekeya's" 9979

"place at the wrong time, the wrong" 9657

"place behind the potting shed, there is a special" 6919

"Place beside the boulevard Saint-Germain" 8949

"Place des Jacobins" 10370

"place for a woman, no" 10836

"Place G." 8368

"place had a look of content and comfort" 3083

"place handy, there was no other" 9520

"place I can't pronounce" 4076

"place in it, have no" 6843

"place in the commercial aristocracy of the East, had its definite" 1021

"place in the forest that is open and green and lovely" 10784

"place in the World" 5552

"place in the world so beautiful" 4041

"place in which Celia lived" 3249

"place in which humans can live" 4905

"place is getting me down, this" 937

"place less important, imagine a" 1116

"place like this" 4329

"place Mickey hasn't got any more" 2896

"Place of Duality" 2635

"place of no importance" 809

"place of wild growth" 3906

"place on the far side of the globe" 4086

"Place Pigalle" 1678

"place to another, from one" 1054

"place to be, what a" 10822

"place to eat, the only good" 7571

"place to place, scurrying from" 4016

"place where he was born" 4572

"place where I was born and brought up" 5119

"place where my legs used to be" 6632

"place where she wanted to be, some distant" 10353

"place where the Little Bird River flowed into the Abanakas" 7669

"place where we have suffered the most" 9277

"place where you can get a vodka martini" 9173

"place you've known forever" 4549

Places 291, 1456, 3083, 3089, 4067, 4086, 4105, 4549, 4705, 4905, 5026, 5975, 6273, 7222, 9173, 9429, 10606

"places, in specific" 1429
"places, in the dry" 4890
"places, one of the very few" 7772
"places, one of those" 3265
"places, one of those lonely run-down" 1080
"places, other times and" 4495
"places, people can describe" 6909
"places, secluded tranquil" 1192
"places along the highway" 1080
"places could speak, if" 6909
"places in the neighbourhood of Shaftesbury Avenue, one of those" 2841
"places like it, there are other" 6922
"Places of Profit, disposed of all" 5883
"places remote from town-life" 7503
"places to escape to, running out of" 3415
"places where I have lived" 3142
"placid" 10788
"placid, politically" 5938
"placidity, continued" 9280
Plagiarism 5502
"Plague, Spanish" 3273
"plague my wife" 360
"plague of flies, suffered a troublesome" 4427
"plague stalked Europe" 169
"Plague was return'd again in Holland" 120
"plague which has swept our country" 1360
"plagued me for three months" 10173
Plagues 120, 4427
"plain, across the drowsy" 9627
"plain, arable rolling" 7260
"plain, city lies in a" 1372
"plain, great midland" 4462
"Plain, high above the" 7810
"plain, high above the yellowing" 757
"plain, Lombard" 5127
"plain, miles of southwestern" 8273
"plain, mountains that ringed this" 6087
"plain, wide lonely" 8391
"plain, wide" 1341, 7649
"plain between the mountains of the north and the plateau of the south" 5152
"plain dominated by the towering peaks of the ancient holy mountain Parnassus" 1439
"Plain of Esdraelon" 9141
"plain rolling away" 9188
"plainings, begin her monotonous" 720
Plains 1372, 1439, 5127, 5128, 5173, 5713, 6087, 7397, 7649, 7669, 8273, 8391, 9141, 10709
"plains, across the" 7669
"plains, bright" 3074

"plains, broad" 4034
"plains, high" 5713
"plains, north central" 1460
"plains, stretched over the" 5173
"plains looked in April, how the" 7397
"plaintively" 1706
"plan, change of" 6945
"plan, decide on some" 6929
"plan, deeply moving" 1449
"plan, execute a" 6928
"plan, Gilbert's" 6940
"plan, here's the" 9960
"plan, I've a" 6938
"plan for a new city in the West" 6935
"plan had been to cross the river at first light" 3687
"plan to stay out of this mess" 6946
"plane, Army" 210
"plane, bush" 1640
"plane, got off the" 10080
"plane, he boarded the" 9594
"plane, just got off the" 9574
"plane, little" 218
"plane, Mexicana" 4580
"plane, my" 6683
"plane, shimmering turquoise" 10
"plane, small twin-engine" 217
"plane, the" 199
"plane, travelling by" 5750
"plane, window of the" 9615
"plane climbed slow and silver into the bright day" 6984
"plane crashed, military" 212
"plane dropped low over the sea" 4580
"plane from Belfast arrived on time" 9595
"plane from Munich to New York" 9570
"plane of the ecliptic" 10571
"plane sped away from Boston" 206
"plane thuds, the" 222
"planes, sleek little" 209
"planes, tilting" 5325
"planes passing overhead" 10222
"planet, war-torn" 4922
"Planet Earth" 532
"planet still shining but dead" 260
"planet which was dying fast" 5827
Planets 532, 537, 6792, 10941
"planets, our Colonies on many" 10941
"planet's circumference, more than a quarter of our" 2516
"planets without history" 6792
"planets without names" 6792
"planked down far south in this 'Yankee state'" 5359
"planking, pine" 8543
"planned from the beginning, as if I had" 5541
"planned it, he had to have" 6942
"planned or intended, no party at

all had been" 6771
"planned to do, what he had" 6930
"planned to stay two weeks" 5053
"planning, no amount of prior" 7824
"plans, drew the" 7760
"plans, so many" 6937
Plans 1449, 2648, 3609, 3687, 4701, 5578, 6197, 7225, 7760, 7824, 7834, 9294
"plans had been running so beautifully" 6931
"plans to go to Texas with the baby" 6944
"plant, pretty fair" 9240
"plant, printing" 1041
"plant, small appealing tulip" 9664
"Plantation, Blue Brook" 7126
"plantation, cottage" 6457
"plantation, help manage her" 3659
"plantation, his" 6569
"plantation, old Gray" 3638
"plantation, Red River" 1269
"plantation, Reed" 8530
"plantation, sugar" 2570
"plantation, the" 3147
"plantation is called Aurora" 3658
"plantation to its original size, restoring the" 3660
Plantations 3147, 3157, 3637, 3638, 3658, 3660, 7126
"plantations" 3075, 4397
"plantations, few houses were on" 3157
"plantations in all that region, one of the best" 3637
"plantations of olives" 5125
"planted a bomb at Heathrow" 883
"planted by Eleanor Bold, elm tree" 9675
"planter, innocent" 4560
"planters and buckets" 7440
"planters liked to live in nearby towns" 3157
"planting potatoes" 3652
Plants 455, 973, 3802, 3803, 3804, 7515, 7818, 9664, 9665, 9666, 9668, 9670, 9671, 9676, 9678, 9679, 9681
"plants, artificial" 4332
"plants, chemical" 5142
"plants, class of" 10899
"plants, plastic" 1846
Plarr, Doctor Eduardo 3774
"plastic plants, always kept" 1846
"plate, everyone had a" 8638
"plate, iron" 1596
"plate, Royal Crown Derby" 1199
"plateau, bluegrass" 3654
"plateau, central" 5609
"plateau, frozen" 10725
"Plateau, Mulligan" 3129
"plateau, on the" 10541
"plateau of the south" 5152
"plateaus, long easy" 5572
"plateaus, valleys and" 6068

"plates stained with old picnics" 6131
"platform, brick" 2017
"platform, flag-draped" 8864
"platform, moved to the margin of the" 7239
"platform, rough landing" 8110
"platform, snow-swept" 9532
"platform, station" 3499, 10069
"platform, wooden" 5323
"platform, wooden station" 7281
"platform breathed like a stove" 4385
"platform of the railway station" 10042
"platform under the gallows beam" 7686
Plato 220, 7897
"Plato's cave" 220
"platoon turned out" 8654
Platt 2069
"Platte" 274
"Platte, on the" 3532
"platter of beans" 3557
"Platz, the" 9542
"Platz der Republik" 10734
"plausible, what then seemed" 6883
Plaxy 2502
Play 292, 299, 305, 315, 324, 328, 329, 959, 4185, 4685, 5084, 5693, 7449, 7710, 10540
"play, began to" 7027
"Play, Chorus of the" 4453
"play, his own aggressive style of" 3971
"play, pretty squalid" 9384
"play, theatre of his" 5398
"play at the pieces, let us" 298
"play in one marathon act, four-pound" 5444
"play Leah, blessed to have had the chance to" 9395
"play music slowly" 5268
"play some for you" 1143
"play the horses" 322
"play the organ a little" 6229
"play the wonderful game of base-ball" 8933
"play there, would sometimes" 7449
"play with their fancies strained" 959
"played a too-delicate Shark" 9397
"played her violin" 6240
"played of a summer night" 6219
"played our games" 327
"played out, going on again when she felt the place had been" 6107
"played out all the best cards in his hand" 3376
"played the piano" 6237
"player, cassette" 10013
"Players, Laurel" 9387
"players are dead" 7388
"Player's Weights, a fourpenny packet of" 5621
Playfair, Virginia 1981

"playful hurt" 6301
"playground" 2722
"Playground, Big" 7113
"playground, large and volumi-nously echoing" 1093
"playground in which some two hundred young children played" 307
"Playground of Millionaires" 8317
Playgrounds 307, 1093, 2722, 7113
"playgrounds, Indians'" 959
"playing, the thing she loved was the" 6240
"playing at children's games" 5693
"playing at work" 8839
"playing ball with His archangels" 2638
"playing basketball" 8913
"playing chess" 310
"playing draughts with Brother Toby" 5653
"playing Frisbee with their mortar-boards" 3283
"playing in a tenth-rate commercial league" 8923
"playing it with a beat urgent as love" 2106
"playing the Fire Highlife" 2106
"playing the half-shift" 4596
"playing there, boys who were" 959
"playing together, children" 5739
"playing upon the sea-bed" 7754
"plays, angry" 390
"plays, trying to put over bad" 9379
"plays heavenly, it" 2102
"playtime is over" 4516
"playwright and fail, rather be a" 9379
"play-writing" 3376
"plaza, broad pink-floored" 307
"Plaza, Shopping" 1122
"plaza of Santa Luz" 1387
"pleaded with her eyes" 1847
"pleasant, almost" 5365
"pleasant, the run in itself was" 7847
"pleasant here, it is very" 6925
"pleasantries, does not understand" 360
"pleasantries, exhausted their stock of" 4916
"please with his Tops, difficult to" 2820
"pleased, I thought you would be" 3929
"pleased him, this" 9470
"pleased with himself, very" 7871
"pleased with my day" 9263
"pleasing and pathetic" 3376
Pleasure 306, 1245, 3740, 3769, 8255, 8536, 9349, 9636
"pleasure, a certain ill-natured" 274
"pleasure, greater" 800
"pleasure, it gives me" 9636

"pleasure, it's a" 7767
"pleasure, long-promised and long-expected" 7491
"pleasure, my" 3979
"pleasure, shivers of expectant" 8536
"pleasure of being driven through a countryside" 2965
"pleasure or pain" 7372
"pleasure soak in, let" 5024
"pleasure to burn, it was a" 3769
"pleasures, the whirl of loose" 5553
Plebesly, Augustus 7851
"pledge their lives their fortunes and their sacred honor" 6995, 6997
"plenipotentiary" 3514
"plentiful, oranges were more" 3650
"plenty, given of his" 3850
"plethora of halves" 4446
Plimsoll, Miss 7561
Plimsoll, Tipton 7140
"plod onwards" 4164
"Plomo" 415
"plot, the old Ricklehouse family" 10564
"plot of this story" 5393
"plot to warm the world" 6567
Plots 1325, 1530, 4251, 5393, 5801, 6567, 6940, 6957, 7054, 7604, 7868
"plotter, main" 5029
"plowed eastward through the Mediterranean" 8112
"plowed my silver-gray Mercedes 450SL" 9821
"ploy, psychological" 6511
Plum, Captain Nathaniel 8563
"plum, frost on a" 1558
"plumber, I liked this" 7738
"plumber, successful" 9423
"plume, she wore her trauma like a" 54
"plume of smoke" 9772, 10718
"plume returned and pulsed" 1606
"plumes of incense rising" 1305
"Plumfield" 953, 1245
"plump bespectacled man" 5208
"plumpness, menopausal" 87
"plunge, fatal" 2374
"plunge, with a sudden" 2209
"plunge into some heated bit of politics or gossip" 4277
"plunged into the cool depths of the river" 9317
"plunging down the waves" 8129
"plunging recklessly" 5462
"plus fours, entrepreneur in" 5170
"Plymouth" 7610, 8056
"Plymouth, a wrecked" 9776
"Plymouth, landed on the rock of" 263
"Plymouth shore" 7594
"Plyn, the hill above" 8258
"pneumonia, caught" 8678

Pnin, Professor Timofey 9564
"poachers of Lincolnshire" 3396
"poaching, night's" 9898
"pocket, his back" 5724
"pocket, his right front" 5724
"pocket, Joseph Champlin's" 3748
"pockets, capacious" 5800
"pockets, many quiet" 9161
"pockets beneath his jowls" 8734
"pockets designed to carry ducks" 5800
"pockets full of money" 8210
"podium, speaker's" 8864
"poem, a" 6272
"poem, beginning of the" 5454
"poem, child played a" 1284
"poem 'Flight to Canada'" 5480
"poem in heroic couplets" 5452
Poems 5452, 5480, 5486
"poems" 5486
"poems, several love" 5413
"poems, such bad" 5471
"poems are equally bad" 5471
"poems by distinguished writers" 5396
"poems in Italian, beautiful" 5527
"poet" 5659
"poet, a" 6617
"Poet, according to the" 289
"poet and novelist, deceased" 5534
"poet Tennyson" 6860
"poet was trying successfully to seduce her" 2794
"poetic reflection" 9515
"Poetical Works of Wordsworth" 5801
Poetry 962, 1284, 1998, 2541, 4455, 5396, 5413, 5448, 5452, 5454, 5457, 5464, 5471, 5480, 5520, 5525, 5527, 5645, 5661, 6272, 8310
"poetry" 5661
"Poetry, Lecturer in" 6491
"poetry, there is" 5645
Poets 281, 2794, 5396, 5448, 5452, 5457, 5471, 5527, 5534, 5659, 6580, 6617, 6860
"poets" 243, 8485
"poets, never for a moment professed to be" 5396
"poets set out, three" 6580
"pogo, the" 8130
"Poictesme, they of" 5213
"Poictiers, the City of" 6089
"Poictou, County of" 6089
"Poieëssa" 5020
"poignancy of those words" 6227
"poignant for its sudden revelations" 4319
"poignantly haunting sound" 8799
Poindexter, J. 4723
Poindexter, Jefferson Exodus 4723
"Point, Blacknose" 1375
"point, eventually to reach a" 3130
"point, final" 6988

"point, gets the" 1801
"Point, Hurlstone" 3692
"point, no" 111
"Point, Nubble" 9136
"Point, Paradise" 5154
"Point, Potts" 10894
"point, reaching a given" 9528
"Point, Shipman's" 9150
"Point, Toros" 2199
"point, vanishing" 7238
"point accusingly at the towering spread of canvas" 8079
"point at which country ended and town began" 4054
"point at which it all starts" 2655
"point at which it begins" 8962
"point of separation" 4085
"point of the blade fixed the old man to the table" 1166
"Point Reyes" 1217
"pointed to the waterfront just ahead" 1441
"pointer, one little" 9009
"pointing across the water" 6913
"pointing of dark boughs, sharp" 9663
"pointless, it would have been quite" 2700
"points of the compass" 3060
"Pointview Connecticut" 8975
Poirot, Hercule 3844, 6023
Poison 1062, 2418, 3408, 4509, 6211
"poison ivy" 1879
"Poison Trade" 1062
"poisoning" 2418, 7802
"poisoning the human soul" 4509
"Poisonings, Blackheath" 2041
"poisonous smoke" 7282
"poisons us dead" 1337
"Poisonville" 10901
Poker 295, 3967
"poker, we were playing" 3967
"poking at the lumpy cutlet on his plate" 3875
"poking out, fingers" 8292
"Poland" 1714, 2592, 4436, 6695
"Poland, born in" 9715
"Poland's deepest autumn" 1714
"Polar Expedition, British South" 5230
"Polchester" 3085, 9214
Poldark, Demelza 9975
Pole, Jill 2077
"pole, his" 10051
"Pole, South" 228
"pole, telephone" 2107, 8913
"Pole, the" 10574
"pole to pole" 6338
"pole to pole like moving arcs" 3044
"pole-axed, as though she had been" 2673
"Poles, castle filled with" 3209
"poles, fallen electric" 3422
"Poles, Sacrifice" 3409

"poles, telegraph" 10604
"poles, telephone" 3044
"Poles have big pricks, us" 346
"Poley, West" 1572
Police 19, 74, 1892, 2022, 2024, 2045, 2304, 2909, 3050, 3408, 3459, 4341, 6184, 6980, 7616, 7835, 8187, 8463, 9303, 9812
"Police, Chief of" 6967
"police, complaining about the" 6956
"police, delayed for two hours by" 883
"police, Greek" 6955
"Police, His Majesty's Royal Northwest Mounted" 5904
"Police, His Most Excellent Majesty's Royal Northwest Mounted" 4341
"Police, New York City" 6274
"Police, Tribune of Secret" 6957
"police, Turkish" 6955
"police and the military, on the run from the" 2024
"police came and found arsenic in the glass" 3408
"police car" 1892
"police car, got down to the" 6962
"police cars" 8187
"Police Commissioner" 6980
"police constables" 6960
"police official" 6950
"police precinct" 3424
"police raid" 6966
"police station" 6971
"police stations, one of New York's popular" 7140
"police-chief, tired" 6947
"policeman, young" 6963
"policeman, the" 3459
"policeman, there was only one" 6962
"policeman followed" 2909
"policeman was watching him" 2909
"policemen, killed eight" 2019
"policemen, traffic" 19
"Policies, Deviation and Dismemberment" 4622
"policies and standards, state certain" 5462
"policy, $127,000 retirement" 7576
"polio, remember" 173
"polish, less of that high" 267
"Polish, not that I was ashamed of being" 9715
"Polish farm community" 3449
"Polish noblemen" 7184
"Polish peasants" 9978
"Polish rage" 6652
"Polish sausage" 4073
"polishes the lenses" 8285
"politely but without enthusiasm, regarded him" 9909
"political ambitions, I have no" 4789

"political and judicial divisions" 6973
"political cafés" 9119
"political matters of the country" 6975
"political pamphlets" 3376
"political perspective" 5209
"political speaking" 6979
"politically placid" 5938
"politician, Irish" 7002
"politician, most approachable" 6987
Politicians 1833, 2009, 2472, 4982, 6509, 6980, 6984, 6985, 6987, 6990, 6991, 6995, 6997, 7000, 7002, 7005, 8864, 8873, 10525
"politicians, frock-coated" 4467
Politics 1139, 2472, 3378, 3468, 5209, 5883, 6260, 6342, 6344, 6509, 7814, 7831, 8005, 10842
"politics" 4277, 10842
"politics, his working definition of" 8005
"politics, think seriously about going into" 6993
"pollards, venerable" 5126
Pollexfen, Sarah 4550
Pollifax, Mrs. 8367
Pollit, Sam 7220
Pollroot, Jacob 6211
"polluted by the tide, not yet" 9738
Pollution 1337, 4580, 7336, 9186, 9738
"pollution" 1931
"Pollux, by" 3812
Polly 5597, 6057, 6370, 6566, 8338
Polly, Mr. 931
Polski, Tiny 286
"Polvosa, valley of" 10693
Polybius, Marcus 5484
Polyclitus 4219
"*Polyolbion*, the" 9575
"pomade, flowery" 8538
"Pomerania" 5016
Pomfret, John 3831
"pomp and glory" 1205
"Pompeii" 3812
"pompously, tell you" 9119
"pond, lily" 3165
"pond, long" 7653
"pond, muddy" 5689
"pond, skating on a" 983
"pond, small" 2894
"pond, stagnant" 2609
"pond, they could see the gray still" 10400
"pond on the Common" 770
"ponder on their value and their strength" 5381
"ponder the awful passage of time" 7896
"pondered" 9411
"pondered, she" 9460

"pondered that which secretly governed man" 3673
Ponderer 9561
"pondering" 5517
"pondering the mystery which dominates vistas framed by a ruined door" 9231
"ponderous explosions" 753
Ponds 5069, 5689, 10400
"ponds, three" 5155
"ponds, three large artificial" 3179
"ponds and puddles glittered in the road's blacktop" 2977
"ponds in the woods at Wood Ibis" 5069
"ponds stocked with fish and water lilies" 3179
"ponies" 3964
"ponies, brown" 5190
"ponies in the world, far more" 427
Ponsonby 2480
Ponsonby, Mrs. 4148
Pont 1048
"Ponte Vecchio" 5614
"Ponte Vecchio, on the" 5830
"Pontiac" 1390
"Pontiff, Sovereign" 9559
"Pontiff, Supreme" 7514
"pontoon, hotel café" 10257
"pony stepped carefully down the rock-strewn path" 10412
"pony-chaises" 9113
"Pooh Bear, furry" 4577
"pool, beside the" 5630, 8578
"pool, game of" 8908
"pool, large kidney-shaped swimming" 6394
"pool, paddling-" 976
"pool, precise" 7806
"pool, small stagnant" 4966
"pool, swimming" 9321, 10292
"pool, water of a" 10448
"pool and cascade" 7652
"pool on the floor" 5326
Poole, A. J. 9026
Pooler 3615
Pools 4643, 5630, 8578, 9999
"pools, clear green" 9561
"pools, hot springs" 6969
"pools, swimming" 7050
"pools and puddles, filthy" 7307
"pools from the night's rainfall" 6574
"pools of emptiness, beyond the deepest" 6001
"pools of green slime" 4073
"poop, pigeon" 4026
"poor, downright cruelly hideously" 7033
"poor, I knew they were" 7040
"poor, know what it is to be" 7033
"poor, people in England were" 7037
"poor, the" 6361

"poor, the better-off" 3237
"poor, very" 7039
"poor, we were very" 7035
"poor condition, scroll is in" 5532
"poor family" 781
"poor farm" 2947
"Poor Farm, county" 2303
"Poor Fork" 436
"poor Gallic goatherder" 6551
"poor in rich America" 7043
"poor they no longer had with them" 7155
"poor whites" 7036
"poorly at Stanford, did" 3526
Pop 2099
"Pop, his" 5841
"Pop and Zam, priests of" 7541
"pop down to my Aunt Agatha's place" 3698
"pope, counselor to a" 1528
"Pope at Rome, setting forth to relieve the" 7510
"Pope Gregory XVII" 1525
"Pope has forgiven the Jews" 8182
"Pope was dead" 1509
Popes 1509, 1525
"Popes, City of the" 9627
Popeye 2890
"poplar, short-lived" 4073
"poplar tree, beneath a" 3165
Poppa 2771, 4177
"popped in my brain, that's what" 6011
Poppie 10074
"poppies that summer were delicate on sunny banks" 3808
"popular minister, never to become a" 1533
"popular with teenage neckers" 1894
"popularity, jeopardize their" 6976
"popularly called" 2041
Population 3362, 5041, 5949, 6828, 10648
"population, feminine" 1012
"population, more numerous" 4533
"population, talked of" 5725
"population explosion, no" 3362
"population of the entire world" 838
"population somewhere near ten thousand" 1363
"population that could be packed away in a corner of Glasgow" 6249
"population there, the" 1340
"population 13,854" 1533
"population was increased by thirty thousand souls" 10648
"porch, cannon on the front" 4262, 4268
"porch, cement" 1554
"porch, front" 3878
"porch, her grandmother's" 8356
"porch, his mother's side" 1769
"porch, on the" 5799
"porch, on the back" 10960

"porch, on the front" 9373
"porch, on the screened" 2001
"porch, screen" 3218
"porch, wedding" 8241
"porch of her house" 3976
"porch swing" 5966
"porch where Hazel had set out swamp flowers" 7440
"porch where his heavy square-built body lounged" 5620
"porch which separates my quarters from the garden" 2536
Pordage, Jeremy 5801
Porgy 3379
Porhoët, Dr. 10334
"pork chops" 3856
"porphyry-tinted twilight" 1300
Porritt, Mr. 9423
"Porsche, black" 9800
"Porsche, it's a" 9784
"Porsche Targa, metallic-gold" 9821
"Port, arrivals from" 1738
"port, coasting" 1355
"port, glass of" 2915
"port, partridge and" 3877
"port, principal" 1392
"Port Amitié" 939
"port and starboard" 8114
"Port Arthur" 3394
"Port Glasgow" 3009
"Port Mahon" 6226
"Port Morris" 9252
"Port Natal" 8116
"Port of Aden" 4257
"port of call, my" 4090
"port of Dar es Salaam" 10442
"port of Mortar" 3275
"Port of Spain" 6435
"Port of Spain, city of" 1419
"Port of Toulon" 8066
"port officials" 8161
"Port Said" 8677
"Port Warwick" 5142
"Port William" 5945
"portals of their home" 4602
"Porte de la Ligne" 487
Portent 8948
"portents, day of" 8948
Porter, Mrs. 7792, 9867
"porter, dozing" 2842
"porter, reluctant" 9532
"porter, third" 4606
"porter attending me" 3737
"porter carrying her suitcase" 10369
"porter in the bowler" 3187
"porter said he'd mind her bag" 9550
"Porterhouse is famous for its food" 3851
"porters, one of the" 5924
"porthole, curtained" 10729
"porthole, view through the" 7307
Portia 6701
Portia, the" 8168
"portico, deep shade of the" 2842

"portico, magnificence of this" 1293
"portico of the *Santa Maria del Pianto*" 1293
"porticos that pockmark the balcony" 6781
"Portland" 1374, 9142
"Portland Oregon" 9486
"portly" 4300
"portmanteau, little black" 9092
"portmanteau, little brown" 9536
"portrait, exquisitely beautiful" 6884
"portrait, large" 493
"portrait, slashed" 496
"portrait of health and independence" 9973
"portrait of itself" 1449
"portrait of the Duchess of Wrexe" 489
"portrait of the King on the opposite wall" 7781
"portrait-painter" 491
Portraits 488, 490, 504, 6884
"portraits, clown" 504
"ports, ranked amongst the most important" 4029
"Portsmouth" 1374, 8128
"Portsmouth Dockyard, rambling expanse of" 8274
"Portsmouth harbour" 10719
"Portuguese commander" 5576
"pose, learning to" 513
"pose against the wall, takes a" 5974
"pose as a man of letters, having no wish to" 9694
"posed" 6401
"*Poseidon*, S. S." 8118
"poses, formal" 6868
"position, assured and enviable" 5423
"position, finds herself in the awkward" 5238
"position, in her" 5276
"position, squat-legged" 6692
"position is not at all eccentric like that of a heart" 4089
"position was in many ways anomalous" 8666
"possess, no man will ever" 10820
"possessed a small landed property" 6611
"possessed my mind" 8494
"possessed what are known as 'qualities of leadership'" 6424
Possession 1380, 1954, 2098, 3551, 3560, 8144
"possession, came into my" 1087
"possession of his house, take" 950
"possessions, my earthly" 7951
"possessive instinct" 3560
"possessive men, more or less" 4309
"possessor of an immense oil fortune, sole" 5659
"possibilities, life's" 5880

"possibility, had they still been a" 1761
"possible or probable, death of the" 5661
"possible, rarely is it" 5596
"possum, harsh cackle of a nearby" 10282
Post, Harriet 3344
"post he had held for more than fifty years" 6436
"post of cast iron, a center" 304
"post office, a large midtown" 6470
"post office in East Shelton" 3430
"post office, the" 3418
"post office was a rack of pigeonholes" 3419
"Post-Dispatch" 3870
"*Post-Dispatch*" 6421
Post Offices 3418, 3419, 3430
"postcard, picture" 1940
"postcard, wrote a" 5747
"postcard addressed in Uncle Giles's neat constricted handwriting" 1921
"postcards of the holiday town" 1936
"postchaise" 2944
Poste, Flora 3273
"poster in front of the closed newsagent's" 10894
"poster on a board, a small" 8322
"poster on the fence rail" 8315
"posterity" 2532
"postillion, leaving the" 9739
"postillion, the" 6316
"postings, frayed and faded" 5166
Postlethwaite, Mr. 8354
"postman, the" 4414
"postman slowly winding his way" 8526
"posts, tall chestnut" 3069
"posture, assumed an unsavory" 5992
"posture of an Egyptian priest-king" 3711
"pot, big blue enamel" 8561
"pot, minding the" 550
"pot of tea" 9353
"potations which had led to his sojourn in the coop" 7140
"potato, shapely yellow sweet" 3814
"potato chips, hair the color of Wise" 4298
"potato skins, stuffed" 3876
"potatoes, planting" 3652
"potatoes were cheaper all right" 3750
"Potcommon" 9138
"Poteau and Arkansas rivers" 7686
"potholes, pock-marked with" 9193
"Potomac, a high rise above the" 3665
"Potomac, alongside the" 195
"Potomac, swamps of the" 7707
"potpourrious suburbs, numerous" 3237

"Potrero and Clybourn, corner of" 5571

"pots banging" 9339

Potter 1229

Potter, Jane 8207

Potter, Johnny 8207

Potter, Mr. 849

"pottery show, one-woman" 511

"Potts Point" 10894

"Poughkeepsie" 1001

Poulter, Mrs. 5258

"pounce upon the cathedral" 1298

"pounding a heavy fist on a table" 6947

"pounding on the bathroom door" 8238

"pounds from the same relative, fifteen hundred" 4926

"pour into it their tributary rivulets" 9738

"pour its warmth" 2257

"poured herself a second cup of coffee" 6638

"pouring out tea" 9350

"pouring round after round into my plane" 6683

"pouring through the open window" 5340

"pours out, it" 7990

Poverty 781, 2292, 3091, 3754, 4131, 4209, 5353, 6361, 6806, 7155

"poverty" 1988

"Poverty" 7032

"poverty, arrogant" 7033

"poverty, steadily increasing" 6806

"poverty that is graceless sordid and miserable" 7033

"powders her arms" 8006

Powell, Owen 1821

Power 5883, 6244, 7043, 10018

"power, already showing incipient" 447

"power, every means in their" 6972

"power, first" 4469

"power, gathering" 9409

"power, gave off such" 6403

"power, her natural" 2765

"power, man of" 4877

"power, source of" 7043

"power, sovereign" 6255

"power, state of formidable" 6244

"Power, studied all Methods for the Encrease of his" 10464

"power, under" 9601

"power, under her own" 4625

"power, very apex of his" 7797

"power behind my voice" 10018

"power in the city, new" 6980

"power of Rachel Arkwright" 2008

"power of saying No" 6613

"power supply failed" 3299

"power that was to give us the world" 4469

"power to end it, those who have the" 8709

"power to them and her, more" 6978

"power to write, perfectly sure of my" 5420

"powered by oil" 2491

"powerful, the" 8904

"powerful emanating, something" 578

"powerful in their own walk" 5392

"powerful Lovers" 6033

Powers, Ben 1116

"powers atrophied" 309

"powers of sensual perception, I withdrew my" 5424

"Powers of the Air" 192

"powwow, solemn family" 3591

"Powwow Highway, The" 9059

Prabha Rani 3278

"practical, who doesn't know which is more" 1273

"practice, ended the day's" 8675

"practice, his humane" 7109

"practice, sound modern" 3660

"practice, target" 10497

"practice board, set up the" 4288

"practiced the end of the world" 3626

"practitioner, amateur" 4460

"practitioner, country" 6887

"practitioner, general" 2616

"Praelector, the" 5851

"Praetorian Guard" 6957

"Praetorian Prefect" 5115

"Prague" 2424

"Prague, Divine Infant of" 8944

Prairie 5132, 6056, 8436, 9563, 9772

"prairie" 4038

"prairie, drift low over the" 8436

"prairie, striding westward across the" 10373

"prairie, the" 8510

"prairie, wild" 789

"prairie, undulating" 9563

"prairie, water courses of a" 8622

"prairie, wide slopes of" 7221

"prairie, wide spring" 9772

"prairie district, ours was the" 4534

"prairie lay that afternoon as it had lain for centuries" 5132

"prairie towns, sprawling" 10341

"prairies, American" 3219

"prairies, beautiful short-turfed" 4036

"prairies, great" 6056

"prairies spread themselves out in vast level reaches" 6056

"prairies would never be plowed" 3399

"praiseworthy" 7163

"pram, lavish silvery" 4753

"pram that felt too small for me" 7443

"prance around like a skittish horse" 4191

Pranks 4250, 8320

"pranks, memory plays its" 7372

Pratap, Maharaja 1930

Pratt, Mr. 8670

"Pravda, Lunaya" 7820

"pray every night" 6750

"prayed for, any blessing ever" 6243

"prayed for a son" 7071

"prayed for the strength" 1541

"prayed God not to let me jump out of the window" 75

"prayed not to become her" 6690

Prayer 52, 75, 83, 650, 1541, 1808, 2296, 3952, 4704, 6243, 6690, 6750, 7071, 7439, 7501, 7506, 7512, 7517, 7522, 7526, 7530, 7540, 7547, 7549, 8155, 8200, 8481, 8504, 8643, 9284

"prayer" 7501

"prayer, as if in" 456

"prayer, audible answer to its" 7506

"prayer, in earnest" 7540

"prayer, Kaddish" 3952

"prayer, midway through the morning" 7549

"prayer, now and then a few words of" 8504

"prayer, summons to evening" 650

"prayer age, he was at the" 83

"prayer cards, gilt" 7533

"prayers, murmured his" 8155

"prayers of the Powers, with the aid of the" 9284

"praying" 7517

"praying for a bathroom lock" 7439

"praying for strength to do as he dreamed" 4704

"preach, books that teach or" 5427

"preacher" 1526

"preacher, Nazarene" 3338

"preacher, son of a" 6535

"preacher, that" 1512

"preacher was singling a particular person out for condemnation" 1533

"preacher when he grew up" 1502

"preaching" 7513

"preaching a sermon" 1538

"preamble to a proclivity" 5992

"precarious" 2278

"precedent, value of" 3955

"precedents, many most excellent" 580

"Precepts, Examples work more forcibly on the Mind than" 7163

"Precinct, Perquimans" 8110

"precincts of the mind" 7373

"precious and dangerous to unscrew and acquire" 9529

"precious stones" 7504

"precipices, mountains and" 5149

"precipitated five travellers into the gulf below" 15

"precipitous fold" 4062
"precipitous rock-cragged shores"
    4071
"precise about the day it began" 604
"precise in what he did" 5954
"precise pool" 7806
"precisely, put more" 2816
"precisely at eight a.m." 6514
"precisely ten o'clock" 9822
"precocious in tragedy" 77
"predawn, darkness of the" 10196
"predicament, golden" 5567
"predicament, greet our" 3372
Predicaments 76, 5567
"predictable, totally" 7975
"predicted, Tarot cards had" 1329
"predicted the hour" 9499
Prediction 3555, 6922, 7011, 7014,
    7023, 7028, 7030, 7031, 9499,
    10599, 10986
Preemby, Mr. 3498
"preface, I use as" 5502
"preface, Jacob's" 5502
"preface, little more than its" 5451
"prefect of studies" 7892
"preferred a day flight" 211
Pregnancy 558, 1998, 2080, 4710,
    5760, 5780, 6049, 7060, 7061,
    7062, 7065, 7066, 7068, 7070,
    7071, 7072, 7073, 7074, 7076,
    7078, 7082, 7084, 7085, 7086,
    7088, 7089, 7091, 7092, 7093,
    7094, 7095, 7098, 7099, 7103,
    7630, 10298
"pregnancy, difficult" 7091
"pregnancy, seven dwarfs of" 7098
"pregnant, announced she was"
    7085
"pregnant, 8½ months" 1998
"pregnant, I'm" 7070
"pregnant, she was" 5780
"pregnant, she was not" 7093
"pregnant, they were both" 7074
"pregnant, young pretty and" 7061
"pregnant body, her heavily" 7630
"pregnant in 1943, when I was"
    7103
"pregnant with me, then you're"
    7070
"pregnant with purpose" 7061
"pregnant with the peril of inva-
    sion" 5026
"pregnant women" 6817, 7099
"prehistoric animal, a melancholy"
    4773
"prehistory, a lost people of" 2605
Preissendorf, Count Viktor von
    6996
"prejudice of any person whatso-
    ever" 5387
"prejudice of human eyes" 5307
"prejudices, aristocratic" 1342
"preliminary, evening's first" 2829
"preliminary, only" 8962
Prelude, Mrs. 5750

"prelude, mere" 5642
"prelude to losing his temper" 4919
Prem 7885
"premeditated crime" 2035
"premier, French" 2491
"premier of this family" 6613
"Premier of France" 9929
"premiership, Beltane's" 7840
"premonition, sigh of his body's"
    2595
"pre-natal influence" 10814
Prentice, Ann 1630
"prenuptial agreement" 5764
"preoccupations, the close fabric of
    her" 9426
"preoccupied, certainly too" 7533
"preoccupying my imagination"
    7234
"prep school" 5869
"prep school in the midlands" 5821
Preparation 200, 273, 1213, 1309,
    1829, 3445, 5115, 5455, 6768,
    8882, 10512
"Preparation, Precise and Particu-
    lar" 6768
"preparation, very little" 273
"preparation, words in the nature
    of" 8964
"preparation of my study" 714
"preparations" 10512
"preparations for our living quar-
    ters" 6122
"preparatory school" 6463
"preparatory schools" 3160
"prepare, we must" 5115
"prepare a critical study of Giotto"
    5465
"prepare other men for death" 1507
"prepare you for what awaits you
    here, I must" 4591
"prepared, found himself poorly"
    5455
"prepared, fully" 1829
"preparing for bed" 5238
"preparing herself" 7490
Presage, Bernard 5936
"Presbyterian church" 314
"preschoolers" 1772
Presence 1690, 1993, 2855, 5825,
    6046, 6672, 8719, 9922, 10304,
    10841
"presence, conscious of his" 4971
"presence, quite so distinctive a"
    5825
"presence, seemed to sense a" 7109
"presence of an untamed thing"
    2796
"presence of the child" 10304
"presences in me, they were hate-
    ful" 6672
Present 3401, 6800
"present, birthday" 898, 4124
"present, future seemed more" 3401
"present, giving myself a" 863
"present, live in the" 9288

"present to you my friend, allow
    me to" 5791
"present waiting for you to unwrap
    it" 1258
"present was always so exciting,
    the" 6800
"*presénter, de vous*" 4795
"presentiment of my future" 7017
"presenting them to the world" 2541
"presents, Christmas" 4512
"presents, many" 4560
"presents, no birthday" 866
"presided at the Council" 5883
"presidency, Calvin Coolidge's" 970
"President" 5892
"president, company" 1925
"president, greatest" 6990
"President, I was with the" 5207
"President, never slept with the"
    8025
"president, the" 9647
"President, the" 6439
"president, when William McKinley
    was" 3394
"President died, the" 2390
"president of the United States"
    1467
"President of the United States,
    ex-" 7000
"President of the United States of
    America" 2310
"President was speaking" 8873
"presidential candidate who died"
    6994
"Presidential Likely" 7831
Presidents 6347, 6990, 8025,
    9375, 9647
"presiding" 5210
"Presidio, Park" 6030
Presley 8765
"press, daily" 6349
"press, goes to" 6318
"press, my" 7771
"press, scandalous" 4104
"Press, the" 9380
"press box" 8920
"pressed an energetic finger against
    the electic-bell button" 9875
"pressed for time, I ain't" 1331
"pressed lightly" 1796
"pressing shoulder to shoulder" 1296
"pressure, being under" 1142
"pressure on the lids of my eyes"
    2611
"pressure within" 5118
"pressures put upon her" 6542
Prest, Mrs. 4696
"prestige, wants the pay and the"
    84
"prestige fell away" 3604
"pretend, I am not going to" 718
"pretend, I cannot" 8979
"pretend that my love affairs are
    not sordid, I don't" 7713
"pretend that they don't" 7527

"pretend that this was any other vacation" 4579

"pretend the girl is an inanimate object" 2107

"pretended to enjoy their bitterness" 9674

Pretending 4902, 5819, 7368, 8711

"pretending, good at" 4902

"pretending, if only I hadn't started" 5819

"pretending, there's no use" 9229

"pretending in front of my wife-to-be" 5819

"pretending that the March sun was stronger than the cruel north wind" 10717

"pretending to be cool" 7229

"pretending to be much healthier than they really are" 55

"pretending to read" 7368

"pretense, lack of" 7903

"pretensions, of some" 3066

"pretext, on the" 1311

"Pretoria" 2475

"pretty, bright and" 3067

"pretty, it is very" 3182

"pretty, she's" 1981

"pretty as a man could sit" 9264

"pretty daughter" 2732

"pretty girl, an extremely" 4139

"pretty Miss Cable" 10036

"pretty sights" 10642

"pretty too, I think it is so" 4850

"pretty woman" 10813

"prevailed, the wind" 6914

"prevaricate a little" 703

"prey, gracefully poised on the neck of her" 10839

Price, H. 10545

Price, Kitty 2112

Price, Martha 9460

Price, Sam 1647

Price, Timothy 8320

Price, Walter 3573

"price 5 cents" 2386

"price not right, is the" 1081

"price of timber and sugar, fall in the world" 2592

"price that sometimes had to be paid for love" 5676

"prices, real estate" 880

"prices for what he could sell, lower" 2592

"prices whitewashed on windshields" 1047

"prick, absolute" 4995

"prick a match with his thumbnail" 7474

"pricking a framed canvas" 484

"pricking the distant clouds" 1299

"prickles of sun glittering came through" 5317

"prickling his scalp" 3714

"pricks, us Poles have big" 346

Pride 9955

Pride 346, 362, 1245, 1415, 3308, 3978, 5430, 7543, 8056, 8571, 9419, 10785

"pride" 3308, 5430

"pride, once a source of" 3978

"pride, quivering with" 7125

"pride and humility" 5699

"pride and pleasure, faces full of" 1245

"pride in his hollow senses" 9296

"pride in our ancestry, take great" 362

"pride of helplessness" 3356

"pride of the town" 3095

"prided herself on her repose of manner" 10785

"pried but she couldn't budge it" 10949

"priest, great" 7541

"priest, high" 8169

"priest, old" 1542

"priest, running for the" 1831

"priest, why I wanted to become a" 1514

"priest, you might as well turn" 5730

"priest, young" 1504

"priest appeared" 1517

"priest had been lacerated" 1537

"Priest of Capitoline Jupiter" 7514

"priest phoned" 2392

"priest pulled the little curtain" 1807

"priest rarely masturbated" 1539

"priest reading Scripture" 2461

"priest shall never darken my doors again" 1489

"priest who had taken a somewhat prominent part" 5194

"priests, full of" 3948

"priests, imagined by" 2492

"priest's face" 1524

"priests of Pop and Zam" 7541

"priests quickly, had to make his new" 1506

"priggish, conceited and" 6977

"priggish, sometimes waking feels" 10314

"prime, feel in his" 82

"prime, in his" 8712

"prime, she approached her" 8637

"prime leather" 2835

"Prime Minister" 2028, 6999, 8866

"prime of life, in the" 8839

"primedonne, Italian" 10788

"primeval, forest" 8209

"primeval, jungle" 10340

"primeval, password" 281

"Primevera, return to" 4542

"primitive people" 1209

"primordial state" 5170

"Primrose Day" 7505

"primroses on her hill, asked us to pick" 9352

"primroses were over" 9673

Prince, Carol 252

"Prince, the" 5345, 10543, 10974

"Prince, the Crown" 8348

"prince and citizen of Rome" 7067

"prince of a divided family" 2398

"prince of Abissinia" 4603

Prince Abi 7799

Prince Albert Frederick George 7805

Prince Bulbo 1902

"Prince Consort standing knock-kneed in a kilt" 1179

"Prince might hear you" 10543

"Prince of Otranto" 6515

"Prince of Prophets" 7521

"Prince of the Captivity" 1565

"Prince of Youth" 4219

"Prince Rupert, a day's sail out of" 8168

"Prince went further and further into the forest" 10784

"princely, this was hardly" 8348

"princes, Carolingian" 1444

"Princes, Courts of the greatest" 10464

"princes, Welsh" 6802

Princess 4647

"Princess, the" 9542

"princess, the" 10430

"princess, there was a beautiful" 5219

"princess and a slave" 5431

"princess named Miranda who had a wish-box" 5219

Princess Elizabeth Mary Alexandra 7805

Princesses 4888, 5219

"princesses as a class are exceedingly attractive" 4888

"Princeton" 8910

"Principal, the" 1200

"Principal of the college" 5832

"Principal of the Edmond Fleg Primary School" 5965

"principal was waiting for the artist to arrive" 10107

"principality of Graustark" 4044

"principle, guiding" 6041

"principle, much the same" 6038

"principles, conforming to certain common" 3242

"principles, formal" 7368

"principles, mistaken" 7888

"principles, on general" 384

"principles of piety and snobbery" 7888

Prine, Bourke 4001

Pringle 3048

Pringle, Ben 3310

Pringle, Doctor 1901

Pringle, Harriet 9916

"print, little" 2714

"print, when I tried to get into" 5477

"printed, pages come to be" 5400

"printed, some years ago was" 5392

"printed in type so blurred and poor that he could scarcely read it" 898
"printed in vermillion ink with a veneer that made it look wet" 8315
"printed with a good prospect of success" 5387
"printer, daisy-wheel" 9314
"printers, the" 7349
"Printer's Devil, Adam was the" 601
Printing 5400, 6318
"printing plant, the little" 1041
"printing the private correspondence of persons still living" 5387
"printing tons of worthless paper" 2023
"Priory, Beliers" 3123, 7060
Pris 7949
Priscilla 10152
Priscus 7518
"prismatic" 5329
"prison, became a" 7149
"Prison, dream about the" 2762
"prison, had come out of" 7131
"prison, he sent me to" 2020
"prison, Jewish" 4370
"prison, open" 2033
"prison, Rose Hill experimental" 2033
"prison, sent to" 2021
"prison, spent a few months in" 7000
"prison, talk of the" 7137
"prison, underground" 7146
"prison, visits to the" 3043
"prison, went to" 6161
"prison, women's" 7152
"prison bus, something sad about a" 9838
"prison cell" 1168
"prison cell into a work chamber, turned a" 7144
"prison run along Swedish lines" 2033
"prison where the Guards had taken Peacock" 7152
Prison 1163, 1165, 1168, 1182, 1505, 2020, 2021, 2027, 2033, 2516, 2762, 3043, 3409, 4024, 4370, 4586, 5564, 6148, 6161, 7000, 7132, 7145, 7152, 9838
"prisoner, his" 2045
Prisoners 1160, 1161, 1164, 1170, 1505, 2020, 2022, 2045, 3409, 3411, 4024, 5399, 5564, 7132, 7133, 7135, 7136, 7137, 7139, 7140, 7141, 7142, 7144, 7145, 7148, 7151, 7152, 7153, 7194, 8227
"prisoners, escorting" 7153
"prisoners, they were" 7133
"prisoner's exhausted mind" 7135
"prisoners in Scottish jails" 7142
"privacies of an upland suburb, the curved and wooded" 10359

Privacy 8313
"privacy, for" 2343
"privacy of my mind" 5424
"private, the" 4803
"private affairs of individuals" 5799
"privet, flowering" 8788
"privet, gardens of" 4627
"privilege of eavesdropping on their private thoughts" 5512
"privilege of tale-tellers" 8951
"privileged, more" 4503
"privileges of the invalid" 125
"privy, a kind of swollen" 8665
"prize-giving was over" 9724
Prizes 2757, 3968, 8242
"prizes, collected" 8242
"prizes in church, giving out the" 2757
Prizzi, Corrado 10664
"Prizzi family" 1068, 10664
"probabilities, several strong" 10724
"probability, in all" 689
"probability, new and nonsensical law of inverse" 1325
"probation officer" 2065
"probationary on both sides" 1986
"probe more deeply into the conflict" 1833
"probing for a splinter under her skin" 7441
"problem" 3579
"problem, old" 5702
"problem, that was the" 590
"problem, this terrible" 7368
"problem in life, the biggest" 5259
"problem is this, the" 2036
"problem was not that I believed in ghosts" 4110
Problems 590, 2036, 3579, 4110, 5259, 5702
"problems, parking" 4627
"problems, two most disturbing" 7154
"problems were solved" 7155
"problems which beset the novelist" 5414
"proboscis, resulting in bent cartilage of someone's" 8934
"proceeded accordingly" 6604
"proceeded to write" 4274
"proceeding at twenty knots toward Gibraltar" 8089
"proceeding in ballast to Cape Town" 8055
"proceedings, the recent" 3341
"process, going through the" 10129
"procession, head of the" 8739
"procession, solemn" 7179
"procession moved up the valleys" 10391
"procession of litters, royal" 1779
"procession of patrons, sparse" 1315
"procession of the senior consul" 7006

"procession which started nearest to their own house" 7006
"proclaim, do hereby" 7801
"proclaim his dynasty" 6646
"proclivities, man of" 5992
"proclivity, preamble to a" 5992
Procrastination 3718, 9017
"procrastinations" 9017
Proctor-Gould 3920
"prodigal mood" 1086
"prodigal sky, a blue" 10590
"prodigiously indifferent" 5617
"producer, the" 9936
"producer, the film" 9723
"production of a rational Being" 6604
"production of *The Dybbuk*, Leon Dalashinsky" 9395
"production of *West Side Story*, junior high school" 9397
Profane, Benny 2839
"profane inquiry, muttered a" 9311
"profanity, he was not given to" 8184
"profession, business or" 10478
"profession, followed his" 6885
"profession, it was his" 1507
"profession, medical" 6407
"profession, my unhappy" 5553
"professional financier" 4460
"professional searcher after truth" 6478
"professionally inappropriate" 4821
"Professnulls, Urban" 6781
"professor, aging emeritus" 9657
"professor, each full" 9335
"professor, the" 7116
"professor at the Hebrew University" 6279
"professor of history" 6022
"Professor of History" 2468
"Professor of the Year" 1950
"professor wondered, the old" 8492
"professors of English Literature, two" 216
"profile, his shadowed" 7699
"profile, New England" 347
"profile in *Fortune*" 8879
"profit, no" 6126
"Profit, Places of" 5883
Profit David 4120
"profit to the United States of America" 6439
"profit which his business afforded himself" 6516
"profuse, cowparsley and campion" 3808
"profusion of late asters, a rich" 3806
Progoff, Christopher 3922
"programs at the Garfield Avenue Theater" 1315
"progress, expectancy of" 9663
"progress, if there is" 5409
"progress, slow shuffling" 10405

"progression, laws of" 3560
"progressive college town" 9233
Prohack, Arthur Charles 9470
"project, God-damned Tumulty" 2479
"projectionist" 1319
"prologue, a" 583
"prologue or epilogue" 9057
"prolonged with cake and cider" 3680
"promenade, forward" 10030
"promenade, whole wide" 10717
"promenade deck" 8072
"Prometheus, golden statue of" 4195
"prominence given to this statement" 4340
"prominent part" 5194
"promise, junior of exceptional" 6432
"promise, fulfilling a" 8982
"promise, I write in fulfilment of a" 5484
"promise, though it be only a" 4607
"promise, vivid with" 4010
"promise and threat" 9389
"promise is given, hope when a" 4607
"promised, because he had" 7115
"promised, he" 9968
"promised, remembered that he had" 7389
"promised end" 3351
"promised himself" 4234
"promised land" 9754
"promised Linc we'd come by" 9958
"promised me a tomorrow like a yummy fruitcake" 2656
"promised to be hot, the day" 2139
"promised to confess" 1815
"promised to dismiss me" 7906
"promised to fly" 9602
"promised to say a Pater an Ave and a Gloria" 1499
"promised you an autobiography" 2550
"promises, love and other" 5649
Promises 1739, 2550, 2743, 3351, 4234, 4607, 5296, 5484, 5649, 6088, 6566, 7115, 7389, 8982, 9602, 9958, 9968
"promises made before birth to be fulfilled" 6088
"promises of youth" 4603
"promises to reward him, believed my" 1167
"promises you at The Four Seasons" 2743
"promising disposition, of no" 6515
"promising with divine assistance" 10651
"promisingly casually" 5775
"promontory, on the extended" 4478
"promontory, salt-washed" 9096
"promontory, shadow of a" 8034

"promontory called Mission Hills" 4060
"promontory is made a peninsula" 4056
"promontory just below Bellagio" 3265
"promontory of the New England coast" 9096
"promotion had finally been approved, his second" 6483
"prompt, determined to be" 9335
"promulgate them in *usum publicum*" 5387
"prone to litigation, she is" 10662
"pronoun *he* and its possessive *him*" 10913
"pronounce, a place I can't" 4076
"pronounced, name was" 4802
"pronounced as Cook" 4871
"pronounced Slade direly" 3969
"pronounces him practically off the hooks" 150
"pronouns teaching the division of earth and sky" 1284
"pronto, get out of here" 5606
Proof 3456, 3457, 3459, 3461, 3464, 3466, 5421, 7053
"proof, living" 6535
"proof, reading a smudgy" 7349
"proof, some sun-foil of" 9696
"proof, that gave the" 3464
"proof of its smartness, sufficient" 11697
"proof of land, I did not feel it was adequate" 3466
"proof of love from an absent one" 5650
"proofs, some elementary" 3456
"prop, some such" 10772
"Propaganda Bureau, German" 5714
"proper place, its" 4468
"proper thing, the" 4988
"properties of mine as are vested in shipping timber or lumber" 4927
"property, her own" 6275
"property, portable form of" 10551
"property, small landed" 6611
"property extended to the bay" 4091
"property of Sir Harry Waring" 3123
"prophecies, out of respect for the" 7505
Prophecy 280, 7012, 7015, 7029, 10513
"prophesied, Armageddon had arrived as" 10513
"prophet of our loves, nasty" 5648
"prophet prophesying Primrose Day" 7505
Prophets 5648
"prophets say will also sink" 280
"propinquity, intimate" 357
"propitious, Neptune was" 7346
"proportioned, perfectly" 6073

Proposals 1073, 5737, 5766, 6988
"proposals, government" 6988
"proposition, my" 1977
"propositions that were being elaborated, the quiet" 8850
"propped against a high mound of pillows" 5623
"propped it against the side of the house" 8618
"propped up on pillows" 3841
"propping her feet against the door" 10949
"proprietor" 2570
"proprietor, sole" 1050
"proprietor and several guests" 7509
"proprietor of the White Horse Inn" 3533
"prosaic, to be entirely" 5431
"proscenium, as if war had a" 8704
"prose, undistinguished" 1118
"prose, verse and" 4455
"prosecution, fear of" 2567
"prosecutions may arise" 5387
"prosecutor, young" 5199
"Prosecutors, Cruelty of their" 6089
"Prospect, back in" 10434
"prospect of three more days of teaching" 2508
"prospect which itself is discreetly separated" 5164
"prospects of money, no" 10834
"prosper, God made him to" 7536
"prosperity" 9209
"Prosperity" 1360
"prosperity, commercial" 1008
"prosperity, single source of its" 1440
"prosperity of the company" 2538
Prospero 7065
"prosperous" 5294
"prosperous, happy and" 2018
"prostitute, that fabled" 10871
Prostitutes 3057, 4821, 7079, 7743, 8777, 10871
"prostitutes, discreet" 2118
"prostitute's dead child" 1538
Prostitution 1538, 1886, 5553, 6480, 8806
"prostrate, lying" 7851
"prostrate by the pain" 3683
"protagonist, principal" 6655
"protagonist becomes suddenly aware of the conspiracy" 1330
"protect her, as though it could" 3030
"protect it from the blowing sand" 10098
"Protector of England" 4554
"protestant face" 822
"Protestant mission schools" 6446
"Protestants, they were" 8220
"Protestants were Banish'd from France" 6089
"protesting wail" 3705
"protests, despite my" 6392

"protests, disregard of his" 4614
"prototype for its hero" 5482
"protruding from hunch-muscles" 6075
"protruding from immense timbered shoulders" 6075
"protuberance jutted out" 4095
"proud, ancestors of whom to be" 362
"proud, good reason to be" 8056
"proud, I used to be" 7543
"proud, I was so" 4223
"proud, stood there" 6085
"proud, very" 7130
"proud appointment" 8102
"proud in my life" 5079
"proud of, I am not particularly" 3393
"proud of, my thoughts are nothing to be" 9419
"proud of his status" 7128
"proud of their antiquity" 358
"proud of this branch of its business" 1015
"proud or ashamed" 5542
"proudly" 7627
"prove a case" 5421
"prove to him that nothing is worthwhile" 3461
"proved him to be a gentleman and a coxcomb" 3812
"proved the world was round, ever since they" 7053
"Provence, a remote part of" 9102
"proverb, runs the" 7724
Providence 36, 1222, 1243, 5556, 6020
"Providence, by direction of" 5139
"providence, luck or" 1243
"Providence, mistakes of" 6020
"Providence, nickname for" 1222
"Providence, rest in" 5562
"Providence has blessed the decline of my life" 5556
"Province, Daji" 4470
"Province, Yunnan" 561
"province of Gascony" 5125
"provinces in Scotland, among all the" 6908
"provinces scheduled for abolition" 4470
"provincial, I am a fifty-eight-year-old" 4844
"provincial of them, it's so" 4986
"provision that is necessary" 4550
"provost of _____" 2088
"prow, stood there in the" 8792
"prowled among the skeleton trees" 324
Prowse, Keith 675
Pru 2447
Prudence 7390, 10789
"prudence" 9260
"prudence, Scotch" 695
"prudent, judging it" 7713

"prudent, more talented than" 5448
"prudent, the" 2466
"prudent to bow to those fashions" 5390
"prudent to scamper back here to before the beginning" 2550
"Prudes" 10764
Prue 342
"Prussia, King of" 7803
"Prussia, Rhenish" 9610
Pryde, Bernie 2359
Pryden, Jack 4703
"p's and q's, mind their" 10538
Psin 4677
"psychiatrist, consulting" 3518
"psychiatrist called Meiss" 6194
"psychic, I wouldn't ever have gone to a" 10977
"Psychical Research, Society of" 10181
Psychoanalysis 7167, 7170
"psychoanalysis is a permanent fad" 7170
"psycho-analysis would help you" 7167
"psychoanalyst, as a" 7177
"psychoanalysts, 117" 7171
"psycho-evolutionary work" 7178
"Psychological Correspondences" 923
"psychological ploy" 6511
"psychologist, Dallas" 2815
"psychologists, amateur" 7840
Psychology 2501, 2815, 3518, 4854, 5265, 5512, 5559, 6194, 6490, 6511, 7735, 7968, 8224, 8490
"psychopath, he was not a" 7173
Ptolemy 535
"Puamahara, town of" 5220
"pub, sandwiches in a" 3832
"pub in Folkestone where I wait for the ferry" 5990
"public, deceiving my" 567
"public, gone" 1817
"public, majority of its" 7003
"public, members of the" 6877
"public, the" 102, 7381, 8061, 9389
"public, they will ever become" 7948
"public affairs, happily subordinate in" 5392
"public and private" 9021
"public curiosity" 9692
"public house, our habitual" 3764
"public house, unpretentious" 4315
"public interest, on the wave of" 499
"public ordinary, one who keeps a" 5385
"public personage" 1313
"public places, you can see them in" 1993
"public property, species of" 9260
"public school" 2374
"public talk" 7825

Publications 2386, 6513
"publicity, widespread favorable and profitable" 8773
"publish one, I must be about to" 705
"published, guidebook to Nihilon was" 912
"published anonymously" 5392
"published for years, novels he had" 5419
"published in duodecimal volumes" 2555
"published last December" 5416
"published notebooks" 5507
"published weekly at Oxbow Village" 8956
"publisher, American" 5419
"publisher, my" 5508
"publisher, placing it with a" 5477
"publisher proclaimed, his" 5423
Publishers 1914, 5311, 5477, 5508
"publishers and birds, activity among" 10980
"publishers first asked me to write his biography" 705
"publishers in America" 1914
Publishing 705, 918, 1006, 5387, 5416, 5419
"publishing, writing and" 5837
"Publishing Company, Mammoth" 5311
"publishing establishment, vast" 1006
"publishing houses" 5537
"publishing their bad novels" 7000
Pubs 3832, 5990
"pucker, feeling only a slight" 7614
"pudding, plum" 3887
"pudding raided from my stores" 3887
"puddle, oblong" 7471
"puddle inset in the coarse asphalt" 7471
"puddles, rime of frost lay thick on the" 10630
"puddles, walked around the deep" 10407
"puddles left by overnight rain" 10407
"pudgy hand" 4414
"Puerto Rican here and there, a fine" 10876
"puffed slowly up the river valley" 7242
"puffing and panting up that grassy hill" 3691
"puffing on his hookah" 6299
"puffs of snout and mews of crack" 6075
"puffs of warm July wind" 2985
"Puget Sound" 400
Pugh, Mr. 6953
"pugnaciously drunk" 2889
"pugs on the dinner table, set her" 10544

"puke, leaned across the railing to" 142

Pulaski, Anna 4180

Pulcifer, Mr. Horatio 4556

"pull himself together" 5947

"pull of the family" 3625

"pull off a big one" 2036

"pull thin and taut" 2066

"pulled by a large dirt-grey horse" 9795

"pulled herself up with a start" 10223

"pulled much too quickly" 9346

"pulled myself together" 6532

"pulled out of San Felipe at day-break" 9762

"pulled out Uncle Jim's costume" 2837

"pulled slowly up" 7265

"pulled the door shut" 4485

"pulled the old Ford into the curb" 2962

"pulling at her dress, I kept" 6694

"pulling corn" 10927

"pulling the pleasure boats up out of the water" 8149

"Pullinstown" 3998

"Pullman, a" 5129

"Pullman car" 1648

"Pullman corridor" 5943

"pulls into Tano's Shop-Rite parking lot" 3032

"pulpit, stood silent and motionless at the" 1532

"pulpit man, never a strong" 1540

"pulsating gaze" 5450

"pulse, sleeper's" 1274

"pulsed through midtown still undiminished" 7569

Pulvertaft, Lalagy 2906

"pump, black satin" 2884

"pump, single rusting gas" 5166

"pumped it in" 3057

"pumpkin, soft as a rotted" 1896

"pumpkins, Marimekko" 7074

"pumps, her red" 2658

"pumps, oil" 1039

"punch line, you're usually the" 4664

"puncher, department" 9310

"punchers, two tired but happy" 1582

"punctual, driver was always" 10093

"punctual, you are always so" 10865

"punctual and reliable of men, the most" 9347

"punctual meal" 4909

Punctuality 1660, 2088, 6200, 6203, 9480, 9992, 10093, 10360, 10865

"punctuality, lets his curiosity interfere with his" 2088

"punctuation, I'll use regular" 9265

"puncture-marks, all dotted and scarred with innumerable" 3047

"pungent, rich and" 1194

"punishing, becomes more" 4407

Punishment 2027, 2043, 2304, 2461, 3353, 6965, 7139, 7143, 7686, 8756, 10542

"punishment, temporal" 7852

"Punjab" 1038, 9847

"puny runt" 7851

"pup, was once a" 399

"pupil, an articled" 3326

"pupil opens wide, at death the" 2378

"pupils, brighter" 4446

"pupils, fellow" 3207

"pupils, gladly have given up taking" 99

"pupils, two" 3931

"pupils' room" 3326

"puppet states" 6256

"puppy, bassett" 6692

"puppy, insolent" 4971

"purchase of a railway-ticket" 9874

"purchased a deluxe semidetached unit" 3264

"purchased a large ledger" 3751

"purchased six hundred acres of land" 6685

"purchased the English soil, could have" 3635

Purchases 681, 1046, 1087, 2841, 3751, 4265, 4289, 9625, 10562

"pure, clear and" 4354

"pure and pellucid as the fountain of Bandusium" 9738

"pure in its pallor" 4157

"purgatory, a little" 1415

"Purgatory, you spend your time in" 9284

"purgatory between land and sea for the traveler" 1415

"Puritania, land of" 963

"puritanical spirit" 6972

"purity of line" 4617

"purity of the beyond" 6145

"purple with evening, cinder piles showed" 8645

"purpling grapes" 1849

Purpose 5427, 5973, 6036

"purpose, came here on" 6831

"purpose, express" 6036, 6441

"purpose, it might have served a better" 9021

"purpose, it will suit my" 3143

"Purpose, mask of" 5973

"purpose, pregnant with" 7061

"purpose, quite another" 7222

"purposeful way, hasty yet" 6301

"purposefulness of long habit" 10421

"purring in the May sun" 5076

"purse, brocade" 6724

"purse, yellow leather snap" 9525

"purser took the last landing card" 9539

"pursue him, terrier began to" 7852

"pursued by threat of war and violence" 3880

Pursuit 297, 2024, 2909, 3030, 4174, 6382, 6582, 6947, 7850, 7852, 7860, 8127, 8130, 8905, 9587

"pursuit of women" 2488

"Purveyors of Leather Fancy Goods" 6448

"Pusan" 10506

"push from behind, gave me a strong" 6708

"pushed almost hard enough to hurt herself" 3689

"pushed an eight-year-old boy off a cliff to his death" 6198

"pushed himself erect, slowly" 10394

"pushed his way among the passengers" 4730

"pushed open a little-used gate" 8212

"pushed open the screen door" 8790

"pushed the balls of her thumbs into her eye-sockets" 3689

"pushed the door open with her behind" 10939

Pushkin, Alexander 2794

"push-up, it was a full" 7989

"put it off, I've" 3718

"Putney Heath" 5928

"putrefaction, sour smell of" 8541

"putting on a dress" 10830

Puttock, Mr. 6977

"puzzle, moral" 5206

"puzzle of winding and oblique streets" 5607

"puzzle persists" 5408

"puzzled" 4158, 10215

"puzzled, evidently much" 6520

"puzzled, he looked" 5369

"puzzled, I am always" 4447

"puzzled about going crazy" 4942

"puzzled hesitation" 5408

"puzzled over" 1731

Puzzles 5206, 5708

"puzzles used in teaching children geography" 5708

"puzzling" 687

Pybus, Mr. Conrad 492

"Pyefield" 6370

"pyjamas, top half of his" 9923

Pyle 9330

Pyle, Homer 2511

Pym, Magnus 1736

Pynsent, Miss 9861

"pyramid" 5971

"pyramid, books were arranged in a tall" 919

"Pyramid, Great" 9293

"Pyramid of Cheops" 8565

"Pyramids" 9239

"pyramids at Giza" 1694

"Pyrenées, majestic" 5125

"pythons" 4685

"Q., remote border town of" 8232
"Q.C. since England had a Queen" 3136
"Quad, Arts" 3283
"quad, garden" 8354
"Quade, Selbury" 3248
"quadrangle" 1596
"quadrant in hand" 8079
"quadrille by seven couples" 2118
"Quadri's in the Piazza San Marco" 8634
"quaffed foaming tankards" 3396
"quagmires, little excursion into the wayside" 2015
"quagmires, stinking" 7323
"quai, along the" 9631
"quai, walk down to the" 5607
"quai, water that slithered against the" 2529
"Quai des Grands Augustins" 6108
"quaint inconveniences" 4644
"quaintly he came" 4936
"qualifications, slightest" 5412
"qualifications, without reference to her personal" 10767
"qualified, well" 5938
"qualities, for all his fine" 5997
"qualities you would expect in a young girl" 4209
"quality, the vast mysterious" 7916
"quarest ting, de" 4716
"quarrel on a staircase, loud unequal" 8769
"quarrel with his wife, having a" 4706
"quarreled once again" 1706
"quarreling at his bedside" 1841
"quarrelled, Margaret and I" 1824
"quarrelled with his barber" 1838
"quarrelling, after a deal of" 3376
"quarrels not their own, fought in" 3557
"quarry, the" 753, 9835
"quarter bordering on Stuyvesant Square" 1012
"quarter-blood" 4358
"quarter-deck, darkness of the" 8060
"quarters, bachelor officers'" 9920
"Quarters, Bachelor Officers" 1551
"quarters, our private inner" 5996
"quarters, winter" 4007
"quarters for the night" 9533
"Quartet, Locatelli's C major" 6226
Quatermain, Allan 3497, 3795, 5412, 10332
"quay, principal" 8066
"quay, stone" 8080
Quayne ladies 10659
"Queasy" 7098
Quebaro, Eugene 7576
"Quebec" 7655, 7658, 10030
"Québec" 2555
"Queen" 4008
"Queen, God Shave The" 8756

"Queen, his" 1902
"Queen, since England had a" 3136
"Queen, the" 127
"Queen, the new" 541
"Queen, the old" 541
Queen Anne 3376
"Queen Anne, county of" 3531
"Queen Charlotte" 8152
Queen Elizabeth 5227, 9391
"queen in England" 3376
"Queen of England" 7604
"Queen of the World" 1216
Queen Victoria 6647
"Queen Victoria, that monstrous dwarf" 6647
Queens 541, 6487, 6561, 7805
"Queens, Borough of" 1884
"Queens, King and" 8991
"Queens New York" 1515
"Queensferry" 9511
"Queensway, formerly" 1040
"queer, acted" 637
"queer and not altogether happy one, my childhood was a" 1268
"queer individuals, two very" 8856
"queer light" 2704
"queer little place" 3418
"queer thing" 11004
"quenched it, until she" 10309
Quentin 7763
Quentin, Mr. Philip 3325
"quest, started on my" 7223
"quest is on again" 7225
"quest separate from the questing after dollars" 7229
"quested after, what he" 7228
"questing after dollars" 7229
"question, another" 7196
"question, asked her grandmother a" 4822
"question, asked himself the same" 4572
"question, begins her memoirs with the" 3679
"question, first" 3913, 7207
"question, fragment of a" 2759
"question, her written" 7197
"question, investigate the nature of this" 7518
"question, key" 7204
"question, most important" 1487
"question, now there was no" 8819
"question, occasional dry" 7200
"question, same" 7211
"question a million times before, asked this" 2096
"question about mathematics" 7202
"question became increasingly perplexing" 4811
"question came to me" 7205
"question here, there is some" 7212
"question in the hall, started her" 7213
"question naturally arises" 1182

"question they asked me, the first" 1514
"question to the parlour-maid, before putting the" 10916
"question was for ten days hourly asked" 1487
"question was settled" 6977
"question will open the way to resolution" 921
"question would not have seemed to him meaningful" 4350
Questions 1487, 1999, 4572, 4811, 4822, 6953
"questions about your life in Cwm Bugail" 6953
"questions, I am often asked a number of" 2067
"questions, I came to ask you some" 6953
"questions, relevant" 7203
"questions, serious" 2570
Quests 253, 723, 2564, 2607, 3466, 4154, 4229, 4379, 4680, 6069, 6927, 6952, 9278, 9930, 10306
"queue, a" 5971
"queue, standing in a bus" 10046
"queue waiting for breakfast" 3968
Quick, Gulliver 6346
Quick, Ralph 9966
"quick, sharp and" 967
"quick for me, he was too" 7518
"quick-bodied" 10804
"quickening of the sap in the trees" 10980
Quickly, Mrs. 4739
"quickly enough, not" 5542
"quickness, birdlike" 4141
"quicksands, crossing the" 9101
"quicksilver, filled to the brim with" 7471
"quicksilver, spilt" 171
"quicksilver of the brain" 2766
"quiescence, a sleeping" 2212
"quiet, deceptive" 7275
"quiet, front was" 10537
"quiet, garden was" 8328
"quiet, he became" 1111
"quiet, house was too" 3163
"quiet, I know of no" 8331
"quiet, room was very" 7789
"quiet, so" 9120
"quiet, spectral" 8119
"quiet, suddenly" 9995
"quiet, things at last were" 8662
"quiet, unpleasantly" 3091
"quiet, usually" 939
"quiet and airy" 7768
"quiet and imaginative" 4892
"quiet as a bank of wildflowers" 1409
"quiet as a grave" 3215
"quiet became dark and threatening" 8332
"quiet discomfort" 4644

"quiet house, completely" 3285
"quiet in Charleston Harbour" 7913
"quiet in her room" 9406
"quiet in my daughter's house" 3121
"quiet in the Saloon Bar of the Crown" 4312
"quiet lay upon the meadow" 8337
"quiet of the early morning" 8795
"quiet quite like that of a men's club, no" 8331
"quiet that had fallen, evening" 664
"quietly, said" 1788
"quietly and carefully" 7766
"quietness" 7670
"quill, bears down on his goose" 5548
"quilt, green eiderdown" 4183
Quin, Mrs. 2330
Quin, Richard 943
Quince, Adam 6319
Quinn 2527, 2972, 3886
Quinn, Daniel 10871
Quinney, Dicken 4085
Quinney, Nicholas Dicken 5667
"quintessence of history" 4489
"Quiquengrogne" 9248
"Quiquenparle" 9248
"quirk of fate, strange" 7453
"quirk of style" 10833
"Quit, if fate says" 2683
"quit in anger when my boss was fired" 6460
"quit my job" 6455
"quit my job, last time I tried to" 6475
"Quito" 6259
"quitter, I've always been a" 3522
Quitting 1493, 2479, 3286, 3334, 3522, 4604, 6434, 6447, 6455, 6460
"quitting time, around" 8776
"quitting time, it was almost" 5809
Quivari, Ethelbert 6968
"quiver, air began to" 8033
"quiver like vaginal lips" 2941
"quivered if one touched them" 303
"quivered in the draught" 5324
"quivering with pride" 7125
"quivers, dress" 1982
"quixotic" 7135
Quorn, Mrs. 8869
"quota, cane" 2570
"quotation I've often heard" 2347
"quote, how it was I" 708
"quoted his long-dead father and mother" 5965
"quoted silently to himself" 8615
"quoted them in Yiddish" 5965
Quoyle 9719

"Rabbi in Israel" 7505
"Rabbi's only son" 6482
"rabbits" 1271
"rabbits, feeding his" 7109

"rabbits, my three hundred" 3463
Rabbitte, Jimmy Sr. 7094
Rabelais 8943
"rabid scavengers" 286
"rabies, epidemic of" 167
Rabinovitz, Leonid 6232
Rabinowitz, Joseph 4942
Race 46, 3137, 4435, 4716, 5933
"race, advisability of perpetuating that" 7056
"race, extreme antiquity of the" 359
"race, her" 9090
"race, inexpressive and speechless" 8841
"race, remnants of a disinherited" 5886
"race, six-day bike" 4702
"race, that emancipated" 8650
"race, the ninth" 1705
"race alongside the late afternoon traffic" 7862
"race of men and women who see all things through this curtain of sea" 7917
"race qualities, persistence of" 4435
"Racecourse, Hazel Park" 1705
"raced down a path" 32
"raced upstairs" 7843
"raced with the steadily ripening fruit" 4374
Races 1684, 7612, 8163, 8924, 10369
"races, Rimi" 3438
"races, Taunton" 1684
"races, to three" 9748
"races, Wallingford" 9919
"Racetrack, World's Most Beautiful" 8317
Rachaeli 6542
Rachel 1953, 9433
"racing, see some" 6939
"racing inexorably around the track" 7851
"racing over country roads" 9774
"racing-season" 8912
"racist cop" 74
"racketing along" 9597
Rackham, Mrs. Barry 9895
"radar screen" 227
Radclif, Sam 9553
"Radcliffe Camera in Oxford" 7772
"Radford Hills" 1908
"radiance, blinding excess of white" 2620
"radiance, its" 5324
"radiance, lacy" 5337
"radiance, streetlights burst into" 2219
"radiant and full-leafed" 423
"radiators, last of the" 9947
"Radich" 4328
"radio, brought home a" 9369
"radio, her" 10810
"radio, Israeli" 1159
"radio, it's a" 9362

"radio, on the" 10085
"radio, shortwave" 9291
"radio, singing on the" 3750
"radio, small Philco" 9366
"radio, someone turned on the" 10147
"radio, tested his" 5716
"radio, transistor" 1046
"radio, turned on the" 10159
"radio communication, I received a" 228
"radio crackled like one emotion too many" 9374
"radio crackled wheezily" 9361
"radio mummy" 7791
"radio *Spider*, secret" 1118
"radio station" 6838
"radio still half-alive from the night before" 2974
"radio still playing to him" 7855
"radio stuttered and crackled" 9363
"radio under the pickup's dash" 6968
Radio 1118, 3750, 4220, 5295, 6810, 6838, 7791, 8320, 9262, 9361, 9362, 9363, 9365, 9366, 9369, 9374, 10085, 10147
"radio-quiet shield" 9756
"radishes, hothouse" 3848
"radium, sparks of everlasting" 785
"radius, causal" 6001
"radius of half a dozen blocks" 6274
"Radnor Pennsylvania" 1188
"R.A.F., I was never in the" 196
"RAF, thrown out of the" 8664
Raffray, Sylvia 10794
Rafi 10297
Raft, Janet 1727
"raft" 9626
"raft, went down the river on a" 5506
"rafters, swung from the" 9839
"rafters, tear down some of the" 1162
"rag, chewing the" 1840
Rage 373, 378, 380, 393
"rage, days of" 5673
"rage, fit of drunken Polish" 6652
"rage, gesture of" 6310
"rage, he liked to feel" 380
"rage, moan aloud with" 3344
"rage, tore off his wig and stamped it under foot in" 373
"rage and frustration, moment of" 5292
"rage hammering through his arteries" 378
"rage suddenly flaring in him" 380
"rages against junk, she" 393
"ragged" 5015
"raging juices, women with" 8993
"raging out of control" 10518
Raglan 6009
"rags an' tags" 4987
"raided from my stores, pudding" 3887

"raiders emerged from the canyon"
  7643
Raids 2854, 6966
"raids, air-" 1282
"raids, recent impact-" 10510
"raiking out of Molesworth Street"
  4936
"railhead, major" 1460
"railhead, nearest" 9586
"railhead at Somkele" 6122
"railing, upper deck's" 8099
"railings, iron" 9153
"railroad, across from the" 2615
"railroad, Burlington" 3087
"Railroad, East & West" 3912
"railroad, embankment of a" 9121
"Railroad, Long Island" 10324
"Railroad, New York Central" 7258
"railroad, there was a" 7273
"railroad car, the all but empty"
  8234
"railroad compartment, first-class"
  1371
"railroad shops near the depot at
  Bonneville" 8765
"railroad station" 1465, 9631
"railroad station, cavernous" 10734
"railroad station, paint me a small"
  7263
"railroad track set for the moon,
  like a" 4635
"railroad tracks" 440, 9300
"railroad tracks, abandoned" 7282
"railroad tracks, mesh of" 10378
"railroad tracks, take me down to
  the" 7270
"railroad trestle, under the" 10230
Railroads 325, 1344, 1365, 1630,
  3087, 3303, 3427, 3649, 4017,
  4047, 4385, 5142, 5709, 6703,
  8765, 9121, 9412, 9529, 9586,
  9596, 9631, 9641, 9761, 10042,
  10069, 10324, 10378
"railroads ran up into the canyons"
  1365
"railroad's thin lines of steel" 4047
"rails, screamed and scraped along
  the" 7278
Railton, Dr. 8518
"railway" 6283
"railway bridge" 9596
"railway carriage, perfectly appointed" 8351
"railway coach, that inexorably
  moving" 9564
"railway, model" 325
"railway platform" 4017, 9657
"railway station" 930, 1368, 2903,
  3427, 9761, 9890, 10042
"railway station, Bramblehurst"
  9092
"railway station, dark arches of
  the" 1618
"railway stations" 7271
"railway, such a" 7253

"railway, Tube" 9381
"railway workers" 10458
"railways" 1344
"Railways, British" 7261
"railway's lights, electric" 8596
Rain 41, 157, 177, 183, 310, 729,
  777, 844, 1055, 1106, 1162, 1399,
  1759, 2132, 2150, 2226, 2272,
  2448, 2469, 2588, 2946, 2990,
  3307, 3314, 3315, 3521, 3836,
  3908, 3940, 4275, 4306, 4421,
  4636, 5033, 5373, 5711, 5778,
  6379, 6567, 6574, 7087, 7706,
  7757, 8033, 8127, 8170, 8406,
  8443, 8471, 8511, 8513, 8519,
  8524, 8786, 9168, 9320, 9617,
  9739, 9828, 9975, 10045, 10085,
  10407, 10409, 10577, 10614,
  10646, 10688, 10690, 10704,
  10711, 10743
"rain, after a day of" 7757
"rain, after heavy" 5169
"rain, air smelled of" 8519
"rain, Amy loves" 5373
"rain, black wall of monsoon" 10533
"rain, braved the" 9828
"rain, burning" 183
"rain, came in out of the" 1759
"rain, carries the" 10690
"rain, chill" 7290
"rain, chill spring" 8443
"rain, chilling April" 10045
"rain, chilly spring" 7341
"rain, cold" 1181
"rain, cold misty" 7315
"rain, cold November" 7322
"rain, day of solid heavy" 4421
"rain, days of" 7706
"rain, drip of the" 3836
"rain, driving" 3307, 10679
"rain, drizzle of" 2226
"rain, drizzling" 7285
"rain, early November" 583
"rain, gazed into the" 5431
"rain, going to" 7306
"rain, harkened drowsily to the"
  7305
"rain, heavy unseasonable" 9168
"rain, in the dark and the" 41
"rain, it became so filmed with"
  2946
"rain, ladled a sprinkle of" 8513
"rain, look of hard wet" 7296
"rain, March" 5778
"rain, mist and drizzle of" 7316
"rain, mizzling" 10577
"rain, night of" 8406
"rain, no ordinary summer" 7311
"rain, occasional flurry of fine" 10606
"rain, overnight" 10407
"rain, pelting" 4636, 7326
"rain, pissing" 7343
"rain, pouring" 1055, 6993
"rain, relentless sleety" 7304
"rain, sits in his car in the" 10085

"rain, slanted slashing" 7300
"rain, squinted at the" 7340
"rain, steady" 9617
"rain, sudden squally" 7298
"rain, summer" 3405
"rain, swathes of" 8127
"rain, swirling" 7288
"rain, today I see the" 7320
"rain, violent shower of" 7284
"rain, voices in the trees betoken"
  10743
"rain, weeks of" 7328
"rain, wind and" 9220
"rain, woodland" 10409
"rain and wet snow" 3810
"rain came down" 7319
"rain ceased" 2150
"rain clouds hung low and dark"
  9228
"rain coming across the harbor in
  swirls and clouds of mist" 7322
"rain darkens the terrace bricks"
  10606
"rain descended through the haze"
  7285
"rain drifting eastwards across the
  Channel" 8127
"rain driven over the mountains
  from the sea" 10711
"[rain] drove with vehemence
  against the windows" 7305
"rain during the night, there had
  been much" 177
"rain fell" 7335
"rain fell across September's highways" 7327
"rain fell steadily from before daylight" 10646
"rain forest, smell of the" 8541
"rain forest of Sarawak" 4109
"rain had been coming and going"
  7337
"rain had been falling for two days"
  7341
"rain had fallen all day" 7312
"rain had fallen, no" 7314
"rain had so distorted visibility"
  7328
"rain had warped" 6698
"rain hammering on the tarpaper
  roof" 6379
"rain in the afternoon" 7308
"rain kept the usual thick seas of
  mud churning" 3653
"rain left off" 2226
"rain on my forehead" 8524
"rain pattered on the rooftop" 8471
"rain pelting in at the open windows" 1162
"rain rain rain" 844
"rain rained, a black oily" 10614
"rain squalls" 10704
"rain stopped" 8170
"rain storm up the Yocona River"
  7301

"rain swept and paused" 7321
"rain that came at dusk" 7288
"rain that had fallen the night before" 9168
"rain that swirled through the Gap" 7290
"rain that turned half into snow" 6567
"rain was . . . condensing in crystal beads on the green snouts of the crocuses" 3521
"rain was falling" 7324
"rain was falling on the campus" 7336
"rain was misting across the lawn" 3521
"rain was rainier" 5033
"rain which drove across the estuary" 7304
"rain would fall" 7289
Rainbird, Captain 4739
Rainbird, Godfrey 5938
Rainbo Woman 2566
Rainbow, Astra 6198
"rainbow, like a" 1273
"Rainbow Center" 2971
"rainbow sheets" 1606
"raincoat, man in the belted" 5927
"raincoat, thin inadequate" 5940
"raindarts splashing white against a jog of umbrellas" 7317
"rained, all day it had" 10688
"rained, for the first four days it" 7338
"rained, when it" 3648
"rained all day" 7302
"rained and I caught the cold" 157
"rained at dawn" 5096
"rained . . . drumming with steel fingers" 7325
"rained for weeks" 7334
"rained in the night" 7332
"rained last night" 7318
"rained lightly" 2469
"rained so heavily that nobody went out" 7303
"rained the entire day" 7344
"rained the night before" 7298
"rained torrentially" 7325
"rained upon" 5911
Rainer, Dr. 8490
"rainfall, the night's" 6574
"rainforest, tropical" 10718
"rainiest lives, like the" 7286
"rainiest nights" 7286
"raining" 2448
"raining, because it was" 8786
"raining, it shouldn't have been" 7309
"raining, it was" 7306, 7319
"raining again" 7330
"raining and blowing" 1106
"raining daily, it had been" 7331
"raining down steadily over all of us" 7329

"raining earlier in the day" 8443
"raining in the forest" 3908
"raining over the city" 7329
"raining since noon" 9320
"raining without stop" 9975
"rains, one of those hard mad" 7294
"rains, tropical" 5052
"rains are over, winter" 7333
"rains began, the" 777, 7313
"rains came gently, the last" 7297
"rains came unexpectedly" 7323
"rains that come down as if with deliberate fury" 7294
"rainstorm, gusty gray March" 3315
"rainstorm skirting the Andes" 7339
"rainstorm that matched his mood" 3315
Raintree, Cassie 2454
"rainy day, on a" 7307
"Rainy River waterway" 4049
"rainy season" 2239, 7287
"raised, where I was" 5528
"raised by decent hypocrites" 9713
"raised his head" 8742
"raised his head on his hands" 7324
"raised in a shuffle of dreary upstate towns" 9719
"raised the cigarette to the sun" 3053
"raised to be, snob that I was" 9714
"raised to the illustrious eminence of a friend" 1
"raised up a son" 6546
"raising a prematurely-wrinkled hand" 7555
"raising France to that state of formidable power" 6244
"raising her by himself" 2934
"raising turkeys" 3662
"Rajas, the" 5715
Raju 9906
Rake, Mr. 2820
"rake the bedroom ceiling in long yellow shafts" 5338
Rakesh 9574
"rakish angle" 5975
Rakonitz family 4142
Raleigh, Walter 7144
"rallying after an uncertain start" 6755
Ralph 132, 2005, 2574, 4375
Ralston, John 5344
Ralstons, the 3561
Ram, Lala Kanshi 3278
"ram, old" 434
"Ram, sign of the" 535
"Ram, time of the" 5458
Raman 3195
Rambam 6431
Rambeau 2669
"ramble, a solitary" 6555
"ramble, begins to" 3056
Rambler, the 6884
"rambler, the" 9519
Ramillies, Lady 4401
"rammed the gunpowder even

harder into the copper pipe" 7048
Ramona 3933
Ramosé 10476
Ramoud, Matussem 10328
"rampaging away, the horde had gone" 1634
"rampant like supporters on a coat of arms" 381
"rampart, Evreux's ancient" 9674
"ramparts of Rosas" 3482
"ramparts of the General Theological Seminary" 3429
"ramparts raised about it frowningly" 1356
Ramsay, Mrs. 6565
Ramsey, Alec 2988
"Ramsgard, small country town of" 9412
"ramshackle, commenced" 3604
"ramshackle barracks" 8699
"ran across the gravel road" 7848
"ran across the polished floor" 4141
"ran along the narrow trail" 4695
"ran around and made one final check" 3245
"ran away" 2148
"ran away, the day before he" 2562
"ran away with Rachel Carter" 6623
"ran for a towel first" 7857
"ran for the bus" 7817
"ran from the room without putting on her shoes" 9916
"ran from words" 9463
"ran into the deep dark taiga" 3413
"ran into the fields" 8429
"ran on and on" 7842
"ran on deck" 2188
"ran out after him so fast" 7860
"ran out of his parents' garden" 963
"ran out of milk" 9736
"ran through the dark quiet streets" 6223
"ran toward the barn" 476
"ran up the concrete steps" 7841
"ran upstairs narrowly ahead of her thoughts" 9409
"ranch, Broderson" 8765
"Ranch, Centipede" 3995
"ranch, JC" 6948
"ranch, JC was a good" 3643
"ranch half the size of a township" 6464
"ranch in South America, my" 4558
"ranch to work for, the Lazy S had been a good" 6418
"ranch which he and Buck Peters jointly owned" 7616
"Ranche, Robles" 5892
"ranchers" 4374
Ranches 3643, 6418, 7636, 8413
"ranches, country of good" 3643
"ranches within a day's ride of the old Bar 20" 3644

"ranchhouse, the Double-Y" 8853
"ranching center" 1460
"rancho of Our Lady of the Little Columns" 8413
"ranch-style" 3208
Randall 8653
Randall, Thomas 5994
"Randolph Junction" 3338
Randon, Lee 8909
Randy 2457
"Ranee's palace" 10509
"rang, phone" 1127
"rang at a little after ten in the morning" 1116
"rang the bell for Jeeves" 656
"rang the bell once" 654
"Range, Bear Tooth" 10570
"Range, Black Spur" 2195
"Range, Blackdown" 1491
"Range, Booradeela" 4084
"Range, Carson" 8729
"range, kitchen" 6024
"Range, Oregon Coastal" 7674
"Range, Pennine" 6060
"range and fall away shoulder to shoulder" 6084
"ranges, rock-ribbed" 1439
"ranges, series of parallel" 6053
"ranges, tangled" 6062
"ranges, two mighty" 6063
"Ranis, the" 5715
"rank of Commodore" 10978
Ranke 6762
"ranks, close" 61
"ranks of apartment houses and business buildings" 5323
"Ranpur, city of" 6446
Ransom 5472, 9890
Ransom, Sir 7166
Ransome 2209
"ranted" 2356
Raoul 3922
"rap, impatient" 5247
"rap on Jesse, the" 5010
Rape 2047, 2048, 2054, 2056, 8020, 9701
"rape" 2054
"rape, this is" 2063
"rape that distresses me" 2048
"raped by two men" 2047
"raped her" 2056
"rapes, these alleged" 9701
"rapes were pure fantasy in one case and an attempted mugging in the other" 9701
"rapid photography" 1314
Rapidan, Thomas 10396
"rapiers, long" 3396
"rapine" 872
"rapist, convicted" 367
Rappaport 2243
"rapping absently on the arm of the chair" 98
"rapping through the fog toward him" 7411

"Rapstone, village of" 6923
"rapt and breathless" 3499
"rapture, utmost pose of" 1521
"rarely is it possible" 5596
"rarely smoked" 8567
"Raritan, the" 7647
"rash to say he would do this job himself" 10947
Raskolnikov 3930
Rasselas 4603
Raste, Dr. 1968
"rat, he was only a small" 458
"rat, the French" 2657
"rat hole" 7176
"rate of four miles an hour" 9757
"ration of life, bound to its miniscule" 9008
"rational Being, production of a" 6604
"rationality, omniscient" 7132
"rationed sky" 10242
"rations, thirty days'" 9576
"Ratnagalla, peak of" 9749
Rats 431, 452, 458, 3962
"rats" 7801
"rats, hardly any demand for" 452
"rats in the rockery" 431
"rats in the walls perked up sniffing" 3962
"rattle, bang and" 3295
"rattle of cartwheels" 8778
"rattle of leaves" 10218
"rattled the tops of garbage cans" 10699
Rattler, Martin 951
"rattler, eyes of a" 10546
"rattles going like hail on a roof" 10546
"rattlesnake, eating a" 459
"rattling around in his rusty wagon" 3035
"rattling her words" 5632
"rattling swiftly now over the bridge" 5142
"rattling the dry palm trees" 10717
Ratty 7114
"ratty beaches" 9181
"ratty jeans" 2872
Rau, Bill 3878
"raucous" 8773
Ravanel, Alice 3931
Raven 6175
Ravenal, Kim 4727
Ravenel, Miss Lillie 5785
"Ravenna, church in" 9353
"ravenous, sudden and" 9071
"raves some" 7231
Ravi 3980
"ravine" 1983
"ravine, across the" 5590
"ravine, deep" 10924
"ravioli, square of" 3344
"ravioli, watched my grandmother make" 1875
"ravishing, she looked" 2832

"raw, *try* them" 3853
"Rawals, the" 5715
"Rawlins, just outside of" 9829
Rawson, Hugh 8099
Ray 3912, 6673
Ray, Mr. 5194
"ray that pierced the eastern shutters, yellow" 10144
Rayborne, David 6048
Rayburn, Kelly 1329
Raymond 8646, 9883
Raymond, George 1660
"rays of golden sunlight" 5309
"rays struck me dead center" 10186
"rays struck the top of the television antenna" 5328
"razed with truly insolent completeness" 4073
"razing of the entire Warsaw ghetto" 2604
Razor, Jake 7187
"razor, finely honed steel" 8044
"razor, long cut-throat" 8043
"razor, sharpening its" 10717
"razor with its ebony handle" 8044
Razumov, Kirylo Sidorovitch 5406
"reach, within their natural and immediate" 10772
"reach for a cigarette, sleepily" 7999
"reach for the orange juice" 595
"reach out, he felt her" 10251
"reached and lifted a quart soft drink bottle" 5118
"reached for a bowl of ocher mud" 2833
"reached for his wife's hand" 4599
"reached for the keys to his apartment" 1263
"reached for the phone" 1131
"reached his desk" 8268
"reached in a hollow place" 2837
"reached its outer rim" 2575
"reached out and switched off the last light" 5336
"reached out both hands" 3714
"reached up to make a tuning adjustment" 9363
"reaches, impenetrable" 455
"reaches of rock and waste, sterile" 9115
"reaching" 10300
"reaching a given point in the shortest possible time, intent on" 9528
"reaching from nowhere" 7855
"reaching out across the miles" 1129
"react to them, see how he would" 5410
"reaction, my" 2522
"reactions, a couple of" 8860
"read, all the world to" 5456
"read, began to" 7355
"read, he seldom" 10051
"read, I cannot" 58

"read, it doesn't matter which you" 1408

"read, learned to" 3282

"read, pretending to" 7368

"read, so I have somewhere" 363

"read, sometimes he" 7354

"read, you may have" 9020

"read a book" 896

"read a lot, I used to" 7353

"read at any hour of the day" 7357

"read *Ferdinand the Bull* as a child" 5455

"read for a fee" 5486

"read it, he could scarcely" 898

"read it, I have never" 914

"read it, would she like to" 5551

"read it, written down when I first" 8999

"read it aloud, he had just" 5473

"read nor write, could neither" 4303

"read or talk a little" 3108

"read slowly" 7350

"read sneakily fifteen years ago" 5502

"read some of my books, you've probably" 908

"read the headlines as he passed by" 10366

"read the *Iliad* of Homer" 5431

"read the King James Version" 7546

"read the letter" 8647

"read the letter again, did not" 1943

"read the lives" 10837

"read 'The Lost Theatre'" 9382

"read the manuscript and gave valuable advice" 714

"read the *New York Times*" 6360

"read the newspapers, Buck did not" 400

"read the paper" 7262

"read *The Powwow Highway*, unless you've already" 9059

"read the two cards" 869

"read them, you never had a chance to" 2534

"read them in silence" 1947

"read these runes" 5545

"read through the papers, having one last" 10486

"read what her mother . . . had written" 4354

"read with pleasure" 5552

"reader" 4218, 5542, 6361, 9038

"reader, apprise the" 8953

"reader, create for the" 5406

"reader, curious" 399

"Reader, Dear" 693, 5523

"reader, interest the" 3986

"Reader, it may suffice the" 778

"reader, no possible consequence to the" 779

"Reader, our" 1408

"reader, the" 1801, 2016, 5386, 5395, 5462, 6604

"reader, undertake to do for you" 4492

"reader acquainted, make the" 4028

"reader is introduced, before the" 6885

"reader may discover" 5435

"reader should be led gently" 8995

"reader should beforehand know every detail" 8961

"reader will excuse me, if the" 1568

Readers 4218, 5435, 5462, 8953, 8961, 8995

"readers, book" 9381

"readers, I will introduce my" 3972

"readers, laying before his" 5557

"readers, many" 6467

"readers, my" 5411, 5693

"readers, surprise our" 7060

"readers, well known to all my northern" 9511

"readers are doubtless aware, our" 696

"readers everywhere, specialized" 8879

"readers unacquainted with the class of facts" 8964

"readiness, lips slightly open in" 5188

Reading 58, 651, 869, 894, 900, 901, 907, 923, 987, 1763, 1943, 1950, 3202, 3070, 4200, 4951, 5311, 5431, 5455, 5486, 5502, 5519, 5520, 6360, 7895, 8647, 8957, 8959, 9016, 9059, 9296, 9382, 10026, 10051, 10219, 10366, 10486, 10837, 10951

"reading, considerable" 5884

"reading, dull enough" 1910

"reading, I wear spectacles for" 4789

"reading, you are not" 7360

"reading a book on music" 6227

"reading a local story" 7367

"reading a smudgy proof" 7349

"reading a story" 5431

"reading aloud to my mother" 5520

"reading class, enriched" 7895

"reading his Bible" 7359

"reading Homer's *Iliad* in three days all at the same time" 9265

"reading in her grandfather's library" 651

"reading *Little Women*" 7348

"reading room" 969, 10951

"Reading Room of the famous Bodleian Library" 7772

"reading the batch of weekly papers" 5311

"reading the morning paper" 3282

"reading the Sunday sports page" 7369

"reading the want ads" 7365

"reading their newspapers" 7352

"reading too long, she had been" 7356

"reading within a cone of yellow light" 7364

"readings of the noon sacrifice" 7514

"reads, the books Nero Wolfe" 907

"ready again, getting" 6287

"ready to come out" 9948

"ready to write" 706

"real, get" 6729

"real, it all seemed so" 7372

"Real Estate" 1033

"real estate, pure planes of" 5178

"real estate mogul" 10559

"real estate prices" 880

"real estate trip" 2971

"real one, until he could get a" 302

Reale, Andrew 4346

"realise how infirm the old rector was" 1536

"realist, I am a" 6835

"realities, cheerless" 10131

"realities of the present hour, unpleasant" 9991

Reality 879, 2763, 3505, 4320, 5436, 6765, 7168

"reality, absolute" 2763

"reality, charged with" 3107

"reality, day-to-day" 9718

"reality, extremely weak grasp of" 7168

"reality, in" 1493

"reality, keeps you in touch with" 079

"reality, presumes itself as" 6765

"reality, their intimations of" 220

"reality in the bar, there was no" 4320

"reality never makes sense" 5436

Realization 2459, 3958, 6166, 10564

"realize, aspire to" 237

"realize, did not" 959

"realize, difficult to" 2538

"realize, long to" 1021

"realize for a long time, I did not" 2459

"realized, should have" 5777

"realized 'Hozomeen is the Void— at least Hozomeen means the void to my eyes'" 6075

"realized at once that he was in for trouble" 6506

"realized he had been in a depression" 2518

"realized it, men seldom" 10793

"realized the whole teenage epic was tottering to doom" 3386

"realizing, suddenly" 6075

"ream, strippling" 7677

"reaping and mowing" 5681

"reappearing in the kitchen" 6160

Reardon 8292

"rear-guard" 2885

Reason 4998, 6806

"reason, age of" 6198

"reason, cold winds of" 6806

"reason, for no apparent" 4236
"reason, for the precise" 1533
"reason, had his" 2501
"reason, looking for a" 687
"reason, no earthly" 616
"reason, no particular" 4229
"reason, right" 9701
"reason, there was no" 10921
"reason and intelligence, gifts of" 4998
"reason at all, for no particular" 6125
"reason for murder, an understandable" 6201
"reason for writing this book" 5427
"reason he took the fatal plunge" 2374
"reason I believe in God" 7542
"reason I have now forgotten, for some" 8664
"reason my younger brother Matthew died, I was the" 8240
"reason to get up in the morning" 6041
"reason why, there was no" 2185
"reason why we should, there was no" 5343
"reason you don't want your wife to know about" 7955
Reasons 687, 690, 5449, 6042, 6049
"reasons, for obvious" 9309
"reasons, for our own" 6047
"reasons, good and sufficient" 4785
"reasons, not very good" 9189
"reasons, ridiculous" 6037
"reasons, three good" 5449
"reasons, two" 6049
"reasons Carl was not able to determine" 5607
"reasons for keeping the engagement a secret" 7953
"reasons never turn out" 6047
"reasons that I'm ashamed of now" 6149
"reassessed her foot-square view of the yard" 5372
"reassuring, negatively" 10184
"reawakening, gradual" 5052
Reba 2863
"rebeginning of his health" 6936
"Rebel Corners" 9145
"rebellion of 1863, the unsuccessful" 7184
"rebellious Babylon" 2636
"rebellious South Carolina" 5785
"reborn, to be" 827
"rebuilt, glad the place had not yet been" 9231
"rebuilt, all that was worthwhile keeping had been" 4178
"recall, could not" 8026
"recall, 'tis a joy to" 7406
"recall, took me a moment or two to" 2982

"recall incidents from my boyhood" 7451
"recall its equal" 3851
"recall so little of his past life, he was able to" 7374
"recall the various details of the affair" 675
"recalled, like a dream not quite" 8676
"recalling" 10139
"recalling, without someone" 6208
"recalling that warm autumn night" 6208
"recaptured all the crushing melancholy, immediately" 3276
"recede a little, they" 7527
"receive a compatriot" 9882
"receive their friends on Monday afternoon" 9859
"received Nona Manford" 9880
"receiver, picked up the" 1144
"receiver pressed against her ear" 1133
"receiver to its cradle, returned the" 1147
"receiver upside down, holding the" 10003
"receptacle, large open metal" 4670
"receptacle of tarnished silver, gorgeous gem-encrusted" 110
"reception in the headmaster's residence, a crowded" 5854
"receptionist" 6506
"recess, during" 7898
"recess, get back in from" 7906
"recesses, bare green" 9742
"recipe for peace in our time" 6807
"recirculation, commodius vicus of" 1175
"recitations were over" 8844
"recite at her funeral, find one that would be appropriate to" 5520
Reckler, Joe 3734
"reckless man, not a" 5988
"reckless thing, I had never done a" 5589
"reckless ways" 2997
Recklessness 5589, 7552
"recklessness, unbelievable placid" 2934
"recklessness, what she called his" 7552
"reckon, do you" 3492
"reckon, I" 2296
"reckon, I don't" 1813
"reckon to be dead by six o'clock, she could safely" 9294
"reclining at his ease" 5613
"reclining in her steamer chair" 9413
"recluse, almost a" 7415
"recluse, the" 6300
"recognise the pain of loneliness, too young to" 10763
Recognition 1759, 8676

"recognition, beyond" 4335
"recognition, sense of impending" 9054
"recognition, teasingly short of" 8676
"recognize her, fail to" 10798
"recognize him" 1759
"recognize it, how would you" 8459
"recognized, easily" 5967
"recognized I" 10184
"recoiled aghast" 10033
"recollect it, can't" 7387
"recollected, only dimly" 4741
Recollection 173, 675, 969, 1267, 1276, 1705, 2116, 2816, 2982, 3390, 3430, 3489, 3491, 3696, 3892, 4741, 4834, 4868, 4904, 5021, 5024, 5117, 5118, 5212, 5460, 6208, 6606, 6741, 6790, 7172, 7207, 7457, 8026, 8166, 8245, 8543, 8890, 9035, 9085, 9238, 10065, 10139, 10143, 10281, 10550
"recollection" 7172
"recollection, my earliest" 7413
"recollection of her, scarcely any" 6606
"recollections, my earliest" 7391
"recollections begin, my" 2291
"recollections of old campfires" 7457
"recollections of others" 9035
"recommended him to me" 6892
"recommended to me by my doctor" 141
"reconciliations" 274
"recondite matter, expounding a" 3267
"reconsider, had that chance to" 1133
"reconstruct it from the recollections of others" 9035
"reconstruct my first whole memory" 6374
"record, complete and accurate" 4929
"record, for the" 4793, 8025
"record, gramophone" 6227
"record, I have a good" 6439
"record, worthy of" 5400
"record for a pilot in civil aviation" 202
"record player" 2111, 6131
"recorded, be it here" 7756
"recorder" 6454
"recorder, tape" 8892
"recount with Impartiality and Faithfulness" 6033
"recover, first to" 7140
"recover, time to" 7462
"recovered, Luterin had" 7464
"recovered very quickly" 7465
"recovers her balance" 475
Recovery 2926, 7165, 10555
"recovery could be gained" 7467
"recreation" 6361

"recruit, young" 3855
"recruited by new comers" 1340
"recruiters, religious" 7544
"recruits had been marched down
   to the post barbershop" 8697
"rectangle, adjoining and still
   larger" 7760
"rectangle of the cabin door,
   sunny" 1556
"rectangular, space was..." 7758
"rectangular in shape" 1122
"Rector, new" 1488
"rector, old" 1536
"Rector of St. Dreots" 2299
"rectory, half-" 1180
"rectory, the" 10643
"recumbent giant women" 2225
"recuperating, sat" 7467
"recuperation from Wall Street, his
   weekly" 1591
Red 6223
Red, Uncle 9944
"red, deep coppery" 2833
"red, everything going" 1481
"red, pure" 10383
"red as blood, moon" 8419
"Red Cross" 10917
"Red Cross, he is our" 7516
"Red Cross, knight of the" 10329
"Red Cross Unit" 4629
Red Elk 6382
"red flag was up" 382
"red people, Oklahoma means" 9015
"Red Rock" 3638
"Red Square" 10350
"red was for British India" 5715
"redargued, may be" 5387
"redbird trilled from the coral
   honeysuckle" 726
"redbud, swelling" 3652
Redcliff, Judith 10144
"Redcliffe" 8481
"Redcoats and Tories are everywhere" 7110
Reddick, Max 2912
"redeem, stout limbs and a fair wit
   scarce" 1228
"redeemed at seventeen" 5671
Redfield, Irene 1913
Reding, Charles 6609
"rediscovered" 5289
Redmond, Eamon 7706
Redmond, Mary Margaret 3521
"red-nostrilled" 7607
"redoubles, rondeaux" 5457
"redoubtable catcher" 8907
Redpath 2888
Redpath, Herman 2358
"redundant, I shall soon be quite"
   7975
"redwoods, under" 8212
"redwoods, wind stirs the" 10683
Reece, Ed 6550
Reed, Alexandra 9035
Reed, Ruth 4419

"Reed City" 4073
"Reed '27" 10656
"Reef, Castle" 8688
"reef, outer" 6933
"reefs, windy" 4319
Reegan, Mrs. 10934
"reek of rotting fruit" 8544
"reeking already of the purity of
   the beyond" 6145
"reelection, campaign for" 7005
Reeves, Darrell 888
Reeves, Mrs. 9509
"referring to the chorus or burden"
   5507
"refilled her fountain pen" 5447
"reflect, retired to the forest to"
   6494
"reflect on my first encounter with
   Fledge" 5870
"reflected as he steered absently"
   2337
"reflected everyone of consequence"
   7481
"reflected images" 2118
"reflected in the air above him, as
   if" 1888
"reflected light" 2118
"reflected on the subject of my
   spare-time literary activities"
   5424
"reflected on the unusual events"
   3443
"reflecting I remember on a line of
   Goethe" 9987
"reflecting the pale light of dawn"
   5142
"reflection, break the" 1751
"reflection, his" 4263
"reflection, periods of" 4233
"reflection, physical" 8568
"reflection, poetic" 9515
"reflection, smiling at her own"
   7485
"reflection in the mirror" 7487
Reflections 450, 855, 2399, 3790,
   4263, 5325, 6304, 9325, 10219
"reflections, shadowed oyster and
   violet" 5146
"reflex, obeying a kind of" 2982
"reform, her talk of" 8880
"reform, social" 5887
"Reformation, in the" 7500
"reforming" 3376
"refrain, aptness she sees in the"
   5507
"refreshed, felt curiously" 10183
"refreshed a man like a flagon"
   10684
"refreshed by the sight, eyes had
   been" 8173
"refreshing or displaying themselves" 7754
"refrigerator, cleaning out the"
   10942
"refuge, secret" 4684

"refuge, take" 7368
"refuge for survivors" 280
"refuge now against hunger or
   darkness" 4684
"refugee, Chilean" 1139
"refugee, Haitian" 9850
"refugee camp" 10532
"refugee from Germany" 8865
"refugee from time, like a battered"
   2903
"refugee on the plane, the only"
   9570
Refugees 263, 1139, 3416, 4682,
   9570, 9792, 10519
"refugees, scrambled with other"
   3416
"refugees, self-devoted and pious"
   263
"refugees rushing out of the city"
   10519
"refulgence of six, the" 9476
"refulgent, rosy and" 854
"Refurbishment Project" 1453
"refusal, emphasizing her" 4069
Refuse 3849, 5700, 7930, 7946
"refuse to take it tragically" 3380
"refused, I" 705
"refused to go back into the mainstream" 4230
"refusing to end" 1060
"regain little, I can" 1267
"regaling herself" 3821
"regally cloaked in pine and piñon"
   6085
"regarded the opposite wall" 8280
"regardless as a shower of millionaires" 4660
"Regent of France" 4554
"regiment, returned to his" 8666
"regiment will advance in squadron
   column" 8679
"regiments, four" 10535
Regina 9393
"region, sylvan and perilous" 6813
"region beyond dreamland, that
   uncharted" 10131
"region called Kona" 5022
"region called the Canine Estates"
   3088
"region first distinguished" 4030
"regions, mysterious" 6267
"register, deftly twirling the" 10920
"registers, parish" 3551
Regret 1410, 6967, 8091, 8123,
   8674
"regret, air of" 6967
"regret, left it with" 1410
"regret, tone of mild" 866
"regret can just wear you away"
   7499
"regret can wash over you like
   water over stone" 7499
"regret nothing, I" 5579
"regret that we hurt each other"
   1820

"regretted, it is to be" 1833
"regretted everything, Abel" 7496
"regretted it, neither of them" 9928
"regretted it at once" 8674
"regular as railings" 10372
"regulars, the" 2936
"regulations, labor" 1319
"regulus, ruled a" 7796
"rehabilitate Austria, help him to" 10486
"Rehavya" 6279
"rehearsal, dress" 9332, 9387
"rehearse his oration" 8894
Rehoboam 5549
"Reich, Third" 223
"Reichholz Bavaria" 2019
"reign, his long and blood-stained" 3721
"reign, in the seventh year of his" 1525
"reign, Rehoboam's" 5549
"reign, Victoria's" 971
"reign of Charles II" 360, 361
"reign of Julian the Apostate" 1447
"reign of Louis XIV, fifty-first year of the" 3837
"reign of Queen Anne, the glorious" 3376
"reign of the last Stuarts" 6972
"reigned nine years in England" 3571
"reigning King of Crim Tartary" 1902
Reiland, Karl F. 10656
Reilly, Catharine 10454
"reined in" 8671
"reined up" 9767
"reined up his bay" 7636
"reined up in back of the tailor shop" 1704
Reinhart 1865, 7480
Reinhart, Corporal Carlo 8665
"reins hung down to the ground" 440
"reinvented . . . *everything*, helplessly" 4901
"reinvented while the whole shimmering world revolved" 4901
"Reiser, The" 5607
"rejector of fantasy" 6478
"rejoice, you will" 7008
"relate, faithfully to" 6096
"relate only through a rat hole chewed in the baseboard" 7176
"relate with Presision, decided to" 3496
"related, he may even have been distantly" 364
"relation, bears a distant" 354
"relation of two step-sisters is unusual" 3556
"relation to Alec Merritt, any" 6699
"relations, very horsy" 6123
"relationship, human" 5203
"relationship, satisfactory adult" 9928

Relationships 4501, 9105, 9928
"relationships, family" 3575
"relative, elderly" 2464
"relative, the same" 4926
"relatively speaking" 3201
Relatives 590, 3590, 4519, 6123, 6613
"relatives, ambitious and bloody-minded" 7802
"relatives, besieging" 6613
"relatives, his" 8641
"relatives, no living" 162
"relatives, visiting" 4519
"relatives they don't talk about" 3590
"relax!" 6547
Relaxation 573, 4119, 5622, 8815
"relaxed, he was" 2599
"release, freedom and" 1616
"release of violent force" 5118
"released from the congestion of narrow streets" 9130
"relentless" 2199
"relentlessly pervasive" 5778
"reliable, less and less" 3057
"relic, as they would look at a" 110
"relic of rare old feudal days, serene" 4044
Relief 1663, 8332, 9938, 10344, 10374
"Relief" 7620
"relief, breathed a sigh of" 1663
"relief, entered with" 10374
"relief, thrown into" 10776
"relief at the silence, he felt" 8332
"relief from the stewpot of summer" 10745
"relieve himself" 6599
"relieve himself, off in the bushes to" 4261
"relieve the dejection of spirits" 9513
"relieved by the *idea* of parting" 2681
"relieved of my rifle company" 10506
Religion 263, 268, 1210, 1294, 1296, 1303, 1309, 1495, 1496, 1499, 1502, 1513, 1516, 1518, 1527, 1533, 1536, 1541, 1807, 1808, 2003, 2336, 2399, 2619, 2622, 2629, 2642, 3338, 4202, 4501, 5114, 5413, 5677, 5697, 6089, 6229, 6546, 6673, 6705, 6807, 7359, 7785, 7798, 8008, 8220, 8303, 8319, 8643, 8646, 8737, 8758, 8944, 9709, 10840, 10896
"religion" 1342, 4501, 7510
"religion, abandoned" 7508
"religion, anything else but" 7525
"Religion, fled for their" 6089
"religion, invented a new" 5413
"religion, I've never given much attention to" 7520
"religion, renouncing her" 7546
"religion . . . died out at last" 7503

"religion lingered latest in the country, the old" 7503
"religion of the villagers" 7503
"religion still had a great deal of the old starch left in it" 7523
"religion was the overpowering concern of all the world" 7531
"religious experience" 5114
"religious parents" 6673
"religious sort, excitement of a" 268
"religious studies" 10896
"relinquished it" 1493
"reluctance, deepest physical" 10234
"reluctance, feel little" 5388
"reluctance, sour heavy" 10121
"remain, it is better I" 1788
"remained, there he had" 6427
"remains, her" 1190
"remains, his wife's mortal" 3941
"remains, my poor" 121
"remark, the following" 6227
"remark, unusual" 2738
"remarkable, that expedition was the most" 6093
"remarkable Fifth Symphony" 6227
"remarkable for a humorous air about the eyes" 5921
"remarkable for exuberance of design" 3122
"remarkable for his abilities in the law" 5193
"remarkable happened, something" 3440
"remarkable medical discoverers" 2616
"remarkable period" 10768
"remarkable person, the most" 10798
"remarkable young woman" 10794
"remarked nervously" 9788
"remarks on the conduct of the characters" 4453
"remarriage of an old widower" 6545
Rembrandt 509
Remedies 3055, 10555
Remedios 1799
"remedy for a bruised heart" 10555
"remember, almost the first thing he could" 7402
"remember, as far as he himself could" 3272
"remember, as far back as I can" 7432
"remember, as they were always afterwards to" 9068
"remember, ever since I can" 2593
"remember, first thing I" 2116, 7417
"remember, I" 7406, 9733
"remember, I am trying to" 4834
"remember, I am what I" 4836
"remember, I don't" 7207
"remember, I try to" 10065
"remember, I used to" 57
"remember, important thing to" 4622

"remember, Lord I" 5117
"remember, loved to" 7414
"remember, must always" 6741
"remember, one thing I" 7435
"remember, she would always" 7429
"remember, things they could" 7379
"remember, we must" 4455
"remember, what I" 10738
"remember a boy" 7542
"remember a time" 2926
"remember an old man, I" 5888
"remember any longer, few could" 10854
"remember anything at all, since I could" 5797
"remember as well as though it were yesterday" 5795
"remember at all, some I can't" 7403
"remember by bits and pieces" 7607
"remember even parts of it, it takes me days to" 7403
"remember everything, I" 7404, 7455
"remember her" 7420
"remember her all at once" 7458
"remember how green the early oat fields were" 7397
"remember it, a minute later could not" 5187
"remember it, too soon for me really to" 5289
"remember it myself, as I" 9035
"remember Lamprias now, not many people" 1034
"remember Link as a little boy" 9425
"remember me?" 3545, 7452, 9957
"remember my dreams" 2816
"remember myself skipping rope" 8747
"remember polio" 173
"remember so much, I can" 7409
"remember that time, we all" 3390
"remember the Alamo" 7447
"remember the day" 8245
"remember the dots of the digital clock" 10290
"remember the Feast of '09" 9051
"remember the first bird" 10290
"remember the island" 5027
"remember the judge leaving" 1705
"remember the night before he died" 7429
"remember the time, I cannot" 10550
"remember the weather" 7422
"remember them, ability to" 7451
"remember them, this was the way to" 2852
"remember to keep on remembering" 7400
"remember to shut the popholes, too drunk to" 2895

"remember very much, could not" 18
"remember when we were seven, do you" 7448
"remember where it began, trying to" 1276
"remember which, no one can" 8934
"remember who they are, no one can" 5434
"remember who they are, we often cannot" 5434
"remembered" 870
"remembered, as he had always" 10002
"remembered, half" 7947
"remembered, he" 3696
"remembered, it will be" 1326
"remembered, she" 8166
"remembered, then she" 5024
"remembered, will be well" 6975
"remembered a swan" 773
"remembered about her, the thing they" 8551
"remembered by all those interested in social reform" 5887
"remembered him, to those who" 6345
"remembered it" 7399
"remembered it as if it still existed" 859
"remembered little" 10285
"remembered my hamster" 859
"remembered my timid confusion" 675
"remembered only three things" 7382
"remembered seeing it later" 5118
"remembered that he had promised" 7389
"remembered the blind man" 7411
"remembered the day after" 9085
"remembered the day I stood at Pleasant Hill" 8512
"remembered this clearly" 4436
"remembered very little of her" 7415
"remembered what she had said" 7412
"remembered with acutest longing" 7392
"remembered with irritation" 1499
"remembering" 5460
"remembering, I started" 1538
"remembering, wake up" 10281
"remembering, would like to forget about" 7444
"remembering how he once lectured" 5971
"remembering they meant, what kind of" 7379
"remembers, before anyone" 9227
"remembers, every one" 8960
"remembers her beginnings, no one" 799

"remembers what he was taught there" 5016
"remembers why, nobody" 3658
"Remembrance, over-busie" 7370
"Remembrance, restlesse" 7370
"remembrance of dear ancestral Britain" 3639
"remembrance of Virginia" 3639
"remind her, nobody would need to" 7412
"reminded, continually" 3356
"reminded himself, he" 3955
"reminded me" 7445
"reminded me of the one" 3430
"reminded me of the one" 3430
"reminder that the great ice-cap was still advancing" 10710
"reminding our Reader" 1408
"reminding us that there are more things to be done" 6088
"reminds me of a finger" 1259
"reminds me of you" 7395
Reminiscence 952, 2303, 2337, 3322, 4277, 5095, 5527, 5552, 5992, 6113, 6787, 7377, 7390, 7398, 7401, 7414, 7425, 7438, 7907, 8551, 8976, 9061, 9394, 11000
"reminiscence, swirling flood of" 2337
"reminiscences of earlier days, moved them to" 7390
"reminiscent of a satisfactory luncheon" 3821
Remmnant 2928
"remnant, decaying" 9662
"remodeled, the terminal was being" 232
Remorse 1802
"remote" 3246
"remote, curiously" 5937
"removal of a stone from his bladder" 1519
"remove from the earthly scene" 2310
"removed the railings" 9243
Rena 6186
"Renaissance surplice" 509
Renault, Jerry 1858
"rendezvous of all travellers, the free" 8951
"renewed, will have to be" 3742
"Renfrew Park" 8934
Rengert, Sarah 5674
Renn 10048
Rennie 1707
Renny 7475
Reno, Jim 8794
"Reno" 2952
"Reno Nevada" 704
Renoir 8027
"renouncing her religion, finally if not formally" 7546
"renovating [homes]" 3241
"renovation, downtown" 1453

"*Renown*, H. M. S." 8098
"renowned, stream which is more"
  7655
"renowned pack, that" 4683
"renowned violinist" 6232
Renshaws, the 3583
Rensselaer, Bret 4993
"rent, could not guarantee his" 2570
"rent, pay the" 7370
"rent the empty upstairs suites"
  3137
"rented for her stay in New York"
  5309
"rented out the little room, I could
  have profitably" 7771
"rent-free, lived" 694
"renting [homes]" 3241
"reorienting himself after a night's
  sleep" 10129
"repair, in bad" 3143
"repair, in the worst possible" 1741
"repartees of jocose ostlers" 9113
"repatriation, his" 4567
"Repeal Association" 5194
"Repeal Movement" 5194
"repeal newspapers" 5194
"repeat after me" 10655
"repeating over and over" 722
"repelled, she was" 1318
"repellent, insect" 8193
"Repetition" 7879
"repetition, made routine by" 1232
"replenishing the earth" 5699
"replied in a faultering tone" 9989
"replied solemnly" 298
"replies, had so many" 4767
"reply, there was no" 8329
"reply, your" 9940
"report" 5544
"report, finished typing his" 2251
"report, I'll make my" 9698
"report, the" 6999
"report cards were handed out"
  3722
"report from patrol car" 6970
"report on the end of one part of
  my life" 5104
"reported that I was in Jerusalem"
  1159
"reporter" 6454
"reporter, I am your" 6338
"reporter, she was a" 6469
Reporters 1107, 6338, 7150
"reporters who questioned him"
  6984
Reports 2251, 5417, 6999, 7355,
  7357, 9698
"reports, a thousand idle exaggerated and mischievous" 3476
"reports read and unread" 9961
"repose, slack" 8386
"repose of manner, her" 10785
"repose upon a manly bosom" 10555
"repossessed" 9793
"representative, customer" 6471

"representative at Lake Success"
  4466
"represented by a star" 3671
"representing the chief branches of
  the law" 5871
"repressively" 676
"reproach, little of" 7092
"reproached him" 7552
"reproduce their kind, do not" 6413
"reproduction, miracle of" 5699
Reproof 5992, 7535, 9003
"republic, trouble with our" 279
"Republic of Aureataland" 6248
"republican government" 6972
"Republican soldier" 8641
"republicanizing" 3376
Reputation 3529, 3544, 5503,
  6034, 6887, 8968
"reputation, evil" 340
"reputation, Nazi by" 4762
"reputation, not of popular" 6213
"reputation, obtained a wide" 6887
"reputation cowered, where that
  thing called his" 5503
"reputation for himself, made a
  great" 3544
"reputation in my hands, I take
  my" 8968
"reputation in society, aimed at a"
  6034
"reputation reached its highest
  point" 3529
"reputations cling closely, three"
  7772
"reputed to be" 9189
"request, complying with your"
  5388
"request, considered the" 7903
"request, I cannot grant your"
  1939
"request, make a most unusual"
  9955
"requested me, you have" 5556
Requests 6074, 7903, 9955
"requite you for my stealing off so
  quietly" 8171
"reread it" 2302
"reread the letter" 1950
"re-restoring" 3376
Rescue 5803, 7934
"rescue the Holy Sepulchre from
  the Infidel" 8646
"rescued from its primordial state"
  5170
"research" 2600
"research, lost in solemn" 794
Resemblance 4292, 5904
"resemblance, bore gayly another"
  9882
"resemblance, close" 4292
"resemblance, disconcerting" 6864
"resemblance, striking physical and
  facial" 5904
"resemblance even more striking"
  9882

"resembles nothing so much as an
  ill-proportioned dumbbell" 8232
"resembles the first in flavour"
  10899
"resentful vehemence" 10927
Resentment 813, 4954
"resentment, anger and" 813
"resentment, watched with" 4954
"reserve all this, you can" 1043
"reserve and despond" 2502
"reserve the three center rows" 1200
"reservoir, searching the" 2564
"resettled himself in his chair" 9405
Residence 337, 500, 694, 775,
  935, 988, 1347, 1348, 1371, 1772,
  1956, 1986, 2061, 2490, 2971,
  3058, 3073, 3081, 3083, 3088,
  3093, 3099, 3101, 3105, 3136,
  3139, 3142, 3153, 3157, 3166,
  3167, 3171, 3172, 3174, 3183,
  3198, 3200, 3204, 3206, 3213,
  3214, 3223, 3228, 3231, 3233,
  3239, 3240, 3247, 3250, 3251,
  3254, 3258, 3262, 3369, 3548,
  3549, 3554, 3637, 3910, 3923,
  4234, 4317, 4461, 4477, 4536,
  4544, 4545, 4551, 4597, 4653,
  4905, 4947, 5049, 5079, 5119,
  5122, 5233, 5279, 5343, 5352,
  6034, 6081, 6108, 6111, 6117,
  6123, 6125, 6128, 6147, 6149,
  6154, 6156, 6163, 6164, 6171,
  6206, 6266, 6275, 6279, 6288,
  6289, 6327, 6416, 6419, 6456,
  6687, 6700, 7793, 7900, 7938,
  8232, 9189, 9711, 10787, 10862
"residence, constant" 6266
"residence, his country" 4555
"residence, nice six-roomed" 3073
"residence, private" 949
"residence, surveyed his new" 6145
"residence, their spacious" 5279
"residence in New Wye" 5452
"residence stood majestic" 3210
"resident in France since 1900" 4567
"resident in this city, I was a" 3910
"resident of Millsburgh, well informed" 1014
"residential, quietly" 9203
"residents, summer" 1375
"residents in Radnage Square" 4166
"residents of Wincaster Row come
  calling on me" 9951
"resignation, sigh of" 10294
"resignation is gazetted, my" 1646
"resigned, then at least" 2429
"resigned, when Nixon" 9375
"resigned from my job" 6447
"resistance to the mother-country"
  10470
"resisted it, he" 10251
"resisting his birth, the foal was" 471
"resolution, your" 9509
"resolution can achieve, a Man's"
  8954

"resolve, inward assertion of unflinching" 2015

"resolved to have things out with her father" 6620

"resort after resort, past" 7264

"resort towns" 9203

"resourceful and patient" 4463

"resources of the known world have been exhausted" 2600

Respect 3329, 3587, 5705, 5998, 6517, 9713

"respect" 6629

"respect, sign of" 4880

"respect and gratitude, earned the" 5998

"respect and love, his unmerited" 6517

"respect for the prophecies" 7505

"respect truth" 9713

"respectability, the" 3589

"respectable" 7714

"respirator unplugged, Mother's" 3623

Respite 9737

"respite, forbidding any" 3690

"responding to the article, I am" 6358

"response, appropriate" 4256

"responsibilities, take over a few of the" 5947

"responsibilities of future office" 6432

Responsibility 242, 2738, 4233, 5474, 5947, 6346, 7562

"responsibility, dignified" 2865

"responsibility, five women attempting to take equal" 6346

"responsibility, share the" 2738

"responsibility, weighted with" 4233

"responsibility, whose was the" 7562

"responsibility was, what the" 7562

"responsible, I am in more than one way" 5474

"responsible party, the really" 5394

"rest, completely at" 10883

"rest, day of" 4333

"rest, no hope of" 8488

"rest, she would never" 7652

"rest awhile in the cool of the evening" 5615

"Rest Home, Pleasant Acres" 3208

"rest of the bleeding bleeders, just like the bleeding" 8661

"rest will do, the" 8751

"restaurant, at the" 3344

"restaurant, expensive" 503

"restaurant, expensive London" 5419

"restaurant, German" 7570

"restaurant, lunched at a" 10334

"restaurant, never takes notes in a" 7583

"restaurant, see everyone who enters and leaves the" 7229

"restaurant below street level" 10392

"Restaurant Chez Pavan" 6433

"restaurant in France" 508

"restaurant slated to open in October" 7579

"restaurant workers, organized" 6477

Restaurants 508, 1474, 2062, 2724, 2992, 3816, 3831, 3858, 3871, 3873, 3876, 3889, 4334, 4511, 5419, 6433, 7754, 8368, 8634, 8640, 8846

"restaurants, a few late" 9828

"rested and ready to roll" 5982

"rested his horse" 9561

"rested in humiliation" 2973

"restful, it's so" 9737

"Restharrow, village of" 1395

Resting 3692, 5615, 9561, 9763, 10458

"resting in the heat of the day" 985

"resting in Z shapes" 9842

"resting on his bed" 6960

"resting place, last" 1190

"resting place in the broom closet, from her" 1828

"restive, grow" 4916

"restive to reach the waiting trains" 4910

"restless, he was" 5937

"restless, White Man's Dog was" 8442

"restless and tense, people are" 9336

"restless and uneasy" 743

"restless in your mind" 743

Restlessness 599, 743, 5937, 8442

"restlessness, ill-subdued" 3863

"restlessness began" 599

"restorative ardor" 7532

"restored a second time to the throne" 10768

"restored with expert care" 496

"restorer, come a" 9103

"restoring" 3376

"restraint is the keynote" 1204

"restricting, it's too" 6816

"restrictions, impolitic" 7814

"restroom, men's" 9583

"Restwell" 786

"result of pressure within" 5118

"results, election" 6991

"results of my investigation" 7548

"resurgence of pain" 7599

"resurrected grass of Memorial Park" 7723

"resurrection and the life, I am the" 3941

"retched, had only" 142

"retched, when he" 3699

Reticence 1167, 1845, 2990, 3727, 4892, 5222, 5746, 6627, 7206, 10334, 10440

"Reticences of Thersites" 5507

"retire mentally to a pleasant place" 4661

"retired, having been" 3511

"retired citizen" 9738

"retired from her post" 6446

"retired into the privacy of my mind" 5424

"retired laundryman and widower" 3498

"retired school teacher" 10809

"retired to bed at one o'clock" 8854

"retired to the forest to reflect" 6494

"retired to the sitting-room" 8214

"retired without heartbreak" 6436

Retirement 309, 3444, 3511, 4134, 6436, 6446, 6494, 6558, 7576, 10809

"retirement, dubious" 3444

"retirement from active service" 6558

"retrace the street, I try again to" 8488

"retreat, during the last" 3416

"retreat, for the last time in" 6109

"retreat, my peaceful" 6510

"retreated to her bedroom" 3629

"retreating" 260

"retreating all day" 5824

"retreating to come again and invade" 980

"retrospect, in" 4711

"return, announce his" 1761

"return, her somewhat inglorious" 6750

"return, secret" 2906

"return any documents, he will promptly" 696

"return from High Mass" 1643

"return from my lunch-hour walk" 1122

"return home" 4559

"return in due season" 2088

"return now, if she should" 2680

"Return of the Bourbons" 9119

"return to Chicago, I must" 1587

"return to Derry and Toms, would always" 2740

"return to Primevera" 4542

"return to the apartment, son did not" 10971

"return to the ocean, trying desperately to" 4652

"return to the place" 9277

"return to the Republic of Venice" 2072

"return to the scene" 2597

"return to your native land" 4591

"return tooth for tooth" 6075

"returned, I have" 1709, 6799

"returned, the day Jerry Renault" 1858

"returned, when she" 1911

"returned from his travels to England" 4554

"returned from Italy, just" 6250

"returned from Rome now" 5670

"returned from Sardinia" 5053

"returned from school" 4179

"returned from school at noon promptly" 4670
"returned from Simla" 1689
"returned from the city" 5249
"returned from the dead" 5027
"returned here several weeks ago" 4598
"returned slowly laboriously and painfully from oblivion" 10156
"returned straight from the University" 6427
"returned to England in 1946" 4567
"returned to his lodgings" 1600
"returned to his regiment" 8666
"returned to New York without a Ph.D." 5546
Returning 1307, 1571, 1590, 1592, 1600, 1633, 1640, 1643, 1644, 1654, 1665, 1666, 1689, 1690, 1709, 1718, 1740, 1755, 1761, 1763, 1768, 1780, 1781, 1858, 2072, 2597, 2680, 2740, 3341, 4179, 4540, 4554, 4559, 4567, 4572, 4595, 4598, 5027, 5037, 5053, 5546, 5784, 6029, 6299, 6670, 6799, 7883, 8201, 8666, 9277, 9820
"returning, time of" 1780
"returning from a show or party or hockey game" 7204
"returning home to lunch" 1654
"returning to the Fitzjohn's Avenue flat" 1665
"returning unexpectedly the day after Christmas" 3496
"returns, each thing" 1666
"returns to the Big House" 4584
"retyped the first three pages, wearily" 8528
Reuben 5978
"Reuters" 4008
"reveal as much as possible" 711
"revealed, his soul he" 7956
"revealed her breasts" 6392
"revealed nowhere and everywhere" 9053
"revealing, whose past she was" 1967
"Revelation, Book of" 6960
"revelation occurred to me" 4708
Revelations 2336, 4708, 5432
"revelations, astonishing" 2336
"revelations, sudden" 4319
"revelations of heaven delivered in catechism class" 2336
Revenge 2393, 4169, 4989, 5397, 6478
"revenge, her" 5397
"revenge, I vowed" 4989
"revenge for your past friendship" 8171
"revenge of my friends" 6478
"revenge that death" 2393
"reverberations of magnitude, sending" 3449

"reverence, deep" 2101
"reverence, treat me with some little" 4458
"reverenced" 358
"reveres me, a son who" 6517
"reverie, Josef Breuer's" 674
"reverie, roused Rogier from his" 5620
"reverie, sitting in an exhausted" 9938
"reversed, things were always" 4436
"reverting to the university at forty" 3276
"review, lively" 5732
"reviewer, book" 6419
"reviewers of books of imaginative matter" 10900
"reviewing the event in slow motion" 5118
"revised and updated Descartes" 6845
"revisit England" 9538
"revive those feudal institutions" 6972
Revolution 2902, 3508, 4457, 6344, 8947, 10516
"Revolution" 3064
"revolution, devoted their lives to the" 10837
"revolution, eternal flame of" 8947
"revolution, student" 5673
"Revolution from coming unglued, my last chance to stop the" 6344
"Revolution has started" 10516
"revolution in the history of the world, greatest" 4457
"revolution started" 2902
"revolutionary women, those great" 10837
"revolutions" 1288
"revolutions, wars or" 3508
"revolver, pointed the" 4263
"revolver shot" 8801
"revulsion" 4256
"revving" 7628
"reward of a penny a page" 7348
"rewarded myself" 5487
"rewarding but still prickly" 1986
Rewards 5487, 7348
Reyes, Narita 714
"Reykjavík Airport" 9653
Reynolds, Mrs. 53
Rezánov 3514
"Rheingold drinking tavern" 3994
Rheinhardt 2911
"Rhenish Prussia" 9610
"Rhine, bank of" 4760
"Rhine, the" 4085, 8705
"Rhine looked narrow sluggish and unimportant" 7660
"Rhine water" 1352
"Rhine-born wife" 3202
"rhinestone tiara" 9729
"rhinestones, encrusted with" 4277
"rhinos, the" 472

Rhoda 1323
Rhode, Anne 7980
"Rhode Island" 6685
"Rhode Island, ancient mart of" 4029
"Rhode Island, Battle of" 713
"Rhode Island Regiment, First" 713
Rhodes, Misty 6305
"Rhodes" 4618
"Rhodesian medical texts" 5607
"rhododendron" 6813
"rhododendron, clumps of" 8788
"rhododendrons, between the" 2984
"Rhondda" 5151
"Rhône, exuberance of the" 9627
Rhubarb Twins 9599
Rhyce, Jack 8177
"rhyme, crazy" 5464
"rhymes, aclang with jarring" 5448
"rhythm, deep unhurried" 7939
"rhythm, the morning's" 7859
"rhythm, the same" 4802
"rhythm ceased, its soft" 2335
"rhythm of a Roman water-clock" 1109
"rhythm that held you to a steady thirty miles an hour" 6030
"rhythmic cadence" 10401
"rhythmic hum of the city" 7569
"rhythmically beating pistons" 7260
Riada 10266
"Rialto, the" 6345
"rib, interment of his" 4683
"rib each other" 4984
"ribbon, plastic" 8892
"ribbon, thin white" 9141
"ribbon, wore a little" 416
"ribbon of dry sand, downward glide of a" 410
"ribbon was cut, when the" 1208
"ribbons of tern and gull, endless" 4587
Ricardo, Mr. 4269
Ricci 10214
"rice paddies" 3664
"rice with milk and brown sugar" 3854
"rice-fields, deserted" 7126
"ricefields, misty sheen hung over the" 7308
"rice-pudding with a blob of jam" 9915
"Riceyman Square" 10338
"Riceyman Steps" 10338
Rich 1527, 9721
Rich, Narciso 10922
"rich" 5555
"rich, as well as very" 10556
"rich, becoming very" 4346
"rich, he was" 7714
"rich, I'm" 10564
"rich, Henry Bech ... is" 5468
"rich, not to be" 250
"rich, she was" 10794
"Rich, The Little Sons of the" 10554

"rich, were not" 1965
"rich America, born poor in" 7043
"rich and pungent" 1194
"rich enough" 5728
"rich home, mother came from a" 6631
"rich lady" 10812
"rich or poor" 5699
"rich women, three" 9420
Richard 3040, 3516, 3720, 5580, 7870, 10761
Richard, Sir 3998
Richards, Joan 10193
Richardson, Commander "Rich" 570
Richardson, Edward G. 4745
"Richelieu, the" 10343
"richer and more distinguished" 4444
"richer friends of their own" 10560
"richer than ourselves" 10560
"richer than the average" 1965
"richer the host, the" 10565
"riches" 1288
"riches, its" 4502
"riches he had obtained in the Californian gold rush" 6104
"richest man in Antioch" 10557
"Richmond" 5142, 9258
"Richmond station" 9187
Richters, Dr. Hendrik 6898
Rick 1794
Ricklehouse 10564
Ricks, Miss Lena 10970
"Ricksey Ball" 9081
"rick-thatcher" 9113
"Ricordanza" 3230
"rid himself of the world, the better to" 1496
"rid myself of a crummy son-of-a-bitch, so I can legally" 2656
"rid of her, get" 6201
"rid of him, get" 9956
"rid of Janice, when I got" 63
Ridd, John 8957
"ride, desperate" 7607
"ride, I cannot" 7641
"ride, thirty-five cent" 6652
"ride, within a day's" 3644
"ride home, offered her a" 6208
"ride like this, a" 7635
"ride on the streetcar" 6583
"ride with her a-maying into the woods and fields" 6561
Rider, Dr. 6034
"Rider, Masked" 1704
"rider came to his senses with a jerk" 9311
"rider slowed and stopped" 9127
"riders, approaching" 8786
"ridge, barren" 6059
"Ridge, Cade's" 664
"Ridge, Cascade" 6075
"ridge, fifteen-acre finger-shaped 750-foot-high limestone" 4080

"ridge, green pointy-fir snake of my own (Starvation)" 6075
"Ridge, Nodd's" 4548
"Ridge, Rosy" 9098
"ridge, steep" 9132
"ridge, tall" 7775
"ridge pointing due south" 4080
"Ridgedale College for Women" 1214
Ridgeley, C. Thomas 7903
"ridges, crest of the" 7221
"ridicule, not from fear of" 2734
"ridiculous, don't be" 7083
"ridiculous, helpless and" 9790
"ridiculous, it is so" 8261
"ridiculous name" 7851
Riding 979, 1582, 1704, 2820, 3307, 4254, 4486, 5190, 5215, 6009, 6561, 7809, 8620, 8671, 8696, 8701, 8794, 9093, 9127, 9304, 9311, 9563, 9648, 9750, 9975, 10405, 10692
"riding, forty hours of steady" 7615
"riding a paint horse" 7625
"riding across the undulating prairie" 9563
"riding along the bottom" 8794
"riding at breakneck speed" 7613
"riding back into the courtyard, he came" 7644
"riding down through a cloud" 7622
"riding high and comfortably" 499
"riding in low" 9436
"riding on to Relief's main four corners" 7620
"riding out of Texas" 5215
"riding the air like an eagle aboard a thermal" 5688
"riding the hundred miles from T'o Tlakai to Tsé Lani" 7612
"riding the sea like an overturned fishing boat" 5039
"riding up the winding road" 1191
"riding with his arms high and wide" 7629
"Ridolfi villa" 3230
"Rien à Declarer" 8312
"rifle, hunts with a" 4347
"rifle, small caliber" 4250
"rifle, thinning flatness made only by a" 8794
"rifle across his forearm" 10098
"rifle [needed] for the Indian" 6100
"rifle reports caught Aaron off guard" 3954
"rifle was real" 4260
"rifles, men carried deer" 4253
"rifles, they crouched with their" 4254
"rifles held up awkwardly high" 8659
Rigden 2965
"rigging, the running" 8086
"rigging giving out musical tones" 8086

"riggings, petrels swarmed their" 8169
"right, as it turned out her Mam was" 10831
"right, do it" 6656
"right, I have to get this" 613
"right, I hope we've done" 2738
"right, nothing ever goes" 60
"right, perhaps it was" 2856
"right, that's about" 10625
"right, wanting her to have what was" 2349
"right about one thing" 8901
"right for Danny, I think she'll be absolutely" 1981
"right from wrong, certain that I knew" 5816
"right now" 3222
"right of birth" 361
"right of law and custom" 4991
"right of seeing people on other days as well" 9859
"right way, the one precisely" 5408
"right way, the only" 5408
"right-minded, who was so" 6104
"rigmarole, it was the same old" 4271
"rigmarole of childhood, the old" 1266
"rigodón de honor" 2118
Rilas, Uncle 4975
Riley, Bubble 2933
Riley, Eden Swift 4902
Riley, Emma Rowena 10436
Riley, Morgan 5782
"Rim, Rainbow" 6564
"rim of earth was tinted rose, flat eastern" 2226
"rim of mud and grass, quaking" 7682
"rime of frost lay thick on the puddles" 10630
"Rimi races" 3438
"rimmed around three sides by blue mountains" 1398
"rims, iron" 9830
"ring, at the end of its first" 1131
"ring, Fisherman's" 1525
"ring, I let it" 1120
"ring, I simply *had* to" 1105
"ring, I wear the" 2858
"ring, let it" 10165
"ring, my emerald-and-diamond" 2861
"ring pierced his study door" 1119
"ring the bell of a tradesman" 9955
"ring you if he shows up" 10059
"ringed about for ever with sea" 5020
Ringelman 6652
"ringing" 655
"ringing, had just ceased" 646
"ringing, kept on" 667
"ringing, wished the phone would stop" 1097

"ringing at an unaccustomed hour" 647
"ringing cut into his dream" 2811
"ringing of the outer bell" 10113
"ringing out in the summer's afternoon" 645
Ringkoping, Peter 1207
Ringo 5710
"rings, hand heavy with" 7555
"rings, jingle of brass" 1807
"rings, jingling their brass" 7707
"rings of previous risings" 10299
Rings'n'Things 8024
"Rio" 3012, 9725
"Rio de Janeiro" 7940
"Rio del Norte" 4673
"Rio Grande do Sul" 800
Rion 3647
Riose, Bel 9557
"riot, a spell of" 901
"riot, decided tendency to run" 266
"Riot of '43, Detroit" 3777
"rioting, noise of the" 8777
"rioting in city after city" 1424
Riots 1424, 3766, 3777, 8777, 10534
"R.I.P." 6472
"ripe" 10808
Ripley, Snake 8452
"ripped off, leather jacket" 2062
"ripple, treacly" 5325
"ripple under the bridge" 8076
"ripples, very little" 5132
"ripples, white crests of" 7930
"ripples cresting away endlessly" 633
"ripples in the creative silence of the First Cause, one of those infinitesimal" 6001
"rippling ran through the leaves" 176
"rippling the bronze-green water" 7684
"rise, all" 5210
"rise, gentle" 1383
"rise, little" 9127
"rise, over the" 7694
"Rise, Upshot" 9164
"rise between the bombed streets" 9175
"rise early" 8479
"rise early, did not always" 2249
"rise from the dark" 8488
"rise it would get, to see what kind of" 10835
"rise like an Arabic exhalation" 9181
"rise of a brilliant young newspaper columnist" 5485
"rise up as if from a swamp" 2796
"risen from the land" 1558
"rises celestially, she" 10316
Rising 1752, 1785, 2188, 2249, 4276, 4285, 6526, 6565, 8479, 8486, 9885, 10128, 10132, 10150,

10168, 10212, 10256, 10268, 10275, 10303, 10308, 10316
"Rising, Easter" 2024
"rising, late in" 8418
"rising, usually associated with" 10183
"Rising, valley of the" 1408
"rising again like herring gulls" 2623
"rising and falling with the peaks and valleys" 9194
"rising bleak and barren out of a sea" 5015
"rising effortlessly to your natural level" 3296
"rising from her desk" 9884
"rising in a lake" 9747
"rising in the world, art of" 238
"rising into one hysterical disembodied note" 5260
"rising to the mellowest highest note" 8748
"risings, rings of previous" 10299
"risk, consideration of the" 10642
"risk, full of" 3405
"risk, looked like a high" 5960
"risks his all including life" 1220
Rites 1206, 1209, 1210, 1212, 1215, 1218, 1506, 1513, 3941, 3954, 10963
"rites" 4502
"ritual, arcane" 1214
"ritual, yearly" 8246
"ritual game of tennis" 10411
Rituals 1214, 8246
"rituals and totems of primitive people" 1209
"Ritz, the" 5840, 8635
"Riva, the" 3709
"rivall, his friendly" 7370
"rivalries, ecclesiastical" 3677
"rivalry, curious spirit of" 125
"*rive gauche*" 1371
"riven stone" 1217
"river, a" 4062
"river, across the" 1194, 4149
"river, along the banks of the" 1478
"River, Arkansas" 9635
"River, Arundel" 1374
"river, at the" 6969
"river, bank of the big" 7189
"river, banks of some" 1443
"river, bed of a great" 9743
"river, bend in the" 7653
"River, Big Blue" 3074
"River, Big Dead" 3129
"River, Big Horn" 7693
"river, boy in the" 998
"River, Bright" 7694
"river, broad" 7657, 8254
"river, broad elbow of the" 976
"river, broad empty" 7658
"river, broad levels of the" 8031
"river, broad tide-" 1336
"River, Bronx" 7688

"River, Calumet" 5139
"river, came back to the" 1640
"River, Cassadaga" 1896
"river, consider a long and famous" 7703
"river, cool depths of the" 9317
"river, cross the" 3687
"river, crossed the" 7662
"River, Cumberland" 436
"river, darkness of the" 7679
"river, door opened . . . to the" 3195
"River, East" 7019, 7672, 7683, 8124, 8516
"River, Eldon" 5088
"river, gurgling waters of the" 5156
"river, Helford" 7661
"River, Hudson" 1012, 1407
"river, in the" 7676
"river, Indian of a" 7670
"River, James" 1465, 5142
"River, Jordan" 831
"river, landscapes . . . stretching along the" 5125
"river, look at us by the" 7705
"river, name of the" 4760
"river, Niagara" 4043
"river, north side of the" 1579
"river, one final glance at the" 10394
"river, pushed off into the" 6576
"river, quick nervous" 7701
"river, road was once a" 9200
"river, sands of the" 9132
"river, silent current of the red" 7654
"river, swirled the shining" 3899
"river, the" 5143, 8512, 9077, 10444
"river, black" 7685
"river, great" 5025
"River, Lachlan" 1466
"River, Little Bird" 7669
"River, Little Grand" 1382
"River, Little Miami" 533
"River, Mattagash" 6155
"River, Mekong" 4094
"River, Merrimac" 7668
"River, Mississippi" 4560, 9635
"River, Mobile" 7907
"River, Mohawk" 4771
"River, North" 1619
"River, Ohio" 1029, 5133, 7232, 9072
"River, Pamunkey" 10451
"River, Patuxent" 5048
"River, Potomac" 9245
"River, Rat" 3104
"River, Red" 1269
"River, Sacramento" 5803
"River, St. Lawrence" 8082
"River, Salinas" 7659, 9751
"River, Scotch" 7651
"River, Sioux" 9140
"River, Still" 2950
"River, Suwanee" 1394
"[River], Tennessee" 7670

"river, there on the" 8164
"river, there was a" 9200
"river, this is the" 7670
"river, throwing myself into the" 2529
"river, trying not to look at the" 9425
"river, two cities divided by a" 1476
"River, Wakonda Auga" 7674
"River, Waso Larok" 7673
"River, Wawanash" 4687
"river, we were approaching the" 7675
"River, Whatsit" 370
"River, wide muddy Ohio" 1029
"river, wide still" 8350
"River, Yarmuk" 5716
"River, Yocona" 7301
"river at their side" 7390
"river bank" 4962
"river became a road" 9200
"river bed, dried" 9546
"River Bend" 3220
"River broad and placid" 7668
"river called Father of Waters" 9198
"river creates a natural boundary between the United States and Canada" 6155
"river Don" 3893
"River drops in close to the hillside bank" 7659
"river enters an infinity of waters and is gone" 7668
"river flowed both ways" 7684
"river flowed quietly through shadow" 7687
"river flowing, slow yellow" 299
"river goes very slowly" 7664
"river had been trapped in the trees and turned to silver" 7696
"river in spring: gentle invisible constant activity" 7697
"river Indus, banks of the" 7808
"river is to be tamed and civilized" 7670
"river . . . isolates and it joins" 7698
"river lapping softly" 8327
"river . . . lies flat as a mirror" 3032
"river Niger" 1429
"River Niyt, slow marshy mosquito-breeding waters of the great" 1308
"river of the aristocrats and paupers" 10871
"River of Time" 2638
"river people" 7748
"River . . . runs deep and green" 7659
"river smelled like hair" 8522
"river succours and impedes native and foreigner alike" 7698
"river suddenly swings about in a wide and peaceful basin" 7668
"river surface, silky" 6401
"river . . . teems with salmon and story" 7703

"river that flowed in a dark narrow channel" 7692
"river that runs through Lethem" 3032
"river that runs widening to the sea" 7657
"River Tillingham" 9134
"river too high and wild" 4690
"river towns" 7323
"river valley" 7242
"river was crowded" 330
"river was in Bengal" 7663
"River was running ice-free and full from bank to bank" 7651
"river which cut so conveniently" 7702
"river which was deep brown after days of rain" 7706
"River winds and twists up the center" 9751
"river with its swamps and deserted rice-fields" 7126
"River Wye, long silver serpent of the" 3155
Rivera, Jésus 4813
"river-boat gambler" 301
"Rivermouth" 6928
"riverrun" 1175
Rivers, Dean 5476
Rivers, John 5436
Rivers, Judson 7523
Rivers 299, 370, 436, 455, 473, 998, 1336, 1382, 1394, 1407, 1479, 1640, 1896, 2529, 3032, 3074, 3082, 3155, 3195, 3687, 3893, 3896, 3899, 4085, 4427, 4673, 4690, 4691, 5048, 5067, 5133, 5139, 5143, 5156, 5169, 5614, 5716, 6155, 6576, 6969, 7301, 8050, 8076, 8082, 8096, 8164, 8254, 8512, 8516, 8522, 8611, 8820, 9076, 9077, 9175, 9200, 9202, 9217, 9317, 9425, 9635, 9738, 9740, 9743, 9746, 9747, 9751, 10356, 10394, 10526, 10683
"rivers, boats and" 4190
"rivers, like" 4825
"rivers, overflowing" 6249
"rivers, seven" 7704
"rivers, two" 1393
"river's bed" 7650
"river's edge, close to the" 3090
"river's icy water" 10871
"rivers of Europe" 10526
"river's passage, only the" 455
"rivers run deep" 5045
"riverward there was the faint moaning of new ice" 10574
"river-watching, years of" 7684
"Riviera, French" 4631
"Riviera coastline was cleaner" 4083
"Riviera morning" 10399
"Riviera sun" 10118
Rivke 2060

"rivulets, tributary" 9738
Ro 9514
"road, across the" 4070
"Road, Alcock" 5145
"road, all along the" 10575
"road, almost perpendicular 'corduroy'" 6057
"road, as if he owned the" 9939
"road, Avonlea main" 7652
"road, bad" 1465
"Road, Bayswater" 8815
"Road, Between Towns" 9160
"Road, Cabot Street" 3666
"road, came down the" 10435
"road, caravan" 9546
"Road, Chepstow" 3213
"Road, Clayborne" 1462
"road, corduroy" 9093
"road, country" 2955
"Road, Crest Ridge" 2971
"road, deserted" 4143
"road, dirt" 2095, 9835
"road, down a long" 9184
"road, down the sliding" 1438
"road, dusty" 1639
"Road, Euston" 494
"Road, Fieldstone" 6774
"Road, Finchley" 3216
"Road, First Lake" 995
"road, first seventy miles of the" 10108
"road, foresaken coach-" 9519
"road, get out o' Mr. Fletcher's" 4970
"road, gravel" 7848
"road, gravelly mountain" 4204
"road, gray wagon" 2949
"Road, Great" 3178
"road, great northern" 7284
"road, gully-washed tobacco" 10347
"Road, Harvard" 3156
"road, her" 9939
"Road, Hertfordshire" 414
"road, high" 2943
"road, high-fell" 3483
"Road, Hillton" 2970
"road, hoof-scarred" 5318
"Road, Hove" 7049
"road, hurried along the" 954
"road, icy slush of the" 10579
"Road, King's Cross" 10338
"Road, Landsdowne" 10189
"road, long straight" 3044
"road, M. 1 slip" 9173
"road, main" 286, 412, 3042, 9115, 9177, 10402
"road, main arterial" 8798
"road, main gravel" 3207
"Road, Market" 7771
"Road, Mornington" 6102
"road, mountain" 3484
"road, narrow" 2969
"road, narrow asphalt" 9174
"road, narrow clay" 2989
"road, new" 2995

"Road, No Bridge" 6297
"road, noisy main" 3227
"Road, Oakmoor" 10862
"Road, Oglethorpe" 6964
"road, old" 3026, 9133
"road, old lumber" 7844
"road, old timber" 5724
"road, on a country" 3119
"Road, on the County" 8765
"road, on the long" 10591
"road, on the narrow" 9767
"road, on the paved" 3225
"road, paved" 3646
"road, pink dirt" 2978
"road, placid country" 10397
"road, point out the" 9647
"road, potholed" 6574
"road, public" 2947, 3036
"road, red ribbons of dirt" 1413
"Road, Reservoir" 7220
"[road], rippling black river" 3011
"road, rising" 9304
"road, river became a" 9200
"Road, Roamin'" 10450
"road, robber-haunted" 4042
"road, rutted" 9813
"road, rutted Vermont dirt" 3036
"Road, San Pedro" 2061
"road, shale" 9782
"Road, Shiraz" 3980
"Road, Shore" 1031
"road, side of the" 9781
"Road, Snake River" 7625
"Road, Somerset" 3153
"Road, Stony" 4150
"road, stretch of muddy" 4145
"road, sunny Virginia" 7131
"Road, Temperance Vale" 9955
"road, the" 7316, 9112, 9148, 9167
"road, there is a lovely" 9146
"road, two-lane" 9194
"road, unevenness of the" 9796
"road, unpaved unnamed" 40
"Road, Warrior" 9202
"road, watched the" 10070
"road, wet black" 3011
"Road, Whitechapel" 9175
"road, winding" 1191
"Road, Wire" 7638
"road, yellow" 10705
"Road, York" 9136
"road again, on this" 9171
"road ahead, view of the" 9194
"road all sun and shadowy with
  trees overhead" 9184
"road and river, moving life by"
  8345
"road branched out to the whole
  world" 9200
"road dipped down into a little
  hollow" 7652
"road down the mountain, followed
  the" 9201
"road drops from the High Moor"
  1361

"road from Boston to Cape Cod"
  9165
"road from the village" 9132
"road from Vinehall meets the road
  from Leasan" 9134
"road from York to London" 7284
"road . . . full of unexplained forks
  and windings and turnings-off"
  9174
"road gets bumpy and narrow" 9176
"road grown dustier and more uneven" 10732
"road had been deserted" 9163
"road in France" 3024
"road is hewn . . . in the cliffs of
  the coast" 9155
"[road] is long and straight and
  ruthless" 9165
"road kept in only fair repair" 9174
"road lay long and black" 10457
"road leading out of the heart of
  the Five Towns" 9118
"road led to the river or to town"
  9202
"road lined with dark telephone
  poles" 3044
"road mounted straight ahead of
  him" 9154
"road of hunger" 4682
"road on a rise that overlooked the
  town" 9717
"road outside his office" 8776
"road ran out toward Chickasaw
  Ridge" 10415
"road ran rich with life" 9136
"road runner flew onto the blacktop" 755
"road runs off westward through
  Harlot's Wood" 9134
"road she loved so much" 4557
"road slippery in places, night frost
  made the" 2990
"road snakes uphill" 3016
"road that appeared to be deserted"
  9187
"road that clung to the contours of
  the land" 9194
"road that led from Kashgar eastward toward Aqsu" 9546
"road that lined the port of Dar es
  Salaam" 10442
"Road that ran south from Bonneville" 8765
"road that runs from Ixopo into
  the hills" 9146
"road that was not the one she inhabited but that led there" 10390
"road that widened at the summit
  into a parking apron" 3005
"road that wound dangerously
  round the high flank of the
  mountain" 2969
"road the woman was traveling"
  9168
"road there is none" 455

"road this afternoon, which" 9182
"road to Boonville" 9128
"road to happiness" 4346
"road to Hastings winds southward
  down the hill" 9134
"road to Paris, hot straight" 9632
"road to the Kennebec" 9758
"road to the municipal airport"
  2337
"road twisted and flowed before
  him" 3011
"road twisted out of the pines, the
  dirt" 1639
"road was a thin streak through the
  rain jungle" 9158
"road was dry [and] dusty" 9193
"road was once a river" 9200
"road went down toward Rome"
  9151
"road which had begun as a rutted
  cart-track" 7609
"road which he failed to cross" 4467
Roads 40, 186, 414, 485, 961,
  1044, 1080, 1191, 1361, 1462,
  2943, 2945, 2947, 2949, 2950,
  2952, 2957, 2959, 2966, 2969,
  2970, 2977, 2978, 2979, 2989,
  2990, 2991, 2994, 2995, 3001,
  3005, 3011, 3016, 3023, 3024,
  3026, 3036, 3041, 3042, 3044,
  3578, 3666, 3723, 3730, 4039,
  4042, 4046, 4073, 4078, 4239,
  4429, 4467, 4548, 4557, 4682,
  4970, 5258, 5318, 5608, 5723,
  5836, 6052, 6057, 6246, 6381,
  7273, 7316, 7327, 7608, 7609,
  7613, 7625, 8303, 8319, 8765,
  9026, 9091, 9112, 9113, 9115, 9116,
  9118, 9121, 9126, 9127, 9128, 9131,
  9132, 9133, 9134, 9136, 9138,
  9140, 9141, 9143, 9145, 9146,
  9148, 9150, 9151, 9154, 9155,
  9158, 9160, 9163, 9165, 9167,
  9168, 9169, 9171, 9173, 9174,
  9175, 9176, 9177, 9180, 9181,
  9182, 9183, 9184, 9185, 9186,
  9187, 9188, 9192, 9193, 9194,
  9198, 9199, 9200, 9201, 9202,
  9204, 9230, 9451, 9546, 9555,
  9577, 9632, 9647, 9758, 9767,
  9781, 9796, 9804, 9812, 9813,
  9817, 9826, 9939, 10093, 10353,
  10377, 10390, 10415, 10425,
  10435, 10442, 10457, 10575,
  10579, 10591, 10732
"roads, all the wild" 4239
"roads, approach-" 883
"roads, back" 4548
"roads, country" 5836, 9774
"roads, dirt" 6137
"roads, iron" 5709
"roads, old coach-" 9113
"roads, river" 9026
"roads, roughest" 9515
"roads, suburban" 5142

"roads, veld" 7036
"roads are busy with cars" 9169
"road's blacktop ahead of me" 2977
"roads cut like slashes through the bush" 7887
"roads dusty" 3396
"roads in Connecticut all look alike" 5608
"roads led to Charley Bland" 4239
"roads meet, two" 4145
"roads of France, the last free" 9792
"roads [of Spain]" 6246
"roads still sluggish and sleepy" 5142
"roadster whose tail light advertised its presence" 9763
"roadway, narrow" 10353
"roaming the flooded fields" 4680
"Roanoke, ten miles out of" 9812
"roar, up the chute with a" 7990
"roar of the laundry vats, sloshy" 1073
"roar of traffic" 8815
"roared" 10025
"roared around" 2997
"roared around the last cloverleaf of new road" 2995
"roared over the loose planks of the swinging bridge" 10203
"roaring, ominous" 10681
"roaring round the bend" 9300
Roark, Howard 6387
Roarty 1863
"roasted, flesh" 4469
"roasted in the flames" 2773
Rob 6, 7110, 9958
Robarts, Mark 6521
"robbed, he was being" 2057
"robbed the hour" 8390
"robbed the world" 10033
"robber-haunted road" 4042
Robbery 2057, 2063, 2869, 9701
Robbins, Sylvan 1073
"robe, folds of his lap" 8461
"robe, hem of his" 7806
"robe, medieval black" 509
"robe, removes her" 8006
"robe, terry-cloth" 7480
"robe, tossed her" 573
"robe, white" 7472
Robert 2532, 2564, 5075, 6008
Robin 837
Robinson 6330
Robinson, Spurgeon 6444
Robinson, Taft 5102
"Robinson's B.E.B., bottle of" 2893
Robison, Anna 7414
"robot, part" 369
Robson, Flora 9391
"robust manner" 10910
"robustness, a return to" 1452
Roche 3000
"Rochester, Bishop of" 1522
Rock, Mr. 10150

"rock, abrupt rise and fall of the promontory" 3205
"rock, awful vaulty blue smoke-body" 6075
"rock, buy a stick of" 10831
"rock, edifice built on the summit of a" 1171
"rock, hundreds of miles of snow-covered" 6075
"rock, made of black" 6075
"rock, overhanging shelf of" 9141
"rock, palm of a" 7680
"rock, shelf of" 4316
"rock, silence and immobility of a great reddish-tinted" 404
"rock, smooth gray" 5154
"rock, stark naked" 6075
"rock, steady as a" 8125
"rock, steps cut in the" 10382
"rock and earth and sweet turf covering it" 5020
"rock and roll songs" 5509
"rock and shell, indentations on" 5044
"rock of sleep" 8467
"Rock River" 1492
"rock star, super" 3545
"rock whose base was in the sea" 1171
"rock-and-roll" 8744
"Rockbottom Pa." 4059
"rocked back on his heels" 1980
"rocked forward and backwards on her sturdily-shod feet" 10859
"rocked on the branches" 723
"Rockefeller Plaza" 1625
"rocker, old rattan" 6859
"rockery, rats in the" 431
Rockets 215, 683, 10519
"rockets, braking" 683
"rockets had fallen on Saigon" 10519
"Rockies, in the shadow of the" 6056
"rocking chair" 6543
"rocking from side to side" 10426
"rocking through wide open country" 1616
"rocks, gray" 1764
"rocks, they were but great" 5015
"rocks of come, big flying" 7990
"rocks planted in green water" 724
"rockslides" 434
"rocky crust" 3903
"rococo manner of speaking" 8640
"rod, glaring-" 7262
"rode a circuit around the herd" 7634
"rode a streetcar" 10367
"rode a taxicab home" 3315
"rode across the hillocks and vales of Missouri" 4486
"rode away beside Lonzo in the ox-cart" 1602
"rode her" 8140

"rode his bicycle with leisurely strokes" 7608
"rode in, three men" 7623
"rode into Dunedin harbour" 8170
"rode into our valley" 9750
"rode into the coast town" 1582
"rode into the dark of the woods" 7633
"rode like fury" 7639
"rode on a mule" 7630
"rode out from Fairoaks" 3307
"rode so far south in Mexico" 9648
"rode through country, cowboy" 7632
"rode up, horsemen" 7606
"rodeo, head like a" 10319
"Rodeo Drive" 7229
Rodney 2967
Rodriguez, Cristo Lorenzo 1612
Rodriguez, Mrs. R. R. 7114
"rods, bare" 5740
Roger 3704, 5634
Rogers, Will 6848
Rogerson 6354
Rogier 5620
"rogue, such a" 4869
"rogues for Ministers" 3376
Rohan 8229
"Rohanda" 5497
"*roka*, the" 2536
Rolandson, Donald 5113
"role they were playing" 4883
"roll, calling the" 7906
"roll around on her tongue like a hard candy" 4419
"roll like a pig" 8118
"roll of the sea, feeling the" 8504
"roll on and on" 3399
"rolled about in the light" 4660
"rolled across the raked pebbles" 2984
"rolled in upon the high-pebbled beach" 7916
"rolled over in her sleep" 8525
"rolled slightly on the water" 8080
"rolled the window down" 2974
"rolling a little" 224
"rolling hills" 1473
"rolling over on top of his mother" 6652
"rolling stock" 9529
Rollow 6958
"rolls, crisp" 3881
"rolls, hard little" 4285
"rolls, steaming-hot" 8530
"Rolls Royce, blue" 9764
"Rolls-Royce, after parking the" 9753
"Rolls-Royce, ancient" 9783
"Rolls-Royce, Company's" 9582
"Rolls-Royce, silver" 9811
"Rolls-Royce, Somerville-bodied" 9822
"Rolls-Royce Silver Wraith" 2899
"roly-poly Kitty, no longer the" 4179

"Romagnat" 9133
"Roman aristocrat" 6551
"Roman Britain" 4056
"Roman Emperor" 4753
"Roman Empire" 5516
"Roman palazzo" 1523
"Roman People, Dictator of the"
    7514
"Roman water-clock" 1109
Romance 322, 704, 1354, 1700,
    1967, 1974, 1981, 1982, 1986,
    1989, 1990, 1997, 2002, 2003,
    2083, 2488, 2502, 2596, 2648,
    3344, 3878, 3965, 4611, 5238,
    5354, 5638, 5652, 5658, 5667,
    5668, 5670, 5674, 5678, 5733,
    5752, 5775, 5852, 5882, 6391,
    6508, 6545, 7461, 7953, 7954,
    7999, 8004, 8011, 8019, 8708,
    9290, 9437, 9509, 10043, 10555,
    10764, 10807
"romance, chivalry and" 3375
"romance, earlier" 7745
"romance (he said) is a word I am
    shy of using" 7711
"romance with one of the river
    people" 7748
"romances, pleasant" 5398
Romanoff, Anastasia 3413
"Romans, by grace of the" 7797
"Romans, one of the modern"
    5345
"Romans were celebrating the end
    of Carnival" 2364
"romantic, excessively" 8799
"romantic, incurably" 6631
"romantic, the young were" 7709
"romantic about love, she was a"
    5678
"romantic adventure, modern" 1354
"romantic enough" 1448
"romantic love, intricacies of" 5238
"romantic myth" 2539
"romantic of cities, the most" 1354
"romantic part of the Highlands, in
    the most" 1171
Rome 1343, 1353, 9593, 9627
"Rome" 1353, 1431, 1494, 2225,
    3406, 4040, 4111, 4499, 4578,
    5670, 5853, 6048, 7067, 7243,
    7754, 8344, 8939, 9151, 9559,
    9720
"Rome, Babylon or" 3275
"Rome, Bishop of" 8848
"Rome, Capitol at" 3986
"Rome, deep in the panting heart
    of" 10486
"Rome, dining in" 5443
"Rome, in the heart of" 9870
"Rome, streets of" 515
"Rome, the Pope at" 7510
"Rome, the younger" 3071
"Rome, uncle from" 10674
"Rome, when in" 1084
"Rome lay asleep" 2280

"Rome of the intelligent foreigner"
    1342
"Rome to call him back again, dar-
    ing" 9593
"Rome was still in a great measure
    its old self" 1343
"Rome welcomed me with lit foun-
    tains" 9582
"Rome within, the" 1342
"Romeo, another and more con-
    spicuous" 7293
"Romes, there are two" 1342
"ROMP, NUDE" 6397
"rondeaux redoubles" 5457
"rondels" 5457
Ronson 2162
Roo, Jenny 9367
"roof, from the" 6140
"roof, gabled" 4328
"roof, green slate" 4698
"roof, holes in the" 3792
"roof, its tin" 7440
"roof, orange" 3001
"roof, red" 3109
"roof, skittery tin" 10740
"roof, slate" 7325
"roof, tarpaper" 6379
"roof, terra-cotta tile" 3113
"roof, under our" 5012
"roof, we need a new" 1239
"roof of a long stone house" 10389
"roof of my mouth" 8216
"roof of the American House" 4632
"roof over it, a" 3149
"roofs, angular" 2225
"roofs, grimy warehouse" 7307
"roofs, slate" 6268, 8448
"roofs, thatched" 4742
"roofs, tin" 1056
"roofs and church spires, jumbled
    dark" 8591
"roofs which radiate out from the
    shipyard" 8448
"rooftop, stood on a" 5964
"rooftops, hundreds of" 5142
Rookwhistle, Adrian 7478
"Room!" 1207
"room, attic" 7782
"room, big" 8857
"room, big dining" 8881
"room, big sitting-" 5959
"room, busy waiting" 7258
"room, cell-shaped" 4635
"room, cold cheerless" 7032
"room, come to see the" 7785
"room, consulting-" 3518
"room, corridor" 5624
"room, cottage sitting" 9943
"room, dark" 5339
"room, dark and silent" 10137
"room, darkened" 6519, 6598
"room, deserted little waiting-" 5617
"room, dim hot airless" 7763
"room, dimly illuminated" 9883
"room, dingy little dining" 3814

"room, dining" 3094, 8265, 8869
"room, dormitory" 8601
"room, downstairs" 7775
"room, drawing-" 3821, 7773
"room, dressing" 7487
"room, emergency" 4623
"room, empty dining-" 9470
"room, familiar" 10753
"room, farthest side of the" 8654
"room, fire-lighted drawing-" 310
"room, flower" 6356
"room, four of us in one" 8706
"room, good" 7784
"room, great empty drawing-" 9873
"room, great pearl-gray slab of a"
    6986
"room, guest" 4921
"room, hadn't been inside the" 7786
"room, handsome dining" 7762
"room, her" 7712, 8353, 9406
"room, her sewing" 8720
"room, her son's" 10949
"room, her superb private draw-
    ing-" 8345
"room, high though very narrow"
    4136
"room, his consulting" 6131
"room, his embalming" 2710
"room, his narrow" 10142
"room, his private" 7752
"room, his private sitting-" 654
"room, his sitting-" 8347
"room, his uncarpeted" 8453
"room, his wife's" 9417
"room, hot little" 7090
"room, hotel" 1116, 4019, 7937
"room, in a handsome" 10782
"room, in a little" 7770
"room, in Fritz's" 668
"room, in her attic" 2776
"room, in her own" 5395
"room, in my" 668, 3787, 9330
"room, in the" 3217
"room, in the next" 7116
"room, in what had been the iron-
    ing" 2419
"room, inner" 5398
"room, instrument-" 8333
"room, Jessie's" 7783
"Room, Jodler" 8553
"room, ladies'" 886, 4480
"room, large" 5429
"room, large reading" 3420
"room, little" 7771
"room, little front" 2915
"room, little three-cornered" 5079
"room, living" 3229, 7040, 7764
"room, lock up the" 10932
"room, lofty dining-" 3084
"room, long empty" 3302
"room, looked round the" 7766
"room, lounging" 4307
"room, Miss Elizabeth's" 1552
"room, morning-" 8839
"room, motel" 4655

"room, music-" 6226
"room, my" 8726
"room, my old" 3701
"room, old Mrs. Maldon's sitting-" 10786
"room, otherwise dingy waiting" 2156
"room, our long work-" 5088
"room, outside her" 161
"room, palm-" 7754
"room, pupils'" 3326
"room, reading" 10951
"Room, Reading" 7772
"room, rear" 3094
"room, reception" 376
"room, rectangle indicating the big" 7760
"room, sat in my" 9404
"Room, Seraglio" 2373
"room, she was actually inside the" 8822
"room, sitting-" 8214
"room, small" 3081
"room, small dark" 1317
"room, small enclosure of her" 9409
"room, small packed" 9336
"room, small-sized reception-" 8719
"room, smoking-" 4305, 8062
"room, sunny dining" 8853
"room, surveyed the" 7125
"room, sombre old" 10670
"room, the" 3796, 3809, 8390
"room, this brown" 8778
"room, Van Gogh's" 7793
"room, vast" 5307
"room, waiting" 6896, 6897, 7781
"room, wasn't really a" 3192
"room, what had once been the Colonel's" 10244
"room, white living" 8724
"room, windowless" 6893
"Room, Zodiac" 7481
"room a chance to work me over gently, gave the" 6503
"room above the stable in the brickyard" 7849
"room after room" 5322
"room at the back of the house" 8248
"room being full of people" 8338
"room could scarcely have been more snug" 3127
"room filled with six beds" 990
"room for another, always seemed" 45
"room for her, what do you mean there's no" 1938
"room full of sunlight" 10225
"room in one of the small dingy houses" 7753
"room in the bachelor officers' quarters" 9920
"room in the Hôtel Milano" 5182
"room made a curious headquarters" 7788

"room of Charlie's and mine" 3192
"room of scarlet hangings and pale brown stone" 7761
"room of the wolfmother wallpaper" 7790
"room of wavering shadows" 5326
"room on Croom's Hill" 6568
"room on the Avenue Gabriel" 7770
"room over Black Ally's Café" 4004
"room overlooking the river" 6316
"room says, the" 7765
"room she called her 'office'" 8528
"room that smelled of honeysuckle" 10180
"room to room, moves from" 5718
"room was crowded" 4016
"room was dark" 10215
"room . . . was in soft gloom" 8353
"room was like a furnace" 7776
"room was long and furnished with anonymity" 7769
"room was long and lofty" 7761
"room was old-fashioned" 7778
"room was practically dark" 7776
"room was so clean, everything in the" 7040
"room was suffused with light" 5335
"room was swaying" 2928
"room was very quiet" 7789
"room . . . which a kindly old lady has lent me" 7770
"room with miniscule kitchenette and stunted bathtub" 3167
"room with my mother and father" 7035
"roommate" 8012
"roommate, her" 2879, 6783
Rooms 185, 190, 1036, 2120, 2129, 2415, 2707, 2803, 2920, 3127, 3192, 3193, 3199, 3217, 3302, 3794, 3796, 3809, 4016, 4019, 4025, 4136, 4477, 4485, 4619, 4634, 4635, 5307, 5316, 5322, 5324, 5326, 5330, 5335, 5338, 5350, 5398, 5429, 5569, 5959, 6226, 6503, 7040, 7125, 7134, 7152, 7258, 7386, 7889, 8062, 8333, 8342, 8353, 8365, 8378, 8390, 8453, 8468, 8537, 8719, 8720, 8778, 8784, 8822, 9880, 9883, 10121, 10215, 10225, 10244, 10278, 10345, 10545, 10580, 10678, 10951
"rooms, attic" 5569
"rooms, don't like about the" 5350
"rooms, drawing-" 7865
"rooms, in airy" 309
"rooms, in other" 2883
"rooms, my" 8787
"rooms, my mother's" 8537
"rooms, nice airy" 9229
"Rooms, Orderly" 8673
"rooms, sitting-" 6296
"rooms, smoky" 2796
"rooms, suddenly blackened" 3299

"rooms, square dark" 185
"rooms, tailor's" 2865
"rooms, these were his" 377
"rooms, two waiting" 4619
"rooms into one, throwing three ground floor" 1180
"rooms of the brick house" 10580
"rooms overlooking the changing sea" 309
"rooms smelled of the jungle and of death" 8537
"rooms that men work in, I like" 7767
"rooms that they rented" 7515
"rooms were like ovens" 4372
"rooms with a view" 7755
Rooney, Andy 6018
"Rooney's Lot was a comma" 6280
Roop, Cecil 4691
Roosevelt 6347
Roosevelt, Colonel Theodore 4689
Roosevelt, Kermit 4689
Roosevelt, President 6652, 6863
"rooster crowed" 8423
"roosters, the crowing of" 2790
"root, eat the" 10899
"roots, black muscular" 3458
"roots, gnarly tap" 10106
"roots, hair" 10106
"roots clutched the earthen bank" 9671
"roots have been pulled out" 7165
"roots . . . sucked life to a gnarled trunk" 9674
"rope, at the end of a" 3353
"rope, end of your" 3339
"rope, holding one end of a long" 8695
"rope, skipping" 8747
Roper, Ned 8994
"ropes were placed on execution day" 7686
Roquebrun, Colonel Pierre 10399
Rosa 5336
Rosalina 9402
Rosamond 10677
Rosanna 1986
"Rosas" 3482
"Roscrea, change at" 9655
Rose 385, 1815, 2070, 2898, 4176, 4774, 5816, 6826, 8843, 9903
"rose, I" 7488
"rose, smelling like a" 8542
"rose and crossed the car" 9526
"rose before the sun" 2188
"rose bushes, new" 8241
"rose by any other name" 8955
"rose early, they" 6133
"rose early that day" 862
"rose from her chair" 6571
"rose from her desk to face the windows" 6900
"rose from his chair" 2924
"rose garden" 10406
"rose high above the Plain" 7810

"rose into the sky" 3300
"rose quite slowly in the heirarchy" 1540
"rose slowly out of the buried night" 10293
"rose with a groan" 10150
"rose with the fog, he" 10256
"rosebush in a canyon, lone" 5859
"rosebushes, rows of" 4286
"Roselands" 3064
Rosenbaum 384
"Rosenberg case" 5207
Rosenbergs, the 680
Roses 3809, 3811, 10315
"roses" 3806
"roses, candy which mimicks" 4850
"roses, rich odour of" 3794
"roses, violent scent of" 10315
"roses, watering his" 10180
"roses, wild" 3396
"roses, wine and" 3397
"roses and wine, summer was" 7709
"roses on the bench, crimson" 3798
"roses past their prime, heady scent of" 3809
"roses roses all the way" 3811
"Rosetta [branch]" 7681
"Rosevalley" 3548
"rose-vines, climbing tangles of" 1349
Roshan 4742
Rosie 631, 3043
Roskov, Dean 2489
Roslyn, Janna 2522
Rosnovski, Abel 7075
Rosnovski, Zaphia 7075
Ross, Abe 10392
Ross, Alan 8228
Ross, Dickie 7913
Ross, Mason 6536
Ross, Yale 489
Rossiter 5346
Rossiter, Miss 3327
Rosso, Marchesa del 10819
"roster, staff" 10958
"rosy and redolent of matzo and milk" 6652
"rosy and refulgent" 854
"Rosy Ridge" 9098
"rosy-brown" 5899
"rot, free of" 275
"rot, it acquires" 275
"rot and win" 10811
"rot began, the" 9243
"rotation, haphazard" 6763
"Roterdam" 120
Roth, Philip 1159
"Rotherhithe" 1346
Rothstein 8599
"Rotonde, the" 7581
Rotondo, Florie 4841
"rotted cucumber" 2656
"rotten, Amelia is" 1897
"rotten, I bet he is" 1897
"rotten, outlandishly rock-bottom" 62

"rotting fruit" 8544
"rotting orangey-red blossoms" 9672
"rotting woods" 4105
"rotund" 5800
Rouault 504
"Rouen" 7709
"rouge" 6958
"rough times ahead" 1994
"Round, Great" 5479
"round, making her early morning" 6459
"round, rising behind it in a gentle" 3421
"round, some old" 4335
"round after round into my plane" 6683
"round the bend" 8799
"roundabout, a" 3069
"rounded and curded" 7945
"rounds, made the" 5537
"rouse yourself" 10128
"roused by the multitudinous silver calling of a world full of birds" 836
"roused from sound sleep before dawn" 10122
"roused himself to fuller consciousness" 10138
"roused Rogier from his reverie" 5620
"roused sharply from that fitful and uneasy sleep" 10132
"Rousseauan society of 'natural men and women'" 9045
"rout her out myself" 2091
"route, paper" 5374
"route, trade" 9198
"Route 81" 1044
"Route 111" 9451
"Route 7 south of Washington" 3665
"route that linked the towns of the Chickasaw nation with the river called Father of Waters" 9198
"Route 31" 9600
"Route 363" 1462
"Route 27" 2994, 9199
"Route 27A" 9203
"route was as familiar to me" 7268
Routes 1175, 3232, 3634, 4548, 5712, 5720, 5723, 6083, 6498, 7268, 8053, 9134, 9138, 9143, 9161, 9175, 9176, 9180, 9184, 9199, 9542
"routes, quirky crosscuts of" 5723
Routh, Mr. Justice 8184
"routine, convenient" 4284
"routine, going through her usual" 564
"Row, Cannery" 6272, 10492
"Row, Hell" 6269
"row, that particular" 1843
"row no further, I could" 3694
Rowan, Laura 4166
Rowan, Lieutenant Tim 8131

Rowan, Lily 7204
"rowboat, in the" 4482
"rowboat, rear of the" 4688
"rowboat bucking the choppy waves" 8164
"rowdy gang of singers" 2901
Rowe, Arthur 6761
"rowers of summer, the last" 4662
Rowhedge, Tom 1852
"rowhouse, front door of the" 1749
Rowley, Emily 5638
"rows of houses with alleys between them" 6277
Roxy 2249
Royal 3183
"Royal Air Force Transport Command" 205
"royal box, sat in the" 8348
"Royal Canadian Air Force North Star" 4674
"royal flagship" 4151
"royal genealogy" 363
"royal palace" 2731
"royal personage" 8872
Royall 1585
"Royallieu" 2820
"royals, the small and distant" 8079
Royalty 127, 354, 541, 798, 927, 1179, 1196, 1197, 1565, 1779, 1902, 2485, 3289, 3375, 4136, 4513, 4583, 4888, 4943, 5082, 5227, 5371, 5451, 6450, 6561, 6647, 7604, 7630, 7794, 7795, 7805, 7812, 8346, 8348, 8872, 8991, 9380, 9892, 10033, 10464, 10669, 10974
"royalty" 9380
Royce, Rupert 709
Rozanov, Sergei 8004
Ruafocus 10196
Ruane, Michael 10674
"rub his nose in her deed" 2684
"rubbed a patch in the pinestraw with his boot toe" 7549
"rubbed itself against his unnerved flesh" 10202
"rubbed the sleep out of her eyes" 10212
"rubber band" 5862
"rubbing hand lotion, carefully" 564
"rubbing her nose with the back of her hand" 7014
"rubbing his head, habit of" 4291
"rubbish, cleared of" 3111
"rubbish, pale spots of imperishable plastic" 7930
"rubbish, tipped the" 6431
"rubbish tip, what seemed to be a" 3227
"rubbish-picker, everybody thought Arp was just a" 6431
"rubble, turned into" 1453
"Rubio City" 9762
Ruby 1154, 2010, 10691
"ruby mine" 7950

"Rubygill" 10641
"rucksack, at the bottom of his"
8708
"ruddy and intense" 5981
"rude end, a sudden" 6510
"rude wonder" 110
Rudolf 4972
Rudolf, King 5082
"rue, something of" 7092
"rue Cambon" 10850
"rue Catinat" 9330
"Rue de Castiglione" 4633
"rue de Rivoli" 10850
"Rue de Rivoli" 10037
"Rue du Coq d'Or" 10792
"Rue François-Villon" 6339
"rue Jacob" 3231
Rueda, Carlos 4129
"ruffling the top of her head" 740
Rufus, Marcus Minucius 7006
"rug, my new blue" 5634
"rug, rich travelling" 5943
"rug of white foam" 7680
"rugby matches" 5329
"Rügen is the biggest island Germany possesses" 5016
"rugged countenance" 5889
"ruggedness of the soil" 9515
Ruggles, Ace 8893
"rugs, tartan" 6039
"ruin, which was by then a depressing" 9253
"ruin standing by itself in the middle of a fourteen-section cattle
pasture" 3253
Ruina! 2570
"ruined, business houses were" 1019
"ruined everything I loved" 9279
"ruined for me, could have been"
10190
"ruined island town" 7467
"ruined once in every generation"
1435
"ruined villages" 6245
"ruining the lives of countless men
and women" 5659
"ruinous for a century and a half"
2636
Ruins 2636, 7282, 9208, 9216,
9230, 9231, 9237, 9255
"ruins, built upon the" 1384
"ruins, continent in" 2262
"ruins, hospital" 1751
"ruins, number of" 9216
"ruins of an Abbey" 9255
"ruins of Berlin and Nuremberg"
2237
"ruins of Ramborough Abbey" 9208
"ruins of which the traveller gazes
with wonder" 6802
"rule, British" 3507
"rule, leg-before-wicket" 7821
"rule, Spanish" 1355
"rule, there is no" 7823

"rule about his house" 7822
"rule for a man's life" 5562
"rule is without them, no" 7815
"rule over each of the directions
upon the earth" 2635
"rule over him, those who" 9704
"rule seems to be no two writers on
the same block" 5529
"rule that people talk about" 7974
"ruled, a few families" 3561
"ruled a regulus or kinglet" 7796
"ruled in simplicity and affluence"
3561
"ruler of Spain, brilliant young"
7800
"Ruler of the Day, Fifth" 4592
Rulers 363, 1444, 1902, 3561,
3571, 3721, 6518, 6697, 7006,
7191, 10473
Rules 5529
"rules of their type, true to the"
5694
"Rum Alley" 957
"rumble, clattering" 10272
"rumble, low brief" 10010
"rumble in the air" 7283
"rumble that isn't meant to be
heard" 10010
"rumbled with theatrical thunder"
9241
"rumbling, clattering and" 8834
Rumbold 6501
"Rumbold Junction" 4130
"rummaged through the boxes of
junk" 6154
"Rummidge campus" 8615
"rumor" 6714
"rumor, any truth to the" 7834
"rumor, heard a" 7836
"rumor, latest wacky" 7831
Rumors 1790, 3968, 5230, 5914,
6346, 6714, 6969, 7949
"rumors, blanketed with smoke
and" 7839
"rumors, curious" 6346
"rumors, Henneker" 5230
"rumour, I heard the first" 7830
"rumoured, it was" 3968
"rumours are the begetters of gossip" 7833
"rump, hams of his" 8266
"rumpled his dress, if he" 3272
"run, his record" 10966
"run, started to" 7858, 9605
"run, they couldn't" 8919
"run after her" 3410
"run around the table" 10656
"run away with the money" 2735
"run for re-election as mayor of the
city" 2472
"run from the police, men on the"
2024
"run in itself was pleasant" 7847
"run into her mother's bedroom"
7213

"run it down, not to" 4445
"run like a goddamn antelope" 7851
"run off, or maybe" 6136
"run off her feet, literally" 3682
"run off with Guy Dupree, my wife
Norma had" 2664
"run over by a double-decker bus"
6319
"run stopped, her eager" 7843
"run the home movie again, I'm
going to" 1331
"run to the pastures" 8933
"runaway slave" 1160
"runes, read these" 5545
Runnels, Phoebe 7197
"runner was seen coming" 7053
Running 32, 2655, 3410, 3484,
4137, 4538, 4695, 5152, 6223,
7712, 8429, 8659, 8789, 8924,
9151, 9463, 9994, 10009, 10893,
10894
"running, desperate" 8789
"running, Fabio was" 9463
"running, still" 4538
"running, woman" 10893
"running a long time, he had been"
7850
"running across the rain-glossed
pavement" 10894
"running as fast as he could" 7845
"running away, they are all" 7801
"running away from one another"
8876
"running down the wooden staircase" 7712
"running fast" 8659
"running flat out, we were" 5293
"running for the porch" 7861
"running for the priest, two cripples" 1831
"running hard and fast over
crumbling highways" 6381
"running in from behind our
house" 320
"running in the still deeper shadow"
5152
"running me down to Murray
Street" 10921
"running out of gas" 9451
"running somewhere early that
morning" 7849
"running through a brilliant light"
7856
"running through the fog across
the snow" 8659
"running through the hills" 9994
"running through the jungle of
southern nights" 6381
"running toward my mother, I am"
7863
"running was a strange thing" 7855
"run-of-the-mill" 4634
"runs in her stockings" 4176
"runt, puny" 7851
"runways of Idlewild Airport" 208

Rupert 8011
Rupert, M. 2101
"Rupert Vermont" 3180
Rupp, Arthur 7852
"rural, became even more quietly"
9203
"rural England" 2193
"rural scene" 5126
"rural tranquillities of middle England" 4139
Rush, Jim 6506
Rush, Peter 2957
"rush of the Grand Central Station" 8173
"rush of the pheasant, coppery"
4105
"rush to the Klondike for gold"
3394
"rushed along by a locomotive"
9515
"rushed over to the Continent"
10768
"Rushes, as often as he comes to
the" 3478
"rushing here and there" 5365
"rushing him to New Haven" 9531
"rushing into their full summer
dress" 9742
"rushing of wings" 2126
"rushlights" 4335
Ruskin, John 716
Russell 1942, 2013, 3911
Russell, Karl 4823
Russell, Superintendent 7108
"Russell Square" 1614
"Russia" 4436, 7001
"Russia, Collective Farm in" 5419
"Russia had occupied Port Arthur
in China" 3394
"Russia in winter" 6263
"Russian Asia" 2257
"Russian bear, the" 3514
"Russian choir, chased by a" 2756
"Russian custom" 5406
"Russian dancer" 2103
"Russian leader" 507
"Russian writer, great" 5466
Russians 287, 8177
"Russians, had not expected to see
the" 8177
"Russians had been a threat" 287
"Russians in San Francisco" 8177
Russo, Alice Blanders 5853
"rust about every man at the beginning, there is some" 7584
"rust therefore will wear off sooner"
7584
"rusted halfway up the doors" 9829
"rusticity, positive" 267
"rustle of her taffeta gown" 376
"rustle sprang through the park, a
sudden" 8033
"rustled, voice that" 10011
"rustling of his servant" 8483
Rusty 6544

Ruth 449, 2351, 3517, 6321, 9164,
9710
Rutherford, Bill 10245
Rutherford, Miss 7877
"ruthless" 9165
"ruthless bastard" 4993
"ruts eroded by spring storms" 2989
"Rutterburg Vermont" 9600
Ryan 1321
Ryan, Eddie 1660, 2155, 7363
Ryan, Edward Arthur 4763
Ryder, Jimbo 3753
Rydock, Mrs. Van 7473
"Rye" 3197

"S held rigid, the deep tumescent"
2851
"'s seemed the black tip of a just-
extinguished match" 6301
"Sabbath, breaking the" 5084
"sabbatical's end" 9614
"Sabine hills" 1494
"Sabine Pass" 8165
"Sabine Pass, Battle of the" 7741
"sabots, feet were stuck into" 10792
"sabra, full-bellied" 2080
"sabre cut" 5012
Sabrina 14
"sacerdotal function" 1527
"sacked" 6435
Sacks, Hamilton 5924
"Sacramento River" 5803
"sacred, it was" 6086
"sacred, swamp that was" 9198
"Sacred Heart, oh" 9904
Sacred Majesty King George 1483
"sacred walls of Ilium" 7810
Sacrifice 2627, 7514, 7813, 8226
"sacrifice, day of" 2627
"sacrifice, Paris hints of" 1366
"sacrifice, the noon" 7514
"sacrifices, offer themselves up as"
7813
"sacristy of a suburban church"
1303
"sad" 5261
"sad, Christmas should ever come
to be" 2504
"sad, people who liked to be" 1454
"sad, why I'd been so" 2675
"sad about a prison bus, there's
something" 9838
"sad and desperate, the day as" 4319
"sad we had to part" 2541
"sadder, there is nothing" 260
"saddest, the rainiest nights . . . are
by no means the" 7286
"saddest story" 8973
"saddest thing she had ever seen"
4197
"saddle, his" 2820
"saddle, in the" 7637
"saddle, light in the" 7629
"saddle, slung his" 7250

"saddle, twisted in his" 7809
"saddle bag" 7361
"saddle had slipped to one side" 440
Sade 7144
Sadie, Aunt 6850
Sadler, Jack 10244
"sadly I have had to stay" 2541
Sadness 275, 970, 1454, 1791,
2494, 2500, 2504, 2510, 2675,
4197, 5261, 6092, 6663, 7286,
8973, 9838
"sadness and wrinkles, acquires"
275
"sadness of any kind, my first experience with" 2510
"safe, believed he was" 1711
"safe, closed the" 8174
"safe, felt" 9808
"safe and sane, sitting here" 2734
"safe conduct through the summer"
6074
"safe in London, they had been"
2149
Safety 1711, 6791, 7516, 9579, 9808
"safety" 7097
"safety, illusions of" 6791
"Safety, we owe allegiance to" 7516
"saffron haze" 1854
"Saffron Park" 1358
Sagamore, Katherine Sherritt 1998
"sagas of courage" 5149
"sage" 9127
"sage, over the" 8768
"sagebrush" 2949
"sagegrass, a stretch of tall yellow"
8366
"sages advise us so, all our" 3845
"sagging barn" 7887
"Saginaw" 4073
"Saginaw Country" 3423
"Saguenay boat" 10030
"*sagûm*, Malay word" 6247
"Sahara, like snowmen found in
the" 1429
"Sahara desert" 2640
"Sahara Desert" 6168
"Sahel" 6256
"said, it is still" 10957
"said, much was" 639
"said, so it was" 4956
"said, something none of us had
ever" 244
"said, what she had" 7412
"said anything, rarely" 4780
"said at those times, should have"
7494
"said for the ten-millionth time"
6566
"said in a moderate tone" 3344
"said in her hasty yet purposeful
way" 6301
"said it to each other" 10828
"said mutely in her sleep" 2786
"said through his fat nose" 6652
"said to herself" 1599

"said to me this afternoon and before" 7598
"said to myself" 4772
"said under his breath" 8108
"said with a pleading gesture" 4986
"said with vehemence" 4983
"said yes when he knew that he ought to have said no" 50
"said you had a car, I thought you" 9836
"Saigon" 2577, 10519
"sail, ship was ready to" 8166
"sail back, I was about to" 9431
"sail down the western coast of Kyushu" 8160
"sail for America, set" 8153
"sail for Europe" 9857
"sail . . . had sickened beneath the violent glare of the August sun" 8079
"sail into Venice" 6345
"sail loft" 3431
"sail struggled lazily into action" 8126
"sail the tour or circle of the globe" 9508
"sailboat, our cruising" 9614
"sailboat, our engineless small" 1998
"sailboat, seeing a" 2285
"sailboat christened *Ketch-22*" 9052
"sailed down onto a secondary runway" 217
"sailed his sloop past the starting-line buoys" 8163
"sailed into Piraeus with my comrades" 10594
"sailed out of Tulagi, never" 406
Sailing 406, 5050, 8053, 8160, 8163, 10594
"sailing" 5050
"sailing, last-minute bustle of" 9431
"sailing high above the waxed corridors" 7096
"sailing the sky in ships" 9745
"sailing their model boats" 8815
"sailing time" 4916
"sailor, a" 8942
"sailor, the" 4315
"sailor, young" 10278
"sailor put down the helm" 8167
Sailors 928, 3997, 5885, 8116, 8137, 8167, 10848
"sailors" 747
"sailors, merchant" 3997
"sailors, sleep hung-over" 8137
"sailors, young" 10848
"sailors in a ship" 6266
"sailors in holiday attire" 3997
"sailors in peril, looked more like" 10754
"sailors term a vessel" 8055
"sailors told each other" 10848
"sails, her two lateen" 8114
"sails, manoeuvred on ropes like glassy" 9253

"sails, snap of the" 8504
"sails, without a flutter of" 8063
"sails set port and starboard" 8114
"saint, soul of a" 8758
"saint and Cabbalistic conjuror" 7505
"St. Ann's" 8632
Saint Antonio 8937
St. Aubert, Monsieur 5125
"St. Augustine" 9973
"St. Augustine's" 1310
"St. Barnabas, old" 9153
"St. Benedict" 8395
"St. Botolphs" 1411, 8604
"St. Bride's, went into" 6161
"St. Catherine, island of" 5052
"St. Clement, Order of" 1303
"St. Cloud's" 556
"St. Columba, church of" 1498
"St. David's churchyard" 1188
"St. David's Head" 4056
St. Dennis, Albert 3506
"St. Dié" 3024
"St. Dreots in South Glebeshire" 2299
"St. Enoch's Church" 3783
"St. Frideswide Hoxton" 1500
"St. Gatien" 6949
St. George, Elizabeth Henry 10926
"St. George, parish of" 6267
"St. George's Channel" 4056
"St. George's registry office" 6622
"St. Giles" 9989
"St. Gregory's" 5653
"St. Helen [Australia]" 6137
"St. Ives, town of" 1764
"St. Ives New Hampshire" 10867
"St. Jago" 9431
"St. James" 6435
"St. James Parish" 9012
"St. James's" 9764
"St. James's Church" 1184
"St. Jean-Cap Ferrat" 3200
"St. John [Virgin Islands]" 9614
"St. John's, church of" 1295
"St. John's Wood" 7415
"St. Julien-le-Pauvre, little church of" 1307
"St. Lawrence, high above the" 7655
"St. Lawrence, the" 10030
"St. Louis" 1349, 4190, 4245, 4424, 8676, 10621
"St. Louis, Château" 7655
"St. Louis, how Eliphalet Hopper came to" 6096
"St. Louis, in the city of" 1567
"*St. Louis*, liner" 3494
"St. Louis Arch" 3038
"Saint Louis Blues, The" 6222
"St. Louis Cardinals" 8934
"St. Louis Missouri" 8852
"St. Louis of the early forties" 8852
"St. Louis tobacco" 899
"St. Maria, harbour of" 8048

"St. Mark's" 1300
"St. Mark's School" 1626
St. Martin of Tours 7539
"St. Martin's-le-Grand" 10079
"Saint Matthew Passion, Bach's" 1746
"St. Matthew's, parish of" 1891
"St. Michael" 8632
"St. Michael Pendeverel is a hamlet" 5144
"St. Pancras church" 6270
"St. Pancras Station" 7261
St. Patrick 4055
"St. Patrick's Cathedral" 7343
Saint Paul 2817
"St. Paul's, dome of" 10079
"St. Paul's, on the way to" 1830
"St. Paul's, spire of" 2214
Saint Peter 5664
"St. Peter's" 7096
"St. Peter's, walked toward" 10439
"St. Peter's foot" 8939
"St. Petersburg" 6039
"St. Petersburg and the outlying beaches" 9616
"St. Petin" 5049
"Saint-Simon, duc de" 5108
"Saint Simon Unawares, parish of" 3498
"St. So-and-so" 110
"St. Sody North Cornwall" 1500
"Saint Swithin" 2150
"St. Swithin" 8395
"sainthood in Judaism, there is no" 7543
"Saintly Gerard" 2336
"Saint-Ouen" 1063
Saints 2623, 7539
"saints" 0405
"saints, chipped plaster" 7533
"saints, Convocation of the" 2623
"Sakhalin" 2516
"Saks opened its doors" 1091
"Sakuyu, Chiefs of" 7801
Sal 8639
Salah-ed-din 7798
Salazar, Josie 9716
"sale held obscurely" 494
"sale room is no place for a woman" 10836
"Salerno" 9155
Sales 1037, 1043, 9439
"salesgirl says" 2845
"salesman, full-time" 1047
"salesman, two-faced hardware" 5769
"salesman, young" 5844
Salesmen 5769, 5844, 8861, 9439
"salesmen at Red Bowers Chevrolet, all the friendly" 6853
Salinger, Donald 3746
"Salisbury" 1486, 1671
"Salisbury, the" 5098
Sallas, Ike 2810
"sallow" 4922, 10933

Sally 1199, 4789, 5658, 6386, 6755, 10071

"salmon therefore not moving" 4690

"salmon wait for Autumn floods" 1336

"Salmon who lies in the pool of Glyn Cagny" 10756

"salon, ushered him into the" 4132

"Salon Carré" 5613

"salon de lecture" 6522

"Salonika" 7459

"saloon" 4324

"saloon, Caraher's" 8765

"saloon, ramshackle" 8852

"Saloon Bar" 4312

Saloons 1365, 4324

"saloons, it had six good" 1387

"saloons, standing in one of the" 3986

"saloons, stores and" 1365

"SALOP, County of" 778

"salt, first sting of" 186

"salt, he tasted" 9075

"salt, ocean" 7657

"salt air, reddened a little by the" 304

"Salt Branch New York" 821

"salt fish" 8512

"Salt Lake City" 9181

"salt water" 5034

Saltana, Professor Cosmo 4644

Salteena, Mr. 9877

Salter, Jim 10460

Saltfleet 10239

"Salud amigos" 4214

"salute my Uncle Oswald, an urge to" 3587

"salvation, I am thy" 7524

"salvation, moment of" 1217

Sam 1121, 2919, 5976, 6218, 7751, 8248

"Sambuco" 9155

"same, it was never the" 5122

"same, they are all exactly the" 1408

"same, they're all the" 10876

"same any more, nothing was the" 2595

"same as now, nothing there was the" 3369

"same now, nothing was the" 1248

Sammler, Mr. Artur 911

Sammy 859, 2973

Sammy, R. 8268

"Samnite mountains" 4040

"sample case, opens his" 5844

"samples of her fudge, as if they were free" 8879

Sams, Jason 5535

Samuel, Mr. 3329

"San Antonio Trace" 5215

"San Diego" 227, 400, 4060, 4064, 8007

"San Elmo" 2660

"San Felipe" 9762

"San Fernando" 9960

San Francisco 1392, 5130, 9611, 10588

"San Francisco" 644, 1020, 2005, 2906, 3524, 4721, 5712, 5787, 5892, 6104, 7079, 7287, 8058, 8104, 8177, 8704, 8945, 9611, 9918, 10446, 10580, 10582

"San Francisco, comes from living in" 9299

"San Francisco, it was sunny in" 10588

"San Francisco, straits of" 3514

"San Francisco, two weeks from" 8084

"San Francisco Bay" 4887

"San Francisco de Juticlan" 230

"San Francisco existed outside the weather" 1472

"San Ignacio del Tule" 9483

"San José" 7238

"San Leandro turnpike" 9116

"San Marco, Piazza" 421, 8634

"San Pedro, liner" 8074

"San Rafael" 2061

"San Roquean" 5699

"San Salvatore" 674

"San Sebastian" 10966

"San Ysidro" 9145

"San Zaccaria pier" 3709

Sanad 6434

Sanchez, Isidro 2570

"sanctity of human life" 6991

"sanctuary, nature" 10422

"Sanctuary, Wild Life" 749

"sanctuary of the Methodist church" 3604

"sand, a thousand feet above the" 234

"sand, beyond a stretch of" 3195

"sand, blowing" 10098

"sand, burning" 2006

"sand, deep white" 10347

"sand, drew pictures in the" 6933

"sand, drifting" 1485

"sand, golden" 4587

"sand, hard-packed" 10379

"sand, multicolored grains of" 8924

"sand, vast stretch of" 7625

"sand and clay broke loose" 5134

"sand at the water's edge" 10421

"sand castles" 1420

"sand clods" 10106

"sand hillocks" 6053

"sand is like shattered ivory" 5174

"sand is white and pure" 5177

"sand on the parlor floor, sprinkles" 10932

"sand was soft" 329

Sandage, Mr. James 2947

"sandals, bright red Italian-style beach" 4277

"sandals, new" 5880

"sandals, tapping of a messenger's" 8330

Sanders, Dr. 7679

"sandes which lie against the Island of Cithera" 7370

Sandifer, Buddy 1047

Sandor 1084

Sandra 2011

Sandro 5775

Sands, Bernard 3741

"sands, miles of empty" 2769

"sands of the river" 9132

"sandstorm, cold" 2957

"sandwich, you also get a" 3280

"sandwiches" 1067

"sandwiches, small cress" 3821

"sandwiches in a pub" 3832

"sandwiches two miles away" 7574

Sandy 8916, 10246

Sandy The Sea Serpent 308

"Sandynugghur" 3067

"sane, sitting here safe and" 2734

"sanely, exist" 2763

"sang, a sweet tenor ever" 8748

"sang, Anne always" 8758

"sang 'Black Lace' on the record player" 2111

"sang a song" 8702

"sang Gibreel Farishta tumbling from the heavens" 2427

"sang like Ledbelly" 8745

"sang that in the hall" 8750

"sang this as lustily as any of his guests" 852

Sanger, Albert 5905

"Sangre de Cristo" 6085

"sanguine self" 5355

Sanity 4948, 7173

"sanity" 1452

Sanjak 2854

Sanjé 5905

"sank a man" 10811

"sank back into the rock of sleep" 8467

"sank forgetfully back" 2495

"sank into a state of mind" 2673

"sank like a stone" 10130

"Santa Barbara" 1039, 4050, 4051

"Santa Chiara, basilica of" 10674

Santa Claus 5918

"Santa Claus, couldn't find anyone who looked more like" 5918

"Santa Claus, too old for" 2586

"Santa Fe" 4214

"Santa Felicia, county of" 5210

"Santa Grazia de Traghetto" 10664

"Santa Luz" 1387

"Santa Margarita del Banana, small town of" 4081

"Santa Maria del Pianto" 1293

"Santa Monica" 4064

"Santa Rosa" 2854, 3211

"Santa Teresa" 3296

"Santa Venetia" 2061

"Santa Vittoria, the history of" 9001

Santangelo, Joseph 3970

"Sante Fe bar towels" 8530

"Santeria" 7533

Santiago 7054

Santinio, Alejo 5841

"Santomaso, town of" 9577

Santos-Dumont, Monsieur Alberto 9940

"Sao Paulo's Congonhas Airport" 217

"sap in the trees" 10980

"sap would some day stir, aboriginal" 4435

"saplings" 3899

"saplings, loblolly" 1879

"saplings, maple" 3036

Sappho, the" 9863

Sara 2458, 8527

"Saracen, it was the" 9399

Saracinesca, Don Orsino 3071

Saracinesca, Ippolito 5730

"Saragossa" 4076

Sarah 4199, 5446, 6101, 8450, 9037, 9560, 10265, 10276

"Sarasota Florida" 6003

"Saratoga" 4371, 8912

"Saratoga Springs" 6939

"Saratoga Springs YMCA" 9320

"Sarawak, rain forest of" 4109

"sarcastically or hopelessly conscious of itself" 8863

"Sardinia" 5053

"sardonic dead, he was as" 2304

"sardonic stories" 8976

"sardonic when alive" 2304

Sarge 10262

"saris tied low showing their navels" 7481

Sarnac 10918

"Sarnia" 10909

"Sarsaparilla" 10812

"Sarthe, the département of" 6571

Sartoris, John 2303

"Sarum" 3400

"sassafras" 973

"sassafras clump" 10940

"sassy, fat and" 5382

"sat, hunched when she" 4196

"sat across from each other at small tables" 309

"sat across the aisle from an Israeli couple" 9630

"sat against a wet grassy paddy dike" 1864

"sat alone by the woodstove" 2456

"sat alone in her room" 8353

"sat alone in Mr. Sniggs's room" 8354

"sat alone now on his sofa" 8332

"sat alone on the back seat" 4168

"sat and waited" 9330

"sat around the fire" 4018

"sat around the table" 4019

"sat at a desk" 970

"sat at a forward angle" 9558

"sat at a table" 4336

"sat at an upper window" 5431

"sat at her writing-table" 8259

"sat at his desk" 1854, 6421

"sat at his ease" 3084

"sat at night in his palace" 7798

"sat at Sunday dinner" 3565

"sat at the base of the big tree" 3759

"sat at the only table they had" 7885

"sat at the open window" 2695

"sat at the roof hole entrance" 8387

"sat at the scattered tables" 2901

"sat at the table in his bedroom" 1952

"sat at the top of the short steep flight of steps" 3976

"sat back in his chair" 5903

"sat before the mirror" 498

"sat Beni Baidoo" 8379

"sat beside his mother" 6238

"sat bolt upright in bed" 8601

"sat by herself at the beginning of the evening" 8725

"sat by the hearth" 2704

"sat by the sea near Palos" 2498

"sat by the window" 7347, 8570

"sat by the window, crying as she" 2071

"sat cross-legged" 8374

"sat cross-legged on the floor" 6143

"sat down" 1496

"sat down, wearily" 4420

"sat down, when he" 1501

"sat down at Alexander's table as he always did" 4274

"sat down on the grass" 3793

"sat down thankfully" 3692

"sat down to breakfast" 7180

"sat down to wait for his friend" 10048

"sat down upon my doorstep" 5615

"sat easy on his motorcycle" 10063

"sat hunched forward" 8270

"sat idle at her desk" 6495

"sat immediately in front of her" 2682

"sat in a low swing chair" 7468

"sat in a position of slack repose" 8386

"sat in a small dark room" 1317

"sat in a solemn unblinking row" 331

"sat in a tiny flat" 2822

"sat in a tonga" 2963

"sat in an old graveyard" 6963

"sat in conference" 5208

"sat in defiance of municipal orders" 2017

"sat in front of the pansy-leaf fire-screen" 8214

"sat in her lodging at Hull" 8342

"sat in her superb private drawing-room" 8345

"sat in her wheelchair" 4922

"sat in his chair" 3690

"sat in his little Italian car" 59

"sat in his oaken stall" 9411

"sat in his office" 3332

"sat in his private room" 7752

"sat in his sitting-room" 8347

"sat in Kensington Gardens" 7953

"sat in my room" 9404

"sat in New York Criminal Court Number 3" 5205

"sat in stunned disbelief" 6232

"sat in the back garden" 5653

"sat in the bath-tub" 567

"sat in the center of the bed" 1923

"sat in the corner of the darkened room" 6519

"sat in the dark" 9374

"sat in the day coach of a train" 9654

"sat in the drawing-room of her house" 3821

"sat in the dressing room" 7487

"sat in the front ground floor consulting-room" 3518

"sat in the green painted gazebo" 301

"sat in the kitchen" 1869

"sat in the last of the lawn chairs" 2348

"sat in the library" 1907

"sat in the lounge" 8125

"sat in the office" 583

"sat in the room of his inn" 8346

"sat in the royal box" 8348

"sat in the shade of the willows" 8350

"sat in the shadows" 520

"sat in the train" 9572

"sat in the train, as she" 10800

"sat in the truck overlooking the school" 4667

"sat knitting upon the beach" 10818

"sat like two Marimekko pumpkins" 7074

"sat looking into the fire" 696

"sat looking out" 10038

"sat morosely upon the back fence" 2497

"sat motionless and inscrutable as a Buddha" 1523

"sat Mrs. Cliff" 10782

"sat next to a young man" 9612

"sat next to Jamie" 2999

"sat on a plain wooden bench" 8280

"sat on a sunny hill-side" 6557

"sat on her grandmother's porch" 8356

"sat on his haunches" 482

"sat on the balcony" 8358

"sat on the bench" 10068

"sat on the edge of his daughter's bed" 6707

"sat on the edge of the table" 8853

"sat on the front seat" 1202

"sat on the front steps in the cool shade" 8038

"sat on the porch" 8371

"sat on the porch of his log house" 2513

"sat on the same high stool" 10041

"sat on the sand under a thorn tree" 4189

"sat on the spongy grass" 7677

"sat on the sty" 8360

"sat on the wedding porch" 8241

"sat once more" 8359

"sat one morning in August" 3987

"sat one morning in the window-bay" 8206

"sat over lunch" 3831

"sat pen in hand" 2535

"sat reading" 7364

"sat recuperating" 7467

"sat shotgun next to Jimmy" 6938

"sat stiffly on the big plush seat of the Cadillac" 3030

"sat the most beautiful girl in Budapest" 10884

"sat there, as he" 2511

"sat there, they" 7352

"sat there in that pitch-dark movie house" 1323

"sat together" 8739

"sat together in the den" 2007

"sat up" 10145

"sat up against the headboard of a bed" 5986

"sat up beside her father" 1617

"sat up in bed" 10134

"sat up in bed abruptly" 10172

"sat up suddenly" 4726

"sat up together all night" 9733

"sat up very straight" 1959

"sat upon, admirably unfit to be" 484

"sat upon a cream-coloured beach of crushed stone" 3582

"sat upon the roadside" 8343

"sat upon the rocking waters" 732

"sat upon the throne" 10474

"sat upright like bankers" 3580

"sat very still" 7781

"sat very upright on a carved oak settle" 10086

"sat very upright on the slippery seat" 9540

"sat waiting for the formation" 8654

"sat white-shirted" 247

"sat William" 8340

"sat with his back against the log wall" 2900

"sat with his head bowed" 9410

"sat with his hearing aid turned off" 2419

"sat with Uncle Miles at Belting" 7677

"sat with young François" 8264

Satan 5810, 9055, 10360

Satan 7990

"satan, blond" 333

"Satan would be, it's like how" 7990

"Satanstoe" 6608

"satchel, cheap imitation alligator-skin" 9525

"satchel bouncing against his fat bottom" 10443

"satchel gave him a *bias*" 10905

"satchel held together by ship rope" 7082

"sate perched on a tree" 719

"satellite dish to the stars" 7030

"satellite whirled around the globe" 531

Satisfaction 1033, 3492, 6433, 9263

"satisfaction, gave her undisguised" 7468

"satisfaction, gave him the great-est" 3741

"satisfaction, greatest" 6433

"satisfaction, long sigh of" 3047

"satisfaction, nothing gives her more" 10194

"satisfaction, said with" 8713

"satisfaction, tender" 1033

"satisfaction, washed away the dull" 2585

"satisfaction never comes" 4676

"satisfactory" 6251

"satisfied, heroic and" 9263

"satisfied after all them adventures" 3492

"satisfied that she was gone from us for good" 3604

"Saturday, could feel in her bones that it was" 10152

"Saturdays was the best day" 2184

"Saturnday" 4282

"saucepan cover lay wrong side" 9351

"saucy and improvident, we were" 1162

Saul 7217

Sauls, Bobby 1260

Saunders, Gil 5622

"saunter, slowed down to a" 10366

"sauntering now in the gardens of the Luxembourg" 10334

"sauntering through the wilderness of this world" 5581

"sausage, Polish" 4073

"sausages, get you" 3832

"Sausalito" 3280

"savage, gesture was vaguely" 8568

"savage hunger" 3304

"savagery of the world" 3366

"savages" 286

"Savannah, the city of" 6275

Savata 3577

"save her, new man she says will" 7744

"save me, he says it will" 5531

"save myself, couldn't reach out a hand to" 3674

"save time by flying at night" 211

"save us O Lord" 8504

"saved for our grandchildren on the plastic ribbon of a tape recorder" 8892

"saved him, perhaps I could have" 7492

"saved him with only a word" 7492

"saved it all afternoon" 2911

"saved us all, perhaps I could have" 7492

"savings, gladly have given his life's" 6322

"Saviour, the sign of its" 2329

"savouring the chill of the other side" 10206

"Savoy" 4269

"saw, first" 7737

"saw, I first" 5853

"saw a large silver cross in the otherwise clear sky" 10320

"saw almost simultaneously two happenings" 3441

"saw anything like it, you never" 4531

"saw at her own head instead of at the bars surrounding her life" 10826

"saw each other, first" 5830

"saw from my window" 3787

"saw her, he" 5878

"saw her, the first morning I ever" 2826

"saw her, the moment she" 5873

"saw her, when I" 7861

"saw her again, next morning he" 5793

"saw her for the first time" 10867

"saw her husband" 1985

"saw him, as I first" 5996

"saw him, she" 5878

"saw him for the first time at the funeral" 3949

"saw him or I didn't, either I" 8278

"saw him years later" 8923

"saw in him, what Nancy" 1974

"saw it, I never" 2088

"saw it, long before they" 683

"saw it, none of us ever" 325

"saw it, not a living soul" 3669

"saw it across three miles of ocean" 5039

"saw it but from the mountain tops or sailing the sky in ships, no man ever" 9745

"saw it coming" 7024

"saw it from a different angle" 9190

"saw Janna Roslyn, first" 2522

"saw Judith Hingham come on deck" 9416

"saw Kester first" 5681

"saw light of day, first" 817

"saw Mr. John Turner first" 5804

"saw most and have said least, it was I that" 7604

"saw myself as a child, things which I" 8965

"saw myself in her" 5510

"saw Ron Galloway, the last time his wife" 2561
"saw the child, when I first" 1286
"saw the enemy" 4198
"saw the girl from a long way away" 4164
"saw the Inheritance, first" 2522
"saw the signboards and the ugliness" 5916
"saw them, first" 8362
"saw them coming along Wire Road" 7638
"saw them first, I don't know who" 1898
"saw with some pleasure" 9962
"Sawley the town" 1394
"sawmill whistles" 7907
Sawyer, Tom 896, 1160, 3492
Saxon 2102
"Saxon blood, taint of" 357
"Saxton, village of" 9795
"say, don't know what to" 8840
"say, easy to" 4732
"say, going to" 4970
"say, I always" 10936
"say, I cannot" 1286
"say, I heard myself" 4229
"say, not much to" 515
"say, often heard her mother" 1827
"say, she had nothing to" 7586
"say, some people" 1459
"say, used to" 3312, 5057
"say, what can you" 2355
"say, what did you" 1552
"say, what do you" 3523
"say, what would you" 281
"say, would often" 6113
"say about it, what humanity had to" 4046
"say all good things to him" 6521
"say at the outset, I may as well" 4258
"say categorically, afraid I must" 1939
"say Davy Jones, before you can" 2820
"say good night to the party people again" 996
"say is this, all I can" 10876
"say it, odd to" 2544
"say it as I hear it, I" 708
"say now, what was it he was about to" 5188
"say of Jenny, the kind thing to" 10878
"say of the two Oliphant brothers" 8208
"say that again, you can" 10516
"say 'the end', can't quite" 8994
"say to her, liked to" 6665
"say to them, wouldn't know what to" 8630
"say to you both, there's something I want to" 2435
"say to yourself" 3622

"say unto him" 1806
"say what, and then" 74
"say what you said" 8868
Sayer, Reverend Samuel 129
Sayer, Rose 129
"saying, as I keep" 7167
"saying 'Hoi! hoil earth!'" 6075
"saying the words to this song" 10912
"saying this, I don't believe I'm" 8027
"sayings that Count Antonio spoke" 5212
"says, what Shanks Caulder" 8892
Sayward 10155
"scaffold, swinging from some" 3353
"scaffolding snapped" 37
Scaggs, Judge Guthrie 388
"Scalado" 10464
"scale, throws off" 114
"scaled, white-" 5624
"scaling cliffs by means of ropes and spikes" 6071
"scalp, digging into his" 575
"scalp, its bare" 5011
"scalp, prickling his" 3714
"scalps, cut" 7409
"Scamander, wells of" 9738
"scamper back here" 2550
Scandal 5091, 5553, 7000
"scandal, a" 5402
"scandal, eclipsed every other" 7065
"scandal, half-forgotten" 5091
"scandal, it had been a great" 7866
"scandal, made a" 7865
"scandal, mild" 7872
"scandal, new-fashioned" 1342
"scandal, the" 7869
"scandal, Watergate" 7000
"scandal, woman who loved" 7867
"scandal cannot touch it, no family so secure that" 7873
"scandal knew no bounds" 7864
"scandalized all Athens by answering him" 4503
"scandalous" 5384
"scandalous press" 4104
"scanned the narrow lane for unseen hazards" 1373
"scanners, newspaper" 9381
"scanning his face" 1610
"scanning the traffic" 2997
"scanty" 5889
"scanty, furnishings were" 7134
"scar most visible to the eye" 5141
"scar of warning" 475
"scared, a little" 3686
"scared, I'm" 8039
"scared, lived" 2599
"scared me to death" 6839
"scared the hell out of him" 34
"scarf, his long red silk" 5996
"scarf, what do you think of this" 3736
"scarf, white flowered" 2826

"scarf dancing about his gracefully modeled limbs" 5996
"scaring Cassie half to death" 8812
Scarlet Creeper 10342
"scarlet fever" 132
"scarp, crest of the" 6574
"scarred earth" 7297
"Scarsdale" 1477
"scattered, they were pretty well" 3643
"scattered around the Arts Quad" 3283
"scattering truth around like pennies" 9702
"scavenger, a madwoman and a" 4945
"scavengers, rabid" 286
"scene, blood-spattered" 10445
"scene, brought us an opening" 583
"scene, mad" 8738
"scene, magnificent" 948
"scene, there's a payoff" 3342
"scene, this earthly" 2310
"scene, whole" 1250
"scene, return to the" 2597
"scene conveying a memorable picture" 2045
"scene in the film, pivotal" 1330
"scene of bitter disputation" 1823
"scene of the offence" 1967
"scene of the telling of this tale" 1390
"scene of this chronicle" 1349
"scene of this narrative" 4045
"scene of tragedy, opening" 5091
Scenery 264, 2989
"scenery, delicious" 1336
"scenery, singular" 9515
"scenery, splendour of the" 9376
"scenery, the subject of American" 264
"scenery, woodland" 3894
"scenery of a country" 9515
Scenes 1330, 2105, 2597, 3342, 4045, 5398, 5450, 6786, 9377
"scenes have been shifted" 7388
"scent, emitting Chanel's wonderful new" 4121
"scent, fresh with the" 3796
"scent in the high pastures is so strong" 8514
"scent . . . makes a man drunk" 8514
"scent of firs, resin" 3405
"scent of pomade and fresh linen" 7409
"scent of roses past their prime, heady" 3809
"scent of roses, violent" 10315
"scent of the lilac, heavy" 3794
"scent of white lilacs" 6499
"scented sibilance" 8526
"scented the languid July day" 8508
"scenting the icy air" 1212
"scents, acrid grease-laden" 4335

"scepter, his long stick-" 3969
"sceptre, wielding the deputy" 6976
Schaeffer, Michael 8322
"schedule, if everything went according to" 9294
"schedule for this narrow-gauge train" 7257
Schedules 2181, 6318, 7257, 9294, 9335
"scheme leads to another, it's how one" 6696
Schemes 258, 4577, 6696
"schemes, his head was full of" 258
"schemes, mind awash with" 4577
Schiff 2685
Schiff, Tevele 7505
Schlifka 3330
Schmertz, Edith 2064
Schmitt, Mr. Wolfgang 7114
"schnapps, maybe a little" 9953
Schnaubelt, Rudolph 2019
Schneider, Paul 5849
Schoessel, Grandma and Granpma 9721
Schoessels, the 9721
Schofield 296
Schofield, Penrod 4670
"scholar bait" 10886
"scholar-gypsy" 1431
"scholars, several hundred" 3333
"scholarship, dance" 1250
"scholarship, pains of" 5448
"scholarship to Oxford" 138
"scholarship voucher" 7907
"scholastic establishment for the sons of gentlemen" 7878
School 579, 657, 837, 2471, 7495, 9274
"school, attend law" 7955
"School, Babbington Grammar" 3722
"school, beaten at" 57
"school, before he went to" 3279
"school, boarding" 4597, 7888
"School, Buntingham Grammar" 298
"School, Carne" 7886
"school, day off from" 837
"school, decided to leave" 2471
"school, dental" 10866
"School, Devon" 7883, 7894
"School, Divinity" 4357
"School, Edmond Fleg Primary" 5965
"school, every one who has been to" 5016
"School, Fern Grammar" 2506
"school, flying" 196
"school, for the first year of" 6651
"school, going to this private" 7900
"school, grade" 7895
"School, Highbury" 7897
"school, his" 4443
"School, Hudson River" 1012
"school, I should of been in" 7495

"school, I was away from this" 3496
"school, Indian Spring" 6408
"School, January" 1945
"School, John Muir High" 7893
"school, junior high" 9397
"school, law" 6750
"School, Marcia Blaine" 977
"school, medical" 4930
"school, no" 2765
"school, obscure private" 6436
"school, old" 2885
"school, prep" 5869
"school, public" 2374
"School, Purlieu Street" 4430
"school, returned from" 4670
"School, St. Louis de France Parochial" 2336
"School, St. Mark's" 1626
"school, seignorial" 7908
"school, Sunday-" 1280
"school, three blocks and all of their lives from" 4876
"School, Tigris" 10987
"school, village" 955
"School, Warrington" 1204
"School, Women's" 2118
"school, your bleeding" 8661
"school again, I'm back at" 3284
"school at Adrianople" 6110
"school at which I was science-master" 7880
"school chapel" 1206
"School Chapel" 9411
"school didn't interfere, when" 5370
"School 50, Public" 970
"school in Vermont, preparatory" 6463
"school 'institution'" 6427
"School of Saint Ignatius, Jesuit Day" 7892
"school stood at the crossroads" 7887
"school . . . was founded" 7891
"school was out" 10623
"school went for a walk, the whole" 6563
"school you went to, what bleeding" 8661
"schoolboy, when he was a" 4284
"schoolboy knows, as every" 10551
"schoolboys, half a thousand" 9411
"schoolboys, procession of" 5788
"schoolboys, troop of" 9816
"schoolgirl" 4183
"schoolgirls, procession of" 5788
"schoolgirls, squealing gray-uniformed" 9641
"school-house" 6408
"schoolhouse" 9219
"schoolhouse, old stone" 864
"schoolhouse stood before the Fire, where the" 3207
"school-master, want to be a" 240
"schoolmaster always wore black" 2862

"schoolmaster was leaving the village" 6092
"school-mastering, this" 6415
"schoolmasters" 6884
"schoolroom" 5316
"school-room" 7877
"school-room at Roselands" 3064
Schools 672, 955, 970, 986, 1204, 1626, 1945, 2724, 3207, 3269, 3270, 3276, 3284, 3496, 3722, 4192, 4216, 4273, 4357, 4430, 4460, 4930, 5821, 5869, 5965, 6110, 6408, 6424, 6436, 6446, 6463, 6563, 6753, 7236, 7336, 7955, 8625, 8661, 8935, 9219, 9250, 9718, 9757, 9945, 10102, 10107, 10866, 10910
"schools, free Council" 7892
"Schools, Nurse Training" 10216
"schools, one of those country day" 6424
"schools, preparatory" 3160
"schools, Protestant mission" 6446
"schools for little boys" 6424
"schoolteacher" 1047
"schoolwork, worry about" 10975
"schooner, little" 8049
"schooner *Castor*, the three-masted" 8058
"schooner *Crab*" 8102
Schreiber, Valerie 7848
Schroeder, Teddy 9049
Schultz 8636
Schultz, Chancellor 5913
Schwartz, Hyman 6514
Schwartz, Ralph 4202
"schwarz" 7572
Schwarzlose 3298
Science 1065, 7164, 10918
"science, miracles of modern" 5699
"science says they are" 7164
"science-master, I was" 7880
"scientific age, this" 10551
"scientific digging" 1384
"Scientist, Mad" 6674
"scientist, young" 2560
Scientists 1065, 2560, 6279, 6409, 6674
"'Scientists', dislike extremely to be called" 6409
"*Scilla nutans*" 3804
"scintillant grass" 10002
"scissors, hair-cutting" 10302
"scolding" 5632
"scooped up his black two-finger ball" 8918
"scooter, old" 2026
"scorched and barren" 730
"scorched the flesh between her cheekbone and her right ear" 8017
"scorching yet, white and" 9163
"scorekeeper" 8918
"scorn, not without" 3516

"scorned by earth and spurned by Heaven" 5165
"scorpion, why didn't I have a" 8021
"scorpions" 10452
"Scorpions, the" 5407
Scorton, Charlie 8683
"Scot, middle-aged" 7918
Scotch Nanny 18
"Scotch peer" 6607
"Scotch prudence" 695
"Scotland" 354, 357, 824, 1171, 1499, 1726, 5761, 6245, 6801, 6884, 6908, 10391
"Scotland, kings of" 3375
"Scotland, northern" 3570
"Scotland, on the north-east coast of" 2173
"Scotland, the north-east of" 9511
"Scotland, the south of" 10679
"Scotland, two-thirds of the size of" 6249
"Scotland, Western Highlands of" 994
"Scotland sniggered, half" 7142
"Scots countryside" 3381
"Scotsman, the" 7142
"Scotsmen, most young" 6398
Scott 8764
Scott, Elizabeth 8349
Scott, Sir William 10658
Scott-King 6427
Scottie 6427
"Scottish gentry" 3550
"Scottish jails, prisoners in" 7142
"Scottish physician" 6901
"Scottish woods, peaceful" 4587
Scott-Williams, Anthony 10200
"scouring of cities" 9738
"Scouting was a funny thing for me to get into" 2004
"scowled, the other half" 7142
"scrambled . . . into a roadside ditch" 3416
"scrambled with other refugees" 3416
"scrambling about upon this whirling globe" 6804
"scrambling and forming into 6:00" 10290
"scrapbook, tucked away in her old" 6861
"scraped a wood match against the wall" 8582
"scraping herself a burrow" 9790
"scraps" 7442
"scraps of paper" 10721
"scraps out of the kindling pile" 1857
"scratch, short of the" 10858
"scratch himself" 5632
"scratched around in the dirt" 3604
"scratched at the bedspread" 2432
"scratched his head" 7646
"scratched there by a cry from the baby" 8115

"scratching around on this limestone peninsula, I was still" 10994
"scratching at a tune on the fiddle" 6218
"scratching comprehensively" 8556
"scratching the underbelly" 6692
"scrawl of gingerbread filigree" 7440
"scrawl of white lines" 495
"scrawled at the end of his farewell note" 2570
"scrawled graffiti" 9253
"scrawled 'Happy Reentry Jesus', someone had" 8318
"scrawled in blood red lettering" 8320
"scrawled it in black marker on the back of my seat" 4779
"scream, she hears Mickey" 10024
"scream, we heard Mother" 7536
"scream and run in" 10066
"scream and scream it does" 540
"scream but there's not even an echo, I" 3706
"scream if I went out on the streets, people would" 73
"scream like that in bed, next time you" 7143
"scream of a brawling harlot" 8777
"scream or faint" 3689
"screamed, cicadas" 4964
"screamed out his anger" 813
"screaming" 4205
"screaming, his sister is" 8238
"screaming, stood" 981
"screaming comes across the sky" 8807
Screams 540, 4964, 7143, 10024
"screams of men" 4469
"screech, half-" 8799
"screen, acting on the" 1317
"screen, I haven't ever been on the" 1316
"screen, in default of a" 122
"screen of bushes" 2890
"screen was abnormally dark" 1323
"screened from the sun by a golden shower creeper" 9668
"screens, winter's white shabby" 10590
"screens had toppled" 10590
"screw just anyone, Harry would not" 7995
"screw this up, no way they could" 7834
"screwing elsewhere, would you mind" 8013
"scribbled a note" 1816
"scribbling spasmodically for some time" 8816
"scribe, a sort of" 6432
"scrimmaging, football team" 8935
"scrimmaging till dark" 9265
"script, in my own" 9262
"Scripture, priest reading" 2461
"scroll, blankest" 514

"scroll curling shut" 8419
"scroll in a curve, the gold" 5647
"scroll is in poor condition" 5532
"scrolls and lyres and marquetry" 8383
"scrolls of words and formulas unfurl in my mind" 8488
"Scrooby" 10086
"scrotum, stuck through his" 1166
"scrub, dried aromatic" 4958
"scrub oak woods" 3907
Scrubb, Eustace Clarence 4740
"scrubby foothills" 10701
"scruples, with so few" 5998
"scrupulous family" 3563
"scrutinise the transient creatures" 519
"scrutinised and studied" 519
"scrutinized his surroundings, swiftly" 9311
"scrutiny, exact" 5307
Scudamore, Joan 8265
"scudded, clouds" 2176
Scudder, Mrs. Katy 9348
"scudding" 7945
"scudding fluffs of cloud" 3667
"scudding off, sent them" 5023
"scudding round my body" 4959
"scuffed the earth with his heavy boot" 8674
"scullery, the back" 4990
"sculpted to resemble a black vine curled into a question mark" 6587
"sculptor, his chief" 6450
"sculptor, I am a" 502
"sculptor, the" 4703
Sculptors 502, 6450
Sculpture 514, 3870
"sculptures wedges from her Howard Johnson hotcakes" 3870
"sculpturing of flesh" 10
"scum, acid-green crust of" 5142
"scurrying forms of the Chinese" 8544
"scurrying from place to place in organized chaos" 4016
"scurrying of mice" 7712
"scuttled up the ladder" 4337
Sea 154, 495, 724, 732, 737, 747, 780, 980, 1480, 2016, 2199, 2598, 2769, 2982, 4056, 4657, 4887, 5011, 5015, 5018, 5023, 5028, 5029, 5030, 5039, 5043, 5045, 5167, 5910, 6061, 6062, 6402, 6403, 6562, 7304, 7647, 7649, 7935, 8034, 8049, 8054, 8057, 8090, 8107, 8122, 8142, 8145, 8147, 8154, 8277, 8394, 8412, 8428, 8491, 8534, 8573, 8722, 8771, 8792, 8835, 8894, 8990, 9069, 9073, 9089, 9319, 9324, 9521, 10014, 10187, 10256, 10449, 10614, 10677, 10696, 10701, 10718, 10719

"sea, above the" 5624
"sea, Aegean" 10716
"Sea, Aegean" 8894
"sea, all the world is" 6062
"sea, alone by the" 2769
"sea, approach it from the" 5038
"sea, approached from the" 8142
"Sea, Baltic" 5016
"Sea, Bering" 4096
"Sea, Black" 4147, 8085
"sea, bounded on one side by the" 6603
"sea, came dripping from the" 10256
"sea, came from the" 7925
"Sea, Caribbean" 4098, 4643
"sea, change in the behavior of the" 737
"sea, changing" 309
"sea, city by the" 1348
"sea, cold" 6402
"sea, cold intoxication of the" 10684
"sea, colour of the" 5330
"sea, Danish" 7914
"Sea, Dead" 4080, 10329
"sea, dim spaces under the" 2946
"sea, distant" 5157
"sea, engulfing waves of a dry" 4377
"Sea, Erythræan" 7648
"sea, fine steep" 1824
"sea, first saw the" 7944
"sea, flowed slowly southward to the" 7666
"sea, follow the" 10354
"sea, gentle" 7929
"sea, gray" 8412
"sea, he came to me from the" 154
"sea, heavy" 6061, 8054
"sea, hills that hemmed the" 6784
"sea, inland" 10329
"Sea, Ionian" 4469
"Sea, Irish" 8090, 9300
"sea, it is almost a" 7664
"sea, land and" 5707
"sea, long blue-green lip of the" 980
"sea, lying low in the" 5031
"sea, mood of the" 5015
"Sea, North" 9208
"sea, oil-smooth" 8122
"sea, on the edge of the" 5233
"sea, on to the" 7668
"sea, primordial Mr. Bubble" 578
"sea, rain driven over the mountains from the" 10711
"sea, riding the" 5039
"sea, rim of the" 8428
"sea, ringed about forever with" 5020
"sea, runs widening to the" 7657
"sea, shallow" 5018
"sea, sharp green Caribbean" 8277
"sea, shelf above the" 5147
"sea, shining" 279
"sea, signs of the" 7931
"sea, six months at" 7910
"sea, soft grey" 8394

"sea, sound of the" 10187
"Sea, South China" 8147
"sea, staring at the" 4224
"sea, straight down to the" 4653
"sea, strange" 9521
"sea, surveying the" 8283
"sea, swept across the" 2237
"sea, the" 665, 3204, 4376, 8534, 10717
"sea, the open" 3181, 7801, 8132
"sea, things that drive men to" 2598
"sea, this curtain of" 7917
"sea, thrust itself out of the" 5028
"sea, to the" 7649
"sea, toward the" 1764
"sea, two legs of" 6390
"Sea, Tyrrhenian" 7909
"sea, unstable" 4034
"Sea, Western" 4572
"sea, whole body of the" 7916
"sea, wrinkled expanse of" 7918
"sea, you are going to" 4117
"sea against the vessel's sides" 8792
"sea and gray sky blend and become one" 7914
"sea and shore, wilderness of" 7228
"sea birds" 774
"sea breaks on the pale line of the shore" 724
"sea breeze" 10014
"sea captains, thousands of hood-eyed" 9247
"sea change" 1254
"sea could be worked up by hand in a few seconds" 1824
"sea falling, sound of the" 8771
"sea falling remotely and eternally" 8771
"sea flat as a plate" 7943
"sea . . . glows rather than sparkles" 7933
"Sea Gull, The" 9393
"sea gulls" 8105
"sea had boomed" 9069
"sea has swallowed her soldiers" 10471
"sea is high again today" 7922
"sea level, the" 7928
"sea licking at his bare brown ankles" 980
"Sea lost nothing of the swallowing identity" 7916
"sea of sheep" 9834
"sea of the city, melted into the" 5790
"sea of vapor" 10260
"sea on one side" 7126
"sea shell, like listening to a" 10002
"sea shifted lazily against the sandy beach" 7930
"sea sparkling in the sun" 5045
"sea that foams and murmurs" 5018
"sea to sea, from" 4825
"sea to shining sea" 279
"sea was a pale elfin green" 6562

"sea was bitter cold" 7920
"sea was very calm" 7912
"sea water, oily" 3693
"sea which heaves and rolls like oil" 6061
"sea which lies before me" 7933
"sea-beach" 6053
"seabird, nimble as a" 8145
"seabird of some kind" 5864
"seabird was flying east" 756
"seabirds, like two enormous" 9324
"Sea-birds that ride on the ninth wave from shore" 747
"seaboard" 6973
"seacoast, many-curved" 4034
"seacoast of Hudson Bay" 4071
"seafaring population" 1346
Seal, Basil 9420
"seal, his" 1525
"seal of secrecy" 5387
"sealer, large" 8048
"sea-loch, tree by the" 9669
"seals, deadly keen on" 10689
"seaman, brown old" 5012
"seaman, experience of a common" 5885
"seaman, Italian" 7934
"seaman, ordinary" 4729
"seamanship, lubberly" 8047
"seamen employed on deck" 8121
"sea-mist was streaming away" 10116
"seamstress, had been a" 6484
Sean 3538
"séance, invitation to assist at a" 2306
"seaplane, commuted to work in a" 231
"seaplanes for hire" 9171
"seaport, great commercial" 3552
"seaport metropolis" 1407
"seaport of the little South American democracy" 6259
"search, began to" 5680
"search, in his long" 7228
"search among the multifarious documents" 5557
"search and hardship, twenty years of" 7216
"search for signs of the sea" 7931
"search of his wife, in" 1591
"search party" 2604
"search the wide slopes of prairie" 7221
"searched for the bell" 9963
"searched long enough, if I" 2607
"searcher after truth" 6478
Searches 470, 953, 991, 1510, 2571, 2604, 2614, 4379, 5557, 5680, 5706, 7216, 7222, 7224, 7228, 7232, 7235, 7717, 7931, 9591
"searching for God knows what" 745
"searching for slugs for his breakfast" 723

"searching for something" 10306, 10421

"searching in the breast pocket of his blue suit" 9591

"searching out my brother" 6797

"searching the reservoir again for Robert" 2564

"searchlight spread upon the Constitutionalists" 4478

"searchlights clustered and hovered" 10494

Sears, Arthur 1110

"seas, asphalt" 4577

"seas, bathwater" 1480

"seas, burdened" 10614

"seas, heaving high" 10614

"seas, stormy" 5011

"seas, unknown" 2016

"sea's flat glittering surface" 8117

"seas of mud" 3653

"seas slanted this way and that" 10614

"sea's slow suck" 8491

"seas together, links two" 1174

"seas were laden with scum" 10614

"seas which surround the Thule of the ancients" 5011

Seascape 5039, 7921, 8132, 8439

"seascape, brisk" 8439

"seasick" 10271

"sea-sick, confoundedly" 126

"sea-sick, feeling rather" 126

"season, against the" 3314

"season, Arctic" 2229

"season, finished off a lousy" 6652

"season, full London" 3813

"season, hasty changing of the" 2235

"season, London" 1337, 9858

"season, long dry" 730

"season, off-" 1778

"season, opening of the" 3417

"season, racing-" 8912

"season, rainy" 2239

"season, stripped by the" 5159

"season, very joyous" 6561

"season after season" 4639

"season as a spotter, my fourth" 8116

"season is also a co-ordinate" 5574

"season more than half over" 9379

"season of Darkness" 3377

"season of dust and languor" 2236

"season of Light" 3377

"season of 1981, during the fall planting" 3449

"season verging upon May" 10773

"season was fast dying of the dust" 9858

"seasoning each morsel of food with the taste of glue" 10831

Seasons 316, 680, 725, 1558, 1563, 1696, 2132, 2156, 2173, 2244, 2305, 3377, 3417, 3801, 3810, 4386, 4400, 4407, 4418, 4424, 4943, 5159, 5574, 5704, 6557, 6801, 7287, 7298, 7312, 7333, 8411, 8584, 8611, 8615, 8623, 9622, 10566, 10567, 10573, 10577, 10587, 10589, 10595, 10603, 10609, 10611, 10618, 10620, 10622, 10624, 10625, 10627, 10631, 10632, 10633, 10638, 10639, 10808

"sea-surrounded nook" 4533

"seat, big plush" 3030

"seat, country" 5067

"seat, his" 8267

"seat, increasingly expensive theater" 10083

"seat, on the high front" 1617

"seat, rickety" 2949

"seat, sheepskin" 2973

"seat, slippery" 9540

"seat, vinyl bucket" 2999

"seat belt decomposes, burnt piece of" 7946

"seat in Parliament" 4339

"seat in the shady side of the bullring" 1549

"seat ... made McKee cold" 1549

"seat of his chair, high crimson velvet" 8348

"seat of the car" 8456

"seat of the concrete bench" 4420

"seat on the left-hand side" 9556

"sea-tangle, quantity of" 7915

"seated a little way off" 8839

"seated at his desk" 1877

"seated at two o'clock in the afternoon on a wooden bench" 8929

"seated gingerly on his Sandy The Sea Serpent rubber lifesaver" 308

"seated in his giant's chair" 3738

"seated myself at the breakfast table" 3698

"seated on a cushion" 3053

"seated on a wooden table" 1166

"seated on the floor of her living room" 8367

"seated with his Queen and only child" 1902

"seating him firmly upon a high straight-backed chair" 3272

Seaton 1767

Seaton, Sir George 3868

"Seatown" 9214

"seats, find your" 630

"seats, one of those ancient but nondescript country" 3160

"seats, wooden" 8150

"seats on the train, the straw" 7274

"seats to rest across" 6584

"Seattle" 1189, 10458

"Seattle, city of" 1391

"seawall, cobbled" 8037

"seawater, handcuffs of" 980

"seawater through the rooms, circulated fresh" 8491

"seaworthy beasts" 8169

Sebastian, Brother 9609

"Sebastian, S." 652

"sec, I've only got a" 10321

"sec left, only a" 10321

"second, fraction of a" 8039

"second coming, the" 8201

"second grade, as far back as the" 10886

"second-hand one" 839

"secrecy, seal of" 5387

"secret, few have been in my" 7948

"secret, is to betray no" 6096

"secret, made it no" 8841

"secret, meditated in" 6928

"secret, Tunis had a" 7962

"secret and desperate society" 2837

"secret is told" 7960

"Secret of a Successful At Home" 6768

"secret of my life, the great" 7951

"secret of the treasure" 7950

"secret servants" 1834

"secretary, Bishop's" 1928

"secretary, deputy" 6999

"Secretary, First" 247

"secretary, his" 3333, 4249, 5311

"secretary, my" 1925

"secretary, perfect" 9880

"secretary hard of hearing, a male" 8636

"Secretary of State" 6995

"Secretary to the Repeal Association" 5194

"secretive, I became" 5226

"secretive, try to be" 975

Secrets 4696, 5480, 6928, 6957

"secrets, all families got" 7961

"secrets, I know more" 7959

"secrets, keeping" 7958

"secrets locked inside its world" 5480

"secrets of pool and cascade" 7652

"section, comfortable but not elegant older" 2001

"secure, scarcely feel" 5082

"security clearance, three have top-" 3626

"security system" 2046

"security wing of Durham Jail" 2033

"sedan, green Jaguar" 9300

"sedan chair was carried in at a run" 1651

Seddon, Miss Florence 3825

Seddon, Reverend Gerald 1500

"Sedgefield" 2033

"seduce her, trying successfully to" 2794

Seduction 2794, 5471

"seductive, how" 7424

"see, asks me what I" 8290

"see, could still" 8297

"see, first thing you" 3259

"see, in the *end* he would" 3345

"see, something to" 2267

"see, suddenly I couldn't" 8187
"see, what do I" 8281
"see any light yet" 5306
"see anyone, we no longer" 5302
"see either way, you can" 9160
"see every detail of the Harcourt place" 4891
"see Gordon, finally I" 1769
"see her, when I" 2812
"see her almost every day" 6291
"see her dimly" 10082
"see her entering the church" 3735
"see her to-day, if I don't" 1578
"see him, I didn't really" 5855
"see him, I don't" 6699
"see him, think I" 4904
"see in it, what do they" 692
"see in the mirror someone on the twenty-fourth floor across the street" 6304
"see into the ground" 8289
"see Iris Allbright again, would not" 6790
"see it ten miles out" 9228
"see Lilia off" 3993
"see me, called to" 6688
"see me, they could not" 9099
"see me in the surgery" 9987
"see me now, if only you could" 7121
"see me now, you should" 4354
"see me the other day, came to" 9986
"*see* my sister's diary, I can still" 2544
"see nothing, I" 8290
"see of it, what you could" 7316
"see one of them, the first to" 2613
"see out of them" 8285
"see the beach below" 2730
"see the strangers" 9099
"see the top of the steps, he could not" 2764
"see there" 4861
"see things as they are" 10761
"see us, Grammy couldn't" 4488
"see what I mean, if you" 9697
"see what it was, to" 9526
"see without my spectacles, I can't" 8261
"see you, he wants to" 9952
"see you, leaning over a bit to" 10408
"see you again, I shall never" 2552
"see you and the world that surrounds you both" 3363
"see you ever again, had not expected to" 8195
"see you in the library" 9871
"see yourself, really" 7484
"seed, spreading" 6398
"seed of desire" 3412
"seed you need, all the" 6126
"seedpods, long black" 9682
"seed-time" 3799

See-ho-kee 4822
"seeing a sailboat, early to be" 2285
"seeing at once, have all of the" 1639
"seeing in a moment of vertigo some terror" 6790
"seeing it, without really" 8296
"seeing Mr. Llewellyn off" 1687
"seeing people on other days" 9859
"seeing through it on a dark Parisian street" 151
"seeing where they had been with me" 7494
"seeings and thinkings, my" 8171
"seek him out" 7446
"seek my fortune in the wide world" 6823
"seek them in the land of the Benjamites" 7217
"seekers in the desert, turbaned disconsolate" 1302
"seeking breakfast" 7235
"seeking the Good Thing" 253
"seemed to do so, he only" 4216
"seemed to me, so it has" 5274
"seems to be, what it" 1430
"seems to me, it" 3704, 7118
"seen anything like it, had never" 8169
"seen before, likes of which had never been" 772
"seen enough, Frankie had" 8291
"seen for more than a year, he hadn't" 7636
"seen from a great distance" 6073
"seen from eye level" 5145
"seen from upsidedown (when I'd do my headstand in the yard)" 6075
"seen Gerry Berger, since I'd" 5951
"seen her, had never" 3540
"seen it, unless you had" 9378
"seen it all, thought she'd" 6469
"seen once before and wanted to see again, what it had" 483
"seen the last of the elephant" 465
"seen through a stand of white birch trees" 5341
"seen you, so many years since I have" 3919
"seep out slowly through a book" 1801
"seep through his eyelids" 10200
"seepage from oil springs" 8165
"sees, first" 5111
"sees, what the boy" 8276
"sees and hears a different world, each generation" 3361
"sees himself spatchcocked" 4897
"seesawing between winter and spring" 10632
Segal, Dr. 813
"Segget, borough of" 4053
"Segovia" 10388
"seignorial school" 7908

"Seine, the" 9286
"Seine, the Thames flowed into the" 9743
"Seine, walking along the" 2529
"seized by a whirlpool of despair" 3705
"seized up altogether, hasn't" 94
"Selampang" 198
"Selbury Quade" 3248
Selby, Mr. 6429
Selden 8173
"selection and elimination" 10995
Self 3845, 5355
"self, a former" 11000
"self, absolutely centered upon his own silly" 5900
"self, conquered the" 3845
"self, its old" 1343
"self, my harmless and sanguine" 5355
"self, recovering his nonsurgery" 4281
"self, why conquer the" 3845
Self-appraisal 846, 5240, 6840, 7469, 7965, 9447
"self-confident and secure" 7980
"self-congratulation of city dwellers is endless" 7129
Self-consciousness 46, 9455
"self-consciousness" 274
Self-control 387, 394, 3320, 5835, 9968
"self-control, unless you have unusual" 5835
"self-criticism, not too much" 9263
"self-deception, masters of" 5241
Self-doubt 2625
"self-emasculation" 1444
"self-indulgence" 8488
Self-knowledge 1974, 2050, 2409, 3522, 5265, 5610, 5922, 10151
"self-preservation, instincts for" 1209
"self-realizing about that, something" 4648
"self-reproach, a feeling of" 2926
"self-sacrifice for a whole" 1209
Self-satisfaction 10759
"self-satisfied" 5296
"self-seeking memoirs" 7000
"self-styled historian" 4503
"selfish, completely" 4354
Selkirk 6434
"Selkirks, the" 8851
"sell a few million paper cups" 9439
"sell back" 10937
"sell eggs and cream" 8893
"sell his house, would not have to" 6124
"sell things, people striving to" 1045
Semana, Miguel 2927
"semester, during the spring" 9290
"seminars, conducts his" 3280
"Seminary, General Theological" 3429
"seminary of learning" 7875

"Senate, U.S." 7831
"Senator, the" 8864
"Senator, The" 40
"Senator, the late" 6994
"send for me so late, didn't usually"
    3474
"send it, I know I'm not going to"
    1957
"send out for pizzas, we can
    always" 2550
"sending the same morse-code
    symbol" 7260
"sending you this account of all that
    I have seen and done" 2552
"senility, beginnings of" 7456
"senility, ripe old" 116
"seniors, in the second row of" 4192
"Senlis" 9929
"sensation, a novel" 9288
"sensation, cause of a" 10126
"sensation is too much the result of
    selection and elimination" 10995
"sensations, alter the ordinary"
    10280
"sensations, unwelcome" 4439
"sense, a strange overpowering
    mystical" 9118
"sense, doesn't make" 8743
"sense, good natural" 5884
"sense, if you got any" 2430
"sense, in a" 4751, 8999
"sense, made no" 5722
"sense, makes too much" 5436
"sense, reality never makes" 5436
"sense, showing more originality
    than" 5803
"sense, the lapping waves of" 10202
"sense a presence" 7109
"sense in it, find even one little
    thread of" 9009
"sense of appetite and glad expec-
    tation" 6311
"sense of circling from nowhere to
    nowhere" 211
"sense of expectancy" 10077
"sense of the wonder of existence"
    9118
"sense of unreality" 10173
"sensed the presence of the child in
    the room" 10304
"*Sensei*" 1081
"senseless fight" 1846
Senses 947, 3361
"senses, bring you to your" 4971
"senses, came to his" 9311
"senses, coming to life of each of
    her" 10148
"senses, lost your" 6619
"senses, sharpens the" 3477
"senses, voluptuous heightening of
    all" 380
"senses had been excited, my" 947
"sensible, I am extremely" 5397
"sensitive to all the lunkheads, be-
    ing too" 9265

"sensitive to his own heartbeats"
    5619
"sensitive to the looks of people"
    10798
"sensitiveness, painful to my" 8299
"sensual perception" 5424
"sent a message" 6014
"sent away from London during
    the war" 1282
"sent by President Jefferson into
    the wilderness" 7232
"sent for the beer" 10921
"sent from her home on a farm in
    Maine" 4186
"sent him a note" 2684
"sent his other children telegrams,
    would have" 1761
"sent me to a boarding-school" 7888
"sent me to her" 1079
"sent on the order" 8734
"sentence, compose the" 5473
"sentence, last" 5541
"sentence, my own first" 711
"sentence, satisfactory opening"
    6357
"sentence, the first" 711
"sentence which I lost, this is the
    opening" 5441
"sentence which used to fascinate
    me" 2379
"sentenced to death" 3407
"sententiæ, quot homines tot" 5013
"sentient being, simple" 10913
"sentiment, backward in" 5889
"sentimental blue eyes" 4438
"sentimentally, ironically or" 1302
"sentries, two" 3482
"Seoul" 10500
"Seoul, main road to" 3416
"Seoul Korea" 6881
"separate from you and from each
    other" 7855
"separated by a ha-ha from the view
    it contemplates" 5164
"separated from Josh" 10857
"separated from the past and the
    future" 9615
"separated so totally from the men
    below" 992
Separation 992, 2681, 10857
"separation, a trial" 2681
"separation, point of" 4085
"sepia sun" 8164
"September" 120, 217, 599, 865,
    1007, 1086, 1382, 1498, 1500,
    1590, 1642, 1653, 1706, 1891,
    2082, 2136, 2143, 2144, 2147,
    2153, 2173, 2185, 2238, 2532,
    2537, 2540, 2616, 2660, 3756,
    4149, 4383, 4386, 4398, 4402,
    4596, 4966, 5098, 5120, 5551,
    5854, 6137, 6323, 6437, 6446,
    6577, 6620, 6881, 7326, 7416,
    7514, 7619, 7763, 7907, 7953,
    8012, 8057, 8413, 8592, 9149,

9328, 9377, 9537, 9546, 9601,
    9674, 9775, 9857, 10143, 10146,
    10185, 10361, 10411, 10433, 10451,
    10477, 10482, 10496, 10613,
    10782, 10794
"September golden and hot" 10622
"September's ominous departure"
    10700
"septic tank" 3983
"Sepulchre, Holy" 8646
"Sepulveda, traffic on" 2986
"sequel will show, as the" 2819
"sequence of events" 2616
"sequestered nook" 4304
"Seraglio, the" 1051
"seraphic face" 969
Seraphine, Sister 1281
"Serbians" 4055
Sercomb, Lady Ann 5930
Serena 9716
"serene and comfortable" 3248
"serene on the doorstep of her
    father's house" 10872
"serene voice" 1281
"serene was a word you could put
    to Brooklyn New York" 1388
"Serenissima of all Serenissime"
    5297
"Serenity of Universes" 2626
Serge 8906
"serge, suit of white" 10336
"sergeant, probably a" 2909
Sergei 7585
"serial formula, I chose the" 6224
"serial work, ninth number of a"
    8955
"serious, might not be anything
    very" 9998
"serious, passionately" 8976
"serious, too" 4201
"serious, you can be" 6532
"seriously, I didn't take him" 10544
"seriously, take themselves too"
    5235
"seriousness, brow furrowed in"
    8873
"sermon" 1533
"sermon, preaching a" 1538
"sermon   was deadly dull" 7513
"sermon-writing" 3376
Sermons 1533, 7513
"sermons, plenty of" 5433
"*Serpent*, gun-boat" 928
"Serpent, still doing service to the"
    5392
"serpent looked like, what do you
    imagine the" 2637
"serpent struck down by a sword"
    1934
"serpentined beneath high clumps
    of gorse" 9153
"serpents, shape of two linked"
    2844
"servant, her Negro" 9955
"servant, his" 8483, 10196, 10649

"servant, how near I came to being her life-long" 5397
Servants 1673, 3325, 10915
"Servants, her" 4221
"servants at Cripplegate" 6457
"servants at the vicarage had gone to bed" 10919
"servants fall silent" 1673
"served him well, I have" 6450
"served sovereigns of foreign countries" 3557
"served under him, not because my father had ever" 364
"served with, so many of the men he" 322
"service, at your" 10007
"Service, Colonial" 8078
"service, constant good" 10900
"Service, Foreign" 4764
"service, too old for the" 2936
"service at Merrion Chapel, the mid-week" 6630
"service in the school chapel in memory of the dead" 1206
"service of the King" 8641
"service station" 1080
"service station, Skelly" 1044
"service stations" 1039
"services, the" 3951
"services for the dead at Dong Xuyen" 3954
"services of the Church" 3680
"services rendered him by Beau Beamish" 7708
"serving a writ" 6948
"serving first with the Balloon Section" 8695
Seryozha 7585
"session, now in" 5210
Sestri Levante, the steamer" 8085
"set a trap" 7741
"set Carney ashore at Packet Harbor" 3534
"set down my thoughts, I want very much to" 3495
"set forth in the year 1855" 6104
"set his foot on God's earth again, he would never" 2311
"set in the college, largest and leading" 7876
"set me up" 7054
"set off at a furious pace" 1626
"set our old nigger Jim free" 1160
"set out, John Brodrick" 1615
"set out from the inn" 6560
"set out on foot" 10431
"set out on the three-mile walk" 9890
Seth 5189, 7801
Seton, Miss Isobel 1916
"sets out down lower Broadway" 8694
"settee, a low" 6519
Setter 141
"setting, has for most of us but one" 5566

"setting, hope it will prove an advantageous" 3360
"setting, incongruous" 5419
"setting out cups and saucers" 9355
"setting sail for the open sea" 7801
"setting sun" 10701
"setting up her loom" 10952
"settings, rural" 5166
"settle, a carved oak" 10086
"settle anything, being dead doesn't" 2437
"settle for life" 6558
"settled" 5294
"settled, long" 3549
"settled down, time he" 425
"settled down again, people" 3303
"settled down on its steady course" 199
"settled himself against the gnarled bole of an olive tree" 5716
"settled in, they" 6156
"settled in our new house" 6094
"settled on America's northeast coast" 7531
"settlement, ancient though not very populous" 7875
"settlement, European" 4030
"settlement, frontier" 6814
"Settlement, International" 6901
"settlement, small" 1397
"settlement, some rare Acadian" 6249
"settlement, the" 1436
"settlement, tiny Spanish" 1392
"settlements, small farm" 4073
"settlement's first days" 2574
"settlements that repose on the edge of nowhere" 5166
"settler, French" 503
Settlers 3641, 4030, 6179, 6813, 7531
"settlers, adventurous" 6813
"settlers, beleaguered" 6179
"settlers, blood and screams of the" 7409
"settlers, invasions of land-hunting" 3105
"settlers in the valley" 3641
"settlers on the American prairies" 3219
"settles slowly into the slip" 8068
"settling down" 5298
"settling himself in his seat" 3711
"seven, Titus is" 972
"seven, when I was" 9321
"seventeen, was just" 1715
"seventeen, when I was" 9279
"seventh, bottom half of the" 8915
"seventies, in the" 9759
"seventies, the early" 8740
"seventy, I am now" 8494
"seventy, when you were past" 2337
"seventy thousand, at least" 3746
"sever this hour from the rest of the day" 3032

"severe outbreaks of cavalry" 296
Severian 4299
"severity of the Christmas of 187-" 8960
Sevier, Lieutenant-Colonel John 2147
Sevillas, Magda 7459
"Seville" 1069, 2558
Sewall, Mr. Horace 1199
"Seward Peninsula" 4096
Sewell 7552
Sewing 4119, 5355, 10934
"sewing, my wife has brought out some" 4119
"sewing magician" 6484
"sewing needle" 8760
"sewing-machine shop" 1609
"sewn by the same dressmaker" 2864
Sex 5670, 7874, 8677, 10186
"Sex" 5489
"sex, father of my" 7554
"sex, no doubt of his" 9839
"sex, not expected to be still compelled by" 8011
"sex, of the wrong" 2936
"sex, when it comes to evading" 7988
"sex acts in the hall" 7984
"sex and adventure" 5453
"sex instinct" 7982
"sex or love, was it" 8028
"sex with Teo" 8016
"sexes, bicycle between the" 977
"sexist" 1214
"sexual alchemy" 7979
"sexual identity, not" 10913
Sexuality 8018, 8026, 8556, 10913
"sexy-looking, they're very" 342
"Sha'ar Hagolan" 5716
"shabbiest suburb in Bonn" 4389
"shack, his" 2095
"shack, lobster" 3431
"shack, two-room" 3857
"shack towns" 1039
"shackled to his seat" 9647
Shadbold, G.F.H. 5507
Shadbolt, Bruno 7219
Shade, John Francis 5452
Shade, Justine 6017
"shade, a more delicate and significant" 10774
"shade, in the cool" 8038
"shade, lounging in the" 5626
"shade, sun-dappled" 9674
"shade, there is no" 4407
"shade, willow" 5121
"shade along the edges of buildings, sought" 4431
"shade of an apple tree" 3119
"shade of old beech woods" 9738
"shade of the big walnut tree" 8739
"shade of the great white pines" 8209
"shade of the sunblinds that screened the shopwindows" 10364

"shade of their messes, escape to the" 8121

"shaded by a sloping terrace roof" 3199

"shaded by big cotton-wood-trees" 1357

"Shades, Associated" 2016

"shadow, before they even made a" 6942

"shadow, grotesquely elongated" 6647

"shadow, I watch a gull's" 9442

"shadow, just a" 8039

"shadow, light and" 3981

"shadow, like a five o'clock" 770

"shadow, mountain's rain-" 7329

"shadow, only a" 8035

"shadow, sun and" 4010

"shadow, thin shaft of" 10157

"shadow, too high for a" 757

"shadow across a hard earth, casting their" 5149

"shadow cast by the wall of the Bibighar Gardens" 5152

"shadow fell, a" 8033

"shadow float among feet on the concrete" 9442

"shadow of a promontory" 8034

"shadow of God on earth" 7807

"shadow of night crept gradually along the Mediterranean" 2202

"shadow of the Confederate monument" 9775

"shadow solidifies in the mist" 8037

Shadows 1036, 2199, 2951, 3981, 4010, 5326, 5632, 7699, 7806, 9442, 10260

"shadows" 5632

"shadows, archaic" 7527

"shadows, be there in the" 8499

"shadows, dim" 8032

"shadows, encased him in" 509

"shadows, he drew back into the" 8899

"shadows, in the slatted" 6744

"shadows, lifted the" 2237

"shadows, lightwire" 10416

"shadows, meager" 5704

"shadows, peripheral" 10260

"shadows, purple" 2199

"shadows, slanting" 1036

"shadows, sucked up their own" 5704

"shadows, the" 523

"shadows, wavering" 5326

"shadows cast on the wall in front" 220

"shadows in the lane, black" 522

"shadows . . . just now overflowed onto the broad levels of the river" 8031

"shadows long gathering in the valleys and the woods" 8031

"shadows of clouds" 3179

"shadows of its orchards" 6249

"shadows of the lime-trees strike obliquely across the gravel" 2951

"shadows of the porch" 5620

"shadows of vine-leaves" 1219

"shadows over the water" 7672

"shadows stretch over the patch of grass" 8038

"shadows toward the center of his life, cast shuddering" 5503

"shadows turned gray and gray turned black" 2199

"shadowy with trees overhead" 9184

Shaffer, Gerda 4777

Shaffer, Mrs. Alec 4777

"shaft, bitter" 392

"shaft, up the" 3295

"shaft blew from the firth" 392

"shafts, long yellow" 5338

"shafts of light" 5314

"shaggy, you're getting a bit" 6681

Shagpat 8040

"Shah brothers" 1038

"shake his head" 2351

Shakely, Ruby 6485

Shakely, Vernon 6485

"shaken hands with her opposite neighbour, she could have" 8342

"Shaker Heights" 4577

Shakespeare 9401

Shakespeare, William 2931

"Shakespeare still meant something to a lot of people, days when" 9401

"Shakespeare's sonnets" 5520

"Shakettes, the" 6485

"shaking, a" 7281

"shaking a lot, my hands were" 4579

"shaking and trembling" 7945

"shaking and trying not to throw up" 151

"shaking him" 305

"shaking my foot" 10179

"shaking their ball trim" 7707

"shako made of white fur" 6967

Shakuntala 3473

"Shalisha, land of" 7217

Shallop, Mrs. Sidney 2608

"sham hero" 4459

Shaman 7281

"Shambles, the" 1027

Shame 3306, 3308, 3393, 3975, 5580, 7748

"shame, felt no" 9422

"shame, what a" 7497

"shame and horror, the confus'd" 6577

"shame forbade Jacob" 3306

"shame me, circumstances which" 497

"shame waiting, there was nothing but" 7748

"shampooed her short slightly graying hair" 564

Shanelle 4210

Shanette 4210

"Shanghai" 773, 3569, 10524, 10536

Shannon, Margy 9147

Shannon, Mrs. 9370

Shannon, Sunny 9687

"shanties" 6570

"shanties, dusty rows of whitewashed" 3238

"shanty along the run" 543

"shanty-town" 2047

"shape, clumsy" 224

"shape, its nonlineal" 4485

"shape, no" 1389

"shape of the leafless trees, delicate" 10414

"shape of the place, something about the" 9999

"shaped, beautifully" 6073

"shaped and tinkered with it" 5539

"shaped like a nice big fat Negro yam" 4100

"shaped them into a people" 7810

"share, more than her" 6652

"share, more than their fair" 7961

"sharecropper's cabin" 826

"shared an umbrella" 3940

"shared it with the boy who sold bibles" 2911

"shared with the six other 'pretty waiter girls'" 7487

Sharfenstein 6514

Sharing 8574

"sharing a cell" 7140

"Shark, a too-delicate" 9397

Sharkey, Canon 2451

"sharking out of lane" 9807

"sharks, the minutes swam by like" 9489

"sharp and quick" 967

Sharpe the taximan 6294

"sharp-pointed" 9681

"Shaston" 10333

"shattered it, whistles" 10503

"shattered over the dresser" 10227

"shattered the deceptive quiet" 7275

"shave him on the verandah" 8046

"shave Shagpat the son of Shimpoor" 8040

"shaved, showered and" 8486

"shaved himself, methodically" 8045

"shaved on holy days" 1503

"shaven, clean-" 4266

"shaven, only partly" 1838

"shaven head" 5971

Shaving 1838, 9920

"shaving, as he was finishing" 9920

"shaving bowl, white" 8044

"shaving stand, mahogany" 8044

Shaw, Emily 4873

Shaw, Kiki 2583

"shawl, her red-brown" 10357

"shawl, his woollen" 8115

"shawl, orange-coloured" 4143

"shawl, paisley" 8376

"shawl with hand-knotted fringes" 8376
Shawn 3538
"she was his" 8144
"sheaf of pages, an unglued and incomplete" 6698
"shed, potting" 6919
"shed, Uncle Billy's" 10547
"shed of unpainted boards" 8665
"shed with copper bulbs on the roof, brick" 3209
"sheds, customs" 8115
"sheds, wooden" 8699
"Sheen, East" 8854
"sheen, sad ruinous" 7345
"sheen created by the Upper Thames" 9076
"sheep, cattle and" 3667
"sheep, sea of" 9834
"sheep and the goats foraged" 5704
"sheep had been skittish with mating" 420
"sheep in a fold" 6266
"sheep pasture" 3634
"sheep-shearing time" 3636
"sheepskin, his" 1548
"sheer massivity" 9221
"sheet, clean white" 131
"sheet bunched at her feet, crumpled" 9355
"sheets, rainbow" 1606
"sheets, shivering wave-like" 9241
"sheets of red-painted tin" 4632
"sheets provided by the Hôtel Meurice" 10119
"Sheffield" 3893, 7261
"shelf, circular" 8044
Shell 7723
"shell of it is still there" 3085
Shelley, Sir Roderick 1971
"shells, three extra" 5724
"shells leaped and crackled round the aircraft" 10505
"shell-shock" 4616
Shelly 8469
"shelter, driven for" 7284
"shelter, free" 2585
"shelter, its" 1298
"shelter, looked around for" 7299
"shelter, providing safe" 5015
"shelter, thatch" 3092
"shelter among the rocks, sought" 4478
"shelter for poor people on the roads" 9230
"shelter from the night wind" 10734
"shelter of a distant village" 6531
"shelter of Gandalf's cloak" 8269
"shelter of the deep round valley" 1433
"sheltered generations of tranquil family life" 3248
"sheltered so many hundreds of Saracinesca" 3071
Shelton 5895

"shelves, names lined up upon her" 903
Shema 4810
Shenstone, Michael 8976
Shep 10049
Shepard, Evan 5671
"Shepford" 9173
"shepheard, hopelesse" 7370
"shepherd up ahead" 5824
"shepherdless" 8400
"Shepherd's Bush" 9778
Sheppard, John 355
Sheridan 10543
"sheriff, the" 2304
"sheriff marched into court" 2045
"sheriff of Cactus County" 6948
"sheriff of Twin River County" 6952
"sheriff reached the jail" 2022
"sheriff's office" 6184
"sheriff's office, hold down the" 7616
Sherman 4019
"Sherman, town of" 4927
Sherrill, Luther 3933
"sherry" 377
"sherry, invariably served him" 4272
Shetland, Joseph 8654
"Shetlands had been raised, where" 3654
"shield, bulbous and curly stone" 3589
"shield, radio-quiet" 9756
"shielded his head with his briefcase" 8179
"shielding their eyes with their hands" 8093
"shields, gilded plaster" 7762
"shields gorgeously emblazoned" 1196
"shieling, the" 3667
"shift, begins slowly to" 5575
"shift a jot, I did not" 8172
"shift and bustle overhead, nervous" 5023
"shift groaning into first" 9201
"shifted awkwardly as though his limbs were hurting him" 2595
"shifty as a shortstop" 9799
"Shikasta" 5497
Shilda 6337
Shilepsky, Tillie 5820
Shillitoe, Samson 5454
"shimmer of soft amber light" 9400
"shimmer off the vat" 189
"shimmering" 3265
"shimmering, heat rises" 9616
"shimmering curtain of snowflakes" 8597
"shimmering in visible waves again" 5340
Shimon 7641
Shimpoor 8040
Shinefeld, Dr. Lulu 6897
"shingle, bare" 10717

"shingles, encasing" 3159
"shining dimly over the details of a cold cheerless room" 7032
"shining fairways" 5627
"shining in the sun, his hard diamondback pattern" 2851
"shining like patent leather" 2727
"shining on the smoother bark" 3894
"shining sea" 279
"shining upon worn tapestries" 5324
"shining wetly through the gathering clouds" 8418
"ship, aboard" 2805
"Ship, Big" 10901
"ship, cargo" 5916
"ship, creak of the" 8504
"ship, deck of the rocking" 6091
"ship, fleet supply" 8121
"ship, hello" 8108
"Ship, His Majesty's Packet" 8152
"ship, light" 8055
"ship, like the hull of a" 7856
"ship, little" 3514
"ship, merchant" 8132
"ship, not a" 7685
"ship, sea-worn and battered" 8066
"Ship, Troop-" 8677
"ship, troop transfer" 8704
"ship, wheelhouse of a" 6501
"ship and dock, green lane between" 8157
"ship as she lay at anchor" 928
"ship came into the bay" 8103
"ship *Cynthia*, the good" 8120
"ship ghosting shoreward through a fogbank" 8142
"ship left Buenos Aires" 9651
"ship of state, made fast his" 7799
"ship rounding the harbor" 4587
"ship swayed uneasily at her anchor" 8086
"ship was ready to sail" 8166
Shipley, Andrew 10051
"ship-of-the-line, Third Rate" 8122
"shipowner's small daughter" 7843
Ships 47, 406, 570, 766, 928, 941, 992, 1069, 1598, 1711, 2188, 2491, 3116, 3494, 3534, 3693, 3791, 4246, 4257, 4270, 4535, 4587, 4730, 4731, 4745, 4916, 5031, 5517, 5628, 6121, 6216, 6363, 6888, 7304, 7307, 7799, 7919, 8504, 8563, 8657, 8677, 8792, 8987, 8990, 9075, 9089, 9247, 9413, 9431, 9508, 9534, 9575, 9603, 9607, 9619, 9651, 10100, 10704, 10729
"ships, calk his" 8165
"ships, masts of the" 3116
"ships, men anchored their" 1069
"ships, one of the" 3550
"ships, passing" 5031
"ships, sailing the sky in" 9745
"ships, thirty years in many" 8075

"ships, two" 8990
"ships, white sails of" 8090
"ships and vessels, His Majesty's" 8102
"ships are sunk or fled" 10471
"ship's armour" 1005
"ships at a distance" 8083
"ships of war, British" 2491
"ship's railing, gripped the" 3593
"ships that have come to grief" 9089
"ship's wake" 4257
"ships were burning in the harbor" 3791
"shipwreck" 1217
"shipyard, the" 8448
Shira 2682
"Shiraz, The" 2373
Shires, Daniel 7702
Shirl 7062
Shirley, Howard 1973
Shirley, Janet 1973
"shirt, blue" 9612
"shirt, blue tee" 4203
"shirt, clean denim" 3646
"shirt, green drill" 2833
"shirt, lime green" 2111
"shirt, loose khaki" 2875
"shirt, textured pink" 2848
"shirt, thin and ragged linen" 1287
"shirt, white" 970, 10421
"shirt a shoit, called his" 10901
"shirt adhered to his back" 8674
"shirt off her back" 1798
"shirts, filthy" 5190
"shirts, my two" 1607
"shirts, put on plaid flannel" 5301
"shirts, sport" 309
"shirts, take off our" 328
"shirts, white cotton" 954
"shirt-sleeved" 4069
"shirtsleeves, clotted" 8864
"shirtwaist, my" 8500
"shit, goat" 7871
"shit, I do not need this" 68
"shit, I don't believe this" 2749
"shit, is a" 4982
"shit, shooting the" 3057
"shit, work in" 8542
"shit in a cardboard box, packing my" 7148
Shiuli 7434
Shiveley, Uncle Preston 3105
"shivered" 6395
"shivered, she" 1556
"shivered in the wind" 10750
"shivering, pronounced" 7281
"shivering and lonely" 1561
"shivering hips and quivering buttocks" 7945
"shivering in the grey dawn" 5940
"shivering wave-like sheets" 9241
"shoals, coral" 1480
"shoals, pebbly" 9740
"shoals, those hungry" 9089
Shock 188, 2795, 3291, 8175, 8183,

8184, 8188, 8193, 8196, 8197, 8201, 8956, 10283
"shock, electric" 10283
"shock, it was that much of a" 2677
"shock, no" 3291
"shock, only a minor" 1925
"shock, shell-" 4616
"shock, welcome" 188
"shock her, said something designed to" 5187
"shock of hearing the telephone ring" 1104
"shock of seeing you" 2795
"shock to me" 8201
"shocked" 8188
"shocked, I was" 8196
"shocked him to be so unready for his own" 1507
"shocker, yesterday was a" 2169
"shocking, nothing is more" 108
"shocking night" 6368
Shockproof 8874
Shodbutt 5943
"shoe, ill-fitting" 5265
"shoe, tip of my" 39
"shoe store, his father's" 9708
"shoe-polish, can of" 10921
Shoes 39, 1601, 2835, 3486, 4277, 4950, 8780, 10457
"shoes, clean his own" 6021
"shoes, dust on his" 10365
"shoes, dusty" 4176
"shoes, frayed tennis" 2875
"shoes, Grandpa's brogan" 8780
"shoes, greasestained tennis" 2690
"shoes, inside one of his" 6871
"shoes, jogging" 3486
"shoes, little white" 4181
"shoes, patent-leather brown and white" 1982
"shoes, tennis" 1002
"shoes, thin soles of their" 10457
"shoes, wearing" 8923
"shoes, without putting on her" 9916
"shoes dropped from his hand, one of the heavy" 1601
"shoes sinking in the sand" 10421
"shone almost blindingly in the sunlight" 5131
"shone and clattered like a street fair" 9191
"shone dazzling white" 6079
"shone hot and clear, morning" 2216
"shone in a white harmony" 8586
"shone like a tangle of red-hot wires" 983
"shone like gold" 8363
"shook hands with the young priest" 1504
"shook his fist" 9310
"shook his younger brother, vigorously" 10115
"shook out a fountain pen" 4274

"shook the hand of Father Urban" 1303
"shook the rusty fringes of palm-leaf" 10701
"shook their heads" 6019
"shook them together so that the edges were level" 5415
Shoolpi 8040
"shoot, youthful" 9660
"shoot the gulls" 4257
Shooting 576, 9842
"shooting" 6965
"shooting, a day's" 10332
"shooting a slingshot" 662
"shooting at his new doghouse with a .44 Magnum" 576
"shooting he was mixed up in" 985
"shooting snooker" 7047
"shooting star of unusual brilliance and duration" 533
"shooting the shit" 3057
Shootings 74, 985, 2028, 2069, 4250, 4261, 4267, 6191, 7024, 9848, 9850, 9854
"shoots, tender" 3979
"shop, a certain" 2290
"shop, antique" 1017, 10399
"shop, bake" 9876
"shop, coffee" 4904
"shop, delicatessen" 3101
"shop, firearm" 4245
"shop, good" 2697
"shop, her" 7529, 10970
"shop, inconspicuous" 1012
"shop, left his" 1010
"shop, modest" 1025
"shop, O'Farrell's tool" 7019
"shop, pastry-cook's" 5079
"shop, poulterer's" 5792
"shop, sewing-machine" 1609
"shop, stumbled out of the" 143
"shop, sweet" 10831
"shop, tailor" 1704
"shop, the" 4127
"shop, tobacconist's" 5398
"shop, went into a" 1046
"shop of the Little Chemist" 9209
"shop so full, why is the" 1048
"shop to shop" 9616
"shop which he managed" 8347
"shopkeeper, every would-be" 7771
"shopkeepers" 8813
"shoppers, last-minute" 3017
Shopping 1024, 1031, 4123, 5365, 7099, 10369
"shopping, a day's Christmas" 10369
"shopping, used to dislike" 5365
"Shopping Plaza" 1122
"Shop-Rite, Tano's" 3032
Shops 675, 1010, 1011, 1012, 1013, 1017, 1025, 1026, 1045, 1046, 1048, 1063, 1064, 1082, 1084, 1088, 1657, 2290, 2697, 2905, 4245, 5398, 5607, 5621, 7237,

7295, 7529, 8308, 9876, 10395, 10399, 10783, 10970
"shops, area of" 5607
"shops, closed and barred florist" 10438
"shops, Jews" 7059
"shops, look at the" 1084
"shops, shuttered" 9828
"shops, souvenir" 4436
"shops, their" 1082
"shops stand three across" 1088
"shops that sell real things close down" 1064
Shore, Eugene 1983
"shore, along the" 4064
"shore, came to" 6155
"shore, down on the" 5315
"shore, on the" 9224
"shore, pleasant" 4631
"shore, Plymouth" 7594
"shore, swerve of" 1175
"shore of a great bay" 1421
"shore of Lake George" 5154
"shore of Lake Superior, rugged and storm-whipped north" 4049
"shore of Lemminjärvi" 5633
"shore of the Sorrentine peninsula" 4037
"Shoreham" 5720
"shoreless ocean" 4533
"shore-party, waiting" 8128
"shores, along the" 5073
"shores, precipitous rock-cragged" 4071
"shores, sandy" 7661
"shores only thinly vegetated" 5035
"short, man so" 5966
"short and stout" 10369
"short and wide" 10821
"short but not stout" 8347
"Short List, I was on the" 7007
"short ones" 349
"short or tall or fat or thin, whether he be" 5426
"short shorts" 4203
"short stories" 5837
"short stories, Latina" 925
"shortcomings, male" 982
"shortcomings, obvious" 10844
"shorts, faded" 2833
"shortsighted, she was slightly" 8265
"shortstop, shifty as a" 9799
"shot, composing a" 8817
"shot, distant pistol" 8777
"shot, got" 8678
"shot, heard the" 8796
"shot, mug" 6872
"shot, revolver" 8801
"shot, rifle" 209
"shot, Vincent was" 7024
"shot, when he heard the" 9845
"shot a Haitian refugee" 9850
"shot a producer" 7050
"shot an elephant in the balls, if I" 4689

"shot dead, a man was" 6191
"shot down my sixth and seventh MIGs" 8656
"shot himself, an hour before he" 9301
"shot himself, my father" 5769
"shot his brother" 2069
"shot in Johannesburg" 2028
"shot inna back" 74
"shot into orbit, as if about to be" 7629
"shot of incurious half-eyes" 5788
"shot of Tzu, a medium" 8388
"shot smash out of the right forward distance" 8794
"shot that boy, when they" 9854
"shot up instantly out of the nest of blankets" 10212
"shot with a *silenced* machine gun" 7004
"shotgun, I sat" 6938
"shotguns in back, three" 4667
"shots, typhus and typhoid" 542
"shots and cries, darkness wild with" 3766
"shots going back and forth" 9842
"shots ring out" 10009
"shoulder blades, pain beneath his" 6593
"shoulder to shoulder" 6084
"shoulderblades, between her" 2107
"shouldered, broad-" 8360
"shoulders, family" 9626
"shoulders, his tired" 5711
"shoulders, hunched his thick" 5029
"shoulders, hunching his" 2588
"shoulders, over their" 1203
"shoulders, round" 7766
"shoulders, slaves'" 9626
"shoulders, slight stoop of the" 5893
"shoulders, thick" 7472
"shoulders squared forward" 8361
"shout" 6231
"shout, hoarsely whispered" 1526
"shout across" 6290
"shout from all the oxcarts" 4214
"shout hung heavily in the shadowed humid jungle air" 1526
"shouted, baby" 555
"shouted again" 9339
"shouted as if they were once more a people" 1565
"shouted at them to make less noise" 986
"shouted into the courtyard" 9370
"shouted *There they go!*, nobody" 6179
"shouting, started" 4318
"shouting 'All right Paul!'" 1132
"shouting at people" 5823
"shouting Hurry on, two dummies" 1831
"shouting in the theatre, when I heard myself" 2477
"shoutings, shrill midnight" 10981

Shouts 1526, 4318, 6552
shouts, hear their" 8710
"shouts came on lulls of the wind" 10002
"shouts of the child" 10111
"shouts the surging crowd" 3006
"shove of her paddle" 4161
"shovelled some earth on to Geoffrey's coffin" 3944
"shovels scraping" 8601
"shoving match, turned first to a" 8934
"Show, Big Bob Travis Night Owl" 9365
"show, in every" 3342
"show, just starting to" 7062
"show, Lord Mayor's" 2639
"show, the Rudy Vallee" 6652
"show, their 3:00 A.M." 4220
"show for my years, more to" 7494
"show that was about ready to begin" 583
"show went out over the air" 9372
"showed up, Uncle Red" 9944
"showed up one July day" 9957
"shower, spring" 7292
"shower of millionaires" 4660
"shower of rain, violent" 7284
"shower stall, cramped officers'" 570
"showered and shaved" 8486
"showerhouse, red wooden" 9235
"showers, their lighter" 7342
"showers of blessing" 844
"showers quickly absorbed by the sun" 7342
"showing up, calling for nothing more than" 4404
"shows up, if he" 10059
"shrank back in terror" 9279
Shrapnel, Henry 7901
"Shrapnel Academy" 7901
"shrapnel cut into Spencer Abbot's thigh" 8693
"shredded his cigarette into the sand" 7549
"shredding the common watchful silence" 5260
"shrewdly suspect" 357
"shrewdness, sacred name of" 4366
Shrewsbury, Irma 10100
"shriek but no one answers, I" 3706
"shrieked through the unlighted Chinese city" 10539
"shrieking drag of pebbles" 8771
"shrieks, piercing" 8769
"shrieks of the bleak December wind" 1907
"shrill thick of it, into the" 5408
"shrilled hideously, alarm clock" 10165
"shrillest" 8773
"shrimp and snapper spawned and thrived" 5170
"shrine, there is a" 1217

"shrinking of all hunted things, instinctive" 8899
"shroud, theatrically flowing grave" 4113
"shroud, white" 4103
"shrouded in dense spectral fog" 9643
"shrouding from view the ancient battlements" 1178
"shrouds, deep bass of the" 8086
"shrub, like some lusty" 11000
"shrubbery at the bottom of the garden" 3983
"shrubs, briars and" 5704
"shrunk into their clothes" 55
"shtetl, came to the" 9978
"shudder" 5129
"shudder, my" 6038
"shuddered as he talked to himself" 10385
"shudders down his frame, running in" 5603
"shuffle of feet" 14
"shuffled along the rows" 986
"shuffled back and forth" 8780
"shuffled the pages of his speech" 8872
"shuffling into his place" 2639
"shuffling progress, slow" 10405
"shuffling round a church in Ravenna" 9353
"shuffling the cards" 301
Shuganan 10453
Shullum 8040
Shultish, Ezra 8133
"shunned by people and trains, railway stations in Italy are" 7271
"shut, always clamped" 8460
"shut, that [door] was" 7843
"shut in with her dead father" 4224
"shut it off" 10165
"shut that thing off" 10137
"shut the door" 3790
"shut the door again" 2721
"shut the front door" 6587
"shut up, wished he would" 8788
"shut up in the closet" 7193
"shuttered against death" 3155
"shuttered windows" 4328
"shutters, dark green" 10257
"shutters, eastern" 10144
"shutters he had just closed, wooden" 10933
"shutters of a certain shop" 2290
"shy, too" 5641
"shy, unbearably" 10064
"shy, very" 952
"Siam, Gulf of" 2188
"Siam is called by its people 'Muang Thai'" 6247
"Siberia, banished to" 7184
"Siberia, France's" 4544
"sibilance, scented" 8526
"Sibley Junction" 1357
Siblings 22, 129, 244, 255, 337,

681, 867, 868, 894, 1157, 1158, 1236, 1239, 1271, 1756, 1906, 2069, 2116, 2393, 2463, 2544, 2573, 3028, 3263, 3287, 3526, 3577, 3602, 3614, 3621, 3756, 3821, 3943, 3965, 4122, 4130, 4138, 4711, 4780, 4930, 4947, 5027, 5110, 5528, 5852, 6106, 6119, 6148, 6218, 6524, 6663, 6797, 7042, 7055, 7058, 7441, 7830, 7832, 7897, 8670, 8675, 8991, 9049, 9334, 9397, 9710, 9716, 10115, 10231, 10422, 10444, 10645, 10660, 10924
"Sicilian octaves" 5457
"Sicily" 2341, 5026
"sick, dog" 151
"sick, fell" 174
"sick, he was going to be" 136
"sick, Mama was" 149
"sick, might have been" 3699
"sick, when he is" 6686
"sick, you're" 153
"sick at heart" 7359
"sick dog" 9340
"sick in this house" 156
"sick man" 122
"sick man, I am a" 146
"sick of the savagery of the world" 3366
"sick or in trouble, if I was" 57
"sick with something I'd never heard of" 174
"sick yesterday on my birthday" 853
"sickened by it, gradually he had become" 6481
"sickened by the miasma of their hideous parasite growth" 324
"sickening" 10892
"sickish green, his face was a" 143
"sickle, like a gleaming" 7665
"sickly" 6515
Sickness 122, 136, 149, 151, 853, 6686, 7850
"sickness came up from his belly in waves" 7850
"sickness in him" 7850
"sickroom" 190
"sideboard, Matilda was reflected in the" 450
"sidelines, sit on the" 10823
"sides, their naked tawny" 6065
"side-saddle" 9559
"sidewalk, crowded" 5800
"sidewalk, wrinkly tar of this" 5445
"sidewalks, dirt" 7220
"sidewalks, quiet" 3402
"sidewalks, their separate blue-slate" 7627
"sidewalks, unpaved" 3156
"sidewalks had not yet been shoveled" 8607
"sidewalls, white" 9786
"sidling, train came" 7255
Sidney 3342

"Siena" 10200
"Sierras, highway of the" 9115
"Sierras, snow-capped" 5144
"sierras to the bays, from the" 171
"sift away eastward like a plume of smoke" 9772
"sifting through a thin screen of fog" 5331
"sigh, gave a last" 7265
"sigh, many an ear-splitting" 9532
"sigh of his body's premonition, let out the" 2595
"sigh of relief, breathed a" 1663
"sigh of resignation" 10294
"sigh of satisfaction, a long" 3047
"sigh tiresomely" 5264
"sighed, stirred and" 10145
"sighed deeply" 8294
"sighed when they fell in love" 7709
"sighing at the little bunches of forget-me-not on the wallpaper" 2343
"sighs, sharp whistling" 9841
Sight 336, 402, 520, 524, 527, 898, 909, 933, 1104, 1172, 1259, 1289, 1419, 1556, 1598, 1638, 1639, 1697, 1751, 1888, 1992, 2396, 2497, 2522, 2588, 2611, 2699, 2704, 2712, 2716, 2722, 2723, 2848, 2856, 2890, 2982, 3259, 3441, 3478, 3656, 3735, 3759, 3773, 3868, 4001, 4082, 4152, 4195, 4198, 4323, 4417, 4549, 4896, 4904, 4969, 5050, 5075, 5083, 5109, 5123, 5357, 5614, 5651, 5792, 5800, 5855, 5874, 5875, 5908, 6291, 6303, 6304, 6691, 6753, 6824, 6889, 6968, 6993, 7087, 7121, 7317, 7324, 7340, 7467, 7484, 7580, 7638, 7646, 7654, 7676, 7686, 7696, 7706, 7766, 7809, 7918, 7937, 7938, 8067, 8079, 8093, 8099, 8131, 8139, 8195, 8311, 8362, 8372, 8403, 8452, 8526, 8676, 8891, 8920, 9099, 9151, 9190, 9259, 9411, 9451, 9634, 9749, 9775, 9894, 10038, 10067, 10160, 10250, 10273, 10278, 10644, 10869, 10871, 10887, 10893, 10959
"sight, came in" 8154
"sight, charming and instructive" 3558
"sight, kept him in" 8546
"sight, lost" 8067
"sight, neither was in" 5050
"sight, no living thing in" 8252
"sight, out of" 8739, 9426
"sight, pretty" 381
"sight, some notable" 9526
"sight, unusual" 9892
"sight, whole" 8279
"sight and sound, preserving" 4507

"sight gave her such pleasure, the" 4344

"sight of her, he had felt pierced by the" 5123

"sight of her, the" 7398

"sight of him, caught" 5800

"sight of him, without" 9325

"sight of himself, catching" 10219

"sight of himself holding a yellow light over his head" 7474

"sight of Marblehead, taking her last" 1598

"sight of Miss Lily Bart" 8173

"sight of that old fool Gladstone" 6993

"sight of the Holy Land, if you wish an early" 8112

"sight of the house" 2223

"sight of the man, my first" 5084

"sight so arresting" 2989

"sight to behold, a" 9324

"sight was beginning to trouble him" 99

"sight was drawing the passengers, some notable" 9526

"sight was so lovely" 8093

"sighted around noontime" 8122

"sighting, made the first" 8275

"sighting an old man in Argentina" 3413

Sightings 478, 782, 1898, 2162, 2824, 5830, 5848, 7737, 8151, 8154, 8267, 8275, 8281, 10235

Sights 2989, 9526

"sights, among other inevitable" 515

"sights, anticipation of the" 3478

"sights, must have been very pretty" 10642

"sightseer, wasn't much of a" 5360

"sightseers" 3439

"sightseers, small party of" 9565

"sightseers, tourists and" 7772

"Sigmaringen" 4017

Sigmund of Lökken, Earl 10796

Sigmundskron, Frau von 79

"sign, a" 8321, 9886

"sign, gave not the slightest" 1624

"sign, green and yellow" 3001

"sign, Grove Chill Tonic" 8308

"sign, huge overhead" 8307

"sign, illuminated" 8314

"sign, jagged tin" 9529

"sign, old" 8317

"sign, Standard Oil" 3733

"sign, street" 7049

"sign, the first" 7161

"sign above the drugstore windows" 8301

"sign for years, had been a" 8309

"sign my name, where shall I" 4717

"sign of Engaine, no" 9329

"sign of the Army and Navy Store" 10628

"sign of the Ram" 535

"sign that he had reached his peroration" 8863

"sign that said *FOR SALE*: A. C. BRADLEY REALTOR" 8305

"[sign] that said *SOLD*: A. C. BRADLEY REALTOR" 8305

"sign that something had gone wrong, the first" 7159

"sign to come and hear de most hurtful part, you'll get a" 4238

"sign to indicate, there was no" 4054

"sign to release her into death, waiting for a" 9298

"sign to tell you so, there's no need of a" 9176

"sign under which she entered Athens" 8312

"sign was granted, now the" 9298

"sign which was said to exhibit the figure of a black lion" 7284

"sign whitewashed high on the blasted cliff-face" 8303

"signal, as though by prearranged" 9841

"signal, at a swift" 7645

"signal, danger" 442

"signal along a wire, like a" 6591

"signal box" 7275

"signal from one of their number" 7645

"signalised himself in behalf of his country" 5193

"signalled for a whiskey" 295

"signals ahead, sent" 7281

"signals of candlepower, first reassuring" 9247

Signatures 917, 4649, 4717, 8804

"signed a suicide pact with her" 9290

"signed an instrument of abdication" 1525

"signed at Paris" 6803

"signed it 'AG'" 4279

"signed the Friend's Book, he" 917

"significance, a lot of" 5807

"significance, feminine" 5083

"significance, town of no" 1463

"significant this was, realized how" 7016

"signify, nothing to" 10965

"Signora, the" 7755

"Signore" 5759

"Signorino, the" 3817

Signs 1596, 3001, 3339, 4315, 5320, 5647, 6028, 6808, 7049, 7284, 10545, 10628, 10748, 10977

"signs, *REFERENDUM*" 10748

"signs, start in with his" 6652

"signs, visible" 5027

"signs along the highway" 8319

"signs external" 1347

"Sikorsky gunships" 230

Silas, uncle 1160

Silence 1017, 1144, 1201, 1297, 1312, 1673, 2122, 2271, 2706, 3091, 3100, 3121, 3163, 3215, 3285, 3384, 3897, 3907, 5073, 5632, 5746, 6505, 7587, 7590, 7599, 7601, 7656, 7789, 8039, 8119, 8181, 8660, 8766, 8777, 8795, 8811, 8813, 8826, 8884, 9120, 9643, 10215, 10334, 10440, 10503, 10515, 10981

"silence" 8324

"silence, after this long" 8181

"silence, after years of" 9957

"silence, and then" 1312

"silence, common watchful" 5260

"silence, complete" 8338

"silence, cutting the" 8795

"silence, dark" 8777

"silence, disturbed the" 739

"silence, full of restless" 8336

"silence, he felt relief at the" 8332

"silence, hollow" 8325

"silence, I can hear the" 8335

"silence, in" 10440

"silence, in dead" 8660

"silence, lapsed into" 10681

"silence, lay on his back in" 5746

"silence, listening in the" 10215

"silence, listening to the" 8826

"silence, long" 5632

"silence, moments of sudden" 7601

"silence, morning is rising in" 2271

"silence, read them in" 1947

"silence, shattered the" 391

"silence, sounds of the" 8766

"silence, spend the two minutes'" 1201

"silence, sudden astonishing" 8811

"silence, there had been a" 5632

"silence, uneasy" 9411

"silence, waited in" 5188

"silence, walked in" 10334

"silence, year begins in" 10981

"silence everywhere" 8333

"silence except for starlings" 10185

"silence of night, the disturbed" 8813

"silence of the First Cause, creative" 6001

"silence was beginning to weigh" 7590

"silence was like glass" 10503

"silent, and are" 5479

"silent, black and" 2205

"silent, cold and" 2420

"silent, hooded and" 3184

"silent, kept Sturgess" 7587

"silent, never" 3904

"silent, quite" 2706

"silent, servants fall" 1673

"silent, the Styx lay" 7656

"silent after the train pulled out of Chicago" 7600

"silent and helpless" 9387

"silent as an ocean" 5132

"silent house" 869

"silent in the sullen noonday heat" 3907

"silent landscape, eerily" 9643

"silent like a forest pond" 1706

"silent men" 9381

"silent now" 7599

"silent time before dawn" 5073

"silent until now, she had kept" 7641

"silent women" 9381

"silently" 1594

"silhouette, gray" 1181

"silhouette, stark" 2959

"silhouetted against the light" 6401

"silhouetted against the magenta sky" 5982

"silhouetted against the sky" 7221

"silhouetted on horseback" 8696

Silhouettes 1181, 6401, 7699, 8114, 8696

"silk, gold wrought" 1198

"silk, like strips of raw" 1706

"silk, lined with red" 6967

"silk hangings, shimmer of the" 4677

Silky 5489

"sill, rotted" 5355

"Silloth" 7617

"silly, banging her" 8024

"silly thing" 5284

"silos, tobacco storage" 7183

"silt, red" 6249

Silva, Flavius 5115

Silver 2384

Silver, Long John 8027

Silver, Patrick 547

"silver, thin streak of" 9224

"silver bullet" 7440

"Silver Dollar, the" 2935

"Silver Smile, The" 1479

"Silver Sun" 2904

"Silverbridge" 2732

"silver-haired" 247

Silverstein, Naomi 158

Silverthrone, Mrs. 4739

Sim 657

"similarities ended, here the" 8237

"similes stretched to the snapping point, string-taut with" 5448

"Simla" 1689

"simmering sun" 9479

Simmons, Chester 2710

Simmons, Mrs. Annie 6399

Simon 2793, 3574, 6303

Simon, W. and S. 6964

Simone, Madame 2048

Simons, Joseph 10751

Simonsky, Stan 1878

Simpkins 7721

"simple, it was" 10954

"simple, nice and" 10954

"simple, she was" 10878

"simple and concise" 7425

"simple person" 10827

"simple really, perfectly" 6257

"simpler, nothing could have been" 3109

"simplicity, elegant" 3296

"simplicity and affluence" 3561

Simpson, Daisy 8854

Simson, Charlotte 10279

"simultaneously, saw almost" 3441

Sin 822, 1803, 1806, 1807, 1808, 1811, 1818, 3364, 5422, 7192, 7511, 7528, 9284

"sin, in a state of original" 822

"sin, mortal" 7528

"sin, my" 10807

"sin, old" 1818

"Sin, old Man in" 355

"sin, punishment due to" 7852

"sin, wages of" 7192

"sin no more, go and" 1807

"sin to miss mass on Sunday" 7511

"sin to write this, it is a" 5422

"Sinai desert" 4080

Sinatra, Frank Jr. 8559

"sincerity, English" 695

Sinclair, Annette Hollander 1951

Sinclair, Lydia 1715

Sinclair, Peter 4809

Sindling, Christian 6241

Sing, Wittman Ah 9299

"sing, myself I" 4800

"sing after we were married, didn't like for me to" 5757

"sing in a lulling voice" 8761

"sing or play for free if the society invites him" 6242

"sing out the familiar melody" 4335

"sing to you" 8759

"sing with it, offered to" 8746

"Singapore" 1443, 8117

"Singapore, battle of" 10507

Singer, Jeremy 10620

"singer, backup" 6485

"Singer Sewing Machines" 6465

Singers 6485, 8752, 8754, 9365

"singers, professional dirge-" 3935

"singers, rowdy gang of" 2901

"singers in the world, greatest" 8754

Singing 563, 567, 571, 852, 5757, 8702, 8738, 8740, 8743, 8744, 8745, 8748, 8749, 8753, 8756, 8757, 8758, 8760, 8762, 9437

"singing, soft feminine sound of" 9437

"singing, somewhere he was" 8748

"singing, three voices" 9995

"singing a rock-and-roll adaptation of *Dink's Blues*" 8744

"singing a song" 8762

"singing a sudden brilliant chorus" 8756

"singing if I remember rightly the 'Toreador Song'" 571

"singing in Faust" 8740

"singing in Happy's Café" 5757

"singing in his dream" 8757

"singing number three on the chart" 9365

"singing of the harp" 8792

"singing on the radio, Eddie Cantor kept" 3750

"singing out of season, warblers" 7025

"singing ... 'Pale Hands I Loved Beside the Shalimar'" 567

"singing splashed out at him" 9437

"singing the evening hymn" 8737

"singing the mad scene in *Lucia*" 8738

"singing the Marseillaise" 563

"singing the Night Office" 1312

"singing to the wounded soldiers" 8767

"singing to your headlights" 8749

"singing voices" 9560

"single file" 10346

"single for several years now" 5995

"single-minded" 9453

"single-shot twenty, his old" 4694

"singling a kid out like that" 4853

"singling a particular person out for condemnation" 1533

"sings, he loudly" 8749

"sings it low and scratchy" 8753

"singular autobiography" 5399

"singular aversion" 5193

"singularity" 5884

"sink far out in the broken water" 5023

"sink her makeshift boat, she would not let me" 1824

"sinking, rapidly" 40

"sinking fast" 2307

"sinking in some gelatinous substance, I am" 4227

"sinking myself down into the East End of London" 6098

"sinned, for I have" 1808, 1811

"sinned, I have" 1803

"sinned against heaven and before thee, Father I have" 1806

"sinner, who has been such a" 5885

Sinnott, John 20

"sins, charity covers no" 3364

"sins, your country's unpunished and punished" 9284

"sins long forgotten" 253

"Sioux, battle with the" 6621

"Sioux City, it is still" 10318

"sipping hot coffee" 4620

"sipping Jose Cuervo by the capful" 2937

"sips from a spritzer" 8883

"sirens from the tarry tidal Thames" 5260

Sirola 10426

Sirovich, John 5537

Sister, Aunt 4437

"sister" 3599, 6666

"sister, brother and" 4780, 8223

"sister, brown-sugared soul" 253

"Sister, Dear" 3472
"sister, didn't know you had a" 8211
"sister, half-" 10771
"sister, her" 894, 1239, 1906, 3287, 5759, 8242, 9716, 9875
"sister, her old" 1923
"sister, her younger" 10035
"sister, his" 734, 2971, 3141, 3207, 3568, 3602, 4122, 4947, 8220, 8238, 9049, 9334, 9420, 10004, 10660
"sister, his half" 4711
"Sister, Little" 8205
"sister, my" 337, 1185, 2544, 3526, 3577, 3623, 4971, 5528, 5781, 6119, 6701, 7900, 8236, 8251, 10231
"sister, my eldest" 8222
"sister, my little" 7042
"sister, my younger" 9710
"sister, my youngest" 8222
"Sister, new night" 5003
"sister, no" 162
"sister, not my" 5110
"sister, our" 244
"sister, twin" 10444
"sister, world didn't begin with my" 8243
"sister, your" 2463, 4130
"sister country" 2087
"Sister home, send" 1158
"sister of Judy the Prudy" 4777
"sister that ran the sweetshop" 8220
"sister who is driving" 3028
"SISTERHOOD magazine" 6513
"sister-in-law, her wicked" 2064
Sisters 2463, 2960, 3028, 3263, 3357, 3562, 3568, 3577, 3623, 4130, 4574, 4777, 8203, 8211, 8222, 8236, 8243, 9334, 10231, 10444
"sister's, at his" 9423
"sisters, elderly McAlister" 8241
"sisters, fourteen" 3263
"sisters, Grimes" 6663
"sisters, her two" 8216
"sisters, his two" 8991
"sisters, my" 5027
"sisters, step-" 3556
"sisters, three lovely and loving" 8232
"sisters, two Aspen" 2960
"sisters, two old" 8214
"sister's address" 9525
"sister's footfall" 7441
"sisters left Darjeeling" 6111
"sisters of seventeen and fifteen" 8212
"sisters-in-law, her" 9710
"Sistine Chapel" 515
"sit, big holes where you're supposed to" 8027
"sit, here I" 2279
"sit, she chose to" 8357

"sit against the window and wouldn't talk" 1845
"sit along the Backs enjoying the October warmth" 5631
"sit and smoke" 8862
"sit at home" 5397
"sit beneath the oak tree" 5337
"sit by the door" 3873
"sit by the fire and be quiet" 9406
"sit fatly, coal tips" 5151
"sit for hours and hours and hours" 8496
"sit in contemplative posture" 8496
"sit in front of my mirror" 6304
"sit in my little cottage" 1444
"sit in the dental chair, liked to" 5351
"sit in the evening dews" 2279
"sit in the rocking chair" 6543
"sit in the tail" 5750
"sit on a bench, accustomed to" 8363
"sit on the banister of his back veranda" 6290
"sit on the bed, I" 8380
"sit on the edge of the bed" 6937
"sit on the sidelines, she never could" 10823
"sit on the steps outside the Laundromat" 4187
"sit or lie down on Desolation Peak" 6075
"sit quietly with her mother" 6744
"sit still, could scarcely" 4913
"sit with a whiskey" 5357
"sit with their backs to the sun" 220
"Sitka" 3514
"sits, a boy" 1001
"sits at her writing-table" 5395
"sits at his desk" 3461
"sits at the water's edge" 4206
"sits by the Virgin of Charity" 10105
"sits in her wicker swing" 8385
"sits in his car in the rain" 10085
"sits in his office" 1982
"sits in his special chair" 8376
"sits in the belfry" 2937
"sits in the woods" 8382
"sits like a blind person in the dark" 8364
"sits on the edge of the mesa" 8273
"sits on the side of his bed" 8384
"sits out there in the porch swing" 5966
"sits up in bed" 10325
Sitting 520, 942, 1001, 1003, 1166, 1444, 1485, 1523, 1549, 1729, 1838, 1907, 1932, 2017, 2279, 2348, 2495, 2498, 2695, 2710, 2739, 2822, 2848, 2937, 3084, 3582, 3692, 3759, 3818, 3848, 3873, 3916, 3984, 3987, 4018, 4019, 4136, 4147, 4187, 4189, 4206, 4308, 4325, 4378, 4420, 4644, 4913, 5337, 5351, 5395,

5459, 5856, 5995, 6010, 6143, 6495, 6501, 6857, 6959, 7347, 7361, 7467, 7752, 7763, 7770, 7781, 8038, 8042, 8125, 8206, 8214, 8264, 8266, 8267, 8273, 8280, 8332, 8450, 8496, 8570, 8579, 8725, 9084, 9114, 9374, 9404, 9411, 9414, 9854, 10008, 10038, 10041, 10048, 10055, 10068, 10086, 10105, 10649, 10782, 10891
"sitting, had taken to" 6501
"sitting, southern method of" 7467
"sitting, two persons were" 9758
"sitting across from the largest woman I have ever seen" 10891
"sitting alone" 2886, 8341
"sitting alone in my study" 9989
"sitting among my abandoned children" 9375
"sitting and rocking" 8355
"sitting around the tea-table" 6850
"sitting at a desk and writing" 5405
"sitting at her desk" 10926
"sitting at her window" 7652
"sitting at my desk" 7770
"sitting at one of the tables in the square" 8377
"sitting at right angles" 8381
"sitting at the edge, couples" 2529
"sitting at the fire by myself" 9854
"sitting at this very moment" 807
"sitting behind his desk" 8572
"sitting benumbed in the bedroom" 10008
"sitting beside the road" 9414
"sitting by her window" 3978
"sitting crying bitterly" 4222
"sitting here, how long have we been" 8373
"sitting here at my desk, I have been" 710
"sitting here in the airplane" 1957
"sitting here safe and sane" 2734
"sitting hunched on the side of his pallet bed" 10196
"sitting hunkered on his heels" 8366
"sitting in a rum shop" 1838
"sitting in a wicker chair" 8473
"sitting in an apartment" 5042
"sitting in an exhausted reverie" 9938
"sitting in an outdoor cafe" 2912
"sitting in deck chairs under the awning" 5019
"sitting in her room" 9445
"sitting in his living room" 7367
"sitting in his veranda" 4378
"sitting in my apartment" 1932
"sitting in my room" 3990
"sitting in the bar" 2919
"sitting in the bell tower" 8579
"sitting in the Guards' Chapel" 10649
"sitting in the lotus position" 6959

"sitting in the middle of a sandpile" 8375
"sitting in the parlor" 8365
"sitting . . . in the parlor" 9114
"sitting in the Small Lounge" 4644
"sitting in the window-seat" 6316
"sitting like a stone in this place" 1729
"sitting naked" 1169
"sitting next to Jim Salter" 10460
"sitting next to them" 5810
"sitting on a bank of shingle" 4147
"sitting on a battered table" 8654
"sitting on a bench" 3848
"sitting on a low wall" 1172
"sitting on a marble bench" 8741
"sitting on a narrow bench" 3299
"sitting on a rock" 7361
"sitting on a stool in a bar in the desert" 2615
"sitting on her accustomed hawthorn" 720
"sitting on her bed" 8450
"sitting on him, we were" 5856
"sitting on his grandmother's knee" 7217
"sitting on his porch" 3282
"sitting on our porch" 4119
"sitting on the beach at Brighton" 4181
"sitting on the doorstep" 8349
"sitting on the edge of a low range of inland cliffs" 1485
"sitting on the north-window side" 9564
"sitting on the porch" 1652, 3757
"sitting on the sea wall" 8362
"sitting on the steps" 10055
"sitting on the verandah" 6010
"sitting opposite Mr. Haddock" 1371
"sitting out in the back yard of the parsonage" 8352
"sitting pretty, I should have been" 9264
"sitting rigidly in a black director's chair" 8388
"sitting side by side" 246, 8344
"sitting up, comes awake" 10300
"sitting up in bed" 4620, 6536
"sitting up until all hours" 8976
"sitting with three other people" 4310
"situated on a strip of dry land, pleasantly" 3058
"situation, cope with a" 1400
"situation, gravity of our" 78
"situation, his mother's sudden" 3591
"situation, our" 76
"situation, their" 3357
"situation, this then was the" 3833
"situation, unfamiliar" 5295
"situation they shall be discovered, in what" 5414

"situations, impossible and romantic" 5410
"situations, melodramatic" 1325
"sivilize me, trying to" 5506
"six, age of" 4270
"Six Towns area" 8934
"six-flat" 9947
"sixpence, newly minted silver" 9431
"sixteen, coming" 979
"sixteen, until I was" 9726
"Sixth" 5880
"sixties, in her early" 2319
"sixty if she was a day" 1432
"size 9½ B" 2835
"size of an open hand" 924
"size of the Cathedral was a surprise" 1306
"sizzling eggs and b." 3839
Skaggs 10098
Skaggs, Taswell 2297
"skateboard, diving off his" 4267
"skated round the dirt sidewalks" 7220
"skating on a pond" 983
"skating rink" 4195
Skeffington, Frank 2472
"skcins, mean lipped" 8616
Skelding, Mr. 4
"skeleton, stone" 9237
"skeleton, 2X4" 1859
"skeleton draped in a theatrically flowing grave shroud" 4113
"skeleton of the empty Greenhouse, massive" 9256
"skeleton trees" 324
"skeletons, weird multitude of" 2190
"Skelly service station" 1044
Skepticism 4116, 9688
"skepticism, trust his own" 9688
"sketching his lean cheeks" 498
"skid row slums" 2906
"skids again, on the" 2898
"skies, blue" 9598
"skies, crystal" 9615
"skies, two" 3032
"skies began to clear" 8443
"skies still hung red with fire" 760
"skiff, boarded a" 10871
"skiff, fished alone in a" 6428
"skiff, work" 4693
Skiing 8916
"skill and invention of an Italian engineer" 3084
"skimming along through a rich English county" 2944
"skims the Post-Dispatch" 3870
"skin, charred" 2463
"skin, exposed" 10717
"skin, fame is a second" 3546
"skin, fine as" 3131
"skin, his smooth bronzed" 10340
"skin, his sunburned" 2833
"skin, I have white" 4789
"skin, metallic silver beneath the" 4509

"skin, my" 1327
"skin, olive" 7485
"skin, rather anemic traditionally indoor" 5629
"skin, soft ribbon of white" 343
"skin, weasel up under your" 6381
"skin crawls suddenly" 8948
"skin flick" 1327
"skin like a mushroom's" 340
"skin of her delicate arms and legs" 4157
"skin on the neck of a chicken, like the" 1166
"skin stretched tight across her sharp bones" 10832
"skin was dyed a deep coppery red" 2833
"skin was loose and wattled" 1166
"skin would feel like leather" 5897
Skinner 3384
"skinny, too" 189
"skins were bronzed" 7036
"skipped down the garden path" 10430
"skipper, the" 8476
"skipper of the submarine" 4745
"skipping rope" 8747
"Skipton Yorkshire" 6448
"skirmish in the war" 3676
"skirmishes, lively" 4906
"skirt, her corduroy" 2348
"skirt, struggles out of her black" 2884
"skirt had a raspberry stain" 2880
"skirt of her new green watered-silk gown" 4921
"skirt slips up to the tops of her stockings" 5471
"skirts, lifting" 6398
"skirts, long" 6868
"skirts, plaid" 4154
"skirts, whipping of silk" 7229
"skirts of a village" 3987
"skittering across the smooth swoop of the gulls" 742
"skitters across the clearing" 475
"skittish, car was beginning to act" 2972
"skittish and apprehensive as squirrels" 3722
"skittish horse" 4191
"skittish with mating" 420
"skivvies, strip to their" 1215
"skivvy, silly little" 4990
"*skreek-skreek* of their clothesline pulleys" 10875
"skule, go to" 3269
"skull, each ant emerged from the" 4963
"skull, Martin Bormann's" 3413
"skull, moon's bleached" 8428
"skull, sounding through her" 8831
"skull collided, his" 24
"skull faded from white to gray" 142

"skull smashed soft as a rotted pumpkin" 1896
"skulls, handled many" 334
"skull-visaged" 169
Sky 38, 175, 222, 522, 523, 529, 531, 533, 729, 757, 1312, 1642, 2150, 2214, 2220, 2225, 2226, 2233, 2242, 2245, 2255, 2850, 3109, 3807, 4015, 4133, 4385, 4409, 4410, 4425, 5051, 5135, 5147, 5286, 5348, 6077, 6373, 7316, 7471, 7701, 7914, 7943, 8326, 8470, 8584, 8597, 8617, 8722, 9081, 9154, 9170, 9228, 9236, 9239, 10242, 10269, 10414, 10454, 10494, 10504, 10590, 10598, 10607, 10614, 10617, 10702, 10732, 10903
"sky, across the bluest" 8447
"sky, against the blue summer" 3109
"sky, against the turquoise" 6085
"sky, all that sweep of" 10702
"sky, black winter" 7701
"sky, blackening" 8442
"sky, blue" 8391
"sky, blue prodigal" 10590
"sky, bomber's" 8422
"sky, brassy noonday" 9154
"sky, brilliant high windless" 8408
"sky, brown" 3209
"sky, bruised and troubled" 771
"sky, Caribbean" 8491
"sky, clearing the" 5051
"sky, cloudless" 2255, 4372, 8448
"sky, cloudless starlit" 6373
"sky, clouds cloaked the" 8401
"sky, cold Virginia" 6077
"sky, colour of the night" 7777
"sky, dark" 6327
"sky, darkening" 5135, 6059
"sky, daylight lingered in the" 2199
"sky, dull" 3044
"sky, eerie orange-tinted" 3792
"sky, enormous" 8441
"sky, far in a clear" 522
"sky, fervor in the" 8398
"sky, filled the" 3665
"sky, flannel" 8326
"sky, flashed blue" 3667
"sky, frozen January" 9244
"sky, ghosts pirouetted across the" 8451
"sky, glow in the" 8396
"sky, granite" 10577
"sky, gray" 7914, 8624
"sky, grey winter" 10160
"sky, half wheel of the" 523
"sky, haze over the" 8416
"sky, high in the reaches of wet" 729
"sky, high up in the pale Flemish" 193
"sky, huge open slab of night" 5952
"sky, huge pane of blue" 6984
"sky, icy star-ridden" 7084

"sky, invisible February" 8597
"sky, it hung under the" 5165
"sky, leaden" 8584
"sky, light had withdrawn from the" 6648
"sky, light the" 8438
"sky, like a mountain" 5147
"sky, looked up at the" 8150
"sky, looking up at the" 2220
"sky, magenta" 5982
"sky, marvelous canopy of the blue northern" 4341
"sky, miracle of blue" 7289
"sky, Northern" 4140
"sky, not a crack in the" 8424
"sky, not even a wisp of it crosses the" 4409
"sky, otherwise clear" 10320
"sky, pale afternoon" 10732
"sky, pale streaks of the cloudy" 2712
"sky, patch of" 5069
"sky, rationed" 10242
"sky, rose into the" 3300
"sky, see the nether" 7471
"sky, sharpened glare of a dry blue" 8417
"sky, slender strip of blue" 8252
"sky, soft blue" 4133
"sky, somber" 8421
"sky, sombrero fell out of the" 2850
"sky, southern" 533
"sky, stainless blue of the" 2225
"sky, starred" 8415
"sky, streaking the" 9300
"sky, strong blue" 10414
"sky, sullen" 2233
"sky, sun teetered in the" 9776
"sky, swelling" 1481
"sky, that's a blue" 8414
"sky, the" 7292, 7316
"sky, thin papery" 8405
"sky, troubled" 3107
"sky, tumultuous" 748
"sky, under a louring" 9170
"sky, under a smoky pink" 8115
"sky, under a sullen November" 7267
"sky, under a white" 9754
"sky, under that leaden" 8434
"sky, under the pale outrage of a breaking" 222
"sky, under the wide" 3664
"sky, vast and brassy" 8410
"sky, vast untroubled" 8400
"sky, watery" 8412
"sky, west" 5348
"sky, western" 8403, 9163
"sky, wide northeastern" 6084
"sky, wind cleared the" 8586
"sky a blue of the first firmament" 5286
"sky a sheet of beaten lead" 9081
"sky above, a flaming blue" 10570

"sky above him gleamed with a cold yet lustrious blue" 8392
"sky already thins, the black of" 8420
"sky and earth faltered" 10598
"sky and the world" 7316
"sky as clear as Eden's" 10454
"sky . . . begins to draw down a translucent dusk" 8470
"sky between bleak clouds, blue strips of" 10607
"sky blue" 4350
"sky came first, the" 8446
"sky charged with metallic frost" 4015
"sky cleared rapidly and then burst into flaming gold and red" 2150
"sky closed in" 8427
"sky collapsed like an old roof" 38
"sky . . . colourless cloudless leafless and pigeonless" 9244
"sky crinkled into a rose colored hollow at its edge" 2242
"sky darkening, the London" 8617
"sky . . . glowed a wondrous lull" 5286
"sky glowed red, the dull" 10614
"sky grew darker and darker" 2245
"sky had a surprise glow" 8433
"sky had cleared" 10585
"sky in ships, sailing the" 9745
"sky is everywhere" 8444
"sky is gray, when the" 5144
"sky is overcast" 7613
"sky is such a solid blue I could touch it" 4425
"sky leaned and ached upon the roof" 4385
"sky looks, know exactly how the" 8414
"sky maybe flame-blue with sun" 9228
"sky of early autumn" 8408
"sky of early autumn, intensely blue" 1849
"sky of its pall, rid the" 7293
"sky of southern Italy, blue" 1219
"sky of summer blue" 10160
"sky of the early autumn afternoon" 8405
"sky of turquoise blue" 3126
"sky opened again" 8435
"sky over London was glorious" 10494
"sky over Rome" 2225
"sky over Stockholm, the autumn" 8470
"sky pressing against the window-panes" 2233
"sky rolled together like a scroll curling shut" 8419
"sky sank down before dawn" 175
"sky sat on top of their hill" 8440

"sky seemed one vast arc of solemn blue" 8394
"sky slowly began to change color" 8432
"sky that held nothing of emergency or love" 4901
"sky that seemed to rest on the hedge" 10617
"sky that was clear and pale like a mountain sky" 5147
"sky the color of smoke" 8722
"sky the grey of Guiseley sandstone" 1642
"sky the same colour as the water" 7943
"sky to the east was black" 9239
"sky unseen, starred" 9236
"sky was as blue as a bottle" 8429
"sky was blue and high" 8426
"sky was changing from a slate gray to a dull blue" 7621
"sky was clouded over" 9077
"sky was luminous with constellations" 7701
"sky was on fire" 10505
"sky was shredded with clouds" 10732
"sky was still dark" 10269
"sky . . . was torn" 8405
"skylight above her, gaze up through the" 8491
"skyline, glorious" 1434
"skyline, proud" 9218
"skyline, steep" 5146
Skypack, Senator 6985
"sky's infinitude, lost in the" 531
"skyscraper, on the top floor of a" 10706
"Skywater" 741
"slab, marble" 4073
"slabs of granite half sunk in the soft ground" 10404
"slack once more, go" 8079
Slade 3969
Slade, Professor 6630
"Slades, the" 3842
"slag, earth rang like" 1547
"slain and the slayers" 6373
"slain and thrown in a ditch" 6185
"Slaka, make the trip to" 1308
"slam it closed behind him, thinking he could" 2714
"slammed the door" 1626
"slammed the door shut" 1663
"slamming and smudging colorful oils onto canvas" 518
"Slane St. Mary's" 3160
"slangy, have to be so" 9011
"slant of Riviera sun" 10118
"slant the chisel just so" 10948
"slanting between the red-brick ranks" 5323
"slapped the face" 5738
"slapped the waves of the gulf" 8092

"slapped up and down by one wake after another " 732
"slash, a bold" 8447
"slashing and clawing" 9086
"slate gray" 6087
"slats of the Venetian blinds" 1020
Slaughter, Dr. 4739
Slaughter, Master Sergeant 8662
"slaughter, their tiresome work of" 927
"Slaughter'd by heaps" 10464
"slaughtering the cow, he had put off" 7331
"slave, nigger" 5506
"slave, runaway" 1160
"slave, with only one" 9969
"slave of women, I am the" 10855
"slave or the outcast of society" 10766
"slave reading a story" 5431
"slave who came to fetch me" 5993
"slavemasters, two merciless" 3690
Slavery 681, 1351, 1827, 3075, 4443, 6806, 10766
"slavery" 1288
"slavery, peaceful semi-" 6806
Slaves 1160, 5993, 9969, 10855
"slaves" 3075
"slaves' quarters, ruined" 9216
Slavin, Lorna 8012
"slayers, the slain and the" 6373
"sleazy motel" 6783
"sled" 9626
Sleep 123, 671, 848, 1102, 1125, 1178, 1656, 2110, 2330, 2759, 2765, 2767, 2771, 2776, 2784, 2785, 2786, 2790, 2799, 2801, 2816, 2972, 3516, 3681, 3713, 4284, 4287, 4496, 5327, 6024, 6205, 6543, 6554, 6671, 6904, 7035, 7152, 8231, 8248, 8324, 8476, 8479, 8483, 8491, 8525, 8653, 8761, 8774, 8818, 8832, 8834, 8907, 10059, 10108, 10129, 10130, 10132, 10139, 10144, 10177, 10180, 10181, 10183, 10186, 10188, 10199, 10213, 10220, 10221, 10232, 10248, 10253, 10264, 10265, 10272, 10300, 10312, 10313, 10318, 10390, 10968, 10969
"sleep, adrift with" 8761
"sleep, afraid of going to" 3713
"sleep, after a night's" 10129
"sleep, amblers who could not" 8813
"sleep, assassination happens in their" 6205
"sleep, before he went to" 4891
"sleep, blackest" 10313
"sleep, came up from" 10301
"sleep, clattering rumble shattered my" 10272
"sleep, clinging to the numbness of" 10188
"sleep, clouds of" 8324
"sleep, couldn't go back to" 8503

"sleep, deep" 10199
"sleep, deep peaceful" 10186
"sleep, died in her" 2330
"sleep, dream-broken" 836
"sleep, even in his" 737
"sleep, face would haunt my" 5084
"sleep, fitful and uneasy" 10132
"sleep, five hours of" 10968
"sleep, get himself calm enough to" 2934
"sleep, he couldn't go back to" 10165
"sleep, he would surely go back to" 10165
"sleep, his right arm went to" 10247
"sleep, I couldn't" 8506
"sleep, in her" 2786
"sleep, in his" 8466
"sleep, in the little death of" 2767
"sleep, in your" 6338
"sleep, instantly out of" 10195
"sleep, laid against his back like" 2973
"sleep, long vertical cylinder of" 8818
"sleep, mist of" 10158
"sleep, nobody could" 8478
"sleep, poor people trying to" 1132
"sleep, rearing into" 7440
"sleep, restless" 10248
"sleep, rolled over in her" 8525
"sleep, roused from sound" 10122
"sleep, rumpled fabric of my" 8832
"sleep, sank back into the rock of" 8467
"sleep, snatch a bit of" 123
"sleep, soundly to" 8481
"sleep, started up from" 9885
"sleep, stirred in its" 4496
"sleep, stirred in your" 2759
"sleep, struggles from" 10300
"sleep, surface of his" 10130
"sleep, sweaty torpor which was" 10264
"sleep, talking in his" 4504
"sleep, thin veil of uneasy" 10245
"sleep, timeless and bottomless world of" 10144
"sleep, unable to" 8486
"sleep, uneasy" 10177
"sleep, untroubled" 10312
"sleep, useless trying to" 8489
"sleep, waited for more" 10123
"sleep, when I'm not able to" 8488
"sleep, why don't you go back and" 10059
"sleep, will not let me" 8494
"sleep again, I cannot and do not wish to" 2536
"sleep any more, he just couldn't" 10163
"sleep drifted across her mind" 10121
"sleep for four hours" 4284
"sleep for weeks, our first decent" 8455

"sleep in her house, wanted me to" 10969

"sleep in the afternoon, a four-hour" 4284

"sleep in the back seat, had gone to" 2972

"sleep like a dog" 8483

"sleep like a weed, yanked out of" 10221

"sleep of summer dawns" 836

"sleep on a pallet made of old coats and comforters" 7035

"sleep out of her eyes, rubbed the" 10212

"sleep seemed not inclined to 'steep her senses in forgetfulness'" 9402

"sleep so sound" 10182

"sleep through Sundays in winter" 2110

"sleep together in the room at the back of the house" 8248

"sleep very much, looked as if he didn't" 8493

"sleep with a young blind woman" 8004

"sleep with Connie whenever I want to dream" 2816

"sleep without dreams, when he sought" 2771

"sleeper in the high old bed" 673

"sleepers, feared to awaken" 7712

"sleepers in Riversley Grange" 10113

"sleepily turned and snapped it shut" 10217

Sleepiness 103, 5201

"sleeping" 2906

"sleeping, cat was only" 6187

"sleeping, I was" 1125

"sleeping, I'm no" 8476

"sleeping, lay" 8471

"sleeping, trouble" 8499

"sleeping, waking or" 2765

"sleeping, where she did her" 1178

"sleeping car, moribund Amtrak" 691

"sleeping dreamlessly and without any jerky movements" 8653

"sleeping husband" 10117

"sleeping husband, her" 6356

"sleeping in the bed, grow used to" 8491

"sleeping in the kitchen" 8706

"sleeping with men" 8007

"sleeping with my sons, I have to stop" 6554

"sleepless" 8490, 8496

Sleeplessness 2536, 8984

"sleeplessness, written testimonies of their" 8485

"sleep-stricken, my voice guttural and" 2776

"Sleepy" 7098

"sleepy, achingly" 9275

"sleepy, deplorably" 5201

"sleepy at times, you get very" 103

"sleepy or not, whether we were" 8221

"sleet, watery" 8085

"sleet, wind and snow and" 9065

"sleet, withering gale of" 9532

"sleety" 6365

"sleeves, puffed" 4181

"sleigh" 9626

"sleigh-bells, sound of" 7380

"slender" 85

"Splendor of Life" 2626

"slept, he hadn't" 8487

"slept, Kendall" 8474

"slept, she had" 10253

"slept, they" 6543

"slept, we" 8468

"slept again" 4496

"slept again, promptly" 10143

"slept badly and restlessly" 10139

"slept in a cell designed for one, six people" 7152

"slept late" 8907

"slept only until the sun entered their room" 10169

"slept or seemed to sleep through the first seventy miles of the road" 10108

"slept poorly" 8497

"slept restlessly" 8475

"slept side by side" 8231

"slept well, had not" 8479

"slept with his mouth open slack" 8460

"slept with the President" 8025

"slew all in the household" 6179

"slewed round on the narrow track" 9791

"slices, tissue-paper" 860

"slicing at the head of a Moor" 9839

"slid around the corner" 2974

"slid in against the high curb like a scared baserunner with his cleats bared" 2995

"slid into my chair" 3850

"slides, giddy skidding" 40

"slides in sideways" 5974

"sliding down over the world" 10574

"slight and seeming frail" 3891

"slim and light, she was very" 8087

"slim as a girl" 10804

"slim like a model" 5970

"slime, earth or" 2346

"sling, forked" 7629

"slingshot, shooting a" 662

"slink and snarl and grin for a bone, they will" 6820

"slip, her black" 2853

"slip away from the roadside" 9649

"slipped along just under the crest of the ridges" 7221

"slipped and hurt themselves" 9394

"slipped away" 1777

"slipped away from the screen" 6587

"slipped easily into the morning's rhythm" 7859

"slipped out the back door of her house" 1782

"slipped out to make a quick telephone call" 1101

"slipper, her silk" 2719

"slipperiness, some sly strip of" 14

"slippers, felt" 10054

"slippers, high-heeled pink satin bedroom" 6399

"slippers, his" 1675

"slippers, pajamas and" 996

"slippers of a rose colour, cross-strapped" 2826

"slips, three small yellow" 1122

"slit of dark grey" 2269

Sloan, Simon 6652

"sloop, sailed his" 8163

"sloop *Elizabeth*" 8146

"sloop *Typhoon*" 8563

"sloops, stealthy" 3396

"slope, at the foot of the white" 8596

"slope, birch-covered" 3129

"slope, gentle" 3146, 9156

"slope, bare grassy" 2006

"slope, down the" 1194

"slope, shale" 4797

"slope, upland" 10697

"slope, western" 8729

"slope below me, steep" 8789

"slope between the sea and the Forêt de Sorède" 3125

"slope of Helvellyn, vast precipitous" 7190

"slope of the Surrey hills" 3076

"sloped down the main road alone" 10402

"sloped in fast" 9807

"slopes, fertile" 3641

"slopes, gently rising" 5572

"slopes, long tree-clad" 10038

"slopes, olive" 9995

"slopes, torn" 5151

"slopes, verdant" 9740

"slopes upwards from its broad tide-river" 1336

"slopped sideways" 5325

"sloppy crowds" 1089

"sloshes roun' de names" 4716

"sloth, giant" 7232

"slouching, perils of" 5992

"Slovenians" 4055

"slow in their movements, men and women" 177

"slow motion" 5118

"Slowburgh" 5080

"slowed down to a saunter" 10366

"slowed down to a stop" 5957

"slowed him down" 9341

"slowness, funereal" 9804

"sluggish, flies" 177

"slugging it out again" 7874

"slugs for his breakfast" 723

"sluices" 9627
"slum, Cairo" 889
"slumber, four hundred years of" 1464
"slumbering on a rough couch" 8453
"slump back into their chairs" 5632
"slums, kids from the" 640
"slums, skid row" 2906
"slung his saddle out into the night" 7250
"slush, greyish" 6294
"slush on the road" 2337
"sluttish in attire, wonderfully" 3554
"sly, on the" 7981
"slyest sneakiest way" 6640
"smaht, Freddy's" 5008
"small, first you are very" 548
"small, I am getting" 1263
"small, Sarah was" 4199
"small, when I was" 9061
"small, when Theresa was" 4197
"small and faint, looking" 3030
"small and tender for her age" 4158
"small for Africa" 6256
"small [shall be] great, the" 4454
Small Henry 2408
"small hours" 1118
"Small House" 3063
"small man" 5978
"small men" 7746
"small talk" 8860
"smaller, there was one" 4436
"smaller, there was one even" 4436
"smaller than Nurse" 4199
"smallest person I ever knew" 7542
Smalley, Tusker 2373
Smart, Jane 6301
"smart, he wasn't very" 5010
"smart behind his eyes, the burn seemed to" 6600
"smart in the grey uniform" 5926
"smart or stupid" 5542
"smart-ass, a real" 3932
"smash against the barracks' concrete wall" 10297
"smash them all, she was going to" 6931
"smash through whatever stood in his way" 5955
"smash yer ter bits, I'm gonna" 1835
"smashed at the arm with a cruel-looking cane" 6652
"smashed it into a mauve pulp" 1868
"smashed the tables and the chairs" 3788
"smashed [her store] up herself" 4945
"smashes the pins for a ten-strike" 313
"smashing his jaw in with my spade" 6182
"smeared the mud over his face" 2833

"smeared with the sweat and foam of a desperate ride" 7607
"smell, clean dusty" 2303
"smell, he's got a sense of" 8535
"smell, warm waxy" 4520
"smell, what is this" 8518
"smell as sweet" 8955
"smell in all the world, no lonelier" 8511
"smell it, we could" 10737
"smell of bleach, high faint" 10875
"smell of clothes boiling" 7441
"smell of his faded overalls" 2303
"smell of linens" 8761
"smell . . . of old matted straw on a rainy November afternoon" 8511
"smell of pine needles in the winter rooms" 4520
"smell of putrefaction, sour" 8541
"smell of smoke" 3780, 8510
"smell of stale urine" 8521
"smell of the factories, ashy" 3184
"smell of the rain forest" 8541
"smell of the soap you have used" 7494
"smell of trees" 8507
"smell of unfamiliar men" 464
"smell of Venice suffused the night" 8523
"smell of wet black earth coming in strong through an open window" 9622
"smell of wet grass" 7308
"smell of wood smoke" 9560
"smell that air" 180
"smell the muscadines" 8531
"smelled faintly of formalin" 5088
"smelled like hair" 8522
"smelled of garbage fires and cooking and diesel fumes and just possibly the sea" 8534
"smelled of goats and hay" 8005
"smelled of honeysuckle" 10180
"smelled of rain, air" 8519
"smelled of smoke and snow" 10720
"smelled sweet, grass" 8513
"smelled the air" 8510, 10255
"smelled the burning fires" 2114
"smelled the onion farms" 5916
"smelled the peculiar odor of new construction" 8543
"smelled the thing" 8517
"smelled the visitors" 9936
"smelled trouble" 8520
"smelling" 5059
"smelling all around him, something powerful's" 10327
"smelling like a rose" 8542
"smelling of clean wood" 3176
"smelling of dew-damp jasmine" 10703
"smelling of oily sea water" 3693
"smelling of rotted fruits" 1480
"smelling you, without him" 8535
Smells 180, 385, 464, 1194, 1524,

2114, 2941, 3176, 3184, 3405, 3478, 3604, 3780, 3794, 3796, 3796, 3800, 3809, 4105, 4121, 4335, 4370, 4427, 5916, 6272, 6499, 6707, 6780, 7308, 7323, 7409, 8005, 8071, 8394, 9560, 9936, 10021, 10255, 10315, 10327, 10575, 10696, 10698, 10720, 10875
"smells, loved the" 8527
"smells like that, what" 8529
"smells of baking" 8540
"smells of cats" 8533
"smells of flowery pomade" 8538
"smells of the place, mingled smothering" 8515
"smelt blossom everywhere" 3800
"smelt of carbolic acid" 8509
"smelt the air" 385
"smelt the breeze salty" 10696
"smelter towns" 9181
"smile, answered with a" 9869
"smile, broke into the loveliest" 8548
"smile, her" 8551
"smile, incredulous" 2492
"smile, little boy's" 8562
"smile, look like idiots when they" 8560
"smile, make you" 253
"smile, never lighted by a" 5889
"smile, odd little" 7475
"smile, off-center" 6241
"smile, only man in France who can" 8550
"smile, queasy" 4210
"Smile, The Silver" 1479
"smile, we" 9926
"smile for a photograph, would not" 8558
"smile for no man" 6820
"smile like applause" 8554
"smile of an angel, soft stone" 1221
"smile softening his lips" 8547
"smile with *a Design upon Us*" 10764
"smiled" 5024
"smiled, although he" 10380
"smiled, she" 8555
"smiled, when Farmer Oak" 8545
"smiled and introduced myself" 8027
"smiled and sweated and spoken for the other" 7882
"smiled at the young woman" 8557
"smiled in return, she" 8027
"smiled mischievously" 2025
"smiled Mrs. Gower" 10865
"smiled to feel the April sun" 8552
Smiles, Mrs. Rensselaer 5080
Smiles, Veronica 2640
Smiles 243, 515, 837, 1235, 2904, 4210, 5308, 5892, 7475, 7485, 8092, 9869, 10133, 10380, 10585, 10865
"smiles" 6842

"smiles, bathing suits and" 8092
"smiles, not unkindly" 5308
"smiles as she stares into the big
   blue enamel pot" 8561
Smiley, George 1816, 5930
Smiley, Mr. George 3444
"smiling" 515, 8546, 10585
"smiling, face moved with" 243
"smiling, settling down into his
   sofa and" 4351
"smiling and pleading" 1661
"smiling at her own reflection" 7485
"smiling at the in-no-way beautiful
   person" 10133
"smiling glances" 9113
"smiling nods, elicited the usual"
   5892
"smiling on a man who risks his
   all" 1220
"smiling on you" 1235
"smiling teeth, insolent flash of"
   8553
"smiling too but with a different intensity" 8546
"smirked a complacent acceptance
   of the epithet" 962
Smith 7222
Smith, Captain John 5227
Smith, Christine 4767
Smith, Emmett 3025
Smith, Father 1499
Smith, George 4276
Smith, Mag 2493
Smith, Miss Charlotte 6104
Smith, Reverend Joshua Sr. 1531
Smith, Roland Lane 9381
Smith, Rona 2758
Smith, Sam 6313
Smith, Valentine Michael 4759
"Smith, graduating from" 3261
Smithers, Mrs. 6094
"Smithport Long Island" 6163
Smiths 1497
"smitten by the sight" 1866
Smitty 4791, 6652
Smock, Mr. Nelson 1591
"smock, sky-blue" 10816
"smog" 5447
"smog, no" 3362
Smoke 771, 1364, 3760, 3763,
   3766, 3767, 3768, 3773, 3774,
   3776, 3780, 3783, 3792, 4412,
   4679, 7258, 7839, 8422, 8510,
   8581, 9505, 10349, 10612, 10718,
   10720
"smoke, a" 10158
"smoke, acrid taste of an ancient"
   10349
"smoke, blanketed with" 7839
"smoke, came through the" 4412
"smoke, cigarette" 6780
"smoke, first saw the" 784
"smoke, fog of its own" 1364
"smoke, foreboding hung like" 7019
"smoke, horizontal plume of" 3774

"smoke, leftover" 10303
"smoke, like a plume of" 9772
"smoke, no" 3108
"smoke, plume of" 10718
"smoke, scrolls of clotted" 3760
"smoke, serpentine plumes of
   gaudy poisonous" 7282
"smoke, sit and" 8862
"smoke, smell of" 3780, 8510
"smoke, smell of wood" 9560
"smoke, swirling ominous cloud of
   acrid black" 3783
"smoke, thicksome bloats of" 771
"smoke, wisps of" 7258
"smoke alive with the flicker of the
   fires" 3766
"smoke and flare of a dying battle"
   786
"smoke below an hour ago, he had
   seen the" 3768
"smoke billowed from broken windows" 3792
"smoke cigarettes to a moderate
   amount" 4789
"smoke coming off the summits"
   8736
"smoke from a grass fire, like" 2952
"smoke from a million chimneys"
   10612
"smoke from his meerschaum" 8573
"smoke from last night's cigarettes"
   10303
"smoke from my cigarette" 9505
"smoke from the cooking fires"
   4679
"smoke furled, far" 3773
"smoke in the valley" 3759
"smoke of the smelter towns" 9181
"smoke rings, like" 7779
"smoke rose a little and then fell
   downward" 3421
"smoke rose from behind the ornate spire of St. Enoch's Church"
   3783
"smoke rose thin and straight, a
   column of" 3763
"smoke sprouting from the wide
   spring prairie" 9772
"smoke that rises from his cigarette" 8581
"smoke was drifting" 3776
"smoked, rarely" 8567
"smoked one cigarette after
   another" 8583
"smokehouse, behind the" 5710
"smokers" 9381
"smokers of pipes" 4335
Smoking 247, 298, 899, 1096,
   2827, 2974, 3990, 4277, 5615,
   5999, 6299, 6730, 6780, 7549,
   7680, 7999, 8895, 8976, 9004,
   9548, 10158
"smoking" 247, 3990
"smoking, chain-" 8578
"smoking a cigarette" 8579

"smoking a cigarette, a lady sat"
   8564
"smoking a pipe" 8572
"smoking in bed" 5960
"smoking in the lobby only" 8569
"smoking joints, casually" 3283
"smoking of an enormous pipe"
   8563
"smoking-rooms, gaunt" 4317
"smoky sunshine" 4571
Smolders, Jackie 5753
Smollett, Arthur 1952
"smooth, very" 181
"smooth as stone" 7685
"smoothly as a dolphin cutting the
   green water" 9811
"smothered quick as kittens" 5332
"smudge or error, without" 4859
"smudging, slamming and" 518
"smudgy proof" 7349
"smug" 5296
"smug bastards" 2527
"smug complacence" 7982
"smuggle him out of court" 1505
"smugglers, beacon set up by" 3671
"smugglers, burly earringed" 3396
"smuggling trade, drug-" 3054
"snake, a dead" 4128
"snake, bitten by a" 633
"snake, from inside like a" 2973
"snake, giant sacred" 529
"snake, like a stub-tailed and
   languorous" 7252
"snake, tail-eating" 5521
"snake between her breasts" 2851
"snake consuming a large Tuscan
   toad" 3882
"snake I saw, the first" 4128
"snake my father brought home"
   4128
"snake sleeping, like a" 9172
"snake this in" 10964
"snaked its way through the
   Adirondacks" 9203
Snakes 449, 633, 2637, 3882,
   4128, 9235, 10205, 10546
"snakes, coupling" 2987
"snakes, fear of" 3714
"snakes, two of them" 3926
"snake's coils about his waist" 10205
"snakes on Ruth's lawns at night"
   449
"snaky feeling" 1878
"snapdragons" 3806
Snape, Reverend Weir 1536
"snapped off, tip of my shoe just" 39
"snapper, shrimp and" 5170
"snapshots" 6849
"Snares and Allurements" 10764
"snarling, clawing and" 9841
"snatching her fingers from the
   piano keys" 6215
"sneak a slug of whiskey" 2892
"sneak in quietly" 2906
"sneakers" 2839

"sneakers, dusty white" 10816
"sneakily" 5502
"sneaking into the neighborhood, coyotes were" 454
"sneaks, moral" 286
"sneer, half determined to" 6896
"sneered" 2356
"sneers and grins and lamby blanks" 6075
Snell, Balso 2603
Snell, Sylvester 997
"snickered nervously" 989
Sniffer 6207
"sniffing, began" 8524
"sniffing gasoline and glue" 6170
"sniffing pinescent" 4704
"sniffing through a pile of her multicoloured knickers" 6707
"sniffs at the counter" 7574
"sniggered, half Scotland" 7142
Sniggs, Mr. 8354
"snipped every radio aerial on the roof of 2094 Brighton Beach Avenue" 6652
"snob that I was raised to be, not the kind of" 9714
"snobbery" 7888
"snooker, shooting" 7047
"Snooks' Club" 10339
"snoop, childhood career as a" 7981
"snooze, fell into a fuddled" 6652
"snore, small" 8496
"snores, she" 8469
"snoring and grunting like a black-man" 8489
"snotnose, he was always a little" 4980
"snout, it's a" 549
Snow, Barney 2162
Snow 178, 221, 983, 1153, 1183, 1727, 2405, 3955, 5383, 5836, 6327, 6567, 6594, 7259, 7318, 7380, 7606, 8779, 8787, 9065, 9239, 9341, 9778, 10075, 10378, 10414, 10570
"snow" 8601
"snow, acres of old" 8588
"snow, bank of" 8607
"snow, beneath the drifted" 9790
"snow, christened" 10009
"snow, covered with" 6073
"snow, crisp" 6594
"snow, crusted" 7318
"snow, drift of" 5772
"snow, driving" 9092
"snow, dry" 8586
"snow, first flakes of" 9778
"snow, first light" 6626
"snow, first winter" 6327
"snow, gentle" 8610
"snow, glittering desolation of" 10570
"snow, grayed with melted" 8611
"snow, hunting" 8592
"snow, iridescent confetti of" 8625

"snow, it feels like" 3955
"snow, it is going to" 8609
"snow, large damp clumps of" 9955
"snow, like an overnight" 1070
"snow, loved the" 5383
"snow, March whistled stinging" 8590
"snow, mostly clear of" 3016
"snow, mountain" 10075
"snow, new" 9341
"snow, patches of" 8603
"snow, pure white bed of" 6594
"snow, several fat flakes of" 8624
"snow, shoveling the" 1701
"snow, silent" 3396
"snow, sudden fall of" 2960
"snow, the fallen" 9239
"snow, the falling" 4143
"snow, the February that it didn't" 8619
"snow, too cold for" 1551
"snow, under a mantle of" 8623
"snow, unseasonable" 8615
"snow, walked through deep" 10378
"snow, wet" 3810
"snow along the curb, dirty lumps of" 10414
"snow and sleet" 9065
"snow and the sound of sleigh-bells" 7380
"snow began quietly this time" 8598
"snow began to fall" 8604
"snow began to fall in the after-noon" 8599
"snow . . . blanketing everything" 8612
"snow blowing around like a bas-tard" 1153
"snow brushed his face" 8610
"snow clung wetly" 8595
"snow covered the airfield" 8605
"snow crusting the lawns and flowerbeds" 8615
"snow drifted against the window" 9778
"snow drifted in mean-lipped skeins" 8616
"snow fall out of a dark sky" 6327
"snow falls like the thick fur of cot-tonwoods" 8622
"snow fell again yesterday" 8612
"snow fell early in Germany" 8602
"snow . . . fell for some hours con-tinuously" 8587
"snow for Christmas" 8613
"snow from yesterday's fall" 178
"snow had been drifted by the wind" 8593
"snow had fallen" 2405
"snow had fallen all night" 8600
"snow had fallen steadily" 8586
"snow had only just stopped" 8787
"snow has melted, when the" 8514
"snow heap, most social" 4322

"snow in an April night, you shouldn't get an inch of" 8621
"snow in the mountains was melt-ing" 78
"snow in the streets is like a dirty worn-out blanket" 8594
"snow into molten gold, dazzle of the sun turned the" 983
"snow . . . lay almost as deep in the towns as in the fields" 8602
"snow lay on the ground" 6626
"snow lay thick on the moorlands" 8616
"snow of the season, first good" 292
"snow . . . sifts from the void" 8625
"snow still fell" 8606
"snow . . . still lay in patches" 178
"snow tarnished by sodium arc light" 8625
"snow that knows no mercy nor feels remorse" 4307
"snow that year, more" 8608
"snow thickening, the falling" 8617
"snow thrown up by the plough" 8607
"snow was almost undisturbed" 9187
"snow was falling, first real" 8606
"snow was falling, light" 7259
"snow was falling, outside the" 8779
"snow was falling over North Lon-don" 8507
"snow winged softly out of the gray sky" 8624
"snow would soon begin falling" 8591
"snowberries which grew under the elms" 4157
"snowed hard the night before" 7606
"snow-fall, ineffectual refreshment of a dull moist" 1183
"snowfall of the year, the last" 9092
"snowfalls, heavy" 8587
"snowfields weep slowly down" 5077
"snowflakes, shimmering curtain of" 8597
"snowflakes eddied, wandering" 8584
"snowflakes fluttered down upon Chicago" 8597
"snowhouse" 10727
"snowing, it must have been" 8614
"snowing, it was" 8618
"snowing steadily for three days" 8593
"snowmen found in the Sahara, like" 1429
"snows of a grim February eve-ning" 8585
"snows . . . were falling in the fine flakes which predict a long storm" 8585
"snowstorm, arrived in Korea in a" 221

"snowy twilight" 8596
Snoxell, Samuel 1294
"snuff, why he took" 6043
"snuffling" 7440
"snug" 3127
"snug little collection" 1349
"snugly around him, tucked" 8376
Soames, Henry 5577
"soaping a meditative foot" 567
"soaping himself, luxuriously" 570
"soar above the murk & smog" 5447
"soared more strongly than ever, spires towers belfries" 10590
"soared over the crude mill town of Magog" 772
"soaring, I was" 7096
"soaring through crystal skies" 9615
"sob, I choked back a" 9063
"sob from his wife, a final" 3566
"sobbing softly" 2084
"sober, still wasn't" 2908
"sober to a fault" 3597
Soby, Arnold 2332
"soccer field" 311
"sociable, so" 1493
"social director" 7727
"social events" 10671
"social frenzy, midday" 8640
"social gatherings" 10798
"social independence of the Bingle family" 7756
"social law that makes the moot guest the early bird" 7816
"social life" 8632
"social map" 5708
"social position, enjoyed a some-what high" 361
"social reform" 5887
"social reputation" 4339
"social round, lame" 8637
"social solitude" 8715
"social standing" 5934
"social worker" 87
Socializing 2886, 4306, 4309, 4322, 4329, 6760, 8715, 9348, 10798
"social-scientist way, your" 8222
"societies, even in small" 7584
"society, almighty secret and des-perate" 2837
"Society, Arcadian" 8344
"society, gentle order of" 4996
"society, high" 2118
"Society, modern" 7378
"society, my rightful place in" 6485
"Society, Noat Art" 2531
"society, slave or the outcast of" 10766
"society, tragic in" 10667
"society applauded Christine Nils-son" 1012
"society from which they had emi-grated" 6147
"society had rallied in force" 1198

"society help and comfort, mutual" 5742
"society here in Vienna" 6242
"society invites him, if the" 6242
"Society of Creative Writers, Australian" 5429
"Society of Psychical Research" 10181
Sociology 4441, 7011, 7164
"sociology" 940
"sock, old woollen" 10934
Socket, Eddie 4438
"socks, gray cotton" 5929
"socks, my other" 1607
"socks, rough woolen" 4154
"socks, tucked carelessly into his" 1501
"socks, white" 4181
"Socorro New Mexico" 6880
Socrates 509
"sod, thick" 8387
"sodden curtains in the tub" 5372
"sodden in rain, azaleas" 3314
"sodomy" 1288
"sofa, black leather" 6131
"sofa, green vinyl" 7085
"sofa beside the Marchesa del Rosso, I found myself on a" 10819
Sofka 6865
"soft, weak" 10811
"soft ones" 349
"soft to touch" 7409
"softball game, final" 2013
"softened to a pliant paste" 2833
Soft-Walker 8510
"Soho, in the heart of" 4319
"soil, adobe" 8038
"soil, American" 277
"soil, clayey" 3653
"soil, English" 3635
"soil, grey clay" 7052
"soil, pebbly" 4380
"soil, ruggedness of the" 9515
"soil, thin blanket of poor" 3903
"soil, 'twas a happy" 6249
"soil of Texas was parched and cracked" 7314
"soil was baked as hard as rock" 3653
"sojourn, disastrous" 6467
"sojourn in the coop, his" 7140
"sojourner from the city, he who is but a" 10566
Sol 9932
"sold cabbages and radishes" 6459
"sold his first house" 1086
"sold insurance" 6482
"sold my Books and Furniture" 10465
"sold off by some peasant father" 366
"sold off the last of our mother's houses" 3756
"sold used cars" 1992

"soldier, brave and honoured Re-publican" 8641
"soldier, half-decent" 4468
"soldier, regular" 8658
"soldier, some Spanish" 8663
"soldier, young" 8692
"soldier, was most singly a" 8698
"soldier alone, a" 2362
"soldier going into battle" 9318
"soldier of God" 7604
"soldiering, vast amount of" 10779
Soldiers 59, 204, 465, 486, 713, 928, 940, 1172, 1529, 2147, 2364, 2560, 2571, 2933, 3676, 4313, 4469, 4590, 4601, 4674, 4803, 5537, 6441, 6733, 6773, 6866, 6881, 7160, 7228, 7246, 7894, 8172, 8767, 9303, 9559, 9755, 10034, 10297, 10465, 10498, 10515, 10533, 10585, 10779
"soldiers" 5971
"soldiers, a number of" 8644
"soldiers, arms of our" 8643
"soldiers, blood of" 4469
"soldiers, foot" 7630
"soldiers, French" 10515
"soldiers, German" 8706
"soldiers, had been" 8688
"soldiers, Indian" 8682
"soldiers, old" 2057
"soldiers, sea has swallowed her" 10471
"soldiers, wounded" 8767
"soldiers arrived, long before the" 9755
"soldiers boarded the train" 8676
"soldiers coming, he could see the" 8710
"soldier's face" 59
"soldiers from England" 8702
"soldiers in blue" 465
"soldier's lung in half, cut the" 2933
"soldiers marched toward them" 8690
"soldiers now embarking" 8643
"soldiers three, only" 8647
"soldiers who had struggled and died" 7228
"sole of his boot down, brought the" 8810
"Soledad, a few miles south of" 7659
"solemn procession" 7179
"solemnity, proper" 6219
"solemnize the nuptials" 10641
"solemnly, replied" 298
"solemnly declare" 9989
"solemnly gliding about" 7709
Solent, Wolf 9412
"soles of his feet" 5686
"solicitor, waiting for his" 10079
"solicitors on the east side of Rus-sell Square" 1015
"solicitous, generally" 3910
"solidity of construction" 3122

"solidity, there was no longer" 4320
"solipsism, discovered" 6839
"solitaire, game of" 301
"solitary life" 6883
Solitude 430, 869, 935, 992,
 2070, 2278, 2362, 2769, 3521,
 3789, 3835, 4227, 5275, 5302,
 6010, 6297, 6428, 6555, 6577,
 6815, 6883, 8332, 8341, 8353,
 8357, 8368, 8491, 9108, 9398,
 9854, 10071, 10237, 10284, 10735
"solitude, blood and women and"
 9285
"solitude, social" 8715
"solitude is limitless" 8732
"solitudes" 9054
Solivan, Tito 2925
Solly 8745
Solomon 2782, 4853
"Solomonlike, totally un-" 362
"solstice slide, long spring" 9776
"solution whatever, no" 2506
"solvent" 5301
"somber sky" 8421
"sombre eyes" 3365
"sombrero, the pushing up of his"
 5899
"sombrero fell out of the sky" 2850
"somebody was calling" 2764
"someday I intended to master" 246
"someone else, I think I became"
 4814
"someone else, it seems" 2111
"someone like myself, to" 5437
"someone very important or very
 fat" 1651
"someone's here" 9980
"someplace bruised and very
 tangled" 9060
"Somerset" 3248, 4567
"Somerset, county of" 8957
"Somersetshire" 1572, 4439
"Somersetshire, West" 9466
"something, is this" 7210
"something, there was" 1350
"something awful coming toward
 him" 2782
"something much more contracted
 and unaccommodating" 10260
"something to do" 937
"something was up" 5777
"Somkele" 6122
Sommer, Bertha 10459
"somnolent hamlets" 7254
"somnolent July afternoon" 3145
Son 2765, 6519
"son, a" 7056
"Son, a" 355
"son, at the sight of her" 8548
"son, concerned about my" 6466
"son, dead man's" 2303
"son, does not deserve to have a"
 6610
"son, eventually had a" 3596
"son, first" 2398

"son, her" 3552, 3582, 3782, 6131,
 6159, 6548, 9931, 10540, 10949
"son, her nine-year-old" 3652
"son, her own" 6610
"son, her young" 9835
"son, his" 2447, 2584, 3553, 3559,
 4254, 5194, 5838, 6516, 6996,
 7006, 7217, 9496
"son, his father's" 4242
"son, his five-year-old" 6851
"son, his older" 6550
"son, his only" 3550
"son, his small" 1627
"son, his twelve-year-old" 1153
"son, married her own" 3628
"son, my" 360, 2576, 3039, 4539,
 4564, 5484, 6552, 6643, 7444
"son, my darling" 1957
"son, my inevitable" 6532
"son, new-born" 549
"son, old woman's" 9659
"son, one" 6515
"son, only" 3356
"son, our" 5296
"son, our youngest" 5779
"son, Peter Dekatha's" 8264
"son, prayed for a" 7071
"son, Rabbi's only" 6482
"son, raised up a" 6546
"son, seventeen-year-old" 3579
"son, stillborn" 4439
"son, their" 2684, 6611
"son, their three-week-old" 5636
"son, thy" 1806
"son, twelve-year-old" 10971
"son, when she saw her" 4108
"son, wished I had a" 6528
"son, younger" 358, 4926
"son and heir of Philip of Macedon
 and of Olympias" 5451
"son blessed with so excellent a disposition" 6521
"son did not return to the apartment" 10971
"son for each farm, one" 3660
"son in affection though not in
 blood" 5484
"son like I have a son, you should
 have a" 6530
"son of a clergyman, the only" 6609
"son of a judge" 6535
"son of a preacher" 6535
"son of a sick mother" 6652
"son of Gerrit" 4760
"Son of God" 2644
"son of my father, the only" 6606
"son of nobody" 366
"son of one of our oldest earls" 6607
"son of Rebecca and Samuel Sternholz" 6472
"son of Richard Courtenay" 4926
"son of Shimpoor" 8040
"son of Shoolpi" 8040
"son of Shullum" 8040
"son who reveres me" 6517

Song 740, 1312, 1614, 2084, 2111,
 3750, 4335, 4474, 4736, 5757,
 6201, 6218, 7833, 8702, 8739,
 8740, 8742, 8750, 8751, 8755,
 8759, 8760, 8762, 8763, 8767,
 9361, 9365, 9560, 9995, 10147,
 10912
"song, begetters of" 7833
"song, common country" 4335
"song, daytime" 8813
"song, good" 8751
"song, loud and sentimental" 10147
"song, my favorite" 4736
"song, passover" 2278
"song, singing a" 8762
"song, skipping rope to that" 8747
"song, South American love" 740
"song, this particular version of
 the" 8755
"'Song, Toreador'" 571
"song, very very funny" 8745
"song, words to this" 10912
"song, Yiddish" 8761
"song about the death of Arthur"
 8762
"song among birds" 10587
"song over the taut wires" 6218
"song to himself, hummed a" 8760
"song written by a former governor
 of Louisiana" 8760
"songs, rock and roll" 5509
Sonia 1565
"son-in-law, her" 10997
"sonnets, Shakespeare's" 5520
Sonny 5355, 8723
"son-of-a-bitch, crummy" 2656
"sonofabitch, you little Fairchild"
 4988
"Sonoma County" 6132
Sons 969, 1806, 2384, 2398, 2576,
 3039, 3550, 3559, 3569, 3579,
 3596, 4108, 4223, 4242, 4254,
 4743, 4753, 5779, 6404, 6466,
 6482, 6516, 6528, 6530, 6532,
 6534, 6544, 6548, 6550, 6590,
 6649, 6716, 6851, 7056, 7071,
 7078, 7385, 7566, 9931, 10540,
 10853
"sons, created four" 2635
"sons, her seven" 2553
"sons, his" 6524, 7554
"sons, his four" 6712
"Sons, I was the Third of five" 6602
"sons, my" 311, 6554
"sons, not being born" 10853
"sons, our two" 6187
"sons, their two" 6140, 6860
"Sons, Three" 7055
"sons, two" 3105, 3569, 7078
"sons and daughters" 640
"son's blood is finally spilled" 6649
"son's coffin, his" 2384
"sons of gentlemen" 7878
"Sons of Italy in America" 3753
"Sons of the Rich, The Little" 10554

"Sony 747" 9594
Sonya 1241
"sooner or later" 3265
"soot, fine black" 1070
"soothe her dear mamma's last
     moments" 8838
"soothe with the sound of names"
     8808
Sophie 4120, 5053, 9397, 9802
Sophie, Grandma 3951
"Sophis, last winter in" 9435
"sophomore, stocky auburn-haired"
     7903
"sopping big ones, you'll get some"
     2279
"Soracte, Mt." 7514
"sorcerer, Egyptian" 4492
"sordid love affairs, I like" 7713
"sordidness" 962
"sordidness of his present exis-
     tence" 5292
"Sorède, Forêt de" 3125
Sorge, Solomon Alexei 5459
"sorority sisters" 1453
"sorrel mare" 437
Sorrell 9536
Sorrell, Mr. 7966
"Sorrentine peninsula" 4037
"Sorrento" 8937
Sorrow 2070, 2079, 2492, 4116,
     5661, 7437, 9402, 10341
"sorrow" 5661
"sorrow, no worldly" 4996
"sorrow, with quiet" 653
"sorrow, worship and" 10341
"sorrowful, thoughts were" 9402
"sorrows, suffer noble" 4454
"sorrows of Evan Shepard's loutish
     adolescence" 5671
"sorry" 162, 341
"sorry, everybody seemed" 6092
"sorry, I'm" 7493
"sorry about all the rows" 1802
"sorry any of it happened, I'm not"
     3509
"sorry for, less much less to be"
     7494
"sorry for myself, I was feeling"
     2505
"sorry for myself, let me be" 1797
"sorry that it happened, not" 1820
"sorry that the press boat was
     alongside" 8091
"sorry to go" 8665
"sorted her mail" 1951
"sorting, the papers she was" 10887
"sorting it all out, job of" 10559
"sotto voce, begin" 622
"Soufrière, Mount" 5052
"sought, township which I" 6069
"sought and found his fortune in
     Malaya" 3152
"sought in vain" 4229
"sought shelter among the rocks"
     4478

"sought the Lord, as long as he"
     7536
"soul" 10757
"soul, energies of the" 5642
"soul, geography of the" 5706
"soul, God rest his" 7002
"soul, harrow the" 4101
"soul, heart and a" 408
"soul, human" 4509
"soul, living" 3669
"soul, longitude and a latitude of
     the" 5574
"Soul, lurked a" 412
"soul, my" 800, 5576, 10807
"soul, my poor" 7057
"soul, not knowing a" 9108
"soul, rang in his" 3514
"soul, sure in his" 4704
"soul, time for nothing but his"
     8979
"soul, whisper unto my" 7524
"soul, winter of his" 5574
"soul has memory of" 800
"soul he revealed, it was his" 7956
"soul of a particular human being"
     6001
"soul of a saint" 8758
"soul of the First Cause of all life,
     the divine-diabolic" 6001
"soul sister, brown-sugared" 253
"soul took a better grasp upon the
     world" 2249
Souls 800, 2249, 5574, 5576,
     5706, 7524, 7956
"Souls" 2286
"souls, 352" 4059
"souls, two human" 5735
"souls, unforgiving" 5914
"souls of the dead" 747
"soul-smiting" 4396
"sound, broken" 10199
"sound, beautiful" 1421
"sound, dog who heard the" 8772
"sound, dropped round globes of"
     661
"sound, faint faraway" 8790
"sound, flopping" 8806
"sound, grave and holy" 653
"sound, great clatter of" 893
"sound, heard the" 8824
"sound, hurricane of" 652
"sound, irregular little" 8784
"Sound, Long Island" 6363
"sound, muted shafts of" 8813
"sound, near-by and indubitable"
     8801
"sound, permit no" 4248
"sound, poignantly haunting" 8799
"Sound, Puget" 400
"sound, she heard the" 8809
"sound, shut out all" 10362
"sound, smoothly continuous
     natural" 8820
"sound, soft" 8809
"sound, soft furtive" 10276

"Sound, the" 8036
"sound, the first" 8823
"sound, there was no" 8330
"sound again, the same" 8833
"sound began suddenly" 8793
"sound came from the engine, no"
     9805
"sound filled the narrow bedroom"
     2352
"sound . . . floated in the air" 665
"sound I heard, the first" 10727
"sound in the great green ferns"
     8809
"sound in the mornings, the first"
     8774
"sound is queer here by the water"
     8835
"sound like nothing he had ever
     heard before" 8817
"sound like the scurrying of mice"
     7712
"sound made my heart race" 8502
"sound merged with her dream"
     10222
"sound naturally surly" 10027
"sound of a farmyard animal" 6224
"sound of a huge emotionless suc-
     tion" 10746
"sound of a motor" 8770
"sound of approaching riders" 8786
"sound of breathing" 8483
"sound of cars" 8798
"sound of chicken frying and pots
     banging" 9339
"sound of church bells" 673
"sound of desperate running" 8789
"sound of his feet touching the
     steps" 8802
"sound of names" 8808
"sound of planes" 10222
"sound of singing" 9437
"sound of sleigh-bells" 7380
"sound of someone knocking" 10295
"sound of the Aegean Sea" 8894
"sound of the Angelus bell" 665
"sound of the applause" 2103
"sound of the explosion" 891
"sound of the name" 7899
"sound of the sea" 8792, 10187
"sound of the sea falling" 8771
"sound of the traffic" 8779
"sound of traffic, there was no" 7135
"sound outdoors arrested her atten-
     tion" 8816
"sound over the coals, hissing" 8810
"sound she makes with her beak
     and claws" 740
"[sound was] desperate and lone-
     some" 8793
"sound was muted and distant"
     8779
"sound was your feet slapping the
     pavement" 7855
"[sound] went high and keening"
     8793

"sound (what he did not know) struck the surface of his sleep" 10130
"sounded . . . like the humming of an insect" 8783
"sounded through Oxford station" 7239
"sounded wild as a storm" 8802
"sounding chain" 9996
"soundlessness of outer space" 8333
Sounds 236, 243, 378, 444, 479, 555, 648, 653, 655, 658, 659, 661, 665, 669, 670, 673, 739, 750, 777, 836, 878, 888, 891, 893, 1073, 1093, 1095, 1102, 1117, 1119, 1123, 1127, 1129, 1155, 1156, 1274, 1532, 1545, 2075, 2085, 2215, 2352, 2697, 2790, 2811, 2964, 3299, 3465, 3478, 3904, 3954, 4248, 4264, 4417, 4657, 4925, 4958, 4964, 5096, 5260, 5619, 5688, 5864, 5916, 6016, 6074, 6214, 6224, 6272, 6964, 7135, 7239, 7261, 7275, 7317, 7380, 7608, 7628, 7712, 7855, 7899, 8033, 8070, 8086, 8111, 8174, 8330, 8335, 8483, 8491, 8502, 8504, 8526, 8601, 8703, 9120, 9276, 9374, 9387, 9472, 9551, 9887, 9898, 9917, 10009, 10021, 10103, 10113, 10130, 10135, 10159, 10164, 10177, 10187, 10188, 10199, 10203, 10210, 10211, 10214, 10218, 10222, 10223, 10229, 10230, 10238, 10245, 10257, 10258, 10260, 10272, 10276, 10277, 10282, 10295, 10297, 10307, 10310, 10405, 10539, 10574, 10598, 10701, 10727, 10746, 10749, 10875
"sounds" 3478
"sounds, aware of" 5619
"sounds, final dying" 9387
"sounds, humming with the phantom" 1129
"sounds, individual" 8335
"sounds, murmured" 10260
"sounds, street" 8773
"sounds, twin" 10245
"sounds issuing from the orchestra" 9376
"sounds of boots stomping" 10297
"sounds of his fellow passengers" 8504
"sounds of life fell with the sun" 8070
"sounds of opening doors" 3299
"sounds of summer, the dry" 10701
"sounds of the silence" 8766
"sounds of their dress rehearsal" 9387
"sounds slowly diminished" 1532
"sounds were dulled, all" 8787
"soup, breathing heavily into her" 4465

"soup, Palestine" 10899
"sour, he was" 6369
"sour in his mouth" 8568
"source of power" 7043
"sources of the Cumberland River, one of the three" 436
"sourly, he decided" 9232
Soutar, Bishop 1504
"South, I suppose we fled the" 1733
"South, the" 2428
"South, the Deep" 4066
"South, The Deep" 2377
"South Africa" 8055, 9638
"South America" 6484
"South American democracy" 6259
"South American ports" 8118
"South Carolina" 331, 3857, 4030, 5785, 6457, 6973, 10469
"South Carolina seacoast" 4397
"South Dakota" 9140
"South Hobart, on the hill of" 1310
"South Kensington" 9381
"South Park" 4439
"South Philadelphia" 2401
"South Pole" 228
"South Square Westminster" 9537
"Southampton" 3476
"Southampton, good town of" 4971
Southby, Allen 1915
"Southern Pacific switching yards" 7269
"southerner nonetheless, he was a" 4543
"Southview Gardens, suburb of" 1856
"southwester, raw" 10698
"souvenir shops" 4436
Souvenirs 7386, 9529
"souvenirs I came upon" 7386
"sovereign, their" 8642
"Sovereign of the East" 7798
"Sovereign Pontiff" 9559
"sovereign power" 6255
"sovereigns, Tudor" 1335
"sovereigns of foreign countries" 3557
"sovereignty of Britain, the nominal" 7795
"Soviet citizens, 2,000" 6232
"Soviet emigrates, no" 6162
"Soviet standards" 6232
"sow, Lord Emsworth's supreme Berkshire" 1178
"sow the summer seeds" 3980
"sowers of hemp" 3639
"sowing" 3640
Space 519, 524, 525, 526, 528, 531, 532, 683, 4549, 4935, 5645, 6792, 6903, 8333, 9500, 9557, 10903
"space" 4935
"space, an uncultivated" 3906
"space, astronaut in" 1690
"space, dark ascensions and black declinations of" 5178

"space, dimensions of" 9500
"space, distant in" 9060
"space, geography of" 526
"space, I need" 8013
"space, illimitable ocean of" 6075
"space, impression of boundless" 10260
"space, intrusions from remote" 7545
"space, just occupying" 8834
"space, monopolised" 9761
"space, poised in" 5645
"space, remote fastnesses of" 528
"space, seeing Colorado from" 4549
"space, soundlessness of outer" 8333
"space, Time is one of the dimensions in" 6903
"space broken here and there by scattered houses and venerable pollards" 5126
"space I needed for my press, all the" 7771
"space pencil belched and lifted free" 215
"space was desultory" 7758
"spaces, curling flower" 9840
"spaces, great" 6249
"spaces, wide open" 1320
"spaceship, big as a" 7990
"Spacey" 7098
Spade, Samuel 333
"spade, one" 318
"spade, throwing aside his" 3793
"spade, with my" 6182
"spaghetti on paper plates" 1003
"Spain" 1098, 3376, 3398, 4592, 5223, 5590, 7626, 7800, 10485
"Spain, inns of" 6246
"Spain, Isabella of" 7630
"Spain, King of" 7124, 10966
"Spain, New" 4502
"Spain, Port of" 6435
"Spain is shattered" 10471
Spaine, Mrs. 5056
"Spaniard" 8165
"Spaniard, Basque Country" 5664
"Spaniard, educated" 9045
"spaniel at his heels, elderly" 2223
"Spanish, half" 4446
"Spanish, speak" 8087
"Spanish border" 7809
"Spanish Calendar" 7502
"Spanish dictator" 4481
"Spanish explorer" 473
"Spanish grant" 3089
"Spanish ladies" 9716
"Spanish Plague" 3273
"Spanish rule, in the time of" 1355
"Spanish settlement, a tiny" 1392
"Spanish soldier, some" 8663
"Spanish Steps" 4111
"spare time" 1710
"spare time, in his" 10559
"spare time, their" 6416
"spare-bodied" 10833

"spareribs" 3876
"spare-time literary activities" 5424
"Spark Iowa" 1676
"sparkled, everything" 5319
"sparkled gold" 7929
"sparkling on the varnish of the new furniture" 2754
"sparkling water" 1481
"sparks in burnt-up paper" 2195
"sparks of everlasting radium" 785
"sparky, atmosphere was" 3132
Sparrow, Caleb 5234
"sparrow, nest of a" 746
"sparrow appeared on the sill" 767
"sparrow than a snail, rather be a" 8749
"sparrows, splash of" 3045
"sparrows strung on barbed wire" 10425
"sparse procession of patrons" 1315
"sparsely populated Upper Peninsula" 4073
"Spartan fox, historic" 9529
"spasm, the final" 2429
"spasmodically, scribbling" 8816
"spasms, last" 10475
"spasms had shaken her" 142
"spat it into a handkerchief" 8882
"spat where his vomit lay" 7956
"spatchcocked, sees himself" 4897
"spatulate full, like a" 7471
"spauldeen bulging fat between her teeth" 1169
Spaulding 6559
"speak, do not" 6212
"speak, he does not" 1167
"speak, his turn to" 2336
"speak, if places could" 6909
"speak, just begun to" 8864
"speak, later we" 6938
"speak, she did not" 7586
"speak, she was meaning to" 5992
"speak, so to" 2550
"speak about the woman" 10558
"speak again, you did not" 2759
"speak early, learned to" 8843
"speak either, he did not" 7586
"speak English, though I" 5446
"speak freely about her past, she would never" 2502
"speak great words" 4454
"speak his name as if you were meditating upon it" 4782
"speak much or often, didn't" 6627
"speak of, things inside of me that I never" 7598
"speak of her, when they" 7527
"speak of instead, she elected to" 5992
"speak out for him after his death" 7584
"speak their little pieces" 8862
"speak to each other again, ever going to" 7589

"speak to her, had not meant to" 7603
"speake, copie of what he would" 7370
Speakeasies 4326
"speakeasy, the" 4326
"speakeasy on Fifty-second Street" 4310
"speaker of our Oklahoma House of Representatives" 2009
"speaking" 1124, 4735
"speaking, old man was" 6917
"speaking, political" 6979
"speaking, President was" 8873
"speaking, relatively" 3201
"speaking, rococo manner of" 8640
"speaking, were not" 7588
"speaking, when they felt like" 8897
"speaking, without" 10368
"speaking as she sometimes does in verse" 1998
"speaking in his customary abstracted and precise manner" 8863
"speaking of her" 10781
"speaking out in fury against man" 9087
"speaks of this story as a biography" 701
"speaks through broken teeth" 5971
"spear, the" 10157
Spearfield, Sylvester 6540
"spearpoint, converging to a" 9228
"spear-shaped clouds" 8404
"special, makes you feel" 879
"special, they were" 3927
"special, was something" 5962
"specialty is woodwind instruments" 6236
Species 5272
"species, female of the" 2559
"species, how many" 5272
"species of black magic" 3534
"species of public property" 9260
"species of the helianthus" 10899
"specific places" 1429
"specifications, made to our" 2835
"specimen, sadly macerated and decomposed" 3804
"specimen of an Irish politician, the perfect" 7002
"specimens, find" 7232
"speck, silver" 225
"speck in the immense whole, an inconsiderable" 4533
"specks of dust" 5339
"spectacle is not at its best" 1183
"spectacles, bifocal" 9314
"spectacles, can't see without my" 8261
"spectacles, he wasn't wearing his" 41
"spectacles, plastic-rimmed" 8758
"spectacles, through his" 6889
"spectacles, through somewhat antique" 1527

"spectacles, two such" 5371
"spectacles for reading, I wear" 4789
"spectacles for the time being" 4153
"spectacles from his nose, took his" 6350
"spectacular, rather" 8287
"spectacular setting" 1391
"spectator, felt like a" 3313
"Spectator, the" 696
Spectators 3313, 8920
"spectral birds" 745
"spectral fog, dense" 9643
"spectral quiet" 8119
"spectres and chimeras" 4101
"speculated in herds of cattle" 3604
"speculated in his rapid and rambling way" 9411
"speculating" 5607
Speculation 8556, 9411
"speculation" 5238
"speculation, interesting" 8556
"speculations about the immediate future" 4616
"speculators, real-estate" 3105
"sped on up the hill" 7846
"sped swiftly up the wide stone steps" 1580
Speech 387, 1677, 1816, 2036, 2435, 2742, 2925, 3243, 3523, 4503, 5188, 5189, 5323, 5363, 5446, 5954, 5997, 6615, 6838, 6979, 6981, 7200, 7412, 7492, 8026, 8296, 8713, 9312, 9603, 9910, 9923, 10107, 10197, 10199, 10543, 10558, 10657
"speech, bridegroom's" 10657
"speech, getting ready to launch into a" 8882
"speech, gift for persuasive" 8026
"speech, hesitating" 8848
"speech, his annual budget" 8866
"speech, it is time for" 8875
"speech, pages of his" 8872
"speech, prepared to make an important" 8859
"speech, rest not day nor night from" 8854
"speech, so that he could begin his" 10107
"speech by the governor" 9729
"speech of farewell, made a curt" 1525
"speech she had just delivered" 8879
"speech that startled him" 8847
Speeches 8875, 10460
"speechless race" 8841
Speed 3621
Speed 9, 5102, 10455
"speed, made" 9130
"speed, steadily increased" 7278
"speed, they got him for his" 5102
"speed I couldn't tell, what" 7990
"speed uncommon for her" 10445

"speeded up and passed the truck" 2973

Speeding 40, 2955, 2979, 2999, 3009, 7639, 7842, 7853, 9770, 10445

"speeding, car was" 2955

"speeding along Memorial Drive" 2999

"speeding along the new through-way" 2979

"speeding along the unpaved un-named road" 40

"speeding through Washington Square Park" 7854

"speeding to the beaches" 9616

"speeding up all the life of folks" 9770

"speeding westward from Chicago" 8564

Speke, Ivor 4831

"spell, its" 1298

"spell, two-week dry" 7031

"spell during the year, a short" 2239

"spell or enchantment, kind of" 9376

"spell that Stuart if you wish" 2797

"spell was broken" 2150

"Spella Ho" 7219

"spelled it" 4831

Spelling 6, 4831

"spelling bee" 6

"spelling of his name, the change in" 3538

Spellman, Elizabeth 10117

Spellman, Francis Cardinal 4661

Spelman, Laura 10414

Spence 8319

Spencer 3576

Spencer, Carol 10800

Spencer, Colonel 4500

Spencer, John 3665

Spencer, Natalie 8629

"Spencer's Mountain" 6077

"spend a quiet Sunday with him" 9858

"spend it, how to" 5259

"spend long on it, you can be sure I won't" 4235

"spend on pilot training" 196

"spend the night at their country place in Pyefield" 6370

"spending the week-end" 9896

"spending the winter in Rome" 9720

Spenlove, Mr. 8075

"spent a lot of time over the past months" 9435

"spent a week in Chicago" 5413

"spent hours each day" 518

"spent my life" 5569

"spent quite a turbulent night" 10285

"spent the last three weeks, where he had" 8091

"spent the most important part of his life" 6500

"spent too many hours" 938

"spermatazoa, paid you a little tribute of" 7996

"sperms, misering his" 7990

"sphagnum, bog marshes of" 4073

"sphere of ours, this whirling" 2218

"sphere of the earth, the great" 525

"sphinx" 5971

"spice on that, this" 7378

Spicer 9988

"spices, herbs and" 8544

"spices, redolent of" 5584

"spicing, a small breeze was" 10586

"Spider, the secret radio" 1118

"spider writing" 5500

Spiegelglass 3600

"spies, foremost" 5309

"spiffy in his patent-leather brown and white shoes" 1982

"spigot open, threw the" 4901

Spike 10099

Spike, Captain Stephen 8047

"spikes, studded with iron" 3985

"spilled wine over our matches" 2129

Spin 7440

"spin and weave both wool and cotton" 1005

"spin of the wheel, another" 10980

"spinach, her own" 3860

"spindrift, day of" 10711

"spine, along my" 2607

"spine against, nothing to prop his" 8257

"spinning on its axis" 2118

"spinning wheels hummed busily" 5886

"spinster, I am a" 4769

"spinster, middle-aged" 2018

"spinster, sixty-five-year-old" 1891

"spinster material" 10886

"spiraling down onto a dying lion" 4778

"spire, half-built minster" 1849

"spire, ornate" 3783

"spire of St. Paul's" 2214

"spire of the church pricking the distant clouds" 1299

"spires and towers of the cathedral and colleges" 9160

"spires, church" 8591

"spires towers belfries soared more strongly than ever" 10590

"spirit" 10757

"spirit, abasement of" 2767

"spirit, broken the" 10525

"spirit, human" 4496

"spirit, some" 6212

"spirit, strict or puritanical" 6972

"Spirit, summoned by the" 3338

"Spirit, Sword of the" 5113

"spirit and flesh" 10774

"Spirit of Des Moines" 7281

"spirit of Galway, all the" 4308

"spirit of the dead man" 2303

"spirited and bright" 10845

Spirits 747, 2303, 2799, 4106, 4109, 4111, 4112, 5704, 9008

"spirits, dejection of" 9513

"spirits, depression of" 8477

"spirits, frozen everyone's" 1563

"spirits, put me in poor" 2444

"spirits contending with one another, winds like" 1706

"spirits high, her" 3019

"spirits of her ancestors would be with her" 4109

"spirits of the desert" 5704

"spiritual, too subliminal to be called" 6001

"Spit, dance club" 4849

"spit away if that's what you feel like" 10560

"spit it out and save himself, a mo-ment to" 6211

"spit of high ground" 6564

"spite of all, in" 2324

"spite of his age, in" 85

"spiteful, 124 was" 3236

"spiteful, she was" 6533

"spiteful man, I am a" 146

Spitefulness 3236, 6533

"spits, He" 2641

"spittin, no point in" 8889

"spitting, neat way of" 246

"spitting distance of millionaires, within" 10560

Spitz, Yussel 7114

"splash!" 5733

"splash of champagne spotted the linen tablecloth" 5186

"splashes of blood" 3798

"splashing, a desolate" 8134

"splayed, legs" 1170

"splayed her fingers" 1760

"splendid, lonely and" 992

"splendour of the scenery" 9376

"splinter under her skin, probing for a" 7441

"splinters falling like hailstones, glassy" 10717

"split on him" 2684

"split up, my wife and I" 5811

"split when I was a child, they" 6699

"splotchy sliding-down grayness" 7316

"spluttering engine" 7628

"spoiling it later on, make up for" 882

"spoke, we hardly" 7591

"spoke as an authority on male shortcomings" 982

"spoke from the foot of the steps" 2765

"spoke in Ann's mind, the phrase" 10967

"spoke in light, they" 8897

"spoke in the garbled mumble" 8895

"spoke lightly, she" 5732

"spoke much of his early life, never" 6127

"spoke of him" 5914

"spoke tenderly of the youth" 11000

"spoke them, but I never" 7492

"spoke to the chauffeur" 4564

"spoke with Altrurian breadth" 5278

"spoken, neither of them had" 7590

"spoken, solemnly" 2311

"spoken as they lingered and slowly moved together" 8847

"spoken intimately, we have never" 8876

"spoken of, it was not openly" 10039

"spoken often" 8876

"spoken to him about it" 9246

"spokes, wooden" 9830

"spoon, dirty plastic" 1864

"Spoonerism, deliberate" 7677

"Sport, A True" 1982

"sport, fine" 317

"sport, outfits for" 2841

"sport, take gentle" 6561

"sport a well-defined mustache" 5301

"Sport of Kings" 8317

"sported with, woman I" 7440

Sports 10, 160, 321, 349, 2013, 2638, 3423, 4448, 4702, 5126, 5245, 5455, 6449, 7159, 7498, 7821, 7837, 8675

"sports and pastimes" 5126

Sports Illustrated 3547

"sports page" 7369

"sportsman, true-bred city" 4683

"sportsmen everywhere, worn and admired" 2835

"sportswriter, I am a" 4837

"sportswriters, shirt-sleeved" 8920

"spot, always on the" 10805

"spot, kindly curious" 6917

"spot, the exact" 2982

"spot, the fairest" 6564

"spot at the back of the house" 069

"spot him, the first to" 1638

"spot on top, a single" 3966

"spotlight he lived under" 1332

"spots, brown water" 5317

"spots, juicy" 4959

"spots, six white" 3966

"spots on my chest" 571

"spots the car" 2994

Spotswood, Tyler 9421

"spotted her" 4210

"spouting and sluicing off grimy warehouse roofs" 7307

"spraddle-legged on the sheepskin seat behind him" 2973

Spragg, Undine 7555

"sprang from the gritty iron of the Pullman car step" 1648

"sprang up on the north central plains" 1460

"sprawled along the counter and on the chairs" 5625

"sprawled before him in an easy-chair" 3916

"sprawled upon his knees is Zuzu" 1982

"sprawls on his stomach" 987

"spray, out of season" 5624

"spray, salt-laden" 8092

"spray flew over the man and the woman" 8092

Sprayberry 6473

"spread, Bar D" 7636

"spread downwards through the foliage" 5314

"spread like wildfire" 6334

"spreading riotous and strange" 7818

"spree, on a truancy" 7898

"sprightly disregard of his protests" 4614

Spring 78, 316, 725, 1177, 1438, 1452, 2244, 2253, 2301, 2305, 2377, 2659, 3314, 3377, 3801, 3805, 3807, 3810, 4382, 5649, 6557, 6561, 7318, 7632, 7650, 7702, 8356, 8411, 8514, 8933, 9068, 9468, 9622, 9683, 9742, 10480, 10496, 10578, 10584, 10587, 10590, 10600, 10603, 10608, 10626, 10627, 10632, 10634, 10638, 10639, 10703, 10737, 10738

"spring" 3314, 10638

"spring, burst forth in" 3979

"spring, cheerful activities of" 7608

"spring, English" 1177

"spring, first really warm day of" 2659

"spring, high country" 1548

"spring, in" 5649

"spring, in the" 6218

"spring, it was" 10584

"spring, it was an uncertain" 10578

"spring, it was the beginning of" 10639

"spring, it was the next" 1160

"spring, long cold" 3807

"spring, mildness of" 1181

"spring, rare sun of" 8411

"spring, sap of" 9468

"spring, since it was" 5141

"spring, small mountain" 4695

"spring, strange false" 10627

"spring, strange withered" 7632

"spring, thunderous" 10603

"spring, wet warm smell of" 7409

"spring again, it was" 10496

"Spring arrived late in 1916" 2305

"spring at last" 3810

"spring came, when" 1438

"spring came blowing gently to us" 10737

"spring came down from the seven hills" 10608

"spring came that year" 4382

"spring down here on the Chatta-hoochee" 2377

"spring . . . fell on him like a curse" 10608

"spring had arrived at the ap-pointed date" 316

"spring had been unusually cold" 9742

"spring has really come" 725

"spring herself, greening" 9622

"spring in memory, the coldest" 3805

"spring in southern New Mexico" 10634

"spring in the city" 10738

"spring is good in this land" 10626

"spring morning" 7887

"spring of 1813" 8356

"spring of 1915" 3825

"spring of 1945, late cheerless" 10526

"spring of 1971" 3751

"spring of 1926" 6447

"spring of hope" 3377

"spring of our times" 9286

"spring of the year" 2244

"spring out upon the Jersey wharf" 4910

"spring poor Ezra Adams died, that was the" 2301

"spring should fairly open, when the" 4555

"spring storms" 2989

"spring sunlight" 2977

"spring was almost done, when" 10480

"spring was in the air" 3801

"spring wind" 10590

Springer 5581

Springfellow, Sir Walter 1758

"Springfield Illinois" 1402

Springrove, Edward 3488

"springs, passing through dozens of" 9622

"springtime" 647

"springtime, early" 3067

"springtime, it is" 2253

"Springwell Harriers" 3998

"sprinkle, after a while it began to" 7299

"sprinkles sand on the parlor floor" 10932

"sprite of memory, flippant" 7373

"spritzer, sips from a" 8883

"sprouted breasts and bellies" 10822

"spruce, red" 6084

"Spruce Harbor Maine" 682

"spruce-trees, file of Norway" 9663

"spumy falls are falling" 7682

"spun in great looping gusts" 9078

"spur of Sha'ar Hagolan" 5716

"spur of the moment" 1816, 9391

"spurned by Heaven" 5165
"spurned Demosthenes' gold" 10871
"spurred his jet black horse" 7627
"spurs, jingling" 3396
"sputter, stopped with a" 9800
"spy, caught a" 8902
"spy, I was never a" 8901
"Spy, worthy of" 5943
"spy at the elbow of the powerful" 8904
"spyhole" 8292
Spying 8899, 8902
"spying on the dark and secret place" 8899
"squab, felt to the touch like a" 416
"squabbles, family" 7510
"squadron, carrier based" 6773
"Squadron, Umptieth" 8649
"squadron column" 8679
"squadron of blue jays" 10310
Squalatush, Mr. 3251
"squalid play" 9384
"Squallacombe" 9081
"squalls, grey" 7279
"squalls, rain" 10704
"squandered the changeless after-
noons" 10051
"square, ancient" 8924
"Square, Baregrove" 1294
"square, be" 9693
"Square, Berkeley" 4304, 9161
"Square, Campden Hill" 3833
"Square, Congo" 2108
"Square, Connaught" 9822
"square, courthouse" 4420
"Square, Harvard" 3186
"Square, Manchester" 9149
"Square, Market" 1629
"Square, Mecklenburg" 8259
"square, old grass-grown" 9214
"Square, Parliament" 2716, 9236
"Square, Pontippy" 9214
"Square, Portman" 8839
"Square, Proclamation" 9820
"Square, Radnage" 4166
"Square, Red" 5971, 10350
"Square, Russell" 1015, 1614, 2699,
3326, 5331
"Square, St. James's" 949, 5747
"Square, Sellway" 6321
"Square, Sheridan" 4108
"Square, Stuyvesant" 1012
"square, the" 6275
"Square, Times" 6274
"square, town" 5342
"Square, Town" 8606
"Square, turned into the" 1606
"square, village" 1462
"Square, Washington" 7756, 7854
"Square, Wellclose" 7505
"square dancing" 4384
"square in build" 6894
"square of about eight feet" 7515
"squared our elbows" 3839
"squash, the" 3973

"squashed than usual, more" 1428
"squat for as long as she could" 7101
"squats on the hill" 4618
"squatted in sullen destitution" 3128
"squatted in the crow's nest" 992
"squatted under a palm tree" 6933
"squatting" 8266
"squatting, men" 9775
"squatting, with the dying wind"
10705
"squawks" 740
"squeak, a very polite" 2697
"squeaked only softly" 7187
"squeeze, it was a tight" 7097
"squeeze fiercely" 1792
"squeezed between the other cars"
10410
"squint, he continues to" 4896
"squinted at Sun" 10311
"squinted at the rain" 7340
"squinted his eyes" 2764
"squinted out the window" 9437
"squinting" 10190
"squinting querulous and famished"
8947
Squires, Claude 10380
"squirrel chattered" 10307
"squirrels, as skittish and apprehensive as" 3722
Sriram 6636
"S.S. *Petrel*, whalecatcher" 8113
"stabbed him with a knife" 70
"stable, came into the" 460
"stable below BB's house" 3782
"stable-block, window of the" 10933
"stableboys" 9101
"stabled his horse" 9142
"stableman came out to greet him"
7644
"stables and outbuildings, picturesque old" 3179
"stabs at it, they have had two"
6998
"staccato, a touching" 1320
Stace, Andrew 7967
Stacey 1662
"staff, editorial" 6815
"staff, members of the" 6763
"staff, thump of a" 8330
"staffed by fairly young biochemists" 1065
Stafford, Paul 712
"Staffordshire" 6268
"stage, baring the" 9141
"stage, landing" 8139
"stage, on the edge of the" 9398
"stage, the great" 9400
"stage, the greatest" 4046
"stage, try their fortunes upon the"
9376
"stage, up on the" 9392
"stage, when I brought the" 2505
"stage driver" 2900
"stage on which we play our little
dramas" 5566

"stage the drowned-man act to
greet him" 6680
"stage was really coming" 9766
"stagecoach" 9626
"stage-coach, dragged by a" 9515
"stagecoach stirred up a long trail
of dust" 9772
"stagecoaches like her were speeding
up all the life of folks" 9770
"stages, its final" 3484
"stagestruck and starstruck" 6274
"staggered out of bed" 8486
"staggered under the load" 4375
"staggering" 10521
"stain, material doesn't" 2845
"stain, raspberry" 2880
"stain, strange incandescent blue"
205
"stained or dyed, as if" 365
"Stainforth estate" 3212
"Stainmoor, valley of" 10450
"stains, green grass" 5317
"staircase, wooden" 7712
"staircase had changed" 1255
"staircase was almost dark" 9406
"stairs, at the top of the" 1661
"stairs, dark" 6759
"stairs, familiar" 1594
"stairs, halfway down the subway"
8521
"stairs, immense cascade of stone"
2225
"stairs, scoured" 7441
"stairs, two flights down the iron"
3050
"stairs, up and down" 9213
"stairs, up three pair of" 9989
"stairs behind a maid, up more"
9873
"stairs that descended from the
Trinita di Monte to the Piazza
di Spagna" 2225
"stairway, great curving" 10368
"stairway, tavern" 10371
"stairway hung delicately between
the floors" 10368
Stairways 1255, 1661, 2005, 3050,
6759, 6770, 8521, 10368
"stairwell, brown-stained" 9887
"staled and pawed by fools" 7711
Stalin 7904
"stalked in the darkness" 8544
"stalking a dame, avidly" 2045
"stalking a hippopotamus" 1610
"stalks of heather" 5305
"stall, her wooden" 463
"stall, lemonade" 10783
"stalled for thirty minutes" 7262
"stalls, cluttered with" 1045
"stalls in the market-place" 906
"stammerer, the" 7802
Stammers, Mrs. 4739
"stamp, all of that" 6605
"stamp, some exact hydraulic"
7989

"stamped her feet to the cadence of the verse" 4474
"stamped on split in two, as if it has been" 5942
"stamped on the steps" 9876
"stamped out by the wilful circumstance of growing up" 4235
"stampede of escape" 8673
"stamps, Minuteman war" 10517
"stand, called to the" 5201
"stand, last forlorn" 7625
"stand, we need a place to" 6926
"stand after swallowing, able to" 2885
"stand and watch" 8093
"stand by the window" 10893
"stand in that court, I shall have to" 6044
"stand just as still as he can, I can" 10104
"stand on a cold floor, after a two-hour" 1215
"stand out the most vividly" 7384
"stand right here" 10066
"stand side-by-side" 2107
"stand still" 4191
"stand there, continued to" 1133
"stand there, could only" 8187
"stand there, nothing to do but" 9387
"stand there on the top-floor landing" 1419
"stand to the Westward" 2543
"*Standard*, looking through his" 7347
"Standard in Cornhill" 4303
"Standard Oil sign" 3733
"standard was different from the later one" 3637
"standards, by her own and her family's" 5744
"standards, Chinese" 3632
"standards, differing 'society'" 1351
"standards, lowered his" 620
"standards, Soviet" 6232
Standing 434, 947, 966, 971, 1185, 1419, 1585, 1641, 1767, 1870, 1980, 2220, 2270, 2455, 2690, 2708, 2719, 2722, 2745, 2827, 3441, 3499, 3774, 3922, 3986, 4109, 4140, 4150, 4155, 4255, 4263, 4298, 4429, 4430, 4532, 4641, 4643, 4678, 4688, 5895, 5898, 5910, 5940, 5944, 5945, 5952, 5959, 5964, 5974, 5979, 6091, 6192, 6719, 6900, 6926, 7529, 7682, 7706, 7918, 8077, 8106, 8246, 8258, 8274, 8277, 8286, 8403, 8452, 8481, 8644, 8684, 8724, 8778, 8792, 8849, 9749, 10042, 10046, 10066, 10072, 10073, 10075, 10079, 10104, 10302, 10716, 10735, 10803, 10850, 10859
"standing, considerable" 6406
"standing, I am" 4532

"standing, where they are" 7682
"standing, where you are" 3664
"standing a young woman" 5799
"standing amid the tan excited post-Christmas crowd" 2447
"standing among the fallen flowers" 7440
"standing around in the summer heat" 8893
"standing at 54th and Sixth" 5880
"standing at the bottom of the government wharf" 2270
"standing at the edge of the hotel porch" 5945
"standing at the edge of the lecture platform" 8555
"standing at the end of the long bar" 4318
"standing back resolutely" 9244
"standing barefoot on an oak stump" 10860
"standing beside her" 2206
"standing beside the bed" 10302
"standing by the bed shaking my foot" 10179
"standing by the Carley float" 8136
"standing halfway up the steps under a streetlight" 1767
"standing here" 4582
"standing here in front of my house" 82
"standing in a bus queue" 10046
"standing in a locker" 4430
"standing in a window" 4904
"standing in front of his dresser mirror" 4263
"standing in front of the Empire Theatre" 8849
"standing in her shop" 7529
"standing in little groups" 7410
"standing in one of the saloons" 3986
"standing in the doorway" 10133
"standing in the hallway" 4626
"standing in the kitchen" 2709
"standing in the knee-high grass, we can see him" 5944
"standing in the middle of the vast Hall" 4895
"standing in the pouring rain" 6993
"standing in the road" 8644
"standing in the runway of Harmony's only livery stable" 3441
"standing in the shadow of the tower" 7133
"standing in the Wonder Bar" 7395
"standing knock-kneed in a kilt" 1179
"standing on a chair" 1870
"standing on a stool in the kitchen" 7402
"standing on a wooden stool" 8260
"standing on station platforms" 5654
"standing on the corner" 4108

"standing on the front porch" 6863
"standing on the front steps" 6971
"standing on Westminster Bridge" 10803
"standing that noon in hot Israeli sunshine" 4704
"standing there" 10872
"standing there, I saw him" 4298
"standing there among the trees" 10564
"standing there watching" 320
"standing there with that queasy smile" 4210
"standing together" 10042
"standing up, she died" 2455
"standing up in the front of his wagon" 2374
"standing where a lane ended and cultivation began" 5152
"standing with legs wide apart" 4154
"standing with my brother" 8246
"stands, white pine" 3423
"stands at six o'clock" 9490
"stands at the edge of the sea" 1799
"stands at the stove" 8561
"stands at the window of the parsonage" 6719
"stands behind the summer-dusty windows" 9451
"stands hesitant" 5927
"stands in front of his bedroom window" 4969
"stands in front of Windsor Castle" 971
"stands looking out the long window" 2719
"stands on the yellow-gold beach" 980
"stands out on Fourteenth Street" 1313
"stands up in the garden" 10890
"standstill, came to a" 9532
"Stanford" 3526
Stanhope, Mrs. 238
"stank between sea and sky" 8071
"stank of drains" 4427
Stanley, Ann Veronica 6620
Stanton, Charles 10141
Stanton, Sabra 5428
Stapie, Uncle 5485
Staples, Robert 6051
"star, going to be a big" 1329
"star, large brilliant evening" 521
"star, represented by a" 3671
"star, shooting" 533
"star, tempestuous Mexican" 3126
"star, evening" 522
"Star, North" 527, 8125
"star, Venus his" 4816
"star, watched for the first" 653
"star, wearing the" 6951
"star glows above the gas pumps, Texaco" 8323
"star like Vico disappears" 1332

"star of his generation, greatest film" 7168

"star shone through a hole" 8401

"star shone with pure brightness" 522

"star you saw and swept onto the tip of your finger to suck" 7437

"starboard, port and" 8114

"starboard quarter" 8053

"starboard wing" 197

"star-crossed lovers" 5588

"stare, a fixed from-under" 5893

"stare, a kind of dreamy" 6548

"stare at them like lanterns" 5788

"stare blankly into the nighttime of his empty cabin" 10278

"stared" 2848

"stared at a piece of white cardboard" 6421

"stared at by the sun at its haughtiest" 5911

"stared at her reflection in the mirror" 7487

"stared at the curtained porthole" 10729

"stared at the flat oblong of stone" 8311

"stared at the harbor" 1711

"stared at what he'd written" 1531

"stared blindly across parkland" 3155

"stared calculatingly upward" 0079

"stared down at his clean sheet of paper" 3728

"stared for a moment or two at his tall windows" 2699

"stared glumly out the window" 2710

"stared out into Mecklenburg Square" 8259

"stared out through the dining-car window" 2595

"stared out upon the broad river and the wharves below" 8254

"stared out upon the river" 5614

"stared pensively through his office window" 8274

"stares, rather embarrassed" 1201

"stares at it for some time" 1730

"stares at me" 5942

"stares at the ceiling" 236

"stares down at the copy of the *Illustrated London News*" 987

"stares through the smoke that rises from his cigarette" 8581

"starfish, broken" 1216

"staring around" 4626

"staring at a blank wall" 220

"staring at the sea" 4224

"staring at the stained-glass window" 1532

"staring at the tick" 5256

"staring due-north through goggles" 2973

"staring eyes" 5971

"staring in through my living room window" 2723

"staring into the eyes of a black panther" 3714

"staring me in the eye" 10911

"staring mournfully" 3995

"staring out over the Mississippi" 8096

"staring out over the wrinkled expanse of sea" 7918

"staring through the darkness" 10250

"staring through the queer light" 2704

"staring up" 909

"staring up at it" 5376

"staring up at the ceiling and down into itself" 10184

"staring up into the blackness of the ceiling" 10220

"stark against a sky of summer blue" 10160

Stark, Hamilton 5482

Stark, Solomon 2337

Starkey, Mrs. B. D. 1107

Starlady Sandra 6478

"starlight, dazzling" 1545

"starlight, in the monstrous" 2105

"starlight, see in" 7440

Starling, Joe 3253

"starlings, silence except for" 10185

Starr, Ron 6231

"starred sky" 8415

"starred sky unseen" 9236

"starred with a flimsy backstroke" 9729

Starret, Lieutenant 8711

"starry-eyed look" 1101

Stars 520, 521, 522, 523, 524, 527, 529, 534, 535, 5051, 7437, 8401, 8420, 8422, 8449, 10149

"stars, ether between the" 2790

"stars, great blinking white" 1584

"stars, his satellite dish to the" 7030

"stars, is our fate in our" 3679

"stars, looked at the" 520, 524

"stars, looking at the" 8579

"stars, pantomime of" 523

"stars, recognize a few" 8422

"stars, there were no" 8449

"stars, three big" 529

"stars, under God's" 10824

"stars, under the first of the" 420

"stars, view of the" 8680

"stars above me were blurred" 6384

"stars hold, though the" 8420

"stars in the heavens, as many as there are" 5272

"stars in the heavens, watching the" 2677

"stars still shone" 10149

"stars to glimmer down on the island below" 5051

"starstruck" 6274

Start, Ben 8515

"start, an uncertain" 6755

"start, just at the" 1797

"start, let me" 5064

"start, right from the" 261

"start, twelfth" 1941

"start a new year, what a way to" 2155

"start here, let's" 1289

"start more swift than weighty, to make a" 5523

"start of each new day" 7109

"start of the whole business, at the" 2841

"start up a new life" 6188

"started, before we get" 6946

"started, hard to get" 621

"started, let's get" 630

"started, when it had" 688

"started as something completely innocuous" 4667

"started badly, the day" 2170

"started here, before we get" 10976

"started it three times" 613

"started on my quest" 7223

"started on the eighth of April" 5117

"started one afternoon, it all" 585

"started two hours before daylight" 8095

"started up from sleep very early that morning" 9885

"started when I was about eleven" 587

"started with Cynthia, things" 635

"starting all over again" 9017

"starting out through the arctic dark" 1213

"starting point, no obvious" 4500

"starting to show, just" 7062

"startled, he looked" 6541

"startled, I was" 8172

"startled by a slight noise" 8174

"startled by God knows what" 10320

"startled cry" 8175

"startled from the newspaper" 6321

"startled the emotions of a small community" 8956

"starts with little girls, everything" 4182

"starvation" 10512

"starved out the three families" 3648

"starving to death" 7802

Stas 9110

"state, ancient" 5345

"state, districts of that" 6973

"State, medium-sized" 4461

"state, Middle Western" 8971

"state, midwestern" 9233

"state, my" 9457

"state, Nne-nne was in a" 3324

"State, Out-Yonder" 280

"state, the" 4068

"State, their" 5020

"state, when Indiana was a baby" 3074

"state, Yankee" 5359

"state, young" 1912
"'State Banner and Delphian
    Oracle'" 8956
"state in the Deep South" 4066
"state need not be Michigan" 1390
"state of fermentation, always in a"
    10801
"state of mind" 2673, 8568
"state-house" 9210
"statement, first made the" 4365
"statement, I am making this" 8709
"statement, prominence given to
    this" 4340
"statement, this is my" 9695
"statement becomes remarkable"
    9001
"Staten Island" 1083, 10628
"states, formation of so many" 7648
"states, mongrelized neo-capitalist
    puppet" 6256
"states, preserve the union of" 269
"States, restless energy of the" 6249
"states, sovereign" 8875
"States, Sugar" 4051
"States, the" 9630
"States, United" 3151
"States of the Union" 7657
"station, Baker Street" 10418
"Station, Belfast" 6970
"station, Blackhawk railway" 2903
"station, clay-colored veranda-
    petticoated little" 4069
"station, come to the" 1504
"station, Doleham Valley" 4385
"Station, Dover" 5895
"station, filling" 1970
"station, gas" 4073
"Station, Grand Central" 6652,
    8173, 9528
"station, Gulf Oil" 9583
"station, I could not say at which"
    9530
"station, Leningrad" 7904
"station, little" 9532
"station, log stage" 9220
"station, lonely" 9211
"Station, McMurdo" 228
"station, Maple City" 9328
"station, outside the" 3303
"Station, Paddington" 9641, 9817
"Station, Pennsylvania" 8565
"Station, Queen Street" 1496
"station, railroad" 1465, 7263,
    9631, 10734
"station, railway" 930, 1368, 3427,
    5709, 6001, 9092, 9890, 10042
"station, run-down old tollbridge"
    3105
"Station, St. Pancras" 7261
"station, service" 1080
"Station, South" 10436
"Station, Union" 4918
"station, vast gloomy Warsaw" 5901
"Station, Victoria" 5817, 8938
"Station, Victoria Coach" 1726

"Station, Washington Square" 3050
"Station, Waterloo" 9412
"station, when it was even with
    the" 7250
"station, your music news and
    sports" 9365
"station of life, highest" 9260
"Station One, Earth" 9756
"station taxicab" 9382
"station wagon, his" 8618
"station wagon, purple and white"
    8925
"station wagons arrived at noon"
    9814
"station where he stopped for gas"
    3007
"station yard" 1227
"stationed himself near the door"
    6330
"stationery, asked for" 4274
"stationery, page of cream" 1963
"stationery was Wedgwood blue"
    4642
"stationmaster" 4069
"stations, a couple of the Los
    Angeles" 9363
"stations, country railway" 7271
"stations, police" 7140
"stations, service" 1039
"stations, stopped at all the" 7241
"stations, switched" 6331
"stations, wireless" 3534
"Stations of the Cross" 503
"stations tried to creep onto the
    same wavelength" 9363
"station-wagon, yellow" 1599
"statuary, cluster of" 6367
"statue, Benjamin Franklin" 8945
"statue, Caesar's" 8948
"statue, Flaubert's" 315
"statue, London" 8938
"statue, small greenish" 8939
"statue of a maid who dared say no
    to Charles the Second" 4069
"statue of a man in a wig on a
    horse" 8939
"statue of Diderot" 8949
"Statue of Liberty" 4654, 8721
"statue of Prometheus" 4195
"statue of the Prince Consort, un-
    speakable" 1179
"statue of the Virgin, gilt-headed"
    5324
"statue on the quay" 8943
"statues, stone" 3230
"statues of the world, famous" 8939
Stature 341, 1263, 4184, 4199,
    4436, 5941, 5956, 5966, 5978,
    6529, 6740, 6753, 7542, 8225,
    10797, 10799, 10885
"stature, heroic" 1391
"stature, his" 6753
"status, proud of his" 7128
Staunton, Mr. 2477
"stay, how long she will" 10808

"stay, let me" 10121
"stay, we didn't" 8668
"stay at the Royal Ocean Hotel"
    9723
"stay for a time with me" 9862
"stay for a weekend" 9949
"stay for nearly five years, he was
    to" 1706
"Stay More" 7194, 10450
"stay of about six months, a" 4558
"stay with her, I was sent to" 3198
"stay with me" 5950
"stay with our aunt and uncle"
    2573
"stayed away from the Acropolis"
    3395
"staying at Beverley Court" 6021
"staying at his aunt's house" 2807
"staying ... at the Devonshire
    Arms" 6448
"staying with her, all four of them
    were" 9893
"staying with his father and two
    elder brothers" 9722
"staying with my friend" 3231
"Stead, Gunnars" 3661
"steadfast" 5015
Steadman 443
"steady as a rock" 8125
"steady himself" 4726
"steak, Kate cut up Hugo's" 3860
"steak on his left eye, put the raw"
    6810
"steal, had first begun to" 2029
"steal, pencil that I managed to"
    2049
"steal for the books" 2014
"steal into the sweet shop" 10831
"steal the aircraft" 2042
"stealing, nurse came" 1770
"stealing from me, my wife was"
    2051
"stealing off so quietly" 8171
"stealthily he prowled" 324
"stealthily parted the branches"
    8899
"steam, turbid" 928
"steamboat" 9626
"steamboat, per" 1349
"steamboat Crescent City" 8096
"steamed the ground" 4404
"steamer, dingy little Greek" 8123
"steamer, fastest" 4270
"steamer, like a huge white paddle-
    wheel" 4652
"steamer, magnificent ocean-" 8051
"steamer, ocean" 4906
"steamer, passengers on the" 6363
"steamer, small white" 8080
"steamer, sunny side of the" 9863
"steamer, the" 8085
"steamer Chow Phya, small Sia-
    mese" 2188
"steamer moved upriver at half-
    speed" 8070

"steamer sat in a bath of grey water" 8109
"steaming like a Cajun bayou" 9083
"steaming low country" 9749
"steamships" 3997
"steamy summer afternoon" 5636
Stecker, Acel 2585
"steed was extremely restless" 8650
"steel, till I hold that" 3485
"steel is an alloy based on iron" 10530
Steele, Cassie 10307
Steele, Tom 5194
"steeling himself against this moment" 1829
"Steeple Bumpleigh" 3341
"steeple of St Augustine's, bruise-coloured" 1310
"steer out of his way" 10375
"steerage, stench and throb of the" 8080
"steered absently through the slush" 2337
"steered along the wet mud bank" 4204
"steered down Borden Street, as she" 4363
"steered through the last-minute shoppers" 3017
"steering wheel" 2975, 8456
"steering wheel, his" 2917
Stein, Irving 3197
Steinberg, Carl 5848
Steiner, Dr. Paul 3518
Steiner, Lexi 8007
Stella 1317
"stellar systems, uttermost" 6001
"stem, parent" 9660
"stems were so thick with flower" 9668
"stench and throb of New York tenements" 8080
"stench and throb of the steerage" 8080
"stench of old fish" 8544
"stench oozed up, a poisonous" 4370
Stenham 1635
"step, heard a" 8781
"step, it was an important" 607
"step, Pullman car" 1648
"step as it were casually into your view" 82
"step in the logic of things, a fresh" 7372
"step up, an appreciable" 3604
Stephen 2747, 4908, 8900
"Stepney" 355
"Stepney, back streets of" 9178
"stepped, he slipped as he" 1601
"stepped back, she" 3780
"stepped daintily" 730
"stepped from his house" 1681
"stepped from the door" 4996
"stepped from the house" 10698

"stepped from the train" 1584
"stepped hesitantly into its huge darkness" 4485
"stepped in" 8256
"stepped into the body of the aeroplane" 220
"stepped into the kettle" 1861
"stepped into the sternsheets of the waiting whaleboat" 405
"stepped off the airplane" 8192
"stepped off the path" 6963
"stepped off the train" 1667, 1723
"stepped onto that train" 1717
"stepped out" 1647
"stepped out from the shelter of a large chestnut-tree" 5711
"stepped out of a taxi" 1653
"stepped out of his house" 1626
"stepped out of the high train" 1645
"stepped out of the warm Burke House bar" 1548
"stepped out onto the concrete apron" 1078
"stepped over the threshold" 6145
"stepped readily enough aside" 10380
"stepped slowly into the pawnshop" 2905
"stepped through the narrow doorway" 8920
"stepped up on the chair" 9292
"stepping off the bus" 1250
"steps, concrete" 7841
"steps, down the" 9528
"steps, long undulant" 2107
"steps, marble" 1293
"steps, quickened his" 3298
"steps, short steep flight of" 3976
"steps, somewhat imposing" 9875
"Steps, Spanish" 4111
"steps, wide stone" 1580
"steps deep in shadows, quick" 10435
"steps leading down from the terrace" 4166
"steps of her sister's Commonwealth Avenue home" 9875
"steps of the Rede Art Gallery" 489
"steps on the moon, first shy" 9733
"step-sisters" 3556
Stern 6124
"*Stern*" 4008
Sterndale 9232
Sternfeld, Susan 9984
Sternholz, Emmanuel Yehoshua 6472
Sternholz, Rebecca 6472
Sternholz, Samuel 6472
"stethoscope around her neck" 2875
Steuben, von 8940
"Steubenville, little town of" 7666
Steven 3026
Stevens, Doctor 6889
Stevens, Dr. Francis 4661
Stevens, Hilary 10191

Stevenson, James 4439
"steward, the" 9650
"steward, Welsh" 9568
"steward advised Dr. Cullinane" 8112
"stewardess, blond" 9579
"stewardess, packet-boat" 1827
"stewards of the big Atlantic liner" 4730
Stewart, Keith 3153
Stewart, William 2797
"stewpot boils over, literary" 8470
"stewpot of summer" 10745
Stick 6579
"stick, shinny" 962
"stick, walking" 6574
"stick, whalebone digging" 10453
"stick leaning against the arm of it" 5903
"stick me, God decided to" 4236
Stiff, Miss 4739
"stiffening straight the other leg" 10206
"stiffness had left her right knee" 5747
"stifles me, it" 175
"stifling" 190
"stifling June day" 5204
Still, Mr. 4739
"still, everything was" 8329
"still, it was very" 1297
"still, unnaturally" 9951
"still as a country Sunday" 9120
"still called Papa John's" 9234
"still here on the twenty-fourth floor" 6304
"still night, the" 8586
"still that night, New York was almost" 1370
"still there, if you were" 1956
"stillborn, their issue is" 10131
"stilled the busyness of their lives" 8093
Stillness 117, 2224, 8334, 10610
"stillness" 117
"stillness, cool foglit" 2119
"stillness, eerie" 10506
"stillness, not absolute" 7930
"stillness, winter" 2224
"stillness in the corridor" 2122
"stillness of a village, immense rife" 4893
"stillness was so absolute" 8334
"Stillwater" 3895
Stillwell, Jessie 4538
"Stilton and coffee" 3877
"stimulating" 2089
"stinging wind" 10572
"Stingray, the" 9799
"stink, a" 6272
"stink, undeniable and inimitable" 4335
"stink from the East River" 8516
"stink of a close crowd" 4335
"stink of rubber" 225

"stink of the unnamable herbs and spices" 8544
"stinking curs" 7801
"stinking quagmires" 7323
"stinking week of torture" 2171
"stint in the Army" 4601
"Stippled Silver Kennel Inc." 1016
"stir of heightened consciousness" 6001
"stirred, I" 10132
"stirred, she" 10121
"stirred, the other never" 1469
"stirred a can of Beef and Potatoes" 1864
"stirred and sighed" 10145
"stirred his brush in the white shaving bowl" 8044
"stirred in its sleep" 4496
"stirred in the broad light of day" 10142
"stirred Mary Hawley awake" 10174
"stirring incident" 5398
"stirring the simmering brown liquid" 8561
"stirring to life" 1464
"stirring with present movements" 9119
"stirs in her bed of sweet clover hay" 463
"stitches in his head" 1512
"stitching up her husband's trouser hems" 6864
"Stobie" 1548
"stock-pens" 7250
"Stockbridge, village of" 9740
"Stockbridge Massachusetts" 510
"stockbroker" 2557
"stockbroker, well-trimmed head of the" 1077
"Stockholm" 8470
"stocking he was wearing" 151
"stockings, her" 2658
"stockings, runs in her" 4176
"stockings, twenty-four black silk" 2830
"stockings, worsted" 5888
"stocks, break in bonanza" 8052
"stocks, set in the" 7505
"stoically, accepts" 9328
"stole from the Gardens" 3977
"stole millions by a stroke of the pen" 2023
"stole the gangster's money" 2684
"stolen a horse" 2025
"stolen canoe" 10960
"stolen car" 1845
"stomach, flat on her" 5145
"stomach, Mother's" 7072
"stomach, playing hide-and-seek inside his" 2901
"stomach, pressed up against my" 6391
"stomach, turned over on his" 10206
"stomach bellied out like a sail" 7072

"stomach buzz, girl who made his" 2111
"stomach rigid with the ache of want" 4678
"stomach was empty" 3699
"stomping, boots" 10297
"stomping around on the roof, blue jays" 10310
Stone, Martin 1644
Stone, Master Orvard 964
Stone, Megan 5495
Stone, Mr. 8179
"stone, as heavy as" 2805
"stone, dazzling freshness of new white" 1849
"stone, fist of" 9304
"stone, flat oblong of" 8311
"stone, great pillars of neolithic" 5149
"stone, grey granite" 9253
"stone, married to a" 5772
"stone, mere black heaps of" 5150
"stone, original" 9223
"stone, pale brown" 7761
"stone, palest cotswold" 3155
"stone, smooth as" 7685
"stone, spongy" 8663
"stone, within the chill grey" 1301
"stone from his bladder, removal of a" 1519
"stone itself, the riven" 1217
"stone telling is my last name" 1729
"stone thrown into the sea, like a" 633
"stone where it was written" 7541
Stonebird, Rupert 9455
"Stonecrop" 9176
"Stonehenge" 1671
"stoneland, grappled in" 8115
Stonelower, R. G. 5466
Stoner, William 7890
"stones, break" 5695
"stones, carrying" 5138
"stones, carved" 7146
"stones, country of sliding" 7068
"stones, crudely heaped pile of" 1212
"stones, damp" 1544
"stones, mossy" 10683
"stones, precious" 7504
"stones, throwing" 957
"stones in a tin, like" 5632
"stones lay before him" 1194
"stones still damp from the outgoing tide" 6648
"stones still lie in the heather" 9230
"stone's throw" 9216
"stone's-throw or so of the riverside, within a" 6558
"stood, from where I" 5981
"stood, from where they" 1176
"stood, there I" 1919
"stood a little apart from his fellows" 7594
"stood alone" 8724
"stood alone at the curb" 10735

"stood and sent my eyes around" 8272
"stood at his study window" 8106
"stood at his tall desk" 8778
"stood at one end of the dusty verandah" 9574
"stood at the altar" 10641
"stood at the back gateway of the abattoir" 4678
"stood at the bathroom window" 8481
"stood at the bend" 4150
"stood at the door of the chapel" 4255
"stood at the fence" 8452
"stood at the kitchen counter" 1871
"stood at the railing" 1711
"stood at the window" 2501, 2831, 4143, 7699, 7706
"stood before a mirror" 7479
"stood before a pier glass" 4921
"stood before his father" 6626
"stood before his mahogany shaving stand" 8044
"stood before his mailbox" 1950
"stood before the minister" 10644
"stood before the mirror" 7470
"stood before the window" 2690
"stood breathing" 9903
"stood by her window" 8283
"stood by the side of an old dilapidated hotel's deserted and dilapidated saltwater swimming pool" 4643
"stood by the table" 3814
"stood close to his mother" 1670
"stood feeding her canary" 3270
"stood for a few minutes" 9749
"stood for a few moments" 6499
"stood for a moment" 1184, 2712
"stood for a moment beside the table" 1641
"stood for a moment on the porch" 2220
"stood for a moment to watch the man go forward" 4246
"stood formally at attention" 7903
"stood gazing out over his domain" 8257
"stood hesitating" 1227
"stood in a circlet of sunlight" 3952
"stood in church" 5774
"stood in front of the house watching her go" 1602
"stood in front of the big picture window" 5959
"stood in front of the full-length mirror" 7477
"stood in front of the partly fogged up mirror" 7485
"stood in her doorway" 8403
"stood in her postage-stamp bathroom" 2879
"stood in his bare studio" 491
"stood in Notre Dame" 3922

"stood in relief" 4140

"stood in the bathroom" 2827

"stood in the chilling April rain" 10045

"stood in the cold" 5979

"stood in the dense cold" 10075

"stood in the door of the barn" 10928

"stood in the doorway to their bedroom" 5772

"stood in the *guérite*" 7918

"stood in the hotel doorway" 10037

"stood in the kitchen" 6192

"stood in the middle of downtown renovation" 1453

"stood in the mine office" 3334

"stood in the muddy field" 5096

"stood in the paddling-pool" 976

"stood in the prow of the boat" 10716

"stood in the rain beside the grave" 3941

"stood in the rear doorway" 566

"stood in the room" 2761

"stood in the small port" 3774

"stood in the third heaven" 7504

"stood leaning on the gate" 4224

"stood leaning on the handle of a broom" 8599

"stood looking doubtfully up" 8692

"stood naked at the edge of a cliff" 6387

"stood near the whipping post" 4155

"stood on a little wooden pier" 5910, 6091

"stood on a long wooden dock" 8153

"stood on a rooftop" 5964

"stood on board the liner" 4535

"stood on the deck of the steamboat" 8096

"stood on the doorstep" 1585

"stood on the far side of their bicycles" 977

"stood on the fox until it died" 2458

"stood on the front lawn" 6550

"stood on the hill" 8258

"stood on the platform" 1575

"stood on the sand" 8277

"stood on the short lawn before her house" 7739

"stood on the side of Highway 82" 4429

"stood on the side of Gladstone Dock" 8131

"stood over the new gopher hole" 968

"stood screaming" 981

"stood sheltered by the doorway" 8786

"stood shivering in the grey dawn" 5940

"stood silent and motionless at the pulpit" 1532

"stood six men" 650

"stood staring" 2723

"stood stiffly with my feet well apart" 8684

"stood still on the station platform" 3499

"stood stooped over" 10405

"stood swaying in the doorway" 4973

"stood tall and forked" 1413

"stood the beautiful virgin" 10786

"stood there and waited" 10072

"stood there in the prow" 8792

"stood there proud and regally cloaked in pine and piñon" 6085

"stood thumbing a ride" 9554

"stood two pleasant houses side by side" 6283

"stood under the dusky lamp" 5901

"stood up and clapped his hands" 5188

"stood up from her desk" 2728

"stood up tall and straight" 9317

"stood very still and very quiet" 4109

"stood watching" 402, 4257, 8648

"stood with his arms folded" 8274

"stood with his elbow on the broad mantel-piece" 8839

"stood with his eyes fixed" 8286

"stood with his eyes shut tight" 8193

"stood with his hands on his hips" 1659

"stool, low bamboo" 3762

"stool, sat on a low" 2874

"stool, small green-painted" 9063

"stool pigeons, devil doll" 3050

"stoop, front" 7122

"stoop, I am on the" 6292

"stop, came to a jerky" 9528

"stop, cry" 5460

"stop, don't he know just when to" 2086

"stop, will you" 2948

"stop again, I have to" 3025

"stop at a stone mill for the night, they had to" 9520

"stop drooling" 2528

"stop instanter whatever you have been doing" 84

"stop it" 9942

"stop me, for who's to" 1819

"stop press, wasn't even in the" 6320

"stop the car" 3033

"stop the mouth of the bottle, it did not pretend to" 5034

"stop you so soon, I'm sorry to" 6235

"stopped" 9773

"stopped, directly it" 1645

"stopped, we" 9640

"stopped at the curb" 9967

"stopped at the premises of the Mammoth Publishing Company" 5311

"stopped before the entrance" 1315

"stopped by a Christian student" 7518

"stopped by his grocery store" 2057

"stopped dead" 5799

"stopped for gas" 3007

"stopped his bay" 7646

"stopped in the bright early-morning sunlight" 7265

"stopped in the midst of the town of New York" 7195

"stopped just long enough" 1629

"stopped short in front of the sidewalk cafe" 10884

"stopped so abruptly that I nearly bumped into him" 1619

"stopped the car" 9676, 9717

"stopped the taxi" 1655

"stopped to eat" 7637

Stopping 136, 1608, 1619, 1655, 2086, 2962, 2987, 2989, 3007, 3034, 4320, 6235, 7249, 7256, 7646, 7669, 7843, 8791, 9640, 9676, 9773, 9785, 9791

"stopping by, telephone before" 7022

"stops before the Place St. Sulpice" 5975

"stops in total darkness" 10462

"*Stor Konigsgaarten*, H.M.S." 1711

"Store, Army and Navy" 10628

"store, decided to go to the" 5637

"store, department" 7099

"Store, Fontaine's Department" 3447

"store, gave up her" 4945

"Store, General" 9111

"store, gift and jewelry chain" 9729

"store, grocery" 1040, 4073

"store, his grocery" 2057

"Store, Jim Hill Cafe & Cigar" 1474

"store, rear of the" 10426

"Store, Rothstein's Discount Liquor" 8599

"store, Sanders'" 4014

"store, shoe" 9708

"store, small confectionery" 8210

"store porch" 8793

"store that sold beer and ice cubes and gas" 6148

"store was there" 1026

"store window" 10392

"store windows" 8606

"storefront addict centers" 1515

"storekeepers" 7295

"storeroom, a sort of" 3094

"storeroom, ell" 7386

Stores 921, 1026, 1040, 1056, 1067, 1091, 1365, 1387, 2057, 2740, 2841, 3447, 4073, 4945, 6148, 7229, 7490, 8191, 8301, 8599, 9111, 9708

"stores" 1082

"stores, backwater country" 5166

"stores, four small white" 1056

"Stores, Guildenstern's" 2511

"stores, small perfect glittering"
7229
"stores, wooden-awninged" 1387
"stores and saloons" 1365
"stores of brushwood and broken
trees" 10710
"storey, on the second" 5628
"storeys high, four" 3153
Stories 633, 698, 701, 704, 709,
1282, 1363, 1406, 1570, 1729,
1799, 1966, 1973, 2018, 2076,
2130, 2148, 2550, 2557, 2567,
2578, 2734, 2896, 3028, 3241,
3298, 3490, 3498, 3504, 3612,
3770, 3972, 4038, 4045, 4186,
4242, 4258, 4453, 4461, 4468,
4500, 4769, 5214, 5384, 5390,
5393, 5404, 5407, 5431, 5432,
5439, 5449, 5461, 5471, 5486,
5489, 5494, 5496, 5506, 5536,
5546, 5563, 5563, 5593, 5619,
5673, 5685, 5837, 5989, 6283,
6317, 6325, 6338, 6349, 6797,
7150, 7217, 7367, 7394, 7703,
7802, 7828, 7838, 7960, 7986,
8075, 8222, 8669, 8789, 8934,
9109, 9522, 9698, 10049, 10323,
10332, 10341, 10470, 10556,
10614, 10851
"stories, countless are the" 5212
"stories, desire to write" 5546
"stories, my first short" 5837
"stories, New York" 3241
"stories, personal" 7150
"stories, short" 5486
"stories, telling strange and sardonic" 8976
"stories, the beginning of many"
6349
"stories, the greater his name the
worse the" 5432
"stories, there are thousands of"
9040
"stories, thirty-four" 8300
"stories, two of the many bizarre"
5536
"stories about me, telling" 7838
"stories into which the reader
should be led gently" 8995
"stories still had power to charm
me" 9034
"stories they tell" 6357
"storm, dust" 9944
"storm, ferocious" 9064
"storm, great gray" 7326
"storm, January" 9065
"storm, last night there was a" 7325
"storm, memories overwhelming
me like a" 7434
"storm, predict a long" 8585
"storm, rain" 7301
"storm, snow" 8589
"storm, sounded wild as a" 8802
"storm, summer" 9080
"storm, the" 9078

"storm, the great" 9085
"storm, the night's" 9082
"storm, tumultuous" 8325
"storm, waiting out the" 748
"storm an imperturbable surl for
cloudburst mist" 6075
"storm and sunshine" 10567
"storm broke, the" 9063
"storm broke and thrashed" 10730
"storm broke over the house" 9079
"storm came down in the night"
9065
"storm clouds" 7019
"storm clouds gathered in the sky"
1757
"storm coming on the horizon" 584
"storm had almost blown itself out"
9082
"storm in his cool hasty blood" 756
"storm of steam and hot water,
small shifting" 1169
"storm off Malta" 853
"storm outside in the ocean" 9069
"storm swept across our town" 9064
"storm was bearing down on our
Cumberlands" 9071
"stormed out of the dustcloud"
10509
"storming, it was" 8588
Storms 221, 584, 748, 853, 1153,
2957, 5033, 5711, 7294, 7301,
7325, 7326, 7339, 8033, 8058,
8118, 8325, 8585, 8588, 8589,
9312, 9944, 10679, 10680, 10704,
10729, 10730
"storms, great autumn" 9089
"storms, so many" 9088
"storms, spring" 2989
"storms blow" 6075
"storm's cold anger" 9087
"storms come from, where most of
our" 9077
"storms were stormier" 5033
"stormy day of early spring" 9068
"stormy seas" 5011
"stormy surging Iris Sea" 9300
Storrs, Bruce 9317
"story" 709
"story, American" 4242
"story, as if I told a" 9698
"story, before telling the" 5563
"story, begin a" 8964
"story, beginning of this" 4038
"story, detective" 1325
"story, difficult for me to relate
this" 10851
"story, each time it was a different"
7828
"story, everyone's" 2130
"story, favorite" 9045
"story, for the purpose of my" 8962
"story, from the fifteenth" 10628
"story, getting ahead of the" 5673
"story, give you the full" 9007
"story, guts-and-glory" 8993

"story, has one" 8978
"story, he is the engine of our" 3298
"story, I am introducing the" 8999
"story, I am obliged to begin this"
10556
"story, I had this" 8972
"story, I have told this" 8968
"story, I may as well begin this"
8970
"story, I told Helen my" 2076
"story, I'm telling this" 8996
"story, impossible" 9018
"story, in the direction of someone's" 1799
"story, in the following" 3972
"story, in the telling of a" 8980
"story, in this" 1973
"story, in writing this" 8982
"story, interminable" 7986
"story, invited to read the" 8959
"story, it is an old" 5471
"story, it was the big" 6317
"story, it's an old" 9032
"story, knew one part of the" 9109
"story, local" 7367
"story, long" 7802
"story, long and true" 8990
"story, may have seen the" 6325
"story, Michael Howell's" 9005
"story, mother in your" 9011
"story, my" 5390, 8789, 8969,
8999
"story, my extravagant" 5384
"story, no part in this" 9522
"story, notes towards a love" 9039
"story, one clear" 3490
"story, open their" 8951
"story, papers carried a" 3770
"story, perhaps she had heard the"
9050
"story, plot of this" 5393
"story, previous to the opening of
the" 698
"story, reading a" 5431
"story, real" 9017
"story, reconstructed the" 9014
"story, sad" 9027
"story, saddest" 8973
"story, scene of our" 8049
"story, serial" 5407
"story, setting of a" 9061
"story, short" 5494
"story, speaks of this" 701
"story, still telling the" 6652
"story, tell a" 8961
"story, tell Annie Jeynor's" 9036
"story, tell my" 6283, 8984
"story, tell the" 8994
"story, tell this" 8983
"story, telling a" 8985
"story, telling this" 9027, 9055
"story, telling you the" 9054
"story, that is another" 4468
"story, the" 8958, 9006, 9029
"story, their simple" 4453

"story, this" 5496, 8955, 8960, 8975, 8977
"story, this ain't no war" 9033
"story, this is a" 9016, 9049
"story, this is a strange" 9013
"story, this is a true" 5494, 9043
"story, this is an old" 9056
"story, this is my" 9004
"story, this is that" 10614
"story, this is the" 704, 1406, 2018, 2578, 3498, 8934, 8954, 8990, 9024
"story, this is the true" 9041
"story, this part of my" 9012
"story, time that I told this" 5461
"story, told as a" 5593
"story, told me his" 10332
"story, told us a" 9051
"story, true" 5214
"story, very old" 8969
"story, waiting for this" 8979
"story, way to open a" 5489
"story, when I came into the" 2896
"story, write the" 2567
"story, write this" 5449
"story, you could say it is also my" 8999
"story, you won't know about this" 9059
"story about how me and Jim went down the river on a raft" 5506
"story about something that happened long ago" 8992
"story about white people" 9015
"story as complex as this" 4500
"story as I lived it" 9047
"story at no point becomes my own, this" 8998
"story began in the Ozark Mountains" 8971
"story began" 8997
"story begins, my" 2148
"story begins, the" 9042
"story begins, the hour this" 9001
"story begins, when this" 4461
"story begins and ends in the dark" 2130
"story begins five years ago" 4769
"story bit by bit from various people" 7828
"story commences, when my" 8952
"story conference" 10049
"story down in black and white, put my" 9009
"story had held us round the fire sufficiently breathless" 8967
"story happened in Corinth" 8971
"story has a beginning, if this" 633
"story has its begnnings, this" 1363
"story has no beginning or end" 8989
"story I am about to tell you" 698
"story I am telling, miss the" 8222
"story I heard years ago" 9034
"story is about A.J. Poole" 9026

"story is about my great-uncle" 8999
"story is about something that happened to them" 1282
"story is as complete as anything can ever be" 9008
"story is crazy, you may think this" 9023
"story is written now, unless this" 2734
"story my father told me every night" 9052
"story my father used to tell" 9045
"Story of a Bad Boy" 8958
"story of a certain Mr. Preemby" 3498
"story of a machine" 5685
"story of a man" 9031
"story of a town that refused to die" 1406
"story of a young life" 8956
"story of Aletheia" 9020
"story of an adventure" 8991
"story of an eye" 9048
"story of Bella" 10323
"story of changes" 9062
"story of Clifford [and] Helen and little Nell" 9038
"story of Danny" 8981
"story of Emmeline Mosher" 4186
"story of guns and trouble" 4258
"story of his emotional life" 7713
"story of how the sun fell in love with the moon" 9010
"story of how Truckbox Al McClintock almost got a tryout" 8934
"story of its movements" 5685
"story of Lovey Childs" 9002
"story of Lucian Dorrit, the real" 10341
"story of Mark Petrie" 5989
"story of me" 8974
"story of mine" 6338
"story of my adventures" 1570
"story of my cousin" 9035
"story of my family" 3612
"story of my friend" 9025
"story of my life" 2550, 5561
"story of my own" 8963
"story of Nicholas, tell the" 6797
"story of Sarah, tell myself the" 9037
"story of the Blitz" 5221
"story of the demon Blue-Shirt" 9053
"story of the little man" 2557
"story of the *Trikkala*" 8987
"story of the war, this is not a" 9022
"story of the whore" 3057
"Story of the World, The One True" 9052
"story of two contests in which I competed" 9024
"story of two men" 8994

"story of Zenia" 9060
"story on tape, put the" 9030
"story opens, my" 8953
"story opens, our" 5619
"story opens, when our" 10470
"story should begin, decide where the" 8988
"story simple, keep the" 9057
"story starts, this is where your" 9044
"story takes place, when this" 1533
"story that ends along the back streets and alleys of Miami Florida" 9027
"story that follows would not have been possible" 3504
"story that might bore you" 8012
"story that must be heard" 9046
"story that must be told, mine is a" 9046
"story that no one wanted told" 9021
"story that tells what happened to young Bob Dubois" 9027
"story to tell, I have a" 1729
"story to tell you, I have a" 9058
"story tonight, there'll be no Mumpkin" 9003
"story was as old as the desert watch fires" 8986
"story which even then was old" 5431
"story which must of necessity tax the powers of belief" 8964
"story will probably run counter to more than one fashion of the day" 5390
"story-books say, as the" 1576
"story teller" 9535
Stourton 3474
"stoutish" 2825
"stove, earthen" 3762
"stove, station" 7567
"stove with its coating of thick grease" 6294
Stover 9529
Stover, Dink 9531
"stowaway child" 4214
"Stowood" 9131
"strafe the neighborhood" 10517
"stragglers, a few" 9426
"stragglers, last of the" 420
"straggling assemblage" 1365
"straight and sharp and converging to spearpoint" 9228
"straight as an arrow" 4303
"straight from the start, let's get that" 5470
"straight through from the beginning" 8994
"straightened itself like a curtain cord drawn taut" 9141
"Strait that links two seas together" 1174
"straitjacket of cloud" 8437

"Straits of Gibraltar" 8112
"Straits of Mackinac" 4073
"Strand, the" 9123
"Strand traffic, the" 2964
"stranded on his bed" 10130
"stranded there by misadventure" 5027
"strands of it that had worked their way loose" 10860
Strange 7411
"strange, anything" 2099
"strange, moment was" 4320
"strange, something" 165
"strange, to come home again is" 4573
"strange and fresh" 3369
"strange and silent" 1584
"strange bed, he was in a" 10259
"strange days indeed" 2174
Strange Disappearance, A 5494
"strange enough" 1221
"strange events, a year of" 10992
"strange had happened, something" 4000
"strange inventions" 5681
"strange land" 3497, 9521
"strange liquid" 8332
"strange long woman" 10885
"strange means" 2538
"strange men and dogs" 9104
"strange one" 8987
"strange quirk of fate" 7453
"strange sea" 9521
"strange tension and insecurity" 3710
"strange then, it did not seem so" 4169
"strange thing" 5402
"strange thing came upon England" 8395
"strange things, likely to do" 8514
"strange things which have happened" 3493
"strange to each other" 9105
"strange world of ours" 6409
"strangeness, pleasant" 10352
"strangeness, the" 8491
"stranger, attractive" 10836
"stranger, intelligent" 6908
"stranger, lived those years with a" 5736
"stranger, middle-aged" 9096
"stranger came asking for him" 9106
"stranger came early in February" 9092
"stranger describing himself" 1099
"stranger . . . dismounted near the cross-roads" 9093
"stranger first came along" 9098
"stranger has yet arrived, no" 9094
"stranger in that part of the country" 9090
"stranger in that still enlarging city" 10798

"stranger in the street, there's a" 9107
"stranger they had picked up at a Bond Street sale room" 10836
"stranger to Kilpeder" 9109
"stranger visiting the United States" 269
Strangers 464, 955, 1099, 1979, 3362, 3506, 5559, 5736, 6144, 6908, 10836
"strangers, half a hundred" 4155
"strangers, hearts and lives of" 5559
"strangers, hospitable to" 3362
"strangers, like drunken" 4504
"strangers, see the" 9099
"strangers, suspicious of" 9102
"strangers, voices and laughter of" 3506
"stranger's eye, every" 3248
"stranger's eyes" 9097
"strangers thrown together fortuitously, like" 8223
"strangers' voices" 6379
"strangers who arrived during the week" 9100
Strangeways, Mr. 1621
Strangeways, Nigel 2964, 10376
"strap, rawhide harness" 7183
"strap cut viciously through the air" 7183
Strategy 6945
"Stratford stank" 4427
Straw, Jack 6031
"straw, old matted" 8511
"straw, prickly" 8475
"strawberries, kneelers find wild" 7227
"strawberries dipped in wine" 4151
Strawbridge, Thomas 9879
"strayed, Gombold had" 9585
"strayed, whither they might have" 7217
"strayed along it to the catch" 10165
"strayed into the wrong season" 4135
Strayhorn, Philip 9301
"streak crossing the foot of his bed, a gold" 10142
"streaked across the southern sky" 533
"streaking the sky, lightning bolts" 9300
"streaking through the trackless dark" 211
"streaks, yellow" 3689
"streaks of grey, faint" 8393
"stream" 5136
"stream, ancient and mighty and famous" 7648
"stream, quiet well-conducted little" 7652
"stream, shallow" 7619
"stream, trout" 9533
"stream, wormy little" 7688

"stream famous for its catfish and the color of its mud" 7688
"stream of salt water on both sides, left passage for a" 5034
"stream that forks in exactly the right position" 5067
"stream that rippled beside us" 7677
"stream that runs past my cabin" 8612
"stream which is more renowned than any other in that hemisphere" 7655
"streamed in smooth shiny infolding waves" 2529
"streaming up from the hot desert floor" 9127
Streams 5136, 8611, 8612
"streams, multitude of smaller" 7647
"streams, narrow running" 7632
"streams, narrow swampy" 5161
"streams, secondary" 5723
"streams, two howling impetuous" 1280
"streams are frozen" 7693
"streams of Surrey, sandy" 9738
"streams of water ran slowly but constantly" 7146
"streams were grayed with melted snow" 8611
"Street, Allen" 7106
"Street, Angel" 2964
"street, any downtown" 5967
"Street, Ashby" 5528
"street, at the end of the" 7683
"Street, Baker" 1055, 10418
"Street, Beacon" 4927, 9859
"Street, Beaufort" 1702
"Street, Berkeley" 10360
"Street, Berners" 7409
"Street, Blue" 3821
"Street, Bond" 489, 6495, 10836
"Street, Borden" 4363
"street, bought his wife a" 4125
"Street, Brattle" 2582
"street, broad Moscow" 7904
"Street, Brougham" 784
"Street, Bucknell" 3156
"street, Carondelet" 10549
"Street, Chestnut" 8255
"Street, Cheval" 1968
"Street, Christopher" 4099, 4108
"Street, Claremont" 1710
"Street, Clifford" 6495
"Street, Clinton" 820
"street, clogged main" 10092
"street, cobbled" 8774
"Street, Colonie" 2183
"Street, Commerce" 1029
"Street, Cork" 1586
"Street, Corliss" 10336
"street, corner of the" 10930
"street, crowded" 10374
"Street, Curzon" 6267, 9232
"Street, D'Arblay" 4330

"street, dark Parisian" 151
"Street, Damjanich" 10534
"street, darkened" 9828, 10833
"Street, Dauphine" 8777
"street, deep solemn massive" 9137
"Street, Delaware" 5757
"street, deserted Brooklyn" 9147
"street, down a side" 9252
"street, down every company" 8673
"street, down the long Brooklyn" 3145
"Street, Dumble" 9425
"street, early November" 10708
"Street, East 92nd" 3261
"Street, East 60th" 7576
"Street, East 68th" 3197
"Street, East Thirty-eighth" 2554
"Street, Ellaman" 3195
"Street, Elsome" 10973
"street, empty shopping" 7315
"street, Eustace Chisholm's" 9166
"Street, Fayette" 8512
"Street, Fiftieth" 9332
"Street, Fifty-second" 4310
"Street, Filbert" 3988
"Street, Fleet" 5311, 6319
"Street, Flower" 652
"Street, Forty-ninth" 3866
"Street, Forty-second" 1767, 7258
"Street, 46th" 5800
"Street, Forty-third" 3031
"Street, Fourteenth" 1313
"Street, Frederick" 8720
"Street, Front" 9142
"Street, Gold" 7061
"Street, Great Britain" 3780
"Street, Grove" 4099, 9206
"Street, Half Moon" 6443
"Street, Halsted" 5908
"Street, Harley" 141
"Street, Hemlock" 775
"Street, High" 3171, 6353, 8397
"street, Holloway" 946
"street, hot bright" 9125
"street, hum of noise from the" 8830
"Street, Iron" 7223
"Street, Kildare" 4936
"Street, La Salle" 9370
"street, lived in a grey shadowy" 3166
"Street, Locust" 8852
"street, long" 8739
"street, long mean" 10046
"Street, Lord North" 1655
"Street, Lower Gardiner" 1600
"Street, Lowery" 1515
"street, London's broadest" 8073
"Street, Macquarie" 5618
"street, main" 1548, 1596, 2961
"Street, Main" 510, 1001, 1064, 1082, 1088, 2850, 2968, 3032, 9203, 9876
"Street, Mango" 3250
"street, maple-bordered" 9120

"Street, Market" 3378
"Street, Marlboro" 10414
"Street, Midland" 1609
"street, miserable main" 1386
"Street, Molesworth" 4936
"Street, Moody" 5445
"Street, Moon" 7753
"Street, Mount Vernon" 790
"Street, Mt. Vernon" 2319
"Street, Murray" 10921
"street, narrow" 5822
"street, narrow cobblestone" 1523
"street, narrow gloomy" 4908
"street, narrow side" 1025, 9144
"Street, Ninety-first" 2867
"street, no" 1389
"street, not a hand-holding" 9164
"street, not in the open" 5418
"street, obscure part of the" 5784
"Street, O'Connell" 1600, 4517
"street, old" 9117
"Street, Oldcastle" 8845
"Street, Olive" 9222
"Street, 119th" 8309
"Street, 116th" 10699
"Street, Opal" 9129
"Street, Orange" 3085
"Street, Orchard" 3330
"Street, Oxford" 776, 1046, 7179, 8347
"Street, Park" 4368
"Street, Payton" 7240
"Street, Peel" 4641
"Street, Pine" 5537
"Street, Pitt" 1896
"Street, Polk" 3816
"Street, Praed" 9817
"Street, Princess" 2711
"Street, Queen" 1496
"street, quiet" 9187
"Street, R" 7220
"street, rain-swept Geneva" 10972
"Street, Rakoczy" 10884
"street, recognized the" 9190
"street, retrace the" 8488
"Street, River" 1727, 4289, 10875
"Street, St. James'" 1569
"Street, St. James's" 3855
"Street, seamy West 69th" 3244
"street, shabby side of the" 9206
"street, sharp stones of the narrow" 8778
"street, she wasn't sure she had the right" 9196
"street, short by-" 6270
"Street, Signal's" 9767
"Street, Sikkim" 6435
"Street, Silver" 1474, 2931
"Street, Siroká" 2424
"Street, Sixth" 9222
"Street, Sixty-third" 7204
"Street, South Audley" 9161
"Street, State" 6496
"Street, Steadman" 3188

"street, steep San Francisco" 10580
"Street, Stockton" 7079
"Street, Straszewskiego" 1714
"street, such a good" 3177
"Street, Swientojerska" 2604
"Street, 3rd" 5814
"Street, Thirty-seventh" 3209
"Street, Thirty-third" 3378
"Street, Tooley" 10394
"street, tree-lined" 10361
"Street, Trinity" 9179
"Street, Troy" 10434
"Street, Twenty-first" 3429
"street, unfamiliar" 7237
"street, unwatched" 876
"street, up and down the" 10032
"Street, Van Buren" 9525
"Street, Vere" 4372
"Street, Vine" 2758
"Street, Wabash" 2831
"Street, Wall" 1028, 1591, 8320
"Street, Washington" 9407
"Street, Waverly" 6306
"Street, Webber" 1419
"Street, Welbeck" 5395
"[Street], West Fourth" 4099
"Street, West 35th" 1619
"Street, West Thirty-fifth" 3132, 9900
"Street, Whitecross" 6361
"Street, Wimpole" 6194
"street, windy side of the" 10396
"Street, Wood" 7501
"street, you may chance upon a quiet by-" 1013
"street again, we would have to be in the" 3206
"street and corner, from every" 6058
"street car" 1579
"street empty, the" 9170
"street in the world, the shortest narrowest" 9189
"street lay like a snake sleeping" 9172
"street led from the Friday mosque down to the park" 9135
"street looked almost deserted" 9125
"street near the Vatican" 1523
"Street of the Cat Who Fishes" 9189
"street of the lower West Side of Manhattan" 3103
"Street of Wells" 9091
"street only a hundred yards long" 1386
"street outside, the" 9195
"street so long, we had been in the" 3206
"street sounds" 8773
"Street stretched away north and south" 9122
"street that led to the hotel" 1045
"street was dark though night had ended" 10708

"street was darkened by a smoky sunset" 3107
"street where I lived, the London" 7268
"streetcar, ride on the" 6583
"streetcar line to the west" 9166
"streetcar to the edge of the city limits" 10367
Streetfield, Bunty 1874
"streetlamp" 5339
"streetlight, pale glare of a" 10298
"streetlights burst into radiance" 2219
"streetlights stepping off into the black distance ahead" 6030
Streets 283, 820, 946, 1013, 1045, 1093, 1368, 1379, 1592, 1762, 2225, 2951, 2963, 2964, 2986, 3065, 3145, 3166, 3206, 3250, 3259, 4125, 4539, 5356, 5822, 6015, 6223, 6270, 6271, 7179, 7220, 7229, 7288, 7315, 7323, 8607, 8616, 9027, 9114, 9117, 9119, 9120, 9122, 9123, 9124, 9125, 9129, 9130, 9135, 9137, 9139, 9142, 9144, 9147, 9149, 9157, 9159, 9161, 9162, 9164, 9166, 9170, 9172, 9175, 9178, 9179, 9187, 9189, 9190, 9191, 9195, 9196, 9197, 9203, 9209, 9767, 9828, 9831, 10046, 10092, 10396, 10416, 10515, 10549, 10580, 10699, 10708, 10875, 10930
"streets, a puzzle of winding and oblique" 5607
"streets, back" 9027
"streets, blue transparency of the narrow" 2225
"streets, bordered by four" 4099
"streets, bright" 1618
"streets, city" 8616
"streets, clammy crowded" 1356
"streets, crowded" 1379
"streets, dark quiet" 6223
"streets, dim two-family-house" 9162
"streets, dirt" 7323
"streets, dirtier" 10446
"streets, dirty" 10352
"streets, East and Markets" 1608
"streets, familiar" 4539
"streets, hilly" 5142
"streets, invisible" 9540
"streets, irregular and ill-paved" 1368
"streets, leafy" 7443
"streets, narrow" 9130, 9765
"streets, one of those" 9114
"streets, pale formal" 9149
"Streets, Princess and Lombard" 1838
"streets, small" 6267
"streets, smaller" 9831
"streets, traffic-clogged" 515
"streets, walk through the" 9524

"streets are empty and unnaturally still" 9951
"streets go, as" 9129
"streets have an atmosphere of their own" 9124
"streets lie black and steaming" 10416
"streets never rebuilt after the war, bombed" 9175
"streets of Rome" 515
"streets of Stepney, back" 9178
"streets of the little city were bright but shadowless" 9139
"streets of the town where I was born" 4539
"streets showed the brilliant colors" 9159
"streets that lead from the Strand to the Embankment" 9123
Streisand, Barbra 8755
Strength 4456, 10018
"strength" 4456
"strength, great" 7056
"strength, their" 5381
"strength, whiteness and" 9416
"strength born of the decision" 2484
"strength ebbing, hard young" 4161
"strength I have become, what" 10018
"strength of chin" 5921
"strength was gone" 2363
Strephon 7370
Stress 1142, 1916
"stress, moments of" 1916
"stress, post-traumatic combat" 9054
"stresses and thrusts" 1314
"stretch, winding" 9168
"stretch her remarkably long and well-made legs out before you" 5471
"stretched herself in the bed" 8476
"stretched himself luxuriously" 10119
"stretched out his arms" 10116
"stretched out on his back" 8517
"stretches a Danish sea" 7914
"stretches out as much as he is able" 5995
"stretching" 10300
"stretching, lazily" 9753
"stretching away to the western horizon" 7878
"stretching far away down the slope and across the river" 1194
"stretching his full length in the lawn chair" 5622
"stretching it out a little" 882
"stretching their muscles" 7410
Strether 3913
Stretton, Julia 883
"strewn about the landscape" 1879
Strickland, Charles 5794
Strickland, Nell 6775
"strict or puritanical spirit" 6972
"stricture, in which" 5434

"stride, athletic" 1757
"stride, dreamy" 10463
"stride, his long hillman's" 10412
"stride, I had reached my" 91
"stride, in time to his" 10443
"stride, without breaking" 4901
"stride ruggedly into the gusts" 55
"strides, a few quick" 4335
"strides down the path" 4203
"striding down toward the train" 10359
"Striding Edge" 5070
"striding westward across the prairie" 10373
Strike 4210
"strike, ready to" 2851
"strike, sweet time for them to" 6179
"strike against God, you are on" 10838
Striker, Eaton 7027
"strikes a martial attitude" 8942
"strikes me as the oddest thing of all" 3374
"striking, a resemblance even more" 9882
"striking, six o'clock was" 9469
"striking enough, not" 304
"striking his little hammer" 5247
"striking on the streets" 5970
"strikingly handsome" 5998
Strindberg 962
"string, tight" 8793
"strings, when the bow first touched the" 6240
"stringybarks, two big" 9773
"strip joint, male" 6966
"strip off her Pig-Pen costume" 6783
"strip to their skivvies, told to" 1215
"stripes, pale orange" 5330
"stripling, tall good-looking" 7195
"Stripling at the University of *Aberdeen*" 10465
"stripped, office was" 6507
"stripped and faced the water" 6680
"stripped by the season" 5159
"stripped down to nothing" 5929
"stripped off his faded shorts and his green drill shirt" 2833
"strippling ream, beside the" 7677
"strode briskly into the lounge of the Repulse Bay Hotel" 10816
"strode through the heavy morning mist" 10352
"stroke, Bob Low had a" 138
"stroke, died of a second and long-expected" 2424
"stroke of the mantel clock, the deep" 3867
"stroke of the pen" 2023
"stroked it lightly" 4256
"stroked the sparse gray hairs of his good arm" 8461
"strokes, affinity of fine brush" 9696
"strokes, booming" 1606

"strokes, leisurely" 7608
"strokes of three o'clock beat out across the town" 1606
"strokes were borne very distinctly" 7180
"stroking the red apples of the sofa" 1788
"stroll, habitual" 4286
"stroll, the" 6274
"stroll hand in hand" 2006
"stroll to work" 10380
"strolled along Park Avenue" 2846
"strolled forward" 6622
"strolled over to the pretty Congress Park" 4371
"stroller along the docks of any considerable seaport" 3997
Strolling 2006, 2223, 2846, 4371, 6622, 10376
"strolling around the babywear department" 7099
"strolling down the hill" 10376
"strolling through the park" 2223
Strong, Kay Leiland 10656
"strong, the" 10522
"strong, try to be" 975
"strong enough to box with" 8239
"strong [came] in platoons, the" 10522
"strong in body" 10845
"stronghold" 3639
"stronghold, evangelical" 3429
"struck by a bolt of lightning, as if" 8560
"struck by a tornado" 8058
"struck nine, it had just" 3815
"struck one off the list of living tailors" 2290
"struck out across the church square" 1736
"struck out due west, he" 1731
"struck ten" 9467
"struck white flames in the hearts of the young bloods" 3965
"struck with his assertion, particularly" 6385
"struck with the singular character of its coast" 5707
"structural collapse" 5599
"structure, adequate stone" 9226
"structure, Elizabethan" 3066
"structure, Gothic" 1171
"structure, survey the" 1293
"Structure, the" 5514
"structure to which it belonged" 1293
Structures 37, 3038, 7190
"structures, oldest business" 1028
"struggle, after so long a" 7154
"struggle, after years of" 3296
"struggle, hopeless as the" 6866
"struggle, hour-to-hour" 4374
"struggle, long and bloody" 10483
"struggle against the fast maturing burden of trees and vines" 4374

"struggled against the station taxicab and extinction" 9382
"struggled through a neck" 7939
"struggled to his feet" 2928
"struggled to point out the road" 9647
"struggled with the deceptive fury" 9841
Struggles 2847, 7154
"struggles" 5558
"struggles to free themselves from each other" 1984
"struggles up from sleep" 10300
"struggling" 2847
"struggling, sun was" 8406
"struggling against the unbendable alloy mesh" 10721
"struggling in every direction" 9319
"struggling to get in" 3996
"struggling to grow up" 4242
"struggling up the gangway" 8072
"strung between heart and clock" 5624
"strung up on rafters" 662
"strut, lunatic" 5286
"strutted aimfully down the east side of Seventh Avenue" 10342
"strutted down her front porch steps" 6399
Stuart 7455
Stuart, Charlie 6086
Stuart, Logan 9142
"Stuartising" 3376
"Stuarts, since the exile of the" 3059
"Stuarts, the" 3375
"Stuarts, the last" 6972
"stub of his cigarette" 298
"stubble, endless" 5181
"stubble, grey three-day" 1838
"stubble, wheat" 2236
"stubborn man" 6698
"stubborn one" 6646
"stubbornly" 3305
"stubbornly, she said" 1842
Stubbornness 2645, 7064
"stubby ones" 349
"stubby red-faced Elof Lofblom" 9554
"stuck, I'm" 7987
"stuck her head in through the open door" 9339
"stuck out on either side like turn signals" 2859
"stuck together, if the family had" 3610
Studdock, Jane 5742
"student, bright gifted" 2568
"student, Christian" 7518
"student, first black" 5102
"student, graduate" 940
"student, I am a" 7884
"student, moneyless young male" 3672
"student, my" 5674
"student in London, art" 6568
"student in Trinity College" 4604

"student of human nature" 6490
"student revolution" 5673
"student there, when I was a" 7883
Students 99, 517, 970, 986, 1214, 2471, 2568, 3207, 3528, 3672, 3722, 3931, 4365, 4604, 5102, 5468, 5631, 5674, 5821, 6144, 6568, 6830, 7495, 7518, 7876, 7881, 7884, 7885, 7889, 7890, 7892, 7898, 7903, 8012, 8752, 8863, 9290, 9729, 10107, 10441, 10953
"students, fellow" 4933
"students, I hate art" 4365
"students (not unlike yourselves)" 5468
"students were assembled in the courtyard" 10107
"students were settling into their rooms" 7889
"studgroom" 2820
"studied, scrutinised and" 519
"studied it" 3773
"studied the book" 7361
"studied the dinner table" 3838
"studied the face of her sleeping husband" 10117
"studied the overhanging bulk of the aircraft carrier" 8131
"studied to be a concert tenor" 8752
"studies, religious" 10896
"studies, seen at his" 5699
"studio, her own" 1869
"studio, his bare" 491
"studio, Pettingill's" 10554
"studio, Superba-Llewellyn" 1687
"studio, Superba-Llewellyn motion-picture" 1324
"studio at WLT, snakebite" 7791
"Studio B" 7791
"studio on East 92nd Street" 3261
"studio was filled with the rich odour of roses" 3794
"Studios, Warner Brothers" 5571
Study 517, 3292, 5639, 7361, 10951, 10953
"study, her" 8313, 9884
"study, her father's" 8174
"study, his father's cave-like" 6231
"study, his private" 6881
"study, I won't" 3268
"study, in my" 9989
"study, Jeffrey's" 3829
"study, my" 714
"study, our projected" 716
"study, upstairs in my" 9987
"study art, thought I would" 517
"study door, her father's" 7843
"study door, his" 1119
"study has been ordered, further detailed" 7514
"study in stark contrast, they were a" 926
"study of Giotto, critical" 5465
"study of his home" 8202

"study vocabulary, tried to" 3292
"stuff, preferred stronger" 2936
"stuff, puffy" 5355
"stuff, there wasn't any of that" 5605
"stuff coming down in sheets" 7307
"stuffed, he wanted to be" 2382
"stuffed his map into his pocket" 5711
"stuffed them into his knapsack" 7858
"stuffy man" 6637
"Stuka, hoping to spot a" 10517
"stumbled back out into the traffic-clogged streets" 515
"stumbled out, I" 1703
"stumbled out of the shop" 143
"stumbling about in open fields" 8695
"stumbling on roots and rocks" 10400
"stump, occasional charred almost petrified" 4073
"stumped down the curving drive" 847
"stunk to high heaven, breath" 1524
"stunning to wake up every morning" 1258
"stupefying decadence" 1464
"stupendous surroundings" 2620
"stupid, far too" 4290
"stupid, smart or" 5542
"stupid, the most" 6570
"stupid talk, too much" 7840
"stupid the young are, how" 11003
Stupidity 4290, 5006, 5009, 5010, 6570, 11003
"stupidly triumphant" 434
"stuporous, still half-" 2905
"sturdy as cliffs" 9212
"sturdy wood-choppers" 3069
Sturgess 7587
Sturgis, Mrs. 6217
"sty, open-air portion of her" 1178
"sty where he had rested so many times" 8360
"Styhead Pass" 8519
"style, boy's quirk of" 10833
"style, Indian" 8156
"Style, Olde Englysshe" 3096
"style and taste, the present fashionable" 3376
"style known to Muscovites as Empire During the Plague" 7904
"style of dormer windows" 5607
"style of play, aggressive" 3971
Styr, Margarethe 5641
"Styx, crossing the" 5029
"Styx, River" 2016
"Styx, the" 1009
"Styx lay silent, the" 7656
"Subaru, her red" 8282
"subconscious minds" 5512
"subdivided in the same manner" 3096

"subdivision, a" 3208
"subdued and cowed by the relentless sleety rain" 7304
"Subiaco lies beyond Tivoli" 4040
"subject, a fitting" 9250
"subject, rather a dismal" 5984
"subject being inescapably personal" 162
"subject of the public talk" 7825
"subject to two most serious drawbacks" 10775
"subjection and slavery, deplorable condition of" 1351
"Subjects, his" 10464
"subjects I never discussed" 7593
"subject's nature, your" 711
"sublime, in form" 7648
"subliminal to be called spiritual, too" 6001
"sublimity connected with vastness" 4032
"submarine, U. S. Navy nuclear ballistic missile" 941
"submarine *Eel*" 4745
"Submarine *Tristram*, His Majesty's" 8128
Submarines 941, 8128, 8140, 8680
"submarine's forward torpedo room" 570
"subordinate in public affairs, happily" 5392
Subservience 10855
"subsidizing public transport" 7003
"substance, thick material" 4377
"substance that was heavy and unwieldy" 9249
"Substantial Boss" 2633
"substantial dream became insubstantial" 10121
"subterranean drain-pipes" 10930
"subtle, conveyed something" 7677
"subtraction is the hardest 'ciphering'" 895
"suburb" 5898
"suburb, early" 1856
"suburb, expensive" 4947
"suburb, its southern" 6283
"suburb, quiet residential" 5754
"suburb, residential" 1362
"suburb, upland" 10359
"suburb, well-to-do" 7367
"suburb in Bonn, shabbiest" 4389
"suburb of Helsinki" 5042
"suburb of Saffron Park" 1358
"suburb on the edge of London" 2041
"suburb region, woodland" 3088
"suburb to the west of London" 3153
"suburban church" 1303
"suburban dwellings" 3242
"suburban end of the new Lincoln Boulevard" 3096
"suburban roads" 5142
"suburban village of Wahwahnissa

Creek" 8515
Suburbs 1358, 1362, 1856, 3088, 3153, 3775, 4063, 4389, 5042, 6141, 10359
"suburbs, fire the" 3775
"suburbs, in the" 10381
"suburbs, numerous potpourrious" 3237
"suburbs, outlying" 1005
"suburbs, the" 6141
"suburbs of London" 6558
"subway, rode the" 9642
"subway, stepped off the" 5454
"subway, walking home from the" 10361
"subway going to work, in the" 5522
"subway tunnel, resembling a miniature" 10462
"succeeded to Spinney Moor" 3212
Success 282, 499, 2035, 2601, 5416, 7125, 7216, 9293, 9378
"success, astonishing and unprecedented" 5416
"success, did not have much" 1510
"success, good prospect of" 5387
"success, great" 5193
"success, preclude the slightest possibility of" 5829
"success, primary Jeeter" 3604
"success, sensational" 9266
"success, Victorian" 3122
"success, West End" 9378
"success' far from being a happy triumph as of old was the sign of doom Himself" 9265
"success of a marriage" 10829
"success of curiosity at least, undeniably a" 9378
"success she had hoped it would be" 6755
"success that destroys, paradox of" 282
"successes" 5558
"successful" 6546
"successful, qualities that have made me quite" 5496
"successful evenings, most" 9270
"succession, third time in" 7817
"succession, three times in" 1132
"succession of the pacific James I" 7794
"successor, nominate a" 6994
"succor, give help and" 8643
"succulent, delicately" 1863
"succumbed to a kidney disease" 2408
Sucette 9029
"Suchard the semi-sweet" 6652
"suck, the sea's slow" 8491
"sucked dry in the hulls by bees" 8531
"sucked in great gulps of air" 1711
"sucked so hard on a Dixie cup" 7051

"sucked up by the midday sun" 5704

"sucked up their own shadows" 5704

"sucked window shades out through the top of opened windows" 10699

"suckered by miscalculation" 3971

"sucking cream, Mary was" 1873

"sucking his mother's milk" 6823

"sucking on his pipe" 6219

"sucks, Texas" 10744

"suction cups" 303

"sudden and ravenous" 9071

"suddenly I'm on my hands and knees" 8949

Sudie 6703

Sue, Auntie 5795

"suffer, can be made to" 6612

"suffer from insecurity" 10844

"suffer noble sorrows" 4454

"suffer so irrevocably" 9279

"suffered a heart attack" 159

"suffered mostly from weak eyesight and poor feet" 158

"suffered the most" 9277

"suffering" 9280

"suffering, emotion and" 8838

"suffering, not far to look for" 9278

"suffering for all your country's unpunished and unrepented sins" 9284

"suffering from strange and unpredictable humors" 10493

"suffering him to remain in ignorance" 6517

"suffering puts a gloss on" 9282

"suffering the pain of a broken heart" 970

"sufficed, the house" 9592

"suffocating, I'm" 9281

"suffocation, a deadly sense of" 4370

"Suffolk" 3165

"Suffolk, after a few days in" 1665

"Suffolk, county of" 4444

"Suffolk, East" 4069

"Suffolk coast" 1883

"suffused the night, smell of Venice" 8523

"Sugar States" 4051

"sugarplum, a good miniature is a" 323

Sugden, Mrs. 10812

"suggested that I should go down to Tralorna" 9723

"suggestion, Colonel Spencer's" 4500

"suggestion, object of enlivening" 1183

"suggestion, put forward my" 7142

Suggestions 7142, 9723

Sugrue 3255

"suicidal ex-patient" 7874

Suicide 75, 2354, 3021, 3519, 5769, 6021, 6187, 6211

"suicide" 9289

"suicide?" 2354

"suicide, forcing to" 7802

"suicide, the moment he decided to commit" 9288

"suicide every day, considered" 9299

"Suicide Notebook" 8816

"suicide pact, signed a" 9290

"suit, biscuit-colored summer" 9753

"suit, blue mohair" 8294

"suit, brushing his" 2831

"suit, crumpled blue" 5208

"suit, glen plaid" 2111

"suit, gray business" 10421

"suit, greasy padded flying" 2847

"suit, green summer" 7045

"suit, his plaid" 1982

"suit, in a three-piece" 4331

"suit, laid out the" 2840

"suit, my best" 1607

"suit, neat brown" 966

"suit, new" 2865

"suit, severe gray" 2658

"suit, shoddy gray" 6950

"suit, striped bathing" 4206

"suit — greyish" 9937

"suit me, it doesn't" 2849

"suit of black garbardine, dressed in a" 10819

"suit of black, his rusty and worn" 8453

"suit of European clothes" 6950

"suit of long trousers, wearing his first" 2827

"suit of white serge" 10336

"suit with a muted red stripe" 2848

"suitcase, carefully packed straw" 2658

"suitcase, holding a" 1702

"suitcase, hugging the little" 3030

"suitcase, rotted cardboard" 10532

"suitcase, Samsonite" 10436

"suitcase, worn cardboard" 1639

"suitcase down, put his" 1659

"suitcase full of books and papers" 10415

"suitcase shut, forced the" 2484

"suitcases, his wife Gracie's" 1783

"suite, Chairman's" 1032

"suite, hotel" 8806

"suite, not in Léon's usual" 4633

"Suite A" 7768

"suites, empty upstairs" 3137

"suites, those vast" 1011

"suites which a merchant designed" 1011

"suits, black business" 2914

"suits, cotton pyjama" 10054

"suits, solemn Sunday" 6868

"suits hanging in the open closet, counted the" 2874

Suki 8008

Sukie 6301

"Sulaco, town of" 1355

"Sulka" 309

"sullen noonday heat" 3907

Sullivan, Billy 1759

Sullivan, Eleanor 9419

Sullivan, Maggie 170

Sully 6652

"sully its perfect whiteness" 3728

"sulphur" 10530

Sultan of Turkey 4172

"sultry, night was" 4384

"sultry after daylong heat" 5068

"sultry August night" 1603

"sultry days" 10567

"sultry heat" 7637

"sum, a foolish" 773

"sum of everything that has happened to them" 3671

"sumac, overgrown with" 3036

"sumac, red spray of" 973

"Sumburgh Head" 5011

Sumitra 10665

Summer 327, 680, 2145, 2152, 2156, 2172, 2200, 2221, 2236, 2691, 2930, 3032, 3180, 3211, 3370, 3501, 3904, 4237, 4372, 4374, 4376, 4377, 4384, 4386, 4388, 4398, 4400, 4402, 4403, 4405, 4418, 4422, 4431, 4656, 4960, 5351, 5364, 5666, 6801, 7312, 7418, 7544, 8594, 8715, 9652, 10146, 10566, 10571, 10576, 10581, 10583, 10593, 10595, 10596, 10600, 10611, 10620, 10621, 10622, 10623, 10625

"summer, all" 10581

"summer, all that" 3137

"summer, both before and after that" 5122

"summer, Chungking's sweltering" 10261

"summer, cloudless Carolina" 1879

"summer, collapse of" 6225

"summer, come the" 6566

"summer, day of" 2172

"summer, decisive" 2988

"summer, dreaded the" 5364

"summer, dry sounds of" 10701

"summer, feel of early" 10600

"summer, first hot days of" 7927

"summer, heat of" 327

"summer, high" 1115, 2236

"summer, hot and sticky in the" 8594

"summer, I spent a large part of every" 9726

"summer, in the" 9747

"summer, in the long-ago" 2771

"summer, Indian" 10597, 10621, 10808

"summer, it was a queer sultry" 680

"summer, it was dry that" 10576

"summer, it was really" 7312

"summer, it was the" 538

"summer, known in London as" 10571

"summer, last" 768, 5035

"summer, last out the" 2672
"summer, once every" 182
"summer, one" 9722
"summer, our usual" 3604
"summer, so it was" 9652
"summer, spend two months of the" 1422
"summer, stewpot of" 10745
"summer, sudden fury of" 4382
"summer, sun shone all" 10596
"summer, that" 5710
"Summer, that" 4237
"summer, that green and crazy" 3501
"summer, that previous" 3196
"summer, that was the" 7544
"summer, the last" 4656
"summer, the last of" 10146
"summer, think of that" 8543
"summer, this" 2152
"summer, this past troubled" 2550
"summer, wet and windy" 30
"summer as children, our last" 1277
"summer darkness" 10730
"summer days, long green" 10623
"summer dress, their full" 9742
"summer freedom" 938
"summer had been passed" 6556
"summer had not yet gone" 4386
"summer has passed" 10593
"summer hesitated sullenly between continued heat and the equinoctial need of change" 4384
"summer in Europe, that first" 515
"summer in her body" 10611
"summer in Montreal, that" 10583
"summer in New York, stifling" 9572
"summer in the Gulf of Eilat" 4418
"summer itself, like" 10622
"summer light" 4118
"summer light, bleached by" 1754
"summer long, all" 9169
"summer morning" 2145
"summer of '89" 9750
"summer of 1296, bright was the" 6801
"summer of 1846" 4427
"summer of 1870, in the heart of the great" 10053
"summer of 1921" 3015
"summer of 1922, for a few weeks in the" 3544
"summer of 1945 or '46" 8934
"summer of 1947" 4388
"summer of 1953" 10506
"summer of 1955" 9321
"summer of 1960" 4403
"summer of 1968" 4405
"summer of 1969" 7418
"summer of 1986, it was the" 3370
"summer of my twelfth year" 7460
"summer of the year, the first" 5704
"summer of weddings, first big" 2930

"summer opening ahead, the long" 5024
"summer Saturdays, hot" 1477
"summer she was fifteen, the" 7969
"summer soaring, young" 4010
"summer term at Oxford" 9569
"summer that year held into September" 10622
"summer vantage point" 847
"summer was perpetual" 2156
"summer was roses and wine" 7709
"summer we lost the bald Jeeter, that was the" 3604
"summer-fall" 9086
Summers, Dick 1713
"summers, forty-three" 7763
"summers, Indian" 4388
"summers at Cold Spring Harbor" 10620
"summer's end" 3904
"summer's green, undone" 10591
"summers in Eastern Tennessee are always hot" 4400
"summer's promise" 10587
"summers were long and warm and drowsy" 3396
"summertime, darkest in" 3211
"summertime, in the" 5370
"summing-up of about four years" 4506
"summit, the" 4478
"Summit Conferences, no" 3362
"summit of the hill" 9738
"summit was wandering and uncertain" 6055
"summits veiled in clouds" 5125
"summon its materiality" 5027
"summoned by the wisdom of Almighty God" 7801
"summoned me to his office" 6509
"summoned to the office of our naval attaché" 6502
"summons, aware of a" 10128
"summons, heralded the" 3444
"summons of that sort" 1118
"summons to evening prayer" 650
"Summulae Logicales" 7879
"sumpter horses" 1779
"sumptuous hotel" 4636
Sun 137, 525, 532, 1188, 1301, 2133, 2158, 2190, 2203, 2280, 2778, 2986, 4133, 4188, 4369, 4372, 4379, 4389, 4397, 4410, 4428, 4429, 5096, 5136, 5143, 5168, 5328, 5340, 5341, 5704, 6395, 7435, 7672, 7757, 7776, 7929, 7942, 8117, 8389, 8392, 8396, 8399, 8402, 8403, 8404, 8405, 8406, 8407, 8409, 8411, 8413, 8417, 8419, 8431, 8437, 8438, 8445, 9276, 9479, 9598, 9776, 10146, 10240, 10329, 10518, 10585, 10586, 10596, 10621, 10700
"Sun" 4008
"sun, afternoon" 2727, 9191

"sun, April" 8552
"sun, bake in the late morning" 8372
"sun, beneath the Southern" 1393
"sun, blazing" 4428
"sun, blazing Mexican" 4379
"sun, blinding midday" 515
"sun, brightly blazed the" 10700
"sun, brutal Mexican" 10883
"sun, burning" 10329
"sun, burning in the" 4367
"sun, Carolina" 7467
"sun, course around the" 525
"sun, devil" 10240
"sun, drying and crumbling in the" 5020
"sun, evening" 8152, 10365
"sun, first beams of the" 9740
"sun, first spot of" 7358
"sun, from the nesting place of the" 9324
"sun, genial generous-minded" 1357
"sun, glint of" 193
"sun, he could see the" 2778
"sun, heart of the setting" 10701
"sun, hot July" 7594
"sun, hot midsummer" 4397
"sun, hot summer" 4374
"sun, late afternoon" 7672, 8034
"sun, late-September" 6986
"sun, late-summer" 8517
"sun, light of the" 92
"sun, like the clock of" 752
"sun, listing toward the" 9678
"sun, long lazy rays of the" 8461
"sun, long-legged" 8214
"sun, low pale lemon grey" 8445
"sun, March" 10717
"sun, midday" 5704
"sun, morning" 1680, 5333, 7942, 9437, 10292
"sun, new" 7929
"sun, not enough" 9299
"sun, orbit about the" 532
"sun, pale" 4133
"sun, rarely touched by the" 5624
"sun, rising" 5964, 8545
"sun, scorching" 3714
"sun, scorching rays of the" 7435
"sun, sepia" 8164
"sun, setting" 1859, 4044, 5341
"sun, should have caught the earliest" 10646
"sun, showers quickly absorbed by the" 7342
"sun, simmering" 9479
"sun, sky maybe flame-blue with" 9228
"sun, slant of Riviera" 10118
"sun, smallish wan" 8406
"sun, soaking up the autumn" 1949
"sun, sounds of life fell with the" 8070
"sun, sparkling in the" 5045
"sun, spring" 7665

"Sun, squinted at" 10311
"sun, summer" 7787
"sun, the" 4188, 5136, 9062
"sun, unwearied" 8392
"sun, violent glare of the August" 8079
"sun, weather bureau forecast" 10599
"sun, willful April" 8437
"sun, wind and rain and summer's" 9220
"sun, yellow" 5149
"sun a red ball dropping slowly" 8403
"sun and shadow" 4010
"sun and wind of thirty-six out-of-door years" 5899
"sun appeared, a moment before the" 5328
"sun at its haughtiest" 5911
"sun at their backs" 1764
"sun beat across the desert sands" 4428
"sun beat down" 10373
"sun beat down mercilessly" 4374
"sun beat down without mercy" 4397
"sun behind, the" 10116
"sun behind one's head slanting down the highway" 4164
"sun blazed" 9239
"sun blazed across the fields" 6395
"sun blazed relentlessly" 8117
"sun blistering her neck" 4429
"sun breaking through the clouds" 10616
"sun broke through" 10585
"sun came in at a slant" 5334
"sun came out suddenly" 7757
"sun came through today" 5330
"sun came up, before the" 8148
"sun came up glaring behind the blue crags" 2986
"sun cracked the day open and hit him in the eye" 2772
"sun cross and recross the carriages" 9605
"sun dark and red" 8404
"sun dropped below the horizon" 2209
"sun entered their room" 10169
"sun fell in love with the moon" 9010
"sun full in his face" 8517
"sun gave a watery promise of warmth and good cheer" 1301
"sun glittering, prickles of" 5317
"sun had already heated the seat" 4420
"sun had been beating down on the houses" 4372
"sun had bleached from red to pink" 6698
"sun had disappeared" 8389
"sun had gone, when the" 8076

"sun had hidden" 5314
"sun had not yet risen" 2203
"sun had sunk below the great stone pile" 2223
"sun had took a clip of his shears along the shadows" 4660
"sun has risen" 5945
"sun having set, the" 9139
"sun hot" 4475
"sun hot on the back of his neck" 10365
"sun hovered behind a pink haze" 10621
"sun hung like an animal's tongue from a sickened blue maw" 5096
"sun hung low in the west" 8431
"sun intended to set right in that room, as if the" 7040
"sun is beaming down" 3622
"sun is setting" 8425
"sun is shining" 2158, 10602
"sun making angular haloes" 8152
"sun no longer strikes my eastern window" 10146
"sun not shining, with the" 7296
"sun of February, pale" 10142
"sun of late afternoon slanted" 5627
"sun of September, in the evening" 1382
"sun of Siena, warm" 10200
"sun of spring, today a rare" 8411
"sun of Syria" 10329
"sun on his tongue" 8239
"sun on it, with the" 4660
"sun on metallic body or translucent wing" 193
"sun outside to prove it" 9598
"sun pale but piercing" 8405
"sun poured brightly into the office" 2511
"sun pours down on a continent aflame" 10518
"sun radiating through clouds" 4319
"sun reluctantly administering sudden jabs of heat, a pale" 137
"sun rose" 5143, 5168
"sun rose higher all through the hot morning" 1188
"sun rose with an upward push of colour" 8409
"Sun runing a most eve course" 7370
"sun . . . settled behind a bank of spear-shaped clouds" 8404
"sun settled into the tawny marshes" 8402
"sun shines, when the" 5144
"sun shining on it" 9425
"sun shone, the" 8407
"sun shone all summer" 10596
"sun shone brightly" 10186
"sun shone brightly down" 1324
"sun shone cloudless" 10569
"sun shone freely" 2190

"sun shone fuller and fuller on that side of the house" 7763
"sun shone gold-brown on the expanse of parquet floor" 5322
"sun shone hazily through a September day" 8413
"sun slanted down through the massive east windows" 6986
"sun slipped down, the February" 9995
"sun stood like a victorious king" 8392
"sun . . . streamed into his narrow room" 10142
"sun strikes it" 7664
"sun struck Norman on his bared head" 5323
"sun swirled in a blinding pinwheel" 2280
"sun teetered in the sky" 9776
"sun . . . threw a golden bar" 7757
"sun tinged with flame" 5149
"sun to sink below the skyline" 483
"sun toward midafternoon, pulled the" 3867
"sun turned black as sackcloth" 8419
"sun turned the snow into molten gold" 983
"sun was a burning yellow fire" 8417
"sun was a gas jet" 9664
"sun was a pale blaze hurting his eyes" 9276
"sun was already reddening the western sky" 9163
"sun was blazing away out there" 7776
"sun was blazing down" 1345
"sun was going down" 1546, 2195
"sun was higher in the sky and a much brighter yellow" 988
"sun was hot, though the" 10337
"sun was hot on Martha's back" 1113
"sun was just beginning to shine down" 4389
"sun was rising" 8438
"sun was setting" 2133, 4422
"sun was shining" 10586
"sun . . . was so fierce that it had stripped the sky of colour" 4410
"sun was struggling through wool tatters of cloud" 8406
"sun was sunnier" 5033
"sun was up, the August" 5340
"sun was warm, when the" 2691
"sun which blazed down" 4410
"sun which shone upon a day" 8399
"sun which warms my face" 4133
"sun will rise in about twenty-five minutes" 2183
"sun won't boil it on you" 9550
Sunbathing 5629
"sunbeams and moonbeams" 4800
"sunbeams slant over the antique gateway" 8937
"sun-blasted desert" 9766

"sun-blistered garage and cafe" 1080
"sunbonnet, her little" 3759
"sunburn, feverish with" 9616
"sunburst, immense" 3001
"Sunbury" 4595
"Sunday sports page, reading the" 7369
"sundown, after" 2911
"sundown, an hour before" 9946
"sundown, dead before" 7934
"sundown, far off" 5314
"sundown, half an hour before" 7292
"sundown, winter" 2704
"sundown and twilight, the hour of" 2234
"sun-drenched" 5026
"sundress, cross-strapped" 6710
"sundry matters" 8886
Sundy 1663
"sunfall, early morning" 1194
"sunflower genus of the *Syngenesia frustranea* class of plants" 10899
"sunflowers" 1376
"sung it better, she had never" 8738
"sung of the deathless exploits of Alice Morell" 4474
"sunglasses, except for her" 6396
"sunglasses, mirrored" 4203
"sunk as deep as he'd been intended to sink, must not have" 1896
"sunk into its grave" 3376
Sunlight 92, 983, 1020, 1177, 1300, 1324, 1379, 1762, 1923, 2132, 2182, 2225, 2264, 2511, 2695, 2754, 2756, 2977, 3126, 4010, 4319, 4406, 4571, 4660, 4704, 5074, 5131, 5168, 5305, 5308, 5309, 5310, 5311, 5313, 5314, 5316, 5317, 5318, 5319, 5322, 5323, 5327, 5328, 5329, 5330, 5333, 5334, 5337, 5340, 5342, 5627, 5945, 6079, 6384, 7040, 7166, 7358, 7619, 7757, 7787, 7933, 8374, 8413, 8431, 8461, 8552, 8937, 9149, 9317, 9425, 9527, 9666, 9740, 10118, 10142, 10144, 10145, 10186, 10193, 10200, 10225, 10267, 10292, 10295, 10310, 10317, 10373, 10384, 10569, 10586, 10588, 10599, 10602, 10611, 10696
"sunlight, a flush of midnight" 6384
"sunlight, American" 290
"sunlight, announce itself in" 10256
"sunlight, breezy sweep of" 1762
"sunlight, bright early-morning" 7265
"sunlight, butter-colored" 980
"sunlight, circlet of" 3952
"sunlight, clear pale October" 1379
"sunlight, dazzling" 10696
"sunlight, early October" 1923
"sunlight, evening" 2991

"sunlight, ghosts of centuries of" 5310
"sunlight, glistening in the" 456
"sunlight, glittered brightly in the" 5074
"sunlight, hot bright" 10145
"sunlight, in the" 6079, 8374
"sunlight, keen February" 9211
"sunlight, pale April" 421
"sunlight, rays of golden" 5309
"sunlight, reflecting golden" 9225
"sunlight, room full of" 10225
"sunlight, shaft of golden" 4319
"sunlight, shafts and freshets of" 5318
"sunlight, shape of" 10121
"sunlight, shone almost blindingly in the" 5131
"sunlight, shone in the blazing" 8121
"sunlight, sparkled in the" 2745
"sunlight, thin" 10295
"sunlight, watery January" 8947
"sunlight, weak" 8386
"sunlight, went out into the" 4406
"sunlight at a December slant" 4412
"sunlight begins to fill the town square" 5342
"sunlight breaking silver" 8710
"sunlight bright in the room" 2754
"sunlight crowded this August afternoon" 5310
"sunlight cut through the windshield" 2977
"sunlight flash" 7067
"sunlight gleaming upon his lithe vigorous body" 9317
"sunlight is on the house" 5327
"sunlight of late September" 9149
"sunlight peeped in like the foremost spies of some advancing army" 5309
"sunlight poured in" 7040
"sunlight poured over her" 10611
"sunlight slipping through the doorway" 4319
"sunlight that filters through the young leaves" 5337
"sunlight through a creeping fig" 10310
"sunlight through tangled branches, break like patches of" 8999
"sunlight would be invisible to him" 5329
"sunlit blue, the" 4559
Sunny 4846
"sunny banks" 3808
"sunny days, looks yellow on" 5154
"sunny in San Francisco" 10588
"sunny rectangle of the cabin door" 1556
"Sunnyside" 1515
"sunray flinging miles of diamonds in the Mediterranean's blue" 4704
"sunrise, at" 1567
"sunrise, pink with" 3652

"sunrise, shortly after" 7230
"suns, a dozen tropic" 10494
"sun's first stretching" 4404
"sun's rays still pour down" 4369
"sun's warmth" 449
"suns were simultaneously setting round the horizon" 10494
Sunset 1546, 5305, 8070
"sunset, at" 10374
"sunset, before the hour of" 4647
"sunset, level light of a summer" 5305
"sunset, ochre" 6327
"sunset, one evening toward" 983
"sunset, out of the" 5215
"sunset, red and ragged as a cloud of" 1358
"sunset, slanting beams of" 2944
"sunset, smoky" 3107
"sunset, the" 1576
"sunset, until" 6085
"Sunset Years" 10606
"sunsets, superb" 1013
"sunsets of the Hudson River School" 1012
"sunshine, after a day of warm" 375
"sunshine, Asian alpine" 247
"sunshine, bland May" 7933
"sunshine, blinding" 1589
"sunshine, bright morning" 3801
"sunshine, delicate" 1177
"sunshine, early spring" 18
"sunshine, flood of morning" 2695
"sunshine, frail spring" 9627
"sunshine, fresh May" 5316
"sunshine, hot Israeli" 4704
"sunshine, hot September" 7619
"sunshine, insects droning in the" 2211
"sunshine, July" 7108
"sunshine, June morning" 2756
"sunshine, much" 9669
"sunshine, smoky" 4571
"sunshine, storm and" 10567
"sunshine, strong white" 1300
"sunshine, warm and balmy" 2264
"sunshine, watery afternoon" 1020
"sunshine, yellow" 2348
"sunshine arrowed through the window" 10317
"sunshine brightening hotly" 2756
"Sunshine Cities for the Sunset Years" 10606
"sunshine . . . fell graciously on London town" 5308
"sunshine flooding the earth" 9527
"sunshine had dried the dew and warmed the ground" 3801
"sunshine had only just penetrated" 9742
"sunshine in ourselves" 7166
"sunshine in the heart, no corresponding" 2511
"sunshine of a fair Spring morning" 5308

"sunshine of June streaming into her window" 10193
"sunshine of Mexican December" 1398
"sunshine pierced the haze" 5311
"sunshine was slanting in through the slats" 1020
"sunshine which is such an agreeable feature of life" 3126
"sunshiny morning" 9757
"sunstroke" 7988
"sun-tan oil, her" 10810
"sunup, since before" 5945
"sup upon myself" 390
"sup with Glaucus to-night, do you" 3812
"superadded by deliberate intent" 8773
"super-bumpers, raspberry" 5184
"superciliousness is not safe after all" 7124
"supercollated, None of us Duvals have been" 360
"superhighway through the woods, cutting a" 8828
"superintendent of the Protestant mission schools" 6446
"Superior, the" 6807
"superiority of mind over matter" 3325
"superiors, his" 1167
"superiors in Québec" 2555
"supermarket, this old A & P" 921
"supernatural paraphernalia of inscrutable Destiny" 1093
"supernumeraries, not counting" 8102
Superstition 1232, 1292
"superstition, dogmas of" 2492
"superstition, origin of" 1232
"superstition reigns with such despotic sway as in Madrid" 1292
"supervision, minimum of" 2033
"supervisor came to fetch her" 7538
"supervisors in white coveralls, a dozen" 307
"supine, immodestly" 1478
"supine, lay" 8209
"supper, after" 450
"supper, at" 9664
"supper, did not wish any" 2495
"supper, give an order in the kitchen about" 3825
"supper, having" 3854
"supper, right after" 6681
"supper, we finished" 8038
"supper, we have had" 4119
"supper, woman who had come over to prepare the" 3835
"supper with his wife and son" 3837
"suppers are the best in Pompeii, they say his" 3812
"supplies, coffee-sack load of" 8360
"support and warmth of some wall" 10772

"support her family" 4186
"supposed himself to be" 6518
"supposed to be, what is this" 3875
"supposed to stay at the beach a week" 9731
"Supreme Court Justice" 5207
"Supremes, the" 5860
"Surat" 8254
"sure, are you" 1719
"sure, could never be quite" 10276
"sure, one thing for" 4107
"sure, she wasn't exactly" 4165
"sure, they could not be" 4947
"sure, we can't be" 2577
"sure how far one could go, nobody seemed quite" 139
"sure in his soul that he could" 4704
"sure of that, I'm" 10398
"sure what had happened, she was not so" 688
"sure-footed" 7630
"sureness recedes, my" 4809
"surf, rippling lacelike" 980
"surf, there had been no" 742
"surf of its own light" 9668
"surface, broken" 5325
"surface, flat glittering" 8117
"surface, grim" 5911
"surface, I" 10299
"surface of Interstate 81, vast desert" 9812
"surface of the globe" 4533
"surge, tremendous" 5011
"surge of the bay mare" 410
"surged a hurrying throng of men and women" 9528
"surged about her" 9409
"surged into mid-March" 10618
"surgeon" 6894
"surgeon, chief" 682
"surgeon, skilled" 8959
"surgeon, the" 8767
"surgeon on the hospital staff" 7539
"surgeons, leave my poor remains to the" 121
"surgeons in the army" 3266
Surgery 607, 1519, 4281, 6183
"surgery, closed the door of the" 2707
"surgery, perform a delicate piece of" 6183
"surgical resident" 2518
"surly, naturally" 10027
"surly act" 8674
"surnames, far more" 4752
"surnames, known by their" 4724
"surplice, white Renaissance" 509
Surprise 288, 410, 891, 1055, 1104, 1219, 1306, 1335, 1507, 1925, 1961, 1985, 2083, 2158, 2169, 2261, 2326, 2451, 2677, 3513, 4123, 4907, 5187, 5731, 5825, 6321, 6467, 6509, 6595, 6940, 7060, 7573, 8171, 8172, 8173, 8174, 8175, 8176, 8177, 8178,

8179, 8180, 8181, 8182, 8183, 8184, 8185, 8186, 8187, 8188, 8189, 8190, 8191, 8192, 8194, 8195, 8196, 8198, 8199, 8200, 8201, 8202, 9311, 10253, 10320, 10708
"surprise, glance with some" 8192
"surprise, I can imagine your" 8171
"surprise, may come as a" 6467
"surprise, more impatience than" 4907
"surprise, my lack of" 8198
"surprise, night comes as a" 2261
"surprise, occasioned little enough" 6135
"surprise, one's" 7573
"surprise, paused in" 8173
"surprise, real" 8188
"surprise, saw with" 8202
"surprise, should come as no" 5379
"surprise, size of the Cathedral was a" 1306
"surprise, to the grocer's" 10708
"surprise and distress" 898
"surprise at my offer" 5731
"surprise for Bitsy, a small" 4123
"surprise our readers" 7060
"surprise than sympathy, more" 4907
"surprised?" 8190
"surprised, can't honestly say I was" 8196
"surprised, cannot be" 150
"surprised, I was" 6509
"surprised, I'm not" 3515
"surprised, should not be" 6461
"surprised a tall old woman" 8186
"surprised and even outraged" 3513
"surprised at the bright sight of himself" 7474
"surprised her" 8183
"surprised him" 6595
"surprised to find it open" 1055
"surprised to find they were there to see it" 8178
"surprised to hear from me" 1961, 8181
"surprised to know that she had slept" 10253
"surprised to see me here" 8200
"surprises, believe in good" 8194
"surprises, full of" 8176
"surprises can only be bad" 8194
"surprises me most, what" 6940
"surprising" 2158
"surprising, hardly" 3660
"surprising, it was not" 10794
"surprisingly enough" 812
Surratt, Buck 7615
"surreal and 'existential' and perhaps even 'anarchist' second novel" 5468
Surrender 1867, 6313
"surrender at Appomattox, Lee's" 6313

"surrender to the stickiness, decided to" 1867
"surrendering natural edges and boundaries" 5265
"surreptitiously collecting them" 7680
"Surrey" 4683, 6568, 9722, 9738
"surrey, the Willing" 5616
"Surrey hills" 3076
"surrogate for pain, fear is the" 3726
"surrounded by the huge smooth yet twisting black marble pillars" 4895
"surrounded by the rolling hills of Umbria" 1473
"surrounded by the split-level houses" 3208
"surroundings, humble" 9974
"surroundings, scrutinized his" 9311
"surroundings, stupendous" 2620
"Surroundings, The" 6768
"surroundings, those" 4079
"survey, slow meticulous" 5716
"survey the Lombard plain" 5127
"survey the structure, travellers were curious to" 1293
"surveyed herself" 7469
"surveyed his new residence" 6145
"surveyed the rolling carpet of grass" 7646
"surveyed the room" 7125
"surveyed the waiting-room without enthusiasm" 7781
"surveyed the wide saucer-shaped valley" 9749
"surveyed the wreckage" 2063
"surveys its windswept acreage" 5975
Survival 75, 3372, 5232, 7802
"survive, lie to" 5232
"survive, the majority of us" 5221
"survive, trying to" 75
"survive by keeping a wall between them" 7176
"survive in the environment" 3372
"survived the passing of less leisurely patrons" 8628
"survived them all, how I" 7802
"surviving their own usefulness" 7819
Survivors 1217, 3413
"survivors, demanding a word with the" 10740
"survivors, two thousand" 8699
"survivors of shipwreck fire and earthquake" 1217
"survivors of the ancient continent of Lemuria" 280
Susan 1282, 1283, 4351, 8375, 8837, 9270
Susannah 4122, 6140
Susie 261, 4009
"suspect, shrewdly" 357
"suspected of insanity" 7505

"suspected strongly" 911
"suspecting myself of a cardiac disease" 141
"suspenders on, his new" 5966
Suspicion 141, 911, 9102
"suspicion, did not hide their" 9302
"suspicion, loathing and" 9304
"suspicion, well-founded" 7056
"suspicion of chill about it" 177
"suspicion that he was in love" 9302
"suspicioned something might happen" 9307
"suspicious of a colleague" 9305
"suspicious of him, they had been" 9306
"suspicious of strangers" 9102
"Sussex" 3549, 4048, 5168, 6327, 9724
"Sussex branch" 3563
"Sussex coast" 2943
"Sussex County town" 485
Sutherland 9454
Sutherland, Mr. 654
Sutton 2392
Sutton, Bowie 1638
Sutton, Martyn 4766
"Suva" 8101
"Swabby" 10978
"swaggered along" 962
Swain 3034
"swale, long narrow" 9751
"swales, four respective" 9186
"swales between the hills" 10623
"swales of broomstraw" 1680
Swallow, Charles 568
"swallowed, it was going to be" 2384
"swallowed up again, I am" 5269
"swallowed up by a tunnel" 9788
"swallowing identity, the" 7916
"swallows were back" 759
"swamp, heart of the" 4021
"swamp, land had been a" 5170
"swamp, light of the" 224
"swamp, on the edge of the" 720
"swamp, rice" 1269
"swamp, rise up as if from a" 2796
"swamp, wild and dark" 9198
"swamp edge, on the" 3651
"swamp flowers" 7440
"swamp that was sacred to the Chickasaw people" 9198
"Swamp Woman, bog-dwelling" 253
Swamps 5170, 7707, 9198, 9217
"swamps, low pelvic mysteries of" 4073
"swamps, river with its" 7126
"swamps close behind" 9217
"swamps dank with brackish water" 4073
"swamps of the Potomac" 7707
"Swan, the" 8056
"Swan Boats" 6678
"swan she had bought many years ago" 773

Swancourt, Elfride 3301
Swann, Adam 847
"swannery, the" 736
Swans 727, 736, 738, 739, 741
"swans, flight of" 739
"swans, something wrong with the" 738
"swans had come of themselves" 736
"swans in slow indignation swam" 727
"swans skimmed across Skywater" 741
"Swansea" 9545
"sward . . . is grass as smooth as velvet" 10784
"swarm, all so much of a" 5788
"swarmed like an epidemic, dwellings that" 5223
"swarming under the trees" 4959
"Swarthmoor Hall" 9101
"swarthy turbaned face" 8850
"swastika" 1714
"swathed in moonlight" 8451
"swathes of rain" 8127
"sway, despotic" 1292
"swayed for a moment" 9771
"swaying, people gently" 8737
"swaying back and forth" 5966
"swaying birches" 5329
"swaying caparisons" 5129
"swaying gently" 8073
"swear, I" 8027
"swear to God" 681
"swear to God, I" 6189
"swearing" 9313
"sweat" 8538
"sweat, the gathered globule of" 1109
"sweat and foam of a desperate ride, smeared with the" 7607
"sweat formed along his spine" 8674
"sweat from my brow, wiped the" 8565
"sweat pouring from her" 10301
"sweated, heavily" 5814
"sweater, her V-neck letter" 2851
"sweater, thick woolen" 2787
"sweaters, fuzzy" 4154
"sweaters, wore" 1554
Sweating 1109, 4414, 4416, 4429, 9924
"sweating" 4416, 6896
"sweating, Dots was" 9924
"sweating a little" 10933
"sweating came easy" 4404
"sweatpants, my dirty" 5637
"sweatshirt, dried-muddy" 6783
"sweatshirt with lettering across the chest" 2872
"sweaty torpor" 10264
"Swedish lines, run along" 2033
Sweeney 8943
"sweep and movement of the Downs" 2228
"sweep it into curlicues" 10932

"sweep of sky, all that" 10702

"sweep the sidewalks in front of their shops" 1082

"sweeping the American coast with wind and snow and sleet" 9065

"sweet, she's really" 7743

"sweet, smell as" 8955

"sweet, tastes" 4850

"sweet, the night was" 6369

"sweet as it used to be, nothing could ever again be as" 2595

"Sweet Caporal" 2827

"sweet shop" 10831

"sweet tooth" 3844

"sweeten all values indefinitely, synthetically" 1448

"sweetened with wild honey" 10196

Sweetie Red, Great-Momma 8530

"sweetshop, ran the" 8220

"sweetspire" 7440

"Sweetwater Tennessee" 1721

"sweet-williams" 1376

"swell, each jade green land" 7919

"swell, unaccountable" 8118

"swell was there, what a" 6212

"swelled straight through August and on into September" 3604

"swelled the dry sounds of summer" 10701

"swelled then burst and dispersed" 893

"swelling, bony" 348

"swelling above the angular roofs" 2225

"swells, tops of the great" 9224

"swells of warm water, gentle" 8057

"sweltered, the city had" 4386

"sweltering, in here it's" 4425

"sweltering summer" 10264

"swept across the sea to Cyprus" 2237

"swept along the floor of the desert" 10707

"swept beneath the Golden Gate Bridge and out of the bay" 8163

"swept down into the South" 3416

"swept into the reception room" 376

"swept northward" 9070

"swept southward" 4871

"swept with hurried hand the strings'" 5396

"swept with sudden speed into the cold stale darkness of a tunnel" 9833

"swerve of shore to bend of bay" 1175

Swift, Jasper 5963

"swift, blundering or" 5542

"swiftness, rolling swinging" 9113

"swig of the beer" 2351

"swigged it" 2925

"swim, it was the same as an early morning" 8092

"swimmer fed on leaf hoppers" 4966

"swimmers, active" 4966

Swimming 3714, 6403, 8092

"swimming, he was" 9322

"swimming, intended to go" 9320

"swimming at night, girls always like to go" 9323

"swimming forever, seemed as if he'd been" 9322

"swimming in Crazy Creek" 3714

"swimming pool" 9321, 10292

"swimming pool, deserted and dilapidated saltwater" 4643

"swimming pool, floor of the" 9999

"swimming pool, municipal" 9729

"swimming pool destroyed, I ordered the" 2470

"swimming suit, in a" 8565

"Swine, The Little" 9908

"swine, you dirty" 4979

"swine in every man, there's a dirty" 4979

"swineherd" 5213

"swing, porch" 5966

"swing, practice" 8927

"swing, red-and-white garden" 9241

"swing young Bobby off my knee" 305

"swinging and arguing" 8241

"swinging his legs" 8654

"swinging the old thumb" 10367

"swings, taking practice" 6550

"swirling like smoke rings" 7779

"swirling next-to-nothingness" 6478

"swirling rain" 7288

"swirling round and round in long columns" 7320

"Swirrel Edge" 5070

"Swirrelsford, market town of" 3124

"switch, felt for the" 10159

"switch on the hall light" 8179

"switch on the light" 9417

"switch to electric" 1079

"switchbacks, the" 9767

"switchboard operator, telephone" 8695

"switched off the last light" 5336

"switching coon tails in everybody's face" 2973

"switch-yards" 1579

"Swithin, Saint" 2150

"Switzerland" 4322, 5066, 8866, 9112

"swivelling his dark glasses round" 2739

Swoboda 8870

"swollen, not particularly" 6596

"swoop of the gulls" 742

"swooped down and hit the concrete" 195

"swooping down" 2950

"swooping low again and again" 772

"swoosh, floom" 7990

"sword, short" 8663

"sword in her heart" 969

"'Sword of Fortune'" 4315

"Sword of the Spirit" 5113

"sword struck fire from metal" 4469

"sword was gallantly drawn" 8641

"sword was thrust into the empty bed" 4469

"swords, flashing" 8642

"swords, hang two crossed" 8641

"swords had Lady Beveridge, how many" 45

"swords out of it, you can make" 10530

"swore profanely and with wonderful command of epithets" 9309

"swore softly" 9310

"swore steadily" 9312

"swore that The Orphan was bad" 9309

"sworn by the most high God" 5411

"swung around the last bend" 9304

"swung from the rafters" 9839

"swung his feet to the floor" 4726

"swung onto the gravel shoulder behind me" 9829

"swung out of bed" 8487

"swung their horses in a semicircle" 7645

"swung up out of the Tube railway" 9381

Sybil 2596, 5806, 8304, 8313

Sybill 1730

"sycamore, fallen-down" 2837

"sycamore, leafy" 5626

"sycamore, prostrate" 9317

"sycamores by the creek" 7025

"Sydney" 202

"Sydney [Australia]" 1758

"syllable which came most readily to John Blaydon's mind" 4744

"syllables of one of the writers, deliberate" 10781

Sylvester 3827, 5017, 6759

Sylvester women 10053

Sylvia 651, 1142, 4118

"symbiotic balance, stable" 9755

"symbol, morse-code" 7260

"symbol of his whole life" 2299

"symmetry, it has a certain" 9186

"symmetry, mistrust" 2741

"symmetry, Oriental" 7229

Symonds, Nick 231

"sympathetic system, cells of the" 10918

"sympathetically, ministering" 3821

"sympathise" 359

Sympathy 580, 1199, 4907, 8966

"sympathy, little gleam of half-humorous half-deprecatory" 1199

"sympathy, more surprise than" 4907

"sympathy, with many expressions of" 8966

"sympathy due to an orphan" 580

"Symphony, his remarkable Fifth" 6227

"Symphony Hall, Boston's" 5851

"symptoms mine produced, the first" 642

"symptoms of affection, never showed any" 6515

"Synagogue, Great" 7505

"synagogue, look at the" 9246

"synapse, this" 9186

"Syngenesia frustranea" 10899

"Syracuse" 1431

"Syria" 10329

"Syrian coast" 7797, 8057

"Syrian day, long sultry" 4370

"syringe, hypodermic" 3047

Syson, Rev. Mr. 1505

"system, security" 2046

"system, stellar" 9557

"systematic, in action" 7648

"systems, other" 528

"Széchy Manor" 10753

T. 2516

T., Jimmy 320

T., John 10063

"Taage, the" 8094

"tabards over something like long underwear" 2855

"Tabernacle of the Eternal Church of the Believer" 1532

Tabidgi 5753

"table, at a little" 10884

"table, at the dinner" 9051

"table, at the kitchen" 8381

"table, at the same" 8223

"table, avocado kitchen" 2852

"table, big mahogany" 5913

"table, big oval" 3847

"table, breakfast" 1587, 1947, 3698, 3839, 3850

"table, candlelit" 1199

"table, damask-covered candle-lit" 3868

"table, deal" 8453

"table, family" 3828

"table, got up from her kitchen" 8278

"table, heavy old Goodwill oak" 5292

"table, I am at a" 3229

"table, kitchen" 1860

"table, merry tea-" 8203

"table, oaken" 2492

"table, small square deal" 7753

"table and chairs in the shade of an apple tree" 3119

"table at lunch, the ideal" 7229

"table beside my bed" 9366

Table Legs 6943

"table to table, might have gone from" 4650

"table's weathered surface" 925

"tablecloth, chenille" 9295

"tablecloth, dirty" 1880

"tablecloth, pristine white" 7020

"tableland, anchored on a windy Nebraska" 10685

"tableland, gently rolling floor of the" 7623

"tables, triple row of white-draped" 4309

"tablet, oblong medicated" 2384

Tabors 542

Tabors, the 1180

"taciturn, at first" 9096

"tacked themselves onto the procession, simply" 7006

"tacking delicately toward 2B" 8013

"tackle box" 10051

Tacs 1885

"tactless person, the most" 5900

"Taenarus" 4082

"taffrail, leaning alone against the" 4730

Taffy 9958

"tag end" 6467

"Tagus" 274

Taheny, Miss Sabina 2451

"Tahlequah Oklahoma" 5598

"Tahoe, South" 8729

"Tai Chi lessons" 10977

"taiga, deep dark" 3413

"tail, disproportionately long" 458

"tail, my" 2656

"tail, wicked twist to her" 8129

"tail tucked in" 9436

"tail up" 10546

"tail wagging" 9342

"tailor shop" 1704

Tailors 2865

"tailors, living" 2290

"tails, forking segmented" 474

"tails regenerate" 474

"taint, known fraction of" 4358

"taint of Saxon blood" 357

"Taipei International Airport" 7128

Taisie 4212

"take him off the support carrier" 8091

"take it, if I should" 2487

"take it, when do you" 3048

"take it after breakfast and dinner, I only" 3048

"take it after every meal, you're supposed to" 3048

"take it very badly, will he" 6330

"take long, this won't" 9501

"take on life" 9463

"take this, I don't have to" 8559

"take this, suppose you" 4117

"take with him, what he meant to" 6112

"taken away, something else was being" 9983

"taken from him, would see her" 1754

"taken long, it had not" 1536

"taken to see the Duke of Wellington" 9881

"take-off, until after" 1943

"takeover, corporate" 2548

"taking a business trip" 9580

"taking leave" 1669

"taking Little Brother to Arkansas" 2436

"taking off, his sudden" 2295

"taking over the criminal end of the business" 6411

"taking their son" 6544

Talbot, Joe 1112

Talbot, Louise 5626

Talbot, Lucienne 7983

Talbot, Mistress 8342

"tale, at the very beginning of the" 5408

"tale, beginning my" 5420

"tale, cautionary" 319

"tale, fairy" 5588, 6829, 9010

"tale, fiddled with our" 9614

"tale, hero of this" 4453, 7293, 8886

"tale, his immortal" 6246

"tale, incidents of this" 263

"tale, interest in a" 8962

"tale, strange" 8967

"tale, tell her" 253

"tale, telling of this" 1390

"tale, the following" 6885

"tale, this" 1486

"tale, very old Celtic" 9007

"tale, you never heard such a" 9045

"tale about bees" 3747

"tale about people" 3747

"tale begins in darkness and ends in darkness" 2119

"tale has its commencement, our" 10467

"tale he could tell his children" 319

"tale I have not told you before" 9028

"tale I might long ago have tried to tell" 5481

"tale is chaotic" 9019

"tale of a book, this is a" 9025

"tale of a meeting" 5827

"tale of action and passion" 8993

"tale of his visit to the future, strange" 5477

"tale of his youth" 7388

"tale of love" 5673

"tale told simply, a simple" 8957

"tale which they narrate in Poictesme" 1966

"talent, greatest natural" 5

"talent, her scenic" 8837

"talent in the earth, burying my" 239

"talent show, competing in a" 9086

"talented than prudent, more" 5448

Tales 253, 340, 2119, 2521, 3747, 4453, 5212, 5219, 5408, 5420, 5477, 5481, 5673, 5827, 6885, 7217, 7388, 8886, 8993, 9007, 9019, 9025, 9028, 9045, 10467

"tales, fabricate" 2521

"tales and legends" 5212
"tale-tellers" 8951
"talk, began to" 8896
"talk, brief" 8886
"talk, if only she wouldn't" 10197
"talk, much" 5749
"talk, our small" 8860
"talk, public" 7825
"talk, slow aimless" 8851
"talk, some tough" 4667
"talk, stupid" 7840
"talk, there was much" 7832
"talk, things about which Mrs. Crump liked to" 7377
"talk, very little" 2990
"talk, Women" 10764
"talk, wouldn't" 1845
"talk about anger" 10842
"talk about anything but Coney Island, he couldn't" 5017
"talk about it" 4536
"talk about Kate, try to" 5243
"talk about Martha" 9910
"talk about the fear, I don't want to" 3727
"talk about the Virgin Mary" 8008
"talk any more to anyone, I can't" 7595
"talk he had had" 10931
"talk like that, he doesn't like it when I" 5363
"talk much anymore, we don't" 7602
"talk of the prison" 7137
"talk of the ship-boat's crew, not choosing to join the" 7594
"talk so much, about whom you" 4788
"talk to, lack of anyone to" 8216
"talk to, someone to" 9923
"talk to him, no one attempted to" 2901
"talk to old Jane" 123
"talk to somebody who knew the old captain" 2328
Talkative Man 4839
"talked about, all they" 8877
"talked about death" 2400
"talked about his craft" 5512
"talked indistinctly" 5004
"talked of population" 5725
"talked to Bilara, while he" 4704
"talked to her, have you" 8895
"talked to him, his father" 9752
"talked to himself" 10385
"talked to the girls" 977
"talker, facile" 5926
Talking 3590, 4041, 5243, 5347, 5926, 7595, 8206, 8630, 8842, 8846, 8874, 10860
"talking" 4230
"talking, about whom they rarely stop" 3590
"talking, generally" 8842
"talking, no use your" 7553

"talking, she was" 10860
"talking, they'll do the" 8630
"talking, to hear people" 4041
"talking, wasn't" 7605
"talking, while still" 8863
"talking, working and" 8206
"talking about, that little girl we had been" 4175
"talking about Ace Ruggles" 8893
"talking about amending" 7821
"talking about himself again" 3573
"talking about how bad we were" 3990
"talking . . . about the cesspool" 8857
"talking about you" 8891
"talking again all at once" 4335
"talking and laughing now, everybody was" 6755
"talking and talking of the cabbie's plight" 6652
"talking dog" 5809
"talking for his countstore or his zoo" 8861
"talking in code again" 8874
"talking in his sleep, like a man" 4504
"talking in the big room" 8857
"talking in the café" 8846
"talking Makar" 8881
"talking of their lives and their loves" 3912
"talking the slow aimless talk of wearied men" 8851
"talking the whole way about savages" 286
"talking to a couple of construction men" 4318
"talking to George" 9925
"talking to Griswold in the railway station at Atlanta" 930
"talking to her, he left the" 7200
"talking to herself" 3695
"talking to himself" 5347
"talking to itself, its way of" 2593
"talking to Moondog" 5880
"talking to two very queer individuals" 8856
"talking together" 1826
"talking together in a large apartment" 8837
"talking with a heavy elderly man" 8865
"talking with the head porter, I started" 10047
"talks, nobody" 5222
"talks to me" 6736
"tall, Eleanor is" 10885
"tall, five feet eleven inches" 5941
"tall, her father was" 6687
"tall, I am" 4789
"tall, only eleven inches" 8944
"tall, six-and-a-half feet" 10891
"tall, six feet" 8360
"tall, thought her too" 10852

"tall, too" 189
"tall and dark and handsome" 8658
"tall and free-striding" 10369
"tall are you, how" 341
"tall as the Venus de Milo" 10797
"tall for his age" 8225
"tall girl, I am a" 4184
"tall massive and noble" 1174
"tall person" 10408
"tall thin one, the" 7140
"taller, a summer" 6876
"taller than his father" 4436
"taller than most men" 10885
"taller than my mother, I am" 6740
"tallest of all" 4436
Talliaferro, Mr. 7982
Tallien 9488
"Tallinn" 6465
"tallish" 2825
Tallmadge, Benjamin 6260
"tallness, his" 10408
"Tally-ho, pea-green" 9113
"Talmud" 9709
"tamarack thickets, impenetrable" 4073
"tamarack trees" 9756
"Tamberlane New York, Catskill village of" 5842
"tamed" 7670
"Tampa" 1148, 9624
"Tampa cousins" 1151
"tamped home, the first layer had been" 8280
Tamsen 6713
Tamsin 1692
Tanaquil 6665
Tancredi 8218
"Tancreds, the" 3603
Tandihetsi, Tarcisius 6697
"tangerine, delicious" 1480
"Tangier" 2416, 10235
"tangle, great" 10106
"tangle of sandbars and willow banks" 8084
"tangled up" 1512
"tangles of rose-vines" 1349
Tangun of Korea 10984
"tank, metal" 5325
"tank was empty, the dipping" 7052
"tankards, foaming" 3396
"tankards, well-polished" 9113
"tanks, three" 6866
"tanks and jeeps, American" 3416
"tanks out of focus" 6866
"tanned, expertly" 2835
"tanned by wind and sun" 5897
"tanned Mr. Jeff Bransford's cheek" 5899
"tanned so deeply by the sun" 6403
Tanner, Carolyn 4301
"Tanniford" 3450
"Tano, the great god" 2627
"tap on his shoulder" 5846
"tape, double-faced Scotch" 6856
"tape, like a length of black" 9167

"tape deck, car's" 3026
"tape recorder" 8892
"tapedeck, my" 9300
"tapestried bowers" 2088
"tapestries, worn" 5324
"tapestry, love weaves its own" 5656
"tapestry, rich and golden as a" 5314
"tapestry screen" 8850
Tapiola 416, 417
"tapped at the door" 9987
"tapped on the viewing window with a quarter" 6730
"tapped the back of his wife's hand" 9934
"tapping her on the shoulder" 3025
"tapping the ivory keys of the piano with her pencil" 6217
"taps on for me, turn those" 10939
Tara 10744
Tardiness 1909, 2359, 3297, 3636, 7243, 7245, 7272, 10032, 10040, 10061, 10078, 10079, 10090, 10967, 10971
Targ 1792
"target, hit the" 3323
"target practice, we have had enough of" 10497
"tariff war against Poland" 2592
"Tarleton twins" 10793
"Tarot cards" 1329
"tarpaulin, large blue" 4026
"tarry tidal Thames" 5260
"Tars, Young" 10978
"tart, notice the strawberry" 7582
"Tartan Army, The" 883
"tartan carpets" 1179
"tarts, all those old girls upstairs are" 6480
Tarvin 4247
Tarwater, Francis Marion 2329
"Tarzan serial" 328
"*Tarzan's Lover, Lady*" 5453
"task, did not like the" 5346
"task, education had become his" 3278
"Task, hard is the" 6033
"task, inconceivable to those who have not done the" 1850
"task, perform this" 5483
"task, sets her husband a" 1998
"task, slightest qualifications for the" 5412
"task, tire of the" 7680
"task, weary" 10927
"task at hand" 5437
"task became impossible" 10953
"Task Force on Crime" 6274
"task in one night's work, do not finish a" 10957
"task often ill judged" 5700
Tasks 663, 686, 1023, 1477, 1850, 1951, 1998, 2823, 2831, 3640, 4161, 4288, 4916, 5346, 5372, 5412, 5415, 5437, 5483, 5683,

5907, 5920, 6021, 6138, 6143, 6160, 6437, 6547, 6579, 6642, 6864, 6948, 7300, 8149, 8561, 9106, 9450, 10887, 10916, 10917, 10919, 10920, 10921, 10926, 10927, 10928, 10929, 10930, 10931, 10932, 10933, 10934, 10935, 10936, 10937, 10939, 10941, 10942, 10943, 10944, 10947, 10949, 10950, 10952, 10953, 10954, 10956, 10957, 10958, 10960, 10962, 10964
"tasks, never the easiest of" 10944
"Tass" 4008
"taste, acquired" 8007
"taste, cold nicotine" 8568
"taste, flat swimming-hole" 2585
"taste, in questionable" 3538
"taste, with good" 139
"taste, wondrously appalling" 3237
"taste in furniture, there is my mother's" 10318
"taste in her mouth, terrible" 10271
"taste of an ancient smoke, acrid" 10349
"taste of autumn, first" 7327
"taste of glue" 10831
"taste of the Dilettanti of Naples, did not please the" 6213
"tasted bitterness, I had" 374
"tasted his death" 6211
"tasted of a wedding" 10645
"tasted salt" 9075
"tasted vile" 7850
"Tastee-Freeze bars" 1039
Tastes 28, 2243, 3845, 4850, 8007, 8517, 8568, 8577, 9075, 10349, 10645, 10831
"tastes bitterly of cream and jam and flaky pastry" 2243
"tastes sweet in my mouth like honey or cane" 4850
"tasting the cherries" 28
"Tatchester" 7244
Tate, Ben 9240
Tatekeya 9979
Tates, the 7318
Tatter, Fred 6777
"tattered cigar" 8568
"tattered few, a" 774
"tattered monkey" 9729
Tattersall 6322
Tattershall, Miles 7335
"tattoo, quick descending" 10371
"tattoo of a thousand hooves" 8776
"tattoo of hammers" 8775
"Tattoo Parlor, Big Dan's" 7237
"taught as a child on my home-world" 9698
"taught by the King" 6450
"taught her how to hyperventilate" 3287
"taught him numbers" 3279
"taught myself" 245
"taught that first" 3291

"taught there, still remembers what he was" 5016
"taut figure, her" 3499
Tave 6331
"tavern, drinking" 3994
"Tavern, Green Leaf" 1152
"Tavern, Yellow Bud" 4311
"tavern stairway" 10371
Taverner, Michael 4832
Taverns 1152, 1387, 2896, 2904, 2936, 3764, 3994, 4303, 4311, 4319, 4326, 4332, 4334, 4335, 4336, 4523, 6178, 9093, 10371
"taverns, kept business lively in" 7865
"tawny marshes" 8402
"tax, no income" 3362
Taxes 3362, 3739
"taxes" 3468
"taxi, airport" 4123
"taxi, got down from a" 1757
"taxi, got into the backseat of the" 4599
"taxi, got out of the" 3959
"taxi, hailed a" 1699
"taxi, I stopped the" 1655
"taxi, in the" 6007
"taxi, jumped into the" 9779
"taxi, lonely cruising" 3402
"taxi, man in the" 9552
"taxi, stepped out of a" 1653
"taxi, the" 1830
"taxi cuts through the rain" 2884
"taxi driver" 4992
"taxi driver in Manhattan" 9801
"taxi drivers" 9161
"taxi drove through a part of north London" 9806
"taxi or a car I can hire, is there a" 9573
"taxi skidding away" 2954
"taxi taking me" 2995
"taxi turned the corner" 9778
"taxi-cab" 6622
"taxicab, dismounted from a" 9537
"taxi-cab, elderly country" 1736
"taxicab, rode a" 3315
"taxicab, station" 9382
"taxied to a hangar" 217
Taxis 1003, 1152, 1227, 1625, 1653, 1655, 1678, 1699, 1736, 1757, 1830, 2044, 2884, 2948, 2954, 2970, 2995, 3315, 3959, 4123, 4992, 6016, 6622, 8320, 9161, 9428, 9537, 9552, 9778, 9779, 9797, 9801, 9806, 9921, 10085
"taxis, scarcely any" 9797
"taxis, station" 9921
"taxis in the station yard" 1227
"taxi's tires are beating out a message" 6016
Taylor, Eric 1654
Taylor, Felicitas Maria 4808
Taylor, Olwen 1100
Taylor, Samuel 3890

Taylor, Virginia 10943
Taylor, Zachary 2310
"Taylor & Haddon" 7099
"tea, afternoon" 9349
"tea, came to" 4008
"tea, China" 3821
"tea, coming to" 4173
"tea, cup of" 9359, 10143
"tea, glass of" 9953
"tea, going to" 9357
"tea, green" 3854
"tea, gulp of his" 3852
"tea, have him to" 1535
"tea, he was preparing" 9355
"tea, her pot of" 9353
"tea, it was just before" 9388
"tea, pouring out" 9350
"tea, some cup of" 9356
"tea, they'd called me for" 9360
"tea at the Ufford" 1921
"tea for everyone, it was time she made" 9358
"tea he was pouring" 8805
"tea is the last meal of the day" 4371
"tea party" 7816
"tea with her, have" 9352
"tea with her, take" 9348
"teach, hi" 4215
"teach, I've always wanted to" 254
"teach as many as possible of those who come after me" 5427
"teach at Brandeis University" 7896
"teach Jen a few human words" 5464
"teach me how to dive into a swimming pool" 9321
"teach or preach, books that" 5427
"teach the great works" 3284
"teacher" 10348
"teacher, Latin" 4273
"teacher, my" 10910
"teacher, my old eighth-grade" 4446
"teacher, Patrick Doyle was a" 6481
"teacher, retired school" 10809
"teacher, substitute" 7895
"teacher Miss Turner, our" 4546
"teacher showed them where to sit" 986
"teacherage" 7887
Teachers 99, 216, 240, 986, 1950, 2468, 2508, 2862, 3270, 4215, 4273, 4446, 4546, 4668, 4876, 5674, 5854, 6092, 6217, 6408, 6415, 6427, 6463, 6481, 6489, 6563, 6651, 6753, 6884, 7459, 7732, 7877, 7880, 7885, 7895, 7896, 7906, 10809, 10910
"teachers, crushes on my" 7732
"teachers, my former" 714
"teachers was my mother in disguise, believed that each of my" 6651
Teaching 2508, 3277, 3284, 3287, 4254, 5427, 5464, 9321
"teaching, three more days of" 2508

"teaching at the Glenkill Academy for Boys" 5854
"teaching children geography" 5708
"teaching of the English language" 7904
"teaching on an exchange basis" 6463
"teaching us the names of the constellations" 536
"tea-hour" 7754
"teahouse, window of a small" 8322
"teak from which the chair was cut" 93
Teakle 9182
"team is sure to win" 6
Teams 6, 8935
"teapot which was perched upon it" 9351
"tear, first" 2070
"tear down some of the rafters" 1162
"tear well up, making a" 7437
"tearful with joy" 4344
"tearing down the little house" 3162
"tearing gates from rusty hinges" 10740
"tearjerker" 7731
"tears, a few" 8400
"tears, break into" 2083
"tears, brought to" 1706
"tears, eyes which can no longer supply" 2287
"tears, full of a child's" 2072
"tears, moved almost to" 6227
"tears, no" 3291
"tears, she drinks her" 2080
"tears, Susan's" 9614
"tears and water" 10811
"tears did not come so easily" 2337
"tears in her eyes" 1859
"tears to lament them" 2287
"teas to freshmen, gave" 2332
"teasing my mind" 7386
"teasing pinches" 8475
"teasingly short of recognition" 8676
Teatime 2089, 4173, 8805
"tea-time" 732
"teatime, by" 8587
"tea-time, dropping darkly down to" 9354
"technique, a bit of simple" 4670
Techniques 5058, 10948
Ted 2840
Teddy 8005
Tedium 5275
Teel, Agatha 9848
"teen-age boy" 2565
"teen-ager, allowing me to become a" 4236
"teenage couple" 1992
"teenage epic" 3386
"teenage marriages" 5749
"teenage neckers" 1894
"teenagers" 1277
"teens, entered his" 949
Teesdale, Bell 4807

"teetering" 1680
Teeth 3861, 4699, 6589, 6675, 9448, 10825, 10831
"teeth, bands of powerful" 7688
"teeth, betel-stained" 5846
"teeth, between her" 1169
"teeth, bone from his" 3861
"teeth, broken" 5971
"teeth, capped" 8559
"teeth, cleaned your" 6675
"teeth, floss your" 2463
"teeth, gnashing his" 962
"teeth, gold" 10054
"teeth, gold front" 6943
"teeth, her" 7743
"teeth, hung on by her" 1842
"teeth, I got my new false" 4699
"teeth, insolent flash of smiling" 8553
"teeth, murderous to the" 10831
"teeth, square yellow" 5292
"teeth, stop grinding my" 10194
"teeth a white scar of warning" 475
"teeth are hard, her yellow" 10825
"teeth gleaming beneath their masks" 3396
"teeth grinding as hers did, my" 2776
"teeth like a saw's" 340
"teeth straight teeth" 9448
"teeth that the good Lord gave you" 10831
"teethed, the fully" 10235
Teitlebaum 6514, 6652
Tejedora, La 10952
Tekakwitha, Catherine 4771
"Tel Aviv" 2251, 6542
"telegram" 6003
"telegram, arranged by" 5801
"telegram, I got Bullivant's" 5999
"telegram, opened the" 6006
"telegram from President Roosevelt" 6863
"telegram from Washington" 8675
Telegrams 1761, 5999, 6003, 6004, 6006, 6007, 8675
"telegrams, would have sent his other children" 1761
"telegraph poles" 10604
"telegraphers" 8920
"telegraphers, small group of" 3534
"telegraphers who had manned the first Canadian wireless stations" 3534
Telemachus, Uncle 10811
"telepathy" 8626
"telephone, into the" 3333
"telephone, long distance" 1107
"telephone, raucous insistence of the" 1123
"telephone, voice on the" 10003
"telephone, voice was indistinct on the" 10654
"telephone, when someone asks for you on the" 1094

"telephone, won't have to answer the" 2460

"telephone, you're wanted on the" 1092

"telephone before stopping by" 7822

"telephone began, depths of the" 1093

"telephone began to ring" 1120

"telephone box, came out of the" 1110

"telephone call, I received a" 1099

"telephone call, make a quick" 1101

"telephone call, received a" 1145

"telephone conversation" 1113

"telephone extension awoke him" 2785

"telephone gave a faint tingle" 1156

"telephone in Ben Powers's hotel room" 1116

"telephone installed, got the" 2162

"telephone line" 1554

"telephone messages on my desk" 1122

"telephone mouthpiece" 1109

"telephone pole" 2107

"telephone pole with a backboard bolted to it" 8913

"telephone poles" 3044

"telephone purred discreetly" 4651

"telephone rang" 1098, 1117, 1128, 1155, 8000

"telephone ring, hearing the" 1104

"telephone ring, let the" 1096

"telephone ringing" 1095, 1138

"telephone ringing, heard the" 1102

"telephone rings, when the" 2439

"telephone seldom rang in Ruby's apartment" 1154

"telephone switchboard operator" 8695

"telephone wakened him" 10182

"telephone woke Anna" 10302

"telephoned me in New York" 1159

"telephoned this morning" 1149

"telephoned to say" 1100

Telephones 1092, 1093, 1095, 1096, 1097, 1098, 1099, 1100, 1103, 1104, 1107, 1109, 1110, 1111, 1112, 1114, 1115, 1116, 1117, 1119, 1120, 1123, 1127, 1128, 1130, 1131, 1133, 1137, 1138, 1139, 1140, 1144, 1145, 1147, 1148, 1149, 1150, 1154, 1155, 1156, 1843, 2162, 2392, 2439, 2460, 2785, 3124, 3333, 4651, 6337, 6937, 7822, 8197, 9393, 10003, 10067, 10132, 10182, 10302, 10654

"telephones, three silent" 10067

"telephoning to a friend" 3124

"telephoning to the Pensione Sofia" 1126

"teleprinter's bell sounded" 1118

Television 321, 1325, 2351, 2388, 2454, 3362, 3982, 5328, 6298, 6331, 6335, 6342, 7398, 7835,

8873, 9297, 9364, 9367, 9368, 9370, 9371, 9372, 9373, 9375, 9733

"television" 1325, 5634

"Television, Amalgamated" 1032

"television, before" 3402

"television, die on" 2388

"television, do it on" 9367

"television, I and half the world saw on" 9371

"television, I think you're on" 9370

"television, Motorola color" 9297

"television, national" 6342

"television, on" 2351

"television, seen and admired on" 3982

"television, watching" 9375

"television, watching the advertisements on" 7398

"television antenna" 5328

"television commercials, no" 3362

"television crews arrived" 7835

"television flickering in front of me" 10318

"television on the wall" 7785

"television screen, black-and-white" 8873

"television set, our brand-new" 9373

"tell, hard to" 4884

"tell, I am going to" 1819

"tell, knew she would have to" 8878

"tell, look and" 1322

"tell, never never" 1819

"tell, wouldn't have been able to" 4327

"tell a patient they are about to die" 10944

"tell a story" 8961

"tell about it, compulsion to" 2036

"tell about mine" 5749

"tell any of Them, Death if you" 1819

"tell Bernie about Harriet Post, wanted to" 3344

"tell Dean Roskov" 2489

"tell her anything, did not" 4437

"tell her ex-husband" 6544

"tell her he was desperate, he couldn't" 7596

"tell him when Hannah Isaacs showed up" 3330

"tell it, at least as I can" 6283

"tell it, but I want to" 8979

"tell it, if I don't" 8983

"tell it, those who presume to" 9046

"tell it again, I *will*" 8227

"tell it to, only Thankful Perkins to" 848

"tell me, can you" 1239

"tell me, can't you" 5350

"tell me, you can't" 1822

"tell me about them" 8211

"tell me her name, won't" 4849

"tell me I was the devil, used to" 8247

"tell me things, women" 7957

"tell me what it was, can't you" 9368

"tell men, they don't normally" 7957

"tell my sister that I'd had Mother's respirator unplugged" 3623

"tell my story" 8984

"tell myself, I" 1881

"tell nobody but God, you better not never" 1805

"tell ourselves" 10710

"tell the story as I watched it happen" 8994

"tell the truth" 2734

"tell the young ones, as I often" 5232

"tell them, tomorrow I shall have to" 6044

"tell them why I did it" 6044

"tell you, anybody ever" 10813

"tell you, I have something to" 1802

"tell you, I shall try to" 43

"tell you, I want to" 8235

"tell you, let me" 1189

"tell you, there is so much I would like to" 3664

"tell you, things I am going to" 8965

"tell you, what can I" 9019

"tell you, what I am about to" 5059

"tell you about the real Rose" 1815

"tell you about the time, did I ever" 8227

"tell you exactly how it was" 8734

"tell you exactly what happened, I can" 7840

"tell you pompously" 9119

"tell you something about myself" 793

"tell you something I've never told anyone before in my life" 7963

"tell you that" 10031

"tell you the story, I am going to" 9038

"tell you these things" 8963

"tell you these things, I want to" 7598

"tell you what" 446

"tell you what the Aegean looks like, I cannot" 7942

Teller, Anna 9570

"telling about us" 1813

"telling herself, kept" 3610

"telling him, on the verge of" 1814

"telling it by means of a journal, he is" 8999

"telling me, they were" 2159

"telling of this tale" 1390

"telling them later, kept" 8296

"telling this story" 9027

"telling this story, it's not me" 9055

"telling you this, I'm only" 5284

"tells herself" 5219

"temper, colossal" 4201

"temper, crusty in" 3554

"temper, I rarely lose my" 379
"temper, indolence in her" 6605
"temper, losing his" 4919
"temper, try not to lose my" 387
"Temperament" 4437
"temperament, depressive" 2507
"temperamental" 497
"temperature, uncomfortable" 4420
"temperature of his body" 6604
Tempers 379, 4201
"tempest-twisted" 6365
"tempestuous Mexican star" 3126
"temples, high flat" 333
Temptation 4670, 5412, 5934, 7727, 9479
"Temptation" 5412
"temptation comes to me" 7727
"temptations and terrors, time's" 9479
"ten, Ralph was" 132
"ten below out there, it's" 1153
"tenacity of the Hound of Heaven" 7852
"tenant of the place" 950
"tenants have gone out, all the lights and" 3244
Tench, Mr. 4379
Tendai 8029
"tendencies, not merely" 5663
"tenderly, had to deal with it" 9536
"tenderness, no gestures of" 8140
"tending New York holdings" 9567
"tendril of land" 5048
"tendrils, creeping with their" 10772
"tenement was over a hundred years old" 9253
"tenements" 6266
"tenements, stench and throb of New York" 8080
"tenements, two great walls of" 7627
"Tenino" 10458
Tennant, Lily 2952
"Tennessee" 1270, 1721, 2947, 4066, 6084, 9365
"Tennessee, Eastern" 4400
"Tennessee, northwestern corner of" 1422
"Tennessee, this is the" 7670
Tennessee Shad 4460
"tennis, ritual game of" 10411
"tennis ball" 302
"Tennis Club" 4321
"tennis court" 2984
"tennis courts" 302
"tennis players" 342
"tennis-players, a quartet of early" 8259
Tenny 4925
Tennyson 6860
"tenor, concert" 8752
"tenor, pure effortless" 8748
"tenor, sweet" 8748
Tenorio, Bishop Rodrigo 9304
"tense, white and" 9318

"tense look, keen" 1610
"tension, could hardly bear the" 8490
"tension, look of" 5048
"tension and anxiety, occasion of some" 7069
"tension and insecurity, full of strange" 3710
"tension had mounted in the street" 3137
"tensions, intangible" 2607
"ten-strike" 313
"tent, dressing" 5317
"tent, everybody in the" 3681
"tent, little muslin" 4954
"tent, oxygen" 2514
"tent, pushed back the flap of his" 524
"tent, stepped out of the" 9739
"tent across the stream" 2574
"tent on a lot near the town square" 331
Tents 4954, 5317
"tents, officers' country" 8684
"tents, rows of" 8699
"tenuous" 2278
"tenuous to be called magnetic, too" 6001
"tenure on living" 6951
Teo 8016
Teresa 9266
"term, first day of" 579
"term, Michaelmas" 7336
"term, second day of" 5631
"Term, Trinity" 1410
"terminal, air" 9591
"terminal was being remodeled" 232
"terminating in a dam" 7653
"termination, Celtic" 10898
"terminus, mainland" 8749
"tern and gull, endless ribbons of" 4587
"Terra Linda" 2061, 3264
"terrace, rooftop" 4286
"terrace dropping down to a prospect" 5164
"terrace of her father's house" 4166
"terraces of a forest garden" 8212
"terra-cotta lunette" 10649
Terrain 5070, 5135, 5180, 6067, 7018, 9995
"terrain" 7018
"terrain, feel out the" 624
"terrain, hides none of its flat" 5038
"terrain, rolling" 7632
"terrain watered by narrow running streams" 7632
"*terrasse*" 7581
"terrestrial globe" 3977
"terrible, far more" 2492
"terrible, I think it's" 4194
"terrible, perfectly" 2650
"terrible [events], some" 10992
"terrible father" 6643
"terrier, white-haired" 8547

"terrier, wire-haired" 419
"terrier, yapping" 7852
"terrier, Yorkshire" 416
"terrier began to pursue him" 7852
"terrified as though a knife offered at her throat" 8793
"terrified of life" 9285
"terrifying" 10004
"terrifying, a nightmare is" 2768
"terrifyingly authentic" 3180
"territories of the United-States, immense and but half-tenanted" 262
"territory, restricted yet tumultuous" 4039
"Territory, the" 1387
Terror 2768, 3699, 5084, 9479, 10004, 10519
"*terror*" 4256
"terror, cold grue of" 5084
"terror, firm spurt of his" 3699
"Terror, Great" 898
"Terror, Holy" 540
"Terror, Master of the" 4457
"terror, shrank back in" 9279
"terror, that hot" 9657
"terror, whimpering" 3722
"terror of the people" 10519
"terror that looks like a joy" 6790
"terrorised the village, the three years he" 8046
"Terrorists" 4457
"terrorists, ambushed a band of" 2026
"terrors, time's temptations and" 9479
"terrors of my childhood" 3701
Terry 1124
"test, wanted to make a" 10938
"Testament for my only Daughter" 5492
"tested his radio" 5716
"tested the temperature of the water" 573
"testes, down low and away from the" 1166
Testicles 4290, 4689
"testify to the antiquity of the family" 3589
"testimony, credible" 3456
"testimony to their restorative ardor" 7532
"testimonies of their sleeplessness" 8485
"testing" 4873
Tests 1918, 5202
"tests, Pacific" 2267
"tethered my horse and buggy" 7223
"Tetragrammaton, Master of the" 7505
"Teutonic fairy tale, a dark" 5588
Tewler, Mr. Edward Albert 4700
Tewler, Young 4700
"Texaco star" 8323

"Texas" 1460, 2138, 4546, 5215, 5967, 6097, 6944, 7509, 8165
"Texas, brown soil of" 7314
"Texas, Clarksville is in" 1418
"Texas, Governor of" 6509
"Texas, plains of" 6061
"Texas, West" 5102
"Texas desert" 10726
"Texas sucks" 10744
"Texas summer morning" 4694
"textile mill" 10838
"textile mills" 1038
Thackeray 3528
Thad 6186
"Thailand, northern" 4094
"Thames, dear pale-tea" 9175
"Thames, hotel near the" 9722
"Thames, river" 8078
"Thames, tarry tidal" 5260
"Thames, the" 5345, 7310, 8050, 8345, 10356
"Thames, Upper" 9076
"Thames bubbling all the way across to the South Bank" 9175
"Thames flowed into the Seine" 9743
"Thames fog, thick" 971
"Thames . . . rolls a clear flood through flowery meadows" 9738
Thangbrand 4456
Thangue, Miss 2089
"thank God" 6497, 10743
"thank you" 2921
"thank you, certainly want to" 6234
"thank you for your letters" 1962
"thank you God" 7530
"thank you so much" 3869
"thankful it had been no worse" 4727
"thankful to say, I am" 17
"thanks, have given" 1217
"thanks for their escape from death" 1217
"thanks neatly, express his" 5457
"thanks to Mr. Kandinsky" 3274
"Thanksgiving, day before" 3576
"Thanksgiving Day" 2661
"Thanksgiving dinner" 1587
"Thassos, island of" 8941
"that's that, then I guess" 3346
"thatched, roughly" 3068
"thatched roofs" 4742
Thayer, Diana 1976
Theater 130, 390, 2477, 3342, 5398, 5444, 5566, 5584, 5892, 8738, 10035
"Theater, Avenue" 8538
"Theater, Garfield Avenue" 1315
"theater, movie" 2040
"theater, Neptuna movie" 5841
"theater in Chinatown" 300
Theaters 300, 1313, 8538, 9377
"theaters" 7896
"Theatre, Auditorium" 10035
"theatre, British" 9378

"Theatre, Cosmopolitan" 5892
"Theatre, Empire" 8849
"theatre, heyday of the" 9382
"theatre, huge" 9389
"Theatre, Royal" 9396
"Theatre, The Lost'" 9382
"theatre abounds with fascination" 9376
"theatre of calamity" 5554
"theatre of his play" 5398
"Théatre St. Philippe, it was in the" 9377
"theatregoers, homing" 9381
"theatre-party" 10035
"theatrical" 5584
"theatrical, above all" 6883
"theatrical costume, hire or sell" 2841
"theatrical thunder" 9241
"theatrically bitten youths" 9376
"Thebes" 7799
"theft of three tarpaulins" 2026
"theme, a happier" 5447
"theme, the main" 5525
Theobold 1017
Theodosius, Emperor 7518
"theologian, noted" 367
"theological exam papers" 6639
Theology 4501
"theology" 4501
Theophano 7641
"theoretically at least" 5086
Theories 3456, 3457, 5977, 6040, 10529
"theories, a number of" 10529
"theories, grand unified" 6907
"theories about why Joe Mondragón did it" 6040
"theory, on the" 4542
"theory, tends to prove a" 3457
"theory I've got about Neil Armstrong" 5977
"theory to which I used to be partial" 3457
"there, and I was" 7120
"there, because I was" 7117
"there, Fanshawe was always" 7118
"there, I was" 7840
"there, it's really" 7066
"there again, she was" 10841
"there because he had promised, he was" 7115
"there from the beginning, Fanny was" 7123
"there she was" 9888
Theresa 4197
"thermometer on the drugstore door" 8308
"Thersites, Reticences of" 5507
"thick of it, into the shrill" 5408
"thicket, stunted" 9116
"thickets" 9084
"thickets, bosky" 3396
Thicknesse, Mrs. 7012
"thief" 2014

"thief, car" 6453
"thief, felt like a" 3311
"thief wants to come in, if a" 2030
Thievery 2016, 2021, 2025, 2026, 2042, 2049, 2051, 2055, 2060, 2062, 2064, 2684, 2760, 3293, 3977
Thieves 2014, 2030, 3311, 6453
"thieves, walled in against" 4328
"thieving gypsies" 6292
"thigh, as big around as my" 10106
"thigh, cream smooth" 5450
"thighs embracing the horse" 8701
"thighs, his" 8266
"thimble, earthy" 5136
"thimble, typhoon in a" 7869
"thin, a little too" 9912
"thin, fair and" 8217
"thin, too" 10852
"thin as a stick" 4301
"thin for comfort, rather too" 425
"Thin Man, the" 221
Thing, Mrs. 4776
"thing, a most unfortunate" 6524
"thing, become a bad" 1259
"thing, dim shadow of the" 8032
"thing, hard" 6536
"thing, it is a great" 5079
"thing, it's just the" 4117
"thing, mysterious" 8028
"Thing, the Good" 253
"thing, there is in me a" 1682
"Thing, This" 10495
"thing, this is a nice" 6415
"thing, untamed" 2796
"thing after another, one" 7378
"thing for him to do, an amazing queer" 729
"thing he did, the first" 4288
"thing he noticed, first" 10869
"thing he saw on waking, the first" 10235
"thing it is, what a silly" 5284
"thing that's happened, most exciting" 3481
"thing was, the" 3684
"things, curious" 3507
"things, her" 6138
"things, I got my" 1695
"things, I haul" 6488
"things, I see" 4898
"things, incredible" 5640
"things, of all" 7525
"things, old" 7214
"things, one of those" 624
"things, ordinary" 500
"things, she liked to make" 1876
"things, such everyday" 7494
"things, the last" 5524
"things, two main" 5085
"things about Elizabeth Ferguson that the people of Bayview disliked" 10852
"things among countless thousands of others" 7616

"things are very different" 97
"things at the bottom of Brother Sebastian's bag" 9609
"things began to occur" 3507
"things grew" 7818
"things I am going to tell you" 8965
"things I wanted to do, I had done almost all the" 9263
"things seem to work out for the best" 1234
"things settled down" 5303
"things that happened to me that day" 1538
"things that happened to them, some" 9049
"things that went through his mind" 9430
"things to be done, more" 6088
"things we had fashioned for ourselves" 1253
"things were always reversed" 4436
"things were going none too well" 49
"things would ever be the same, I wondered if" 2423
"think, as so many people seem to" 10555
"think, I" 146, 6841, 7999
"think, I cannot" 58
"think, I often like to" 3457
"think, I really do" 3853
"think, I used to" 10849
"think, she would" 8491
"think, sometimes I" 9438
"think, what do you" 2317
"think, you" 3014
"think about, everything he least wanted to" 9432
"think about it" 4536
"think about it, if one bothered to" 4752
"think about it, makes herself" 42
"think about Link, she would begin to" 9425
"think about Manfredi" 9454
"think about marriage" 5776
"think about them afterward" 4153
"think about what country it is in, no one bothers to" 4081
"think after all, I don't" 157
"think after all that the first constant was water" 9442
"think for a moment" 4866, 8249
"think I see him" 4904
"think I wouldn't come" 1728
"think in Hindustani" 5446
"think of Alex always as I first saw him" 5996
"think of getting married" 5746
"think of him, I used to" 5953
"think of it, had come to" 6275
"think of it, I still have only to" 9008
"think of it as curved, he would always" 9238

"think of something else" 6816
"think of that summer, she would" 8543
"think of the future" 7953
"think of the man named Kirby Frye" 9427
"think of the picture better, stop to" 5445
"think of ways to kill my daddy" 6197
"think of words, dont stop to" 5445
"think seriously about death" 2323
"think that nothing happens in it" 1374
"think things over" 9406
"think this thing over" 9403
"think this unique, impossible not to" 9585
"think what else I might have done" 7494
"think what had awakened him" 10170
"thinker, before he was a" 4242
Thinking 58, 312, 685, 8249, 8485, 9403, 9411, 9421, 9427, 9431, 9438, 9461, 10170, 10352
"thinking, before" 7474
"thinking, clear-" 6815
"thinking, his" 3285
"thinking, I had been" 9447
"thinking, I keep" 4894
"thinking, I remember" 6747
"thinking, I amly kept" 8660
"thinking, not" 2973
"thinking, Shep was" 10049
"thinking, what do you imagine they could be" 9461
"thinking, what you" 2788
"thinking, without even" 3718
"thinking about Coyote when it happened" 9821
"thinking about insomnia" 8485
"thinking about my early childhood" 1276
"thinking about the kid" 10262
"thinking about the wisdom of the Church" 7539
"thinking about what happened to Tom McMann and me" 9435
"thinking about your family is like gardening" 3622
"thinking all the while" 24
"thinking and saying, what they were" 477
"thinking back" 3384
"thinking how I should tell my story" 8984
"thinking in Central Park" 9434
"thinking it over" 9305
"thinking like other men" 5215
"thinking of anything, not" 5619
"thinking of Cluny Brown" 9423
"thinking of going home" 4537
"thinking of Harry" 9413
"thinking of her troubles" 2070

"thinking of how I learned to drive" 6683
"thinking of real estate prices" 880
"thinking over it a little now and then for weeks" 7403
"thinking over many things" 9404
"thinking that I may have to hide now" 4484
"thinking that nothing was the same any more" 2595
"'thinking' things, go about" 6173
"thinking to climb to the benchland" 8429
"thinkings, seeings and" 8171
"thinks about, whatever she" 9445
"thinks as he stands behind the summer-dusty windows" 9451
"thinned and distorted by the sea breeze" 10014
"thinner and thinner" 10116
Thirkield, Nick 3584
Thirst 2940, 4672, 4673, 7561
"thirst of information" 1292
"thirsted for the jungle shade" 3714
"thirsty trail herd" 2215
"thirteen, when he was barely" 3504
"thirteen, when he was nearly" 22
"thirties, in my early" 4113
"thirty, I'm" 7987
"thirty, she was less than" 10804
"thirty-five, at" 7978
"thirty-seven, today I am" 855
"this morning" 4349
"thistles, thorns and" 993
Thomas 2008, 2096, 3902, 6679
Thomas, Andy 9705
Thomas, Brother 139
Thomas Aquinas, Sr. 10859
Thompkins, Rollin 6730
Thompson, Dick 9907
Thompson, Doc 2156
Thompson, Nel 5844
Thompson, Oliver 4624
Thor 404
Thorgrimur 4456
Thorn 6026
Thorn, Beany 4336
"thorn, pink-flowering" 3794
Thorn the Mannamavi 5545
"thorn tree" 4189
Thornby, Nicholas 7580
Thornhill, Edward 2339
"thorns, as though they concealed" 10428
"thorns, circle of" 6808
"thorns, longest fiercest" 9671
"thorns and thistles" 993
"thoroughfares, business" 9114
Thorpe, Mr. Templeton 5734
Thorpe, Mr. Zachary 1294
"Thorsday" 4282
"those, who's" 2098
"thought, Catherine" 4552
"thought, cut off his world of" 5620
"thought, deep in" 9452

"thought, discovered in my mind
the" 9431
"thought, gave no" 9213
"thought, he" 220, 7635
"thought, head bowed in frowning"
9410
"thought, I turn my every" 2287
"thought, Jeannie Laird Colter"
2157
"thought, Joshua" 9449
"thought, lost in" 9402
"thought, Mrs. Beneker" 1511
"thought, moment of" 9407
"thought, my first" 2397
"thought, nice" 4642
"thought, offspring of his" 2632
"thought, orgy of concentrated"
9412
"thought, protection from free" 223
"thought, wrongly" 1309
"thought about her grandfather"
3022
"thought about him, still" 2676
"thought about the Conway twins"
9440
"thought about the dead girl" 10239
"thought about what he was going
to do" 10098
"thought all babies ugly" 554
"thought as a child" 3592
"thought as dispassionately as he
could" 9437
"thought as he made the turn onto
Park Presidio" 6030
"thought at first that the seedpods
were centipedes" 9682
"thought at the time" 5106
"thought first and mainly of Basil
Seal" 9420
"thought first came to him" 9415
"thought flatteringly of himself"
1856
"thought for a long time, had not"
9424
"thought for a moment" 9923
"thought he had offended me" 4992
"thought he might not have heard"
5746
"thought he was never going to see
Palster Manor again" 7392
"thought how fine it was to be an
American woman" 9464
"thought I would study art" 517
"thought in mind, with but one"
9439
"thought it was dead funny" 4660
"thought Laura" 6566
"thought Margy Shannon" 9147
"thought now I am a beetle" 4895
"thought occurred to her, a funny"
9456
"thought of, first thing he" 277
"thought of, not to be" 9458
"thought of a passage from the
Bible" 8921

"thought of Cary anymore, I
rarely" 2800
"thought of Daniel" 9433
"thought of her in the midst of pure
and delicate colours" 9441
"thought of herself, always" 7980
"thought of himself as a 'confirmed
bachelor'" 5765
"thought of it, how I" 9950
"thought of it as a tiger" 422
"thought of it as an anniversary,
no longer" 10439
"thought of that child, whenever
he" 6890
"thought of the Abnaki Indians of
the Algonquin tribe" 7457
"thought of the void" 6075
"thought of them, when he" 4436
"thought once again of his father
and mother" 6648
"thought only people I did not
know died" 2410
"thought Rupert Stonebird" 9455
"thought sadly, I" 3862
"thought she might scream or faint
or kill someone" 3689
"thought she was dying" 2435
"thought she'd seen it all" 6469
"thought struck him that it was
time I learned to read" 3282
"thought surfaced" 9448
"thought the woman was being
murdered" 6173
"thought to poisoning, I had never
given a" 2418
"thought when she stuck out her
tongue" 10645
"thoughtful, very" 7130
"thoughtfully" 5344, 9444
Thoughtfulness 7130
Thoughts 42, 49, 128, 220, 277,
674, 687, 880, 1186, 1276, 1327,
1438, 1871, 1888, 2157, 2287,
2323, 2595, 2621, 2632, 2676,
2788, 2800, 3014, 3022, 3282,
3495, 3689, 3862, 4537, 4661,
4674, 4778, 4894, 4895, 5021,
5424, 5446, 5512, 5620, 5870,
5996, 6011, 6173, 6494, 6747,
6775, 6841, 6890, 7539, 7599,
7600, 8180, 8278, 8480, 8491,
8936, 8984, 9353, 9821, 9987,
9989, 10063, 10098, 10156,
0239, 10262, 10479, 10873,
10967
"thoughts, crude" 9457
"thoughts, dark as the" 1186
"thoughts, innermost" 2533
"thoughts, lost in her own" 7599
"thoughts, narrowly ahead of her"
9409
"thoughts, secret" 10873
"thoughts, set down my" 3495
"thoughts, their private" 5512
"thoughts, these" 7663

"thoughts, too much occupied with
his" 9417
"thoughts and actions of Pericles
the Athenian" 707
"thoughts and dreams jostled in
disorder" 10156
"Thoughts are ever turn'd upon appearing *Amiable*" 10764
"thoughts are nothing to be proud
of, my" 9419
"thoughts . . . chafe mercilessly"
9446
"thoughts down on paper, attempt
to put my" 9446
"thoughts for company" 128
"thoughts were sorrowful" 9402
"thoughts which hung heavily at
the back of his mind" 9418
Thought-Woman 9445
"thousand hooves" 8776
"thousands, pious" 2555
"thousands came back" 1592
"Thracian Tchermen" 6110
"thread, spins its own golden" 5656
"thread of sense" 9009
"threadbare pedlars" 3396
"threading their way toward the
sea" 1764
"threads, massive and tarnished
gold" 7056
"threads of adventure" 10051
"threads on the needle, catching
the" 10934
"threat, promise and" 9389
"threat of death, live under the"
1163
"threat of disaster" 2599
"threat of the long stifling midday
hours" 4378
"threat to the icehouse, posing
some" 3604
"threatened to paralyse him" 3721
"threatening, dark and" 8332
"threatening Afric's fires and savagery" 8642
Threats 287, 1163, 1835, 3621,
3880, 4974, 8315
"three, when I was" 3282
"three of them" 3008
"Three Sands" 3044
"three to a township, no more
than" 5529
"three-card monte players" 6274
"threes, why" 2100
"threshold, carry me over the" 1996
"threshold, picturesque" 4047
"threshold, stepped over the" 6145
"threw, only Helen" 1203
"threw an ornament at him, Bentley's father" 6682
"threw at my feet" 4128
"threw back the blanket" 10116
"threw down her cards" 4976
"threw down the magazine section"
6351

"threw him into a far corner of the room" 3325
"threw him out, when Bentley's father" 6682
"threw it down" 396
"threw it inaccurately at the dust-bin" 8575
"threw me off the hay truck, they" 9541
"threw up, she just" 2677
"threw very straight, she" 4147
"thrill that overcame me" 5476
"thriller, the" 1325
"thrilling, unbearably" 5881
Thrills 5476, 5881
"thrills" 5489
"thrive with exclamation marks" 10843
"thriving river-town" 8956
"throat, cleared his" 8872
"throat, cutta the" 2014
"throat, I cleared my" 7518
"throat, like something caught in his" 7456
"throat, she cleared her" 4901
"throat, stuffed in his" 10303
"throat, took him cheerfully by the" 3325
"throat decomposing to fat" 8883
"throats, delicate white" 4129
"throats, tearing at their" 3381
"throb and shudder, comforting" 8811
"throbbing like the gills of a river bass laid out in a pail" 8734
"throbbing south-east" 9575
Throckmorton 3604
Throckmorton, Braxton Porter III 3604
"throne, his" 5082
"throne, lounged amiably on his" 3396
"throne, sat upon the" 10474
"throng, no such" 3991
"throne of his fathers" 10768
"throne of our ancestors" 7801
"throng of ancient memories" 5617
"throng of bearded men" 3985
"throng of men and women, a hurrying" 9528
"thronged" 1295
"thronged, standing closely" 1296
"thronged with auditors" 1292
"thronging bronze" 1606
"through, you don't know what I've been" 71
"through it all before, I have been" 52
"through with him, she was" 7988
"throughout the world" 5040
"throw, stone's" 487, 9216
"throw crumbs of wedding cake" 10657
"throw herself into the Seine" 9286

"throw herself off the Great Pyramid, tried to" 9293
"throw him in the river if he says a word too much" 4974
"throw Newt Hardbine's father over the top of the Standard Oil sign" 3733
"throw up, trying not to" 151
"throwing a cloak from her shoulders, as if she were" 6587
"throwing aside his spade" 3793
"throwing icicle darts" 10740
"throwing myself into the river" 2529
"throwing off his midshipman's jacket" 8642
"throwing pebbles into the Black Sea" 4147
"throwing their champagne glasses" 1203
"thrown from one side to another" 762
"thrown out of bed" 10227
"thrown out of the RAF" 8664
"thrown up there, as if it had been" 5165
Thrush, Elijah 5659
"thrush, a" 10209
"thrush, note of the" 8788
"thrust, lunge and" 8027
"thrust a brown paper parcel into her arms" 851
"thrust again with one hand" 8027
"thrust from the bloody bowels of woman" 9285
"thrust itself out of the sea" 5028
"thrust of Ware Neck" 8067
"thrust the sharp point home" 3047
"thrust them against the city" 10726
"thrusts, stresses and" 1314
Thucydides 99
"Thucydides, weary of" 99
"thud of hoofbeats" 10405
Thudbury 1401
"thuds, the plane" 222
"Thule of the ancients" 5011
"thumb, open and shut with his" 5621
"thumb, prodded it with an expert" 4132
"thumb, swinging the old" 10367
"thumb is stiff, my left" 6596
"thumbed his way from New York to Worcester Mass." 9584
"thumbing a ride on an Iowa high-way corner" 9554
"thumbs, balls of her" 3689
"thumbs, called to talk about" 9301
"thumped her Gladstone bag down" 9878
"thunder, cracks of" 9088
"thunder, first clap of" 9067
"thunder, grumbling his" 9066
"thunder, no" 7514
"thunder, theatrical" 9241

"thunder burst above Black Valley" 9067
"thunder enough to deafen you, soundless" 8948
"thunder grumbled along" 9077
"thunder of the waters" 9208
"thundercloud, piled-up" 9070
"thundered through the open door" 10108
"*Thunderer, The*" 5743
"thundering down the alley" 313
"thundering knock" 9920
"thunderous spring" 10603
"thundershower, last drops of the" 5711
"thunderstorm, after a warm" 9083
"thunder-storm, suddenly as a tropical" 7009
"thunderstorm broke very suddenly" 7294
"thunderstorm frightened a great many people" 9074
"thunderstorms" 1998
"thunderstorms, heavy" 9072
Thurmond, Doan 5754
Thurs 7299, 9555
"Thursday, an ordinary" 4524
"Thursday, that hot August" 2177
"tiara, rhinestone" 9729
"Tiber, the" 5345, 7678
"Tiberian eye" 7011
"Tiberias, Lake of" 5716
"tick that was sucking the life from the hoary grey ear of the donkey" 5256
"ticket, Bevan" 3742
"ticket, bought the" 9625
"ticket, no return" 7907
"ticket, owned the" 3968
"ticket, railway-" 9874
"ticket in one of those public carriages" 9511
"ticket seller" 1319
"ticket taker" 1319
"ticket with baggage claim checks attached" 9653
"ticket-seller, the usual shabby bored lonely" 5617
"ticket-taker" 1313
"ticking" 10503
"ticking of the second hand" 9495
"tickling her stomach" 740
"tidal abyss" 435
"tidal Thames, tarry" 5260
Tiddyboo 4785
"tide, incoming" 10719
"tide, on the high" 8170
"tide, outgoing" 6648
"tide, loving" 7649
"tide, retreating" 6053
"tide flowed east towards the sun, the running" 5167
"tide makes, as soon as the" 8047
"tide of man's life on earth pauses and begins slowly to shift" 5575

"tide on the flats, low" 10277
"tide went out, when the" 7926
"tides, beneath the" 14
"tides, oversurging" 6249
"tides, the" 7657
"tides that he could hear" 7913
"tides that raced up the Yangtze" 10524
"tidied away the tea-things" 8214
"tidings, evil" 6307
"tie, blue" 970
"tie, carefully knotted" 10421
"tie, maroon and gold" 2848
"tie, regimental striped" 1942
"tied hand and foot" 10327
"tied him at its barred side door" 7620
"tied to for life" 5242
"tied up at the dock" 8168
Tierney, Rev. Mr. 5194
"ties, knitted" 4789
"tiffs, one of our Darby-and-Joan" 1142
Tigellinus 6957
Tiger 9752
"tiger, he *thought* of it as a" 422
"tiger, Thomas Tracy had a" 422
"Tiger John" 8750
"Tiger Stadium" 7498
"tight, his morning coat was getting" 2838
"tightest pants" 2834
"tightrope his way back" 6372
"tigress, caged" 10345
"Tijuana, Jake is in" 8731
Tilbury, Lord 5311
"tile, the fallen" 1217
"tiles, bathroom" 5333
"tiles and platters, bobbing" 4691
"tiles underfoot seem cool" 7076
"Tilling" 1826, 8378, 10525
"Tillingham, River" 9134
Tilney, Clara 2738
"tilt the little print hanging beside it" 2714
"tilt to it, a strange" 10746
Tim 3584
"Timbali" 6483
"timbered, well-" 5067
"timbered house" 9674
"timbered out, long since" 5161
Timberlake, Asa 3107
"timberlands" 9084
"Timbuctoo" 4076, 7663
"Timbuctoo on the river Niger" 1429
Time 103, 526, 621, 1331, 1606, 1650, 2064, 2187, 2274, 2335, 2968, 2981, 3433, 3499, 4320, 4510, 4923, 4935, 5097, 6903, 7120, 7579, 9331, 9342, 9412, 9438, 10625, 10815, 10980, 10993
"time" 4935, 9483
"Time" 4008
"time, after much" 9639

"time, after that first" 6075
"time, all the" 10689
"time, as if for all" 215
"time, at any" 9287
"time, at that" 7607
"time, at the same" 6705
"time, awful passage of" 7896
"time, best" 827
"time, born before my" 796
"time, checkout" 7097
"time, chose a bad" 6544
"time, cold with" 7388
"time, course has been forward in" 9493
"time, creeping hours of" 3301
"time, dark chaotic unfathomable pool of" 1706
"Time, Daylight Saving" 9491
"time, deadly" 3629
"time, definite span of" 5572
"time, dirty" 10634
"time, eastern" 9486
"Time, Eastern Standard" 2559
"time, even if they got the" 2967
"time, events produce the effects of" 3433
"time, every" 384, 9983
"time, extended periods of" 7463
"Time, fantastic store-house of" 5307
"time, first" 840, 865, 967, 1059, 1210, 1318, 1512, 1988, 2435, 2582, 2807, 2899, 3491, 3630, 3656, 3715, 4584, 4832, 5107, 5651, 5795, 5796, 5805, 5807, 5810, 5813, 5821, 5823, 5833, 5840, 5848, 5856, 6086, 6757, 7280, 7382, 7522, 7676, 7679, 7751, 7764, 8005, 8024, 8749, 9724, 10867
"time, fixed in" 2156
"time, for a long" 2459, 6700, 7440, 9440
"time, for any length of" 6391
"time, for the third" 3739
"time, fourth" 10541
"time, good deal of" 5360
"time, great deal of" 10561
"time, hard" 6927, 10961
"time, having scarce" 2088
"time, I ain't pressed for" 1331
"time, I spent my" 187
"time, I've got plenty of" 621
"time, impaired by" 1293
"time, in a moment's" 9279
"time, in his" 334
"time, in men's" 9747
"time, in that" 3389
"time, it was a bad" 66, 3391
"time, it was at that" 6635
"time, it wasn't the first" 7193
"time, it's" 9504
"time, it's almost" 9485
"time, just in" 3413
"time, killing" 10092

"Time, Killing" 9502
"time, last" 494, 1570, 1887, 1929, 2013, 2561, 3015, 4813, 7201, 8738, 8799, 8909
"time, long" 7983, 8876
"time, minutes that are not reckoned as" 3499
"time, nature's" 836
"time, not sure you could spare the" 9865
"time, now is the" 6989
"time, occupied her" 3320
"time, odd" 3709
"time, on" 1660
"time, one and only" 2322
"time, only" 10676
"time, owned all" 8862
"time, particular" 6260
"Time, River of" 2638
"time, sailing" 4916
"time, sheep-shearing" 3636
"time, shortest possible" 9528
"time, spent all his" 6239
"time, take your" 624
"time, ten-millionth" 6566
"time, the" 7653
"time, there was" 9475
"time, there was a" 3388, 7120, 7531, 9422
"time, these things take" 9506
"time, they were of old" 5015
"time, this third" 1754
"time, this was the" 3601
"time, torpid" 2236
"time, very awkward" 2451
"time, very decisive" 86
"time, very first" 5843
"time, wasting" 4923
"time, we all remember that" 3390
"time, we was in plenty of" 10360
"time, we were right on" 9480
"time, worst" 10160
"time ago, long" 28, 3554, 9181
"time already remote enough to make fables seem possible" 1025
"time and a windless noon" 9479
"time and again" 1814
"time and bad conditions do not favour beauty" 10815
"time and energy, want all your" 10876
"time and money, a considerable expenditure of" 1030
"time and season" 10589
"time as any, as good a" 2540
"time before dawn, it was the silent" 5073
"time before steamships, in the" 3997
"time began, where" 10751
"time being, at least for the" 8013
"time between day and evening, that lingering" 2276
"time came, when my" 796
"time came, when the" 7058

"time caught up with history" 5097
"time comes, when the" 5397
"time could have stopped, if only" 9438
"time doing it, one spends more and more" 9502
"time Elmo was home, isn't it" 9339
"time for earlier romance, no" 7745
"time for hurricanes is past" 10743
"time for nothing but his soul, he nowadays has" 8979
"time for them to strike, it was a sweet" 6179
"time had stopped" 4320
"time has always lagged, historical" 3383
"time Hymie, it's" 10254
"time I saw him, the first" 5855
"time I saw them, here is the first" 5833
"time immemorial" 7266
"time immemorial, from" 357, 4741, 6085
"time in a week, for the second" 5774
"time in his life" 2515
"time in his life, the first" 3567
"time in my life, for the first" 5295
"time in my life, for the second" 8494
"time in the world, all the" 377
"time in this place, spends a lot of" 8200
"time is not a line but a dimension" 9500
"Time is one of the dimensions in space" 6903
"time is so forever" 4510
"time is the only measure of change" 526
"time it is now, such a" 5704
"time it was, didn't ask himself what" 2981
"time it was, to see what" 9492
"time lies coiled there" 9503
"time limit, there is no" 7357
"time must come" 5776
"time now, for some" 165, 9306
"time now, so any" 10084
"time of changes, think of it as the" 8543
"time of day, during the mystery-laden" 2278
"time of his departure" 2359
"time of inexplicably happy marriages" 5755
"time of moral bankruptcy" 2023
"time of my end approaches" 3336
"time of returning" 1780
"time of the war, it told the" 10503
"time of the year, as folk do at that" 6561
"time of this in its beginning" 9747
"time of tragedy" 5947
"time of year, sweet genial" 6557

"time of year, the wrong" 10638
"time of year, this" 5663
"time on, from that" 6532
"time on this earth was over, his" 9846
"time or two" 6469
"time out of mind" 694
"time remaining, neither he nor his wife had much" 3751
"time so long ago, that mellow" 7709
"time spent curled up within its pages" 5462
"time that came afterwards" 5124
"time that evening, for the third" 10953
"time that morning, for the third" 2765
"time that was before" 5124
"time to be young, the best" 9382
"time to beware" 10858
"time to go" 1650, 9516
"time to time, from" 6244, 9949
"time to wake up" 10124
"time touches all things with destroying hand" 9468
"time traveling" 5297
"Time Traveller" 3267
"time trusts no one and so it disappears before us" 9505
"time was coming, another" 3206
"time was of the essence" 7579
"time was starting to melt and mix like a thick liquid" 9498
"time wears on" 3490
"time when neither of them had spoken" 3384
"time when the world was a colder and darker place" 3400
"time which he didn't know how to spend" 10561
"time which passes over our heads so imperceptibly" 9465
"time with Frank Birdsong, her" 7490
"timebound, less" 10377
"timed perfectly" 3425
"timekeeper the moon, our" 10822
"timeless, lazy and" 5024
"times, at different" 3426
"times, best of all possible" 4170
"times, better" 1675
"times, countless" 1799
"*Times*, crumpled" 6356
"times, good" 5936
"times, happier" 5057
"times, happiest of" 4353
"times, how many" 9201
"times, in former" 7179
"times, in the very earliest" 359
"times, it was the best of" 3377
"times, it was the worst of" 3377
"times, modern" 3529, 10033
"times, more prosperous" 4073
"times, old" 7765

"times, our" 3627
"*Times, Penarth*" 6352
"*Times*, Sunday" 6351
"*Times, The*" 4008, 5735
"times, these ridiculous" 84
"times, troubled" 1475
"times ahead, rough" 1994
"times and incomes change" 6654
"times and places, different" 7718
"times and places, other" 4495
"times before, many" 2789
"times in which we live" 2532
"times long since past" 2885
"times of ours, in these" 8050
"times of unperceived cataclysm" 3403
"Times Square" 6274, 9157
"time's temptations and terrors" 9479
"times were finely changed" 9113
"timid confusion" 675
"timidly" 6308
"timing, sense of" 2685
"timing was off" 1778
Timon 10853
"Timon of Athens" 390
"Tin of Kings, Phoenix the" 4632
"tin roofs" 1056
"tingle, faint" 1156
"tingled, her body" 10283
"tingled with a wonderful sense of freedom" 9615
"tinker" 4987
"tinker beneath their car hoods" 1477
"tinkered with it" 5539
"tinkety-tink" 4987
"tint, deep bluish" 7288
"tint of the first light of dawn, under the bluish" 1433
"tint which is so widely condemned" 7288
"tinted a lemony yellow" 8245
"tinted purple" 8323
"tinting a cloudless sky" 2255
Tiny, Wm. 9959
"tip, twenty pence" 2044
"tip of my shoe just snapped off" 39
"tip of the newest and oldest continent, the southernmost" 4087
"tip to tip of the island" 171
"tipple, coal mine" 1018
"tips, we depend on" 6652
"tips, we work for" 6652
"tipsy father" 2942
"tire, putting air in a" 3733
"tire of the task" 7680
"tired, he was" 3683
"tired and very cold, I was" 3686
"tired even to undress, too" 3685
"tired of being a character" 945
"tired of being so busy" 1493
"tired of sitting, beginning to get very" 894
"tired to the roots of his eyes" 3695

"tires, heaps of discarded" 5982
"tires, warped" 9600
"tires taking their own erratic paths" 2989
"Tiresias, this patrician parrot of a" 6039
"tiring day, had a" 3697
"tiring yourself out" 956
Tish 4792
"Titicaca, lake" 1567
"title, came to his" 950
"title, I take my" 5516
"title of this work" 2466
"title to this work" 8953
"title-page" 5394
Titles 897, 904, 2466, 2824, 5394, 5516, 8955
"titles, all my" 5567
"titles for chapters, books with" 904
"tits, girl with the big" 4620
"tits, world of the" 4200
"titter under their breath" 2118
"tittlefaces and parallel lumps" 6075
Titus 972, 5115
"Tiusday" 4282
"Tivoli" 4040, 7514
"T'o Tlakai" 7612
"toad, large Tuscan" 3882
"toadstools, handful of obnoxious black-gilled" 1863
"toast, one slice of buttered whole-wheat" 3852
"toast, piece of" 9923
"toast, slice of" 4349
"toast at breakfast had been burnt" 2333
"toast him brown while he was very new" 6519
"toast 'n' coffee" 3871
"toasting himself unmercifully" 5629
Toasts 1199, 1203, 1975, 2916, 6809
Tobacco 246, 6043, 7350, 7680
"tobacco" 3641
"tobacco, black St. Louis" 899
"tobacco, chew of" 246
"tobacco, rolled his quid of" 7350
"tobacco factories" 5142
"tobacco storage silos" 7183
"tobacconist's shop" 5398
"tobacco-roller, the" 3559
Tobit 4780
"toboggan" 9626
Toby 4120, 5631
Toby, Brother 5653
"tobyman, gallant" 3396
"to-day, at half-past one" 6410
"today is my birthday" 855
"today is the day" 7076
"today was no day for stirring abroad" 7025
Todd 10303
"toddies, hot" 3394
Toddy 5809
Todhunter, Mr. 99
"toe, her big" 4277

"toe, slipped his" 10206
"toe of Zivanias had failed him, the big" 350
"toenails" 115
"toenails, cut her" 564
"toes, break someone's" 8944
"toes, curled webbed" 5624
"toes, her tiny pink" 4181
"toes were coated and dark" 8371
"Toft End" 9118
"together, how long we've been" 1999
"together, in here" 4813
"together, they could be seen" 3483
"together, they were always" 3917
"together, we are gathered" 10672
"together on the water" 5242
"toggery, hunting" 2820
Toil 1621, 1850, 2853, 3683, 4375, 4693, 10924, 10946, 10961
"toil, unrewarded" 3683
"toiled up flight upon flight" 6759
"toiled up the hill" 9872
"toilers, weary" 6361
"toilet bowl, poised over the" 7540
"toilet for each member of the family" 284
"toilet-room, the women's" 8564
"toiling in a deep ravine" 10924
"toiling near to each other" 10946
"toils, great are the" 1850
"token, offered some" 1217
"Tokyo" 9816
"Tokyo, I come from" 4553
"told, if not as it ought to be" 6283
"told, should first be" 5560
"told about water and women" 10811
"told all of it, he should have" 9005
"told each other how much they were in love" 7712
"told from between firm lips" 3272
"told her back" 4437
"told him she was two months along" 7088
"told him so, everyone" 1229
"told him so, Guru had" 1231
"told himself, he" 6030, 6490
"told his builders to build gigantic pavilions" 7808
"told his four sons that he wished to see them" 6712
"told his wife" 3278
"told in another book" 1283
"told in verse and prose" 4455
"told me I was a Negro, no one sat me down and" 7981
"told me it would be" 3141
"told me not to, he never" 1813
"told me that one day I'd marry, if anyone had" 5783
"told me to behave and not make noise" 6632
"told me to tell you that" 10031
"told over and over again to keep out of it" 3898
"told Thad she was dead, who" 6186

"told us one morning during catechism class" 9853
"told you already, I" 2877
"told you in detail, could have" 6127
"told you not to do that" 643
"Toledo, cooking fires of" 4679
"Toledo, towers and battlements of" 5590
"tolerate, I've learned to" 3864
"Tolland New York" 1401
"tolled for five minutes, abbey-bell" 1292
"tolling of an Angelus bell" 650
Tom 3183, 4530, 4685, 4715, 5369, 6370, 9516, 10226, 10251
"Tomahawk, low-slung" 9807
Tomasso, Dino 2987
"tomatoes, so were" 3750
"tomb of Hannah and her seven sons" 2553
"tomb of the radio mummy" 7791
"tomb was recently discovered" 4494
"tomb-gray" 9228
"tomboy, every bit a" 5861
"tombs" 6661
"tombs, altar" 2300
"tombstone, often cracked butternuts on your" 2312
"tombstones" 725
"tombstones, mouldy" 1183
"tomcat, my" 3139
Tommie 1667
Tommy 2448, 6094, 8525
Tomorrow 490, 2154, 2166, 6565
"tomorrow, if it's fine" 6565
"tomorrow is First Pasturing Day" 2154
"tomorrow like a yummy fruitcake" 2656
"tomorrow mornin', it's" 7385
"tomorrow the man I love is to die" 7182
"tomorrow was Friday" 2166
"tone, a" 6272
"tone of mild regret" 866
"tones, Hilda's" 9998
"tonga, sat in a" 2963
"tongue, animal's" 5096
"tongue, brandy trickle over his" 2939
"tongue, hold" 975
"tongue, my infant" 4714
"tongue, put out his" 4216
"tongue, roll around on her" 4419
"tongue, stuck out her" 10645
"tongue, sun on his" 8239
"tongue, tip of his" 7456
"tongue has been stuck to the roof of my mouth" 8216
"tongue rather too large for his mouth" 4282
"tongued the barn match" 3778
"tongue-tied, got a little" 8894
"Tonic, Grove Chill" 8308

"tonic, Maud's favorite stomach" 1024

Tonio 6873

"Tonkawa" 3044

"tons, eighteen thousand" 8089

"tons, seventeen thousand" 8074

Tony 6992, 9060, 9471

"too late" 2537

"took a leak" 437

"took almost everything with them" 6131

"took his wife Lulah to the window" 2073

"took it for granted" 5799

"took the street car" 1579

"took them an hour" 1745

"took to his bed" 4907

"took up his position in the lobby" 4659

"tool, this splendid" 271

Tools 271, 10948, 10962

"toothbrush, firm as a new" 9670

"toothpaste" 1067

"toothpick" 6943

"toothsome eggs and bacon" 3850

"tooting midnight" 2968

"top of Bleakridge" 2496

"top of the bank, from the" 414

"top of the covers" 10265

"top of the hill" 8652, 9141

"top of the tree, at the very" 4522

"top of the tulip-shaped wineglass, placed her hand over the" 2921

"top the rise, when you" 3259

"topography which has otherwise become a jungle" 5572

Topouzoglou, Isaac 2398

Topouzoglou, Stavros 2398

"topped the little rise" 9127

"topper, glossy" 2842

"Tops, difficult to please with his" 2820

"tops at about five thousand feet" 197

"tops of the mountains" 9070

"tops to them now, there weren't any" 9242

"topsails, closely-reefed" 8054

"topsails, lower" 8152

"topsy-turvy" 1831

"Torbay" 8093

Torbett, Jonas 3617

"torches, flaming" 3775

"tore like wild and savage hunger, ache that rose in him and" 3304

"tore them apart" 5023

"'Toreador Song'" 571

"Tories, Redcoats and" 7110

Torment 4598, 10874

"torment, in a state of dull" 4598

"torment mankind" 253

"torment of her life, the very" 951

"tormentor, my" 10874

"torments, mental and physical" 3514

"torn by the stiff piercing wind" 7945

"torn from a Sunday magazine advertisement" 6864

"torn from his lips, the words were as" 8184

"torn in some long past convulsion of nature" 1174

"torn it, that's" 9790

"torn slopes" 5151

"torn to fragments" 8400

"tornado, struck by a" 8058

"Toro y Plata domaine" 455

"Toroella de Sta. Barbara, village of" 2339

"Toronto" 807, 4125, 7272

"Toros Point, ridge of" 2199

"torpid time" 2236

"torpor which was sleep" 10264

Torr, Mr. 6429

"Torre Fiore, rooftops of" 660

"torrent, the scarlet" 9849

"torrid day" 7637

Torrigiani 3084

"torso, her" 2107

"torso dipped, his" 7989

Torture 1166, 9853

"torture, 26 miles and 385 yards of cruelest" 8924

"torture was ended, another stinking week of" 2171

"tortured by the Indians in America" 9853

"tortured his eyebrows in the heat" 189

"tossed about by waves of ocean" 4463

"tossed her briefcase to the floor" 7085

"tossed it like a juggler from right to left hand" 8918

"tossed out of the door, bundle of blankets is" 1738

"tossing about like a tiny cockleshell" 8132

"tossing them in little piles behind her" 10927

"totems, rituals and" 1209

Totman, Mr. 6353

"touch, at her first warm" 8438

"touch, forbidding" 10313

"touch, get in" 3920

"touch, I have lost" 6984

"touch, sense of" 5897

"touch, soft to" 7409

"touch cold tile, whenever I" 7439

"touch 'em, he'll never" 2820

"touch of an unexpected branch or flower" 8766

"touch the maze of slate roofs" 8448

"touched by that dark miracle of chance" 1221

"touched cold metal" 10165

"touched the lungs, she" 9579

"touched the top of his head" 8461

"touches, those final" 2823

"touching" 5059

"touching her face" 7385

"touching it, you're" 343

"touching staccato" 1320

"touching their people, all things" 2621

"touching up her makeup" 2879

"tough and horny" 5382

"tough talk" 4667

"tough time when I'm gone, he'll sure have a" 2296

"Toulon, Port of" 8066

Toulouse 6932

"touohkomuk" 3906

"tour, short Highland" 9513

"tour, on" 1190

"tour guides" 6274

"tour had begun" 9577

"tour into the adjacent frontier of the sister country" 2087

"toured a personal future" 9604

Tourism 3072

"tourist, curiosity of the" 4920

"tourist, general" 9515

"tourist bus" 1671

"Tourist Corporation, South African" 1420

Tourists 1084, 1293, 1832, 5066, 7527, 9251, 9353, 9559, 9565, 9569, 9577, 9610, 9616, 9621, 9636

"tourists" 6274

"tourists, American" 9636

"tourists, English" 9353

"tourists, entertainment of" 5066

"tourists, legend to beguile the" 7527

"tourists, with the rest of the" 1832

"tourists and sightseers" 7772

"tourists are having lunch" 3873

"tourists had begun to appear like crocuses" 9569

"tourists hurry" 9616

Tours 3190, 9577, 9604, 9658

"tours, book" 2067

"Tours, St. Martin of" 7539

"tours of inspection, on one of his" 9658

"Tov, Baal Shem 2278

"towel first, ran for a" 7857

"towel in his mouth" 2876

"towels, ancient faded rainbow-colored Mississippi-spun bathing" 8530

"towels, her roommate's designer" 2879

Tower, Alwyn 81

"tower, cathedral" 667

"Tower, Dwight-Richardson" 7319

"Tower, English Cathedral" 9207

"Tower, High" 5233

"tower, red-and-white candy-striped" 9247

"tower, shadow of the" 7133

"tower, the" 9228
"Tower, the" 1196
"tower, turquoise" 3001
"tower, University" 5088
"tower, water" 1215
"tower of St. Pancras church" 6270
Towers 9207, 9248
"towers" 10590
"towers, austere" 9212
"towers, concrete" 5859
"Towers, Greenwood" 5238
"towers, grey" 7390
"towers, one of the four" 8663
"towers and battlements" 5590
"towers of steel and cement and limestone" 9212
"towers of Zenith aspired above the morning mist" 9212
Towle, Craig 5768
"town, American commercial" 4029
"town, American county seat" 1425
"town, ancient Hohenzollern" 4017
"town, assize-" 1335
"town, beautiful little" 5078
"town, beyond the edge of" 3422
"town, bright streets of the strange" 1618
"town, could see the" 10718
"town, crude mill" 772
"town, drive through the" 3014
"town, Earth's most famous" 1380
"town, edge of" 8246
"town, every little Southern" 7038
"town, first glimpse of the" 9548
"town, flank of the" 7668
"Town, French" 3262
"town, grubby harbor" 1407
"town, had come to" 6036
"town, hand . . . poised above the" 10582
"town, holiday" 1936
"town, home" 5359
"town, in a certain" 779
"town, in a small Southern" 2560
"town, in our" 7771
"town, incongruous Indiana" 8586
"town, inland" 10696
"town, it's a nice" 1432
"town, little" 665
"town, little agricultural" 1385
"town, little ancient" 1375
"town, little corn-shipping" 960
"town, Midwestern university" 8485
"town, my" 1520
"town, nearer to the" 6080
"town, nice part of" 5292
"town, obscure little" 6436
"Town, Old" 4060
"town, old river" 1411
"town, one-storey" 6241
"town, only" 9563
"town, only a small" 1497
"town, our" 1698
"town, out of" 2018
"town, outskirts of" 9799

"town, pastoral country" 6137
"town, pleasant" 1352
"town, pleasant county-" 1965
"town, pleasant Sussex County" 485
"town, prairie" 1377
"town, predominantly Hindu" 5822
"town, pretty" 3070
"town, pride of the" 3095
"town, remote border" 8232
"town, right in the centre of the" 7880
"town, river" 6004
"town, ruined island" 7467
"town, see a" 1480
"town, shanty-" 2047
"town, small" 1465, 3007, 4081, 4241, 5601, 6199, 9205
"town, small Arizona" 596
"town, small bleached" 331
"town, small but increasingly flourishing" 1038
"town, small college" 4858
"town, small railroad" 4089
"town, south Devon coastal" 1736
"town, spired and watery" 8470
"town, sprung-up counter-jumping" 1420
"town, textile" 8923
"town, the" 1416, 4521
"town, this" 1478
"town, tiny jerkwater" 7262
"town, usually quiet old" 3467
"town, thriving river-" 8956
"town, up-to-date progressive college" 9233
"town, went to" 8893
"town, within the walls of a large" 6556
"town began" 4054
"town beneath the Southern sun" 1393
"town but Forks, any other" 1223
"town called Valley Forge" 1457
"town full of aristocratic prejudices" 1342
"town had a name but no shape" 1389
"Town Hall" 2214
"town hall, out-of-date" 9233
"Town Hall Annexe" 6291
"town he had just left" 7616
"town house, perfectly appointed" 3961
"town houses, Georgian" 309
"town in Maine, small" 6695
"town in Poland, small" 6695
"town in question" 1486
"town in the hills of western Catawba" 10042
"town itself is dreary" 1386
"town lay sprawled at his feet" 1412
"town life, mechanism of" 6199
"town limits" 3604
"town located inside the green zone" 230

"town near my grandparents' summer home in Maine" 3430
"town of a certain shire" 6406
"town of almost five thousand people" 1422
"town of Bideford, little white" 1336
"town of Dawson's Landing" 1349
"town of Desert D'Or" 4061
"town of Fonthill" 1533
"town of iron-works" 175
"town of Leah" 8606, 9964
"town of Libya Hill" 5914
"town of Manhattan, the goodly" 1334
"town of no significance" 1463
"town of Ottsville" 3104
"town of Pedro" 1365
"town of St. Ives" 1764
"town of the middle class" 8971
"town of the Middle West" 1821
"town shone in the snowy twilight" 8596
"town slept" 7687
"town square" 1732, 5342, 9775
"Town Square" 8606
"town that refused to die" 1406
"town they have helped to make" 1415
"town was occupied" 10481
"town was oven hot" 4390
"town was there, the whole" 3945
"town where he was born and bred" 9717
"town where he'd lived" 2001
"town where I grew up" 4598
"town where I was born" 4539
"town where you lived when you were a kid" 4536
"town which bears its name" 9205
Towne, John 6467
"town-house" 8340
"townhouse, five-storied brick" 808
"townie, a" 8012
"townlet, sea-skirted" 9091
"town-life, in places remote from" 7503
Towns, Harry 3525, 5630
Towns 175, 182, 230, 272, 278, 505, 596, 665, 772, 809, 954, 960, 1038, 1049, 1223, 1335, 1336, 1338, 1339, 1340, 1344, 1347, 1349, 1350, 1352, 1355, 1362, 1363, 1365, 1374, 1375, 1377, 1380, 1384, 1385, 1386, 1387, 1389, 1393, 1394, 1400, 1402, 1403, 1406, 1407, 1410, 1410, 1411, 1412, 1413, 1415, 1416, 1418, 1422, 1423, 1425, 1428, 1430, 1431, 1432, 1440, 1445, 1454, 1456, 1457, 1460, 1462, 1463, 1465, 1468, 1477, 1478, 1480, 1481, 1482, 1486, 1497, 1618, 1679, 1736, 1755, 1764, 1821, 1936, 2490, 2560, 3007, 3014, 3061, 3087, 3097, 3467,

3605, 3766, 3945, 4017, 4029,
4040, 4046, 4053, 4054, 4061,
4068, 4069, 4070, 4075, 4081,
4089, 4241, 4308, 4376, 4390,
4518, 4521, 4536, 4539, 4544,
4546, 4675, 5078, 5119, 5130,
5220, 5359, 5601, 6004, 6080,
6099, 6137, 6199, 6241, 6267,
6416, 6556, 6695, 6831, 7194,
7244, 7262, 7273, 7371, 7666,
7668, 7687, 8232, 8509, 8586,
8596, 8971, 9126, 9159, 9202,
9424, 9548, 9563, 9717, 9719,
10092, 10420, 10481, 10484,
10648, 10685, 10718, 10742, 10769
"towns, bathed-in-light" 1481
"towns, buried" 1384
"towns, dotted with presumptuous
   mushroom" 4046
"towns, in those small" 10957
"towns, its sister" 1387
"towns, nearby" 3157
"towns, old soot-and-sweat factory"
   5982
"towns, one of our New England"
   3060
"towns, one of the wealthiest of our
   great English" 6886
"towns, one of those grey" 3087
"towns, quaint old" 9159
"towns, river" 7323
"towns, shack" 1039
"towns, shuffle of dreary upstate"
   0710
"towns, smelter" 9181
"towns, sprawling prairie" 10341
"towns, tiny down-at-the-heels resort" 9203
"towns, wheat sheep and cattle"
   2988
"towns have sprung up" 1344
"town's north edge" 2489
"towns of brief stay" 4046
"towns of the Chickasaw nation"
   9198
"towns on the island of Kaua'i"
   10957
"towns standing on our seacoast"
   1344
"towns . . . that have remained unchanged for years" 10957
"towns they had come from" 8976
Townsend, Mrs. 7760
"Township, Richland" 3642
"township which I sought" 6069
"townspeople, the" 3095
"townspeople still talk of Lucy
   Gayheart" 3532
"toxicity, characteristic sign of amphetamine" 6170
"toy, triggerman who looked like
   a" 4260
"toy department" 4708
"toy spinning wheels of polished
   oak" 5886

"toying with a Pernod" 2912
"Toyota, the rented" 40
Toys 303, 323, 325, 981, 1075,
   1271, 2614, 4260
"toys" 1271
"toys, grown-up" 1420
"'Tra-la-la' as I did the lathering"
   4349
"trace, moved up the" 10357
"Trace, San Antonio" 5215
"trace of someone, indistinct" 3465
"trace on a map" 5713
"trace survives, no" 10131
"traced a pattern of erratic beetles"
   5627
"track, a single car-" 7240
"track, at the end of a dirt-" 2480
"track, desert" 9127
"track, long lines of dusty level"
   7238
"track, narrow" 9791
"track, noticed the small" 2606
"track, racing inexorably around
   the" 7851
"track, two hundred miles of" 9642
"track coach" 8675
"track me, trying to" 8130
"track stretched away in a flat line"
   7275
"track which led from the shanty-
   town to the house above it" 2047
"trackless continents" 4539
"tracks, stay off the" 8703
"tracks, these railroad" 9300
"tracks in which my mind used to
   run, avoid the" 7400
"tracks of the invading forces" 6052
"tract of grass" 7878
"traction device" 10228
"tractor, wrestling with the" 10925
Tracy 6171
Tracy, Hugh 7614
Tracy, Thomas 422
"trade, destroyed the" 7814
"trade, drug-smuggling" 3054
"Trade, Poison" 1062
"trade in ox-hides and indigo" 1355
"trade routes, confluence of" 1443
"trader" 10348
"trader, Mexican" 8852
"trader, the" 3914
"traders" 3635
"trades big, Luke" 1074
"tradesman, wealthy" 6516
"tradesman named Phineas Cutter"
   9955
"tradesmen" 2290
"trading-post" 1400
"tradition, according to" 4880
"tradition, appears from" 3551
"traditions, elegant and dignified"
   1314
"traditions of the world of literature" 1314
Traffic 1012, 2964, 2993, 2996,

2997, 3017, 3021, 3041, 3723,
   4078, 7135, 7862, 8320, 8410,
   8749, 8773, 8779, 8798, 9119,
   9130, 9160, 9169, 9332, 9451,
   9828
"traffic, din of" 8773
"traffic, early morning" 5142
"traffic, human" 6433
"traffic, in the" 8320
"traffic, Labor Day" 3041
"traffic, late afternoon" 7862
"traffic, roared and glittered with
   celestial" 8410
"traffic, scanning the" 2997
"traffic, sound of the" 8779
"traffic, stop-and-start" 9616
"traffic, water-" 1126
"traffic and pedestrians" 5308
"traffic began to slow and thicken
   ahead of her" 2996
"traffic behind you, long line of"
   8749
"traffic go by, watching the" 9451
"traffic jam" 9332
"traffic lights" 2993
"traffic lights at the intersections
   holding and changing" 6030
"traffic moved at the pace of the
   drooping horse-car" 1012
"traffic of a single city" 9160
"traffic of Dockland" 9130
"traffic on Sepulveda, light early
   morning" 2906
"traffic policemen" 19
"traffic somehow thin and scared"
   9451
"traffic turned north" 4078
"traffic was legendary" 3041
"traffic was sparse" 9828
"tragedies of life, the overwhelming" 5799
Tragedy 77, 2510, 4116, 4225,
   4557, 5091, 5261, 5799, 10902
"tragedy" 10341
"tragedy, darkness of the" 11004
"tragedy, family" 2510
"tragedy, in time of" 5947
"tragedy, intolerable" 4225
"tragedy, last murmur of futile"
   10902
"tragedy, opening scene of" 5091
"tragedy, precocious in" 77
"tragedy, we went because of a"
   2510
"tragedy having turned my basic
   languor to indolence" 4116
"tragedy more than a delight, was
   a" 4557
"tragic" 5261
"tragic death" 2360
"tragic in society" 10667
"tragically, less" 274
"tragically, refuse to take it" 3380
"trail, buffalo" 9126
"trail, lower swamp" 7639

"trail, moved up the" 10401
"Trail, Old California" 6948
"trail, old cattle" 2949
"trail, paused on the" 8510
"trail, stony rut-lined" 2947
"trail, vaguely marked" 9152
"Trail, Wilderness" 1912
"trail rides up the Chisholm" 3399
"trail that is nobody knows how
    old" 8971
"trail that led beside the shore"
    4695
"trailer, hired a U-Haul" 6169
"trailer, house" 6165
"trailer, shabby aluminum" 4073
Trails 8971, 9121, 9126, 9150, 9152
"trails, seared and cross-barred
    with grave-lined" 4046
"train" 9626, 10099
"train, afternoon" 7272, 10063
"train, almost empty" 9545
"train, Amtrak" 9597
"train, arrived by" 7082
"train, boarded the" 8676
"train, boarded the afternoon" 9525
"train, by" 1721
"Train, Christmas" 4131
"train, compartment of an almost
    empty" 6639
"train, day coach of a" 9654
"train, early afternoon" 7254
"train, entered the" 9530
"train, fast" 5673
"train, first freight" 136
"train, first time I've been on a"
    7280
"train, go around the country by"
    9932
"train, got off the" 9571
"train, got out of the" 1649, 8507
"train, he always somehow missed
    his" 9347
"train, he had said *the*" 7245
"train, helped from the" 2903
"train, high" 1645
"train, I'll catch the first" 1578
"train, in and out like the E" 10324
"train, it was a gay" 1612
"train, last" 4594
"train, Missouri Pacific" 7262
"train, Morehaven" 9641
"train, narrow-gauge" 7257
"train, New York-Montreal passen-
    ger" 7283
"train, nickname of the" 7251
"train, on the" 4579
"train, Paris" 7245
"train, passenger" 9328
"train, presage of a" 7239
"train, receding" 1575
"train, same long slow-coach of a"
    7266
"train, sat in the" 10800
"train, shaking out a proud white"
    8082

"train, some day he would take
    that" 243
"train, southbound" 582
"train, Sunday morning accommo-
    dation" 7242
"train, special" 7265
"train, stepped from the" 1584
"train, stepped off the" 1667, 1723
"train, stepped onto that" 1717
"train, straw seats on the" 7274
"train, striding down toward the"
    10359
"train, taking the" 9618
"train, the" 2967, 7252
"train, uptown A" 3050
"train, waiting for the" 10094
"train, westbound" 9586
"train, work-passenger" 7247
"train becomes an elevated" 7282
"train begins to pick up speed" 5142
"train bore them onwards and
    downwards" 9627
"train call" 9385
"train came in between the pillars"
    9605
"train came sidling through the
    scattered lights" 7255
"train clacked slowly" 7269
"train compartment" 8574
"train crawling down the shore"
    1640
"train dragged itself across the flat
    Dutch countryside" 7246
"train drew up in the meadow and
    stopped" 7256
"train from Baltimore puffed and
    panted" 7248
"train from Kilcoole" 9300
"train from London" 7587
"train from London, the twelve-
    nineteen" 6001
"train from Mexico City pulled
    into Cìudad Juárez" 7259
"train from New York" 9612
"train from New York, took the"
    6370
"train from Paddington to Here-
    ford" 7268
"train from Paris, southbound"
    7266
"train from the North, the long"
    9528
"train from upstate" 7265
"train future society-page ladies
    and discreet prostitutes" 2118
"train had just begun its leisurely
    journey" 7254
"train I was riding" 7262
"train in the Pennsylvania Station"
    8565
"train labouring" 9545
"train of future events" 6244
"train of the night, the one great"
    7245
"train passed the stock-pens" 7250

"train pulled endlessly across flat
    stretches" 7267
"train pulled out of Chicago" 7600
"train reached Westport" 1624
"train . . . rolled into the Grand
    Central Station" 9528
"train route, village" 7276
"train seat, green plush" 9558
"train slowed" 7249
"train slowed before drawing into
    the station" 9523
"train sped through the night" 2467
"train starts pulling out of the
    camp" 1738
"train stopped, when the" 1703
"train swaying and rocking" 9572
"train that first carried me into
    Rome" 7243
"train that trundled west" 8457
"train that was carrying him to his
    execution" 3407
"train to San Francisco" 8704
"train traveling from Milan to
    Turin" 9659
"train waiting in Queen Street Sta-
    tion" 1496
"train was a little late" 10032
"train was an hour late" 9524
"train was beginning to slow down
    again" 9562
"train was carried slowly through
    the night" 7260
"train was late" 9333
"train . . . was late overcrowded
    and cold" 7243
"train was late that day" 1909
"train was nearing its destination"
    9548
"train was rocking" 1616
"train was travelling northwards"
    7279
"train which carried Cristo Lorenzo
    Rodriguez into Calumet" 1612
"train which had roared through a
    withering gale of sleet" 9532
"trained, intent on being" 3483
"trainer, dog" 470
"training, basic" 10297
"training, pilot" 196
"trainload of men" 9638
Trains 243, 691, 1201, 1371, 1575,
    1577, 1584, 1612, 1616, 1624,
    1640, 1645, 1648, 1649, 1667,
    1703, 1717, 1721, 1723, 1738,
    1750, 1909, 2359, 2467, 2595,
    2903, 2967, 3050, 3407, 4131,
    4139, 4579, 4594, 4910, 5129,
    5142, 5181, 5360, 5673, 5924,
    5943, 6368, 6370, 6372, 6639,
    7082, 7239, 7241, 7242, 7243,
    7244, 7245, 7246, 7247, 7248,
    7249, 7250, 7251, 7252, 7254,
    7255, 7256, 7257, 7258, 7259,
    7260, 7261, 7262, 7264, 7265,
    7266, 7267, 7268, 7269, 7271,

7272, 7274, 7275, 7276, 7278, 7279, 7280, 7281, 7282, 7283, 7474, 7587, 8234, 8351, 8457, 8507, 8564, 8574, 8596, 8676, 8799, 8812, 9300, 9328, 9333, 9347, 9385, 9516, 9523, 9524, 9525, 9526, 9528, 9529, 9530, 9531, 9532, 9543, 9545, 9548, 9551, 9558, 9562, 9564, 9571, 9572, 9596, 9597, 9605, 9612, 9618, 9627, 9638, 9641, 9642, 9654, 9659, 9932, 9973, 10032, 10063, 10094, 10099, 10359, 10800

"trains, all the" 7241
"trains, buses and" 5360
"trains, lightning limited" 1360
"trains, necessary for him to change" 9543
"trains, shunned by people and" 7271
"trains, the waiting" 4910
"train's hooter shattered the deceptive quiet" 7275
"trains roll by, watch the" 7270
"trains which percolate" 4139
"trait, inherited from his mother every" 4434
"trait . . . that made him worth while" 4434
"trajectory of the teeming droplets" 4901
"Tralorna" 9723
"tram, took the" 6630
"tram that runs with a few inland incursions along the coast" 7264
"tramp, mistaken for a" 7215
"tramped toward the Indian village" 10451
"tramping over a ridge of down" 9533
"tramway, Darlinghurst" 4315
"tramways" 1342
"trance-like aspect" 10566
"Trangloek" 5158
Tranmore, Lady 9326
"tranquil family life" 3248
"tranquil together, we are" 1972
"tranquillities of middle England, rural" 4139
"tranquillity" 223
"tranquilly dozed the village" 10700
"transaction, in this" 5394
"transactions, certain peculiar" 5417
"transactions, record of their inward" 9422
"Transactions of the Pickwick Club" 5557
"transactions which took place in Japan and China some months ago" 5417
"Trans-Canada Air" 1640
"transcendence, achieving a moment of" 7624
"transcontinental journey" 9571

"transcript, turn the pages of the" 10026
"transcription, resist" 5238
"transfer that barn" 512
Transformation 1259, 1261, 1263, 1264, 2616, 5121, 6168, 6546, 8026, 10877
"transformed by its gaiety" 1250
"transformed Dr. Charles Peruzzi" 2616
"transformed from a heavy nightmare to freedom" 1250
"transforming, believed it would be" 5121
"transistor radio" 1046
"transistors" 3402
Transition 1245, 5095
"transition, momentous and most difficult" 5115
"transition, not an abrupt" 8412
"transitions, intriguing in its" 304
"transitory, however" 9928
"translating forty lines of Greek" 10953
"transparent membrane" 2066
"transparent sides of some insects" 9467
"transplanted in her time" 5762
"transport, bizarre lines of" 9792
"transport, public" 7003
"transportation free, get your" 6126
"transports had sneaked up from the south" 8107
"Trantor" 4738
"trap, drove up in her" 10036
"trap, set a" 7741
"trap-line, body" 1213
"trapeze, perched on her" 4180
Trapped 2803, 3319, 9565
"trapped" 33
"trapped, city-" 6883
"trapped, he was" 2803
"trapped, party of sightseers found itself" 9565
"trapped, you're" 3502
"trapped in one way or another" 3319
"Traquhair" 10898
"trash cans" 3787
Trask 3002
Trask, Ivy 3197
Trask, Sheila 5854
"trauma like a plume, she wore her" 54
"traumas, troubled by the" 6444
"traumas of human history, accumulating" 4509
Travel 136, 179, 226, 229, 276, 515, 595, 691, 693, 1052, 1190, 1201, 1326, 1479, 1575, 1615, 1616, 1639, 1640, 1662, 1668, 1676, 1722, 1726, 1750, 1764, 1771, 1832, 1957, 1991, 2004, 2087, 2421, 2467, 2477, 2481, 2510, 2640, 2653, 2755, 2839, 2911,

2943, 2949, 2950, 2959, 2996, 3015, 3025, 3037, 3306, 3469, 3511, 3693, 3711, 3730, 3993, 4011, 4073, 4190, 4269, 4270, 4393, 4423, 4495, 4556, 4559, 4563, 4579, 4606, 4672, 4731, 4920, 5297, 5360, 5477, 5609, 5711, 5750, 5787, 5838, 5943, 6048, 6101, 6162, 6210, 6230, 6250, 6251, 6265, 6363, 6372, 6385, 6584, 6639, 6875, 6925, 6939, 7026, 7062, 7171, 7243, 7253, 7262, 7264, 7266, 7268, 7271, 7272, 7277, 7279, 7280, 7466, 7474, 7600, 7605, 7612, 7614, 7615, 7618, 7630, 7637, 7662, 7824, 7955, 7966, 8123, 8167, 8293, 8304, 8312, 8457, 8504, 8574, 8620, 8731, 8765, 8854, 8865, 9101, 9171, 9182, 9251, 9358, 9385, 9439, 9723, 9762, 9764, 9789, 9798, 9815, 9826, 9834, 9874, 9918, 9923, 9932, 9970, 10108, 10192, 10341, 10422, 10458, 10464, 10563
"travel" 5533
"travel, book of" 5477
"travel, fresh from" 1184
"travel, marks of" 10784
"travel, way both Alice and I felt about" 2004
"travel between Edinburgh and the Queensferry" 9511
"travel cross-country" 5609
"travel direct to the borders of North Wales" 9874
"travel in the good old Asiatic style" 9515
"*Travel Light*" 5468
"travel on horseback" 8620
"travel to Aix-les-Bains" 4269
"traveled a long way to reach it" 1640
"traveled between Chicago and Kansas City" 9654
"traveled by canoe down the Mississippi River" 9635
"traveled on foot through the sprawling prairie towns" 10341
"traveled so ill he could not stand" 4469
"traveled steadily northward" 9549
"traveled without escort" 9557
"traveler" 1415, 9553
"traveler, our" 10894
"traveler, solitary" 9512
"traveler, weary" 9115
Travelers 15, 1184, 1293, 1335, 1764, 2595, 2911, 2955, 2959, 3267, 4303, 4559, 4630, 4920, 5066, 5129, 5609, 5711, 5787, 6901, 7171, 7279, 7284, 7600, 7610, 8351, 8620, 9115, 9168, 9512, 9515, 9522, 9527, 9528, 9529, 9530, 9531, 9532, 9539,

9543, 9546, 9548, 9550, 9553, 9554, 9555, 9558, 9562, 9564, 9571, 9585, 9599, 9612, 9628, 9629, 9632, 9643, 9653, 9654, 9657, 9659, 9864, 10108
"travelers, lonely" 9657
"travelers' checks" 9653
"traveling, road the woman was" 9168
"traveling, she liked" 5360
"traveling, three people" 9551
"traveling, time" 5297
"traveling, you are" 693
"traveling back and forth across America" 3037
"traveling farther south" 9581
"traveling fast" 7614
"traveling north" 9622
"travelled, seldom" 9152
"travelled much, a man who" 4920
"travelled with broad slow wing" 4034
Traveller 468
"traveller, drowsy" 10108
"traveller, modern" 1335
"traveller, railway" 7279
"traveller, tall and sharp-boned" 2595
"traveller, the" 9515, 10199
"Traveller, Time" 3267
"traveller gazes with wonder" 6802
"traveller in the eastern part of Berkshire Mass." 9515
"travellers, European" 7950
"travellers, five" 15
"travellers, forlorn little group of" 9628
"travellers, four" 7284
"travellers, modern" 6246
"travellers, modest" 4630
"travellers, rendezvous of all" 8951
"travellers, unagrarian Eastern" 5129
"travellers, weary" 3396
"travellers in Italy, English" 1293
"travellers stopping at the Astor House Hotel" 6901
"travelling" 2943
"travelling by plane" 5750
"travelling from Calais" 9632
"travelling south from New Orleans to the Islands" 9521
"travelling through Natal" 9522
"travelling through the country" 9520
"travelling together in the East" 9514
"travels, after arduous" 9657
"Travels, European" 10464
"travels, returned from his" 4554
"travels of *Moryson*, the quaintly-written" 6385
"travels toward the setting sun" 6101
"traverse them with expert knowledge" 9161

Travis, Big Bob 9365
"trawlers" 732
Traylor, Samson 6101
"treacly ripple" 5325
"treading softly" 8456
Treadup, David 821
Treason 2032, 6263, 6983
"treason" 6263, 6983
"treason is, do you know what" 2032
Treasure 4491, 5012, 5828, 7950, 9656
"treasure, secret of the" 7950
"Treasure Island" 5012
"'Treasure Island' given to him by his father" 898
"treasure may be hard to find" 4491
"treasure not yet lifted, there is still" 5012
"treasure while life should last" 8093
"treasurer, assistant" 6426
"treasurer, state's" 368
"treasures, bag of" 9656
"treasures together, gathered his" 6112
"Treasury Chambers" 6974
"Treasury's final confirmation" 3741
"treat, private or eleemosynary" 5385
"treated as befitted her nobility" 3413
"treated by at least six of them" 7171
"treatment, when you finish your" 10049
Treatments 3417, 6589
Treats 248, 5184, 8377
"treble of the running rigging" 8086
"Treblinka" 1159
"Treblinka, thinking of" 9459
Tree, Emma 8471
Tree, Jesse 8471
"tree, acacia" 475
"tree, aged" 9660
"tree, apple" 3119
"tree, banyan" 7030
"tree, big walnut" 8739
"tree, celerywood" 687
"tree, cherry" 28, 9683
"tree, climb the mimosa" 328
"tree, climb up in this" 7710
"tree, cottonwood" 10929
"tree, crab-apple" 9674
"tree, dead cypress" 9084
"tree, deciduous" 5740
"tree, dogwood" 8512
"tree, elm" 9675
"tree, forbidden" 5064
"tree, from the top of a" 6225
"tree, giant silk-cotton-" 933
"tree, gum" 3559
"tree, high up in the" 9677
"tree, horse chestnut" 2647
"tree, kapok" 2084
"tree, nonexistent" 8528

"tree, old and curiously gnarled cherry" 9662
"tree, olive" 5716
"tree, one tall" 9677
"tree, palm" 6933
"tree, pear" 746
"tree, pepper" 10937
"tree, poplar" 3165
"tree, reached the top of the" 4198
"tree, Roussillon" 9662
"tree, shade of the" 4416
"tree, thin shade of a dying peach" 3616
"tree, thorn" 4189
"tree, twenty objects hidden in the" 9680
"tree, walnut" 7059
"tree always bore a few wrinkled black-spotted apples" 9674
"tree by the sea-loch, it was a good" 9669
"tree fell, the" 2325
"tree . . . fell last night" 9675
"tree has its voice" 9661
"tree of knowledge" 5064
"tree of the avenue" 8770
"tree of the knowledge of good and evil" 2633
"tree trunks hollowed out by burning" 8156
"tree which dominated the ragged lonesome hollow" 3458
"tree which is full and thick and green and artificial" 4522
"treeless side of Phosphate Mountain" 8458
Trees 27, 28, 299, 746, 933, 973, 1061, 2266, 2325, 2633, 3092, 3177, 3221, 3663, 3895, 3899, 4073, 4198, 4371, 5033, 5064, 5153, 5171, 5179, 5314, 5740, 6065, 6085, 7662, 7692, 7710, 8266, 8321, 8431, 8434, 8507, 8526, 9084, 9156, 9186, 9479, 9660, 9661, 9662, 9663, 9667, 9669, 9672, 9674, 9675, 9677, 9680, 9682, 9683, 9742, 10372, 10414, 10590, 10601, 10681, 10730, 10753, 10923, 10929
"trees, alder" 3082
"trees, banyan" 2209
"trees, ber" 5704
"trees, bower of" 3119
"trees, camphor" 3411
"trees, Christmas" 1061
"trees, cotton-wood-" 1357
"trees, dark" 10400
"trees, dark multitude of olive" 9995
"trees, darker blackness of the" 6030
"trees, distant" 5074
"trees, dry palm" 10717
"trees, elm-" 5314
"trees, few peach" 1386
"trees, few scattered" 9742
"trees, flame" 9672

"trees, full-fledged" 9479
"trees, gets like a lot of little grey" 4660
"trees, huge" 10753
"trees, in the center of a ring of" 8374
"trees, leafless" 2214
"trees, leafless beach" 3421
"trees, lime-" 2951
"trees, man was bracing" 10923
"trees, maple" 3095
"trees, monkeypod" 9682
"trees, moss-hung" 5069
"trees, motionless line of" 8790
"trees, naked" 10572
"trees, narrow grove of" 10461
"trees, new young" 3177
"trees, old oak" 3894
"trees, olive" 5357
"trees, palm" 1417, 9598
"trees, pine" 8526
"trees, pipal" 730
"trees, ragged pattern of" 9076
"trees, sad little clump of" 2722
"trees, scrub" 5153
"trees, shape of the leafless" 10414
"trees, skeleton" 324
"trees, smell of" 8507
"trees, spindly little" 10738
"trees, stand of white birch" 5341
"trees, taken over by" 5171
"trees, tall" 7692
"trees, tamarack" 9756
"trees, through the" 3190
"trees, turning" 9159
"trees, two gingko" 3232
"trees, two sets of" 3032
"trees, wide-branched limbs of" 3899
"trees already scattered hard with bud" 10590
"trees and bushes" 5020
"trees and garden, veiling" 10646
"trees at the back of the yard" 2266
"trees bent and writhing in the wind" 10730
"trees bent with wind" 1481
"trees enclosed the hockey field" 9672
"trees growing over a couple of smooth mountains" 4660
"trees in a soft breeze" 8737
"trees in the garden" 10601
"trees in the little valley" 10681
"trees of the garden" 3794
"trees of the jungle, towering" 4895
"trees pointing upwards like dark fingers" 8434
"trees pressing in on either side" 9156
"trees reach in the windows" 2883
"trees standing there as they always have" 761
"trees stocked with impossible fruit" 9436

"trees sway in the breeze that came off the ocean" 8248
"trees were motionless" 10736
"trees which everywhere embower and stifle" 4371
"trees which rose nearly two hundred feet" 4073
"tree-tops began to tremble" 176
"trek, panicky" 3416
"trek along the main road to Seoul" 3416
Trelawney, Squire 5012
"tremble, felt his body" 10097
"tremble, making the city seem to" 5331
"tremble, tree-tops began to" 176
Trembles, Tralee 3968
"trembling, delicate" 7281
"trembling, shaking and" 7945
"trembling had frozen into a single shrieking note" 3716
"trembling to the sex, cause of much" 10779
"trembling under the wind" 7945
"trembling with fright" 10140
"tremendous surge" 5011
"tremor, feeling the" 7086
"tremor under his feet" 10706
"tremulous fire, points of" 8394
"trenches, up in the" 2305
"trenches, zigzag patchwork of" 10537
"trenches and bunkers along the front line" 10506
Trend, Mrs. Cortlandt 8627
"Trenton" 8533
"Trenton station" 9529
"trepidation, looked with some" 6330
"TRESPASS AND FIND OUT" 8315
Tressilian, Sir Oliver 3084
Trevalla, Trix 5083
Trevelyan, Louis 5638
"Trevi fountain" 9593
Trevize, Golan 2745
Trevor, Mrs. 10813
Trewly, Roger 5769
"trial, live-together" 1997
"trial began, when the" 1744
"trial of John Demjanjuk" 1159
"trial of men charged with murder" 5200
"trial on charges of extortion" 5209
"trial was a half-forgotten scandal" 5091
Trials 1159, 1744, 2027, 3486, 5091, 5194, 5196, 5198, 5200, 5204, 5206, 5209, 5210, 5430, 6044, 10838
"trials, a time of" 273
"Trials, the State" 5194
"trials by association" 9696
"triangle, broad flat" 9141
"Triangle, Golden" 4094
"triangle of benches and trees" 4099

"'Tribal War in Western Uganda'" 1833
"tribe, remote Australian" 7545
"tribe of head hunters, modern white-collar" 1077
"tribe who dwelt near Bangor a thousand years ago" 7457
"tribes, Frankish" 1444
"tribespeople question" 7545
"tributaries, hysterical crashing of" 7674
"tributaries of the Amazon" 473
"tributary of the Mohawk" 370
"tribute, day of" 1565
"tribute from my fantasy" 2795
"tribute of chips" 3969
"tribute of spermatazoa" 7996
Tributes 1565, 2795, 7996
"tributes to his greatness, as so many" 6308
"trick, more or less adroitly performed the" 14
"trick, played a cruel" 7053
"trick, scurvy" 3812
"trick of the rubber, final" 4000
"trick prearranged with Consolidated Edison" 5321
"tricked in some way" 1801
"trickles and splashes, drying in" 7052
Tricks 3287, 3293, 7045, 7053
"tricky, it's very" 506
Tridib 6159
"tried for the murder of Breckenridge Lansing" 3407
"tried somebody else, he might have" 1106
"tried to get my little brother off the chain gang" 8227
"tries, it took eight" 2873
"Trieste, on his way to" 8865
"Trieste harbor" 8106
"trifles, events are decided by" 4468
"triggerman who looked like a toy" 4260
"*Trikkala*, the" 8987
"trilled, redbird" 726
"trim, carpenter-Gothic" 3218
"trim, what they call cream" 9162
"trim, white stone" 3113
Trinh, Corporal 3371
"Trinidad" 2239
"Trinidad Rise, towering" 7940
"Trinita di Monte" 2225
"Trinity, tutor of" 3376
"Trinity Term" 1410
"trinkets, old" 2021
"Trinovantes, Paramount Chief of the" 5431
"trip, business" 9580
"trip, end of the" 4493
"trip, planned a" 6939
"trip, this is an ill-fated" 7026
"trip, this the" 9645
"trip, took a miniature" 9646

"trip every time I pass the house" 4278

"trip to Africa" 9566

"trip to Kentucky, real-estate" 2971

"trip to the moon, Theodor Herzl's" 9040

"tripe, poring over that" 7358

"tripods hung with red hurricane-lamps" 10930

"Tripoli" 155

Tripp, Richard 6465

"tripped up the somewhat imposing steps" 9875

"tripper on a low-fare excursion to the Delphic Oracle" 6896

Trips 1308, 6939, 7026, 9566, 9645, 9646

Tristan 1151

Tristessa 7996

"Tristram, Submarine" 8128

"trite but true" 7163

"triumph, day of" 1565

"triumph, day of his" 3741

"triumph in the world, the most civil" 9510

"triumph of Christianity" 7503

"'Triumph of Death, The'" 962

"triumphant" 652

"triumphant, law and order" 2045

"triumphant, stupidly" 434

"triumphant the execution, the more" 2035

"triumphant throughout the colony" 10469

"triumphantly, threw it" 6669

"trodden into rags" 7753

"troika, they were in a" 2794

"Troizen, Citadel of" 9227

"Trojans, wives and daughters of the" 9738

"Trojans washed their splendid garments in the days of peace" 9738

"trolls and hobgoblins" 5588

"troop of first-class passengers" 8072

"troops, carried among his" 4469

"troops, French" 9559

"Troops, O. C." 8677

"troops drilling, Imperial" 8700

"Troop-Ship *Georgic*" 8677

"tropic suns, a dozen" 10494

"Tropical Disturbance, Miss" 9086

"tropical rainforest" 10718

"tropical rains" 5052

"tropical rainstorm" 7339

"tropics, in the" 2261

"trots eager ahead" 10377

Trott, Miss 6144

"trotted the huge mahogany-and-snow collie" 412

"trotters" 246

Trouble 50, 61, 279, 400, 620, 628, 631, 1475, 1490, 2426, 3297, 3608, 4159, 4221, 4258, 5802,

5868, 6173, 6506, 6711, 6929, 8191, 8520, 9902, 10487

"trouble, are you in" 6421

"trouble, grinning face of" 50

"trouble, guns and" 4258

"trouble, he smelled" 8520

"Trouble, I have great" 4221

"trouble, I've never been anything but" 6711

"trouble, in" 1490

"trouble, in for" 6506

"trouble, knew I was in" 5868

"trouble, never expected" 8191

"trouble, show some sign of being in" 9902

"trouble, sick or in" 57

"trouble, start of this" 631

"trouble, that was the" 10487

"trouble, the" 5705

"trouble, their" 5802

"trouble, then there was" 3608

"trouble, they may get into frightful" 6173

"trouble, you're giving us" 2426

"trouble began with their parents' divorce" 6663

"trouble comes, when" 61

"trouble got started" 620

"trouble himself" 1833

"trouble of thinking or acting for myself, save me the" 3356

"trouble placing it with a publisher" 5477

"trouble started, the" 628

"trouble was brewing" 400

"trouble with an Orphanage upbringing" 9718

"trouble with fiction, the" 5436

"trouble with our republic, having all this" 279

"trouble with the lift" 3297

"trouble working with patients" 7174

"trouble you were after, if it was" 4159

"troubled if it had known, in the least" 1373

"troubled me, it" 10969

"troubled summer" 2550

"troubled times" 1475

Troubles 56, 67, 9265

"troubles" 6163

"troubles, concealing his" 56

"troubles, everybody in the world's had his own" 9265

"troubles, thinking of her" 2070

"troubles began in January" 67

"troubles I had to go through, recitation of the" 9265

"troublesome summer" 6026

"troubling dream" 10127

"trousers, baggy looseness of his" 5901

"trousers, corduroy" 4789

"trousers, dropped his" 7858

"trousers, fine wool" 7229

"trousers, she nearly always wore" 10833

"trousers of blue jeans" 954

"trousers were creased" 2840

Trout 7834

Trout, Eva 6913

Trout, Kilgore 7145

Trout, Mr. Ephraim 1687

"trout, curving like a" 10299

"Trout Fishing in America" 8945

"Trout Wapshott and Edelstein" 1687

"Trovatore, an aria from" 4121

"Troy" 1431, 4463

"Troy, city of" 2603, 10871

"truancy spree, on a" 7898

"Truce of God" 6361

"truck, burnt-out" 3056

"truck, canoe on top of the" 10960

"truck, drove the" 3411

"truck, falling off the top of a" 9769

"truck, farm" 1775

"truck, gentian blue home-painted thirty-hundredweight" 5184

"truck, giant orange garbage" 9823

"truck, hay" 9541

"truck, parked the" 5724

"truck, pickup" 3933

"truck, rattling old" 1191

"truck, Sanitation Department" 3002

"truck, swerved the" 3045

"truck, United States Army" 9813

"truck, watching the" 6165

"truck, wouldn't fit in the" 6150

"truck carrying a number of migratory workers" 25

"truck coming from the opposite direction" 3040

"truck driver stopped on a highway" 3023

"truck missed us by two feet or less" 9803

"truck rocking and pitching" 1680

"truck sliding on the ice" 9823

"trucker picked him up" 10912

Trucks 25, 1191, 3002, 3023, 3040, 3411, 5184, 6165, 7328, 9769, 9791, 9798, 9803, 9813, 9817, 9823, 9967

"trucks, abandoned" 9539

"trucks, gravel" 9201

"trucks, sad rusted carcasses of cannibalized" 5982

"trucks, the" 3615

"trucks, two stake" 10076

"trucks in Highway 52, heard the" 5916

Trudel, Jack 2970

"trudge, began the" 6574

"trudge from claim to claim" 5456

True 10673

"true, if it were only" 3340

"true, it is" 2399

"true, it may be" 3633

"true, it would not be strictly" 7588
"true, not strictly" 5486
"true, pretty much" 10508
"true, that had not been" 3777
"true, what I now know to be" 2734
"true life experience" 7884
"true story" 9041
"true to the rules of their type" 5694
"trump, leading a" 6308
Trumpelman, I. C. 1698
"trumps, pour in their" 3376
"truncheon, special constable's" 6993
"trundled west from Hereford" 8457
"trunk, gnarled" 9674
"trunk, small" 9525
"trunks" 3094
"trunks, ragged" 3894
"trunks, tangle of great" 3899
"trunks and boxes, opened" 4154
"Truro" 6894, 8632
"Trust, National" 3160, 3692
"trust a one of them, I don't" 9684
"trust each other" 9685
"trust his own skepticism" 9688
"trust in God" 7447
"trust me" 9686
"trust nothing, you can" 9689
"trust that man and herself" 9687
"trust them anymore, she didn't" 9690
"trust water, I" 9691
"trusted, a morning not to be" 2277
"trustees, her two" 10771
"trusting her natural power to wake him" 2765
Truth 496, 625, 1684, 2734, 4240, 4490, 4501, 5212, 5216, 5345, 5562, 5595, 5950, 6798, 9007, 9041, 9713, 9890, 10508, 10882, 10999
"truth" 4501
"truth, awkward but undeniable" 625
"truth, convincing image of the" 5345
"truth, full" 9692
"truth, herein set down the" 9694
"truth, honesty enough to tell the" 4490
"truth, I shall never have the courage to tell the" 2734
"truth, if you want to know the" 9706
"truth, in" 10882
"truth, in literal" 2403
"truth, only sad" 5595
"truth, professional searcher after" 6478
"truth, rarely the whole" 5226
"truth, respect" 9713
"truth, say the" 288
"truth, supposedly unassailable" 6798
"truth, tell the" 1984

"truth, tried to find out the" 9700
"Truth, turn upon the poles of" 5562
"truth, youth is" 10999
"truth about a man's life, I will tell you the" 5950
"truth about Hector Cabot" 9700
"truth about his love for women, I will tell you the" 5950
"truth about the man I was going to visit" 9890
"truth about the slashed portrait" 496
"truth around, scattering" 9702
"truth as an old hobbled unicorn" 9696
"truth as I saw it" 9694
"truth enough for everyone else" 9702
"truth enough for one family, if its" 9702
"truth is, the" 1684
"Truth is a matter of the imagination" 9698
"truth is more compelling" 5216
"truth lies, harder to discern where" 5212
"truth of it, knew the" 4108
"truth of it, the" 9007
"truth of it, whatever the" 1167
"truth of the matter" 4573
"truth of this odd matter" 9692
"Truth Seekers did to us there" 9435
"truth stood tall on battlements of commonsense and right reason" 9701
"truth to the rumor" 7834
"truth universally acknowledged" 5726
"truth was held in about the same esteem as anyone's old partner" 4240
Truthfulness 6634
"truths, those sad" 6517
Truttwell, John 6503
"try" 1542
"try, I will" 9697
"try, thought I'd give it a" 8027
"*try* them raw, we should at least" 3853
"try to be honest, I honestly will" 9697
"trying to cross Avenida Atlântica" 1762
"trying to explain" 6051
"tryout with the genuine St. Louis Cardinals" 8934
"Tsar, helped assassinate the" 10837
"Tsar's incontiguous and barbarous northeastern possessions" 3514
"Tsé Lani" 7612
Ts'its'tsi'nako 9445
Tu 6327
"tub, hot" 573

"tubbed, after he had been" 3272
"Tube railway" 9381
"tubs, large wooden" 4286
"tubs, you've got the blue" 9899
Tuby, Dr. Owen 4644
Tuby, Owen 6443
"tuck them under a rug of white foam" 7680
"tucked away in a narrow side street, too modestly" 1025
"tucked carelessly into his socks" 1501
"tucked snugly around him" 8376
"tucked the bedcovers about his shoulders" 3705
"tucked under the right arm" 413
Tucker 1277
Tucker, Ike 9106
tuckoo, baby 961
"Tucson" 6058
"Tudor sovereigns" 1335
"Tuesday, wet and soggy" 3657
"tug, black" 8104
"tug, old converted coal-fired steam" 8135
"Tug Hill country" 9128
"tug was pushing midriver" 1479
"tugged hugely by the whole might of ocean" 435
"tugs swarming about her" 8072
"Tuileries, the" 3144
"Tuileries gardens" 10037
"tuition, my" 10910
"Tulagi" 406
"tulasi, divine" 7515
"Tule, San Ignacio del" 9483
"tulip plant, small appealing" 9664
"Tulip Tree, the" 7079
"tulips made a brave show" 8259
Tull, Pearl 9456
Tully 7257
"tumbleweed field" 4694
"tumbling down the stairs" 24
"tumbling from the heavens" 2427
"tumult, in a" 373
"tumultuous territory" 4039
Tunbridge, Freddy 9873
"Tunbridge" 2943
"tundra, thawing" 2227
Tune, Cousin 4595
"tune, out of" 4335
"tune, tinselly Hawaiian" 6216
"tune, words of the" 8739
"tune lacked, all that the" 6218
"tune on the fiddle" 6218
"tune that came drifting back" 8739
"tuned up tonight" 8867
"tunes, fragments of old" 7386
"tunes in to himself with both ears" 7628
"tunic, wore his" 3812
"tuning their instruments" 1680
Tunis 7962
"tunnel, cold stale darkness of a" 9833

"tunnel, dark dank dead-ended subterranean" 4319
"tunnel, down the" 10190
"Tunnel, Holland" 10912
"tunnel, swallowed up by a" 9788
"tunnel in my chest" 4894
"tunnel they were passing through" 7474
"tunnelled carefully through the blankets" 10190
"tunnels, engulfed in" 7279
"Tunxis village green" 4155
Tuppence 913
"tuppence" 1085
"Tupperware party" 10559
"turban to match" 2832
"turbans, hair in" 5190
"turbulent night" 10285
"turbulent twilight" 8789
"turbulent white-capped frenzy" 7304
"turf, bracken-free spread of close-cropped" 3692
"turf, short fine elastic" 3634
"turf, sweet" 5020
"Turin" 9659
"Turkey, Sultan of" 4172
"Turkey Fleet" 120
"turkeys, raising" 3662
"turkeys, twenty young" 9753
"Turkish bath" 4504
"Turkish craftsman" 717
"Turkish police" 6955
Turmoil 2177, 5105
"turmoil and self-destruction" 2177
"turn, Father O'Flynn's" 1511
"turn, in your" 2337
"turn, it's Frank's" 8
"turn, whose" 3028
"turn and look" 10004
"turn it in" 10049
"turn my head, made me" 1104
"turn off and drive through the town" 3014
"turn signals, like" 2859
Turnbull 5919
Turnbull, Bunny 1840
"turned around and went home" 1784
"turned away from me" 10025
"turned away from the window" 4160, 9326
"turned away to take the delectable Lida's slender arm" 2044
"turned back, then" 9635
"turned back to Dr. Vollmer" 10010
"turned carefully off the main road" 3042
"turned down on the grounds that I was incompetent" 6475
"turned from a simple pest into a dangerous man" 6168
"turned from her daughter's face" 6784

"turned from one steep muddy lane to another" 8212
"turned from the stove to face him" 4983
"turned his head to dart a glance at me" 10010
"turned his office into his home" 6140
"turned in at about this time, she always" 1178
"turned into the Square" 1606
"turned into Upshot Rise" 9164
"turned like a defensive animal" 8174
"turned off Great Road" 3178
"turned off the motor" 2974
"turned off the Turnpike" 2978
"turned on her pillow" 10117
"turned out" 372
"turned out, man well" 2823
"turned out in the end, the way the thing" 1225
"turned out of Midland Street" 1609
"turned out the light" 1078
"turned over" 10116
"turned over and opened one eye" 10224
"turned over on his stomach" 10206
"turned over to her husband" 10174
"turned round, when I" 5109
"turned the corner" 5321
"turned the ignition key of his car" 9805
"turned the wicks down" 5332
"turned to her left" 10439
"turned up the gravel path" 2984
Turner 9300
Turner, Big Joe 8744
Turner, Emily Stockwell 2146
Turner, Job 2726
Turner, Mary 6177
Turner, May 10809
Turner, Miss 4546
Turner, Mr. John 5804
Turner, Richard 6177
"turning abruptly to the violinist" 6215
"turning again in her chair" 4118
"turning around, without even" 2402
"turning at will" 5604
"turning back, no" 1743
"turning back again to plod onwards" 4164
"turning down Cinnamon Alley" 9175
"turning from his books" 98
"turning her head briefly" 4164
"turning his face towards the wall" 2343
"turning once more to the morning's news" 6311
"turning over and over" 4660
"turning over in bed" 10128
"turning over in my mind" 6625

"turning quick upon me" 9510
"[turning] skepticism to sorrow" 4116
"turnips, sack of winter" 10347
Turnlung 4786
"turn-out, good" 3599
"turnovers, buy one of them" 7567
"turnpike, along the" 4137
"turnpike, San Leandro" 9116
"Turnpike, turned off the" 2978
"turnpike stretches its dusty hot and interminable length" 9116
"turns, taking the" 40
"turns, wild tender and distant by" 1986
"turns on the lavatory, waited their" 8869
"turnstile, came through the" 10054
"turnstile where the tickets were taken" 9215
"turn-to-the-sun" 10899
"turpentine, dripped" 3760
Turtle, Mr. 3297
"turtle" 1271
"turtle, old man" 7235
"turtle, snapping" 4691
"turtle as big as a saddle" 4691
"turtleneck, old cotton" 6547
"Tuscany" 2236
"Tuscaroras" 3902
Tussy 7592
"tutor of Trinity" 3376
"tutor read the *Iliad* of Homer" 5431
"tutorial session, first" 7459
"tuxedo, satin-lapel" 2863
"TV, watching loud" 6783
"TV audience" 6478
"Tweed" 274
"tweeds, changed hurriedly into his" 9724
"tweeds, form-fitting" 1610
"twelve twice, he was" 871
"twenties, in his early" 4291
"twentieth-century nightmare" 3392
"twenty, hardly more than" 5993
"twenty today, I am" 848
Twentyman 10935
"Twickenham" 1112
"twigs outside the bathroom window, bare elm" 7318
Twilight 1770, 2189, 2212, 2219, 2234, 2239, 5149, 8390, 8443, 8596
"twilight" 2234
"twilight, approaching the time of" 2189
"twilight, cool porphyry-tinted" 1300
"twilight, early" 521
"twilight, in the" 7699, 8940
"twilight, it was the hour of" 8263
"twilight, long" 960
"twilight, midwinter" 8584
"twilight, pale in the" 2219
"twilight, savage violet" 5149
"twilight, snowy" 8596

"twilight, steel and silver" 2196
"twilight, there is no such thing as" 2239
"twilight, thickening" 1770
"twilight, turbulent" 8789
"twilight, troubled" 1184
"twilight, vast web of" 5620
"twilight, with the" 8443
"twilight between darknesses, a grudged measure of" 2273
"twilight comes between the sudden shift from light to dark" 2239
"twilight had been forgotten, as though" 2235
"twilight in the island" 2239
"twilight in the rain forest of Sarawak" 4109
"twilight lay upon the landings" 9406
"twilight of his house" 10180
"twilight translucent" 5620
"twilight was like deep pale water" 2212
"twilight's tranquil charm" 8390
Twillig, Little Billy 9594
"twin, bad" 8239
"twin, hadn't known he was a" 8228
"twin, his" 8213
"twin, with her came her" 7058
"twin brother, my" 255
"Twin Cities" 9730
"twin dies, if one" 8244
"twin elements" 8412
"twinkle, in his eye a" 7505
"twinkle in her cornflower eyes" 4176
"twinkled her eyes and teeth" 1432
"twinkling of an eye" 7536
"twinkling with water" 5141
Twins 255, 7058, 8207, 8213, 8228, 8233, 8239, 8244, 9440
"twins" 8207
"twins, Conway" 9440
"twins, in to see the" 543
"twins, inseparable" 7164
"twins, mistaken for" 8233
"twins, the" 1236
"twirling the eye end between his fingers" 8760
"twirling the register, deftly" 10920
"twist, came with a nasty" 9289
"twist, with a sliding" 1110
"twisted and danced in an everchanging mirage" 4410
"twisted in his saddle" 7809
"twisted the dial" 6331
"twisting and turning like sheets that are squeezed and wrung out" 7320
"twisting its way among fat bluffs" 9140
"twitch, gave the ignition a resigned" 2974
"twitched in his muscles" 5603
Twitchel, Deacon 9348

"two of them" 1987
"Two Medicine country" 9494
"two-by-four nailed across the doorway" 10949
"two-faced place" 6920
Twombly, Mr. 10169
"Tyburn, England had her" 7179
"Tydd" 4069
Tyler, Edward 867
Tyner, McCoy 10085
Tyner, Nolen 5960
"type, I'm not the" 8200
"type, in smaller" 1915
"type easily, I" 13
"type so blurred and poor, printed in" 898
"typed the last sentence of the novel" 5541
"typescript, two piles of" 9961
"typewriter, his" 5292
"typewriter, my portable" 10415
"typewriter, portable" 1629
"typewritten foolscap" 5415
"typhoid fever" 1342
"*Typhoon*, sloop" 8569
"typhoon in a thimble" 7869
"typical, it was" 6345
"typical, least" 3122
"typical act" 8674
"typing, closely covered with" 7355
"typing his report" 2251
"tyranny, vigilance of" 5554
"Tyrant of the Seas" 7801
Tyrell, Major 3097
"Tyrol" 1396
"Tyrol, the" 8596
"Tyrolean Alps, summits of the" 8389
Tyrrell, Miss Paula 3989
"Tyrrhenian Sea" 7909
Tzu 8388

U Po Kyin 4378
"Uast, mighty city of" 7799
Udal, Magister 8346
Udal, Magister Nicholas 4668
"Ufford, the" 1921
"Uganda" 2605
"Uganda, Western" 1833
Ugliness 554, 5916, 6534, 9229
"ugliness, restless" 1379
"ugliness, saw the signboards and the" 5916
"ugly, his is very" 6534
"ugly, thought all babies" 554
"ugly one, a peculiarly" 3153
"UK, living in the" 6147
"Ukari, plain of" 10709
"ulaq, entrance of the" 8387
"ulcerated danger zone" 286
Ulevik, Nils 6219
Ulli 7074
Ulrich, His Royal and Religious Highness Crown Prince 4583

"Ulster" 2386
Ultima 5156
Ultima, La 10871
"ultimate historical value" 2532
"ultimo, 13th" 5387
"ultramarine, change into an" 9542
Ulysses 4465
Umberto 6655
"umbrella, shared an" 3940
"umbrella, without an" 1055
"umbrellas, jog of" 7317
"umbrellas under his arm, three" 1294
"Umbria" 1473
"unaccustomed hour" 647
"unaddicted" 8841
"unagrarian Eastern travellers" 5129
"unanimous voice of our people" 7801
"unanswered, her written question" 7197
"unavoidable, it is indeed" 5414
"unaware, caught" 891
"unaware, completely" 6467
"unawareness, pass their lives in" 3671
"unbearably thrilling" 5881
"unborn, the yet" 6991
"unborn, to the as-yet-" 5266
"unborn Sternholzes, innumerable" 6472
"unburdened" 5077
"uncanny agility" 5997
"uncertain as to what they were supposed to be doing" 686
"uncertain start" 6755
"uncertain thing, it was such an" 3466
Uncertainty 2751, 4809, 10498
"uncertainty, already there is an" 4809
"uncertainty, new" 4549
"uncertainty, wandered in labyrinths of" 10498
"uncertainty of sublunary enjoyment" 9989
"uncertainty touched one and then another of her friends" 10121
"unchaperoned" 7772
"uncharted region beyond dreamland" 10131
"uncle, an" 6170
"uncle, aunt and" 2573
"uncle, dying" 4604
"uncle, her" 3025, 5428
"uncle, her defrocked" 10894
"uncle, his" 3451, 10426
"uncle, just like your" 5925
"uncle, maternal" 5753
"uncle, my" 1955, 3221, 3233, 3275, 4719, 6496, 6568, 6939, 9514
"uncle, my maternal" 1050
"uncle, Peter's" 798
"uncle, your" 9903

"uncle from Rome" 10674
"uncle had been dead for only half a day" 2329
"Uncle Junk" 5848
"Uncle Sam ain't no woman" 8745
Uncles 138, 1050, 10674
"uncles, his" 837
"uncles began to come home" 1277
"uncomfortable" 3584, 9275
"uncomfortable, made him feel" 3486
"uncomfortable, most" 7513
"uncomplaining" 7290
"uncomplaining who have gone to Sabrina beneath the tides" 14
"unconcerned" 7229
"unconscionably, he kept her" 9325
"unconscious" 32
"unconscious, man had lain" 2405
"unconscious for sixty-three days" 2353
"unconsciously lifted, faces all" 8072
"unconsciousness, state of" 10286
"unconstitutional way, acting in an" 7817
"uncouth an appellation" 8955
"uncultivated space" 3906
Uncumber 4167
"Undead, land of the" 324
"undemocratic, so you think it" 10558
"under the maples" 10383
"under water, as if from" 10300
"underbelly of Europe, soft" 5026
"underbrush" 3458, 3899
"underclothes were white, her" 2864
"underdeveloped country" 6262
"underdrawers, young girl's" 5355
"underfoot the earth was half frozen" 521
"undergraduate condition, crushing melancholy of the" 3276
"undergraduate paper" 5530
"undergraduates, black-gowned" 10441
"undergraduates, seventy or eighty" 7876
"undergraduates, young" 7772
"undergraduates who were waiting" 7239
"underground, discover something" 2607
"Underground, he came out of the" 10375
"underground and up the chute with a roar" 7990
"underground prison" 7146
Underhill, Captain John 356
"underprivileged children" 10826
"undershorts, white Jockey" 8384
"underside of the world, on the precarious" 2966
"understand, could never" 684
"understand, did not" 372
"understand, I never could" 1340

"understand, one must try to" 5060
"understand, thing I can't" 6038
"understand, you got to" 9372
"understand, you would" 4354
"understand America" 271
"understand and forgive" 10762
"understand him, he didn't always" 5664
"understand how it happened" 5123
"understand machinery, she could never" 5690
"understand me, you never" 6721
"understand pleasantries, does not" 360
"understand the gravity of our situation" 78
"understand the meaning" 7194
"understand the world, I do not" 2399
"understand this, she could never" 8717
"understand what has happened to us, I am trying to" 7400
"understand why, I can't" 676
"understand why I don't" 7353
"understand you, I don't" 3929
"understandable" 3307
Understanding 78, 91, 477, 2675, 3345, 3524, 4884, 5002, 5060, 5123, 5664, 5676, 5690, 6635, 7194, 7400, 9009, 10077, 10761, 10762, 10849, 10872
"understanding all at once why I'd been so sad" 2675
"understanding grin" 837
"understanding I had, offer the little" 1929
"understanding of my narrative, may help you to a better" 698
"understatement" 4418
"understatement, it's no" 5595
"understood, but have never" 4549
"understood, everyone" 2918
"understood, he partly" 10872
"understood, I have never" 2671
"understood, investigated and" 2600
"understood the foundation-work of a House" 6613
"understood the meaning of 'bad' and 'good'" 6635
"understood the price" 5676
"understood them, liked the words because he" 8760
"understood what they were thinking and saying" 477
"undertake the expedition" 7234
"undertaker" 6420
"undertaker, red-haired" 2349
"undertaker's mute, unemployed" 6993
Undertakings 242, 1542, 4457, 7216
"undertakings, adventurous" 5018
"undertakings established in France" 1015

"undertone of the breeze, a whispered" 8499
"underwater light, glittery" 2782
"underwear, cheap" 10395
"underwear, long" 5929
"underwear, magician's" 2609
"underwear, something like long" 2855
"underwear has just been found in a cardboard suitcase" 2609
"underworld, darkness of the" 1593
"Undir Hofdi church" 3661
"undisguised satisfaction" 7468
"undone by love" 10765
"undress, too tired even to" 3685
"undressed before climbing into the tub" 568
"undressed slowly" 8027
Undressing 1215, 2884, 6386, 6388
"undressing, left Tony" 9471
"undressing in the bushes" 6388
"undressing just outside the pale pool of candle-light" 6386
"undulant steps" 2107
"undulations of buttock" 7985
"uneasiness, sense of vague" 135
"uneasy, restless and" 743
"uneasy feeling" 1675
"uneasy sleep" 10132
"unenslaved, a morrow" 6361
"unessentials, mounting collection of" 6150
"unexpected obstacle" 44
"unexpectedly, arrived so" 8180
"unexpectedly, quite" 794
"unexpectedly one cold March night" 1985
"unexplored, long" 6066
"unfair, life was monstrously" 5250
"unfamiliar situation" 5295
"unfit, had suddenly become" 796
"unfit to be sat upon, admirably" 484
"unforgiving souls" 5914
"unfortunately for him" 119
"unfurl in my mind" 8488
"unfurling its million waves" 7921
"ungrateful" 6884
"unGreek" 8894
Unhappiness 1268, 2500, 6165
"unhappiness, happiness and" 1342
"unhappy" 6165
"unhappy day, it had been an" 2500
"unheard behind the scrubby foothills" 10701
"unhygienic" 1376
"unicorn, old hobbled" 9696
"unicorn, the" 430
"unicorn when he saw one, knew a" 3274
"uniform, blue" 3190
"uniform, brown and yellow" 4183
"uniform, gaudy" 8650
"uniform of the company" 5926

"uniform shirt, unfamiliar black and green" 8674
"uniforms, gray cotton" 7133
"uniforms of Yankee blue" 4486
"unilluminated as yet" 7761
"unimpeachably erect" 215
"unimportant, joined the ranks of the" 9744
"uninitiated, the" 1008
"Union, States of the" 7657
"union meeting" 4013
"Union Square is surrounded" 6061
"Unionville Tennessee" 1422
"unique, each in its own way was" 3450
"unique, in our own way we were rather" 6288
"unique, think this" 9585
"unique in its way, each" 3242
"unison, going green in" 3402
"united in resistance" 10470
"United Nations" 6986
"United States" 269, 3151, 5713, 6155, 6407, 7007, 8875, 9518
"United States, Army of the" 8672
"United States, ex-President of the" 7000
"United States, history of the" 4030
"United States, left the" 9517
"United States, on my way to the" 10506
"United States, people of the" 10495
"United States, president of the" 1467
"United States, territories of the" 262
"United States Army" 1529, 6441
"United States Army truck" 9813
"United States Navy" 5417
"United States of America" 268, 361, 1360, 2310, 6439, 6982, 10193
"United States Ship *Eel*" 570
"unity is a figment of the imagination" 6906
Universe 528, 534, 2630, 5479
"universe, close to the center of the" 3605
"Universe, Creator of the" 8501
"universe, crepuscular buzz of the" 8333
"universe, dead center of the" 3592
"Universe, Lord of the" 2638
"universe, lovable human" 6883
"universe, mad dogs of the" 3716
"universe, navel of the" 4646
"universe, this astronomical" 6001
"universe known to me in the year 1864" 3359
"universe like our own, each a" 528
"universe of stench and shrill" 10377
"Universities, matriculating at the" 3528
"Universities, Oxford and Edinburgh" 9076

"university" 8880
"university, American" 9657
"University, Brandeis" 7896
"University, Centennial State" 7881
"University, Grant" 2568
"University, Harvard" 3333, 6491
"University, Hebrew" 6279
"university, left our" 10500
"University, Louisiana State" 7498
"University, Oxford" 7801
"university, reverting to the" 3276
"university, the" 6630
"University, the" 6427, 6451
"University, The" 8886
"University, Winona" 8907
"University, Winthrop" 7899
"University, Yale" 9531
"University of California" 940
"University of London" 3266
"University of Missouri" 7890
"university of Oxford, just left the" 2087
"University's West Bank" 10896
"unjust, just people and" 1342
"unkempt, not at all" 6894
"unknown, he was not" 3531
"unknown, in source" 7648
"unknown, it can never be" 5061
"unknown, tramp my fifteen miles into the" 6560
"unknown to me then" 5580
"unknown to the general tourist" 9515
"unleashing waves" 7939
"unlike so many of the men he served with" 322
"unloaded at a dock in Montreal" 10935
"unlock his front door" 1784
"unlocked his front door" 1574
"unlucky, I was so" 1161
"unlucky, lucky or" 5542
"unmarried and being chased by a Russian choir" 2756
"unmarried daughters" 6545
"unmindful of the inquisitive glances" 3499
"unmitigatedly hideous house" 3123
"unnoticed, not entirely" 4446
"unobtrusively trying to maneuver himself" 989
"unpacked" 9592
"unpacked in her new lodgings" 6116
Unpacking 6116, 9609
"unpardonable gesture" 6232
"unpaved, remained" 9148
"unpleasant, not in themselves" 5607
"unpleasant, something quite" 9965
"unprecedented" 5416
"unpretentious" 5416
"unpretentious architecture" 5607
"unpretentious public house" 4315
"Unpromised Land" 6136

"unpropitious, my birth was" 358
"unquestioning" 7198
"unreachable by camel caravan" 1429
"unread, better lay it aside" 5401
"unreality, mysteriously enveloped by" 10352
"unreality, that curious sense of" 10173
"unreality, this world is the" 6842
"unreason, bent hairpins of" 7516
"unreliable" 4201
"unrepentant" 4583
"unrolled slowly, it" 5717
"unsaid, once said it cannot be" 8898
"unseasonably warm" 9774
"unsheathed his knife" 10541
"unsociable, perpendicular and" 8841
"unsophisticated" 9102
"unspotted from the world" 1375
"unsteadily, a little" 2924
"unsuccessful rebellion" 7184
"unsure of the implications" 10233
"untamed hearts" 8993
"untamed thing" 2796
"unthreading itself from the knotted mass of gray-green mountains" 9141
"untidy, so" 6431
"untidy man, a very" 5985
"untoward was to happen to him, anything" 405
"untravelled" 9102
"untroubled sleep" 10312
"untrue, being" 9893
"untrue to say, it would be" 8657
"unturned, hoped to remain" 4613
"unusual, facing anything" 10800
"unusual, one of the more" 7461
"unusual activity" 641
"unusual associations" 7772
"unusual happened, nothing" 1261
"unwatched" 5295
"unwealthy" 9381
"unwell, his wife Anne was" 135
"unwillingly" 813
"unwon, a war worth leaving" 10535
"unwrapped himself" 7480
"unwrapping glassware" 6143
"up, what's" 2094
"up at dawn, you must be" 8112
"up before me" 7984
"up earlier than usual" 10268
"up or down, no" 9319
"up to down, change in the wind from" 4871
"up to her scant eyebrows" 5372
"up with the lark, you'll have to be" 6565
"up yonder" 7316
Upbringing 3365, 3671, 4240
"upbringing, Orphanage" 9718

"upbringing, puppyish protected" 9708
"upchuck" 7990
"upchucked, she ran into the downstairs bathroom and" 2677
"upheaval, extreme" 5118
"upholstery, interior" 5129
"upland, remote" 9628
"upland on the west, pleasant" 1336
"upland valleys of Tuscany" 2236
"Uplands, Southern" 10391
"upper deck, the" 9556
"upper deck, they were gone from the" 10831
"Upper Peninsula" 4073
"upperclassmen" 1214
"upriver, moved" 8070
"uproar, the general" 8773
"uproar of iron-shod wheels and hooves on granite blocks" 9130
"Upshot Rise" 9164
"upstairs, come" 2317
"upstairs, sent" 8756
"upstairs, went slowly" 9406
"upstairs for a little, I am going" 9866
"upstairs she went, straight" 9873
"up-to-date" 9233
Upton, Donald 8686
"Upton-on-Severn" 5067
"Urals, the" 6061, 10518
Urban, Father 1303
"urban development" 1931
"urchins, howling" 957
"urged their mounts into the forest" 10541
"urgencies and agonies, the city's vast" 3429
Urgency 4918, 9998
"urgency of contradicting a dream" 4701
"urgency too, a certain" 9017
"urgent, always" 9998
"urgent, made my need more" 10102
"urgent as love" 2106
"urgent domestic business" 8694
"urgent voices in the trees" 10743
"urging her to hasten" 4162
"urging him monotonously on" 3690
Urgrossmuttchi 7403
Urination 380, 437, 3023, 4177, 7047
"urine, smell of stale" 8521
"urn, crumbling stone" 5162
"uroboros" 5479
"urologist in New York, the best" 6892
Ursula 2658
"us, about" 7954
"us, each and every one of" 5699
"*us*, not quite one of" 5919
"U.S. 40" 4577
"U.S. Senate, run for the" 7831
"U.S. 61" 3730

"U.S. Virgins" 9614
"U.S.A." 276, 5452
"U.S.A., old violent beloved" 7205
Usaph 1985
"use, of little" 6551
"use it, if you can not" 271
"use of my limbs, lost the" 2894
"used to Clay County, just barely getting" 6136
"used to it" 3374
"used to it, she was never able to get" 4754
"used-car lot" 1047
"useful, I consider it at least" 4929
"usefulness, outlived its" 3184
"usefulness, surviving their own" 7819
"ushered him into the Assistant Secretary's office" 6506
"ushered in the day" 3680
"ushered into the waiting-room" 949
"usurping space" 6512
"Utah, southwest" 10452
Utch 3277
Utchka 3277
"ute going outside, Dad has the" 9818
"utility, got into the" 2961
"utility company, a large" 6471
"utilize instead of use" 8870
"Utopia" 7816
"Uttamussack, Indian village of" 10451
"utter exhaustion" 8455
"utterance, so scornful an" 10900
"uttering this indignant exclamation" 6610
Utterson, Mr. 5889
Utz, Kaspar Joachim 2424

"Vaal, the" 5456
"vacancy, aimed at" 215
"vacant and preoccupied expression" 5424
"vacation, pretend that this was any other" 4579
Vacations 929, 932, 938, 1422, 2018, 2906, 3180, 3398, 3496, 3515, 3601, 3621, 4269, 4376, 4579, 4581, 4639, 4656, 4893, 5024, 5035, 5053, 5122, 6003, 6544, 6911, 7130, 8642
"vacations were automatic" 9735
"Vacaville, little town of" 4374
"vaccination, tenth day of" 3683
"vacuity of the empyrean" 10903
"vagabond" 4970
"vagabond, idle" 4971
"vaginal lips, quiver like" 2941
"vagrant, branded and denounced as a" 358
"vagrants" 8886
"vague as a headache" 260

Vaiden, Colonel Miltiades 6979
Vaiden, Jimmie 3098
Vail, Susan 500
"vainglory, in hidden" 3516
Val 10404, 10713
"vale, shallow" 1576
"Vale, Blackmoor" 3072
"Vale, Blakemore" 3072
"Vale of Blakemore or Blackmoor" 10333
"valedictory letter" 6439
"*Valencia*, my favorite song is" 4736
"Valenciennes" 3931
Valentine 1093
Valentino, Rudolph 1982
"vales, hillocks and" 4486
"valet parking attendants" 1705
"valetudinarian" 6896
Valide, The Sultane 2411
"Valle del Sole" 633
Vallee, Rudy 6652
"Valletta, by the main gate of" 5229
"valley, along the rim of the" 9204
"valley, Athabaska" 9747
"valley, away down the" 10016
"valley, beautiful blue" 9748
"Valley, Bendigo" 9634
"Valley, Black" 9067
"valley, blue wide" 2949
"valley, channeled" 1713
"valley, chased Red Elk out of the" 6382
"Valley, Cherry" 7409
"valley, dark" 1353
"Valley, Doleham" 4385
"valley, far below in the" 8682
"valley, floor of the" 4374
"valley, from the" 650
"valley, gravel and cinder floor of the" 3422
"Valley, Happy" 4356
"valley, his beloved little" 9753
"valley, hot dry but immensely productive" 1357
"valley, in a little" 1421
"valley, in the" 5898, 7887
"valley, life forms of the" 9755
"valley, little" 7775, 9744, 10681
"valley, lofty" 8052
"valley, lonely Westmoreland" 9742
"valley, long" 9740
"valley, looking down into the" 3757
"Valley, Miracle" 6040
"valley, Penowell" 9545
"valley, protected" 9756
"valley, reaching the" 6069
"valley, river" 7242
"valley, rode into our" 9750
"Valley, Salinas" 9751
"Valley, Santa Brigida" 3089
"valley, shallow" 9533
"valley, shelter of the deep round" 1433
"Valley, Shoestring" 3105

"valley, situated in a" 9741
"valley, tawny Jabalón" 9995
"valley, the" 9219
"Valley, the" 6713
"valley, through a wooded" 7668
"Valley, Two River" 3676
"valley, unfertile" 4073
"Valley, Walden" 10623
"valley, went to see the" 9752
"valley, wide saucer-shaped" 9749
"valley below" 5142
"valley below, down into the night-ridden" 7290
"valley cup" 1398
"valley fairer than the Fairy Glen, there is no" 9745
"Valley Fields" 7109
"valley floor, flat" 7625
"Valley Forge" 1457
"valley . . . had lain unnoticed" 9744
"valley not very remote from the sea" 780
"valley of Polvosa, the rocky" 10693
"valley of the Big Dead River" 3129
"Valley of the Red Cedar" 9746
"valley of the Rising" 1408
"valley of the River Tillingham" 9134
"valley of the Whatsit River" 370
"valley spread out below, you can see the whole" 9754
"valley which had been the bed of a great river" 9743
Valleys 780, 1357, 4027, 5898, 9204, 9219, 9512, 9995, 10693
"valleys" 4027
"valleys, hills and" 3893
"valleys, in one of those beautiful" 9738
"valleys, moved up the" 10391
"valleys, portions of three" 4062
"valleys, rich" 6249
"valleys, rich green" 2950
"valleys, two" 6697
"valleys and plateaus" 6068
"valleys in Westmoreland, one of the wildest" 10767
"valleys of Tuscany, upland" 2236
"valleys of Westchester, one of the numerous little" 9512
"valleys through which the Thames . . . rolls a clear flood" 9738
Valoroso XXIV 1902
"valour was in the spring wind" 10590
"Valparaiso" 8058
"valuables" 1775
"valuables, in search of" 6177
"value, their" 5381
"value of precedent, he knew the" 3955
"value the artists and craftsmen" 5440
"valued, will come to be" 5440

"values, dispensed traditional" 8879
"values, sweeten all" 1448
"vampire, the" 9444
"vampire Lestat, I am the" 92
"Vampire Lestat here" 9058
"Vampire Lestat, I'm the" 3545
"vampire who became a super rock star" 3545
"vampires were knocking" 4114
"van, mail" 7328
"van, the" 9817
"van, removal" 6139
Van Leer, Rupert 2443
"vanaprasthi, I am now a" 6494
Van Brunt, Walter 6796
"Vancouver" 202
van der Rohe, Ludwig Mies 7882
Van de Weyer, Mario 6289
Vandover 7374
Vane, Harriet 8259
Vane, John 5080
Vane, Mr. Hilary 8970
Van Eyck, Mr. 10561
Van Gogh 7793
Van Gogh, Monsieur 10124
"Van Gogh's room" 7793
"vanilla" 5184
"vanish quickly in either direction if need be" 7221
"vanished, the female of the species" 2559
"vanished from this earth altogether" 2575
"vanished into the bush again" 6179
"vanished like a puff of grey smoke" 2557
"vanishing act" 2579
"vanishing into the belly of a petrified whale" 9788
"vanishing point, unnatural" 5180
Vanity 2634, 5885, 7964, 10765
"vanity" 2634, 5885, 10765
"vanity, height of" 362
"vanity, her mother's" 7482
"vanity is eager" 7964
"vanity is seldom successful" 7964
"vans and lorries" 9130
"vantage point, favourite summer" 847
"vantage slot" 6228
Vanya 5329
"vapor, faint opacity of" 2225
"vapor, sea of" 10260
"vaporetto to the Giudecca" 3709
"vaporous" 189
"vapour, acrid" 1356
"vapour streaming up from the clammy crowded streets" 1356
"vapours, swaying" 324
"vapours rolled along, partial" 5125
Vardoe, Mrs. 9426
"variance of light and shadow, a pleasing" 3981
"variation, end each" 6224
"variation in the style" 5607

"variations in serial form, a set of" 6224
"varied, most" 6908
"variety of objects, vast" 947
"varnish, many coats of" 1057
"varnished by the cold November rain" 7322
Vartan 1071
"Varva, Upper" 3901
"vassal" 6972
"Vassar '33" 10656
"vast as an ocean" 5132
"vast Hall" 4895
"vastness, sublimity connected with" 4032
"vasty heights and distances" 7754
"vat, shimmer off the" 189
"Vatican" 1523
Vaughan 2361
Vaughan, Bronwen 6953
Vaughan, Dennis 1088
"vault, sepulchral" 3984
Veasy, Al 4013
Vedh, Jai 365
"veers toward the dry lake bed" 9181
"vegetable" 3973
"vegetable, in the hospital for being a" 34
"vegetable, we have an excellent old" 10899
"vegetable nature, observers of" 9660
"vegetable rows, neatly spaced" 9430
"vegetable world" 2190
"vegetables, most intense of" 9679
"vegetation, examined the" 9676
"vehemence, resentful" 10927
"vehemence against the windows, [rain] drove with" 7305
"vehicle, curious" 9759
"vehicle, jolting of the" 10108
"vehicle, swaying and lurching" 9769
"vehicle, this" 9832
"vehicle left Farmer Councill's door" 9759
"vehicles, three" 9765
"veil, behind her rosy" 2188
"veil, lit up the talcum" 6304
"veil of darkness is drawn across a continent in ruins" 2262
"veil of transparent steel" 8035
"veil of uneasy sleep, thin" 10245
"veiled, water" 7917
"veiling trees and garden" 10646
"veils, shadows of their" 8891
"veins, blood of her" 2799
"veins, raised blue" 352
"veins at the base are prominent" 6596
"veins in his neck" 9849
"veld roads" 7036
Velde, Clara 4302
"velocity of 1200 miles per hour" 216

"velvety calm" 1011
Venable, Lucy Bondurant Chastain 2428
Venables 3565, 7737
"Vence" 10399
"Vendôme side of the Ritz" 5840
"vendor, market" 773
"vendors, public food" 7820
"veneer, cheap birch" 1119
"veneer that made it look wet" 8315
"venerable appearance" 3140
"venerable from its antiquity" 1171
"venerable from the virtues which it enclosed" 1171
"venerable lump, this" 8506
"venerable name" 4179
"venerable virginity" 357
"veneration, entitled to the utmost" 7772
"Venetian blind" 8481
"Venetian blinds" 1020
"Venezuela" 2341
Vengeance 583, 5205
"vengeance, getting" 583
"vengeance on the men" 5205
"Venice" 1069, 1126, 4064, 6345, 8252, 9575
"Venice, a suburban" 1416
"Venice, azure" 5297
"Venice, gondoliers of" 8754
"Venice, Republic of" 2072
"Venice, smell of" 8523
"Venice, so this is" 1450
"Venice, somewhere near" 8865
"Venice book, my" 5508
"Venice California" 1454
"Venice is burning" 505
Venn, Miss Ella 4344
"venture, joint" 716
"Venus de Milo, tall as the" 10797
"Venus, planet" 537
"Venus his star" 4816
Vera 5522, 10439
"veracity, testimony in favor of his" 3456
Veracruz, President 7979
"Veracruz" 8733
"Veracruz, port town of" 1415
"veranda, his back" 6290
"veranda, sitting in his" 4378
"veranda which overlooked a lovely flower-garden" 3064
"veranda would break, I figured the" 445
"verandah" 4698, 9668
"verandah, sat on the" 2209
"verandah, shave him on the" 8046
"verandah, sitting on the" 6010
"verandah, the" 6632
"verandah of Palam airport" 9574
"verandahs, deep-set" 9229
"verandahs, wooden" 3103
"verbal or other embroidery" 8841
"verbena" 8508
"verbs, conjugate" 6698

"verbs, gentle" 1284
"verdict, consider their" 5196
"verdict on the custody of Ari their son" 2682
Verdicts 2682, 5196, 5198
"verdin, a tiny gray" 442
"Verdun" 7196
"verdure, mountains covered with" 8192
"verdure, remarkable for its" 4031
Vere de Vere, Lady Clara 10788
"verge of fifteen, on the" 2827
"Vergennes Vermont" 6101
Verger 6767
"Vergil class, in his" 4273
Verheiden 1599
"verify experimentally, difficult to" 6907
"verisimilitude, needed no" 959
"Verity, town of" 2069
Verloc, Mr. 1010
"Vermont" 218, 1367, 1462, 3036, 3104, 3180, 4073, 6101, 6463, 6626, 7334, 9600
"Vermont border" 772
"Vermont line, across the" 6783
Verna 10939
Vernell 8670
Vernon, Blanche 3320
"Verona" 9969
Veronica 4597
"veronica flowers" 2072
"Versailles" 9882
"verse, cadence of the" 4474
"verse, stepped back to gain perspective on his" 8310
"verse and prose" 4455
"verses, compose a set of formal" 5457
"versifying, knack of" 5448
"version, condensed" 5530
"Version, King James" 7546
"version, my" 5417
"version of what happened" 8669
"versions, fabulously fractured" 7440
"vertigo, moment of" 6790
Vesey, Peter 9076
"vessel, I first saw the" 8151
"vessel, large" 8056
"vessel, merchant" 8057
"vessel, trading" 8056
"vessel filling with a strange liquid, like a" 8332
"vessel that stands high upon the water" 8055
"vessel to hold experience, curious" 3499
"vessel toward a convenient disaster, direct a" 3671
"vessels lying at anchor" 8106
"Vestal" 1431
"Vestal Virgins" 7514
"vestibule" 969
"vestibule, cramped" 3695

"vestibule, in his" 8186
"vestibule, inner" 10035
"vestments, freestone" 8937
"vestry, his" 1541
"vests, wear" 2866
"Vesuvio, planned to climb" 10674
"Vesuvio's on South Collins" 2062
"veterans, last of the" 8739
"veterans of the old school of good fellows" 2885
Veterinarians 9684
Vettori, Sam 5908
"Vévey, little city of" 9112
"Vevey, little town of" 5066
"vexation, Prince was in a" 10974
"vexed and worried at the look of things below" 2623
"VFW lodge, on his way to the" 2057
"via a rationed sky" 10242
"Via Condotti" 1084
"Via della Conciliazione" 10439
"Via Sistina" 10819
"Viatech" 1065
"vibrant body" 9141
"vibrating in the wind angrily" 10721
"vibrating noisily as if eager to be off again" 9785
"vibration, a" 6001
"vibration, felt the" 5686
"vibrations, frightening" 762
"vibrators, getting it off with one of their" 7874
"Vibraye" 6571
"Vicar, a glance at the" 6308
"vicar, her" 1309
"vicar, the" 2757
"Vicar General" 1928
"Vicar of Hatch End" 5743
"vicar thought, the" 49
"vicarage" 10919
"Vicarage, Eastwold" 3165
"vicarage in Surrey, my uncle's" 6568
"vicar's wife" 7864
"vice, actor's secret" 1332
"Vice Squad" 6274
"Vice-Chancellor's motives" 9305
"vice-consul, Her Britannic Majesty's" 4982
"Vicegerents, God's" 10033
"vice-president of the United States" 7007
"Viceroy was to make an important announcement" 3278
Vices 1332
"Vichy government, fallen" 4017
"vicious inclination" 10765
Vico 1332
"victim, a born" 4196
"victim, accident" 4281
"victim, fellow" 5355
"victim, helpless" 6761
"victim of his own tendency to fool around" 1111

"victim was his youngest, fourth" 6203

Victims 4507, 6203, 7179

"victims" 4507

"victims of justice" 7179

Victor 1278, 6878

Victoria 4797, 7083

Victoria, Queen 6647

"Victoria, platform at" 1630

"Victoria and Albert, yacht" 8119

"Victoria Australia" 6137

"Victoria Coach Station" 1726

"Victoria Cross, winning the" 248

"Victoria Station" 5817, 8938

"Victorian gloom of the front parlour" 7757

"Victorian latticework" 3225

"Victorian success, a monument to" 3122

"Victorian-baronial style" 3179

"Victorianisms" 10910

"Victoria's reign" 971

"victories, born in the year of" 792

Victorine 3815

"Victorious, The" 1351

Victory 792, 1839, 1955, 6669, 7447, 10471, 10481

"Victory!" 192

"VICTORY!" 1955

"victory, given us the" 10471

"victory is certain" 7447

Vida 2921

Vida, Aunt 2414

"Vienna" 1210, 3166, 6132, 6242, 9524, 10486

"Vienna, flight to" 7171

"Viennese orchestra" 6220

"Viennese woman" 7056

"Vietnam" 4590

"Vietnam War was 'over'" 7000

"view, coming into full" 4587, 8652

"view, contemplating the" 5357

"view, everybody is guaranteed a Mount Tamalpais" 3264

"view, get a" 233

"view, loomed into" 3038

"view, marvelous" 2005

"view, panoramic" 1932

"view, privileged" 5723

"view, rooms with a" 7755

"view, the" 1849

"view, triangular" 10190

"view embraced four counties" 3092

"view from here, always loved the" 6678

"view I once adored" 5357

"view it contemplates" 5164

"view of it, since my last" 1255

"view of it that he remembered with acutest longing" 7392

"view of the colleges can be obtained" 7772

"view of the fountain" 7771

"view of the road, a long clear" 9141

"view of the road ahead, never enough" 9194

"view of the yard, foot-square" 5372

"view or vista that the squinting eye now beheld" 8287

"view the magnificence of Blenheim" 2088

"view through the porthole was not encouraging" 7307

"view was bounded by the majestic Pyrenées" 5125

"view which had made this hotel loved" 3831

"viewed from the back windows" 7878

"viewed three worlds" 3365

"viewing the place with a heavy kinde of delight" 7370

Views 233, 1932, 2699, 2718, 2730, 3038, 3092, 3776, 3810, 3831, 5125, 5155, 5164, 5181, 5357, 5908, 6678, 7307, 7392, 7655, 7699, 7755, 7771, 8090, 8259, 8274, 8287, 8345, 8573, 9076, 9131, 9634, 9754

"views mistaken, many of my" 10998

"views on the foreign loans" 7505

"vigil on the mountain" 6960

"vigilance, casual" 2045

"vigilance from the beleaguered settlers, drained the" 6179

"vigilance of tyranny" 5554

"vigilant eyed" 10115

Vigneron, Dr. Jean Claude 6892

"vigor, found and spent its first" 7667

"vigor, I sensed their" 10313

"vigor of her movements" 376

"vigorously" 10401

"vigour, moved with equal" 8121

"Viking warrior, a great" 5981

Vile, Miss 4739

"vile" 5701

"vile, it tasted" 7850

Villa, Pancho 6344

"villa" 10001

"villa, castellated" 9738

"villa, decaying old" 3200

"villa, Döbling" 5935

"villa, gardens of a" 1494

"villa, her underground" 9291

"villa, his" 10399

"villa, in a snowy" 3552

"villa, Joyce" 3265

"Villa, Kent" 484

"villa, Ridolfi" 3230

"villa, the" 1659

"Villa Borghese" 935, 10783

"villa by the sea, his cool" 9858

"Villa Byrsa" 5251

"villa gates" 9671

"villa of a retired citizen" 9738

"Villa Paradiso" 3879

"Villa Ribar" 10562

"Villa Rubein" 9869

"villa . . . stood above the little town and port" 3125

"villa stood on the top of a hill" 3112

"villa with a sloping lawn" 3552

"village" 8975

"village, ancestral" 4741

"village, ancient" 9896

"village, came to the" 7222

"village, Catskill" 5842

"village, country" 9012

"village, county-seat" 954

"village, dozed the" 10700

"village, escapes being an overgrown" 1425

"Village, Friendship" 10917

"village, in the" 9573

"village, incorporated" 821

"village, Indian" 8168

"village, large mining" 6268

"village, leaving the" 6092

"village, little" 4033

"village, little Baralong" 1427

"village, Mediterranean seaside" 1481

"village, nearly forgotten in the" 9150

"village, northern French" 2198

"village, our" 1381

"Village, outskirts of the" 10687

"village, people in the" 9102

"village, remote" 561

"village, road from the" 9132

"village, scattered" 1346

"village, scruffy little crossroads" 5720

"village, seaside" 2441

"village, shelter of a distant" 6531

"village, squalid little" 831

"village, terrorised the" 8046

"village, the" 79, 2219, 4224

"Village, The" 4742

"village climbed the steep hill" 9460

"village described in the Benedictine's manuscript" 10898

"village doctors" 6884

"village far in the country, a little" 6266

"village free of fog" 5882

"village half hidden" 5158

"village in a valley" 1491

"village in the hills" 3416, 3987

"village in the hollow below the house" 1376

"village in the valley of the Rising" 1408

"village in Yunnan Province" 561

"village is finally coming out of winter" 1452

"village laced with irrigating ditches" 1357

"village lay in a valley" 9743

"village like a cross" 4145

"village of Brinthorpe" 3599

"village of Caplin Bight" 1421

"village of Chakrata" 1446

"village of Chiang Saen" 4094
"village of Denboro" 1373
"village of Forchheim" 1444
"village of Garth in Garthdale"
    1361
"village of Hasnapur" 7030
"village of Kravasaras" 1439
"village of London, retired" 4304
"village of North Bath" 9203
"village of Rapstone" 6923
"village of Restharrow" 1395
"village of Saxton" 9795
"village of 352 souls" 4059
"village of Toroella de Sta. Bar-
    bara" 2339
"village of Valle del Sole" 633
"village of West Meadows" 1367
"village square" 1462
"village stood on a wide plain" 1341
"village that looked across the
    river" 3093
"villager, Latino" 1737
"villagers, religion of the" 7503
"villagers were permitted to walk
    in the park and woods" 10419
Villages 804, 1341, 1346, 1350,
    1357, 1361, 1367, 1373, 1376,
    1381, 1383, 1392, 1395, 1396,
    1408, 1421, 1425, 1427, 1436,
    1439, 1444, 1446, 1452, 1466,
    1491, 2198, 2219, 3093, 4059,
    4094, 4145, 4893, 5139, 5158,
    5168, 5720, 5882, 6092, 6245,
    6266, 6268, 9012, 9102, 9133,
    9203, 9581, 9740, 9741, 9743,
    9795, 10402, 10687, 10700, 10898
"villages" 3535, 9133
"villages, cheerful" 263
"villages, dowery of ruined" 6245
"villages, fishing" 1344, 8093
"villages, in the" 272
"villages, maritime" 1350
"villages, New England" 6249
"villages, weathered disassembled"
    6167
"villages were small and poor" 9581
"villain" 3911
"villain, nor was I even its" 3393
"villainously cold" 6365
"villanelles" 5457
"villa-residences" 3122
Villas 3112, 3125, 3230, 3265,
    9738, 10562
"Ville Marie de Montréal" 1397
"Vincennes, beautiful little city of"
    9662
Vincent 6932, 7024
"vine leaves, some richly tinted"
    1849
"Vinehall" 9134
"vines, thickly hanging" 3714
"vines that hung over the narrow
    path" 3714
"vines that spread illimitably" 3899
"vineyards" 1059

"vineyards were painted with fresh
    green" 10587
Vinny 3937
"vintage, class and" 10863
"vintage, wines coming to" 2236
"vintage year, it was a" 10988
"violation, this is" 2063
Violence 34, 74, 957, 1166, 1321,
    1328, 1512, 1831, 2040, 2069,
    2370, 3325, 3455, 3755, 3880,
    4260, 4267, 4623, 5874, 6179,
    6182, 6207, 6682, 7004, 7024,
    7187, 7368, 7409, 7553, 8693,
    8917, 10157, 10445
"violence, diffuse form of" 7368
"violence, strange" 5572
"violence, war and" 3880
"violence in which he died" 9846
"violence inexcusable, find all
    direct" 7368
"violence lies always beneath the
    quietness" 7670
"violence lies very close to the sur-
    face in the Punjab" 9847
"violent for me, this movie's much
    too" 1328
"violent force, release of" 5118
"violent like the furious breath of
    an ice-dragon" 10725
"violently" 813
Violet 7362, 10004
"violets bloomed all year" 5033
"violin, a" 6101
"violin, high-pitched on a" 3716
"violin, played her" 6240
"violin lessons" 4089
"violinist, renowned" 6232
"violinist, turning abruptly to the"
    6215
"vipers" 9235
Virek, Josef 3414
Virgil, Old 7716
"virgin, a" 2054
"Virgin, altar of the" 1210
"virgin, beautiful" 10786
"virgin, most beautiful" 6515
"virgin, return to her homeland
    a" 4172
"Virgin, statue of the" 5324
"virgin, was not a" 2056
"virgin, while I was still a" 7731
Virgin Joseph 8008
"virgin martyr" 4808
Virgin Mary 8008
"Virgin of Charity" 10105
"virginal, deceptively" 6145
Virginia 2748, 10298
"Virginia" 786, 1465, 2839, 3639,
    6053, 8673, 9245
"Virginia, colony of" 6211
"Virginia, fragrant" 3396
"Virginia, Old" 3637
"Virginia family, prominent" 4824
"Virginia for the summer" 9727
"Virginia hills" 3665

"Virginia road" 7131
"Virginia sky" 6077
"Virginian pioneers" 6813
Virginity 7731, 8008, 8012, 8022
"virginity, chronicles of venerable"
    357
"virginity, lost her" 8012, 8022
"virginity was on its last legs, my"
    7731
Virgins 1886, 2054, 2056, 4172,
    4505, 10786
"Virgins, two" 4505
"Virgins, Vestal" 7514
"virgins sold into the penny
    brothels" 1886
"viridian green, dark" 9681
"virile and pregnant with purpose"
    7061
"virtually no berries" 9681
"virtu vinci, in" 4642
"virtue, monotonous but safe stride
    of" 2015
"virtue, privately consider a" 7982
"virtue of consistency, make a"
    5427
Virtues 2310, 6812
"virtues, her" 6605, 6606
"virtues, most disturbing of all"
    6812
"virtues of said Hugh McGehee
    were no less great" 2310
"virtues which it enclosed" 1171
"virtuoso with any neighborly love"
    6242
"virtuous impecunious tub-dweller"
    10871
"Viscount Castlewood, fourth" 950
"Viscount Mauley, Seventh" 5984
"Viscountess, Lady" 950
"visibility and fame, desire for"
    3545
"visible, barely" 1433
"visible for miles around" 1310
"visible from the hilltop" 4482
"visible signs" 5027
"vision, breadth of" 1032
"vision, his line of" 8701
"vision, Leo's" 7216
"vision, what I saw seemed to
    smear" 7317
"vision began, the" 5335
"vision of Babette at fifteen" 4142
"vision of earth, my first" 7917
"vision of mapmakers, idealized"
    5719
"vision of the future" 7021
"vision on the Spanish Steps" 4111
Visions 4111, 4112, 4904, 5335,
    7021, 10320
"visions, golden" 3550
"visions, soft" 10108
"visions of Joe" 4112
"visions of steak" 4674
"visions of the past, far-reaching"
    4492

"visions that allured" 3550
"visit, Christmas" 3488
"visit, decided to pay a" 8662
"visit, farewell" 9950
"visit, her" 9896
"visit, her mother's" 5570
"visit, his most unpleasant" 9971
"visit, just returned from a" 6282
"visit, last" 9928
"visit, man I was going to" 9890
"visit, my father's second" 5563
"visit, my first" 7409
"visit, paid his annual" 1500
"visit, paid his official" 8102
"visit, proposed" 1902
"visit, to" 9935
"visit a young woman" 3022
"visit from the Premier of France"
    9929
"visit Grandma and Grandpa
    Schoessel" 9721
"visit her grandparents, went
    downstairs to" 9984
"visit his old boys" 9932
"visit me in San Francisco" 9918
"visit of three solid weeks" 3698
"visit some parts of the north of
    England" 2087
"visit the grave, how would she"
    2436
"visit to a notable landowner of
    those marches" 9874
"visit to Africa, my first" 9371
"visit to England, Mr. Direck's
    first" 6251
"visit to the Apostolic Church" 1309
"visit to the future" 5477
"visit to the Mandersons" 5747
"visit your mother" 4600
"visitant of thirteen years standing"
    9941
"visitants appeared" 9941
"visitation, some midnight" 9008
"visitation had fallen on a child,
    such a" 8967
"visited, had never" 10420
"visited Cate Conboy" 9897
"visited her son" 9931
"visited me last night" 4484
"visited my sister underwater" 8251
"visited once again" 1307
"visiting Arlington Cemetery" 9621
"visiting friends" 9860
"visiting grandsons" 985
"visiting relatives, fed up with"
    4519
"visitor, English" 3046
"visitor, her" 9861
"visitor, her occasional" 3552
"visitor, our" 7767, 9886
"visitor, out-of-town" 9977
"visitor, periodical" 3552
"visitor, the" 5039
"visitor, their" 3989
"visitor approaching him" 9894

"visitor from Dragoon Arizona"
    9977
"visitor from France" 9606
"visitor there, every casual" 6974
"visitor to San Francisco" 9611
"visitor walked into the coffee-
    house" 9962
"visitor was her husband" 3552
Visitors 44, 290, 418, 651, 668,
    856, 949, 985, 989, 1126, 1181,
    1257, 1303, 1307, 1309, 1500,
    1535, 1572, 1605, 1613, 1618,
    1635, 1652, 1659, 1661, 1684,
    1693, 1720, 1727, 1728, 1853,
    1902, 1985, 2001, 2303, 2313,
    2701, 2709, 2720, 2725, 2726,
    2770, 2784, 2842, 2871, 2930,
    3022, 3043, 3141, 3161, 3309,
    3488, 3552, 3698, 3974, 3989,
    4075, 4114, 4132, 4173, 4176,
    4193, 4249, 4253, 4272, 4484,
    4519, 4558, 4619, 4677, 4698,
    4703, 4767, 5563, 5570, 5683,
    5747, 6047, 6200, 6282, 6316,
    6506, 7122, 7151, 7415, 7490,
    7638, 7767, 7780, 7822, 8102,
    8251, 8256, 8359, 8380, 8662,
    8706, 8781, 9094, 9099, 9104,
    9348, 9352, 9538, 9606, 9610,
    9611, 9621, 9721, 10008, 10039,
    10135, 10295, 10420, 10568, 10815
"visitors" 3060, 4619
"visitors, off-season" 1126
"visitors, several generations of"
    4644
"visitors, smelled the" 9936
"visitors to Belgium" 7264
"visitors to Rhenish Prussia" 9610
"visits, insidiously time their" 4712
"visits to the prison, monthly" 3043
"visits two old women" 10845
"Visoka, small town of" 4360
"visor, imaginary" 4896
Vista, Al 2102
"vistas, magnificent" 1013
"vistas framed by a ruined door"
    9231
"visualize" 512
"visualize the words" 2541
"viva Santa Fe" 4214
"vivacious" 7584
"vivacity" 2820
"vivacity, youth and" 1432
Vivian 3911
"vivid, images more" 7460
"vivid, steadily were becoming
    more" 9076
"vivid afternoon" 6127
"vivid painful adolescence" 2539
"vividly perceived" 5558
"Vliss, town of" 809
"vocabulary, study" 3292
"vocalist in the nation, finest fe-
    male" 9365
"vodka martini" 9173

Vogel, Anita 6512
"voice, aerated tone of" 6038
"voice, angry" 6619
"voice, awe and astonishment in
    her" 6529
"voice, boy with a wrecked" 7542
"voice, came the" 10014
"voice, coaxing" 8205
"voice, crackling" 8753
"voice, disconsolate" 10568
"voice, eunuch's" 10001
"voice, every species of tree has its"
    9661
"voice, flat" 6968
"voice, fling out with his" 6218
"voice, friendLee" 10007
"voice, her serene" 1281
"voice, his father's" 10122
"voice, his grandmother's" 10162
"voice, his smooth" 8499
"voice, his wife's high loud" 9997
"voice, husky" 7132
"voice, I heard a shrill small" 9989
"voice, it was a pleasant" 8742
"voice, low" 4914
"voice, Marie's" 10008
"voice, Marjorie Carling's" 9992
"voice, power behind my" 10018
"voice, raising her" 8613
"voice, rough" 10112
"voice, Sam's quiet" 1121
"voice, singsong" 10026
"voice, singsong holier-than-thou"
    10672
"voice, still not raising her" 2765
"voice, top of his" 7393
"voice, unmistakable" 10013
"voice, well-known shrill" 9991
"voice, Willy's" 10027
"voice, youthful female furious" 6727
"voice again, I hear your very"
    10022
"voice answered" 9989
"voice as soft as the river's easy
    breeze" 6917
"voice began to call" 10005
"voice . . . boomed across the air-
    port waiting room" 10006
"voice comes to one in the dark, a"
    10015
"voice distending raw and clear
    and black as christened snow"
    10009
"voice eager with malice" 7518
"voice from the sound truck" 6126
"voice guttural and sleep-stricken,
    my" 2776
"voice of a domestic" 6285
"Voice of Faith" 7506
"voice of Father" 10028
"voice of our people, unanimous"
    7801
"voice of the announcer" 10006
"voice of the man, monotonous"
    9996

"voice of the woman" 5632
"voice on the other end" 1138
"voice on the telephone" 10003
"voice rising, her pure" 8758
"voice rose above" 10012
"voice rose as usual upon the phrase" 7512
"voice rose in a protesting wail" 3705
"voice said into the phone" 6727
"voice sang out impatiently, a woman's" 10137
"voice splitting the quiet hum of late night" 8753
"voice still astonished" 2570
"voice that clanged like dustbin lids" 817
"voice that implied" 986
"voice that made all but his sister Violet turn and look" 10004
"voice that rustled" 10011
"voice was calling me" 10020
"voice was indistinct on the telephone" 10654
"voice was quiet" 3918
"voice was reaching a pitch it had never reached before" 2063
"voice was something to dream about" 9994
"voice which he'd affected since he was at Oxford" 1121
"voice which was smoother than dirt" 10027
"voiced, dulcet-" 5998
"voiceless" 7440
Voices 555, 622, 813, 986, 1121, 1138, 1281, 1526, 2477, 2764, 2765, 2776, 3461, 3506, 3568, 3706, 3918, 3935, 4205, 4214, 4335, 4908, 5182, 5632, 6126, 6218, 6379, 6917, 6968, 7132, 7225, 7512, 7542, 7991, 8175, 8205, 8499, 8613, 8742, 8753, 8758, 8769, 8823, 8862, 8885, 8895, 9560, 9619, 9661, 10111, 10121, 10122, 10137, 10162, 10231, 10654, 10672, 10743, 10792
"voices, chanting" 1305
"voices, do you hear" 10000
"voices, excited women's" 7294
"voices, frog-" 10701
"voices, hearing the wrong" 3461
"voices, magic of singing" 9560
"voices, noise of" 4335
"voices, our children's" 10021
"voices, strangers'" 6379
"voices and laughter of strangers" 3506
"voices died away" 10121
"voices hoarse" 4154
"voices in the trees betoken rain" 10743
"voices ring, made their" 9999
"voices that I heard, two" 9993
"voices to hear, many" 7225

"voices trickled insistent but subdued in the open air" 10023
"void, it's but a small step to enter the" 2575
"Void, not the" 6075
"void, they love the" 5521
"void, thought of the" 6075
"void of storks and lions" 1429
"volcanic dust" 760
"volcanic mountains" 8192
"volcano, active" 5052
Volcanoes 5052, 10718
"Volga limousine" 9833
Volkbein, Hedvig 7056
"Volkbein arms" 7056
"Volkswagen, heart the size of a" 3618
"Volkswagen, small blue" 1031
"Volkswagen headliners" 9925
"Volkswagen's upholstery, the" 6400
"volleyball, her rubber" 10810
Vollmer, Dr. 10010
Vollmer, Francis 9845
Voltaire 2629
Volterra, Baroness 9870
"voluble, became" 9096
"volumes, duodecimal" 2555
"volunteer, Debbie is a" 1149
"voluptuary" 8577
"voluptuous look of tension" 5048
"Volvo, Hudson's brown" 3036
"vomit lay, spat where his" 7956
"vomit out his intimate feelings" 7956
Vosper, Miss 9908
Voss 4482
Vost, Konrad 5954
"vow solemnly spoken" 2311
"vowed, he had" 3516
"vows, exchanged" 3604
"voyage, almost too pleasant" 7966
"voyage, odd" 7276
"voyage, on her homeward" 8051
"voyage, sabbatical" 9614
"voyage from Odessa, drawn-out" 4011
"voyage hard to believe, many who find our" 2744
"voyage of discovery" 2600
"voyage of exploration and discovery" 6564
"Voyage on which we are embarked" 2543
"voyaged back from the asphalt seas" 4577
Voyages 47, 126, 853, 992, 1598, 1628, 2188, 2368, 2543, 2600, 2744, 3494, 3514, 3593, 4270, 4535, 4559, 4701, 4731, 4916, 5029, 5223, 6091, 6121, 6135, 6155, 6576, 7919, 7966, 8051, 8053, 8061, 8064, 8067, 8073, 8075, 8088, 8089, 8100, 8101, 8107, 8112, 8118, 8120, 8123, 8124, 8125, 8132, 8134, 8136,

8145, 8160, 8166, 8504, 8680, 8792, 9431, 9508, 9517, 9534, 9575, 9601, 9603, 9607, 9614, 9619, 9857, 10729
"voyages, some" 4701
Voyolko, Senator 6985
"*vrai, pas*" 9291
"*vrouw*, old Boer" 5402
"vulgarest thing there is" 7127
"vulnerability, the suggestion of" 7472
"vulnerable as a small child" 1706
"vulpine" 1089
"vulture, I am the chosen" 4778
"vulture, some giant mythical Ulsterian" 10740
"vulture spiraling down onto a dying lion" 4778
"vulva, my" 343
Vyuko 8701

"Wa, the Tame" 6820
"Wa, the Wild" 6820
"Wabash, the" 9662
"Wabash Steel" 1070
"wacky city" 7831
"wacky rumor" 7831
"waddled sideways" 5907
Wade, Luther 5966
Wade, Sapphira 5222
"Wadi Parek of southen Israel" 8275
"wafted him toward his haven of bliss" 7346
"wager, on a" 5738
Wages 3329, 6464, 6494
"wages, Government still pays my" 6494
"wages from him, accepted" 3329
"wages of sin" 7192
"wagging, its tail" 9342
Wagner, Fred 6470
Wagner, Lauren 2813
"wagon, big" 9762
"wagon, brightly painted green and red and blue" 7645
"wagon, canvas-covered freight" 9617
"wagon, heavy" 2959
"wagon, heavy farm" 9759
"wagon, his" 2374
"wagon, one-horse" 9758
"wagon, patrol" 6959
"wagon, rusty" 3035
"wagon, toy" 9626
"'Wagon and Horses'" 6566
"wagon drawn by oxen, a double" 6101
"wagon mount the hill, watching the" 9414
"wagon swaying through forest and swamp" 4144
"wagon that'll run without a hoss" 4937

Wagoner, Summer Deer 5598
Wagons 3035, 4144, 9758, 9759, 9762, 9792, 9832
"wagons, ice" 2210
"wagons moved slowly" 6099
"Waianae and Koolau mountain ranges" 10616
"Waikiki" 5859
"wail, half-" 8799
"wail, long" 10539
"wail, protesting" 3705
"wailed, her mother" 7555
"wailing and thundering among our tall trees and ivied chimneys" 10678
"Wailing Wall, catch a glimpse of the" 9251
"waistline, her almost nonexistent" 4300
"wait, having to" 10033
"wait, I could hardly" 7906
"wait, nothing to be done but" 2625
"wait, should not be able to" 4909
"wait, write and" 5475
"wait a minute" 95
"wait and see" 1763
"wait between trains, the" 9586
"wait calculated to the second" 6506
"wait for baggage, there was a long" 9595
"wait for her" 9622
"wait for his friend" 10048
"wait for instructions on how to write what they want you to write" 10049
"wait for Leo Hermann to arrive, I could hardly" 9956
"wait for that unique contribution to art" 10049
"wait for the assignment" 10049
"wait for the ferry" 5990
"wait for your agent to make the deal" 10049
"wait impatiently" 7262
"wait outside the great man's office" 10049
"wait thirty seconds more, you can" 1120
"wait three years for a phone call" 1120
"wait to get inside the gate" 10049
Waite, Mr. Arnold 3572
"waited" 10068
"waited, man had" 10057
"waited, she" 9325
"waited, stood there and" 10072
"waited, three men" 10088
"waited, watched the house and" 10087
"waited, we" 4488
"waited and waited and waited" 2669
"waited at the curb for her father" 10036

"waited behind the thick Osage orange hedgerow" 10043
"waited by her mailbox" 8624
"waited chin on hand" 9405
"waited for another conveyance" 8566
"waited for justice" 5205
"waited for Madame de Malrive" 10037
"waited for Poppie to return" 10074
"waited for Pyle" 9330
"waited for Skaggs to come down the beach" 10098
"waited for the bus" 10045
"waited for the innocent moment" 6899
"waited in silence" 5188
"waited in the early grey morning" 10751
"waited in their parlour" 10053
"waited over her, he" 7989
"waited their turns on the lavatory" 8869
"waited till he had left" 1736
"waited till his father . . . fell into a fuddled snooze" 6652
"waited two weeks" 1953
"waited until it was dark" 10056
"waited until the kids were in bed" 2677
"waited with its doors yawning" 7887
"waiter, arrival of the" 654
"waiter, celebrated head" 4305
"waiter, the" 1101
"waiter, was a" 6472
Waiting 482, 654, 667, 1003, 1120, 1169, 1714, 1775, 1953, 2295, 2363, 2365, 2395, 2444, 2625, 2664, 2669, 2682, 2993, 3037, 3338, 3499, 4007, 4102, 4155, 4183, 4204, 4310, 4488, 4906, 4909, 4921, 4922, 4925, 5188, 5205, 5459, 5475, 5654, 5957, 5990, 6200, 6380, 6503, 6506, 6532, 6971, 7156, 7239, 7262, 7283, 8078, 8316, 8498, 8505, 8566, 8624, 8654, 8691, 8724, 9244, 9298, 9325, 9326, 9329, 9330, 9331, 9334, 9335, 9336, 9338, 9341, 9343, 9405, 9406, 9595, 9622, 9670, 9678, 9822, 9889, 9905, 9956, 10433, 10749, 10751, 10967, 10971
"waiting" 4007, 10073, 10086
"waiting, as if" 8724
"waiting, car that was" 4204
"waiting, city is" 10096
"waiting, formal" 10032
"waiting, he was" 10051
"waiting, I am here" 10065
"waiting, it's the" 10049
"waiting, looked back" 5957
"waiting around for the credit card billings" 2664

"waiting at the door of number 32 Connaught Square" 9822
"waiting at the door of my office" 10050
"waiting at the fortress" 4183
"waiting at the office door" 10058
"waiting by the mailbox" 10103
"waiting customers" 1048
"waiting for, he had been" 4224
"waiting for, we had been" 6380
"waiting for, what they had been" 7742
"waiting for a sign to release her into death" 9298
"waiting for Ambrose all day" 10090
"waiting for Caleb Gare" 10039
"waiting for her, hoped they weren't" 10089
"waiting for her lover" 10041
"waiting for her to sleep, gargoyles" 2799
"waiting for him" 9905, 10080
"waiting for him, she is" 10044
"waiting for him for twenty years, she was" 10044
"waiting for his quartz alarm clock to bleep" 8498
"waiting for his secretary" 10040
"waiting for his wife" 5459
"waiting for it to dock" 8078
"waiting for Mr. Balducci" 10081
"waiting for me" 10082, 10433
"waiting for me at the corner" 7156
"waiting for Nora" 4310
"waiting for some archer to shoot them down" 9667
"waiting for some highly idiosyncratic pay-off" 2589
"waiting for something" 10038
"waiting . . . for something momentous to occur" 10083
"waiting for the alarm" 8505
"waiting for the artist to arrive" 10107
"waiting for the ferry" 10054
"waiting for the lines of faces to pull out" 5654
"waiting for the men to decide" 10105
"waiting for the old lady" 2365
"waiting for the rest of the theatre-party" 10035
"waiting for the train" 10094
"waiting for the train from Kilcoole" 9300
"waiting for their carriages" 6751
"waiting for them" 10064
"waiting for them to come" 10091
"waiting for them to go green" 2993
"waiting for us, is there anything" 6323
"waiting for us, where Pappie was" 6122
"waiting for you" 10101

"waiting for you in the foyer of that superb hotel" 10047
"waiting impatiently" 4921
"waiting in the Lyceum cafe" 9334
"waiting in the outer room of his offices" 6503
"waiting on the curb" 10749
"waiting out the storm" 748
"waiting outside his father's house" 667
"waiting parents, asterisks of" 5096
"waiting patiently" 10099
"waiting patiently, about sixty of them" 10076
"waiting room" 6896, 6897, 7781, 10006
"waiting shore-party" 8128
"waiting so long for death" 2444
"waiting the return of a courier" 10034
"waiting there, I preferred" 10095
"waiting to be found for a day and a night" 1169
"waiting to be watered" 9678
"waiting to flow in" 3302
"waiting to round up wood-chucks" 4155
"waiting to see her" 10075
"waiting to see him" 9889
"waiting to share her astounded contemplation" 9409
"waiting while she fought out the difficult words" 7200
"waiting with various combinations of dread hope and ennui" 10083
"waitress, long-distance" 7574
"waits for the next great event" 9951
"wake, as I" 10146
"wake, before they" 5327
"wake, had never gone to a" 3955
"wake, his father's" 3950
"wake at four and take dictation, no responsibility to" 1118
"wake belonging to the barge" 8076
"wake her, forced her mind to" 10220
"wake him, trusting her natural power to" 2765
"wake in the night and know why we have become what we are" 10151
"wake Isabelle, knocking on the door did not" 9885
"wake of the taxi-cab" 6622
"wake of the watertrucks, in the" 10416
"wake ready for the day" 4284
"wake suddenly from a doze on the couch" 10318
"wake the dead" 6338
"wake the poor people trying to sleep" 1132
"wake today panting, as I" 10321
"wake up" 283, 9017, 10112
"wake up, it's time to" 10124

"wake up all woebegone and goopy" 2906
"wake up and mover over" 10213
"wake up cold" 2250
"wake up every morning" 1258
"wake up for the twenty-sixth consecutive New Year's Day of your life alone in bed" 10237
"wake up I think I'm there, when I" 10263
"wake up one fine morning" 5467
"wake up remembering, I always" 10281
"wake very slowly" 10148
"wake with a headache" 8514
"waked first, she had" 10226
"waked first, would have" 10226
Wakefield, Luke 4833
"wakeful, many were" 7797
"wakefulness, disquieting" 10251
"wakefulness, stirred into" 10216
"waken all at once, did not" 10130
"waken easily" 10172
"waken in their beds" 3381
"wakened, we have just" 8455
"wakened as usual by the slant of Riviera sun" 10118
"wakened as usual by the flutter of pigeons" 10210
"wakened by the knotting of the snake's coils about his waist" 10205
"wakened from a charming dream" 2752
"wakened him, telephone" 10182
"wakened quickly, I" 10172
"wakens, when Aggie" 10280
Wakes 3950
"wakes, as she" 10279
"wakes as she always does" 2814
"wakes to finish his book" 10219
"wakes to the gentle pressure of Mark's hand" 10298
"wakes up" 10322
"wakes up, when he" 10327
Waking 243, 283, 463, 560, 670, 671, 673, 737, 836, 862, 995, 1102, 1125, 1128, 1132, 1137, 1208, 1258, 2249, 2250, 2752, 2754, 2756, 2762, 2772, 2773, 2779, 2782, 2784, 2785, 2802, 2804, 2814, 2906, 3381, 3516, 3701, 3714, 3732, 4177, 4284, 4578, 5024, 5121, 5329, 5374, 5467, 5605, 6041, 6593, 6598, 7013, 7158, 7324, 7385, 7407, 7731, 7907, 7998, 8015, 8438, 8455, 8467, 8472, 8484, 8503, 8514, 8795, 8813, 8819, 8832, 8854, 9017, 9104, 9432, 9739, 9885, 10727, 10968
"waking" 10292
"waking beneath the vine" 10308
"waking feels *priggish*" 10314
"waking from a state of unconsciousness" 10286

"waking her" 10180
"waking him" 1128
"waking in the morning" 10160
"waking me up in time to see the cows milked" 10324
"waking or sleeping" 2765
"waking out of a dream" 4578
"waking up" 5374, 10139, 10204
"waking up at least twice a night" 560
"waking up begins with saying *am* and *now*" 10184
"waking up in a secret cave" 3714
"Wald, dark" 7624
Walden, Katherine 5291
"Waldorf-Astoria" 4654
"Wales" 9560, 9743
"Wales, citizen of" 5972
"Wales, New South" 11004
"Wales, North" 9874
"Walham Green" 8636
"walk, asked to go for a" 6698
"walk, blue brick" 2602
"walk, called a" 5788
"walk, he takes a" 2030
"walk, his usual solitary afternoon" 4275
"walk, I took a" 6559
"walk, I was well able to" 7443
"walk, impetuous" 6577
"walk, no possibility of taking a" 10330
"walk, started to" 10367
"walk, such a long and as you can now hear applauseless" 10460
"walk, take a country" 4996
"walk, three-mile" 9890
"walk, three-minute" 3186
"walk, went for a" 6563
"walk, when John was able to" 963
"walk among the old tombstones" 725
"walk around the Shopping Plaza" 1122
"walk around the world" 1676
"walk away smelling like a rose" 8542
"walk down the Via Condotti" 1084
"walk down them arm-in-arm" 9123
"walk down to the quai" 5607
"walk far, you will not have to" 3232
"walk forth into the fields" 10566
"walk in a day of my life with a bell" 9442
"walk in the park and woods" 10419
"walk march" 8679
"walk miles in fog" 3832
"walk of a tall person, the lean-to" 10408
"walk off the unfenced yard during recess, all you do is" 7898
"walk past the farmhouse" 995
"walk save you, no soul shall" 10416
"walk slowly as she turned into Dumble Street" 9425

"walk slowly enough to read the headlines" 10366

"walk swiftly across the room" 1792

"walk the clipped horses" 10032

"walk the forest" 6569

"walk the half mile to the White-laws" 10411

"walk through all the dim two-family-house streets" 9162

"walk through burnt grass" 437

"walk through the streets" 9524

"walk toward Tooley Street" 10394

"walk unsteadily to the head of the stairs" 2901

"walk up" 10358

"walk westwards" 1610

"walk with me" 6361

"walked, as he" 10453

"walked, lurched when she" 4196

"walked a familiar forest" 3902

"walked a far piece" 10398

"walked across the fields" 7591

"walked across the Lincolnshire up-lands" 10386

"walked across the room towards the window" 9444

"walked across the square faster than he would have liked" 10455

"walked across the still-soggy ground" 3959

"walked across the wide stretch of lawn" 10355

"walked alone to an abandoned farmhouse" 9950

"walked along a street" 10388

"walked along Holywell" 10335

"walked along the evening avenue" 10372

"walked ... among the apparitions on the bowery" 10463

"walked and walked in the rain" 6567

"walked around bouncing it off the sidewalks and off walls" 302

"walked around the deep puddles" 10407

"walked as steadily as he could" 2909

"walked at once to the Doctor's house" 121

"walked away hunching his shoulders" 2588

"walked back" 10461

"walked back to the office after lunch" 6443

"walked behind him" 4677

"walked briskly" 2842

"walked down Berners Street in London" 7409

"walked down Fulham Broadway" 10395

"walked down River Street every afternoon" 4289

"walked down the hallway" 8007

"walked down the road" 10459

"walked down the steps" 10370

"walked down the street" 10440

"walked down the wing" 8292

"walked fast" 10427

"walked for an hour or more, as if she had" 10353

"walked heavily" 10426

"walked heavily up the Park Street mall" 4368

"walked home along the Embank-ment to my wife" 4571

"walked home from school" 10443

"walked in front" 7585

"walked in silence" 10334

"walked in single file" 8682

"walked in the street" 8607

"walked into the art gallery" 10867

"walked into the coffeehouse" 9962

"walked into the dock" 1829

"walked into the empty old house" 1148

"walked into the house" 3206

"walked into the lighted lobby" 1638

"walked into the windowless room" 6893

"walked into the woods to take a leak" 3023

"walked on, when he" 2909

"walked on his own" 10437

"walked on in the belief" 2308

"walked on the width of Welburn Field" 5916

"walked out of the cottage" 1683

"walked out of the hospital grounds" 4615

"walked out of the house" 2934

"walked out on to the third-floor porch" 5920

"walked out without waiting" 1838

"walked over from the university" 6630

"walked over my grave" 10385

"walked over to the french win-dows" 2402

"walked rapidly along Piccadilly" 10360

"walked round and round the Red Square" 10350

"walked round the corner of the house" 3882

"walked slowly" 1649

"walked slowly across Clerkenwell Green" 1184

"walked slowly down the road" 10365

"walked slowly in long strides from the hip" 10441

"walked slowly to the door" 8278

"walked slowly up Western Avenue" 4149

"walked so swiftly" 4145

"walked the granite canyons" 9197

"walked through deep snow" 10378

"walked through the cool October night" 10421

"walked through the dark with the accuracy of habit" 9417

"walked through the hospital Emergency doors" 4625

"walked through the town" 3800

"walked through the wilderness" 1530

"walked to the beach" 6403

"walked to the end of the disused pier" 5039

"walked to the river" 2278

"walked to the window" 2728

"walked to Woolworth's" 3751

"walked toward her twin sister" 10444

"walked toward his apartment" 10413

"walked toward St. Peter's" 10439

"walked twice around the cave" 7541

"walked two blocks to the overpass" 10415

"walked up and down the platform" 3912

"walked up Corliss Street" 10336

"walked up the dun slope" 10454

"walked up the lane" 9430

"walked upright on his hind legs" 1882

"walked with her friend" 8546

"walked with his eldest daughter" 6616

"walked with the arrogance of a young untried eagle" 8918

"walked with the dreamy stride of a noctambulo" 10463

Walker, Mary 2732

Walker, Mickey 2896

Walker, Mr. George 2732

Walker, Samuel 7232

Walker, William 9954

"walkers, busy" 10380

"walkers, solitary" 9828

Walking 14, 96, 421, 538, 876, 960, 994, 995, 999, 1084, 1106, 1184, 1498, 1576, 1610, 1649, 1657, 1676, 1685, 1731, 1732, 2083, 2223, 2278, 2493, 2529, 2582, 2603, 2811, 2909, 3232, 3298, 3310, 3482, 3681, 3691, 3692, 3703, 3714, 3800, 3902, 3912, 4145, 4149, 4203, 4275, 4278, 4286, 4289, 4368, 4371, 4411, 4413, 4539, 4571, 4615, 4625, 4797, 4918, 5321, 5495, 5607, 5724, 5814, 5824, 5867, 5888, 5916, 6160, 6402, 6434, 6443, 6555, 6559, 6560, 6562, 6563, 6564, 6567, 6569, 6571, 6574, 6622, 6648, 7099, 7221, 7290, 7390, 7564, 7585, 7591, 8212, 8278, 8292, 8512, 8546, 8607, 8660, 8679, 8682, 8780, 8845, 8918, 9091, 9092, 9120, 9123, 9142, 9144, 9162, 9164,

9197, 9414, 9417, 9425, 9430, 9442, 9455, 9890, 9950, 9982, 10032, 10092, 10566, 10724
"walking" 10396
"walking, began" 5724
"walking, came briskly" 4918
"walking, children were" 10424
"walking, I saw him" 10408
"walking, just" 10348
"walking, my time for" 96
"walking, start" 1227
"walking, you keep" 10403
"walking a large dog, like a woman" 5239
"walking a narrow roadway" 10353
"walking across it" 10389
"walking across the campus" 10433
"walking along" 10387
"walking along Portage Avenue" 10392
"walking along the beach of a nature sanctuary in Israel" 10422
"walking along the deserted beach" 5495
"walking along the river wall" 9869
"walking along the Seine" 2529
"walking along the side of the Square" 4411
"walking as it seemed from Bramblehurst railway station" 9092
"walking briskly and elegantly" 10351
"walking by the creek together" 2677
"walking by the Thames, I was" 10356
"walking deep in the ocean, like" 10449
"walking demurely" 4142
"walking down a bombed-out block" 2811
"walking down Fayette Street" 8512
"walking down Marlboro Street in Boston" 10414
"walking eyes up" 10452
"walking fast past the waiting customers" 1048
"walking from room to room" 6160
"walking home from the subway" 10361
"walking home together" 10332
"walking homeward" 10333, 10450
"walking in Mediterranean sunlight" 10417
"walking in right after we open up" 1657
"walking in that direction" 6136
"walking in the college garden before dinner" 7390
"walking in the garden" 6860
"walking in the rose garden" 10406
"walking in the suburbs" 10381
"walking in the tall grass" 2603
"walking on Brattle Street" 2582
"walking on waves, Christ" 1302

"walking out" 8559
"walking out of a cloud, he came" 5867
"walking past the Sharanpur Club" 6434
"walking rather listlessly" 6562
"walking rather too slowly down the road" 9455
"walking round the couples" 2529
"walking slowly down Troy Street" 10434
"walking stick" 6574
"walking ten paces behind" 10412
"walking the earth under the stars" 10377
"walking three hundred feet into the earth" 10462
"walking through pouring rain without an umbrella" 1055
"walking to the bank" 1106
"walking toward the woman in her dream" 10444
"walking under the wing" 7564
"walking unhurriedly among the rows of rosebushes" 4286
"walking up and down" 3482
"walking up and down the platform" 8565
"walking up Park Avenue" 10432
"walking with my son" 4539
"walking-stick, chose her favourite" 6571
Walkinshaw, Claud 3550
"walks down the street" 10429
"walks in fear" 2362
"walks the dirtier streets of San Francisco" 10446
"walks to South Station" 10436
"walks with downcast eyes" 2493
"wall, acoustically perfect" 9474
"wall, against the white-washed" 6321
"wall, blank" 220
"wall, burgundy brick" 3113
"wall, cracking" 5521
"Wall, escape over the" 7004
"wall, George Lockwood's" 1853
"wall, high brick fruit-" 6283
"wall, low stone" 5162
"wall, my" 9854
"wall, old tumbled-down" 10404
"wall, on the library" 8641
"wall, opposite" 8280
"wall, red bricks of the" 495
"wall, rosy brick" 2984
"wall, stone" 8349
"Wall, The" 9218
"wall, there was a" 1855
"wall, thin" 6296
"Wall, Wailing" 9251
"Wall, Western" 1722
"wall between their sitting-rooms" 6296
"wall between them, survive by keeping a" 7176

"wall flowers at the parties" 2332
"wall is straight at that point" 9238
"wall mellow with age, a brick" 10355
"wall of a hut, corrugated-iron" 10164
"wall of bulging green, high leafy" 9672
"wall of snow-white sand" 5138
"wall of the Leprosarium, solid" 4622
"Wall Street" 1591
"wallaby" 5277
Wallace 1053
Wallace, Dave 9766
Wallace, Luther 2009
Wallace, Margaret 4354
"Wallah" 5753
"walled in against thieves" 4328
"wallflowers, prize-winning beds of" 4069
Wallin, Benecia 10651
"Wallingford races" 9919
"walloper, kopje" 5456
"wallpaper, bathroom" 5376
"wallpaper, faded flowered" 5024
"wallpaper, forget-me-not on the" 2343
"wallpaper, like the" 4642
"wallpaper, murky brown" 6511
"wallpaper, wolfmother" 7790
Walls 1853, 1855, 2941, 3230, 4622, 5138, 5152, 5317, 6296, 8037, 8280, 9223, 9238, 9242, 9251, 9474, 10404
"walls" 9242
"walls, a few dry" 5150
"walls, barked at by sudden brick" 7279
"walls, blackened" 1368
"walls, brick" 8590
"walls, canvas" 5317
"walls, glass-topped" 6501
"walls, limestone" 7146
"Walls, Outer" 9223
"walls, pink" 2941
"walls, rain-swept" 5431
"walls, red" 5330
"walls, splintered plank" 8068
"walls, surrounding" 3230
"walls, whitewashed" 2463
"walls again, chewing the" 445
"walls billowed" 7856
"Walls of China, these" 5138
"walls of Ilium, sacred" 7810
"walls of tenements" 7627
"walls of the National Academy of Design" 1012
"walls of the underground prison" 7146
"walls quiver like vaginal lips" 2941
"walls were dripping in fog" 10349
"walls were mirrors" 4309
"walls were stained and grimy" 7134

Wally 2876
Walmer, Augustus 4820
"Walmouth" 1894
"walnut tree" 8739
Walsh, Ellen 6296
Walsh, Helen 174
Walsingham, Miss 7491
Walter 4564, 5469, 5682, 9645
Waltz, Harry 3950
Wanda Gay 8241
"Wanda, Lord of" 7801
"wander only twenty paces" 1272
"wander out the door" 1003
"wandered through our state" 1431
"wandered through the dream city of London" 6584
"wanderers and gentlemen adventurers" 3557
"wandering around the lot where he sold used cars" 1992
"wandering around the yard during the night" 3465
"wandering forever" 3799
"wandering in those deserts of Africa" 7648
"Wandering Jew" 3055
"wandering over the hills" 10609
"wandering through the halls of heaven" 2644
"wandering through years briefer than the blink of an eyelid" 7084
"wanders up and down the hall" 7231
"waned I wined" 2913
Wang Lung 2309, 3567, 10647
Wang the Tiger 3567
Wang Yuan 3567
"Wanstead Flats" 5928
"want, ache of" 4678
"want, everything anyone could" 3607
"want, what we" 929
"want, whatever it is they" 10835
"want him, did not" 781
"want more, you" 2530
"want them to come, I even" 10091
"want to do, something that I did not" 9431
"wanted, the man she" 7741
"wanted posters, acquired a few more" 6952
"wanted something other" 255
"wanted the same thing, you could say we both" 5506
"wanted them, I" 2522
"wanted to and tried, though I" 6508
War 155, 209, 223, 236, 322, 786, 833, 873, 888, 920, 1099, 1206, 1277, 1279, 1282, 1482, 1735, 1985, 2305, 2491, 2811, 3150, 3198, 3233, 3362, 3416, 3434, 3508, 3662, 3676, 3880, 4042, 4252, 4387, 4468, 4469, 4629, 5221, 5226, 5654, 5662, 6446,

6531, 6621, 6683, 6774, 6779, 6801, 6803, 6806, 6811, 6866, 7000, 7110, 7155, 7196, 7228, 7246, 7730, 7792, 7853, 7894, 8172, 8178, 8503, 8641, 8643, 8648, 8653, 8656, 8658, 8659, 8668, 8671, 8675, 8678, 8681, 8686, 8689, 8693, 8694, 8695, 8699, 8701, 8704, 8705, 8709, 8711, 8712, 8713, 8767, 8807, 9022, 9033, 9344, 9420, 9792, 10034, 10539
"war, a good" 10478
"war, a year or two before the" 5799
"war, after the end of the" 2604
"war, ancient causes of" 7155
"war, at night in the" 8703
"war, back from the" 8581
"war, beautiful madness of" 10527
"war, born in a" 10531
"war, British ships of" 2491
"war, by the end of the" 8686
"war, came late to the" 9344
"War, Civil" 1279, 3665, 4073, 6097, 7792, 10467
"war, day I left for the" 8503
"war, during the" 1282
"War, during the" 3049
"War, during the whole" 3233
"war, end of the" 3171
"war, first skirmish in the" 3676
"war, first world" 6806
"War, First World" 1464
"war, founded on" 1482
"War, Great" 8678
"war, greatest people's" 10483
"war, grew up in a" 10531
"war, he proceeded to wage" 5662
"war, in one of the years of" 8178
"war, in the first years after the" 6289
"war, in the second year of the" 1985
"war, last of the" 1277
"war, looks like a long" 10516
"war, love and" 7730
"war, love flourishes in time of" 5654
"war, my father was in the" 3359
"war, never felt the same again about" 10507
"War, no Cold" 3362
"war, not as yet been worn down by" 8653
"War, old French" 3434
"war, outbreak of" 10479, 10525
"war, outbreak of the" 1590
"war, peace and" 3071
"war, probably I was in the" 10490
"War, Second World" 9420, 9654
"war, second year of the" 6114
"war, simplified by the" 10485
"war, since the end of the" 2518, 3136

"War, Six Weeks" 3139
"war, state of undeclared" 10520
"war, story of the" 9022
"War, Th'" 8712
"War, Third World" 5203
"war, this is" 10499
"war, time of the" 10503
"war, tired of" 10498
"war, towards the end of the" 5930
"War, Tribal" 1833
"war, two years after the end of the" 1099
"War, Vietnam" 7000
"war, within which we" 5479
"war, years immediately following the" 6811
"War, Zulu" 9522
"war against Germany" 10496
"war against Poland, German tariff" 2592
"war against the French" 10493
"war all along" 10531
"War and Trade" 10464
"war and violence in the streets" 3880
"war began, before the" 9722
"war began in earnest" 10480
"War being proclaimed with *Holland*" 10466
"War Between the States" 8694
"war broke out" 10182
"war broke out, before the" 3662
"War broke out, when the" 8658
"war came early one morning in June of 1950" 10500
"war came to an end late one evening" 10506
"war came to Monterey, when the" 10492
"war came to the Dutch East Indies" 10523
"war effort, know one's place in the" 10517
"war ended, Korean" 1277
"war ended last night" 10528
"war finished" 10481
"War for Independence, long before the" 6100
"war had a proscenium, as if" 8704
"war had begun, to see if the" 10536
"war had just begun" 6446
"war had made him what he was" 10498
"War hero, Revolutionary" 8940
"war in Europe ended, after the" 1206
"war is being deliberately prolonged" 8709
"war is ever popular at first" 10473
"war is over" 10489
"war of independence" 10470
"War of Independence" 8641
"War of Independence, not undistinguished in the" 361
"war parts, the" 10508

"war pipe, carrying a" 7853
"war story, this ain't no" 9033
"war surplus, purchased as" 8135
"war that has been raging out of
    control" 10518
"war to end wars" 10495
"War II, World" 6531
"war was done" 10483
"war was everywhere and nowhere"
    10501
"war was over, when the" 322
"War which agitated Britain during
    the seventeenth century" 10467
"war which had desolated Scotland
    was then at an end" 6801
"war worth leaving unwon, at last
    found a" 10535
"war would end" 10503
"warblers singing out of season"
    7025
"war-cry of the Amangtakwena"
    8789
Ward, Jane 3824
Ward, John 4002
Ward, Miss Maria 5727
"ward, emergency" 4621
"Ward, Toshima" 9816
"ward, our" 4626
"Ward Four" 4057
"ward of the court" 1725
"Warden, Sub-" 3468
Wardrobe, Miss 4739
"wardrobe, a" 3217
"warehouse, abandoned" 3192
"warehouse, abandoned cotton"
    3788
"warehouse, Davenant's" 8775
"warehouse, Number Two bonded"
    1912
"warehouses, gloomy" 1368
"warfare, mountain" 8682
"warhead, pearly" 7990
Waring, Lady Cora 7060
Waring, Sir Cecil 7060
Waring, Sir Harry 3123
Warleggan, Elizabeth 7069
"Warley, I came to" 1642
"warlike neighbors" 6802
Warlock 6954
"warm, it is" 10602
"warm, unseasonably" 9774
"warm, you are kept very" 548
"warm after the drip of the winter
    night" 7758
"warm and salty on the breeze"
    10737
"warm day" 3806
"warm the morning" 2348
"warmed by the sun, not yet" 10616
"warmed, I never really" 4290
"warmest, that winter was the"
    10640
"warmth" 7097
"warmth, forcing its foul" 10727
"warmth, its heartening" 5308

"warmth, October" 5631
"warmth, sun's" 449
"warmth had opened the buds"
    9683
"warmth of a rare jewel" 3076
"warmth to the steam-heated
    living-room" 7756
"warn the fishing-fleet" 8062
"warn you, I should" 10548
"warned away from Uncle Billy's
    shed" 10547
"warned inland" 756
"warned me, they" 1819
"warned me about Washington"
    10544
"Warner Brothers Studios" 5571
"warning, howling their" 9104
"warning, never heeding my" 10546
"warning, ten-second" 2829
"warning, white scar of" 475
"warning, with no" 40
"warning and example to all" 10542
"warning flash" 10541
"warning of being different from
    many other days, gave no" 2165
"warning of the night, first air-
    raid" 10539
Warnings 319, 442, 475, 1819,
    2165, 2394, 8062, 9299
"warped out of her berth by a
    black tug" 8104
Warren, Eleanor 8084
"warrior, great Viking" 5981
"Warrior King" 4743
"warriors, more than a hundred"
    10535
"Wars, Gallic" 920
"wars, literary" 5535
"wars, old colonial" 4467
"wars, period between the" 10495
"Wars, Persian" 4503
"wars came early" 10524
"wars of any respectable size" 10512
"wars of North America, colonial"
    10468
"wars or revolutions, covered six-
    teen" 3508
"Warsaw" 5901, 7277
"Warsaw, citizen of" 9578
"Warsaw, sixty kilometers south of"
    4328
"Warsaw ghetto" 2604
"warships and auxiliaries, lines of
    moored" 8117
"war-sick" 5026
"war-time, in her house it seemed
    to be" 3198
"wartime, life began in" 833
"war-torn Middle Eastern capital"
    2811
"warts, cure" 6338
"Warwickshire" 4574
"wary, so" 6698
"wary of its people" 6920
"wash, hanging out the" 10875

"wash was hastily taken off" 7294
Washburne, Elihu B. 9497
"washdays, hated" 5372
"washed away as usual" 9168
"washed away with old dishwater"
    7316
"washes her hands" 8006
"washing, like a line of dark and
    white" 3645
"washing down, she was" 3824
"washing greens" 10960
"washing his shirt" 10922
"washing machine" 10963
"washing up at the water trough"
    566
Washington 269
Washington, G. 8940
Washington, George 1401, 1442,
    10516
Washington, John 4588
"Washington" 247, 1437, 1787,
    3078, 3306, 3449, 4555, 6370
"Washington, captured" 4468
Washington, D.C. 1442, 1455,
    1467
"Washington, growing city of" 2710
"Washington, north of" 7751
"Washington, south of" 3665
"Washington, the rue" 8858
"Washington, warned me about"
    10544
"Washington correspondents" 794
"Washington D.C." 1467, 4921,
    6037, 9245
"Washington *Evening Star*" 7831
"Washington is a market" 1455
"Washington Monument Grounds"
    6995, 6997
"Washington receptionists" 6506
"Washington Square" 7756, 8945
"Washington Square Station" 3050
"Washona" 6324
"washout, a" 2606
"washstand, deal" 10142
"wasp in the kitchen" 4965
"wasps as big as flying tigers" 5033
Waste 396, 2634, 5700, 7561
"waste, disposal of" 5700
"waste, obsessed with" 1261
"waste, unexplored" 2605
"waste and vanity" 2634
"waste not want not" 7561
"waste of good water" 7561
"waste product" 5700
"waste too much time, you dont"
    2430
"wasteland, panorama of" 3668
"wasting everyone's time, stop"
    2464
"wasting it, passionately enjoy"
    9483
Wasum, Otis 4988
"watch, boredom of his" 8663
"watch, Bulova" 8314
"watch, consulted his" 1201

"watch, gold" 4134, 9497
"watch, gold fob" 2335
"watch, looked at her" 163, 9294
"watch, looked at his" 10143
"watch, old royal" 9488
"watch, silver" 4273
"watch fires, desert" 8986
"watch him, stopped their games to" 7627
"watch him with silent admiration" 7627
"watch of eyes, ominously anxious" 6613
"Watch of the Fifth Ruler of the Day" 4592
"watch out for life" 5266
"watch the game" 8920
"watch the Imperial troops drilling" 8700
"watch the news on national television" 6342
"watch the people as he rode along" 9556
"watch the white-power demonstration" 6586
"watch the woman running" 10893
"watch whatever he did, everyone could" 3584
"watched, over her shoulder" 5428
"watched a patrol of police cars" 8187
"watched and mourned" 3962
"watched back" 8271
"watched by his mother" 976
"watched everything within range" 2095
"watched from the quarterdeck" 4417
"watched from the window" 5083
"watched helplessly" 2773
"watched her father descend the hillside into the Valley" 6713
"watched her own figure acting on the screen" 1317
"watched his visitor approaching" 9894
"watched its doing" 1850
"watched keenly and closely, this world was being" 519
"watched my grandmother make ravioli once" 1075
"watched party after party of armed men" 1172
"watched the *Annie Conser*'s bow" 8099
"watched the golf carts" 5627
"watched the house and waited" 10087
"watched the muddy boys" 8921
"watched the Pi-Ume-Sha dancers" 2114
"watched the stage driver get drunk" 2900
"watched the three vehicles" 9765
"watched the work going on in the camp" 10940

"watcher, Coles was a" 5936
"watcher, the" 10093
"watcher on the hilltop" 5716
"watchers of the night" 6373
"watches a Western" 1326
"watchfulness, indolent" 2295
Watching 214, 320, 1172, 3774, 4195, 4254, 6719, 7707, 8003, 8029, 8271, 9765, 10041, 10070, 10087
"watching, river-" 7684
"watching a baseball game through half-closed eyes" 8929
"watching a movie, as though he were" 5118
"watching a small boat" 1751
"watching at the classroom window" 8747
"Watching Father Die" 2396
"watching fireflies" 4969
"watching her go" 1602
"watching her grandmother" 1870
"watching him expectantly" 8268
"watching his father" 6719
"watching its growth" 2630
"watching loud TV" 6783
"watching me, they are" 9455
"watching mesmerized" 5636
"watching Ryan beat up the Mexican crew leader" 1321
"watching shadows" 8038
"watching television" 9375
"watching The Bad Czech, they were all" 4523
"watching the moon" 8450
"watching the night Tendai was conceived" 8029
"watching the North Star brighten" 527
"watching the receding train" 1575
"watching the shadowy fish" 402
"watching the stars in the heavens" 2677
"watching the swing door" 10041
"watching the thick red moon" 8452
"watching the traffic go by" 9451
"watching the truck" 6165
"watching things that don't move much" 7467
"watching those first moon-men" 9733
"watching two delivery men carry our brand-new television set" 9373
"watchman, night" 8520
"watchtower of York Factory" 7918
"watch-tower over a camp of fear" 1310
Water 1447, 5325, 6087, 7671, 7695, 7941, 9691, 10811
"water, black" 8111
"water, black rushing" 40
"water, blue" 1598, 9863
"water, brim with brown" 5169
"water, broken" 5023

"water, bronze-green" 7684
"water, channels of dark" 727
"water, clear" 5154
"water, eyes are the color of" 7917
"water, filthy" 5372
"water, first constant was" 9442
"water, gentle swells of warm" 8057
"water, glass of" 6809
"water, glittering floor of the" 8082
"water, gritty" 976
"water, half-covered by a skim of" 525
"water, here by the" 8835
"water, hot running" 8760
"water, I trust" 9691
"Water, Indal" 9561
"water, it is about" 7941
"water, let himself into the" 9318
"water, live within sight of salt" 7938
"water, long sluggish" 5025
"water, miles of crinkling" 10696
"water, movement of the" 7677
"water, night" 5952
"water, oil-smooth" 8125
"water, shining" 4133
"water, sky the same colour as the" 7943
"water, sparkling" 1481
"water, streams of" 7146
"water, swiftly moving but heavy" 2529
"water, tears and" 10811
"water, to his knees in" 9997
"water, twinkling with" 5141
"water, warm tropic-blue" 8147
"water, waste of good" 7561
"water, wealth of clear" 1447
"water and women" 10811
"water ballet" 9729
"water boiled and roared in a hissing fury" 7939
"water broke through the ground, the first bit of" 3669
"water cascading as if from some jagged rupture" 9837
"water churning up phosphorescence in the river" 6942
"water courses of a prairie" 8622
"water dripping from sheets and halyards" 8142
"water flowing in upon the Syrian coast" 8057
"water for a civilization" 7695
"water forming the oceans" 525
"water from a copper jug, added hot" 8044
"water in a haunch of the crouching mountains" 6087
"water in the beginning, it was about" 7941
"water in the metal tank" 5325
"water is yellow with the mud of half a continent" 7664
"water lies broken" 7685

"water line" 9224
"water meters" 3020
"water of a blue more deep" 5177
"water of a pool, pale green" 10448
"water of the brook, icy" 10943
"water on the first floor, only a foot or two of" 7291
"water ran down and away from it" 3648
"water slanting" 10730
"water sour" 8101
"water splashed or slapped, protect herself from" 8491
"Water Star" 8783
"water supply controlled their location" 3643
"water that slithered against the quai" 2529
"water veiled" 7917
"water was slack at the inner bank" 7671
"water was streaked with great patches of crimson and gold" 8076
"water was too oily for waves to break" 7930
"Waterbath" 4909
"watercolor landscape" 3665
"watercourse, shallow" 5169
"watered, waiting to be" 9678
"watered, well-" 5067
"watered by narrow running streams" 7632
"watered by the river Don" 3893
"watered them after each senseless fight" 1846
"waterfall, began at the" 7689
"waterfall, close beside the great" 424
"waterfall, insubstantial" 2118
"waterfall spilling upon the dancing pairs" 2118
"Waterford" 1173
"waterfront just ahead" 1441
"Watergate scandal" 7000
"watering his roses" 10180
"watering hole" 5462
"Waterloo Station" 9412
"waterman, the" 8035
"watermelon, brought in the halved" 3815
"watermelon, I owned a" 3822
Watermelon Kid 9026
"watermelon patch" 5121
Waters, Elizabeth 6863
"waters, bleak" 5071
"waters, brown" 5133
"waters, frigid gray" 5030
"waters, great" 7507
"waters, green-gray" 7666
"waters, in the" 457
"waters, its great outer mass of" 7916
"waters, rocking" 732
"waters, still" 1751

"waters, still green" 5074
"waters, thin" 7507
"waters, upstream" 6155
"waters, yellow-brown" 742
"waters as angry as an intemperate man and grayer than death" 8722
"waters become troubled and disturbed, the shining" 7661
"waters falling into it, along the other" 9747
"waters of the Gareloch" 5071
"waters of the globe, on most of the" 8075
"water's rush and hiss" 8817
"waters yielded us our earliest civilisation" 7648
"watershed, crossed the" 10709
"water-side, at the" 1567
"water-traffic" 1126
"waterway, frozen" 3896
"waterway, Rainy River" 4049
"waterways, various winding" 9521
Watkins, Sally 4970
Watson, Amos 9971
Watson, Jim 2304
Watters, Katherine 3032
"Wattleborough parish church" 7180
Wave 7942
"wave, a" 6001
"wave, character of each particular" 7916
"wave, the ninth" 747
"wave and wind unfailingly, they broke" 5015
"wave breaks again, till the long" 7945
"wave of unexpected optimism" 10622
"waved above the towers of the Louvre" 9892
"waved at and You knowed all over again, she got" 4437
"waved her hand gently in the air" 1760
"waved her hand in the air like usual" 4437
"waved the cook" 4602
"waved to the neighbours" 1617
"waved wildly" 6730
"wave-flung" 435
"wavelength, the same" 9363
"wavelengths of hidden pressures, when I receive those" 2607
"wavelets made by the incoming tide" 10719
"wave-like sheets" 9241
"wavering and thinning in the quivering iridescence of heat waves" 9127
Waves 7916, 7936, 8068, 8145
"waves, choppy" 8164
"waves, grey" 7304
"waves, heat" 9127
"waves, its million" 7921
"waves, longest reach of the" 7945

"waves, plunging down the" 8129
"waves, shimmering in invisible" 5340
"waves, small" 7928
"waves, smooth shiny infolding" 2529
"waves, unleashing" 7939
"waves beat angrily upon the sandy shores" 7661
"waves climbed the slope of the beach" 7936
"waves of the gulf" 8092
"waves of the Jordan" 10329
"waves ... pour themselves into an inland sea" 10329
"waves run in to the foot of the hills" 724
"waves slip back into their element, only very little" 5132
"waves spume, green" 8068
"waves swelled high" 8132
"waves to break, too oily for" 7930
"waves within him, words became" 8894
"waving" 1630
"waving all gayly and expressively his hat and stick" 8546
"waving his arms" 7393
"waving one arm over his head" 8671
"waving round the office a mildly revolted hand" 6497
"waving to her from the shore" 4587
"waving your car down the ramp" 8749
Waxman-Weissman, Benno 6132
"way, American" 289
"way, best" 233, 5058
"way, dies in his own" 2331
"way, finding his" 4895
"way, found her" 4420
"way, have its" 9450
"way, I was on my" 5787
"way, if I had my" 7553
"way, in a queer" 7009
"way, in a vague and hazy" 8297
"way, in her brisk" 7493
"way, in his sneaky" 8499
"way, knew he was on his" 1785
"way, lost his" 6491, 10421
"way, picked his" 9144
"way, superficial casual" 1246
"way, we are on our" 1773
"way along the country lane, made their" 3578
"way back, on their" 7552
"way down the Paddington platform, making its lordly" 5943
"way from Woodhorn to Potcommon, the only" 9138
"way home, on his" 4556
"way in, one" 6829
"way in or out of the Hamptons, it is the only" 9199

"way it happened, thats the" 9702
"way it has to be, thats the" 9702
"way led along" 9121
"way or another, in one" 10492
"way out, knew there was no" 2506
"way out, on his" 3326
"way out, the only" 7396
"way out of the house, on our" 1619
"way the thing happens to be done
  here and now" 7718
"way they entered the General
  Store, considering the" 9111
"way to bed, on his" 6543
"way to do it, the only natural"
  7718
"way to some fishing, on his" 3511
"way to the Double Y, on his" 7616
"way to the mine" 7950
"way you were going, which" 9202
Waycaster, Laviny 6417
Waycaster, Marshall 6417
Wayde, Willis 4891
"Waye, Daemon Wente" 9175
"*Wayfarer*, the" 8094
"wayfarers, local" 9091
Waymarsh 3913
Wayne 283, 8499
Wayne, Joseph 6626
Wayne, Mr. 4564
Wayne, Mr. and Mrs. 6525
"Waynesboro Female College" 9250
"ways, not many make new" 249
"ways, their hoggish" 3864
"ways about it, no two" 6257
"weak, blood" 8487
"weak, the" 10522
"weak came in droves, the" 10522
"weak soft" 10811
"weakened, as he" 6549
"weakling, though no" 3341
"weak-minded enough to give up"
  129
"weakness" 9928
"weakness, he has one" 5925
"weakness, moment of" 5834
"weal or woe" 7372
Wealth 1965, 3569, 3607, 4346,
  5468, 6104, 6516, 7000, 7714,
  8712, 10769, 10782, 10794
"wealth, add considerably to the
  kingdom's" 1005
"wealth, commercial or professional" 3122
"wealth, commodities represent"
  10551
"wealth, main road to" 10549
"wealth, supply new sources of"
  2600
"wealth, sudden acquisition of"
  10555
"wealth and cultivation, increased
  so rapidly in" 6245
"wealth monopolized" 2600
"wealth of empty ruled pages" 5517
"wealthy, real" 369

"wealthy sixty-four-year-old American" 10422
"wealthy tradesman" 6516
"wealthy Zagreb banker" 10562
"weapon, concealed" 6207
"weapon, one day out with his"
  7990
"weapon of a brave and honoured
  Republican soldier" 8641
"weapons" 10521
"weapons, in hand as" 990
"wear, don't know what to" 2860
"wear, Grandma used to" 4154
"wear over their faces to distort
  and disguise" 2066
"wear them always, she would not
  have to" 4153
"wearied men" 8851
"wearing, what are you" 2882
"wearing a clean denim shirt" 3646
"wearing a picture of Christ" 7538
"wearing a wrinkled sort of colorless jumpsuit" 5118
"wearing an imaginary baseball
  cap" 302
"wearing black" 3956
"wearing black levis" 2839
"wearing it up on her shoulders
  like a cape" 10860
"wearing new sandals" 5880
"wearing orange clothes" 6546
"wearing pink today, I am" 2849
"wearing shoes and an assumed
  name" 8923
"wearing the starry-eyed look" 1101
"wearing tonight, what jewels will
  you be" 2868
"wears a thin and ragged linen
  shirt" 1287
"weary, old healer is" 1799
"weary from the cold and the dust
  and the stares" 9649
"weary might sit" 7896
"weary of Thucydides" 99
"weary task" 10927
"wearying of his job" 1493
"weasel up under your skin like
  hookworm" 6381
Weather 182, 183, 277, 765, 829,
  1002, 1399, 1472, 1544, 1547,
  1551, 1555, 1559, 1563, 1564,
  1727, 2062, 2070, 2132, 2138,
  2139, 2147, 2151, 2173, 2182,
  2197, 2244, 2264, 2275, 2279,
  2402, 2405, 2440, 2448, 2659,
  3805, 3908, 4275, 4306, 4367,
  4368, 4369, 4370, 4371, 4372,
  4373, 4377, 4378, 4379, 4380,
  4381, 4383, 4387, 4388, 4391,
  4392, 4393, 4394, 4396, 4397,
  4398, 4400, 4402, 4407, 4409,
  4412, 4413, 4419, 4424, 4426,
  4428, 5068, 5550, 5630, 5631,
  5704, 5747, 6315, 6567, 6654,
  7031, 7287, 7289, 7293, 7294,

7295, 7298, 7299, 7300, 7302,
  7306, 7307, 7312, 7314, 7320,
  7321, 7322, 7325, 7326, 7329,
  7330, 7335, 7337, 7338, 7341,
  7345, 7422, 7661, 7912, 8085,
  8129, 8136, 8330, 8442, 8584,
  8585, 8587, 8590, 8591, 8600,
  8601, 8608, 8612, 8613, 8615,
  8617, 8625, 8779, 8877, 9001,
  9063, 9066, 9068, 9069, 9073,
  9074, 9076, 9082, 9086, 9088,
  9098, 9195, 9220, 9320, 9341,
  9354, 9730, 10256, 10567, 10568,
  10576, 10577, 10578, 10579,
  10585, 10586, 10592, 10594,
  10597, 10599, 10601, 10602,
  10605, 10606, 10607, 10609,
  10610, 10612, 10614, 10615, 10616,
  10617, 10618, 10619, 10627, 10628,
  10629, 10630, 10632, 10637,
  10677, 10678, 10679, 10680,
  10681, 10682, 10685, 10686,
  10688, 10690, 10698, 10703,
  10705, 10709, 10711, 10712, 10714,
  10715, 10717, 10722, 10724,
  10729, 10730, 10732, 10733,
  10734, 10736, 10737, 10738,
  10740, 10743, 10746, 10747,
  10748, 10750
"weather" 2533
"weather, a long run of raw" 2264
"weather, about the" 5550
"weather, absolutely perfect" 5630
"weather, aware of the" 10628
"weather, bitter cold" 765
"weather, calm" 2543
"weather, connoisseur of" 6654
"weather, dirty" 2607
"weather, dolphin" 10594
"weather, earthquake" 10619
"weather, fine" 10615
"weather, glorious summer Adriatic" 9575
"weather, good corn-growing" 9098
"weather, hottest" 4383
"weather, I even remember the"
  7422
"weather, in hot" 5351
"weather, in just such" 9881
"weather, in this" 1560
"weather, look at the" 10568
"weather, outside the" 1472
"weather, provide himself against
  the" 10579
"weather, pursued by harsh" 9657
"weather, strange" 10733
"weather, sudden burst of gold and
  silver" 10585
"weather, the" 277, 2501, 7312,
  8877
"Weather Bulletin" 9086
"weather bureau forecast sun" 10599
"weather charts of the world" 9073
"weather exist, did" 10605
"weather front is moving in" 10606

"weather had a different feel" 4388
"weather had been seesawing between winter and spring" 10632
"weather had changed" 8442
"weather had changed overnight"
10577
"weather is known, state of the"
9001
"weather is not unusual, when the"
3126
"weather is what it should be, if
the" 8053
"weather perpetually changing"
10578
"weather report" 829
"weather showed a lack of character" 10601
"weather vane" 2214
"weather was fair" 9730
"weather was mild and sunny" 5631
"weather was not unusual, when
the" 1324
"weather was rainy" 5747
"weather was very bad" 1162
Weatherby, George 8976
"weathercock, as sure a" 2607
"weathers, out in all" 8220
"weave, pattern to" 5439
"weave, spin and" 1005
Webber, George 5914, 8263
Weber 4288
Weber, Philip 5840
Webster 3465, 6414
Webster, George 2554
"wed, newly" 8745
"wed December, May might" 6249
"wedded an old flame" 5728
Wedderburn, Alexander 917
"wedding, Aunt Helen's garden"
10676
"wedding, day after his" 7737
"wedding, day of my" 5108
"wedding, going to a" 1100
"wedding, her" 1243
"wedding, his" 1157
"wedding, my sister's" 4574
"wedding, never missed a" 10663
"wedding, no carriages for her"
10653
"wedding, strange" 10666
"wedding, tasted of a" 10645
"wedding, Tilney-Studdart" 10646
"wedding, unusual fact to set down
of any" 10652
"wedding, your father's" 10654
"wedding cake, throw crumbs of"
10657
"wedding day" 10643
"wedding day, Duke of Windsor's"
10669
"wedding I ever went to, the best"
10675
"wedding in the basilica of Santa
Chiara" 10674
"wedding night" 7059

"wedding of a girl called Fitzgibbon" 10649
"wedding reception" 8745
"wedding to Ben Berliner" 10671
"wedding was one of the worst
events in my experience" 10667
"wedding went without a hitch"
10652
Weddings 952, 1100, 1157, 1243,
1995, 1996, 2930, 3599, 3604,
4119, 4574, 5108, 5732, 6865,
7059, 7737, 8745
"weddings, baby-" 10642
"weddings, first big summer of"
2930
"wedged with her Best Friend" 982
"Wedgwood blue" 4642
"weeds, fertile for" 6811
"weeds of the borrow pit" 437
"week, all" 641
"week, last" 72
"week, twice a" 6587
"week of summer, in every" 6587
"week of torture, stinking" 2171
"weekday, on every ordinary" 1626
"weekday bleached by summer
light" 1754
"weekend, over the" 10970
"weekend break" 2508
"weekend two, her usual" 10320
Weeks, Snowy 660
"weeks, six pale-blue fluorescent"
8680
"weeks old, four wet and wintry"
9569
Weenie 4530
"weeping" 2406
"weeping, came" 2079
"weeping one will not turn to salt"
2080
"weeps most, which mother" 6649
"Weepy" 7098
"weevils, like bloodstained" 6225
"weevils napping comfortably inside curled poplar leaves" 5272
"wegiwa" 7599
"weighed and considered all this"
6604
"weighed down by millenniums"
9503
"weighed one thing against
another" 1069
Weigholtz, Mrs. 6652
"weighs a little more" 10797
"weight, throwing their" 8940
"weight coming from all directions"
33
"weight of a tremendous surge" 5011
"weight of obligation" 9951
"weight on one side, it meant a"
10905
"weight thirteen stone three
ounces" 5941
"weighted with passionate words"
2311

"weights, ankle" 3487
"Weights and Measures" 6974
Weiller, Monsignor Hans 1523
Weinstock, Martin 6491
"weir, roaring softly behind him
like a" 2964
"weird dream" 2773
"weirdest, the very" 3497
Weiss, Dr. 5493
Weiss, Dr. Jeffrey 6511
Weissburg 6372
Welches 3183
Welchman, Dr. Hugh 3861
"welcome home" 4599
"welcome the guests who were just
beginning to arrive" 6330
"welcome to Mt. Hope" 8317
"welcome us home" 6008
"Welcome Wagon lady" 1432
"welcome you back to-day" 9884
"welcomed in lofty rooms by millionaires and poets and actresses"
243
"welcomed the intrusion" 9906
"welfare center, the" 3424
"welfare of his two daughters" 6523
"well, all is" 1788
"well, did very" 6930
"well, that's all very" 3746
"well as could be expected" 4013
"well born" 4442
"well enough to bear it, when I
was" 9047
"well met" 3812
"well rising into grey film and
vapour" 2754
"well with herself, had done very"
9261
"well woman, not a" 170
Welles, Thomas 10366
"Wellesley and Sable" 3296
"Wellesley Massachusetts" 6774
Wellingborough 4117
Wells, Esther 5356
Wells, Myra 3334
"Wells" 1486
"Wells, arrival at the" 7708
"wells of Scamander" 9738
"well-wishers on the dock" 4916
"Welsh glens, black" 10574
"Welsh Marches beyond, the distant" 3155
"Welsh princes maintained their independence" 6802
"Welsh steward" 9568
Welton, Gilbert 4350
Wendell, Karen 2783
Wendover 5940
Wendy 4770
"went away with the Nawab" 1689
"went back to Ivers" 1755
"went back to Oxford recently" 1740
"went down, *Niome*" 3693
"went down town" 1579
"went flat into a balustrade" 733

"went for it" 8369
"went forth, quietly" 1574
"went forward slowly in a steady pace" 10353
"went in" 2688
"went in her spare time" 1710
"went in overnight" 166
"went into a shop" 1046
"went off for the day" 6640
"went on in the Manor, what" 7840
"went one morning to Harley Street" 141
"went out, whenever they" 7208
"went out into the garden" 4224
"went out that way, nobody ever" 2700
"went out to India to die" 2421
"went out to the upper deck" 8115
"went slowly upstairs" 9406
"went that night, wherever he" 7952
"went through Oxford together" 8207
"went to Bermuda in early May" 9732
"went to France in 1917" 8695
"went to Ghaleh Bagh, three nights before he" 6014
"went to live with his half brother" 6148
"went to Los Angeles" 6172
"went to New York City on an Amtrak train" 9597
"went to the back door of her home" 2702
"went to the flower room to iron it" 6356
"went to the library" 3426
"went up it, that day we" 9143
"went when I was young, where I" 1729
Wentworth 1593
Wentworth, Andrew 3846
Wentworth, Madge 3846
"Wentworth" 10687
"wept, you" 2337
"wept and trembled" 2751
"were not at all, you" 4878
"werewolf, born a" 337
Werner 2517
Wertheim, Eduard 554
Wes 8810
Wess, Aunt 10035
"Wessex" 2190
"Wessex, Gibraltar of" 9091
"Wessex, Upper" 10331
"Wessex coast" 10779
"Wessex town" 4996
"west, almost painfully blue" 7775
"West, Far" 2956
"West, in the Old" 1460
"west, middle" 5709
"West, Middle" 1821, 1965
"West, mountain" 1581
"West, news swept out of the" 6333
"West, open in the" 9860

"West, out" 4534
"West, raw and mighty" 4046
"West, she went" 2615
"West, Wild" 1320
"West Bank of the Jordan River" 831
"West Coast" 9918
"West Condon" 3338
"West End" 9378
"West End, in the heart of the" 9161
"West Indian islands" 9216
"West Meadows" 1367
"West Poley" 1572
"West Side Story" 9397
"West Virginia" 3586
"Westbourne Terrace" 8341
"Westchester" 4577, 10564
"Westchester, county of" 6608
"Westchester, valleys of" 9512
"Westchester County New York" 4425
"Western, watches a" 1326
"Western civilization" 10083
"Western Front" 8678
"Western Isles, dark nakedness of the" 4034
"Western movie, as in a" 9842
"Western Union" 6004
"Western world, Christ-forgetting Christ-haunted death-dealing" 7205
"Westland helicopter" 2847
"Westminster" 5126, 9537
"Westminster, Dean of" 7513
"Westminster Abbey" 8942
"Westmoreland" 10767
"Westmoreland valley, lonely" 9742
Weston, Mrs. Vance 4730
Weston, Vance 5413
"Weston Massachusetts" 8372
"Westport" 1624
"Westport Connecticut" 5352
"Westward, stand to the" 2543
"wet and glitters, everything is" 7318
"wet day, dark" 2150
"wet from swimming in Crazy Creek" 3714
"wet with fog and surf" 5015
Wetherby, Della 9875
Wetherford, Lee Virgina 1581
"Wexford, county of" 2024
"Weydon-Priors, village of" 10331
"Weymouth" 6524
"wha'?, you're" 7094
"whale, breed of" 3618
"whale, petrified" 9788
"Whale Back, hills of the" 32
"whale lined with jagged basalt" 9788
"whaleboat, waiting" 405
"whalecatcher, the" 8113
"whaled a boom of delight" 444
Whales 444, 480, 3618
"whales, happy Blue" 444

"whales went to the great bay, each year the" 480
"whaling brig" 5628
"whaling fleet" 8116
"wharf" 3431
"Wharf, Circular" 9934
"wharf, government" 2270
"wharf, his" 4693
"wharf, huge shed of the" 6216
"wharf, Jersey" 4910
Wharton, George 5111
Wharton, Miss Emily 1891
"wharves" 8254
"what am I" 6840
"what art thou" 9989
"what else to do" 5515
"what happened" 3452, 3510, 9006
"what happened to him" 709
"what is it" 2782
"what *is* this" 5519
"what it takes, he had" 6424
"what it was" 4072
"what now" 2090
"what on earth" 5438
"what she was" 4804
"whatever it was" 3285, 6582, 8539
"what's happening" 3454
"what's this" 2092
"what's up" 2094
"wheat, newly blossoming" 6395
"wheat stubble" 2236
"wheat-growing" 1383
"wheat-rust" 3105
"wheel, at the" 2989, 3046
"wheel, hands off the" 3004
"wheel, spin of the" 10980
"wheel, steering" 2942, 8282, 8456
"wheel chair" 10832
"wheel hummed, the" 6958
"wheelchair, dozed in his" 8461
"wheelchair, from its" 6039
"wheelchair, in her" 4922
"wheeled me out on to the verandah" 6632
Wheeler 971
Wheeler, Claude 10115
Wheeler, Obadiah 1147
Wheeler, Ruth 10833
Wheeler, Uncle Charlie 9876
Wheeler, Zoyd 10310
"wheelhouse" 10147
"wheels, big heavy wooden" 9830
"wheels and hooves, iron-shod" 9130
"wheels churning in a mixture of dirty snow and loose stones" 9791
"wheels cocked absurdly up on the bank" 9790
"wheels of solid steel, five hundred" 7278
"wheels of the Coronation Special" 7261
"wheels of the stagecoach" 9772
"wheels of the wagon rolled . . . over his unconscious neck" 2374

"wheels on the soaked gravel" 6624
"wheels . . . screamed and scraped along the rails" 7278
"wheeze of the black engine car" 7283
"when now?" 7198
"When the Saints" 5468
"where am I" 5024
"where are we" 5612
"where I am" 10243
"where I was, that's" 2872
"where is he" 5969
"where is there to go" 1737
"where it was" 4072
"where now?" 7198
"where they had gone, so I could see" 2664
"where we are, you know" 3617
"where were 'they'" 7208
"wherever it is that I am" 5606
"whiff of fall, detected the last" 8528
"whiff of salt fish" 8512
"whiff or two, give 'er another" 10114
"whiffing" 6652
"whig, moderate" 6607
"Whileaway" 803
"whim" 5884
"whim, not entirely a" 5815
"whimper, animal" 10199
"whimsical, some things" 5884
"whimsy, inappropriate" 4897
"whined again, collie" 9898
"whining" 2913
"whining with its own weight" 1129
"whip, cracking his" 3009
"Whippet Georgia" 826
"Whipping, Public" 7186
"whipping of silk skirts" 7229
"whipping the grey waves into a turbulent" 7304
Whippy Bird 1474
"whip-poor-will" 720
"whirled my chair to face him" 9909
"whirling course" 9841
"whirling in a violent wrestle with the wind" 7320
"whirling like a dancer" 410
"whirling up the brisk little hills" 2950
"whirlpool of despair" 3705
"whirlpools in the quiet water, a trail of" 8155
"whirlwind, the failing" 10705
"whirr of grass-mowers droned" 8800
"whisker, his gray fringe of chin" 8079
"whiskers, powerful" 462
"whiskey, pint of" 2911
"whiskey, pint bottle of" 2925
"whiskey, signalled for a" 295
"whiskey, sit with a" 5357
"whiskey, sneak a slug of" 2892

"whiskey and cakes, had put out" 3947
"whiskey into water in a glass, like" 2265
"whisky, moonshine" 899
"whisky and soda, sipped a" 574
"whisky he had had that morning, the bad" 2905
"whisky poured over it, a small" 8377
"whisper, crisp" 376
"whisper, in a" 4994
"whisper in the bedchamber" 7949
"whisper it to make you smile" 253
"whisper unto my soul" 7524
"whispered" 8027
"whispered to my mother" 1763
"whispering, inside the house they were" 8888
"whispering began, wondering" 7835
"Whispering Death painted on its side" 230
"whispers, it was still in" 7712
"whispers of fancy" 4603
Whistle, Sam 6420
"whistle, steam" 8765
"whistle, to" 7202
"whistle, urgent" 243
"whistle of the Manhattan Flyer" 243
"whistle westward down through the mountains" 10741
"whistled in the bed of pachysandra" 8788
Whistler, The 6203
"whistles, sawmill" 7907
"whistles always woke Mazie" 10238
"whistles shattered it" 10503
"whistles were tooting midnight" 2968
"whistles which I was never awake to hear" 8774
Whistling 1614, 6353, 7202, 8741, 10062
"whistling" 8741
"whistling, bus-driver was" 10062
"whistling, stopped" 6408
"whistling abstractedly to himself" 1614
"whistling round the bend" 8799
"whistling to warn the fishing-fleet" 8062
"whistling vociferously through his teeth" 6353
"Whit, the" 6283
"Whitbury" 6283
White, Gary Cooper 802
"white, buried deep in" 8592
"white, cry of" 7685
"white, fishbelly-" 1480
"white, subtle and tender" 10774
"white, they were all" 6830
"white American features" 4438
"white Americans" 4643

"white and colossal" 3665
"white and dirty white" 7945
"white and tense" 9318
"white as snow" 2820
"white beggars" 7036
"white boys, the first" 959
"white cashier" 1048
"white doctor" 10442
"white enough in all conscience" 2819
"white folks" 5729
"white girl, she was a very" 4157
"White House" 2161, 5404
"white in the face as the snowberries" 4157
"white indeed, very" 8587
"White Man" 9522
"white man, like a" 4347
White Man's Dog 8442
"white men, lonesome skinny fairly old" 5827
"white people" 3137, 9015
"white people did, so the" 61
"white people, we" 5055
"white person, still be a" 3262
"white sidewalls" 9786
"white skin, I have" 4789
"white woman, made love to a" 10186
"white women" 21
"white world" 5753
"whitecaps, speckled with countless tiny" 5071
"whitecaps of the bay" 4417
"Whitechapel" 1428
"Whitechurch, small town of" 786
"white-collar tribe" 1077
"Whitehall" 8801, 9882
Whitelaw 10411
Whiteleather, Miss 4739
"white-power demonstration" 6586
"whiten the streets and sidewalks, began to" 8617
"whiteness, half-seen" 10121
"whiteness, its perfect" 3728
"whiteness and strength" 9416
"whiteness that covered the ground" 1648
Whiteoak, Finch 1251
Whiteoak, Maurice 4562
Whiteoak, Renny 8547, 10579
Whiteoak, Wakefield 7842
"Whites, arms of the" 3413
"whites, poor" 7036
"whitethorn, scented" 9671
"whitewashed exteriors" 1349
Whiting, Jasper 3695
Whiting, Ruth 1645
Whitman, Alan 4789
Whitman, Walt 281
Whitney 8578
Whitney, Perdita 2421
"Whitsun holiday" 6568
Whitten, Calvin 3676
Whittington, Mrs. 9948

Whittle, Robert 2468

"whittling, looked up from their" 9775

Whittredge, Nancy 1091

"who am I" 4746, 4822

"who are you" 4771

"who I am" 4866

"who I am, begin with" 609

"who I am, simple just to say" 4851

"who is he" 5969

"who is it" 9976

"who is John Galt" 4750

"who knows Miss Rosamond Lacey" 4758

"who now" 7198

"who she was, the muddle of" 4804

"who was I before all this happened" 4834

"who was she" 4811

"who were they?" 4796

"*Who's Who in America*" 900

"whole of it, got the" 4437

"whole thing, the" 10904

"wholesale raising of silver foxes" 1016

"wholesale without paying for it" 583

"whoop bouncing back and forth against the hillsides" 10016

"whoosh, loud" 8111

"whore, drink and" 322

"whore, story of the" 3057

"whore, this one" 7743

"whorehouse on Stockton Street" 7079

"whoring thieving gypsies" 6292

"whorls shot across the blue film" 3689

"why, I can't think" 2539

"why I am writing this" 6045

"why I did it, tell them" 6044

"why I did these things" 2354

"why I wanted to become a priest" 1514

"why must we do this" 10932

"why they were there, that's" 6046

"why threes" 2100

"whys and wherefores" 7652

"Wichita" 1044

"wicked, exotic or" 1288

"Wickenburg" 2340

Wicker, Dr. 2478

Wicklow 1976

Wicklowe, Silas 8192

Wickwire, Morgan 4125

"wide, and easily as" 10891

"wide open country" 1616

"wide open spaces" 1320

"wide-awake in a world of cheerless realities" 10131

"widen and narrow widen and narrow" 10841

"widow, a" 6623

"widow, genteel young" 10768

"widow, leaving me a" 2368

"widow, rich" 5892

"widow, spirited Yugoslav" 9931

"widow, the" 4840

"widow, young" 6113

"widow and millionaire" 10782

Widow Douglas 5506

"widow of a nephew of his father" 9857

"widow of a wholesale New York grocer" 5080

"widow of Martino Consalvi" 6019

"widow of the beloved Nazarene preacher" 3338

"widow well on in years" 3104

"widowed" 3599, 5762

"widowed mother, his" 6110

"widower" 2726, 3498

"widower, old" 6545

"widower in public, longtime" 7721

"widower of forty-five" 3831

"widowhood, first on the block to reach" 77

"widowhood, my" 7030

Widows 77, 2368, 4840, 6113, 9931, 10782

"widows, group of professor's" 7074

"widows, musicians'" 6242

"wife, academic" 2332

"wife, could no longer live with his" 2486

"wife, Deacon Twitchel's" 9348

"wife, got rid of his" 6636

"wife, he had a" 6414

"wife, he'd take a" 5782

"wife, her High Mightiness my" 360

"wife, his" 125, 135, 1086, 1112, 1224, 1591, 1658, 1757, 1783, 1969, 1970, 1983, 1991, 2001, 2009, 2061, 2073, 2373, 2508, 2561, 2684, 2757, 2971, 3194, 3278, 3338, 3416, 3498, 3566, 3572, 3751, 3828, 3837, 3878, 3941, 3955, 3970, 4125, 4225, 4338, 4599, 4706, 4976, 5636, 5748, 6279, 6308, 6851, 6860, 6893, 6979, 7515, 7714, 8479, 8525, 9027, 9417, 9732, 9934, 10062, 10135, 10180, 10241, 10328, 10510

"wife, his beautiful" 5970

"wife, his ex-" 6140

"wife, his good" 6094

"wife, his lady" 9090

"wife, his pretty" 2942

"wife, his Rhine-born" 3202

"wife, his young" 2949, 7979

"wife, I need a" 8734

"wife, in want of a" 5726

"wife, kill his" 6201

"wife, Lao Li's" 1782

"wife, look for a" 4931

"wife, looked at his" 5772

"wife, man and" 10661

"wife, Mor's" 3744

"wife, must be his" 10434

"wife, my" 360, 597, 1142, 1185, 2051, 2349, 2664, 2681, 3200, 3277, 3579, 4119, 4571, 4789, 5456, 5547, 5777, 5811, 6187, 9036, 9517, 10406, 10651

"wife, my brother's" 4972

"wife, my dead" 7593

"wife, my dear" 3073

"wife, my dear good" 1971

"wife, my ex-" 5858

"wife, my second" 10433

"Wife, one" 7055

"wife, outlasting a" 3105

"wife, she was still someone else's" 5819

"wife, splendid" 9054

"wife, the" 2920, 8078

"wife, told his" 2663

"wife, vicar's" 7864

"wife, waiting for his" 5459

"wife, your" 7955

"wife and child, deserted his" 5914

"wife and I split up" 5811

"wife asleep on top of the sheets" 5777

"wife commit adultery" 1988

"wife had killed our two sons and taken her own life" 6187

"wife in a card game, won his" 3970

"wife of another man, sat with the" 7576

"wife of Bernard Amedroz" 6612

"wife of Earl Sigmund of Lökken" 10796

"wife of George Page" 5250

"wife of only four years" 2681

"wife of Richard Turner" 6177

"wife of Sir Cecil Waring" 7060

"wife reproached him" 7552

"wife so ill these past few weeks" 2508

"wife threaten to bring suit for sixty-five dollars" 7012

"wife was Mrs. Fountain's half-sister" 10771

"wife was stealing from me" 2051

"wife went off with a young and penniless man" 7864

"wife who gave teas to freshmen" 2332

"wife-left feller" 2651

"wife's high loud voice, his" 9997

"wife-to-be, my" 5819

"wifey, all right" 9265

"wig, Governor tore off his" 373

"wig, hat and" 9757

Wiggen, Henry 793

Wiggins, Bubbles 2852

Wiggins, Bud 2808

Wiggins, Hartley 3820

"wigs, very large full-bottomed" 3376

Wigton, Mrs. 3328

Wilcox, Victor 8498

"wild, gone" 7631
"wild, too" 189
"wild, vast tract of unenclosed" 2189
"wild and savage hunger" 3304
"wild as a storm" 8802
"wild growth, place of" 3906
"wild horse" 6814
"wild hyacinth" 3804
"wild part of Arizona" 869
"Wild West Exhibition" 1320
Wilde 7144
Wilder, Janice 64
Wilderness 263, 455, 783, 959,
    1543, 2189, 2194, 3086, 4035,
    4047, 4049, 4144, 5581, 6057,
    6100, 8379, 8682, 10343, 10468
"wilderness" 4035
"wilderness, Canadian" 1543
"wilderness, eyes scanning a" 5981
"wilderness, flows through" 9747
"wilderness, green" 2194
"wilderness, in the heart of a great"
    3086
"wilderness, many a broad waste
    of" 263
"wilderness, Ohio" 4144
"wilderness, primeval" 6057
"wilderness, the" 4047
"wilderness, toils and dangers of
    the" 10468
"wilderness, walked through the"
    1530
"wilderness, Western" 3639
"wilderness between the Ohio
    River and the Gulf of Mexico"
    7232
"wilderness of maple trees" 3095
"wilderness of rails and points" 9539
"wilderness of sea and shore" 7228
"wilderness of the French frontier"
    10343
"wilderness of this world" 2751,
    5581
"Wilderness of Zin" 5831
"Wilderness Trail" 1912
"wilderness world" 4049
"wildfire, spread like" 6334
"wildflowers, quiet as a bank of"
    1409
Wildlife 423, 8275, 9755
"Wild-Water" 10683
Wilhelm, Tommy 56
Wilibald 4456
Wilkes, Darren 1891
Wilkins, Mr. 6406
Will 4530
Will, Sara 10435
"will, damned silly" 4934
"will, free" 10409
"will, God's" 36
"will, he sent for his" 2302
"will and testament, last" 713
"will of its own" 3546
"will of my late grand-uncle" 4929
"will power, human" 5702

"will you or will you not" 7201
Willa 10390
Willemse, Agent 8463
William 298, 2007, 7016, 8018,
    8340
William, Uncle 7232
William the Conqueror of England
    6518
William the Lyon 3381
William the Norman 6090
Williams, Aunt Hager 8403
Williams, Fanny 5498
Williams, Marc 1193
Williams, Ralph Vaughan 6227
Williams, Sarah 1741
"Williamsburg" 373, 3531, 10352
"Williamsburg Bridge" 8798
Williamson 3648
"Williamstown" 4410
Willie 3247, 7437
"willies, I get the" 2705
"willing to admit" 3308
"Williston North Dakota" 10092
"will-less, brittle and" 7968
"will-o'-the-wisp" 4906
Willoughby 6613
Willoughby, Sophia 9881
"willow, shade of a lonely" 7662
"willow shade" 5121
"Willow Springs" 5222
Willowes, Laura 6106
"willows, stand of" 8790
"willows beside the wide still river"
    8350
"willows that gesture in tepid Au-
    gust airs" 299
"willow-trees" 6249
Willpower 5702
Wills 2302, 4929, 4934
Willy 1143, 10027
"Wilmington Delaware" 5486
Wilson 1959, 8358
Wilson, Professor Lucius 8255
Wilt 3397
Wilton, Jerry 4757
"Wiltshire" 3563, 8702
Wimsey 7107
Wimsey, Lord Peter 7376, 9790,
    10119
"win, anxious to" 5200
"win, rot and" 10811
"win it at any cost" 1839
"win this fight, she wanted to" 1839
"Wincaster Row" 9951
"winced" 6810
"Winchelsea church" 2300
"wincing whenever a new step
    rushed up to meet him" 24
Wind 14, 55, 176, 184, 673, 983,
    1002, 1106, 1447, 1481, 1554,
    1606, 1706, 1727, 1907, 2985,
    3696, 3794, 3895, 3909, 4133,
    4306, 4307, 5051, 5068, 5071,
    5138, 5550, 6354, 6365, 6914,
    7229, 7320, 7321, 7638, 7661,

    7684, 7685, 7854, 7922, 7943,
    8047, 8085, 8086, 8126, 8129,
    8136, 8248, 8422, 8516, 8528,
    8533, 8541, 8586, 8588, 8590,
    8593, 9078, 9082, 9215, 9239,
    9241, 9619, 9742, 9771, 9789,
    10014, 10146, 10574, 10579,
    10586, 10590, 10598, 10600,
    10606, 10614, 10616, 10846
"wind, backing" 10577
"wind, biting" 4306, 9092
"wind, bitter" 8584
"wind, bitter north" 10719
"wind, bleak December" 1907
"wind, blowing like a summer" 4610
"wind, brisk little" 10714
"wind, change in the" 4871
"wind, Chrissy heard" 10749
"wind, close-hauled upon the in-
    creasing" 8069
"wind, cocked her ears to the" 8764
"wind, cold November" 10692,
    10699
"wind, cold upper" 8586
"wind, cracked from the" 7685
"wind, cruel north" 10717
"wind, cry beat against the" 9619
"wind, damp" 8533
"wind, dawn" 9082
"wind, driven onward by the" 2337
"wind, dying" 10705
"wind, dying away of" 5068
"wind, east" 9742
"wind, fierce" 10679
"wind, fighting the" 3696
"wind, freshet of" 6381
"wind, good strong" 10728
"wind, groans sounded in the"
    10598
"wind, harsh late March" 10735
"wind, I am carried away by the
    same" 10723
"wind, I lost my" 6134
"wind, I need a" 10728
"wind, late October" 10753
"wind, light breath of a fair" 8093
"wind, light summer" 3794
"wind, lulls of the" 10002
"wind, masterful" 10682
"wind, moaning" 10755
"wind, most disagreeable" 10724
"wind, mostly the" 10752
"wind, muffler danced in the" 983
"wind, puffs of warm July" 2985
"wind, rising" 10700
"wind, sharp" 10692
"wind, shrieking" 4307
"wind, shuddering" 2337
"wind, skirts whipping in the
    warm" 7229
"wind, slightly chilling" 7854
"wind, soft fingers of the" 5138
"wind, soft summer" 10683
"wind, spring" 10590
"wind, stiff piercing" 7945

"wind, stiff south-westerly" 5071
"wind, stinging" 10572
"wind, strong north" 8110
"wind, the" 1002, 1393, 4133
"wind, there was no" 7943, 10702, 10736
"wind, thrilling flush of" 7922
"wind, vibrating in the" 10721
"wind, west" 7180
"wind, wild March" 10711
"wind, without" 1550
"wind, write a book about the" 5550
"wind . . . already clawed" 10708
"wind and rain" 9220
"wind and snow and sleet" 9065
"wind back to it" 9022
"wind be so strong, how could the" 10754
"wind . . . beat vainly and with savage insolence against the staid windows" 4307
"wind blew" 10687
"wind blew across empty miles of Texas desert" 10726
"wind blew . . . cold off the snowy mountains" 10751
"wind blew from the northern ranges" 10720
"wind blew gently, the east" 8510
"wind blew hard" 9241
"wind blew hard through the canyons" 10751
"wind blew in the tops of the pine trees" 10695
"wind blew its guts out" 9789
"wind blew lightly" 8588
"wind blew through Europe" 10739
"wind blew . . . with a sweep uninterrupted by dwelling houses or other obstacles" 10687
"wind blow her hair wild, let the" 10716
"wind blowing through 116th Street" 10699
"wind blows, when the east" 7661
"wind blows flat and strong" 10690
"wind blows in Trenton" 8533
"wind blustering down" 8085
"wind bore up from the Firth of Clyde" 5071
"wind built a wall of snow-white sand" 5138
"wind came in from the sea" 10718
"wind came up and swept along the floor of the desert" 10707
"wind . . . catches the outhouse door" 10743
"wind circling the earth" 10614
"wind cold from the north-east" 8129
"wind enough to clear the smoke" 8422
"wind from the east" 8516
"wind from the high ground struck it" 9771

"wind from the southwest" 1598
"wind had blown savagely from the northeast, all day the" 10688
"wind had quickened to a fury" 10722
"wind has risen early tonight" 10743
"wind howled round her" 8086
"wind . . . howls and shrieks and circles" 10740
"wind in New Mexico" 10744
"wind in port, waiting for a" 8047
"wind in the black locusts" 7638
"wind inarticulate meaningless" 10755
"wind is rising" 10677
"wind its way through the people" 3006
"wind knifing down Third Avenue" 10750
"wind laboured so mightily to build the barrier" 5138
"wind marked September's ominous departure" 10700
"wind messenger of death" 10740
"wind might have blown them" 7763
"wind moans in the trees" 10747
"wind moved over the river" 3405
"wind of mid June, the soft" 673
"wind prevailed" 6914
"wind pulled back" 10746
"wind push her head back, Ruby let the" 10691
"wind . . . rode up the main mast" 8126
"wind sharpening its razor on exposed skin" 10717
"wind shuttled, a lazy dry" 10693
"wind sifted out of the black Welsh glens" 10574
"wind sneaked into the convertible, the cold" 10713
"wind so high, the" 10706
"wind sprang high, a" 10684
"wind stirred amidst the trees of the garden" 3794
"wind stirs the redwoods" 10683
"wind swept across the wide confines of Portsmouth harbour" 10719
"wind swirled, cold" 9239
"wind swirled up strong and then died" 9077
"wind swirling through the hedges" 10733
"wind that bit sharply at their flesh" 8136
"wind that blows all these people down the street" 10723
"wind that came with the night" 522
"wind that lashed and whirled about the house" 8593
"wind that sent chills to the marrow" 4306
"wind that smelled of smoke and snow" 10720

"wind that whipped across the Platz der Republik" 10734
"wind that whistled about the corners of the house" 1907
"wind that . . . whistled with icy tongues" 10734
"wind thick with the sleety snow" 4307
"wind used to blow in the night" 10738
"wind usually came from the south" 7684
"wind was as icy as in winter" 10579
"wind was blowing" 1698, 10692
"wind was cold" 4475
"wind was increasing" 10681
"wind was particularly bitter" 10742
"wind was rising again" 8126
"wind was south-west" 10689
"wind was up and out" 10682
"wind which butts it and drives it" 7320
"wind whispering and moaning" 10727
"wind worried" 10748
"windbreak along the north side of the yard" 8790
"windbreaker, her" 10833
"windbreakers, grease-stained" 5982
Winderman 3601
"windless noon" 9479
"windless sky" 8408
"window, at the" 10753
"window, at the open" 8257
"window, bathroom" 8481
"window, big picture" 5959
"window, birds flew past the" 9426
"window, blue-moon" 2727
"window, how of the" 8850
"window, calling from the" 10231
"window, classroom" 2722, 8747
"window, come to the" 2696
"window, dirty" 3238
"window, fell out of the" 2520
"window, from her" 2730
"window, from his classroom" 8935
"window, from my" 9137, 10959
"window, going to the" 10952
"window, her bedroom" 9964
"window, high-set" 8260
"window, his" 5155
"window, his back" 8263
"window, his bedroom" 8262
"window, his cabin" 2701
"window, his office" 8274
"window, his small" 98
"window, I was at the" 3246
"window, large central" 6499
"window, large latticed" 8342
"window, like a Christmas" 8596
"window, long" 2719
"window, looked out of the" 9856
"window, looked out through the" 7324
"window, looks out his" 6303

"window, lower berth" 7474
"window, my" 767
"window, my living room" 2723
"window, obscure college" 7335
"window, office" 1751
"window, open" 5340
"window, open French" 7348
"window, open the" 2120
"window, opens the" 10325
"window, our little" 9063
"window, outside the" 10318
"window, outside the club car" 5181
"window, put her head through the" 844
"window, sat at her" 9460
"window, saw from my" 3787
"window, screenless iron-barred" 10320
"window, single show-" 1012
"window, sitting at her" 7652
"window, sixth-floor" 6321
"window, small crossed" 7849
"window, stained-glass" 1532
"window, stood at the" 7706
"window, stood by her" 8283
"window, store" 10392
"window, study" 8106
"window, tall narrow" 1849
"window, the" 2692
"window, through her unwashed" 8421
"window, through the north" 2704
"window, through the open" 8568
"window, to the" 9526
"window, trying to raise a stuck" 20
"window, turned away from the" 4160, 9326
"window, uncurtained" 10269
"window, up in the" 9678
"window, vast" 9411
"window, walked to the" 2728
"window between the kitchen and the pantry" 2689
"window blurred by out of season spray" 5624
"window in the dining-room" 7347
"window means so much to me" 2717
"window of a hockshop" 2760
"window of a small teahouse, inside the front" 8322
"window of her bedroom" 2695
"window of her flat" 5083
"window of his law office" 2501
"window of his private office" 8254
"window of his room" 9894
"window of his room in the attic" 8090
"window of Pedlar's store" 4143
"window of Rothstein's Discount Liquor Store" 8599
"window of the bedroom" 4082
"window of the box office" 10035
"window of the Château St. Louis" 7655

"window of the fire-lighted drawing-room" 310
"window of the German Propaganda Bureau" 5714
"window of the house next door" 6303
"window of the Maison du Poirier" 8742
"window of the parsonage" 6719
"window of the picturesque garden-room" 8378
"window of the plane" 9615
"window of the stable-block" 10933
"window of the tall house" 3053
"window of their new apartment" 2073
"window overlooking the Palisades" 7699
"window shades, the lowered" 2756
"window so multifaceted so prismatic" 5329
"window that looks on the street" 3810
"window that opened on the park" 3831
"window was a hard edged block" 7777
"window where the glass had been smashed" 2715
"window which overlooked the Embankment and the Thames" 8345
"window which was common in Paris" 2686
"windowless room" 6893
"windowlight, heavenly" 347
"window-panes, diamond" 3242
"windowpanes, grimy" 8615
Windows 20, 75, 735, 767, 844, 1020, 1036, 1084, 1601, 1849, 2120, 2219, 2269, 2501, 2686, 2689, 2690, 2692, 2693, 2695, 2696, 2697, 2699, 2701, 2703, 2704, 2709, 2710, 2712, 2715, 2716, 2717, 2718, 2719, 2722, 2723, 2727, 2728, 2730, 2760, 2822, 3158, 3165, 3166, 3209, 3238, 3246, 3776, 3787, 3792, 3810, 3978, 4143, 4160, 4281, 4332, 4393, 4514, 5133, 5155, 5181, 5182, 5309, 5316, 5329, 5338, 5340, 5959, 6160, 6303, 6310, 6316, 6371, 6499, 6548, 6719, 6900, 7315, 7335, 7347, 7581, 7655, 7696, 7699, 7706, 7707, 7777, 7834, 7902, 8065, 8090, 8106, 8254, 8257, 8260, 8262, 8263, 8274, 8304, 8342, 8345, 8378, 8421, 8481, 8502, 8935, 9137, 9253, 9451, 9460, 9533, 9545, 9856, 9894, 10193, 10210, 10231, 10256, 10269, 10317, 10324, 10592, 10696, 10703, 10863, 10893, 10933, 10959
"windows, banks of wide" 9225
"windows, beneath our" 750

"windows, calm" 1302
"windows, church" 1312
"windows, cut stone round all the" 3131
"windows, dormer" 5607
"windows, drawing-room" 735
"windows, dusty" 4004
"windows, face the" 6900
"windows, four dirt stained never opened" 3166
"windows, french" 2402, 7766
"windows, glowing caverns of the" 5338
"windows, high" 5316
"windows, hotel" 10257
"windows, its old" 9253
"windows, leaded glass" 5329
"windows, lights shone from" 6323
"windows, massive east" 6986
"windows, no" 4332
"windows, opened" 10699
"windows, petition" 4609
"windows, rattling frail" 10740
"windows, staid" 4307
"windows, store" 8606
"windows, streaking the" 7315
"windows, summer-dusty" 9451
"windows, tall and mullioned" 1177
"windows, three closed" 10139
"windows, through the curtained" 5309
"windows, trees reach in the" 2883
"windows and embrasures were few and narrow" 9304
"windows began to show yellow" 2219
"windows closed" 4407
"windows full of beautiful things" 1084
"windows full of ocean" 4354
"windows into the garden" 7766
"windows looked out to the disordered garden" 3165
"windows of a gloomy-looking inn" 1183
"windows of a neighbor's living room" 4250
"windows of Fleet Street" 6319
"windows of his ebony and teak paneled office" 7319
"windows of the Holyhead mail" 10108
"windows of the room" 2716
"windows of the small perfect glittering stores" 7229
"windows open, keeping both of the" 4614
"windows open to the garden" 8857
"windows open to the long-legged sun" 8214
"windows overlooked Hyde Park" 2822
"windows overlooking Russell Square" 2699
"windows rattle, old" 10738

"windows reaching from floor to ceiling" 3064
"windows showing black" 9833
"windows that opened onto Ridgeway Avenue" 8583
"windows were little fists of bluish light" 3209
"windows with their miracles" 1302
"winds, lost in the cool high" 6084
"winds, stirred by innumerable frenzied" 1706
"winds, trade" 10616
"winds are changeable and gusty" 10606
"winds blew high over Jersey" 5051
"winds blew strongly from the North" 10710
"winds came" 7321
"winds cold at the source" 10709
"winds like spirits contending with one another" 1706
"winds of April blew the fountain out" 1606
"winds of autumn, first chill" 10146
"winds of Heaven blow, when the" 55
"winds reverse, sometimes the" 10741
"windshield, bug-spattered" 3038
"windshield, sunlight cut through the" 2977
"windshield was closed, when the" 2946
"windshorn Booradeela Range" 4084
"Windsor, Duke of" 10669
"windswept acreage" 5975
"windy" 10733
"windy, it was" 10732
"windy day" 4943
"windy day, it was a" 10846
"windy side of the street" 10396
Wine 2236, 2915, 6654
"wine, always drank sherry" 2936
"wine, bowl of hot" 10196
"wine, connoisseur" 6654
"wine, could transform it to" 6809
"wine, drank cool" 8027
"wine, drink" 6752
"wine, glasses for the" 3847
"wine, goblets [hold]" 785
"wine, Irish" 9300
"wine, over their" 2886
"wine, palm-" 5281
"wine, roses and" 7709
"wine, spilled" 2129
"wine, strawberries dipped in" 4151
"wine, warmth and light of old" 9527
"wine and roses, days of" 3397
"wine and yuppies, days of" 3404
"wine in the world, drink all the" 2933
"wine sweetened with wild honey" 10196

"wined, I" 2913
"wineglass, tulip-shaped" 2921
"wineglasses balanced on knees" 4018
"wines coming to vintage" 2236
Wing, Isadora 5536
"wing, eternally on the" 7584
"wing, new one-story trauma" 2401
"wing, our starboard" 197
"wing, shadow of his" 724
"wing, translucent" 193
"wing covers all its extent" 724
"wing of *Archangel*, under the" 686
"wing-and-wing" 8114
Wingate, Joe 10680
"winged, still-" 729
Winger, Newt 4955
"wings, bifurcated" 7056
"wings, rudimentary" 8941
"wings, rushing of" 2126
"wings, till we rate a pair of" 5255
"wings of the evening breeze" 650
Winifred 6212
Winifrede, Sister 8903
"winking and blinking" 3413
Winlake, Agatha 10495
"Winnebago" 10787
"Winnebago, sitting on the bumper of the" 6875
"winner, backed a long-priced" 1101
Winnette 5378
"winning of a dance scholarship" 1250
"Winona Mississippi" 8005
"Winona University" 8907
Winslade, Ruth 3692
Winslow, Hooker 8482
Wint, Alan 247
Winter 1168
Winter, Lucy 9572
Winter 178, 292, 765, 1301, 1452, 1543, 1563, 1734, 2062, 2110, 2224, 2229, 2244, 2305, 3154, 3377, 3807, 4412, 5574, 6037, 6263, 6327, 6626, 7285, 7333, 7380, 7651, 7690, 7696, 7729, 8445, 8585, 8587, 8592, 8594, 8595, 8596, 8600, 8601, 8603, 8607, 9468, 10570, 10572, 10574, 10577, 10589, 10590, 10595, 10598, 10606, 10607, 10609, 10617, 10618, 10624, 10627, 10630, 10631, 10632, 10636, 10639, 10639, 10640, 10678, 10725, 10742
"winter, almost" 4412
"winter, another" 3807
"winter, Bristol" 7865
"winter, cold" 1543
"winter, cold strong heart of" 2244
"winter, decided to" 7130
"winter, dry leaves and bare branches of" 9468
"winter, finally coming out of" 1452

"winter, here it might have been the dead of" 10639
"winter, in the" 5287
"winter, it was" 10572, 10678
"winter, its long stretch of" 6249
"winter, let lodgings in the" 3154
"winter, like the unexpected coming of" 375
"winter, long cold" 7729
"winter, official beginning of" 5033
"winter, pass the" 6037
"winter, record-breaking" 1563
"winter, Russia in" 6263
"winter, sure foreknowledge of" 1301
"winter, that" 10598
"winter, that memorable" 9454
"winter afternoon" 9354
"winter and spring, seesawing between" 10632
"winter came late that year" 8603
"winter camp" 8851
"winter comes gradually to northern New England" 10589
"winter entrenched across the remote midlands of Ireland" 10607
"winter evening, pallor of a" 10577
"winter had been fierce and relentless" 10618
"winter had been relatively easy" 765
"winter had broken early" 7651
"winter had come in early that year" 10609
"winter had set in early" 8592
"winter in the upper heights of the Bear Tooth Range" 10570
"winter is memory" 10624
"winter morning, like every other" 10945
"winter mornings" 1477, 2250
"winter night, London" 7285
"winter night, long" 2229
"winter now, it was" 10636
"winter of despair" 3377
"winter of her discontent, the horrid" 8356
"winter of his soul" 5574
"winter quarters" 4007
"Winter Palace" 4583
"winter rains are over" 7333
"winter stillness" 2224
"winter sundown, cracked and dusty square of" 2704
"winter term" 10312
"winter that comes in June" 10595
"Winter was come" 10574
"winter was the warmest in a hundred years" 10640
"winter wood was cut" 6626
"Winter would last for ever" 2305
"winters, one of their off-and-on cold" 2062
"winters are long in Mattagash Maine" 10631

"winters on his back, fifty or more" 5299

"winter's white shabby screens" 10590

"wintertime, go off in the" 4169

Winthrop, George 10968

Winton, Charles Clare 6622

"Winton, city of" 7892

"wipe your feet" 4193

"wiped his forehead" 4414

"wire, live" 6338

"wire, sometimes you can hear the" 1129

"wire, twisted phone" 1111

"wired to her folding chair" 1169

"wireless operator" 6461

"wireless stations, Canadian" 3534

"wireless, turned off the" 8338

"wires, break a song over the taut" 6218

"wires, like a tangle of red-hot" 983

"wires rising and falling in sweet regular curves" 3044

"wiring of some . . . diabolical brain" 9019

"Wisconsin" 3359, 5838, 6414

Wisdom 275

"wisdom, fresh arrogance of his" 10759

"wisdom, it was the age of" 3377

"wisdom, troubled in her" 3562

"wisdom of Almighty God" 1496, 7801

"wisdom of the Church" 7539

"wisdoms, corrupt" 275

"wise about her hair" 4297

"wise and foolish" 5381

"wise ones at Oxford" 10910

"wise people, a very" 10757

"wise to get married, too" 10763

"wiser than anything else in the world" 10756

"wiser than we know" 10757

"Wisewoman, the" 3204

"wish, every man's" 8083

"wish, fluttering" 9861

"wish, if she should only" 8027

"wish, if such was their" 7142

"wish most heartily that something would happen" 928

"wish on the part of Government, an anxious" 6972

"wish that finally comes true, like a long-sought" 659

"wish you would, I" 2737

"wish-box" 5219

"wished he would shut up" 8788

"wished it were Saturday" 2250

"wished one could live slowly as one can play music slowly" 5268

"wished the phone would stop ringing" 1097

"wished to see me, you" 5876

Wishes 241, 653, 659, 928, 1097, 2250, 2449, 5219, 8083, 9593

"wishes, make their" 653

"wishes sincerely to help me" 1167

"wishing he could be different" 241

"wishing that Catholics had been encouraged to read the King James Version" 7546

"wisp off" 7317

"wisps of fog" 7779

"wisps of undifferentiated nothingness" 5266

"wisteria" 1480, 9665

"wistful dog" 2497

Wiswell, Seaton 6423

"wit, a fair" 1228

"wit, her" 10781

"witch, mother could have been a" 6476

"Witch of the West, brig" 8069

"witchdoctor, evil" 9045

Witches 6476

"with them all the time, I was" 9588

"withdrew into a cloud of reserve and despond" 2502

"withdrew to a side table" 5443

"withering away of heat and brightness" 2119

"withering the young crops" 4382

Witherspoon, Arthur 8530

"withy binders?" 3092

"witness, I will be her" 3462

"witness, turned out to" 3439

"witness, we shall now" 2389

"witnessed her father's murder" 6181

"witnessed to the respectability" 3589

Witnesses 3462, 7604

"witnesses of another colour, thirty-seven" 9941

Wittgenstein 6844

Wives 135, 597, 1112, 1224, 1782, 1783, 1966, 1970, 1971, 1988, 2000, 2001, 2008, 2009, 2051, 2073, 2332, 2349, 2373, 2486, 2508, 2561, 2651, 2663, 2664, 2678, 2681, 2684, 2949, 3194, 3277, 3278, 3498, 3566, 3572, 3878, 3941, 3955, 3970, 4119, 4571, 4599, 4706, 4931, 5239, 5250, 5459, 5547, 5636, 5726, 5736, 5772, 5773, 5777, 5782, 5811, 5829, 5845, 5970, 6187, 6201, 6635, 6851, 7515, 7552, 7576, 7593, 7714, 7749, 7864, 7954, 8078, 8476, 8479, 8525, 8734, 9027, 9036, 9090, 9417, 9997, 10062, 10180, 10202, 10241, 10328, 10406, 10433, 10434, 10651, 10796, 10843

"wives, advice on the subject of" 5773

"wives, four" 7749

"wives, married three" 6635

"wives, their" 7481

"wives, three or four successive" 5829

"wives, two" 3596

"wives and children, their various" 3608

"wives and daughters" 9738

"wives passed, young" 8815

"WLT" 7791

"WMFT, this is" 9365

"wobbled diagonally across the envelope" 1948

"wobbled drunkenly" 10445

"Wobblies" 285

"Wodensday" 4282

"woe, weal or" 7372

"woebegone and goopy" 2906

"woke, as he" 10202

"woke, child" 10317

"woke, city" 10264

"woke, Heriot" 10164

"woke, she" 7998, 10283

"woke, when he" 7407, 10285, 10289

"woke agreeably" 10296

"woke and groaned softly" 10208

"woke and lay with her eyes closed" 10266

"woke Anna, telephone" 10302

"woke at daybreak from a pitch of familiar dreams" 10291

"woke at exactly quarter past seven" 10189

"woke at first light" 10195

"woke at six" 8503

"woke at 3:45 A.M." 10297

"woke before dawn" 10143

"woke each morning before day came" 10195

"woke first, usually Cynthia" 10169

"woke from the dream-broken sleep of summer dawns" 836

"woke her every time" 10261

"woke her from a dream" 2756

"woke him" 10169, 10267

"woke him, the phone" 1137

"woke him from untroubled sleep" 10312

"woke him up, pounding on the door" 10135

"woke in the dark yet glimmering grey of some later hour" 8854

"woke it from an uneasy sleep" 10177

"woke Mazie, whistles always" 10238

"woke me some time before dawn" 10218

"woke me up, lousy blue jays that" 10207

"woke me up, she" 10175

"woke simply by opening his eyes wide" 10185

"woke simultaneously when the light came" 10242

"woke slowly" 10270

"woke soon after dawn" 10161

"woke the boy" 243
"woke to a morning of warm and balmy sunshine" 2264
"woke to find the room full of sunlight" 10225
"woke to hear his grandmother's voice" 10162
"woke to hear my sister calling" 10231
"woke to the sound of the sea" 10187
"woke two hours earlier than usual" 10275
"woke up" 7731, 10211, 10244, 10320
"woke up, Colman Brady" 10247
"woke up, Fanny felt the warm wetness and" 4177
"woke up, the King" 10288
"woke up, when he" 5605
"woke up, when I" 10179, 10197, 10304
"woke up a little earlier than usual" 10282
"woke up abruptly" 10131
"woke up afraid" 2804
"woke up alone" 10284
"woke up backwards" 10221
"woke up crying" 10240
"woke up hearing, chimes you" 7907
"woke up hearing a word" 10167
"woke up in the dark" 10236
"woke up in the middle of the night" 10239
"woke up in their new bedroom" 10305
"woke up one morning" 10323
"woke up one morning earlier than he wanted" 10311
"woke up slowly" 10142
"woke up the way he did every morning" 10262
"woke up with a head like a rodeo" 10319
"woke up with the curious sense of unreality" 10173
"woke with a terrible taste in her mouth" 10271
"woke with the first ting of the alarm" 10293
"woken by the methodical chipping of steel tools" 10257
"woken to thin sunlight" 10295
"woken up to turn on the water" 7158
"Wolcott Rhode Island" 6685
Wolf 2135, 8655
"wolf from the door, keep the" 5542
"wolf travels, moved as the" 7221
"wolf-beast, great" 3381
Wolfe 583, 4271, 7588, 9886, 10010, 10485, 10921
Wolfe, Nero 907, 1619, 2322, 3132, 3738, 8860, 9900, 9902
Wolfgang 4853

"wolfmother wallpaper" 7790
"wolves, abandoned me to the" 6551
"woman, a" 1724, 2002, 2976, 3012, 3891, 5609, 5851, 7082, 8256, 8283, 9982, 10038, 10291, 10353
"woman, American" 3959, 9464, 10374
"woman, another" 2677, 5914
"woman, any" 1706
"woman, aristocratic old white" 7435
"woman, beautiful" 9546
"woman, beautiful single" 6298
"woman, blond young" 10816
"woman, bloody bowels of" 9285
"woman, born a" 10766
"woman, born of a" 5583
"woman, colored" 964
"woman, curious foreign" 8959
"woman, every" 8978
"woman, every third" 7061
"woman, fair" 5344
"woman, fat rich" 2697
"woman, fiercely ruffled angry-eyed old" 5571
"woman, frail elderly Japanese" 10887
"woman, good" 10775
"woman, greet the" 9884
"woman, he found a" 3695
"woman, heavy Irish" 9370
"woman, heavyset" 8298
"woman, his high-yellow" 8458
"woman, I know that" 10889
"woman, if Homer had been a" 4474
"woman, Indian summer is like a" 10808
"woman, invariably depends on the" 10829
"woman, it had to be a" 7995
"woman, L.A." 7731
"woman, lay the blame upon a" 7554
"woman, lilac-eyed" 4901
"woman, little" 10799
"woman, little weather" 4197
"woman, married" 7721, 7995
"woman, met a beautiful" 6650
"woman, middle-aged" 3216, 6412
"woman, Muslim" 5822
"woman, Negro" 1272
"woman, never felt less like a" 3480
"woman, no place for a" 10836
"woman, noble" 1185
"woman, not a beautiful" 10882
"woman, not a well" 170
"woman, old" 97, 114, 147, 773, 1075, 3099, 4420, 5632, 7222, 8561, 9316, 9659
"woman, old Gullah granny" 118
"woman, old ill" 4508
"woman, old Indian" 10026
"woman, old serving-" 6002
"woman, older" 10387

"woman, one remarkable young" 10794
"woman, pretty" 10858
"woman, proud angry" 10791
"woman, second" 10856
"woman, seeing a" 7736
"woman, slim" 10883
"woman, small black" 10815
"woman, sprightly young" 838
"woman, sturdy steely haired" 6722
"woman, sturdy young" 9641
"Woman, Swamp" 253
"woman, tall old" 8186
"woman, the" 1622, 1954, 3882, 4922, 4970, 5632, 5961, 6388, 7737, 7860, 8092, 8361, 8799, 9168, 9530, 9963, 10188, 10558
"woman, very noisy" 2589
"woman, very old" 5283
"woman, very strange long" 10885
"woman, well-bred" 238
"woman, when she became a" 10872
"woman, where there is a" 10847
"woman, white" 10186
"woman, who was that" 10812
"woman, with a" 10434
"woman, young" 1629, 2529, 2533, 2919, 2966, 5471, 5799, 6562, 8557, 9659, 10134, 10800, 10806, 10850
"woman, young blind" 8004
"woman, younger" 7590
"woman, you're a mighty pretty" 10813
"woman at all, not a" 10856
"woman at the open window" 10863
"woman by the name of Roberta Hightower" 7741
"woman changes to a beast" 10877
"woman crushing ice cream cones" 776
"woman drove me back to Rio" 3012
"woman for four years, hadn't been to bed with a" 7997
"woman for whom I have always had the deepest affection" 10851
"woman from the Milk Marketing Board trying to kill me" 73
"woman has been at the bottom of it" 10770
"woman he had not met" 3022
"woman he'd been seeing on and off" 7963
"woman his father loved" 4588
"woman I have ever seen, largest" 10891
"woman I sported with" 7440
"woman I was introduced to" 6032
"woman in a tight green skirt" 6702
"woman in bed" 5324
"woman in her dream" 10444
"woman in her early thirties" 10894
"woman in love" 8002
"woman in middle years" 2581

"woman in our freshman dental class, the only" 10866
"woman in the chaise lounge" 8578
"woman in the middle of life's youth" 4901
"woman in the rocker" 2804
"woman in the white silk dress" 10441
"woman is the slave or the outcast of society" 10766
"woman like that, kiss a" 6038
"woman named Benna" 6302
"woman named Carla" 10896
"woman named Mrs. Cortez" 3170
"woman now approaching middle age" 10038
"woman of forty, sensible-looking" 10780
"woman of taste" 6607
"woman rode like fury" 7639
"woman running" 10893
"woman stood on her back step" 10073
"Woman taken in the raid" 2854
"woman to help hear Annie" 5782
"woman was an ancient thing" 118
"woman who died of a heart attack" 8030
"woman who had come over to prepare the supper" 3835
"woman who lived in the shoe, unlike the old" 5056
"woman who looks very tired and worn for twenty-nine" 6702
"woman who loved scandal" 7867
"woman who married her own son" 3628
"woman who was far from pale" 5799
"woman who was turning nineteen that day" 838
"woman whose presence turned men into spittling masturbating pigs" 10871
"woman with ample breasts" 10062
"woman with her skirts hitched up, like a" 1478
"woman with the bunned hair" 8761
"womanhood, girl to be approach-ing" 4170
"woman's bare backside" 6391
"Woman's Christian Temperance Union" 1911
"woman's cry, a" 7067
"woman's life, in every" 5776
"woman's mendacity is limitless" 7988
"womanised for far longer than ap-pears credible" 150
"womaniser approaching eighty" 150
"womb" 9626
"womb, he was already felt in the" 4011
"womb, her mother's" 7097
"womb, in the waters of her" 7078

"womb, smooth week in the" 7462
"womb, still yet in the" 558
"womb, stopped moving inside her" 7095
"womb, world" 5262
Women 21, 45, 46, 54, 55, 79, 118, 238, 253, 261, 376, 563, 564, 635, 776, 903, 1185, 1214, 1432, 1477, 1706, 1724, 1841, 1967, 1977, 1981, 1982, 2018, 2020, 2332, 2488, 2493, 2559, 2598, 2777, 2793, 2812, 2824, 2826, 2832, 2854, 2879, 2881, 2898, 2919, 2963, 2976, 3012, 3030, 3204, 3216, 3272, 3314, 3362, 3480, 3499, 3599, 3695, 3891, 3963, 3965, 3976, 4006, 4171, 4230, 4296, 4300, 4302, 4474, 4505, 4508, 4588, 4611, 4620, 4724, 4771, 4772, 4773, 4785, 4830, 4849, 4901, 4922, 5056, 5083, 5118, 5123, 5250, 5344, 5354, 5392, 5471, 5555, 5571, 5583, 5640, 5644, 5654, 5659, 5678, 5776, 5782, 5822, 5950, 6104, 6346, 6396, 6399, 6412, 6422, 6459, 6650, 6686, 6690, 6900, 6931, 6956, 7056, 7057, 7061, 7073, 7074, 7082, 7176, 7187, 7237, 7435, 7476, 7485, 7554, 7599, 7639, 7724, 7736, 7737, 7741, 7743, 7747, 7825, 7860, 7867, 7945, 7949, 7950, 7957, 7988, 7995, 7997, 8001, 8002, 8018, 8019, 8021, 8026, 8027, 8030, 8244, 8283, 8361, 8381, 8385, 8556, 8561, 8564, 8629, 8837, 8954, 8993, 9027, 9037, 9261, 9282, 9293, 9416, 9420, 9445, 9455, 9464, 9509, 9668, 9859, 9912, 9982, 10038, 10053, 10073, 10126, 10293, 10353, 10357, 10364, 10434, 10441, 10558, 10611, 10659, 10716, 10939, 10952
"women" 2598, 3599
"women, all I've learned about" 10835
"women, American" 10848
"women, as it comes to" 7068
"women, beautiful" 4309
"women, black" 10876
"women, blood and" 9285
"women, brave single-minded" 10837
"women, certain" 9282
"women, certain rare" 10774
"women, down among the" 10822
"women, dozens of" 10796
"women, famous Sylvester" 10053
"women, five young" 7645
"women, half-naked" 516
"women, high-waisted and muslin-gowned" 10779
"women, his love for" 5950

"women, I am the slave of" 10855
"women, I understood" 10849
"women, I'm tired of" 10876
"women, inscrutable and silent" 9381
"women, intermixed with" 3985
"women, invisible" 10875
"women, like innumerable other mid-life" 10844
"women, like many" 6690
"women, made love to five different" 8001
"women, most of the seven o'clock" 10293
"women, old" 1149, 10845
"women, older" 1977
"women, one of those young" 10777
"Women, perversity of view re-garding" 5392
"women, pregnant" 6817, 7099
"women, pretty" 4045
"women, pursuit of" 2488
"women, recumbent giant" 2225
"women, shrouded" 8891
"women, soft-bodied" 2772
"women, some men and" 10527
"women, still he looked at" 7749
"women, surrounded by young" 1051
"women, the" 10869
"women, those great revolutionary" 10837
"women, three nice young" 10862
"women, three rich" 9420
"women, two" 2095, 4006, 4224, 5337, 8381, 9455
"women, two elderly" 1889, 9668
"women, two white" 21
"women, two young" 8837, 10364
"women, very personable" 4432
"women, water and" 10811
"women are all kittens or cats" 7176
"women are beautiful" 3362
"women are billowy, the foam" 7945
"women are hanging out the wash" 10875
"women are mortal" 10867
"women bear only daughters" 7073
"women cleaning up with the girls helping" 3591
"women didn't work" 10880
"women do not clean their own houses or do their own nails" 1477
"women ever learned the way, none of the" 7950
"women feel guilty in not being born sons" 10853
"women gave birth" 7057
"women get together, when" 10892
"women give birth to murderers, some" 10790
"women had gone, after the" 2793
"women in the wegiwa" 7599

"women must do, other" 6686
"women of Fada, young" 10795
"women of her mother's village" 8244
"women of no note" 4454
"women of the past" 10837
"women on their own" 10895
"women pain, heterosexual fucking gives" 8021
"women peered at her" 8891
"women severely coiffed in long skirts and billowing blouses" 6868
"women standing on station platforms" 5654
"Women talk" 10764
"women tell me things" 7957
"women tend to crccp about" 55
"women to the arms of men" 7735
"women wanted to talk about anger" 10842
"women were dead, the five" 10864
"women were jealous of how well her clothes hung on her" 10852
"women were quarreling at his bedside" 1841
"women were undone by love than vanity, fewer" 10765
"women who cannot grow alone as standard trees" 10772
"women who were loved by Bob Dubois" 9027
"women with ivory skin and fine dark hair" 2772
"women with raging juiccs" 8993
"women workers from a textile mill" 10838
"womenfolk" 1604
"womenrain, some things are not" 7342
"women's voices" 7294
"won his wife in a card game" 3970
"won it, Dunlavin had" 3968
Wonder 2465, 5661
"wonder, a drift of" 4582
"wonder, certainty destroys" 5661
"wonder, gazed in" 8093
"wonder, I" 3271
"wonder, it was always a matter of" 7374
"wonder, love of" 5212
"wonder, pcople must" 1974
"wonder, soul-shaking" 7216
"wonder, the same rude" 110
"Wonder Bar" 7395
"wonder if Connolly is content now" 7532
"wonder if I can" 5501
"wonder of existence" 9118
"wonder of moving from one space to another" 9213
"wonder of the world, eighth" 8938
"wonder they might feel for the knucklebone of St. So-and-so" 110
"wonder what he meant by it" 4118
"wonder whence came the multitudes of pictures" 2753

"wonder who I really was" 2354
"wonder why they had ever dreaded their return home" 4559
"wondered" 9411
"wondered, I" 7589
"wondered, sometimes Jake" 8460
"wondered about women's breasts all the time" 9453
"wondered if he would ever have a reason to laugh again" 9454
"wondered later, he sometimes" 9424
"wondered what 'home' meant" 4552
"wondered where to lay down blame, he no longer" 7562
"wondered who she was" 4772
"wonderful, how" 194
"wonderful, some" 10992
"wonderful party" 6771
"wonderful place" 9524
"wondering, point of" 9289
"wondering, tried to stop" 2465
"wondering if anything might have happened that made me become what I am" 1276
"wondering if he was dead or alive" 10977
"wondering in a time" 7084
"wondering what he had forgotten" 3838
"wondering what she will say" 699
"wondering where he was" 5605
"wondering whether to inquire directions" 1227
"wonders of curiosity explored" 2600
"wonder-smitten with the trance-like aspect of the green and golden world" 10566
"wondrous occurrences" 3403
"wont, as was her" 9291
"wont, as was his" 10043
Wood, Jonah 2584
Wood, Myrtle 511
Wood, Philip Sidney 10168
"wood, a lilac" 430
"wood, a load of" 3069
"wood, a small" 5155
"Wood, Alton" 3894
"wood, an ancient" 2754
"wood, bosom of an old" 9738
"wood, dim shadows of the" 8032
"Wood, Duncton" 7326
"wood, dwellers in a" 9661
"wood, edge of the" 3559
"Wood, Harlot's" 9134
"wood, in a" 8718
"wood, in the low" 8701
"wood, long stretches of soft" 9128
"wood, many different kinds of" 3906
"wood, smelling of clean" 3176
"wood, soft greyness of weather-beaten" 3159

"wood, spluttering dry" 10678
"wood, the" 9673, 10344
"wood, wasn't carrying any" 867
"wood bell" 3804
"wood called Coilla Doraca" 10756
"wood crashing" 10297
"Wood Eaton" 9131
"wood fire" 869
"wood hyacinth" 3804
"Wood Ibis" 5069
"wood was cut, winter" 6626
"wood which rose with a steep but not precipitous ascent" 9738
Woodard, Leon 10447
"Woodbrook Green" 3134
"wood-choppers, sturdy" 3069
"woodchucks, round up" 4155
Woodcock, Sir Bussy 2306
"wooded combes, green" 3248
"wooded with leafless beech trees" 3421
"Woodedge" 1894
"wooden horse, famous" 2603
"Woodford Wells" 3498
"Woodhorn" 9138
Woodhouse, Emma 5555
Woodhouse, Guy 3170
Woodhouse, Rosemary 3170
"woodland" 6923
"woodland scenery" 3894
"woodlands, extensive" 9519
Woodley, Charles Alistair Wentworth 5984
Woods 959, 3024, 3894, 5069, 6212, 7316, 7619, 8507, 9666, 10344, 10354, 10404
"woods, backed by" 3184
"woods, Big Sur" 2906
"woods, black" 7260
"woods, dark" 7619
"woods, dark of the" 7633
"woods, darker" 6327
"woods, darkness began to settle over the" 3720
"woods, deep" 9666
"woods, dew-pearled" 3396
"woods, drove through the" 2989
"woods, edge of the autumn" 10404
"woods, followed the" 10354
"woods, great beech" 9533
"woods, gunfire in the" 4264
"woods, her deadened" 9946
"woods, I went out in the" 2837
"woods, in the" 7652
"woods, luxuriant" 5125
"woods, musk of rotting" 4105
"woods, old beech" 9738
"woods, out of the" 65
"woods, peaceful Scottish" 4587
"woods, pine" 6408
"woods, scrub oak" 3907
"woods, the" 973, 4684, 7316, 7695, 8382, 8600, 9201
"woods, these" 6212
"woods, through the" 9150

"woods all about her" 8507
"woods beyond, into the" 5142
"woods by the boy's house" 825
"woods collided" 10009
"woods of fir and birch" 3024
"woods were as the Indians had left them" 959
"woods which had long since engulfed an ochre sunset" 6327
"woodshed, came back from the" 867
"Woodside" 1152
"Woodstock, town of" 2088
"Woodville" 2310
"woodwind instruments" 6236
"Woof! Woof Woof! *Woof! Woof!*" 3706
"wool, tinted" 484
"wool of my gown" 5096
"Woollam Chersey" 3698
Woolley, Bernadette 4821
Woolsey-Beans 1775
"Woolworth's" 4069
"Woolworth's, walked to" 3751
Wooster, Bertram 3341
Woosters 3698
"Worcester Mass." 9584
"Worcester Park" 9711
"Worcestershire field" 3640
"Worchester" 9890
"word, added one" 8663
"word, following each" 7350
"word, for which the Germans probably have a" 4598
"word, in the beginning was the" 601
"word, loud clear" 2759
"word, man of his" 3572
"word, most overworked" 7519
"word, produced the" 913
"word, serene was a" 1388
"word, spit out the" 7456
"word, such a grandiose" 10911
"word, that was the" 10905
"word, the first" 10908
"word, they received" 3170
"word, we got the" 1693
"word around town" 6969
"word basked under the light" 10202
"word break like a wave on the shells of my ears, hearing a" 10167
"word comes down the line" 8651
"word fall, let a" 8862
"word 'fantastical' is accentuated in our tongue" 10900
"word I am shy of using" 7711
"word in edgewise, get a" 3883
"word in the language, best" 10502
"word just with just this customer's personal brand of justness" 2589
"word like a bean, clipping each" 3832
"Word of God" 7534
"word out of Joe Mundy, get a look or a" 7136
"word right, if I've got the" 3850

"word spread quickly" 6329
"word to her father, she carried a" 10914
"word to say, a farewell" 1677
"word too much, says a" 4974
"word was set in a circle of thorns" 6808
"word 'wife', the" 10202
"wordplay, cue for further" 8027
Words 6, 383, 601, 913, 1230, 1284, 1388, 2311, 2589, 2759, 3268, 3832, 4598, 5341, 5464, 5505, 6247, 6302, 6808, 7200, 7350, 7456, 7492, 7597, 7711, 8184, 8651, 8838, 8843, 8862, 8883, 8889, 8890, 8894, 8898, 9015, 9313, 9416, 9606, 10051, 10167, 10202, 10502, 10548, 10814
"words, a few human" 5464
"words, about ninety thousand" 10904
"words, customary bald form of" 5735
"words, difficult" 7200
"words, exchanging" 4971
"words, first" 9606
"words, graven" 8947
"words, groping careless anguished" 1706
"words, his exact" 10521
"words, hold back hot" 383
"words, I have only recently begun to use" 10910
"words, ill" 7505
"words, liked the" 8760
"words, my" 9062
"words, rattling her" 5632
"words, speak great" 4454
"words, tell you in a few" 5355
"words, that is the thing with" 8898
"words, thems were my very" 8889
"words, Thorn's own" 5545
"words, torrent of" 8852
"words, weighted with passionate" 2311
"words, what were the" 10907
"words, with these" 2545
"words, without intelligible" 10199
"words and formulas, scrolls of" 8488
"words and memories" 116
"words are sometimes very poor exponents of such an event" 8838
"words became waves within him" 8894
"words came clearly enough" 8742
"words can convey, no" 1397
"words coming out obliquely" 9004
"words concerning my own history" 698
"words fail me" 7597
"words had a grave resonance" 10902
"words I am writing" 5505

"Words in England, by the usual corruption of" 6601
"words in the nature of preparation" 8964
"words looked strange, the simplest" 10051
"words mumbled by a disreputable old Irishwoman" 10814
"words of a dead man" 10548
"words of a great musician" 6227
"words of her own, strange" 8843
"words of love, soft" 8140
"words of the passover song" 2278
"words of the tune" 8739
"words on the printed page" 901
"words or any telling, beyond" 4582
"words out of my mouth, two" 7492
"words popped into Mr. Melton's mind" 9416
"words scattered by chance" 1230
"words spoken by himself quite without intention" 8847
"words to each other, couldn't say two" 3614
"words to me, first" 8890
"words to this song" 10912
"words were as torn from his lips" 8184
"words were like strips of raw silk rubbed violently together" 1706
"words were pinched through a throat" 8883
Wordsworth 5801
"wore a hunting costume" 2878
"wore a little ribbon on top of his head" 416
"wore a thick woolen sweater with three bone buttons on the left shoulder" 2787
"wore black, always" 2862
"wore bras, we all" 2881
"wore himself out" 3684
"wore his tunic in those loose and effeminate folds" 3812
"wore in the great War of Independence" 8641
"wore nothing else except a towel in his mouth" 2876
"wore the tightest pants" 2834
Work 135, 166, 1233, 1654, 2548, 3326, 3329, 3682, 4941, 5688, 6206, 6856, 7144, 7215, 7767, 8121, 8202, 8206, 8542, 8801, 9418, 9450, 10016, 10380, 10442, 10555, 10880, 10890
"work, after" 1233
"work, apply himself to his" 9450
"work, began this" 4499
"work, commuted to" 231
"work, did not" 7158
"work, dirty" 10950
"work, domestic" 10915
"work, enabling his to" 166
"work, going to" 5522
"work, good day's" 3326

"work, happily at" 3973
"work, hard at" 485
"work, he was truly seeking" 7215
"work, his" 3285
"work, his morning's" 1654
"work, honest" 10555
"work, I had no other" 5281
"work, if it's not and never has
  been your line of" 2036
"work, if only to end the" 8121
"work, long drive in to" 5104
"work, look at the" 6858
"work, Mr. Deacon's" 494
"work, on his way to" 7421
"work, playing at" 8839
"work, pleasant place to" 1065
"work, psycho-evolutionary" 7178
"work, stroll to" 10380
"work, there was" 1070
"work, title to this" 8953
"work, without pausing in her"
  10016
"work, women didn't" 10880
"work at the corner of the street"
  10930
"work better when surrounded by
  young women" 1051
"work chamber" 7144
"work clothes" 1952, 2852
"work for, good ranch to" 6418
"work for the YW-YMHA" 6452
"work going on in the camp" 10940
"work in shit all day long" 8542
"work it, tried to" 3648
"work me over gently" 6503
"Work of Nature, Checquer" 5552
"work of our archaeologists" 2605
"work of the day being over" 5615
"work off that fruit cake" 3487
"work on foot, came to" 10442
"work on the plant" 3484
"work out, not going to" 3525
"work that follows, responsible for
  the" 5474
"work up the nerve, trying to" 4210
"work was over, the day's" 1007
"work where I work" 6206
"worked, where he" 6319
"worked, where she" 7079
"worked all day" 6133
"worked all night on the engines"
  10938
"worked almost continuously for
  the better part of a year" 10918
"worked at a small café" 10896
"worked at the station" 3007
"worked for a year in a tiny art
  gallery" 6474
"worked for the same firm" 2011
"worked hard for him" 3329
"worked his heart out on a good
  book" 5476
"worked in a grocery shop" 6437
"worked out fine, everything" 3285
"worker, dock" 4315

"worker, skilled clerical" 5938
"workers, cement" 8813
"workers, migratory" 25
"workers, railway" 10458
"workers, restaurant" 6477
"workers, women" 10838
"workhouse" 779
"working, for a time not" 3619
"working, garden where she has
  been" 10890
"working a seventy-two-hour week"
  5286
"working and talking" 8206
"working at his side" 135
"working at midnight, still" 6856
"working at seat G16" 10951
"working at the hay" 10946
"working for the Mayflower Dairy"
  8515
"working himself off both-handed"
  7990
"working his row-boat out to sea"
  7913
"working in a cotton mill" 4186
"working in the kitchen" 1968
"working off the temporal punishment due to sin" 7852
"working on a perfect game" 8918
"working on our house" 6941
"working quietly in his room" 8801
"working such long hours" 2548
"working very hard all the morning" 401
"working very well anymore, it
  isn't" 7162
"workmanship, please be tolerant
  of the" 5439
"workmen, bunch of" 5618
"workmen, two" 10929
"Workmen's Circle" 6652
"works, great" 3284
"works, motor" 9160
"works of Mr. Todhunter" 99
"workshirt, blue cotton" 5814
World 1258, 2468, 2623, 3354,
  3361, 3366, 3368, 3510, 3678,
  4509, 4533, 5383, 5698, 6062,
  6604, 6842, 6843, 6848, 7053,
  7090, 7316, 7965, 8243, 8979,
  9062
"world, all over the" 5097, 8470
"world, all people in the" 1285
"world, all the" 5456, 7531
"world, all the countries of the"
  6109
"world, all the time in the" 377
"world, allowed in the" 9260
"world, alone in the" 8714, 8716
"world, alone upon the" 8736
"world, art of rising in the" 238
"world, bad" 5698
"world, bottom of the" 4087
"world, came into the" 4346
"world, centre of the whole" 8299
"world, cognizance of the" 4496

"world, corners of the" 1211
"World, Crossroads of the" 6274
"world, different" 3361
"world, do not understand the"
  2399
"world, dusty" 1221
"world, eighth wonder of the" 8938
"world, end of the" 874, 3354,
  3510, 3626, 4544
"World, End of the" 3338
"world, entered the strange" 6017
"world, entering this" 828
"world, every part of the" 5743
"world, everything else in the" 8863
"world, face the" 3360
"world, for all the" 4524, 9324
"world, from a happier" 6212
"world, futility and sordidness of
  the" 962
"world, give us the" 4469
"world, gleaming" 522
"world, got his first real look at
  the" 407
"world, grain-of-sand" 7084
"world, grasp upon the" 2249
"world, greatest in the" 1434
"world, green and golden" 10566
"world, her" 1288
"world, his new" 5629
"world, history of the" 4046, 4508
"world, I came into the" 358
"world, in all the" 914, 8511
"world, in an entirely different"
  6867
"world, in the" 4041, 5402, 8754
"world, in the whole" 9147
"world, in today's" 1273
"world, into the" 7077, 7090
"world, knock over the" 10408
"world, lay before the" 5885
"world, leak in the" 3678
"world, learned about the" 3275
"world, left the" 8423
"world, lived in the" 5082
"world, loosed upon the" 10474
"world, lord of the" 7807
"world, made good to the" 5384
"world, made some noise in the
  gay" 5386
"world, most of those who enter
  this" 813
"world, most people in this" 5694
"world, much of the" 10083
"World, New" 1392, 6121
"world, new and untried" 2600
"world, niche in the" 5998
"world, novel-reading" 5393
"world, of the" 5884
"World, Old" 1392, 4441, 10012
"world, one aspect of the" 7924
"world, one place in this" 8191
"world, own the" 2491
"World, place in the" 5552
"World, Queen of the" 1216
"world, regarded the" 8649

"world, savagery of the" 3366
"world, saved the" 8686
"world, secrets locked inside its" 5480
"world, section of the" 8111
"world, shown the" 5404
"world, sliding down over the" 10574
"world, somewhere in this" 4841
"world, strike up for a new" 281
"world, sugary" 7711
"world, that part of the" 8444
"world, the" 4339, 4805
"World, The" 6792
"world, the great" 267
"world, the grown-up" 2593
"world, the known" 2600, 10628
"world, the modern" 1360, 5383
"world, the neutral if not coopera-tive" 70
"world, the new" 9613
"world, the outside" 5043
"world, the real" 5077
"world, the sky and the" 7316
"world, the wide" 6823
"world, this" 6842
"world, this blackened" 1714
"world, three-colored" 3371
"world, throughout the" 5040
"world, to all the" 3583
"world, to most of the outside" 9245
"world, took him around the" 9052
"world, twenty-one years in the" 5555
"world, underside of the" 2966
"world, understood this" 5002
"world, unspotted from the" 1375
"world, upon the" 2292, 10759
"world, vain pomp and glory of the" 1205
"world, walk around the" 1676
"world, warm the" 6567
"world, weather charts of the" 9073
"world, Western" 7205
"world, what in the" 7107
"world, what remained of the" 1530
"world, when in the" 4972
"world, who in the" 2983
"world, who make up this" 9062
"world, wilderness of this" 2751, 5581
"world, You gave the" 8021
"world about which they received reports" 2623
"world all around me, pea-green" 10114
"world around her, outgrowing the" 6876
"world as flat as an eighteenth-century Arcadia" 7711
"world as it appeared to the peo-ple" 7531
"world at large, announce to the" 5735

"world before him, he had all the" 5638
"world began, since the" 5069
"World Cup, 1923" 5607
"world didn't begin with my sister" 8243
"world down upon us, you have called the" 7563
"world full of birds" 836
"world gone mad" 6837
"world had been buried deep in white" 8592
"world had ever known" 10483
"world has long been looking for" 9692
"world he hasn't yet met" 260
"World Headquarters" 8321
"world is compressed, my" 3373
"world is purple" 745
"world is sea, all the" 6062
"world is waiting for this story" 8979
"world is what it is" 6843
"world itself came to be, how the" 9062
"world knows nothing about it" 8979
"world may last, as long as the" 5562
"world much older" 9397
"world of cheerless realities" 10131
"world of his time, edge of the" 7808
"world of Jims Johns and Jenni-fers" 4853
"world of literature" 1314
"world of new beginnings" 5092
"world of our own, a little" 6266
"world of ours, this strange" 6409
"world of sleep" 10144
"world of the breasts" 4200
"world of the tits" 4200
"world of thought" 5620
"world pauses, when the" 9951
"world revolved, while the whole shimmering" 4901
"world sat on the edge of an in-creasingly expensive theater seat" 10083
"World Series began, just before the" 9932
"world set high above the dark earth" 522
"world takes people very willingly" 7965
"world that surrounds you both" 3363
"world to revolve around them, want the" 10876
"World Trade Center" 3332
"world turned on Mr. Raleigh W. Hayes" 70
"World War, First" 1464
"World War One and Two dead" 4073

"World War II, in the first weeks of" 6531
"world was a colder and darker place" 3400
"world was a vast gloomy cavern" 3358
"world was backing him into a corner" 3415
"world was being watched keenly and closely" 519
"world was coming to an end" 2468
"world was in a frenzy of mating" 7740
"world was mad, a sense that the" 5183
"world was nothing but a sad dan-gerous junk pile" 6848
"world was right" 4339
"world was round, proved the" 7053
"world was small, the" 3368
"world we know, the" 10758
"world where there was any mercy" 2397
"world without end" 7507
"world womb" 5262
"world would be beautifully changed" 1260
"world would perish" 4509
"worlds, viewed three" 3365
"worlds, you see different" 9160
"world's brand-new again, the whole" 1258
"world's people" 6833
"worlds ... that before today had been closed" 5121
"worlds that lie so many years away" 6792
"worldwide" 4648
Wormold, Mr. 7395
"worn and admired by sportsmen everywhere" 2835
"worn itself out in the Carolina Low Country" 9078
"worn out" 3648, 3683
"worn out from fighting the wind" 3696
"worn with powder" 3376
"worried, Tapiola was" 417
"worried, vexed and" 2623
"worried about my sick old grand-mother" 8721
"worried his expression" 189
"worries, conflicts and" 9263
"worries rested enough by five hours of sleep" 10968
Worry 189, 417, 1153, 1795, 2623, 2803, 3415, 7563, 8721, 10163
"worry, began to" 10971
"worry, did not" 2955
"worry, not to" 7563
"worry, this great" 10976
"worry a great deal, I" 10979
"worry about, that was something extra to" 10973
"worry about dinnertime" 10163

"worry about Link" 9425
"worry about schoolwork, never
  had to" 10975
"worry furrows" 2803
"worry that everyone has" 10976
"worry the events in his mind"
  7411
"worse, but still" 358
"worse, doesn't look any" 3185
"worse, expect the" 3583
"worse, good deal" 9287
"worse, it was always" 2863
"worse, then got" 2170
"worse for much wear" 5911
"worse off" 6535
"worse pursue, and yet the" 3911
"worse than Martin Stone had
  anticipated" 1644
"worship, Him whom I" 10476
"worship, your" 4217
"worship and sorrow, his boyish"
  10341
"worship Aphrodite" 7527
"worship false gods" 4459
"worshiped, divine tulasi that his
  wife" 7515
"worshipped me, lover of mine
  who" 2381
"worshippers, the departing stream
  of" 7505
"worst, prepared for the" 9603
"worst of times" 3377
"worst week in my life" 63
"Worsted Skeynes" 9761
Worth, Colonel 6310
Worth, Jefferson 9762
Worth, Mark 9471
Worth, Stephen 4568
"worth, whether he has seen my"
  1167
"worth while, it has all been" 5579
"worth while, simply not" 10653
"worthless, I am" 2542
"worthless paper, tons of" 2023
"worthwhile, nothing is" 3461
"worthy of Spy" 5943
"worthy to be called thy son, no
  more" 1806
"wound, head" 10156
"wound of kingship, exile is the"
  7191
"wound which went deep and ran
  even, like a lancet" 9158
"wounded, dark and" 9503
"wounding a man in a movie
  theater" 2040
Wounds 155, 6649, 10156
"wounds, open untended" 2784
"wounds, our" 7516
Wozzeck, Jerzy 6237
"wrack in the thickets and timberlands" 9084
Wragg, Mr. 7493
"wrapped from the edge of his eyes
  to the edge of his collar" 1524

"wrapped her body in a chenille
  tablecloth" 9295
"wrapped in a rain-repellent leather
  cloak" 7630
"wrapped in his woollen shawl"
  8115
"wrapped in rags and old clothes"
  2604
"wrapped it, paper and silence
  which have" 4154
"wrapped me in this garment" 7539
"wrapped the tails of his overcoat
  round his knees" 2974
"wrath, in high" 4971
"wrath, stern ecclesiastical" 9087
"wreaths, going in with the" 3937
"wreck I am, what a fucking" 73
"wreck it for ever if she should
  only wish" 8027
"wreck the hearts of the youth of
  Rouen" 7709
"wreckage, entangled in the" 33
"wreckage, surveyed the" 2063
"wreckless with his life" 2381
"wrecks and junks" 769
Wren 6971
Wren, Finnley 9285
Wren, Russel 4798, 4826
"Wren, big blonde" 8306
"wren in a cloud" 2230
"wrench, metric" 9834
"wrenched from the depths of some
  complex troubling dream" 10127
"wrenched my knee" 128
"wrenched off the full ears with a
  resentful vehemence" 10927
"wrenching John Moore out of the
  sweaty torpor" 10264
"wrestle with each other, the forces
  of history" 4504
"wrestling on Saturday nights,
  watches" 321
"wrestling with the catch" 2726
"wrestling with the tractor" 10925
"wrestling with Walter Butler" 7409
"wretched food" 8544
"Wrexham" 9599
"wriggle through a crowd of people" 2940
"wriggling to it" 6075
Wright, Lieutenant Jerry 4313
Wright, Mr. 2026
Wright, Mr. Benjamin 9872
Wright, Mrs. Drusilla 1239
"Wrigley Field" 4448
"wrinkled expanse of sea" 7918
"wrinkled hand, prematurely-" 7555
"wrinkles, diverging" 8545
"wrinkles, sadness and" 275
"wrinkles of old age" 9468
"wristlets, detachable black" 6495
"wrists bound" 1170
"wristwatch" 9342
"writ, serving a" 6948
"writ before this one, book I" 5506

"write, all but ceased to" 5503
"write, as I" 7933
"write, as I sit down to" 1219
"write, began to" 5443, 5460
"write, country where I" 5177
"write, first I will" 9162
"write, I cannot" 58
"write, medium with which to" 5511
"write, now later than when I began to" 9493
"write, power to" 5420
"write, proceeded to" 4274
"write, ready to" 706
"write, what am I now about to"
  5391
"write a book, beginning to" 5402
"write a book about the wind" 5550
"write a book analyzing the emotions of this day" 5472
"write a book of travel, if I were
  ever to" 5477
"write a full account of the events"
  5528
"write a funny book" 5419
"write a history" 4493
"write a love-story, I am to" 5404
"write a novel" 2527, 5482
"write a novel in the first person,
  never" 5513
"write a paragraph exclusively
  about myself" 700
"write a tale of his youth" 7988
"write about, what on earth am I
  to" 5438
"write about Bigfoot" 5522
"write about the Jewish experience"
  5486
"write all those beautiful poems in
  Italian" 5527
"write an account of our experiments" 5497
"write an essay" 5412
"write and wait, so I" 5475
"write anything so long as this may
  be" 5433
"write as brilliantly on a happier
  theme" 5447
"write at my wife's behest" 5547
"write down for the instruction of
  future ages" 707
"write down here" 8240
"write down his adventures" 5397
"write down the whole particulars
  about Treasure Island" 5012
"write eight interrelated books on
  the same theme" 5541
"write everything down, Peter says
  I should" 5531
"write his biography" 702
"write his biography, publishers
  first asked me to" 705
"write his life and memoirs" 697
"write his memoirs" 703
"write his mother" 1926
"write his own memoirs" 4490

"write in fulfilment of a promise, I"
5484
"write in the third year of Rehoboam's reign" 5549
"write in the time of the Ram" 5458
"write it" 4982
"write it, came to" 5536
"write it, not I who" 4453
"write it down, I am going to" 5501
"write Jack Straw, don't" 6031
"write my mother's autobiography,
I'll never" 5499
"write or speak of circumstances"
3435
"write stories, desire to" 5546
"write the letter on onionskin
paper" 1958
"write the story" 2567
"write them down, I'll" 5538
"write these lines, I" 5481
"write this, asked me to" 5417
"write this, it is a sin to" 5422
"write this book, helped me to"
5446
"write this History of my Life and
Adventures" 5492
"write this memoir" 718
"write to inform Your Excellency"
7548
"write to them before the evening
light had withdrawn from the
sky" 6648
"write to you" 4591
"write two books, I shall" 5456
"write what they want you to
write" 10049
"write you a letter" 2549
"writer" 5773
"writer, a" 9460
"W R I T E R, a" 9265
"writer, copy-" 3327
"writer, doesn't make me a" 5470
"writer, her most gifted" 2360
"writer, I am a" 4872
"writer, its" 1910
"writer, old" 3235
"writer, only another" 5476
"writer, says a great Russian"
5466
"writer, the" 100, 2824, 5822
"writer by profession" 1590
"writer of fiction" 5398
"writer of this singular autobiography" 5399
"writer seldom extolled, women
whom the" 5392
Writers 100, 257, 274, 349, 695,
696, 710, 794, 1587, 1590, 1910,
2360, 2527, 3231, 3235, 3545,
4274, 4453, 4872, 5233, 5385,
5392, 5396, 5398, 5399, 5414,
5415, 5420, 5423, 5429, 5433,
5440, 5442, 5446, 5448, 5452,
5456, 5465, 5466, 5468, 5470,
5472, 5476, 5485, 5486, 5503,

5504, 5508, 5512, 5522, 5529,
5534, 5535, 5536, 5537, 5541,
5546, 5550, 5551, 5565, 5773,
5837, 6404, 6421, 6454, 6580,
8641, 9265
"writers" 2906
"Writers, Australian Society of
Creative" 5429
"writers, distinguished" 5396
"writers, field of contemporary"
5565
"writers, Old World" 274
"writers, so many" 5442
"writers, syllables of one of the"
10781
"writers, winter" 5529
"writers are spread out like pieces
in a game" 5529
"writers of America, one of the
most famous" 8641
"writers on the same block, no
two" 5529
"writes a great deal about the
nature of love" 5233
"writes a record of a series of
events, when a man" 5426
"writes his own history, he who"
695
"writes such bad poems" 5471
"write-to-Miss-Lonelyhearts-and-
she-will-help-you" 6421
"writhing and kicking knot of his
own body" 9319
Writing 58, 252, 624, 695, 696,
697, 699, 700, 702, 703, 705,
706, 707, 709, 710, 715, 716, 718,
1167, 1219, 1531, 1587, 1588, 1912,
1923, 1926, 1931, 1932, 1937,
1941, 1942, 1952, 1957, 1958,
1959, 1961, 1963, 2294, 2532,
2533, 2535, 2536, 2537, 2538,
2540, 2543, 2545, 2547, 2548,
2549, 2550, 2567, 2734, 2924,
3051, 3231, 3435, 3495, 3545,
3670, 3728, 3887, 4274, 4292,
4425, 4490, 4493, 4499, 4508,
4656, 4829, 4982, 5012, 5177,
5233, 5388, 5389, 5391, 5395,
5397, 5401, 5402, 5403, 5404,
5405, 5406, 5407, 5411, 5412,
5414, 5415, 5416, 5417, 5419,
5420, 5421, 5422, 5426, 5427,
5428, 5432, 5433, 5437, 5438,
5441, 5443, 5444, 5445, 5446,
5447, 5449, 5450, 5451, 5456,
5458, 5459, 5460, 5461, 5462,
5463, 5465, 5470, 5472, 5473,
5475, 5478, 5480, 5481, 5482,
5483, 5484, 5485, 5486, 5487,
5488, 5490, 5491, 5497, 5499,
5500, 5501, 5503, 5505, 5508,
5509, 5510, 5511, 5513, 5514,
5515, 5517, 5522, 5524, 5526,
5527, 5528, 5530, 5531, 5535,
5536, 5538, 5541, 5545, 5546,

5547, 5548, 5549, 5551, 5567,
5837, 6035, 6045, 6348, 6383,
6404, 6956, 7375, 7388, 7802,
7885, 7933, 7948, 7951, 8816,
8957, 8982, 8999, 9162, 9446,
9493, 9644, 10049
"writing" 2906, 5459
"writing, busy" 1048
"writing, I dislike confessional"
5461
"writing, I must get back to my"
1587
"writing, left off" 2924
"writing, Paul Hobbes was" 7968
"writing, play-" 3376
"writing, sermon-" 3376
"writing, sitting at a desk and" 5405
"writing, spider" 5500
"writing, longish piece of" 5462
"writing, up to this present" 8171
"writing, words I am" 5505
"writing a book, just because I'm"
5470
"writing a history of the world"
4508
"writing about and talking about,
what people are" 7351
"writing about them" 5510
"writing an introduction is something I know little about" 5483
"writing and complaining about
the police" 6956
"writing and publishing my first
short stories" 5837
"writing any account of my life" 699
"writing books" 5509
"writing business, book-" 5490
"writing case, morocco" 717
"writing in Paris" 3231
"writing in pencil" 1948
"writing letters" 1931
"writing letters in my head" 1932
"writing materials, he brings me"
1167
"writing my usual Christmas letter"
1937
"writing of this book" 5462
"writing the following pages" 7951
"writing the life of Mrs. Aubyn"
696
"writing the long story" 7802
"writing this, why I am" 6045
"writing this book" 5427, 5432
"writing this for myself, I am" 5488
"writing this in Westchester County
New York" 4425
"writing this letter" 4542
"writing to Emma Howe" 1952
"writing to you, I had put off" 1956
"writing to you this letter" 1957
"writing under the name of Uncle
Stapie" 5485
"writing very meek political pamphlets" 3376
"writing-table" 5395, 8259

"written, among the dullest books ever" 920
"written, freshly" 7509
"written, much has been" 5565
"written, quaintly-" 6385
"written, what he'd" 1531
"written, what is here" 5401
"written a book, he had" 5551
"written about me in these pages, what is" 2737
"written about Paul Stafford" 712
"written account, better if you were to let me have a" 6953
"written and sent under the seal of secrecy" 5387
"written at all, would not have been" 5508
"written by myself" 5416
"written by Russell Atha, should have been" 5505
"written clearly without smudge or error" 4859
"written down when I first read it" 8999
"written from memory" 7375
"written in a foreign language" 6784
"written in a hurry" 5508
"written nothing for seven whole days" 5403
"written now, unless this story is" 2734
"written plenty of sermons" 5433
"written question unanswered" 7197
"written 'The End', having" 2550
"written to ask" 9862
"written to prove a case, this book has not been" 5421
"written to you earlier, I have" 1955
"wrong, as though nothing was" 9608
"wrong, but she was" 6469
"wrong, but they were" 6031
"wrong, didn't see where he had done anything" 2065
"wrong, everything began to go" 64
"wrong, it's all" 4634
"wrong, knowing they were all" 3562
"wrong, lived my life all" 5586
"wrong, nothing was" 10967
"wrong, something had gone" 7156, 7159
"wrong, something was" 1256, 2371, 3958, 7157, 7161
"wrong, what's" 1794
"wrong, whether or not they go" 7713
"wrong, without having done anything" 5246
"wrong dead cat" 6032
"wrong in the kitchen, something went" 2550
"wrong place at the wrong time" 9657
"wrong side up" 9351

"wrong times, at the" 2997
"wrong track, you think I'm on the" 5950
"wrong turn, on the day she made a" 1242
"wrong way, doing everything the" 6018
"wrong with Manya, something was" 130
"wrong with the projector, something was" 1323
"wrong with Turnbull" 5919
"wrongs himself extremely" 2088
"wrote, Peterson" 5463
"wrote, she" 5524
"wrote a letter to the editor, I never even" 6348
"wrote a postcard to her daughter" 5747
"wrote Betty Flanders" 1588
"wrote down years later, something he" 319
"wrote in blue ink" 1963
"wrote in her diary" 252
"wrote in his diary" 2535
"wrote in his journal to the crown" 3466
"wrote the autobiography" 3545
"wrote the poem 'Flight to Canada'" 5480
"wrote the story" 709
"wrote this first chapter of my secret history" 5451
"wrote to anyone, most exciting letter I ever" 3472
"wrote you for the last time" 1929
"wrought iron" 2987
"wrung the door on its hinges" 6587
Wu 3569
"Wudgewunda" 1466
Wulf, General 10753
Wursup, Frederick 6140
"Wyandotte, the" 3078
Wyatt, Colonel 6524
Wyatt, Rob 7467
Wybrow, Doctor 3529
Wylie 10
Wylie, Sir Andrew 9703
Wyndham, Mrs. Sam 9859
Wynn, Frank 6127
"WYNN" 8320
"Wywurk" 1669

"Xerox" 3402
Xerxes 2636
"XK-E" 9787
Xman 1743
Xorander 5856

"yacht" 9460
"yacht ... approached the harbor mouth and lay to" 8119

"yacht *Victoria and Albert*, His Majesty's" 8119
"Yale University" 9531
"Yalta in troubled times" 1475
"yam, nice big fat Negro" 4100
"Yangtze, the" 10524
"yanked it open, smartly" 2720
"Yankee blue, uniforms of" 4486
"Yankee state" 5359
"yard, back-" 9241
"Yard, Big" 7147
"yard, the" 8336
"yard walled in against thieves" 4328
"Yardley slicker lipstick" 4192
"yards and sheds of the motor works" 9160
"Yarmouth, town of" 4222
"yarn, a" 9000
"yarn to spin" 5439
"yarns drawn from his thirty years in many ships" 8075
Yasai 6002
Yasha 3777
"yat yot" 8883
"yawl, cruising" 8063
"yawl, fourteen-ton" 8065
"yawn, tried to stifle a" 942
"yawn and stretch" 5632
"yawned" 2974, 6351
"yawned, Cleopatra" 934
"yawned, sat up in bed and" 10136
"yawning, doors" 7887
"yawning, I wasn't" 4148
"yawp, barbaric" 281
"Yazoo-Delta" 7251
Yazzie, Adjiba 10952
"year, another" 10980
"year, another dull and lurid" 10985
"year, cold dark part of the" 67
"year, completed his twenty-first" 834
"year, every" 9932
"year, fresh start of a new" 1086
"year, his twenty-first" 10341
"year, in a" 6905
"year, in her thirtieth" 5250
"year, in his fifty-third" 877
"year, in his forty-fifth" 70
"year, moon" 10983
"year, my twelfth" 7460
"year, Nathaniel's eleventh-grade" 10312
"year, new" 2155, 4524, 8045
"Year, New" 10982
"year, new academic" 7889
"year, it's been a hell of a" 10989
"year, once or twice a" 1720
"year, palmy" 6163
"year, solar" 10983
"year, that blessed" 5576
"year, that strange and crazy" 10991
"year, the" 10984
"year, vintage" 10988
"year ago" 10336

"year ago, over a" 1929
"year as it was marked by some Spanish soldier" 8663
"year began, that singular" 10987
"year began in the last hot days of August" 10991
"year begins in silence" 10981
"year for dying, this has been a" 10990
"year gone, another" 10994
"year has turned again, the" 10993
"year I was born" 6685
"year in prep school, my next-to-last" 5869
"year later, exactly a" 496
"year now, more than a" 1154
"year of grace" 1339
"year of his age, eighty-first" 2072
"year of my life, fifty-fourth" 5481
"year of my life, that final" 2776
"year of our life, twenty-fourth" 7801
"year of the Christian era, four hundred and thirteenth" 1485
"year of the war, in the second" 6114
"year that the locusts came" 9993
"yearbook" 4192
"year-old, eight-" 4180
"year-old, thirty-eight-" 5947
"year-old, twenty-five-" 2355
Years 792, 1019, 5576, 10980, 10980
"years, after so many" 1819, 4703
"years, after two" 6311
"years, almost a hundred" 436
"Years, Dark" 7956
"years, during the last fifty" 1395
"years, eight hundred" 8347
"years, for a great many" 5587
"years, for fifty" 4734
"years, for many" 1072
"years, for some two hundred" 1180
"years, for thousands of" 220
"years, for twelve straight" 4236
"years, for twenty-four" 8019
"years, for twenty-one" 6427
"years, fourteen hundred" 1353
"years, getting on in" 103
"years, growing-up" 3293
"years, had been there for two" 6437
"years, her own earlier" 7377
"years, in a few feverish" 1392
"years, in a hundred" 10640
"years, in his middle" 5503
"years, in the best" 4400
"years, in the lush" 309
"years, in the next hundred" 5440
"years, in the past three" 4561
"years, in the twenty" 1255
"years, it had been five" 5951
"years, it was twenty" 4547
"years, it's been almost thirty-five" 9505

"years, more than three thousand" 5458
"years, most of its ninety" 3186
"years, my younger and more vulnerable" 6625
"years, navel string of the" 11000
"years, nearly five billion" 532
"years, not after so many" 6790
"years, over twenty" 859
"years, seven rough" 7892
"years, six months short of twenty-one" 10794
"years, some hundred-and-twenty-odd" 1910
"years, spent three" 1495
"Years, Sunset" 10606
"years, the last few thousand" 7928
"years, the middle" 2023
"years, the most awful" 7216
"years, these warring" 5226
"years, thirty-six out-of-door" 5899
"years, thousand" 1444
"years, two thousand million" 7990
"years, wild postwar" 6767
"years, within his first four" 4737
"years after it had ended, for some" 3233
"years ago" 2145, 3635, 6788, 6917, 7054
"years ago, a good many" 3437
"years ago, a hundred or a thousand" 4105
"years ago, about a billion" 4095
"years ago, about fifteen" 10042
"years ago, about thirty" 3085
"years ago, all those" 4202
"years ago, as recently as two" 2872
"years ago, fifteen" 5502, 7690
"years ago, fifty-eight" 10662
"years ago, forty" 9513
"years ago, four" 10645, 10819
"years ago, it was many" 1706
"years ago, just a few" 10402
"years ago, many" 25, 6785
"years ago, millions upon millions of" 7924
"years ago, more than thirty" 2982
"years ago, more than twenty" 5837
"years ago, not many" 5052
"years ago, one million" 6259
"years ago, one morning" 6880
"years ago, over twenty" 794
"years ago, quite a number of" 9214
"years ago, seven" 9047
"years ago, several" 3915
"years ago, some" 3066, 6502, 7178
"years ago, some three thousand" 8399
"years ago, some twenty" 10862
"years ago, thirty" 82, 10534
"years ago, two" 5593
"years and years ago" 9370
"years are longer, where the" 7068
"years as a whole, can see our" 5568

"years back, a few" 3680
"years before" 5152, 6208
"years before, about thirty" 7955
"years before, twenty" 2971
"years before the war broke out, during the" 3662
"years briefer than the blink of an eyelid" 7084
"years have gone by, more than twenty-five" 912
"years have passed, many" 9517
"years have passed, some three-score" 5269
"years immediately following the war" 6811
"years in the life of Quoyle, a few" 9719
"years later" 1431
"years later, many" 4209
"years later, more than a hundred" 3557
"years later, that many" 7907
"years of age, about ten" 1492
"years of age, between thirty and forty" 9749
"years of age, I am eighty-two" 8965
"years of age, I was close to thirteen" 4176
"years of age, I was then twenty-three" 6448
"Years of Age, Seventeen" 10465
"years of age, ten" 5281
"years of age, was but eight" 7607
"years of his decline, the thirty" 2513
"years of hope deferred" 3683
"years of marriage, after some thirty" 5750
"years of our lives, for the first fifteen" 6293
"years of river-watching" 7684
"years of silence" 9957
"years of slumber, after four hundred" 1464
"years old, about fifteen" 974
"years old, couldn't have been much more than sixteen" 967
"years old, eight" 4177
"years old, eighteen" 8716
"years old, forty" 9538
"years old, I was seven" 6382, 6635
"years old, I'm nineteen" 4736
"years old, Maria was ten" 4153
"years old, not yet eight" 964
"years old, one hundred" 119
"years old, only twenty-one" 10998
"years old, over a hundred" 9253
"years old, seventy-five" 7359
"years old, she was seven" 6295
"years old, sixteen" 1896
"years old, ten" 3931
"years old, till he was sixty" 202
"years old, twenty-four" 5638

"years old, twenty-nine" 4809
"years old, when he was about two" 425
"years old, when he was seven" 6110
"years old, when I was fifteen" 3330
"years old maybe, fourteen" 4210
"years on end" 8799
"years passed, many" 4477
"years since I have seen you, it has been so many" 3919
"yeasting up like sudden blood" 10018
"Yedo" 9188
"yelled, she" 28
"yelled at, I'm getting" 7564
"yelled 'get a horse' at the first motor cars" 3394
"yelled out so loudly" 7991
"yelling" 7848
"yelling at the top of his voice" 7393
"yellow, dusty" 7108
"yellow, pure" 10383
"yellow, sulphurous" 8403
"Yellow Copse" 8536
"Yellow Dog, the" 7251
"yellow for the India of the princes" 5715
"Yellow Jacket's post office" 3419
"yellow men, gangs of" 5138
"yellowest part of a clear flame" 10774
"yellowish and dun" 7945
"Yellowstone, up here on the" 2279
"yells, a succession of furious choking" 10792
"yells AJ" 7990
"yells from the street" 10792
Ye Lui 4677
Yelverton, Sir Henry 8483
"yeoman" 8957
"yeoman, English" 4303
"yeomanry blood, remains of our good" 4432
Yeovil, Cicely 7468
"yes, said" 50
"Yes, he would have said" 4350
"yesterday" 5849
"yesterday, as if it were" 5084
"yesterday, as though it were" 5795
"yesterday, day before" 860
"yesterday, how well you did it" 84
"yesterday, only" 3402
"yesterday, two pieces of" 7407
"yesterday at our notary's house" 317
"yesterday was a shocker" 2169
"yesterdays, forgetful of their" 9119
Ygraine 5662
"Yiddish" 9709
"Yiddish, he quoted them in" 5965
"Yiddish curses, mumbled" 6958
"Yiddish song" 8761
"yielded without fee to Diogenes" 10871
"YMCA" 9320

"yokels in spotless smocks, beaming" 3396
"Yokohama" 5787
"Yokohama, fishing hamlet of" 7908
"yolk, blue-black" 8470
"Yom Kippur 1955" 6514
"yonder, blue" 7467
"yonder, up" 7316
"yoo-hoo" 9370
"yore, days of" 4303
York, Noah 1052
"York" 7284
"York, City of" 6601
"York, county of" 9694
Yorke, Waldo 4927
"Yorkshire" 4401, 6448, 10391
"Yorkshire, low hill-land of south" 9795
"Yorkshire, South" 497
"Yorkshire, West Riding of" 316, 1518, 5163
"Yorkshire terrier" 416
"Yorkville" 384
Yossarian 5651
Yost, Charlie 9919
"you are all you have" 6846
"'You Are My Sunshine'" 8760
"young, always" 8194
"young, best time to be" 9382
"young, coach captain was" 5926
"young, die" 113
"young, he was" 8653
"young, I am very" 10998
"young, I can remember when I was" 7436
"young, I have been" 106
"young, I was very very" 6384
"young, it is no longer" 275
"young, night was" 6369
"young, one" 7133
"young, so many and mostly so" 1637
"young, supple flat-stomached" 7481
"young, too" 2586, 10763
"young, when China was" 93
"young, when I was" 1729, 9118
"young, when we were" 2539
"young, when you were" 2337
"young America" 10007
"young are, how stupid the" 11003
"young as when I moved into it" 82
"young blood" 6943
"young bloods" 3965
Young Elk 7221
"young enough" 5728
"young enough to be very active" 1484
"young have such moments, only the" 10996
"young in body, the" 11001
"young in 1913" 5659
Young Lance 2606
"young life, a" 8956
"young nation" 275
"young ones, tell the" 5232

"young people" 9759
"young people, we're neither of us" 5731
"young pretty and pregnant" 7061
"young were romantic, the" 7709
Youngdahl, Dr. 3869
"younger, looked" 88
"younger, three years" 6515
"younger people, something amiss with the" 10997
"younger son, I was a" 358
"younger than I remember" 2796
"youngest of us" 8230
"youngster" 10112
"youngsters, as" 8233
"youngsters, her five" 428
Yount, Great-uncle Cyrus Barnard 4437
"your honor" 5198
"yours, are they" 6541
"yours, it's all" 6497
"yourself to be, do you more seem to" 4799
Youth 82, 84, 88, 97, 106, 639, 697, 1637, 2586, 3514, 4339, 4603, 4800, 4901, 4977, 5370, 5648, 5798, 6369, 6384, 6625, 7388, 7424, 8194, 9468, 10763
"youth" 4339
"youth, a certain kind of" 958
"youth, a fair" 948
"youth, a homely" 6515
"youth, as a" 8965
"youth, bells of" 3514
"youth, bestow the bloom of" 9468
"youth, early" 3553
"youth, everything has had" 11002
"Youth, Harshest Events of" 5492
"youth, in her" 8637
"youth, in the days of his" 5370
"youth, in the flower of" 5553
"youth, in the middle of life's" 4901
"youth, lithe with" 4203
"youth, memories of one's" 7424
"youth, memories of our" 11004
"youth, Monica's early" 639
"youth, my" 97
"youth, prime assurance of his" 10759
"youth, promises of" 4603
"youth, tale of his" 7388
"youth, throughout our" 5648
"youth, when I was but a mere" 6656
"youth allows itself, it is not often that" 10995
"youth and death I sing" 4800
"youth and vivacity, working at" 1432
"Youth both in Age and Person" 355
"youth he had been" 11000
"youth in the seat beside him" 2947
"youth is truth" 10999
"youth lay sprawled" 6594
"youth of Rouen" 7709

"youth of still tender age" 949
"youth with a lean face, a fidget-
    ing" 5208
"youthful" 9882
"youthful conceit" 5816
"youths, theatrically bitten" 9376
Yozip 3035
"Yucatán" 9614, 10994
"Yugoslav widow" 9931
"Yugoslavia" 4055
Yulch, Adam 2906
Yuli 6146
"Yuma" 9333
"yummy fruitcake" 2656
"Yunnan Province" 561
"yuppies, days of wine and" 3404
Yurovsky 3413
"yurt of her half-brother" 6002
Yussel 6482

Zachary 3275
Zack 8171
"Zagreb" 4055
"Zagreb banker, wealthy" 10562
Zali, Zeev 4859
Zalushioon, Matty 9436
"Zam, Pop and" 7541
"ZAMBO!!" 8949
"Zam-Zammah, the gun" 2017

"Zanj" 6256
Zapata, Emiliano 6344
Zareef, Captain Ali 203
Zbyszek, Wanda 2056
"zeal, educational" 7886
"zebec, Moorish" 7346
Zedé 6484
"zeitgeist" 879
Zeljko 10316
Zelli, Marya 7568
Zen 3221
Zenia 9060
"zenith, toward the" 8409
"Zenith" 2104, 9212
"Zenkali, island of" 5043
"zephyr so light and caressing it
    seems man made" 7229
"Zephyrfield" 5754
"Zero-1 medium bomber" 219
"zest, midlife" 6241
"zest for life, an infinite" 8976
"zest to the make-believe of their
    games" 959
Zeta 8561
"Zetland, Mainland of" 5011
Zeus 2628
Ziegler, Adrienne 4611
"ziggurat of Bel-Marduk" 2636
"Zimmerdale" 1044
"Zin, Wilderness of" 5831

"zinging like crazy" 4959
Zinn, Miss Deirdre Louisa 6577
Zinn, Mr. and Mrs. John Quincy
    6577
"zinnias" 3806
"Zion, walled city called" 4080
Zita 1257
Zivanias 350
"Zodiac" 535
"Zodiac Room" 7481
Zoe Mae 7283
"zombies, served" 4324
"zone, sub-tropic" 1357
"Zoo, don't want to go to the" 5361
"zoo, go back to the" 852
"zoo, the extent of this" 4886
Zooey 5843
"zooming quietly over the sky"
    4587
Zoos 4886, 5361
"Zopocomapetl, the top of" 10718
Zorzi 9302
"Zouaves, service in the" 486
"Zulu War" 9522
"Zululand" 4518, 6122
"Zulus" 4685
"Zurich" 4659
"Zürich" 2477
Zuzu 1982
Zweck, Norman 10206

Index of
Authors and Titles

A.B.C. Murders, The 4558

a.k.a. Katherine Walden 5291

Aaron's Rod 521

Abandoned, The 18

Abandoned Woman, The 7483

Abba Abba 4799

Abbess of Crewe, The 8903

Abbey, Edward 4065, 4845, 7235, 8875

Abbey, Lloyd 7940

Abbey in the Wood, The 9255

Abbot, The 9465

Abbott, Raymond H. 6582

Abeng 5044

Abercrombie, Barbara 4925

Aberration of Starlight 6855

"Abiding Vision, The" 2073

Abish, Walter 9606, 10511

Able McLaughlins, The 5132

Ableman, Paul 3316, 3454

Abortion, The 3425

About Harry Towns 5630

About Tilly Beamis 3410

Above Ground 6650

Abrahams, Peter 209, 335, 1192, 3371, 5645, 6377, 8111, 9472

Abrams, Linsey 1942

Absalom, Absalom! 7763

Absent in the Spring 8265

"Absentee, The" 6751

Absolute Beginners 3386

Abu-Jaber, Diana 10328

Academic Question, An 2868

Acceptable Losses 2785

Acceptance World, The 1921

Accident, The 2529

Accidental Man, An 5752

Accidental Tourist, The 9731

According to Mark 3022

Accounting, The 3745

Achebe, Chinua 530, 1829, 3535, 4923, 6987

Acker, Kathy 369, 2034, 2404, 4710, 5680, 6666, 6932, 7992, 8021, 10834

Ackroyd, Peter 1307, 2431, 5514, 6799, 7233, 8464

Acolyte, The 2739

Acorn Plan, The 2933

Acrobat Admits 936

Across Five Aprils 3652

Across the Barricades 4790

Across the River and into the Trees 8095

Act of Darkness 987

Act of Terror, An 2006

Action at Aquila 6063

Action by Night 9549

Actor's Daughter, An 1545

Acts of Faith (Koning) 9962

Acts of Faith (Segal) 1218

Acts of Love 4407

Aczel, Tamas 10763

Ada 5466

Ada Dallas 9228

Adam and Eve 5697

Adam and the Serpent 8899

Adam Bede 4492

Adam Blair 4338

Adam Johnstone's Son 6784

Adamic, Louis 4055

Adams, Alice 2005, 5111, 6394, 7971, 9336, 10627

Adams, Andy 6097

Adams, Arthur 3238

Adams, Frank Davis 4917

Adams, Glenda 6166

Adams, Henry 1295, 6037

Adams, Richard 1465, 3904, 5325, 8820, 9673, 10733

Adams, Samuel Hopkins 3796, 4314, 5136, 7258, 7618, 8595, 9211

Adams, Thomas 4126

Adaptable Man, The 4069

Addie Pray 5218

Addis, Faith 115

Address Book, The 887

Address Unknown 2515

Ade, George 294, 5789

Adèle and Co. 10120

Adele at the End of the Day 3810

Adeline Mowbray 3548

Adios, Scheherazade 6989

Adjacent Lives 9337

Adler, Renata 5293

Admirable Woman, An 7973

Admiral Hornblower in the West Indies 8102

Adrift in Soho 8664

Adult Education 7074

Adult Life of Toulouse Lautrec, The 6932

Adultery, An 10867

Adventure 7559

Adventurers, The (Haycox) 4916

Adventurers, The (Robbins) 9846

Adventures in the Alaskan Skin Trade 6693

Adventures of a Young Man 273

Adventures of a Younger Son 358

Adventures of Augie March, The 245

Adventures of Captain Horn, The 8058

Adventures of Elizabeth in Rügen, The 5016

Adventures of Gerard 8846

Adventures of God in His Search for the Black Girl, The 2629

Adventures of Goodnight and Loving, The 2172

Adventures of Hajji Baba of Ispahan, The 6405

Adventures of Harry Richmond, The 10113

Adventures of Hiram Holliday 4731

Adventures of Philip, The 6610

Adventures of Robina, The 824

Adventures of Roderick Random, The 5193

Adventures of Sally, The 6755

Adventures of Sir Launcelot Greaves, The 7284

Adventures of Wesley Jackson, The 4736

Adventures with Julia 10668

Adversary in the House 2831

Advise and Consent 7013

Advocate, The 5574

Ægypt 2639

Aerodrome, The 2894

Affair, The 8633

Affair at Honey Hill, The 4412
Affair of Men, An 9156
Affectionately, Eve 1414
Affirmation, The 4809
Affliction 2578
Afghanistan 8503
Afloat and Ashore 780
African Queen, The 129
African Witch, The 3438
After Claude 2657
After Dark, My Sweet 10367
After Eli 10087
After Goliath 345
After House, The 4930
After Julius 10189
After Leaving Mr. Mackenzie 6108
After London 1244
After Many a Summer Dies the Swan
   5801
After Moondog 5880
After Roy 475
After Shocks/Near Escapes 2452
After the Act 4576
After the Death of Don Juan 2558
After the First Death 4894
After the Reunion 8194
After the War (Marius) 4948
After the War (Raphael) 3401
After-Dinner's Sleep, An 9963
Afterlife 2445
Aftermath 3973
Afternoon Men 3048
Afternoon of a Faun 7484
Afternoon of a Good Woman 2659
Afternoon Sun, The 3543
Against a Darkening Sky 3976
Against Entropy 2245
Against the Season 3314
Against the Stream 6679
Agatite 1460
Age 8011
Age of Consent 4423
"Age of Grief, The" 10866
Age of Innocence, The 8740
Age of Iron 7449
Age of Miracles, The 36
Age of Wonder, The 6717
Agee, James 1270, 3516
Agee, Jonis 1772, 3045
Agents and Patients 7713
Agnes Grey 4491
Agnes of Sorrento 8937
Agony and the Ecstasy, The 498
Agrippa's Daughter 6181
Ah, but Your Land Is Beautiful 5959
Ahmed and the Old Lady 8682
Aiken, Conrad 2948, 4912, 7010,
   8743, 10759
Ainsworth, William Harrison 948,
   1196, 3984, 7501
Air 4331
Air and Angels 330
Air That Kills, An 2561
Airman Mortensen 10634
Aissa Saved 9217

Aitken, Will 1859, 10964
Akins, Ellen 6714, 7746
Alabaster Egg, The 798
Alamo House 1997
Alas, Babylon 6004
Alaska (Harris) 1052
Alaska (Michener) 4095
Albert, Gail 3928
Albert Angelo 1862
Alberts, Laurie 4924
Albion Walk 5584
Album, The 6288
Alchymist's Journal, The 3290
Alcorn, Alfred 456
Alcott, Louisa May 292, 953,
   1245, 2070, 3065, 4231, 4512,
   4906, 8390, 8584, 9516, 10029
Alder, Ken 7902
Alder Gulch 3405
Aldington, Richard 10475
Aldiss, Brian W. 378, 428, 1426,
   1882, 3046, 3776, 3811, 5288,
   6146, 6230, 6770, 7464, 7818,
   7928, 7936, 10417, 10510, 10512,
   10601
Aldrich, Bess Streeter 1377, 2533,
   3823, 4377, 7469, 8980, 9126,
   9328, 9746
Aldrich, Thomas Bailey 1490,
   2293, 3895, 6928, 8958
Aldridge, James 203, 205, 709,
   2847, 3200, 3579, 5206, 6137,
   7844, 8566, 9006, 10485, 10581
Alexander, Kate 3599
Alexander, Lynne 5969, 8759
Alexander's Bridge 8255
Alexandra Freed 3319
Alfau, Felipe 3288, 8982
Alfie Darling 6391
Alger, Horatio 4035, 10112
Algerine Captive, The 356
Algren, Nelson 372, 2651, 2829,
   2897
Ali, Tariz 4528
Alice Adams 4614
Alice Alone 6722
Alice at 80 110
Alice in Bed 6687
Alice of Old Vincennes 9662
Alice's Adventures in Wonderland 894
Alien Heat, An 3582
Alive and Kicking 2464
All About H. Hatterr 5226
All Around Me Peaceful 6969
All Fall Down 3151
All for Love 10620
All Good Women 4363
All Hallows' Eve 10803
All Heaven in a Rage 4074
All I Have Is Blue 8295
All in a Lifetime 6529
All in the Family 2510
All Manner of Riches 3907
All My Friends Are Going to Be
   Strangers 5658

All New People 4598
All Night Long 375
All of It, The 4690
All or Nothing 10853
All Our Fault 8448
All Our Yesterdays 9130
All Over Again 7269
All Passion Spent 102
All the Best People 5154
All the Conspirators 10689
All the Gods and Goddesses 5217
All the King's Ladies 10288
All the King's Men 9143
All the Little Live Things 7313
All the Pretty Horses 3790
All the Time There Is 2917
All the Western Stars 1813
All This, and Heaven Too 2312
All Under Heaven 1434
All We Need of Hell 9459
All You Need 6340
Allan and the Holy Flower 3795
Allan and the Ice-Gods 5412
Allan Quatermain 4223
All-Bright Court 3890
Alldritt, Keith 7726
Allen, Edward 537
Allen, Hervey 2218, 2959, 3900,
   6063, 9133
Allen, James Lane 2194, 2495,
   3973, 10569
Allen, Walter 5347, 6529
Alley Jaggers 7628
Alleys of Eden, The 10519
Allingham, Margery 703, 2557,
   6174
Alma 6877
Almanac Branch 8897
Almanac of the Dead 8561
Almayer's Folly 9991
Almighty Me 1960
Almost Dark 10989
Almost Family 6822
Almost Famous 6845
Almost Innocent 6689
Almost Japanese 4834
Almost Midnight 8757
Alnilam 10746
Alone 3789
Along the Arno 10160
Alp 8553
Alphabetical Africa 10511
Alroy 1565
Also Georgiana 5177
Altar in the Fields, An 3103
Alter, Stephen 7537
Alteration, The 10012
Alternative, The 4307
Alther, Lisa 2366, 3927, 8282,
   9826
Alton Locke 4440
Alvarez, A. 2448, 7728
Alvarez, Julia 5635
Always Coming Home 1729
Always Young and Fair 5644

Amadi, Elechi 4686, 9177
Amalgamemnon 7975
Amanda 908
Amanda/Miranda 3204
Amazing Interlude, The 5566
Amazing Marriage, The 927
Ambassador, The (Brink) 2475
Ambassador, The (West) 6439
Ambassadors, The (James) 3913
Ambient 6938
Ambler, Eric 198, 884, 1222, 1544, 2026, 2563, 3008, 4982, 5003, 6318, 6949, 6955, 6983, 7803, 8085, 9005, 9764
Ambrose Holt and Family 1599
Ambush 3768
Amelia 1964
America America 6073
America, My Wilderness 983
American, The (Fast) 5917
American, The (James) 5613
American Ambassador, The 2053
American Appetites 515
American Beauty (Ferber) 2950
American Beauty (Hribal) 9639
American Blood 10527
American Blues, The 9022
American Brat, An 4602
American Claimant, The 2193
American Cowboy, The 1380
American Dream (Foster) 899
American Dream, An (Mailer) 5818
American Dreams (Klein) 8238
American Earthquakes 7539
American Falls 7272
American Girl 9973
American Gold 4180
American Love Story, An 7789
American Made 6658
American Memory, An 4113
American Mischief 7724
American Politician, An 9859
American Prophet, An 755
American Psycho 8320
American Rose 3203
American Scrapbook 210
American Senator, The 1340
American Tragedy, An 2200
American Tropic 992
American Visitor, An 10348
Americana 10985
Ames, Jonathan 7743
Amis, Kingsley 3, 148, 1256, 1874, 3742, 5932, 5972, 6022, 6118, 6157, 6988, 7358, 7573, 9270, 9907, 10012, 10387
Amis, Martin 1124, 3193, 9043, 9807, 10255, 10313
Ammahabas 7693
Among Birches 4018
Among Friends (Tiersten) 7041
Among Friends (Wright) 2167
Among Malay Pirates 928
Among the Cinders 9000
Among Thieves 7776

Amongst Women 6549
Amos 5968
Amrita 2963
Anagrams (Moore) 6302
Anagrams (Slavitt) 3712
Anarchy of Love, The 1663
Anatolian, The 2398
Anatomy Lesson, The 6686
Anatomy of a Murder 2968
Anaya, Rudolfo A. 5156, 8571, 10248
Ancestors 2089
Ancient Allan, The 3497
Ancient Child, The 9972
Ancient Enemies 6682
Ancient Evenings 9457
Ancient Highway, The 6837
Ancient History 9922
Ancient Law, The 7131
Ancient Lights 343
And Again? 5488
And Be a Villain 3739
And Chaos Died 365
And Do Remember Me 4429
"...And Ladies of the Club" 9250
And Now Tomorrow 7386
And the Ass Saw the Angel 771
And the Desert Shall Blossom 8447
...And the Wife Ran Away 5356
And the Wild Birds Sing 9619
And Then We Heard the Thunder 8745
And They Didn't Die 7052
And Wait for the Night 7306
And We Were Young 8686
Anderson, Barbara 4025
Anderson, Edward 2585
Anderson, Jessica 1436, 4295, 6539, 7442, 9937
Anderson, Jim 1166
Anderson, Linda 9851
Anderson, Sherwood 100, 960, 5133, 6414, 6627, 7034, 9876
Anderson Question, The 9815
Andersonville 6569
Andrew and Tobias 3589
Andrews, Raymond 870, 2449, 2613
Andromeda Strain 596
Angadi, Patricia 2486
Angel (Collins) 8336
Angel (Taylor) 10903
Angel at the Gate, The 9296
Angel Child 826
Angel in the Corner, The 9354
Angel Landing 8432
Angel Loves Nobody 10721
Angel of Light 2393
Angel of the Revolution, The 192
Angel Pavement 8073
Angell, Pearl and Little God 6891
Angels 9620
Angels All Over Town 4110
Angels Falling 2844
Angels on Toast 2893
Anger 5765

Angle of Repose 9268
Anglo-Saxon Attitudes 2507
Angry Tide, The 10732
Angry Wife, The 1224
Animal Farm 2895
Animal Game, The 2966
Animal Wife, The 7749
Ann Veronica 6620
Ann Vickers 299
Anna Apparent 3581
Anna Delaney's Child 10949
Anna L·M·N·O 10302
Anna of the Five Towns 1280
Anna Papers, The 2002
Anna Teller 9570
Anna's Book 7734
Annals of the Parish 1483
Anne of Geierstein 3432
Anne of Green Gables 7652
Anne's Head 503
Anne's Youth 7042
Annette 5754
Annie Chambers 1538
Annie John 2410
Annie Kilburn 1571
Annie Magdalene 3872
Annie Parsons 4990
Annunciation, The 7420
Anointed, The 2828
Another Country 9157
Another Good Loving Blues 4077
Another Kind 9596
Another Pamela 3472
Another Part of the Wood 10064
Another Roadside Attraction 2609
Another Street, Another Dance 575
Another Time 9647
Ansa, Tina McElroy 7090
Anstey, F. 8341
Answer As a Man 670
Answered Prayers 4841
Antagonists, The 3460
Antarctica Cookbook, The 8732
Ante-Room, The 5313
Anthem (Rand) 5422
Anthem, The (Gerson) 7519
Anthills of the Savannah 4923
Anthony, Michael 8914, 9917
Anthony Adverse 9133
Antic Hay 9411
Anticipation 9493
Anti-Death League, The 10387
Antiquary, The 9511
Antique Collector, The 1797
Antiquity Street 5996
Antoni, Robert 10961
Antonia Saw the Oryx First 10442
Antonietta 2281
Antonina 6052
Antrim, Donald 1480
Any Four Women Could Rob the Bank of Italy 7271
Any God Will Do 9845
Any Minute I Can Split 10826
Any Old Iron 10530

Any Woman's Blues 5536
Anya 6657
Anything for Billy 5867
Anywhere But Here 1845
Apaches 5190
Apartment in Athens 3500
Ape and Essence 3439
Apes and Angels 3402
Apes of God, The 6367
Aphrodite's Cave 7527
Apostles of Light 3185
Appetites 1871
Apple, Max 9819
Apple of the Eye, The 8402
Appleman, Philip 3402, 5655,
 9799
Applewhite, Cynthia 2863
Appointment in Samarra 5619
Apprenticeship of Duddy Kravitz, The
 2508
Approaching Priests 7546
April Hopes 6753
April, June and November 1981
April Morning 6642
April's Grave 9440
Apropos of Dolores 4343
Aquaboogie 7236
Arabian Jazz 10328
Arabian Nightmare, The 4287
Aransas 8691
Ararat 8004
Arc d'X 6211
Arcadia (Crace) 1278
Arcadia (Sidney) 7370
Arcadio 1940
Archer, Jeffrey 507, 1085, 2485,
 3752, 7075
Architect, The 3591
Arden, John 10521
Ardizzone, Tony 8928
Are We There Yet? 6134
Are You Hungry Are You Cold 1271
Are You Listening Rabbi Löw 8617
Are You Mine? 8030
Arensberg, Ann 2258, 3228
Arfive 1667
Argonauts of North Liberty, The 646
Arigato 4123
Aristocrat, The (Richter) 10969
Aristocratic Miss Brewster, The 10688
Aristocrats, The (Atherton) 6057
Arlen, Michael 2824
Arlen, Michael J. 10738
Arm and the Darkness, The 8325
Arm of Gold, The 5910
Armada 8158
Armadale 3417
Armah, Ayi Kwei 1666, 9781
Armed with Madness 3091
Armitage, G. E. 7427
Arms of Nemesis 5997
Arnold, Catharine 7335
Arnold, Edwin L. *See* Arnold, Ed-
 win Lester Linden
Arnold, Edwin Lester Linden 5640

Arnold, Emily 6701, 9802
Arnold, Jean 7044
Arnold, June 4840
Arnold, Madelyn 4626
Arnow, Harriette Simpson 7108,
 7350, 10066, 10362
Around the World in Eight Days 9023
Arrangement, The 678
Arrow of God 530
Arrow of Gold, The 9124
Arrowing of the Cane, The 3349
Arrows of Desire 6967
Arrowsmith 4144
Art 8837
Art Lover, The 4206
Arthur, Elizabeth 9308, 10099
Arthur Mervyn 3910
Arthur Rex 5662
Artie 294
Artificial Princess, The 9542
Artist of the Floating World, An 3232
Artist Type, The 10197
"Artist's Life, An" 5864
Arts and Sciences 10953
Arundel 9694
As I Lay Dying 10346
As I Was Going Down Sackville Street
 4936
As If by Magic 7779
As Max Saw It 3265
As Music and Splendour 2078
As Soon as It Rains 8888
As Summers Die 5161
As the Crow Flies 1085
As the Earth Turns 8588
As Towns with Fire 5260
As We Are Now 107
Asa, as I Knew Him 5974
Ascent, The 3909
Asch, Nathan 9219
Ascher, Carol 6380
Ashenden 1590
Asher, Marty 3510
Ashford, Daisy 9877
Ashour, Linda 1798, 7276
Ashton, Winifred 3564
Ashworth & Palmer 7270
Asimov, Isaac 1861, 2370, 2745,
 3305, 3520, 4416, 4738, 7804,
 8268, 8784, 9557
Ask for Me Tomorrow 8461
Ask for Nothing More 1993
Ask Me Now 2514
Ask Me Tomorrow 1611
Askew, Rilla 9056
Asmodeus at Large 121
"Aspern Papers, The" 4696
Asphalt Jungle, The 6980
Asphodel 9534
Assassination of Jesse James, The 3214
Assassins (Mosley) 10389
Assassins, The (Kazan) 1677
Assassins, The (Oates) 801
Assistant, The 10708
Assyrian, The 10747

Astley, Thea 457, 687, 1478, 2029,
 2739, 4521, 5180, 6241, 6842
Astonishing History of Troy Town,
 The 6308
Astonishment of Heart 9496
Astor, Brooke 10100
Asya 1777
At Bertram's Hotel 9161
At Fault 2295
At Fever Pitch 1412
At Freddie's 9394
At Heaven's Gate 8408
At Lady Molly's 364
At Mrs. Lippincote's 2317
At Paradise Gate 7414
At Play in the Fields of the Lord 4956
At Risk 4965
At Sunrise, the Rough Music 1231
At Swim Two Birds 5424
At the Border 10434
At the Jerusalem 10393
At the Sign of the Naked Waiter 8450
At the South Gate 3761
At the Villa Rose 4269
At Weddings and Wakes 6587
Athas, Daphne 3580
Atheist, The 10763
Atherton, Gertrude 101, 2014,
 2089, 2830, 3268, 3514, 3935,
 4928, 5014, 5130, 5641, 5738,
 6057, 9379, 9868
Atlantic Fury 2474
Atlas, James 3951
Atlas Shrugged 4750
Atonement of Ashley Morden, The 4674
Attachments 5833
Attoe, David 643
Atwood, Margaret 1707, 5290,
 5578, 8468, 9060, 9171, 9500,
 10201
Auchincloss, Louis 108, 493, 715,
 1028, 2537, 2548, 3148, 3173,
 3197, 3537, 4234, 5108, 5515,
 5570, 5806, 6135, 6163, 6512,
 6992, 7729, 9280, 9289, 9734,
 10855
Auerbach, Jessica 1953, 9341
August 6897
August Break 6899
August Heat 10875
August Is a Wicked Month 10599
August People 3601
Augusta Cotton 174
Augustus 4469
Auntie Mame 7302
Aunt's Story, The 2318
Aurora Dawn 4346
Aurora 7 7946
Austen, Jane 2943, 3549, 4439,
 4451, 5555, 5726, 5727
Austen, Michael 7173
Auster, Paul 538, 1138, 3037,
 5524, 6825, 7118
Austin, Jane Goodwin 7949
Austin, Mary 699

Authentick Memoirs of the Life, Intrigues, and Adventures of the Celebrated Sally Salisbury 10764
Author Bites the Dust, An 5429
Autobiography of an Ex-Coloured Man, The 7951
Autobiography of Henry VIII, The 2412
Autobiography of Miss Jane Pittman, The 2151
Autobiography of My Body, The 1262
Autobiography of My Mother, The 6572
Autocracy of Mr. Parham, The 2306
Automotive History of Lucky Kellerman, The 864
Autumn (Mojtabai) 8149
Autumn (Nathan) 653
Autumn Equinox 8362
Available Light 2669
Avalanche (Boyle) 9551
Avalanche, The (Poole) 1370
Avenue, Clayton City, The 1078
Avenue of Eternal Peace 5722
Avenue of Stone, An 7011
Aviator, The 7018
Awakening, The 722
Awakening of Helena Richie, The 9872
Away from Home 9725
Awfully Big Adventure, An 2085
Ayala's Angel 2292
Ayesha 7216
Ayrshire Legatees, The 1901
Ayrton, Michael 5458
Azadi 3278
Aztec 4502

B. F.'s Daughter 6370
Bab 3496
Babbitt 9212
Babble 546
Babel 7574
Babitz, Eve 4802, 7731
Baby, Come On Inside 5605
Baby Houston 4840
Baby Love 4187
Baby of the Family 7090
Baby Sweet's 2613
Baby Teeth 6710
Baby Todd and the Rattlesnake Stradi varius 3953
Babylon South 1758
Bach, Richard 2631, 5865, 7929
Bache, Ellyn 10301
Bacheller, Irving 43, 411, 655, 1353, 1378, 3822, 5411, 5796, 6093, 6101, 6250, 6617, 7385, 7613, 8975
Bachelors, The 5928
Bachelors Anonymous 1687
Bachelors' Bride, The 5860
Bacho, Peter 235
Back 1620
Back in the Blue House 4995
Back to China 742

Backward Place, A 3841
Backward Shadow, The 599
Backwater 8850
Bad Angel, The 623
Bad Boy 7391
Bad Guy (Drexler) 2263
Bad Guys (Arthur) 10099
Bad Man, A 4249
Bad Man Ballad 7025
Bad Seed, The 2506
Bad Sister, The 5761
Badanes, Jerome 6906
Badge of Glory 4415
Bag, The 3424
Bagnold, Enid 5135
Bagthorpes Unlimited 5105
Bailey, Anthony 6260
Bailey, Charles W. 7454
Bailey, Hilary 4330
Bailey, Paul 2594, 10393, 10602
Bailey's Cafe 3294
Bainbridge, Beryl 1035, 1702, 2085, 2365, 2915, 3780, 5004, 5834, 9334, 9591, 10064, 10403
Baker, Elliott 2356, 5454, 6355, 7050, 8686, 9335
Baker, Nicholson 1748, 2882, 3888
Baker, Sharlene 9649
Balance Wheel, The 4272
Balancing Acts 6145
Balcony of Europe 6294
Baldur's Gate 4703
Baldwin, James 144, 1502, 4792, 6371, 9157, 9849
Balisand 8067
Ballad and the Source, The 9352
Ballad of Castle Reef, The 8688
Ballad of Love, A 7770
Ballad of Peckham Rye, The 4979
Ballad of T. Rantula, The 6670
"*Ballad of the Sad Café, The*" 1386
Ballantyne, R. M. 399, 951, 2187, 8049
Ballantyne, Sheila 6857
Ballard, J. G. 283, 2042, 2361, 2998, 3443, 4392, 7679, 10524, 10536, 10712
Balthazar 5146
Bamboo Bed, The 9291
Bamboo Cannon, The 256
Banana Cat 9252
Band of Angels 4746
Band of Brothers 7128
Bandicoot 10079
Bandits 164
Banerji, Sara 7601
Bang the Drum Slowly 1103
Bangs, John Kendrick 1009, 2016, 6094
Bank Shot 1043
Bankrupts, The 4348
Banks, Iain 33, 3409, 8831
Banks, Lynne Reid 599, 1843, 2697, 3149, 3216, 4124, 4777, 7049, 9935, 10234

Banks, Russell 478, 2578, 5482, 9012, 9027
Banner by the Wayside 8595
Banners of Gold 392
Bannister, Don 1868
Banquet, The 10091
Banshee 10430
Banto, Mykal Mayfield 8235
Banville, John 146, 606, 1238, 6841, 6904, 7597
Bar Stories, The 2727
Bar 20 Days 1582
Bar 20 Rides Again, The 5907
Barabbas 4370
Barbarous Coast, The 4316
Barbary Light, The 5746
Barbary Shore 10490
Barber, Phyllis 8447
Barchester Towers 1487
Baree, Son of Kazan 3358
Barefoot Boy with Cheek 2217
Barefoot Brigade, The 388
Barefoot in the Head 1426
Barefoot Man, The 2704
Barfoot, Joan 10280
Barker, A. L. 2736, 4566, 6501, 6667, 7590
Barker, Elspeth 833
Barker, Pat 111, 2715, 3217, 8709
Barn Blind 2125
Barnaby Rudge 4303
Barnard, A M (pseud.). *See* Alcott, Louisa May
Barnard, Judith 5459
Barnes, Djuna 7056, 7507
Barnes, Julian 315, 472, 1988, 3452, 7455, 7823
Barnes, Margaret Ayer 1199, 1379, 2650, 3824, 9413
Barr, Joel 5533
Barr, Pat 4255
Barr, Robert 3994
Barracks, The 10934
Barracks Thief, The 6543
Barren Corn 4406
Barren Ground 4143
Barrett, Andrea 534, 4021, 7839
Barrett, William E. 499, 5216
Barrie, James M. 4232
Barrier, The (Beach) 3914
Barrier, The (Maugham) 750
Barrier Island 766
Barry Lyndon 10770
Barry, Sebastian 8889
Barstow, Stan 305, 3398, 4596, 7721
Barth, John 94, 1998, 4751, 4768, 5437, 5448, 9614
Barthelme, Donald 2367, 2793, 4861, 10817
Barthelme, Frederick 1481, 2001, 3218, 5296, 9624
Bartlett, Hall 9398
Bartlett, Neil 6874
Basic Black with Pearls 2261
Basil 5391

Basque Hotel, The 1082
Bat, The 6947
Batchelor, John Calvin 631, 4818, 6263, 6384, 7272
Bates, H. E. 730, 2960, 3645, 4753, 5184, 6067, 7219, 9753, 10653
Bates, Ralph 9995
Bathing Machine Called the Twentieth Century, The 1536
Battle, Lois 1765, 3593, 6275, 6490
Battle Lost and Won, The 1694
Battle of the Villa Fiorita, The 9671
Battle-Ground, The 4137
Battling Prophet, The 5926
Bauer, Douglas 3933, 5192
Bauer, Laurel 4524
Baumbach, Jonathan 546, 4227, 7177, 8877
Baumgartner's Bombay 10445
Bausch, Richard 1445, 2934, 8730, 9061, 9981
Bausch, Robert 885, 1960, 6189
Bawden, Nina 138, 248, 1416, 2659, 2663, 2738, 2860, 3505, 3581, 5525, 5810, 5933, 8871, 8896, 9357, 9780
Baxter, Charles 777, 4526
Baxter, John 8527
Bay of Arrows 8169
Bay of Noon, The 212
Bay of Silence, The 6920
Bayer, Valerie Townsend 5302
Baylis, Sarah 5237
"Be My Guest" 2011
Beach, Edward L. 570, 4745, 9245
Beach, Rex 1392, 3914, 3995, 7134, 10686
Beachcomber, The 6368
Beachmasters 457
Beachy, Stephen 578
Beacon at Alexandria, The 764
Beagle, Peter S. 430
Bealby 6413
Bean, Henry 3717
Bean Trees, The 3733
Beano, The 6870
Beans of Egypt, Maine, The 3224
Bear 5287
Bear Flag, The 10454
Beard's Roman Women 9593
Bearkeeper's Daughter, The 1461
Bears of Blue River, The 3074
Beasley's Christmas Party 9120
Beast in the Jungle, The 8847
Beast in View 3918
Beastly Beatitudes of Balthazar B, The 797
Beatrice 2192
Beattie, Ann 4795, 8499, 8755, 9677
Beaty, David 207, 213, 1030, 1225, 1409, 5813, 8138, 8668, 9073, 9428, 10057, 10245
Beauchamp's Career 8642

Beaufort Sisters, The 342
Beautiful 10828
Beautiful and Damned, The 5086
Beautiful Empire, The 800
Beautiful Greed, The 10378
Beautiful Islands 4549
Beautiful Lady, The 8299
Beautiful Losers 4771
Beautiful Room Is Empty, The 5869
Beautiful Visit, The 6631
Beautiful Women; Ugly Scenes 10849
Beauty Beast 2608
Beauty Queen, The 2157
Beautyful One Are Not Yet Born, The 9781
Be-Bop, Re-Bop 8638
Because It Is Bitter, and Because It Is My Heart 1896
Bech: A Book 5468
Bech Is Back 5503
Bechard, Gorman 7097
Becker, Stephen 249, 1886, 2362, 5626, 6820, 8672, 8699, 10542, 10705
Beckett, Mary 9854
Beckett, Samuel 708, 2324, 7198, 8267, 8407, 9588, 10015
Beckham, Barry 6589, 9485
Bed Rest 157
Bed/Time/Story 10408
Bedford, Sybille 6117, 6125, 7203, 7443
Bedford Village 2218
Bedrock 9826
Beds in the East 10166
Beef Wellington Blue 4830
Been Down So Long It Looks Like Up to Me 4577
Beerbohm, Max 7239
Beet Queen, The 7273
Beethoven Conspiracy, The 2405
Before Adam 2753
Before and After 8562
Before Lunch 8262
Before Midnight 8860
Before My Life Began 6694
Before My Time (Howard) 3715
Before My Time (Tucci) 796
Before She Met Me 1988
Before the Crossing 10048
Before the Dawn 5312
Before the Fact 10790
Beggarman, Thief 2542
Begin to Exit Here 6032
Beginners, The 85
Beginner's Book of Dreams, The 3609
Beginning of Sorrows, The 10624
Beginning of Spring, The 7277
Beginning the World Again 3546
Begley, Louis 3265, 5299, 9347
Behan, Brendan 3968, 9904
Behaving Badly 1309
Behind a Mask 10029
Behold the Man 993
Being Invisible 6470

Being There 7112
Bel Ria 9792
Bela Lugosi's White Christmas 7990
Believers, The 4748
Belinda 238
Bell, Christine 4364
Bell, Eric Temple 5312
Bell, Madison Smartt 2618, 4288, 6239, 8281, 8501, 9283, 9812
Bell, The 2652
Bell for Adano, A 10484
Bell Jar, The 680
Bellamy, Edward 782, 8966, 9740
Bellamy, Guy 3864, 7737
Bellarosa Connection, The 7444
Bellefleur 1706
Belles Lettres Papers, The 5530
Bellow, Saul 56, 245, 911, 915, 4302, 4381, 4665, 4939, 6456, 7444, 9422, 9566
Beloved 3236
Beloved Gravely 5509
Below the Salt 4892
Belshazzar 10476
Belt of Gold, The 7641
Belting Inheritance, The 7677
Belton, Don 8757
Belton Estate, The 6612
Bemelmans, Ludwig 58, 1271, 1396, 4163, 10966
Ben 9830
Ben Preserve Us 9779
Benard, Robert 7528
Benatar, Stephen 1889, 7415
Benchley, Nathaniel 2540, 2710, 4326, 4541, 7269, 8425, 9167, 9914
Bend in the River, A 6843
Bend in the Ganges, A 3771
Bend Sinister 7471
Bender, The 10180
Benedict, Elizabeth 3609, 7751, 8007
Benedict, Helen 8292
Benedictus, David 1508, 2038, 5070, 10381
Benefactor, The 1252
Beneficiaries, The 4934
Benet, George 2873
Ben-Hur 6054
Benítez, Sandra 1799
Benito Cereno 8048
Bennett, Arnold 654, 675, 784, 958, 1011, 1092, 1280, 1354, 1362, 1595, 1968, 2496, 2752, 2825, 3326, 3357, 4305, 4309, 5642, 5695, 5898, 6495, 8174, 8345, 8347, 8845, 9118, 9351, 9378, 9381, 9470, 10338, 10538, 10571, 10786, 10915
Bennett, James Gordon 6729
Bennett's Angel 4858
Benson, E. F. 80, 1826, 2196, 4225, 4226, 5279, 10337, 10351
Benson, Robert Hugh 9405
Benson, Stella 7585

Bentley, E. C. 10758
Bentley, Phyllis 5095
Bentley, Ursula 3487, 9711
Benton's Row 5215
Beowulf 10159
Bereavements 4108
Beresford, J. D. 9530
Beresford-Howe, Constance 254, 661, 2781, 8188, 10583
Berg 5624
Berger, John 4967, 6655
Berger, Thomas 1047, 1057, 1865, 2920, 2936, 4798, 4826, 5662, 5780, 6200, 6470, 6798, 7480, 8665, 8940, 9707, 10229
Bergland, Martha 2003
Bergner, Daniel 7544
Berk, Ann 7540
Berl Make Tea 9915
Berlin Game 8373
Berlin Wild 2518
Bermant, Chaim 1999, 2344, 3590, 3596, 3945, 6139, 7423, 8603, 9243, 9598, 9715, 9779, 9915
Bernard Clare 3420
Bernays, Anne 887, 3333, 10987
Bernhard, Virginia 10451
Bernstein, Aline 1545
Berry, Wendell 1036, 1058, 5611, 5945
Best Intentions 9037
Best Is Yet to Be, The 5110
Best Laid Plans, The 5231
Best There Ever Was, The 8931
Bester, Alfred 872, 3385, 8130
Bethel Merriday 840
Beti 5446
Betrayed by F. Scott Fitzgerald 7558
Betrothed, The 6802
Betsey Brown 10621
Betsy, The 4620
Betty Alden 7949
Between Eternities 5269
Between the Acts 8857
Beverly of Graustark 4044
Beware of the Mouse 10587
Beyond 6622
Beyond Defeat 9277
Beyond Deserving 6944
Beyond the Aegean 2491
Beyond the Bedroom Wall 8488
Beyond the Bridge 8726
Beyond the Chocolate War 1858
Beyond the City 6285
Beyond the Glass 9724
Beyond the Mountain 3451
Beyond This Horizon 7155
Beyond This Place 6630
Beyond This Point Are Monsters 2564
Bezzi, Tom 5526
Bhattacharya, Bhabani 4739, 4743, 10192, 10540
Bidders, The 8527
Big As Life 6223

Big Barn, The 4950
Big Bounce, The 1321
Big Boys, The 2161
Big Clock, The 6763
Big Fish 8315
Big Fisherman, The 2221
Big Hype, The 3323
Big Laugh, The 5228
Big Life, A 7106
Big Man 5282
Big Mogul, The 7760
Big Money, The 2891
Big Nickel, The 282
Big Pink Kite, The 5682
Big Rock Candy Mountain, The 1616
Big Score, The 2285
Big Sky, The 8781
Big Sleep, The 7296
Big Story, The 6317
Big Sur 2906
Bigamist's Daughter, A 2746
Bigfoot Dreams 5522
Bigger Light, The 1931
Bijou 3714
Bilgewater 5832
Billany, Dan 1919
Billarooby 1466
Billing, Graham 746, 6074
Billington, Rachel 555, 1873, 4355, 5830, 6007, 6669, 8446, 10828
Billion Dollar Brain, The 846
Billy Bathgate 6942
Billy Brazil 9274
Billy Budd 3997
Billy Liar 9429
Billy Liar on the Moon 9173
Billy Phelan's Greatest Game 8918
Binchy, Dan 5876, 8294
Binchy, Maeve 12, 5334, 7362, 8540, 9462
"Bindlestiff, The" 9030
Bingham, Charlotte 2551
Bingham, Sallie 4532, 8505
Binstead's Safari 1991
Biodegradable Soap 1261
Biography 1155
Birchwood 6841
Bird, Carmel 233
Bird of Night, The 7046
Bird of Paradise 2440
Bird of Prey 421
Bird, Sarah 1997, 7098
Birdcage (Canning) 9796
Birdcage, The (Bowen) 8634
Bird-Eyes 4626
Birds Fall Down, The 4166
Birds of a Feather 3692
Birds of America 749
Birds of Paradise, The 740
Birds of Passage 6296
Birds of the Air (Salisbury) 9360
Birds of the Air, The (Ellis) 8613
Birds of Winter 4082
Birds on the Trees, The 2738
Birdsong Ascending 7490

Birdy 9942
Birmelin, Blair T. 7332
Birney, Earle 1918
Birstein, Ann 4846
Birth of a Grandfather, The 5024
Birth of the People's Republic of Antarctica, The 4818
Birthday King, The 8333
Birthmark, The 6797
Birthplace 4542
Bishop, The (Helwig) 5191
Bishop, The (Marshall) 1928
Bishop's Apron, The 7965
Bishop's Mantle, The 9552
Bishop's Progress 4168
Bishop's Wife, The 272
Bissoondath, Neil 4612
Bitter Creek 6065
Bitter Ground 7623
Bitter Orange 8430
Bittersweet 1782
Bittinger, Billy 8010
Black April 3090
Black Arrow, The 647
Black Baby 2641
Black Book, The 1825
Black Buttes 9312
Black Coconuts, Brown Magic 8192
Black, David 6400, 7416
Black, Kathy 4351
Black Dogs 6742
Black Dwarf, The 7606
Black Hood, The 3996
Black House, The 1833
Black Is My Truelove's Hair 10353
Black Is White 1907
Black Laurel, The 9894
Black List, Section H 5155
Black Marble, The 1305
Black Mischief 7801
Black Money 4321
Black Moon, The 7069
Black Mountain 2322
Black Mountain Breakdown 4962
Black Narcissus 6111
Black Oxen 9379
Black Prince, The 5474
Black Robe 10097
Black Room, The 8555
Black Rose, The 9329
Black Spring 5418
Black Summer 8481
"Black Swan" 4843
Black Tower, The 9928
Black Water 40
Blackballed 6468
Blackboard Jungle, The 9225
Blacker, Irwin R. 4673
Blacker the Berry . . . , The 46
Blackheath Poisonings, The 2041
Blackmailer, The 2
Blackmore, R. D. 1491, 2887, 4041, 8957
Blackwood, Caroline 1932, 2387, 3198, 9952

Blades 4728
Blades, John 4265
Blair 1754
Blair, Sydney 2937
Blaise, Clark 4688, 6458
Blake, Michael 10634
Blake, Nicholas (pseud.). *See* Day-Lewis, Cecil
Blakeslee, Mermer 6479
Blanche and Nicky 2171
Blanche of Brandywine 2492
Blandings' Way 1547
Blanket of the Dark, The 9131
Blauner, Peter 560
Blaze of Noon 8513
Blazed Trail, The 270
Blazing Air, The 449
Bleak House 8339
Blechman, Burt 5259, 7926, 8721
Bleeding Heart, The (French) 10252
Bleeding Heart, The (Shriver) 189
Bless Me, Ultima 5156
Bless the Beasts and Children 6914
Bless This House 1852
"Blessed Art Thou" 1534
Blessed McGill 10626
Blessed, The 10315
Blessing, The 4915
Blind Date 4284
Blind Heart, The 10717
Blind Man with a Pistol 8309
Blind Raftery and His Wife, Hilaria 4308
Blind Tongues 10306
Blindfold, The 4904
Blindness 2531
Bliss 2389
Bliss, Corinne Demas 8143
Bliss, Eliot 10575
Bliss Case, A 6546
Blithedale Romance, The 5784
Bliven, Naomi 6721
Blix 3815
Bloch, Don 3695
Block, Lucienne S. 1236
Blockbuster 8805
Blood and Guts in High School 6666
Blood Dance 8836
Blood for Blood 4831
Blood Libels 8495
Blood Meridian 1287
Blood of Paradise, The 443
Blood of the Lamb, The 6120
Blood of the Martyrs 7715
Blood Oranges, The 5656
Blood Red, Sister Rose 3189
Blood Sisters 2082
Blood Solstice 6195
Blood Star, The 4133
Blood Tie 6080
Bloodbrothers 8525
Bloodhunt 9898
Bloodsmoor Romance, A 6577
Bloodstream 10448
Bloodworth Orphans, The 9793

Bloody Marko 10316
Bloom 4192
Bloom, Robert S. 4022
Bloomer, The 4926
Blow Your House Down 3217
Blown Figures 6817
Blue Bel Air 10896
Blue Calhoun 2683
Blue City 4536
Blue Crystal 5342
Blue Dreams 5469
Blue Eyes 4794
Blue Fruit 2552
Blue Guitar, The 1127
Blue Hammer, The 3005
Blue Heaven 6940
Blue Hill Avenue 5942
Blue Knight, The 6958
Blue Moon 1482
Blue Moon in Poorwater, A 4131
Blue Mountain 9190
Blue Mountains of China, The 7403
Blue Movie 7986
Blue Nature, The 8472
Blue North 3871
Blue Pastoral 8886
Blue Rise 3597
Blue River 4487
Blue Ruin 2450
Blue Skies, No Candy 1327
Blue Star, The 3226
Blue Streak, The 2811
Blue Voyage 2948
Bluebeard 2550
Bluebird Café, The 233
Bluebird Canyon 3598
Blue-Eyed Shan, The 6820
Bluegrass 3656
Blueprints 1846
Blues 8159
Bluest Eye, The 3182
Blum, Carol O'Brien 503
Blume, Judy 573, 7993, 10246
Blumenthal, Michael 6491
Blunt, Wilfrid 4769
Blunted Lance 7361
B-Movie 3398
Boarding-House, The 2343
Boat, The 3124
Boat of Stone 8506
Boat off the Coast, A 2526
Boats Against the Current 3029
Bobbin Up 7062
Bobby Rex's Greatest Hit 6337
Bobby-Soxer, The 5768
Bodenheim, Maxwell 6903
Bodey, Donald 344
Bodhrán Makers, The 3042
Bodies and Souls 1558
Bodily Harm 1707
Bodsworth, Fred 737, 2227, 4071, 4674
Body 7093
Body and Soul 6237
Body in Four Parts, The 8251

Body in the Library, The 2757
Body's Memory, The 5531
Bogarde, Dirk 4651, 5162, 8811
Bogeyman, The 5817
Bogmail 1863
Bogner, Norman 8798
Bohemians, The 6576
Bohjalian, Christopher A. 5245
Bold Rider 10693
Bomb, The 2019
Bombardier, The 875
Bomber 8422
Bonanno, Margaret Wander 1773, 2388, 3958
Bonaventure 4036
Bone 3632
Bone of My Bones 1857
Bone People, The 10429
Bones 10322
Bones of Coral 2454
Bonfire (Fisher) 9218
Bonfire, A (Johnson) 7561
Bonfire of the Vanities, The 74
Bonner Boys, The 9392
Bonnet, Theodore 971
Bonney Family, The 8352
Bonnie Prince Charlie 1007
Bonsai Tree, The 3929
Bontemps, Arna 1269
Bony and the White Savage 105
"Booby Trap" 1619
Book 482
Book and the Brotherhood, The 2871
Book Class, The 10855
Book of Absent People, The 6014
Book of Carlotta, The 5642
Book of Common Dread, The 926
Book of Common Prayer, A 3462
Book of Daniel, The 9584
Book of Ebenezer Le Page, The 10909
Book of Eve, The 8188
Book of Jamaica, The 9012
Book of Lights, The 221
Book of Mamie, The 4551
Book of Marvels, The 1760
Book of Merlyn, The 1522
Book of Phoebe, The 6049
Book of Ruth, A (Leahy) 10237
Book of Ruth, The (Hamilton) 395
Book of Saints, The 633
Book of Songs, A 2717
Books Do Furnish a Room 3276
Boomerang 3663
Boomfell 1086
Boon Island 1410
Boorstin, Paul 8689
Border, The 9953
Border Country 7847
Border Station, A 9193
Border Trumpet, The 8084
Borderline 7824
Borgman, C. F. 2422
Borich, Michael 9492
Boris, Martin 2177
Borisch, Sarah Allan 6593

Born Brothers 1956
Born Burning 93
Born of the Sun 8762
Borrow, George 5078, 9739
Borrowed Lives 6971
Borstal Boy 9904
Borsten, Rich 6466
Boss, The 6618
Bosse, Malcolm 1774, 5543, 5689, 8574
Boston 1877
Boston Adventure 7035
Bostonians, The 10031
Boswell 2338
Boswell, Robert 8576, 10461
Bosworth, David 1067, 3205
Bosworth, Sheila 95, 6689
Bottle Factory Outing, The 2365
Bottle in the Smoke, A 9502
Bottom Dogs 6107
Bottoms, David 4968
Bought With a Gun 1387
Bounty Guns 1223
Bounty Hunters, The 8042
Bourgeau, Art 1749
Bourjaily, Vance 2560, 2678, 3384, 7225, 7353, 7681, 9386, 9607
Bowden, Charles 10026
Bowen, Elizabeth 727, 1589, 2954, 5143, 6220, 6913, 8770, 10382, 10646
Bowen, John 3368, 3983, 4275, 5031, 8634, 10856
Bower, George 7327
Bowering, Marilyn 2432
Bowl of Cherries, A 5171
Bowles, Jane 6628
Bowles, Paul 1635, 3842, 8097, 10153
Box Socials 8934
Boy Almighty 131
Boy, Girl, Boy, Girl 3756
Boy Knight, The 1172
Boy's Own Story, A 6578
Boy's Pretensions, A 891
Boyd, Blanche McCrary 328
Boyd, Brendan 2450
Boyd, James 3097, 3760, 6065, 7611, 9415
Boyd, Shylah 6658
Boyd, Thomas 2198, 3899, 7292
Boyd, William 828, 2922, 4290, 4689, 10432
Boyd, William Young 9813
Boyds of Black River, The 246
Boylan, Clare 2641, 3678, 4530, 10424
Boylan, James Finney 2064
Boyle, Kay 736, 3141, 6388, 6959, 9087, 9430, 9551, 10806
Boyle, T. Coraghessan 3522, 6398, 6796, 8298, 9322
Boys and Girls Together (Goldman) 7064

Boys and Girls Together (Saroyan) 8365
Boys and Their Baby, The 9257
Boys from Brazil, The 217
Boys Like Us 2580
Boys of Winter, The 5529
Brace, Gerald Warner 4294
Bracewell, Michael 4365
Brackenridge, Hugh Henry 5884
Bradbury, Malcolm 278, 1308, 3370, 4581, 5877
Bradbury, Ray 978, 1454, 1469, 3769, 6265
Braddon, Russell 7352
Bradfield, Scott 10873
Bradford, Richard 3847, 4253
Bradley, David 1129, 9172
Bradley, John Ed 7498, 8931, 9982
Bradley Beach Rumba, The 2512
Bradshaw, Gillian 764, 1461, 6487, 7538
Bradshaws of Harniss, The 6889
Brady, Joan 11003
Braestrup, Kate 559
Bragg, Linda Brown 9359
Bragg, Melvyn 1731, 3483, 4685, 8043, 9102, 10202, 10209, 10397
Braided Lives 860
Brain, Robert 8489
Brain Child 9718
Brain 2000 6375
Braine, John 137, 316, 1642, 2655, 4980, 5098, 5579, 5669, 5939, 7224, 10175
Branch, Kip 4806
Brand New Life, A 2653
Brandons, The 8261
Bransford of Rainbow Range 6564
Brantwood 716
Brass 4374
Brat Farrar 4465
Brathwaite, Errol 9156
Brautigan, Richard 2383, 2395, 2850, 3425, 4067, 4254, 6326, 8945
Brave Bulls, The 1398
Brave New World 8300
Brave Talk 1215
Braverman, Kate 4875, 9689
Bravest of the Brave, The 4971
Bravo, The 8389
Brawley, Ernest 2123, 4182
Brazzaville Beach 4290
Breach of Immunity 8296
Bread 6217
Bread and Circus 10950
Bread and Stones 163
Bread of Exile, The 2168
"Bread of Time to Come, The" 224
Bread Upon the Waters 10259
Bread-Winners, The 9467
Breaker Boys 3728
Breakfast at Tiffany's 3142
Breakfast in the Ruins 2740
Breakfast of Champions 5827

Breakfast with the Nikolides 1385
Breaking and Entering 3247
Breaking Gentle 1796
Breaking of Bumbo, The 8661
Breaking the Rules 10864
Breaking Wave, The 197
Breaks, The 3283
Breast, The 600
Breath of Air, A 8783
Breath of French Air, A 4753
Breathe Upon These 1390
Breathing Lessons 3957
Bredes, Don 5499, 6449
Breed of Heroes, A 6257
Breem, Wallace 6010
Brendan 825
Brenna, Duff 4551
Brent, Joanna 3856
Breskin, David 10752
Breslin, Catherine 9965
Breslin, Jimmy 2925, 4092, 4702, 7695
Brethren, The 7798
Brewster's Millions 10554
Breytenbach, Breyten 9044
Briary-Bush, The 5709
Brick People, The 10751
Bricks Without Straw (Norris) 4889
Bricks Without Straw (Tourgée) 4716
Bride of Israel, My Love 5286
Bride of Lammermoor, The 7948
Bride of Liberty 10932
Bride of Lowther Fell, The 7325
Bride Price, The 2708
Bride Who Ran Away, The 2596
"Bridegroom's Body, The" 736
Brides of Price 10221
Brideshead Revisited 8652
Bridge, The (Banks) 33
Bridge, The (Mano) 878
Bridge of Birds 1211
Bridge of San Luis Rey, The 15
Bridge of Years, The 3119
Bridgeport Bus 9162
Bridgers, Sue Ellen 10435
"Bridges at Toko-Ri, The" 7920
Bridges of Madison County, The 1787
Bridgwood, Caroline 3234, 3611, 7099
Brief Candle 2177
Brief Lives 2438
Briefing for a Descent into Hell 10728
Brien, Alan 2413
Briggs, Desmond 8154
Bright Blue Sky, The 5667
Bright Candles 4541
Bright Day 9723
Bright Feather 9841
Bright Flows the River 3011
Bright Journey 5068
Bright Lights, Big City 4329
Bright Pavilions, The 7617
Bright Prison, The 2229
Bright Procession 4568
Bright River Trilogy 7694

Bright Shawl, The 9410
Bright Skin 10122
Brighten the Corner 1202
Brighten the Corner Where You Are
   2175
Brightening Day, The 6648
Brightness Falls 2013
Brighton Rock 6176
Brill Among the Ruins 7681
Brimming Cup, The 5617
Brimstone Club 8122
Brindel, June Rachuy 7175
Bring Down the Sun 3716
Bring Me Children 10462
"Bring Me His Ears" 8852
Brink, André 2006, 2475, 4796,
   4961, 5060, 5953, 7117, 7970,
   9039, 9324
Brinkmanship of Galahad Threepwood,
   The 7140
Briskin, Mae 9978
Bristow, Gwen 8120
Britannia Mews 3120
British Museum Is Falling Down, The
   9432
Brizzolara, John 4332
Broder, Bill 612
Broderick, John 452, 1649, 2451,
   8900, 10293
Brodkey, Harold 10314
Brodsky, Michael 1743, 4229, 9625
Brody, Jean 2414, 6859
Broken Barriers 2467
Broken Bubble, The 1074
Broken Ground 9967
Broken Penny, The 8302
Broken Places 10534
Brokenhearted 9736
Bromell, Henry 3866
Bromfield, Louis 1099, 1601, 1911,
   1917, 2209, 3101, 3102, 3383,
   4000, 4293, 4376, 6756, 6757,
   7252, 7380, 7716, 7919, 8357,
   8777, 8779, 8858, 10925
Bronc People, The 9842
Broner, E. M. 2080, 7070
Broner, Peter 1814
Brontë, Anne 239, 4491
Brontë, Charlotte 1484, 1903, 3061,
   10330
Brontë, Emily 6282
Bronze Mirror 7489
Brook Kerith, The 7217
Brooke-Rose, Christine 588, 5441,
   5856, 7975
Brooker, Barbara 71
Brooker, Bertram 4382
Brookfield, Amanda 6722, 10672
Brooklyn Boy 8761
Brookner, Anita 1961, 2438, 2581,
   2718, 3320, 4132, 4812, 5061,
   5493, 5863, 6865, 8577
Brooks, Gwendolyn 5348
Brooks, Jeremy 4954, 5648
Broome Stages 3564

Brophy, Brigid 423, 1651, 1974,
   2629, 4583, 8185
Brothel in Rosenstrasse, The 7463
Brother, The (Manfred) 7299
Brother, The (Wilson) 9141
Brother Cain 1646
Brother of the More Famous Jack 5502
Brother Owl 7409
Brother Saul 3562
Brotherhood of the Grape, The 2660
Brotherly Love (Dexter) 1002
Brotherly Love (Fielding) 4744
Brothers (Goldman) 6403
Brothers (Rubens) 8614
Brothers, The (Barthelme) 1481
Brothers, The (Strong) 9132
Brothers and Sisters 7967
Brothers in Arms 10443
Brothers K, The 7369
Brothers Keepers 1803
Broughton, T. Alan 446, 6190,
   7560
Browder, Catherine 2805
Brown, Alice 1860
Brown, Cecil 2127
Brown, Charles Brockden 3910,
   5388, 5389, 6404, 7964
Brown, Christy 5629, 8815, 8947
Brown, Dee 5160, 7150, 9617
Brown, Frederic 1029, 2760
Brown, Geoff 4770
Brown, George Mackay 8036
Brown, Hob 9297
Brown, James 1725
Brown, James Ambrose 1557, 9637
Brown, James William 8836
Brown, Joe David 5218
Brown, Larry 9645, 10457
Brown, Michael David 7564
Brown, Rita Mae 799, 1840, 2460,
   2927, 10101
Brown, Rosellen 6572, 8005, 8562
Brown Girl, Brownstones 3145
Browne, Gerald A. 9484
Brownstein, Karen 1795, 9367
Bruce 408
Bruggen, Carol 2166, 4217, 8557
Brunner, John 7691, 7930
Bruno's Dream 10204
Brunton, Mary 695, 6555
Bryan, C. D. B. 1551, 10849
Bryant, Will 229, 10230
Bryers, Paul 5973
Bryher 2231, 2242, 3700, 8329,
   8330, 9080, 9667, 10159, 10177,
   10187
Brynhild 10131
Bubble Reputation, The 4230
Buccaneers, The 8912
Buchan, James 2576, 2930
Buchan, John 585, 1576, 3916,
   4141, 4342, 4435, 4497, 5084,
   5249, 5999, 6350, 6560, 7009,
   7609, 7711, 8851, 8968, 9131,
   9418, 9533

Buck, Pearl S. 300, 842, 849, 1117,
   1177, 1224, 1434, 2143, 2248,
   2309, 3567, 3569, 3762, 4003,
   4568, 4607, 4638, 4999, 5137,
   5741, 6066, 7356, 8090, 8328,
   9997, 10193, 10210, 10496, 10539,
   10584, 10647, 10706, 10983, 10984
Buckeyes, The 7637
Buckmaster, Henrietta 86
Budd, Virginia 257, 2423
Buddha of Suburbia, The 4864
Buddies 8693
Budding Prospects 3522
Buddwing 10183
Buechner, Frederick 825, 1207,
   1656, 2358, 3130, 3388, 3926,
   6984, 7472, 8521, 8950, 9049,
   10013
Buell, John 2970, 2992, 9196, 10241
Buff 409
Buffalo 2937
Buffalo Afternoon 3664
Buffalo Girls 2279
Buffalo Nickel 9648
Bugles in the Afternoon 1389
Builders, The 1909
Building, The 9254
Building of Jalna, The 9383
Bukowski, Charles 1150, 1688,
   6025, 7417, 7997
Bull, Bartle 4337
Bull from the Sea, The 10594
Bullet Park 7263
Bulwark, The 10651
Bumblebee Flies Anyway, The 2162
Bunch from Bananas, The 4081
Bunker Bean 241
"Bunner Sisters" 1012
Bunyan, John 2751
Burden, The 1301
Burdick, Eugene 9158
Burger's Daughter 4183
Burgess, Anthony 200, 223, 856,
   1109, 1973, 2043, 2473, 2587,
   2589, 2624, 2910, 2931, 3392,
   4799, 4881, 5516, 6039, 6393,
   8306, 8377, 8518, 8996, 9313,
   9488, 9575, 9593, 10166, 10235,
   10530
Buried Alive 10571
Buried Land, A 664
Burke, Fielding (pseud.). *See*
   Dargan, Olive Tilford
Burke, James Lee 7927, 8696, 9782
Burmese Days 4378
Burn, Gordon 6877
Burnett, W. R. 1399, 2758, 2956,
   5214, 5814, 5908, 5915, 6980,
   7137, 7621, 7623, 9072
Burney, Fanny 6307
Burnford, Sheila 9792
"Burnham Camp" 7275
Burnham, Sophy 9201
Burning 4402
Burning Bright 5317

Burning Houses 3231
Burning of the Rose, The 9047
Burning Questions 10837
Burning Woman, The 154
Burning Women of Far Cry, The 5769
Burns, Alan 7574, 7675
Burnshaw, Stanley 2159
Burnt-Out Case, A 2535
Burr 10662
Burroughs, Edgar Rice 4103, 8032, 8972, 10340
Burroughs, William S. 3049, 3050, 3235, 5848
Burroway, Janet 31, 2345, 3162, 4940, 5181, 6537
Burton and Speke 4257
Burton, Gabrielle 3428
Burton, Philip 2363
Buruma, Ian 1564
Busch, Frederick 2265, 2375, 2384, 4876, 6133, 6548, 8440, 8702, 9054, 10256
Bushwhacked Piano, The 4250
Busman's Honeymoon 5740
Buster Midnight's Cafe 1474
But We Didn't Get the Fox 9582
Butcher's Boy, The 4013
Butcher's Crossing 9777
Butler, David 8144
Butler, Francelia 8375
Butler, Gwendoline 1435, 5584
Butler, Margaret 1691
Butler, Octavia E. 4585
Butler, Robert Olen 888, 1070, 3486, 4851, 6507, 10519
Butler, Samuel 1568, 5563, 5888
Butlin, Ron 6778
Buttenwieser, Paul 1144
Butterfield 8 10126
Butterflies of the Province, The 10936
Butterfly (Loewen) 8160
Butterfly, The (Rumaker) 302
Butterfly Chair, The 3607
Butterfly Man, The 8627
Butterfly Plague, The 981
Butts, Mary 3091, 4698
Buyer's Market, A 494
Buzbee, Lewis 9197
Buzzards, The 4940
By England's Aid 8643
By Love Possessed 5647
By Pike and Dyke 1346
By Right of Conquest 8056
By the Green of the Spring 2262
By the Pricking of My Thumbs 1978
"By the Sea" 608
By the Waters of Whitechapel 1428
Byatt, A. S. 917, 922, 1661, 2117, 3158, 4903, 9391
Bylow Hill 9117
Byrne, Donn 837, 3562, 4308, 4557, 5903, 5906, 6000, 8741
Bystander, The 7719
Byzantium Endures 89

Cabala, The 7243
Cabalist, The 162
Cabell, James Branch 1966, 3378, 3898, 4102, 5213, 5565, 7510, 10796
Cabin Fever 6304
Cable, George W. 4036, 4042, 4045, 5793, 8398, 9117, 9377, 10549
Cabot Wright Begins 3363
Cactus and the Crown, The 8106
Cactus Garden, The 7696
"Cadena de Amor" 714
Cadillac Cowboys, The 2340
Cadillac Jack 10544
Cadnum, Michael 37, 2282
Café Nevo 6472
Cage, The 9338
Cahan, Abraham 1246
Cain, James M. 1023, 5803, 5845, 9541, 10923
Caine Mutiny, The 5921
Cajun 3867
Cakes and Ale 1094
Cal 4678
Caldwell, Erskine 375, 659, 1024, 1226, 1422, 1546, 2074, 2235, 3654, 4394, 5134, 5751, 5754, 6003, 10055, 10135, 10347, 10600, 10697, 10703
Caldwell, Joseph 2266, 2869, 10674
Caldwell, Taylor 338, 380, 670, 1521, 1614, 1926, 2079, 2212, 2315, 2622, 2626, 3011, 3115, 3843, 4272, 4514, 4661, 6002, 6113, 6315, 6534, 6590, 7135, 7866, 8325, 8722, 10760, 10902
Caleb Williams 5554
Caliban's Filibuster 1322
Calico Bush 1598
Calico Palace 8120
California Time 1326
Californians, The 3268
Calisher, Hortense 1273, 1975, 3177, 4281, 5768, 7129, 8011, 9696, 10605
Call, The 821
Call for the Dead 5930
Call Girls, The 9788
Call Home the Heart 6417
Call in the Night 1115
Call It a Canary 8616
Call It Sleep 8080
Call It Treason 10489
Call Me Captain 9428
"Call Me Larry" 4473
Call of the Wild, The 400
Call the Darkness Light 7782
Callaghan, Mary Rose 10095
Callaghan, Morley 1059, 1983, 4641
Callanish 762
Callbacks 2388
Calling of Dan Matthews, The 8971
Calm at Sunset, Calm at Dawn 187
Cambio Bay 10311

Cambridge 8166
Cambridge, Joan 1561
Camera Always Lies, The 3052
Cameron, Carey 6723
Cameron, Peter 1766
Camerons, The 10220
Camomile Lawn, The 6356
Campbell, Bebe Moore 6243
Campbell, Will D. 9084
Camperlea Girls, The 982
Camping Out 1560
Can You Forgive Her? 10775
Can't Quit You, Baby 8381
Canaan 4543
Canadian Brothers, The 9205
Canal Dreams 8831
Canal Town 5136
Canberran, The 1738
Candle for St. Jude, A 9665
Candle in the Wilderness, A 7613
Candleford Green 1617
Canin, Ethan 4487
Cannaway Concern, The 10084
Cannaways, The 5159
Cannery Row 6272
Cannibal, The 3422
Cannibal Galaxy, The 5965
Cannibal in Manhattan, A 2084
Cannibals and Missionaries 7526
Canning, Victor 421, 2990, 3692, 5157, 8782, 9081, 9114, 9796, 9943, 10266
Cannon, Taffy 6335
"Canyon, The" 5713
Canyon Passage 9142
Cap'n Eri 6020
Capable of Honor 7831
Cape Ann, The 6941
Cape Cod 480
Cape of Storms 9324
Capital 5041
Capital City 1382
Capote, Truman 3142, 4841, 8785, 9553
Caprice 652
Captain and the Enemy, The 865
Captain Archer's Daughter 1375
Captain Bennett's Folly 9086
Captain Blackman 4252
Captain Caution 8079
Captain from Connecticut, The 8086
"Captain Hendrik's Story" 4091
Captain Horatio Hornblower 3482
Captain Lightfoot 5214
Captain Macedoine's Daughter 5019
Captain Macklin 697
Captain Newman, M.D. 204
Captain Nicholas 2206
Captain of Company K, The 5891
Captain of the Sands 3657
Captain of the Gray-Horse Troop, The 10570
Captain Singleton 353
Captain Vinegar's Commission 994
Captain with the Whiskers, The 2328

Captains and the Kings 6590
Captains Courageous 8062
Captain's Doll, The 4476
Captain's Wife, The 10134
Captive and the Free, The 1505
Captive in the Land, A 205
Captives, The 2299
Captivity Captive 1812
Caputo, Philip 2274, 5955, 8817
Car 4352
Car Thief, The 9786
Caracole 6698
Caraganis, Lynn 718, 6164
Caravan 3293
Caravans 6502
Card, Orson Scott 7566
Card, The 784
Card from Morocco, A 4540
Cardigan 7650
Cardinal's Snuff-Box, The 3817
Cards of Identity 3832
Care of Time, The 884
Carey, Peter 1535, 2389, 3335,
    4827
Caribbean 4098
Caribbean Mystery, A 6254
Caribbee 8156
Carillo, Charles 6359
Carkeet, David 160, 551, 3038,
    9626
Carleton, Captain George (pseud.).
    See Defoe, Daniel
Carlile, Clancy 9944
Carlisle, Henry 8124, 8151, 9239
Carlson, Ron 7558
Carmen Dog 10877
Carmichael's Dog 9658
Carnac's Folly 297
Carnovsky's Retreat 6939
Caroline, Caroline 2777
Caroline's Daughters 2005
Carpathians, The 5220
Carpenter, Don 1061, 1732, 3239,
    6081, 9800
Carpenter's Gothic 763
Carr, Caleb 8190
Carr, J. L. 1703
Carroll, Gladys Hasty 84, 1604,
    2148, 2154, 3121, 3135, 4758,
    4914, 5283, 5439, 8588, 9136,
    9224, 11001
Carroll, James 29, 504, 1470,
    1844, 6924, 9608, 10247
Carroll, Jonathan 2096, 2646,
    5053, 6684, 9301
Carroll, Lenore 1538
Carroll, Lewis 894, 3468, 5275,
    7551
Carson, Michael 10443
Carter, Angela 817, 1476, 6533,
    7039, 7404, 7969, 7996
Carter, Forrest 6660
Carter, Michelle 2870
Cartiér, Xam 6781, 8638
Cartomancer, The 768

Carvic, Heron 10907
Cary, Joyce 966, 1185, 1505, 2020,
    2021, 3438, 4344, 4470, 5432,
    6527, 7512, 9217, 9695, 10348,
    10356, 10696, 10795
Casa Braccio 4040
Casanova's Chinese Restaurant 9231
Cascone, Gina 5114
Case of Curiosities, A 1087
Case of General Ople and Lady
    Camper, The 6558
Case of Jennie Brice, The 7291
Case of Mr. Crump, The 7377
Casey, John 4693
Casey, Juanita 433
Cashel Byron's Profession 7878
Cashelmara 7593
Casing the Promised Land 8190
Caspers, Nona 10315
Cass Timberlane 5201
Cassandra Singing 10203
Cassata 3879
Cassidy 7002
Cassill, R. V. 345, 500, 542, 1329,
    2903, 4797, 7360, 8667, 8901
Cast of Smiles, A 10672
Castaway 3699
Castedo, Elena 6585
Castillo, Ana 9960
Casting Away of Mrs. Lecks and Mrs.
    Aleshine, The 5787
Casting the Circle 9308
Castle, Frederick Ted 9493
Castle Corner 7512
Castle Craneycrow 3325
Castle Garac 10366
Castle Gay 6350
Castle in the Air 2044
Castle in the Swamp 5069
Castle Keep 6389
Castle of Otranto, The 6515
Castle Rackrent 694
Castle Richmond 5393
Castles of Athlin and Dunbayne, The
    1171
Casual Brutality, A 4612
Casual Commentary, A 10980
Casuals of the Sea 8587
Casualties 1843
Casualties of Peace 10390
Cat and Shakespeare, The 3164
Cat and the King, The 5108
Cat Chaser 5960
Cat of Bubastes, The 1345
Cat Who Walks Through Walls, The
    6193
Cat-Nappers, The 571
Cat's Cradle 4765
Cat's Eye 9500
Cat's Pajamas, The 6322
Catalina 2140
Catamount Bridge 10447
Catastrophe Practice 1209
Catch a Brass Canary 909
Catch a Falling Spy 180

Catch the Wind 3676
Catcher in the Rye, The 9706
Catch-22 5651
Cates, David 1003
Catfish Man, The 7688
Cathedral, The 787
Cather, Willa 1494, 3087, 3532,
    3828, 4462, 5797, 6105, 7658,
    8255, 8908, 10115, 10685
Catherine 3376
Catherine Carmier 1652
Catherine Carter 7389
Catherine, Her Book 9281
Catherine Wheel, The 10051
Catherwood, Mary Hartwell 2191,
    4135, 4718, 7911
Catholic, The 9853
Catholic Education, A 7528
Catholic Girls 4202
Catholics 5039
Catlin 4185
Catling, Patrick Skene 9083
Caudle, Neil 10914
Caught 10482
Cause for Alarm 1544
Cause for Wonder 593
Caute, David 1412, 3901, 4597,
    7988, 10498
Cautious Heart, The 1105
Cavalier, The 4042
Cavalier of Tennessee, The 5199
Cavanagh: Forest Ranger 1581
Cave, Emma 8334
Cave, Nick 771
Cave, Robert Haynes 3493
Cave, The 2835
Cave Girl, The 8032
Cave of Ice 1645
Caves of Steel, The 8268
Cawthorn Journals, The 5072
Caxtons, The 6520
Cebu 235
Cecilia 8344
Celebrant, The 8926
Celebration (Settle) 10291
Celebration (Swados) 2775
Celebrity, The 3530
Celestial Navigation 5947
Celia 8260
Celt and Saxon 9874
Cement Garden, The 6668
Centaur, The 9844
Centenary at Jalna 4158
Centennial 5476
Center of the Green, The 4275
Centurion, The (de Hartog) 5779
Centurion, The (Wibberley) 10196
Century's Daughter, The 111
Century's Ebb 281
Ceremony 9445
Ceremony in Lone Tree 2696
Ceremony of the Innocent 1521
Certain Kinds of Loving 4198
Certain Mr. Takahashi, A 8756
Certain Rich Man, A 959

Certain Women 8168
Chabon, Michael 6715
Chace, Susan 2058
Chad Hanna 4311
Chain of Voices, A 5060
Chainbearer, The 6608
Chains, The 5956
Challenging Heights, The 10736
Chamberlain, Diane 3792, 4902, 7344
Chamberlain, Elwyn 1757
Chambers, George 2439
Chambers, Robert W. 2734, 2826, 4973, 7650
Chameleons, The 8900
Champagne, John 5872
Champagne for One 1106
Chance (Conrad) 8065
Chance (McAulay) 3016
Chance Acquaintance, A 10030
Chand, Meira 3929, 4237
Chandler, Raymond 2899, 3113, 6271, 7296, 9222, 10003
Chandler Heritage, The 10070
Chaneysville Incident, The 1129
Change of Air, A 10033
Change of Luck, A 1242
Change of Scene, A 387
Changeling, The (Williams) 2919
Changelings, The (Sinclair) 3137
Changes and Chances (Elmblad) 10307
Changes and Chances (Middleton) 1000
Changing Heaven 5550
Changing Places 216
Changing States 4188
Changing the Past 6798
Channings, The 645
Chant of Jimmie Blacksmith, The 5753
Chantic Bird, The 5284
Chapel Street 3260
Chapin, Kim 4828
Chaplet of Pearls, The 10642
Chaplin, Gordon 9803
Chapman, Robin 7595
Chappell, Fred 1791, 2175, 3223, 7063, 7775, 8366
Chapters and Verse 5533
Charade (Mortimer) 6911
Charades (Hospital) 6907
Charioteer, The 9477
Charisma Campaigns, The 6504
Charity Girl 306
Charlatan, The 2865
Charles, Gerda 1922, 4063, 4774, 5825
Charley Bland 4239
Charley Is My Darling 966
Charleyhorse 6464
Charlie and the Chocolate Factory 6645
Charlie, Come Home 7185
Charmed Life, A 20
Charmers, The 4767
Charms for the Easy Life 6492
Charnel House, The 1770

Charters, Samuel 2617, 6234, 9372
"*Charwoman's Daughter, The*" 3081
Charyn, Jerome 210, 339, 445, 547, 1442, 1510, 2052, 3209, 4794, 6128, 6132, 6276, 6530, 7688, 8750, 8919, 9436
Chase, Joan 5166
Chase-Riboud, Barbara 2411, 7701, 9939
Chasing Dad 10082
Chasing Shadows 9641
Chasm, The 9144
Château, The 8105
Chatterton 7233
Chatwin, Bruce 2424, 3588, 8231
Cheap Shot 7834
Checker and the Derailleurs 7027
Checkmate 6772
Cheek, Mavis 2674, 2679, 3249
Cheer Leader, The 6861
Cheever, Benjamin 8321
Cheever, John 1165, 1411, 7263, 8604, 9016
Cheever, Susan 4852, 6451, 7602, 7935, 9338
Chehak, Susan Taylor 5119, 7702
Chekhov's Sister 1475
Chelsea Girl, A 1075
Chelsea Murders, The 2853
Cheong, Fiona 329
Chequer Board, The 5804
Chernin, Kim 3523
Chernoff, Maxine 1847
Cherry 7373
Cherry, Kelly 9650
Cherry Pit, The 7262
Cherton 5984
Chesapeake 9306
Chesire, Jimmy 9
Chesnutt, Charles Waddell 123, 9468
Chester A. Arthur Conspiracy, The 8694
Chesterton, G. K. 1358, 5693, 6562, 10684
Cheuse, Alan 6576, 8243, 9032
Chevigny, Bell Gale 5873
Chewsday 5462
Chez Charlotte and Emily 8877
Chez Cordelia 5491
Chez Pavan 6433
Chibka, Robert 7092
Chicago Loop 10456
Child Across the Sky, A 9301
Child Buyer, The 6985
Child from the Sea, The 10212
Child in Time, The 7003
Child of God 1680
Child of Storm 5055
Childermass, The 1372
Childlike Life of the Black Tarantula, The 2034
Children, The 8072
Children at the Gate (Banks) 4777
Children at the Gate, The (Wallant)

10384
Children of Dynmouth, The 1440
Children of God 1497
Children of Light 10292
Children of Men 6552
Children of Sisyphus, The 5256
Children of the Albatross 1250
Children of the Ghetto 1347
Children of the King 8053
Children of the Sun, The 4505
Children Sing, The 1832
Children Who Sleep by the River, The 8029
Children's Bach, The 6860
Childress, Alice 3857
Childress, Mark 4205, 6921, 8465
"*Child's Play*" 9950
Childwold 2776
Chilly Scenes of Winter 4795
Chin, Frank 2115
Chin Music 3725
China Boy 38
China Court 2330
China Flight 4003
China Saga 8700
China Sky 10539
Chinchilla Farm, The 2676
Chinese Bandit, The 10542
Chinese Whispers 1955
Chirundu 7143
Chisholms, The 3947
Chita: A Memory of Last Island 9521
Chloe and Olivia 5873
Chocolate Soldier, A 7435
Chocolate War, The 8917
Choice, The 6639
Choice of Enemies, A 5209
Choice of Nightmares, A 6051
Choir Invisible, The 2194
Choirboys, The 8681
Choiring of the Trees, The 7194
Chokeberry Tree, The 9554
Chopin, Kate 722, 2295
Chosen, The 6293
Chosen Country 792
Chosen People 10206
Chosen Place, the Timeless People, The 9168
Chowder, Ken 812, 8437
Christ in Concrete 8590
Christian, Paula 908, 1031, 7672, 10713
Christie, Agatha 913, 1301, 1630, 1978, 2103, 2238, 2347, 2693, 2757, 3110, 3740, 3844, 3978, 4280, 4558, 6023, 6252, 6254, 6353, 7381, 7387, 7405, 7473, 8265, 9161, 9380, 9891, 10369
Christie Malry's Own Double-Entry 10827
Christina Alberta's Father 3498
Christmas at Fontaine's 3447
Christmas at Thompson Hall 8960
Christmas Carol, A 2288
Christmas Holiday 3471

Christmas Pudding 7218
Christmas Tree, The 4520
Christmas Without Johnny 4914
Christopher and Alexandra 8028
Christopher Homm 2342
Christopher Park Regulars, The 4099
Chromos 3288
Chronicles of Count Antonio, The 5212
Chronicles of Doodah, The 3727
Chu, Louis 8795
Churchill, Winston 783, 1360,
　3530, 3531, 4720, 5404, 6096,
　8970
Chute, Carolyn 769, 3224
Chymical Wedding, The 8444
Cider House Rules, The 556
Cigarette-Maker's Romance, A 5398
Cigarettes 6050
Cimarron 3565
Circle Home, The 10171
Circle of Friends (Binchy) 8540
Circle of Friends, A (Mitchell) 3167
Circle of Love 5957
Circle of Reason, The 991
Circle Tour, The 289
Circles in a Forest 7230
Circles of Deceit 5525
Circles of Time 3015
Circuit Rider, The 895
Circuits 9625
Circular Staircase, The 2018
Circumstance 6363
Cisneros, Sandra 3250
Citadel, The 9545
Citizen Tom Paine 9889
City and the Pillar (revised), The 4320
City Boy, The 970
City of Anger, The 1404
City of Childhood 5302
City of Discontent 1402
City of Fading Light 4447
City of Glass 1138
City of God 2256
City of Gold 7153
City of Illusion (Fisher) 10924
City of Illusions (Le Guin) 2121
City of Light 2942
City of Masks, The 10916
City of Pleasure, The 10538
City of Spades 6497
City of the Mind 5338
City of Trembling Leaves, The 704
City on a Hill, A 439
City Primeval 1705
Civil to Strangers 10865
Civil Wars 8005
Claiborne, Sybil 628
Claire Ambler 1591
Clairvoyant 8386
Clam Shell, The 8609
Clansman, The 8767
Clapperton 10296
Clara's Heart 4238
Clarence 5892
Clarence and Corinne 3070

Clarise Cumberbatch Want to Go Home
　1561
Clarissa 7825
Clark, Eleanor 218, 1560, 4703,
　8368
Clark, Tom 4017
Clark, Walter Van Tilburg 704,
　2075, 9547
Clarke, Austin 1931, 6440, 9924
Clarke, Lindsay 8444
Clarke, Terence 9504
Clarke, Thurston 391
Clarkson, Ewan 5167, 8431
Clash, The 4997
Class of '49, The 1061
Class Porn 624
Class Reunion 4012
Claudelle Inglish 10055
Claudius the God 7802
Claverings, The 3972
Claw of the Conciliator, The 4296
Clay that Breathes, The 2805
Clayhanger 5898
Clea 3650
Cleaning House 10942
Clear Horizon 3302
Clear Light of Day 758
Clearance, The 4959
Clearing, The 8434
Cleary, Jon 342, 1631, 1758, 1900,
　2160, 2178, 4008, 4447, 6540,
　9331, 9737, 10157
Cleland, John 5386, 5553
Clem Anderson 2903
Clemens, Samuel See Twain, Mark
Clement, Aeron 8536
Clemmons 1141
Cleopatra 4494
Cleopatra's Sister 6493
Clergyman's Daughter, A 10127
"Clever One, The" 5002
Clewlow, Carol 4666, 10670
!Click Song 8883
Cliff, Michelle 4421, 5044
Cliff Walk 2275
Cliff-Dwellers, The 4039
Clock Winder, The 3184
Clock Without Hands 2331
Clockers 4210
Clocks, The 2238
Clockwork Orange, A 2473
Clockwork Testament, The 10235
Cloister and the Hearth, The 4454
Cloning of Joanna May, The 10992
Clonk Clonk 8554
Close Quarters (Golding) 863
Close Quarters (Heinemann) 8684
Close Quarters (Thirkell) 4752
Close Sesame 10268
Close to Home 1226
Closed Eye, A 1961
Closer 5377
Closest Possible Union, The 5272
Close-Up 8804
Closing 3027

Closing Arguments 9054
Closing Distance 5995
"Cloud, The" 4010
Cloud Chamber, The 5575
Cloud Cuckoo Land 5020
Cloud Howe 4053
Cloud Nine 5845
Cloud on Sand, A 9651
Clouds and Sunshine 1337
Clouds of Witness 10119
Cloudstreet 7705
Clowns of God, The 1525
Cluny Brown 9423
Coal War, The 6079
Coale, Howard 5243
Coast of Bohemia, The 293
Coat of Varnish, A 4411
Coates, Robert M. 6419
Cobb, Irvin S. 1912, 4723
Cobb, William 8936
Cobbler's Dream 9670
Cobwebwalking 7601
Cochrane, Ian 3213
Cock Jarvis (Unfinished) 4470
Cockatrice 6438
Cockpit 8876
Cockroaches of Stay More, The 10450
Cocksure 2987
Coconut Book, The 9031
Coconut Kiss, The 10973
Code of the Woosters, The 656
Cody, Robin 5010
Coe, Christopher 8558
Coetzee, J. M. 2857, 3694, 6664,
　7077, 7449
Cofer, Judith Ortiz 7091
Coffin Tree, The 5267
Cogan's Trade 2848
Cohen, Arthur A. 1232, 6196,
　6996, 7973
Cohen, Jon 2647, 3616
Cohen, Leonard 4771
Cohen, Matt 3229, 4679
Cohen, Richard 3240
Cohen, Robert 4898
Coin of Carthage, The 10177
Colbert, James 8295
Cold Comfort 1128
Cold Comfort Farm 3273
Cold Dog Soup 2720
Cold Feet 10869
Cold Heaven 8150
Cold Is the Sea 9245
Cold Moons, The 8536
Cold Spring Harbor 5671
Cold Times 2283
Colegate, Isabel 2, 2838, 2843,
　3517, 4866, 7872, 10529, 10596
Coleman, Bob 4218
Coleman, Terry 10086
Collaborators 5236
Collector, The 6291
Collier, Zena 8895
Colliers Row 2254
Collignon, Jeff 9316

Collins, Clive 10449
Collins, Merle 8336
Collins, Wilkie 1294, 2289, 2291, 3417, 3529, 5196, 5391, 5559, 6035, 6052, 6362, 8954, 8959, 9466, 9517
Colombo, Judith Woolcock 2642
Colonel Jack 5552
Colonel Mint 215
Colonel Quaritch, V.C. 3491
Colony 8835
Color of Blood, The 9820
Color of Evening, The 4064
Color of Light, The 2083
Color of Murder, The 905
Color Purple, The 1805
Colorado 7252
Colorist, The 516
Colors of Vaud, The 9080
Colquhoun, Keith 6357
Colter, Cyrus 2942, 3343, 3805, 7435
Columbus Avenue 1869
Colwin, Laurie 2368, 3585, 3594, 6485
Come and Get It 3826
Come Back to Erin 9139
Come, My Beloved 4638
Come Nineveh, Come Tyre 6995
Come Out to Play 7139
Come Sunday 8825
Come, the Restorer 9103
Come Winter 8916
Come with Me Home 4758
Comedians, The 4467
Comfort, Alex 1986, 7139
Comfort Me with Apples 7012
Comfort of Strangers, The 10257
Comforters, The 10162
Comforts of Madness, The 4613
Comic, The 4941
Coming Back Up 91
Coming First 5973
Coming from Behind 9269
Coming Home 9235
Coming in with the Tide 6352
Coming of Cassidy - and the Others, The 9310
Coming of Rain, The 4400
Coming Race, The 361
Coming Through Slaughter 4077
Coming to Life 545
Coming to Terms 3322
Coming Up for Air 4699
Command 10788
Command the Morning 10496
Commandant, The 1436
Commitments, The 7209
Committal Chamber 7352
Committed Men, The 5940
Commodore, The 1142
Commodore Hornblower 565
Common Heart, The 2957
Common Wilderness, The 4471
Companion, The 1999

"Company" 10015
Company K 4119
Company Man 1962
Company of Women, The 4808
Compass Error, A 7203
Complicity 10868
Compton-Burnett, Ivy 82, 734, 1971, 3360, 3574, 3767, 4148, 4985, 6415, 6526, 6528, 7166, 7201, 7556, 7967, 8215, 9419, 9884, 9901
Compulsion 3337
Computer Connection, The 8130
Comrade Jacob 10498
Comrades (Dixon) 6310
Comrades (Irving) 6866
Comyns, Barbara 735, 2076, 6123, 6480, 7059, 9187
Conan Doyle, Arthur 648, 1008, 2686, 3047, 3266, 3490, 3818, 4458, 5410, 5900, 6285, 8061, 8395, 8846, 10568
Conceived in Liberty 8651
Concerning the Eccentricities of Cardinal Pirelli 1198
Concertina 7084
Concluding 10150
Concrete Island 2998
Condon, Richard 1068, 1073, 1125, 1528, 2149, 2846, 3584, 4005, 4121, 4123, 6180, 6800, 7168, 7483, 7570, 7576, 9489, 9845, 9848, 10079, 10588, 10664
Condor Passes, The 6840
Conduct of the Game, The 4196
Cone of Silence 1030
Cone-Gatherers, The 9669
Confederacy of Dunces, A 2859
Confederate General from Big Sur, A 4067
Confederates 1985
Confession of Jack Straw, The 6031
Confession of Joe Cullen, The 1759
Confessions of a Homing Pigeon 7413
Confessions of a Prodigal Daughter 10095
Confessions of a Taoist on Wall Street 6862
Confessions of Elisabeth Von S., The 10986
Confessions of Josef Baisz, The 009
Confessions of Nat Turner, The 3476
Confessions of Summer 3393
Confessions of the Nun of St. Omer 6517
Confidence 9720
Confidence-Man, The 1567
Confidential Agent, The 728
Congo 3905
Congressman's Daughter, The 7959
Coningsby 949
Coniston 5404
Conjugal Rites 2671
"Conjugial Angel, The" 4903
Conley, Ellen Alexander 163, 3865
Connaughton, Shane 8710, 9193
Connell, Evan S. 3290, 4754, 4918,

5099, 8946, 9443, 10194
Connoisseur, The 8946
Connolly's Life 7532
Connor, Ralph 5910, 6056, 7651, 8209
Conquered, The 10116
Conquering Horse 10056
Conqueror, The (Atherton) 5014
Conqueror, The (Marshall) 5451
Conquest, The 373
Conquest of Canaan, The 8586
Conrad, Joseph 1010, 1355, 2015, 5018, 5406, 5893, 6059, 6060, 8063, 8065, 8066, 9124, 9991, 10551, 10996
Conroy, Jack 1018
Conroy, Pat 2858, 4090, 6773
Conroy, Sarah Booth 7707
Conscience of the Rich, The 5202
Conscience Place 10913
Consenting Adult (Hobson) 1802
Consenting Adults (De Vries) 6671
Consequences of Loving Syra, The 6832
Conservationist, The 751
Consider Sappho Burning 747
Consider the Lilies 1514
Consider This, Señora 1090
Consolidator, The 10464
Conspiracy, The 6957
Conspiracy of Knaves 7150
Conspirators, The 7133
Constable's Tower, The 1174
Constance 9248
Constance Trescot 9871
Constant Nymph, The 5905
Consul at Sunset, The 5919
Contarini Fleming 7648
Contenders, The 8994
Continent 4933
Continental Drift 9027
Contract with the World 4942
Contre-Jour 8195
Control 8191
Conversation 8743
Conversation Piece 3998
Conversations with Lord Byron on Perversion 7788
Convert, The (Robins) 9873
Converts, The (Warner) 10998
Convictions 6335
Conyngham, John 3349
Cook, David 453, 1793, 6538
Cook, Judith 2185
Cook, Thomas H. 919
Cooke, Elizabeth 10868
Cook-Lynn, Elizabeth 9979
Cool Million, A 3104
Cooler by the Lake 2068
Cooler Climate, A 8895
Cooling Off 7860
Coomer, Joe 5175, 10281, 10425, 10636
Cooper 9499
Cooper, Dennis 1170, 5377
Cooper, J. California 4510

Cooper, James Fenimore 262, 263, 264, 265, 266, 267, 780, 1334, 2619, 3433, 3434, 3456, 4027, 4028, 4029, 4031, 4032, 4555, 5885, 6246, 6556, 6608, 7647, 7814, 7909, 8047, 8389, 9112, 9512, 9514, 10468
Cooper, Jamie Lee 4960
Cooper, Lettice 9961
Cooper, Rand Richards 393
Cooper, William 90, 2716, 7880, 8304
Cooter Farm, The 8542
Coover, Robert 1890, 3338, 5207, 8915, 9657, 10669
Copper Beech, The 12
Copperhead, The 835
Corbett, Christopher 620
Corbin, Steven 8705
Cordelia? 5501
Cordell, Alexander 4481, 9599
Corelli, Marie 649, 1351, 1356, 2294, 3435, 4370, 7033, 8324, 8392, 8477
Cork Street, Next to the Hatter's 381
Corleone 5730
Corman, Avery 3323, 4207, 6511, 8189, 10517
Cormier, Robert 1858, 2162, 2334, 4894, 5094, 6868, 8917, 9600
Corn King and the Spring Queen, The 4147
Cornelisen, Ann 7271
Corner of Rife and Pacific, The 1468
Corner That Held Them, The 7586
Cornered 10186
Cornet of Horse, The 2101
Coromandel Sea Change 2181
Coronation 7261
Coronation Summer 902
Corpus of Joe Bailey 4060
Corregidora 5757
Corrida at San Feliu, The 2339
Corridors of Power 1655
Corrigan 9952
Corrington, John William 875, 4422, 7306, 7311, 7337
Corson of the JC 3643
Corvo, Frederick Baron (pseud.). *See* Rolfe, Frederick William
Cosmetic Effects 1763
Costain, Thomas B. 1397, 4002, 4892, 5029, 7624, 8988, 9329, 9768, 9892, 10493, 10557
Cotrell, Georgia 622
Cotton Comes to Harlem 6126
Cottonwood Gulch 9744
Couch Trip, The 1516
Couloumbis, Audrey 1277
Coulter, Hope Norman 3617, 3659
Count Belisarius 6110
Count Robert of Paris 9660
Counterlife, The 166
Counterpoint 533
Country, The 9612

Country Beyond, The 4049
Country Cousin, The 7729
Country Divorce, A 5782
Country Doctor, A 10567
Country Girls, The 10172
Country House, The 9761
Country of Marriage, The 9331
Country of Strangers, A (Richter) 4165
Country of Strangers, A (Shreve) 3665
Country of the Pointed Firs, The 1350
Country People 3642
Country Place 5426
Country Such as This, A 9621
Countrymen of Bones 888
County Road, The 1860
County Woman 1056
Coup, The 6256
Coup d'Etat 2571
Couple of Comedians, A 6081
Couples 1979
Courage of Captain Plum, The 8563
Courage of Girls, The 483
Courtenay, Bryce 3453
Courtesy of Death, The 3168
Courting Emma Howe 1952
Court-Martial of George Armstrong Custer, The 7322
Courts of Illusion, The 7422
Courtyard of Dreams, The 4880
Cousin Claire 2449
Cousin Henrietta 8334
Cousin It 6164
Cousin Phillis 5079
Cousin Rosamund 943
Coven of Women, A 2414
Covenant, The 5073
Covenant of Grace 7531
Covenant with Death, A 5626
Cover Artist, The 2528
Cover Her Face 5091
Covered Wagon, The 6103
Covington, Vicki 2440, 8578, 9202
Coward, Noël 9229
Cowardice Court 4974
Cowell, Stephanie 2461
Cowley, Joy 2849
Cox, Elizabeth 1721, 2007
Coyle, Beverly 1540
Coyote (Gadol) 9050
Coyote (Vannucci) 9821
Cozzens, James Gould 106, 1096, 1611, 3699, 4563, 5200, 5647, 8074, 8589
Crace, Jim 348, 1278, 4933
Cracking India 3373
Cradle of Life 4055
Cradle of the Copperheads 8893
Craik, Dinah Maria Mulock 8203
Craik, Mrs. *See* Craik, Dinah Maria Mulock
Crampton Hodnet 2272
Crane, Stephen 957, 7288, 10472
Cranford 10769
Craque-o'-Doom 4135
Crash 2361

Crater, The 266
Cravens, Gwyneth 2483, 2802, 8441
Craving, A 9802
Craving for Women, A 628
Crawford, Dean 8236
Crawford, F. Marion 79, 98, 99, 486, 488, 1296, 1342, 1343, 2133, 2584, 3071, 3556, 4037, 4040, 4118, 4136, 4443, 4717, 5247, 5344, 5398, 5708, 5730, 6019, 6523, 6752, 6784, 6835, 6909, 7504, 7950, 8053, 8344, 8738, 8963, 9302, 9859, 9863, 9870, 10783
Crazy Cock 291
"Crazy Hunter, The" 6388
Crazy in Berlin 8940
Crazy in Love 231
Cream of the Jest, The 5565
Creation 4503
Creator 616
Creed for the Third Millenium, A 10742
Creek Called Wounded Knee, A 4610
Creek Mary's Blood 5160
Crescendo 10863
Cress Delahanty 4156
Cresswell, Helen 5105
Cressy 6408
Crewe Train 1493
Crews, Harry 1423, 2851, 2874, 4352, 4793, 7093, 7603, 8458, 8803, 9459, 9583, 9925
Crichton, Michael 596, 3292, 3905, 4621, 7521
Crichton, Robert 9001, 10220
Cricket on the Hearth, The 7550
Crime at Vanderlynden's, The 193
Criminal Trespass 3427
Crimson Gate, The 4391
Crimson Wind, The 8887
Crippled Lady of Peribonka, The 8977
Crisis, The 6096
Croatan 7610
Crock of Gold, The 10756
Crome Yellow 7241
Cromie, Alice 341
Crone, Moira 6702
Cronin, A. J. 1498, 1618, 1927, 2228, 5088, 6630, 7892, 9545, 10060, 10125, 10592
Cronin, Justin 8932
Cronley, Jay 2113, 5112, 7834
Crooked Hearts 8576
Croquet Player, The 8856
Cross, Ian 1789
Cross Currents 9528
Crossing, The 783
Crossing Blood 3262
Crossing Borders 3255
Crossing in Berlin 10734
Crossing Point, The 4063
Crossing to Safety 10299
Crossover 2184
Crossroads (McConkey) 2521

Crossroads (Morris) 6508
Crosstown Sabbath 1072
Crotchet Castle 9738
Crow Eaters, The 5998
Crowley, Aleister 2499
Crowley, John 2639, 10420
Crown in Candlelight 756
Crown Jewel 1632
Crown Oklahoma 6342
Crows 5075
Crozart Story, The 5572
Crucial Conversations 10411
Cruel Madness, A 7149
Cruel Sea, The 8990
Crumbs Under the Skin 2166
Crusade of the Excelsior, The 8054
Crusader, The 4170
Crusoe's Daughter 4838
Cruz Chronicle, The 5595
Cry of Absence, A 4986
Cry of Angels, A 10730
Cry of Crickets, A 5357
Cry of the Peacock 7152
Cry, the Beloved Country 9146
Crying Game, The 5098
Crying Heart Tattoo, The 7733
Crying of Lot 49, The 10559
Cryptozoic! 7928
Crystal Cup, The 101
Crystal Garden, The 10236
"*Crystal River*" 10960
Crystal Vision 2923
Crystal World, The 7679
Cuba Libre 1612
Cuisine Novella 5975
Cullen, Brian 4829
Cullinan, Elizabeth 387, 2352
Cumberland Vendetta, A 4684
Cummings, Betty Sue 4822
Cummins, Maria Susanna 2186
Cunningham, Elizabeth 1876
Cunningham, Laura 3859
Cunningham, Michael 454, 9827
Cuomo, George 7776, 9837, 10426
Cup of Gold 10574
Cup of Tea for Mr. Thorgill, A 2965
Cupboard, The 9295
Curious Street, A 818
Curley, Daniel 1193
Curran, Mary Doyle 4057
Curranne Trueheart 5771
Current Climate, The 3525
Currey, Richard 867, 8703
Currie, Ellen 2669
Curtain 7405
Curtain Going Up 2277
Curtin, Michael 1856
Curwood, James Oliver 403, 404,
    407, 1543, 3086, 3358, 3897,
    4047, 4049, 4341, 5902, 5904,
    6214, 6837, 8563, 8977, 10343
Custom House, The 2536
Custom of the Country, The 7555
Customs 6455
Cuts 3370

Cutter, The (Suarez) 236
Cutters, The (Aldrich) 3823
Cutting Edge, The 549
Cutting Stone 5181
Cutting Through 6332
Cybele 2381
Cytherea 8909

Dad 1054
Daddy Boy 6723
Daddy Was a Number Runner 2770
Dagon 7775
Dahl, Roald 3587, 6645
Dahl, Tessa 8197
Dahlberg, Edward 6107, 7496
Dahomean, The 681
Dain Curse, The 2602
Daisy Miller 5066
Daitch, Susan 516
Dale Loves Sophie to Death 156
Dallas, Sandra 1474
d'Alpuget, Blanche 8433, 9633
Dalva 5271
Daly, John 8310
Damage (Hart) 5706
Damages (Worthen) 7
Dames 10843
Damnation of Theron Ware, The 3991
Dance Down the Mountain 6086
Dance of the Mothers, The 117
Dance on a Sinking Ship 2276
Dance the Eagle to Sleep 3538
Dancer from the Dance (Holleran) 2377
Dancer from the Dance, The (Burro-
    way) 3162
Dancer of Fortune, A 5188
Dancers in Mourning 703
Dancers in the Scalp House 752
Dancing at the Rascal Fair 288
Dancing Aztecs 7226
Dancing Bear 7423
Dancing Floor, The 7711
Dancing in the Dark 2929
Dane, Clemence (pseud.). *See*
    Ashton, Winifred
Danger Tree, The 8685
Dangerous Ages 836
Dangerous Days 8629
Dangerous Woman, A 6208
Dangling Man 9422
Daniel Deronda 10778
Daniel Martin 8279
Dann, Patty 7534
Dann, Sam 5849
Danny and the Boys 3129
Dansville 5861
Danvers, Dennis 9258
Danziger, Jeff 8711
Darby, Catherine 169
Darconville's Cat 2862
Darcy's Utopia 5677
Dargan, Olive Tilford 6417
Dark, The 8868
Dark Arena, The 4570

Dark Dancer, The 7308
Dark Dawn, The 10341
Dark Flower, The 10335
Dark Forest, The 5901
Dark Glasses, The 10997
Dark Horse (Knebel) 6994
Dark Horse, The (Godden) 447
Dark Labyrinth, The 9565
Dark Lady, The 3197
Dark Laughter 5133
Dark Night's Work, A 6406
Dark Sister, The 3625
Dark Summer 1900
Dark Thirty 8531
Dark Traveler, The 10715
Dark Tunnel, The 8594
Darken Ship 2385
Darkening Island 4789
Darker Brother, The 1248
"*Darker Days Than Usual*" 672
Darkness and Day 7166
Darkness and the Dawn, The 7624
Darkness and the Deep 526
Darkness at Ingraham's Crest, A 8810
Darkness Visible 4079
Darlin' Bill 445
Darling 7458
Darling Buds of May, The 5184
Darling Daughters 4361
Darrell 8305
Darrow, Clarence 1579
Darwin's Secret 473
Daughter Buffalo 4786
Daughter of Anderson Crow, The 5896
Daughter of Bugle Ann, The 10052
Daughter of Earth 7914
Daughter of Eve 5227
Daughter of Silence 2236
Daughter of the Hills 9071
Daughter of the Legend 3475
Daughter of the Middle Border, A 1587
Daughter of the Red Deer 4695
Daughters 3355
Daughter's a Daughter, A 1630
Daughters and Sons 4148
Daughters of Albion 5679
Daughters of Memory 5521
Davenport, Guy 999
Davenport, Marcia 2321, 4149, 10148
David Balfour 9737
David Copperfield 4452
David the King 420
Davidson, Lionel 2853, 4663,
    7720, 8275, 8524, 9576, 9908
Davidson, Max 318, 394, 574, 4830
Davies, A. A. T. 10394
Davies, Pete 3251
Davies, Robertson 51, 918, 1708,
    2477, 3938, 4020, 5100, 5948,
    6207
Davies, Valentine 5918
Davin, Dan 10221
Davis, Burke 4387
Davis, Christopher 7436, 7450
Davis, Clyde Brion 529, 1401, 2313,

2828, 3967, 4516, 5087, 5139,
5682, 6839, 7351, 9303
Davis, George 9235
Davis, H. L. 274, 3105
Davis, J. Madison 10316
Davis, Kathryn 4116, 7437
Davis, Margaret Thomson 3009,
7083, 8132, 10543
Davis, Rebecca Harding 175
Davis, Richard Harding 697, 9867
Davis, Terry 4823
Davis, Thulani 6167
Davis-Gardner, Angela 7020, 8502
Davita's Harp 6695
Davy Chadwick 2576
Dawe, Margaret 10324
Dawid, Annie 7283
Dawkins, Cecil 6464
Dawkins, Louisa 9641
Dawn (Bacheller) 5411
Dawn (Haggard) 5225
Dawn (Porter) 898
Dawn's Left Hand 7245
Dawson, Carol 10962
Day, Douglas 6344
Day After Sunday, The 8802
Day Before, The 8775
Day in Shadow, The 7481
Day Must Dawn, The 8592
Day No Pigs Would Die, A 7495
Day of Atonement 2448
Day of the Dog, The 1578
Day of the Locust, The 8776
Day of the Scorpion, The 5822
Day of Their Wedding, The 9523
"Day Off, A" 10121
Day the Money Stopped, The 2694
Daydreams 1169
Day-Lewis, Cecil 676, 738, 1621,
2964, 5461, 6178, 8307, 10376
Days of Vengeance 2165
Days Without Weather 2127
Dead, The 3682
Dead Babies 3193
Dead Father, The 2367
Dead Languages 8894
Dead Man Leading 9996
"Dead Man Range" 9563
Dead of the House, The 1518
Dead Secret, The 2289
Dead Voices 1264
Deadeye Dick 5266
Deadline (Heidish) 3291
Deadline (Stacey) 4333
Deadlock 9409
Deadwood 4261
Deagon, Ann 8312
Deal, Borden 1413, 1639, 1682,
2249, 3656, 4009, 4068, 4393,
4675, 5574, 6129, 7157, 7559,
7670, 8793, 9028
Dean's December, The 6456
Dear Beast 1107
Dear Deceit, The 588
Dear Digby 6513

Dear Friends 9454
Dear James 1963
Dear Mr. Capote 1941
Dear Rafe 5518
*Death and Birth of David Markand,
The* 10123
Death and Life of Harry Goth, The 308
Death at St. Anselm's, A 10093
Death by Dreaming 1132
Death Comes for the Archbishop 1494
Death Committee, The 6444
Death Grows On You 6970
Death in Don Mills 3852
Death in Kashmir 10276
Death in the Castle 1177
Death in the Family, A 1270
Death Is a Lonely Business 1454
Death Kit 9580
Death of a Doxy 8272
Death of a Dude 4279
Death of a Ghost 6174
Death of a Hero 10475
Death of a Politician 1125
Death of a Swagman 5138
Death of an Expert Witness 1123
Death of Attila, The 1885
"Death of Descartes, The" 3205
Death of Donna-May Dean, The 5301
Death of Felicity Taverner 4698
Death of Jim Loney, The 8921
Death of Men, The 5958
Death of Nora Ryan, The 2155
Death of the Detective, The 1685
Death of the Fifth Sun 4592
Death of the Fox 8483
Death of the Heart, The 727
Death of William Posters, The 10386
Death Out of Season, A 9587
Death, Sleep & the Traveler 2658
Death Walked in Cyprus 3702
"Deaths at Sea" 1733
Death's Darkest Face 5539
de Bernières, Louis 7979, 9273
de Boissiere, Ralph 1632
de Breffny, Brian 4932
Debt of Dishonour 3624
Debut, The 5493
Decatur Road, The 10425
Deceits of Time 10529
Deception 5538
de Chair, Somerset 7188
"Decision" (Boyle) 3141
Decision (Drury) 3484
Decline and Fall 8354
Decline of the West, The 3901
de Combray, Richard 6047
"Decoration Day" 7337
Dee, Jonathan 8474
Deep Silence, The 5071
Deep Sleep, The 8788
Deepening Stream, The 7379
Deeping, Warwick 492, 1597,
8772, 9536
Deepwood 3207
Deer at the River, The 2266

Deer Park, The 4061
Deerslayer, The 3433
Defects of the Heart 10735
Defending Civilization 5981
De Ferrari, Gabriella 9651
Defoe, Daniel 120, 353, 354, 355,
778, 3527, 5384, 5552, 6089,
6601, 9508, 10464, 10465, 10466
De Forest, John W. 5080, 5785,
10777
DeGrazia, Emilio 9274
De Haan, Tom 184
de Hartog, Jan 190, 1142, 5779,
6898, 8463, 9101, 10523
De Haven, Tom 988
"De Havilland Hand" 5598
Deighton, Len 180, 744, 846, 1168,
1417, 1467, 2517, 2916, 3021,
4993, 6005, 6999, 7004, 7153,
8373, 8422, 8541, 8680, 8804,
9332, 9804, 10597
Deirdre 9535
Delafield, E. M. 639, 1914, 2532,
3974, 5416, 5419
de la Mare, Walter 6312
Deland, Margaret 1367, 1375,
7240, 7710, 9872, 10643
de la Peña, Terri 925
de la Roche, Mazo 1251, 1970,
3127, 3150, 4158, 4562, 7475,
7842, 8082, 8547, 9215, 9383,
9548, 10154, 10579
Delbanco, Nicholas 747, 1555,
2779, 2913, 3180, 3773, 4584,
4618, 9592
DelCorso's Gallery 8817
Del-Del 10638
Delderfield, R. F. 847, 2357,
2842, 2982, 5092, 6316, 6570,
7185, 9586, 10509
Delicate Geometry 812
Delicate Monster 10791
Delilah 8087
DeLillo, Don 290, 3395, 3539,
4648, 5102, 6818, 9594, 9642,
9814, 10985
Deliverance 5717
Dell, Floyd 5709, 8976
Dell, George 10043
Deloria, Ella Cara 6158
Delphinium Girl, The 1837
Delta Star, The 4523
Delta Wedding 7251
Deluge, The 363
Del Vecchio, John M. 2803, 9755
DeLynn, Jane 75, 3241, 7732
Dem 3169
DeMarinis, Rick 997, 5769
Demetz, Nana 2059
Democracy (Adams) 6037
Democracy (Didion) 2267
De Mojo Blues 225
Demolished Man, The 872
Demon, The 7995
Denis Duval 360

Denning, Candace 10444, 10668
Dennis, Nigel 3832
Dennis, Patrick 7302
Dennison, George 1139, 10021
Departing as Air 7783
Depths of Glory 9631
Derleth, August 657, 2219, 2234, 5025, 5068, 8510
de Rosa, Peter 8580
Desai, Anita 758, 5846, 8526, 10445
Desani, G. V. 5226
Descendant, The 8343
Descending Order 8376
Descent from Xanadu 6900
Desert, The 9278
Desert Drama, A 8061
Desert Fabuloso 7579
Desert of the Heart 7819
Desert Rose 3019
Deserters, The 9920
Desierto 10026
de Silva, Colin 7021
Desmonde 7892
Desolation Angels 6075
Despair 5420
Desperate Remedies 3488
Dess, G. D. 690
Dessa Rose 1742
Destination Biafra 3210
Destinies of Darcy Dancer, Gentleman, The 10607
Destiny Bay 8741
Destiny Express 8382
Destiny Makers, The 7840
Destiny Waltz, The 5825
Destroyers, The 10407
Detling Secret, The 9458
Deuce, The 4851
Devices and Desires 6203
Devil at Home, The 8287
Devil by the Sea 5810
Devil in the Dooryard, The 2051
Devil Is Loose, The 3775
Devil Loves Me, The 10650
Devil of a State 1109
Devil on Lammas Night, The 2769
Devil Tree, The 7683
Devil with Love, The 665
Devil's Advocate, The (Caldwell) 7135
Devil's Advocate, The (West) 1507
Devil's Alternative, The 7934
Devil's Dream, The 4531
Devil's Hand, The 7267
Devil's Laughter, The 7983
Devil's Wind, The 1930
Devilseed 7487
Devine, Laurie 2163, 9687
Devoted Ladies 6759
DeVoto, Bernard 3830
De Vries, Peter 379, 568, 1114, 1235, 4324, 4446, 5090, 5467, 5660, 5701, 5705, 5820, 5934, 6120, 6322, 6634, 6671, 6776, 7012, 7170, 7172, 7722

Dew, Robb Forman 156, 182, 3629
Dewhurst, Keith 3657
Dexter, Pete 167, 1002, 2401, 4261
Dexterity 3933
Dialogues with the Devil 2626
Diamond 3309
Diamond Jo 5456
Diamond Lane, The 4450
Diamond Wedding 4737
Diana of the Crossways 10781
Diary of a Drug Fiend 2499
Diary of a Good Neighbour, The 4506
Diary of a Lost Boy 2556
Diary of a Mad Housewife 4398
Diary of a Nobody, The 3073
Diary of a Provincial Lady 3974
Diary of a Rapist, The 10194
Diary of a Yuppie 2548
Diary of an Old Man 2344
Dick, Philip K. 1074, 3280
Dick, R. A. 10799
Dick, The 4984
Dick Gibson Show, The 4784
Dickens, Charles 96, 359, 779, 2288, 3377, 4303, 4367, 4452, 4714, 5054, 5557, 5728, 6519, 7550, 8050, 8339, 9207
Dickens, Monica 23, 55, 324, 1110, 2349, 2691, 3339, 4951, 8717, 9165, 9354, 9670, 10586
Dickey, James 5717, 8713, 10746
Dickinson, Charles 3950, 4994, 5075, 8290
Dickinson, Peter 1258, 2725, 4778, 6401
Dickson, Margaret 2275, 6331, 6691
Diddakoi, The 4987
Didion, Joan 2267, 3462, 7169, 8796
di Donato, Pietro 2327, 8590
Die the Long Day 1433
Diehl, Margaret 8016
Dieter, William 3451, 7696, 10267
Difference of Design, A 5109
Different Drummer, A 4066
Different Face, A 1633
Different Kind of Christmas, A 7903
Different World, A 3012
Difficulties with Girls 6157
Digger's Game, The 9787
Digs 6964
Dillard, Annie 8167
Dillon, Eilis 4931
Dillon, Millicent 117
Dime to Dance By, A 3753
Dimple Hill 1298
Dinner at the Homesick Restaurant 9456
Dinner Party, The 10294
Dintenfass, Mark 3595, 3876
Diplomat, The 8566
Diplomat's Daughter, The 7213
Dipper, Alan 5103
Dirty Story 4982

Dirty Work 9645
Disaffection, A 6481
Disappearance, The (Guy) 10250
Disappearance, The (Wylie) 2559
Disappearing Acts 10876
Disappearing Moon Cafe 3696
Discipline 695
Discovery 6341
Discovery of Light, The 2284
Disenchanted, The 10049
Disinherited, The 1018
Disorderly Knights, The 10658
Dispossessed, The (Carpenter) 1732
Dispossessed, The (Le Guin) 1855
Disraeli, Benjamin 834, 949, 952, 1265, 1565, 1569, 3059, 3964, 6090, 6267, 7648
Dissent of Dominick Shapiro, The 4070
Dissenter in the House of God, A 6514
Distant Kingdom, The 2421
Distant Trumpet, A 5057
Disturbances in the Field 7174
Disturbing the Peace 64
Ditto List, The 7736
Diva's Ruby 7950
Diver's Tomb, The 8312
Divided Lady, The 3474
Divina Trace 10961
Divine Comedy of John Venner, The 6833
Divine Concepts of Physical Beauty 4368
Divine Days 4601
Diviner, The (Harris) 7530
Diviners, The (Laurence) 7684
Divining Blood 1479
Division of the Spoils, A 10514
Divorce Sonnets, The 5005
Divorcing Daddy 5304
Dixiana Moon 6937
Dixie Association, The 7148
Dixie Riggs 7211
Dixon, Stephen 1195, 1328, 5850
Dixon, Thomas Jr. 2687, 3996, 6310, 7800, 8767, 10034
Do Black Patent Leather Shoes Really Reflect Up? 4236
Do Butlers Burgle Banks? 9919
"*Do Clams Bite?*" 9949
Do, Lord, Remember Me (Garrett) 1657
Do Lord Remember Me (Lester) 1531
Do With Me What You Will 2035
Doane, Michael 7086, 10452
Dobyns, Stephen 2452, 2526, 2720, 3880, 6926, 9320
Doc's Legacy 5116
Doctor, The 10129
Doctor Blues 5586
Doctor Claudius 98
Doctor Cobb's Game 8901
Doctor Copernicus 606
Doctor Criminale 5877
Doctor De Marr 9957

Dr. Excitement's Elixir of Longevity 10290
Doctor Fischer of Geneva 4359
Doctor Frigo 5003
Doctor Grimshawe's Secret 3554
Dr. Gruber's Daughter 4922
Dr. Haggard's Disease 9987
"Dr. Heart" 8368
Doctor Is Sick, The 8518
Doctor Love 10261
Doctor Luke of the Labrador 5015
Dr. North and His Friends 6095
Doctor of Desire, The 10300
Dr. Rocksinger and the Age of Longing 5608
Doctor Sax 5445
Dr. Sevier 10549
Doctor Slaughter 9108
Doctor Sleep 8501
Doctor Thorne 6885
Doctor Zay 4927
Doctors 6830
Doctors & Women 7602
Doctor's Family, The 6034
Doctor's Wife, The 9595
Doctorow, E. L. 820, 2904, 3191, 6223, 6596, 6672, 6942, 9584
Dodd, Susan 114, 8233
Dodge, Jim 830
Dodsworth 2104
Doerr, Harriet 1090, 5609
Dog Crusoe, The 399
Dog Days 2679
Dog Horse Rat 7450
Dog Named Chips, A 413
Dog of the South, The 2664
Dog Soldiers 8369
Dog Tags 2362
Dogeaters 8538
Do-Gooders, The 10008
Dogs, Dreams, and Men 671
Dogs of March, The 9448
Dogwood Afternoons 4828
Doherty, P. C. 3353
Doig, Ivan 288, 6875, 8145, 9494
Doin' the Box Step 4600
"Doing and Undoing" 2818
Doings of Raffles Haw, The 10568
Dollarville 3251
Dolliver Romance (unfinished), The 10111
Dollmaker, The 10362
Dolly and the Nanny Bird 6821
Dombey and Son 6519
Domestic Arrangements 386
Domestic Life 4925
Domestic Pleasures 2453
Dominic 6551
Don Bueno 7692
Don Juan in the Village 75
Don Juan's New World 9085
Don Orsino 3071
Don Quixote 4710
Don't Stop the Carnival 5032

Don't Touch Me 8655
Donald, Anabel 7026, 7465
Donald Duk 2115
Donleavy, J. P. 797, 3166, 4276, 7315, 8411, 8426, 8617, 8636, 9618, 10607
Donnelly, Frances 2748
Donnelly, Gabrielle 4093, 8758
Donnelly, Nisa 2727
Donnington Legend, The 1225
Donofrio, Beverly 3039
Doolittle, Hilda 490, 9534
Doomed Oasis, The 1108
Doom's Caravan 8902
Doomsters, The 426
Door, The 128
Door Into Summer, The 3139
Doorbell Rang, The 594
Dorfman, Ariel 5866
Dorit in Lesbos 7942
Dork of Cork, The 636
Dorothy Vernon of Haddon Hall 698
Dorris, Michael 8380
Dos Passos, John 273, 281, 792, 2141, 2891, 5927, 6216, 7196, 7768, 8068, 8630, 8645, 8650, 9421, 10377
Doting 9384
Double Affair, A 5743
Double Double 5189
Double for Death 3646
Double Honeymoon 9443
Double Indemnity 1023
Double Negative 551
Double Vision 1942
Double Yoke 8880
Doubleman, The 1310
Dougall, Lily 268
Douglas, Colin 6895
Douglas, Ellen 3185, 3718, 5744, 8381, 10415
Douglas, Lloyd C. 2221, 3100, 4233, 7829
Douglas, Norman 126
Dove 1190
Dove in the Eagle's Nest, The 1849
Down Among the Women 10822
Down and Out in Paris and London 10792
Down There on a Visit 706
Down Where the Moon Is Small 5650
Downing, Michael 5610
Doyle, Arthur Conan see Conan Doyle, Arthur
Doyle, Lynne 5442
Doyle, Roddy 7094, 7209
Drabble, Margaret 438, 754, 3350, 3674, 3860, 4574, 4775, 5540, 5573, 7398, 8445, 10072
Dracula 9524
Dragon and the Raven, The 3068
Dragon Harvest 1098
Dragon Seed 9997
Dragon's Teeth 8719

Dragon's Wine 8793
Dranow, John 4628
Dream, The 10918
Dream Dredger, The 2573
Dream Journey, A 10242
Dream Life, The 9057
Dream Life of Balso Snell, The 2603
Dream Merchants, The 1625
Dream of Destiny 9381
Dream of Kings, A (Grubb) 9099
Dream of Kings, A (Petrakis) 2244
Dream Years, The 1063
Dreamhouse 5970
Dreaming 7836
Dreaming in Cuban 8385
Dreaming of Babylon 6326
Dreaming of Heroes 6863
Dreamland 9601
Dreams Like Thunder 9985
Dreams of an Average Man 10990
Dreams of Leaving 3956
Dreams of Long Lasting 2812
Dreams of Sleep 5327
Dreams of the Kalahari 4189
Dred 3736
Dreiser, Theodore 1359, 1363, 2200, 5564, 6412, 7154, 9525, 10651
Drexler, Rosalyn 2263
D'ri and I 6617
Drifters, The 10999
Drinkard, Michael 4853
Driver's Seat, The 2845
Drop of Patience, A 3163
Drowning Pool, The 10804
Drown, Merle 10088
Drowned World, The 4392
Drowning 10959
Drowning of a Goldfish, The 5381
Drowning Season, The 8371
Druid Time 4219
Drummer of the Eleventh North Devonshire Fusiliers, The 999
Drums 3760
Drums Along the Mohawk 9544
Drury, Allen 258, 531, 2390, 3484, 4277, 5046, 5062, 6450, 6661, 6986, 6995, 6997, 7013, 7354, 7813, 7831, 9364
Dry Bones 3617
Dry White Season, A 5953
Duberstein, Larry 3041, 5773, 6939
Dubin's Lives 5836
Dubious Legacy, A 9836
Dubus, Andre 1733, 2666, 2670, 2932, 3485, 6826
Dubus, Elizabeth Nell 3867
Duchess of Milan 7104
Duchess of Wrexe, The 489
Duchess's Diary, The 7595
Duck and Cover 3626
Ducks 770
Ducornet, Rikki 4509
Dud Avocado, The 2144
Due, Linnea A. 1214

Due East 4289
Due North 2458
Duet for Three 10280
Duff, Gerald 8925
Duff, Stephen 8155
Duffy, Bruce 1333
Duffy, Maureen 795, 2346, 4074, 4783, 5041, 5460, 6677, 7985
Duggan, William 7643, 9638
Duke of Stockbridge, The 9740
Dukes, Carol Muske 4026, 6513
Duke's Children, The 8714
Dukore, Margaret Mitchell 4192
Duluth 1451
Dumachas and Sheba 7146
Dumas, Henry 7320
du Maurier, Daphne 179, 1615, 2755, 4978, 6571, 7181, 7661, 8076, 8258, 8551, 9480, 10146, 10222, 10370, 10577
du Maurier, George 2132, 5399
Dunaway, Laramie 6971
Dunbar, Paul Laurence 3075, 8393
Dunbar's Cove 7670
Duncan Campbell 354
Duncan, David James 7078, 7369
Duncan, Jane 5261, 5449, 5816, 9431
Duncan, Norman 5015
Duncton Wood 7326
Dundy, Elaine 2144, 4319
Dunedin 8170
Dunfords Travels Everywheres 10213
Dunn, Katherine 10955
Dunn, Nell 850, 10214, 10395
Dunn, Suzannah 672
Dunne, Dominick 3809, 8640
Dunne, John Gregory 886, 1744, 5684
Dunne Family, The 10832
Dunnett, Dorothy 535, 569, 1069, 3719, 4172, 6345, 6772, 6821, 8620, 9314, 10658
Dunphy, Jack 450, 9461
Dunster 10979
Duplechan, Larry 170
du Plessis, Menán 7329
Durable Fire, A 10451
Durandal 524
Durham, Marilyn 2772, 9945
During the Reign of the Queen of Persia 5166
Durrell, Gerald 5043, 7478
Durrell, Lawrence 1825, 2914, 3650, 4317, 5146, 6327, 6432, 7266, 7922, 8459, 9248, 9565, 9627, 10974
Dust on the Beach 570
Dust on the Paw 247
Dusty Answer 6287
Dutch Shea, Jr. 886
Dutiful Daughter, A 10603
Dutton, Geoffrey 8808
Dwarfs, The 3257
Dworkin, Andrea 4862, 7431

Dworkin, Susan 1071
Dyad 4229
Dye, Eva Emery 373
Dying Young 1769
Dylanist, The 5678
Dynasty of Death 2212

Each Man's Son 8034
Eagle and the Iron Cross, The 10503
Eagle Eye 10605
Eagle in the Sky 5428
Eagle Song 10737
Eagles Gather, The 2315
Eagle's Heart, The 1492
Eagles' Wings to the Higher Places 9020
Eagleton, Terry 7151
Earl, Maureen 6346, 8506
Earl, The 8484
Early Autumn 6757
Early from the Dance 2800
Early Life of Stephen Hind, The 3711
Earnshaw Neighborhood, The 5751
Earth Abides 6982
Earth Abideth, The 10043
Earth Is the Lord's, The 6002
Earthbreakers, The 7300
Earthly Possessions 2662
Earthly Powers 856
Earthworks 1882
Ease 8637
Easeful Death 9465
East and West 9816
East Is East 9322
East Lynne 8340
East of Eden 9751
East of the Setting Sun 9095
East of the Giants 9416
East Side, West Side 10148
East Wind, Rain 8809
Easter Egg Hunt, An 5494
Easter Parade, The 6663
Easter Weekend 4968
Easterbrook, Gregg 8316
Eastlake, William 752, 6389, 8271, 9291, 9475, 9842, 10516
Easton, Robert 1989, 9045
Easy Keeper 2814
Easy to Kill 6252
Easy Travel to Other Planets 8491
Easy Way Out, The 1157
Eat a Bowl of Tea 8795
Eaters of the Dead 7521
Eaton, Vincent 4854
Eben Holden 6093
Eberhart, Dikkon 1696
Ebersohn, Wessel 2391
Eberstadt, Fernanda 260, 2667
Eberstadt, Isabel 10850
"Ebony Tower, The" 9589
Echewa, T. Obinkaram 3324
Echo of Lions 7701
Echoes of Celandine 2654
Echoing Grove, The 9899
Eckert, Allan W. 989, 4300, 5030,

7206, 7599
Ecstasy Business, The 7168
Edelson, Julie 6153
Eden and Honor 7087
Eden Close 185
Eden Passion, The 1181
Eden Prairie 4957
Eden Rising 2784
Edgar Huntly 5389
Edge of Eden 8539
Edge of Sadness, The 8998
Edge of the Alphabet, The 5700
Edgerton, Clyde 462, 469, 1995, 6488, 8384
Edgeworth, Maria 238, 694, 947, 2885, 3356, 3911, 6751, 7491, 9855, 9856, 10677, 10766
Edible Woman, The 10201
Edisto 7898
Edmonds, Walter D. 246, 1827, 1944, 4311, 4950, 6425, 8077, 9128, 9544
Edna His Wife 1379
Education of Don Juan, The 572
Education of Harriet Hatfield, The 5596
Education of Little Tree, The 6660
Education of Patrick Silver, The 547
Edwardians, The 5414
Edwards, G. B. 10909
Edwards, Junius 9478
Edwards, Louis 1848
Edwards, Page 2547, 9973
Edwards-Yearwood, Grace 8824
Edwin Mullhouse 2360
Egan, Pierce 9376
Eggleston, Edward 240, 895, 954, 955, 4038, 5729, 5890, 7371
Eggleston, George Cary 2494
Egoist, The 6613
Egremont, Max 3252, 9806
Ehle, John 4824, 5378, 9946
Ehrlich, Gretel 8704
Ehrlich, Max 1446, 1683, 2161
Eight Corners of the World, The 1081
Eight Cousins 2070
Eight Days 2762
1876 1441
Eighth Day, The 3407
Eighty-Minute Hour, The 10512
Eighty-Sixed 1539
Einstein's Dreams 9507
Eisenhower, My Eisenhower 9436
Ekaterina 4878
Elbowing the Seducer 8466
Elders and Betters 3360
Eleanora Duse 3365
Elect Mr. Robinson For a Better World 1480
Elegy for September, An 5724
Elena 919
Elephant, The 8027
Elephant Walk 9749
11 Edward Street 4530
"Eliduc" 9007

Eliot, George 3336, 4034, 4492, 5886, 7649, 9113, 10776, 10778
Elissa 8399
Elixir, The 1671
Elizabeth Alone 6793
Elizabeth Appleton 3156
Elizabeth Cole 4852
Elkhorn Tavern 7638
Elkin, Stanley 1817, 2338, 2685, 3001, 4249, 4709, 4784, 4885, 5178, 7456, 7793
Ellen Foster 6197
Ellerman, Winifred *See* Bryher
Elliott, Janice 890, 1205, 2844, 3688, 4922, 6144, 6809, 9460
Elliott, Summer Locke 1767, 3410, 7119
Ellis, Alice Thomas 2409, 5666, 8613
Ellis, Bret Easton 3723, 8012, 8320
Ellis, Mel 748
Ellis, Peter Berresford 8237
Ellison, Emily 3618, 6692
Ellison, James Whitfield 8693
Ellison, Jane 6580
Ellison, Ralph 5922
Ellmann, Lucy 3242
Elman, Richard 479
Elmblad, Mary 3907, 10307
Elmer Gantry 2889
Elsie and the Child 1968
Elsie Dinsmore 3064
Elsie Venner 4441
Elvis Presley Calls His Mother After The Ed Sullivan Show 9372
Elward, James 1993
Ely, David 1650, 1676, 2032, 5544, 6505, 9577, 10714
Elysian Fields 6871
Embarrassment of Riches, An 7232
Embassy House, The 1166
Ember Lane 9138
Embezzler, The 3537
Emecheta, Buchi 1049, 1697, 2708, 2774, 3210, 4855, 8880, 10223
Emergency Exit 5263
Emerson, Sally 7977
Emilia in England 10773
Emma 5555
Emmeline (Rossner) 4186
Emmeline (Singmaster) 5616
Emmons, Della Gould 10140
Empathy 9374
Emperor of Ice-Cream, The 8944
Emperor's Ladies, The 3144
Empire 10528
Empire City, The 7032
Empire of the Senseless 369
Empire of the Sun 10524
Empty Lot, The 9983
Empty Meadow, The 10020
Emshwiller, Carol 10877
Enchanted, The 1622
Enchanted Voyage, The 8081
Enchantment (Dickens) 324

Enchantment (Merkin) 5520
Enchantress, The 5076
End of All Songs, The 3853
End of Chapter 2964
End of Eternity, The 1861
End of My Career, The 5277
End of My Life, The 3384
End of Solomon Grundy, The 2975
End of the Affair, The 8989
End of the Battle, The 8666
End of the Dream, The 6915
End of the Empire 2465
End of the House of Alard, The 2300
End of the Line, The 3339
"End of the Road, The" (Bromfield) 1917
End of the Road, The (Barth) 4751
End of the Rug, The 595
End of the World, The 5729
End of the World News, The 223
"End of Tragedy, The" 8639
End Zone 5102
Enderby Outside 2589
Enderby's Dark Lady 2931
Ending Up 148
Endless Love 9279
Endless Night 2347
Endymion 1569
Enemies 10224
Enemies of the System 6230
Enemy Camp, The 4159
Enemy Gods, The 2621
Enemy in the Blanket, The 200
Engel, Marian 4125, 5287, 7462, 9938
Engel, Monroe 4593
Engine of Owl-Light, The 8889
England Made Me 10041
English, Isobel 591
English Creek 9494
English Governess at the Siamese Court, The 2188
English Music 6799
English Patient, The 10890
"Enigma, The" 2565
Enigma of Arrival, The 7338
Ennis, Michael 7104
Ennui 3356
Entail, The 3550
Enter Sir Robert 1408
Entered from the Sun 4335
Entering Ephesus 3580
Entrance to Porlock, The 1207
Entwining, The 9489
Envoy Extraordinary 10001
Ephron, Amy 1261
Ephron, Nora 2164
Episode in Palmetto 659
Episode of Sparrows, An 3977
Epitaph for a Spy 6949
Epps, Garrett 1455
Epstein, Jacob 3858
Epstein, Leslie 1698, 5223, 6236, 7735, 8314, 9393
Epstein, Seymour 1699, 4507,

6156, 10629
Equal Affections 2435
Equality 8966
Erdrich, Louise 2425, 7273, 10092
Erewhon 1568
Erewhon Revisited 5563
Erhart, Margaret 174, 8890
Eric Brighteyes 4456
Erickson, Steve 1734, 5050, 6211
Erie Water 8077
Erik Dorn 520
Ermelino, Louisa 7100
Errand of the Eye, The 3659
Error of Judgement, An 141
Erskine, John 4463, 5697, 7248
Escape Artist, The 7045
Escape from Dade City 2876
Escape from Five Shadows 8790
Escape from Sonora 10230
Esmond in India 3473
Espey, John 6738
Establishment, The 4919
Estate, The 145
Estate of Memory, An 7141
Esther 1295
Esther Waters 1575
Estuary, The 1562
Et Tu, Babe 6170
Eternal Lover, The 10340
Ethan Frome 7828
Europe 7848
Europe After the Rain 7675
Europeans, The 1183
Eustace and Hilda 1300
Eustace Chisholm and the Works 9166
Eustace Diamonds, The 9261
Eutaw 720
Eva 6641
Eva Trout 6913
Eva's Man 3408
Evan Harrington 2290
Eve 5064
Eve of Saint Venus, The 9313
Eve's Longing 10325
Eve's Tattoo 7237
Evelina 6307
Even Cowgirls Get the Blues 2372
Even Now 2729
Evening in Byzantium 309
Evening in Spring 657
Evening of Brahms, An 6235
Evening of the Holiday, The 8218
Evening Star, The 3043
Ever After 10548
Everett, Percival 4590, 4863
Everlasting 4552
Every Little Crook and Nanny 2152
Everything in the Window 6452
Everything Must Go 9003
Everything That Moves 313
Everything to Live For 251
Evidence of Love (Grau) 808
Evidence of Love (Jacobson) 9685
Evil Genius, The 5196
Evil Under the Sun 3110

Evolution Man, The 10710
Ewings, The 10661
Excellency 10245
Excellent Women 10805
Excelsior 6847
Except the Lord 1185
Execution 5026
Executioner's Song, The 27
Executive Suite 134
Exes 5691
Exhibitionist, The 1790
Exile, An (Jones) 4983
Exile, The (Kotzwinkle) 7120
Exile of Céline, The 4017
Exiles, The 5815
Exit 8978
Exit Lady Masham 715
Exotic 7895
Expecting 7076
Expecting Miracles 552
Expedition of Humphry Clinker, The 5387
Expensive Habits (Howard) 1807
Expensive Habits (Vigfusson) 2783
Expensive People 2031
Expensive Place to Die, An 744
Experiments with Life and Death 34
Exploits of Brigadier Gerard, The 4458
Explorer, The 7912
Exposure 2884
Extraordinary Means 6711
Extraordinary People 6733
Extras, The 10532
Eye for an Eye, An (Darrow) 1579
Eye for an Eye, An (Trollope) 3066
Eye of God, The 1396
Eye of Love, The 5145
Eye of the Storm, The (Hearne) 2232
Eye of the Storm, The (White) 147
Eye of the Heron, The 8374
Eyeless in Gaza 6849
Eyes 2345
Eyes of the World, The 10572
Ezekiel, Tish O'Dowd 1842

F.N.G. 344
Fabian, Warner (pseud.). *See* Adams, Samuel Hopkins
Fable, A 10491
Fablesinger, The 2642
Fabricator, The 367
Fabulous Clipjoint, The 2760
Fabulous Englishman, The 9025
Face 32
Face Beside the Fire, The 5089
Face of Jalanath, The 8611
Face of Terror, The 1934
Face of Time, The 6633
Face Value 3695
Faces in the Water 7516
Facial Justice 5203
Facing Death 6268
Facing the Tank 10951
Factotum 1688

Fade 6868
Fade Out 10169
Fading, My Parmacheene Belle 8734
Faessler, Shirley 6452
Faggots 5949
Fahrenheit 451 3769
Failure to Zigzag 2100
Faint Perfume 6624
Fair, The 3387
Fair and Tender Ladies 4850
Fair Bride, The 1503
Fair Day's Work, A 7307
Fair Game 5455
Fair God, The 7502
Fair Land, Fair Land 1713
Fair Maid of Perth, The 6908
Fair Margaret 6835
Fair Sister, The 3577
Fair Stood the Wind for France 6067
Fairbairn, Ann 3748
Fairbairns, Zoë 3027, 5168
Fairly Good Time, A 3804
Fairly Honourable Defeat, A 4782
Fairoaks 3307
Fairy Tale of New York, A 8426
Fairyland 1767
Faith and the Good Thing 253
Faith Doctor, The 5890
Faith of a Collie, The 1910
Faithful Are the Wounds 3685
Faithful Servants, The 150
Falconer 1165
Fall & Rise 5850
"Fall and Rise of Mrs. Hapgood, The" 2976
Fall from Grace 9943
Fall of Kelvin Walker, The 1726
Fall Quarter 9654
Fallen Leaves, The 5559
Falling (Schaeffer) 5755
Falling (Thubron) 8199
Falling Angels 3620
Falling in Place 9677
Falling Up the Stairs 6475
Falls the Shadow 9643
False Coin 5252
"False Dawn (The 'Forties)" 8508
False Entry 9696
False Match 3717
False Messiah, The 1841
False Premises 1719
Falstaff 805
Falter-Barns, Suzanne 4600
Familiar Ground 1721
Familiar Passions 2663
Families and Survivors 6394
Family (Cooper) 4510
Family (Gold) 284
Family (Leavitt) 3606
Family, The (Emechita) 4855
Family Affair, A 668
Family and a Fortune, A 7556
Family and Friends 6865
Family Arsenal, The 3053
Family Business 3033

Family Feeling 7932
Family Fictions 1776
Family Happiness 3594
Family Honor 10426
Family Laundry 7535
Family Life 10749
Family Likeness, A 9339
Family Linen 1730
Family Madness, A 1064
Family Man, The 1866
Family Money 8896
Family Myths and Legends 6192
Family Night 6171
Family of Max Desir, The 9183
Family Pictures 868
Family Planning 1761
Family Secrets 9590
Family Skeletons 10440
Family Ties 2864
Family Trade 504
Family Trouble 4565
Family Truths 9623
Family's Affair, A 5744
Famine 9067
Famished Road, The 9200
Famous Last Words 6678
Fan 7753
Fan Man, The 8727
Fanatic, The 276
Fancy Dancer, The 6229
Fanny 5492
Fanny Herself 10787
Fanny Hill 5553
Fanshawe 7875
Fantasy, The 5857
Fantasy and Fugue 3701
Fantazius Mallare 4935
Fante, John 2660
Far Afield 9653
Far Country, The 2961
Far Cry from Kensington, A 8826
Far from Cibola 6064
Far from the Madding Crowd 8545
Far from the Sea 7937
Far in the Forest 8585
Far Off Place, A 2124
Far Pavilions, The 810
Far Side, The 3969
Far Side of the Dollar, The 7309
Far Side of Victory, The 6595
Far Tortuga 2252
Far-Away Bride, The 7585
Farah, Nuruddin 550, 8496, 9014, 10268
Faraway 298
Faraway Drums, The 2160
Faraway Places 8619
Farewell Companions 6854
Farewell, My Lovely 6271
"Farewell, Summer" 4595
Farewell to Arms, A 3093
Farewell to Europe 6330
Fariña, Richard 4577
Farish, Terry 4629
Farm, The 7380

Farm Under a Lake, A 2003
Farmer, Penelope 5064
Farmers Hotel, The 4059
Farnham's Freehold 9362
Farrell, J. G. 1443, 4075, 4645, 6225
Farrell, James T. 1660, 1878, 2155, 2653, 2827, 3420, 3566, 4763, 6633, 6851, 7363, 7511, 8210, 8417, 8421, 9266, 10136, 10832
Farrell, M. J. (pseud.). *See* Keane, Molly
Farrelly, Peter 6716
Farthing's Fortunes 807
Fashionable Adventures of Joshua Craig, The 3078
Fast, Howard 813, 861, 1517, 1529, 1759, 4883, 4919, 4953, 5594, 5917, 6181, 6642, 7388, 8135, 8651, 9611, 9889, 10139, 10294, 10388, 10483
"Fast and Loose" 310
Fatal Crown, The 1779
Fatal Light 8703
Fate of Mary Rose, The 2387
Fate of O'Loughlin, The 7189
Father Abraham 411
Father and His Fate, A 6528
Father and Son (Farrell) 10136
Father and Son (Maas) 2176
Father Hilary's Holiday 6807
Father Hunt, The 7204
Father Malachy's Miracle 1496
Father Melancholy's Daughter 5120
Father Stafford 4339
Fatherland 10637
Fathers (Budd) 257
Fathers (Gold) 9918
Fathers, The (Tate) 8512
Fathers and Children 4328
Fathers and Crows 2555
Father's Day 9437
Father's Words, A 9713
Faulkner, William 1400, 2022, 2027, 2303, 2690, 2890, 4052, 5710, 5931, 7394, 7763, 7982, 8649, 9414, 9840, 9887, 10346, 10491
Fault Lines 9608
Faultline 3463
Faulty Ground 4093
Fauset, Jessie Redmon 9129
Faust 5363
Faust, Irvin 5, 331, 602, 613, 1515, 6372, 6990
Favorite, The 10265
Favourite of the Gods, A 6125
Favours 9294
Fawcett, E. Douglas 5081
Fear of Flying 7171
Fearful Joy, A 6527
Fearing, Kenneth 5572, 6763
Fearless 2599
Feast, The 1500
Feast of Ashes, A 4285

Feast of Saint Barnabas, The 9234
Feast of Snakes, A 2851
Feats on the Fjord 5707
Federigo 3671
Federman, Raymond 1230, 9017, 9029
Feel Free 2351
Feikema, Feike (pseud.). *See* Manfred, Frederick
Feinberg, David B. 1539, 3889
Feinstein, Elaine 3299, 3881, 6340, 9953, 10236
Feld, Ross 5367
Feldman, Ellen 691, 2671, 5291
Felice 7020
Felicity 9701
Felix Holt, the Radical 9113
Fellow Passengers 9734
Fellowship of the Ring, The 5435
Female Complaints 4611
Female Friends 10762
Female Man, The 803
Female of the Species, The 945
Female Quixote, The 5883
Fence Walker, The 7428
Fenella Phizackerley 3675
Ferber, Edna 1391, 2950, 3565, 3826, 4725, 4727, 6314, 7061, 8410, 10787
Fer-de-Lance 10921
Ferdinand Count Fathom 4490
Fergus, Charles 9315
Fergus Lamont 7142
Ferguson, Patricia 6192
Ferguson Affair, The 589
Ferlinghetti, Lawrence 5673
Ferrell, Anderson 3225
Ferret Fancier, The 9479
Ferris Beach 6305
Ferriss, Lucy 3542
Ferro, Robert 3226, 3243, 9183
Festival at Farbridge 1629
Feud, The 1057
"Feudists, The" 8794
Few Days in Weasel Creek, A 3856
Few Fair Days, A 4173
Few Flowers for Shiner, A 660
Few Foolish Ones, A 9136
Few Green Leaves, A 10419
Fiddle and Bow 4356
Fiddlefoot 7667
Fiddler's Green 8094
Fiedler, Leslie 142, 742
Fiela's Child 2572
Field Full of Folk, A 2399
Field of Honor (Byrne) 4557
Field of Honor (Murari) 4413
Field of Stars 9984
Field of Vision, The 1549
Field, Rachel 725, 1017, 1598, 2312, 4998, 6787, 7386
Fielding, Gabriel 1042, 2762, 4157, 4744, 5936, 8333, 9568
Fielding, Henry 1964, 2286, 4489, 5385, 7163

Fielding, Sarah 6033
Fielding Gray 1206
Fields, Jeff 10730
Fields, The 10357
Fields of Fire 1864
Fiend, The 938
Fierce Dispute, The 3095
Fifth Business 5100
Fifth Child, The 7742
"Fifth Head of Cerberus, The" 8221
Fifth Horseman, The 4478
Fifth Queen, The 4668
Fifth Queen Crowned, The 8848
Fifth Station, The 8240
50 6511
54-40 or Fight 4605
Fifty-Two Pickup 7725
Figes, Eva 4649, 5326, 7438, 8335, 9974, 10269
Fighting Littles, The 2756
Fighting with Shadows 2099
Figures of Earth 5213
File on Fraulein Berg, The 5839
File on Stanley Patton Buchta, The 1515
Filene, Peter 634
Final Beast, The 1656
Final Club, The 10312
Final Deduction, The 4761
Final Glass, The 9828
Final Harbor (Homewood) 8140
Final Harbor (Martin) 3023
Final Heat 8452
Final Hour, The 3115
Final Opus of Leon Solomon, The 6906
Final Passage, The 557
Final Payments 3948
Final Things 10971
Financial Expert, The 4741
Financier, The 1359
Finders Keepers 1236
Finding Brendan 1898
Finding Signs 9649
Findley, Timothy 440, 981, 4656, 6334, 6678, 8482
Fine 5270
Fine and Private Place, A 1983
Fine Excess, A 6580
Fine Madness, A 5454
Fine Time to Leave Me, A 5118
Finger of Saturn, The 5157
Finished Man, The 8864
Finishing School, The 2791
Fink, Jon Stephen 4867
Finley, Martha 3064
Finnegans Wake 1175
Finney, Ernest J. 2010, 4488, 10103
Finney, Patricia 7604
Finnley Wren 9285
Firbank, Ronald 127, 652, 933, 1198, 2945, 4292, 5732, 9542
Fire 9070
Fire Along the Sky 5274
Fire and Rain 3792
Fire Child 7977
Fire Down Below 10025

Fire from Heaven 10205
Fire in Heaven 5689
Fire in the Morning 9684
Fire on the Mountain (Abbey) 4065
Fire on the Mountain (Desai) 8526
Fire Sale 8486
Fire Sermon 8276
Fire Will Freeze 1916
Firebird 1470
Firecrest 2990
Firedrake's Eye 7604
Fire-Dwellers, The 5464
Firefly Summer 5334
Fireman's Fair, The 7467
Fire-Raiser, The 3784
Fires in the Sky 7810
Fires of Spring, The 4913
Firm of Girdlestone, The 1008
Firm Word or Two, A 9914
First Among Equals 2485
First and Vital Candle 10392
First Blood 2505
First Claim 3441
First Confession 6878
First Day of Friday, The 7305
First Family of Tasajara, A 10680
First Ladies 9965
First Light (Ackroyd) 2431
First Light (Baxter) 4526
First Light (Ellison) 6692
First Man in Rome, The 7006
First Men in the Moon, The 1219
First Nights 10897
First Papers 3159
First to Land, The 5172
First Wine 450
Fish Tales 6399
Fisher, Carrie 8022
Fisher, Dorothy Canfield 962,
  3080, 4461, 5617, 7379, 9218
Fisher, M. F. K. 9893
Fisher, Vardis 336, 526, 1497,
  2949, 5603, 5643, 7717, 8266,
  8517, 8746, 8786, 8899, 10141,
  10924
Fisher King, The 7191
Fisher's Hornpipe 761
Fiskadoro 5174
Fit, The 1204
Fitzgerald, F. Scott 1316, 4434,
  4631, 5086, 6625
Fitzgerald, M. J. 7084
Fitzgerald, Penelope 1051, 3230,
  7277, 7870, 9244, 9394, 10754
Five for Sorrow, Ten for Joy 2856
Five Gates of Hell, The 2807
Five Hundred Scorpions 6709
Five Red Herrings, The 6416
Five Smooth Stones 3748
Fixer, The 7849
Flag, The 3165
Flag for Sunrise, A 2924
Flambard's Confession 9945
Flame 1329
Flame, The 8217

Flame Bearers, The 3523
Flame for Doubting Thomas, A 5646
Flame of Life, The 1046
Flaming Forest, The 4341
Flaming Youth 3796
Flamingo Feather 8789
Flanagan, Mary 1815, 9343
Flanagan, Thomas 1700, 9109
Flanagan's Run 7858
Flanigan, Sara 6703
Flash 7439
Flash and Filigree 4617
Flash for Freedom! 6993
Flashman and the Dragon 10858
Flashman and the Mountain of Light
  3289
Flashman and the Redskins 3281
Flashman at the Charge 6009
Flashman in the Great Game 1179
Flashman's Lady 7821
Flat-Land Fable, A 5175
Flats 10398
Flaubert's Parrot 315
Flavin, Martin 1622, 5800, 6629
Flawless Jade 10531
Fleetwood 6606
Fleming, Berry 663, 4412, 9086,
  10576
Flesh 1974
Fletcher, Inglis 2214, 2222, 3116,
  8110, 8213, 8409, 9152
Flett, Una 2795
Flickers 7323
Fliegelman's Desire 9197
Flight from Fiesta 6085
Flight from the Enchanter 2471
Flight into Camden 3940
Flight of Peter Fromm, The 6325
Flight of the Falcon, The 9480
Flight to Canada 5480
Flight to Landfall 10595
Flights 10976
Flint 10582
Flint, Helen 116
Flint Spears 10692
Flipping for It 8013
Flirt, The 10336
Flivver King, The 4937
Floaters 1842
Floating in My Mother's Palm 7095
Floating Island, The 1455
Floating Opera, The 5437
Floating World, The 10874
Floatplane Notebooks, The 469
Flood (Warren) 6912
Flood, The (Ascher) 6380
Flood, The (Broderick) 10293
Floodtide 8096
Flook, Maria 6171
Florence, Ronald 7786
Florentine Dagger, The 332
Florey, Kitty Burns 3982, 5491,
  6154
Florry of Washington Heights 6278
Flower Beneath the Foot, The 127

Flower Garden, The 10944
Flower of May, The 10652
Flower of the Chapdelaines, The 5793
Flower of the Republic, The 7116
Flower Shadows 4629
Flower That's Free, A 9495
Flowering, The 3806
Flowering Mimosa 6713
Flowering Thorn, The 6021
Flowering Wilderness 8938
Flowers, Arthur 225, 4877
Flowers for Lilian 312
Flowers for the Judge 2557
Flowers of the Forest, The 4483
Flowers on the Grass 2691
Flute-Player, The 7158
Fly Away Home (Piercy) 6690
Fly Away Home (Tindall) 2539
Flyers, The 4306
Flying Hero Class 7545
Flying in to Love 2815
Flying Inn, The 6562
Flying Lessons 9503
Flying to Nowhere 10427
Flynn, Robert 6029
Flynt, Candace 3028, 7365, 10082
Foe 3694
Foggage 10617
Folded Leaf, The 9999
Folks, The 2136
Folks That Live on the Hill, The 1874
Follow Me Down 4383
Follow the River 1556
Follower, The 3866
Folly 6945
Fombombo 9879
Fong and the Indians* 1040
Fontes, Montserrat 6878
Food of the Gods, The 6409
Fool and His Money, A 4975
Fool of the Family, The 8771
Foolish Gentlewoman, The 3122
Foolish Immortals, The 5571
Fools Crow 8442
Fools Die 5950
Fools of Fortune 3215
Fools Paradise 4803
Fools' Gold 4096
Fools' Parade 4399
Fool's Progress, The 4845
Fool's Sanctuary 2519
Foolscap 9400
Foolscap Rose, The 3328
Football Dreams 8922
Foote, Mary Hallock 8052
Foote, Shelby 2226, 2320, 3391,
  4383, 10585
Footstool in Heaven 9397
"For Better For Worse" 2025
For Ever Wilt Thou Love 9068
For Love 42
For Love of the Game 4658
For Mary, with Love 7896
For My Great Folly 4002
For Name and Fame 721

For the Love of Robert E. Lee 4243
For the Sake of All Living Things 2803
For the Temple 956
For They Shall Inherit 7048
For Want of a Nail 4685
For Whom the Bell Tolls 10695
Forayers, The 6973
Forbath, Peter 7700, 10215
Forbush and the Penguins 6074
Force Majeure 2808
Force of Gravity 1263
Ford, Elaine 816, 4184, 8285, 10956
Ford, Ford Madox 1093, 2204,
 3092, 4668, 7758, 7966, 8346,
 8351, 8848, 8973, 10040
Ford, Jesse Hill 2907, 6222, 9234,
 10409
Ford, Kathleen 2722
Ford, Paul Leicester 5401, 7346,
 8842
Ford, Richard 3619, 4837
Foregone Conclusion, A 8252
Foreign Affairs 1724
Foreign Bodies 9282
Foreign Devils 602
Foreign Husband, The 10449
Foreign Land 2273
Foreign Matter 10304
Foreigner, The 9712
Forest and the Fort, The 3900
Forest Hearth, A 6812
Forest of Arden, The 112
Forest of the Night 5318
Forester, C. S. 129, 177, 565,
 2701, 3482, 7349, 7513, 8086,
 8098, 8100, 8102, 8412, 8653,
 10655, 10704, 10922
Foretaste of Glory 1393
Forever... 7993
Forever Panting 7170
Forever Street, The 3600
Forge, The 3098
Forgetting Elena 10233
Forgive Us Our Virtues 5643
Forgiving 389
Forgotten Life 3811
Forgotten Smile, The 8941
Fork River Space Project, The 2611
Forms of Shelter 8502
Forrest Gump 5006
Forrest, Leon 4601, 8530, 9793
Forsaking All Others 2925
Forster, E. M. 1369, 1906, 3993,
 6563, 6836, 7755
Forster, Margaret 1959, 2840,
 3675, 5519, 5817, 6768, 7016,
 7325, 7412, 7774
Forsyth, Frederick 2251, 7934
Fort, The 3111
Fortitude 5248
Fortress, The 1788
Fortunate Lives 3629
Fortunate Pilgrim, The 7627
Fortune Is a Woman 5807
Fortune's Daughter 10619

Fortunes of Nigel 7794
Fortunoff's Child 553
Forty Lashes Less One 9333
42nd Parallel, The 8650
Foster, Michael 899, 2759
Found, Lost, Found 8572
Foundation 4738
Foundation and Empire 9557
Foundation's Edge 2745
Founder's Praise 6662
Founding Father, The 2098
Foundling, The 2223
Fountain, The 7246
Fountain Overflows, The 7589
"Fountainblue" 1576
Fountainhead, The 6387
Fountains of Neptune, The 4509
Four Days 8690
Four Feathers, The 3076
480, The 9158
"Four Seasons, The" 7891
Four Swans, The 6894
Four Voices 591
Four Ways of Computing Midnight
 6358
Four Winds, The 9073
Four-Chambered Heart, The 6221
Four-Gated City, The 2703
1492 (Frohlich) 7809
1492 (Johnston) 2498
Fourteen Sisters of Emilio Montez
 O'Brien, The 3263
"Fourteen Years After" 4000
Fourteenth of October, The 9667
Fourth Angel, The 7723
Fourth Codex, The 6968
Fourth Horseman of Miami Beach, The
 6791
Fourth K, The 119
Fourth King, The 7644
Fourth of June, The 1508
Fowler, Connie May 1243
Fowler, Karen Joy 10458
Fowler, Robert H. 5240, 5517
Fowles, John 1325, 2565, 4010,
 6291, 6647, 8279, 9007, 9589,
 9628, 10260, 10724
Fox 10885
Fox, John Jr. 176, 3759, 4684,
 7289, 9210, 9527
Fox, Paula 2441, 2570
Fox, William Price 214, 6937, 8308
"Fox, The" 4724
"Fox and the Clam, The" 3282
Fox and the Hound, The 429
Fox from His Lair, The 8136
Fox in the Attic, The 739
Foxes of Harrow, The 7664
Foxfire 1819
Foxglove Saga, The 139
Foxybaby 1945
Fragile Peace, A 4525
Fragment of Life, A 2754
Fragments (Armah) 1666
Fragments (Fuller) 3347

Fragments of Light 1212
Frame, Janet 1284, 2230, 2379,
 4069, 4786, 5033, 5220, 5700,
 5938, 7516, 8364
Frame, Ronald 1892, 3877, 4708,
 9824
Framley Parsonage 6521
Franchise Affair, The 4537
Franchiser, The 3001
Francis, Richard 5176
Francisco, Patricia Weaver 10869
Frank, Pat 6004
Frank, Waldo 10123
Frankenstein 7008
Frankenstein Unbound 10510
Franklin, Miles 5277, 6366, 6588
Franklin Scare, The 1442
Franklin's Crossing 7646
Franks, Lucinda 1775
Franky Furbo 1473
Franzen, Jonathan 8249
Fraser, George MacDonald 1179,
 3281, 3289, 3396, 4468, 6009,
 6993, 7821, 8139, 10858
Fraternity 8397
Fraud 2581
Frayn, Michael 351, 1032, 2245,
 2993, 3920, 4167, 9259, 9970
Fraze, Candida 2415
Freaks of Mayfair, The 5279
Freaky Deaky 892
Freckles 7215
Freddy's Book 5838
Frederic, Harold 835, 3555, 3991
Free Air 2946
Free Fall 906
Free Frenchman, The 3931
Free Man, The 4734
Free, Suzanne Hamilton 8472
Freed, Lynn 1288
Freedman, Nancy 10887
Freedom Road 10483
Free-Lance Pallbearers, The 3172
Freelands, The 3640
Freely, Maureen 9700
Freeman, Gillian 303, 798, 5494,
 5756, 10986
Freeman, Huey 10286
Freeman, Judith 2676, 6598
Freeman, Mary E. Wilkins 1573,
 4475, 9663
French, Marilyn 113, 4480, 10252
French Admiral, The 8162
French Lieutenant's Woman, The 10724
Frenchman's Creek 7661
Freud, Esther 3631, 7605
Freydberg, Margaret Howe 5851,
 6402, 6832
"Frida" 2887
Friday 10423
Friedman, B. H. 2396
Friedman, Bruce Jay 1272, 3525,
 4984, 5630, 6124, 10282
Friend, Dorie 7535
Friend from England, A 5863

Friendly Young Ladies, The 7766
Friends Along the Way 5853
Friends and Heroes 9916
Friends and Relations 10646
"Friends in the Country" 1745
Friends of Eddie Coyle, The 4251
Frieze 10948
Frigor Mortis 9194
Fringe of Heaven, The 9107
Fringe of Leaves, A 9934
Frisk 1170
Frobisch's Angel 4111
Froese, Robert 3908
Frog 1195
Frog Who Dared to Croak, The 5232
Frohlich, Newton 7809
From a Distant Place 3239
From a View to a Death 2951
From Here to Eternity 5920
From My Father, Singing 1067
From Ponkapog to Pesth 2293
From Sea to Shining Sea 4825
From the Heart of the Country 6664
From the Heat of the Day 5485
From the Housetops 5734
From the Realm of Morpheus 8929
From the River's Edge 9979
From the Teeth of Angels 5053
From the Terrace 3329
Front Runner, The 604
Frost in May 9540
Frozen Music 8288
Frozen Pirate, The 8055
Frucht, Abby 4424, 8030, 8039
Frye, Ellen 1462
Fuchs, Daniel 6445, 7294, 7295, 10352
Fugard, Athol 5632
Fugard, Sheila 2128
Fugitive 5661
Fugitive Nights 5881
Fugitives, The 1649
Full Catastrophe, The 3038
Fuller, Henry B. 4039, 4907
Fuller, Iola 1022
Fuller, Jack 3347
Fuller, John 10427
Fuller, Roy 3701, 5923
Fulton County 4097
Fun with Dirk and Bree 3404
Funeral Games 2636
Funeral in Berlin 10597
Funeral Makers, The 6155
Funerals Are Fatal 2693
Funny Farm 5112
Funny Papers 988
Fur Masters, The 7918
Fur Person, The 425
Furies, The 6883
Furman, Laura 4195, 7856
Furors Die 10
Further Adventures 4867
Further Adventures of Huckleberry Finn, The 5506

G. 6655
Gaan, Margaret 1062, 3868, 8884, 9190
Gabo Djara 827
Gabriel, Eric 7862
Gabriel Tolliver 1904
Gabrielle 5994
Gabriel's Lament 2594
Gaddis, Sarah 6730
Gaddis, William 763, 6765, 10011
Gadol, Peter 9050
Gaines, Ernest J. 1652, 2151, 2709, 2983, 10019
Gainham, Sarah 597, 6008, 9389
Gaitskill, Mary 6017
Gala 4479
Galápagos 6259
Galbraith, John Kenneth 7905
Gale, Patrick 1311, 8637, 10295, 10951
Gale, Zona 6624, 9664, 10917
Galford, Ellen 7958
Gallacher, Tom 3693, 6149, 9036
Gallagher, Mary 2481
Gallagher, Rachel 3321
Gallant, Mavis 3804, 4178, 6610, 7891
Gallico, Paul 18, 4007, 4104, 4313, 4731, 5571, 6852, 7261, 8118, 8859, 9286, 10067, 10181, 10399
Gallie, Menna 10437
Gallions Reach 8070
Gallison, Kate 8533
Galloway, David 10428
Galloway, Jack 5379
Gallowglass 1084
Galsworthy, John 1586, 2134, 2307, 3558, 3560, 3640, 5182, 5307, 5895, 6622, 7378, 8078, 8397, 8938, 9537, 9761, 9869, 10335, 10339
Galt, John 357, 1483, 1901, 3550, 7500, 8476, 9260, 9703
Galton Case, The 3296
Galusha the Magnificent 4556
Galvin, James 5077
Gambit 9911
Game, The (Byatt) 1661
Game, The (Hastings) 9153
Game and the Ground, The 1641
Game in Heaven with Tussy Marx 10391
Game Men Play, A 9607
"Game of Spirit" 6927
Game Player, The 6141
Games Were Coming, The 8914
"Ganado Red" 10952
Ganesan, Indira 8244
Gang That Couldn't Shoot Straight, The 4702
Gann, Ernest K. 623, 1405, 3460, 5115, 5712, 6375, 7018, 7128, 8094, 8101, 8513, 8669, 10017, 10615
Garcia, Cristina 8385

Garcia, Lionel G. 6731
Gardam, Jane 1801, 3946, 4173, 4807, 4838, 5832, 8224, 8277
Garden, The (Perutz) 2333
Garden, The (Summers) 10226
Garden of Earthly Delights, A 25
Garden of Eden, The 4653
Garden Path, The 3982
Garden State 7345
Gardens of Stone 5688
Gardiner, John Rolfe 11, 5674
Gardner, John 340, 434, 1187, 2039, 3749, 5292, 5577, 5838, 7631
Gardner, Martin 6325
Gardner, Mary 3399
Garfield, Leon 2081, 9789
Garfield Honor, The 140
Garish Day, The (Billington) 555
Garish Days (Caraganis) 718
Garitano, Rita 5373
Garland, Hamlin 1357, 1492, 1581, 1587, 3359, 4910, 4911, 6099, 8626, 8843, 8907, 9759, 10570
Garmaise, Freda 3317
Garments the Living Wear 9399
Garner, Helen 4283, 6860
Garner, Hugh 3852
Garnett, Henrietta 10440
Garretson Chronicle, The 4294
Garrett, George 1657, 2994, 4335, 5702, 6467, 7199, 8483, 8861, 8885, 9699
Garrick Year, The 7398
Gascoyne, the Sandal Wood Trader 8049
Gaskell, Elizabeth 97, 1266, 1335, 1338, 3634, 4033, 5079, 6091, 6406, 8454, 10769
Gaskell, Mrs. *See* Gaskell, Elizabeth
Gass, William H. 1037
Gate of Angels, The 10754
Gate of Rage 4599
Gate to the Sea 2231
Gates of Ivory, The 5540
Gates of Paradise, The 2802
Gates of Wrath, The 8345
Gateway to Empire 4300
Gathering Home 8578
Gathering of Old Men, A 10019
Gathering of the West, The 8476
Gatherings 10676
Gaudy, The 1255
Gaudy Night 8259
Gaudy Place, The 1791
Gault, Peter 7486
Gavin, Catherine 287, 8106, 10515
Gavin, Thomas 1332
Geary, Patricia 5500
Gedge, Pauline 188
Gee, Maggie 6905, 8028
Gee, Maurice 2392, 3784, 8003
Geek Love 10955
Geeslin, Campbell 9392
Gehman, Christian 5509

Gelb, Alan 1869
Geld, Ellen Bromfield 8612
Gellhorn, Martha 608, 1658, 1880,
    2025, 2918, 2976, 3568, 5002,
    7470, 7660, 7832, 8326, 8552,
    9483, 9905, 10690, 10691
General, The 7260
General Ludd 3862
Generation of Leaves, A 4022
Generation Without Farewell 9430
Generous Man, A 2765
Genetha 8229
"Genius," The 1363
Genius and the Goddess, The 5436
Genteel Poverty Bus Company, The
    5180
Gentian Hill 8093
Gentle Infantryman, The 9813
Gentle Julia 7124
Gentle Knight of Old Brandenburg, A
    4888
Gentle Occupation, A 8811
Gentleman and Ladies 1304
Gentleman from Indiana, The 5129
Gentleman's Agreement 2503
Gentleman's Guide to the Frontier, A
    8163
Gentlemen, I Address You Privately
    9087
Gentlemen in England 1947
Gentlemen in Their Season 5936
Gentlemen of Adventure 10615
Genuine Article, The 4358
George Beneath a Paper Moon 3505
George, Margaret 2412, 6383
George Mills 4885
George's Mother 7288
Georgie Winthrop 10968
Georgina and Georgette 3450
Georgy Girl 2840
Gerald's Party 1890
Gerard, Philip 5047
Gerber, Merrill Joan 1216, 7122
Gerhardie, William 4535, 4615
German Requiem, A 9284
Geronimo Rex 6228
"Geronimo's Ponies" 8038
Gerontius 7279
Gershon, Karen 2168
Gerson, Noel B. 1188, 3144, 4170,
    4171, 4397, 4981, 5227, 6121,
    7110, 7183, 7314, 7519, 10413
Gertler, T. 8466
Gervais, Paul 6733
Gess, Denise 6724, 8753
Get Home Free 6767
Get Ready for Battle 6766
Get Shorty 2062
Getbacks of Mother Superior, The 4692
Getting It Right 9948
Getting of Wisdom, The 10784
Getting Together 2743
Ghose, Zulfikar 800, 1038, 3012,
    4286, 5576, 7692
Ghosh, Amitav 991, 6159

Ghost, The 675
Ghost and Mrs. Muir, The 10799
Ghost of Henry James, The 8607
Ghost of Monsieur Scarron, The 3837
Ghost of the Sun 10633
Ghost Waves 8905
Ghost Woman 7105
Ghost Writer, The 5837
Ghosts (Auster) 6825
Ghosts (Figes) 7438
Ghostwright 2282
Giant 8410
Giant, The 9555
Giants' Bread 9380
Giardina, Anthony 891, 9808
Giardina, Denise 558, 5371
Gibbon, Lewis Grassic 3381, 4053,
    10349
Gibbons, Kaye 3885, 6197, 6492
Gibbons, Stella 937, 3273, 4767,
    9896
Gibbs, Henry 4391
Gibson, Elizabeth 7366
Gibson, Graeme 2126
Gibson, Tom 5368
Gidding, Joshua 5762
Gideon Planish 243
Gideon's Band 8398
Gideon's House 6859
Gidley, Charles 30, 8158
Gifford, Barry 4336, 8731
Gift of Asher Lev, The 3258
Gift of Stones, The 348
Gift of the Golden Mountain 2577
Gilbert, Anna 312, 7445, 10231,
    10666
Gilbert, Sarah 7211
Gilbert, Stephen 431
Gilchrist, Ellen 2002, 4872, 5534,
    5598, 7420, 9652
Gilda Stories, The 8475
Gilden, K. B. 7399
Gildner, Gary 3878
Giles, F. T. 135
Giles, Janice Holt 973, 1512, 4161,
    4748, 5745, 8361, 10170, 10371
Giles, Jeff 4995
Giles Goat-Boy 4768
Gill, Brendan 2694
Gillian 4573
Gilliatt, Penelope 549, 1112, 1750,
    2786, 9578
Gilligan's Last Elephant 7673
Gillott, Jacqueline 8183
Gilman, Charlotte Perkins 7375
Gilman, Dorothy 3293, 4094,
    7028, 8367
Gilmour, David 2938
Gilmour, H. B. 5961
Ginger Man, The 8411
Ginger Tree, The 853
Gingher, Marianne 6337
Giniger, Henry 2416
Giovanni's Room 6371
Gipson, Fred 2586, 4747

Gipsy in the Parlour, The 10053
"Girl" 9936
Girl Among the Anarchists, A 9404
Girl from Lübeck, A 8602
Girl from Storyville, The 4177
Girl Green as Elderflower, The 6936
Girl in a Swing, The 10733
Girl in Blue, The 2511
Girl in May 1504
Girl in the Head, A 6225
Girl of Forty, A 8008
Girl of the Limberlost, A 6619
Girl on the Boat, The 5309
Girl, 20 3
Girl Who Loved Garbo, The 3321
Girl Who Trod on a Loaf, The 4116
*"Girl with the White Fur Muff,
    The"* 3722
Girls, The (Bowen) 3983
"Girls, The" (Summers) 5547
Girls at Play 9672
Girls in Their Married Bliss 2509
Girls' Night Out 9968
Girls of Slender Means, The 7037
Girls Turn Wives 7557
Girls, Visions, and Everything 2050
Girzone, Joseph F. 1563, 4014,
    4428, 8337
Gissing, George 1184, 1574, 3989,
    5403, 6361, 6616, 7180, 7877
Gittelson, Celia 1155
Give and Take 9958
Give Me Liberty 7183
Give Me Possession 10495
Give Me the Stars 10145
Give Me Time 1214
Give Them Stones 9854
Give Us This Day (Barstow) 4596
Give Us This Day (Delderfield) 847
Givens, John 2665
Glad Rags 5988
Glad River, The 9084
Gladiator 1969
Gladstone, Frances 7042
Glaister, Lesley 8829
Glamorous Powers 5335
Glamour, The 1276
Glance Away, A 4676
Glanville, Brian 3309, 3502, 4348,
    4578, 4941, 5001, 5357, 5823,
    9438, 10160, 10197
Glasgow, Ellen 965, 1909, 2501,
    3107, 3270, 4137, 4143, 5197,
    5736, 7131, 7348, 7757, 8343,
    9063, 9093, 9277
Glaskin, G. M. 10595
Glaspell, Susan 1599, 3108, 4634
Glass, Joanna McClelland 10436
Glass Cage, The 8519
Glass Key, The 3966
Glass of Blessings, A 1104
Glass People 1980
Glass Slippers Always Pinch 138
Glass-Blowers, The 6571
Glassblower's Breath, The 2463

Glasscock, Sarah 10302
Glassy Sea, The 9938
Glastonbury Romance, A 6001
Glazebrook, Philip 994
Glendinning, Victoria 8023
Glickman, Gary 3605
Glimpse, The 1011
Glitter Dome, The 4256
Glittering Images 1145
Glittering Prizes, The 9933
Glitz 7024
Gloag, Julian 2335, 3861, 4831,
  5364, 6320, 8724, 10287, 10729
Gloria Mundi 218
Glorious Third, A 3201
Glory and the Lightning 2079
Glory for Me 5916
Glory of Hera, The 2628
Glory of the Hummingbird, The 5660
Glory Road 3362
Glover, Douglas 5548, 5777
Glowstone 6339
Glynn, Thomas 3786, 9254
Gnawing at My Soul 4806
Go 7968
Go in Beauty 9475
Go Tell It on the Mountain 1502
Go to the Widow-Maker 4643
Goat Song (Yerby) 7850
Goatsong (Holt) 1471
Go-Between, The 6789
God Against the Gods, A 6661
God and Harvey Grosbeck 6896
God and His Gifts, A 7201
God and My Country 1634
God and Sarah Pedlock 548
God Bless the Child 10061
God Bless You, Mr. Rosewater 3747
God Boy, The 1789
God in the Car, The 8253
God in the Mountain, The 8134
God Is an Englishman 10509
God Knows 8006
God of Mirrors, The 5331
God of Nightmares, The 2441
God of the Labyrinth, The 9486
God on the Rocks 8224
God Sends Sunday 1269
Godchild, The 7537
Goddard, Robert 2680, 3624,
  7960, 8833
Godden, Jon 759, 1659, 8103,
  8600, 8682, 9921
Godden, Rumer 447, 1385, 2181,
  2330, 2856, 3117, 3834, 3977,
  3980, 4120, 4987, 5878, 6111,
  6808, 7663, 8783, 9396, 9665,
  9671
Goddess Abides, The 7356
Goddess Letters, The 2054
Goddess Named Gold, A 10540
Godfather, The 5205
God-Fearer, The 5601
Godmother, The 1205
Godric 3926

Gods Arrive, The 4730
God's Country - The Trail to Happiness 3086
God's Ear 6482
God's Grace 10614
God's Little Acre 5134
God's Men 10706
God's Pocket 2401
God's Snake 4128
Gods Themselves, The 3520
God-Seeker, The 2224
Godwin, Gail 501, 1980, 2791,
  5036, 5120, 6775, 8485, 9966
Godwin, Parke 10750
Godwin, William 237, 5554, 6606
Goebbels & Gladys 6357
Goethe, Ann 1818
Gog 6390
Gogarty, Oliver St. John 4056,
  4936, 10138
Going After Cacciato 66
Going All the Way 8676
Going Blind 152
Going Down 4893
Going for Broke 5990
"Going Home" 6584
Going Some 3995
Going to California 6376
Going to Jerusalem 6128
Going to Patchogue 5341
Gojiro 632
Gokhale, Namita 5510
Gold 100
Gold, Alison Leslie 0306
Gold, Herbert 284, 940, 975,
  1987, 2711, 3389, 3508, 4297,
  5649, 5652, 7836, 8008, 8861,
  9794, 9918
Gold, Ivan 5535
Gold Flake Hydrant, The 9823
Gold Hunters, The 3897
Gold of Malabar, The 8114
Gold Tip Pfitzer, The 7682
Goldberg, Gerald Jay 505, 10504
Goldberg, Philip 6280
Golden, Marita 3612, 4429, 7899
Golden Age, The 10682
Golden Age Hotel, The 4652
Golden Apples 726
Golden Bowl, The (James) 5345
Golden Bowl, The (Manfred) 9140
Golden Calves, The 6512
Golden Child, The 9244
Golden Days 6867
Golden Gate, The 5523
Golden Gizmo, The 5809
Golden Hawk, The 10702
Golden Honeycomb, The 6998
Golden Journey, The 10368
Golden Moment, The 3770
Golden Notebook, The 4006
Golden Orange, The 4220
Golden Ripple, The 9361
Golden Rooms, The 8266
Golden Salamander, The 8782

Golden Sickle, The 10722
Golden Snare, The 5902
Golden Soak, The 9237
Golden Spiders, The 9900
Golden Spur, The 4642
Golden States 454
Golden Virgin, The 5103
Golden Warrior, The 3571
Goldeneye 7689
Goldenrod 7486
Golding, William 863, 906, 2545,
  4079, 5185, 6378, 7312, 7845,
  8424, 8554, 9319, 10001, 10025,
  10363
Goldman, James 4097, 5828
Goldman, Laurel 2417, 4813
Goldman, William 384, 914, 1830,
  2083, 6403, 6637, 7064, 8191,
  8662, 8754, 9437, 9686, 9852,
  10081
Goldreich, Gloria 3952, 5337,
  6395, 7835, 8690
Goldseekers, The 5814
Goldsmith, Bruce 2723
Goldsmith, Oliver 5725
Goldstein, Lisa 1063
Goldstein, Rebecca 3625, 5241,
  5767
Gomez, Jewelle 8475
Gondar 1537
Gone the Dreams and Dancing 7425
Gone the Sun 829
Gone to Earth 8400
Gone to Soldiers 1951
Gone with the Wind 10793
Gonzales, Laurence 7822
Gooch, Brad 10303
Good Apprentice, The 1806
Good as Gold 5486
Good Baby, A 4204
Good Behavior (Westlake) 2721
Good Behaviour (Keane) 385
Good Child's River, The 8984
Good Companions, The 6060
Good Confession, A 63
Good Day to Die, A 10232
Good Deeds 8753
Good Earth, The 10647
Good Family, The 8359
Good Hearts 5336
Good Husband, The 854
Good King Harry 5371
Good Listener, The 5631
Good Luck On Your Downward Journey 4259
Good Man in Africa, A 2922
Good Men and True 5899
Good Morning, Midnight 7765
Good Mother, The 3430
Good, Protected Life, A 6168
Good Republic, The 2806
Good Riddance 4325
Good School, A 8752
Good Shepherd, The 8412
Good Soldier, The 8973

Good Son, The 6683
Good Spirit of Laurel Ridge, The 8360
Good Terrorist, The 3227
Good Time Gospel Boys, The 8010
"Good Will" 3757
Good Woman, A 1911
Goodbye Europe 6047
Goodbye, Janette 10972
Goodbye, Karl Erich 5849
Goodbye Look, The 6503
Goodbye, Mickey Mouse 9804
Good-bye, Mr. Chips 103
Goodbye to Berlin 9137
Goodbye Un-America 3200
Goodbye Without Leaving 6485
Goodness 6735
Goodrich, Marcus 8087
Goodwin, Stephen 443
Goosefoot 4414
Gor Saga 6677
Gordimer, Nadine 751, 1100, 4183,
    4538, 4842, 5065, 5353, 6006,
    9356, 10211
Gordon, Barbara 10735
Gordon, Caroline 2628, 3647,
    8327, 8479, 9765
Gordon, Jaimy 6204
Gordon, Mary 2462, 3352, 3513,
    3724, 3948, 4808, 9659
Gordon, Noah 3602, 6444, 7281,
    10188, 10249
Gordon, Richard 3863
Gordon Liddy Is My Muse 6263
Gorilla Hunters, The 2187
Gormenghast 972
Goshawk Squadron 8678
Gospel Hour 5992
Gospel Singer, The 1423
Goss Women, The 500
Gossamer Fly, The 4237
Gossip from the Forest 9929
Gotlieb, Phyllis 7321
Goudge, Elizabeth 8093, 10212
Gould, John 3219, 5235
Gould, Lois 4130, 4619, 8025,
    10839
Gourse, R. Leslie 10593
Gover, Robert 640, 1424
Governor's Lady, The 4390
Gowdy, Barbara 3620
Gown of Glory, The 9771
Goy, The 1668
Goyen, William 1940, 3577, 6567,
    9103
Grabien, Deborah 2644
Grace Abounding 10845
Graced Land 4873
Graduate, The 4575
Grady, James 3676
Graham, John (pseud.). *See* Phil-
    lips, David Graham
Graham, Winston 712, 2588,
    4576, 4943, 5807, 6194, 6891,
    6894, 7069, 8146, 8152, 8632,
    9975, 10732

Grahame, Kenneth 401, 10682
Grain of Truth, The 8871
Grand Babylon Hotel, The 4305
Grand Design, The 2141
Grand Life, The 6471
Grand Opening 3730
Grandfathers, The 543
Grandissimes, The 9377
Grandmother and the Priests 338
Grandmothers, The 81
Grandmothers' Club, The 9032
Grapes of Wrath, The 7297
Grass Crown, The 3481
Grass Harp, The 8785
Grass Is Singing, The 6177
Grasse 3/23/66 2913
Grasshopper Summer 4960
Grateful to Life and Death 9263
Grau, Shirley Ann 301, 808, 2240,
    6840, 7923
Graustark 1577
Graves, Ralph 1091, 3601, 9971
Graves, Robert 841, 1162, 2323,
    4499, 5567, 6110, 7802, 8985
Graveyard for Lunatics, A 1469
Gravity's Rainbow 8807
Gray, Alasdair 1726, 3758, 7577,
    7784
Gray, Francine du Plessix 1274,
    3479
Gray, John 2308
Gray, Spalding 7947
Gray Dawn 6365
Graysons, The 4038
Great American Jackpot, The 940
"*Great American Novel --, The*"
    (Davis) 5087
Great American Novel, The (Roth)
    4791
Great American Novel, The (Wil-
    liams) 5409
Great Auk, The 5030
Great Black Russian 7029
Great Blizzard, The 10982
Great Circle 4912
Great Days, The 5927
Great Divorce, The 10046
Great Equalizer, The 6466
Great Expectations 4714
Great Fire of London, The 8464
Great Fortune, The 8865
Great Gatsby, The 6625
"*Great God Pan, The*" 9865
Great God Success, The 6348
Great Granny Webster 3198
Great Indian Novel, The 6262
Great Jones Street 3539
Great K. & A. Robbery, The 5401
Great Letter E, The 9345
Great Lion of God 6534
Great Man, A 8347
Great Meadow, The 6218
Great Mischief 1025
Great Occasion, The 2838
Great Ponds, The 4686

Great Pretender, The 3951
Great Pursuit, The 6043
Great Santini, The 6773
Great Son 1391
Great Steamboat Race, The 7691
Great Thirst, The 7643
Great World, The 10878
Greatest Breakthrough Since Lunchtime,
    The 6895
Greatest Crime, The 3054
Greatest Enemy, The 8121
Greatest Performance, The 6264
Greatest Slump of All Time, The 160
Green, Gerald 311, 713, 755, 2478,
    2614, 3002, 4015, 4623, 5321,
    5478, 5956, 8480, 8805, 8943,
    9816, 9936
Green, Hannah (pseud.). *See*
    Greenberg, Joanne
Green, Henry 733, 1592, 1620,
    2316, 2531, 3831, 9384, 10150,
    10482
Green, Jesse 352
Green, Lewis W. 10618
Green Bananas 4853
Green Bay Tree, The 6756
Green Centuries 3647
Green Days by the River 9917
Green Desire, A 10421
Green Earth 3854
Green Flesh, A 6194
Green, Green My Valley Now 4582
Green Hat, The 2824
Green Island 10263
Green Journey, A 1727
Green Man, The (Amis) 7573
Green Man, The (Jameson) 10360
Green Mansions 1820
Green Shadows, White Whale 6265
Green Water, Green Sky 6640
Green Years, The 1618
Greenberg, Eric Rolfe 8926
Greenberg, Joanne 1518, 4423,
    5365, 5979, 6083, 6595, 6662,
    9159, 10068
Greenburg, Dan 5462, 6597
Greencastle and the Denizens of the
    Sacred Crypt 319
Greene, Annie 7694
Greene, Constance C. 6966
Greene, Gael 1327, 10261
Greene, Graham 728, 865, 2535,
    3446, 3774, 3855, 4359, 4379,
    4467, 5798, 6175, 6176, 6465,
    6761, 7395, 8358, 8939, 8989,
    9330, 9539, 10041, 10344
Greene, Harlan 5063, 7944
Greene, Sheldon 10908
Greenfeld, Josh 506, 7837
Greenfield, Robert 8045
Greengage Summer, The 3834
Greenhouse, The 9256
Greening of Thurmond Leaner, The
    4655
Greenlanders, The 3661

Greenleaf, Stephen 7736, 9249
Greenlee, Sam 7005
Greenmantle 5999
Greenvoe 8036
Greer, Ben 2376, 8009, 8579, 10410
Greifenstein 79
Grendel 434
Grenelle 7869
Grenville, Kate 629, 5970, 7080
Grey, Anthony 8147, 8289
Grey Granite 10349
Grey, Zane 124, 1584, 4433, 7654, 8768
Greybeard 428
Greyling, The 2028
Grieg, Michael 6717
Griffin's Way 10813
Griffith, Bill 9947
Griffith, George 192, 3494, 4457
Griffith, Patricia Browning 2591
Griffith Gaunt 1489
Grifters, The 143
Griggs, Sutton E. 3269
Grimes, Roberta 371
Grimes, Tom 2179, 3547
Grimus 4282
Gringa 6873
Gringos 10994
Grisanti, Mary Lee 2049
Grisly Wife, The 11004
Grizzly King, The 404
Groom, Winston 829, 5006, 5161, 7367
Groseclose, Elgin 2854, 3677
Gross, Joel 1722, 4199, 7787, 10270, 10840, 10943
Gross, Polly 7497
Grossman, Alfred 936, 4395, 7015, 10008
Grossman, Judith 3480
Grossmith, George and Weedon 3073
Grotesque, The 5870
Grotto, The 1290
Group, The 10656
Group of Noble Dames, A 3072
Group Sex 3228
Group Therapy 3220
Grove, Lee 6462, 10959
Grove of Fever Trees, A 6632
Groves of Academe, The 1920
Growing Up Bronx 819
Grown-Ups, The 8023
Grubb, Davis 343, 495, 2704, 4399, 5929, 6373, 9099, 9481, 10558, 10722
Grudin, Robert 482
Grumbach, Doris 2719, 5592, 6454
Grumley, Michael 2116
Grunwald, Lisa 5612, 7207
Gryll Grange 10899
Guard of Honor 4563
Guardian Angel, The 8956

Guerard, Albert J. 5569, 5815, 5994, 7719
Guerrillas 3000
Guest, Judith 1712, 6041
Guest, Lynn 6594, 9188
Guest in the Jungle, A 7339
Guest of a Sinner 8763
Guest of Honour, A 10211
Guest of Quesnay, The 9119
Guide, The 9906
Guide for the Perplexed, A 693
Guild, Nicholas 4133, 10747
Gulliver Quick 6346
Gulliver's Travels 6602
Gun Garden, The 8668
Gundy, Elizabeth 6150
Gunn, Neil M. 334, 2090, 4639, 7915, 9069, 9898
Guns for Rebellion 7187
Gunsights 7871
Gunther, John 5935
Gupta, Sunetra 776, 2463
Guralnick, Peter 1836
Gurganus, Allan 2433, 8712
Gurnah, Abdulrazak 3785
Gurney, A. R. Jr. 2112
Gurr, David 9490
Gutcheon, Beth 2453
Guthrie, A. B. Jr. 1667, 1713, 2048, 4358, 6184, 6961, 7298, 8781, 8862, 9240
Guy, David 1262, 5374, 8922
Guy, Rosa 1717, 5045, 10250
Guy Mannering 2087
Gypsy Man, The 7786
Gypsy Storyteller, The 4969
Gypsy's Curse, The 4793

H. D. (pseud.). *See* Doolittle, Hilda
H. M. Pulham, Esquire 6424
H.M.S. Saracen 10719
Haas, Ben 7038, 8490, 10070
Hacey Miller 7520
Hack, The 2974
Hackenfeller's Ape 423
Haddad, Carolyn 2056
Hadrian the Seventh 3683
Hagar's Daughter 269
Hagedorn, Jessica 8538
Haggard, H. Rider 785, 1006, 1267, 1352, 2192, 3489, 3491, 3497, 3670, 3795, 4223, 4373, 4456, 4493, 4494, 4977, 5055, 5225, 5400, 5402, 5412, 5792, 6364, 7216, 7506, 7797, 7798, 7799, 8394, 8399, 8974, 9208, 9522, 10332, 10471, 10473, 10474, 10476, 10757
Haien, Jeannette 4690
Haig-Brown, Roderick L. 5316
Hail the Conquering Hero 6506
Hailey, Elizabeth Forsythe 6, 2549, 4529, 8002
Hair of Harold Roux, The 3461

Hale, Nancy 1107, 2695, 3183, 4150, 8481, 9148
Haley, Albert 7895
Haley, Alex 804, 7903
Haley, Russell 7897
Half a Hero 6977
Half a Marriage 65
Half of Paradise 7927
Half the Gladness 4217
Half-Mother, The 5330
Halfway Home 8247
Hall, James B. 9776
Hall, James Baker 8881
Hall, James W. 2454, 4263
Hall, Oakley 4060, 4505, 5190, 6954
Hall, Radclyffe 5067
Hall, Richard 1776
Hall, Rodney 1812, 4868, 7529, 10748, 11004
Hall of Mirrors, A 2911
Hallapoosa 7278
Hallberg, William 8930
Hallinan, Nancy 3003
Halloween 2376
Halper, Albert 6061, 6791
Halt During the Chase, The 4175
Ham on Rye 7417
Hamill, Desmond 8430
Hamill, Pete 4657
Hamilton, Hugo 10459
Hamilton, Jane 395
Hamilton, Virginia 3902
Hamilton, William 508, 2865
Hamilton Stark 5482
Hamilton-Paterson, James 7279, 10308
Hamlet, The 4052
Hamlet Had an Uncle 10796
Hamlin, Liz 4200
Hammer, Richard 6086
Hammer on the Sea 9482
Hammett, Dashiell 16, 333, 2602, 3966, 4310, 10901
Hamner, Earl 3576, 6077, 9727
Hampdenshire Wonder, The 9530
Hand in Glove (Goddard) 8833
Hand in the Glove, The (Stout) 10794
Hand-Made Gentleman, The 43
Hand-Me Downs 4360
Hand of Ethelberta, The 4996
Hand of Glory 7190
Hand of Mary Constable, The 10181
Handful of Dust, A 17
Handful of Rice, A 2909
Handl, Irene 2094, 7682
Handling Sin 70
Handmaid's Tale, The 8468
Hands of Cantú, The 7626
Handsome Man, A 7935
Handy Andy 6018
Handyman, The 2402
Hanging Garden, The 7596
Hangman's Beach 5034
Hangman's Children, The 5117

Hangsaman 3572
Hankla, Cathryn 4131
Hanky of Pippin's Daughter, The 2525
Hanley, Clifford 575, 598, 1662, 10182
Hanley, Gerald 1026, 3507, 5919, 6806, 7673, 10507
Hanley, James 6679, 10242
Hanley, William 5469
Hannah, Barry 1279, 3018, 3663, 6185, 6228, 6673, 7433
Hannah Fowler 8361
Hannah's House 8222
Hannay, Allen 2612
Hannie Richards 4330
Hanrahan, Barbara 1075, 1190, 3872, 5264, 10531
Hans Cassebeer and the Virgin's Rose 6996
Hansen, Joseph 1718, 2883
Hansen, Ron 1312, 3214
Hanta Yo 757
Happenstance 3344
Happy All the Time 3585
Happy Ending 1554
Happy Land 8301
Happy Parrot, The 2826
Happy Prisoner, The 4951
Happy Return 7060
Happy Tree, The 4058
Harbourmaster, The 8075
Hard Blue Sky, The 7923
Hard Cash 3552
Hard Feelings 6449
Hard Laughter 3202
Hard on the Road 4988
Hard Rain (Abrahams) 3371
Hard Rain, The (Smith) 10085
Hard Times for These Times 5054
Hardcase 3419
Hardcastle 985
Harder They Come, The 10016
Harder They Fall, The 2896
Harding, Alison 5177
Harding, William Harry 28, 1559
Hardscrub 6731
Hardwick, Elizabeth 5582, 9226
Hardy, Robin 572, 9085
Hardy, Ronald 3411, 6574, 8611, 10709
Hardy, Thomas 1572, 2189, 2190, 3072, 3301, 3488, 4996, 6092, 8545, 8737, 9091, 9519, 9661, 10331, 10333, 10779
Harford, Henry (pseud.). *See* Hudson, W. H.
Haring, Jo 2098
Harington, Donald 4878, 7194, 7262, 10450
Harker, Herbert 4078
Harland, Henry 3817
Harland's Half Acre 4086
Harlequin 3925
Harlot's Ghost 7457
Harmer John 9064

Harmony 5119
Harnack, Curtis 5663
Harnessing Peacocks 1946
Harold 10109
Harold and Maude 9292
Harp into Battle 8792
Harp of a Thousand Strings 274
Harper, Frances E. W. 4211
Harper, M. A. 4243
Harpoon in Eden 5628
Harriet Hume 7712
Harriet Said 10403
Harrigan, Stephen 8691, 10273
Harrington 947
Harris, Frank 2019
Harris, Jana 1052
Harris, Joel Chandler 1904, 3418, 7214
Harris, John 4085, 5667, 7361, 8136, 8311, 8887, 10736
Harris, MacDonald 814, 3690, 4879, 5988, 6339, 7581, 9817
Harris, Marilyn 1140, 1181, 2784, 3540, 4625, 4804, 7087, 7101, 7186, 7530
Harris, Mark 793, 1103, 1402, 1668, 1701, 3298, 3306, 3621, 3869, 4640, 5444
Harris, Norma 5874
Harris, Robert 10637
Harris, Wilson 9296
Harrison, Barbara Grizzuti 9282
Harrison, Carey 7838
Harrison, Claire 7161
Harrison, Jim 3445, 4073, 5271, 9622, 10232
Harrison, Kathryn 2884, 10882
Harrison, M. John 5940
Harrison, Sam 1260, 7490
Harrison, Sarah 9495
Harrison, Sue 8387, 10453
Harrison, William 2875, 4257
Harry and Catherine 6548
Hart, Josephine 5706, 10888
Hart-Davis, Duff 1156, 9082
Harte, Bret 646, 1339, 2195, 2601, 5128, 5892, 6408, 7238, 7287, 8054, 9115, 9116, 10680, 10681
Harley, L. P. 1300, 1318, 2091, 3124, 5203, 6789, 7165, 8211, 8658, 9998
Hartmann the Anarchist 5081
Haruf, Kent 161, 1768
Harvest, The 4011
Harvester, The 1583
Harvesting Ballads 7047
Harvey, Andrew 1275, 1949, 3231
Harvey, John 2571
Has Anybody Seen My Father? 2562
Hasford, Gustav 8687, 10533
Hasluck, Nicholas 1127, 9603
Hassler, Jon 1727, 1963, 3730, 5875
Hastings, March 9843
Hastings, Michael 7592, 9153
Hatter Fox 3540

Hatteras Light 5047
Hattersley, Roy 1541
Haunted Bookshop, The 1013
Haunted Hotel, The 3529
Haunted Lady, The 564
Haunted Land, A 3138
Haunting of Hill House, The 2763
Hauptman, William 6739
Hauser, Thomas 2405, 5857, 7270, 7980
Hausman, Gerald 9062
Havannah 5294
Have His Carcase 10555
Haven's End 6420
Haviaras, Stratis 4680
Hawaii 7924
Hawbuck Grange 8764
Hawbucks, The 7244
Hawk Is Dying, The 9925
Hawkes, John 2658, 3004, 3154, 3422, 5355, 5656, 5759, 5954, 6693, 6869, 9018
Hawkesworth, John 4787
Hawkline Monster, The 4254
Hawksmoor 5514
Hawley, Cameron 134
Hawthorne, Nathaniel 3060, 3554, 3985, 3986, 5784, 6557, 7875, 10111
Hawthorne Group, The 7980
Hay, John 9467
Haycox, Ernest 1389, 2952, 3405, 3649, 4001, 4916, 6951, 7247, 7300, 7614, 7615, 7625, 7662, 8084, 8099, 8794, 9142, 9220, 9549, 9563, 10694, 10698
Hayden, Sterling 8428
Hayden, Thomas 2939
Hayduke Lives! 7235
Hayfield, Nancy 10942
Haynes, David 1004
Hays, Donald 5117, 7148
Haywood, Eliza 10765
Hazard and the Five Delights 10954
Hazard of New Fortunes, A 9403
Hazeley Family, The 3814
Hazo, Samuel 8573
Hazzard, Shirley 212, 6328, 8218, 8870
Hazzard's Head 5670
He Got Hungry and Forgot His Manners 4092
He Knew He Was Right 5638
He Sent Forth a Raven 2311
He/She 1987
He, She and It 2682
He Who Rides a Tiger 4743
Head, Ann 5749
Head, Bessie 1427, 5703
"Head of the Mountain" 8099
Head to Toe 9585
Headlong Hall 10108
Headsman, The 9112
Heal, Edith 6899
Healers, The 4623

Health and Happiness 4627
Healy, Dermot 2099
Healy, Sophia 9110
Hear Us O Lord from Heaven Thy Dwelling Place 10711
Heard, Nathan C. 4323, 7147
Hearing Secret Harmonies 753
Hearn, Lafcadio 9521
Hearne, John 2232, 8141, 8362
Hearne, Vicki 470
Hearon, Shelby 513, 3220, 3873, 4884, 5300, 6709, 7071, 7484, 7931, 8222
Hearsay 10326
Heart Failures 7999
Heart for the Gods of Mexico, A 7010
Heart in the Desert, The 705
Heart Is a Lonely Hunter, The 3917
Heart Mountain 8704
Heart of a Distant Forest, The 2271
Heart of a Dog, The 1016
Heart of a Goof, The 2201
Heart of Aztlán 8571
"Heart of Darkness" 8063
Heart of London, The 1110
Heart of Mid-Lothian, The 7179
Heart of Princess Osra, The 4908
Heart of Rome, The 9870
Heart of the Country (Matthews) 1457
Heart of the Country, The (Weldon) 7192
Heart of the Matter, The 8358
Heart of the Order 8928
Heart of the River 9615
Heart of the Sunset 10686
Heart of the Valley, The 765
Heart of the World 5400
Heart of War 10518
Heart Payments 505
Heartbeat Drumbeat 2809
Heartbreak Hotel (Burton) 3428
Heartbreak Hotel (Siddons) 9729
Heartburn 2164
Hearts 5719
Hearts and Lives of Men, The 9038
Heart's Desire 8441
Hearts of Glass 3735
Hearts of Three 3436
Heartstones 2418
Heat 9852
Heart and Dust 1689
Heat of the Day, The 6220
Heat Storm 9980
Heat's On, The 3921
Heath, Catherine 1309, 5289
Heath, Roy A. K. 1838, 5485, 8225, 8229
Heather Blazing, The 7706
Heaven and Earth 6152
Heaven and Hardpan Farm 2695
Heaven and Hell and the Megas Factor 10513
Heaven's My Destination 7509
Heavy Feather, A 6667
Heavy Weather 5311

Hebert, Ernest 5008, 8882, 9448
Hecht, Ben 332, 520, 523, 4477, 4935
Heckler, Jonellen 4525, 8818
Hedges, Peter 8246
Hegarty, Frances 10317
Hegi, Ursula 5495, 7095
Heidenmauer, The 6556
Heidish, Marcy 1060, 2742, 3291, 3512, 7785, 10243
Heights of Rimring, The 9082
Heinemann, Larry 2068, 8684, 9033
Heinlein, Robert A. 3139, 3362, 3781, 4501, 4759, 5000, 6193, 6674, 7111, 7155, 7778, 7820, 9362, 10423, 10488
Heirs of Columbus, The 3466
Helen (Edgeworth) 9856
"Helen" (Summers) 13
Helen of the Old House 1014
Helen with the High Hand 5695
Helena 5431
Hell Hath No Fury 9655
Hell of a Woman, A 7861
Heller, Joseph 509, 2705, 5486, 5651, 8006
Heller, Steve 864
Helliconia Spring 6146
Helliconia Summer 7936
Helliconia Winter 7464
Hello America 283
Hello Down There 7549
Hell's Bells 7023
Héloïse and Abélard 8646
Helprin, Mark 1449, 2280
Helwig, David 2442, 2712, 2928, 3300, 5191, 10433, 10611
Hemenway, Robert 10434
Hemingway, Amanda 2443, 5047
Hemingway, Ernest 2210, 3093, 3181, 4653, 6428, 8095, 8910, 10695
Hemingway, Lorian 5303
Hemingway's Suitcase 7581
Hemley, Robin 10027
Hemlock and After 3741
Hemphill, Paul 5982, 10740
Henderson, Laurence 9828
Henderson the Rain King 9566
Hendin, Josephine Gattuso 2426
Hendrie, Don Jr. 7938
Henley, Gail 10663
Hennessy, Max (pseud.). *See* Harris, John
Henrietta Temple 6090
Henry and Cato 9596
Henry for Hugh 10040
Henry in Love 7096
Henry Ryecroft 5403
Henry's War 4954
Henty, G. A. 579, 721, 928, 956, 1007, 1172, 1173, 1344, 1345, 1346, 2101, 3067, 3068, 3467, 4222, 4369, 4971, 6268, 6524,

6615, 6929, 7553, 8056, 8643, 8644, 8840, 9741, 9860, 9862, 10679
Hepatica Hawks 4998
Her 3256
Her First American 2615
Her Living Image 4301
Her Monster 9316
Her Mothers 7070
Her Mother's Daughter 113
Her Native Colors 6544
Her Own Terms 3480
"Her Sense of Timing" 2685
Her Victory 2097
Herald, The 181
Herb 'n' Lorna 370
Herbert, Xavier 984
Herbs and Apples 7242
Herbst, Josephine 7764
Herdman, John 1050, 5285, 10296
Herdsman, The 8986
Here Be Dragons 6258
Here Lies the Water 8622
Hereward the Wake 4455
Hergesheimer, Joseph 562, 3328, 6813, 8067, 8909, 9408, 9410
Heritage and Its History, A 3574
Heritage of Hatcher Ide, The 1384
Heritage of the Desert, The 124
Herland 7375
Herlihy, James Leo 3151, 5257, 6653
Herman, Michelle 2060
Hermit of 69th Street, The 3244
Hernández, Irene Beltrán 2809
Hero, The 7347
Hero Continues, The 6071
Hero for Regis, A 10178
Hero Jesse 4816
Heroes 1453
Heroes and Villains 6533
Heroic Age, The 4680
Herrick, Amy 8450
Herrick, Robert 3077, 10644
Herrick, William 109, 9030
Herriges, Greg 4664, 8469
Herrin, Lamar 6550, 7446
Herring, Robert 6084, 6917
Herron, Carolivia 4115
Hers the Kingdom 6045
Herself Surprised 2020
Hersey, John 821, 2281, 2604, 2979, 3708, 4155, 4609, 6138, 6430, 6957, 6985, 8159, 10167, 10198, 10484
Hershman, Marcie 2490
Herzog 4939
Hesper 4910
Hessian, The 1517
Hetty Wesley 8254
Hewett, Dorothy 7062
Hey Jack! 7433
Heyen, William 621
Heyer, Georgette 306, 2223, 4406
Heyward, Du Bose 1593, 1603, 3379

Hickory Cured 8892
Hickory Dickory Death 6023
Hidden Flower, the 8328
Hidden Part, The 7721
Hidden Pictures 9680
Hidden River, The 1636
Hidden Symptoms 4197
Hide and Seek 1294
Hideous Kinky 7605
Hiding Place, The 4389
Higgins, Aidan 5320, 6294
Higgins, Colin 9292
Higgins, Don 4185
Higgins, George V. 68, 439,
  2848, 3194, 4251, 5209, 5487,
  6453, 8372, 9601, 9787
Higgins, Jack 2488
Higgins, Joanna 1542
High 5463
High Adventure 4194
High and the Mighty, The 5712
High Command 942
High Cost of Living, The 8370
High Cotton 7981
High Hearts 10101
High Holiday 8212
High Place, The 3898
High Road, The 893
High Sierra 2956
High Stand 685
High Towers 1397
High Wind in Jamaica, A 9216
High Window, The 3113
Higher Ground (Phillips) 4896
Higher Ground (Trapido) 3954
Higher Ground (Willis) 3592
"Highland Widow, The" 9513
Highlights of the Off-Season 7900
Highly Flavoured Ladies, The 2486
High-Rise 3443
Highwater, Jamake 5246
Hijuelos, Oscar 3263, 5841, 9370
Hilda Lessways 10915
Hilda's Letter 7165
Hill, Carol 10009, 10075
Hill, Donna 909
Hill, Eugenie 669
Hill, Niki 6970
Hill, Rebecca 3597, 4018
Hill, Russell 6489
Hill, Ruth Beebe 757
Hill, Susan 330, 1304, 2706, 3713,
  6130, 7046
Hill, Weldon 2250, 3672
Hill of Dreams, The 8396
Hill of Many Dreams, A 4704
Hill of Summer, The 2390
Hiller, Catherine 9051
Hillmore, Susan 9256
Hills Stand Watch, The 2234
Hilton, James 103, 1201, 3999,
  6788, 6888, 10143, 10931
Himalayan Concerto, The 10412
Himes, Chester 60, 419, 2908,
  3743, 3801, 3921, 4345, 6126,

8309, 8744
Hinde, Thomas 5463, 6026
Hind's Kidnap 8186
Hine, Al 7409
Hine, Daryl 7517
Hines, Alan 9809
Hines, Barry 986, 7777
Hinojosa-Smith, Rolando 5518
Hinton, Nigel 765
Hired Man, The 10202
Hireling, The 8658
Hirsh, M. E. 460
His Father's Son 10630
His Little Mother 8203
His Little Women 4240
His Majesty's U-Boat 8128
His Majesty's Yankees 8264
His Master's Voice 5340
His Own Man 8552
His Own People 7754
His Vision of Her 690
*History and Adventures of an Atom,
  The* 9989
History Man, The 4581
History of David Grieve, The 2821
History of Henry Esmond, The 950
History of Luminous Motion, The
  10873
History of Miss Betsy Thoughtless, The
  10765
History of Mr. Polly, The 931
History of Pendennis, The 3813
History of Sir Charles Grandison, The
  9509
*History of the Remarkable Life of John
  Sheppard, The* 355
*History of the World in 10½ Chapters,
  A* 472
Hite, Molly 624, 8296
Hitty 1017
Hjortsberg, William 8553, 8570
Hoagland, Edward 3310, 4691,
  10171
Hoban, Russell 441, 857, 4819,
  5361, 6591, 8196
Hobbie, Douglas 1086
Hobbit, The 3106
Hobhouse, Janet 347, 2929, 5265,
  6883
Hob's Daughter 6190
Hobson, Laura Z. 1794, 1802,
  2503, 3159, 5101, 7525
Hobson, Mary 5369
Hochman, Sandra 2109
Hocus Pocus 4865
Hodges, Hollis 367, 510
Hodgins, Eric 1547, 3118
Hodgins, Jack 8749
Hodgman, Helen 770
Hoffenberg, Jack 939, 10178
Hoffman, Alice 775, 2069, 3211,
  4965, 6303, 6573, 8371, 8432,
  10619
Hoffman, Roy 6822
Hoffman, William 10, 3778

Hogan, Desmond 818, 1438, 9013
Hogan, Linda 7031
Hogan, William 1130, 7893
Hogg, James 3375, 3551
Holbrooke, Blythe 6710
Hold Autumn in Your Hand 2138
Hole in the Head, A 5104
Holiday Friend, The 7264
Holinger, William 7428
Holland, Cecelia 1885, 2182, 2256,
  4677, 4991, 5980, 7641, 8438,
  8484, 8671, 10454
Holland, Isabelle 5106, 7869, 10093
Holland, Jack 4219, 6329
Hollaran's World War 5375
Holleran, Andrew 2110, 2377
Holley, Marietta 637, 5017
Hollinghurst, Alan 4594
Hollow Land, The (Gardam) 4807
Hollow Lands, The (Moorcock) 603
Hollow of Her Hand, The 9532
Hollywood (Bukowski) 1150
Hollywood (Vidal) 8383
Holmes, John Clellon 6767, 7968
Holmes, Oliver Wendell Sr. 4441,
  8956, 8964
Holocaust 311
Holt, Isabella 3770
Holt, Tom 1471, 4366, 8378, 10525
Holy Mother 8758
Holy Pictures 10424
Holy Terror, The 540
Homage to Blenholt 10352
Hombre 592
Home, The 6131
Home Again 1148
Home and Away 634
Home as Found 4555
Home at the End of the World, A 9827
Home Bodies 3032
Home Boy (Chesire) 9
Home Fires Burning 464
Home Free (Hailey) 4529
Home Free (Wakefield) 7115
Home from the Hill 9775
Home Ground 1288
Home Mountain 6087
Home Movie 6714
Home of the Brave 10943
Home Place, The 10928
Home Thoughts 5775
Home to Harlem 8071
Home Truth 1158
Homeboy (Morgan) 8024
Homecoming, The 6077
Homecoming Game, The 8863
Homecomings 4571
Homeplace 3732
Homer's Daughter 2323
Homesick 2801
Homesman, The 7088
Homestead, The 9702
Homeward Bound 4031
Homewood, Harry 219, 941, 8140,
  10616

Homework 10632
Honest John Vane 5080
Honey Badger, The 4396
Honey for the Bears 6039
Honey in the Horn 3105
Honeycomb 8507
Honeymoon in Space, A 3494
Honig, Donald 8920
Honkytonk Man 9944
Honor at Daybreak 8165
Honor of the Big Snows, The 6214
Honorable Men 5515
Honorable Peter Stirling, The 8842
Honorable Profession, An 8935
Honorary Consul, The 3774
Honour and Obey 9822
Honour Thy Father 8829
Honourable Schoolboy, The 1834
Honours Board, The 4216
Hood, Ann 3610, 6172, 6240, 7466
Hood, Christopher 9252
Hood, Hugh 677, 3052, 9241
Hood, Stuart 2173, 6581
Hooker, Richard 682, 6441
Hooks, David 8284
Hoopla 5587
Hoosier Chronicle, A 651
Hoosier School-Boy, The 955
Hoosier School-Master, The 240
Hoover, Paul 4847
Hoover, Thomas 4417, 8156
Hopalong Cassidy 4046
Hopalong Cassidy and the Eagle's Brood 10920
Hopalong Cassidy Serves a Writ 6952
Hopalong Cassidy Takes Cards 7616
Hopalong Cassidy's Protégé 8853
Hopcraft, Arthur 2926
Hope, Anthony 580, 1197, 2822, 4339, 4444, 4908, 4972, 5013, 5082, 5083, 5212, 5562, 5894, 6248, 6977, 8253, 10033
Hope, Christopher 614, 1530, 2866, 4843
Hope Diamond Refuses 9956
Hope of Happiness, The 9317
Hope of Heaven 8983
Hopeful Monsters 3372
Hopkin, Alannah 684, 7330
Hopkins, Pauline 269, 4043, 8844
Horgan, Paul 251, 584, 1976, 2504, 2957, 5057, 5058, 5580, 6064, 7228, 10495, 10761
Horn 4779
Horn of Africa 5955
Horn of Life, The 2830
Hornblower and the Atropos 8100
Hornblower and the Hotspur 10655
Hornblower During the Crisis 2701
Horowitz, Eve 5781
Horowitz, Gene 1143, 6575
Horse and His Boy, The 8991
Horse Crazy 9646
Horse Hunters, The 471
Horse of Selene, The 433

Horse Soldiers, The 8568
Horse Under Water 1417
Horsecatcher, The 7221
Horseman, Pass By 7397
Horsemaster, The (Broughton) 446
Horsemasters, The (Wolf) 191
Horse's Head, A 24
Horse's Mouth, The 10356
Horses of Heaven 6487
Horses of the Sun, The 8593
Horses of War 1156
Horses of Winter, The 10394
Horse-Shoe Robinson 6053
Horwood, Harold 1421, 8125
Horwood, William 760, 762, 7326
Hospital, Janette Turner 390, 6907, 7824, 9105
Hostage Heart, The 3002
Hostage: London 3477
Hostages to Fortune 8193
Hot Air 6486
Hot Blue Sea, The 10938
Hot Month, The 1662
Hot Properties 6777
Hot Water 10106
Hot Wire 1725
Hotchkiss, Bill 7693
Hotchner, A. E. 5840
Hotel, The 1589
Hotel du Lac 2718
Hotel New Hampshire, The 8230
Hothouse by the East River, The 3340
Hottentot Room, The 2866
Hough, Emerson 271, 638, 1800, 4212, 4605, 6103, 8647, 10038
Hough, John Jr. 4196
Houng-dog Man 2586
Hound of Earth, The 2560
Hound of the Baskervilles, The 3818
Hour Before the Dawn, The 10355
Hour of Blue, The 3908
Hour of the Bell, The 1439
House Above the River 2759
House and Its Head, A 6526
House at Old Vine, The 7182
House Behind the Cedars, The 9468
House Divided (Williams) 10927
House Divided, A (Buck) 3567
House for Mr. Biswas, A 6435
House in Bloomsbury, A 9866
House in Clewe Street, The 1299
House in Paris, The 2954
House in the Hamptons, A 9199
House in the Uplands, A 10697
House Made of Dawn 3175
House Mother Normal 3924
House Next Door, The 6819
House of a Thousand Candles, The 1905
House of All Nations 4633
House of Breath, The 6567
House of Cards, The 2081
House of Children, The 10696
House of Christina, The 8490
House of Dies Drear, The 3902
House of Dolls, The 6480

House of Earth 4742
House of Egremont, The 3557
House of Five Talents, The 3148
House of God, The 6396
House of Gold 2352
House of Hope 2697
"House of Hunger, The" 1695
House of Incest 7917
House of Mirth, The 8173
House of Real Love, The 2816
House of Slammers 7147
House of Stairs, The 4992
House of the Arrow, The 1015
House of the Four Winds, The 4497
House of the Prophet, The 108
House of the Seven Gables, The 3060
House of Women, A (Bates) 3645
House of Women, The (Bermant) 3596
House on Coliseum Street, The 301
House on Mango Street, The 3250
"House on the Beach, The" 6976
House on the Mound, The 5025
House on the Sound, A 3161
House on the Strand, The 179
House Tibet, The 8020
House-Boat on the Styx, A 1009
Houseguest, The 6200
Household, Geoffrey 1709, 2397, 2567, 3168, 3477, 6967, 7396, 8902, 11000
Household Saints 3970
Householder, The 7885
Housekeeping 9710
Houston, James 2797, 9104, 10727, 10737
Houston, James D. 862
Houston, Robert 6968, 9954
Hoving, Thomas 6341, 9271
How Boys See Girls 2938
How German Is It? 9606
How Green Was My Valley 1607
How He Saved Her 5668
How I Got Him Back 2677
How It Is 708
How Jerem Came Home 10609
How Like a God 1594
How Like an Angel 2972
How Many Miles to Babylon? 5475
How Much? 8721
How Old Was Lolita? 8
How Right You Are, Jeeves 3839
How She Died 10228
How the García Girls Lost Their Accents 5635
How to Leave a Country 7162
How to Make an American Quilt 517
How to Save Your Own Life 2661
Howard, Elizabeth Jane 3833, 6631, 8338, 9287, 9923, 9948, 10189, 10309, 10660
Howard, Linda U. 552
Howard, Maureen 1807, 3715, 5723, 8997, 9162, 10845
Howards End 1906

Howatch, Susan 1115, 1145, 2522, 2597, 2769, 5335, 7424, 7593, 8198, 8219, 9433, 9440, 10963
Howe, Edgar Watson 4534
Howe, Fanny 2406
Howe, George 10489
Howell, Barbara 5764, 7744
Howells, William Dean 293, 1341, 1571, 1821, 1965, 2648, 3641, 3912, 3987, 4368, 4371, 5278, 5614, 5731, 5786, 6055, 6753, 7552, 8252, 8715, 9114, 9403, 9523, 9864, 10030, 10032
Hower, Edward 3026
Hoyer, Linda Grace 476
Hoyle, Fred 6224
Hoyle, Peter 716, 6300
Hoyt, Richard 473
Hoyt's Child 4797
Hribal, C. J. 9639
Hub 6917
Hubble Time 5526
Huckleberry Finn 896
Hudson, Christopher 3603, 8821
Hudson, Helen 3427, 8317
Hudson, W. H. 1820, 5561, 7753
Hudson River Bracketed 5413
Hufford, Susan 539
Hug Dancing 5300
Huge Season, The 4273
Hugger Mugger 318
Hugh Wynne 9704
Hughart, Barry 1211
Hughes, David 5858, 8457, 10274, 10499
Hughes, Glyn 1797, 3731, 5163
Hughes, Langston 8403
Hughes, M. E. 3660
Hughes, Mary Gray 9983
Hughes, Richard 739, 4958, 7384, 9216
Hughes, Thomas 3528, 7876
Hugo 2752
Huie, William Bradford 3312
Hull, Helen R. 4145
Hulme, Keri 10429
Human Being 701
Human Comedy, The 968
Human Factor, The 3855
Human Season, The (Rossiter) 626
Human Season, The (Wallant) 8332
Human Voices 1051
Humbler Creation, The 4662
Humboldt's Gift 915
Humes, H. L. 874
Humphrey, William 1418, 3583, 7447, 8193, 9775
Humphreys, Emyr 377, 10654
Humphreys, J. R. 7541
Humphreys, Josephine 5327, 5593, 7467
Humpty Dumpty 523
Hunger in America 1003
Hungry Hearts 9395
Hungry Hill 1615

Hungry Men 2585
Hunnicutt, Ellen 463
Hunt, Irene 3652
Hunt, Marsha 7961
Hunt (Alvarez) 7728
Hunt, The (Aczel) 10753
Hunter, Evan 24, 2152, 2233, 3311, 3313, 3803, 3947, 4589, 5035, 5059, 6183, 6856, 7769, 7937, 8601, 8878, 8916, 9225, 10183
Hunter, Jim 5150, 8217
Hunter, Kristin 1033, 2156, 10061, 10970
Hunter, The 7844
Hunter and the Whale, The 8116
Hunter's Horn 7350
Hunter's Moon, The 8425
Hunter's Orange 10267
Huntingtower 4141
Hurling, Joan 5686
Hurnard, Hannah 9020
Hurry Home 3849
Hurry On Down 5350
Hurry Sundown 7399
Hurston, Zora Neale 1394, 7057, 8083, 9066
Husbands of Edith, The 3819
Husband's Story, The 3915
Hussar, The 1463
Husted, Darrell 7410
Huston, Bo 9057
Huston, James 533
Hustvedt, Siri 4904
Huth, Angela 2008, 10275
Hutton, Malcolm 2515, 3450
Huxley, Aldous 969, 3439, 5436, 5801, 6849, 7241, 8300, 9411, 9992, 10005
Hyams, Edward 1027
Hyde, Elisabeth 6544
Hyde-Chambers, Fredrick R. 5511
Hyman, Mac 3684
Hypatia 1485

I Am Elijah Thrush 5659
I Am Mary Dunne 7401
I Am One of You Forever 3223
I Am the Cheese 9600
I Am the Clay 3416
I Am Zoë Handke 6740
I Been in Sorrow's Kitchen and Licked Out All the Pots 6744
I Been There Before 9626
I, Claudius 5567
I Come as a Thief 6992
I Dreamt I Was a Nymphomaniac 7992
I, Eve 3351
I Follow Saint Patrick 4056
I for Isobel 866
I Get on the Bus 1771
I, Giorghos 1136
I Hardly Knew You 6044

"'I Have a Thing to Tell You'" 10132
I Hear America Swinging 4324
I Hear the Reaper's Song 7231
I Hear Thunder 2239
I Hear Voices 3454
I Like It Here 6118
I Lock My Door Upon Myself 8164
I Look Divine 8558
I Never Promised You a Rose Garden 9159
I Pass Like Night 7743
I Remember Valentine 4200
I Saw the Sky Catch Fire 3324
I Saw Three Ships 3680
"I Say No" 6362
"I See a Long Journey" 5852
I Sent a Letter to My Love 10831
I Shall Not Hear the Nightingale 10497
I Visit the Soviets 5419
I Want It Now 6988
I Want What I Want 4770
I Was a Teen-Age Dwarf 7884
I Was Dancing 10185
I Will Fear No Evil 7778
Ice Age, The 754
Ice and Fire 7431
Ice Brothers 6774
Ice House, The 9357
Ice in the Bedroom, The 7109
Ice Palace 7061
Ice Saints, The 7773
Ice-Cream War, An 4689
Ice-Shirt, The 9053
Ida 7058
Idea of Home, The 4905
Ideal, Genuine Man, The 7340
Idell, Albert E. 10982
Ides of March, The 7514
Idiot at Home, The 6094
Idol Hunter, The 7807
Idols of the Cave, The 8033
If Beale Street Could Talk 4792
If Birds Are Free 2260
If Death Ever Slept 7588
If He Hollers Let Him Go 419
If Morning Ever Comes 4122
If Not on Earth, Then in Heaven 10635
If the Old Could... 1723
If We Must Die 9478
Ignatieff, Michael 1777
Ikon Maker, The 1438
Iles, Francis 10790
I'll Never Be Young Again 8076
I'll Storm Hell 1188
I'll Take It 3734
Illumination Night 6303
Illusionist, The 5964
Illusions 2631
Illustrator, The 4849
Illywhacker 4827
I'm Dying Laughing 8157
I'm Expecting to Live Quite Soon 1429
I'm the King of the Castle 6130
Image of Josephine 7127

Images of Rose 10231
Imaginary Crimes 6857
Imaginary Friends 9435
Imaginary Life, An 1286
Imaginative Qualities of Actual Things
  5471
Imagining Argentina 4129
Imago 10872
Imago Bird 2593
"Immaculate Man" 3513
Immaterial Murder Case, The 6762
Immaturity 1596
Immediate Prospect of Being Hanged,
  The 1894
Immigrants, The 4883
Immigrant's Daughter, The 861
Immortal Marriage, The 3935
Immortal Wife 376
Imperative Duty, An 8715
Imperial Governor, The 2350
Imperial Palace 1595
Imperial Purple 7538
Imperial Woman 10983
Imperium in Imperio 3269
Impossible Marriage, An 6790
Impossible Object 5654
Impossible Vacation 7947
In a Certain Light 9367
In a Dark Wood 7806
In a Far Country 5505
In a Free State 8123
In a High Place 448
In a Hollow of the Hills 10681
In a Summer Season 2142
In a Year of Grace 6255
In Another Country 2407
In Any Case 6643
In Chancery 3560
In Country 3025
In Custody 5846
In Dubious Battle 2208
In Every Woman's Life . . . 5776
In Freedom's Cause 9741
In Full Possession 116
In Hazard 7384
In Her Garden 759
In Her Own Image 3782
In Memoriam to Identity 8021
In Memory of Junior 6488
In My Father's House 2709
In My Mother's House 2554
In Orbit 7629
In Pale Battalions 7960
In Pious Memory 5750
In Praise of Older Women 1977
In Pursuit of Evil 5819
In Search of Love and Beauty 5962
In Search of the Perfect Ravioli 1875
In Search of the Unknown 2734
"In Sickness and in Health" 9905
"In the Act" 3285
In the Beginning 605
In the Best Families 9895
In the Blue Light of African Dreams
  234

In the Cage 5276
In the Castle of My Skin 844
In the City 7274
In the City of Fear 2046
In the Clear Light 10090
In the Company of Eagles 8669
In the Country of Last Things 5524
In the Dark 10947
In the Days of Good Queen Bess 3493
In the Days of Poor Richard 5796
In the Days of the Comet 5405
In the Ditch 10223
In the Eye of the Sun 3374
In the Falcon's Claw 2645
In the Flesh 5760
In the Forest at Midnight 6728
In the Heart of the Whole World 5674
"In the Highlands" 2918
In the Hollow of His Hand 9307
In the Land of the People Apart 8155
In the Middle Distance 3773
In the Middle of a Life 2773
In the Middle of Nowhere 2406
In the Mood 3369
In the Night Café 2579
In the Palace of the King 4136
In the Palomar Arms 8529
In the Reign of Terror 8840
In the Secret State 7411
In the Shadow of the Peacock 8824
In the Skin of a Lion 995
In the Spanish Ballroom 173
In the Springtime of the Year 2706
In the Suicide Mountains 340
In the Sun 1659
In the Time of Greenbloom 4157
In the Twelfth Year of the War 5655
In the Wet 5433
In the Year of Jubilee 1574
In Their Wisdom 4
In These Promiscuous Parts 10437
In This House of Brede 6808
In This Our Life 3107
In This Sign 10068
In Thrall 7732
In Three Minds 5983
In Times of Peril 3067
In Transit 8185
In War Time 3988
In Youth Is Pleasure 9722
Incandescence 6027
Incas, The 7811
Incident at Badamyâ 7028
Inclinations 4292
Incline, The 6536
Incline Our Hearts 3884
Incredible Brazilian, The 5576
Incubator Ballroom, The 11
Incurable, The 10214
Indecent Exposure 4518
Indecent Obsession, An 8692
Indian Affairs 9111
Indian Country 2274
Indian Giver 8925
Indian in the Cupboard, The 4124

Indian Lawyer, The 3455
Indian Summer (Howells) 5614
Indian Summer (Knowles) 10502
Indiana, Gary 9646
Indifferent Children, The 493
Indigo (Warner) 10327
Indigo (Wiley) 10107
Indiscretion in the Life of an Heiress,
  An 8737
Indiscretion of the Duchess, The 580
Indoctrinaire 10725
Indoor Boy, The 10321
Infants of the Spring 9883
Infinity of Mirrors, An 4121
Informer, The 7841
Ingalls, Rachel 1534, 1745, 1991,
  2011, 2672, 3285, 4019, 4091,
  5770, 5852, 5864, 6151, 7421,
  8250, 8639
"Inheritance" 2672
Inheritors, The (Golding) 7845
Inheritors, The (Robbins) 1120
Inimitable Jeeves, The 4213
Injured Party, The 5772
Injury Time 5004
Ink Truck, The 2766
Inkling, The 8366
Inman, Robert 464, 3259
Inn of the Hawk and Raven, The 838
Inner Tube 9297
Innes, Hammond 615, 685, 1108,
  1751, 2474, 2538, 2513, 3686,
  4755, 8129, 8623, 8987, 9170,
  9237
Innocence 3230
Innocent, The (Jones) 9154
Innocent, The (Kim) 10506
Innocent, The (McEwan) 8707
Innocent Blood 87
Innocent Darkness 5383
Innocent Eye, The 4637
Innocent Millionaire, An 5590
Innocents, The (Sharp) 6654
Innocents, The (Slaughter) 944
Inquisitor, The 8405
Inside Mr. Enderby 2910
Inside of the Cup, The 1360
Inside, Outside 6510
Insolent Breed, The 1413
Instant Enemy, The 2986
Instant in the Wind, An 4796
Instrument, The 6024
Insular Possession, An 7698
Insurrection 4517
Intensive Care 1284
Intercom Conspiracy, The 2563
Interim 9878
Interloper, The 6685
International Episode, An 9518
International Garage Sale, The 4260
Interpreters, The 8797
Interstate 2249
Intertidal Life 2270
Interview with the Vampire 9444
Interviewing Matisse 2455

Intimacy 2058
Intimations of Eve 5603
Into the Blue 2680
Into What Far Harbor? 7813
Into Your Tent I'll Creep 7722
Intruder in the Dust 2022
Intrusions 5495
Intrusions of Peggy, The 5083
Invasion, The 10477
Inventing Ivanov 5329
Inventing the Weather 1478
Invention of the World, The 8749
Inventor, The 2575
Inverted World, The 2707
Investigator, The 4947
Invisible Man (Ellison) 5922
Invisible Man, The (Wells) 9092
Invisible Mending 2265
Invisible Swords 6851
Invisible Worm, The 10893
Invitation to the Married Life 2008
Invitation to the Waltz 1376
Iola Leroy 4211
Iowa Baseball Confederacy, The 4448
Ipcress File, The 6005
Ireland, Ann 8756
Ireland, David 5284, 7072
Irish, Lola 9619, 9634
Irish, William (pseud.). *See*
   Woolrich, Cornell
Irish Magdalen, The 2451
Irish Wine 9300
Iron Heel, The 10683
Iron Stallions, The 8311
Iron Woman, The 7710
Ironweed 1191
Irreversible Decline of Eddie Socket,
   The 4438
Irvine, Lucy 6161
Irving, Clive 6866, 10522
Irving, John 556, 2040, 3277,
   3848, 6892, 7542, 8230
Irwin, Margaret 4151
Irwin, Robert 4287, 7368, 7488
Is He Popenjoy? 8961
Is This What Other Women Feel Too?
   2881
Isaac and His Devils 260
Isherwood, Christopher 48, 706,
   4735, 5912, 6764, 8181, 9097,
   9137, 10184, 10689
Ishiguro, Kazuo 3232, 4814, 7234
Island (Huxley) 10005
Island (Perry) 3030
Island Death, An 1792
Island Harp, The 3667
Island in the Sun 8567
Island of Apples, The 7676
Island of Dr. Moreau, The 8059
Island of Sheep, The 7009
Island of the Innocent, The 7717
Island Pharisees, The 5895
Island Within, The 5280
Islanders 4145
Islandia 6760

Islands in the Stream 3181
Islas, Arturo 9716
Israel, Philip 1152
Israel Potter 9515
Isvik 8623
It Can't Happen Here 7762
It Is Always Summer 10611
It Is Never Too Late to Mend 3635
It Is Time, Lord 7063
It Looked Like For Ever 1701
It's a Battlefield 5798
It's All in the Family 10152
It's All Zoo 9484
It's an Old Country 3846
It's Raining in Mango 687
Italian, The 1293
Italian Girl, The 2698
Italian Lesson, The 890
Italian Wife, The 10654
Item from the Late News, An 4521
Ivanhoe 3893
Ivory Bright 8285
Ivory Grin, The 10050
Ivory Swing, The 9105
Iyayi, Festus 7324

J C Saves 1424
J. Poindexter, Colored 4723
J R 10011
Jack and Jill 292
Jack Archer 579
Jack Gance 9735
Jack in the Box 1704
Jack Rivers and Me 8813
Jack Tier 8047
Jackson, Charles 901, 2348
Jackson, Guida 2713
Jackson, Helen Hunt 3636
Jackson, Shirley 337, 2763, 3133,
   3572, 3939
Jacob's Ladder (Rawlings) 4384
Jacob's Ladder (Williams) 7939
Jacob's Room 1588
Jacob's Well 10273
Jacobson, Dan 85, 809, 5601, 7036,
   7868, 7991, 9685
Jacobson, Howard 1452, 9034, 9269
Jacobson, Mark 632
Jacobson, Sidney 9647
Jade 4255
Jadis 8437
Jaffe, Rona 252, 2371, 2568, 3308,
   4012, 7789, 8194, 9590, 9725
Jaffe, Susanne 6143
Jaffee, Annette Williams 6829, 7074
Jailbird 7145
Jake's Thing 1256
Jalna 7842
Jamaica Inn, The 10577
Jambeaux 7822
James, Donald 10441
James, George P. R. 3062
James, Henry 1183, 2649, 3913,
   4696, 4909, 5066, 5085, 5276,

   5345, 5613, 6036, 6286, 6407,
   6522, 6754, 8546, 8841, 8847,
   8967, 9094, 9325, 9349, 9518,
   9720, 9857, 9861, 10031
James, P. D. 87, 1123, 1883, 1891,
   2359, 3518, 5091, 6028, 6203,
   9928, 10216
James, Will 4380, 9705, 10692
James, by the Grace of God 10946
Jameson, Storm 1636, 2965, 3111,
   3382, 3711, 4997, 5812, 6436,
   6786, 7222, 9487, 9894, 10048,
   10121, 10134, 10199, 10360, 10717,
   10791
Jampot Smith 5648
Jane and Prudence 7390
Jane Cable 10036
Jane Eyre 10330
Jane Talbot 7964
Janeway, Elizabeth 10361
Janice Meredith 7346
Janowitz, Tama 2084, 5637
Janus Island 1116
Jarman, Rosemary Hawley 756,
   3979, 5324, 7422
Jaro, Benita Kane 9969
Jarrell, Randall 7882
Jarrett's Jade 3147
Jasmine 7030
Java Head 9408
Jazz 10889
Jazz, Jazz, Jazz 9083
Jealous God, The (Braine) 4980
Jealous Gods, The (Atherton) 5738
Jealousies 5843
Jeeves and the Feudal Spirit 567
Jeeves and the Tie That Binds 3850
Jeeves in the Morning 3341
Jefferies, Richard 1244, 3793
Jeffords, Nicole 3735
Jeffrey County 2722
Jelly Roll Morton's Last Night at The
   Jungle Inn 6234
Jen, Gish 4242
Jenkin, Len 6338
Jenkins, Elizabeth 9149
Jenkins, Robin 247, 1285, 7142,
   9669
Jenkins, Victoria 3334
Jennie Gerhardt 6412
Jennifer 2712
Jennifer Lorn 1
Jennings, Dana Andrew 10547
Jennings, Gary 465, 4502, 5545,
   7634, 10022
Jenny by Nature 2235
Jeremiah 8:20 10009
Jeremiah Martin 5240
Jeremy 3085
Jeremy and Hamlet 2689
Jeremy at Crale 7125
Jeremy Bell 5139
Jeremy's Version 5359
Jericho Mosaic 1464
Jericho Sleep Alone 8603

Jerome, Jerome K. 929, 3990
Jerome, A Poor Man 4475
Jerry of the Islands 405
Jerusalem Diamond, The 10249
Jerusalem the Golden 4775
Jessie and Jesus 870
Jessup, Richard 88, 10938
Jest of God, A 8747
Jesus Tales 5664
Jewel 7103
Jewel in the Crown, The 5152
Jewel of Seven Stars, The 7372
Jewels 455
Jewett, Sarah Orne 485, 1350, 3992, 10567
Jezebel's Daughter 2291
Jhabvala, Ruth Prawer 255, 1689, 2963, 3473, 3841, 5360, 5962, 6766, 7178, 7885
Jigsaw 7443
"Jim" 3568
Jim Dandy 331
"Jiru Road, The" 10886
Jitterbug Perfume 9679
Jo Stern 5951
Joan Haste 9208
Joan Makes History 629
Joanna 6876
Joanna and Ulysses 10716
Joanna Godden 4048
Joanna's Husband and David's Wife 2549
Job 3781
Job's Year 1718
Jocelyn 3184
Joe 10457
"Joe and Pete" 10690
Joe Hill 1189
Joe Jones 7333
Joe the Engineer 3020
Joey Dee Gets Wise 7100
John and Anzia 8500
John and Mary 4772
John Baring's House 8349
John Barleycorn 4697
John Caldigate 3553
John Cornelius 3533
John Dollar 1764
John Halifax, Gentleman 4970
John Macnab 3916
John Sherwood 6621
John Ward, Preacher 10643
John Wood Case, The 10168
John-Juan 1675
Johnnie Cross 5508
Johnno 6659
Johnny Got His Gun 1097
Johnny Logan 7599
Johnny Nelson 9311
Johnny Osage 10170
Johnson, B. S. 1862, 3924, 5479, 10827
Johnson, Charles 253, 2598, 6457
Johnson, Denis 183, 1778, 5174, 9620

Johnson, Diane 4402, 4627, 4882, 5455, 6442, 8891
Johnson, Hillary 1259
Johnson, James Weldon 7951
Johnson, Josephine W. 4152, 5568, 10715, 10981
Johnson, Joyce 2579
Johnson, Mrs. A. E. 3070, 3814
Johnson, Nora 3509, 5049, 10564
Johnson, Owen 4460, 9529, 9531
Johnson, Pamela Hansford 141, 381, 418, 839, 843, 854, 2207, 3174, 4216, 4662, 5631, 6253, 6790, 7011, 7264, 7303, 7389, 7561, 10383
Johnson, Samuel 4603
Johnson, Susan 7106, 9503
Johnson, Wayne 4667
Johnston, Jennifer 2158, 2519, 2541, 4520, 5475, 10893, 10911
Johnston, Mary 786, 2498, 3559, 5615, 7610
Joke Goes a Long Way in the Country, A 7330
Joke of the Century, The 5858
Jolis, Alan 5179
Jolley, Elizabeth 1710, 1945, 2259, 4127, 5504, 6261, 6304, 6725, 10545, 10739
Jolly Rogerson 6354
Jonah Man, The 8151
Jonah's Gourd Vine 9066
Jonathan Livingston Seagull 7929
Jonathan Wild 4480
Jones, Ann T. 5782
Jones, Carol 8286
Jones, Douglas C. 388, 1076, 1735, 4610, 6918, 7322, 7425, 7638, 7640, 7686, 8892
Jones, Ellen 1779
Jones, Gayl 3408, 5757
Jones, Glyn 7676
Jones, J. B. 5306
Jones, James 873, 1693, 2995, 4643, 5920, 8107, 8659, 9390
Jones, Kaylie 6726, 8245, 8888
Jones, Louis B. 2061, 3264
Jones, Madison 664, 4983, 4986, 5318, 7418, 7523, 9154
Jones, Mary 8493
Jones, Matthew F. 8542
Jones, Mervyn 1692, 1939, 3188, 4772, 5583, 5941, 7355, 9441, 10505
Jones, Nettie 6399, 8017
Jones, R. S. 1263
Jones, Robert F. 8142
Jones, Rod 6901
Jong, Erica 2661, 5297, 5492, 5536, 7171, 10857
Jonoah and the Green Stone 7320
Jordan, Neil 1936
Jordan County 2226
Jordanstown 10981
Jorrocks' Jaunts and Jollities 4683

Jo's Boys 1245
José, F. Sionil 714, 5496, 10851
Jose, Nicholas 5722
Joseph 7355
Joseph Andrews 7163
Josh Lawton 3483
Joshua 4014
Joshua and the Children 8337
Joshua in the Holy Land 4428
Joshua Then and Now 9449
Josiah Allen's Wife (pseud.). *See* Holley, Marietta
Josipovici, Gabriel 8195
Journal of Nicholas the American, The 4484
Journal of the Flood Year, A 5544
Journal of the Plague Year, A 120
Journey (MacLachlan) 6879
Journey, The (Ganesan) 8244
Journey from Prague Street, The 2059
Journey from This World to the Next, A 2286
Journey Homeward, The 6806
Journey in the Dark 6629
Journey into Fear 8085
Journey of Tapiola 416
Journey to Matecumbe, A 2837
Journeyer, The 10022
Journeyman 6149
Jovanovich, William 5537, 5989
Joy 7961
Joy Baby 1798
Joy Club, The 771
Joy in the Morning 9233
Joy Ride (Howell) 7744
Joyce, James 961, 1175, 3682, 8041
Joyful Condemned, The 4315
Joyful Delaneys, The 10133
Joyride (Chaplin) 9803
"Joy-Ride, The" (Barker) 6501
Joys of Motherhood, The 1697
Jubb 1881
Jubilee 743
Judas, My Brother 3655
Judas Tree, The 10592
Judd, Alan 1943, 6257, 8018
Judd Rankin's Daughter 4634
Jude the Obscure 6092
Judge, The 2071
Judge, Jury and Executioner 10286
Judgment Day (Farrell) 1878
Judgment Day (Lively) 6916
Judgment of Deke Hunter, The 3194
Judgment of Paris, The 54
Judgment on Deltchev 6983
Judith 9266
Judith Paris 3099
Juggling the Stars 10455
Julia Bride 8546
Julia Paradise 6901
Julian 7518
July 7th 10912
July's People 9356
Jumping the Queue 641
Junghyo, Ahn 6459

Jungle, The 9760
Jungle Lovers 10402
Junior Bachelor Society, The 2852
Juniper Tree, The 9187
Junk-Drawer Corner-Store Front-Porch Blues, The 10891
Junkers, The 3503
Junky 3049
Jurgen 1966
Just, Ward 1437, 2046, 2053, 5224, 6078, 9022, 9735
Just Above My Head 9849
Just Across the Street 725
Just and the Unjust, The 5200
Just Before Daybreak 1277
Just Causes 1447
Just Relations 7529
Justin Bayard 10157
Justin Moyan 10501
Justine 7922
Jutland Cottage 5434

K. 9122
Kabul 460
Kadohata, Cynthia 10874
Kagami 7908
Kahawa 4963
Kahn, Alice 3404
Kahn, Roger 7857
Kahuna 1542
Kalki 611
Kalpakian, Laura 4873, 10741, 10863
Kamitses, Zoë 1867
Kane, Henry 10217
Kane, Rod 4449
Kanfer, Stefan 4260
Kangaroo 5618
Kanin, Garson 26, 1234, 2479, 3332, 5501
Kansas in August 10295
Kanthapura 1381
Kantor, MacKinlay 1200, 1612, 1634, 1832, 2608, 4154, 4162, 5916, 6569, 7138, 7406, 8301, 8359, 8654, 8655, 9098, 9543, 9994, 10052
Kaplan, David Michael 6734
Kaplan, James 35
Kaplan, Johanna 6962
Kappillan of Malta, The 5229
Karan 10285
Karate Is a Thing of the Spirit 8803
Karbo, Karen 4450, 6162
Karlin, Wayne 10532
Karmel, Ilona 7141
Karpov's Brain 4015
Kaser, Paul 10609
Kashner, Rita 157, 6542
Kata, Elizabeth 7908, 8414
Katana, The 916
Kate and Emma 23
Kate Fennigate 10798

Kate Vaiden 5591
Katharine Lauderdale 5344
Katherine's House 6402
Kathleen 5407
Kathy Goes to Haiti 10834
Katz, Bob 6486
Katz, Steve 607, 6278, 7357
Kaufelt, David A. 858, 992, 1323, 2512, 2590, 10089, 10271
Kauffman, Janet 5236, 8251
Kaufman, Bel 1984, 4215
Kaufman, Joan 671
Kaufman, Joseph 6168
Kaufman, Pamela 392, 10272
Kaufman, Sue 4398
Kaufmann, Myron S. 1990
Kavan, Anna 5909, 10802
Kay, Susan 458, 7102
Kay, Terry 477, 8531, 10087
Kaye, M. M. 810, 3702, 10276, 10814
Kaye-Smith, Sheila 2300, 4048, 4058, 4385, 7253, 7392, 9134, 9138
Kaysen, Susanna 5974, 9653
Kazan 403
Kazan, Elia 678, 1677, 2398, 2491, 3342, 4407, 6073
Keane, John B. 3042
Keane, Molly 385, 3131, 3998, 4498, 5963, 6759, 7745, 8718, 10789
Keasey, Ken 7984
Keeble, John 9967
Keeley, Edmund 7459, 10096
Keenan, Joe 4712, 6940
Keene, John 1780
Keep the Aspidistra Flying 5621
Keep the Change 3253
Keeper of the Bees, The 4726
Keeper of the Light 7344
Keepers of the House, The 2240
Keeping Secrets 8471
Keeping the Faith 10670
Keeping Up Appearances 8854
Keeping Warm 3399
Kees, Weldon 9654
Keillor, Garrison 7791
Kelleher, Victor 10638
Kellerman, Jonathan 1146
Kelley, Edith Summers 7267
Kelley, Emma Dunham 6309
Kelley, William Melvin 3163, 3169, 4066, 10213
Kellogg, Marjorie 3923
Kelly, Jack 4266
Kellys and the O'Kellys, The 5194
Kelman, James 6481
Kelton, Elmer 4805, 8165
Kenan, Randall 2643
Keneally, Thomas 1064, 1513, 1714, 1985, 2574, 2633, 2988, 3189, 5230, 5753, 5831, 7545, 9371, 9929, 9931, 10603, 10894
Kenilworth 8951

Kennedy, Adam 5505, 10861
Kennedy, Eugene 9453
Kennedy, John P. 6053
Kennedy, John Pendleton 8171
Kennedy, Leigh 4484, 9717
Kennedy, Lena 9178
Kennedy, Margaret 1500, 3160, 3515, 5905, 7953, 8771, 8941, 9074, 9230, 10809
Kennedy, Raymond 7116, 8026, 10870
Kennedy, Teresa 3953
Kennedy, Thomas E. 3255
Kennedy, William 1191, 2183, 2369, 2766, 8918, 10871
Kennedy for the Defense 6453
Kenney, Susan 2407, 3431
"Kenny" 10925
Kent, Louise Andrews 3134, 10797
Kentish Manor Murders, The 4334
Kentons, The 1965
Kentuckians, The 9210
Kentucky Cardinal, A 10569
Kentucky Love 10281
Kepler 6904
Kept in the Dark 5560
Kerouac, Jack 2336, 2906, 5445, 5657, 5811, 6075, 7575, 7668, 9265
Kerr, Philip 7582, 9284
KES (A Kestral for a Knave) 7777
Kesey, Ken 2810, 7674
Key, The 9969
Key of the Chest, The 9069
Key to the Door 976
Keys of the Kingdom, The 1498
Khaled 7504
Kick the Can 320
Kid for Two Farthings, A 3274
Kidman, Fiona 10090
Kidnapped 1570
Kiefer, Warren 831, 2434, 5211
Kiely, Benedict 2328, 9629
Kiely, Kevin 7598
Kiker, Douglas 461
Kildeer Mountain 9617
Kilgore, Kathryn 2861
Kilian, Michael 118, 2276, 2285, 8297
Kill Hole 5246
Kill Memory 109
Kill Price, The 10731
Killeen, The 10859
Killens, John Oliver 5097, 7029, 8745
Killer Angels, The 7633
Killer Diller 8384
Killing Everybody 3298
Killing Fields, The 8821
Killing Frost, The 2939
Killing Ground, The 9491
Killing Mister Watson 774
Killing of the King, The 4179
Killing of Yesterday's Children, The 3783

Kill-Off, The 7867
Killshot 2935
Kim 2017
Kim, Richard E. 10500, 10506
Kimball, Philip 7047
Kincaid, Jamaica 2180, 2410
Kincaid, Nanci 3262
Kincaid's Battery 4045
Kind Are Her Answers 9417
Kind of Anger, A 6318
Kindling, The 3688
Kindling and Ashes 6525
Kindly Ones, The 10933
Kindness Cup, A 6842
Kindness of Women, The 10536
Kindred 4585
Kinds of Love 2095
Kinflicks 2366
Kinfolk 300
King, Florence 4815
King, Francis 987, 2536, 4899,
    8223, 8288, 8313, 10997
King, Roger 7053
King, Tabitha 4548, 8625
King, The 4861
King Coal 1365
King Coffin 10759
King Hereafter 3719
King Jesus 4499
King Must Die, The 9227
King of Hearts 4405
King of Kings 4080
King of Pirates, The 5384
King of Schnorrers, The 7505
King of Spades 6649
King of the Fields, The 9042
King of the Jews 1698
King - of the Khyber Rifles 6978
King of the Mountain 6922
King of the Road 5982
King of the World 1216
King Richard's Land 5314
King Silky! 6011
King Solomon's Mines 4493
King Who Was a King, The 1314
Kingdom of Brooklyn, The 7122
Kingdom of Evil, The 4477
Kingdom of the Wicked, The 5516
Kingfishers Catch Fire 4120
King's Coat, The 4711
King's Commission, The 4869
King's Evil, The 3300
King's General, The 10146
King's Grey Mare, The 5324
Kings in the Countinghouse 9756
Kings in Winter, The 8671
King's Mirror, The 1197
King's Oak 3403
Kings of Vain Intent, The 3772
King's Orchard, The 277
King's Pleasure, The 7630
King's Privateer, The 4511
Kingsblood Royal 6426
Kingsford Mark, The 9081
Kingsland, Rosemary 3879

Kingsley, Charles 1336, 1485,
    4440, 4455, 5390, 6283
Kingsolver, Barbara 3733, 10895
Kingston, Maxine Hong 9299
Kinney, Harrison 2562
Kinsella, W. P. 4448, 8923, 8934
Kinsolving, William 7213
Kinstler, Clysta 9046
Kiowa, The 2854
Kipling, Rudyard 2017, 4244,
    8062
Kirkland, Joseph 1850, 5891
Kirkwood, James 62, 2036
Kirn, Walter 5879
Kirshenbaum, Binnie 10675
Kiss Before Dying, A 6931
Kiss of Kin, The 8303
Kisses of the Enemy 10748
Kit Brandon 6627
Kitchen God's Wife, The 6736
Kitchen Man, The 8904
Kite 9959
Kiteley, Brian 4966
Kith 9293
Kitto, Crispin 8732
Kitty Foyle 2892
Klane, Robert 8486
Klansman, The 3312
Klass, Perri 1065, 4900
Kleber Flight, The 8001
Klein, Colleen 6397
Klein, Edward 1524
Klein, Elizabeth 158
Klein, Norma 300, 545, 1135,
    1241, 1992, 6541, 7557, 8238,
    9272, 9958
Kleinzeit 6591
Kluge, P. F. 3348, 8534
Kluger, Richard 285, 7812
Klynt's Law 9335
Knebel, Fletcher 2980, 3178, 3971,
    5186, 5859, 5937, 6994, 10734
Kneeling Bus, The 1540
Knight, Eric 10480
Knight, The 3903
Knight of the Cumberland, A 9527
Knight on the Bridge, The 5165
Knights & Dragons 3406
Knock on Any Door 83
Knockout Artist, The 2874
Know Nothing 10811
Knowles, John 3331, 3586, 6794,
    7883, 7889, 7894, 9035, 10176,
    10502
Knowlton, Christopher 5234
Knowlton, Winthrop 1719
Knox, Alexander 8608
Kocan, Peter 9184
Koch, C. J. 1310, 5835
Koch, Stephen 5860
Koestler, Arthur 9769, 9788
Kogawa, Joy 10610
Kohan, Rhea 4360
Kolb, Ken 1516
Kolonialagent 8489

Kona 5022
Konadu, Asare 2627
Kondoleon, Harry 2556, 6474
Konecky, Edith 4856
Koning, Hans 8001, 9962
Königsmark 5913
Kops, Bernard 1428, 4070, 10385
Kornblatt, Joyce Reiser 1728
Kosinski, Jerzy 2482, 3244, 4284,
    6531, 7112, 7683, 8876, 9581,
    9805
Koster, R. M. 1164, 9604, 9658
Kostoff, Lynn 6051
Kotker, Norman 9040
Kotker, Zane 10841
Kotlowitz, Robert 5340, 10622
Kotzwinkle, William 1704, 3447,
    7022, 7120, 8728
Kovic, Ron 9023
Kraft, Eric 370, 3282, 3722, 3930,
    4430, 4473, 6297, 7583, 9024,
    9366, 9949, 10978
Kram, Mark 8924
Kramer, Larry 5949
Kramer versus Kramer 8189
Kranes, David 8522
Krasner, William 8516
Krauth, Nigel 1536
Krawiec, Richard 3754
Krich, A. M. 1450
Krich, John 2130, 5687
Kriegel, Leonard 4504
Krippendorf's Tribe 6707
Kroetsch, Robert 432
Kropp, Lloyd 319, 7408
Kruger's Alp 1530
Kubicki, Jan 3728
Kuhlken, Ken 8729
Kuniczak, W. S. 9021, 10195
Kunstler, James Howard 5842,
    6195, 7232
Kupfer, Fern 1870, 7499
Kureishi, Hanif 4864
Kurtén, Björn 6704
Kurzweil, Allen 1087
Kwitney, Alisa 3892

L. A. Woman 7731
Labors of Love 7360
Labrador 7437
LaBrava 6858
Labyrinth, The 5251
Lad of Sunnybank 412
Ladders to Fire 10801
Laddie 8205
Ladies, The 2719
Ladies' Man, The 9806
Ladies of Levittown, The 6575
Ladies of Missalonghi, The 1239
Ladies Whose Bright Eyes 7966
Lady, The 2735
Lady Baltimore 7554
Lady Chatterly's Lover 3380
Lady in the Lake, The 9222

Lady of Fort St. John, The 7911
Lady of Rome, A 10783
Lady of Situations, The 6163
Lady of Spain 3044
Lady of the Aroostook, The 3987
Lady of the Heavens, The 4373
Lady of the Shroud, The 4929
Lady on the Burning Deck 5289
Lady Oracle 5578
Lady Washington 4191
Lady with the Alligator Purse, The 2010
"Ladybird, The" 45
Lady's Maid 1959
La Farge, Oliver 2621, 4246, 7612, 9275
Laidlaw 7855
Laidlaw, Brett 1752, 10896
Laing, Kojo 8239, 8379
Lakestown Rebellion, The 2156
Lama 5511
Lamb, Harold 524, 4669, 9135
Lamb, Robert 7750
Lamb, Wally 9373
Lamb 9609
Lamb in His Bosom 1602
Lamb's War, The 8463
Lambdin, Dewey 4511, 4711, 4869, 8162
Lambert, Betty 3716
Lambert, Gavin 7600
Lambton, Antony 9255
Lament for a Silver-Eyed Woman 6360
Lamming, George 201, 844, 8126, 10604
Lamming, R. M. 317, 10947
Lamott, Anne 3202, 4598, 7333, 10852
Lamplighter, The 2186
Lanark 7577
Lancaster, Bruce 1851
Lancaster, G. B. 6386
Lancelot 7780
Land 10926
Land Beyond the Mountains, The 10371
Land Beyond the River, The 10074
Land God Gave to Cain, The 4755
Land Is Bright, The 6121
Land Leviathan, The 5477
Land of Laughs, The 2096
Land of Mist, The 5410
Land Remembered, A 9811
Land That Drank the Rain, The 3778
Land Was Ours, The 7454
"Land Where My Fathers Died" 2932
Land Where the Sun Dies, The 9239
Landing on the Sun, A 351
Landlocked 1113
Landlord, The 1033
Landlord at Lion's Head, The 6055
Landlord's Daughter, The 2349
Lane, James Allen 3639
Lane, Rose Wilder 4054, 5739
Lange, Oliver 6872, 8287, 9798
Langley, Dorothy 7639

Langrishe, Go Down 5320
Language in the Blood 6880
Languages of Love, The 3689
Lansbury, Coral 1290, 4474, 4832, 9701
Lantern in Her Hand, A 9126
Lap of Luxury, The 508
Lapatine, Kenneth A. 6656
Lapin, Mark 7906
Lapsing 1811
La Puma, Salvatore 5382
Laqueur, Walter 6330
Lardner, Ring Jr. 10620
Lardners and the Laurelwoods, The 7253
Lark Rise 1383
Larsen, Eric 4113, 6740
Larsen, Ernest 9801
Larsen, Jeanne 514, 7489
Larsen, Nella 1913, 8353
La Salle 9635
Lasher 10028
Lassalle, Caroline 10864
Last Adam, The 8589
Last and First Men 4496
Last and the First, The 4985
Last Angry Man, The 8480
Last Armenian, The 7434
Last Battle, The 424
Last Blossom on the Plum Tree, The 10100
Last Blue Whale, The 444
Last Campaign, The 8416
Last Catholic in America, The 9439
Last Chance, The 2371
Last Chronicle of Barset, The 2732
Last Convertible, The 6934
Last Dance 6462
Last Days of Pompeii, The 3812
Last Days of Louisiana Red, The 280
Last Duty, The 3006
Last Exile, The 203
Last Exit to Brooklyn 5625
Last Film of Emile Vico, The 1332
Last Gentleman, The 9434
Last Good Time, The 8730
Last Great Love, The 4625
Last Great Season, The 8920
Last Hero, The 7700
Last Hours of Sandra Lee, The 5450
Last Hurrah, The 2472
Last Laugh, Mr. Moto 5021
Last Love, The 5029
Last Lovers 8949
Last Loves 7747
Last Magic, The 10608
Last Man, The 4533
Last Man Standing, The 2439
Last Mandarin, The 1886
Last Night at the Ritz, The 8635
Last Night of Summer, The 4394
Last of How It Was, The 4437
Last of Mr. Norris, The 9097
Last of Summer, The 9550
Last of the Barons, The 5126

Last of the Country House Murders, The 3190
Last of the Crazy People, The 8482
Last of the Curlews 2227
Last of the Golden Girls, The 327
Last of the Lairds, The 357
Last of the Mohicans, The 10468
Last of the True Believers, The 4846
Last of the Wine, The 57
Last One Home 4824
Last Picture Show, The 8723
Last Post, The 3092
Last Puritan, The 6289
Last Resort (Summer) 1716
Last Resort, The (Binchy) 8294
Last Resort, The (Johnson) 7303
Last Resorts (Boylan) 3678
Last Respects 1884
Last Romantics, The 1740
Last Room, The 4100
Last Room in Manhattan, The 1077
Last Score 5812
Last September, The 8770
Last Shot, The 10459
Last Stand at Saber River 8270
Last Station, The 10993
Last Studebaker, The 10027
Last Summer 5035
Last Supper, The (Bermant) 3945
Last Supper, The (McCarry) 2787
Last Testament of Oscar Wilde, The 1307
Last Things 6323
Last to Go, The 393
Last Tycoon, The 1316
Last Unicorn, The 430
Last Valley, The 9240
Last Virginia Gentleman, The 8297
Last Voyage, The 2543
Last Voyage of Somebody the Sailor, The 94
Last Waltz, The 7873
Last Whales, The 7940
Late Bloomer 2590
Late Bourgeois World, The 6006
Late Call 3653
Late George Apley, The 790
Late Mrs. Null, The 3069
Late Night Muse, The 2066
Latecomers 8577
Later Adventures of Tom Jones, The 4218
Late-Summer Passion of a Woman of Mind, The 5241
Lathe of Heaven, The 435
Latin Jazz 171
Latin Moon in Manhattan 7282
Latiolais, Michelle 2729
Laugh Lines 7540
Laughing Boy 7612
Laughing Matter, The 4672
Laughing Sutra, The 561
Laughing Whitefish 7223
Laughlin, Ruth 4214
Laughter in the Dark 7714

Laughter of Carthage, The 7976
Laura 4228
Laurence, Margaret 2106, 5464, 6646, 7684, 8747
Laurent, Antoine 5975
Laurents, Arthur 10823
Lauterstein, Ingeborg 1210, 2129
Lavengro 5078
Lavin, Mary 1299, 5140
Law, Janice 10288
Law at Randado, The 9427
Law for the Lion, A 5570
Lawd Today! 2764
Lawrence, D. H. 45, 402, 521, 3082, 3380, 4476, 4724, 5131, 5618, 6215, 6269, 7864, 8206, 8911
Lawrence, Josephine 52, 6638
Lawrence, Karen 3622, 7697
Lawrence, Kathleen Rockwell 1077, 7081
Lawrence Clavering 487
Law-Yone, Wendy 5267
Laxalt, Robert 1082
Lay of the Land, The 8236
Lazarre 4718
Lazarre, Jane 4201, 5599
Lazarus 5987
Lea, Sydney 998
Lea, Tom 1398, 1648, 7626, 10707
Leader, The 303
Leader of the Band 6478
Leafy Rivers 2702
League of Frightened Men, The 583
Leah's Children 7835
Leah's Journey 6395
Leahy, Syrell Rogovin 2864, 3959, 4654, 5957, 9623, 10237
Leamon, Warren 8581
Leanna 4408
Leap in the Dark 10562
Leap Year 1766
Learning About God 9040
Learning Tree, The 4955
Least One, The 6129
Leatherwood God, The 3641
Leaton, Anne 4419
Leave Cancelled 10047
Leave It to Psmith 8257
Leave of Absence (McInerny) 10439
Leave of Absence (Morrison) 9450
Leaves in the Wind 6069
Leaves on Grey, The 9013
Leavetaking, The 9442
Leaving Brooklyn 9048
Leaving Cheyenne 10179
Leaving Home 10361
Leaving Losapas 3415
Leaving the Land 6811
Leavitt, Caroline 1937, 2569, 3606, 5843
Leavitt, David 2435, 10438
Leavy, Jane 349
Lebanon 729
LeBaron, Charles 1212

Le Carré, John 1684, 1736, 1816, 1834, 2246, 2991, 3444, 3464, 4659, 5930, 7886, 7904, 8605, 10059
LeCompte, Jane 4203
Le Comte, Edward 3351
Lederer, William J. 1136
Ledger, The 5686
Led-Horse Claim, The 8052
Lee 8736
Lee, Andrea 3541
Lee, C. Y. 832, 4599, 8700
Lee, Gus 38
Lee, Harper 22
Lee, Sky 3696
Lee, Sophia 2287
LeFanu, J. Sheridan 2944, 5305, 10678
Left Hand of Darkness, The 9698
Left-Handed Spirit, The 5484
Legacy (Kay) 458
Legacy (Michener) 1240
Legacy, A (Bedford) 6117
Legacy, The (Fast) 9611
Legend of Montrose, A 10467
Legend of the Yellow River 7188
Leggett, John 3429
Legion of Noble Christians, The 8943
Legs 2369
Le Guin, Ursula K. 435, 1729, 1855, 2121, 6792, 7407, 7687, 7945, 8374, 9698, 10720
Lehman, Dennis 4692
Lehmann, Rosamond 1376, 4647, 6287, 8631, 9352, 9899, 10128
Lehner, Christine 7076
Lehrer, Jim 320, 398, 2009, 6342, 7007
Lehrer, Kate 6347, 9037
Leila 9618
Leimbach, Marti 1769, 6169
Leitch, Maurice 10190
Leland, Christopher T. 1760, 4586, 5332
Leland, Mary 7546, 10859
Lelchuk, Alan 2999, 5483, 7724, 8761, 9630
Lemann, Nancy 6925, 10667
Lemprière's Dictionary 5051
L'Engle, Madeleine 130, 1306, 3949, 4749, 8168, 8110, 9783
Lenin 2413
Lennox, Charlotte 5883
Leonard, Elmore 164, 592, 892, 1321, 1705, 2062, 2065, 2935, 3013, 5153, 5960, 6579, 6586, 6853, 6858, 7024, 7725, 7871, 7963, 8042, 8270, 8559, 8790, 9333, 9427, 9850, 10076
Leonard, Hugh 325, 4023
Leonard, Phyllis G. 6592
Leonora (Bennett) 8845
Leonora (Edgeworth) 10766
Leonowens, Anna 2188, 6247
Leopard, The 6179

Leopard and the Cliff, The 6010
Leopard's Spots, The 10034
Leopold, Christopher 4083, 4803
Leprosarium, The 4622
Lerman, Rhoda 6482
Lesbia Brandon 10774
Lesley, Craig 2114, 7642
Less Than Angels 9353
Less Than Zero 3723
Lesser, Ellen 2811, 3245
Lessing, Doris 1113, 1723, 2703, 3227, 3390, 4004, 4006, 4506, 5497, 6177, 7742, 7833, 9668, 10073, 10364, 10728, 10941
Lessons 2394
Lester, Julius 1531
Let It Come Down 8097
Let Love Come Last 10902
Let Me Alone 5909
Let Me Count the Ways 5701
Let No Man Write My Epitaph 3802
Let Noon Be Fair 980
Let the Emperor Speak 920
Let the Hurricane Roar 5739
Let the People Sing 1609
Let's Fall in Love 10075
Letourneau's Used Auto Parts 769
Lette, Kathy 9968
Letter from Peking 2143
Letter Left to Me, The 1954
Letter to Sister Benedicta 610
Letting Go 3051
Levanter, The 9005
Leven, Jeremy 616, 9019
Leverson, Ada 125, 8769, 9327
Levi, Jonathan 693
Leviant, Curt 2278, 8133
Levin, Donna 6711
Levin, Elizabeth 511
Levin, Ira 217, 307, 1432, 3170, 6931, 7874
Levin, Jenifer 4418, 10262, 10297
Levin, Meyer 276, 3337, 3591, 4011, 6641, 10077, 10824
Levin, Michael 630, 1950, 2464
Levin, Sheila 6232
Levine, Faye 10975
Levinson, Deirdre 3284
Levinson, Norma 8575
Levkas Man 9170
Levy, Norman 1237
Lewes, George Henry 7285
Lewis, Alfred Henry 6618
Lewis, C. S. 104, 424, 963, 1282, 1283, 2077, 4740, 5711, 5742, 8991, 8992, 9890, 10046
Lewis, Cecil 8088
Lewis, Georgina 8435
Lewis, Janet 3421, 3837, 3976, 10477
Lewis, Matthew G. 1292
Lewis, Roy 10710
Lewis, Sinclair 19, 243, 299, 840, 1313, 2104, 2224, 2889, 2946,

2955, 4140, 4144, 4375, 4632, 5201, 6426, 7762, 9212
Lewis, Wyndham 903, 1366, 1372, 2105, 5911, 5943, 6367, 7132, 8035, 9476
Lewis Percy 4132
Lewis Rand 3559
Lewisohn, Ludwig 1390, 2142, 3103, 5280, 7377, 8778, 9068
Leyner, Mark 3623, 6170
L'Heureux, John 1217, 2527, 5472, 8935
Li, Leslie 1782
Liberated, The 2997
Liberation of Lord Byron Jones, The 2907
Liberty Lad, The 10190
Libra 9642
Licorice 8039
Lidchi, Maggi 3922
Lie Down in Darkness 5142
Lie of the Land, The 3886
Lie to Me 8382
Lies Boys Tell, The 6550
Lies of Silence 10958
Lieut. Gullivar Jones 5640
Lieutenant Hornblower 8098
Lieutenant's Lady, The 2533
Life, A 5944
Life Among the Savages 3133
Life and Death of Liam Faulds, The 5512
Life and Gabriella 7757
Life and Loves of a She-Devil, The 5233
Life and Times of Buckshot South, The 4917
Life and Times of Captain N., The 5548
Life & Times of Michael K 7077
Life at the Top 10175
Life Before Man 5290
Life Drawing (Arnold) 6701
Life Drawing (Grumley) 2116
Life During Wartime 230
Life Everlasting, The 3435
Life Force 9986
Life I Really Lived, The 9011
Life in the Iron Mills 175
Life in the Land of the Living 1747
Life in the West 10417
Life of an Actor, The 9376
Life of Byron Jaynes, The 5842
Life of Helen Alone, The 7697
Life of the Party, The 9700
"Life on the Bolotomy" 3930
"Life Sentence" (West) 5799
Life Sentences (Hailey) 8002
Lifelines 2569
Life's Lure 295
Life-Size 8834
Lifestyle 9714
Lifetime Burning, A 3718
"Lifted Veil, The" 3336
Light (Epstein) 10629

Light (Figes) 10269
Light a Penny Candle 7362
Light and the Dark, The 3800
Light Here Kindled, The 5283
Light in August 9414
Light in the Clearing, The 3822
Light in the Forest, The 974
"Light in the Piazza, The" 10374
Light in the Window, A 4564
Light of Day, The 6955
Light of the Star, The 4911
Light of Western Stars, The 1584
Light Possessed, The 8243
Light That Failed, The 4244
Light Years (Gee) 6905
Light Years (Salter) 7685
Light Years, The (Howard) 10309
Lightman, Alan 9507
Lights Across the Delaware 7197
Lights Out in the Reptile House 9831
Like China 8248
Like Men Betrayed (Mortimer) 5349
Like Men Betrayed (Raphael) 5824
"Likely Story, A" (Barker) 2736
Likely Story, A (Westlake) 5513
Lilac and Flag 4967
Lilacs out of the Dead Land 6007
Lileks, James 6475
Lilian 6495
Lilian's Story 7080
Lilies of the Field, The 5216
Lilith 6559
Lime Twig, The 3154
Limestone Tree, The 6813
Limited Partnerships 3254
Limits of Glory, The 10755
Limits of Love, The 590
Limits of the Land 5663
Limits of Vision, The 7488
Lincoln 9497
Lincoln, C. Eric 1078
Lincoln, Joseph C. 1373, 4340, 4556, 6020, 6889, 7567, 7760, 7827, 8401, 10688
Lincoln's Dreams 468
Lincoln's Mothers 4811
Lind, Jakov 1055, 2575
Lindbergh, Reeve 6741
Lindbergh's Son 627
Linden Hills 4088
Lindmann 8109
Lindner, Vicki 8528
Lindop, Audrey Erskine 1163
Line of the Sun, The 7091
Linett, Deena 4588
Lingard 2033
Lingard, Joan 4790, 4959, 5839, 6191
Linn, Merritt 2717
Linney, Romulus 5664
Lion at My Heart 8599
Lion at the Door 643
Lion Country 8521
Lion in the Stone 86

Lion of Boaz-Jachin and Jachin-Boaz, The 441
Lion of Christ, The 1691
Lion of Pescara, The 8532
Lion of the North, The 10679
Lion, the Witch and the Wardrobe, The 1282
Lion's Share, A (Steadman) 8427
Lion's Share, The (Bennett) 8174
Lionel Lincoln 7814
Lions and Shadows 5912
Lip Service 2012
Lipman, Elinor 1088, 6732
Lippard, George 2492, 7032
Lipsett, Suzanne 91, 9191, 10883
Lise Lillywhite 4567
Lish, Gordon 1941, 9368, 10460
List, Shelley 389
Listen Ruben Fontanez 1664
Listen to the Nightingale 5878
"Listener, The" 8357
Listening to Billie 9336
Listening Walls, The 1828
Listfield, Emily 5976
Little, Loyd 6381
Little, Big 10420
Little Big Man 9707
Little Bit Married, A 1994
Little Bits of Baby 1311
Little Brown Jug at Kildare, The 930
Little Caesar 5908
Little Dorrit 4367
Little Drummer Girl, The 3464
Little Girls, The 10382
Little King, The 4513
"Little Kingdom of J. Franklin Payne, The" 8202
Little Love, a Little Learning, A 248
Little Men 953
Little Men, Big World 1399
Little More Than Kin, A 8882
Little Orvie 964
Little Peg 9976
Little People, The 9817
Little Raw on Monday Mornings, A 2334
Little Red Rooster 5977
Little Shepherd of Kingdom Come, The 7289
Little Sister 8884
Little Stockade, The 7569
Little Union Scout, A 7214
Little Woman 7746
Little Women 4512
Littlefield, Bill 2004
Littlejohn, David 6376
Littlepage, Layne 2879
Litvinoff, Emanuel 1644, 1934, 8800, 9587
Live Free or Die 5008
Live from Golgotha 2817
Lively, Adam 2552
Lively, Penelope 3010, 3022, 3960, 4508, 5164, 5338, 6233, 6493, 6916, 10251

Lively Lady, The 1374
Lives and Times of Bernardo Brown, The 11000
Lives of Cleopatra and Octavia, The 6033
Lives of Girls and Women 4687
Lives of Rachel, The 1722
Lives of Riley Chance, The 6189
Lives of the Dead, The 8293
Lives of the Poets 6596
Lives of the Saints (Lemann) 10667
Lives of the Saints (Slavitt) 7543
Lives of the Twins 5238
Livesey, Margot 10632
Livia 6327
Living (Green) 1592
Living, The (Dillard) 8167
Living Alone 2665
Living and the Dead, The 3303
Living Arrows 6675
"Living at Home" 2462
Living in Ether 5500
Living in the Maniototo 2379
Living in the Present 9288
Living Is Easy, The 10358
Living Reed, The 10984
Living Upstairs 2883
Livingston, Harold 10537
Liza of Lambeth 4372
Lizzie 4589
Llewellyn, Richard 595, 660, 1231, 1607, 2625, 4582, 4660, 4704, 5286, 5646, 5650, 6433, 7317, 7494, 8187, 8415, 9151, 9175, 9560, 9582, 9940, 10002
Lloyd-Jones, Robin 9185
Locked Room, The 7118
Locke-Elliott, Sumner 1208
Lockhart, J. G. 4338
Lockridge, Ernest 6374
Lockridge, Ross Jr. 1515
Lockwood Concern, The 1853
Locos: A Comedy of Gestures 8982
Locusts Have No King, The 7952
Lodge, David 216, 692, 7402, 8498, 8615, 9432, 10612
Loewen, Paul 8160
Loewenstein, Andrea Freud 2268
Loewinsohn, Ron 451, 6030
Lofts, Norah 1852, 7182, 7630
Log of a Cowboy, The 6097
Logan, Ben 10020
Logical Girl, A 4774
Logue, John 3029
Lois the Witch 6091
Loitering with Intent 6963
Lolita 10807
Lolly Willowes 6106
London, Jack 400, 405, 406, 581, 2102, 2688, 2753, 3436, 3896, 4495, 4697, 4721, 6098, 9121, 10683
London End 6443
London Fields 9043
London Match 2517

Lone Star Ranger, The 4433
Lone Stars 9110
Lonely, The 4313
Lonely Crusade 4345
Lonely for the Future 1660
Lonely Girl, The 6437
Lonely Passion of Judith Hearne, The 6116
Lonesome Dove 459
Lonesome Traveler 2250
Long, Jeff 3909
Long Afternoon of Earth, The 7818
Long and Happy Life, A 2973
Long Day's Dying, A 7472
Long Distance 9926
Long Distance Life 3612
Long Distances 7051
Long Division 2656
Long Dream, The 3705
Long Goodbye, The 2899
Long Hot Summers of Yasha K., The 3777
Long Hunt 3097
Long Knife 2513
Long Live the King! 8348
Long Lost Journey, The 3887
Long Love, The 4999
Long March, The 1879
Long Naked Descent into Boston, The 10516
Long Pennant 4246
Long Remember 9543
Long Road Home 1080
Long Shadow, The 10666
Long Storm 10698
Long Summer Day 2842
Long Talking Bad Conditions Blues 5607
Long Time Dying, A 1456
Long View, The 3833
Long Voyage Back 4016
Long Way From Home 4876
Long Way from Verona, A 1801
Long Way Home, The 1715
Long Way to Go, A 7157
Longest Journey, The 6836
Longest Road, The 9683
Long-Haired Boy, The 8000
Longing 3524
Longleg 6166
Longstreet, Stephen 368, 548, 1627, 2767, 3394, 5747, 6779, 8439, 9784, 10853
Look at Me 5061
Look at the Harlequins! 5829
Look Away, Look Away 7038
Look Homeward, Angel 1221
Look Under the Hawthorn 1462
Looker 118
Looking Backward 782
Looking for Atlanta 4949
Looking for Bobby 5589
Looking for Leo 8451
Looking for Love 691
Looking for Mr. Goodbar 802

Looking for Work 6451
Looking Glass War, The 8605
Looking on Darkness 7970
Looking-Glass Lover, The 7448
Lookout Cartridge 880
Looks and Smiles 986
Loon Feather, The 1022
Loon Lake 6672
Loop, The 10636
Loop's End 4268
Loop's Progress 4262
Loot of Cities, The 1092
Lopate, Phillip 1746, 3393
Lord, Bette Bao 618
Lord, Gabrielle 5169
Lord Byron's Daughter 5597
Lord Elgin's Lady 4587
Lord Grizzly 586
Lord Hornblower 7513
Lord Jim 5893
Lord of the Dance 9185
Lord of the Flies 10363
Lord of the World 9405
Lord Ormont and His Aminta 5788
Lord Raingo 2825
Lord Richard's Passion 9441
Lordan, Beth 10875
Lorde, Audre 10018
Lords of Discipline, The 2858
Lords of High Decision, The 8204
Lords of Vaumartin, The 5980
Lorenz, Tom 2057
Lorenzo Bunch, The 1315
Lorna Doone 8957
Lortz, Richard 4108
Los Angeles Without a Map 5868
Los Cerritos 2014
Los Gusanos 10105
Loser, The 4068
Loser Takes All 8939
Losing Battles 8423
Loss and Gain 6609
Loss of Flight 1472
Loss of Heaven, The 8579
Lost and Found (Gloag) 5364
Lost & Found (Greene) 10908
Lost and Found (Harris) 7101
Lost and Found (Lehrer) 2009
Lost Book of Paradise, The 5549
"Lost Boy, The" 1606
Lost Boys 7566
Lost City, The 5935
Lost Colony, The 4766
Lost Ecstacy 2302
Lost Empires 3942
Lost Europeans, The 1644
Lost Father, The (Simpson) 5600
Lost Father, The (Warner) 7441
Lost Flying Boat, The 6461
Lost Get-Back Boogie, The 8696
Lost Heir, The 8644
Lost Horizon 3999
Lost Lady, A 3087
Lost Lands, The 10598
Lost Language of Cranes, The 10438

Lost Morning 1603
Lost Sister, The 2436
Lost Skiff, The 10207
Lost Sunrise 1608
Lost Time 7335
Lost Traveller, The 1626
Lost Weekend, The 901
Lost World, The (Doyle) 5900
Lost World, The (McDowell) 3031
Lot to Make Up For, A 9196
Lothair 952
Lott, Bret 3246, 7103, 7738
Lottman, Eileen 10318
Louisa Brancusi 7410
Louisiana Black 2617
Love 7040
Love Affair (Epstein) 1699
Love Affair (Leahy) 4654
Love Always 8755
Love Among the Cannibals 10810
"Love Among the Haystacks" 5131
Love Among the Ruins 3123
Love and Death in a Hot Country 1720
Love and Friendship 2146
Love and Glory 2111
Love and Mr. Lewisham 5639
Love and Money 6003
Love & Obits 9982
Love and Other Natural Disasters 2612
Love and Work (Cravens) 2483
Love and Work (Price) 1119
Love at All Ages 427
Love at Arms 650
Love at Second Sight 8769
Love Bites 3317
Love, Bones and Water 1895
Love Child 4783
Love, Dad 6856
Love Department, The 5653
Love Eaters, The 5924
Love, etc. 1984
Love Eternal 785
Love Feast 3388
Love for Lydia 2960
Love in a Dry Season 2320
Love in a Cold Climate 10556
Love in All Its Disguises 1131
Love in Idleness 9863
Love in the Days of Rage 5673
Love in the Ruins 7205
Love in the Temperate Zone 5778
Love, Infidelity and Drinking to Forget 6150
Love Is Eternal 7476
Love Is Where You Find It 7672
Love Junkie 3679
Love Knot, The 169
Love, Let Me Not Hunger 4007
Love Letters, The 8418
Love Life 862
Love Me Little, Love Me Long 10771
Love Me Tender 8014
Love Medicine 10092
Love of Elspeth Baker, The 1990
"Love of Seven Dolls" 9286

Love Passed This Way 4559
Love Pavilion, The 3152
Love Queen of the Amazon, The 4209
Love Story 2355
Love Unknown 10862
Love-Act 7173
Loved One, The 10701
Lovel the Widower 4453
Lovelace, Earl 69, 1419
Loveland 2107
Lovelock Version, The 2634
Lovely Time Was Had by All, A 3346
Lovenheim, Lisa 7579
Lover, Samuel 6018
Lover for Estelle, A 6122
Lover Next Door, The 7726
Lover of History, The 8474
Lovers (Klein) 1135
Lovers (Standún) 6599
Lovers and Strangers 3704
Lovers and Tyrants 1274
Lovers of the African Night 9638
Love's Cross-Currents 5887
Love's Mansion 5882
Love's Shadow 9327
Lovey Childs 9002
Loving 2316
Loving Attitudes 1873
Loving Cup, The 8152
Loving Daughters 2408
Loving Hands at Home 6442
Loving Little Egypt 3544
Loving Place, A 3876
Loving Roger 5634
Loving Spirit, The 8258
Loving Wife, A 211
Loving Women 4657
Lovingkindness 767
Low Company 7295
Low Tide 2667
Lowell, Susan 10952
Lowest Trees Have Tops, The 9483
Lowry, Beverly 466, 1796
Lowry, Malcolm 1669, 4729, 6068, 10711
Loyalties 6699
L-Shaped Room, The 3149
Luard, Nicholas 1537
Lucas, John 5986
Lucas, Russell 2012
Lucia in London 4225
Lucia in Wartime 10525
Lucia Triumphant 8378
Lucid Stars 534
Luck and Pluck 1681
Luck of Huemac, The 2635
Luck of the Vails, The 2196
Lucky Jim 6022
Lucky Piece, The 8375
Lucky to Be Alive? 341
Lucy 2180
Lucy Boomer 6489
Lucy Carmichael 7953
Lucy Church Amiably 8355
Lucy Gayheart 3532

Ludwig, Jack 6650
Luisa Domic 1139
Lulu Incognito 10870
Lumpkin, Grace 10648
Lunar Attractions 4688
Lurie, Alison 1724, 2120, 2146, 3179, 5219, 7318, 9435, 9690
Lurie, Morris 2243
Lusitania 8144
Lust for Life 10124
Lusts 6458
Lusty Wind for Carolina 3116
Luvaas, William 7432
Lux the Poet 3056
Lydia Bailey 5427
Lying Days, The 1100
Lying in Bed 3869
Lying Together 923
Lykiard, Alexis 2354
Lynchers, The 8748
Lyons, Paul 5990, 6943
Lyre of Orpheus, The 4020
Lysbeth 1352
Lytle, Andrew 2325, 3143
Lytton, Edward Bulwer 121, 361, 3812, 5126, 6213, 6520, 6607, 6886, 8953, 10109

*M*A*S*H* 6441
*M*A*S*H Goes to Maine* 682
MF 6393
"*M.H.*" *Meets President Harding* 1149
Maas, Peter 2176, 9246
Mabel Parker 4035
McAlmon, Robert 10687
MacArthur's Ghost 8534
Macaulay, Rose 49, 836, 1493, 1643, 3125, 6104, 8207, 8854, 10980
McAulay, Sara 3016
Macauley, Robie 8948
MacBeth, George 916, 7734, 8532
McCaig, Donald 256, 10289, 10945
McCall, Dan 1153, 3598, 3874
McCampbell's War 6084
McCandless, Anthony 10562
McCarry, Charles 2787
McCarthy, Cormac 1287, 1680, 3790, 9163, 10416
McCarthy, Dudley 7189
McCarthy, Mary 20, 749, 1920, 7526, 7816, 10656
McCauley, Stephen 1157, 7085
McCauley, Sue 1133, 10024
McClanahan, Ed 5370
McCloy, Kristin 2796
McClure, James 10872
McCluskey, John Jr. 7859
McConkey, James 2516, 2521
McConnel, Malcolm 1447
McCool, J. M. 7860
McCorkle, Jill 6305, 6861, 10298, 10912
McCormack, Eric 8473

McCormmach, Russell 8492
McCorquodale, Robin 5783, 5861
MacCoun, Catherine 36
McCoy, Maureen 1479, 2668, 5774
McCreary, Lew 7704, 11002
McCrum, Robert 7411, 9025, 10639
McCullers, Carson 1386, 2331, 3501, 3917, 6805
McCullough, Colleen 851, 1239, 3481, 7006, 8692, 10742
McCutcheon, George Barr 788, 838, 1577, 1578, 1580, 1822, 1907, 2297, 2888, 3079, 3325, 3819, 4044, 4306, 4307, 4728, 4974, 4975, 5056, 5346, 5734, 5896, 5897, 6525, 6623, 7290, 7293, 7756, 8350, 8627, 8766, 8849, 9095, 9532, 10036, 10554, 10916
McDade, Charlie 10989
McDermott, Alice 2746, 6587, 7739
McDonald, Frank 1523
MacDonald, George 6559, 6611, 10110
Mcdonald, Gregory 990, 7176, 7563
MacDonald, John D. 766, 1532
MacDonald, John Ross (pseud.). See Millar, Kenneth
McDonald, Julie 815
Macdonald, Malcolm 7048, 7689, 9655, 9022, 10630
McDonald, Roger 5585
Macdonald, Ross (pseud.). See also Millar, Kenneth 426, 589, 2986, 3005, 3296, 4316, 4321, 4580, 6503, 7309, 9754, 10058, 10218, 10804
McDonough, James 10755
McDougall, Colin 5026
MacDougall, Ruth Doan 3346, 4483, 6783
McDowell, Edwin 3031
McElroy, Joseph 688, 880, 1954, 3367, 4106, 8186, 9922
McEwan, Ian 6668, 6742, 7003, 8707, 10257
McEwen, Todd 761, 7703
McFall, Lynne 9052
McFarland, Dennis 2681
McFee, William 4565, 5019, 6368, 8075, 8089, 8587, 10788
McGahan, Andrew 635
McGahern, John 6549, 8868, 9442, 9605, 10934
McGarry, Jean 483
McGehee, Peter 2457, 2580
McGill, Gordon 2778
McGinley, Patrick 1863, 4414, 6082, 6712, 10617
McGonigle, Thomas 5341
McGrath, Eamonn 1770
McGrath, Patrick 5870, 7451, 9987
McGrath, Thomas 10628

McGuane, Thomas 279, 1783, 3253, 3318, 3423, 4250, 5107, 8436
McGuffin, The (Bowen) 10856
MacGuffin, The (Elkin) 7456
McHale, Tom 9454
Machen, Arthur 522, 2754, 6311, 8396, 9865
Machine Dreams 7426
Machlis, Joseph 10884
McIlvanney, William 7855, 10319
McIlvoy, Kevin 8240, 9976
McInerney, Jay 2013, 2749, 4329
McInerny, Ralph 3465, 6354, 7532, 7852, 9194, 10439
MacInnes, Colin 1228, 3275, 3386, 6115, 6497, 7925
McKay, Claude 8071
McKay, Deborah 10325
Mackay, Shena 5171, 8170
McKay's Bees 6935
McKenna, Richard 8108
Mackenzie, Henry 6516, 7584
McKenzie's Hundred 8234
McKnight, Reginald 1771
Mackerel Plaza, The 379
Mackintosh, Elizabeth 658, 4465, 4537, 7255
MacLachlan, Patricia 6879
McLaurin, Tim 2933, 7341
MacLaverty, Bernard 4678, 9609
McLaverty, Michael 6639, 6648, 8214
MacLean, Robert 10304
McLeave, Hugh 5512, 10418
MacLeish, Roderick 10613
MacLennan, Hugh 3807, 4072, 8034, 8995, 10151
McMahon, Thomas 3544, 6935
McManus, James 3725, 8905
MacMathúna, Seán 10763
MacMillan, Ian 4024, 8701
McMillan, Terry 6782, 10876
McMinnies, Mary 7493
McMurtry, Larry 459, 576, 2279, 3019, 3043, 5658, 5867, 6727, 7397, 8723, 8725, 10179, 10544, 10829, 10835
McNab, Tom 7858
McNamee, Thomas 9198
McNickle, D'Arcy 1406
McPherson, William 8927, 9732
McTeague 3816
McX 7703
Mad Carews, The 5310
Mad Dog 4266
Mad Grandeur 10138
"Madame de Fleury" 9855
"Madame de Treymes" 10037
Madame Sousatzka 3707
Madden, David 3714, 7998, 8227, 9365, 10203, 10378
Madden, Deirdre 4197
Madder Music 7172
Maddon's Rock 8987

Maddy's Song 6691
Made in America 9246
Madness of a Seduced Woman, The 7331
Madness of May, The 1908
Madonna of the Astrolabe, The 852
Magdalene 855
Maggie (Crane) 957
Maggie (Kennedy) 9178
Maggie - Her Marriage 2622
Maggie-Now 2834
Maggot, A 9628
Magic 9686
Magic Christian, The 9567
"Magic Flute, The" 8314
Magic Garden, The 4146
Magic Kingdom, The 4709
Magic Moment, The 8316
Magic Step, The 4628
"Magic Striptease, The" 5702
Magic Toyshop, The 7969
Magic We Do Here, The 5721
Magician, The (Maugham) 10334
Magicians, The (Priestley) 6429
Magician's Girl, The 5592
Magician's Nephew, The 8992
Magistrate, The 10017
Magnetic Field(s) 451
Magnificent Adventure, The 10038
Magnificent Ambersons, The 10553
Magnificent Obsession 7829
Magnificent Spinster, The 8494
Magnolia Gardens 3234
Magog 6810
Magus, The 6647
Mahatma and the Hare, The 5792
Mahoney, Tim 5375, 10446
Maia 8820
Maid in Waiting 2307
Maid Marian 10641
Maid of Buttermere, The 1731
Maiden, Cecil 8792
Maiden Rites 4298
Mailer, Norman 27, 4061, 5818, 7457, 8478, 9457, 10007, 10277, 10490
Maillard, Keith 6332
Main Chance, The 7826
Main Line West 584
Main Street 1140
Mainland (McCrum) 10639
Mainland (Schaeffer) 6696
Maitland, Sara 2047, 3689, 3697
Maiwa's Revenge 10332
Major, Charles 362, 698, 1220, 3074, 3965, 4459, 4513, 4719, 4888, 6812
Major, Clarence 72, 1079, 4485, 5263, 10830
Major, The 10499
Major André 6260
Make Me an Offer 587
Make-Believe Ballrooms 2520
Maker's Mark, The 1541
Making Believe 3429

Making Good Again 4663
Making History 5009
Making It 6872
Making of a Saint, The 5791
Malacia Tapestry, The 3776
Malafrena 7687
Malamud, Bernard 3035, 5465, 5836, 7474, 7849, 9571, 10219, 10614, 10708
Malcolm 8363
Malcontents, The 667
Male Child, A 8657
Male Cross-Dresser Support Group, The 5637
Malefactors, The 8479
Malenov's Revenge 6196
Malgonkar, Manohar 1930, 3771, 5715
Malign Fiesta 2105
Malliol, William 823
Mallock, William H. 8051, 9858
Mallon, Thomas 7946, 10953
Mallory, Carole 7439
Mallot Diaries, The 6076
Malone, Michael 70, 3448, 6848, 9400
Malone Dies 2324
Malouf, David 224, 1286, 4086, 6659, 9950, 10878
Maltese Falcon, The 333
Mama Day 5222
Mamaw 114
Mamba's Daughters 1593
Mambo Kings Play Songs of Love, The 9370
MAMista 8541
Man and Boy 2761
Man Could Stand Up --, A 1093
Man for the Ages, A 6101
Man from Brodney's, The 2297
Man from Glengarry, The 7651
Man from Greek and Roman, The 5828
Man from Marseille, The 1330
Man from Next Door, The 9009
Man from the North, A 958
Man Had Tall Sons, A 3835
Man in a Mirror, A 8415
Man in Lower Ten, The 6411
Man in the Brown Suit, The 2103
Man in the Glass Booth, The 8182
Man in the Gray Flannel Suit, The 5352
Man in the Iron Mask, The 6300
Man in the Saddle 4001
Man in the Window, The 2647
Man Next Door, The 8800
Man of Earth 3922
Man of Feeling, The 7584
Man of His Time, A 5095
Man of Honor, A 2494
Man of Mark, A 6248
Man of Nazareth 2043
Man of Power, A 3517
Man of Property, The 3558
Man of the People, A 6987

Man of the World, The 6516
Man Off Beat 8457
Man on the Mountain 2148
Man on the White Horse, The 8772
Man That Corrupted Hadleyburg, The 6785
Man Who Cried I Am, The 2912
Man Who Fell in Love with the Moon, The 9055
Man Who Killed the Deer, The 3765
Man Who Knew Kennedy, The 7353
Man Who Lived at the Ritz, The 5840
Man Who Lost His Wife, The 4350
Man Who Loved Cat Dancing, The 2772
Man Who Loved Children, The 7220
Man Who Made Friends with Himself, The 10359
Man Who Made the Devil Glad, The 10289
Man Who Owned Vermont, The 7738
Man Who Thought He Was Messiah, The 2278
Man Who Was Late, The 9347
Man Who Was Not with It, The 8861
Man Who Was There, The 6114
Man Who Was Thursday, The 1358
Man Whose Dreams Came True, The 10200
Man with the Chocolate Egg, The 8419
Man with the Golden Arm, The 2897
Man Within, The 10344
Man, Woman and Child 6012
Manalive 10684
Manchester, William 1404
Manchurian Candidate, The 10588
Mandala 10210
Mandel, Sally 2867, 6780
Mandelbaum Gate, The 5457
Mandragon 9604
Mandrake Root, The (Cowley) 2849
Mandrake Root, The (Ostenso) 8511
Man-Eater of Malgudi, The 7771
Manfred, Frederick 131, 586, 741, 3854, 4957, 6649, 7299, 7622, 7853, 7962, 8228, 8933, 9140, 9554, 9555, 10056, 10929
Manfroné 9402
Mangione, Jerre 244
Mangled Hands 6697
Manguel, Alberto 2730
Manhattan Transfer 8068
Manila Galleon 9076
Mankowitz, Wolf 587, 3274, 6431, 6438
Manley, Joey 5301
Manly-Hearted Woman, The 7853
Manning, Olivia 155, 982, 1633, 1694, 5714, 8685, 8865, 9916
Mannix, Daniel P. 429
Manny and Rose 8467
Mano, D. Keith 39, 308, 878, 4168, 4779, 7989, 8674
Mano Majra 4388
Manœuvring 7491

Manor, The 7184
Manrique, Jaime 7282
Man's Estate, A 377
Man's Woman, A 3681
Manservant and Maidservant 3767
Mansfield Park 5727
Mansion, The 2027
Mantee, Paul 1875
Mantel, Hilary 76
Manticore, The 2477
Mantis Carol, A 9008
Mantissa 10260
Mantrap 4375
Manual Labor 6133
Many a Green Isle 1425
Many Colored Coat, The 4641
Many Marriages 6414
Many Slippery Errors 4395
Many Things Have Happened Since He Died and Here Are the Highlights 1897
Many-Forked Branch, The 8431
Mao II 290
Maori and Settler 6929
Mapp and Lucia 4226
Maps 8496
Marathon Man 384
Marble Faun, The 3986
March, William 2506, 4119
Marching Men 9876
Marching On 7611
Marden, Hal 6846
Marechera, Dambudzo 1695
Marek, Richard 5007
Margaret 10473
Margaret in Hollywood 9401
Margins (de la Peña) 925
Margins (Kranes) 8522
Mariana 8717
Marie Beginning 7015
Marie Blythe 10431
Marie Laveau 2108
Marietta 9302
Mariette in Ecstasy 1312
Marilyn the Wild 339
Marilyn's Daughter 396
Marion Darche 5708
Marital Rites 7412
Marius, Richard 4400, 4948
Marius the Epicurean 7503
Marjorie Morningstar 7718
Mark, Jan 4897
Mark Coffin, U.S.S. 9364
Mark of the Warrior, The 3687
Markandaya, Kamala 1972, 2909, 6998, 7515, 8148
Markfield, Wallace 1254, 6652, 9833
Marking Time 8338
Markson, David 4893, 5581, 6015
Markson, Maud Carol 3613
Markus, Julia 1242, 3203, 5853, 8226
Marling Hall 3114
Marlowe, Derek 2654, 4353

Marlowe, Lara 5983
Marlowe, Stephen 4527, 4650, 5072
Marmot Drive, The 4155
Marne, The 4270
Marquand, John P. 790, 1021, 1915, 3457, 3573, 3829, 4891, 5021, 5417, 6370, 6420, 6424, 6950, 8091, 8177, 9262, 9424
Marriage 4139
Marriage Bed, The 2781
Marriage Hearse, The 5773
Marriage Machine, The 5756
Marriage of William Ashe, The 9326
Marriages Between Zones Three, Four, and Five, The 7833
Married Look, The 528
Married Man, A 5208
Married to a Stranger 7485
Marrow of Tradition, The 123
Marry Me 9174
Marryers, The 6250
Marsh, Fabienne 7051, 9088
Marsh Island, A 485
Marshall, Alexandra 8879
Marshall, Bruce 1496, 1499, 1503, 1504, 1506, 1928, 3474, 3745, 5453, 6807, 7805, 8602, 10486
Marshall, Edison 1628, 4756, 4766, 5069, 5451
Marshall, James Vance 4109, 8113
Marshall, Joyce 3704
Marshall, Paule 2484, 3115, 3355, 9168
Marshall, Tom 3810
Marshall-Andrews, Bob 326
Martha, Eric and George 1654
Martha in Paris 9910
Martha Quest 9668
Martin, David 3023, 7733, 8382, 10462, 10624
Martin, Gillian 6675
Martin, Kay 5217
Martin, Malachi 4080, 10526
Martin, Russell 4549
Martin, Valerie 6583, 7193
Martin, William 480, 1808, 5328
Martin and John 2086
Martin Chuzzlewit 359
Martin Eden 2688
Martin Rattler 951
Martineau, Harriet 5707
Martlet's Tale, The 4618
Martyred, The 10500
"Maruja" 7238
Mary 6605
Mary Anne 8551
Mary Barton 4033
Mary Dove 7632
Mary Marie 4722
Mary Midthorne 3079
Mary O'Grady 5140
Mary of Marion Isle 4977
Mary Queen of Scotland and the Isles 6383

Mary Reilly 7193
Mary Wakefield 10154
Marya 6379
Mary's Neck 9096
Marzio's Crucifix 5247
Mascara 5866
Masefield, John 2500, 4050, 4051, 7244
Mask of Apollo, The 1034
Mask of Dimitrios, The 1222
Maso, Carole 4206
Mason, A. E. W. 487, 1015, 3076, 4269, 5913, 8979
Mason, Anita 5964, 9463
Mason, Bobbie Ann 3025, 8319
Mason, F. van Wyck 242, 2147, 5428, 5628, 7187, 8122, 8591, 9076
Mason, Philip 8514
Mason, Richard 1623, 10054
Mason, Simon 2444
Massachusetts 8504
Massacre at Fall Creek, The 10940
Massie, Allan 920, 5958, 5991
Master, The 6249
Master and Commander 6226
Master and Servant 4409
Master of Ballantrae, The 9692
Master of Chaos, The 655
Master of Jalna, The 8547
"Master of the Inn, The" 3077
Master of the Return 2553
Master-Christian, The 640
Masterclass 7978
Masterpiece 9271
Master-Rogue, The 10550
Masters, Dexter 5575
Masters, Hilary 1141, 4264, 9499
Masters, John 942, 2257, 2262, 5158, 8679, 10412, 10518
Masters, Olga 1456, 2408
Masters, The 8787
Masters of Atlantis 8695
Mate in Three 9164
Mather, Berkely 8114
Mathews, Harry 6050
Mathews, John Joseph 789
Matilda 10067
Matilda, Rosa 6517
Mating 2530
Matriarch, The 4142
Matter of Conviction, A 3803
Matter of Honor, A 507
Matter of Life and Sex, A 5244
Matter of Paradise 4989
Matter of Time, A 1924
Matters of Chance 3928
Matthee, Dalene 2572, 7230
Matthew, Christopher 8000
Matthews, Greg 1457, 5506, 5977, 9344, 9823
Matthews, Jack 876, 1044, 6504, 7974, 8726
Matthiessen, Peter 774, 2252, 4956, 8104, 9150

Mattison, Alice 9984
Maturin, Charles Robert 4604
Maud Gone 7081
Maud Martha 5348
Maugham, Robin 750
Maugham, W. Somerset 897, 1094, 1249, 1590, 1605, 2140, 2197, 3112, 3437, 3471, 4372, 5425, 5791, 5794, 7347, 7912, 7965, 8175, 10334, 10355
Maundy 8724
Maura's Dream 10840
Maurice 6563
Mavericks 8273
Mavor, Elizabeth 7014
Max 813
Max Jamison 8569
Max Lakeman and the Beautiful Stranger 3616
Maximum Bob 2065
Maxwell, William 50, 8105, 9999, 10130
Maya Red 7541
Maybe 5259
Mayerson, Evelyn Wilde 2260, 2880, 5170
Maynard, Joyce 261, 4187
Maynard, Richard 9031
Mayne, William 6536
Mayor of Casterbridge, The 10331
Maze Maker, The 5458
Mazes and Monsters 2568
Mazza, Cris 7162
Me an' Shorty 2304
Me and Brenda 1152
Meadow, The 5077
Meaker, Marijane 8874
Mean Spirit 7031
Mean Time 4586
Meanwhile 7761
Measure of Time, A 1717
Meditations in Green 9678
Medoff, Mark 2812
Medusa 1751
Medusa Frequency, The 8196
Medusa's Gift 8025
Meet Me at the Morgue 5808
Meet Me in the Green Glen 7316
Meeting by the River, A 8181
Meeting Evil 5780
Meeting Point, The 6440
Meeting Rozzy Halfway 1937
Mefisto 1238
Meg 2392
Megda 6309
Meggs, Brown 4989, 8812
Mehta, Gita 6494
Melincourt 10767
Melmoth the Wanderer 4604
Melodeon, The 5481
Melville, Herman 1566, 1567, 2819, 3997, 4117, 4713, 7910, 8048, 9515, 10566
Melville Goodwin, USA 9262
Member of the Wedding, The 3501

Memento Mori 5447
Memoir of a Gambler 7144
Memoirs of a Cavalier 778
Memoirs of a Dance-Hall Romeo 2488
Memoirs of a Fox-Hunting Man 1268
Memoirs of a Midget 6312
Memoirs of a Survivor, The 3390
Memoirs of an English Officer, The 10466
Memoirs of an Ex-Prom Queen 2741
Memoirs of an Infantry Officer 2305
Memoirs of an Invisible Man 7121
Memoirs of Christopher Columbus, The 4527
Memoirs of Major Alexander Ramkins, a Highland Officer, The 10465
Memoirs of Many in One 717
Memoirs of Maria Brown 5386
Memorial, The 48
Memorial Bridge 6924
Memorial Day 1795
Memorial Service, A 7522
Memories of Amnesia 642
Memories of Another Day 1887
Memories of Rain 776
Memories of the Ford Administration 9375
Memories of the Future 1976
Memory Board 2419
Memory of Departure 3785
Memory of Old Jack, The 5945
Memory of Snow and of Dust 9044
Men 8016
Men and Angels 3724
Men and Brethren 1096
Men and the Girls, The 41
Men and Wives 82
Men at Arms 9559
Men Die 874
Men from the Bush, The 10709
Men in Trouble 3883
Men Like Gods 932
Men of Iron 7607
Men Who Loved Evelyn Cotton, The 8019
Men with Debts 9808
Menorah Men, The 9576
Men's Club, The 10842
Men's Room, The 8827
Mercedes & the House of Rainbows 5179
Mercedes of Castile 6246
Mercier and Camier 9588
Merciless Ladies, The 712
Mercy 4862
Mere Formality, A 5764
Meredith, Christopher 1753
Meredith, George 14, 927, 2290, 4432, 5127, 5392, 5788, 6558, 6613, 6976, 7708, 8040, 8642, 9874, 10113, 10773, 10781, 10900
Meredith, Isabel 9404
Merely Players 7176
Meridian 3007
Merington, Rippeth 2876

Merivales, The 5056
Meriwether, Louise 2770
Merkin, Daphne 5520
Merlin 609
Mermaid (Millar) 10846
Mermaids (Dann) 7534
Merrill, James 496
Merriman, Henry Seton 3364
Merry Month of May, The 9390
Merry-Go-Round 6746
Merry-go-round in the Sea, The 304
Merton, Thomas 10723
Merton of the Movies 5408
Merullo, Roland 3415
Meschery, Joanne 448, 8163
Mesquite Jenkins 9127
Mesquite Jenkins, Tumbleweed 6418
Message to the Planet, The 4946
Messenger, The 6292
Messer Marco Polo 6000
Messiah of Stockholm, The 8470
Metalious, Grace 10589, 10808
Metcalf, John 3862
Meteors in August 6382
Metroland 7823
Mettle of the Pasture, The 2495
Metz, Don 6922, 10447
Metzger, Deena 4857
Metzger's Dog 8819
Mewshaw, Michael 6048, 6468, 8832
Mexico 6210
Mexico Bay 7228
Mexico Days 3526
Mexico Set 3021
Meyer, Nicholas 7413
Meyers, Harold Burton 8038
Mezzanine, The 1748
Mia 9169
Micah Clarke 3490
Michael, Brother of Jerry 406
Michael Forth 786
Michael O'Halloran 9693
Michaelis, David 3756
Michaels, Leonard 5546, 10842
Michalos, Peter 6553
Michener, James A. 532, 1240, 3449, 4095, 4098, 4913, 5073, 5476, 5541, 6210, 6502, 6509, 7920, 7924, 8112, 8656, 9306, 10999
Mickelsson's Ghosts 5292
Mickle, Shelley Fraser 6747, 10991
Micou, Paul 2528, 6483
Microcosm, The 2346
Midcentury 10377
Mid-Century Men 2926
Middle Age of Mrs. Eliot, The 7817
Middle Class Education, A 9569
Middle Ground, The 3860
Middle Kingdom, The 7839
Middle of the Journey, The 1624
Middle Passage 2598
Middleman, The 2607
Middlemarch 10776

Middlepost 4859
Middleton, Haydn 625, 3886
Middleton, Stanley 1000, 2726, 9195, 9963, 10023
Midheaven 8729
Midlander, The 8208
Midnight Clear, A 7160
Midnight Cowboy 5257
Midnight Folk, The 2500
Midnight Lace 4154
Midnight Lemonade 1818
Midnight Suppers 159
Midnight Sweets 4848
Midnight's Children 811
Midwinter 7609
Midwood, Barton A. 4858
Might as Well Be Dead 9902
Mighty and Their Fall, The 8215
Migrant Souls 9716
Miguel Street 6290
Milagro Beanfield War, The 6040
Milburn, Frank 6685, 8697
Mild Route 8515
Mildred Pierce 10923
Mile High 2149
Mile Zero 7941
Miles, Richard 10721
Miles to Go 8924
Military Philosophers, The 1118
Milk and Honey 10739
Milk, Sulphate and Alby Starvation 73
Milkbottle H 2030
Mill on the Floss, The 7649
Mill Song 1559
Millar, Kenneth *See also* Macdonald, Ross 4536, 5808, 8594, 10050
Millar, Margaret 938, 1828, 1916, 2561, 2564, 2898, 2972, 3918, 3919, 5210, 5351, 8461, 10152, 10430, 10561, 10650, 10846
Millar, Martin 73, 3056
Miller, Alicia 3032
Miller, Caroline 729, 1602
Miller, Henry 291, 935, 2314, 2832, 3706, 5418, 5805, 10463
Miller, J. B. 8560
Miller, Richard 3055
Miller, Sue 42, 868, 3430
Miller of Old Church, The 9093
Miller's Dance, The 8146
Millhauser, Steven 1182, 2360, 4800, 8202, 8929
"Millionaire of Rough-and-Ready, A" 2601
Millman, Lawrence 4816
Mills, Hugh 5819
Millstein, Gilbert 6896
Millstone, The 5573
Mimic Men, The 3171
Mind and Body Shop, The 7336
Mind Parasites, The 4500
Mind to Murder, A 3518
Mind-Body Problem, The 5767
Minds 7416

Mindspell 10854
Mine Boy 9472
Mine with the Iron Door, The 6058
Miner, Robert 5691
Miner, Valerie 2082, 3017, 4363
Miniature Man, The 4964
Minister's Charge, The 7552
Minister's Wooing, The 9348
Ministry of Fear, The 6761
Minot, Steven 2744
Minot, Susan 6705, 6945
Minus, Ed 9959
Minus Man, The 7704
Minute for Murder 1621
Miracle on 34th Street 5918
Miracles (Heidish) 7785
Miracles (Hufford) 539
Miraculous Day of Amalia Gómez, The 10320
Mirage 188
Miriam at Thirty-four 2999
Miriam in Her Forties 9630
Mirror Crack'd, The 3978
Mirror for Princes, A 184
Mirror Images 10283
Mirror, Mirror 4171
Mirror of the Giant, The 5718
Mirsky, Mark 910, 5358, 5942
Mirthful Haven 7657
Misalliance, The 3320
Mischief Makers 8017
Misfortunes of Elphin, The 7795
Miss Billy 8716
Miss Bishop 1377
Miss Harriet Townshend 8413
Miss Herbert 9730
Miss Lonelyhearts 6421
Miss Lulu Bett 9664
Miss MacIntosh, My Darling 10062
Miss Mamma Aimee 10600
Miss Mapp 80
Miss Marjoribanks 8838
"*Miss Mehaffy*" 3101
Miss Morissa 9772
Miss Owen-Owen 6768
Miss Peabody's Inheritance 5504
Miss Pickthorn and Mr. Hare 4773
Miss Pinkerton 1095
Miss Pym Disposes 658
Miss Ravenel's Conversion from Secession to Loyalty 5785
Miss Seeton Sings 10907
Miss Willie 973
Missed Connections 816
Missing 2060
Missing Children 3608
Missing Person, The 6454
Missolonghi Manuscript, The 10819
Mistaken Identity 8161
Mr. America's Last Season Blues 7859
Mr. American 8139
Mr. and Mrs. Bo Jo Jones 5749
Mr. and Mrs. Haddock Abroad 3469
Mr. and Mrs. Haddock in Paris, France 1371

Mr. Armitage Isn't Back Yet 5941
Mr. Bingle 7756
Mr. Blandings Builds His Dream House 3118
Mr. Blettsworthy on Rampole Island 3563
Mr. Bone's Retreat 7016
Mr. Bridge 5099
Mr. Britling Sees It Through 6251
Mr. Crewe's Career 8970
Mr. Field's Daughter 2934
Mr. Fortune's Maggot 1495
Mr. Gallion's School 2985
Mr. Hamish Gleave 10002
Mr. Hodge and Mr. Hazard 9538
Mr. Isaacs 4443
Mister Johnson 10795
Mr. Littlejohn 5800
Mr. Love and Justice 7925
Mr. Majestyk 10076
Mister Margolies 7477
Mr. Meeson's Will 1006
Mr. Midshipman Hornblower 10704
Mr. Moto Is So Sorry 6950
Mr. Nicholas 6505
Mr. Pratt 7027
Mr. Prohack 9470
Mr. Right Is Dead 3308
Mr. Sammler's Planet 911
Mr. Scarborough's Family 8962
Mr. Scobie's Riddle 10545
Mr. Sermon 5092
Mr. Smith 1099
Mr. Standfast 9533
Mr. Stone and the Knights Companion 8179
Mr. Tasker's Gods 10919
Mr. Thistlewood 9632
Mister Touch 1774
Mr. Wakefield's Crusade 4833
Mr. White Eyes 3508
Mr. Whittle and the Morning Star 2468
Mr. Witt's Widow 4444
Misterioso 921
Mistress Masham's Repose 4153
Mistry, Rohinton 7547
Mitchell, Julian 3167, 5821
Mitchell, Ken 8323
Mitchell, Margaret 10793
Mitchell, S. Weir 3988, 6095, 6100, 6363, 6621, 8031, 8064, 8585, 9704, 9871
Mitchell, W. O. 1213
Mitchison, Naomi 541, 4147, 5020, 7715, 10116
Mitchner, Stuart 9358
Mitford, Mary Russell 6266
Mitford, Nancy 4915, 6850, 7218, 10479, 10556
Mitgang, Herbert 9247, 9756
Mittee 4347
Mixquiahuala Letters, The 9960
Mixture of Frailties, A 3938
Mo, Timothy 1053, 6147, 7698
Moby Dick 4713

Moccasin Ranch, The 6099
Mockery Bird, The 5043
Mockery in Arms 2847
Modarressi, Taghi 1958, 6014
Modern Baptists 6148
Modern Chivalry 5884
Modern Chronicle, A 4720
Modern Hero, A 1601
Modern Instance, A 1341
Modern Mephistopheles, A 8584
Modus Vivendi 3284
Moggach, Deborah 4425, 6919
Moghul, The 4417
Mohawk 2724
Moise and the World of Reason 3192
Mojtabai, A. G. 2877, 8119
Moll Cutpurse, Her True History 7958
Moll Flanders 3527
Molloy, Frances 822
"*Molly*" 2670
Moloch 10463
Molton, Stephen 1215
Mom Doth Murder Sleep 6209
Mom Kills Kids and Self 6187
Mom Meets Her Maker 8200
Momaday, N. Scott 3175, 9972
Moment in Peking 2137
Moment in the Sun, A 2747
Moments of Favor 7544
Mommy Club, The 7098
Monahan, Brent 926
Monardo, Anna 4880
Monastery, The 10090
Monday's Warriors 10535
Monette, Paul 2445, 8247
Money 9807
Money Is Love (Condon) 7576
Money Is Love (Glanville) 9438
Money Magic 1357
Money Master, The 3083
Moneyman, The 9892
Monikins, The 3456
Monk, The 1292
Monk Dawson 7888
Monkey Bay 10956
Monkey Grip 4283
Monkey King, The 1053
Monkey Wrench Gang, The 8875
Monkeys 6705
Monninger, Joseph 1866, 6706, 7548, 8618
Monsarrat, Nicholas 199, 1420, 2024, 2385, 3155, 4160, 4164, 4318, 4764, 5229, 7307, 7594, 8872, 8990, 10047, 10366
Monsieur 7266
Monsieur Beaucaire 6930
Monsignor Quixote 3446
Monsky, Susan 159
Monstre Gai 8035
Montana 1948 7460
Montauk Fault, The 9247
Monte Walsh 979
Montezuma's Daughter 10471
Montgomery, L. M. 7652

Montgomery, Marion 3651, 5661, 8305
Month in the Country, A 1703
Month of Sundays, A 1520
Month of the Falling Leaves, The 5453
Month Soon Goes, A 7222
Monumental Sculptor, The 1232
Moods 8390
Moody, Rick 7345
Moon, Bucklin 1248
Moon and Sixpence, The 5794
Moon Is a Harsh Mistress, The 7820
Moon Is Down, The 10481
Moon Lamp, The 4107
Moon of Israel 8974
Moon Palace 538
Moon Passage 4203
Moon Pinnace, The 9964
Moon Tiger 4508
Moon Under Her Feet, The 9046
Mooncranker's Gift 1045
Moondreamer 1867
Mooney, Bel 9815
Mooney, Ted 4901, 8491
Moonlight, The 4344
Moonlighter, The 10217
Moonshine Light, Moonshine Bright 8308
Moonstone, The 6035
Moorcock, Michael 89, 603, 2740, 3582, 3853, 5221, 5477, 7463, 7976
Moore, Barbara 442, 4988
Moore, Brian 1938, 4134, 5039, 6116, 7401, 8150, 8944, 9595, 9820, 10097, 10958
Moore, Elizabeth Jordan 2283
Moore, George 122, 1575, 7217, 8646
Moore, Lorrie 6302
Moore, Oscar 5244
Moore, Richard 4947
Moore, Sandra Crockett 8535
Moore, Susanna 3779, 9682, 10957
Moorland Cottage, The 3634
Morales, Alejandro 2731, 10751
Moralist of the Alphabet Streets, The 9088
More Die of Heartbreak 4665
More Innocent Time, A 669
More Than Allies 9204
More Women Than Men 9884
Morgan, Berry 149, 2981
Morgan, Charles 7246, 7587
Morgan, Clay 7054
Morgan, Lady 6385
Morgan, Seth 8024
Morgan's Passing 314
Morganstern, S. (pseud.). *See* Goldman, William
Morier, James 6405
Morley, Christopher 194, 701, 1013, 1380, 1613, 2892, 3088, 3271, 5407, 7759, 10359

Mormon Prophet, The 268
Mornin, Daniel 8448
Morning 8015
Morning After Death, The 8307
Morning and the Evening, The 1319
Morning at Jalna 3150
Morning in Antibes 10176
Morning Is Near Us, The 3108
Morning Light 7843
Morning Noon and Night 106
Morning Star 7799
Morning Tide 7915
Morning Watch, The 3516
"Morpho Eugenia" 2117
Morris, Mary 6508
Morris, Mary McGarry 6208, 9041
Morris, William 1348, 7796
Morris, Wright 593, 877, 1549, 2241, 2332, 2611, 2696, 2761, 4273, 4890, 5944, 6114, 7073, 7629, 8276, 10810, 10928
Morrison, Theodore 9450
Morrison, Toni 1711, 3182, 3236, 6273, 9602, 10889
Morrow, Bradford 8825, 8897
Mortadella 346
Mortal Antipathy, A 8964
Mortal Flesh 5946
Mortal Friends 10247
Mortal Matters 2786
Morte d'Urban 1303
Mortimer, John 2792, 3882, 5349, 6911, 6923, 9318, 10979
Mortimer, Penelope 1645, 2229, 2402, 6131, 9579, 9697, 9926, 10365
Morton, Brian 5678
Morton, Frederic 1072, 3600, 4322
Moses, Edwin 6681, 9496
Moses, Man of the Mountain 7057
Moses the Lawgiver 5831
Mosher, Howard Frank 3614, 10431
Mosley, Nicholas 220, 1209, 2593, 3372, 5654, 9236, 10389
Mosquito Coast, The 286
Mosquitoes 7982
Moss, Robert 5274
Most Likely to Succeed 7768
Most Private Intrigue, A 2737
Mother, The 3762
Mother and Son 9901
Mother and Two Daughters, A 6775
Mother Earth, Father Sky 10453
Mother Hunt, The 9912
Mother Is a Country 3519
Mother Load, The 5862
Mother London 5221
Mother Love 3028
Mother Mason 7469
Mother Night 4762
Mother of Gold 8647
Mother of Pearl 8241
Motherland 8537
Mothers (Goldreich) 5337

Mothers, The (Fisher) 10141
Mothers and Daughters 8601
Mother's Girl 3881
Mother's Kisses, A 1272
Mother's Little Helper 5114
Mother's Recompense, The 10118
Mother's Secret, A 2056
Mothersill and the Foxes 7854
Motley, Willard 83, 980, 3802
Mottram, R. H. 193, 8648
Mount Allegro 244
Mount's Mistake 11002
Mountain Europa, A 176
Mountain Lion, The 132
Mountain Man 8746
Mountain Meadow 9418
Mountain Path 7108
Mountain Road, The 6070
Mountain Time 3830
Mountains of Gilead 6222
Mountolive 6432
Mourners Below 5366
Mouse on the Moon, The 8866
Mouse That Roared, The 4062
Mouse That Saved the West, The 9452
Moviegoer, The 3840
Moving On 8725
Moving Parts 607
Moviola 3332
Mowat, Farley 5262
Mowry, Jess 4267, 9838
Mozart and the Archbooby 6242
Mphahlele, Es'kia 6324, 7143
Mrs. Appleyard's Year 10797
Mrs. 'Arris Goes to Moscow 6852
Mrs. Beneker 1511
Mrs. Blood 4776
Mrs. Bridge 4754
Mrs. Caliban 7421
Mrs. Cliff's Yacht 10782
Mrs. Craddock 897
Mrs. Dalloway 3797
Mrs. Demming and the Mythical Beast 5855
Mrs. Eckdorf in O'Neill's Hotel 4781
Mrs. Gailey 4385
Mrs. Henderson 4545
"Mrs. Maddison" 7470
Mrs. Palfrey at the Claremont 1674
Mrs. Panopoulis 8103
Mrs. Parkington 8779
Mrs. Pollifax and the Golden Triangle 4094
Mrs. Randall 5332
Mrs. Reynolds 53
Mrs. Starr Lives Alone 9921
Mrs. Stevens Hears the Mermaids Singing 10191
Mrs. Wallop 5467
M31 7210
Muckle Annie 4193
Mudlark, The 971
Muggeridge, Malcolm 10350
Muhanji, Cherry 3256
Muir, Helen 946

Muir, R. 4964

Mukherjee, Bharati 4646, 5758, 7030

Muldoon 5499

Mule on the Minaret, The 10006

Mulford, Clarence E. 410, 1582, 2304, 3643, 3644, 4046, 5907, 6418, 6948, 6952, 7616, 8549, 8852, 8853, 9127, 9309, 9310, 9311, 9312, 9744, 10920

Mulock, Dinah Maria 4970

Mulwa, David 4409

Mumbo Jumbo 1982

Mummer's Wife, A 122

Mummy 1193

Munchmeyer and Prospero on the Island 9004

Mundy, Talbot 934, 6970

Mungo's Dream 3187

Munonye, John 5188

Munro, Alice 4687

Munro, H. H. 3821, 7468

Munson, Linda Chandler 9980

Muñoz, Elías Miguel 6264

Muntz, Hope 3571

Murari, Timeri 4413

Murder at the ABA 2370

Murder by the Book 3440

Murder in the English Department 3017

Murder Is Announced, A 6353

Murder Must Advertise 3327

Murder of Aziz Khan, The 1038

Murder of Miranda, The 10561

Murder of Quality, A 7886

Murder on Clam Pond 461

Murder Song 2178

Murder with Mirrors 7473

Murderer, The 8225

Murderer Invisible, The 8404

Murderer Next Door, The 6206

Murderous McLaughlins, The 9461

Murdoch, Anna 3033, 3322, 3782

Murdoch, Iris 1552, 1806, 2471, 2652, 2698, 2871, 3744, 3941, 4706, 4782, 4946, 5474, 5752, 6844, 7156, 7933, 7954, 8801, 9573, 9596, 9728, 9927, 9930, 10204

Murfy's Men 713

Muriel at Metropolitan 1048

Murphy 8407

Murphy, Louise 4887

Murphy, Tom 1871

Murphy, Walter F. 2380, 9640

Murray, Albert 7907

Murther & Walking Spirits 6207

Muse-Echo Blues 6781

Museum Pieces 10744

Music for a Broken Piano 8881

Music for Mohini 4739

Music of Chance, The 3037

"*Music of the Spheres*" 7735

Music of the Swamp 5121

Music Programme, The 6483

Music Room, The 2681

Mutual Friend, The 2375

My America! 10254

My Amputations 4485

My Ántonia 4462

My Argument with the Gestapo 10723

My Blue-Checker Corker and Me 4084

My Boy John That Went to Sea 8113

My Brilliant Career 6588

My Brother Tom 3579

My Brother's Keeper 2321

My Cousin, My Gastroenterologist 3623

My Cousin Rachel 7181

My Dearest Friend 3036

My Death My Life 2404

My Father in Dreams 6160

My Father in the Night 9504

My Father's Geisha 6729

My Father's Moon 6725

My Fellow Devils 1318

My First Naked Lady 4932

My Friend Annie 5449

My Friend, Cousin Emmie 9431

My Friend Judas 10372

My Friend Matt and Hena the Whore 3932

My Friend, My Father 2159

My Friend Rose 5816

My Friend Sashie 5261

My Friend Says It's Bulletproof 9579

My House in Umbria 4870

My Lady Greensleeves 661

My Lady Ludlow 97

My Life and Dr. Joyce Brothers 9650

My Life as a Man 9708

My Life as a Whale 4874

My Life in Action Painting 8560

My Life in the Bush of Ghosts 6635

My Life with Darwin 924

My Life with Goya 3233

My Love, My Love 5045

My Main Mother 9485

My Mortal Enemy 5797

My Mother 5680

"*My Mother Takes a Tumble*" 6297

My Name Is Asher Lev 4788

My Old Sweetheart 3779

My Own Ground 3330

My Petition for More Space 4609

My Present Age 5295

My Romance 10460

My Search for Warren Harding 4707

My Secret History 7043

My Sister the Moon 8387

My Son Africa 9355

My Son and Foe 5023

My Son the Jock 5478

My Son's Story 5065

My Thomas 371

My Uncle Oswald 3587

Myra Breckinridge 10820

Myrer, Anton 3442, 6934, 10421

Myron 5606

Mysteries of Algiers, The 7368

Mysteries of Pittsburgh, The 6715

Mysteries of Udolpho, The 5125

Mysteries of Winterthurn 9955

Mysterious Ways 4823

Mystery of Edwin Drood, The 9207

Mystery of Metropolisville, The 7371

Mystery Ride 10461

Mystic Adventures of Roxie Stoner, The 149

Mystic Masseur, The 4466

Mystical Paths 10963

Nabokov, Vladimir 791, 2523, 5420, 5452, 5466, 5829, 7471, 7714, 9564, 10807

Nachman, Elana 2566

Nada the Lily 9522

Nadine 3229

Nagy, Gloria 1448, 7429, 8451, 9199

Nahai, Gina Barkhordar 7152

Nahal, Chaman 3278

Naipaul, Shiva 1720

Naipaul, V. S. 21, 3000, 3171, 4466, 6290, 6435, 6843, 7338, 8123, 8179

Naive and Sentimental Lover, The 2991

Najarian, Peter 5521

Naked and the Dead, The 8478

Naked Came I 6644

Naked in Garden Hills 8458

Naked Lunch, The 3050

Naked Sun, The 3305

Name for Evil, A 3143

Name of Annabel Lee, The 2403

Names, The 3395

Names of the Lost, The 9323

Names of the Mountains, The 6741

Nana's Ark 9492

Nancy Flyer, The 9770

Nanny, The 6597

Napoleon of Notting Hill, The 5693

Napoleon Symphony 9488

Narayan, R. K. 259, 3195, 3845, 4741, 4839, 4886, 6498, 6636, 7771, 9263, 9906

"*Narrow Boat, The*" 7590

Narrow Corner, The 3437

Narrow House, The 9125

Narrow Rooms 2378

Narrow Time, A 5610

Narrowing Stream, The 9318

Narrows, The 9425

Nash, N. Richard 993, 1134, 7527, 8809, 10608

Natalie Natalia 9236

Nathan, Robert 272, 416, 417, 528, 653, 665, 710, 1019, 1671, 2213, 2237, 2301, 2468, 2605, 2623, 3361, 3387, 4064, 4637, 4671, 5147, 6076, 6109, 6112, 7256, 7656, 7666, 8081, 8788, 9169, 9561, 10406, 10513

Nation Thief, The 9954

National Standard, The 10504

"*National Velvet*" 5135

Native, The 577
Native Air, The 673
Native Moment, The 10591
Native Son 10137
Natives of My Person 8126
Natural, The 7474
Natural Curiosity, A 8445
Natural History 5723
Natural Man, The 5370
Natural Order (Penner) 8621
Natural Order, The (Bentley) 9711
Natural Selection (Barthelme) 5296
Natural Selections (Nagy) 7429
Natural Shocks 6140
Natural Victims 10850
Naughton, Bill 6391
Naumoff, Lawrence 1784, 3040, 6201
Navigator, The 6933
Naylor, Gloria 3294, 4088, 4705, 5222
Naylors, The 6336
Nebraska Coast 2313
Nebula Maker 2630
Necessary Doubt 9778
Necessary End, A 2540
Nectar in a Sieve 1972
Ned Myers 5885
Nedra 1580
Needle, The 8223
Needle's Eye, The 10072
Needleman, Jacob 1459
Neider, Charles 228, 3511, 6242
Neighbor to the Sky 1604
Neighbors 2920
Neihardt, John G. 295, 3128
Nell 10284
Nellie Without Hugo 5265
Nelly's Version 4649
Nelson, Gillian 7430
Nelson, Indiana 9977
Nelson, Kent 6880, 6969
Nemerov, Howard 3671, 8863
Nemesis 4280
Neon Bible, The 7280
Neon Madonna, The 5876
Nephew, The 2971
Nero 7067
Nerve Endings 5328
Nest of Simple Folk, A 7382
Net of Jewels 4872
Nether World, The 1184
Neugeboren, Jay 1664, 4436, 5282, 6694, 9932, 10422
Never Come Morning 2829
Never Die 1279
Never Victorious, Never Defeated 7866
Never-Fail Blake 8256
New Axis 6532
New Centurions, The 7851
New Confessions, The 828
New Day 6981
"New Eden?, A" 7740
New Grub Street 7180
New History of Torments, A 4286

New Hope 2216
New Jersey 6706
New Jerusalem 6338
New Leaf Mills 1821
New Life, A 9571
New Men, The 7830
New Paul and Virginia, The 8051
"New Queens for Old" 1042
New Republic, The 9858
New Voyage Round the World, A 9508
New Year, The 1117
"New Year's Day (The 'Seventies)" 1967
New Year's Eve/1929 8421
New York Time 5763
New Yorkers, The 3177
Newby, P. H. 59, 5746, 6352, 6956, 8180, 9293
Newcomer, The 7351
Newcomes, The 719
Newlove, Donald 5771
Newman, Charles 6532, 9186, 9267
Newman, John Henry 6609
News 3180
News from a Foreign Country Came 2730
Newspaper of Claremont Street, The 1710
Newsreel 613
Newton Letter, The 7597
Next of Kin (Carroll) 2154
Next of Kin (Lange) 9798
Next of Kin (Zeitlin) 3668
Next to Nature, Art 5164
Nexus 3706
Ng, Fae Myenne 3632
Ngcobo, Lauretta 7052
Niccolò Rising 1069
Nice and the Good, The 8801
Nice Murder for Mom, A 1957
Nice Work 8498
Nicholas Cooke 2461
Nicholas Nickleby 5728
Nichols, John 5724, 6040, 7000, 9290, 10063, 10527
Nichols, Ruth 3521, 4780, 5484, 9047
Nicholson, Meredith 651, 930, 1905, 1908, 2467, 3820, 4138, 5199, 7826, 8204, 8628, 9317, 9763
Nicholson at Large 1437
Nick the Greek 9180
Nickel Mountain 5577
Nicol, Mike 5124, 8046
Nielsen, Alfred 1083
Nigger Heaven 10342
Nigger of the "Narcissus," The 8060
Night 1831
Night and Day 9350
Night and Silence, Who Is Here? 10383
Night Falls on the City 9389
Night Fishers of Antibes, The 4083
Night in Bombay 7919

Night in Cold Harbor, A 9230
Night Is a Child, The 7317
Night Journey 5569
Night Manager, The 4659
Night of Bright Stars, A 9940
Night of Camp David 5186
Night of the Aurochs 1444
Night of the Broken Glass 1814
Night of the Hunter, The 495
Night of the Weeping Women, The 6201
Night of the White Bear 8608
Night of Their Own, A 8111
Night of Wenceslas 9908
Night Over Day Over Night 397
Night Ride Home 9202
Night Rider 7249
Night Song 2905
Night Studies 3343
Night Swimmers 3003
Night Thoughts of a Classical Physicist 8492
Night Time Losing Time 2437
Night Travellers, The 481
Night Unto Night 10967
Nightclimber 2247
Night-Comers, The 198
Nighthawk Blue 1836
Nightingales Are Singing, The 10586
Nightmare Abbey 3058
"Nights at the Alexandra" 4844
Nights at the Circus 817
Nights in Aruba 2110
Nightshade 4353
Nightspawn 146
Nightwatchmen 6185
Nightwood 7056
Nightwork 8728
Nile 2163
Nile Shadows 889
Nin, Anaïs 1102, 1250, 1317, 4635, 4701, 6221, 7917, 10044, 10801
Nine Days to Mukalla 7921
Nine Months in the Life of an Old Maid 2768
Nine Tailors, The 9790
1985 3392
Nineteen Eighty-four 9473
1982, Janine 7784
1959 6167
1919 7196
98.6 8037
Ninety-Two in the Shade 279
Nirvana Blues, The 7000
Nissenson, Hugh 1066, 3330
Nissequott 10324
Nix, Shann 3633
Nixon, Cornelia 9834
No Ceiling but Heaven 8235
No Clouds of Glory 7462
No Country for Young Men 2386
"No Door" 3799
No Earthly Notion 8233
No Easy Place to Be 8705
No Enemy but Time 5170

No Face in the Mirror 10418
No Fond Return of Love 7461
No Fun on Sunday 8933
No Hero 5417
No Laughing Matter 1320
No Longer at Ease 1829
No Mate for the Magpie 822
No More into the Garden 4519
No More Parades 7758
No Name 9466
No News Is Good 6153
No Nudes Is Good Nudes 1178
No One Hears But Him 3843
No Other Life 4134
No Other Place 3219
No Place for an Angel 5187
No Place to Cry 10861
No Regrets 7499
No Resting Place 7447
No Roof but Heaven 9832
No Second Wind 6961
No Star Is Lost 8210
No Telephone to Heaven 4421
No Time for Sergeants 3684
Noah's Ark 6864
Noble Descents 3507
Nobody Does You Any Favors 7066
Nobody Knew They Were There 6183
Nobody's Angel 3318
Nobody's Fault 1692
Nobody's Fool 9203
Nocturnal Minstrel, The 6212
Nocturne 9469
Nocturnes for the King of Naples 5952
Noël, Christopher 10954
"Noise of Strangers" 2994
Nomads of the North 407
"No-Man's-Land" 6560
None But the Lonely Heart 4660
None Shall Look Back 9765
Noone, John 8419
Nop's Trials 10945
Nordan, Lewis 5121
Nordhoff, Charles 2199, 3089
Norfolk, Lawrence 5051
Norman, Howard 9369
Norman, Philip 9179
Norman Rockwell's Greatest Painting 510
Norris, Charles G. 1020, 3272, 4374, 4889, 6217, 6313, 10582
Norris, Frank 3681, 3815, 3816, 7374, 8765, 10035
Norris, Gloria 5589
Norris, Kathleen 1281, 1608, 3827, 5250, 5622, 6422, 8212, 8413, 10580
North, Elizabeth 6682, 10843
North, Sam 3260
North and South 8454
North Gladiola 4544
North of Hope 5875
North of 36 4212
North of Welfare 8516
North Star 8129

Northanger Abbey 4451
Northern Lights (O'Brien) 8487
Northern Lights, The (Norman) 9369
Northwest Passage 5421
Norwood 8670
Nostromo 1355
Not a Penny More, Not a Penny Less 3752
Not a Through Street 9801
Not a Word About Nightingales 8997
Not Honour More 9695
Not in Newbury 2940
Not in the Calendar 3160
Not in Vain 2614
Not Now but Now 9893
"Not Quite Dead Enough" 195
Not So Quiet... 8455
Not That Sort of Girl 7500
Not the End of the World 4208
Not to Disturb 1673
Not Wanted on the Voyage 6334
Not Without Laughter 8403
Not Working 6188
Note in Music, A 8631
Notebook of Gismondo Cavalletti, The 317
Nothing 3831
Nothing but Blue Skies 1783
Nothing but the Night 10163
Nothing for You, Love 946
Nothing Happens in Carmincross 9629
Nothing Like the Sun 2624
Nothing Man, The 6815
Nothing So Strange 6788
Nova, Craig 3630, 3787, 6027, 6683, 7959, 10825
Novak, Jan 4089, 6471
Novel, The 5541
"Novelette" 4566
November 347
Now and Another Time 7071
Now for the Turbulence 5844
Now, God Be Thanked 2257
Now I Lay Me Down to Sleep 10966
Now in November 5568
Now Newman Was Old 6139
Now Playing at Canterbury 7225
Now You Know 9259
Now You See Her 2583
Now You See It 9834
Nowhere 4826
Nowhere City, The 2120
Nowra, Louis 2000
Nuclear Age, The 4944
Nudists, The 7737
"No. 55" 3102
Number of the Beast, The 6674
Number of Things, A 3838
Number One 9421
Numbers 745
Nunn, Kem 1147, 4291, 9106
Nunquam 8459
Nuns and Soldiers 6844
Nutmeg Tree, The 563
Nye, Robert 609, 805, 5363, 7808

Nylon Pirates 4160
Nymph and the Lamp, The 3534

O Beautiful 352
O Beulah Land 3458
O Caledonia 833
O God of Battles 10616
O, How the Wheel Becomes It! 5507
O K*A*P*L*A*N! MY K*A*P*L*A*N! 7114
O Master Caliban! 7321
O My America! 6962
O Pioneers! 10685
O River, Remember! 10045
O Shepherd, Speak! 4636
Oak Openings, The 2619
Oakley, Ann 8827
Oasis, The 7816
Oates, Joyce Carol 25, 40, 515, 801, 1672, 1706, 1819, 1896, 2031, 2035, 2381, 2393, 2776, 3506, 3578, 5238, 5854, 6379, 6577, 7479, 7524, 7565, 8164, 9298, 9955, 10014
Oath and the Sword, The 10405
Obasan 10610
Obedient Wife, The 7328
Oberland 4606
Object Lessons 8543
Object of My Affection, The 7085
O'Brian, Patrick 6226, 6953, 8127
O'Brien, Dan 3755
O'Brien, Darcy 9015, 9401
O'Brien, Edna 893, 1831, 2509, 6044, 6437, 8220, 8898, 10172, 10390, 10599
O'Brien, Flann 5424, 6182
O'Brien, Kate 2078, 5313, 9550, 10652
O'Brien, Tim 66, 4944, 8487, 8708
"Obsession" 5496
Occasion for Loving 4538
Occasion of Sin 4355
Occupation, The 7988
O'Connor, Edwin 2472, 2510, 4386, 8998, 10185
O'Connor, Flannery 2329, 9558
O'Connor, Philip F. 1898, 5981
O'Connor, Sheila 6205
O'Connor, Varley 8248
Octavia's Hill 6331
October Blood 3479
October Ferry to Gabriola 1669
October Light 2039
October the First Is Too Late 6224
Octopus, The 8765
Odd Girl Out 9923
Odd John 702
Odd Woman, The 8485
Odd Women, The 6616
Ode to Billy Joe 4404
Odessa File, The 2251
Odor of Sanctity, An 9276
Odtaa 4051

Odyssey of a Nice Girl, The 9721
Odyssey of Kostas Volakis, The 5149
Of Age and Innocence 201
Of Desire 2442
Of Human Bondage 2197
Of Lizards and Angels 7962
Of Love and Dust 2983
Of Many Men 10485
Of Mice and Men 7659
Of Mortal Love 4615
Of One Blood 8844
Of Such Small Differences 5979
Of the Farm 2978
Of Time and the River 10042
O'Faolain, Julia 2386, 7328, 10071
O'Faolain, Sean 5488, 7382, 9139
Off for the Sweet Hereafter 3604
Office, The 1029
Office Politics 2700
Officers and Gentlemen 10494
Offshore 7870
O'Flaherty, Liam 1600, 4517, 7841, 9067, 9745, 10926
O'Grady, Timothy 8537
Oh! 10258
Oh, Money! Money! 10552
Oh, Susannah! 9616
Oh What a Paradise It Seems 9016
O'Hagan, Howard 9747
O'Hara, John 1853, 2469, 3156, 3329, 4059, 5228, 5619, 6024, 8331, 8720, 8983, 9002, 9726, 10126, 10661
O'Hehir, Diana 2596
Ohio, Denise 2465
Okpewho, Isidore 3006
Okri, Ben 6088, 9200
Old Boys, The 3297
Old Colts, The 4835
Old Curiosity Shop, The 96
Old Devils, The 5972
Old Devotions 6299
Old Dogs and Children 3259
Old English Baron, The 4554
Old English Peep Show, The 4778
Old Gentleman of the Black Stock, The 5790
Old Girl, The 5762
Old Gods Laugh, The 10718
Old Hickory 7110
Old Home Town 4054
Old Jest, The 2158
Old Ladies, The 9214
"Old Maid (The 'Fifties), The" 3561
Old Man and Me, The 4319
Old Man and the Sea, The 6428
Old Men at the Zoo, The 6499
Old Mortality 6972
Old Neighborhood, The 10517
Old Powder Man 6127
Old Pybus 492
Old Reliable, The 3126
Old Saint Paul's 7501
Old Soldier 2678
Old Soldiers Never Die 6431

Old Tom, Young Tom 4126
Old Wives' Tale, The 3357
Old World, New World 3595
Old Yeller 4747
Older Love, An 7268
Oldest Confession, The 7570
Oldest Living Confederate Widow Tells All 2433
Old-Fashioned Girl, An 9516
Oldham, Perry 3954
Oldtown Folks 5558
Olga Romanoff 4457
Oliphant, Margaret 1488, 6034, 8838, 9206, 9866
Oliphant, Mrs. *See* Oliphant, Margaret
Olive Field, The 9995
Olive of Minerva, The 7496
Oliver, Jim 5995
Oliver October 788
Oliver Twist 779
Oliver Wiswell 6423
Oliver's Story 153
Olivieri, David (pseud.). *See* Wharton, Edith
Olmstead, Robert 321
Olsen, Tillie 10238
Olshan, Joseph 2798, 4238, 5527
Olson, Toby 6795, 7562, 7699, 7942
Olympia 3677
Olympian, The 5823
O'Malley of Shanganagh 5906
Omar 4769
Omar Khayyam 9135
Omensetter's Luck 1037
Omoo 1566
On Common Ground 4588
On Distant Ground 3486
On Glory's Course 1533
On Her Own 6721
"On Ice" 6151
On Keeping Women 7129
On Mermaid Avenue 10675
On Other Days While Going Home 2870
On Strike Against God 10838
On the Beach 10161
On the Big Wind 9365
On the Black Hill 8231
On the Darkening Green 1510
On the Highest Hill 5316
"On the Mountain" 7832
On the Plantation 3418
On the Road 5811
On the Stroll 6274
On the Third Day 6279
On the Trail of the Tumbling T 8549
On the Verge 1696
On the Way Home 885
Once a Gentleman 10441
Once an Eagle 3442
Once More the Hawks 4085
Once upon a Droshky 6530
Once Upon a Time on the Banks 10631

Ondaatje, Michael 995, 4077, 10890
One 5865
One Big Bed 2130
One by One 1112
One Clear Call 8092
One Day 2241
One Day in the Afternoon of the World 1653
One Fat Englishman 5932
One Fine Day 2139
One Flew Over the Cuckoo's Nest 7984
One Generation 1838
One Hand Clapping 1973
One Hell of an Actor 2479
158-Pound Marriage, The 3277
One Hundred Times to China 7408
One Is One 6161
One Last Glimpse 6137
One Last Mirror 1275
One Man's Initiation 6216
One More River 8078
One More Spring 1019
One More Sunday 1532
One of Our Conquerors 14
One of Ours 10115
One of the Founders 8180
One of the 28th 9862
One on One 8625
"One Red Rose for Christmas" 2504
One Smart Kid 6681
One True Story of the World, The 9052
One True Thing 9344
One Way Home 6554
One White Star 3135
Ones You Do, The 2684
Onion 559
Onion Eaters, The 7315
Onionhead 3672
Only 7367
Only Children (Lurie) 5219
Only Children (Yglesias) 7089
Only Daughter, The 6539
Only Fade Away 7805
Only Problem, The 3024
Only Shorter 5367
Only Son, The 10433
Only the Best 10279
Only When I Laugh 9332
Only Yesterday (Gloag) 10287
Only Yesterday (Leahy) 3959
Open Heart 2358
Open Prison, An 6463
Open-Eyed Conspiracy, An 4371
Opening Nights 31
Operation Shylock 1159
Opie, Amelia 3548
Opie, Mrs. *See* Opie, Amelia
Opportunity of a Lifetime, The 1935
Optimist, The 975
Optimist's Daughter, The 6893
Opus 21 133
Oracle, The (O'Connor) 4386
Oracles, The (Kennedy) 9074

Oral History 5966
Orange and Green 1173
Oranges Are Not the Only Fruit 6700
Orbit of Darkness 4024
Orchard Keeper, The 9163
Orchestra and Beginners 2984
Ordeal 8456
Ordeal of Gilbert Pinfold, The 5440
Ordeal of Richard Feverel, The 5392
Orderly Life, An 1925
Orders of Chivalry 1302
Ordinary Families 1824
"Ordinary Love" 6547
Ordinary Lunacy, An 4295
Ordinary Money 2061
Ordinary People 6041
Ordinary Time 2877
Ordways, The 1410
Organ Builder, The 4898
Origin, The 8044
Origin of the Brunists, The 3338
Original Sins 3927
Orion 1091
Orlando 9839
Orlando King 2843
Orley Farm 8955
Orlock, Carol 2054
Orlovitz, Gil 2030
Ormond (Brown) 6404
Ormond (Edgeworth) 2885
Orphan, The 9309
Orphan Angel, The 8069
Orphan Island 6104
Orphans of the Sky 7111
Orphan's Tale, An 9932
Orrie's Story 2936
Orton, Joe 9585
Orwell, George 2895, 4378, 4699,
 5621, 8774, 9473, 10127, 10792
Osborn, Karen 4426
Osborn, Susan 7863
Oscar and Lucinda 1535
O'Shaughnessy, Erin 1737
Ostenso, Martha 3499, 3835, 4559,
 5310, 6219, 8406, 8511, 8515,
 9666, 10039, 10045, 10341, 10645
Other Anne Fletcher, The 6143
Other Garden, The 4681
Other Gods 6066
Other Halves 1133
Other Hand Clapping, The 5333
Other House, The 6286
Other Landscape, The 4639
Other Lips and Other Hearts 8816
Other Men's Daughters 3186
Other People 10255
Other People's Worlds 3808
Other Plans 6966
Other Room, The 1682
Other Side, The 3352
Other Side of Desire, The 1031
Other Side of the Fire, The 5666
Other Side of the Sun, The 9783
Other Voices, Other Rooms 9553
Other Woman, The (Jaffe) 252

Other Woman, The (Lesser) 3245
Other Women 8282
Other Women's Children 4900
Otherwhere 1773
Otto, Whitney 517, 2583
Ouida 2131, 2820
Our Choice of Gods 2799
Our Deal 1237
Our Exploits at West Poley 1572
Our Father (Hinde) 6026
Our Father (Rubens) 2640
Our Father's House 8439
Our Gang 6991
Our House in the Last World 5841
Our Man in Havana 7395
Our Mr. Wrenn 1313
Our Mother's House 2335
Our Mutual Friend 8050
Our Nig 2493
Our Spoons Came from Woolworths
 2076
Our Village 6266
Ouroboros, The 5243
Ourselves to Know 9726
Out 879
Out After Dark 325
Out of Danger 9191
Out of the Shelter 7402
Out of the Silent Planet 5711
"Out of the Whirlpool" 5692
Out of This World 9733
Out of Time 9506
Out of Town 4644
Outcast of the Islands, An 2015
Outcasts, The 249
Outcry, The 9094
Outer Banks 9089
Outer Mongolian, The 6816
Outerbridge Reach 10640
Out-haul, The 684
Outlaw 2434
Outlaw Games 8528
Outrider, The 7265
Outside Providence 6716
Outside the Dog Museum 2646
Outsider, The (Fast) 1529
Outsider, The (Wright) 8597
Over and Above 7525
Over My Dead Body 9888
Over the Edge 1146
Over to Candleford 6566
Overflight 228
Owens, Iris 2657, 9956
"Owl, The" 5759
Owls Do Cry 2230
Owning Jolene 513
Ox-Bow Incident, The 9547
Oxherding Tale 6457
Ozick, Cynthia 4945, 5096, 5965,
 8470
O-Zone 7208

P. S. Wilkinson 1551
P. S. Your Cat Is Dead! 62

Pacific Interlude 10848
Pacific Street 2182
Packard, Cindy 5862, 7023
Paco's Story 9033
Pagan King, The 4756
Pagan Place, A 8220
Pagan's Pilgrimage 1050
Page, Myra 9071
Page, Thomas Nelson 3637, 3638,
 5790
Paint It Today 490
Painted Bird, The 6531
Painted Devil, A 5830
Painted Dresses 4884
Painted Turtle 1079
Painted Veil, The 8175
Painter of Signs, The 3195
Painting Classes 8286
Painting on Glass 1953
Pair of Blue Eyes, A 3301
Palace of Wisdom, The 326
Palace Without Chairs 4583
Paladin, The 9674
Palais-Royal 4591
Pale Criminal, The 7582
Pale Fire 5452
Pale Moon 7621
Pale View of Hills, A 4814
Palliser, Charles 5339, 5871
Palm for Mrs. Pollifax, A 8367
Palm Latitudes 9689
Palmer, William 2806
Palm-Wine Drinkard, The 5201
Palomino 2259
Palu 2000
Pamela 4221
Panama 5107
Panic Blood 10881
Panna Maria 3209
Panter-Downes, Mollie 2139
Panther in the Sky 4682
Papa You're Crazy 845
Paper Doll 686
Paper Dragon, The 3311
Paper Men, The 6378
Paper Moon see Addie Pray
Paper Sheriff 5204
Parachutes & Kisses 10857
Parachutists, The 1524
Paradise (Barthelme) 2793
Paradise (Castedo) 6585
Paradise Bum, The 5255
Paradise Man 2052
Paradise Motel, The 8473
Paradise News 692
Paradise Postponed 2792
Paradox Players, The 5460
Paragon, The 7889
Parasites, The 4978
Pardoner's Tale, The 9676
Parent, Gail 1994, 5231, 6198
Parents and Children 9419
Parini, Jay 4546, 8169, 10993
Paris Trout 167
Parish and the Hill, The 4057

Parish of Rich Women, A 2930
Park 2308
Park, Jacquelyn Holt 7342
Parker, Gilbert 297, 3083, 5198, 7195, 7655, 8172, 9209, 9743, 10573
Parker, Michael 7549
Parker, Robert B. 2111
Parkin, Frank 6707, 7336
Parks, Gordon 4955, 7019
Parks, Tim 1761, 5113, 5634, 5775, 6735, 10455
Parlor Games 3249
Parnassus on Wheels 3271
Parnell and the Englishwoman 4023
Paro, Dreams of Passion 5510
Parotti, Phillip 7810
Parris, P. B. 10104
Parrish, Richard 2799
Parsons, G. M. T. 4228
Parsons, Rupert 1738
Part of Fortune, The 2417
Particles and Luck 3264
Partisan, The 10469
Partners of the Tide 7567
"*Party at Jack's, The*" 9221
Party Dress, The 562
Party Going 733
Pasaquina 1737
Pascarel 2131
Pasmore 10225
Pasó por Aquí 7815
Passage of Arms 2026
Passage of Hawks, A 3157
Passage Through Gehenna 7523
Passage to India, A 1369
Passenger 2633
Passing 1913
Passing Bells, The 2255
Passing On 3960
Passing Through 2713
Passion, The 1872
Passion Artist, The 5954
Passion of New Eve, The 7996
Passion Play 2482
Passionate Friends, The 3495
Passionate Journey, The 527
Passions of the Mind, The 10401
Past, The 1936
Past All Dishonor 5803
Past and Present of Solomon Sorge, The 5459
Past Is Another Country, The 1765
Past the Bleachers 5245
Pastoral 10142
Pastors and Masters 6415
Pastures of Heaven, The 7508
Patch Boys, The 4546
Patch of Blue, A 8414
Patchett, Ann 3669
Patchwork 4426
Pater, Walter 7503
Path of Dalliance 666
Path of the King, The 8851
Path to the Silent Country 9935

Pathfinder, The 4032
Pathfinders 8088
Paths of Peace 3599
Paton, Alan 5959, 7492, 9146
Patriarch, The 3590
Patric, Beth S. 8318
Patrician, The 5307
Patrick, Vincent 2714
Patriot Game, The 8372
Patriot, The (Buck) 3569
Patriot, The (Connell) 4918
Patron Saint of Liars, The 3669
Patronage 10677
Patterson, Orlando 1433, 5256
Paul Patoff 6909
Pause Between Acts 2674
Pavilion of Women 842
Pawn in Frankincense 569
Pawnbroker, The 10379
Pay the Piper 5376
Payne, David 2800, 6862
Payne, Peggy 3034
Payofski's Dyscovery 6846
Peace 9675
Peace Breaks Out 7894
Peace in Friendship Village 10917
Peace Shall Destroy Man 7887
Peaceable Kingdom, The 9101
"*Peacetime*" 1291
Peach Groves, The 5264
Peachtree Road 2428
Peachy 2582
Peacock, Thomas Love 3058, 7795, 9738, 10108, 10641, 10767, 10899
Peacock Spring, The 3980
Peacock's Tail, The 3310
Peake, Mervyn 972, 5604, 9223
Pearl (King) 4548
Pearl (Leaton) 4419
Pearl, The (Steinbeck) 10149
Pearl Lagoon, The 3089
Pearl of Orr's Island, The 9758
Pearl-Maiden 7797
Pearl's Progress 35
Pearson, T. R. 3604, 4437, 5992, 10860
Peck, Dale 2086
Peck, George W. 6614
Peck, Richard 3204, 5763, 6333, 10939
Peck, Robert Newton 471, 7278, 7495
Peck's Bad Boy 6614
Peckham's Marbles 6776
Peculiar People, The 190
Pedler, Margaret 5735
Pedlock & Sons 5747
Pedlock Inheritance, The 9784
Pedlock Saint, Pedlock Sinner 2767
Pedlocks, The 1627
"*Peep Show*" 6400
Peeping Tom 1452
Peerless Flats 3631
Peg Woffington 8453
Peggy Salté 2547

"*Pegnitz Junction, The*" 4178
Pei, Meg 4553
Peking 8289
Pelham 6607
Pelletier, Cathie 4230, 6155, 8624, 10631
Pemberton, Margaret 10944
Pembroke 1573
Pembroke Colors, The 3394
Pemmican 8517
Penelope's Hat 9824
Penelope's Man 4463
Penitent, The 9251
Penknife in My Heart, A 6178
Penman, Sharon Kay 3720, 6258, 8449, 9643
Penmarric 2522
Penner, Jonathan 152, 8621
Penny Wars, The 6355
Penrod 2497
Penrod and Sam 296
Penrod Jashber 4670
Pentagon 5046
Peony 10584
People, The 3035
People in Glass Houses 8870
People in the Picture, The 625
People in Trouble 3354
People Like Us 8640
People of the Abyss, The 6098
People of the Valley 9748
"*People to People*" 4019
People Versus Kirk 2045
People Will Always Be Kind 9238
Perchan, Robert 172
Perchan's Chorea 172
Percy, Walker 165, 3840, 7159, 7205, 7780, 9434
Perdue, Tito 8736
Peregrine Pickle 6603
Perelandra 9890
Pérez Family, The 4364
Perfect Gallows 2725
Perfect Happiness 6233
Perfect Lover, The 883
Perfect Sonya, The 466
Perfect Spy, A 1736
Perfect Timing 8201
Perfect Woman, A (Hartley) 2091
Perfect Woman, A (Slaughter) 8283
Perfectionists, The 5036
Pericles the Athenian 707
Perimeters 4482
Period of Confinement, A 6702
Perlycross 1491
Perpetual Motion 2126
Perpignon Exchange, The 831
Perrin, Ursula 6299, 7448, 7999
Perry, George Sessions 2138
Perry, Thomas 3030, 4013, 8315, 8322, 8819
Persian Boy, The 366
Persian Nights 8891
Personal Recollections of Joan of Arc 8965

Personality Surgeon, The 2616
Persuasion 4439
Peru 9368
Perutz, Kathrin 2333, 3161, 3519
Pesetsky, Bette 2066, 4848, 6964
Petals of Blood 6960
Peter Abelard 8742
Peter Doyle 3962
Peter Ibbetson 5399
Peter Nevsky and the True Story of the Russian Moon Landing 6384
Peter Pan 4232
Peterkin, Julia 3090, 7126, 10122
Peters, Daniel 2635, 5074, 7811
Peters, Joan K. 8467
Peterson, Brenda 3626
Petesch, Natalie L. M. 3777, 4622, 6713
Petrakis, Harry Mark 1439, 2165, 2244, 5149, 8599, 9180, 10633
Petrie, Glen 7190, 7644
Petrovics-Ofner, László 10534
Petry, Ann 5426, 9425, 10699
Pett, Stephen 9829
Pettibone's Law 1780
Petting Zoo, The 2382
Peveril of the Peak 6518
Peyton, Jim 10625
Peyton Place 10808
Phaedra 7175
Phantastes 10110
Phantom 7102
Phantom Blooper, The 10533
Phantom Lady 6369
Phantom of the Sacred Well 6592
Phases of Harry Moon, The 1756
Phelan, Francis 6358
Phelps, Elizabeth Stuart 4927, 7286
Phelps, Gilbert 705, 5946, 8999
Philadelphia Fire 350
Philip's Girl 3542
Philipson, Morris 2637, 3412
Phillips, Caryl 557, 4547, 4896, 8166
Phillips, David Graham 363, 2298, 3078, 3915, 6348, 6410, 10550
Phillips, Dee 10973
Phillips, Jayne Anne 7426
Philosopher's Pupil, The 4706
Philosopher's Stone, The 6227
Phineas Finn 6887
Phineas Redux 6975
Photographing Fairies 7212
Phroso 5013
"*Phyllis of the Sierras, A*" 9115
Physical Culture 1259
Physician, The 3602
Pianoplayers 8377
Pic 5657
Pícaro 2199
"*Piccadilly*" 4309
Pickwick Papers, The 5557
Picoult, Jodi 6882

Picture Makers, The 3618
Picture of Dorian Gray, The 3794
Picture Palace 9447
Picture This 509
Pictures from an Institution 7882
Pictures of Fidelman 5465
Pictures of the Journey Back 1044
Picturing Will 8499
Piece of Cake 9810
Pied Piper 4733
Piercy, Marge 860, 1951, 2682, 2921, 3538, 6690, 7482, 8278, 8370, 8828
Pierre 10566
Pietro Ghisleri 3556
Pig Iron 6313
Pigeon Pie 10479
Pigs in Heaven 10895
Pike, Christopher 2813, 10879
Pilcer, Sonia 4298
Pilgermann 4819
Pilgrim Hawk, The 5802
Pilgrim's Progress, The 2751
Pilgrim's Regress, The 963
Pilgrim's Rules of Etiquette, The 1958
Pillar of the Sky 8438
Pillow Fight, The 1420
Pilot, The 4028
Pilpel, Robert H. 5269, 7359
Pinball 9805
Pincher Martin 9319
Pinchot, Ann 2747
Pinckney, Darryl 7981
Pinckney, Josephine 1025, 2326, 5023, 10144
Pinder, Leslie Hall 9498
Pineapple Bay Hotel, The 8277
Pineda, Cecile 32, 4209, 10948
Pink Marsh 5789
Pinktoes 60
Pinocchio in Venice 9657
Pinter, Harold 3257
Pinto and Sons 5223
Pioneers, The 4027
Pious Agent, The 7224
Pipe Dream, The 4757
Piranhas, The 7343
Pirate, The 5011
Pirates of Venus 4103
"*Pistol, The*" 679
Pit, The 10035
Pitch Dark 5293
Place at the Table, A 4856
Place Called Estherville 10703
Place for Outlaws, A 5676
Place in England, A 10209
Place in Flowers Where Pollen Rests, The 2429
Place in Mind, A 998
Place in the Country, A 597
Place of Greater Safety, A 76
Place of Stone, A 5150
Place of the Lion, The 414
Place of the Swan, The 9634
Place on Earth, A (Berry) 1036

Place on Earth, A (Revised) (Berry) 1058
Place to Come To, A 2374
Place Where the Sea Remembers, A 1799
Place with Promise, A 7741
Places to Stay the Night 6172
Plagiarist, The 8321
Plague Dogs, The 5325
Plain Grief 1847
Plain Jane 5781
Plain Man, The 6500
Plain Song 2644
Plains of Abraham, The 10343
Plains Song, for Female Voices 7073
Planet of Exile 10720
Planets, The 2064
Plans for Departure 3875
Plante, David 577, 1888, 2529, 8607, 9612, 9712, 9853, 10400, 10404
Plath, Sylvia 680
"*Platinum*" 10851
Play a Lone Hand 566
Play It as It Lays 7169
Playback 10003
Player Piano 1403
Players 4648
Players and the Game, The 5826
Player's Boy, The 3700
Playground 10241
Playhouse, The 1104
Playing Catch-Up 2048
Playing Tahoe 2109
Playing the Game 1564
Playing the Mischief 10777
Playmaker, The 2574
Playroom, The 10317
Playtime is Over 4516
Please Pass the Guilt 10010
Pleasure-Dome 8227
Pledge, The 5594
Pledge of Allegiance 7906
Plexus 2832
Plot It Yourself 907
Plot That Thickened, The 1324
Plough the Sea 8663
Plowing Up a Snake 10088
Plum Bun 9129
Plumed Serpent, The 8911
Plunder 4314
Plunket, Robert 3679, 4707
Plunkett, James 6854, 8119
Plus 3367
Plutocrat, The 9065
Pnin 9564
Pocho 7259
Pocketful of Rye, A 1927
Pocock and Pitt 2356
Poet and Dancer 7178
Point Counter Point 9992
Point of No Return 9424
Pointed Roofs 9406
Points of Light 512
Poison Heart, The 2443

Poison Pen 6467
Poker Game 3971
Poland 3449
Polite Sex 3261
Pollyanna 10785
Pollyanna Grows Up 9875
Polonaise 2592
Polster, James 7339
Polyglots, The 4535
Pomona Queen 4291
Pomp and Circumstance 9229
"*Ponder Heart, The*" 5925
Ponsonby Post, The 2480
Poole, Ernest 1370, 9770
Poor Boy and a Long Way from Home 10094
Poor Cow 10395
Poor Dear Charlotte 7026
Poor Devils 2032
Poor Fellow My Country 984
"*Poor Koko*" 1325
Poor Miss Finch 8959
Poor No More 1647
Poor Things 3758
Poor Tom 5369
Poor Wise Man, A 1368
Poorboy at the Party 640
Poorhouse Fair, The 2092
Pope of Greenwich Village, The 2714
Popo 502
Popovac, Gwynn 3729
Poppa John 5665
Population of One, A 254
Pop. 1280 9264
Porgy 3379
Pork Butcher, The 10274
Pornographer, The 9605
Port of Missing Men, The 2878
Portage to San Cristóbal of A. H., The 4810
Portent, The 6611
Porter, Connie 3890
Porter, Eleanor H. 898, 4722, 8716, 9528, 9875, 10552, 10785
Porter, Jane 6801
Porter, Katherine Anne 1415
Porterhouse Blue 3851
Portion of Labor, The 9663
Portis, Charles 2664, 4169, 8670, 8695, 10994
Portnoy's Complaint 6651
Portrait in Brownstone 9289
Portrait of a Lady, The 9349
Portrait of a Marriage 5137
Portrait of a Married Woman 2867
Portrait of a Romantic 4800
Portrait of a Scoundrel 2710
Portrait of an Artist with Twenty-six Horses 8271
"*Portrait of Bascom Hawke, A*" 6496
Portrait of Jennie 4671
Portrait of My Desire, A 4879
Portrait of the Artist as a Young Man, A 961

Portrait of the Artist with My Wife 2444
Portrait of the Artist's Wife 4025
Portygee, The 8401
Poseidon Adventure, The 8118
Possessing the Secret of Joy 2459
Possession (Byatt) 922
Possession (Delbanco) 1555
Post Captain 8127
Post Office 6025
Postcards 1785
Postcards from Pinsk 3041
Postern of Fate 913
Postman Always Rings Twice, The 9541
Potato Baron, The 3615
Potatoes Are Cheaper 3750
Potok, Andrew 3233
Potok, Chaim 221, 605, 1253, 3258, 3416, 4788, 6293, 6695
Potter, Dennis 2595
Potter, Jennifer 3887, 10743
Potterism 8207
Poverman, C. E. 2782, 6160
Powell, Anthony 178, 364, 494, 753, 1118, 1921, 2841, 2951, 3048, 3276, 5415, 5507, 7191, 7713, 8523, 9231, 10649, 10930, 10933
Powell, Dawn 2893, 4274, 4642, 7952
Powell, Padgett 3286, 7898
Power, M. S. 3783
Power, The 4938
Power and Glory (Easton) 9045
Power and the Glory, The (Greene) 4379
Power and the Glory, The (Parker) 7655
Power of One, The 3453
Power-House, The 585
Powers, J. F. 996, 1303
Powers, John R. 4236, 9439, 10891
Powers, Richard 536, 1458
Powers of Charlotte, The 4201
Powers That Be, The 8046
Pownall, David 4081, 6718
Powwow Highway, The 5685
Powys, John Cowper 6001, 7916, 9412
Powys, T. F. 10919
Practice, The 1227
Prager, Emily 7237
Prairie, The 262
Prairie Child, The 6038
Prairie Mother, The 10114
Prairie Wife, The 5733
Praise 635
Praise Singer, The 8751
Praise the Human Season 3751
Praisesong for the Widow 2484
Prancing Nigger 933
Prantera, Amanda 162, 7788
Prater Violet 4735
Praxis 4181
Prayer for Fair Weather, A 452

Prayer for Owen Meany, A 7542
Prayer for the Ship, A 7304
Preacher's Boy, The 6719
Precious Bane 5681
Precious in His Sight 3660
Precious Jeopardy 3100
Precipice, The 10151
Predator, The 476
Prelude 130
Preparing for Sabbath 6295
Present and the Past, The 734
Presenting Lily Mars 9382
Preserve and Protect 7354
President, The 8667
Presidenta, La 10839
Presidential Mission 2958
President's Child, The 9951
President's Lady, The 7619
Prester John 5084
Presto! 7229
Pretty Girl, The 3485
Pretty Girls 6016
Pretty Lady, The 9378
Pretty Leslie 542
Price, Reynolds 1119, 2446, 2683, 2765, 2973, 5336, 5591, 6186, 6680
Price, Richard 3283, 4210, 7113, 8525
Price of Diamonds, The 7036
Price of Love, The 10786
Prick of Noon, The 5705
Pride 6277
Pride and Prejudice 5726
Pride and the Anguish, The 8117
Pride's Castle 2023
Pride's Fancy 3766
Pride's Harvest 9737
Priest, Christopher 883, 1276, 2707, 4789, 4809, 6448, 10725
Priest, The 7852
Priestley, J. B. 298, 1609, 1629, 2145, 2699, 3846, 3942, 4312, 4644, 6060, 6429, 6443, 8073, 8572, 9232, 9723, 10904
Primadonna, The 8738
Primal Yoke, The 1648
Prime Minister, The 4442
Prime of Miss Jean Brodie, The 977
Primitive, The 10929
Primitive People 7792
Prince, The 1164
Prince and the Page, The 3894
Prince and the Pauper, The 781
Prince and the Tobacco Lords, The 10543
Prince Caspian 1283
Prince Elmo's Fire 6374
Prince of Darkness & Co., The 7517
Prince of Graustark, The 1822
Prince of India, The 8057
Prince of Peace 29
Prince of Tides, The 4090
Prince Ombra 10613
Prince Otto 5396

Princes, The 5715
Princess Bride, The 914
Princess Casamassima, The 9861
"Princess, the Dwarf, and the Dungeon, The" 1182
Principia Martindale 5967
Pringle, Terry 5118, 6719, 7452
Printer of Malgudi, The 6498
Prison Notebooks of Ricardo Flores Magón, The 6344
Prisoner of Grace 5432
Prisoner of Zenda, The 4972
Prisoner's Base 3132
Prisoner's Dilemma 536
Prisoners of Twilight 3788
Prisoner's Wife, The 6329
Prisons 848
Pritchett, V. S. 9996
Private Accounts 3487
Private Acts 1477
Private Life, A 2264
Private Life of Axie Reed, The 9035
Private Memoirs and Confessions of a Justified Sinner, The 3551
Private Papers 5519
Private Woods 8535
Private Worlds 6008
Private Wound, The 5461
Privates 1143
Privy Seal 8346
Prized Possessions 4207
Prizzi's Family 1068
Prizzi's Glory 1073
Prizzi's Honor 10664
Proceed, Sergeant Lamb 1162
Proceedings of the Rabble 5358
Prodigal Child, A 3212
Prodigal Daughter, The 7075
Prodigal Parents, The 2955
Prodigal Women, The 4150
Professor, The 1903
Professor of Desire, The 7727
Professor Romeo 3333
Professor's Daughter, The 4174
Professor's House, The 6105
Proffitt, Nicholas 1166, 5688, 8539
Progress of a Crime, The 7571
Project, The 1203
Prokosch, Frederic 983, 2119, 4105, 5315, 7133, 7308, 7770, 7921, 8033, 9546, 10816, 10819
Prologue to Love (Ostenso) 3499
Prologue to Love, A (Caldwell) 8722
Promenade 6386
Promise, The (Buck) 4607
Promise, The (Potok) 1253
Promise of Joy, The 6997
Promise of Light, The 3791
Promise the Earth 10522
Promisekeeper, The 9267
Promises of Alice, The 1367
Promising Career, A (Brown) 8815
"Promising Career, A" (Gellhorn) 1658
Pronto 7963

Proof of the Pudding, The 8628
"Proofs" 6600
Proper Marriage, A 10364
Property Of 6573
Propheteers, The 9819
Proprietor, The 4820
Prose, Francine 2108, 3970, 5522, 7792, 9395
Proselytizer, The 7989
Prospect 2004
Prospects Are Pleasing, The 8660
Proteus 4920
Protocol, The 6593
Proud and the Free, The 7388
Proud Flesh 3583
Proud Monster 8701
Proud Sheriff, The 6062
Proulx, E. Annie 1785, 9719
Provenance 1523
Providence (Brookner) 4812
Providence (Wolff) 6469
Providence Island 1854
Provincial Lady in America, The 1914
Provincial Lady in London, The 5416
Provincial Lady in Wartime, The 2532
Proving Flight, The 1409
Provost, The 9260
Prudence Palfrey 1490
Pryce-Jones, David 3543
Psyche 6553
Public Burning, The 5207
Public Image, The 5322
Pudd'nhead Wilson 1319
Puffball 2780
"Pull of the Earth, The" 456
Pumpkin Eater, The 9697
Puppet Masters, The 5000
Purdy, James 1533, 2378, 2971, 3363, 5359, 5366, 5659, 8363, 9166, 9307, 9399
Puritan, The 1600
Purple Land, The 5561
Purple Parasol, The 5346
Purple Plain, The 730
Pursued by the Crooked Man 6202
Pursuit 2981
Pursuit of Happiness, The 5542
Pursuit of Love, The 6850
Pursuit of the House-Boat, The 2016
Pursuit of the Prodigal 4234
Put Out More Flags 9420
Put Yourself in His Place 1005
Putting on the Ritz 4712
Puzo, Mario 119, 4570, 5205, 5950, 7627, 8153
Pyle, Howard 6561, 7607, 9520
Pylon 2690
Pym, Barbara 1104, 1501, 2272, 2868, 3426, 7390, 7461, 9353, 9455, 10419, 10805, 10836, 10865
Pynchon, Thomas 2839, 8807, 10310, 10559
Pyramid, The 7312
Pyrates, The 3396
Pyx, The 2970

Q (pseud.). See Quiller-Couch, Arthur
Quade Inheritance, The 3248
Quake 10227
Quality of Mercy, The 10032
Quarantine 9603
Quartet 7568
Quartet in Autumn 3426
Quartzsite Trip, The 7893
Quednau, Marion 3607
Queen Bee 9453
Queen Cleopatra 934
Queen Dolley 2055
Queen Emma of the South Seas 8808
Queen Lear 7745
Queen Lucia 10337
Queen of a Distant Country, The 2655
Queen of Hearts (McCall) 3874
Queen of Hearts (Shreve) 7082
Queen of October, The 10991
Queen of Sheba, The 6928
Queen of Swords 7022
Queen of the Damned, The 3545
Queenie 1273
Queer 5848
Quentin Durward 6244
Question of Guilt, A 3863
Question of Power, A 5703
Question of Upbringing, A 10930
"Quick, The" 6281
Quick and the Dead, The 7536
Quicksand 8353
Quiet American, The 9330
Quiet End of Evening, The 5040
Quiet Life, A 9334
Quiller-Couch, Arthur 3680, 5397, 6308, 8254
Quill's Window 8350
Quimby 3238
Quin, Ann 5624, 6321
Quincunx, The 5871
Quindlen, Anna 8543
Quinn's Book 10871
Quintesse 7598
Quinx 9627
Quisanté 2822
Quite the Other Way 6726
Quitting Time 4504

Raban, Jonathan 2273
Rabbi, The 10188
Rabbi of Lud, The 5178
Rabbi's Wife, The 2038
Rabbit at Rest 2447
Rabbit Is Rich 9451
Rabbit Redux 1041
Rabbit, Run 8913
Rabble in Arms 10478
Rabe, David 518
Race of Scorpions 8620
Race Rock 9150
Racers to the Sun 9776
Rachel Ray 10772
Rachel, the Rabbi's Wife 67

Rachlin, Nahid 7485
Racket, The 9463
Radcliffe, Ann 1171, 1293, 5125
Radcliffe, Mary-Anne 9402
Raddall, Thomas H. 1640, 3534,
    3766, 4248, 4390, 4561, 5034,
    8264
Radiance 1134
Radiant Way, The 3350
Radical Surgery 9833
Raditzer 8104
Radley, Paul John 4084, 8813
Rag Doll Plagues, The 2731
Rag Woman, Rich Woman 7083
Rage in Harlem, A 3743
Rage of the Vulture, The 3721
Rage to Live, A 2469
Ragged Dick 10112
Ragged Way People Fall Out of Love,
    The 2007
Raging of the Sea, The 30
Ragtime 3191
Raider, The 10409
Railway Station Man, The 10911
Rain and the Fire and the Will of God,
    The 2967
Rainbow and the Rose, The 202
Rainbow Roun Mah Shoulder 9359
Rainbow, The (Buck) 849
Rainbow, The (Lawrence) 3082
Rainbow Walkers 2169
Rains Came, The 2209
Raintree County 4515
Rainy Day Man 5373
Raker, The 6319
Raleigh's Eden 2214
Rally Round the Flag, Boys! 8993
Ralstons, The 6523
Rambling Rose 4176
Ramgobin, Mewa 4362
Rami, Sonia 5996
Ramona 3636
Ramrod 9767
Ramsey Milholland 8739
Rancho of the Little Loves, The 2623
Rand, Ayn 4750, 5422, 6387, 8509
Randall and the River of Time 8653
Random Harvest 1201
Raney 1995
Ranthorpe 7285
Rao, Raja 1381, 3164
Rap, The 2123
Rape of Tamar, The 7868
Rape of the Rose, The 3731
Raphael, Frederic 590, 1326, 1981,
    2984, 2996, 3401, 5699, 5824,
    6152, 8109, 9933
Rapoport, Nessa 6295
Rappaport 2243
Raptor 5545
Rare Earth 2049
Rash Act, The 2204
Rasselas 4603
Rat Man of Paris 9189
Rat on Fire, The 68

Rates of Exchange 1308
Rathbone, Irene 3825
Ratner's Star 9594
Raucher, Herman 4404, 5037
Raven, Simon 1206, 1646, 3746,
    7572, 8677
"Ravenswing, The" 4304
Ravi Lancers, The 8679
Raving Wind 10266
Raw Material 601
Raw Silk 6537
Rawlings, Marjorie Kinnan 726,
    1186, 2205, 3763, 4384
Ray 6673
Raymo, Chet 636, 2645
Rayner, Richard 5868, 8027
Razor's Edge, The 5425
Reaching Tin River 6241
Read, Piers Paul 1519, 2592, 3414,
    3503, 3931, 4174, 5208, 6279,
    7888, 10391, 10520
Reade, Charles 484, 1005, 1337,
    1489, 3552, 3635, 4454, 4630,
    4926, 8453, 8837, 8839, 10771
Reading Turgenev 3891
Ready to Catch Him Should He Fall
    6874
Real Cool Killers, The 8744
Real Estate 3241
Real Illusions 7897
Real Life 6154
Real Life Diary of a Boomtown Girl,
    The 10752
Real Life of Sebastian Knight, The 791
Real People 3179
Real Presence 1445
Real World, The 5234
Realms of Gold, The 438
Reasons of the Heart 2416
Rebecca 2755
Rebel Angels, The 1708
Rebel Powers 9061
Rebels 8580
Recapitulation 9181
Recent History 6829
Recent Martyr, A 6583
Recess, The 2287
Rechy, John 396, 745, 3478,
    7723, 10320, 10726
Recital of the Dog 518
Reckless Eyeballing 6827
Reckoning, A (Sarton) 10414
Reckoning, The (Penman) 8449
Recognitions, The 6765
Recombinations 1065
Reconciliations 158
Recovery 2726
Re-Creation of Brian Kent, The 5795
Rector, The 1488
Rector of Justin, The 2537
Red and the Green, The 9728
Red Anger 2567
Red Ashes 5735
Red Badge of Courage, The 10472
Red Barbarian 3868

Red Box, The 9886
Red City, The 8064
Red Earth, White Earth 1948
Red Eve 10474
Red Harvest 10901
Red Lamp, The 6349
Red Likker 1912
Red Men, The 6712
Red Pony, The 2220
Red Priest, The 903
Red Republic, The 4973
Red Rock 3638
Red Rover, The 4029
Red Sky at Morning 3847
Red Threads 3295
Red Truck, The 2420
Red Whiskey Blues 6724
Red White and Blue, The 1744
Redback 9034
Redburn 4117
Redemption 4528
Redemption of Elsdon Bird, The 1893
Redgauntlet 9990
Red-Haired Bitch, The 598
Redmon, Anne 5528
Redon, Joel 3963, 10448, 10635
Redskins, The 9514
Reed, Ishmael 280, 1982, 3172,
    5480, 6013, 6827, 8735
Reed, Kit 4202, 6670
Reed, Paul 3524
Reef, The 44
Reeman, Douglas 4410, 4415,
    5071, 5172, 7304, 7781, 8117,
    8121, 8128, 8131, 8274, 8280,
    9785, 9791, 10407, 10719
Reeve, Clara 4554
Reeves, Rosser 502
Refinements of Love 7707
Reflections in a Golden Eye 6805
Reflex and Bone Structure 10830
Refugees, The 2686
Refugio, They Named You Wrong 10546
Regeneration 8709
Regent, The 2496
Regiment of Women 10229
Regina 9393
Reich, Tova 2553
Reid, Victor Stafford 6179, 6981
Reign of Law, The 3639
Reilly, Robert 5331
Reincarnation of Peter Proud, The 1683
Reinhart in Love 8665
Reinhart's Women 1865
Reivers, The 5931
Relations 9446
Relative Distances 3334
Relatives 10404
Remains of the Day, The 7234
Rembrandt 4760
Remember Jack Hoxie 4008
Remember Me (Lipsett) 10883
Remember Me (Weldon) 8462
Remember Santiago 1076
Remember This 2728

Remembering 5611
Remembrance Day 3046
Renault, Mary 57, 366, 731, 1034, 2636, 7766, 8751, 9227, 9417, 9477, 10205, 10594
Rendell, Ruth 1084, 2418, 4992
Rendezvous in Haiti, A 8699
Rendezvous - South Atlantic 9785
Renegade 8778
Renek, Morris 10950
Renifleur's Daughter 2415
Renny's Daughter 3127
Repent in Haste 8091
Repent, Lanny Merkel 10844
Replacing Dad 6747
Replay, The 1856
Report on Probability A 10601
Representing Super Doll 10939
Republic of Love, The 6743
Requiem for a Nun 1400
Rescue, The 5018
Reservations Recommended 7583
Resistance 8493
Resonating Bodies 8759
"Rest of Life, The" 9659
Rest of Our Lives, The 9398
Restoration 5985
Resurrection, The 1187
Resuscitation of a Hanged Man 1778
"Retread" 4293
Return Journey 2982
Return of a Fighter 3649
Return of Ansel Gibbs, The 6984
Return of H*Y*M*A*N K*A*P*L*A*N, The 794
Return of Jeeves, The 1101
Return of Lanny Budd, The 6838
Return of Mr. Hollywood, The 506
Return of the Goddess, The 1876
Return of the Indian, The 7049
Return of the King, The 8269
Return of the Native, The 2189
Return of the Sphinx 4072
Return to Jalna 4562
Return to Night 731
Return to Peyton Place 10589
Return to Thebes 6450
Reuben 5978
Reuben, Reuben 5934
Revelation (Payne) 3034
Revelations (Burnham) 9201
Revenge for Love, The 7132
Reverberator, The 6522
Reversible Santa Claus, A 9763
Revisiting Empty Houses 2795
Revolution and Roses 59
Revolution of Little Girls, The 328
Revolutionary Road 9387
Revolutionary Woman, A 2128
Revolving Lights 9213
Reynolds, Clay 1460, 4420, 7646
Rezánov 3514
Rhine Journey 9610
Rhine Maidens 7972
Rhinehart, Luke 4016

Rhoda Fleming 4432
Rhodes, Eugene Manlove 415, 5899, 6062, 6564, 7815
Rhys, Jean 61, 6108, 7383, 7568, 7765
Ricci, Nino 633
Rice, Anne 92, 2804, 3545, 9058, 9444, 10028
Rice, Linda Lightsey 5122
Rice, Luanne 231, 1482, 4110, 9464, 9656
Riceyman Steps 10338
Rich in Love 5593
Rich Like Us 10565
Rich Man, Poor Man 8675
Rich Pay Late, The 3746
Rich Rewards 7971
Richard A. 7419
Richard Carvel 3531
Richards, Caroline 9797
Richard's Feet 7838
Richard's Things 2996
Richardson, Dorothy M. 1298, 3302, 4606, 6102, 6270, 7245, 8507, 8850, 9213, 9406, 9409, 9878
Richardson, Ethel Florence Lindesay 10784
Richardson, Henry Handel (pseud.). *See* Richardson, Ethel Florence Lindesay
Richardson, Jack 7144
Richardson, John 9205
Richardson, Samuel 4221, 7825, 9509
Richer Dust, A 6786
Richer Than All His Tribe 8872
Riches and Fame and the Pleasures of Sense 4351
Richler, Mordecai 772, 2508, 2987, 8460, 9449, 10935
Richmond, Grace S. 3761
Richter, Conrad 543, 974, 2735, 3673, 4165, 4572, 4734, 5644, 6814, 10155, 10354, 10357, 10969
Ricochet River 5010
Riddle of Genesis County, The 5442
Riddley Walker 857
Ride a Cockhorse 8026
Ride the Man Down 7250
Ride with Me 9768
Ride with Me, Mariah Montana 6875
"Rider of the High Mesa, A" 7625
Riders in the Chariot 10812
Riders of Judgment 7622
Riders of the Purple Sage 8768
Ridge of Gold 1557
Riding in Cars with Boys 3039
Riding the Dolphin 689
Rienzi 8953
Right Bitch, The 10892
Right by My Side 1004
Right of Way, The 5198
Right Thing to Do, The 2426
Right to an Answer, The 8996

Right to Die, A 9913
Rim of the Prairie, The 9328
Rimrock 1638
Rinehart, Mary Roberts 128, 564, 1095, 1247, 1368, 2018, 2302, 2470, 3094, 3496, 4564, 4930, 5566, 6288, 6349, 6411, 6947, 7291, 8348, 8629, 9122, 10129, 10800
Ring of Endless Light, A 3949
Ring of Truth, The 6638
Ringan Gilhaize 7500
Ringarra 4832
Ringed Castle, The 4172
Ringer (Slavitt) 4327
Ringer (Terry) 4112
Riotous Assembly 1430
Ripoff, The 8822
Ripple from the Storm, A 4004
Rise of David Levinsky, The 1246
Rise of Gerry Logan, The 5001
Rise of Life on Earth, The 7565
Rise of Mr. Warde, The 4427
Rise of Silas Lapham, The 5786
Rising, The 1289
Rising Like the Tucson 8711
Rising of the Moon, The (Ellis) 8237
Rising of the Moon, The (Martin) 1808
Rising Sun 3292
Rising Tide, The (Deland) 7240
Rising Tide, The (Keane) 4498
"Risi's Wife, The" 4422
Risk Pool, The 322
Risks 3958
Rites of Passage 2545
Ritter, Margaret 154, 2777, 4921, 9388
Ritual in the Dark 10375
Rituals 10988
Riven Realm, The 8556
River, The 7663
River and the Wilderness, The 275
River in Winter, The 6902
River Journey, The 7666
River Line, The 7587
River Road 2422
River Song 2114
River Sutra, A 6494
River Why, The 7078
Riverfinger Women 2566
Riverman, The 7653
River's End, The 5904
Rivers of Darkness 6574
Rivers of Eros, The 3805
Riverside Villas Murder, The 7358
Rivet in Grandfather's Neck, The 3378
Rivington Street 7001
Road from the Monument, The 6436
Road Grows Strange, The 84
Road of Ages 6109
Road to Avalon, The 8443
Road to Lichfield, The 3010
Road to Many a Wonder, The 1686
Road to Wellville, The 8298

Road to Wigan Pier, The 8774
Road to Zena, The 3963
Roads of Earth, The 5062
Roanoke Hundred 2222
Roaring Queen, The 5943
Rob Roy 5556
Robber, The 4382
Robber Bride, The 9060
Robber Bridegroom, The 4560
Robbins, Harold 1120, 1526, 1625, 1887, 3726, 4620, 6900, 7343, 9846, 10972
Robbins, Susan Pepper 6554
Robbins, Tom 2372, 2609, 7790, 9679, 10083
Robe, The 4233
Robert and Arabella 7645
Robert Elsmere 9742
Robert the Bruce 383
Roberts, Cecil 5251
Roberts, Elizabeth Madox 2311, 6218, 10353
Roberts, Kenneth 1374, 1410, 5421, 5427, 6423, 8079, 9694, 10478
Robertson, Don 112, 275, 3751, 3788, 7340
Robertson, E. Arnot 1824
Robertson, Mary Elsie 8434, 10749, 10977
Robins, Elizabeth 9873
Robinson 5027
Robinson, Derek 5720, 8678, 9810
Robinson, Frank M. 4938
Robinson, Jill 5608, 10408
Robinson, Kathleen 6551
Robinson, Margaret A. 1952
Robinson, Marilynne 9710
Robinson, Rony 6870
Robinson Crusoe 6601
Robison, James 4849
Robison, Mary 10258
Robots of Dawn, The 4416
Rocannon's World 6792
Rochelle 7680
Rochlin, Doris 173, 4111
Rock 136
Rock, Phillip 2255, 3015, 7323
Rock and the River, The 8209
Rock Cried Out, The 10415
Rock Wagram 5698
Rockland, Michael Aaron 6546
Roderick Hudson 9857
Rodman, Howard A. 8582
Rogan, Barbara 3627, 4188, 6472
Roger Sudden 4561
Rogers, Jane 4301
Rogers, Lettie 5141
Rogers, Paul T. 7533
Roger's Version 4357
Rogue Herries 724
Rogue Justice 2397
Rogue's Harbor 8110
Roiphe, Anne 767, 2656, 5542
Rolbein, Seth 1809

Rolfe, Frederick William 3683
Roll of Thunder, Hear My Cry 10078
Roll River 9415
Roll-Call, The 3326
Rolt, Francis 7434
Roman 1735
Roman Blood 5993
Roman Marriage, A 4578
Roman Singer, A 8963
Roman Spring of Mrs. Stone, The 2225
Roman Wall 8329
Romance of a Plain Man, The 9063
Romance of Rosy Ridge, The 9098
Romance of Two Worlds, A 8477
Romantic, The 10305
Romantic Comedians, The 5736
Romany Rye, The 9739
Rome Haul 9128
Romelle 2758
Romeo in Moon Village 7293
Romola 4034
Ron 6231
Ronalds, Mary Teresa 7067
Ronan, Frank 8019
Rooke, Daphne 2028, 4347, 5446, 5456, 6122, 6632, 8791
Rooke, Leon 4204
Rookwood 3984
Room, The 2122
Room at the Top 1642
Room Temperature 3888
Room Upstairs, The (Dickens) 9165
Room Upstairs, The (Levinson) 8575
Room with a View, A 7755
Rootie Kazootie 3040
Roots 804
Roots of Bondage 8132
Rope of Gold 7764
Roper, Robert 3526, 9835
Rosa (Sharp) 4401
"*Rosa*" (Ozick) 4945
Rosalie 3965
Rosalind Passes 2153
Rosalynde's Lovers 7608
Rosamund's Vision 9358
Rosca, Ninotchka 2118
"*Rose*" 6826
Rose, Daniel Asa 8013
Rose and the Key, The 5305
Rose and the Ring, The 1902
Rose and the Yew Tree, The 9891
Rose for Ana María, A 151
Rose for Marianne, A 135
Rose in Bloom 4906
Rose in the Ring, The 7290
Rose of Dutcher's Coolly 8843
Rose of Tibet, The 7720
Rose of Yesterday, A 4118
Rose Reason 1815
Rose Theatre 467
Rosemary's Baby 3170
Rosen, Gerald 819
Rosen, Norma 8500
Rosenberg, David 5549
Rosenblatt, Paul 1762

Rosenblum, Helen Faye 8376
Rosenbluth, Sally 4285
Rosenfeld, Alvin 6514
Rosenheim, Andrew 232
Rosenthal, Chuck 34, 4262, 4268
Rosenthal, Lucy 6460
Rose's Last Summer 2898
Rosie 10852
Ross, Glen 8416
Rossi, Agnes 6281
Rossiter, Sarah 626
Rossner, Judith 802, 2768, 4186, 4240, 4278, 5833, 6897, 10826
Rosten, Leo 204, 794, 2737, 5489, 6011, 7114
Rosten, Norman 1131, 3176
Rosy Is My Relative 7478
Roth, Henry 8080
Roth, Henry H. 5595
Roth, Philip 166, 250, 600, 1159, 3051, 4791, 5538, 5837, 6651, 6686, 6991, 7727, 9708, 10563
Rough Strife 2524
Rough-Hewn 962
Roughneck 2962
Round the Bend 196
Rounds 2384
Round-Up, The 6948
Rover, The 8066
Roxana 6089
Roxy 954
Royal Flash 4468
Royal Gentleman, A 7752
Ruan 8330
Ruark, Robert 1647, 2833, 4396
Rub of the Green, The 8930
Rubber Band, The 6351
Rubens, Bernice 2480, 2640, 3575, 3707, 4833, 5470, 5490, 6296, 8614, 9164, 9294, 10206, 10831
Rubicon Beach 1734
"*Ruby*" 10691
Ruby Red 214
Rubyfruit Jungle 799
Rudder Grange 5343
Rude Awakening, A 5288
Rudner, Lawrence 5721
Rudnick, Paul 1739, 3734
Rug Merchant, The 1746
Ruggles of Red Gap 2823
Rule, Jane 1929, 2419, 3314, 4942, 7819, 10833
Rule Brittania 10222
Rulers of Kings 4928
Rules of Attraction, The 8012
"*Rules of Life, The*" 2174
Rules of the Knife Fight 7578
Rum Punch 6586
Rumaker, Michael 302
Rumbin Galleries 7164
Rummage Shop, The 4436
Rumor Has It 4994
Rumours of Rain 4961
Run Man Run 2908

Run of the Country, The 8710
Run River 8796
Run Silent, Run Deep 4745
Runagates Club, The 4435
Runaway 8976
Runaway Soul, The 10314
Runner in the Sun 1406
Runner Mack 6589
Running 7327
Running Dog 6818
Running Proud 7594
Running Time 7600
Running to Paradise 2423
Running West 2797
Rupert of Hentzau 5082
Rush, Norman 2530
Rushdie, Salman 811, 2127, 4202, 8232
Rushes 3478
Rushing, Jane Gilmore 4258, 7531, 7632
Russ, Joanna 365, 803, 2855, 10838
Russell, Paul 1001
Russell, William Clark 8055
Russia House, The 7904
Russian Interpreter, The 3920
Russo, Richard 322, 2724, 9203
Rust, Marina 10676
Rustlers' Valley 410
Ruth 1335
Rutherfurd, Edward 3400
Ryan, William 10290
Ryder 7507

S. 9644
S. S. San Pedro 8074
Sabatini, Rafael 650, 3084, 5183
Sabbatical 9614
Sabotage 5859
Sabre Squadron, The 7572
Sacajawea of the Shoshones 10140
Sackville-West, V. 102, 5414
Sacred and Profane 544
Sacred and Profane Love Machine, The 9927
Sacred Fount, The 6754
Sacred Hoop, The 612
Sacred Hunger 6834
Sacred Monster 9501
Sacrifice, The 9562
Sad Variety, The 676
Saddest Summer of Samuel S, The 3166
Saddle and Ride 10694
Saddle by Starlight 7620
Sadler's Birthday 10244
Sadness of Witches, The 9460
Sadoff, Ira 6298
Safe Conduct 7751
Safe Houses 5969
Safe Passage 10301
Safekeeping (Mcdonald) 990
Safekeeping (Heckler) 8818
Saginaw Paul Bunyan, The 4464
Sahgal, Nayantara 3875, 6434,

7481, 8161, 9574, 9847, 10565
Saigon 8147
Saigon, Illinois 4847
Sailing 3431
Sailing Out, The 815
Sailor Song 2810
Saint, H. F. 7121
St. Aubin de Terán, Lisa 1715, 5173, 6876, 6920
Saint Hiroshima 9717
St. Ives 1161
Saint Jack 711
St. Leon 237
Saint Maybe 6306
St. Ronan's Well 6245
St. Urbain's Horseman 8460
Saints and Scholars 7151
Saint's Progress 2134
Saki (pseud.). *See* Munro, H. H.
Salamanca, J. R. 5048
Salamander, The 2364
Salaryman 4553
Salazar Blinks 168
Salem Chapel 9206
Salinger, J. D. 9706
Salisbury, Ray 2269, 9360
Sally Hemings 9939
Salt (Gold) 5652
Salt (Norris) 3272
Salt Line, The 6824
"*Salt of the Earth, The*" 2953
Salt Point, The 1001
Salter, James 7685
Salvage 8183
Salzman, Mark 561
Sam Bass 2789
Sam Holman 7363
Sam Houston 7314
Samantha at Coney Island and a Thousand Other Islands 5017
Samantha at the St. Louis Exposition 637
Same Blood 6479
Same River Twice, The 8143
Sams in a Dry Season 5535
Samuel Drummond 7292
Sanchez, Thomas 7941
Sanctuary (Faulkner) 2890
"*Sanctuary*" (Wharton) 10995
Sanctuary V 10065
Sand, Froma 9355
Sand Pebbles, The 8108
Sandcastle, The 3744
Sandel 10905
Sanders, Joan 8816
Sanders, Scott R. 7025
Sanditon 2943
Sandlin, Tim 644, 1810, 8760
Sandmouth 1892
Sandoz, Mari 1382, 2606, 7221, 7665, 8598, 9772, 10373
Sanity Matinee, The 6473
Sansom, William 1105, 5450
Sant' Ilario 486
Santayana, George 6289

Santiago and the Drinking Party 7054
Santmyer, Helen Hooven 3095, 4595, 7242, 9250
Saperstein, Alan 8, 6187
Sapia, Yvonne V. 9505
Sapphira and the Slave Girl 3828
Sapphire, The 8979
Sara Will 10435
Saraband 10575
Saracen Blade, The 1176
Saracinesca 1343
Sarah 4199
Sarah Canary 10458
Sarah Phillips 3541
Saraswattee 5704
Saratoga Swimmer 9320
Saratoga Trunk 6314
Sard Harker 4050
Sardines 9014
Saroyan, Aram 10305
Saroyan, William 422, 845, 968, 1653, 4672, 4736, 5698, 8365
Sarsen Place 1435
Sarton, May 107, 425, 2095, 2319, 3119, 3685, 4569, 4773, 5024, 5596, 5765, 8494, 9572, 10191, 10411, 10414, 10716
Sartoris 2303
Sarum 3400
Sassafras 7974
Sassafrass, Cypress & Indigo 10847
Sassoon, Siegfried 1268, 2305, 4616
Satan 9019
Satan and Cardinal Campbell 1506
Satanic Verses, The 2427
Satanstoe 265
Sati 10879
Satterthwait, Walter 8544
Saturday Night and Sunday Morning 2901
Saturn Over the Water 10904
"*Satyr Shall Cry, The*" 9699
Sauce for the Goose 1235
Saudi 9687
Saul's Book 7533
Savage 8689
Savage, Elizabeth 63, 1554, 4801, 7130, 8635
Savage, Georgia 1562, 8020
Savage, Thomas 1468, 7896
Savanna 4161
Save Me, Joe Louis 2618
Savic, Sally 6871
Saville 9795
Saving Grace 3627
Saving St. Germ 4026
Saviors, The 9192
Savory, Teo 9176
Saw 7357
Say Goodbye to Sam 10738
Say These Names (Remember Them) 4822
Say You Want Me 3240
Sayer, Paul 4613

Sayers, Dorothy L. 3327, 3798, 5740, 6173, 6416, 7107, 7376, 8259, 9790, 10119, 10555
Sayers, Valerie 2677, 4289
Sayles, John 10105
Saylor, Steven 5993, 5997
Sayonara 8656
Scales of Gold 6345
Scandal 4821
Scandalous Risks 2597
Scapegoat, The (du Maurier) 10370
Scapegoat, The (Settle) 6676
Scar Lover 7603
Scaramouche 5183
Scarbrough, George 10623
Scarlet Letter, The 3985
Scarlet Mansion, The 989
Scarlet Plague, The 9121
Scarlet Plume 741
Scarlet Sister Mary 7126
Scarlett Greene 10102
Scarperer, The 3968
Scary Kisses 10303
Scenes from Later Life 90
Scenes from Married Life 8304
Scenes from Metropolitan Life 2716
Scenes from Provincial Life 7880
Scent of the Gods, The 329
Scented Gardens for the Blind 8364
Schaefer, Jack 979, 2505, 5713, 8273, 9750
Schaeffer, Susan Fromberg 2544, 3664, 5755, 5772, 6657, 6696, 7040, 7331, 10897
Scheme of Things, The 4624
Schine, Cathleen 5298, 6687
Schinto, Jeanne 6552
Schirmer Inheritance, The 7803
Schlee, Ann 4820, 9610
Schmidt, Michael 10263
Schmitt, Gladys 420, 4760
Schindler's List 1714
Schofield, Susan Clark 10546
School Book, The 10987
School for Hope 8214
School for Pagan Lovers 7459
Schoolgirl Murder Case, The 10239
Schor, Sandra 9345
Schott, Max 9830
Schreiner, Olive 8391
Schulberg, Budd 313, 967, 1407, 2896, 10049, 10065
Schulman, Helen 9506
Schulman, Sarah 2050, 3354, 9374
Schultz 8636
Schultz, James Willard 4245
Schwamm, Ellen 5668, 9337
Schwartz, Lynne Sharon 2524, 6145, 7174, 9048
Schwerin, Doris 2169, 4408
Scissor Man, The 7044
Scofield, Sandra 4431, 6873, 6944, 9204
Scoop 5423
Scorpio Rising 1331

Scorpion God, The 8424
Scorpion in the Fire 3009
Scotswoman, The 8213
Scott, Carolyn 2277
Scott, Evelyn 7913, 9125
Scott, Joanna 5272, 8734
Scott, John A. 1754
Scott, Mary 2940
Scott, Natalie Anderson 7569
Scott, Paul 740, 2339, 2373, 3152, 3687, 5152, 5822, 6446, 8657, 10180, 10514
Scott, Sir Walter 2087, 2088, 2466, 3432, 3893, 5011, 5556, 6244, 6245, 6518, 6802, 6884, 6908, 6972, 7179, 7606, 7794, 7948, 8951, 8952, 9465, 9511, 9513, 9660, 9990, 10329, 10467, 10898
Scottish Chiefs, The 6801
Scott-King's Modern Europe 6427
Scout, The 10470
Screenplay 814
Scudders, The 8975
Scumbler 3222
Sea and the Stars, The 5627
Sea Beggars, The 4991
Sea Change, The (Howard) 9287
Sea Changes (Kotlowitz) 10622
Sea Lady, The 2733
Sea Level 7053
Sea Lions, The 267
Sea of Grass, The 6814
Sea of the Ravens, The 4669
Sea Runners, The 8145
Sea, the Sea, The 7933
Sea Within, The 4887
Sea Wolf, The 581
Seaborn, Captain Adam (pseud.). *See* Symmes, John Cleves
Sea-Grape Tree, A 4647
Seagull on the Step, The 10806
Sea-Hawk, The 3084
Seals, David 5685, 9059
Sealy, I. Allan 323
Search, The 3470
Search Sweet Country 8379
Searching for Caleb 9597
Searoad 7945
Season for War 3348
Season in Purgatory 9931
Season in the West, A 3414
Season of Delight, A 5365
Season of Mists, A (Tracy) 10004
Season of Mists, A (Woodhouse) 5372
Season of Passage, The 2813
Season of Peace, A 7427
Season of the Jew 8698
Season of the Owl 3014
Season of the Stranger, The 10705
Season of the Strangler 7418
Season of the Witch, The 6653
Season of Yellow Leaf 7640
Seasons' Difference, The 3130
Season's End 3547

Seats of the Mighty, The 8172
Seaview 7562
Seawell, Molly Elliot 3557
Sebastian 10974
Second Bridegroom, The 4868
Second Bridge, The 3878
Second Brother 5374
Second Chances 10627
Second Coming, The 7159
Second Confession, The 7767
Second Curtain, The 5923
Second Dune, The 7931
Second Ending 7769
Second Fiddle 6238
Second Foundation 7804
Second Generation (Fast) 8135
Second Generation (Williams) 9160
Second Greatest Story Ever Told, The 7097
Second Heaven 1712
Second Home, A 3502
Second Inheritance, The 8043
Second Marriage 3218
Second Mrs. Whitberg, The 9243
Second Season 8618
Second Sight (Redmon) 5528
Second Sight (Tannen) 2487
Second Skin 5355
Second Son 3243
Second Son of Heaven, The 832
Second Stone, The 142
Second Time Round 10182
Second Victory, The 2969
Secondary Attachments 8469
Second-Class Citizen 2774
Second-Hand Life, A 2348
Seconds 1650
Secret Agent, The 1010
Secret Annie Oakley, The 1060
Secret Anniversaries 7748
Secret Glass, The 2915
Secret Glory, The 522
Secret Harmonies 4021
Secret History, The 78
Secret History of Time to Come, A 8948
Secret Isaac 8750
Secret Life, A 7430
Secret Lives (Chamberlain) 4902
Secret Lives (Egremont) 3252
Secret of Santa Vittoria, The 9001
Secret of the Marshbanks, The 1281
Secret Pilgrim, The 1816
Secret Places 6144
Secret Understandings 2637
Secret Words 6745
Secrets 3183
Secrets of Harry Bright, The 227
Secrets of Paris 9464
Sedges, John (pseud.). *See* Buck, Pearl S.
Seduction, The 1749
Seduction by Light 2430
Seduction of the Minotaur 4701
Seductions of Natalie Bach, The 7432
See, Carolyn 5009, 6867, 7972

See the Old Lady Decently 5479
See You in Yasukuni 10507
Seebohm, Caroline 1740
Seed and the Sower, The 7591
Seeds of Anger 9637
Seeman, Ernest 4180
Seese, June Akers 2881, 10880
Segal, Erich 153, 1218, 2355, 6012, 6830
Segal, Lore 2615
Seide, Michael 4471
"Seize the Day" 56
Selby, Hubert Jr. 2122, 5625, 7995
Selena 4182
Self Condemned 9476
Self-Control 6555
Self-Portrait of Someone Else 4854
Selling Out 226
Selvon, Samuel 2239, 9752
Senator North 9868
Send a Fax to the Kasbah 9314
Sennett, Richard 4591, 5232, 6235
Sensationist, The 5339
Sense and Sensibility 3549
Sense of Honor, A 8814
Sense of Shadow, A 2546
Sense of the Past, The 5085
Sense of Values, A 10173
Sensible Life, A 7943
Sent for You Yesterday 2788
Sentence of Life, A 6320
"Sentimental Education, A" 10014
Sentimental Journey 9510
Señor Vivo and the Coca Lord 7979
Separate Checks 9321
Separate Development, A 614
Separate Hours 7177
Separate Peace, A 7883
September Faces 6156
September September 3391
Septimius Felton 6557
Seraglio, The 496
Seraph on the Suwanee 1394
Serenissima 5297
Sergeant Lamb's America 8985
Serious Living 2057
Serote, Mongane 3206
Serpent 220
Serpent Amongst the Lilies, The 3353
Serpent and the Staff, The 10165
Servant's Tale, A 2570
Set for Life 6598
Set on Edge 3575
Set This House on Fire 9155
Seth, Vikram 5523, 6748
Seth's Brother's Wife 3555
Seton, Cynthia Propper 2264, 3201
Setting Free the Bears 3848
Setting the World on Fire 4895
Settle, Mary Lee 848, 3458, 4239, 5924, 6080, 6676, 8303, 8609, 9491, 10291, 10811
Settled in Chambers 8184
Settlers, The 10824
Settling the Score 630

Seven Ages, The 8335
Seven Men of Gascony 6316
Seven Rivers West 4691
Seven Seasons 10215
Seven Sisters, The 4105
Seven Who Fled, The 9546
Seventeen 9407
17 Morton Street 9051
Seventh Avenue 8798
Seventh Babe, The 8919
Seventh Game, The 7857
Seventh Heaven 775
Seventh Stone, The 10887
Several Perceptions 7039
Severed Head, A 7954
Severed Wasp, A 1306
Sex and Rage 4802
Sex and Sunsets 1810
Sexing the Cherry 4860
Sexton, Linda Gray 512, 1477, 10283, 10988
Sexus 5805
Shaara, Michael 181, 4658, 7633
Shabby Genteel Story, A 10768
Shacochis, Bob 5052
Shadbolt, Maurice 1678, 2634, 8698, 9000, 10535
Shade of Difference, A 6986
Shadow Catcher 9315
Shadow Flies, The 49
Shadow from Ladakh 10192
Shadow Knows, The 4882
Shadow Line, The (Conrad) 10996
Shadow Line, The (Furman) 7856
Shadow Lines, The (Ghosh) 6159
Shadow Master, The 3299
Shadow of a Tiger 6839
Shadow of a Man 2319
Shadow of a Sun 3158
Shadow of My Brother 6373
Shadow of the Earth, The 8497
Shadow of the Long Knives 3899
Shadow of the Torturer, The 7017
Shadow on Summer, A 5629
"Shadow Partisan" 8706
Shadow Play 777
Shadow World, The 8626
Shadows on Our Skin 2541
Shadows on the Rock 7658
Shady Grove 1512
Shainberg, Lawrence 642
Shaitan 1446
Shake Down the Stars 2748
Shalimar 8148
Shallows 4087
Shaman 7281
Shame 8232
Shame the Devil 9799
Shane 9750
Shange, Ntozake 10621, 10847
Shankman, Sarah 8471
Shannon 7019
Shannon's Way 5088
Shape of Illusion, The 499
Shapes of Sleep, The 9232

Shapiro, Anna 10892
Shapiro, Jane 5880
Shapiro, Lionel 1637
Shardik 3904
Share of Honor 9971
Sharp, Margery 150, 563, 1180, 1654, 3109, 3120, 3122, 4401, 4567, 5145, 5319, 5354, 5750, 6021, 6654, 9423, 9910, 10053
Sharp, Paula 5239
Sharpe, Tom 1430, 3397, 3851, 4518, 6043
Shaving of Shagpat, The 8040
"Shavings" 4340
Shaw, George Bernard 1596, 7878, 10780
Shaw, Irwin 309, 382, 1233, 1550, 2542, 2785, 8596, 8675, 8727, 9474, 10259
Shaw, Robert 3165, 4389, 4540, 8182, 9075
Shawno 10021
She 3489
She and Allan 10757
She and I 10318
She Drove Without Stopping 6204
She Needed Me 5879
She's Come Undone 9373
Sheard, Sarah 4834
Shears, Sarah 4990
Sheed, Wilfrid 1804, 2700, 2974, 5529, 7310, 8569, 9230, 9569
Sheehan, Edward R. F. 5383
Shelby, Graham 3772, 3775, 5159, 10084, 10405, 10541
Sheldon, Dyan 4522, 4874, 10990
Shelley, Mary Wollstonecraft 4101, 4533, 6605, 7008
Shelter 3510
Sheltered Life, The 7948
Sheltered Lives 8697
Sheltering Sky, The 10153
Shem, Samuel 5270, 6396
Shepard, Jim 686, 9831, 10976
Shepard, Lucius 230
Shepherd, The 1563
Shepherd Avenue 6359
Shepherd of the Hills, The 8969
Sher, Antony 4859, 10321
Sherbrookes 4584
Sherburne, James 436, 1679, 7520, 10094
Sheriff of Nottingham, The 7812
Sherrods, The 8766
Sherry 2888
Sherston's Progress 4616
Sherwood, Frances 7123
Shield of the Valiant, The 2219
Shield of Three Lions 10272
Shields, Carol 2872, 3344, 6743
Shields, David 1453, 8894
Shifts 1753
Shikasta 10941
Shiloh 10585
Shimoni's Lover 10297

Shine Hawk 7440
Shine On, Bright and Dangerous Object 2368
Ship Must Die, A 4410
Ship of Fools 1415
Ship of the Line 7349
Ship to Shore 8089
Shipping News, The 9719
Shipway, George 2350, 3199, 3903, 9674
Shirley 1484
Shockproof Sydney Skate 8874
Shoeless Joe 8923
Shoes of the Fisherman, The 1509
Shooting Party, The 7872
Shooting Star, A 7200
Shootist, The 7635
Shores of Paradise, The 10673
Short, Luke 566, 1223, 1387, 1548, 1638, 2215, 2900, 3419, 3441, 3768, 5204, 7250, 7257, 7265, 7620, 7636, 7667, 8867, 9766, 9767, 9920, 10069, 10693
Short Dance in the Sun, A 2873
Short History of the Long Ball, A 8932
Short History of a Small Place, A 10860
Short List 7007
Short of Glory 1943
Short Reign of Pippin IV, The 3140
Short Time to Live, A 5583
Short Walk, A 3857
Short-Timers, The 8687
Shosha 9709
Shoulders 622
Show Boat 4727
Show Business 2750
Shower of Summer Days, A 4569
Show-Piece, The 6890
Shrake, Edwin 8806, 10626
Shrapnel Academy, The 7901
Shreve, Anita 185, 2067
Shreve, Susan Richards 3665, 6863, 7082
Shrewsdale Exit, The 2992
Shrimp and the Anemone, The 9998
Shrine at Altamira, The 1217
Shrinking 5483
Shriver, Lionel 189, 945, 7027
Shroud for a Nightingale 10216
Shrouded Walls, The 8219
Shulman, Alix Kates 2741, 5776, 6274, 10837
Shulman, Max 2217, 3750, 7884, 8993
Shute, Jenefer 8834
Shute, Nevil 196, 197, 202, 2961, 3153, 4733, 5433, 5804, 7772, 8456, 10142, 10161
Shuttle, Penelope 5718
Shuttlecock 859
Siamese Harem Life 6247
Sicilian, The 8153
Siddons, Anne Rivers 2428, 3403, 3732, 6819, 8835, 9089, 9729
Sidhwa, Bapsi 3373, 4602, 5998

Sidney, Philip 7370
Siege, The 2093
Siege of Krishnapur, The 4075
Siege of the Seven Suitors, The 3820
Siege of the Villa Lipp, The 3008
Siesta 10576
Sigal, Clancy 497, 1690
Sigh for a Strange Land 2902
Sightings 5672
Sign of Four, The 3047
Sign of Jonah, The 9148
Sign of the Eighties, A 6198
Signal Thirty-Two 8654
Signed with Their Honour 10581
Silas Bradford's Boy 1373
Silas Marner 5886
Silber, Joan 7274
Silence in the Garden, The 4550
Silence of Desire, A 7515
Silence of History, The 4763
Silence of Snakes, The 10618
Silent Gondoliers, The 8754
Silent Partner, The 7286
Silent Sea 219
Silent Song 617
Silent Speaker, The 3738
Silk Road 514
Silken Net, The 9102
Silko, Leslie Marmon 8561, 9445
Silky! 5489
Sillitoe, Alan 601, 912, 976, 1046, 1835, 2097, 2901, 4235, 5692, 6461, 7260, 7747, 8115, 8683, 10386
Silman, Roberta 2573, 3546
Silmarillion, The 2632
Silver 2675
Silver Bough, The 334
Silver Chair, The 2077
Silver Chalice, The 10557
Silver Desert, The 2952
Silver Light 869
Silver Rock 7257
Silver Rose 10089
Silver Spoon, The 9537
Silver Spooner, The 9015
Silver Wedding 9462
Silvis, Randall 6847
Simmons, Charles 3279, 5530
Simmons, Diane 9985
Simms, William Gilmore 720, 4030, 6803, 6973, 10469, 10470
Simon Dale 5562
Simon Says 9388
Simple Gifts 6083
Simple Honorable Man, A 3673
Simple Truth, The (Hardwick) 9226
Simple Truths (Levin) 6232
Simpleton, A 484
Simpson, Mona 1845, 5600
Simpson, Thomas William 4969, 6946
Sin 10888
Since Daisy Creek 1213
Sincerely, Willis Wayde 4891

Sinclair, Andrew 1203, 5255, 6319, 6390, 6810, 8661, 10372
Sinclair, Clive 1763, 8495
Sinclair, Harold 8568
Sinclair, Jo 3137, 9570
Sinclair, Marjorie 5022
Sinclair, May 1361
Sinclair, Upton 1098, 1365, 1414, 1877, 2958, 3146, 3472, 3936, 4636, 4732, 4937, 6079, 6838, 8092, 8550, 8719, 9760
Sing Out the Glory 5439
Singapore Grip, The 1443
Singer, Brett 2382, 9397
Singer, Isaac Bashevis 145, 7184, 9042, 9251, 9709, 10224
Singh, Khushwant 4388, 10497
Singh, Kit Puran 5704
Singing Sands, The 7255
"Single Heart, The" 3382
Single Man, A 10184
Single Pebble, A 6430
Singletusk 6704
Singmaster, Elsie 5616, 8349
Singular Man, A 4276
Sinjohn, John (pseud.). *See* Galsworthy, John
Sinner's Congregation, The 3864
Sins of Omission 7365
Sins of the Father, The 5991
Sioux, The 2094
'Sippi 5097
Sir Andrew Wylie 9703
Sir Henry 9561
Sir Michael and Sir George 2699
Sir Nigel 8395
Sirens 9829
Sirens of Titan, The 5253
Sirian Experiments, The 5497
Sirius 2502
"Sis and Bud" 8250
Sissie 206
Sisson, C. H. 2342
Sister Carrie 9525
Sister Hollywood 9825
Sister Wolf 2258
Sisters by a River 7059
Sisters by Rite 6191
Sitting Pretty 6042
Six Miles to Roadside Business 10452
Six Months with an Older Woman 1323
Six Out Seven 9838
Sixkiller Chronicles, The 10740
Sixth Column 10488
Sixth Heaven, The 8211
Sixth of June, The 1637
Sixth Seal, The 1121
Sixty Seconds 6903
Skaters' Waltz, The 9179
Skating in the Dark 6734
Skating Party, The 7690
Skeletons 5362
Skin Chairs, The 6123
Skinny Legs and All 7790
Skull Beneath the Skin, The 6028

Sky and the Forest, The 177
Sky Changes, The 5748
Sky Pilot, The 6056
Slade's Glacier 8142
"Slain By the Doones" 4041
Slammer 10410
Slanting Light, A 1922
Slapstick 2253
Slaughter, Carolyn 855, 944, 4189, 8283, 9446, 9615, 10091
Slaughter Informer, The 1027
Slaughterhouse-Five 10508
Slave (Malliol) 823
Slave, The (Amadi) 9177
Slave Girl, The 1049
Slave Trade 2711
Slavitt, David R. 110, 168, 1128, 1463, 1790, 2351, 2997, 3712, 4179, 4327, 4405, 5602, 5951, 6816, 7543, 7680, 8873
Sleath, Eleanor 6212
Sleep Has His House 10802
Sleep of Reason, The 4539
Sleeping Beauties (Moore) 9682
Sleeping Beauty (Macdonald) 4580
Sleeping Beauty, The (Taylor) 3937
Sleeping Dogs 8322
Sleeping Dogs Lie 3861
Sleeping Fires 5130
Sleepless Moon, The 10653
Sleepless Nights 5582
Sleepwalker 37
Sleepwalking 2400
Slesinger, Tess 3975
Slicing Edge of Death, The 2185
Slides 10400
Slight Lapse, A 7092
Sligo, John 6584, 7275, 7740
Slipping-Down Life, A 10821
Slipstream (McDonald) 5585
Slipstream, The (Cochrane) 3213
Slipway, The 746
Sliver 7874
Slouching Towards Kalamazoo 4446
Slow Dancing 8007
Slow Fade 1137
Slow Motion Riot 560
Slow Natives, The 2029
Slow Poison 95
Slow Suicide, A 5989
Smack Goodness 6343
Small, David 3789, 6845, 6902
Small Changes 7482
Small Game 4265
Small House at Allington, The 3063
Small Rain 9592
Small Room, The 9572
Small Tales of a Town 6831
Small Town (Wilson) 10080
Small Town, A (Hearon) 3873
Small Town Girls 4241
Small Town in Germany, A 2246
Small Victories 8505
Small World 8615
Smart Hearts in the City 77

Smart Women 573
Smash 1234
Smedley, Agnes 7914
Smile, Honey 7465
Smiles on Washington Square 9029
Smiley, Jane 2125, 3661, 3666, 3757, 6547, 7414, 10866
Smiley's People 3444
Smith 7510
Smith, Betty 1388, 2834, 9147, 9233
Smith, C. W. 3870, 9648
Smith, Charles 871, 3628, 10960
Smith, Charlie 4543, 7440, 8293
Smith, Dinitia 2728, 10085
Smith, Emma 1935
Smith, Gregory Blake 2051, 6833
Smith, H. Allen 4785
Smith, Helen Zenna 8455
Smith, Iain Crichton 2399, 9253
Smith, J. P. 1330, 2284, 6237
Smith, Kay Nolte 5123, 10854
Smith, Lee 1730, 4531, 4579, 4850, 4962, 5966
Smith, Mark 1685, 1837, 2607, 2977, 4107, 5586, 10278
Smith, Mary-Ann Tirone 2878, 6049, 6360
Smith, Mitchell 1169, 2458
Smith, Patrick D. 9811
Smith, Peter J. 2520, 7900
Smith, Rita Pratt 6728
Smith, Rosamond (pseud.). *See* Oates, Joyce Carol
Smith, Rukshana 10665
Smith, Vincent 444
Smith and Jones 4764
Smith's Gazelle 8275
Smoke Bellew 4721
Smoke Street 10278
Smokehouse Jam 6381
Smollett, Tobias 4490, 5193, 5387, 6603, 7284, 9989
Smoodin, Roberta 5329, 6720, 7229
Smugglers, The 10413
Smuggler's Bible, A 4106
Snail 3055
Snake Game, The 4667
Snake Pit, The 10000
Snakes 679
Snap 4424
Snapper, The 7094
Snare, The 6771
Sneaky People 1047
Snooty Baronet 5911
Snow 4418
Snow, C. P. 4, 667, 1655, 3470, 3764, 3800, 4411, 4539, 4571, 4952, 5202, 6323, 7830, 8633, 8787
Snow Ball, The (Brophy) 1651
Snow Ball, The (Gurney) 2112
Snow Gods 4322
Snow Walker, The 5262
Snow White 10817

Snowy 6783
So Big 4725
So Far from Heaven 4253
So Help Me God! 7730
So Little Time 3829
So Long, Daddy 5961
So Long, Princess 71
So Love Returns 5147
So Red the Rose 2310
So the Wind Won't Blow It All Away 2395
So Well Remembered 10143
Social Disease 1739
Social Secretary, The 6410
Socratic Method, The 1950
Soft Water 321
Sojourner, The 1186
Soldier Erect, A 6770
Soldier in the Rain 8662
Soldier of Arete 5532
Soldier of Fortune 1405
Soldier of India, A 5368
Soldier of the Great War, A 2280
Soldier's Art, The 2841
Soldier's Daughter Never Cries, A 8245
Soldiers in Hiding 9636
Soldier's Joy 6239
Soldiers of Fortune 9867
Soldiers of Misfortune 10345
Soldier's Pay 8649
Sole Survivor 8003
Solid Mandala, The 5258
Solomon, Barbara Probst 77
Solomon Gursky Was Here 772
Solomons Ikey jun. (pseud.). *See* Thackeray, William Makepeace
Solomon's Daughter 2782
Solomons Seal 615
Solstice 5854
Sombrero Fallout 2850
Some Angry Angel 4005
Some Buried Caesar 8176
Some Came Running 8659
Some Can Whistle 6727
Some Do Not . . . 8351
Some Kind of Hero 2036
Some Tame Gazelle 1501
Somebody Else's Life 3412
Somebody in Boots 372
Somebody's Baby 7161
Somebody's Darling 10835
Some-Day Country, The 8867
Someone Else 1665
Someplace Safe 4664
Somerlott, Robert 4592
Somers, Jane (pseud.). *See* Lessing, Doris
Something About a Soldier 3306
Something About Eve 4102
Something Blue 7466
Something for Nothing 2861
Something Happened 2705
Something in Disguise 10660
Something in the Wind 4579
Something Light 5354

Something Like a Love Affair 1899
Something New 5308
Something of Value 2833
Something on the Wind 442
Something to Answer For 6956
Something to Be Desired 8436
Something to Die For 6881
Something to Hide 4164
Something Wicked This Way Comes 978
Sometimes a Great Notion 7674
Sometimes I Live in the Country 8440
Sommer, Scott 8291
Son at the Front, A 491
Son of a Hundred Kings 8988
Son of Laughter, The 8950
Son of Royal Langbrith, The 5731
Son of the Gamblin' Man 10373
Son of the Hawk 4248
Son of the Middle Border, A 3359
Son of the Morning 7524
Song in the Night 52
Song of Daniel, The 1194
Song of Sixpence, A 10060
Song of Solomon 9602
Song of the Cardinal, The 723
Song of the Lark, The 8908
Song of the Pearl 3521
Song of the Wild 7206
Song of Years 9746
Songs My Mother Taught Me 1431
Songs of Enchantment 6088
Songs of the Humpback Whale 6882
Sons (Buck) 2309
Sons (Hunter) 3313
Sons and Daughters 6779
Sons and Lovers 6269
Sons of Adam 8228
Sons of Darkness, Sons of Light 10208
Sontag, Susan 1089, 1252, 9580
Soon to Be Immortal 3865
Sooner Spy, The 398
Sophie's Choice 6142
Sorcerers 1459
Sorrell and Son 9536
Sorrentino, Gilbert 467, 921,
    2923, 3961, 5471, 5748, 6855,
    8886, 10906
Sorrow Floats 644
Sorrows of Satan, The 7033
Sort of Rich 5380
Sot-Weed Factor, The 5448
Soueif, Ahdaf 3374
Soul of a Bishop, The 1823
Soul of Kindness, The 10657
Souls and Bodies 10612
Sound and the Fury, The 9840
Sound Like Laughter, A 2928
Sound of Coaches, The 9789
Sound of Drums and Cymbals, The 9363
Sound of My Voice, The 6778
Sound the Retreat 8677
Sound Wagon, The 8773
Sounding the Territory 4813

Sour Sweet 6147
Source, The 8112
Source of Light, The 6680
South, The 8830
South African Quirt, The 1944
South Moon Under 2205
South of the Angels 2836
South Street 9172
South Will Rise at Noon, The 5777
South Wind 126
Southern, Terry 4617, 4694, 7986, 9567
Southern Discomfort 1840
Southern Exposure 5122
Southern Family, A 9966
Southern Light 5048
Southern Women 6275
Southpaw, The 793
Souvenir 10271
Sováková, Lidmila 5381
Sowers, The 3364
Soyinka, Wole 8797
Space 532
Space Machine, The 6448
Space Vampires, The 683
Spackman, W. M. 5109
Spanbauer, Tom 8619, 9055
Spangle 465
Spangled Road, The 4393
Spanidou, Irini 4128
Spanier, Muriel 7334
Spanish Doctor, The 4679
Spanish Farm, The 8648
Spark, Muriel 977, 1126, 1673,
    2063, 2845, 3024, 3196, 3340,
    4979, 5027, 5322, 5447, 5457,
    5928, 6963, 7037, 8826, 8903,
    10162
"Spark (The 'Sixties), The" 4976
Sparks Fly Upward 9275
Sparrow's Fall, The 4071
Spartina 4693
Speak Now 3459
Speakeasy 4326
Speaking in Tongues 7276
Spearfield's Daughter 6540
Special Destiny, A 4507
Special Providence, A 8673
Spectator Bird, The 10606
Speed 3621
Spell of Time, The 10077
Spella Ho 7219
Spellbinder 1526
Spence + Lila 8319
Spencer, Colin 1663, 10818
Spencer, Elizabeth 481, 3406,
    5187, 6771, 6824, 7301, 9684,
    9774, 10374
Spencer, Scott 1741, 7748, 9279
Spencer's Mountain 3576
Spend It Foolishly 2481
Spender, Stephen 5675
Sphinx 5971
Spider 7451
Spider Webs 5210

Spider's House, The 1635
Spielberg, Peter 10326
Spillard, Anne 768
Spire, The 5185
Spirit in the Flesh 7787
Spirit Lake 4162
Spirit Lost 4114
Spirit of Bombatse, The 6364
Spirit of the Hills 3755
Spirit Wrestler 9104
Splendid in Ashes 2326
Splendid Spur, The 5397
Splendor and Misery 10975
Splintered Eye, The 8318
Split Images 9850
Spoil of Office, A 9759
Spoilers, The 8284
Spoils of Eden, The 5517
Spoils of Poynton, The 4909
Spoilt City, The 5714
Spontaneous Combustion 3889
Spook Who Sat by the Door, The 7005
Sport of Nature, A 4842
Sport of the Gods, The 3075
Sporting Club, The 3423
Sporting Proposition, A 9006
Sportsman's Paradise 6925
Sportswriter, The 4837
Sporty Creek 8429
Spreading Fires 3331
Spring, Howard 5093, 5144
Spring Came on Forever 8980
Spring Moon 618
Spring of the Ram, The 535
Spring Sonata 5490
Springer's Progress 5581
Springs of Living Water 3622
Sproat, Robert 1955
Sprott, Duncan 4427
Spy, The 9512
Spy Hook 1467
Spy in the House of Love, A 1102
Spy in the Ointment, The 5683
Spy Line 7004
Spy Sinker 4993
Spy Story 8680
Spy Who Came in from the Cold, The 10059
Spy Who Spoke Porpoise, The 8520
Spyglass Tree, The 7907
Square Dance 9809
Square Peg 5347
Square's Progress 7310
Squeak 3368
Squeeze Play 349
Squire of Bor Shachor, The 9598
Squirrel-Cage, The 3080
Staats, Marilyn Dorn 4949
Stacey, Tom 4333
Stafford, Jean 132, 7035, 10051
Stalin's Shoe 6708
Stambaugh, Sara 7231
Stamboul Train 9539
Stampfer, Judah 4328
Stand Like Men 436

Stand We at Last 5168
Standard Dreaming 4281
Stand-In, The 4425
Standing Fast 5323
Standing into Danger 8154
Standish, Robert 9749
Standún, Pádraig 6599
Stanley and the Women 9270
Stanton, Johnny 6697
Stanton, Paul (pseud.). *See* Beaty, David
Stanton Succession, The 5211
Stapledon, Olaf 374, 702, 2502, 2630, 4496
Star in the Wind, A 2237
Star in the Family, A 5
Star Maker 374
Star of Peace 6898
Star Rover, The 4495
Star Turn 4836
Staring at the Sun 3452
Stark, Sharon Sheehe 3955
Starlight Rider 7614
Stars and Bars 10432
Stars at Noon, The 183
Stars Incline, The 9303
Stars, Like Dust, The 8784
Stars Look Down, The 10125
Stars My Destination, The 3385
Stars on the Sea 8591
Starship 378
Start in Life, A 4235
Start of the Road, The 7248
Starting Over 1229
Starting with Serge 8906
State of Change, A 9578
State of Fear, A 7329
State of Independence, A 4547
State of Peace, A 6809
State of Siege, A 5033
State of Stony Lonesome, The 3221
State's Evidence 9249
States of Emergency 9039
Statesman's Game, The 709
"Static of the Spheres, The" 9366
Statues in a Garden 10596
Statutes of Limitations 4593
Staying Afloat 7334
Staying On 2373
Staying out of Hell 10098
Stead, C. K. 9825
Stead, Christina 4633, 7220, 8157, 9730
Steadman, Mark 826, 8427
Steagle, The 6372
Steele, Wilbur Daniel 4737, 7136, 7881
Steelwork 10906
Steen, Marguerite 7865
Stefan in Love 10884
Stegner, Wallace 1189, 1616, 7200, 7313, 9181, 9268, 10299, 10606
Stein, David Lewis 4652
Stein, Gertrude 53, 7058, 8355
Stein, Harry 5587

Stein, Toby 2743, 2917, 10279
Steinbach, Meredith 8622
Steinbeck, John 2208, 2220, 3140, 5317, 6272, 6626, 7297, 7508, 7659, 8981, 9145, 9751, 10149, 10174, 10481, 10492, 10574
Steiner, George 4810, 6600
Steinke, Darcey 186, 2941
"Steinway Quintet, The" 6236
"Stella" 1317
Stella Fregelius 8394
Stella Landry 5783
Stepdaughter, The 1932
Stepford Wives, The 1432
Stephen Morris 7772
Stephens, Jack 474
Stephens, James 3081, 9535, 10756
Stepping 5042
Stepping Westward 278
Steps 9581
Sterile Cuckoo, The 9290
Stern 6124
Stern, G. B. 4142
Stern, Richard G. 1039, 3186, 3709, 6140, 6643, 7848, 9713
Sterne, Laurence 6604, 9510
Stevens, James 4464
Stevenson, Robert Louis 647, 1161, 1570, 3737, 5012, 5396, 5889, 9090, 9692
Stewart, Angus 10905
Stewart, Donald Ogden 1371, 3469
Stewart, George R. 525, 6982, 9070, 9416, 10158
Stewart, J. I. M. 852, 1255, 1527, 3187, 3589, 6336, 6463, 7522
Stewart, Jean 5531
Stewart, Mary 6476, 7065
Stick 6579
Stick Your Neck Out 10935
Stiff Upper Lip, Jeeves 4349
Still, James 8429
Still Glides the Stream 1395
Still Life 917
Still Life with Insects 4966
Still Life with Woodpecker 10083
Still Lives 8291
Still Waters 4109
Stillmeadow Seasons 2692
Stillness 2779
Stillwater Tragedy, The 3895
Sting of the Bee 1809
Stirling, Monica 2902
Stitch 3709
Stockton, Frank R. 3069, 5343, 5787, 8058, 10782
Stoic, The 7154
Stoker, Bram 4929, 7372, 9524
Stolen Goods 1071
Stolen Jew, The 10422
Stolen Past, A 6794
Stone, Alma 5844
Stone, Irving 376, 498, 527, 1923, 2831, 7476, 7619, 8044, 9631, 10124, 10401

Stone, Laurie 8906
Stone, Robert 2911, 2924, 8369, 10292, 10640
Stone Angel, The 6646
Stone Field, The 8406
Stone Gone Mad, A 7342
Stone Heart 9656
Stone Junction 830
Stone of Chastity, The 3109
Stone of the Heart, A 2179
Stone Virgin 1167
Stonecliff 710
Stonecrop 9176
Stoner 7890
Stones for Ibarra 5609
Stones of Bau, The 3658
Stones of the Dalai Lama 8323
Stonor Eagles, The 760
Stop at a Winner 6570
Stopover: Tokyo 8177
Store, The 6979
Store Up the Anger 2391
Storey, David 3212, 3940, 4076, 9795, 10225
Storm 525
Storm and Echo 5315
Storm Cloud, The 5141
Storm from Paradise, A 6581
Storm in Chandigarh 9847
Storm of Fortune 9924
Storm Season, The 6739
Storming Heaven 558
"Story, A'" 7068
Story Catcher, The 2606
Story Like the Wind, A 3504
Story of a Bad Boy, The 8958
Story of a Country Town, The 4534
Story of a Happy Woman, The 511
Story of an African Farm, The 8391
Story of Annie D., The 7702
Story of Deep Delight, A 9198
Story of Dr. Wassell, The 6888
Story of Esther Costello, The 2024
Story of Julia Page, The 5250
Story of My Life 2749
Story of Sir Launcelot and His Companions, The 6561
Story of the Outlaw, The 638
Story of Tonty, The 2191
Storyteller, The (Robbins) 3726
Storyteller, The (Sillitoe) 1835
Storyville (Battle) 6490
"Storyville" (Smith) 3628
Stout, Janis 1158, 9339
Stout, Rex 195, 583, 594, 668, 900, 907, 1106, 1594, 1619, 2322, 3132, 3295, 3440, 3646, 3738, 3739, 4271, 4279, 4761, 6351, 7204, 7588, 7767, 8176, 8272, 8565, 8860, 9886, 9888, 9895, 9900, 9902, 9909, 9911, 9912, 9913, 10010, 10794, 10921
Stover at Yale 9531
Stow, Randolph 304, 3138, 4445, 6936, 9941, 10164

Stowe, Harriet Beecher 2886, 3736,
   5558, 6284, 8937, 9348, 9758
Stowe, Rebecca 4208
Straight, Susan 6744, 7236
Straight and Narrow Path, The 5438
Straight Cut 9283
Straight Through the Night 537
Strange Ailments; Uncertain Cures 2723
Strange Alphabet 2354
Strange Angels 3045
Strange Business 9056
*Strange Case of Dr. Jekyll and Mr.
   Hyde, The* 5889
*Strange Case of Miss Annie Spragg,
   The* 4376
Strange Children, The 8327
Strange Fits of Passion 2067
Strange Loyalties 10319
Strange Meeting 3713
Strange One, The 737
Strange Peaches 8806
Strange Story, A 6886
Stranger from the Sea, The 4943
Stranger in a Strange Land 4759
Stranger in My Grave, A 3919
Stranger in the Kingdom, A 3614
Strangers and Brothers 3764
Strangers and Journeys 1678
Strangers' Banquet, The 5903
Stranger's House, A 3246
Strangers When We Meet 2233
Stratton, Richard 6343
Stratton-Porter, Gene 723, 1583,
   4146, 4726, 6619, 7215, 8205,
   9693, 10117
Straus, Dorothea 6797
Street, Pamela 1755, 4934
Street, The 10699
Street Where the Heart Lies, The 4163
Streets of Gold 5059
Streets of Night 8630
Streshinsky, Shirley 2577, 6045,
   10673
Stribling, T. S. 582, 2947, 3098,
   6979, 8773, 9879
Stricken Field, A 7660
Strickland 4264
Strike from the Sea 7781
Strike the Bell Boldly 368
Strike the Father Dead 9305
Striking Out 7750
Stringer 6078
Stringer, Arthur 5733, 6038, 8256,
   10114
Strode Venturer, The 2538
Stroke of Luck 9351
Strong, Jonathan 2818, 6745, 6927
Strong, L. A. G. 5314, 9132
Strong Motion 8249
Strong Poison 3798
*Struggles of Brown, Jones, and Robin-
   son, The* 5394
Strumpet City 8119
Stuart, Alexander 5242
Stuart, Francis 3836, 5104, 5155

Stuart, Jesse 1393, 2985, 3475,
   4247, 8360, 8780, 8893, 10074
Stuart, Sarah Payne 3883, 6750
Stubbs, Jean 3365
Studhorse Man, The 432
Study in Scarlet, A 3266
Stumbling on Melons 8557
Sturdy and Strong 6615
Styron, William 1879, 3476, 5142,
   6142, 9155
Suarez, Virgil 171, 236
Subject to Change 4130
Success (Adams) 9211
Success (Amis) 1124
Succession, The 8885
Such a Long Journey 7547
Such Good Friends 4619
Such Was the Season 72
Suckow, Ruth 2136, 2216, 3642,
   8352, 9721, 10168
Sudden Death 2927
Suddenly, in Rome 394
Sudie 6703
Suffrage of Elvira, The 21
Sugar Cage 1243
Sugar House, The 9385
Sugar Mother, The 6261
Suicide Blonde 2941
Suicide's Wife, The 7998
Suitable Boy, A 6748
Suite for Calliope 463
Sukenick, Ronald 879, 1553, 5607,
   8037
Sula 6273
Sullivan, Alan 7918
Sullivan, Faith 5855, 6941, 9340,
   10844
Sullivan, Thomas 93, 1756
Sum of Things, The 155
Sumitra's Story 10665
Summer (Grunwald) 7207
Summer (Wharton) 1585
Summer, Scott 1716, 5670
Summer After the Funeral, The 3946
Summer Ago, A 10623
Summer Before the Dark, The 10073
Summer Bird-Cage, A 4574
Summer Boy, The 1868
Summer Crossing 4817
*Summer Dreams and the Kleig Light
   Gas Company* 2863
"*Summer in Maine, A*" 9652
Summer in the Greenhouse 7014
Summer in the Twenties, A 1258
Summer in Williamsburg 7294
Summer Meadows, The 10406
Summer Moonshine 2211
Summer of '42 5037
Summer of the Paymaster, The 1083
Summer of the Red Wolf 3366
Summer of the Royal Visit, The
   4866
Summer People 8828
Summer Place, A 5028
Summer to Decide, A 843

Summer Visits 1180
Summer Will Show 9881
Summers, Hollis 13, 904, 1202,
   5547, 8802, 10226
Summer's Lease 3882
Summertime 5774
Summertime Island 1422
Summit 2794
Summon the Bright Water 1709
Summoning, The 7364
Summons to Memphis, A 6545
Sun Also Rises, The 8910
Sun and the Moon, The 9010
Sun Chemist, The 8524
Sun Dial Street 6169
Sun Doctor, The 9075
Sun Dogs 6507
Sun in Capricorn, The 1762
Sun in Scorpio, The 5319
Sun Is My Shadow, The 5623
Sun Is My Undoing, The 7865
Sun Maiden, The 9346
Sun Virgin, The 7800
Sunday Best 5470
Sundial, The 3939
Sundog 9622
Sundown 789
Sundown Jim 9220
Sundowners, The 1631
Sunflower 5690
Sunlight Dialogues, The 7631
Sunne in Splendour, The 3720
Sunrise to Sunset 7618
Sunrising 453
Sunset Dream, The 287
Sunset Graze 9766
Sunset Song 3381
Sunset Tree, The 9666
Superintendent, The 7332
Superior Women 5111
Superstition Corner 9134
Supply of Heroes 1844
Sure Hand of God, The 2074
Sure Salvation, The 8141
Surface of Earth, The 6186
Surface with Daring 9791
Surfacing 9171
Surgeon's Daughter, The 6884
Surprise of Burning, The 7086
Surrender the Pink 8022
Surtees, Robert Smith 4683, 8764
Survey of the Atlantic Beaches, A 7938
Survival of the Fittest, The 3174
Surviving the Flood 2744
Surviving the Seasons 1870
Surviving the Wreck 7863
Survivor (Gallacher) 3693
Survivor, A (Jones) 10505
Survivor, The (Keneally) 2988
Survivors, The (Hunter) 10970
Susan Lenox 2298
Suspects 7079
Suspense 6059
Susy 9116
Sutherland, Margaret 9107

Sutton, Henry (pseud.). *See* Slavitt, David R.
Suttree 10416
Suyin, Han 5076, 10264
Swados, Harvey 2337, 2775, 5252, 5323
Swag 6853
Swallow (Haggard) 5402
Swallow (Thomas) 5633
Swallow Barn 8171
Swallow Hard 6730
Swamp Angel (Langley) 7639
Swamp Angel (Wilson) 9426
Swamp Fox, The 4397
Swan, Susan 327
Swan Song 7378
Swann 2872
Swann, Lois 3906
Swanson, Walter S. J. 3207
Swansong 5176
Swap, The 1992
Swarthout, Glendon 1681, 2107, 2340, 4835, 5148, 5254, 5362, 5473, 5481, 6914, 7088, 7635, 10503
Sweatman, Margaret 10885
Sweet Adelaide 10253
Sweet Alice 4474
Sweet and Sour Milk 550
Sweet Country 9797
Sweet Desserts 3242
Sweet Dove Died, The 10836
Sweet Dreams 2993
Sweet Eyes 1772
Sweet Hereafter, The 478
Sweet Medicine 9059
Sweet Morn of Judas' Day 2625
Sweet Thursday 10492
Sweet William 9591
Sweetheart (McGehee) 2457
Sweethearts (Krich) 1450
Sweet-Shop Owner, The 3345
Sweetsir 1839
Swift, Edward 4099, 5967, 7741, 8241
Swift, Graham 859, 3345, 6823, 9733, 10548
Swift, Jonathan 6602, 7055
Swiftie the Magician 3389
Swimming in the Volcano 5052
Swimming Pool, The 2470
Swimming Pool Season, The 8823
Swimming-Pool Library, The 4594
Swinburne, A. C. 5887, 10774
Swing in the Garden, The 9241
Swinnerton, Frank 2153, 9469
Swiss Family Manhattan 194
Swiss Summer, The 9896
Switch, The 3013
Sword in the Stone, The 7879
Sword Maker, The 3994
Sword of Hachiman, The 6594
Sword of Honour 207
Sword of the Lictor, The 4299
Sybil (Auchincloss) 5806

Sybil (Disraeli) 3964
Sycamore Tree, The 5441
Sylvia 5546
Sylvia's Lovers 1338
Sylvie and Bruno 3468
Sylvie and Bruno Concluded 5275
Symmes, John Cleves 2600
Symons, Julian 905, 1899, 2037, 2041, 2403, 2975, 4334, 4350, 4757, 5539, 5826, 6500, 6762, 7571, 7677, 8302, 9458, 10200, 10253
Symposium 2063
Symzonia 2600
Szanto, George 6188
Szilagyi, Steve 7212
Szydlowski, Mary Vigliante 617

Taber, Gladys 2692, 10145
Table Legs 6943
Table Money 7695
Tables 5986
Taine, John (pseud.). *See* Bell, Eric Temple
Take a Girl Like You 9907
Take It or Leave It 1230
Take Me Where the Good Times Are 5094
"Take the Long Way Home" 9024
Take This Man 10256
Take Three Senses 3117
Takeover, The 3196
Taking of Agnès, The 10743
Taking Shelter 7442
Taking the Biscuit 115
Tale for Midnight, A 2119
Tale of a Lonely Parish, A 99
Tale of a Tub, A 7055
Tale of Asa Bean, The 876
"Tale of Chloe, The" 7708
Tale of the Body Thief, The 9058
Tale of the Wind, A 5123
Tale of Two Cities, A 3377
Tale of Valor 336
Talent for Loving, A 6180
Tales of the Master Race 2490
Talisman, The 10329
Talkative Man 4839
Talking It Over 7455
Tallant, Robert 3703
Tallent, Elizabeth 10744
Taller Women 1784
Tallien 6477
Tamsen 10428
Tan, Amy 773, 6736
Tanaquil 6665
Tancred 6267
Tangerine Tango Equation, The 2489
Tangled Up in Blue 170
Tango 8018
Tannen, Mary 475, 2487, 2814
Tantalus 5847
Taos 4673
Tapiola's Brave Regiment 417

Tapping the Source 9106
Taps for Private Tussie 8780
Taquisara 4717
Tar 7034
Tar Baby (Morrison) 1711
Tar Baby, The (Charyn) 6132
Tar Beach 479
Targan, Barry 2489
Tarkington, Booth 296, 964, 1315, 1364, 1384, 1591, 2497, 2756, 3096, 4614, 4670, 5129, 6804, 6890, 6930, 7124, 7127, 7164, 7373, 7657, 7709, 7754, 8208, 8299, 8586, 8739, 9065, 9096, 9119, 9120, 9382, 9407, 9882, 10336, 10553, 10798
Tarr 1366
Tarr, Herbert 5273, 7730
Tartt, Donna 78
Tarzan of the Apes 8972
Taste for Death, A 1891
Tate, Allen 8512
Tattooed Countess, The 8564
Tax, Meredith 7001, 10671
Tax Inspector, The 3335
Tay John 9747
Taylor, David 7197
Taylor, Debbie 8029
Taylor, Elizabeth 732, 1674, 2317, 3937, 10657, 10659, 10903
Taylor, Erika 9346
Taylor, Harry H. 3608, 5005
Taylor, Mildred D. 10078
Taylor, Peter 2534, 6545
Taylor, Robert Jr. 4356
Taylor, Robert Lewis 662, 2837, 9077
Taylor, Robert Love 2436, 3044
Taylor, Ronald B. 1080
Taylor, Sheila Ortiz 3463
Tear His Head off His Shoulders 850
Teetallow 2947
Tefuga 6401
Teitlebaum's Window 6652
Telfair, David 5984
Tell Me How Long the Train's Been Gone 144
Tell Me Now, and Again 9175
Tell Me That You Love Me, Junie Moon 3923
Telling of Lies, The 4656
Temper the Wind 3967
Tempest-Tost 51
Temple 8045
Temple, The 5675
Temple of Gold, The 6637
Temple of My Familiar, The 6484
Temple Tree, The 213
Temples of Delight 3934
Temporary Kings 8523
Temporary Life, A 4076
Temporary Residence, A 8317
Temptation of Eileen Hughes, The 1938
Temptations 6749
Tempting Fate 4924

Ten Commandments, The 1597
Ten North Frederick 8720
Ten Seconds 1848
Tenant of Wildfell Hall, The 239
Tenants, The 10219
Tenants of Moonbloom, The 1111
Tenants of Time, The 9109
Tender 4205
Tender Is the Night 4631
Tender Offer (Johnson) 10564
Tender Offer (Marshall) 8879
Tender Victory 4661
Tenderloin 7258
Tending to Virginia 10298
Tenement, The 9253
Tenement of Clay 4608
Tennant, Emma 824, 1257, 3190,
    5330, 5761
Tennant, Kylie 4315
Tennenbaum, Silvia 67, 554
Tennessee Shad, The 4460
Tennis Handsome, The 3018
Tent Peg, The 222
Tenterhooks 125
Tenth 3690
Tenth Man, The 6465
Tenth Month, The 5101
Tents of Wickedness, The 568
Tenured Professor, A 7905
Teresa of Watling Street 1354
Terhune, Albert Payson 408, 409,
    412, 413, 1016, 1910, 2135, 6365
Terminal Man, The 4621
Terms of Endearment 10829
Terre Haute 1859
Terrible Teague Bunch 7634
Terrible Temptation, A 8839
Terrible Threes, The 8735
Terrible Twos, The 6013
Territorial Rights 1126
Terror, The 6311
Terry, Bill 9026
Terry, Marshall 4112
Tesich, Nadja 8706
Tesich, Steve 4817
Tess of the D'Urbervilles 10333
Tester, William 7458
Testimonies 6953
Testimony of Two Men 1926
Testing the Current 8927
Tetrarch 1986
Texas 6509
Texas Summer 4694
Texasville 576
Texier, Catherine 8014, 10881
Textures of Life 1975
Textures of Silence, The 10910
Tey, Josephine (pseud.). *See* Mac-
    kintosh, Elizabeth
Thackeray, William Makepeace
    360, 719, 950, 1902, 3376, 3813,
    4304, 4453, 6610, 8641, 9757,
    10768, 10770
Thanatos Syndrome, The 165
Thank Heaven Fasting 639

Thank You, Jeeves 10965
Thank You, Mr. Moto 3457
"Thankful Blossom" 1339
Thanksgiving 10086
Tharoor, Shashi 2750, 6262
That Day in Gordon 6582
That Eye, The Sky 9818
That Hideous Strength 5742
That Night 7739
That Printer of Udell's 2296
That Summer 4277
That Time in Malomba 10308
That Uncertain Feeling 3742
That's How it Was 795
That's My Baby 1241
Thayer, Nancy 1558, 3036, 4114,
    4354, 4552, 5042, 8015, 10284
Theatre 1605
Theft, A 4302
Their Eyes Were Watching God 8083
Their Pride and Joy 1144
Their Town 7881
Their Wedding Journey 2648
Theirs Be the Guilt 3146
Theirs Was the Kingdom 2357
Thelma 8392
Thelwell, Michael 10016
them 7479
Then Again 10024
Then and Now 1249
Then She Found Me 6732
Then Spoke the Thunder 1757
Theo and Matilda 8446
Theophilus North 6447
Theory of Everything, The 5612
Theory of War 11003
There Is Another Heaven 7656
"There Is No Conversation" 8855
There Will Be a Short Interval 9487
Thereafter Johnnie 4115
Therefore Be Bold 5649
There's Always Another Year 6219
Theroux, Alexander 2862, 10867
Theroux, Joseph 8192
Theroux, Paul 286, 711, 1040,
    1833, 3053, 7043, 7208, 9108,
    9447, 9672, 9957, 10402, 10456
These Golden Days 5669
These Latter Days 10741
These Lovers Fled Away 5144
These Thousand Hills 8862
These Twain 1362
They Both Were Naked 208
They Came Like Swallows 10130
They Came to Baghdad 3740
They Came to Cordura 5148
They Stooped to Folly 2501
They Went on Together 6112
They Were Also Strangers 9028
Thicker Than Water 10882
Thief of Dreams 6165
Thieves in the Night 9769
Thin Man, The 4310
Thin Mountain Air, The 5580
Thin Red Line, The 8107

Thing of Beauty, A 2228
Thing of It Is . . . , The 1830
Things as They Are 10761
Things Fall Apart 3535
Things Invisible to See 2638
Things They Carried, The 8708
Think Fast, Mr. Moto 1021
Thinking Reed, The 9885
Thiong'o, Ngugi wa 6960, 10815
Third Generation, The 3801
Third Girl 3844
Third Life of Grange Copeland, The
    1670
Third Parties 3859
Third Policeman, The 6182
"Third Time Lucky" 5770
Thirkell, Angela 427, 902, 1408,
    3114, 3123, 3136, 4752, 5434,
    5743, 7060, 8261, 8262
Thirteen at Dinner 7381
Thirteen O'Clock 391
13th House, The 3237
13th Valley, The 9755
31st of June, The 2145
Thirty-nine Steps, The 5249
This Above All 10480
This Animal Is Mischievous 5070
This Bed Thy Centre 2207
This Coffin Has No Handles 10628
This Crooked Way 7301
This Day and Age 5124
This Day's Death 10726
This Family of Women 6333
This Gun for Hire 6175
This Is Next Year 6280
This Is Not for You 1929
This Is Your Life 3287
This Island, Now 209
This January Tale 2242
This Other Eden 7186
This Perfect Day 307
This Place 2268
This Promised Land 1989
This Proud Heart 5741
This Real Night 5268
This Rough Magic 7065
This Side Jordan 2106
This Side of Innocence 6315
This Side of Love 10713
This Side of Paradise 4434
This Strange Adventure 3094
This Sweet and Bitter Earth 9599
This Thing Don't Lead to Heaven 9583
This Time of Morning 9574
This Very Earth 1546
This Way Madness Lies 6946
This Year in Jerusalem 10270
Thom, James Alexander 1556,
    2513, 4682, 4825, 10098
Thomas, Amanda 689
Thomas, Audrey 1431, 2270, 4776,
    6817, 9004
Thomas, D. M. 923, 2794, 2815,
    5633, 5971, 7158, 8004, 9613
Thomas, Elean 4100

Thomas, Elizabeth Marshall 7749
Thomas, Gwyn 5151, 6069, 9304
Thomas, Hugh 5294
Thomas, Leslie 2172
Thomas, Maria 10442, 10886
Thompson, David 869
Thompson, Flora 1383, 1395, 1617, 6566
Thompson, Jean 619
Thompson, Jim 143, 2962, 5809, 6815, 7391, 7861, 7867, 8822, 9264, 10367
Thompson, Joyce 6746, 10322, 10913
Thompson, Maurice 7608, 9662
Thompson, Rupert 2807
Thompson, Sandra 1996
Thomson, David 7079
Thomson, Rupert 3956
Thon, Melanie Rae 6382
Thorn Birds, The 851
Thorndike, John 3615, 10949
Thornton, Lawrence 4129, 7105
Thornyhold 6476
Thorofare 1613
Thorpe, Adam 1786
Those Who Love 1923
Thou Worm Jacob 910
Thousand Acres, A 3666
Thousand Hour Day, The 10195
Thousand Summers, A 26
Threat 88
Three 6321
Three Cheers for the Paraclete 1513
Three Children 9691
Three Circles of Light 2327
Three Clerks, The 6974
Three Continents 255
Three Daughters of Madame Liang, The 2248
Three Farmers on Their Way to a Dance 1458
Three Fates, The 2584
Three for the Money 10069
Three Graces, The 8242
Three Harbors 242
Three Hostages, The 4342
Three Hunters 2875
Three Lovers 10071
Three Men in New Suits 4312
Three Men in a Boat 3990
Three Men on Wheels 929
Three Mustangeers, The 9705
Three Nights in the Heart of the Earth 1752
Three O'Clock Dinner 10144
Three Partners 2195
Three Perils of Man, The 3375
Three Sisters, The 1361
Three Soldiers 8645
Three Times Table 3697
Three Women 9843
Three Women at the Waters' Edge 4354
Three Years to Play 1228
Three-Legged Horse 6240

Three-Pipe Problem, A 2037
Throne of Saturn, The 531
Through a Glass Darkly 5622
Through Russian Snows 6524
Through Streets Broad and Narrow 9568
Through the Arc of the Rain Forest 7453
Through the Eye of the Needle 5278
Through the Fields of Clover 5090
Through the Looking-Glass and What Alice Found There 7551
Through the Wheat 2198
Thubron, Colin 1781, 7149, 8134, 8199
Thudbury 1401
Thunder at Dawn, A 939
Thunder at Sunset 5158
Thunder on the Left 7759
Thurm, Marian 5636, 7096, 9342
Thurman, Wallace 46, 9883
Thursday's Children 9396
Thyrza 3989
Ticket for a Seamstitch, A 4640
Ticket Out, The 6460
Ticket to Ride 2595
Ticonderoga 3062
Tidewater Tales, The 1998
Tidings 9681
Tie that Binds, The 161
Tiersten, Irene 7041
Tiffany Street 7955
Tiger, The 5173
Tiger for Malgudi, A 4886
Tiger in the Tiger Pit, The 390
Tiger's Daughter, The 4646
Tight White Collar 5472
Tikal 5074
Tiktin, Carl 6231
"Till Death Us Do Part" 1880
Till Morning Comes 10264
Till the Fat Lady Sings 3892
Till We Have Faces 104
Time After Time 5963
Time and Tide 8898
Time and Time Again 10931
Time Before This, The 4318
Time Enough for Love 4501
Time for a Tiger 4881
Time for Frankie Coolin 9947
Time for Heroes, A 229
Time for Judas, A 1059
Time for Wedding Cake, A 5382
Time in Its Flight 2544
Time Is Noon, The 10193
Time Loves a Hero 8009
Time Machine, The 3267
Time Must Have a Stop 969
Time No Longer 4514
Time of Her Life, The 182
Time of Hope 4952
Time of Peace 9471
Time of the Angels, The 1552
Time Out of Mind 6787
Time Sharing 3754

Time to Be Happy, A 6434
Time to Sing, A 6780
Time Will Darken It 50
Timeless Moment, The 1755
Time's Arrow 10313
Time's Witness 6848
Tin Can Tree, The 3943
Tin Lizzie Troop, The 5473
Tin Men, The 1032
Tindall, Gillian 1665, 2539, 6119, 7400
"Tinian" 871
Tinker, Tailor, Soldier, Spy 1684
Tinniswood, Peter 2353, 8616
Tinsel 10081
Tinsley, Molly Best 924
Tirra Lirra by the River 9937
Titan, The 5564
Titch 9715
Titmuss Regained 6923
Titus Alone 5604
Titus Groan 9223
Tlali, Miriam 1048
To a Distant Island 2516
To a God Unknown 6626
To All Appearances a Lady 2432
To Asmara 9371
To Be a Pilgrim 2021
To Brooklyn with Love 5321
To Dance with the White Dog 477
To Die For 261
To Every Birth Its Blood 3206
To Have and to Hold (Johnston) 5615
To Have and to Hold (Moggach) 6919
To Have and Have Not 2210
To Hear a Nightingale 2551
To Kill a Mockingbird 22
To Leeward 1342
To Let 1586
To Reach a Dream 4323
To Risks Unknown 8274
To Serve Them All My Days 9586
To Slay the Dreamer 4481
To the Birdhouse 5298
To the Bright and Shining Sun 9782
To the Honor of the Fleet 7359
To the Indies 10922
To the Islands 10164
To the Lighthouse 6565
To the Precipice 4278
To the Sargasso Sea 9732
To the Tenth Generation 6542
To the Victors the Spoils 6115
To the White Sea 8713
Tobacco Men, The 4675
Tobacco Road 10347
Tobias and the Angel 9242
Together 10644
Together and Apart 3515
Tóibín, Colm 7706, 8830
Toil of the Brave 8409
Toilers of the Hills 2949
Tokens of Grace 6205
Tokyo Woes 10282

Tokyo-Montana Express, The 2383
Tolkien, J. R. R. 2632, 3106, 5435, 7846, 8269
Tom Brown at Oxford 7876
Tom Brown's School Days 3528
Tom Jones 5385
Tom Sawyer 4715
Tom Sawyer Abroad 3492
Tom Sawyer, Detective 1160
Tomaso, Carla 2816
Tomin, Zdena 6708
Tomlinson, H. M. 7843, 8070, 8178, 8775, 9130
Tomorrow! 7669
Tomorrow Will Be Better 9147
Tomorrow Will Be Sunday 1421
Tomorrow's Another Day 5915
Tom-Walker, The 7665
Tongues of Angels, The 2446
Tongues of Fire 6377
Tongues of Flame 5113
Tonks, Rosemary 4175, 7987
Tonner, Leslie 553, 4611
Tono-Bungay 5694
Tontine, The 10493
Tony and Susan 5551
Too Dear for My Possessing 839
Too Far to Walk 2979
Too Late 1328
Too Late the Phalarope 7492
Too Many Clients 9909
Too Many Cooks 8565
Too Many Ghosts 4104
Too Many Women 4271
Too Much, Too Young 7099
Toole, John Kennedy 2859, 7280
Tooth and Claw 5169
Toothache Tree, The 5379
Toots in Solitude 2790
Top of the Hill, The 1233
Topless 39
Toppel, Lori 9691
Torching, The 3512
Tormenting of Lafayette Jackson, The 232
Torn Covenants 3906
Tornado Alley 3787
Tornado Pratt 3316
Toro! Toro! Toro! 8570
Torpedo! 941
Torpedo Run 8280
Torquemada 10388
Tortilla Flat 8981
Tortoise and the Hare, The 9149
Tortoise by Candlelight 1416
Tortuga 10248
Tory Lover, The 3992
Totally Free Man, A 5687
Touch 8559
Touch of Danger, A 2995
Touch of Daniel, A 2353
Touch the Sky 10537
"Touchstone, The" 696
Touchstone of Fortune, The 1220
Tough Guys Don't Dance 10277

Tour, The 9577
Tourgée, Albion W. 4716, 7752
Tourist (Green) 2478
Tourists (Wright) 6965
Tourmaline 4445
Tournament, The 10590
Tours of the Black Clock 5050
Toward the End 7130
Toward the Morning 2959
Toward What Bright Glory? 258
Tower Abbey 5106
Tower of Babel, The 5716
Tower of Ivory 5641
Tower of London, The 1196
Towers, Robert 7364
Towers of Silence, The 6446
Towers of Trebizond, The 1643
Town, The (Faulkner) 7394
Town, The (Richter) 10155
Town and the City, The 7668
"Town Crier Exclusive" 1817
Townsman, The 8090
Toyland 2977
Tracer 9624
Track of the Cat, The 2075
Tracker 882
Tracks 2425
Tracy, Honor 3838, 5040, 5438, 6255, 7305, 8184, 8660, 8688, 9009, 10004, 10936
Tracy's Tiger 422
Trade Wind 10814
Traffic and Laughter 4901
Tragic Comedians, The 10900
Tragic Ground 1024
Tragic Muse, The 8841
Trail Dust 3644
Trail of the Lonesome Pine, The 3759
Trail of the Serpent, The 10523
Trail of the Sword, The 7195
Trail Smoke 7615
Trail Town 6951
Train in the Meadow, The 7256
Traitor, The 2687
Traitor's Gate 10515
Transatlantic Blues 1804
Transit of Venus, The 6328
Translator, The 5224
Transmigration of Timothy Archer, The 3280
Transparent Things 2523
Tranter, Nigel 383, 3691, 8556, 10946
Trap, The (Billany) 1919
Trap, The (Richardson) 6270
Trap, The (Treherne) 2170
Trapido, Barbara 3934, 5502, 6864
Trapper 3208
Trapper's Last Shot, The 4403
Travel Light 541
Traveler from Altruria, A 9864
Travelers (Jhabvala) 5360
Traveller (Adams) 1465
Travelling Woman, A 7167
Travels in Nihilon 912

Travels of Jaimie McPheeters, The 662
Travels of Maudie Tipstaff, The 7774
Travels to the Enu 1055
Traver, Robert 2045, 2968, 3129, 7223
Travesty 3004
Treasure Hunt (Buechner) 10013
Treasure Hunt (Keane) 3131
Treasure Island 5012
Treasure of Heaven, The 1356
Treasure of Pleasant Valley, The 3304
Treasures of Time 10251
Treatment and the Cure, The 9184
Tree Full of Stars, A 9481
Tree Grows in Brooklyn, A 1388
Tree of Knowledge, The 9974
Tree of Life, The 1066
Tree of Man, The 9773
Tree on Fire, A 8115
Tree Still Stands, The 9978
Trees, The 10354
Trees of Heaven 4247
Treherne, John 2170
Trelawny, Edward John 358
Tremain, Rose 610, 5985, 8823, 9295, 10244
Trembling Upon Rome, A 1528
Tremor of Intent 9575
Trent's Last Case 10758
Trespass 3178
Trespasser, The (Lawrence) 6215
Trespassers, The (Roper) 9835
Trespassers Welcome Here 6162
Trespasses (Bailey) 10602
Trespasses (Bridgwood) 3611
Trevor, William 1440, 2343, 3215, 3297, 3808, 3891, 4550, 4781, 4844, 4870, 5653, 6793
Trial by Terror 8859
Trial by Water 9837
Trial of Sören Qvist, The 3421
Trials and Tribulations of Aaron Amsted, The 6656
Triangulation 474
Tribe That Lost Its Head, The 199
Trick of It, The 9970
Trick of the Ga Bolga, The 6082
Trilby 2132
Trilling, Lionel 1624
Triphammer 1153
Tripmaster Monkey 9299
Tristan and the Hispanics 1151
Tristram of Blent 5894
Tristram Shandy 6604
Triumph (Wylie) 7202
Triumph, The (Gann) 5115
Trojan Horse, The 1380
Trojans, The 8420
Trollope, Anthony 1340, 1486, 1487, 2292, 2732, 3063, 3066, 3553, 3972, 4442, 5194, 5393, 5394, 5395, 5560, 5638, 6521, 6612, 6885, 6887, 6974, 6975, 8714, 8955, 8960, 8961, 8962, 9261, 10772, 10775

Trollope, Joanna 41
Trombone 3630
Troop, Elizabeth 4361
Tropic of Cancer 935
Tropic of Capricorn 2314
Trot 10714
Trott, Susan 5304, 5672, 6202
Trotter-Nama, The 323
Trouble 9988
Trouble Country 7636
Trouble for Lucia 1826
Trouble in July 10135
Trouble Shooter 7247
Troubled Air, The 9474
Troubles 4645
Trout Fishing in America 8945
Time with Time, A 10750
True American, The 806
True Confessions 5684
True Crime 8832
True Detective, The 6199
True Grit 4169
True Love 4297
True to the Old Flag 9860
Trumbo, Dalton 1097, 1444
Trumpet Shall Sound, The 8178
Trumpet-Major, The 10779
Trumpets of Silver 5874
Trust (Flanagan) 9343
Trust (Ozick) 5096
Trustee from the Toolroom 3153
Trusty Knaves, The 415
Truth About Lorin Jones, The 9690
Truth About Them, The 5038
"Truth Lover, A" 5285
Truxton King 5897
Tsotsi 5632
Tsukiyama, Gail 6737
Tucci, Niccolò 796, 2341, 9010
Tuck, Lily 2455
Tunc 2914
Tunkashila 9062
Tunnel, The 6102
Tunnel of Love, The 6634
Tuohy, Frank 2966, 7773
Tupelo Nights 7498
Turkey Hash 10825
Turkey War, The 3662
Turkish Delights 5602
Turmoil, The 1364
Turn Again Home 4078
Turn Again Tiger 9752
Turn of the Screw, The 8967
Turnaround 9800
Turnbull, Agnes Sligh 277, 1425,
  2150, 2476, 3806, 3981, 8592,
  9552, 9771, 10368
Turnbulls, The 1614
Turner, George 7840, 9718
Turning Back the Sun 1781
Turtle Beach 8433
Turtle Diary 5361
Turtle Moon 2069
Turvey 1918
Tussy Is Me 7592

Tuten, Frederic 6477
Tutuola, Amos 5281, 6635
Tuxedo Park 4195
Twain, Mark 781, 896, 1160, 1349,
  2193, 3492, 4715, 6785, 8965
Tweedie, Jill 455
Twice Blessed 2118
Twilight for the Gods 8101
Twilight of the Day 3188
Twilight Sleep 9880
Twisted Sword, The 9975
Two Admirals, The 3434
Two Against One 2001
Two Bishops, The 3981
Two Days in Aragon 8718
*Two Deaths of Señora Puccini,
  The* 3880
Two Destinies, The 9517
"Two Drovers, The" 8952
Two Girls, Fat and Thin 6017
Two Is Lonely 10234
"Two Little Confederates" 3637
Two Mrs. Grenvilles, The 3809
Two Much 7994
Two of Them, The 2855
Two of Us, The (Braine) 316
Two of Us, The (Johnson) 3509
Two on a Tower 2190
Two People 7678
Two Roads to Guadalupé 9077
Two Serious Ladies 6628
Two Sisters 6392
Two Towers, The 7846
Two Vanrevels, The 7709
Two Weeks in Another Town 1550
Two Wings to Veil My Face 8530
Two Women and Their Man 1939
Two Worlds and Their Ways 1971
Two Years Ago 6283
Twofold Vibration, The 9017
Twyborn Affair, The 9182
Tycoon 7452
Tyler, Anne 314, 2662, 3184,
  3943, 3957, 4122, 5947, 6306,
  9456, 9597, 9731, 10821
Tyler, Royall 356
Typee 7910
Typical American 4242
Tyranny of Love, The 10818

Ucko, Barbara 10102
Ullmann, Alex 8503
Ultimate Prizes 8198
Ultramarine 4729
Ulverton 1786
Ulysses 8041
Un-American Activities 285
Unapparent Wounds 1448
Unassigned Territory 1147
Unbalanced Accounts 8533
Unbearable Bassington, The 3821
Uncalled, The 8393
Uncharted Places 5049
Uncivil Seasons 3448

Unclassed, The 7877
Uncle 8226
Uncle Dynamite 7254
Uncle Fred in the Springtime 1610
Uncle from Rome, The 10674
Uncle Peel 1378
Uncle Silas 10678
Uncle Tom Andy Bill 4719
Uncle Tom's Cabin 2886
Uncommon Danger 9764
Unconditional Surrender 8942
Uncoupling 6298
Under Cover of Daylight 4263
Under Heat 7564
Under the Apple Tree 4472
Under the Boardwalk 3176
Under the Dog Star 2869
Under the Eye of the Storm 10198
Under the Greenwood Tree 9661
Under the House 9498
Under the Lilacs 3065
Under the Net 7156
Under the Shadow 3961
Under the Skin 5933
Under the Volcano 6068
Under Two Flags 2820
Under Western Eyes 5406
Underdog 7137
Underground Man, The 10218
Underground Woman, The 6959
Understood Betsy 4461
Understudy, The 3342
Undiscovered Country, The (Howells)
  9114
Undiscovered Country, The (Mitchell)
  5821
Undying Fire, The 2620
Unexplained Laughter 2409
Unfinished Cathedral 582
Unfinished Funeral 2341
Unfinished Portrait 7387
Unfortunate Woman, An 8731
Unger, Douglas 3662, 6811, 10745
Unhealthful Air 7050
Unheard Melodies 8581
Unholy Loves 3506
Unholy Uproar 529
Unicorn Rampant 3691
Uniform, The 9573
Union Square (Halper) 6061
Union Square (Tax) 10671
Union Street 2715
*Universal Baseball Association, Inc., J.
  Henry Waugh, Prop., The* 8915
Unknown to History 8342
Unless You Die Young 11001
Unlimited Dream Company, The 2042
Unnamable, The 7198
Unnatural Causes 1883
Unnatural Death 6173
Unofficial Rose, An 3941
*Unpleasantness at the Bellona Club,
  The* 7107
Unpossessed, The 3975
Unreasoning Heart, The 10583

Unsocial Socialist, An 10780
Unspeakable Skipton, The 6253
Unsuitable Attachment, An 9455
Unsuitable Job for a Woman, An
  2359
Unsworth, Barry 1045, 1167, 3721,
  6834, 7807
Until the Day Break 8858
Until the Sun Falls 4677
Untold Millions 1794
Untouchable Juli, The 5206
Unusual Behaviour 9961
Unusual Company 8890
Unvanquished, The (Fast) 10139
Unvanquished, The (Faulkner) 5710
Unwritten Chronicles of Robert E. Lee,
  The 7446
Up 1553
Up Above the World 3842
Up at the Villa 3112
Up, into the Singing Mountain 7494
Up the Country 6366
Up the Down Staircase 4215
Up Through the Water 186
Upchurch, Michael 4331
Updike, John 1041, 1520, 1979,
  2092, 2447, 2978, 4357, 5468,
  5503, 6256, 6301, 8913, 9174,
  9375, 9451, 9644, 9844
Upfield, Arthur W. 105, 5138,
  5429, 5926
Upon This Rock 9640
Upper Hand, The (Corrington) 7311
Upper Hand, The (Hood) 2173
Upstairs, Downstairs 4787
Upstart, The 1519
Upstate 4532
Urdang, Constance 1154, 1291, 7539
Urquhart, Jane 5550
Utah 7699
Utrillo's Mother 5237
Utz 2424

V. 2839
V for Victor 6921
"V. R. T." 2610
Vacant Places 9195
Vacationland 620
Vacillations of Poppy Carew, The 2673
Vainglory 5732
Valdez Is Coming 5153
Vale of Laughter, The 1114
Valedictory (Kantor) 1200
Valedictory (Kuniczak) 9021
Valentino's Hair 9505
Valiant Wife, The 8356
Valide 2411
Valkyrie Encounter, The 4650
Valley, The 9219
Valley Forge 7406
Valley of Bones, The 178
Valley of Decision (Middleton) 10023
Valley of Decision, The (Davenport)
  4149

Valley of Decision, The (Wharton)
  1297
Valley of Silent Men, The 4047
Valley of the Moon, The 2102
Valley of the Shadow 7436
Valley of Vision, The 8786
Valmouth 2945
Vampire Lestat, The 92
Vandenburgh, Jane 2100
Vanderhaeghe, Guy 2801, 5295
van der Post, Laurens 2124,
  3504, 5089, 7591, 8116, 8789,
  9008
Vandover and the Brute 7374
Vanessa 8548
"Van Gogh's Room at Arles" 7793
Vanguard, The 654
van Herk, Aritha 222
Vanished (Knebel) 5937
Vanished (Morris) 9041
Vanity Fair 9757
Vanity of Duluoz 9265
Vanity Row 9072
Vannucci, Lynn 9821
Van Peebles, Melvin 806
Vansittart, Peter 1302, 1641, 2093,
  10590, 10598
Van Vechten, Carl 8564, 10342
Variable Winds at Jalna 7475
Variations in the Night 5976
Varmint, The 9529
Vassi, Marco 5333
Vast Memory of Love, The 5543
Vatican 10526
Vaughn, Elizabeth Dewberry 1897
Vector 8873
Vein of Iron 965
Vein of Riches, A 3586
Velocity 2796
Velvet Horn, The 2325
Venables, The 10580
Vendetta 2294
Vendor of Sweets, The 3845
Venerable Bead, The 6800
Venetia 3059
Venetian Glass Nephew, The 2072
Vengeance Valley 1548
"Veni, Vidi . . . Wendt" 1039
Ventura, Michael 2437
Venture in the East 1851
Venus Envy 2460
Venus in Sparta 1028
Venusberg 5415
Vera 4224
Veracruz 8733
Vergilius 1353
Vernon, John 627, 3962, 9635
Veronica 4597
Vertical Hold 4524
Vertical Smile, The 2846
Very Air, The 5192
Very Good, Jeeves! 3698
Very House, The 8082
Very Old Bones 2183
Very Private Life, A 4167

Very Rich Hours of Count von Stauffen-
  berg, The 7227
Vespers in Vienna 10486
Vestal Virgin Room, The 3870
Veteran's Day 4449
Via Crucis 2133
Vic Holyfield and the Class of 1957 621
Vicar of Christ, The 2380
Vicar of Wakefield, The 5725
Vice Versa 8341
Viceroy of Ouidah, The 3588
Victim, The 4381
Victim of Love 4522
Victim of the Aurora 5230
Victim's Daughter, The 8583
Victor Ollnee's Discipline 8907
Victors and Vanquished 3836
Victory 10551
Vida 2921
Vidal, Gore 54, 611, 1441, 1451,
  2817, 4320, 4503, 5606, 6392,
  7518, 8383, 9079, 9497, 10147,
  10528, 10662, 10820
Vienna Girl 2129
View from Chivo, The 4785
View from Coyaba, The 1192
View from the Parsonage, The 7392
View from Tower Hill, The 5939
View of the Harbour, A 732
Vigfusson, Robin 2783
Vigil, The 4420
Viking, The 1628
Vile Bodies 47
Villa Golitsyn, The 10520
Villa in France, A 1527
Villa in Summer, A 10365
Villa Rubein 9869
Village 10687
Village of Stars 10057
Villarreal, José Antonio 4478, 7259
Villette 3061
Vilmure, Daniel 1747
Vindication 7123
Vine, Barbara (pseud.). See Ren-
  dell, Ruth
Vineland 10310
Vintage, The 10156
Viola Gwyn 6623
Violated, The 9386
Violence (Bausch) 9981
Violence (Iyayi) 7324
Violent Bear It Away, The 2329
Violet Clay 501
Viper Tree, The 7548
Virgin and the Gypsy, The 7864
Virgin in the Garden, The 9391
Virgin Territory 2047
Virginia 3270
Virginian, The (Wister) 9526
Virginians, The (Thackeray) 8641
Virginie 9018
Virtue, Noel 1893
Virtuous Woman, A 3885
Visa for Avalon 10187
Vision of Battlements, A 8306

Visions of Cody 7575
Visions of Gerard 2336
Visit Home, A 10964
Visit to Yazoo, A 3511
Visitants 9941
Visitation of Spirits, A 2643
Visitors, The 7493
Vital Parts 7480
Vittoria 5127
"*Vivian*" 3911
Vivian Grey 1265
Vivisector, The 10937
Vixens, The 10487
Vizenor, Gerald 1264, 3466
Vizinczey, Stephen 1977, 5590
Vliet, R. G. 1331
Vodi, The 137
Vogan, Sara 1472, 1846
Voice, The 4635
Voice at the Back Door, The 9774
Voice of Bugle Ann, The 9994
Voice of Our Shadow 6684
Voice of the People, The 5197
Voice Through a Cloud, A 6568
Voices from Home 10914
Voices from the Moon 2666
Voices in an Empty Room 8313
Voices in the Garden 5162
Voices in Time 3807
Voices of a Summer Day 382
Voices of Glory, The 10558
Volcano Lover, The 1089
Volk, Patricia 6020
Vollmann, William T. 2555, 3057, 3413, 9053
von Arnim, Elizabeth 4224, 5016
Vonnegut, Kurt 1403, 2253, 2550, 3747, 4762, 4765, 4865, 5253, 5266, 5827, 6259, 7145, 10508
Voodoo Queen, The 3703
Vorster, Gordon 10910
Voss 9903
Vox 2882
Vox Pop 10521
Voyage 8428
Voyage in the Dark 7383
Voyage of the Franz Joseph, The 6769
Voyage of the Dawn Treader, The 4740
Voyage of the Destiny, The 7808
Voyage Out, The 9123
Voyage to Sante Fe 5745
Voyage to the First of December 8124
Voyage Unplanned, The 7319
Vrettos, Theodore 4082, 4587, 9482
Vreuls, Diane 6134

Wabash 1070
Wachtel, Chuck 3020
Waddell, Helen 8742
Wade, Brent 1962
Wagmam, Fredrica 2582
Wagner, Bruce 2808
Wagner, Eliot 10254

Wagoner, David 136, 882, 1686, 5605, 6136, 6535, 7045, 7596
Waif of the Plains, A 5128
Wain, John 3710, 3944, 5350, 7167, 8994, 9288, 9305, 9676
Waiting for Childhood 7119
Waiting for Cordelia 9794
Waiting for Rain 9977
Waiting for Sheila 5579
Waiting for the Barbarians 2857
Waiting for the End of the World 9812
Waiting for the Mahatma 6636
Waiting Sands, The 9433
Waiting to Exhale 6782
Waiting to Live 4362
Waiting to Vanish 3610
Wake in Ybor City, A 8216
Wake of the Storm, The 5167
Wake Up, Stupid 5444
Wakefield, Dan 226, 1229, 4472, 7115, 8676
Wakefield's Course 10579
Waking 5326
Waking Spell, The 10962
Waking the Dead 1741
Waldrop, Rosmarie 2525
Walg 6688
Walk in the Wood, A 7445
Walk Me to the Distance 4590
Walk on the Wild Side, A 2651
Walk Out of the World, A 4780
Walk Proud 8878
Walk Through Fire, A 8936
Walk Through the Valley 1639
Walker, Alice 1670, 1805, 2459, 3007, 6484
Walker, Charles 10764
Walker, David 7671
Walker, George Lee 3727
Walker, Margaret 743
Walker, Walter 1894, 3753, 7578
Walking Across Egypt 462
Walking After Midnight 2668
Walking Davis 1676
Walking Distance 9342
Walking Dunes 4431
Walking into the River 5303
Walking Naked 2860
Walking Papers 2113
Walking Stick, The 2588
Walking the Cat 631
Wall, The (Hersey) 2604
Wall, The (Rinehart) 1247
Wall of the Plague, The 7117
Wall to Wall 10380
Wallace, Don 10106
Wallace, Lew 6054, 7502, 8057
Wallace, Pamela 4241
Wallant, Edward Lewis 1111, 8332, 10379, 10384
Walled Orchard, The 4366
Waller, Robert James 1787
Walls 8310
Walls of Blue Coquina 1260
Walnut Door, The 6138

Walpole, Horace 6515
Walpole, Hugh 489, 724, 787, 1788, 2206, 2299, 2689, 3085, 3099, 3533, 5248, 5737, 5901, 7125, 7617, 8405, 8548, 9064, 9214, 10133
Walsh, Jill Paton 1811
Walter 6538
Waltz in Marathon 3950
Waltzing in the Attic 10104
Wambaugh, Joseph 227, 1305, 4220, 4256, 4523, 5881, 6958, 7851, 8681
Wanderer of the Wasteland 7654
Wanderer Springs 6029
Wanderers, The (Mphahlele) 6324
Wanderers, The (Price) 7113
Wanderers Eastward, Wanderers West 9100
Wanderer's Necklace, The 1267
Wandering of Desire, The 3651
Wanting 10275
Wanting Seed, The 2587
Wanton Mally 9882
Wanton Summer Air, The 8573
Wapshot Chronicle, The 1411
Wapshot Scandal, The 8604
War and Remembrance 8137
War Babies 8702
War Between the Tates, The 7318
War Brides 3593
War Cries Over Avenue C 6276
War Games 877
War Is Heaven! 8674
War Lover, The 10167
War of Camp Omongo, The 7926
War of Don Emmanuel's Nether Parts, The 9273
War of Dreams, The 7404
War of the Worlds, The 519
War on the Cimarron 2215
War Story (McGill) 2778
War Story (Robinson) 5720
War Train, The 8812
War Zone, The 5242
Ward, Mary Augusta 2821, 9326, 9742
Ward, Mary Jane 10000
Ward, Mrs. Humphry *See* Ward, Mary Augusta
Ward of the Golden Gate, A 7287
Warden, The 1486
Warden of the Smoke and Bells 9151
Warleggan 8632
Warlock (Hall) 6954
Warlock (Harrison) 3445
Warlord, The 8574
Warmer Season, A 5527
Warner, Marina 7441, 7690, 7806, 10327
Warner, Peter 9714
Warner, Rex 707, 2894, 5443, 10998
Warner, Susan 5195

Warner, Sylvia Townsend 1495, 2558, 6106, 7586, 9881
Warning Bell, The 3216
Warren, Patricia Nell 604, 2157, 6229
Warren, Robert Penn 2374, 2835, 4746, 5430, 6072, 6912, 7249, 7316, 8408, 9143
Warrick 1140
Warrior in Bronze 3199
Wars, The 440
Wars of Heaven, The 867
Wartime Lies 5299
Washington, D.C. 9079
Washington Square 6407
Washington Square Ensemble, The 8281
Wasp Factory, The 3409
Watch and Ward 6036
Watch Dog 9340
Watch That Ends the Night, The 8995
"Watcher by the Threshold, The" 8968
Watcher in the Shadows 7396
Watchers on the Shore, The 305
Watchfires 9280
"Watching Father Die" 2396
Watching the Body Burn 3786
Watching TV with the Red Chinese 8388
Watchman, The 5929
Water Castle, The 1210
Water Dancer 10262
Water Is Wide, The 7366
Water Music 6398
Water Under the Bridge 1208
Water with Berries 10604
Waterboys 7862
Waterfall, The 3674
Waterfront 1407
Waterhouse, Keith 1881, 3369, 9003, 9173, 9429
Waterland 6823
Waterlily 6158
Waterline, The 2798
Watermelon Kid, The 9026
Water-Method Man, The 6892
Waters, Frank 3765, 5620, 6085, 8799, 9748, 10700
Waters of Kronos, The 4572
Waters Under the Earth, The 10645
Watership Down 9673
Water-Witch, The 7647
Watkins, Paul 187, 234, 397, 3791
Watmough, David 4519
Watson, Larry 7460
Watson, Sterling 10306
Watson, William 5165
Watson's Apology 3780
Watt 8267
Waugh, Alec 8567, 9361, 10006
Waugh, Auberon 139, 666, 1514, 8869
Waugh, Evelyn 17, 47, 5423, 5431, 5440, 6427, 7801, 8354,

8652, 8666, 8942, 9420, 9559, 10494, 10701
Wave, The (Scott) 7913
Waverly 2466
Waves, The (Woolf) 2203
Way Men Act, The 1088
Way of a Man, The 1800
Way of All Flesh, The 5888
Way Out of Berkeley Square, The 7987
Way Past Cool 4267
Way to Fort Pillow, The 1679
Way to the Gold, The 7136
Way to the Lantern, The 1163
Way to the West, The 271
Way We Live Now, The (Thurm) 5636
Way We Live Now, The (Trollope) 5395
Way We Were, The 10823
Way West, The 7298
Ways of the Hour, The 1334
Wayward Bus, The 9145
We and Our Neighbors 6284
We Can't All Be Heroes, You Know 9851
We Have Always Lived in the Castle 337
We Speak No Treason 3979
We That Were Young 3825
We the Living 8509
Weans, The 2605
Weather in the Streets, The 10128
Weather of February, The 904
Weather Shelter, The 3654
Weather Tomorrow, The 6046
Weave of Women, A 2080
Weaver, Gordon 1081
Weaver, Will 1948
Weavers, The 9743
Web, The 1949
Web and the Rock, The 5914
"Web of Earth, The" 9993
Webb, Charles 4575
Webb, James 1864, 6881, 8814, 9621
Webb, Mary 5681, 8400
Webb, Paula 4925
Weber, Nancy 9736
Webster, Jan 2254, 4193
Webster, Susan 6831
Wedding, The 10648
Wedding Bargain, The 2476
Wedding Group, The 10659
Wedding Journey, The 1827
Weedkiller's Daughter, The 10066
Weedy Rough 6918
Weekend, The 10323
Weekend in Dinlock 497
Weekend Man, The 1122
Weekend with Claude, A 1035
Weep Not, Child 10815
Weesner, Theodore 6199, 9786
Weidman, Jerome 1884, 4159, 7955
Weight of Winter, The 8624
Weingarten, Violet 65, 211, 1511

Weinstock Among the Dying 6491
Weinzweig, Helen 2261
Weir, John 4438
Weir of Hermiston 9090
Weiss, David 544, 6644, 10501
Welch, Denton 6568, 9722
Welch, James 437, 3455, 8442, 8921
Welcome to Hard Times 2904
Welcome to Xanadu 9167
Weldon, Fay 2174, 2780, 4181, 5233, 5356, 5677, 6478, 7192, 7901, 8462, 9038, 9951, 9986, 9988, 10560, 10762, 10822, 10992
Well, The 4127
Well and Truly 2880
Well at the World's End, The 7796
Well of Loneliness, The 5067
Well-Beloved, The 9091
Wells, H. G. 519, 540, 931, 932, 1219, 1314, 1823, 2306, 2620, 2733, 3267, 3495, 3498, 3563, 4139, 4343, 4700, 5405, 5639, 5694, 6251, 6409, 6413, 6620, 7761, 8059, 8856, 9092, 10131, 10918
Welsh Eye, A 5151
Welt, Elly 2518
Welter, John 6032
Welty, Eudora 4560, 5925, 6893, 7251, 8423
Wept of Wish-Ton-Wish, The 263
"We're Friends Again" 8331
We're Not Here 10446
Wescott, Glenway 81, 3500, 5802, 8402
Wesley, Mary 641, 1121, 1946, 2673, 6238, 6356, 7580, 7943, 9836
West, Anthony C. 5260, 9479, 10591
West, Anthony P. 9556, 10156
West, Dorothy 10358
West, Elliot 2171
West, Jessamyn 1924, 2702, 2836, 3221, 4156, 9011, 9897, 10940
West, Morris 1507, 1509, 1525, 2236, 2364, 2969, 3366, 3925, 4920, 5588, 5716, 5987, 6317, 6439, 6933, 7002, 7978
West, Nathanael 2603, 3104, 6421, 8776
West, Paul 215, 1322, 1429, 2429, 4479, 4608, 4871, 5597, 5882, 7227, 7628, 7990, 9189
West, Rebecca 943, 2071, 2073, 2953, 4166, 5268, 5690, 5799, 7589, 7712, 8855, 9885
West, Stanley Gordon 5968
West, William 10186
West of Sunset 4651
West of the Hill 9224
West of the Rockies 6445
West to Eden 3952
Western 4190

Western Lands, The 3235
Western Motel 7497
Western Swing 8760
Westlake, Donald E. 1043, 1803, 2044, 2721, 4194, 4963, 5513, 5683, 6989, 7226, 7994, 9501
Westmacott, Mary (pseud.). *See* Christie, Agatha
Westward Ho! 1336
Westward Passage 9413
Westward to Laughter 3275
Westways 6100
Wet Paint 3729
Wetherell, W. D. 1475
Wetzel, Donald 2967, 10207
Weymouth Sands 7916
Weyr, Garret 6016
Wharton, Edith 44, 310, 491, 696, 1012, 1297, 1585, 1967, 3561, 4270, 4730, 4976, 5413, 7555, 7828, 8072, 8173, 8508, 8740, 8912, 9880, 10037, 10118, 10995
Wharton, William 1054, 1473, 3222, 6277, 7160, 8949, 9681, 9942
What a Way to Go 2332
What Became of Anna Bolton 3383
What Comes Next 4227
What Did It Mean? 3136
What Dinah Thought 4857
What Happened Was This 7837
What I Have to Tell You 10977
What I'm Going to Do, I Think 2989
"What Maisie Knew" 2649
What Makes Sammy Run? 967
What Mrs. McGillicuddy Saw! 10369
What Niall Saw 4829
What the Dead Remember 7944
What Time Collects 8417
What Waiting Really Means 10880
Whatever Happened to Gloomy Gus of the Chicago Bears? 10669
What's Become of Waring 10649
What's Bred in the Bone 918
What's Eating Gilbert Grape 8246
What's the Big Hurry? 7393
What's-His-Name 8849
Wheat That Springeth Green 996
Wheatcroft, John 9281
Wheaton, Philip D. 5110
Wheel of Fortune, The 7424
Wheelis, Allen 4624, 9278, 10300
When a Man's a Man 6910
When All the Woods Are Green 8031
When I Was Otherwise 1889
When Knighthood Was in Flower 362
When Nietzsche Wept 674
When Rain Clouds Gather 1427
When She Was Good 250
When Sisterhood Was in Flower 4815
When the Boys Came Out to Play 2269
When the Green Woods Laugh 9753
When the Parrot Boy Sings 5872
When the Tree Flowered 3128
When the War Is Over 8672

When the World Shook 3670
When They Took Away the Man in the Moon 6347
When Valmond Came to Pontiac 9209
When We Get Home 3613
When We Had Other Names 6119
When William Came 7468
Where All the Ladders Start 6030
Where Angels Fear to Tread 3993
Where Do You Stop? 4430
Where I Used to Play on the Green 5163
Where Is My Wandering Boy Tonight? 6535
Where She Was 3225
Where the Blue Begins 3088
Where the Boys Are 5254
Where the Cherries End Up 10663
Where the High Winds Blow 7671
Where the Rainbow Ends 3603
Where There's a Will 900
Where You Once Belonged 1768
Which Ones Are the Enemy? 7199
While Gods Are Falling 1419
While the Angels Sing 3121
Whip, The 2900
Whipple's Castle 8606
Whisnant, Luke 8388
Whisper of the Axe, The 9848
Whistle 1693
Whistle and I'll Come to You 2150
Whistlejacket 6869
Whistling Song, The 578
White, Antonia 1626, 9385, 9540, 9724
White, Curtis 4905
White, Edgar 1289
White, Edmund 5869, 5952, 6578, 6698, 10233
White, Jon Manchip 1132, 2247
White, Kenneth 3871
White, Patrick 147, 717, 2318, 3303, 5258, 9182, 9773, 9903, 9934, 10812, 10937
White, Stewart Edward 270, 700, 3570, 7653
White, T. H. 1522, 4153, 7879
White, Terence de Vere 5508
White, Theodore H. 6070
White, William Allen 959
White Budge 6459
White Bird Flying, A 4377
White Bus, The 7902
White Company, The 648
White Crow, The 10199
White Cutter, The 6718
White Dawn, The 10727
White Eagles over Serbia 4317
White Eskimo 8125
White Fang 3896
White Figure, White Ground 677
White Flag, The 10117
White German Shepherd, The 470
White Horse Cafe 6720
White Horse to Banbury Cross 8187
White Horses 3211

White Hotel, The 9613
White Jazz 9186
White Light 6828
White Lotus 3708
White Monkey, The 10339
White Noise 9814
White Peacock, The 402
White People 8712
White Poppy 1062
White Rajah, The 3155
White Rhino Hotel, The 4337
White Rising 10841
White Sea Bird, The 8138
White Sister, The 488
White Water 1728
White-Jacket 2819
Whiteness of Bones, The 10957
Whiteoak Brothers, The 1251
Whiteoak Harvest 1970
Whiteoak Heritage 9548
Whiteoaks of Jalna 9215
Whitewater 5058
Whitlock, Brand 7637
Whittemore, Edward 889, 1464
Whitten, Dr. Kathryn M. 8593
Who Are the Violets Now? 8869
Who Is Angelina? 10240
Who Is Teddy Villanova? 4798
Who Was Changed and Who Was Dead 735
Who Was Oswald Fish? 5498
Whole Hog 6136
Whom God Hath Joined 9110
Whore of Tjampuan, The 6474
Whores for Gloria 3057
Whose Body? 7376
Whosoever Shall Offend 6019
Why Are We in Vietnam? 10007
Why We Never Danced the Charleston 5063
Wibberley, Leonard 4062, 8866, 9452, 10196, 10587
Wichelns, Lee 8497
Wicked Angel 380
Wicked Pavilion, The 4274
Wickford Point 1915
Wide House, The 6113
Wide Is the Gate 3936
Wide Sargasso Sea 61
Wide, Wide World, The 5195
Wideman, John Edgar 350, 2788, 3849, 4676, 5978, 8748
Widower's Son, The 8683
Widows' Adventures, The 8290
Widow's Cruise, The 738
Widow's Trial, The 5378
Wiebe, Rudy 7403, 7887, 10392
Wiegand, William 8694
Wieland 5388
Wieland, Liza 9323
Wier, Allen 5676, 7783
Wife 5758
Wife to Mr. Milton 841
Wifey 10246
Wiggins, Marianne 1764, 9321

Wilber, Alix 2456
Wilcox, James 3261, 4544, 5380, 6148, 8763
Wild Apples 1775
Wild at Heart 4336
Wild Bananas 1996
Wild Bunch, The 7662
Wild Conquest 5645
Wild Country, The 7716
Wild Earth's Nobility, The 5620
Wild Geese (Dillon) 4931
Wild Geese (Ostenso) 10039
Wild Geese Calling 3570
Wild Goose, Brother Goose 748
Wild Grow the Lilies 8947
Wild Horizon 2147
Wild Irish Girl, The 6385
Wild Is the River 8777
Wild Nights 1257
Wild Oats 3858
Wild Palms, The 9887
Wild Pitch 6184
Wild Surmise, A 5699
Wild Swan, The 10809
Wild Sweet Witch, The 8514
Wild Western Scenes 5306
Wildcatting 3633
Wilde, Oscar 3794
Wilde West 8544
Wilder, Robert 5623, 5627, 8663, 9078, 9363, 9841
Wilder, Thornton 15, 2202, 3407, 6447, 7243, 7509, 7514
Wilderness (Danvers) 9258
Wilderness (Warren) 6072
Wilderness, The (O'Flaherty) 9745
Wilderness Called Peace, A 10096
Wilderness-Stone, The 3361
Wildlife 3619
Wildwood 4152
Wiley, Richard 4096, 9636, 10107
Wilhelm, Kate 2546, 9616, 10311
Wilkes, Paul 6749
Wilkinson, Sylvia 1857
Will, The 2337
Willard 431
Willard, Nancy 2638
Williams, Ben Ames 9471, 10927
Williams, Bob 4259
Williams, Charles 414, 10803
Williams, Dennis A. 2184
Williams, Jeanne 3667, 6087, 9683, 9832
Williams, Joan 1056, 1319, 2771, 5376, 6127
Williams, John 4469, 7890, 9777
Williams, John A. 206, 2852, 2905, 2912, 4252, 7854, 7939, 8883, 10208
Williams, Joy 2919, 3247
Williams, Nigel 4836
Williams, Philip Lee 1194, 1813, 2271, 5342, 8201, 8452
Williams, Raymond 6699, 7847, 9160

Williams, Sherley Anne 1742
Williams, Tennessee 2225, 3192
Williams, Thomas 3461, 8606, 9964
Williams, William Carlos 5409
Williams, Wirt 3157, 3969, 8420, 9228
Williamson, Chilton Jr. 9702
Willingham, Calder 282, 1854, 4176
Willis, Connie 468
Willis, Meredith Sue 3592
Williwaw 10147
Willowwood 4801
Willy Remembers 6990
Willys Dream Kit, The 4089
Wilson, A. N. 1947, 3884, 4821, 5498, 5679, 5766, 9502, 10862
Wilson, Angus 1320, 2507, 3653, 3741, 4895, 6499, 7779, 7817
Wilson, Barbara Ker 3248
Wilson, Colin 683, 2033, 2616, 4500, 6227, 8519, 8555, 8664, 9486, 9778, 10239, 10375
Wilson, Dorothy Clarke 2055, 4191, 4742, 4811, 8986, 9141
Wilson, Ethel 9426
Wilson, Harriet E. 2493
Wilson, Harry Leon 241, 2823, 5408
Wilson, Margaret 5132, 8356
Wilson, Robley 8583
Wilson, Rudy 2420
Wilson, Sloan 1116, 3054, 5028, 5154, 5352, 6774, 10080, 10173, 10848, 10968
Wilson, William S. 4542
Wilson, Z. Vance 7536
Wilt on High 3397
Wimmer, Dick 9300
Winchester, Stanley 1227
Wind Bloweth, The 837
Wind Cannot Read, The 1623
Wind from Nowhere, The 10712
Wind from the Carolinas 9078
Wind in the Forest, The 9152
Wind in the Willows, The 401
Wind Leaves No Shadow, The 4214
Wind off the Sea, The 5813
Wind on the Heath, The 9036
Wind Over Wisconsin 8510
Windham, Donald 6071, 6665, 7678
Winding Stair 7686
Winds of Blame 4258
Winds of God, The 7385
Winds of Heaven, The 55
Winds of Sinhala, The 7021
Winds of the Day 5093
Winds of War, The 3315
Windsor Castle 948
Windy McPherson's Son 960
Wine and the Music, The 858
Wine of Astonishment, The (Gellhorn) 8326

Wine of Astonishment, The (Lovelace) 69
Wines of Pentagoët, The 5235
Winesburg, Ohio 100
Wing-and-Wing, The 7909
Winged Escort 8131
Wings of Night, The 1640
Wings of the Dove, The 9325
Wings of the Wind, The 3411
Winner, The 4009
Winning of Barbara Worth, The 9762
Winona 4043
Winsor, Kathleen 7645, 9100
Winston Affair, The 4953
Winter (Deighton) 1168
"Winter" (Gilchrist) 5534
Winter Concert 5851
Winter Doves 1793
Winter Garden 1702
Winter in April 2213
Winter in Jerusalem 9633
Winter in Moscow 10350
Winter in the Blood 437
Winter in the Hills, A 3944
Winter Journey (Broughton) 7560
Winter Journey (Frame) 4708
Winter Kills 3584
Winter of Artifice 10044
Winter of Our Discontent, The 10174
Winter People, The (Ehle) 9946
Winter People, The (Phelps) 8999
Winter Quarters 418
Winter Return 6738
Winter Rider, The 663
"Winter Thunder" 8598
Winter Tree, The 8435
Winter Wife 9341
Winterchill 10103
Wintering, The 2771
Winterkill 7642
Winter's Love, A 4749
Winter's Reckoning, A 8612
Winter's Tale (Helprin) 1449
Winter's Tale, A (Godden) 8600
Wintersmoon 5737
Winterson, Jeanette 1872, 4860, 6700
Winthrop, Elizabeth 2554
Winthrop Covenant, The 6135
Wintle, Justin 346
Winton, Tim 4087, 7705, 9818
Wirecutter 4332
Wisdom's Gate 2650
Wise, Leonard 5116, 7146
Wise Blood 9558
Wise Children 1476
Wise Virgin (Wilson) 5766
Wise Virgins, The (Woolf) 5696
Wiseman, Adele 9562
Wiser, William 289
Wish Her Safe at Home 7415
Wister, Owen 7554, 9526
Witch Diggers, The 9897
Witch of Merthyn, The 9560
Witch of Prague, The 1296